PREMIER

REFERENCE

SERIES

ZONDERVAN NIV

BIBLE

COMMENTARY

VOLUME 1: OLD TESTAMENT

An abridgment of *The Expositor's Bible Commentary*

KENNETH L. BARKER &

JOHN R. KOHLENBERGER III

CONSULTING EDITORS

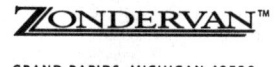

GRAND RAPIDS, MICHIGAN 49530

ZONDERVAN™

Zondervan NIV Bible Commentary: Volume 1: Old Testament

Copyright © 1994 by Zondervan

Requests for information should be addressed to:

Zondervan, *Grand Rapids, Michigan 49530*

Library of Congress Cataloging-in-Publication Data

The Zondervan NIV Bible Commentary / Consulting editors, Kenneth L. Barker and
    John R. Kohlenberger III
        p.   cm.
    An abridgment of The expositor's Bible commentary, retaining the interpretative mate-
    rial but missing the text of the NIV and the detailed scholarly notes and discussions.
    Includes indexes.
    Contents: v. 1. Old Testament — v. 2. New Testament.
        ISBN: 0-310-57850-7 (v. 1). — ISBN 0-310-57840-X (v.2)
        1. Bible–Commentaries..   I. Barker, Kenneth L.   II. Kohlenberger, John
R.   III. Expositor's Bible commentary.
BS491.2.Z65   1994
220.7—dc20   94-6885

Printed in the United States of America

---

    03 04 05 06 /❖ DC/ 19 18 17 16 15

Contents

Acknowledgments

The publisher of the *Zondervan NIV Bible Commentary* wishes to thank the two editors who undertook the massive task of reducing eleven volumes of Bible commentaries into two: Richard Polcyn, who did the Old Testament, and Verlyn D. Verbrugge, who did the New Testament. Thanks also to Dr. Kenneth L. Barker and John R. Kohlenberger III, who offered invaluable assistance as consulting editors.

The publisher also deeply appreciates the assistance of Neal and Joel Bierling, who served as consultants for, and provided, most of the pictures used in this two-volume commentary. Unless otherwise noted, all pictures are theirs. Finally, thanks to the Bible Department of Zondervan for allowing us to use many of the charts and maps from their best-selling study Bibles.

About the Editors

John R. Kolenberger III is the author or coeditor of more than three dozen biblical reference books and study Bibles, including *The Strongest Strong's Exhaustive Concordance of the Bible, NIV Interlinear Hebrew-English Old Testament, NRSV Concordance Unabridged, Greek-English Concordance to the New Testament, Hebrew-English Concordance to the Old Testament,* and the award-winning *NIV Exhaustive Concordane* and *NIV Bible Commentary.* He has taught at Multnomah Bible College and Western Seminary in Portland, Oregon.

Kenneth L. Barker (Ph.D., Dropsie College for Hebrew and Cognate Learning) is presently serving on the Committee for Bible Translation of the International Bible Society (the committee that oversees the New International Version of the Bible), is the general editor for the upcoming revised *NIV Study Bible,* and authored the commentary on "Zechariah" in *The Expositor's Bible Commentary.*

Preface

The NIV Bible Commentary has been in the making for a long time. In 1976 the first volume of The Expositor's Bible Commentary (Volume 10) was released, containing commentaries on Romans to Galatians, under the general editorship of Frank E. Gaebelein. The final volume in this series was published in 1992, with commentaries on Deuteronomy to 2 Samuel.

Contributors for The Expositor's Bible Commentary were solicited from among the best evangelical scholars on both sides of the Atlantic. Each expositor was committed to the divine inspiration, complete trustworthiness, and full authority of Scripture as God's Word. Each author's work aimed to provide preachers, teachers, and students of the Bible with insights into the Scriptures that were scholarly yet practical to everyday life. The full text of the New International Version of the Bible was printed along with the commentary section. The units of discussion were often followed by technical notes of interest mainly to scholars.

The Expositor's Bible Commentary has fulfilled its goal admirably, judging from the positive reviews it has received, the awards it has earned, and the tens of thousands of sets that have been purchased. It was felt that this excellent series could serve well as the basis for a two-volume commentary set designed primarily for lay persons. Consequently, the commentaries from Genesis to Revelation in the Expositor's Bible Commentary have now been abridged, retaining all the important interpretative material of the larger set but without the text of the NIV and the detailed scholarly notes and discussions.

This two-volume commentary has two additional features not found in the original set. First, both volumes are replete with maps, charts, tables, and pictures that are relevant to the passages under discussion. Secondly, throughout the commentary, where specific biblical words are discussed at some length, the Goodrick-Kohlenberger numbers (abbreviated GK) have been added. These numbers, which appeared first in The NIV Exhaustive Concordance, are based on the numbering system for each Hebrew, Aramaic, and Greek word in the Bible developed by Edward W. Goodrick and John R. Kohlenberger III (a numbering system similar but superior to the ever-popular Strong's numbering system). An index of the words that are referred to is found in the back of each volume.

It is the hope of the publisher that just as The Expositor's Bible Commentary has served so well the needs of pastors and teachers, this two-volume commentary will serve the needs of average lay persons in the church who want to learn more about the Bible in their personal study or prepare themselves to lead a Bible lesson in a small group study.

The Bible is the greatest and most beautiful book of all time, the primary source of law and morality, the fountain of divine wisdom, the infallible guide to life, and above all, the inspired witness to Jesus Christ. May this work fulfill its function of expounding the Scriptures with grace and clarity, so that its users may find that both Old and New Testaments do indeed lead us to our Lord Jesus Christ, who alone could say, "I have come that they may have life, and have it to the full" (John 10:10).

Pictures, Maps, and Charts

Abbreviations

Books of the Bible

Ge	Genesis
Ex	Exodus
Lev	Leviticus
Nu	Numbers
Dt	Deuteronomy
Jos	Joshua
Jdg	Judges
Ru	Ruth
1Sa	1 Samuel
2Sa	2 Samuel
1Ki	1 Kings
2Ki	2 Kings
1Ch	1 Chronicles
2Ch	2 Chronicles
Ezr	Ezra
Ne	Nehemiah
Est	Esther
Job	Job
Ps	Psalms
Pr	Proverbs
Ecc	Ecclesiastes
SS	Song of Songs
Isa	Isaiah
Jer	Jeremiah
La	Lamentations
Eze	Ezekiel
Da	Daniel
Hos	Hosea
Joel	Joel
Am	Amos
Ob	Obadiah
Jnh	Jonah
Mic	Micah
Na	Nahum
Hab	Habakkuk
Zep	Zephaniah
Hag	Haggai
Zec	Zechariah
Mal	Malachi
Mt	Matthew
Mk	Mark
Lk	Luke
Jn	John
Ac	Acts
Ro	Romans
1Co	1 Corinthians
2Co	2 Corinthians
Gal	Galatians
Eph	Ephesians
Php	Philippians
Col	Colossians
1Th	1 Thessalonians
2Th	2 Thessalonians
1Ti	1 Timothy
2Ti	2 Timothy
Tit	Titus
Phm	Philemon
Heb	Hebrews
Jas	James
1Pe	1 Peter
2Pe	2 Peter
1Jn	1 John
2Jn	2 John
3Jn	3 John
Jude	Jude
Rev	Revelation

Other Abbreviations

c.	about
cf.	compare
ch(s).	chapter(s)
EBC	Expositor's Bible Commentary
e.g.	for example
etc.	and so on
ff.	following verses
Gk.	Greek
GK	Goodrick/ Kohlenberger number
Heb.	Hebrew
i.e.	that is
lit.	literally
NT	New Testament
OT	Old Testament
v(v).	verse(s)
ZPEB	Zondervan Pictorial Encyclopedia of the Bible

Genesis

INTRODUCTION

1. Background

Little is known about the origin and authorship of the book of Genesis. It is part of the Pentateuch, which Jewish tradition and the NT have ascribed to Moses (cf. Jn 1:17; 5:46; 7:19, 23). Generally, the question of the authorship of Genesis is taken up within the context of theories regarding the literary history of the Pentateuch as a whole.

We must distinguish at least two kinds of background material in the book of Genesis: (1) the historical background in which the book was written, and (2) the historical background of the context of the events recorded in the book. The first concerns a specific time and place for the composition of the book. The second covers a wide-ranging array of settings (e.g., the Garden of Eden, the Flood, the city of Babylon, Canaan, and Egypt).

Genesis records two types of events: those that happened on a global or even cosmic scale (e.g., Creation, the Flood) and those that happened in a relatively isolated, localized way (e.g., Noah's drunkenness, Abraham's vision). By far most events in Genesis happened in a limited sphere of time and location and can best be described as "family matters."

2. Unity

The book of Genesis is characterized by both an easily discernible unity and a noticeable lack of uniformity. Much like the writers of the NT Gospels and the later historical books of the OT, the writer of Genesis appears to have composed his work from "archival" records of God's great deeds in the past. We know from references within the early historical books that such records were maintained at an early stage in Israel's history (Ex 17:14; Nu 21:14; Jos 10:13); so perhaps similar records were kept at far earlier stages within the individual households of the patriarchs and their tribal ancestors. The narratives within Genesis appear to be largely made up of small, self-contained stories worked together into larger units by means of various geographical and genealogical tables. Thus one should not expect to find absolute uniformity of style, vocabulary, etc., among all the individual narratives, any more than an absolute uniformity can be expected in the later historical books. Indeed, we would more likely expect the writer, working under the direction of God, to have preserved his records just as he had received them, sacrificing uniformity for the sake of historical faithfulness.

3. Authorship

The question naturally arises as to who wrote or composed the final account of the book of Genesis. Who put all the narratives together? The composer of Genesis, which is part of the Pentateuch, seems most likely to be the same as that of the Pentateuch as a whole. Nowhere in the work does the author refer to himself or identify himself. Early and reliable tradition has ascribed the authorship to Moses; and it is a fact that throughout the pentateuchal narratives it is Moses who is most closely associated with the writing of the material contained in the Pentateuch (Ex 17:14; 20:1; cf. also Jos 8:31–32). It appears certain that Jesus and the writers of the NT believed that Moses was the author of the Pentateuch (e.g., Jn 5:46).

4. Purpose

Since the purpose of the book of Genesis is intricately bound up with the purpose of the Pentateuch, we shall address briefly the question of the overall purpose of the Pentateuch. The task of discovering the purpose of a work that is so large and diverse is best achieved by means of compositional analysis, which basically describes the method and techniques used by an author.

The final shaping of the canonical Pentateuch involved the sorting and placement of material consisting of at least four distinct literary types: narrative, poetry, law, and genealogy. The genealogical texts play an important role in the early sections of the Pentateuch, especially in the book of Genesis, but do not lead to fruitful conclusions about the shape or structure of the Pentateuch as a whole. A similar verdict can be drawn from a consideration of the large legal collections within the Pentateuch. The importance of such collections is beyond dispute, but they do not appear to be the means by which the whole of the Pentateuch has been shaped.

A close study of the author's use of narrative and poetic texts, however, sheds considerable light on the final shape of the work. The technique of using a poetic speech and a short epilogue to conclude a narrative is well known in biblical literature and occurs frequently within recognizable segments of the Pentateuch itself. The Creation account in Ge 1 and 2 concludes with the short poetic discourse of Adam (2:23) followed by an epilogue (v.24). The account of the Fall in ch. 3 concludes with a poetic discourse (vv.14–19) and an epilogue (vv.20–24). The account of Cain in ch. 4 concludes with a poetic discourse (vv.23–24) and an epilogue (vv.25–26).

That this same pattern can be found throughout Genesis suggests that it was an important part of the compositional technique of the author. Most notable is the occurrence of this pattern in the Joseph story (chs. 37–48), which concludes with the poetic discourse of Jacob's blessing of Ephraim and Manasseh (48:15–16, 20). More importantly, however, the poetic speech–short epilogue pattern recurs at a much higher level within the entire Pentateuch, suggesting that the technique was extended as part of the structure embracing the whole of the five-volume work.

Another literary seam in the Pentateuch can be expressed by the term *narrative typology*. One cannot read the Pentateuch without recognizing definite similarities among narratives (e.g., Ge 12:10–20; 20:1–18; and 26:1–11). It is even possible that the sojourn of Abraham in Egypt and later in Gerar (both because of a famine), and Isaac's sojourn in Gerar (also because of a famine), foreshadow Ge 41–Ex 12, Israel's sojourn in Egypt that came about as a result of the famine recorded in the Joseph story. What the author wants to show is that the events of the past are pointers to those in the future.

5. Literary Form

Except for scattered poetic sections in Genesis, its overall literary form is historical narrative, which is the re-presentation of past events for the purpose of instruction. Two dimensions are always at work in shaping such narratives: the course of the historical event itself and the viewpoint of the author who recounts the events. Thus we must not only look at the course of the event in its historical setting, but we must also look for the purpose and intention of the author in recounting the event.

No historical narrative is a complete account of all that occurred in a given event or series of events. The author must select those events that most effectively relate not only what happened but also the meaning and significance of what happened.

A close study of Ge 1:1–2:4a shows that the author made a careful and purposeful selection in the composition of the Creation account. Rather than give details about the creation of the angels, stars, and galaxies, the author has chosen to concentrate on the creation and preparation of the land. In fact, he has only three specific subjects in his account of Creation: God, man and woman, and the land. Although the creation of the sun and moon is given considerable attention, neither of these bodies is mentioned in its own right but only as it relates to the affairs of humans on earth (1:14–15). What, then, does Ge 1:1–2:4a tell us about the land? It tells us that God is its owner. He created and prepared the land, and he can give it to whomever he chooses (Jer 27:5).

Another interrelationship between structure and selection that Ge 1:1–2:4a shows is in the view of God. He is the Creator of the universe. Because Israel came to know God in a close and personal way, a certain theological pressure existed that tended to localize and nationalize God as the God of Israel alone (Mic 3:11). Over against this lesser view of God stands the message of Ge 1 with its clear introduction to the God who created the universe and who has blessed all humanity. From the point of view of the author of the Pentateuch, the Creator of the universe has a plan of blessing for all people. This is the theological foundation of all subsequent missionary statements in the Bible.

Finally, Ge 1:1–2:4a serves as a backdrop for the central theme of the Pentateuch. The most prominent event and the most far-reaching theme in the Pentateuch is the covenant between God and Israel established at Mount Sinai. That covenant relates directly back to God's initial desire to bless the human race. About that theme we can say three things: (1) The covenant at Sinai was God's plan to restore his blessing to the human race *through the descendants of Abraham* (Ge 12:1–3; Ex 2:24). (2) However, the covenant at Sinai failed to restore that blessing because Israel failed to trust God and obey his will. (3) But the author goes on to demonstrate that God's promise to restore the blessing will ultimately succeed because God himself promised to give Israel, at some future date, a heart that would trust and obey him (Dt 30:1–10). In other words, the entire outlook of the Pentateuch is "eschatological," for it looks to the future as the time when God's faithful promise (blessing) would be fulfilled.

To summarize, therefore, Ge 1:1–2:4a: the author of the Pentateuch intends his Creation account to relate to his readers that God, the Creator of the universe, has prepared the land as a home for his special creature, the human race, and that he has a plan of blessing for all of his creatures.

EXPOSITION

I. Introduction to the Patriarchs and the Sinai Covenant (1:1–11:26)

Chapters 1–11 introduce both the book of Genesis and the Pentateuch. They set the stage for the narratives of the patriarchs (Ge 12–50) as well as provide the appropriate background for understanding the central topic of the Pentateuch: the Sinai covenant (Ex 1–Dt 34).

A. The Land and the Blessing (1:1–2:24)

1. The God of creation (1:1)

1 The Creator is identified as "God" (Heb. *Elohim*; GK 466), the God of the Fathers and of the covenant at Sinai. The proper context for understanding 1:1 is the whole of the book of Genesis and the Pentateuch. By identifying God as the Creator, a crucial distinction is introduced between the God of the Fathers and the gods of the nations (i.e., idols). This verse also explains the origin of all that exists in the universe, affirming that

God alone is eternal and that all else owes its origin and existence to him. The term "beginning" marks a starting point of a specific duration (cf. Dt 11:12), namely, the beginning of the story of God and his people.

2. Preparation of the land (1:2–2:3)

a. First day (1:2–5)

2a Verse 2 describes the condition of the land just before God prepared it for the human race. The immediate context suggests that the land was "formless [GK 9332] and empty [GK 983]" because "darkness" was over the land, and it was covered with water. It was in its "not-yet" state, i.e., not yet inhabitable for humankind (cf. Isa 45:18). Thus the remainder of the account portrays God's preparing the land for man and woman. When Israel disobeyed God, the land became again "uninhabitable" (GK 9332), and the people were sent into exile: "I looked at the earth, and it was formless [GK 9332] and empty [GK 983] and at the heavens and their light was gone.... the fruitful land was a desert" (Jer 4:23–26). In other words, the *land* after the Exile was depicted in the same state as it was before God's gracious preparation of the land in Creation. The land lies empty, dark, and barren, awaiting God's call to light and life.

2b The second part of v.2 describes the work of God, or the Spirit of God, in the initial stages of Creation, hovering over the "not-yet" world like an eagle "hovering" (cf. Dt 32:11) over its young with great concern. There is an interesting parallel between the Creation account (Ge 1) and the account of the construction of the tabernacle in Exodus. In both the work of God (Ge 2:2; Ex 31:5) is to be accomplished by the "Spirit of God." As God did his "work" of creation by means of the "Spirit of God," so Israel was to do their "work" by means of the "Spirit of God."

3–5 Verse 3 has often been taken to mean that God created light before he had created the sun, since not until v.16 does the narrative speak of God making the sun. But the sun, moon, and stars are all to be included in the usual meaning of the phrase "heavens and the earth," and thus according to the present account these celestial bodies were all created in v.1. Verse 3 describes the appearance of the sun through the darkness (cf. 44:3; Ex 10:23;

Ne 8:3). The division between "the day" and "the night" leaves little room for an interpretation of the "light" in v.3 as other than that of the sun.

The frequent repetition of "And God saw" (vv.4, 10, 12, et. al.) describes the "seeing" activity of God. This is obviously an element that the author wishes to emphasize about God. The first name given to God within the book is that of Hagar's: "El Roi" (the "God who sees," 16:13; cf. 22:1–19, where the verb "to see" is rightfully translated in its secondary sense of "to provide"). Other significant places where the author records God seeing are 6:5; 11:5; 18:21; these verses, however, record a tragic reversal of Ge 1, where God sees what is good.

The "good" (GK 3202) is that which is *beneficial* for the human race. On the second day (vv.6–8) the narrative does not say that "God saw that it was good," for on that day nothing was created or made that was directly "good" or beneficial for humankind. The heavens were made and the waters divided, but the land where people were to dwell remained hidden under the "deep." Only on the third day, when the sea was parted and the dry land appeared, does the word "good" (GK 3202) again appear (v.10). Throughout ch. 1 God is depicted as the one who both knows what is "good" for the human race and is intent on providing the good for them. Thus the author prepares the reader for the tragedy of ch. 3, where the rebellious attempt by man and woman to gain the knowledge of "good and evil" for themselves is seen not only as sin but also as folly.

b. Second day (1:6–8)

6–8 The sense of the account of the second day is largely determined by one's understanding of the term "expanse" (GK 8385). Does it reflect a cosmological perspective or an immediate, everyday experience (e.g., the "clouds" that hold the rain)? The text assigns it the meaning "to separate water from water" and calls it the "sky" (GK 9028), a term that refers not only to the place of the sun, moon, and stars (v.14) but also to where the birds fly (v.20). Is there a single word or idea that would accommodate such uses of the term "expanse"? The word "sky" appears to cover this sense well. The "waters above" the sky is likely a reference to the clouds (cf. 7:11–12; 2Ki 7:2; Pss 104:3; 147:8; 148:4).

c. Third day (1:9–13)

9–13 There are two distinct acts of God on the third day: the preparation of the dry land and the seas, and the furnishing of the dry land with vegetation. Unlike the work of the second day, both acts are called "good," doubtless because they are for the benefit of humankind. Both acts relate to the preparation of the land (see comment on vv. 3–5), a central concern of the author (cf. 12:7; 13:15; 15:18; 26:4). Water is an obstacle standing in the way of inhabiting the dry land; it must be removed before humans can enjoy God's gift of the land (cf. the Flood, chs. 6–9, and the parting of the "Red Sea," Ex 14–15).

In his second act on the third day, God furnished the land with bushes and fruit trees. If in fact the author intended a connection to be drawn between God's furnishing the land with fruit trees in ch. 1 and his furnishing the "garden" with trees "good for food" in ch. 2, the focus of the Creation account, then, is on the part of God's creation that ultimately becomes the location of the Garden of Eden. The selectivity of the Creation account can be seen in the fact that it focuses only on the "seed-bearing plants" and "fruit trees," plants that are designed for human food. No other forms of vegetation are mentioned.

d. Fourth day (1:14–19)

14 The narration of events on the fourth day raises several questions. If the text states that the sun, moon, and stars were created on the fourth day, how could "the heavens and the earth," which would have included the sun, moon, and stars, have been created "in the beginning" (v.1)? Could there have been a "day and night" during the first three days of Creation if the sun had not yet been created? Were there plants and vegetation on the land (created on the third day) before the creation of the sun? A common viewpoint is that though "the heavens and the earth" were created "in the beginning," they were not completed until the fourth day or were even possibly obscured by the waters until the fourth day.

There is another way to look at this text that provides a coherent reading of 1:1 and 1:14–18. First, if "the heavens and the earth" means "universe" or "cosmos," as is most probable, then (as already suggested) the whole of the universe—including the sun, moon, and stars—was created "in the beginning" and not on the fourth day.

The second step concerns the syntax of v.14. Verse 6 suggests that when God said, "Let there be an expanse," he was in fact creating an expanse where there was none previously ("creation out of nothing"). So clearly the author intended to say that God created the expanse on the second day. In v.14, however, God does not say, "Let there be lights ... to separate," as if there were no lights before this command and afterward the lights were created. Rather the Hebrew text reads, "And God said, 'Let the lights in the expanse of the sky separate.'" In other words, God's command assumes that the lights were in existence and that in response to his command they were given a purpose, namely, "to separate the day from the night" and "to mark seasons and days and years."

15–19 A third observation comes from the structure of vv.15–16. At the end of v.15, the author recounts, "and it was so." This expression marks the end of the author's "report" and the beginning of his "comment." Thus v.16 is not an account of the creation of the sun, moon, and stars on the fourth day but a remark that draws out the significance of what has previously been recounted: "So God [and not anyone else] made the lights and put them into the sky" (pers. tr.). Behind this narrative is a concern on the part of the author to emphasize that God alone created the lights of the heavens, and thus no one else (and certainly no other god) is to be given the glory and honor due only to him.

e. Fifth day (1:20–23)

20–23 The creation of living creatures is divided into two days. On the fifth day God created the sea and sky creatures. On the sixth day (vv.24–28) he created the land creatures—including man and woman. The word for "created" (GK 1343) is used six times in the Creation account (1:1, 21, 27; 2:3). Elsewhere the word "to make" (GK 6913) is used to describe God's actions. Why is "created" (GK 1343) used with reference to the "great creatures of the sea" (v.21)? One suggestion is that here we have the beginning of a new stage in Creation, namely, of "living beings" (cf. vv.1, 2, 26). The orderliness of the account is evident, as the author shows the

creation of all living creatures in three distinct groups: on the fifth day, sea creatures and sky creatures, and on the sixth day, land creatures.

For the first time the notion of "blessing" (GK 1385) appears. The blessing of the creatures of the sea and sky is identical with the blessing of the human race, with the exception of the notion of "dominion," given only to man and woman. As soon as "living beings" are created, the notion of "blessing" is appropriate because the blessing relates to the giving of life.

f. Sixth day (1:24–31)

24–25 The account of the creation of the land creatures on the sixth day distinguishes two types: the "living creatures" that dwell on the land and humanity. In turn, the former are divided into three groups: "livestock," "creatures that move along the ground," and "wild animals" (v.24). Humanity is distinguished as "male" and "female" (v.27).

Once again the author begins with the divine command—"And God said"—and then follows with a comment—"God made." Verse 25 adds the important clarification that although vegetation was produced from the land, the living creatures were made by the Lord God himself (cf. ch. 2).

26–27 The beginning of the creation of the human race is marked by the usual "And God said." However, God's command that follows is not an impersonal (third person) "Let there be ... " but rather the more personal (first person) "Let us make." Second, whereas throughout the previous account the making of each creature is described as "according to its kind," in the account of the creation of humankind it is specified that the man and the woman were made "in our [God's] image," not merely "according to his own kind." Their image is not simply that of the human being; they share a likeness to the Creator. Third, the creation of humankind is specifically noted as a creation of "male and female." Previously gender was not considered to be an important feature of the creation of the other forms of life, but for humanity it takes on importance. Thus the fact that God created "man" as "male and female" is stressed. Fourth, only human beings have been given dominion in God's creation. This dominion is expressly stated to be over all other living creatures: sky, sea, and land. Thus the text portrays humanity as a special creature different from the rest of the creatures but like God, made in the image and likeness of God.

Many attempts have been made to explain the plural forms: "Let *us* make man in *our* image, in *our* likeness": e.g., (1) the plural is a reference to the Trinity; (2) the plural is a reference to God and his heavenly court of angels; (3) the plural is an attempt to avoid the idea of an immediate resemblance of humans to God; (4) the plural is an expression of deliberation on God's part as he sets out to create the human race. The singulars in v.27 ("in his own image" and "in the image of God"; cf. 5:1) rule out explanation 2, since in the immediate context the creation of man and woman is said to be "in *his* image," with no mention of them in the image of the angels. Explanations 3 and 4 are both possible, but neither explanation is specifically supported by the context. Verse 27 states twice that "man" was created in God's image and a third time that man was created "male and female." The same pattern is found in Ge 5:1–2a. The singular "man" is created as a plurality, "male and female." In a similar way the one God ("And God said") created humankind through an expression of his plurality ("Let us make man in our image"). Following this clue the divine plurality expressed in v.26 is seen as an anticipation of the human plurality of the man and woman, thus casting the human relationship between man and woman as a reflection of God's own personal relationship with himself.

28–31 The importance of the "blessing" (GK 1385) cannot be overlooked since it remains a central theme throughout the book of Genesis and the Pentateuch. The living creatures have already been blessed on the fifth day (v.22); thus the blessing here extends to the whole of God's living creatures, including human beings. The blessing itself is primarily posterity. Thus already the fulfillment of the blessing is tied to man's "seed" and the notion of "life"—two themes that will later dominate the narratives of Genesis.

g. Seventh day (2:1–3)

1–3 The seventh day is set apart from the first six because God "sanctified" it. On this day God does not "speak," nor does he "work"

as he had on the previous days. On this day he "blessed" (Gk 3385) and "sanctified" (NIV, "made it holy"; GK 7727), but he did not "work." The reader is left with a somber and repetitive reminder of only one fact: God did not work on the seventh day. While little else is recounted, it is repeated three times, emphasizing God's "rest." If the purpose of pointing to the "likeness" between humans and their Creator was to call on the reader to be more like God (e.g., Lev 11:45), then the seventh day stresses the very thing that they elsewhere are called on to do: "rest" on the seventh day (cf. Ex 20:8–11; cf. Ps 95:11; Heb 3:11).

3. The gift of the land (2:4–24)

a. Creation of man (2:4–7)

4–6 This account begins with a description of the condition of the land before the creation of the first man (cf. 1:2). The focus is on those parts of the land that will be directly affected by the Fall (3:8–24). The narrative points to the fact that before man was created (in v.7), the effects of his rebellion and the Fall had "not yet" been felt on the land. In the subsequent narratives, each part of the description of the land in vv.4–6 is specifically identified as a result of the fall of humankind. The "shrub of the field" and "plant of the field" do not refer to the "vegetation" of ch. 1 but anticipate the "thorns and thistles" and "plants of the field" that come (in 3:18) as a result of the curse. Similarly, when the narrative states that the Lord God had not yet "sent rain on the earth," we can sense the allusion to the Flood narratives (7:4).

The reference to "no man to work the ground" points to the time when the man and the woman are cast from the garden "to work the ground" (3:23). Thus, as an introduction to the account of man's creation, we are told that a land had been prepared for him. In the description of that land, however, we catch a glimmer of the time when humans would become aliens and strangers in a foreign land.

7 At first glance the description of the creation of the first man here is quite different from that of ch. 1. No two descriptions could be more distinct. Though made in God's image, man did not begin as a "heavenly creature"; he was made of the "dust of the ground." This anticipates his destiny in the Fall, when he would again return to the "dust" (3:19). In Creation man arose out of the dust; in the Fall he returned to the dust.

b. Preparation of the garden (2:8–14)

8 An inordinate amount of attention is given to the description of the "garden." We are told that the Lord God planted the garden and "put" man there. Later this is repeated with significant differences. Then, too, the garden was planted "in the east, in Eden." The word "Eden" (GK 6359) appears to be a specific place; it means "delight" and evokes a picture of idyllic delight and rest. "In the east" is striking because elsewhere in Genesis "eastward" is associated with judgment and separation from God (e.g., 3:24; 11:2; 13:11). For example, when the man and woman were expelled from the garden, the cherubim were placed "on the east side" (3:24) of the garden, giving the impression that the garden itself was not in the east. Such an apparent difficulty in the coherence of the passage may account for the fact that in v.8 the garden is not actually called the "garden *of* Eden" but rather the "garden *in* Eden," a designation found only here. Thus the garden was planted in Eden, which apparently was a location larger than the garden itself; and, if "in the east" is taken with reference to Eden itself, the garden was on its eastern side.

9–10 In the garden were beautiful, lush trees, including the elusive "tree of life" and "tree of the knowledge of good and evil," as well as a river with four "headwaters." Care is given to locate the rivers and to describe the lands through which they flowed. The lands were rich in gold and precious jewels, and their location was closely aligned with the land later promised to Abraham and his descendants. Later on associations were made between the Garden of Eden and the land promised to the fathers (cf. Isa 51:3; Eze 36:35; Joel 2:3).

11–14 The location of the Garden of/in Eden has long been a topic of debate. Two rivers mentioned can be identified with certainty, the Euphrates and the Tigris. It is difficult to identify the other two. Since the "land of Cush" is identified in the Bible as Ethiopia, the "Gihon" is most likely the river that passes through Ethiopia, perhaps the "river of Egypt." "Havilah" cannot be identified.

Most attention in the narrative is given to the "Pishon," but there is little certainty about its identification and location. On the other hand, the narrative merely states that the River Euphrates is the fourth river. The mention of the Euphrates and Tigris rivers can be linked to the identification of the Garden of Eden and the Promised Land. It can hardly be a coincidence that these rivers, along with the "River of Egypt," again play a role in marking boundaries of the land promised to Abraham (15:18).

c. Man's place in the garden (2:15–24)

15–24 The author had already noted that God "put" (GK 8492) man into the garden (v.8b). Now he gives the purpose for this. Two important points are in danger of being obscured by the English translations. The first is the change from the Hebrew word for "put" to a term that the author elsewhere has reserved for God's "rest" or "safety" (GK 5663), a safety that he gives to people in the land (e.g., Ge 19:16; Dt 3:20; 12:10; 25:19), and the "dedication" of something in the presence of the Lord (Ex 16:33–34; Lev 16:23; Nu 17:4; Dt 26:4, 10). Both senses appear to lie behind the word here. Man was "put" into the garden where he could "rest" and be "safe," and he was "put" into the garden "in God's presence" where he could have fellowship with God (3:8).

A second point is the specific purpose for which God put man in the garden. Most translations have "to work it and take care of it." Although that translation is as early as the LXX (2d cent. B.C.), there are serious objections to it. For one, the suffixed pronoun in the Hebrew text rendered "it" in English is feminine, whereas the noun "garden" is masculine. Only by changing the pronoun to a masculine singular, as the LXX has done, can it have the sense of the EVs, namely "to work" and "to keep." Moreover, later in this same narrative (3:23) "to work the ground" is said to be a result of the Fall, and the narrative suggests that the author had intended such a punishment to be seen as an ironic reversal of the man's original purpose. If such was the case, then "working" and "keeping" the garden would not provide a contrast to "working the ground."

In light of these objections, a more suitable translation would be "to worship and to obey." Man is put in the garden to worship God and to obey him. His life in the garden was to be characterized by worship and obedience; he was a priest, not merely a worker and keeper of the garden. Such a reading not only answers the objections raised against the traditional English translation, it also suits the larger ideas of the narrative. Throughout ch. 2 the author has consistently and consciously developed the idea of man's "likeness" to God along the same lines as the major themes of the Pentateuch as a whole, namely, the theme of worship and Sabbath rest.

A further confirmation is the fact that in v.16 we read for the first time that "God commanded" (GK 7422) the man whom he had created. Enjoyment of God's good land is contingent on "keeping" God's commandments (cf. Dt 30:16). The inference is that God alone knows what is good for the man and what is not good for him. To enjoy the "good" man must trust God and obey him. If he disobeys, he will have to decide for himself what is good and what is not good. To people today such a prospect may seem desirable, but it is the worst fate that could have befallen the human race; for only God knows what is good for them.

Having put this in general terms in vv.16–17, the author turns in the remainder of the chapter to set forth a specific example of God's knowledge of the "good"—the creation of the woman. When he sees man alone, God says, "It is not good for the man to be alone." At the close of ch. 2, the author puts the final touch on his account of what it means for man to be "in God's image and likeness." In the first chapter the author intimated that the creation of the human race in the "image of God" somehow entailed being male and female (v.27). In the narrative of the creation of the woman in ch. 2, the author returns to develop this theme by showing that man's creation "in God's image" also entails a "partnership" (NIV, "a suitable helper [GK 6469]") with his wife. The "likeness" that the man and the woman share with God in ch. 1 finds an analogy in the "likeness" between the man and his wife in ch. 2.

For the first time since the account of the creation of the man and the woman in ch. 1, there is divine deliberation. The plural "Let us make" is replaced by the singular "I will make," perhaps because only the woman is being created. In ch. 1 the divine plurality found its analogy in the creation of "male and female," whereas here the divine singular appears to be a curious reflection of man's being

alone. The divine intention for the woman is that she be a "partner." The point is that there is no helper to correspond to man. A special act of creation of the woman is necessary. Man needs a helper to care for the garden and to provide support in a general sense. But in light of the importance of the blessing in 1:28, most likely the "help" envisioned is in the bearing of children. Furthermore, the woman's judgment relates specifically to her role in bearing children (3:16).

Just as at other crucial points when a new relationship is initiated (e.g., 15:12; 28:11), the recipient of God's provision sleeps while God acts. The purpose of the sleep is not merely anesthetic but portrays a sense of passivity and acceptance of the divine provision (cf. Ps 127:2). A homiletic midrash says that "just as the rib is found at the side of the man and is attached to him, even so the good wife, the rib of her husband, stands at his side to be his helper-counterpart, and her soul is bound up with his." The man's jubilant response— "bone of my bones and flesh of my flesh"— goes beyond the narrative account in vv.21–22, where only "rib" is mentioned. "One of the ribs" anticipates "bone of my bones." Moreover, the mention of the closing of the "flesh" anticipates "flesh of my flesh," and "the rib and the flesh" show the woman to be in substance the same as the man.

Clearly the naming of the animals is part of the story of the creation of the woman, for in the conclusion of v.20 the author remarks, "But for Adam, no suitable helper was found." The author saw in man's naming the animals his search for a suitable partner. That no suitable partner was found shows that man was *not like* the other creatures. In contrast, his words "bone of my bone and flesh of my flesh" show that he recognized his own likeness in the woman.

B. The Land and the Exile (2:25–3:24)

1. Disobedience (2:25–3:7)

A more-studied attempt to treat the problem of evil and temptation to sin cannot be found in all the Scriptures.

a. The transition (2:25)

25 Verse 25 clearly links the account of the land and the blessing (1:1–2:24) with that of the Fall (2:25–3:24). The reference to the "two of them" (NIV, "both") looks back to

the previous narrative, while their description as "naked, and . . . no shame" anticipates the central problem that follows.

Two different but related words are used to describe the "nakedness" of the man and his wife. The choice of *arom* ("naked"; GK 6873) at the beginning of the narrative is likely motivated by the alliteration between *arom* and *arum* ("crafty," 3:1; GK 6874). This provides an immediate connecting link with the previous narrative and a presage to the events and outcome of the subsequent story. It also gives an immediate clue to the potential relationship between the serpent's "cunning" and the innocence implied in the "nakedness" of the couple.

Second, there is a difference in meaning between *arom* ("naked"; GK 6873) in 2:25 and *erom* ("naked"; GK 6567) in 3:7. The latter is used in Dt 28:48 to depict Israel's exiles who have been punished for their failure to trust and obey God's word (cf. Eze 16:39; 23:29). In distinguishing the first state of human nakedness from the second, the author introduces a subtle yet perceptible clue to the story's meaning. The effect of the Fall was not simply that the man and the woman came to know they were "naked" but that they were "naked" in the sense of being "under God's judgment."

b. The tempter (3:1)

1 The author discloses an important clue about the snake: he was more "crafty" (GK 6874) than any of the creatures. This word is not primarily a negative term but suggests wisdom and adroitness. This description suggests a relationship between the Fall and humankind's quest for wisdom. Man's disobedience is not so much an act of great wickedness or a great transgression as much as it is an act of great folly. He had all the "good" he would have needed, but he wanted more—he wanted to be like God.

The forbidden tree is the tree of the knowledge of "good and evil." When the woman and the man took of the tree and ate, it was because she "saw that the tree was desirable for gaining wisdom" (v.6). Thus even the serpent is represented as a paragon of wisdom, an archetypical wise man. However, the serpent and his wisdom lead ultimately to the curse (v.14). It should not be overlooked that the serpent is said to be one of the "wild animals" that God had made (cf. 1:25; 2:19). It was not a supernatural being.

c. The temptation (3:2–7)

2–7 The story of the temptation is told with subtle simplicity. The snake speaks only twice, but that is enough to offset the balance of trust and obedience between the man and the woman and their Creator. The centerpiece of the story is the question of the knowledge of the "good and evil." The snake implied that God was keeping this knowledge *from* the man and the woman, while the sense of the narratives in the first two chapters has been that God was keeping this knowledge *for* the man and the woman (e.g., 1:4, 10, 12, et al.). In other words, the snake's statements are a direct challenge to the central theme that God will provide the "good" for the human race if they will only trust and obey him.

The woman's thoughts in the last moments before the Fall were that she "saw that the . . . tree was good." Up until now the expression has only been used of God. Thus the temptation is not presented as a general rebellion from God's authority but rather a quest for wisdom and "the good" (GK 3202) apart from God's provision. How quickly the transgression comes once the decision has been made! The thrust of the story, with all its simplicity, lies in its tragic and ironic depiction of the search for wisdom. Ironically, that which the snake promised did, in fact, come about: the man and the woman became "like God" as soon as they ate of the fruit. The irony, however, lies in the fact that they were already "like God" because they had been created in his image (1:26).

The possibility that they would know only the "evil" and not the "good" is not raised in the narrative prior to their eating the fruit. Yet when they ate of the fruit and their eyes were opened, it was not the "good" that they saw and enjoyed. Their new knowledge was that of their own nakedness. Their knowledge of "good and evil" that was to make them "like God" resulted in the knowledge that they were no longer even like each other: they were ashamed of their nakedness, and they sewed leaves together to hide their differences from each other. They sought wisdom, but found only vanity and toil.

2. Judgment (3:8–20)

a. The scene (3:8)

8 The judgment scene opens with the "sound" (GK 7754) of the Lord's coming, a common form of expression for the Lord's call to obedience (cf. Dt 5:25; 8:20; 13:18; et al.). Appropriately the scene of the curse opens with a subtle but painful reminder of the single requirement for obtaining God's blessing.

The coming of the Lord at the mountain of Sinai is foreshadowed here. There too the people "heard the sound of the LORD our God." In both instances fear prevailed. In the present instance, Adam and his wife fled at the first sound of the Lord in the garden. They fled to the trees. Trees play a central role in depicting humanity's changing relationship with God. In chs. 1–2 fruit trees symbolize God's bountiful provision. In ch. 3 they become the ground for inciting the man and the woman to rebellion and the place where they seek to hide from God. Finally, when the man and the woman are cast out of the garden, their way is barred from "the way to the tree of life" (v.24; cf. Dt 21:22–23; Gal 3:13).

b. The trial (3:9–13)

9–13 Before meting out the judgment, God's only words to the rebellious pair come as questions (cf. 4:9–10; 18:21). Skillfully, by the repetition of "naked," the author allows the man to be convicted with his own words. Then, to show that alienation between the man and the woman as a result of their sin went far beyond the shame that each felt in the presence of the other, the man cast blame on the woman and, obliquely, on God. The man's words are an ironic reminder of God's original intention in 2:18. As a measure of the extent of man's fall, he now sees God's good gift as the source of his trouble.

c. The verdict (3:14–20)

Although much can be said about the curse of the snake, the woman, and the man, very little is written. We get the impression that this is not their story but the story of humankind. With great skill the author presents these three participants as the "heads" of their race. The snake, on the one hand, and the man and the woman, on the other, are as two great nations embarking on a great struggle, a struggle that will find its conclusion only by an act of some distant "seed" or "offspring."

14–15 Whereas once the snake was "crafty" (*arum*, v.1; GK 6874), now he was "cursed" (*arur*; GK 826). His "curse" distinguished him "above all the livestock and all the wild animals"—he must "crawl on [his] belly and ... eat dust all the days of [his] life." This curse does not necessarily suggest that previously the snake had walked as the other land animals. The point is rather that for the rest of his life, when the snake crawls on his belly, he will "eat dust," an expression of "total defeat" (cf. Isa 65:25; Mic 7:17).

As representatives, the fates of the snake and the woman embody the fates of their seed. At first in v.15 the "enmity" (GK 368) is said to be between the snake and the woman and between the "seed" (NIV, "offspring"; GK 2446) of the snake and the "seed" of the woman. The second half of v.15, however, says that the "seed" of the woman ("he") will crush the head of the snake ("your head"). The woman's "seed" is certainly intended to be understood as a group (or individual) that lies the same temporal distance from the woman as the "seed" of the snake does from the snake itself. Yet in this verse it is the "seed" of the woman who crushes the head of the snake himself. That is, though the "enmity" may lie between the two "seeds," the goal of the final crushing blow is not the "seed" of the snake but rather the snake itself; *his* head will be crushed. In other words, it appears that the author seems intent on treating the snake and his "seed" together, as one. When that "seed" is crushed, the head of the snake is crushed. More is at stake in this brief passage than the reader is at first aware of. No attempt is made to answer the question of the snake's role in the temptation over against that of a higher being—Satan. Later biblical writers, however, certainly saw Satan behind the deed of the snake (cf. Ro 16:20; Rev 12:9).

Verse 15 contains a puzzling yet important ambiguity: Who is the "seed" of woman? The purpose of this verse has not been to answer that question but rather to raise it. The remainder of the book is the author's answer.

16 The judgment against the woman relates first to her sons and then to her husband. She will bear sons (children) in increased pain or toil. Her "desire" will be for her husband, and he will "rule over" her. The sense of this judgment within the larger context of the book lies in the role of the woman that is portrayed in chs. 1 and 2. The woman and her husband were to have enjoyed the blessing of children (1:28) and the harmonious partnership of marriage (2:18, 21–25). The judgment relates precisely to these two points. What the woman once was to do as a blessing—be a marriage partner and have children—had become tainted by the curse. In those moments of life's greatest blessing—marriage and children—the woman would sense most clearly the painful consequences of her rebellion from God.

We should not overlook the relationship between the promise of v.15 and the words to the woman in v.16. In that promise the final victory was to be through the "seed" of the woman. In the beginning, when the man and the woman were created, childbirth was at the center of the blessing that their Creator had bestowed on them (1:28). Now, after the Fall, childbirth is again to be the means through which the snake would be defeated and the blessing restored. In the pain of the birth of every child, there was to be a reminder of the hope that lay in God's promise. Birthpangs are not merely a reminder of the futility of the Fall; they are as well a sign of an impending joy (Ro 8:22–24; cf. Mt 24:8).

17–20 Because of the curse the man could no longer "freely eat" of the "good land" provided by the Creator. Throughout chs. 2–3, humankind's ongoing relationship with the Creator is linked with the theme of "eating." At first God's blessing and provision for man are noted in 2:16. Then it was exactly over the issue of "eating" that the tempter raised doubts about God's ultimate goodness and care for the man and his wife (3:1–3). Finally, the pair's act of disobedience is that "she ate it . . . and he ate it" (3:6). Significantly, then, "eating" is related to the judgment on the man. (On "eating" and the relationship of man to God, see Lev 11 and Dt 14 on clean and unclean food and Lev 23 on eating as participation in the feasts of God.)

The description of the "land" is a reversal of that in ch. 2. The present condition of the land is not the way it was intended to be but is the result of human rebellion (see comment on 2:4–6). This opens the way for the motif of "a new heaven and a new earth" (Rev 21:1; cf. Isa 65:17; Ro 8:22–24). Similarly, v.19 shows the reversal for the man's condition. Before the Fall he was taken from the ground and given the "breath of life" (2:7). Now he must return to the dust he was taken from. Thus the verdict of death had come about (2:17). A further reminder of the effect of the Fall is the connection between the man's name, "Adam" (*adam*, v.20; GK 134), and the "ground" (*adamah*; GK 141) from which he was taken. Adam again named his wife, this time calling her "Eve" (GK 2558) and pointing to her destiny ("the mother of all the living [GK 2645]"), whereas her previous name (cf. 2:23) pointed to her origin ("out of man").

3. Protection (3:21)

21 The mention of the type of clothing that God made—"garments of skin," i.e., tunics—is perhaps intended to recall the state of the man and the woman before the Fall: "naked" and "no shame" (2:25). The author may also be anticipating the notion of sacrifice in the animals slain for the making of the skin garments (cf. Ex 28:42).

4. Exile (3:22–24)

22–23 The verdict of death consisted of being cast out of the garden and barred from the tree of life (Ex 31:14), cut off from the protective presence of the community in the garden (cf. Ge 4:14). Ironically, when the human race, who had been created "like God" (cf. 1:26), sought to "be like God" (vv.5–7), they found themselves after the Fall no longer "with God." Their happiness does not consist of their being "like God" so much as it does their being "with God" (cf. Ps 16:11).

In 2:15 (see comment) the man was put into the garden for "worship" (*leobdah*; GK 6268) and "obedience" (*leshomrah*; GK 9068); but here in v.23, after the Fall, he is cast out of the garden "to work [*laabod*; GK 6268] the ground," and he is "kept" (*lishmor*, NIV, "to guard"; GK 9068) from "the way to the tree of life" (v.24).

24 The depiction of the garden and of the tree of life after the Fall guarded by cherubim anticipates God's plan to restore blessing and life to the human race in the covenant at Sinai and in the law (Ex 25:10–22; cf. Dt 31:24–26).

Only through the covenant can human fellowship with God be restored (Ex 25:22). In the covenant humans return to the state enjoyed in Ge 2:15, as people who serve God, obey his will, and enjoy his blessing. At this point in the narrative, "east" only signifies "outside the garden" (but cf. 11:2; 13:11).

C. Life in Exile (4:1–26)

1. Worship (4:1–8)

1–2 Eve's first words after the Fall raise many questions. Her acknowledging God's help makes it look as though she were hopeful that the promise of a "seed" to crush the head of the serpent (3:15) might find its fulfillment in this son. Her words, however, can also be read in a less positive light as a boast that just as the Lord had created a man, so now she had created a man, expressing her confidence in her own ability to fulfill the promise of 3:15. The latter interpretation is more likely. First, the recurring theme in the narratives of this book is that of human effort in obtaining a blessing that only God can give (cf. ch. 11; 16:1–4). A second consideration is the contrast in Eve's words. At the beginning Eve said, "*I* have brought forth a *man*," whereas at the close of the narrative she acknowledged, "*God* has granted me another *seed*"(v.25). Moreover Eve did not say that Seth was given to replace Cain, but he was to replace Abel, which suggests that she had not placed her hope in Cain but in Abel.

3–4 The narrative of Cain and Abel teaches a lesson on the kind of worship that is pleasing to God—that which springs from a pure heart. How does the narrative teach a lesson about a pure heart? The difference between the two offerings is not explicitly drawn out by the author. Contrary to the popular opinion that Cain's offering was not accepted because it was not a blood sacrifice, it seems clear from the narrative that both offerings, in themselves, were acceptable—they are both described as "offerings" (GK 4966) and not "sacrifices." Furthermore, they were both "firstfruits" offerings; thus Cain's offering of "fruits of the soil" was as appropriate for a farmer as Abel's "firstborn of his flock" was for a shepherd.

5–7 Whatever the cause of God's rejection of Cain's offering, the narrative focuses our attention on Cain's twofold response: (1) anger

against God (v.4b) and (2) anger against Abel (v.8). By stating the problem in this way, the author surrounds his lesson on "pleasing offerings" with a subtle narrative warning: "by their fruit you will recognize them" (Mt 7:20). God pled with Cain to "do what is right" or face the consequences of shedding innocent blood and exile from the land (cf. v.12; cf. Jer 7:5–7).

8 Possibly the present narrative is to be read in light of the legislation of the "cities of refuge." The purpose of the cities was to ensure that "innocent blood will not be shed in your land" (Dt 19:10), which, of course, is the central point of the Cain and Abel narrative (v.10).

The law (Dt 19:11) specifies that a guilty murderer is one who lies in wait for his neighbor, "rises up" (NIV, "assaults") against him, and slays him. Here it states that "while they were in the field, Cain attacked [lit., rose up (against)] Abel and killed him." According to Deuteronomic law, Cain's offense was punishable by death. That God showed mercy on Cain and that later in the story God's mercy was connected with Cain's building a city suggest more than coincidental relationship between the story of Cain and the cities of refuge.

2. Repentance (4:9–15a)

9–12 Again (cf. ch. 3) when the Lord came in judgment, he first asked questions (v.9) and then meted out the punishment (vv.11–12). The picture of Cain's judgment is remarkably similar to the exile Israel was warned of in Dt 28:16–18 (cf. Isa 26:21; ch. 27).

13–14 Both the sense of "bear" (GK 5951) and the Lord's response to Cain in v.15 suggest that his words are not to be understood as a complaint about his punishment but rather as an expression of remorse over the extent of his "iniquity." In v.14 Cain acknowledged that God's punishment (v.12) would result in his own death since he would not have the protection of an established community. Like his parents, Adam and Eve, who were driven out of their home, the penalty of death was to be carried out against Cain by banishment from a protective community.

15a By themselves Cain's words do not necessarily suggest repentance, but the Lord's response implies that Cain's words in v.13 are words of repentance.

3. Protection (4:15b–24)

15b–18 The background of the cities of refuge (Nu 35:9–34) may provide a clue to the sense of the "sign" or "mark" (GK 253) given to Cain. Its purpose was to provide Cain with protection from vengeance. Most English versions state that the "mark" was put "on" Cain, though the passage states that the sign was given "to" or "for" Cain (lit., "and he appointed to Cain a sign"; cf. 21:13, 18; 27:37; 45:7, 9; 46:3 with 21:14; 44:21). Though the sign is not explicitly identified, the narrative continues with an account of Cain's departure to the land of Nod, "east of Eden," where he built a city. In light of the purpose of the later cities of refuge, it may be significant that the "sign narrative" is followed by the "city narrative." Cain's city may have been intended as the "sign" that gave divine protection to him, since the purpose of the "sign" was to provide protection for Cain from anyone who might attempt to avenge Abel's death (cf. Nu 35:12). Even in Lamech's day Cain's city was a place of refuge for the "manslayer" (see comments below). Thus Cain's city may be viewed as a "city of refuge" given to him by God to protect him and his descendants from blood revenge (see Dt 19:11–13). The remainder of the chapter is devoted to the "culture" that developed in the context of the "city" that Cain built.

19–24 The primary components of city life were animal husbandry (Jabal, v.20), arts (Jubal, v.21), craftsmanship (Tubal-Cain, v.22), and, apparently, law (Lamech, vv.23–24). Lamech's words to his two wives are frequently read as an example of a boasting arrogance and rebellion. But in the context of the Mosaic law and the teaching regarding the cities of refuge, Lamech's words appear to be an appeal to a system of legal justice. The Mosaic law provided for the safe refuge of any "manslayer" until a just trial could be held (Nu 35:12). Lamech, by referring to the "avenging of Cain" (cf. v.24), made it known that in his city he too had been "avenged."

To show that he had not shed innocent blood, Lamech appealed to the fact that he killed a man "for wounding" and "for injuring" him. He did not "hate his neighbor, lie in wait for him, rise up against him, and kill him" (cf. Dt 19:11), as Cain had done, but rather based his appeal on a plea of self-defense. Lamech's appeal bears striking resemblances to the principle of lex talionis (Ex 21:25). The force of the principle was to ensure that a given crime was punished only by a just penalty. Thus Lamech killed a man for wounding him, not because he "hated him" (Dt 19:4–6). If Cain, who killed his brother with malice, could be avenged, then Lamech would surely be avenged for a killing in self-defense, that is, for "wounding" him. The point is not that Lamech's sense of justice was correct or even exemplary but that Cain's city and descendants had a system of law and justice representative of an ordered society.

4. Blessing (4:25–26)

25–26 Though Cain's sons have prospered and have become the founders of the new world after the Fall, the focus turns from the line of Cain to the new son born "in place of Abel." In such narratives as these, the author betrays his interest in the "seed" of the woman. A pattern is established that will remain the thematic center of the book. The promised seed will come not through the heir apparent but through the one whom God chooses. Cain takes his place as one of those who were not to become a part of the line of the "seed" (cf. Japheth, 10:2–5; Ham, 10:6–20; Nahor, 11:29; 22:20–24; Ishmael, 17:20; Lot, 19:19–38; Esau, ch. 36). The importance of the line of Seth is underscored by the fact that in his days people already practiced true worship of God.

D. The Story of Noah (5:1–10:32)

A major break is signaled at the beginning of ch. 5 by the new heading: "This is the written account of Adam's line." This section, which concludes at 9:29, is built around a list of ten of the descendants of Adam, concluding with Noah. After the death of Noah is recorded (9:29), a new list of his sons begins, ending with the birth of Abraham (11:26). Several narrative passages, varying greatly in size, are interspersed within these lists of names. The interweaving of narrative and genealogical lists is a characteristic feature of Genesis.

1. Prologue (5:1–3)

1–3 The prologue first redirects the reader's attention back to the course of events in ch. 1, reiterating the "likeness" of God motif. Second, vv.1–3 tie ch. 5 together with 4:25–26 by continuing the pattern of "birth" and "naming." There is a similarity between the picture of the first parents and their sons and that of God and Adam. God's naming of Adam appears here for the first time in Genesis, casting God in the role of a father who names his son. This role of God as a father is heightened even further by the parallels between his creating Adam "in the likeness of God" and Adam's giving birth to a son "in his own likeness, in his own image." Clearly, although Adam is the father of Seth and Seth the father of Enosh, etc., God is the Father of them all. The return to the theme of God's "blessing" (GK 1385) humankind (cf. v.2) recalls a father's care for his children, a recurring theme in Genesis. The picture that emerges is of a loving father ensuring the future well-being of his children through an inherited blessing. God's original plan of blessing, though thwarted by human folly, will be restored through the seed of the woman (3:15), the seed of Abraham (12:3), and the "Lion of the tribe of Judah" (49:8–12; cf. Rev 5:5–13).

2. The sons of Adam (5:4–32)

4–32 The genealogical list in ch. 5 is nearly identical in form to that of 11:10–26, the genealogy of Shem. A comparison of the two shows that the only difference between them is the inclusion of the clause "and then he died" (ch. 5). The reason is because Enoch *did not die.* The death of each patriarch in ch. 5 is underscored to highlight the exceptional case of Enoch. He "walked [GK 2143] with God." The phrase is used of Noah (6:9) and of Abraham and Isaac (17:1; 24:40; 48:15).

In Enoch the pronouncement of death is not the last word. A door is left open for a return to the tree of life. Enoch found that door by "walking with God" and has become a paradigm for all who seek to find life. Significantly, this theme recurs at the opening of ch. 17, where God establishes his covenant with Abraham. "Walking with God" is the way to life, not just a mere "keeping" of a set of laws. This theme is associated with those who could not have had a set of "laws,"

which shows that there is a better way to live than merely a legalistic adherence to the law.

The genealogical list in ch. 5 has been purposefully restructured at its conclusion to accommodate the Flood narrative, which has been inserted into the genealogy between the notations of Noah's age at the time he begat his three sons (5:32) and the total length of his life and his death (9:29). Two points in particular call for attention. First, we are told that Noah will bring comfort from the labor and painful toil of the curse (v.29). Likely the comfort Noah brought was the salvation of humankind in the ark as well as the reinstitution of the sacrifice after the Flood (cf. 8:21). Second, it is then significant that the narrative of the Flood is inserted into the genealogical list just before the final word about Noah's death, where it, in effect, is part of the following table of nations (ch. 10). The same explanation for Enoch's rescue from death ("he walked with God") is made the basis for Noah's rescue from death in the Flood.

By means of a brief genealogical note, the story of Noah's drunkenness is appended to the close of the Flood account (9:18–27). This strikingly different picture of Noah provides a basis for the final word concerning him: "and he died" (v.29). Noah's deed was one of disgrace and shame (he took of the fruit of his orchard and became naked), which parallels that of Adam and Eve (who took of the fruit of the garden and saw that they were naked).

This tablet contains a Babylonian flood account. Now located in the British Museum. Courtesy Howard F. Vos.

3. Epilogue (6:1–4)

1–2 At the conclusion of the list of patriarchs and before the account of the Flood, the author summarizes the state of affairs of Adam's descendants (cf. 10:31–32; 11:27–32; Ex 1:7.) Historically there have been three primary views of vv.1–4. The "sons of God" are (1) angels (the oldest); (2) royalty (also very old); and (3) pious men from the "line of Seth." The first view has not been widely held since it appears to contradict Mt 22:30. The commonly accepted view is that the "sons of God" refer to the godly line of Seth. This assumes that vv.1–4 introduce the account of the Flood and are to be understood as its cause. If, however, vv.1–4 summarize ch. 5, there is little to arouse our suspicion that the events recounted are anything out of the ordinary. This little narrative, therefore, is a reminder that Adam's children had greatly increased in number, had married, and had continued to have children; i.e., a picture of everyday affairs (cf. Mt 24:38–39).

3 The sense of v.3 is clear if read within the context of what precedes and follows. After creating humans as male and female, God "called them man [*adam*; GK 134]" (5:2), which obviously had a wider scope than the personal individual of ch. 4. In the remainder of ch. 5, the focus was on the lives of individual men again. Here in v.3 God speaks a second time, again speaking of "man"(GK 132) as "humankind." Between these two statements of God about humankind is the list of ten great individual men, whose length of life stands in stark contrast to the "one hundred and twenty years" of the life of humankind. The inference is that it was God's Spirit dwelling with these men that gave them their long lives. The sad reality is that such long lives belonged to another age and that they were exceptions rather than the rule. The shorter life marks humankind's fall and separation from the Creator. Thus the author continues to show the ages of the men of the book and notes that generally their ages grow increasingly shorter (cf. 11:10–26). At the close of the Pentateuch we finally reach an individual who is specifically mentioned as dying at the age of 120 years (Dt 34:7).

The 120 years was taken by Luther and others to refer to a time of reprieve granted by God to humankind before sending the Flood. This apparently is an attempt to resolve the discrepancy between the limit of 120 years and the record of 11:10–26. The reprieve interpretation may also reflect the influence of 1Pe 3:20, which many take to refer to the period of 120 years in Ge 6:3.

4 "Nephilim" (GK 5872) elsewhere in the Pentateuch refers to the great men who were in the land of Canaan at the time of the Exodus (Nu 13:32–33). Here "Nephilim" appears to refer to the great men of antiquity. Since the author has just referred to ten such great men (ch. 5), perhaps these were the "men of renown." Numbers 13:33 indicates that there were still survivors of the "Nephilim" in the days of the Exodus, which would appear to conflict with our taking them as the ten great men of ch. 5, unless the word is a generic term that means "great men."

4. The Flood (6:5–9:17)

a. The decree (6:5–12)

5–8 These verses form the introduction proper to the Flood story. The cause for the Flood is tied directly to the earlier account of the fall of humankind (ch. 3). Although humans had obtained the "knowledge of good and evil," it had not been beneficial. They were far better off when they had to trust God for "the good." The grief and pain of human sin were not something that only people felt. God himself was grieved over it. The purpose of v.8 is to say no more than that Noah found favor with God. Verses 9–12 explain why God found him to be an exception.

9–12 The Flood account begins with the description of Noah's being "righteous" (GK 7404). It seems that the main purpose of the story is not to show why God sent a flood but rather why God saved Noah. Noah's "righteousness" is contrasted with the "violence" of "all flesh." The message is quite straightforward. God saved Noah because he "walked with God" and did not "corrupt" God's way (cf. 5:22–24). The picture of Noah that emerges becomes a model of the kind of life that finds grace in the sight of God. It is simple obedience to God's commands and trust in his provision by faith (cf. Heb 11:7).

b. The command to build the ark (6:13–22)

13–15 The list of specifications for the ark is not so much that we might be able to see what the ark looked like but rather that we might appreciate the meticulous care Noah exercised as he obeyed God's will. The size and shape are described only in general terms. The word rendered "ark" here is an Egyptian loan word that means "palace" (not "chest" or "coffin") and is a different word than "ark" in Ex 2:3, 5. The term focuses on the structure as an abode.

The exact nature of the material the ark was made from is unknown. NIV's "cypress wood" rests on the doubtful association of a Latin word and a Hebrew word as well as on the fact that such wood was commonly used for shipbuilding. The exact meaning of the term remains a mystery. This wood was sealed with "pitch," another rare word found only here. For a wooden vessel, the ark was enormous. By modern standards it is comparable to a small cargo ship.

16 The ark was constructed with three stories, or decks, of "rooms" (v.14) or separate compartments; it had an opening for light and a door in its side. Obviously the structure consisted of more features than those enumerated in this brief description. We should not conclude from the brevity of the narrative that Noah and his sons built such a vessel on their own.

c. The command to enter the ark (7:1–5)

1–5 The command to make the ark had been given and followed to its completion (6:22). The next scene opens with the command to enter the ark before the coming rains. The emphasis of the section lies in the special provisions for the "clean animals" to be taken into the ark. The specific mention of the "clean animals" suggests that while in the ark Noah and his family ate only "clean meat" (cf. Lev 7:19–21). As entrance into the tabernacle was possible only with an offering of unblemished animals, so too Noah's entry into the ark is tied to his taking with him "seven pairs" of every clean animal. The sacrificial importance of these "clean animals" is seen in 8:20–21.

d. The floods (7:6–24)

6–24 What is most apparent in the description of the onset of the Flood is the focus on the occupants of the ark. With great detail the procession of those entering the ark passes by the impatient eyes of the reader. Facts like

Noah's age, the month and the day of the beginning of the rain, the source of the waters, the kinds of animals and their number suggest that first and foremost this is a picture of Noah's salvation. It is only at the conclusion of ch. 7, when the ark is resting safely over the highest mountains in the surging flood, that the author casts his glance in the direction of those who did not seek refuge in the ark (vv.21–23). But even then the author's attention on those who did not survive the Flood is motivated by the reason why they perished: "Only Noah was left, and those with him in the ark" (v.23). Thus when it is repeated four times that those who survived the Flood were those who had done "as God had commanded" (7:9, 16; cf. v.5; 6:22), the point is clear. Obedience to the Lord is the way to salvation.

e. The floods abate (8:1–14)

1 While those in the ark may have been safe, they had not yet been saved. The author does not finish his story until Noah and his family are back on dry ground (v.14). But those in the ark had to wait before God sent his deliverance. So the story passes over the time of waiting in the ark and proceeds immediately to the decisive moment when "God remembered Noah and all . . . that were with him in the ark."

2–14 Again it is noticeable how the author has prolonged the picture of God's deliverance. God is depicted at work stopping the flow of the waters and removing the sources of the floods. But it still takes time before Noah can be back on dry land. He still has to wait. With this picture of God at work as background, the author turns his attention to Noah inside the ark and focuses on his patience as he waited on God's deliverance. At the end of forty days, Noah began to look for signs of his impending deliverance. He sent out a raven and a dove, but no signs of dry land appeared. Noah continued to wait. When the sign of the return of the dry lands finally appeared and the dove did not return, Noah had waited exactly one year (cf. 7:6, 11 and 8:13–14). But even then Noah could only open the window to look out of the ark. He still had to wait for God's command before leaving the ark (vv.15–17).

The image that emerges from this portrait of Noah is that of a righteous and faithful *remnant* ("Only Noah was left," 7:23), patiently waiting for God's deliverance (cf. Isa 8:17–18; 40:31; Jas 5:7–11). Henceforth "the Flood" is synonymous with eschatological judgment (Isa 8:7–8), and Noah's deliverance is an image of the salvation of the faithful (Mt 24:37–39).

f. The command to exit the ark (8:15–19)

15–19 Noah left the ark only at God's command. The description, though condensed, closely follows the Creation pattern in Ge 1. The picture is of a return to the work of Creation "in the beginning." Significantly, at this point the author takes up a lengthy account of the *covenant* (8:20–9:17). The restoration of God's Creation was founded on the establishment of a covenant.

There is a striking thematic parallel between the picture of God's calling Noah out of the ark (8:15–20) and the call of Abraham (12:1–7). Both Noah and Abraham represent new beginnings. Both are marked by God's promise of blessing and his gift of the covenant.

g. The altar and the covenant (8:20–9:17)

8:20–9:17 In the account of Noah's altar and covenant, the author continues his close associations with ch. 1. As a result of this altar and offering, the whole of the state of humankind before the Flood is reestablished. The human race is still fallen (9:21), but through an offering on the altar they may yet find God's blessing. It is significant that just as in Ge 1, the focus of the author's interest in "man" after the Flood is his creation in God's image (9:6).

Just as significant as the associations of this passage with the Creation account, however, are the several close associations between Noah's altar and Moses' altar at Mount Sinai following the Exodus (Ex 24:4–18). These similarities between God's "covenant" (GK 1382) with Noah and the covenant at Sinai suggest that God's covenant at Sinai is not a new act but rather a return to God's original promises. The covenant with Noah plays an important role in the restoration of blessing, for it lies midway between God's original blessing of all humankind (1:28) and God's promise to bless "all peoples on the earth" through Abraham (12:1–3).

5. Noah's drunkenness (9:18–29)

18–19 These verses conclude the Flood story and introduce the short episode of Noah's drunkenness. What should not be overlooked in this particular transitional unit is the identification of Canaan as one of the sons of Ham. This is crucial to what follows (cf. vv.22, 25).

20–21 Just as in the Creation God planted a garden for people to enjoy, so now Noah plants an orchard. The outcomes are remarkably similar. Noah ate of the fruit of his orchard and became naked. That is, even after the salvation from the Flood, enjoyment of God's good gifts by the human race could not be sustained. Noah, like Adam, sinned, and the effects were felt in the generations of sons and daughters to follow. As in ch. 3, the effect of Noah's sin is seen in his "nakedness" (cf. 2:25; 3:7).

22–29 Ham looked on his father's nakedness. Shem and Japheth instead covered it without looking on him. All speculation concerning the nature of Ham's sin aside, what the author apparently wants to show is simply the contrast between the deeds of Ham and those of Shem and Japheth. That contrast becomes the basis for the curse and the blessing that follow. The significance of the contrast between the actions of the sons is seen from the author's account of the Fall in ch. 3. In covering their father's nakedness, Shem and Japheth were like Adam and Eve (3:7) and God (3:21), who did not look on human nakedness but covered it (cf. 2:25). Ham did not follow that lead. His actions were more like those of whom God warned later in the Torah, those who "expose their own nakedness" before God and others (cf. Ex 20:26). Since some scholars interpret Ex 20:24–26 as a prohibition of Canaanite forms of worship, there may be an intended link between Ham and the Canaanites in the notion of "nakedness." The sons of Noah belong to two groups of humankind, those who like Adam and Eve hide the shame of their nakedness, and those who like Ham, or rather the Canaanites, have no sense of their shame before God. To the one group, the line of Shem, there will be blessing (v.26); but to the other, the Canaanites (not the Hamites), there can only be curse. These three sons—as later the "seed of Abraham" and the "nations"—

represent two responses to human guilt and disobedience. It is not simply because one is born into a certain family line that he or she is blessed or cursed.

6. The line of Noah (10:1–32)

The author's purpose in giving a list of names at this point can be seen in the statement at 10:32. These names give a panoramic view of the nations as a backdrop for the rest of the book and beyond. There are exactly seventy nations represented in the list, which symbolizes the totality of nations. In other words, "all nations" find their ultimate origins in the three sons of Noah.

Though he is on the verge of narrowing his focus to the "seed of Abraham" and the "sons of Israel," the author first lays a solid foundation for his ultimate purpose in God's choice of Abraham: through his "seed" God's blessing will be restored to "all people on earth" (12:3). It is not without purpose that the author reminds his readers that the total number of Abraham's "seed" at the close of Genesis is also "seventy" (46:27; cf. Ex 1:5). Before Abraham, the nations numbered "seventy." After Abraham, at the close of Genesis, the seed of Abraham numbered "seventy." He who was taken from the nations has reached the number of the nations.

a. The sons of Noah (10:1)

1 Chapter 10 is bracketed at either end with an identification of the list of names as "Noah's sons" and the temporal marker "after the flood." The author was concerned that the list in ch. 10 not be read outside its context. Such conspicuous attention to context is another indication that the author has a plan to unfold and that he did not want the reader to lose sight of it.

b. The sons of Japheth (10:2–5)

2–5 The list begins with those nations that are considered the "islands of the nations" (cf. v.5), i.e., those that make up the geographical horizon of the author, a kind of "third world" over against the nations of Ham

TABLE OF NATIONS

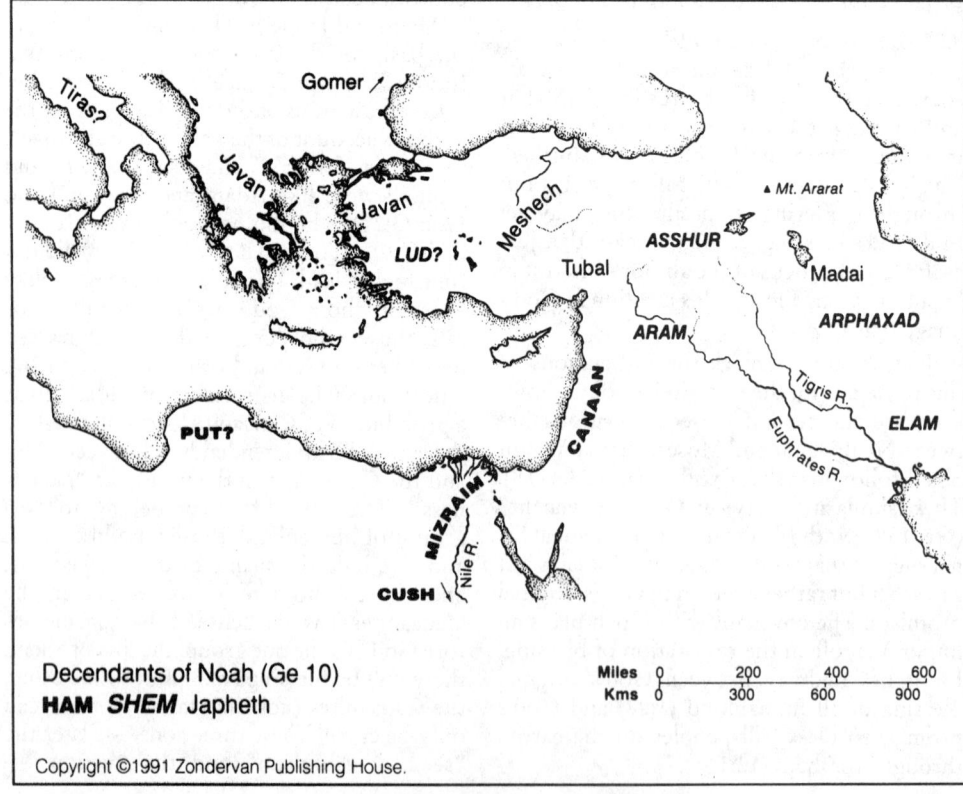

Decendants of Noah (Ge 10)
HAM SHEM Japheth

Miles	0		200		400		600
Kms	0	300		600		900	

(Canaan) and Shem. Later, when the focus is on the establishment of God's universal kingdom, these nations again come into view to show that his plan includes all peoples (Ps 72:8, 10).

A pattern in the author's selection is clearly discernible in the list of the sons of Japheth. Fourteen names are listed in all: seven sons of Japheth, then seven grandsons. The author has omitted the sons of five of the seven sons of Japheth (Magog, Madai, Tubal, Meshech, and Tiras). He lists only the sons of Gomer and Javan. Thus his intention is not to give an exhaustive list but rather a "complete" list, one that for him is obtained in the number "seven."

c. The sons of Ham (10:6–20)

6–12 The list of the sons of Ham begins as the list of the sons of Japheth does, with the simple naming of Ham's four sons. Then, as also in the Japheth list, the grandsons of the first listed (Cush) are given. But before going on to the next son (Mizraim), the great grandsons (sons of Raamah) are listed. The end result is a list of "seven sons"—a complete list. Immediately following are the exploits of Nimrod and his cities, introducing the city of Babylon, the subject of 11:1–9.

The deliberate association of Assyria with Babylon is significant because it takes Assyria out of its natural associations with Shem and identifies it with Babylon. Thus the way is opened for an association and identification of any city with the city of Babylon (Isa 13–14; Rev 17:5). The prophet Micah can already speak of Assyria as the "land of Nimrod" (Mic 5:6).

13–20 The genealogy of Ham continues with a list of the sons of Mizraim, again seven names. This is the last list of the numerical pattern "seven." The remainder of the lists of names appear to be influenced by no particular numerical pattern except that of the total number of "seventy nations" that dominates the list of names as a whole. The focus of the "non-seven" lists (vv.15–29) is more comprehensive because the Canaanites and the sons of Shem play prominent roles in the book of Genesis and the Pentateuch. The exact boundaries of the area of Canaan are singled out since that area lay at the heart of the purpose of the book. This was the land promised to Abraham, though "at that time the Canaanites were in the land" (12:6).

d. The sons of Shem (10:21–31)

21–31 The reference to Shem and Japheth without Ham recalls Noah's blessing of Shem and Japheth in 9:26–27, where there also Canaan is excluded. The mention of the "sons of Eber" anticipates the genealogy that yet lies ahead and results in the birth of Abraham (11:10–26).

The list of descendants of Shem is also highly selective, going to the two sons of Eber and then following the line of the second son, Joktan. Significantly, another genealogy of Shem is repeated after the account of the building of Babylon (11:1–9), and there the line is continued to Abraham through the first son of Eber, Peleg (11:10–26). Thus a dividing line is drawn through the descendants of Shem on either side of the city of Babylon, falling between the two sons of Eber, Peleg and Joktan. One line leads to the building of Babylon and the other to the family of Abraham. A hint to this division is in v.25. Typically, the "earth" refers to the "inhabitants of the land." Thus not only is the land divided in the confusion of languages (11:1), but two great lines of humanity diverge from the midst of the sons of Shem: those who seek to make a name (*shem*; GK 9005) for themselves in the building of the city of Babylon (11:4) and those for whom God will make a name (*shem*, 12:2; GK 9002) in the call of Abraham.

e. Epilogue (10:32)

32 The final verse of ch. 10 again takes up the theme of the division of the nations, providing a context for the narrative of the city of Babylon that follows. What has been described "geographically and linguistically" in ch. 10 is described "theologically" in ch. 11, namely, God's judgment of Babylon and his dispersion of the nations.

E. The City of Babylon (11:1–9)

1–9 The oneness of the people up to this point divides in the two sons of Eber (10:25). One line ends in Babylon, the other in the Promised Land. The first scene opens with a movement "eastward" to the "plain in Shinar." Thus the starting point of the events of the story was a land west of Babylon. Both the man and woman and Cain moved eastward after being cast out from the presence of God (3:24; 4:16). When Lot divided from Abraham, he moved "toward the east" (13:10–12). When a man goes "east," he leaves the land of blessing (Eden and the Promised Land) and goes to a land where his hopes will turn to ruin (Babylon and Sodom).

The word "name" (*shem;* GK 9005) plays a central role here. First, the builders of the city wanted "to make a name [*shem*]" for themselves. Second, the conclusion of the story returns to the "name" (*shem*) of the city, ironically associating it (Babylon/Babel) with the confusion of their language. "Scattered" (GK 5880) is another key word. The purpose of the city was so that its inhabitants would not "be scattered over the face of the whole earth." Ironically, at the conclusion of the story it is the Lord who "scattered" the builders from the city "over the face of the whole earth," a fact repeated twice at the conclusion. The expression "the whole land" is a third key term in the story. The people had left "the whole land [NIV, world]" to build a city in the east. The purpose of the city was to keep them from being scattered throughout "the whole land." But in response the Lord reversed their plan and scattered them over "all the land."

The focus of the author since the beginning chapters of the book of Genesis has been both on God's plan to bless humankind by providing them with that which is "good" and on human failure to trust God and enjoy the "good" God had provided. The characteristic mark of this failure has been the attempt by humans to grasp the "good" on their own. The author has centered his description of God's blessing on the gift of the land (1:28). The good land is the place of blessing. To leave this land and to seek another is to forfeit the blessing of God's good provisions. It is to live "east of Eden."

F. The Line of Shem (11:10–26)

10–26 This list of ten descendants of Shem, like that of Adam in ch. 5, draws the line of

A model of one of the ziggurats or staged towers of ancient Babylonia. On top of this particular tower stood the temple of Marduk, the chief god of Babylon in 600 B.C. These ziggurats were later counterparts to the Tower of Babel. Courtesy Oriental Institute of University of Chicago.

the "faithful" (Noah to Abraham) and by-passes the "unfaithful" (10:26–30). In ch. 5 the list of ten patriarchs from Adam to Noah provided the link between the "offspring" promised to the woman (3:15) and the off-spring of Noah, the survivor of the Flood (7:23). Not only does the list mark the "line of the promise," it also bypasses the line of Cain (4:17–22)—the line of the builders of the city (v.17) and the civilization (vv.20–24) that was destroyed in the Flood.

Verses 10–26 show that God's promise concerning the seed of the woman cannot be thwarted by the confusion and scattering of the nations at Babylon. Though the seed of Noah were scattered at Babylon, God pre-served a line of ten great men from Noah to Abraham.

II. Abraham (11:27–25:11)

A. The Line of Abraham (11:27–32)

27–32 The genealogy that precedes the narra-tive of Abraham provides the necessary background for understanding the events in his life. Thus far the author has followed a pattern of listing ten names between impor-tant individuals, but this short list has only eight names. This raises the question of who the ninth and, more importantly, the tenth names will be. As the narrative unfolds, the ninth and tenth names are shown to be the two sons of Abraham, "Ishmael" (16:15) and "Isaac" (21:3). The genealogical introduc-tion, then, anticipates the birth of Isaac, the tenth name.

Interspersed in the list of names is the brief notice that Terah and his family, includ-ing Abraham and Lot, had left Ur of the Chaldeans and traveled as far as Haran, en route to the land of Canaan. There is no men-tion of the call of God until 12:1, and that ap-pears to be after the death of Terah (v.32b). The initial impression is that while in Haran Abraham was called to leave his homeland—after the death of his father, Terah, and not while in Ur of the Chaldeans. That impres-sion is further sustained by the narrative in 12:4–5, which recounts Abraham's obedient response to the call of God and explicitly states that he "set out from Haran," not men-tioning Ur of the Chaldeans. A second look, however, suggests that the author intended us to understand the narrative differently.

Verses 27–32 show that it was Ur of the Chaldeans, not Haran, that was the place of Abraham's birth. Thus the command given to Abraham to leave the place of his birth (12:1; NIV, "your country") could only have been given at Ur of the Chaldeans. Putting the call of Abraham within the setting of Ur aligns this narrative with themes in the later prophetic literature and connects the call of Abraham (12:1–3) with the dispersion of the city of Babylon (11:1–9), thus making Abra-ham prefigure all those future exiles who, in faith, wait for the return to the Promised Land (cf. Mic 7:18–20).

Marked similarities are evident between the introductions to the Abraham and the Isaac narratives (25:19–26). Abraham's brother, Haran, died "before" his father; Isaac's brother Ishmael died "before his brothers" (25:18b). Abraham took a wife, and she was barren; Isaac took a wife, and she was barren (25:20–21). Both narratives con-tain an element of struggle between brothers. Abraham was accompanied by Lot from birth, and Jacob was accompanied by Esau from birth (25:22–24). In the struggles that ensued, Abraham was "separated" from Lot (13:9, 11, 14) and Jacob was "separated" from Esau (25:23).

B. The Call of Abraham (12:1–9)

1–5 Abraham, like Noah, marks a new begin-ning as well as a return to God's original plan of blessing "all peoples on earth" (cf. 1:28). Notable is the frequent reiteration of God's "blessing" throughout the narratives of Abraham and his descendants (12:1–3; 13:15–16; 15:5, 18; et al.). Abraham is here repre-sented as a new Adam, the seed of Abraham as a second Adam, a new humanity. Those who "bless" (GK 1385) him, God will bless; those who "curse" (GK 826) him, God will curse. The way of *life and blessing*, which was once marked by the "tree of the knowl-edge of good and evil" (2:17) and then by the ark (7:23b), is now marked by identification with Abraham and his seed.

The identity of the seed of Abraham is one of the chief themes of the following narra-tives. At the close of the book (49:8–12), a glimpse of the future seed of Abraham is briefly allowed. This one seed who is to come, to whom the right of kingship belongs, will be the "lion of the tribe of Judah" (cf.

49:9); and "the obedience of the nations is his" (49:10).

6–9 The account of Abraham's entry into the land of Canaan is selective. Only three sites are mentioned: Shechem, a place between Bethel and Ai, and the Negev. Significantly, these are the same three locations visited by Jacob when he returned to Canaan from Haran (chs. 34–35), as well as the same sites occupied in the account of the conquest of the land under Joshua.

C. Abraham in Egypt (12:10–13:4)

12:10–13:4 Verse 10 opens with a notice that a famine forced Abraham to seek refuge in Egypt. The recurring theme of the threat to God's promise in 12:1–3 is first noted in the present story. In nearly every episode that follows, the promise of a "numerous seed," "blessing to all peoples on earth," or the "gift of the land" is placed in jeopardy by the actions of the characters of the narrative. The promise looks as if it will fail. In the face of such a threat, however, God remains faithful to his word and safeguards the promise. God can bring about his promise, despite human failures.

The account of Abraham's sojourn in Egypt parallels in many respects the account of God's deliverance of Israel from Egypt (Ge 41–Ex 12). Both passages have a similar message. The past is not allowed to remain in the past. Its lessons are drawn for the future. That is, Abraham's stay in Egypt prefigures Israel's later stay in Egypt (both initiated by a famine). Behind the pattern stands a faithful, loving God. What he has done with Abraham, he will do for his people today and tomorrow. In light of such parallels we should also understand the close similarity between the accounts of Abraham's sojourns in Egypt (ch. 12) and Gerar (ch. 20) and Isaac's in Gerar (ch. 26). The similarities have long been recognized, though not always appreciated.

D. The Lot Narratives (13:5–19:38)

1. Abraham and Lot (13:5–18)

5–18 The narrative here is governed by the theme of "struggle" and shaped around the "separation" (vv.9, 11, 14) that ensues. At its conclusion stands the second statement of God's promise to Abraham. Just as the first statement of the promise was preceded by

Abraham's separation (10:32; 12:1), so the second statement of the promise is put in the context of Abraham's separation from his closest kin, Lot. Significantly, the final statement of the promise to Abraham comes immediately after he has demonstrated his willingness to be separated from his only son and heir, Isaac (22:15–18).

Abraham's separation from Lot also carries the theme of the promise into jeopardy. Ironically, Abraham is on the verge of giving the Promised Land to Lot, who later (19:37–38) became the father of the Ammonites and the Moabites. These people throughout Israel's subsequent history (Dt 23:3–6; Ezr 9:1) were the primary obstacle to the fulfillment of the promise. Thanks to Abraham the promise seems to teeter on the whim of the father of the Moabites. But Lot "chose" to go "east"; so Abraham remained in the land. Thus God's promise was secure, in spite of Abraham's passivity.

The land Lot chose was "like the garden of the LORD" and "like the land of Egypt," a positive description within the context of Genesis. But there is a subtle foreshadowing of the fatal results of Lot's choice in the geographic marker "toward Zoar." That was where Lot fled for safety from the destruction of Sodom and Gomorrah (19:22). Lot's choice of a land "toward the east" forebodes disaster.

Definite ties connect Lot's separation from Abraham to the separation (10:32) of the nations at Babylon (11:1–9) and the judgment of the nations at Sodom (19:1–29). The ties between ch. 13 and the destruction of Sodom (ch. 19) can be seen in v.10b and vv.12b–13.

The account of the dispersion of the nations closes in 10:32b with a reference to the nations being "spread out [i.e., separated; GK 7233] over the earth after the flood." Then the narrative of the dispersion of Babylon opens with the people of the land traveling "eastward" (11:2). Similarly, Lot traveled "toward the east" when he "parted" (GK 7233) from Abraham (13:11). Following the separation of the nations at Babylon, the narrative resumes with Abraham traveling throughout the land of Canaan, receiving it as a promise, and then building an altar in response to God's promise (12:1–9). So also, after Lot separated to Sodom, Abraham traveled throughout the land of Canaan, received it a second time as a promise, and built an altar in response.

2. Abraham and the nations (14:1–24)

1–11 At first glance the ties between chs. 13 and 14 seem meager. Abruptly the narrative begins in the time frame marked as "In the days of Amraphel" (NIV, "At this time Amraphel"). Just as abruptly the location moves from Hebron (13:18) to an international arena and the wars of four kings. Again, Lot is the link between the two accounts. Immediately following the report of Lot's capture, the narrative returns to Hebron (14:13b). At that point Abraham is brought into the center of the account of the battle with the four kings (vv.14–17). The mention of "Mamre" at v.24 returns us to the scene at the close of ch. 13.

"The LORD" (GK 3378), the God Abraham worshiped at Hebron (13:18), is the "Creator of heaven and earth" (14:22) who delivers the four kings of the east into Abraham's hands. Abraham, who asks nothing and wants nothing from the kings of this world (vv.22–23), is the only one who proves able to dwell peacefully in the land. As 12:3 has forecast, those who join with Abraham (v.13b) will enjoy his blessing (v.24b); but those who separate from him, as Lot had done (13:12), will suffer the same fate as Sodom and Gomorrah (14:11–12).

Shinar has already been identified as Babylon (10:10; 11:2, 9). The author has deliberately put the king of Shinar's name first in the narrative, thus aligning the account with the theme of "Babylon" introduced in chs. 10 (v.10) and 11 (v.2). Elsewhere throughout the chapter Kedorlaomer is always first among the four kings (vv.4, 5, 9, 17).

Although very little information is given about the actual battles other than that the kings of Sodom and Gomorrah were soundly defeated and completely routed, the account is overladen with geographical and political details. What emerges as certain from this feature of the narrative is that the events recounted were global in scope and ended in the disgraceful defeat of the kings of Sodom and Gomorrah.

12 The perspective changes markedly from the war with the four eastern kings to the fate of Lot. The ultimate cause of Lot's unfortunate fate was that "he was living in Sodom," a reminder of the blessing in the land (12:1–3; 13:14–17) and the fate of all those who separate themselves from Abraham.

Lot's fate is the first stage in a lesson that will bring him still further in need of the intercession of Abraham (18:23–32). Twice Abraham intercedes for Lot: here he rescues Lot in the war with Babylon, and later (chs. 18–19) Abraham's intercession (18:23–32; 19:29) effects Lot's deliverance. The picture of Abraham that emerges here is the same as that in 20:7: "He is a prophet, and he will pray for you and you will live."

13–16 The scene returns to Abraham and his three friends at Hebron, strangely unaffected by the events of the previous narrative. In this brief scene Abraham musters a select army, defeats the four kings, and returns Lot with the rest of the captives.

17–20 After his return from battle, Abraham was met by two kings in the "King's Valley." Suddenly Melchizedek appears as if out of nowhere and just as quickly is gone, not to be encountered again or subsequently explained. The insertion of the encounter with Melchizedek into the section dealing with the king of Sodom suggests that it is to be read as the background to the encounter with the king of Sodom. Thus a contrast is established between Abraham's responses to the king of Salem and the king of Sodom. One is positive, the other negative. Lying behind Abraham's responses is the contrast between the offers of the two kings. The king of Salem brings "bread and wine" as a priestly act and acknowledges that it was the "God Most High, Creator of heaven and earth," who delivered the adversaries into Abraham's hand. The king of Sodom offered Abraham the booty of the battle (v.21; see next comment). Abraham's response to Melchizedek is an appropriate recognition of the validity of his offer as well as of his priesthood: Abraham paid a tithe (see Nu 18:21).

21–24 The king of Sodom offered Abraham all the "goods" recovered in the battle. Abraham would have nothing to do with an offer of reward from him. Abraham's reward would come from "the LORD, the Creator of heaven and earth" (cf. 15:1, 14b). Although he rejected the offer from the king of Sodom, Abraham laid claim to rightfully own what his young men had eaten (cf. Dt 20:14b). Abraham also recognized that his three friends had their own rightful share in the spoil. But Abraham flatly refused to take anything from the king of Sodom (cf. Dt 20:17). Abraham is a man of faith.

3. Abraham and the covenant (15:1–21)

1–4 God's address to Abraham is in the elevated style typical of later prophetic literature (vv.1, 4; cf. Jer 34:12). Like the seer Balaam (Nu 24:4, 16), Abraham saw the word of the Lord "in a vision." For the first time it is recorded that Abraham spoke to God. Previously when God spoke to him, Abraham obeyed but did not speak in return. Abraham raised a question of how the promise would be fulfilled. In fact, he raised so many questions that we are reminded of his unwavering faith (v.6).

Abraham's questions provide the backdrop for the central issue of the chapter: God's apparent delay in fulfilling his promises. The issue at stake is the same one faced by Jeremiah. God's people, instead of enjoying the promised blessing, would find themselves about to enter captivity in Babylon. The promise appears to have come to naught (cf. Jer 25:11). But in Jeremiah's warning there is the promise of ultimate blessing. The time of exile has a limit (v.12). Abraham's predicament is like that of later generations of God's people. He too must wait in faith for the fulfillment of the promise, being counted righteous in his faith (v.6), but realizing that the promise was far off to another generation (vv.15–16; cf. Heb 11:13).

What was Abraham afraid of? What "reward" (GK 8510) did God have in mind? Were the military events in ch. 14 still posing a threat to Abraham? Since ch. 15 makes a major break with ch. 14 ("after this"; cf. 22:1; 39:7; 40:1), God's first words to Abraham probably do not relate to the immediate context of ch. 14. Apparently Abraham had begun to fear for the final outcome of God's promise to make his "offspring like the dust of the earth" (13:16; cf. v.2).

The questions Abraham raised betray the fact that such a fear lay behind God's first words of comfort. Not only do his questions betray the fear that lay within him, but also the Lord's continued assurances point in the same direction (v.4). From all appearances around him, Abraham has little to give him

hope that God will remain faithful to his word. It is significant that the next words Abraham spoke to the Lord (17:18) appear to reveal doubt. On the other hand, when he is silent, his actions always exhibit faith.

5 The appeal to the number of the stars of "the heavens" recalls Abraham's own words in 14:22, where his hope for reward was based solely on the "Creator of heaven and earth." If the Lord was the Creator of the great multitude of stars, he was able to give Abraham an equal number of descendants (cf. 22:17; 26:4; Ex 32:13; Dt 1:10; 28:62). God's faithfulness in the past was the basis for Abraham's trust in the future.

6 God was about to enter a "covenant" (GK 1382) with Abraham that would be the basis of all God's future dealings with him and his offspring (vv.7–21). Verse 6 sets the record straight: Abraham had believed in the Lord and had been accounted righteous. The "covenant" did not make in him "righteousness" (GK 7407); rather, it was through his "faith" that he was reckoned righteous.

7–16 These verses recount the establishment of a covenant between the Lord and Abram. The opening statement is virtually identical to that of the Sinai covenant (Ex 20:2). "Ur of the Chaldeans" refers to 11:28 and 31, grounding the present covenant in a past act of divine salvation from "Babylon" (cf. Ex 20:2). The coming of God's presence in the awesome fire and darkness of Mount Sinai (Ex 19:18; 20:18; Dt 4:11) appears to be intentionally foreshadowed in Abram's pyrotechnic vision (vv.12, 17). In the Lord's words to Abram, the connection between Abram's covenant and the Sinai covenant is explicitly made by means of the reference to the four hundred years of bondage of Abram's descendants and their subsequent exodus.

17 The act of dividing the animals and walking through the parts was apparently an ancient form of contractual agreement (cf. Jer 34:18). While the meaning of the details may remain a mystery, fortunately the writer of Genesis has explained the custom: "On that day the LORD made a covenant with Abram."

The sudden and solitary image of the birds of prey that Abram must drive away (v.11) give a fleeting glimpse of the impending doom that awaits Abraham's seed but in the same moment points to the protective care of God's promises (cf. Mt 24:28). The imagery of the birds of prey surrounding the carcass is followed by a reference to the darkening of the sun (Ge 15:12; cf. Mt 24:29) and the promise of future redemption (Ge 15:14; cf. Mt 24:30).

18–21 The author again draws the promise of the land back into the narrative by concluding with a description of the geographical boundaries of the covenant land. The borders of the Promised Land appear to coincide with those of the Garden of Eden (cf. 2:10–14).

4. Hagar (16:1–16)

1–6 The mention of Hagar's geographical origin ("Egyptian") links this account to 15:18b–21. Twice we read that Hagar, *the Egyptian,* "despised" Sarai (cf. 12:3). As a consequence, Hagar was forced into the "desert" (v.7), where she was to stay until she submitted herself again to Sarai. Only then did the Lord offer Hagar a blessing (v.10; cf. 17:2, 20).

To deal with her barrenness, Sarai's plan of offering her maid to Abram to bear him an heir was apparently acceptable within the social custom of the day. Sarai's plan, however, was one more example of the futility of human efforts to achieve God's blessing. Although successful, Sarai's plan does not meet with divine approval (17:15–19; cf. 11:1–9; 12:10–20; 13:1–12; 14:21–24).

7–12 The location shifts to the wilderness, to the "spring that is beside the road to Shur." Hagar was returning to Egypt (see 25:18). The angel of the Lord greets Hagar with a question (cf. comment on 3:9). Then he offers a blessing to the distraught handmaid. The child to be born to her will be named "Ishmael" because the Lord "has heard" (a play on words, since both terms are built on the same Heb. root) her "misery" (GK 6715). The key term throughout the chapter is "misery," which occurs as a noun in v.11b and as a verb in v.6 ("mistreated"; GK 6700) and v.9 ("submit"; GK 6700). Hagar was afflicted by Sarai (v.6); she was told to put herself back under that affliction (v.9); and the Lord heard her affliction (v.11).

The second half of Hagar's "blessing" did not portend well for her son: he would be a "wild donkey of a man." There is a wordplay between "donkey" and "Paran," the later lo-

cation of the tribes of Ishmael. The sense of the last statement in the blessing can perhaps be gained from 21:21, where it is said that Ishmael "was living in the Desert of Paran." Ishmael was to dwell on the outskirts of civilization, i.e., in the wilderness.

13–16 The final section of the narrative consists of Hagar's naming of God and the birth of Ishmael. The two events go together in that the birth of the child was the confirmation of the name given to God in this section: "the God of seeing."

5. Abraham, Sarah, and Ishmael (17:1–27)

1a Abram was eighty-six years old when Ishmael was born (16:16). At the beginning and close of ch. 17, his age is given as ninety-nine. Thus his age functions as a framework.

1b–2 The Lord's first speech to Abram establishes the interpretive boundaries for the rest of the chapter and establishes the fact that the events of the chapter represent the making of a covenant between the Lord and Abram. The substance of the covenant is the promise of abundant descendants.

God is immediately identified as the "Lord" (GK 3378), the God of the covenant at Sinai (Ex 3:15). Within the narrative, however, God identified himself to Abram as "God Almighty." An insight into the faith of Abram is that he worshiped the covenant God, "the Lord," but knew him as "God Almighty" (see Ex 6:3). After identifying himself, the Lord gives a brief synopsis of the covenant, stressing Abram's obligation: "Walk before me and be blameless" and the divine promise: "[I] will greatly increase your numbers." Had not God already "made" a covenant with Abraham in 15:18? Why did he establish a covenant with Abram a second time? The two covenants are, in fact, two distinct aspects of God's covenant with Abraham—one stresses the promise of the land (15:18–21) and the other the abundance of descendants (17:2).

3a The report of Abram's response is also brief: Abram "fell facedown," a sign of deep respect. Comparing Abram's response to the Lord's second speech (v.17), we see that he not only "fell facedown" but also "laughed." When Abram heard that God would greatly increase his descendants, he responded with respect and submission. But when he heard *how* God would carry out his plan, his respect contained a tinge of laughter.

3b–16 The second divine speech is divided into three sections by the clause "and God said." Each section deals respectively with one of the parties of the covenant (the Lord, Abram, and Sarai). The substance of each section is memorialized by a specific sign within that section: the change of Abram's name, the circumcision of all males, and the change of Sarai's name. God's part of the covenant consists of two promises: abundant descendants and eternal faithfulness. The descendants of Abraham who belong to this covenant will owe their existence to God alone. The promise of abundant descendants is memorialized in the change of Abram's name to "Abraham," which is interpreted to mean "father of many nations."

The choice of the word "be fruitful" (GK 7238) in v.6 and "multiply" in v.2 ("increase your numbers"; GK 8049) recalls the blessing of all humankind in 1:28 and its reiteration in 9:1, showing the covenant with Abraham to be the means God uses to channel his blessings to all people.

A new element is added in v.6b: "kings will come forth from you." This anticipates not only Abraham's descendants recorded in Samuel and Kings but, more importantly, provides a link between the general promise of blessing through the seed of Abraham and the subsequent focus of that blessing in the royal house of Judah (Ge 49:8–12; Nu 24:7–9). The notion that the blessing would come from a king is not new (cf. 14:18–19), but the idea that this king would come from the seed of Abraham is.

The focus of vv.7–8 lies in the repetition of the term "everlasting" (GK 6409). The covenant promised is "everlasting" and the possession of the land is "everlasting." The promises in these verses were given before (cf. 13:14–15; 15:18–21); however, here the everlasting nature of promises is in view. Eternality was certainly implied in the "forever" of the land promise (13:15); but when the covenant was granted in ch. 15, there was no mention yet of its being "eternal." Thus as God reiterated his role in the covenant, the focus was centered on his everlasting faithfulness.

Abraham's part in the covenant consisted of his obedience to the covenant. What this involved immediately was that "every male among you shall be circumcised." To keep the covenant was to faithfully practice circumcision; to "break" the covenant was to be "uncircumcised." But the whole of the covenant was not simply the rite of circumcision, for that was to "be the sign of the covenant."

Sarai's part in the covenant was to be the mother of nations, and "kings of peoples will come from her." As with Abraham, her new name—Sarah—was a sign of her part in the covenant. In Hebrew "Sarah" means "princess."

17–18 Abraham's response—"fell facedown" and "laughed" (GK 7464)—is unexpected. Abraham's own words uncover the motivation behind his laughter. In 18:12, when Sarah also responded to God's promise with laughter, her laughter was met with divine disapproval. The absence of such a rebuke here suggests that Abraham's laughter does not so much reflect a lack of faith as it does a limitation of his faith. Abraham's faith must grow if he is to continue to put his trust in God's promise. One clear purpose in Abraham's laughter is that the Hebrew expression "he laughed" foreshadows the name "Isaac."

The irony of Abraham's response is evident. His laughter became a verbal sign marking the ultimate fulfillment of the promise in Isaac. Throughout the remainder of the narratives surrounding the birth of Isaac, a key word within each major section is "laughter." Sarah "laughed" (18:12); Lot's sons-in-law laughed (19:14); all who heard of Sarah's birth to Isaac would "laugh" (21:6); the son of Hagar laughed (21:9b; NIV, "was mocking") at Isaac. Finally, Isaac's own failure to trust in God (26:7) was uncovered when the Philistine king saw him "laughing" (26:8b; NIV, "caressing"). Thus the power of God and the limitations of human faith are embodied in that most ambiguous of human acts, laughter.

19–22 The third divine speech extends the covenant to include Isaac, who is to be born of Sarah, and consequently excludes Ishmael, the son of Hagar. Thus Isaac is here brought to the level of a participant in the original covenant, and the identification of the covenant "offspring" of Abraham is made more specific. The descendants of Abraham who are heirs of the covenant are those through

Sarah, that is, the "offspring" of Isaac, anticipating 26:3b.

Although Ishmael has been excluded from the covenant with Abraham, Ishmael and his descendants are still to live under the blessing of God. In fact, in his blessing of Ishmael, God reiterated both his original blessing of all humanity in 1:28 and his blessing of Abraham in 12:2. Just as the "offspring" of Isaac would form a great nation of twelve tribes (49:1–27), so the "offspring" of Ishmael, under God's blessing, would form a great nation of twelve rulers (cf. 25:13–15).

23 Abraham's final response shows that he obeyed the covenant; he circumcised all the male members of his household "as God told him." Abraham's obedience reflects the injunction given in v.1: "Walk before me and be blameless." "Blameless" (GK 9459) occurs in Genesis only here and in 6:9 (Noah). "Walk before God" occurs more frequently (5:22, 24; 6:9; 17:1; 24:40; 48:15). Thus Abraham and Noah are examples of those who obeyed the covenant and were therefore "blameless" before God.

24–27 The ages of Abraham and Ishmael mark the closure of an *inclusio* (see comment on v.1). The final word at the close restates Abraham's obedient response to the covenant.

6. Three visitors (18:1–33)

a. Abraham's hospitality (18:1–8)

1a The narrative begins in the same way as ch. 17, with the report that "the LORD appeared to Abraham." The importance of this comment should not be overlooked, for it helps clarify who the three men were who visited Abraham and what their mission was. In some (albeit unexplained) way, the three men represented the Lord's "appearing" to Abraham.

The mention of the "great trees of Mamre" reestablishes the location of Abraham during these events (cf. 13:18). Since the identification of "Abraham" within ch. 18 does not occur until v.6 (in v.1 NIV supplies his name but the Heb. has only "to him"), the opening of ch. 18 is closely bound with the end of ch. 17 and the account of the circumcision of Abraham and his household.

The final verse (v.33)—which recounts that after the Lord had finished speaking, "he left"—shows that the whole chapter is to be understood within the context of the Lord's appearance to Abraham (cf. 17:1 and 22; 35:9 and 13).

1b–8 The narrative of the arrival of three men at Abraham's tent is complicated by several uncertainties. First, the relationship between the three men and the appearance of the Lord (v.1a) is not explicit. Second, there appears to be a conscious shift in the verbal forms between v.3 (sing. masc.) and vv.4–9 (pl. masc.). Finally, there is the question of the nature of the relationship between the uncertainties just raised in ch. 18 and their apparent counterparts in ch. 19, where the relationship between the "two angels" (or "messengers," 19:1a; GK 4855) and the Lord ("LORD"; GK 3378) remains unexplained (e.g., the two "men" [19:12] tell Lot they will destroy Sodom [19:13], but the text states that "the LORD rained down burning sulfur on Sodom and Gomorrah" [19:24]). The verbs and pronouns in Lot's greeting are all plural masculine (19:2) and continue to be so until the end of the story, where the same sort of unevenness found in ch. 18 reappears (e.g., 19:17: "as soon as they [pl. masc.] had brought them out, one of them said [sing. masc.]"; or 19:18: "Lot said to them [pl. masc.], ... Your servant ['your' is sing. masc.]"). Also, unlike 18:3b, the Masoretes' vocalization of "my lords" (NIV) in 19:2 reflects an address to persons other than God, whereas when the same persons are addressed in 19:18, the Masoretic form of "my lords" (NIV; GK 123) is again the form used only to address God (see NIV note).

Such irregularities as exist in the narrative are the result of a conscious attempt to stress at one and the same time the theological relevance of the promise of God's *presence* along with his transcendent, sovereign *power.* Thus the final unevenness results from the need to reconcile two equally important views of God.

There are close similarities between the account of Abraham's visit by "three men" and Lot's visit by the "two angels/men" (19:1–2). In ch. 18 Abraham is sitting "at the entrance to his tent," whereas in ch. 19 Lot is "sitting in the gateway of [Sodom]" (v.1). Second, when Abraham "saw" the men, he ran "to meet them" and "bowed low to the ground" and said, "O Lord, if now" (see

NIV note); so also Lot in ch. 19, when he "saw" the angels/men, he got up "to meet them" and "bowed down with his face to the ground" and said, "Behold now, my lords" (NIV, "My lord"). One primary difference between the two accounts is the way the visitors are greeted. Abraham addressed them as "Lord" and appropriately used the singular to address all three men in v.3 (see above). Lot, however, addressed the visitors as "lords" and thus used the plural to address the two angels/men. Abraham, who had just entered the covenant (ch. 17), recognized the Lord when he appeared to him, whereas Lot, who then lived in Sodom, did not recognize the Lord. Abraham knew God, but Lot did not.

The interchange between the singular and plural in v.3 and vv.4ff. appears to be one way to clarify the nature of the divine-human relationship. God makes himself known intimately and concretely to his covenant people through "speaking," "in a vision" (15:1), or through his "angel" (16:7) who speaks for him. He even can "appear" to individuals (12:7; 17:1; 18:1). Those narratives that speak of God's making himself known through words, visions, and angels pose no difficulty in light of the strict prohibition against the presentation of God in any physical form (Dt 4:15). But passages where it is expressly stated that God "appeared" to someone (12:7; 17:1; 18:1) would naturally raise difficult questions. How is it that God can "appear" and yet his form not be seen (Dt 4:15)? How can God "appear" and yet say "my face must not be seen" (Ex 33:23)? By carefully identifying and distinguishing the characters in the narrative by means of the singular and plural verbal forms, the author is able to show that the Lord's appearing to Abraham and the visit of the three men are one and the same event. God appeared to Abraham, but not "face to face" in his own physical form. Rather, the singular and plural forms are so arranged that the three men always represent God's presence and can be identified with his presence but at the same time remain clearly distinct from him.

The explanation seems to be that the three men, as such, are to be understood as the physical "appearance" of the Lord to Abraham. Although God himself did not appear to Abraham in physical form, the three men are to be seen as representative of his presence (cf. Ex 3:2–3). In such a way the actual presence of God among his covenant people was assured but without leaving the impression that God may have a physical form.

b. The promise of a son (18:9–15)

9–11 The three men inquired about Sarah but spoke only to Abraham. Abraham and Sarah were too old to have children. Sarah, as all women her age, no longer was physically capable of even conceiving a child. Thus, although Abraham's age was a factor to be reckoned with, the main obstacle to the fulfillment of the promise was Sarah's age (cf. 25:1–4). The primary importance of her age can also be seen in v.12, where she listed her limitation first and then that of Abraham's. Finally, Sarah's thoughts are revealed in v.13 with no mention of Abraham's old age. Thus it is repeatedly stressed that for her to have a child was not simply unlikely; it was impossible (v.14; NIV, "too hard")!

12–15 The key to the sense of this short passage lies in the Lord's question to Abraham about Sarah's laughter. The subtle changes in the wording of Sarah's thoughts reveal that the Lord was not simply restating her thoughts but was interpreting them as well. First, the Lord restated Sarah's somewhat ambiguous statement—"After I am worn out, . . . will I now have this pleasure?"—as simply "Will I really have a child?" Then he took Sarah's statement about her husband—"my master is old"—and reshaped it into a statement about herself: "now that I am old." Finally, he went beyond her actual words to their intent: "Is anything too hard for the LORD?" The underlying issue, then, is the physical impossibility of the fulfillment of the promise through Sarah.

Once the physical impossibility of Sarah's giving birth was firmly established, the Lord repeated his promise to Abraham. At this point Sarah, who had only been "listening," entered the conversation with a terse reply: "I did not laugh." The author then quickly puts her response aside as a lie and states that she lied because "she was afraid." This brief narrative concludes with the Lord's reiteration of what the reader by now certainly knows to be the truth—Sarah did in fact laugh.

c. Sodom in the balance (18:16–22)

16 As the three men arose and looked out toward Sodom, Abraham accompanied them to send them off. With a seemingly insignificant gesture, the three men "looked down toward Sodom," the doomed city of the next chapter.

17–19 The Lord's words reveal the inner motivation for his actions ("what I am about to do"). Verse 18 looks back to the original promise that Abraham would become a "great . . . nation" (cf. 12:2a) and that "all the nations on earth will be blessed through him" (cf. 12:3b).

Verse 19 seems to be an expansion on the ideas of 17:1. The Lord puts into words what has been a central part of the narrative, namely, Abraham's election: "I have chosen him" (GK 3359). Second, the Lord expresses his purpose in choosing Abraham. Here attention is directed internally ("to keep the way of the LORD") with the end in view that Abraham and his descendants do "what is right and just." Only then will the Lord fulfill what he had promised to Abraham. The notion of an internalized obedience is remarkably close to the terms of the "new covenant" (Jer 31:33) and is deeply rooted in the theology of Dt 30:6.

20–21 Apparently in vv.17–19 the Lord was speaking to himself. Here, however, Abraham was most certainly the one being addressed. The Lord's words answer the question in v.17. Thus the Lord revealed to Abraham that he would go down to investigate the wickedness of Sodom and Gomorrah.

22 Notice that the narrative first states that the "LORD (GK 3378) said, "I will go down and see" (v.21); then "the men turned away and went toward Sodom." Once again the Lord and the men are brought into close association. If "the men" are the emissaries of the Lord and represent his presence amid everyday affairs, then when they journey to Sodom and Gomorrah, it can rightly be said that the Lord himself was visiting these cities.

As has been the case throughout this narrative, "the men" represent the Lord's appearance but are not actually identified as the Lord. Thus the fact that the Lord remained behind after two of "the men" had left is no more a surprise than the fact that the Lord was again present with Lot in Sodom along

with two of "the men" (19:12, 16). So when the Lord said, "I will go down and see," it stands to reason that, as in ch. 18, "the men" in ch. 19 represent the Lord's presence with Lot.

One question remains, however. If the three men left Abraham, why did only "two messengers" (19:1) arrive in Sodom? Clearly the two messengers who visited Lot are two of the "three men" who visited Abraham, especially since in ch. 19 the "messengers" are subsequently referred to simply as "the men." But what happened to the other "man"? The most common explanation is that the "man" is a "christophany," i.e., an appearance of the Second Person of the Trinity in human form, before the Incarnation. Thus when the text says that "the men turned away and went toward Sodom" and that the Lord remained with Abraham, and then further that only "two messengers" (19:1) came to Sodom, one of the men must have stayed behind with Abraham. Since we know that the Lord stayed behind, that man must have been the Lord. Abraham was then visited by the preincarnate Christ who was accompanied by two "angels."

Clearly the two men in Sodom represent the carrying out of the Lord's intention to "go down and see if what they have done is as bad as the outcry." But how did the Lord investigate the "outcry of Gomorrah"? Since the narrative records only the events of the men's visit to Sodom, and since at the conclusion of ch. 19 the mention is made not only of the Lord's destruction of Sodom but also of Gomorrah (v.24a), apparently the third man went to Gomorrah and carried out a similar task in that city. By specifying the number of men who visited Sodom, the author has left us with an answer to the question of the Lord's righteous and just treatment of Gomorrah. Thus "the Judge of all the earth" (v.25) has "dealt justly" (cf. 19:15b).

d. Abraham's intercession (18:23–33)

23–33 The central issue of the discourse between Abraham and the Lord is expressed in Abraham's question at the end of v.25. The Lord's answer is a resounding yes. Abraham started with a question about fifty righteous people in a city and concluded with the question of ten righteous ones. Why stop at ten? Did he not care about Lot and his family who only numbered four? One possible solution is that the sequence fifty down to ten, in units of ten, would naturally end with ten. Abraham would not have gone to zero righteous people, since he was concerned only with the salvation of the righteous amid the unrighteous, not with the destruction of the wicked. Abraham had his answer in general terms and did not need to pursue the question to the exact number.

In Abraham's concern for Lot, the narrative addresses the larger issue of God's treatment of any righteous person in his judgment of the wicked. While the city of Sodom was destroyed, Lot was taken out of it. Thus we have the answer to what God would do if less than ten righteous were found in the city. It should also be pointed out, however, that though Sodom was not spared for Lot's sake, the little city of Zoar was spared on Lot's behalf (see comments on 19:17–22).

7. Lot and Sodom (19:1–38)

a. Two angels at Sodom (19:1–14)

1a According to vv.10, 12, 15–16, the two "angels" were "men" (v.10), specifically, the men who had visited Abraham (18:3). More important is that toward the end of the narrative, the men are represented as a visitation of the Lord (v.18; cf. NIV note). They came to carry out the Lord's retribution against the wickedness of the city (v.13b); but in response to Abraham's prayer for the righteous (18:23–32), they also had come to rescue Lot (19:29).

Below is an overview of the southern end of the Dead Sea with a fertile oasis—the most likely location for Sodom and Gomorrah. To the right is a memorial by the Dead Sea, with salt visible on the water in the background.

1b–11 The depiction of the events at Lot's house on the eve of the destruction of Sodom and Gomorrah justifies the divine judgment on the two cities. Even Lot, the righteous one who was ultimately rescued, was tainted by his association with Sodom. Unlike Abraham, Lot appears quite insensitive to God's presence with the messengers, addressing them only as "sirs" (v.2; NIV, "lords"; GK 123). Though Lot was just as hospitable as Abraham and can certainly not be put in the same class as the men of Sodom, his suggestion that the men of the city take his own daughters and do with them what they please can hardly be taken as a sign of his good character. In fact, in an ironic turn of events, Lot himself later inadvertently carried out his own horrible proposal (vv.30–38).

12–14 The messengers clearly stated their twofold purpose: they had been sent to destroy the city and to rescue Lot and his family. The response of the two "sons-in-law" shows that they are at one with the rest of the men of the city. This provides a further vindication of the divine punishment that was to follow.

b. Lot's deliverance (19:15–28)

15–16 In contrast to the men of Sodom who blindly groped for the door of Lot's house,

Lot and his family were taken by the hand and led out of the city to safety at the break of day. The rescue of Lot was in response to the prayer of Abraham, for the angels' words explicitly recall the words Abraham used (cf. 18:23; 19:15, 17; see esp. 19:29).

This section pictures Lot as a righteous man living amid the unrighteous, who is rescued from the fate of the wicked through the intercession of God's chosen one. Surprisingly, however, the basis of God's saving Lot was not his righteousness but because "the LORD was merciful." Lot's "righteousness" (cf. 2Pe 2:7) comes only from the connection established between Abraham's prayer "for the righteous" in ch. 18 and the events of Lot's rescue in ch. 19. In the account of the rescue itself, the emphasis is on God's compassion. Lot acknowledges in v.19 that he had found "favor" and "kindness" before God.

17–22 At the conclusion of Lot's rescue, he requested shelter in the nearby city of Zoar. In granting the request, the Lord saved that city from destruction. Thus Lot's rescue is a result of prayer—Abraham's and his own. God had promised not to destroy the city "on behalf of" the righteous in it. So now, though Sodom was destroyed, Zoar was saved from the destruction on account of Lot, the righteous one living in it.

23–28 Before the onset of the description of God's judgment, we are reminded of two things. First, "the sun had arisen over the land," and second, "Lot reached Zoar [safely]." The mention of the sun ties this section together with Lot's early morning rescue (v.15) and with the larger biblical picture of the "sunrise" as an image of divine salvation for the righteous and divine judgment on the wicked (Isa 9:2; Mal 4:1–2). With that as an introduction, we come to the classic image of the fate of every wicked person: "The LORD rained down burning sulfur on Sodom and Gomorrah."

Lot's wife and Abraham both "looked" at the destruction of the cities, but with very differing consequences. Lot's wife became a "pillar of salt" because she "looked back," thus disobeying the words of the rescuers (v.17). Abraham, on the other hand, looked from a vantage point consistent with the men's words in v.17. They said, "Don't stop anywhere in the plain," and so Abraham "returned to the place where he had stood be-fore the LORD. He looked down toward Sodom and Gomorrah, toward all the land of the plain" (vv.27–28). Unaware of the warning to Lot and his family, Abraham obeyed and escaped the destruction.

c. Lot's incest (19:29–38)

29–38 Verse 29 is a clear reminder of Abraham's role in Lot's rescue. This carries through the theme of God's promise—in Abraham and his offspring "all peoples on earth will be blessed" (12:3). Ironically, in his own drunkenness Lot carried out the shameful act that he himself had suggested to the men of Sodom (19:8): he lay with his own daughters. The account is remarkably similar to the story of the last days of Noah after his rescue from the Flood (9:20–27). There, as here, the father becomes drunk and uncovers himself in the presence of his children with negative consequences. Thus at the close of the two great narratives of divine judgment, those who were saved from God's wrath subsequently fell into a form of sin reminiscent of those who died in the judgment.

Lot is mentioned as the father of the Moabites and the Ammonites in Dt 2:9, 19, the passage that stresses their relationship to Israel, and not in Dt 23, where they are excluded from the congregation. Both the Moabites and the Ammonites continued to play an important role in later biblical history.

E. Abraham and Abimelech (20:1–18)

The focus of chs. 20 and 21 is the relationship between Abraham and the nations. Abraham's role is as a prophetic intercessor, as in the promise "all peoples on earth will be blessed through you" (12:3). He prayed for the Philistines (20:7), and God healed them (v.17). In the narrative Abimelech plays the role of a "righteous Gentile" with whom Abraham could live in peace and blessing. There is an implied contrast in the narratives between chs. 19 (Lot, the one who pictures the mixed multitude) and 20 (Abimelech, the righteous sojourner).

1 Abraham left the "great trees of Mamre" (18:1, 33) and traveled into "the Negev" (i.e., "southward") to sojourn in Gerar, which is in the "land of the Philistines" (21:34).

2 Sarah was taken into Abimelech's house. The narrative here is much briefer than the similar event in ch. 12. Clearly the focus is not so much the fate of Sarah as it is that of the Philistines. Many of the details are withheld until Abraham is given an opportunity to speak on his own behalf (vv.11–13). At that point his actions cast more light on the Philistines' inner motives than on his own. Abraham's words show that he had mistakenly judged the Philistines to be a wicked people, but their actions proved otherwise.

3–16 The narrative goes to great lengths to demonstrate the innocence of Abimelech, making it clear that "Abimelech had not gone near her." Thus Abimelech's claim to be "innocent" (lit., "righteous"; GK 7404) and his appeal to his innocence contrast sharply with Abraham's deception. Indeed, in v.6 God himself concurred with Abimelech's plea of innocence. Abimelech, however, was in immediate need of a warning lest he lose his innocence by his mistreatment of Abraham's household. Abraham's wife was to be returned, and Abraham the prophet must pray in behalf of the life of Abimelech. The surprising outcome of God's visit of Abimelech is that he responded immediately by rising early in the morning and declaring his dream to his servants and then to Abraham. The Philistines responded quickly and decisively to God's warning (cf. Jnh 3:6–9).

Abraham's reply seems intended not only to justify his action with Sarah in the present narrative but also to provide a larger picture for understanding his similar actions while in Egypt in ch. 12. At the same time, by tracing the plan back to the very beginnings of his sojourning from his father's house, he showed that the plan in this instance was not based on an actual assessment of the Philistines' religious life; rather, it was simply a part of a larger scheme. Thus an explanation is given as to why Abraham misjudged the Philistines. Though we have followed the life of Abraham closely since he left his father's house in ch. 11, this is the first we have heard of such an overarching strategy on Abraham's part or of this aspect of his relationship with Sarah. In the last analysis we are left only with the opinion of Abimelech himself, who undoubtedly accepted Abraham's explanation and faulted only himself in this unfortunate situation. Just how sincerely Abimelech accepted Abraham's story can be seen in the fact that in speaking to Sarah he called Abraham "your brother," showing that he accepted the explanation and in turn was attempting to restore the broken relationship with expensive gifts.

17–18 Abraham accepted the gifts from the Philistines and offered a prayer on their behalf in return. Only at this point do we discover the nature of God's words to Abimelech in v.7. The Lord had "closed up every womb in Abimelech's household."

F. Abraham and Isaac (21:1–25:11)

1. The birth of Isaac (21:1–7)

1–7 Verse 1 picks up a central line of narrative from 18:10. Strangely, the news of the birth of Isaac has been delayed and treated anticlimactically. More attention was paid to the *announcement* of the birth of the son in ch. 18 than to the report of the *accomplished fact*. The birth of Isaac came about "as [the LORD] had said," stressed three times within the first two verses. Thus the narrative calls attention to God's faithfulness to his word and to his careful attention to the details of his plan.

The importance of the announcement of Isaac's birth is seen in the statement that "the LORD was gracious," which focuses on his attentive care and concern. Also important is the reminder that Isaac was the "son . . . in [Abraham's] old age" and that he was born "at the very time God had promised him," reiterating the key themes of the earlier promise narratives (e.g., 18:10–14). The narrative also emphasizes Abraham's obedience (cf. 17:12). Abraham was a hundred years old when Isaac was born (cf. 17:1, 24). Sarah's words in v.7 emphasize his age.

2. Hagar and Ishmael (21:8–21)

8–21 The celebration of Isaac's coming of age was the occasion for the expulsion of Ishmael. The similarities between this chapter and the events in ch. 16 are notable. The writer's close attention to the similar details in the two chapters is perhaps best explained by his frequent use of "foreshadowing" to draw connections between important narratives. In this case the Lord's promise to Hagar (16:11–12) was recounted in a strikingly similar fashion to that of the fulfillment of the promise (vv.18–21). The promise foreshadows the fulfillment.

3. Abraham and Abimelech (21:22–34)

22–34 The recurrence of Abimelech shows that Abraham was still living with the Philistines (cf. v.34). This is a reminder that Abraham did not live out all his days in the Land of Promise but spent many days in exile. Even Isaac, the son of the promise, was not born in the Land of Promise. He was born in exile and had to sojourn there with his father who "wandered from nation to nation, from one kingdom to another" (Ps 105:13). Hebrews 11:8–13 recalls that though Abraham had left his father's land and had come to the Land of Promise, he lived there "like a stranger in a foreign country. . . . They were aliens and strangers on earth." Abraham in exile typifies God's care of the righteous who must suffer while waiting to enter the land. The servants of Abimelech had stolen Abraham's wells. But because God was with Abraham in all that he did, Abraham made a covenant with their king; and all was restored to him.

4. The binding of Isaac (22:1–14)

1–14 The clear statement that "God tested Abraham" reveals the Lord's real purpose in this incident. There is no thought of an actual sacrifice of Isaac in the narrative, though in the mind of Abraham within the narrative that was the only thought that was entertained. The abruptness of God's request surprises us as much as it would have Abraham. Without any further explanation, the request is made in three simple imperatives: "Take," "go," and "sacrifice him."

Although, unlike Abraham, we know that this was a test, we are as much in the dark about the intention of God's ways as Abraham was. Noteworthy is the way the narrative excessively and deliberately details Abraham's preparation for the journey and the journey itself. Without explicit commentary, we are left to ponder the thoughts of Abraham as he so matter-of-factly carried out God's directions. When at last someone in the narrative speaks, it is Isaac, not God, who breaks the silence; and the question he raises serves only to heighten the anguish of the Lord's request. When Abraham finally speaks, his reply to Isaac's question anticipates precisely the final outcome of the story: "The LORD will provide."

Abraham's words cast a new light on his silence. Amid the anguish that can be read into his silence emerges a confidence in the Lord who will provide. Abraham's words are not merely an attempt to calm the curious Isaac but are a settled expression of his trust in God. Few narratives can equal the dramatic tension of the last moments before God interrupts the action and calls the test to a halt. Abraham's every action is described in exaggerated detail. At the last dramatic moment the Lord intervened and, as Abraham had already anticipated, provided a substitute. Abraham therefore named the altar he had built "The LORD will provide."

5. The angel of the Lord (22:15–19)

15–19 At the end of the narrative is a "second" encounter between Abraham and the angel of the Lord. Since in v.19 Abraham returns to the two young men who had accompanied him, apparently this "second" encounter occurred on the same occasion as the first, though at a separate time (after Abraham had finished the burnt offering). The reason why it is called a "second" encounter is to show that the renewal of God's original promises to Abraham was not based on Abraham's specific actions in carrying out the test but on the faith and obedience of Abraham that showed through this test.

The promise reiterated here is similar to that of the earlier chapters. The promise of "blessing" recalls 12:2. The increase of Abraham's "descendants" is similar to 13:16; 15:5; and 17:2. The view of the "nations' " enjoyment of and participation in Abraham's blessing is similar to 12:3 and 18:18. The reference to Abraham's act of obedience as the basis of the promise is similar to 18:19. Perhaps, also, the reference to Abraham's descendants possessing the "cities of their enemies" (v.17) is to be taken as a reference to the gift of the "land" (12:7; 13:15; 15:18; 17:8).

6. The relatives of Abraham (22:20–24)

20–24 Immediately after the reiteration of the promise of a great multitude of descendants comes a notice regarding the increase of the family that Abraham and Sarah had left behind in their homeland. The twelve names in the list suggest that the writer intended to draw a comparison of these names with the twelve sons of Jacob or the twelve sons of

Ishmael in 25:12–15. In any event, the central purpose of listing the names is to introduce the future bride of Isaac, Rebekah, and to show that she was of the lineage of Milcah and not of her concubine.

7. Machpelah and Sarah's death (23:1–20)

1–20 Sarah died in Hebron, and Abraham apparently came there from Beersheba (cf. 22:19) to mourn her death. The point of ch. 23 is to show how Abraham fairly and squarely first came into legal possession of a parcel of land in Canaan. Through what appears to be a hard bargain, Abraham bought not only a cave for the burial of his wife but also a large field with many trees. This became an important burial site for the patriarchs and their wives (cf. 49:30–32; 50:13). As Abraham would not accept a gift from the king of Sodom lest it be said that the king had made Abraham wealthy (14:23), similarly here Abraham refused to accept the parcel of land as a gift. Apparently against the wishes of the Hittites, he paid the full price. God, not a human being, was the source of Abraham's hope of blessing. He would not seek to become wealthy or to own land apart from the promises of God. Abraham's purchase of land embodied his hope in God's promise that one day all the land would belong to him and his descendants (cf. Jer 32:6–15).

8. A bride for Isaac (24:1–67)

1–9 Abraham's concern that God's promise come to the descendants of Isaac is evidenced in the oath Abraham made with his servant. Two important points are made regarding the future of Abraham's descendants. First, they were not to be mixed with the inhabitants of Canaan, which appears to be a further expression of the notion of the two lines of blessing and curse (cf. 9:25–27). The seed of Abraham must be kept separate from the seed of Canaan. Second, Abraham's descendants are not to return to the land of their fathers. Canaan is their home, and Abraham is careful to ensure that Isaac not be taken back to the ancestral home.

This section once more portrays the faith of Abraham. The questions raised by the servant provide the occasion. As so many times before, Abraham's reply proves to be both prophetic (anticipating the final outcome of the story) and thematic (providing the central motive of the narrative): "The LORD, the God of heaven, . . . will send his angel before you so that you can get a wife for my son from there." The key idea is God's going before the servant to prepare his way.

10–27 The servant spelled out specifically the nature of the sign he sought from the Lord. God prepared the way, bringing the young girl in question on the scene even before the servant finished speaking. All the details of her background are given as soon as she enters the picture. While the servant is unaware of the actual identity of the girl, we know that she is Rebekah, the daughter of Bethuel, the son of Milcah. Clearly, the Lord has answered the servant's prayer. From the type of information given, there is no doubt that this was the girl the servant had asked for and that God had indeed sent his messenger out ahead of him to prepare the way. Such divine preparation for the descendants of Abraham and the line of the blessing must be accompanied by the kind of appreciation seen in the servant in vv.26–27.

28–49 After meeting Laban and his household, the servant retells the episode. Rather than a mere repeating, however, the retelling reasserts the central points of the first narrative. Originally Abraham is recorded as saying, only generally, that God would send a messenger and that the servant would find a wife for Isaac (v.7). When he retold the story, however, the servant included the idea that God would send the angel and also added that the angel would make his journey a success by gaining a wife for Isaac from his own family. The further details make the miracle of God's provision even more grand than suggested in the original incident itself.

50–61 At the conclusion of the servant's account, Laban and Bethuel acknowledge that it was the Lord who prepared the way for the servant to meet Rebekah. Thus several witnesses testify that these events were the work of God: the narrator (vv.15–16), the servant (vv.26–27), and Laban and Bethuel (v.50). The final witness is Rebekah herself, who, against the wishes of her brother and her mother, returned with the servant to Isaac. The simplicity of her response (v.58) reveals the nature of her trust in the God of Abraham (cf. Ruth 1:16).

62–67 The importance of the blessing of Rebekah by her family lies in the similarity of this blessing to that given to Abraham by the Lord in 22:17. This reveals the careful attention to detail the Lord has shown in choosing this wife for Isaac. In God's plan the same blessing is given to both Isaac and his bride.

For the first time in the story, Isaac enters the narrative, just as the servant is bringing the young woman to him. They both lift up their eyes and see the other in the distance. The narrator, along with the readers, knows who it is that Isaac and Rebekah see, but they themselves do not.

Verse 66 shows that the writer knows just how long to tell the story and stops short of going beyond that point. He says merely that the servant "told Isaac all he had done." The final remarks again show that God's guidance in the mundane areas of life is good for those who put their trust in him. When Isaac took Rebekah as his wife, he loved her and was comforted with her after the death of his mother. So Rebekah follows Sarah in the line of the descendants of Abraham.

9. Abraham's death (25:1–11)

1–6 The narrative reads as though after the death of Sarah, Abraham took another wife by the name Keturah. Because the Chronicler called Keturah a "concubine" (1Ch 1:32), some have suggested that she was one of the "concubines" mentioned in v.6, and hence these sons were born to Abraham and Keturah while Sarah was alive. Though Keturah is called a "concubine" in Chronicles, she is called a "wife" here, which seems to preclude her from being a mere concubine during the time Sarah was alive.

The picture that emerges of Abraham's life after the death of Sarah is that of a complete rejuvenation of the old man of the previous narratives. He continued to be rewarded with the blessing of many offspring. But only Isaac had any share in the promised blessing.

7–10 Surprisingly little attention is given to the details of the death of Abraham. The length of his life is given, which connects him to the patriarchs (cf. 11:32). That Abraham died "at a good old age" recalls the word of the Lord in 15:15. The mention of Abraham's "good old age" contrasts to Jacob's "few and difficult" (lit., "evil") years (47:9). This narrative thus picks up the "good" and "evil" theme begun in the first chapters of the book

and carried through to the end (cf. 50:20). The final resting place of Abraham was in a portion of the Promised Land that he rightfully owned—the field that he purchased from Ephron the Hittite.

11 There are relatively few narratives devoted to the theme of "blessing" in the life of Isaac. Most are woven into the busy tapestry of ch. 26. All the more important, then, is this brief statement that God blessed Isaac, a reminder that his was the line of the divine blessing (cf. 17:21).

III. The Account of Ishmael (25:12–18)

12–18 The Isaac stories open (cf. v.11) with a final statement regarding the line of Ishmael. The statement consists of a genealogy of the twelve leaders of Ishmael's clan, a report of the length of Ishmael's life, and a report of his death. The number twelve appears again to be a deliberate attempt to set these individuals off as founders of a new and separate people (see comment on 22:20; cf. 17:20). No mention is made of the blessing of Ishmael recounted in 17:20, and we hear nothing more about him in Genesis. The descendants of Ishmael, however, continue to play a part in the Genesis narratives (28:9; 36:3; 37:27–28; 39:1).

IV. The Account of Isaac (25:19–35:29)

A. The Birth of Jacob and Esau (25:19–28)

19 The "account of Abraham's son Isaac" almost immediately turns out to be about the sons of Isaac rather than Isaac himself. Although an important link in the line of Abraham, as an individual character Isaac is given little attention (but cf. ch. 26).

20–28 Isaac, like Esau (26:34), was forty years old when he took a wife, Rebekah. Like Sarah (11:30), Rebekah was barren. Like Abraham (20:17), Isaac prayed for his wife, the Lord answered, and she bore two sons. The barrenness of both Sarah and Rebekah, as well as Rachel (29:31) and Leah (29:35), reiterates the point that the promised blessing through the chosen seed of Abraham is not to be accomplished merely by human effort. The fulfillment of the promise at each crucial juncture requires a specific act of God.

A central theme of Genesis—the struggle between brothers—occurs here in the womb of Rebekah. The conflict between brothers began with Cain and Abel and continues throughout the book (cf. 9:20–27; 13:7–12; 21:9; chs. 29–31; 37–50), perhaps stemming from the first words of judgment in the book (3:15). The point is not that the struggles were necessary for the accomplishment of the will of God but that God's will was accomplished in spite of the conflict.

Another important motif is that "the older will serve the younger." From ch. 4 the narrative has portrayed God choosing and approving the younger and the weaker through whom he would accomplish his purpose and bring about his blessing (cf. 4:1–5, 26–5:8; 17:18–19; 29:18; 37:3; 49:8). The blessing was not a natural right but was extended solely by God's grace (cf. Mal 1:1–5; Ro 9:10–13).

B. Selling the Birthright (25:29–34)

29–34 The story of Esau's rejection of his birthright is a narrative example that God's choice of Jacob over Esau did not run contrary to the wishes of either. Esau "despised" (GK 1022) his birthright, while Jacob went to great lengths to gain it. Esau, though he had the right of the firstborn, did not value it over a small bowl of stew. Thus, when in God's plan Esau lost his birthright and consequently his blessing, there was no injustice dealt him.

C. Isaac and Abimelech (26:1–35)

There are several similarities between the events of this chapter and those in the life of Abraham (12:10–20; 20:1–18). Each brief narrative of Isaac parallels a similar situation in the life of Abraham. The short span of one chapter shows how the whole life of Isaac is a retelling of what happened to Abraham. The lesson conveyed is of God's continuing faithfulness.

1–5 The present famine was not the one that forced Abraham to go to Egypt (12:10). At first we are told only that Isaac went down to Gerar to Abimelech; but in the warning Isaac received in the vision of v.2, we are informed that he was on his way to Egypt. No explanation is given why he should not go to Egypt, except that he is to "live in the land." The Lord's warning, however, became the occasion for a formal restatement of the blessing. In the face of the impending famine, the Lord promised to be with Isaac, to bless him, and

to bring about all that had been promised to his father, Abraham. Essentially the same promise given to Abraham was given to Isaac. His seed would be great in number (cf. 12:2), the land would be his (12:7), and all the nations of the land would be blessed in him (12:3).

The Lord then added a remarkable note: Abraham "kept my requirements, my commands, my decrees and my laws" (cf. Dt 11:1). Did Abraham know the law? If so, how? If not, what was the meaning of the Lord's words? At several points Abraham acted in accordance with the law—particularly the law as recorded in Deuteronomy; yet he never actually had a knowledge of the law itself. For example, in ch. 14 Abraham's actions followed quite closely the stipulations of Dt 20; he obeyed the law from the heart (cf. Dt 30:6; Jer 31:33). He is the ultimate example of true obedience. Thus, Abraham, a man who lived in faith, could be described as one who kept the law.

6–11 There are several similarities between Isaac and Abraham in this section. Just as Abraham "stayed in Gerar" (20:1), so also did Isaac. Just as Abraham once devised a scheme with his wife Sarah, calling her his "sister" (20:2), so also did Isaac with Rebekah. Just as Abraham was rebuked by the Philistine king, Abimelech, for the great shame he might have brought on his people (20:9), so also was Isaac. Such similarities can hardly be coincidental. Unlike the same incident in the life of Abraham, however, it was not God who warned Abimelech not to touch Abraham's wife (20:6); Abimelech himself forbade anyone to touch Isaac's wife. It was not God who protected the wife with the threat of capital punishment (20:7); Abimelech himself said that anyone who molested Isaac or his wife "shall surely be put to death."

Though earlier Abimelech was said to have been "pure of heart" (20:6; NIV, "clear conscience"), in ch. 26 his actions alone show that his heart was right. Abimelech did not need to be warned in the dream. All that was necessary was to discover that Rebekah was not Isaac's sister; that was enough for him to fear that a great shame (NIV, "guilt") may come upon his people. Clearly the picture of the Philistine king that emerges is of a righteous, even pious, Gentile who did what was right; by contrast, Isaac is shown to be less righteous than he. A wider picture of the nations emerges here—both as wicked and deserving judgment and as righteous and capable of entering into covenant with the chosen offspring (21:27, 32; 26:28). The Philistines also caused great hardship for Isaac in the controversies over the wells (vv.14–22).

12–13 Just as Abraham prospered while sojourning among the Gentiles (12:16; 20:14), so Isaac prospered while sojourning with Abimelech. The source of Isaac's prosperity was that "the LORD blessed him." This is the second reference to Isaac's blessing, apparently to underscore the connection between Isaac's prosperity and God's promise to Abraham in 12:2. What God had promised to Abraham was fulfilled with Isaac.

14–22 Just as Abraham's prosperity became the occasion for the conflict between his shepherds and Lot's (13:5–7), so Isaac's wealth angered the Philistines. The statement that "the herdsmen of Gerar quarreled with Isaac's herdsmen" (v.20) parallels the narrative of the "quarreling" (13:7) that broke out between the herdsmen of Abram and of Lot. As the name that was given to the well—"Rehoboth"—shows, there was a progressive resolution of the conflict as Isaac continued to move away from the Philistines and dig new wells. After finding no conflict at Rehoboth, they said, "We will flourish in the land" (cf. 1:28).

23–25 Just as the Lord had spoken to Abraham after he had separated from Lot (13:14–17) and renewed his promise of land and great prosperity, so now after Isaac had returned to Beersheba, the Lord appeared and renewed the promise. For a third time it is said that the Lord would bless Isaac (vv.2, 12). Like his father (12:7; 13:3–4), Isaac responded by building an altar and worshiping God.

26–31 Earlier Abimelech, acknowledging God's presence with Abraham (21:22), sought to enter into a covenant with him. Likewise, Abimelech acknowledged the Lord's presence with Isaac and sought to enter into a covenant with him. Isaac, like Abraham, was the source of blessing to those who sought him out. Isaac, like Abraham, trusted God and lived "in peace" with his neighbors.

32–33 The final picture of Isaac here concludes with the account of the discovery of a new well "on the same day" (NIV, "that day") that Isaac had made peace with his neighbors. Consequently the writer associates the name of the city, "Beersheba" (lit., "well of the seven/oath"; cf. 21:31), with the "oath" (NIV, "[they] swore an oath").

34–35 Initially the short notice of Esau's marriage to two Hittite women seems insignificant. But as an introduction to ch. 27, it casts quite a different light on the events of that chapter. Just before the account of the mischievous blessing of Jacob, we are told that Esau, from whom the blessing was stolen, had married Hittite women and that they were a source of grief to both Isaac and Rebekah. These verses, along with vv.29–34, form the background to the central event of ch. 27, the blessing of Jacob. These preliminary notices put into perspective the cunning deed of Jacob and Rebekah and demonstrate that Esau was not fit to inherit the blessing.

D. The Stolen Blessing (27:1–40)

1–26 In recounting this story of Isaac's "blessing" (GK 1385), close attention is given to those elements that heighten the suspense and highlight the deception of Jacob. Thus Jacob's name, which means "the deceiver" (cf. v.36), has been appropriately chosen. Isaac is depicted as too old and too blind to distinguish between his two sons. Perhaps this is an attempt to ease Isaac's culpability. Isaac's insistence on a "good meal" before the blessing recalls Esau's own trading of the birthright for a pot of stew and thus casts Isaac and Esau in similar roles. Isaac's blindness makes the story more believable and more suspenseful. Thus the events of the story make sense and the suspense is real. The suspense is carried right to the end, where Jacob is shown leaving "at the same moment as" (cf. v.30) Esau returns from the hunt. The plan is in danger of not succeeding right up to the end.

27–29 The goal of Jacob's strategy was to wrest the blessing from Isaac. Although he did not appear completely convinced, in the end Isaac blessed Jacob. The theme of "blessing" points out the relationship of this narrative both to those that precede and those that follow. The promise to Abraham (12:2–3) is alluded to in the final words of the blessing.

Similarly, Isaac's blessing foreshadows Jacob's later prophecy concerning the kingship of the house of Judah (cf. 49:8). Thus the words of Isaac are a crucial link in the development of the theme of the blessing of the seed of Abraham. So too Jacob's daring scheme is a link in the chain connecting the blessing of the offspring of Abraham with the rise of kingship in the house of Judah.

30–40 The reverse side of the blessing of Jacob is the disappointment and anger of Esau. He is presented as a tragic figure, a victim of his more resourceful and daring brother. His anguish on hearing about his misfortune of losing the blessing recalls the events of 25:21–34 and his loss of the birthright. Esau lost everything, and Jacob gained it all. Within the narrative, Isaac recounted the main points of the blessing a second time, underscoring the fact that he had blessed Jacob rather than Esau. Finally, weepingly, Isaac answered Esau's pleas for a blessing with a third reiteration of the central point of Jacob's blessing: "You will serve your brother." These reiterations underscore the irretrievability of the lost blessing and hence the certainty of the fulfillment of the blessing itself.

E. Jacob's Flight From Beersheba (27:41–28:5)

27:41–28:5 Jacob's scheme not only resulted in his obtaining the blessing that Isaac had intended for Esau, it also became the occasion for Jacob's journey to the house of Laban in search of a wife. The picture of Esau at the conclusion of this story is that of a bitter, spiteful brother and son. He made plans to kill Jacob and regain by force his birthright and blessing. Again Rebekah thwarted the plans, having Isaac send Jacob back to her homeland to find a wife. As in many of the narratives of Genesis, Isaac's words of blessing to the departing Jacob precisely anticipate the eventual outcome of the ensuing story: Jacob would visit Laban "for a while," Esau's anger would subside (see ch. 33), and Jacob would find a wife and return as a great assembly of people. Within Isaac's farewell blessing is a final reiteration of the central theme of the preceding narrative: The blessing of Abraham was to rest on the family of Jacob. The promises of Abraham and the promises of Isaac were now the promises of Jacob.

F. Esau's Bitterness (28:6–9)

6–9 The final picture of Esau in this narrative is that of a bitter son seeking to spite his parents through deliberate disobedience. The marriage of Esau to the daughter of Ishmael reminds us that the promised offspring of Abraham was determined, not by the will of human beings, but by the will of God. The families of the two "older" sons (Ishmael and Esau) were united in the marriage, but neither received the blessing promised to Abraham. The families of the "younger" sons (Isaac and Jacob), however, did.

G. Jacob at Bethel (28:10–22)

10–22 Jacob, like Abraham (ch. 15), received a confirmation of the promised blessing while asleep in the night. Abraham received God's word "in a vision" (15:1), and Jacob saw the Lord in a dream. Both times a divine confirmation was given regarding the establishment of the same covenant of promise. In a remarkably similar fashion, both chapters turn to the future "exile" of Abraham's descendants and the promise of a "return." Abraham's vision looked forward to the sojourn of God's people in Egypt and also to the Lord's deliverance in the Exodus. Jacob's dream looked forward to his own sojourn in Haran and to the Lord's eventual return of Jacob to the land promised to Abraham. In both cases the promise was that God would not forsake them and would return them to their land.

The Lord's words in v.15, "I am with you and will watch over you wherever you go, and I will bring you back to this land," become the guiding principle that governs the course of the narrated events. So when Jacob returned from Laban's house after many years, he went back to the same place, Bethel, where God again blessed him and promised to give him the land he had already promised to Abraham (35:12); God also reaffirmed his promise to make Jacob's descendants into a great nation (35:11). Just as Jacob erected a "pillar" at the outset of his journey and then named the place "Bethel," so also when he returned, he erected another "pillar" and named the place "Bethel" (35:14–15). At either end of the Jacob narratives is the reminder that God was with him in all that he did and that God was faithful to his promises.

H. Jacob and Rachel (29:1–14a)

1–14a In keeping with the picture of Jacob's sojourn as an exile from the Promised Land, the account opens with the words "Jacob continued on his journey and came to the land of the eastern peoples." Jacob's journey to find a wife was similar to that of Abraham's servant who sought a wife for Isaac. In ch. 24 the words of the servant guide the narrative and show that it was God alone who directed him to the right young woman for Isaac. In this chapter Jacob is relatively silent. He does not reflect on God's guidance nor on the Lord's promise to be with him wherever he goes (28:15). It is Jacob's actions, not his words, that tell the story of God's help and guidance. First, as with the servant in ch. 24, God directs Jacob to the well where Rachel is watering her flocks.

The description of the size of the rock covering the well and the number of shepherds already on hand hint that Jacob was going to do a mighty deed. Only when all the shepherds are present are the men able to lift the rock from the well and water the flocks, because the rock was big. When Jacob saw Rachel, however, and the shepherds identified her as the daughter of Laban, he singlehandedly removed the rock and watered her sheep. Then, in a great show of emotion, Jacob kissed Rachel and cried with a loud voice. Clearly Jacob saw in these circumstances the guiding hand of God (cf. 24:27). Jacob's physical strength was perhaps meant as further evidence that God was with him and that he had not forsaken his promises (28:15; cf. 24:27).

I. Jacob's Marriages (29:14b–30)

14b–30 For the first time Jacob was the object of deception. Laban turned the tables on him. In the case of the blessing (ch. 27), Jacob was able to exchange the younger for the older, whereas here Laban reversed the trick and exchanged the older for the younger. Jacob was getting what he deserved. The seven extra years that Jacob had to serve Laban appear as a repayment for his treatment of Esau.

Jacob was indignant. But he was left speechless by Laban's reply in v.26. After that the narrative says only that Jacob conceded. Unknown to him, Laban's words had deftly expressed the very circumstances that had led

Jacob on his present journey. Jacob's past had caught up with him, and he could do no more than accept the results and serve Laban seven more years. At first it had looked as if Jacob's journey was in fact following the course that Rebekah had anticipated (27:44). Thus we are not surprised to read that Jacob's first seven years of working for Laban seemed as if they were "only a few days." But with the discovery of Laban's trick, seven more years are added to Rebekah's "few days"; and Jacob's—and Rebekah's—plans begin to unravel.

J. The Birth of Jacob's Sons (29:31–30:24)

29:31–30:24 In a way that recalls the beginning of the Abrahamic narratives (11:30), the central problem is introduced: The Lord opened Leah's womb, "but Rachel was barren." It is at first surprising that the Lord was behind Rachel's barrenness. In the preceding chapter God had promised that Jacob's descendants would be more numerous than the "dust of the earth." Now Rachel, Jacob's intended wife, was barren; and it appeared to be the Lord's doing. Again Jacob's plans have come to naught. He had planned to take Rachel as his wife, but God intended him to have Leah. Jacob sought to build a family through Rachel, but she was barren; and God opened Leah's womb.

Jacob's schemes, which had brought him fortune thus far, were beginning to crumble. Schemes will not be sufficient to carry out the plans of God. Jacob too will have to depend on God to bring about the divine blessing. In the conflict that ensued between Jacob and his two wives over the birth of their sons, the pattern is set for the remainder of the narratives in Genesis. One of Leah's sons was Judah, while Rachel was the mother of Joseph.

Though all twelve sons are important, Joseph and Judah stand out markedly in the narratives that follow. Both are used by God in important ways, but each has a different role to play in the accomplishment of God's blessing. Here, at the beginning, it appears that ultimately Judah, the son of Leah, was given the place of preeminence. Counter to Jacob's plans, God had opened the womb of Leah and not Rachel.

In the end the Lord did hearken to Rachel, and her son Joseph was born (30:22). But as Jacob's words to Rachel underscore, God

JACOB'S JOURNEYS

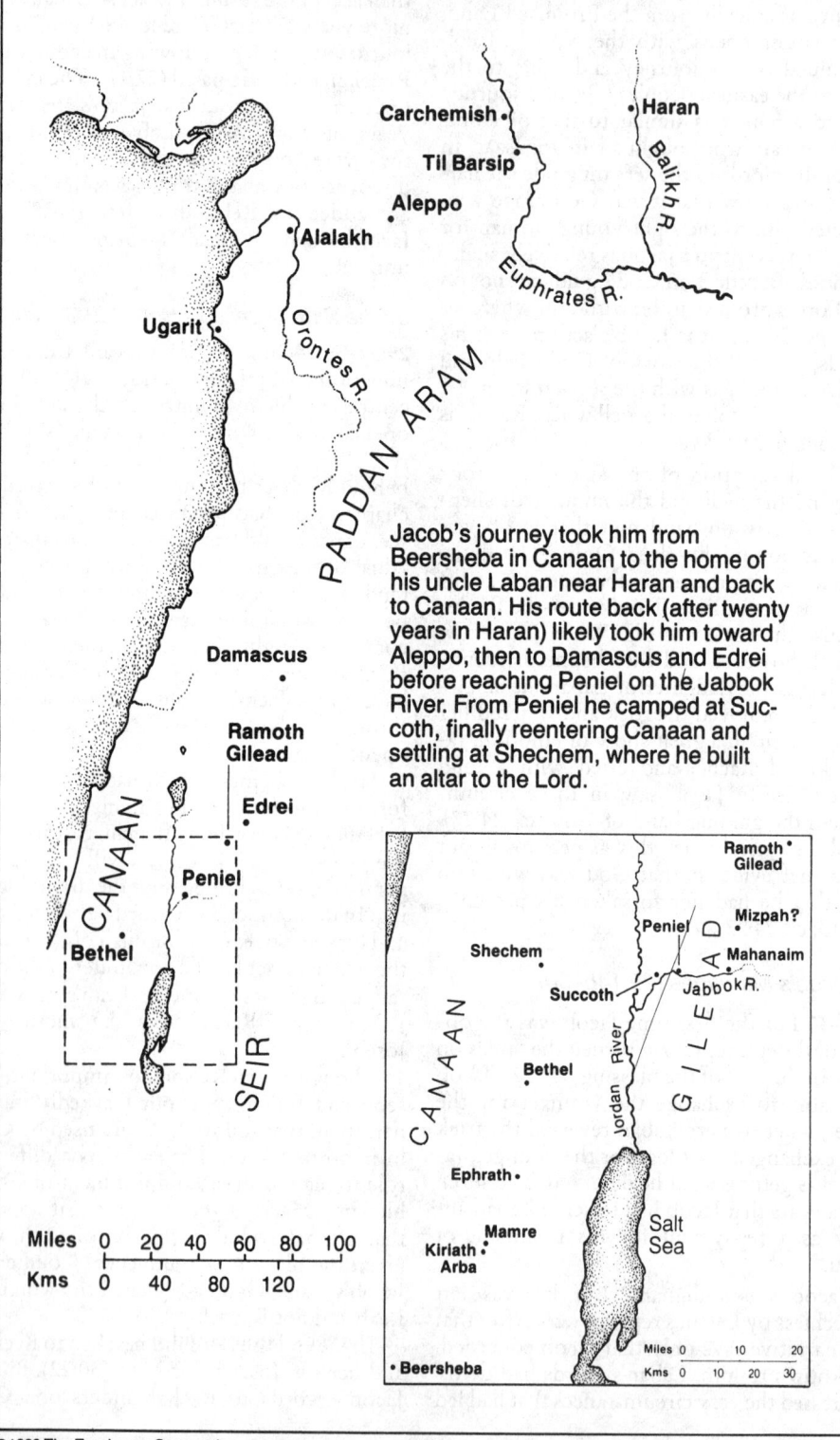

Carchemish

Haran

Til Barsip

Balikh R.

Aleppo

Alalakh

Euphrates R.

Ugarit

Orontes R.

PADDAN ARAM

Jacob's journey took him from Beersheba in Canaan to the home of his uncle Laban near Haran and back to Canaan. His route back (after twenty years in Haran) likely took him toward Aleppo, then to Damascus and Edrei before reaching Peniel on the Jabbok River. From Peniel he camped at Succoth, finally reentering Canaan and settling at Shechem, where he built an altar to the Lord.

Damascus

Ramoth Gilead

Edrei

CANAAN

Peniel

Bethel

SEIR

Ramoth Gilead

Peniel

Mizpah?

Shechem

Mahanaim

Succoth

Jabbok R.

Jordan River

GILEAD

CANAAN

Bethel

Ephrath

Salt Sea

Mamre

Kiriath Arba

Miles 0 20 40 60 80 100

Kms 0 40 80 120

Miles 0 10 20

Kms 0 10 20 30

Beersheba

had withheld sons from Rachel so that the descendants of Abraham would be built from Leah (30:2). Even after Leah had ceased bearing children, she managed to have two more sons and a daughter by Jacob. Just as Jacob had purchased the birthright for a pot of stew (25:29–34), so also Leah purchased the right to more children by Jacob with the mandrakes of her son Reuben. All the conflict and tension that existed between Joseph and his brothers—and particularly Joseph and Judah—in the narratives that follow are anticipated and foreshadowed here.

K. Jacob and Laban's Sheep (30:25–43)

25–43 After the account of the birth of the sons, we have the first mention of Jacob's departure from Haran. Laban, seeking the Lord's blessing on behalf of Jacob, attempted to settle his account for the work Jacob had done for him over the years. So Laban asked Jacob to name his wages. Laban's offer apparently contained a request that Jacob stay on with him and continue to watch over his herds. Jacob struck a bargain with Laban that resulted in great blessing and wealth for Jacob.

The blessing did not come from Laban; rather, it was a gift from God (cf. 14:21). What Jacob took instead was the right to stay on and shepherd Laban's flocks and to keep part of the herd that he raised. After the deal was struck, Jacob was to keep all the speckled or spotted goats and all the black sheep. From this he would build his own herds.

The passage is surely to be read as an example of the Lord's promise in ch. 28 to be with Jacob during his sojourn in the East. Jacob's clever use of the peeled poplar branches was not so much intended to demonstrate his resourcefulness as it was to further the theme of God's continued faithfulness to his word. The clue to the meaning of the passage is in v.43, where a summary of the whole narrative is given. The summary recalls quite clearly God's blessing of both Abraham (12:16) and Isaac (26:14); it thus puts the events of this chapter within the larger context of the themes developed throughout the book, namely, God's promise of blessing and his faithfulness to that promise. Jacob's wise dealings with Laban then are an example of the way God caused him to prosper during this sojourn. Further confirmation that such is the sense of the narrative comes from the

words of Jacob himself in the next chapter. Looking back he told his wives that it was God who had taken Laban's herds and given them to him (31:9).

L. Jacob's Flight From Laban (31:1–21)

1–3 Just as Isaac's wealth had made the Philistines jealous (26:14), so Jacob learned that Laban was now angry and jealous of his wealth. At this time the Lord also directed Jacob to return to the land of his fathers. We are again reminded of the Lord's promise to be "with" (28:15) Jacob on his journey; and thus the direction of Jacob's life again points toward Bethel, the place of the original promise.

This seems to be the middle point of the narrative and life of Jacob. He was on his way back to Bethel. Later on (32:10), when Jacob looked back at this point, he repeated the Lord's words of comfort and promise. However, instead of the promise "I will be with you," Jacob recalled God's words as "I will make you prosper" (32:10). Thus Jacob's own words offer an expansion and commentary on the sense of God's promise to be "with" him.

4–13 Jacob's words of explanation repeat the primary events of the preceding chapter. Though the events of ch. 30 give the appearance that Jacob was getting the best of Laban, from another perspective Jacob's actions are to be understood as the Lord's enabling him to be repaid for Laban's mistreatment. The events were all part of the outworking of God's plan, the plan that began with Jacob's vow at Bethel and the Lord's promise to be with him. Now even Laban's change of attitude toward Jacob and the jealousy of his sons are seen as part of the plan of God.

14–21 Jacob's wives were willing to leave their own family and go with him to the land of Canaan (cf. 24:58; Ruth 1:16). More important, they were ready to put their trust in God and seek his blessing. Despite the wives' positive response to Jacob, an ominous note is sounded about Rachel's stealing of Laban's "household gods." It is unclear whether Rachel's actions are to be viewed favorably or reveal a weakness of character. There is a similarity and contrast between Rachel's stealing her father's "household gods" when fleeing from home with her husband and Jacob's stealing his father's blessing when fleeing from home to find a wife (ch. 27). In both cases the younger stole what rightfully belonged to the elder. As we see later (v.32), Jacob did not know that Rachel had taken the gods. It is through Rachel's resourcefulness alone that Laban's prized possessions were successfully taken. In addition, Rachel's covert action is matched by Jacob's deception in departing from Laban secretly.

M. Jacob Overtaken by Laban (31:22–55)

22–42 The dispute over the stolen household gods gives an occasion for the writer to restate his central theme, which is expressed in Jacob's words to Laban in v.42: Jacob's wealth had not come through his association with Laban but through God's gracious care during Jacob's difficult sojourn.

43–55 The narrative concludes with an account of a covenant between Jacob and Laban. Just as Isaac parted ways with Abimelech by entering into a covenant (26:28–31), so also Jacob and Laban parted ways with a covenant.

N. Jacob's Meeting With Angels (32:1–2)

1–2 The events of this chapter are couched between two accounts of Jacob's encounter with angels (vv.1, 25). Jacob's meeting with angels on his return to the land recalls a similar picture of the Promised Land in the early chapters of Genesis, when the land was guarded on its eastern borders by angels (3:24). It can hardly be accidental that as Jacob returned from the east, he was met by angels at the border of the Promised Land. This brief notice may be a clue to the meaning of Jacob's later wrestling with the "man" at Peniel (vv.25–30), who too may have been an angel.

O. Messengers Sent to Esau (32:3–22)

3–12 The emphasis of this chapter and the next is on the wealth of Jacob and the restoration of Jacob and Esau. Much suspense surrounds Jacob's reunion with his brother, Esau. Like Jacob, we are not sure of Esau's intentions in gathering four hundred men to meet Jacob on his return. The last we heard from Esau, his intention was to slay Jacob in revenge for the stolen blessing (27:41). Jacob's fear that Esau had now come to do just that seems well founded. In light of this, Jacob's prayer plays a crucial role in reversing

the state of affairs. Jacob prayed for safety and then appealed to the covenant promises God had made earlier.

13–22 True to form, Jacob made elaborate plans to save himself and his family in the face of Esau's potential threat. He provided his servants with abundant gifts for Esau and instructed them carefully on how to approach Esau when they met. In it all his desire was to "pacify" Esau and deliver his family from his hand. Again we see Jacob the planner and the schemer. As he had taken Esau's birthright and blessing, as he had taken the best of Laban's herds, so now he had a plan to pacify Esau. However, it was not Jacob's plan that succeeded but his prayer. When he met with Esau, he found that Esau had had a change of heart. Running to meet Jacob, Esau embraced and kissed him and wept (33:4). Jacob's plans and schemes had come to naught, for God had prepared the way.

P. Jacob's Wrestling Match (32:23–32)

23–32 Jacob's wrestling with an angel epitomizes the whole of Jacob's life. He had struggled with his brother (chs. 25, 27), his father (ch. 27), and his father-in-law (chs. 29–31), and now he struggles with God (ch. 32). Jacob's own words express the substance of these narratives about him: "I will not let you go unless you bless me." Here is a graphic picture of Jacob struggling for the blessing— struggling with God and with a man (v.28).

Significantly, Jacob emerges victorious in his struggle. His victory, even in his struggle with God, came when the angel "blessed him." The importance of the name "Peniel" is that it identifies the one with whom Jacob was wrestling as God. Jacob's remark that he had seen God face to face did not necessarily mean that the "man" he wrestled with was in fact God. Rather, when one saw the "angel of the Lord," it was appropriate to say that he had seen the face of God (e.g., Jdg 13:22; but cf. Hos 12:2–4).

Q. Jacob's Meeting With Esau (33:1–17)

1–17 When Jacob saw Esau and the four hundred men approaching, he divided his entourage again (cf. 32:7–8). He showed his preference for Rachel and Joseph by putting them last. Esau's greeting was totally unexpected. Jacob had expected revenge from

Esau, or, if not revenge, then heavy bargaining and appeasement. But, seemingly in response to Jacob's prayer (cf. 32:11), Esau had had a change of heart.

The change in Esau is depicted graphically in the contrast between Jacob's fearful approach and Esau's eager excitement to see his brother. All of Jacob's plans and preparations pale in the light of Esau's joy. Ironically, the four hundred men accompanying Esau turned out not to be for battle with Jacob's household and for taking his spoils, but for safeguarding the final stage of Jacob's journey. Once again Jacob is portrayed as one who has gone to great lengths to secure his own well-being but whose efforts have proved pointless. Jacob continued to scheme and plan; yet God's own plans ultimately made Jacob's worthless.

This reconciliation of the brothers and Esau's partaking of the blessing that Jacob had received (v.11) picture the ultimate fulfillment of God's promise to Abraham: "All peoples on earth will be blessed through you" (12:3).

R. Jacob at Shechem (33:18–34:31)

33:18–20 These last verses form a transition in the narrative between Jacob's sojourn in the east and the events of the later years of his life in the land of Canaan. As he left Canaan in ch. 28, Jacob vowed that if God would be with him and watch over him so that he returned to the land "in peace" (NIV, "safely" GK 8969), he would give to God a tenth of all he had (28:20–22). The narrative has been careful to follow the events in Jacob's life that have shown the Lord's faithfulness to this vow. Thus Jacob returned "safely" to the land of Canaan. God had been faithful.

Jacob returned to Bethel in ch. 35 and built an altar there (v.7). No mention is made of Jacob's giving a "tenth" to the Lord. But perhaps the erection of an altar here and in ch. 35, along with the offerings, represented his "tenth." It may be also that the "hundred pieces of silver" represent a part of that "tenth." The portion of land purchased by Jacob plays an important role in the later biblical narratives. This was the land where the Israelites buried the bones of Joseph (Jos 24:32) and thus represented their hope in God's ultimate fulfillment of his promise of the land.

34:1 The birth of Dinah was recorded without much comment in 30:21. But once Jacob and his descendants had departed from Paddan Aram and settled in the vicinity of Shechem (vv.18–20), Dinah became the center of the conflict between Jacob and the inhabitants of Canaan. The point of the narrative is to reiterate the portrait of Jacob that has been central throughout these stories: he was a man who planned and schemed for what appears to be his own ends, but who in the end actually accomplished God's purposes. In the present narrative God's purpose in setting apart the descendants of Abraham comes into jeopardy with the proposal of marriage between Dinah and Shechem. Twice we are informed that the purpose of the marriage was that the family of Jacob should become "one people" (vv.16, 22) with the inhabitants of Canaan. This runs counter to Abraham's admonition (24:3), Rebekah's fear (27:46), and Isaac's command (28:1).

While the story operates at a level of family honor and brotherly concern for a ravished sister, it nevertheless also carries along the theme that God works through and often in spite of the limited, self-serving plans of human beings.

2–4 Though the Hivite son genuinely loved Dinah, the point is that he lay with her, apparently against her will, and thus humiliated her. Simeon and Levi's final words express clearly how they viewed the situation: "Should he have treated our sister like a prostitute?" (v.31).

5–24 Jacob was curiously silent about the incident. When he heard what had happened to Dinah, he waited for the return of his sons. The reason behind Jacob's silence is not clear at the beginning of the story. It is significant that it was the sons of Jacob, not Jacob himself, who carried out the deception; and at the end of the story Jacob admonished his sons for their actions. The plans and schemes no longer were Jacob's; they were the plans and schemes of his sons. Jacob's last words to Simeon and Levi concerning the events of this chapter were very harsh: "Let me not enter their council, let me not join their assembly, for they have killed men in their anger. . . . Cursed be their anger, so fierce, and their fury, so cruel!" (49:6–7).

That Simeon and Levi had a plan of deception to repay the offense is suggested in the report of their anger at hearing the news of Dinah. The bitterness of their anger shows that they would not let such an act go unpunished. In ch. 17 the rite of circumcision was to be a sign (v.11) of the unity of the covenant people and their separation from the rest of the nations. Circumcision was not limited to Abraham's descendants but was rather given as a sign of one's joining in the hope of God's promises to Abraham. It was, in fact, a sign given of the covenant promise that Abraham would become the father of "many nations" (17:5). But in the way the sons of Jacob carried out the request that these Canaanites be circumcised, it offers a curious reversal of God's intention. They offered circumcision as a means for the two families to become "one people." The Canaanites were not joining the offspring of Abraham; rather, the descendants of Abraham were joining with the Canaanites. This point is stressed in Hamor and Shechem's report to their countrymen: "Won't their livestock, their property and all their other animals become ours?"

25–31 When the sons of Jacob carried out their deception to the end, their actions did not go unrebuked. Jacob's words in v.30 express his final judgment on their actions. That the sons' reply stands as the last words of the narrative shows that their motive had not been mere plunder but the honor of their sister.

S. Jacob's Return to Bethel (35:1–15)

1–5 The chapter opens with a reference back to the appearance of the Lord to Jacob at Bethel (28:10–15). As Jacob had once fled to Bethel to escape the anger of his brother Esau, so now the Lord has told Jacob to return to Bethel and dwell there in the face of the trouble that his two sons, Simeon and Levi, had stirred up. When Jacob obeyed and went to Bethel, the Lord delivered him from the anger of the Canaanites who dwelt nearby. It is significant that Jacob called God the one "who answered me in the day of my distress and who has been with me wherever I have gone." That epithet is a fitting summary of the picture of God that has emerged from the Jacob narratives. Jacob was in constant distress; yet in each instance God remained faithful to his promise and delivered him.

The only previous mention of the "gods" that Jacob's household might have had is the "household gods" (31:19) that Rachel stole from her father. These may be included in the term "foreign gods"; but in light of the fact that the writer mentions that they buried the "rings in their ears" along with these "foreign gods," it is likely that Jacob's household had picked up other religious objects while living in Shechem. The point is that Jacob and his family were leaving such things behind and purifying themselves in preparation for their journey to Bethel.

6–15 The arrival at Bethel marked the end of Jacob's journey and the final demonstration of the faithfulness of God. He had been with Jacob throughout his journey, and now Jacob had returned to Bethel in safety. As Abraham and Isaac had done on numerous occasions, Jacob built an altar and named it in commemoration of the Lord's appearing to him there when he left for Haran (cf. 28:10–22). In response the Lord appeared again to Jacob and "blessed him." For a second time Jacob's name was changed to "Israel" (cf. 32:28). The point of the second renaming was to give the name "Israel" a more neutral or even positive connotation. It does so by removing the notion of "struggle" associated with the wordplay in 32:28 and letting it stand in a positive light, contrasting it with the name "Jacob," a name frequently associated throughout these narratives with Jacob's deceptions. Jacob's successive names reveal his standing before God.

The importance of God's words to Jacob in vv.11–12 cannot be overemphasized. First, God's words recall clearly the primeval blessing of Creation (1:28) and hence show God to be still "at work" in bringing about the blessing to all humanity through Jacob. Second, for the first time since 17:16, the mention is made of royalty in the promised line. Third, the promise of the land, first given to Abraham and then to Isaac, was renewed here with Jacob. Thus within these brief words several major themes come together. The primeval blessing of humankind was renewed through the promise of a royal offspring and the gift of the land.

In the course of the narrative, this section represents a major turning point and thematic focus. Two lines that have thus far run parallel are about to converge, and out of them both will emerge a single theme. Jacob has two wives, each representing a possible line through which the promise will be carried on. Just as Abraham had two sons and only one was the son of promise, and just as Isaac had two sons and only one was the son of the blessing, so now Jacob, though he has twelve sons, has two wives (Leah and Rachel), and each has a son (Judah and Joseph) who can rightfully contend for the blessing. As the Jacob narratives have already anticipated, in the end it was Judah, the son of Leah, not Joseph, the son of Rachel, who gained the blessing (49:8–12).

T. Benjamin's Birth and Rachel's Death (35:16–20)

16–20 Rachel, Joseph's mother and Jacob's favorite wife, died giving birth to her second son, Benjamin. The account of the birth of this youngest son is separated from the rest of the sons in 29:32–30:24, but it follows closely on that passage. The last son to have been born was Rachel's first son, Joseph. At the time of his birth, Rachel had said, "May the LORD add to me another son" (30:24). Apparently looking back to that request, Rachel's midwife said, "Don't be afraid, for you have another son." As she was about to die, Rachel named the son "Ben-Oni," meaning "son of my trouble." Jacob, however, making a wordplay on "Oni," which can mean either "trouble" or "wealth," named him "Benjamin" (lit., "son of my right hand"), reinterpreting the name given by Rachel to mean "son of my wealth or good fortune."

The site of Rachel's burial, Ephrath, was clearly identified with the city of Bethlehem, an important place in biblical history (cf. 1Sa 17:12; Mic 5:2). This site is further identified by the pillar that Jacob set up to mark Rachel's grave (cf. 1Sa 10:2). This passage continued to play an important role in later biblical texts (cf. 48:7; Jer 31:15; Mic 5:2; Mt 2:18).

U. The Sons of Jacob (35:21–26)

21–26 Because of their horrendous conduct, the three oldest sons of Jacob fell from favor. The writer has already recounted the violence of Simeon and Levi (ch. 34); now he briefly notes the misconduct of Reuben. As the list that follows shows, the next brother in line was Judah, the son of Leah. With the older sons out of the way, the stage is set for

the development of the lines of Judah and Joseph, which continues throughout much of the rest of the OT. The Genesis narratives that follow are devoted primarily to Joseph, but that is no indication of the final outcome. The last word regarding the future of these two lines of Abraham's descendants is not heard until chs. 48 and 49.

V. The Death of Isaac (35:27–29)

27–29 The end of the Jacob narratives is marked by the death of his father, Isaac. This notice is not simply to record Isaac's death but to show the complete fulfillment of God's promise to Jacob (28:21). According to Jacob's vow, he had asked that God watch over him during his sojourn and return him safely to the house of his father. Thus the conclusion of the narrative marks the final fulfillment of these words as Jacob returned to the house of his father, Isaac, before he died.

V. The Account of Esau (36:1–43)

1–8 The separation of Jacob and Esau is cast in the same form as the separation of Abraham and Lot (ch. 13). The possessions of the two brothers were too great, and the land was not able to sustain both of them (cf. 13:6); so just as Lot parted from Abraham and went eastward, so Esau parted from Jacob and went to Seir. The heirs of the promise remained in the land, and the other sons moved eastward. The parting of ways was beneficial to both Jacob and Esau.

In the remainder of this chapter, the writer shows the progress and well-being of the line of Esau. He is particularly careful to note that Esau is, in fact, "Edom" (GK 121). The repeated identification of Esau as "that is, Edom" throughout the chapter prepares us for the future importance of Edom during Israel's later history.

9–19 The unusually long "genealogy" of Esau is made up of several smaller lists. The first list, of the sons of Esau, is largely dependent on the brief narratives regarding Esau's wives (26:34; 28:9; 36:3). Verse 10 divides the sons of Esau into two groups: the sons of Adah and the sons of Basemath. Adah's sons (and grandsons) are listed in vv.11–12, then Basemath's in v.13, and finally Oholibamah's in v.14. Verses 15–19 list the tribal "chiefs" of the sons of Esau, beginning with the eldest,

Eliphaz, and again grouped according to their mothers. The term "chief" (GK 477) is used in the Bible only for the tribal leaders of Edom, with the exception of Zec 12:5–6, where it is also used of the leaders of Judah. Outside the Bible the word refers to the leaders of foreign nations. The title then would have denoted primarily a political or military function.

20–30 To the two above lists is added a list of "the sons of Seir the Horite, who were living in the region," and then a list of their tribal "chiefs." Seir is ordinarily the name of the geographical territory occupied by the Edomites, but here it refers to an individual. He and his descendants are listed here because they occupied the territory of Edom. In 2Ch 25:11, 14, the "sons of Seir" are called "Edomites." The list identifies Seir as a "Horite," which earlier commentators interpreted as "cave dwellers"—deriving the sense from the similarity of the word "Horite" to the Hebrew word meaning "cave."

31–43 The list of Edomite kings is introduced by the heading, "These were the kings who reigned in Edom before any Israelite king reigned." This presupposes a knowledge of the kingship in Israel, or at least an anticipation of the kingship. Thus it is a part of those texts (e.g., 17:6, 16; 35:11) that look forward to the promises of Ge 49:10; Nu 24:7, 17–18; and Dt 17:14–20 (cf. 1Sa 2:10).

The chapter closes with a final list of the tribal "chiefs" of Esau's clan. Several names in this list overlap with those in vv.10–14.

VI. The Account of Jacob (37:1–49:33)

A. Jacob in the Land (37:1)

1 Jacob is back in the Land of Promise but is still dwelling there as a sojourner, like his father (and grandfather) before him (cf. Heb 11:13). As his ancestors, he was awaiting the fulfillment of the promises of God. The verse is a fitting transition to the narratives that trace the course of events by which the sons of Jacob left the Land of Promise and entered the land of Egypt. According to 25:11 Jacob's father, Isaac, dwelt in Beer Lahai Roi, which evidently is where Jacob lived at this time.

B. Joseph's Dreams (37:2–11)

2–3a The formal title "This is the account of Jacob" obscures teh fact that the remaining narrative is not about Jacob but about Joseph and, later, Judah. Joseph, at seventeen years of age, is (along with his brothers) a shepherd of his father's sheep. He is only a young lad compared with his other brothers. We are told that Joseph brought a "bad [GK 8273] report" about his brothers to his father and also that his father, Jacob, loved him more than the other brothers because he was the son born to him in his old age. Jacob's special love for Rachel (29:30) has carried over to that of her son, Joseph. Since the story of Joseph is filled with wordplays and reversals, it seems likely that the reference to the "bad report" foreshadows the brothers' intended "evil" (NIV, "harm"; same word in Hebrew) spoken of in 50:20.

3b–11 The "richly ornamented robe" Jacob made for Joseph illustrates the father's preferential love for Joseph. The repeated references to the coat throughout the story remind us that Joseph's preferred status was the central problem that angered his brothers and turned them against him. Eventually their anger resulted in a plan to do away with him altogether. But first, adding to their hatred, Joseph recounted two dreams, both of which end with the image of his brothers "bowing down" to him. This foreshadows the conclusion of the story where, because he is ruler of the land of Egypt, his brothers "bowed down" (42:6) to him, and Joseph "remembered his dreams about them" (42:9).

The reason for the two dreams is to be understood in light of Joseph's own words in ch. 41, where he explained to the Pharaoh that the twofold occurrence indicates that the matter has been firmly decided by God (41:32). So too here God will surely bring to pass the fulfillment of Joseph's dream. The significance of the dreams is seen in the words of Joseph's brothers: "Will you actually rule us?" This reveals the sense of the "bowing down" to be an acknowledgement of royalty and kingship. The irony of the narrative composition is that in the end such royal honor does not reside in the house of Joseph but in the house of Judah (49:10).

C. Joseph's Journey to Egypt (37:12–36)

12–18 After a minor difficulty in which he temporarily lost his way and had to seek help from a stranger, Joseph found his brothers in Dothan. The purpose of this small account can be seen by comparing it with the brief and similar prelude to the second part of the story, where he met his brothers in Egypt (chs. 42–44). The symmetry reinforces the sense that every event is providentially ordered. Here at the beginning of the Joseph story, when Joseph's brothers "saw him" approaching, they "plotted to kill him." In the same way midway through the narrative, when Joseph first "saw his brothers" in Egypt (42:7), he eluded them by disguising himself so that they did not recognize him and then planned a scheme that, at least on the surface, looked as if he intended to kill them.

19–36 Both the details of the brothers' plans and their motivation are given. Behind those plans lie Joseph's two dreams. Little did they suspect that the very plans that they were then scheming were to lead to the fulfillment of those dreams. The first plan was simply "to kill him," throw his body in a pit, and then tell their father that a "ferocious" (lit., "evil"; GK 8273) animal had eaten him. Again, the brothers punctuated their plan with a reference to Joseph's dreams in an obviously ironic statement: "We'll see what comes of his dreams" (cf. 42:9). This initial plan is interrupted by Reuben, who saved Joseph from their hands.

The reference to Reuben is countered later by a similar reference to Judah. It was not merely Reuben who saved Joseph from the plan of his brothers, but Judah also played an important role. Again we can see the central importance of Jacob's last words regarding Judah in 49:8–12. In the end it is Judah who is placed at the center of the narrative's focus on the fulfillment of the divine blessing. It is the descendants of Judah who will ultimately figure in the coming of the Promised Seed. Reuben's plan is to persuade the brothers merely to throw Joseph into a pit and, apparently, leave him to die. His actual plan, however, was to return later and rescue Joseph. Reuben's plan was partly successful. The brothers threw Joseph into the pit alive and left him there. The reference to Joseph's coat highlights the central point of the story, that the present plan is part of a larger divine plan foreshadowed in Joseph's dreams.

An important turn of events occurs with the arrival of the "Ishmaelites." They become the occasion for Judah to enter the story with the suggestion that the brothers could "sell [Joseph] to the Ishmaelites." Only a cursory account of Joseph's fate follows in the text. The Ishmaelites, who are also called "Midianites" in this narrative, arrive, and Joseph is sold to them for twenty shekels. They then take him to Egypt with them.

When the focus of the narrative returns to Reuben and to the outcome of his plan to deal with Joseph, ironically it serves only to underscore the role of Judah in the actual rescue of Joseph. Verse 29 suggests that Reuben had no part in the plan to sell Joseph to the Ishmaelites. He returned to the pit, expecting to find Joseph there and to rescue him, but Joseph was not there. He was surprised and angry that Joseph was gone. Thus in no uncertain terms we learn that it was Judah, not Reuben, who saved the life of Joseph. Ultimately the brothers must fall back on their original plan of telling their father that a "ferocious" (lit., "evil") animal had killed Joseph.

Once again the coat provides the narrative link in the story. The symbol of the brothers' original hatred for Joseph becomes the means of the father's recognition of his loss. In the end the blood-stained coat is all that remains of Joseph; on seeing it Jacob tore off his own coat and exchanged it for sackcloth. Thus Jacob's own fate and that of his sons are briefly sketched out in this opening narrative. What happens to Joseph foreshadows all that will happen to the sons of Jacob. They will be carried down into Egypt and will be put into slavery. In this sense, then, Jacob's final words set the focus of the narratives to follow: "in mourning will I go down to the grave [Sheol] to my son." Ironically, the Joseph narratives conclude with Jacob's going down (46:3–4) to Egypt to see his son and then to die (50:24–26).

D. Judah and Tamar (38:1–30)

1–11 The narrative of ch. 38 has only a loose connection with the Joseph story. The first verse notes only that these events occurred "at that time." Without this remark we would have little basis for relating these events to the story of Joseph. In the overall strategy of the book, however, this chapter plays a crucial role.

The narrative begins with the mention of three sons (cf. the three sons of Adam, Noah, and Terah). Two sons died because of the evil they did. The point of this introductory information is to show that the continuation of the house of Judah lay in Judah's hands. The narrative that follows shows that he does nothing to further his own household. It takes the "righteousness" (GK 7405) of the woman Tamar (v.26) to preserve the seed of Judah. The story is much like the other patriarchal narratives outside the story of Joseph, which show the promised offspring in jeopardy and the patriarch showing little concern for its preservation. Just as in ch. 20, where the seed of Abraham was protected by the "righteous" (NIV, "innocent") Abimelech, here it is the woman Tamar, not Judah the patriarch, who is ultimately responsible for the survival of the descendants of the house of Judah.

The text is not clear from whose house Jacob originally took Tamar for his son's wife. Since we are told that Judah's own wife was a Canaanite, had Tamar also been a Canaanite, a similar statement presumably would have been mentioned. Since she was likely not a Canaanite, this introduction shows another point at which the promise to Abraham was in jeopardy. By marrying the daughter of a Canaanite, Judah had realized the worst fears of Abraham (24:3) and Isaac (28:1); so the promise regarding the descendants of Abraham and Isaac was in danger of being unfulfillable. Through Tamar's clever plan, however, the seed of Abraham was preserved by not being allowed to continue through the sons of the Canaanite, the daughter of Shua. The line was continued through Judah and Tamar. The genealogy at the close of the narrative underscores this point.

12–26 Tamar's plan resembles that of Jacob and Rebekah (ch. 27). Through a disguise she obtained a part in the blessing of the firstborn. In so doing, just as with Jacob and Rebekah, she obtained what the patriarch should have rightfully given. Shelah, the son of Judah, was of age, and Tamar should have been given to him as a wife. Thus, in the end, the continuation of the line of Judah was not due to the righteous actions of the patriarch Judah, but lay in the hands of the "righteous" Tamar.

27–30 The whole of the Jacob narratives reaches a fitting summary in this brief account of the birth of the two sons Perez and Zerah. As the Jacob narrative began with an account of the struggle of twins (25:22), so now the conclusion of the Jacob narrative is marked by a similar struggle. In both cases the struggle resulted in a reversal of the right of the firstborn and the right of the blessing. The result of both struggles was that the younger gained the upper hand over the elder. As Jacob struggled with Esau and overcame him, so Perez overcame Zerah, the elder, and gained the right of the firstborn (cf. Nu 26:20, where Perez is regarded as the firstborn). The brevity and austerity with which the narrative is recounted leaves the impression that the meaning of the passage is self-evident to the reader. Indeed, coming as it does on the heels of a long series of reversals in which the younger gains the upper hand over the elder, its sense is transparent.

E. Joseph in the House of Potiphar (39:1–23)

1 Fully conscious of the intervening Judah narrative, the text resumes the account of Joseph, taking up where ch. 37 left off. As in 37:27, those who have brought Joseph into Egypt are called "Ishmaelites," while in 37:28, 36, they are known as "Midianites."

2–6 Verse 2 establishes the overall theme of the narrative: "The LORD was with Joseph and he prospered." Verses 3–6 relate the theme to the specific series of events to follow: Joseph's blessing from the Lord is recognized by his Egyptian master, and Joseph is put in charge of his household. Joseph's sojourn in Egypt, like that of his father, Jacob (30:27), has resulted in an initial fulfillment of the Abrahamic promise that "all peoples on earth will be blessed [GK 1385] through you" (12:3). Thus we are told that "the LORD blessed [GK 1385] the house of the Egyptian because of Joseph." Such a thematic introduction alerts the reader to the underlying lessons intended throughout the narrative. This is not a story of the success of Joseph; rather, it is a story of God's faithfulness to his promises. The last note about Joseph in this introductory section sets the stage for what follows.

7–20 This story about Joseph reverses a well-known plot in the patriarchal narratives. Whereas before it was the beautiful wife (12:11; 26:7) of the patriarch who was sought by the foreign ruler, now it was Joseph, the handsome patriarch himself who was sought by the wife of the foreign ruler. Whereas in the earlier narratives it was either the Lord (12:17; 20:3) or the moral purity of the foreign ruler (26:10) that rescued the wife, rather than the patriarch, here it was Joseph's own moral courage that saved the day. Whereas in the preceding narratives, the focus had been on God's faithfulness in fulfilling his covenant promises, in the story of Joseph attention is turned to the human response.

Abraham, Isaac, and Jacob repeatedly fell short of God's expectations, though, of course, they continued to have faith in God. Joseph, however, is a striking example of one who always responds in total trust and obedience to the will of God. The Joseph narratives give expression to that part of the promise found in 18:19: "that they may do righteousness and justice so that the LORD may fulfill what he has promised to Abraham" (pers. tr.). There was a human part to be played in the fulfillment of God's plan. When God's people respond as Joseph responded, then their way and God's blessing will prosper. Significantly, in all the book of Genesis only Joseph is described as one who was filled with the Spirit of God (41:38). In fact, the narrative is explicit in its emphasis on his total uprightness throughout the attempted seduction by the Egyptian's wife. He was in jail because of false witness brought against him.

21–23 The emphasis of the epilogue is clear. God has turned an intended evil against Joseph into a good. God was with Joseph and prospered his way. Lying behind the course of events is the lesson that all the Joseph narratives teach: "You intended to harm me, but God intended it for good" (50:20). Like Daniel during the Exile, Joseph suffered for doing what was right, but God turned the evil into a blessing.

F. Joseph in Jail (40:1–23)

1–23 Chapter 40 represents an intermediate stage in the development of the plot of the Joseph story. Joseph had been cast into jail and had risen to a position of prominence there. Apparently Joseph's position was responsible for his being assigned to wait on the two incarcerated royal officials. They each had a dream that Joseph correctly interpreted, but ultimately to no avail, since the surviving official soon forgot the matter. Later, when the Pharaoh himself had a dream, the butler remembered the events of this chapter and told the king about Joseph. The picture of Joseph that comes through these events is of one who, like Daniel, is an interpreter of dreams and mysteries. He discerns the course of future events that to others lies in total darkness.

The sense of the cupbearer's dream may seem self-evident, but as the sense of the baker's dream shows, such apparently self-evident meanings are by no means certain. Who could, on the face of it, discern between the meanings of the two dreams? One is favorable and the other is not. There is clearly more to the dreams than a plain reading of each would suggest. The picture of Joseph that emerges from this narrative is precisely that which the Pharaoh himself later expresses: Joseph is "one in whom is the spirit of God" (41:38). Joseph knows the interpretations of dreams, which, in his own words, "belong to God" (40:8). He is set apart from all those who have preceded him in the book. He is "discerning and wise" (41:39), and "things turned out exactly as he interpreted them" (41:13). Whereas Abraham was a "prophet" (20:7), Joseph is a "wiseman" (cf. 41:39). Whereas Abraham sees the course of future events "in a vision" (15:1), Joseph discerns (41:39) the course of the future in the mysterious dreams of others.

G. Joseph's Interpretation of Pharaoh's Dreams (41:1–36)

The central theme of ch. 41 is expressed by Joseph in v.32: "The matter has been firmly decided by God, and God will do it soon." "Two" dreams with the same meaning show that God will certainly bring about what was foreseen in the dreams. In the previous chapter the "two" officials of the king each had a dream. One dream was good, the other bad. The dreams and their interpretations are repeated twice, once in the narrative of ch. 40 and then again by the cupbearer before the Pharaoh in vv.9–13. After "two years" the king himself had "two" dreams; one part of each dream was good (v.29) and the other bad (vv.27, 30). Within the narrative, each dream is repeated twice, once by the writer and again by Pharaoh. Such symmetry in human events is evidence of a divine work.

1–8 Pharaoh's two dreams are more transparent than those of the two officials. The sense of the two dreams can be seen in the elements of the dream. Seven good cows and seven good heads of grain are seven good years. Seven ugly cows and seven blighted heads of grain are seven bad years to follow. To show that the dreams' simplicity conceals rather than reveals their meaning, the writer tells us that all the king's magicians and wise men were unable to give their meaning (cf. Dan 2:4–12). Joseph not only had to forecast from the dreams what was to happen, but, more important, he advised Pharaoh how to prepare for what was to come. Joseph's wisdom in dealing with the situation forecast in the dreams is portrayed as of equal importance to the interpretation of the dreams. His wisdom consisted more in planning and administration than in a knowledge of secret mysteries.

9–13 Though the cupbearer had forgotten about Joseph, he now recalled that Joseph's interpretation had stood the test of time. As it turns out, even the cupbearer's forgetfulness worked in Joseph's favor since just at the opportune moment he remembered Joseph and recounted his wisdom before the king. By drawing the reader's attention to the events of the previous passage, both the wisdom of Joseph and the sovereign workings of God are emphasized. Joseph's wisdom is highlighted by the fact that in contrast to the wise men of Egypt, the interpretation of Joseph, "a young Hebrew," proved true. God's sovereign power is highlighted in the fact that though the cupbearer did forget Joseph at the time, he remembered just at the right moment and thus served as the means for Joseph's ultimate rise to power.

14–36 When the Pharaoh repeated the dreams, he added only two major parts—the comments about the ugly cows and these cows looking just as "ugly" (lit., "evil"; GK 8273) after they ate the good cows as before. In both cases the repetition seems to stress the "evil" of the appearance of the cows in contrast with the "good" cows of the first group.

The emphasis on the "good" and "evil" represents Joseph's ability to distinguish between the "good" and the "evil." It is clear that ultimately such knowledge comes only from God (v.39). Thus the lesson of the early

chapters of Genesis is artfully repeated in these last chapters. In light of such considerations, it can hardly be accidental that Joseph's plan seemed "good" to the Pharaoh and all his servants.

H. Joseph's Exaltation Over Egypt\ (41:37–57)

37–57 The account of the king's appointment of Joseph over all his kingdom presents a picture of Joseph that recalls Adam in Ge 1. Just as Adam was dependent on God for his knowledge of "good and evil," so Joseph also is portrayed here in the same terms. Just as Adam is made God's "vicegerent" to rule over all the land, so Joseph is portrayed here as the Pharaoh's "vicegerent" over all his land. As Adam was made in God's image to rule over all the land, so the king here gave Joseph his "signet ring" and dressed him in royal garments. Just as God provided a wife for Adam in the garden and gave the man all the land for his enjoyment, so the king gave a wife to Joseph and put him over all the land.

At many points in the story, Joseph appears to be represented as an "ideal" of what a truly wise and faithful man is like. He is a model of the ideal man, the ideal king. He accomplishes all that Adam failed to do. The story of Joseph is a reflection of what might have been had Adam remained obedient to God and trusted him for the "good." At the same time the picture of Joseph anticipates what might yet be, if only God's people would, like Joseph, live in complete obedience and trust in God. The picture of Joseph, then, looks back to Adam, but even more looks forward to one who was yet to come, the one from the house of Judah to whom the

These are scarab rings, similar to what Joseph would have received from the pharaoh (41:42). Courtesy Nahum Slapak.

kingdom belongs (cf. 49:10). Thus the tension between the houses of Joseph and Judah is resolved by making the life of Joseph into a picture of the one who is to reign from the house of Judah.

I. Joseph's Brothers in Egypt (42:1–28)

The preceding chapter recorded Joseph's rise to power. The present chapter turns to the divine purpose behind his miraculous rise.

1–2 The narrative returns to Jacob, who has been out of the picture since 37:34. As so frequently in biblical narratives, the words spoken at the beginning of a story foreshadow the outcome. Jacob, sending his sons to Egypt, said, "Go down there . . . so that we may live and not die" (cf. 45:5).

3–13 The "twelve" sons of Jacob are divided into two groups throughout the narrative. There are the "ten of Joseph's brothers" and then the "two" sons of Jacob by Rachel—Joseph and Benjamin. These two sons are contrasted with the two sons of Leah—Reuben and Judah. Both Reuben and Judah play an important and similar role in the narrative. They speak on behalf of the other brothers and are the catalysts in the resolution of the plots instigated by Joseph. It was Judah, however, who saved the day by offering himself as a pledge for the young lad Benjamin; and it was Judah who repeated Jacob's own thematic words "that we and you and our children may live and not die" (43:8; cf. 42:2). Finally, it was Judah who spoke before Joseph and offered himself as a substitute for Benjamin, lest he cause any evil to come on his father, Jacob (44:33–34).

Throughout the narrative the plot is woven around the interplay between Joseph and Judah, and in the end it is Judah who resolved the conflict. By the same token it is Joseph who created the conflict and tension throughout the narrative. When his brothers approached him to buy grain, he "pretended to be a stranger" and spoke harshly, accusing them of being spies. Verse 9 reveals that Joseph's schemes and plans against his brothers were motivated by the dreams of the earlier narratives and not by the things his brothers had done to him.

In response to Joseph's accusation that they were spies, the brothers defended their integrity by saying, "Your servants are twelve brothers"; but lest their integrity be gainsaid, they were forced to add: "and one is no more." Joseph's schemes have provoked the first hint that their evil deed accomplished long past may yet rise up against them. When the brothers recounted this event to their father (v.32), they reported their own words in a different order than that of the narrative in v.13. Here they mentioned first the "one who is no more"; but when they tell their father about Joseph's accusations and their response, they mention last the "one [who] is no more" and then tell of Benjamin who is home with their father. Though subtle, such a reversal suggests that the memory of what they did to Joseph was beginning to rub on their consciences.

Another reminder that reveals Joseph's motives in perplexing his brothers is the conclusion they draw from his trick of having their money returned to them in their grain sacks. When they saw their money, they asked, "What is this that God has done to us?" (v.28). However they might have meant it, their words have a ring of truth about them. Though we know it was Joseph who had had the money put back into their sacks, their words point us to the work of God, confirming the direction the narrative as a whole appears to be taking.

14–24 Joseph devised two plans to test his brothers. The first was that "one" of the brothers should return for the youngest and the rest remain in prison. After three days the second plan was announced; "one" of the brothers was to remain behind and the others were to return to get the youngest. The focus is on the "one" brother who rescues the others. Within the narrative this "one" brother appears to be an echo of the "one [who] is no more." No wonder, then, that the brothers' own conclusion is that their present distress has been caused by the distress that they had brought on Joseph. When they begin to talk about this distress, we catch a glimpse of where Joseph's plans are leading. Reuben's words focus on the central point: "Now we must give an accounting for his blood." Joseph's plans were not in revenge for how his brothers once treated him; rather, they were to show how, in God's world, the "guilt" of the brothers came back on them and called for justice. The remarkable message of the narrative, however, is that Joseph had already forgiven his brothers of the evil they had done to him, for he had to turn away from them to hide his sorrow for the distress his plan caused. What awaited the brothers was not the "evil" they intended for Joseph but the "good" God intended for them through Joseph (50:20).

25–28 Joseph's next plan was to fill the brothers' sacks with the money they had brought to buy grain (see comment on vv.3–13). God was behind it all, and through it all was working out his purposes.

J. Joseph's Brothers Return for Benjamin (42:29–38)

29–38 The events of this chapter are now retold in an abbreviated form by the brothers. Their focus was on the plan of Joseph for the return of the youngest son. As if he knew all that had in fact happened between his sons and Joseph, Jacob's words in v.36 ring truer than he would ever have suspected. The brothers had deprived him of Joseph, and it was because of them that Simeon was not now with them and that Benjamin was to be taken away. Thus in the words of their father, there was a reminder of the guilt that lingered over their treatment of Joseph.

In the face of Jacob's words, Reuben's response was unusual. He certainly meant his words to ensure confidence in his own resolve to return Benjamin; but within the context of the narrative, it appears only to add insult to injury. Jacob's reply to Reuben not only summarily dismissed Reuben's pledge, but it raised one more time the matter of the loss of Joseph.

K. Joseph's Identity (43:1–45:28)

1. The second trip to Egypt (43:1–34)

1–14 In keeping with the general motif of "pairs" of events throughout the Joseph narratives, the story now begins the "second" journey of the sons into Egypt. The famine was still in the land, and the grain purchased earlier was gone; so the father sent his sons back for more. This time Judah insisted on taking Benjamin back with them in accordance with Joseph's demands.

In persuading his father, Judah offered to take full responsibility for Benjamin if he was allowed to accompany the brothers to Egypt. That both Reuben and Judah had suggested ways Benjamin could be safely taken to

Egypt recalls the events of ch. 37 and the brothers' maltreatment of Joseph. There both Reuben and Judah attempted to save Joseph's life (37:21, 26). Here they attempt to save Benjamin from the plan Joseph had initiated against the brothers. Judah expresses his impatience with Jacob by making explicit reference to the fact that this was the "second" time a journey to Egypt had been made (cf. 41:32).

Jacob gave in. Just as it was Judah's plan that ultimately saved the life of Joseph (37:26), so now his plan saved the life of Simeon and, in the end, of Benjamin. Jacob's farewell words in v.14 (note especially the word "mercy") provide the narrative key to what follows. At the conclusion of the narrative, when the sons reached Joseph and he saw Benjamin, we are told that "his mercy" (v.30; part of "deeply moved" in NIV) was kindled toward his brother. It is important that in these words of Jacob the compassion that Joseph was to find toward his brothers was given by "God Almighty."

15–25 Curiously, the whole problem of the brothers' being "spies" (42:9) is not raised again. Their fears and misgivings as they were ushered into the royal house of Joseph reveal their conviction that nothing good was going to come of this. We are told at the start, however, that the brothers were being taken into the house for a great feast. We know that their fears in v.18 were misguided. They need not have feared becoming Joseph's slaves.

When the brothers repeat to the steward how they found the money in their grain sacks, we see why they were so anxious and just how misguided they actually were. The purpose of the retelling is to get the steward's response. Joseph's steward brushed off their explanation. The reader surely knows that the steward's words cannot be taken seriously, for there was no mention of money given to the steward. Apparently the steward has been in on Joseph's secret plan all along. But unwittingly the steward expresses one of the central themes of the book: "Your God, the God of your father, has given you treasure."

26–34 Joseph was conspicuously careful to ask about the well-being of the brothers' father and the lad, Benjamin, whom they had brought back with them. It is only when we see Joseph hurry to another room to hide his tears that we are sure his identity was still unknown. One wonders what the brothers themselves thought about Joseph's questions and their treatment in his house. They had come expecting to be made into servants, but it was they who were being served. The text simply states that the brothers were "dismayed" (NIV, "in astonishment"). They asked no questions and seemed to accept the words of Joseph's steward (v.23) and Joseph's words to Benjamin (v.29) as the most plausible solution.

2. The silver cup (44:1–34)

1–13 Once more Joseph tricked his brothers by having his cup and Benjamin's money returned in Benjamin's sack of grain. The purpose is clear from what Joseph instructed his men to say. If we are to judge by the brothers' response when the servants reached them with Joseph's message, the word that the servants spoke was more detailed than what we are given in the narrative. The brothers immediately made reference to the silver and gold that were supposedly in their sacks. Perhaps Joseph's words were reported only in general terms because they expressed the central issue of the Joseph narratives: the contrast between the "evil" done by the brothers and the "good" intended and accomplished by God (cf. 50:20).

Joseph's question appears to include the issue of the brothers' treatment of him in ch. 37, which raises again the matter of their guilt in their treatment of Joseph. A residue of guilt still hung over their heads; and almost everywhere they turned, they heard an echo of their mistreatment of Joseph.

Joseph's plan worked as if every detail had been carefully planned out ahead of time. Not knowing that the cup and money were in Benjamin's sack, the brothers made a rash vow, putting the life of Benjamin and their own freedom in jeopardy. When the cup was discovered, their response was one of complete hopelessness. "They tore their clothing in a rage" (lit. tr.) and returned to the city. There was nothing else to do. Curiously, their response mirrored their father's response to hearing their earlier report of the loss of Joseph (37:34). The grief they had caused their father had returned on their own heads.

14–17 While it had looked as if Joseph was working a slow revenge on his brothers, his purpose was not revenge but repentance. Through his schemes his brothers were coming to an awareness of their guilt and were ready to acknowledge it. Their utter frustration is expressed in their questions and their expression of guilt. The rhetorical answer to their questions is that they have nothing to say or cannot show themselves to be right. Thus the conclusion they drew was that "God has uncovered your servants' guilt."

Though the brothers have only the immediate issue of the lost "cup" in mind, within the compass of the whole of the Joseph narrative, their words take on the scope of a confession of their former guilt as well. We know that the brothers did not take the cup; Joseph had it put into Benjamin's sack. We also know that the brothers know they did not take the cup. So when they speak of God "uncovering [their] guilt," we are forced to generalize their sense of guilt within the context of the entire narrative. In his response Joseph steered the matter in a direction that even more closely resembles his brothers' treatment of him. The young lad was to be sold into slavery in Egypt, and the brothers were to return to their father.

18–34 In Judah's final speech, he retold the whole of the Joseph story. His own retelling reveals the brothers' perception of the events as well as the hopelessness of their situation. The overall sense of Judah's version is that the brothers have been mistreated. He implies that if anyone was to blame, it was Joseph. According to Judah's version, Joseph had initiated the series of mishaps that led to the present predicament. All the brothers had done was follow his instructions and the instructions of their father. Judah's words, however, reveal something more to the reader than even he intended; they show that the fault did not lie with Joseph but with the "evil" intention of the brothers toward Joseph. Once again his words raised the issue of the brothers' mistreatment of Joseph.

Curiously, at this point Judah said of Joseph, "[He] is dead," rather than what was said of him on other occasions, namely, that "[he] is no more" (42:13). The meaning of "he is no more" does not imply that one is dead (cf. 5:24; 42:36). Thus, in retelling the story Judah added a dimension that was not previously there. The story now resembles the original intention of the brothers (37:18), and it corresponds to the story that the brothers gave to Jacob. What in real life would have perhaps been a "slip of the tongue" is a clue to the state of mind of the brothers as well as to their guilt.

But Judah's account raises even further the issue of the brothers' guilt regarding Joseph when he recounted Jacob's response to the demand that Benjamin be taken to Egypt. On that occasion Jacob had said, "You know that my wife bore me two sons. One of them went away from me, and I said, 'He has surely been torn to pieces.' " How could Judah recount the story this way? He surely knew that Jacob's words were mistaken. It was not a wild animal that killed Joseph; the brothers themselves had sold him into slavery. But to tell the story the way it actually happened would be to admit to a guilt even greater than that of which they were presently accused. Thus even when retelling the story to demonstrate his own innocence, Judah gave testimony of his own guilt and the guilt of his brothers. Though it is through Judah's speech that the reader is again reminded of the brothers' guilt, it was Judah who intervened on behalf of Benjamin and ultimately his words that saved the day.

After this speech Joseph could contain himself no longer. He felt compelled to unveil his identity to his brothers.

3. Joseph's revelation (45:1–28)

1–8 Joseph had taken no personal enjoyment in deceiving his brothers. When he could hold back no longer, he revealed his true identity. In his words of explanation and comfort to his brothers, Joseph returned once again to the central theme of the narrative: though the brothers were responsible for Joseph's being sold into Egypt, and though they intended "harm," God was ultimately behind it all and had worked it out for the "good." As he told his brothers, "It was to save lives that God sent me ahead of you," and, "God sent me ahead of you to preserve for you a remnant on earth and to save your lives." In the narrative thus far, this theme has been expressed by Jacob (42:2) and Judah (43:8) and has also been indirectly alluded to by Joseph himself (42:18). Here, however, and in 50:20, the theme is given its full expression in the words of Joseph.

Furthermore, it was not the brothers who sent Joseph to Egypt; it was God. And God had a purpose for it all. Joseph, the one ultimately responsible for initiating the plots and subplots of the preceding narratives, reveals the divine plan and purpose behind it all. Through it all he saw God's desire to accomplish a "great deliverance." In describing how God had taken care of him, Joseph alluded to the brothers' initial question regarding his dreams as a young lad (37:8). He reminded them that he had been made "ruler of all Egypt."

9–20 In the second part of his speech, Joseph made plans to bring his father to Egypt. He twice repeated that the brothers were to go to Jacob and with all haste bring him down to Egypt. In the midst of the famine, the sons of Israel were to be well provided for in Goshen. When the Pharaoh restated Joseph's offer and "twice" gave the brothers the "good" (vv.18, 20; NIV, "best") of the land of Egypt, it is hard not to see an allusion to the "good" (1:31) land given to Adam. Joseph pictures restoration, not just of the good fortune of Jacob, but of the blessing that was promised through the offspring of Jacob.

21–28 At first, when Jacob heard the news that Joseph was alive, "his heart grew numb" (NIV, "Jacob was stunned") and "he did not believe." But when he heard everything that Joseph had said and saw all that he had sent to take him back to Egypt, "the spirit . . . of Jacob revived," and he set out to go to him. A new dimension in Jacob's faith is the contrast between his "numbed heart" and his "revived spirit." Jacob's lack of faith is identified with his "numbed heart"; when his spirit was renewed, however, he believed.

L. Jacob's Journey to Egypt (46:1–7)

1–4 Before Jacob went to Egypt, he traveled to Beersheba, built an altar there, and offered sacrifices to the God of his father, Isaac. The patriarchs all worshiped the same God. The Lord had said to Isaac, "Do not go down to Egypt" (26:2); but he now said to Jacob, "Do not be afraid to go down to Egypt." Such a change in attitude toward the patriarchs' traveling to Egypt indicates that the Lord was following a specific plan with regard to his people.

The words spoken to Jacob in the night vision reiterate the promise to Abraham

(12:2), but they also add that God would perform this in Egypt. He would bring his people into Egypt and be with them there; and after they had become a great nation, he would bring them back to the Promised Land. This was the second "vision" in which God revealed his future plans with the offspring of Abraham (cf. 15:1, 13–14).

5–7 Special attention is given to the journey of Jacob and his household into Egypt. Just as Abraham had left Ur and journeyed to Canaan (12:4–5), so now Jacob left Canaan and journeyed to Egypt. Both men were leaving the land of their birth in obedience to the will of God, and the obedience of both plays a pivotal role in God's election of the seed of Abraham. Thus vv.6–7 emphasize by repetition that "all his offspring" went with Jacob into the land of Egypt. To graphically demonstrate the importance of this point, the writer lists the names of "all his offspring," numbering them at "seventy" (see next comment).

M. Jacob's Sons in Egypt (46:8–27)

8–27 The list of names in these verses appears to have been selected so that the total numbers "seventy" (v.27). It can hardly be coincidental that the number of nations in Ge 10 is also "seventy." Just as the "seventy nations" represent all the descendants of Adam, so now the "seventy sons" represent all the descendants of Abraham, Isaac, and Jacob, the sons of Israel. What we see is a demonstration of the theme in Dt 32:8, that God apportioned the boundaries of the nations (Ge 10) according to the number of the sons of Israel. Thus the new nation of Israel is portrayed as a new humanity and Abraham as a second Adam. The blessing that is to come through Abraham and his offspring is a restoration of the original blessing of Adam, a blessing that was lost in the Fall.

N. Settling in Goshen (46:28–47:12)

28–34 Curiously, it was Judah, not Joseph, who led the sons of Israel into the land of Goshen. Once again Judah is singled out for special attention over against Joseph. Although in the Joseph story as a whole it was Joseph who was responsible for the preservation of the sons in Egypt, here, within this detail of the passage, it is Judah who "pointed out the way" (NIV, "to get directions") to the

land of Goshen. Such a special focus on Judah highlights his crucial role in God's plan to bring about Israel's deliverance. The prominence of Judah is seen most clearly in Jacob's words of blessing to his twelve sons (49:8–12).

The chapter ends with Joseph's plan to secure the land of Goshen as a dwelling place for the sons of Israel. The plan was simply to tell the Pharaoh that they were shepherds. The Egyptians hated shepherds and thus would allow the Israelites to dwell by themselves in Goshen. Joseph's plan succeeded, and his family was given the land of Goshen. In these two brief narratives, Joseph and Judah are placed in marked contrast. Judah led the brothers to the land of Goshen, but it was Joseph's wise plan that resulted in their being able to live there.

47:1–12 Joseph's wisdom resulted in the sons of Israel dwelling safely in the land of Goshen while there was severe famine in the land of Canaan. Pharaoh's response was even more generous than the previous narrative would have suggested. Not only did he grant their wish and allow Joseph's brothers to settle in Goshen, he also put the brothers in charge of his own livestock, a result reminiscent of Joseph's own rise to power in the house of Pharaoh (cf. 41:41). Thus Joseph's fortune was duplicated in the fortune of his brothers. The land of Goshen is called the "best part of the land," which perhaps is a wordplay on the "good" that God intended in all of these recorded events (50:20).

Significantly, the central concern of this narrative is to show that Jacob "blessed Pharaoh" (vv.7, 10) when he was brought before him. Lying behind such an emphasis is God's promise to Abraham that he would bless those who blessed the offspring of Abraham. The passage shows that in Joseph and Jacob, the promise to Abraham was being fulfilled with the nations around them.

Jacob's words to the Pharaoh in v.9 sound unusual in the way they contrast with the two accounts of his blessing Pharaoh. They seem a deliberate contrast to the later promise in Deuteronomy that one who honors his father and mother should "live long and that it may go well with you in the land" (Dt 5:16). Jacob, who deceived his father and thereby gained the blessing, must not only die outside the Promised Land, but we also learn here that his years were few and diffi-cult, perhaps a recompense for his earlier ac-tions. Abraham obeyed God and lived long in the land (Ge 26:5), but Jacob's years were short and difficult. In spite of such a final ver-dict, Jacob lived out his remaining years "in the good [NIV, best part] of the land," though not the Promised Land; and Joseph, his son, provided for him and his household.

O. Joseph's Rule in Egypt (47:13–27)

13–27 The narrative returns to the story line of 41:57 with an account of the affairs of Jo-seph in Egypt and his work on behalf of the Pharaoh. The brothers are no longer the cen-ter of attention; the focus is on Joseph and his sons.

Perhaps the account of Joseph and his brothers (chs. 42–46) is inserted in the midst of the narratives dealing with Joseph's rise to power in Egypt (chs. 39–41, 47) because of the way this final narrative resembles the story of Joseph and his brothers. Through-out those narratives the theme was repeat-edly expressed that Joseph's wisdom and administrative skills saved the life of his brothers and father. Thus at the beginning of the story, Jacob had told his sons to go down to Egypt to buy grain "that we may live and not die" (42:2). Then Judah, "in the second year" (45:6), told his father to let them return to Egypt "that we may live and not die" (43:8). Finally, when he revealed himself to them, Joseph told his brothers that God had sent him to Egypt "to save life" (45:5; NIV, "to save lives").

In keeping with that emphasis, the present narrative opens with the statement of the Egyptians to Joseph as they seek to buy grain from him: "Why should we die before your eyes?" Then it continues with the account of their return to Joseph "the second year" (NIV, "the following year"), when they again said, "Why should we perish?" and then again, "that we may live and not die." Such repetitions suggest that a thematic strategy is at work. First with his brothers and then with the Egyptians, Joseph's wisdom is seen as the source of life for everyone in the land. Furthermore, through God's wisdom given to this descendant of Abraham, the nations are receiving a blessing (cf. 12:2–3).

A further evidence of a distinct strategy behind the present narrative in ch. 47 can be seen in the ironic twist given the earlier nar-ratives by the outcome of this chapter. The whole of the story of Joseph and his brothers began with Joseph being sold (37:28) into sla-very (39:17) for twenty pieces of silver (37:28). Now, at the conclusion, Joseph is shown selling the whole of the land of Egypt into slavery and taking their "money" (v.18). In the end, because of the wisdom of Joseph, the offspring of Abraham became "fruitful," "increased greatly in number," and were dwelling safely and prosperously in the "re-gion" of Goshen. Such a picture appears to be an obvious replication of the intended blessing of the early chapters of Genesis (1:28).

P. Jacob's Deathbed (47:28–49:33)

1. Jacob's burial instructions (47:28–31)

28 The initial impression from this verse is that the Jacob narratives are coming to a close, but such is not the case. Two crucial chapters remain. Verse 28 provides continu-ity within the Jacob narrative that had been broken into by the account of Joseph's fur-ther rise to power (vv.13–27); it also moves the narratives to a new time frame, seventeen years later. Perhaps the underlying assump-tion is that by now the famine was over and Joseph's position in Egypt has been well es-tablished.

29–31 As he approached death, Jacob's only request was that he not be buried in the land of Egypt. The manner of the request alludes back to Abraham (cf. 24:2). As he ap-proached death (24:1), Abraham did not want his son to take a wife from among the people in the land where he was then dwell-ing (24:3–4). In the same way, as Jacob ap-proached death (v.29), he did not want to be buried among the Egyptians but with his fa-thers in his own land. The same theme is taken up in ch. 50, when Joseph makes his sons swear that they will carry his bones back to the Promised Land, a request carried out in Jos 24:32.

A central element of the covenant with Abraham was the promise of the land. The request of the patriarchs to be buried in the land "with their fathers" emphasizes their trust in the faithfulness of God to his word. Henceforth a key symbol of Israel's faith in the promises of God is the bones of the faith-ful offspring that lie buried in the Promised Land. One other chapter of the Bible, Eze 37, with its prophecy of the "dry bones," pays specific attention to this symbol.

As early as the rivalry between Leah, Judah's mother, and Rachel, Joseph's mother (ch. 30), the question of the preeminence of one of the brothers over the other has occupied a central role. In chs. 48 (the blessing of Joseph) and 49 (the blessing of Judah) the issue comes to a final resolution in the choice of one from the tribe of Judah who will reign over the rest of the brothers (49:8–10). Similarly in Eze 37 the prophet returns to the theme of the Joseph narratives and the rivalry between the brothers. There, as here, the brothers are reunited under the king from the tribe of Judah, David (Eze 37:15–17, 22–24).

2. Ephraim and Manasseh blessed (48:1–22)

The phrase "some time later" suggests an important break from the events that have preceded. Chapter 48 fittingly concludes the Joseph narratives. As in the earlier patriarchal narratives, the blessing of the father is passed along to the next generation. Two features stand out. First, as earlier, it was the younger son, Ephraim, who was blessed as the firstborn rather than the older, Manasseh (v.19), thus continuing the well-worn theme that the blessing did not follow the lines of natural descent or natural right. The blessing was a gift bestowed on those who could not claim it as a right. Second, the blessing recorded here is largely subordinated and superseded by the blessing of Jacob in ch. 49.

Curiously, Judah rather than Joseph ultimately gained preeminence among his brothers. As important as Joseph is in the structure of the Genesis narratives, his role is subordinate to that of Judah. Consequently, not the blessings of the sons of Joseph, but the blessing of Judah plays the dominant role in the continuing story of the promise and the blessing. From Judah comes the house of David, and from David comes the Messiah. Ephraim and Manasseh play an important role in the texts dealing with the divided northern kingdom, but the importance of that kingdom, which ultimately was exiled and lost in the Dispersion, pales quickly in the light of the rising star of David.

1–4 The frailty of Jacob foreshadowed that his life was drawing to a close. As soon as he saw Joseph and his two sons, however, Jacob was revived, and he prepared to bestow God's blessing on the house of Joseph. Jacob's recollection of God's promise to him at Bethel (35:9–13) is significant. He repeated the Lord's words almost verbatim; but in the minor alterations we can see not only Jacob's assessment of the promise but also the writer's perspective. As he had acknowledged in 35:9, so now Jacob recalled that God had "blessed him." When he recounted what God had said, Jacob brought out a nuance to God's words that helps clarify our understanding of the Lord's promised blessing.

In 35:11 the Lord had said, "Be fruitful and increase in number. A nation and a community of nations will come from you." In essence he was saying, "May you be fruitful and increase," as in Ge 1:28. But as Jacob retold the story to Joseph here, he stressed that God was the one who would bring about all that had been promised: "I am going to make you fruitful and will increase your numbers. I will make you a community of peoples, and I will give this land as an everlasting possession to your descendants after you." As he reflected back on the blessing and recounted it to his sons, Jacob brought out just that aspect of the blessing that had been the theme of the Joseph narratives: God ultimately will bring about all that he has promised.

A second nuance noticeable in Jacob's recounting God's promise of the land is that he again did so verbatim: "I will give this land . . . to your descendants after you" (cf. 35:11). But there is a significant addition to Jacob's retelling. He has added "as an everlasting possession." Only one other time is the promise of the land called an "everlasting possession" (17:8; cf. 13:15).

5–7 Ephraim and Manasseh were taken into the family of Jacob and were to be treated as his own. They, along with the other sons of Jacob, would inherit the promise of Abraham. Henceforth the families of Ephraim and Manasseh were counted among the sons of Jacob and later became two of the most important tribes of Israel. Later these two names became synonymous with the northern kingdom of Israel, which stood in bitter opposition to the kingdom of Judah.

The mention of Rachel and her burial site could be prompted by the fact that just as she had borne Jacob "two sons" (44:27, Joseph and Benjamin) at a time when he was about to enter (48:7) the land, so also Joseph had given Jacob "two sons" just at the time when he was about to enter Egypt. Such symmetry suggests that Ephraim and Manasseh are seen as replacements of Joseph and Benjamin, which furthers the sense of divine providence behind Jacob's life.

Furthermore, Jacob's recollection is virtually verbatim to that of the account of Rachel's death in 35:16–19. Both passages stress the site of "Ephrath," which is identified as Bethlehem. As in the earlier cases of the concern for the burial of the patriarchs in the Promised Land, Jacob's mention of Rachel's burial is tied to the promise that the land would be an "eternal possession" of the seed of Abraham, a reminder of the faithfulness of God to his covenant promise.

8–14 The blessing of Ephraim and Manasseh is recounted in great detail. In the account of Jacob's blessing his sons (ch. 49), these two sons are not mentioned. In other words, the present account augments ch. 49. Great care is taken to emphasize that in the blessing of these two sons, Ephraim, the younger, was given the blessing of the firstborn (v.20b).

The first blessing (vv.15–16) appears to be of Joseph rather than the two sons ("Then he blessed Joseph," v.15). In the blessing itself, however, reference is made to the "young sons" (v.16), and the blessing of Joseph ultimately focuses on them. Before Jacob went on to address the two sons specifically in the blessing, Joseph interrupted him, attempting to get his father to place his right hand on Manasseh rather than Ephraim, thus giving the right of the firstborn to Manasseh, the older son. After objecting to Joseph's attempt (v.19), Jacob went on to bless the two sons specifically ("He blessed them," v.20), thus giving Ephraim preeminence over Manasseh.

15–16 Jacob's blessing is a storehouse of key thematic terms. God is identified as the "God before whom my fathers Abraham and Isaac walked." Not only does the mention of Abraham and Isaac connect Jacob's faith in God to his immediate forefathers, but it also helps tie together the faith of the earliest patriarchs in Genesis with that of Abraham, Isaac, and Jacob. At two earlier points in the book, the faith of the primeval patriarchs is described as those who "walked with God" (5:22, 24; 6:9). The faith of the early fathers

was at one with that of the patriarchs—they walked with God.

God is also described as the "God who has been my shepherd all my life to this day" and as the "Angel who has delivered me from all harm." It is unusual that God himself should be described as "the Angel," since earlier in the book it is said that God sent "his angel" (24:7) or simply that one of the patriarchs was visited by "the angel of the LORD" (22:11).

The blessing of the two sons picks up the theme of the promise to Abraham. They are to be called by Jacob's "name" and the "name" of Abraham and Isaac, just as God had promised Abraham: "I will make your name great" (12:2). They were to "increase greatly," just as God had promised Abraham, "I will make you into a great nation" (12:2).

17–20 The central concern here is to underscore that Ephraim, the younger son, was given preeminence over Manasseh. Though nearly blind himself (v.10), Jacob appeared to be making the same mistake that his father, Isaac, had when Jacob deceived him in ch. 27. When Joseph attempted to correct him, he stated his intentions clearly: "His younger brother will be greater than he." Why so much concern over whether Ephraim or Manasseh was put first, especially since neither Joseph nor his two sons but Judah received the preeminence? The issue of preeminence is meant to address the larger question that receiving the blessing offered by God does not rest with one's natural status in the world. On the contrary, it is based solely on God's grace. The one to whom the blessing did not belong has become heir of the promise.

21–22 Throughout these narratives Jacob has been pictured, not as a man of "sword and . . . bow," but as "a quiet man, staying among the tents" (25:27). Elsewhere Jacob has said of the inhabitants of the land of Canaan, "If they join forces against me and attack me, I and my household will be destroyed" (34:30). Now, suddenly, on his deathbed, Jacob revealed another picture of himself as he bequeathed to Joseph the portion of land he had taken by force. Though he spoke to Joseph, his use of the plural pronouns ("with you," pl. Heb.) shows that he was addressing a larger audience. That larger audience appears to be the house of Joseph that was to be represented in the tribes of Ephraim and Manasseh.

3. Jacob's sons blessed (49:1–28)

1–2 Jacob's last words to his sons are the occasion for a final statement of the book's major theme: God's plan to restore the lost blessing through the offspring of Abraham. The key to the writer's understanding of Jacob's last words lies in the narrative framework that surrounds them. We are explicitly told that Jacob was speaking about those things that would happen "in the last days" (NIV, "in days to come"; see also Nu 24:14–24; Dt 31:29). On all three occasions the subject matter introduced by the phrase "in days to come" is that of God's future deliverance of his chosen people. At the center of that deliverance stands a king (Ge 49:10; Nu 24:7; Dt 33:5). In Ge 49 that king is connected with the house of Judah.

At the close of Jacob's discourse (v.28), the writer draws a line connecting Jacob's words in this chapter to the theme of "the blessing" that has been a central concern of the book since 1:28. He does this by repeating the word "blessing" (GK 1385) three times in the short span of v.28, which literally reads: "And he blessed them; each according to his blessing he blessed them." Jacob's last words look to the future—"in days to come"—and draw on the past—God's blessing of humanity. The order of the sons follows roughly the order of the record of their birth (chs. 29–30).

The sons of Leah lead the list, followed by the sons of the handmaidens, Bilhah, Zilpah, and again Bilhah, and then the sons of Rachel.

3–4 The key to the saying regarding Reuben is the statement "you will not excel" (NIV, "no longer excel"). The word "excel" (GK 3855) is a play on the two statements that have preceded it: "excelling in honor" and "excelling in power." Though Reuben has excelled, he will no longer excel. The reason given is brief but to the point: "for you went up onto ... my couch and defiled it" (cf. 35:22). Reuben no longer had the right of the firstborn because he violated the honor of his father (cf. 1Ch 5:1–2 for the right of the firstborn being transferred to Joseph).

5–7 Simeon and Levi are grouped together because they instigated the bloodshed against the city of Shechem (34:25). At that time Jacob protested vehemently against the two sons and their attack on the defenseless city (34:30). Here Jacob gave his final verdict on their action: the two tribes of Levi and Simeon would not have their own portion in the inheritance of the land. The fulfillment of Jacob's words can be found in the facts that the tribe of Simeon virtually disappears from the biblical narratives after the time of the Conquest (because they "received their territory within the territory of Judah"; Jos 19:9) and the tribe of Levi was given the responsibility

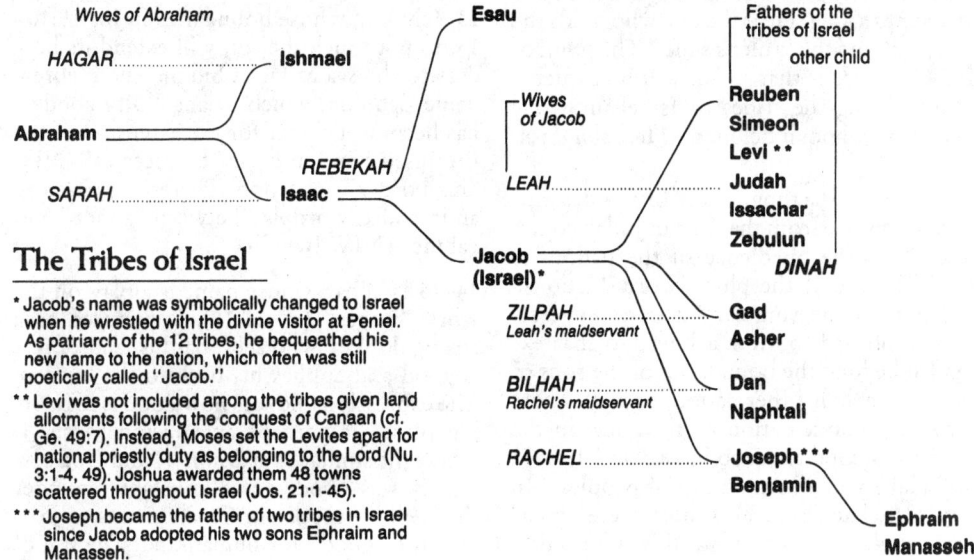

The Tribes of Israel

* Jacob's name was symbolically changed to Israel when he wrestled with the divine visitor at Peniel. As patriarch of the 12 tribes, he bequeathed his new name to the nation, which often was still poetically called "Jacob."

** Levi was not included among the tribes given land allotments following the conquest of Canaan (cf. Ge. 49:7). Instead, Moses set the Levites apart for national priestly duty as belonging to the Lord (Nu. 3:1-4, 49). Joshua awarded them 48 towns scattered throughout Israel (Jos. 21:1-45).

*** Joseph became the father of two tribes in Israel since Jacob adopted his two sons Ephraim and Manasseh.

© 1985 The Zondervan Corporation

of the priesthood and hence received no inheritance in the apportioning of the land.

8–12 Having eliminated the older brothers as rightful heirs of the blessing, Jacob foretold a future for the tribe of Judah that pictured him as the preeminent son. We have seen that the right of the firstborn, according to Ge 48:5, belonged to Joseph (see above and 1Ch 5:1–2). Though not having the right of the firstborn, Judah had been chosen over all the others as the royal tribe. According to 1Ch 5:2, Judah "prevailed" (NIV, "was the strongest") over his brothers and thus became heir to the throne (cf. Ps 78:67–68).

Unlike the imagery used of the other sons, the words of Jacob regarding Judah are transparent. Judah is described as a victorious warrior who returns home from battle and is greeted by the shouts of praise from his brothers. The parallelism of v.8 is extended by the statement "your father's sons will bow down to you." It is difficult not to see in this an intentional allusion to the dream of Joseph (37:10). What happened to the house of Joseph has been picked up by way of this image and transferred to the future house of Judah.

The image of the victorious warrior is extended with the picture of Judah as a "young lion" (NIV, "lion's cub"). The young lion is pictured as sleeping in its den after having just devoured its prey. The question at the end of v.9 speaks for itself. In v.10 the picture is filled out with a description of the young warrior as a king. He is the one who holds the "scepter" and the "ruler's staff." The point of Jacob's words is that Judah will hold such a status among the tribes of Israel until one comes "to whom it belongs" (Heb. *shiloh*; cf. Eze 21:27).

The most startling aspect of the description of this one from the tribe of Judah comes next: "and the obedience of the nations is his." The use of the plural word "nations" rather than the singular "nation" suggests that Jacob had in view a kingship that extended beyond the boundaries of the sons of Israel to include other nations as well. There may be an anticipation of this view in the promise of God to Jacob in 28:3 and 48:4: "I will make you a community of peoples." In any case, later biblical writers were apparently guided by texts such as this in formulating their view of the universal reign of the future Davidic king (e.g., Ps 2:8; Dan 7:13–14; Rev 5:5, 9).

Verses 11–12 draw an extended picture of the reign of this one from the tribe of Judah. In his day there will again be plenty for everyone. Poetically this idea of plenitude is expressed with the images of the donkey tethered to the choicest of vines and clothing washed in vintage wine. The sense of the imagery is that wine, the symbol of prosperity and blessing, will be so plentiful that even the choicest vines will be put to such everyday use as tethering the animals of burden and vintage wine will be as commonplace as wash water. Verse 12 returns to the picture of the king of Judah. His eyes are darker than wine and his teeth whiter than milk. He is a picture of strength and power. Later writers drew heavily from the imagery of this short text in their portrayal of the reign of the coming Messiah (cf. Isa 63:1–6; Rev 19:11, 13, 15).

Jacob's words regarding the remaining sons, with the exception of Joseph, are noticeable not only for their brevity, but also for their cryptic allusions to epic events that at the time lay yet in the future. The destinies of the remaining sons are, in most cases, based on a wordplay of the son's name. The central theme uniting each image is that of prosperity. Just as the victorious king from the tribe of Judah will reign over all nations in a time of rich blessing, so also each of the remaining brothers will experience the same sort of prosperity and blessing.

13 Zebulun, whose boundaries in Jos 19:10–16 do not touch the sea, will extend its borders to the sea as far as Sidon. The Hebrew name Zebulun, which means "lofty abode," has become a cipher for the extension of the Promised Land into the "far recesses" (NIV, "his border") of Sidon. There is apparently an intended wordplay between "abode" and "abide" (NIV, "will live").

14–15 Issachar, whose name is a play on the word "wages" (cf. 30:18), is pictured as a strong donkey who sees that his land of rest is good and applies his back to the burden. The expression "he sees how good is his resting place" is perhaps an allusion to ch. 1, where the similar expression—"and God saw that it was good"—is a constant reminder that God's purpose in Creation was to provide the "good" for humankind. The use of the term "resting place" or "land of rest" aligns the words of Jacob with the theme of the future rest that God will give his people in the Promised Land (cf. Ps 95:11).

16–18 Dan, whose name is a play on the expression "he will judge," is the one who will judge his people. He is likened to a snake along the path that attacks the heels of the horse and cunningly defeats the horseman. Though the sense of the image itself is unclear, Jacob's final words regarding Dan show that the image was meant in a positive way: "I look for your deliverance, O LORD" (v.18). Breaking in, as it does, on the increasingly terse poetic images, this expression of hope in the Lord's deliverance provides the much-needed clue to the meaning of Jacob's words. In the individual and future destiny of the sons is embodied the hope of all Israel. That hope is of a future prosperity for the nation and a future victory over their enemies. At the center of that hope is the king from the tribe of Judah.

19 The brief statement regarding Gad contains a wordplay on nearly every word: "Gad [*gad*] will be attacked [*yegudennu*] by a band of raiders [*gedud*], but he will attack [*yagud*] them at their heels." Again, though it is very brief, the saying falls in line with the others, following in the path of the prophecy regarding Judah in that it gives expression to the hope of the final defeat of the enemy.

20 The statement regarding Asher has no clear wordplays, and its meaning is self-evident. In the future Asher's sons will enjoy great abundance and rich delicacies.

21 The words regarding Naphtali are also brief. The picture they present, which is similar to the others, is of a time of great future prosperity and abundance.

22–26 Jacob has much to say about the future of the tribe of Joseph. In substance Jacob's statements repeat much of what was said about the other brothers after Judah. The difference, however, is the repetition of the word "blessing." Whereas Jacob's words regarding the other brothers paint a picture of the future well-being of the sons and thus figuratively speak of a future blessing, Jacob's words to Joseph explicitly refer to this future well-being as a "blessing." These words to Joseph, therefore, fall in line with all those earlier passages that speak specifically of the promised "blessing" and prepare the way for the final remarks about Jacob's words in v.28: "he blessed them; each according to his blessing, he blessed them" (lit. tr.). The reference to the "Shepherd" in v.24 appears to be an allusion to Jacob's earlier blessing of Ephraim and Manasseh (48:15).

27 The picture of Benjamin is similar to that of Judah. Both depict the patriarch's future in terms expressing a victorious conquest over the enemy. In both the conqueror is a vicious predator, the lion and the wolf. The stark simplicity of these words to Benjamin, however, brings out the sense of sudden victory and conquest in much stronger terms than the imagery of Judah.

28 The writer sums up Jacob's words to his sons. They are an expression of the theme of the blessing that was to be passed along through the seed of Abraham, Isaac, and Jacob. Within Jacob's words to each son (after Judah), the theme of blessing has been evident in two primary images. First, the reverse side of the blessing is stressed in the imagery of the victorious warrior. The defeat of the enemy is the prelude to the messianic peace. Second, the positive side of the blessing is stressed in the imagery of great prosperity and abundance. Behind such imagery is the Garden of Eden—the Paradise lost. The focus of Jacob's words has been the promise that when the one comes to whom the kingship truly belongs (v.10), there will once again be the peace and prosperity that God intended all to have in the Garden of Eden.

4. Jacob's burial instructions repeated (49:29–33)

29–33 As he lay dying, Jacob once more made a request that his sons bury him in the Land of Promise with his fathers. The specific place he had in mind was "Machpelah," the burial place purchased by Abraham in ch. 23. Although Jacob had made a similar request earlier (47:29–30), this final one was far more specific. He wanted to be buried with Abraham, Sarah, Isaac, Rebekah, and Leah. The request renews our awareness of the promise of the land—that Jacob's seed would live in peace in the land promised to Abraham and Isaac. Jacob's faith in God's promises remained firm to the end. With such an expression on his lips, "he ... breathed his last and was gathered to his people."

Q. Jacob's Death and Burial (50:1–14)

1–14 Over half of the final chapter is occupied with a description of the mourning for and burial of Jacob. Joseph himself mourned and then the Egyptians. Great preparations were made both by Joseph and the Egyptians. A special request was granted by the Pharaoh to bury Jacob in his homeland, and a large entourage was provided as a burial procession to carry Jacob's body back to Canaan. "All Pharaoh's officials . . . and all the dignitaries of Egypt" along with Pharaoh's chariots and horsemen accompanied Joseph on his journey back to Canaan. Even the Canaanites recognized this as "a very large [lit., heavy; NIV, solemn] ceremony of mourning."

Why such detail over the burial of Jacob when the deaths of the other patriarchs are simply recounted in the bare facts that they died and were buried? Even the account of the death of Joseph consists only of the brief notice that he died and was embalmed and entombed in Egypt (v.26). It is appropriate to seek a motive for such an emphasis within the narrative.

The writer has been focusing on God's faithfulness to his promise of the land and on the hope of God's people in the eventual return to the land. In later prophetic literature, a recurring image of the fulfillment of the promise to return to the land pictures returning Israel accompanied by many from among the nations. The prophets of Israel saw the return as a time when "all the nations will stream to" Jerusalem, and "many peoples will come and say, 'Come, let us go up to the mountain of the LORD, to the house of the God of Jacob' " (Isa 2:2–3; Zec 8:23).

It is difficult not to see the same imagery at work in the present narrative. Jacob, in his final return to the Land of Promise, was accompanied by a great congregation of the officials and elders of the land of Egypt. With him also was the mighty army of the Egyptians. Thus the story of Jacob's burial in the land foreshadows the time when God "will bring Jacob back from captivity and will have compassion on all the people of Israel" (Eze 39:25).

VII. The Final Joseph Narrative (50:15–26)

A. Joseph's Forgiveness (50:15–21)

15–21 The narrative turns once more to the scene of Joseph and his brothers and to the central theme of the Joseph narratives: "You intended to harm [lit., evil; GK 8288] me, but God intended it for good . . . [to] the saving of many lives." Behind all the events and human plans recounted in the story of Joseph lies the unchanging plan of God. It is the same plan introduced from the very beginning of the book, where God looks at what he has just created for humankind and sees that "it is good" (1:4–31). Through his dealings with the patriarchs and Joseph, God had continued to bring about his good plan. He had remained faithful to his purposes.

The last description of Joseph's dealings with his brothers is the statement that "he comforted [NIV, reassured; GK 5714] them and spoke kindly to them." It is again difficult not to see in this picture a foreshadowing of the future community of the sons of Israel in exile awaiting their return to the Promised Land (cf. Isa 40:1–2).

B. Summary of Joseph's Life and Death (50:22–26)

22–26 Though his words are few, the final statement of Joseph to his sons gives the clearest expression of the kind of hope taught in these narratives. As had his father Jacob, Joseph wanted his bones returned to the Promised Land. Also like Jacob, he saw to it that his sons swore to return his bones when they returned to the land. Though he knew he would die and not see the time when his sons returned to the land, he nevertheless expressed clearly the hope and trust that he had in God's promise: "God will surely come to your aid and take you up out of this land to the land he promised on oath to Abraham, Isaac and Jacob." As has been characteristic of the literary technique of the Joseph narratives, Joseph repeated a second time (cf. 41:32) his statement of trust in God's promise: "God will surely come to your aid, and then you must carry my bones up from this place."

The book of Genesis ends with the Israelites "in Egypt." The narrative, however, does not end here. As in earlier segments of the book, the death of the patriarch is followed immediately in the next book by a list of names that begins a narrative of the events in the lives of the next generations (cf. Ge 50:26–Ex 1:5 with Ge 35:29–36:43).

The Old Testament in the New

OT Text	NT Text	Subject
Ge 1:3	2Co 4:6	Creation of light
Ge 1:27	Mt 19:4; Mk 10:6	Creation of humans
Ge 2:2	Heb 4:4	God rested the seventh day
Ge 2:7	1Co 15:45	Creation of Adam
Ge 2:24	Mt 19:5; Mk 10:7; 1Co 6:16; Eph 5:31	Institution of marriage
Ge 5:2	Mt 19:4; Mk 10:6	Creation of humans
Ge 12:1	Ac 7:3	Call of Abraham
Ge 12:3	Gal 3:8	Gospel to Abraham
Ge 13:15	Gal 3:16	Offspring of Abraham
Ge 14:18–20	Heb 7:17, 21	Melchizedek
Ge 15:5	Ro 4:18	Offspring of Abraham
Ge 15:6	Ro 4:3, 9, 22; Gal 3:6; Jas 2:23	Faith of Abraham
Ge 15:13–14	Ac 7:6–7	Prophecy to Abraham
Ge 17:5	Ro 4:17	Abraham as a father of many
Ge 18:10, 14	Ro 9:9	Promise for Sarah
Ge 18:18	Gal 3:8	Gospel to Abraham
Ge 21:10	Gal 4:30	Expulsion of Ishmael
Ge 21:12	Ro 9:7; Heb 11:18	God's choice of Isaac
Ge 22:17	Heb 6:14	God's oath to Abraham
Ge 22:18	Ac 3:25	Nations blessed in Abraham
Ge 24:7	Gal 3:16	Offspring of Abraham
Ge 25:23	Ro 9:12	God's choice of Jacob
Ge 26:4	Ac 3:25	Nations blessed in Abraham

Exodus

INTRODUCTION

1. Title

The name "Exodus" means "exit," "departure." In the Hebrew, this book begins with the conjunction "and"; this emphasizes that it was thought of as a continuation of Genesis and an integral part of the five books making up the first division of the Hebrew canon, the Torah (meaning "law," "instruction," "teaching"; GK 9368). Since the second century A.D., these first five books have been called "the Pentateuch" (i.e., "the five books").

2. Authorship

The several internal claims that directly ascribe authorship to Moses (17:14; 34:4, 27–29; 24:4; 20:22–23:33) are supported by a strong association of Mosaic authorship with these same materials in other OT books (cf. Jos 1:7; 8:31–32; 1Ki 2:3; 2Ki 14:6; et al.). The NT writers likewise support Mosaic authorship (cf. Mk 12:26 and Ex 3:6; Lk 2:22–23 and Ex 13:2; Mk 7:10 and Ex 20:12; 21:17).

3. Date of Writing

Since Moses first became involved with leading the Israelites after his eightieth birthday (7:7), the date for the composition of the book of Exodus must fall between his eightieth birthday and his one hundred and twentieth birthday, when he died, just as the wilderness wandering was drawing to a close (Dt 34:7). Thus the approximate date for the composition rests on the date set for the Exodus from Egypt.

4. Date of the Exodus

The book of Exodus nowhere gives us enough data to link definitively biblical events with Egyptian chronology. We only know about "a new king, who did not know about Joseph" (1:8) or an anonymous "Pharaoh" (1:11, 19, 22; 2:15), or a "king of Egypt" (1:15; 2:23). It is noteworthy that "Pharaoh," which means "great house" and

designates the king's residence and household, became, for the first time in the Eighteenth Dynasty of Egypt, a title for the king himself. Thus, even though Ex 2:23 tells us that the king or "Pharaoh" of the oppression died and therefore could not have been the Pharaoh of the Exodus (cf. 4:19), we have no internal evidence to identify either of them specifically.

The identity of these two Pharaohs has generally centered on two views: (1) placing the Exodus under the Pharaohs of the Eighteenth Dynasty (c. 1580–1321 B.C.) and (2) placing it under Pharaohs of the Nineteenth Dynasty (c. 1321–1205 B.C.). For a discussion of this issue, see either EBC, 2:288–91 or ZPEB, 2:432–36. Generally, conservative scholars have held to the earlier date for the Exodus, which is the position taken here.

5. Theology

Exodus contains some of the richest theology in the OT. Preeminently, it lays the foundation for a theology of God's revelation of his person, redemption, law, and worship. It also initiates the great institution of the priesthood and the role of the prophet, and it formalizes the covenant relationship between God and his people.

Exodus contains detailed disclosures of the nature of God and the significance of his presence (as given by his name Yahweh ["the LORD"] and his glory). His attributes of justice, truthfulness, mercy, faithfulness, and holiness are highlighted.

God is also the Lord of history, for there is no one like him, "majestic in holiness, awesome in glory, working wonders" (15:11). Thus neither the affliction of Israel nor the plagues in Egypt were outside his control. In this book God begins to fulfill the promises that he had uttered centuries ago to the patriarchs.

The theology of deliverance and salvation is a strong emphasis of the book. The heart of redemption theology, as acknowledged by the NT (see Jn 1:29; 1Co 5:7), is best seen in the Passover narrative (ch. 12) along with the sealing of the covenant (ch. 24).

Exodus also tells us how we should live. The foundation of biblical ethics and morality is laid out first in the gracious character of God and then in the Ten Commandments and the ordinances of the Book of the Covenant.

The book concludes with an elaborate discussion on the theology of worship. The tabernacle was very costly in time, effort, and monetary value; yet in its significance and function it pointed to the chief end of human beings: to glorify God and to enjoy him forever.

EXPOSITION

I. Divine Redemption (1:1–18:27)

A. Fulfilled Multiplication and Forced Eradication (1:1–22)

1. The promised increase (1:1–7)

The three prominent subjects of Exodus are (1) God's plan for deliverance, (2) God's guidance for morality, and (3) God's order for worship. As the book opens, another prominent fact is immediately set forth: vv.1–7 are a virtual commentary on the ancient promise made to Abraham, Isaac, and Jacob about their seed (Ge 15:5; 22:17).

1–4 In the Hebrew, the book of Exodus begins with the words "And these are the names of" (which is the Heb. name for the book; cf. Ge 46:8). This is the first example of a practice common to most of the historical books of the OT: the use of the simple copulative "and" to begin a book (cf. Joshua, Judges, Ruth, 1 and 2 Samuel, et al.), which indicates an ongoing sequence of revelation and narration. The sons of Jacob's wives, Leah and Rachel, are placed in order of their seniority ahead of the sons of his two concubines, except for Joseph, who is omitted because he was already in Egypt.

5 The family list in Ge 46 gives this tally: the six men of Leah had twenty-five sons and two grandsons, totaling thirty-three; the two sons of Rachel had twelve sons, totaling fourteen; Bilhah's two sons had five sons, contributing seven to the sum; and Zilpah's two sons had eleven sons, one daughter (appar-

ently counted here), and two grandsons, making sixteen; therefore, thirty-three plus fourteen plus seven plus sixteen equals "seventy." Genesis 46:26–27 starts with the figure of sixty-six (apparently dropping out Er and Onan, since they died in Canaan, as well as deleting Joseph and his two sons, since they were already in Egypt, but adding Dinah, feeling she could not be deleted). To this total of sixty-six, it added Joseph, his two sons, and Jacob himself, for a total of seventy.

6–7 With the vocabulary of God's promised blessing of multiplication and increase as given to Adam (Ge 1:28), Noah (Ge 8:17; 9:1, 7), Abraham (Ge 17:2–6; 22:17), Isaac (Ge 26:4), and Jacob (Ge 28:3, 14; 35:11; 48:4), Moses recorded that God had been fulfilling his plan during the 430 years Israel was in Egypt.

2. The first pogrom (1:8–14)

8 The "new king" who was ignorant of Joseph's contribution to Egypt has been variously identified. The most logical choice favors a Hyksos king. The Hyksos were foreign invaders who drove the Egyptians south and did not use Egyptian hieroglyphic writing on their scarabs. They too were Semites.

9–10 Israel was called "a people" (GK 6639) for the first time here. The situation called for an extremely delicate balance: Pharaoh needed to maintain the Israelite presence as an economic asset without thereby jeopardizing Egypt's national security.

11 The term "masters" (*sar*; GK 8569) is common to both Hebrew and Egyptian. The same official Egyptian name appears on the famous wall painting from the Theban tomb of Rekhmire, the overseer of the brick-making slaves during the reign of Thutmose III. The painting shows such overseers armed with heavy whips. Their rank is denoted by the long staff held in their hands and by the Egyptian hieroglyphic determinative of the head and neck of a giraffe. The two storehouse cities Israel built were for the storage of provisions and perhaps armaments. The location of Pithom may be equated with Tell er-Retabeh ("Broomhill"), which some equate with Heliopolis (cf. ZPEB, 4:803–4). Rameses has most recently been located at or near Qantir ("Bridge").

12–14 Pharaoh's challenge—"or they will become even more numerous" (v.10)—was quite foolish in view of v.12. The result was a frightful dread that came over the Egyptians. Ironically, the God-intended instrument for the salvation of both nations (cf. Ge 12:3) became instead, through the hardness of human hearts, the source of crippling fear. Thus the Egyptians "made [Israel's] lives bitter," a fact later commemorated in the Passover meal's "bitter herbs" (12:8). The emphasis of vv.8–14 falls on the "ruthlessness" of the work and servitude imposed on Israel.

3. The second pogrom (1:15–22)

15–16 The two midwives were probably representatives of or superintendents over the whole profession. The delivery stools were literally "two stones" (dual form).

17–21 The midwives "feared God" more than they feared the king of Egypt. If they were not Hebrews but Egyptians, their God-fearing ways reveal the presence of God's common grace and the residue of earlier divine revelation that their ancestors shared but had gradually left in whole or part (cf. Ge 20:11; Dt 25:18; Mal 3:5). The midwives had respect for life, as God wanted them to have. Even though they lied to Pharaoh, they are praised for their outright refusal to take infant lives. Their reverence for life reflected a reverence for God. Thus God gave them "families." The midwives may also have attempted to avoid answering Pharaoh's question directly, and therefore they commented on what was true without giving all the details.

22 A single concluding and transitional verse summarizes ch. 1. Pharaoh needed to openly command by decree what had proved abortive by mere speeches. "All his people" were made agents of this crime in order to nullify the divine work of increased Hebrew children (cf. Herod's action at the birth of Christ). Thus the third pogrom began.

B. Preparations for Deliverance (2:1–4:26)

1. Preparing a leader (2:1–10)

1–4 An unnamed couple from the family of Levi became the parents of Moses. Moses was not the firstborn, for his brother Aaron was three years older and his sister Miriam was a young girl already. That he was a "fine child" may relate to his physical appearance (cf. Ge 39:6) as well as to the qualities of his heart. When Moses' mother could hide him no longer, she fashioned a basketlike watertight boat from papyrus reeds. Clearly, Moses' mother had something else in mind besides child abandonment or exposure, for her actions denoted love and hope.

5 The Hebrew text does not say the royal party went "into" the river (as did Naaman in 2Ki 5:14) but that they were "at" or "by" the river, since normally royal personages did not bathe in a river. Ancient historians tell us that the waters of the Nile were regarded as sacred, and such washing was more of an ablution with its health-giving and fructifying effects.

6–9 The princess discovered the reed basket and opened it to find a beautiful Hebrew baby boy, crying. Her heart was immediately moved with compassion. Miriam emerged from her hiding place, perhaps acting as if she were just casually passing by. If her words were not according to the careful plan and instruction of her mother, then her inward prompting must have come from God—not a moment too soon or too late, with not a word too many or too few! Not only was the child returned to his own mother, but she was paid wages for nursing the child she feared she might never see alive again. Thus Moses' mother and father had an opportunity to teach him about the God of his fathers.

10 When the Hebrew lad "grew older," he was brought to Pharaoh's daughter, who adopted him and named him Moses. The

These are papyrus plants in Cairo, which were used to make the basketlike boat in which baby Moses was placed.

name is generally considered to be Egyptian, but the attached phrase—"I drew him out of the water"—points to a Hebrew origin. However, since the Egyptian princess is credited with naming him, and because of the similarity of Egyptian names such as Ptahmose, Thutmose, Ahmose, and Ramose, it is now universally regarded as Egyptian. The Hebrew root "to draw out" (GK 5406) is used perhaps because of the assonance it shared with the Egyptian name.

2. Extending the time of preparation (2:11–22)

11–12 In time Moses became aware of his Hebrew descent. When he was forty years old (Ac 7:23; cf. Heb 11:24–25), he struck and killed an Egyptian for beating a fellow Hebrew. It was his impetuosity that was wrong, not his sense of justice or his defense of the downtrodden. This cost him another forty years of education before he was ready for the task of delivering Israel. Moses' conscience revealed that he had no legal authority to do what he did, for he first looked "this way and that" and then buried the corpse in the sand. The very impulse that led Moses to avenge wrongdoing apart from due process of law was developed to do the work of God.

13–14 The champion of the oppressed and underdogs went forth the next day—this time to settle a dispute between two of his own people. But Moses was thoroughly rebuffed and his motives impugned by the one who ought to have been practicing neighborly love. He thoroughly disarmed Moses by announcing that he knew what Moses had done on the previous day—he was a murderer, and now he was meddling in someone else's business! Moses surmised that it must have become public information, and he wisely decided to leave Egypt as quickly as possible.

15–19 Pharaoh's wrath was not so much to avenge the death of an Egyptian as it was to deal with his discovery that Moses was acting as a friend and possible champion of his sworn enemy, the oppressed Israelites. So Moses fled to Midian, in the Arabian Peninsula along the Gulf of Aqaba, only to be aroused by another scene of injustice. The seven daughters of a Midianite priest named Reuel were being harassed and chased from watering their flocks at the troughs by un-scrupulous shepherds, but Moses rescued them. Since Moses still had his Egyptian clothing on, they judged him to be Egyptian.

20–22 The offer of hospitality led to Moses' marriage to Reuel's daughter Zipporah (which means "bird"; i.e., "Lady Bird"). Subsequently she gave birth to a son. Moses betrayed his loneliness by naming his son Gershom; for he explained, "I have become an alien in a foreign land."

3. Preparing a people for deliverance (2:23–25)

23 The king of Egypt who died was probably the same one who sought Moses' life for murdering an Egyptian (2:15; 4:19). The only pharaohs who ruled for more than thirty years in the Eighteenth and Nineteenth Dynasties were Thutmose III (1483–1450 B.C.), Amenhotep III (1410–1372 B.C.), Haremhab (1349–1315 B.C.), and Rameses II (1301–1234 B.C.). Thutmose III was probably the pharaoh of the oppression who had gained control after the death of his aunt-stepmother-mother-in-law.

Misery finally found a voice, and so the pain of bodily senses of the Israelites preceded their recognition of the poverty of their spiritual condition. Thus God prepared the audience and people who would be delivered while he prepared the deliverer himself. No longer did Egypt symbolize delightful foods, wealth, and fatness; instead, it now meant slave-masters, forced labor, and bondage. So Israel cried out to God.

24–25 God was pleased to respond to even those first lisps of faith, but he was also moved by his own word that he had promised to the patriarchs Abraham, Isaac, and Jacob (Ge 17:7, 19; 35:11–12; et al.). It was a remembrance that was more than a mental act; it also included a performance of his word (cf. Ge 8:1; 1Sa 1:19). In four consecutive verbs, the divine action is charted: God heard, God remembered, God looked (i.e., considered), and God knew (i.e., was concerned).

4. Calling a deliverer (3:1–10)

1–4 While Moses was actively engaged at one task, God called him to another—the very one he had felt himself so eminently qualified for forty years earlier, when he had struck out against the abuses of power he had witnessed in Egypt.

The valley of er-Raha lay between the three summits traditionally identified with the "mountain of God" (so named in retrospect because God had appeared there). There the Lord appeared "in the form of a flame of fire." What took place was a "strange sight" to Moses. The burning bush was not consumed; that was the miracle.

God chose the small and the despised burning bush as his medium of revelation, and he waited to see how sensitive Moses was toward the insignificant things of life before he invested him with larger tasks. The fire symbolized God's powerful, consuming, and preserving presence (cf. 19:18; 24:17; et al.). When Moses went over to inspect this unusual sight, God issued his call by repeating Moses' name to express the urgency of the message (cf. 1Sa 3:10).

5–6 The presence of God demanded a holistic preparation of the one who would aspire to enter his presence. Therefore, to teach Moses this lesson, God set up admittedly arbitrary boundaries—"Do not come any closer"—and commanded that he should also remove his sandals. This was to prevent him from rashly intruding into the presence of God and to teach him that God was separate and distinct from humans (cf. 19:10–13; 2Pe 1:18). Because God was present, what had been ordinary became "holy ground" and consequently "set apart" for a distinct use. The place where sheep and goats had traveled just a short time ago was transformed into "holy ground" by God's presence. This is the first occurrence of the noun "holy" (GK 7731) in Scripture (cf. Ge 2:3 for the verb form).

When the condition for meeting God had been satisfied, he revealed himself as the "God of your father." The collective singular "father" had a special point in that it was through the *one* man of promise that the *many* were to receive the blessing of God. Thus God assured Moses that the God of his father had not forsaken his repeated word of promise (Ge 15:1–21; 26:2–5; 35:1–12) or his people.

7–10 The anthropomorphisms of God's "seeing," "hearing," "knowing" (i.e., "be concerned about"), and "coming down" are graphic ways to describe divine realities in terms of partially analogous situations in the human realm. But these do not imply that God has limitations; rather, he is a living person who can and does follow the stream of human events and who can and does at times directly intervene in human affairs.

Three times v.8 mentions the "land." The often-repeated promise to the patriarchs was about to become a reality after over half a millennium! Two facts described the land: it was a good land and a spacious land (cf. Dt 8:7–9)—good because it was "flowing with milk and honey," and spacious because six nations were living there. And Israel would possess it all.

The call of Moses comes to a double conclusion in vv.9–10 with the phrase "And/so now." Verse 9 essentially repeats v.7 by summarizing the preceding speech and by restating the grounds on which this divine call is issued: namely, Israel's present need and God's solution. Verse 10, however, is the bottom line to the whole incident of the burning bush: It is the formal commissioning of Moses as God's emissary to lead Israel out of Egypt.

5. Answering inadequate objections (3:11–4:17)

a. Who am I to go to Pharaoh? (3:11–12)

The first of five protests against accepting God's commission reflects the great change that had come over Moses after forty sobering years of reflection and development. He who had been only too eager to offer himself as a self-styled deliverer earlier was now timid, unsure of himself, and devoid of any self-assertiveness that his divine commission demanded of him.

11 Moses repeated the twofold divine commission of v.10: that he should personally go to Pharaoh and that he should bring Israel out of Egypt. He prefaced this comment with the familiar idiom of the Near East that stresses the magnitude of the inequity between the agent and the mission, "Who am I?" (cf. 6:12; 1Sa 18:18; et al.).

12 God's response to Moses was twofold: he would personally accompany him, and he would give him a sign. As God had promised fourteen times to be "with" the patriarchs Isaac and Jacob, he now assured Moses that he would be actively present as he continued to fulfill his promised word of blessing.

This "sign" (GK 253) given to Moses is confirmatory and appeals to faith rather than to immediate evidence or to the presence of the miraculous. It is not the same as Gideon's (Jdg 6:17), for Gideon requested the sign; Moses did not. Moses' sign belongs in the same class as other signs about the future (1Sa 2:34; 10:2, 3, 5; 2Ki 19:29, et al.). Thus while God gave "signs" as "proofs" to the people (Ex 4:1–9), interestingly enough he gave no such "signs" to Moses himself but asked him to believe and trust in his word and promised to be present (cf. Mt 28:20). There was also more than a hint in this sign that the mission of Moses went beyond a mere deliverance of a nation from bondage; Israel was to be set free to "worship" God.

b. What if they ask what your name is? (3:13–22)

13 Moses did not anticipate being asked, "By what name is this deity called?" Rather, he feared that if he announced that the God of their fathers, the patriarchs, had sent him to them, the people would bluntly ask him, "What is his name?" The Hebrew seeks the significance, character, quality, and interpretation of the name. Therefore, what they needed to know was "What does that name *mean* or *signify* in circumstances such as we are in?"

14–15 God gave *two* answers to the problem posed by Moses. The second answer builds on the basic explanation of the meaning of the Lord's name and links that name with previous and all future generations.

Perhaps the most natural explanation that does fullest justice to the meaning of "I AM" is that this name is connected with some form of the verb "to be" and is to be seen as expressing the nature, character, and essence of the promise in v.12: "I will be with you." What, then, was his name? The answer was that "[my name in its inner significance is] I am, for I am/will be [present]." While it may sound to Western ears that God was deliberately trying to avoid disclosing his name, the context shows that he was actually doing the opposite. Often this construction is used to express a totality, intensity, or emphasis. Therefore, the formula means "I am truly he who exists and who will be dynamically

present then and there in the situation to which I am sending you."

This was no new God to Israel; it was the same God of Abraham, Isaac, and Jacob who was sending Moses. His name was Yahweh (= LORD; GK 3378). For the first time God used the standard third-person form of the verb "to be" with the famous four consonants YHWH. This was to be his "name" (GK 9005) forever. His "name" was his person, his character, his authority, his power, and his reputation. So linked was the person of the Lord and his name that both were often used interchangeably (e.g., Dt 28:58; Ps 18:49). This name was to be a "memorial"; it was to be for the act of uttering the mighty deeds of God throughout all generations.

16–18a The "elders of Israel" were the heads of various families (6:14–15, 25; 12:21; Nu 2) or tribes. Moses was to deliver God's message to this body of men and to get them to accompany him when he went to Pharaoh. The message came in the name of "the LORD," who was the same as the God of the patriarchs. It began with a repetition of the words used by Joseph on his deathbed: lit., "I have surely visited you" (NIV, "I have watched over you"), and "I have promised to bring you up out of your misery in Egypt." Joseph had prophesied the very deliverance announced by Moses (see Ge 50:24). Thus the repetition here was equivalent to saying that the Lord would complete and fulfill what he had begun to do as spoken by Joseph. In fact, the very word used for misery in v.17 was used in the original promise to Abraham in Ge 15:13 that the Egyptians would "mistreat" them for four hundred years. Moses was assured of a sympathetic hearing from the elders, for the hearts of human beings are in the hands of God.

18b–20 Moses and the elders were instructed first to make only a moderate and limited request of Pharaoh for a temporary leave to offer sacrifices to the Lord their God. This was not an example of a half-truth or a ruse and an attempt to deceive Pharaoh. God deliberately graded his requests of Pharaoh from easier (a three-day journey with an understood obligation to return) to more difficult (the total release of the enslaved people) in order to give him every possible aid in making an admittedly difficult political and economic decision. God certainly knew this king of Egypt well enough to know what his reactions would be. Therefore Moses was cautioned not to misconstrue any rejection he received as a sign that God had not called him or that God was not with him—all to no avail; for Moses later raised those very complaints (5:22–23).

21–22 God had promised Abram that after Israel had served for four hundred years, they would "come out with great possessions" (Ge 15:14). Thus the early chapters of Exodus systematically record the fulfillment of one patriarchal promise after another to make the connection clear. The taking of spoils from the Egyptians was to be explained by a simple request and by granting divine favor to the Israelites' request. The Israelites themselves were to live by this same principle of providing a present to a slave who was to be released every seven years (Dt 15:13). Charges of fraud, deception, deceit, and villainy against Israel are all misplaced. The fact is that the ignominy of their slavery is reversed in this sign of the recovery of their personhood—why even the children were to be decked in the jewels and the gifts of clothing!

c. What if they will not believe me? (4:1–9)

1 Moses did not flatly contradict God's assurance in 3:17. Both the Hebrew and the LXX make his question a hypothetical situation. But it does indicate that Moses was by no means a shining model of faith and trust in God. At the same time, neither could Moses have been certain as to the response of his fellow Israelites in Egypt. Moses stalled for time by posing further nuances to what he had already been told.

2–5 *The first sign.* God's prophets were accredited by "signs and wonders" (cf. Dt 13:1–3) with the sole purpose of validating the messenger and the message—that both were truly from God. Accordingly, Moses was given a "sign" (see comment on 3:12) to perform "so that they may believe that the LORD . . . has appeared to you."

The staff in Moses' hand was ordinary and unspectacular, but when it was thrown on the ground, as God commanded, it became a snake. It is perhaps too much to connect this snake directly with the uraeus (or cobra) worn on the headdress of Pharaoh (as if Moses had Egypt's king by the tail). In order

to underscore its supernatural nature, Moses was instructed to grasp the serpent by its tail to further prove the divine source of this miracle; for one would normally pick up a serpent by the neck.

6–7 *The second sign.* The Hebrew word for leprosy covered a number of assorted diseases. Actually, leprosy, or Hansen's disease, was known in antiquity. But leprosy in the Bible apparently also covered cases of psoriasis, vitiligo, ringworm, syphilis, mildew, and the rot—all affecting garments and houses as well as people in some cases. Which was involved here is uncertain, but the condition of the skin was such that its color resembled snow. Any small or ordinary skin annoyance would hardly be of any "sign" value. It had to pose a greater threat to the life and health of Moses if the instantaneous cure was also to reflect the greatness and majesty of God's power. The significance of this power to take away the health of the body and then to restore it again so that the affected part was "like the rest of his flesh" was to warn Pharaoh that this God, who had sent Moses, had the power to inflict or to save whatever he wanted with just a word or a gesture from his ambassador.

8–9 *The third sign.* The Lord next seized the initiative by using almost identical terms to those used by Moses in v.1. What was not being heeded in each case was literally "the voice" of these two signs. But their "voices" would leave Israel just as accountable as the "voice" of the words of Moses (v.1). Israel was to be confronted by God through the "voice" of his word and the "voice" of his miracles. This indicates that an appropriate significance would attach itself to each sign.

In this third sign Moses was to take some water *from* the river (the first plague would later be performed *in* the Nile) and turn it into blood. The Nile, which flowed with the blood of innocent Hebrew victims, would itself witness to its involuntary carnage with this miracle. Would the point of the "sign" be wasted on any Hebrew—or Egyptian? Like Abel's blood that cried out from the ground, so would the infants' whose lives had been demanded by Pharaoh (1:22). Egypt's mighty god, the Nile, was dominated by the Lord God of Abraham, Isaac, and Jacob.

d. What about my slow tongue? (4:10–12)

10 Moses began with yet another objection: "I have never been eloquent" (lit., "a man of words"). Then in a truly Oriental phrase, he added, literally, "not since yesterday and not since the third day," which adds up to simply "never before." Not even the experience at the bush had remedied this problem. Moses summed it all up: he was "slow of speech and tongue." Scarcely could this imply that he had a natural speech impediment or that he was a stammerer (cf. Ac 7:22). Thus Moses' complaint was not in a defective articulation but in his inability to take command of Hebrew and Egyptian with a ready and copious supply of words and thoughts to beat back all objections from his brothers and Pharaoh—though he does quite well with God!

11–12 God answered Moses with a question that takes on proverbial status (Ps 94:9). The gifts of speech, sight, and hearing are from the same Lord who was sending this hesitant leader. While God was not to be blamed for directly creating any defects, his wise providence in allowing these deprivations as well as his goodness in bestowing their ordinary functions mirror his ability to meet any emergency Moses might have suggested. So God announced, "I will help you speak" (lit., "I will be with your mouth") "and will teach you what to say."

e. Why can you not find someone else? (4:13–17)

13–14a Moses' groundless opposition angered God. Moses could think of no more good objections, for God had met every one point by point. So God's unwilling servant revealed the true nature of his heart: literally he said, "Send, I beg you, by the hand [of whom] you will send," which is a delightful Hebraism for "choose any other man, not me!" (NIV, "please send someone else").

14b–17 Nevertheless, God mercifully decided still to use his reluctant servant by sending his brother, Aaron, to supply any deficiency Moses might have felt. However, Moses had a price to pay for his intransigence: Aaron would receive the honor of leading the priesthood, which appears to be the reason for including this reference to "the Levite" (cf. 1Ch 23:13). Once more the omniscience of God is seen in that Aaron was

"already on his way to meet [Moses]," having begun at the special prompting of God (v.27). Whether Aaron came with the news that the king who sought Moses' life was dead (2:15) or for some other reason is not known.

The arrangement was that Moses was literally "to become God" to Aaron, and Aaron was to become Moses' mouth (or "prophet," according to 7:1). Nothing defines more accurately the intimate relationship between God and his prophet than 4:16 and 7:1. There were to be no more excuses or discussions: "You shall speak to him and put words in his mouth." Further, God would teach both of them what they were to do. As for action and deeds, it would be the very humble staff in Moses' hand that God would use to perform the miracles he already had begun to speak about (3:20) and to show to Moses (4:2–8).

6. Preparing a leader's family (4:18–26)

18 Moses left the region of Sinai and went to Midian to ask Jethro's permission to return to Egypt. Even the call of God did not erase the need for human courtesy and respect. Interestingly, Moses did not share the real reason for his desire to return to Egypt. The reason he gave was "to see if any of [my own people] are still alive." So Jethro granted Moses permission to go and wished him well.

19–20 This short section informs us that Moses' conversion took place in Midian, not in Sinai where God had appeared to him, and that Moses had made his decision to return before he heard that the Pharaoh who had sought his life had already died. The news of the passing of his enemies may have influenced him to decide to take along his wife, Zipporah, and their two sons. Up till now only one son, Gershom, has been mentioned (2:22). Eliezer, though unmentioned in this text, probably had been born (18:4); thus the plural is correct here. Moses' family is not mentioned again until Jethro's visit with Moses and the Israelites camped at Sinai (ch. 18).

Moses took along the "staff of God." What had once been ordinary became extraordinary by virtue of its use in the service of God. So equipped, Moses prepared to return to Egypt.

21–23 By way of summary, the Lord rehearsed the key features of his previous directives to Moses: (1) you will perform miracles before Pharaoh; (2) Pharaoh will harden his heart and not release the people; (3) you are to inform him that since Israel is "my firstborn son," the Israelites must be set free so that they might worship me; and (4) Pharaoh's refusal will lead to the death of his firstborn son.

The expression "I will harden [Pharaoh's] heart so that he will not let the people go" is used here for the first time. In all, there are ten places where "hardening" (GK 2616 & 3877) of Pharaoh is ascribed to God (4:21; 7:3; 9:12; 10:1, 20, 27; 11:10; 14:4, 8, 17). But it must be stated just as firmly that Pharaoh hardened his own heart in another ten passages (7:13, 14, 22; 8:15, 19, 32; 9:7, 34, 35; 13:15). Thus the hardening was as much Pharaoh's own act as it was the work of God. Even more significant is the fact that Pharaoh alone was the agent of the hardening in the first sign and in all the first five plagues. Not until the sixth plague was it stated that God actually moved in and hardened Pharaoh's heart (9:12), as he had warned Moses in Midian that he would have to do.

The announcement that Israel was God's "son" (GK 1201), yes, even his "firstborn" (GK 1147), may have stunned Pharaoh; for he was accustomed to regarding himself alone as the "son of the gods." But for a whole people to be a "son" of the deity was a little surprising. Added to this filial relationship was the declaration that Israel was God's "firstborn," which does not mean "first" in chronological order, because Jacob (renamed Israel) was actually born *after* his twin, Esau. Here God meant "first in rank," firstborn by way of *preeminence*, with all the rights, privileges, and responsibilities of a "firstborn." Thus what had previously rested on natural rights of primogeniture now rested on grace. With it went the privilege given by God to the seed of Abraham, namely, that by means of this "firstborn" all the nations of the earth would be blessed. The penalty that Pharaoh would ultimately pay for his refusal to acknowledge Israel as the Lord's son and firstborn, however, would be aimed at his own firstborn. Just as 3:12 had included an adumbration of Moses' return to Sinai, so vv.21–23 intend to show the future work of God, beginning with the "wonders" of the plagues and ending climactically with a threat to Pharaoh's firstborn.

24–26 This paragraph has continued to baffle interpreters. The place to begin to solve these problems is with the explanation given in the text itself. Verse 26b explains that this whole episode—what Zipporah did, what she said, and on whom she operated—all have reference to the rite of circumcision. The link with the context must revolve around Pharaoh's "son," his "firstborn" (v.23), and Moses' "son," *perhaps* also his "firstborn," along with the fact that all Israel was God's son, his firstborn. The Lord had attacked Moses as he was en route to accomplish the mission of God in Egypt. The nature of this nearly fatal experience is not known. That Moses was the object of the divine action is clear from the fact that the otherwise unspecified son would need to be identified as belonging to someone other than Moses. The sudden introduction of Zipporah's action leads us to believe that she instinctively connected her husband's peril (a malady so great that it left only her hands free to act) with their failure to circumcise their son. This she immediately proceeded to do. But her words of reproach indicate that the root of the problem of not circumcising the boy earlier lay in her revulsion and disgust with this rite.

The narrative was included at this point to demonstrate that an additional factor was needed in the preparation of God's commissioned servant: the preparation of his family. In Ge 17:10–14 God had commanded Abraham to circumcise every male on the eighth day as a sign of the covenant; any uncircumcised male was to be cut off from his people. However, in this case the father was suffering for his refusal to circumcise his son. Thus for one small neglect, apparently out of deference to his wife's wishes, or perhaps to keep peace in the home, Moses almost forfeited his opportunity to serve God and wasted eighty years of preparation and training! To further underscore this connection between Moses' grave condition and the circumcision of his son, Zipporah took the excised prepuce and touched Moses' feet. The Lord let Moses go, and the grip of death was lifted.

C. First Steps in Leadership (4:27–7:5)

1. Reinforced by a brother (4:27–31)

27–28 At God's command Aaron, now eighty-three years of age, was to meet Moses midway en route to Egypt at the "mountain of God" (i.e., Horeb; see 3:1). As predicted in v.14, Aaron "kissed" Moses. The men had much to share as to what had happened during the forty years they were apart, but Moses' words about God's liberating directives and miraculous signs were most prominent.

29–31 Immediately the narrative jumps ahead to the meeting with the elders that Moses had been instructed to convene when he arrived in Egypt. Evidently God wished to see duly constituted authority respected; therefore an appeal needed to be made to Israel's existing leadership and their consent obtained before initiating any requests of Pharaoh. Aaron acted as chief spokesman in relaying all that God had said to Moses. In addition, though Moses alone had been told (v.17) to perform the signs God had given in vv.1–9, both Moses and Aaron performed the miracles.

Since the elders represented the people and subsequently reported to them what they had heard and seen from Moses and Aaron, the text quickly compresses each of these steps in v.30 by saying all this was done "before" (lit., "in the sight of") the people. The response was just as had been predicted in 3:18—"they believed." The pressure of physical hardship had made this people more receptive than would be their custom in later years. Whether the signs were needed, as Moses had feared in v.1, the text has no comment. Especially heartening was the fact that God cared about them and their misery. Their response was immediately to worship the Lord, for he was the One who had "visited" (NIV, "was concerned about") them and "had seen" their trouble.

2. Rebuffed by the enemy (5:1–14)

1–2 Some time later Moses and Aaron, perhaps accompanied by the elders (cf. 3:18), went to Pharaoh and boldly demanded that he release the people. They wished to celebrate a festival to this God in whose name the demand was being made, namely, "the LORD, the God of Israel" (see comment on 3:14–15). Pharaoh's retort to this affront to his sole right to command these slaves was crisp and cynical. Indeed, if God chose to identify himself with such a hapless and hopeless lot of slaves, and if he was so powerless to effect their deliverance, why should Pharaoh fear

him or obey his voice? Pharaoh's answer was clear: "No!"

3 Perhaps stunned by Pharaoh's insolence and arrogance, Moses and Aaron recast their request in milder terms. Acting now as representatives of the people and in language given at the burning bush, the demand is changed to a humble request. God's servants warned Pharaoh that should he disallow this temporary release, he could suffer untold losses; for this God might allow all sorts of pestilence to break out, or he might even send an invader across the eastern frontier where Israel lived in vulnerable exposure.

4–14 Pharaoh was unmoved by any of these requests or threats. In his judgment the people were much too lazy or too idle, and Moses and Aaron were disturbers of the peace at best and plotters of sedition against the throne at worst. His question to them was in essence, "Why are you encouraging this?" There were already too many people (another witness to God's covenantal faithfulness), and should he give them rest from their labors to further increase their numbers?

The Egyptian slave drivers were to instruct the Israelite "foremen" that straw would no longer be provided for the bricks Israel had to produce. From then on Israel was to rummage the countryside for what stubble and straw they could find without decreasing their daily quota of bricks. Chopped straw was mixed in with the clay to make the bricks more pliable and stronger. So the people were scattered all over Egypt while the slave drivers kept beating the Israelite foremen and pressuring them to meet their daily quota of bricks.

3. Rebuffed by the enslaved (5:15–21)

15–16 The Hebrew foremen, unaware of the total deterioration of their position due to Moses and Aaron's request of Pharaoh, personally appealed the "No straw policy." In a courteous but bitter complaint, they asked, "Why have you treated your servants this way? We are given no straw; we are constantly pressed to keep making bricks; we are beaten—and the fault, sir, lies with your own people." This last charge seems to deferentially use the words "your people" in a circumlocution for Pharaoh himself.

17–18 Pharaoh's analysis of the situation has been reduced to a single word: "lazy." He repeated the word for emphasis (cf. v.8). If their request was "Let us go . . . now," then he was ready to render his conclusion: "Get to work." No straw would be supplied, and no falling behind in quotas would be allowed either.

19–21 Only now did the real untenability of their position begin to come home to the foremen. Moses and Aaron had deliberately "stationed" (NIV, "waiting") themselves so as apparently to be the first to debrief the men as they emerged from their meeting with Pharaoh; for they had had a fairly good idea of what would be the outcome of the foremen's audience with the king of Egypt. What they may not have expected was the full venting of the foremen's anger when they "found" them.

Instead of earning respect from these Hebrew foremen for all their efforts to alleviate their brutal condition, Moses and Aaron felt, in no uncertain terms, the heat of the foremen's anger. They asked God to judge these two troublemakers, for they were making Israel's reputation to stink. The words of vv.20–21 reflect those of v.3. Instead of a plague "striking" Israel and a "sword" coming, Moses and Aaron, not an enemy, had put a sword in Pharaoh's hands. So it happened that they "struck," or as we would say, "happened to bump into," Moses and Aaron.

4. Revisited by old objections (5:22–23)

22–23 Even though Moses had been forewarned from the start that Pharaoh would not accede to God's requests, he was not prepared for the effect this refusal would have on his own fellow Israelites. Filled with an "I told you so" attitude, it was Moses' turn to ask "Why?" (cf. Pharaoh in v.4, the foremen in v.15): "Why did you ever send me [in the first place]?" (lit. tr.). Fortunately, Moses did not vent his wrath on the foremen, but he did pour out to God the keenness of his resentment. Moses did not charge God directly with authoring this evil, for the idiom only means that God allowed and permitted such trouble as Pharaoh had thus spawned.

The clincher for Moses was v.23. His prayer (in essence) was, "O Lord, why is all this happening? Why did you ever send me?" Then he concluded: "Besides, you haven't done what you said you would anyway—deliver them! I've done nothing but bring/make trouble since I arrived here!" Obviously, Moses was again wrestling with some of his old objections (cf. 3:11–4:17). In his estimation things were moving too slowly, and the suffering was intensifying rather than letting up.

5. Reinforced by the Name of God (6:1–8)

1 There were no direct answers to Moses' questions, for these were to be gathered from his experience as their leader. But Moses' complaint about the time could now be answered, for God announced his "now"—he would delay no longer. The promised show of God's power would commence immediately with a show of his "mighty hand" (cf. 3:19).

2–5 The heart of God's response to Moses and the people was a fresh revelation of God's character and nature. One phrase stands out: "I am the LORD," which appears four times from v.2 to v.8. Once again God reminded Moses that he was the God who had promised the land of Canaan to the patriarchs and that he had also seen the affliction of his chosen people. Moreover, whereas in the past the patriarchs had known him in the character of and in his capacity as El Shaddai ("God Almighty"; cf. Ge 17:1; 28:3; et al.)—the name that disclosed his power to impart life, to increase the goods of life, and to deal with all unrighteousness—now he would be known as "the LORD" (i.e., Yahweh; GK 3378).

Moses and Israel (and even the Egyptians later) would shortly know what "I am the LORD" meant. This would not be the first instance of the use of that name, for it had already occurred some 162 times in Genesis. Significantly, people "began to call on the name of the LORD" as early as Ge 4:26. The Lord is the God who would personally, dynamically, and faithfully *be present* to fulfill the covenant he had made with Abraham, Isaac, and Jacob. The patriarchs had only the promises, not *the things* promised. The fullness of time had come when God was to be known in the capacity and character of his name Yahweh, as he fulfilled what he had promised and did what he had decreed. These deeds are further enumerated and spelled out in the seven promises of vv.6–8.

6–8 The contents of God's ancient promises are brought together and arranged so as to explain what "I am the LORD" means.

1. There were three first-person verbs with God's *promise of redemption* (v.6): (1) "I will bring you out"; (2) "I will free you"; (3) "I will redeem you." God promises to "redeem" Israel with the same "mighty acts of judgment" he had alluded to in 3:20 and 4:23 and had predicted long ago to Abraham in Ge 15:14. The plagues were to be judgments for crimes as well as spectacular wonders to instill faith.

2. Two more first-person verbs detailed God's *promise to adopt Israel* as his own people (v.7): (1) "I will take you as my own people"; (2) "I will be your God." These two promises will serve as two parts of the tripartite formula to be repeated in the Old and New Testaments almost fifty times: "I will be your God, you shall be my people and I will dwell in the midst of you" (cf. Ge 17:7–8; 28:21; Ex 29:45–46; et al.).

3. The last two promises focused on God's *promise of the land* (v.8): (1) "I will bring you to the land"; (2) "I will give it to you." This he pledged with the oath of his uplifted hand (cf. Ge 22:16; 26:3) so that by two immutable things—his word of promise and his oath—Israel (and *all* subsequent believers; cf. Heb 6:17–18) might have a strong encouragement and a solid confidence in the future. Then, as if to remind Israel once again, God concluded with his signature: "I am the LORD."

6. Reminders of Moses' lowly origins (6:9–7:5)

9–12 In spite of the grandeur of what "I am the LORD" meant for Israel, the people did not listen "for shortness of breath" (NIV, "their discouragement"). It was the inward pressure caused by deep anguish that prevented proper breathing—like children sobbing and gasping for their breath. This made such an impact on Moses that he had another attack of self-distrust and despondency. How could he persuade Pharaoh when he failed so miserably to impress his own countrymen who presumably would have had a naturally deep interest in what he had to say, given their circumstances. Anyway, his lips were "faltering" (cf. NIV note, "uncircumcised") in the job they had been given to do. Thus Moses returned to his fourth objection (4:10).

13–30 The stage has been set in 1:1–6:12 for the main action to begin. However, before that happens, it is important to know just who were "Aaron and Moses to whom the LORD" had spoken. In fact, the whole genealogy of vv.14–25 is surrounded and framed by the near verbatim repetition of vv.10–13 in vv.26–30 and v.14a in v.25b. Therefore, the genealogical list concentrates on two men and how it was that they happened to be at this precise and momentous juncture in the history of humans and nations.

Everything in the list suggests that God's choosing of Moses had nothing to do with natural advantage or ability. The list stops after naming only three of Jacob's sons—Reuben, Simeon, and Levi—for its object had been reached. Moses and Aaron sprang, not from the "firstborn," Reuben, but from Levi, Jacob's third son, and not even then from Levi's oldest son but Kohath, his second son. And Moses was not even the oldest son of his father, for Aaron was older. Moses' calling and election of God were a gift of grace and not based on rights and privileges of birth.

So wicked were Jacob's three older sons that they each inherited a curse: Reuben lost his birthright as "firstborn" (Ge 49:3–4), and Simeon and Levi were denied an inheritance with the tribes and were scattered instead (vv.5–8). But while Reuben's and Simeon's descendants did morally follow in their fathers' footsteps, Levi's descendants, with devotion to God, turned what was a curse into a blessing and used their dispersion through the tribes as an avenue of blessing to all through the priesthood and service at the sanctuary of God. This honor, however, did not prevent Levi's descendant Korah (vv.21–24) from destroying himself by his own rebellion (Nu 16); yet his descendants were not thereby forever adversely determined for evil, for they later rose to a place of high position in the temple and in composing Pss 42–49, 84–85, and 87. So the *making* of "this same Moses and Aaron," as well as the *uses* they were put to after they were made, were totally the work of God. Nevertheless, the record also made plain that there was a congruity between the experiences and all the endowments that had accrued to Moses during these eighty years of life; thus election worked in the natural realm as well as the spiritual.

Pharoah Ramses II, one of the proposed pharaohs of the time of the Exodus, here shown in a wall relief indicating victory over an enemy.

The text returns to repeat the words of vv.10–13 in vv.26–30, as if to say, "Look who is talking back to God! A man of few credentials except those given him in the providence and grace of God!" But never mind that, v.28 seems to affirm; it is now a whole new game. The hour had come, and the name of the LORD would be all the equipment Moses would need.

7:1–5 While the LORD had made Moses as "God" to Aaron and Aaron in turn as his "prophet" (GK 5566) to the people, Moses was also ordained as "God" to Pharaoh in that he would speak and act with authority and power from above and Aaron would be Moses' "prophet" addressing Pharaoh (cf. 4:15–16). But again this team was warned that Pharaoh's heart would be "hardened" (see comment on 4:21), even though God would graciously provide him with supporting evidence by way of signs and wonders. Nevertheless, after God had judged Egypt with his "mighty acts of judgment," Israel would come out by its "divisions."

Not only would Israel know what was meant by the name "LORD," but so would the Egyptians. In addition to understanding the

significance of that name (Heb. YHWH or Yahweh), these miracles would also be an invitation for the Egyptians to personally believe in Israel's Lord. Thus the invitation was pressed repeatedly in 7:5; 8:10, 22; 9:14, 16, 29; 14:4, 18—and some apparently did believe, for there was "a mixed multitude" (12:38 KJV) that left Egypt with Israel.

D. Judgment and Salvation Through the Plagues (7:6–11:10)

1. Presenting the signs of divine authority (7:6–13)

6–9 After eighty years of preparation, Moses began his life work. He and Aaron were directed to reappear before Pharaoh, who in turn would request them to perform a miracle, presumably to assure him that they were messengers of Israel's God.

Significantly, Scripture judges Pharaoh's demand for validation of such claims as reasonable. The Lord informed Moses to use the first of the three signs he had drawn on to convince Israel that he was indeed an accredited messenger of God (see 4:2–9, 30–31). However, in this instance Aaron's staff (it was the same as Moses' staff or the staff of

God; cf. 4:17; 7:15, 17, 19–20), when cast down, became a *tannin* (GK 9490; "great serpent," "dragon," or "crocodile"; in 4:3–4 it became a *nahash,* "snake"; GK 5729). The connection of the name *tannin* with the symbol of Egypt is clear from Ps 74:13 and Eze 29:3.

10–13 Moses and Aaron did exactly as God instructed them—only to learn that Pharaoh's wise men, sorcerers, and magicians were able to imitate the same feat by their magical arts. The use of magic in Egypt is well-documented in the Westcar Papyrus, where magicians are credited with changing wax crocodiles into real ones only to be turned back to wax again after seizing their tails.

The relation between Aaron's miracle and the magical act of the magicians, whom Paul knew by the names of Jannes and Jambres in 2Ti 3:8, is hard to define. Possibly by the use of illusion and deceptive appearances they were able to cast spells over what appeared to be their staffs but which actually were serpents rendered immobile (catalepsy) by pressure on the nape of their necks and by the use of magical spells. Or perhaps it was by demonic power. However, as evidence of God's greater power, Pharaoh's magicians lost their "staffs" when Aaron's "swallowed [them] up." But Pharaoh was unaffected. His heart "became hard."

2. First plague: water turned to blood (7:14–24)

14–18 Moses was instructed by God to go early (so in 8:20) in the morning with his brother, Aaron, to intercept Pharaoh and his officials as they went out to the Nile (cf. v.20). Pharaoh's purpose for going here remains unknown, perhaps to worship the Nile River god, Hapi. Moses and Aaron, however, were there to remind Pharaoh that "the LORD, the God of the Hebrews" had sent them (5:1); yet the king of Egypt remained resolute in his defiance of this Lord. Therefore God would help Pharaoh "know" who he was (cf. 5:2). God would change the water of the Nile River into blood when Moses struck the Nile with his staff.

19–21 When Aaron stretched out his staff and struck what the Egyptians regarded as sacred, the Nile and the water all over Egypt turned to blood. What was the "blood" (GK

1947)? Some scholars suggest that since all the plagues followed a natural cycle and all happened in one year, this first plague could be connected with an unusually high Nile flood in July and August. The sources for the Nile's inundation are the equatorial rains that fill the White Nile, which originates in east-central Africa (present-day Uganda) and flows sluggishly through swamps in eastern Sudan, and the Blue Nile and the Atbara River, which both fill with melting snow from the mountains and become raging torrents filled with tons of red soil from the basins of both these rivers. The higher the inundation, the deeper the color of the red waters. In addition to this discoloration, a type of algae, known as flagellates, comes from the Sudan swamps and Lake Tana along the White Nile, which produces the stench and the deadly fluctuation in the oxygen level of the river that proves to be so fatal to the fish. Such a process, at the command of God, seems to be the case for this first plague rather than any chemical change of the water into red and white corpuscles (cf. Joel 2:31: "the moon [will be changed] to blood"; or 2Ki 3:22, where, however, the water looked "like blood"). Unlike other plagues and in agreement with this natural phenomenon, this plague did not stop suddenly. This change affected the "streams" (= seven [in Herodotus] branches of the Nile), the canals (to fertilize the fields), the ponds (left from the overflowing Nile), and the reservoirs (artificially made to store water for later use).

22–24 Once again Pharaoh's magicians applied their "secret arts" and imitated the miracle sufficiently to blunt the force of it on Pharaoh's conscience. The question where they found any unblemished water if the fourfold water system in "all Egypt" (vv.19, 21) was affected, is answered in v.24—from subterranean water from freshly dug wells. But Pharaoh remained unmoved and merely returned to his palace from the bloody river's edge: his heart grew rigid and hard in spite of this evidence.

3. Second plague: frogs (7:25–8:15)

25–8:5 Seven days after the first plague had begun, Moses and Aaron were instructed by God to take their demands to the king's palace. If he refused to grant their repeated request to go to the desert to worship the Lord, they were to announce in the set formula, "I will plague your whole country with frogs." This was not to be a "sign" but a "plague" only. In comparison with what was to come, this was only a trivial annoyance.

6–7 On Aaron's signal the frogs emerged from the water and "covered" the land. These pesky creatures, though regarded as sacred to the Egyptians, were God's scourge to whip the Egyptians into facing the living God. The intensification of the nuisance by Pharaoh's magicians was totally ignored by him. The fact was that tons of croaking, crawling, creeping intruders were everywhere.

8–15 Why should the frogs so suddenly abandon their natural habitat in August during a high Nile and invade the homes, bedrooms, ovens, kneading troughs, and even the palace itself? And why should they likewise die off so suddenly? Perhaps the frogs abandoned all the polluted and overflowing waterways (cf. 7:19) and sought cover from the sun on dry land in homes where possibly the presence of some unadulterated water attracted them. However, since they had already been exposed to spores of *bacillus anthracis* from the death spread along the waterways, the frogs also suddenly collapsed and died.

Pharaoh had finally been forced to acknowledge the power of the Lord, not by human armies, but by squadrons of loathsome little frogs. Now he knew who this "Lord" was (cf. 5:2), and he acceded to Moses and Aaron's request—only to renege later on.

Moses' response to Pharaoh's desperate or, as some think, cynical plea was to dare Pharaoh to test his prophetic credentials and, more important, the power of God by setting the time when he wished to be rid of this plague. Pharaoh's quick response of "tomorrow" led Moses to enter into some intensely earnest prayer. Moses' freedom to negotiate on his own terms and then, as it were, to have God back him up is remarkable. The frogs dropped dead all over the place—in the houses, fields, and open courtyards. Frogs were piled up in heaps, and there was a firm reminder to aid Pharaoh's wavering memory—the stench of dead frogs. Nevertheless, that faded and so did Pharaoh's permission. This "relief" was worse than the plague for this proud king. People do not often learn the righteousness of God when he

grants them his mercy and his favor (Ps 78:34–42; Isa 26:10).

4. Third plague: gnats (8:16–19)

16–17 The third plague began without warning to Pharaoh or his magicians. God again used the outstretched staff in the hand of Aaron to initiate this plague. Aaron struck the dust of the ground, just as he had struck the Nile in the first plague (7:20), and "all the dust throughout the land of Egypt became gnats." The word "gnats" occurs five times in this passage and nowhere else except in the parallel passage of Ps 105:31. It is debatable whether this word means "lice" (so KJV et al.) or "gnats" or "mosquitoes," as we favor (with most interpreters).

18–19 On their fourth attempt to duplicate the miracles of Moses and Aaron, the Egyptian magicians admitted defeat. In spite of what success they did or did not experience in the previous three encounters (and it could well have been through sleight of hand—given the advance notice of the nature of the plague or sign in those cases—or perhaps it was just plain demonic, supernatural empowerment to mimic God's power), they now realized that the plague of the gnats was the "finger of God," i.e., the result of his power. But Pharaoh was not so persuaded in his heart and mind—he remained adamant and opposed to any Israelite demands.

5. Fourth plague: flies (8:20–32)

20–21 As in the first plague, Moses was sent to intercept Pharaoh again as he went down to the Nile early in the morning. This time Pharaoh and all his people and their houses were threatened with a plague of "flies." It seems best to say that the fly *Stomoxys calcitrans* best fulfills all the conditions of the text. This fly multiplies rapidly in tropical or subtropical regions (hence the delta with its Mediterranean climate would be exempt) in the fall by laying its six hundred to eight hundred eggs in dung or rotting plant debris. When it is full grown, the fly prefers to infest houses and stables, and it bites both humans and animals, usually in the lower extremities. Thus it becomes the principal transmitter of skin anthrax (see plague six), which it contracts by crawling over the carcasses of animals that have died of internal anthrax.

22–24 By inaugurating a "distinction" (GK 7151) between Moses' people and Pharaoh's people, God intended to aid those hardened Egyptian hearts who suspected that nothing more than chance or difficult times had been involved in the preceding three plagues. This distinction is found in the fourth, fifth, seventh, ninth, and tenth plagues. The purpose of this preferential treatment to Israel was to teach Pharaoh and the Egyptians that the Lord God of Israel was in the midst of this land doing these works; it was not one of their local deities. Gods were thought by ancient Near Easterners to possess no power except on their own home ground. But not so here! The innocent were being delivered and the guilty afflicted because this God was in their midst. He would again do a "miraculous sign" designed to evoke faith in him from the Egyptians and the release of Israel.

In another innovative feature Moses announced in advance when the plague was due to strike, giving the Egyptians time to repent. This advance notice is found in the fourth, fifth, sixth, eighth, and tenth plagues. Moreover, Pharaoh and his court were again singled out as the first victims of this plague because of the heavy responsibility they bore for their intransigence.

25–32 Moses' claim—that if Israel sacrificed animals in Egypt, it would be extremely offensive to the Egyptians—has been challenged by some commentators as a clever ruse on Moses' part. Thus Moses rejected Pharaoh's counteroffer to allow Israel to sacrifice in Egypt. Finally Pharaoh conceded the long-denied permission. With a note of self-importance he pontificated, "*I* will let you go ... but you must not go very far." And as if to show what his real thoughts were all along, he quickly added, "Now pray for me."

Moses was not to be put down, for his mission likewise had dignity; so he too began with the pronoun "I": "*I* am leaving you, and *I* will pray" (lit. tr.). Moses, with an obvious rebuke, said in effect, "Don't you 'however' me when you are in such a poor bargaining position." But then on a courteous note, with a switch to the third-person form of address, he continued, "Only be sure that Pharaoh does not act deceitfully again."

The plague was removed through Moses' prayer (cf. 1Ki 18:42; Am 7:2, 5). So effective was the power of prayer and the evidence that God was in their midst that "not a fly remained." But Pharaoh once again (cf. second plague, 8:15) returned to his hard-nosed stand once he obtained the physical relief he desired.

6. Fifth plague: cattle murrain (9:1–7)

1–4 The fifth plague was patterned after the second: Moses was to go to Pharaoh's palace and announce the next pestilence. A "terrible plague" would be brought, not by God's "finger," as the Egyptian magicians had put it in 8:19, but by his "hand." It would fall on all the cattle in the field. There is no need to press the expression "all the livestock" to mean each and every one and then find there are no Egyptian cattle left for the seventh plague (vv.19, 25), for it is already plain in v.3 that the plague affected only those cattle "in the field." Normally the Egyptian cattle were stabled from May through December, during the flood and the drying-off periods when the pastures were waterlogged. Thus some of the cattle were already being turned out to pasture down south; so it must have been sometime in the month of January. These cattle were then affected when they came into contact with the heaps of dead frogs left from the second plague and died of *bacillus anthracis,* the hoof and mouth disease.

The Israelite cattle were exempted from the plague, possibly because the delta would have been slower in recovering from the effects of the flood, which was farther downstream. Also, the Israelites' different attitude toward corpses—they took precautions to deal with the heaps of dead carcasses—may have spared their own cattle. This was the second plague where God placed a distinction between the Egyptians and the Israelites.

5–7 The interval between the announcement and the morrow, when the fifth plague was to take effect, was to allow time for a believing response from Pharaoh and the Egyptians. Presumably some believed and attempted to rescue their animals by bringing them in from the fields. Others purposely delayed turning their cattle out to pasture.

When Pharaoh heard that all the Israelite cattle had miraculously escaped the cattle plague, he sent envoys to Goshen to investigate. The rumor was true. Pharaoh must have had his own explanations and rationalizations, for his position and heart again became resolute and unyielding. Meanwhile, another part of Egypt's wide array of gods was hard hit: the Apis, or sacred bull Ptah; the calf god Ra; the cows of Hathor; the jackal-headed god Anubis; and the bull Bakis of the god Mentu. The evidence was too strong to be mere coincidence: (1) the time was set by the Lord, the God of the Hebrews; (2) a "distinction" was made between the cattle of the two peoples; and (3) the results were total: all Egyptian cattle "in the field" died; not one head of Israelite livestock perished.

7. Sixth plague: boils (9:8–12)

8–9 Like the third plague, this one was sent unannounced. For the first time human lives are attacked and endangered, and thus it was a foreshadowing of the tenth and most dreadful of all the plagues. With a touch of divine irony and poetic justice, Moses and Aaron were each to take two handfuls (the form is dual) of soot from a limekiln or brick-making furnace, the symbol of Israel's bondage (see 1:14; 5:7–19). The soot must have been placed in a container and carried to Pharaoh's presence, where Moses then tossed it into the air. The act was to be a symbolic action much like those of the latter prophets (Jer 19 or Eze 4–5). There was also a logical connection between the soot created by the sweat of God's enslaved people and the judgment that was to afflict the bodies of the enslavers.

10–12 When the soot was tossed skyward, festering boils broke out on all the Egyptians and their animals. Attempts to identify this malady have produced various suggestions: (1) small pox, (2) Nile-blisters similar to scar-

The bull, an important animal to the Egyptians, experieneced one of the plagues. This relief shows an Egyptian leading a bull.

let fever, (3) skin anthrax, and (4) inflammations or blains that become malignant ulcers. Skin anthrax seems the most probable, since Dt 28:35 limits this plague principally to the lower extremities of the body. Furthermore, the black soot is especially suited, for anthrax (cf. anthracite coal) is a sort of black, burning abscess often occurring with cattle murrain.

The flies of the fourth plague have generally been blamed as the carriers of the anthrax spores, but they were totally removed at the conclusion of that plague. Presumably this was another generation of flies (depending on the temperature, another batch can come in twenty-seven to thirty-seven days). After animals or humans are bitten on the legs by these flies, a small bluish-red pustule with a central depression in the middle of the swelling appears after two or three days. The center of the boil dries up only to have new boils swell up, and the skin festers as if it had been burnt and then peels off.

In a humorous aside, v.11 notes that the magicians (who bowed out in plague three and are unnoticed, though possibly present, in plagues four and five) literally (and vocationally) "could not stand" before Moses. The same could be said for all the Egyptians. Here for the first time God hardened Pharaoh's heart—a seconding, as it were, of his own motion made in each of the preceding five plagues.

8. Seventh plague: hail (9:13–35)

13–19 As in the first (7:15) and the fourth (8:20) plagues, Moses was to begin this plague by rising early in the morning to confront Pharaoh with the Lord's message. From these early days in February until the time of the tenth and climactic plague, Pharaoh would spend approximately eight of the most dreadful weeks he had ever known.

To further underscore the theological significance of these weeks and their events, Moses was prompted by God to preface his latest announcement of divine judgment with a long message filled with doctrinal instruction. This unprecedented message was calculated to move Pharaoh and his subjects from rebellion to belief in the God of the Hebrews. Its ominous contents included (1) an announcement that God would vent the "full force" (i.e., "all the remaining plagues") of his plagues on Egypt so that no one would doubt that there was anyone like this God in all the earth; (2) a reminder that previous pestilences and plagues might well have swept both king and people off the face of the earth had not God deliberately and purposely spared them for one very important reason: that God's power and name would be heralded throughout the earth by means of Pharaoh's stupidity; (3) a declaration that in denying the release of Israel Pharaoh had acted as an obstructionist against Almighty God himself; (4) a threat that Egypt would experience the worst hailstorm it had ever seen in its history; and (5) an extraordinary feature that provided for those Egyptians who believed Moses' words were a means of escape from the effects of the storm.

The seventh plague was to be judgment with the expectation that it might result in the blessing of belief and trust. Had not Abraham been given this mission to be a means of blessing to "all peoples on earth" (Ge 12:3)? And has not the theme "that the Egyptians might know that I am the LORD" (or slight variations) appeared frequently in the midst of these plagues (7:5; 8:10; 9:14, 16, 29–30; and later in 14:4, 18)? Moses, like his Lord, would sigh of Israel (Nu 14:11): "How long will these people treat me with contempt? How long will they refuse to believe in me, in spite of all the miraculous signs I have performed among them?" The same words could apply just as well to Egypt.

The months of leniency were about over. Now the full blast of the ensuing plagues would penetrate directly to Pharaoh's "heart" (v.14; NIV, "against you"). The "heart" (GK 4213) does not signify "his person" but rather his inner being, nature, and seared conscience. His pride and arrogance would be tossed to the wind as the terrors of these new plagues forced him in perplexed and desperate sorrow of soul to literally beg that the Israelites leave his presence immediately. Yet Pharaoh was no mere pawn to be toyed with at will, for the object was that he too might come to experience personally and believe ("know") the incomparability of God's person and greatness. The very superlative rating of his deeds—none "like it" (of the hailstorm in vv.18, 24; of the locusts in 10:6)—should have led the king and his people to the identical rating of God's person (no one "like you" in 15:11 and "like me" in 9:14).

20–26 Rainfall comes so occasionally in Upper Egypt that the prediction of a severe hailstorm accompanied by a violent electrical storm must have been greeted with much skepticism. Only the delta receives on the average about ten inches of rainfall per year while Upper Egypt has one inch or, more often, none. But there were some who "feared the word of the LORD" and acted accordingly. Some Egyptians must have received Moses' words as being from God himself; for they became a part of that mixed company who left Egypt with Israel (see 12:38).

Moses apparently lost his shyness and diffidence, for he was the one who now stretched forth his staff and his hand (cf. Aaron's leading role in the first three plagues: 7:19–20; 8:6, 17). Hail joined by unannounced thunder and balls of fire that ran along the ground provided Egypt with the most spectacular display in her history. The destruction was devastating. Five times in vv.24–25 the word *kol* ("all," "everything") is used; yet it is used hyperbolically and not literally because the first two *kol*s ("in all Egypt," vv.24–25a; NIV, "throughout Egypt") are immediately qualified to exempt the land of Goshen where Israel lived. Nevertheless, even though the storm did not take every single tree, herb, or creature in the field, it was tragic enough to impress the most callous individual.

27–30 Pharaoh, obviously shaken, conceded the point: "I have sinned," though he included the face-saving qualifier "this time." What made this plague any different from the rest—except its severity? Only when the Lord began to hurt Pharaoh did he (momentarily) seek him (cf. Ps 78:34). Like Jeremiah (Jer 12:1), Pharaoh declared that "the LORD" (i.e., Yahweh, not Elohim!) was in the right and that he and his people were in the wrong!

Moses' reply was simple, confident, and noble. He would spread out his hands in prayer (a gesture of request and appeal to God) once he was back with his own people, and the hail and thunder would stop—to prove once again (in this repeated apologetic and evangelistic refrain) that the whole earth belongs to the Lord. "But," Moses added, "I know that you and your officials still do not fear the LORD God."

31–35 Since in Egypt flax is usually sown in the beginning of January and is in flower three weeks later while barley is sown in August and is harvested in February, both would be exceedingly vulnerable if this plague occurred in the beginning or middle of February (probably a little later than usual with a high Nile year). Wheat and spelt were also sown in August but were not ready for harvest until the end of March. That Goshen was unaffected by this storm matches the agricultural observations; for the Mediterranean temperate zone has these storms only in late spring and early autumn but not from November to March. Flax, of which there were several kinds, was used for linen garments. The vicinity of Tanis was ideal for producing it. Barley was used in the manufacture of beer (a common Egyptian drink), as horse feed, and by the poorer classes for bread.

After Moses' prayer was answered, Pharaoh once again rescinded his offer and forgot all about his confession of sin and wrong.

9. Eighth plague: locusts (10:1–20)

1–2 For the first time we are told that Egypt's officials were also as obstinate as Pharaoh; therefore the Lord had hardened all of them as well. But Moses was to find a lesson in this divine work of hardening. There follows, then, another theological preface to the eighth plague, just as Pharaoh had been served in 9:14–16 with a similar lesson prior to the seventh plague. The lesson for Israel was to be twofold: (1) to educate succeeding generations in how the Lord "dealt harshly" with the Egyptians and performed his miracles in their land, and (2) to thereby bring Israel to faith in the Lord.

3–6 Moses proceeded to the palace and announced to Pharaoh the next plague. The message began with a question: "How long will you refuse to humble yourself before the Lord?" His act of self-condemnation and abject humility in 9:27 was just that—an act. But here was the consummate question of all questions that God finally raises against all obstinate sinners: "How long?"

The demand for Israel's release was again laid down along with a time lag that provided ample opportunity for reflection and repentance: "tomorrow." Moses informed Pharaoh that God would "bring locusts into your country." Joel 2:25 calls locusts God's "great army." They would finish off every

living green thing, leaving destruction in their wake. It would exceed any locust invasion Egypt had ever known in the past. With that, Moses and Aaron turned their backs on Pharaoh (an amazing gesture for normal protocol) and stalked out.

7–11 Pharaoh's officials picked up Moses' "How long?" with a "How long?" of their own. Out of loyalty to their king and country, they blamed Moses; but it was obvious that they were beginning to become impatient with Pharaoh's intransigence. Could Pharaoh not see the "snare" this man was setting for them, and did Pharaoh not realize that Egypt was about ruined? Someone had to give in. They urged Pharaoh to yield: "Let the people go."

In another first, Pharaoh had Moses and Aaron return to the palace for some negotiations related to the imminent pestilence. Clearly as a sop to his frightened officials, Pharaoh half-heartedly gave Moses permission to take Israel to sacrifice in the desert. However, he coyly asked (as if he did not remember Moses' original request or the advice just given him by his own officials), "Just who will be going [on this religious trip]?" Moses responded out of a position of strength: "We all are going to celebrate this festival to the LORD" (cf. v.9). "Oh no you are not," was Pharaoh's decisive rejoinder. "You take only your 'men'; that will be enough for religious purposes." It is true, of course, that later Israel required only her males to attend these three yearly festivals (23:17; 34:23; Dt 16:16), but the artificiality of this limitation at this time is evident since women normally accompanied the men at Egyptian religious festivals.

The contempt Pharaoh felt for Moses' request and for the Lord himself can be seen in his biting sarcasm and veiled threat of v.10: "The LORD be with you [i.e., 'May God help you']—if I let you go, along with your women and children!" To Pharaoh it was plain that Moses and his people were up to no good. Pharaoh did not yield to this moderate first-step request for fear of what was to be (though unknown at the time to him) the ultimate request. Moses and Aaron were then insulted by being chased from the premises—another in a string of wicked firsts.

12–15 So the plague was ordered to begin as Moses again stretched out his hand and staff over Egypt. Swarms of locusts from the bumper crop produced due to the exceedingly wet summer in Ethiopia were swept away from natural breeding grounds around Port Susa and Jidda (on the west side of the Red Sea across from the Arabian Peninsula) by an east wind that blew all day and all night (cf. 14:21). Thus these locusts (now ready to migrate in February or March after hatching during the winter from the eggs laid in September) were driven into Egypt by a sirocco (a hot wind) from the Arabian Peninsula, instead of into Canaan, had the winds been from the southwest. They came in droves (lit., "exceedingly heavy"). They finished off everything the hail had left.

16–20 Hastily Pharaoh summoned Moses and Aaron and, without any qualifications as in 9:27–28, confessed his sin against the Lord their God and against these men. But he still insisted on having the upper hand. "Now," he added, as if to organize Moses' conclusion, "forgive my sin once more [i.e., this one more time]." No more would he change his mind, no more tricks! Just ask your God, he pled, "to take this deadly plague away from me."

Once again God graciously answered Moses' prayer. He sent a strong "sea breeze," which for people in Canaan would have been a "west wind" but for those in Egypt was a north or northwest wind, which drove the locusts into the Reed Sea. The results at the palace, however, were the same.

10. Ninth plague: darkness (10:21–29)

21–23 Unannounced, like the third and sixth plagues, the ninth plague came in the month of March, as Moses once again stretched out his hand. No doubt God used the yearly phenomenon known as the *Khamsin,* meaning the "fifty"-day wind that blows off the Sahara Desert from the south and southwest usually about the time of the vernal equinox. During two or three of those days, it blows with great force, picking up sand and dust. Given the unusually high Nile with the red dirt it had spilled over the fields now barren and baked after the hail and locusts had destroyed all the vegetation that would hold the soil in its place, this was no ordinary *Khamsin.* The polluted air got so thick—"no one could see anyone"—that the sun itself was blotted out for "three days." Israel mean-

while was somewhat protected by the hills on the south side of the Wadi Tumilat and by the fact that the red silt would not have dried out as much since their fields were later in clearing the effects of the flood.

24–29 Pharaoh decided to compromise further: Israel could take their families to this festival celebration, but they must leave their flocks and herds. But Moses yielded nothing. "Not a hoof is to be left," he affirmed, for they needed them in worshiping God. The festival was brand new, and it was as yet unannounced, explained Moses. But Pharaoh had had enough. Rudely he demanded they leave and never darken his presence again on penalty of death. But did he think that would prevent further disasters? Had not plagues three, six, and nine come without warning? Was it not strange for him to be threatening Moses with death when the smell of death was all over his court and Egypt?

11. Tenth plague: death of the firstborn (11:1–10)

1–3 These verses are parenthetical; for Moses had one last message to communicate to Pharaoh before he left his presence after the ninth plague in 10:29, and thus he knew that Pharaoh had "spoken correctly" (cf. 10:28) in halting any further audiences. God had informed Moses before he went in to see Pharaoh concerning the ninth plague that this contest was about to end abruptly. One more plague and he would send Israel away, "in the manner of one's sending away a slavegirl who had been promised to be one's daughter-in-law" (probably a better rendering of the Heb. than NIV's "when he does"), i.e., filled with gifts on her release from slavery. This interpretation leads easily and naturally into their requests of the Egyptians for gold and silver articles. The reasons for the extraordinary generosity of the Egyptians are (1) the LORD made them "favorably disposed" toward Israel (cf. Ps 106:46), and (2) "Moses himself was highly regarded." The greatness of the man was not because of his personal qualifications but because of the esteem he had accumulated from the magicians (8:18–19), the court officials (9:20; 10:7), and Pharaoh himself (9:27; 10:16).

4–8 Moses' speech continues the remarks he began in 10:29. Unlike all the other plagues, this time the LORD himself would march through the land of Egypt. The firstborn of all Egyptian families—slaves and cattle—would die at midnight (the exact day was not specified). An unprecedented outpouring of grief would follow, but among the Israelites there would be such tranquility on that evening that not a dog would have occasion to bark! Moses' final word was that the Egyptians on bent knee would beg the Israelites to leave immediately. Moses said, "After that I will leave." But the stupidity and waste of all those lives just because of stubborn human sinfulness made Moses exceedingly angry.

9–10 Therefore, as a recapitulation of all Moses' negotiations beginning in 7:8, we are reminded that all had taken place as God had predicted it. No amount of evidence had persuaded Pharaoh's hard heart, and Israel was still enslaved.

E. The Passover (12:1–28)

1. Preparations for the Passover (12:1–13)

1–2 The instructions for the Passover and the Unleavened Bread feasts were the only regulations given while Israel was still in Egypt. The phrase "in Egypt" indicates that the contents of this chapter were written after the Exodus. This event was so significant that henceforth the religious or ecclesiastical year was to begin in the month of Abib (13:4), the month when "the barley had headed" (the Canaanite name for the month). Later the Babylonian month name of Nisan was substituted (Est 3:7), matching our present calendar time of late March to the beginning of April (Ne 2:1).

3–11 The following instructions, communicated through the elders (see v.21), were given to the "whole community of Israel": (1) Preparations were to begin on the tenth day of Abib; (2) the head of each household was to select a "lamb" or "kid" according to the number of people who would be present; (3) the animal was to be a year-old male without any defects; (4) each animal was to be slaughtered at twilight on the fourteenth day; (5) the blood from the animals was to be applied to the doorframe of each house; (6) that night each family was to eat the roasted lamb or kid along with bitter herbs and unleavened bread; (7) the meat was to be roasted whole with the head and legs intact and the washed

internals left inside; it was not to be eaten raw or boiled in water; (8) all leftovers were to be burnt; nothing was to be allowed to become profane by putrification or superstitious abuse (i.e., before daybreak, according to 23:18; 34:25; Dt 16:4); (9) the meal was to be eaten with an air of haste and expectancy. Therefore, the people's robes were to be tucked in their belts, their sandals were to be worn, and their staffs were to be ready and on hand.

Thus the whole nation was to be a nation of priests (see 19:5–6; cf. 1Pe 2:5; Rev 1:6). The apparent intervention of the Levites in 2Ch 30:17–18 and 35:5–6 was contrary to the original design of the Passover. Here there were no priests, no altar, no tabernacle; families were communing in the presence of God and around the sacrificial lamb that was the substitute for each member of that family. The lamb was to be a year-old male because it was taking the place of Israel's firstborn males who were young and fresh with the vigor of life. The bitter herbs were to recall the bitter years of servitude (1:14), and the unleavened bread was to reflect this event's haste on that first night. This was the Lord's Passover, and this was how Israel was to eat it.

12–13 On that same night, the fifteenth of Abib, the Lord would pass through Egypt and strike down the firstborn of all men and animals whose household had not been placed under the blood. Like the other "signs" or "miracles" Pharaoh had seen, the blood also was to be a pledge of God's mercy. The Lord would "pass over" (GK 7173) these marked homes, and no "plague" would touch them. Indeed, even "all the gods of Egypt" would be judged by this final plague of God. Obviously, those deities whose representatives were linked with beasts were dealt direct blows—the bulls, cows, goats, jackals, etc. There could be little doubt that this would be interpreted as a direct blow to the gods of Egypt themselves.

2. Preparations for the Unleavened Bread (12:14–20)

14–16 The connection between the Passover and the Feast of Unleavened Bread is close yet distinct. The OT uses both names to refer to the same feast: "Passover Feast" (GK 7175) in Ex 34:25; Eze 45:21; and "Feast of

Unleavened Bread" (GK 5174) in Dt 16:16; 2Ch 30:13, 21; Ezr 6:22. Yet the two rites are treated separately, even if in sequence, in Lev 23:5–6; Nu 28:16–17; 2Ch 35:1, 17; Ezr 6; Eze 45:21.

"This day" refers to the same day in view in vv.1–13. The slaying of the paschal lamb "between the evenings" that divide the 14th and 15th of Abib (Nisan) looks forward to the festive celebration that night, the day of the Exodus (i.e., the night of the Passover; Abib 15). The Israelites were to "commemorate" (i.e., make it a memorial; GK 2355) that day as a "festival" and a "lasting [i.e., perpetual] ordinance."

For seven days they were to eat "bread made without yeast" (Heb. *matzo*, GK 5174), in order to remember Israel's haste in leaving Egypt (v.39) and to underscore again that impurity and corruption (which leaven sometimes symbolizes) disqualified persons from religious services. The whole household needed to be pure and clean of heart; therefore, all yeast was to be removed from the entire house (v.19). The first and the seventh days of that week beginning with the celebration of the Passover were to be holy convocations.

17–20 "I brought your divisions out" reflects a post-Exodus stance. Verse 19 is not an empty repetition of v.15 but adds the important notice that Gentiles may be celebrants along with Israel even as was contemplated in the Abrahamic covenant (Ge 12:3c). The "alien" (GK 1731) must have included the "mixed multitude" (v.38, KJV) who left Egypt with Israel, the Kenites who joined them in the desert (Nu 10:29–31; Jdg 1:16), and those who were converted later, like Rahab's family (Jos 2:10–14). Those "native-born" (GK 275) were, no doubt, Abraham's descendants who are here regarded as the true natives to the land of Canaan, since it was assigned to them by God some six hundred years prior to the Exodus.

3. Celebration of the Passover (12:21–28)

21–23 When the instructions for the preparation of the Passover had been completed, the elders were briefed on what each Israelite family was to do. Two new items are included here: (1) Blood was to be applied to each doorframe by a "bunch of hyssop"

dipped into a basin of blood, and (2) no one was to leave the house "until morning."

The lamb or kid to be slaughtered by each family is called "the Passover" itself (NIV, "the Passover lamb"). Blood from this animal was placed in a basin and with "a bunch of hyssop" was "slapped" on the doorframe. Israel would know the grounds and means of their deliverance and redemption.

"The destroyer" (GK 5422) was not a demonic power that rivaled God but probably an angel of the Lord who expedited his will. In Ps 78:49, however, where God lets loose on the Egyptians four different words for his anger, this wrath is collectively called "a band of destroying angels." Thus whether an angel was the mediating agent or the term was a figurative personification of the final judgment of God on Egypt, it was still God's direct work (cf. 1Co 10:9–10; Heb 11:28).

24–28 Once again provision was made for the annual observance of this ceremony and for the parental obligation to instruct children in the meaning and significance of this reenactment. The section closes with one of those rare notices in Israel's history: they did exactly what the Lord had commanded—and well they might after witnessing what had happened to the obstinate king and people of Egypt!

F. The Exodus From Egypt (12:29–51)

1. Death at midnight (12:29–32)

29–30 The final stroke came at midnight of Abib 15. While the previous plagues may have utilized some of the natural and secondary agencies of nature, vv.23 and 29 attribute this tenth plague solely to the LORD. The Lord went through the land of Egypt, and death touched every "family" (lit., "house")—from Pharaoh to the prisoner (cf. 11:5).

31–32 How Pharaoh "summoned" Moses and Aaron is unknown. The release granted Israel was for more than a three-day journey to worship the Lord. Previously when Pharaoh had given permission to leave (only to immediately rescind it or place unacceptable restrictions on it), he had said: "Go, worship the LORD your God" (10:8, 24), or "Go, sacrifice to your God" (8:25); but now the command was: "Up! Leave my people!" In fact, God had predicted that the effect of this tenth blow would be so hard that Pharaoh would "drive [them] out completely" (11:1). As Moses was taking leave of the king and Egypt, Pharaoh had one final request. "Bless me," he begged. Pharaoh, the god of Egypt, entreated Moses' God to bless him!

2. Preparations for the Exodus (12:33–36)

33–34 The Egyptians urged the people most vehemently that they should leave immediately, for no Egyptians would be left if things continued as they were going. The Israelites wrapped the unleavened lumps of dough in sacks and slung them over their shoulders along with their kneading troughs and whatever other incidentals they planned to take with them.

35–36 On the spoiling of the Egyptians, see 3:21–22 and 11:2–3.

3. The Exodus and the mixed multitude (12:37–51)

37 The wilderness itinerary actually begins in this verse. Rameses is best identified with Qantir instead of the remoter but more popular Tanis (seventeen miles northeast), since Qantir was situated near the water—as Egyptian documents observed, on the "Waters of Ra," the Bubastite-Pelusiac eastern arm of the Nile River. Succoth is now generally identified with Tell el Maskhuta near modern Ismailia. With the number of fighting men at 600,000, the total number of Israelites could well be 2 million.

38 The "many other people" (KJV, "mixed multitude") were Egyptians (cf. 9:20), perhaps some of the old Semitic population left from the Hyksos era, and slaves native to other countries. Some of this group must be part of the "rabble" mentioned in Nu 11:4. Thus the promise to Abraham in Ge 12:3c received another fulfillment in this swarm of foreigners who left Egypt with Israel. Another reason for God's display of his power was so that the Egyptians could be evangelized (7:5; 8:10, 19; 9:14, 16, 29–30; 14:4, 18).

39 As the Lord had predicted in 11:1, the Israelites "had been driven out of Egypt." Indeed, they left so quickly that they had no time to prepare anything, much less set the yeast in the dough; so they left with unleavened bread and made unleavened cakes during those early days (see v.34).

40–42 Appropriately, now that the Exodus had begun, the narrator took a moment to reflect on the total Egyptian experience. Twice he commented that it had been 430 years, "to the very day." That "night" was to be observed by all future generations as a "Watchnight Service," for on that night the Lord "preserved" or "kept" the destroyer from touching them.

43–49 The question arises concerning the "mixed multitude" who came out of Egypt with Israel and all such persons who might join them thereafter. Were they to keep the Passover also? Thus it was necessary to repeat and elaborate on the instructions already given.

No male was to participate in that meal unless he was circumcised and thus was a member of the community of faith. This excluded temporary residents, hired workers, aliens, and all foreigners. Furthermore, each lamb was to remain in one house (as implied in vv.3–10). Its parts were not to be divided and eaten in separate homes; it was to be the basis of a fellowship meal stressing the unity and joy of the participants. In addition, no bones of the paschal lamb were to be broken (cf. Ps 34:20 and Jn 19:33–36). This was the Lord's Passover and not the table of Israel; therefore, the same requirement was made of all, whether native-born or alien.

50–51 The concluding notice is that Israel "did just what the Lord had commanded" (cf. v.28); and "on that very day" (cf. vv.17, 41) the much-delayed Exodus finally took place as the Lord brought Israel out by their "divisions." Surprisingly, the desert journey began on the Sabbath!

G. The Consecration of the Firstborn (13:1–16)

1–2 Closely linked with the account of Israel's release from Egypt and the Passover was the consecration of all the firstborn in Israel. The sanctification of all firstborn was commanded by God probably at Succoth, the first stopping place after the Exodus (12:37); and it fell within the seven days set aside for the Feast of Unleavened Bread (12:15).

The general principle is that every "firstborn" (GK 1147) male of both humans and animals (cf. vv.12–13) belongs to the Lord and is therefore "to be set apart" from common usage for holy purposes. Thus God set aside the seventh day, the tabernacle, the tribe of Levi—and here all firstborn. The basis for God's claim was that he had already set apart to himself the firstborn in Israel on the day he smote all the firstborn of Egypt. God's adoption of Israel as his "firstborn" led to his delivering them. From that time onward, that spared nation would dedicate the firstborn of its people and animals in commemoration of God's acts of love and his deeds that night.

3–10 Further directions are given relating this consecration of the firstborn to the Feast of Unleavened Bread. When Israel possessed the land promised to her, this ceremony was to be observed annually. The Israelites were to explain to their children that they ate unleavened bread and set apart the firstborn to the Lord because of what he had done personally for each subsequent Israelite (and believer)—"for me"—when he brought Israel out of Egypt. Likewise, in v.16 subsequent generations would be taught that he brought "us" out of Egypt. This festival and consecration were to be a "sign" on the people's hands and a "reminder" (GK 2355) or "memorial" between their eyes. No doubt this injunction was a figurative and proverbial mode of speech (cf. Pr 3:3), for the law of the Lord was "to be on [their] lips."

11–16 As the destroyer "passed over" their firstborn and Israel later "passed over" the Red Sea, so now they were "to cause to pass over" or "give over" (GK 6296) to the LORD all their firstborn when they entered the land. Only two slight modifications were made to this principle: (1) all firstborn male humans (firstborn females were exempted) were to be redeemed or "bought back at a price" (fixed at five shekels in Nu 18:16; cf. also Nu 3:46–47), and (2) donkeys were to be "bought back" or "redeemed" (GK 7009) by a lamb or kid, since donkeys were unclean animals and therefore unfit for sacrifice. To prevent any refusal to follow this command to ransom their animals, the Israelites were to kill them by breaking their necks.

The obligation of the firstborn to serve the LORD in some nonpriestly work around the sanctuary was later transferred to the Levites who became God's authorized substitutes for each firstborn boy or man (Nu 3). When the number of Levites was exhausted, additional males could be ransomed or re-deemed at the price of five shekels apiece. Verses 15–16 again reiterate the explanation: the firstborn were owned by the LORD; for he dramatically spared them in the tenth plague, *and* he had previously called them to be his firstborn (4:22).

H. Journey to the Red Sea (13:17–15:21)

1. Into the wilderness (13:17–22)

17–18 There were three possible routes of escape: (1) a northeast route going to Qantara through the land of the Philistines to Gaza and Canaan; (2) a middle route heading across the Negeb to Beersheba, which incorrectly assumes Mount Sinai is Jebel Halal near Kadesh-Barnea; and (3) a southeast route leading from the wilderness east of modern Ismailia to the southern extremities of the Sinai Peninsula. Israel was warned not to take the shorter route through Philistia, for the prospects of fighting the bellicose Philistines would so demoralize Israel that they would change their minds and return to the servitude in Egypt. This judgment was proven correct when Israel was threatened with war in Nu 14:4.

Thus God led Israel around by the "desert road" or the "way of the wilderness" toward the "Red Sea" or, better, "Sea of Reeds" (*Yam Suph*, see NIV note). Israel camped on the west coast of the Sinai Peninsula by *Yam Suph* on their way to Horeb/Sinai (Nu 33:10–11), and later on *Yam Suph* is also used to refer to the salt waters of the Gulf of Aqaba (Dt 1:1; 1Ki 9:26; et al.). Thus nothing prevents our linking *Yam Suph* with the Red Sea.

19 The records in this verse are a verbatim report of Joseph's words in Ge 50:25 except for the additional words "with you." God's promise of the land is never far from sight in any of these passages.

20 The exact location of Etham is unknown. It is described as a region in Nu 33:6 and appears to be equated with the Desert of Shur (Ex 15:22).

21–22 How God led the Israelites (v.17) is now explained. This single "pillar" (14:24), which was a cloud by day and a fire by night, and whose width at the base was sufficiently large to provide cover for Israel from the intense heat (Ps 105:39), was a visible symbol of the presence of the Lord in their midst. The

THE EXODUS

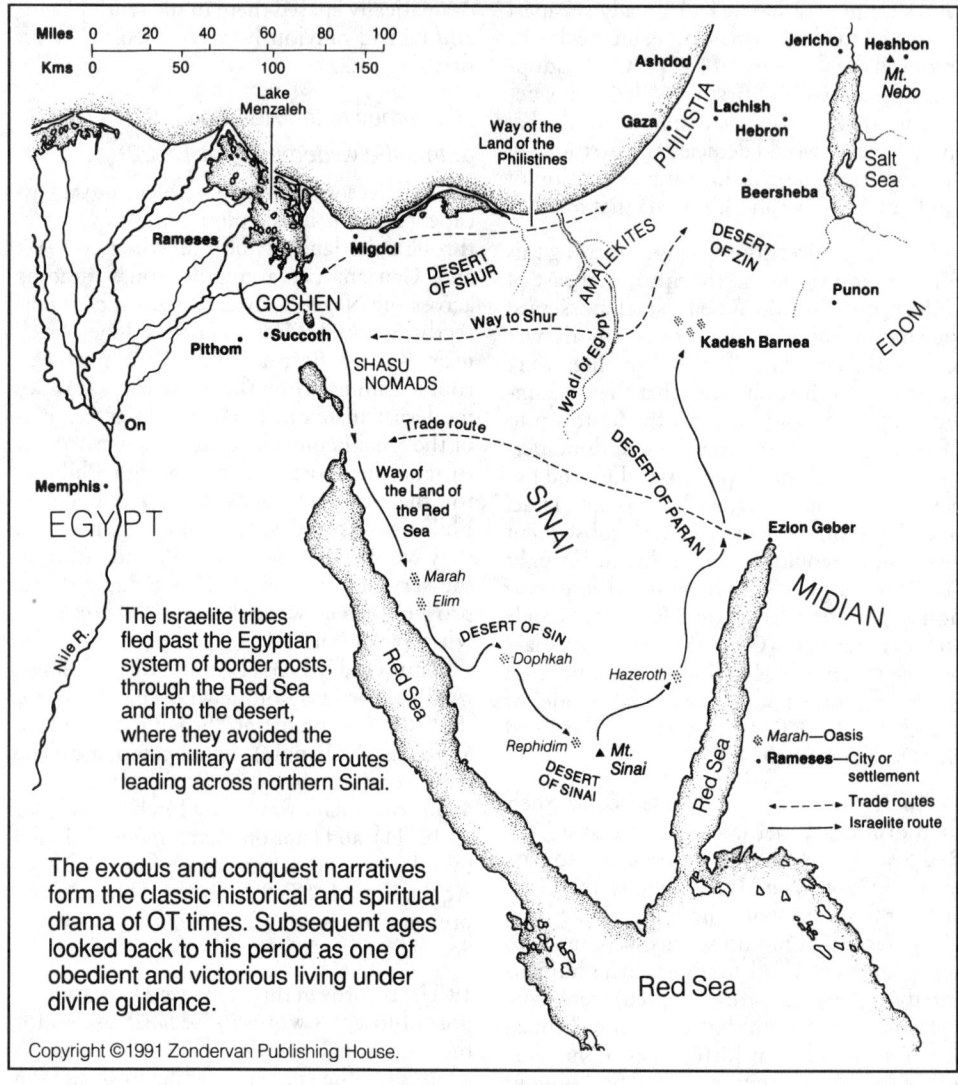

Miles 0 20 40 60 80 100
Kms 0 50 100 150

Lake Menzaleh

Jericho
Heshbon
Mt. Nebo

Ashdod

Way of the Land of the Philistines

PHILISTIA
Gaza
Lachish
Hebron

Salt Sea

Beersheba

Rameses

Migdol

DESERT OF SHUR

AMALEKITES

DESERT OF ZIN

GOSHEN

Way to Shur

Punon

Pithom

Succoth

SHASU NOMADS

Kadesh Barnea

EDOM

On

Trade route

Memphis

EGYPT

Way of the Land of the Red Sea

Wadi of Egypt

DESERT OF PARAN

Ezion Geber

SINAI

MIDIAN

Nile R.

Marah
Elim

DESERT OF SIN

Dophkah

Red Sea

Hazeroth

Marah—Oasis
Rameses—City or settlement

Red Sea

Trade routes
Israelite route

Rephidim
Mt. Sinai
DESERT OF SINAI

The Israelite tribes fled past the Egyptian system of border posts, through the Red Sea and into the desert, where they avoided the main military and trade routes leading across northern Sinai.

The exodus and conquest narratives form the classic historical and spiritual drama of OT times. Subsequent ages looked back to this period as one of obedient and victorious living under divine guidance.

Red Sea

Copyright ©1991 Zondervan Publishing House.

pillar of the cloud and fire was but another name for "the angel of God," for 14:19 and 22:20–22 equate the two. In fact, God's Name was "in" this angel who went before them to bring them into Canaan (23:20–23). He was the "angel of his presence" (Isa 63:8–9). Malachi 3:1 calls him the "messenger of the covenant," who is equated with the Lord, the owner of the temple. Obviously, then, the Christ of the NT is the shekinah glory or the Lord of the OT (see comment on Jn 1:14). Through this cloudy pillar the Lord spoke to

Moses (33:9–11) and to the people (Ps 99:6–7). Such easy movement from the pillar of cloud and fire to the angel and back to the Lord himself has already been met in the same interchange between the burning bush, the angel, and the Lord in ch. 3.

2. At the Red Sea (14:1–14)

1–4 The command "to turn back" (GK 8740) meant a change in direction and perhaps even a temporary setback for Israel, but which way did they go? According to Nu 33:7, Pi

Hahiroth was opposite Baal Zephon and between Migdol and the sea. The site of Pi Hahiroth has not been identified as yet. A possible location for Migdol ("tower") is either Migdol near Succoth, mentioned in a papyrus of Seti I's time, or the ruins of a square tower on a height known as Jebel Abu Hasan overlooking the southern part of the small Bitter Lake.

Pharaoh assumed that Israel's divine help had run out and that they were hopelessly entangled on a dead-end trail since the desert, the sea, and marshes surrounded them. God, however, had commanded Moses to take this impossible route to show the Egyptians once more that he was God (see 7:17; 9:14) and to show Israel his great power (vv.30–31). Nevertheless, God would receive glory from Pharaoh and his army. That glory would have come to God whether Pharaoh had yielded or had rebelled and said in effect, "Those Hebrews will leave this place over my dead body!"

5–12 Shortly after Israel left, Pharaoh and his officials quickly put aside the terrors of that awful night when they lost their firstborn and decided to go after the Israelites, who had marched out of Egypt "boldly." When they saw the Egyptian troops, the Israelites cried out in despair to the Lord, but not for long. Moses was a much more immediate target than the Lord, so they complained to him. Were there "no graves at all in Egypt?" They mocked in the most satirical tone possible (since Egypt specialized in graves and had about three-fourths of its land area available for grave sites). Then followed the "I-told-you-so" pseudoprophets. Suddenly the hardships of their Egyptian bondage were forgotten.

13–14 The former quick-tempered Moses patiently answered the people's hasty accusation with three directives: (1) "Do not be afraid"; (2) "Stand firm" and see the salvation, i.e., the "deliverance of the LORD," for "the LORD will fight for you"; and (3) "Be still," i.e., stop all action and become inactive, for "he LORD will fight for you.

3. Across the Red Sea (14:15–31)

15–18 If God had promised to bring Israel out of Egypt and to give them the land of Canaan, then Moses and Israel had best stop their crying and begin to move on. The contrast between v.16 and v.17 is clear: "You," Moses (emphatic position), use the staff in your hand to "divide" or "form a valley" so that Israel may go through the sea "on dry ground"; "I" (again the emphatic position), the Lord, will harden the hearts of the (pursuing) Egyptians (cf. 9:12)

19–20 The identity of the angel of God is clarified in the second part of v.19: the pillar of cloud and fire (see 13:22). The reality of God's promised presence may be stated in the symbol of his presence (the pillar of cloud and fire), in his messenger (the angel of the Lord), or in the Lord himself, who "went ahead of them" (13:21; cf. 14:24). But when the presence of God "withdrew," he went behind them to protect Israel's rearguard. What was light for Israel became darkness for the Egyptians. The double nature of the glory of God in salvation and judgment could not have been more graphically depicted.

21–22 With the single gesture of Moses' upraised hand over the sea, the Lord "drove . . . back" the sea by means of a "strong east wind all that night" (lit. tr.; cf. 15:8). The exact location of this "Reed Sea" crossing is unknown; but it would seem best to place it somewhere between the southern end of the Bitter Lakes and the Gulf of Suez or even in the northern tip of the Gulf of Suez itself. Meanwhile the waters formed a "wall" on the right and on the left. They were piled up like a "heap." The event, while incorporating the natural element of the wind, has the element of the exceptional (cf. Dt 4:32, 34) accompanying it, which strongly suggests the presence of God.

23–28 Sometime during the morning watch the Lord "looked down" (GK 9207) at the Egyptian army as it began to pursue Israel across the recently formed valley in the sea and "threw it into confusion." This "look" of God took on concrete proportions, for the pillar of fire must have suddenly lit up the sky with such a flash that the chariots careened against one another.

Meanwhile a spectacular display of thunder, lightning, rain, and earthquake struck terror in the boldest and most arrogant of Egypt's charioteers (cf. Ps 77:16–20). By this time the thoroughly distracted Egyptians had another problem: God made the chariot wheels "come off" (NIV) or "jam" (cf. NIV note) against one another. The Egyptians had enough and were willing to forget about Israel altogether, but it was too late. The Lord had begun his fight against Egypt as promised in v.14, described in vv.27, 31, and celebrated in the song of 15:3. Israel had only to stand still and watch the victory won on their behalf; for with the upraised hand of Moses, the walls of water cascaded toward each other to resume their usual place just as dawn broke.

Pharaoh lost all the men and chariots he had committed to that engagement. Ps 136:15 records that God "swept Pharaoh and his army into the Red Sea." The destruction of the "entire army of Pharaoh" is qualified by the clause "that had followed the Israelites into the sea." But all involved in the chase certainly perished: "Not one of them survived."

29–31 The Lord had "saved" (GK 3828) Israel that day, for Israel saw the corpses of the Egyptians floating by. Above all, Israel saw with what great powers the Lord had delivered them, and they feared him and believed him and his servant Moses. Their response was back to where it was in 4:31 and the goal stated in 9:29–30: "that you [in this case, Egyptians] might know that the earth is the Lord's . . . [and] fear [him]."

4. Song at the sea (15:1–21)

The song in vv.16–18 is one of three composed by Moses (see also Dt 31:22; Ps 90). It is a victory ode that hymns the spectacular power and unrivaled supremacy of God over Pharaoh's chariots. The focus of the song is "the Lord" himself (the divine name appears ten times). The general outline of the song is divided between two themes: vv.1b–12, a retrospective description of the overthrow of the Egyptian forces; vv.13–18, a prospective prediction of Israel's entrance into the Promised Land.

As we see it, the song has four strophes. Each strophe is then divided into three parts.

Exodus 15: Victory at Sea

Strophe I   vv.1b–5
Part A: Introit—v.1b:
        "I will sing to the Lord"
Part B: Confession—vv.2–3

Part C: Narration—vv.4–5
Concluding simile: "like a stone," v.5b
Strophe II   vv.6–10
Part A: Introit—v.6:
        "Your right hand, O Lord"
Part B: Confession—vv.7–8
Part C: Narration—vv.9–10
Concluding simile: "like lead," v.10b
Strophe III   vv.11–16a
Part A: Introit—v.11: "Who . . . is like
        you, O Lord?"
Part B: Confession—vv.12–13
Part C: Anticipation—vv.14–16a
Concluding simile: "as a stone," v.16a
Strophe IV   vv.16b–18
Part A: Introit—v.16b: "Until your
        people pass by, O Lord"
Part B: Confession—v.17
Part C: Anticipation—v.18

1 *Part A: Hymnic introit.* The first person— "I will sing"—is not unusual for such invocations when the whole community praises God as *one* collective person; yet each individual also makes such praise/confession personally his or her own. The motivating reason is given immediately: "for he is [lit.] gloriously glorious" in that "the horse and its rider he has hurled into the sea."

2–3 *Part B: Confession.* The two themes of the introit's two bicola are now treated in sequence: (1) the Lord (in vv.2–3) and (2) the overthrown enemy (the narration in vv.4–5). In this confession five attributes of the Lord) are given—all in the first person: "my strength," "my song," "my salvation," "my God," and "my father's God." Then v.3 continues in the third person: "The Lord is a warrior;/ the Lord is his name."

The title in v.3 has caused many Christians to ask, "How can this 'man of war' [cf. Isa 42:13] be related to the God and Father of our Lord Jesus Christ?" The fact that he acts at all in wars speaks only to the point of his immanence and presence in the fabric of life, but it does not tell us any more about the moral character of God than "the Lord is our rock" or "stone" or "high tower" does.

4–5 *Part C: Narration* (of the work of God). The concern shifts to the enemy, and the four key words focus on the water: "sea," "Red Sea," the "deep waters," and the "depths." Just as the verbs of the confession in Part B were parallel ideas—"I will praise him," "I will exalt him" (cf. the introit: "I will sing")—so here they are synonymous: "he has hurled into the sea . . . are drowned. . . . The deep waters have covered them . . . they sank." Then the strophe ends with a simile: "they sank to the depths like a stone."

6 *Strophe II: Part A: Introit.* With repeated use of "Your right hand, O LORD," the song announces the beginning of the second strophe using a descriptive metaphor for the omnipotence of God (cf. Moses' song at Dt 33:2 and numerous Psalms). In this strophe more details and the mode of the enemy's destruction are given.

7–8 *Part B: Confession.* The first line of four bicola recalls the phrase "highly exalted" of the introit (v.1). In the "greatness of your majesty," you "pulled them down" (NIV, "threw down"; usually of demolishing buildings), those "risers up against you" (NIV, "opposed you"; here of those who wanted to destroy the building of God). God, with the burning heat of his wrath and a fiery look from the pillar of cloud, "consumed them like stubble." The "strong east wind" of 14:21 is here represented in theological terms as "the blast of your nostrils," thus confirming the divine agency behind the wind. The result was that the "waters piled up" and the "running, surging, flowing ones" stood "like a heap" (cf. Ps 78:13). (Later on the Jordan River will also "heap" up [Jos 3:13, 16].) Meanwhile the waves "congealed," as if turned to solid ice. This was the power of God that Israel confessed.

9–10 *Part C: Narration* (of the work of God). Five bicola narrate in dramatic form the staccato phrases that almost simulate the heavy, breathless heaving of the Egyptians as, with what reserve of strength is left, they vow: "I will pursue" or "I will overtake," "I will divide the spoils," "I will gorge myself," "I will draw my sword," and "my hand will destroy [lit. and ironically, 'dispossess'] them." But v.10 changes all that; with a mere gust of God's "breath" or "wind" (cf. v.8a), "the sea covered them," and they "sank." Like the first strophe (v.5), the second strophe ends with a simile: "They sank like lead in the mighty waters."

11 *Strophe III: Part A: Introit.* The song now turns to the theological interpretation and the significance of all that was done. Using the formula for incomparability—"Who is like you"—Israel proclaims that God's exclusive uniqueness had been demonstrated and "proven powerful by his [NIV, 'majestic in'] holiness" and his "awesome . . . wonders" or "miracles." No other "gods" (whose reality is neither affirmed nor denied at this point; cf. 12:12) could do what the Lord had done.

12–13 *Part B: Confession.* The second-person address of these verses matches vv.7–8 and v.17; therefore, these verses belong together and mark the three great works of God in three bicola: the victory at sea, guidance in the wilderness, and the destination of God's "holy dwelling" in Canaan. Thus the heroic deeds at the sea were a pledge that God would fulfill his promise of giving the land. The "earth" may here signify Sheol, the grave (cf. 1Sa 28:13; Isa 29:4), for it was actually the sea that "swallowed them." But it was God's "grace" or "unfailing love" that would lead those who had been "redeemed." The alliterative sequence of the Hebrew verbs ("you stretched out," "you will lead," and "you will guide") adds to the majesty of the form and unity of the thought.

"Your holy dwelling" (lit., "your holy pasture or encampment") cannot refer to Sinai since the nations in vv.14–15 would not have been affected by that mountain. Nor is Canaan alone meant; but v.17 clearly indicates that Moses had in mind that place in Canaan where God had promised him he would "put his Name" (Dt 12:5, 11, 21; et al.) in a place he had chosen (Dt 12:14, 18, 26; et al.), i.e., his temple on Mount Zion.

14–16a *Part C: Anticipation* (of the work of God). Once again the song shifts from the second person to the third person (cf. vv.4 and 9). A summary statement in v.14a precedes vv.14b–15, where four of Israel's future enemies are listed: Philistia, Edom, Moab, and Canaan. Thus the "nations" of v.14a may be the Egyptian designation for the "Asiatics" who occupied southern Palestine. That news of Israel's sensational deliverance from the Egyptian army got around is clearly attested by Rahab (Jos 2:10–11). Canaan is here named by its residents along the southwestern coastal strip. The "chiefs" or "princes" of Edom introduces another piece of Mosaic identification, for the term is useful in the proto-dynastic era of Edom (cf. Ge 36:15–16), as is the local term of "leaders" or "rams" of Moab. But all these peoples and leaders shared one thing in common: fear. Seven expressions for fear are climaxed with the strophe, concluding with a simile for "stone"-cold "silence."

16b *Strophe IV: Part A: Introit.* Once more the repetitive parallelism introduces the past and the climactic word—this time the outcome of God's great work at the sea: "Until your people pass by" or "cross over" into Canaan (or perhaps the Jordan), even the people who had been "bought."

17 *Part B: Confession.* Based on God's parallel handling of Pharaoh and the nations that would oppose their entrance into Canaan, Israel may now anticipate the fulfillment of the patriarchal promise that they would be given—in that future day when the Lord would reign forever—the land of Canaan as an inheritance (on the figure of "planting," see Pss 44:2; 80:8–16). The text moves from the "mountain of [his] inheritance" to a "place . . . for [his] dwelling," even the "sanctuary" his "hands established" (see v.13).

18 *Part C: Anticipation* (of the work of God). In one final burst of unbounded joy, Moses and Israel rejoice in the prospect of God's universal rule and reign lasting forever. How temporary in comparison were the reigns of such hardened rulers as Pharaoh and the leaders of state in Canaan and its environs!

19–21 A narrative interlude separates the Song of Moses from Miriam's song in v.21. Miriam is called a "prophetess" (cf. Nu 12:2) and a "sister" of Aaron, even though she was also Moses' sister. But apparently she ranked only with Aaron and not with Moses. There would be other prophetesses in Israel (Jdg 4:4; 2Ki 22:14; Ne 6:14; et al.). As a prophetess and a leader in Israel (Mic 6:4), Miriam led the women perhaps in an antiphonal response, repeating the song at the conclusion of each part or strophe, accompanied by timbrels and dancing.

I. Journey to Sinai (15:22–18:27)

1. The waters of Marah (15:22–27)

22–23 The "Desert of Shur" is the whole district ranging from Egypt's northeastern frontier eastward into the northwestern quarter of the Sinai Desert and extending southward to the mountains of Sinai. Shur, meaning "wall," is mentioned several times in Genesis (16:7; 20:1; 25:18). In Nu 33:8 this area is called the "Desert of Etham." Perhaps Etham reflects the old Egyptian word for "fort."

Israel's first stop is traditionally placed at Ain Musa, the "Springs of Moses," a site not mentioned in any biblical text. It was a source of sweet water about sixteen to eighteen hours' journey north of Marah ("bitter"), Israel's first-mentioned stop. This traditional site for crossing the Red Sea is about ten miles south of the northern end of the Red Sea and about one-half mile inland from the coast. The journey from Ain Musa to Marah was about forty miles.

At first the Israelites contended with a stony desert, bounded by the deep blue waters of the Gulf of Suez on their right and the mountain chains of El Ruhat on their left. After nine more miles, they came into the desert plain called el Ati, a white, glaring stretch of sand that turned into hilly country with sand dunes rolling out to the coast. But water was nowhere to be found. Marah is usually identified with Ain Hawarah, a site several miles inland from the Gulf. Ain Hawarah's waters are notoriously salty and brackish.

24 The people's grumbling is strong evidence of the historical truthfulness of the wanderings narrative. As a general pattern the grumblings that preceded the golden calf incident are raised by genuine need, but those that follow are mainly illegitimate forms of murmuring. The unpalatable waters at Marah made a strong enough impression so as to obliterate all the miracles of Egypt and the parting of the Red Sea—or so it appeared.

25a The Lord "showed" (GK 3723) Moses a tree. The verb "showed" is from the root that means "to teach" or "instruct" and is the same root from which we derive the word "Torah" ("instruction," "law"; GK 9368). Israel was to learn that the *instruction* they needed, after being freed from Egypt, would come from heaven. This, in turn, would prepare them for the reception of the precept of the laws. The text is clear that God gave Moses special instructions in response to the despair of the people. The tree may have had little more to do with the actual temporary healing of the waters than did the salt in Elisha's healing of the Jericho spring in 2Ki 2:19–22. In both cases it may only be the power of God and a test of obedience that are present.

25b–27 This miracle was connected with a promise: From now on obedience to commands and statutes would bring healing, both physically and morally. God allowed Israel to go three days without water to "test" them. God later tested Israel at Meribah (17:1–7), at Sinai (20:20), at Taberah (Nu 11:3; 13:26–33), and elsewhere; but it was "to humble [them] and to test [them] in order to know what was in [their] heart[s]" (Dt 8:2). On the other hand, the "diseases" God "brought on" the Egyptians would afflict Israel if they disobeyed and rebelled against God (Dt 28:27).

Israel journeyed to "Elim," located in the large and beautiful valley of Gharandel, about seven miles south of Ain Hawarah. This tract of land lies between the wilderness of Shur and the wilderness of Sin and contains two other wadis besides the Wadi Gharandel. In the rainy season a constant torrent of water runs down to the Red Sea. The grass is thick and high, and there are many trees there.

2. The manna and the quail (16:1–36)

1–3 The "fifteenth day of the second month" was exactly one month after Israel had left Egypt (12:6, 31). Since Nu 33:5–11 mentions only seven places of encampment and only one journey of three days' duration (Ex 15:22), it is evident that either Israel stayed at several of these places for a number of days or that they camped in a number of other unmentioned places. The Hebrew text implies that they may have left Elim in various detachments and finally assembled as a complete group when they all reached the Desert of Sin. The location of the Desert of Sin is problematic.

This time the people "grumbled" about the amount of food and the lack of meat. Suddenly Egypt seemed all peaches and cream (actually pots of meat and all you could eat) rather than bondage and slave drivers. With a twisted piety and a condescending reference to the Lord's name, the Israelites pretended that they would have preferred being victims at God's hand in Egypt to being the recipients of so many miracles—

and all this hardship. The provisions from Egypt may have lasted these thirty days, but their supplies were undoubtedly exhausted.

4–5 God would graciously answer the Israelites' grumbling by raining down on them "bread from heaven" (cf. Ne 9:15; Ps 78:24; Jn 6:31–51). But there was to be a "test" (GK 5814) to see whether Israel would obey and trust God by faith. Already prior to the giving of the Ten Commandments, the seventh day was to be set apart to the Lord because of the Creation ordinances in Ge 2:2–3. On the sixth day, the people were to gather twice the daily amount. It was not to be left or eaten in the form they gathered it; instead, it was to be prepared by milling and baking (cf. Nu 11:8).

6–8 The first part of v.8 explains that Israel's lapse of memory would be restored that very evening, when God sent them food in a way yet to be announced; then they would *know* (here is that evangelistic word from the plagues) that it was the Lord! The second part of v.8 elaborates on the inner meaning of the words in v.7b: your grumbling is not directed at your leaders, but ultimately your complaint is against God. Hence we have the theology and abiding principles to be gained from Israel's appreciation (and ours!), for what God did here is placed in front of the actual narration of the events.

9–12 Moses instructed Aaron to summon the congregation to "come [near] before the LORD." Verse 10 explains that they were to look toward the desert where the Lord appeared in the cloud. The meaning of this symbol of the real presence of God connected with the splendor of this cloud and fire will be clarified in 24:15–17. Once again, as in vv.6 and 8, Israel "will know that I am the LORD your God."

13–18 The events describing the gift of quail is similar in form but separate in time from the narrative in Nu 11:4–22, 31–33 (that event took place in the second year of the wanderings, Nu 10:11). Quail (not locusts or flying fish, but "feathered fowls" as Ps 78:27–31 makes clear) are well-known migratory birds. They usually fly in vast numbers in the spring to the northern regions and return in the fall. Because of their prolonged flight over the Red Sea, they landed exhausted on the shore of the Sinai Peninsula.

Not only did the quail "come up" from the horizon, but so did the dew "come up." When the dew evaporated, beneath it appeared "thin flakes like frost on the ground, . . . on the desert floor." The peoples' question "What is it?" (Heb., *man hu*) shows why Israel called this bread from heaven "manna" (GK 4942; see v.31). Various natural explanations have been suggested for the origin of the manna, but they all run into trouble when trying to fully explain its miraculous occurrence. In the final analysis, it was a unique substance, miraculously created for a special purpose. Each family unit was to gather "an omer," about two quarts or one-tenth of a bushel (v.36), for each person in their tent.

19–21 In spite of his warning that God was testing (v.4) the people by ordering them not to leave any manna until the next morning, "some . . . paid no attention to Moses." This test was to remind Israel that they did not live by bread alone but by "every word that comes from the mouth of the LORD" (Dt 8:3). Furthermore, it taught Israel that even their daily bread was a gift from God; therefore, they were to live in daily dependence on him.

22–30 The day of rest, a holy Sabbath to the Lord, did not originate with the Sinaitic legislation; for even in 20:8–11 it was grounded in the ordinances of Creation (Ge 2:2–3; cf. also 29:27). This pattern of six days for gathering and one day of rest was ordered by God (v.5). The seventh day was to be a "day of" cessation or "rest"; therefore, food preparations for the morrow were to be made on the sixth day. But when some failed to obey, the Lord groaned: "How long will you [pl.] refuse to keep my commands and my instructions?" Only then did the people "rest" (lit., "stop," "cease") on the seventh day.

31 The name and description of manna are given also in Nu 11:6–9. Coriander seed is a small, lobular grain that is white or yellowish gray and is used for seasoning (cf. our use of caraway and sesame seeds). Numbers 11:7 adds that it "looked like resin" and, according to the older versions, that it had the color of "bdellium" (KJV; = pearl?). Its taste was like wafers made of honey or "something made with olive oil" (Nu 11:8); and it could be ground in a mill, crushed in a mortar, cooked in a pot, or made into cakes (Nu 11:8).

32–36 At some subsequent time, Moses ordered that the manna be memorialized by placing some of it into the ark of the testimony. The ark had not been revealed, much less constructed, at this time. In support of this position is the historical note in v.35, which describes the eating of manna over the next forty years; therefore, these verses were written by Moses at the end of the wanderings.

3. The waters of Meribah (17:1–7)

1–2 Before Israel came to Rephidim, the people rested at Dophkah and Alush (Nu 33:12–14). Rephidim is best identified as the large Wadi Refayid, in southwest Sinai, instead of Wadi Feiran. They had hoped to find water, but the wadi was already dry. This situation presents us with a third narrative on the Lord's provision for Israel's needs in the desert.

As a result of this disappointment, the people "quarreled" with Moses, demanding: "Give [pl. form] us water to drink." The verb "to quarrel" (GK 8189; from the root *rib*) explains one of the names for this place, "Meribah" (v.7), which means "quarrel," "strife," or "argument." What had been a gracious gift of God through Moses' hands was demanded as a magical solution to their problem: "Give it to us."

Significantly, Israel had traveled to Rephidim specifically "as the LORD commanded" (lit., "at the mouth of the LORD"). Thus God in his wisdom had directed his people to move from the Desert of Sin (where they hungered but afterward were satisfied) to Rephidim (where they thirsted).

Instead of submitting to the *tests* God was conducting for them (15:25; 16:4), Israel began to *test* the Lord (Pss 78:56; 106:7, 14, 25, 29)! God's people tempt or test their Lord when they distrust his kindness and providential care and grumble against him and/or his leaders. Moses would later warn (Dt 6:16) that the people were not to put God to the test as they did at Massah.

3 Biblical narrative often leads off the story with a general statement (here, v.2) and then by means of a coordinate clause explains in more detail the theme announced in the previous verse(s). Accordingly, it might be better to translate v.3: "Since the people were thirsty for water."

4–7 Moses took his difficulties to the Lord (15:25; 32:30; et al.). In his exasperation he pled, "What am I to do with these people?" Thus they were ready to stone Moses—an angry mob's solution to an irritating problem.

The Lord's response was to move directly to sending relief. Moses, with a few elders, was to go in front of the people—presumably farther down the wadi. There, where the pillar of the cloud stood as the symbol of God's own presence, Moses was to "strike [on] the rock" just as he had "struck" the Nile River. Striking the Nile (7:17, 20) in the first plague, however, signaled an interruption in that nation's water supply, whereas this striking would signal the commencement of the flow of waters.

This incident is not to be confused with a similar episode that comes near the conclusion of Israel's forty years of journeying in Nu 20:1–13. In this later account, the glory of the Lord is not present; and Moses is explicitly instructed that he is *not* to strike the rock but only *to speak* to it.

Thus we have the dual name that brought out both the people's testing of God (*Massah;* i.e., "test") and their quarreling (*Meribah;* i.e., "contention," "strife"). In less than six months the Israelites had witnessed ten plagues, the pillar of cloud and fire, the opening and shutting of the Red Sea, the miraculous sweetening of the water, and the sending of food and meat from heaven; yet their real question came down to this: "Is the LORD among us or not?"

4. The war with Amalek (17:8–16)

8 The Amalekites lived in the desert, south of Canaan around Kadesh (Ge 14:7), otherwise known as the northern part of the Negev (Nu 13:29; 14:25, 43). Amalek was the son of Eliphaz (Esau's eldest boy) by a concubine named Timna (Ge 36:12) and became a "clan" or "chief" in the tribe of Esau (Ge 36:15). Thus the Amalekites were distant cousins to the Israelites.

Amalek's assault on Israel drew the anger of God because they failed to recognize the hand and plan of God in Israel's life and destiny and because the first targets of their warfare were the sick, aged, and tired of Israel who lagged behind the line of march (Dt 25:17–19). Thus Amalek became the "first among the nations" (Nu 24:20)—in this case,

to attack Israel. They are juxtaposed with another group of Gentiles in the next chapter (Jethro's Midianites) who believed in Israel's God. These two chapters illustrate two kingdoms and two responses to the grace of God from the Gentile world.

9 To direct the battle against the Amalekites, Moses commissioned a young man (perhaps about forty-five) from the tribe of Ephraim (Joseph's son) named Hoshea (Nu 13:8) the son of Nun (1Ch 7:27), who later was renamed Joshua. He was to muster an army to fight against the Amalekites while Moses, with the staff of God in his hand, would stand on top of one of the nearby hills overlooking the plain. Both elements were to be operating: the sword in Joshua's hand and the staff (symbol of divine intervention) in Moses' hand.

10–13 Aaron and Hur went with Moses up the hill. Hur is again mentioned with Aaron in 24:14. Whether this is the same Hur who descended from Judah through Caleb (1Ch 2:18–20) and whose grandson Bezalel built the tabernacle (Ex 31:2) is difficult to say. Tradition says that Hur was the husband of Moses' sister, Miriam.

"As long as" Moses held up his hands, Joshua and his men were victorious. However, "whenever he lowered his hands" through weariness, the Amalekites forged ahead in the battle. This gesture was not merely for psychological effect to inspire the troops every time they glanced up the hill. Nor does the text specifically claim that Moses prayed while his hands were raised. Rather, Moses' outstretched arms primarily symbolized his appeal to God. Finally the lengthy battle came to an end, with Joshua as victor and with the help of Aaron and Hur in holding Moses' hands up.

14 The account of this battle, in which the powerful presence of the Lord played an important role, was to be written down on a scroll and continually reiterated for Joshua's benefit. Amalek would pay dearly for its awful deed. The psalmist (Ps 83:4, 7) links Amalek's motives with those of other nations: " 'Come,' they say, 'let us destroy them as a nation, that the name of Israel be remembered no more.' " But what they had threatened to do to Israel would be measured out to them. This sentence of total extinction was not yet carried out in Saul's day (1Sa 15), for Saul failed to do what God had said. David continued the action (2Sa 1:1–8:12); and it may still have been going on in Esther's day, if Haman indeed is proven to have been an Amalekite.

15–16 Whether "The LORD is my Banner" is the name of the altar (cf. Jacob in Ge 33:20) or a title for God himself cannot be known for certain. The result is the same in either case. The Hebrew word for "banner" reflects the root "to be high," "raised," or "conspicuous." The allusion is to lifting up the staff as a standard and a testimony to his power. The victory, then, was the Lord's, just as the war had been his.

The interpretation of v.16 is difficult because of the unusual spelling of the word "throne" (*kes*). The best solution (taking the more difficult textual reading) is to see *kesyah* as a shortened form of *kisse'-yah* ("throne of Yah[weh]"). The text would then read: "Truly, the hand is towards the throne of the Lord," i.e., in a supplicating position. An alternative rendering is "because a hand is against the throne of the LORD" (see NIV note). This latter reading fits the context of v.14 better.

5. The wisdom of Jethro (18:1–27)

1–5 Jethro, Moses' father-in-law, met Moses and the Israelites in the desert at the "mountain of God" (see 3:1). Moses must have sent his wife and children on ahead to Midian to bring Jethro back to Sinai for a visit. Zipporah, Gershom, and Eliezer may have been sent back to Midian after the family dispute in 4:20–26. But it would have been most important for Eliezer as the next high priest to be a firsthand witness of all that God had done for Israel in the Exodus.

6–8 Jethro announced his arrival by means of a messenger, and Moses went out to meet him (cf. Ge 18:2; 19:1; 32:6; 33:1) and to exchange the usual Oriental greetings. Moses then recounted "all" that "the LORD" (the personal and covenantal name of God is used instead of the generic name Elohim, which depicts God's relationship to all creation) had done. As the psalmist exhorted (Ps 145:5–7, 12), so Moses acted, recounting the awesome work and abundant goodness of the Lord both in Israel's rescue from Egypt and in their subsequent "hardships" along the way.

9–12 The news evoked an instinctive "Praise the LORD" from Jethro, thereby showing either that he had continued believing in the God of his fathers (cf. Ge 25:2) or that he had spiritually benefited from Moses' forty-year stay in his house. Jethro continued, "Now I know that the LORD is greater than all other gods." This confession formula is a clear statement to the Lord's incomparable greatness above all the gods of Egypt.

Jethro then "took" or "brought" a burnt offering and fellowship offerings (NIV, "other sacrifices") to God (*Elohim*). "Brought" (GK 4374) is the customary word for proffering or providing an animal for sacrifice; it is never used in the OT in the sense of "to offer." Accordingly, he did not officiate as priest by "offering" these sacrifices, but he did worship and fellowship with Moses and Aaron "in the presence of God."

The generic name for God (Elohim) is used instead of the covenantal, personal name (Yahweh), perhaps because God was relating to the Gentile and the Jewish world simultaneously. Clearly Jethro was an outsider, an alien (a *ger*, like the name Moses gave to his son—*Ger*shom), even though he had made a strong declaration of faith in vv.10–11. "In the presence of God" may simply reflect the phrase "the glory of God," and thus we may have a covenant meal eaten in the presence of the God who dwells in the midst of his people.

13–16 Jethro is depicted as an efficiency expert who wisely suggests a modification in Israel's leadership structure (cf. vv.17–23), which Moses then adopted with divine permission. Prior to this the people came to Moses for instruction and judicial settlements.

17–23 Jethro's solution to this lengthy process, which was wearing out both the people and their leader, was to give Moses that portion of the work that involved a twofold office: an advocate on behalf of the people and an interpreter on behalf of God to teach the people. Jethro warned that his plan needed to be executed only if God was pleased with this advice.

Moses' work was to be supplemented with additional help. He was to "select capable men." While it may seem from this passage that Moses autocratically chose his own staff, the actual election was the work of all

This picture was taken from the top of what is considered by most scholars to be Mount Sinai, looking down into the valley below, where the nation of Israel would have been camped. The building in the valley is the St. Catherine monastery.

the people, as Dt 1:9, 13 affirms. Their leadership course was to include instruction in "decrees" (i.e., specific enactments), "laws" (i.e., general enactments), the "way to live" (i.e., lifestyle and the path of duty), and the "duties" (or jobs) each was to perform.

The qualifications for these men were that they should be "capable men" (i.e., men with a native aptitude for judging), "men who fear [in reverence and belief] God," men of truth (i.e., "trustworthy"), and men who hated all "dishonest gain." These were to be arranged in a decimal system of a graduated series of groups in multiples of ten, with Moses being the court of final appeal.

24–27 Amazingly enough, Moses listened to his father-in-law, having been taught by a man who was not even an Israelite.

II. Divine Morality (19:1–24:18)

A. The Eagles' Wings Speech (19:1–8)

1–2 In the third month Israel left Rephidim (see 17:1, 8) and came to the Desert of Sinai. "The desert in front of the mountain" is called er-Raha (meaning "the palm [of a hand]") in that it is a flat plain about five thousand feet above sea level that stretches over four hundred acres. Several mountains have been associated with Sinai. Most scholars prefer Gebel Musa (7,363 feet elevation at the southern end of er-Raha) because of its relation to the plain (20:18: "they stayed at a distance") and because of its imposing granite formations.

3–6 The "sign" given to Moses in 3:12 is fulfilled here: he has returned to the "mountain of God" (3:1). When Moses "went up" the mountain, the Lord delivered his "eagles' wings speech." A twofold title is used for the people of God: "house of Jacob" (a reminder of their humble beginnings; cf. Ge 28:13; 35:11; 49:7) and "the people of Israel" (a statement as to what they had become: a nation).

The metaphor of the eagles' wings could refer to one of the eight species of eagles found in Syria, Palestine, and Arabia in addition to the Palestinian vulture. Here it is probably the latter one. This metaphor is developed most extensively in Dt 32:11, where the loving compassion, protection, strength, and watchfulness of God are compared to the majestic bird's attributes. As the young eagles were carried on the adult wings and brought out of their nests and taught to fly, so the Lord had lovingly carried and safely delivered Israel.

The covenant mentioned here, first given to the patriarchs, was unconditional in its transmission and bestowal, but it was indeed conditioned with regard to its enjoyment and personal participation. The presence of the "if" in v.5 did not, however, pave the way for Israel's declension from grace into law any more than an alleged presence of a condition paved an identical fall for the patriarchs (Ge 22:16–18; 26:5) or for David (2Sa 7:14–15; 1Ki 2:4; 8:25; et al.).

Three titles summarize the divine blessings that an obedient and covenant-keeping Israel will experience: they would be a "treasured possession" (GK 6035), "a kingdom [GK 4930] of priests [GK 3913]," and "a holy [GK 7705] nation [GK 1580]." The first signified that Israel would be God's valuable property and distinct treasure (Dt 7:6; 14:2; 26:18; Ps 135:4; Mal 3:17; cf. Tit 2:14; 1Pe 2:9), set aside for a marked purpose. Furthermore, they were to be at once priest-kings and royal-priests (Isa 61:6; cf. 1Pe 2:5, 9; Rev 1:6; 5:10; 20:6)—everyone in the whole nation. This expression was not a parallel phrase or a synonym for a "holy nation"; it was a separate entity. The whole nation was to act as mediators of God's grace to the nations of the earth (cf. Ge 12:3c). The last title designated Israel as a separate and distinct nation because her God was holy, separate, and distinct, as were his purposes and plans (Dt 7:6; 14:2, 21; 26:19; Isa 62:12; cf. 1Pe 2:9).

This whole synopsis of God's suzerainty treaty with his vassal Israel is remarkably personal. It begins and concludes with "to the sons of Israel." Its first and last clauses are introduced by an emphatic "you" along with two other references to "you" in v.4.

7–8 The people responded, "We will do everything the LORD has said." Some commentators have criticized Israel for speaking rashly by agreeing to do all that God said; for they went off the promise, so it is alleged, and onto a law standard. On the contrary, the Lord approved of their response in glowing terms: "Everything they said was good. Oh, that their hearts would be inclined to fear me

and keep all my commandments always" (Dt 5:28–29).

B. The Advent of God on Sinai (19:9–25)

9 To forestall all future pretext for saying that the law Moses was about to give to Israel was of his own devising, God conferred on Moses the highest possible honor and deference ever given to mortals. The "you" in this verse is singular, but the event of the advent or coming of God in a dense, dark cloud was public. Ordinarily God dwelt with his people in a pillar of cloud and fire; but here it turned dense and pitch black, perhaps with a roar of thunder and the flash of lightning as God's voice pierced his creation. The voice of God speaking to Moses (cf. Dt 4:32–33) would be audible in the camp so that Israel and all her true descendants would trust in Moses' words both then and for all time.

10–15 As a token of their inward preparation for meeting with God on the third day, the people were to wash their clothes, stay off the mountain, and abstain from sexual relations. The theology of this passage is fitness for meeting with God and preparation for the worship of God (see on 3:5). This is not to say that there was intrinsic virtue in the mere act of washing clothes or abstaining from marital relations, but the outward act was to signal that the inner work of sanctification had also been sought.

Sealing off the mountain was as much a temporary and arbitrary boundary as it was in 3:5, but it was introduced as an aid for the proper worship of a holy God. The penalty for intruding on such a holy scene was death, since anyone who dared to transgress so explicit a divine precept was already a profane and sacrilegious person whose presence would pollute the rest of the worshiping community. This was tantamount to what Nu 15:30–31 calls "sinning defiantly" or what the NT regards as blasphemy against the Holy Spirit (Heb 10:26–31). After the "ram's horn" sounded a long, drawn-out blast, the people could once again ascend the mountain (v.13b).

16–19 The advent of God took place amid a most impressive display of cosmic disruptions: thunder and lightning (cf. Ps 77:18; Heb 12:18–19; Rev 4:5; 8:5; 11:19), an exceedingly loud trumpet blast (cf. Rev 1:10; 4:1), and a thick cloud (Ex 19:9; 2Ch 5:14). A deep moral impression was made on the people, for they were in the presence of the glorious majesty of the holy God who was about to reveal his person and character in his law.

20–25 Moses' reaction to this awesome sight is not given here, but in Heb 12:21 his response is, "I am trembling with fear." God's response came in v.21. Moses was to warn the people not to intrude rashly on the presence of God. The triple emphasis (vv.12–13, 21–22, 25) is a standard literary practice when the text wants us to notice an important subject. Thus the boundary between the human and the divine was not to be taken lightly by mortals.

"Even" the priests who approached the Lord were to consecrate themselves. Certainly this was not the Aaronic priesthood, because that had not yet been established. It must be a reference to the "firstborn" of every family who were dedicated and consecrated to God (13:2). Only later was the tribe of Levi substituted for each firstborn male (Nu 3:45). Should the people fail to observe this request, the Lord would "break out against them."

C. The Decalogue (20:1–17)

The purpose of the law of God was threefold: (1) to show the awful sinfulness of humans in their moral distance from God, (2) to demonstrate humanity's need for a mediator if they were ever to approach God, and (3) to outline how humans should live more abundantly by using as their guide the unchangeable perfections of the nature of God as revealed in the moral law.

The grammatical form of these commandments needs some comment. There are only three positive statements in vv.2–17—all without a finite verb (vv.2, 8, 12). These phrases might be rendered thus:

1. "I, *being* the LORD your God . . ."
   [Therefore observe commandments one to three]
2. "*Remembering* the Sabbath day . . ."
   [Therefore do vv.9–11]
3. "*Honoring* your father and your mother . . ."
   [Therefore observe commandments six to ten]

The resulting outline would be as follows: (1) Right Relations With God (vv.2–7), (2) Right

Relations in the Worship of God (vv.8–11), and (3) Right Relations With Society (vv.12–17).

1–2 God's commandments are simply labeled "all these words." The title "Ten Commandments" comes from Ex 34:28 and Dt 4:13, while Heb 12:19 speaks of "a voice speaking words." God himself is the speaker and source of these commandments (cf. Dt 5:12–13, 32–33).

The lawgiver places his law in the environment of grace, for it was his gracious act of redemption and deliverance from Egypt that revealed his name, "the LORD." The "I" is both emphatic and the subject; "the LORD" is the predicate. The introduction of the Lord's name at this point brackets both ends of the Exodus event: In Ex 3:14 and 6:2, God tied the promise of his deliverance of Israel from Egypt with his name. Now that that promise had become reality, the Lord proclaimed his name once again. All that the Lord is, says, and does is embodied in this one affirmation: "I am the LORD." The rest of the statement is one of the great formulas of Scripture, used 125 times to describe the character and graciousness of the Lord.

3 In the first commandment there is only one difficult expression, the phrase "before/besides me." Nowhere does this phrase in the Hebrew mean "except me." It is perhaps best translated, "You shall not prefer other gods to me." The result, however, is the same: The Lord is the only true God.

4–6 The second commandment discusses the *mode* rather than the *object* of worship. It has two parts: the precept (vv.4–5a) and the penalty (vv.5b–6).

The OT is replete with synonyms and words (there are fourteen) for idols and images. Verse 23 explains the proscribed idols as "gods of silver or gods of gold." "Idol" also includes images carved from stone or wood and later those made from metal. Since *pesel* ("idol"; GK 7181) refers to statues, "resemblance" or "form" applies to real or imagined pictorial representations. None of these is to be made *with the intention to worship it*. This word was not meant to stifle artistic talent but only to avoid *improper* substitutes that, like the idols of Canaan, would steal hearts away from the true worship of God. One need only to consider the tabernacle with its ornate appointments—all under divine instruction—to see that making representations is not absolutely forbidden.

"You shall not bow down to them or worship them" is a figure of speech called hendiadys, where two expressions are used to convey a single idea, namely, "to offer religious worship." This expression is only used with respect to giving worship to foreign deities forbidden to Israel.

The sanctions attached to this command begin with the majestic reminder that "I, the LORD [Yahweh] your God, am a jealous God." The term "jealous" (or "zealous"; GK 7862) must not be understood in such popular misconceptions as God is naturally suspicious, distrustful, or wrongly envious of the success of others. When used of God it denotes (1) that attribute that demands exclusive devotion (Ex 34:14; Dt 4:24; 5:9; 6:15), (2) that attitude of anger directed against all who oppose him (Nu 25:11; Dt 29:20; Ps 79:5; et al.), and (3) that energy he expended on vindicating his people (2Ki 19:31; Isa 9:7; 37:32; et al.). Thus all idolatry, which Scripture labels elsewhere as spiritual adultery, that raises up competitors or brooks any kind of rivalry to the honor, glory, and esteem due to the Lord will excite his zealousness for the consistency of his own character and being.

Children often repeat the sins of their fathers by personally hating God; hence they too are punished like their fathers. Moses made it plain in Dt 24:16 that such punishment is the result of the children's own sin. The effects of disobedience last for some time, but the effects of loving God are far more extensive: "to a thousand [generations]."

7 The third commandment deals with the profession of the mouth in true adoration of God. The "name" (GK 9005) of God stands for so much more than the mere pronouncing of his title of address. It includes (1) his nature, being, and very person (Ps 20:1; Lk 24:47; Jn 1:12), (2) his teaching or doctrine (Ps 22:22; Jn 17:6, 26), and (3) his moral and ethical teaching (Mic 4:5) (see ZPEB, 4:360–66).

To "take up" the name of the Lord on one's lips "in vain" meant to "misuse" it, i.e., to use it for no purpose. Some vain uses of God's name on the lips of his people (1) express mild surprise, (2) fill in the gaps in speeches or prayers, and (3) confirm something that is false. This commandment does not exclude legitimate oaths, for they appear frequently (e.g., Dt 6:13; Ps 63:11; Isa 45:23; Jer 4:2; 12:16; Ro 1:9; 9:1; 1Co 15:31; Php 1:8; Rev 10:5–6).

8–11 The fourth commandment invokes the remembrance of the Sabbath. The term "Sabbath" (GK 8701) is derived from the Hebrew verb "to rest or cease from work." The Hebrews were to set aside each seventh day as belonging to the Lord their God. The command to remember the Sabbath is *moral* insofar as it requires of a person a due portion of his or her time dedicated to the worship and service of God, but it is *ceremonial* in that it prescribes the seventh day. The sanctity of the first day in honor of God's new deliverance, which the Lord Jesus accomplished in his death and finally in his resurrection, was already signaled in the symbolism of the feasts in Lev 23—"the day after the Sabbath" (v.15); "on the first day hold a sacred assembly" (v.7); "the first day is a sacred assembly . . . on the eighth" (vv.35–36). Indeed, these were the very feasts that pointed forward to the same events that Christians now celebrate on Sunday!

The reason for memorializing this day rested on two works of God: one retrospective (v.11 links it with the Creation), which pointed to the new Rest of God in the end times; the other prospective in the plan of redemptive history (Dt 5:15 links it with the Exodus from Egypt), which pointed to a new Exodus in the final day. This interpretation is borne out by the fact that the Sabbath was another "sign" of the covenant (see on 31:12–17).

12 The fifth commandment, to "honor" (GK 3877) one's parents, involves (1) prizing them highly (cf. Pr 4:8); (2) caring, showing affection for them (Ps 91:15); and (3) showing respect or fear, or revering them (Lev 19:3). Parents are to be shown honor, but nowhere is their word to rival or be a substitute for God's word. The promise in Eph 6:2–3 attached to this commandment to revere one's parents is unique, even though there is a sense in which the promise of life stands over all the commandments (Dt 4:1; 8:1; 16:20; 30:15–16). The captivity of Israel would be caused, in part, by a failure to honor their parents (Eze 22:7, 15).

13 The sixth commandment forbids murder. The ethical theology that lies behind this prohibition is that all humans have been created in the image of God (Ge 1:26–27; 9:6). While Hebrew possesses seven words for killing, the word used here (*rasah;* GK 8357) appears only forty-seven times in the OT. This is the one word that could signify "murder" where premeditation and intentionality are present. Thus this prohibition does not apply to beasts (Ge 9:3), to defending one's home from night-time burglars (Ex 22:2), to accidental killings (Dt 19:5), to the execution of murderers by the state (Ge 9:6), or to involvement with one's nation in certain types of war. It does apply, however, to self-murder (i.e., suicide), to all accessories to murder (2Sa 12:9), and to those who have authority but fail to use it to punish known murderers (1Ki 21:19).

14 The seventh commandment forbids adultery. The verb "to commit adultery" can be used of either men or women. Since the punishment for adultery is death (Dt 22:22) while the penalty for the seduction of a virgin is an offer of marriage or money (Ex 22:16–17; Dt 22:23–29), adultery is distinguished from fornication in the OT.

15 The eighth commandment prohibits stealing either a person or an object. This commandment recognizes that the Lord owns everything (cf. Pss 24:1; 115:16), and only he can give it or take it away. Therefore no one must despotically enslave or kidnap his fellow human being or usurp the rights to property he has not owned or been given.

16 The ninth commandment calls for sanctity of truth in all areas of life, even though the vocabulary primarily reflects the legal process in Israel. To despise the truth was to despise God, whose very being and character are truth.

17 The tenth commandment disallows covetousness, namely, "to desire earnestly," "to long after," or "to covet" (GK 2773; cf. Dt 5:21). This commandment deals with one's inner heart and shows that none of the previous nine commandments could be observed merely from an external or formal act. Every inner instinct that led up to the act itself was also included (cf. 1Ti 6:6).

D. The Reaction of the People to the Theophany (20:18–21)

18 The awe-inspiring phenomena that heralded the theophany (i.e., the appearance of God) terrified the people. What had been depicted in 19:16–19 is here restated anew from the perspective of the people's reactions to these same phenomena. The "mountain [was] in smoke" because it was "ablaze with fire" (Dt 5:23).

19 The people suddenly had no desire to approach God's holy presence (cf. Heb 12:19). They instinctively sensed their need for a mediating priesthood or representative person to approach God on their behalf. Out of this realized need came one of the greatest revelations in a long line of OT promises of the Messiah. He would be a "prophet" like Moses who would speak God's word to them (see Dt 18:15–22). As a result of this arrangement, the people "stayed at a distance," and Moses delivered God's word to them.

20–21 "Do not be afraid," Moses told the people (cf. 14:13); for God had not come to kill Israel (cf. Dt 5:24–25) but to test her. This verse contrasts two types of "fear": tormenting fear (which comes from conscious guilt or unwarranted alarm and leads to bondage) or salutary fear (which promotes and demonstrates the presence of an attitude of complete trust and belief in God; cf. Ge 22:12). This second type will keep us from sinning (cf. Pr 1:7; Ecc 12:13; et al.).

Sunrise as seen from Jebel Musa, in the Sinai range where Moses received the Ten Commandments.

Israel's newly appointed mediator "drew near" or "approached" the thick darkness where God was and received the directives contained in the Book of the Covenant.

E. The Book of the Covenant (20:22–23:33)

The title for this section derives from 24:7. The laws may be arranged into two basic types. The conditional form, where the main condition and additional subheadings are introduced by "if" or "when," is called the casuistic or case law (laws based on actual precedents: "if a person . . ." or "when a person . . .") formulations. The second type takes a categorical, unconditional form and is in the second person (most frequently the singular), often with a negative command or prohibition. This is the form used for most of the Ten Commandments and called the apodictic (i.e., expressing what is always true) formulation.

Some scholars would isolate a third group of laws from within the apodictic. These laws are located in 21:12, 15–17; 22:19–20. They usually are very brief (around five short words), carry the death penalty, and all begin with a Hebrew participle. They are called the "Hebrew participial laws," but actually they are unconditional and apodictic in function. We may speak, then, of two basic types of law in the covenant code.

1. The prologue (20:22–26)

22–23 The connection is this: Since all of you witnessed the Lord speaking from heaven even though you saw no visible shape, form, or representation, therefore totally abandon any thought of ever trying to embody me in a material image. First and foremost, then, the worship of God must be without idols (see 20:4–6; cf. Dt 4:14–16).

24–26 These modest earthen altars were temporary in form and occasional in usage (cf. Ge 12:7; 13:18; 22:9). Stone altars were not to be hewn with a "tool," possibly so that no one could turn it into an image or some other fetish. Likewise, steps were not to be built up to the altars, to preclude the possibility of the worshiper exposing himself as he descended the steps. Later on, when altars with steps were allowed (Lev 9:22; Eze 43:13–17), the priests were instructed to wear linen undershorts (Ex 28:40–42; Eze 44:18).

2. Laws on slaves (21:1–11)

1 It is strange that the title (for v.1 appears to be such) comes after the section on the altar law (20:22–26). Since 22:18–23:19 consists mainly of moral and sapiential exhortations along with the ritual calendar in an appendix-like fashion, it is best to regard the title as referring to 21:2–22:17. These "laws" (or better, "judgments") are given as precedents to guide Israel's civil magistrates. While they deal mainly with temporal matters, they nevertheless are based on one or another express commandment in the Decalogue. It is most appropriate, therefore, that these judicial and political regulations should be set alongside the Decalogue.

2–4 Laws on the Hebrew slave are mentioned only in 21:1–11; Lev 25:39–43; Dt 15:12–18; and Jer 34:8–22. But there are differences in these laws. In Dt 15:12 the Hebrew slave is sold, while in Lev 25:39 he sells himself and the servitude is determined by the year of Jubilee. In Ex 21:2 and Dt 15:12, the servitude is for six years. In Ex 21:6 and Dt 15:17, it is for life when the slave desires it. The word "buy" (GK 7864) in judicial terms means to acquire as one's own property. After six years of service, the slave is to go out "free" (GK 2390 & 3655). The term seems to mean a "freeman" in the sense that he was a citizen once again. A slave left his master either single or married depending on what he was when he entered. Where a wife had been given to a slave, that wife and any children that resulted from that union belonged to the master.

5–6 "I love my master . . . wife and children" has legal rather than romantic overtones (cf. Dt 21:15–17: "does not love," i.e., "hates"). The "judges" changed the slave's status from temporary to permanent by a ceremony at the doorpost of the master's house. The perforation of the ear was a humiliating punishment in the Middle Assyrian Laws.

7–11 This pericope pertains to a girl who is sold by her father, not for slavery but for marriage. Nonetheless, she is designated a "servant." Should the terms of marriage not be fulfilled, it is to be considered a breach of contract, and the purchaser must allow the girl to be redeemed; she must not be sold outside that family. Always she must be treated as a daughter or a free-born woman, or the forfeiture clause will be invoked.

3. Laws on homicide (21:12–17)

12–14 This is a list of offenses that demanded the death penalty: murder, striking one's parents, kidnapping, or cursing one's parents. Homicide contravenes the divine order in Ge 9:6. Since humans are made in the image of God, no money or property settlement can atone for the premeditated destruction of the image of God in them. Accidental death is distinguished from intentional murder. In the case of accidental death, a place of asylum was to be provided (cf. Nu 35:6–34; Dt 19:1–13). But no sanctuary was to be given to the deliberate murderer. Notice the unusual first-person references to God.

15–17 Parental authority is so highly valued in biblical law that striking and cursing parents was a criminal and capital offense. Verses 15 and 17 are illustrations of the fifth commandment. Notice that the father and mother are mentioned together, thereby stressing their basic equality. Kidnapping draws a capital punishment because it is the theft of a human.

4. Laws on bodily injuries (21:18–32)

Following five cases that could involve the death penalty are five cases involving assault and bodily injury.

18–19 The first example concerns a man who is severely injured in a dispute but recovers sufficiently to be able to walk outdoors with the help of a cane or crutches. This injury will not carry the talionic punishment (cf. vv.23–25), but the assailant must recompense the injured for his "loss of time," loss of income, and all medical expenses.

20–21 The second case concerns a slave who is struck by his master and then dies after lingering for "a day or two." The master is given the benefit of the doubt and judged to have struck the slave with disciplinary and not homicidal intentions. When this law is considered alongside that in vv.26–27, which acted to control brutality against slaves at the point where it hurt the master's pocketbook, a whole new statement of the worth of the personhood of the slave is introduced. The aim of this law was to restrict the master's power over the salve.

22–25 The third situation describes a pregnant woman who gives birth prematurely as a result of an injury sustained from men who are fighting. This law envisions two alternatives: (1) "she gives birth but there is no serious injury," and (2) "there is serious injury."

Even though both mother and child survive, the offender must still pay some compensation (cf. vv.18–19). The fee would be set by the woman's husband and approved by a decision of the court. Should the pregnant woman or her child suffer serious injury, equal recompense is invoked, demanding "life for life." The talion principle invoked here appears to preclude exemption from death for an accident fatality as per v.13 because the punishment must match, but not exceed, the damage done. However, Nu 35:31 permits a substitute to ransom all capital offenses in the OT except in the one case of willful and premeditated murder. Thus the defendant must surrender to the deceased child's father or wife's husband the monetary value of each life (notice v.30) if either or both were harmed. The *lex talionis* does impose a strict limit on the amount of damages anyone could collect.

26–27 The fourth case concerns any slave who suffered a permanent injury from his owner; he won his freedom immediately (but cf. vv.20–21). Thus a slave was not to be treated as if he were mere chattel. The economic sanctions were designed to give the owner plenty of reason to resist any abusive tactics for the sake of his financial investment even if he totally disregarded the slave's dignity and worth as a human.

28–32 A fifth example of bodily injury involved goring oxen. People were responsible for the injuries their oxen caused to other people. The Bible's concern was not economic but moral and religious (cf. Ge 9:5–6). It made no difference what the age, social status, or gender of the person was.

5. Laws on property damages (21:33–22:15)

33–34 Culpable negligence (such as leaving a pit uncovered) that results in loss or damage to the property of another demands full restitution. The dead animal becomes the property of the person who is negligent and who must pay to replace that animal.

35–36 A second property damage case concerned a cattle fight, where one animal killed a neighbor's animal. In this case they were to kill the surviving animal, sell its meat, and divide the price as well as the dead animal. But if the animal that survived had a reputation for goring, then its owner must take total responsibility for the animal.

22:1–4 This third example of property damage, which illustrates the morality of the eighth commandment, also contains a group of five cases. In cases of theft the penalty is much greater than those of negligence involving another person's property. The reason for the fivefold penalty in the case of stealing an ox is probably because one man stole the means of another man's subsistence. The principle would extend to any of the man's livelihood implements.

Breaking and entering a home in the night could expose the intruder to the loss of his life (justifiable homicide), in which case the householder would not be held responsible (cf. Jer 2:34). Such invasion during the daylight hours would be a different situation since there would be witnesses and the scope of the intruder's intentions (whether just to steal or also to kill) could be assessed.

When stolen goods have been sold or consumed and the thief has nothing with which to repay his crime, he must be sold into servitude—presumably until he has repaid the debt. But if the goods are still in his possession, then there is hope of repentance and voluntary restitution. At least the original owner can be reunited with his own animal, and the penalty would be that the thief must provide a similar animal. When the thief voluntarily confessed, Lev 6:4–5 required that he add only one-fifth to the theft (cf. Nu 5:6–7).

5–6 A fourth type of property damage involved letting livestock graze in another man's field and letting a fire get out of control so that it burns over a neighbor's field. Both v.5 and v.6 begin with "if," meaning that they are treated as separate laws. Thus people are held responsible, not only for the harm they *do*, but also for the harm they *occasion*, even though they may not have purposely designed the damage that ensued. The restitution will be the top yield that that field has ever produced if the whole field was ruined, or, if not, the choicest sections left will be the standard for the whole field.

7–15 The last section on property damage treats four classes of goods entrusted to other persons for their custody or use.

The first case (vv.7–9) involves leaving valuable articles for safekeeping only to discover a thief stealing them. The thief is to make a double restitution (cf. v.4). The same situation appears in vv.8–9, only the identity of the thief is not known, and thus there is a suspicion that the keeper may have embezzled these securities. The bailee must appear before "the judges," where a deposition of innocence is taken as an oath before God in court. Though this text does not specifically mention an oath, the term "whether" is used elsewhere so frequently as the oath formula that we cannot take it as anything else here (the oath is mentioned explicitly in v.11). Verse 8 is the general rule, and v.9 specifies charges of misappropriation or breach of trust.

The second case (vv.10–11) deals with animals entrusted to another that are mutilated in the pasture, injure themselves, or are driven off by robbers. The same oath in court is required since there are no witnesses and only God can finally decide the keeper's culpability.

In the third case (vv.12–13), the animal given for safekeeping is stolen. Since the bailee is negligent in guarding the animal, he must make restitution by giving the owner an animal for the one stolen. But if the animal given for safekeeping is torn to pieces by wild animals, he need only produce the evidence of this fact, and no payment is required.

The last case (vv.14–15) treats the problem of a hired beast being injured or dying while the owner is not present. Since neglect is presumed, a full replacement is required. However, if the owner is present, the wages agreed on are regarded as sufficient to offset the hazard run by the owner in renting out his property; and his firsthand witness to the deed will take away all suspicion of negligence.

6. Laws on society (22:16–31)

16–17 The law on the seduction of a maiden not yet engaged is different from that dealing with the seduction of the betrothed girl in Dt 22:23, where violence is also involved. The penalty here is that the seducer must pay the bride-price and agree to marry her. Should this offer of marriage be rejected by the girl's father, the man must still pay the bride-price. This payment and offer do not clear the guilt of sin committed, for cleansing is needed by repentance.

18 "Sorceress" is the feminine form of a Semitic word that means "magician" or "sorcerer." The intensive form of the Hebrew verb means to use incantations, magic, sorcery, or the arts of witchcraft. Our English "witch" is alleged to have come from "to wit," i.e., "to know." The LXX rendered our word by *pharmakos* ("poisoners"), since sorcerers dealt in drugs and pharmaceutical potions.

19 This law forbids bestiality (cf. Lev 18:23; 20:15–16; Dt 27:21). The Hittite laws proscribed this evil with the threat of a sentence of death unless pardoned by the king. This offensive act apparently was prevalent among the Canaanites.

20 All who sacrifice to any god other than the Lord "will be dedicated for destruction" (pers. tr.). Notice Dt 17:2–5 for a parallel law.

21–27 These verses treat various forms of oppression against the poor, the widow, the orphan, and the alien. Since these have few or no natural protectors, they are to be shielded in their vulnerable estate. Both the sojourner or resident alien and the widows and orphans are to be protected (see 23:11; Lev 19:9–10; Dt 14:21; et al.).

The laws regulating interest on loaned money are dealt with more fully in Lev 25:35–37 and Dt 15:7; 23:19–20 (cf. Job 24:9; Pr 28:8; et al.). The righteous man may be defined as the one "who lends his money without usury" in Ps 15:5 and "does not lend at usury or take excessive interest" in Eze 18:8 (cf. vv.13, 17). On the other hand, Dt 23:20 declares, "You may charge a foreigner interest, but not a brother Israelite." This law is not dealing with "usury" in our modern sense of the word, i.e., exorbitant or illegal interest, but interest of any kind to a fellow Israelite.

Apparently even an interest-free loan required some type of pledge or security, but retaining one's outer garment (temporary collateral) overnight was strictly forbidden. This cloak or poncho, which doubled as a blanket at night, was needed when evening came.

28 Any word or deed that detracts from the glory of God is a reviling or cursing of his name (see on 20:7). Similarly, care must be taken not to curse any who are in authority, for the penalty for cursing God and the king is death (cf. Lev 24:15–16; 2Sa 16:9; 1Ki 2:8–9; 21:10).

29–30 The law of the firstfruits requires that "the fullness of your harvest and the outflow [lit., 'the tear'] of your presses" (lit. tr.), the firstborn of their children, and the firstborn of the cattle be offered to God. The children are to be redeemed by a money payment or by the substituted service of one Levite for each firstborn (13:13; Nu 3:46–48). They are not to "hold back" or "delay" to do these things, even though the text seems to be aware of a natural reluctance on the part of men. On the seven days that the young firstborn were allowed to stay with their mother, see Lev 22:27.

31 Underlining all these instructions on societal relations is this call to service: "You are to be my holy people." Such a noble calling as the Lord's firstborn son (4:22) or his "treasured possession . . . a kingdom of priests and a holy nation" (see comments on 19:5–6) demands noble living. Animals killed by another are unclean because the carnivorous beasts that tear it are unclean and because the blood of such a slain animal would remain in its tissues, leaving it unclean. Such meat is to be fed to dogs. "Men of holiness" (lit. tr.) are to be separate in inward principle and outward practice—one of which is illustrated here.

7. Laws on justice and neighborliness (23:1–9)

1 This prohibition against slander (whether in court or not) is an amplification of the ninth commandment. Compare Lev 19:16 and the cases of Dt 22:13–19 and 1Ki 21:10–13. The clause "Do not help a wicked man" is the NIV's rendering of "do not set your hand with."

2–3 Justice demands impartiality rather than unwarranted compliance with the "many" (NIV, "crowd") or favoritism to the poor (cf. Lev 19:15).

4–5 Deuteronomy 22:1–3 gives fuller details on a man's responsibility to his brother in the matter of restoring a lost animal or helping someone in difficulty. This act of compassion is owed to another regardless of whether the man is an enemy or one who hates him (cf. Job 31:29; Pr 25:21–22).

6–8 Possibly "your poor people" is better understood here as "your opponent, adversary" (a synonym for "your enemy," v.4, and "the one hating you," v.5). Thus the suffix "your" is more easily understood and the meaning would be thus: When called to testify or to adjudicate between your enemy and someone else, do not pervert the judgment against your enemy just because he is your enemy. Justice demands that people distance themselves from any false charges (cf. v.1). God will not hold such persons or judges guiltless.

Verse 8 is repeated almost verbatim in Dt 16:19. Bribery must have been a common temptation, for numerous passages warn against it.

9 This verse is similar in wording and the motivation to 22:21, but it is placed here because this should be one of the great motivators for all Israelites to exercise justice: Remember how you felt when you were aliens (and all that that implies) in Egypt.

8. Laws on sacred seasons (23:10–19)

10–12 Every seventh year was to be a "Sabbath of sabbaths to the land, a sabbath to the LORD" (cf. Lev 25:4). The land was to lie fallow and to rest. The motivation for this legislation is to favor the poor and the wild animals. In Lev 25:1–7, 18–22, the reasons are more theological than civil: "a sabbath to the LORD" (25:4).

Verse 12 repeats the fourth commandment so that no one would gain the impression that once the sabbatical year was observed, all ordinary observances of the regular Sabbath would no longer be required. This repetition of 20:8–9 adds an additional reason for its observance: so that humans and animals alike might "be refreshed."

13 The caution against idolatry here appears to summarize all the divine precepts given above: literally, "in all things that I have said to you." "Do not let them be heard on your lips" is paralleled by "you shall not cause [all

these things] to be remembered" (NIV, "do not invoke"). There would come a "day" when God would cut off the names of the idols out of the land, and they would "be remembered" no more (Hos 2:17; Zec 13:2). This was the practice of David in Ps 16:4 (note Ex 20:3; Jos 23:7).

14–17 This section deals with the three great annual pilgrimage feasts: Unleavened Bread at the beginning of the barley harvest in the spring, commemorating the Exodus (v.15); Harvest (also called Weeks in 34:22) at the end of the spring harvest of grain, commemorating the giving of the law (v.16a); and Ingathering of the summer crops of olives and grapes in early autumn, commemorating the wilderness wanderings (v.16b; cf. 34:18–26; Lev 23). All three feasts were at once agricultural and historical, and required annual attendance of all men. On the Unleavened Bread Feast, see 12:34 and Lev 23:5–8, 10–14. This feast began with Passover and lasted seven days with a holy convocation on the first and last days. The rule for all the feasts was "No one is to appear before me empty-handed."

Fifty days after the offering of the barley sheaf as the "firstfruits" of the harvest, the Feast of Harvest, known later as Pentecost, was to be celebrated (cf. Lev 23:15–22; Dt 16:9–11).

The Feast of Ingathering or Tabernacles (cf. Lev 23:33–36; Dt 16:13; 31:10; Jn 7:2) was a kind of thanksgiving festival. It was grossly neglected for many periods of Israel's history (Ne 8:17).

18 The first part of this verse has nothing to do with eating anything leavened. Rather, it means that individual Israelites were not to kill the Passover lamb while leaven was still in their houses. The second half of the verse makes no reference to fat as such; but as the parallel verse in 34:25b says, the "sacrifice from the Passover Feast" (here lit., "sacrifice of my feast") shall not "remain until morning" (cf. 12:10). If the word "fat" is retained over the parallel text in 34:25b, which would make "fat of my feast" parallel to "sacrifice of my feast," then the householders are being told to destroy the intestinal fat by morning. But the first explanation (i.e., the presence of leaven) is preferred.

19 The law of firstfruits and its theology have already been discussed in 4:22; 11:5; and 12:29. This was to be brought into the house of God yet to be described.

The prohibition of cooking a young goat in its mother's milk (see also 34:26; Dt 14:21b) has been explained since 1933 by a reference in a broken passage of a thirteenth-century B.C. Ugaritic text called "The Birth of the Gods Pleasant and Beautiful" (text 52, line 14). It is generally agreed that the reference is to a fertility rite that entails boiling a kid in milk; but there is no sure reference to the milk of its mother in the broken Ugaritic text. The matter is basically that the young dead kid is being cooked in the very milk that had sustained its life.

9. Epilogue (23:20–33)

An epilogue concludes the Covenant Code. Israel is promised the angel of God, every protection, and success, provided they remain faithful to the covenant (cf. 33:1–3; 34:11–16; Lev 26:3–11; Dt 7:13–15; 28:1–14).

20–22 The angel mentioned here cannot be Moses, God's messenger, or an ordinary angel; for the expressions are too high for any of these: "he will not forgive your rebellion" (who can forgive sin but God alone?) and "my Name is in him." This must be the Angel of the Covenant (cf. Isa 63:9; Mal 3:1), the Second Person of the Trinity. Just as the Lord's name resided in his temple (Dt 12:5, 11; 1Ki 8:29), so this Angel with the authority and prestige of the name of God was evidence enough that God himself was present in his Son. Obedience to the Angel would result in all of the blessings listed in the text. Israel was commanded: "Do not rebel against him"; yet they did just that (Nu 14:11; Ps 78:17, 40, 56).

23–26 On the nations listed here, see comment on 3:8. All these nations God's Angel would "wipe . . . out," i.e., remove from their national, not necessarily personal, existence; for surely David had Hittites in his army (2Sa 23:39) and was friendly with a Jebusite (2Sa 24:18–24). It was the worship and practices of the gods of these nations that were strictly forbidden. Instead, Israel was to demolish these gods and smash their "sacred stones," which apparently were free-standing stones that were associated with the veneration of deities, particularly the male deity.

The worship of God would affect the Israelites' water and food. No wonder the prophets connected a series of agricultural reverses with the judgment of God on a particular culture (e.g., Hag 1:5–11). Moreover, unlike the wicked who fail to live out half their days (Ps 55:23), the worshiping obedient will have full life spans.

27–30 God promised (in addition to his Angel in vv.20, 23) to send panic and confusion to every nation that Israel would face. He would also send "the hornet," a word that occurs only here, in Dt 7:20, and in Jos 24:12. Perhaps "the hornet" is a symbol of Egypt, just as Isa 7:18 uses the "fly" and the "bee" as symbols of Egypt and Assyria, respectively.

The speed of the conquest is stated differently in several texts. Like this one, Jdg 2:20–3:4 also argues for gradual progress in conquering the land; yet Dt 9:3 promises that it will be done "quickly." The answer lies in noting that the general sweep of the land and its conquest in principle were accomplished speedily. Because of mopping-up operations, however, the need to have people settle in the areas rid of Canaanite influence, and the threat of wild animals infesting them (cf. 2Ki 17:25), the completion of that task would designedly be slow.

31–33 The borders God promised to establish would be from "the Red Sea" (here an eastern boundary), the Gulf of Aqaba with its port city of Elath; to the "Sea of the Philistines," the Mediterranean Sea on the west; from the desert in the south, the Negeb; to "the River" in the north. Rather than equate the Euphrates with "the River," it would appear better to equate it with a river that preserves the same name in Arabic today, currently serving as the boundary between Lebanon and Syria. This description traces out limits already given to Abraham in Ge 15:18 and comes close to matching the extent of the United Kingdom under David and Solomon (2Sa 8:3–14; 10:6–19; 1Ki 4:21, 24; 2Ch 9:26).

No covenant was to be made with these people (though the Gibeonites did succeed in making one, Jos 9:3–15). The potential snare of their gods, practices, and worship was too great; thus there was to be no peaceful coexistence between these nations and Israel in Canaan.

F. Ratification of the Covenant (24:1–18)

The narrative, temporarily interrupted for the contents of the "Book of the Covenant" (20:22–23:33), is resumed from 20:21. Moses and his aides were to ascend the mountain *after* the actions mentioned in vv.3–8 were completed.

1 Nadab and Abihu, Aaron's two eldest sons, would have been the next high priests in the line. They died, however, under God's judgment (Nu 3:4) because of their perverse deed (Lev 10:1–2; Nu 3:4). The official "seventy elders" of Nu 11:16 had not been formally appointed yet. They were selected here to represent the twelve tribes, perhaps representing Jacob's seventy descendants.

2 Moses alone was to function as the mediator between God and the Israelites, just as Christ is designated the second Moses in Heb 3:1–6 and thus is the Mediator of the new covenant (Heb 12:24).

3 When the people promised to obey and to observe all that the Lord had said, they did not exchange the blessings of promise for the law. The keeping of the "Lord's words and laws" was to be based on the prior provision of sacrificial blood. The blood cleansed men and women so that "doing" and "obeying" became possible for them. This was *not* "doing" in order to merit favor or salvation.

4 This passage testifies to Moses' direct involvement in the composition of the book of Exodus. That "Moses then wrote down everything" agrees with his recording the account of the war on Amalek (17:14) and the writing of the Ten Commandments by the "finger of God" (31:18) (see comment on 17:14). The "twelve stone pillars" represented the twelve tribes (Jos 4:5, 20; 1Ki 18:31).

5 The "young Israelite men" were the firstborn who officiated until the Levites were appointed in their place in Nu 3:41 (see 19:22, 24).

6 Both the altar and the people were sprinkled with half of the blood, each in an act of dedication or consecration. Hebrews 9:19 does not mention the altar but speaks of the "book" or "scroll" of the covenant as also being sprinkled with blood. It is probably not correct to speak, as some do, of the altar as

representing the Lord (cf. Ge 15:9–10, 17). The rite mentioned here is a rite of purification (not the water, scarlet wool, and hyssop of Lev 14:6–7 and Heb 9:19–20). The division of the blood points to the twofold aspect of the blood of the covenant: The blood on the altar symbolizes God's forgiveness and acceptance of the offering; the blood on the people points to a blood oath that binds them in obedience. In other words, the keeping of the words and laws was made possible by the sacrificial blood of the altar.

7 The Book of the Covenant includes in its narrowest meaning words from 20:22–23:33 but more fully, here, the contents of ch. 19, the Decalogue of ch. 20, and the case laws of 20:22–23:33.

8 The blood by which the covenant was ratified and sealed was the basis for the union between the Lord and the people. This phrase becomes most important in the NT (Mt 26:28; Mk 14:24; Lk 22:20; 1Co 11:25; Heb 9:20; 10:29; also Heb 12:24; 13:20; 1Pe 1:2).

9–10 That Moses and his company "saw the God of Israel" at first appears to contradict 33:20; Jn 1:18; and 1Ti 6:16; but what they saw was a "form ['similitude'] of the Lord" (Nu 12:8; cf. Eze 1:26; Isa 6:1). There is a deliberate obscurity in the form and details of the one who produced such a splendid, dazzling effect on these observers of God's presence.

Under God's feet was a "pavement made of sapphire," a deep blue or, more accurately, lapis lazuli of Mesopotamia, an opaque blue precious stone speckled with a golden yellow-colored pyrite. True sapphire, the transparent crystalline of corundum, was unknown in Egypt around 1400 B.C. It symbolizes the heavens (cf. Eze 1:22).

11 "God did not raise his hand against [lit., stretch out his hand; cf. 9:15] these leaders" who saw him. "Leaders"(GK 722) probably comes from the verb "to be deeply rooted," hence, "eminent ones," "nobles," or "chief men." In one of the most amazing texts in the Bible, these men saw God. Verse 11 uses another word than v.10; here it stresses inward, spiritual, or prophetic vision.

"They ate and drank" describes a covenant meal celebrating the sealing of the covenant described in vv.3–8. There is, however, no mention of God's participation in the eating or drinking!

12 Once again Moses was told to "come up" (cf. v.1). This is the first mention of the "tablets of stone."

13–14 In response to the call of God to Moses, Joshua accompanied him as they went farther up the mountain. Aaron and Hur, appointed as Moses' deputies in 17:10 and apparently as judges in 18:22, were left in charge. It is noteworthy that Hur does not appear in the golden calf incident (ch. 32).

15–16 As Moses ascended the mountain, all he could see was a cloud. When the glory of God "settled" on the mountain, the Bible uses the same word (*shakan*; GK 8905) as the one underlying the "shekinah" glory (cf. Jn 1:14, the Word "tabernacling" among us; see comment).

17 On "the glory of the LORD looked like a consuming fire," see comment on 16:10. The three symbols of God's glory, i.e., of his presence, are the cloud, the fire, and the voice of God. The radiance of his presence is like a fiery furnace (cf. Heb 12:18, 29).

18 Once Moses entered the "cloud," he would not be seen again for "forty days and forty nights" (cf. Mt 4:2). During this time Moses received all the instructions on the tabernacle and its furnishings in chs. 25–31. Not until ch. 32 do Moses and Joshua come down to face Israel's apostasy.

III. Divine Worship (25:1–40:38)

The final sixteen chapters of Exodus center on the worship of God. The only interruption of this theme is the episode of the golden calf (chs. 32–34), a section that contrasts the divinely appointed worship established in connection with the tabernacle with humanly devised worship that leads to debauchery.

The most important question about the tabernacle deals with its significance. My view is that the tabernacle primarily embodies the theology of worship. It thereby assumes that God is the Great King who reigns and is therefore worthy of our praise and adoration. Even more specifically, the meaning of the tabernacle is that God has come "to dwell," "to tabernacle," in the midst of Israel, as he would one day come in the Incarnation

This is a model of the tabernacle, built by the Israelites in the desert at Mount Sinai. Prominent in the picture is the altar of burnt offering and the Tent of Meeting, with the cloud hovering above it. Courtesy Zondervan Corporation © 1984.

(Jn 1:14) and will come in the Second Advent (Rev 21:3). The Lord who dwelt in his visible glory in his sanctuary among his people (Ex 25:8) will one day come and dwell in all his glory among his saints forever.

A. The Tabernacle (25:1–31:18)

1. Collection of materials (25:1–9)

1–2 The "offering" (or "contribution"; GK 9556) mentioned here is not a "heave offering" (KJV, ASV mg.) but one separated for a sacred purpose as a gift to be consecrated to the Lord. See the translation "special gift" in Dt 12:6, 11, 17. It was also a voluntary gift, as v.2b stresses.

3–7 The fourteen components or materials that went into the tabernacle are listed. They include (1) gold, (2) silver, and (3) bronze. Then follow three colors of yarn. (4) "Blue" is derived from a dye of a shellfish, variously described as sky blue, deep dark blue, blue-purple, or bright violet. Its significance, though not stated, is perhaps of the heavenly character of Christ. (5) "Purple" is derived from the secretion of a gland of the murex snail and was supplied primarily by the Phoenicians. It is a purple-red and speaks of royalty. (6) "Scarlet," or crimson, is derived from the eggs and bodies of the worm *coccus ilicis*, which attaches itself to the leaves of the holly plant. Their maggots are collected, dried, and pulverized; and the powder produces a bright red (or yellow-red) dye. It is a part of the contribution. It may refer to the earthly aspect of the Son of Man.

(7) "Fine linen" translates an Egyptian loan word in Hebrew. Some linen found in Egyptian tombs has 152 threads per inch in the warp as compared to only 86 threads per inch in the most finely woven modern techniques. It is usually white, representing purity and righteousness. (8) The "goat hair" came from long-haired goats and most likely was black. It was a coarse material often used to weave tents. Felt would be a modern equivalent. (9) The "ram skins" had all the wool removed and then were dyed red; they were like our morocco leather. (10) The "hides of sea cows" no doubt came from the East African sea cows ("porpoise" or "dolphin") found in the Red Sea.

(11) "Acacia wood" is a species of the mimosa, whose wood is darker and harder than oak and therefore avoided by wood-eating insects. It is common in the Sinai Peninsula. (12) There was also "olive oil," made from crushing the olives, for light. (13) The word for "spices" is derived from the Hebrew word *basam* (GK 1411; "to be fragrant"). The four best species for anointing oil are identified in 30:22–25 as "myrrh" (sap of a balsam bush), "cinnamon" (bark of the cinnamon tree), "cane" or sweet calamus (a pink-colored pith from the root of a reed plant), and "cassia" (from the dried flowers of the cinnamon tree). The four species for incense are identified in 30:34–38 as "gum resin" or "stacte" (KJV; a powder taken from the middle of the hardened drops of the myrrh bush, rare and very valuable), "onycha" (from the shell of a type of clam [mollusks] similar to the purple murex snail and found deep in the Red Sea), "galbanum" (a rubbery resin of thick milky juice from the roots of a flowering plant thriving in Syria and Persia), and "frankincense" (a resin from the bark of *boswellia carteri* growing in southern Arabia). The *boswellia carteri* resin dripped spontaneously from the plant in the fall and was "pure," without any foreign matter—pure "white"—hence its Hebrew name "whiteness."

(14) The "onyx stones" cannot be positively identified. The LXX translates it as "beryl," mostly a sea-green color. Another suggestion is a chrysoprase quartz ranging in color from blue-green to yellow-green and apple-green. The Egyptians knew chrysoprase. For other gems mounted in the ephod and breastplate, see 28:6–25.

8 The "sanctuary" (GK 5219) means "holy" place or "the place set apart." Everything about the tabernacle was holy. The same word in 1 and 2 Chronicles refers to the temple. Hebrews 9:1 calls the sanctuary "the sanctuary of this world" (NIV, "earthly sanctuary").

9 The most important word about the sanctuary was that it was to be built according to the "pattern" God would show Moses. The word "pattern" (GK 9322) signals the fact that typology is present, for this is only a "model" or "pattern" of the real thing (see v.40).

The word "tabernacle" (GK 5438) appears here for the first time in the OT. It is from the word "to dwell" and is the place where God dwells among his people (cf.

29:42–46; Lev 26:9–12; Eze 37:26–28; and in the NT, Rev 21:2–3).

2. Ark and mercy seat (25:10–22)

The first item in Moses' list of instructions in the tabernacle was the ark of God with its "atonement cover" (GK 4114). Tyndale rendered this word as "mercy seat." However, the ark was the place of atonement or propitiation, hence the place where God was rendered favorable to his people.

10a The "chest" or "ark" (GK 778; English word from the Lat. *arca*) is called "the ark [of] the Testimony" (v.15), "the ark of the covenant of the LORD of all the earth" (Jos 3:11), "the sacred ark" (2Ch 35:3), and "the ark of your might" (Ps 132:8). It is the throne of God. God begins at the heart of things rather than working from the outside in (cf. also Heb 9:4).

10b–17 The ark was $3\,^3/_4$ feet long by $2\,^1/_4$ feet wide and high. It was to be overlaid with "pure gold." It had a type of "molding" or "collar" around it, and four gold rings were attached there. The "acacia wood" poles were slid through the rings for transporting the chest. The "Testimony" (GK 6343) or "laws" of the Ten Commandments were placed inside the ark. In Egypt, Babylonia, and the Hittite Empire, important documents were deposited in the sanctuary "at the feet" of the deity.

The verb that lies behind the noun "atonement" in the expression "atonement cover" (GK 4114) means "to ransom or deliver by means of a substitute." (There is no word for "lid" or "cover" here.) The LXX has "propitiatory covering" or "mercy seat," as does Heb 9:5 (see NIV note). This place of expiating the sins of humanity is an adumbration of Christ's propitiatory work (Ro 3:25; Heb 9:23–24; 1Jn 2:2) and is at the heart of our worship of the one who died for us.

18–22 A cherub (pl. "cherubim") is usually depicted as a composite creature with wings, a human head, and a body combining elements of an ox, a lion, or an eagle (cf. Ge 3:24; Eze 1; Rev 4). In Egypt the sphinx was prevalent. In Assyria the same root word was used to describe one who functioned as a temple guardian. The two cherubim were to be made from the cover itself and as part of it. These were hardly made in relief, since they were "looking toward the cover" (cf. 1Pe 1:12).

Verse 22 gives the theological relevance of the ark and cherubim, indeed, of all our worship of God: "There ... I will meet with you." The living God is continually present in his tabernacle and walks among his people there (Lev 26:11–12). It was from his throne above the cherubim that he spoke and met with his people (cf. 1Sa 4:4).

3. Table of the bread of the Presence (25:23–30)

The table of the Presence was one of three pieces of furniture in the Holy Place. It was made of acacia wood overlaid with gold on which twelve loaves of bread were placed. The table with its bread presented two sides of the same truth: a Godward side and a human side. First, it stood before God, reminding Israel that they were ever open to the omniscience and protection of God. Next, it was where the priests served and found their bread. That bread pointed to the Bread that would come down from heaven and give to men and women everlasting bread (cf. Jn 6).

23–28 The "table" measured 3 feet long by $1\,^1/_2$ feet wide by 27 inches high. The table taken from the second temple by Antiochus Epiphanes is depicted on the Arch of Titus among the items the Romans took back to Rome in A.D. 70. The description of the table is similar to the ark, overlaid with gold, with a molding or encircling rim and four gold rings to hold the transporting poles.

29 "Its plates and dishes ... its pitchers and bowls" were not for the purpose of serving God food as in pagan nations. Even the sacrifices set apart for God were not to be boiled or roasted; they were to come up before him in vapors and odors, not in substance or as food. Of course, some of the offerings were to be shared with the priests, and the fellowship offerings were shared in part with the people.

30 "The bread of the Presence" is referred to here and also in 1Sa 21:6 and 1Ki 7:48. In this phrase "Presence" (lit., "faces"; GK 7156) stands for the Divine Person himself, just as the "angel of his presence" (lit., "face[s]") in Isa 63:9, or in Ex 33:14–15, "my Presence [lit., 'my face'] shall go with you," is an OT designation of Christ. The twelve loaves

symbolize the twelve tribes of Israel as constantly being under the scrutiny, care, and preservation of God (cf. Jn 6:32–38). Just as that bread supplied the needs of priests on the Sabbath in the Holy Place (see Lev 24:5–9), so Jesus meets the needs of his children in this generation (Jn 6:32–35).

4. Golden lampstand (25:31–40)

31 The third article in the Holy Place was "a lampstand [*menorah*; GK 4963] of pure gold" fashioned all in one piece. It was placed on the south or left side of the Holy Place.

The lampstand's design—"flowerlike cups, buds and blossoms"—was patterned after an almond tree (v.33), the first tree of spring in the Near East, awakening as early as mid-December and decking itself in radiant white blossoms before leafing. The triad of its parts cannot be identified with final certainty. The "cups" were either the calyx (outer covering of the flower; cf. the same word translated "cup" in Ge 44:2) or the almond nut whose medical and cosmetic properties are described as perfect. The "bud" is also rendered as the knop or bulb, the round object on the branch (same word as the capitals or chapiters on the pillars in Solomon's temple, 1Ki 7:18). The "blossoms" of the almond tree render the same word used of Aaron's almond rod that budded and blossomed (Nu 17:8).

The expression "hammer it out" is difficult. Josephus claims it was "cast gold [and] hollow," made in a mold. The verb is used of fashioning the cherubim, the lampstand (vv.31, 36; 37:17, 22; Nu 8:4), and the two silver trumpets (Nu 10:2).

32–36 The total number of ornaments—i.e., "six branches . . . three cups . . . on the lampstand . . . four cups . . . one bud," etc.—would be 69 (6 branches times 3 sets times 3 figures plus 1 branch times 4 sets times 3 figures plus 3 buds under each set of branches equals 69).

37–39 The ancient lamp was a kind of small, round (clay) saucer with the rim pinched together to form a spout from which protruded the top of the wick dipped in the oil of the saucer. Examples of seven-pinched-rim lamps come from the age of Moses (Late Bronze). Beth Shan and Meggiddo have supplied examples of metal pedestals designed to carry a lamp, consisting of an upright three-foot-long shaft dividing into three feet and joined in a ring to be placed on the ground on top of which is a ledge for the lamp. "A talent of pure gold" was about seventy-five pounds.

40 "According to the pattern [GK 9322]" is once again a key word warning Moses and all subsequent readers that what he was really building was only a model (see comment on v.9), not the real, or the archetype, that lay behind the model. Therefore, it was "only a shadow of the good things that are coming—not the realities themselves" (Heb 10:1). Thus there was a built-in obsolescence in this revelation and the models exhibited in the whole tabernacle and its service as contained in Ex 25–Lev 9. The archetype remained with God while these earthly models merely pictured what was yet to come.

5. Curtains, framework, veil, and screen (26:1–37)

a. The tabernacle's curtains (26:1–14)

There are two sets of coverings and two sets of curtains. The two coverings were an outer one of hides of sea cows and an inner one of ram skins dyed red. The two curtains were an outer set of goat hair and an inner set of fine linen with blue, purple, and scarlet yarn. Within the sanctuary, moving from the inside out, the curtains of fine linen were visible only to the priests who served in the presence of him who is purity and righteousness itself. The curtains of goats' hair were reminders of the daily sin offering that was a kid from the goats (Nu 28:15) and of our cleansing from sin (Lev 16). The covering of rams' skins also recalled the sacrifice used in consecrating the priesthood (Lev 8); and it was deliberately dyed red, showing that the priesthood was set apart by blood. Finally, the protective coating of the sea cows' hides marked a protective separation between the dwelling place of God and the world.

1–3 On the "linen" see 25:4. Each of the "ten curtains of finely twisted linen" was about forty-two feet long and six feet wide. They were sewn together in two sets of five. The curtains were more important than the tabernacle's frame, for they are described first—thus setting up the same priority we saw in the ordering of the description of all the tabernacle's parts.

4–6 After stitching each five-sectioned curtain together, two curtains were coupled together by fifty loops on one side and fifty loops on the other side. These were then to be joined by fifty golden clasps or hooks (cf. v.11). The beauty of these white, fine linen curtains with blue, purple, and scarlet yarn (see 25:4) was enhanced with cherubim (see 25:18) embroidered on them.

7–13 Of the eleven "curtains of goat hair," six were sewed in one portion and five in another, and again the fifty loops on one side were joined to the fifty loops on the other by fifty clasps. Goat hair in the Eastern world is black, not white (cf. SS 1:5; cf. on 25:4). Since the "tent curtains" were larger than the curtains of the tabernacle (vv. 1–6), there would be material left on the end and on either side to "hang down the rear" and to "hang over the sides of the tabernacle so as to cover it."

14 See comment on 25:5.

b. The tabernacle's framework (26:15–30)

15–25 On "acacia wood" see comment on 25:5. The command to "make upright frames" (cf. vv.19, 26) introduces the three elements that made up the "walls." The traditional rendering "boards" has led many to the idea that the walls were solid; but if this were so, it would have obscured the inner linen curtains from sight. These frames formed a trellis-like structure over which the four curtains were draped.

Each frame was to be 15 feet long by 2 1/4 feet wide. The framework of the tabernacle consisted of twenty boards each on the north and south sides with six on the western end with a post at each of the two corners. The "two projections" (lit., "hands") are probably the two tenons at the bottom of each frame to be inserted into the bases. The frames were fitted into a foundation of "forty silver bases" or sockets on each side. Israel contributed one hundred talents of silver for these bases (38:25–28), which was described as atonement money (30:11–16). Thus it may be said that the foundation of the tabernacle rested on a ransom or redemption, just as the church was "bought with his own blood" (Ac 20:28).

The Hebrew word for "corner" apparently means "angle." Thus one frame was cut down the center on a miter, and the two pieces would form the "corner" or "angle" frame on the two sides of the corner.

26–29 Fifteen "crossbars" were to be fitted on the outside of the structure to strengthen the trellis framework: five on each of the two sides (north and south) and five on the back (west). One of the five was full length down the middle of the wall; the other four extended only half the length of the wall, making three rows of bars on the outside of the frame. The "gold rings" were to serve as holders (lit., "houses") for the bars (cf. 25:26–27).

30 Once more we are reminded that all was to be done "according to plan" (see comment on 25:40; cf. Heb 8:5).

c. The tabernacle's veil (26:31–35)

31–35 The inner veil (NIV, "curtain") separating the Most Holy Place from the Holy Place was to be made of the same material and design as the inner curtain and was to be supported on four gold-covered acacia wood pillars. The "curtain" (GK 3749) is called the "veil of covering" or "shielding curtain" (39:34; 40:21; Nu 4:5) or the "curtain that is in front of the Testimony" (Ex 27:21). At the death of Christ, this inner curtain of the temple was torn in two, thereby giving the believer permanent access to the presence of God (Mt 27:51; Mk 15:38; Lk 23:45; Heb 6:19; 9:3; 10:19–22).

d. The tabernacle's screen (26:36–37)

36 "The entrance . . . curtain" was like the curtain dividing the two inner rooms (v.33) of the tabernacle and the inner curtain of v.1. The same Hebrew word is used for the curtain at the entrance to the courtyard (27:16) as the screen for the entrance to the tent (here).

37 Since this curtain went to the outside and to the corners of the wall, it had "five posts of acacia wood overlaid with gold" instead of just four (v.32).

6. Altar of burnt offering (27:1–8)

1–2 The first and largest piece of equipment that a worshiper would meet on entering the court of the tabernacle was the "altar" (GK 4640) the altar of burnt offering in Lev 4:7, 10, 18). Its position just inside the gate made it easily accessible, unavoidable, and unmistakable. It was made of acacia wood (see comment on 25:5) and measured $7\frac{1}{2}$ feet square by $4\frac{1}{2}$ feet high. It was overlaid with bronze. There was but one altar just as there is but one way of salvation, and this Jesus fulfilled (see Jn 1:29; Heb 9:13–14, 22–28). The "horns" (GK 7967), i.e., "a horn at each of the four corners," were projections of the four corner posts but of one piece with the altar. They symbolized power, help, and sanctuary (cf. 1Sa 2:1, 10; 2Sa 22:3; 1Ki 1:50; 2:28; Pss 89:17; 112:9). The reason the horns symbolized the atoning power of the altar was that in the atonement ritual some of the blood was put on the horns before the rest was poured out at the base of the altar (29:12; Lev 4:7, 18, 25, 30, 34; 8:15; 9:9; 16:18).

3 The "pots" (or pans) were to hold the fat-soaked ashes when they were removed from the hearth by the "shovels." The "sprinkling bowls" (or basins) were to catch the blood of the animals slain beside the altar to be sprinkled on the altar's base later on. The three-pronged "meat forks" (fleshhooks) were for arranging the sacrifice or retracting the priests' portion (1Sa 2:13). The "fire pans" (or possibly "censers") were probably for carrying fire from the altar of incense inside the Holy Place (Lev 10:1; 16:12; 1Ki 7:50).

4–8 A "grating" was placed midway between the top and the bottom of the boxlike structure. This grating divided the altar into a lower and an upper part, a division necessitated by the sprinkling of the blood. Since any fire built inside the upper half would have eventually destroyed the altar from the intense heat, perhaps the altar box was designed to be filled with earth when it was in use. Perhaps this is why it was to be made "hollow."

"A bronze ring at each of the four corners" was attached to the bronze grating through which the acacia wood staves were placed when the altar had to be moved. The "ledge" was a projection or a collar around the altar halfway up its side.

7. Court of the tabernacle (27:9–19)

9–11 The "courtyard for the tabernacle" was a perfect rectangle, 150 feet long by 75 feet wide. Its purposes were fourfold: (1) to prevent unlawful approach; (2) to keep out all wild animals; (3) to be a positive line of demarcation between the world and the holy

presence of God; and (4) with its single gate, to be a way of approach to God.

The courtyard was to be shielded by a curtain made of the same fabric and colors (v.16) as the entrance, the dividing curtains, and the inner curtains of the tabernacle (26:31–33, 36–37). It was to be high enough ($7\frac{1}{2}$ feet, v.18) to block the view of all persons. Each long side was to have "twenty posts and twenty bronze bases." In all there would be sixty posts (or fifty-six if the corner posts were counted twice as belonging to each side from an observer's point of view). The posts were spaced $7\frac{1}{2}$ feet apart, with a frame or rod going through the top of the silver capitals or "bands" (v.17), providing a frame or guy rod to give stability to the posts. They were also anchored by guy ropes and pegs.

12–19 The courtyard was divided in half. The tabernacle occupied the central position in the west half, and the altar and laver were probably somewhat centered in the eastern half (see the various pictures of the tabernacle). The entrance was invitingly wide; "curtains fifteen cubits long" were to flank the entrance, which would be about thirty feet wide (cf. 6:36–37). The entrance too marked a division between the world and the dwelling place of God. All the poles surrounding the courtyard had silver fillets or "bands," which apparently were narrow strips of binding metal used as decoration.

8. Priesthood (27:20–28:5)

Only Aaron and his four sons were to serve as priests in standing before God. The priest was the indispensable mediator in the life of fellowship with God.

20–21 The "clear oil of pressed olives" was extracted from unripened olives that were beaten and pounded in a mortar rather than crushed in a mill. The pulpy mass was then placed in a basket; and the oil, without any mixture of other parts of the olive, dripped through the basket, giving a clear, pure oil that burned with little or no smoke. The lamps were to be kept burning "from evening till morning" (cf. 30:8; 1Sa 3:3). Significantly, the people were to provide this oil continuously; otherwise there would be darkness in the dwelling place of God.

1 Nadab and Abihu were two of Aaron's four sons who later offered unauthorized fire before the Lord and were consumed (Lev 10:1–2), leaving only Eleazer and Ithamar. Aaron and his sons were to "serve . . . as priests." They were to stand before the Lord (applied to *all* Levites in Dt 10:8) "to offer gifts and sacrifices for sins" and "to deal gently with those who are ignorant and are going astray" (Heb 5:1–2). They were to teach the people (Ne 8:2, 9) and serve as intercessors for them.

2–5 The garments of the high priest were "to give him dignity and honor," i.e., they were to exalt the office and function of the high priest as well as beautify the worship of God. "The skilled men" were to make priestly garments for Aaron. Eight garments are mentioned: the four inner garments worn by all priests—tunics, linen undergarments or breeches, girdles or sashes, and headbands (vv.39–42). The four overgarments that were to be especially worn by Aaron were the breastpiece, ephod, robe, and turban (miter).

9. Garments of the priests (28:6–43)

6–14 The ephod probably was a high priestly waistcoat woven of blue, purple, scarlet, and white linen thread—all entwined with gold thread. Instead of having sleeves or being joined at the sides, it was hung from the shoulders by straps on which one onyx stone was mounted on each strap on top of a golden clasp with the names of the six younger sons of Israel engraved on one stone and the six elder sons engraved on the other stone. The names symbolize that the high priest represented all Israel when he ministered in the tabernacle. A "waistband" made of the same material and style as the ephod held the front and back of the ephod to the priest's body. It had no significance of its own.

15–30 The "breastpiece," a square piece of cloth made the same way as the ephod, was folded in half upward to form a sort of pouch in a square, 9 inches by 9 inches. Two rings at the inside lower corners attached the breastpiece to the rings of the ephod with a blue cord. Two golden rings on the top of the breastpiece fastened it to the shoulder pieces of the ephod with two golden chains. Twelve stones, one for each tribe, were set in four rows of three stones: the name of each son of Jacob was engraved on its respective stone in the proper birth order of the sons. Thus the nation was doubly represented before the Lord.

The "Urim and the Thummim" (lit., "lights and perfection") often were used in times of crisis to determine the will of God (Nu 27:21), but just how they functioned and what they looked like are unknown. Perhaps they only symbolized the special revelation open to the high priest rather than being the necessary means of achieving that information. See also Lev 8:8; Nu 27:21; Dt 33:8; et al.

31–35 Under the ephod was a long, sleeveless blue "robe," woven without a seam, which reached a little below the knees. It had slits for the arms and a hole for the head to pass through. Along the hem were blue, purple, and scarlet alternating pomegranates and golden bells. The bells, which jingled as the high priest served in the tabernacle, assured all who listened that he had not died in the Holy Place and that he continued to minister on their behalf.

The high priest's garments, with twelve stones set in the breastplate (one for each tribe). Courtesty Zondervan © 1984.

115

36–39 The most conspicuous and important feature of the "turban" (miter) was the golden plate with the engraving "HOLY TO THE LORD." The plate stretched over the forehead from ear to ear and was attached with a blue band going through two holes at the ends of the plate and then over the top of the head to a hole in the center of the plate.

The "tunic of fine linen" no doubt referred to a long white linen coat worn over the linen drawers or breeches (v.42), which perhaps reached down to the ankles and was close-fitted to the body as were the sleeves.

40–43 The attire for the ordinary priests is described next. Its purpose was to give "dignity and honor" (lit., "glory and beauty") to them in their office. Verse 41 forms a transition to ch. 29, which speaks of the ordination of the priests. On the linen garments see comment on 20:26.

10. Ordination of the priests (29:1–46)

The instructions given to Moses in 28:41 are here elaborated in greater detail and are implemented in Lev 8. The consecration of Aaron and his sons in an act of ordination stressed the seriousness and central mission they had been given in the whole act of worship of our holy God.

1–9 Aaron and his sons were installed as high priest and ministering priests, respectively. This service of consecration uniquely marked them for the service of the tabernacle. The sacrifices for this occasion were to be "without defect" (cf. 12:5). Similarly, the consecrating sacrifice must be "without yeast" (cf. 12:15). Then Aaron and his sons were to be washed. The investiture of the high priest involved nine acts (Lev 8:7–9), but for ordinary priests it involved only three. Washing symbolized the removal of uncleanness resulting from sin (cf. 40:12–13; Lev 8:6–9; notice Heb 10:22).

Aaron and his sons were next dressed in the clothes described in ch. 28 and then anointed. The manner in which the high priest Aaron was anointed was different from that of his sons (cf. v.21; cf. also Lev 21:10). For the composition of the anointing oil, see comment on 30:22–25.

10–12 A bull was brought as a sin offering to atone for Aaron and his sons' past sins. This was accomplished in symbol by laying their hands on the bull's head, in effect transferring their sins to the sin-bearer (cf. Lev 4:1–5:13; 16:11, 15, 21). The bull was next slaughtered in the presence of the Lord as an act of appeasement. Applying blood to the horns and the base of the altar sanctified the offering place as well as the offering.

13–14 After the sacrifice was killed, the choicest parts were burned on the altar, the enveloping fat adding fuel to the fire (cf. Lev 3:4–5, 16; 7:23–25). The "flesh and its hide and its offal," however, were thought of as being permeated with sin and were thus burned outside the camp. Similarly, Christ our Sacrifice offered up his spirit to the heavenly Father, but his flesh went into the tomb, outside the "camp" (cf. Heb 13:11–13).

15–18 As with the bull, Aaron and his sons were to identify with one of the rams by laying on their hands. This ram was completely offered to the Lord. Entire and wholehearted dedication of everything they were or hoped to be to God was called for. This constituted the "pleasing aroma" to the Lord (cf. Lev 1:9).

19–21 The second ram was also to be identified with, but it was to be used to consecrate Aaron and his sons. After slaughtering the ram, they were to "take some of its blood" and consecrate "the lobes of their [right] ears," the organ that hears the Word of God. Next blood was to be applied to "the thumbs of their right hands," organs by which the mediatorial work was to be performed on behalf of the people. Then Aaron and his sons were to apply blood to the "big toes of their right feet," so that the sanctified walk of the priests would be examples to the people. Lastly, some of the blood of the altar was to be mixed with the anointing oil and sprinkled on Aaron and his sons and their clothes. This represented the full consecration of the priests.

22–26 The second ram was called "the ram for the ordination," which is literally "the ram of filling." The choice parts of this ram, along with the unleavened bread, oiled cake, and wafer, were to "fill" the hands of Aaron and his sons and to be used as a "wave offering." The origin of the idiom "to fill the hand of" is unknown, but the idea of "filling" came to mean "ordination." The waving was not from side to side but toward the altar and back, showing that the sacrifice was given to God and then received back by the priest for his use (cf. Lev 7:30; 23:20). Everything that had been waved except the "breast of the ram" was then to be burned on the altar.

27–28 "The breast that was waved and the thigh that was presented" of animals given as fellowship offerings were to be given to the priests.

29–30 The ordination garments of Aaron and his sons were to be passed down for future ordinations. The priest who would follow Aaron as high priest would wear these garments for seven days, perhaps symbolizing the completeness of his consecration.

31–34 The "ram for the ordination" (i.e., the breast and thigh, v.27) was to be cooked in a "sacred place," namely, in the tabernacle courtyard. Then Aaron and his sons were to partake of the various foodstuffs in a type of communion meal. This was a closed communion, and all leftovers were to be burned and not passed on.

35–37 Again obedience is emphasized. The full consecration of the altar required the sacrifice of a bull for seven days running. After seven days of consecration, the altar would be "most holy," as meaning that whatever touched it would likewise be made holy (cf. Mt 23:19).

38–41 Next Moses was instructed as to the nature of the daily offerings. Two yearling lambs a day were to be sacrificed, one in the morning and the other at evening (cf. Nu 28:3–8; cf. also 2Ki 16:15; Eze 46:13–15). The morning and the evening sacrifices were accompanied by a mixture of about two quarts of flour and one quarter of a hin of olive oil and a drink offering of a quart of wine. Once again the Lord reminded Moses that the offering was a pleasing aroma for him.

42–43 The Lord gave Moses a prophetic glimpse into Israel's future by referring to the obligation "for the generations to come." He promised to meet with the priests and Israel as regularly as the sacrifices were made. The Hebrew for "the place will be consecrated" is literally "it will be consecrated," perhaps meaning that "Israel" would be sanctified, since fellowship was based on atonement.

44–46 After the Lord has consecrated the priests and paraphernalia, he "will dwell among the Israelites and be their God." In fact, the divine side of the Exodus was so that God "might dwell among" his people. The real significance of the tabernacle theology is explicitly stated as God's "tabernacling" or "dwelling" among people so that they could recognize that he indeed was God.

11. Altar of incense (30:1–10)

a. Building instructions (30:1–6)

The altar of incense also stood in the Holy Place. Whereas the altar inside the gate to the court was overlaid with bronze and was the place of continual bloodshed, this altar was overlaid with gold and had perpetual incense on it to symbolize continual intercession to God.

1–6 The altar was to be made of "acacia wood." This square structure with horns on each corner was considerably smaller than the altar of burnt offering (cf. 27:1). The incense altar was to be overlaid with gold. The altar had the usual rings for the transporting poles. The altar was to be located directly in front of the curtain that shielded the "ark of the Testimony" from view.

b. Operating instructions (30:7–10)

7–10 The incense that was to be burned every morning and evening symbolized the prayers of the saints and communion with God (cf. Ps 141:2; Lk 1:10; Rev 5:8; 8:3–4). What was not to be used on the altar of incense is explicitly pointed out (v.9). Failure to follow this would result in the altar's desecration. Also, it was necessary that once a year the altar be cleansed with blood from the atoning offering.

12. Census tax (30:11–16)

11–16 The precise reason for taking a census is not given. Perhaps it was to obtain a register of citizens for public duties in the Lord's service. Previously 13:13 stated that the firstborn son belonged to God and had to be redeemed by a sacrifice. Likewise all firstborn belonged to God, and he accepted the tribe of Levi in lieu of all the firstborn (4:22; Nu 3:12). Verse 12 extends the principle. The word for "ransom" (GK 4111) or "atonement" signifies "to deliver or redeem by a substitute." In this case the substitute was money by taking a census. Usually a census was equivalent to mustering troops; that is why it was so dangerous in David's case (2Sa 24). It is clear, however, that those who were numbered under the proper circumstances would be under divine protection.

The "shekel" (GK 9203) was mentioned in 21:32. A "half shekel" would be about one-fifth of an ounce. This tax was to be paid by adults of military age. The fact that the rich were to give the same amount as the poor shows that it was not how much one had that obtained atonement for his life. The proceeds from the census tax were to be used by the Levites in their service for the Lord and were also to serve as a memorial for the Israelites (v.16).

13. Bronze basin, anointing oil, and incense (30:17–38)

17–21 The "bronze basin" was made from the bronze mirrors of the women (38:8) given as a freewill offering. Its exact shape is uncertain, but perhaps the "stand" was separate since it is always mentioned separately (cf. 31:9; 35:16; et al.). It was vital that the priests washed their hands and feet whenever they entered the "Tent of Meeting" and when they approached the altar to make an offering to the Lord by fire. Performing service to God in a state of ritual impurity risks death (cf. Lev 10:1–2).

22–38 On the spices and anointing oils, see comment on 25:6. The anointing of the various furniture pieces and other accoutrements served to consecrate them to the Lord's service. The "sacred anointing oil" was to be unique, in both its makeup and its use. To merchandise it or duplicate it without proper authorization would result in excommunication from the nation. The incense was likewise to be unique and was considered most sacred. Failure to properly consider it would similarly result in excommunication from the nation.

14. Appointment of craftsmen (31:1–11)

1–11 Bezalel means "in the shadow of God's [protection]." He was a descendant of Caleb (1Ch 2:19). His ability to work in the arts and his skills as a craftsman were gifts of the Holy Spirit. Oholiab, Bezalel's assistant, was from the tribe of Dan. His name means "tent of the father" or "the (divine) father is my tent."

These two skilled craftsmen were responsible for all that pertained to the tabernacle and its service, though they themselves possibly only supervised the construction.

15. Sabbath rest (31:12–17)

12–17 Even though the construction of the tabernacle and its furnishings was a sacred work, the workmen were not to overlook the sacred institution of the Sabbath. "You must observe my Sabbaths" is emphatic. To violate the Sabbath even for the sake of working on the tabernacle would result in death. "Desecrates" contrasts sharply with "makes you holy." As God's covenant people, the Israelites were to carefully observe the sign of that covenant. The Sabbath was the sign of "a lasting covenant" (lit., "a perpetual covenant"), as were the rainbow (Ge 9:16), circumcision (Ge 17:7, 13, 19), and the table of the bread of the Presence (Lev 24:8). The Sabbath was thus a gift to Israel signifying their separateness as a people.

16. Conclusion to the instructions (31:18)

18 This verse is transitional to the golden calf scene. The forty days (see 24:18) had come to an end. The "two tablets of the Testimony" contained the Ten Commandments (cf. 32:15–16; 34:28; Dt 4:13; 5:22; 10:4). On the "finger of God," see comment on 8:19.

B. False Worship of the Golden Calf (32:1–34:35)

1. Golden calf (32:1–29)

While chs. 32–34 continue the narrative interrupted after 24:18, their appearance at this point in the text deliberately contrasts the authorized worship of God set forth in the tabernacle instructions with the fabricated human worship of the golden calf. One could hardly conceive of two greater opposites. There is another contrast between what is taking place on the mountain and what is happening on the desert floor: the contrast between the presence of God and the insidious force of sin (cf. Dt 9:8–21; Ne 9:18; Ps 106:19–23). Therefore, chs. 32–34 form a terrible and ignominious interlude between the instructions on Israel's worship and their implementation.

1Without proper visible leadership, people fail. Sometimes even the holiest of men, such as Aaron, can be persuaded to do things con-

118

trary to their testimony. The people's cry, "Come, make us gods who will go before us," revealed their inadequate faith in a time of waiting. The clause "as for this fellow Moses who brought us up out of Egypt" is deliberately cast in coarse language, thus revealing the attitude of the people who had relegated God's works to a mere mortal.

2–4 Aaron instructed the people to "take off" (lit., "tear off") their "gold earrings." No doubt these were part of the booty-gifts brought from Egypt (see 3:21–22; 11:2–3; 12:35–36). Aaron then "cast [them] in the shape of a calf," probably by applying gold leaf over a wooden form, which thus could be burned (cf. 32:20). Or he may have rough cast it in solid gold and then shaped it by hand. The idol was a calf, i.e., a young bull, the symbol of virile power. On completion Aaron—and probably his sons—had the audacity to proclaim to Israel, "These are your gods," a direct violation of the recently given second commandment (cf. 1Ki 12:28).

5–6 Apparently the altar built (of field stones and earth as in 20:24–25) in front of the calf and the "festival" were to act as sops for Aaron's conscience. After making an attempt to honor the Lord with their offerings, the people satisfied their own desires and proceeded to "indulge in revelry," namely, drunken, immoral orgies and sexual play (cf. Ge 26:8; 39:14, 17).

7–10 In response to Israel's behavior, God charged Moses, "Your people whom you have brought up ... have become corrupt." God deliberately changed the possessive pronoun, thereby indicating that he was disowning Israel (contrast "my people" in 3:10 et al.). "Have become corrupt" (GK 8845) renders the same verb found in Ge 6:12 for the apostasy or corruption in Noah's day; it means "to go to ruin or destruction" (cf. Dt 9:6; 10:16; Ps 75:5; Jer 17:23; Acts 7:51). The fact that they were "quick to turn away" shows Israel had apostatized from the revealed truth in word and events that they had witnessed. The "stiff-necked people" would not bow under God's authority (cf. Jer 27:11–12), even though they had readily "bowed down" to the calf and worshiped it.

God was very angry with the people. The God who seemed unmerciful, however, is the same God who had mercifully prepared

Moses for just such an occasion as this. So God said, by way of testing Moses, "Leave me alone." But God would allow himself to be bound, as it were, by prepared persons doing prepared work in God's way.

11–14 In his role as a divinely raised-up mediator, Moses appealed to the Lord. First, he reminded the Lord of his special covenantal relationship with his people, which he manifested in the Exodus. Then he appealed to God's need to keep his name holy and trustworthy. Finally, he referred to the great patriarchal promises. As Moses championed the Lord's cause, "the LORD relented [GK 5714]." God's repentance or "relenting" shows that he can and does change in his actions and emotions to humans when given proper grounds for doing so, and thereby he does not change in his basic integrity or character (cf. Pss 99:6; 106:45; Jer 18:8; Am 7:3, 6; Jnh 3:10; Jas 5:16). In Scripture, three grounds are given for the Lord's "repenting": intercession (cf. Am 7:1–6); repentance of the people (Jer 18:3–11; Jnh 3:9–10); and compassion (Dt 32:36; Jdg 2:18).

15–16 This is the only passage that informs us that the "two tablets of the Testimony" were inscribed "on both sides." That "the tablets were the work of God" emphasizes their divine origin. In 31:18 they are said to be "inscribed by the finger of God," though 34:28 says that "Moses ... wrote on the tablets the words of the covenant—the Ten Commandments" (see comment on 34:1–3).

17–18 According to 24:13, Joshua had ascended the mountain with Moses, perhaps halfway up. Joshua mistook the "noise of the people shouting" for war cries. Moses, however, discerned otherwise. The phrase "sound of" is literally "the sound of answering." There is a play on the word "answer" used in two senses: it was not the "shout" of the victor with its corresponding racket of the vanquished, but it was the antiphonal song of singers.

19–20 The wickedness of the people he had just pled to the Lord to preserve angered Moses when "he saw the calf and the dancing." Not only were the stone tablets broken, symbolizing the breaking of God's covenant by the people, but Moses quickly broke up the calf and the festivities, bringing an end to the people's covenant with carnality. Moses took the calf and "burned it," "ground it to powder," and "scattered it on the water and made the Israelites drink it," a fitting conclusion for a shameful act (cf. 2Ki 23:15).

22–24 Aaron had to do some quick thinking to extricate himself from guilt as an accomplice in the people's reveling. He tried four excuses: (1) "you know how prone these people are to evil"; (2) "they said to me"; and (3) "we don't know what has happened to [Moses]." The flimsiest excuse came last: (4) "out came this calf!" Was Aaron trying to say that a miracle had occurred?

25–26 The people had cast off all restraint (cf. Pr 29:18). The idea of "to cast off all restraints" is of loosening or uncovering. Apparently there was a type of religious prostitution connected with the people's worship of the golden calf. Moses realized that decisive action was required. So he challenged the people (cf. Jos 24:14–15; 1Ki 18:21; Mt 6:24). "All" is undoubtedly a generalization, since Dt 33:9 implies that some Levites were slain in the action that followed (v.28).

27–29 The Levites who chose to follow God were commanded to arm themselves and "go back and forth . . . killing." This was not the command of a prophet but of a holy God. No small number of people had to pay the consequences for their stiff-neckedness (cf. Ac 2:41). Following God now sometimes requires denying one's family (cf. Lk 12:51–53;

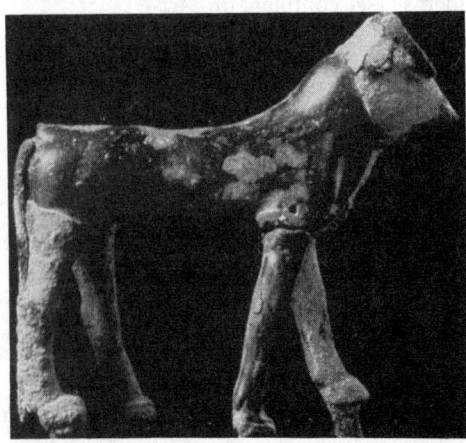

This bronze bull calf, originally covered with silver, was found in a Canaanite sanctuary at Ashkelon, dating to 1550 B.C. The Israelites experimented with calf worship here in Exodus 32.

14:26). A necessary part of consecration is being obedient to the Lord's command, which always results in his blessings. The Levites wholeheartedly followed God (Jos 14:8) and counted other ties of kinship as nothing in comparison (Dt 33:9).

2. Mediation of Moses (32:30–35)

30 Even though the people had repented, atonement for sin was still needed. Moses would attempt to ransom or deliver the people from the certain judgment of their sin by offering a substitute—himself.

31–32 Moses ascended the mountain once again and proceeded to intercede in prayer on Israel's behalf a second time. The sincerity of Moses' devotion to his people is seen in his request: "Blot me out" (cf. Ro 9:1–3). The "book" or "scroll" is called the "book of the living" in Ps 69:28 and is referred to in Isa 4:3: "recorded among the living" (cf. Eze 13:9; Da 12:1; Mal 3:16; cf. Php 4:3; Rev 3:5; 20:12, 15; 21:27).

33–34 Moses' offer was refused by the Lord, who replied, "Whoever has sinned . . . I will blot out of my book" (cf. Pss 9:5; 51:1). Thus the OT principle is reaffirmed: the person who sins is accountable for his or her own sin (cf. Dt 24:16; Eze 18:4, 13, 17). Whereas in the past the Lord had led (12:42, 51; 13:17; 15:13; 20:2) and Moses was only his servant, from then on Moses and an angel were to lead. "The time comes for me to punish" is literally "in the day of my visitation." Perhaps this is the beginning of the "Day of the LORD" warnings.

35 The order of events is probably not in strict chronological sequence; hence the plague may well be the slaughter of the three thousand mentioned in v.28. The plague came on the people because they caused the calf to be made or asked for it. Frequently in Scripture events may be directly attributed to people when they only occasioned them since the one could implicate the many as a member of a community, just as today one traitor can compromise a whole army or nation.

3. Threatened separation and Moses' prayer (33:1–23)

1–3 The Lord issued the command to move on, promising to "send an angel" before them (cf. 23:20, 23; 32:34). The angel promised here is altogether different from "the angel of his presence" in Isa 63:9, since God declared that his "Name is in him" (23:21). Thus that angel was a christophany, an appearance of Christ in the OT. Although the Lord promised to send his personal representative, he himself would "not go with [them]." This withdrawal of the divine presence assured in 23:20–23 was because of the presence of sin.

4–6 The people would rather risk the danger of divine chastisement than be deprived of the divine presence; hence "they began to mourn" and desisted from putting on any further ornaments. Reminded once more of their stubbornness, the people were asked to "take off [their] ornaments," i.e., the ones they were already wearing, as a test of their repentance. Akin to putting on sackcloth and ashes, the people "stripped off their ornaments" as a sign of mourning for their sin (cf. Ge 35:4; Eze 26:16).

7–11 The "tent ... outside the camp" was different from the tabernacle or "Tent of Meeting" with its ark and other furniture where the Lord permanently dwelt. This "tent of the meeting" was outside the camp, a temporary structure used until the more permanent shelter was constructed (cf. 27:21 et al.). The verbs in v.7 show that Moses customarily erected this tent. Moses visited this tent whenever he desired a meeting with the Lord. When Moses entered it, "the pillar of cloud would come down," an indication that the Lord was communicating with him "as a man speaks with his friend" (cf. Nu 12:8; Dt 34:10). A similar descent later caps the completion of the tabernacle (40:33–34; see 13:21). The presence of the pillar of the cloud at the tent entrance evoked a spirit of worship from the people.

12–14 As the time approached for Moses to take up the lead of the Israelites, he became concerned as to the identity of the companion God had promised him (32:34; 33:2). He believed that a mere angel was no substitute for the presence of God. "I know you by name" is tantamount to saying, "I have singled you out" or "I have chosen/selected you." Moses asked the Lord for a demonstration of his love so that he might know and serve him better. The Lord responded by promising, "My Presence [lit., 'my face'; GK 7156] will go with you." With this new word, the Lord reinstated the angel of his presence in whom he invested his "Name" (23:20–21) as the leader of Israel's way to Canaan.

15–18 Moses beseeched God not to send the people out without his "Presence" to lead them. Moses knew that God's presence was essential to Israel's testimony, in order to keep them distinct from the rest of the world. That was the response the Lord was waiting for; but Moses sought one further thing: God's "glory."

19–20 In response to Moses' request to see God's "glory," God said that he would "cause all [his] goodness to pass" before Moses. By his "goodness" (GK 3206) is meant his whole character and nature. A further aspect of God's glory was the proclamation of his name. The name of God includes his nature, character, person (Ps 20:1; Lk 24:47; Jn 1:12), doctrine (Ps 22:22; Jn 17:6, 26), and standards of living (Mic 4:5). Here his name includes his "mercy" and his "compassion." The one restriction was that Moses would not be permitted to see the Lord's face. In fact, "no one may see me and live" (see Jn 1:18; 6:46; 1Ti 1:17; 1Jn 4:12).

21–23 To see God's glory Moses was to stand on a "rock" (cf. Mt 7:24–27). When the glory passed by, Moses would be hid in the "cleft in the rock" and covered by the Lord's hand. Then the hand of God would be removed so that Moses might see God's back. But since God is Spirit and has no form, and since no one can see him and live (v.20), the word translated "back" could just as well and more accurately be rendered "the after-effects" of his radiant glory, which had just passed by.

4. Renewal of the covenant (34:1–35)

1–3 Since Moses had broken the former tablets (32:19), which "were the work of God" (32:16), it was appropriate that he "chisel out two stone tablets like the first ones." No contradiction exists between God's statement that he "will write on them the words that were on the first tablets" and vv.27–28, where Moses did the actual writing. Apparently these are alternate ways of saying the same thing. The law is the direct expression of the mind and will of God.

4–7 Moses obediently followed the Lord's directions and prepared two new stone tablets. Early the next morning he brought them to the Lord on top of Mount Sinai. The Lord once more appeared before Moses and proclaimed his name: "the LORD" (see 33:19; cf. 20:2). Then the Lord "passed in front of Moses." The Lord's self-disclosure is prefaced by the repetition of his name, perhaps to emphasize his unchangeableness.

Verses 6b–7 are essentially repeated in Nu 14:18; 2Ch 30:9; Ne 9:17; Jnh 4:2; et al. On "compassionate" (GK 8157), see comment on 33:19. The "gracious [GK 2843] God" bestows his unmerited favor on those who have no claim whatsoever on it. His graciousness is explicated by "slow to anger, abounding in love and faithfulness, maintaining love to thousands, and forgiving wickedness, rebellion and sin." But his grace is balanced, for "he does not leave the guilty unpunished." His chastisement will be felt to the "third and fourth generation." The full formula (see 20:5) includes the important qualifier "of those who hate me."

8–9 The revelation of God's person and character humbled Moses and caused him to once more plead for his grace to be given to his people, even though they were stiff-necked and wicked.

10–14 The Lord's statement "I am making a covenant with you" is not to be understood as the instituting of a second covenant in vv.10–27 but is best seen as a renewing of the same covenant after the events of ch. 33. The word "wonders" is used of the plagues sent on Egypt (3:20). They would be so outstanding that the people would be awestruck. For Israel to benefit from God's miraculous display, however, they had to be obedient to his commands.

The Lord further warned the Israelites not to become involved in unholy alliances (cf. 2Co 6:14). More than that, they were to take the initiative and eliminate the pagan "altars, . . . sacred stones and . . . Asherah poles." The Asherim were probably sacred trees or wooden poles placed alongside Baal's altar (Jdg 6:25; 1Ki 15:13; 2Ki 21:7). With the pagan religious objects removed, there would be less temptation to "worship any other god." The word "jealous" is mentioned twice for emphasis (see comment on 20:5). This particular Hebrew word is used only of God

and illustrates the parallel between idolatry and adultery (cf. Dt 22:22).

15–16 Once more the warning against unholy alliances is sounded. This time some of the "snares" (cf. v.12) are given: (1) "they will invite you and you will eat their sacrifices," and (2) "you [will] choose . . . their daughters as wives." Both actions lead to idolatry.

17 The prohibition against making "cast idols" is most relevant (cf. ch. 32; see also 20:4–6).

18–26 For these verses see comments on 23:14–19. The way of obedience balances prohibitions with admonitions: "Celebrate the Feast of Unleavened Bread" (see comments on 12:14–20). For "the first offspring . . . belongs to me" see comments on 13:11–16. See comments on 20:8–11 for laboring six days and resting one. In 23:16 the "Feast of Weeks" is called the "Feast of Harvest."

The Lord added a special promise for the pilgrim to the three annual feasts that required his presence. The Lord would protect the pilgrim's land from his ungodly neighbor who might move the boundary markers or steal from the land while the pilgrim was absent. The statement "when you go up three times each year" looks forward to the time when the people were settled in the land; it need not imply that this verse was written later (cf. Dt 16:16). On v.25 see comment on 23:18. For the law and theology of "firstfruits," see comment on 23:19 (cf. 4:22; 11:5; 12:29).

27–28 For the Lord's commanding Moses to "write down these words," see comment on v.1. For "forty days and forty nights," see comment on 24:18. That Moses was able to go for this length of time without food or water was a miracle requiring the Lord's supernatural care (cf. Dt 9:9, 18; Mt 4:2).

29–32 Spending an extended period of time in the Lord's presence had a telling effect on Moses. The verb "to radiate" is related to the noun for "horn." The Vulgate confused these two, which thus led to the representation in European medieval art of Moses wearing two horns! The manifestation of the divine countenance struck fear in the Israelites. A word from Moses, however, encouraged Aaron, the leaders, and all the Israelites to approach him; and he thus delivered the word of the Lord to them.

33–35 Moses' radiance was only visible to the people when he was acting as the oracle of God. At other times he kept his face veiled. This was not a priest's "mask," for Moses left the veil off when speaking to the people as God's messenger or when he was alone in the presence of God (cf. 2Co 3:7–18).

C. Building the Tabernacle (35:1–40:38)

1. Summons to build (35:1–19)

1–3 Since he had gathered the Israelites together, Moses relayed to them the commands of the Lord. The Sabbath, the sign of the covenant, was mentioned first, an indication of its importance. On "a Sabbath of rest," see comments on 20:8–11 and 31:12–17. Although the prohibition against lighting a fire on the Sabbath is not mentioned elsewhere, it is implied in part in 16:23.

4 Almost every item in 25:1–30:10 is repeated in 35:4–40:38 in identical or similar words, except here the verbs are mainly in the past tense. In the ancient Near East it was customary to repeat the instructions by a literal repetition of the terms except for change in verb forms.

"This is what the LORD has commanded" repeats v.1 to revert back to the primary theme after the prefatory words about observing the Sabbath (cf. Lev 23:2, 4).

5–9 See comments on 25:3–7. The differences are negligible except for the introductory words in 25:3, which would have been out of place here.

10–19 See comments on 25:1–28:43; 30:1–10, 17–38; cf. 31:7–11.

2. Voluntary gifts (35:20–29)

20–29 After Moses' instructions, the people left to set about doing their tasks. Those whose hearts were moved brought offerings for the tabernacle and its related service. The willingness of the people is mentioned repeatedly. "Men and women alike" are specifically mentioned to avoid the misapprehension that "everyone" excluded women even though vv. 25–26 mention them in another connection. On the various gifts of the people, see 25:1–7.

3. Bezalel and his artisans (35:30–36:7)

For further comments on these verses, see also comments on 31:2–6.

30–35 God's selection and equipping of Bezalel was so that he could "engage in all kinds of artistic craftsmanship" (lit., "engage in every work of thought"). This would include implementing the plan or thought previously given for the project (cf. 31:4–5). Verse 34 adds that Bezalel and Oholiab were given "the ability to teach others," a capability of training and guiding assistants who would work with these two artificers. Verse 35 is almost entirely new.

36:1–7 The chapter division here is unfortunate, for no break is signified by the verb, as though the account now turns to the execution of the work by these craftsmen. The willingness of the people exceeded the requirements of the craftsmen; so the order was given to the people to make no further offerings for the sanctuary. This is a noteworthy illustration of generosity for the Lord's work.

4. Progress of the work and Moses' blessing (36:8–39:43)

8–19 The start of the actual work on the tabernacle begins here. The order is different from the order of the instructions. The work of the curtains repeats 26:1–13.

20–34 On the frames and crossbars, see comments on 26:15–30.

35–38 For the inner curtain, see comments on 26:31–35.

37:1–9 On the ark, see comments on 25:10–22. Bezalel is specifically mentioned with the work of the holiest of tabernacle objects.

10–16 On the table of the bread of the Presence, see comments on 25:23–30.

17–24 On the lampstand, see comments on 25:31–40.

25–29 On the altar of incense, see comments on 30:1–6. On the "sacred anointing oil," see comments on 25:6.

38:1–7 On the altar of burnt offering, see comments on 27:1–8.

8 On the bronze basin, see comments on 30:17–21.

9–20 On the tabernacle courtyard, see comments on 27:9–19.

21–39:1 These verses are an inventory of the tabernacle materials. Verses 25–26 give an insight into the population of Israel at this time. There are 3,000 shekels to a talent; therefore 3,000 times 100 equals 300,000 plus 1,775 equals 301,775. Since each man (from twenty years and older) was valued at a half shekel, the total number of men able to bear arms was over 600,000 (301,775 times 2 equals 603,550), a number very similar to the later count of Nu 1:46 (603,550) or Nu 26:51 (601,730). Such a tally for the army would more than justify estimates of 2 million for the total population.

"As the LORD commanded Moses" is the emphasis of chs. 39–40. The clause occurs nine times in ch. 39 and seven times in ch. 40.

2–31 See comments on 28:6–43. "The sacred diadem" is a new designation here, not found in 28:36–37.

32–41 The statement "so all the work . . . was completed" is reminiscent of Ge 2:1–2, the concluding words of the Creation account. This section emphasizes that the Israelites completed their work "just as the LORD commanded." The workmen, on behalf of all the people of Isarael, "brought the tabernacle to Moses." Once again the list of articles is repeated (cf. 35:11–19; a shortened form occurs in 31:7–11). "With its row of lamps" is a new

A view of the inner part of the tabernacle, showing the ark, the lampstand, the basin, and the table. Courtesy Zondervan © 1984.

term for the lamps set in order on the lampstand.

42–43 "Moses . . . saw that they had done it just as the LORD had commanded" is again parallel to the expression in Ge 1:31. The conclusion was, "So Moses blessed them" (cf. Ge 1:22, 28; 2:3).

5. Erection of the tabernacle (40:1–33)

1–5 The tabernacle was erected on the "first day of the first month." Verse 17 adds that this was the beginning of the "second year" of the wilderness wanderings. Since the nation of Israel entered the Sinai Desert in the third month after the Exodus (19:1) and Moses was on Mount Sinai for two forty-day periods (24:18; 34:28) plus the events covered in 19:1–24:11 and chs. 32–33, the building of the tabernacle took less than six months to build.

Once again, as in 25:10–22, the ark, the most prominent object in the tabernacle, is first to be mentioned. This was God's throne in the midst of Israel. The "curtain" and how it shielded the ark is further described in v.21 (cf. also 26:31–35; 36:35–38).

On the "table," see comments on 25:23–30; 37:10–16; on the "lampstand," see comments on 25:31–40; 37:17–24; on the "gold altar of incense," see comments on 30:1–10, 34–38; 37:25–29.

6–8 On the "altar of burnt offering," see comments on 27:1–8; 38:1–7; on the "basin," see comments on 30:17–21; 38:8; on the "courtyard," see comments on 27:9–19; 38:9–20.

9–11 On the "anointing oil," see comments on 25:6; 30:22–33. These instructions were carried out in Lev 8:10–12. "Consecrate it" is literally "sanctify it" in the sense of setting it apart for the service of the Lord.

12–16 The anointing and consecrating of the priesthood included Aaron and his sons. The institution of the priesthood was "for all generations to come" (cf. 12:24; 27:21). Even though the hereditary priestly office of the Aaronic line ended, Christ would carry it out perpetually.

17–33 Verse 17 parallels v.2 in almost every detail. Verses 18–33 contain seven subsections, each concluding with the formula "as the LORD commanded him/Moses."

1. "Moses set up the tabernacle."

2. "He took the Testimony and placed it in the ark" (see 25:14, 16, 21).

3. "Moses placed the table" (26:35; 40:4).

4. "He placed the lampstand" (26:35; 40:4).

5. "Moses placed the gold altar" (30:6; 40:5).

6. "He put up the curtain" and "he set the altar of burnt offering."

7. "He placed the basin" (30:18; 40:7).

6. Dedication of the tabernacle (40:34–38)

34–38 The tabernacle had been constructed and set in order as the Lord had commanded Moses; yet something was lacking. Form must be invested with divine life; so "the glory of the LORD filled the tabernacle." On the Lord's glory, see comments on 16:7, 10; 24:16–17; 33:18, 22. With the arrival of the glory of the Lord, the nation of Israel was ready to move on. The promise of the divine messenger to lead the people was fulfilled (23:20, 23; 32:34; 33:2). The Lord now lived in the midst of his people as their King, and he continued to lead them throughout the next forty years in the desert. The signal for them to continue their journey was "whenever the cloud lifted" (cf. 13:21; see also 17:1; 25:22).

The Old Testament in the New

OT Text	NT Text	Subject
Ex 1:8	Ac 7:18	King who did not know Joseph
Ex 2:14	Ac 7:27–28, 35	Moses in Egypt
Ex 3:5	Ac 7:33	Moses at the burning bush
Ex 3:6	Mt 22:32; Mk 12:26; Lk 20:37; Ac 7:32	The living God
Ex 3:7–8, 10	Ac 7:34	God promises to deliver Israel
Ex 9:16	Ro 9:17	Purpose of Moses
Ex 12:46	Jn 19:36	No broken bones
Ex 13:2, 12	Lk 2:23	Dedication of the firstborn
Ex 16:4	Jn 6:31	Bread from heaven
Ex 16:18	2Co 8:15	God provides enough
Ex 19:12–13	Heb 12:20	Not touching the mountain
Ex 20:11	Ac 4:24; 14:15	God the creator
Ex 20:12	Mt 15:4; Mk 7:10; Eph 6:2–3	Fifth commandment
Ex 20:13	Mt 5:21; Ro 13:9; Jas 2:11	Sixth commandment
Ex 20:14	Mt 5:27; Ro 13:9; Jas 2:11	Seventh commandment
Ex 20:15	Ro 13:9	Eighth commandment
Ex 20:17	Ro 7:7; 13:9	Tenth commandment
Ex 21:17	Mt 15:4; Mk 7:10	Cursing parents
Ex 21:24	Mt 5:38	Eye for Eye
Ex 22:28	Ac 23:5	Cursing rulers
Ex 24:8	Heb 9:20	The blood of the covenant
Ex 25:40	Heb 8:5	Pattern of the tabernacle
Ex 32:1, 23	Ac 7:40	Asking for idols
Ex 32:6	1Co 10:7	Sin of idolatry
Ex 33:19	Ro 9:15	Mercy of God
Ex 34:33, 35	2 Co 3:13	Veil of Moses

Leviticus

INTRODUCTION

1. Historical Background and Contents

Leviticus, the middle book of the Pentateuch, is largely limited to material revealed at Sinai after the Exodus and before Israel's wandering in the desert. Genesis gives the patriarchal background of the people of Israel. They were molded into a nation, however, at the time of the Exodus by Moses, the great lawgiver. The Israelites left Egypt in the spring on the fourteenth of Nisan, the month that begins the spring season. This was a datum point, the "first month of your year" (Ex 12:2). On the fifteenth of the second month, they came to the Desert of Sin (Ex 16:1). In the third month (Ex 19:1), they arrived at Sinai and encamped before the mountain. There they stayed for about one year. The second Passover was celebrated at Sinai (Nu 9:5).

The people were "numbered" on the "first day of the second month of the second year" after leaving Egypt (Nu 1:1). On the twentieth day of the second month of the second year, the Israelites marched on from Sinai toward Kadesh Barnea, the southern gateway to the Promised Land (Nu 10:11).

The Israelites thus encamped before Mount Sinai just short of a year. During that time Moses spent eighty days on the mountain with God. Then the people of Israel, at Moses' instruction, built the tabernacle. During this year Moses also organized the nation, built up the army, established courts and laws, and ordered formal worship. It was a busy year. Although most of the laws that Moses drew up at that time are found in Exodus and Numbers, Leviticus is the law book *par excellence*. It mainly emphasizes Israel's worship of God and the instructions for the priests. Undoubtedly for this reason the LXX called the book *Levitikon* ("pertaining to the Levites").

The book of Leviticus, presuming the construction of the tabernacle as detailed in Ex 25–31; 35–40, begins with a description of the offerings for the great bronze altar (chs. 1–7) and continues with the consecration of the first priests and the start of the tabernacle worship (chs. 8–10). The chapters that follow largely set forth those laws for the conduct of the people that were administered by the priests. It is difficult to generalize, however, because the priests were concerned with instruction for and regulation of many aspects of Israel's life, not just the sacerdotal—for instance, chs. 18 and 20 cover laws of incest. The laws of cleanliness come in ch. 11–15, followed by the law of the great national sin offering on the Day of Atonement in ch. 16. The next section (chs. 17–26) is sometimes called the Holiness Code, because it emphasizes God's moral standards for his people. Included is a description of the other annual feasts of Israel (ch. 23) and further miscellaneous regulations concerning the sabbatical year and laws of land inheritance (ch. 25). Chapter 26 includes extensive warnings of punishment if Israel departs from the Lord, and the book ends (ch. 27) with regulations concerning property given to the Lord's work.

2. Date and Authorship

The view taken of the date and authorship of Leviticus depends largely on one's view of the Pentateuch as a whole. The tradition of Israel unanimously declares that the ritual laws of Leviticus—and the other Pentateuchal material as well—were given by God through Moses. See the discussion of these issues in the introduction to Exodus.

3. Literary Form and Classification

The study of Israel's laws is important because the will of God is found in them. They must be studied with care, however, because obviously not all of them apply to the Christian today (cf. Heb 7:12). Some of the laws of Israel (e.g., the Ten Commandments) carry over into the present age and are repeated in the NT (Ro 13:9); some are abrogated (Ac 10:14–15).

The nation of Israel was unique in that it was a theocracy; God was its Head. He had chosen Israel and channeled his grace particularly through that nation. To Israel he gave his revelation, including the order of true worship. In Israel things that we call sacred and profane were mingled together. Before the monarchy virtually all administration of the nation was in the hands of the priests. There were physical penalties—even capital punishment—for religious offenses.

Israel's laws have customarily been classified as moral, civil, and ceremonial—the commandments (e.g., you shall not murder), judgments (e.g., a person guilty of manslaughter may flee to a city of refuge), and ordinances (e.g, prescribing a sin offering for a repentant sinner). Such a classification implies that the ceremonial legislation is done away in Christ, the civil legislation changes with the civil government, and the moral legislation continues ever in binding force.

A better approach, however, is to see the law as defining (1) our relationship to God and (2) our relationship to our fellow beings. These laws can be further divided into eternal principles and temporary manifestations. Thus, for example, the first four of the Ten Commandments give the eternal principles of divine worship. Other laws also stress God's holiness, hatred of sin, and love issuing in redemption. These eternal principles were manifested in the temporary laws of worship that occupy much of Leviticus. They typify the holiness of God, the uncleanness of humans, the necessity of blood redemption, and the restoration of fellowship with God. They also point forward to Jesus Christ, the Lamb of God, who came to take away the sins of the world (Jn 1:29). Today these same eternal principles find temporary manifestations in baptism, the Lord's Supper, and other aspects of Christian worship.

Similarly, the last six of the Ten Commandments express God's will for our relations with our fellow beings, being manifested in civil law. The civil laws of modern cultures reflect more or less the eternal principles that God has implanted in the consciences of humans and set forth in his Word.

A third recent classification of Israel's laws is as case laws and categorical laws (casuistic and apodictic legislation). The case laws apply to a particular situation and are of the form, "If someone does such and such, then you shall punish that person in such and such a way." The categorical or apodictic laws are "You shall not ..." or "Whoever does such and such shall surely suffer." This difference in form between case law and categorical law does not seem to be too significant in Leviticus. For example, ch. 18 is largely categorical law; ch. 20 repeats many of these items in case law formulation, but the laws in ch. 20 include a penalty. Practically all the laws of the surrounding cultures were of the case-law type.

The Pentateuchal legislation does not cover all possible situations, but it covers enough; and the judges on whom God placed his Spirit were competent enough to handle all other cases on these principles. God had providentially given Moses training in the royal academies of Egypt. And God used Moses to give the Israelites such precedents and case laws as were necessary and helpful in establishing the infant nation. Moses served as chief justice of Israel for forty years, and many cases came before him for judgment. He was knowledgeable on legal principles, and the important cases were collected at his direction and under the Spirit's inspiration during these forty years and were given for the guidance of the nation ever after.

There is no evidence that Israel's ritual law was derived from the rituals of the nations in which they lived. Eighteen of the chapters in Leviticus begin with the words "The LORD said to Moses." Israel's worship, like Israel's theology, was of divine origin; and the prescriptions for ritual were God-given. The Bible makes it plain that the sacrificial system of the OT began as soon as our first parents had sinned. The specialized institutions of national worship, however, were given by God through Moses at Sinai.

4. Theology

a. Sin

Underlying Leviticus is the biblical doctrine of sin. This seems clear both from specific words used (e.g., "sin" in 18:25; 19:22; "sins" in 16:16, 21–22; the verb "to sin" in 4:2–3; "guilt" in 10:17; 22:16) and from the punishments prescribed for offenses committed. Human beings have a problem with sin; they violate God's law. Such sin had to be atoned for—i.e., to have the penalty paid and the guilt removed—in order for fellowship between God and his people to be renewed. God revealed the sacrificial system as the means of atonement.

b. Sacrifice

The most important matter discussed in the book of Leviticus, therefore, is the sacrificial system of ancient Israel. It begins with a description of five major sacrifices, together with their regulations (chs. 1–7). Chapter 16 discusses the rituals of the great Day of Atonement. While no passage of Leviticus discusses the meaning of sacrifice in a formal manner, many things are said that give us considerable guidance. In ch. 16 the principle is clearly stated that sin is atoned for by sacrifice and the guilt is taken far away (cf. Ps 103:12). The historic view of the OT sacrificial system is that the death of the sacrificial victim is the God-given type of the death of Christ and that the blood shed by the lamb or goat points forward to the blood shed by Christ on Calvary to atone for our sins (see especially Heb 8–10; also Ro 3:25–26).

c. Cleanness

Large sections of this book deal with the topic of cleanness and its relationship to holiness. There are two main things to consider: the concept of *ethical* holiness as separation from sin and the concept of *ritual* holiness as separation from various defilements. God's own holiness involves both ethical and ritual holiness.

Regarding ethical holiness, the Holiness Code (chs. 17–26) outlines numerous ethical commands that were applicable in many areas of Israelite life. These are all subsumed under one general principle, repeated in several places of this book: "Be holy because I, the LORD your God, am holy" (19:2; cf. 11:44–45; 20:7–8; 21:8).

Regarding ritual holiness, in order to approach the holy God, the priest, the articles of worship, and the worshipers all had to be cleansed. Only in that way could God preserve his holy name in the midst of an elect but sinful nation. The animals used for sacrifice had to be perfect, in order to meet the requirements of a perfect God. The Lord also revealed to Moses numerous ritual cleanness laws regarding diet, health, and habits. Why? God had promised that he would defend his people from the diseases of Egypt (Ex 15:26; Dt 7:15); in other words, the health of his

people was a major concern. Sickness and death are ultimately the result of sin. Rules of diet, washing, and quarantine were therefore necessary to promote Israel's health; these rules were also naturally given the religious sanctions requiring sacrifices and other rituals for their enforcement.

EXPOSITION

I. Description of the Five Major Offerings (1:1–6:7)

A. Burnt Offering (1:1–17)

1 These directions for sacrifice were not given to Moses while he was on Mount Sinai but while he was at work arranging for Israel's worship. The "Tent of Meeting" is the usual name of the movable tabernacle constructed by Moses at Sinai (Ex 40:2). Most likely, however, the reference here is to a temporary tent of worship set up during the time at Sinai (cf. Ex 33:7–10; 38:8). God would hardly leave Israel for a year without a place of worship.

2 The "herd" would be cattle; the "flock" would include both sheep and goats. Although the Israelites were a nomadic people, their mainstay was their cows, sheep, and goats. It is probable that during the extended wandering in the desert the cows, which needed more pasture, were reduced in number; and the people kept the hardier sheep and goats. The ruminant animals digest cellulose. Goats, especially, can live on dried grass, stalks, and bushes. The directions for sacrifice included all the animals that might be offered both in the desert and later in the settled country.

3–17 In brief, the "burnt offering" (GK 6592) was to be made of a clean animal; and all of it was to be burnt on the altar, except the feathers and crop of a bird and the hide of an animal. The hide was for the priest (7:8). The hand of the offerer was to be placed on the animal's head in symbolic acknowledgment of the substitution of the animal for the worshiper (v.4); this is specified also in the fellowship offering (3:2, 8, 13) and the sin offering (4:4, 15, 24, 29, 33). The ritual seems to be self-explanatory but is interpreted clearly in connection with the Day of Atonement (16:21). When hands are laid on the animal and sins are confessed, the sins are in symbol transferred to the animal. The scapegoat carried the sins off into the desert, signifying their total removal. In the cases where the animal was slaughtered, laying on of hands signified the substitution of the sacrifice in judgment on sin.

The blood was to be sprinkled on the altar to emphasize substitution by death (cf. 17:14). Various animals were used in the ritual depending on the choice and ability of the worshiper. The rich would bring a young bull, the poor a bird, the average person a sheep or a goat.

The burnt offering, sometimes called a "holocaust" (total) offering, was completely consumed on the altar. It was not the most common sacrifice. When thousands of sacrifices were offered, they were usually fellowship offerings, which were partly eaten.

The special meaning of the burnt offering is nowhere explicitly given. It included atonement by the giving of life for life, as did the other sacrifices. It seems probable that the additional meaning of the burnt offering was worship, symbolized by the ascending smoke. It is also legitimate to see the idea of surrender.

A burnt offering was given for all Israel every morning and again in the evening. On the Sabbath the burnt offerings were double (Nu 28:9), and there were extra offerings on the various feast days. The directions of this chapter refer especially to voluntary burnt offerings that any Israelite might be led to offer in special worship to God.

B. Grain Offering (2:1–16)

1–16 The "grain offering" (GK 4966) is sometimes called a meal offering or cereal offering, for it consisted of flour or baked goods. Four kinds of grain offerings are specified: uncooked flour, bread baked in an oven, bread prepared on a griddle, and bread cooked in a pan.

The meaning of the grain offering is not explicitly given. It has a practical value in that a "memorial portion" of the offering was burnt on the altar and the rest was given to the priests for their food (cf. 1Co 9:13). Only males who were priests could eat it in the Holy Place (6:16–18). The rest of the priest's family would eat ordinary yeast bread. Apart from the practical value that this offering gave the priests bread to eat with their meat,

the symbolism of the grain offering possibly emphasizes thanksgiving. A grain offering was specified to accompany other various types of offerings on the altar (23:13–20; Ex 29:40; Nu 28–29; et al.). The drink offering, which was to accompany various sacrifices, is not mentioned in this section. It was a libation offering, poured on the altar—not drunk (cf. Nu 28:7).

The size of the grain offering is not given here. Elsewhere various amounts are specified—the smallest is one-tenth measure of flour (about two quarts if a "measure" is an ephah) mixed with one-fourth hin of oil (about a pint and a half; cf. Nu 28:11–14).

The grain offering was to be accompanied with oil, incense, and salt. The familiar olive oil was often used as a shortening, as an ointment, and as an ingredient in perfume. Only a portion of the flour was to be burnt, but all the incense was consumed on the altar. The proscription of yeast with the sacrifices that are burnt on the altar is frequent. The reason for forbidding yeast with the Passover meal was that when Israel left Egypt, there was no time to use yeast to make the bread rise. This incident may have determined the symbolic meaning in other sacrifices. The law against honey appears only here (perhaps because under some circumstances this will also ferment). Yeast and honey were indeed edible and were suitable gifts as an offering of firstfruits for the priests' food, but they were not to be burned on the altar.

C. Fellowship Offering (3:1–17)

1–17 In the phrase "fellowship offering," the word translated "fellowship" (GK 8968) includes the ideas of health, wholeness, welfare, and peace. It is reflected in the common Jewish greeting "Shalom!" This offering apparently symbolizes peace with God because the worshiper joins in the sacred meal. The fellowship offering was brought to the priest, the worshiper laid his hand on the head of the animal in symbolic identification and transfer of guilt, then the priest dressed it, handling the blood in the same way as was done for the burnt offering. In this case, however, only the fat and kidneys were burned on the altar. Elsewhere it is specified that the priest is to be given the right breast and the right thigh as his portion (see 7:34). The balance was for the worshiper and his family to eat.

Old Testament Sacrifices

NAME	OT REFERENCES	ELEMENTS	PURPOSE
BURNT OFFERING	Lev 1; 6:8-13; 8:18-21; 16:24	Bull, ram or male bird (dove or young pigeon for poor); wholly consumed; no defect	Voluntary act of worship; atonement for unintentional sin in general; expression of devotion, commitment and complete surrender to God
GRAIN OFFERING	Lev 2; 6:14-23	Grain, fine flour, olive oil, incense, baked bread (cakes or wafers), salt; no yeast or honey; accompanied burnt offering and fellowship offering (along with drink offering)	Voluntary act of worship; recognition of God's goodness and provisions; devotion to God
FELLOWSHIP OFFERING	Lev 3; 7:11-34	Any animal without defect from herd or flock; variety of breads	Voluntary act of worship; thanksgiving and fellowship (it included a communal meal)
SIN OFFERING	Lev 4:1-5:13; 6:24-30; 8:14-17; 16:3-22	1. Young bull: for high priest and congregation 2. Male goat: for leader 3. Female goat or lamb: for common person 4. Dove or pigeon: for the poor 5. Tenth of an ephah of fine flour: for the very poor	Mandatory atonement for specific unintentional sin; confession of sin; forgiveness of sin; cleansing from defilement
GUILT OFFERING	Lev 5:14-6:7; 7:1-6	Ram or lamb	Mandatory atonement for unintentional sin requiring restitution; cleansing from defilement; make restitution; pay 20% fine

When more than one kind of offering was presented (as in Nu 6:16, 17), the procedure was usually as follows: (1) sin offering or guilt offering, (2) burnt offering, (3) fellowship offering and grain offering (along with a drink offering). This sequence furnishes part of the spiritual significance of the sacrificial system. First, sin had to be dealt with (sin offering or guilt offering). Second, the worshiper committed himself completely to God (burnt offering and grain offering). Third, fellowship or communion between the Lord, the priest and the worshiper (fellowship offering) was established. To state it another way, there were sacrifices of expiation (sin offerings and guilt offerings), consecration (burnt offerings and grain offerings) and communion (fellowship offerings—these included vow offerings, thank offerings and freewill offerings).

A fellowship offering could be voluntary as a special offering of thanks to God or could be given as the result of a vow or as a freewill offering (7:12–26). This offering was given by the thousands at special celebrations when many people joined in the sacred meal (1Ki 8:63). If a man was too poor to bring a voluntary fellowship offering, he would probably be given a share in the offerings of others. Neither fat nor blood was to be eaten (see 17:10–14). It generally is not realized that eating the fat was also prohibited (see 7:22–25). It was the special part of the animal that was offered to the Lord and was therefore sacred.

D. Sin Offering (4:1–5:13; cf. Nu 15:22–31)

4:1–35 The "sin offering" (GK 2633) and the guilt offering (5:14–6:7) are similar. Indeed, 7:7 says, "The same law applies to both the sin offering and the guilt offering." They are offered in a somewhat similar way, though different animals are specified and the blood was handled differently.

The purpose of the sin offering was to give a specific way for a penitent sinner who was convicted of sin to attain full restoration of fellowship with God. It was both a confession of sin and an assurance of pardon. There were representative sin offerings prescribed for leaders of the people as well as offerings for the individual. A type of sin offering was available for the poorest sinner in the land (5:7, 11).

The difference between the sin offering and the guilt offering was in the nature of the sin. The former was for what might be called general sins; the latter was for sins that injured other people or detracted from the sacred worship. The guilt offering thus involved not only a sacrifice but also restitution plus a fine of 20 percent (6:5). The sins for which the sin offering was prescribed are called "unintentional sins"; the same expression is used in connection with the guilt offering (5:15). The sins concerned are not so strictly limited, however.

The expression "to sin unintentionally" (GK 8706) calls for some comment. The NIV reading may give the impression that there was no sacrifice for intentional sins. This presents a problem, for many of our sins are more or less intentional (though not necessarily deliberate). The word basically means "to err," "go astray," "wander," or "stagger."

That is, the notion of intent or lack of intent is not basic to the meaning of the Hebrew word and ought not to be imported.

The usual sins we fall into are covered by the sin offering and the guilt offering. For instance, lying, stealing, cheating, and false swearing are surely intentional; yet they are specifically covered by the guilt offering (6:2–3). There is one place where these words seem at first to refer to unintentional sins (Nu 15:22–31). There the "unintentional" sin is contrasted with sinning "defiantly" (NIV) or, as the Hebrew expresses it, "with a high hand." Here the NIV has correctly caught the sense of the unpardonable sin—not one done intentionally, but one done "defiantly," i.e., in rebellion, sinning against light (cf. Mt 12:31–32), which results in separation from God. No sacrifice is specified for that.

The sense will be adequately caught if, in all the verses concerned here in Lev 4–5, the phrase "sins unintentionally" is rendered by "goes astray in sin" or "does wrong" or the like. "Unintentional" seems better only in the manslaughter passages (Nu 35:11–22; Jos 20:3–5), and even there "inadvertently" or "by mistake" would actually fit better.

In the case of the sin offering, there was special emphasis on substitutionary atonement. For the sin of a prominent person—e.g., an anointed priest (4:3)—or the whole congregation (v.13), an expensive offering was demanded ("a young bull"). Substitution was typified by laying hands on the offering just prior to its being slain (cf. v.24). Some of the young bull's blood was to be taken into the Holy Place and sprinkled seven times before the veil and also put on the horns of the altar of incense. The rest of the blood was poured out at the base of the bronze altar, presumably on the ashes. In such cases the fat was to be burned on the bronze altar and the carcass burned outside the camp in the place of ashes (cf. Heb 13:11).

In the case of an offering for the sin of an ordinary individual, blood was applied to the four horns of the bronze altar and the rest of the blood poured out as in the previous cases. The fat also was to be burned on the altar, but the meat was to be eaten by the priests in the sacred precincts (7:22–27).

Special sin offerings for the congregation were ordained for particular feast days (Nu 28–29). Particular solemnity was attached to the Day of Atonement in the autumn, when the ritual centered around the goat for a sin offering and the scapegoat (see on Lev 16). All the offerings of the tabernacle included the idea of atonement by blood. The sin and guilt offerings symbolized this basic idea most emphatically.

5:1–13 Verses 1–4 give examples of sins that required a sin offering. Far from the modern idea, it was the duty of a witness to come forward and give his testimony in the interest of truth and justice. In Israel all the people were to be involved in seeing that justice was done. Not to witness was a sin.

The laws of cleanness were partly for public health (cf. chs. 11–15), but they were given sanction in the tabernacle. The priests were the public health officers. Uncleanness demanded ritual cleansing.

An unlawful oath should not be made and should not be kept. Jesus' teaching on oaths emphasized that a person's word is sacred. Jesus himself went on oath before the high priest (Mt 26:63–64). In certain circumstances an oath is not wrong, but an oath should not be necessary. A Christian's word should be as good as his bond (Mt 5:33-37).

One must not suppose that every Israelite who ever sinned intentionally was cut off from the congregation or that no sacrifice availed for him. David at least did not think so (Ps 51:19). The sin offering was available for any tender soul convicted of wrongdoing. Compassionate provision was made for the poor. Atonement is without money and without price. It is true, however, that there were sins recognized under the old covenant as unpardonable because they were defiant, just as in the NT (see comments on 4:1–35).

When a pigeon or chicken has its neck wrung (i.e., rapidly twisted), the neck is broken and the bird killed; but the head is not necessarily severed. A somewhat similar procedure is given in 1:17 in connection with the burnt offering, where it is said specifically that the priest should not sever the bird. The NIV reads as if the sin-offering bird has its head still attached though its blood is to be drained out. The other bird, used as a burnt offering, is said specifically (1:15–17) to have the head wrung off and burned first, then the blood sprinkled and the carcass cleaned but not "divided" and then burned. Although the details are not clear, it would seem more probable that the two birds were handled

alike and that ch. 5 has not repeated the details of the cleaning and opening of the carcass. The priest would presumably have the bird of the sin offering to eat (cf. v.13). The other bird would be put on the altar as a burnt offering.

An "ephah" (v.11) seems to have been about three-fifths of a bushel (twenty-two liters), though there is some uncertainty. Jars marked as containing one bath (= one ephah) have been found; but since they are in pieces, the total capacity is not known. Apparently a tenth of an ephah would be about two quarts. This would be an offering that even the poor should be able to give. It was distinguished from the fellowship offering in that it should have no oil or frankincense and was not to be cooked. Presumably, in accordance with 2:11–13, it also was to have no yeast or honey but would have salt added. Though it was a bloodless offering, a portion of it was burned on the altar and thus associated with the sacrifices offered with blood. The balance of the flour was for the priest.

E. Guilt Offering (5:14–6:7)

5:14–6:7 As explained above (see comment on 4:1–35), the "guilt offering" (GK 871) and the sin offering were similar in ritual and meaning. Even the names sometimes interchange. The guilt offering had more reference to sins that had done definite damage to the tabernacle service or to a neighbor. This required repair of the damage and a penalty of 20 percent in addition (5:16; 6:5). It is not entirely clear what sort of damage is referred to. Probably it could include withholding tithes or firstfruits or other required offerings.

The guilt offering required without exception a male sheep plus restitution plus a 20 percent fine. Like the fines for stealing given in the civil law of Ex 22, there was no remission of fines for the poor. Presumably, as in Ex 22:3, the poor man had to get the money or be sold into bondage. There is a distinction between the sins mentioned as examples in Lev 6:1–5 and outright stealing. These sins are more on the edge of dishonesty. They concern things obtained by false representation, keeping a lost-and-found article, etc. These things also are sins but are not so easily established in court. If a man was guilty of such things and his conscience convicted him, however, he needed to confess and bring his guilt offering and the penalty, too. For cases of outright lawbreaking, such as those given in Exodus, the fines would vary according to the circumstance and as assessed by the judge. A repentant lawbreaker, however, would also presumably offer his guilt offering. In any kind of sin involving damage, full restoration must be made. Forgiveness does not allow us just to forget the damage done but requires us in repentance and with confession to make right as far as possible the wrong done. That forgiveness is free does not mean that it is free of obligation. And there is also a 20 percent penalty. Apparently the fine was given to the person wronged along with the full payment of damage done.

Regarding "unintentional," see comments on 4:1–35.

Guilt in the biblical sense is not just a feeling but a condition. There may be known transgressions that bring feelings of guilt, but there is also the condition of guilt before God, caused by sins known or unknown. Sometimes a hardened sinner has few feelings of guilt when he is the most guilty. Any sinner must bear the guilt of his transgression.

The guilt offering differed from the sin offering in that blood was never sprinkled in the Holy Place. Rather the blood was sprinkled on the altar of burnt offering in the manner of the burnt and peace offerings. The fat parts were to be burned on the altar and the meat eaten by the priests as in the case of the ordinary sin offering. This offering is one of those specified for the cleansing of a "leper" in Lev 14:12–28. It was a special sacrifice also for a Nazirite who had accidentally become unclean during his period of consecration (Nu 6:9–12).

In the great prophecy of Isaiah, the predicted Servant is said to suffer and die as a "guilt offering" (Isa 53:10; GK 871). In this significant verse the messianic hope of Israel is associated with the sacrificial system. The Lamb that God would supply for the sacrifice was the coming Messiah. It is worth adding that in the context of Isa 53, the glorious results of the suffering and death of the Servant are given in ch. 54, climaxing in the Davidic covenant (55:3): "I will make an everlasting covenant with you, my faithful love promised to David." In this central portion of Isaiah, the sacrificial system, the suffering and dying Servant to come, and the

promised Son of David are in close association. These lines of prophecy and typology thus interpret one another. The Christ was both to suffer and to die as a sin and guilt offering and yet would reign as great David's greater Son.

II. Directions for the Priests in Their Service (6:8–7:38)

A. Burnt Offering (6:8–13)

It should be remembered that the Bible does not tell us every detail of the methods of sacrificing. There was no need, for example, to tell an ancient priest how to skin a sheep. But enough was given to be self-explanatory to the Israelites and to give us the general outline and meaning of the ritual. The section on the prescribed ritual of the five major offerings gives mainly instructions for the officiating priests. Leviticus was a directory for worship for the priests from which they in turn were to instruct the people.

8–13 There is an emphasis here on the perpetual fire on the bronze altar. Actually, the sacrifices required not a little work. Wood had to be secured and cut. A good bit of wood was needed to get the roaring fire that would burn the sacrifices completely and carry the odor skyward so as not to be offensive. The care of the ashes is detailed in vv.10–11. Leviticus 1:16 says that the place of the ashes was east of the altar, i.e., toward the front of the tabernacle court (cf. Ex 27:13–15; Nu 3:38). The sacrifices were killed on the north side, i.e., to the right as the worshiper faced the tabernacle. It was helpful that the prevailing winds came from the west.

The reason for the use of linen is given in Eze 44:18. No garment "that makes them perspire" was to be worn by the priest while officiating. Linen made a fine cloth, easily washed and comfortable. The linen garments were to be kept clean. For disposing ashes outside the camp, ordinary clothes were to be worn.

B. Grain Offering (6:14-23)

14–23 Much of this section repeats material already given in ch. 2. The additional directions concern the grain offering to be given by the priests themselves. This offering differs from the usual in that it was to be burned up entirely. It was given every morning and was to accompany the burnt offering (Nu

28:5) and the fellowship offerings (Lev 7:12). It represented the thanksgiving of the priests and, through them, all Israel.

C. Sin Offering (6:24–30)

24–30 The description of this section adds little to the previous treatment at 4:1–5:13 except to emphasize the holiness of the offering. Offerings whose blood was not taken into the tabernacle could be eaten by the officiating priest, but only by him and the males of his family. It was to be eaten within the sacred precincts, and the vessels it was cooked in were to be broken or scoured. It was apparently the most solemn sacrifice of Israel and was thus an especially fitting type of Christ's atoning death (Heb 13:12).

D. Guilt Offering (7:1–10)

1–10 As v.7 says, the guilt offering was similar to the sin offering, especially as regards ritual. The main difference was that the blood of the guilt offering was treated like that of the burnt and fellowship offerings rather than like the sin offering. A difference is made between the cooked and uncooked grain offerings. The former belonged to the officiating priest. The latter, because it was in flour that could be preserved, was distributed among the priests.

E. Fellowship Offering (7:11–38)

Several other instructions were given for this most common sacrifice. There were two varieties of the fellowship offerings. The first expressed thanksgiving for God's general benefits (vv.12–15); the second served as a fulfillment of a vow or as a freewill offering (vv.16–18). Slight differences were made in the eating of the remainder from these varieties of offerings. Since, of all the sacrifices of the tabernacle, only fellowship offerings might be eaten by those who were not from priestly families, special warnings are given with regard to cleanness on the part of those who eat them. The prohibition of fat and blood is repeated (cf. 3:17), and details are given as to the portion of the animals that was given to the priests for food. On these verses see the remarks on 3:1–17.

11–18 The standard grain offering is specified to accompany the burnt offering and the meat of the fellowship offering. The description of the grain offering repeats the term of 2:4 and 6:14. A "memorial portion" was burned on the altar.

A second kind of breadstuff is specified, an offering of yeast bread. This was not burned on the altar. A portion was given the priest, who would present it before the Lord as an "offering" and then eat it. The rest of the bread, like the rest of the meat, was for the worshiper.

All of the thanksgiving offering was to be eaten on the same day to encourage sharing it with the poor. The other types of fellowship offering could be eaten on the second day, but by the third day it was prohibited as unsafe (cf. 19:5–8; 22:30).

19–21 As mentioned above, only the fellowship offerings were eaten by laypersons. Rules for guarding their sacredness were therefore needed. They must be kept clean. An unclean person must absolutely not eat of the sacred meal (cf. 1Co 11:28).

The phrase "cut off [GK 4162] from his people" is used over twenty-five times, usually with regard to some ceremonial violation. It is clearly associated with capital crimes only three times (17:14; 18:29; Ex 31:14). Similar phraseology is used repeatedly of cutting off enemies. The phrase here may have meant only some kind of excommunication from the people of the Lord.

22–27 The carcass of an unclean animal was not to be touched; but a sheep or goat that died a natural death or was killed by a wild beast could be used—only not for food. Its hide and wool were usable. Its fat also was usable, perhaps mostly for fuel.

28–34 The priest's portion of every fellowship offering was the right breast and the right thigh. The breast was "waved" before the Lord, i.e., presented and then taken by the priest. Similarly, the thigh, being heavier, was lifted up before the Lord as a "contribution" and then taken by the priest and his family (10:14).

For "the right thigh" it is difficult to know whether the hindquarter or forequarter is meant. If the Hebrews observed their comparative anatomy (the word when used for people means "leg"), the hindquarter would be intended. Also, the hindquarter is much better meat than the forequarter, and it is probable that the choicer portion was given to the priests; the rest was for the worshipers.

35–38 These offerings were allocated to the priests from "the day they were presented to serve" and onward. There need be no problem between the statement "on Mount Sinai" and 1:1, which says God spoke to Moses from "the Tent of Meeting." The Hebrew preposition *b* (GK 928) can mean "in," "on," "at," etc. Or the phrase "Mount Sinai" may have included more than the mountaintop itself. And some of these regulations may indeed have been given to Moses during his two periods on the mount while others may have been added during the year of establishing the worship of Israel.

III. The Beginning of the Tabernacle Worship (8:1–10:20)

Chapter 8 shows in a very interesting way the relationship of Leviticus to Exodus. They are parts of a unified whole. The consecration of the priests here is the fulfillment of the commands in Ex 29 (cf. vv.1–37).

The last part of Exodus consists largely of the directions for setting up Israel's worship (Ex 25–28, 30), followed by the record that the worship was set up in just that way (Ex 37–39). There is much repetition, with a difference only in tenses. For instance, the instructions for building the ark in Ex 25:10–21 are repeated almost verbatim in the past tense in Ex 37:1–9.

In the same way, the directions for the consecration of the priests in Ex 29:4–20, 22–26, and 31 are very closely paralleled by the record of the consecration in Lev 8:6–9, 12–19, and 31. It is rather obvious that Leviticus is a continuation of Exodus. Exodus ends with the setting up of the tabernacle. Leviticus proceeds with the directions for the offerings. Then Leviticus tells how the priests began their ministry, using the terms of the directions already given in Exodus.

Moses first acted as priest to consecrate the tabernacle, the altar, and Aaron and his sons. It is hard to overemphasize the work of Moses, the man of God. As the first priest, Moses is a type of Christ, the Great High Priest. As the greatest of the OT prophets, he was a type of Christ who spoke the word of God (Dt 18:15–19; Jn 7:40). As the great lawgiver, he received God's revelations face-to-face and was faithful as a servant in all God's house (Nu 12:7–8). Here too he was but a type and a shadow, far inferior to Christ, who was faithful as a Son over all God's house (Heb 3:1–6).

A. Consecration of Aaron and His Sons (8:1–36; cf. Ex 29:1–37)

1–13 The service of consecration was carried on according to the Lord's command and was done in the presence of the congregation. The people had given to the building of the tabernacle, and many had worked on it. Now it and its ministers were ready for the consecration of the priests and the dedication of the house of God.

The steps of the consecration of Aaron and his sons were solemn and meaningful. Aaron first was washed and clothed anew with the holy garments. He wore the ephod, the breastplate with its twelve-jeweled symbols of the tribes, the Urim and Thummim, and the priest's turban with the golden plate and its inscription "HOLY TO THE LORD" (Ex 28:36; 39:30). Then he, his sons, the altar, and its accouterments were anointed with oil. This was a special perfumed oil described in Ex 30:23–25. Psalm 133 says the oil ran down to the skirts of Aaron's garments.

It is generally agreed that the anointing oil typifies the Holy Spirit. When kings were anointed, the Holy Spirit came on them (1Sa 10:1–6; 16:13). The word "messiah" comes from the Hebrew word for "anoint" (GK 5417), and the work of Christ began with such an anointing of the Holy Spirit. There is no statement in the OT as to why oil typified the Holy Spirit. Oil was widely used in lamps. As the lamp burned, the oil seemed to vanish into the air. Such a connection of oil and air possibly may have made the typology natural in the Hebrew culture. The Hebrew word *ruah* (GK 8120) means either "spirit" or "wind, air, breath." The seven-branched lampstand, perpetually fed with oil, is called a symbol of the Spirit in the OT (Zec 4:2–6).

14–30 After being anointed, Aaron and his sons offered first for themselves (Heb 7:27) and then for the consecration of the altar. Then came a burnt offering of worship and consecration. Next they offered a ram of "ordination." This is an unusual term, used idiomatically in the sense of "filling the hand" of a priest, i.e., installing him in his office or ordaining him (cf. v.33).

The ram was sacrificed as a fellowship offering with special application of the blood to the priests' right ears, right thumbs, and right great toes. This doubtless symbolized their new total obedience and service.

31–36 The ram of ordination was then eaten at the door of the tabernacle in a new communion with God. So for seven days Aaron and his sons stayed at the tabernacle in contrition, worship, consecration, and fellowship. The whole OT ritual is given without any prescribed prayers except the Aaronic benediction of Nu 6:24–26.

B. Divine Acceptance of the First Worship (9:1–24)

1–4 After one week of ordination service, Aaron and his sons had fulfilled the complete ritual of consecration and were then ready to begin their priestly service. This chapter tells of a sin offering, burnt offerings, fellowship offerings, and a grain offering for the priests and the people.

5–6 It seems at first sight that this promised manifestation (which occurred at v.23) was a second one, different from that recorded in Ex 40:34. However, it is difficult to see why, if God had already accepted the tabernacle then, the priests would here have to consecrate it again with offerings and anointings. It is perhaps best to see the event mentioned here as the same one as the event recorded in Ex 40.

7–14 These verses give the details of Aaron's offering for himself the sacrifices of v.2. As mentioned in 8:15, the blood of the sin offering of the priest was put on the horns of the golden incense altar in the Holy Place; the rest of the blood was poured out at the base of the large bronze altar of burnt offering.

15–21 The details of Aaron's sacrifice of the offering of the people mentioned in vv.3–4 are given here. Notice that in v.21 Aaron presented the wave breast and the right thigh to the Lord but then took them for food for himself and his sons. The people's sin offering, however, being a sin offering for the congregation, was burned outside the camp (4:13–21).

22–24 After the offerings had been duly made, Aaron lifted up his hands in benediction and blessed the people. He probably spoke the prescribed benediction of Nu 6:24–26. The material in this section need not be strictly chronological. The symbolic presence of God was evidenced by the reality of his glory (see comment on vv. 5–6). There had been fire on the altar during the week of the priests' consecration. But miraculous fire came from the Lord to consume the offerings and to show the divine acceptance. That this was miraculous fire could easily be distinguished by its suddenness, intensity, etc. It emphasized the fact that when the sacrifices were burned year after year, God himself accepted them and blessed the people accordingly. The fire was sacred and was not to be allowed to go out.

The immediate response of the people— "they shouted for joy and fell facedown"— was gladness at God's acceptance. Mingled therewith, however, was awe at the presence of the supernatural manifestation of the holy Lord who had promised to live with them, to be their God, and to take them for his people.

C. Nadab and Abihu's Profanation (10:1–7)

1–7 Unfortunately humans are feeble and frail, and no amount of oil on the outside will change the heart. Two of Aaron's own sons, Nadab and Abihu, profaned the sanctuary with strange fire and died before the Lord. Judgment was harsh (cf. Ac 5:1–11). Aaron and the congregation needed to know that God was real and that the priests were not playing at religion.

D. Explicit Instructions for the Priests (10:8–20)

8–11 Apparently Nadab and Abihu profaned the Lord's house because they were drunk. At least a prohibition of fermented drink while serving in the Lord's house was immediately given. From here on the priest entering the tabernacle was to drink no alcohol.

12–20 It appears that Nadab and Abihu were the elder sons of Aaron. When Moses was on the mountain, God invited Aaron, Nadab, Abihu, and seventy elders to come partway to meet the Lord (Ex 24:1–2). Possibly Eleazer and Ithamar were under the age of thirty (cf. Nu 4:3, 23, 30). As Aaron, however, was about eighty at this point and had been married about forty years, his youngest sons may indeed have been over thirty. The text does not say whether all four sons were consecrated at the same time.

After the death of Aaron's older sons, Moses found that Aaron and his two remaining sons had not eaten the meat of the sin offering as was normal. But Aaron replied that though he was forbidden to mourn, he could not eat in good conscience that day. With that Moses was content; for Aaron had acted, not in negligence or mechanically, but in responsible sincerity. The heart attitude is more important than the mechanics of all the sacrifices (1Sa 15:22; 2Ch 30:19).

"The goat of the sin offering" was not the people's sin offering mentioned in 9:15. When such an offering was made with a male goat, the blood was sprinkled in the Holy Place, and the meat was not to be eaten by the priests (4:13–21). In the present instance there had been further offerings. Individuals had apparently also brought sin offerings whose blood was not sprinkled in the Holy Place and whose flesh could be eaten by the priest. Aaron, however, had directed the flesh of this sin offering also to be burned outside the camp, as was prescribed for a young bull whose blood had been sprinkled in the Holy Place.

IV. Laws of Cleanness (11:1–15:33)

The Levitical laws of cleanness symbolized spiritual cleansing and set Israel apart from the surrounding nations. The spiritual and the hygienic reasons for the laws are remarkably valuable in the area of public health. In general they protected Israel from bad diet, dangerous vermin, and communicable diseases. Only recently have better laws of health been possible with the advance of medicine. These were rule-of-thumb laws that God gave in his wisdom to a people who could not know the reason for the provision.

First, the laws protected Israel's diet. Some of the food forbidden was good some of the time, but not unless it was properly prepared. Pigs spread trichinosis; rabbits spread tularemia. The fish classified as clean are normally free-swimming, whereas scaleless and finless fish are usually bottom feeders and therefore susceptible to a great many more parasites. Cows, goats, and sheep are safe to eat under all ordinary circumstances and are economical to raise. The horse and camel were too uneconomical to use for meat.

The Hebrews were not only to avoid eating unclean animals; they were not to touch their dead carcasses. Thus the laws automatically helped control vermin. Common unclean animals would be spiders, flies, bugs, rats, and mice. A dead rat in a Hebrew house was not overlooked. It was carefully taken out and buried. In an effort to avoid such problems, the Hebrew housewife would normally keep a clean house.

The word "leprosy" used in older translations of chs. 13–14 is now generally recognized to include several "skin diseases" (GK 7669) showing a rash, such as measles, smallpox, and scarlet fever. For any such disease there was a quarantine period with weekly examination until the patient was well. Likewise, the laws on sexual uncleanness protected Israel from venereal diseases and from childbed fever.

A. Clean and Unclean Food (11:1–47) (cf. Dt 14:4–21)

1–8 Deuteronomy 14:6–19 is almost a verbatim copy of Lev 11:3–20. The difference between clean and unclean food is clearly as old as the time of Noah. It was to some extent tied in with sacrifice, for parts of some of the sacrifices were eaten. Noah's purpose in taking extra pairs of the clean animals aboard the ark was to have meat available for his family. There is no reference to clean and unclean items in the history between Noah and Moses, though Job, whose date is uncertain, does frequently mention the difference. Abrahamic sacrifices were of clean animals as far as they are specified (Ge 15:9). The need for extensive laws on these matters concerning public health would only arise when Israel became a nation under Moses.

The phrase "a split hoof completely divided" is obscure. The precise meaning of the terminology is not sure.

The clean animals are further limited to those that "chew the cud." The ruminants are peculiar in that they can exist on a rough diet. Cows, sheep, goats, and camels actually digest cellulose such as found in straw, leaves, twigs, bushes, etc. Horses and pigs require more nourishing food. Deuteronomy 14:4–5 names nine animals that are clean, including the wild deer and the antelope.

Contrary to general opinion, the use of the camel was not characteristic of ancient Israel. Camels are mentioned twenty-four times in connection with the patriarchs who traveled widely along the caravan routes. The rest of the Pentateuch mentions them only three times. From Moses to the Exile, the use of camels by the Israelites is only mentioned twice. They were more a desert animal; apparently the life of Israel did not nearly so much revolve around the camel as does life for the Arab today.

Neither the "coney" (GK 9176; see NIV note, "hyrax or rock badger") nor the "rabbit" is a ruminant. The coney is a vegetarian and an ungulate (i.e., has hoofs). Though small like a rabbit, it is related to the elephant. Both the coney and the rabbit wiggle their noses in a chewing action that resembles the chewing of a cud. The description is not scientifically precise but one of external appearances. Outlawing the rabbit protected the nation from tularemia.

9–12 Fish with fins and scales are free swimming and generally free of parasites. Scaleless fish are more likely carriers of parasites since they are scavengers and mud-bottom dwellers. Clams in current times have carried hepatitis—though this may be due to modern pollution problems. Crabs are scavengers, and some of their meat is said not to be good. Snail fever from infested waters has been a curse in Egypt.

13–19 There was no easy rule of thumb for clean birds. A negative list is given that in cases is difficult to translate with certainty. The different modern versions vary in detail. In general carrion-eating and fish-eating birds were forbidden, just as they are not used for food today. Chickens are not mentioned in the OT. The eating of bird eggs and the mother bird together is forbidden in Dt 22:6, apparently for conservation reasons. If the eggs are taken, the mother bird will lay more; but if the mother bird is taken, there will be no more eggs! Doves, their eggs, and their young were eaten.

20–23 "Flying insects that walk on all fours" include such pests as cockroaches, flies, or even mosquitoes. Verses 21–22 allow the locust/grasshopper family as food. The distinction is that they have strong hind legs for springing. Evidently in the category of insects, the hind pair of legs was not counted; so these insects are described as creeping on all fours.

The "locust" (GK 746) is not the cicada or the seventeen-year locust but a large grass-

hopper-type of insect. These locusts could be great pests in antiquity. A plague of them could eat every green thing in a field in a very short time. Travelers in the Near East tell of having seen the sun obscured by clouds of locusts. When they are present in more normal numbers, they are used as food to this day. Only the muscular portion is used and when fried is said to be a delicacy. John the Baptist ate locusts and wild honey. No one in the OT is mentioned as eating locusts, but this silence does not prove that they were not eaten.

24–43 The words for "weasel," "great lizard," "gecko," "monitor lizard," "wall lizard," and "skink" occur only in these verses in Leviticus. It is impossible to be sure of their identification. Some of these names of animals have parallels in later Arabic or Aramaic literature. Fortunately the details are not important.

The basic meaning of the word "moves about" is to multiply. The little animals like mice, lizards, etc., multiply rapidly if they are not controlled. The word is used again in vv.41–42 to refer to snakes, lizards, centipedes, etc. The word also is used in Ge 1:21 to refer to animals that multiply in the water and in Ge 9:7 in the command to people after the Flood to multiply and fill the earth. The small animals mentioned here are thus rapid movers and reproducers.

The laws of cleanness apply as much to touching the carcasses of vermin as to eating them. Even a part of the carcass of an unclean animal was defiled. This was not true of the carcass of a clean animal killed for food. Dead vermin were a problem in the Hebrew house. Dead bugs in an earthen pot meant the pot was to be broken. Food contaminated by dead bugs or mice was to be thrown out. A carcass on dry seed was all right but on damp seed was contaminating. Even the carcass of a clean animal that had died a natural death (i.e., by a disease) was unclean. Such laws resulted in prompt burial of carrion and certainly promoted public health.

44–47 The phrase "be holy [GK 7705], because I am holy" is interesting because it is like the words of 19:2, which are said to be characteristic of the Holiness Code (chs. 17–26). Actually, the words are characteristic of the laws of holy conduct wherever found. The use of the phrase here unifies stylistically the laws of cleanness and the laws of holiness.

B. Purification After Childbirth (12:1–8)

1–8 Fuller details with regard to sexual impurity are given in ch. 15. Childbirth, like menstruation, rendered the mother unclean. The period was seven days for a boy, twice that for a girl. There may be more reasons than one for such a law. First, it would put the mother in sufficient isolation to assist in bringing her back to normal health. Being unclean she could not do the cooking or keep the house. Also, it is possible that such a provision would help prevent the spread of childbed fever, which in former days took many lives. If the mother was unclean, presumably any midwife would have to wash in water and be unclean until the evening, which would prevent the direct transmission of this disease.

Circumcision was instituted by God in Abraham's family and distinguished his descendants from all others. Although some ancient peoples practiced circumcision as a puberty rite, infant circumcision appears to have been peculiar to Israel. It had one extra virtue by precluding any licentious puberty circumcision rites that other nations may have observed. The spiritual import of circumcision is clear from Dt 10:16; Jer 4:4; and Ro 2:29.

There was an additional period of semi-isolation during which a newly delivered mother could not yet make the journey to the sanctuary for her offering. Travel in ancient days was more strenuous than now. It would be a physical blessing for a mother to wait for about a month. Breast-feeding was then a must as now it still is a desideratum. It was a natural and wise provision for a mother to have time at home with her baby until the child was stronger and her milk established.

It is not at all clear why the time of uncleanness and seclusion is doubled for a female child. There may be the symbolism of the uncleanness that the daughter would eventually suffer in her turn. Or it may be that circumcising the male child at the end of one week was considered symbolically to reduce the attendant uncleanness. There is no statement that the baby is ceremonially unclean. That the child is also a sinner is plain in the OT (cf. Ps 58:3)—else why the ritual of circumcision that is said to be symbolic of circumcision of the heart?

There may have been good reasons in that culture why the journey to the temple was delayed for a baby girl. Girls are usually smaller at birth. More girls are born than boys, but even now the mortality rate is greater for girls so that the sexes are soon numerically even. To allow a longer time to let a baby girl grow and get established would be a good thing! There may also have been cultural influences. In many countries girls are less desired than boys. Thoughtless husbands might have taken better care of baby boys and their mothers; so a longer time at home might have been a positive help for a mother with a baby girl. No difference is made in the temple ritual between the birth of a boy or a girl. The only difference is in the periods of uncleanness and seclusion.

The prescribed offering for the new mother was a burnt offering and a sin offering that was normal for a woman with any unnatural discharge (15:30). The OT does not state that conception and birth are sinful; but all who conceive and bear are sinners, and the end of all such uncleanness was accomplished by ritual laws of cleansing. The laws were for public health, but there was also the religious sanction. Doubtless the physical uncleanness was typical of spiritual uncleanness as well.

C. Cleanness and Skin Diseases (13:1–46)

Clearly chs. 13–14 are not limited to what is now termed leprosy or Hansen's disease. The Hebrew word translated "skin diseases" (GK 7669) is used only in connection with sickness and mildew, and its use elsewhere gives no great light on the identification. The word is used in connection with the miracles of Moses' hand (Ex 4:6), Miriam's plague (Nu 12:10), and Naaman's healing and Gehazi's plague (2Ki 5:1–27). These all refer to the whiteness of skin and thus would be true leprosy. Uzziah's curse, being a continuing disease (2Ki 15:5; 2Ch 26:21), also could be true leprosy. The other references are general and do not add to the picture (22:4; Nu 5:2; Dt 24:8; 2Sa 3:29).

The symptoms listed in ch. 13 are more applicable to the communicable diseases characterized by skin rash, such as measles, smallpox, scarlet fever, etc. Hansen's disease does not change the hair color but causes loss of hair. It makes no pocks in the skin. The different symptoms listed in the chapter are hard to follow in detail; but the main consideration is whether the sore is virulent,

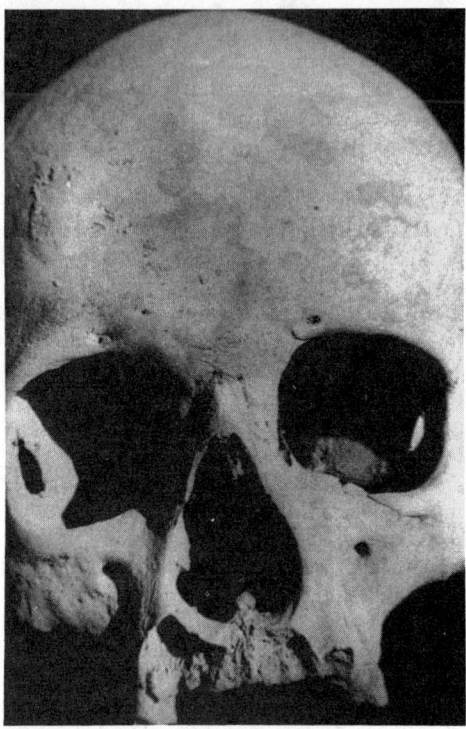

The disfigurement on this skull gives evidence that this person had leprosy. Courtesy Israel Antiquities Authority.

spreading, and deeper than the skin. Such a disease would be watched for seven days and if necessary seven days more. By that time, if the disease were serious, the person would likely be either well or dead. Hansen's disease is slow in onset and does not improve in seven days. Of course, the references to the disease affecting a garment or a house (vv.47–49; 14:33–53) cannot apply to Hansen's disease.

No medication is prescribed because in those days there was nothing appropriate. The only weapon the people had to prevent the spread of disease was quarantine, and this was applied as sensibly as it could be in those times. No other ancient law code has these quarantine prescriptions or even approaches the questions of public health.

Some damage may have been done by the translation "leprosy." Some of the diseases here referred to are highly communicable. Leprosy is not easily communicable; but partly because of these biblical references, people with leprosy, even in modern days, have been more isolated than necessary. It is true that leprosy is more communicable

among children. With modern treatment, however, it can be controlled without the strict quarantine that was usually added to the pitiable state of the victims. Such unfortunate hardships were perhaps overbalanced by the beneficial results of an ancient quarantine for measles, smallpox, scarlet fever, and other such communicable diseases.

1–11 That the victim "must be brought" indicates that he would be too sick to walk. Leprosy in its incipient stages does not incapacitate a person. No details are given about the type of "isolation" required. The sick person was probably not confined at home, and no quarters were available around the tabernacle. His family would probably avoid him. He would stay outside the camp (see v.46). The implication is that a "rash" was a temporary thing. At least there was no serious disease. He was to wash and be clean. True leprosy does not change enough in fourteen days to be recognized by such an examination. Some other affliction is intended.

The details of these symptoms and the examinations by the priest escape us. It appears that the main questions were, Is the sore more than skin deep? Is there raw flesh? Is the infection spreading? A temporary disease meant quarantine; a chronic disease meant segregation; an abated disease meant cure—the individual was clean.

12–17 Any disease that would leave the whole body white after a couple of weeks would not be serious. Apparently it means that the rash had gone, leaving the skin white. Perhaps the whiteness would refer to new skin, not as sun-bronzed as usual. However, if raw flesh appeared, the person was unclean.

18–23 The word "boil" (GK 8825) is used of Job's affliction, and boils were one of the ten plagues of Egypt. The similar Arabic word refers to inflammation. That the person is pronounced "unclean" means that the boil has not healed. The test is, Is the infection more than skin deep? Again, leprosy is too specific for the disease.

24–28 The case of a "burn" (GK 4805) is more clear. This sore is caused by fire. Burns are not contagious, but they can become infected; in that case, for his own good as well as for others, the infected person would be quarantined. Again the key questions are, Is it deep? Is the hair dead? Is it spreading?

29–37 The "itch" (GK 5999) is possibly a scab that is complicated by the hair of the head or the beard. The patient is to shave the hair around the sore and watch it. Such open sores were not allowed to fester without care. And the person with the sore was not to spread the infection.

38–46 The dull white spot, it must be remembered, is against the background of the darker skin of the tanned Jew of Palestine. The spots are not active, raw, or deep. They are a "harmless rash," possibly a scar. From the context, at least, it was harmless.

The word for "unkempt"(GK 7277) is difficult and may derive from a word referring to long hair such as a Nazirite had (Nu 6:5) or from a word meaning "a bit loose," "untied" (a turban). In 21:10 the priest was forbidden thus to take off his turban (or let his hair grow long) as a sign of mourning. The unclean man was to do what a priest was forbidden to do.

The quarantined person in Israel was not quarantined in his house; that would endanger the family. He was to warn others of his illness by dress and action and was to stay outside the camp. He probably got little care except from a mother who was willing to share his uncleanness. Till relatively recent years many a country town had a pest house where victims of communicable diseases were put. The author's grandfather once nursed a relative in such a pest house. Mortality was high; but it would also have been high at home, and the well people were preserved. It is hard for modern people to imagine the severity of ancient epidemics. The black death (bubonic plague) killed a quarter of Europe's people in about 1350. Whole villages would move away from those stricken with the disease. Quarantine was the only available relief. The OT specified such quarantine already in the days of Moses.

D. Mildew (13:47–59)

47–59 Obviously leprosy is not in view here but some kind of rot, fungus, or "mildew" (GK 7669; cf. 14:33–53). Palestine has a winter rainy season that could generate mildew. One unfortunate result of this presence of mildew is that we have few remnants of the writings of ancient Israel. If the Israelites had written on clay tablets, we might have had an abundance of preserved writings; but except for those found in the dry, hot Jordan valley, the leather and papyrus copies have perished through the rot mentioned here.

Leather was used for clothing, as these verses point out (cf. Heb 11:37); but leather clothing is not often referred to in the OT, being, perhaps, the clothing of the poor. It would seem to be durable but hot and uncomfortable. As v.48 shows, leather was also used for other objects: belts (2Ki 1:8), skins for liquids (Jos 9:4), etc. Leather was cheap and versatile but subject to decay. Linen and woolen objects likewise would mildew if stored in a damp place. Such mildew could be irritating to the lungs and certainly would be damaging to the articles. The law that declared such objects unclean was good for both hygiene and economics.

The ancient housewife could not spray the item with a disinfectant or bleach. The Lord did not instruct Moses in the biology of fungi. He did prescribe, however, practical public health measures to be administered under the priest-physician. The article was to be shown to the priest who isolated it for seven days; then if the fungus had not spread, the article was to be washed and watched for another week. If the fungus was gone, the garment was safe to wear; if not, the spot was to be cut out or the whole article was to be burned up. If the mildew was caused by storage in a damp place, the transfer to the priests' quarters would probably fix an ordinary problem. Probably a housewife would go over stored clothes rather often to prevent such trouble and loss. If the garments were frequently inspected and aired, that alone would be a good thing. The principle of quarantine was a practical means to control mildew in clothes or houses as well as to control sickness.

To wash the item was a logical treatment. If washing did not fix the trouble, nothing more could be done—better to burn it and keep any problem from spreading. Much was left to the priests' judgment. If washing helped, cutting out the spot would cure. Then watch it again, wash it again, and the garment was safe to wear.

Verse 59 summarizes the matter of mildew only. Similar summaries for other regulations appear in 11:46–47; 14:57; and 15:32.

E. Cleansing From Skin Diseases (14:1–32)

1–7 The priests were the public health officers, but they served in their priestly capacity. Israel was a holy nation, and even her cleansing from sickness was done with religious ceremony. Sickness was symbolic of sin, and even now it should not be forgotten that sickness and death are part of God's curse on the sin of Adam and the human race. Therefore, cleansing the diseased person required sacrifices (cf. Lk 5:12–15).

It is difficult to see in detail the symbolism of the two live birds. The ritual of cleansing a house in vv.49–53 is so similar to the cleansing of a diseased person that the latter passage may be used to explain the former. Verse 52 makes it quite explicit that the fresh water was mingled with the small amount of blood of the slaughtered bird and used in the cleansing. When the bird was killed over the fresh water, its blood dripped into the water. The wording of vv.51 and 53 is so similar to that of vv.6–7 that we may use v.52 to interpret the action of the earlier verses to include the fresh water also in the sprinkling. The live bird was identified with the blood of the dead bird so that both penalty for and removal of sin are symbolized (cf. 16:21–28). The scarlet yarn, hyssop, and cedar wood were presumably used in the sprinkling. Hyssop is a plant that can be used like a paint brush, and the wood may have served as a handle around which to wrap the yarn.

8–20 The rather unusual practice of shaving was a real help in cleansing the body and showing up any remaining scabs. After seven days of semiisolation and a final bath, the man was clean and must offer his sacrifice. The order of the offerings was first a guilt offering, then a sin offering, then the burnt offering. The grain offering was three-tenths of an ephah, indicating that one-tenth should be offered with each sacrifice. The same extremities are touched with blood and oil that were consecrated with blood at a priest's ordination (Ex 29:20). The ear, thumb, and great toe stand for the whole person who is cleansed and anointed with the "log of oil"— a little over one cup of olive oil.

21–32 As usual in the case of a necessary offering, there is provision for the poor, but the principles of the offering are maintained.

Verses 24–31 are almost a duplicate of the regulations of vv.12–18 with the changes of the two doves instead of two lambs. This illustrates the usual Hebrew style that loves duplication.

F. Cleansing Houses From Mildew (14:33–57)

33–57 As remarked above, the word used to describe infection in houses as well as infection of skin proves that its meaning is not restricted to leprosy. "Mildew" surely is preferable. Verse 34 shows that the Israelites had the expectation of being in Canaan within the year. This law of mildew in a house was obviously not for the desert journey. It is equally obvious, however, that God did not expect Israel to live forever in tents.

In dealing with this problem, the house was first to be emptied because it was suspect and may be pronounced unclean. For all the contents to be pronounced unclean unnecessarily would be quite a loss. As would be expected, the symptoms of "greenish or reddish depressions" are not very clear. The words for the colors are used elsewhere, but the word "depressions" is used only here. It may mean "hollow," "crack," "spot," etc. The main thing is that it is not a surface stain.

The procedure for dealing with the mildew in the house is again isolation (v.38). If the house is emptied of its contents and the mildew continues or spreads, the affected stones must be removed and the area scraped and replastered. If the mildew persists, the house must be condemned. If the mildew is cured, the house is clean. We see once more a useful procedure for public health. A house with such mildew conditions would normally not be a healthy place to live because of dampness, allergens, etc.

The procedure for purifying the house is similar to that of cleansing persons (vv.2–7). This time it is clear that fresh water was used in the cleansing, mixed with the blood that had dripped into it. The symbolism of blood atonement and removal of defilement is maintained, but no further guilt, sin, or burnt offering was required. The problem of the house's mildew was impersonal.

G. Uncleanness From Emissions (15:1–33)

Various matters are taken up in this chapter: defilement from normal sexual activity, abnormal sexual discharge, and, probably, diarrhea (cf. Dt 23:9–14).

1–3 The words "any man" may indicate that the first section applies to both men and women. The question involves the nature of the "bodily discharge [GK 2307]." This is not the normal male emission that is specifically mentioned in vv.16–18 and that involves only washing and temporary uncleanness. This discharge, like a woman's unnatural discharge of blood (vv.25–30), requires a sacrifice. It may therefore be a virulent male discharge such as in the case of gonorrhea. Or it may not be a sexual discharge at all. Diarrhea is common still in the Near East and is sometimes a symptom of many serious diseases. It is perhaps safest to say that this section is all-inclusive, and both diarrhea and any unnatural male discharge are covered.

4–12 The regulations covering the uncleanness of a person in this case are very stringent. Anything he touches is unclean, and anyone who touches anything he touches is unclean. These prohibitions better fit diarrhea. For instance, the scourge of cholera is very serious. It involves diarrhea and is very contagious. Venereal diseases, on the other hand, are almost always transmitted by sexual contact rather than by infected items.

13–15 Examination by the priest was not required because there were no external symptoms such as 13:1–44 mentions. A waiting period of seven days, however, was required in this case also, then a bath, and then offerings. The offerings specified are only the sin offering and burnt offering, and only doves or pigeons are required, not lambs. After all, diarrhea may sometimes be a serious symptom, but it may also be common and not at all serious.

16–18 Normal sexual activity resulted in temporary uncleanness requiring washing, but no guilt was attached and no offering was required. The Bible says a good bit about sex. It heavily condemns extramarital and perverted sex. Marriage, however, is plainly said to be honorable (Heb 13:4). A Christian perhaps may not speak much of sex, not because it is shameful, but because it is intimate, wonderful, and holy.

19–24 Notice the emphasis on washing, which is good hygiene. No offering is prescribed for cleansing after a woman's regular period. The natural result of the stipulation in v.24 is to protect a woman with cramps and some weakness from the unwelcome advances of an unfeeling husband. The penalty is not severe; the situation is probably different from 20:18, which should be compared.

25–33 The ancient law distinguishes between normal flow and abnormalities causing a discharge, possibly because of disease. The net effect of the quarantine imposed would be to prevent contagion and to give the woman a real rest from housework, marital relations, and family care. A person perpetually unclean could hardly prepare the food and do the housework.

The offering prescribed for a woman's sickness was exactly the same as that for the "discharge" of a man or the diarrhea of either sex (cf. vv.13–15, 28–30).

V. The Annual Sin Offering of the Day of Atonement (16:1–34) (cf. 23:27–32; Nu 29:7–11)

The Day of Atonement is not mentioned in Ex 23:14–17 and 34:18–23. Nor does it appear in Dt 16:1–16. These places mention only the three so-called pilgrimage festivals when the males of all Israel were to assemble before the tabernacle. The Day of Atonement was not such a pilgrimage festival. The ordinary Israelite remained at home, and the priests carried out the ritual. It was the only day of fasting enjoined on Israel and was to be a special Sabbath of rest and solemnity. It was a time of special contrition, special sin offerings, and atonement. It is kept to this day by the Jews and is called Yom Kippur ("Day of Atonement"). The biblical term is plural, "Day of Atonements."

This day had a special symbolism. Two goats were taken to bear the people's sins. One was killed as a sin offering; the other was sent off into the desert to bear away the sins of the people. The two goats thus symbolized both propitiation for sins by death and complete removal of the sins for which atonement was made. Clearly the Day of Atonement was to symbolize for Israel every year the substitutionary atonement God provided for their sins and the total removal of their guilt.

1–10 The mention of the death of the two sons of Aaron shows that chronologically this law of the Day of Atonement was not given until near the end of the stay at Sinai, which is one good reason why it is not found in Exodus. The occasion of the institution was the necessity to protect the priests in their ministry. It appears probable that Nadab and Abihu had entered the Most Holy Place. This privilege and duty were now limited to the high priest who "entered the inner room, and that only once a year, and never without blood, which he offered for himself and for the sins the people had committed in ignorance" (Heb 9:7). Christ, as Hebrews emphasizes, has entered heaven itself once for all with his own blood, "having obtained eternal redemption" (Heb 9:12).

The "Most Holy Place" (GK 7731) behind the curtain was the inner shrine where the ark was kept. The golden lid of the sacred chest, the "atonement cover" (GK 4114; called the "mercy seat" in KJV), is better translated "the atonement place." The emphasis is on the atonement rather than on the mercy lying behind the atonement. In the symbolism of the tabernacle, this inner shrine was the dwelling of God; and the place above the ark was the place where he would meet with humans. But the holiness of God was so awesome that for sinners to approach him carelessly and without an atoning sacrifice could be fatal—as it was for Nadab and Abihu (cf. Jn 14:6).

A young bull was the sin offering specified for a priest (4:3). This was to be followed by a burnt offering. These offerings were for Aaron himself, that he might be cleansed and consecrated afresh before acting as priest for the people. Hebrews 7:27 declares that Christ had no need of this first cleansing sacrifice. Christ is the perfect Priest. Aaron was but a human type.

What is the "scapegoat" (GK 6439)? In later Jewish theology the Book of Enoch uses the word as a name for one of the fallen angels, Azazel. Enoch's extensive demonology is demonstrably late (c. 200 B.C.). It often uses late Aramaic forms for names of the demons, which suggests that they were of postbiblical invention. Enoch is dependent on Lev 16 rather than vice versa and is no guide to the interpretation of Leviticus.

A much simpler view goes back to the LXX of 200 B.C. The first part of "Azazel" can mean "goat" and the last part is from a verb that means "go away." Compound nouns like this are rare in ancient Hebrew, but new evidence for them is turning up in Ugaritic. It is simply the designation of the goat to be taken away, the escape goat. In Nu 29:11 the escape goat is called "the sin offering for atonement."

11–14 The formula for the "fragrant incense" is given in Ex 30:34–38. It was not to be used for private perfume, for it was holy. This incense was not burned on the altar of incense in the Holy Place but in the censer that Aaron was to carry into the Most Holy Place. The smoke of the incense in the dark shrine would add to the awesomeness of Aaron's work in the annual blanket atonement for Israel's sins.

The "Testimony" (GK 6343) was the tablets of the Ten Commandments (Ex 25:16; 31:18); thus the tent is called the tabernacle of the Testimony. The phrase "ark of the Testimony" is used eleven times in Exodus, twice in Numbers, and once in Joshua. The more usual name is the "ark of the covenant," used twice in Numbers, four times in Deuteronomy, and often in the later histories, Joshua–2 Chronicles. It is clear that the tablets of the law are also called the "testimony" and the "covenant," and this is the reason for the phrase "ark of the covenant" (2Ch 6:11). Studies of ancient treaties draw attention to the nature of the Ten Commandments as sharing parts of the treaty form of early times.

In this most solemn act of worship in the inner shrine, the blood sprinkled before God symbolizes the substitutionary atonement. "Without the shedding of blood there is no forgiveness" (Heb 9:22).

15–19 The same ritual is now repeated by Aaron for the people. The newly cleansed priest representatively bears the nation before God for atonement. The shrine, the whole tent, and the bronze altar must be cleansed by the sin offering because these things dwell among an unclean people. It is clear that the ritual cleansing of the tabernacle furniture was not due to its physical uncleanness. Rather, it stemmed from the Israelites whose sin and rebellion defiled the tabernacle when they worshiped.

20–28 Attention has already been called to the part of the ritual for sacrifice wherein the symbolism of transfer of sins is prominent (cf. 1:4 et al.). In this special case the symbolism is quite clear. The priest confesses Israel's sins over the goat, putting them on the goat, who then bears them away. Of course, this was only symbolic. The NT antitype is our union with Christ (Ro 6:5), in virtue of which "he himself bore our sins in his body on the tree" (1Pe 2:24). The divine order set forth here is, first, sins must be dealt with; then comes worship and consecration. Aaron's own burnt offering was delayed until the sin offerings were all completed; then both Aaron's and the people's burnt offerings were acceptable. The sin offering for a priest and the sin offering for the nation were to have the carcasses burned outside the camp (cf. 4:12, 21). Hebrews 13:11–12 applies this principle to the death of Christ, who suffered outside the gate as a sin offering.

29–34 A series of holy days clusters in the fall in the Jewish calendar. The phrase "deny yourselves" (GK 6700) probably signifies fasting (NIV note). It is used in conjunction with fasting in Ps 35:13 and in parallel with fasting in Isa 58:3 (where in both instances it is referred to as humbling). But as the context in Isa 58 shows, God's injunction was not for mere external fasting but for fasting as an accompaniment of true repentance and new obedience. The title "high priest" is not common in the OT, but this verse shows that a hereditary succession is in view. The conclusion to the whole chapter does not mention the cleansing of tabernacle furniture but specifies that atonement was thus "made once a year for all the sins of the Israelites."

VI. Laws of Personal Holiness (17:1–22:33)

A. One Place of Sacrifice (17:1–9) (cf. Dt 12:1–27)

1–2 Chapter 17 is a hinge chapter between the public and private regulations. It deals with the requirement for central sacrifice, as does Dt 12:1–27, and it likewise forbids eating blood. These matters concerned the general public.

3–7 Of the several Hebrew words for "kill," the one used here practically always is used for killing animals for sacrifice, except that it also refers to the slaughter of people. As Dt 12:15 makes plain, people could kill animals at home but not for sacrifice. Animals sacrificed elsewhere would not have God's blessing, and bloodguilt would be imputed to the offerer. It is unnecessary to hold that *butchering* was not done at home. The alleged contradiction of Lev 17:3–5 and Dt 12:15 disappears if "sacrifice" is adopted in Lev 17:3–5.

8–9 The prohibition against sacrificing away from the central tabernacle repeats the law of v.3, except that it adds mention of the major kind of sacrifice—the burnt offering. Repetition is not surprising in Hebrew; indeed, it is characteristic. A double prohibition also is given in Dt 12:4–6 and 13–14, which is probably dependent on the earlier command in Leviticus, giving, however, a few extra details—the mention of wild animals as examples of legitimate butchering at home (v.15). Deuteronomy 14:23–26 takes up the further question of converting tithes into money if the central sanctuary is too far away to carry gifts to it.

The expression "must be cut off from his people" (cf. v.4) is not easy to identify. It usually refers to ceremonial offenses (Passover, Ex 12:15, 19; Nu 9:13), being uncircumcised (Ge 17:14), eating of unclean foods, or failing to be cleansed after defilement (Lev 17:4, 9, 10, 14; Nu 19:13, 20, et al.). The times when it may refer to judgment on moral matters are Lev 18:29, where it refers to all the previous matters of incest; Nu 15:30, the unpardonable sin; Ex 31:14, Sabbath desecration; and Lev 20:3, 5–6, idolatry and spiritualism. It is hard to think that all these instances involve capital punishment—though some may. Another view is that they involve excommunication.

B. The Sanctity of Blood (17:10–16)

10–16 Blood, so obviously necessary to life, plays the major role in the sacrificial system and did so from the first sacrifice of Abel. God told Noah that human blood was sacred, for it stands for the life of a human being made in God's image (Ge 9:4–6). That animal blood was forbidden as food further emphasizes this fact. The additional reason for its sacrificial meaning is given in the present passage (cf. Dt 12:23).

C. Laws Against Incest (18:1–18)

The laws of ch. 18 and much of ch. 20 are not against indecent exposure (as the KJV and NRSV phrase "You shall not uncover the nakedness of" might suggest); rather, they deal with sexual relations, and this chapter forbids incest. Chapter 20 covers much the same ground, giving the penalties for such actions. As mentioned in connection with ch. 17, the ground for these laws is found in the lordship of God (ch. 18) and his holiness (ch. 20). The Lord had brought the Israelites out of Egypt where such practices were common. In their new land they were to avoid these common sins of pagan society.

1–5 A frequent emphasis of critics is that Israel borrowed her religion from her neighbors. Doubtless some faithless Israelites did borrow, but the constant emphasis of the Law and Prophets was for Israel's faith to be kept unique. Their religion was to be different from the practices of Egypt and Canaan. Its greatest distinction was expressed in the refrain "I am the LORD your God."

Verse 5—"Keep my decrees and laws, for the man who obeys them will live by them. I am the LORD"— is quoted in Eze 20:11, 13, 21; Ne 9:29; and in Lk 10:28; Ro 10:5; and Gal 3:12. There is some difference of opinion how it should be taken. Ezekiel and Nehemiah use the verse to condemn Israel. God's people had violated his ordinances and were exiled. Christ told the questioning lawyer to keep the commandments, and he would live. It is sometimes said that Christ here allowed a hypothetical salvation by works. But he then told the parable of the Good Samaritan in order to search out the lawyer's sin and bring conviction.

Rather than teaching salvation by works, v. 5 teaches that the OT believers who trusted God and obeyed him from the heart received life abundant both here and hereafter. It would seem that the things required to be done include all the laws of God— including keeping the laws of morality and the rituals of atonement and worship in the tabernacle. Observance of these laws in an attitude of faith resulted in spiritual life and power for the godly Israelite. But, as Lev 19:17 and other verses show, the Lord required more than mere external obedience and ritual. The Lord desired a circumcised heart (Dt 30:6). Therefore, it is best to take Lev 18:5 as a command to keep all God's laws by faith and thus attain a full spiritual life.

6–18 The forbidden degrees of relationship are given here. Some of these provisions seem unnecessary because the marriage is impossible anyway (i.e., with a daughter-in-law, she being already married), but the law would be in point if the person were widowed or divorced.

Two items call for special mention: v.16, marriage with a brother's wife, and v.18, with a wife's sister. The problem with v.16 is that it seems to forbid the levirate marriage of Dt 25:5. It is usually supposed that levirate marriage was an old and acknowledged exception (Ge 38:6–11). It was in force only if the widow was childless. Was it also required only if the surviving brother was single (Dt 25:5, if brothers were living together)? As to v.18, at the very least it forbids this special case of polygamy. This does not mean that polygamy in general is approved—only that its excesses are curbed.

The reason for forbidding these relationships is because extensive intermarriage results in tragic abnormalities and also destroys the freedom of the family that should be able to have normal love and intimacy without sexual overtones. In a polygamous society such rules were the more necessary. And incest was common in antiquity under certain circumstances. For three generations just prior to Moses, the kings of Egypt had married their half-sisters to maintain the kingship in the royal family. The laws of incest as given in this chapter are those recognized in civilized society. Marriage with first cousins is not forbidden.

D. Sexual Purity (18:19–30)

19 As argued at 15:24, the restriction of this verse is a general protection for a woman against an inconsiderate husband's approach. The penalty in 15:24 is a seven-day period of uncleanness. In view of that regulation, it seems that here to "be cut off from their people" (v.29) does not involve death but perhaps excommunication, perhaps divine displeasure.

20 This verse defines adultery as specifically forbidden in the seventh commandment (Ex 20:14; Dt 22:22). Other sexual aberrations are mentioned and various penalties given. Intercourse with a single girl required marriage (Dt 22:28–29). But violation of another man's wife broke the marriage bond and destroyed the home. People lightly call it "cheating" today, but in God's sight it is a capital offense.

21 "Sacrificed to Molech" is literally "to cross over, or through, to Molech." It seems to be an abbreviation of the phrase used elsewhere (2Ki 23:10), "to make one's child pass through the fire to Molech" (of unwanted or illegitimate children?). On Molech see the comments on 20:1–5.

22 Homosexual acts are clearly denounced as hateful to God. The penalty given at 20:13 is capital punishment. Homosexuality is denounced also in Ro 1:26–27. This sin was well-known in Canaan—witness Sodom (Ge 19:5) and Gibeah (Jdg 19:22)—but it was no less wicked in God's sight. Clearly "gay churches," where homosexuality is rampant, can exist only where people have cast off biblical authority.

23 Bestiality is likewise punishable by death (20:15–16; Ex 22:19 [18 MT]; Dt 27:21). This wicked perversion of the holy sexual relationship given for marriage and the home shows how deeply the human race has fallen!

24–30 People forget that God judges nations when iniquity runs rampant. The Canaanites had no covenant relationship with God. Yet for their excess of abominations, God punished them, and the land vomited out its inhabitants. There comes a day when God's patience runs out. Evil brings its own reward, though not immediately or infallibly in this life. But at last when the cup of iniquity is full, evil brings God's judgment. This eternal principle of justice applied also to Israel, as she found out in the days of the judges.

E. Miscellaneous Laws (19:1–37)

These laws of varied content show how intimately the moral and ceremonial legislation was mixed in ancient Israel. A number of these laws have parallels elsewhere. It is difficult to classify the laws of this chapter and perhaps unnecessary to try. Ancient law codes do not always follow an arrangement we think of as logical.

1. Parents, Sabbaths, and idols (19:1–4) (cf. Dt 27:15–16)

1–3a Verse 2 was alluded to by Christ (Mt 5:33–35) and quoted in 1Pe 1:16 (cf. Lev 11:44; 20:26). The character of God is behind his commandments. Among the sensual and foolish deities of antiquity, no god could ground all moral duty in his divine character; only the God of Israel could. The word "respect" (v.3a; GK 3707) is frequently used of the fear of God; the principle is the same as the fifth commandment (Ex 20:12) and is stated negatively in the curse ritual at Dt 27:16.

3b The word "Sabbath" (GK 8701) refers to the annual feasts and the sabbatical years as well as the weekly Sabbaths. All parts of the Bible emphasize the Sabbaths. Attempts to explain away the Jewish Sabbath without reference to revelation are unsatisfactory. No other nation of antiquity observed a seven-day week. Efforts are made to derive the Sabbath from Assyrian unlucky days and from the phases of the moon, but the twenty-nine and a half days of the lunar month are not so divisible.

Whether the Sabbath is for Christians to observe has been much debated. Some say the Sabbath law is part of the moral law and must be kept today. But they do not keep the day as the OT believers did, resting at home. And the NT emphasizes the Lord's Day, the first day of the week, as did the early church. Others say that the Sabbath was wholly ceremonial and is done away in Christ. These also seem to neglect some NT data and the witness of the early church.

Most Christians, with varying emphases, agree that the Sabbath day, the various feasts called Sabbaths, and the sabbatical years were part of Israel's ceremonial worship. However, these days were based on eternal principles of rest. The spiritual significance of the OT law is kept in the NT by its setting apart of the Lord's Day. The ceremonial part of the law specifying the seventh day and certain feast days and sabbatical years is done away (cf. Gal 4:10 et al.). It should be noted that the OT ceremonies were not exactly "done away" in Christ. They were fulfilled and their principles continue to be represented in the simpler NT ceremonies.

4 The word "cast" means "poured out" and refers to the process of casting metals—an ancient invention. The proscription of idolatry is pervasive in the OT. This matter also is emphasized in the Ten Commandments and in the curse ritual at Dt 27:15. The basis for the prohibition is given extensively in Dt

4:15–19. God has no form or likeness. To represent the Deity by any material object is to represent the Creator by his creation—and thus to limit him. In the words of Christ, God is spirit (Jn 4:24). Such teaching is unique in antiquity. In all the excavations of Palestine no idol of Israel's God has ever been found.

2. Fellowship offerings (19:5–8)
(cf. Dt 24:19–22; 27:18)

5–8 This is really a rule about eating the fellowship offering. The same thing is said in more detail in 7:15–18 (see comments on those verses). There it requires a thanksgiving fellowship offering to be eaten on the same day and allows other fellowship offerings to be eaten on the second day. That passage is a rubric for priests especially. The reason is clear. Meat quickly spoils without refrigeration. Meat that could not be eaten was to be promptly shared with others or else burned up.

3. Help of the unfortunate (19:9–14)

9–10 These verses are almost identical with 23:22. Chapter 19 has an added phrase referring to vineyards. Deuteronomy 24:19–22 gives the same law in different words. Deuteronomy 23:24–25 adds a further thought that a person may eat his fill in a neighbor's vineyard or field but must not carry anything away in a vessel. This last law, incidentally, is still followed among the Arabs of Palestine.

11 "Steal . . . lie . . . deceive" are standard ethical prohibitions given in the Ten Commandments and elsewhere. In this particular setting they may have special reference to defrauding the poor. The word "another" (GK 6660) is used only a dozen times—eleven in Leviticus and once in Zec 13:7. It is translated twice in the KJV as "another," once as "fellow," and nine times as "neighbor." It is handled similarly in the NIV, except "countryman" is used at 25:14–15.

12 Verse 12 probably sheds light on the third commandment, though the wording there is slightly different. To take the name of God in vain (KJV) is not merely to use it as a curse word but to invoke the name of God to support an oath that is not going to be kept. A false oath profanes the name of God as does idolatry (20:3) or violation of God's commands for worship (22:32).

13 Evidently hired servants, at least the poor, were paid daily (cf. Mt 20:1–8). To keep their wages until later would work a hardship. Deuteronomy 24:15 gives the explanation that the laborer is poor and needs his pay daily.

14 To curse the deaf might have been fine sport, for they could not hear the cursing! But God would hear, and he is the Protector of the unfortunate. Likewise, such a callous attitude toward the blind—and there was much blindness in antiquity—comes under God's condemnation. Again there is a parallel to the curse ritual of Dt 27:18.

4. Fairness and neighborly love (19:15–18)

15 Justice is not justice unless the scales of the balance swing even. King Jehoshaphat's instruction for his judges rather closely parallels this verse (see 2Ch 19:7). Deuteronomy 27:19 also treats this subject, recognizing, however, that it is usually the "alien, the fatherless or the widow" who gets the small end of justice. Nonetheless, partiality for the poor is also not justice.

16 The word for "slander" (GK 8215) is used also in Pr 11:13 and 20:19, where it is translated "gossip." The translation "slander" is preferable in each case (cf. Jer 6:28; 9:4; Eze 22:9, where slander and murder are again connected).

17 This significant verse shows that the OT law did not concern itself only with outward obedience. Jesus in the Sermon on the Mount was not giving a new spiritual meaning to the law, as is often supposed, for it already had the spiritual meaning in the OT. He was protesting against the Pharisaic interpretation of the law that limited it to externals.

18 Verse 18 is quoted often in the NT (Mt 5:43; 19:19; 22:39; Mk 12:31; Lk 10:27; Ro 13:9; Gal 5:14). From the passage in Luke, it seems that Jesus was not the first or only one to couple this verse with Dt 6:5 as the greatest commandments. The error of the lawyer who tempted Jesus was not that he did not know the law but that he did not apply it to himself. The law is plain and gives a noble teaching. As Paul says, it sums up the commandments of our duty to our fellow human

beings. The same law is given requiring love for aliens in v.34.

The great parable on this verse is the story of the Good Samaritan (Lk 10:30–37). Its usual interpretation is that to love your neighbor is to help the unfortunate as the Good Samaritan did. Another view notes that the Good Samaritan is the hero of the story. Jesus asked who had become neighbor to the wounded man. The obvious answer is, the Samaritan. Then, Jesus implies, "Love the Samaritan." This the lawyer never did. He did not really keep the law and thus needed God's grace. This is somewhat more limited than the Levitical law that forbids revenge and anger against any "one of your people."

5. Forbidden mixtures (19:19)
(cf. Dt 22:9–11)

19 The reason for these provisions is not clear but could refer to keeping pure a superior breed of cattle brought from Egypt. The reference to mixed seeds or cloth is difficult to understand without more background. It might be an effort to reduce adulteration of a good product. Mixing wheat and barley would make harvest difficult because of different times of ripening. Or possibly the prohibition is against using good seed mixed with weed seed.

Similar laws are given in Dt 22:9–11. In Deuteronomy the clothing mixtures are specified as wool and linen. Why these should not be mixed is not clear. Flax and wool are spun differently. Whether weaving them together was difficult for people of antiquity we cannot say. Or perhaps different threads in warp and woof would cause difficulties in washing—surely they would shrink differently. They also take dyes differently.

Regarding the prohibitions of mixtures in Dt 22:9–11, the first, about mixed seeds (v.9), is parallel with the second of Leviticus. The third of Deuteronomy, mixed cloth materials (v.11), is parallel with the third of Leviticus. One would expect the second of Deuteronomy ("Do not plow with an ox and a donkey yoked together," v.10) to be parallel with the first one of Leviticus ("Do not mate different kinds of animals"). The trouble is that Deuteronomy seems to speak of mismatching animals, Leviticus of mismating them.

Is Leviticus, however, so clear? Different kinds of animals just do not mate. The only exception is the horse and donkey, which produce the sterile mule. The mule was not forbidden in Israel. Mules are mentioned seventeen times in the OT, often in a favorable context (e.g., 1Ki 1:44). This law can hardly forbid mules. Either the Leviticus law refers to keeping breeds of cattle pure, or the usual translation is faulty.

"Do not mate different kinds of animals" is the NIV rendering. But the word for "mate" (GK 8061) means "lie down" (cf. Ps 139:3). It is only used elsewhere in Lev 18:23 and 20:16, where it refers to bestial relations. The word is an Aramaic cognate to the common Hebrew word that many times means "to lie down to rest." Once the word is used for a donkey fallen down under a burden (Ex 23:5). It is never used for copulation.

Possibly the figure in Lev 19:19 is not sexual at all but more naturally would forbid causing different animals to bear a load in such a way that it would be an unequal load under which they would fall. If this interpretation is adopted, the law would fit beautifully its parallel in Deuteronomy. Indeed, the LXX on Lev 19:19 can be read, "You shall not hold down your animals with an unequal yoke." The word "hold down" is rare and is translated here sexually by some, but its derivatives usually refer to "restraint" in general. We suggest, therefore, something like, "Do not make your animals fall down with an unequal yoke."

6. Protection of slave girls (19:20–22)

20–22 The expression "due punishment" (GK 1334) is troublesome. The situation could be reconstructed thus: a slave woman is *betrothed* to a man, i.e., is assigned in advance, but not yet given her freedom (the man presumably was a free man); and then a different man sleeps with her. In such a case normally the penalty was death. But the slave girl was presumed to be not free to resist or not so guarded by a father. So the penalty was not death, but she is not marriageable to the original man. Therefore, the original suitor must be reimbursed; the damages would be a fine (NIV, "due punishment") paid to the original suitor or slave owner. Then the moral offense would be dealt with by the sacrifice, and presumably the slave girl, after being freed, would be married to the second man.

7. Fallow fruit trees (19:23–25)

23–25 The common fruit trees of Palestine were the olive, fig, and date palm. The details of Israelite horticulture are unknown. Does this verse mean that fruit may be eaten in the fifth year of the tree or in the fifth year of its fruit bearing? Probably the latter. Olives are slow-growing trees. Date palms reach full maturity in thirty years but last for nearly two hundred years. The main idea, probably, is that the first three crops are light and that the firstfruits given to the Lord should be a good crop, such as would be borne in the fourth year.

8. Against heathen practices (19:26–31) (cf. Ex 22:18; Dt 18:9–13)

26 The emphasis and frequent prohibition of blood suggest that in this context eating blood or the flesh with the blood was a common heathen practice. The words for practicing divination and sorcery involved heathen worship. To engage in such practices was a capital offense (cf. Ex 22:18; Dt 18:9–13). In ancient Israel as a theocracy, false religion was not to be tolerated. Those who apostatized were free to leave. But those who were Israelites remained bound to Israel's religion. On the other hand, the errors of the English and the New England witch trials were multiple. The definition of witchery was wrong, the court procedure—extorting confession by torture—was poor, and, in any case, the state should have been kept separate from the church so that there would not have been civil trials for religious offenses.

27–28 There was nothing morally wrong with cutting the hair or the beard or with tattooing. But these practices then, and also now in some places, were parts of heathen ritual.

29 Probably in the context to degrade a daughter by making her a prostitute means to make her a religious harlot, a devotee of a heathen shrine.

30 The command to "observe my Sabbaths" is identical with 26:2 (see comments on that verse).

31 "Mediums" and "spiritists" were common and very degrading in the surrounding religions (see v.26).

9. Protection for the old, the stranger, and the poor (19:32–37) (cf. Dt 25:13–26)

32–34 Verse 32 seems to be unique in the Pentateuch, though it is implied in the fifth commandment that honor be given to parents. Proverbs 20:29 and 16:31 give similar thoughts. Verse 34 is a complement to v.18. The neighbor is not to be treated differently from the alien. Both are to be loved as ourselves because the Lord God loved Israel when she was a stranger in Egypt and us while we were yet sinners (Ro 5:8).

35–37 There are more ways to steal than by thievery. And the poor are usually the defenseless ones who suffer most. The emphasis on just weights and measures is given again in Dt 25:13–16 and finds an echo in Pr 11:1; 16:11; 20:10, 23. Without a central bureau of weights and measures, it was all too easy to cheat the poor. Exodus 30:13, 24 et al. show that the priests served to some extent as such a bureau of weights and measures. In Egypt we find examples of a "royal cubit." There the king established the standard. Genesis 23:16 appeals to common, well-known standards. God here reminds them of his constant presence and concern: "Keep . . . all my laws . . . I am the LORD."

F. Punishments for Various Sins (20:1–27)

1. Against the Molech cult (20:1–5)

1–5 The giving of children to Molech seems clearly to be human sacrifice and is strictly forbidden. It is mentioned in the OT in 2Ki 23:10; Jer 32:35 (in the days of Josiah and Jeremiah) and in 1Ki 11:7 (which, however, may be *Milcom* as in v.5 [cf. NIV note]). In the past it was supposed that the name was a false vocalization for *melek* ("king"; GK 4889), i.e., a divine king-idol, and that the consonants were mixed with the vowels for "shameful thing," which were written in by a later pious Jewish scribe. The deity Molech was equated with *Melkar* ("Melech of the city"), a deity of of the city of Tyre. The cult came later into northern Israel in force with Queen Jezebel.

Evidently the sacrifice of children was a dreadful reality among Israel's neighbors and a danger to Israel herself. A bystander is also guilty if he fails to inform on a neighbor performing this monstrous sacrifice (v.4).

2. Various sexual sins (20:6–21) (cf. Ex 21:17; 22:19; Dt 22:30; 27:20)

6 "Mediums and spiritists" are the same evil pair mentioned in 19:31; 20:27; and elsewhere. Verse 27 implies that the persons are inhabited by these evil spirits (lit., "in whom shall be a medium"). Isaiah 8:19 and the report of the witch of Endor (1Sa 28:3–11) show that these people claimed contact with the dead. Of course, this was common in the heathen religions.

7–8 Following the call to consecration, v.8 nicely associates the ideas of human responsibility—"Keep my decrees"—and divine grace—"I am the LORD, who makes you holy."

9 This verse is quoted in Mt 15:4 and Mk 7:10. Cursing one's parents was a capital offense (so also in Ex 21:17; cf. Pr 20:20). Also, striking one's parents was a capital crime (Ex 21:15); and a "stubborn and rebellious son," "a profligate and a drunkard," was to be stoned (Dt 21:18–21). This appears to be severe punishment. What parent would wish to have a son stoned to death for being "stubborn and rebellious"? It is probable that there is more to these verses than meets the eye.

The phrase "stubborn and rebellious" is applied to wayward sons in Dt 21:18. It is applied to Israel's apostasy from God in Ps 78:8 and Jer 5:23. From this we may surmise that the connotation of the phrases included apostasy and idolatry. As to the duty of parents to accuse such a son, the implication is that parents should not shield even their own children who descend to apostasy and black magic (cf. Dt 13:6–11).

Likewise, cursing father and mother here surely does not refer to the angry response that a child might give in a fit of temper. The word is widely used. It includes blaspheming the name of God (24:11–16). Shimei cursed David in open rebellion (2Sa 16:5–13). Gaal, the son of Ebed, cursed Abimelech (Jdg 9:27). Cursing in ancient times sometimes involved a malevolent operation of magic against the person cursed. The modern equivalent is to put a hex on someone. It could thus include an appeal to false religion. Such cursing of parents (or anyone in authority, Ex 22:28), if it were a determined and aggravated offense, was punishable by death.

The place of this sin at the head of a list of sexual crimes may or may not be significant. Many times the laws recorded in the Pentateuch are not according to a system we would expect. It may be that the law has closer affinity with the law forbidding "mediums and spiritists" in v.6.

In vv.9–16 death is specified as the penalty. The method of execution was usually by stoning. This was the penalty for idolatry (Dt 13:10; 17:5; Lev 20:2, 27), adultery (Dt 22:21, 24), blasphemy (Lev 24:13–16), profligacy (Dt 21:21), and Sabbath breaking (Nu 15:35). Often the method of execution is not named. Burning (Ge 38:24) was apparently rare.

10 Compare 18:20. The law of Israel took very seriously the sacredness of marriage. Both parties who broke that bond were judged guilty of death. In Deuteronomy this law is put in connection with the one in Ex 22:16–17 on forcible rape of a betrothed or married woman. In such a case only the man was guilty and had to die.

11–12 Compare 18:8, 15 (cf. also Ex 22:19; Dt 22:30; 27:20). These more serious cases of incest received the death penalty. At first glance it seems that adultery would also be involved, and it may have been. More likely this refers to marriage after the death of the woman's husband.

13 Compare 18:22. Homosexuality was quite common among the Greeks of a later time. The Bible is emphatic that it is a serious sin. Here the death penalty is specified. The NT condemns homosexual acts as shameless perversion (Ro 1:27).

14 Compare 18:17. The Hebrew phrasing shows that marriage is under consideration, and this would be impossible with a wife and her mother unless the mother were widowed or divorced. Theoretically in a polygamous society such a marriage would be possible, but it was strictly forbidden as was also marriage with two sisters (18:18). As mentioned above, the reason for such prohibitions is reinforced by the necessity to keep the areas of family love and affection among children in the house from the overtones of possible sexual attraction that could lead to incest and promiscuity.

"Burned in the fire" is a peculiar provision. The method of execution is mentioned only two other times (Ge 38:24; Lev 21:9). In both cases it is punishment of grave harlotry. Evidently this type of incest was regarded as especially reprehensible.

15–16 Bestiality is mentioned also in 18:23. There it is forbidden; here it has the death penalty attached. Also in Ex 22:19 it is listed among capital offenses; and in Dt 27:21 it is included among the curses at Mount Ebal. The stories of the gods and goddesses of Ugarit frequently exhibit such practices. Israel's pagan neighbors probably followed their gods in these revolting practices.

17 Compare 18:9. This incest with a full or half-sister was forbidden but apparently did not receive the death penalty.

18 The prohibition of intercourse during menstruation was given earlier (15:19; 18:19; see comments on 18:19). It seems probable that here the phrase "cut off from their people" does not refer to execution.

19–21 These verses cite various cases of incest, all of which were covered in ch. 18. The penalties added here are minor and apparently are to be executed by divine providence. "They will be held responsible; they will be childless." See the discussion of levirate marriage on 18:16.

3. Exhortations to holiness (20:22–27)

The strong emphasis on holiness in these verses and this whole section of Leviticus is noteworthy. In the midst of an immoral age and in an era of false religion, the demands of Israel's God stood out in bright light.

22–23 To dwell securely in the Promised Land, it was necessary for the Israelites to shun "the customs of the nations." The word for "customs" (GK 2978) is literally "statutes." The morals and worship of the surrounding nations were low. Therefore, the Lord required Israel to be separated and different from them. He had cast out the Canaanites because they did all "these things," i.e., the incest, perversions, and immoralities referred to in the previous chapters. Israel was to be holy because the Lord is holy (v.26).

24 The expression "flowing with milk and honey" is used fourteen times in the Pentateuch and five times in the rest of the OT. It is, of course, symbolic of the agricultural plenty of Palestine. Palestine today is far from attractive, agriculturally speaking; the rainfall is seasonal, and the summers are dry. It is probable that a similar climate obtained in Moses' day, though the subject is debated. A little more rain would have made a great difference. At least a cover of trees would have better conserved the winter rains. The mention of honey is perhaps lost to modern ears. To us honey is a dispensable condiment. Then it was the only sweetener at hand.

25–26 In the midst of moral prescriptions and warnings on false religion, there is an emphasis again on the laws of cleanness. There is here a reminder that all God's laws for Israel were intertwined and all had a religious sanction. It is convenient to divide the laws into moral, ceremonial, and civil; but the Bible itself makes no such distinction. They were all God's laws and were given in wisdom for the regulation of the life and worship of his people.

27 The two words "medium" and "spiritist" usually go together (see v.6). In the Pentateuch they are forbidden in Lev 19:26, 31; 20:6, here; and Dt 18:11. The latter verse is the inclusive one and should be compared for discussion of the terms. Only in the present verse is the penalty assigned. Since all such practices involved pagan worship, the penalty naturally was death (see 19:26).

G. Special Holiness for Priests (21:1–22:16)

The thrust of this section is twofold: the office of a priest is holy, and the office is above the man. A "priest" (GK 3913) must be holy in body, upright in conduct, and ceremonially clean; for he is the representative of God. The OT priest was a type of Christ. We see this from the priest's work of mediation, which was nevertheless not perfect or final (cf. Heb 9). We see this also from the priest's official character: he was to be cleansed and more holy than other men. His perfection pointed to a perfect priesthood. We see the priesthood as a type of Christ, especially from the references to a Melchizedekian priesthood in Ps 110 and to a king-priest to come (mentioned in Ps 110; Zec 6:11–14).

1–4 To touch a dead body brought uncleanness for seven days (Nu 19:11). The prohibitions in this chapter include more than just touching the dead body of a friend. They also refer to visible signs of mourning. Aaron was not to tear his clothes in mourning even for his two sons (10:6). The case there, however, was somewhat different; for they had died under the judgment of God, and Aaron was the high priest (cf. v.11). The verses here allow mourning by an ordinary priest for death in the immediate family.

Curiously, the priest's wife is omitted in vv.2–3! Surely this omission is insignificant, and the wife is implied. The Hebrew word for "relative" means flesh-and-blood kin, and the degree of this relationship is here specified.

5–6 The practices of self-disfigurement were forbidden to all Israelites (19:27–28). They were apparently heathen signs of grief, which were forbidden to Israel and especially to Israel's priests (cf. 1Ki 18:28).

7–8 One special reason for the prohibition in v.7 is that there should be no question of paternity about the next generation of priests. For the same reason the high priest must marry a "virgin from his own people" (v.14).

9 On "burned in the fire," see 20:14. As the priest is to be holy, his family also is to be holy. Sin is more heinous on the part of those chosen by God for special service.

10–15 The phrase "the anointing oil poured on his head" designates the high priest and his sons who were called to a special sanctity of service. The anointing is commanded for Aaron in Ex 30:30, and the anointing of Aaron as high priest is recorded at Lev 8:12. There are not many references to the high priest (Heb.: "great priest") in the OT; Aaron is called simply "the priest" (Ex 31:10; Nu 25:11), as well as "chief priest" (or "high priest"; Nu 35:25, 28).

In v.10 and at Nu 35:25, the phrase "high priest" (GK 1524 & 3913) is explained as the anointed priest, which is the term used in Lev 4:3, 5; 6:22, and 16:32. The latter verse further qualifies this anointed priest as the high priest. In Nu 20:28 and Dt 10:6, the high priesthood was transferred from Aaron to his son Eleazer and in Nu 25:11 to Phinehas. Deuteronomy 26:3 refers to the "priest in office." Outside the Pentateuch the office is referred to using various terms; and prominent men like Eli, Jehoiada, and Hilkiah occupied it. The office gathered importance after the

Exile, when the high priest eventually assumed governmental functions.

The curious provision that the priest must not "leave the sanctuary" is not clear. There were no living quarters in the tabernacle or its court. Actually the phrase is more general. It forbids the high priest from going away from the tabernacle on any business. It was a twenty-four-hour job! Numbers 3:38 says that Moses, Aaron, and his sons should encamp in front of the tabernacle to the east. After the temple was built, the officiating priests lived in the rooms built in three stories against the outside walls of the temple.

As explained above, a priest's children also were to be holy and above reproach. If the high priest married only a virgin from his own people, the legitimacy of his successor to the holy office could not be questioned.

16–24 It is difficult to translate some of the terms of these verses with certainty, but it is clear that the priest was to be physically perfect. This is an understandable provision for priests who stood in a public relation; but even more, as remarked earlier, it carries out the typology of Christ the perfect Priest.

Blindness was common in antiquity. With improper setting of broken bones as well as no way to correct birth defects, lameness was also common. "A crippled foot or hand" surely refers to common deformities when broken bones would have been poorly set. The word *gibben* (GK 1492) is used only here, but its derivation makes "hunchbacked" probable. The word *daq* (GK 1987) means "thing" or "small" and could refer to someone "dwarfed," though the evidence is scanty. "Eye defect" is literally "blurred or spotted in his eye," but what kind of defect is intended is beyond our information. "Festering . . . sore" is used only here and in similar contexts in 22:22 and Dt 28:27. Surely it refers to some long-continuing disease or scab. "Running sore" is used only here and at 22:22. The exact meaning is unsure.

The term translated "damaged testicles" is used only here, and the precise meaning is uncertain, though the word for "testicle" is clear from neighboring languages. If this is the correct reading, why was the ordinary word for eunuch not used? Perhaps because that word was not specific enough and was also applied to high court officials who were not eunuchs. Could a eunuch officiate as a priest? Clearly not. Deuteronomy 23:1 is translated similarly but has totally different Hebrew words and is subject to some obscurities. Leviticus 22:24 rejects castrated animals as offerings.

The unfortunate cripple in the priest's family could not serve in office but received his regular food like others of the family. He could even eat the most holy things, which shows that there was no superstitious or callous attitude inculcated toward the disabled person.

22:1–3 Chapter 22 continues the directions for sanctity and cleanliness that govern the priesthood. The translation "treat with respect" (GK 5692) is the verb from which the word "Nazirite" (GK 5693) is derived. A Nazirite not only kept away from certain things, he kept himself holy in respect to those things. In v.2, however, it seems that the priests were not to separate themselves from the sacrifices—which, after all, they were to offer—but were to consecrate those sacrifices, to treat them with respect. As the following verses explain, the priest was to keep the holy things inviolate when he himself had some uncleanness.

4–8 The standard causes of uncleanness listed in vv.4–5 have been given before. The emphasis is further given that an unclean priest not only must not minister but also must not eat of the holy offerings. The unclean priest should bathe and be unclean the rest of the day. He would again be clean "when the sun goes down." The Hebrew day then, as now, began at sundown. This was usual in the Orient. The Romans began the day at midnight.

9 It was no small matter to be a priest of God. The institution was divine and not to be trifled with. The judgment on Nadab and Abihu was supernatural, as it later was on Korah and his company (Nu 16). On the other hand, the judgment on Eli's sons was providential. Many a faithless priest escaped catastrophe in his lifetime, but the threat of judgment was always there.

10–13 The definition of an "outsider" (GK 2424) is interesting. He was a temporary visitor or worker. The slave was considered family. The principle is that an outsider should not eat of the holy things. A married daughter with a nonpriest husband was no longer in the priest's family. A widow or divorced daughter with children might bring a stranger's children into the family. This was not allowed. But a priest's daughter without children would revert to her childhood status.

14–16 To "eat a sacred offering by mistake" would be one of the sins that required the guilt offering. There too a 20 percent penalty was specified (cf. 5:16).

Verses 15–16 are somewhat obscure. The meaning chosen by the NIV is that these verses oblige the priests to enforce the rules against the practice of the sacred portions being eaten by the people who offered them. This unites vv.15–16 with the preceding verses. The KJV seems to take v.15 to require the priests to maintain their sanctity, and v.16 requires the priests to preserve the people from profaning the holy things. The NIV reading seems to fit the context better.

H. Perfection Required in Sacrifices (22:17–33)

The principle of a perfect sacrifice has been already stated at Lev 1:3. It is emphasized here with details. Other laws on the subject are in Dt 15:21 and 17:1. Malachi reproached the people after the Exile for offering their worthless and blemished animals (though the words he used are somewhat different). He complained that Israel offered to the Lord animals that would not be acceptable for taxes and that their God, the "great king, . . . the LORD Almighty," was displeased (Mal 1:14).

17–25 Numbers 15:14–15 says that if an alien wishes to join in worship, he must do so in the same way as the Israelite. The "alien" (GK 1731) was probably not just a visitor. He was a foreigner living temporarily in Israel without full rights. Abraham was a sojourner (alien) among the Canaanites. He has been likened to a man having taken out first papers for citizenship. Doubtless the legal status of an alien varied over the centuries.

The word "defect" (GK 4583) is the same one used in 21:18. It is defined in the context as well as by common sense. If the offering was to mean anything, it should be an offering of perfection. As the priesthood symbolized Christ the Perfect Priest, so the offering symbolized Christ the Perfect Sacrifice.

As at 21:18, the words "blind, the injured or the maimed" are sometimes obscure. The words "blind" and "injured" are obvious. The word "maimed" probably means "cut." The word "warts" is used only here, but similar words suggest a running sore (see 21:20).

At 7:15–16 the fellowship offerings are divided into thanksgiving, votive, and voluntary or "freewill offerings." Here it is explained that a stunted or overgrown animal (if not diseased or blemished) can be used for a freewill offering regardless of its market value. However, an offering made in consequence of a vow would require the standard market value of a standard animal. The words "deformed" and "stunted" are uncertain, but the general sense is clear. These animals are not normal in growth, but neither are they diseased. They are all right for some purposes.

There is no word here in the Hebrew for "testicles." There may be truth in the translation, however, that would forbid the offering of an emasculated animal. The LXX takes it so.

Animals purchased from a foreigner were apparently not forbidden as sacrifice, but such purchased animals as were defective were unacceptable. Deuteronomy 15:21–22 explains that defective animals may be eaten for food at home but must not be offered to the Lord.

26–33 The reason for the law in v.27 is not entirely clear. But even today newborn calves are not usually slaughtered. The meat improves with age. Also, it probably is better for the mother that the calf not be taken at once. We might add that to transport a calf under a week old for some distance to the tabernacle or temple would likely in some cases kill the calf.

Similar provisions to v.28 are found in the thrice-repeated law, "You shall not boil a kid in its mother's milk" (Ex 23:19; 34:26; Dt 14:21), and also in the law not to kill a mother bird with her young (Dt 22:6–7). The provisions are curious. To boil a kid in its mother's milk is probably a Canaanite ritual, and this heathen practice was therefore to be avoided. It is barely possible that Dt 22:6–7 gives the key. Those verses forbid the killing of the mother bird when the young are taken. The mother bird is easily caught with her fledglings, but then the goose that lays the golden egg is killed. The mother must be preserved so that the species will not become extinct.

Possibly the thrust of the phrase "on the same day" is general and means "at the same time." The mother cow especially should not be slaughtered just when she "comes in fresh" with plenty of milk.

"That same day" is slightly different from the phrase in v.28; it repeats the law of 7:15. Leviticus 19:5 gives the general law of the fellowship offerings. Repeatedly in this section the character of God is given as the basis of his will for Israel. Verse 33 (as Ex 20:1) also gives the basis of God's saving work in bringing Israel out of Egypt. Because he has redeemed us, and because he is the holy God, therefore we are bound to keep his commandments.

VII. The Feasts and Worship of the Lord (23:1–24:9)

A. Introduction (23:1–2) (cf. Ex 23:10–17; 34:18–23; Nu 28:9–29:39; Dt 15:1–16:17)

1–2 A directory for Israel's worship would not be complete without a catalog of the annual feasts. Leviticus has so far given the rules for offerings, ordination of priests, public health, and personal holiness. Now the religious ceremonial seasons are given. The emphasis is on the things the general public would need to know. Numbers 28–29 is more technical and for the use of the priests. Two feasts celebrated by Jews today do not appear in these Pentateuchal lists because their origin was much later—Purim, which was established in Esther's day, and Hanukkah, which celebrates the rededication of the temple in 165 B.C., after it had been desecrated by the Syrian invaders. Of the five major feasts, three required the presence of all grown men at the tabernacle, later at the temple (Ex 23:17; 34:23; et al.). These are often called the pilgrimage festivals. They were the special times when offerings would be brought in great numbers.

B. The Sabbath (23:3)

3 All the festivals are properly called Sabbaths, but the weekly Sabbath gains great emphasis in the Pentateuch and many other places in Israel's instruction and history (cf. Ex 20:8–11; 23:12; 31:12–17; 34:21; 35:2; Nu 15:32–36; 28:9–10; Dt 5:12–15). The basis for the Sabbath is God's Creation activity. It might indeed be that God ordained the weekly Sabbath on the basis of Creation to

OLD TESTAMENT FEASTS

Name	OT References	OT Time	Today	Description	NT References
Sabbath	Ex 20:8-11; 31:12-17; Lev 23:3; Dt 5:12-15	7th day	Same	Day of rest; no work	Mt 12:1-14; Mk 2:23-3:5; Lk 4 4:16-30; 6:1-10; 13:10 -16; 14:1-5; Jn 5:1-15; 9:1-34; Ac 13:14-48; 17:2; 18:4; Heb 4:1-11
Sabbath Year	Ex 23:10-11; Lev 25:1-7	7th year	Same	Year of rest; fallow fields	
Year of Jubilee	Lev 25:8-55; 27:17-24; Nu 36:4	50th year	Same	Cancelled debts; liberation of slaves and endentured servants; land returned to original family owners	
Passover	Ex 12:1-14; Lev 23:5; Nu 9:1-14; 28:16; Dt 16:1-3a, 4b-7	1st month (Abib) 14	Mar-Apr	Slaying and eating a lamb, together with bitter herbs and bread made without yeast, in every household	Mt 26:1-2, 17-29; Mk 14:12-26; Lk 22:7-38; Jn 2:13-25; 11:55-56; Jn 13:1-30; 1Co 5:7
Unleavened Bread	Ex 12:15-20; 13:3-10; 23:15; 34:18; Lev 23:6-8; Nu 28:17-25; Dt 16:3b,4a,8	1st month (Abib) 15-21	Mar-Apr	Eating bread made without yeast; holding several assemblies; making designated offerings	Mt 26:17; Mk 14:1,12; Luke 22:1,7; Ac 12:3; 20:6; 1Co 5:6-8
Firstfruits	Lev 23:9-14	1st month (Abib) 16	Mar-Apr	Presenting a sheaf of the first of the barley harvest as a wave offering; making a burnt offering and a grain offering	Ro 8:23; 1Co 15:20-23
Weeks (Pentecost)\(Harvest)	Ex 23:16a; 34:22a; Lev 23:15-21; Nu 28:26-31; Dt 16:9-12	3rd month (Sivan) 6	May-June	A festival of joy; mandatory and voluntary offerings, including the firstfruits of the wheat harvest	Ac 2:1-41; 20:16; 1Co 16:8
Trumpets (Later: Rosh Hashanah–New Year's Day)	Lev 23:23-25; Nu 29:1-6	7th month (Tishri) 1	Sept-Oct	An assembly on a day of rest commem- orated with trumpet blasts and sacrifices	
Day of Atonement (Yom Kippur)	Lev 16; 23:26-32; Nu 29:7-11	7th month (Tishri) 10	Sept-Oct	A day of rest, fasting and sacrifices of atonement for priests and people and atonement for the tabernacle and altar	Ac 27:9; Ro 3:24-26; Heb 9:1-14, 23-26; 10:19-22
Tabernacles (Booths)\(Ingathering)	Ex 23:16b;34:22b; Lev 23:33-36a, 39-43; Nu 29:12-34; Dt 16:13-15; Zec 14:16-19	7th month (Tishri) 15-21	Sept-Oct	A week of celebration for the harvest; living in booths and offering sacrifices	Jn 7:2-37
Sacred Assembly	Lev 23:36b; Nu 29:35-38	7th month (Tishri) 22	Sept-Oct	A day of convocation, rest and offering sacrifices	Jn 7:37-44
Dedication		9th month	Dec	A commemoration of the purification of the temple in Maccabean era (166-164 B.C.)	Jn 10:22-39
Purim	Est 9:18-32	12th month (Adar) 14,15	Feb-Mar	A day of joy and feasting and giving presents	

Copyright ©1991 Zondervan Publishing House.

protect the Israelite from the pagan unlucky days associated with moon worship in the surrounding cultures. At least the Sabbath is never called unlucky or sinister as in the Assyrian tablets. It is a "holy convocation" (KJV) or day of "sacred assembly" (see 19:3).

C. The Passover and Firstfruits (23:4–14)

4–5 The Passover was probably the greatest feast of the year, commemorating as it did the deliverance from Egyptian bondage (cf. Ex 12:14–20; 43–49; 23:14–15; 34:18; Nu 9:1–14; 28:16–25; Dt 16:1–8). In type it represents Christ our Passover sacrificed for us (1Co 5:7). The Jews today, because of the destruction of the temple in A.D. 70, celebrate the Passover using only a dry bone instead of the paschal lamb. The ancient Passover ritual, like most all of the other sacrifices, emphasizes redemption through the blood of the slain lamb. It was against this background that John the Baptist proclaimed Christ as "the Lamb of God, who takes away the sin of the world!" (Jn 1:29). The Jews today celebrate the Passover far differently from the OT regulations. The Jewish liturgy changed greatly at A.D. 70.

For "at twilight" the Hebrew has "between the evenings." This curious phrase is explained, however, in Dt 16:6 as "in the evening, when the sun goes down."

6–8 More details on the Feast of Unleavened Bread are given elsewhere (cf. esp. Ex 12; Dt 16). In the latter passage unleavened bread is called the "bread of affliction" (Dt 16:3). It commemorated the fact that the Israelites left Egypt in haste with no time to let their dough rise. The Passover and the time of Unleavened Bread were so closely intertwined that in the NT the whole week is called the Passover (Ac 12:3–4; cf. Jn 19:14). Directions for the special sacrifices to be offered on this and on the other feast days are given in Nu 28–29.

9–14 Allied to Passover and Unleavened Bread was the Feast of Firstfruits celebrated at the same time. The firstfruits at Passover would be barley, which ripens in the warmer areas as early as March.

The presentation of the sheaf "on the day after the Sabbath" symbolized the dedication of the whole year's crop; and until this was done, none of the new grain was to be eaten. In Nu 28:27 other offerings are specified for this day; but as the context shows, they are the standard offerings for every day of Unleavened Bread. This "burnt offering" is an extra one for the firstfruits ceremony.

An "ephah" was about three-fifths of a bushel. Two-tenths would be about four quarts (dry measure; see 5:11). The value of the "hin" is possibly about one gallon (see ZPEB, 5:916). A "quarter of a hin" would then be about a quart. The name "drink offering" (GK 5821) is a misnomer. The Hebrew word refers to pouring. The drink offering was never drunk but was poured out over the sacrifice at a holy place (Ge 35:14; Nu 28:7; 2Ki 16:15).

D. The Feast of Weeks (23:15–22)

15–21 The Feast of Weeks is called the Feast of Harvest in Ex 23:16 and the "firstfruits of the wheat harvest" in Ex 34:22 (cf. Nu 28:26–31; Dt 16:9–12). It always occurred on the first day of the week and fell seven weeks and one day after the Sabbath after the full moon of the Passover (14 Nisan). From the day after the Passover Sabbath to the day after the Pentecost Sabbath is "fifty days" by inclusive reckoning, counting both the first and last days. It would therefore be around the end of May to mid-June.

It should be remembered that there is a wide latitude of seasons in Palestine from the seacoast to the mountains to the Jordan Valley. This feast was a dedication of the wheat harvest to the Lord. Special sacrifices were specified. The fellowship offering was normally prepared without yeast. Here in v.17 it is different. It is the first part of the harvest prepared as a Hebrew housewife would prepare it. The "seven male lambs" and other offerings were to sanctify Israel and cleanse her anew for the new season's work and rejoicing.

All the males were to appear at the tabernacle; but, in this time when the harvest was beginning, they would not stay long. The NT antitype to this feast is Pentecost, which was, as a consequence, on Sunday, and was the day of the outpouring of the Holy Spirit in a new phase of God's saving work extending the harvest to the Gentiles also.

22 This rule is appropriate for a harvest festival. In all Israel's life, the poor in Israel were helped and protected. Christians should search their hearts to be sure they have a similar attitude toward the unfortunate in our day. There is much talk of the church's duty to the poor. It is obvious that in a time of famine, emergency, or tragedy, no Christian should withhold his means if he or she is able to help. Still, the NT examples and teaching emphasize the church's duty toward the poor *in the church* (Ac 6:1; 11:29; 24:17; 1Ti 4:9–10). The law on gleaning with mention also of the treatment of vineyards is stated in 19:9–10.

E. The Feast of Trumpets (23:23–25)

It is interesting that this ancient fall feast was not given the extra emphasis that its equivalent, the New Year (Rosh Hashanah), is given among Jews today. Neither was the New Year given the emphasis that it had in Babylon, where it was a week-long celebration. This feast was a one-day celebration with special sacrifices, and that was all. Actually, the phrase Rosh Hashanah occurs only once in the OT (Eze 40:1), where it is used of the "beginning of the year" (NIV) without reference to what month is in question; and it just as well could be in the spring. The Hebrew year began in the spring (Ex 12:2). The "turn of the year" of Ex 34:22 and the "going out of the year" of Ex 23:16 need not mean the "end of the year" but only the turn of the season (cf. below).

23–25 Every new moon in Israel began with a special celebration marked by blowing the trumpets (Nu 10:10; 28:11; Ps 81:3; et al.) and by offering special sacrifices (Nu 28:11–15). It was of some importance for business as well as for religious observances for the new month to be fixed definitely, and this announcement was made by the priests with the blowing of trumpets. Since a lunar month is twenty-nine and a half days long, there is some possibility for variation in the calendar. Probably, as in surrounding nations, the decision to start a new month was arrived at partly by observation, partly by calculation. It is not improbable that the beginnings of the months of Israel were integrated with the dates decided by the surrounding nations, at least in later years. It seems clear that the blowing of trumpets reechoed the signal across the hills of Palestine. It was helpful to know when the seventh month started since it included important religious festivals. The prescribed offering for the Feast of Trumpets is given in Nu 29:1–6.

F. The Day of Atonement (23:26–32)

26–32 The Day of Atonement has been discussed in connection with the ritual prescribed for it in Lev 16 (cf. Lev 16:1–34; Nu 29:7–11). It was to be a day of fasting. People were to remain in their houses and remember that on this day their high priest was to enter the Most Holy Place bearing the name of their tribe on his breastpiece. Verse 32 underlines the fact that any of the annual feasts could also be called a Sabbath. There seems to be no special reason why the tenth of the month was chosen for this Sabbath. It was a proper and convenient time for repentance and spiritual preparation for the Feast of Tabernacles of the following week.

G. The Feast of Tabernacles (23:33–44)

33–44 The Feast of Tabernacles (or Booths; cf. Ex 23:16; 34:22; Nu 29:12–40; Dt 16:13–17) is also called the Feast of Ingathering "at the end of the year" (Ex 23:16). As noted above, this does not necessarily mean the end of the calendar year—just as we have other years: school years, fiscal years, etc. The usual expression "turn of the year" always means "spring" (2Sa 11:1 = 1Ch 20:1; 1Ki 20:22, 26; 2Ch 36:10). The present Jewish new year starts in the fall, but the biblical text nowhere calls this Rosh Hashanah (head of the year). The biblical new year began in the spring. From these references some have concluded that there were two new years in Israel—spring and fall—but the fall new year is probably a later Jewish development.

Like Passover and the Feast of Weeks, Tabernacles was a pilgrimage festival when all the men were to appear at the tabernacle or temple. Of course, in many cases the whole family came. The offerings are detailed in Nu 29. A peculiar feature is that the burnt offering on the first day of the feast includes thirteen bulls and that each subsequent day the number is reduced by one until the last day, when seven bulls are offered (Nu 29:13–32). The other offerings stayed the same in number every day.

Autumn was a convenient time to bring an offering from the year's harvest. Even the grapes, olives, and dates would have been ripe by then. The weather would have been mild and clear, ideal for the temporary stay in booths. There is a problem in v.40 in the relation of fruit and branches. It is probable that eating the good fruit of fruit trees was part of the festivities of rejoicing during the eight days. The waving of the palms and branches, perhaps in processions, would be another part of the rejoicing. The branches were used in any case to make the booths (Ne 8:15–17).

The feast was a reminder of the Exodus from Egypt and the long trek to Sinai with the people living in tents. It would in future days be a reminder of the simple desert life when they walked with God at their head. The Hebrew name is Sukkoth, which in modern Hebrew is changed in pronunciation to Sukkos.

In contrast to the fast and repentance of the Day of Atonement, the Feast of Booths was an occasion of joy—a thanksgiving day (cf. Zec 14:16–19). Indeed, it is clear that when the Puritans proclaimed their Thanksgiving Day in New England, they had in mind the OT harvest festival.

H. The Care of the Lampstand (24:1–4)

1–4 In a sense this section, like ch. 8, is a complement to the book of Exodus. Exodus 25:31–40 has the directions for making the seven-branched lampstand; 37:17–24 records Moses' having made the lampstand. Then Ex 27:20–21 gives directions for the care of the light. Here in vv.1–4 these directions are to be carried out. The wording of this section (vv.2–4) is almost identical to that in Ex 27:20–21. This is not surprising if we recognize that Leviticus is part of the larger structure of the Pentateuch. Many times in Ex 35–40 the description of the building of the tabernacle and its furniture is almost word for word the same as the instruction for its building in Ex 25–29.

The fire on the altar was never to go out. But it seems from the phrase "from evening to morning" and the similar one in Ex 27:21 that the lamps were to burn every night but not through the day. This arrangement may explain the statement in 1Sa 3:3: "The lamp of God had not yet gone out," i.e., it was toward morning but still dark. On the meaning of "Testimony," see comment on 16:13.

I. The Bread of the Presence (24:5–9)

5–9 This is the only place where the details of the offering of the bread of the Presence are given (cf. Ex 25:30; 40:23). It was the priests' grain offering. It was set out before the Lord every Sabbath and eaten at the end of the

week. Presumably it was hard baked and would not spoil in the interim. On the other hand, the text does not strictly say that the bread would stay on the table a week. It may have been taken off at a convenient time—after the Sabbath was over—and eaten by the priests. This is the background of the famous incident when David ate the consecrated bread (1Sa 21:6; cf. Mt 12:4).

"Two-tenths of an ephah" is about four quarts of flour (the ephah being about twenty quarts), which seems to be an impossibly large amount for each loaf or cake. Actually, the Hebrew says "two-tenths" to each cake. The measure is not specified. Probably some smaller measure like the seah (five quarts) or the omer (four pints) is intended. The flat, round, pancakelike loaf of bread would not take very much flour.

"Along each row put some pure incense" is a better translation than KJV's "upon each row." The incense was not eaten, for it is not edible. It was burned with the "memorial portion" of the bread. The meaning of the ritual, like the ordinary grain offering, surely includes communion as the bread was eaten before the Lord in the Holy Place.

VIII. Identical Laws for the Stranger and the Israelite (24:10–23)

10–23 Not much of Leviticus is narration. The whole year's stay at Sinai is told in a few chapters in Exodus and Numbers. But the incident of the son of Shelomith gave rise to legislation and therefore finds a place in Leviticus. His offense was plain and called for execution, just as if he had been an Israelite. His father was one of the mixed multitude who went out with the Israelites, probably because he had married a woman of the tribe of Dan.

Just what the crime was is hard to say. It may well have been more than thoughtless profanity. The Hebrew does not have the Tetragram (*YHWH*, "Lord"; GK 3378) here at v.11 or at the end of v.16. It is, however, at the beginning of v.16. Clearly the sacred Name is intended. The word "curse" (GK 7837) is used when Balak hired Balaam to curse Israel so that he might conquer the nation. The man may have engaged in some curse procedure to injure his opponent by a kind of hex in the name of the Lord, or it may have been an angry cursing of the Israelite man and his God. Blasphemy, of course, was strictly forbidden and punishable by death. The man was stoned.

The decision in the case established the principle that one who lived in Israel's company was counted as an adherent of their faith. The alien already had been made subject to Israel's laws of offering and cleanliness (17:8–15). Likewise, the alien enjoyed the protection of the law (Ex 23:9). But the sojourner who blasphemed would have to pay the extreme penalty.

The stoning of the blasphemer is taken as the occasion for the summation of the principles of justice. Here again the principle of lex talionis or retaliation is stated as a form of justice. The principle similarly appears in Ex 21:23–25 and Dt 19:21. Christ quoted the law in Mt 5:38–42 and seems to have opposed it, though he was actually not contradicting the OT but was denouncing the Pharisaic use of these verses to justify personal revenge.

It is another question whether this law was taken literally or is an emphatic statement of the principle that the punishment must fit the crime. If a man killed a beast, his own beast was not killed (v.21). There is no example in the OT of a judge exacting literally an eye for an eye. The usual penalties of Hebrew law were capital punishment for a limited number of serious offenses and fines and restitution for the remainder. There were no prisons in the early days, and none is mentioned in the Pentateuchal legislation. Apparently we have here an emphatic legal idiom meaning that the punishment must be commensurate with the offense.

IX. Laws of Land Use (25:1–55)

There are three subdivisions to this section: the sabbatical year, the Jubilee, and the laws of indebtedness. The basis of the land laws God gave to Israel is his statement that "the land is mine" (v.23). When Joshua conquered Palestine, the land was divided by sacred lot, not secured by individual military prowess. The people, therefore, could not sell their land. Society was agricultural; and the farms belonged, under God, to the people in perpetuity. The question was, How do you keep such a system working? The constant tendency is for the rich to increase their holdings at the expense of the poor. To obviate this danger the Lord instituted a land reform of return to the old homestead every fifty years. Actually, the Jubilee was one of the first land reforms known in history.

The sabbatical year likewise was a humane and advanced social program. Imagine all debts forgiven and slaves released every seven years! Ingrained into Israel's laws and faith was a concern for the poor and unfortunate. It is observable in many of the laws already noticed and is made most emphatic in this chapter. It is not by accident that v.10 of this chapter is the motto on the Liberty Bell that hangs in front of Independence Hall in Philadelphia, Pennsylvania.

A. The Sabbatical Year (25:1–7)

1–7 The sabbatical year is mentioned also in Ex 23:10–11 and Dt 15:1–18. In the former passage, however, it is described as a year to leave the land fallow (as here in Lev 25) without the year being specifically named. In the Deuteronomy passage the year is described as a year of canceling debts and freeing slaves, not as a year of rest from the tillage of the land. However, in Ex 23:11 the NIV has "let the land lie unplowed." It appears from the combination of these two ideas that the seventh year was both a fallow year for the land and a year of canceling debts. For the further matter of liberating slaves, see the Jubilee below.

As far as Moses knew at this time, the occupation of Canaan would begin in a few months, and Israel would begin this program of land tenure at once. Though Israel was in the wilderness, she was looking toward a settled condition within a year, similar to what they had known in Egypt—without the slavery! The adoption of such a law does not imply that the legislation is late, long years after the Conquest. Indeed, v.2 says it is a law adopted to cover future circumstances.

The terminology "the land itself must observe a sabbath" apparently comes from the weekly Sabbath that was already in force. The emphasis of the Sabbath was the resting. The land "I am going to give you" (notice the proprietorship) will have its rest as well. Presumably no one then knew why this would be good for the land. Principles of crop rotation were not known, and God did not give them such advanced wisdom. But he did give them the idea of the land lying fallow, and he gave it religious sanction. Seemingly no other nation had any custom like this.

Verse 5 at first appears to contradict v.4. The solution seems to be that there is to be no normal work of harvest or grape-gathering that would involve servants and include storage. It was all right to eat and gather directly from the fields (v.11), but regular harvest work was forbidden. The idea was twofold. First, the produce of the sixth year would be so abundant because of the Lord's blessing that there would be a surplus. Second, the natural produce of the land would feed the poor (Ex 23:11). It would even give wildlife a chance to repopulate itself. The natural crop would be public property.

There is an additional reason for the sabbatical year that does not appear in this chapter. In the Feast of Booths of the sabbatical year, the law was to be read to the people. The whole nation was to have a short-term Bible institute (Dt 31:10–13). There would be opportunities for other instruction during the rest of this vacation year.

B. The Jubilee (25:8–34)

8–12 The word "Jubilee" (GK 3413) means "blowing the ram's horn," which was done in announcing the year. Thus the root occurs also in the name Jubal, the father of musicians (Ge 4:21). The identifying name *Jubilee* occurs only in Leviticus and in Nu 36:4. But the idea of release of those enslaved for debt occurs, not only at v.10, but also at Isa 61:1; Jer 34:8, 15, 17; and Eze 46:17. From this word the idea of celebration has come into English, especially the celebration of a fiftieth anniversary.

In v.8 the Hebrew is "seven sabbaths" of years, not "seventy sevens" as in Dan 9:24–27, though there too the word "seven" is used for a sabbatical-year period. Probably it was well that the announcement came "on the Day of Atonement," that solemn day of contrition. Otherwise many a hard-hearted, rich Israelite would have refused the obligations of the release. Indeed, the Jubilee and sabbaticals were not always observed (2Ch 36:21). It was suggested above that the new moon trumpet reechoed through the land as others took up the signal of the start of a new moon. Here, clearly, there was such an arrangement for the word to get around.

It seems rather impractical to have had two fallow years in succession, namely, the forty-ninth and the fiftieth, though, of course, God could have simply compounded the blessing for the forty-eighth year. A suggestion to relieve the problem comes from the Book of Jubilees. This book, written perhaps about 200 B.C., is a reworking of Genesis with every event dated. The dates are counted from Creation and are given in terms of jubilees, sabbaticals, years, months, and days. But the Jubilees are only forty-nine years long. This may have been a mistake on the part of the author of Jubilees, or it may give a clue to a better translation of v.10. Just as seven weeks from Sunday to Sunday is called fifty days by inclusive reckoning in 23:15–16, so in the present sense the last of the forty-nine years might be called the fiftieth year by inclusive reckoning.

"To proclaim liberty" for the slaves was characteristic of every sabbatical year. The return to the family homestead was a special feature of the Jubilee. The word for "liberty" (GK 2002) is used in Jer 34:8–17 of the freeing of slaves in the sabbatical year. The inference is as suggested above, that the seventh sabbatical year was the Jubilee.

13–17 The arrangement for buying or selling considering the number of years since the Jubilee was simple. A field that could be possessed forty years before the Jubilee was worth more than one that would be possessed only ten years. A man might speculate in land for temporary advantage, but no family could be permanently disadvantaged. In all this social legislation, successful operation really must proceed on the basis of the cooperation of the citizens. And Israel's regard for the poor was supported by the knowledge that the Lord is God and that he has respect for the poor (Ex 22:27).

In a sense Israel had a kind of communism. The wealth was partially redivided every few years. But it is unfair to call this communism, just as it is inaccurate to call the communal living of the early church communism. It was a communal sharing that works well in a family where all have the strongest ties of love and interest. Even in families the system breaks down if the common bond is not there. Israel, like the early church, was a community of people united in worship of the true God and sanctified in him. In times of revival, at least, the bulk of Israel's citizens would have been God-fearing men and women who earnestly desired to obey God's law.

18–28 The success of laws such as these depended on the people's obedience; but the system still would not work except for the special blessing of God, who owned both the land and the people and had his sovereign purposes for both. Verse 21 underlines the importance of the providential blessing of God. It was doubtless good for the land to lie fallow one year. God would bless an obedient nation with rains, and pests would cease under his hand. Unfortunately the nation turned to other gods, and God vacated the land until it had "enjoyed its sabbath rests" (2Ch 36:21).

Verses 23–24 spell out the details of the Jubilee. There are certain exceptions and special regulations. The NIV's "must not be sold permanently" presents well the idea of the Hebrew text. This law of land reform is perpetual, but the land when sold was to be sold for a limited time only, not permanently. Not only was the land to return to its original family in the Jubilee, but a man who had been forced to sell his land out of necessity could buy it back at any time that he could raise the money. If his near kin could do it, he should. If the man's fortunes increased, he could do it himself (cf. the book of Ruth).

29–31 To "refund the balance" is to pay back the price of the field at the later date, which would be less than the price at the earlier date. The translation "balance" is more accurate than the RSV's "overpayment" or KJV's "overplus."

The city is different from the country. To live in a walled city was a privilege, not a right. Real estate in the walled city was at a premium. Its value was not just its land but the improvements in terms of house and fortifications. A man temporarily in need could sell the house and redeem it in a year, but after that time the buyer was protected. As explained in v.16, when a man sold his farm, he was selling so many crops until the Jubilee. In contrast to walled cities, the villages, which were unrestricted in extent, were counted in with their respective fields. They were released in the Jubilee.

32–34 The point of v.32 is that many, if not all, of the Levitical cities listed in Jos 21 were walled, where normally the right of redemption was limited to one year. Levites usually did not have any property outside these cities. Thus, except for this provision, the Lev-

ites eventually could have lost their cities and, therefore, all their holdings. But in these cities the Levites could redeem their property at any time.

The Hebrew of v.33 is somewhat involved, but the total meaning is clear. No Levitical house can be bought in perpetuity. It will go out in the Jubilee.

C. Protection of the Poor (25:35–55)

In this section there are three cases that are covered by the Mosaic law on loans (cf. Ex 22:25; Dt 23:19–20). Usually they have been treated as (1) loans without interest, (2) indentured servitude for debt, and (3) indentured servitude to an alien.

35–38 "Help him" is not a proper translation of the Hebrew, which literally says, "you shall seize him." The supposition is that a creditor has seized his debtor like a resident alien while he works off the debt. While the debtor was working off the debt, he himself served as a pledge for its payment, and no further interest or second interest could be charged. That would be "excessive" interest or usury. Verse 36 is a conclusion to v.35. If you seize him, you will not make further charges but must treat him like a brother. The implication is that it is wrong to treat him like a resident alien. After enslavement no further interest should accrue. Otherwise the poor man could never work off his debt. The word "interest" (GK 5968) is from the root "to bite." The rate of interest mentioned in Ne 5:10–11 is 1 percent—probably 1 percent a month.

Verses 36–37 do not forbid a loan to the poor man, for Ex 22:25–27 pictures a loan to a poor man with his garment as collateral. (Or was it really not collateral but a token that was taken before witnesses and restored promptly?) The passage in Dt 24:10–13 on pledges specifies that the creditor could not enter a house to choose the pledge he desired. The pledge chosen by the borrower must be accepted by the creditor, then recorded and restored promptly. In case of default, temporary enslavement would result. It seems strange in such a context to assume that no interest at all could be charged. But in any case, no excessive interest could be charged— interest beyond the usual regulations. The poor were to be protected.

39–46 The situation in v.39 is similar to that in v.35, only more extreme. The two verses begin with exactly the same words. In this instance a man has no credit to obtain a loan. His case is hopeless, and he takes the initiative. But he has his rights; he is not a slave. "A hired worker or a temporary resident" is perhaps better translated "resident laborer," i.e., not a resident alien.

The notice "until the Year of Jubilee" would apply equally well to case 1 of v.35, if that man's debt were not worked off before the Year of Jubilee. The mention of "resident laborers" brings up the contrasting positions of "slaves." Hebrews could not be enslaved by their compatriots. Slaves of the nations were permitted, and these were not released in the Jubilee. The most that could be exacted of a brother Israelite was indentured servitude. Of course, slaves too had their rights. Indeed, a runaway slave was not to be returned to his master (Dt 23:15). This would tend greatly to affect a master's attitude toward his slaves.

47–55 "An alien or a temporary resident" who bought a Hebrew slave did so under the stipulations of Hebrew law. The redemption of such a slave was a kinsman's duty. Or the slave might grow rich and redeem himself. This says a good bit about the relative independence of such a slave. His time with his owner was counted like that of a hired servant. In any event, the slave with his children would be freed at the Jubilee. Of course, if a man died in slavery, his children would not be slaves forever. They would benefit by the Jubilee.

Verse 55 is remarkably like the thought of Col 4:1. All Israelites were God's servants. They therefore should be compassionate masters—an attitude that Christians should remember even though the institution of physical slavery is happily over.

X. Warnings Against Apostasy (26:1–46)

A. Conditions of Blessing (26:1–13)

This chapter has strong affinities with Dt 28–30 (cf. esp. Dt 28:1–14; 30:1–10). It is a solemn reinforcement of the preceding laws with an appeal to Israel to obey God's laws and so be blessed rather than to turn away to disaster. The warnings in Dt 28–30 are more extensive than the promises, but the chapters end with a reminder of God's enduring mercy and the ancient covenants he made with the patriarchs.

The conditions given here are only summarized. The things specified are avoiding idols, keeping the Sabbath, and revering the sanctuary (vv.1–2). Beyond that the broad statement is "Obey my commands" (v.3). The promises, which are emphatic and detailed, largely concern material blessings; but the crowning spiritual blessing—"I will walk among you and be your God, and you will be my people"—is included (v.12; cf. Jer 30:22; Hos 2:23; et al.).

The physical blessings and curses characterize Israel's establishment as a nation. Even in God's dealings with the patriarchs, the promised material blessings were largely not for the present. Abraham died only having seen the promises afar off (cf. Heb 11:13). He owned only a sepulcher in the Promised Land. Abraham grew rich, but Isaac probably grew poor; and Jacob certainly had a hard life. Material blessings such as favorable rains, health, peace, etc., were appropriate promises for Israel as a nation living in one area with unified culture, laws, and worship. In other situations the people of God shared the common lot of human beings. God sends his "rain on the righteous and the unrighteous" (Mt 5:45). Today when God punishes a nation with war, the innocent must suffer with the guilty.

1–5 The ban on idols is sharp and pervasive throughout the OT. The reason is plainly given in Dt 4:15–19. God has no form and is not a part of his creation. Any material god is less than God. The prohibition of idolatry was so emphatic that ancient Israel made no images of God, at least as far as archaeological evidence goes. The idols that Israel worshiped were of the heathen gods. The word for "idols" (GK 496) is a word of scorn ("worthless things"). The word for "image" (GK 7181) is a general word for any image constructed or sculptured of wood, stone, metal, etc. The word "sacred stone" (GK 5167) refers to a monumental stone stele or slab with or without inscription. Some such monuments apparently associated with the temple of Baal Berith in Shechem (Jdg 9:6, 46) have been found.

The word for "carved stone" (GK 74) is less certain but refers to some kind of sculptured figure. It may be added that the absence of idols was wonderful for the advancement of faith, though it is troublesome to the archaeologist. Much can be learned of the surrounding cultures' religion, history, and art by the carved work that often bears inscriptions. Palestine digs are sadly (or happily) lacking in these idolatrous materials.

As mentioned in the comments on ch. 23, the Sabbaths include the set feasts as well as the weekly Sabbath. The word "sanctuary" (lit., "holy place"; GK 5219)) is used many times in the OT from Ex 15:17 on and usually refers to the tabernacle or the later temple. Verse 2 repeats 19:30, but here it serves well as a summary of God's will for his worship.

Significantly, the first blessing mentioned is "rain." Palestine is water conscious. In those days farmers and housewives were totally dependent on the rain and the perennial springs. There are two views of the amount of rainfall in antiquity. The first argues that the climate in Palestine has greatly changed, while the other argues that it has not. Actually, Jerusalem has about the same average annual rainfall as London. But in Palestine the rain is all concentrated in the months from October to April. If the rains have a good spread, i.e., including early and latter rains, then crops grow well. Also forestation and irrigation can conserve the water for a longer growing season. It was a very small matter for the Lord to give better rains and rains spread out in a better way so as to bless a faithful nation.

It would be quite a harvest that would last from June to September! Actually, with ancient methods of harvesting and threshing, this may not have been much hyperbole for a really good year (cf. Am 9:13).

6–8 There is a causal connection as well as a providential connection here. Decent living and decent government to an extent produce peace. Immoral, reckless government invites wars, both civil and foreign. In the years from the division of the kingdom to the fall of Samaria, the two kingdoms had a diverse character. The northern kingdom openly encouraged idolatry and in its national life apostatized from the Lord. During those two hundred years, the northern kingdom saw nine different dynasties fight for the throne. In the southern kingdom, which in general maintained the faith, the dynasty of David continued with one small interregnum at the time of Athaliah. God often uses wars as an instrument of punishment (Isa 10:6).

Dangerous animals ("savage beasts"), except for snakes and scorpions, have not been much of a problem in Palestine for many years. In biblical times, however, both lions and bears are mentioned repeatedly. There must have been a somewhat different situation (cf. v.4 above). Egyptian pictures show pharaohs hunting lions where now there are only deserts. Such animals require lesser game for food. The lesser game require some grass and woodland. Palestine in ancient times clearly must have been different from what it is today, for "savage beasts" were a real danger to Israel. In fact, God promised to drive out the Canaanites gradually so that the dangerous animals would not multiply unduly (Ex 23:30).

The same sort of expression as "five of you will chase a hundred" is found in Dt 32:30. Of course, there is hyperbole here, but it is true even today that small things can turn the tide of history. Gideon's 300 men defeated 135,000 Midianites; Jonathan and his armor-bearer alone defeated a Philistine force. When David killed Goliath, all the Philistines fled. In ancient warfare, even more than in modern times, a little incident such as the death or prowess of a hero could turn the whole tide of battle. God promised the Israelites victory if they would remain faithful to him.

9–13 "Will keep my covenant" is literally "will cause to rise up my covenant." This is probably legal language. The covenant referred to in the present verse is probably the covenant God made with Israel on Mount Sinai. Verses 1–2 refer to prominent parts of that covenant. However, this chapter should not be pressed into a covenant-treaty mold, as has been proposed in recent covenant-treaty studies. There is no historical prelude; the commands or "stipulations" are brief if they can be found at all, nor are the copies specified, as is usual in treaties. The chapter is a logical presentation of the consequences of obedience or disobedience to God's law.

God promised to dwell among his people in the tabernacle spiritually, not materially. From the word for "dwelling place" (GK 5438) and its root (GK 8905) , the later Israelites developed a name for the presence of God in the Most Holy Place—the Shekinah.

The expression "I will walk among" is not to be literalized in this connection. It refers to life, fellowship, and behavior. Enoch, Abraham, and others were said to "walk with God." God would continually fellowship with his people if they obeyed his word; he would *live* among them. The thought repeats that of the promised dwelling at v.11. The promise "and be your God" is repeated in Jer 30:22; Eze 11:20; Hos 2:23; and Ro 9:26.

Ten times in Leviticus and over a hundred times in the rest of the OT, God's miraculous deliverance of Israel from Egyptian bondage is emphasized. The event made an indelible impression on the Hebrew mind and record. The expression "enabled you to walk with heads held high" (lit., "upright") is an interesting commentary on how the ancient mind regarded slavery—about as we do today.

B. Threatened Punishments (26:14–39) (cf. Dt 28:15–68; 29:18–28)

14–17 A long list of threatened punishments to Israel if they disobeyed God's laws follows (cf. Dt 28:15–68; 29:18–28). These punishments and the preceding blessing sound like the imprecations and benedictions of a Hittite treaty. Yet in this section the whole of a covenant-treaty structure is not easily observable. This should perhaps be a warning against too mechanical an approach to the covenant format. It was not always followed nor slavishly observed, and appropriate parts could be used alone for particular emphasis. The more extensive presentation of imprecations and benedictions is in Dt 28 and 30.

Similar words to "but if you will not listen to me" introduce the corresponding section in Dt 28:15, which adds "I am giving you today." Here we do not have the conclusion of a long sermon, as Deuteronomy was, but a code of laws and rituals. In one sense, all the legislation of Exodus and Leviticus is part of the covenant God ordained at Sinai. The summary was the Ten Commandments that were engraved in stone as a witness and testimony. The sacred chest that contained them was therefore often called the "ark of the covenant" or the "ark of the Testimony." The curtain separating the holy shrine where the ark was kept was even called the "curtain of the Testimony [or Covenant]" (24:3).

The word "covenant" (GK 1382) as used in such biblical phrases is somewhat like the word "contract" or "treaty"—only it was a

one-sided treaty imposed on the nation chosen for God's blessing. To break the covenant or contract meant not only to forfeit all God's promised blessings but to incur his curse. The word "covenant" as used in these biblical phrases is somewhat different from the theological formulation of "covenant" when the word is used in such contexts as "covenant theology." In such contexts the covenants of works and grace embrace a representative principle that some would and others would not find so extensively in God's dealings with his people.

The phrase "sudden terror" does not seem to require the idea of surprise but means "to be terrified" or "to be confused." The words "wasting diseases and fever" are used only here and in Dt 28:22. They refer to physical ailments. The Arabic equivalent of "wasting diseases" is the disease formerly called consumption—tuberculosis. Quite likely the words "that will destroy your sight and drain away your life" are not adjectival in referring to previous "wasting diseases." The normal result of fever is not to "destroy the sight." The words are participles and probably substantival in use: "a destruction of sight" and "a draining away of life."

Palestine was situated on the land bridge between the great powers of antiquity. And there were local enemies, too. The threat of enemy domination was very real. The Midianites of Gideon's day are likened to grasshoppers who devour everything.

Verse 17 is picked up by Pr 28:1. How different the situation if Israel were obedient (v.8)!

18–26 Verse 18 is a surprisingly rare usage of the number seven. It is apparently restricted to this chapter (vv.21, 24, 28) and is a threat of multiple punishment.

The expression "sky . . . like iron and the ground . . . like bronze," which refers to a rainless sky and dried ground, is used only here and in Dt 28:23, where the symbols of iron and bronze are reversed! Obviously they are figures of speech. No Israelite thought the heavens were solid metal. The Deuteronomy passage adds further description of the dryness of the ground.

Bronze is an alloy of copper and tin and was used early, but how early is hard to tell. ("Brass," used in KJV, was not much used until nearly the time of Christ.) The first bronzes were probably accidental, for tin and copper occur together in some minerals. Bronze is a practical metal. It can be cast and hammered easily and makes good hard tools and weapons. Its properties vary according to the amount of tin used.

Verse 19 is only the second mention of iron in the Bible. The first mention (Ge 4:22) is a special case and perhaps refers to meteoric iron or even an ironlike stone that first received the name. Nothing in the tabernacle was made of iron. A little iron was found in the tomb of the Pharaoh Tutankhamun (c. 1360 B.C.). Deuteronomy 3:11 mentions it in connection with Og's bedstead (which was probably a sarcophagus trimmed with iron). But the secret of successful iron-working and tempering into steel did not come into Palestine until about 1180 B.C., when the Philistines introduced iron weapons and implements and brought in the Iron Age (1Sa 13:19–22). This verse only refers to iron as a hard metal and would fit well the pre-Philistine period. The crop failure obviously would be because of a drought so harsh as to affect the trees. The roads would not be much traveled because of danger from wild animals and enemies.

The Hebrew of v.25 is emphatic. The sword will "avenge the vengeance" of the covenant. The broken covenant cannot be passed over by God without awful judgment. The Israelites will "withdraw into [their] cities" (a phrase that indicates a state of siege). In time of war people living in the countryside fled to the cities for protection. In the crowded cities hunger and pestilence took their awful toll. "Ten women will be able to bake your bread" indicates that there would be many people but very little bread to go around. Every crumb would be weighed and conserved, and still people would go hungry.

27–35 The horrors of ancient sieges are matched perhaps only by the modern siege of Leningrad in World War II. There also cannibalism occurred. There are biblical references to these horrors in the sieges of Samaria (2Ki 6:28–29) and Jerusalem (La 4:10). Josephus (*War* 6.15–32 [3–4]) tells dreadful stories of the siege of Jerusalem by the Romans.

So horrible would be God's judgments that even the enemies around would be "appalled" (v.32). These references to captivity have been used to argue that this chapter could not have been written until after the Exile. It seems like a strange argument. By the same token, the blessings of vv.4–13 are so wonderful that one might think they could not have been written until after the Millennium! Actually, anyone in antiquity who could write a treaty of the Hittite suzerainty type could write such maledictions. The anguish of famine, conquest, and siege were well enough known in Moses' time.

"Enjoy its sabbath years" (v.34) is quoted in 2Ch 36:21 and combined with Jeremiah's prophecy (25:11) that the Captivity would last seventy years. There is no need to be mechanical and hold that the sabbatical-year provision was neglected for just 490 years. But it was evidently neglected for a long time. "Enjoy" is the regular translation of the Hebrew word used again at v.43.

36–39 One can argue that v.36 repeats v.17. The words "as though fleeing from the sword, and they will fall" may be parenthetical. The point is that the people will flee at the sound of a driven leaf—when none pursues. The wording is somewhat different from v.17, but the thought is similar. This section ends with an emphasis on their end and the unreasoning panic that God will put in their hearts. Proverbs 28:1 probably alludes to v.37 as well as v.17.

C. God's Perpetual Covenant (26:40–46)

God had promised the land of Palestine to Abraham, Isaac, and Jacob (Ge 15:18) by a covenant. God's promises are inviolable. God remembered the promise to Abraham as the people groaned in Egyptian bondage (Ex 3:15–17). The promise of vv.40–46 is similar to that in Dt 30, and there too God remembers the word he "swore to . . . Abraham, Isaac and Jacob" (v.20). Two other passages give somewhat similar promises. Solomon prayed that the Lord would hear the people's prayer of repentance when they would be in captivity (1Ki 8:46–53). Nehemiah prayed (Ne 1:8–9) that the Lord would remember his promise to Israel through Moses, probably referring to Lev 26 and Dt 30, that if they returned to God, he would regather them.

The 1 Kings and the Nehemiah passages, however, have an element not found in the Pentateuch. In his prayer Solomon included the idea that the dispersed people should pray toward the holy temple he had just built in Jerusalem. And Nehemiah's prayer assumes that God would regather Israel to the place where God's name dwelt, Jerusalem. Such ideas are proper in the later books, but in Moses' time Jerusalem had not yet been chosen for the sanctuary. It was not even conquered until David's day. This chapter therefore makes no mention of Jerusalem. Indeed, the only possible mention of Jerusalem in the whole Pentateuch is in Ge 14:18.

40–45 Confession is essential if we would be rid of sin and right with God. The word in Dt 30:2 is "return to the LORD . . . with all your heart and with all your soul." The idea of the circumcised heart is thought to be characteristic of Deuteronomy and Jeremiah. And it is true that the phrase is found in Dt 10:16 and 30:6, as well as in Jer 4:4; but the Leviticus passage has the equivalent thought in negative expression and is in fact similar to Jer 9:25, which complains that Israel is uncircumcised in heart like the heathen round about.

Actually, God's law never emphasized the merely external, though there was far more of the external in the OT than in the NT. Proverbs 23:26 expresses the eternal desire of God in the words, "My son, give me your heart." Circumcision was not just a physical mark of national origin. Paul says real circumcision is a matter of the heart (Ro 2:29; more lit., "circumcision . . . is of the heart").

In Lev 25:23 God said, "The land is mine," and he promised to remember his promises to the patriarchs to give them that land. Incidentally, the promises given here to Israel are not limited to the time of the judges or the Babylonian captivity. Paul declares that the promises to Israel and the fathers are "irrevocable" (Ro 11:28–29). But the Jews will not reinherit Palestine in peace and blessing until they return to the Lord.

Verse 36 stated that only some of the people of the Captivity will be left. But God will spare some and use their punishments to bring them back to him. A sad commentary on human nature is that in prosperity people tend to forget God, and he must often punish them to bring them back to him. The wise child of God will stay close to him in the first place and rejoice in the blessings without having to get the punishments.

46 The mention of the mutuality of the covenant is interesting, though it is also stated that God "gave" the laws. This verse is really a summary of the material of Leviticus, though some additional material on vows is given before Numbers begins with the order to break camp and move on toward the land of Canaan.

XI. Laws Concerning Gifts and Endowments (27:1–34)

It is difficult to understand this section fully because we know so little about the details of dedicating things to the Lord in ancient Israel (cf. Ex 34:19–20; Dt 23:21–23). The chapter discusses dedicated persons, clean animals, unclean animals, houses, and lands. Firstborn animals cannot be dedicated because they belong to the Lord already. Then comes an enigmatic paragraph on devoted things and people. These are apparently the spoils of certain types of war that belong absolutely to the Lord. This is followed by a brief section on tithes.

It seems clear that a person normally would dedicate to the Lord some person or thing, not an amount of money. It was not an age of money exchange; coinage was not yet invented. But often, if not usually, the person or thing given was redeemed, and its value in silver was given instead. The person given would presumably become a temple slave, so the values are those of a slave. They may be given in tabular form:

Age	Value of Male	Value of Female
1–5	5 shekels	3 shekels
5–20	20 shekels	10 shekels
20–60	50 shekels	30 shekels
60 plus	15 shekels	10 shekels

A silver coin of Seleucid King Demetrius II, bearing the dating formula for 144 B.C. A coin like this may have been used to pay the necessary temple tax at that time. Courtesy of the Tell Gezer Excavations, 1972.

We may *not* conclude from these figures that women were considered of less worth in the OT. It is merely that adult males were more capable of and valuable for the heavy work of the tabernacle. Note that a bride was purchased in ancient Israel; a groom cost nothing! This proves nothing! Also, the value of a slave, male or female, gored to death by a vicious ox is thirty shekels (Ex 21:32).

The "devoted" (GK 3051) things and persons mentioned in vv.28–29 are quite different. These are not things vowed to the Lord by an individual but spoils of war devoted to destruction by the Lord. The best-known examples are the spoils of Jericho (Jos 6:24) and of the Amalekites of Saul's day (1Sa 15:3–9). Such spoils and captives could not be redeemed, sold, or ransomed.

Numbers 18:14 is in line with this interpretation. At first sight it might seem that the devoted thing there promised to the priests is the firstborn of man or beast mentioned in v.15. But actually there is in this section of Numbers a list of items to be given to the priests. First-ripe fruits are mentioned in v.13. Devoted things under the ban come next as another category; then come firstborn animals and men. There is therefore no problem between the Numbers statements and the Leviticus laws that devoted things, animals, or men may not be redeemed; that firstborn animals may be redeemed; and that it is obligatory that firstborn men must be redeemed (Ex 13:13; Nu 18:15–16). The redemption price of firstborn men is five shekels of silver according to Nu 18:16, which is the valuation of a male up to five years of age according to Lev 27:6.

1–8 The rendering "special" (GK 7098) is strange. The underlying word is used many times to mean "wonderful" or even "miraculous"; but here and in Nu 15:3, 8, it is used in the sense of making a vow that is special or particular. Nothing in the contexts of these verses indicates that this type of vow was out of the ordinary. It was just the special reaction of a consecrated heart to the goodness of God. The LXX has "whoever shall vow a vow." The Hebrew word order differs a little from the English: "a special vow in valuation of persons." The presence of the word "valuation" or "equivalent value" in this connection suggests that a common practice was to

give the money equivalent, not the person, for the tabernacle service. It was otherwise when Hannah vowed to give her son to the Lord (cf. 1Sa 1). There was no thought of redemption there. On the other hand, Jephthah's vow (Jdg 11:32–40) was very different and was an evil vow that never should have been made or kept.

On "fifty shekels of silver" see the table of values of a dedicated tabernacle slave given above.

Apparently "if a man is too poor" refers to a man who wanted to make a vow but was too poor to redeem the person (slave or child?) whom he had vowed. In this case the priest was not to take the one who made the vow as a slave in lieu of the money but was to reduce the evaluation to what the man could afford.

9–13 In the case of clean animals, the vow of an animal was supposed to be final. The case was quite different from the dedication of men. A man might dedicate to the Lord the next male sheep born in his flock. If so, he should give it regardless of whether it looked especially good or bad. And if he tried to exchange it for another animal, both animals would be forfeited.

The "unclean animal" might or might not be given to the tabernacle. There was a need for such animals. Priests used donkeys, too. But such an animal could be redeemed. It is not clear why the animal was valued by the priest if the animal, and not the monetary equivalent, was actually being given. Perhaps the priest's evaluation would be a factor in the worshiper's decision whether or not to add 20 percent and redeem the animal.

14–15 The law for dedicating a house is similar to that for an unclean animal. Notice that if the man adds 20 percent and redeems the house, "the house will again become his." Otherwise the house is the property of the tabernacle. Nothing is said about the house going out in the Jubilee. Probably this case applied to houses in fortified cities that were sold absolutely (25:30).

16–21 The law for other land acquired by purchase is given in vv.22–25. Land values were determined by formula depending on the area of what we would call tillable land. Rock outcroppings, ravines, etc., did not count. The area that would normally be sown by a homer of barley (about six bushels) cost fifty shekels. Modern planting calls for about a bushel and a half of seeds per acre, which would mean that land values would be fifty shekels for four acres of arable land—twelve and a half shekels per acre.

"The priest will determine the value." For instance, if twenty-five years had passed since the last Jubilee, the value of the land would be reduced by half. If a man had redeemed a field by paying an extra 20 percent, the field would be his. But if he gave it to the tabernacle without redeeming it, it would be an irrevocable gift. Also, the gift would be irrevocable if he had promised it eventually to the tabernacle but had sold it to another person until the Jubilee. When it went out in the Jubilee, it would then not revert to the owner but to the tabernacle to which it was promised. By this method the tabernacle lands could greatly increase over the years. Whether they did or not, we cannot tell. Such increase of church properties was a great problem in late medieval times.

22–25 It was impossible for anyone to dedicate perpetually to the Lord a part of some other family's inheritance. Perhaps his own line of heirs might run out, and he could properly give his own land. But bought land must revert to its owners at the Jubilee, and even the tabernacle could have no claim on it. "The sanctuary shekel" was an established weight. Present-day governments have effective control over weights and measures to keep them standard. Such standardizing in antiquity was difficult. There are many references in the OT to the sin of using false weights and measures.

26–27 The principle that "the firstborn already belongs to the LORD" is first stated in Ex 13:2. God had killed the firstborn of men and animals of the Egyptians but had spared the firstborn of the Israelites. Therefore, he claimed a special ownership of the firstborn. The firstborn of men and animals that could not be offered were to be redeemed (Ex 13:13). All the firstborn of clean animals were to be the Lord's (Ex 13:12). In consequence of this principle, the clean firstling was already the Lord's and obviously could not be given by a vow.

Verse 27 adds another option to Ex 13:13. There it is said that every firstborn donkey should be redeemed with a lamb. Here it says that the animal may be redeemed with its money value plus 20 percent, or, if not redeemed, the priest may take it and sell it. The law in Ex 13:13 says that if a man does not redeem it, he must break its neck. That is, the owner cannot keep the animal in any case. The law in Leviticus is in full agreement; the animal, if not given to the Lord's work, must be redeemed either by a lamb (Ex) or money (Lev), or it must be killed.

28–34 See the discussion on devoted things at the introduction to this chapter. The word for "devoted thing" (*herem*; GK 3051) has the curious double usage of referring to the totally holy and the totally evil. It is used especially of the holy war of conquest of Canaan that put the spoils of war "under the ban," as it is sometimes translated. The spoils of Jericho, for instance, that were perishable were devoted to the flames (Jos 6:17, 21, 24). The spoils that could stand the fire belonged absolutely to the Lord. This principle in the Conquest kept the Israelites from fighting for the sake of the spoils, as was so often done in ancient warfare. The individual got no personal reward for his fighting.

The "tithe" (GK 5130) belonged to the Lord. It also could not be dedicated by a vow, though that point is not raised here. The tithe of grain and fruit was sufficiently uniform to be redeemed by adding 20 percent. Perhaps also this provision was used because some fruits were too perishable to transport to the tabernacle.

Some animals are strong and healthy; other are scrawny and poor. An unscrupulous herdsman could easily have given to the Lord the worst, as the priests did later (cf. Mal 1:8). Or an overzealous herdsman could injure his own flock by always giving the best breeders to the tabernacle. The Lord gave a wise provision that every tenth animal regardless of its condition should belong to the Lord.

This last chapter adds a footnote, as it were, to the main body of laws concluded in ch. 26. There were yet a few more laws to be given at Mount Sinai that were included in the early chapters of Numbers, but this section is concluded by the formula that had been used with variation before (7:38; 25:1; 26:46). The opening verses of Numbers begin the directions preparing for the march from Sinai to the Promised Land.

The Old Testament in the New

OT Text	NT Text	Subject
Lev 5:11	Lk 2:24	Offering of the poor
Lev 11:44–45	1Pe 1:16	Holiness commanded
Lev 12:8	Lk 2:24	Offering of the poor
Lev 18:5	Ro 10:5; Gal 3:12	Living by the law
Lev 19:18	Mt 5:43; 19:19; 22:39; Mk 12:31; Lk 10:27; Ro 13:9; Gal 5:14; Jas 2:8	Love your neighbor as yourself
Lev 20:9	Mt 15:4; Mk 7:10	Cursing parents
Lev 24:20	Mt 5:38	Eye for eye
Lev 26:11–12	2Co 6:16	God living with us

Numbers

INTRODUCTION

1. Historical Background and Purpose

The book's name comes from its title *Arithmoi* in the LXX (the Greek translation of the Old Testament), through the Latin *(Numeri)*; this name is based on the census lists found in chs. 1–4 and 26. One Jewish designation for the book is taken from the fourth word in v.1, lit., "In the Desert"—a particularly apt description of its contents, for it describes what happened during the thirty-eight years of wandering in the desert after the Exodus.

The original recipients of the book were the people of Israel in the second generation from the Exodus, awaiting the command of God to cross the Jordan to conquer the land of Canaan. The book describes the affairs of the people of the first generation, but its teaching is for those who were about to enter Canaan.

The purpose of the book is to compel obedience to the Lord by the new community by reminding them of the wrath of God on their parents because of their breach of covenant; to encourage them to trust in the ongoing promises of the Lord as they follow him into their heritage in Canaan; and to provoke them to worship God and to enjoy their salvation. In other words, it is designed to encourage spiritual confidence on the part of the people who were about to leave the desert to cross over into Canaan.

2. Authorship and Date

The book of Numbers traditionally has been ascribed to Moses, the great prophet of God. This conclusion is based on (1) the statements concerning the writing activity of Moses (Nu 33:1–2; Ex 17:14; 24:4; 34:27; et al.); (2) the assumption that the Pentateuch is a unity and comes from one writer; (3) the excellent training of Moses in Egypt that would have prepared him for this great literary task (see Ac 7:22); (4) the involvement of Moses as the principal human protagonist in

the record of the deliverance and desert experiences of Israel; and (5) the NT citations that speak of Moses as the one responsible for the books of the Torah (Mt 19:8; Jn 5:46–47; Ro 10:5; et al.).

We may style the book of Numbers "The Memoirs of Moses in the Desert." The varied styles and seeming inconsistencies of the book may have been produced in part by its occasional nature in the lifetime of Moses. Further, this book may have received some editorial additions following the lifetime of Moses, though this material may have reached back to the time of Moses. Additions to the book under the direction of the Holy Spirit may have occurred at a later time, or the book may have been compiled by another hand using Mosaic material. This would also explain the origin of the Balaam story in chs. 22-24, much of which was outside Moses' observation (see comments). All in all, however, we take the position that the essential content of this book did come from Moses, the servant of the Lord, prior to the conquest of Canaan.

3. Theological Themes

a. The old and the new

The book of Numbers presents the concept of the chastening wrath of God on his own disobedient people. The entire generation that had been delivered from formidable foes by the direct intervention of the Lord, that had formed a holy community, and that had been allowed to participate in his holy worship lost their enjoyment of the Promised Land because of their rebellion against God's grace and their disbelief in his power to deliver them. Thus Numbers presents a sobering, chilling reality. The God of Israel was also a consuming fire—a wrath that extended equally to his errant children and to the enemy nations of Egypt and Canaan. Not even Moses was exempt from God's wrath because of his disobedience.

Yet in his wrath the Lord remembers mercy; a new generation arises to inherit the land. The association of the Lord's wrath and mercy, his anger and his love, is a marked feature of this book as part of the Law and the Prophets.

b. Balaam

No doubt thoughts came to a people who had experienced the miraculous hand of God but now sensed his wrath: Is God indeed finished with us? Is he done with the nation as a whole? Have we no hope? In one of the most remarkable sections of the Bible, the Lord worked providentially and directly to proclaim his continued faithfulness to his people, despite their continuing unfaithfulness. This section is the story of Balaam.

In Balaam we have the pagan counterpart to Moses the man of God. Balaam was an internationally known prophet, who thought that the Lord God was like any other deity whom he thought he could manipulate by mantic acts. But Balaam learned that an encounter with the God of Israel was fundamentally different from anything he had ever known. When he finally began to utter his words of cursing on the nation of Israel at the instigation of Balak, king of Moab, he found his mouth unable to express anything but blessings for God's people and the most ferocious cursings on their enemies. It is the blessing of God on Israel that is the heart of the book of Numbers.

c. Worship

The book of Numbers has a great deal to contribute to the theology of worship. The NT concept that in worship all things should be done in an orderly and fitting manner (1Co 14:40) finds its basis in Numbers. We also learn of pageantry and procession, festival and fasting, mandatory sacrifices and freewill offerings, restrictions and blessings. In it the ongoing purposes of God for his covenant people are reaffirmed. It contains important materials for the specific worship patterns of Israel, such as the Aaronic Benediction (ch. 6) and instructions on Passover (ch. 9). If God's people respond in faithfulness and obedience, he will fulfill his promises and his blessings.

But the book of Numbers also *is* the worship of God by Moses and those who align themselves with him. By God's grace it may become a book of worship for us as well.

d. Numbers

What seems to some to be the most embarrassing element of the book—the numbers that seem impossibly inflated for a small nation at the beginning of its existence—is its crown and glory. These numbers are a mark of God's blessing. They are a fulfillment of his covenant. They anticipate numbers of peoples who will be like the stars of the heavens, the sand of the seashore. The numbers extol the glory of God in his people.

4. The Large Numbers

a. The problem

The numbers of the tribes of Israel stated and implied in this book just seem to be far too large to be historically credible. If the numbers of the men who are mustered for war from the age of twenty and up actually add up to over 600,000, then the total populace would have had to be at least two million persons—perhaps considerably more! This does not seem to be an excessively large number for our own crowded days, but it seems to be nearly an impossibly large sum for Israel in the very beginning of its existence.

The mid-1988 estimate for the population of Israel was 4,400,000, roughly twice the size of the nation at the Exodus. Currently, the population of Israel is mixed between scattered rural settlements, small towns, and three large cities. As we look at the modern cities with their sprawling size and multistory buildings, we wonder how the ancient farmlands, towns, and cities might have accommodated such numbers. Since the testimony of the wicked Hebrew spies was an exaggerated report of the size of the cities, their towering walls, and hulking men—all the stuff of fear—the implication at the least is that the Canaanite population was significantly larger and more powerful than the approaching Hebrew populace (see Dt 4:38; 7:1). The more we think of them, the more these numbers boggle our minds.

Then we may wonder what the population of Canaan was in the biblical period. Since presumably the population of Canaan was as least as dense in the eighth century under Hebrew settlement as in the fifteenth century during Canaanite times, it is just not possible to imagine an invading force of Hebrews that might number several millios having any reason to trust in the Lord for the conquest of the land. By sheer numbers they would overwhelm the native population.

A well-worn problem in the large numbers of the families of Israel in the book of Numbers has to do with the growth from seventy persons to more than two million in just four centuries. Scripture assures us that the growth of the population of the Hebrew people was a dramatic outworking of God's grace, a fulfillment of his promise. The narrative of growth in Ex 1:7 is emphatic: "but the Israelites were fruitful and multiplied greatly and became exceedingly numerous, so that the land was filled with them." This unprecedented growth was in fulfillment of numerous promises of God to the fathers (see Ge 17:2, 6; 22:17; 26:4; 28:14; 35:11; 48:4). Moses is able to use the patriarchal phrase of abundance as he recounts his experience as their leader: "The LORD your God has increased your numbers so that today you are as many as the stars in the sky" (Dt 1:10; cf. Ex 32:13).

Yet there are counterindications to this immense size. One points to just two midwives in Ex 1:15—certainly some very overworked women in a nation so large! Another points to the rhetorical underplaying of the size of the nation in Dt 7:7: "for you were the fewest of all peoples." Another has to do with the sheer logistics of two million people or more crossing the Red Sea in one night and their organization and provision in the desert for a generation.

Now all this is possible within the wonder of the work of the Lord. We have no doubt of his ability to provide for two million or two billion persons. But we still wonder at these large numbers in terms of the lands and cities of the ancient world. Were the Canaanite cities of the Late Bronze Age sufficiently large to be a formidable threat to the millions of Hebrews about to descend on them from the desert? Would the ten spies have been so fearful of the residents of the land if they themselves represented a people so very large in numbers? And could the land of Canaan have absorbed such a huge company in biblical times, right at the beginning of Israel's experience? We do not doubt that the population of Israel under her great kings David and Solomon might have numbered one million. But we pause at the thought of more than twice that many persons right at the beginning of her history.

So there we have it: The numbers of the book of Numbers are just too large!

b. A suggestion

I suggest that the large numbers in the census lists are deliberately and purposefully exaggerated as a rhetorical device to bring glory to God, derision to enemies, and point forward to the fulfillment of God's promise to the fathers that their descendants will be innumerable, like the stars.

It appears that the figure given in the two census lists for the army of Israel may possibly be a magnification by a factor of ten. An army of about 60,000 men would fit the criteria of the region and the times. A rhetorical exaggeration by a factor of ten has much to commend it. It takes into account the "round" number nature of each integer. It fits in nicely with the approximation of 600,000 as a multiple of 50,000 times 12, the number of the tribes. It results in an army in excess of 60,000 men, with a total population of about 250,000 to 300,000. This sum seems to fit the requirements of the social, geographical, and political realities without diminishing at all the sense of the miraculous and providential care of God.

An army of 60,000 is not an insignificant force, but it was likely considerably smaller than the combined armies of the city-states of Canaan at the time. In this way the peoples of Israel must have seemed to be a "swarm" as they lived in Egypt, but they were still "the smallest of nations" when ranked with combined great world powers. This smaller number accords with the large (but not supernatural!) force that the Egyptian Pharaoh sent in pursuit of them to the Sea of Reeds. Six hundred chariots (Ex 14:7) is a considerable force and would surely be a death threat against the unorganized people of Israel. This approach also allows for the drama of the conquest of the book of Judges, where battles were won by the armies of Israel in league with the Lord, their Great Warrior. This smaller number fits as well for the failures to occupy the full land as that book also details. It also accords well with the well-known Mernepthah stele that records Israel as among the peoples of Canaan during his raid, which we may place during the period of the judges. A population of several million would have more of an impression on this pharaoh!

Again, this smaller number does not diminish the miraculous. It enhances it; for we confront now a cluster of miracles that we may embrace readily rather than shun from some sense of embarrassment, as some do! The supernatural increase of the people in Egypt, the crossing of the Red Sea in one night, the gathering of the people at Mount Sinai, their daily provision of food and water in the desert, their entry into the Promised Land—all miracles! Only the Lord could so provide for this vast number of people in this manner; and a population of over one-quarter million is indeed vast. But now we can envision a series of miracles that fits the geography, the topography, and the times. The "myth" of the Exodus becomes the history of redemption.

The principal objection that may come to the position I advance is the observation that the number 603,550 is in general agreement with the similarly large number in the second census in 26:51 (601,730); and it is in accord with other statements in the Torah of a population of about 600,000 men (see again, Ex 12:37; 38:26). We may observe that the same deliberate rhetorical function occurs in the second census. In fact, it is even more important that the new generation be regarded in the same significance as the first. The words of Balaam (Nu 23:10) emphasize the "mystique" of the immense numbers of Israel. But what to him was but "mystique" was to Moses nothing less than the power of God. As to the numbers in Exodus, they must be based on the numbers in the census lists of Nu 1:46; that is, the interpretation of the numbers in the book of Numbers has priority over the interpretation of these same numbers in Exodus. This means that the interpretation we derive in Numbers will work as well for the round figure of 600,000 in Ex 12:37. Exodus 38:26 is more difficult because of the very specific numbers used for weights (vv.25–31). Yet if the pattern of 600,000 (strictly 603,550) is established as the power number for Israel, then the payment of the redemption price would be rhetorically inflated to fit the established number. The "truth" of the passage is that there was the exact payment of one-half shekel for each of the numbered men in the census, whatever that exact number might have been.

The one problem remaining is the payment of the half-shekel in Ex 38:25–26. This 100 talents plus 1,775 shekels is the one number that does not easily arise from a purposeful tenfold increase. I suggest, with some temerity, that the numbers in this passage may have been inserted into the text of Exodus on the basis of the census of Nu 1–4. The number 603,550 in Ex 38:25 is certainly based on the census total in Nu 1:44. That is, once the factor of a tenfold magnification was established in Numbers, then the payment of the redemption price, to be consistent, would be presented in such a way as to agree with this larger number.

It appears to me that the numbers of the census are real figures. They are treated like real integers; there is no confusion of hundreds and thousands. Here are numbers that are internally consistent and coherent. Yet I propose that they may have been deliberately magnified by a factor of ten for rhetorical reasons. The promise was that the people of God would be in number like the stars. Six-hundred thousand must have seemed like an "astronomical" number in these early biblical times. Certainly the "real" number of 60,000 men was very large, particularly for the desert sojourn. But the 60,000 would still not be an overwhelming force for the task ahead of conquering the peoples of the land, who are seven in number and far more numerous than Israel. To have any success in their task, this army would need to have the help of the Lord along every step of their path. From the abortive battle in the first generation with the Amalekites (14:44–45) to their decisive victories a generation later with Arad (21:1–3) and the small kingdoms of Sihon and Og (21:21–31), these numbers fit the situation. Here is a seasoned army of approximately 60,000 men, ready to march across the (dry bed of the) Jordan and to take the ancient city of Jericho as the firstfruits of conquest in the land—an offering to the Lord.

The obvious objection one may bring—that people do not use numbers this way today—is not overwhelming. In ancient times numbers were used with deliberate exaggeration for rhetorical effect. The ancient Sumerian king list affords an example that long predates the time of Moses. In this list the reigns of kings from remote antiquity were vastly exaggerated, no doubt to indicate their tremendous importance. An even more common use of rhetorical language is in battle braggadocio and mottoes of heroes: "Saul has slain his thousands, and David his tens of thousands" (1Sa 18:7).

I am aware that some may regard the concept of "rhetorical use of numbers" as a departure from "literal interpretation." In fact, it is not. Literal interpretation of numbers includes understandings that extend from mathematical exactitude, through general approximation, to literary license. The only demand of literal interpretation (better, "normal" interpretation) is that the reader seek to find the use he or she believes the text itself presents and demands. It is an abuse of literal interpretation to insist that the way we use numbers in our digital and pocket-calculator age is the way that biblical persons ought to have used numbers in their day.

In summary, the book of Numbers is just that! It is a book that uses numbers to celebrate the work of the Lord! And in these numbers is his praise.

EXPOSITION

I. The Experience of the First Generation in the Desert (1:1–25:18)

The book of Numbers appears to be a bifid of unequal parts. The two censuses (chs. 1–4, 26) are key to understanding the structure of the book. The first census (chs. 1–4) concerns the first generation of the Exodus community; the second census (ch. 26) focuses on the experiences of the second generation, the people to whom this book is primarily directed. The former were prepared for triumph but ended in disaster. The latter had an opportunity for greatness—if only they would learn from the failures of their fathers and mothers the absolute necessity for faithfulness to the Lord despite all obstacles.

A. The Preparation for the Triumphal March to the Promised Land (1:1–10:36)

1. Setting apart the people (1:1–10:10)

As the book as a whole presents itself as a bifid of unequal parts, so chs. 1–10 also form a bifid of unequal sections: 1:1–10:10 records the meticulous preparation of the people for their triumphal march into Canaan; 10:11–36 describes their first steps under the leadership of Moses.

a. The census of the first generation (1:1–4:49)

(1) The muster (1:1–54)

(a) The command of the Lord (1:1–4)

1 The opening words set the stage for the chapter and, indeed, for the entire book. The phraseology "the LORD [Yahweh] spoke to Moses" presents a point of view that will be repeated throughout this book, a phrase that is important to the self-attestation of the divine origin of the book of Numbers. The expression "the Tent of Meeting" speaks of the revelatory and communion aspect of the tent. Other terms and phrases used for this tent in Numbers are "the tabernacle" (v.51) and "the tabernacle of the Testimony" (vv.50, 53). The term "tabernacle" points to its temporary and transitory nature; it is a movable, portable shrine, specially designed for the worship of God by a people on the move.

The first verse also gives a specific time notice for God's command to take a census of the nation. The book begins thirteen months after the Exodus. Israel had spent the previous year in the region of Mount Sinai receiving the law, erecting the tabernacle, and becoming a people. Now they were to be mustered as a military force and formed into a cohesive nation to provide the basis for an orderly march. The events of Numbers cover a period of thirty-eight years and nine or ten months, i.e., the period of Israel's desert wanderings. The second month in the Hebrew calendar corresponds roughly to our April. This pattern of dating events from the Exodus signifies its centrality in the experience of the people of God. Time will hence be measured from their leaving Egypt (cf. B.C. and A.D.). Time for Israel had its beginning with the Exodus, God's great act of deliverance of his people from bondage.

2 The Hebrew verbs "take" and "number" (v.3) are in the plural, indicating that Moses and Aaron were to complete this task together (see v.3), but the primary responsibility for the task lay with Moses. The purpose of this census was to form a military roster. Other reasons are (1) to demonstrate to the people the extent of God's faithfulness to the provisions of the Abrahamic covenant (Ge 12:2; 15:5; 17:4–6; 22:17); (2) to provide a clear sense of family and clan identity for the individual; and (3) to provide the means for an orderly march of the people to their new home in Canaan.

3 The point of the census was to prepare the armies of Israel for their triumphal war of conquest against the peoples of Canaan. Tragically, all the peoples who are numbered for military duty in this chapter—save only Joshua and Caleb—died without facing the war in which God demanded they become engaged.

Those mustered for war at the end of the desert period (ch. 26) are entirely different persons from those listed here. Except for Joshua and Caleb, the total died in the desert between slavery and liberty, between cursing and blessing, between there and here, with hopes dashed and desires never fulfilled. But in the new roster of Nu 26 there is a new generation, a new beginning, a new hope.

4 By having a representative from each tribe assist Moses and Aaron, not only would the task be more manageable, but the resultant count would be regarded as legitimate by all. No tribe would have a reason to suggest it was under- or over-represented in the census.

(b) The names of the men (1:5–16)

5–15 The names of these luminaries occur again in chs. 2, 7, and 10. Most are built by compounding one of the designations for God into a name that is a significant banner of faith in the person and work of God. The antiquity of the list of names is revealed by the fact that many are built on the names *El*, *Shaddai*, *Ammi*, *Zur*, and *Ab*. At a later time many names were based on the covenant name *Yahweh* because of the revelation of a new significance of that name in the Lord's encounter with Moses (Ex 3; 6) and his subsequent teaching of these truths to Israel.

16 The Hebrew word underlying the phrase "the men appointed" (GK 7924) is a technical term for representatives. Verse 16 is legal, formal, and precise in tone. Three phrases are used to give sanction to each of these leaders. Levi is not represented in this listing (see 1:47).

(c) The summary of the census (1:17–19)

17 The leadership of Moses and Aaron in the task is indicated here, as is their obedience to the Lord. This chapter is marked by a studied triumphalism. Numbering the tribes and mustering the army are sacred functions that prepare the people for their war of conquest, under the right hand of God, who is their warrior (see Ex 15:3).

18 The expression "twenty years or more" indicates that one who was under the age of twenty would still be regarded as a member of his father's house; one over the age of twenty was morally and civilly responsible.

19 Hebrew prose often gives a summary statement and then the details that explicate that summary. So here v.19 is the summary statement, and vv.20–43 give the details.

(d) The listings of the census by each tribe (1:20–43)

20–43 For each tribe there are two verses in repetitive, formulaic structure giving (1) the name of the tribe, (2) the specifics of those numbered, (3) the name of the tribe restated, and (4) the total enumerated for that tribe.

Certainly one of the most difficult issues in the book of Numbers concerns the large numbers of these lists (see the introduction for comments on this). The numbers for each of the tribes are round numbers; each unit is rounded off to the hundred (but Gad to the 50 [1:25]). The same numbers are given for each tribe in ch. 2, where there are four triads of tribes with consistent use of numbers, sums, and grand totals. Further, the total might have been rounded off to 600,000 but was not (see 1:46; 2:32).

Because the descendants of Levi were excluded from the census (see on v.47), the descendants of Joseph are listed according to the families of his two sons, Ephraim (vv.32–33) and Manasseh (vv.34–35). In this way (1) the traditional tribal number of twelve is maintained, and (2) Joseph is given the "double portion" of the ranking heir of Jacob (cf. Ge 49:22–26; Dt 33:13–17).

(e) The summary of the census (1:44–46)

44–46 There appears to be no textual difficulty in the Hebrew tradition in the soundness of this large number for the census of the fighting men of Israel. The mathematics of these numbers is accurate and complex—complex in that the totals are reached in two ways: (1) a linear listing of twelve units (1:20–43), with the total given (1:46); (2) four sets of triads, each with a subtotal, and then the grand total (2:3–32), which equals the total in 1:46. These numbers are also consistent with the figures in Ex 12:37–38 and 38:26. Further, they relate well to the figures of the second census in Nu 26 (601,730 men) at the beginning of the new generation. This large number of men conscripted for the army suggests a population for the entire community in excess (perhaps considerably in excess) of two million people.

Most importantly, the numbers of the people may also be regarded as a fulfillment of the particular blessing of God in the unusual growth of the people of the family of Jacob in Egypt. Exodus 1:7 describes in five Hebrew phrases the stunning growth of the Hebrew people in Egypt during the four centuries of their sojourn. The growth of the nation was God's benediction on them. But we are still drawn back to the problem of logistics in these large numbers. So I return to the position suggested above (see Introduction: The Large Numbers).

(f) The reason for the exclusion of the Levites (1:47–54)

47–49 The Levites, because of their sacral tasks, were excluded from this military listing; they were to be engaged in the ceremonies and maintenance of the tabernacle. Chapter 3 is given over entirely to their families, numbers, and functions.

50 As in Ex 38:21, the sanctuary is here called "the tabernacle of the Testimony." The "Testimony" (GK 6343) refers to the Ten Words written on stone tablets (Ex 31:18; 32:15; 34:29). These tablets were placed in the ark (Ex 25:16, 21; 40:20), leading to the phrase "the ark of the Testimony" (Ex 25:22; 26:33–34; et al.).

51–52 The Hebrew word rendered "anyone else" (GK 2424) is often translated "stranger," "alien," or "foreigner" (Isa 1:7; Hos 7:9). Thus a non-Levite Israelite was considered an alien to the religious duties of the tabernacle (see Ex 29:33; 30:33; Lev 22:12). The punishment of death is reiterated in Nu 3:10, 38; 18:7, and was enacted by divine fiat in 16:31–33 (see 1Sa 6:19). The sense of the Divine Presence was both blessing and cursing in the camp: blessing for those who had a proper sense of awe and wonder at the nearness of deity; cursing for those who had

no sense of place, no respect for the Divine Presence.

53 The tents of the Levites are detailed in 3:21–38. The encampment of the Levites around the tabernacle was a protective hedge against trespass by the non-Levites to keep them from the wrath of God; it was a measure of God's grace and a reminder of his presence.

54 In view of Israel's great disobedience in the later chapters, these words of initial compliance to God's word have a special poignancy. Israel began so well, then failed so terribly that her experience remains a potent lesson to all people of faith who follow them. Ending well is the desire.

(2) The placement of the tribes (2:1–34)

(a) Summary command (2:1–2)

1 This chapter begins with the announcement of the word of the Lord to Moses and Aaron. The more usual phrasing in the Torah is "And the LORD spoke to Moses, . . . saying," as in 1:1. The reference to Aaron along with his illustrious brother indicates the strong focus on the shrine of God's presence in the center of the camp. Aaron, as will be detailed in ch. 3, has the principal task of maintaining the purity, order, and organization of the work respecting the central shrine.

2 The Hebrew word order stresses the role of the individual in the context of the community; each one was to know his exact position within the camp. The repetition of the verb "will encamp" is for stately stress. Here is the meaning of the individual in Israel, and here is the significance of his family.

The people of Israel were a community that had their essential meaning in relationship to God and to one another. But ever in the community was the continuing stress on the individual to know where he belonged in the larger grouping. Corporate solidarity in ancient Israel was a reality of daily life; but the individual was also very important.

The dwelling of the tribes was in a circuit about the shrine but at some distance from it. The protective grace of God demands a sufficient distance to serve as a protective barrier from untoward approach to the Divine Presence and the judgment of God that such an approach might provoke. Too casual an approach betrays too minimal a reverence.

Each tribe had its banner and each triad (group of three) of tribes had its standard. Jewish tradition suggests that the tribal banners corresponded in color to the twelve stones in the breastplate of the high priest (Ex 28:15–21) and that the standard of the triad led by Judah had the figure of a lion, that of Reuben the figure of a man, that of Ephraim the figure of an ox, and that of Dan the figure of an eagle (see Eze 1:10; cf. Rev 4:7).

(b) Details of execution (2:3–33)

In ch. 1 the nation is mustered, and the genealogical relationships are clarified. In ch. 2 the nation is set in structural order, and the line of march and the place of encampment are established.

3–9 The eastern encampment. Judah, Issachar, and Zebulun were the fourth, fifth, and sixth of the six sons born to Jacob by Leah. It is somewhat surprising to have these three tribes first in the order of march since Reuben is regularly noted as Jacob's firstborn son (1:20). However, because of the perfidy of the older brothers (see Ge 49:3–7), Judah is granted pride of place among his brothers (Ge 49:8). Judah becomes the royal line of the Messiah (Ge 49:10; Ru 4:18–21; Mt 1:1–16).

Further, the placement on the east is significant. East is the place of the rising of the sun, the source of hope and sustenance. Westward was the sea. Israel's traditional stance was with its back to the sea and the descent of the sun. The ancient Hebrews were not a sea-faring people. For Israel the place of pride was on the east. Hence there we find the triad of tribes headed by Judah, Jacob's fourth son and father of the royal house that leads to King Messiah.

10–16 The southern encampment. Reuben, Jacob's firstborn son, leads the second triad, on the south. As one's stance in facing east has the south on the right hand, one senses a secondary honor given to the tribes associated with Reuben. He is joined by Simeon, the second son of Jacob by Leah. Levi, Leah's third son, is not included with the divisions of the congregation but is reserved the special function of the service of the tabernacle and the guarding of the precinct from the untoward actions of the rest of the community (see v.17 and ch. 3). This triad is completed by Gad, the first son of Leah's maidservant Zilpah.

17 The tent in the middle, representing God's presence within the heart of the camp, is a change from Ex 33:7–11. Here the tent is inside the camp, and all Israel is positioned around the tent. Here he is continually in their midst. There is a sense here of the progressive manifestation of the presence of God in the midst of the people. First he is on the mountain of Sinai; then he comes to the tent outside the camp; then he indwells the tent in the midst of the camp. One day he would reveal himself through the Incarnation in the midst of his people (Jn 1:1–18); and, on a day still to come, there will be the full realization of the presence of the person of God dwelling in the midst of his people (Rev 21:1–4).

This verse relates not only to the manner of encampment but especially to the manner of march. On the line of march the Judah and Reuben triads would lead the community; then would come the tabernacle with the attendant protective hedge of Levites (see 1:53); last would come the Ephraim and Dan triads. In this way there was not only the sense of the indwelling presence of God in the midst of the people, there was as well the sense that the peoples in their families and tribes were protecting before and behind the shrine of his presence.

18–24 The western encampment. The Rachel tribes were on the west. Joseph's two sons, Manasseh and Ephraim, received a special blessing from their grandfather Jacob; but in the process the younger son, Ephraim, was given precedence over Manasseh (Ge 48:5–20). Here, true to Jacob's words, Ephraim is ahead of Manasseh. Last comes Benjamin, the last-born son of Jacob, Joseph's younger brother, on whom the aged father doted after the presumed death of Joseph.

25–31 The northern encampment. Dan was the first son of Bilhah, the maidservant of Rachel. Asher was the second son of Zilpah, the maidservant of Leah. Naphtali was the second son of Bilhah. These, then, are secondary tribes and are positioned on the north side of the shrine of the presence, as it were, on the left hand. Here again we need to read these texts with the values of the people who first experienced them. Our orientation tends to be to the north, but Israel's orientation was to the east. In the final settlement of the land, these three tribes situated to the north of the shrine actually settled in the northern sections of the land of Canaan.

32–33 These verses conform to and summarize 1:44–53. The total number is the same as in 1:46, and the distinction of the Levites is maintained (see 1:47–53). The arrangement of the numbers of the tribes in triads, each with subtotals, and the grand total for the whole suggest the concept of the stability of these large numbers in the text.

(c) Summary conclusion (2:34)

34 These words of absolute compliance contrast with Israel's later folly. This verse also speaks of significant order—a major accomplishment for a people so numerous, so recently enslaved, and more recently a mob in disarray. The text speaks well of the administrative leadership of Moses, God's reluctant prophet, and of the work done by the twelve worthies who were the leaders of each tribe. It may have been the beauty of the order of this plan of encampment that led the unlikely prophet Balaam to say, "How beautiful are your tents, O Jacob,/ your dwelling places, O Israel!" (Nu 24:5).

(3) The placement and the numbers of the Levites and firstborn of Israel (3:1–51)

The notion of order continues to lace itself unabatedly through this chapter. These early chapters have about them a stately grace and a sense of presence. When the modern reader attempts to envision the magnitude of the task the Lord gave to Moses to bring order to an immense number of people who were so recently slaves and now so newly free, the resulting sensation is one of overwhelming burden. But these chapters do not speak of burden at all but have about them a sense of calm control—the control of God himself.

(a) The family of Aaron and Moses (3:1–4)

1–2 At first blush the wording "the family of Aaron and Moses" seems out of order because normally Moses is placed before Aaron. But the emphasis is correct: it is the family of Aaron that is about to be described. Aaron's wife was Elisheba, the daughter of Amminadab and sister of Nahshon, prince of the tribe of Judah (see Nu 1:7; 2:3), and the mother of the four sons noted in this chapter (see Ex 6:23).

The accentuation indicates that Aaron may still have been in grief for his firstborn son, Nadab. The accents lead to the following punctuation (lit.): "Now these are the names of the sons of Aaron: the firstborn, Nadab; also Abihu, Eleazar, and Ithamar." Nadab is given double "honor," being identified as the firstborn, and the accents set his name off from those of his brothers.

3 Exodus 28:41 records God's command to Moses to anoint his brother, Aaron, and his sons as priests of the Lord (see Ex 30:30; Lev 8:30). This solemn act gave recognition of a special consecration to the Lord and a particular knowledge on their part that they were

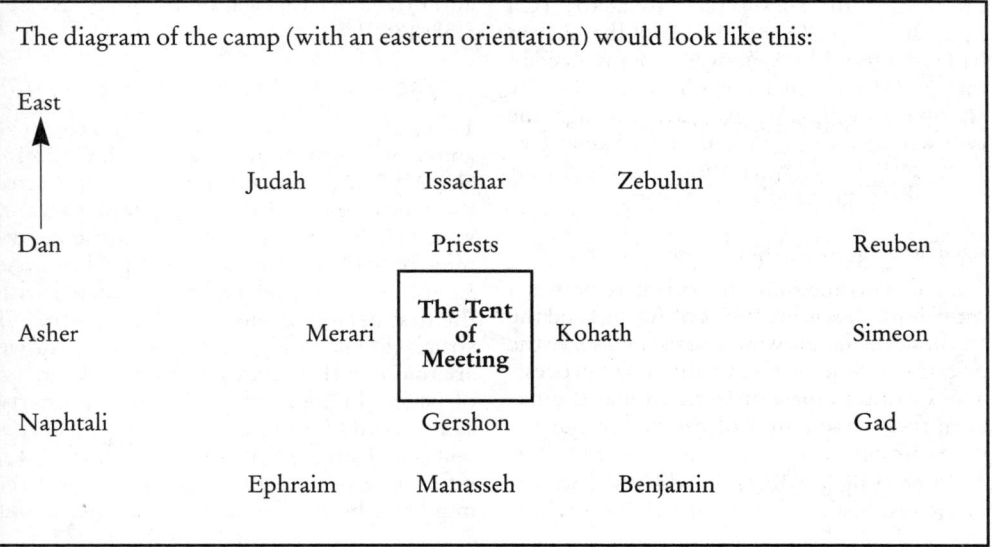

The diagram of the camp (with an eastern orientation) would look like this:

East

	Judah	Issachar	Zebulun	
Dan		Priests		Reuben
Asher	Merari	The Tent of Meeting	Kohath	Simeon
Naphtali		Gershon		Gad
	Ephraim	Manasseh	Benjamin	

no longer ordinary—they were now special to God. This anointing led naturally to being ordained. The Hebrew idiom "who were ordained" literally means "to fill the hand" (Heb. of Ex 32:29). The hands of the anointed were filled with a sense of the presence of the divine mystery. These were men of moment, servants of God.

4 Nadab and Abihu used fire that the Lord had not commanded (Lev 10:1). The pain of this account is strengthened by its brevity and mystery. We are left at a loss to explain their motivation, just as we do not know the precise form of their error. Because of the prohibition of wine and beer among the priests in their priestly service in Lev 10:8–11, these sons of Aaron may have committed their offense against God while in a drunken state.

Verse 4 states the matter of the death of these errant priests of the Lord succinctly: "[They] fell dead before the LORD." More fully: "Fire came out from the presence of the LORD and consumed them, and they died before the LORD" (Lev 10:2). This suggests a bolt of lightning (cf. 1Ki 18:38). There is a certain sense of poetic justice in the fact that these wicked priests who used unauthorized fire in the worship of the Lord were themselves destroyed by fire from his presence. Nadab and Abihu's fate is made even sadder in that they did not leave sons after them to continue their names among the priestly rolls in Israel. When they died, their story was over. Each time they are mentioned in the Bible, it is with sadness (cf. Nu 26:61; 1Ch 24:2). It is also the mercy of God that Aaron had two other sons who were not involved in the perfidy of their brothers. Hence the Aaronic priestly line extended through the two younger sons, Eleazar and Ithamar (see 1Ch 24:1–4), who continued to minister throughout the lifetime of Aaron.

(b) The duties for the Levites (3:5–10)

5–8 Clear distinctions are made here between the priestly house (the sons of Aaron) and the Levites. The latter were to assist and serve the priests—and the whole nation in the process. The Levites come out from among the nation; they were a part of the nation but are now distinct.

Interestingly, Moses is addressed in v.5. He is responsible for the nation as a whole

and, hence, for the faithful obedience of the Levites in their service of the priestly house of Aaron. Moreover, the tribe of the Levites was to be "brought near," terminology for the approach of the Divine Presence. Only Moses had an open invitation to draw near to God in a direct manner. Now he is presented with the task of drawing these other ministers near to their work before the Lord. This work consisted of service to Aaron and the guarding of the ministry relating to him and the whole congregation. Moreover, they were responsible for the tasks of moving the furnishings of the tabernacle at times when the camp was on the move.

The key to the work of the Levites may be in the words "perform [GK 9068] duties for him." The basic meaning of the Hebrew is "to keep watch," "to guard." Hence the Levites were to guard the holy things from foolish people and to care for the holy things when the people were to be on the move.

9 That the Levites are subsidiary to the priests is made quite clear ("wholly given"). It appears that the issue here is service to Aaron (and through him to the Lord); in 8:16 the service is to the Lord.

10 The warning of the death penalty of 1:51 is repeated. The Hebrew term is literally "stranger," i.e., anyone lacking authorization. Service at the tabernacle may be done only at the express command of God. If the sons of Aaron were put to death at the commencement of their duties, how dare an unauthorized person even think to trespass (see 3:38; 18:7)!

(c) The separation of the Levites (3:11–13)

11–13 The words "in place of" are a clear example of substitution in the OT (cf. Ge 22:13; also Mt 20:28). The Hebrew text emphasizes the word "mine" by using it four times in vv.12–13, by the emphatic "I" at the beginning of v.12, by the concluding "I am the LORD," and by three verbs constructed with the first person pronoun ("I have taken," "I struck down," and "I set apart"). Again we are told that the Levites were from the midst of Israel but are now the exclusive property of the Lord (see 13:2). The last phrase of this section, "I am the LORD," adds authority, significance, and weight to the text. It is a reminder of both what has been revealed about his blessed person and work and what he has shown himself to be in relation to his people.

(d) The census of the Levites (3:14–39)

14–20 The enumerating of the Levites corresponds to that of the other tribes but is to be done of males from the age of one month rather than from twenty years. In summary, the Levites, who were not being mustered for war but for special service of the Lord, were distinct from the rest of the tribes in several aspects: (1) they had their service in and about the holy things and the holy place of God; (2) they were not numbered among the tribes but were to be distributed among them; (3) they are numbered differently than the other tribes; (4) they are not the fighting men of Israel but her ministers, subject to the leadership of the priests; and (5) they had certain restrictions of behavior and manner that marked off their office as distinct from the rest of the people.

21–26 The words of 1:53—"their tents around the tabernacle of the Testimony"—are detailed by four paragraphs in vv.21–38.

The description of the Levitical clans leads up to the most favored: Gershon to the west (vv.21–26), Kohath to the south (vv.27–32), Merari to the north (vv.33–37), and Moses and Aaron and sons to the east (v.38). The secular tribes, by contrast, began with the most favored: Judah on the east (2:3), Reuben on the south (2:10), Ephraim on the west (2:18), and Dan on the north (2:25)

The leaders of the Levitical houses correspond to the leaders of the secular tribes (see 1:5–15). As in the case of the names of the other tribal leaders, these names are theophoric (built on compounds of terms for God): Eliasaph ("[My] God Has Added") son of Lael ("Belonging to God"; 3:24); Elizaphan ("[My] God Has Protected") son of Uzziel ("My Strength Is God"; v.30); Zuriel ("My Rock Is God") son of Abihail ("My Father [God] Is Might"; v.35).

Under the leadership of Eliasaph, the clan of Gershon was to camp on the west side of the tabernacle (i.e., away from its entrance). Their particular charge was the structure itself: the tent, its coverings, and the varied curtains and ropes. This was a significant charge for the people of the house of Gershon, whose male members over the age of one month were 7,500.

There were three curtains or covering screens of the tabernacle: (1) one at the gate of the court (v.26; 4:26); (2) a second at the entrance of the tent (vv.25, 31; 4:25); and (3) a third dividing off the Most Holy Place within the tent (4:5).

27–32 The Kohathites under the leadership of Elizaphan were to encamp on the south side. This clan, the largest of the Levitical families, had particular concerns for the care of the principal furnishings of the tabernacle along with many implements of their service. Aaron's son Eleazar, "the chief leader," was placed over this group of Levites, probably because of the inordinately sensitive nature of their work.

The term "Amramites" reminds us of the family of Aaron and Moses. Aaron is an Amramite (see Ex 6:20). The presence of the family of the Amramites suggests that Amram was not the direct father of Aaron, Miriam, and Moses but an ancestor. Hence, Aaron and Moses were from the family of Kohath, of the tribe of Levi. The Kohathites were responsible for the care of the most holy things (4:4–18).

33–37 The house of Merari, camped on the north of the tabernacle, was led by Zuriel and numbered 6,200 males from the age of one month. Their particular charge was the care of the frames, posts, bases, and crossbars of the tent, as well as all auxiliary materials. It is fitting that this clan of Levites was stationed on the north, as their work is not nearly as glamorous as that of the other two companies of Levites. There is a consistency in that this house of the Levites is on the same side of the tent as the triad led by Dan.

38 Moses and Aaron had the most honored location. They guarded the entrance to the Tent of Meeting, and they did so facing the sun, and it was the direction of the encampment of the people. Later on, the entrance to Solomon's temple also would face east.

Moses and Aaron were not placed on the east side of the tabernacle because of arrogance; rather, they were placed there for a representational ministry. Theirs was an exclusive work but beneficent to the entire community. The sovereignty of God was evident in his limitations on the means to approach him. The "stranger" (NIV, "anyone else"; GK 2424) could be a better man or woman, more pious and devout than a given son of Aaron; but he or she would still face death based on presumption (cf. 1:51; 3:10, 38; 18:7).

39 The total of Levites given in v.39 is 22,000, which is 300 less than the total of 7,500 Gershonites (v.22), 8,600 Kohathites (v.28), and 6,200 Merarites (v.34) (= 22,300). Many scholars believe that there has been a textual corruption in the number in v.28, that the correct number of the Kohathites is 8,300 (as in the LXX).

Concerning the grand sum of 22,000 Levites, we observe that this is a bit small compared with the numbers given for the other tribes in ch. 1. There is a consistency, however, when this number is compared to the 23,000 Levites in the second census (26:62). It is particularly small when we realize that the 22,000 included all males in the tribe of Levi who were over the age of one month rather than over the age of twenty years as in the other tribes.

(e) The census and redemption of the firstborn (3:40–51)

40–43 The basic teaching of this text is that the male Levites over the age of one month were regarded by the Lord as a redemption for the "firstborn" (GK 1147) of the nation. The firstborn of animals were to be sacrificed to the Lord; but God never countenanced the sacrifice of humans on his altars. Hence a substitution was done; a male Levite was regarded as a substitution for the firstborn member of a secular tribe. The firstborn of the livestock were also included in the substitutionary arrangement; Levites for firstborn of Israel and Levite's livestock for firstborn livestock of Israel.

The command of God seems to be distinct in this text. Not only was there to be a count of a discrete group of people, but the names were to be written down (cf. 1:2). The number of the firstborn of the Israelites came to 22,273. This number stands out from all the other numbers we have seen thus far. All other numbers are rounded off, including the number of the Levites, 22,000. Yet this specific number of the firstborn of Israel is related to the rounded number of the Levites, to provide a surplus of 273 firstborn, for whom a redemption price had to be made.

The number of the firstborn sons of Israel (22,273) seems to be much too small for a population in excess of 2 million. In fact, this number accords very nicely for a population of about 250,000. My suggestion is that the unexpectedly small number of the firstborn in the first generation is an impressive clue to the size of the population as a whole and that there may be two different uses of numbers in this passage. Moses here presents a comparison of numbers of different sorts. The one number is specific—exactly 22,273; the other is rounded, inflated, rhetorical (22,000 Levites of a certain age). The first number is the surest figure for calculating the numbers of the whole community; the extrapolation of 250,000 is considered fitting for this number of firstborn persons. Against this specific figure (22,273) is pitted a rhetorical figure (22,000, the number of Levites of a certain age) in order to provide an analogy of redemption. The "surplus" of these two discordant types of figures affords the opportunity to deal with the problem of a surplus. The payment of a redemption price of five sanctuary shekels per "surplus" individual teaches us that every individual needs to be accounted for, no matter how these numbers are used. Possibly the point of the passage is not the numbers per se but the importance of paying the redemption price for each individual firstborn person in the young nation.

44–51 To make up for the number of the firstborn Israelites beyond the number of the Levites, a special tax of five shekels (see Lev 27:6) was to be paid for each of the 273 supernumeraries. This is the payment of a redemption price, according to the heavier sanctuary shekel. That silver was then paid to Aaron and his sons, as commanded by the Lord, so that the full complement of the firstborn sons of the community might all be redeemed together.

The redemption of the firstborn is a marvelous expression of the grace of God. Never since the story of the binding of Isaac (Ge 22) has God demanded the firstborn son of any of his people as a sacrifice to his majesty. Nor does God demand that his people enslave themselves to him (cf. Ro 12:1–2). Nevertheless, the firstborn sons are the special possession of the Lord. God does not demand the life of these sons; such would be abhorrent to the Hebrew faith. God does not demand their enslavement; such would be a slight on his mercy. But he does demand their redemption—and provides the means for bringing that to pass. The resultant weight of the shekels so collected is given (1,365 shekels) as a statement of the impressive nature of the transaction and as a witness to its accuracy (5 x 273).

(4) The numbers of the Levites in tabernacle service (4:1–49)

(a) The command for the census and a description of duties (4:1–33)

1–2 When the sons of Levi are mentioned in 3:17, their order is Gershon, Kohath, and Merari; this order also informs the structure of the balance of ch. 3: Gershonites (vv.21–26), Kohathites (vv.27–32), and Merarites (vv.33–37; cf. Ge 46:11; Ex 6:16; 1Ch 6:1, 16).

The order of the listing of sons in the Bible is not necessarily that of birth order; but the consistent pattern Gershon, Kohath, Merari suggests that birth order is intended here. This makes the order of the Levitical families in Nu 4 somewhat unexpected, as the families of Kohath (the presumed second son) are mentioned first (vv.2–20), then the families of Gershon (vv.21–28), and finally the families of Merari (vv.29–33). The same pattern is recapitulated in the numbering listed at the end of the chapter (vv.34–45).

The reason for this elevation of the second son over his older brother seems to be based on the sovereign selection of the Lord and the favored work he gives this family in proximity to the holiest things. Further, we find here a recurring pattern in the Hebrew text: the surprising elevation of a lesser son over his older brother. These are examples of the grace of God that reaches out in sovereign selection, bringing blessing to whom he wishes to bring blessing, elevating whom he desires to elevate, for reasons of his own will (cf. Isaac over Ishmael, Jacob over Esau, Joseph over Reuben, Moses over Aaron, Saul and David over their respective brothers).

3 The census here is of all males "from thirty to fifty years," in contrast to ch. 3, where all males over the age of one month are listed (v.15). This chapter lists those Levites who were of the age to serve in the tabernacle. Of the 22,000 Levite males mentioned in 3:39, there were 8,580 of service age (v.48). From 8:24 we learn that the beginning age for ser-

vice was twenty-five; perhaps the first five years were something of an apprenticeship.

4–5 The paragraphs detailing the work of the Kohathites in their care of the most holy things come to the modern reader as truly from another time. The attention to care and detail for holy things is, lamentably, a lost art. Even though the primary care of these holy things was given to the Kohathites, they were forbidden to touch them (v.15)—or even to look on them (v.20)—lest they die. All the work of the Kohathites was to be strictly supervised by Aaron and his sons, and only the priests themselves were to touch and look on the unveiled holy things. We presume that even they had to be extremely careful in this regard (see 3:2–4).

6–15 Translators have difficulty in identifying the precise nature of the "hides of sea cows" (i.e., the outer covering of the ark) and the other items of holy furniture. The Hebrew word rendered "sea cow" is similar to the Arabic term for the dolphin; hence, porpoise-hide or hide of sea cows seems correct.

The manner of the transport of the holy things was by foot, with the six packages of holy things suspended between carriers by poles (see vv.6, 8, 11, 14) or kept on a carrier frame (vv.10, 12). The sad story of Uzzah is an unwitting self-test of the profound significance of these words (2Sa 6:6–7).

16 The special functions of the high priest are specified in this section both as a delimitation and as a mercy to the other sacral persons. The priest had certain duties peculiar to his office that none other might ever do. But the mercy of God was that there was a person who could draw near to the most holy things on behalf of the people. Were the high priest unable to attend to the holy things, there could be no worship from any of the community. Hence, his welfare ought to have been the concern of the people, for theirs was certainly tied to him.

17–20 The final section relating to the Kohathites in this portion concerns their ongoing service before the Lord in the context of the ongoing people of God; but it also presents a significant warning: any improper approach toward, touch of, or glance at the sacred things would mean death. The underlying reason on God's part may well have been mercy. It was a mercy of God that he had made himself known to anyone; it was the continuing mercy of God that he did not destroy more persons more quickly because of their wickedness; and it was a condescending mercy of God that he presented himself in their midst. The revelation of God's word brings with it demands, some of which seem harsh and difficult. But God is near. Some seem to be so judgmental; yet God has not destroyed all. Some seem to be so threatening; yet God by his mercy allows some sense of his presence to remain known in the camp. His manifestation is based on his mercy; his strictures allow his mercy to continue to be realized.

21–28 The Gershonites cared for the outer curtains and hides of the tabernacle. They and the Merarites were permitted to touch the things they were responsible for (cf. vv.15–20); the men of Kohath were not even to look at or touch the things of the Most Holy Place. But the Gershonites and the Merarites were not to do their work alone. Even with them Aaron was to be the chief responsible agent, but he was able to delegate some of that responsibility to his son Ithamar.

29–33 Similar phrasing to the two other family units graces this section, with the instructions that the Merari family was to have their principal duties with the frames, crossbars, posts, bases, pegs, ropes, and other equipment. Their work was as important as that of any other family group; for without it the more desirable, prestigious work of the tabernacle could not be done. Hence the Merarites could take an interest even in the placing of a post, a peg, or a rope, not because each of these items is a distinct, suitable "type of Christ," but because the worship of God could not proceed—nor could the camp move out—unless these people were doing their holy work.

(b) A description of the census of Kohath, Gershon, and Merari (4:34–45)

34–45 The most notable thing in the census of the Levitical families in this section is the use of numbers. They still appear to be rounded off; but since the numbers are smaller than those in ch. 1, the rounding off is done to the tens level: 2,750 from Kohath, 2,630 from Gershon, and 3,200 from Merari.

(c) A summary of the census and the work of Moses in the census (4:46–49)

46–49 Here we find the seemingly routine use of a summary text in which notice is given of compliance on the part of the leaders. Further, the total number of the men from the three Levitical families from the age of thirty to fifty who worked in and about the Tent of Meeting was 8,580. These summary texts give a sense of completion to the unit. Hebrew style seems to allow the reader to enjoy a sense of "going full-circle."

b. Diverse commands and rituals in preparation for the triumphal march (5:1–10:10)

(1) The test for purity and the law of jealousy (5:1–31)

(a) The expulsion of the impure from the camp (5:1–4)

1–2 In biblical times skin diseases, especially open sores, were among the three prominent factors (along with oozing discharges and contact with dead bodies) that rendered one unclean and hence unfit to be with the community; such a person was also a possible contaminate to the tabernacle and the pure worship of the Lord. It is not clearly indicated (despite the NIV rendering) that the offending skin diseases are infectious, for some of the diseases that might cause the disorders described in Lev 13 are not infectious. A preferable, nonspecific translation is "[to suffer] a serious skin disorder." The OT concept of "uncleanness" is hard for many modern readers to understand. For more on "skin disease," see Lev 13–14 and comments.

The second problem rendering a person ritually unclean is a discharge of any kind (see comments on Lev 15). These discharges were primarily from the sexual organs and were chronic in nature.

The third factor rendering a person unclean in ancient Israel was contact with a dead body. The ultimate tangible sign of uncleanness in ancient Israel was the corpse. Processes of decay and disease in dead flesh were evident to all. Physical contact with a corpse was a sure mark of uncleanness and quite possibly a source of infection.

3 The modern reader should be impressed that these various disorders that render one unclean, and hence to be expelled from the camp, include male and female alike. The concept of clean versus unclean cuts across sexual lines. Women are excluded along with men, and women may be released of exclusion along with men. The essential issue in all laws of purity in Israel was not magic or health or superstition; the great reality was the presence of the Lord in the camp; there can be no uncleanness where he dwells.

4 Israel fully complied with this law when it was initiated (cf. 1:54; 2:34; 3:16, 42, 51; 4:49). In view of the dramatic phrase "I dwell among them" (v.3), the essential reason for the importance of "uncleanness" in the camp is the indwelling presence of the Lord. His commands that the unclean be expelled from the camp are essentially expressions of his mercy.

(b) Restitution for personal wrongs (5:5–10)

5–7 Here Moses discusses a person within the camp who wrongs another. The connection of vv.5–10 (personal wrongs) to the first paragraph (ritual uncleanness) may be one of moving from the outward and visible to the inward and more secret faults that mar the community. Those with evident marks of uncleanness are to be expelled for the duration of their malady. But more insidious are those people who have overtly sinned against others and think that they may continue to function as though there were no real wrong.

The particulars of the text demand a procedure for restitution in the case of unspecified personal wrongs. Of first importance is the recognition that such wrongs are not slight offenses between people only but are in fact acts of treachery against God. The steps for restitution include (1) a condition of guilt—that person is guilty, which excludes that person from active participation in the community as surely as a serious skin disease or contact with a dead body; (2) a public confession of that sin—presumably in the precincts of the sacred shrine, before witnesses and priests; (3) full restitution plus one-fifth to the one wronged (see Lev 22:14; 27:11–13, 31); (4) a sacrifice to the Lord of a ram offering for atonement.

8 Each above step is enumerated in Lev 6:1–7 in the initial presentation of the law of defrauding. However, Nu 5 has an additional provision: What if a person has defrauded another but that person is no longer living and

has no living relative to whom restitution might be paid? Verse 8 adds the next proviso: (5) the payment of restitution is to be made to the priest when there is no suitable relative to whom such payment might otherwise be made. In this way the debt is paid fully, no matter who of the injured family has survived. The term for "close relative" (GK 1457) means "the protector of the family rights" and sometimes is translated "kinsman-redeemer" (e.g., Ru 4:3).

9–10 Finally, a note is added that the offerings presented to the priests truly belong to the priests. The offering is not a sham that is withdrawn secretly after a public presentation. The intent of this law on defrauding is clear in the context of this chapter: purity among the people is essential for their successful journey through the desert and their eventual triumph over the inhabitants of the land. Just as the physically impure needed to be expelled from the camp, so those attitudes and jealousies one might have against another of a petty or serious nature also had to be dealt with equitably for the camp to remain pure.

(c) The law of jealousy (5:11–31)

Yet another element that will lead to impurity within the camp is undetected marital infidelity. The law concerning jealousy is best read in the context and flow of the two earlier laws in this chapter. Moses moves from issues of purity established with the physical marks (vv.1–4), to those of interpersonal relationships (vv.5–10), and then to the most intimate of relationships, that of purity of a man and woman in their marriage bed (vv.11–31). As with the first two, so the unexposed but treacherous act of marital infidelity also brings harm to the camp as a whole.

11–15 A test for marital fidelity is far harder to prove than a test for a skin disorder; hence the larger part of the chapter is given over to this most sensitive issue. The husband's "feelings of jealousy" may have been provoked on the basis of good cause, and the issue must be faced; the concern is ultimately based on the reality of God's dwelling among his people (v.3). The gravity of the ritual shows that the Law regards marital infidelity most seriously. Such was not just a concern of a jealous husband; the entire community was affected.

Two sides need to be discussed. On one hand, the husband may shame his wife publicly and force her to a rigorous, demeaning religious trial merely on the (unfounded) suspicion of marital faithlessness. She may have presented no evidence whatsoever. Further, there is no mention of the guilt, trial, and judgment of the man that this woman is supposedly involved with—all guilt, shame, trial, and judgment rest on her shoulders.

On the other hand, there is a limitation on the husband—a protection of the wife from his abusive hand. Were there not such a provision in a male-dominant culture, an angry, suspicious husband might strike out against his wife without any sure reason, harm her physically and mentally, and even take her life. But God reaches out through Moses and has a means of escape for a woman under suspicion of unfaithfulness. The trial she is taken to is not a kangaroo court; it is in the precincts of the tabernacle, under the jurisdiction of the priests, in concert with a solemn sacrifice—she places herself under the hand of the Lord.

The woman brought to such a place will not take this issue lightly. Public humiliation, shame, anger with her spouse, and exposure before priests and people were all terrifying prospects. But then neither would her husband take these issues lightly. For he was not just spreading rumors nor digging at his wife in the privacy of their home. He too was coming before the Lord, and he too might be judged. Hence we have another expression of the mercy of God to women who are so often abused by prideful men. Here is a means of escape from suspicion and evasion of punishment. If the woman was indeed guilty, then the husband was vindicated. This was important, not just for the pique he might be feeling, but for the sense of the ongoing stability of the family. If a woman was unfaithful to her husband, she might be carrying the child of another man; and the rights of inheritance might become hopelessly enmeshed in the complexities of family relationships.

But if the woman was innocent, then her husband would have his reasons for jealousy alleviated. Again, this is a limitation on his jealous nature. Most men would be very careful before pressing the issue. The results could be disastrous for themselves.

16–18 The central phrasing of this text is that the priest shall bring the woman to stand before the Lord. The repetition in v.18 is for emphasis. The biblical phrasing demands a theological understanding of the woman's judgment. Further, that she is brought before the Lord helps again to demonstrate the concept of purity and the proper connection of this law with the two earlier laws of the chapter.

Taking holy water, adding dust, and then mixing a doubtful drink seems to be a world away from things we understand. It seems most unlikely that the addition of dust from the floor to the holy water is what makes that water "bitter" (GK 5253). It was added to holy water, not to change the taste, but to emphasize the holiness of the matter.

Next the woman is made to loosen her hair, perhaps a sign of openness on her part. She is to be presented before the Lord. This loosening of the hair would be for the guilty woman an expectation of judgment and mourning (see Lev 13:45; 21:10). For the innocent wife, who had nothing to fear but the glory of the Lord to demonstrate, the loosening of her hair is a strengthening action of feminine personhood in the Holy Place.

The terminology that bitter water brings a curse is problematic. It is not just that the water was bitter tasting but that it had the potential of bearing with it a bitter curse. That this potion was neither simply a tool of magic nor merely a psychological device to determine stress is to be seen in the repeated emphasis on the role of the Lord (vv.16, 18, 21, 25). The verdict of the woman was precipitated by her physiological and psychological responses to the bitter water, but the judgment was from the Lord. The phrase may be rendered in a somewhat expansive manner: "the water that may result in bitterness and provoke a profound curse."

19 The priest presents two possibilities. First, the woman is truly innocent. In this case his specific prayer to the Lord is that the water with the potential of bitterness will not harm her. The priest's words to the innocent woman assure her of no harm from the bitter water. If she is truly guilty of the deed that her husband suspects, then the full onus of the curse-bearing waters will come to her, enter her body, descend through her intestines, and be the physical means the Lord will use to produce a physical change in her body.

20–22 The other possibility is that the woman has been unfaithful to her husband, in which case the priest pronounces a curse on her from the Lord. The NIV note has "causes you to have a miscarrying womb and barrenness." The figurative language here (and in v.27) speaks of the loss of the capacity for childbearing (and, if pregnant at the time of her judgment, the miscarriage of the child). For a woman in the ancient Near East to be denied the ability to bear children was a personal loss of inestimable proportion.

The woman who was guilty may return to her home to await the outcome of the oath. If she was innocent of infidelity, she should count on progeny. If she was guilty but not caught in the act, then she would suffer debilitating physical symptoms that would prohibit successful pregnancies. She would then bear her guilt in her body and the inner chambers of her heart. In either case the woman was to hear the words of the curse in the midst of the solemn precincts, and then to bring that potential curse on herself by saying to the Lord and his priest, "Amen. So be it." The double "Amen" (lit. Heb.; GK 589) is her signal that she understands the issues and is in agreement with the judgment—or escape from judgment—that will come into her body.

23–28 After the words of the cursing had been announced, the priest would write them on a scroll and then blot the letters off into the water. The woman was not only going to hear the words but in a dramatic, figurative sense drink them; thus the awful sense of taking the curse into one's own body was realized. The NIV suggests the very drinking of the water would cause suffering. The bitterness was not in taste, convulsions, or physical shock but in the latent sense of the potential judgment of childlessness. "Bitterness" is a most appropriate term for just this potential judgment. The innocent woman, however, would not suffer the bitterness of the water and its curses.

29–31 The summary statement of this law concerns the woman who has been rightly accused by her husband. The chapter has a cohesion to it of instances relating to the maintaining of purity within the camp. The importance of marital fidelity is further supported by numerous NT texts (especially 1Co 5), which point to God's continuing affirmation of the seventh commandment: You are not to commit adultery.

(2) The vow of the Nazirite and the Aaronic Benediction (6:1–27)

(a) The vow of the Nazirite (6:1–21)

1–2 It is not generally recognized that these vows of special devotion to God could be made by a woman as well as a man; that is, women were not precluded from this vow (cf. 30:1–16). The vow described here is not a routine matter; rather, it is an act of unusual devotion to God, based perhaps on an intense desire to demonstrate one's utter separation to the Lord.

"Nazirite" (GK 5687) describes the person who has marked out a special time of separation or consecration to God. The Nazirite had to face three demanding limitations: (1) absolute abstinence from all produce of the vine (whether intoxicating or not; see vv.3–4), (2) total forswearing of trimming of the hair (v.5), and (3) utter separation from contact with a dead body (vv.6–8). For the Nazirite one major clean food (any form of grape products) was prohibited during the course of one's vow. After the period of the consecration was over, wine and all grape products were permitted again (v.20).

3–4 The term "fermented drink" (*shekar*; GK 8911) is often used in association with "wine" (*yayin*; GK 3516) and is found in texts condemning drunkenness (see 1Sa 1:15; Pr 20:1; Isa 5:11, 22; et al.). But *shekar* is also used in other texts describing the normal, moderate drinking (along with wine) that was part of the expected common food of the people of Israel. Further, *shekar* could be used in the drink offering (Nu 28:7) in the worship of the Lord. Since *yayin* is the fermented product of the vine, presumably *shekar* is the fermented product of the field, i.e., beer. The Nazirite was to abstain from both wine and beer and from everything associated with the wine grape, not just the fermented beverages, but even the vinegar that results when such products sour. Moreover, the prohibition included fresh grape juice, grapes either fresh or dried, and even the seed and skin of the grape. It is unclear why grape products are specifically forbidden to the Nazirite.

5 A second voluntary prohibition for the Nazirite was the normal and expected trimming of the hair (cf. Jdg 13:5). The unexpectedly long hair of a Nazirite man was a physical mark of his vow of special "separation" (GK 5694) to the Lord. Since women in most cultures wear their hair longer than men do, presumably the Nazirite woman might not only have let her hair grow long but may have allowed it to remain relatively unkempt (cf. "untended vines," Lev 25:5, 11), or perhaps she let it hang loose as opposed to putting it up. Otherwise, it is difficult to see how the (unusually) long hair of a woman would be a distinctive sign of her period of vow. In this way, the Nazirite was to be "holy."

6–8 The third prohibition for the Nazirite concerned any physical contact with a dead body—even within his own family. Here a person faced heart-rending decisions not to do normal things in times of great grief because of intense consecration to the Lord. Even a priest was expected to care for the dead body of a close relative (Lev 21:1–3). But the Nazirite could not care for such a body, no matter how beloved the person, or he would bring contamination on himself.

9–12 The accidental death of a person in the proximity of the Nazirite makes him unclean, guilty of sin before the Lord. This section deals with the unexpected and the unplanned events of daily living. The special focus of the person's contamination is his dedicated hair, which was to be shaved on the seventh day of the Nazirite's rite of purification. Then, following obligatory offerings of birds (the less expensive offerings) for sin (v.8) and burnt offerings and a lamb (the more expensive) for guilt offerings, the person would rededicate himself to the Lord for the period of time that had originally been planned; the time spent up to that point would no longer count because of the contamination. No wonder this vow is termed a "hard vow" (v.2; cf. Pr 20:25).

13–20 The public presentation of the Nazirite by the priest at the Tent of Meeting before the Lord shows that this type of vow was not just an intensely personal and private act of relationship with the Lord. Any such public rite suggests that the vow was also a matter of public knowledge. Presumably, the community could be supportive of the person during the time of his vow. But more important is the personal presentation before the Lord at the Tent of Meeting (see vv.13–14, 16–17, 20). Through this vow, one had a profound sense of one's coming into the presence of the Holy One.

Burning the hair signified the completion of the vow and demonstrated that the act of the Nazirite was in devotion to the Lord. Since the Nazirite was prohibited any contact whatsoever with wine and vine products during his vow, one might conclude that such things are essentially evil in themselves. However, a wine offering ("drink offering"; GK 5821) was presented on the altar to the Lord along with the clean animals and the associated grain offerings. The conclusion respecting the prohibition of wine and beer to the Nazirite during his vow must take into account the use of wine in the rite of vow-completion as well as the notice that he was then free to drink wine again (v.20).

21 The costs of the Nazirite vow were considerable and varied. It was not a demand of God on his people but a provision for men or women to voluntarily show their devotion to him.

(b) The Aaronic Benediction (6:22–27)

22–23 The words of the prayer of vv.24–26 are termed the Aaronic Benediction. Perhaps the most impressive aspect of this prayer is that it is a provision for God's desire to bless his people. Blessing is his idea. It is not something his people must beg for, but the outreaching of his grace.

The pattern of the prayer is exquisite; the language is poetic and emotive. There are three lines each with the divine name "Lord"; the repetition of the divine name gives force to the expression of v.27 and is certainly fitting with the (later) Christian revelation of the Trinity. Each line conveys two elements of benediction, and the lines are progressively longer. Not counting the threefold use of the divine name, there are twelve words to the prayer, which suggest the twelve tribes of Israel.

This prayer speaks of the light of the presence of the Lord; but there is a sense that the prayer itself is light-giving. Prayed in faith, it expects God to respond by drawing near and enfolding one in his grace. In fact, the concluding words promise that he will bless his people.

24 While these words are directed to the entire community, the pronouns are singular. The Lord blesses the whole by blessing individuals; he blesses individuals by blessing the whole. "The LORD bless you and keep you" are words of reminder, of attestation of promise. The buttressing words "and keep you" further explain his blessing. God's intention for his people is their good; he will preserve them to enjoy that good.

25 The words "make his face shine upon you" recall the experience of Moses on Mount Sinai (see Ex 34:29–35). As his glory had caused Moses' face to shine, so the Lord desires to make his presence known to all his people. When Moses was on the mountain, it was in the context of terror. But God had come down in grace; his revelation was of mercy. Hence we have the splendidly suitable tie of the light of his face and the grace of his presence.

26 The Hebrew word *shalom* ("peace"; GK 8934) is here seen in its most expressive fullness, not just as an absence of war, but as the positive state of rightness and the fullness of well-being. This kind of peace comes only from the Lord. The expression "turn his face" suggests pleasure and affection and is functionally equivalent to "smile."

27 The Lord says that this prayer is the means of placing his name on his people. Since "the LORD" itself is a term of blessing whereby the eternal God states his relatedness to his people, these words of blessing could not be more appropriate. The prayer is designed to help the people experience the reality of the blessing of the Lord.

(3) The offerings at the dedication of the tabernacle (7:1–89)

(a) The presentation of carts and oxen (7:1–3)

1 With much repetition of language, ch. 7 records the magnificent (and identical) gifts given to the Lord for tabernacle service by the leaders of each of the Twelve Tribes. It is wonderfully fitting that the record of these gifts follows the Aaronic Benediction (6:24–26): in response to God's solemn promise to bless his people, they bring their blessing to him—magnificent gifts in twelve sequential days of celebrative pageantry.

The focus in the chapter is on the tabernacle, the "dwelling place of God," and the altar, the point of approach to God's dwelling. After Moses had completed supervising the construction and erection of the sacred tent and its altar, he "anointed" and "consecrated" them for the Lord's special services. "Anoint" (GK 5417) is the same term used for the anointing of special persons. "Consecrate" (GK 7727) means that those present recognize that the tabernacle and its furnishings and the altar and its implements are no longer common items but are now marked out as special, distinct, and other—set apart to the worship of God.

2–3 Then the leaders of the tribes (cf. chs. 1–2) come forward with their first gifts. There are six carts, each drawn by a pair of oxen, for the special use of the priests in transporting the elements of the sacred tent and its

The picture above shows various utensils used by priests; the picture to the right shows the altar. Courtesy Zondervan Corporation © 1984.

furnishings when the people set out on their march toward Canaan. The Hebrew used here has traditionally been understood to describe a covered wagon, which would certainly be appropriate for transporting the sacred items.

(b) The distribution of the carts and oxen (7:4–9)

4–9 Following the command of God, Moses takes these six covered carts and their pairs of oxen and distributes them to the three Levitical families based on their need and their particular responsibilities. Two of the carts and their four oxen he gives to the families of Gershon for their work in transporting the varied curtains of the tabernacle and the courtyard (see 4:24–28); the other four carts and their pairs of oxen go to the families of Merari for their work in transporting the frames, crossbars, etc., of the tabernacle and the courtyard (see 4:29–33). The Kohathites are not given any carts; they must carry the holy things on their shoulders, with staves placed through the carrying loops (see 4:4–20; esp. vv.6, 8, 11–12, 14). This prohibition of the use of carts for the holiest objects was not followed by David (see 2Sa 6:3–13).

(c) The plan of the tribal offerings (7:10–11)

10–11 The literal Hebrew reads "one leader for one day, one leader for one day." The repetition shows the pacing that God required. Each leader's gift was worth a day's celebration. None of the gifts were to be grouped, none of the leaders bunched. Each leader, and the people he represented, was to have his day of approach with significant gifts to the presence of the Lord.

(d) The offerings of the Twelve Tribes (7:12–83)

12–83 The leaders of the Twelve Tribes have already been named in 1:5–15 and 2:3–32. The order of the presentation is the same as the order of march: first the tribes camped to the east of the tabernacle; then those to the south; then those on the west; finally those on the north.

The gifts of each of the twelve worthies were the same:

one silver platter weighing about 1.5 kilograms

one silver sprinkling bowl weighing about 0.8 kilogram
one gold ladle weighing about 110 grams
the plate and bowl containing flour mixed with oil for a grain offering
the ladle filled with incense
one young bull, one ram, and one male lamb for a burnt offering
one buck goat for a sin offering
two oxen, five rams, five buck goats, and five male lambs for a fellowship offering

These gifts were to be used in the worship patterns of the temple service. The "silver plate" may have been used in association with the bread of the Presence. The sprinkling bowls were for the blood that would be sprinkled on the altar. The gold "dish" might have been used for incense, as this is the way it was presented to the Lord. The shekel used to weigh the silver and gold gifts is termed the "sanctuary shekel," as against the half-value shekel sometimes used. The weight of the sanctuary shekel was established in Ex 30:13 as "twenty gerahs" (= .403 ounce or 11.4 grams; see EBC, 1:379). Certainly these gifts were regarded as substantial, particularly coming from a people so recently slaves. They had despoiled the Egyptians (Ex 12:35–36) to enrich the worship of their God. The incense that filled the dishes was the prescribed, fragrant incense of Ex 30:34.

Obviously the writer might more easily have said that each of the twelve leaders brought the same magnificent offerings to the Lord on his appointed day during the twelve-day celebrative period. How are we to regard his seeming excess of repetitive detail throughout the long chapter? Is it not possible that in this listing we catch a glimpse of the magnificent pomp and ceremony attending these gifts? Do we not see the genuine spirit of worship of each of the successive tribes as their turn came to bring gifts to the Lord? And finally, do we not see the joy of the Lord in his reception of these gifts? This chapter has a stately charm, a leisurely pace, and a studied sense of magnificence as each tribe in its turn was able to make gifts to God that he received with pleasure.

(e) The totals of the offerings (7:84–88)

84–88 At long last the twelve-day procession of givers and gifts came to its conclusion. Each tribal leader had his moment, each tribe its opportunity, and on each day there was experienced the smile of the Lord. In characteristic Hebrew style, this paragraph gives the sums of the twelve sets of gifts, a further witness to the opulence of the offerings, the festive nature of the ritual of presentation, and the sense of celebration each tribe had in its part.

(f) Moses' conversation with God (7:89)

89 The climax is Moses' hearing the voice of the Lord speaking to him from the central shrine, amid the cherubim and over the atonement cover. Communion is established between the Lord and his prophet; the people have an advocate with the Lord.

(4) Setting up the lamps and the separation and age of service of the Levites (8:1–26)

(a) Setting up the lamps (8:1–4)

1–2 The words "The LORD said to Moses" serve a double purpose: they present a new topic and remind the reader of the divine origin of the words and of the role Moses had as the intermediary between God and man. The seven lamps and the lampstand are described more fully in Ex 25:31–40. The lamps were to be positioned so that they would light the area in front of the lampstand, that is, the area where the bread of the Presence was displayed. Thus there would always be "light" on the bread.

On entering the Holy Place, the golden lampstand would be on the left side and the table of the bread of the Presence on the right side, with the altar of incense straight ahead. Beyond that altar was the veil leading into the Most Holy Place with the ark, the mercy seat, and the cherubim.

3–4 Aaron is reported to have obeyed the command of God in the proper focusing of the lamps; then a reminder of the beauty of the design of the lampstand is given. The most remarkable aspect of this section is the note that the lampstand was made in exact accordance with the pattern the Lord had given to Moses (see Ex 25:40; also cf. Heb 8:5; Rev 1:12–20).

(b) The separation of the Levites (8:5–22)

5–10 The Levites were distinct from the other tribes (see vv.6, 14, 16, 19): they were to have no tribal allotment; their places of living would be spread throughout the other tribes, but they were drawn from the tribes to have a special service before the Lord in assisting the priests.

The cleansing process of the Levites began with a sprinkling of water on them rather than with a sprinkling of blood (cf. Ex 29:20–21). In the Hebrew this water is termed "water of sin," a phrase taken to mean "water of cleansing" or "purification from sin" (cf. "bitter water" in 5:18). Next the Levites shaved their entire bodies, which speaks of the fullness of their cleansing (cf. Lev 14:8; see Nu 5:2). Shaving the body is in some ways a return to innocence and an initiative symbol of purity. Bodily hair needs to be cleansed regularly, for the follicles tend to collect and hold dirt. The cleansing of the Levites seems to be an initial rite of purification. Since Semitic men in the ancient world generally wore beards and had ample bodily hair, shaving must have been regarded as a remarkable act of devotion to God. The third factor in cleansing the Levites was washing their garments. The verb used for washing means "to tread," "to walk" (i.e., "to wash garments by treading"). This pictures the ancient form of washing clothing.

Following the sprinkling, shaving, and washing, the Levites were ready for the next step in their purification, the presentation of offerings and sacrifices to God: two bulls along with the fine flour mixed with oil that constitutes the grain offering. This would then be presented by Moses before the Tent of Meeting, with the nation gathered to witness the event. The people (their representatives) would then place their hands on the Levites as a means of identifying with them. The Levites had come from among the people; now they were standing in their place before the Divine Presence. This was a solemn act, worthy of reflection. The Levites were the substitutes for the nation; by placing hands on them, the people of the nation were dramatically acknowledging this substitutionary act (see 8:16–18).

11–14 Our text makes a subtle move from the placing of the hands of the people on the Levites to the placing of the hands of the Levites on the two bulls. This is a double substitution. The Levites substitute for the people, the bulls substitute for the Levites. The bulls, with this double signification, are then sacrifices of sin offering and burnt offering to provide atonement for the Levites.

Aaron comes more directly into the picture, as he is to present the Levites as a "wave offering" (GK 9485) before the Lord. The notion of "wave offering" is somewhat obscure to us. The idea was to hold an object, usually the part of the offering that would be the food for the priests, before the Lord, to wave it back and forth, and then to keep it for one's own use. In the case of the Levites, perhaps Aaron and his sons would place hands on their shoulders and then cause them to move from side to side in a symbolic way to represent that they were a living sacrifice presented before the Lord and that they now belonged to the priests to assist them. In this way the Levites were separated from the rest of the community; they belonged to the Lord, and in turn they would belong to the priests.

15–19 The Levites were next acknowledged by the Lord as his particular possession. They substituted for the firstborn of every mother in Israel. The story line of salvation comes strongly here: Passover! Israel was in Egypt. The tenth plague was imminent. Faithful people had slaughtered a lamb, roasted it, and were eating it along with bitter herbs and matzo bread. When the angel of death was passing over the camp, the angel looked for blood on the posts and lintel of each home. Where that blood was found, the angel moved on to the next home. No one died. All lived. But in those homes that lacked the prescribed blood, there came blood. Instead of the blood of an animal on the door bracing, there was blood in the bed of the oldest child; for the angel of death had extracted the most vicious toll, the death of the firstborn. But for the firstborn of the faithful Israelites, who were not killed, a price was to be paid; and that price was the Levites. They were given to the Lord for his exclusive use (cf. v.14). In turn the Lord gave his Levites to the priests as aids for the work of the ministry.

20–22 This section serves two functions: it reports the completion of the act of separation as a literary device; it also reports the obedience of the people as a mark of their initial compliance to the will and work of God (see 1:54; 2:34; 3:16, 51; 4:49; 5:4; 8:4, 20, 22; 9:5, 23). The implicit obedience of Moses and the people of Israel to the commands of God leaves us quite unprepared for their complaints against his loving character and their outrageous breaches of faith in the rebellions that begin in ch. 11.

(c) The age of service of the Levites (8:23–26)

23–26 At 4:3 the age for the service of the Levite is said to be from thirty to fifty. The present paragraph has the same upper limit but a new lower limit: twenty-five. We do know that the age for entering service for the Levites was reduced to twenty by David (1Ch 23:24, 27), as the circumstances of their work had greatly changed by the time of the monarchy (v.26). Apparently no contradiction was seen in these numbers at the time these words were written. The rabbis harmonized these two texts by surmising that a five-year period of apprenticeship was included in one number.

After a Levite had reached the mandatory retirement age of fifty, he was still free to assist his younger coworkers as long as he was able to do so (perhaps at the great festivals), but he no longer was to do the hard and difficult work he had done in his prime. Again, in these regulations we sense the holiness and the mercy of God. His holiness demands that his ministers be fully able to do the work that is required for them. His mercy precludes a man doing the work when he was no longer physically able.

(5) The celebration of the Passover (9:1–14)

(a) The command to keep the Passover (9:1–5)

1–2 The arrangement of materials in the book of Numbers is not strictly chronological. The events of this chapter actually preceded the beginning of the census of 1:2 (cf. 1:1). There are two discreet emphases here. The first concerns the appropriate time and the proper regulations for the Passover; the second is found in the verb "to celebrate" (GK 6913). One term focuses on the demands, obligations, and rites of worship in Hebrew Scripture and the other on the ability to reach out for the celebrative, enjoyable, and festive nature of that worship. To lose sight of the regulation is to trespass in presumption. To forget the celebrative is to lose the joy and heart of worship; only to follow the obligation is to slip into the dreary work of "religion."

3–4 In traditional Hebrew practice, "twilight" is regarded as the end of one day and the beginning of the next. The official determination of the precise moment was when one could no longer distinguish between a white or a black thread when standing outside in the growing darkness.

In addition to the emphasis on the appropriate timing of the Passover is the necessity for complete obedience to all the statutes and judgments of the celebration. The latter can lead in two directions: (1) to the obedience of faith that regards the minute details as important and compliance to them as that which will bring the pleasure of the Lord; (2) to legalism that finds itself so preoccupied with the details and the regulations as to lose the primary sense of the meaning God had in the legislation in the first place.

5 This report of compliance is yet another example of the obedience of Israel to the demands of the Lord in these early chapters of Numbers. Yet these reports ill-prepare us for the dreadful rebellion of Israel at Kadesh, described in the following chapters.

(b) The ceremonially unclean (9:6–8)

6–8 A crisis developed within the community because of ritual impurity on the part of some, who had come in contact with a dead body. Such contact rendered a person ritually unclean and no longer able to participate in the community until rites of purification had been completed (see 5:2). Hence such a person would not be permitted to participate in the celebrative Feast of the Passover. The section points to two issues: (1) the desire of these people to obey God fully in worship and festivals and (2) the formidable obstacle of participation based on ritual uncleanness.

Being "ceremonially unclean" (GK 3238) was not simply being physically soiled but was also a teaching device to remind the people of the holiness of God. The idea that any person at all might have the effrontery to approach the Lord is audacious in itself. Only by his grace may anyone come before him to worship. By developing a concept of ritual purity, an external symbol, the notion of internal purity might be presented.

Moses promised the people that he would seek an answer from the Lord regarding this situation of ceremonial uncleanness.

(c) Divine permission for a legitimate delay (9:9–13)

9–11 The grace of God is seen, not only in the words of his response to Moses, but in that he responded at all. God's gracious provision for those who were ritually unclean was an alternative opportunity to celebrate the Passover one month later, so that they would not be excluded totally from its observance. The text thus presents the reality of the distancing that uncleanness brings between a believer and his participation in the worship acts of the community; it also provides a merciful alternative from the Lord. Further, the answer of the Lord made provision also for those who might be away on a trip. Even when the Passover was celebrated a month later, it was still to be done fully in order. The text emphasizes the essentials of the meal and the ritual. There was to be the lamb (noted by the word "Passover"), the unleavened bread, and the bitter herbs.

12 The strictures for the Passover include two additional items: none of the feast is to be left over until morning, and the bones of the sacrificial lamb are not to be broken. Eating the Passover lamb and its attendant foods is to be done entirely in one evening (cf. Ex 12:10, 46; 16:19; 23:18). When the Lord Jesus ("our Passover lamb," 1Co 5:7; cf. Jn 1:29) was crucified, none of his bones were broken, in fulfillment of the Scripture (Jn 19:36; see 9:12; also Ex 12:46; Ps 34:20).

13 Grace is generally accompanied by presumption. Those who had no reason not to celebrate the Passover and simply failed to do so were to be cut off from the community. God's gracious provision for the distressed to have an alternative time of celebration was not to be license for the careless to ignore the Passover altogether. Such ones by their own neglect show that they are not part of the community and are not deserving of further union with it. The obdurate is to be "cut off" (GK 4162), which signifies either death by divine agency or perhaps banishment, a severe judgment indeed (cf. 1Co 11:28–30).

(d) The rights of the alien at Passover (9:14)

14 The alien first had to be circumcised before he was able to participate in the Passover celebration (cf. Ex 12:48). But there was an opening for the non-Israelite who had come to faith in the God of Israel to participate fully with the Israelites in holy worship. This is the point of the Abrahamic covenant (Ge 12:3).

(6) The covering cloud (9:15–23)

15 The cloud was the dramatic symbol of the presence of the Lord hovering above the tabernacle (cf. Ex 13:21; 40:34). That this was no ordinary cloud is attested not only by its spontaneous appearance at the completion of the setting up of the tabernacle but also by its appearance as fire by night. It was by means of the cloud that the Lord directed the movements of his people.

16 The mystic cloud, the fiery heaviness, and the enveloping presence must have been an extraordinary sight. The words "this is how it continued to be" suggest the permanent abiding of the cloud over the camp. The cloud and fire were both reversals of the expected phenomena of the time. To relieve the heat of the desert sun, there was a cloud by day. To reverse the cold darkness of the desert night, there was the comforting fire overhead.

17 Two significant verbs describe the presence of the cloud as the symbol of God's nearness. One means "to cover" (v.15; GK 4059); the other means "to settle" (8905). The expression "wherever the cloud settled" contains the significant verb *shakan,* which is the basis for the idea of the "Shekinah glory." The English rendering "shekinah" is built on the verb meaning "to dwell" and the shortened form of the divine name *Yahweh* (i.e., *shakan-yah*). This symbolizes God's nearness and remoteness. He is present as a cloud but hovers above; he is near as a fire, but one cannot draw very close.

18 The words "at the LORD's command" are literally "by the mouth of the LORD." The cloud was one way that the Lord spoke to his people; it was the means he used to direct the movements and the resting times of his people Israel.

19–22 The movement of the cloud and its presence were unpredictable, without discernible pattern. This was to impress on the people the sense that it was God who was leading them. The cloud might linger only a

day or so, or it might linger in one spot nearly indefinitely. The wording of these verses indicates a very lengthy stay, a briefer stay, or a very short stay. Whatever it might be, the people were to move or to encamp based on the movement or settling of the cloud.

23 This verse gives a report of compliance. The repetitious nature of this section (vv.15–23) enhances the expectation of continued complete obedience to the sure direction of the Lord in Israel's movements through the desert. The role of Moses is mentioned for balance: He was the agent of the Lord who interpreted the movement of the cloud signaling the movement of the people. The level of the tragedy of their subsequent disobedience is heightened by this paragraph of great obedience.

(7) The two silver trumpets (10:1–10)

(a) The command to fashion two silver trumpets (10:1–7)

1–2 The Bible speaks of two types of trumpets: the silver trumpet, as here (cf. 31:6; 1Ch 13:8; 2Ch 13:12; 29:26; Ps 98:6) and the ram's horn trumpet (the *shofar;* GK 8795), as in Jos 6:4. Both instruments are far removed from the modern trumpet, as they produced notes of only certain intervals such as fourths or fifths. The silver trumpet was a long, straight, slender metal tube with a flared end. Trumpets were blown for order and discipline, as required by the immense number of people.

3–7 Two trumpets were blown for assembly of the people and one for assembly of the leaders. Trumpets were also blown for a signal to the people to set out on the line of march, at times of battle (v.9), and during festivals of worship (v.10). Obviously different signals would be used; hence, we may presume the development of a guild of priestly musicians was demanded (v.8). These were professionals whose making of music was as serious as the work of a soldier on the battlefield and as sacred as any task done by a sacrificing priest.

(b) The ordinance for the silver trumpets (10:8–10)

8 The role of the sons of Aaron as the sole players of these silver trumpets further signals the sacral function of this music. These instruments were like the lampstand and the censers, implements in the worship of God.

9 In times of battle the distinctive Israelite trumpet signal for war would be blown so that (1) Israel would be remembered before the Lord and (2) the people might be rescued from their enemies. The trumpet blast was analogous to prayer, a means of participation in activating the will of God. By blowing the trumpets before the battle, Israel expected God's active presence in the battle scene.

10 As in the case of battle, it appears that the blowing of the trumpets was a means of knowing that the people were remembered by the Lord. The trumpets were blown as an introit to prepare the people for an active confrontation with God. Trumpets were used in times of festive worship, including feasts, New Moon festivals, burnt offerings, and fellowship offerings. They served as a memorial of the people to God and of him to them. The text ends with the solemn assertion that marks the importance of a text and the completion of a major unit of the book.

2. Setting forth of the people on the triumphal march (10:11–36)

a. The march begins (10:11–13)

11–13 After eleven months near Mount Sinai, the people moved out for the first time led by the Lord in his wondrous cloud. Israel, on the move from the Desert of Sinai, was on a journey that in a few weeks could lead them into the conquest of the land of Canaan. This was a day not to be forgotten: the second year, the second month, the twentieth day. At last the Israelites were on their way to Canaan!

The journey this text describes is not detailed fully here. It is not until 12:16 that the destination of the Desert of Paran is achieved. More specifically, the people settled at Kadesh in the Desert of Zin (20:1). There are at least three stops on this initial journey: Taberah (11:3), Kibroth Hattaavah (11:35), and Hazeroth (11:35).

The Desert of Paran is a large plateau in the northeastern Sinai, south of what later would be called the Negev of Judah, and west of the Arabah. This forms the southernmost portion of the Promised Land, the presumed staging area for the assault on the land itself. Israel's staging for attack in the Desert of Pa-

ran was a brilliant strategy. They would avoid the fortified routes to the west, presumably under the control of Egypt. This unusual line of attack from the south would stun the inhabitants of the land. They would come like a sirocco blast from the desert, and the land would be theirs, under the hand of God.

b. The grand procession of tribes and Levites (10:14–28)

14–28 The names of the leaders of the Twelve Tribes are given for the fourth time in the book (see 1:5–15; 2:3–31; 7:12–83); the order for the tribes in the line of march is the same as was presented in ch. 2. The new detail is that the Gershonites and the Merarites bearing the tabernacle followed the triad of the Judah tribes in the line of march. The Kohathites carrying the holy things followed the triad of the Reuben tribes. Each of the four triads of tribes had a banner for rallying and organization (cf. 2:3, 10, 18, 25).

c. The request for Hobab to join the march (10:29–32)

29–32 Hobab was Moses' brother-in-law, the son of Reuel (Jethro; see Ex 2:18; 3:1). Reuel had been most helpful to Moses earlier (see Ex 18); now his son, with expertise in the desert lands of the Sinai, would be a great help in locating water and pasturage. Several reasons made this appeal to Hobab appropriate: one was likely Moses' relatedness to him through marriage; another is based on the goodness of God that is promised to Israel and in which Hobab may participate; and another is the above-mentioned expertise of Hobab. In this latter instance Moses says that Hobab might become the "eyes" of the people. Moses then reinforces the benefits that will come to Hobab; he will share in the benefits the Lord is about to bring on the nation.

Hobab refused at first, citing the need to care for his own family, following the traditional ancient Eastern pattern of adherence to family and place. No doubt there was also a tie to his family gods. Moses continued to urge Hobab to join Israel. Hobab did not come easily, but he did eventually come (see Jdg 1:16). Coming with Moses was not just a change of address; it was a radical reorientation of life itself, a new family, a new land, and a new God.

Although Hobab's descendants received a share in the land (Jdg 1:16), Hobab himself apparently only experienced the goodness of God in the same way that the rest of the people did: in God's providential care of his erring people in the desert of their banishment. The few weeks' journey was to last a lifetime.

d. The three-day procession behind the ark of the Lord (10:33–36)

33–34 The journey began with a three-day march. Eleven months earlier the people were a rag-tag group of former slaves, gathered in the desert in the first rush of deliverance. Now they were prepared for the march, the battle, and the victory.

35–36 The sense of a victory march is enhanced by what we may call the "Battle Cry of Moses" (cf. 11:11–15). This little poem rests ultimately on the notion of cursing and blessing that goes all the way back to the Abrahamic covenant (Ge 12:2–3). The words of v.35 are a cursing of the enemies of the Lord and his people; the words of v.36 are a blessing on the people of his promise.

B. The Rebellion and Judgment of a Fearful People (11:1–25:18)

1. A cycle of rebellion and atonement and the record of death (11:1–20:29)

These ten chapters balance and contrast with the ten chapters that present the record of Israel's preparation. Barely had the march begun before the rebellion was underway—a rebellion of the spirit of the people that manifested itself in a variety of ways. But always it came down to this: God's demand of complete obedience and robust faith, a devotion of the whole person, was infrequently found in his people. Many of the people of God in all ages seem to display similar traits of irreligion and apostasy. This is one reason the book of Numbers is so important for readers today.

a. The beginning of sorrows (11:1–35)

(1) A judgment of fire (11:1–3)

1 Only three days into their march, the people reverted to the disloyal complaining they had expressed a year earlier, three days after their deliverance from the waters of the Red Sea (Ex 15:22–27). The people again expressed the ingratitude that marked their early experience. The response of the Lord to this outbreak of murmuring was one of wrath. The purging fire was limited to the outskirts of the camp, an evidence of the Lord's mercy.

2 In the midst of his wrath, the Lord remembers mercy. The people truly deserved God's considerable wrath. But the survivors of his anger cried out to Moses for help in their behalf. Moses prayed, and the fire subsided.

3 The place name "Taberah" comes from a Hebrew noun meaning "burning" (cf. Dt 9:22). Because of the raging fire of God in their midst, the people named that place of awful memory "Taberah," Burning.

(2) A surfeit of quail (11:4–34)

4 This account appropriately begins with the "rabble" (GK 671), the non-Israelite people who followed Israel from Egypt. Those who did not know the Lord and his mercies too easily incited those who did know him to rebel against him. The murmuring soon spread throughout the camp, and the people began to complain about their diet, forgetting what God had done for them (Ps 106:14). By romanticizing the past, the people tended to minimize earlier discomforts when in a new type of distress. The verb "to crave" leads to the name of the location of the subsequent judgment, Kibroth Hattaavah, "Graves of Craving" (v.34).

5–6 The vegetables and fruit mentioned in this verse are suggestive of Egypt. Further, the poor in Egypt were able to supplement their diet with fish. The contrast was sure: there are no fish or vegetables in the desert. That there should have been any food at all to eat was solely by God's mercy.

7–9 The description of the manna would be meaningful only to people who lived later (cf. also Ex 16). As with the cloud and fire (9:15–23), the nature and appearance of manna would have been familiar to the persons of this story. In fact, that is the point: they were sick of it!

Several factors suggest that the manna was a unique provision from the Lord, not just a natural substance in greater abundance: (1) The very Hebrew word *manna* ("What [is it]?") suggests something unknown by the people at the time (see Ex 16:15); (2) the description of it suggests that it was not experienced by other peoples; (3) the daily abundance and periodic increase and decrease (Ex 16:22, 27) hardly suggest a natural phenomenon; (4) its ample supply for the entire desert experience, no matter where the people were (Ex 16:35), goes against the idea of a natural substance; (5) the keeping of a sample in the ark for future generations (Ex 16:33–34) suggests a unique food, a holy provision.

10–15 The rejection of his heavenly food was extremely evil to the Lord. God had said that the reception of the manna by the people would be a significant test of their obedience (Ex 16:4). In their spurning the manna, the people had contemned him. Their action was greatly troubling to Moses as well. Instead of turning to the Lord to ask that he understand the substance of their complaint, Moses turned to the Lord to ask why he was given such an ungrateful people to lead.

This leads to what we may call "Moses' Lament," a studied contrast with the "Battle Cry of Moses" (10:35–36). There are elements in this section similar to the lament psalms in the Bible. The lament begins with Moses asking God why he has brought calamity on him and ends with him begging the Lord not to let him see the full extent of his calamity. Moses would rather die than continue to be so very troubled by this obdurate people. One should note, however, that the people were ultimately ranting against the Lord.

16–17 The response of the Lord was twofold—mercy and curse. There was mercy to Moses in that his work load was now to be shared. There was a curse on the people that was in kind with their complaint: they asked for meat and would now become sick with meat (vv.18–34). The reference to the Spirit is noteworthy. God tells Moses that he will take of the Spirit that is on Moses and put that Spirit on the seventy. They will share the same Holy Spirit who empowers Moses.

18–20 The people's distress at the lack of variety in the daily manna led them to challenge the goodness of the Lord. They had screamed for meat. They claimed that manna was a boring diet, that they could not live without variety, without some meat to eat. Now they were going to receive a diet of constant meat, for a full month, until it spewed from their nostrils. The principal issue was not meat at all. The people "have rejected the LORD."

21–23 Moses reminds God (!) of the numbers involved: six hundred thousand men on foot. Moses' distress at providing meat for this immense number of people is nearly comical—the task is staggering; it is an impossibility. The response of God is, "Is the LORD's arm too short?" The human impossibility is an occasion to demonstrate the wonder of the Lord.

24–25 Sovereignly, mysteriously, graciously, the Lord apportioned the same Spirit that was on Moses on the seventy elders. The taking of "some" of the Spirit from Moses suggests the release of some of the burden that he bore. They will share in that work with him. These elders prophesied, but they did not continue to do so. The temporary gift was primarily to establish their credentials as Spirit-empowered leaders rather than to make of them ongoing agents of the prophecy of the Spirit. Their principal task will be to help in the administration of the population, especially in the context of the increasing impiety of the people.

26–30 Two of the designated elders did not meet with the others when the Spirit of God came on the group; but they also received the Spirit and began to prophesy. A young man who was devoted to Moses informed him of this and begged his master to have them cease. The prophesying of Eldad and Medad was perceived as an opportunity for further personal attacks on Moses. But Moses desired that all the people might have the full gifts of the Spirit. The "young man," so protective of the reputation of Moses, is likely Joshua son of Nun. Perhaps it was this close association with Moses that emboldened Joshua, along with Caleb, to take his stand with the promise of God rather than with the fears of the people (chs. 13–14).

31–34 The sickening feast of the plague of quail ends this chapter. The people had begged for meat; the Lord supplied more quail than the people possibly could eat. The NIV suggests that the quail were borne along by the wind at the height of about three feet and hence were low enough to be seized by people quite readily. The supply of birds was stupendous. The least successful gatherer still captured "ten homers" worth (nearly sixty bushels). The drama is exquisite: "while the meat was still between their teeth," the plague of the Lord struck them down. Before they could swallow, God made them choke. So this place took on an odious name: "Graves of Craving." These graves marked the death camp of those who had turned against the food of the Lord's mercy.

(3) A journey note (11:35)

35 Surely there was a sense that the people could not leave Kibroth Hattaavah quickly enough. "Hazeroth" means "enclosures." This was a location that allowed them a temporary residence on their journey northward. But it also became the locus of yet another place of trouble, the attack on Moses by Miriam and Aaron (12:1–15).

b. The opposition of Miriam and Aaron (12:1–16)

1 Grammatical clues indicate that Miriam was the principal in the attack against Moses. Miriam was not judged because she was a woman but because she sinned. The story of her attack is included because of how important she really was. She preserved the life of the helpless infant who later became the great Moses (see Ex 1). She made it possible for Moses' true mother to become his nurse. She led the singing of the first psalm we find recorded in the Scriptures (Ex 15). It is precisely because she is such a magnificent person that her act of rebellion is recorded.

The initial attack on Moses concerns his wife, though Moses' marriage to a Cushite woman was not the real issue. The real issue concerned Moses' prophetic gift and special relationship with God. Cush was the first son of Ham, the father of the peoples living in the southern Nile valley (Ethiopia). If Moses' wife, Zipporah, is intended (see Ex 2:15–22), then her foreign ancestry is attacked by exaggeration. Maybe her skin was more swarthy than the average Israelite. More likely, however, Moses had taken a new wife, perhaps after the death of Zipporah; the language of 12:1 indicates a recent marriage of a Cushite woman. So at issue here is not "woman versus woman" or "woman against man"; rather, it is basic resentment of race against race. In any case, the attack on the woman was a pretext for the real issue at stake.

2 Miriam and her brother Aaron ask, rhetorically, "Has the LORD spoken only through Moses? Has he not spoken as well through us?" Of course, he had (cf. Mic 6:4). God spoke through Aaron and Miriam; but his principal spokesman was ever Moses. The prophetic gifting of the seventy elders (11:24–30) seems to have been the immediate provocation for the attack of Miriam and Aaron on their brother.

3 It is not likely that a truly "humble" (GK 6705) person would write in such a manner about himself. It is possible, though not likely, that Moses authored such a line under inspiration, just as it is possible that he might have recorded the account of his death and burial by prophetic insight (Dt 34). Secondly, Moses was not really an exceptionally meek man. He was given to rage, self-pity, questioning, and debate. Evidence from etymology and usage suggests that "miserable" is a possible reading, and the context indicates that it is the preferred meaning here. The basic meaning of the Hebrew root is "to be bowed down." One could be bowed down by force (i.e., subdued) or with submissiveness (i.e., humble) or with care and trouble (i.e., miserable or afflicted).

Ever since 11:1, one thing after another has brought pressure on Moses so that in 11:14 he whimpers to God that he is not able to bear the load any longer. He even asks that he might die to be relieved of the pressures. Now with this assault of his sister and brother, it was simply too much. He was now the most "miserable" man on earth. He had found his lot so difficult, his task so unmanageable, his pressure so intense that he called out to God saying, "It is too much!" (cf. 11:14). At this point he is utterly speechless; he is a broken man. "Now the man Moses was exceedingly miserable, more than any man on the face of the earth!" (pers. tr.).

4 The association of the Lord to his servant Moses is so strong that here suddenly he comes to redress the wrong done to his friend. That God speaks to Moses along with Aaron and Miriam suggests that he was present when they were berating Moses so unfairly.

5–9 When the trio came to the Tent of Meeting, according to the command of the Lord, he descended to them in the cloud (cf. 11:25).

When the Lord appeared from the midst of the cloud, he spoke to Aaron and Miriam. The Oracle of the Lord in vv.6–8 is in poetic format. Some salient features of this poem may be noted. The poem stresses in an unusual manner the sovereignty of the Lord in the way he deals with prophets and other persons. He decides how he shall speak, to whom, and in what manner. The poem also powerfully presents the distinctiveness of Moses as against all other agents of divine disclosure. To other prophets God may speak in a variety of ways (cf. Heb 1:1; 1Pe 1:10–11). But to Moses there is a one-on-one relationship. Only Moses could approach the holy mountain and gaze on the Divine Person. Only his face radiated following these encounters. The one sure thing in this text is to insist that while God has spoken through Aaron, Miriam, and a host of others, there was none who was on such a familiar ground with God as was Moses (cf. Dt 34:10). In feigned incredulity God asks, "Why are you not very afraid?" Clearly, the ax of his wrath is about to fall!

10 The immediate effect of the wrath of God was seen on the body of Miriam. That Miriam was "leprous" (GK 7665) and Aaron was not is a signal that she was the principal offender. She broke out with the type of infectious skin disease that excluded persons from the community (see 5:1–4). The result of this judgment was that Miriam became an outcast.

11–13 The repentance of Aaron for the sin of presumption is touching both in its intensity and in its concern for their sister. His description of the appearance of Miriam's skin is ghastly but effective. Moses then calls out to God to heal her. His prayer is remarkable in its urgency and simplicity.

14–15 The response of God is graciousness mingled with sobriety. He grants Miriam healing but demands a period of time of public shame. Seven days apparently was the briefest period of such shame before any restoration might be accomplished (see 19:11, 14, 16).

16 At last, the destination of the grand march was achieved. The Desert of Paran was the staging area for the attack on the land of Canaan. Despite numerous terrible events that marred the dream of the triumphal march, at last the people were at their destination. Glory awaits. Or at least that is what should have been the case.

c. The twelve spies and the mixed report (13:1–33)

(1) The command of the Lord (13:1–2)

1–2 Comparing the account in Dt 1:21–23 with Nu 13:1–2, we see that the command to send spies came from the Lord. Likely Deuteronomy presents the story from the level of the people and Nu 13:1–2 presents the divine perspective. When the people requested that spies be sent, Moses decided, on the basis of the will of God, to accede to their request. By putting the two accounts together, we see that the very idea of sending spies to the land was a further example of the grace of God. The specification of the type of men to be selected reminds us that God does use select persons for his leadership tasks. Yet ten of the twelve men turn out to be dismal failures. That they were each leaders of their tribes did not guarantee that they were adequate for the leadership role God desired they would have.

(2) The roster of names (13:3–16)

3 As in the records of chs. 1–10, the story begins with the compliance of Moses to the will of God. The names listed in vv.4–15 are different from the tribal leaders given in chs. 1, 2, 7, and 10. Presumably the tribal leaders were older men. The task called for younger and more robust men, but no less respected by their peers. The travel of the spies began in the Desert of Paran and came full circle geographically (v.26). But the men who returned were not the same as those who left. Presumably they left in confidence, with a spirit of divine adventure; but they returned in fear, groveling before men, no longer fearful of God.

4–15 The significance of listing the names is multiple: (1) they add a certain historical verisimilitude, (2) they provide a level of accuracy, (3) they should give the occasion for pride, (4) they become markers of sadness (cf. Taberah and Kibroth Hattaavah), and (5) they remind us of the significance of names to God (Rev 20:12).

16 Joshua's name was first known as Hoshea, but Moses changed it as a mark of a special relationship between the two men. This change is a fatherly action, as though Moses has adopted his young aide and marked him for greatness (cf. Ge 17). In Hebrew, "Hoshea" means "salvation"; the new form of the name Joshua means "The LORD saves"; the latter form is the Hebrew spelling for Jesus.

(3) The instructions of Moses (13:17–20)

17–20 The instructions of Moses to the twelve spies were comprehensive, for he had some sense of the lay of the land of Canaan. The scouts were to give special attention to the people and the produce of the land, to the cities and towns, to the soil and the presence or absence of forests. Since the journey was at the time of the harvest of grapes, there is a personal note that they were to show themselves courageous in taking some of the fruit, words that would later come to haunt the nation.

(4) A summary of the reconnaissance (13:21–25)

21–25 The journey of the spies began in the southernmost extremity of the land (the Desert of Zin) and took them to the northernmost point (Rehob near Lebo Hamath; see 34:8). The first city the spies came to was Hebron. The parenthetical comment may have been prompted by their amazement at the size and fortification of the city. According to their ancestors, Hebron had not been a great city but a dwelling and trading place for shepherds and herdsmen. The size of the grape cluster that the spies found led them to name the location "the valley of the cluster" (i.e., Eshcol). The very size was a mark of the goodness of the land that God was giving

This familiar tourist symbol used by Israel today is taken from the story of the report of the spies.

them. To think of clusters of grapes so large that two men would transport the cluster on a pole—the people should have thought they had discovered Eden! The grapes, which were wine grapes, were a symbol of the joy the land would provide.

(5) The mixed report (13:26–33)

26–29 The first portion of the report was truthful, if timorous. The spies did give assent to the bounty of the land; it was a land flowing with milk and honey (cf. Ex 3:8). But immediately the spies lamented its people and cities. The cities were described as being inaccessible, impregnable. The listing of the nations that inhabited the land became a new reason for terror. Yet this listing could as well be taken as an indication of the victories that God was going to give his people in fulfillment of his promise in Ge 15.

30 The report of the majority must have caused the people to become frightened. Only Caleb and Joshua returned a report prompted by faith in God. Caleb's words, "We can certainly do it," were not merely bravado; they were the words of one who really believed that the Lord was giving the land to the people. Boldly, confidently, Caleb assured the people that they could take the land.

31–33 But the evil report prevailed. At last the ten state explicitly what they had implied. They were in a state of denial that included the power and presence of God, the promises and assurances of God, their own resources—indeed, even their own names. Those wonderful names—most of which speak of the blessing of being the people of God—were being denied as they spoke their words of calumny (see Ge 37:2; Jer 20:10).

The Land of Promise was a good land, a gracious gift of the Lord. By speaking evil of it, the faithless spies were speaking evil of him. At this point their words became exaggerations and distortions. The Anakites (who were of large size) were now said to be "Nephilim" (GK 5872), the race of giants described briefly in Ge 6:4. This word seems to be deliberately provocative of fear. The exaggeration of the faithless led them to their final folly, comparing themselves to "grasshoppers."

d. The rebellion of the people and defeat by the Amalekites (14:1–45)

(1) The final rebellion of the faithless people (14:1–4)

1–2 The threefold emphasis on the extent of the rebellion—"all the people of the community," "all the Israelites," and "the whole assembly"—is important; for the judgment of God will extend to the entire community. Moses and Aaron became the central targets of the anger of the people, who "grumbled" against them even as they grumbled against the Lord and began to wish that they had already died. It would have been preferable to have died in Egypt or even in the desert than to come this close to their goal, only to discover that it was unattainable.

3–4 The more the people wailed, the more excessive their words. Then they began to aim their anger more directly at the Lord himself. Moses and Aaron were the fall guys, but the Lord was the one really to blame; he had delivered them from Egypt. The people worked themselves into such a frenzy of fear that they wished that God had not brought them there at all. The most reprehensible charge against the grace of God concerned their children (see vv.31–33). But in the end, only they survived. All the rest died in the desert they had chosen over the Land of Promise.

(2) The words of the faithful warning against rebellion (14:5–9)

5 In the midst of this rebellion, a few voices still spoke of God's grace and remembered his power. Moses, Aaron, Caleb, and Joshua's passion for truth in the midst of error caused Moses and Aaron to prostrate themselves before the enraged leaders of the people. They were aware that the anger of the Lord was likely to burst on the people in a moment.

6–7 Joshua and Caleb tore at their clothing, mourning out of faith because of the death of hope. Yet even as they mourned, Joshua and Caleb extolled the land and its virtues with extravagant language. They had been there and reminded the people that the land still flowed with milk and honey.

8 Then these righteous men presented the posture of faith. It was still possible to gain the land and to enjoy its fruit. The only thing necessary was that "the LORD is pleased with us."

9 Two things were needful: the people had to stop their rebellion against the Lord and to cease being afraid of the people of the land. The word translated "protection" (GK 7498) is often rendered "shadow" or "shade." God had served as a protecting shadow for the peoples of the land of Canaan; now that protection was gone. The Lord was with his people, and they could swallow their foes alive!

(3) The appearance of the Lord to withstand the rebels (14:10–12)

10 Despite the impassioned language of Joshua and Caleb and the prostrate forms of Moses and Aaron, the people were deaf to mercy, blind to truth. In the midst of the peoples' rage, God in an awesome display of his wonder burst into their midst at the entrance of the tabernacle. Moses and Aaron had a foreboding this would happen; likely this is why they were prostrate (v.5).

11–12 When God appeared, he did not thunder against the people; but he spoke to his servant Moses about the people's outrageous behavior. By refusing to believe in the power of the Lord, they were holding him in contempt. The anger of God was at fever pitch. In a moment he would destroy them all. And God could begin again, with Moses as the head of a new family of God (see Ex 32:10).

(4) The pleading of Moses (14:13–19)

13–16 Not for a second did Moses mull the possibility of a new people of God. Zealous for the honor of God, Moses burst with protest. There was no God like the Lord; never had a deity done for his people what the Lord had (see Dt 4:32–40). And the nations were watching! Moses was aghast at the thought that word would go back to Egypt that God was not able to deliver his people.

17–19 Moses then affirmed the splendors of the character of God, particularly his grace. He moved from the reputation of the Lord to his character, presenting a composite quotation of his own words of loyal love for and faithful discipline of his people (see Ex 20:6; 34:6–7). Moses knew God intimately. He knew him as a consuming fire; he also knew his warm embrace. While the wrath is real, it is long delayed.

(5) The judgment of the Lord against the rebels (14:20–35)

20–21 In response to Moses' request, God declared that he had forgiven the people. But the forgiveness was not complete. The people who had behaved so intolerably would not be put to death, but neither could things go back to the way they were. A sentence had to be paid.

22–23 The judgment was mitigated. The people were not put to death, but neither would they be allowed to see the land. Since all the people were in rebellion, not one would escape the mitigated judgment.

The Lord speaks of ten times when the people tested him. A possible list of these is as follows: (1) at the Red Sea, where it seemed that Pharaoh's army would destroy them (Ex 14:10–12); (2) at Marah, where they found bitter water (Ex 15:22–24); (3) in the Desert of Sin, as they hungered (Ex 16:1–3); (4) in the Desert of Sin, as they paid no attention to Moses concerning the storing of the manna until the morning (Ex 16:19–20); (5) in the Desert of Sin, as they disregarded Moses concerning the gathering of the manna on the seventh day (Ex 16:27–30); (6) at Rephidim, as they complained for water (Ex 17:1–4); (7) at Mount Sinai, as Aaron led the people in making the golden calf (Ex 32:1–35); (8) at Taberah, where the people raged against the Lord (Nu 11:1–3); (9) at Kibroth Hattaavah, in the grumbling provoked by the rabble for quail (Nu 11:4–34); (10) at Kadesh in the Desert of Paran, when the people refused to receive the good report of Joshua and Caleb but rather wished themselves dead (Nu 14:1–3). It was a dismal record indeed.

24–25 The Lord calls Caleb "my servant" and remarks with affection on his "different spirit." Caleb's ultimate vindication came forty-five years later (see Jos 14:10). The Lord then reminded Moses that there were Amalekites and Canaanites in the land; hence the people needed to turn back to the desert. They had lost their opportunity.

26–35 The rash words of the people asking to die in the desert become in a sense the judgment of the Lord. All those who were above the age of twenty, who were counted in the census, were to die in the desert—except Joshua and Caleb. God's sharpest rebuke of his errant people came in response to their charge that he wanted to kill their children (v.3). God simply would not tolerate the accusation that he had brought the people into the desert to destroy their children. So a further element in God's justice here was the notice that the children would be the only ones actually to enjoy the land. The rest of the people's bodies would "fall in this desert."

The forty days of the travels of the spies became the numerical paradigm for the suffering of the people: one year for one day, so that for forty years the people over twenty would be dying. Thus, when the time was fulfilled, only the young generation would enter the land.

(6) The death of the evil spies (14:36–38)

36–38 The people as a whole received a commuted sentence, but not those responsible for the attitudes that led to this debacle of doubt! They had to be put to death. The judgment on the ten evil spies was immediate; the generation they influenced would live out their lives in the desert. Only Joshua and Caleb were exempt from this judgment.

(7) Defeat by the Amalekites (14:39–45)

39–45 Too late the people determined to go up and take the land. They confessed that they had sinned, but their confession was partial at best, as their actions were rash and foolish. Not only was the Lord not with them now; he was against them. In fact, he had warned them not to go this way but to turn back to the desert (v.25). Their subsequent defeat was another judgment the rebellious people brought on their heads. In fact, any soldiers who died in this abortive warfare only hastened their own punishment for the rebellion at Kadesh.

e. Laws on offerings, the Sabbath, and tassels on garments (15:1–41)

(1) Teaching on special offerings (15:1–16)

1–2 The conjunction of these verses with the sad ending of the narrative of Nu 14 is dramatic. The sins of the people were manifold; they would be judged. The grace and mercy of the Lord are magnified as he points to the ultimate realization of his ancient promise to Abraham (Ge 12:7) and his continuing promise to the nation that they would indeed enter the land.

3–12 The offerings in Nu 15 relate more to the desire of the believer for a spontaneous, grateful response to the wonder of knowing God. Grain and wine offerings were to accompany the offerings by fire; the grain was to be mixed with oil. The grain and wine offerings increased in amounts with the increase of size of the sacrificial animal. These passages are the first to indicate that wine offerings must accompany all burnt or fellowship offerings. The provision of "fine flour" speaks of luxurious food (cf. Ge 18:6; 1Ki 4:22; Eze 16:13). Only the best was good enough for the Lord.

The system of sacrificial worship in ancient Israel was very complex. Some of the sacrifices God demanded were presented in the context of a mournful admission of sin, a guilt-laden expression of repentance. But many sacrifices were presented in contexts of joyful celebrations and heartfelt expressions of one's delight in knowing the Lord.

Another element in worship is the pleasing "aroma" (GK 8194) to the Lord (cf. Lev 1:9). The odor of sacrifice would be heavy, acrid, and pungent. Flour, oil, and fine wine would add an exotic element to the smells. It was not the mere smell, however, that made God happy but the offerer (see Ps 40:6–8; Mic 6:8–10). The smells and the smoke, the flesh and the flour made the offering "real" by adding substance and action to the feeling of worship.

13–16 The "alien" (GK 1731) had the same regulations as the native-born Israelite. Because the one who sojourns with Israel was under the same Torah, he also was able to bring pleasure to the Lord. If the alien continued to please God, he could become a part of the community as a whole. While still an alien, the proselyte had to learn to worship in the same manner as the native populace; and together they needed to learn their worship from the Lord.

(2) Instructions on the cake offering (15:17–21)

17–21 This law also looks forward to when the Israelites would be in the land. Since the book of Numbers presents two generations, we need always to remember who is addressed. The plural "you," though spoken to the community as a whole, is addressed to the children who will actually enter the land.

The concept of the firstfruits symbolizes that all blessing is from the Lord and all increase belongs to him. This offering was made of coarse grain. Right at the time of the threshing of the grain, a cake was to be made in worship of God and held high from the threshing floor. The idea seems to be one of immediacy. This was a perpetual ordinance; for the further removed the people became from the events of their salvation, the more likely they would forget the nature of their salvation. The first generation was not able to remember much longer than three days (11:1–3)!

(3) Instructions on offerings for unintentional sins (15:22–29)

22–29 God's attitude toward his law is complex: he is serious about his commands. But he is also gracious. God made high demands and expected compliance, but he also provided avenues for redress when one did not comply fully. Hence sins may be unintentional, but they still needed to be covered (cf. Lev 4:2). As with other sacrifices, the alien and the citizen had the same demands of compliance.

(4) Instructions for defiant sins (15:30–31)

30–31 For one who set his hand defiantly to despise the word of God and to blaspheme his name, the punishment was one of death, not just banishment or exile (cf. Heb 10:26–39). This injunction dealt with the outrageous behavior of blasphemy, not mild infractions. However, what the law regarded as outrageous behavior may be surprising to us.

(5) A man who violated the Sabbath (15:32–36)

32–36 This account illustrates vv.30–31. The point is that Sabbath breaking is defiance of the Lord; the offense strikes at the very center of Israel's responsibility before him. The ones who discovered the man in Sabbath violation did not quite know what to do. The answer came from the Lord: The penalty for breaking the Sabbath was death (Ex 31:15; 35:2).

(6) Instructions for tassels on garments (15:37–41)

37–40 To bring fear to all people lest they too be led to the breaking of the demands of the

Lord in his law, a most practical device was given: the wearing of tassels on one's garment as a perpetual reminder of God's demands. The swirling tassels would be excellent memory prods to keep faith with the law, to obey the commands of God.

41 The chapter begins and concludes with the continuing promise of God to bring his people into the land. He was still at work in the process of completing their redemption from Egypt.

f. The rebellion of Korah and his allies (16:1–50)

(1) The beginning of revolt (16:1–3)

1 This is the second presumptuous, unprincipled rebellion against Moses by leading figures under his leadership. Korah's paternity is traced through Izhar and Kohath to Levi. His name is later famous for the role his descendants had in music in the time of David and following. Korah's cohorts in this evil plan of insurrection were the Reubenites Dathan and Abiram, sons of Eliab, and On (a man mentioned only here).

2 The principals were joined by another 250 men, who were constituted officials, men of name. These dignified leaders were not content with the privilege they had received by God's grace; they wanted more.

3 Aaron also was under attack. Perhaps Korah's real desire was not only to demean Moses but to make himself priest instead of Aaron. Both Moses and Aaron were in their eighties. The nation was under a sentence of God's judgment, and these men knew that they were a part of the doomed community. "They came as a group" suggests an organized, well-planned conspiracy.

The conspirators' words are literally, "Much to you" (i.e., Moses and Aaron arrogated to themselves too much; they have presumed on their power for self-aggrandizement). When Korah and his cohorts said that the entire congregation was holy, they emphasized the word "all." They also insisted that the Lord was in the midst of the whole community, not just residing in the Tent of Meeting. They appeared to be arguing for a democratization of the divine privilege. But in fact they merely desired a shift of power—to themselves. The pattern of leadership the Lord established in Israel was theocratic—a

rule of God—mediated through a divinely sanctioned regent. The Lord was present with all the people. The leaders had more privilege than the common people, and Moses and Aaron were the most privileged and had the greatest responsibilities.

(2) Moses' rejoinder (16:4–7)

4 Moses fell to his face on the ground, in obeisance to the Lord, whose regent he was and to whom his sole allegiance belonged. The baselessness of the attack of Korah and his company is superbly demonstrated by Moses' action. Although Aaron was also under attack, all focus is on Moses. If he stumbles, Aaron stumbles as well.

5 When Moses rose, he spoke decisively. His words were now the Lord's words. Tomorrow would be the day of reckoning. Once and for all the role of Moses would be defined. Moses' term for the choice one of God is "the holy" (GK 7705), perhaps "the holiest." The Lord will bring near to himself the one who is the holiest, based on his own choice in that one. The enemies were asking for a showdown. Now they would get their chance, but it would be to their ruin.

6–7 Only the initial provisions for the test are laid out here. Moses tells those involved to take a censer, fire, and incense. This is remarkable since the priests alone were to hold the censers. While Korah was of the house of Levi, he was not a member of the priestly family. The others as Reubenites were not even remote possibilities. But Moses dared them to do as he demanded. Then the Lord would make his choice known to all. In an arresting turn of phrase, Moses shouts to these detractors that it is they who "have gone too far" (cf. v.3).

(3) Moses' warning to the rebels (16:8–11)

8 Although the text says "Korah," Moses is addressing all the assembled insolent men. Since the principals along with Korah are Reubenites, it is difficult to know whether Moses' words "you Levites" are inclusive of other Levites who are joined with Korah or are meant to include Dathan, Abiram, and On in a sarcastic manner.

9 Moses asks the rebels whether in their judgment it is nothing that the Lord has marked them out as distinct from the entire community for a special work. They were in a special place in God's economy, but they were not satisfied. Korah was the ringleader, but all in his company were culpable. The issue was gratitude versus pride.

10 It became clear to Moses that the conspirators were really after the priesthood. It was not that he was in error or that Aaron was at fault. It was simply that these wicked men wanted their positions.

11 The phrase "banded together" shows the determination of Korah and his followers as a congealed body. Moses added literally, "And Aaron!" after "against the LORD." His language is incredulous, as though to say, "What did he ever do to you that you should strike out against him?"

(4) Confrontation with Dathan and Abiram (16:12–14)

12–14 The behavior of Dathan and Abiram is even more intolerable than that of Korah: (1) they refuse to appear before Moses; (2) they mock his words; (3) they abuse the language of choice for Canaan to describe contemptuously the land of Egypt; (4) they accuse Moses of their plight in the desert; (5) they mock him as a strutting prince; (6) they blame him that they do not possess the fields and vineyards of Canaan; (7) they taunt him with such a misuse of power that he attempts to blind others to his faults; and (8) they repeat their outrage of disobedience, "We will not come!"

(5) Judgment on his enemies (16:15–35)

15 In his wrath Moses asks God not to turn his face with gracious favor on their offering; he proclaims himself innocent of misuse of his office for personal gain; he proclaims himself guiltless of any harm. He has not enriched himself by one donkey nor brought harm to one person.

16–18 The trial was to be by fire: Which men would the Lord accept as his priests in the holy tabernacle? The 250 men allied with Korah came with arrogance to withstand Moses and Aaron at the entrance of the Tent of Meeting. Seemingly with Aaron now quite old, Korah wants his position. Even though the "job" is the service of the Lord in his holy precincts, Korah apparently believes he will

be able to wrest that service by force, with the Lord acquiescing to his demands!

19–22 Suddenly the glory of the Lord bursts into their midst. The Lord speaks again that he has had it with the people. He is about to wipe out the nation again. Moses and Aaron understand that it is all the people, not just the foolish rebels, whom God is about to destroy. Again we see the character of Moses and Aaron who pray to God to preserve the nation despite yet another outrageous attack. Moses and Aaron ask whether it is right that the whole nation be destroyed just because one man has sinned.

23–30 The Lord seems to accede to the reasoning of these words, for he demands that the people move away from the tents of Korah, Dathan, and Abiram. The judgment of the Lord was going to be severe, but he did not wish to have it lash out on the bystanders. Moses wished to assure the people that the judgment that was coming was certainly the direct work of the Lord. The opening of the earth to swallow the rebels was a sure and evident sign of the wrath of God and the vindication of Moses and Aaron. The earth is pictured as a ravenous monster.

31–35 As soon as Moses finished speaking, the earth split open and swallowed the rebels, with their households. Apparently the sons of Korah did not join their father in his rash plan and hence did not die (cf. 26:11; see Pss 42; 44–49; 84–85; 87–88; cf. Ex 6:21, 24; 1Ch 6:22–31). The men and all with them were under the ban (cf. Achan in Jos 7). The children, wives, and even toddlers died with their wicked fathers. The 250 men were then devoured by fire (perhaps lightning). The horror of the story is that the punishment included women and children. No easy answer presents itself to deal with this issue. But we do know that the God of Israel will do right (Jdg 18:25)!

(6) The aftermath of the contest—more distress (16:36–50)

36–40 After the terrible conflagration of Korah and his cohorts, Moses is told to have Eleazar son of Aaron take the censers from the midst of the smoldering remains. A chilling scene is that of the true priests taking the censers of the 250 deceased impostors from their charred remains and employing these holy instruments in hammered bronze sheets for the altar. Even with the death of the false priests, the holy things had to be treated as holy things! From that time on the sheet of bronze over the altar would be a memorial of the utter folly of the self-proclaimed priests of the most holy God. God has established his personnel; he will allow none to breach their ranks.

41–45 On the next day following the terrible judgment of God, the whole Israelite community grumbled against Moses again. They who had seen the judgment of God in such a remarkable manner still did not interpret things correctly. Again they blasted Moses, unfairly charging him with the death of "the LORD's people." Verse 42 speaks of the men turning toward the Tent of Meeting, which may mean that the crowd was about to take over the territory, to seize the tent as their own holding. At once, as before, the glory of the Lord was in the midst of the people—in judgment. Fear must have seized them. The Lord had come! Again, but for the intervention of Moses and Aaron (see vv.4, 22), the entire nation might have been destroyed by the Lord because of the people's continued rebellion. The Lord spoke to them to depart so that he might destroy the nation; instead they fell to the ground (cf. v.4), bowing down to seek the Lord's mercy, to turn away his wrath.

46–50 This chapter has turned on the account of holy censers being used by unholy men in mock piety. Now Aaron, whose right it was, was to take his censer and do the work of the true priest to stay the plague of the Lord and to bring mercy to the people. The wrath of God had already burst out in indiscriminate slaughter by means of a virulent, rapidly spreading plague. Moses calls to Aaron to do his priestly work. What poetic justice! The very implement used by the enemies to force God's hand to wrath now has to be used by his true priest to force his hand to mercy. Moses knows that the plague may be stemmed; only they must hurry. So Aaron ran! He stands in the breach between the dead and the living. He stops the plague. Thousands died needlessly (14,700), in addition to those who died in the incident of Korah. At last the plague is stemmed. Moses and Aaron meet again at the entrance to the Tent of Meeting, vindicated in the role that God had given to them.

g. The budding of Aaron's staff (17:1–13)

(1) The test for the true priest (17:1–7)

1–7 Moses is commanded to collect twelve staffs, one from each of the tribes of Israel, and write the name of each leader thereon. This is the third vindication of the Aaronic priesthood against all opposition (16:1–50). The test needed to be unequivocal. The staff of the tribe of Levi had to have Aaron's name written clearly on it. This staff had to be chosen over the other staffs because of the trans-community support given to the rebellion of Korah. The staffs were to be placed "in front of the Testimony," which means that they were brought within the Most Holy Place. Moses must have realized that he was doing a most unusual act. The intention was to rid the nation from the grumbling concerning the validity of the priests. The trial was to identify the "right" staff by having it sprout. It is clearly not possible for a wooden staff that is long dead to sprout again. This demanded a miracle.

(2) The outcome of the ordeal (17:8–13)

8–11 On the next morning, Moses found that Aaron's rod had not only sprouted, it had "budded, blossomed and produced almonds"! God exceeded the demands of a test so that there might be no uncertainty (cf. 1Ki 18:24, 38). Miracles of this sort (natural events that occur in unnatural conditions, timing, and/or placement) often occur in the Bible.

It must have been humbling for the men from the other tribes to take back their dead staffs. But only those who aspired to an office that was not theirs would feel shame. Aaron's rod was to be a perpetual reminder of the choice of God in his priest. Hence, it was to remain in front of the Testimony in perpetuity. Aaron's rod joined the stone tablets of the law of Moses (see Ex 25:16) and the jar of manna (Ex 16:33–34) within the ark of the Lord.

12–13 At last the enormity of the arrogant sin of the people in challenging the role of Aaron hit them. Their remorse was justified; death was deserved. Any untoward approach to the holy tabernacle would result in disaster.

This depicts the ark of the covenant and its contents. On the left is the atonement cover with the two gold cherubim. Inside the ark were placed the tablets of the Ten Commandments, a jar of manna, and Aaron's rod that budded. Courtesy Zondervan Corporation © 1984.

h. The priests and the Levites (18:1–32)

(1) Their general duties (18:1–7)

1–7 The Lord's choice of Aaron and his family as the true priests presented an onerous task. Without proper priests, there would be only death among the sinning community. The priests were to be assisted by the tribe of Levi; but the assistants were not to usurp their serving role. Were they to do so, not only would they die, so would the priests who were responsible. Aside from the Levites, no one else could come near. The only people who had a right to work in the shrine were the Levites under the supervision of the priests. The frightful obligations were balanced in the sense of the importance and honor of the work. They of all men were able to approach the Holy Place and minister before the Lord. The Lord's gift of the priesthood was also to the people, an act of his mercy. On their shoulders rests the protection of the nation.

(2) Their offerings and support (18:8–13)

8–11 The priests were to be supported (see Lev 6:14–7:36). Since the Levites as a whole and the priests in particular had no part in the land, it was necessary that the means for their provision be spelled out fully. The offerings not put through fire would be given to the priests. Something is regarded as holy, not because of some mysterious inner quality, but because it had been presented to the Lord for his use. Among the gifts he gave to the priests was holy food. The basic meaning of the word "holy" (GK 7731) is "set apart for special use in the service of God." These holy foods were specifically restricted to the males and could be eaten only by those who were ritually clean. The wave offerings were for the entire family to eat. Provision was made not only for the priests themselves but also for their families. Only the ceremonially unclean family members were forbidden to eat the gifts and offerings (cf. v.13).

12–13 Since the very best items of produce were to be given to the Lord, they became the special foods of the priests and their families. The grace of God is manifest in this provision for his servants, but so are the demands of God: the priests and their families were to be in a state of ritual purity when they ate sacred foods. The idea that God gets "the best of the first" occurs throughout the Bible.

(3) The firstborn offerings and redemptions (18:14–19)

14–16 Things under the ban belong to the priests (unless such things are destroyed). The firstborn were to be consecrated to the Lord (Ex 13:2); they were a means of supporting the priests. They would receive the firstborn of animals and man or their redemption price. There was to be no sacrifice of a human being and no sacrifice of unclean animals. These needed to be redeemed. The price set for the redemption of the firstborn of women (five shekels) was a considerable sum. Seemingly the reason for paying a redemption price for a firstborn son and unclean animals and the sacrifice of the firstborn of clean animals was to provide a perpetual reminder that conception, birth, and life are gifts of God.

17–19 The firstborn of clean animals were not to be redeemed; they were devoted to the Lord by being sacrificed (see ch. 15 on offerings by fire), though the meat would belong to the priests. This was a permanent obligation, symbolized by salt—a lasting compound. Salt was used in some of the sacrifices to the Lord (Lev 2:13; Eze 43:24) and in special incense that was used in the worship of God (Ex 30:35). Its mention here speaks of eating and, hence, of communion (see Ge 31:54; Ex 24:5–11; Ps 50:5).

(4) Aaron's special portion (18:20)

20 Special blessings were given to Aaron. While he did not have a part in the land that the rest of the people would inherit, he had more—a peculiar relationship to the Lord.

(5) The tithes and the Levites (18:21–24)

21–24 Giving tithes to the Levites was a gift of God in return for their work of ministry. Only Levites could approach the Tent of Meeting. The precincts were now sacred, fitted only for sacral people. The wrong people who approached for even a "right" reason would die. The Levites were cared for with a double portion: they were related to the Lord in a special way, and they were provided for by him from special sources.

(6) The contributions of the Levites (18:25–32)

25–32 The instruction of this section, which Moses was to relate to the Levites, is impressive: those who make their living by contributions for the Lord's work shall themselves be responsible for giving to the Lord. As others give, so must the Levites give. The offerings that they render to the Lord are not themselves fresh. Their grain is not new; neither is their wine. But since they themselves are not doing the harvesting of their own lands, the produce of others will be regarded as their own. As in the case of the people, the Levites are to render to the Lord "the best and holiest part of everything." By keeping faith in these matters, the Levites will escape judicial death.

i. The red heifer and the cleansing water (19:1–22)

(1) The statute of the red heifer (19:1–10)

1–4 Western readers have little understanding of or appreciation for ritual, and the slaughter of a magnificent animal is repugnant. The ritual of the cleansing waters is a direct requirement of God. The heifer was to be perfect, without defect, and unused as a draft animal. Only the very finest animals, ordinarily used for the improvement of the herd, were acceptable. The color of the heifer was to be red, presumably because of the color of blood. The animal involved was not a sacrificial beast. It was a cow, not a bull (cf. Lev 1:3). It was to be slaughtered, not sacrificed, outside the camp, not at the holy altar. In contrast to the sacrificial animals (see Lev 1:5), some of the blood of the heifer was to be sprinkled from the priest's finger seven times toward the front of the Tent of Meeting.

5–8 Instead of separating hide and offal from the meat and fat (cf. Lev 4:3–12), the heifer was to remain intact while it was burned. The fire of the offering was to be augmented with cedar, hyssop, and scarlet stuff (perhaps scarlet-colored wool). These elements were associated with cleansing properties (see Lev 14:4) and help us see the cleansing association that the resultant ashes were to have in the Hebrew consciousness. It is striking and unprecedented in the OT (cf. Lev 1:3–9) that the animal was to be burned in its entirety. The priest who officiated at the burning was ceremonially unclean for the rest of the day, as was the one who did the actual work at his command; both were considered clean after washing their bodies and clothes.

9–10 The priest and the worker, because they were unclean, were not to handle the ashes. A third person, who was ritually clean, was to gather the ashes and put them in a ceremonially clean place outside the camp. The ashes could not be brought into the camp, but they were holy. Only the clean could touch them; but whoever did so became unclean because of his contact with the dead remains. He was unclean for the rest of the day and had to bathe before returning to the camp. This was a lasting statute, pertaining to both the native-born and the aliens.

(2) Application of cleansing waters (19:11–13)

11–13 The ashes from the red heifer were kept outside the camp in a ritually pure place. Then a portion of these ashes would be mixed with water for cleansing from contact with dead bodies. The period of uncleanness was to be seven days; acts of purification were to be done on the third and seventh days. Willful neglect of the provision for cleansing brought not only judgment on the person but a pollution of the tabernacle itself. There was an issue of responsibility here. The person who was contaminated had to initiate the action. For the community the individual's state of uncleanness would pollute the dwelling place. One person's sinful state could endanger God's continuing presence in the midst of his people. The second danger was for himself. One who refused the provision of cleansing was to be a castoff (cf. 1Co 5:5).

(3) Specifics of uncleanness (19:14–16)

14–16 Touching a corpse rendered a person unclean. The individual might have died in battle or expired of a natural death. In either case the corpse was unclean and made all who touch it unclean. Thus the situation concerned a corpse out in the open in a tent, or in a container. If the container was open, then the result was uncleanness for persons in the room; it was as though the corpse was in the room with them. If the container was fastened, then there was no effect on others nearby. There would be many occasions for a person to become unclean, not because of a deliberate act of contact with a dead body, but just by being in the proximity of one who died. The cleansing water was a gift of grace, allowing family members to minister to the bodies of their deceased loved ones, knowing that their ritual impurity could be removed.

(4) Application of the cleansing waters for uncleanness (19:17–22)

17–22 The ritual application of the cleansing waters for purification rites is detailed in this section. First was the preparation of the water. Ashes from the heifer were placed in a clay pot. Then fresh water was added and mixed. This was not magic but ritual. The water was still water, the ashes were still ashes. Hyssop, a plant long associated with cleansing (e.g., Ex 12:22) and already associated with the ashes of the heifer (v.6), was used to sprinkle the water on all that was unclean—persons and things. It took a ceremonially clean person to sprinkle the ceremonially unclean person or thing. Following the sprinkling, the person being cleansed would then bathe and wash all his clothes. Failure to avail oneself of these provisions would result in his being cut off from the community, for his failure affected both himself and the sanctuary. The cleansing water of the ashes of the red heifer is specifically related to the cleansing property of the blood of Christ in the NT (Heb 9:13) and is a portrait of the cleansing of the believer (1Jn 1:7–9).

j. The ultimate rebellion in the sin of Moses (20:1–13)

1 The chronological notice indicates that this was the "first month" but does not give us the year (cf. 9:1). A comparison of 20:22–29 and 33:38, however, indicates that this chapter begins in the fortieth year from the Exodus. After challenging the authority of Moses, Miriam, along with her brother Aaron (ch. 12), nearly disappears from the scene. She may never have fully recovered the position of trust and privilege that she had enjoyed before this rebellion. It really was true: all those over the age of twenty at the time of the rebellion would die; even Miriam was buried in the sands of the desert instead of being given the opportunity to enter the Land of Promise.

2–8 Forty years earlier at Rephidim the people screamed to Moses to give them water to drink (Ex 17:1–3). Moses was instructed by the Lord to take the staff he had used to strike the Nile in the curse of plague (Ex 7:20) and to strike the rock at Horeb to initiate a flow of the water of blessing. Now, at the place of Israel's worst act of rebellion, the story was being rerun. The people now desired to die with those who had already passed away in earlier judgments of the Lord (see 14:22; 16:31–35). Moses and Aaron went to the entrance of the Tent of Meeting and fell down in obeisance to the Lord (see 14:5; 16:4, 22, 45). Then, as anticipated, there was the appearance of the Lord, in glory and in wonder. However, there was no fire, no judgment, no anger—just a gentle word to Moses to take his staff and to go with Aaron to bring water from the rock for the thirsting community. The instructions were quite clear: "Speak to that rock." While he was to take his staff, the symbol of his power through the Lord, he was merely to speak to the rock; and it would give its water for the people.

9–12 Moses began by doing exactly as the Lord had instructed him. Suddenly, Moses exploded against them—and against the rock. The accumulated anger and frustration of forty years bore down on Moses. The death of his sister was the end of an era. Yet nothing had changed; the children were as rebellious as ever. Moses' words—"Must we bring you water out of this rock?"—express the intense level of his exasperation and pain. At this point he reached out with the rod and struck the rock twice. In his rage Moses disobeyed the clear instructions of the Lord (v.8). While the water was released and the people and their livestock were refreshed, the rash action of Moses brought a stern rebuke from the Lord. The judgment of God had not flashed out against the people, but now it burst against his (usually) faithful servants. The end result was sure: neither Moses nor Aaron would enter the Land of Promise. The inclusion of Aaron in this verse demonstrates his partnership with his brother in the breach against the holiness of the Lord.

13 Once again a name of judgment was given to a place of Israel's journey: Meribah, "a place of strife" or "quarreling" (see NIV note). The same name had been used forty years earlier (Ex 17:7; also called Massah, "testing"). Psalm 95:8 laments the rebellion at Meribah and Massah, and Ps 114:8 celebrates both occasions of God's grace. For Meribah/Massah is both: a reminder of the rebellion and a symbol of celebration of God's mercy.

k. The resistance of Edom (20:14–21)

14–17 The nation was about to begin their last trek in the desert that would lead them to the land. The first nation whose land they would cross was Edom, a brother nation to Israel (see Ge 36:1). Moses diplomatically sent messengers to the king of Edom, requesting passage through his land. Moses used language designed to bring the most favorable decision: he called Edom a brother; he rehearsed their experience in Egypt and in the desert; he spoke of the deliverance of the Lord; he stated their present condition; and he asked permission to pass through the land of Edom. In all this Moses betrayed no desire for military aggrandizement; his only request was passage through their land.

18–21 The response of Edom was unusually hostile. Moses countered with an elaboration of his purpose. Again he assured Edom that he had no intention of conquest. Again Edom refused, backing up its haughty behavior with a show of force. With a sigh, Israel turned away to the east to make a broad circuit of the territory. The rebuff and its aftermath must have been especially galling to Moses and Aaron; it was another step in their decline.

l. The death of Aaron and the succession of Eleazar (20:22–29)

22–24 At last the people were on the move, north and east from their long stay in the desert near the oasis of Kadesh. As Israel came to the region of Mount Hor on the bor-

The hills that once belonged to Edom appear in the distance. In a color picture, these hill have a reddish hue.

der of Edom, the word of the Lord came to Moses and Aaron that Aaron, the aged priest, was about to die. The reason for his death is stated, a reminder of the sin at Meribah. The interests of Moses and Aaron in the transfer of power were also the interests of God. Even in the death of his servant, the Lord showed his continuing grace.

25–29 Before Aaron died, he was to see that his son Eleazar was his sure successor. In a dramatic symbol of this transfer of power, Moses took the garments from his brother, the insignia of his divine office, and placed them on his dutiful son Eleazar. At this point Moses did precisely as the Lord commanded.

Three men ascended the mountain; two returned. Aaron died there, apparently buried by his brother and his son. From the mount there was a sense of looking out to the land to the northwest; this was as close as Aaron would get. Later Moses would have a view of the land from another hill; he too would see the land only from a distance. Both brothers are associated with mountains on their dying; their sister Miriam with the oasis of Kadesh.

2. A climax of rebellion and hope and the end of their dying (21:1–25:18)

a. The destruction of Arad (21:1–3)

1–3 The first battle against the Canaanites was provoked by the king of Arad. The vow of the people speaks of their dependence on God for their victory. The verb translated "totally destroy" (GK 3049) means "to devote to the ban" and is related to the place name "Hormah" ("to devote to destruction"; see the NIV note on v.2). This ruthless action was determined from a sense that the people were engaging in holy war, where the extermination, not just the subjugation, of their enemies was their spiritual goal in the conquest of Canaan. The cup of iniquity was now full (see Ge 15:16); Israel was to be the instrument of the Lord's judgment. The success of the military action against the king of Arad was thorough. The new generation faced a new day; victory ahead seemed assured.

b. The bronze snake (21:4–9)

4–5 The people had to detour because of the intransigent attitude of Edom. They rejoined the road to the Sea of Reeds to make a broad circuit around Edom. They had been so very near the land and had even tasted the sweet wine of victory. But now they were wandering again, and they seemed to be as far away from "real" food as ever. With Moses' determination not to engage Edom in battle, the people began to speak against God and Moses. As their fathers, they asked why they had not been left back in Egypt and why they should be brought to this awful place to die. Again they complained about the lack of food and water. But then they went beyond their fathers and not only spoke of the monotony of manna, but they described it as "miserable food."

6–7 Once more God was rejected by his people; again he brought judgment on their heads. This time it was snakes, with "fire" in their venom. The virulent poison led to horrible, agonizing deaths. There was a change of sorts in the people as they asked for forgiveness. They were sinners, but they confessed their wrong. So Moses prayed for them as he had prayed before (11:2). And God answered in a most unusual way.

8–9 Instead of losing the snakes, the people had to get their fill of them (cf. 11:31–34). Moses, who had transmitted to Israel God's prohibition against making images, was told to make a graven image of a snake! In biblical thought snakes are not only detestable in themselves but are symbolic of the prince of darkness himself (Rev 12:9; 20:2). Think of the enormity of what Moses was asked to do! Verse 9 does not speak of eternal salvation but of physical healing. Many would die in the desert of the fiery snake venom, but not all had to die. God would keep alive those who would do as he demanded (cf. Jn 3:14–15).

c. The journey toward Moab and the Song of the Well (21:10–20)

10–15 At last the people were on the march; they skirted Edom and made their way to the Arnon, the wadi border between the region of Moab and that of the Amorites. This portion of the itinerary led to a quotation from a fragment of an ancient book termed "the book of the Wars of the Lord" (cf. Jos 10:13; 2Sa 1:18), mentioned only here in the OT. This book was presumably an ancient collection of songs of war in praise of God; the poem fragment attests to the variety of sources used by the author of the book. In biblical times one might well use song to set in the memory various places of encampment in the desert.

16–18a The quest for water had been a constant problem during the desert experience (see Ex 17; Nu 20). At this new promise of water from the Lord, the people burst forth into the triumphant words of the "Song of the Well"—a dramatic departure from their earlier behavior! When the people came to a likely spot, the Lord instructed Moses to have a well dug. The place received the happy name "Beer," meaning "well" in Hebrew. Here came also happy words from the Lord: "Gather the people together and I will give them water." How fitting it is that this was a place of song! Quite possibly this song came from the same collection as the Song of Places, the "Book of the Wars of the LORD" (see v.14). In this song there is a sense of the joy of knowing God, even though the name of God is not mentioned.

18b–20 From Beer the people journey ever onward, finally coming to the valley of Moab, where Pisgah was a fine spot to spy out the land of Canaan. Only later (Dt 34:1) do we associate this peak with Moses' final moments.

d. The defeat of Sihon of Heshbon (21:21–31)

21–26 The victories over Sihon and Og are the true beginning of victories. The Amorites, unlike the Edomites, were not related to the Israelites. As in the case of Edom (20:14–19), Israel first requested a right of passage. When Sihon tried to meet Israel with a show of force, he suffered an overwhelming defeat. The land of the Amorites was in Transjordan, extending from the Arnon River at the midpoint of the Dead Sea to the Jabbok River, which flows into the Jordan River some twenty-four miles north of the Dead Sea. Among Israel's conquests were the cities of Heshbon and its dependent settlements. It was this victory that cast such a pale of fear into the Moabites (see 22:2–3).

27–30 A third song is now included, possibly also from the "Book of the Wars of the LORD" (see v.14). This one was originally an Amorite taunt song celebrating their earlier victory over Moab. Heshbon, the capital city

of Sihon, had been wrested by the Amorites from a former Moabite king, perhaps Zippor, the father of Balak (see 22:2). Its reuse by Israel must have been particularly galling to Moab and the principal reason for Moab's call for Balaam. It was not just the people of Moab who had been defeated; it was their god Chemosh as well. But now a new God had come on the scene, and his power was not limited by geography.

31 After forty years of sojourn in the Desert of Sinai, the people had entered the land of the Amorites—the land that would become theirs.

e. Israel's defeat of Og of Bashan (21:32–22:1)

32–35 The region of this king and his people was east of the Sea of Galilee. By defeating Og, Israel was victor of Transjordan from the region of Moab to the heights of Bashan. The victories over Sihon and Og were matters for singing (Pss 135:11; 136:19–20) and regular parts of the commemoration of the works of the Lord in the Passover celebration.

Significantly, this section begins with a notice that Moses sent spies to scout out the land before he began his attack on the region of Bashan. These spies must have done as they were instructed, in contrast to the rebellious spies of chs. 13–14. It is also notable that the battle was joined with the army of Og only after the word of the Lord had come to Moses assuring him of a divine victory. This is to be the pattern of holy war, an obedient people following the sure word of their great God. The victory was complete because God's ways were followed.

On this hill the ruins of the city of Heshbon are being excavated by archaeologists. Courtesy Bastiaan Van Elderen.

22:1 This section ends with the statement of the journey of Israel to the plains of Moab and the subsequent encampment near the Jordan River across from the city of Jericho. This verse also sets the stage for one of the most remarkable stories in the Bible: the dramatic encounter of Balaam, the pagan mantic, with the God of Israel (22:2–24:25).

f. Balak and Balaam (22:2–41)

(1) The "call" of Balaam (22:2–20)

2–3 The story of Balaam begins with the gut-wrenching fear of Balak son of Zippor, the king of Moab. With the vast army of Israel encamped on the edge of his territory, he feared the very worst. Balak's fear was intensified because of Israel's victories over his northern enemy neighbors (see 21:10–31). A new, stronger enemy was present, before whom Balak and his people seemed to be powerless. Balak was not aware that Israel had no designs on the land of Moab. As the Lord was about to give Canaan to Israel, so the Moabite land was a gift of the Lord to Moab. In fact, the Lord had prohibited Israel from attacking the territorial integrity of Moab in their wars of conquest (Dt 2:9). Yet there was a reason for the fear of Moab: the events of the Exodus salvation of Israel were designed to provoke fear in all nations (see Dt 2:25).

4 The image of Israel as an ox is an emphatic symbol of her strength and power. The association of Moab with the Midianites in this verse is more significant than we might first think (cf. ch. 25).

5–7 Since Balak believed that there was no military means available to withstand the forces of Israel, he sought to battle Israel on the level of pagan divination. He sent for a diviner of renown. Balaam was an internationally known prophet, an expert in examining the entrails of animals and observing natural phenomena to determine the will of the gods. He thought that the Lord God of Israel was like any other deity whom he imagined he might manipulate by mantic acts. The letter of Balak to Balaam indicates his intent: to bring a curse on a people who were under a blessing of a god. This story thus takes us into the mysterious world of blessing and cursing in the ancient Near East. If God's blessing of the Israelites could be destroyed, then they would no longer be a threat.

8–11 Balaam is altogether outside Israel's prophetic tradition. He was a pagan, foreign national whose mantic acts centered on animal divination, including the dissection of animal livers, the movement of animals, and the flight of birds. He believed that he had a way with the gods, a hold on them. To him Israel's Lord was not the Lord of heaven but just another deity whom he might manipulate. He was in for the surprise of his life. That God did speak to Balaam is not to be denied; it is just that Balaam did not yet realize that the God of Israel was not like the supposed deities of his usual machinations.

12–20 Israel was under the blessing of the Lord as the heritage of the Abrahamic covenant (Ge 12:1–3). Balaam was being sought by Balak to bring Israel under a divine curse; this God would not allow, for Israel was "blessed" (GK 1385). The first words of God to Balaam are a prohibition for him to accompany the emissaries of Balak. But when these emissaries returned to Balak, he refused to listen to their report of Balaam's refusal to return with them. He sent grander and nobler representatives, with greater and finer promises of gifts for this mantic to come with them. Balaam first said that nothing could change his mind. Then in a dream he was given permission to go with them.

There seems to be a contradiction in the permission God granted Balaam in v.20 with the prohibition he had given earlier (v.12) and the anger of the Lord that was displayed against Balaam on his journey (v.22). The difficulty is best seen as lying in the contrary character of Balaam rather than in God. God first had forbidden him to go to Moab to curse Israel; then God allowed Balaam to go to Moab, but only as he would speak at the direction of the Lord. Balaam's real intentions, however, were known to the Lord, and hence by his severe displeasure he confronted the pagan mantic on the road.

(2) The donkey story (22:21–41)

21–28 The pagan mantic, the donkey, and the angel of the Lord are brought together in this truly tragicomic scene. The donkey has been depicted from the earliest times as stupid and contrary. Yet here the "stupid" ass saw the angel of the Lord and attempted to protect her rider from God's drawn sword. Three times the hapless Balaam beat his donkey. Then the donkey spoke. The donkey did not give a prophetic oracle; she merely said what a mistreated animal might say to an abusive master if given the chance. What keeps this story from the genre of legend or fairy tale is that the animal did not speak of its own accord but as it was given the power to do so by the Lord. Before he revealed himself to Balaam, the Lord first "got his attention." Balaam had to learn from a donkey before he could learn from God.

29–33 The point of the story is furthered by Balaam's words, "If I had a sword in my hand, I would kill you right now." The ridiculous picture of the hapless Balaam looking for a sword is precious; there was a sword very near, but the object was not about to be the donkey (vv.23, 31–33)! All the donkey said was that she had been a good donkey. In some ways the opening of the eyes of the pagan prophet to see the reality of the living God was the greater miracle. The animal was but a brute beast; the prophet was a man bent on trafficking with idolatrous gods.

34–35 The words of Balaam to God lead us to think that he was truly repentant. Only the later outcome of the story shows this to be false (see chs. 25; 31). The Lord told Balaam to continue on his journey but to "speak only what I tell you." This is the point of the whole chapter: Balaam would not be able to speak cursing as he had planned. Instead, he would be the most remarkable instrument of God in blessing his people, Israel.

36–38 We are led by the narrative into the enemy camp. Balak was so anxious to have Balaam begin his curse-work that he went to some distance to meet him at the border of his land, and then he upbraided his visitor for the delay in his journey. Doubtless Balak puzzled over the words that Balaam greeted him with: "I must speak only what God puts in my mouth." Ordinarily Balaam probably believed he could say pretty much what he pleased to say, if the price was right, with the belief that the will of the gods would in some manner correspond with his words. But not this time! We learn of the consternation of the enemy over the power of God in the camp of Israel.

39–41 Balak and Balaam engaged in animal sacrifices as they prepared for the mantic acts. The pieces given to Balaam presumably would have included the livers, for he was a specialist in liver divination. Numbers 24:1 reports that Balaam subsequently gave up on his acts of sorcery as the power of the word of the Lord came on him. But at the beginning he started his procedures as he always had. Yet never did he speak as he was about to speak.

g. Balaam's seven oracles (23:1–24:25)

(1) Balaam's first oracle (23:1–12)

1–6 The elaborate sacrificial actions of Balaam and Balak are pagan. The number seven was held in high regard among Semitic peoples in general. The many animals would provide abundant liver and organ materials for the diviner. Balaam was in charge; Balak was now his subordinate. Despite the pagan and unsavory actions, the Lord deigned to meet with Balaam and to speak through him. We often say that God will never use an unclean vessel. However, God may use whatever vessel he wishes. Those who had sent for Balaam were standing by the altar, hoping for a word from heaven that would destroy their presumed foe. They received a word from heaven all right, but not what they expected.

7–8 The Hebrew word translated "oracle" (GK 5442; normally translated "proverb") establishes the distinctive nature of the prophecies of Balaam; none of the prophecies of the true prophets of Israel is described by this term. The two verbs "to curse" and "to speak against with indignation" work together to give the sense of anger and indignation. "Jacob" and "Israel" are interchangeable words marking out the people of God's covenant. The words of v.7 represent Balak's desire for the Lord to break his promise to the fathers. Yet Balaam was unable to do what he had been hired to do. The blessing of Israel was inviolable; Balaam had no power to attack their blessing.

9–10 Balaam explained that Israel was unique among the nations. Her distinction was in her relationship with her God. As he is holy, so his people were holy. Balaam's wistful desire was to share in Israel's blessing! He who had come to curse wished himself to be blessed. But just as Balaam could not "get their number," so he realized that he was not a part of Israel's destiny, for he never participated in the death of the righteous (31:8, 16).

11–12 Balaam was unable to curse Israel; Israel was unique because of her blessing from the Lord. Balak was furious—and the Lord is sovereign. The words of consternation of Balak and the response of Balaam are marvelous.

(2) Balaam's second oracle (23:13–26)

13–17 Trying to cover all the angles, Balak attempted to reduce the power of the people by selecting a point where their immense numbers would be obscured. Alas for Balak, the oracle that followed exceeded the first in its blessing on Israel. If one is confronted only with a small percentage of the whole, Balak reasoned, then the enormity of the nation would not cause the gods to bless when they were requested to curse Israel. The result of all this frenetic activity was the same as the first time. Again the Lord met Balaam and gave him a new word, to the consternation of Balak who was piously pretending at his pagan altar.

18–20 The naming of Balak in the second line as "son of Zippor" is a fine use of parallelism. The words "God is not a man, that he should lie" describe the immutability of the Lord and the integrity of his word. Balaam is himself a foil for God. Balaam is constantly shifting, prevaricating, equivocating, changing—he is himself the prime example of the distinction between God and humans. Balaam's view of gods was based on his own human failings. Now he confronts God who is not like a man in his failures at all. All others may change; God—even with all his power—cannot change, for he cannot deny himself (cf. 1Sa 15:29; Ps 89:35–37). God must fulfill his promise, for he has bound his character to his word. The blessing of God is thus irrevocable.

21 It is because God is the King that he was able to use Balaam for his own ends—to bless his people in a new and wonderful manner. The whole course of Israel's experience in the desert was one evil after another, one misery on another. Yet it is evidently the standing of Israel that is in view here, not her state. It is also possible that the words "evil" and "misery" are not used to refer to moral issues but

to mantic concerns. That is, God does not look on his people with "an evil eye" or a hostile glance. When Israel is presented in the context of a hostile environment, then it is the blessing of Israel that is maintained. Only in the family is the sinfulness of the people addressed. Since the Lord is in their midst, they are invincible from outside attack.

22 The wild ox is a traditional image of power (also 24:8). The Hebrew expression speaks of two horns (which the NIV paraphrases as "strength"). God is in the process still of bringing his people from Egypt; he will complete his work soon by bringing them into his land. And along the way he is their strength.

23 The reason for Israel's eventual triumph is because there can be "no sorcery against Jacob." Balaam had no tricks to withstand the blessing of Israel. Since there is no possibility of the use of magic either for or against Israel, whatever comes of Israel will truly be regarded as the work of God. Balaam had come to use magic, but he could not "get their number" (v.10). God was in control, and Balaam was his puppet.

24 Israel was about to arise and devour its foes, as a lioness on the hunt (see 24:9). At this point the would-be victim of the curse of Balaam and Balak became the instrument of the destruction of its own enemies. As a lioness (the huntress), Israel was about to rouse herself and bring her foes down to destruction. She would not rest until the enemy was devoured, its blood lapped clean at the end of the chase.

25–26 The tragicomic nature of the story is again seen in the aftermath. Balak appears incredulous. He gasps, "What have you done to me!" in v.11. Now he says, in essence, "Stop it all together." But Balaam is indefatigable in his mission from the Lord.

(3) Balaam's third oracle (23:27–24:14)

23:27–24:2 Balak then tried another tack. Perhaps a change of place would lead to a change of words. The mention of Peor takes on a horrible association in Nu 25; apparently this was the center for the worship of Baal. Again seven altars and sacrifices were prepared, but this time with a significant change. Balaam did not go about his normal routine of sorcery. This time "the Spirit of

God came upon him." This unexpected language prepares us for the heightened revelation about to come from the unwitting messenger. The oracles build in intensity and in depth of meaning.

3–4 The introduction to this oracle is extensive and descriptive of Balaam's experience in the presence of the Lord. Now Balaam's eyes were opened (cf. 22:31). The repeated use of the term "oracle" adds significant solemnity to his words. Balaam's experience included a revelation. He had now heard God and seen the vision of him. Balaam lay prone before him, but his eyes were now opened to wonders he had not dreamed of. But the seer still was not a man of faith; he was not a member of the family (see again 23:10: "Let me").

5–6 Balaam, speaking prophetically, looked down on the tents of Israel, but he thought of their future. He saw the orderliness of the encampments, but he was given a vision of their coming grandeur. He spoke in general but luxuriant terms of the blessings that would fall on Israel as they settled in their new land. The people would have a sense of Eden in the lushness of their blessing from the Lord.

7 This verse speaks of luxuriance of productivity as well as of the majesty of the coming king of Israel. It is prophetic in tone. The most problematic issue is the reference to "Agag." Agag was the opponent of King Saul in the tenth century, hundreds of years later. Possibly "Agag" was a common name among the Amalekite kings (cf. Abimelech in Philistia and Ben-Hadad in Aram). In this case the use of this name may grow out of the attack on Israel by Amalek (see Ex 17:8–13) and again when Israel first came against Canaan (see Nu 14:45). But it is also possible that here we confront a specific, predictive prophecy of a victory of a king of Israel over a great enemy. The words "their king will be greater than Agag" may be a historical continuity that begins with the attacks of Amalek in Israel's recent past, leads to the future victory of Saul over his nemesis, Agag (1Sa 15:32–33), and culminates in the victory of Israel's greatest King (Jesus) over all her enemies. This is certainly in keeping with the prophecies that follow in the fourth oracle (see v.17).

8 The broad interpretation suggested for v.7 fits with the direction of v.8. It is stunning to

hear the central words of Israel's salvation ("God is bringing him out of Egypt") recited by one who was an outsider and a hostile foe. The imagery of victory is in the manner of a lion (as in v.9).

9 The theology of blessing and cursing (Ge 12:2–3) is now made an explicit part of the oracle of blessing. The idea of the lion is taken from the second oracle (see 23:24). The stunning climax is in the blessing of God on all who bless Israel. The irony cannot be missed by Balaam or by any who hear his words. In his actions he brings a curse on his own head, even as he speaks blessing!

10–14 The oracles could well have ended with the great third word from Balaam. But they do not; there is one grander yet to come. Balak is beside himself. He rages in anger, strikes his hands, and rants. He observes that at this point Balaam has given three distinct blessings of Israel. At least Balak has got this right. In his disgust with the failure of Balaam to curse Israel, Balak dismisses him without pay—the ultimate insult to his greed (2Pe 2:15). Balaam is ready to leave; the whole thing must have been uncomfortable for him as well! But before he goes, he is constrained by the Lord to speak again, his greatest oracle. In the phrase "in days to come" we recognize the signal for the distant future.

(4) Balaam's fourth oracle (24:15–19)

15–16 As in the third oracle, the introduction to the fourth oracle is lengthy, preparing the reader for the startling words of the prophecy to come. Comparing this section with vv.3–4, we find one new phrase: "Who has knowledge of the Most High." This expansion intensifies the anticipation of the blessing that follows; the repetition helps tie these oracles together, giving a sense of crescendo and climax.

17 Without question this is the most debated and the most important verse in the oracle corpus. The theme is that Israel has a coming deliverer. In agreement with many in the early church and in early Judaism, we believe this text speaks unmistakably of the coming of the Messiah. That this prophecy should come from one who was unworthy makes it all the more dramatic and startling. The terms "star" (GK 3919; cf. 2Pe 1:19; Rev 22:16) and "scepter" (GK 8657; cf. Ge 49:10) certainly may speak of the promise of a king like David, Israel's greatest king in the historical period. But ultimately these words reach beyond him. The setting for the text is "in days to come" (see again v.14), an eschatological notice. The inclusion of these words in the text is for the final victory over the enemies of Israel. The section reaches to the end because it reaches all the way to the Savior.

18–19 In the time of Moses, Edom was a nation that Israel was forbidden to attack (cf. 20:14–21). The future projection of the text assumes a time of enmity of Edom against Israel (cf. Obadiah), for which they finally received their penalty for the shabby treatment of Israel. David became a victor over Edom (2Sa 8:14). But after the division of the kingdom, Edom became independent (2Ki 8:20–22) and remained an implacable foe of Israel, awaiting the final wrath of God (Isa 63:1–6). In the eschaton, words such as Edom and Seir stand for any enemies of the people of God and of their Messiah. The contrasting words to the ultimate downfall of Edom at the end of v.18 must be stressed: Israel will grow strong while her enemies languish.

This is also the point of v.19. There is no subject for the verb "will come out"; the likely referent is the Star-Scepter of v.17. The Star-Scepter makes Israel triumphant as he gains dominion over the enemies of God's people. The theme of this oracle is sustained: Israel's ultimate blessing centers in her Deliverer from all enemies.

(5) Balaam's fifth oracle (24:20)

20 The first defeat of Israel in the desert was at the hand of the Amalekites, when Israel went against them foolishly without the blessing of God (see 14:44–45). A day of reckoning would come on Amalek that would be dreadful. The Amalekites were defeated by Saul (1Sa 14:48; but see 15:1–35) and David (1Sa 30:18; 2Sa 8:12). But there is also the possibility that this verse has an extension into the days of the Messiah's final victory over all enemies.

(6) Balaam' sixth oracle (24:21–22)

21–22 The spotlight of judgment turns from Amalek to the Kenites. Why they come under attack here is not certain; perhaps it is because they became associated with the Midi-

anites who came under the scourge of Israel (Nu 31). The mention of Assyria is also a surprise, as its ascendancy to power was centuries away from Balaam's day; yet Assyria was known as a powerful city-state even in Abraham's day. This text may be a powerful insight into the way of the prophets—the taking of familiar things and juxtaposing them in startling ways.

(7) Balaam's seventh oracle (24:23–25)

23–25 Balaam's last oracle is more difficult than any of the others to interpret. The relative obscurity of the words compels attention; clarity may come as the time of the oracle is realized. Its meaning falls in line with the lesson taught throughout the oracles: the sense of the utter dependence on the Lord; no one is able to live, except God establishes it. The mention of Asshur connects v.24 with the preceding oracle. The identification of Kittim in the early period of Israel's history seems to be Cyprus. But ultimately the word was applied to Rome (cf. Da 11:30). The resulting meaning may refer to the final battle between forces of the west (the Kittim) and forces of the east (Asshur and Eber)—a battle in which both will be destroyed, presumably before a greater power than either (the Lord of glory). One nation will rise and supplant another, only to face its own doom. With the promises of a future deliverer ringing in their ears, the defeated collaborators Balaam and Balak depart.

h. Israel's final rebellion with the Baal of Peor and the death of the first generation (25:1–18)

This chapter presents a formative encounter with Baal worship, a miniature of the disaster that would one day engulf and destroy the nation. The time is the end of the forty-year period of Israel's desert experience. The place is the staging area for the conquest of the land of Canaan. The issue is that of apostasy from the Lord by participation in the debased, sexually centered Canaanite religious rites of Baal worship. This chapter is an end and a beginning. It marks the end of the first generation; it also points to the beginning of a whole new series of wicked acts that will finally lead to Israel's punishment (see on 33:50–56). All the rebellions up to this point have centered in murmurings against the Lord and his servants Moses and Aaron. But this chapter describes Israel's involvement in the worship of another deity.

(1) The involvement of Israel in the worship of Baal Peor (25:1–3)

1–2 "Shittim" is another name for the region of Israel's staging for the conquest of the land; it was in Transjordan, across from Jericho (see Jos 2:1). From 31:8, 16 we learn that the principal instigator of the apostasy of the Israelites was Balaam son of Beor. Failing to destroy Israel by the means of the mantic curse, Balaam then seduced Israel by the Canaanite practices of the sexually centered worship of the god Baal. The phrase "Moabite women" ties this chapter to the preceding ones (chs. 22–24). What the fathers of Moab could not do, their daughters were able to accomplish. Always in the ancient Near Eastern context, references to sexual imagery such as this suggest interconnecting circles of sexual immorality tied to sacral rites of prostitution, essential parts of pagan religious systems of the day. The phrase "to the sacrifices of their gods" reminds us that the true worship of the Lord, which was sacrificial in nature, was easily compromised in the minds of the people because of the sacrificial systems of their neighbors (see Ex 34:15; Dt 32:38; Jdg 16:23; et al.).

3 The verb "to be joined in worshiping" (GK 7537) is literally "to be yoked," as oxen are yoked in a common task. In this case, Israel was "yoked" to pagan peoples in the worship of their god. The verb speaks of adapting to the worship patterns of a foreign people, an abhorrent concept from which Israel was prohibited (see Dt 22:10; cf. 2Co 6:14). "Peor" describes a mountain in Moab (see 23:28) where the manifestation of Baal was worshiped. In v.18 Peor is used alone of the god (see 31:16; Jos 22:17). The wrath of the Lord is a "reddening of his nose" (lit. Heb.), a flashing of his rage. God has his flash point; his rage has a trigger. It should have been expended against Moab and Balaam because of their effrontery; but here it is directed against Israel. They have deflected his rage from others to themselves by their folly.

(2) The judgment of the Lord on his errant people (25:4–5)

4–5 God's rage against his people provoked a terrible judgment. The gravity of the sin called not only for death but for a special display of the corpses so that the survivors would be strongly warned of the consequences. "In broad daylight" speaks of something done openly, publicly (so 2Sa 12:12). The execution of the leaders was designed to divert God's anger from the populace as a whole. So Moses commanded the judges of Israel to kill those persons who had attached themselves to Baal Peor. This may be one of the most indelicate texts of Scripture, where Israel's judges are commanded to kill their own people who are engaged in the worship of Baal. If they are not excised, they will soon ruin the entire nation.

(3) The zeal of Phinehas (25:6–9)

6 The wording of v.6 is somewhat problematic. Perhaps it is best read: "Then a certain Israelite man brought *the* Midianite woman to *the Tent [of God]* right before the eyes of Moses and the eyes of all the congregation of Israel; *and they were sporting* at the entrance of the Tent of Meeting." The last phrase in the NIV indicates that it was Moses and the congregation of Israel who were "weeping" (GK 1134; see below) at the entrance to the holy precincts. No doubt the outrage of the events might have driven Moses and pious persons to weep and to beg God for forgiveness. It seems to me, however, that the subject of the verb "weeping" is not Moses and the congregation but the sinning Israelite and his Midianite partner. The focus is on them, not Moses. What they did was to engage in a sexual embrace in the manner of Baal worship, before Moses, at the entrance of the holy Tent of God!

What I am suggesting is that the author made a deliberate substitution of an opposite word, "weeping," to connote "caressing," an unusual form of euphemism to stress the heightened enormity of this act. They are not weeping; they are engaged in delirious lovemaking (cf. Ge 26:8; Ex 32:6). The contempt for the holy things and the word of the Lord shown by Zimri and his Midianite lover, Cozbi (v.15), is unimaginable. In joining the sexual frenzies of the sacrificial feasts of Baal, the man and his partner act to transform the worship of the Lord into the type of sexual rites that were the mode of Canaan. Had this outrage not been stopped, there could never have been true worship in the Holy Place again.

The person is identified in the Hebrew as "the Midianite woman" which suggests that she was a person of prominence. Perhaps she was the high priestess of the religion at Baal Peor. While priests were always male in Israel, priests could be women in the pagan religions that surrounded Israel. In fact, the sexually centered religions would have catered to women in their priesthood. Perhaps this is the principal reason that Israel had no women priests. The brazenness of these two made them not just sinners but an abomination to the Lord.

7–8 When Phinehas the son of Eleazar grandson of Aaron (Ex 6:25) saw what was happening at the entrance of the tent, he reached for a "spear" (GK 8242) and drove it through the licentious couple. Possibly the implement he used was a spear that he took from a soldier nearby. It is also possible that the Hebrew word used here might mean "knife," a more expected tool for a priest. Phinehas was a man of valor and a true servant of the Lord. Ultimately, he is typical of Christ the Victor (see Pss 2; 110; Rev 19). He is an early embodiment of "star" and "scepter" of 24:17, the smiter of Moab.

Verse 8 says that Phinehas pursued the couple into the "vaulted canopy" (NIV, "tent"). It is possible that the term refers to some canopy at the entrance of the Tent of Meeting and that the couple were not actually in the Most Holy Place. That Phinehas pierced through both of them indicates that the knife or spear could not have been little and that tremendous force would have been needed to plunge the knife or spear through both bodies. The staying of the plague indicates that this was not just an outrageous instance of debauchery, but likely the couple were the instigators of the pagan rites!

9 The number who died because of the flagrant actions of the people in their worship of the Baal of Peor (24,000; see 1Co 10:8) exceeded even those who died in the rebellion of Korah and his allies (14,700; see 16:49).

(4) The Lord's covenant with Phinehas (25:10–13)

10–13 The zeal of Phinehas for the honor of the Lord became the occasion for the Lord's covenanting with him and his descendants as God's true priests. Since the hero of our story is a priest, our estimation of priests and

priesthood should be enhanced. Then we remember that Christ is priest. The best in priests points to Christ. The Lord now institutes his covenant with the priests through Phinehas. He was priest by divine right, being descended from the right family in an immediate line. He showed himself to be the rightful priest by his interest in divine righteousness. He is now confirmed priest by the rite of the divine covenant. This covenant is God's doing; it involves his "seed," and it is lasting. In the case of Abraham, God first chose him; then by Abraham's action of faith, the Lord confirmed his covenant with him (see Ge 12; 15; 22). In the case of Phinehas, he was already chosen by God; but in his action, God's covenant with him is confirmed. Surprisingly, by the action of Phinehas, "atonement" was made for the people: the plague was stopped (v.9).

(5) The aftermath of the rebellion (25:14–18)

14–18 Only after the role of Phinehas has been suitably celebrated are the names of the antagonists given. The Israelite was a prince of the house of Simeon, Zimri son of Salu. He was not an insignificant individual. As the great pride of Eleazar must have swelled over the actions of his son that day, so there must have been extraordinary shame among the members of Zimri's family. Zimri ("My Remembrance") had been named in praise of God. However, he has come to be forever remembered as the one who nearly destroyed his people in his flagrant, wanton attack on the pure worship of God. The name of his Midianite partner is given as Cozbi daughter of Zur. "Cozbi" means "My Lie" or "Deception." She stands forever memorialized as a prime example of the deception of the allure of pagan worship. From a noble house of her own people, she was likely a priestess of her religion, a prototype of Jezebel who would later be instrumental in bringing Baal and Asherah worship into the center of the life of Israel.

Because of their active participation in the seduction of the sons of Israel, the Midianites were put under the curse of God and were henceforth to be treated as enemies. The Midianites had been in league with Balak from the beginning of the confrontation (see on 22:4); they now became the objects of a holy war of Israel to declare the glory of the name the Lord (see ch. 31).

II. The Prospects for the Second Generation to Enter the Promised Land (26:1–36:13)

The book of Numbers is rightly named and its organization is simple. There are two grand sections: (1) the census and preparation for march of the first generation and their subsequent failure and judgment (chs. 1–25); (2) the census and preparation for march of the second generation and the hope that they will not repeat the sins of their fathers and mothers (chs. 26–36).

A. The Preparation for the Triumphal March to the Promised Land, the Second Generation (26:1–32:42)

1. The second census of the new generation that will enter the land (26:1–65)

a. The command of the Lord to take the census (26:1–4)

1–4 The plague of ch. 25 was the final judgment of God on the first generation. The first census, taken over thirty-eight years earlier, was for conscription to the army for the conquest of the Land of Promise. That first generation of people over the age of twenty had died. It was now time for the new generation to be numbered and mustered. It was the same task: number the able-bodied men over the age of twenty to conscript them for the army of Israel, though the place had changed from Sinai to Moab. More importantly, the people had changed. The aged Moses was joined in this task by his nephew Eleazar. Aaron was dead (20:28). Miriam was dead (20:1). And Moses was soon to die.

The words of v.4b serve as the section heading for the listing of tribe by tribe that follows. The reference to the departure from Egypt indicates that this generation is regarded as the Exodus people. It is as though their parents had not lived. The story begins anew, as though the people had just left bondage in Egypt.

b. The enumeration of the people by their ancestral tribes and clans (26:5–50)

(1) The tribe of Reuben (26:5–11)

5–7 Pride of place is given to Reuben, firstborn of Jacob. Four clans are descended from his four sons (cf. Ge 46:9). From the seventy persons of Ge 46:27 to the quarter million (or two and one-half million!) of Nu 26:51 is an enormous increase, despite the conditions in Egypt for four hundred years, coupled with the experience in the desert for another forty years.

8–11 The listing of the families of Reuben becomes an occasion to remind us of the part that certain of their number (esp. Dathan and Abiram) had in the rebellion of Korah (16:1). The overwhelming judgment was to remain "a warning sign" to succeeding generations. The tribe of Reuben numbered a decrease of 2,770 from the 46,500 of the first census (a loss of about 6 percent). Their further history is in 1Ch 5:1–10.

(2) The tribe of Simeon (26:12–14)

12–14 The greatest loss was among the tribe of Simeon. The exceedingly wicked Zimri (ch. 25) was of the house of Simeon. Perhaps the larger number of the 24,000 who died in the fairly recent plague were of the house of Simeon. Ohad of Ge 46:10 and Ex 6:15 is not mentioned in Numbers; perhaps he died childless. This tribe experienced a decrease of 37,100 from the 59,300 of the first census (a decrease of about 63 percent). The later history of the family is in 1Ch 4:24–43.

(3) The tribe of Gad (26:15–18)

15–18 There are several problems in parallel passages with the names of these sons of Gad. When we compare the names in Ge 46:16, we find some variations of names. There are several explanations: (1) different spellings for the same name, (2) different names for the same person, and (3) confusion of scribes and hence mistakes in the copying of the names. The tribe of Gad numbered a decrease of 5,150 from the 45,650 of the first census (a decrease of about 11 percent). Their further history is in 1Ch 5:11–17.

(4) The tribe of Judah (26:19–22)

19–22 The family of Judah was unique in that two sons died childless in Canaan before their father left for Egypt. Now, hundreds of years later, the sordid story of Er and Onan is alluded to, to cause the people to remember. The twin sons of Judah by his son's wife, Tamar, each fathered a clan. The firstborn, Perez, has two subclans. Likely the listing of these subclans makes up for the loss of the two deceased older sons. Perez has the double honor; his line includes king David (Ru 4:18–22) and David's Greater Son, Jesus (Mt 1:3; Lk 3:33). The tribe of Judah numbered an increase of 1,900 from the 74,600 of the first census (a gain of less than 3 percent). Their further history is in 1Ch 2:3–4:23.

(5) The tribe of Issachar (26:23–25)

23–25 There is a difficulty with the spelling of Puah (cf. Ge 46:13; 1Ch 7:1), and the name Job is mistakenly written in the Heb. of Ge 46:13 for Jashub. The tribe of Issachar numbered an increase of 9,900 from the 54,400 of the first census (a gain of about 18 percent). Their further history is in 1Ch 7:1–5.

(6) The tribe of Zebulun (26:26–27)

26–27 Sered, Elon, and Jahleel, sons of Zebulun, founded the three clans of this tribe. The tribe of Zebulun numbered an increase of 3,100 from the 57,400 of the first census (a gain of over 5 percent). Their further history is not recorded in 1Ch 2–8; only the name of the tribe is given in 2:1. This is a strange omission (see also the comment on Dan, vv.42–43).

(7) The tribe of Manasseh (26:28–34)

28–34 Joseph received the double honor of his father, Jacob, by having two sons receive equal status with his brothers among the tribes of Israel. With the removal of the tribe of Levi from the lay tribes, this "bonus" to Joseph maintained the sacred number twelve for the fathers' houses. The tribe of Ephraim was superior in numbers to Manasseh in Nu 1; the reverse is true in Nu 26. Later in Israel's history, Ephraim becomes the counterpart in the north to the importance of Judah in the south. Yet at this point the tribe of Ephraim is among the smallest (only Simeon with 22,200 is smaller).

There are a couple of unusual things in the roster of the clans of Manasseh. First, only one son of Manasseh is listed: Makir (see Ge 50:23; Nu 27:1; 32:39–40; Dt 3:15; Jos 13:31; 17:1, 3). The tribe of Manasseh did not divide into subclans until the fourth generation. The last named presents the second unusual factor; Zelophehad, actually the grandson of Gilead, "had no sons, only daughters." While the descendants of Jacob have a remarkable propensity to father sons, surely there were

daughters along the way! Yet Zelophehad's daughters are nearly the only ones mentioned in this chapter (v.46). Since the chapter is a roster of men being mustered for war, the lack of the mention of daughters elsewhere is understandable. The reason for mentioning Zelophehad's daughters is to set the stage for the narrative of ch. 27 (cf. ch. 36).

The tribe of Manasseh numbered an increase of 20,500 from the 32,200 of the first census (a stunning gain of 64 percent). Their further history is in 1Ch 7:14–19.

(8) The tribe of Ephraim (26:35–37)

35–37 The clans of Ephraim are listed in three sons and one subclan (Eran is not mentioned elsewhere). The tribe of Ephraim numbered a drop of 8,000 from the 40,500 of the first census (a decrease of about 20 percent). Their further history is in 1Ch 7:20–29.

(9) The tribe of Benjamin (26:38–41)

38–41 The lists of the names of sons and clans in the earlier rosters have presented some problems of spelling and identification when those in Nu 26 are compared with similar ones in Genesis and 1 Chronicles. But in the case of the tribe of Benjamin, we come to nearly insurmountable problems of correlation. Apparently the listings of the clans of Benjamin is quite fluid, perhaps depending on differing purposes of our sources, as well as considerable confusion in the transmission of these names. The most hopeful thing one can observe is that scribes did not attempt to go through these lists to harmonize them.

The tribe of Benjamin numbered an increase of 10,200 from the 35,400 of the first census (a gain of 29 percent). Their further history is in 1Ch 7:6–12; 8:1–39.

(10) The tribe of Dan (26:42–43)

42–43 The briefest of all the tribal notations is given for Dan; only one clan (Shuham) is listed. Yet the total population is large, with only Judah being larger. In Ge 46:23, the only son listed for Dan is Hushim. The relationship of the words Shuham and Hushim is unknown. The tribe of Dan numbered an increase of 1,700 from the 62,700 of the first census (a gain of about 3 percent). Dan is not mentioned at all in the tribal genealogies of 1Ch 1–8 (see also comment on vv.26–27, with respect to Zebulun).

(11) The tribe of Asher (26:44–47)

44–47 One name has dropped in Nu 26 from the listing of the names of the sons of Asher in Ge 46:17 and 1Ch 7:30, the name Ishvah. Perhaps he did not found a clan and so is not listed in Numbers. The mention of Serah, daughter of Asher, is remarkable (cf. Ge 46:17; 1Ch 7:30). Is it possible she was the only daughter born to the twelve sons of Jacob, even as Jacob himself had only one daughter, Dinah? The tribe of Asher numbered an increase of 11,900 from the 41,500 of the first census (a gain of 29 percent). Their further history is in 1Ch 7:30–40.

(12) The tribe of Naphtali (26:48–50)

48–50 Naphtali numbered a decrease of 8,000 from the 53,400 of the first census (a drop of 15 percent). There are four clans. The tribe of Naphtali is in the twelfth rank in both census lists. The names of the sons of Naphtali, but no further history of the tribe, are in 1Ch 7:13.

c. The grand celebrative number, to the praise of the Lord (26:51)

51 Despite all those who died during the desert experience, the total—601,730—was nearly the same as those who were first numbered (on the large numbers, see the introduction). The loss of 1,820 persons from the first census is a drop of only 0.3 percent—a negligible sum! It is utterly remarkable that the total number has remained nearly unchanged even though the people have lived under the most trying conditions for a period of thirty-eight years. God's faithfulness to his people is grandly celebrated with this triumphant chapter of census; the number glorifies God and anticipates the time when the Israelites will be as countless as the sand on the seashore.

A final note: The listing of the clans in the second census would later be very important for the nation for purposes of tribal inheritance. Not all those who were part of Israel were genetically descended from Jacob through his twelve sons. From the beginning there was a joining of destiny with the people of Israel of persons of varied backgrounds. However, to have their part in the land, they had to have a tie with a tribe and a family.

d. The allotment of the land on the basis of the names of the families of Israel (26:52–56)

52–56 In the first census the emphasis was fully on preparation for warfare (see 1:3, 45). The second census relates not only to military service in the conquest of the land but to inheritance rights once the land was secured. It is a section of promise designed to impel the people to faithfulness as well as to ensure the equitable distribution of land. Larger tribes would receive larger shares, but the decisions of place would be made by lot. The land is God's gift to his people; hence their shares in it are their inheritance from him.

e. The families and numbers of the Levites (26:57–62)

57–58a This pericope corresponds to the separate counting of the Levites in the first census (see 1:47–53; 3:1–39; cf. Ex 6:16–25). A comparison of the line of Levi in Ex 6 shows that not all the sons of Gershon, Kohath, and Merari founded families that were reckoned among the Levites.

58b–61 The parenthetical section on Kohath, Amram, and Jochebed is likely inserted here to assert anew the lineage of Aaron and to remind the priests of the debacle of Nadab and Abihu. The record of Amram and Jochebed is compressed. Kohath must have lived at least 350 years before Moses, as he was born before Jacob went down to Egypt (see Ge 46:11). Further, there is a family of Amramites that numbered several hundred at the time of Moses (see comment on 3:27). Most probably Amram and Jochebed are celebrated ancestors of Aaron, Miriam, and Moses rather than their immediate parents. On Amram see also 1Ch 6:1–3; contrast Ex 2:1.

62 The number of male Levites over the age of one month increased from 22,000 in the first census (3:39) to 23,000 in the second (26:62), an increase of about 5 percent. This section ends with the restated reason for the separate numbering of the Levites: they were neither part of the army nor would they be inheritors of the land; they were a tribe holy to the Lord. But they are a part of the nation, and their families need to be listed along with the names of the other family names in Israel.

f. A recapitulation of the point of the census: this is the new generation (26:63–65)

63–65 These verses form a fitting conclusion to the section begun in vv.1–4a, with numerous ties: (1) the mention of Moses and Eleazar the priest, (2) the location on the plains of Moab, (3) the words "after the plague" in v.1, tying to the notice in v.64 that not one of the original group of rebels was still alive, save only Caleb and Joshua. Their survival reminds us of the grace of the Lord, who keeps his promise to save, even as he remembers his oath to punish.

2. The inheritance of women on entering the land (27:1–11)

1–4 The question brought to Moses by the five daughters of Zelophehad, whose genealogy is traced back to Manasseh (cf. 26:33), concerned the securing of the inheritance and the preservation of their father's name in the land. Their action in approaching the leaders of the nation was unprecedented, a great act of courage, conviction, and faith. When the women made their claim to Moses, they specified that their father had not died because of participation in the rebellion of Korah (see Nu 16) but only because he was part of the entire doomed first generation. It appears from this verse that the rebels associated with Korah not only lost their lives in the judgment of God but that their survivors may have lost their inheritance as well. So the women came asking for a decision from the Lord, that their father's name not disappear from among the clans of his family. These verses clearly demonstrate the tie of name to land in the expectation of Israel. One's meaning in the community is dependent on the survival of his name in the distribution of land in the time of conquest.

5 The leadership of Moses is seen in how he hears the women's complaint and then takes their case before the Lord. In the Heb. "their case" is highlighted to bring special attention to the fact that this was an appeal from women.

6–11 This section gives an indication of how case law might have operated in Israel. The general laws would be promulgated. Then legitimate exceptions or special considerations would come to the elders and perhaps be brought to Moses himself. He then would await a decision from the Lord. In this case the Lord gave a favorable decision to these women. In fact, he went beyond their request. They had requested a landed property (v.4). The response of the Lord was for a hereditary possession of landed property. Not only would they receive the property, they could transfer it to their heirs as well. It is as though their father had had sons!

The following pattern is then laid out. The first in line for inheritance is the son. If the father has no son, then his daughter will inherit in his stead. If there is no daughter, then the inheritance will pass to nearest relatives: brothers, uncles, or other kin. The intent is to keep the inheritance as close as possible to the deceased man's family line. The section closes by saying that the decision was mediated through Moses but originated from the Lord.

Numbers 36 provides an appendix to this account. This deals with the complicating factor of women who are now inheritors of the land and who might marry outside their families and thus muddle the subsequent inheritance claims of Israel.

3. The successor to Moses (27:12–23)

12–14 Provisions are made for the exceptions and the irregularities of the inheritance laws, but there is no provision for Moses, the (usually) faithful servant of the Lord. His sin at Meribah at Kadesh (20:1–13) was always before him. Aaron had already died; Moses was soon to die. He would be allowed a glimpse of the land from a distant mountain, but not even he would be allowed a footfall in the land itself (cf. Dt 3:23–25). The mountain from which Moses would see the land is not specified in Nu 27; Dt 3:27 and 34:1 describe it as Mount Nebo and the top of Pisgah.

The sin of Moses is tied to Aaron (cf. Nu 20); hence, both had to die before the people could enter the land. The ominous name "Meribah" reminds us of the rebellion of the leader of the people against the Lord (see comment on 20:13). The assault on the holiness of God by Moses and Aaron was disastrous. The fact of Aaron's death adds a level of certainty to Moses' own soon demise.

15–17 In the light of his impending death, Moses requested the Lord to appoint someone to succeed him (see 20:22–29). The successor was not chosen because of a blood relationship to Moses; he was not a king. Nor was he chosen by a popular election, for Moses had not been elected by the people (cf. 14:4). The successor was to be appointed directly by God. The Lord is King; Moses was only an agent. The successor is pictured as a shepherd, one needed by the flock.

18–23 As with Aaron (20:22–29), the true successor of Moses had to be established. Joshua and Caleb were the two heroes in the darkest day of Israel's apostasy (Nu 13–14). It was fitting that the Lord selected one of them. Furthermore, from his early youth Joshua had been an aide of Moses (11:28), which made him especially well suited to follow his master's steps. Moses was to be the one to single out Joshua. "Spirit" can refer to Joshua's own leadership capacity or to the Holy Spirit, which seems more likely (see Dt 34:9).

The succession procedure included the laying on of hands, a visual representation of the transfer of power while Moses was still alive (cf. Ac 6:6). This action would forestall any doubts as to the legitimacy of the transfer of power among the people. This investiture was to be done before Eleazar and the whole congregation. Moreover, the transfer was to be put into operation on a gradual but immediate basis. Some of Moses' authority was to be given to Joshua so that the people might begin to obey him. Joshua was to stand before Eleazar while Moses was alive so that there would be no priestly objections either. Joshua would go before the priest for consultation and for the decision of the Urim (see comment on Ex 28:30) before the Lord. Joshua was to begin leading the congregation as well. Moses followed the command of God to the letter.

4. Commands for the second generation on regular offerings, festival offerings, and vows (28:1–30:16)

As the first generation was given numerous laws in preparation for its entry into the Land of Promise (chs. 5–10), so now the second generation receives its own new "laws" (chs. 28–30). The change of leadership does not indicate a change in the worship patterns of Israel. These extended chapters attest to the all-pervasiveness of sacrifice in the life of the people and the enormity of the work of the priests on their behalf.

a. Regular offerings (28:1–15)

(1) The daily offerings (28:1–8)

1–8 This paragraph reiterates the laws of sacrificial worship in the daily offerings in their order (see Ex 29:38–41; Lev 1–7). The most significant issue is the wording of these commandments. The personal involvement of the Lord, the emphasis on his speaking, and the direction of worship are the paramount issues. The wording makes it abundantly clear that this is the *law of God*. The overwhelming emphasis on sacrificial worship points to the enormity of sin, the need for grace, and—in some mysterious way—the coming cross of Savior Jesus.

In the daily offerings the following factors are emphasized:

1. The "appointed time." Sacrifices are a part of the rhythm of worship. All of time is marked by sacrifice.

2. The "acceptable gift." A specified offering is to be presented (cf. Lev 22:17–33). Not just any animal or thing may be used; all is according to pattern.

3. The "pleasing aroma to the LORD." The acrid odor of the burning sacrifices is the physical symbol of the spiritual reality; obedient people bring pleasure to the Lord.

4. The enormity of it all. The yearly sacrifices at a minimum would include 113 bulls, 32 rams, 1,086 lambs, more than a ton of flour, and a thousand bottles of oil and wine. God would bless his people to allow them to do all that he demanded.

(2) The Sabbath offerings (28:9–10)

9–10 The Sabbath offerings, which were in addition to the daily offerings, mark that day out as "holy." This does not mean that the Sabbath was to be the "day of worship." It was to be a day of rest—except for the priests, who had additional service to perform. Each day was a day of worship; this is the reason for the daily offerings.

(3) The monthly offerings (28:11–15)

11–15 The sacrifices at the beginning of the month were of great proportion. Whereas two lambs were specified for the daily offerings (and two more on each Sabbath), the animals for the New Moon sacrifices included two bulls, one ram, and seven lambs. Each animal sacrifice was accompanied with flour, oil, and wine; in addition, a goat also was to be offered as a sin offering. Each month was a marker of his blessing, a time for special rejoicing.

b. Festival offerings (28:16–29:40)

(1) The Passover (28:16–25)

16–25 The focus of these passages is on the work of the priests. Passover is the spring feast at which the nation celebrates the marvel of redemption from Egypt. It is also associated with the Feast of Unleavened Bread (see Ex 12:15; Lev 23:4–8). This paragraph is studded with the number seven (and its multiple of fourteen). On the Passover the people were not to do any work, which gives rise to the idea of "holy days."

(2) The Feast of Weeks (28:26–31)

26–31 The Festival of Firstfruits (also called the Feast of Weeks; see Ex 23:16; 34:22) came fifty days after the Feast of Unleavened Bread (see Lev 23:9–22); the Greek term Pentecost comes from this number (Ac 2:1). This came shortly after the beginning of the grain harvest. Each feast is associated in some way with the agricultural year. The Lord used the cyclic agricultural events as a basis for his people to worship him. Two things should be noted: (1) the special offerings of these feasts are in addition to the regular daily sacrifices; and (2) the animals had to be without defect (cf. Heb 9:14).

(3) The Feast of Trumpets (29:1–6)

1–6 This feast came at the beginning of the seventh month, a busy month for holy festivals (see Lev 23:23–25). Later this feast became the time of the new year (Rosh Hashanah). The sacrifices were one bull, one ram, and seven male lambs, each along with the requisite grain and libation offerings. The goat for the sin offering and the daily offerings were to accompany these celebrative whole burnt offerings. Again both the soothing aroma of the sacrifices and the fact that the male animals must be without defect are noted.

(4) The Day of Atonement (29:7–11)

7–11 The Festival of Trumpets leads into the Day of Atonement, or Yom Kippur. Yom Kippur ("the day of atoning") was a time of confession, contrition, and celebration (see Lev 16; 23:26–32). This is the most solemn of Israel's holy days. It is a time of fasting rather than of feasting, of solemnity rather than rejoicing. "You must deny yourselves" (GK 6700) means to deny oneself by fasting (see Lev 16:29, 31; 23:27, 32; Ps 35:13; Isa 58:3, 5). In the NT, Yom Kippur is fulfilled in the death of the Savior who made atonement for us (see Ro 3:24–26; Heb 9:7; 10:3, 19–22).

(5) The Feast of Tabernacles (29:12–38)

12–38 The Feast of Tabernacles (or Booths) began on the fifteenth day of the seventh month and lasted for seven more days (see Lev 23:33–44). This feast demanded the most animals to be sacrificed. On each of the first seven days, two rams and fourteen male lambs were to be sacrificed, along with their requisite grain and libation offerings. In addition, thirteen bulls were sacrificed on the first day, twelve on the second, and one less on each of the days leading to seven bulls on the seventh day—a total of seventy bulls for the seven days. On the eighth day one bull, one ram, and seven male lambs were sacrificed along with requisite grain and libation offerings. In each day of this festival, a male goat was also offered as a sin offering, along with the normal daily offerings (see also Ex 23:16; 34:22; Dt 16:13–15; Zec 14:16–19).

(6) Summary (29:39–40)

39–40 The sacrifices that have been elaborated on in Nu 28–29 are in addition to any voluntary offerings that one might bring (see ch. 15), as well as any vow that one might make to the Lord (see ch. 30). Thus we understand that there was to be a regular pattern of sacrifice without regard to the special offerings one might bring because of a heart overflowing with joy to God or because of a desire to make a special need known to him.

c. Vows (30:1–16)

(1) The issue of vows to the Lord (30:1–2)

1–2 This chapter is a significant OT text on the subject of the "vow" (GK 5624; see Dt 23:21–23). The principal issue is that a vow is not to be made rashly (see Ecc 5:1–7), but once made, a vow to the Lord must be kept.

(2) The vows of a woman who lives with her father (30:3–5)

3–5 The vow of an unmarried woman who was still under her father's protection might be nullified by him. Presumably this and the next law were to protecti the woman, who in ancient Near Eastern society was subject to strong societal pressures. This text protects her father as well, who might have to come up with whatever the vow entails if his daughter is remiss in fulfilling her vow.

(3) The vows of a (newly) married woman (30:6–8)

6–8 The vow of a married woman might be nullified by her husband. The comparison of this section with vv.10–15 suggests that these verses relate to young couples who have recently married, as these are cases where the woman brings a vow into her marriage that may be heavily restrictive on her husband. Again, there is something protective in this for the woman (she has an escape clause) as well as for the husband (who would have to pay if the vow was not fulfilled). The woman in this case is treated like a minor child, not having independent authority to enter into a vow or an obligation on her own right. She was either under her father's home or under her husband's home. In both cases, her vows may be released by a man, but only if he acts immediately on the information he has.

(4) The vows of a widow or a divorced woman (30:9)

9 A widowed or divorced woman is her own agent in the taking of vows. She is no longer under the household of her father, and she is no longer under the household of her husband. This verse clearly indicates that a divorced woman (Lev 21:7, 14; 22:13; Eze 44:22) has the legal status of one who is a widow. She has become an independent agent. Like the widow, her former husband is in a sense "dead" to her. She is not under the protection of her father (unless she were to seek that out again). So this woman, along with the widow, is able to negotiate contracts, take vows, make promises—to function like any man in society. However, some restrictions are placed on her just by virtue of her gender and her status as one who is divorced (see Lev 21:7 again).

(5) The vows of a married woman (30:10–15)

10–15 These verses deal with those who have been married for a while. Possibly these sev-

eral complications arose much as the case of the daughters of Zelophehad (27:1–11). That is, one case after another presented itself; the resulting chapter is the final codification. Presumably in the centuries leading up to the NT, the legal decisions on the subject of vows became even more complex. Jesus' words in Mt 5:33–37 are quite liberating. He forswore oaths and vows altogether for his disciples and urged them to let their words speak for themselves.

(6) A summary statement (30:16)

16 Clearly this chapter has to do specifically with the making of vows by women. Much like ch. 27, it deals with the feminine exceptions to the general rule of men.

5. The reprisal against Midian, Moses' last campaign (31:1–54)

Chapter 31 picks up on the story line of ch. 25, the account of the debauchery of Israel at Baal Peor. Midian was placed under interdict by the Lord because of their part in the failure of Israel (25:17). This chapter tells the story of the holy war of Israel against these enemies. In the midst of terrible wrath, God remembers mercy, which is also the story of this chapter.

a. The report of the battle (31:1–24)

(1) The instructions for the battle (31:1–6)

1–2 This, the last war of Moses before God brings his life to an end, was to be a war of vengeance against Midian. It is announced by the Lord, not Moses. It was "the LORD's vengeance" because of the wickedness of the Midianites, who caused the seduction of the Israelites (25:16–18).

3–4 On hearing the command of the Lord, Moses turned to the people and called for a strike force. This was a limited, contained, special task calling for a limited army of special forces. One thousand men were to come from each of the tribes of Israel, a representative army for the whole nation.

5–6 In biblical thought a blood relative may take vengeance on the killer of the slain (see ch. 35). There is a sense that the Lord is the kinsman of his people who issues a command for his own holy vendetta. The war is one of divine reprisal for the near destruction of his people by the Midianites. The mention of

Phinehas is especially noteworthy. His zeal for the honor of the Lord led him to spear Zimri and Cozbi (25:8). Now his leadership in the sacral aspects of the battle demonstrates that this was truly holy war. He took to battle the holy implements and the priestly trumpets (see 10:9). The implements from the sanctuary do not seem to include the holy ark. Whatever implements he took, the belief was sure: as the Lord was with his people in the sacred place, so he was with them in war. The trumpet was a long, straight metal tube with a flowing bell; it was not the shofar, the ram's horn of ancient Israel. The blowing was an act of celebrative worship.

(2) The report of the victory (31:7–12)

7 The Lord commanded the conquest and extermination of all the peoples in Canaan (see Dt 20:1–16) because of their gross wickedness and the threat they represented to the integrity of Israel and to their very survival in the land. The cup of the Amorites was full (see Ge 15:16). Israel fought as they were taught, with faithfulness, courage, and obedient trust. The report that they "killed every man" means that there was a complete defeat; that is, they killed the men only (cf. v.9).

8 The five chieftains that the Israelites killed are memorialized forever as enemies of the Lord who were impotent before his armies. There is here a vindictiveness of the sacred, a display of triumph—a celebration of God who has given glorious victory. Among the names are two surprises. One is Zur, the father of Cozbi (see 25:15), the Midianite woman who was stabbed to death with Zimri by Phinehas. That she was a significant person is now confirmed. Cozbi is like Jezebel, a priestess-princess of paganism. The other surprise is Balaam. The story of ch. 25 lacks the name of the principal instigator of the seduction of the men of Israel. But here he is found among those killed; what Balaam failed to accomplish by the mantic arts of chs. 22–24, he was able to achieve by his advice to the Midianites (v.16).

9–12 While the men of Midian were killed by the victorious Hebrew soldiers, the women and children were spared as plunder. Moses commanded that only the virgin women (who were thus innocent of the indecencies at Peor) could be spared; the guilty women and the boys (who might endanger the inheritance rights of Israelite men) were to be put to death (vv.15–17).

Jericho, the first city west of the Jordan that Israel would win by warfare, had all its inhabitants and their possessions placed under the ban. The strike on Midian, however, was punitive. Therefore, many items of plunder (including surviving people) were to be distributed among the men of the army and the people who had remained in camp. The burning of the cities precluded their being inhabited by the Hebrews and would greatly impede their being reinhabited by enemies.

In a sense of poetic justice, the Midianites who had conspired to destroy Israel through the licentious behavior of their priestess cult functionaries were now to have their wives and daughters added to the families of Israel.

There is an episodic nature to the book of Numbers, for this story ties up three loose ends: Cozbi's father, Balaam, and the meaning of the story of Baal Peor. The tone so far in this story is one of victory march.

(3) The destruction of the women and boys (31:13–18)

13–18 Surprisingly, the people face anger from Moses instead of approval. The meeting outside the camp is an omen; something is unclean. Moses does not come to bless the officers of the armies in their victory but to vent his rage at the victories. Moses asks almost incredulously about the status of the very women whom Balaam had used to bring about the seduction of Israel.

The brutality demanded by vv.17–18 is nearly unimaginable. It is one thing to kill a woman in battle, even to kill children in a frenzy of hatred. But this verse demands the purposeful killing of women and children after the battle was over. Those girls who were to be kept alive (demonstrable virgins) would have to be rather young, and their mothers would have had to be killed. The only way to understand such a ghastly command is to realize what was at stake in the story of Baal Peor. Numbers 25 records an altogether new type of sin and rebellion—one that bears within itself the threat of the doom of the nation as a whole. It was this very type of evil that finally destroyed the Hebrew kingdoms in the land. Objectively, the destruction of the women and the boys was an act of God's mercy—for Israel. Divine judgment is sure for the nations who are a threat to the existence of God's people or who have rejected his grace.

(4) The purification of the soldiers (31:19–20)

19–20 Since this was holy war (see 19:11–13), both people and things (vv.21–24) had to be cleansed. The rites of purification from contact with a dead body would demand the waters of cleansing from the ashes of the red heifer (see 19:12). All were addressed here who had been involved in killing the enemies of God. The death of any person made one who came in contact with that corpse unclean, even when the killing was commanded by God. Thus even in a text of judgment, there are still the lessons of ritual cleansing for the people of God.

(5) The purifying of the goods (31:21–24)

21–24 Things that are ritually impure will contaminate people who are otherwise clean. Metal objects had to be purified by having them pass through fire, then be cleansed with the waters of cleansing. Some of these metal objects then became gifts to the Lord (see v.50). Those items that could not withstand fire had to be cleansed in the water alone (cf. 1Co 3:10–15). In the cleansing of soldiers, they had to wait until the seventh day, then wash their clothes, and then they could enter the camp. This pattern of seven days of exclusion from the camp because of uncleanness is well established in Israel (see Miriam in ch. 12).

b. The division of the spoils (31:25–54)

(1) The share for the soldiers (31:25–41)

25–41 The book of Numbers delights in lists. Here the Lord commands Moses to have the sum taken of the spoils of the battle, both people and animals. The term "people" relates only to the little girls who were spared the ban; the animals include sheep, cattle, donkeys, and goats. Eleazar and heads of the father's houses were to aid Moses in taking this toll. The task must have been enormous, given the numbers involved.

The division of the spoil was in two sections, one for those who had fought in the war and the other for the rest of the congregation. The two halves were equal, but their distribution was deliberately unequal—there were far fewer soldiers than those who remained in the camp. Since the soldiers had risked their lives, theirs was the larger personal share. Before the men of war could enjoy their spoil, a tribute to the Lord was required. The ratio in this case was 1 unit of 500. The tax share of the soldiers who had risked their lives was smaller than the share demanded of the people. The "tax" or "tribute" for the Lord was given to Eleazar the priest as a sacred offering. From the half of the booty to be distributed to the congregation, 1 unit of each 50 was to be given as a tribute to the Lord, to be used by the Levites in return for their service at the tabernacle. Thus the people's tax was ten times that of the soldiers.

The numbers listing the plunder were enormous; the victory was staggering. This was just the beginning; on the other side of the Jordan lay the rest of the land of God's promise. Again, the section concludes with a statement of the obedience of Moses.

(2) The share for the people (31:42–47)

42–47 The statistics of the half share for the people follow in much the same procedure as that for the soldiers. The numbers of this half are the same but are listed in a celebrative manner. Again, Moses followed faithfully in the distribution of the Lord's share.

(3) The extra share for the Lord (31:48–54)

48–54 The spontaneous extra gift of the officer corps to the Lord went beyond the tax that they were required to give of the booty of the war. The captains of thousands and of hundreds approached Moses and made a magnanimous offering of numerous beautiful objects of gold that the soldiers had taken for their own use as they looted the camps. This gift was in gratitude for the most remarkable fact that not one soldier of the elite Hebrew corps had died in the war! The only explanation for this is the presence of the Lord among his people. Moses and Eleazar weighed the gold items and found the cumulative weight to be about 420 pounds! This enormous gift came from grateful men to an all-protective God. The gold became a "memorial" of the victory that the Lord had won.

The motivation of the chiefs was "to make atonement . . . before the LORD." This was prompted by overwhelming gratitude for battle losses that were nil—not one Hebrew soldier died! The making of atonement was an offering of expiation for the lives of those who ordinarily would have died.

6. The settlement of the Transjordan tribes (32:1–42)

a. The request of Reuben and Gad to settle in Transjordan (32:1–19)

(1) The original request (32:1–5)

1–5 The chapter begins with the approach of petitioners to Moses. The abundance of fertile grazing land in Transjordan prompted the leaders of Reuben and Gad to request of Moses and Eleazar the right to settle there and not cross the Jordan. These tribal leaders found that the lands they had won from the people of Sihon and Og were ideal for the running of large flocks and herds. Only later (v.33) do we find that some clans of Manasseh were involved as well. The nobles of Gad and Reuben do more than to add place names; they place the issue of the land in the realm of divine gift.

The repetition of the word "livestock" indicates that their herds must have been exceptionally large, perhaps out of proportion to the other tribes. They needed the room that Transjordan seemed to provide. But it was not just the matter of livestock that animated them; God in his power provided the land as a gift for his people. So the two tribes requested of Moses that the land of Transjordan be given to them as their singular possession. Possibly, however, their polite words were covering a rebellious spirit. That is, these two tribes may have been abandoning their place in the league as a whole, saying something such as, "We have ours, good luck with yours." This was the way Moses read their words.

(2) The angry response of Moses (32:6–15)

6–8 Moses rages against the two tribes that they have become no better than their fathers, for they also were not willing to go to the land to fight the battle of conquest. Moses' words may have been provoked by his anger, but they became the opportunity to review the basic theology of the desert period. He was able to contrast the first and second generation, to warn the second on the basis of the experience of the first. Moses charged these tribal leaders with posing an intolerable situation. By granting them the right to settle outside Canaan proper, not only would these tribes be lost from the battle plans, but their absence would be a means of hindering the other tribes from crossing the Jordan as well. The entire nation might have become discouraged. This would lead perhaps to an ominous replay of the failure of their parents. Moses' fear was that the failure of these two tribes to stay with the whole community in the war of conquest of Canaan would be the beginnings of a general revolt among the people against entering the land. It would be the failure of Kadesh (chs. 13–14) all over again.

9–13 Moses presents an example of a biblical use of history (especially chs. 13–14, the rebellion of the first generation at Kadesh Barnea) for the instruction of the people of God. The new generation had a new opportunity to be other than their parents. They could be the people who succeeded. They did not have to repeat the failure of their parents.

Numbers is a book of worship. Worship is not just responding to grace; it is also remembering past disaster—and learning to avoid it in the present. Verse 11 recalls the covenant that was promised and rebuffed. But the promise is still there. God's oath was not just a past oath. Since he lives, so does the promise. The only question in the generation that stands before him now is: Will they be the ones, or must he wait for another? The reference to twenty years and upward speaks of the generational change that these emissaries from Reuben and Gad represented.

14–15 Moses' words were unusually harsh. There was a moral culpability in the action of disunity that might bring the ruin of God on the entire community. His words were expressive of his deep, personal feelings (cf. Paul in 2Co 1–3). This was an intensely personal moment for the great prophet of God. Rightly or wrongly, he had been provoked to vent his deepest feelings. But the deep feelings were based on his experience—and the deep feelings of God that he had experienced as none other in his day.

(3) The assurances of Reuben and Gad (32:16–19)

16–19 The men who were addressed so angrily attempted to assure Moses that they did not wish to shirk from their part in the conquest of the land. They would join their brothers in battle but wished to leave their families and livestock behind in the portion of their choosing. Their promises were sound; they had met the demands implicit within the charge of Moses.

b. The decision of Moses for their settlement (32:20–30)

20–30 Moses was not easily calmed. He spoke to the people as a father to an errant but repentant child. He gave them words of comfort and also words of strong warning. Moses' adjuration also reminded Gad and Reuben that it is not just their participation that he desired but their commitment to the affirmation of faith. They needed to prepare for battle, but they also had to know that the Lord was going to win the battle. The actions were the Lord's; the people were partners with him in his holy war.

The bargain was struck, but not without strong warnings of the seriousness of the matter if the people failed to live up to their word. In the permission that Moses granted, we sense the negotiation that was possible in Israel, even from the hand of the Lord (cf. Ge 18:16–33). In a sense the bargain with Moses was a bargain with God. When they agreed with Moses, they were also saying that they would do as the Lord commanded. The specifying elements—children, wives, livestock, and cattle—were a part of the bargain. The language is like that of a contract; agreement is full and complete.

c. The public declaration of the agreement (32:31–32)

31–32 These two verses serve as a public declaration of the decision to which the men of Gad and Reuben had come before the presence of Moses. Now it is made formal and binding before the congregation.

d. The territories of Reuben and Gad (32:33–42)

33 Apparently after the principle of Transjordan settlement was established with Reuben and Gad, a portion of the tribe of Manasseh joined with them in their agreement to settle in Transjordan and then to participate in the battle for Canaan.

34–42 The happy record of the rebuilding and settling of the people of the Lord in that portion of the land that he had given to them includes notices about continuing conquests, a mark of the Lord's continuing pleasure. This land was now really theirs. The cities that had been destroyed were now being rebuilt, and in some cases they were being renamed to show new relationships and to evince the new reality. The old gods were not in control any longer; this was now the land of the people of the Lord. The exploits of the family of Makir and their conquest of Gilead, along with the heroic exploits of Jair and Nobah, are a further expansion of the people in Transjordan. This aggression was a part of the plan of God in further dispossessing the Amorites from the region.

B. A Review of the First Generation's Journey and Words of Warning and Encouragement to the Second Generation (33:1–56)

Numbers 33 is a somewhat curious piece in the book. Principally, it is a listing of places, much like some chapters have been listings of numbers and names. It is the one chapter in which we read that Moses was commanded by the Lord to write an account of his experience in the desert (v.2).

1. The stages of the journey in the desert (33:1–49)

a. Introduction (33:1–2)

1–2 The listing of the numerous places (significantly forty in number between Rameses in Egypt and the plains of Moab) in Israel's desert experience is a rather straightforward listing that might easily be charted on a map. Most of the sites were desert encampments, not cities with lasting archaeological evidences. Many of the places are not recorded elsewhere in Exodus and Numbers. The book of Numbers as a whole is a travel narrative; this chapter is just a routing list.

b. The point of departure (33:3–4)

3–4 Only at the beginning of the journey and at one point along the way does the listing of places give way to narrative. Both the specific notation as to the time of the Israelites' departure and a description of the manner of their leaving Egypt (see Ex 12:37) are included. They left with disdain (see Ps 114:1–2), not watching the burial details of the many grieving Egyptian families whose firstborn had been slain by the hand of the Lord, but relishing the victory that the Lord had won over the gods of the land. This section is a triumphant taunt; yet even the mention of the dead adds a gentle note of sadness.

c. The stages of the journey from Rameses to Mount Hor (33:5–37)

5–37 Succoth, Etham, and Pi Hahiroth were in Egypt, to the west of the Sea of Reeds. The other sites are all in the Desert of Sinai.

d. The events at Mount Hor (33:38–40)

38–40 Unexpectedly, the staging area of Mount Hor is singled out for special mention. It becomes the setting for a memorial notice to Aaron the high priest, brother of Moses, who died here at the age of 123. Not only is his age given, but so is the date: the first day of the fifth month of the fortieth year. This is the second date in the list (the first being the date of their leaving Rameses on the fifteenth day of the first month of the first year, v.3). This means that the journeying from Tanis/Rameses to Mount Hor completes the forty years of desert wanderings.

The death of Aaron marks a pivotal date in the history of Israel. His death is regarded as having an atoning effect (see ch. 35). Aaron was three years older than Moses (see Ex 7:7; cf. Dt 1:3; 34:5–7). His great age was a mark of God's blessing in his life. By the mercy of the Lord, his time was extended to the very last year of Israel's desert experience, though his own sin (Nu 20) kept him from living into the time of the conquest of the land.

The second notice given with respect to Israel's time at the staging area of Mount Hor is word concerning the king of Arad. Even the king who dwelled in the Negev of the land of Canaan knew of the coming of the people of Israel; the reference is to the story of 21:1–3, the first of Israel's victories on the military field—promise for a new generation being different from their fathers.

e. The stages of the journey from Mount Hor to the mountains of Abarim (33:41–47)

41–47 The listing of place names continues in these verses.

f. The encampment in Moab as the staging area for the assault on the land of Canaan (33:48–49)

48–49 After forty years, the people were situated on the plains of Moab across from the city of Jericho—the firstfruits of the land; only the Jordan River separated them from their goal, the Promised Land. The encampments of the thousands of Israel stretched from Beth Jeshimoth ("Place of Desolation"; see Jos 12:3; 13:20) to Abel Shittim ("Field of Acacias"; see Nu 25:1; Mic 6:5), in the lowlands of Moab. The distance from these two sites, north to south, was over five miles—a suitable spread for the thousands of the tribes of Israel.

2. Words of warning and encouragement to the second generation (33:50–56)

50–54 The instructions of the Lord to the new generation came at the climax of the record of their triumphal march. They were now at their last staging area. Before them was the land, behind them an exceedingly long and tortuous journey. The commands of the Lord are expressed in several significant verbs: (1) they were to *dispossess* the present inhabitants, (2) *destroy* their idolatrous symbols, (3) *destroy* all their molten images, and (4) *shatter* their high places. Verse 53 repeats the verb "take possession" (GK 3769) and then speaks of living in the land as God's divine grant to the people. The land was his to give; he chose to give the gift to his people. The manner of the distribution of the land was to be by lot, with the assurance that the lot would not be by chance but by the disposition of the Lord. In this way the people would be able to take possession of the land as a lasting inheritance. As in 35:8, consideration would be given to the size of the clans of Israel.

55–56 These verses form the true climax of the book of Numbers. If the people failed in their divine commission to dispossess the pagan inhabitants, they would find two things to be true: the natives who remained would be perpetual trouble, and the Lord would bring on Israel the dispossession he demanded them to accomplish. The description of trouble is sadly prophetic. The remaining Canaanites did become barbs in the eye and pricks in the side (see Jos 23:13). These expressions describe constant annoyance (at the least) to terrible pain (at the most). The most chilling words, however, came from the Lord: "I will give you trouble." These words were threatening indeed. But the prospects were good. The second generation had fully replaced their erring fathers and mothers. And with them is the eternal Lord!

C. An Anticipation of the Promised Land (34:1–36:13)

These last three chapters have the sense of appendages. Chapter 33, with its itinerary, final blessing, and warning, really serves as the climax of the book. The prospects for conquest and the warning of failure were just what the new generation need to be the people of God.

1. A preview of the land (34:1–29)

a. The boundaries (34:1–12)

(1) Introduction (34:1–2)

1–2 The listing of the four boundaries is given, not only for information purposes, but also to display again the dimensions of God's great gift to his people in the Land of Promise. The initial covenant specified the land in terms of the peoples who lived there (see Ge 15:18–21). This chapter presents the land in terms of an outline of its borders.

The presentation of the boundaries follows an orderly format. Even geography is a matter of worship in Numbers. This chapter is a celebration of God's gifting. It presents a trust deed, a legal document from God to his people. Prophetically, it points to realization in Jos 15. These chapters were designed to build confidence in the people and also to provoke their continuing worship of the Lord.

(2) The southern boundary (34:3–5)

3–5 The southern boundary does not run on a straight line on an east-west basis; it forms a rough, broad angle with the southernmost point south of Kadesh. Similarly, the northern boundary forms a rough, broad angle. The resultant picture of the land is somewhat ideal, jewellike, giving a dynamic shape to the outline of the land. However, the land was a real entity, not just an ideal in the mind. Hence the exotic place names are of signal importance.

The line of the border begins with the south, which was more familiar to the people from their desert environment. In a sense movement is from the known to the unknown. The southern border would include part of the Desert of Zin near Edom, with the Dead Sea as the easternmost extension. The line moves southwest through Scorpion Pass, traverses Zin, and extends to the south of Kadesh Barnea. Then the border moves westward and northward passing through Azmon to the Wadi of Egypt on the Mediterranean.

(3) The western boundary (34:6)

6 The Great Sea is the Mediterranean and its coastlands. Certainly there was no misunderstanding of the western boundary.

(4) The northern boundary (34:7–9)

7–9 The northern boundary is something of a bloated, mirror image of the southern. It does not form a straight line west to east but moves northeast to Lebo Hamath, where it turns, either dropping sharply to the eastern area north of the Sea of Galilee or, more likely, moving even more northerly as it reaches to the sites of Zedad, Ziphron, and Hazar Enan. Mount Hor here is not to be confused with the Mount Hor in the south where Aaron died (see 33:37); this is a mountain in the region of Lebanon.

(5) The eastern boundary (34:10–12a)

10–12a The line from the northernmost point that traverses to the south finally to join the southern tip of the eastern side of the Sea of Galilee is the most precarious to attempt to draw. Perhaps a grand curve is intended that includes the sweep of much of southeastern Syria (Aram). The sites Shepham and Riblah are unknown today. The Sea of Kinnereth (another name for the Sea of Galilee) and the Jordan form the traditional eastern border for the southern part of the line.

(6) Summary (34:12b)

12b These are words of grand gifting; the role of God as the Giver of the land cannot be stressed too highly. At no time in Israel's history did she ever realize the full extent of the land these verses present (but cf. Jos 23:14). But the ideal was ever there.

b. The inheritance in Transjordan (34:13–15)

13–15 The new realities that the settlement of Reuben, Gad, and the half-tribe of Manasseh in Transjordan brought about (see ch. 32) demand that this section be added. Since the Jordan River is the traditional eastern boundary of the land of Canaan, these tribes are outside the boundaries in a strict sense. Yet it is possible to see them as deliberately extending the borders of the Land of Promise. Again in these verses we find the obedience of Moses to the word of God.

c. The personnel of the inheritance (34:16–29)

16–29 The listing of the new tribal leaders recalls that of the first generation (1:5–16). This time the promise would be realized; these new leaders would assist Eleazar and Joshua in actually allotting that land. The chapter ends in the report of accomplishment: "These are the men." These are the names of the second generation; the leaders of the earlier listings were dead. But with the outlines of the land in mind, and with new leaders of the tribes now in place, soon the new generation would begin its long-anticipated conquest of Canaan under the hand of God.

2. Levitical cities and cities of refuge (35:1–34)

a. The Levitical cities (35:1–5)

1–3 The notation of the Israelite location across from Jericho adds pungency to the account. In their final staging area for their assault on the land, the people needed to have a perspective of how the land was to be apportioned. Since the Levites would not receive an allotment with the other tribes (1:47–53), they would need towns to live in and places to care for their livestock. The Levites were to be spread throughout the land, receiving certain cities and territories. The term "pasturelands" (GK 4494) includes open land for agriculture as well as for herds and flocks (see Jos 14:4; 21:2).

4–5 The description of the allotment of land in each of these cities is not very clear. Verse 4 speaks of a distance of one thousand cubits (fifteen hundred feet) from the town wall round about for the open land; v.5 speaks of a measurement of two thousand cubits (three thousand feet) on each side of the city for the open land. The simplest suggestion is that the city is regarded as a point encompassed by a square that is two thousand cubits to a side. From the point of the city, each direction would be one thousand cubits. That this suggests a very small city is not really a difficulty, for most of the towns and settlements of the

land of Canaan were small—often just a matter of acres. Were this provision of open lands not made, a grudging tribe might allow some Levitical families to live within a small settlement but not give them any room (except at great cost) for their flocks, herds, and farming needs. A city apart from arable land and sufficient pasturelands was no great gift.

b. The cities of refuge (35:6–34)

(1) The basic concept of the cities of refuge (35:6–8)

6–8 Six Levitical cities were to be stationed strategically in the land—three in Transjordan and three in Canaan proper—as cities of refuge, or asylum cities, where a person guilty of unintentional manslaughter might escape blood revenge (cf. Jos 20). These six cities were to be in addition to forty-two cities for the Levites, giving a total of forty-eight cities. Further, the ideal was that the selection of the cities would be based on the relative size of the holdings of the various tribes and their relative populations.

(2) Further details on the cities of refuge (35:9–15)

9–15 The Lord through Moses commanded the people who were about to enter the land to personally select special cities of asylum for a killer from the avenger of blood. The provision of these cities was to be for one who had killed another person accidentally (cf. 15:30). The "avenger [GK 1457] of blood" was a relative of the slain who would take it on himself to protect the family rights and to avenge his relatives of the loss suffered by the family. In fact, the term often translated "redeemer" has this basic idea (see Lev 25:48; Ru 3:13). A redeemer is one who redeems the loss sustained by the family. This could be by payment of a price or by taking of life. In the latter case, one was an "avenger of blood" (vv.19, 21).

In his rage against the loss of a family member, the redeemer might rashly kill the offender before he found out the circumstances of the death. If the death was not premeditated, or was quite accidental, then the killing of the offending party would add wrong to wrong. Basically, then, the provision of the cities of asylum was another instance of Lord's mercy in his provisions for

Cities of Refuge

The idea of providing cities of refuge (Jos 20:1-9) for capital offenses is rooted in the tension between customary tribal law (retaliation or revenge, in which the blood relative is obligated to execute vengeance) and civil law (carried out less personally by an assembly according to a standard code of justice).

Blood feuds are usually associated with nomadic groups; legal procedures, with villages and towns. Israel, a society in the process of sedentarization, found it necessary to adopt an intermediate step regulating manslaughter, so that an innocent person would not be killed before standing trial. Absolution was possible only by being cleared by his hometown assembly, and by the eventual death of the high priest, which freed the offender from ritual pollution.

• Kedesh
• Acco
• Golan
• Dor
Beth Shan•
• Ramoth
Shechem •
Peniel
Gezer
• Gibeon
• Bezer
Heshbon
Hebron •

The six cities of refuge are shown in bold type.

Miles 10 5 0 10 20
Kms 10 5 0 10 20 30

Beersheba •

the needs of his people in the world setting in which they lived.

There seems to be no significance to the number of the cities (six), but there is certainly a significance to the placement of them. Three would be on each side of the Jordan River, providing accessibility from any point in the land. Also, the inclusion of three cities of asylum in Transjordan further legitimized the holdings of the two and one-half tribes in the expansion territories. Verse 15 explains that there would be equal access to these cities by all persons who were in the land, free citizen as well as sojourner or even temporary alien. This provision is another aspect of the grace of God.

(3) Basic stipulations concerning the taking of life and the cities of refuge (35:16–21)

16–21 Various descriptions of the taking of life are presented that would indicate willful murder. The provisions of this section are based on the notions of evident intent. The manner of a person's death could be suggestive of willful intent. If the person was killed by a lethal instrument, then there was a presumption of guilt on the part of the one who killed him. In these cases the party was presumed guilty, as the means of death would seem purposeful. Further, if the person died by a physical blow that was made by hatred or in the context of an ambush, then the party is guilty and had to die. For such a one was a killer.

(4) Cases to be decided concerning the taking of life and the cities of refuge (35:22–32)

22–32 The cities of refuge were to be established for persons who had committed an act of involuntary manslaughter. But such cases were not always simple to determine. Killing an individual by a lethal weapon brought a presumption of guilt on the slayer. Yet it is possible that this death was inadvertent. In cases of doubt, judgments would have to be made by the town elders. If the council decided the death was premeditated and deserving of death, then the guilty party would be delivered over to the blood avenger. But if there was no premeditated malice, then the slayer would have to go to the asylum city to be protected from the avenger. He would be protected from the avenger only so long as he remained within the asylum city; if he were to leave the city for any reason, the avenger was allowed to slay him without any consequence to his own person.

The one who sought asylum had to stay for protection in that asylum city until the death of the high priest (vv.25, 28). There was an atoning significance for the entire populace when the high priest died (cf. Heb 5–10). If the high priest died during the period of the slayer's exile in the asylum city, then he was not only free to leave the city, but he could resume his normal life again, including his stake in his ancestral land.

A further provision of mercy was the necessity for witnesses, so that the possibility of an innocent party being accused and sentenced to death on insufficient evidence might be avoided. Two witnesses (at least) were required to preclude malevolent falsehood from one isolated voice.

The stipulations concerning ransom payments were also designed as acts of mercy. Conceivably, a wealthy person might take the route of paying ransom as a means of getting out of a sticky situation, while the poor person, who could not afford a ransom payment, would be at the mercy of the avenger or be forced to live years in an asylum city. Hence, no ransom was to be paid by either the deliberate killer or the accidental killer.

(5) The divine perspective on murder and the land (35:33–34)

33–34 The shedding of human blood pollutes the land. The crime of murder is not only an offense against the sanctity of life; it is a pollutant to the Lord's sacred land (Ge 4:10). The point is not just that there were to be cities for the Levites to inhabit or cities of asylum for the inadvertent killer to find refuge. All the theology of the chapter culminates in the last words of v.34: "For I am the LORD, who dwells in the midst of the people of Israel" (pers. tr.). If God is to liveamong his people, then the land may not be polluted.

3. A review of the inheritance of women (36:1–13)

a. Concerns of the Gileadites for the daughters of Zelophehad (36:1–4)

1–4 The family of the daughters of Zelophehad brought their petition to Moses. They did not dispute the former decision of the Lord that the daughters might inherit, in the absence of brothers, to carry on their father's line. Their distress resulted the problems that would eventuate if these daughters married outside their clan and tribe. At issue was a concern for the continuity of the lines of inheritance within the tribes. At the year of Jubilee, when all problems of lines of inheritances were to be resolved, this one would not be resolvable because of the twin lines of right to the land, through wives and husbands from different tribes.

b. The law for the marriages of the women who inherit familial land (36:5–9)

5–9 Again, in great grace, the word of the Lord came through Moses to present a decision. The women were permitted to marry whomever they choose, but they must choose their husbands from within their own clans. The issue was not just their personal happiness but the solidarity of the larger family unit. The destiny of the family in Israel was tied to the land. The instance of these women became a law that was applicable in other similar cases. The basic issue was to keep the inheritance of a family in the clan and the tribe of the fathers.

c. The compliance of the daughters of Zelophehad (36:10–12)

10–12 The women were married within their families, paternal "cousins." In this manner the inheritance of their father stayed within the clan. The book of Numbers, which so often presents the rebellion of God's people against his grace and in defiance of his will, ends on a happy note. These noble women, who were concerned for their father's name and their own place in the land, obeyed the Lord. Significantly, there is a final statement of obedience; and it is in the lives of these noble daughters of Zelophehad. We likely would never have heard of him had he had sons instead of daughters!

d. A summary statement of the law of the Lord (36:13)

13 The book of Numbers is far more than a record of commands and regulations. The climax of the book is in 33:50–56. Yet there is a salutary feeling in this chapter of theoretical issues being put to practical work. There is hope in the actions of the daughters of Zelophehad that they will be representative of the nation: this generation will do well.

The Old Testament in the New

OT Text	NT Text	Subject
Nu 12:7	Heb 3:2, 5	Faithful Moses
Nu 16:5	2Ti 2:19	God knows his own

Deuteronomy

INTRODUCTION

1. Name

The name Deuteronomy results from a mistranslation of Dt 17:18. For the Hebrew "a copy of this law," the LXX and the Vulgate have terms meaning "the second law" or "a repetition of this law." Internal data locate the book as beginning in the desert east of the Jordan in Moab on the first day of the eleventh month of the fortieth year—forty years after the Exodus from Egypt (1:3). This was after Moses and the Israelites had defeated Sihon and Og, kings of the Amorites in Transjordan (1:4).

2. Character and Author

In addition to the many statements about Moses' speaking these words are statements made within the book itself that indicate he was the author (cf. 1:5; 31:9, 22, 24, 30). Other OT books assert Mosaic authorship of Deuteronomy (1Ki 2:3; 8:53; 2Ki 14:6; 18:6, 12), as do Jesus and writers of the NT (Mt 19:7–8; Mk 10:3–5; 12:19; Jn 5:46–47; Ac 3:22; 7:37–38; Ro 10:19).

Deuteronomy can be approached from several angles: (1) as a "Book of the Law"; (2) as a series of addresses given by Moses, repeating much of the earlier legal material in the Pentateuch and adding various other elements; (3) as a covenant-treaty between the sovereign Lord and his people, similar in both form and content to other covenant-treaties that have been found in the ancient Near East (having a preamble, historical prologue, various laws, arrangement for depositing treaty copies and for regular reading of the treaty, witnesses, and curses and blessings); (4) as a compendium of directives that the Lord gives through Moses to the Israelites as they are about to enter Canaan. Of these four, it is primarily a covenant renewal document, to prepare the new generation of God's covenant people to live responsibly and joyfully under the Lord's rule in the Promised Land (i.e., the third purpose).

3. Purpose

The purpose of Deuteronomy is distinctly stated as "Hear, O Israel," "These are the commands," and "Be careful to do" (4:1–2, 5–6,9–14, et al.). Such exhortations are often followed by reasons for obedience to the Lord. The basic existential occasion grew out of the rescue of the people from Egypt and their position on the southeastern border of Canaan—poised to enter and to occupy that land as their own in fulfillment of the promises first made to Abraham, Isaac, and Jacob, and now reiterated to the descendants of the patriarchs. It was the intention of God to form their nation and give Canaan to them as their national homeland (cf. 6:18).

The book of Deuteronomy calls for the enactment (renewal) of the covenant as the Israelites prepared to enter Canaan to conquer and occupy it, and it presents the way of life that they were to follow in the Promised Land. Incidental to this covenant enactment are the curses that would fall on Israel if they failed to observe the stipulations and the blessings they would receive when they obeyed the Lord.

4. Theological Values

The theological values of Deuteronomy can hardly be exaggerated. It stands as the wellspring of biblical historical revelation. It is a prime source for both OT and NT theology. When the prophets speak of God, they speak of the God and the message of Deuteronomy and of the relationship embodied in its covenant-treaty. The warnings of doom in the prophets (esp. Jeremiah) are the warnings and curses of Deuteronomy. The promises of blessing for the Israelites when they live in faith, love, and obedience to the Lord are the blessings of Deuteronomy.

The way of life for the people of God forms the basis of all subsequent revelation of the way of life that is acceptable to him. God has redeemed his treasured inheritance from the bondage of Egypt, and he is about to fulfill his promise to Abraham, Isaac, and

Jacob by giving them the Promised Land. The later NT teachings on the love of God, the redemption offered through Christ, the saved as the inheritance of God, and the fulfillment of the promises of God to the saved as their inheritance from him rest on Deuteronomy.

God in this book is personal, eternal, omnipotent, sovereign, purposeful, loving, holy, and righteous. The knowledge of his person and will is communicated by propositional, directive, exhortative, informative, and predictive revelation. No other god exists.

The most important element of subjective theology in Deuteronomy is that of absolutely unqualified, total commitment of the people of the Lord. Nothing else is acceptable, especially no syncretism with other gods or other religious practices. The people belong to the Lord alone!

EXPOSITION

I. Preamble (1:1–5)

1–5 The terms used here indicate the nature of the book. "These are the words" suggests a suzerain-vassal treaty preamble. "All that the Lord had commanded him" indicates the source of the material in the book, the nature of Moses' ministry as communicator of the Lord's commands rather than that of an author, and the authoritative character of the addresses as commands of the Lord.

"The Lord [GK 3378]," "The Lord our God," "The Lord your God," "The Lord, the God of your fathers" (1:3, 6, 10, 11, et al.) all signify a strong emphasis on the Lord as the originator of everything that follows in Deuteronomy. He transcends any king (or any god) in the suzerain-vassal treaties (where gods are mentioned as empowering the kings), because he is not only superior to all other gods but he is the supreme author, enactor, and benefactor of the covenant-treaty.

A crucial, stirring moment in the experience of the new nation was at hand. It was time for the Israelites to realize the Lord's promises from the past—a time for the fulfillment of the hope that began at the Exodus. The Lord's concern—and Moses'—was to prepare the people for the conquest and occupation of Canaan. Now, on the brink of

crossing the Jordan, Moses reviewed the salient historical events and Israel's covenant-treaty with the Lord.

The geographical references in these verses were evidently known in Moses' time. Perhaps these locations identify a few of the places where Moses had earlier imparted some of "these . . . words" to the people. Laban and Hazeroth appear to be two stations on the journey from Egypt to Canaan (Nu 33:18, 20–21). Mount "Horeb," which is interchangeable with Mount Sinai, is used more often in Deuteronomy (1:2, 6, 19; 4:10, 15; et al.) but also occurs elsewhere in the OT. "In the fortieth year" marks the terminal point of the generation that disobeyed the command at Kadesh.

Sihon and Og were kings of Amorite peoples (cf. 2:24–3:11; ZPEB, 1:140–43). Heshbon was the capital city of Moab, but Sihon had captured it and made it his capital. Bashan was the territory east of the Lake of Galilee. Ashtaroth, Og's capital, was a little more than twenty miles east of the Lake of Galilee while Edrei, where Israel defeated Og, was a little less than twenty miles southeast of Ashtaroth. Canaan proper, west of Jordan, is labeled "the hill country of the Amorites" (vv.7, 19, 20, et al.). Sihon controlled southern Transjordan and Og the northern sector, mainly the area east of the Lake of Galilee. So here, "east of the Jordan," Moses began his sermon.

II. First Address: The Historical Prologue (1:6–4:43)

A. Experiences From Horeb to the Jordan (1:6–3:29)

1. The command to leave Horeb (1:6–8)

6–8 Moses began by reciting God's order to leave Horeb and go to Canaan, though what the Lord commanded the people was a new bit of information (its content is given only here; cf. Nu 10:11–13). The Lord's gift of Canaan to Israel and his command to them to enter and to possess the land are cardinal elements of the book. The description of the extent of the land coincides with that promised on oath to the fathers (Ge 15:18). The geographical terms delimit the land by sections: "The Arabah" is the Jordan Valley from Lake Galilee to the area south of the Dead Sea; "the mountains," the central hill country; "the western foothills," the slopes toward the

Mediterranean; "the Negev," the area north of the Sinai peninsula but south of the central hill country; "the coast," the land along the Mediterranean; "the land of the Canaanites" and "Lebanon, as far as . . . the Euphrates," the northern section.

The promise of the land was given "to Abraham, Isaac and Jacob—and to their descendants." The land, then, first promised to Abraham, was given Isaac as the "only" son of Abraham and Sarah and then limited to Jacob and his sons, the heirs of the promise (Ge 12:7; 15:18; 26:3–4; 28:4, 13–15). This promise was reaffirmed at the burning bush (Ex 3:8, 17).

2. The appointment of leaders (1:9–18)

9–14 The increased number of Israelites presented too many problems for Moses to care for alone. Consequently, political and juridical appointments were initiated. No mention is made here of the instigation of this procedure by Moses' father-in-law (cf. Ex 18:13–26); here Moses simply stated that he saw the need for "judges" [GK 9149] in political and judicial activity as his assistants. While Exodus suggests that Moses himself appointed these leaders, it is apparent from v.13 that the people chose the leaders as representative of the various tribes, and then Moses appointed them to their several tasks (vv.15–18). The leaders were to be characterized by wisdom, understanding, and experience.

15–18 The use of the word "commanders" [GK 8569] and the size of the groups—thousands, hundreds, fifties, and tens—suggest a military arrangement. The need, however, was for assistant judges, not for military men. The context begins and ends with reference to a judicatory. The designation of these men as commanders, tribal officials, and judges seems to indicate three distinct classes. This arrangement seemed to be satisfactory to the people.

Four matters regarding the administration of justice are mentioned: (1) disputes between fellow Israelites or with foreign inhabitants in the land were to be arbitrated; (2) directives for making decisions include no partiality—small and great were to be heard on an equal basis; (3) judges were not to fear human beings because juridical process rested on the realization that "judgment belongs to God"; and (4) cases too difficult for the judges were to be referred to Moses.

3. The spies sent out (1:19–25)

19–23 After leaving Horeb, the Israelites went "as the LORD . . . God commanded" (cf. v.7) toward the hill country of the Amorites. This difficult journey of more than 150 miles through the Desert of Paran brought them to Kadesh Barnea on the southern perimeter of the Land of Promise. "That vast and dreadful desert" was a forbidding limestone plateau: hot, dry, rugged, and usually bare of any sustainable vegetation. There Moses reiterated the Lord's command (v.8) to take possession of the land God was giving them and exhorted them not to be afraid, obviously indicating that the Israelites were afraid. The people suggested that some men be sent into the land to scout it out. In light of Nu 13:1–3, apparently the people first suggested that this reconnoitering be made; Moses then approved the idea, referred the request to the Lord who agreed to it, and ordered that each tribe send out one representative.

24–25 Moses, recalling that event, left out details and descriptions, saying only that the spies returned with a report that the land was good and that they brought back some fruit from the Valley of Eshcol as evidence (cf. Nu 13:3–33).

4. The rebellion against the Lord (1:26–46)

26–31 In spite of the good report and evidence of the productivity of the land, the people refused to enter because the rest of the report discouraged them. The size and strength of the inhabitants, the high fortifications of their large towns, and the presence of the Anakites made the Israelites so fearful that they rebelled against the Lord, misconstrued his attitude toward them, and refused to believe in his promises. Grumbling in their tents, they said, "The LORD hates us," when in truth he loved them. They claimed that the Lord brought them from Egypt to have them destroyed by Amorite hands; but the contrary was true. Again Moses urged the people not to be afraid, asserting that the Lord their God would go ahead of them as he had in Egypt and Sinai. Before their very eyes God had carried them along (cf. Nu 11:12).

32–36 In spite of the promise of the Lord's leadership, the people refused to enter the land; so the Lord declared that they would not see that good land. Out of the vast throng of Israelites, only those under twenty, plus Caleb and Joshua, would enter it (cf. Nu 14:30–31). Caleb "followed the LORD wholeheartedly"; he was totally committed to the Lord and obeyed him fully. God promised him the area he had explored.

37–38 Moses told the people that the Lord was angry with him also "because of you"; so Moses himself would not be allowed to enter the land. This must refer back to the experience of the Israelite quarrel with the Lord at the waters of Meribah (Kadesh). There the Lord said that Moses and Aaron would not enter the land because they did not honor him (Nu 20:12). Moses here looked behind his own failure and referred to the cause of his action: the people's criticism of the Lord's provision of food. Joshua is called Moses' assistant (lit. Heb., "he who stands before you"); he would lead the Israelites in taking the land.

39–40 The children of this rebellious generation would acquire the country that that generation had faithlessly failed to invade and possess. That generation was condemned to return to the desert. The way of the Red Sea was doubtless a well-known route through Sinai and does not necessarily imply destination.

41 Being sent back into the vast, dreadful desert (v.19) was more than the people could take; so they confessed their sin, put on their weapons, and presumptuously went up into the hill country. This admission of their guilt was frivolous. Without due consideration of the Lord's later command, their action of going up into the hill country, now without the Lord's approval, was foolhardy.

42–43 Not only did the Lord declare that he would not go with the people, he also prophesied their defeat. But the Israelites' obstinacy was such that they would not listen; so they marched up to battle against the Amorites in an action of presumption, rashness, and arrogance.

44–46 The Amorites met the Israelite army somewhere north of Kadesh Barnea and then routed the Israelites toward the south or southeast. The Amorites' pursuit "like a swarm of bees" describes numerical greatness, persistence, and ferocity. "You came back and wept before the LORD" means that the Israelites returned to the tabernacle of the Lord and wept there. The Hebrew time phrase in v.46 expresses a long, indefinite period and suggests that a large part of the next thirty-eight years was spent there.

5. The journey from Kadesh to Kedemoth (2:1–25)

1–7 In obedience to the Lord's command in 1:40, the chastised Israelites returned to the desert, between Kadesh and the Seir range. The period probably encompassed both departures from Kadesh recorded in Nu 14:25 and 20:22. The phrase "for a long time" (cf. 1:46) suggests that the time spent at Kadesh and around Seir took up the period between the abortive attempt to enter Canaan from Kadesh and the end of the wanderings that brought them to the Jordan River opposite Jericho. It was a "long time" because the Lord had decreed punishment on the nation for their disobedience at Kadesh.

If the command to go northward was given in Kadesh, then the order gives the general direction only, for it was necessary to go south and east before marching north. With the exception of Caleb, Joshua, and Moses, the generation of men twenty years old or more who had refused to enter Canaan at the Lord's command were now dead (vv.14–15); and Moses also would die soon. Therefore, the Lord said that they had gone around the hill country long enough.

Approaching Edomite lands brought Israel in or near the area the Lord had promised to Esau and his descendants. So the Lord commanded the Israelites not to make war on their Edomite relatives; neither were they to take their land or anything in it; they were to buy food and drink with "silver." Before this the Israelites had lived off what the Lord had supplied. Manna did not completely cease until the day after the first celebration of the Passover in Canaan under Joshua (Jos 5:10–12; cf. Ex 16:35).

8–9 The order of the journey reviews the travel from Ezion Geber or Elath at the head of the Gulf of Aqaba northward to the plains of Moab. As the Lord had forbidden Israel to attack the Edomites because they were blood brothers, so now he warned them not to fight with the Moabites. They were descendants of Lot, and he had given them the land they controlled.

10–12 The mention of these territories elicited historical references to former inhabitants, which the Moabites (vv.9–11), Ammonites (vv.19–21), Edomites (vv.12, 22), and Caphtorites (v.23) had displaced. These ancient nations are described as numerous, tall, and strong. Yet they were destroyed by invading brothers of the Israelites—surely a suggestion that Israel too would succeed in conquering the land they were about to invade. The reference to Israel's destruction of former inhabitants may indicate the point of view of Moses referring to the conquest of Transjordan.

13–15 Since the fighting men of the generation that had failed to enter the land had died off, the Lord's hand was no longer against Israel. He directed the new generation to cross the Zered, which flows into the southern end of the Dead Sea from the east, and then to cross the Arnon (v.24). This brought them into the area controlled by the Amorites.

16–19 When the Israelites came near the northeastern border of Moab at Ar, they were next to the territory occupied by the Ammonites, who at that time lived east of the Amorites. Sihon controlled the area between the Arnon River on the south, the Jordan on the west, the Jabbok on the north, and the border of the Ammonites on the east. The Israelites were not to disturb the Ammonites but were to turn northwestward into the country of Sihon. The Ammonites were the descendants of Lot, and the Lord had given that country to Lot and his descendants (see comment on v.9).

20–23 This parenthetical portion mentions how the Lord had destroyed the Zamzummites (a nation of large people who could be called giants; cf. 3:11) and had given their land to the Amorites. He had also destroyed the Horites, the Avvites, and the Caphtorites and had given their land to the descendants of Esau. Evidently the Lord through Moses was establishing belief in his control over the Canaanite groups of the past to inspire Israel for the conquest ahead.

24–25 While Israel was not to disturb the Edomites, Moabites, or Ammonites, such prohibition did not extend to the Amorites. The Lord declared that he had put Sihon and his kingdom into Israel's hands. The conquest was certain; it was only for Israel to accomplish it. They were to cross the Arnon into Amorite territory and confidently engage Sihon's army in battle. God would put the fear of Israel into all the nations in the area (Cf. 11:25; also Ex 15:15–16; 23:27).

6. The conquest of Transjordan (2:26–3:20)

a. The defeat of Sihon (2:26–37)

26–35 Though the Lord had said that he had given Sihon into Israel's hands (v.24), Moses approached Sihon with messengers bearing a request to pass peaceably through his country. But Sihon, from a heart made stubborn by the Lord, refused the request and came out to battle against the Israelites. Sihon, his sons, his army, his people, and his towns were destroyed. So southern Transjordan was subjected to total destruction, except that the Israelites kept for themselves the "plunder" instead of giving it over to the Lord by destruction. Such exceptions were not allowed when the Lord required a strict following of the total-destruction principle (cf. Jos 7; 1Sa 15).

36–37 So all the territory from the Arnon Gorge on the south to Sihon and Og's boundary in Gilead on the north, and from the upper course of the Jabbok River on the east to the Jordan on the west fell to the Israelites. They did not, however, encroach on any of the Ammonite land, which the Lord expressly commanded them to avoid (see v.19).

b. The defeat of Og (3:1–11)

1–3 The conquest continued by pressing north to engage Og king of Bashan in battle because the Lord had signified that his army and territory would also become Israel's. Og was vanquished; and both population and cities were destroyed, but the livestock and valued goods were kept by the Israelites (v.7).

4–7 The geographical limits of the country of Og that was conquered are in general clear, though certain specific designations are not. The description of the sixty cities as "fortified with high walls and with gates and bars"

The oasis of Kadesh Barnea is located in the narrow valley of the Wadi el-'Ain. The Israelites may have camped here for an extended period. Courtesy Ze'ev Meshel.

indicates that they were formidable obstacles and that their capture was a remarkable success (cf. Nu 32:33; Jos 9:10; Pss 135:10–11; 136:18–22). "City" (GK 6551) need not imply a place with a large population; some cities had a population of only a few hundred.

8–11 Prior to allocating the captured lands to the Reubenites, Gadites, and the half-tribe of Manasseh, Moses described the whole area taken from the Amorite kings. The names Sirion and Senir for Mount Hermon occur elsewhere in the Scriptures (1Ch 5:23; Ps 29:6; SS 4:8; Eze 27:5). Salecah and Edrei apparently fix the southern border of Bashan. His iron bed might have been a black basalt sarcophagus, many of which have been found in that country.

c. The division of the land (3:12–20)

12–15 The geographical description of the territories given to the two and a half tribes is difficult to follow in its entirety. In the NIV this half of the tribe of Manasseh is called "the half-tribe of Manasseh"; Makir was their progenitor (cf. Nu 26:29; 32:40). The other half, which received its allotment in Canaan proper, is not mentioned as often and is not designated "the half-tribe of Manasseh." The Geshurites and Maacathites were two smaller kingdoms that Israel did not drive out. Those people continued to live on their land under Israel (Jos 13:11, 13).

"The rest of Gilead" (v.13; a northern part other than that given to Reuben and Gad) is

given to the half-tribe of Manasseh (simply "Gilead" in vv.15–16). Gilead sometimes refers to the area between the Jabbok and the Yarmuk (the northern sector), sometimes to the central area south of the Jabbok but north of Heshbon and the Dead Sea, and sometimes to the area including both sections. Jair's area was in the northern sector of Gilead, beyond the Yarmuk Valley up to the territory of the Geshurites and Maacathites who occupied the land east of Lake Galilee and the Waters of Merom. The boundary between Gilead and Bashan is not clearly defined. The territory of Jair seems to be in both Gilead and Bashan.

16–17 Verse 12 says that the Reubenites and Gadites' area included half the hill country of Gilead. This makes the southern part of Gilead the northern part of Reuben and Gad, the southern border of Reuben and Gad being the Arnon Valley, and the eastern border being the Jabbok River from its headwaters in the south. The eastern border continues northward until the river bends and flows westward to the Jordan. Its western border was that part of the Jordan River and the Dead Sea that closed the gap between the northern and southern borders.

"Kinnereth" (cf. Gennesaret in Lk 5:1) is an older name for Lake Galilee, a town on its northwest perimeter, or the entire area. The western border of the Gadites and Reubenites' allotment extended from Kinnereth along the Jordan and the eastern side of the

Dead Sea as far as the Arnon Gorge, approximately half the length of the sea.

18–20 Moses reminded the men of the two and a half tribes of their responsibility to cross the Jordan with the rest of the Israelites to win the land there before they settled down in their Transjordanian possessions. All the "able-bodied men" had to represent a special body of soldiers. Surely some men, also armed, must have remained in Transjordan to protect the women and children.

7. Moses forbidden to cross the Jordan (3:21–29)

21–29 After encouraging Joshua with the assurance that God would fight for him in Canaan as he did in Transjordan, Moses referred to his appeal to God that he might go into "the good land beyond the Jordan." The Lord refused this request (cf. 1:37; 3:26; 4:21) and directed him to ascend to the top of Pisgah so that he might look over the Promised Land, even though he would not enter it; this was fulfilled after Moses had delivered the messages of Deuteronomy (see 31:7–8, 14, 23). Joshua, not Moses, was to lead the people in conquering the land.

B. Israel Before the Lord (4:1–40)

1. Exhortation to obey the Lord's commands (4:1–14)

1–2 Moses next turned to the stipulations of the covenant-treaty. This beginning section is largely hortatory, though what the Israelites were exhorted to do necessitates introductory reference to the stipulations. Moses emphasized the importance and necessity of adhering to the codes that the Lord had given the people. What he declared was sufficient to guard their lives and to guarantee their possession of the land. The phrase "I am about to teach you" indicates the nature of the Deuteronomic messages. Coupled with these expositions of the law are the exhortations to "follow" (GK 6913) the laws and to "keep [GK 9068] the commands of the LORD."

3–6 Failure to follow the Lord would result in death (cf. Nu 25; cf. Ps 106:28; Hos 9:10). "Baal Peor" designates both the place and the god of the place. The worship of the Canaanite Baal involved sexual acts and continued to be a serious breach of the first commandment

among the Israelites and, consequently, of the covenant. Loyalty to the Lord was an absolute requirement for those who would follow him; failure to heed the warnings about the "other gods" of Canaan would result in immediate destruction. Only those who held fast to the Lord could expect to remain alive. Obeying the Lord's codes would also make them known to the nations, who would esteem the Israelites as wise and understanding people.

7–8 Moses pointed up the distinctive character of these codes: the Lord was near them when they prayed, and no other nation had such righteous laws. Since these laws were communicated through prayer, the giving of them brought Israel close to God. The Lord's presence in the center of the camp was symbolized in the glory over the ark of the covenant and the tabernacle (tent) in which the ark was placed and in the pillar of cloud by day and of fire by night (Ex 40:34–38; Nu 23:21).

9–14 Moses was concerned that the generations to follow would be taught what he was teaching to the people; this communication involved memory and observance. But knowledge was not enough; the people had to "follow them" (vv.1, 5, 13–14) and "observe [GK 6913] them carefully" (v.6). Active obedience was essential. Israel was called on to remember the day at Horeb (Sinai) when the Lord spoke to them "out of the fire." They were to remember his presence through "the sound of words . . . only a voice." This is elaborated further by such terms as "his covenant [GK 1382], the Ten Commandments," and as what was written "on two stone tablets." The "Ten Commandments" epitomize all the commands that the Lord gave to Israel through Moses. The "two stone tablets" are two tablets, each inscribed with the list of commands. This coincides with the two copies of a suzerain-vassal treaty, which each participant was to have.

2. Idolatry forbidden (4:15–31)

15–18 As an introduction to the exhortation to shun idolatry, Moses repeated his observation (v.12) that the people saw no form when the Lord spoke to them from Horeb. Because he has no physical form, no physical representation could be tolerated. The description of the forms of creatures is slightly more explicit than that in the second command-ment (Ex 20:4; Dt 5:8) and reminiscent of the Creation narrative (Ge 1:20–26). The Lord is not like the idols of Canaan.

19 Neither were the Israelites to worship the sun, the moon, and the stars. "Things the LORD your God has apportioned to all the nations under heaven" cannot mean that God gave these celestial bodies to the nations as objects of worship. Rather, these were given to all humankind for the physical benefit of the earth and were not proper objects of wor-ship at all (Ge 1:14–18).

20 The use of metal by heating certain ores and then hammering the metallic residue or welding it to other parts while still hot may have appeared in the Near East in the first half of the third millennium B.C., but the man-ufacture of iron objects (usually weapons) was limited till 1500 B.C and later. Bringing Is-rael out of Egypt was like bringing her out of an iron-smelting furnace—the heavy bond-age of Egypt with its accompanying difficul-ties and tensions being likened to the hottest fire then known. Israel had been brought out of Egypt "to be the people of his inherit-ance," as they indeed were (cf. Ps 78:62, 71; Isa 19:25).

21 Moses, however, was to die in Moab; and for the third time he referred to the Lord's re-fusal to let him cross the Jordan and enter Canaan proper (1:37; 3:26–27). Each time he spoke of the Lord's anger toward him "be-cause of you." Moses seemed to feel that the Israelites were to bear the blame for his pre-dicament. Certainly the repetitious reference to the Lord's prohibition reflects his keen disappointment.

22–24 Since the people were about to enter the land, Moses reiterated his exhortation that they be very careful not to forget the covenant the Lord made with them. The cen-tral character is the Lord himself, who is "a consuming fire," intolerant of idols in any form (5:9; 6:15; Ex 20:5; 34:14; cf. Jos 24:19; Na 1:2).

25–29 The spirit of the prophets moved in Moses as he looked into the future of Israel relative to idol worship. Seeing that the gen-erations to come might become corrupt through idolatry, he called heaven and earth as witnesses of his warning of destruction

against the Israelites, the scattering of them among the nations, and their extremely lim-ited numerical survival. He seemed sure that such a situation would prevail because he proceeded to tell how, in those foreign lands, the Israelites would "worship man-made gods" but eventually would seek and find the Lord their God. The Lord would not aban-don, destroy, or forget them—or forget his covenant with them (cf. vv.29–31). This in-dictment of idolatry portrays the spiritual nature of Deuteronomy. Idols have no senses but are only human fabrications using com-mon, insensate materials. The only way out of any future predicament resulting from in-fidelity rested on unequivocal recommittal to the Lord (cf. 6:5; 10:12; 11:13; 26:16; 30:2, 6, 10).

30–31 The nation may fail to uphold the cov-enant; the people may forget their Lord; but when they turn back to him in faith and obe-dience, he will mercifully accept them. He will not forget the covenant based on his promises.

3. Acknowledgment of the Lord as God (4:32–40)

32 Waxing eloquent as he tried to press home the greatness of the Sinaitic experience, Moses grandly asserted by a series of ques-tions that the revelation of the Lord at Horeb was the greatest event of history. From the creation of humanity until that time, no-where else on earth had such an observable event happened.

33–38 God had spoken to the people out of the fire, and they still lived! Moses described what the Lord had done for them in Egypt and through the deserts. The "testings" (GK 4999) probably relate primarily to the plagues or "great trials" (cf. 7:19). This "test-ing" is immortalized in the experience at Rephidim where the Israelites tested the Lord's patience by asking, "Is the LORD among us or not?" (Ex 17:7). The more or less synonymous expressions in v.34 indicate the extraordinary display of the Lord's power. They all indicate that the Lord is God and that he is stronger than the gods of Egypt. Moreover, all these "awesome deeds" had been done for them "before [their] very eyes" with a specific intent. They were to (1) learn that he was the only true God, (2) be corrected of any false notions or wrong behavior, and (3) be prepared for entrance into the land of their inheritance.

The Lord's love for his people finds its first mention here. The reference to the Lord's choice of Israel, based on his love for their forefathers, and the reference to his gift of Canaan to them as an inheritance go back to the covenant with Abraham and to the promises of that covenant (Ge 12:3; 17:4–8; 18:18–19).

39–40 Moses again emphasized personal commitment to the Lord, based on the fact that he is the only God and that he exists both in heaven and on earth. Such a commitment would result in prosperity and continued possession of the land that the Lord was giving them. The Hebrew structure of the last clause in v.40 suggests purpose rather than result—in order that you may continue to live in the land.

C. The Transjordanian Cities of Refuge (4:41–43)

41–42 Bezer, Ramoth Gilead, and Golan are designated as sanctuaries—elsewhere "cities of refuge"—for whoever unintentionally and without premeditation killed someone (cf. 19:1–13; Nu 35:9–28). Only here are the names of the Transjordanian cities of refuge expressly mentioned (but see Jos 20:8).

43 The desert plateau extends eastward from the upper part of the Dead Sea. Bezer lies about twenty miles east of the northeast corner of the Dead Sea. Ramoth Gilead was about thirty miles southeast of Lake Galilee, and Golan, twenty miles east of a centerpoint on the east bank of Lake Galilee. Bezer, then, was accessible to the people in southern Transjordan, Ramoth Gilead to those in the central part, and Golan to the ones in the north. The identification and location of these places are not certain.

III. The Second Address: Stipulations of the Covenant-Treaty and Its Ratification (4:44–28:68)

A. Introduction (4:44–49)

44–49 As an introduction to the stipulations, this paragraph presents something of the character of what follows—namely, "stipulations, decrees and laws." It mentions also the people, the time, the place, and a brief description of the extent of the lands they had captured.

Why another introduction? (Notice 1:1–5.) Perhaps this follows the procedure of updating the treaty at treaty renewal time. It may be an instance of the repetitive character of Deuteronomy as a device for emphasis and instruction.

B. Basic Elements of Life in the Land (5:1–11:32)

1. The Ten Commandments (5:1–33)

a. Exhortation and historical background (5:1–5)

1–2 Moses' main address begins much as his introduction to the historical prologue (4:1). He urged the people personally to learn these decrees and laws and to adhere to them. He reminded them that they themselves had received the covenant from the Lord who had spoken to them out of the fire on Mount Horeb. Though the people he was then talking to were less than twenty years old (except for Caleb and Joshua) at the time of the Horeb experience, they were there and were now representative of Israel. The covenant-treaty was made by the nation represented at Horeb, and the covenant remained in force to all succeeding generations until abrogated or qualified by the Lord.

3 The "fathers" (GK 3) were not the people's immediate fathers but their ancestors, i.e., the patriarchs (see 4:31, 37; 7:8, 12; 8:18).

4–5 The immediacy of the Lord's relationship with the people is pointed up in the phrase "face to face" (cf. 34:10; Ex 33:11; Ge 32:30; Jdg 6:22). However, Moses explained that this relationship came through his mediatorship, because of their fear of the fire on the mountain. The character of Moses' mediation can be seen in the contrast between the Israelites' hearing the sounds of the voice of God (4:12, 15; 5:4, 22, 24; 10:4) but not with sufficient clarity to distinguish the words (Ex 19:7, 9; 20:19, 21–22; cf. Ac 9:7).

b. The commandments (5:6–21)

6–7 The Ten Commandments sit appropriately at the beginning of Moses' elucidation of the basic legislation for the Israelites. These commands are not only to be learned but also to be obeyed. They come directly from the Lord their God, who brought them up from Egypt. Their relationship with God is rooted in history, and that history is one of God's interventions for their benefit. The phrases "other gods" and "before me" also speak of the relationship of the people to God. God does not allow his people to have "other gods"—whatever they might be.

8–10 The proscription of making or using idols is total. Nothing in Israel's environmental experience may be the basis for an idolatrous form to be honored and worshiped as God. The reason is definitely personal, both on the part of the Lord and on the part of the people. The people either hate the Lord or love and obey him, and they receive from him punishment or love commensurate with their hate or love and obedience. Those who adhere to the covenant-treaty stipulations get its promised benefits; those who do not adhere to them get its punishments.

The children of Israel are not punished for the sins that their fathers committed; they are punished for their own sins (cf. 24:16). The punishment, however, goes on "to the third and fourth generation of those who hate me," just as his love continues toward "a thousand [generations] of those who love me and keep my commandments." The distinction between punishment to the third and fourth generation and love extended to thousands suggests that God's love far surpasses his retribution.

11 The third commandment concerns the use of the name of the Lord God in oaths or vows. Oaths were part of the common process of making authoritative and firm statements or promises. The Israelites were not to use the Lord's name to seal such declarations in a light or frivolous manner or without the intention of fulfilling the oath, vow, or promise. The "misuse" of the name of the Lord for an unworthy cause or in an unworthy manner destroys the proper use of that name in prayer, praise, and thanksgiving; and it substitutes a blasphemous manipulation of witchcraft and other supposed sources of power for a holy invoking of God's name (cf. 18:9–14; cf. also Mt 5:33–37; Jas 5:12).

12–15 In the commandment on the Sabbath day, the emphatic statement "as the LORD your God has commanded you" looks back to the initial declaration in Ex 20. The prohibition against making animals work on the Sabbath is also more emphatic here than in Ex 20:10. All the Israelite animal holdings are included in "any of your animals." Moses' concern for the lower strata of society is tied to the exhortation to remember that the Israelites themselves were slaves in Egypt. The Lord's bringing them out of Egypt does not preclude other reasons for the law of the Sabbath—as God's rest on the seventh day (after Creation; Ex 20:11). The words "may rest, as you do" indicate concern for others' well-being.

Ideas involved in the observance of the Sabbath are perpetuated in the NT by the analogy of the creating of a new people of God through the ministry of the Lord Jesus. The ritual elements of the Jewish Sabbath are superseded by the work of Christ and by faith in him. And the time reference has changed to the first day of the week, now called the Lord's Day, to focus on the new life effected and epitomized by the resurrection of Christ Jesus (Mt 28:1–7; Mk 16:1–6; Lk 24:1–6; 1Co 16:2; Rev 1:10; cf. Eph 2:4–10; 4:24). However, even now the observance of the Lord's Day must be in keeping with Col 2:16–17 (cf. Jn 20:1, 19, 26; Ac 2:1; 20:7).

16 To "honor" (GK 3877) one's parents is to respect, glorify, and venerate them. Children are to hold parents in high regard because of their position in the family, a position not only in God's scheme of authority in human relationships, but also in the covenant relationship that called for continuation of the people's status with the Lord. Children's regard for their parents led to regard for their parent's relationship to God. Both father and mother are to be honored. The results of failure to honor parents can be seen in the law concerning an incorrigibly rebellious son (21:18–21).

The apostle Paul referred to the fifth commandment as "the first commandment with a promise," the promise being "that it may go well with you and that you may enjoy long life on the earth" (Eph 6:2–3; see comment). The honoring of father and mother, together with its promise, carries over into all time and everywhere. However, the promise of an ultimate resting place (homeland) reaches its greatest fulfillment in "a new heaven and a new earth" (2Pe 3:13; Rev 21:1).

17 The NIV correctly translates the sixth command as a prohibition of murder rather than of killing. Murder is a personal, capital crime. Killing may be done as representative of the nation in judgment on a criminal or in war. In OT times persons were put to death in obedience to the command of God, but private or personal killing is murder and is proscribed.

Capital punishment is the penalty for willful homicide (Ge 9:6; Ex 21:12; Nu 35:16; Dt 19:12), the worshiping of other gods (Dt 17:2–7), and other acts of disobedience to the Lord (Dt 22:22; Jos 8:24–26; et al.). The Ten Commandments do not allow pandering the criminal who takes the life of a fellow human. Yet the person who accidentally kills another is protected (4:41–42). So the covenant-treaty restricts the passions that lead to murder but requires proper punishment of criminal homicides.

18 The starkly simple sentence "You shall not commit adultery" carries an immense load of social and spiritual implications and provides the basis for the later development of these implications. The marriage relationship continues throughout the OT as a figure of the covenant relationship between the Lord and his people (cf. Jer 3:8–9; Eze 16:15–63; Hosea). Apostasy is spiritual marital infidelity (figuratively), and total commitment must be Israel's relationship to the Lord; human marriage under the covenant must be marked by the same faithful commitment (cf. Lev 20). Jesus declared that lustful thoughts also constitute adultery (Mt 5:27–28).

19 Throughout Scripture thievery is condemned. The right to personal property is basic to the whole Mosaic economy. The indictment of the eighth commandment extends to both kidnapping (stealing a person) and the theft of goods. The protection granted by the eighth commandment is still essential to a free society; the freedom from involuntary servitude and the right to hold property are protected by this law against theft. The commandment involves spiritual values also, which rest on the covenant relationship that the Lord proffers to his people.

20 Truth was an important matter in Israel. God is "the God of truth" (Isa 65:16; cf. Ps 119:142, 151), and he hates "a lying tongue" and "a false witness" (Pr. 6:17, 19). Judges were required by the Lord to make their decisions on the basis of truth (1:16–17). False

testimony brought severe penalty (cf. 19:15–21). Both here and in Ex 20:16 this commandment is directed to bearing false witness against one's neighbor (i.e., another Israelite).

21 The last commandment goes beyond what people do; it probes into their minds and desires. The prohibition against coveting catches wrongdoing at its source. Coveting stems from the seat of one's soul, from one's intentions, from one's motivations, from one's "heart." The prohibition against coveting a neighbor's land would have no meaning if family rights in marriage ties, domestic tranquility, and property ownership did not exist. To ensure family rights after Canaan was allotted, the Lord forbade coveting not only a neighbor's wife, servants, animals, and whatever other goods he owned, but also his house and land, neither of which any of them had at that time.

c. Ratification of the covenant-treaty (5:22–33)

22 Moses' declaration that these commands alone were spoken to the Israelites directly by God makes them more emphatic. The rest of the stipulations were given to Moses, who in turn gave them to the Israelites. The Ten Commandments constitute the basic behavioral code of the people and of all succeeding generations as well. No other short list of commands begins to compare with the effect that these have had in world history. In spite of being constantly broken, they stand as the moral code par excellence.

23–28 Moses referred to a strange inconsistency of the leaders of Israel that necessitated his mediatorial ministry. They acknowledged that they had seen the Lord's glory and majesty and had heard his voice and yet remained alive. Nevertheless, they were afraid that continuous exposure would cause their death. No reason for this contradiction was offered, but they wanted Moses to be their intermediary. They asserted that they would do whatever God told Moses they should do. Moses reminded them that the Lord had accepted this arrangement, and Moses became the intermediary for the establishment of the covenantal stipulations. The people accepted that covenant (Ex 20:19; 24:3).

29–31 The best interests of his people are deep in the heart of God. He is a God of compassion, not vindictiveness. This glimpse into his heart is in harmony with the most compassionate depictions of Christ in the NT. The Israelites were directed to return to their tents. However, at the direction of God, Moses stayed to receive additional commands, decrees, and laws for the people to follow in the land.

32–33 Before once again stating and explaining the specific laws, Moses urged the people to do exactly what the Lord had commanded. The result of obedience would be long residence in the land of Canaan. Individual longevity may not be precluded from this promise for following the Lord, but the main reference was to the national welfare (cf. 6:2).

2. The greatest commandment: Love the Lord (6:1–25)

a. The intent of the covenant (6:1–3)

1–3 As the intermediary between the Lord and the people, Moses began to teach them what the Lord wanted them to do in the land across the Jordan. They and their descendants should "fear" (GK 3707) the Lord throughout their lifetimes. Standing in awe of God and holding him in utmost reverence and respect are essential to the understanding of "fearing God." The reason for Moses' teaching is elaborated by explaining why the people should hear and obey: to insure the nation's well-being and to increase in number and wealth. "A land flowing with milk and honey" describes a land of plenty, a land of fertility.

b. The greatest command: total commitment (6:4–5)

4–5 The ineloquent Moses (cf. Ex 4:10) was used of the Lord to give the world some of the most eloquent declarations in all the history of speech when he extolled the being and nature of the Lord and described the relationship that his people should have with him. Various interpretations have been given to the *shema* (lit., "Hear"; GK 9048). Does the text teach monotheism? or monolatry for Israel? Or does it teach only a uniqueness in the Lord as over against various Baals and gods of other peoples? Some of the Israelites believed in the reality of other deities, but this declaration of the nature of the Lord does not admit of the real existence of other gods. The Lord is the only deity.

While the primary assertion is that there is only one true God, it is also asserted that this true God is Israel's God. Thus, the Israelites should acknowledge no other god. The Lord cannot be known or acknowledged in many forms like the Canaanite Baals. There is only one Lord, and he alone is God, and they have entered into a covenant-treaty with him.

The exhortation to love "with all your heart and with all your soul and with all your strength" indicates the totality of one's commitment in the purest and noblest intentions of trust and obedience toward God. The words taken together mean that the people are to love God with their whole selves.

Jesus taught that Dt 6:4–5 constituted the first, the greatest, and the most important commandment, and that by obeying it one would live (Mt 22:37–38; Mk 12:29–30; Lk 10:27).

c. Propagation of the command (6:6–9)

6–9 The people were not to concern themselves only with their own attitudes toward the Lord but were to impress them on their children as well. They were to talk about God's commands always, whether at home or on the road. Since in Ex 13:9–16 the consecration of the firstborn is said to be "like a sign on your hand and a reminder on your forehead that the law of the LORD is to be on your lips" (v.9), it would seem that here also the tying of these words as symbols on their hands and binding them on their foreheads and writing them on their doorframes and gateposts should be taken metaphorically or spiritually rather than physically. The symbols drew attention to the injunctions in vv.5–7.

d. Ways to preserve the command (6:10–25)

10–12 Again Moses gave a warning in the context of history. The land that was to be Israel's had been promised years before to Abraham, Isaac, and Jacob. This promise was to be fulfilled in Israel's experience. It involved much wealth: barns, houses, wells (cisterns), vineyards, and olive groves that they had not built, provided, dug, or planted. When they would eat and be satisfied, they might "forget" (GK 8894) the Lord who brought them out of Egypt, the land of slavery. The warning was wise, for the people later did exactly what Moses warned against.

13–19 The warnings continue, focused on the necessity of recognizing and obeying their God because of who he is and what he would do if they did not acknowledge and obey him. The people must adhere to him so that it may "go well" with them and so that they may thrust their enemies from the "good land." If they do not devote themselves to him ("fear" him), worship and work for him only ("serve" him), and speak of him in their daily relationships to one another ("take your oaths in his name") but instead follow other gods, his "jealous" (GK 7862) anger will destroy them as a nation. Many find the jealousy ascribed to God very difficult to understand because jealousy can be such a vicious sin in human beings, producing much grief and animosity. But one must recognize that the provocations that give rise to the Lord's anger are most severe. Biblical history shows that such provocations frustrate the love of God until his patience with idolatry ceases to be a virtue. Only then does his jealousy call for redress (cf. 32:16–26).

20–25 The answer to a son's query, "What is the meaning of the stipulations?" is a historical recounting of the Exodus, the making of the covenant-treaty, and the giving of the legislation for the nation, together with the Lord's commands to obey and reverence him. The Lord had been active on their behalf in freeing them from Egypt and from the control of Pharaoh by his mighty hand, by miracles that taught lessons, and by wonderful acts that were great and terrible—an appropriate description of the plagues. God had brought them out of Egypt in order to bring them into Canaan, the country that he had promised to their forefathers. Obedience was necessary for their prosperity and continuance as a people in that land. Obedience to all the Lord's legislation would constitute their "righteousness" (GK 7407; see 24:13). These items must be impressed on each succeeding generation.

3. Problems of achieving the covenant of love in the land (7:1–26)

a. Relations with the people of the land and with the Lord (7:1–10)

1–2 The Hittites mentioned here were remnants of the great Hittite Empire that began about 1800 B.C. and continued to 1200 B.C. Smaller Hittite states existed prior to this and after. The Girgashites were an otherwise unknown group; they are mentioned in Ugaritic literature. The Amorites were situated west of the Jordan near the Canaanites who were on the southwest coast on the Mediterranean (Jos 5:1). Canaanites lived farther north also (Jos 11:3; 13:4).

Apparently the Perizzites lived in the southern area allotted to Judah and Simeon (Jdg 1:4–5). However, they also appear to be in the area of Ephraim in the center of the country (Jos 17:15). At this time the Hivites were found in Gibeon (Jos 9:7; 11:19; cf. 2Sa 24:7). The Jebusites lived in Jerusalem and its surroundings (Jos 18:28; Jdg 1:21).

Israel would win the land from its inhabitants by driving them out and destroying the ones remaining (cf. 7:1, 22). The Lord would drive out the Canaanites and "deliver them over to" Israel (vv.2, 16, 23); but the Israelites would be the instrument used to accomplish this destruction—though the Lord might use other persuaders also, such as the hornet (v.20). The inhabitants who were not driven out of the country were to be destroyed. No treaty was to be made with them, no mercy shown to them. The covenant-treaty of the Lord with Israel excludes other treaties.

3–5 The young Canaanite men were not to be given Israelite daughters as wives, and young Canaanite women were not to be taken by Israelite men as wives. This would lead to forsaking the Lord and to worshiping other gods. Only by total commitment to the Lord and to the covenant-treaty could the unique status of Israel be preserved. The prohibition of intermarriage was not absolute. The regulation for the marriage of an Israelite man to a foreign woman taken as a prize of war is given in 21:10–14 (but cf. Ezr 9–10; Ne 13:23–27). "Destroy them totally" and "show them no mercy" (v.2) are explicated more fully by "break down their altars, smash their sacred stones, cut down their Asherah poles and burn their idols in the fire."

6–10 The Israelites were the Lord's "treasured possession" (GK 6035; a people of great value owned completely by him). Moses, concerned that Israel keep the right perspective in her relationship with the Lord, pointed out that the large number of people in the Israelite community was not the reason for the Lord's choice of them as his people. They were few in number (in contrast to the large Near Eastern empires, or even in comparison with the seven nations they were to displace; cf. 4:38; 9:1; 11:23)—or perhaps the reference is to their small beginnings. Elsewhere Israel is said to be "as many as the stars in the sky" (1:10; 10:22) and "a great nation" (4:6; 26:5)—doubtless in fulfillment of the promise to Abraham.

Because he loved them and kept the promise of his covenant, the Lord brought the Israelites out of Egypt. It is the character of God rather than any excellence in the people that accounts for the choice. This is more evident by the reiterated assertion that the Lord their God was God, was faithful and true in himself and true to his covenant-treaty, and would be true in his covenant love toward his people into the distant future—"to a thousand generations of those who love him and keep his commands." But those who hate him, who do not love and obey him, he will repay with destruction "to their face." Both the singular suffix on "face" and the figurative use of "face" (GK 7156) suggest the meaning "to each one personally."

b. Blessing of the conquest (7:11–26)

11–16 If the Israelites followed the Lord's stipulations, he would keep his "covenant of love" with them (cf. vv.13–15). He would love and bless them with many children and with productivity in crops and animal husbandry. These blessings were of things close to the soil and natural productivity. Good health too would come to the obedient Israelites. Those terrible diseases they knew in Egypt would not come on them (Ex 15:26; 23:25) but would be inflicted on their enemies. To secure these advantages, the Israelites were to destroy without pity the Canaanites and their gods (cf. Ex 23:33; Jdg 2:3; Ps 106:36; cf. also Ex 34:12; Jos 23:13).

17–26 The Israelites were not to be intimidated by thinking that the nations of Canaan were stronger than they, making it impossible for them to drive out the Canaanites. They were to "remember" (GK 2349) what the Lord had done to Pharaoh and all Egypt. With their own eyes they had seen how the Lord had brought them out (cf. 4:34). He would do to the Canaanites what he had done to other enemies. He would also send the "hornet" among them so that even those

who survived the onslaught and hid themselves would die (this likely refers to a sense of fear, panic, or discouragement that the Lord would inflict on the Canaanites; cf. 11:25). Moses reminded the people that the great and awesome Lord was among them; so they should not be terrified by the Canaanites. However, their driving out the Canaanites would be little by little because of the wild animals (cf. Ex 23:30–31).

Though the conquest was not to be immediate over the whole land, the Lord, nevertheless, would deliver the Canaanites into Israel's hand. They would wipe out their kings' names from under heaven, i.e., remove them from the earth. The destruction of the Canaanite idols was to be complete. Even their silver and gold were detestable to the Lord. "Utterly abhor and detest it" indicates the abhorrence the people were to hold toward the idols.

4. Exhortation not to forget the Lord (8:1–20)

a. The discipline of the desert and the coming Promised Land (8:1–9)

1–5 Moses first focused on the necessity of following every command of the Lord so that Israel would be able to enter and possess the Land of Promise. They were to remember the discipline of the forty years of the Lord's leading in the desert, in order to teach them that "man does not live on bread alone but on every word that comes from the mouth of the LORD" and that "as a man disciplines his son, so the LORD . . . disciplines" them. He had made them hungry, then fed them with manna (see Ex 16). Under his providence during those forty years, their clothes did not wear out and their feet did not swell, in spite of the desert.

6–9 The Israelites were urged to walk in the ways of the Lord and to revere him, not only as in the past days of hunger and thirst, but also when the affluence of Canaanite productivity became theirs. The country he was leading them into had great natural benefits. This contrasted both with Egypt proper and with Sinai. This good land would sustain them; they would lack nothing. The iron was probably that in southern Lebanon, in the mountains of Transjordan, and, perhaps, in the Arabah south of the Dead Sea.

b. Remembrance of the Lord who led them from Egypt to Canaan (8:10–20)

10–18 When the Israelites had eaten and were satisfied, after they were settled in the land, they were to praise the Lord for his goodness. In their prosperity they were not to forget him. They had lived through the hard life of that desert by God's providence, but the future prosperity in a better land might lead them astray. In that desert experience the Lord had brought water out of the hard rock (cf. Ex 17:1–7; Nu 20:2–13); in Canaan they would find streams and pools. In that desert the Lord gave them manna. In Canaan bread would not be scarce. In their prosperity they might claim that their hands produced their wealth, not remembering that the Lord their God gave them the ability to produce wealth in confirmation of his covenant.

19–20 Once more Moses warned that forgetting and disobeying the Lord and turning to follow other gods to worship and bow down before them would mean the destruction of Israel as surely as those who followed other gods were destroyed by the Israelites.

5. Warning based on former infidelity (9:1–10:11)

a. The coming defeat of the Anakites (9:1–6)

1–6 Moses recognized the difficulties that the people would face in the country they were about to possess. The current inhabitants were greater and stronger than the Israelites (4:38), with large cities with walls up to the sky (cf. 1:28). But Moses had an adequate answer to the proverbial Anakite strength: The Lord would go across ahead of them (cf. Ex

13:21; Dt 1:30, 33, et al.). Almost in the same breath, Moses said that Israel would drive out the inhabitants and that the Lord would drive them out, indicative again that Israel's abilities were from the Lord. At best they were the Lord's instruments.

One of the most important things for the people to remember was that not Israelite righteousness but Canaanite wickedness was causing this Canaanite dispossession (Lev 18:1–30). As a matter of fact, Israel was an intractable people and, consequently, not deserving of the good land. They were receiving it by God's grace.

b. The golden calf provocation (9:7–21)

7–14 Moses sought to impress strongly on the people that they must not provoke the Lord by disobedience as they began the conquest of Canaan. Continuing his warnings, Moses reminded Israel of their behavior from the time they left Egypt till they arrived at Jordan. He exhorted them to remember how they had rebelled against the Lord, provoking his anger and arousing his wrath. He had been angry enough to slay them at Horeb. Moses had gone up on the mountain to receive the Ten Commandments (Ex 19–20; 31:18). After forty days, the Lord told Moses to go back down to the people who had become corrupt with idolatry. God told Moses that the people were stiff-necked (cf. v.6) and asked Moses not to interfere with his intention to destroy them, offering to make Moses into an even stronger and more numerous nation.

15–17 Moses proceeded to tell how he went down from the fiery mountain, carrying the two stone tablets in his hands, or perhaps one

The stone basin on the left was used for crushing olives in the process of producing olive oil. The two pictures on the right show the pomegranate flower and fruit. The Israelites were promised these and many other earthly blessings as part of their inheritance in Canaan (Dt 8:8).

in each hand. When he saw that the people had sinned against the Lord by making an idol, Moses threw down the two tablets, breaking them before the people's eyes. The nature of their sin is indicated not only by the indictment of making the calf-idol but also by their turning away quickly from the Lord's commands. The first two commands on the tablets that were physically broken by Moses had already been broken by the people.

18–21 Moses spoke of the second period of forty days and nights and also referred to two prayers on their behalf. Those two prayers are telescoped, a reference to the destruction of the calf-idol being at the end of the narrative. Moses said he feared the anger and wrath of the Lord because he was angry enough to destroy the Israelites (cf. v.8). But Moses' intercession was successful both for the people and for Aaron. Moses destroyed the calf by heating it, grinding it to fine dust, and throwing the dust into a mountain stream. "That sinful thing of yours, the calf you had made" contrasts with the Lord himself as the Almighty Creator. Exodus 32:20 adds that Moses threw the dust into the stream and "made the Israelites drink" from the stream—surely an ignominious exercise!

c. Israel's rebellion and Moses' prayer (9:22–29)

22–24 Repeatedly the people had showed themselves rebellious and stiff-necked, and thus they angered the Lord. So Moses made the overall indictment: "You have been rebellious against the LORD ever since I have known you." The source of this rebellion was their lack of trust in the Lord and, consequently, their disobedience to him.

25–29 Again Moses mentioned how he had interceded successfully for Israel (cf. Nu 14:13–19). From a most humble position, Moses addressed God as "Sovereign LORD" and prayed eloquently, reminding God that these were his people, his own "inheritance" (GK 5709), and that he had redeemed them from Egypt by his great power and mighty hand. He called on the Lord to remember Abraham, Isaac, and Jacob—doubtless a reference to the covenantal promises. If God's people were destroyed, the Egyptians would indict him for his inability to bring Israel into the land and for his trickery of leading them

into the desert to slaughter them (because he hated them). Moses did not at all deny the people's guilt but pled with the Lord to overlook their stubbornness, wickedness, and sin.

When he spoke to Moses about the people's sin while he was on Horeb the first time, God called the Israelites "your people whom you brought out of Egypt" (v.12); but when Moses prayed, he said that they were "your people, your (own) inheritance." Why this change of identification? God was probably trying to evoke Moses' concern for his people by identifying them as Moses' people whom Moses had brought from Egypt. Moses did show his concern by his great intercessory prayer in which he insisted that the people belonged to the Lord, and this brought the desired result.

d. New tablets (10:1–11)

1–5 Moses next rehearsed the second experience regarding the two stone tablets of the covenant (Ex 34:1–4). "At that time" refers to the period when Moses offered the prayer of 9:26–29. At the Lord's command he had chiseled out two stone tablets similar to the first ones. God said that he would write on them the words that had been on the first tablets. Moses was also to construct a wooden chest for the tablets. In deference to tradition NIV uses the term "ark" (GK 778) for this particular chest. Exodus 37:1–9 reveals that the ark was built by Bezalel after Moses' return, rather than that Moses made it himself before he went up the mount the second time, as could be implied here. It is not uncommon that a leader of a venture is said to do something when the actual physical accomplishment of it is done by someone else.

6–9 The "wells of the Jaakanites" is to be identified with Bene Jaakan, Moserah with Moseroth (Nu 33:31), and Gudgodah (v.7) with Hor Haggidgad (Nu 33:32). It appears that after leaving Kadesh, Israel went toward Edom and then later returned to Kadesh before starting on the last trip around Edom and up onto the plains of Moab. Consequently the order here is the reverse of that in Nu 33:31–33. Moserah was evidently a larger area that included Mount Hor. So it was correct to identify Aaron's place of death as either Mount Hor (Nu 20:22–29; 33:38–39; Dt 32:50) or Moserah (Dt 10:6). Moserah means "chastisement" and might be Moses' designation of the area, not a generally used name. None of the places mentioned has been located with certainty.

Verses 6–9 are a historical aside. Moses' mind moved along the course of events relating to the ark and then proceeded to the Israelites' journey beginning just before the death of Aaron and includes Aaron's death, the succession of Eleazer, the ministry of the Levites relative to the ark, as well as their broader ministries and their special situation regarding landed inheritance (GK 5709; cf. 9:29). The Lord himself in a special way—not land—was to be their inheritance.

10–11 The climax of this recital is Moses' declaration that the Lord listened to his plea on the Israelites' behalf. It was not the Lord's will to destroy them. The grace of God—not because they were numerous or righteous—kept them from destruction (cf. 7:7–9), and by his grace Moses' orders were renewed to "lead the people on their way" to occupy the Promised Land.

6. Exhortation to revere and love the Lord (10:12–11:32)

a. The requirement of allegiance (10:12–22)

12–13 In answer to the question "What does the LORD your God ask of you?" five familiar phrases are piled one on the other. The people are urged to (1) "fear the LORD [their] God"; (2) "walk in all his ways"; (3) "love him"; (4) "serve" him; and (5) "observe [his] commands and decrees." More or less synonymous with "observe" are the words and phrases "keep," "obey," "fix in your hearts and minds," and "teach his commands, requirements, laws, and decrees." All this was for their own good.

14–16 Although God, to whom the Israelites were to give their fealty, owns the farthest reaches of the "heavens, the earth and everything in it," yet he set his affection and love on their forefathers and "chose" (GK 1047) these, their descendants, above all other nations. Because of this gratuitous position they had in relation to the true God, the Israelites were urged to circumcise their hearts and cease being stiff-necked (cf. 30:6; Jer 4:4). The circumcision of the heart—i.e., being open, responsive, and obedient to the Lord—contrasts with being "stiff-necked" (GK

6902 & 7997)—i.e., being stubborn and rebellious.

17–22 The majestic sovereignty of the Lord is portrayed by the names ascribed to him as well as by the characteristics and acts attributed to him. "God of gods" and "Lord of lords" are Hebrew superlatives. The designations do not suggest that there are in reality other divine gods or lords over whom God rules. Rather, as God and Lord he is supreme over all. As the great, mighty, and awesome One, the Lord performed the "great and awesome wonders" that the people had seen with their own eyes. The majesty of the Lord extends to righteous behavior, showing no partiality, accepting no bribes. He defends the fatherless and the widows and loves the aliens, giving them food and clothing. The people were to be like the Lord; they too were to love aliens, for they had been aliens in Egypt.

Not only were the people to reverence and worship the Lord, they were also to hold fast to him and make oaths only in his name. Moreover, the Lord was to be the object of their praise because he had brought up out of Egypt the descendants of the seventy (Ge 46:27; Ex 1:5), who, while there, had become "as numerous as the stars in the sky." In contrast to the few who went down into Egypt with Jacob, this generation had become numerous indeed.

b. Love and obedience toward the Lord (11:1–25)

1–7 The exhortations to love, remember, observe, worship (serve), obey, teach, and walk in the Lord's ways are all here. The dominant personnel in the nation were those who had seen what the Lord had done for them in Egypt and in the desert. They were not of the generation doomed to die in the desert for their disobedience at Kadesh Barnea (1:35–36) but those who ranged from infancy to the age of twenty (Nu 14:29–30).

Moses focused his attention on those who were the leaders, repeating the exhortation formula: "Love the LORD . . . and keep his requirements." Then, in a semi-negative way, he built up the responsibility of those who were under twenty years of age at Kadesh Barnea (1:35–36). They themselves had had the experiences in the Exodus and the desert and that should have taught them to love the

Lord and to keep his requirements. Though Korah was a leader of the rebellion described in Nu 16:1–35, he is not mentioned with Dathan and Abiram here. Perhaps Korah is not named because his sons were not destroyed (Nu 26:9–11).

8–15 In order to be able to conquer the land and to live long in it as a nation, the people were to observe the Lord's commands. The description of the land has a new element. Not only was it "flowing with milk and honey"; it was a land that drank "rain from heaven." It was not like Egypt, where the planted seed was irrigated by foot because water had to be brought from the Nile. Possibly an Egyptian would use his feet to clear a channel for the flow of water to where he wanted it in his garden. In Egypt water for growing grains, vegetables, and fruits depended on the people's labors. In Canaan the water came in its season from the heavens by the providence of God; and if the people faithfully obeyed him, he would send the rain.

16–21 However, if the Israelites were enticed to turn away from the Lord and to worship other gods, he would shut the heavens so that it would not rain. Baal (Hadad) did not control the rains that brought fertility to Canaan; rather, it was the Lord who governed the incidence of rainfall. If the people did not worship and obey him, he would shut the heavens (28:23–24; Lev 26:19–20; cf. Mal 3:10).

22–25 The land that the people would acquire by obedience to the Lord under the covenant was limited in two ways: by "every place where you set your foot" and by geographic boundaries. The Lord confirmed this promise to Joshua (Jos 1:3). He also had made a particular promise of this sort to Caleb (1:36), a promise that was fulfilled in Jos 14:9–13. The geographical boundaries are generalized, in harmony with other such promises and prophecies (1:7; Ge 15:18).

c. Directives for the blessing and curse recital (11:26–32)

26–32 The most important addition to the highly repetitive directives of ch. 11 is that of the blessing and curse recital to be proclaimed from Mounts Gerizim and Ebal. The blessing was to be theirs for obedience and the curse for disobedience (cf. 27:9–28:68).

The basic element is adherence to the Lord as God, and the basic error is following other gods. No doubt Gerizim and Ebal were chosen because of their centrality and natural adaptability for such an event. They are close to each other and are both about 3,000 feet above sea level. "West of the road" refers to the main north-south road, and "near the great trees of Moreh" indicates a location a little south of the center of the valley between the two mountains.

C. Specific Stipulations of the Covenant-Treaty (12:1–26:19)

1. For worship and ceremony (12:1–16:17)

a. At the place of the Lord's choosing (12:1–32)

1–14 Chapter 12 presents some crucial elements for the Israelites' national and individual spiritual lives. (1) The people were to worship the Lord their God in the place he chose to put his Name, the place he identified himself with and where his presence would be manifested (contrast vv.2, 5, 11, 13–14, 26, et al.). (2) The people were not to worship the gods of the Canaanites but were to destroy them, their articles, and their places of worship. (3) Israel was not to worship the Lord in the way or with the means that the inhabitants of Canaan worshiped their gods. (4) Israel's burnt offerings, sacrifices, tithes, special gifts, vows, freewill offerings, and the firstborn of their flocks and herds were all to be brought to the place in the Promised Land where the Lord chose to put his Name.

"The resting place" (v.8; GK 4957) as a description of the land begins with Jacob's blessing when he called the allotment of Issachar "his resting place" (Ge 49:15). Psalm 95:11 becomes the source for vital NT teaching; the psalmist says that the Lord had declared of the people who disobeyed him in the desert, "They shall never enter my rest." According to the author of Hebrews, those who disbelieved, disobeyed, and rebelled did not enter his rest (ch. 3). To fulfill the promise of God, a rest was still to be provided. That rest was for the soul in Jesus as Savior from sin (Heb 4:3). Jesus is the "the resting place" for the believer.

15–28 While sacrificial offerings were to be brought to the central sanctuary, the butchering and eating of meat for regular sustenance could be engaged in anywhere. The only restriction on eating nonsacrificial meat (except for the rules relative to unclean foods) was the prohibition on eating blood (cf. Lev 3:17; 7:26–27; 19:26; and esp. 17:10–14). The blood was to be poured out on the ground like water. The nonsacrificial meat may be eaten by anyone—unclean or not.

The freedom enunciated in v.15 and repeated in vv.20–22 is conditioned by the prohibitions of vv.17–19. The life of the creature is its blood; so the spilling of the lifeblood is the giving of its life as the atoning sacrifice. This central characteristic of the sacrificial system in the OT becomes all important in the NT, where the typical aspects of the OT sacrifices are fulfilled in Christ by the shedding of his blood on the cross as atonement for sin (Ac 20:28; Ro 3:25; Eph 1:7; Heb 9:11–28; et al.)

Tithes, vows, and certain offerings were to be eaten only in the place the Lord chose. Notice that "you, your sons and daughters, your menservants and maidservants, and the Levites" fall under the prohibition.

29–32 The Israelites were to resist the influences of the Canaanite culture and were not to conform to Canaanite religious practices. Death was the penalty for anyone who sacrificed a child by passing him through the fire (Lev 18:21; 20:2–5). This section on the place of worship ends with Moses' warning neither to add to nor to subtract from all that he had said (cf. 4:2; Pr 30:6; Rev 22:18–19).

b. Worship of other gods forbidden (13:1–18)

1–5 In order to hinder and thwart rebellion against the Lord and adherence to the deities of the country that they were soon to enter, Moses gave the Israelites directions on how to deal with insurrectionists from the Lord's authority. Dreams were used in prophecy both legitimately (Nu 12:6) and illegitimately (Jer 23:25). Moses said that illegitimate prophets were used by the Lord to test the people's love for him. They were not to be followed (cf. v.4) but were to be put to death so that the evil would be purged from among the people. This test of the prophet overrides all others. The *sine qua non* of life is total love, commitment, and allegiance to the Lord. Elsewhere the fulfillment of prophecy establishes a prophet as a prophet. In such a case, however, the one who claims to be a

prophet does so in the name of the Lord (18:19–22; Jer 28:9).

6–11 Not only rebellious prophets, but one's closest relatives or friends who said, "Let us go and worship other gods," were to be put to death, whether the enticement had been made secretly or openly. Moses spoke of the gods of the people who would be around the Israelites as "gods you have not known" or as "gods that neither you nor your fathers have known." Neither the Israelites nor their fathers had ever acknowledged them as gods. They were not to yield to, listen to, show pity to, spare, or shield an enticer. Not only was the defector to be stoned to death, but the first stone was to be thrown by the near relative or friend that the defector had attempted to drive from the Lord. This extreme punishment was expected to produce good results. Clearly punishment—especially capital punishment—is a deterrent to crime.

12–18 Towns that defected to other gods were to be punished also. Allegations were to be investigated thoroughly and proven before a town was destroyed. Inhabitants, livestock, and all plunder were to be a whole burnt offering to the Lord, and the town was never to be rebuilt. This doom indicates how serious the Lord considered any defection from him. In other circumstances some alleviation of these rigorous rules for destruction was allowed, but under these circumstances no "condemned things" could be salvaged. If Israel kept the Lord's commands and did what was right in his eyes, he would have compassion on them.

c. Clean and unclean foods (14:1–21)

1–2 Earlier, Moses had referred to the Lord as Israel's father and to Israel as his son (1:31; 8:5). He had also said that they were holy to the Lord and were his treasured possession (4:20; 7:6). Now, on the basis of this relationship, they were commanded not to follow the ways of mourning for the dead that the nations of Canaan practiced (Lev 19:27–28; 1Ki 18:28).

3–21 Because the Israelites were the Lord's children, they were not to eat any "detestable thing" (GK 9359; cf. Lev 11). As the chosen people of God and as his holy possession, they were to follow God's injunctions to distinguish themselves from the surrounding peoples, because the pagan Canaanite culture was inimical to the holiness of the Lord and to the holiness required of his people. The reason for these injunctions about foods is basically spiritual, though there may be psychological and sanitary considerations as well. Some unclean animals had associations with Canaanite religions. Eating anything dead probably relates to the prohibition of eating blood. The meat would not be worth selling to a foreigner or giving to an alien if it were not edible.

In Lev 17:13–16 both Israelite and alien were not to eat meat with blood in it; yet here an Israelite was allowed to give such meat to an alien, and he could eat it. In Deuteronomy Moses prepared the people for the situation in Canaan, where they would be in a head-on clash with pagan culture in which the alien would not yet be integrated into Israelite culture. In Leviticus the alien comes within the culture of Israel and has the benefits of adhering to that culture.

The prohibition against cooking a young goat in its mother's milk is apparently in reaction to an ancient Canaanite and Syrian custom dated as early as the fifteenth century B.C.

d. Tithes (14:22–29)

22–29 The "tithe" (GK 5130) is to be taken to the place the Lord shall choose as a dwelling for his Name, and there it is to be eaten joyfully in the presence of the Lord. Moses had already mentioned in 12:6 the tithes along with the other things that the people were to bring to the chosen sanctuary, where they should eat and rejoice. Surely the people in a few days would not consume a tenth of their total annual production! Having already given directions for the support of the Levites by the tithes (Nu 18:21–28), Moses here spoke of the festal communal meals that the people were to enjoy when the tithes were brought to the tabernacle.

Every three years these tithes were to be brought to local city centers where they were stored for the use of the Levites, the aliens, and the poor. This care for nonlanded people would lead to God's blessing on the work of their hands. This garnering of tithes was to come during the third year and the sixth year. After the sixth year, the sabbatical year was

observed as a year when the fields lay fallow, after which the cycle commenced again.

The logistics of transporting the tithes would be difficult—perhaps impossible—for families living at a distance from the tabernacle. Thus the people could turn the tithe into cash and then, at the place the Lord would choose, convert it into food and drink desired for the celebration of God's blessing.

e. The year of canceling debts (15:1–11)

1–4 Israel was to have a very special internal relationship of brotherhood in its citizenry. If followed, there would be no poor or needy person among them because of the Lord's blessing (vv.4–6, 10). The cancellation of debt itself would go a long way toward producing that blessing, and it would result in limiting the centralization of monetary assets in the hands of the more well-to-do. No evidence exists that the Mosaic economy in its details was ever fully implemented with its sabbatical years and years of Jubilee.

The assertion that "there should be no poor" among them at first glance may seem to conflict with v.7 and especially v.11. But apparently Moses proclaimed and urged the ideal while being doubtful that the ideal would be fully realized (cf. the same thing in 1Jn 2:1).

5–6 Israel would realize the ideal situation only if the people would fully obey the Lord. Obedience would not only bring rich blessings so that no poor would be among them, but they would also have monetary superiority over the nations around them.

7–11 Moses moved into the subjective bases for the Israelites' behavior—their thoughts and emotions—when he said that they should not be hardhearted, but should freely lend a brother whatever he needs. They must exercise care not to harbor a base thought that would limit generosity, such as "the year for canceling debts is near." They must give generously without a grudging heart. A warning is appended: the brother can appeal to the Lord, and the grudging-hearted will be found guilty of sin. The indictment "You will be found guilty of sin" may be one made directly by the Lord to the conscience or a formal one made by a priest (23:21–22; 24:15; cf. Lev 20:20; Nu 9:13; 18:22).

f. Freeing servants (15:12–18)

12–18 Those in servitude should go free after no more than six years of bondage (cf. Ex 21:2–6). But one's liberality should go beyond manumission, for those freed should be given liberal supplies from their former owner's flock, threshing floor, and winepress. If a servant did not want to be set free, the master was to push an awl through the lobe of his ear and into the door or doorpost, thereby marking him for a life of servitude (cf. Ex 21:6). Two reasons for this choice of life servitude are love for the master and the well-being of the servant under the master. In Ex 21:5 love for one's wife and children acquired during servitude constitutes an additional reason. The servant who does not want to leave his wife and children, as the law required, chooses life servitude instead.

Anticipating possible reaction to the largess required of the master, the Israelites were to realize that the indentured servant during his six years of servitude has been worth twice as much as a hired hand. Perhaps what is meant is that through the years the servant's labor was equivalent to that of a hired hand, yet he had not received the daily wage of a hired hand. Thus the servant was worth double because the owner not only had the service of the servant, but also did not have to pay out anything for that service.

g. Firstborn animals (15:19–23)

19–23 In addition to earlier directives on the firstborn (cf. 12:6–7, 17; 14:23–26), here it is said that the firstborn of herds should not be worked and the firstborn of sheep not sheared. They belong to the Lord and are not for private gain.

All the people were to eat and rejoice together at the annual festivals. The regulations of Deuteronomy are, generally, given to all the people, including the priests. The logistics of consuming all the specified parts of all the firstborn of herds and flocks annually might well demand the participation of the whole populace. Animals with serious defects were not to be sacrificed but were to be eaten as common food by the people, ceremonially clean or unclean, being careful to properly dispose of the blood. These regulations emphasize anew that God's people were to follow a holy way of living.

h. Passover (16:1–8)

1–4 In Deuteronomy the whole Passover (GK 7175) Festival is in mind (cf. Ex 23:14–19; Lev 23; Nu 28:16–29:38), including the Feast of Unleavened Bread, and so the sacrificing of the Passover animal (or animals) includes animals from the herd as well as from the flock for the main Passover meal. Moreover, when they were settled in the land, the Passover was to be held in the place the Lord would "choose as a dwelling for his Name." The historical occasion for the Passover would have an added significance—that of the agricultural year.

Yeast suggests decay and was unsuited for the symbolism of the Passover. Thus here bread without yeast, the bread of affliction (cf. Ex 3:7), was to be eaten because the Israelites had left Egypt in apprehensive haste. The statement "so that . . . you may remember the time of your departure from Egypt" makes it clear that the date of the Passover Feast rests on a historical basis rather than on the agricultural year. "On the evening of the first day" would be the beginning of the fifteenth of Nisan (March/April) (Lev 23:6).

5–8 After eating the Passover, the people were to return to their temporary residences where they were staying during their visit to the place the Lord would choose. The Passover meal was complete in itself; none of the meat sacrificed in the evening was to remain until the morning. The Passover-Unleavened Bread Festival ended with a special closing assembly.

In the NT the last Passover that Jesus ate with his disciples became the Lord's Supper (Mt 26:17–29; Mk 14:12–25; Lk 22:7–22), and Christ's death on the cross became the Passover sacrifice to take away sin (1Co 5:7–8; cf. Jn 1:29).

i. Feast of Weeks (16:9–12)

9–12 This feast was to begin seven weeks from the time the sickle was put to the standing grain. According to Lev 23:15, the count was to be made from "the day after the Sabbath, the day you brought the sheaf of the wave offering," i.e., on the second day of the Passover Festival. The phrase "fifty days" in Lev 23:16 in the LXX led to the designation of the Feast of Weeks as Pentecost. In the NT the Feast of Weeks becomes significant as the time of the outpouring of the Holy Spirit in fulfillment of the prophecy of Joel 2:28–32 and the beginning of the NT church. The Feast of Weeks was a harvest celebration, and the freewill offering made at that time was to be commensurate with the blessing the Lord had given the people (cf. vv.16–17).

j. Feast of Tabernacles (16:13–17)

13–17 The Feast of Tabernacles or Booths was celebrated for seven days after the processing of the grain at the threshing floor and the grapes in the winepress. In Ex 23:16 and 34:22, it is called the Feast of Ingathering; and the time of the feast is more explicitly given in Lev 23:34, 36, 39, and Nu 29:12 as extending from the fifteenth to the twenty-first of the seventh month, which is Tishri (Sept./Oct.). It was followed by an additional day with a closing assembly. This seven-day feast was to be a joyful occasion for everybody, because of God's blessing on the work of their hands.

A summary and reiteration of the command that all Israelite men were to appear before the Lord for these three festivals annually concludes this review. One was not to attend the festivals empty-handed but was to bring a contribution proportionate to the Lord's blessing on his labor.

2. National concerns (16:18–19:21)

a. Judges (16:18–20)

18–20 This section really belongs with ch. 17. Contemplating the new settlement in Canaan, Moses instructed the people to appoint "judges" (GK 9149) and other "officials" (GK 8853) in the towns the Lord would give them. The judges were civil magistrates, and the officials were subordinate leaders who implemented the decisions of the judges. The judges were to "judge the people fairly"; and the people were admonished to follow justice alone, so that they would be able to continue living as a nation in possession of the land. The judges were not to pervert justice or show partiality. Bribes blind the wise and twist the words of the righteous. The Lord demands pure justice.

b. Asherah poles, sacred stones, and flawed animals (16:21–17:1)

16:21–17:1 Moses once more warned of the idolatry Israel would find in Canaan. The worship of the Lord must not be with the paraphernalia of the gods of Canaan. An important element in proper worship was the quality of the offerings brought to the Lord; the firstborn offered had to be without "serious flaw" (15:21) and "without defect" (Lev 1:3 et al.); i.e., it had to be perfect. This rule is here applied to the sacrifice of any ox or sheep.

c. Procedures for punishment of covenant violators (17:2–13)

2–3 Deviations from the worship of the Lord are called "doing evil in the eyes of the LORD," a "violation of his covenant," and "contrary to my command." Israel was not to worship the sun, moon, and stars of the sky either as physical entities or as representations of pagan deities. The sun, moon, and stars along with other physical elements show the glory of the Lord but are by no means idolatrous representations of him (Pss 8:3; 19:1; Ro 1:18–21; et al.).

4–13 Any alleged deviation from the worship of the Lord is to be thoroughly investigated. If it proves true (as in 13:14) on testimony of two or three witnesses—one witness being insufficient—the guilty party must be stoned to death, the witnesses being the first to throw stones. The seriousness of this defection and the purpose of the punishment are seen in the declaration, "You must purge the evil from among you (Israel)."

"The place the LORD will choose" is to be the juridical as well as the spiritual, social, and political center of the nation (cf. 16:18–20). All cases too difficult for local court decision were to be taken to the priests and the current judge at that chosen center. Their decision was final and was to be followed in detail. Contempt of court was a capital offense. When these procedures are followed, "all the people will hear and be afraid." As in 13:11, capital punishment would be a deterrent to crime.

The local judges were not to decide in the cases that were appealed to the higher court; the higher court decision was then implemented by the local judges. The responsibility for the application of the law is on the whole populace. "The man who shows contempt" may be anyone in Israel—as is obvious from the idea that none of the people will be "contemptuous" when they learn of the one in contempt being put to death.

d. Appointment of and rules for a king (17:14–20)

14–15 The possible future institution of kingship does not rise out of the Lord's immediate plan for government but out of a supposition that the people will want a king because of the surrounding peoples (see 1Sa 8:4–9). In developing revelation, the Lord revealed his eternal plan of using kingship as the vehicle of central importance in messianic prophecy and fulfillment. Given the desire for a king, the people were to find the one the Lord would choose, who must be a brother Israelite.

16–17 Restrictions too were placed on the king (cf. vv.18–20). The accumulation of horses is linked to the prohibition that the people were not to return to Egypt. Having many horses signified either riches or military resources or both. Doubtless both indicated a reliance on one's own resources rather than on the Lord. A large harem also represented a likeness to the Oriental courts of other kingdoms, and having many wives envisaged the usual procedure of sealing treaties by marriage. Such wives would bring foreign cultures and idol worship into the palace and so lead the heart of the king astray. The accumulation of silver and gold would also tend toward reliance on riches rather than on the Lord (cf. 1Ki 10:1–11:13).

18–20 Following the procedures for vassal treaties, a copy of the covenant-treaty was deposited in the dwelling of the Lord. From this the king was to make a copy for himself and keep the copy with him, reading it regularly. This preoccupation with the "words of this law" had a threefold purpose—that the king may (1) learn to serve the Lord, (2) follow carefully all the words of the law, and (3) keep on the same level as his brothers before the law of the Lord. The result of this behavior would be a long reign.

e. Shares for priests and Levites (18:1–8)

1 A wide, sweeping presentation, telling of the support of the Levites, is added to the stipulations relative to judges and possible kings. The designations the "priests," the "Levites," and the "whole tribe of Levi" indicate that the priests and Levites were not always coextensive terms; the "priests" were those Levites who were the descendants of

Aaron, and the "Levites" included all those who belonged to the tribe of Levi, whether or not they were descendants of Aaron (Nu 18:20, 23–24).

2 The Levites as a tribe were not to have a tribal allotment in Canaan, as the other tribes would have. The Lord was their inheritance, as far as material possessions were concerned. They would have certain cities and, under certain situations, could also have private holdings (see v.8; Nu 35; Jos 20–21). The Levites' daily sustenance came from the offerings made to the Lord and from the firstfruits. Particular portions of the offerings were to be given to the priests, i.e., the sons of Aaron (Lev 7:31–35).

3–5 The word for "sacrifice" (GK 2284 & 2285), which normally refers to sacrificing animals for religious feasts, here includes the meals of the festivals that are in addition to the fellowship offerings (cf. 12:15, 21). "The share due the priests" was the portion established by the Lord for them because of their office and service. Designations of the Levites as the priestly tribe sometimes refer to their tribal position as a whole and at other times to the sons of Aaron, a more limited group.

6–8 When a Levite from elsewhere in Israel desired to move to the place the Lord would choose in order to engage in priestly service, he could do so; and he was to have an equal share in the benefits of his position. The benefits accrue to any Levite even though he may have other assets from the sale of family possessions—whatever they may be.

f. Detestable practices of Canaan (18:9–13)

9–13 References to these "detestable ways" (GK 9359) are not uncommon, but the list in vv.10–11 is fuller than elsewhere. Precise identifications cannot always be clearly discerned by the terms used. Comparison with other such prohibitions shows that several of the words are sometimes generalizations and at other times more specific or discrete. Not only was adherence to the false gods of Canaan proscribed, but also the means by which the Canaanites attempted to communicate with them were to be abhorred totally and rejected completely.

g. The prophet like Moses (18:14–22)

14–19 Israelite reliance was to be wholly on the Lord, who would send them "a prophet" (GK 5566) like Moses. These prophets would be selected by the Lord from their own brothers, and the Lord would put his words in their mouths. Being the spokesman for God is the central characteristic of a prophet. The Lord would call to account anyone who did not listen to the words spoken in his name. In the NT, this promise of the "prophet like you from among their brothers" was seen as prophetic of Jesus Christ (cf. Jn 1:21; 6:14; 7:40; Ac 3:22–23).

20–22 The prophet who presumed to speak in the Lord's name (without authorization) or who spoke in the name of other gods was to be put to death. The latter broke the first commandment and merited capital punishment. But the former could be difficult to determine. The prescribed test was that if the prediction did not happen, the message was not from the Lord. This answer speaks of only one of the ways to determine the validity of a prophet and a prophecy; predictive proof alone cannot be used to distinguish a true prophet from a false one, because prediction that comes true when spoken in the name of another god is a capital offense (cf. ch. 13:1–5). Verse 14 clearly states that sorcery and divination were not permitted, which is the main way pagans get messages from their gods. Adherence to the Lord and his written word is the highest law; one should not be afraid of any false prophet or his predictions.

h. Cities of refuge (19:1–14)

1–4 Bezer, Ramoth, and Golan had already been established as cities of refuge for Reuben, Gad, and the half-tribe of Manasseh east of the Jordan (4:41–43). Now Israel is commanded to set up three cities of refuge in Canaan proper when they occupy it. If Israel's control would extend over the whole Land of Promise, which according to the oath to their forefathers apparently extended from Egypt to the Euphrates (Ge 15:18), three more cities were to be chosen (vv.8–9), making nine in all. But the third set of cities of refuge was never appointed because the people never fully controlled the larger territory.

The cities were to be centrally located in three divisions of the country so that any slayer would have reasonably close sanctuary. Cities of refuge constituted a means to thwart a hasty application of blood revenge, which might result in the death of an innocent man—one who killed another unintentionally and without malice aforethought (cf. Ex 21:12–14; Nu 35:6–34; Jos 20–21).

5–13 The shedding of innocent blood in Israel would bring guilt on the nation (v.10). It would be wrong to allow the innocent to be killed and the guilty to go unpunished (v.13). The process of determining the innocence or guilt is not given here—other than that the elders of the town of the accused should send for the killer to be returned from the city of refuge to which he had fled. If guilty, he was to be handed over to the avenger of blood for execution. Acquittal or guilt would be determined on bases indicated elsewhere (cf. v.15; Nu 35:9–34). That deliberate capital offenses were to be punished by capital punishment rigorously applied is seen in the declaration "Show him no pity" (cf. v.21).

14 Moses looked ahead to the time when Israel would be settled in the land within the tribal and family boundaries and when these boundaries could be subject to dispute. The boundaries once allotted in the original division of the land were to be inviolate; the Lord had given the land to the people. Their descendants were never to disturb the boundary stones. The right to hold property was a cornerstone of Israel's inheritance from the Lord. It is still a primary right of free people on the earth.

i. Witnesses to a crime (19:15–21)

15 Jurisprudence must have rules of evidence, and in Israel witnesses were required to supply evidence or be punished (Lev 5:1). The rule for witnesses in capital offenses (17:7) is here applied to any crime or offense. Two or three witnesses are required (17:6; Nu 35:30; Mt 18:16; 2Co 13:1).

16–20 The designation of a false witness as "malicious" probably indicts one who uses harsh and injurious language. When one accuses another after this fashion, the two of them are to stand in the presence of the Lord before the incumbent priests and judges. "In the presence of the LORD" refers to the tribunal meeting in the place in the central sanctuary designated for this purpose (17:9). The investigation must be "thorough" (cf. 13:14; 17:4); and if the accuser is proved to be a liar, the punishment for the accused will be meted out to the accuser.

21 The "lex talionis" (cf. Ex 21:23–25; Lev 24:18–20) is given as the guide to punish offenders. Jesus seemingly negated this rule for his disciples in Mt 5:38–42 and substituted the turning of the other cheek. It must be remembered, however, that Deuteronomy is the law that the officials of the nation were to follow to protect the public, to punish offenders, and to deter crime. Jesus, on the other hand, spoke to individuals about reacting to violence against themselves personally.

3. Rules for warfare (20:1–20)

1–4 The Israelites were not to be frightened by the panoply of their enemies, because the Lord who had brought them up from Egypt would be present with them. The priest was to prepare the army for battle by assuring the troops of the Lord's presence to give them victory. The fourfold expostulation is dramatic: (1) Do not be fainthearted; (2) do not be afraid; (3) do not be terrified; (4) do not give way to panic.

5–9 The officers too were to speak to the inductees and articulate the ways to be excused from service. Only men ready and willing for battle were wanted. This was no conscripted army. The exemptions—acquiring a home and having the opportunity to live in it first; being able to enjoy the fruit of one's vineyard; being able to enjoy a recent marriage (cf. 24:5)—generally relate to settled society and indicate settled life in Canaan. So that discouragement would not infect the ranks, the fearful and fainthearted were also exempt. When the troops were psychologically ready for battle, commanders were appointed. It is unclear as to who was to do the appointing.

10–15 When in the more distant future Israel would attack a city beyond the boundaries of Canaan proper, different rules would apply. The cities of Canaan were to be totally destroyed, but the distant cities were first to be offered peace. If they accepted that offer, they were to become a work force for the Israelites. In cities that refused a peace offer, the men were to be executed; but the women, children, livestock, and everything else were to become booty for Israel.

16–18 In contrast to this treatment, the cities within Canaan proper were subject to *herem* (cf. 7:26, "set apart for destruction"; GK 3051). "Anything that breathes," as elsewhere (except in Ge 7:22), refers to human beings. All the inhabitants that remained in the conquered cities of Canaan were to be completely destroyed so that Israel would not be enticed into the supreme sin of defecting from the Lord and turning to other gods.

19–20 When Israel needed logs for building siege works, the immediate need was not to outweigh the long term value of fruit trees. Thus, they were not to be used for this purpose because of their value in producing food. Orchards were not common and were considered valuable.

All warfare is filled with violence, anguish, and inhumanity. These directions given to Israel must be measured relative to the world they lived in and to the heinousness of the sins of the cultures of Canaan.

4. Interpersonal relationships (21:1–25:19)

a. Atonement for unsolved murder (21:1–9)

1–5 When murder or manslaughter has been committed (Nu 35:32–33), the justice of God is affronted. There is an identification of the criminal with both the land and the people; and unless the criminal is punished, justice is not met. When the perpetrator of the crime cannot be detected, some method of removal of the guilt must be secured. First, the guilty area is determined by the elders and judges who measure the distance from the body to the nearby towns. Then the elders of the nearest town must make atonement for the bloodshed. An unworked heifer is to be led into an uncultivated valley that has a flowing stream. Presumably the place where the heifer is led is as near as possible to where the body lay. The priests need to be present, for they represent the Lord (10:8; 18:5).

6–9 Atonement is made for the bloodshed when the elders break the heifer's neck and wash their hands over the heifer's body while they declare that they, representing the people, are innocent of the homicide. Then they pray that the Lord's redeemed people will be held guiltless. This action purges the people

Major Social Concerns in the Covenant

1. Personhood
Everyone's person is to be secure (Ex 20:13;
Dt 5:17; Ex 21:16-21,26-31; Lev 19:14;
Dt 24:7; 27:18).

2. False Accusation
Everyone is to be secure against slander and
false accusation (Ex 20:16; Dt 5:20; Ex 23:1-3;
Lev 19:16; Dt 19:15-21).

3. Woman
No woman is to be taken advantage of within her
subordinate status in society (Ex 21:7-11,20,
26-32; 22:16-17; Dt 21:10-14; 22:13-30; 24:1-5).

4. Punishment
Punishment for wrongdoing shall not be
excessive so that the culprit is dehumanized
(Dt 25:1-5).

5. Dignity
Every Israelite's dignity and right to be God's
freedman and servant are to be honored and
safeguarded (Ex 21:2,5-6; Lev 25; Dt 15:12-18).

6. Inheritance
Every Israelite's inheritance in the promised land
is to be secure (Lev 25; Nu 27:5-7; 36:1-9;
Dt 25:5-10).

7. Property
Everyone's property is to be secure (Ex 20:15;
Dt 5:19; Ex 21:33-36; 22:1-15; 23:4-5;
Lev 19:35-36; Dt 22:1-4; 25:13-15).

8. Fruit of Labor
Everyone is to receive the fruit of his labors
(Lev 19:13; Dt 24:14; 25:4).

9. Fruit of the Ground
Everyone is to share the fruit of the ground
(Ex 23:10-11; Lev 19:9-10; 23:22; 25:3-55;
Dt 14:28-29; 24:19-21).

10. Rest on Sabbath
Everyone, down to the humblest servant and
the resident alien, is to share in the weekly rest
of God's Sabbath (Ex 20:8-11; Dt 5:12-15;
Ex 23:12).

11. Marriage
The marriage relationship is to be kept inviolate
(Ex 20:14; Dt 5:18; see also Lev 18:6-23;
20:10-21; Dt 22:13-30).

12. Exploitation
No one, however disabled, impoverished or
powerless, is to be oppressed or exploited
(Ex 22:21-27; Lev 19:14,33-34; 25:35-36;
Dt 23:19; 24:6,12-15,17; 27:18).

13. Fair Trial
Everyone is to have free access to the courts
and is to be afforded a fair trial (Ex 23:6,8;
Lev 19:15; Dt 1:17; 10:17-18; 16:18-20;
17:8-13; 19:15-21).

14. Social Order
Every person's God-given place in the social
order is to be honored (Ex 20:12; Dt 5:16;
Ex 21:15,17; 22:28; Lev 19:3,32; 20:9; Dt 17:8-13;
21:15-21; 27:16).

15. Law
No one shall be above the law, not even the king
(Dt 17:18-20).

16. Animals
Concern for the welfare of other creatures is to
be extended to the animal world (Ex 23:5,11;
Lev 25:7; Dt 22:4,6-7; 25:4).

from the guilt of spilling innocent blood. The atonement mentioned is not an atonement within the sacrificial system, for the blood of the heifer is not offered. It is rather an atonement for justice; the heifer suffers death in place of the unknown criminal, to clear the land of guilt.

b. Family relationships (21:10–21)

10–14 Suppose in warfare with nations that were "at a distance" (20:15) an Israelite man desired to marry a foreign, unmarried woman captured in warfare. Since she would not be under the ban of *herem* (20:16–18), she and the man would be subject to the rules regarding the marriage of Israelites. This legislation would restrain the man from rape and allow the woman time to become adjusted to their new condition. Symbolic of casting off her former life, the woman was to remove her native clothing, shave her head and trim her nails, and put on new clothes. These cleansing rites (cf. Lev 14:8; Nu 8:7; 2Sa 19:24) initiated the woman into the Israelite family, but she would have a full month to mourn her separation from her natural family before she became the wife of the Israelite. She was also protected from being sold for money or treated as a commodity. After marriage, if her husband was not pleased with her, he must let her go free because he had intercourse with her.

15–17 Polygamy, while not officially approved, was condoned in ancient times; so problems relating to the responsibilities and privileges of succession would arise (cf. Ge 29:15–30:24). The rule here established for Israel existed elsewhere in the ancient Orient (cf. Middle Assyrian law). In Israel the responsibilities and privileges of the firstborn stayed with the firstborn regardless of the father's desires. A father was not to make a will to frustrate this law or otherwise dispose of his property. The Hebrew idiom for "double share" (GK 9109 & 7023) became indicative of the position of successor (cf. 2Ki 2:9). "The first sign of his father's strength" describes the first son as the first result of the father's procreative power.

18–21 The rules for behavior in domestic and civil life generally provided protection for the less fortunate. In the case of a recalcitrant son, however, no mercy was allowed. This son was "stubborn" (GK 6253) and "rebellious" (GK 5286) in the face of remonstrance. These words describe incorrigible wickedness. Moreover, when the parents leveled charges against the son before the elders, they made the specific accusations of his being both a drunkard and a profligate. No hope remained for such a person.

His parents made their accusation before the elders sitting in the place of judgment in the gate of the city, and the punishment of being stoned to death was meted out by the townspeople so that evil would be purged from among them. The fear of punishment was expected to restrain each filial rebelliousness (13:11; 17:13; 19:20). This kind of rebelliousness was strictly forbidden by the fifth commandment (5:16; Ex 20:12; cf. Ex 21:15).

c. Relations to land, animals, and things (21:22–22:12)

22–23 The body of a person put to death for wrongdoing and hung on a tree must not remain exposed overnight: the body is under God's curse, and more exposure would desecrate the land. Hanging (cf. Jos 8:29; 10:26–27) exhibited the person to public humiliation. The criminal was under the indictment of death by God's judgment.

The meaning of "under God's curse" is not certain. Since judgment basically is God's (1:17), the judgment that takes one out of the covenant community as a criminal and displays that judgment by the humiliation of hanging in public shows that that person is under God's curse. The exposure of his body was the utmost desecration. But continued exposure would desecrate the land, possibly because of the effect the continual remembrance of the crime and its punishment

would have symbolically on the land. Paul's citation of this verse to illustrate the extent of Jesus' humiliation is very apt (Gal 3:13).

22:1–4 Straying domestic animals are not to be ignored but must be returned to their owner. When an owner does not live nearby, or for any other reason is unknown, the one who saw the stray must take it to his own place for safekeeping until the owner comes searching for it. Then the animal is to be restored to the owner. This same rule applies to anything one loses and another finds. Concern for an animal fallen on the road requires that anyone passing by should help it to its feet. This does not necessarily refer to an animal that had strayed; more likely it envisages an animal fallen under a load with the owner beside him (Ex 23:5). Because of the weight of the load, the owner alone is unable to assist the animal to its feet.

5 The prohibition against a woman wearing men's clothing and vice versa can scarcely refer to transvestism. Most probably illicit sexual practices—including homosexuality (Lev 18:22; 20:13)—are included in this prohibition. Scripture considers the natural differences between male and female to be the Lord's creation and so should not be disregarded.

6–7 The injunction here relates to a mother bird on her nest with eggs or newly hatched young. Concern of the "be kind to animals" type or for animal parenthood or for saving the mother in the interest of continuing productivity may have occasioned this legislation (but cf. Ge 1:28; 9:9–10). Long life and well-being follow obedience to this command (cf. 5:16).

8 Protection of self and property from the guilt of bloodshed underlies the concern for persons who may be on the flat roof of one's house (Jos 2:6; 2Sa 11:2). A railing was to be built as a safety precaution. The roofs of houses were often used for various purposes. Consequently, without some kind of restraining wall, one could easily fall off and be hurt.

9–10 The prohibitions of mixing seeds for planting, plowing with diverse animals, and wearing clothes woven of differing threads expand slightly on Lev 19:19. The ancient rationale for these regulations is not known.

Perhaps the distinctions that God ordained in Creation are to be preserved. Israelite behavior was to be differentiated from that of its neighbors. Possibly the mixing of animals pulling plows was thought to be unkind because of the differing strengths of the animals or ways of pulling under harness (see comment on Lev 19:19). Verse 9 declares that when vines and other plants are mixed, both the grapes and the other crop are "defiled" and no longer permissible for personal use. The aim of the legislation again seems to be to maintain the natural distinctiveness of Creation.

11–12 The mixing of kinds of thread is prohibited in Lev 19:19, but here the specific kinds of thread—"wool and linen"—are mentioned. Perhaps these are illustrative. In Nu 15:38–40 the regulation for the wearing of tassels includes the reason: "You will have these tassels to look at and so you will remember all the commands of the LORD. . . . Then you will remember to obey all my commands and will be consecrated to your God" (vv.39–40).

d. Marriage violations (22:13–30)

13–21 Divorce, though not God's will (cf. Mk 10:5–9), was permitted under certain circumstances and restrictions. A husband's charge of premarital infidelity on the part of his newly acquired wife followed certain procedures. If the husband, after lying with his bride, disliked her and declared that she was not a virgin when she came to him, her parents could come to her aid by displaying the proof of her virginity (apparently the blood-spotted bedclothes) to the town elders. If they decided that the man was guilty of defaming his bride, he must give a hundred shekels of silver to the girl's father, and she must remain as his wife, never to be divorced. If no acceptable proof of virginity was presented, she was to be stoned at the door of her father's house.

The law protected the innocent bride from the caprice of her husband and discouraged premarital infidelity among young women. It did not, however, protect young women from getting a husband who had previously had sexual relations. But other laws do concern themselves with men's extramarital relations (e.g., vv.22–29).

22 The injunction "You must purge the evil from among you" or "from Israel" is given three times (vv.21, 22, 24) in this series of capital offenses—an indication of the seriousness of crimes against marital fidelity. Under the conditions expressed, adultery was not only forbidden but, as a capital offense, demanded the death penalty.

23–27 If one of the adulterous persons was a woman "pledged to be married" to someone else and the act occurred in a town, without any voiced protest by the woman, stoning was required. If rape occurred in the country, where a girl's screams could not be heard, only the man's life was required; the girl went free.

28–29 The law was more lenient with a man who forced a virgin who was not pledged in marriage to another. The penalty, however, was not light. The offender had to pay a fine of fifty shekels of silver, marry the girl, and keep her as his wife as long as he lived. It was customary to pay a purchase price for a wife (Ge 34:12; Ex 22:16; 1Sa 18:25; Hos 3:2).

30 The prohibition of intercourse with one's father's wife undoubtedly refers to a wife other than one's own mother, since a father's wife in this sense is in view elsewhere (27:20; Lev 18:8, 11; 20:11). Jacob condemned Reuben for his incest with Bilhah (Ge 35:22; 49:3–4). In Leviticus death was decreed for both persons involved in such incest (Lev 18:8, 29; 20:11).

e. Family, neighborhood, and national relationships (23:1–25:19)

1–2 Chapter 23 begins its miscellany of laws with three categories of persons who are excluded from the assembly of the Lord: eunuchs, illegitimate children, and Ammonites and Moabites. The assembly is expressly called "the assembly of the LORD" (vv.1–3, 8) and is probably restricted to the religious community. Any bodily defect was considered unacceptable to God—as were the results of sinful acts, whether personal (as illegitimacy) or national (as the behavior of the Ammonites and the Moabites).

The excluded eunuchs were those who were deliberately made eunuchs—probably those in dedication to foreign gods and those who had official positions under foreign governments; these rules were also against any deliberate mutilation abhorrent to the position of God's people as holy. Isaiah predicted that in the future eunuchs who did what pleased the Lord would have a better name than the sons and daughters of Israel (56:4–5; cf. Ac 8:26–39).

Precisely who comes under the ban of those born out of wedlock is not clear (see NIV note, KJV). The passage hardly refers to all persons born out of wedlock because prohibited marriages are clearly delineated and fornicators were put to death, required to be married, or in some cases required to remain in protective custody of a family. This regulation might well be aimed at the offspring of cult prostitutes or of other promiscuous sexual practices related to the fertility religions of Canaan. It seems possible, however, that the law covers the offspring of all "forbidden marriages." The reference "to the tenth generation," as v.6 indicates, means as long as the nation exists.

3–6 Ammonites and Moabites were excluded because they failed to show concern for the Israelites when they moved toward Canaan. Israel had sought nothing except the right to purchase food and water (2:28–29). Because of a refusal, Israel skirted their lands and showed no hostility toward them (2:9, 16–19). But Moab hired Balaam, a Mesopotamian sorcerer, to curse Israel; and even though the Lord turned the curse to blessing (Nu 22–24; cf. Ge 12:3), Moab came under the indictment of not supporting the Israelites. The act of the king is naturally the responsibility of the whole kingdom because he represents and acts for the people.

Israel as a nation was never to seek peace or good relations with these two nations. The prophets also denounced the Ammonites and Moabites (Isa 15:1–16:13; Jer 48:1–49:6; et al.). Ruth, a Moabitess whose descendants included the Davidic line eventuating in the Messiah, was a notable exception.

7–8 Though Edomites and Egyptians also failed in kindness toward the Israelites—and even oppressed them—these two nations were not to be abhorred; Edom because of near kinship, and Egypt because Israel lived as an alien there. Great grandchildren could be integrated into the assembly of the Lord.

9–14 Rules for the holiness and cleanliness of the camp during military engagements are in mind here. A man who has an emission at night must go outside the camp and remain there until the next evening when, after washing himself, he may reenter at the going down of the sun. For the disposal of excrement, a place outside the camp was to be chosen. In addition to weapons, some sort of instrument like a spade was to be used for digging a hole. The excrement was to be covered over so that the Lord would not be offended as he went through the camp; this reference is most likely to the Lord's personal, spiritual presence. Holiness is identified with cleanliness. Only the clean person can approach the Lord in worship (Ex 19:10–11; 30:18–21; Jos 3:5; Ps 51:7, 10).

15–16 A fugitive slave was not to be handed over to his master but was to be given asylum and the freedom to go anywhere he desired within the domain of Israel. These slaves had fled from foreign parts; they were not to be oppressed as the Israelites themselves had been oppressed in Egypt (Ex 22:21; Lev 19:33–34).

17–18 Temple prostitution was practiced among Baal worshipers. Israel was strictly forbidden to indulge in this demoralizing practice. The earnings of prostitutes are tainted and are not to be offered to the Lord to pay any vow ("vow" covers any contribution to the Lord). Whatever is acquired by evil means as well as what is evil in itself is not to be offered to the Lord.

19–20 When the nation was first established, the Israelite economy was by no means mercantile; loans were made primarily to help persons too poor to support themselves. Such assistance was to be given without interest. But since merchants from other nations might come for business reasons to Israel or might make loans on interest to Israelites, foreigners could be charged interest. This rule alleviated the plight of the poor and made it more possible for them to work themselves out of their low estate. Interest is also regulated in Ex 22:25 and Lev 25:36–37. The Lord's blessing on the labors of God's people in the land was contingent on following this directive.

21–23 Vows were common in the OT world. They became a part of the OT system of offerings and are mentioned frequently with the sacrificial offerings. Vows were never

required, however, but properly handled would have the Lord's approval. Sometimes the payment of a vow was contingent on the occurrence of some specific event (cf. Jdg 11:30–31). Moses urged the people to fulfill vows with dispatch and stressed that the payment of vows cannot be escaped (cf. Nu 30:2). The Lord requires it; failure to pay is sinful. In Nu 30 certain persons within the family structure are not under responsibility to pay their vows unless certain conditions prevail.

24–25 The right to pick a few grapes from a neighbor's vineyard or a few kernels of grain in his field appears to stand on somewhat the same level as gleaning during harvest. It is based on a concern for the immediate need for food. This advantage was not to be abused by putting grapes in a basket or putting a sickle to the neighbor's grain. According to one Jewish tradition, these verses refer only to persons who were hired to work in the vineyard or field.

24:1–4 Divorce (GK 4135) appears as a fact of social life; while under certain circumstances it was permitted, it was to be regulated (Lev 21:7, 14; 22:13; Nu 30:9). Divorce could be initiated only by men, not by women. Verses 1–3 set the stage: a man marries a woman who subsequently displeases him because of some indecency. The man divorces the woman, and she remarries another man who also dislikes her and divorces her—or dies, leaving her without a husband. This law says that the first husband cannot remarry the woman because she has been defiled by the second marriage. This act of remarriage would be detestable in the Lord's eyes and would bring sin on the land (cf. Jer 3:1; Mt 5:31–32).

The man who desires to divorce his wife must show that there is "something indecent" about her. Something less than adultery must be meant since the punishment for adultery is death (22:22–27; Lev 20:10). When grounds for divorce existed, the man must have "a certificate of divorce" served on his wife. Only then may he send her from his home.

5 In 20:7 a man engaged to a woman is exempt from military duty. Here exemption is extended to the newly married and lasts for one year, doubtless because in war he might

be killed. Happy family life and family continuity were held in great respect in the Mosaic economy.

6 The millstones that ground the grain for a family were not to be taken as security for a loan. The family's life was involved.

7 The death penalty would be exacted of one who kidnapped a brother Israelite for involuntary servitude or as merchandise. The victim's free life was involved; so the death penalty was decreed for the culprit—life for life. Once more the relationship of crime to the responsibility of the commonwealth and to its moral condition is emphasized by the demand: "You must purge the evil from among you."

8–9 Twice the people are exhorted to exercise special care to follow the commands of the Lord regarding skin diseases. The reference to leprous diseases presupposes acquaintance with Lev 13–14 (see comments).

10–13 The grant of a loan to a neighbor should be made discreetly. The security is to be chosen by the neighbor privately and brought to the one granting the loan. If the neighbor is so impoverished that his cloak, which serves as his bedclothes at night, has to be given as security, the cloak must be returned to him by sunset. God will approve this act as a righteous one, and the debtor will thank his creditor.

14–15 One was not to take advantage of the poor working man living in any Israelite town. Wages were to be paid each day because the worker needed to cover his daily expenses. In contrast to the thankfulness of the man whose garment was returned at sunset, the man who was denied his daily wage at sunset might cry to the Lord against his employer, and sin would be registered against him.

16 The law of individual responsibility under which the courts decreed punishment inflicts that punishment only on the criminal. Though shame and other consequences of crime fall naturally on one's family and descendants according to the governance of God, the punishment to be exacted for a crime falls on the perpetrator alone. Therefore the Israelites as a community are not to put fathers to death for their children's crime, but "each is to die for his own sin." However, in some situations the group as a whole is implicated (cf. Jos 7), and the individuals in the group are either punished with the group or are benefitted by union with it.

17–18 Concern for the underprivileged (cf. 10:18–19; 14:29; 16:11; 24:6, 10–15) is based on Ex 22:21–24; 23:6, 9; and Lev 19:9–10; 23:22. Israel's slavery in Egypt is said to be the reason for God's commands that they act kindly toward the alien, the widow, and the orphan. The alien and fatherless are not to be deprived of justice, and the widow's cloak must not be taken in pledge (but cf. vv.12–13).

19–22 The overlooked sheaf of grain was to be left for the underprivileged so that the Lord's blessing may rest on the owner's endeavors. Only once are the olive trees to be beaten with poles to harvest olives. The remaining olives were for the alien, the widow, and the orphan. In grape harvest also the vines were gone over only once so that the needy could have the remainder. Again, the Israelites were to remember that they had been redeemed from Egypt.

25:1–3 When a dispute arises between persons, they are to take the matter to court. The judge has been given the responsibility and the authority to make decisions and to make sure that the punishment, if any, is inflicted on the guilty party. The guilty must be beaten with the number of blows commensurate with the nature of the crime. Moreover, the number of blows must not exceed forty lashes because that would be inhumane; the person would be humiliated publicly. The guilty is to lie down in front of the judge and is to be flogged there so that the punishment will conform to the judge's decision.

4 Animals too must be treated with kindness, keeping in mind their need of food. In the threshing process heavy animals were led around a threshing floor. The stalks of grain were laid on the floor, and the hoofs of the animals and sometimes a sledge drawn by animals would separate the kernels from the stalks (Isa 28:28; 41:15; Hos 10:11; cf. 1Co 9:9–10; 1Ti 5:18).

5–6 Levirate marriage, under which a brother (or nearest relative by marriage) takes a childless brother's widow into his home to raise up a descendant, was of considerable importance to the continuity of the family and the distribution of landed property. Moses had already established that when no male heir existed, daughters would be heirs of their father's property (Nu 27:1–8). So a basic reason for levirate marriage did not exist if a man died without a male heir but did have a daughter. The rule that the widow must not marry outside the family is similar to that which grew out of the experience of Zelophehad's daughters (Nu 36:10–12). If the husband's brother fulfilled the law of the *levir*, the first son (child?) the widow bore was to carry on the name of the dead brother; the estate would belong to him.

7–10 If the man did not want to marry his brother's wife, the widow could bring the matter before the elders. There she would indict her husband's brother for his refusal to carry on her late husband's name. If the elders failed to break the man's persistence, she was to take off one of his sandals, spit in his face, and denounce him as one who would not build up his brother's family line. His family line would then be known as "The Family of the Unsandaled." This procedure is given as law only here, but the narratives in Ge 38 and Ru 4 indicate similar practice. The legislation makes possible the release of the brother-in-law from his duty, while definitely discouraging such failure by shame.

11–12 Indecency in sexual situations is illustrated by the law against a woman laying hold of the private parts of an assailant of her husband. The circumstance would not be common but is rather a case law that would cover all such actions. The punishment was severe, necessitating the additional statement: "Show her no pity." Once again the law and punishment appear to be used as a deterrent.

13–16 An Israelite was to be honest in any commercial dealing (Lev 19:35–36). A large weighing stone for buying (to acquire more for one's money) and a small weighing stone for selling (to give less) were unlawful. Neither were the people to have differing quantitative measures in their homes—"one large, one small." The Lord detests those who deal dishonestly, but those who follow his ethical standards will be rewarded with long life in the land (cf.Lk 6:38).

17–19 The Amalekites, descendants of Esau (Ge 36:15–16; 1Ch 1:36), were a nomadic tribe living in upper Sinai who attacked the Israelites at Rephidim (Ex 17:8–16). The Israelites eventually won those battles (Ex 17:16). Later, after Israel rejected the directive of the Lord to enter Canaan from the south, Israel suffered defeat at the hands of the Amalekites and the Canaanites (Nu 14:39–45). Moses called the Israelites to remember that the Amalekites attacked the "weary and worn" stragglers. In those attacks, the Amalekites showed "no fear of God." The call to remember what the Amalekites had done and the Lord's directive concerning them are emphasized by the totality of the destruction decreed: "You shall blot the memory of Amalek from under heaven," and by the additional admonition: "Do not forget!"

The Amalekites disappeared from history after the time of Hezekiah (1Ch 4:43). Their incorrigible wickedness was such that annihilation was necessary. Besides, by their attacks on God's people, the Amalekites indicated that "they had no fear of God."

5. Firstfruits and tithes (26:1–15)

1–4 When the people were settled in the land, each family leader was to take some of the first produce to the place the Lord would choose. There each man was to say, in essence, to the priest, "I have received my part of the land as an inheritance according to the promise of God." The landowner then was to present to the priest the produce as a token of the land's fruitfulness, and the priest was to set the basket down in front of the altar. Since only priests were allowed in the tabernacle, that altar must be the altar of sacrifice outside the tent.

These tokens of the first produce together with the declarations, while similar to the regular offering of firstfruits (Ex 23:19; 34:26), surely refer to an initial offering after the first harvest in the land—subsequent, of course, to the years required by Lev 19:23–25.

5–6 The terse historical review (vv.5–9), replete with phrases and descriptive clauses used elsewhere, witnesses to the Israelites' faith in the Lord their God. Jacob, the wandering Aramean, went down into Egypt with a few individuals but became a numerous and powerful people, who, after mistreatment and suffering, were brought out of Egypt by the Lord.

7–11 When he was to appear before the enslaved Israelites in Egypt, Moses was to identify the God who spoke to him and who directed him to lead his people out of Egypt as "the LORD, the God of your fathers" (Ex 3:16). The Israelites were to assert now that they cried out in distress to the God of their history, not to any newly found or newly revealed God, and that the God of their fathers had brought them out of Egypt and into the Promised Land. Israel's escape from the oppression in Egypt and the trials of the Exodus and the blessings of residence in the land "flowing with milk and honey" (cf. 6:3) were all credited to the Lord with thankfulness, worship, and rejoicing. Levites and aliens were to be included as participants in this festivity.

12–15 Appended to this initial giving of the firstfruits is the rule for the setting aside of the tithe of every third year for the support of the Levites and the underprivileged. In substance the declaration says that the tenth of the produce had been removed from the donor's premises and was given to the Levites and the underprivileged—aliens, orphans, and widows. Because the donor had obeyed the Lord's command, he could pray for the Lord's blessing on the people and on the land the Lord had given to the people.

The part of the produce of the land given to the Levites and the underprivileged is called the "tenth" or "tithe" (GK 6923 & 5130; see 12:6) and the "sacred portion." This sacred tithe was not conceived of as a secular tax for the welfare of the poor but as an act inspired by the Lord. Both the giving of it and the reception of it were spiritual acts and were to be recognized as holy.

Several specific situations illustrate the speaker's assertion that he himself had not eaten any of the tenth. He had not eaten any while in mourning (i.e., while he was unclean for that reason). In fact, he had not removed any of it while he was unclean for any reason. Neither was any of the food ever offered to the dead (putting food in a grave with a dead body was a common Egyptian and Canaanite practice, which the Israelites were not to emulate).

The worshiper reiterated that he had obeyed the Lord's commands to the letter.

The affirmation ended with prayer recognizing that God's dwelling place is in heaven and that he had given the Israelites the land flowing with milk and honey as he had promised to their forefathers. Thus continued blessing on both people and land was requested.

6. Concluding exhortation and the declaration of the covenant-treaty compact (26:16–19)

16–19 This whole section (12:1–26:19) concludes with an exhortation to adhere carefully to the stipulations of the covenant-treaty the Lord has given to the Israelites. "This day" points to a particular day when the command to follow God's decrees and laws with heart and soul was reiterated on the plains of Moab and when the people declared that the Lord was their God and the Lord declared that they were his people.

The Lord declared that the Israelites in a special sense were his people and were his "treasured possession" (GK 6035; see 7:6; 14:2). As the Lord was to be the object of their praise (10:21), so his people would be the object of the praise of the nations. They would have a name with a fame high above other nations.

D. Ratification of the Covenant-Treaty (27:1–26)

1. The law and the altar on Mount Ebal (27:1–8)

Chapters 27–28 constitute the instruction for impressing the covenant-treaty on the Israelites by two specific programs: (1) the setting up on Mount Ebal of stones on which the law was written and the building of a fieldstone altar on which burnt offerings and fellowship offerings were to be sacrificed for this event; (2) the presentation by the people of the curses and blessings on Mounts Ebal and Gerizim.

1 According to this verse, not Moses alone, but Moses and the elders of Israel commanded the people. Perhaps the elders are associated with Moses because of his imminent death and consequent absence from the ceremony at Gerizim and Ebal.

2–4 The temporal focus of being on the verge of entering Canaan is mentioned again. Large stones set up on Mount Ebal were to be coated with plaster and then inscribed with "all the words of this law." What is meant by "all the words of this law" cannot be definitely determined. Most likely the salient parts of the laws reiterated in Deuteronomy would be all that was necessary. "Today" (v.1) limits the commands to what Moses had said to them in that twenty-four-hour period.

5–8 In addition to the stones to be set up on Mount Ebal for displaying the law, an altar of fieldstones was to be erected. In agreement with Ex 20:25, no iron tool was to be used in building this altar. This altar was for temporary use on a special occasion, like the altars erected by the patriarchs. "Burnt offerings" and "fellowship offerings" were to be sacrificed there, and the people were to eat the fellowship offerings while rejoicing in the presence of the Lord. Just as the people were instructed at the incidence of the giving of the law at Sinai, so now, at the renewal of the covenant-treaty, burnt offerings and fellowship offerings were to be made.

2. The curses from Mount Ebal (27:9–26)

a. The standing and the stance of the tribes (27:9–13)

9–11 The authority of the elders coupled with that of Moses began this series of directives (v.1); now that of the priests is added. The repetition of the declaration of the people becoming the people of the Lord their God is noteworthy. Basically three occasions of this declaration occurred or were about to occur: at Horeb (Sinai) (Ex 19:3–8), on the plains of Moab (Dt 26:16–19; 27:9–10), and on Mount Ebal (Jos 8:30–35). In every instance the important aspects of the treaty for-

These stones are the ruins of an ancient altar on top of Mount Ebal. Courtesy Zev Radovan.

mula are present. Most notable is the relationship established between the Lord and Israel. Not only is the Lord the Creator of the people as human beings, but he is also the Creator of Israel as a political entity. Rewards and punishments stem from this relationship.

12–13 The tribes to stand on Mount Gerizim to bless the people are all descendants of Jacob's two wives, Leah and Rachel, while the tribes that uttered curses were Reuben and Zebulun, both sons of Leah, plus the tribes of the sons of the handmaids Zilpah and Bilhah. Preference is given to the sons of the wives of Jacob who had higher standing than the sons of the handmaids, though the division into two groups of six necessitated putting two sons of Leah with those of the handmaids.

b. Curses and response (27:14–26)

14 While vv.12–13 reveal that six tribes were to stand on Mount Gerizim to bless the people and the other six on Mount Ebal to pronounce curses (GK 826), here we learn that the Levites were to recite the words and the people were to say, "Amen." The Levites voicing the blessings and curses were apparently priests who cared for the ark of the covenant (Jos 8:33). The rest of the tribe of Levi was on Gerizim (v.12). The list of curses in vv.15–26 tells on whom and why the curses would fall. The actions that evoke the curses are illustrative rather than comprehensive.

15 The first curse covers an Israelite's relationship to the Lord. No one was to make an idol, either carved of wood or cast in metal. This was detestable to the Lord God (cf. Ex 20:3–4).

16 The second curse falls on the one who dishonors his parents (cf. Ex 20:12; Dt 5:16).

17 The third curse relates to the division of the land. Each family's allotment was to be respected; consequently, moving boundary stones came under God's curse (see 19:14).

18–19 The next two curses concern the disabled and the underprivileged. Leviticus 19:14 prohibits putting "a stumbling block in front of the blind." Here the curse falls on the one "who leads the blind astray on the road." The next curse is on the man who withholds justice from the disadvantaged: the alien, the fatherless, or the widow. The requirement of equal justice for everyone is frequently stated (Ex 22:21–24; 23:9; Lev 19:33–34; Dt 10:17–19; 24:17).

20 Here the first of four curses involving incest is indicative of the importance of sexual morality in the Mosaic order. The "father's wife" refers to someone other than one's mother. The euphemism "dishonors his father's bed" may mean that he violates his father's marriage. Sexual relations are only for those lawfully married.

21 Having sexual relations with animals was not unknown in the ancient Near East. Among the Hittites bestiality was practiced to bring people into union with their gods. Exodus 22:19 and Lev 18:23; 20:15–16, as well as the reiteration by Moses here, indicate that was practiced in Canaan. When this sin was discovered, death was the penalty. If not discovered, the participants were nevertheless under the curse of God.

22–23 Curses eight and nine fall on those who commit incest with a half-sister or one's mother-in-law (cf. Lev 18:9, 17; 20:14, 17).

24–25 The tenth and eleventh curses fall on those who kill secretly and those who accept fees for killing innocent persons. These actions, along with the preceding, appear to place a curse on criminal actions that are not publicly known. The Lord denounces that person, and the Lord's curse ever hangs over him, eventuating in unknown punishment. Only here is a curse placed on anyone who accepts a bribe.

26 The last of the twelve curses sums up them all but includes more than the curses specified. The Israelites must "uphold," or make effective (GK 7756), this law by following it. This covers all the law as enunciated by Moses on the plains of Moab. To the recitation of each curse, the people were to respond with a definite "Amen" (GK 589), a solemn assertion confirming the validity of the curses. The people declared that they were placing themselves under the consequences of breaking the covenant stipulations, which was tantamount to saying, "We formally accept the terms and agree to all the provisions."

The Deuteronomic curses were warnings not to break the law, given with the intent that paying heed to the warning would keep

Israel in good relationship with the Lord. Those living in OT times who were faithful to the Lord were not under the curse but had the witness from the Spirit of God that they were acceptable to him.

E. The Blessings and the Curses (28:1–68)

1. The blessings (28:1–14)

1–2 The oft-repeated reference to the "commands I give you today" (cf. vv.9, 13, 14, 15, 45, 58, 62) introduces "all these blessings" (GK 1388) for obedience. Full obedience to the Lord would result in blessing for his people. Among these blessings is eminence. If Israel obeyed the Lord, she would be set high above all the nations of the world (26:19). The blessings would come to the people and go with them, much like goodness and love in Ps 23:6.

3–4 Two sections of blessings and curses balance each other in vv.3–6 over against vv.16–19. The blessing or the curse would be nationwide, covering "city and country" (vv.3, 16). Every productivity would be under either the blessing or the curse: children, crops, and livestock, including both herds and flocks. The blessing of reproduction had been in the promise to Abraham and was repeated throughout the revelation through Moses (Ge 15:5; Ex 32:13; Dt 1:10).

5 Blessing or curse would extend to the Israelites' daily sustenance (vv.5, 17), the basket and kneading trough being used to gather food products and to prepare them for meals. Among a desert-dwelling people food products were scarce, and hunger and thirst common. Abundant foodstuffs were a notable blessing indeed!

6 The Lord's goodness would cover the Israelites' daily labor. Going out and coming in is a common description of going about one's daily tasks.

7–8 Further specification of the Lord's blessing under the covenant tells of victory over enemies and utopian prosperity in the land. When enemies would come from one direction, they would flee in defeat in seven directions. External foes would be decisively disoriented and scattered, unable to carry on warfare. The Lord would eagerly command blessing to be on the Israelites' barns (granaries) and everything they put their hands to.

9–11 Once again Moses conditioned Israel's blessed relationship to the Lord on keeping his commands and walking in his ways. If Israel would do this, the Lord would fulfill his sworn promise to establish them. This establishment as the Lord's holy people would make other people recognize that the Israelites were "called by the name of the LORD," and this would make the nations afraid of them. The blessing of v.4 to be experienced in the land is expanded into "abundant prosperity."

12 The particular blessing of rain would provide fertility to the soil and an abundance of crops to the farmer. The Lord promised to bless the people by opening the treasure house of the skies (cf. Job 38:22; Pss 33:7; 135:7). The prosperity of v.8 is now the Lord's "bounty," describing the goodness and sufficiency of his treasures of rain. Moses insisted that it was the Lord who would either bless Israel with abundant rain or withhold rain because of her disobedience. Because of the blessing of the Lord, Israel was destined to be rich and would "lend to many nations but borrow from none."

13–14 Israel would move upward from her current status to that of the head among the nations. But this would be determined by the adherence of the people to the stipulations of the covenant-treaty that they had accepted from the Lord. They must "carefully follow them" and "not turn aside . . . to the right or to the left" from any of the commands Moses was rehearsing to them that day.

2. The curses (28:15–68)

15 As the blessings of the Lord seem to be personalized (v.2), so also the curses take on personal action; they would come and overtake a disobedient Israel (cf. v.45).

16–19 After the basic coverage of the curse, following the same plan as that of the blessings (vv.3–6), Moses developed—with about six times the length—the description of the disaster that would follow when Israel was disobedient to the Lord. Curses, confusion, and rebuke would fall on everything disobedient Israel did—until destruction and sudden ruin enveloped her.

20–21 The Lord would send plagues of many kinds. Some would attack the Israelites physically, and others would affect their lands and goods.

22–24 The bodily aspects of the curse that would come on the people include illnesses of various sorts and the shameful desecration of their dead bodies (v.26). Disturbance of their emotional and mental balance would follow. A precise identification of the diseases listed here is not possible. And not only were diseases to be the people's punishment, but the physical land too would suffer. The nature of that curse is developed as drought and its accompanying evils. Just as the specific diseases mentioned relate in some way to the excessive heat of fever or inflammation, so the curse of the land mentions the heat of drought and its consequences: scorching heat from a bronze sky, drought producing dust rather than rain from the Lord, and soil made as hard as iron by the hot east wind off the desert (cf. Ge 41:6, 23, 27).

"Blight and mildew" is an idiom signifying disaster to the crops by contrasting degenerative actions. Together the words depict the dearth of productivity and the destruction of the crops.

25 Israel under the curse of disobedience would also suffer defeat in warfare. Under the blessing their enemies would come from one sector but flee in seven directions (v.7). Under the curse the opposite would be true. Israel would attack her enemies from one direction and flee in seven. Seven depicts complete, disorganized rout.

26 The Israelites' dead bodies would not be given burial but would be eaten by the birds and wild animals, a shameful desecration. Jeremiah similarly portrayed the frightful future in the Valley of Hinnom, after which it would be called the Valley of Slaughter (Jer 7:32–33; cf. 1Sa 17:44, 46; 1Ki 14:11; Ps 79:2; et al.).

27 The "boils of Egypt" doubtless refers to the sixth plague (Ex 9:9–11). This may have been a form of leprosy. The "tumors" (GK 6754) were like those the Philistines later contracted when the ark of the covenant was held by them (1Sa 5–6). The Hebrew word is usually thought to be hemorrhoids, tumors, bubonic plague, or leprosy. The "festering sores" appear to be some kind of eruptive sore (cf. Lev 21:20; 22:22). The "itch" is some sort of skin disorder that induces scratching. These skin eruptions will be incurable.

28–29 Following on these diseases afflicting the skin come debilitating dysfunctions: madness, blindness, and mental confusion. This blindness will be so complete that in the brightness of noon the people will grope about. They will be unsuccessful in everything they do. Continually, they would be oppressed and robbed of whatever they labored for; and there would be no one to rescue them from their plight.

30 From this verse on, Moses portrayed the miserable existence and utter destruction of Israel as a nation. The possibility of a blessed future remained, but the possibility of the horrors of Israel because of infidelity seemed more sure.

To be pledged to be married was a more certain relationship than modern engagement; so having that status broken, probably by being taken captive and forced into sexual compliance, would be a very trying experience. Building a house would be useless labor. The same frustration would follow attempts at viticulture; not even the beginning of the enjoyment of the fruit would be experienced (cf. 20:6).

31–32 One's ox would be slaughtered in plain view, but the Israelite owner, obviously helpless, would have none of it to eat. So also his donkey would be forcibly taken from him and never returned, and his sheep given to his enemies. Sons and daughters would be taken captive; and parents helplessly would wear out their eyes watching for the return of those who would never come back.

33 Instead of the abundance that an obedient Israel would receive from the soil (vv.4–6, 8, 11–12), disobedient Israel would have the people of an unknown land eat what their "land and labor" produced while they themselves would experience cruel oppression throughout their lives. "Another nation" in v.32 and "a nation unknown to you" in v.36 both signify foreign people.

34–35 Blow upon blow continues. What the people would see would drive them insane. The specifics of this dirge are picked up again. Painful, incurable boils that particularly afflicted the knees and the legs would spread from the soles of their feet to the top of the head (cf. Job 2:7–8; 7:3–5; et al.). This may have been a kind of elephantiasis.

36–37 So far Moses has said that disobedient Israel would be plagued until they were "destroyed . . . from the land" (v.21) and that their children would be given to another nation. Here he announces the fact of national captivity and then describes their situation in the foreign land in bold outline. The Lord would drive the Israelites and their king to a distant, foreign nation unknown to them or their fathers, and there they would worship idols. Among the nations they would become an object of horror, scorn, and ridicule (1Ki 9:7; 2Ch 7:20; Jer 24:9).

38–42 Again the curse on the land, resulting in unproductive farming, is elaborated. This time the produce itself is attacked, and the harvest is lost. Grain would not be harvested because grasshoppers would eat it. Grapes would not be gathered, and people would not drink the wine that might have been made—worms would eat the grapes. Olive oil would not be available. The locust swarms would take over the land. In this scene of unproductivity, the Israelites would not be able to keep their children either, because they would go into captivity.

43–44 In contrast to vv.12b–13a, aliens would lend to the Israelites, and they would be the head and Israel the tail. The Israelite condition under the curse would be more of a curse than their blessing would be a blessing, because of their continual deterioration.

45–48 All these curses would not only come on the people and overtake them but would pursue them until they were destroyed for their disobedience. The Lord who had brought the Israelites out of Egypt by signs and wonders (4:34) would make the curses to be "a sign and a wonder" to them and their descendants forever. Because the people did not serve the Lord, they would serve the enemies he would send against them. In their prosperity, the people neglected to serve the Lord joyfully and gladly. Since they did not under these conditions serve the Lord, they would experience the dire consequences of the curse: hunger, thirst, nakedness, poverty, and servitude would come on them like an iron yoke, until they were destroyed.

49 The destruction of disobedient Israel was to come from a distant, foreign nation. This distant enemy would strike swiftly and unerringly like an eagle swooping on its prey (cf. Hos 8:1; Jer 48:40; 49:22). This foreign nation would have a language not understandable to the Israelite population (cf. Isa 28:11; 33:19).

In 1Co 14:21 Paul quotes Isa 28:11–12 and Dt 28:49 in reference to the tongues problem in the Corinthian church. The tongues mentioned in Isaiah and Deuteronomy were the regular languages of foreign peoples that were unknown by the Israelites.

50–52 This "fierce-looking nation" (cf. Da 8:23), without regard for either the aged or the young, would mercilessly eat up the choice livestock and the crops. That they would "besiege all the cities throughout the land" seems to include cities of any size or importance; however, only walled cities were subject to siege. Israel's misplaced trust would be evident when the walls fell down.

53–57 The frightful horrors of the siege included children, given to the people under the blessing of God but now eaten by their parents. And when the flesh of children was insufficient to go around, there would be no sharing of flesh with a starving brother or sister. Women, raised in delicate fashion, at the time of giving birth would begrudge their husbands and older children the afterbirths of their wombs and the children themselves who were born during the siege, eating them as food. Not only rough, coarse characters would do such things, but the most gentle and sensitive would descend to this debased state (cf. 2Ki 6:24–31; La 2:20; 4:10). All these frightful experiences would result "because of the suffering that your enemy will inflict on you during the siege." Three times this phrase occurs (vv.53, 55, 57), bearing down on the terrible experience the Israelites could expect if they disobeyed their Lord.

58–61 The Israelites would experience not only the diseases of Egypt but every other sickness or disaster as well—even all those "not recorded in this Book of the Law." The people are told that they would fall under the curse if they did not carefully follow "all the words of this law, which are written in this book." The capitalization of "this Book of the Law" signifies that a definite, particular written document is meant. While its precise contents are uncertain, it covered the basic laws and the historical episodes relating to the establishment of the covenant-treaty—so far as it was written. Failure to follow all the stipulations would result in failure to revere the glorious and awesome name: "the LORD your God." This glorious and awesome name speaks of his essence, character, and reputation as the God of the promises, the true and living God revealed to the people, particularly at Horeb (Sinai).

62–64a Israel's growth as a nation would also be reversed. Under the covenant flowing from the promise to Abraham, Isaac, and Jacob, Israel had increased and would continue to increase in number as the stars in the sky (1:10; 10:22; 26:5); but under the curse a reversal would return them to being few in number. The promise of the land as their very own was central in the promise to Israel—a promise repeated again and again in this book. But under the curse the few people left would be torn from the land and scattered worldwide.

64b–68 Instead of following the Lord exclusively, the Israelites would turn from him and engage in idolatrous worship. Instead of the repose of the Promised Land, anxiety, wearisome longing, fear, constant suspense, and despair would be their lot among the nations. In the Promised Land under the blessing of the Lord, the nations would fear them (v.10); but under the curse in foreign lands, the Israelites would be in constant fear of the nations. So low would they sink that the offering of themselves as slaves in Egypt would be rejected. The psychological state of the people dispersed among the nations is depicted with no less descriptive power than the foregoing calamities.

IV. Third Address: The Terms of the Covenant (29:1–30:20)

The rest of the book of Deuteronomy concerns the ratification (renewal) of the covenant-treaty (29:1–15), the results of acceptance or rejection of it (29:16–30:20), Moses' Song (31:19–32:43), his final blessing on the tribes (33:1–29), Joshua's induction as Moses' successor (31:1–8, 14–15, 23; 32:44; 34:9), and Moses' death (34:1–12).

A. Recapitulation of Historical Background (29:1–29)

1. Introduction (29:1)

1 Moses differentiated between the two declarations of the covenant (Moab, Horeb). The covenant is one; the affirmations or renewals of allegiance to the Lord and the terms of the covenant could be several.

2. Recapitulation of desert situation (29:2–8)

2–3 In these culminating addresses of his life, Moses at first identified the people with the whole immediate past history. Many of those in front of him had not been in Egypt; they were born in the desert. However, many were under the age of twenty at Kadesh, two years after leaving Egypt, and were eighteen years of age or younger at the time of the Exodus (they were now thirty-nine to fifty-six years old). These had seen the "miraculous signs and great wonders" (4:34; 7:19) that the Lord had loosed on the Egyptians during the plagues, though the youngest of them would have no memory of what happened when they were infants. Moses' message, however, was directed to the nation. The community had been in Egypt and had seen the wonderful things that the Lord had done for them. Even the specific mention of "your own eyes" is doubtless directed to the whole community comprising the nation, as vv.10–11 indicate.

4 When Moses said that the Lord had not given the Israelites the realization of his intervention in the experiences of their history, he did not deny that they had knowledge of his part in the action; rather, he was asserting that the ultimate directive and operative power in all their national life was the Lord himself. This, he said, they had not yet fully realized.

5–6 The Lord's providence (cf. 8:4; Ne 9:21) included provisions of clothing and food. Specific miracles of supplying clothes and of keeping clothing from falling from their bodies in tatters are not mentioned, but uniting the durability of their clothing and sandals with the giving of manna and water puts this supply from the Lord on the same plane for the same purpose—"that you might know that I am the LORD" (cf. Ex 6:7; 7:5, 17; 10:2; 14:4, 18).

7–8 "When you reached this place" refers to the area immediately north of the Arnon, controlled by Sihon (2:24–37); so the plains of Moab were in Amorite hands until Moses conquered that area. Og had been king of the northern sector of Transjordan. He also was defeated by Moses (3:1–11). The allotment of these areas to Reuben, Gad, and the half-tribe of Manasseh followed the defeat of the Amorites (3:12–17).

3. Clarification of covenant-treaty situation (29:9–21)

9–13 Moses emphasized the importance of adopting the covenant and following its stipulations in order to experience prosperity. All the Israelites standing in the presence of the Lord were called on to enter into the covenant-treaty with the Lord, who was sealing it with an oath. In this renewal the central characteristic and purpose of the covenant was again affirmed as the establishment of the people as the people of the Lord and their acceptance of him as their God in accordance with what he had promised to Abraham, Isaac, and Jacob by an oath. The "oath" (GK 8678) in v.12 is like the oath to Abraham, and the formation of Israel as the people of God is in fulfillment of the promise to Abraham.

14–15 To focus on the national character of this covenant renewal—and the future benefits to the nation and the responsibilities of the national entity—Moses declared that not only those who were standing there at that time (notice the frequent "today") but those who were not there at that time but would appear in later generations were involved in making this covenant-treaty (cf. 5:3; Ac 2:39).

16–18 The statements "how we lived in Egypt" and "how we passed through the countries on the way here" provide the locale and historic background for the people's knowledge of the gods in those places and the nature of their worship. This is evident from the definite reference to the detestable images and idols that they saw among the people there. The Israelites were exhorted to "make sure" that no one's heart turned away from the Lord and that there was no source in them to produce such "bitter poison." The source of "bitter poison" was the person or persons who turned away from the Lord to worship the gods of Egypt and those of the

other nations through which the Israelites passed on their journey from Egypt to the plains of Moab.

19–21 Moses, by the Spirit of God, expressed the thoughts of such a "bitter-poison" person when he heard "the words of this oath"; that is, the terms of the covenant-treaty, perhaps with special reference to its curses as a specific warning. Such a person invokes a blessing on himself saying, "I will be safe, even though I persist in going my own way."

The punishment the Lord would send is noteworthy in two respects. (1) From the "no man or woman," an individual apostate condition is considered. Individual apostasy could not hide in the blessed state of the believing community. One's apostasy would bring disaster on the innocent. The individual apostate would feel the result of the Lord's burning wrath and zeal. (2) No more dreadful state can be imagined than "the LORD will never be willing to forgive him" (cf. Heb 6:4–8; 2Pe 2; 3:16–17). The appalling results of apostasy would be heaped one on the other: all the curses in the book, the blotting out of one's name on earth (cf. 25:19; Ex 17:14), and being singled out for disaster. All these results would fall on the apostate.

4. Results of the Lord's anger on those who abandon the covenant (29:22–29)

22–24 Both the inhabitants and foreigners from distant lands would see the devastation and diseases resulting from the Lord's punishment—a punishment likened to that of Sodom and Gomorrah (Ge 14:2; 19:24–29). Utter desolation would prevail. No more would the land flowing with milk and honey be so productive that "abundant prosperity" would be present (28:11). The Promised Land would become a burning waste of salt and sulfur—"nothing planted, nothing sprouted, no vegetation growing." The pictorial representation is dramatized further by the reaction of later generations of Israelites and of the nations, who would ask the universal question when confronted by events that adversely affected lives or properties: "Why? Why did the Lord do this? Why was he so angry?" (cf. v.24).

25–28 The answer contains (again) the warning that Israel "abandoned the covenant of the LORD," though the answer is cast in the form of accomplished prediction. The people did abandon the covenant; they did go off and worship other gods. Therefore, the Lord's "furious anger" and "great wrath" uprooted them from their land and thrust them into another land.

29 The "secret" (GK 6259) or hidden things are at least the future experiences of Israel whether they are obedient or disobedient—experiences then hidden but eventually realized by future fulfillment. The hidden things of the future are known only to the Lord, but his people, nevertheless, have reason for great expectations allied with great responsibilities; they have the "things revealed" (GK 1655). These are within the area of their knowledge and that of their children forever, and for a definite, specific reason—that they should "follow all the words of this law." So God knows all things, and human knowledge in comparison is severely limited (cf. Isa 55:8–9).

B. Prosperity After the Return to the Lord (30:1–10)

1–3 Moses looked beyond the period when Israel had a time of blessing and after a subsequent time when Israel would be under the curse of the Lord while dispersed among the nations. It is not clear whether the destruction by a nation whose language they would not understand (28:36, 49) is the same experience as the scattering among the nations in 28:64; 29:22; and 30:1. Neither is it clear that there would be two basic dispersions, as later Scriptures and history have shown—one after the destruction of the kingdom(s) culminating in 586 B.C. and another after A.D. 70. When the people dispersed among the nations returned to the Lord in obedience to the covenant with all their heart and soul, then the Lord, in compassion, would restore their fortunes after regathering them.

4–8 The hypothetical particle translated "even if" is often used to make a very strong assertion (cf. Nu 22:18). So here from the most extreme distance, the Lord will regather his people. This future return will be occasioned by the resolve of their heart and will be characterized by their wholehearted love for him and by their obedience to his commands. The Lord's compassion makes possible the return from the most distant lands. That compassion not only returns the people to their land; it also rehabilitates them and

makes them more prosperous and more numerous than their fathers.

The curses of disobedience will then fall on Israel's enemies, not on Israel herself. The Lord will circumcise the people's hearts so that they will love him with heart and soul. This work of God in the innermost being is characteristic of the spiritual nature of Deuteronomic revelation (6:5–6; 10:16; see comment on 10:14–16).

9–10 The initial promises that the Lord had been giving the Israelites as they were being prepared for entrance into Canaan will be renewed. They will be prosperous in everything they do. Fecundity will again mark their families, livestock, and crops (28:11). The Lord will again delight in his people; he will return to being pleased to make them prosper. This look into the future ends with a warning that prosperity will come only if the people return to the original demands of the covenant-treaty—obedience to the Book of the Law, i.e., total allegiance to the Lord their God.

C. The Covenant Offer of Life or Death (30:11–20)

11–14 Moses turned to the options for Israel as they stood by the Jordan facing the future in Canaan. He first set before them the availability of the resources for responding affirmatively to the commands he was giving them. The commands were neither too difficult nor beyond their reach. Their proximity and intimacy are illustrated by assertions and rhetorical questions. Even in these Moses emphasized the necessity of obedience. The positive assertion of the nearness of the revelation is even more specific: the word is in their mouth (i.e., they can repeat it) and in their heart (i.e., they can think it and understand and react to it). Obedience is possible!

15–20 Starkly clear, the Lord through Moses set the choice before his people: life and prosperity (for obedience) or death and destruction (for disobedience). The route of obedience is twofold. It requires one "to love [GK 170] the LORD" and "to walk [GK 2143] in his ways." As in a covenant-treaty, the "love" required is the committal in loyal devotion to the Lord. It relies on faith in his saving grace and walking "in his ways" (GK 2006), i.e., obeying his precepts. That will lead to life; it will increase the size of the nation and bring the Lord's blessing on them in the land. However, if the people turn their hearts away from the Lord, disobedient Israel will be destroyed. The nation separate from the Lord will not live long in the Promised Land.

After invoking both heaven and earth to witness that he has placed the options of life and death, blessings and curses, before Israel (4:26), Moses made his final appeal to his people. "Choose life!" (GK 1047 & 2644; see also comment on 32:44-47) he exhorted. Then they and their children will live; and they will love the Lord, listen to him, and hold fast to him. When they are committed wholly to him, he will give the nation many years in the land he promised to Abraham, Isaac, and Jacob.

V. Concluding Narratives (31:1–34:12)

A. Charge to Joshua and Deposition of the Law (31:1–29)

1. Joshua to be leader (31:1–8)

1–2 Moses was 120 years old and unable to lead the people. This inability was not because his natural strength was gone (34:7) but because the time for Israel's entrance into Canaan had come. Moses' entrance was precluded by his arrogance at Meribah (Nu 20:24).

3–6 Though Moses himself was not to cross the Jordan, he encouraged the Israelites that the Lord himself would cross over ahead of them and that he would destroy the nations of the land as he had destroyed Sihon and Og. He exhorted them not to be afraid of the Canaanites. The Lord would not only go with them, he would never leave them nor forsake them. Moses would soon remind them, however, that this promise was contingent on their allegiance to him.

7–8 In the presence of "all Israel," Moses repeated to Joshua personally what he had just said to the people, adding that Joshua was to divide the land among the people. What land each would receive would be that family's inheritance. The exhortation "Be strong and courageous" given to Joshua and to the people by Moses at the end of his career is repeated by the Lord to Joshua after the death of Moses (Jos 1:6, 9) and also urged on Joshua by the people (Jos 1:18).

2. Recitation of the law at every seventh Feast of Tabernacles (31:9–13)

9 The time when Moses wrote down the law and what "law" is meant in each of the cases mentioned here cannot easily be determined. The "law" surely included all that was essential to the covenant-treaty documents referred to in Deuteronomy—and that includes historical, hortative, and legal elements, substantially all of Deuteronomy. The priests (designated as the sons of Levi) are also designated as those "who carried the ark of the covenant of the LORD," which was apropos especially to the wandering and residence in the desert.

10–13 The stated time for reading "this law" was at seven-year intervals, at the time of canceling debts (15:1; i.e., the sabbatical year). More specifically, it was to be during the Feast of Tabernacles of the sabbatical year, when all Israel was "to appear before the Lord at the place he [was to] choose" (i.e., where the tabernacle was placed).

Attendance at the feast was to be a joyous occasion for all (16:14). The law was to be read before all the people. The children were singled out for special mention because they did not know the law. This septennial reading does not obviate the teaching ministry of the home (6:1–9) or that of the priests (17:11; 24:8; Lev 10:11). It is meant, rather, to strengthen these other teaching procedures. It would also dramatize the learning of the law for those children and others who had not been reached by the other teaching procedures in home and tabernacle.

The reading of the law was to inspire the people to revere the Lord and to follow carefully all the covenant stipulations. That this process should go on "as long as you live in the land" is not to suggest that elsewhere knowledge of the Lord and his word was not necessary. Rather, the process of making known the revelation of God should never cease so that reverence for the Lord and obedience to his word would never cease.

3. Some last words on leadership transfer (31:14–23)

14–15 At the commissioning of Joshua, Moses and Joshua presented themselves before the Lord at the "Tent of Meeting"; and the Lord spoke of the future apostasy of Israel, not only to Moses, but in the hearing of

Joshua as well. Thus Joshua too was warned to resist the tendency of the people to turn to foreign gods. The solemnity of the event is apparent in the description of the Lord appearing in the "pillar of cloud," with the cloud standing over the entrance to the tent.

16–18 After mentioning that Moses was soon to rest with his fathers, the Lord told him and Joshua that the people would soon prostitute themselves to the foreign gods of the land they were about to enter. Turning to Canaanite gods had its counterpart in forsaking the Lord and breaking the covenant-treaty. When the people forsook the Lord, he would forsake them in anger against their wickedness and would hide his face from them. This is the converse of making his face to shine on his people and turning his face toward them (Nu 6:25–26). Many disasters and difficulties would come on them; and they would wonder about the reason for the disasters, indicating that they knew that the disasters came because God was not with them.

19 In view of the apostasy to come, the Lord told Moses and Joshua to write down this song. "Teach it to the Israelites and have them sing it" implies sufficient repetition to fix it in the minds of the people. Only then would they be able to sing it, and only then would it be a witness to the Lord's admonition, not only to that generation, but to their descendants (v.21).

20–23 The apostasy was to come after the fulfillment of the promise made to the fathers concerning possession of the land flowing with milk and honey (Ex 3:8, 17; 13:5; et al.). Under affluence they would become apostate, turning to other gods, rejecting the Lord, and breaking the covenant-treaty. So when the disasters and difficulties come, the Song of Moses would testify against them.

Moses had shown his pessimistic view of Israelite allegiance to the Lord before. Here he reported that the Lord himself had the same expectation. The Lord said that he knew their disposition toward disobedience, which appeared even before they entered the Land of Promise. Therefore, this song was given and taught to the Israelites. The succession of Joshua, the writing down of the law, the prediction of the people's rebellion with its attendant results, and the Song of Moses are intertwined in ch. 31.

4. The deposition of the law book and its witness (31:24–29)

24–29 Moses finished writing the book from the beginning to the end, a statement not made before. The command of the Lord to write down the song was given so that it would be a witness against sinning Israel (v.19). The Book of the Law as a witness (cf. v.26) suggests that the Song of Moses is included in this completed book.

The procedure for making the song known to the people seems to have three steps: Moses wrote it down (vv.19, 22), then he spoke these words in the hearing of the elders and officials (v.28), and finally he recited them in the hearing of the whole assembly (v.30). The instruction that the Lord gave Moses indicates that initially Moses directly taught the song to the Israelites (vv.9, 22; 32:44–45). Whether the song was recited originally as a poem or sung as a song is not certain. Moses' last words are replete with warnings against apostasy, directed to all the Israelites (29:2, 16–28; 30:17–19; 31:30–32:47), to Joshua (vv.14–22), to the Levites (the priests) (vv.24–27), and to the elders and officials (vv.28–29).

The Book of the Law was to be placed beside the ark as a witness against the people, because the Lord knew how rebellious and stiff-necked the people were. The Lord had said to Moses (vv.14–18) that after his death the people would soon become apostate. Here Moses conveyed this pessimism in a more direct and personal way to the people by telling them that after he was gone they would be even more rebellious than when he was alive. His pessimism was well founded in experience and in predictive warnings from the Lord.

B. The Song of Moses (31:30–32:47)

After the call to listen (vv.1–2), the Lord is proclaimed and praised (vv.3–4). Then the people are chided for their reaction to the Lord (vv.5–6). This leads the speaker into a recital of the Lord's goodness to Israel (vv.7–14), Israel's response to that goodness (vv.15–18), his rejection of them (vv.19–20), and their estrangement and future punishment (vv.21–30) and that of their enemies (vv.31–35). The poem ends with the Lord's salvation for his people and his judgment on his (and their) enemies (vv.36–43).

1. Moses' recitation before the assembly (31:30)

30 The command to write down the song, to teach it to Israel, and to have them sing it (v.19) is said to have been obeyed (v.22). This is now made more explicit as an introduction to the song itself.

2. Literary introduction (32:1–2)

1–2 In his introduction Moses called heaven and earth to listen to what he was about to say (cf. Isa 1:2; 34:1; Mic 1:2; 6:1–2). Yet the message of the song is directed to the nation of Israel. The call to the heavens and the earth to listen is a poetic way of emphasizing the importance of the song's themes. All creation is a witness to the covenant-treaty between the Lord and Israel.

The remainder of the introduction expresses Moses' wish that his song would have a beneficent and pleasing reception and result. To this end he revealed his desire in four references to the beneficial results of water coming onto the land. Like rain, dew, showers, and abundant rain bringing fertility to the new grass and tender plants, Moses hoped that his words would prove pleasant and beneficial.

3. The theme: the proclamation of the Lord (32:3–4)

3 The song proper begins with the declaration that Moses proclaimed "the name" (GK 9005) of the Lord and called on others to ascribe greatness to him. Moses has proclaimed the name of the Lord throughout Deuteronomy. He has transmitted the third commandment and warned that such misuse of his name would bring punishment (5:11). The people were to make oaths only in the Lord's name (6:13; 10:20). The priests were to bless the people in the Lord's name (10:8; 21:5; cf. Nu 6:22–27); they were also to minister in the Lord's name always (18:5, 7). It is this name, the glorious and awesome name, that Moses called the people to revere (28:58). Basically, the name of the Lord signifies his person.

The most common reference to "the Name" (cf. 26:2) in Deuteronomy speaks of the place the Lord would choose as a dwelling for his Name (12:5, 11, 21; 14:23–24; 16:2, 6, 11). In these places the Name most significantly relates to his person, his being. Consequently, the NIV in these places capitalizes

Name. This not only signifies that the Lord (*YHWH*, "Yahweh"; GK 3378; NIV "Lord") is God but that the he is the God of history, the God of the promises, the God who was fulfilling the covenant promises, the God whose people they were, under the covenant-treaty.

4 The metaphor "the Rock" (GK 7446) declares that the Lord is strong and stable, one who can be relied on. The following four parallel lines indicate how the Lord as "the Rock" stands in contrast to Israel who acted corruptly toward him (vv.5–6). The rest of the song suggests that the main "works" of the Lord are activities of creating, aiding, and guiding Israel. These "works are perfect, and all his ways are just" (cf. Ps 18:30). His character is marked by faithfulness; no wrongdoing exists in him.

4. The indictment of Israel (32:5–6)

5–6 The Lord's governing of his people is on the highest moral and ethical level, but in contrast the Israelites "have acted corruptly." While the Lord is always right in his handling of Israel, Israel has been wrong and devious in rejecting him. The idolatry of the golden calf illustrates this corruption that broke their relationship to the Lord so that they were "no longer his children." This condition of no longer being his children was to their shame and disgrace. The people are described further by two synonyms that speak of twisting and turning from the right path. Though the Lord is their Father (i.e, the progenitor and originator of the nation as well as the one who has matured and sustained them), the Israelites turned from him to idols and consequently lost their status of sonship.

5. Israel as God's inheritance (32:7–9)

7 The song calls on Israel to remember the past, to remember the divine acts of kindness. The people are urged to ask for information from their fathers and their elders (4:32; Job 8:8). They would "tell them" what had occurred. Then, supposing the people had asked for this explanation, the song proceeds to give it.

8–9 When speaking of God's allocating geographical areas for the nations, he is the "Most High" (GK 6610; used only here in Deuteronomy), which is in contrast to his name "LORD" (see comment on v.3) as the God of Israel. Most High is an elative form (cf. Ge 14:18–20, 22). That Canaan was Israel's inheritance by the Lord's decree, based on the promise to Abraham, is of major importance in the developing doctrine of the Lord's relationship to his people and his redemption for them and providence toward them. This inheritance was soon to be divided among the tribes. Thus ownership of landed property becomes a basic right of Israelite social structure and economy. And much more, ownership on the basis of inherent right describes the relationship of Israel to the Lord—and sometimes of the Lord to Israel. Israel is the Lord's "inheritance" (GK 5709).

However, not only did the Lord give Canaan to Israel, he also gave certain lands to other nations. The Lord rules over the disposition of land to all nations in the sovereign exercise of his will in every generation (ch. 2). The latter part of v.8 probably means that the boundaries of the nations were determined with the intent that Israel would have Canaan because her numbers could be supported in that area. The use of Jacob for Israel contributes to the poetic style of the song.

6. The Lord's early care of Israel (32:10–12)

10–11 In a bold, dramatic way it is said that Israel was found "in a desert land" and "a barren, howling waste." This is part of the moving description of how the Lord found Israel in a desolate and desperate plight in the Sinai Desert (cf. Jer 2:2; Hos 9:10). Moses focused on the people as an unorganized body in an inhospitable environment at the time God entered into the covenant-treaty with them. There the Lord "shielded" them by surrounding them with his protection, and he attentively thought of them and concerned himself with them.

The Lord exercised his loving care for Israel like an eagle caring for its young, especially as they are taught to fly. The eagle by stirring up the nest thrusts the eaglets out into the air to try their wings but does not leave them altogether on their own resources. The parent eagle catches the fluttering little ones on its outspread wings and again deposits them in the nest. Similarly, the Lord took Israel out from Egypt into the deserts of Sinai but did not leave them without his help. His widespread wings supported them throughout the learning years in Sinai.

12 The gods of the Egyptians, the desert tribes, and the Canaanites were multiple. Not so the Lord! He was alone as the leader and supporter of Israel.

7. The Lord's care of Israel in Canaan foreseen (32:13–14)

13 The Lord fed Israel with the finest foods, that which comes directly from God's natural provisions. Causing Israel to ride on the high places of the land pictures their advance and conquest of Canaan, which was known as a high, mountainous country. The song views Israel as fed and nourished with the fruit of the fields (food, produce), honey from the rock, and olive oil from the trees in the flinty crags. Bees in Canaan often built their combs between the rocks. Olive trees flourished and produced bountiful crops of olives in the unlikely limestone soil in rocky places.

14 The animals too contributed to this good life, with curds and milk and the meat of the best of lambs and goats. Curds might refer not only to the curds of cattle's milk but also to cream (Job 29:6) and butter (Pr 30:33). The fat of lambs describes the best of lambs, which is the meaning of "fattened lambs and goats." Bashan produced fine livestock, being noted for bulls and cows (Ps 22:12; Am 4:1) as well as rams. In addition the people were to have the "fat of the kidneys of the wheat"—i.e., the choicest, richest, or finest wheat—and fine wine of the blood of grapes (blood indicating the red grapes of Canaan).

8. Affluent Israel's rejection of God (32:15–18)

15 Israel's condition sets the stage for their sinfulness. After eating fine foods and drinking choice red wine, Israel the Righteous (see NIV note on Jeshurun) grew fat, i.e., became affluent and then, rather than being thankful, kicked! Where there should be thankfulness and obedience, there is open recalcitrance. The last half of v.15 and on through v.18 shows how Israel kicked: you grew fat (NIV, "filled with food"), you became heavy, you became obese ("sleek"). In this state Israel "abandoned," "rejected," "angered," "deserted," and "forgot" the Lord and "made

him jealous." The God who had made Israel, who had fathered him and had given him birth, was maltreated in this way. Though he was called "God," "Rock," "Savior," "Creator" (see v.6), and Sustainer of the nation, they made him jealous with their foreign gods and angered him with their detestable idols.

16–18 The gods they turned to were "foreign," "detestable idols," "demons," "no gods," and, "worthless idols" (v.21). They were gods they had not before acknowledged. In contrast to the Lord who as Creator is the God of history and the God their fathers worshiped, these gods appeared recently and were gods their fathers had not feared (i.e., reverenced).

9. God's rejection of Israel (32:19–30)

19 The indictment of both sons and daughters for angering the Lord is unusual since it is common to include both sexes under the term "sons" (which could be "children"), as at the end of v.20. Perhaps this more sharply indicates the total participation of the people in worshiping other gods—the women being implicated as much as the men.

20 In his anger the Lord says, "I will hide my face [GK 7156] from them" (cf. 31:17–18). "I will . . . see what their end will be" does not suppose that the Lord did not know what would transpire. It is rather a declaration that he will see that those punishments do come. The two clauses—"I will hide my face from them" and "I will . . . see what their end will be"—are explicitly parallel. These two actions follow from the condition of the people—from their being a perverse generation, unfaithful children.

21 As the Lord has been roused to jealousy and anger by Israel's worship of worthless no-gods, so he will rouse Israel to jealousy, anger, and humiliation by foolish, vile non-people. No specific nation seems to be intended, and several nations have fitted the description and fulfilled the prediction.

22–23 The result of the Lord's anger is described as a world-embracing cataclysm of fire adversely affecting three entities: the realm of death, the earth and its harvests, and the very foundations of the mountains (Ps 18:7). The calamities of v.23 are those experiences that affect people adversely. These disasters will be heaped on Israel, and the Lord's arrows will be used up against his people.

24 This general description is followed by specific calamities: famine, pestilence, plague, attacks by wild animals and snakes, as well as warfare. Each calamitous situation is further defined by appropriate descriptive words—not only famine (or hunger), but "wasting" famine (probably from desiccation, having all one's flesh and energy sucked out by total lack of fluids and malnutrition); not only pestilence, but "consuming" pestilence. It is the fangs of the wild animals and the venom of vipers that will attack them.

25–27 Moreover, the sword (i.e., warfare) will reach Israel both "out in the streets" and "in their homes," allowing them no place of safety. All ages will succumb; those who remain will be scattered so that no one will remember them as a nation. This is the punishment the Lord said he would send on the Israelites for their disloyalty. However, because Israel's enemies might understand what was happening and attribute the devastation of Israel to their own prowess in warfare, there seems to be an unvoiced suggestion that this would in a measure stay God's hand. The Lord's compassion for his people in v.36 also affects the full application of his anger.

28–30 It seems best to interpret Israel as the subject of the poem in these verses. This section gives the reasons for the calamities described in the preceding section: the obtuse stupidity on the part of Israel and the wickedness on the part of their enemies. Israel's stupidity derives from its lack of sagacity or wisdom, i.e., "without sense." "No discernment" indicates that they could not discern what their end would be.

Because of their lack of wisdom, the people could not detect or understand their destiny. They did not believe what Moses had already told them and doubted that the Lord was the source of the miracles that brought them out of Egypt and through Sinai. In later years, however, for a long while the people had insufficient knowledge of the message of Deuteronomy to make a sound judgment, though they were never wholly without some revelation from the Lord.

The only answer to the rhetorical question of v.30, if any answer could be given, was, "There is no way one enemy warrior could chase a thousand Israelites if the Lord was on Israel's side." So when this happened, it was obvious that their Rock, whom they had abandoned, rejected, deserted, and forgotten, had now sold them (cf. Ge 37:36; 45:4–5) and "had given them up." Israel would experience this rejection repeatedly (see Jdg 2:14; 3:8; 4:2; 10:7).

10. The punishment of Israel's enemies (32:31–35)

31 The antecedent of "their" changes from Israel to the enemies of Israel. The pronoun "their" in v.30 is Israel; in v.31 it is their enemies. In v.30 "their Rock" is the Lord; in v.31 "their rock" is the enemies' god, and even the enemies concede that the Lord is superior to "their rock" (cf. Ex 14:25; Nu 23–24).

32–33 Under the figure of vines, grapes, and wine, the wickedness of Israel's enemies is described. Their vine (character) has its source in the vine of Sodom and Gomorrah—those wicked cities annihilated by the Lord (Ge 19:24–25). Their grapes were lethal, bitter, and venomous.

34–35 Once again the text of the song reverts to the first person, to the Lord speaking. He has kept in reserve the history of the acts of wicked nations against his people and has sealed this wicked history in his vaults. God's avenging wrath rests on his sense of righteousness. He will mete out righteous judgment whether in punishment or in defense. "I," God says, "will repay" (GK 8966; Ro 12:19 and Heb 10:30 interpret this as teaching that personal revenge against any wickedness is prohibited). The enemies may think that it was their decision and their strength that brought terrible punishment on the Lord's people (v.27), but that was not really so. They were only the instruments of God's punishment. But because they willfully and wickedly acted within the providence of God, their time of punishment would also come. It would come when the Lord's time for it had arrived, the time when their foot slips (cf. Pss 17:5; 38:16).

The time when God acts against the wicked is indicated as near and soon. Even though he is a God of patience, he nevertheless moves quickly to punish the wicked. "In due time" does not contradict "their day of disaster is near" or "their doom rushes upon them" but rather explains it. When their foot slips, disaster and doom rush in (Heb 2:3).

11. The Lord's compassion toward Israel and vengeance on the enemies (32:36–43)

36 "The Lord will judge his people" is not a declaration of punishment but expresses his vindication of them, having compassion on them and making atonement for both his land and his people (v.43; cf. Ge 30:6). (In the Hebrew, the first two lines of v.36 are quoted verbatim in Ps 135:14.) The Lord's vindication comes when his people have no more strength and, hyperbolically, no longer exist (actually, they would no longer exist as a nation). From the following verses "no strength" doubtless labels the gods that they had relied on as likewise utterly impotent. "Slave or free" conveys the sense that the nation is so decimated that all classes of people are destroyed.

37–38 The Lord asks his people, in this dreadful condition, where those gods they took refuge in are—those gods that they thought were a rock and they worshiped. The fat of sacrifices and wine of drink offerings should have been offered to the Lord instead of to gods that could not help them. In irony, the Lord suggests that those gods should arise and help them and give them shelter.

39 The Lord speaks of himself as the only true God who controls all life and history. This section of the song (vv.39–42) begins with a personal assertion. "See now" (GK 8011) suggests strong feeling on God's part; the word here means "understand." What was Israel to understand? That the Lord is God! This statement is made the more emphatic by the repetition of the first person pronoun, "I, even I" and the simple but profound assertion, "I am he"—an assertion of the reality and uniqueness of the Lord as God. This reality is seen in what he does: he puts to death at his will and he gives life—a reference to his creative power and his power to rescue from death. The Lord stated that he was the one who had wounded Israel and that he would also heal his people. Moreover, no one would be able to rescue Israel's enemies from his "hand" (i.e., power; see Job 10:7; Isa 43:13; Hos 5:14).

40 In a strong anthropomorphism the Lord applied to himself the taking of an oath by raising the hand toward heaven (Ge 14:22; Ex 6:8; Nu 14:30) and declaring, "As the LORD lives, I will" (cf. Jdg 8:19; 1Sa 14:39; et al.). The traditional oath formula is adjusted to the occasion by the Lord himself declaring, "As surely as I live forever" (cf. Nu 14:21, 28; Isa 49:18; Jer 22:24; Eze 5:11; et al.).

41–42 What the Lord declared as he used this strong figure must be taken as a statement of absolute certainty and received with the greatest seriousness. The Lord presented himself as a warrior, and the dramatic portrayal represented the terrible punishment to be meted out to his enemies. When he grasps his sharpened, flashing sword, it devours flesh, the heads of the enemy leaders; and he makes his arrows drunk with the blood, not only of those slain, but of the captives as well—signifying that no one will escape. The arrows that were before spent against Israel (v.23) now are turned on his enemies with devastating effect. None can withstand the Lord.

43 The song ends with a call to the nations to rejoice with Israel because the Lord will punish his enemies for what they have done against his land and his people.

12. Moses' presentation of the song and his exhortation to obey the law (32:44–47)

44–47 The narrative about the Song of Moses comes to its conclusion here, which repeats 31:30 with an additional admonition to the people to command their children to obey "all the words of this law." In 31:30 Moses is said to have recited "the words of this song." In 32:44 Moses, with Joshua son of Nun, spoke "all the words of this song." In v.45 Moses finished his recitation. It is evident that Joshua had been with Moses, since, at the command of the Lord, Moses had called Joshua and the two of them had presented themselves before the Lord at the Tent of Meeting for Joshua's commissioning. Moses' spiritual emphasis again appears in his admonition that the people "take to heart" all that he had said.

Previously Moses had said that the Lord was the people's life (see comment on 30:20); here he said that "all the words I have solemnly declared to you," "all the words of this law," are their "life." These words were

not to be taken lightly. The Lord their God was their life, and his words were their life. Commitment to the Lord and to his word would ensure a long national life for Israel in the Promised Land.

C. Directives for Moses' Death (32:48–52)

48–50 There was no lapse of time. On the very same day that the song was recited, the Lord's directives regarding Moses were received. The Lord commanded him to ascend Mount Nebo, look over the land, and then die there (see also Nu 27:12–14, which has some slight variations). Mount Nebo is in the Abarim Mountains, a range running in a general north and south direction about ten miles east of the most northern part of the Dead Sea. It is 2,631 feet above sea level. From Nebo Moses could see Canaan in the north, on the west the mountains of Judea, and toward the south as far as the area south of the Dead Sea (Zoar). On Nebo Moses was to die "and be gathered to" his people (an idiom for death; see Ge 25:8, 17; 35:29; et al.), as Aaron had died on Mount Hor (Nu 20:22–29; 33:37–39).

51–52 The reason for the prohibition against Moses' entrance into the Promised Land is more explicit here than in Nu 20:24, where it is simply stated that he and Aaron had rebelled against the Lord at Meribah. Here it is said that they "broke faith" with the Lord in Israel's presence and "did not uphold my holiness among the Israelites." Instead of speaking to the rock, they called the people rebels and struck the rock twice. The Lord denounced this action on the spot as a failure to trust him enough to honor him as holy.

The mountain in the distance is Mount Nebo, seen from Heshbon in Moab. Courtesy Bastiaan Van Elderen

Thus, they were not permitted to bring Israel into the land (Nu 20:7–12; Ps 106:32–33), though Moses was to see the land "from a distance."

D. The Blessing of Moses on the Tribes (33:1–29)

1. Introduction (33:1–5)

1 The blessings that Moses pronounced on the tribes is placed after his Song and between God's directives to him regarding his death and the actual narrative of that death. This chapter presents these blessings as recorded by someone other than Moses. While Moses speaking or writing of himself in the third person is common in the Pentateuch, this chapter has every appearance of being reported by someone else.Very fittingly Moses is called "the man of God." Never before in the Pentateuch had this designation been used. The second occurrence of this phrase also refers to Moses (Jos 14:6).

2 The encomium to the Lord begins with the theophany at Sinai. Deuteronomy usually speaks of Horeb as the mountain of the giving of the law, but here it is Sinai. The coming of the Lord on Mount Sinai was like the sun flooding the desert area bounded by Sinai, Seir, and Paran. The locations are not certain. The figure could be taken from the surrounding mountains and metaphorically related to the giving of the law on Mount Sinai with its thunder, lightning, earthquake, and darkness. In these meteorological elements the Lord is presented as the brightness of light. The Lord came not only as the light-giving sun but from the tens of thousands of his holy ones, that is, from heaven—or with myriads of his angels. The last line is especially difficult. The NIV interprets the Hebrew "from his right hand" as geographic, meaning "from the south" (cf. 1Sa 23:19, 24; Ps 89:12; et al.).

3–4 The encomium moves on to state the Lord's love toward his people and their worshipful response to his instruction. It is the Lord, not some other god, who loves his people, "the holy ones" that are in his hand—a hand that both controls and supports them. At his feet they bow down and worship, and at his feet they receive the law that Moses gave them—the law that was their possession. Moses spoke of himself in the third person in v.4, a fairly common practice in this kind of literature.

5 In praise of the Lord, his kingship at the assembly at Sinai is declared—his kingship over Jeshurun, Israel the Righteous. The Lord's kingship assumes supreme importance in the Mosaic economy. Without a hereditary monarchy or any other means than direct revelatory selection by the Lord, the Israelites had no way of recognizing a leader with the exception of the leadership invested in the high priest—a leadership that did not cover the power and responsibilities of Moses. Succession to Moses was established charismatically by the Lord's choice of Joshua, but no evidence exists that the Lord revealed to Joshua who was to be his successor.

2. Reuben (33:6)

6 The order of the tribes in the blessings is not the order of the patriarchal blessings of Jacob, nor the order of birth of the tribal fathers, nor the order of their encampments, nor the order of either list in the census narratives in Numbers, nor the order of their tribal allotments in Transjordan and Canaan. For various reasons—some known and some unknown—all these differ from one another.

As in Jacob's blessings, Reuben, the eldest, is mentioned first, though he had lost his birthright because of fornication with Bilhah, his father's concubine (Ge 35:22; 49:4). Then comes Judah, who had been given the birthright, then the other sons of Jacob and his wives (Leah and Rachel), and finally the sons of Jacob with the handmaids. Simeon is not mentioned; for the most part the Simeonites found their future together with Judah and never realized a tribal patrimony except for certain cities in Judah (Jos 19:1–9). At least some of the Simeonites, however, did continue their tribal identity (see 1Ch 4:24–43). Though the tribe of Reuben lost its preeminent position, it was not to die but continued to live, though reduced numerically.

3. Judah (33:7)

7 As with Reuben, the blessing of Moses for Judah comes as a prayer couched in very general expressions. The cry of Judah, the defense by his own hands, and the plea for the Lord's help all suggest a military situation. The hand of Judah, according to Jacob's blessing, was to be on the neck of his enemies, and for this victory his brothers would praise him. The prayer of Moses that Judah should be brought to his people may relate to his victorious return to his people from battle.

4. Levi (33:8–11)

8–10 In Jacob's blessing, Simeon and Levi are considered together. In Moses' blessing, however, the status of Levi has changed remarkably because of the choice of Levi as the priestly tribe, the only appointment that gives every person in the tribe a special position in Israel. Not only all the men, but the women and the children too become beneficiaries of the support generated by the tithes and other emoluments. But the blessing of Moses speaks of Levi's status of caretaker, teacher, and revealer of the covenant and will of God, and of bearing the priestly responsibility of offering the sacrifices of the ritual system, representing the people before the Lord and the Lord and his revelation to the people. Not only did the Levites have charge of the physical, inscripturated word placed beside the ark of the covenant and of the Thummim and Urim, but they were also to teach that word to the people at regular intervals (Lev 10:11; Dt 31:9–13). The one that the Thummim and Urim belonged to is called the godly man or "the man [God] favored."

The strife that arose at Massah and Meribah over water points out the difficulties that Moses, Aaron, the leaders of Israel, and the leaders of the tribe of Levi suffered on the journey from Egypt to Moab. The special devotion of Levi to the Lord is said to be portrayed by the action of the Levites in purging the community of sin by killing many of their own relatives after they had worshiped the golden calf (Ex 32:26–29). Because of the Levites' loyalty to the Lord on that occasion, they were set apart to him as the priestly tribe (Ex 32:29; Dt 10:8). Offering incense and whole offerings to the Lord are together descriptions of the entire sacrificial system.

11 Moses concluded his blessing on Levi with a prayer that Levi's use of his skills may be blessed with accomplishments that result in the Lord's being pleased with him. Moses also prayed that the power of Levi's enemies would be destroyed—never to rise again.

5. Benjamin (33:12)

12 The blessing for Benjamin has a tenderness that differs markedly from the description of the Benjamites in Jacob's last words (Ge 49:27). Moses asked that Benjamin as the one loved of the Lord and shielded continually by him would have a secure rest between the Lord's shoulders, as a father might carry a son—a figure already used to describe how the Lord carried the Israelites all through the desert journeys (1:31). "The one the LORD loves" is a repetition of "the beloved of the LORD," a device to signify the subject of the last line.

6. Joseph (Ephraim and Manasseh) (33:13–17)

13–16a When Jacob blessed his sons just prior to his death, he included Joseph rather than Ephraim and Manasseh, even though he had placed his blessing on them and had made a particular point of indicating that these two sons of Joseph were to be reckoned as his (Ge 48:5–20; 49:22–26). Moses also blessed Joseph, but he mentioned the two tribes at the end of his statement about Joseph (v.17).

The blessing desired for Joseph is expressed in considerable poetic beauty. The words "precious," "best," "finest," "fruitfulness," and "best gifts" are all from the same Hebrew word (GK 4458). This blessing would be achieved by the application of the precious things from heaven and from under the earth—the dew, the springs, and the rivers. The "ancient mountains" and "the everlasting hills" exemplify the land of the Joseph tribes across the middle of Canaan. The fertility of the land would cover the mountains with eternal productivity.

All this is summed up in v.16a—"with the best gifts of the earth"—with the further explanation that this productivity would be in all fullness possible (the same phrase as occurs in 1Ch 16:32; Pss 24:1; 50:12). The Lord, the one who presented himself to Moses in the burning bush, is the one who will favor Joseph with this blessing of abundance (see Ex 3).

16b–17 The remainder of the Joseph blessing describes the character and prowess of these two tribes. The blessing is to rest as a crown on the head and brow of Joseph, "the prince among his brothers." The reference to the majesty of the firstborn bull links v.17 with Joseph being prince among his brothers. And the end of v.17 explicitly says that the goring of the nations by the one metaphorically called the firstborn bull and wild ox refers to both Ephraim and Manasseh. Contrary to the usual poetic usage of citing thousands before ten thousands (1Sa 18:7), the ten thousands of Ephraim are mentioned before the thousands of Manasseh. So it is obvious that Moses recognized the superiority of Ephraim, though Joseph, not Ephraim, is the firstborn bull.

Manasseh was really the firstborn son, but here this prominence has become Ephraim's later prominence. Ephraim became the dominant tribe in the northern kingdom and was often militarily the more powerful kingdom in Canaan in the ninth, eighth, and seventh centuries B.C. The extent of the military victories of Joseph, however, should best be taken as poetic hyperbole, signifying the greater relative strength and prowess predicated of the Joseph tribes.

7. Zebulun and Issachar (33:18–19)

18 Zebulun and Issachar, the last two sons of Leah, are mentioned together, the younger being placed first. The poetic parallelistic structure of the first two lines is to be understood as a play on the fairly common expression of one's daily activity as "going out and coming in," with "in your tents" being equivalent to "coming in." So then the sense is "Rejoice, Zebulun, and you, Issachar, in all your activities."

19 These tribes together were to "summon peoples to the mountain" and "there offer sacrifices of righteousness." "Mountain" may simply designate a place of sacrifice and worship. The "peoples" would certainly include other Israelites but may not be limited to them. Their sacrifices would be those Moses had given to them. No other sacrifices could be called righteous, nor could righteous acts by themselves apart from the sacrificial system be considered as sacrifices at this time.

These two tribes were to feast on "the abundance of the seas" and "the treasures hidden in the sand." The boundaries of Zebulun and Issachar as allotted by Joshua did not give either Zebulun or Issachar access to the Mediterranean; but Moses is in harmony with the vision of Jacob, who saw Zebulun living by the seashore, a haven for ships, with his border extending toward Sidon (Ge 49:13). The influence of the tribes and the actual boundaries did not always remain where the original allotment placed them. Since sand is almost invariably the sand of the sea, that is, the seashore, it is likely that the two phrases are in synonymous parallelism referring to the same source of riches—maritime wealth.

8. Gad (33:20–21)

20 The blessing on Gad focuses first on the Lord himself, who enlarges Gad's territory by giving the tribe what it requested after the conquest of the area east of the Jordan, which had been under the Amorite rulers Sihon and Og (Nu 21:21–35; 32:33; Dt 3:1–20; 29:7–8). Gad was known as warlike and aggressive. The tribe was able to hold onto the territory and to keep its tribal identification on the east of Jordan until it succumbed to Tiglath-pileser in the latter part of the eighth century B.C. (1Ch 5:23–26). This warlike character is portrayed as a lion that tears an arm and even the head of its prey. Jacob too saw Gad attacking its enemies (Ge 49:19), and 1 Chronicles describes some Gadites as having faces of lions (12:8), the least of which "was a match for a hundred, and the greatest for a thousand" (1Ch 12:14).

21 Gad chose the best of the land, or the leader's part. Moreover, Gad was to fulfill the Lord's righteous will that the assembly of Israel had required of Reuben, Gad, and the half-tribe of Manasseh, that is, their cooperation in subduing the peoples of Canaan before they returned east of Jordan (Nu 32:1–33; Dt 3:18–20; Jos 1:12–18; 22:1–8).

9. Dan (33:22)

22 The blessing on Dan is a metaphor describing at least the inherent, ravenous character of a lion's cub that springs on its prey. Jacob had likened Dan to a serpent, a viper. The reference to Bashan is not to Dan directly but to the lions of Bashan, an area somewhat removed from the area around Laish that was later occupied by Dan. Moses saw the Danite tribe leaping out of ambush like a ravenous lion to secure its prey.

10. Naphtali (33:23)

23 As with Dan, little is said of Naphtali; but what is said of Naphtali is approval. Naphtali will have the Lord's favor in abundance and will be full of blessing—blessing that will be his because of the excellent and fertile land the tribe will inherit. His land will extend from the north of Galilee to the area west and south of the lake.

11. Asher (33:24–25)

24–25 Asher, declared to be a most blessed of sons, is to be favored above his brothers. Bathing his feet in olive oil (probably mixed with fragrant unguents) and having a secure residence behind gates bolted with iron and bronze bars, the tribe of Asher will grow in strength as its days increase in number.

12. Peroration of God and Israel, his people (33:26–29)

26 Moses' final blessing returns to Israel as a whole—commencing with praise to the Lord as the God of Jeshurun (cf. v.5). The God of Jeshurun has a unique greatness—he rides on the heavens and on the clouds in his majesty to help his people (see also Pss 18:9; 68:33; Isa 19:1).

27–28 The "eternal God" was the God of their fathers. In many places Moses emphasized that he was sent by the God of their fathers. The Lord is the God who is the Creator of all things, the God of history, and the God of the promises to the patriarchs. The Lord was the dwelling of his people, and his everlasting arms were beneath them to keep them from harm, discouragement, and failure. They would not be left to rely on only their own strength. The Lord was to drive out the enemy before them with the command "Destroy!"

The promise that God would go before Israel to conquer the land has always in it the participation of the people in obedience to the Lord's commands, but that participation is always to be understood as effective only as the Lord works with them and through them. The result will be victory that will leave Israel as a secure nation living in "safety," relying on the Lord, who would give them victory and would sustain them.

Israel, Jacob's spring (i.e., the descendants that flowed from Jacob), would live safely and securely in the land whose supply of grain and wine was symbolic of rich productivity and where the dew of heaven, representative of sufficient precipitation, would nourish their crops.

29 The blessing of Moses on the tribes ends with an exclamation, a rhetorical question, and a twofold affirmation of the Lord's strength and help and of Israel's triumph over her enemies. The exclamation "Blessed are you, O Israel!" comes as a fitting climax. The rhetorical question reinforces the exclamation by its obvious answer: No other nation was like Israel, the nation saved by the Lord. And the affirmation that follows reinforces the thrust of both the exclamation and the question.

As shield and helper, the Lord would defend the Israelites; as their sword of majesty or glory, he would give them victory over their enemies, thus indicating their superiority. The enemies will present themselves as vanquished in battle and consequently as inferior to their conquerors. Israel would be victorious over the enemies they would face on the other side of the Jordan.

E. The Death of Moses and the Succession of Joshua (34:1–12)

1–4 Before he died, Moses climbed from the plains of Moab up to the top of the Pisgah range, to the top of Mount Nebo, and from there the Lord showed him the whole land. The description indicates the area one would see from Nebo when looking first northward (from Gilead to Dan), turning his gaze northwest (all of Naphtali; the territory of Ephraim and Manasseh), and west (all the land of Judah as far as the western sea), and then looking southward (the Negev and the whole region from the Valley of Jericho, the City of Palms, as far as Zoar).

As Moses viewed Canaan from Nebo, the Lord told him that this was the land he had promised to Abraham's descendants (see Ge 12:7; 13:14–17; 15:18; 17:8; 26:3; 28:4, 13). The Lord let Moses see the land with his eyes, but he did not permit him to cross over the Jordan into it. At 120 years of age, Moses looked out with eyes that "were not weak" (v.7), and—though he was still vigorous—his mission came to an end. What drama! What pathos! What sense of accomplishment mixed with disappointment must have been in Moses' mind as he looked over the land the Lord had promised to Israel!

5–8 The "servant of the LORD" died and was buried in an unknown way, in an unknown grave, in the valley facing Beth Peor, where the Israelites were encamped (3:29). The thirty-day mourning for Moses conformed to the mourning period for Aaron (Nu 20:29).

9 Before the writer closed his remarks about Moses with a final eulogy, he mentioned Joshua the successor as one whose ability to lead rested on his ordination by Moses, an ordination that filled him with the spirit of wisdom. So Israel listened to (i.e., obeyed) Joshua—doing what the Lord had commanded them to do through Moses.

10–12 Deuteronomy closes eulogizing Moses as the greatest of all prophets, the one whom the Lord knew intimately, and the greatest miracle-worker. The acts of the Lord through Moses are said to be miraculous signs, wonders, and awesome deeds performed with mighty power (the terms used here are common in the narratives of Exodus and the desert journeys (see Ex 7:3; Nu 14:11, 22; Dt 4:34; 6:22; etc). These were done before Pharaoh, his officials, his people, and in the sight of all Israel. These were done to accomplish the task the Lord had called Moses to do in Egypt and on the journey to Canaan.

Not until the Lord Jesus Christ came (the one whom Moses spoke about, Jn 5:46) was there anyone greater than Moses, the emancipator, prophet, lawgiver, and father of his country.

The Old Testament in the New

OT Text	NT Text	Subject
Dt 4:24	Heb 12:29	God is a consuming fire
Dt 4:35	Mk 12:32	No other God
Dt 5:16	Mt 15:4; Mk 7:10; Eph 6:2–3	Fifth commandment
Dt 5:17	Mt 5:21; Ro 13:9; Jas 2:11	Sixth commandment
Dt 5:18	Mt 5:27; Ro 13:9; Jas 2:11	Seventh commandment
Dt 5:19	Ro 13:9	Eighth commandment
Dt 5:21	Ro 7:7; 13:9	Tenth commandment
Dt 6:4	Mk 12:29, 32	Only one God
Dt 6:5	Mt 22:37; Mk 12:30, 33; Lk 10:27	Love God
Dt 6:13	Mt 4:10; Lk 4:8	Serve God alone
Dt 6:16	Mt 4:7; Lk 4:12	Do not test God
Dt 8:3	Mt 4:4; Lk 4:4	Not by bread alone
Dt 9:19	Heb 12:21	Moses' fear
Dt 17:6	Heb 10:28	Two or three witnesses
Dt 17:7	1Co 5:13	Purge out evil
Dt 18:15, 18–19	Ac 3:22–23; 7:37	The prophet
Dt 19:15	Mt 18:16; 2Co 13:1	Two or three witnesses
Dt 17:7	1Co 5:13	Purge out evil
Dt 18:15, 18–19	Act 3:22–23; 7:37	The prophet
Dt 19:15	Mt 18:16; 2Co 13:1	Two or three witnesses
Dt 21:23	Gal 3:13	Curse of the cross
Dt 24:1	Mt 5:31	Certificate of divorce
Dt 25:4	1Co 9:9; 1Ti 5:18	Not muzzling an ox
Dt. 25:5	Mt 22:24; Mk 12:19; Lk 20:28	A brother's widow
Dt 27:26	Gal 3:10	Curse of the law
Dt 29:4	Ro 11:8	A misunderstanding mind

The Old Testament in the New

OT Text	NT Text	Subject
Dt 29:18	Heb 12:15	No root of bitterness
Dt 30:12	Ro 10:6	The word not in heaven
Dt 30:13	Ro 10:7	The word not in deep
Dt 30:14	Ro 10:8	The word near you
Dt 31:6	Heb 13:5	Faithfulness of God
Dt 32:21	Ro 10:19	Making Israel envious
Dt 32:35	Ro 12:19; Heb 10:30	God avenges sin
Dt 32:36	Heb 10:30	God judges his people
Dt 32:43	Ro 15:10; Heb 1:6	Rejoice, O nations

Joshua

INTRODUCTION

1. Background

The Pentateuch provides the background both historically and theologically for the book of Joshua. The call of Abraham was God's initial response to the predicament of humankind as portrayed in Ge 1–11. God was preparing a people through whom the Messiah would come. As part of that preparation, he promised to give them a land of their own (Ge 12:7; 13:14–17; 15:7; et al.). The fulfillment of that promise is the primary focus of the book of Joshua. The author has gone to great lengths to demonstrate that the work of Moses and the work of Joshua are related to each other as preparation and fulfillment.

The book of Joshua is closely related to the book of Deuteronomy; even the language is similar. Deuteronomy seeks to prepare Israel for entry into the Promised Land; Joshua describes that entry. In other words, in Exodus, Moses was called by God to mold the people into a mighty nation and to lead them out of slavery. The central feature of his leadership was the mediation of the law as the guide for Israel. Now Joshua has been appointed as Moses' successor. Like Moses, his position involved him as the religious, military, social, and civil leader. He had been prepared for the various aspects of this role during the forty years that Israel was in the desert (see Ex 17:8–16; 24:12–13; Nu 13:1–25; 32:28–29; Dt 31:1–8).

The date of the Conquest continues to be debated. The traditional date (c. 1400 B.C.) is based on 1Ki 6:1, which specifies that the fourth year of Solomon's reign was the "four hundred and eightieth year" after the Exodus. It is fairly well established that the fourth year of Solomon's reign was around 966 B.C. This would put the Exodus at about 1446 B.C. and the Conquest forty years later. These figures appear to be corroborated also by the total number of years that the various judges ruled. Other evangelical scholars, however, argue for the thirteenth century B.C., based on the Rameses of Ex 1:11 being the city named for Rameses II (who lived around 1290 B.C.). They argue that the 480 years in 1Ki 6:1 represent twelve generations (12 generations times 40 years in a traditional generation); if an actual generation is closer to twenty-five years, then the number of years before Solomon's reign was 300, making the Exodus in 1260 B.C. and the Conquest in 1220.

2. Authorship

In the Talmud Joshua is named as the author of the book of Joshua. This view is appealing because the book bears his name. Furthermore, it lends more credibility to the narratives if they are the report of an eyewitness. Those who hold this view attribute to Eleazer or Phinehas the account of the death of Joshua and other short passages that Joshua could not have written. The book itself does not specify who the author was, nor is the author named anywhere else in the OT.

The name of the book is derived from the principal character, Joshua, whose name means either "Save, Yahweh!" or "Yahweh saves" (see comment on 3:13). It is an appropriate name for the man the Lord chose to lead his people triumphantly into the Promised Land. The Grecized form of Joshua is "Jesus."

3. Date

If Joshua was the author, then the date of writing the book is a fairly simple matter: it must have been written before his death and after the last event narrated in the book. Joshua was 110 years old when he died (24:29). If Joshua was nearly the same age as Caleb, then his death and the writing of the book would have taken place about thirty years after the Conquest began. This would have been around 1370 B.C. according to the earlier dating. Other evidence, however, suggests a later date.

The phrase "to this day," which occurs frequently (4:9; 5:9; 6:25; et al.), indicates the passing of time between the event and the recording of the event. In 6:25 the statement that Rahab "lives among the Israelites to this day" suggests that Rahab was still living at the time of writing, but it probably refers to her descendants.

4. Occasion and Purpose

Apparently the author had two complementary purposes in writing: (1) to show that God had been faithful in fulfilling his promise to Abraham to give the land of Canaan to him and to his descendants; (2) to demonstrate that the covenant-keeping God is also righteous and that he would bless his covenant people only if they were obedient to his word.

5. Theological Values

The book of Joshua, like all other books of the Bible, is primarily a book of theology. Through it God has revealed himself in various aspects: (1) God is the God of Israel. In giving Israel the land, he was fulfilling the promises that he made to Abraham and which he reaffirmed to the people of Israel at the time of the Exodus. Thus he entered into covenant with some human beings, but not all. Here we see elements of a doctrine of election.

(2) God is holy. He does not tolerate wickedness and rebellion. The Canaanites are driven out because of their sin and wickedness; God treats the Israelites according to the same principle (cf. ch. 7; cf. also Dt 28–29).

(3) God is gracious. All who are willing to turn from their pagan ways and acknowledge him are spared (e.g., Rahab, the Gibeonites).

(4) God is the God of creation. All creation is subject to his sovereign control, and he therefore can work mighty miracles in nature (such as those recorded in this book: 3; 6; 10:9–14; et al.).

(5) God is a God of the entire universe. He can choose to accept into his people the prostitute Rahab upon her testimony of his universal reign (2:11). The land is his, and he can give it to whomever he chooses.

(6) God is a man of war. He fought for Israel by commanding the attack, providing the strategy, assisting with supernatural acts, and giving the victory to Joshua.

6. Special Problems

The single greatest problem in the book of Joshua is the extermination of the Canaanites. Men, women, and children were included among the things that were to be "devoted [GK 3051] to the LORD" (6:17; cf. NIV note). This was not the first instance of the practice in Israel. In Nu 21:2–3, the Israelites vowed to "totally destroy" the cities of the Canaanites in the Negev if God would give Israel victory over them. But how can we justify this seeming mass slaughter of humanity?

God was careful to point out that he was not arbitrarily destroying the Canaanites just to give the land to Israel. The wickedness of the Canaanites was the reason God was removing them; and if Israel proved unfaithful, she too would be removed from the land (as happened in the Exile; cf. Ge 15:16; 2Pe 2:9).

The extermination of the Canaanites is but one of the many evidences in the Bible that evil is real and that the Devil exists. That struggle actually took the Son of God to the cross, and only by his suffering and death has God overcome evil once and for all. Those who choose not to be separated from their sin by repentance will be destroyed with their sin (cf. Jn 8:24). Thus God's severity in his treatment of sin and of sinners is but the obverse side of his grace and love. Sin and evil destroy the people he loves and prevent the full establishment of his glorious kingdom. In the *Wisdom of Solomon* it is stated that God chose to annihilate the Canaanites little by little rather than all at once in order to give them a chance to repent.

The most difficult thing to understand is the slaughter of innocent children. But we must remember that death is not the ultimate destiny of the human race, nor is it the greatest evil. Someday God will give a full explanation of his actions, which is something that only he can do.

EXPOSITION

I. Conquering the Promised Land (1:1–12:24)

A. A New Leader for Israel (1:1–18)

1. Joshua's commission (1:1–9)

1 Moses' death separates the book of Joshua from the Pentateuch, for, obviously, Moses'

leadership had ended. However, everything Joshua accomplishes is the fulfillment of what God had begun with Moses. Observe the many links between Moses and Joshua in this chapter alone (vv.1, 3, 5, 7–8, 13–15, 17).

"Servant [GK 6269] of the LORD" is a title of honor used most frequently of Moses (Ex 14:31; Nu 12:7–8; Dt 34:5; and 13 times in Joshua). With the words "The LORD said to Joshua," leadership is transferred from Moses to Joshua. Joshua is called the "son of Nun" ten times in this book, but nothing is known about his father. Already in the Pentateuch Joshua was called "Moses' aide" (Ex 24:13; 33:11; Nu 11:28). Only at the end of his life was he too honored with the title "servant of the LORD" (24:29).

2–3 Moses' death was the occasion for God to renew his command for Israel to enter the land. The crossing of the Jordan marked Israel's entrance into the Promised Land. Flood conditions made this a formidable undertaking. The promise of the land, which was first given to Abraham in Ge 12:7, is a major theme throughout patriarchal history. The fulfillment of that promise is one of the major themes in Joshua.

4 The promise in Dt 11:24 (cf. Dt 1:6–8) is reiterated here, although the territory that Joshua and Israel actually conquered was not nearly so vast. The literal and complete fulfillment of this promise was not experienced by Israel until the reigns of David and Solomon (see 1Ki 4:21, 24) and then once again in the time of Uzziah and Jeroboam II. The word "desert" refers to the Negev in the south, and "Lebanon" (lit., "the Lebanon") refers to the Lebanese mountains. Palestine was referred to as "the Hittite country" by both Egypt and Babylonia even after the Hittites had withdrawn from the area (cf. Jdg 1:26). "The Great Sea" is the Mediterranean.

5 Israel's failure to observe the conditions for the promise, "No one will be able to stand up against you" (vv.6–9), caused their humiliating defeat at Ai (7:1–5). God's promise, "I will be with you" (cf. Dt 31:6–8), was the secret of Moses' success and would be the secret of Joshua's success also (cf. Mt 28:19–20). The conditions for this promise are found in vv.7–8 (cf. 7:12). The statement "I will never leave you nor forsake you" is an example of the doubling of synonyms for emphasis, a common feature in this chapter (cf. vv.7–9, 18).

6 The command to be "strong [GK 2616] and courageous [GK 599]" is repeated three times in God's charge to Joshua (vv.6–9) and again in the people's reply to Joshua (v.18). Perhaps Joshua was intimidated by the greatness of his predecessor Moses and the awesomeness of his own responsibility. For this reason courage is emphasized in the Lord's charge to him. This passage introduces the two major parts of the book: the conquest of the land (chs. 1–12) and the division of the land (chs. 13–21).

7 "The law my servant Moses gave you" was probably some part or all of the book of Deuteronomy (cf. Dt 1:5; 31:9–13). The many parallels that the book of Joshua has with Deuteronomy show that the author of Joshua was familiar with the latter's contents. The covenant relationship between Israel and God was contingent on Israel's obedience to the law. The expression "to the right or to the left" shows that no deviation would be permitted.

8–9 Verse 8 is the theme verse of Joshua. The phrase "from your mouth" refers to the custom of muttering while studying or reflecting. "Meditate" (GK 2047) literally means "mutter." When people continually mutter God's word to themselves, they are constantly thinking about it. But knowledge of God's law is not enough; one must also "be careful to do" what it commands. "Everything written in it" must be observed, because obedience to certain parts only is no obedience at all (cf. Jas 2:8–13).

2. Joshua's orders to the officers (1:10–11)

10–11 Joshua had a well-organized chain of command by which orders could quickly be passed to the people. The supplies would have included the manna that God continued to provide until Israel crossed into the land of Canaan (5:12). Each man was responsible for his own supplies since there was no regular quartermaster's corps. Once the Israelites were in the land, they found a ready food supply standing in the fields, for the invasion was begun during the harvest season (3:15). "Three days" simply means "the day after tomorrow" or "in a few days" (2:16, 22; 3:2; 9:16).

3. Joshua's orders to the Transjordanian tribes (1:12–15)

12 Throughout the book special attention is given to "the Reubenites, the Gadites and the half-tribe of Manasseh" (4:12–13; 13:8–32; 22:1–34). Although their territory was included in the larger boundaries promised to Israel (1:3–4), the narrative at times seems to place the two and one-half tribes outside the Promised Land (cf. 22:19).

13–15 Moses' command referred to here is recorded in Dt 3:18–20 (cf. Nu 32:20–22). "Rest" (GK 5663) implies secure borders and peace; it is an important concept in the OT (cf. Ru 1:9; 3:1 NIV note; Heb 4:1–11).

The phrase "all your fighting men" presents some difficulty, for Nu 26:7, 18, 34 indicates that these tribes had as many as 110,000 men capable of bearing arms. Yet Jos 4:13 states that only 40,000 warriors from the two and one-half tribes entered Canaan. Perhaps only the ablest fighting men participated in the Conquest while the others cared for the women, children, elderly, and domestic animals (cf. 22:8). For the return of these tribes to their own land, see 22:1–4. The account of Moses' assigning Transjordan as their inheritance is in Nu 32.

4. Joshua confirmed as leader (1:16–18)

16–18 This paragraph apparently deals with all Israel, not just the Transjordanian tribes. The people pledged to Joshua the same allegiance that they had shown Moses. The words "may the LORD your God be with you" seem to be a condition for their allegiance rather than a prayer, as if they were saying: "We will follow your leading so long as there is evidence that you are being led by God." The severity of the punishment threatened in v.18 was in keeping with the military situation where strict discipline was required. This punishment was actually carried out in the case of Achan (ch. 7).

B. Gaining a Foothold: Jericho and Ai (2:1–8:35)

1. Rahab and the spies (2:1–24)

a. Sending the spies (2:1–7)

1 Joshua was determined to keep the spy mission secret from the Israelites, perhaps because a negative report (cf. Nu 13–14) might again demoralize the people. The sending of spies was not an act of unbelief, for the promise of divine aid never rules out human responsibility. Apparently Joshua sent spies before every major battle (cf. 7:2). The words "especially Jericho" indicate that this espionage mission was focused on Jericho, a formidable fortress guarding the pass leading westward. Jericho was particularly important as the scene of Israel's first military engagement in the Promised Land.

The house of the prostitute Rahab was the only place where the men could stay with any hope of remaining undetected and where they would be able to gather the information they were seeking. Moreover, her house afforded an easy way of escape since it was located on the city wall (v.15).

2–3 For the most part the towns of Palestine were independent city-states, and their rulers were called kings. The spies had failed in their attempt to remain undetected. The report that "some of the Israelites have come" was the worst news conceivable, for the citizens of Jericho were in terror of the Israelites (see vv.9–11; cf. Ex 15:15c). The word "tonight" must refer to late afternoon, because the spies would not have been able to enter the city after dark. The king would naturally have assumed that the spies were staying with Rahab. In antiquity prostitutes frequently were involved in intelligence activities. The king expected Rahab to do her patriotic duty and turn the spies in.

4–5 Rahab lied as much in what she did by hiding the spies as in what she said. Deception is an important strategy in warfare. By hiding the spies, Rahab was siding with Israel against her own people. It was an act of treason! Rahab told the king's men to "go after them quickly," making it clear that if they tarried, the spies would escape. She could not risk having her house searched, because she knew that anyone suspected of collaborating with the spies would be put to death.

6–7 The flat-roofed houses of that era were suitable for drying grain or stalks. Rahab used her flax stalks to good advantage. The road mentioned here led from Jerusalem to Jericho and then eastward across the Jordan River. The "fords" were places where the river was normally shallow enough to cross on foot. Though the river was at flood stage, the spies were able to cross without a miracle.

When the pursuers went out, "the gate was shut"; i.e., it was closed again (see v.5), underscoring the predicament of the spies who were trapped inside the city.

b. Rahab's covenant with the spies (2:8–21)

8 The spies may have intended to "[lie] down for the night," but before they settled in for the night and went to sleep, their rest was interrupted by Rahab.

9 It is truly remarkable how much Rahab knew about Israel's history and God's plans for Israel's future. Rahab spoke of the takeover of the land as if it were an accomplished fact. What God had done for Israel in Egypt and in Transjordan convinced her that God was able to give Israel this land, too. The "great fear" that had fallen on all the people had been predicted in Ex 15:15b–16.

10 On the Lord's drying up the "Red Sea," see Ex 14:21–31. For "Sihon and Og," see Nu 21:21–35. "Amorites" is a general term designating the inhabitants of the mountainous regions on both sides of the Jordan. "Completely destroyed" renders the Hebrew word *herem* (GK 3049); the ancient practice of completely destroying the spoils of warfare was a way of devoting them to a deity (cf. 6:17).

11–12 Morale is always a major factor in warfare. Fear is contagious and can even cause the defeat of an army that is superior in all other respects. Rahab's confession of her faith is remarkable for a pagan and is evidence of her conversion to faith in Israel's God (cf. Heb 11:31). "Kindness" (GK 2876), often translated "love" in the NIV, designates a reciprocal relationship of caring. In delivering the spies from the king's officers, Rahab risked her life and set herself against her own people. In return for this, she deserved to be assured of her own safety and the safety of her family.

13 When Rahab requested that the spies "spare the lives" of her family, she may have been asking no more than that they be taken alive as prisoners. Eventually, however, they were assimilated into the nation (6:25). In Scripture salvation is frequently a family matter (Ex 12:3; 24:15; cf. Ac 16:31). The family members would demonstrate their personal faith by gathering in Rahab's house and remaining there.

14–15 In the statement "If you don't tell" the pronoun is plural: Rahab and her entire family would have to guard this secret. Houses, such as Rahab's, constructed within the wall have been discovered by archaeologists in the ruins of ancient Jericho.

16 Undoubtedly the conversation in vv.16–21 occurred before Rahab lowered the spies to the ground. For "three days," see 1:11. The hills to the west of Jericho are a barren wasteland. The king's officers had gone in the opposite direction.

17–21 The spies laid down three conditions: (1) the scarlet cord must be placed in Rahab's window; (2) Rahab's whole family must stay in her house; and (3) the covenant between Rahab and the spies must be kept secret. These were practical ways for Rahab and her family to demonstrate their faith. The "scarlet cord" would identify Rahab's house. The spies no doubt anticipated a house-to-house battle in which the Israelites would have been instructed to spare the house so marked. The statement "his blood will be on his own head" means that all who disobey the instruction to stay in the house will be responsible for their own death.

Since the spies did not know at this time that God would use a miracle to capture the city, they may have arranged a plan for Rahab to deliver the city into Israel's hands. This could be the secret that Rahab was not to tell anyone. The statement "she tied the scarlet cord in the window" forms a fitting conclusion for this section because it points to Rahab's faith in action.

c. The report of the spies (2:22–24)

22–24 It is remarkable that the spies trusted Rahab so implicitly as to follow her instructions. Since the spies told Joshua "everything," we must assume that v.24 is only a summary of what they said. The narrative ends triumphantly. The spies learned two important facts: God had been faithful to his promise, and the inhabitants of the land were totally demoralized.

a. Instructions for crossing (3:1–13)

1–3 The journey from Shittim to the Jordan (c. ten miles) must have taken the better part

This is the OT site where Jericho stood, viewed from the west and looking east across the Jordan River.

of the day. "After three days" is a Hebrew idiom meaning "on the third day" (see 1:11). The presence of the "ark of the covenant," which symbolized God's presence among his people (cf. Ex 25:10–22), indicates that the crossing of the Jordan was a religious procession. When it was carried across the Jordan by the priests, the Lord was marching in to claim his land. "From your positions" refers to the specific locations assigned to the various tribes whenever they set up camp (cf. Nu 2).

4 The people, warned to "keep a distance" of about "a thousand yards" from the ark while crossing the Jordan, would have had to cross one-half mile upstream or one-half mile downstream. Perhaps they maintained this distance only until the priests were stationed with the ark in the middle of the river.

5 The people were to be holy because God is holy, the ark was holy, and the event itself was holy. Consecration involved bathing, washing one's clothing, and abstinence from sexual activity (cf. Ex 19:14–15). "Amazing things" means miraculous things.

6 The priests were commanded to take up the ark and cross over but were not told how they would be enabled to cross the river, which was overflowing its banks (v.15). God often waits for us to step out in faith before he opens the way for us.

7–8 The appointment of Joshua as leader of the people would now be confirmed in action. One major reason for the great miracle was to demonstrate that God was with Joshua as surely as he had been with Moses. The command "Go and stand in the river"

builds the suspense. There is still no indication how the people would get through the water.

9–10 In the phrase "the living God" emphasis is on the fact that Israel's God is *living* (GK 2645). Joshua is affirming that the God who marches with Israel is able to act and to perform mighty deeds in contrast to the pagan gods that have eyes but cannot see, etc. (cf. Ps 115:3–7). Either "Canaanites" or "Amorites" can be used to designate the whole population of Canaan. Strictly speaking, however, the Canaanites were the people living in the lowlands of the sea coast and the Jordan valley (Nu 13:29), while the Amorites lived in the mountainous areas. For "Hittites" see 1:4. The "Perizzites" lived in the central highlands in the time of Abraham and Jacob (Ge 13:7; 34:30). The "Gergashites" are mentioned here although they are not always included in the lists of the Canaanite populations. The "Jebusites" inhabited Jerusalem (15:63), which was formerly called Jebus. Jebusites lived also in the hill country of northern Palestine (11:3).

11 The way the people would cross the Jordan still had not been revealed. The ark would go before them, which signifies that God would go with them and prepare the way.

12 The command to "choose twelve men" interrupts the flow of the narrative, and there is no explanation here of why they were to be chosen or what they were to do. Perhaps this verse indicates when the men were actually selected, and 4:2–3 (where the command is repeated) is the point in the narrative where the mission of the twelve was carried out.

13 In the phrase "the LORD—the Lord of all the earth," the first occurrence of "lord" is printed with one large and three small capitals, representing the sacred name "Yahweh" (GK 3378). The Jews, out of reverence for God's holy name, regularly substituted the Hebrew equivalent for "Lord," "Adonai" (GK 123), when they came to the name "Yahweh" in the Scriptures. The second occurrence of "Lord" actually means "lord," "ruler," or "owner." One of the great themes in the Exodus and the Conquest is that Israel's God is the Lord of all the earth (cf. Ex 9:29). This gave Israel the right to take over the land.

Here finally we are told how the people would be able to cross. The regular flow of the river would be cut off upstream, where the waters would collect in a heap.

b. Crossing on dry ground (3:14–17)

14–16a After the Israelites "broke camp," the priests led the way bearing the ark of the covenant. That the Jordan was at "flood stage" builds the suspense by suggesting the natural impossibility of what was about to happen. The statement that "as soon as . . . their feet touched the water's edge, the water . . . stopped flowing" may be an example of narrative heightening to convey a true sense of wonder at the great miracle that was taking place. The flow of the water had to have stopped upstream prior to the moment that the priests approached the river, or else it would have taken time for the water to flow away downstream after they stepped into the river's edge.

16b–17 The waters began to collect "in a heap" upstream. "Adam" was a city located about twenty miles upstream from where the Israelites crossed the Jordan. The water stopped too far upstream for the Israelites to have seen it; so the timing had to be perfect for the waters to be exhausted at the precise moment that the priests stepped into the river. "The Sea of the Arabah" is the Dead Sea. With the water from upstream "completely cut off," the water flowing downstream was soon emptied into the Dead Sea. "Dry ground" does not mean that the riverbed was powdery dry but simply that it was no longer covered with water.

c. Memorials to the crossing (4:1–24)

1–3 The frequent repetition of the phrase "the LORD said to Joshua" emphasizes the fact that everything was done in obedience to God's commands. If the narrative followed a strict chronological order, it would mean that these men crossed all the way over and were then sent back into the riverbed. The command was actually given, however, before the people began to cross; and it is recorded here at the point in the narrative when the men actually picked up the stones on their way across the river (see 3:12). Stones taken from the middle of the riverbed were remarkable evidence that the river had actually stopped flowing to allow Israel to cross over.

4–6a The twelve men found their stones near the place where the priests carrying the ark were standing. The stones were "to serve as a sign" for future generations (v.6a).

6b–9 Raising stones as a memorial is common in the OT (cf. 7:26; 24:26–27; Ge 28:18–22; 31:45–47; 1Sa 7:12). These memorials were intended to provoke questioning so that the story of God's miraculous interventions might be told over and over. Remembering was a way for future generations to participate in the great acts that God had done for Israel.

10–11 The statement "just as Moses had directed Joshua" reminds us again that Joshua's ministry was subservient to that of Moses. There is no record of Moses giving Joshua explicit instructions for crossing the Jordan, although such a crossing is implied in Dt 31:7. "The people *hurried* over" because the river was stopped for a limited time only. It is clear that the priests did not march out of the river until *after* the people had crossed over.

12–13 Again we see how important it was to our writer that the Transjordanian tribes had a primary role in the conquest of the land of Canaan (cf. 1:12). They went ahead of the other Israelites. For "forty thousand," see comment on 1:14. They were "armed for battle" and thus were prepared in the event that the inhabitants of the land should attack while Israel was crossing the river.

14 "The LORD exalted Joshua" as he had promised (3:7). Joshua was now firmly established as leader in the place of Moses (cf. Ex 14:31).

15–18 The following order is customary in Joshua: The Lord told Joshua, Joshua told the people, and the command was obeyed. Clearly obedience is the prerequisite for God's blessing. "Dry ground" here refers to the river bank as distinct from the riverbed (cf. 3:17). The miraculous element is heightened by stressing that the waters were cut off just long enough for Israel to cross over, and then they "returned to their place."

19–20 The parallels between Moses and Joshua are obvious (cf. both crossed a body of water on dry ground, and both gave commands on "the tenth day" of the first month; cf. Ex 12:3). "Gilgal" was a strategically located town. The Jordan provided security on one side, and the open plain prevented any surprise attack from the other side. An abundant water supply was provided by the river. Joshua may have piled the stones in a heap (cf. 7:26) or he may have placed them in a circle (Gilgal sounds like the Hebrew word for circle).

21–23 Joshua foresaw the importance of these stones for future generations, as a memorial to the miraculous crossing. Again the term "dry ground" is mentioned to emphasize the supernatural aspect of the crossing. The crossings of the Red Sea and the Jordan were mighty miracles that were to be celebrated by Israel forever (cf. Ps. 114). They marked Israel's exodus from the land of bondage and entrance into the Land of Promise. They were a sign of Israel's transition from slavery to freedom.

24 This verse gives two additional reasons for this great miracle: to impress the power of Israel's God on the nations and to confirm Israel's reverence for their God.

It is possible that a landslide caused by an earthquake stopped the flow of the Jordan River. Landslides are common in the soft clay banks of the Jordan. At least two such landslides, each of which resulted in a damming of the river, are recorded in history: in A.D. 1267 and again in 1927. In the latter instance the slide occurred near the town of Adam (cf. 3:16), and the flow of the river was interrupted for about twenty-one hours. The Jordan Valley lies along one of the major faults on the earth's surface. Evidences of earthquake activity have been found in the excavations of Jericho. Moreover, there are indications in the Bible that earthquakes accompanied Israel's march into the Promised Land (Jdg 5:4–5; Ps 114:3–4, 7). If an earthquake was responsible for stopping the Jordan River, it was still a miracle. The discovery of secondary causes only serves to explain how God did what he did, and only God's intervention can account for the miraculous timing.

3. Renewing the covenant with Israel (5:1–15)

a. The covenant sign (5:1–9)

1 This transitional verse sums up the effect that the miraculous crossing of the Jordan had on the inhabitants of Canaan and explains how Israel could have been secure enough to observe the covenant ceremonies that follow. News traveled fast, even in those times (cf. 2:9–10). "Their hearts melted" with fear, but this did not result in their conversion (cf. 2:9–11; 9:9–1T).

2–3 This was the Bronze Age, when bronze implements were common; yet Joshua was commanded to make "flint knives." Religious ceremonies tend to preserve ancient customs. When God reaffirmed his covenant with Abraham, promising him the land of Canaan, he warned him that anyone who was not circumcised would be violating the covenant (Ge 17:7–14). Consequently, Israel could not claim the covenant land until the sign of the covenant had been restored (cf. Ex 4:24–26). In the instructions God gave Moses for the Passover meal, no uncircumcised males were allowed to participate (cf. Ex 12:48–49). Circumcision may have been a puberty rite in some nations, but for Israel it marked one's entrance into the covenant community. Joshua was reinstituting circumcision after it had been neglected during the forty years in the desert.

The name "Gibeath Haaraloth" has a rather grotesque meaning: "the hill of the foreskins." Throughout the Promised Land there were monuments and place names that served to remind Israel of their history.

4–6 It is strange that none of the males who were born in the desert was circumcised. The fact that Israel was always on the move is not an adequate explanation. Perhaps the sign of the covenant had been suspended while a whole generation rejected the covenant in disobedience and unbelief. Israel had disobeyed the Lord thirty-eight years earlier when they stood on the southern border of the Promised Land (Nu 13–14). The stereotyped phrase "a land flowing with milk and honey" describes the fruitfulness of the land (cf. Dt 11:9–12).

7 God was fulfilling his promise in Nu 14:31. This was a new beginning for the nation: The crossing of the Jordan symbolizes death and rebirth, and the renewal of circumcision constituted Israel anew as the people of God.

8 The Conquest had to be delayed until the men recovered, for the Israelite warriors were temporarily rendered helpless by circumcision (cf. Ge 34:25). That circumcision had to be performed at this crucial moment shows how foundational the covenant relationship was between God and Israel. It is, of course, possible that a few males were living who had been circumcised in Egypt and who were under the age of twenty at the time of Israel's disobedience (cf. v.6).

9 Since the Egyptians practiced circumcision, "the reproach of Egypt" probably means that the Israelites, now reestablished as the covenant people in the Land of Promise, had been delivered from their national disgrace of enslavement and homelessness, not that they had been unable to practice this rite in that land (cf. v.5). The name "Gilgal" sounds like the Hebrew word that means "to roll" (cf. 4:20). There are other instances in Scripture where a certain locality was given the same name on more than one occasion (cf. Ge 21:31 with Ge 26:33; Ge 28:19 with Ge 35:14–15).

b. The covenant meal (5:10–12)

10 It was the first month (cf. 4:19); consequently "the fourteenth day" was the official day for observing the Passover (see Ex 12:2, 6, 18). Though the Passover had been observed at Sinai (Nu 9:1–5), it had been neglected during the years of rejection and wandering, just as circumcision had been.

11 Another sign of a new beginning was that "they ate some of the produce of the land." "Unleavened bread" was prescribed for the entire week following the Passover (Ex 12:14–20). They had no leaven anyhow, since for nearly forty years they had been living on manna and quail.

12 Since it was no longer needed, "the manna stopped." Extraordinary means are only temporary. Now the Israelites would experience the miracle of regular harvests in the land of milk and honey.

c. The true leader of the covenant people (5:13–15)

13 On the eve of Israel's attack on Jericho, Joshua personally surveyed the area surrounding the city and inspected the fortifications. The words "he looked up" convey the element of surprise. "A man" is what Joshua thought he was seeing, but subsequent events reveal that it was no ordinary man. The man's "drawn sword" was symbolic of God's participation in the coming battle. Seeing the man standing there ready for combat provoked Joshua to inquire whether he was friend or foe.

14 The stranger's response put everything in proper perspective: God is sovereign. The stranger came as "commander of the army of the LORD"; Joshua was to be subservient to him. Though he does not reappear in the story of the Conquest, the stranger was a heavenly being who fought behind the scenes in the spiritual realm. His presence was a sign that the Lord was the real military leader of the Conquest. Many identify this person as "the angel [GK 4855] of the LORD (cf. Ex 3:2–4:17; Jdg 6:11–23; et al.) The army of the Lord was an angelic host, and they assured victory to Israel if Israel was obedient (cf. Ge 32:1–2; 2Ki 6:17).

Though "Joshua fell facedown," we cannot be sure that he realized he was in the presence of a supernatural being. In that culture persons would prostrate themselves before anyone in authority. Moreover, when Joshua said "Lord," he did not use the divine name "Yahweh," which is rendered "LORD" (see comment on 3:13). The purpose of this encounter was to inspire Joshua with humility and reverence and to instill in him the confidence that God was with him and was in control (cf. 1:9).

15 The command "Take off your sandals" does not indicate that this incident occurred at an ancient shrine. Rather, any place where God reveals himself is hallowed by that revelation (cf. Ge 28:10–22; cf. also Moses' experience in Ex 3:1–6). The events of this chapter are further evidence that the Conquest was to be accomplished by God's power. From a human point of view, it would seem to have been wiser to fulfill the rituals of circumcision and the Passover on the other side of the Jordan. But celebrating them in the Promised Land symbolized that the covenant relationship between God and Israel was a prerequisite for possessing the land.

4. The conquest of Jericho (6:1–27)

a. The Lord's instructions (6:1–5)

1 The inhabitants of Jericho were paralyzed by fear of the Israelites and of Israel's invincible God (cf. 2:9–11; 5:1). Fear of infiltration

or trickery by the enemy kept them from allowing anyone to enter. That no one was let out indicates how desperate the situation was. It was not uncommon in a time of siege to send warriors out to harass the enemies or to engage them in battle. Sometimes a small party was sent out secretly in search of help or supplies.

2 With the words "I have delivered Jericho," Joshua was reminded that victory comes only from the Lord (cf. Ps 108:12–13). Moreover, the tense of the verb indicates that the battle had already been won (cf. 2:9). The conquest of a walled city was a major challenge. The Israelites had not encountered walled cities before; and after their many years of wandering in the desert, they were not equipped for such an undertaking. High walls had discouraged the spies forty years earlier (Nu 13:28).

3 The command to "march around the city once" seems senseless and required faith that God would keep his promise to deliver the city into their hands (Heb 11:30). The stratagem of waiting seven days has a number of biblical parallels (cf. Ex 24:16; 1Ki 20:29; 2Ki 3:9; et al.)

Inside Jericho all routine pursuits had been given up, and every effort was aimed at defense. When the armed men of Israel merely marched around the city day after day, the vigilance may have relaxed. On the other hand, this senseless marching may have completely demoralized the defenders, who would have been totally confused about what was going on. The march around the city too was another expression of God's grace, giving the people one last opportunity (an entire week) to repent. Only "the armed men" were involved.

4 Seven is the number of divine perfection or completeness. The emphasis on the number seven (fourteen times in this chapter), the use of ceremonial trumpets (made from ram's horns), the presence of priests, and the prominence of the ark all indicate that the conquest of Jericho was more than a military campaign; it was a religious event. Israel must always remember that the land was God's gift to them.

5 "A long blast" was a signal distinct from the continual blowing of the trumpets. The phrase "all the people" means "the whole army," excluding women and children. The "loud shout" was a war cry intended to encourage their fellows and intimidate the enemy. In v.10 we are informed that Joshua had ordered the people to be silent during all the marching up to this point. The way that God would give them the city is now revealed: "The wall of the city will collapse." That "every man [went] straight in" means that from their positions all around the city, the Israelites were able to go directly in—though not necessarily in a perfectly straight line—so that the city would be attacked in every quarter at the same time.

b. The attack on Jericho (6:6–21)

6–7 Though repetitious, the account is not tedious. The suspense builds until it reaches its climax in v.20. The orders Joshua passed on to the people are summarized here (cf. vv.2–5). Separate orders were given to the priests and to the people.

8 The phrase "before the LORD" is a vivid reminder that the ark symbolized God's presence. The parallel statement in v.4 says that the seven priests were to carry seven horns *before the ark.*

9–10 The presence of warriors before and behind the ark indicates that the Israelites would have to fight. Perhaps the "armed guard" mentioned here consisted of the two and one-half tribes from Transjordan (cf. 4:12–13). Because of the privileges granted them, they were to lead the others into every battle. Joshua's instructions here recall the orders he had given earlier (vv.6–7.; cf. v.5).

11 No details are given as to how the march was conducted. Jericho occupied only about five or six acres of land. Even though the Israelites must have maintained sufficient distance from the city to be safely beyond the range of enemy arrows, it is possible that the head of the column had arrived back at the camp before the last of the rear guard left.

12–14 This repetitious narrative conveys something of the tedium of marching around the city day after day for six days.

15 On the seventh day the Israelites set out "at daybreak" because of all that needed to be accomplished that day. Considering the size of Jericho and the number of Israelite troops, it is likely that when "they circled the city seven times," the column doubled over on itself again and again until the city was surrounded many columns deep.

16–17 The eagerly awaited command to shout was given. Before telling us what happened, details are inserted (vv.17–19) concerning commands that Joshua must have given earlier (vv.6–7). "Devoted" represents the Hebrew word translated "completely destroyed" in 2:10 (see comment on 2:10). Jericho was Israel's first conquest in the land of Canaan, a kind of firstfruits; therefore everything in it was holy—humans, animals, and property—and was to be consecrated to the Lord (cf. Ex 23:31–33; 34:11–14; Dt 2:32–35; 3:3–7; 20:16–18; et al.).

Rahab's profession continues to be mentioned here and in vv.22 and 25 to emphasize that she was a trophy of God's grace. Her hiding of the spies is stated as the reason for her deliverance (cf. Heb 11:31; Jas 2:25). The themes of judgment and salvation often appear side by side in Scripture (cf. Ge 6–8; 19:1–29; see also Jn 3:16–21).

18–19 Joshua had made it plain that the whole nation could be devoted to destruction through the action of a single person. This verse prepares us for the story of Achan (ch. 7). Metals are not destroyed by fire. They had to be removed from common use by being placed in the treasury of the sanctuary to provide for the necessities of the sanctuary and the priests.

20–21 The narrative, which has been interrupted by the instructions concerning the things devoted to destruction, is now resumed. To emphasize the divine intervention, no secondary causes for the collapse of the wall are mentioned. The destruction of the defenders of the city together with their women and children involved the Israelites in hand-to-hand combat. Their enemies were not able to fight effectively because they were demoralized, outnumbered, and taken by surprise. Everything in the city was devoted to the Lord.

c. Rahab rescued and Jericho cursed (6:22–27)

22–23 Evidently the part of the wall where Rahab's house was located was miraculously preserved. Rahab and her family were put in "a place outside the camp" as a kind of ritual

quarantine. The camp of Israel was holy, and nothing unclean could be allowed to enter (cf. Lev 13:46; Nu 5:3; 31:19; Dt 23:3, 14). After the passage of time and the observance of appropriate rituals, they were received into the congregation (see v.25).

24–25 The term "the LORD's house" is generally applied only to the temple, though the Bible often applies later terminology to an earlier institution. The statement "she [Rahab] lives among the Israelites to this day" most likely means that Rahab lived on in her posterity, not that this account was written during her lifetime. Thus concludes the two themes of ch. 2: the capture of Jericho and the salvation of Rahab.

26 The city of Jericho was to remain an object lesson of God's great victory in Israel's very first battle. Though the city was soon resettled (18:21; Jdg 3:13–14; 2Sa 10:5), the curse uttered here was not fulfilled until the time of King Ahab, when Hiel, a resident of Bethel, rebuilt *the wall* around Jericho to make it a fortress once again (see comment on 1Ki 16:34).

27 Joshua was firmly established as leader in Israel (cf. 1:1–9; 2:9–11; 4:14; 5:1–3). The statement "The LORD was with Joshua" marks the climax of his rise to leadership, fulfilling God's promise in 1:5. The people had pledged their loyalty to Joshua on the condition that the Lord would be with him (1:17). This triumphant summary statement in no way prepares us for the disaster in ch. 7.

5. The conquest of Ai (7:1–8:29)

a. Achan's sin (7:1–26)

1 Israel's sin, a violation of their covenant with the Lord, was serious. Though the crime was committed by one person, the whole nation was considered guilty and was charged with the punishment of the offender (cf. 1Co 5:6–13).

However unfair it may seem, experience shows that the wrongdoing of a single individual has adverse effects on others (cf. Dt 5:9). Moreover, this was a time of war, and strict discipline had to be maintained. God's judgment on sin was viewed as a result of his anger (cf. Ro 1:18–32). His judgment on the Canaanites was not arbitrary; it was the consequence of their sin, and now, when God's chosen people sin, they too must be judged.

2 "Ai" (GK 6504) means "a ruins." This may not have been the name of the city, since it is a term that could be applied to any ruins; to specify which ruins is meant, the text states that it was near Bethel (cf. 12:9). "Beth Aven" means "house of wickedness" (cf. Hos 4:15; 5:8; 10:5). Joshua confined most of his military exploits to the mountainous areas where the inhabitants were unable to use chariots. The conquest of Ai and Bethel seems to be part of a strategy to divide the central mountains in the middle and thus prevent any united defense.

In planning his attack, Joshua sent out spies as he had done earlier at Jericho. This was the first time in the Conquest that Joshua did anything on his own initiative, and it was doomed to failure. It is ominous that nothing is said about Joshua seeking guidance from the Lord. The great victory at Jericho made him overly confident of God's help.

3 The total population of Ai was estimated to be about twelve thousand (8:25). With armies of equal size, the defenders inside the city walls would have a considerable advantage. The confidence of the spies was inspired by their memory of Israel's great victory over Jericho and of God's intervention. The climb to Ai was 3,300 feet.

4–5 In spite of Joshua's sending the larger number of troops suggested by the spies, the Israelites suffered a humiliating defeat. While thirty-six casualties out of three thousand troops is not a great loss, it was symbolic of Israel's resounding defeat. In the type of warfare that was fought in those days, it was not uncommon for the victor to have no casualties at all (cf. Nu 31:48–49). The very same words that Rahab had used to describe the demoralized population of Jericho (2:9, 11; cf. 5:1) are here applied to Israel.

6 Joshua and the elders went into mourning, expressing great grief at Israel's defeat. Joshua immediately turned to God. He was able to approach the ark more freely than the high priest (cf. Lev 16:2). He, not the high priest, was responsible to intercede for the people. The actions of Joshua and the elders were not indications of repentance; they were expressions of anger, frustration, and distress.

7–8 Joshua addressed God in a reverent manner, but that did not keep him from arguing with God. If victory was to be attributed to God's help, then defeat must come from God's failure to intervene. Joshua accused God of wanting to destroy his people. He was struggling here as a man of faith who was brutally honest with God and was seeking answers to his urgent questions. Yet his comment about Israel being content to dwell on the east of the Jordan (cf. Ex 16:3) came dangerously close to the way Israel had reasoned at Kadesh Barnea (Nu 14:1–4). Had he forgotten that God himself had commanded them to cross over into Canaan? In self-pity Joshua charged God with capriciousness. He believed that the defeat of Israel meant the end of his leadership.

9 Joshua was well aware that the report of Israel's victories had demoralized and immobilized the people of Canaan. The worst part of their defeat was that Israel had lost this great advantage; now their enemies would be encouraged to fight back. Moreover, if Israel was destroyed, God's name would be disgraced. In OT times a "name" (GK 9005) was more than just an identity. It stood for one's person and reputation. This was not special pleading; Joshua was showing genuine concern (cf. Ex 32:12–13; Nu 14:13–19; Dt 9:26–29).

10 The Lord's command for Joshua to "stand up" was not a rebuke but a response to an honest and reverent prayer. This was no time for self-pity; it was time for action.

11 Since the gift of the land was part of God's covenant with Israel, Joshua should have known that defeat was not due to any fickleness on God's part but had been caused by Israel's failure to be faithful to the covenant. In God's eyes the whole nation was implicated in the sin of Achan; his crime was their crime: "they have lied." They had taken as their own things that had been dedicated to God.

12 God's warning had come true (see comment on 6:18); now the Israelites themselves must be devoted to destruction. No more dreadful threat is imaginable than that God would no longer be with Israel (cf. climax of chs. 1–6 in 6:27), but that is exactly what is being threatened here. If, however, the people will take action to "destroy whatever among you is devoted," they will demonstrate their innocence and preserve their relationship with God (cf. 2Co 7:5–12).

13 The people had to be consecrated again (cf. 3:5)—an act that was necessary whenever God was going to act in some special way. Now he was coming in judgment to remove the defilement from his people.

14 The people were to present themselves to the Lord by appearing before the sanctuary by family units. There is no specific statement as to how the Lord would single out the culprit (cf. 1Sa 10:19–24; cf. 14:36–43), but presumably it was by lot. The decision was placed solely in the hands of God (cf. Pr 16:33).

15 Though corporate responsibility was stressed, individual responsibility and guilt were not overlooked: The culprit "shall be destroyed," absolving the nation of guilt. The death penalty here was made even more offensive by burning the offender's body (cf. Ge 38:24; Lev 21:9). "All that belongs to him" is ambiguous; in v.24 both persons and possessions are included.

16–18 In the selection process each tribe, clan, and family was represented by a single individual. To us the procedure seems to leave everything up to chance. For them it left everything in the hands of God, and, in the final analysis, the right person was chosen.

19 Though Joshua deals gently and fairly with Achan, some indignation and vindictiveness are apparent in v.25. The expression "give glory [GK 3883] to the LORD" is an appeal for an honest confession (cf. Jn 9:24). Confession of sin is a way of honoring God. Joshua did not rely solely on the selection by lot. Personal confession and the gathering of evidence were also required (vv.22–23).

20 Achan confessed his sin but was not forgiven because he did not confess willingly (cf. Ps 32; 1Jn 1:9). His silence during the long process of casting lots gave evidence of the hardness of his heart.

21 Achan called what he took "plunder" (GK 8965)—as something customarily divided among the victors. "Shekel" denotes a measure of weight, not a coin. "Wedge" indicates an ingot or a bar. Coveting is often the beginning of a sinful action. The same three verbs "I saw," "I coveted," "I took" are found in the story of the Fall (Ge 3:6; cf. Jas 1:13–15).

Achan hid the things he took because he knew he had sinned.

22–23 The messengers located the hidden booty, brought it to Joshua, and spread everything "before the LORD," i.e., at the Tent of Meeting (cf. v.14), because God is the final Judge.

24 Representatives of the entire nation participated in punishing Achan to remove the guilt from all the people. Apparently Achan did not have a wife at this time. The punishment of children for the sin of their father is an offense to our sense of justice, but Achan's family was implicated in his crime because he could not have hidden his loot under his tent without their knowing it. Moreover, this punishment is an example of the severe discipline necessary in time of war. Judging by his possessions, Achan had little need for what he stole. "Achor" (a pun on Achan's name; cf. 1Ch 2:7) means "disaster."

25–26 Once again "all Israel" refers to representatives from the whole nation, acting in accord with their promise to Joshua in 1:18. Achan and his family were stoned and burned, and stones were heaped on them. After Achan's sin had been judged, "the LORD turned from his fierce anger," and Israel was restored to favor (cf. also Ac 5:1-11 and comments).

b. The second attack on Ai (8:1–29)

1 Now that the sin of Achan had been dealt with, God reassured Israel of his presence and help (cf. 1:9). But Joshua would still have to use common sense and the best military strategy. It is not clear how many men constituted "the whole army" (cf. the numbers in vv.3, 12). Perhaps the 30,000 in v.3 is the size of the whole army whereas the 5,000 in v.12 is the number of troops in the ambush. The rest of the army would have been held in reserve.

2 Only the king and the people were to be devoted to destruction (see comment on 6:17); the plunder and livestock from Ai and all subsequent cities could be kept by Israel and would be their means of support throughout the years of conquest. God explicitly commanded Joshua to "set an ambush." Surprise is a necessary strategy in warfare. "Behind the city" probably means behind it from the standpoint of Israel's base of operations (on the west, v.12). This would be the least suspected area from which to stage an attack.

3 Most likely only five thousand constituted the actual ambush (v.12). It would be difficult even for a detachment of that number to avoid detection between Ai and Bethel. Presumably vv.10–13 report the carrying out of what was commanded in vv.3–9. The movement of troops "at night" was one of Joshua's successful strategies (cf. 10:9).

4–5 Joshua's men were to be ready to move at a moment's notice. Israel's new strategy required careful coordination and quick action. By drawing a sufficient number of the defenders away from the city, they could make its capture relatively easy. This involved a great risk, however, because a fleeing army was far more likely to suffer casualties.

6–7 The ruse depended on making the attack appear similar to the previous one. The troops waiting in ambush were to move in when the defenders were drawn from the city. Verses 18–19 suggest that the troops waited for a signal from Joshua.

8 The troops in ambush were to "set it on fire" to notify Joshua and the Israelites that the city had been taken. This would demoralize the enemy. With their wives and children killed and their homes destroyed (cf. v.28), what would they have left to fight for? This time the Israelites must "do what the LORD has commanded."

9 Joshua set up the ambush "between Bethel and Ai" to avoid the main route between the two cities. He did not try to prevent Bethel from assisting Ai, because any engagement with the army from Bethel would have exposed the ambush. Joshua spent the night with the main army.

10–13 It was night when "they set up camp" (cf. v.3); so the army's presence was not detected until the next morning. Though the numbers are difficult to harmonize, v.12 repeats the action described more fully in vv.3–9. Joshua went into the valley when everything was ready. Apparently he spent the night scouting the valley in preparation for battle the next day (cf. 5:13–15).

14–15 Eager for victory and overly confident, the king of Ai "hurried out." The "Ar-

abah" is a desert area (this word commonly refers to the Jordan Valley). "Toward the desert" likely refers to a road leading from the vicinity of Ai (or Bethel) to Aphek.

16–17 The proximity of Bethel may have encouraged that army to come to the aid of Ai. Thus, the Israelite ambush had to be hidden from the main road to keep the troops coming from Bethel also from discovering them. In their confidence of an easy victory, "they left the city open" without anyone there to defend it.

18–19 Joshua's use of the javelin is another indication that God was directing the army of Israel (cf. Ex 17:8–12); Joshua did not bring his hand down until the victory over Ai was complete (v.26). This action symbolizes that victory comes from the Lord. Apparently holding out the javelin was a prearranged signal. The men in ambush would not have been able to see it, but they could have had scouts posted.

20–21 The statement "they had no chance to escape in any direction" suggests that the men of Bethel and Ai lost their will to fight when they saw that their families and possessions were gone. The smoke rising from Ai was the signal to Joshua that the ambush had been successful.

22–23 No distinction should be made between "survivors" and "fugitives." The key captive, "the king," was not killed in the battle but was taken to Joshua.

24–27 We are surprised to learn that there were still survivors in the city. Evidently the troops in ambush had not destroyed all the inhabitants of the city before setting it on fire. The chapter is silent about what happened to the army from Bethel, though they must have also been destroyed (cf. 12:16; "destroyed," the same word as used in 6:17; see comment on 2:10). Joshua was careful to do everything in conformity with God's commands. Clearly the Lord was in control this time.

28 "Heap" (GK 9424) refers to a particular kind of mound formed by the ruins of a walled city. The phrase "to this day" indicates that Ai had not been rebuilt at the time the narrative was composed. Apparently it was never rebuilt, though Joshua did not pronounce any curse against Ai as he had Jericho (6:26).

29 The king of Ai was not executed by hanging, yet his body was impaled on a tree or pole to add to his disgrace. To display the lifeless body of the king whom they had feared was another way of bolstering the morale of the Israelites. They were forbidden to leave a body hanging overnight because it would desecrate the land (Dt 21:23). This law required also that the body be buried the same day. The king of Ai's body was entombed in a pile of rocks so that it might serve as a vivid object lesson for future generations.

6. Covenant renewal at Mount Ebal (8:30–35)

30 By building the altar and offering sacrifices on it, Joshua acknowledged the Lord as the source of every victory and blessing and claimed this territory in the name of the Lord. It was an appropriate time to worship now that Israel had established a foothold in the central highlands. Mount Ebal became the place of worship at this time in Israel's history.

Because the narrative says nothing about any Israelite conquest of the area around Mount Ebal and Mount Gerizim, perhaps the inhabitants were friendly to Israel, or it is possible that the battle of Ai is symbolic of the conquest of the entire mountainous area in central Palestine. The Israelites could celebrate this ritual of covenant renewal in peace because God had placed the fear of Israel in the hearts of the natives.

31 The use of "uncut stones" in constructing the altar (cf. Ex 20:25) is either a reaction to pagan culture or another example of the conservatism of religion (see 5:2), since the use of iron tools was a recent innovation.

32 The law "copied on stones" (special stones covered with plaster that Moses had commanded to be prepared for this purpose; Dt 27:4) was to be the basis of Israel's life in the land. The people's faithfulness to this law would determine their fortunes.

33 From the time of the Exodus, aliens who chose to live and worship with Israel were assimilated into the nation (cf. 1Ki 8:41–43), and they participated in the covenant renewal. "The ark of the covenant" was placed in the center of the assembly as a symbol of God's presence. Everything was done as Moses "had formerly commanded" (cf. Dt 11:29; 27:11–26). The emphasis here is on the positive blessings, even though Moses' command included both blessing and cursing (cf. v.34).

34–35 The public reading of the law had both a practical and a ceremonial function. It impressed the people with their responsibility to obey. The Israelites were always to be considerate of "the aliens who lived among them" because they too had been aliens living in slavery in Egypt (Ex 22:21; 23:9; Dt 24:17–22).

C. The Southern Campaign (9:1–10:43)

1. The Gibeonite deception (9:1–27)

a. The treaty with Israel (9:1–15)

1–2 All the city-states in mountainous regions of southern Palestine joined forces against Joshua. No longer would he be able to conquer one city at a time. No longer would the reports of earlier victories lead them to suppose that Israel was invincible. In resisting Israel, however, they were resisting God. Their stubborn rebellion was eloquent testimony that the sin of the Amorites had reached its full measure (cf. Ge 15:16).

3–5 Gibeon (see 10:2 for its importance) and several other cities (see v.17) joined together and spared no effort in trying to deceive and convince Joshua and Israel that they lived in a faraway country. Somehow they must have known that God had forbidden Israel to make any treaties or to save alive any of the inhabitants of the land (Dt 7:1–3; 20:16–18). "Dry and moldy" bread probably means "dry and crumbly," since dry bread is not likely to become moldy.

6 "Gilgal" is where Israel had had its base of operations since first entering the land (4:19). It is surprising that Joshua continued to use this as his base camp even after he had established a foothold in the mountainous region at Ai because of the arduous climb from Gilgal to the central mountain range. Perhaps Gilgal provided a more secure place for their families and livestock. The phrase "men of Israel" refers to the same group of officers who are called "leaders of the assembly" in vv.15 and 18 and "elders" in 8:33.

7 The narrator identifies the inhabitants of Gibeon as "Hivites." This was one of the nations God had promised to drive out of the land before Israel (3:10). The leaders' question—"perhaps you live near us"—indicates suspicion.

8 When the Gibeonites said, "We are your servants," they were offering to become Israel's vassals. In return they expected Israel, the stronger party, to protect them from their enemies (cf. 10:6). Their offer provoked Joshua to ask, "Where do you come from?" Joshua and the leaders were persistent in their attempt to carry out the Lord's command, even though they did not seek the Lord's guidance.

9–10 The Gibeonites' statement that they had come "because of the fame [or "name"; GK 9005] of the LORD your God" is the key statement. Though the incident is filled with tension and contradiction, the Gibeonites were drawn by the great name of the Lord and were spared. They admitted that God's mighty acts on behalf of Israel had made his great name known far and wide (cf. 2:9–11). Just as Rahab had done, the Gibeonites believed the reports about the God of Israel; and fear drove them to seek to come under his protection and to scheme in order to escape annihilation at the hand of the Israelites. In rehearsing the mighty acts of the Lord, the Gibeonites carefully omitted recent events that they would not have known about had they really come from a far country. Yet the matters they omitted were the very things that motivated them to seek a treaty with Israel (cf. v.3).

11–13 The Gibeonites spoke of their "elders," but not their king—possibly because they did not have a king. They presented their contrived evidence to the Israelites to prove that they had come a very long way.

14 Strangely, the Israelite leaders "sampled their provisions" in spite of the fact that they were dry and moldy. Eating together was often a part of making a treaty (cf. Ge 31:54). How tragic that the leaders were so impressed by the Gibeonites' stale provisions that they (including Joshua!) failed once again to seek God's guidance! Joshua especially should have known better. He had gone up the mountain of revelation with Moses (Ex 24:13–14); and in his preparation for leadership, he had been trained in the use of the Urim and Thummim for determining the will of God (Nu 27:18–21). How easy it is even in the service of the Lord to take God's guidance and blessing for granted!

15 Joshua made an alliance with the Gibeonites and concluded a treaty with them to protect their lives. This treaty committed Israel to more than simply sparing the Gibeonites' lives. They would have to come to their defense in all kinds of danger. This treaty was not valid until "the leaders of the assembly ratified it."

b. The ruse discovered (9:16–27)

16 Scarcely had the treaty been concluded when the Israelites learned that they had been deceived. As their "neighbors," the Gibeonites were some of the very people whom Israel had been commanded to exterminate and with whom they were to make no treaties, lest they be tempted into idolatry (Dt 7:1–6; 20:16–18).

17 Some of the Israelites were intent on violence against the cities in league with the Gibeonites, but they were restrained by their leaders (v.18).

18 "The whole assembly grumbled," possibly because they were resentful of the plunder that had been denied them. On the other hand, they may have been fearful of another judgment like that at Ai, because they had failed to keep God's command.

The Gibeonites, who became "water carriers" for the Israelites, were known for their excellent wells, which are being excavated today. Courtesy Werner Braun.

19 The "oath" (GK 8678) was made in the name of the Lord. Consequently fidelity was owed, not to the Gibeonites, but to the Lord. The form of the oath called on the Lord to punish the Israelites if they failed to keep their agreement (cf. vv.18–20). This explains why Israel felt bound to the treaty even though it had been made under false pretenses (cf. Ge 27:35; Ps 15:4).

20 The word for "wrath" (GK 7912) usually has the idea of divine retribution that inevitably follows the violation of some divine decree (cf. 22:20; Nu 1:53; 18:5). Many years later God's wrath did fall on Israel when King Saul violated this treaty (2Sa 21:1–9).

21 The Gibeonites were reduced to menial service as "woodcutters and water carriers" (cf. Dt 20:10–15; cf. Jos 16:10; 17:13; et al.). There is some confusion whether they were to serve "the entire community" or to serve "the house of my God" (see v.23); in v.27 both ideas are combined. Possibly they were to cut the wood and draw the water needed for the temple ritual, a duty that normally fell to the community.

22–23 At first Joshua's question seems humorous, if not ridiculous. Obviously the Gibeonites did what they did to save their lives! Even Joshua's curse of subservience does not seem to be serious, since the Gibeonites had escaped the sentence of death. For pagans to come and serve at the Lord's sanctuary is surely a blessing (cf. Ps 84:10).

24–25 The Gibeonites did not anticipate the degrading sentence imposed on them, but they preferred to live. As in the case of Rahab, fear led to their salvation. The statement "Do to us whatever seems good and right to you" was not simple resignation on the part of the Gibeonites. They knew the Israelites would be duty bound to treat them kindly.

26–27 Joshua, being a leader of integrity, accepted the Gibeonites' surrender. Worship was to be limited to one central sanctuary as a testimony to the fact that there was only one Lord (Dt 6:4) and in order to preserve the unity of the nation. This central sanctuary was located successively at Shechem, Shiloh, and Gibeon. Ultimately, of course, the site of the one sanctuary would be located in Jerusalem.

2. Israel's victory over the southern coalition (10:1–43)

a. The rescue of the Gibeonites (10:1–15)

1 One of the principal kings in the south gathered the whole region together to fight against Israel. News of Israel's victories at Jericho and Ai, with the extermination of all their inhabitants, struck fear into the heart of Adoni-Zedek (whose name means "Lord of Righteousness"). "Jerusalem," formerly called Jebus (Jdg 19:10), was a stronghold of the Jebusites, one of the seven nations the Israelites were to drive out of the land (3:10). Though the king and his army were killed by Joshua and Israel, the city itself was not captured until after Joshua's death (Jdg 1:8; cf. 2Sa 5:6–9).

2 The defection of the Gibeonites was cause for great alarm for three reasons: (1) it was discouraging to see such a large city with an excellent army surrender to the enemy, (2) without Gibeon the southern coalition was severely weakened, and (3) they constituted a fifth column that would fight with Israel in time of war. Gibeon was obviously a strong and influential city-state (cf. 11:12).

3–5 The kings of four other cities south and west of Jerusalem joined forces with Adoni-Zedek to attack the traitor city of Gibeon. They had to be punished to prevent any further defections to Israel and to eliminate the threat of their siding with Israel in time of war.

6 The Gibeonites turned to Joshua for help because the treaty of peace (9:15) obligated Joshua to defend them as his vassals.

7–8 The march from Gilgal to Gibeon involved an ascent of 3,300 feet. It is not clear whether "all the best fighting men" is descriptive of the whole Israelite army or only a special division of elite troops. The Lord assured Joshua that victory would be theirs.

9–10 A forced march under the cover of darkness was another of Joshua's well-planned strategies. The march, which covered a distance of about twenty miles, would have taken eight to ten hours. Joshua took the enemy by surprise, and the Lord used this to create disorder. Again human efforts and divine intervention worked hand in hand. The pass at Beth Horon, about five miles northwest of Gibeon, was an important point of access to the hill country and to Jerusalem.

11 Joshua pursued his enemy along the ancient road that went from Lachish to the Valley of Aijalon. In disarray the enemy fled down from the mountains through the pass at Beth Horon and headed south. God then intervened on behalf of his people with "large hailstones," a miracle that dwarfed the accomplishments of Israel's army. It was the Lord who won the victory. The Canaanites, who worshiped nature deities, must have thought that their own gods were aiding the Israelites.

12 This miracle is often called "Joshua's long day." It is the third and last great miracle in the book and the most bewildering. The NIV is correct in arranging vv.12b–13a as poetic, and they must be interpreted accordingly. The Hebrew word translated "stand still" (GK 1957) is often translated "be silent." Joshua may have been requesting that the sun not shine with its normal brightness and heat. Joshua desired favorable conditions so as to be able to make the most of the victory. After an all-night march, the sun's heat would have sapped the strength of the weary Israelites; and relief from that heat would have helped just as much as extended daylight. (At a certain time of the month the moon is visible in the daytime. Its mention here provides a poetic parallel to the sun.)

13 The Hebrew word for "stood still" (GK 1957) was used in 3:16 to say that the waters of the Jordan "stopped flowing." In a poetic passage like this, it could mean "stop moving" or even "stop shining." "The Book of Jashar" (i.e., "the book of the righteous") is mentioned also in 2Sa 1:18. Like other ancient books (cf. 1Ki 14:19, 29), this bit of ancient Hebrew literature has been lost. All of vv.12–15 may have been quoted from that source. The final statement in this verse does clearly favor the interpretation that the sun stood still or that it slowed down in its course across the sky.

14–15 "There has never been a day like it before" (cf. 2Ki 18:5; 23:25) shows something very spectacular occurred that day that elevated Joshua as a man of God: his prayers were unusually effective. This episode reminds us again that Israel was not winning the land by their own strength; God was giving it to them.

Verse 15 seems out of place here. The events of vv.16–27 are part of the battle, and it is very unlikely that Joshua returned to Gilgal in the middle of it all. There are two plausible suggestions: (1) This verse may conclude the quotation from the Book of Jashar. (2) Verses 7–14 may describe the battle in terms of the supernatural assistance, and vv.16–42 may go over the same ground supplying details about the fate of the various kings and their cities. In this case v.15 and v.43 describe the same event.

b. The execution of the five Amorite kings (10:16–28)

16–18 "The five kings" are named in v.3. "Large rocks" were placed at the entrance of the cave to prevent the kings who "had been found hiding" there from escaping and thus to free the warriors to pursue the enemy.

19–20 The warriors were encouraged to fight hard, "for the LORD your God has given them into your hand." As many as possible of the enemy were to be slain in the open fields, because it would be nearly impossible to capture them once they had reached their fortified cities. There were indeed a few survivors who managed to get to the cities, but by and large the enemy was totally annihilated.

21 The statement that "The whole army then returned safely" implies that the Israelites suffered no casualties. Apparently the campaign took longer than this abbreviated account might lead one to suppose. The observation that "no one uttered a word" provides another parallel in the careers of Moses and Joshua (cf. Ex 11:7).

22–24 Joshua did all he could to bolster the morale of his troops, so he humiliated the five kings before they were killed. When the officers placed their feet on the necks of these great kings (a widespread practice in ancient times; cf. 1Ki 5:3; Ps 110:1), they recognized that they were frail human beings like everyone else.

25–26 The words "be strong and courageous" remind us of ch. 1 (vv.6–7, 9, 18). The bodies of the kings were hung on trees to make them an example and to add to their humiliation (see comment on 8:29).

27 The bodies of the kings were taken down "at sunset" to keep from defiling the land (cf. Dt 21:23). The cave provided a convenient place for their burial. Piling large rocks at the entrance, the Israelites created a memorial to keep alive the memory of another victory God had given Israel.

28 "That day" most likely means "at that time." For "totally destroyed" see comments on 2:10; 6:17. This comparison with the king of Jericho is strange because no details were given as to how Joshua treated him (cf. 6:20–21, 24).

c. The completion of the southern campaign (10:29–43)

29–30 Libnah, Makkedah, and Debir were not included in the coalition. Joshua was beginning to secure the foothills before invading the mountains. Joshua devoted the entire population to God by destruction (cf. v.28; 2:10).

31–33 The words "On the second day" suggest that the campaign in the south continued for several days or weeks. "Gezer" is near the entrance to the Valley of Aijalon, about a day's march north of Lachish. Joshua destroyed the king and his army, though he did not follow through to capture the city itself (cf. 16:10).

34–39 Leaving the foothills Joshua moved into the highlands and captured the two principal cities with their surrounding villages. By this time Hebron may have already enthroned a new king (cf. vv. 25–26). Joshua "totally destroyed it and everyone in it."

40 This comprehensive statement of Joshua's victories in the south demonstrates that the accounts of the capture of a few cities is only a sketchy summary of the more important victories in an extensive campaign. "The hill country" is the central mountain range principally in Judah and Ephraim. "The Negev" is the desert in southern Palestine. "The western foothills" is the area between the hill country of Judah and the coastal plain. "The mountain slopes" refers to the steep descent from the mountains to the Jordan Valley. Neither Jerusalem (Jdg 1:8) nor Jarmuth were conquered at this time, but the Con-

quest was extensive enough to give Israel control of the area. Probably the expression "all who breathed" did not include the livestock, which the Israelites were permitted to take as booty.

41–43 The phrase "from Kadesh Barnea to Gaza" denotes a large area in southern Palestine. We have no way of determining the length of this "one campaign," but it must have taken a considerable amount of time. Victory in the south clearly demonstrated that "the LORD, the God of Israel, fought for Israel." The Israelites did not occupy these cities immediately. Instead they returned to their families and livestock in their base camp "at Gilgal."

D. The Northern Campaign (11:1–15)

1. The northern coalition formed (11:1–5)

1 "Jabin" may have been a dynastic name assumed by all kings of Hazor (cf. Jdg 4:2). "Hazor" was by far the most imposing city in all of Palestine, covering about two hundred acres (cf. the five or six acres of Jericho). With its allies and armaments, Hazor confronted Joshua and Israel with their last and most awesome challenge.

2 The cities named in v.1 were south of Hazor, but Jabin also summoned "the northern kings." The thirty-one kings named in 12:9–24 are probably only the more important ones. Jabin assembled the kings of the Jordan Valley ("the Arabah"), the area around the Sea of Galilee ("Kinnereth"), and the coastal plain south of Mount Carmel ("Naphoth Dor").

3 Since "Canaanite" was a generic term for all who lived in the lowlands, "the Canaanites in the east" must refer to the people living in the Jordan Valley (cf. Nu 13:29). The Amorites, Hittites, Perizzites, and Jebusites lived in the hill country. The inhabitants of Jerusalem were Jebusites. Joshua destroyed the army of the "Jebusites" (10:9–14) and killed Adoni-Zedek their king (10:22–27), but he did not capture their city. Possibly survivors from the southern campaign rallied to the support of the northern coalition. "Hermon" is the highest mountain in the Anti-Lebanon range.

4–5 Though Palestine at this time was made up of independent and hostile city-states, the presence of a common enemy caused them to rally to Jabin's call. The northern coalition was Israel's most formidable foe. "Horses and chariots" posed an awesome challenge to the Israelites, whose army was made up solely of foot soldiers. All previous battles had been on terrain where the use of chariots was not feasible. The kings apparently gathered in the mountainous area of Wadi Meiron (4000 foot elevation) to develop their strategy, not to do battle.

2. The major battle (11:6–9)

6, 9 Before this last and most challenging battle, Joshua did not fail to consult the Lord. Disabling the horses and burning the chariots showed disdain for modern weaponry; Israel's confidence was to be in God alone (cf. Ps 20:7). Early Israelite tradition is consistently negative toward the use of horses and chariots (cf. Dt 17:16; 2Sa 8:4; Isa 31:1).

7–8 Joshua again resorted to a surprise attack (cf. 10:9). The enemies were caught unprepared and were driven into the mountains where chariots could not be used. Once again victory was God's gift to Israel. The defeated enemy fled in a northerly direction. Sidon is on the Phoenician coast north of Mount Carmel. "The Valley of Mizpah" must have been in the north in the vicinity of Sidon and Misrephoth Maim.

3. The capture of the northern cities (11:10–15)

10 The phrase "at that time" may denote the same day or later. After he defeated the combined armies, Joshua "turned back" from pursuing his enemies in the north and concentrated on individual cities, beginning with the city of Hazor. The execution of the king, as usual, is mentioned separately. Perhaps the kings were killed with some special ceremony as in 10:22–27.

11 Joshua faithfully carried out the command that all the inhabitants of the land be devoted to the Lord by totally destroying them (cf. comments on 2:10; 6:21). As in 10:40, "anything that breathed" refers only to human beings. Archaeological excavations indicate that Hazor was destroyed sometime in the late fifteenth century B.C. and was not rebuilt until the time of Solomon (cf. 1Ki 9:15).

12–15 Following Moses' command, Joshua took the "royal cities," i.e., city-states each of which had its own king (cf. 10:2). The burning of the cities had not been commanded by God (cf. Dt 7:1–6; 20:16–18); consequently, they were ready immediately for reoccupation by Israel. As the Lord had promised, the Israelites would live in cities they did not build and would have food that they had not worked for (Dt 6:10–11).

Once again we are reminded that victory and blessing are the outcome of obedience. Joshua had done everything the Lord commanded Moses. The writer uses extravagant language—"he left nothing undone"—to celebrate Joshua's obedience and Israel's great victories even though he does not hesitate in succeeding chapters to indicate that the Conquest was still incomplete (cf. 13:1–5, 13; 15:63; 16:10; 17:12).

E. A Summary of the Conquest (11:16–23)

16–17 Joshua gained control of the whole region even though he did not take every individual city. The last of the Canaanites were not subjected to Israel's authority until the reign of David. The author describes in great detail the geography of the Promised Land that Joshua had captured—from north to south and from east to west. The western coastal plains where the Canaanites were able to use their chariots are not mentioned (cf. 9:1) because Joshua did not conquer those areas (cf. 17:16; Jdg 1:19). The southern coastland was the stronghold of the Philistines, who continued to harass Israel until they were finally subdued by David.

18 Though creating the impression of a lightning-quick campaign, the Conquest really took "a long time" (cf. God's statement to Moses in Ex 23:29–30). Undoubtedly the Conquest involved many battles not mentioned.

19–20 The surrender of the Gibeonites was one small exception to the general rule of totally annihilating the population of Canaan. God hardened the Canaanites' hearts, not to keep them from repenting, but to prevent them from surrendering to Israel in unrepentance. The examples of Rahab and the Gibeonites demonstrate the unchanging purpose of God that "Everyone who calls on the name of the Lord will be saved" (Ro 10:13). God was patient as long as there was any hope of

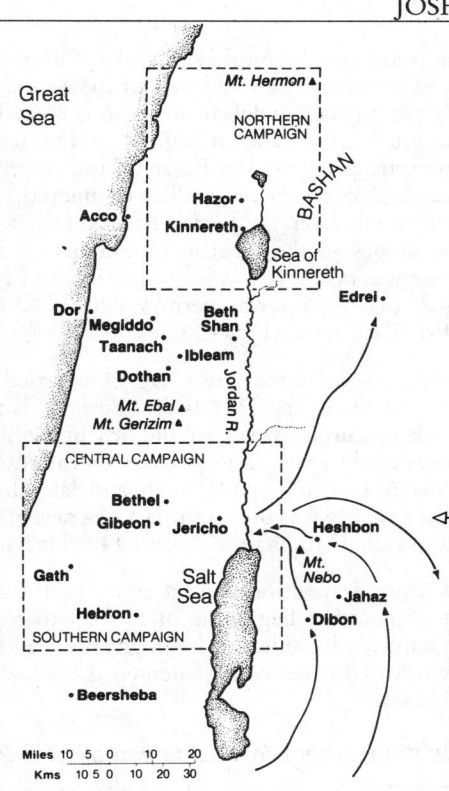

Great
Sea

Mt. Hermon ▲

NORTHERN
CAMPAIGN

BASHAN

Hazor •
Acco •
Kinnereth •

Sea of
Kinnereth

Edrei •

Dor •
Megiddo •
Taanach •
Beth
Shan
• Ibleam

Dothan •

Mt. Ebal ▲
Mt. Gerizim ▲

CENTRAL CAMPAIGN

Bethel •
Gibeon • Jericho •
Heshbon •
▲
*Mt.
Nebo*

Gath •
Salt
Sea
• Jahaz

Hebron •
• Dibon
SOUTHERN CAMPAIGN

• Beersheba

Jordan R.

Miles 10 5 0   10   20
Kms 10 5 0 10 20 30

4. THE NORTHERN CAMPAIGN

Late Bronze Age Hazor was burned by Joshua (Jos 11:13). Excavations have revealed three clearly datable destruction layers, one of which may provide the strongest evidence yet for a historically verifiable date for the conquest.

The excavator thought Joshua burned the latest level (c. 1230 B.C.), but others argue that it must actually have been the earliest of the three levels, c. 1400 B.C.

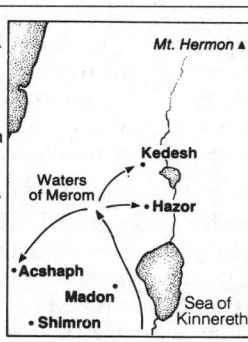

Mt. Hermon ▲

Kedesh •
Waters
of Merom
• Hazor

• Acshaph
Madon •
• Shimron

Sea of
Kinnereth

Conquest of Canaan

1. ENTRY INTO CANAAN

When the Israelite tribes approached Canaan after four decades of desert existence, they had to overcome the two Amorite kingdoms on the Medeba plateau and in Bashan. Under Moses' leadership, they also subdued the Midianites in order to consolidate their control over the Transjordanian region.

The conquest of Canaan followed a course that in retrospect appears as though it had been planned by a brilliant strategist. Taking Jericho gave Israel control of its strategic plains, fords and roads as a base of operations. When Israel next gained control of the Bethel, Gibeon and the Upper Beth Horon region, she dominated the center of the north-south Palestinian ridge. Subsequently, she was able to break the power of the allied urban centers in separate campaigns south and north.

2. THE CENTRAL CAMPAIGN

The destruction of both Jericho and Ai led to a major victory against the Canaanites in the Valley of Aijalon—the "battle of the long day"—which then allowed Joshua to proceed against the cities of the western foothills.

Archaeological evidence for the conquest is mixed, in part because the chronological problems are unsolved. On the one hand, clay tablets containing cuneiform letters to the Egyptian court have been found at Tell el-Amarna

in Egypt from c. 1375 B.C. These mention bands of *Habiru* who threaten many of the cities of Palestine and create fear among the Canaanite inhabitants.

On the other hand, numerous towns were destroyed c. 1230 B.C. by unknown assailants, presumably the "Sea Peoples," but possibly including the Israelites as well. The Biblical chronology based on 1Ki 6:1 seems to demand an even earlier dating, near the end of the 15th century (see Introduction to Joshua: Historical Setting).

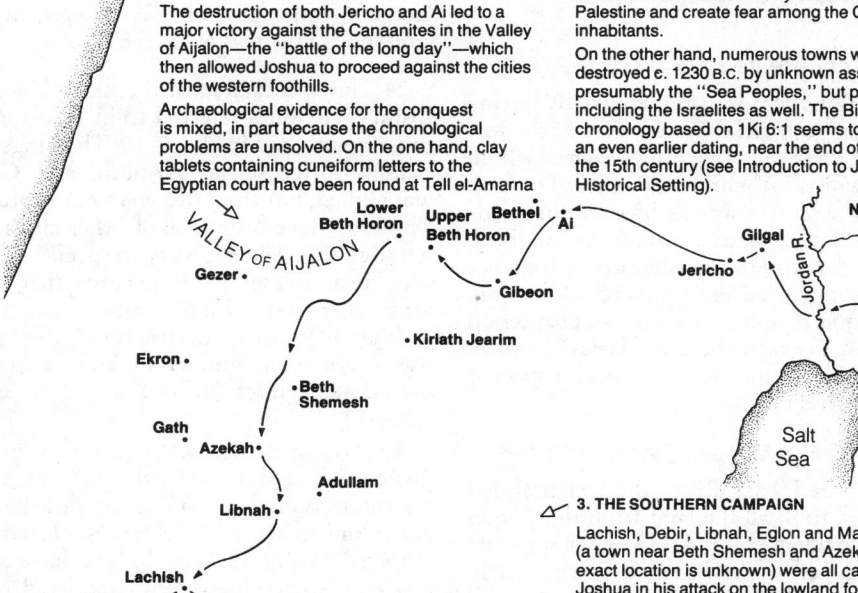

VALLEY OF AIJALON
Lower
Beth Horon
Upper
Beth Horon
Bethel •
Ai •
Gilgal •
Beth
Nimrah

Gezer •

• Gibeon

Jericho •
Jordan R.
Abel
Shittim

Ekron •

• Kiriath Jearim

• Beth
Shemesh

Gath •
Azekah •
• Adullam

Libnah •

Salt
Sea

MEDEBA PLATEAU

Lachish •

Eglon •
• Hebron

3. THE SOUTHERN CAMPAIGN

Lachish, Debir, Libnah, Eglon and Makkedah (a town near Beth Shemesh and Azekah, whose exact location is unknown) were all captured by Joshua in his attack on the lowland foothills controlling the approaches to the Judahite plateau.

Several of these towns, most notably Lachish, contain destruction evidence that might possibly be correlated with the Israelite conquest, but with Jericho and Ai, the historical implications are not clear.

Miles 5   0   10
Kms 5   0   10

• Debir

309

repentance (Ro 2:4), but the sin of the Amorites had reached its full measure (Ge 15:16). The annihilation of the Canaanites was the only way that God's gracious purpose could be fulfilled.

21–22 The report of Anakites in the land had earlier discouraged Israel from entering while they were encamped at Kadesh Barnea (Dt 1:19–33). Now, in summarizing the victories of the Israelites, they triumphed over these very people. Joshua as leader of the army is credited with the accomplishments of his subordinates (cf. 15:13–14, 17–19). "Gaza, Gath and Ashdod" were three of the five Philistine cities that were located in the southern coastal plain. This verse places that whole region outside Israelite territory.

23 On the statement "Joshua took the entire land," see comment on v.16. "He gave it as an inheritance" is a transitional statement: with the Conquest completed (chs. 1–12), the author turns to the division of the land (chs. 13–19).

"Then the land had rest from war" is a profound declaration and a fitting conclusion for the first section of the book. It is prophetic of the "rest" that will come when all evil has been conquered and Christ is made King of Kings and Lord of Lords (Rev 11:15; 19:16).

F. A List of Defeated Kings (12:1–24)

The Conquest is summarized by listing the kings that Israel defeated. East of the Jordan there were only two kings, each of whom ruled a wide area with many cities. The land west of the Jordan was divided into individual city-states. Israel's conquests on both sides of the Jordan are mentioned together here to emphasize the unity of the nation. The conquests summarized in this chapter do not begin to reach the boundaries stated in 1:4. Consult the map for the exact location of the territories taken.

1. Kings whom Moses defeated (12:1–6)

1 East of the Jordan River, the Israelites, led by Moses, took all the land from the Arnon River, which enters the Dead Sea at about its midpoint, to Mount Hermon in the north. "The Arabah" refers to the Jordan Valley.

2–3 Most of that territory is either mountainous or high plateau; accordingly the inhabit-

ants are called Amorites (cf. 3:10). Sihon and Og are called the two kings of the Amorites (2:10; 9:10). The defeat of Sihon is recorded in Nu 21:21–31 and Dt 2:26–37, and his territory from the Arnon River on the south to the base of the Sea of Galilee (Kinnereth) on the north, from the Jordan River on the west to slopes of the Abarim mountains on the east was taken. It was from the slopes of Pisgah that Moses was permitted to view the Promised Land (Dt 34:1).

4–5 Israel's victory over Og is recorded in Nu 21:33–35 and Dt 3:1–11. "Bashan" is the rich pastureland east of the Sea of Galilee, bordered by the Yarmuk River on the south, Mount Hermon on the north, and Salecah on the east. Og was one of the last of a race of giants called "Rephaites" (cf. Ge 14:5; Dt 3:11).

6 Moses is mentioned at the end of vv.1–6 and Joshua at the beginning of vv.7–24 to place them side by side and highlight the way the work of Joshua complemented the work of Moses.

2. Kings whom Joshua defeated (12:7–24)

7–8 The boundaries of the territory that Joshua conquered are mentioned here. All this territory is west of the Jordan River. Consult a map for what is covered in this land. For "Hittites" et al., see 3:10.

9–24 This is a catalog of the kings killed by Joshua. The ones referred to in vv.6–13a are those mentioned in chs. 6–10. The kings and armies of Jerusalem, Jarmuth, and Gezer were killed, but the cities were not captured. This may have been true of other cities also (cf. Jdg 1:27). The necessity to specify that Ai was "near Bethel" (v.9) suggests that there were other ruins with this same name. "Hormah" (v.14) means "destruction"; this name was given to a number of cities that had been destroyed (cf. Nu 14:44–45; 21:1–3; Jdg 1:16–17).

Regarding Bethel (v.16), the army of Bethel participated in the battle of Ai (cf. 8:17), but the account does not record the killing of either king or army. The conquest of Bethel is reported in Jdg 1:22–26. As we have seen, however, some cities were conquered more than once. With the name of Bethel, the list turns to cities in the central and northern parts of Palestine.

"Tirzah" (v.24) was the capital of the northern kingdom of Israel until the time of Omri (1Ki 14:17; 15:21, 33; 16:6–24).

II. Dividing the Promised Land (13:1–21:45)

A. The Command to Divide the Land (13:1–7)

1 Perhaps Joshua was about the same age as Caleb, whose age is given as eighty-five years in 14:10. This notice concerning Joshua's advanced age is evidence that the Conquest took a long time. The Lord had to remind Joshua of his unfinished task. The division of the land (v.7) was a part of his original commission from the Lord (1:6; Dt 31:7), and it had to be completed before Joshua died.

2–5 A description follows of large areas that remained unconquered along the coast and in the far north (the many cities scattered here and there that had not been captured are not taken into consideration here). "The regions of the Philistines and Geshurites" is the southern coastland along the Mediterranean Sea. The Philistines continued to oppress and harass the Israelites throughout the period of the Judges and the reign of Saul, until they were subdued by David. "Shihor" refers to the River of Egypt, which flows from the Sinai Peninsula into the Mediterranean Sea about forty-five miles southwest of Gaza and marked the boundary between Egypt and Palestine.

"Ekron" was the farthest north of the five major Philistine cities; it was regarded as "Canaanite," for although the Philistines were not Canaanite, they had taken this area from the Canaanites. Gaza, Ashdod, and Ashkelon were near the coast, whereas Gath and Ekron were farther inland. "Canaanite" refers here to any people, irrespective of origin, who lived in the lowlands. "Sidonian" here includes all the residents of the northern coastal plains.

6–7 The Lord reaffirmed his promise to drive out the inhabitants of the land (cf. 3:10). From this point on, however, further conquests would be the concern of the individual tribes. Moreover, the promise was conditional and was never completely fulfilled because Israel was disobedient to the command of the Lord (cf. v.13).

Joshua was to divide all the land promised to Israel, whether or not Israel possessed all of it at this time. The word translated "allocate" (GK 5877) refers to the casting of lots. The use of lots placed everything in the hands of God and freed Joshua and the elders from any possible charge of favoritism. The concept of "inheritance" (GK 5709) was very important in Israelite society. One's inheritance was a piece of real estate that was the inalienable possession of one's family. A large portion of OT legislation is dedicated to regulating and protecting the rights of inheritance (cf. 17:3–6).

B. Division of the Land East of the Jordan (13:8–33)

1. Introduction (13:8–14)

8 The Transjordanian tribes receive a disproportionate amount of attention in this book that records the Conquest and division of the land *west* of the Jordan (cf. 1:12–15; 4:12; 12:1–6; 13:8–33; 22:1–34). The author was eager to uphold the unity of the Twelve Tribes in spite of the geographic separation.

9–13 The author describes the land east of the Jordan River that became the inheritance of Reuben, Gad, and the half-tribe of Manasseh. It covered all the land that had been ruled by "Sihon king of the Amorites" (see 12:2–3) and Og king of Bashan (see 12:4–5). The area stretched from the Jordan to the mountainous plateaus to the east. For Moses' victory over Og and Sihon, see Nu 21:21–35; Dt 2:26–37. Though this book celebrates God's great promises and Israel's mighty victories, it does not conceal the fact that sometimes the fulfillment of the promises was limited by Israel's failure to obey fully the command of the Lord.

14 The Levites had been set apart for the service of the tabernacle and the altar (Ex 32:29; 38:21; Nu 3:45; see comment on 14:3–4 for how this affected the numbering of the twelve tribes).

2. The inheritance of Reuben (13:15–23)

15–21 Beginning with Reuben in the south, a slightly more detailed description is given of the inheritance of each of the two-and-a-half tribes. The distribution "clan by clan" is in agreement with the principle laid down that the larger tribes were to receive a larger territory (see Nu 26:52–56). "Bamoth Baal" (v.17), near Medeba, was one of the places from which Balaam attempted to curse Israel (Nu 22:41). Sihon fought with Israel at "Jahaz" (v.18; cf. Nu 21:23; Dt 2:32).

"Beth Peor" (v.20) was another place from which Balaam tried to curse Israel (Nu 23:28). It was here that the Israelites engaged in sexual immorality with Moabite women and in idolatry (Nu 25:1–3). This was the place Moses delivered his farewell address to Israel (Dt 3:29), and he was buried nearby (Dt 34:6). The defeat of the "Midianite chiefs" (v.21) is recorded in Nu 31:8, where they are called "kings."

22–23 When the Israelites were traveling north from the desert into Transjordan, Balaam was hired by Balak king of Moab to curse them. Each time he tried, the Lord made him bless Israel instead (Nu 22–24; cf. Jos 24:9–10). Balaam's death is reported in Nu 31:8. Though the OT does not give the reason why Balaam was slain, Rev 2:14 makes him responsible for the sin of Israel recorded in Nu 25:1–5 (cf. Dt 23:4–5; Ne 13:2; Mic 6:5). The word "villages" (v.23) often refers to unwalled settlements outside a fortified city. Few cities in Transjordan had walls; therefore it is more likely that it refers to land around the city that was under cultivation or was used for raising livestock.

3. The inheritance of Gad (13:24–28)

24–28 Gad received the central region in Transjordan. "Jazer" became a Levitical town (21:39). Since the Israelites had been forbidden to take any of the Ammonite territory (Dt 2:19, 37), "half the Ammonite country" may refer to land first taken from the Ammonites by Sihon and then taken from Sihon by the Israelites. "Rabbah" (v.25) was the principal city of the Ammonites. "Mahanaim" (v.26) is on the Jabbok River on the border between Gad and Manasseh (see v.30); it was there that Jacob was met by two angels on his way back from Paddan Aram to Canaan (Ge 32:2). At the River Jabbok Jacob wrestled with God (Ge 32:22–30). "Sea of Kinnereth" (v.27) is the Sea of Galilee.

4. The inheritance of the half-tribe of Manasseh (13:29–31)

29–31 The territory allocated to the half-tribe of Manasseh is the northern part of Transjor-

dan and is not described in as much detail as the territories of Reuben and Gad. Here the name "Makir" is used to designate the tribe of Manasseh (cf. Ge 50:23).

5. Summary (13:32–33)

32–33 Verse 32 brings down the curtain on the account of the distribution of the land east of the Jordan. Verse 33 repeats the statement in v.14, because of its importance.

C. Division of the Land West of the Jordan (14:1–19:51)

1. Introduction (14:1–5)

The amount of space devoted to the description of the territory of each of the tribes and the order of presentation correspond to the importance of each particular tribe in Israel's history. Accordingly, Judah—the tribe of David, Solomon, and their successors—is treated most thoroughly. Then the tribes of Joseph are considered, who so predominated the northern kingdom that Ephraim became one of its names. The third and last tribe to be given special treatment is Benjamin, the tribe of Saul, Israel's first king.

1 Only the territory west of the Jordan was called the land of Canaan. Though at times the dimensions of the land promised to Israel are described as reaching from the River of Egypt to the river Euphrates (e.g., 1:4), there is a strong, persistent tradition that the Promised Land was much more restricted. "Eleazar the priest" was to assist Joshua in dividing the land. As priest he was the one who wore the ephod with the Urim and Thummim by means of which the will of God was determined (Nu 27:21). "The heads of the tribal clans" had been chosen by Moses, as commanded by the Lord, to help in the division of the land (Nu 34:17–29).

2 The land was to be "assigned by lot [GK 1598]." Presumably the priest Eleazar employed the Urim and Thummim (cf. Nu 27:21; 34:17). For Israel the use of lots left the choice completely in the hands of God (see 7:14). The old refrain "as the Lord had commanded through Moses" is repeated again to drive home the point that obedience is the key to God's blessing.

3–4 Once again material about the two-and-a-half tribes is repeated (cf. 1:15; 12:6; 13:8–32). Since "the Levites" had been set apart to serve in the tabernacle (Nu 35:1–8), Ephraim and Manasseh were treated as separate tribes to preserve the full number twelve (cf. Ge 48:5). They were to be apportioned towns and agricultural lands throughout the territories of all the other tribes (ch. 21).

5 Typical of OT narrative style, the introduction ends in a statement summarizing what the following account relates in detail.

2. The inheritance of Judah (14:6–15:63)

a. Caleb's inheritance (14:6–15)

6 Caleb and Joshua were the two faithful spies who believed God was able to give Israel the land of Canaan (Nu 14:6–9, 30). The receiving of their inheritances frames the story of the dividing of the land among the nine-and-a-half tribes, with Caleb's at the beginning and Joshua's at the end (19:49–50). Caleb and Joshua are living examples of God's faithfulness in fulfilling his promises made more than forty years earlier.

In Ge 15:19 the Kenizzites are listed as one of the pagan nations whose land God was giving to Israel. When Caleb is called a Kenizzite, it may mean no more than that one of Caleb's ancestors was named Kenaz (cf. 15:17; 1Ch 4:13, 15). This title "man of God" is ascribed to Moses also in Dt 33:1; Ezr 3:2, and in the title of Ps 90. For what God said to Moses about Caleb and Joshua, see Nu 14:30.

7–9 The spy mission Caleb participated in is recorded in Nu 13. Caleb's report was characterized by bold confidence in God (Nu 13:30; 14:6–9). The statement that Caleb "followed the LORD my God wholeheartedly" is found three times in this brief passage (vv.9, 14). It describes him as one who really lived out the theme of this book and is the reason he was still alive and would inherit part of the land (cf. Dt 1:36).

10–11 Of all who were twenty years and older when Israel left Egypt, only Caleb and Joshua lived to enter the Promised Land. Caleb was now "eighty-five years old." From this passage we can calculate the approximate number of years involved in the Conquest. Forty years old at the time of the spy mission plus thirty-eight years of wandering leaves seven years for the Conquest.

12 The "hill country . . . Anakites . . . cities . . . large and fortified" are the very things that the ten faithless spies used to discourage the Israelites from entering the Promised Land (Nu 13:28–29). Caleb viewed them as a challenge. By faith Joshua and Caleb triumphed over the formidable foe who intimidated the unbelieving Israelites.

13–15 Some believe that when Joshua blessed Caleb, he bestowed on him the spiritual qualities needed for this dangerous venture. For "Then the land had rest from war," see 11:23. In Jdg 1:9–10 the conquest of Hebron is credited to the men of Judah. Hebron is only one of many cities that had to be captured more than once (e.g., Jerusalem; see comment on 15:63).

b. The borders of Judah (15:1–12)

1 Judah, the tribe of the great Davidic dynasty, was the first tribe to receive its allotted territory in Canaan. God had commanded that when the land was divided the size of the territory should correspond to the size of the respective tribe or clan (Nu 33:54). In the process of carrying out the command, Joshua gave Judah a territory larger than her numbers merited (19:9). The "territory of Edom" was east of the Arabah. Here, however, Edom may refer to Amalekites living in the Sinai Peninsula and the southern Negev (cf. Ge 36:12). "The Desert of Zin" is around Kadesh Barnea (see Nu 20:1). Judah's lot was "in the extreme south." The description of Judah's southern boundary is in close agreement with the southern boundary of Canaan as described in Nu 34:3–5.

2–5 The word "bay" here refers to the extreme northern and southern ends of the "the Salt Sea" (i.e., the Dead Sea). "Zin" and "Kadesh Barnea" are both localities within the Desert of Zin. The latter would have been the staging point for the Israelite's invasion of the land of Canaan had they trusted in God (cf. Nu 13:26–33). "The Wadi of Egypt" is the River of Egypt that flows from the Sinai Peninsula into "the sea" (i.e., the Mediterranean Sea). "The northern boundary" of Judah corresponds to the southern boundaries of Benjamin (18:14–19) and of Dan (19:41–46).

6–7 The expressions "go up" and "go down" are used in the OT with reference to the elevation of the land. Here the border of Judah ascends from the Valley of Achor, which borders on the Dead Sea. "Gilgal" is a different Gilgal from the one on the plains of Jericho which Joshua made his base of operations when he entered Canaan (4:19).

8-11 "The Valley of Ben Hinnom" is the wide, deep valley on the south and east of the old city Jerusalem. "The Valley of Rephaim" is west of Jerusalem. The border around Jerusalem is described in greater detail, perhaps to make clear that Jerusalem was not included in the territory of Judah. "Mount Seir" (v.10) was on the west side of Jerusalem (not to be confused with Mount Seir in Edom); "Mount Jearim" is about ten miles west of Jerusalem. "Ekron" is one of the cities of the Philistines (see 13:3).

12 "The Great Sea" is the Mediterranean. With the Mediterranean as her western boundary, Judah's allotment included Philistine and Geshurite territory that had not been conquered yet (cf. 13:1–3). This was in conformity with the Lord's command (13:6) that the entire land of Palestine be allotted in the confidence that some day all would belong to Israel.

c. The inheritance of Caleb's daughter (15:13–19)

13 God promised Caleb that he would inherit the land he had explored (14:9; Nu 14:24). In the providence of God, this area fell within the borders of his own tribe.

14–17 The "three Anakites" (cf. Nu 13:22) were living in Hebron at the time of the first spy mission; there are three accounts of their defeat (11:21–22; 14:10–15; 15:13–14). Caleb led the attack on Debir, but Othniel captured it. As in the case of Hebron, this victory is also credited to Joshua as commander-in-chief (10:36–39). It was not uncommon to offer special incentives for acts of bravery (cf. 1Sa 17:25; 18:17, 25; 1Ch 11:6). Othniel later became one of the judges of Israel (Jdg 3:7–11). The phrase "Caleb's brother" can refer to any male member of the same clan or tribe. The word "brother" (GK 278) can mean simply "relative" or "ally"; but Jdg 1:13; 3:9, where Othniel is called "Caleb's younger brother," seems to favor the idea of "blood brother."

18–19 The word "a special favor" (GK 1388) is commonly translated "blessing." Perhaps Caleb's daughter was asking her father for a wedding gift. She needed "springs of water." Land in the Negev is of little value without water, but it is very productive when irrigated. Othniel recognized the validity of her request.

d. The towns of Judah (15:20–63)

20 Possibly the list of towns assigned to Judah comes from an administrative register where the southern kingdom of Judah was divided into twelve districts for such purposes as taxation and military conscription. The towns of Judah made up ten and one-half districts and the towns of Benjamin made up the other one and one-half (cf. 18:11, 21). This list described the homeland that God had given to the tribe of Judah. It is another evidence of the historical, down-to-earth nature of God's redemptive program (cf. Jn 1:14).

21–32 "The southernmost towns" are mostly in the Negev (esp. those in vv.26–32)—towns that are also ascribed to Simeon in 19:1–9. There it is stated that the territory given to Judah was "more than they needed" (19:9). Consequently some of it was reassigned to Simeon. The distribution of the land was not all completed at once; rather it took place over an extended period of time (see 18:1–10). Thirty-six towns are named here. Even if some of the names are combined or accounted for in other ways, it seems impossible to reduce the list to "twenty-nine towns." The solution to the problem is not clear.

"Ziklag" (v.30) is the town that Achish, king of Gath, gave David as a place for him and his men to live during his time of exile from King Saul (1Sa 27:6). This was therefore one of the towns that was assigned to Judah but not occupied by them until years later.

33–47 "Zorah" is the highest point in the Shephelah. This town and Eshtaol were the scenes of some of Samson's exploits (Jdg 13:25; 16:31). "Lachish" and "Eglon" were the main towns of two of the southern kings allied with Adnoi-Zedek (see 10:1–5). "Beth Dagon" (v.41) means "house of Dagon," the god of the Philistines (see 1Sa 5:2–7).

"Ekron," "Ashdod," and "Gaza" (vv.45–47) were three of the five major Philistine cities (see comment on 13:1–5). Though assigned to Judah, these three were not possessed until many years later. The style of these three verses differs markedly from all the others in this list of towns assigned to Judah, both in the inclusion of the phrase "its surrounding settlements and villages" and in the omission of the concluding statement that gives the total number of cities.

48–60 The cities in this section were located in the vicinity of Hebron (cf. 10:3–5, 36, 39; 14:13–15). Hebron became a city of refuge (20:7) and a Levitical town (21:11). "Carmel" (v.55) must not be confused with Mount Carmel on the Mediterranean seacoast. It is seven and one-half miles south-southeast of Hebron. Nor should "Jezreel" (v.56) be confused with the town of the same name in the Valley of Esdraelon.

61–62 "The desert" refers to the desert area on the eastern border of Judah along the shore of the Dead Sea. In the title of Ps 63, it is called "the Desert of Judah" (cf. 12:8). "The City of Salt" may be Khirbet Qumran, the center of the Essene community made famous through the discovery of the Dead Sea Scrolls. "En Gedi" is near the midpoint of the Dead Sea.

63 The statement "Judah could not dislodge the Jebusites" is strange because Jerusalem was part of the territory assigned to Benjamin (18:28), and the description of the northern border of Judah so carefully excludes Jerusalem (see comment on vv.8–11). Judges 1:8 records that the men of Judah did capture the city. Then in v.21 we have the same statement as here, only it states that Benjamin did not capture Jerusalem. The final conquest of Jerusalem was accomplished under the direction of King David (2Sa 5:6–10). Some cities seem to have changed hands several times before they were securely in Israel's control. The admission that Judah was unable to dislodge the Jebusites is strange in a book that exalts the supernatural power of God, who gave victory to his people over all their enemies. Joshua records a remarkable mixture of miracle and human effort—a combination of divinely aided victory and of failure that resulted from Israel's disobedience and unbelief. Thus God is revealed as sovereign. He responds to the needs of his covenant people but is not subject to their whims.

3. The inheritance of the Joseph tribes (16:1–17:18)

a. Introduction (16:1–4)

1–3 "The allotment for Joseph" was divided between the tribe of Ephraim (vv.5–10) and the half-tribe of Manasseh (17:1–13; for the other half-tribe of Manasseh, see 13:8–13). The importance of the tribe of Joseph is reflected in their lot being drawn second and in the comparatively large amount of space devoted to the description of their territory. The southern border of Joseph is actually the northern borders of Benjamin (18:11–14) and Dan (19:40–48). "The Jordan of Jericho" designates the Jordan near Jericho. Jericho itself was in the allotment of Benjamin (18:12), as was Bethel (18:22).

Nothing is known about the "Arkites" (v.2) except that David's counselor Hushai was from that clan (2Sa 15:32; 16:16). The "Japhletites" (v.3) were another non-Israelite clan about which nothing is known (but cf. 1Ch 7:32–33). "The Sea" is the Mediterranean.

4 The order in which "Manasseh and Ephraim" are mentioned is the actual order of birth. The order in which their respective territories are described reflects the ascendancy of Ephraim (cf. Ge 48:12–20). The descriptions of the inheritances of the Joseph tribes contain no lists of towns.

b. The inheritance of Ephraim (16:5–10)

5–9 Although much space is devoted to Ephraim and Manasseh, the description of their territories is fragmentary and difficult to follow. Apparently vv.5–6a are a severely abbreviated restatement of the southern boundary. Then, beginning at "Michmethath," the point farthest north, the boundary is traced east and south until it joins the southern boundary forming the eastern border. Beginning again at the far north, the northern boundary is followed to the Mediterranean Sea, which formed the western border.

10 On Israel's failure to "dislodge the Canaanites," see comment on 15:63. The king and the army from "Gezer" were defeated by Joshua (10:30). Many natives of Canaan who survived were conscripted as "forced labor" for Israel (Jdg 1:28–30, 33, 35). The commands of God allowed Israel to

LAND OF THE TWELVE TRIBES

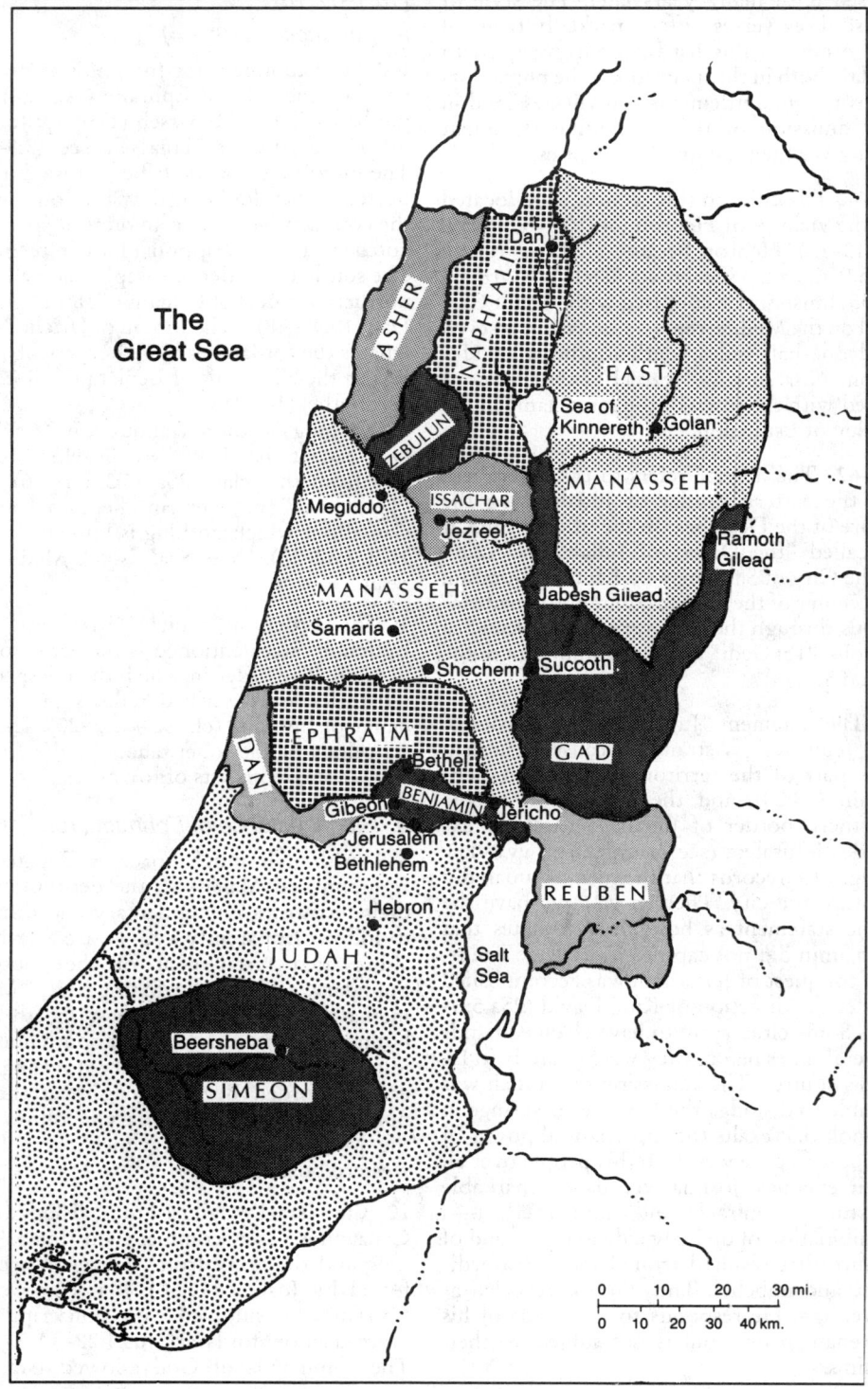

The
Great Sea

ASHER

NAPHTALI

Dan

EAST

Sea of
Kinnereth • Golan

ZEBULUN

MANASSEH

Megiddo •

ISSACHAR

Jezreel •

Ramoth
Gilead

MANASSEH

Jabesh Gilead •

Samaria •

Shechem •

Succoth

EPHRAIM

DAN

Bethel •

GAD

Gibeon •

BENJAMIN

Jericho •

Jerusalem •
Bethlehem •

REUBEN

Hebron •

Salt
Sea

JUDAH

Beersheba

SIMEON

| 0 | 10 | 20 | 30 mi. |
| 0 | 10 | 20 | 30 | 40 km. |

subject the people from cities outside Palestine to forced labor, but the population of the cities inside the Promised Land were to be put to death without pity and without exception (Dt 20:10–18). Because they failed to do so, the Israelites were corrupted by intermarrying with these pagans and engaging in their perverse and idolatrous worship (Jdg 2:1–3; 3:5–6; 10:6).

c. The inheritance of Manasseh (17:1–13)

1–2 Manasseh was "Joseph's firstborn" son (Ge 41:51). "Makir" is called "Manasseh's firstborn" when, as it appears, Makir was Manasseh's only son (Ge 50:23). At times Makir's name is used to designate the half-tribe of Manasseh that settled east of the Jordan.

From the records we have (Nu 26:29–34; cf. 1Ch 7:14–19), it is difficult to unravel the genealogy of Manasseh. The phrase "the rest of the people of Manasseh" (v.2) designates the half-tribe that did not receive its inheritance in Transjordan. "Male descendants" are specified because the following paragraph deals with the inheritance of the daughters of Zelophehad.

3–6 "Hepher" (cf. 12:17) and "Tirzah" (cf. 12:24) were also the names of Canaanite towns whose kings Joshua killed. The presence of those same names in the genealogy of Manasseh gives evidence that Canaanites were assimilated into Israel.

In the four instances in this book where Joshua and Eleazar are mentioned together, Eleazar is always named first, perhaps out of respect for his crucial role as high priest (see 14:1; 19:51; 21:1). The daughters of Zelophehad based their claim on what "the LORD commanded Moses." An unusual privilege and a remarkable measure of equality were granted to these women. On brothers, see comment on 15:14–17. The "ten tracts" (v.5) are one each for five of Gilead's sons and one each for the five daughters of his sixth son.

7–13 The description of "the territory of Manasseh" is very confusing. It provides little more than a clearer definition of the border with Ephraim. "Shechem," between Mount Ebal and Mount Gerazim, is mentioned frequently in the patriarchal stories in Genesis. It was chosen to be a Levitical town (21:21) and one of the cities of refuge (20:7). Joshua

gathered all Israel in Shechem for his farewell address and covenant renewal (ch. 24).

"Tappuah" (v.8) was one of several towns within the boundaries of Manasseh that belonged to Ephraim (cf. 16:9). For "bordered Asher on the north," see 19:24–31; for "Issachar on the east," see 19:17–23. While Manasseh's northern boundary was the Valley of Esdraelon, a few of their towns lay "within Issachar and Asher."

d. The complaint of the Joseph tribes (17:14–18)

14 The relative sizes of the various tribes as recorded in Nu 26 indicate that Ephraim and Manasseh should have qualified for one allotment each. However, considering the relative size of the territory granted to each tribe, it becomes apparent that the first two lots in the territory west of the Jordan were disproportionately large (i.e., Judah and Joseph). Moreover, their land was the most fertile in all Palestine. The Joseph tribes had little reason to complain.

15 Joshua was certainly justified in resisting their request. He challenged them instead to occupy the area already assigned to them. "The hill country of Ephraim" is the central mountainous region. The "Rephaites," like the Anakites, were a people of unusually large stature (cf. 12:4). As Caleb defeated the Anakites, so, with God's help, a great tribe like Ephraim should be able to conquer the Rephaites.

16–18 The Joseph tribes' response shows that their difficulty was not the size of the allotment nor the forested condition of the highlands; it was the presence of other inhabitants in the plain whom they felt unable to drive out because of their "iron chariots" (actually constructed of wood with iron points and iron reinforcements). In response, Joshua again reminded them that they were "numerous and very powerful" and able to provide for their needs within the area already assigned to them.

4. Division of the rest of the land (18:1–19:51)

a. Joshua's rebuke of the seven tribes (18:1–10)

1 "The whole assembly" refers to the seven tribes who had not yet received their specific inheritance (cf. v.3). The Tent of Meeting, mentioned explicitly only twice in Joshua (cf. 22:19), had been moved from Gilgal to Shiloh. This transfer was symbolic of the completion of the Conquest, for Shiloh was in the center of Canaan; it now became the center of national life, and here the final allotments of land were made. Yet even though the Israelites had the land "under their control," they still did not possess it all (cf. 13:1–5; Jdg 1:30–36).

The expression "in the presence of the LORD" occurs a number of times (e.g., vv.6, 8, 10) and means "before" or "near the ark of the covenant," which was housed in the "Tent of Meeting." When the Israelites moved the Tent of Meeting to Shiloh, they moved the ark of the covenant there, too, which remained there until it was captured by the Philistines (1Sa 4:1–11).

2 The statement "there were still seven Israelite tribes who had not yet received their inheritance" implies that a significant amount of time had elapsed. Apparently the remaining tribes had grown complacent. They were satisfied with nomadic life in the fertile land of Ephraim and Manasseh and were not eager to be involved in the warfare required to claim their own territory.

3 The word "Israelites" here refers only to those tribes who had not received their land. Joshua reproved them for the ingratitude and unbelief manifested in their failure to take what God had already given to them. Joshua was eager to complete his commission, which included the division of the land among the tribes.

4–5 The appointment of "three men from each tribe" was part of a new system devised for dividing the remainder of the land. The phrase "according to the inheritance of each" means that the land was to be divided into equitable portions that could then be assigned by lot. Those portions that were already assigned (to Judah and to Joseph) were to stand.

6–7 The casting of lots was done under Joshua's authority, though Eleazar actually did it (14:1–2; 19:51; cf. Nu 27:21). On casting lots "in the presence of the LORD," see comment on v.1. Joshua repeats the information about the Levites and the two-and-a-half tribes (cf. 13:8–32; 14:3–4). The two-

and-a-half tribes from east of the Jordan must have become impatient to have the division of the land completed so that they could return home to their families and possessions.

8–10 The men were to describe each area "town by town" because the number and nature of the towns were more important to them than the precise borders or the number of square miles. Once again "Israelites" refers only to the seven tribes who as yet had not received any inheritance (cf. v.1). For a quick perspective on where these territories were, consult the map of the land of the twelve tribes.

b. The inheritance of Benjamin (18:11–28)

11 Benjamin was not the largest of the seven tribes receiving their allotments; yet theirs is described in greater detail than most others. Perhaps the author had more information about Benjamin. If these lists came from an administrative register (see comment on 15:20), that in itself might account for the amount of detail.

12–13 "The north side" of Benjamin corresponds to the southern border of Ephraim (16:1–3). Beth Horon belonged to Ephraim.

14–20 "Along the western side" means the western boundary of Benjamin. "The southern side" of Benjamin was the northern boundary of Judah (15:5–9). Many of the places mentioned here are referred to in 15:5–8 (see comments).

21–28 The towns allotted to Benjamin are divided into two lists. The first records twelve cities in the east (vv.21–24); the second, fourteen cities in the west (vv.25–28).

22–28 Many of these cities lie between Bethel to the north (see 7:2; cf. Jdg 1:22–23) and Jerusalem (also called "the Jebusite city"; see 15:8, 63) to the south.

c. The inheritance of Simeon (19:1–9)

1 All the towns allotted to Simeon had been given first to Judah. The text clearly states (v.9) that because Judah's portion was too large, some of the towns were reassigned to Simeon. According to the blessing Simeon and Levi received from Jacob shortly before his death (Ge 49:7), their descendants were destined to be scattered among the other

tribes as punishment for their violent revenge against the Shechemites (Ge 34).

2–6 The first group of the towns of Simeon (thirteen in all) are in the Negev. "Beersheba" was an important fortress on Judah's southern border in the time of the divided kingdom.

7–8 In the second group of the towns of Simeon (four in all), two are in the Negev and two in the foothills (see also 15:28–32).

9 All the towns assigned to Simeon were located within the borders of Judah; thus the tribe of Simeon was soon assimilated by Judah. Apparently 1Ki 19:3 reflects a period when the assimilation was complete, because Beersheba is called Beersheba in Judah.

d. The inheritance of Zebulun (19:10–16)

10–16 Though Zebulun was the younger brother of Issachar, he received his inheritance first (cf. 17:1). Their cities are in the vicinity of Nazareth (in Galilee) and Mount Tabor. "Bethlehem" (v.15) is Beth Lahm east of Mount Carmel and should not be confused with Bethlehem in Judah. To arrive at a total of "twelve towns," some of the towns named in defining the border of Zebulun would have to be included.

e. The inheritance of Issachar (19:17–23)

17–23 No description of the borders of Issachar is given, only a list of towns. Their inheritance lay mostly in the plain of Jezreel and was bounded on the west by Zebulun, on the north by Naphtali, on the east by the Jordan River, and on the south by Manasseh. "Beth Shemesh" (v.22) is to be distinguished from Beth Shemesh in Judah (15:10) and Beth Shemesh in Naphtali (v.38).

f. The inheritance of Asher (19:24–31)

24–31 Asher's territory was located primarily on the western slopes of the mountains of Galilee and bordering on the Mediterranean Sea.

g. The inheritance of Naphtali (19:32–39)

32–39 The territory given to Naphtali lay between Asher and the Jordan. Its southern tip lies at the foot of Mount Tabor (where Zebulun, Issachar, and Naphtali came together). "Kinnereth" (v.35) is on the northwest shore of the Sea of Galilee. Naphtali reached almost to Mount Hermon in the north.

h. The inheritance of Dan (19:40–48)

40–48 The inheritance of Dan lay between the inheritance of Judah and that of Ephraim. To form this territory Judah gave up some of its northern towns (e.g., "Zorah" and "Eshtaol"; see 15:33), and Ephraim gave up some of its southern towns. Dan's allotment overlapped Philistine territory, a situation that is reflected in the Samson stories. "Leshem" is also known as Laish (Jdg 18:29). The rather gruesome tale of the capture of this town by men from the tribe of Dan is related in Jdg 18.

5. Joshua's inheritance (19:49–51)

49–50 The description of the inheritances allotted to Caleb (14:6–15) and Joshua provided a framework within which land was allotted to the nine-and-a-half tribes. They were men of faith; therefore this arrangement symbolizes the spiritual truth that the gift of the land to Israel is predicated on faith. The words "as the LORD had commanded" must be a reference to Nu 14:24, 30.

51 The dividing of the land among the various tribes was complete. All that remained was to designate the cities of refuge (ch. 20) and the Levitical towns (ch. 21). This summary is similar to the introduction in 14:1, with which the division of the land began.

D. The Cities of Refuge (20:1–9)

1. The rationale (20:1–6)

1–2 Murder is regarded as a very serious crime in the OT (Ex 20:13; Dt 5:17). Capital punishment is prescribed in all cases of murder to uphold the sanctity of all life (Ge 9:4–6). The land itself is defiled whenever murder goes unpunished (Nu 35:33). Blood vengeance can be traced back to Cain, who expected to be killed in revenge for the murder of Abel (Ge 4:13–14). The provision of "cities of refuge" was without parallel among the civilizations of the Near East. The provision was made to distinguish between murder and accidental killing (manslaughter) and to grant the right of trial to suspected murderers.

3 God's law distinguished between willful murder and manslaughter (Nu 35:6–34; Dt 19:1–13). In either case one had to leave his family and possessions and go immediately to the place of asylum to avoid being killed without a proper hearing. The elders of the cities of refuge were to provide protection and a trial for such people (Nu 35:25). Even though the law made provision for a strong centralized government to enforce the laws, at various times in Israel's history this was lacking. Thus the responsibility to protect rights to property or to avenge a murder fell to the victim's closest relative, who was called "the avenger of blood." Vengeance was to be a deterrent to murder.

4 The city gate controlled all traffic in or out of the city and thus facilitated its defense. Normally there were benches where the elders would sit to adjudicate cases of various kinds (cf. Ru 4:1–12). The accused had to "state his case," for sanctuary was not granted indiscriminately. A person was to be regarded innocent until proven guilty, and a minimum of two witnesses was required to condemn one accused of murder (Nu 35:30). The elders of these cities must "admit him . . . and give him a place to live," and presumably also a means of livelihood.

5 The command "they must not surrender" indicates that the accused murderer must be assumed to be innocent. The goal of the trial was to determine if the killing was intentional or "without malice aforethought."

6 Protection from the avenger of blood was promised only so long as the accused remained in the city of refuge (Nu 35:26–28). Even if he was only guilty of manslaughter, he had to remain in the city "until the death of the high priest." One who killed another accidentally was held responsible and had to forfeit his freedom for a period of time. It is difficult to understand why the "death of the high priest" was chosen as the time for the sentence to be ended. This may have been a time of general amnesty. The words "then he may go back" suggest that his old situation awaited him on his return. Nothing is said about what would be done for his family and his possessions while he was detained.

2. The selection (20:7–9)

7 Three cities of refuge were selected in the territory west of the Jordan. They were strategically located so that a person would have ready access to one of them. "Kedesh" (see 12:22) is in the north, "Shechem" (see 8:30;

cf. 8:33; Jdg 9:7) in the center, and "Kiriath Arba" or Hebron (see 14:15) in the south. The last one was given to Caleb as a reward for his unwavering faithfulness (14:6–14). In 21:12 we are told that the agricultural land and the villages remained in Caleb's possession. Perhaps he shared the city with the Levites (see 21:1).

8 The cities of refuge in Transjordan had already been selected (Dt 4:41–43). This passage may refer to the implementation of Moses' selection. This time the three cities are named from south to north (cf. Dt 4:43). "Bezer" was in the south; "Ramoth in Gilead" was in the center; "Golan" was in the north.

9 Asylum in the cities of refuge was offered to "any alien" living within the borders of Israel. This provision is based on the memory of Israel's many years as aliens in Egypt and is a testimony to God's concern for all humanity. Though the Israelites stood against the pagan societies around them, their hearts were to be open to receive any foreigner who would adopt their religion and their customs.

E. Towns for the Levites (21:1–42)

1. Assignment of the towns by lot (21:1–8)

1–3 With the land apportioned to the various tribes, "the family heads of the Levites" felt it was time for them to be given towns to live in, as they had been promised (see comments on Nu 35:1–8). Apparently they would live in them without actually owning them, because their inheritance was to be the service of God (cf. 14:4). Thus they approached Eleazer (he is again named before Joshua here) at "Shiloh" (see comment on 18:1). "The heads of the other tribal families" complete the group of elders entrusted with this important task.

Some towns were assigned to the Levites even though they were still held by the Canaanites. Joshua assigned many portions of unconquered land, apparently confident that God would give Israel possession of these areas also. Four towns from each tribe were set apart for the Levites with the exception that only three were from Naphtali and nine were from the combined territories of Judah and Simeon. Though Levitical towns were selected from every tribe, they were not evenly distributed but seem to have been clustered on the frontiers and in other endangered areas.

4–8 The will of the Lord was determined by lot (see 7:14; 14:2). The "descendants of Aaron" mentioned here are the "Kohathites" (the family of the high priest). Because the temple would be built in Jerusalem, their towns were located in the territories of Judah, Simeon, and Benjamin. The number of towns set apart for the descendants of Aaron is indicative of God's providence. At the time of selection, there were only three or four generations of the descendants of Aaron; they would scarcely have needed thirteen towns. The number of towns for each of the Levite clans (thirteen, ten, thirteen, twelve) was cleverly arranged without dividing the towns from any one tribe other than Manasseh, which had already been divided into two half-tribes.

2. The towns of the Kohathites (21:9–26)

a. Towns of the descendants of Aaron (21:9–19)

9–19 "The first lot fell" to the descendants of Aaron, presumably through the providence of God. There was no question in the minds of the Israelites that God controlled the outcome of the casting of lots. The cities of this clan were located in Judah, Simeon, and Benjamin. On the inheritance of Caleb, see 14:6–15. The "villages" were the small settlements outside the walls of the towns.

b. Towns of the remaining Kohathites (21:20–26)

20–26 The towns for this part of the clan of the Kohathites were found in the territory of Ephraim, Dan, and the western half of Manasseh.

3. The towns of the Gershonites (21:27–33)

27–33 The towns of the Gershonite clan of the tribe of Levi were located in the eastern half of Manasseh and in Issachar, Asher, and Naphtali.

4. The towns of the Merarites (21:34–40)

34–40 The towns of the Merarite clan of the tribe of Levi were located in Zebulun, Reuben, and Gad; that is, most of them were east of the Jordan.

5. Summary of the Levitical towns (21:41–42)

41–42 No new information is given in this summary of the preceding verses.

F. God's Promises Fulfilled in the Division of the Land (21:43–45)

43 The statement "the LORD gave Israel" emphasizes God's sovereign action, but Israel's obedient participation was essential. All Canaan was not yet in Israel's possession, nor were all the enemies destroyed; nevertheless Israel was in control of "all the land." God's oath to Abraham had now been fulfilled.

44 The "rest" that "the LORD gave them" was a cessation of hostilities, with the result that the people dwelt securely and serenely in the land (cf. Dt 12:9–10; cf. Heb 4:1–11). "Not one of their enemies withstood them" is a generalized statement. The Gibeonite deception and the existing pockets of resistance do not contradict the fact that Israel was victorious over every enemy that they faced in battle. God had not promised immediate destruction of the Canaanites but only their gradual extermination (Ex 23:30; Dt 7:22).

45 On this note of victory and celebration, the story of the Conquest and the division of the land is completed.

III. Preparation for Life in the Promised Land (22:1–24:33)

A. The Eastern Tribes Return Home (22:1–34)

1. The dismissal of the eastern tribes (22:1–9)

1 The role played by the eastern tribes in the Conquest and their place in the nation and in the worship of the Lord are prominent concerns throughout the book of Joshua. The Jordan River was a formidable natural barrier that isolated the two-and-a-half tribes from the rest of Israel, which would later prove to be a serious threat to the political and religious unity of the nation. Seeds of disunity are already apparent in this chapter.

2–3 The phrase "Moses the servant of the LORD" recalls 1:1–2, and 7. Joshua's words "you have obeyed me" show that they had accepted him as Moses' rightful successor (cf. 1:16–18). Joshua commended these tribes for the great sacrifice they had made, having been separated from their families and unable to work on their newly acquired lands. Their help of their fellow Israelites was regarded as "the mission . . . God gave you," i.e., as service to God.

4 "Rest" means the freedom to live in one's own land without the fear of war (see comment 21:44). "Your homes" (lit., "tents"; GK 185) has a broad usage; when the Israelites settled in the land, they began to live in houses.

5 This is the key verse in this chapter. In order to urge the Transjordanian tribes to continue to be faithful, Joshua reminded them of the way God had rewarded their faithfulness during the Conquest. The "law that Moses . . . gave you" is probably all or part of the book of Deuteronomy (see comment on 1:7). The emphasis here on loving the Lord, walking in his ways, and serving him "with all your heart and all your soul" recalls Dt 6:1–5. This is not legalism (which is rigid obedience to law for its own sake). The law is an expression of God's will for his people and must be obeyed with wholehearted devotion (cf. Jn 14:15).

6 Ritual blessing was an effective means of guaranteeing the well-being of another. The one pronouncing the blessing was acting on behalf of God.

7 The reference to the two divisions of the tribe of Manasseh is strange here. Apparently the circumstance of a tribe being given land on both sides of the Jordan was unusual enough to merit special mention. Perhaps the shorter form "Reubenites and Gadites" (vv. 25, 32–34) is a more convenient way of referring to the two-and-a-half tribes.

8 The Israelites had been enriched with the spoils taken in battle. The command "divide with your brothers" probably means they were to share the booty with those who had remained in Transjordan to guard the v omen, children, and elderly and to care for the livestock (see 1:14; cf. Nu 31:27; 1Sa 30:23–25).

9 "Shiloh" (see comment on 18:1) was in the hill country of Ephraim; it had been selected as the place of worship. The name "Gilead" designates all Israel's land east of the Jordan. "Israelites" here means, as it does elsewhere,

a major portion of the Israelites as distinguished from some smaller portion (see comment on 18:3). Joshua emphasized once again that their land had been given to them by the Lord.

2. The altar of witness (22:10–34)

a. The crisis (22:10–14)

10 At "Geliloth" (either the name of a place or a reference to Galilee or Gilgal), the two-and-a-half tribes built an enormous altar, large enough to be seen easily. Its function was to be a witness, not a place for sacrifice.

11–12 We do not know how much time elapsed before "the Israelites heard" about this project, but the warriors had sufficient time to complete the altar and return to Gilead (v.15). Representatives of the nine-and-a-half tribes gathered at "Shiloh," the political and religious center of the nation. The whole assembly was ready immediately "to go to war." They were not unmindful that the Transjordanian tribes had served them at great personal sacrifice; nevertheless, they would not tolerate what appeared to be a flagrant act of apostasy. They expected dire consequences for the entire nation (vv.17–20; cf. ch. 7) if they did not obey Moses' command to deal severely with any such acts (cf. Lev 17:8–9; Dt 13:12–15).

13–14 The zeal of the Israelites for the honor of God and the purity of his worship might have ended in terrible disaster had they not obeyed God's command to always investigate carefully before taking action (Dt 13:14). In this episode Phinehas is the central figure. He had already distinguished himself as a zealous defender of true worship at Peor (Nu 25:6–18; Ps 106:30), and he could be trusted to confront these tribes. With him went a representative of each of the other tribes, because the investigation and any subsequent action were concerns for the whole nation.

b. The confrontation (22:15–20)

15–16 Building this altar had been viewed as an act of unfaithfulness to God. When the nine-and-a-half tribes pressed for repentance and reconciliation before declaring war, it gave the two-and-a-half tribes an opportunity to explain. Tragedy was averted by the willingness of both sides to dialogue. They did not accuse these men of turning away from the Lord to serve other gods but of deviating from the revealed will of the Lord. Even sacrifices offered in the name of the Lord were viewed as acts of rebellion when they were offered on an unapproved altar (cf. 1Ki 12:26–30).

17–18 The delegates appealed to the mistakes of the past (cf. also v.20). The "sin of Peor" had drawn some Israelites into pagan worship and immorality, and about 24,000 died in a plague that the Lord sent as judgment (Nu 25). "We have not cleansed ourselves from that sin" means that its consequences continued to be experienced. Israel had to struggle continually against idolatry among her own people (cf. 24:23). Any such rebellion would have dire consequences for the entire nation.

19 The word "defiled" (GK 3238) refers to ritual uncleanness and does not necessarily imply anything inherently evil or sinful. The delegates insinuate here that perhaps Transjordan lay outside the sphere of the Lord's blessing and that the two-and-a-half tribes were building this altar to offer sacrifices and to sanctify it. When the nine-and-a-half tribes called Canaan "the LORD's land," it is clear that they did not regard Transjordan as part of the Promised Land. The presence of "the LORD's tabernacle" was further evidence that the land west of the Jordan was especially blessed. Their willingness to "share the land" reveals a beautifully generous spirit and is proof of the sincerity of their concern for orthodox worship.

20 For "the devoted things," see comments on 2:10; 6:17. The Israelites, fearing that the sin of a few would bring judgment once again "upon the whole community," manifested a strong sense of corporate responsibility. If the unfaithfulness of a single individual such as Achan had such dire consequences (7:5, 24–26), what would happen if the two-and-a-half tribes rebelled?

c. The explanation (22:21–29)

21–22 The warriors from Transjordan appealed to God as their witness, using a name that emphasized his omnipotence and sovereignty (cf. Ps 50:1). The repetition of this solemn name indicates how serious they considered the situation to be. If they were

guilty, they would not object to being punished.

23–25 The Transjordanians agreed that any departure from the pure worship of the Lord deserved severe judgment; however, they fervently rejected the idea that they had built an altar as a rival to the one at Shiloh. Joshua had expressed fear that the isolation caused by the Jordan might lead to the Transjordanians' turning from the worship of the Lord (v.5). Now they were afraid that this isolation might cause their descendants to be rejected by the rest of Israel.

26–27 In the estimation of the two-and-a-half tribes, the very presence of the altar would be a silent "witness" (GK 6332) to those on the west side of the Jordan that the Transjordanian tribes had every right to be included in the people of Israel and the worship of the Lord (cf. 24:27, where a stone serves as a witness).

28–29 The altar was a "replica" of the Lord's altar because its shape was an integral part of its witness, linking it to the true altar at the Tent of Meeting. Apparently the design of an altar indicated what deity was worshiped at that altar (cf. 2Ki 16:10–16; 2Ch 28:22–25).

d. The resolution (22:30–34)

30–31 The Israelites "were pleased" when they realized that no bloodshed would be necessary, which proves that they were not motivated by a vengeful spirit but were distressed by what appeared to be a flagrant act of apostasy. The faithfulness and unity of God's people were taken as evidence of God's presence and blessing.

32–33 No doubt the leaders of Israel returned from their Transjordanian meeting with joy in their hearts, eager to inform the rest of the community of the good news. Not only were the people "glad to hear the report," they also "praised God." All talk of war ceased.

34 This altar was to be a witness that the Lord was the God of the Transjordanian tribes and the rest of Israel and that they shared a common form and place of worship. Later history reveals that the Israelites in Transjordan were subject to repeated attacks by enemy armies and that they were tempted to worship foreign deities. Ultimately their land was taken from them and their few survivors were assimilated into the rest of Israel.

B. Joshua's Farewell to the Leaders (23:1–16)

1. God's blessing: the reward for faithfulness (23:1–11)

1 Apparently the words "After a long time" mean a long time after Joshua had assumed leadership in Israel. The events of chs. 23–24 probably occurred shortly prior to his death at the age of 110 (24:29). At least twenty-five years had passed since the end of the Conquest because Joshua was the same age as or younger than Caleb (see 14:10).

"Rest" (GK 5663)), a common theme in Joshua, was the goal of the Conquest. It was realized when the major battles were ended and Israel was at peace with "all their enemies," even though all those enemies had not yet been driven out (cf. vv.4–5).

2 In ch. 22 (v.12; cf. v.16) "the whole assembly of Israel" designated representatives of the nine-and-a-half tribes. Joshua could hardly have addressed the whole nation at one time. Most likely 22:1–8 was Joshua's farewell to the Transjordanian tribes. Here the words "all Israel" refer only to those tribes living west of the Jordan. Perhaps the leaders, judges, and officials were subdivisions of the elders (cf. 24:1). The place of assembly is not stated. Joshua's advanced age was his reason for delivering his farewell address at this time.

3 The Israelites had been eyewitnesses of God's mighty acts (cf. 24:31). The theme of Joshua's address is a call for loyalty to the Lord because of all he had done for Israel. Ultimately it was the Lord who had defeated and dispossessed the Canaanites. In this holy war the Israelites did participate with sword and shield; nevertheless the victory was credited to God alone (cf. Dt 1:30; 3:22; 20:4).

4–5 In 13:1–7 the Lord commanded Joshua to divide all of Canaan among the nine-and-a-half tribes (his remarks are limited to the land "between the Jordan and the Great Sea"), even though much of it was yet to be conquered. Israel's lethargy in driving out the last of their enemies is difficult to understand, but it contributed to the fulfillment of God's promise to drive them out "little by little" (Ex 23:30).

6 The command "Be very strong" recalls the words of encouragement directed to Joshua in ch. 1 (vv.6–7, 9, 18). The exhortation to courage and obedience to the Book of the Law in 1:7 is repeated here almost word for word. God's promise was not unconditional; Israel's faithfulness was required.

7 Because Israel replaced a people whose culture was advanced beyond their own, the temptation to worship the pagan gods of the Canaanites must have been overwhelming. Yet if the Israelites adopted any of their wicked practices, they too would be subject to punishment (Dt 8:19–20). God does not show any partiality.

8 The word translated "hold fast" (GK 1815) is used in Ge 2:24 to describe the intimate and binding relationship between husband and wife. Here it is used to describe a close relationship between Israel and God (cf Dt 4:4; 10:20; 11:22; 13:4). In spite of occasional lapses, Israel's behavior was characterized as holding fast to the Lord.

9–11 The motive for faithfulness to the Lord was that he was the God who had given Israel the land. The statement "no one has been able to withstand you" seems to overlook the Israelite defeat at Ai. This, however, was not due to the superiority of that army but to Israel's unfaithfulness. As long as Israel was faithful, the Lord would continue to fight for them. The command to "love the LORD" that was given to the Transjordanian tribes in 22:5 is repeated here for the rest of Israel.

2. God's judgment: the consequences of unfaithfulness (23:12–16)

12 The danger of apostasy was Joshua's great concern here. Thus the people must not "ally" (GK 1815; cf. v.8) themselves to any pagan nations. Alliances with other nations frequently involved intermarriage (cf. Ge 34:9–10) and respect for their gods (cf. 1Ki 11:1–6). Because of the great danger involved in intermarriage, it was strictly prohibited for Israel (Ex 34:12–16; Dt 7:1–6).

13 Just as faithfulness had been essential for Israel to acquire the land, so now it was indispensable if they were to continue to live in the land (cf. Ex 23:30–33; 34:11–12; Nu 33:55).

14 "The way of all the earth" emphasizes the universality of death in human experience (cf. 1Ki 2:2; Ro 5:12). "All the good promises" of the Lord had indeed come true. Israel's victories had been so all-pervasive that pockets of resistance remaining in the land did not detract from their appreciation of God's faithfulness.

15–16 God's faithfulness to his promises meant that he would keep his threats as well. Israel should not suppose that being the recipients of God's blessings made them immune to his judgment. The threats contained here were fulfilled in the Babylonian exile.

Although the concept of a "covenant" (GK 1382) between the Lord and Israel is foundational to the book of Joshua, it is not explicitly referred to often (cf. the ark of the covenant in chs. 3–4; 6; the covenant rites of circumcision and Passover in ch. 5; the ceremony of covenant renewal in 8:30–35). Chapter 24 contains a final ritual of covenant renewal. All this indicates that the Conquest was a religious event and not simply a military exploit.

C. The Covenant Renewed at Shechem (24:1–28)

There are three important elements that are new in this chapter and have no counterpart in ch. 23: (1) the review of Israel's history from the call of Abraham to the present; (2) the responses by the people with their solemn pledge to be faithful to the Lord; (3) the covenant that Joshua drew up for the Israelites. This ceremony of covenant renewal is similar in form to the suzerainty treaties that were common in the ancient Near East (cf. comment on Dt 1:1–5).

1. A recitation of Israel's sacred history (24:1–13)

1 "Shechem," located in the hill country of Ephraim, was one of the towns of Ephraim that were given to the Levites (21:21); it was also a city of refuge (20:7). Shechem may have been chosen as the site for Joshua's last great act of covenant renewal because of its illustrious history (cf. Ge 12:6–7; 35:4).

2 "The River" is the Euphrates, but precisely where the forefathers lived is not indicated (Ge 11:31 specifies Ur in Chaldea). Genesis is strangely silent about the existence of any pa-

This excavation is of biblical Shechem; the altar in the foreground may be that of Jos 24. Courtesy Garo Nalbandian.

gan gods (except for Laban's "household gods" [Ge 31:19]); so it comes as a surprise when we are told they "worshiped other gods."

3–4 Abraham was brought up in pagan idolatry. We know nothing of his conversion to the Lord. Abraham's call required that he go "from the land beyond the River" to "Canaan." Abraham was constantly on the move in that land, where all he ever possessed was the Cave of Machpelah, which he bought as a place of burial (Ge 23). Land and "many descendants" were the major elements in God's promise to Abraham (Ge 15:5, 7, et al.), but neither materialized for several generations. Isaac's son Esau was given a land of his own (the mountains of Seir, south of the Dead Sea), while Jacob and his sons left the land they expected to possess and went into bondage in Egypt.

5–6 Moses and Aaron were the principal figures in the deliverance from Egypt (Ex 3:1–4:17). The second person pronoun "you" is surprising. Though some of his audience may have experienced the Exodus, most had not. In the very next sentence the reference is changed to "your fathers." A bewildering oscillation between second and third persons follows until the climax is reached in the words "you saw with your own eyes" (see comment on v.7). The "sea" is the Red Sea (lit., "the Sea of Reeds"; see comment on Ex 13:17–18).

7 Most of those listening to Joshua had not seen these things. The alternation of pronouns from second to third person expresses Joshua's conviction that all Israel participated in every crucial event in their national history, whether or not they had actually been present. The events during the forty years of wandering are covered in a single sentence: "you lived in the desert for a long time."

8–10 For the defeat of the Amorites, see Nu 21 and Dt 2 and 3. Balak did not actually fight with Israel; the only resistance he offered was the hiring of Balaam to curse them (Nu 22–24; Dt 23:4–5).

11 That the "citizens [GK 1251] of Jericho" (likely a reference to the landowners) had fought against Israel is not reported in ch. 6. The list of these seven nations (see comment on 3:10) stands in apposition to "the citizens of Jericho."

12–13 Possibly the hornet is the terror that the Lord sent to demoralize and immobilize the enemy (cf. 2:9–11, 24; 5:1; see also comment on Ex 23:27–30). The two Amorite kings are examples of those who were driven out by the hornet. The statement "you did not do it with your own sword and bow" does not mean that they did not do any fighting (cf. v.11). Their efforts alone, however, would not account for the victory—it was a gift from God. Verse 13 is clearly the fulfillment of Dt 6:10–11.

2. Joshua's charge and the people's response (24:14–24)

14 At this point the Lord's message (cf. "I" in vv.3–13) to Israel has ended. Joshua challenges the people to "fear [GK 3707] the LORD." Fear may be either destructive or saving (cf. Heb 12:28–29). The very first commandment is "You shall have no other gods before me" (Dt 5:7). Hence, we are shocked to read that Joshua had to command the Israelites to "throw away the gods" of their ancestors (see v.2; cf. Eze 20:7; 23:3, 8). Apparently the Israelites were still worshiping idols in spite of experiencing so many of the Lord's great miracles and victories. Joshua called the people to give undivided loyalty to the Lord as the only way to experience his presence and blessing in the future.

15 Joshua wanted Israel to be honest with themselves and declare their allegiance. Though he said, "Choose" (GK 1047), he did not intend to encourage idolatry but was confident that the very thought of making a commitment to an idol would be so abhorrent to them that they would take a stand against all such worship. Joshua left no doubt as to the choice he had made for him and his household (cf. Ac 16:31).

16–18 Joshua's appeal produced the effect he was looking for: "Far be it from us" was a response involving both the will and the emotions. In denying the charge of idolatry, the Israelites asserted that the Lord had always been and always would be the object of their worship. The people added their personal affirmation to Joshua's recitation of the mighty acts God had done for them. With the words "brought us and our fathers" they identified with their fathers in God's saving purpose.

19–20 Joshua's response is unexpected. After encouraging the Israelites to make a commitment to the Lord, he told them they would be unable to keep it. His purpose was not to discourage them but to lead them to count the cost and to mean what they said (cf. Lk 14:25–35). They did serve God faithfully for many years (cf. v.31). Of course, they were only able to do this by the grace of God. To be God's people they too must be holy (GK 7705; see Lev 11:44). Because the Lord "is a jealous God," he would not tolerate any rival deities or condone any apostasy (Ex 20:5; 34:14; Dt 5:9). Joshua wanted to caution the people not to speak carelessly, because God would hold them accountable.

21–22 When the people said, "No! We will serve the LORD," Joshua could see that his exhortation was producing the desired result. The people's own words would condemn them if at any time in the future they turned from the commitment they had made that day.

23–24 Joshua called for action to substantiate the Israelites' commitment to the Lord. Nothing could be tolerated that might lead to their return to idolatry. The outward expression of discarding their idols was essential, but it had to be accompanied by loyalty from their hearts.

3. Sealing the covenant (24:25–28)

25–26 The covenant that Joshua made was likely a copy of the law of Moses (1:8; 22:5; 23:6). Since commitments are easily forgotten, Joshua memorialized this important transaction in both the written word and a visible object to preserve the memory for future generations. "The Book of the Law of God" was a collection of the laws and regulations that Joshua delivered to the people and as such was distinct from "the Book of the Law of Moses" (1:8 et al.). The reference to "the holy place" suggests that they had erected the Tent of Meeting here temporarily for this very occasion.

27–28 The stone Joshua set up would be a constant reminder ("witness"; GK 6338) of the covenant promises made by Israel that day. It may have borne some appropriate inscription.

D. Three Burials in the Promised Land (24:29–33)

29–30 For the first time the title "the servant of the LORD" was granted to Joshua, elevating him close to the stature of Moses (see comment on 1:1). At his death, Joshua was ten years younger than Moses, thus indicating that he never became fully equal to Moses. A certain style of leadership also came to an end at that time. The words "in the land of his inheritance" present an important contrast with Abraham and Jacob, who possessed nothing more than a few burial plots in a land where they lived as aliens. Now the Israelites lived in a land of their own.

31 That the people were faithful "throughout the lifetime of Joshua" is eloquent testimony to the power of Joshua's influence. The memorials, confessions, and rituals of covenant renewal were designed to keep the people loyal, but these were not adequate forever (cf. Jdg 2:10–15).

32 The burial of "Joseph's bones" symbolized the completion of an era and the fulfillment of God's promises to the patriarchs. When he gave instructions for his remains to be buried in Canaan, Joseph manifested great faith in the promises of God (Ge 50:24–25; cf. Ex 13:19; Heb 11:22). The burial of Joseph's remains provides a fitting conclusion to the long saga that began with the call of Abraham.

33 When "Eleazar son of Aaron died," the whole generation of those who had left Egypt came to an end. In the Hebrew text, "Gibeah" is literally "Gibeah of Phinehas" and may be the full name of the town (cf. "Gibeah of Saul," 1Sa 11:4).

Judges

INTRODUCTION

1. Title

The English title of this book reflects the MT ("judges"), the LXX ("judges"), and the Vulgate ("Book of Judges") titles. God brought these "judges" to deliver Israel from oppression. Although they were divinely empowered leaders, they did not become hereditary rulers.

Eight men in this book are said specifically to have "judged" or "led Israel" (GK 9149; 3:10; 10:2–3; 12:7, 8–9, 11, 13–14; 15:20; 16:31). Even though others, such as Ehud (3:12–30) and Gideon (6:1–8:32), were judges, it is not specifically said that they "judged" or "led" Israel. Also "leading" Israel was one woman, Deborah (4:4–5). Elsewhere in Scripture the leaders of the period from Joshua's death to King Saul are also called "judges" (Ru 1:1; 2Sa 7:11). Eli and Samuel were the last two judges. In all there were fifteen judges, if Barak is considered a co-judge with Deborah and if Eli and Samuel are added to the thirteen judges in the book of Judges.

2. Historical Background

The book of Judges covers the period from the death of Joshua to the dawn of the monarchy. Political and religious turmoil accompanied Israel's attempts to occupy the land that had been conquered and divided by lot under the leadership of Joshua. Apart from the struggle against the Canaanites at the time of Deborah, Israel's adversaries came from outside the land. Most of these, such as Moab, Midian, and Ammon, were content periodically to plunder the land. The Philistines, however, who at this time entered Palestine in greater numbers, contested with Israel for permanent possession of the land.

Tragically, the Israelites even fought among themselves. Ephraim was ravaged by Manasseh (ch. 12), and Benjamin was almost annihilated by the other tribes (chs. 20–21). Between the days of Joshua and Samuel, Israel plummeted to moral and spiritual disaster. Over and over the pattern of sin followed by oppression was repeated. Occasionally God raised up a Deborah or a Gideon to turn the people back to himself, but the intervals of revival were all too brief.

The events narrated in Judges cover a period of 410 years if viewed consecutively. Such a lengthy time does not, however, fit any accepted chronology of the early history of Israel. Consequently some of the judgeships must have overlapped. Samson and Jephthah, for example, may have ruled simultaneously—one in the west (in Canaan), the other in the east (in Transjordan; 10:7). Most of the data can be worked into a satisfactory historical framework if we adopt the early date of the Exodus (c. 1446 B.C.) and Conquest (which began forty years later).

3. Authorship and Date

The writer of the book of Judges is unknown. Although he may have been an associate of Samuel, unlike Samuel he did not focus attention on the dangers inherent in the monarchy. The book is a unified whole, divided into three parts: (1) the success and failure of the Israelites in Canaan (1:1–2:5); (2) the period of the judges' rule (2:6–16:31); and (3) two stories denoting sin and corruption (17:1–21:25).

Several factors show that the author lived and wrote during the early monarchy (c. 1030 B.C.). The hectic events in this book are viewed from the perspective of a united, stable rule: "In those days Israel had not king; everyone did as he saw fit" (21:25; cf. 18:1; 19:1). This statement suits the time of the united kingdom best; and 1:21 points to a period before David's capture of Jerusalem, for the Jebusites were living there "to this day." The mention of Canaanite control of Gezer (1:29) implies that the king of Egypt had not yet captured the city and given it to King Solomon as a dowry for his Egyptian bride (c. 970 B.C.).

4. Purpose

The primary purpose of the book of Judges is to show that Israel's spiritual condition determined its political and material situation. When the Israelites disregarded Joshua's warnings and worshiped the gods of Canaan, they felt the wrath of an angry God, who allowed the nation to come under the control of tyrants and invaders. Few books of the Bible show human depravity as does this one. When in the midst of their suffering the nation repented of their sin, cried to God for mercy, and turned to him in renewed obedience, God graciously sent deliverers to rescue the people from oppression.

This book also shows that Israel failed to realize her divinely intended goal without a king. The Israelites were unable to govern themselves according to the law of Moses and thereby proved that they needed a king. To this author, monarchy was definitely better than anarchy. The implication is that a nation led by a godly king would experience prosperity under the blessing of God.

The events recorded in Judges also serve in general to fill the gap between the time of Joshua and that of Samuel.

5. Special Problems

One problem that perplexes the reader of Judges is the apparent approval of cruelty and gruesome killing. But such actions as performed by Ehud and Jael are not necessarily sanctioned either by the author or by the Lord. Long neglect of the Mosaic law had left the Israelites with many mistaken notions about God's will.

Another problem closely related to the above is how God's Spirit could use men like Jephthah and Samson, whose motives and behavior were open to such serious question. That God worked through Samson need not denote his approval of an immoral lifestyle. In God's sovereignty the Holy Spirit came on people for particular tasks, and this enduing was not necessarily proportionate to one's spirituality. The Spirit's power enabled people to inspire Israel (6:34; 11:29) and to perform great feats of strength (14:6, 19; 15:14). But it was a temporary enduement, and Samson and later Saul tragically discovered that the Lord had left them. The NT experience of the permanent indwelling of the Holy Spirit was not known in the OT.

EXPOSITION

I. The Success and Failure of the Tribes in Canaan (1:1–2:5)

A. The Capture of Adoni-Bezek (1:1–7)

1–2 The first chapter presents supplementary material on the conquest of Canaan viewed from the standpoint of individual tribes. Most of the episodes occurred after the death of Joshua. Before conducting further military action, the people consulted the Lord, probably through the Urim and Thummim handled by the high priest (Nu 27:21). As in the order of march in the desert (Nu 2:9), Judah was designated to be first (cf. also Jdg 20:18). Judah was also the tribe leading the march against Benjamin in the civil war at the end of the book (20:18). Though the Joseph tribes (Ephraim and Manasseh) received the birthright (1Ch 5:1), Judah had been destined to lead the nation (Ge 49:10).

"Canaanites" applies to all the peoples found in the land of Palestine, but at times it is restricted to the inhabitants of the valleys and coastal plains (Nu 13:29). God's promise that he had "given the land into [Judah's] hands" parallels his encouraging words to Joshua after the death of Moses (Jos 1:3).

3 Judah invited their full-brother tribe Simeon to join them, especially since Simeon's territory was surrounded by Judah's (Jos 19:1) and that tribe was undoubtedly gradually absorbed into Judah. The tribe of Simeon was greatly reduced in numbers during the wilderness wanderings, probably as punishment for their sins of idolatry and fornication in Moab (Nu 25:1–14).

4–5 The Lord fulfilled his promise to Judah, who won a great victory at Bezek (cf. 1Sa 11:8). Adoni-Bezek means "lord of Bezek" (cf. Jos 10:1–3). Adoni-Bezek died in Jerusalem (v.7).

6–7 The severing of Adoni-Bezek's thumbs and big toes incapacitated him as a warrior and as a priest, a dual function common to many kings. In their ordination service the priests had blood applied to their thumbs and big toes (Lev 8:23–24). Adoni-Bezek admitted that he had similarly mutilated the thumbs and toes of seventy rulers of cities, making beggars out of them; so he deserved to be paid back (cf. Ex 21:24).

B. The Capture of Jerusalem, Hebron, and Debir (1:8–15)

8 The city of Jerusalem did not become an integral part of Israel until David stormed the fortress of the Jebusites (2Sa 5:7). Hence the successful attack of Judah was either a temporary or partial capture.

9 From Jerusalem the men of Judah went south and west to continue their conquest. The three areas mentioned are the major geographical divisions of southern Palestine. The "hill country" is the central mountainous region, the "Negev" is the dry ground in the southern part, and the "western foothills" represent the region between the mountains and the coastal plain.

10 Hebron (some nineteen miles south of Jerusalem) has the highest elevation (3,000 ft.) of any city in Judah and is famous as the home of Abraham (Ge 13:2; 23:2, 19). Sheshai, Ahiman, and Talmai were descendants of Anak, who had terrified the spies (cf. Nu 13:22–33). This time, however, the men of Judah conquered them. Fittingly, Caleb, one of the two believing spies, was allotted Hebron as his inheritance (Jos 14:13–14); he directed its capture (Jdg 1:20; see also Jos 15:13–19).

11–13 Debir is located eleven miles southwest of Hebron. Its king was listed among the thirty-one kings captured by Joshua (Jos 12:13). Like Hebron it was a residence of some Anakites (Jos 11:21). This city was captured by Caleb's younger brother Othniel after Caleb offered his daughter Acsah as the prize. Normally young men paid a brideprice to the father of the bride, but the military triumph was considered payment enough (cf. 1Sam 18:25). As relatives of Kenaz, Othniel and Caleb were apparently associated with an Edomite clan (Ge 36:11). Their rise to prominence in Judah and Israel demonstrates the degree to which other people were assimilated by the chosen nation.

14–15 Caleb's daughter needed the permission of her husband before she could ask her father for a gift. Since Caleb had given them land in the arid Negev, she requested a field with "springs of water." Caleb agreed, and this gift may have been her dowry.

C. The Additional Success of Judah and Simeon (1:16–18)

16 The Kenites, an ancient Canaanite people (Ge 15:19) connected with the Amalekites, had been friendly to Israel during the wilderness wanderings. Moses had, in fact, married a Kenite girl. The Kenites left Jericho, the "City of Palms" (3:13), and joined some people of Judah living near Arad, an important city sixteen miles directly south of Hebron. Moses had defeated the king of Arad as Israel skirted southern Palestine (Nu 21:1–3), and Joshua later counted Arad's king among his victims (Jos 12:14).

17 Judah together with Simeon successfully captured Zephath, renaming it Hormah—a city that was allotted to Simeon (Jos 19:4). Since the name means "total destruction," it may be the same Hormah demolished by Moses near Arad (Nu 21:1–3). The complete destruction recalls the Lord's command to wipe out the Canaanites and their livestock and give all the articles of silver and gold to the sanctuary (Dt 7:1–2; 20:16–17; Jos 6:17–19).

18 The capture of Gaza, Ashkelon, and Ekron by Judah must have been temporary (cf. v.19). These were Philistine cities along the coast, though the main migration of the Philistines did not reach Palestine until 1200 B.C. The order of the three cities suggests an invasion from the south.

D. A Summary of Success and Failure (1:19–21)

19 While notably successful in the hilly regions of central Palestine, Judah failed to control the plains. The Israelites were no match for the iron chariots that functioned effectively on the level terrain along the coast (see especially chs. 4–5).

20 Taking Hebron represented the key achievement of Judah, and v.20 attributes its capture to Caleb (cf. also v.9). Hebron became a city of refuge belonging to the priests (Jos 20:7; 21:11), but its fields and suburbs were Caleb's own possession (Jos 21:12).

21 Benjamin's main city was Jerusalem, but neither Benjamin nor Judah could dislodge the Jebusites (see comment on v.8). An alternate name for Jerusalem is "Jebus" (19:10),

Five Cities of the Philistines

Like a string of opulent pearls along the Mediterranean coast, the five cities of the Philistines comprise a litany of familiar Biblical names: Gaza, Ashkelon, Ashdod, Ekron and Gath.

Each was a commercial emporium with important connections reaching as far as Egypt along the coastal route, the "interstate highway" of the ancient world. The ships of Phoenicia, Cyprus, Crete and the Aegean called at Philistia's seaports, which included a site today called Tell Qasile, where a Philistine temple has been found, on the Yarkon River just north of modern Tel Aviv.

The Philistine plain itself was an arid, loess-covered lowland bordering on the desert to the south—a stretch of undulating sand dunes adjacent to the sea—and the foothills of the Judahite plateau on the east. No area in Biblical history was more frequently contested than the western foothills (the Shephelah region), lying on the border between Judea and Philistia. Beth Shemesh, Timnah, Azekah and Ziklag were among the towns coveted by both Israelites and Philistines, and they figure in the stories of Samson, Goliath and David.

The area to the north of Philistia, the plain of Sharon, was also contested at various periods: During Saul's reign the Philistines even held Beth Shan and the Esdraelon valley. Later, from about the time of Baasha on, a long border war was conducted by the Israelites at Gibbethon. Originally a part of Judah's tribal allotment, the coastal area was never totally wrested away from the Philistines who may have begun their occupation as early as the time of Abraham.

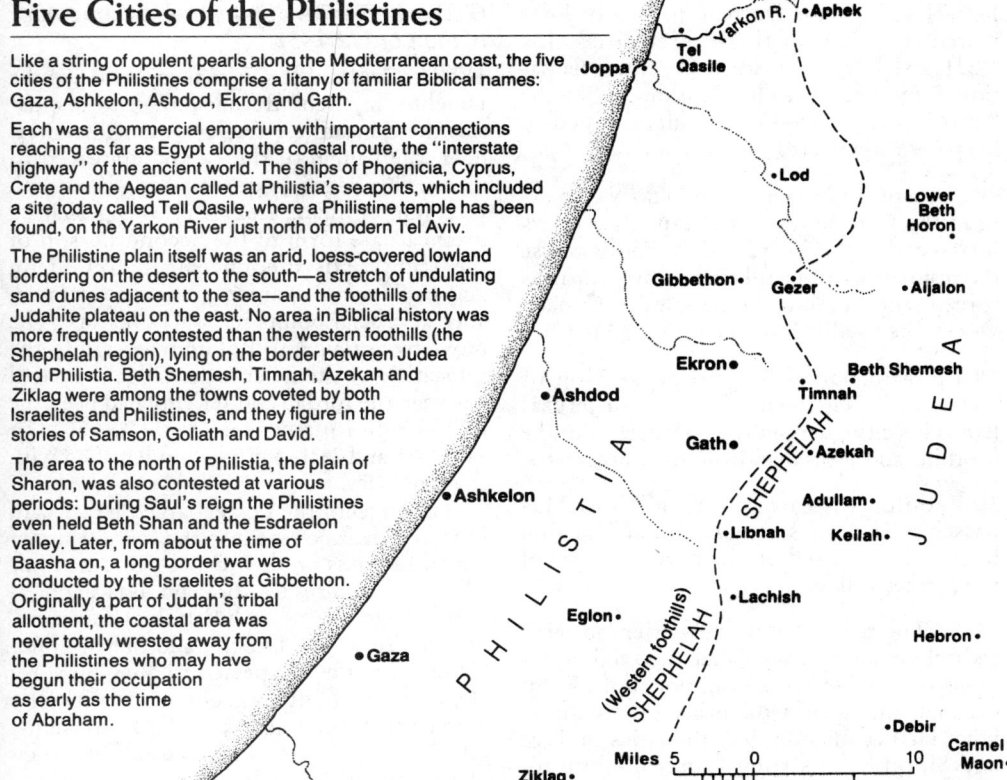

which attests to the long attachment of the Jebusites to this natural stronghold.

E. The Capture of Bethel (1:22–26)

22 Next to Judah, the most important tribe was Ephraim; and vv.22–29 describe the activities of Ephraim and his brother, Manasseh. The two tribes may have cooperated in the capture of Bethel (about twelve miles north of Jerusalem), since the attack is attributed to "the house of Joseph"; but the city lay within Ephraim's territory. Bethel means "house of God," a name given by Jacob after God's revelation to him there (Ge 28:19). As God promised to protect the patriarch, so he "was with" the Joseph tribes here. Bethel was to become a key religious center during the divided kingdom.

23–25 To capture Bethel, Israel followed the strategy used at Jericho. Spies were sent there, and they found a man willing to show them the entrance to the city. In return for his cooperation, the spies promised safety for the informer, just as Rahab and her family

had been protected at Jericho. When the Israelites captured the city, they released the man and his family.

26 These survivors headed north, "to the land of the Hittites," a term applied to Syria (Jos 1:4). The Hittite Empire was based in Asia Minor but extended its control over wide areas west of the Euphrates.

F. Additional Failures of the Tribes (1:27–36)

27 The remainder of ch. 1 records the inability of the other tribes to occupy territory. Manasseh's allotment included several key cities in the Valley of Jezreel. Joshua 17:16 mentions the problems in this area because the Canaanites had "iron chariots." Beth Shan was an important fortress controlling a trading route across the Jordan.

Taanach was five miles southeast of Megiddo, a city that controlled the pass at the entrance to the Jezreel Valley. Dor lies along the Mediterranean coast south of Carmel; Ibleam is situated at the southern end of the

Jezreel Valley near Dothan. Joshua had defeated the kings of these three cities (Jos 12:21, 23), but a permanent Israelite occupation did not follow. The Canaanites, like the Amorites in vv.34–35, were determined to keep their living areas and resist Israel.

28 The most the Israelites could do was to exploit the Canaanites as a cheap labor force. Moses earlier had instructed the nation to use the residents of peaceful cities near Canaan as forced laborers, but the peoples of Canaan were to be totally destroyed (Dt 20:11–17).

29 Ephraim failed to gain possession of Gezer, a city eighteen miles west of Jerusalem. This city guarded the approaches to the foothills and Jerusalem from the northwest.

30 Zebulun's territory was north of Manasseh's. The cities of Kitron and Nahahol likely were situated on the northern edge of the Jezreel Valley.

31–32 The tribe of Asher experienced wide setbacks against Acco, Aczib, and Sidon, regions on the Mediterranean north of Mount Carmel, and against the other towns somewhat farther inland. Here the cities of Tyre and Sidon led a strong Canaanite culture with its vigorous Baal worship. Their culture and religion had a strong influence on Israel, especially during the reigns of Solomon and Ahab.

33 The Naphtalites, whose region lay to the east of Asher, failed to dislodge the residents of Beth Shemesh and Beth Anath. Beth Shemesh ("house of the sun") may have had a sanctuary devoted to the worship of the sun god; Beth Anath contains the name of Anath, the Canaanite goddess of war and both consort and sister of Baal.

34–36 The fortunes of the tribe of Dan have a certain prominence in Judges (see ch. 18). Their difficulties stemmed from Amorite pressure to keep them out of the plains and valleys, where most of their inheritance lay. The Amorites kept control of Aijalon, eleven miles northwest of Jerusalem, and nearby Shaalbim. After the Danites migrated north, the nearby tribe of Ephraim finally subjugated the Amorites. The "Scorpion Pass" is located south of the Dead Sea, at the southern border of the Promised Land (Jos 15:2–3).

G. Disobedience Condemned by the Angel of the Lord (2:1–5)

1–2 The deplorable spiritual condition of the Israelites lay behind their failure to dispossess the Canaanites. To expose Israel's sinfulness, the "angel of the LORD" appeared to them. This angel, frequently identified with God himself (6:22; 13:21–22), was perhaps a preincarnate form of the Second Person of the Trinity. His announcements to Gideon and to Samson's parents promised deliverance at crucial points in Israel's history. The move from Gilgal to Bokim may signify the relocation of the tabernacle. Gilgal, situated between the Jordan and Jericho, had been the initial religious center (Jos 4:19–20). In 20:18–28 and 21:1–4, Bethel is identified with the sanctuary.

The angel of the Lord charged Israel with breaking their covenant with God in spite of his faithfulness on their behalf. God had fulfilled his promises to Abraham, Isaac, and Jacob. He would "never break [his] covenant" (cf. Lev 26:42–44; Dt 7:9); and out of gratefulness Israel was expected to obey him. Yet they entered into agreements with the Canaanites, including marriage covenants (cf. Pr 2:16–17), and did not tear down their altars (Ex 34:12–13).

3 God therefore did not help the Israelites drive out their enemies but left some to trap them through pagan customs and religions. Israel had been repeatedly warned that the Canaanites could become irritants in their eyes and thorns in their sides (Nu 33:55; Jos 23:13).

4–5 The response of the people to the angel's sad pronouncement was to weep loudly. Like the weeping of Nu 14:1, when the spies announced that Canaan could not be captured, here the crying does not necessarily imply repentance. They offered sacrifices, however; and the burnt offerings and fellowship offerings sacrificed at Bethel not long after (21:1–4) did connote national mourning. "Bokim" means "weeping."

II. The Rule of the Judges (2:6–16:31)

A. Introduction (2:6–3:6)

1. The passing of godly leaders (2:6–9)

After the summary of the incomplete wars of occupation, we meet the threatening wars of liberation that characterize the period of the judges. To explain how Israel fell prey to powerful oppressors, the author reviews events since the death of Joshua.

6–9 Just before his death, Joshua had led the people in renewing the covenant with the Lord (Jos 24). Then he sent them away to finish occupying the land. What they did about this is described in ch. 1. Joshua was buried on the land allotted to his family in Timnath Heres. He received the exalted title of "servant of the LORD" (see comment on Jos 24:29). During the lifetime of Joshua and the leaders who outlived him, Israel was relatively faithful to the Lord. These men had experienced God's miracles.

2. The pattern of the period of the judges (2:10–23)

10 After the death of Joshua's contemporaries, the new generation accelerated down the highway to destruction. They did not know God in a vital way nor had they seen the miracles their fathers had talked about. Each generation must personally experience the reality of God.

11–13 History repeated itself as Israel went through the fivefold pattern of sin, slavery, supplication, salvation, and silence. The *sin* phase is always introduced with the words "The Israelites did evil in the eyes of the LORD" (3:7, 12; 4:1; 6:1; 10:6; 13:1). They deserted the very God who had delivered them from Egypt and had saved them from Pharaoh and his host (cf. v.1). They worshiped Baal—an epithet of the Canaanite storm god Hadad, the god of rain and agriculture, and the leading deity in the pantheon. There were also "Baals" associated with particular places (see Nu 25:3; Jdg 9:4). Israel's earlier encounter with the Baal of Peor had been disastrous (Nu 25). The "Ashtoreths" were deities such as Astarte, who was goddess of the evening star and renowned for her beauty. She was a goddess of fertility, love, and war, and was often linked with Baal (10:6).

14–15 The Lord became angry at Israel's apostasy and turned the Israelites over to their enemies, thus initiating the *slavery* phase of the cycle. God "sold them" as one sells a slave (3:8; Dt 32:30). Israel's crops, supposedly guaranteed by the worship of Baal, were carried off year after year. The strong hand of the Lord now acted to secure Israel's defeat (cf. Dt 28:25). In their distress the people entered the *supplication* stage; they cried out to the Lord.

16–19 *Salvation* came through the judges raised up by God. Some fifteen individuals could claim this designation, though six are "minor" judges who are mentioned only briefly (Shamgar, Tola, Jair, Ibzan, Elon, and Abdon). Not long after gaining Israel's freedom, the people forgot what the Lord had done (the *silence* stage), and the judges would find them newly enmeshed in sin. Their religious prostitution meant that they were forsaking the nation's true "husband," the Lord ("Baal" means "husband" or "owner"). Moreover, the worship of the Canaanite gods literally involved sexual conduct with temple prostitutes supposedly to promote the fertility of the soil.

The Lord spared the people throughout the lifetime of a given judge, even though they deserved to be resubjugated. The words "groaned" and "oppressed" (v.18) relate back to the Egyptian bondage (cf. Ex 2:24; 6:5; 3:9). Then after the death of a judge, the corruption of the people increased; they became "stubborn" (GK 7997), repeating their stiffnecked attitude in the desert (cf. Ex 32:9; 33:3, 5).

20–23 Again the anger of the Lord is mentioned (cf. vv.12, 14). There is a note of contempt as the Lord addressed the people as "this nation" rather than as "my nation" (cf. Hag 1:2). The summary here closely resembles the stern pronouncement of vv.1–3 by the angel of the Lord. Violating the covenant meant a slower conquest of Canaan. The nations would be left there to test Israel's desire to obey the Lord. The constant pressure from a pagan culture would prove who the genuine believers really were.

3. The people left to test Israel (3:1–6)

1–2 The nations left in Canaan to test Israel had another purpose: they afforded practical experience in warfare, for these new generations of Israelites had not participated in Joshua's wars of occupation. Israel would one day confront major powers like Egypt and Assyria; so the smaller wars provided valuable training. Part of God's sovereign action was to use the Canaanites both to punish and to teach Israel.

3–4 The Philistines (who had migrated from Caphtor of the Aegean area) are mentioned first, perhaps because they were to become the primary opponents of Israel. Their five-city cluster along the Mediterranean included Gaza, Ashdod, Ashkelon, Gath, and Ekron. The "Sidonians" refers to the Phoenicians, whose leading port city was Sidon (cf. 1:31). The Hivites were located in northern Israel in Jos 11:3, but Shechem (cf. Ge 34:2) and Gibeon (Jos 9:3, 7) in central Palestine were also Hivite cities.

5–6 The Hittites may not be the same north Syrians of 1:26 but another Canaanite people well known at Hebron in the hills of Judah (Ge 23). Intermarriage with the peoples of Canaan had been forbidden (Jos 23:12) since it would lead directly to idolatry. It was into that very trap, however, that the nation fell (cf. 2:1–3).

B. The Victory of Othniel Over Cushan-Rishathaim (3:7–11)

7 The first cycle, though brief, follows the pattern delineated in ch. 2. Israel sinned by forgetting God and worshiping foreign deities. "Asherah" was the wife of both El and Baal, and some confuse her with Ashtareth/Astarte (2:13). An "Asherah" was also a symbol of the goddess, a sacred tree (Dt 16:21), or a carved pole set up beside an altar to Baal (Jdg 6:25).

8 Israel's sin angered the Lord, who sent Cushan-Rishathaim, king of Upper Mesopotamia, to oppress them. The king's name seems to mean "Cushan of double evil," a rather strange designation but perhaps intended to be an intimidating one. "Cush" (Ge 10:8) was the father of Nimrod, founder of Babylonian civilization.

9–10 When the Israelites appealed to God for help, Othniel was commissioned to rescue them. This relative of the illustrious Caleb has already been introduced in 1:11–15 as a successful warrior. His selection shows that the oppression followed Joshua's death quite closely, perhaps about 1375–1367 B.C. When the Spirit of the Lord came on him, Othniel won a great victory. The empowering of the Spirit is crucial in Judges, and down to the time of David it remained the mark of God's chosen vessel.

11 Othniel's triumph ushered in a forty-year peace, the first of several peace periods given in multiples of forty (v.30; 5:31; 8:28).

C. The Victory of Ehud Over Moab (3:12–30)

1. Israel oppressed by Moab (3:12–14)

12–14 When Israel again fell into sin, God used their perennial enemy Moab to subdue them. Usually the Lord gave strength to the Israelites (e.g., 16:28), but here the Lord was on the side of Israel's foe. In Moses' day the Moabites had attempted to thwart Israel by hiring Balaam to curse them, and along with the Midianites they had actually involved God's people in idolatry (Nu 25). Now Moab had allies such as the Amalekites, who had bitterly opposed Israel in the desert (Ex 17:8–16).

Moabite forces crossed the Jordan and occupied Jericho ("City of Palms"). This means that they had first defeated the tribe of Reuben, which had inherited territory east of the Dead Sea. Because of their locale, the Transjordanian tribes were especially vulnerable to enemy attack. Jericho had been cursed by Joshua (Jos 6:26) and was probably unoccupied when King Eglon moved in. From this strategic base Eglon dominated the Israelites for eighteen years.

2. King Eglon slain by Ehud (3:15–25)

15 God's choice to end the Moabite oppression was a man from Benjamin. Ehud was a left-handed man of the same mold as the seven-hundred expert slingers from Benjamin who fought in the civil war (see 20:13b–16, 43–47).

16–17 Ehud's task was ostensibly to make the yearly tribute payment to Eglon to assure him of Israel's subjection for another year. Since the payment was carried by a number of men, it may have been food or wool. For the occasion Ehud had made a small sword or dagger, about eighteen inches long. It was well concealed, and the fact that he was left-handed enhanced his stratagem.

18–23 Apparently Ehud and his men left Jericho before Ehud returned alone to strike his fatal blow. "The idols near Gilgal" were most likely a well-known landmark. After the other Israelites were safely en route home, Ehud came back to seek a private audience with Eglon. The king wanted to hear this secret message, so he requested his officials and attendants to leave. With Eglon sitting in the cool upper room of his palace, Ehud presented the "message from God." The king stood up reverently to hear the divine oracle, and Ehud drew his sword and delivered the fatal "message." Perhaps the huge size of the king (cf. v.17) and the unexpected use of the left hand prevented him from seeing Ehud's move, for it is clear that no cry of alarm was heard outside. Ehud left the dagger completely buried in Eglon's abdomen and made his escape, locking the doors of the room to prevent quick detection of his crime.

24–25 Eglon's officials hesitated to unlock the doors, assuming that their master might be seeing to his bodily needs. Finally they became suspicious and took a key to remove the bolt from the doors. They found the king lying on the floor, the victim of assassination. God did not necessarily approve of the method used by Ehud, for the Spirit of the Lord did not come on Ehud, and he was never described as "judging Israel" (cf. 2Sa 4:11).

3. The Moabites defeated by Ehud (3:26–30)

26 The reluctance of the Moabite officials to break into the king's room gave Ehud the time he needed to escape. He followed the same route he had started to take earlier (cf. v.19), heading for the unidentified "Seirah." His goal was to reach the hill country of Ephraim. Ephraim was one of the most powerful tribes of Israel and occupied the territory adjacent to Benjamin on the north.

27–29 Ehud knew that the death of Moab's king would throw the officials and troops at Jericho into confusion—an opportune time to strike the hated invaders and end their rule. Using the ancient alarm system of a trumpet (Nu 10:9), Ehud quickly assembled Israelite men to help him follow up his personal triumph. Ehud's bravery and enthusiasm inspired a large following, for all sensed that the Lord was handing the enemy over to them. Under Ehud's command the Israelites took control of the fords of the Jordan and cut off Moab's line of retreat (cf. 7:24; 12:5–6). Ehud led the rout of ten thousand Moabites, who probably represented Eglon's crack troops.

30 Israel's victory restored her independence as Moab was "made subject" (GK 6268) or "subdued." This verb is used at the end of several cycles in Judges (4:23; 8:28; 11:33) to indicate a thorough defeat. Eighty years of peace (1309–1229?), the longest "rest" in the book, followed Ehud's triumph.

D. The Victory of Shamgar Over the Philistines (3:31)

31 The reference to Shamgar is brief but intriguing. As with some of the other minor judges, there is no mention of the sin of Israel (10:1–5; 12:8–15). Shamgar's work was explicitly military. He won an astonishing victory over the Philistines by means of an oxgoad (cf. 15:16)—a stout stick tipped with bronze and used for prodding animals. Shamgar's use of this weapon implies that the Philistines were already disarming neighboring people (cf. 5:8; 1Sa 13:19–22).

Shamgar is a foreign name. His name is mentioned in 5:6, along with Jael, as a hero of Israel. He may have been a contemporary of Ehud, since the latter's death is not cited till 4:1.

E. The Victory of Deborah and Barak Over Jabin and Sisera (4:1–5:31)

1. The prose account (4:1–24)

Somewhat in the form of Hebrew parallelism, Judges has two supplementary accounts of the victory over the Canaanites. The first is in narrative fashion; the second is a majestic poem.

a. The oppression (4:1–3)

1–3 The next major oppression came at the hands of a coalition of Canaanite forces led by Jabin and Sisera, and it affected primarily the northern tribes. Jabin lived in Hazor, once the largest city in Palestine, some nine miles north of the Sea of Galilee on the main route between Egypt and Mesopotamia. Joshua had defeated a Jabin king of Hazor (cf. Jos 11:1–11). Sisera's strength lay in his 900 chariots, a sizable force for this early period. With this military advantage, he terrorized the tribes living near the Valley of Jezreel.

b. Deborah's challenge to Barak (4:4–10)

4–5 Deborah was a prophetess, like Miriam (Ex 15:20) and Huldah (2Ki 22:14), and also a judge. Because the rule of women was not normal in Israel, her prominence implies a lack of qualified men. Deborah sat as judge at the southern end of Ephraim's territory. The reference to a palm tree may allude to the stateliness and gracefulness of women (SS 7:7–8).

6 The Lord commanded Deborah to challenge Barak of Naphtali to confront Sisera's troops, whose oppression was felt even in Ephraim and Benjamin. Naphtali and Zebulun, the first tribes to be summoned, covered most of Israel's territory north of the Jezreel Valley. Cone-shaped Mount Tabor rises some thirteen hundred feet from the valley and afforded an unmistakable meeting place. Barak was told to "lead the way"; if he did so, God would lead the enemy into the trap.

7 Deborah revealed that the site of the battle would be near the Kishon River. This river flowed in a northwesterly direction through the Valley of Jezreel and emptied into the Mediterranean north of Carmel. During the summer months it dwindled to a mere stream. The surrounding valley was excellent terrain for deploying chariots. During the spring, however, the rains caused the river to overflow its banks and flood the low-lying areas nearby.

8–10 Barak expressed his willingness to go, but only if Deborah accompanied him. Her presence as a prophetess would assure contact with the Lord, just as the presence of Moses and the ark of the covenant brought victory in battle (Nu 10:35), while their absence meant defeat (Nu 14:44). Barak's lack of faith prompted Deborah to predict that the honor of killing Sisera would belong to a woman (see v.11). So Deborah went along, and her support helped Barak raise the necessary troops. They began the search for troops in Kedesh, Barak's hometown.

c. Jael's husband introduced (4:11)

11 This seemingly intrusive verse acquaints the reader with the family of the woman Deborah had just alluded to in v.9. Jael, the wife of Heber, belonged to the nomadic Kenites, most of whom lived in the arid regions of southern Judah (1:16). As relatives of Moses, this people had a strong tie with Israel. The "great tree" in Zaanannim (cf. Jos

19:33) lay on the escape route taken by Sisera after the battle.

d. Sisera's army routed by Barak (4:12–16)

12–14 When Sisera learned of Israel's troop movements at the northeastern end of the valley, he called out his entire chariot force and a large army to advance against them from the west. The presence of a sizable enemy force at Mount Tabor cut off the line of communication between Sisera and King Jabin in Hazor. Humanly speaking Barak's hastily gathered army had no chance against such might, but Deborah said that this was the opportune moment. She encouraged Barak by announcing that "the LORD [had] gone ahead [GK 4200 & 7156] of [him]." This is a technical term used of a king marching at the head of his army (1Sa 8:20). The Lord would take the lead in striking down the enemy (2Sa 5:24).

15–16 The Lord's role is even clearer as he "routed" (GK 2169; cf. Ex 14:24; 1Sa 7:10) Sisera's army. This routing probably took place by a rainstorm (cf. "thunder" in 1Sa 7:10; cf. also Jos 10:10–11), for Deborah's song shows that a sudden downpour overwhelmed Sisera's chariots (5:20–21). Even Sisera was forced to abandon his useless chariot and flee north, away from the heated action. The main conflict took place at Taanach, some five miles south of Megiddo (5:19).

The Lord's control of the forces of nature showed his superiority over Baal, the Canaanite storm god. Sisera would certainly not have tried to depend on chariots during the rainy season; so this storm probably struck some time after the spring rains that normally end in May. The lightly armed Israelites quickly demoralized the bogged-down Canaanites, who turned and fled westward. It was a decisive victory, for the Canaanites never again formed a coalition against Israel.

e. Sisera slain by Jael (4:17–24)

17 Sisera headed north away from the main line of pursuit. He may have hoped to reach Hazor, but his strength was running out. When he arrived at Zaanannim, he decided to take advantage of the hospitality of the friendly Kenites. He knew of their cordial relationship with Jabin but was clearly unaware of their intermarriage with Israel (v.11).

18–20 Jael greeted Sisera as "lord" (GK 123), in deference, he thought, to his lofty military title. Her offer of refuge was tempting, for who would search for him in a woman's tent? Besides, the law of hospitality among nomads guaranteed the safety of one's guests. Jael put a covering over the exhausted leader and gave him some milk (probably a kind of yogurt or curdled milk; 5:25). Though Jael's kindness convinced Sisera of his safety, he took one more precaution by asking her to mislead any potential searching party.

21 When Sisera had fallen into a deep sleep, Jael picked up a wooden mallet and a tent peg and drove the peg into his temple, with enough force to hammer the tent peg into the ground. Women normally did the work of putting up and taking down the tents; so Jael knew how to handle her tools. Although Jael's action was a startling violation of hospitality, Sisera was a man who had "cruelly oppressed the Israelites for twenty years" (4:3). Since he had had no mercy on God's covenant people, Sisera probably lay under the sentence of "total destruction" placed on the Canaanites in general (Dt 7:2; Jos 6:17; see comment on Jos 2:10). Victory over the enemy was usually not considered complete until the leaders were eliminated, and in specific cases the Lord demanded that their lives be taken.

22 When Barak finally tracked Sisera down, Jael showed him the dead commander. Deborah's prediction had come true; Barak lost the honor of vanquishing his chief rival. Sisera had died at the hands of a woman—in that culture a disgraceful death (cf. 9:54).

23–24 The rout of Sisera's army broke the power of Jabin, king of Canaan. Without his commanding general, he succumbed to the Israelite forces. His eventual destruction doubtless includes the loss of his capital at Hazor.

2. The poetic version—the Song of Deborah (5:1–31)

The victory over the Canaanites was also commemorated in a poem of rare beauty. Called the "Song of Deborah," this masterpiece expresses heartfelt praise to God for leading his people in triumph. It is a hymn of thanksgiving, a song of victory like Ex 15 or Ps 68. The poetry itself is magnificent, featuring many examples of climactic parallelism (vv.7, 19–20, 27) and onomatopoeia (v.22). Deborah is usually considered the author; the connection between prophetess and music is a natural one (cf. Ex 15:20–21).

a. Praise to God for his intervention (5:1–5)

1 A prose verse similar in form to Ex 15:1 introduces the song. Both songs commemorate the supernatural overthrow of horses and chariots.

2 The opening line can also be translated "When locks of hair grow long in Israel," alluding to the practice of leaving hair uncut to fulfill a vow (Nu 6:5, 18). This then connotes dedication to the Lord in participating in a "holy war" (cf. Dt 32:42). The willingness of the people to fight for the Lord is emphasized in the second line. "Praise" (GK 1385) is literally from the verb "to bless."

3 Out of deep gratitude for God's motivating work among the people, Deborah lifted her heart to the One worthy of praise. She wanted "kings" and "rulers" (GK 8142) to hear about the God of Israel and his magnificent victory. The song is directed to "the LORD" (GK 3378), the name of God that expresses his covenant relationship with Israel.

4–5 These two verses describe a theophany (a visible, temporal manifestation of God), a characteristic of songs of victory (Ps 68:7–8). God's intervention is compared with his awesome appearance at Sinai, where the covenant with Israel was established to the accompaniment of thunderstorm and earthquake (Ex 19:16–18). This is an apt reference, for the rains had been Sisera's undoing and again revealed God's transcendent power.

b. Conditions during the oppression (5:6–8)

6 Conditions were deplorable as Canaanite robbers roamed the highways, making travel dangerous. Commercial trading was likewise stopped, and the economy was being adversely affected.

7–8 Agriculture also was disrupted by the marauders. Life in unwalled villages was unsafe, and crops had to be abandoned. God had sent war and oppression because of their sin; now they were being effectively disarmed as well (or perhaps the large army did not dare to use their weapons against Sisera and his chariots). This lamentable situation continued until Deborah came on the scene. Her deep concern for the nation and her abilities as prophetess and judge inspired the people to take action. But first they had to give up the "new gods" they had chosen.

c. Challenge to recount the Lord's victory (5:9–11)

9 Oppression and defeat have given way to triumph, as travelers can once more move about freely, and normal activities are resumed. The author's heart goes out to the volunteers and leaders whose courage made this possible.

10–11 All classes of travelers are told to listen as the singers recount God's great acts. Whether rich or poor, all would stop at the wells and have an opportunity to hear about the Lord's "righteous acts." The final two lines present the reverse of v.8: instead of war coming to the gates, people could now congregate there for normal judicial and business activities.

d. The roles of the individual tribes (5:12–18)

To throw off the Canaanite yoke, it was important for the tribes to cooperate in battle. Those who participated are commended, while the tribes who shirked their responsibility are condemned.

12 The section begins with a call to Deborah herself to awake. Normally "wake up" (GK 6424) is a plea to take action (Ps 44:23; Isa 51:9), and apparently Deborah had to be roused from her complacency as a judge (4:5). The song she is asked to "break out in" may have been a war song (cf. 2Sa 1:18). Barak (son of Abinoam; 4:6) too is called on to take captives, implying a convincing victory (cf. Ps 68:18; Eph 4:8).

13 The years of oppression had taken a heavy toll in lives. The verse may reflect a two-stage gathering of troops. First, volunteers may have joined their tribal leaders, before journeying together to the rallying point at Mount Tabor. The last phrase could be translated "against the mighty," meaning the enemy.

14–15a Ephraim and Benjamin, two southern tribes, are mentioned first, perhaps because of their association with Deborah. The reference to Amalek is probably a geographical one (cf. 12:15). Makir usually refers to the half-tribe of Manasseh east of the Jordan, but here the western half is clearly intended (Jos 13:30–31) since the battle occurred within its borders. Zebulun is highly praised for its bravery. Along with Naphtali, they had responded to Barak's initial summons (4:10). Issachar, located at the eastern end of the Jezreel Valley, also participated enthusiastically.

15b–16 Several tribes somewhat distant earned the author's wrath for their inactivity. Apparently Reuben at least seriously considered sending some men, for their "searching of heart" is mentioned twice. The tribes from Transjordan had made an important contribution to the conquest under Joshua (cf. comment on Jos 1:12), but pressure from the Moabites may have influenced Reuben's decision. The mention of campfires and flocks presents a tranquil picture in contrast with war cries and clashing armies.

17 Gilead was a common designation for much of Transjordan. The tribe of Gad possessed most of Gilead (Jos 13:24–25), though the half-tribe of Manasseh also lived there (Jos 13:31). "Reuben" and "Gilead" would thus include all three of the tribes across the Jordan.

The tribe of Dan had encountered difficulty in taking possession of their inheritance ever since the time of Joshua (cf. 1:34). It is not surprising, then, that they did not help solve this largely northern problem. The reference to "ships" implies that Dan had not yet migrated to the north. Asher, situated along the coast north of Carmel, had also failed to dislodge the Canaanites. Yet Asher was close enough to the oppressed area to have offered some assistance.

18 The aloofness of these tribes is sharply contrasted with the wholehearted efforts of Zebulun and Naphtali. Judah and Simeon are not mentioned, presumably because of their location far to the south.

e. The battle described (5:19–23)

The vividness of the poetry increases as the author uses repetition, satire, and concrete imagery to paint a lively picture. This poetic account should be closely compared with the description of the battle in 4:12–16.

19 The armies clashed at Taanach, near Megiddo, and the kings of Canaan were supremely confident of victory. With a touch of sarcasm, the author says that this time there was no plunder. They had robbed and oppressed the Israelites for the last time.

20–22 The Canaanites' downfall came as God intervened. The reference to the participation of the stars may be a slap at astrological readings used by the Canaanites. As the rains fell, the river Kishon overflowed its banks; and chariots and riders were swept away. The surging river encouraged the Israelites to "march on" in pursuit of the enemy. The mighty horses of the foe were no match for the people of the God of Israel. In the context "thundering hoofs" seems to relate to a frantic retreat. The repetition of "galloping" (GK 1852) is a striking example of onomatopoeia in Hebrew.

23 The city of Meroz came under God's curse, pronounced by the angel of the Lord, for failing to fight. Meroz was undoubtedly located in the heart of the oppressed area; so the condemnation of that community was more severe than that of the distant tribes. Since elsewhere in Judges cities refusing to participate in urgent battles were destroyed (8:15–17; 21:8–10), Meroz may have shared the same fate.

f. Jael praised for her deed (5:24–27)

24–27 In sharp contrast to the curse against Meroz is the blessing reserved for Jael, a woman who refused to remain neutral (see comments on 4:19–21). She initially treated Sisera in accord with his noble standing. But this once magnificent leader was quickly struck down. This heroine is compared to an expert archer, for the verbs "shattered" and "pierced" are used of arrows in Nu 24:8 and Job 20:24.

In v.27, the words "sank" and "fell" occur three times each, and "feet" occurs twice. This repetition builds up to the final and climactic word of the verse: "dead" (lit., "destroyed"). Sisera had been a mighty and devastating force against Israel, but now the destroyer was himself destroyed (cf. Isa 33:1).

g. Sisera's mother's futile wait (5:28–30)

28–30 The scene shifts from Jael's tent to the luxurious home of Sisera. With a skillful, dramatic touch, the author reflects on the agonized waiting of Sisera's mother for the return of her son. The long delay could mean that the illustrious warrior had tasted defeat, but his mother and her ladies-in-waiting console themselves with visions of plunder. It was common for soldiers to carry off beautiful maidens as trophies of victory (cf. 21:12). "Garments" were a special prize of war (cf. Jos 7:21; Zec 14:14), and Sisera as commander was sure to secure the most beautiful for his family.

h. Conclusion (5:31)

31 As in another song of victory (Ps 68:1–2), there is rejoicing over the fall of the wicked (cf. Nu 10:35). Reference to the sun and its strength closely parallels Ps 19:4b–6; Mal 4:2. The stunning defeat of Sisera resulted in forty years of peace for Israel.

F. The Victory of Gideon Over the Midianites (6:1–8:32)

The Gideon cycle is the longest segment of the book. Chapter 9 might also be counted as part of the Gideon story, since it describes the rule of his son. Under the inspiring leadership of this judge, the Israelites won a victory even more astonishing than that of Deborah and Barak.

1. Israel's land devastated by the Midianites (6:1–6)

1–4 For the fourth time in Judges, the Israelites fell into sin. This time they found themselves at the mercy of invading Midianites. These desert dwellers, descended from Abraham and Keturah (Ge 25:2), lived generally to the south of Palestine. For seven years the camel-riding Midianites swept across the Jordan into the Valley of Jezreel at harvest time. With their speedy, wide-ranging mounts, they roamed all the way to Gaza, helping themselves to crops and animals. The Midianites were joined by the Amalekites—who had earlier assisted King Eglon of Moab (3:12–13)—and by other eastern peoples. Israel was helpless to resist the invaders and literally took to the hills to save their lives. It was a time of judgment comparable to the Day of the Lord (Isa 2:12, 19; 9:4).

5–6 The destruction was so great that it could be described in terms of a plague of locusts. Both in numbers and in effect, the invasion of the nomads matched the work of those devastating insects earlier mentioned as the inevitable outcome of disobedience (Dt 28:38; cf. Joel 1:4). The staple products of the land were no doubt hard hit by this yearly destruction (cf. Joel 1:11), including sheep, cattle, and donkeys (cf. Dt 28:31). The main areas affected had borne the brunt of the preceding Canaanite oppression. Manasseh suffered most, along with other tribes adjacent to the Jezreel Valley: Asher, Zebulun, and Naphtali (v.35).

2. Israel's disobedience condemned by a prophet (6:7–10)

7–10 In their distress the Israelites once more cried out to the Lord. The last time this happened, God used the prophetess Deborah to bring deliverance (4:3–4). On this occasion the Lord sent a "prophet" (GK 5566) to pinpoint the cause of the oppression in words similar to those of the angel of the Lord in 2:1–4. Once again God reminded the people of their release from Egypt's slavery, which should have resulted in perpetual devotion to the Lord. Instead, the Israelites had been worshiping the gods of the Amorites. Here "Amorites" is used generally of all the inhabitants of Palestine (cf. Ge 15:16). Israel refused "to listen to" (GK 9048) the Lord, a Hebrew idiom for disobedience (cf. 2:2).

3. Gideon challenged by the angel of the Lord (6:11–24)

11 The Lord's instrument of deliverance was a young man from the tribe of Manasseh named Gideon. While he was threshing wheat in Ophrah, the angel of the Lord appeared to him there and sat under the oak tree (cf. 4:5). To hide the wheat and himself from the Midianites, Gideon was threshing in a winepress, a pit carved out of rocky ground. Normally threshing floors were located in exposed areas so that the wind could easily blow away the chaff.

12 The angel's words seemed out of line with the timid actions of Gideon, and Gideon himself challenged their validity. Actually, the promise of the Lord's presence was intended to encourage Gideon, just as the same assurance led Moses to take the Israelites out of Egypt. "The LORD is with you" is in fact the basic meaning of the name Yahweh (see comment on Ex 3:12–14). Gideon was called a "mighty warrior," perhaps in anticipation of his remarkable bravery, or else a term that means he was of the upper class, the warriors who became the landed aristocracy.

13 Gideon did not recognize the visitor and complained that the oppression proved that the Lord was not with Israel. Like the psalmist (Ps 44:1–3, 9–16), Gideon contrasted the miracles everyone had heard about with the current inactivity of the Lord. Apparently Gideon was unaware of the prophet's explanation in vv.8–10.

14 The heavenly guest is identified as the Lord himself, who was sending Gideon as Israel's deliverer (cf. Ex 3:12; Isa 6:8–9). The strength Gideon possessed was the promise of the Lord's presence with him.

15–16 It is difficult to know whether "Lord" (GK 151) means "sir" or "Lord," for either is possible; in any case, Gideon came to recognize the supernatural character of the visitor only gradually. Gideon belonged to the weak clan of Abiezer, and his own position in his family division was not a prominent one. Yet God delights to use those who are young or humble and bring them to prominence (see 1Co 1:26–27). Gideon's fears were somewhat relieved by the reassurance that with the Lord's help he would be able to defeat the Midianites.

17–21 To obtain proof that God or his messenger was really talking to him, Gideon requested that his guest perform a miraculous sign, the first of three signs that Gideon was to see. First, however, Gideon received permission to bring his guest an offering. Since "offering" can mean "gift," the food prepared by Gideon was partially an expression of hospitality. Unleavened bread is, of course, involved in many offerings; but it is sometimes served in quickly prepared meals (Ge 19:3). This was a substantial meal for such a time of scarcity, since the "ephah" of flour was about half a bushel. The angel instructed Gideon to use the rock—perhaps part of the winepress—as an altar. The fiery consumption of the meat and bread indicated the acceptance of Gideon's offering and, together with the disappearance of the angel, provided the sign Gideon was seeking.

22–24 Gideon's response was one of fright, for he knew that no one could see God face to face and live (Ex 33:20; cf. Jdg 13:22). Gideon was quickly assured that he would live, since the Lord promised him "peace" (GK 8934) and well-being. This peace included not only his personal welfare but also the restoration of Israel's freedom and prosperity. Gratefully, Gideon built an altar to commemorate the Lord's promise.

4. The altar of Baal destroyed and Gideon's life imperiled (6:25–32)

25–26 Almost immediately the Lord asked Gideon to respond to his call to deliver Israel from Midian by taking decisive action in his own family. Even his father had espoused the Baal cult, leading the community in the worship of this pagan deity. Through Moses, God had said that altars to Baal and their accompanying Asherahs must be torn down (Ex 34:12–13; Dt 7:5; cf. Jdg 2:2). Baal worship was popular, however, and Gideon knew he was risking his life by obeying the Lord.

Part of Gideon's task was to sacrifice a bull on a new altar dedicated to the Lord. Bull worship was closely associated with Baal and his father, El, and this particular bull was doubtless reserved for the Baal cult. If two bulls were intended, one might have been used to break down the pagan altar. The altar of the Lord was to be set up on top of a "height" (i.e., a "bluff" or "stronghold"), a prominent place where the city residents may have found refuge from the Midianites. Pieces of wood from the sacred pole would supply fuel for the burnt offering.

27–30 Gideon followed the Lord's orders at night, correctly anticipating that his deeds would arouse the anger of the populace and his own relatives. Apparently one of Gideon's ten servants revealed the identity of Baal's enemy to the townspeople, and they demanded Gideon's death. How different from Dt 13:6–10, where Moses commanded that even close relatives must be stoned for

idolatry! The heresy had become the main religion.

31 Joash refused to put his son to death, arguing that a deity like Baal could defend himself. To interfere was an insult to Baal punishable by death. Joash's seemingly honest appeal to Baal may reflect his own doubt in the power of a deity who could not deliver them from the Midianites.

32 Gideon was probably called Jerub-Baal ("Let Baal contend [with him]") as a derogatory name, indicating the certain judgment the people expected him to face. When no harm came to him, the name became a reminder of Gideon's great victory over Baal.

5. Gideon's army (6:33–35)

33 The crisis in Ophrah was soon eclipsed by the annual invasion of the Midianite coalition. This was their eighth incursion into the fertile Valley of Jezreel, and it came during the wheat harvest in May or June (v.11).

34–35 This time, however, the enemy was not to feast without a fight. The Spirit of the Lord "came upon" (lit., "clothed"; GK 4252) Gideon (cf. 2Ch 24:20–21; Isa 51:9; Lk 24:49), already encouraged by his initial obedience. Like Ehud (3:27), Gideon sounded the trumpet of alarm to gather the troops. The men of his own clan of Abiezer were the first to follow him—an indication that they now shared Gideon's attitude toward Baalism. Then the rest of Manasseh and the other northern tribes came to oppose the Midianites. Ephraim was not invited, perhaps because Gideon feared that this powerful "brother" tribe would not accept his leadership (cf. 1:22; 8:1–3).

6. The fleece (6:36–40)

36–38 Gideon's confidence in God's promises was far from complete and needed to be bolstered frequently. As in the previous instance (v.17), Gideon again asked for a sign to confirm God's favor and word (cf. Ge 24:12–14). Gideon felt that if the fleece only was wet with dew and not the surrounding ground, that meant the Lord was with him. As Gideon requested, so it was: the fleece was saturated with dew, but the ground was dry.

39–40 The wool fleece would absorb the dew more readily than the hard ground of the threshing floor; so the second test required an even greater miracle. When Gideon made the second request, he knew the Lord would be unhappy with his weak faith. The wording of v.39 is remarkably close to Abraham's final plea on behalf of Sodom (Ge 18:32).

Like Gideon, many a believer whose faith needed bolstering has "put out the fleece" to help him find the Lord's will. If this "fleece" consists of a careful observation and interpretation of God's leading through circumstances, the procedure can be a healthy one. But Gideon's method was to make purely arbitrary demands of God and insist on immediate guidance. Despite Gideon's lack of faith and insistence on a second sign, God in mercy not only chose to withhold punishment but condescended to answer him.

7. Gideon's army reduced (7:1–8a)

1 With his hastily assembled army, Gideon set up camp at En-Harod, at the foot of Mount Gilboa. The Midianite hordes were located some four miles north of them in the Jezreel Valley, at a place about ten miles west of the Jordan. The invaders knew about this 32,000-man army and their leader (v.14), but apparently they did not view them as a serious threat.

2–3 The Lord's instructions probably came as a surprise to Gideon, who was already outnumbered four to one. But the size of the army was not the crucial factor: God could give victory to a few men as easily as to a large army (cf. 1Sa 14:6). Lest Israel take credit for her achievements, the Lord began to remove all ground for boasting. The first stage in the troop reduction was to allow the cowardly to go back home. Their fear might prove contagious and ruin the campaign (cf. Dt 20:8). More than two-thirds of Gideon's army left the scene.

4–6 The Lord, however, informed Gideon that the army had to be reduced even further. A special "screening" was set up based on the way the 10,000 drank water. This strange procedure netted a total of 300 men who

Gideon's Battles

The story of Gideon begins with a graphic portrayal of one of the most striking facts of life in the Fertile Crescent: the periodic migration of nomadic people from the Aramean desert into the settled areas of Palestine. Each spring the tents of the *bedouin* herdsmen appear overnight almost as if by magic, scattered on the hills and fields of the farming districts. Conflict between these two ways of life (herdsmen and farmers) was inevitable.

In the Biblical period, the vast numbers and warlike practice of the herdsmen reduced the village people to near vassalage. Gideon's answer was twofold: (1) religious reform, starting with his own family; and (2) military action, based on a coalition of northern Israelite tribes. The location of Gideon's hometown, "Ophrah of the Abiezrites," is not known with certainty, but probably was ancient Aper (modern Afula) in the Valley of Jezreel.

The battle at the spring of Harod is justly celebrated for its strategic brilliance. Denied the use of the only local water source, the Midianites camped in the valley and fell victim to the small band of Israelites, who attacked them from the heights of the hill of Moreh.

The main battle took place north of the hill near the village of Endor at the foot of Mount Tabor. Fleeing by way of the Jordan Valley, the Midianites were trapped when the Ephraimites seized the fords of the Jordan from below Beth Shan to Beth Barah near Adam.

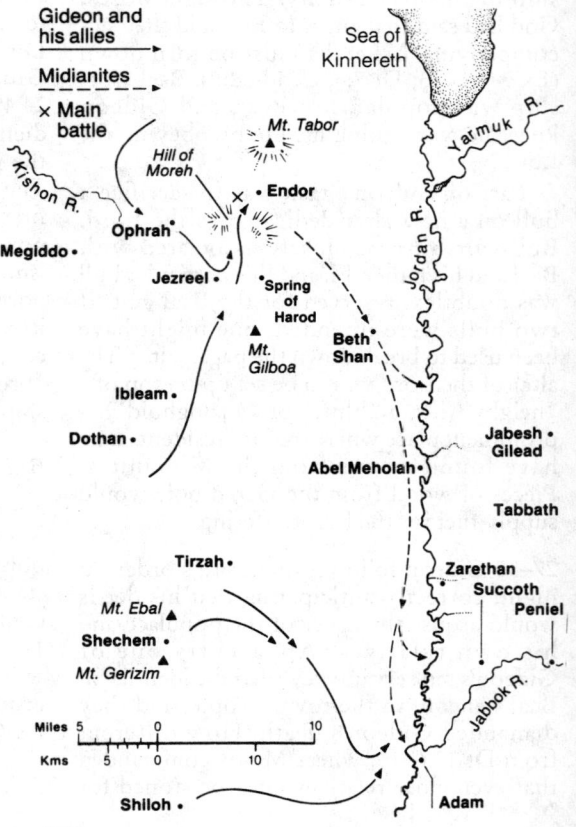

342

apparently crouched down to scoop up water by using their hands as a dog uses its tongue. All the others dropped to their knees before drinking.

7–8a Possibly the 300 displayed a greater alertness in staying on their feet, but in actuality they may have been no more courageous than the 9,700 others. When v.8a says that Gideon "kept" (GK 2616) the 300, it implies that they too had a strong urge to vanish with their colleagues (this expression is used in 19:4 for a person detained against his will). If these 300 men were beginning to tremble, the need for God's intervention became even greater. Before departing the 9,700 gave the remaining soldiers their provisions and their trumpets. The large number of trumpets that Gideon acquired (cf. v.18) implies that a surprise attack was in the planning.

8. Gideon's victory confirmed by a dream (7:8b–14)

8b–12 With less than one percent of his original army, Gideon's faith again began to waver. For the third time God gave him a sign, and at last Gideon was thoroughly convinced. Any promise or action repeated three times was regarded as the surest confirmation (16:15; Nu 24:10). Before he attacked, Gideon and his aide Purah, who was probably his armor-bearer (9:54), paid a visit to the Midianite camp. What he was to hear would encourage him tremendously.

The foe spread out before them seemed innumerable (cf. Jos 11:4; 1Sa 13:5), while Gideon could count the available Israelites all too easily.

13–14 Gideon and his servant overheard two of the enemy soldiers discussing a dream. In the ancient world dreams were considered an important means of divine communication (1Sa 28:6; cf. Ge 20:3–6; 37:6–7; et al.). The enemy soldier was able to interpret the dream and predict Gideon's victory. Barley bread could represent Israel as a cultivator of the soil. The key to the interpretation of the dream is that the word translated "came tumbling" (lit., "overturning"; GK 2200) can be applied also to swords (cf. its use in Ge 3:24). The "overturning" or "overthrow" of the tent represented the collapse of the nomadic forces.

9. Preparation for the battle (7:15–18)

15 Gideon realized that what he had heard was far more than a coincidence; so he immediately prostrated himself in grateful worship before the Lord. Now ready to fight, Gideon returned to prepare his men for the historic battle.

16–18 The only orthodox part of Gideon's instructions was to divide the men into three groups (cf. 1Sa 11:11; 2Sa 18:2). By spreading out around the Midianites, Gideon's troops would create the impression of being a much larger army. The "trumpets" (GK 8795) were the same ram's horn type used by Ehud and Gideon (3:27; 6:34) to summon the troops. Only the leaders would give signals on the trumpets, so three hundred trumpets normally represented a sizable army. When Joshua captured Jericho, only seven priests had trumpets (Jos 6:6).

The empty jars were used to hide the light of the torches until the proper moment arrived. The soldiers may have been mystified as to the actual purpose of such unusual weapons, but their orders were to follow Gideon's example carefully. After blowing the trumpets, they were to shout the war cry (v.20).

10. The Midianites routed (7:19–25)

19–20 Gideon and his men disrupted the Midianite camp sometime between ten o'clock and midnight, striking just after new guards had been posted. The Israelites' main weapon was noise; and between the trumpet blasts and the smashing of jars, they achieved the intended effect of demoralizing the Midianites. Once the jars were broken, three hundred torches lit up the night, apparently at the head of vast columns of troops. To add to the nightmare, a ringing battle cry pierced the night air.

21–22 These startling developments quickly produced panic, a normal occurrence when God led his people into battle. The Midianites were convinced that a powerful army was about to massacre them. The people ran about, shouting and trying to escape as fast as possible. In all the confusion they began fighting among themselves, thinking that enemy forces were already in their camp. Finally, to avoid the slaughter, the Midianite hordes fled toward the Jordan and the safety of the desert beyond.

23–25 To help in the pursuit, Gideon summoned reinforcements, perhaps including many of his original 32,000. Their courage restored, they gladly rushed after the foe. Gideon also called on the powerful tribe of Ephraim to cut off the Midianites at the fords of the Jordan (cf. 3:28). Many of the enemy forces had not yet crossed when the men of Ephraim attacked them and captured Oreb and Zeeb, probably leading generals of the army. The two were promptly put to death at sites later named to commemorate the occasion (cf. Isa 10:26). When the Ephraimites met with Gideon in 8:1–3, they brought along the heads of these leaders.

11. The Ephraimites' complaint (8:1–3)

1–3 The tribe of Ephraim had a proud heritage (see 1:22) and felt insulted by Gideon's failure to call on them earlier. They had cooperated honorably with Ehud (3:26–29) and Barak (5:13–14a) and wondered why they were left out this time. Gideon decided to adopt a course of appeasement. He praised them for their great victory over Oreb and Zeeb, assuring them that in comparison his accomplishments were small. In a sense Ephraim received the "leftovers" (NIV, "gleanings"). These, however, were more substantial than the initial victory ("harvest") won by his little Abiezrite clan. Gideon's flattery calmed their anger and avoided the civil war that later flared up between Ephraim and Manasseh (12:4–6). "A gentle answer turns away wrath" (Pr 15:1).

12. Lack of cooperation from Succoth and Peniel (8:4–9)

4–6 The narrative now shifts back to the exploits of the "three hundred." Gideon was faced with an attitude exactly the opposite of Ephraim's as two cities completely rejected his request for help. The tiny army was now some forty miles from the hill of Moreh when they came to Succoth, just north of the Jabbok River. Worn out from the long chase, Gideon asked these residents of Gad for some provisions. The men of Succoth reasoned that the fleeing Midianites would soon regroup and easily defeat the makeshift army thrown together by Gideon. Any assistance given to Gideon would implicate Succoth

and bring certain retaliation from the feared nomads. The question in v.6 apparently refers to the custom of cutting off the hands of dead victims as a convenient body count (1Sa 18:25; cf. Jdg 1:6).

7 The sarcastic, unpatriotic response of the leaders of Succoth brought a sharp retort from Gideon. Perhaps the tribes of Transjordan could be excused for failing to aid Deborah and Barak (5:17), but neutrality was impossible when the conflict was on their soil (cf. 5:23). Gideon promised that when he returned in victory, he would severely punish the city.

8–9 Moving six miles east, Gideon received the same response from the people of Peniel. In the very place where Jacob had met with God and had his name changed to Israel (Ge 32:28–30), these descendants of his refused to believe that God could give victory over the Midianites. Gideon vowed that he would soon demolish the fortified tower that had made Peniel an important city.

13. The capture of the kings of Midian (8:10–12)

10–12 True to his word, Gideon pressed farther into Transjordan, following the caravan trail taken by the Midianites. By this time the remnants of the Midianite army were in Karkor, east of the Dead Sea. No doubt the Midianites believed they were safely out of range of the pursuing armies, but again Gideon surprised them and routed them.

Gideon's main goal was the capture of Zeba and Zalmunna, Midian's two kings, for without leadership the eastern hordes were not likely to resume their raids. The two kings probably belonged to different tribal groups.

14. Retaliation against Succoth and Peniel (8:13–17)

13–17 The resounding victory over Midian did not deter Gideon from severely disciplining these two delinquent cities. A young man from Succoth was compelled to write down the names of the "princes" or "elders." The seventy-seven men who were registered on this death list heard Gideon repeat their earlier taunt before carrying out the punishment. Like their neighbors in Peniel, the men of Succoth doubtless died for their guilt.

15. The Midianite kings slain (8:18–21)

18 The scene probably shifts across the Jordan, so that Gideon could display his captives to the main body of Israelites. The presence of his young son, Jether, also points to a location nearer home. After viewing the vengeance taken by Gideon on fellow Israelites, the Midianite kings did not hold out much hope for their own survival. In fact, they seemed to prefer death by admitting they had killed Gideon's full brothers—a slaughter that may have occurred during one of their earlier campaigns, when opportunity for revenge seemed remote.

19 Gideon had considered sparing the kings' lives, but the additional element of personal revenge made their death certain. Moreover, the death of enemy leaders almost always accompanied total military victory (3:21–25; 4:21–22; 9:55; Jos 10:26).

20–21 Gideon gave the honor of executing the kings to his firstborn son, Jether. The lad shunned this gruesome task, and the kings quickly pointed out that this was a man's job. For them it would be more honorable and less painful to be killed by a renowned warrior like Gideon. Death at the hands of a boy or a woman was considered a disgrace (5:24–27; 9:54). Gideon complied with their final request.

16. Gideon's ephod (8:22–27)

22–23 Gideon's celebrated victory brought him an invitation to become king over Israel and establish a ruling dynasty. Under unified rule, the Israelites felt they could better prevent any future oppression. Gideon rejected the offer, for God was their king, and the people needed to renew their allegiance to him.

24–26 While refusing the throne, Gideon did in fact assume many of the prerogatives of a king; he established a large harem (v.30), amassed a fortune (v.26), acquired royal robes, and made an ephod to consult God (v.27). He also accepted gifts from his grateful soldiers. Most of the items given to Gideon were those usually worn by women in Israel: "earrings" (perhaps "noserings"; cf. Ge 24:47; Eze 16:12), "pendants," and "chains" or "necklaces" (cf. SS 4:9). This vast repertoire of jewelry may have been a factor in Gideon's accumulation of wives.

Verse 24 contains the only reference in Judges to the Ishmaelites. Apparently this was an inclusive term for Israel's nomadic relatives and alternated freely with "Midianites" (cf. Ge 37:25–28; 39:1).

27 With the gold Gideon surprisingly made an ephod that was to lead Israel into idolatry. The high priest wore an ephod, an apronlike garment made of linen, various colors of yarn, and gold thread (Ex 39:2–5). The breastpiece attached to it contained the mysterious Urim and Thummim (Ex 28:28–30), used to consult God (1Sa 23:9–10); this may have been Gideon's purpose in making a golden replica. Gideon seems to have wrongly assumed priestly functions. The ephod eventually served an idolatrous purpose and is described in the same terms as the gods of Canaan (2:2, 17). Gideon, who had boldly broken up his father's altar to Baal, was now setting a trap for his own family.

17. Gideon's accomplishments and death (8:28–32)

28–31 Midian had been thoroughly disgraced and caused no further trouble. Gideon himself spent the remainder of his life in Ophrah. His many wives and sons reflected his prosperity (cf. 2Ki 10:1, 4; 12:9, 14). The hatred and murder that plagued Gideon's family after his death (cf. ch. 9) are characteristic of OT polygamous situations. Among Gideon's wives was a concubine from Shechem. Apparently she continued to live in her hometown and remained under the authority of her father. In such marriage relationships the husband was expected to visit from time to time (cf. 15:1). It is the son of this low-ranking wife who rises to prominence in the next chapter.

32 Gideon's death notice further attests his importance; only he and Samson were buried in the tomb of their fathers. To die "at a good old age" implies a long and full life (Ge 15:15; 25:8; 1Ch 29:28).

G. The Brief Reign of Abimelech (8:33–9:57)

1. Apostasy after Gideon's death (8:33–35)

33 Abimelech is not called a judge, nor was he raised up by God to rescue Israel. Since he was the son of Gideon, this period stands in a unique relationship with the preceding one.

Again the Israelites became enamored with Baal worship, and particularly Baal-Berith (cf. 2:11), whose worship was centered at Shechem. Baal-Berith means "Baal of the covenant" and may indicate that they had made a covenant with Baal.

34–35 By worshiping Baal-Berith, Israel deserted the God who had made a covenant with them at Sinai and who had repeatedly been their Savior. They also quickly forgot the benefits won for the nation by Gideon. Calling Gideon Jerub-Baal here recalls Baal's inability to "defend himself" against Gideon (see 6:27–32).

2. Abimelech's rise to power (9:1–6)

1 In a polygamous society the relatives of one's mother can provide refuge and support for an ambitious prince. Abimelech was probably spurned by his half-brothers because of his mother's lowly status (cf. 11:1–2); so he appealed to his mother's brothers for help.

Shechem (between Mount Ebal and Mount Gerizim) lay on important caravan routes. Since no mention is made of the capture of Shechem during Joshua's conquest of Canaan, possibly a treaty was made with that city soon after the invasion (see Jos 8:30–35; 24:1–27—two covenant renewal ceremonies that took place at Shechem). The people of Shechem maintained a link with the Canaanite founders of the city, and perhaps Abimelech's mother herself was a Canaanite.

2–4 Abimelech's appeal was based on the tenuous claim that his step-brothers' rule would not have Shechem's best interests at heart. In fact, it is unlikely that Gideon's sons intended to dominate an area thirty miles south of Ophrah. The residents of Shechem, however, agreed to his plan and provided a substantial sum to carry it out. Temple treasures were often used for military and political ends (cf. 1Ki 15:18). The individuals hired were a worthless band (cf. 11:3; 2Ch 13:7).

5–6 Treacherous and unstable, these mercenaries helped Abimelech commit wholesale fratricide. But mass murders are rarely a total success, and Jotham managed a narrow escape (cf. 2Ch 22:10–12). Nevertheless, Abimelech became the first person ever to be crowned as king in Israel. His abortive rule ran roughshod over the divine requirements

for that office (cf. Dt 17:14–20). His coronation ironically took place near the tree in Shechem where Joshua had solemnly placed the "Book of the Law" (Jos 24:26). Beth Millo (lit., "house of the fill") is likely the same as the "tower of Shechem" of v.46. The word "fill" comes from the huge earthen platform on which these structures were built.

3. Jotham's fable (9:7–21)

The sole survivor of Abimelech's purge delivered an incisive evaluation of his half-brother's rule. Presented in allegorical form, this story of the trees effectively lays bare Abimelech's true character and the utter disregard of the people of Shechem for Gideon's memory.

7–9 Jotham traveled to Shechem and climbed Mount Gerizim's eight-hundred-foot slope south of the city. There, at a safe distance from his audience, he pronounced a powerful curse (cf. v.57).

The introduction to the fable contains an unusual reference to God as the One who listened to them. By this statement Jotham may be asking the hearers to present to God a response to his arguments. For the comparison of kings to trees, see also Isa 10:33–34. In recognition of Israel's lowly status, Jotham began, not with a cedar, but with an olive tree. Olives were used for food, ointment, and medicine; they were one of Israel's most valued crops (Dt 11:14). Olive oil kept the lamps in the Holy Place burning constantly, thus "honoring" the Lord. In view of its important functions, the olive tree declined the offer to become king.

10–11 The fig tree likewise passed up the opportunity to rule. Like olives, figs were a key agricultural product. Israel's picture of the ideal age was for every man to sit under his vine and under his fig tree (Mic 4:4; cf. 2Ki 18:31).

12–13 Predictably, the vine also refused. Its fruit was the main beverage of the land, and libations of wine accompanied many sacrifices at the sanctuary (Nu 15:10).

14–15 At last "the thornbush" was called on; and, having nothing better to do, the surprised shrub gladly agreed to reign. This plant was a menace to agriculture and had the quality of burning quickly (Ps 58:9). Since it provided little if any shade, its "refuge" is spoken of sarcastically. It could only threaten to destroy, if its rule were not accepted.

16–20 By this time Jotham's main point was clear, but he gave a detailed interpretation. Gideon probably represented one of the good trees invited to become king (8:22), though exact identifications are not needed. Noble, capable leaders like Gideon believed that the theocracy, not a monarchy, was the best form of government. Abimelech was the thornbush king. Along with the Shechemites, he was guilty of a terrible crime against Gideon, who had saved them at the risk of his own life. He really had nothing to offer the people. Abimelech's mother is called a "slave girl," a term usually referring to a wife's servant who is also a concubine (Ge 21:12; 30:3).

The reference to acting "honorably and in good faith" (v.19) with Gideon and his family implies that an agreement of some kind had been made with Gideon (cf. 8:35). A judge and his family had certain privileges that the revolt completely ignored. The supposition in v.20 is actually a grim prediction that the parties to the crime would mutually destroy each other. True to its nature, the thornbush would ignite a deadly blaze.

21 Before the hostile audience could intercept him, Jotham ended his short speech and fled.

4. The revolt of Gaal and Shechem (9:22–29)

22 Abimelech's rule of Shechem, Arumah (v.41), and Thebez (v.50) was a brief one. The word for "governed" (GK 8606) is unique to the book and is perhaps chosen to distinguish Abimelech's ill-fated rule from that of the true judges. He ruled like a tyrant, and he soon encountered opposition in Shechem itself.

23–25 The Lord was at the source of the conflict, for he "sent an evil spirit" to disrupt the relationship between Abimelech and Shechem. If "spirit" is to be taken in the sense of a supernatural being, this situation would be comparable to Saul's (1Sa 16:14; cf. 1Ki 22:19–23). The citizens of Shechem and Abimelech had committed murder, and the friction between them arose as a result of their guilt.

"To act treacherously" (v.23) is to break an agreement with someone. Shechem's citizens betrayed Abimelech by ambushing the caravans that passed through the ideally located city. No longer could Abimelech receive revenue from these welcomed traders. With travel so dangerous and the lost income, the economy began to suffer greatly (cf. 5:6).

26–27 A certain Gaal came to Shechem to exploit the situation and to deepen the rift between Abimelech and Shechem. He was probably a Canaanite strongly opposed to Israelite rule. Gaal and his men arrived near the time of the summer harvest, when the Canaanites had a religious festival similar to Israel's Feast of Tabernacles (Lev 23:34–43). The Canaanite celebration often included excessive drinking and immorality, hardly conducive to true religious expression. Yet the "festival" of v.27 is literally a "praise," when the gods (especially Baal-Berith; cf. v.4) would be honored for providing an abundant harvest (cf. 16:24).

28–29 Gaal took advantage of the occasion to advocate open rebellion against Abimelech. Whereas Abimelech had earlier stressed his descent from a woman of Shechem (vv.1–2), Gaal noted that Abimelech's father was an Israelite. How could a city that traced its heritage back to the Hivite prince Hamor (Ge 34:2) give its allegiance to an Israelite intruder? Gaal boldly asserted that he would be a far better leader and threw out a challenge to Abimelech. Part of Gaal's appeal lay in the fact that Abimelech did not reside in Shechem; instead, he had appointed Zebul (a Canaanite name meaning "prince") to govern the city, and the Shechemites may have resented this.

5. Gaal's defeat (9:30–41)

30–33 When Zebul heard about Gaal's slanderous remarks aimed at Abimelech and him, he moved quickly before the rebel forces could decide to restrict his activities. He secretly sent messengers to inform Abimelech of the dangerous situation and to offer some sound advice. If Abimelech struck quickly, he could still save the day; for Gaal had not yet had time to organize the Shechemites into a solid army. Zebul recommended an ambush—a strategy that had worked at Ai (Jos 8:2; cf. Jdg 20:37).

34 Abimelech took Zebul's advice and used the tactics of his father, Gideon—moving at night and dividing his forces into several companies. By morning Abimelech's army was ready to make a sudden dash to Shechem and surprise the enemy.

35–37 Gaal, in his new role of leader of Shechem, was stationed at the city gate when he noticed the approaching men. But Zebul was there to ease Gaal's fears in an effort to keep him from preparing his troops. Finally, it became clear that people were coming from all over, including a company from the soothsayers' tree. Gaal may have wished he could have consulted a practitioner there, though his fate seemed sealed already.

38–39 At this point Zebul reminded Gaal of his earlier taunt and challenged him to make good his boast. Gaal probably was not prepared for a siege; so he had little choice but to leave the city walls behind and confront Abimelech in the open. It is difficult to know whether Gaal had the support of the fighting men of Shechem in the battle or had to rely only on his personal supporters (the alternate translation of v.39 in NIV note., "Gaal went out in the sight of the citizens of Shechem," is equally valid). Shechem's residents were mainly involved in battles on the following day (vv.42–45).

40–41 Whatever its composition, Gaal's army soon headed back to the city, and many more were killed or wounded along the way. Abimelech himself did not try to enter the city, but his capable governor drove the disgraced Gaal and his remaining men out of Shechem.

6. The capture of Shechem and the tower of Shechem (9:42–49)

Apparently the people of Shechem were eager to resume their normal activities. Abimelech, however, wanted to punish them further for their lack of loyalty. But his vindictive action destroyed the main city of his "kingdom" and left him with little to rule (cf. Pr 30:21–22).

42–44 Since the fields were outside the city, the people had to go outside its walls to bring in the rest of the harvest. They likely did not have any military plans, nor did they anticipate further problems from Abimelech—at least not so soon. However, for the second day in a row, Abimelech set an ambush and surprised the people in the fields. He cut off their line of retreat to the city while the rest of his troops slaughtered those who were stranded.

45 Already weakened by the loss of so many able-bodied men, the people left in Shechem were unable to ward off Abimelech's full-scale attack. He forced his way into the city and put the rest of the people to the sword. Then he tore down the main buildings and sowed the ground with salt to symbolize the utter destruction of the city and its perpetual infertility (Dt 29:23; Ps 107:34). Indeed, Shechem was not rebuilt until the reign of Jeroboam I, almost two centuries later (1Ki 12:25).

46 The tower of Shechem was probably the same as Beth Millo (see comment on v.6). Normally the tower or fortress was located within the city proper, as at Thebez (v.51). At Shechem the fortress-temple of El-Berith (an alternate name for Baal-Berith; cf. 8:33) may have been this inner citadel. People could have taken refuge within its walls to defend the citadel independently of the rest of the city (cf. 1:8).

47–49 This time Abimelech decided to build a huge fire to destroy his victims. He and his men got some branches or brushwood from nearby Mount Zalmon and carried them to the tower. Abimelech's command to have his soldiers follow his example sounds like Gideon (7:17), who himself had destroyed a tower at Peniel (8:17). After the usual long, rainless summer, the wood was like tinder; so a blazing fire was soon underway. The temple gave the people no protection. With the collapse of the fortress, all resistance at Shechem came to an end.

7. The death of Abimelech (9:50–57)

50–53 Dissatisfaction with Abimelech's rule was widespread, for he next traveled ten miles northeast of Shechem to punish Thebez. The city proper was easily taken, but a strong fortress within it proved more formidable. The people of Thebez heard of Abimelech's strategy at Shechem; so they climbed to the roof where they could offer some resistance. When Abimelech tried to set another fire, he was struck by an upper millstone thrown with amazing accuracy by a woman. The "upper millstone" was an easily held stone, about ten inches long, that rode back and forth over the larger lower millstone as the grain was crushed (cf. Dt 24:6). Grinding wheat was the work of women, and the woman doubtless took the stone with her as a potential weapon. Her success was surprising (cf. 1Ki 22:34); it was unmistakably a divine retribution.

54 Since dying at the hand of a woman was considered a disgrace (cf. 4:17–24), Abimelech commanded his armor-bearer to kill him immediately. Yet long after his death, the credit continued to be given to the woman (cf. 2Sa 11:21; 1Sa 31:4).

55 With Abimelech dead, the Israelites gave up their campaign and returned home. Similarly, later in Israel's history, the slaying of a leader led to the disintegration of Sheba's revolt against David (2Sa 20:22) and to the dispersal of Ahab's armies at Ramoth Gilead (1Ki 22:34–36). Each example illustrates the power of individual leaders and the desperate need for godly, capable rulers.

56–57 Both Abimelech and Shechem had been guilty of murder and ultimately had to pay for their crimes. Jotham's curse was fulfilled in a remarkably literal way (vv.15, 20). The fire that destroyed the tower of Shechem may have been partially fed by thornbushes, the very designation used for Abimelech in the fable.

H. The Rule of Tola and Jair (10:1–5)

1–2 Little is known about the rule of the minor judges mentioned here and in 12:8–15. The reference to "save" implies a military victory over some oppressor. Except in the reference to Shamgar (3:31), none of the references to the other minor judges identifies the oppressor of Israel. Since the word "led" (or "judged") appears most often with the lesser judges, some believe that these judges functioned primarily to handle judicial decisions (cf. its use in 4:4).

Tola son of Puah was, like his father, named after one of the sons of Issachar (Ge 46:13). Shamir was located in central Palestine. By maintaining a base there, Tola may have exercised control over much of the land.

3–5 Tola's twenty-three-year rule probably overlapped that of Jair, though Tola's began first. Jair was in charge of Gilead, east of the Jordan, and his rule provides a transition to the more important exploits of another Gileadite, Jephthah. Like Tola, Jair was named after a renowned figure—Jair, a great-great-grandson of Manasseh, who captured sixty cities in Bashan (Nu 32:39–41; 1Ch 2:22–23). These cities were called "Havvoth Jair" (the "settlements of Jair"), and thirty of them were still controlled by Jair the judge. That Jair had a total of thirty sons shows he was wealthy (cf. 8:30), as does his possession of thirty donkeys. Kings rode donkeys of this kind (Ge 49:11; Zec 9:9).

I. The Victory of Jephthah Over the Ammonites (10:6–12:7)

1. Oppression and supplication (10:6–16)

The scene now shifts to Transjordan as the Ammonites exerted tremendous pressure from the east. The author uses the occasion of this renewed suffering to detail again the phases of the cycle (cf. 2:6–3:6). These verses also introduce the Philistine oppression, which probably ran concurrently with the Ammonite invasion (cf. v.7).

6–7 This is the final and most extensive list of Israel's sins; it may apply to the whole period. The Baals and Ashtoreths (cf. 2:11–13) were worshiped by most of the nations mentioned here, but other deities also were served. Moab's main god was Chemosh (Nu 21:29), Ammon served Milcom (1Ki 11:5), and Dagon was the leading deity of the Philistines (16:23). By mentioning the gods of the Ammonites and the Philistines last, the author emphasizes that Israel deserved to be enslaved to these two nations.

8–9 The opening clause of v.8 refers to the Ammonites and their severe oppression of Israel. "That year" can be placed about 1096 B.C. The oppression lasted as long as the Moabite one (3:14) and was concentrated in Gilead (i.e., central and northern Transjordan (cf. 5:17). Tribes in south-central Palestine also came under Ammonite domination, and the mention of Ephraim is important for understanding 12:1–3.

10–14 Faced with mounting difficulties, the Israelites finally confessed their sin and cried out for help. The Lord, however, is not to be called on only in emergencies; so he withheld assistance. After all, he had faithfully rescued them at least seven times, only to have them turn quickly to other gods. He released them from Egypt's iron furnace and enabled them to defeat Sihon and Og, the two kings of the Amorites (Jos 2:10) who lived in Transjordan. The Ammonites had earlier aided the Moabites (3:13), and Shamgar was renowned for defeating the Philistines (3:31). The Sidonians may have helped Jabin and Sisera during the "Canaanite" oppression (4:1–3), and the Amalekites already opposed Israel twice in Judges, supporting the Moabites (3:13) and the Midianites (6:3). The Midianites themselves may be the seventh nation mentioned.

15–16 God's people demonstrated the genuineness of their repentance by throwing out the idols they were worshiping and by being willing to return to God on his terms. Persistent prayer finally brought an answer from Israel's compassionate Lord (cf. 2:18). Expressed in human terms, God "could bear [them] no longer," as he watched them suffer.

2. Gilead's predicament (10:17–18)

17–18 Israel's deliverance came in the campaign that followed. At first, however, it looked as if another Ammonite victory was imminent. Their army had once more assembled to attack Israel. The Israelites, determined to stop the Ammonites, gathered at Mizpah to plan their strategy (a town near the territory of the Ammonites; see 11:29). The leaders of Gilead had no outstanding general; so as an incentive they offered to make any commander who proved successful against the Ammonites the ruler of their entire territory (cf. 11:9).

3. Jephthah's exile and recall (11:1–11)

1–3 The opening paragraph is a parenthesis introducing Jephthah son of Gilead. Gilead too was named after a famous ancestor, in this case the grandson of Manasseh. Without doubt his family belonged to the "upper class," one reason why Jephthah was called a "mighty warrior" or "man of valor." Jephthah was certainly a capable fighter, but his social position also was important. Because of his mother's status, he was an illegitimate son and ranked at the bottom of his family. But in spite of this, the Lord saw fit to use him in a remarkable way.

Apparently Gilead was not a polygamist. Only one wife is mentioned in v.2, and the reason for Jephthah's expulsion was that he was the son of "another woman." His half-brothers had little sympathy for him, especially in the matter of inheritance. Unlike Abimelech (9:1–5), Jephthah did not have the protection of his mother's family; so he was forced to flee to Tob, some fifteen miles east of Ramoth Gilead. In this desolate region Jephthah roamed with a band of "adventurers" and fellow misfits (cf. 9:4).

4–6 Jephthah established such a reputation as a skilled fighter and leader that the men of Gilead turned to him in their search for a commander. Presumably "some time later" brings the reader back to 10:17–18 and the Mizpah gathering.

7–11 With understandable bitterness, Jephthah reminded the leaders of Gilead of his ostracism (cf. 10:14). The elders swore before the Lord that his banishment was over and that they would in fact make him ruler over all Gilead after the battle. This offer astonished Jephthah, but he was convinced by their willingness to take an oath. His years of wandering had served to deepen his faith in the Lord. He knew that if victory lay ahead, it would be from the Lord's hand (v.9). When Jephthah returned with the leaders to Mizpah, he confirmed his intentions "before the LORD" as the agreement with Gilead was sealed. The ceremony at Mizpah had the makings of a coronation as the people installed their new leader.

4. Jephthah's presentation of Israel's territorial claim (11:12–28)

12–13 Jephthah's first move as commander was to get in touch with the Ammonites in an attempt to negotiate peace. The reply from the king of the Ammonites contained hope for peace, but only on the condition that Israel return "occupied territory."

14–15 Since the disputed land lay between the Arnon and the Jabbok rivers, Jephthah sent back a detailed explanation of how Israel had obtained possession of that region. This historical summary attempts to prove that Israel captured this land from the Amorites without violating the territorial rights of either Moab or Ammon (who were now allies; cf. 3:13).

16–18 Jephthah first referred to Israel's stay at Kadesh, when they requested permission to travel through Edom (Nu 20:14–17) and Moab. Neither Edom nor Moab allowed Israel to pass through; so the people detoured south of Edom and then east of Moab, stopping at the eastern end of the Arnon River. The Lord specifically commanded Israel not to fight against Edom, Moab, and Ammon because these peoples were all related to Israel; and God had given them their own territory (Dt 2:5, 9, 19).

19–22 No such prohibition applied to Sihon, however. So when the Amorite king also refused the Israelites passage, there was a battle at Jahaz. God gave the Israelites a decisive victory, and they took possession of the precise parcel of land then claimed by the king of Ammon (v.13). Based on the borders at the time of Israel's conquest, Jephthah's case is a strong one. Moses had seized only Amorite territory and had avoided any open conflict with either Moab or Ammon.

23–24 In OT times war often was viewed as a contest between the gods of the nations involved (cf. v.27). The Lord had clearly defeated the gods of the Amorites, giving Israel clear title to the land. The Ammonites, therefore, had no right to take it away. They should have been content with the territory Chemosh had given to them. Indeed, land itself was considered the property of the deity (cf. 2Ki 5:17). Ammon was thus guilty of stealing real estate belonging to the God of Israel.

Jephthah's reference to Chemosh raises a problem, since Chemosh was the god of Moab while Milcom was the Ammonites' deity. The Ammonites may have joined in the worship of Moab's gods, just as the Midianites did in Nu 25. Possibly "Chemosh" and "Milcom" were viewed as alternate names of the same deity.

25–26 Jephthah's final argument is based on the length of time Israel had possessed the disputed territory. Balak was the king of Moab who hired Balaam to curse the Israelites. After the curses turned out to be repeated blessings (Nu 24:10), Balak made no attempt to regain the area held by Sihon and then Israel. He clearly recognized the legitimacy of Israel's claim to the land. During the next "three hundred years," neither Moab nor Ammon succeeded in retaking the land. Did not such a long occupancy prove Israel's right to that area?

27–28 Insisting on his innocence, Jephthah appealed to the Lord to decide the issue (this is the only explicit reference in the book to the Lord as Judge). But Jephthah's detailed arguments failed to impress the king of Ammon. Convinced that at least might was on his side, the king prepared for war with Israel.

5. Jephthah's vow and victory over Ammon (11:29–33)

29 As in the case of Gideon (6:34), the Spirit of the Lord empowered Jephthah in preparation for battle (cf. 6:34). Thus strengthened, he traveled north through Transjordan, gathering troops from the tribes of Gad and Manasseh. These two tribes actually split Gilead between them (Jos 13:25, 31), with Gad receiving the larger share.

30–31 Jephthah's desire to defeat the Ammonites was so intense that he made a special "vow to the Lord." Though intended as an act of devotion, it showed a lack of faith in God's enabling power. Scholars continue to debate whether or not Jephthah had a human sacrifice in mind. The phrases in question can be translated "whatever comes out" or "whoever comes out" and "I will sacrifice it," but it is hard to see how a common animal sacrifice would express unusual devotion.

Human sacrifice was strictly forbidden by the Mosaic law (Lev 18:21; Dt 12:31); so Jephthah should have known that God's favor could not be gained in this terrible way. Yet Israel's neighbors—ironically, especially the Ammonites—sacrificed their children (see 2Ki 3:27); and this custom might have influenced Jephthah. Although Jephthah did not originally plan to sacrifice his daughter, he would gladly have offered up anyone else if it helped bring victory.

32–33 The Lord gave Israel a stunning victory over Ammon, and Israel was able to capture twenty cities. Thus the bulk of the region between the Arnon and the Jabbok once again belonged to Israel. Verse 33 indicates that a very large number of Ammonites died in the battle.

6. Jephthah's vow fulfilled (11:34–40)

34–35 The flush of victory gave way to bitter despair when Jephthah was greeted by his daughter, leaping and dancing, like Miriam and the women of Israel who had celebrated the triumph at the Red Sea (cf. Ex 15:20). But as the first to leave his house, she came under the terms of his vow. How strange for this happy young girl to notice the response of her father! He behaved like a defeated soldier, not the victorious commander he really was. The death of his only child would mean the end of his family line. Jephthah's lament describes the situation as an unmitigated disaster. Both he and the Ammonites were humiliated and subdued. His own daughter unknowingly brought calamity to herself and her father.

36–39 Jephthah's daughter sensed the implications of her father's vow but made no attempt to get him to break it. Her willingness to yield herself resembled that of another only child, Isaac (Ge 22). Even if victory over Ammon meant her life, it was worth it; and she gently encouraged her father to perform his vow. First, however, Jephthah's daughter requested a two-month period in which she could literally weep because she would never marry. The goal of every Hebrew girl was to marry and have children (Ge 30:1), but Jephthah's daughter would do neither. Accompanied by her friends, she spent two months on the mountains, weeping and meditating, preparing for her ordeal. When she returned, Jephthah carried out his solemn vow.

40 The yearly commemoration of this noble girl makes sense only if she died at the hands of her father. No other interpretation is satisfactory. The death of this innocent girl came because of a rash vow. Jephthah knew that it was a sin to break a vow (Nu 30:2), but in this case it was an even greater sin to fulfill it. Jephthah was treating his daughter as a "person devoted to destruction" (Lev 27:29). This type of punishment was a strong curse reserved for the enemies of God (cf. Jos 6:17), but Jephthah's daughter had done nothing to deserve such a fate. According to Pr 26:2, "an undeserved curse does not come to rest" (cf. 1Sa 14:28, 43–45). Though Jephthah sincerely believed God required him to go through with his promise, he was badly mistaken.

7. Jephthah's defeat of Ephraim (12:1–7)

1–3 The proud and powerful tribe of Ephraim had earlier denounced Gideon for failing to invite them to participate in the victory over Midian (8:1–3). Gideon had soothed them by involving them in the campaign and praising their contribution. Now Ephraim challenged Jephthah, voicing their complaint after crossing the Jordan and coming to Zaphon. They threatened to burn down Jephthah's house, as if he were no more than a petty prince (cf. 15:6). This time the exchange did not end so amicably.

Understandably, Jephthah was greatly irritated by the Ephraimites' arrogance. During the eighteen-year oppression, the people of Gilead had doubtless asked for help from Ephraim and other affected tribes (cf. 10:9), but no assistance was forthcoming. In the recently completed campaign, there was no mention of an invitation to Ephraim (11:29), though Jephthah indicated that a general call may have gone out. The fight against the Ammonites was a perilous one. Yet Jephthah defeated them and gave God the credit. Why should the Ephraimites complain about a victory accomplished through God's intervention for the benefit of all the tribes? It was a strange jealousy that spurred on Ephraim.

4–6 The civil war was triggered when the men of Ephraim called the Gileadites "renegades." This insult may have been partially aimed at Jephthah's former position as a brigand chief, but more likely it stemmed from the division between the eastern and western tribes (cf. 5:15–17). Ephraim looked down on these relatives across the river, who no longer even spoke the same dialect.

For the third time in Judges, the capture of the fords of the Jordan was crucial (3:28; 7:24–25). Apparently these were the same fords where the Ephraimites had cut down the Midianites in ch. 7. But this time Jephthah's army slaughtered the Ephraimites, who were trying to flee from the skillful Gileadite fighters. The clever test faced by the disgraced soldiers was to pronounce the word "Shibboleth," which means either "an ear of grain" or "a flowing stream." The Ephraimites were identified when they managed to say only "Sibboleth" (cf. Mt 26:73).

With the loss of 42,000 men, Ephraim's military capability was virtually wiped out (cf. Nu 1:33). Jephthah was vindicated and his position as leader of Gilead was strengthened. Nevertheless, the intertribal warfare illustrated the serious problems that confronted the nation as a whole.

7 Jephthah "led" or "judged" (see the introduction) Israel for only six years, most likely only in Transjordan. He was buried in Gilead, perhaps in Mizpah where he had made his home.

J. The Rules of Ibzan, Elon, and Abdon (12:8–15)

Before his detailed discussion of Samson's life, the author inserts brief notices about the last three minor judges. They ruled for comparatively short periods of time and were probably contemporaries.

1. Ibzan (12:8–10)

8 Ibzan ruled from Bethlehem, which may refer to the famous town south of Jerusalem or to a city in the territory of Zebulun (Jos 19:15). The Zebulun location is favored because the southern city is usually identified as "Bethlehem in Judah" (17:7–9; 19:1–2, 18).

9–10 Ibzan's large family reveals his wealth and polygamous practices (cf. 8:30; 10:4). He gave his daughters away in marriage to people outside his clan (cf. Dt 25:5). Marriages were often contracted within one's tribe (14:3); the fact that Ibzan's marriage policy is mentioned suggests a break with tradition.

2. Elon (12:11–12)

11–12 Elon ranks with Tola (10:1–2) as a judge about whom almost nothing is known. He was named after one of the sons of the founder of the tribe (Ge 46:14).

3. Abdon (12:13–15)

13 Pirathon was the home of Benaiah, one of David's mighty men (1Ch 11:31) from Ephraim (1Ch 27:14). The site is close to the border between Ephraim and Manasseh.

14–15 The mention of Abdon's forty sons and thirty grandsons seems out of proportion with his short period as judge. Counting sons and grandsons, Abdon's offspring equaled Gideon's (8:30). For the significance of the donkeys, see comment on 10:4.

K. Samson's Victory Over the Philistines (13:1–16:31)

In chs. 13–18, the author concentrates on the tribe of Dan, one of the largest and most prominent tribes during the desert march (Nu 2:25–31). In the period of the judges, however, Dan seemed helpless against the Amorites (1:34) and moved northward to find new territory (chs. 17–18). Contrasted with these failures are the exploits of Samson. Yet his own life was a strange mixture of the strength and weakness that epitomized the tragic conditions within the tribe itself.

1. The angelic announcement of Samson's birth (13:1–14)

1 The primary introduction to this cycle was in 10:6–16, where it was linked with the sins that brought on the Ammonite invasion. Now the author, having described the defeat of Ammon, turns to the enemy that proved to be a thorn in Israel's side until David mastered them. The Philistines had lived in Palestine since Abraham's time (Ge 21:32–34; 26:1–6); but since 1200 B.C., they had settled along the coast in increasing numbers (cf. 3:3). Shamgar had won a great victory over them (3:31), halting their advance at least temporarily.

The Philistines, however, were warlike and powerful, and by 1100 B.C. they were exerting considerable pressure from their five cities in the west. The start of their forty-year oppression of Israel—the longest in the book—followed about five years later, and the tribes of Dan and Judah were the first to come under Philistine rule (cf. 15:11).

2–5 The epic story of Samson begins in the city of Zorah, located in the foothills about fifteen miles west of Jerusalem (cf. v.25; 16:31; 18:2, 8, 11). The plight of Manoah's wife was one shared earlier by the renowned Sarah and Rachel (Ge 11:30; 29:31). Since the Israelites considered children as a gift of God (cf. Ps 127:3), barrenness was a mark of divine disfavor. To die childless was tragic indeed (cf. 11:37–40). Manoah's wife would have been overjoyed to have just an ordinary baby, but the angel of the Lord informed her that she would have a special son.

The son promised to Manoah's wife would be a Nazirite (GK 5687; a word meaning "dedicated" or "consecrated"). According to Nu 6:1–12, the Nazirite vow was voluntarily taken for a limited time, but Samson's was lifelong. Nazirites had three special restrictions: (1) they were to abstain totally from "fermented drink" and could not eat any grapes or raisins; (2) they could not have their hair cut; and (3) they could not come near a corpse. Violation of all these plays an important part in Samson's life, though the second restriction is particularly emphasized.

Samson's mother was commanded here to observe the Nazirite vow at least during the course of her pregnancy. The prohibition against eating unclean food applied to all Israelites. It was, however, especially important for her because carcasses were used as food and could contaminate—or make ceremonially unclean—whatever they came in contact with (cf. Lev 11:32–40), including her unborn son.

The dedication of the child was to have military implications also, for he would gain victories over the Philistines. Yet since he would only "begin the deliverance," the conquest would be an incomplete one.

6–7 Manoah's wife shared the amazing news with her husband but had difficulty describing the visitor. "A man of God" is a term normally applied to prophets (Dt 33:1; 1Sa 9:6; cf. 2Ch 8:14). The man's impressive or "awesome" (GK 3707; cf. Pss 66:5; 76:12) appearance caused him to wonder whether he was an angel. To establish the authenticity of the message, it was important to know the name of the messenger (cf. Ex 3:13).

8–14 Manoah's motivation in praying for a second visit by the man of God apparently lay in his anxiety about rearing so unusual a child. He seemed overwhelmed by the responsibility, which may explain why his wife had said nothing to him about the child's involvement with the Philistines. The Lord answered Manoah's prayer and sent the angel back. This time Manoah was able to confer with him (vv.11–18). Yet he said nothing more about how to raise the child; the boy's manner of life and his mission in life had been adequately explained in v.5. Verse 14 does, however, add the detail about avoiding any product of the grapevine, not just wine (cf. Nu 6:3). That the angel did not directly answer Manoah's question may imply that his request for a confirming visit showed lack of faith. He was not easily convinced by the word of God (cf. 6:36–40).

2. The angel's miracle (13:15–23)

15–17 Proper etiquette demanded that Manoah provide a meal for his guest, as Abraham had done on a similar occasion (Ge 18:1–8). So Manoah prepared a young goat. Since Manoah and his wife had not fully realized who the angel was, they did not intend to sacrifice the goat. When the angel asked that a burnt offering be presented to the Lord, Manoah wondered about the identity of this man. Besides, Manoah wished to "honor" the man who predicted the birth of the long sought-after son.

18–22 The angel avoided a direct answer to the question. In the phrase "beyond understanding," however, there is a clear indication of his divine nature. Proof that this was the angel of the Lord came when Manoah presented the burnt offering and its accompanying grain offering. As the flame rose, the angel ascended in it before the couple's startled eyes. This was even more spectacular than the disappearance of the angel who talked with Gideon (6:21). Manoah's reaction to the miracle, however, matched Gideon's; he too thought he would die as a result of seeing God (6:22; cf. Ge 16:13).

23 The Lord had calmed Gideon's fear of dying (6:23), but here Manoah's wife relieved his anxiety. Using good common sense, she reasoned that the Lord would not have taken the trouble to come down twice and promise them a child if they were to die immediately. Besides, the Lord had requested and accepted an offering from them.

3. The birth and growth of Samson (13:24–25)

24–25 The faith of Manoah's wife was rewarded when the Lord blessed the couple with a baby boy. The name "Samson" is formed from the word for "sun," perhaps to signify that God, like the sun, had brought new light into their lives (cf. Mal 4:2).

The early years of Samson's life are covered swiftly (cf. Lk 1:80; 2:40, 52). God gave him a sound mind and a strong body as he grew to maturity. For a while he lived in Mahaneh Dan ("camp of Dan")—possibly a temporary home because of Philistine pressure on the cities.

More than any other judge, Samson was moved by the Spirit of God (see also 14:6, 19;

15:14). On this occasion an unusual verb (GK 7192) describes the Spirit's activity—a word elsewhere used of men whose spirits are disturbed by dreams (cf. Ge 41:8; Dan 2:1, 3). Perhaps the Lord used the same means to speak to Samson and to stir him to "begin the deliverance . . . from the hands of the Philistines" (v.5).

Contrasted with Jephthah, Samson had every advantage as a boy. His birth was predicted by an angel; he had godly parents who loved him greatly; he was uniquely dedicated to God as a Nazirite; and he experienced the power of God's Spirit as a young man. Despite all these favorable factors, Samson's life as it unfolds in the next three chapters is marked by tragedy.

4. Samson's engagement to a Philistine (14:1–9)

1–2 The saga of Samson begins and ends with Samson displaying a fatal weakness for Philistine women. In this first episode Samson traveled some four miles southwest of Zorah to Timnah, a city on the border between Judah and Dan, which apparently was assigned to the latter tribe (Jos 15:10; 19:43).

The presence of Philistines at Timnah reveals their occupation of Israelite territory. Their rule was more subtle and peaceful than the other periods of oppression, since Samson and presumably others were free to intermarry with the Philistines. Even the tribe of Judah was content to let the Philistines control them, a sign that a fairly normal life was possible (15:11).

At Timnah a Philistine woman captivated Samson, and he wished to marry her. Normally in Israel parents decided whom their children should marry (Ge 24:4; Ex 21:9; cf. Ge 28:1–2) and were responsible for making arrangements with the bride's parents (Ge 24:34–38). Samson was willing to let his parents approach the woman's parents as long as he selected the woman (cf. Ge 34:4).

3–4 Samson's parents objected strenuously to his choice, for Israel had been warned not to intermarry with the Canaanites (Dt 7:1–3; cf. Jdg 3:6). Although the Philistines were not listed among the seven nations of Canaan in Dt 7:1–3, the same objections given there applied to them. They were foreigners whose idolatry would lead their spouses astray (cf. Ge 26:34–35; 1Ki 11:1–6; Ne 13:27). Moreover, the Philistines were the one nation near Israel that did not practice circumcision of any kind (cf. also 15:18; 2Sa 1:20).

The pleading of Samson's parents did not sway him, and reluctantly they gave in. From the divine perspective, however, Samson's contact with the Philistines gave an opportunity for God to use him. It may seem paradoxical that the Lord would work through Samson's willful decision, but this aspect of his sovereignty appeared before in Judges (cf. 3:1–2).

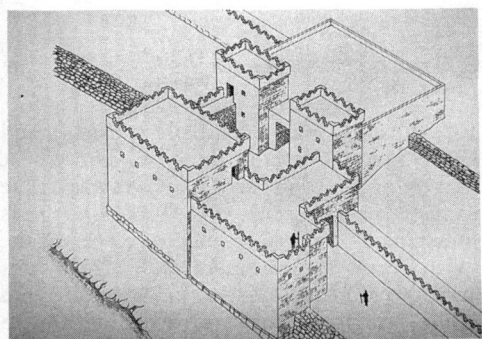

The picture to the right shows excavation in process at Timnah. The picture above is artist Ray Weisel's drawing of the gateway to that city (taken from Neal Bierling, *Giving Goliath His Due* [Grand Rapids: Baker, 1992]). Used by permission.

5–6 Samson and his parents were traveling to Timnah to discuss marriage arrangements when his great strength was first displayed. He had evidently left his parents briefly and rejoined them later on the main road. Attacked by a lion, Samson was enabled by the Spirit of God to kill the lion easily. Samson likely said nothing to his parents about his feat because such contact with the dead lion violated his Nazirite vow (cf. Nu 6:6, 9). The mention of the vineyards in v.5 may mean that Samson broke another Nazirite law by eating some grapes (Nu 6:3).

7–9 This additional meeting with the woman reinforced Samson's desire to marry her; so at the specified time he returned to Timnah for the wedding feast. On the way he took the same path he had followed in v.5 and noticed that there was a honeycomb in the lion's carcass. Heedless of the Nazirite vow, he scooped out some delicious honey and shared it with his parents. It was the unusual location of the honey that gave Samson the idea for the riddle of vv.12–14.

5. The marriage feast and the riddle (14:10–20)

10 Arriving at Timnah, Samson made preparations for the wedding feast. "Feast" is literally "a place of drinking," and doubtless the forbidden fruit of the vine passed between the lips of Samson the Nazirite. Samson's father is singled out, perhaps because he was paying for the feast, or perhaps because he was a witness to this marriage covenant (cf. Ge 24:50; Eze 16:8).

11 The thirty companions were probably provided by the bride's family (cf. Mt 9:15; Mk 2:19). In some instances these companions were a kind of bodyguard for protection against marauders. At this feast their function was to match wits with Samson.

12–13 Though the riddle was designed as a form of entertainment, it may have been related to the lack of proper wedding attire also (cf. Mt 22:11–12). Samson's offer was an attractive one, since clothes were highly regarded in the Near East. Possibly also the Philistines wanted to prove that they were smarter than the Israelites.

14–17 Solving the riddle turned out to be more difficult than anticipated; so by the middle of the week the Philistines realized what this wedding might cost them. In desperation they threatened Samson's wife, and the festal atmosphere turned into a battle of nerves. The bride was asked to use any means possible to get the answer from Samson, or she and her family faced destruction and death (cf. 15:6). To save her family, Samson's wife pled for him to show his love by confiding in her; she wore him down by weeping for a week (cf. 16:15). Samson was good at keeping secrets (cf. vv.6, 9), but he eventually gave in to his wife's nagging.

18–20 Given the answer by Samson's wife, the Philistines triumphantly presented it before the deadline. Samson replied with another bit of verse that showed how they got the answer. Heifers were not normally used for plowing; so the thirty had not played fair. In retaliation Samson traveled over twenty miles to the coastal city of Ashkelon, one of the five key Philistine centers. There, again empowered by the Spirit (v.6), he waylaid thirty well-dressed men and robbed them of their clothes to pay off the debt. Apparently he hoped to conceal his actions by going such a long distance from Timnah.

Still angry with his wife, Samson avoided her for a time and returned to his father's home. If Samson had not had relations with his wife, the marriage was not fully legal; and the bride's father wondered whether it ever would be consummated. Therefore, because he did not want his daughter to be abandoned in disgrace so soon after the wedding, he gave her to Samson's best man (cf. 1Sa 25:44).

6. Samson's revenge for the loss of his wife (15:1–8)

1–2 Samson's anger eventually subsided, and he decided to reclaim his wife. The wheat harvest occurred in early June and was a time of festivity. The word "visit" in v.2 suggests that Samson's marriage may have been of the "visit" type (see comment on 8:31). By this arrangement the Philistine bride could avoid the in-law problems that her presence in an Israelite household would cause.

If this was a "visit" marriage, the young goat was considered an acceptable present for the enjoyment of marital relations (Ge 38:17). Samson also wanted to atone for his apparent desertion of his wife. When he announced his intention of going to her room and consummating the marriage, her father told him that she was no longer his wife. Knowing that Samson had legally purchased his bride, the father offered him his more beautiful younger daughter.

3–6 Samson was not impressed with the "Rachel" of this family and flatly rejected the offer. His claim of being the true husband of the older daughter was correct, for even the Philistines referred to him as "the Timnite's son-in-law" (v.6). True, he had not immediately consummated the marriage, but was this sufficient ground for the divorce effected by the father? Samson held all the Philistines responsible for the affront and felt he had the right to take revenge.

The "foxes" Samson used may actually have been jackals. The fire spread with incredible speed, and soon the Philistines' crops were ruined. The fire destroyed the sheaves of stacked grain and also the grain ready to be harvested in the fields (Dt 23:25). Grapevines and olive trees were also ruined. Under the law (Ex 22:6), burning crops and fields was considered a serious offense; and the Philistines were distressed at this blow to their economy. They retaliated by burning Samson's wife and her father, a fate that ironically she had tried to avoid by wheedling out of Samson the key to his riddle (14:15).

7–8 Quickly the feud with the Philistines assumed national proportions as Samson sought to avenge the death of his wife. Though he intended to stop when he got even, neither side quit seeking revenge till Samson and thousands of Philistines were dead (cf. 16:28). Presumably the slaughter took place in the Timnah area, but it served to arouse all Philistia. Anticipating the Philistines' reaction, Samson took refuge in a "cave" or cleft of a rock.

7. Samson's victory at Lehi (15:9–20)

9–13 Aroused by Samson's outbursts, the Philistines assembled as an army and moved into Judah near "Lehi" (lit., "jawbone"), the name given to the area after Samson's victory. The presence of an army prompted a quick investigation, for the men of Judah were anxious to keep the peace. Aware of Samson's hideout, three thousand men went to extradite him. Their action betrays the strange complacency with the status quo that made them willing to accept continued domination by the godless Philistines. They meekly handed Samson over to face almost certain death. Samson's justification of his behavior was the same as that used by the Philistines: They deserved to be paid back! Samson agreed to let the men of Judah tie him up after being assured that they would not harm him. He had no desire to fight and kill his own countrymen. Uncertain of his attitude toward them, they tied him securely with new ropes.

14–15 The Philistines' battle cry was a sign that they sensed victory over their hated foe. Shouting provided a psychological advantage over one's enemy (cf. 1Sa 4:5). In this instance the shouting only served to arouse Samson. Empowered again by the divine Spirit (cf. 14:6), he easily snapped the ropes that bound him. He seized a fresh jawbone of a donkey, one that was moist and not brittle, and killed a thousand men. Any of the Philistines who survived probably fled the scene in astonishment. Again, the men of Judah had a chance to follow up this victory and throw off Philistine domination, but they remained strangely inactive.

16–17 To commemorate the triumph, Samson composed another short poem. Like the couplet in 14:18, this poem uses repetition, and it also includes a play on words (cf. NIV note). Carcasses of donkeys were usually thrown outside the city wall (Jer 22:19), and this kind of disgraceful burial had befallen the Philistines. Samson's single-handed victory resembles that of Shamgar (see 3:31). The importance of the jawbone and what Samson did accounts for the name "Jawbone Hill" (see NIV note).

18–20 Samson acknowledged that God was responsible for his victory, but, like Elijah (1Ki 19), he was physically and emotionally drained following the conflict. As he had done for the Israelites in the wilderness (Ex 17:6), God provided water for Samson from the "hollow" in Lehi. The spring was thereafter called "Caller's Spring" because of God's wonderful answer to prayer. By referring at this point in the Samson story to his twenty-year prominence as judge (cf. 16:31), the author suggests that his effectiveness ended prior to the tragic events of ch. 16.

8. Samson's feat of strength at Gaza (16:1–3)

1–3 The final episodes in Samson's story confirm both his great physical strength and his great weakness for women. A number of years passed before he ventured into Philistine territory again. This time he went to Gaza, some forty miles west of Hebron and twelve miles south of Ashkelon. Even at this southernmost Philistine city, his reputation was well known; and the residents showed great caution in their attempt to capture him.

Samson's sensual nature led him to involvement with a prostitute, one of many at centers such as Gaza. Still not married, Samson was especially susceptible to temptations of the flesh (cf. Ge 38:12–15). Thinking they had him trapped, the men of Gaza hid outside and made plans to surprise Samson in the morning. They probably fell asleep, confident that the locked city gates had hemmed in their prisoner.

Sometime during the middle of the night, when the Philistines least expected it, Samson left his shelter and tore loose the city gate. He carried off the heavy wooden doors, the posts on which they hung, and the crossbar of wood or metal that reinforced the doors. He proceeded to haul the whole gate assembly to a hill opposite Hebron.

9. Samson and Delilah (16:4–20)

4–5 Delilah lived near Samson's hometown, for Zorah and Mahaneh Dan (cf. 13:25) were situated by the Sorek Valley. Delilah is never called a Philistine woman (cf. 14:1–2), but her proximity to the Philistine-occupied area and her close contact with their leaders indicate that she probably was.

The Philistine leaders were determined to find out the secret of Samson's strength. Instead of threatening the woman he was infatuated with, the five rulers (cf. 3:3) promised Delilah a fortune—fifty-five hundred shekels of silver (more than 140 pounds)! No wonder Delilah did not give up till she had discovered the secret of Samson's strength. The Philistines' goal was to "subdue" Samson; they hoped to harness his strength and put it to good use.

6–9 Delilah's objective must have been obvious to Samson. He knew how well his Philistine wife had kept a secret (14:17) of far less importance than this one. Confident that he would never tell her the truth, he toyed with her for his own amusement. The first clue dealt with "thongs" made from animal intestines. These were "fresh," much like the fresh "jawbone" he so effectively had used in battle (15:15). But their moistness was of no more help than the perfect number seven; Samson easily broke them (cf. 15:14), and the Philistines made no attempt to seize him.

10–12 Delilah claimed that Samson had deceived or cheated her. His second clue was a variation of the first one, though the Philistines should have learned from previous experience that new ropes could not shackle him (15:13). Perhaps they felt that the men of Judah had not tied him securely enough the first time. But special tying was ineffective as Samson once more broke free.

13–14 Again Delilah complained of being mistreated, and her third plea to Samson took on a new intensity. The Hebrew suggests that Delilah shouted, "Tell me!" as Samson's irritation grew. This time he came dangerously close to the truth as he linked his strength with his hair, and his explanation was so different that it might have given Delilah hope that he was not lying this time.

It is difficult to determine the kind of loom Samson's hair was woven to. That Samson was sleeping suggests the horizontal kind. Having woven Samson's hair into the fabric and fastened it with a pin, Delilah thought she had him trapped. Samson had no more difficulty "pulling up" the pin and the whole loom than he had tearing loose the gate of Gaza (cf. v.3).

15–17 By this time Delilah was frustrated. Yet though she had failed to learn the secret and the Philistines had undoubtedly grown impatient and had gone home (cf. v.18), she was not yet ready to give up. Instead, she did as Samson's wife had done and began to question his love (cf. 14:16). Samson's continued deception disturbed Delilah because it confirmed his intention to keep the secret. Lying once or twice might have been forgiven, but this was the third time. Yet Delilah kept after Samson, who became so tired of her nagging that he finally gave in, as he had during the wedding feast (14:17). Rather than break his relationship with Delilah, he allowed it to break him.

Samson's career as a Nazirite was an inconsistent one. He had been careless about keeping his distance from the fruit of the vine or from dead bodies (see comments on 14:6–10). Yet he kept his long hair as the symbol of his dedication to God. This was the specific point the angel had spoken of (13:5), and it may have exceeded the other Nazirite restrictions in importance (cf. 1Sa 1:11).

18–20 Knowing that she had finally arrived at the truth, Delilah persuaded the Philistine rulers to return one final time so that she might betray him to them. While they knew that shaving beards and pulling out hair was a sign of mourning (cf. Jer 41:5), they hardly dared believe what cutting off Samson's hair would do to him.

Samson himself could not believe the inevitable, planning to elude the Philistines as always. But the bonds of sin are not so easily shaken off. When the Spirit of the Lord leaves someone, the results are indeed disastrous.

10. The capture and punishment of Samson (16:21–22)

21–22 Moving in quickly, the Philistines seized Samson and blinded him. The Jews considered loss of eyesight a terrible curse (Pr 30:17; cf. 1Sa 11:2). Samson's feet were fettered by bronze shackles (cf. 2Sa 3:34), and he was forced to work in a prison in Gaza, the very city from which he had once escaped (v.3). Grinding at the mill was a woman's job (9:53), which added to Samson's humiliation. It is unclear whether he used a small handmill or was forced to turn a large circular stone, a job normally given to donkeys (the latter task would avenge Samson's earlier treatment of the Philistines; cf. 15:16). While in prison, Samson's hair began to grow again.

11. Samson's final revenge at the feast of Dagon (16:23–31)

23–25 The capture of Samson led to great rejoicing; and the Philistines had a national festival in honor of Dagon, their god of grain and chief deity. They attributed Samson's downfall directly to Dagon, and it was this theological error that led to the destruction of Dagon's temple. Samson had fallen into their hands, not because Dagon had defeated the Lord, but because Samson's sinfulness had caused the God of Israel to abandon him.

How vividly the Philistines remembered Samson's "reign of terror"! It had been a time of devastation and death, and even Dagon's grain was put to the torch (15:5). But this was replaced by laughter and feasting as the drunken Philistines called for the once invincible Samson to appear before them and to "entertain" (GK 8471) or "amuse" them. Clearly the Philistines intended to mock Samson as he performed for them (cf. Ge 21:9).

26–30 From the noise around and above him, Samson could tell that he was near the center of the building. With help from the young man assigned to attend him, Samson located the main columns of the temple. It was his turn to get revenge on the Philistines (15:7); so he called on the Lord for assistance, as he had done at Lehi years earlier (15:18). The Philistines apparently had no inkling of Samson's intentions. Indeed, he may not have fully regained his strength until the Lord empowered him this one last time.

With a mighty effort Samson dislodged the pillars from their bases, bringing down the roof on top of the dignitaries assembled inside. Thousands of spectators on the roof also perished in the fall, and the number killed proved to be Samson's greatest slaughter. He gladly died with them rather than continue his pitiful existence among them.

31 The "brothers" who buried Samson may have been relatives from the tribe of Dan (cf. 14:3). The "father's family" was a more restricted group than a clan but broader than our Western conception of a family. Samson was laid to rest in the region where he had grown up and was given the honor of burial in his father's tomb (cf. 8:32).

Samson was ranked among the heroes of the faith (Heb 11:32). Yet he failed to live up to his great gifts. Unable to conquer himself, he was ruined by his own lusts. He stands as a tragic example of a man of great potential who lacked stability of character. Still, God in his sovereignty used him.

III. Two Appendixes (17:1–21:25)

The final five chapters of Judges constitute two nonchronological appendixes to the book, omitting any reference to judges or times of oppression. Both episodes recounted in this section occurred early in the whole period of the judges and illustrate the moral and religious decay that eventually led many to call for the appointment of a king. The key expression in these chapters is "In those days Israel had no king" (17:6; 18:1; 19:1; 21:25).

A. Micah's Priest and the Migration of Dan (17:1–18:31)

1. Micah's mother and idolatry (17:1–6)

1–2 The bizarre and violent events in the appendixes are closely linked with the hills of Ephraim, the highlands of central Palestine beginning some twelve miles north of Jerusalem (the region that played an important role in the success of Ehud, Deborah, and Gideon; see 3:27; 4:5; 7:24). In tune with the moral chaos of the day, a man named Micah stole a substantial sum of silver from his own mother (a yearly wage was ten shekels; cf. v.10). No wonder Micah's mother cursed the thief! Since a well-founded curse was dreadfully effective—even within one's own family (Ge 9:25)—Micah was frightened into confessing his guilt. Immediately his mother pronounced a blessing on him to undo the curse.

3–4 Out of gratitude for getting her silver back, Micah's mother decided to consecrate it to the Lord (cf. Ex 28:38). Yet the desire to make an idol was diametrically opposed to God's command and, in fact, made Micah's mother liable to God's curse (Dt 27:15). Strangely, she dedicated only two hundred of the original eleven hundred shekels. Both her motivation and her activity are questionable.

With the two hundred shekels of silver, the silversmith made an idol for Micah's mother (cf. v.3–4; 18:14, 17–18). This idol was possibly cast in the form of a calf (cf. Ex 32:4). Later the same idol was associated with the city of Dan (cf. 18:30; 1Ki 12:29).

5–6 In addition to the carved image, Micah had *teraphim* ("idols"; GK 9572)—one or more household gods (cf. Ge 31:19; 1Sa 19:13, 16). Like the "ephod" (cf. 8:27), the *teraphim* could be used for divination purposes (Eze 21:21). Since the ephod was a priestly garment, Micah went one step further by ordaining one of his sons as priest. Thus Micah boldly set up a "shrine" (lit., a "house of God") right in his home. It was a sad perversion of the true worship of the Lord, leading the author of Judges to bemoan

the fact that in those days "everyone did as he saw fit" (cf. 21:25).

2. Micah's Levite (17:7–13)

7–9 The law had specified that priests were to come from the tribe of Levi; so Micah was quick to "upgrade" his religious establishment when the opportunity arose. The Levite he hired had been living in Bethlehem (cf. 19:1). Bethlehem was not one of the forty-eight Levitical cities mandated by Moses (Nu 35:6–8) and assigned by Joshua (Jos 21). The Levites were doubtless scattered because of lack of support, a situation that prevailed all too often in Israel's history (cf. Ne 13:10). In an attempt to improve his situation, the young Levite traveled north and found Micah eager to hire a more "legitimate" priest.

10–12 The Levite became both a "father" and a "son" to Micah. "Father" is a term of honor used of Joseph's position in Egypt (Ge 45:8) and of Elisha as a respected prophet (2Ki 6:21; 13:14). Micah promised to give him enough to live on, including the clothes needed to carry on his priestly functions. Content with these terms, the Levite agreed to serve Micah, who thereupon carried out the second ordination ceremony in the chapter (cf. v.5). The new priest was a descendant of Moses (18:30); since the priesthood was restricted to the descendants of Aaron, his attempt to minister was abortive.

13 Equipped with a shrine, a Levitical priest, and an assortment of idols, Micah felt that this strange combination would bring God's blessing. His smug assertion ranks with Aaron's announcement about a "festival to the LORD" the day after the golden calf was made (Ex 32:5).

3. Danite spies and Micah's priest (18:1–6)

1 Again it is mentioned that Israel had no king (cf. 17:6; 19:1; 21:25)—the only thing that might stop the chaos described in chs. 17–21. Despite the monarchy's drawbacks, kingly rule would improve general conditions at least temporarily.

Caught in a squeeze between the Amorites (1:34–35) and the Philistines to the west and Judah's territory to the south, the Danites sought out a new homeland. Their desire to move revealed a lack of faith in the

Lord who had allotted to them their original territory (see Jos 19:40–48).

2–3 Five spies were sent from the same area where Samson grew up, Zorah and Eshtaol (cf. 13:2). They were assigned to search for a new location to the north, much like the twelve men commissioned by Moses (Nu 13:2). En route they stopped at Micah's house, which must have been near a main road. They were attracted by the voice of the recently hired Levite. Their questions imply that they knew him personally, or at least recognized his "Judean" accent. Their repetitive questions reveal their surprise at finding a Levite in that locale.

4–6 When they learned his occupation and resources, the Danites decided to consult the Lord through the Levite. The inquiry was successful, for "Go in peace" implies they would be victorious over the enemy.

4. The report of the spies (18:7–10)

7 The spies traveled straight north till they arrived at the city of Laish, some one hundred miles from their original inheritance and farther north than any territory allotted to the tribes of Israel. There, at the foot of Mount Hermon, they discovered a highly desirable location, a long distance from potential enemies and furnished with an excellent supply of water. The Lebanon range protected it from interference from either Syria or Phoenicia. The residents of Laish enjoyed their secure position and had not built any defenses against invaders. It was an ideal situation for the land-hungry Danites.

8–10 The account the spies gave to the rest of the tribe was most promising. Their positive and unanimous report, recommending an immediate attack, contrasted sharply with the pessimistic majority opinion of the spies sent by Moses to explore the entire land (cf. Nu 13:25–33). The claim of divine approval, however, based on the consultation of v.6, was hardly justifiable.

5. The abduction of Micah's priest (18:11–21)

11–12 Responding to the challenge of the spies, the Danites quickly set out for this new "promised land." Yet one wonders why only six hundred are mentioned. From the Samson narratives it is clear that not all the Dan-

ites moved north. The first stop on the journey was near Kiriath Jearim, a city about eight miles from their original homeland of Zorah and Eshtaol.

13–17 The next leg of the journey brought the Danites to the home of Micah. They had recalled the favorable oracle of v.6 and were planning to make more extensive use of the priest and his paraphernalia. The young Levite must have been surprised to see the men again, and at first he was dismayed at the theft of the ephod and idols (cf. 17:4–5). With a six-hundred-man army poised outside, there was little the priest could do to prevent the robbery.

18–21 The priest's mild protest was countered by an offer that he join the Danites and enjoy an expanded ministry to an entire tribe. With the prospect of a higher salary and increased influence, he quickly forgot his loyalty to Micah and agreed to their terms. Instead of losing his religious equipment and perhaps his life, he gained a new position.

6. Micah's futile pursuit (18:22–26)

22–24 When Micah discovered the loss of his idols and his priest, he hastily gathered some friends and pursued the thieves. The Danites were forced to travel at a moderate pace because of the children and the livestock; so they were easily overtaken (cf. Ge 31:23). The Danites pretended to be innocent of the charge hurled by Micah; but they did not invite a search. Micah's protest has an almost humorous ring to it. He had good reason to be upset, and the Danites knew it.

25–26 With their superior manpower, the Danites threatened to attack Micah's forces and put an end to his complaints. They claimed to be fierce or desperate men (2Sa 17:8). Faced with almost certain defeat and death, Micah sadly gave up the cause and returned home. Micah stood face to face with the weakness of his gods. They were taken captive, unable to effect their own escape (cf. 6:31; Isa 46:1–2).

7. The capture of Laish (18:27–31)

27–28 Moving straight north, the Danites successfully attacked and destroyed Laish. Because of its isolated location and the people's desire to remain independent, they could not find help against the invaders.

29–30 The new city was renamed "Dan" and became the northernmost outpost of Israel in the proverbial "from Dan to Beersheba." There Micah's idols were set up and Jonathan son of Gershom, the son of Moses (Ex 2:21–22), served as priest.

31 The events of this chapter must have occurred before 1075 B.C., since the Philistines destroyed Shiloh at about that time (cf. Jer 7:12–15). The tabernacle had been set up at Shiloh, some twenty miles north of Jerusalem, by Joshua (Jos 18:1); and the site continued as a religious center during the period of the judges. In those days Israel had no king and no Jerusalem sanctuary to unify the people.

B. The Atrocity at Gibeah and Civil War (19:1–21:25)

The second appendix relates one of the most shocking episodes of Israel's history. It occurred quite early in the period of the judges, because Phinehas, the grandson of Aaron, was still ministering as high priest (20:28; cf. Nu 25:7, 11), and because the tribes were still able to function as a unit (cf. Jos

This picture shows the excavation of the gate to Dan in the 19/18 centuries B.C. The metal roof was to prevent erosion after the rains.

22:9–34). There is also a need for a long time span between the disgraceful behavior of the tribe of Benjamin and the choice of a Benjamite, Saul, as Israel's first king (1Sa 10:26)!

1. The reconciliation of the Levite and his concubine (19:1–8)

1–2a The major characters come from the hill country of Ephraim and from Bethlehem in Judah. This time it was the Levite who lived in Ephraim and had a concubine from Bethlehem. Evidently she was unhappy with her status as a secondary wife; for she committed adultery and then returned to the refuge of her father's home in Bethlehem rather than face an angry husband.

2b–4 Four months later the Levite attempted to recover his concubine. Using tender, comforting words, he tried to persuade her that reconciliation was the best policy. Her father was very happy to see him, probably because the breakup of the relationship had meant social disgrace for the family. Anxious to please his son-in-law, the father insisted that the Levite stay in Bethlehem a few days. The laws of hospitality play an extremely important role as the story unfolds (cf. 4:17–23).

5–8 The Levite's attempt to get an early start on both the fourth and fifth day was thwarted by his father-in-law. The enjoyment mentioned in vv.6 and 9 is often associated with food and drink (cf. v.22). The concubine was apparently not present during the meals, for "the two of them" refers to the Levite and the father. She is ignored through most of the narrative, and there is no indication that she even wanted to rejoin her husband. The delay on the fifth day proved to be as dangerous as Lot's hesitation in Ge 19:16.

2. The journey to Gibeah (19:9–15)

9–10 When his father-in-law requested that the Levite delay his departure for a third time, the Levite refused the offer and insisted on leaving. Perhaps he felt that he had stayed too long already. Unfortunately it was the kindness of the girl's father that led to her fatal overnight stay in Gibeah. The travelers headed north toward Jerusalem, six miles from Bethlehem. They left mid to late afternoon, since daylight was almost gone when they reached Jerusalem.

11–14 The road the Levite and his company took passed just to the west of Jebus; so it would have been a convenient lodging place. But the Levite refused his servant's suggestion due to the foreign residents of the city (cf. 1:8, 21). He feared the possibility of danger there and wanted to reach an Israelite city where, ironically, he expected good hospitality. Gibeah lay four miles beyond Jebus. Gibeah belonged to the tribe of Benjamin. Up to that time apparently the Benjamites' immorality was not well known.

15 The city square was an open area just inside the city gate, and it was the logical place for visitors to wait. They would have had to spend the night there if no invitation was forthcoming (cf. Ge 19:2). After the lavish hospitality of Bethlehem, it must have seemed strange that no one offered them lodging. But it was too late to venture out onto the dark roads.

3. The hospitality of the old man (19:16–21)

16–17 In a culture where inns or hostels were nonexistent, it was incredible that anyone would refuse hospitality to a stranger. Yet the Levite and his party were ignored till an old man from the same tribal area as the Levite came on the scene. This Ephraimite was residing in Gibeah on a temporary basis. Like Lot, the old man did not share the morals of the townspeople.

18–19 The Levite explained the situation, though he added that he was going to the house of the Lord (located at either Bethel or Shiloh). He made it clear that he had plenty of provisions; so the old man would not find his visit burdensome. Normally the host supplied the needs of the traveler (Ge 24:25), but the Levite was taking no chances.

20–21 The old man warmly welcomed the Levite to alleviate his nervousness about the strange reception of Gibeah. Spending the night in the square was far too dangerous; so the three were taken into his house. The crisis was over—or so it seemed. The friendly man performed the normal duties of a host, politely refusing the Levite's offer to use his own supplies. The old man fed the animals and provided water for the trio to wash their feet (cf. Ge 18:4; 24:25). Then they enjoyed a meal together.

4. The sexual perversion of the Gibeahites (19:22–28)

22–24 Before long it became evident that the Levite and his company had relaxed prematurely, and the Levite must have soon understood why no one else had offered hospitality. Gibeah had imbibed the morals of Canaan and had become another Sodom. Just as the worship of Baal had brought about a near catastrophe in the plains of Moab (Nu 25:1–9), so the Baal cult was probably responsible for subverting the Benjamites. This must have been comparatively soon after the earlier incident, for the same priest Phinehas intervened on both occasions (Nu 25:7–8; Jdg 20:28).

The "wicked men" (lit., "sons of Belial") are worthless scoundrels bent on evil. They were active homosexuals engaging in practices condemned in Scripture (Lev 18:22; 20:13). The old man felt a deep sense of responsibility to protect his principal guest, and in desperation he offered the townspeople his own daughter and the Levite's concubine instead of letting them assault his guest (cf. Ge 19:8). In those days the place of a woman was often very low, and the "disgraceful thing" was to molest the man. Nevertheless, the Israelites normally considered the rape of a woman disgraceful (Ge 34:7), and women who were promiscuous were also condemned to death for their behavior (Dt 22:21).

25–26 One can easily see why the concubine had left her husband in the first place. She was virtually sacrificed to save his skin as the men sexually "abused" her all night. The concubine survived till dawn, but by actual sunrise the ordeal had taken her life.

27–28 The Levite had not anticipated the mass assault his concubine had succumbed to, but his words seem callous nonetheless. Should he not have shown concern for her long before daybreak? And did he really expect her to be in any condition to travel? It is little wonder that he is called her "master" rather than "husband" (vv.26–27).

That night of horror made a powerful impact on the nation, and centuries later the prophet Hosea recalled the depth of Gibeah's corruption (Hos 9:9; 10:9).

5. The crime report to Israel (19:29–20:7)

29 The shocking murder influenced the Levite to take drastic action. He cut up his concubine's body as one divides the carcass of a sacrificial animal (Ex 29:17; Lev 1:6) and sent a part of her body to each of the twelve tribes, including the leaders of the offending tribe, Benjamin. Apparently the recipients of this gruesome parcel were expected to respond to the appeal or else risk being struck with the sword themselves (cf. 21:10; cf. 1Sa 11:7).

30–20:1 Predictably, the nation reacted with burning indignation. The Israelites had been guilty of numerous sins since the Exodus, but never of anything so repulsive as this. They needed to appraise the situation and then plan a course of action. The nation then "came out as one man," even from the distant borders of Israel. Mizpah, an important religious center in the days of Samuel (1Sa 7:5, 16) that was only a few miles from Gibeah, was the rallying center.

2–3 The leaders of "the people of God" bore the solemn responsibility of meting out the proper punishment for the crime, and a large army supported them. Benjamin's forces of 26,700 (v.15) seemed little in comparison to the 400,000 of Israel.

4–7 The Levite related the shocking details of the murder, claiming that his own life had been in danger that night. He may have exaggerated this point to place himself in the best possible light before the assembly. Then he explained his decision to dismember the concubine's dead body lest the deed go unnoticed. Such "lewd" behavior as that of the men of Gibeah deserved swift and harsh punishment, and the Levite pled that the leaders would hand down a guilty verdict.

6. Israel and Benjamin: preparations for war (20:8–18)

8–10 The response to the Levite's plea was a positive one, and all Israel resolved to take punitive action against Gibeah. This decision was clearly God's will, though they cast lots to find out which tribe should lead the way (cf. v.18). Ten percent of the troops were set apart to gather supplies in case a lengthy campaign was necessary. No effort was to be spared to deal with the "vileness" or "disgraceful thing" (cf. 19:23–24) of the men of Gibeah.

11 For the third time in the chapter, the expression "as one man" occurs (cf. vv.1, 8). The Israelites were knit together as a unit, in marked contrast to the days of Deborah and Barak (5:15–17).

12–13a As originally intended, the anger of the nation was directed only against Gibeah. Since Gibeah belonged to the tribe of Benjamin, however, the leaders of that tribe were of necessity involved. Capital punishment was clearly prescribed, and the Israelites confronted the Benjamites with the Mosaic passages (Dt 13:5; 21:21).

13b–16 Rather than surrender the guilty men, the leaders of the tribe chose to be loyal to the town of Gibeah. What had begun as a punitive operation against one city now turned into full-scale civil war. The men of Benjamin had a good reputation as excellent soldiers (cf. Ge 49:27); their prowess with the bow and the sling was well known (cf. 1Ch 8:40; 12:2). If many of the soldiers of Gibeah were among the elite left-handed (cf. 3:15) slingers, one can understand why the whole tribe would be reluctant to hand them over without a battle. Apparently seven hundred slingers formed a unit within the army, much like the chariotry or the light infantry (cf. 2Ki 3:25; 2Ch 26:14). Stones propelled at speeds up to ninety miles per hour were extremely effective.

17–18 The forces of Israel comprised a powerful army, the largest the nation had ever assembled (cf. v.2). The nation sought guidance from God (cf. 1:1), and the Lord directed that the prominent tribe of Judah should lead the way (cf. Nu 2:9). Gibeah's proximity to the territory of Judah insured familiarity with the terrain.

The mention of Bethel poses a problem, since the tabernacle was located at Shiloh (cf. 18:31). Bethel had been a revered location ever since the Lord revealed himself to Jacob at that site (Ge 28:11–19); so, like Mizpah (v.1), Bethel could have been one of several suitable holy places. The ark of the covenant may have been moved from Shiloh to Bethel (cf. vv.26–27) to be nearer to the scene of battle (cf. Nu 10:35). Since Phinehas the high priest stayed with the ark, it was possible to inquire of the Lord wherever Phinehas happened to be.

7. The first battle (20:19–23)

19–21 Confident of victory, the Israelites moved their forces and equipment near Gibeah and lined up for battle. But the hilly terrain gave the advantage to the defending Benjamites, who used their expert slingers and swordsmen to kill 22,000 of the enemy. The men of Benjamin fought with the determination of those who knew that their very existence as a tribe was at stake. Apparently they struck quickly and withdrew into the city, leaving the Israelites to mourn their losses the rest of the day.

22–23 The startling defeat brought Israel to its knees. On other occasions such slaughter had followed blatant national sin (Nu 25:6; Dt 1:45). The tribes wondered whether perhaps the defeat was punishment for attacking a "brother" tribe—perhaps they had misinterpreted the Lord's will. So this time they asked the question the answer to which they had assumed in v.18. The Lord again answered affirmatively, and the army received a much-needed boost to their morale (cf. 1Sa 4:9; 2Sa 10:12).

8. The second battle (20:24–28)

24–25 Early the next day a more determined Israelite army took the field only to fall back once more before the invincible men of Benjamin. This time fewer were killed, but the 18,000 casualties brought the two-day total to a staggering 40,000, ten percent of their entire force (cf. v. 2)! It seemed catastrophic; but by reducing the size of the army, God was showing them that numbers alone do not guarantee victory. They needed to trust God to accomplish the impossible (cf. 7:7).

26 Deeply discouraged, the army retreated eight miles north to Bethel. The weeping and fasting revealed their desperation, for it appeared that the Lord was ignoring their just cause. The combination of burnt offerings and fellowship offerings was usually an expression of devotion and commitment. The absence of any sin offering implies that the people were innocent of wrongdoing.

27–28 Ministering at Bethel was Phinehas, the zealous grandson of Aaron who had stopped the terrible plague on the plains of Moab, where 24,000 Israelites had perished in the worship of the Baal of Peor (Nu 25:9). Once more he was called on to intercede in a time of national disaster. The sacred ark (its only mention in Judges) was also there, symbolizing the presence and power of God (cf. 1Sa 4:3). The Israelites were prepared to give up the fight against Benjamin, but the Lord again advised them to attack. This time he gave assurance of victory!

9. The third battle (20:29–41)

29 The third time for any event or activity is often the decisive time. If Israel lost this battle, the war against Benjamin would have ended in disgrace. To strengthen their attack, the Israelites changed their strategy. They decided to set an ambush, a strategy successfully used at Ai (Jos 8:2) and Shechem (Jdg 9:33–44). The men of Benjamin were overconfident after two easy victories, and the ruse might work.

30–36a For the third consecutive day, the Israelites lined up against Gibeah, and once again the Benjamites sensed victory. They pursued the men of Israel, who were retreating to the north, and thirty more soldiers died. The death of these men actually made the strategy more effective. When most of the defenders were some distance from Gibeah, the 10,000 men in ambush attacked the city. This sizable force (twice that at Ai [Jos 8:12]) was well able to capture Gibeah. The success of the ambush turned the tide of the battle.

36b–41 The sudden assault on Gibeah brought death to all in the city. Gibeah was quickly set on fire as a signal that the city had been captured. When they saw the smoke, the other Israelites turned and began to fight in earnest. They probably pointed to the fire so that the Benjamites would turn around and see what had happened. As in the case of Ai (Jos 8:20), the psychological impact was tremendous. The Benjamites could not believe their eyes, and they lost all incentive to fight. Disaster had caught up with them because of their evil deeds. The word "whole" (v.37; GK 3972) is often used of "whole burnt offerings" (Dt 33:10). The entire wicked town literally became a burnt offering (cf. Dt 13:16)!

10. The flight of Benjamin (20:42–48)

42 Caught between the inspired main force of Israelites and the ten thousand troops used in the ambush, the Benjamites' only recourse was to flee. They headed east toward the desert area extending from Bethel to Jericho (cf. Jos 16:1). Perhaps they hoped to cross the Jordan and escape into the deserts beyond, but the sheer numbers of Israelites made this impossible. The pursuing forces were augmented by men from nearby cities. Whenever Israel had the enemy on the run, it seemed that volunteers flocked to join in the pursuit (cf. 7:23–24; 1Sa 14:22).

43–47 The Benjamites were surrounded not far from Gibeah and suffered tremendous losses as the Israelites seemed intent on wiping them out. The term "cut down" (vv.42, 45; GK 8845) has the idea of killing or capturing the enemy down to the last man (cf. Dt 24:21 [NIV, "go over"]; Jer 6:9). In one day some 25,000 elite warriors died.

. The total slain, given more exactly as 25,100 in v.35, still does not seem to account for the 26,700 mentioned in v.15. If only 600 survived (v.47), 26,100 must have been killed. The other 1,000 men apparently died during the first two days of fighting, where the author of Judges only supplies the number of Israelites who were killed. The last 600 men of Benjamin found refuge at the rock of Rimmon, a conical limestone hill surrounded by wadis and located about four miles east of Bethel. Numerous caves provided hiding places from the relentless pursuers.

48 Methodically, the Israelite soldiers captured and destroyed all the defenseless towns of Benjamin. According to Dt 13:12–18, any Israelite city that harbored idolaters was to be burned—people as well as animals. The sin of Gibeah was considered as serious as idolatry.

11. Concern for Benjamin's survival (21:1–4)

1–2 Unlike most victorious armies, the men of Israel mourned rather than celebrated. The terrible judgment against Benjamin had all but eliminated that tribe. So Israel went to Bethel to weep before the Lord, just as they had done after being defeated in the two earlier battles (20:23, 26). Did the nation suddenly realize that the punishment had gone further than they intended, or were they simply lamenting the judgment that the Benjamites fully deserved?

It appeared that the tribe would become extinct because of the oath that had been taken when the Israelite army assembled at Mizpah (cf. 20:1–10). The low morality exhibited at Gibeah was sufficient reason for banning intermarriage with that tribe; the men of Benjamin had become Canaanites (cf. 3:6). But the people later regretted that they had taken an oath.

3 When Israel had won battles in the past, sometimes very few men were missing in action (cf. Nu 31:49). No wonder they bemoaned the fact that an *entire tribe* was missing after this conflict. The tribes of Israel were twelve in number, but Jacob's youngest son was about to lose his posterity completely.

4 To renew their commitment to the Lord and to seek his help, the people presented the same kinds of offerings mentioned in 20:26. This time they built another altar (cf. 6:24, 28).

12. Wives from Jabesh Gilead (21:5–14)

5–7 The dilemma posed by the first oath was partially solved by reflecting on another, more important oath the Israelites had taken. When the pieces cut off from the concubine had been sent throughout Israel, the implication was that any city that did not respond to deal with this atrocity would itself be subject to death. If it had not been for their grief over Benjamin, the Israelites might never have discovered which regions were delinquent.

8–9 The search revealed that the city of Jabesh Gilead was guilty. This town was located nine miles southeast of Beth Shan and two miles east of the Jordan. Perhaps these residents of Manasseh refused to oppose a tribe related to them through Rachel.

10–12 The leaders of Israel decided that Jabesh Gilead deserved the same fate as the cities of Benjamin in 20:48. According to Nu 31:17–18, it was permissible in a war of revenge to save the lives of the virgins. They alone could be spared, and it was this provision that was used to secure wives for Benjamin. Four hundred girls were taken to Shiloh (the place where the tabernacle was located) on the Canaan side of the Jordan River. Situated about nine miles north of Bethel and the rock of Rimmon, Shiloh afforded a temporary refuge where the captive girls could mourn the loss of their loved ones.

13–14 Four months had passed since the six hundred Benjamites had been in hiding. The anger stirred by the war had now subsided, and the men were doubtless eager to give up their precarious existence. When the offer of peace was combined with a promise of wives, the men of Benjamin decided it was safe to accept the terms. Thus the sole survivors of a city were married to the remaining refugees of a tribe. Since there were only four hundred women, however, two hundred men were still left without spouses.

13. Wives from Shiloh (21:15–23)

15–18 The grief of the nation is again mentioned (cf. v.6); and it seems as if the "elders of the assembly" were unaware of the four hundred women obtained from Jabesh Gilead. Perhaps the plan being devised to abduct the maidens of Shiloh was formed before the outcome of the campaign against Jabesh Gilead was known. After the four hundred Jabesh Gilead virgins arrived on the scene, it would be difficult to worry about the tribe being "wiped out." By v.22 the results of the war with Jabesh Gilead had become available.

The "gap" was literally a "breach," usually associated with an outburst of the Lord's anger (2Sa 6:8). It also refers to a break in a wall, suggesting the incompleteness of Israel without Benjamin. For the third time in the chapter, reference is made to the oath that forbade the giving of daughters to Benjamin (cf. vv.1, 7). In the absence of wives, the breach seemed irreparable.

19 A solution was suggested by the approaching festival in Shiloh, when a large number of people would gather. During the celebration perhaps the Benjamites could find the girls they needed. The festival was likely the Feast of Tabernacles (see Dt 16:13–15), since vineyards are mentioned and the grape harvest comes in August and September. It was a joyous harvest festival.

The detailed directions about Shiloh's location may have been given to assist the Benjamites in making the fastest escape possible. Probably they were not familiar with the region, since it lay in the middle of Ephraim's territory to the north. In view of the spiritual condition of Gibeah and most of Benjamin, it is unlikely that they had bothered to attend any recent religious festival in Shiloh.

20–23 Ironically, the men of Benjamin were told to set an ambush ("hide"; GK 741) for the girls, the same technique used by the Israelites against the Benjamites at Gibeah (20:37). The strategy worked flawlessly, and each man obtained his wife. This highly unorthodox method of obtaining a wife was sure to disturb the relatives of the women greatly. Fathers and brothers usually received a bride price from the prospective groom and had an important voice in arranging the marriage (cf. Ge 24:50–53). The Israelites promised to intercede for Benjamin on the grounds that there was no other way to save the devastated tribe. The fact that the Benjamites *stole* the maidens absolved the parents from the curse against *giving* their daughters to Benjamin! These arguments may have been less than convincing, but the leaders of Israel prevented the relatives from retaliating against the Benjamites (cf. 18:22–26).

Restored to their property, the surviving Benjamites began the long task of rebuilding and repopulating their cities. It is a tribute to their hard work and to the resiliency of Israel as a whole that a member of the Benjamite tribe was selected to be their first king (1Sa 9:1–2).

14. Conclusion (21:24–25)

24–25 Since the Israelites had dealt with the sin of Benjamin (cf. 20:8) and yet had provided for the future of that defeated tribe, the soldiers felt free to disband. The task had been far more difficult than they had anticipated, and the whole affair constituted one of the most tragic chapters of Israel's history.

The last verse repeats the somber words with which these appendixes began in 17:6. From the standpoint of the monarchy, the period of the judges was indeed a time of anarchy and upheaval. The often leaderless people wallowed in idolatry, immorality, and hatred. Sin abounded on both a personal and a national level, and God repeatedly allowed the enemy to overwhelm his people. The reigns of David and Solomon were a far happier time. Yet it was the last of the judges, Samuel, whom God used to call the people to repentance.

Ruth

INTRODUCTION

1. Background

By any standards the book of Ruth is a classic short story. It has been called the most beautiful short story ever written. It deals with a plot that naturally emerges through conversations between the major characters: Ruth, Naomi, and Boaz.

The setting of the book is the time of the judges. Chronological uncertainties, however, make it impossible to date this period more precisely than the last third of the second millennium B.C.—the period between the initial conquest of Palestine under Joshua and the establishment of the monarchy under Saul. It was a time of moral and political chaos in Israel. There was no strong central government or leader, the people repeatedly turned away from God, and neighboring peoples constantly harassed and invaded the disorganized nation (Jdg 2:14–15; 21:25).

2. Authorship and Date

Jewish tradition in the Talmud accepted Samuel as the author of the book of Ruth. The similarity of the language of Ruth to that of Judges and Samuel was probably responsible for linking it to Samuel. But there is nothing in the book of Ruth itself that helps us to identify the author, though we do know that he was a literary artist and a skillful teacher. The book was almost certainly written during or after the time of David, since one of the main purposes of the book is to point out that Ruth, a woman from Moab, was an ancestor of King David (4:18–22).

3. Theological Values

The book of Ruth does not deal with the major events or the institutions in Israel's history but with the problems and concerns of a single family in Bethlehem. Through the story of the experiences of this family, Ruth presents unobtrusively but powerfully the concept of divine providence. There are no direct conversations with God or appeals to him, though God is mentioned in the book in various places, and the solemn oath "As surely as the LORD lives" (3:13) is invoked. Clearly divine providence is behind everything that happens in the book—the famine, the deaths, Ruth's choice of Boaz's field as a place to glean, his attraction to her, and their eventual marriage.

The covenant relationship that bound the people of Israel to God and to one another underlies much of the book. Though the word "covenant" is not found in Ruth, it is a significant factor in the book's unfolding plot. Ruth's eloquent commitment to the God of her mother-in-law (1:16–17) was her acceptance of a relationship voiced earlier by Israel at Mount Sinai (Ex 24:3). When Boaz commended Ruth's loving care of Naomi (2:12), he was echoing Deuteronomic theology (Dt 28:2). Even Naomi's bitter complaint (1:21) was based on the presupposition of his faithfulness and trustworthiness by reason of his covenant relationship with his people.

EXPOSITION

I. An Israelite Family's Sojourn in Moab (1:1–5)

A. Famine in Judah (1:1–2)

1 The story opens during "the days when the judges ruled." The judges functioned as military leaders in times of crisis; they also served as local rulers, administering political and legal justice (Jdg 4:4–5). The time of the judges was a period of lawlessness and chaos in Israel (cf. Jdg 21:25).

The story begins in a time of famine, a natural catastrophe that occurred often in Palestine, where crops were dependent on the rainfall in its proper season (cf. Dt 28:15, 23–24, 38–40). The famine was probably widespread. "Bethlehem in Judah" is located about six miles south of Jerusalem. The name means "house of bread" and suggests the fertility of the region. Bethlehem is best known as the birthplace of both David and Jesus

Christ. Rachel had been buried near there (Ge 35:19).

The severity of the famine caused a certain man and his family to leave their home in Bethlehem and to journey to Moab in the expectation of a fuller life. Permanent migration was not their intention. The "country of Moab" was a land that lay east of the Dead Sea. A large part of this area is fertile and receives adequate rain.

2 The head of the family was Elimelech, whose name means "God is king" or "my God is king." As a kinsman of Boaz, his ancestry could be traced to the tribe of Judah (2:1; 4:20–21; Nu 1:7). His wife's name, Naomi, derives from a word that means "pleasant" or "lovely." The meaning of the two sons' names, Mahlon and Kilion, is uncertain.

The family is identified as Ephrathites from Bethlehem in Judah. Bethlehem was also known as Ephrath (Ge 35:19) and as Bethlehem Ephrathah (Ru 4:11; Mic 5:2). Ephrathah has been understood to have been either an older settlement that became absorbed into Bethlehem or the district where Bethlehem was located.

B. Deaths of Naomi's Husband and Children (1:3–5)

3–4a We are not told how long the family was in Moab before Elimelech died. Naomi's sons married Moabite wives named Orpah and Ruth (4:10 reveals that Ruth was married to Mahlon). Marriages with Moabites were not specifically forbidden by the law (Dt 7:1, 3), though Moabites were not allowed in the congregation of the Lord to the tenth generation (Dt 23:3; Ne 13:1–3). The name "Ruth" is traditionally derived from a word that means "friend" or "friendship"; the meaning of Orpah is less certain.

4b–5 The Hebrew is not clear whether the sons lived in Moab for ten years or were married for ten years before their deaths. For a woman to be "left without" her husband and "her . . . sons" was serious enough in her own community, but in another land she would be in desperate straits. It was only natural that Naomi's thoughts would turn to her homeland at such a time.

II. Naomi's Return to Judah (1:6–22)

A. Naomi's Appeal to Her Daughters-in-law (1:6–15)

6 Naomi heard that the Lord "had come to the aid of" his people in Canaan, so she made preparations to return to Judah. Orpah and Ruth did not question their duty to accompany their mother-in-law, though it meant leaving their own land.

7–8 Apparently the party had not traveled far on the road to Judah when Naomi realized the difficulties that faced her daughters-in-law. Therefore she released them from all obligation to her by encouraging them to return to their "mother's home." As returning to their "father's house" would have been more usual, the reference here is probably to the women's quarters of the home where comfort would be forthcoming and preparations for another marriage initiated. Naomi's parting wish was that the Lord would show "kindness" (GK 2876) to her daughters-in-law as they had shown to her.

9 Naomi also expressed the hope that her daughters-in-law would find "rest" (GK 4957) in the home of another husband. This word refers to the security that marriage gave a woman, not to freedom from work. Naomi kissed them in a parting gesture, but they began to weep loudly.

10 Both Orpah and Ruth refused to be separated from Naomi. They pledged themselves to return to Judah with her, abandoning their families, friends, homeland, deities, and prospects for remarriage. Their devotion, while remarkable in the light of what they were giving up to remain with Naomi, was at the same time high commendation of Naomi's character.

11 Naomi attempted to show her daughters-in-law the irrationality of their determination to remain with her. The verse assumes the law of levirate marriage (Latin *levir,* "brother-in-law") and cannot be understood apart from it. This law (Dt 25:5–10) provided for the marriage of a childless widow to a brother-in-law. If the daughters-in-law went with Naomi, as foreigners there would be little or no hope for them to remarry and have homes of their own. Naomi reminded them that she was not pregnant with sons who, as the younger brothers of Mahlon and Kilion, would be obligated to marry their widowed sisters-in-law according to the levirate law. Naomi's rebuke of their offer was not harsh but considerate. Observe her tender address: "my daughters." Her unselfish placing of her daughters-in-law's welfare above her own shows her noble character.

12–13 Naomi pointed out further absurdities of the situation they were creating. She reminded them that she was too old to find a husband. Then, even if she did find one and married that same night, it would be asking too much for them to wait till her sons were grown in order to marry them.

Having sized up the situation, Naomi concluded that her lot was far more bitter than that of her daughters-in-law. Because of their younger ages, they could remarry and find happiness and security in their homeland. But the true bitterness of Naomi's lot was that she believed the Lord was punishing her. Naomi offered no explanation as to why she thought God was her enemy. Perhaps she could not really understand the calamities that had struck her.

14 The daughters-in-law wept again because of the hopeless situation Naomi had described to them. Orpah then took leave of her mother-in-law with a parting kiss. Ruth, however, refused to leave Naomi. Orpah has frequently been described as unfeeling because she deserted Naomi; but a careful reading of the text shows that, though reluctant to leave, she was obeying Naomi's wishes. Nevertheless, by returning to her land she returned to her gods (v.15). So she stood in marked contrast to Ruth's faith (v.16).

15 In ancient times it was believed that a deity had power only in the geographical region occupied by his or her worshipers. Thus to leave one's land meant separation from one's god(s). Naomi, though a worshiper of the Lord, encouraged Ruth to join her sister-in-law and return to her land and to her own "gods." The OT does not acknowledge the genuine existence of other gods, but it does admit their reality as objects of worship.

B. Ruth's Pledge to Remain with Naomi (1:16–18)

16–17 Ruth's answer to Naomi has become a classic expression of devotion and loyalty. Ruth's commitment to go and "stay" (lit., "spend the night"; GK 4328) wherever Naomi went was not limited to the journey back to Bethlehem but was a commitment to share her home and circumstances, whatever they might be, after they returned to Judah. Ruth's renunciation of her people and gods was total.

By first naming the people and then God, Ruth revealed that she could not relate to God apart from his people. Nothing but death would separate her from Naomi. She swore a solemn curse on herself if she did not keep her promise, invoking the covenant name of God (Lord). Her commitment of no

The Book of Ruth

Set in the dark and bloody days of the judges, the story of Ruth is silent about the underlying hostility and suspicion the two peoples—Judahites and Moabites—felt for each other. The original onslaught of the invading Israelite tribes against towns that were once Moabite had never been forgotten or forgiven, while the Hebrew prophets denounced Moab's pride and arrogance for trying to bewitch, seduce and oppress Israel from the time of Balaam on. The Mesha stele (c. 830 B.C.) boasts of the massacre of entire Israelite towns.

Moab encompassed the expansive, grain-filled plateau between the Dead Sea and the eastern desert on both sides of the enormous rift of the Arnon River gorge. Much of eastern Moab was steppeland—semi-arid wastes not profitable for cultivation, but excellent for grazing flocks of sheep and goats. The tribute Moab paid to Israel in the days of Ahab was 100,000 lambs and the wool of 100,000 rams.

separation even by death probably refers to the Israelite custom of burying members of the same family in a family tomb.

18 Naomi obviously realized the determination of her daughter-in-law and saw that it would do no good to argue further with her. The solemnity of Ruth's curse was itself sufficient to deter Naomi from further protestations.

C. Arrival of Naomi and Ruth in Bethlehem (1:19–22)

19 Nothing is told of events along the road back to Bethlehem; but considering that thieves frequently lurked along the roads, it must have been a dangerous trip for two unaccompanied women (cf. Ezr 8:22, 31; Jer 3:2; Lk 10:30). When they arrived back in Bethlehem, "the whole town was stirred" with the news of their arrival. The commotion caused by Naomi's return may have been from the joy of seeing her again or it may describe the women's shocked whispering about her abject, changed appearance.

20 Naomi's reply to the women involves a play on names. Following a common practice of changing a name to reflect changed circumstances (cf. Ge 17:5, 15; 32:28; 35:18; 41:45; Nu 13:16; 2Ki 24:17; Dan 1:7), Naomi asked that her name be changed from Naomi ("Pleasant") to Mara ("Bitter"). Her reason for changing her name was that God had "made [her] life very bitter" (cf. Job 27:2). The name for God used in this verse is "the Almighty" (*Shaddai*; GK 8724)—the name of God that the patriarchs knew before he revealed himself to Moses (Ex 6:3). Naomi's concept of the sovereignty of God caused her to attribute her ill fortune to him, not to chance or to other gods. She did not mean it as an accusation but as an acknowledgment of his total control of all things.

21 Naomi further contrasted her former and current states: "I went away full" (i.e., rich with a husband and two sons). The position of "I" is emphatic and is intended to heighten the contrast with her current condition caused by the Lord—"empty" (i.e., widowed, childless, and poor). Naomi insisted that she should not be called "Pleasant" since the Lord himself had "afflicted" (GK 6700) her. She believed that God was showing his displeasure with her by the misfortunes she

had experienced. Naomi probably shared the Israelite belief that God blessed the righteous and brought calamity on the unrighteous (Dt 28:1–2, 15; Job 11:13–20). Again she named "the Almighty" as the one who had brought misfortune (lit., "caused evil") on her.

22 This verse summarizes the preceding events of the first chapter with one additional bit of information—the two women "returned" at the beginning of the season of barley harvest, i.e., in the eighth month of the agricultural calendar (April/May). This verse prepares the reader for the events to follow in the harvest field.

III. Ruth the Gleaner (2:1–23)

A. In the Fields of Boaz (2:1–3)

1 This chapter opens a window on the hardships of the poor in ancient Palestine. The first verse immediately establishes the relationship of Boaz to Naomi: he was a "relative" of Elimelech, specifically, he was from Elimelech's "clan." He was also a "man of standing," meaning that he was either a good warrior (cf. Jdg 6:12; 11:1) or a distinguished, honored person. The origin of the name Boaz is uncertain. It is the name of one of the pillars in front of Solomon's temple (1Ki 7:21). If the pillars were named for two of Solomon's ancestors, the meaning of the second pillar, Jachin, is unknown.

2 Ruth requested that Naomi allow her to go into the fields to "pick up [or glean] the leftover grain." God's law expressly allowed the poor the right to glean in the fields (Lev 19:9–10; 23:22; Dt 24:19–21), but the owners of the fields were not always cooperative. A hard day's work under the hot sun frequently netted only a small amount of grain (cf. Isa 17:5–6). Aware of that attitude of the landowners, Ruth hoped she would locate a field in which she would "find favor"; such a desire probably reflects her awareness of how either the poor or foreigners were frequently treated by hostile landowners. Naomi granted Ruth's request and added an affectionate "my daughter."

3 By chance Ruth found herself gleaning in the fields that belonged to Boaz. From the perspective of Ruth and Boaz, the meeting was accidental, but not from God's perspective. Once again the writer reminds the reader that Boaz was from the family of Elimelech.

B. Boaz's Notice of Ruth (2:4–7)

4 Boaz came from Bethlehem to see how the work was going. He greeted his workers with a typical Israelite greeting: "The LORD be with you!" which gives immediate insight into his character (cf. Jdg 6:12; Ps 129:8). They responded with a similar greeting. This kind of salutation would rarely be heard in fields today!

5 Boaz's question to his foreman, "Whose young woman is that?" suggests an attraction to Ruth, a woman he had not noticed previously working in his fields. The question suggests that he was seeking information about her ancestry or clan (cf. Ge 32:17–18; 1Sa 17:55–58; 30:13).

6–7 The foreman identified Ruth as the Moabitess who had returned with Naomi. Boaz had surely heard about the return of the two women, though he apparently had not yet met them. The foreman further told of Ruth's courteous request for permission to glean after the reapers had completed their work, even though the law allowed her the right to glean (cf. v.15, which makes it clear that the privilege of collecting grain from among the sheaves could only be granted by the field's owner). He described her as hard working, taking little time to rest.

C. Boaz's Provision for Ruth (2:8–16)

8–9 The good report the foreman gave concerning Ruth could only increase Boaz's interest in her. His greeting reminds the reader of the disparity of their ages. He encouraged her not to go to other fields to glean but to remain with his servant girls and work alongside them. The men wielded the sickles, and the women followed along, tying the sheaves in bundles. As further proof of his concern for her and his desire to protect her from harm, Boaz told Ruth that he had ordered the men not to "touch" her. She could also drink from the "water jars" that the men had filled for their use. This was a privilege not ordinarily permitted the gleaners.

10 Ruth's response is typical of ancient Near Eastern expressions of gratitude and humility (Jos 7:6; Jdg 13:20; 1Sa 20:41; 2Sa 14:4). She bowed herself with her face to the ground before Boaz and asked in amazement why she, a foreigner, had found favor in his eyes.

11 Although Boaz did not recognize Ruth when he first saw her (v.5), he had already heard about her. He informed her that he knew of her kindness to Naomi and of her abandonment of her own people and land in order to come to live with a people whom she had not previously known.

12 Boaz pronounced a blessing on Ruth, not only for her sacrificial loyalty to Naomi, but especially for her acceptance of the God of Israel. A vivid idiom describes her faith. It pictures a tiny bird snuggling under the wings of its mother (cf. Dt 32:11). Figuratively the idiom symbolizes God as her Protector (Pss 36:7; 57:1; 91:4).

13 Ruth responded with true humility and undoubtedly with some surprise that Boaz could speak such comforting and kind words to one who did not even have the standing of a servant girl before him. Ruth's calling Boaz "my lord" was a common way of showing respect. The phrase "have spoken kindly" may be understood as an expression of confidence about the future (cf. Ge 50:21; Isa 40:2). Ruth was not pleading with Boaz to be kind; she was grateful that he was kind.

14 Boaz showed his increasing interest in Ruth by inviting her to share the noon meal with his reapers. The meal consisted of bread (or in a broader sense, food), wine vinegar, and roasted grain. Boaz himself served her as she sat with his reapers. Ruth ate till she was satisfied, with food left over. Then she left to return to the fields.

15–16 After Ruth went back to continue her work, Boaz ordered his reapers to let her glean among the sheaves (not just picking up grain that they accidentally dropped as they reaped) and not to "embarrass" her. Moreover, they were to pull stalks from their bundles that had not yet been tied up by the women and leave them for her to pick up. Boaz's instructions were generous, far beyond what the law required that allowed gleaners in the fields only after the reapers had finished their work. His actions showed that he already had a special interest in Ruth.

D. Ruth's Conversation with Naomi about Boaz (2:17–23)

17 Ruth gleaned in the field till evening and then beat out what she had gleaned (i.e., separated the grain from the chaff). Her gleanings measured about one-half to two-thirds of a bushel (twenty-nine to fifty pounds). Such a large quantity could not have been acquired in a day by an ordinary gleaner. It shows how Boaz's instructions to his reapers aided Ruth and also how diligently Ruth had worked. Ruth probably gathered enough to last Naomi and her for several weeks.

18 Ruth returned to Bethlehem and proudly showed her mother-in-law what she had gleaned that day. She also gave Naomi some of the food she had saved from her noon meal with the reapers.

19 Naomi must have been amazed by what she saw, for her words tumbled out in rapid succession. There was a question concerning where Ruth had worked and a hasty blessing pronounced on the benefactor, unknown as yet to Naomi. Ruth identified him as Boaz.

20 On learning the name of their generous benefactor, Naomi pronounced a second blessing on him but acknowledged that it was the Lord who had not stopped showing his "kindness" to the living and the dead (cf. Ge 24:27; 2Sa 2:5). She added for Ruth's benefit that Boaz was a "close relative." As such, he qualified as a "kinsman-redeemer" (GK 1457), a man who under the levirate law could fulfill the duty of preserving the name of the dead by marrying Ruth. The responsibilities of the kinsman-redeemer included avenging the death of a murdered relative (Nu 35:19), marrying a childless widow of a deceased brother (Dt 25:5–10), buying back family land that had been sold (Lev 25:25), buying a family member who had been sold as a slave (Lev 25:47–49), and looking after needy and helpless members of the family (Lev 25:35).

21–22 Apparently interrupted by Naomi before her account was complete, Ruth continued by telling of Boaz's instruction to her to remain close to his servants till the harvest was finished. Naomi expressed approval that Ruth was allowed the protection of going to the fields with Boaz's maidens. She was aware that a woman of Ruth's status could meet with harm if she worked alone in other fields.

23 Ruth accepted Naomi's counsel and stayed close to Boaz's servant girls in the fields till both barley and wheat harvests were finished. She continued living with her mother-in-law, to whom she returned from the fields each evening. The two harvest seasons would have lasted for from late April to early June (cf. Dt 16:9).

IV. Encounter at the Threshing Floor (3:1–18)

A. Naomi's Advice to Ruth (3:1–5)

1 Naomi asked whether she should "try to find a home" for her daughter-in-law—i.e., find security and benefits for her in marriage. Parents customarily arranged marriages in the ancient Near East (Ge 24:3–4; 34:4; Jdg 14:2). Naomi's motive was unselfish: "where you will be well provided for." If Ruth remained an unprotected widow in a foreign land, life could go very hard for her.

2 Naomi knew that Boaz was a kinsman (though not the nearest, cf. v.12) who could satisfy the levirate law of marriage. She interpreted Boaz's kindness to Ruth that allowed her to work alongside his servant girls as an indication of a favorable disposition on his part toward Ruth and possibly a willingness to do the kinsman's part. Naomi knew that Boaz would be winnowing barley at the threshing floor that same night, and she had devised a plan whereby he might know of Ruth's willingness to marry him.

3–4 Naomi instructed Ruth to beautify herself according to the custom of the times by washing (cf. Isa 1:16) and perfuming herself. Then after putting on her "best clothes," she was to "go down to the threshing floor." Naomi cautioned Ruth not to reveal herself to Boaz till he had finished eating and drinking. Ruth was to "note" where Boaz lay down and then to go in, uncover his feet, and lie down. She would then wait for Boaz to tell her what to do. Naomi probably had in mind that Boaz would recognize Ruth's action as an appeal to marry her as the next of kin. Though some scholars claim that Naomi was encouraging Ruth to offer herself sexually to Boaz, we must caution against interpreting her advice as an act of such boldness and immorality. It is important to note that only the place of Boaz's feet was involved in the uncovering.

5 Ruth agreed to do exactly as her mother-in-law had instructed her (cf. Ex 19:8; 24:3; 2Ki 10:5). Verse 9 suggests, however, that Ruth did not wait for Boaz to tell her what to do after he awoke, as Naomi had instructed her. Divine providence does not eliminate human activity.

B. Ruth at the Feet of Boaz (3:6–13)

6–7 Ruth carried out the plan that Naomi had proposed to her. As Naomi had anticipated, Boaz ate and drank. He was happy and contented. Boaz lay down at the end of the pile of grain that had been threshed and winnowed and went to sleep. Ruth entered "quietly" (lit., "in secrecy"; cf. Jdg 4:21; 1Sa 24:4), uncovered his feet, and lay down.

8 Some time must have passed. At midnight Boaz awoke suddenly (perhaps from a bad dream or from the cold caused by his uncovered feet) and discovered that a woman was lying at his feet. In the darkness he did not immediately recognize Ruth.

9 Boaz did recognize the shadowy figure as a woman, as his question "Who are you?" uses a feminine singular pronoun. Ruth immediately identified herself as his "servant" Ruth. Then she asked him to spread the corner of his "garment" over her since he was a kinsman-redeemer. Ruth's request has been interpreted as a request for protection or perhaps even for marriage (cf. Dt 22:30; Eze 16:8). Marriage, however, was only one function of the kinsman-redeemer; he was also to serve as protector of needy members of the family. It is an arbitrary judgment to insist that Ruth was proposing marriage. It may be significant that she said, "You are *a* kinsman-redeemer," instead of, "You are *my* kinsman-redeemer," as there was a closer relative (3:12; 4:1). Naomi could not have been ignorant of the existence of the nearer kinsman, though Ruth may have been.

10 Boaz was flattered by Ruth's kindness in seeking him out. If there had been doubt earlier about his age, it is now clear that Boaz was much older than Ruth. It pleased him that she turned trustingly to him rather than to a younger man, "whether rich or poor." It

is increasingly clear that Boaz interpreted Ruth's bold actions as a request for marriage.

11 Boaz allayed Ruth's concern that she might have acted presumptuously or offended him by her forwardness. He assured her that he would do all that she requested. Everyone in Bethlehem knew that she was a "woman of noble character" (cf. Pr 31:10). He assured her that all would know there was nothing wrong in the fact that Ruth had come to him with the request to marry him.

12 Boaz then informed Ruth that there was a barrier to his serving as the kinsman-redeemer—there was a nearer kinsman on whom the legal duty fell. Why Naomi sent Ruth to Boaz instead of to the other man can only be surmised. She may have preferred Boaz or perhaps did not feel free to approach the other kinsman directly and hoped that Boaz would serve as a "go-between."

13 Boaz requested that Ruth remain at the threshing floor the rest of the night after assuring her that he would contact the nearer kinsman the next morning to see whether he would accept his obligation to her. If he would not, Boaz swore with an oath that he would be Ruth's kinsman-redeemer. Not to carry through his commitment after invoking the Lord's name would have been a violation of the third commandment (Ex 20:7).

C. Ruth's Return to Naomi (3:14–18)

14–15 Ruth remained at Boaz's feet till morning but arose to leave before daybreak with Boaz's encouragement, lest it be known that "a woman" had spent the night there. Town gossips would put the worst construction on the incident, thereby destroying Ruth's reputation and perhaps his own. But before Boaz allowed her to leave, he asked Ruth to hold out the "shawl" she was wearing. He filled it with six "measures" of barley. Then she returned to the city.

16–17 Naomi's question to Ruth on her daughter-in-law's return seems strange: "Who are you, my daughter?" It can be understood as initial lack of recognition in the early morning darkness, but more likely the question means "How did it go?" Ruth told her mother-in-law all that had happened. She pointed to the barley Boaz had given her and repeated his admonition, "Don't go back to your mother-in-law empty-handed" (her "empty" days were about to end; cf. 1:21). These are the last recorded words of Ruth in the book.

18 On learning what had happened, Naomi advised, "Wait ... until you find out what happens." She was convinced that Boaz was the kind of person who would not rest till the matter of the right of the nearer kinsman was settled that day. Also, her advice to "wait" reveals a stance of faith—a confident, expectant belief that only God could bring the venture to a successful conclusion.

V. A Transaction at the City Gate (4:1–12)

A. A Kinsman's Refusal to Redeem Naomi's Land (4:1–6)

1 Naomi was correct in her assessment of Boaz's determination to settle the matter as quickly as possible. He went to the city gate, a kind of outdoor court where judicial matters were resolved by the elders and those who had earned the confidence and respect of the people (Dt 22:15; 2Sa 15:2; Pr 22:22; Jer 38:7; Am 5:10). The location also served as a place for transacting business. Boaz waited for the nearer kinsman, who had prior rights and duties toward Naomi and Ruth, to pass that way. In a town the size of Bethlehem, the best place to encounter friends was to station oneself at the city gate. Sooner or later everyone passed that way. Boaz did not have long to wait. He saw the man he was seeking and hailed him. His attention gained by Boaz's greeting, the man stopped and sat down at the gate with Boaz.

2 Boaz called ten elders who were already nearby to serve as witnesses to the legal brief he was about to set forth. The elders exercised important roles—both judicial and political—in all the periods of Israel's history (see Dt 19:12; 21:2; 22:15; 25:7–9; Jos 20:4; Jdg 11:7–8; et al.). In matters of dispute they sat and listened to the opposing parties present their cases, heard witnesses, weighed evidence, and then made their decision. In the matter between Boaz and the other kinsman, they primarily were serving as witnesses.

3–4 Boaz proceeded to set forth his case. He explained that Naomi, who had returned from Moab, was selling a piece of land that belonged to their relative, Elimelech. The reader is not told why she was selling it or what her legal claim to it was. According to law, land passed from a man to his son or to his kinsmen; property could pass from father to daughter if there was no son, but the law did not make specific provision for passing an inheritance from husband to wife.

It was important in Israel that land remain within the family (cf. Lev 25:23–28; Nu 27:1–11; 36:1–12; Dt 19:14; 1Ki 21; Jer 32). Boaz urged the kinsman to make his intentions known before the people and before the elders who were witnessing the exchange. Would he redeem the property as the nearest kinsman? The man immediately agreed to redeem the property. He must have felt that it would be to his advantage to buy it.

5 Boaz had a plan to discourage the kinsman from buying the land, so he reminded him of a condition he must satisfy to redeem the land. He must marry Ruth the Moabitess to bear children to restore the name of Elimelech to his inheritance in accordance with the levirate law (see Dt 25:5–9). The firstborn son of their marriage would legally be Mahlon's son and eventually own the land.

This case differs from the levirate law on several counts: (1) here a more distant relative than a brother was expected to marry the widow; (2) the kinsman removed his own shoe (see comment on v.8) instead of the rejected widow doing it; and (3) apparently no disgrace was involved, as the significance of removing the shoe here was to seal a legal transaction.

6 On hearing Boaz's inclusion of Ruth in the transaction, the kinsman refused to redeem the land. His justification was that it would "endanger" his own estate. In the presence of the witnesses, he forfeited his right of redemption to Boaz, the next nearest kinsman, by refusing to honor his obligation. Perhaps the kinsman was aware that he would be paying part of what should be his own children's inheritance to buy land that would revert to Ruth's son as a legal heir of Elimelech. Or maybe he was reluctant to intermarry with a Moabite woman (cf. Dt 23:3–4).

B. Boaz's Purchase of the Land (4:7–12)

7 "In earlier times" introduces the author's parenthetical insertion to describe a custom that was no longer practiced at the time the book was written (cf. Jer 32:9–12). The origin of the custom has been traced to an ancient practice of taking possession of property by walking on the soil that was being claimed (cf. Dt 1:36; 11:24; Jos 1:3; 14:9). Removing the sandal and handing it to another became a symbol of the transfer of the land.

8 In the presence of the gathered witnesses, the kinsman renounced his right to the land and invited Boaz to buy it. In a time when few written records were kept, attestation by a number of witnesses made transactions legally secure. The Hebrew is not clear as to whose sandal was transferred. The practice of removing a sandal described here is different from that described in Dt 25:9 (which suggests contempt by the widow for a husband's brother who refused to fulfill his duty). Here it appears to be a ritual used to confirm the ratification of a transaction.

9–10 Boaz addressed the elders and all the people who had assembled, reminding them that they were witnesses to what had transpired. He had "bought" from Naomi all that belonged to Elimelech and to his sons, Kilion and Mahlon. In addition he "acquired" Ruth (only here is it said that Ruth had been Mahlon's wife) to become his wife, in order that Elimelech's name would not disappear from among his people (cf. 2Sa 18:18; Isa 56:4–5). Boaz began and ended his remarks to the elders and the people with the same words: "Today you are witnesses" (cf. Jos 24:22).

11–12 The people answered with what must have been an established legal response: "We are witnesses" (cf. 1Sa 12:5). Moreover, they pronounced a blessing of fertility on Ruth, that she would be like Rachel and Leah, who had twelve sons between them (Ge 29:31–30:24).

The people then pronounced a dual blessing on Boaz—a desire that he "have standing" (likely a phrase that he might achieve wealth) and that he would become "famous" in Bethlehem. In the parallel blessing of fertility in v.12, the people wished that his family would be like the family "of Perez, whom Tamar bore to Judah" (cf. Ge 38:29; 1Ch 2:5; 4:1; cf. Ps 127:4–5). Perez is intentionally named because he was an ancestor of the house of Judah (Ge 38:26, 29). Since the first son of Boaz and Ruth would be reckoned as Mahlon's, the people were expressing a hope

that Boaz would have many other children, who would legally be his.

VI. Birth of a Son to Boaz and Ruth (4:13–17)

13 Boaz and Ruth were married. We are not told how much time elapsed between their marriage and the birth of their first son. Attributing to the Lord Ruth's conception after ten years of sterility (1:4) may be the writer's subtle way of explaining why Mahlon, living in a land that worshiped Chemosh, was unable to have children. Both fertility and barrenness were attributed to the Lord (Ge 29:31; 30:2).

14 The women of the community, who earlier had witnessed Naomi's bitter lament, now gathered around her to share her happiness. They praised the Lord, giving him credit for providing a redeemer for Naomi. Their statement suggests that the child is the kinsman-redeemer, though this statement should be understood in the context as a blessing pronounced over the child, just as the men had previously prayed for blessing on Boaz (v.11). Boaz is indeed the redeemer (cf. 2:20; 3:9, 12–13; 4:10). The women blessed the child and expressed a hope that he would become famous throughout Israel.

15–16 According to the women's perspective, this child took away Naomi's reproach of childlessness and would take care of her in her old age. The women foresaw the child as a restorer of life for Naomi and as the one who would sustain her in her old age. They also had a word of praise for Ruth; she was better to Naomi than seven sons might have been. The tribute to Ruth is striking in light of the importance placed on sons in the OT (cf. 1Sa 1:8; 2:5; Job 1:2; 42:13). Naomi took the newborn child, laid him in her bosom, and cared for him as his guardian.

17 This verse gives the only example in the OT of a child being named by someone other than the immediate family (cf. Ex 2:10). The women who named this grandchild of Naomi called him Obed ("servant"; perhaps it meant he would serve his grandmother as a kinsman-redeemer). A genealogical fragment concludes the verse by linking Obed to David as the father of Jesse and thus as the grandfather of David.

The story of Ruth has shown how a Moabite woman obtained an exalted place in Hebrew history. There is later evidence that David did not forget his Moabite roots. During the period of flight from Saul's wrath, David asked the king of Moab to let his parents stay there for refuge (1Sa 22:3–4).

VII. The Genealogy of David (4:18–22)

18 Perez, the son of Tamar (Ge 38:29), and Hezron are mentioned in Ge 46:12 (cf. Mt 1:3). The genealogy in Ruth is traced back to Perez, who was the founder of a family of Judah that was named for him, called the Perezites (Nu 26:20), to which Elimelech and Boaz belonged. The list is composed of ten names. It appears that there are gaps (i.e., unimportant names are omitted) in order to preserve the number ten. The first five names cover the period from the time of the entry into Egypt (Perez, Ge 46:12) to the time of Moses (Nahshon, Ex 6:23; Nu 1:7), while the remaining five belong to the period of the early settlement in Canaan to the closing years of the judges.

19–21 For other listings of the genealogy that is recorded here, but with different spellings for some of the names, see Ge 46:12; Nu 1:7; 26:21; 1Ch 2:4–12, 25–27, 51, 54; 4:1; Mt 1:3–5; Lk 3:31–33.

With the naming of Boaz, the rest of the genealogy falls into focus. Neither Mahlon nor Elimelech is included, however, as the "legal" father of Obed; instead, Boaz, his natural father, is listed.

22 The link to David has now been established. Obed is presented as the father of Jesse and thus the grandfather of David.

It is difficult to know precisely why the book of Ruth ends with a genealogy. It is unlikely that the only purpose of the story was to lead up to the genealogy, and yet it is improbable that the book of Ruth would have found its way into the OT canon apart from its connection with David. Perhaps the genealogy was included to remind the reader of the hand of God in the direction and continuity of history. Two people brought together by a highly unlikely series of circumstances became ancestors of the great king of Israel, David, who in turn for Christians provides an integral link in the genealogy of our Lord.

1 Samuel

INTRODUCTION

1. Title

In the Jewish canon the two books of Samuel were originally one. Like Kings and Chronicles, each of which is slightly longer than Samuel, the scroll of Samuel was too unwieldy to be handled with ease and so was divided into two parts in early MSS of the LXX. Not until the fifteenth century A.D. was the Hebrew text of Samuel separated into two books. It is understandable that the ancient Hebrew title of the book was "Samuel," since the prophet Samuel is the dominant figure in the early chapters.

2. Authorship and Date

According to the Babylonian Talmud, the judge and prophet Samuel wrote the first twenty-four chapters of 1 Samuel (1Sa 25:1 reports his death), and the rest of the Samuel corpus was the work of Nathan and Gad (the latter theory is based on 1Ch 29:29). But we cannot say for certain that this is the case. The priests Ahimaaz (cf. 2Sa 15:27, 36; 17:17, 20; 18:19, 22–23, 27–29) and Zabud (cf. 1Ki 4:5), among others, have also been proposed as possible candidates. All arguments about authorship fail to convince. In sum, we must remain content to leave the authorship of Samuel in the realm of anonymity. Ultimately, of course, the Holy Spirit is the Author.

A statement in 1Sa 27:6 has often been referred to in discussions of authorship: "Ziklag . . . has belonged to the kings [pl.] of Judah ever since." This verse suggests that Samuel was not written until after the division of the kingdom of Israel following the death of Solomon in 931 B.C. But we must reckon with the possibility of a modest number of later editorial updatings and/or modernizations of the original work. With respect to the date of the books of Samuel, all that can be said for certain is that since they report "the last words of David" (2Sa 23:1), the final chapters could not have been written earlier than the second quarter of the tenth century B.C. (David died c. 970).

3. Historical Context

After the conquest of Canaan by Joshua, the people of Israel experienced the normal range of problems that face colonizers of newly occupied territory. Exacerbating their situation, however, was not only the resilience of the conquered but also the failures—moral and spiritual as well as military—of the conquerors. Their rebellion against the covenant that God had established with them at Sinai brought divine retribution, and the restoration that resulted from their repentance lasted only until they rebelled again (cf. Jdg 2:10–19; Ne 9:24–29). By the end of Judges the situation in the land had become intolerable. Israel was *in extremis,* and anarchy reigned (Jdg 17:6; 21:25). More than three centuries of settlement (cf. Jdg 11:26) did not materially improve Israel's position, and thoughtful people must have begun crying out for change.

If theocracy implemented through divine charisma was the hallmark of the period of the judges (cf. Jdg 8:28–29), theocracy mediated through divinely sanctioned monarchy would characterize the next phase in the history of the Israelites. In the days of the judges "Israel had no king" (Jdg 17:6; 18:1; 19:1; 21:25), and it was becoming increasingly apparent to many that she desperately needed one. Not until the accession of Saul did the people have a king in the truest sense of the word—and even then they expected him to "judge" them (cf. 1Sa 8:5–6, 20).

Historically, the division of the monarchy occurred in 931/30 B.C., following Solomon's death. If we interpret the biblical figures literally, Solomon reigned from 970 to 931 (forty years, 1Ki 11:42), David from 1010 to 970 (forty years and six months, 2Sa 5:5), and Saul from 1052 to 1010 (forty-two years, 1Sa 13:1). Assuming that Samuel was about thirty years old when he anointed Saul as king of Israel, we arrive at the approximate dates of

1080 (the birth of Samuel) to 970 B.C. (the death of David) as the time span covered in the books of Samuel.

4. Purpose

In the books of Samuel, monarchy becomes a reality. Three figures dominate the book—Samuel the king-maker, Saul the abortive king, and David the ideal king. A major purpose of Samuel, then, is to define monarchy as a gracious gift of God to his chosen people. Their desire for a king (1Sa 8:5) was not in itself inappropriate, despite Samuel's initial displeasure (v.6). Nor were they necessarily wrong in wanting a king like "all the other nations" had (vv.5, 20). Their sin was that they were asking for a king "to lead us and to go out before us and to fight our battles" (v.20). They were willing to exchange humble faith in the protection and power of "the LORD Almighty" (1Sa 1:3) for misguided reliance on the naked strength of "the fighting men of Israel" (2Sa 24:4).

5. Literary Form

Justifiable concern for the inspired truth and moral excellence of Scripture should not blind us to its consummate beauty. For the most part the books of Samuel are composed of prose narratives that serve well in presenting a continuous historical account of the advent, establishment, and consolidation of monarchy in Israel. It is possible to isolate various literary units within the larger whole—e.g., the Ark Narratives (1Sa 4:1b–7:17), the Rise of Saul (chs. 8–12), the Decline of Saul (chs. 13–15), the Rise of David (16:2–28:2), etc.—although debate is vigorous concerning their parameters.

In recent years various sections of the books of Samuel have been subjected to close reading in order to uncover aspects of Samuel's exquisite literary structure. While manufacturing chiasms where there are none is a constant temptation that the exegete must avoid at all costs, the author of Samuel seems to have used the technique on numerous occasions. A clear example is the Epilogue, in which the Song of David (2Sa 22) and David's Last Words (23:1–7) nestle between two warrior narratives (21:15–22; 23:8–39) that are framed in turn by reports of divine wrath against the people of God (21:1–14; 24).

Second Samuel 1–20 displays a four-part architectonic structure that is impressive indeed. David's Accession to Kingship Over Judah (1:1–3:5) ends with a four-verse listing of the sons born to David in Hebron (3:2–5); David's Accession to Kingship Over Israel (3:6–5:16) ends with a four-verse listing of the children born to him in Jerusalem (5:13–16); David's Powerful Reign (5:17–8:18) and David's Court History (chs. 9–20) each end with a four-verse roster of his officials (8:15–18; 20:23–26). A symmetrical literary edifice of such magnitude can hardly be accidental.

When poetry punctuates the corpus here and there, it does so in memorable and striking ways. For example, the Song of Hannah and the Song of David—the first near the beginning of the work (1Sa 2:1–11) and the second near its end (2Sa 22)—remind us that the two books were originally one by framing their main contents, by opening and closing in similar ways, and by highlighting the messianic horizons of the Davidic dynasty through initial promise (1Sa 2:10) and eternal fulfillment (2Sa 22:51).

6. Theological Values

In terms of the political scene, Israel at the beginning of 1 Samuel was a loosely organized federation of anemic tribal territories scarcely able to keep the Philistines and other enemies at bay. By the end of 2 Samuel, however, Israel under David had become the most powerful kingdom in the eastern Mediterranean region, strong at home and secure abroad. As far as the religious picture is concerned, the opening chapters of 1 Samuel find Israel worshiping at a nondescript shrine presided over by a corrupt priesthood. The last chapter of 2 Samuel, however, records David's purchase of a site in Jerusalem on which the temple of Solomon would be built. Sweeping change, then, is a hallmark of the Samuel narratives—changes guided and energized by the Lord himself through humans like Samuel, Saul, and David.

Election is also important in the books of Samuel. The Lord's elective purpose embraced Samuel (cf. 1Sa 1:19–20), Saul (cf. 10:20–24), and David (cf. 16:6–13). 2 Samuel 7 describes God's choice of the dynasty of David as that through which future kings (including the Messiah) would come. In 2Sa7, kingship and covenant kiss each other.

Reversal of fortune as an index of divine sovereignty and grace is another significant theme. Hannah, a barren woman, becomes the mother of six children (cf. 1Sa 1–2). Men of privilege (such as Eli's sons) die in shame (cf. 4:11). An unheralded donkey wrangler (cf. 9:2–3) and an obscure shepherd boy (cf. 16:11) are anointed as the first two rulers of Israel.

A key theme of the ark narratives is that God refuses to be manipulated. Carrying the ark into battle does not guarantee an Israelite victory (cf. 4:3–11), placing the ark in a Philistine temple does not ensure divine blessing (cf. 5:1–6:12), and looking into the ark brings death (cf. 6:19; 2Sa 6:6–7). The ark, with its tablets of the covenant, served as a continual reminder to the Israelites of God's demands on their lives.

The Deuteronomic theme of blessing for obedience and curses for disobedience is furthered in the books of Samuel. To the extent that David understood that his role as human king was to implement the mandates of the Divine King (Israel's true ruler), blessing would follow (cf. 2Sa 6:11–15, 17–19; 7:27–29). When he deliberately flouted God's will, however, he could count equally on the fact that he would be under the curse (cf. 12:1–18). If the Davidic covenant was eternal in the sense that his line would continue forever (cf. 7:12–16, 25–29; Ps 89:27–29, 33–37), it was also conditional in that individual participants in it would be punished when they sinned (cf. 1Ki 2:4; 8:25; Pss 89:30–32; 132:12).

The offices of king and prophet arose simultaneously in Israel. Saul, the first king, was anointed by Samuel, who stands at the head of the prophetic line (cf. 1Sa 9:6–10, 19; Ac 3:24; 13:20) as promised to Moses (Dt 18:15–18). If the task of the king was to administer the covenant, that of the prophet was to interpret its demands. To the end of the monarchy, the prophets protected with holy zeal their divinely authorized claims over kingship.

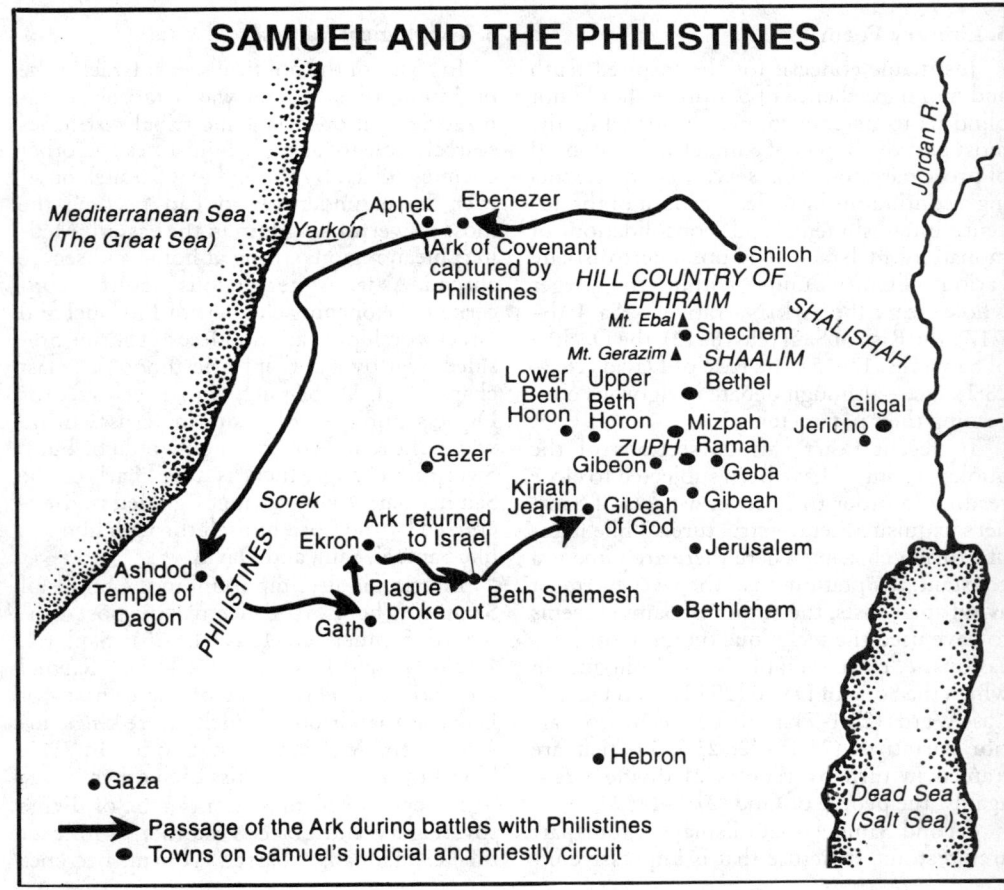

SAMUEL AND THE PHILISTINES

→ Passage of the Ark during battles with Philistines
● Towns on Samuel's judicial and priestly circuit

EXPOSITION

I. Prelude to Monarchy in Israel (1:1–7:17)

First Samuel introduces us to Israel's last two judges (Eli, a failure; Samuel, a success) and first two kings (Saul, a failure; David, a success). Appropriately the story of Israel's monarchy begins with an account of the early life of Samuel: prophet, priest, judge, and, most significantly, king-maker. God chose Samuel to anoint Israel's first two kings. Each was to be the "leader" over his people (10:1; 13:14; 16:13).

A. The Childhood of Samuel (1:1–4:1a)

1. The birth and dedication of Samuel (1:1–28)

1–2 "Ramathaim"—the town of Samuel's birth, official residence, and burial—means "Two heights." Elsewhere the town is called simply Ramah, "Height" (1:19; 2:11; 7:17; et al.).

Samuel's father is called a "Zuphite" who lived in the area assigned to Ephraim. The Chronicles genealogies identify Samuel as a member of the Kohathite branch of the tribe of Levi and an ancestor of tabernacle and temple musicians (1Ch 6:16, 22, 31–33). Allotted no patrimony of their own, the Levites lived among the other tribes (see Jos 21:20–22). "Elkanah," a popular name in ancient Israel, means "God has created [a son]." He is the only commoner in the books of Samuel and Kings specifically mentioned as having more than one wife. Although polygamy was not God's intention (cf. Ge 2:24; Mal 2:15), having "two wives" accords with the polygamous culture of the ancient world.

Hannah (lit., "Grace") initially has pride of place, probably because she was Elkanah's favorite. Later, however, Peninnah (lit., "Ruby") is mentioned first, no doubt because she was a prolific childbearer (cf. v.4). Barrenness was the ultimate tragedy for a married woman (cf. Ge 11:30; 15:2–4; 16:1–2; 25:5; et al.).

3–8 Three times a year all Israelite men were required to go to the central sanctuary to offer sacrifices at the main religious festivals (Ex 34:23; Dt 12:5–7; 16:16; cf. Lk 2:41). Shiloh (sixteen miles east of Ramah) had been the location of the tabernacle and the ark of the covenant (4:3–4; Jos 18:1; Jdg 18:31). Eli

("Exalted is [the Lord]"), the priest at Shiloh (v.9; 2:11) and a judge in Israel (4:18), was descended from Aaron's son Ithamar (14:3; 22:20). Each of Eli's two reprobate sons—unfortunately also priests—had an Egyptian name: Hophni ("Tadpole") and Phinehas ("The Nubian").

The festival in view here is probably the Feast of Tabernacles. Sacrifices were offered to the "the LORD Almighty" (or "the LORD of hosts"). Festival celebrations were times of rejoicing in God's blessings, especially that of a bountiful harvest. Elkanah distributed portions of sacrificial meat (cf. Ex 29:26; Lev 7:33; 8:29) to Peninnah and her children, since family members shared in certain of the sacrificial offerings (cf. Dt 12:17–18; 16:13–14). Elkanah provided Hannah with a double portion because of his love for her. Hannah's sterility likely prompted Elkanah to take Peninnah as his second wife, who thus became Hannah's "rival." She "kept provoking" Hannah to "grief" (v.16). The devout Hannah was content to allow the Lord to avenge the wrong committed against her (cf. 2Sa 3:39).

The "house of the LORD" refers to the tabernacle but apparently also includes more permanent auxiliary structures that had doors (3:15) and therefore doorposts (v.9). These sacred buildings are called "the LORD's temple" (cf. 3:3).

Elkanah, mindful of Hannah's grief, asked her (lit.), "Why is your heart bad?" To do something "with a bad [GK 8317] heart" means to do it resentfully (cf. Dt 15:10). Apparently he thought she was angry or spiteful because she did not have children. Thus Elkanah was asking Hannah, "Why are you resentful? Don't I [your husband, who loves you very much] mean more to you than ten sons?"

9–11 Hannah's misery peaked at Shiloh during an annual pilgrimage. Her sadness and "bitterness of soul" led her to pray and make a vow to the Lord for herself and a son. The Nazirite vow (supposed here) included (1) abstaining from the use of grapes in any form, (2) not shaving the hair on one's head, and (3) avoiding dead bodies (Nu 6:3–7). The Nazirite vow was not usually taken by proxy and was rarely lifelong.

Hannah humbly calls herself "your servant" (GK 563), a word that indicates her submissive in the presence of a superior (cf. v.16; 3:9–10), and requests that God "look upon [her] misery" (cf. Ge 29:32; cf. 2Sa 16:12). God's remembrance is not a matter of recalling to mind but of paying special attention to or lavishing special care on someone (cf. Ps 8:4). Hannah recognizes that children are always a gift of God. If he will "give" (GK 5989) her a son, in gratitude she will "give" him back to the Lord (but cf. Ex 22:29).

12–18 Hannah's prayer reveals her intimate relationship with God. She prayed "to" the Lord; she prayed "in her heart"; and she prayed silently. Eli misunderstood Hannah's actions. Prayer in the ancient world was almost always audible (cf. Pss 3:4; 4:1; 6:9; Da 6:10–11), and drunkenness was not uncommon at festal occasions. He can hardly be excused for his spiritual insensitivity and should have realized that Hannah's moving lips signified earnest prayer rather than intoxicated mumbling. He therefore mistakenly rebukes her.

Hannah justly protests that she has been "pouring out [her] soul to the LORD," a vivid idiom for praying earnestly (cf. Pss 42:4; 62:8; La 2:19). She declares herself to be "deeply troubled" and does not want Eli to mistake her for a "wicked woman."

Satisfied with Hannah's explanation, Eli tells her to "go in peace" (cf. 25:35). Eli's hope that God would grant Hannah's request is soon fulfilled in the birth of Samuel (v.27; cf. 2:20). Being assured by Eli's response, she breaks her self-imposed fast, and her face is "no longer downcast."

19–20 The next day Elkanah's family worshiped the Lord, which had special meaning for Hannah this time. After their return from Shiloh to Ramah, Elkanah "lay with" (lit., "knew"; cf. Ge 4:1, 17, 25) Hannah. The Lord "remembered [GK 2349] her" by enabling her to bear a son. Hannah called him Samuel (lit., "Name of God") and then punned on the name by saying that she had "asked" the Lord for him (the Hebrew for "asked" is found in the word "Samuel").

21–23 After Samuel was born, Elkanah continued taking his family to Shiloh to sacrifice to the Lord (1:3; 2:19). On at least one occasion he had the additional purpose of fulfilling a "vow," perhaps in support of Hannah's

earlier vow (v.11). Hannah decided not to make the trip this time. She preferred to wait until Samuel was weaned. Then she could leave him there to serve the Lord for the rest of his life, as she had promised. After Samuel's weaning, Hannah intended to "present him before the LORD." Elkanah agreed with his wife's desire to follow through with her vow.

24–28 The big day finally arrived, and Hannah was ready. For the trip from Ramah to Shiloh, they took ample provisions. The three-year-old bull was doubtless meant to be sacrificed to the Lord. The purpose of the flour and wine remains obscure (cf. 28:24; Jdg 6:19). When the official slaughterers at the tabernacle had sacrificed the bull, Hannah and Elkanah brought Samuel before Eli the priest. In addressing Eli, Hannah used a common oath formula: "As surely as you live." She thus solemnly affirms that she is indeed the same woman he first had met a few years earlier and that the boy, Samuel, given in answer to her prayers, is now to be given back to the Lord. Eli responded by worshiping the God whom they both served.

2. The Song of Hannah (2:1–11)

1–2 Verses 1–10 are commonly referred to as the "Song of Hannah" because of similarities to other ancient OT hymns (e.g., Ex 15:1–18, 21; Dt 32:1–43; Jdg 5; and esp. 2Sa 22). It may have originated as a song of triumph at the Shiloh sanctuary in connection with Israel's victory over an enemy. Such songs would have been taught to worshipers, and this one perhaps became a personal favorite of Hannah. Therefore she sang it as a means of expressing her gratitude and praise to the Giver of life (cf. esp. v.5). Hannah's song may have been the seedplot for Mary's Magnificat (Lk 1:46–55; cf. also the Song of Zechariah in vv.68–79).

The song begins on a note of grateful exuberance: Her heart rejoices in the Lord—and in his "deliverance" (or "salvation"; GK 3802) as well (see Pss 9:14; 13:5; 35:9; Isa 25:9). The metaphor of one's "horn" (GK 7967) being lifted high perhaps comes from the animal world, where members of the deer family use their antlers in playful or mortal combat. "Horn" thus symbolizes strength.

For Hannah, the Lord is holy, unique, and mighty. She therefore celebrates God's holiness in righteous victory. She then connects his uniqueness with the metaphor of the Rock (cf. 2Sa 22:32; cf. also Ge 49:24; Dt 32:4; Isa 26:4; et al.)

3–8d After describing God's majesty and power, Hannah warns all who would vaunt themselves in their pride (including Peninnah!). Arrogance is both foolish and futile (Pss 31:18; 75:4; 138:6). God judges the heart and weighs it rather than external appearances (cf. 16:7). The "broken" bows are echoed by the "shattered" opponents of v.10. Making the strong weak and the weak strong is what God does (cf. Heb 11:32–34).

The last half of v.5 had special meaning for Hannah, who had once been barren (cf. Jdg 13:2–3). "Seven" here means simply "many," but at the same time also represents the ideal (cf. Job 1:2; 42:13). Just as she who has had many "pines away," so the mother of seven will "grow faint." The formerly barren Hannah eventually had a total of six children (v.21).

The Sovereign God ultimately blesses some and curses others (cf. vv.9c–10c). Verse 6a contrasts death with life; possibly the second half does too, though it may also refer to rescue from the brink of death after a serious illness (therefore contrasting sickness with health; cf. Ps 30:2–3).

The Lord can—and does—reverse the fortunes of poor and rich (Zec 9:3–4), of the humble and the proud (Job 5:11; Ps 75:7; and esp. 2Sa 22:28). He can lift a Baasha "from the dust" and later consume him (1Ki 16:2–3); he can ensconce a Job on an ash heap (Job 2:8) and later restore him (Job 42:10).

8e–10 The "foundations of the earth" (cf. 2Sa 22:16) refers pictorially to the firmness and stability of God's creation—which is always under his sovereign control. How much more is he able to protect his people (Pr 3:26) and confound his (and their) enemies (Dt 32:35)!

The word often translated "saint" (GK 2883) means "one to whom the Lord has pledged his covenant love [GK 2876]" (cf. Pss 12:1, 8; 50:5, 16; 97:10; 145:10, 20). The final destiny of the ungodly, however, is the silence of Sheol, the "grave" (GK 8619; v.6), where all is darkness (Job 10:21–22; 17:13; 18:18; cf. also Mt 8:12).

Hannah learned that in the battles of life it is not physical strength that brings victory.

Whether through human agency or directly, God always shatters the enemy (cf. Ex 15:6; Ps 2:9). Peninnah may have "thundered against" (1:6, lit.) Hannah, but Hannah knew full well that the Lord would ultimately "thunder against" Peninnah and all others who oppose him.

The Song of Hannah ends as it began, by using the word "horn" in the sense of "strength." Hannah voices the divine promise of strength to the coming "king"—initially David, who will found a dynasty with messianic implications. The king—the "anointed" one (GK 5431)—will rule by virtue of God's command and will therefore belong to him body and soul. The king will be "his" (2Sa 22:51).

11 With Samuel's dedication and Hannah's song complete, the family returned to Ramah—except for Samuel, who began what was to be a continuing ministry.

3. The wicked sons of Eli (2:12–26)

12–17 The reference to Hophni and Phinehas as "wicked men" (GK 1175) contrasts them with Hannah, who did not consider herself a "wicked woman" (1:16). Furthermore, the sons of Eli "had no regard for the LORD"—unlike Samuel, who "did not yet know" (3:7) the Lord.

Not content with the priests' portions of the sacrificial animals (cf. Lev 7:34), the servant of Eli's sons "would take for [themselves] whatever the fork brought up." And not only that, "even before the fat was burned" (Lev 7:31), Hophni and Phinehas demanded raw meat. On occasion they even preferred roasted meat to boiled—as if in mockery of the necessarily hasty method of preparing the first Passover feast (Ex 12:8–11). They wanted their unlawful portion before the Lord received what was rightfully his. Their rebellion, impatience, and impudence were great sins. These premonarchic priests treated the Lord's offerings with contempt, which could only lead to disaster (cf. Nu 16:30–32).

18–26 As a young apprentice priest under Eli's supervision, Samuel wore the "linen ephod," a priest's garment. Indeed, the little "robe" that Samuel's mother made for him annually as he was growing up may well have been an example of the "robe of the ephod" (Ex 28:31). By providing Hannah with additional children, the Lord continued to be gracious to her (cf. Ge 21:1). Samuel's continued growth in the Lord's presence, in stature and in favor with God and people, anticipates Luke's portrayal of Jesus' youth (Lk 2:40, 52).

The hapless Eli, whose advanced age is stressed from this point on (4:15, 18), was unable to restrain the sinful conduct of his sons. To their earlier callous treatment of their fellow Israelites (vv.13–16), they added sexual promiscuity—and with the women who served at the tabernacle (cf. Ex 38:8)! Such ritual prostitution was specifically forbidden to the people of God (Nu 25:1–5; Dt 23:17; Am 2:7–8). Eli's rebuke, justified in the light of widespread and public reports of his sons' evil deeds, fell on deaf ears. His theological arguments, weak at best, were to no avail, especially since God had already determined to put Hophni and Phinehas to death. What is eminently clear is that God's decision to end the lives of Eli's sons was irrevocable. Hannah had already expressed her willingness to leave such decisions within the sphere of divine sovereignty (v.6)—and so must we!

4. The oracle against the house of Eli (2:27–36)

27–36 The chapter concludes by expanding on the Lord's intention to put Eli's sons to death (v.25). The prophetic oracle to (and against) Eli uses the messenger formula ("This is what the LORD says") and mediates the divine word through an anonymous "man of God." The term "man of God" occasionally refers to an angel (cf. Jdg 13:3, 6, 8–9) but is usually a synonym for "prophet" (cf. 1Sa 9:9–10). This man of God reminds Eli that God had revealed himself to his ancestor Levi's house (in Aaron; see Ex 4:14–16) before the Exodus. Indeed, Aaron had been the object of special divine election to serve the Lord as the first in a long line of priests (Ex 28:1–4). Aaron would go up "to" the Lord's altar and would wear the ephod in the course of his divinely ordained work (cf. Lev 8:7).

Recipients of such privilege, Eli and his sons nevertheless "scorn" (GK 1246) the Lord's prescribed sacrifices. Literally, the verb means "to kick" and is found only once elsewhere in the OT (Dt 32:15). Although the Hebrew words for "fat" and "heavy" are different there than the word for "fattening" here, the parallel is striking: Like Israel centuries earlier, the house of Eli has "kicked at" the Lord's offerings by gorging themselves on the best parts of the sacrifices (vv.13–17). By condoning the sin of Hophni and Phinehas, Eli has demonstrated that he loves his sons more than he loves God and that he is therefore unworthy of the Lord's continued blessing (see Mt 10:37).

The Lord had promised that Aaron's descendants would always be priests (cf. Ex 29:9), and he had confirmed that promise on covenant oath (Nu 25:13). They would "minister [GK 2143] before" the Lord forever. But because of flagrant disobedience, the house of Eli would be judged by God. Although the Aaronic priesthood was perpetual, individual priests who sinned could thereby forfeit covenant blessing. The description of divine judgment, when translated literally, is vivid: "I will chop off your arm and the arm of your father's house." Furthermore, Eli would be the last "old man" in his family line, because God's execution of his death sentence would be swift and sure (4:11, 18; 22:17–20; 1Ki 2:26–27).

Examples of the predicted distress in God's "dwelling" (GK 5061; the tabernacle is meant) are the capture of the ark by the Philistines (4:11) and the destruction of Shiloh (cf. Jer 7:12, 14; 26:6, 9). Although in Eli's line there would "never" be an old man, in the line that would replace his there would "always" be a faithful priest. The only member of Eli's line to "be spared" was Abiathar, and he was later removed from the priesthood (1Ki 2:26–27).

Hophni and Phinehas would die "on the same day" (4:11), a prophetic sign to Eli not only of his own impending death but also of the fulfillment of the other components in the oracle of the man of God. The Lord would bring a "faithful" priest on the scene, who would be privy to the very thoughts of God and obedient to him.

"Faithful" (GK 586) contrasts strongly with the rebellion of Eli's sons and plays an important role in the succeeding context, both near and remote. In this same verse the Lord says, "I will firmly [GK 586] establish his house"—lit., "I will build for him a faithful house" (cf. 2Sa 7:27). In the present context the faithful priest whose house the Lord would establish refers initially to Samuel (3:1; 7:9; 9:12–13; cf. esp. 3:20). Later, however, the line of Zadok would replace that of Abiathar,

Eli's descendant (2Sa 8:17; 15:24–29; 1Ki 2:35)—a replacement that would constitute a greater fulfillment of the oracle of the man of God. Zadok and his descendants would thus "always" minister before the Lord's "anointed one"—David's son Solomon (1Ki 2:27, 35) and his descendants. Ultimate fulfillment would come only in Jesus the Christ, the supremely Anointed One, "designated by God to be high priest" (Heb 5:10) "forever, in the order of Melchizedek" (6:20).

As for the members of Eli's house, once fattened on priestly perquisites, soon not even the least benefit of priestly office would be theirs.

5. The call of Samuel (3:1–4:1a)

1 Special revelation was rare in the days of the judges. The few visions that did exist were not widely known (cf. Am 8:11–12). The word "vision" (GK 2606) means "divine revelation mediated through a seer."

2 Eli's aging eyes were so "weak" (cf. Dt 34:7) that he could barely "see" (he would eventually go completely blind; cf. 4:15). How different from Samuel, whose eyes saw clearly in a physical and a spiritual sense (v.15)!

3 The lamps on the seven-branched lampstand (Ex 25:31–37) were filled with olive oil, lit at twilight (30:8), and kept burning "before the LORD from evening till morning" (27:20–21; cf. Lev 24:2–4; 2Ch 13:11). Thus Samuel's encounter with the Lord on his bed in the tabernacle compound took place during the night, since the "lamp of God had not yet gone out."

4–10 Although Samuel did not yet know that it was the Lord who was speaking to him, his answer was typical of the servant who hears and obeys the divine call (Ge 22:1, 11; Ex 3:4; Isa 6:8). Samuel's openness to serving God would soon enable him to know the Lord in a way that Eli's sons never did (2:12). Although the word of the Lord had not yet been revealed to Samuel, that would soon take place (v.11); and as God continued to speak to Samuel through the years (v.21), the Lord's word would so captivate him that it would be virtually indistinguishable from "Samuel's word" (4:1). Samuel the priest would become Samuel the prophet (v.20).

Samuel thought that Eli was calling him. Twice Eli told Samuel to go back to bed, but the third time it finally dawned on the aged priest that it must be God who was calling the boy. He therefore told Samuel that he should respond the next time by saying, "Speak, LORD, for your servant is listening." This time the Lord "came and stood there," suggesting that Samuel could see him as well as hear him. Again the Lord called out Samuel's name twice, imparting a sense of urgency and finality. Samuel responded as Eli had instructed, though he left out the word "LORD."

11–14 The Lord's word to Samuel not only had immediate reference to Eli's house but also pointed forward to the more remote future (2:27–36). The disaster to overcome Eli and his sons (including the destruction of Shiloh) would "make the ears of everyone who hears of it tingle." Death was the penalty for showing contempt for the priesthood (Dt 17:12) as well as for disobeying one's parents (21:18–21), and Eli was implicated because he did not "restrain" (GK 3909) Hophni and Phinehas. The house of Eli had thus committed blatant sins against God and showed no signs of remorse. They were now subject to the divine death sentence (2:25; cf. Heb 12:16–17), and no sacrifice or offering could atone for their guilt.

15–18 When Samuel arose in the morning, he opened the doors of the tabernacle compound and doubtless busied himself with other tasks to avoid telling Eli what he had seen and heard. The aged priest was not to be denied, however, and demanded a full report. Indeed, he swore an oath of imprecation, calling down God's judgment if the boy refused to tell everything he knew. Samuel's obedient response in v.18 echoes key words from v.17 (pers. tr.): "Samuel told him all the words; he did not hide [anything] from him." Eli's reaction is both devout and submissive; he resigns himself to divine sovereignty.

3:19–4:1a As the Lord's presence would later be with David (16:18; 18:12), so the Lord was with Samuel, a fact evident to all the Israelites. That God "let none of [Samuel's] words fall" means that he made sure that everything Samuel said with divine authorization came true. Although earlier God's word had not been revealed to Samuel (v.7), it now was; and as the Lord had appeared to him earlier (vv.10–14), so he "continued to appear at

Shiloh." The Lord's word became equivalent to "Samuel's word" (4:1; see comment on 3:4–10).

The focus of this section is thus the Lord's sentence of judgment against the house of Eli. The boy Samuel, having become a "man of God" (9:6–14), has confirmed in no uncertain terms the prophecy earlier proclaimed by the anonymous "man of God" (2:27–36).

B. The Ark Narratives (4:1b–7:17)

1. The capture of the ark (4:1b–11)

1b The "Philistines" (GK 7149), inveterate enemies of Israel, are mentioned nearly 150 times in 1 and 2 Samuel alone. They were so entrenched and dominant in the coastal areas and the foothills of Canaan that they eventually gave their name (Palestine) to the entire land. Although their connections with various Aegean cultures have been verified through decades of intensive research, their origins remain somewhat obscure. The OT relates them to Caphtor (Ge 10:14 = 1Ch 1:12; Jer 47:4; Am 9:7), which was probably Crete. The aggressive, expansionist ancestors of the Philistines of the time of Samuel apparently arrived in Canaan shortly after 1200 B.C.

It is impossible to say who was the aggressor in this first-recorded battle between Israel and the Philistines. The Philistines camped at Aphek, an important site inhabited during the entire biblical period. Ebenezer, where the Israelites camped, is about two miles east of Aphek on the road to Shiloh.

2–3 The Israelites were defeated not once but twice in this chapter (vv.2, 10). Not until 7:10–11 did they defeat the Philistines on the battlefield and then only (as always) with divine help. The Israelites lost "four thousand" men, a terrible tragedy. The Israelite elders were puzzled by the debacle on the battlefield. Their solution was to bring the ark of the covenant into the camp to guarantee the Lord's presence with his people. The "ark" (GK 778) is a significant thematic element in this section.

The elders doubtless remembered the account of Joshua's victory over Jericho (Jos 6:2–20; cf. also Nu 10:35). What they failed to understand, however, was that the ark would not ensure victory. If God willed defeat for his people, a thousand arks would not bring success. The elders understood clearly that if God was not "with" them, defeat was inevitable (Nu 14:42; Dt 1:42). They mistakenly assumed, however, that wherever the ark was, the Lord was.

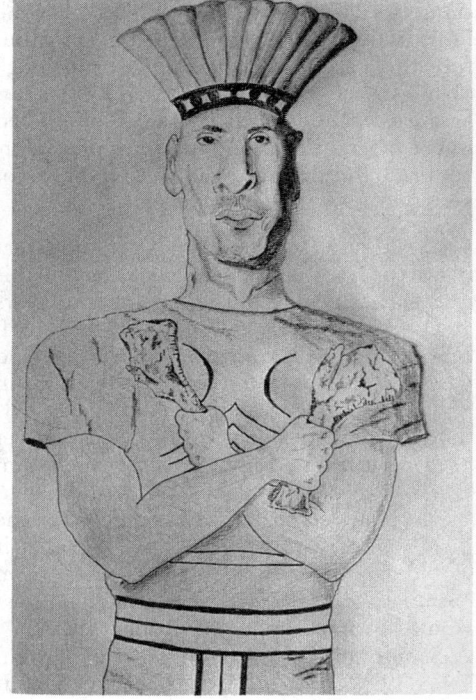

The Israelites camped at Ebenezer and the Philistines at Aphek, the site shown above. A Turkish citadel is visible, which was built on the ruins of a Crusader castle. Philistine and Israelite ruins are within the walls. The picture to the right shows a Philistine soldier wearing his corselet and "feathered" headdress (details based on relief drawing of Philistines found in Egypt). Drawing by Rachel Bierling.

4–9 So men were sent to Shiloh from the Israelite camp at Ebenezer to bring back the ark, here impressively described as "the ark of the covenant of the LORD Almighty, who is enthroned between the cherubim" (cf. 2Sa 6:2; 2Ki 19:15). In ancient Near Eastern art a king was often pictured sitting on a throne supported on each side by a cherub (winged lions with human heads.) One function of the ark of the covenant was to serve as the symbolic cherub-throne of the invisible Great King.

The ark, accompanied by Hophni and Phinehas, caused a great commotion upon reaching the Israelite camp. The people gave a loud shout (cf. Jos 6:5, 20). The uproar aroused the Philistines camped nearby, and their superstitious response echoed that of the Israelite elders. They believed that the arrival of the ark heralded the coming of whatever god or gods its owners worshiped. To avoid being enslaved by the Hebrews, as the Hebrews had been by them (cf. Jdg 13:1), they encouraged one another to be strong and fight like men.

10–11 The result of the ark's presence was another Israelite defeat, this one far more severe and described as a "slaughter" (GK 4804). The Philistines' own turn would come (14:13; 19:8; 23:5), but in the meantime Israel suffered heavy losses. The sins of Eli's sons produced appalling casualties among Israel's foot soldiers (cf. Dt 28:15, 25). As foretold by the man of God (2:34), Hophni and Phinehas died. The elders' folly was revealed as the Philistines captured the ark, and the destruction of Shiloh—and perhaps the tabernacle itself—was not far behind.

2. The death of Eli (4:12–22)

12–18 No sooner was the second battle with the Philistines over than the tragic news of Israel's defeat reached Shiloh. A Benjamite messenger, with his clothes "torn and dust on his head" (cf. Jos 7:6; Ne 9:1), reports Israel's flight from and slaughter by the Philistines as well as the death of two prominent priests.

Eli is sitting on his chair beside the road (cf. 1:9). Perhaps no longer considering himself to be the priest he once was, he nevertheless trembles with fear for the ark's safety.

The messenger first told his story to the townspeople at Shiloh, who "sent up a cry" when they learned that the ark had not brought them victory and was no longer with them. Mere possession of the ark enabled neither Israelite nor Philistine to manipulate the God whose presence it symbolized.

Hearing the uproar in the city, Eli wanted to know its meaning. Ninety-eight years old, obese, and totally blind, Eli was probably unable to go into town without considerable help; so the messenger went to him. The news was bad indeed. That his sons were dead did not seem to faze Eli, who may have already given them up as hopeless. But the shock of hearing that the ark had been captured was too much for him. He "fell" off his chair, broke his neck, and died. The tragedy of Eli's life matches that of Saul: sometimes serving God faithfully, at other times not measuring up to even the most moderate of standards. Priest at Shiloh for most of his adult life, Eli had judged Israel forty years.

19–22 Eli's death did not end the tragedy, even in his own family. The message of Eli's and Phinehas's deaths, combined with the report of the ark's capture, caused Phinehas's pregnant wife to go into premature labor. The distressing report caused her to be "overcome by her labor pains." The combination was fatal: She died in childbirth. Before she died Phinehas's wife named her newborn son Ichabod ("No glory"; cf. 14:3): "The glory [GK 3883] has departed [lit., 'has gone into exile'] from Israel, for the ark of God has been captured." After the Exodus the Lord promised to consecrate the tabernacle by his glory (Ex 29:43); after it was set up, his glory filled it and the cloud covered it (Ex 40:34–35). "Glory" represents the Presence of God dwelling in the tabernacle (Ps 26:8; cf. also Ex 25:8; 29:44–46), giving rise to the later theological term the "Shek(h)inah Glory" (cf. also Heb 9:5). Perhaps the wife of Phinehas, in her dying hour, spoke better than she knew.

3. The Lord's affliction of the Philistines (5:1–12)

1–5 From the battlefield at Ebenezer, the Philistines took the ark to Ashdod, apparently the chief city (6:17). Ashdod was located three miles from the Mediterranean coast about thirty miles southwest of Ebenezer. The ark was brought into the temple of Dagon, the Philistine national deity, and placed near a large idol representing him. The next day the statue of Dagon had fallen face-down, vanquished by Israel's God (see 17:49) and lying prostrate before the ark in a posture of worship. The people of Ashdod put the idol back in its "place" (cf. v.11).

The next morning Dagon was again face-down before the ark—this time with its head and hands "broken off" (cf. 17:51). In the ancient world severed heads and hands (cf. Jdg 8:6) were battlefield trophies. The Lord had therefore vanquished Dagon in his own temple. The head and hands of Dagon's statue landed on the temple threshold, rendering it sacred (in the minds of his worshipers) and therefore untouchable (cf. Zep 1:4, 9).

6–12 With the reference to Dagon's hands being rendered helpless, a major motif is introduced in the account: "the LORD's hand." The first reference here to the hand of the Lord comes from the lips of the Philistines, who related the divine hand to the plagues of Egypt (4:8)—and rightly so (see Ex 9:3; cf. also Jer 21:5–6). They did not take lightly the possibility that the fate of the Egyptians might befall them also (6:6).

"Tumors" (GK 6754) were one of the many potential curses that would be inflicted on the Israelites if they disobeyed God (Dt 28:58–60). Here that affliction descended on the Philistines, who realized that the hand of the Lord was heavy on them (cf. v.11). Their five rulers (6:18) advised them to get rid of the ark—which all recognized as the visible counterpart for the Israelite deity and therefore the cause of the plague—by moving it to Gath (about twelve miles east-southeast of Ashdod). The Lord's hand was then against Gath (cf. 7:13) and brought "an outbreak of tumors" on its inhabitants.

The ark was quickly shipped to Ekron (about six miles due north of Gath). But the arrival of the ark in Ekron had the same effect there as the news of its capture had in Shiloh: The people sent up a cry for help, fearful that the God of Israel would "kill" them—a power that he certainly possessed (cf. 2:6, 25). The people of Ekron told their rulers to send the ark away. Even those who did not die were afflicted with tumors; no one escaped the dreaded plague.

4. The return of the ark (6:1–7:1)

1–6 Chapter 4 tells of the capture of the ark, ch. 5 of its movement from place to place in Philistia, and ch. 6 of its return to Israel after being in Philistine territory for several months. The Philistines, eager to rid themselves of the ark and its sinister influence, sought supernatural guidance as to the best way of sending the ark back to "its [proper] place." "Tell us how," they said to their pagan counselors.

Ancient religious protocol mandated that the worshiper not approach his god(s) empty-handed (cf. Ex 23:15; Dt 16:16). Thus the Philistine priests and diviners advised that a guilt offering accompany the ark back to Israel. Although such an offering was normally an animal sacrifice, occasionally money or other valuables were acceptable. If the Lord accepted the Philistines' offering, their people would be healed; then they would know that his hand had been responsible for their misery.

The linking of tumors, rats, and plague suggests that the tumors were symptoms of bubonic plague spread by an infestation of rats, which were capable of destroying a country (cf. Jer 36:29; Da 11:16). The Philistine advisers recommended gold models of tumors and rats to serve as the guilt offering to placate the God of Israel. Perhaps the Philistines intended the models to function in the realm of sympathetic magic also, so that by sending them out of their land the genuine articles would depart as well.

The word "plague" (GK 4487) recalls the Egyptian plagues in Ex 9:14, further heightening the parallel between the earlier disaster and this (cf. again v.6). The lesson is clear: Hardening one's heart only brings divine retribution, resulting in the victory of God's people over their enemies (Ex 12:31–32). The Philistines are thus well advised to cut their losses as soon as possible.

7–12 A new cart pulled by two cows "that have calved and have never been yoked" was to be used to transport the ark. The cows would later be sacrificed by the Israelites (v.14) in faint reminiscence of the slaughter of the red heifer by Eleazar (Nu 19:2–3). The Philistines were to "take" the calves from their mothers, "send" the gold objects as a guilt offering to the Lord, and "return" the ark to him and his people (v.21).

The first destination of the ark was Beth Shemesh, just inside Israelite territory. Beth Shemesh had a pagan past (its name means

"Temple of the sun-god"). The Philistines of Samuel's day acknowledged that Beth Shemesh was under Israelite control. They hoped that the cows would take the ark there, reasoning that if cows new to the yoke would desert their newborn calves—even temporarily—to pull a cart all the way to Beth Shemesh, that would be a supernatural sign that the divine owner of the ark had sent the plague against them. But if the ark did not reach Beth Shemesh, they would take that fact as proof that the Lord's hand had not struck them and that mere chance was responsible.

Against natural instinct ("lowing all the way" because their calves were not with them) and under divine compulsion (not turning "to the right or to the left"—i.e., staying on the main road), the cows pulled the cart straight to Beth Shemesh. The five Philistine rulers, following the cows to the border, stayed only long enough to make sure that the ark was securely in Israelite hands.

6:13–7:1 The ark arrived at Beth Shemesh in June, during wheat harvest, after the spring rains (cf. 12:16–18). Rejoicing to see the ark, the people decided to use the cart for fuel and to sacrifice the cows as a burnt offering. They "chopped up the wood" (cf. Ge 22:3). A large rock in a field belonging to Joshua of Beth Shemesh became the temporary locale for the ark. The Levites, who alone were permitted to handle the ark (cf. Jos 3:3; 2Sa 15:24), had removed it from the cart and set it on the rock, which served as a witness of the ark's homecoming.

Ancient Near-Eastern oxcarts, such as the one used to transport the ark, have been reconstructed from archaeological remains.

Meanwhile, the five Philistine rulers returned to their five cities (cf. Jos 13:3). Each one was fortified and was supported by a number of nearby "country villages" (cf. similarly Dt 3:5; Est 9:19).

Divine retribution continued to overtake those who misused the ark. This time some men of Beth Shemesh "looked into" (GK 8011) the ark, a sin punishable by instant death (Nu 4:5, 20; cf. also 2Sa 6:6–7). The mourners sensed that the ark symbolized the presence of a "holy God" (cf. Lev 11:44–45), whose sanctity they could not approach. They therefore hoped he would depart from them.

Kiriath Jearim (about ten miles northeast of Beth Shemesh) was the ark's location for the next twenty years (7:2). More specifically, it resided at "Abinadab's house on the hill" (7:1; 2Sa 6:3). Eleazar son of Abinadab was then consecrated to guard it. The downgraded status of the ark may have been partially due to the Philistine destruction of Shiloh (presupposed by Ps 78:60; Jer 7:12, 14; 26:6, 9) and perhaps the tabernacle as well. Not until David's accession as king in Jerusalem would the ark once again be restored to its rightful place of honor (2Sa 6).

5. Samuel the judge (7:2–17)

2–4 The "twenty years" that the ark remained at Kiriath Jearim may be figurative for "half a generation," during which time the "people" (lit., "house"; GK 1074) of Israel "mourned," apparently with sincere remorse. They were bemoaning the reduced status of the ark, no longer housed in a tabernacle. Samuel encouraged them to repent and to serve the Lord wholeheartedly, as he would do later (12:20, 24).

Samuel urged the people to get rid of the foreign gods (GK 466; cf. "the Baals and the Ashtoreths" in 12:10) that they were so prone to worship (cf. also Dt 12:3; Jdg 10:16; 2Ch 19:3; 33:15). Baal and Ashtoreth were the chief god and goddess in the Canaanite pantheon during this period. Samuel pleaded with them to commit themselves wholeheartedly to the Lord. God's people are to serve him exclusively (see Dt 6:13).

5–6 The assembly of "all Israel" did not necessarily include every single Israelite living in the land but most likely consisted of representatives from all the tribal territories.

Convocations at Mizpah in Benjamin were not uncommon in the days of the judges and early monarchy (cf. 10:17; Jdg 20:1; 21:8). There Samuel prayed for the people (cf. also vv.8–9; 8:6; 12:19, 23; 15:11; Jer 15:1), and there they "poured ... out [water] before the LORD," perhaps a symbol of contrition (cf. 2Sa 23:16).

The notice of Samuel's judgeship is followed immediately by a report of Philistine intention to attack Israel. The function of a "judge" during this period was more executive than judicial. "Judge" often paralleled "ruler" or "prince" (cf. Ex 2:14), and one of the most common roles of the judge was to repel invaders (Jdg 2:16, 18).

7–9 Cowed by Philistine might, Israel typically reacted with fear to news of impending warfare with them (17:11; 28:5). But when the Philistines "came up" to attack, Samuel prayerfully "offered ... up" a burnt offering to the Lord. The sacrifice was a suckling lamb at least eight days old (cf. Lev 22:27).

10–12 While the sacrifice was still in progress, the Philistine troops marched forward. Before the battle could be joined, however, the Lord "thundered" against the enemy (see 2:10; 2Sa 22:14–15). He demonstrated that he, not the Philistine Dagon, not the Canaanite Baal son of Dagon, was truly the God of the storm, the only one able to control the elements whether for good or ill (cf. 12:17–18). "With loud thunder" highlights the vivid OT image of thunder as the voice of God (see Ps 29:3–9).

The ensuing panic in their ranks (cf. 2Sa 22:14–15) drove the Philistines into full retreat, enabling the Israelites to pursue and slaughter them. The Ebenezer of v.12 is almost certainly not the Ebenezer of 4:1 and 5:1, since the latter is too far to the northwest for Mizpah to be used as a benchmark for its location. Ebenezer ("The stone of [divine] help"), the stone set up by Samuel, paid tribute to the God apart from whom victory is inconceivable (cf. Ge 35:14; Jos 4:9; 24:26).

13–17 The second half of v.13 assumes continued Philistine pressure (though greatly reduced) against Israel and thus cautions us not to understand the first half as meaning that the Philistines no longer bothered the Israelites (cf. esp. 9:16). The Amorites, who preferred to live in the hilly regions of the land

(cf. Nu 13:29; Dt 1:7) as compared to the Philistines who lived along the coast, were also relatively nonbelligerent during this period.

The circuit of Samuel's judgeship was relatively restricted: Bethel, Gilgal, and Mizpah were all within a few miles of one another. All three towns served as shrine centers at one time or another, as did Ramah, Samuel's hometown. The latter was not far from the other three (about fourteen miles northwest of Mizpah). The local nature of judgeship in ancient Israel subtly introduces us to the need for a king.

II. Advent of Monarchy in Israel (8:1–15:35)

Monarchy was a significant factor in God's plans for his people from the days of Abraham (Ge 17:6, 16). The blessing of Jacob hints at the establishment of a continuing dynasty (Ge 49:10). Israel was to be "a kingdom of priests and a holy nation" (Ex 19:6). Balaam's fourth oracle refers to monarchical rule (Nu 24:17–19), and Moses outlines the divine expectations Israel's kings were to meet (Dt 17:14–20).

However, from the earliest days it was recognized that ultimately God himself was King (Ex 15:18; Nu 23:21; Dt 33:5); he alone possessed absolute power and authority (Ex 15:6, 11; Jdg 5:3–5). Any king of Israel would have to appreciate from the outset that he was to rule over Israel under God. Only on the basis of this fundamental theological premise can the narratives of the advent of monarchy in Israel be properly understood.

A. The Rise of Saul (8:1–12:25)

1. The demand for a king (8:1–22)

1–3 With reference to Samuel's advanced age (vv.1, 5; 12:2), the old order (of the judges) is passing, the new (of the monarchy) is dawning. While Samuel continued as judge at Ramah and nearby towns (7:15–17), he appointed his two sons to serve in the same capacity at Beersheba on the southern boundary of the land (cf. 3:20). Their actions and reputations (v.5) belied their names— Joel ("The Lord is God"); Abijah ("My [Divine] Father is the Lord")—but at least their geographical distance from Samuel (Beersheba is about fifty-seven miles southsouthwest of Ramah) absolved him from any direct complicity in their evil deeds.

Whether Samuel should have appointed his sons as judges in the first place is highly questionable, since judgeship was usually a divine charisma. In any event, they did not follow in their father's footsteps. "Turned aside" and "perverted" (both GK 5742) tie their three sins together. Failing to emulate their father (12:3–4) or their God (Dt 10:17), Joel and Abijah accepted bribes, a crime inseparable from the perversion and denial of justice (Pr 17:23). Ironically, Samuel's two sons were as wicked in their own way as were Eli's two sons.

4–9 Old men ("elders") confront the old man and—perhaps unwittingly—remind him of the cruel parallel between himself and the deceased Eli (cf. 2:22). Because of Samuel's age, and because they want nothing to do with a dynastic succession that would include his rebellious sons, the elders decide that a king would best suit their needs. Samuel had "appointed" his sons as "judges"; the elders wanted him to "appoint" (GK 8492) a king to "judge" Israel.

This king was to lead them, "such as all the other nations have." Verse 20 reveals their hidden agenda: The king would "go out before us and fight our battles." They were looking for a permanent military leader who would build a standing army powerful enough to repulse any invader (cf. Dt 17:14, 15–17). Samuel, fully aware of those dangers, was "displeased" with the elders' request—and he was convinced that the Lord too was displeased (12:17; cf. also 15:11).

But Samuel, as he sought God's mind in the matter, was doubtless surprised when the Lord told him to "listen to" (or "obey"; GK 9048) the people's request mediated through their elders. Israel was not rejecting the Lord's chosen leader but the Lord himself (see also 10:19). Since the days of the Exodus, the people had consistently preferred other gods and other leaders to God himself and his chosen servants.

God, graciously condescending to the people's desire (a desire not in itself wrong but sullied by the motivation behind it), told Samuel to warn them what the "regulations of the kingship" (10:25) would demand of them, particularly their loss of freedom in (absolute) monarchy.

10–18 The "regulations of the kingship" described by Samuel (with God's prompting and approval) were totally bereft of redeeming features and consisted only of oppressive requirements. Among the latter was forced labor, including compulsory induction of both raw recruits and laborers in field and foundry.

The palace-to-be would acquire horses in great numbers (cf. Dt 17:16), and the king's chariots would need front runners (cf. 2Sa 15:1; 1Ki 1:5). Reference to commanders "of thousands and . . . of fifties" implies a huge standing army, with "weapons of war." Women would not be exempt from conscription into royal service. Even in desperate times the king would always get his share (Am 7:1)—a minimum of 10 percent of the income from field and flock.

Key words in the "regulations of the kingship" are "take" (GK 4374) and "best" (GK 3203). By nature royalty is parasitic rather than giving, and kings are never satisfied with the worst. Samuel's regulations followed contemporary semifeudal Canaanite society. In the light of Samuel's own record of fairness and honesty during his judgeship (cf. esp. 12:3–5), it is no wonder that he was alarmed at the prospect of setting up a typical Oriental monarchy in Israel.

If these "regulations of the kingship" attained full authority, the average Israelite would soon be little more than a chattel at the disposal of his monarch. The frequent occurrence of "servant" and "slave" thus sounds an especially ominous note. In v.17 Samuel warned the people that they would "become" their king's "slaves" (GK 6269), terminology employed elsewhere of bondage imposed by a conqueror (17:9). Too late the Israelites would cry out to a God who would not answer—unlike the days when Samuel was judge (7:8–9).

19–22 Samuel's best efforts were futile. Despite his totally negative delineation of the royal "regulations," the people refused to "listen to" (or "obey"; GK 9048) him. They wanted a king—a demand that Samuel hurled back in their teeth twice in the context of their rejection of divine rule (10:19; 12:12). They clung doggedly to their original request (v.5). The implicit military component of their idea of monarchy now becomes explicit: Their king would "fight our battles"—although a godly Israelite king would know from the outset that it was the Lord's joyful duty to do just that for his people (2Ch 32:8).

As the Lord had told Samuel earlier (v.7), so he told him now: "Listen to them and give them a king." On that negative (for Samuel) note the chapter ends, and Samuel's farewell oration to Israel begins (12:1).

2. The anointing of Saul (9:1–10:16)

1–2 Saul's father, Kish, is called a "man of standing" (cf. Ru 2:1; 1Ki 11:28). The term often has military connotations and is translated "brave man" in Saul's servant's description of David (16:18). It is nowhere used of Saul himself. The family line of Kish is from Benjamin, the smallest of the tribes. Israel's first king came from these humble origins. The Hebrew root for the name "Saul," which means "Asked (of God)," occurs in 8:10, where the people were "asking" for a king (GK 8626).

Saul is introduced as an "impressive" young man (cf. Ge 39:6; 2Sa 14:25), "without equal" among the Israelites. That would eventually change, however; his kingdom would be torn from him and given to "one better than" he—to David (15:28). Saul was also "a head taller" than his fellow Israelites, a characteristic noteworthy enough to be mentioned again (10:23–24). Of regal stature, he had the potential of being every inch a king. Saul's subsequent failure as king makes the well-known divine admonition in 16:7 all the more poignant.

3–14 The Lord used straying donkeys to bring Saul into contact with Samuel. Searching for the lost donkeys, Saul and his servant crisscrossed the borderlands between Benjamin and Ephraim, but to no avail. They began and ended their search in the "hill country of Ephraim" since Zuph is associated with the hill country in 1:1. The unnamed town in v.6 is therefore probably Ramah.

Saul, not wishing to cause his father needless worry, wants to give up the search and return to Benjamin. The servant, however, points out that there is a "man of God" nearby who might be able to help them. The servant appears to be more persistent and imaginative than Saul himself—a fact that may not speak well for Saul's future attempts at leadership. Although the man of God is not named at first, we are later informed that he is indeed Samuel.

Saul continued to protest, reminding the servant that they had no gift for the prophet; their "sacks" were empty. When consulting a prophet, it was common courtesy to bring a gift (Am 7:12), whether modest (1Ki 14:3) or lavish (2Ki 8:8–9). The servant responded that he had "a quarter of a shekel of silver" to give to the prophet. Although coinage was not invented until the seventh century B.C., it is likely that much earlier there were pieces of silver of fixed weight.

Verses 9–10 bring together the three main terms to describe the prophetic office: "seer" (GK 8014), "prophet" (GK 5566), "man of God" (GK 408 & 466). Samuel is often (and fittingly) called the "last of the judges and first of the prophets"—the latter in the sense that the formal office of prophet began with the monarchy and ended shortly after the monarchy did (for Samuel's unique role, cf. 2Ch 35:18; Ps 99:6; Jer 15:1; and esp. Ac 3:24; 13:20; Heb 11:32).

"Seer" means just what its Hebrew (and English) root implies: one who sees—but with spiritual eyes—beneath the surface of the obvious, focusing on the divine dimension. A seer was a man of (spiritual) vision (cf. Isa 1:1; 6:1–5; Jer 1:11–19; Am 7:7–9; 8:1–2; Zec 1:7–6:8).

A "prophet" was "called" in the sense of being summoned by God to be a spokesman for God (cf. Ex 4:16; 7:1–2). A prophet was to be God's "mouth"; that was his "calling." Prophecy was by calling, not by choice.

Saul and his servant went "up the hill" to the town (probably Ramah, which means "height"). It was early evening, since girls were coming out to the well to draw water (see Ge 24:11; cf. also v.19). When asked whether the seer was there, they informed the men that he had arrived only recently to participate in a sacrificial ritual at the "high place." Almost always on conspicuous elevations and often located outside of town (vv.14, 25), high places were open-air sanctuaries, sometimes with shrines or other buildings (v.22), where worship was conducted. The association of high places with idolatry had contributed to the divine rejection of Shiloh and the capture of the ark (Ps 78:58–61).

Verses 12–13 are charged with urgency: "He's ahead of you. Hurry now; he has just come. . . . Go up now."

15–24 The divine encounter with Saul was mediated through Samuel, to whom the Lord had "revealed" (lit., "uncovered the ear of," as if to speak in secret) his will (cf. 2Sa 7:27; 1Ch 17:25). As an act of gracious condescension to the people's request (Ac 13:21), the Lord promised to send an obscure Benjamite to Samuel, emphasizing the divine initiative in the matter. Samuel was to "anoint" him (with oil; cf. 10:1; cf. also 15:1, 17).

Anointing was by prophet and/or people, both acting as agents of the Lord (cf. 16:12–13; 2Sa 2:4; 5:3). It symbolized the coming of the Holy Spirit in power (16:13; Isa 61:1–3). Especially at the beginning of the monarchy, anointing was to the office of "leader" (GK 5592) rather than "king" (cf. 10:1; 13:14; 25:30; 2Sa 5:2; 6:21; 7:8). Beyond the likelihood that it represents Samuel's understandable reluctance to establish a full-fledged kingship (with all its negative implications; cf. again 8:10–18), the term might have been a title for "king-designate, king-elect" (cf. 2Ch 11:22) with military connotations.

In language strongly reminiscent of the Exodus, God had looked on the people of Israel (cf. Ex 2:25), whose cry had reached him (cf. Ex 3:9). The new leader would have the potential of delivering Israel from the Philistines (cf. 4:3)—although some seriously doubted that Saul would be able to accomplish that formidable task (10:27).

The seer Samuel "caught sight of" Saul, raised up as leader because God had "looked upon" his people. "This is the man," the Lord said to him, in a scene that would be replayed with only modest variations a few years later (cf. 16:12). Samuel then identified himself to Saul. As the Lord had promised to "send" Saul to Samuel, so Samuel would soon "let" Saul "go" (lit., "send" him on his way, as in v.26) after his divine commissioning (10:9). Samuel the seer authenticated his prophetic role by revealing Saul's inmost thoughts and relieved Saul's mind by informing him that his father's donkeys had been found. He then told Saul that all Israel was eagerly awaiting his benevolent reign.

Saul respectfully demurred. He pointed out that Benjamin, his tribe, was the smallest in all Israel (doubtless due to the terrible massacre decades earlier; cf. Jdg 20:46–48) and that his clan was the weakest in his tribe (cf. Jdg 6:15). Saul's humility (cf. 10:22) was in the grand tradition of prophets and judges.

Samuel, however, knowing that Saul was God's choice, brushed aside his objections and led him and his servant into a "hall" (GK 4384), in a building on the high place outside Ramah. This Hebrew word almost always denotes a room in a sanctuary or temple. Such rooms were normally used as apartments for sanctuary personnel or as storerooms (cf. Ne 10:39; Jer 35:2, 4). The hall at Ramah was large enough to seat thirty people.

Saul and his servant, guests of honor, were seated at the head of the table. The special "piece of meat" brought to Saul was perhaps the "share" of the sacrifice normally reserved for priests (cf. Lev 7:33). It was a special "occasion" (GK 4595) indeed, a time for celebration—unlike a future "set time" (13:8, 11) when Saul's impatience and disobedience would initiate his downfall (13:13–14).

25–27 After what must have been a sumptuous if solemn meal, eaten in a house of worship on a sacred site, Samuel, Saul, and Saul's servant retired to Ramah and conversed for a while on the "roof" of Samuel's house. Samuel was preparing Saul for his divine commissioning as ruler of Israel. Sleeping overnight on the roof of a house is a common practice even today in the Middle East. The following morning Samuel told Saul to dismiss his servant temporarily (see 10:14). Saul himself, however, was to stay briefly at Ramah (10:2) to receive a communication from God and to be anointed leader over the Lord's inheritance (10:1).

10:1–8 Saul's rise to kingship took place in three distinct stages: He was (1) anointed by Samuel (9:1–10:16), (2) chosen by lot (10:17–27), and (3) confirmed by public acclamation (11:1–15). The Lord had told Samuel to anoint Saul as leader over his people Israel (9:16). Samuel now proceeded to fulfill that command, being careful to inform Saul that the anointing was from the Lord. The Israelites are here called the Lord's "inheritance" (GK 5709) in the sense that they inhabited his territorial patrimony and belonged uniquely to him as Creator, Redeemer, and Conqueror (Dt 4:20; 9:26; 32:8–9; Ps 78:70–71). The anointing oil was a distinctive formula (Ex 30:23–33); it was "sacred" (Ps 89:20). Samuel also kissed Saul as an act of respect and submission (cf. Ps 2:11–12).

Verses 7 and 9 speak of three "signs" (GK 253) that would confirm the Lord's choice of Saul. (1) Samuel said that Saul would "meet" two men who would verify that Kish's donkeys had indeed been found and that therefore Saul's father could now devote his attention to his son's welfare. (2) Three men would meet Saul and offer him two loaves of bread, which he would accept. The men were "going up to God" to worship and commune with him. On their way they would "greet" Saul. (3) This sign, because of its significance, is described at greater length. Whereas the first sign involved two men and the second involved three men, the third focused on a "procession"—a larger band or group—of prophets (vv.5, 10). Saul would meet them outside "Gibeah of God."

The beginnings of the Israelite monarchy witnessed the emergence of a prophetic movement known as the "sons of the prophets" (cf. 1Ki 20:35). "Sons" is used here in the sense of "members of a group" (cf. 2Ki 2:3, 5, 7, 15). The companies were often large in number ("fifty," 2Ki 2:7; "one hundred," 1Ki 18:4, 13; 2Ki 4:43). They were frequently associated with time-honored places, such as Ramah (19:18–20), Bethel (2Ki 2:3), Jericho (2:5), and Gilgal (4:38). Their characteristic activity was "prophesying," usually interpreted to mean "uttering ecstatic praises/oracles." The actions and activities of prophetic bands were sometimes accompanied by music (2Ki 3:15; 1Ch 25:1–7).

Individual or group prophesying was often induced when the Spirit of the Lord came on a person in power (19:20, 23; Nu 11:25, 29). At such times the prophet would experience an altered state of consciousness and would be "changed into a different person" (cf. also v.9). Such ecstasy was often contagious (19:20–24). Similar ecstatic phenomena, though in a negative sense, were sometimes induced when an "evil" or "injurious" spirit came on a person (18:10; cf. also 16:14–16, 23). Members of prophetic bands were often young (2Ki 5:22; 9:4); they frequently lived together (2Ki 6:1–2), ate together (2Ki 4:38), and were supported by the generosity of their fellow Israelites (2Ki 4:42–43). Samuel provided guidance and direction for the movement in its early stages. At the head of a particular group of prophets would be the "father" (2Ki 2:12) or "leader" (19:20).

Samuel told Saul that after the three signs were fulfilled, he was to do whatever his hand found to do (cf. Ecc 9:10). Samuel assured Saul that God was with him, implying that therefore he could not fail (cf. Jos 1:5).

Then came a sober warning: At a later time Samuel would meet Saul at Gilgal. A preliminary meeting would first be held there to reaffirm Saul's kingship (11:14–15), with the appropriate fellowship offerings and accompanying celebration. Then on a later occasion Samuel would meet Saul again at Gilgal, this time to sacrifice burnt offerings (cf. Lev 1:3–17; 6:8–13) and fellowship offerings (cf. Lev 3:1–17; 7:11–21). On this latter occasion Saul was to wait seven days, until Samuel came and told him what to do. Saul faithfully fulfilled the former obligation (13:8), but impatience got the better of him. He failed to await Samuel's arrival with further instructions, and his act of disobedience was the beginning of the end for his kingdom (13:9–14).

9–16 Meanwhile, however, Saul was open to Samuel's instructions and the Lord's leading. He "turned" to leave, and as he did so, God "changed Saul's heart" (cf. the third sign; v.6). The arrival of Saul and his servant at Gibeah of God (cf. v.5) was followed by the Spirit of God coming on Saul in power, resulting in his joining the prophetic band in their ecstatic behavior (cf. 11:6).

Gibeah of God was scarcely four miles northeast of Gibeah of Saul, the hometown of the new Israelite ruler. When his fellow townsmen learned of Saul's arrival, they turned out in force to see what had happened to the "son of Kish." The Spirit of the Lord, coming on Saul in power, authenticated him as Israel's next ruler and produced the visible evidences of ecstatic behavior. To question the genuineness of that behavior was to question Saul's legitimacy in his new office.

"And who is their father?" was asked to find out the identity of the leader of the "procession of prophets" (cf. 2Ki 2:12). Although perhaps prompted by the reference to Saul as "son of Kish," the question was not so banal as to be requesting information about Saul's physical paternity.

Verses 14–16 conclude the theme of Kish's concern for Saul's whereabouts and welfare. Saul's "uncle" was doubtless seeking information for Kish and himself. The story of finding Kish's lost donkeys is once again related, but Saul did not tell his uncle anything about Samuel's view of kingship or his own participation in it (cf. 8:6–22). Rule over Israel would soon be his in truth (11:14), but it would not be long before he would be convinced that he was about to lose it to a man after God's own heart (18:8).

3. The choice of Saul by lot (10:17–27)

17–24 Assembling the Israelites at Mizpah, Samuel addresses them in words strongly reminiscent of those of the prophet in Jdg 6:8–9a. The Lord is called the God of his chosen people Israel. He then speaks in the first person, using the emphatic pronoun "I" in strong contrast to the emphatic "But you." The familiar Exodus redemption formula is followed by a reminder that God had delivered his people not only from Egypt but also from the "kingdoms" that "oppressed" them. Although the Lord had saved them out of all their "calamities and distresses," they had rejected him (echoing 8:7; cf. also Nu 11:20). The Israelites continued to insist in no uncertain terms that they wanted a king (see 8:5, 19). Samuel, reluctantly acquiescing, told the people to present themselves before the Lord by their tribes and clans.

The lots, known as Urim ("Curses," providing negative responses) and Thummim ("Perfections," providing positive responses), were stored in the breastplate attached to the ephod of the high priest (Ex 28:28–30) and were brought out and cast whenever a simple "yes" or "no" would suffice. Although casting lots was perhaps not unlike throwing dice, God himself guided the results (Pr 16:33). Verses 20–21 show that Benjamin was chosen by lot from the Twelve Tribes, Matri (unknown elsewhere) from the Benjamite clans, and Saul—God's man for this season—from the Matrite families. Ironically, like the lost donkeys that had earlier consumed so much anxious time for their searchers (9:3–5, 20; 10:2, 14–16), "when they looked for [Saul], he was not to be found."

Another divine oracle was therefore necessary, but this time the question demanded more than a "yes" or "no" answer. So in a more direct way the people "inquired" (GK 928 & 8626) of the Lord to discover Saul's whereabouts. The reluctant "leader" was subsequently found hiding among the military supplies (cf. 17:22; 25:13; 30:24).

Anxious to hail their new king, the people ran to bring him out from his hiding place. He came out and presented himself in their midst; his impressive height is again stressed (9:2). Samuel reminded the Israelites that the Lord had "chosen" (GK 4334) Saul.

The public acclamation "Long live the king!" represents now, as it did then, the enthusiastic hopes of the citizenry that their monarch would remain hale and hearty in order to bring their fondest dreams to fruition. The people of Saul's day "shouted" their approval.

25–27 After the people's acclamation of Saul as their king, Samuel outlined for them the "regulations of the kingship," which he then wrote down on a scroll (cf. Ex 17:14; Jos 18:9). He deposited the scroll in a safe place "before the LORD"—i.e., in the tabernacle, probably located at Mizpah at that time (cf. v.17)—in order (1) to preserve it for future reference and (2) to have it serve as a witness against the king and/or people, should its provisions ever be violated (cf. Dt 31:26; Jos 24:26–27).

Samuel then permitted all the people to return to their homes. Saul, the recently anointed king, went to his home in Gibeah. With the formal festivities over, two opposing reactions to Israel's new leader surface: "Valiant men," apparently eager to affirm God's choice, accompanied Saul to Gibeah, while "troublemakers" despised him. The latter group unwittingly echoed to Saul the earlier words of Gideon about himself: "How can I save Israel?" (Jdg 6:15). Neither Gideon nor the troublemakers understood—at least not at first—that it is God, not a human being, who saves (Jdg 6:16; 1Sa 10:19).

4. The defeat of the Ammonites (11:1–11)

1–2 The Ammonite siege of Jabesh Gilead under Nahash produced a conciliatory response in its inhabitants. They asked Nahash to "make a treaty" with them, as a result of which they would recognize him as their suzerain and become his vassals (cf. Eze 17:13–14). The phrase "cut a covenant" is almost universally understood to refer to the sacrifice ("cutting") of one or more animals as an important element in covenant solemnization ceremonies in ancient times. Nahash's threat to gouge out the right eye of every Jabeshite may imply their rebellion against a previously established overlordship. In the ancient Near East, the physical mutilation, dismemberment, or death of an animal or human victim could be expected as the inevitable penalty for treaty violation.

3 Nahash's threat (v.2) received a plaintive response from the elders of Jabesh, who functioned as representatives of the community (cf. 4:3; 8:4; 16:4). They tried to buy some time to send for help. Nahash appears to have acceded to the elders' request, apparently sure of his own military superiority.

4 When the Jabeshite messengers arrived at Gibeah of Saul with the terms of Nahash's demands, its people "wept aloud," a common display of grief, distress, or remorse (cf. Jdg 2:4; 1Sa 24:16; 2Sa 3:32; 13:36). Apparently Saul's fellow citizens in his own hometown despaired of leadership at this critical juncture in their history.

5–6 But at that very moment, Saul was returning from plowing in the fields, and he asked two questions: "What is wrong with the people? Why are they weeping?" Upon hearing the Jabeshites' report, Saul was energized by a powerful accession of God's Spirit. He had already experienced a similar accession earlier (10:6–10). This time, in the tradition of the judges, the Spirit of God filled him with divine indignation and empowered him as a military leader. Although the earlier accession had been temporary, this one was somewhat more permanent, apparently lasting until Samuel anointed David to replace Saul as king (16:13–14).

7 Rallying the troops to defend a covenant suzerain, vassal, or brother was a common stipulation in ancient treaties. Similar to the earlier action of the Levite of Jdg 19:29; 20:6, Saul cut two of his oxen into pieces and sent them throughout Israel as a graphic illustration of what would happen to any tribe that failed to commit a contingent of troops (cf. Jdg 21:5, 10). The "terror of the LORD" that here fell on the people is not to be understood as fear of divine punishment.

8 The mustering or counting of the troops (cf. 13:15; 14:17; 2Sa 24:2, 4) took place at Bezek. The numbers represent substantial contingents of troops. Their being listed separately as "men of Israel" and "men of Judah" anticipates the eventual division of the kingdom into north and south.

9 Saul and his troops told the messengers to return to Jabesh Gilead and inform its frightened citizens that divine deliverance (cf. v.13) would come to them the very next day—"by the time the sun is hot" (cf. Ex 16:21; Neh 7:3), a phrase that almost surely refers to high noon. The messengers' report caused the men of Jabesh to become "elated" (cf. v.15).

10 Confident of victory, the Jabeshites promised the Ammonites that they would surrender to them the following day and that the Ammonites would then be free to do "whatever seems good to you" (lit., "whatever seems good in your eyes," an ironic pun on Nahash's earlier threat to gouge out the right eye of any rebellious Jabeshite; cf. 14:36).

11 Saul wasted no time in deploying "his men" for the attack on Ammon. "The next day" probably refers to the evening of the day on which Saul's message reached the Jabeshites (v.9), since among the Israelites each new day began after sunset. Saul, following a military strategy common in those days (see 13:17–18), divided his men into three groups. Offensively it gave the troops more options and greater mobility, while defensively it lessened the possibility of losing everyone to a surprise enemy attack. The Israelites under Saul's leadership broke into the Ammonite camp "during the last watch of the night" (cf. Ex 14:24). Saul's attack obviously caught the Ammonites by surprise, and—as promised (v.9)—by high noon God had defeated them and delivered his people, routing the enemy survivors by scattering them in every direction (cf. also Nu 10:35; Ps 68:1).

5. The confirmation of Saul as king (11:12–12:25)

12–15 Saul's troops and the people of Jabesh Gilead, having witnessed God's victory over Ammon under Saul's leadership, demanded from Samuel the death penalty for all the troublemakers who had questioned his ability to save them from foreign rule (10:27). Saul, however, showing how magnanimous he could be when given the opportunity, asserted that the divine deliverance was a cause for gratitude, not vengeful retribution (cf. 2Sa 19:22).

Saul's demonstration of the leadership qualities necessary to be Israel's king led Samuel to convoke an important meeting at Gilgal. The OT records three meetings of Samuel and Saul at Gilgal, each fateful for Saul: (1) In the flush of his victory over Ammon, Saul was reaffirmed as king (11:14–15); (2) because of his impatience while awaiting Samuel's arrival, Saul was rebuked by his spiritual mentor (13:7–14); and (3) because of his disobedient pride after the defeat of the Amalekites, Saul was rejected as king (15:10–26).

The purpose of the first meeting is to "reaffirm the kingship" of Saul, who had already been anointed at Ramah (10:1) and chosen by lot at Mizpah (10:17–25). The reaffirmation was a confirmation by public acclamation and is the last of the three stages comprising his rise to monarchy over Israel.

Samuel's invitation to the people to reaffirm Saul as king was greeted with enthusiasm. "In the presence of the LORD" they confirmed their earlier choice, and "before the LORD" they brought their sacrifices. Fellowship offerings were the appropriate response of the people of Israel, who by sacrificing them were expressing their desire to rededicate themselves to God in covenant communion and allegiance. Saul's ascent to the throne was now complete, and the "great celebration" that accompanied the sacrificial ritual more than matched Israel's earlier elation upon their receiving the messengers' report of the imminent doom of the Ammonites (v.9).

12:1 Samuel begins his farewell speech by reminding the people that he has "listened to" (meaning "obeyed"; GK 9048) them and has set a king over them (cf. vv.14–15). This phrase echoes 8:7, 9, 22, and highlights Samuel's commitment to God's will despite his own personal reservations. After all, Saul is "the man the LORD has chosen," the king affirmed by public acclamation (10:24).

2 However reluctantly, Samuel formally acknowledges the transfer of Israel's leadership from himself to Saul. Although Samuel has been the recognized "leader" of the people from his youth until the present (cf. 3:10; 3:19–4:1; 7:15–17), King Saul is now their "leader." Samuel's reference to himself as "old and gray" is probably a modest claim to wisdom (cf. Job 15:9–10). His mention of his

sons emphasizes the length of time it has been his privilege to serve the people of Israel—and perhaps also provides them with an unwelcome reminder of their earlier refusal to allow his sons to succeed him as judge (8:5).

3 "Here I stand" echoes an important servant motif (e.g., Ge 22:1, 11) in Samuel's first recorded words (cf. 3:4, 5, 6, 8, 16). Samuel invites the people to "testify against" him about covenant stipulations he might have violated. As though in a courtroom, the inquiry takes place "in the presence of" Samuel's heavenly and earthly superiors.

Aware that testifying on his own behalf could well result in self-incrimination (cf. 2Sa 1:16), Samuel nevertheless launches into a brief series of protestations of innocence. The key verb is "taken" (GK 4374), which Samuel consciously uses as a powerful means of contrasting his admirable behavior with the potentially oppressive demands of a (despotic) king that he had earlier warned about (8:11, 13–17). Doubtless alluding to the covenant stipulations of Ex 20:17, Samuel challenges the people to accuse him of having taken from any of them so much as an ox or a donkey (contrast 8:16; 22:19; 27:9; cf. Nu 16:15; Ac 20:33).

Samuel goes on to affirm that he has neither "cheated" nor "oppressed" anyone. Samuel's refusal to cheat/oppress others looks backward to his specific denial of having engaged in bribery. Accepting bribes is universally condemned in Scripture, and Samuel carefully distances himself from a practice that has already made his own sons infamous (8:3; cf. Ps 15:5; Am 5:12). If such were the case, Samuel promises to make restitution (cf. 2Sa 9:7).

4 The people readily accepted and agreed with Samuel's declaration. Samuel declared his determination not to make merchandise of the prophetic office (cf. Mic 2:6–11; 3:11).

5 After solemnly affirming his innocence of any wrongdoing, Samuel declares that the Lord and Saul (cf. v.3) are witnesses to the truthfulness of his words. The people's response, "He is witness," could refer either to the Lord or to Saul and may be intentionally ambiguous.

6 Verses 6–12 summarize the history of Israel from the time of Moses and the Exodus through the period of the judges and their sinful request for a king, stressing divine leadership and Israel's idolatrous disloyalty while challenging them to the same covenant faithfulness. By highlighting the name of the Lord from the outset, Samuel leaves no doubt that, in the final sense, Israel's leader has always been the Lord. God, working through and in concert with Moses and Aaron, freed his people from Egyptian bondage (cf. Ex 6:13, 26–27). The exodus of Israel from Egypt was remembered as the greatest of all divine acts of redemption for the nation (see Ex 20:2).

7 Samuel continues to use the language of the courtroom as he commands the people to "stand" (GK 3656) at attention and in anticipation before the bar of God's justice. He intends to "confront [them] with evidence" of God's blessing on their history, all the more casting their apostasy in darker relief. Samuel's evidence is "the righteous acts performed by the LORD" (cf. Jdg 5:11; Da 9:16; Mic 6:5).

8–9 Verses 8–12 recapitulate and expand on 8:7–8. "Jacob" refers to the patriarch himself and also, by extension, to the nation of Israel. The Lord (cf. also v.10) graciously answered (Ex 2:25) their cry for help (Ex 2:23–24). He sent Moses (Ex 3:10) and Aaron to lead Israel out of Egypt (cf. 1Sa 10:18)—a fact acknowledged even by their enemies (1Sa 6:6)—and to bring them to the borders of the Promised Land. The dreary cycle of the book of Judges is reprised in vv.9–11: rebellion (v.9a), retribution (v.9b), repentance (v.10), and restoration (v.11).

Rebelling against their God, the Israelites "forgot" (cf. Jdg 3:7) what he had done for them in the past and ignored him personally as they worshiped other gods (cf. v.10). In response to his people's apostasy and in retribution against them for their sin, the Lord "sold them," as though on the slave market, "into the hand[s] of" their enemies, including Sisera (Jdg 4:2; cf. Ps 83:9), the commander of the army of the city of Hazor, the Philistines (Jdg 3:31; 10:7; 13:1), and Eglon king of Moab (Jdg 3:12–14).

10 Samuel now describes repentant Israel sporadically throughout the period of the judges. Although they often forsook the Lord and violated his covenant with them by serving the Baals (male deities) and the Ashtoreths (female deities), they pled for his deliverance and promised to serve him alone if only he would release them from the shackles of enemy oppression.

11 God did restore the Israelites to their former covenant relationship by sending judges to their rescue. Jerub-Baal (Gideon) is perhaps mentioned first (1) because he is the central figure in the book of Judges and arguably the most important of the judges themselves; (2) because his very name (cf. Jdg 6:32 and NIV note there) means "Let Baal Contend"; and (3) because he specifically refused to establish dynastic as opposed to divine rule over his countrymen (Jdg 8:22–23)—for which refusal he must surely have been one of Samuel's heroes (cf. v.13). Samuel then refers to Barak, Deborah's general in the successful war against Sisera's Canaanite army (Jdg 4:6–7), and Jephthah (Jdg 11:1), victor over the Ammonites. Finally, Samuel mentions himself as the last of the judges as well as the most recent victor over the Philistines (7:6, 11–15). He then summarizes the Lord's triumphant deliverance of his people from all their enemies through his chosen leaders.

12 Three times the people express their determination not to have God as their King but rather to have a human king like "all the other nations" (8:5–7): (1) after Samuel's earlier warning about the dangers inherent in their demand (8:19–20), (2) during the public assembly at Mizpah (10:19), and (3) in the face of the Ammonite threat (12:12).

13 Serving as the hinge of the chapter, this verse focuses once again on the gracious, permissive will of God, who has given his people the king they "asked for" (another pun on the name "Saul"; cf. also vv.17, 19). In successive stages Saul had acceded to that office. The Lord's eventual rejection of the very king the people demanded is eerily echoed later in a similar situation in Hos 13:10–11 (cf. esp. v.11).

14–15 To "fear [GK 3707] the LORD and serve [GK 6268]" him (Jos 24:14) brings his blessing; to "rebel [GK 5277] against his commands" (Dt 1:26, 43; 9:23; Jos 1:18) brings his curse. "Fear of God/the LORD," a common expression in OT wisdom literature (cf. Job 28:28; Pr 1:7; 9:10), was the generic term for "religion" in ancient Israel. In the OT, fearing God had more the connotation of reverence and awe (cf. Dt 17:19) than of terror or dread—although the latter was not totally lacking. To "serve" means not only to work and minister but also to worship (cf. already 7:3–4). If Israel and her new king would fear, serve, and obey God by carefully following his law, they would receive his blessing (for the king, see Dt 17:18–20). Disobedience and rebellion "against his commands," however, would result in his curse against them in the future (cf. 1Ki 13:21–26; La 1:18) as it had been against their "fathers" in the past (cf. Nu 20:24–26; 27:12–14).

16 Earlier (v.7) Samuel had told the people to "stand" and see the evidence of God's righteous acts in the past on their behalf. Now he commands them to "stand" and be awed by divine omnipotence (cf. also Ex 14:31). The divine act then results in natural inversion. In that part of the world not only is "rain in harvest . . . not fitting" (Pr 26:1), it is so totally unexpected that it could easily be interpreted as a sign of divine displeasure.

17 "Thunder" represents thunder as the loud and powerful voice of God manifested in storms (cf. 7:10; Ps 29:3–9). The driving rain that often accompanied such thunder could be especially destructive to crops (Pr 28:3), and when it occurred unseasonably, it could leave those who depended on it destitute (cf. Jdg 15:1–5). Thus Samuel's rhetorical question in this verse served as an ominous reminder to the people that all their hard work had the potential of being wiped out in an equally brief period of time. The people would then "realize" how evil their motives had been in asking for a king.

18–19 Samuel's prayer for a storm out of season was answered "that same day," and all the people "stood in awe" of both God and Samuel (cf. Ex 14:31). The reputation of Moses and Samuel as being especially close to God's counsel (Jer 15:1) was justly deserved; the people's plea to Samuel—"Pray to the LORD"—is a clear echo of Ex 9:28. That the people should ask Samuel to pray to the Lord "your" God (rather than "our" God) indicates a recognition of their own apostate condition. They admit that asking for a king was an evil that "added to" all their other sins (cf. similarly 2Ch 28:13; Job 34:37; Isa 30:1).

20 Samuel concludes his address to the people of Israel by encouraging them to do good (vv.20–24) and warning them not to do evil (v.25). He reminds them that they were the ones who asked for a king (cf. v.19); thus they have only themselves to blame if Saul proves to be either weak or despotic. All is not lost, however, if only the people will acknowledge that their true King is the Lord himself. Samuel further urges Israel to "serve the LORD with all your heart," an often expressed covenant requirement (cf. Dt 10:12–13; 11:13–14; cf. also 30:9–10).

21 By contrast, the people are not to follow "useless idols." The reference in this context seems to denote any defection from serving the Lord—including, of course, preference for a human king. Only God can do the people good; no one else can "rescue."

22 The Lord's elective purposes for his people would not be denied. His intention to make Israel his own covenant people (Ex 19:5; cf. 1Pe 2:9) was not because of any merit on their part (Dt 7:6–7). Rather, he chose them because of his love for them and to fulfill his oath that he had sworn to their forefathers (Dt 7:8–9; cf. Ge 15:4–6, 13–18; 22:16–18). In addition, and perhaps most important, he chose them "for the sake of his great name" (cf. also Jos 7:9–11).

23 Taking his rightful place among the giants of intercession (Ex 32:30–32; Da 9:4–20; Ro 1:9–10; et al.), Samuel declares his unwillingness to sin against God (cf. 14:33–34) by failing to pray for Israel (cf. also v.19; 7:5, 8–9; 8:6; 15:11; Jer 15:1). To help the people live a life pleasing to God, he promises to "teach" them "the way that is good and right" (cf. also 1Ki 8:36 = 2Ch 6:27).

24–25 The rest is up to the people themselves; so ch. 12 ends with encouragement to faith and obedience (which summarizes Dt 10:20–21) and warning against the consequences of disobedience appropriate to a covenant renewal document (cf. Ecc 12:13). After all, the Lord had done "great things" for his people, which should have been a cause for rejoicing on their part (Ps 126:2–3; Joel 2:21). Samuel feels constrained to remind them, however, that pursuing their penchant for evil will surely result in their destruction.

B. The Decline of Saul (13:1–15:35)

1. The rebuke of Saul (13:1–15)

1 This verse is doubtless the defective remnant of the formal introduction of Saul's reign. Such formulas are common in later portions of the Deuteronomic history of the southern kings. However, two notable exceptions to the regnal formula must be mentioned: that of Saul in v.1 and that of Ish-Bosheth son of Saul (2Sa 2:10). After the murder of Ish-Bosheth (2Sa 4), the regnal formula is reserved exclusively for southern kings. As for Saul, the mutilated condition of v.1 may reflect later scribal antipathy toward him. The two NIV footnotes to v.1 summarize the text-critical reasons for the numbers the NIV restores there.

2–10 The people had "chosen" a king to lead them into battle (8:18–20), and now their king obliged them: Saul "chose" (GK 1047) three thousand Israelite men to serve in his standing army (cf. 8:11–12). Two thousand were under his command at Micmash and in the high country at Bethel, while one thousand were at Gibeah in Benjamin (his hometown) under the command of his son Jonathan (which means "The LORD has given"). Apparently feeling confident in the size of his two military units, Saul sent the rest of the men home.

The smaller unit under Jonathan started a war against the Philistines by attacking their outpost at Geba in Benjamin, about five miles north-northeast of Jerusalem. Saul, ultimately responsible for the attack and realizing that the main Philistine army had heard about it, entertained second thoughts about his own troop strength. He therefore had the ram's-horn trumpet blown throughout Israel to summon additional men (cf. Jdg 3:27; 6:34).

To state that Israel had now become a "stench to the Philistines" was tantamount to affirming that the Philistines would muster their troops to fight Israel, and so they did. In the meantime, Saul's call to arms was answered by the "people," who assembled at Gilgal.

The Philistines were feared far and wide for their wooden chariots armed with iron fittings. The present account uses hyperbole to emphasize the magnitude of the Philistine threat. Besides being able to put three thousand two-man chariots into the field, the enemy had summoned troops "as numerous as the sand on the seashore"—a simile not only familiar to a believing community who traced their allegiance to the Lord back to the Abrahamic covenant (Ge 22:17; cf. also 1Ki 4:20–21) but also useful in describing huge numbers of fighting men (2Sa 17:11; Jos 11:4).

Since the Philistines set up camp at Micmash, Saul either hastily retreated to Gilgal or perhaps had earlier decided to make his headquarters there. The Philistine deployment there caused mass desertions in the Israelite army. Like their ancestors before them (Jdg 6:2), some of the Israelites hid in whatever out-of-the-way places they could find (14:11, 22). Others fled eastward across the Jordan River, seeking safety in Gad and Gilead. David would later discover that caves (23:23; 24:3, 7–8, 10) would afford safe protection from Saul and other enemies.

The greatly reduced number of men who remained with Saul at Gilgal were understandably frightened. Saul, remembering Samuel's earlier command (10:8), waited seven days for his arrival. When the prophet failed to appear at the appointed time, even more of Saul's troops began to defect. Desperate, Saul decided to seek the Lord's favor (v.12) by sacrificing the offerings that Samuel had told him he himself would make. Samuel arrived on the scene just after Saul had offered up the burnt offering but before he had had time to sacrifice the fellowship offerings. Upon Samuel's arrival Saul went out to "greet" (lit., "bless"; GK 1385; cf. Ge 47:7) him, which would not mollify him in this situation any more than in similar circumstances later (15:13).

Saul's sin was not that as king he was forbidden by God's law to sacrifice burnt offerings and fellowship offerings under any and all circumstances. David (2Sa 24:25) and Solomon (1Ki 3:15) later made the same kinds of offerings, and there is no hint of divine rebuke in either case. Saul sinned because he disobeyed God's word through the prophet Samuel—a sin that he would commit again (15:26).

11–15 Saul's motivation to offer the sacrifice seems genuine and appropriate: The Philistines were gathering for battle against Israel, his men were deserting him, and Samuel had not arrived on the scene when he had said he would. Saul therefore felt the urgent need to seek God's favor. What he apparently failed to realize, however, is that animal sacrifice is not a prerequisite for entreating God. Clearly, Saul had not heeded the divine word through the prophet, and obedience is always better than sacrifice (15:22).

But there is more. It would seem that in ancient Israel, rituals associated with the holy war were not to be performed by the king unless a prophet was present. In chs. 13 and 15 Saul acted without the presence of Samuel, and in both cases his transgression was related to holy war ritual (15:3, 7–11, 17–19). For these offenses he was rebuked by Samuel and rejected by God.

Had Saul obeyed, his "kingdom" over Israel would have been divinely established "for all time." Such a promise presents a difficulty in light of the Davidic covenant since the Lord affirms that David's throne will be established "forever" (2Sa 7:13, 16; cf. also Ge 49:10). It is possible, of course, that God's original choice of Saul (9:15–17; 10:1, 24) carried with it a genuine (though hypothetical) promise of a continuing dynasty that was never in danger of being fulfilled, given Saul's character.

Saul, reminded twice that he had not obeyed the Lord's command, is told that he would be replaced by a man "after [God's] own heart" (Ac 13:22), i.e., a man who truly has God's interests at heart.

Saul now takes a census of his fighting men to assess their numerical strength (cf. 11:8; 14:17). In spite of the original two thousand men (or perhaps three thousand) mentioned earlier (v.2) and the general call to arms to supplement them (vv.3–4), wholesale defections had reduced his troops to "about six hundred" (cf. 14:2).

2. The struggle against the Philistines (13:16–14:23)

16–22 The combined forces of Saul and Jonathan at Gibeah numbered only in the hundreds (14:2), while those of the Philistines at Micmash scarcely four miles to the northeast numbered in the thousands (v.5). Philistine "raiding parties" (14:15) left camp in three detachments, a common military strategy in those days (11:11; Jdg 7:16; 9:43; 2Sa 18:2) since it provided more options and greater mobility. They headed off in three different directions: One group went toward Ophrah in Benjamin (cf. Jos 18:23), a second went toward (Upper) Beth Horon in Ephraim (cf. Jos 16:5), and the third went an undetermined distance eastward toward the Valley of Zeboim.

As an effective method of denying weapons to the beleaguered Israelites, the Philistines had apparently deported all the Israelite blacksmiths (cf. 2Ki 24:14, 16; Jer 24:1; 29:2). Hebrew fighting men were not to have swords or spears (Saul and Jonathan, either with Philistine permission or by subterfuge, were the sole exceptions; v.22).

Since Philistia was located on the coastal plains west of the foothills of Judah, Israelites who visited the Philistines for any purpose "went down" to them (see Jdg 14:19; 16:31; Am 6:2). As in the days of Deborah (Jdg 5:8), the Israelites were woefully outgunned as the battle against the enemy loomed before them. Despite their lack of weapons, however, with God's help (14:6) they would rout the mighty Philistines just as David would later defeat the giant Goliath (17:45, 47).

13:23–14:14 The stage having been set in 13:16–22, the drama of Israel's victory over Philistia begins with a remarkably courageous attack by two men, who win a skirmish with a heavily armed enemy against overwhelming odds.

A "detachment" of Philistines had left their main camp at Micmash (13:16) and had gone out to defend a pass leading to it. It is Saul's son Jonathan who takes the initiative against the enemy. He suggests to his armor-bearer that they attack the recently established Philistine outpost. Armor-bearers in ancient times had to be unusually brave and loyal, since the lives of their masters often depended on them. The function of Jonathan's armor-bearer was especially important because of the scarcity of weapons in Israel (13:22). Jonathan decided not to tell his father about his plans, perhaps not to worry him needlessly or because he felt that Saul would forbid him to go.

Meanwhile, Saul's modest army of six hundred men (13:15) was with him near Gibeah, his hometown. Although the statement that Saul himself was sitting "under a pomegranate tree" contrasts his timidity and relative ease/luxury with Jonathan's willingness to sacrifice his very life for Israel, it may simply be intended as an allusion to his role as leader (cf. Jdg 4:5).

Among the men with Saul was the priest Ahijah, grandson of Phinehas and great-grandson of Eli (v.3). Reference to Ahijah's ancestors recalls the divine curse on the house of Eli (2:30–33) and the deaths of Eli (4:18) and Phinehas (4:11). Later the text will describe the deaths of Ahitub and his fellow priests (22:11–18) at the command of Saul himself. The apparently needless reference to Ichabod recalls yet another tragedy in Eli's family. Thus the rebuked King Saul is in the company of the priest Ahijah of the rejected house of Eli, and neither is "aware" that the courageous Jonathan son of Saul is on his way to fight the Philistines.

When Jonathan repeated his suggestion of v.1 to his armor-bearer, he made a significant change by calling the Philistines "those uncircumcised fellows," a term of reproach used elsewhere (17:26, 36; 31:4; 2Sa 1:20) and designating them as nonparticipants in the Abrahamic covenant (Ge 17:9–11). Jonathan is confident that the Lord will fight for Israel and that nothing can keep God from saving them (cf. 17:47). He knows that with God on his side, even an insignificant number of men can achieve victory (cf. Jdg 7:4, 7). The armor-bearer's response to Jonathan shows the extent of his loyalty. Their two hearts beating as one, the men march into battle together.

A brief comment by Jonathan introduces the sign and its sequel. As the dew on the fleece would give Gideon the faith to believe that God would save Israel by Gideon's hand (Jdg 6:36–37), so the appropriate Philistine response to the approach of Jonathan and his armor-bearer would give Jonathan the faith to believe that the Lord would give the enemy into their hands.

When the Philistines caught sight of the two men, they assumed them to be Israelite deserters who had earlier hidden in caves and holes (13:6). Confident that they had nothing to fear, the Philistines shouted the fateful words: "Come up to us." Wasting no time, Jonathan and his companion climbed up to the outpost and began the slaughter. Although outnumbered about ten to one, Jonathan and his armor-bearer dispatched "some twenty men" in a "[furrowed] area" (cf. Ps 129:3) of a field small enough to be plowed by a yoke of oxen in half a day—that is, the Philistines were killed in a brief time and a short distance.

15–23 Confusion struck the Philistine troops (cf. vv.20, 22) whatever their location: in the camp at Micmash (13:16), out in the field, at the various outposts, with one or another of the three raiding parties (13:17–18). The panic, sent by God, was of the kind promised to Israel against her enemies when the people trusted him (Dt 7:23). During such times of terror, the ground may shake, as when the Lord led his people through the Sea of Reeds while at the same time overthrowing the Egyptians (Ps 77:18).

So total was the Philistine panic and so noisy their flight that Saul's watchmen on the walls at Gibeah could see—and perhaps hear—many of the enemy soldiers as they scattered in all directions. The "melting [away]" of an enemy force is a vivid metaphor describing full retreat (cf. Isa 14:31; cf. also Ex 15:15; Jos 2:9, 24). Curious about what was causing the Philistine flight, and perhaps considering the possibility of helping to turn it into a total rout, Saul decided once again to take a census of his troops (see 13:15)—but this time to see whether any of them had left the camp and were perhaps responsible for the Philistine panic. Amazingly enough, it was not until the census was complete that Saul became aware of the absence of Jonathan, his own son.

Still not quite ready to go to Jonathan's aid, however, Saul told the priest Ahijah to bring the ark of God before him. A special point is made of the fact that it was "with the Israelites" at that time (presumably having been brought to Gibeah from Kiriath Jearim; cf. 7:2), and Saul may well have wanted to carry it into battle against the Philistines in a superstitious attempt to guarantee victory (cf. 4:3–7).

Hearing the increasing tumult in the Philistine camp, Saul apparently changed his mind about the need to make use of the ark and told Ahijah to stop the ritual proceedings. Together with his men he then marched into battle, presumably without benefit of priestly blessing of any kind. The Philistines, meanwhile, had become filled with total "confusion." Brother was wielding sword against brother (cf. Eze 38:21).

Saul, Jonathan, and the Israelite army were soon joined by two groups of reinforcements. Some were Hebrews who had previously gone to the Philistine camp, perhaps either to have their agricultural tools sharpened (cf. 13:20) or, disgruntled with Israelite rule, to hire themselves out as mercenaries (cf. 29:6). The second group of reinforcements consisted of Israelite deserters who had been hiding (cf. 13:6) in the hill country of Ephraim, a large, partially forested plateau (Jos 17:15–18) north and west of Micmash. The "hot pursuit" of the combined Israelite forces under Saul and Jonathan would be tragically reversed in the final relentless attack of the Philistines against the king and his son (31:2).

The Hebrew expression translated "So the Lord rescued Israel that day" is a verbatim quotation of Ex 14:30. Its deliberate use stresses the importance of Saul's victory while also giving all the glory to God (as Saul apparently also did; cf. v.39). The Israelite forces, however, were not satisfied with the results of their own efforts until they had driven the Philistines some distance west of Beth Aven toward their own homeland beyond Aijalon (v.31).

3. The cursing of Jonathan (14:24–46)

24–30 The scenes recorded here constitute a flashback to events simultaneous with the battle description in vv.20–23. Saul had bound the troops under an oath of abstaining from food for the entire day of the battle, an understandable religious demand in a "holy war" context. The result, however, was that they were "in distress" from hunger. Thus Saul's motivation, however praiseworthy, resulted in his men's becoming "faint" and "exhausted." Accompanying the fulfillment of the oath, intended to implement a religiously motivated fast that would energize the men and fill them with fighting zeal, would be the opportunity for Saul to take vengeance on his enemies.

As with Samson (Jdg 14:8–20), honey in a Philistine context almost cost Jonathan his life. Upon entering a forest, Saul's troops noticed a honeycomb on the ground. Although it was filled with honey, no one so much as tasted any of it because they "feared" the oath (cf. Pr 13:13). But Jonathan, unaware of the oath, used the end of his staff (perhaps to avoid being stung by bees) to dip some honey from the comb. When Jonathan ate it, his

eyes "brightened," implying renewal of strength (cf. Ps 19:8–10).

One of Jonathan's fellow soldiers warned him about his father's oath, adding the observation that obeying it had caused the troops to become "faint." Jonathan's rebuttal, based on his refreshment after eating food, is that Saul "has made trouble for the country." Jonathan concludes by arguing that even more Philistines would have been killed if Saul's men had eaten some of the food they "took" as plunder.

31–35 Saul's men were no longer under his oath of abstinence because it was after evening and the Philistines were totally routed. The Israelites had devastated them and driven them westward all the way to Aijalon, which had originally been assigned to the tribal territory of Dan (Jos 19:40–42).

Famished, the Israelite troops seized sheep, cattle, and calves from the Philistine plunder, butchered them, and ate the meat without waiting for the blood to drain from it. Since eating meat with the blood still in it was forbidden to the people of God throughout their history (cf. Lev 17:10–14; 19:26; et al.), it is not surprising that Saul, on hearing of his men's sinful deed, would immediately act to absolve them of guilt. He first accused them of having betrayed their promise to God. He then demanded that a large stone be rolled over to him so that animals could be properly slaughtered on it, not on the ground as before. In this way he is making a commendable attempt to right a sinful wrong perpetrated by his understandably hungry troops.

Spiritually sensitive Israelite leaders built altars as a matter of routine (cf. 7:17; 2Sa 24:25; 1Ch 21:18; Jdg 6:24). In Saul's case a special point is made of the fact that this was the "first time" he had done so, probably a negative comment directed at Saul's lack of piety.

36–46 Initially Saul determined to plunder and slaughter the Philistines until nothing and no one remained. The decision to attack at night and plunder till dawn reflects the common practice of conducting military operations in the dead of night, when the number of attackers was small and the element of surprise was important (cf. 2Sa 17:22; Jdg 16:3). Saul's men, apparently satisfied that he had their best interests at heart, were ready to follow him.

The priest Ahijah, however, sensed the need to "inquire of" God (lit., "draw near to"; GK 448 & 7928; cf. Zep 3:2), perhaps by making use of the sacred lots stored in the ephod (v.3). Agreeing, Saul "asked" the Lord whether the defeat of the enemy was imminent (cf. 7:8–9; Jdg 20:23). When he received no answer, he sensed that something was amiss in the army.

Saul called for the army "leaders" (cf. Jdg 20:2) to come before him to ascertain what sin had been committed and who had committed it. Pronouncing the solemn oath "As surely as the LORD lives" (cf. v.45; 19:6; 20:3, 21; 25:34; 26:10, 16; et al.), Saul affirmed that whoever had sinned "must die." If necessary, he was even prepared to give up the life of his son Jonathan (cf. Ge 22:10, 12, 16; Jdg 11:31, 39; Heb 11:17). Respectful even in the face of Saul's shocking announcement, knowing that Jonathan had (however innocently) violated his father's imposed oath, aware that the brave Jonathan would likely die through no fault of his own, doubtless sympathizing with Jonathan's position as over against Saul's folly—none of his men "said a word" during those dramatic moments.

Anticipating the casting of lots to determine who had committed the sin that imperiled further war against Philistia, Saul made the first division by lining up his troops on one side and himself and Jonathan on the other. The casting of lots proceeds swiftly, and the rest of the men are eliminated as "Jonathan and Saul" are taken (that Jonathan's name appears first is an ominous sign). As the final lot is cast, Saul is cleared and Jonathan taken. Saul's statement to Jonathan echoes Joshua's to Achan centuries earlier (Jos 7:19). Jonathan then admits tasting a little honey with the end of his staff, but also says he is ready to die. Even more solemn than the oath Saul had taken earlier (v.39) is the one he now takes (v.44; cf. also 25:22), and it seems that Jonathan's doom is sealed.

Unable to contain themselves any longer, Saul's men remind him of how cruel it would be to execute Israel's deliverer. Because he was able to achieve victory with God's help (cf. Ge 4:1), not a single hair of his head would fall to the ground (cf. 2Sa 14:11; 1Ki 1:52; Ac 27:34). Finally persuaded, Saul re-

scinds his order, and thus Jonathan is "rescued" (lit., "ransomed"; GK 7009; cf. Job 6:23) by the fervent pleas of the troops. Distracted by his determination to execute his own son, Saul loses his best opportunity to deal the Philistines a lethal blow.

4. Further wars of Saul (14:47–52)

47–48 Although for the most part we do not know the times or extent of Saul's wars against his enemies, we read that he was successful wherever he turned. In anticipation of Saul's fiasco in ch. 15, the narrator reserves the Amalekites for special attention. On one or more occasions (otherwise unrecorded) during his reign, Saul "fought valiantly" against Amalek and defeated them. He also saved Israel from the hands of "those who had plundered" them. But Saul's incomplete victory in ch. 15, caused by his disobedience, led to divine rejection and the loss of his kingdom (15:28; 28:17–18).

49 The names of Saul's children are recorded here, and those of other family members appear in vv.50–51. In addition to his firstborn, Jonathan, Saul had at least two other sons: Ishvi (probably Ish-Bosheth) and Malki-Shua ("My King is noble," 31:2). Saul also had a fourth son, not mentioned here (Abinadab; cf. 31:2). Saul's two daughters, Merab (2Sa 21:8) and Michal (cf. 19:11–17; 2Sa 6:16–23), are listed in their proper genealogical order. Both would later be offered in marriage to David (18:17–27).

50–51 Saul's wife was Ahinoam ("My Brother is pleasant") daughter of Ahimaaz. Saul also had a concubine named Rizpah (2Sa 3:7). The commander of Saul's army was his cousin Abner. Saul's father Kish and uncle Ner were both sons of Abiel (cf. 9:1).

52 Chapter 14 concludes with reminders of the never-ending and all-pervasive Philistine threat and of the king's continuing need for fresh troops (cf. 8:11). The final verse of the chapter also sends forth literary rays into the future. One of the "brave" men Saul will conscript is David (18:17).

5. The rejection of Saul (15:1–35)

Chapter 15 concludes the account of Saul's decline (chs. 13–15). As in ch. 13, Saul's intention to offer an unauthorized sacrifice in the context of holy war leads to God's rejection—this time, a final rejection. If at that earlier time Saul was denied a dynasty, now he is denied his kingship. Thus ch. 15 is climactic.

1–3 Samuel stresses his role as the representative through whom God anointed Saul as king and through whom he now proclaims a further message to him. Soon to wrest the kingship from Saul's grasp, the Lord—the only true King in Israel's theocratic monarchy—is described as "the LORD Almighty," a specifically royal name (see 1:3). His message to Saul is that the time has come for the final destruction of the Amalekites, predicted and reiterated long ago (Ex 17:8–16; Nu 24:20; Dt 25:17–19). The geographical clues scattered throughout the chapter make it clear that the Amalekites referred to here are the traditional southern marauders rather than a smaller Amalekite enclave occupying an area in the hills of western Samaria.

The significance and uniqueness of the divine command to annihilate the Amalekites is underscored by *herem* (GK 3049; see NIV note for its meaning). In this case it means "attack," "do not spare," and "put to death" (see v.3). It is furthermore clear that "everything that belongs to them" here means "everything among them that breathes" (cf. Dt 20:16–17). Representative pairings of animate creatures doomed to destruction conclude the verse. The command is specific: "Do not spare them"; later, Saul rationalized his disobedience of that command (vv.9, 15).

We should not be surprised that Saul did not flinch at the prospect of killing innocent women and children. Wars in the ancient Near East always had a religious dimension, and the battlefield was an arena of divine retribution. The Amalekites, in their persistent refusal to fear God (Dt 25:18), sowed the seeds of their own destruction. God is patient and slow to anger, "abounding in love and faithfulness" (Ex 34:6); he nevertheless "does not leave the guilty unpunished" (v.7). The agent of divine judgment can be impersonal (e.g., the Flood or the destruction of Sodom and Gomorrah) or personal (as here), and in his sovereign purpose God permits entire families or nations to be destroyed if their corporate representatives are incorrigibly wicked (cf. Jos 7:1, 10–13, 24–26).

4–9 Saul summoned from Judah "ten thousand" men. In addition he mustered "two hundred thousand foot soldiers," probably from Israel. Saul's troop strength had declined considerably since the battles against Nahash and the Ammonites (11:8), but it was more than adequate for the present task.

Before Saul's main attack against the Amalekites, he urged the Kenites living in or near Amalekite territory (cf. 27:10; 30:29) to move out (at least temporarily) to avoid getting killed in the crossfire. The Kenites had shown "kindness" to the Israelite spies centuries earlier and had thus been spared in return (Jos 2:12–14).

The Israelites attacked the Amalekites throughout their homeland. The description of the total destruction of "all" the people is hyperbolic, since the Amalekites survived to fight again (cf. 30:1). In any event, Saul spared Agag—but perhaps with the intent of later putting him to death, since the idiom "take alive" often describes an action preparatory to subsequent execution (cf. 2Ki 10:14; 2Ch 25:12; and esp. Jos 8:23, 29).

Besides sparing Agag, Saul and his troops also set aside the best of the enemy's animals. When reproved by Samuel for not slaughtering even the best animals (vv.14, 19), Saul gave the excuse that his "soldiers" (vv.15, 21) intended to sacrifice them to the Lord. If Saul is sincere at this point, his reluctance to accept responsibility and his haste to shift the blame to his men are disquietingly reminiscent of similar situations (Ge 3:12–13; Ex 32:21–24). The text, however, states that Saul and his men were "unwilling" (GK 14) to destroy—a verb specifically linked elsewhere with the sin of rebellion (Dt 1:26).

10–21 The phrase "the word of the LORD came to" is used of God's revelation to a prophet only three times in the books of Samuel (see 2Sa 7:4; 24:11; cf. 1Sa 3:1). In each of two stages in this section (vv.10–15, 16–21), Samuel brings the condemning word of God to Saul for having disobeyed the divine command.

Whether Samuel had by this time become reconciled—however reluctantly—to Saul's kingship is difficult to say. After all, God's role in making Saul king is stressed over and over in these chapters (9:17; 10:1, 24; 12:13; 13:13; 15:1). Although Samuel did not yet know it, Saul had "turned away" from the Lord (GK 8704), an action fraught with the most serious of consequences (cf. Nu 14:43;

32:15; Jos 22:16, 18, 23, 29; 1Ki 9:6–7). The Lord's "word" to Samuel was clearly disturbing to him, causing him to be "troubled" and to cry out (for help; cf. 7:8–9; 12:8, 10; GK 2410) to the Lord all night long. During his night-long wrestling with God in prayer he received the divine message of irreversible doom for Saul's kingdom (cf. v.16). God has now spoken; throughout the rest of the chapter Samuel mediates the divine word to the rejected Saul.

Samuel was told that Saul had gone to Carmel and set up a monument (probably an inscribed victory stele) "in his own honor" (apparently not giving credit to the Lord). Having built the monument, Saul then went to Gilgal—the very place where Samuel had earlier rebuked him for sacrificing to the Lord (13:7–14; cf. v.21).

When Samuel arrived at Gilgal, Saul—either genuinely or pretending innocence—greeted him in the traditional way (cf. 23:21; 2Sa 2:5; Ru 2:19–20; 3:10) and then told him that he had carried out the Lord's "instructions." But Samuel, not to be denied, wanted to know why he heard sheep and cattle in the background. Saul's meek retort in v.15 fails on two counts: (1) However commendable his declared motive, Saul had been told to destroy every living thing and therefore should not have spared even the best of the animals; (2) even if his soldiers were primarily responsible for saving the animals, Saul was their leader and therefore should not have tried to shift the blame to them. Especially stark is the contrast between "they spared" and "we totally destroyed." Notice that in speaking to Samuel, Saul referred to "the LORD your God" (rather than "the LORD our God"; cf. vv.21, 30).

Samuel would have none of Saul's self-righteous protestations. With all the force of divine authority, he told Saul to "stop" (v.16) and to listen to what God had revealed to him the previous night. He reminded Saul that despite the fact that Saul had once considered himself too insignificant to be Israel's ruler (cf. 9:21; 10:22), the Lord had nevertheless anointed him as king. He then reminded Saul of the divine commission regarding the wicked Amalekites. Saul has no better defense against Samuel's onslaught than to repeat in detail what he had already said (v.13). Although he stresses his own obedience by speaking in the first person several times in

v.20, he also tries to justify the actions of his troops by attributing to them the worthy intention to sacrifice to the Lord the animals they had spared.

22–31 The poetic format of Samuel's well-known condemnation of Saul's objection in no way blunts its severity (cf. v.33). As at the time of the Fall (Ge 2–3), the matter at stake is one of obedience, and Saul failed as miserably as did Adam and Eve.

Verse 22 is a classic text on the importance of obedience, moral conduct, and proper motivation in animal sacrifice (cf. Pss 40:6–8; 51:16–17; Isa 1:11–15; Hos 6:6; Mk 12:32–33). To Samuel, himself both prophet (3:20) and priest, the issue is not a question of either/or but of both/and. Sacrifice must be offered to the Lord on his terms, not ours. Saul's postponement of the commanded destruction, however well meaning, constituted flagrant violation of God's will.

Just as Saul's earlier impetuous disobedience had brought the full force of Samuel's rebuke (13:14), so now his halfhearted fulfillment of the divine command removes him from royal office. Rejection begets rejection.

The note of finality in Samuel's voice finally brings Saul to his senses. Saul says—twice—"I have sinned." He confesses to having "violated the LORD's command," apparently not having learned the lesson of his earlier failure (13:13). Fearing the people more than God (cf. Pr 29:25; Isa 51:12–13), Saul "gave in to them"—lit., "listened to their voice"—when all along he should have been obeying the voice of God through the prophet (vv.19, 22).

At first Saul's plea to Samuel for forgiveness falls on deaf ears. As far as Samuel is concerned, the conversation is over; so he turns to leave the scene. At this point Saul in desperation seizes the hem of Samuel's robe. Saul may not have been aware of the full implications of his spontaneous act. But since a man's robe may symbolize his power and authority (cf. 2:19), the tearing of Samuel's robe implies an irreparable breech between Saul and Samuel as well as the more obvious sundering of the kingdom from Saul and his descendants (cf. 1Ki 11:11–13, 29–31).

The "neighbor" destined to receive Saul's kingdom (cf. 13:14) is David. As obedience is "better than" sacrifice, so David is "better than" Saul. It is ironic that Saul himself had originally been considered "better than" his peers (9:2).

The general statement in Nu 23:19 concerning the immutability of God's basic nature and purpose is now applied in v.29. Samuel gives to the unchangeable God a unique name by calling him the "Glory" of Israel.

Perhaps by now reconciled to the irreversible divine determination to reject him finally as king of Israel, Saul poignantly repeats his earlier statements of confession and of his desire for Samuel to "come back" with him. Saul wanted to save face before the elders and people of Israel by publicly worshiping the Lord and so demonstrating his allegiance to him. Samuel—a man, not God—this time relented.

32–35 There was one piece of business still to take care of, however. Using the language common to the ritual procedure of sacrifice, Samuel said, "Bring me Agag." The Amalekite king feels that his life will be spared. In Samuel's mind, however, Agag is an offering to be sacrificed to the Lord. Quickly dispelling Agag's optimism, Samuel applies the lex talionis to him (cf. Jdg 1:7) and reminds him that bloodshed begets bloodshed (Ge 9:6). Without further ado Samuel then executes Agag, probably by hacking him in pieces for the treaty violation implications of such an act (cf. 11:12).

Following the death of Agag, Samuel and Saul go their separate ways—Samuel to his hometown of Ramah, just as he does after anointing David (16:13), and Saul to his hometown of Gibeah. Although after this time Saul would go to see Samuel again on more than one occasion (19:23–24; 28:10–11), never again would Samuel initiate such a meeting. Samuel nonetheless "mourned" for Saul (cf. also 16:1)—the language used here suggests mourning for one who is dead.

The chapter ends with a doleful echo of v.11: "The LORD was grieved that he had made Saul king." Saul's rejection of God's word through his prophet had led to God's rejection of Saul's rule over his people. To end this part of our discussion on a relatively positive note, however, we do well to remember that the divine rejection of the kingship of Saul does not imply a rejection of the person of Saul.

III. Establishment of Monarchy in Israel (16:1–31:13)

Although monarchy in the person of Saul had long since arrived in Israel, only with the anointing and rapid rise of David can it be said to have been truly established. Unlike Saul's abortive rule, David's reign was sovereignly instituted by God alone. Chapters 16–31 are as much the story of the decline and ultimate fall of Saul and Jonathan as they are of the rise of David.

A. The Rise of David (16:1–28:2)

1. The anointing of David (16:1–13)

In addition to being the middle chapter of 1 Samuel, ch. 16 is pivotal in another way as well: Its first half (vv.1–13), ending with a statement concerning David's reception of the Spirit of God, describes David's anointing as ruler of Israel to replace Saul; its second half (vv.14–23), beginning with a statement concerning Saul's loss of the Spirit and his replacement with an "evil spirit" sent by God, describes David's arrival in the court of Saul. Thus the juxtaposition of vv.13 and 14 delineates not only the transfer of the divine blessing and empowerment from Saul to David but also the beginning of the effective displacement of Saul by David as king of Israel. It serves as the literary, historical, and theological crux of 1 Samuel.

1–5 This chapter begins where ch. 15 ends: Samuel is still mourning for Saul. Ironically, the divine "how long" serves as a prophetic rebuke to the prophet Samuel. Since God had rejected Saul as king over Israel, a change of leadership was in order. The Lord tells Samuel to go to "Jesse of Bethlehem." At Bethlehem one of Jesse's sons would become the next ruler of Israel by being anointed with oil. Jesse of the tribe of Judah (cf. Ru 4:12, 18–22) and his hometown, Bethlehem in Judah, would forever become associated with the Messiah (Isa 11:1–3, 10; Mic 5:2; Mt 1:1, 5–6, 16–17; 2:4–6).

The Lord also tells Samuel that he has "chosen" a son of Jesse. Samuel was understandably afraid that the rejected Saul would kill him if he learned that Samuel was on the way to Bethlehem to anoint Saul's successor. The Lord therefore reminded Samuel of an accompanying reason for making the journey: to sacrifice a heifer (presumably as a fellowship offering; cf. Lev 3:1) in conjunction

DAVID'S FAMILY TREE

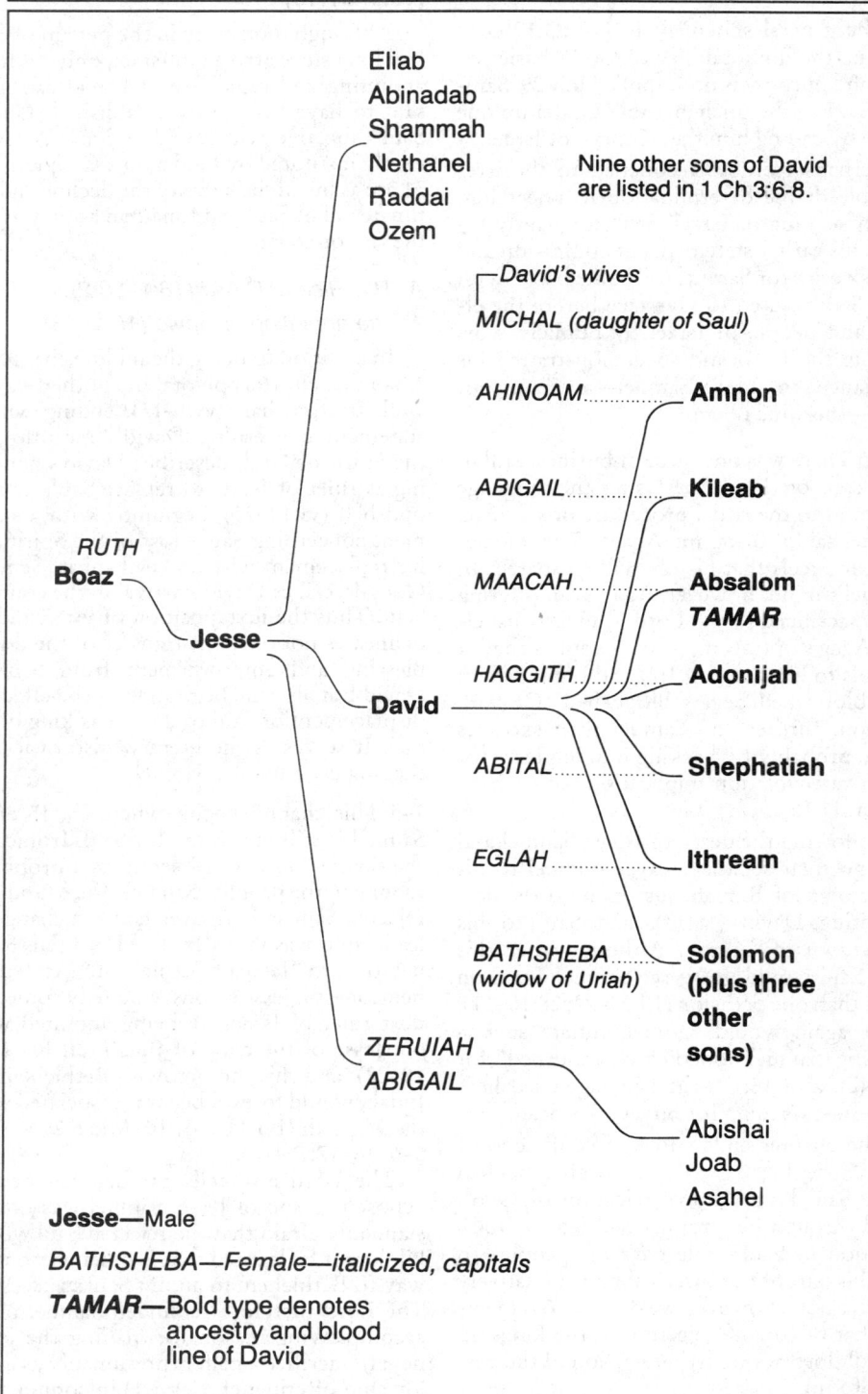

Eliab
Abinadab
Shammah
Nethanel
Raddai
Ozem

Nine other sons of David
are listed in 1 Ch 3:6-8.

David's wives

MICHAL (daughter of Saul)

AHINOAM .... **Amnon**

ABIGAIL .... **Kileab**

MAACAH .... **Absalom**
TAMAR

HAGGITH .... **Adonijah**

ABITAL .... **Shephatiah**

EGLAH .... **Ithream**

BATHSHEBA .... **Solomon**
(widow of Uriah) **(plus three
other
sons)**

RUTH
Boaz

Jesse

David

ZERUIAH
ABIGAIL

Abishai
Joab
Asahel

Jesse—Male

BATHSHEBA—Female—italicized, capitals

TAMAR—Bold type denotes
ancestry and blood
line of David

with the ritual of anointing (cf. 9:11–10:1; 11:15).

The sacrificial ceremony was for a select few (including Jesse, his sons, and the elders of Bethlehem) and was therefore by invitation only (cf. 9:24). God's promise to Samuel in v.3 leaves no doubt concerning God's sovereign role in the choice of Saul's successor: Samuel must anoint for the Lord the one whom the Lord indicates (cf. Dt 17:15).

Obedient to the Lord's command, Samuel went to Bethlehem. Perhaps awed by his formidable reputation, the town elders "trembled when they met him" (cf. 21:1). They asked Samuel the customary question in such circumstances: "Do you come in peace?" (cf. 1Ki 2:13; 2Ki 9:22). Samuel's cordial response allayed their fears as he told them (part of) the reason he had come. In preparation for entering into God's presence, he had the elders consecrate themselves; then he personally consecrated the specially designated celebrants (Jesse and his sons).

6–10 Samuel, apparently eager to get on with the anointing of Israel's next king, saw the oldest son, Eliab, and felt sure that he was the Lord's "anointed." The divine response to Samuel's musings immediately eliminates Eliab. God rejects him (as he had rejected Saul, v.1). What Samuel saw externally was Eliab's "appearance," but what man "looks at" (GK 8011) is not what God looks at (cf. 15:29). Human beings are impressed—and therefore often deceived—by what their eyes tell them, while God looks at the "heart" (cf. 1Ki 8:39; 1Ch 28:9; cf. esp. Lk 16:15).

Abinadab and Shammah, the second and third sons of Jesse (17:13), fared no better than Eliab had. Regarding both of these, "The LORD has not chosen this one either." Verse 10 summarizes the rest of the proceedings with respect to the divine rejection of David's brothers. None of the seven is acceptable.

11–13 Samuel, knowing God's determination that one of Jesse's sons will be king (v.1), but also knowing that God has not chosen any of the first seven (v.10), asks Jesse whether he has any other sons. Jesse informs him that there is one more, the "youngest" (cf. also 17:14).

When we first met Saul, he was looking for his father's donkeys (9:2–3); when we first meet David, he is tending his father's sheep.

At Samuel's request, Jesse sends someone to bring David in from the fields. Ironically, David, while presumably not a tall man, immediately presents a striking appearance. No sooner was David brought into Samuel's presence than the Lord commanded Samuel to anoint him as Israel's next ruler.

Samuel's anointing of David ("in the presence of his brothers," so that there might be witnesses that he is truly God's choice) is linked with David's accession of the Spirit of the Lord. Anointing with oil thus symbolized anointing with the Holy Spirit (cf. Isa 61:1). In David's case the divine accession was permanent ("from that day on"; cf. 30:25), while elsewhere the Spirit comes and goes (twice for Saul, 10:6, 10; 11:6; three times for Samson, Jdg 14:6, 19; 15:14).

Verse 13 concludes with Samuel's prophetic departure for his home in Ramah. Although he makes additional appearances later on, he no longer plays an active role in 1 and 2 Samuel. The anointing of David was the capstone of Samuel's career.

2. The arrival of David in the court of Saul (16:14–23)

14–18 The Spirit's coming on David and the Spirit's leaving Saul were two climactic events that occurred in close sequence to each other (cf. esp. 18:12). Just as the accession of the Spirit by David was an expected accompaniment of his anointing as Israel's next ruler (v.13), so the departure of the Spirit from Saul should be understood as the negation of effective rule on his part from that time on.

The "evil spirit," the divinely sent scourge that "tormented" (GK 1286) Saul, returned again and again (18:10; 19:9; cf. Jdg 9:23). Although the "evil" spirit may have been a demon that embodied both moral and spiritual wickedness, it is more likely an "injurious" (see NIV note) spirit that produced harmful results for him. It was responsible for the mental and psychological problems that plagued Saul for the rest of his life. That God used alien spirits to serve him is taken for granted in the OT (cf. esp. 2Sa 24:1 with 1Ch 21:1). Saul's "attendants," aware that their king was being tormented by an evil spirit, were ready and eager to help (cf. v.17; 17:32, 34, 36; 18:5 et al.).

Perhaps sensing the soothing effect of music, Saul's attendants offered to look for someone to play the "harp" to make their master "feel better." Saul agreed with his attendants' counsel, and one of his "servants" suggested that a certain son of Jesse would meet Saul's needs admirably. In the course of doing so, the servant gave as fine a portrayal of David as one could wish: a good musician, a "brave man," a "warrior," an articulate speaker, and a handsome man as well. The servant's final descriptive phrase reminds us that just as the Lord was with Samuel (3:19), so also he was with David. Although unwittingly, Saul's servant has just introduced us to Israel's next king.

19–23 Again Saul, influenced by a servant's suggestion, sent for the man described. Saul's reference to David as being "with the sheep" identifies him as a shepherd (cf. v.11). Unwittingly, he too characterizes David as Israel's next king.

Jesse sent David to take bread, wine, and a young goat to Saul (cf. Pr 18:16). Obviously impressing Saul, David "entered his service" as an armor-bearer. Although skilled men can expect to be pressed into service by kings (Pr 22:29), Saul also "liked" David personally. David's skill as a harpist brought soothing "relief" that drove the evil "spirit" from the disturbed king. The chapter ends with a gifted young man, Israel's future king, coming to serve a rejected and dejected ruler who is totally unaware of the implications of his welcoming David into his court.

3. The death of Goliath (17:1–58)

Just as Samuel's anointing of Saul (10:1) was followed by Saul's defeat of Nahash and the Ammonites (11:1–11), so also Samuel's anointing of David (16:13) is followed by David's defeat of Goliath and the Philistines (ch. 17). Each victory demonstrated the courage, determination, and military expertise of the newly anointed leader. The exciting story of David and Goliath is an excellent example of representative warfare effected by means of a contest of champions. The purpose of such contests was to decide the strength of a country without massive loss of life.

1–3 The Philistines were Saul's inveterate enemies throughout his reign (14:52). On this occasion they gathered "their forces" between Socoh and Azekah, two towns in the western foothills of Judah (Jos 15:20, 33, 35). The Israelite camp was on the northern slopes of the valley. The contest between David and Goliath took place on the floor of the valley itself, about halfway between the two opposing campsites.

4–7 In vv.4 and 23 Goliath is called a "champion." By any standard of measure, the Philistine champion was a giant of a man, "over nine feet tall." His armor and weapons are described at length. A coat of mail such as Goliath's was fashioned from several hundred small bronze plates that resembled fish scales and had to meet the needs of protection, lightness, and freedom of movement. The weight of Goliath's armor is impressive. Greaves protected the legs below the knee, and javelins were probably used to fend off attackers as often as they were used in offensive maneuvers. Goliath's most formidable offensive weapon seems to have been his spear, whose heavy "point" was made of iron (cf. 13:19–22). Goliath's sword, although not mentioned until vv.45, 51, doubtless had an iron blade. Receiving added protection from the large shield carried by his aide, the Philistine giant must have felt—and appeared—invincible.

8–11 Goliath hurls the challenge of representative combat into the teeth of the Israelite army. The Philistines (so Goliath thinks) will win a quick and easy victory over Israel, who will then be enslaved by them. Having thrown down the gauntlet, the Philistine challenger at first had no takers. In fact, Saul and his troops were "dismayed and terrified." Barring the response of an Israelite hero, Goliath would win by default, and the Philistines would continue to be Israel's masters.

12–16 Again we are introduced to David, Jesse's son (16:19). His three oldest sons, loyal warriors all, "followed" Saul into battle. Although having entered Saul's service earlier (16:21), David was currently engaged in his main task, tending his father's sheep—in preparation for a more important shepherding task later. Goliath came forward twice a day for forty days in continuing, taunting defiance. He "took his stand," like the kings of the earth in Ps 2:2, "against the LORD and against his anointed one" (Ps 2:2, NIV note).

17–22 The urgency of Jesse's command ("Hurry") underscores his concern for his sons' well-being and safety. Jesse sent along the staple items of roasted grain and bread for David's brothers, while for the commander of their unit he provided a gift of "ten cheeses."

The rest of ch. 17 describes David's transformation from being a shepherd of flocks to becoming a leader of people. When he reached the battle lines, David "greeted" his brothers (lit., "asked concerning [their] welfare/well-being"; cf. the same expression in v.18).

23–30 Even from a distance Goliath's defiant challenge appears to have been loud enough to interrupt David's conversation with his brothers. The mere sight of the giant was enough to cause the men of Israel to flee in panic. Nothing had changed in more than a month (v.16).

Notice the contrast between the attitudes of David and the men of Israel: The men of Israel call Goliath "this man," David calls him "this uncircumcised Philistine"; they say that Goliath has come out to "defy Israel," David says that he has come out to "defy the armies of the living God"; they refer to Goliath's potential victor as "the man who kills him," David refers to him as "the man who kills this Philistine and removes this disgrace from Israel." In short, the men of Israel see a fearsome giant who is reproaching Israel; David sees merely an uncircumcised Philistine who is defying the living God.

Giving one's daughter in marriage as a reward for faithful service was not unprecedented in Israel (cf. Jos 15:13–17). In addition, Saul promised great wealth to Goliath's victor as well as making his father's family "exempt . . . from taxes."

In righteous indignation David implicitly offers himself to fight Goliath, an offer that becomes explicit in v.32. In David's eyes the Philistines' god Dagon is a dead idol (5:3–4). By contrast "the LORD is the true God; he is the living God, the eternal King" (Jer 10:10). David's oldest brother, Eliab, misunderstood and angrily questioned David's motives for coming down to the battlefield (cf. Ge 37:4–36).

31–33 David's expressions of bravado were reported to Saul, who then decided that he wanted to talk to the young shepherd. Knowing that the Lord is on his side, David offers to fight Goliath in spite of the over-whelming odds against him (cf. Dt 20:1–4). But Saul, unimpressed, insists that a fight between David and Goliath would be a mismatch. As for Goliath's reputation as a "fighting man," David has already been referred to as a "warrior" earlier in the text (16:18). The odds are therefore much more even than either Saul or Goliath might imagine, especially when the divine element is added to the equation.

34–35 In vv.34–37 David demonstrates beyond cavil that he "speaks well" (16:18). Though others may flee from lions and bears (Am 5:19), David does not. As a shepherd "keeping his father's sheep" (cf. 16:11), David often rescued them from the mouths of dangerous animals (cf. Am 3:12).

36–37 The comparison between David as a herder of sheep and David as a leader of people is made even more explicit. Goliath will be "like" the lion or the bear, both of whom David had killed. As David routinely "rescued" sheep from wild animals (v.35), so also God had "delivered" David from them and would thus "deliver" him from Goliath. Deliverance from enemies depicted as predatory animals is not an uncommon motif in Scripture (Ps 22:21; cf. also 2Ti 4:17).

Saul, again impressed by David's bravado (cf. v.31), tells him to "Go." Saul's added expression of encouragement ("the LORD be with you") echoes 16:18 and unwittingly calls attention to the tragically disparate spiritual conditions of Saul and David (16:13–14).

38–40 Saul, desirous of giving David every advantage, clothed him in the same kind of armor. Since it was generally believed that to wear the clothing of another was to be imbued with his essence and to share his very being, these latter acts were probably calculated to enable Saul to take credit for, or at least to share in, David's victory.

David, however, denied Saul his potential moment of glory. He insisted that he could not "go" while wearing Saul's heavy armor. After taking the armor off, he selected five sling stones from the streambed in the Valley of Elah. Such stones were part of the normal repertoire of weapons in the ancient world (cf. 2Ch 26:14). Armed only with his shepherd's staff and the five sling stones, David the Israelite shepherd strides forth to do battle with Goliath the Philistine champion.

41–44 Together with his aide carrying a large shield, the huge Goliath must have considered himself invincible. He failed to understand, however, that he and his shield bearer were no match for David and his God. Apparently ignoring David's sling, Goliath perceived that David was coming to fight against him with "sticks." Such weapons, he implied, would be appropriate for beating a "dog," the lowest of animals. He then cursed David "by" his "gods."

45–47 David's responding taunt begins and ends with reference to the ineffectiveness and irrelevance of "sword and spear" when the God of Israel is involved in the battle. David fights Goliath "in the name of" the Lord. Goliath is on perilous ground. He has "defied" (GK 3070) "the armies of Israel," thus defying "the armies of the living God" (v.36; cf. v.10); this is tantamount to defying God himself.

Anxious to get on with the contest, David asserts that Goliath will be killed "this day" and he will "cut off" the giant's head. All who hear will know that the God of Israel is the only true God. In addition, they will know that the Lord, not weapons of war or a human instrument, is the true Deliverer, a fact already understood by Jonathan (14:6). "The battle" belongs to him alone (2Ch 20:15). David concludes by warning that God would give "you" (pl.) into "our" (pl.) hands, thus reminding Goliath of his own earlier intention that their battle was indeed representative warfare, the results of which would have profound implications for the Philistines and Israelites as a whole (vv.8–9).

48–49 Undeterred, Goliath moved closer to "attack" David, who in turn wasted no time in running forward to "meet" him. One sling stone sufficed; it felled the Philistine, who toppled to the ground facedown (cf. 5:4).

50–51a With only a sling and a stone, not with a sword, David vanquished Goliath. As David had earlier "struck ... and killed" wild animals threatening his father's sheep (v.35), so now he "struck down the Philistine and killed him." The actual killing did not take place with an Israelite sword; irony of ironies, David killed Goliath with his own sword.

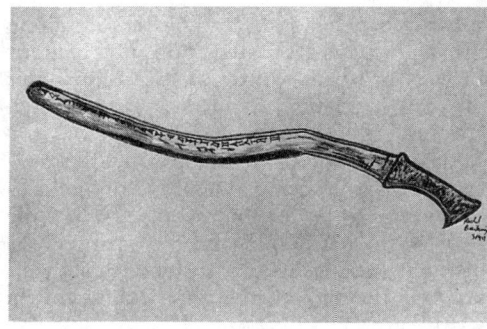

This is a *kophesh* sword, common in the Near East and perhaps similar to the one Goliath used. Drawing by Rachel Bierling.

That David "ran" to the Philistine after felling him indicates that he wanted to kill Goliath before he regained consciousness. As he had promised (v.46), he cut off the Philistine's head (cf. 5:4). Goliath's head was later displayed as a trophy of war (v.54); his sword as well became a battlefield trophy (owned by David; cf. 21:9).

51b–54 The death of Goliath produced panic in the Philistine ranks, and they fled in disorder. Goliath's original defiant challenge of representative warfare was now forgotten or ignored or both. The men of "Israel" and "Judah" set out in hot pursuit, chasing the Philistines all the way to Gath (Goliath's hometown, v.4) and Ekron (about six miles north of Gath).

On returning from the slaughter of the Philistines, the Israelite army plundered the enemy camp. David's role in the plundering operation is perhaps summarized in v.54b, which informs us that he put Goliath's weapons in "his" own tent. He proceeded to put Goliath's head on public display. That he took it to Jerusalem, a city not yet under Israelite control (cf. 2Sa 5:6–10), perhaps was a way of putting the Jebusites on notice that just as the Philistine had fallen victim to David, Jerusalem's demise was only a matter of time. Perhaps under cover of night to avoid detection, David may have affixed Goliath's head to Jerusalem's wall (cf. 31:10).

55–58 The events recorded in v.54 postdate vv.55–58, as v.57 makes clear. Indeed, vv.55–56 synchronize with v.40, while vv.57–58 follow immediately on v.51a. Determined to know who the boy is, Saul says to Abner, "Find out." Abner brought David to Saul, and David identified himself as the son of "Jesse of Bethlehem."

4. The jealousy of Saul (18:1–30)

Up to the events recorded in ch. 18, Saul had apparently been favorably disposed toward David. The scene that unfolds in vv.6–9, however, changed all that.

1–4 Some time after David's conversation with Saul that concludes ch. 17, Saul's son Jonathan entered into a covenant with David. The ambiguous verb "loved" (GK 170) describes the covenantal relationship. That intimate friendship made Saul all the more determined to make David a permanent member of the royal household. The covenant between Jonathan and David was only one of many such agreements made over a long period of time, until David's kingship was firmly established (20:16–17; 23:18; 2Sa 3:13, 21; 5:3). And when Jonathan took off his robe (a symbol of the Israelite kingdom; cf. 15:27–28) and gave it to David, he was in effect transferring his own status as heir apparent to him. Saul had earlier tried to put his tunic and armor on David, but to no avail (17:38–39). Jonathan now gives his own tunic and armor (including a type of belt that was often used to hold a sheathed dagger; cf. 2Sa 20:8) to David, who apparently accepts it without further ado.

5 This verse anticipates and summarizes David's continued successes as a warrior after his victory over Goliath. Having experienced repeated military success himself (14:47), Saul appreciated its importance and honored David accordingly by giving him command over one or more army units. David's skill as a warrior "pleased" all the "people." After David became Israel's king, his ability to please his subjects would continue (2Sa 3:36).

6–8 When David the conquering hero returned to the Israelite camp (17:57) after killing Goliath, and after the Israelite army had defeated their Philistine counterparts (17:52–53), all the troops (including Saul) returned home to be greeted by their fellow countrymen. Such victory celebrations were normally led by women, who came to meet the triumphant warriors with "dancing" accompanied by "tambourines" (cf. Ex 15:20; Jdg 11:34) and "singing" (cf. Ex 15:21; Jdg 5:1). Saul's reaction to the contents of the refrain was not surprising: He became angry (cf. 20:7), assuming that David was receiving ten times more praise than himself. Saul now fears for his kingdom.

9–16 Saul's formerly positive attitude toward his young armor-bearer now became decidedly negative. His paranoia was exacerbated by the frequent arrival of "an evil spirit from God." To bring relief to Saul when an evil spirit was tormenting him, David would play the harp (16:15–16, 23; cf. 19:9).

There would be at least one other time (cf. "twice," v.11) when Saul would try to pin David to the wall with a spear (19:10). Although Jonathan at first could not believe that Saul was determined to kill David (20:9), Saul's attempt to impale even his own son finally convinced him (20:32–33).

Apparently fearful because God was with David but had "left" him (cf. esp. 16:13–14), Saul "sent away" David. He made him commander of a "thousand." His purpose was sinister: He intended to place David at the head of the front rank of troops, where he would be sure to be killed by the Philistines (v.17; cf. 2Sa 11:14–15). David's military exploits, possible only because the Lord was "with him," bound him all the more closely to "Israel and Judah" in covenant relationship. But Saul became increasingly afraid of David.

17–19 As a further means of assuring David's death at the hands of the Philistines, Saul offered him the distraction of his "older daughter Merab" in marriage. But David declined to marry Merab and later became the husband of her younger sister Michal (vv.26–28), although David is never described as loving Michal.

Saul's mandate to David—essentially "be brave and fight"—echoed the common battle cries of those days (cf. 4:9). David had already proven himself to be just the sort of man that Saul was eager to press into service in his army (14:52). His duplicity, however, is evident in his intention to place him in situations that would guarantee his death at the hand of the Philistines.

20–26a Every time either Merab or Michal appears in this chapter, she is referred to as the "daughter" of Saul (vv.17, 19–20, 27–28). David's marriage to one or both could not escape the political implications of their being the daughters of the reigning king: If Saul (and Jonathan) should die, David's claim on the throne of Israel would be all the stronger. In addition, when political marriages were arranged, it was usually the daughter of the ostensibly weaker ruler who married the stronger (cf. Ge 34:9; 1Ki 3:1; 2Ch 18:1). David's relentless climb to Israel's throne was thus proceeding apace.

Michal's "love" for David parallels that of Jonathan (vv.1, 3) and perhaps carries the same covenantal nuances. What is certain is that these two siblings evidence more love to David than to their father.

In spite of David's plea of poverty as an excuse not to marry Michal, Saul would hear none of it. A mere "hundred Philistine foreskins" would suffice as compensation for her. In asking David to kill one hundred Philistines, Saul of course was hoping that David himself would be killed. Saul gave another reason, however, for his demand: that he might "take revenge" on his enemies by decimating them (cf. 14:24; Jdg 15:7). Ironically, David himself has become one of Saul's "enemies" (v.29; cf. also 19:17; 20:13; 24:4, 19; 25:26, 29).

26b–29 David's "men" (first mentioned in v.27) accompany him on this venture. The verbs "went out," "killed," and "brought" are singular in number, stressing David's leadership in fulfilling Saul's demand. "Presented," however, has a plural subject and involves David's men, without whose help he surely would have failed in the overall success. Saul, true to his word, gave his daughter to his enemy. The combination of the evidence of God's help for and presence with David and of Michal's love for David increased Saul's fear of David (cf. v.12), with the result that "he" (Saul) remained "his" (David's) enemy for the rest of his "days" (cf. 23:14).

30 The final verse of ch. 18 repeats the theme of David's success (cf. vv.5, 14–15). He soon proved that he was more than a match for the Philistine commanders; and even when they later joined in common cause against Saul, they would justifiably remain wary of David (29:3–4, 9).

5. David the refugee (19:1–24)

1–7 Although Saul is earlier described as desiring David's permanent residence at the

palace (18:2), ch. 19 records the final break between the two men. Despite being Saul's wise and successful "servant," David is the object, not of the king's delight, but of his murderous intent, asking his servants and even his son Jonathan to find an opportunity to kill David. But Jonathan is "fond of" David and will therefore do everything in his power to save the life of his covenanted friend (cf. 18:1–3).

Jonathan tells David to "go into hiding and stay there." From this time on and for a long period of time, the man after God's own heart would be a hunted fugitive. Jonathan's personal interest in helping David is underscored by his agreement to stand "with" his father as David's advocate (cf. v.4). The venue was the "field" where David was hiding, perhaps not far from Saul's fortress in Gibeah. Jonathan further promised to keep David fully informed (cf. 20:10).

The plea of Jonathan in vv.4–5 begins and ends with his hope that Saul would not "do wrong to" David, especially since the latter had not "wronged" the king (cf. also 24:11). Jonathan further reminds his father that David's deeds have helped Saul, that David "took his life in his hands" in Goliath's challenge, and that Saul himself had been pleased with the outcome (17:55–58). There is therefore no reason to kill "an innocent man," and such a crime could only bring bloodguilt on Saul (Dt 21:8–9).

Jonathan's rebuke of his father brought him to his senses, at least temporarily: He "listened to" Jonathan and took the most solemn of all oaths (cf. 14:39), promising that David would not be put to death—a promise that he quickly forgot (v.11). In the meantime, however, David was once again made a member of Saul's court in good standing (cf. 16:21; 18:2).

8–10 David's continued military success against the Philistines evoked the repetition of a familiar scene (see 16:14, 16; 18:10–11).

11–17 Tradition claims vv.11–17 as the original setting of Ps 59. Although the mission of Saul's men was to kill David "in the morning," God's strength and love preserved him "in the morning" (Ps 59:16).

The human agent assuring David's rescue was Michal, his loving wife (18:20, 28). After warning him to flee the home they shared, she helped him escape by lowering him "through a window" (cf. Jos 2:15; 2Co 11:33). To give David time to put sufficient distance between himself and his pursuers, Michal fashioned a crude dummy to take his place in his bed. She further stalled for time by telling Saul's men that her husband was ill, thus implying that they should not disturb him.

Michal's dummy is described as "an idol," a Hebrew word that is usually translated "household gods" (GK 9572). Since these gods are presumably always small (Ge 31:19, 34–35; et al.), the dummy was almost certainly not a single, man-sized idol. Michal probably piled clothing, carpets, or the like on David's bed and covered it with a garment, allowing only goats' hair at the head to show. She did not place the household idols "in" the bed but "beside" it, to enhance the impression of David's illness.

Michal's ruse worked to perfection; Saul's men were deceived. Saul, however, not satisfied with their report, sent his men back for another look, this time with orders to "bring [David] up" to Gibeah, bed and all, so that he might be killed there. By the time they arrived, of course, David was long gone.

In v.5 Saul's son asks him "why" he would want to kill David, and in v.17 Saul asks his daughter "why" she would "deceive" him and keep David from being killed. Michal tells Saul that David had warned her that if she did not let him flee he would kill her. Saul's own words identify David as his mortal "enemy" (cf. 18:29), barring forever his return to Saul's court at Gibeah. David's days as an outlaw, now begun in earnest, would continue until Saul's death.

18–24 Verse 18 reverts to the time when David had escaped after Michal's warning (v.12). He went to Ramah, Samuel's hometown, to inform the prophet about what Saul had done. Saul heard where David was and, in relentless pursuit, sends men to Naioth to capture him. The Spirit of God, however, protects David by causing three successive contingents of Saul's messengers to prophesy under a divinely induced trance (see 10:5).

Finally realizing that his men were not going to apprehend David, Saul took matters into his own hands by going to Ramah himself. As soon as he found out the exact whereabouts of Samuel and David, Saul continued on his way and began "prophesying" him-

self, after receiving an accession of the Spirit of God. His laying aside of his robe is symbolic of his rule, demonstrating once again his forfeiture of any claim to be Israel's king.

In addition, the rhetorical question demanding a negative answer—"Is Saul also among the prophets?"—underscores that forfeiture and thus takes an ironic twist: To question the genuineness of Saul's prophetic behavior was to question his legitimacy as king of Israel. The use of this proverb in 10:11–12 and now here brackets the narrative descriptions of Saul's first and last encounters with Samuel as well as with the Spirit of God. Neither legitimate king nor genuine prophet, Saul continues to stumble toward his doom at the hands of the Philistines, when he will be "stripped" of his garments for the last time (31:8–9).

6. Jonathan's friendship (20:1–42)

1–4 David's flight from Saul at Naioth takes him back to the Gibeah fortress and to his friend Jonathan, the only one he can trust. David wants to know the nature of the terrible sin he has supposedly committed that would bring on such frantic pursuit of him. Jonathan, trusting son as well as loyal friend, thought it incredible that Saul really intended to harm David (vv.2, 9; cf. also Saul's oath in 19:6)—until it became painfully obvious to him (v.33). Jonathan encouraged David by assuring him that Saul did nothing without "confiding in me."

David, however—more sensitive to Saul's unpredictability and changes of mood—responds by suggesting that he go and hide in the field. He swears with the most solemn of oaths that there is "only a step" between him and death at the hands of Saul. David affirms that Saul, who knows of the high regard in which Jonathan holds David (cf. v.29), does not want his son to know of his evil designs on David's life or he would be "grieved."

5–7 David's plan is simple: If Saul accepts Jonathan's explanation for David's absence from the forthcoming New Moon festival celebration, then David is safe; but if Saul becomes angry, then Jonathan will know that Saul is bent on harming David. David would hide in a "field" (near Saul's fortress in Gibeah) until the evening of the third day, by which time he would presumably expect to receive word from Jonathan concerning

Saul's reaction toward his absence from the festival.

David's excuse for not attending is relayed by Jonathan to Saul in vv.28–29. David's desire to participate in an "annual sacrifice" with his family would not have been considered unusual (1:21; 2:19). During Samuel's boyhood days the normal venue was Shiloh (1:3), the site of the tabernacle. By David's time, however, Shiloh had been destroyed (see 4:11), and the tabernacle had no fixed location. Thus it was only to be expected that annual sacrifices would be offered in the celebrants' hometowns.

Understandably, David was risking Saul's wrath by pretending to substitute a competing festival for the one the king had invited him to. David surely was not serious in asserting that Saul's ready agreement to allow him to go to Bethlehem would mean that he would then be back in the king's good graces. David knew that Saul was determined to kill him; and although Jonathan had not yet brought himself to admit that cold fact (vv.9, 13), he soon would (v.33).

8–17 Reminding Jonathan of the covenant that they had made (18:3), David asks him to demonstrate covenant loyalty ("kindness"; GK 2876). David voiced his preference for dying at the hand of his covenanted friend Jonathan instead of his sworn enemy Saul. But Jonathan avowed that if he had "the least inkling" that his father intended to harm David, he would surely tell his friend. David, still wary, wants to know whether Jonathan would really tell him if Saul answered "harshly."

David and Jonathan went to the field "together," using the privacy the field afforded to reaffirm their undying loyalty. In accord with David's wishes to learn of Saul's response by "the evening of the day after tomorrow" (v.5), Jonathan promises on oath to send David word no later than that time—whether the news is favorable or unfavorable. In Jonathan's closing statement, he acknowledges David's divine calling and recognizes that David, not he himself, will be the next king of Israel.

Jonathan has David reaffirm his side of the covenant they have made. Covenant friendship is the basis of Jonathan's plea that neither he nor his descendants be executed by David after he becomes king. By now

Jonathan surely perceives that among David's "enemies" is his own father, Saul (cf. 18:29; 19:17). Thus Jonathan extends in perpetuity his previous covenant with David to his house/family/descendants.

18–23 Jonathan's suggested ruse begins by echoing the time and place of the venue that David had originally proposed (v.5). He agrees that David will be "missed" because his seat will be "empty." On the third day David is to go to the field where he was hiding. There he is to "wait" by a stone called Ezel. Jonathan then goes on to explain how the message of Saul's reaction to David's absence will be communicated. If the arrows are beyond where the boy is at the time of Jonathan's shout, then David's life is in danger, and he must flee in response to the will of "the LORD."

24–34 Playing out the charade to humor his friend, David hid in the field. When the celebrants gathered for the New Moon festival, Saul took his customary seat "by the wall," where he could feel relatively secure from surprise attack. Jonathan and Abner, Saul's army commander (and cousin) (14:50; 17:55), occupied places of honor at the table, but David's place was "empty" (as Jonathan and David had planned, v.18).

When David did not appear on the first day of the New Moon festival, Saul assumed that something had happened to make him "ceremonially unclean" (cf. Lev 15:16, 18) and therefore disqualified from participating in a religious feast (cf. Nu 9:6). But when David's seat was empty on the second day also, Saul naturally wanted to know why. In referring to David as the "son of Jesse" (cf. also 22:7–9, 13, and esp. 25:10), Saul probably intended at least a mild insult.

Jonathan responded to Saul's question essentially as he and David had discussed. As David had feared (v.7), Saul became violently angry when Jonathan told him the reason for David's absence. For all intents and purposes, Jonathan and David were indistinguishable to Saul as he exploded. Saul curses Jonathan by a vile epithet hurled at his son. He accuses Jonathan of having "sided with" David, and that not only to his own shame but also the shame of the "mother who bore you."

Saul further reminded Jonathan that so long as David remained alive, neither Jonathan nor Jonathan's kingdom could survive. History would prove Saul's fears to be prophetic beyond his worst nightmares: Although the kingdom of Saul and his son would not be established (13:13–14), the kingdom of David and his son would be (2Sa 7:16, 26; 1Ki 2:12, 46).

Saul's demand for David's death brings a predictable response from Jonathan: "Why?" (cf. 19:5). Saul, though placated before (19:6), would not be denied this time. Not having David as his target, Saul tried to pin David's surrogate Jonathan to the wall with his spear. Jonathan needed no further convincing that Saul indeed intended to kill David (cf. v.7) and that the spear had really been meant for his covenanted friend. In Saul's eyes, Jonathan and David had momentarily become one.

It was Jonathan's turn to fly into a rage. Knowing of his father's murderous designs on and mistreatment of David caused Jonathan to be "grieved" (GK 6772; see David's statement in v.3). On the second day of the New Moon festival, neither David nor Jonathan ate at the king's table (vv.29, 34).

35–40 Jonathan had told David to wait by the stone Ezel on the second day of the New Moon festival "toward evening" (v.19). The boy Jonathan takes with him (vv.21–22) is "small" and thus less likely to ask embarrassing questions about the orders he is given.

Jonathan tells the boy to find the "arrows" he shoots; but, since his aim is true, he discovers that he needs to shoot only one "arrow." The arrow's landing beyond the running lad, loudly confirmed by Jonathan so that David would be sure to hear it, was a signal to David that it was God's will for him to remain a fugitive from Saul (v.22). After the boy retrieved the arrow, Jonathan sent him back to town with all the weapons, assuming (and doubtless hoping) that David might want a private moment to bid his friend farewell.

41–42 Getting up from his hiding place near "the stone," David bowed down more than once to acknowledge Jonathan's (covenant) superiority. Jonathan's "Go in peace" reflects the "safe(ly)" of vv.7, 13, 21 and is generally spoken by a superior to an inferior (cf. 1:17; 25:35). At the same time Jonathan magnanimously uses the emphatic "we" as he reminds David of their mutual and everlasting oath of friendship (cf. vv.17, 23), sworn "in the name of the LORD." The covenant between Jonathan and David included their "descendants forever" (cf. v.15; cf. also 24:21).

The two friends parted after Jonathan's farewell speech. Apart from one other brief meeting (23:16–18), this was the last time they would see each other.

7. David and the priest of Nob (21:1–9)

Chapters 21–22 apparently record events later than those in the preceding chapters since by this time David has gathered around him a sizable body of "men" (21:2, 4–5; 22:6) and has become their "leader" (22:2).

1–6 David, needing help in his continued flight from Saul, went to Nob, where there was a large contingent of priests (22:11, 18–19); it may have been the location of the tabernacle. Ahimelech, one of the more prominent of Nob's priests and mentioned several times in these chapters, "trembled" when he "met" David, thus fearing his reputation and perhaps also recognizing his authority (cf. 16:4).

Ahimelech's two questions—"Why are you alone?" and "Why is no one with you?"—may seem to be saying much the same thing, but David answers them separately. He is alone because there is a secret matter that he wishes to discuss with the priest, and his men are not with him because he will meet them later.

David next asks Ahimelech two questions (vv.3, 8), each of which is followed by the priest's answer (vv.4, 9a) and then David's response (vv.5, 9b). The first question is, "What do you have on hand?" David follows it up with a request: "Give me five loaves of bread"—a modest amount at best (cf. 17:17).

Echoing David's request, Ahimelech tells him what he has and does not have "on hand": No "ordinary" bread is available, but "there is" some "consecrated" (lit., "holy") bread that David and his men may eat. There was a condition, however: The men must not recently have had sexual relations with women, which would have rendered them ceremonially unclean (Ex 19:14–15; Lev 15:18) and therefore temporarily unfit to partake of the holy food. David assured Ahimelech that women had indeed been "kept" from himself and his men, and they are thus clean.

Satisfied with David's rationale, Ahimelech gives him this bread of the (divine) "Presence." Such bread, after it had performed its symbolic function, became "a most holy part" of the customary share given to the priests, who were to eat it in a "holy" place (Lev 24:9). Since priestly perquisites were for priests and their families only (cf. Ex 29:32–33; Lev 22:10–16), how could Ahimelech in good conscience give the consecrated bread to David and his men, who were not priests? The answer provided by Jesus (Mt 12:1–8; Mk 2:23–28; Lk 6:1–5) seems to be that human need may take precedence over ceremonial law.

7 Doeg the Edomite, perhaps a mercenary pressed into service as a result of Saul's war(s) against Edom (14:47), is introduced parenthetically in anticipation of his sinister role later (22:18–19). He had been detained "before the LORD" (i.e., at the tabernacle). His official role in Saul's employ was as his "head shepherd."

8–9 David's request for bread (v.3) is followed by one for weapons. What is not in his own hand he hopes is in Ahimelech's. The urgency of the "king's business" is David's excuse for his lack of weapons. As in v.2, the identity of the king remains shrouded in studied ambiguity.

The only weapon Ahimelech has to offer to David is the sword of Goliath, whom—as was apparently widely known—David had killed (cf. 17:2, 19, 48–51). Although he first took the giant's sword as part of his share of the Philistine plunder (17:54), he must have eventually brought it to the sanctuary of the Lord. Ahimelech thus tells David that it is in a storage place behind the "ephod," where David can find it protected in a "cloth" (cf. Ex 12:34; Jdg 8:25).

8. David the fugitive: Gath, Adullam, Mizpah (21:10–22:5)

10–15 Immediately after departing from Nob with the sword of Goliath, David went to Gath (ironically Goliath's hometown, 17:4), possibly to seek employment as a mercenary soldier. The king of Gath was Achish son of Maoch (27:2). Whatever David's intentions in going to Gath, the "servants" of Achish were sufficiently impressed by David's reputation—as reflected in the ditty composed after he and Saul had defeated the Philistines

(18:7; cf. 29:4–5)—to be wary of him. David took the servants' words seriously. Having fled "from" Saul, he was now very much afraid "of" Achish. Sensing danger, David extricates himself from the situation by feigning madness. The manifestations of David's pretended insanity were "making marks" on the doors of the (city) gate and letting saliva run down his beard—hardly the picture of a recently anointed king!

Achish has seen enough. Sarcastically declaring that he already has sufficient madmen of his own, he makes it clear that he wants nothing more to do with this Israelite refugee. David's deception of Achish worked—as it would again (ch. 27) and again (ch. 29).

22:1–2 Leaving Gath David "escaped" (a reference to his continuing flight from Saul; cf. 27:1) to a cave near Adullam. His brothers and other family members went "down" (presumably from the higher ground at Bethlehem, their hometown) to join him there. They may have feared royal reprisal if they remained in Bethlehem, where Saul would be sure to come looking for the fugitive David.

Those who had gathered around David numbered about "four hundred" (in itself a formidable force; cf. 25:13; 30:10, 17) even in the beginning; the ranks of David's men eventually swelled to as many as six hundred (23:13; 27:2; 30:9). United by adverse circumstances of all sorts, they were attracted to the charismatic David as their "leader" (GK 8569; cf. 2Sa 4:2; 1Ki 11:24). Such bands of malcontents and other social misfits were not uncommon in the ancient Near East (cf. Jdg 9:4; 11:3).

3–5 The "forest of Hereth" was located on one of the heights of the tableland east of the Dead Sea. It was understandable that David should seek refuge for his "father and mother" in Moab (which he would later conquer, 2Sa 8:2), since Moabite blood flowed through the veins of his ancestors on his great-grandmother's side (Ru 1:4; 4:13, 16–17). In being solicitous of the needs of his parents, David was following common ancient practice (Jos 2:13, 18; 6:23; 1Ki 19:20) as well as obeying the fifth commandment (Ex 20:12; Dt 5:16). The location of David's "stronghold" is unknown, though it could not have been the Cave of Adullam since that "stronghold" was not in Judah. David's true stronghold, of course, was ultimately God himself (2Sa 22:2–3).

As the prophet Samuel had helped and advised Saul, so from now on "the prophet Gad," among others, would perform the same functions for David (cf. 2Sa 24:11). It was through such prophets that the word of God was mediated to Israel's leaders during the days of the monarchy.

9. The slaughter of the priests of Nob (22:6–23)

6–8 Saul knew both David's whereabouts and the identity of the men with him. They "had been discovered." Saul demands of his fellow Benjamites an answer to the question of whether the "son of Jesse" can provide for them more possessions and privileges than they already have as associates of Saul himself. Would David be able to make them "commanders of thousands and commanders of hundreds" (which, if true, would mean that David had become king; cf. 8:12)? After all, David himself was merely a "leader" of a few hundred men.

In his paranoia Saul assumes that all his men—indeed, the priest Ahimelech as well (v.13)—are co-conspirators with David against him. Saul complains that no one "tells" him about his son Jonathan's perceived acts of treachery: making a covenant with David (cf. 18:3; 20:16) and inciting David to ambush Saul. All this, Saul insists, demonstrates his servants' lack of concern for their master.

9–10 Like Saul's officials (v.6), Doeg the Edomite was "standing" near him. Imitating Saul's reference (v.7) to David as the (despised) "son of Jesse," Doeg informs Saul that he witnessed David's meeting with Ahimelech, "son of Ahitub" (see 14:3), at Nob (see 21:7) and intimates that Ahimelech had "inquired" of the Lord for David, a fact not mentioned in 21:1–9 but readily admitted to by the priest (v.15). In addition, Doeg continues, Ahimelech gave David "provisions" and "the sword of Goliath the Philistine." Doeg is suggesting that Ahimelech was committing treasonable acts by assisting Saul's enemy.

11–17 Doeg's report to Saul resulted in the king's sending for Ahitub's "whole" priestly family, who "all" responded by coming from Nob to Gibeah, scarcely two miles to the northwest. Upon their arrival Saul addressed Ahimelech in words that echo vv.7–8. In response Ahimelech's "Yes, my lord" is appropriately servile and obedient.

Saul's retort combines the elements of Doeg's report in v.10 and the substance of his own accusations against his officials in v.8. But whereas Saul was of the opinion that his men had conspired among themselves, he insists that Ahimelech is overtly in league with his enemy David. Ahimelech's response to Saul is polite but firm. He defends David's character by suggesting that none of the king's servants is as "loyal" as David (cf. 2:35). After all, David is Saul's "son-in-law" (cf. 18:18). In addition, he is the captain of Saul's "bodyguard" (cf. 2Sa 23:23) and "highly respected" (cf. 9:6).

Having evaluated David's reputation positively to his own satisfaction, Ahimelech emphatically denies that this was the first time he had consulted God on David's behalf. Ahimelech claims to know nothing at all of the crimes that Saul attributes to David. Believing Ahimelech to be a liar, however, Saul tells him that he and his family "will surely die" (cf. 14:39, 44).

Saul then issues orders for the execution of the priests of Nob. He first commands the "guards" at his side to kill them for their failure to tell Saul about David's whereabouts and perhaps also for being in league with David. But Saul's orders fall on deaf ears, thwarted by the religious scruples of his officials. The officials are adamant: They are "not willing" to kill the Lord's priests.

18–19 When Saul, not to be denied, issues his ominous order to Doeg, the doom of the priests is sealed. An Edomite, Doeg has no qualms about massacring Israelite priests. Not satisfied with killing the eighty-five priests of Nob, Doeg extends the slaughter by putting the entire town "to the sword" (cf. the similar threat against Jerusalem in 2Sa 15:14). The doleful list of victims at the end of the verse recalls once again the contrast to Saul's earlier reluctance to totally destroy the Amalekites (see 15:3). David's response to this massacre is found in Ps 52.

20–23 Probably unknown to Saul at the time, one son of Ahimelech, Abiathar, "escaped" and joined David's fugitive band. He performed priestly functions for David for the rest of David's life (cf. 23:6, 9; 30:7; 2Sa 8:17), eventually to be replaced by Zadok under Solomon's reign (1Ki 2:27, 35). When he informs David about Saul's massacre, David tells him that he had anticipated Doeg's act of betrayal ever since their earlier encounter at Nob (cf. 21:7). David then confesses that he himself, however unwittingly, is ultimately accountable for the massacre. He therefore offers refuge to Abiathar, telling him not to "be afraid" (cf. 23:17). Saul now seeks the life of both of them; so they become partners in flight. King-elect and priest-elect have joined forces as fellow fugitives.

10. The rescue of Keilah (23:1–6)

1–6 The Philistine threat returns to menace a town in Judah. Just as Saul had saved Israel from "those who had plundered" them (see 14:48), so also David would save the people of Keilah from the Philistines who were "looting" their threshing floors, which often served as storage areas (2Ki 6:27; Joel 2:24).

David's repeated inquiries to God concerning whether he should go to Keilah and attack the Philistines are reminiscent of similar inquiries and responses during the period of the judges (Jdg 20:23, 28). Such inquiries usually made use of the sacred lots, the Urim and Thummim, stored in the priestly ephod (cf. v.6). When David's men learned that the Lord had responded affirmatively to his first inquiry, they demurred out of fear.

David therefore inquired of the Lord again, and this time God told him that he himself would guarantee David's victory over the Philistines. The promise of divine help apparently reassured David's men, who then joined him in defeating the enemy. Thus David "saved" the people of Keilah, as God had commanded and promised. Once again, the Lord chooses not the rejected king Saul but the fugitive king-elect to deliver his people from the Philistines.

11. The pursuit of David (23:7–29)

In contrast to David's seeking and receiving divine guidance, which brings him victory (vv.1–6), Saul relies totally on human messages and reports (cf. vv.7, 13, 19, 25, 27), which bring him frustration and failure (vv.7–29).

7–13 Whether sincerely or in a false display of piety, Saul affirms that God has "handed" David over to him (cf. v.20). Saul assumes

that David is trapped, that he has "imprisoned himself" in a walled town from which there may be only one exit. Preparing to attack David at Keilah, Saul "called up" his troops.

David soon found out about the evil that Saul was "plotting" against him. He therefore told Abiathar to bring the ephod so that he might use the Urim and Thummim to inquire of the Lord (cf. vv.1–6; 30:7–8). David begins and concludes his plea with the words "O LORD, God of Israel," acknowledging the Lord as the true Sovereign of his people. He expresses his concern that Saul "plans" to destroy Keilah because of him.

Although David asks two questions, the Lord answers only the second one. David therefore repeats the first one, this time expressing his concern for the safety of his men also. The Lord now answers it as well. That the citizens of Keilah would even think of surrendering their deliverer and his men to Saul might seem like the height of ingratitude, but perhaps they feared royal retribution if they harbored fugitives. In any case, David and his men leave Keilah and frequently change their location. Although since the last count (22:2) the number of his men has increased to "about six hundred" (cf. also 25:13; 27:2; 30:9), David understandably feels that they are still no match for Saul and his army (cf. 24:2). For his part, Saul changes his mind about going to Keilah when he learns that the fugitives have left.

14–24a Knowing that Saul was relentlessly continuing his search for him, David hid in various "strongholds" in the Desert of Ziph and elsewhere. In spite of God's gracious and providential care, David was afraid, because Saul came out to take his life (cf. 20:1; 22:23). So Saul's son Jonathan went to Horesh to remind David of the Lord's concern for him and to encourage him. Jonathan said, "Don't be afraid, because" Saul will not "lay a hand on you."

Jonathan vigorously continues to encourage David: "You will be king," while "I will be second to you"—an inevitable truth that Saul also knows. "The two of them"—as equals—then make a covenant in the presence of the Lord, perhaps invoking his blessing and taking an oath in his name. It is better to understand this covenant as a fresh, bilateral covenant defining their new relationship (see 18:3) rather than simply renewing their previous covenant. Having comforted his friend, Jonathan returns home to Gibeah—perhaps never to see David again.

Certain "Ziphites" go to Gibeah and reveal David's whereabouts, perhaps to ingratiate themselves to Saul (cf. the title of Ps 54, whose traditional setting is the narrative in vv.19–24a). The Ziphites invite Saul to come to them "whenever it pleases you," at which time they promise to hand David over to him.

Saul's reply to the Ziphites, "The LORD bless you," is a stereotyped expression that tells nothing about his piety (or lack of it; see v.7). Always the investigator relying on human ability, Saul tells the Ziphites to "find out" (cf. 14:38; lit., "know and see") where David usually hides. David will later hurl Saul's phrase back at him (24:11) in protestation of his own innocence.

Saul is determined to track David down no matter where he goes or what it takes; he will not permit the "crafty" David to outwit him. The Ziphites are to pinpoint every potential hiding place that David might use and then report back to Saul "with definite information." Obedient to their presumed overlord, they return to Ziph and begin to search for David and his men.

24b–29 On the run as usual (v.13), David and his men go to "the Desert of Maon, in the Arabah south of Jeshimon." Like the Desert of Ziph (see v.14), the Desert of Maon was named for a town that had been allotted to Judah in the hill country west of the Dead Sea after Joshua's conquest of Canaan (Jos 15:48, 55).

Upon hearing that Saul had once again embarked on his relentless "search" for him (cf. v.14), David retreated with his men to "the rock" in the Desert of Maon. Informed of this (probably by the Ziphites), Saul pursued his quarry. He probably divided "his forces" into two groups so that they could attack both flanks of David's men "on the other side" of the mountain, thus "closing in" on them. Although David had been able to "get away" from Saul on several occasions (cf. 18:11; 19:10), it appears that this time all was lost—at least from a human standpoint. Providentially, however, a messenger arrived with the unsettling news that Philistines were raiding part of Saul's sovereign territory. Sensing a greater threat from the Philistines,

Saul had no choice but to postpone his pursuit of David. The "rock" therefore was called "Sela Hammahlekoth," "The rock of parting," apparently referring to the timely retreat of Saul's men from David's men on that occasion.

God used the distraction of Philistines, rather than the aid of Ziphites or other Judahites, to rescue David from the tentacles of Saul. For his part David moved himself and his men to strongholds in the vicinity of the En Gedi oasis (cf. SS 1:14; Eze 47:10, 18–19; 48:28).

12. Sparing Saul's life (24:1–22)

1–7 On a previous occasion when the Israelites "returned from chasing the Philistines," they plundered their camp (17:53). This time, after Saul "returned from pursuing the Philistines" (cf. 23:28), he was told about David's general location and set out with "three thousand chosen men" (see also 26:2) that outnumbered David's motley band five to one. The term "chosen men" (GK 1047) refers to warriors who were especially skilled (Jdg 20:16) and courageous (Jdg 20:34).

David hid in a cave in En Gedi, perhaps in Crags of the Wild Goats—a lush area with waterfalls, surrounded by the Judean desert.

The "sheep pens" Saul came to probably consisted of one or more enclosures made of low stone walls flanking the entrance to a cave. Thus Saul would have entered the pens to gain access to the cave. His purpose in going into the cave was to "relieve himself" (cf. Dt 23:12–13; Jdg 3:24).

Unknown to Saul, David and his men were "far back in" that very cave; compare Pss 57 and 142 in this connection. In both psalms David cries out for divine "mercy" (57:1; 142:1), and in both he affirms that the Lord, not the cave, is his true "refuge" (57:1; 142:5).

David's men see in the presence of Saul inside the cave a golden opportunity to get rid of him once and for all: David now has a chance to eliminate his "enemy" (vv.4, 19; see also 18:29). Out of respect for Saul's divine anointing, and therefore not willing to kill him, but at the same time wanting to let him know that he was not in control of his own destiny, David crept up behind him "unnoticed." In cutting off the corner of Saul's robe, David may have been symbolically depriving Saul of his royal authority and transferring it to himself (cf. v.11).

That David was "conscience-stricken" for what he had done is to be understood as recognition on his part that he had sinned (cf. 2Sa 24:10). Using a solemn oath, David—himself also the Lord's anointed—affirms to his men that he will never do harm to his master Saul, who is "the LORD's anointed" (used seven times in chs. 24 and 26).

8–15 The brief *apologia* of David recorded here should be compared with that of Samuel (ch. 12) in terms of persuasive power. Moreover, David's speech is echoed at the end of ch. 26, where it functions in much the same way as that of Samuel, serving as a kind of farewell speech to Israel's king. After Saul left the cave (v.7), David, after a short time, himself emerged and "called out" to Saul (the verb often implies physical distance between sender and receiver, as in 20:37; GK 7924). Addressing Saul as his acknowledged superior, David "bowed down and prostrated himself with his face to the ground" (cf. 28:14).

David begins his protestation and defense with a "Why?" He assures Saul that he is not intent on "harming" him, nor is he guilty of "wrongdoing." Unlike those who spread false rumors about his murderous plans, David refuses to listen to all who would incite him to vengeance against Saul. Indeed, the king himself knows that David has just now had a unique opportunity to kill him, but David has refused to seize it.

Pressing his advantage, David says to Saul, "See . . . look . . . recognize." When he addresses Saul as "my father," he is probably not simply using a term of respect but is reminding the king that he is, after all, Saul's son-in-law (cf. 18:17–27; 22:14) and thus holds him in high regard (Saul will later respond to David as "my son," v.16).

Continuing to protest his innocence, David wants Saul to "understand and recognize" that he is not guilty of "wrongdoing," a plea that he will repeat later (26:18). David reminds Saul that he has not "wronged" him (cf. also Jonathan's strong objections to his father in 19:4). There is therefore no reason, says David, that Saul should be "hunting" him down. Unwilling to submit their dispute to human arbitration, David invokes the help of the Lord, the only fair and impartial Judge (cf. Jdg 11:27). But no matter what happens, David assures his king, "My hand will not touch you."

David concludes his apology by entreating the Lord to decide between himself and Saul. Confident of the outcome, David affirms his belief that the Lord will "uphold" his "cause" against Saul, using a phrase that he would use again after the death of Nabal, Saul's alter ego (25:39). He prays to the Lord to "vindicate me [by delivering me] from" Saul (v.15).

16–22 It is no more necessary to deny Saul's sincerity here than in 26:21, 25. In each case Saul begins with the plaintive "Is that your voice, David my son?" (v.16; 26:17; cf. also 26:21, 25). Saul, distressed and conscience-stricken, "wept aloud" when confronted by David's innocence. Saul says to his son-in-law David, "You are more righteous than I." He then draws a contrast between David's exemplary conduct and his own deplorable actions. David has treated Saul "well." Saul admits that what David has done to him is "good," and Saul desires that the Lord will reward David "well" for what he has done, since no one ever lets his enemy get away "unharmed." Saul admits to David, "I have treated you badly."

Saul's recognition that the Lord had "delivered" (GK 6037) him into David's hands is later echoed by Abishai (26:8). Understanding that David has every right not to let his "enemy" (cf. v.4) get away, Saul—with words reminiscent of Boaz's to Ruth (Ru 2:12)—prays that God will reward David richly for what he has done.

Earlier Samuel had told Saul that, because of his rebellion against God, his "kingdom" would not endure but would be given to a man after God's own heart (13:14). Now Saul emphatically acknowledges that David will be ruler over the "kingdom" of Israel (cf. also 15:28; 18:8; 23:17).

Like Jonathan before him, Saul is concerned that David not "cut off" his "descendants." And as David had sworn that he would show unfailing kindness to Jonathan and his family (20:14–17), so now he swears that he will not harm Saul's offspring or wipe out his name. Having secured David's oath, Saul returns to Gibeah. David, however, wisely continues to distrust Saul and therefore retreats to his "stronghold" (see 22:4–5).

13. David, Nabal, and Abigail (25:1–44)

1a Loved and respected by his people, Samuel was mourned by them at his death (cf. 28:3). Notices of the burials of Samuel and Saul in v.1 and 31:13 frame the final seven chapters of the book.

1b–3 The difference in social status between David and Nabal becomes immediately apparent: David "moved down" to the "Desert of Maon," but he told his men to "go up" (v.5) to Nabal at "Carmel." Like David's later friend Barzillai (2Sa 19:32), Nabal was very "wealthy." Sheepshearing was a time for celebration (cf. 2Sa 13:23–24).

The contrast between Nabal (meaning "fool") and his wife Abigail (meaning "My [Divine] Father is joy") could scarcely be more stark. Not only "beautiful" (GK 3637 & 9307; cf. Ge 29:17; Est 2:7), Abigail was also "intelligent" (GK 3202 & 8507). Nabal, however, was "mean" (GK 8273)—and thus a polarity between "good" and "evil" is set up at the beginning of ch. 25. Together they underscore one of the major themes of the story: Good brings its own reward, while evil recoils on the head of the wicked.

The beautiful and intelligent Abigail, though mismatched with Nabal, is a perfect match for David, whose commendable qualities complement hers (cf. 16:12, 18). In all respects she is David's equal. In fact, she should perhaps be identified with one of David's two sisters, the only other Abigail mentioned in the Bible (1Ch 2:15–16). At the same time, since David was the son of Jesse, Abigail would then have been only his half sister, which would have made it possible for him to marry her (v.42; cf. Ge 20:12). If the two Abigails are thus identified, her first husband would have been Jether (2Sa 17:25; 1Ch 2:17)—perhaps Nabal's real name.

4–13 After hearing that Nabal is shearing sheep, David sends ten young men to him. David's message to Nabal begins by telling them to "greet him" in David's name (i.e., as his representative). They are instructed to wish him "well-being/welfare/peace/good health" (GK 8934). David continues in his persuasive tone as he seeks a favor from Nabal. He senses that sheep shearing time would put Nabal in a good mood, because it is a "festive" occasion. Utilizing the ancient equivalent of the protection racket, David observes that his men did not mistreat Nabal's shepherds or steal anything from them, perhaps implying that there were plenty of opportunities to do so (see also vv.14–16). David's concern for the welfare of Nabal's shepherds had in fact extended over a long period of time.

David's request that Nabal should "be favorable toward my young men" is the epitome of courtesy. He is simply requesting for himself and his men "whatever" supplies (primarily food; cf. v.11) Nabal might be willing to give them, since they depend on the generosity of others for the protection they provide (v.16).

Arriving in Carmel, David's men act as faithful messengers by reporting to Nabal David's message. Nabal's repeated "Who?" is uttered with scorn, like that of David with respect to Goliath (17:26). Nabal also uses "son of Jesse" in an insulting and belittling way, as did Saul before him. In so doing Nabal rejects David's courteous reference to himself as Nabal's "son."

Nabal's contention that "many servants are breaking away from their masters these days" is at least double-edged and perhaps even triple-edged. (1) He may be referring to David, who is fleeing from his master Saul;

(2) he may be subtly suggesting to David's servants that they would be well advised to break away from their master; and (3), ironically, he speaks better than he knows, since he will shortly find himself as a master whose servants break away (cf. vv.14–17). Nabal is even unwilling to give to David and his men "bread and water," the most basic food and drink (Nu 21:5; Dt 9:9, 18; 1Ki 13:8–9, 16–17)—much less the meat he had slaughtered for his workers.

Upon receiving Nabal's response, David's men "turned" (GK 2200) and reported back to David. His immediate reaction was to retaliate by arming himself and his men with swords—a poignant contrast to his earlier repudiation of the sword before his contest with Goliath (17:39, 45, 47). Splitting his six hundred men into two groups of unequal size, David sets out for Carmel with four hundred and leaves the rest behind with the "supplies."

14–19 Nabal's servant describes to Abigail the shoddy treatment David's men received at Nabal's hands. He especially stresses the physical proximity of Nabal's shepherds to David's men ("near them") during "the whole time" they were in the fields. Like the fortress "wall" enclosing a city, the protection provided by David and his men continued around the clock. The servant concludes his appeal by observing that no one can talk to Nabal, implying that perhaps his wife Abigail may be able to persuade him of the folly of his ways. Otherwise, disaster may happen.

Abigail's response to the servant's report was a "gift" (lit., "blessing," v.27; GK 1388) of substantial proportions for David. Nabal's sloth is more than compensated for by Abigail's speed in meeting David's needs. She "lost no time," she acted "quickly" by supplying him with "two hundred loaves of bread" in addition to large amounts of other provisions. "Cakes of raisins" and "cakes of pressed figs" were especially prized, not only for their sweetness and nutritive value, but also because they could be kept for some time without spoiling (cf. 30:1, 11–12).

20–31 Having sent her servants ahead with the provisions for David and his men, Abigail follows on a donkey, a common means of transportation in ancient times (Ex 4:20; Jos 15:18). She intercepts David near a mountain "ravine," an out-of-the-way place reminding us that he is still a hunted fugitive. David was feeling cheated by Nabal's action (or inaction). Although guaranteeing that none of his property was "missing" (cf. also vv.7, 15), David has been "paid . . . back evil for good." He was intending to retaliate by killing every male in Nabal's household by daybreak—although he later expresses his gratitude that the Lord (and Abigail) kept him from doing so (vv.33–34).

In preparation for responding at some length to David's threat against her husband and in contrast to Nabal's treatment of David and his men (vv.10–11), Abigail bows down respectfully before him. Her speech is a masterpiece of rhetoric, appealing not only to reason and the emotions, but also to her own credibility. Beginning with a formal introduction and ending with a formal conclusion, the main body of the speech treats matters of the past, present, and future.

Riding alone to meet a band of four hundred armed men bent on violence, the defenseless Abigail knows that she has very little time to change their minds. She immediately demonstrates an attitude of submission to David, referring to him as "my master" in every verse of her speech and to herself as "your servant" in all but vv.26, 29, and 30. The contrast between her attitude toward David and that of Nabal could hardly be more striking. Abigail pleads for an opportunity to "speak to" David.

To save Nabal's life, Abigail assumes his guilt (v.24). The urgency and insistence clearly detectable throughout her speech are modulated by a tone of courtesy and politeness. She characterizes Nabal as a "wicked man" and a "fool"; her action is wise and calculating, for David would hardly have been eager to marry (vv.39–40, 42) a woman known for disloyalty to her husband, even though wealthy and beautiful, since she would be a continual threat to his rule. At the same time her integrity prevents her from pulling any punches. Since Nabal is a "wicked man," one should "pay no attention" (cf. also 4:20) to him.

Abigail disavows having seen the "men" (v.25) David had sent to him (v.5). She senses that God has "kept" David from harming Nabal and his men, a truth that David later acknowledges (v.34). At the same time David asserts the important role of Abigail herself in keeping him from "bloodshed" (v.33), recognizing in her the mediator of the Lord's intentions. Since vengeance belongs to God alone (Dt 32:35), David must not avenge himself (vv.26, 31, 33) and so usurp God's prerogatives. Abigail expresses her desire that David's "enemies" (among whom Saul counts himself, 18:29; cf. also 26:8) and all who "intend to harm" him might "be like Nabal"—thus apparently anticipating the death of her husband and also, by implication, foreshadowing the death of Saul.

Though Nabal may be stingy, not so Abigail. She describes the generous supply of food that she brings to David and his men as a "gift" (GK 1388). Continuing to accept the blame for Nabal's folly (v.28), she begs David's forgiveness for her own "offense" and pleads with him not to do anything rash—anything that might endanger or even destroy the "lasting dynasty" that God will give him. Unlike the king desired by the people of Samuel's day, a king who would "fight our battles" (8:20), David is to be a man who "fights the LORD's battles."

Continuing to look into the future, Abigail alludes (v.30) to the Davidic covenant of 2Sa 7. She refers to the time when the Lord will have done for David "according to every good thing he promised." Although God has already "appointed him leader," a fact earlier announced to Saul by Samuel (see 13:14), David would not exercise effective rule over Israel until after Saul's death. In the meantime, however, Abigail does not want David to do anything to jeopardize his future or endanger his throne. Abigail ends her plea by asking that David "remember" her when the Lord "has brought . . . success" to him.

32–35 Although David was on his way to destroy Nabal's household, Abigail's sevenfold use of the divine name YHWH (vv.26 [bis], 28 [bis], 29, 30, 31) has perhaps reminded him of the spiritual dimensions of his calling. David sees in Abigail the Lord's envoy. He recognizes that "good judgment" is an admirable quality in a woman (cf. Pr 11:22). He also understands that God has used Abigail to keep him from bloodshed and from attempting to avenge himself. The oath "As surely as the LORD . . . lives" is frequently used where life and death hang in the balance (see 14:39). Mass killings of the kind that David had contemplated often occurred at

night, giving point to his statement that not a male in Nabal's household would have survived till "daybreak" (cf. v.22; 14:36).

David then gratefully accepts Abigail's gift of food for himself and his men. He makes it clear that she has succeeded in assuaging his wrath: "Go . . . in peace." His final words must have been like music to her ears: "I have . . granted your request," guaranteeing that he would not be the instrument of Nabal's death.

36–38 Abigail went to Nabal's "house," doubtless in Carmel (cf. v.40), where his sheep shearing celebration was taking place. He was presiding at a banquet fit for a "king"—a cruel irony when it is remembered that his wife has just declared her allegiance to Israel's king-elect. At his feast Nabal was "in high spirits" from wine. Realizing that he was in no condition to understand what she might say to him, Abigail decided to tell him "nothing" until "daybreak"—the time by which, ominously, David had originally sworn to kill every male in Nabal's household (cf. also v.22).

As it turns out, Nabal's folly was his own worst enemy. By the next morning "Nabal was sober." Feeling that the time is now ripe, Abigail tells her husband "all these things"— perhaps the entire story of her meeting with David, but doubtless including the list of provisions that she had so generously given him and that Nabal would surely begrudge. The shock is too much for him in his materialistic greed. Nabal the "fool" now suffers from a heart that goes bad. Since the heart is the seat of courage, Nabal is depicted as a coward as well.

The description of Nabal's becoming "like a stone" should not be diagnosed as a specific illness but understood figuratively (cf. Ex 15:16). The narrator may be presenting Nabal as receiving a "heart of stone" in exchange for his heart of flesh (contrast Eze 36:2). Though not immediate, Nabal's death was not long in coming. After about ten days "the LORD struck" him. Thus Nabal "died" at God's hand.

39a David greets the news of Nabal's death with an outburst of praise (cf. v.32). As he had earlier entreated the Lord to "uphold" his "cause" against Saul (24:15), so now he expresses his gratitude to the Lord for having "upheld his cause" against this Saul-like person. The Lord's dealings with David and Nabal could hardly be more diverse: As for David, God has "kept his servant from doing wrong," while in Nabal's case he has "brought [his] wrongdoing down on his own head."

39b–43 Nabal now dead, David "sent" his servants to Abigail to "take" her to become his wife. Abigail, by no means unwilling, nevertheless continues to characterize herself as David's "maidservant." Adopting the same posture of servile obedience with which she had first met him (v.23), Abigail then expresses her readiness to go so far as to "wash the feet of my master's servants." Since footwashing normally was a self-administered act (Ge 18:4; 19:2; 24:32; et al.), Abigail demonstrates her joyful willingness to be "slave of all" (Mk 10:44; cf. Jn 13:5–17). "Attended by her five maids," she hurries back with David's messengers to become his wife (see v.3).

Verse 43 calls attention to David's marriage to Ahinoam, which occurred before he took Abigail as his wife (Ahinoam is always mentioned before Abigail when the two names occur together; 27:3; 30:5; 2Sa 2:2; 3:2–3). The only other Ahinoam mentioned in the Bible is the wife of Saul (14:50), and thus possibly before David took Abigail to become his wife, he had already asserted his right to the throne of Israel by marrying Queen Ahinoam—a tactic perhaps hinted at in Nathan's speech to David (2Sa 12:8).

44 Whether or not Ahinoam of Jezreel is to be identified with the wife of Saul, he "had given" his daughter Michal, David's wife, to another man. The name of Michal's second husband was Paltiel, who was from Gallim.

14. Sparing Saul's life again (26:1–25)

1–5 This chapter narrates the final confrontation between Saul and David, and its speeches are animated by the mutual irreconcilability of the two men. Once again Saul goes "down" from the high ground at Gibeah with his "three thousand chosen men" (see 24:2) to the "Desert of Ziph," where he continues to "search . . . for" David. David, sensing that Saul has followed him to the desert, sends scouts to confirm that fact.

After his scouts have pinpointed the exact location of Saul's camp, David waits until Saul and his men have retired for the night

and then goes to look over the situation for himself. Saul's apparent invulnerability is detailed: (1) Abner, his cousin (see 14:50–51) and the commander of his army, is lying beside him; (2) he is safely inside the "camp" (vv.5, 7); and (3) the rest of his army is encamped "around him" (v.7).

6–12 "Ahimelech the Hittite" (mentioned only here) and "Abishai son of Zeruiah, Joab's brother" are asked whether they are willing to join David to go down to Saul's camp. Zeruiah, David's sister, was the mother of Abishai and Joab (1Ch 2:15–16), who both figure prominently in 2 Samuel, especially after David becomes king following Saul's death. Portending his later importance, Abishai volunteers to go down with David into the camp of Saul.

The two men arrive after dark, when everyone is asleep, and leave before anyone wakes up (v.12). Since Saul and his men are in a "deep sleep" brought on by the Lord (cf. Ge 2:21; 15:12), David and Abishai can move about undetected and speak to one another without being heard. Like a scepter symbolizing the royal presence, a "spear" is stuck in the ground near Saul's head. Abishai, anxious to be rid of Saul once and for all, wants to kill him. He envisions himself as the instrument of divine deliverance: "Let me pin him to the ground." Not characterized by restraint, Abishai is always quick to act (cf. 2Sa 16:9–10; 19:21–23).

David does not allow any of his men to press their advantage against the unsuspecting Saul. Because he is the "LORD's anointed," no one—including David himself—is to "lay a hand on" him (vv.9, 11, 23; cf. 24:6, 10).

David intones the solemn oath—"As surely as the LORD lives" (cf. v.16). Then David describes potential ways that Saul might die: (1) The Lord will "strike" him (with a fatal disease), "or" (2) when his "time" comes he will die (i.e., a natural death), "or" (3) he will "perish" in battle. In any of these, of course, the Lord is the ultimate cause of Saul's death, because vengeance belongs to him (25:32, 39).

Reflecting the language of 24:6, David uses another oath to underscore his refusal to kill Saul. In 24:4 he had taken "a corner of Saul's robe," a symbol of royal authority. Here he orders Abishai to take Saul's spear (a symbol of his authority but also of death)

nd water jug (a symbol of life; cf. 1Ki 19:4–
). As Saul was unprotected and unsuspect-
ng in 24:3, so also here—indeed, he and his
men are unable to awaken because of divinely induced slumber. Thus David and
Abishai, unseen and unheard, steal away into
he night. Although Abishai doubtless
obeyed David's command to take the spear
and the water jug, he did so on David's behalf—and so the text attributes the act to
David.

13–16 After leaving Saul's camp, David places
a safe distance between himself and his enemy. Then David calls out to Saul's army in
general and to its commander, Abner, in particular. Abner finally replies, "Who are you
who calls to the king?" David's first two
questions in v.15 seem to be scornful. His
third question rebukes Abner for dereliction
of duty, a failing in which he also implicates
Abner's men. The "someone" who came to
"destroy" the king was of course Abishai,
whom David had already kept from doing so.

17–20 Saul's initial question—"Is that your
voice, David my son?"—is a verbatim echo
of 24:16. But whereas there David had addressed Saul not only as "my lord the king"
(24:8) but also as "my father," here Saul is
simply "my lord the king." Saul has already
acknowledged David as his legitimate successor (24:20), and therefore David no longer
needs the rejected "king" as his "father."
David is firm in his conviction that he is innocent of any "wrong[doing]" (cf. 24:11). By
deciding again not to "lay a hand" on the
Lord's anointed, David refuses to make his
guiltless hands guilty of wrongdoing.

In vv.19–20a David sets forth two possible
sources of Saul's dogged pursuit of him. First,
God may have "incited" Saul against him.
Second, men may be at fault. In that case
David pronounces a solemn oath against
them: "May they be cursed before the
Lord!" (cf. Jos 6:26). David's sense of urgency is underscored by his use of "now." He
is concerned that his fugitive status would
prevent his participation in "the Lord's inheritance" (i.e., the land of Israel). David thus
prays that Saul will not cause him to die "far
from the presence of the Lord"—in this case,
in Philistia.

In a reprise of 24:14, David concludes his
statement to Saul by stressing the incongruity of Saul's enterprise. The most powerful

man in the land ("king of Israel") has taken it
upon himself to "come out" (cf. also 23:15) to
look for something trivial, something unworthy of his time and energy—a single
"flea." Looking for a single flea is compared
to hunting a single "partridge" in the mountains, something no one in his right mind
would take the time or make the effort to do.

21–25 Saul responds to David with words
that he has felt a need to utter before: "I have
sinned" (cf. 15:24). Recognizing that David
has "considered" his "life precious," Saul
promises not to harm him. Apparently Saul's
repentance is sincere this time: He admits
that he has erred "greatly" and that—like
Nabal—he has "acted like a fool" (cf. 13:13).

David's retort to Saul offers to return his
spear, the symbol of death, but not the water
jug, the symbol of life. The argument of
David to the effect that God "rewards" all
who are characterized by "righteousness"
(GK 7407) and "faithfulness" (GK 575) is
perhaps as much a condemnation of Saul's
conduct as it is a commendation of his own.
As before so also now David refuses to lay a
hand on Saul, the Lord's anointed. It is the
Lord who has "delivered" Saul into David's
hands, and as recompense for his respect for
Saul's life he prays that the Lord will "deliver" him from "all trouble."

Strangely enough, Saul's final words to
David are good wishes for his greatness and
triumph. Three times Saul has called David
his "son" (vv.17, 21, 25), and Saul now apparently knows that David will be his successor
on Israel's throne as well (cf. 24:19–20). His
blessing on David virtually assures as much.
David had prayed that any potential enemies
of his might be "cursed" (v.19); Saul now
leaves David after praying that he might be
"blessed." Since there is nothing more to be
said, David and Saul part (cf. 24:22), never to
see each other again.

15. Achish the Philistine (27:1–28:2)

27:1–4 Long a fugitive, David decides to flee
to Philistia where he will be free of Saul's relentless pursuit once and for all. David
knows that it is only a matter of time before
he will be "destroyed" (lit., "swept away";
GK 6200) by Saul. David thus comes to the
conclusion that "the best thing I can do is" to
go to Philistia. If he does so, Saul will "give
up" his pursuit. Saul does stop "searching"

for him, ceasing what he had relentlessly done while David was still in Israelite territory (23:14, 25; 24:2; 26:2, 20).

So David and his six hundred men seek refuge in Philistia with Achish son of Maoch king of Gath, to whom David had earlier fled for help (see 21:10). Since Gath is some thirty rugged miles northwest of the Desert of Ziph, where David had been hiding earlier (26:1–2), the task of moving himself, his two wives Ahinoam and Abigail, and his men and their families (v.3) must have involved considerable hardship.

5–7 David's settlement in Gath would doubtless be temporary, however, since he is not sure that it would be advisable to live with a man who had earlier given him reason to fear him (21:11–12). David therefore hopes that if he has "found favor" in the "eyes" of Achish—implying that Achish can now trust him (see 20:29)—the Philistine ruler will not insist that he live in the "royal city." David would be content to be assigned a country town; so Achish gives him Ziklag, which originally had been part of the tribal patrimony of Simeon "within the territory of Judah" (cf. Jos 19:1, 5; cf. Jos 15:21, 31). Achish doubtless placed David in Ziklag to protect Philistia against marauders from the south. His settlement there anticipates the subsequent ownership of Ziklag by the "kings of Judah," of whom he would become the ideal dynastic ancestor (2Sa 2:4). Altogether David lived in Philistine-controlled territory for "a year and four months."

8–12 While vv.1–7 describe David's settlement in Philistia, vv.8–12 outline his raiding operations, in connection with which—for the second time—he succeeds in deceiving Achish (cf. 21:12–15). Since the Philistines themselves were often raiders (23:27), it is not surprising that a Philistine vassal or ally like David would also engage in raiding campaigns. Among those whom David and his men raided were the Geshurites, the Girzites, and the Amalekites. All these peoples had lived in southern Canaan and northern Sinai "from ancient times." Saul had conducted a fateful campaign against the Amalekites (ch. 15), and David would soon fight them again (ch. 30).

David's "practice" whenever he attacked an area was not to "leave a man or woman alive." Unlike the situation in 15:3, however,

where total annihilation of the population was for religious purposes, David here kills everyone so that no survivors would be left to report to Achish what has really happened. In addition to garments, he "took" as plunder only animals, a procedure to be expected as a matter of course from kings (8:16) but not from prophets (see 12:3).

Although David was raiding Geshurites, Girzites, and Amalekites, he told Achish that he was raiding various subdistricts of the Negev that belonged to or were controlled by Judah (30:26–29). Far enough away from Gath so that Achish would be ignorant of his movements, David can lie to him with impunity—especially by leaving no survivors who might be able to contradict him. David thus has the best of both worlds: He implies to Achish that Judahite hostility toward David is increasing, and at the same time he gains the appreciation and loyalty of Judah toward himself by raiding their desert neighbors.

To his detriment, Achish trusts David and is therefore deceived by his report. He is confident that David the Israelite has become "odious" (GK 944) to his own people and will thus be forced to be a "servant" (GK 6269) of Achish the Philistine for life.

28:1–2 Still laboring under the assumption that David is his faithful vassal, Achish forcefully reminds him that he and his men are expected to "accompany" the Philistines to fight against Israel. David appears to acquiesce by responding that Achish would then "see" for himself what David was capable of doing. In referring to himself as Achish's "servant," David reflects the thoughts of Achish concerning him (27:12)—although David intends nothing more than a polite expression equivalent to the personal pronoun "I." Continuing to misjudge David, Achish announces his desire to make him "my bodyguard." Achish, however, fails to see that David and his men constitute a dangerous fifth column inside Philistine territory.

B. The End of the Reign of Saul (28:3–31:13)

1. Saul and the medium at Endor (28:3–25)

The strange story of the meeting of Saul with Endor's "witch" (better "necromancer" or "medium"; GK 200), resulting in the announcement that Saul would die at the hands of the Philistines (v.19), is preceded (27:1–

Exploits of David

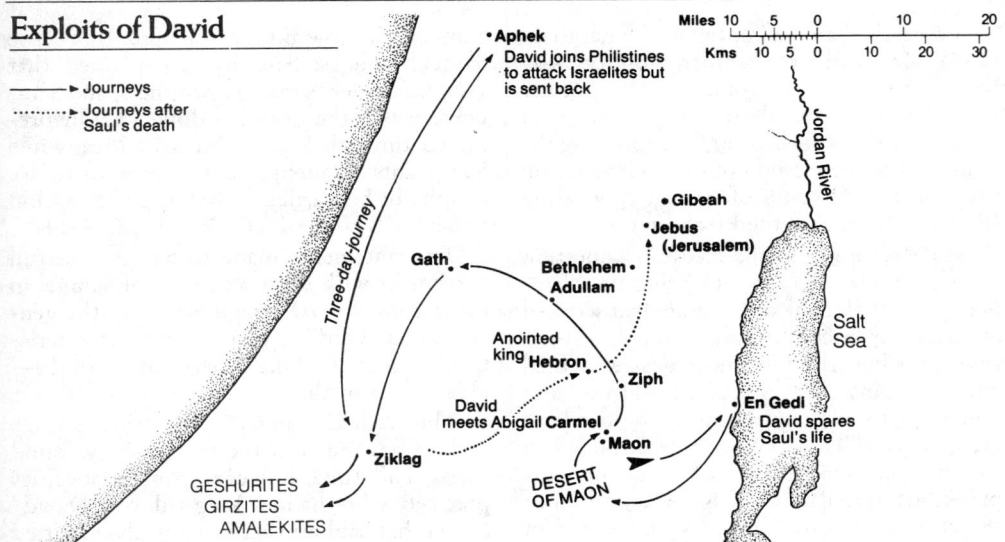

——▸ Journeys
·······▸ Journeys after
    Saul's death

• Aphek
David joins Philistines
to attack Israelites but
is sent back

Miles 10 5 0   10   20
Kms 10 5 0   10   20   30

Jordan River

• Gibeah

**• Jebus
(Jerusalem)**

Gath •   Bethlehem •
          Adullam

Three-day journey

Salt
Sea

Anointed
king Hebron •
         • Ziph

David
meets Abigail Carmel •
         • Maon

• En Gedi
David spares
Saul's life

• Ziklag

DESERT
OF MAON

GESHURITES
GIRZITES
AMALEKITES

© 1985 The Zondervan Corporation

28:2) and followed (29:1–11) by accounts of David's friendly relationships with the Philistines through Achish king of Gath.

3 Verse 3a reprises 25:1a. The reminder that Samuel had died is coupled with the observation that Saul (cf. Lev 19:31; 20:6–7; Dt 18:11) had expelled the mediums and spiritists from Israel; both events figure prominently in the rest of the chapter.

4–6 Skillfully and tersely v.4 describes the opposing forces: The Philistines "assembled" and "set up camp" at Shunem (in the territory of Issachar), while Saul "gathered" his forces and "set up camp" at Gilboa (a mountain ten miles south-southeast of Shunem). When Saul "saw" (GK 8011) the Philistines, he became "afraid" (cf. 17:11, 24; 23:3). Given the situation, it is understandable that Saul "inquired of" the Lord. For all Saul's efforts to receive an "answer" (cf. v.15) from the Lord, none came. The normal modes of divine communication were silent: "dreams" (cf. v.15), "Urim" (the sacred lots stored in the priestly ephod), and "prophets" (cf. v.15).

7–14 Under such circumstances it is not surprising that Saul, out of sheer desperation, would resort to a forbidden source of information—a "medium." Fearful of Philistine strength, he wanted to know how to proceed (v.15). An element of mystery suffuses ch. 28, and it would be presumptuous to claim to have successfully plumbed its depths.

"Find" a medium, the king says, thus violating his own earlier intention (v.3). Endor was located dangerously close to where the Philistines were encamped (v.4). That Saul should prefer a "woman" as a medium is not surprising (cf. Na 3:4). Although he was obviously convinced that if he "disguised himself" he would be able to conceal his identity, he was wrong—and in any event the information he received through the medium's efforts was hardly what he wanted to hear (vv.17–20).

Since the netherworld is a place of darkness (Job 10:21–22; 17:13; Pss 88:12; 143:3), "night" provided the proper setting for communicating with one of its denizens. In addition, necromancers probably preferred to do their work at night, and Saul would have found it easier to conceal his identity under cover of darkness. Taking two men with him, the king went to the woman and asked her to "consult" a "spirit" on his behalf, a practice universally condemned as a pagan abomination (6:2; cf. Dt 18:10, 14; 2Ki 17:17). King Saul is now commanding a necromancer to "bring up" for him one who dwells in the "realm of death below" (Dt 32:22).

Not yet recognizing Saul, the woman reminds him that Israel's king has "cut off"- (either killed or expelled) all the land's mediums and spiritists. Her words to Saul drip with irony: "You know" that "spiritists" are no longer allowed here. Saul will later compound the irony by asking the wraith that he believes to be Samuel "to tell me" what to do (v.15). Meanwhile the woman wonders why her nocturnal visitor would want to put her life in jeopardy by begging her to do what royal decree has forbidden. In promising the woman that she would not be punished, Saul uses the most solemn of oaths by swearing (for the last time) in the Lord's name.

Saul's response to the medium's question is specific: He wants her to bring up "Samuel." Although Saul and Samuel had worked at cross-purposes throughout much of their time together, the king now desires a final word from his prophet. How—and whether—the woman engaged the dead we are not told. The medium's reaction when Samuel appeared was one of shock and surprise: She "cried out" (GK 2410), an emotional outburst often linked with feelings of fear and dismay (cf. 4:13; 5:10). At the very least the woman must have been clairvoyant, because while in her trancelike state she was able to penetrate Saul's disguise and recognize him.

The irony continues: Saul, previously afraid because of the Philistine threat (v.5) and soon to be afraid "because of Samuel's words" (v.20), tells the necromancer not to be afraid. He then asks her what she sees, thus indicating that he is not privy to the apparition itself. She responds that she sees "a spirit." Saul asks what he looks like. When the medium describes him as "an old man wearing a robe," Saul is convinced that the apparition is Samuel, who in Saul's mind has always worn the robe of the prophet (15:27; cf. 2:18–19).

15–19 Saul now speaks (probably via the medium) to what he believes is the "spirit" of Samuel. The apparition begins the interchange by complaining that Saul has "disturbed" him (see Isa 14:9). Saul's claim to be in "great" distress reflects his desperate emotional state. He knows full well that "God" had long ago abandoned him (see 16:14; cf. also 18:12), and therefore he felt it necessary to consult a spirit.

In v.6 the Lord did not answer Saul "by dreams or Urim or prophets"; in v.15 Saul tells "Samuel" that God does not answer him "either by prophets or by dreams," perhaps omitting "Urim" to hide his slaughter of the priests of Nob (22:11–19) and perhaps listing "prophets" first in his hope that the prophet

Samuel will now fill that vacuum. In a sense Samuel obliges: Saul has complained that God no longer speaks by prophets, and Samuel says that the Lord has done what he predicted through Samuel himself. Meanwhile Saul wants Samuel to "tell" him what to do, in spite of his earlier refusal to pay attention to Samuel's counsel (cf. 10:8 with 13:8–14).

The statements made to Saul are in full agreement with what we know of Samuel in other contexts. Although Saul uses the general word "God" in v.15, Samuel characteristically refers to "the LORD" in vv.16–19—seven times in all.

The prediction in v.17 refers back to 15:28 and echoes much of the terminology found there. This time, however, Samuel specifies precisely who the new king will be: "David" (a fact that Saul himself had already admitted earlier; cf. 24:20).

Verse 18 summarizes the two fateful decisions made by Saul that prompted the Lord to wrench the kingdom from his grasp: (1) He disobeyed the Lord's command through his prophet (see ch. 13), and (2) he refused to fully carry out the divine wrath against the Amalekites (see ch. 15). Obeying God had never been easy for Saul (cf. 15:19, 22), and his impatient insistence on his own way cost him the kingdom.

Although throughout Samuel's lifetime the Israelites had been delivered "out of the hand/power of the Philistines" (cf. 7:3, 14), the Lord would now "hand over" Israel to them. Samuel predicts the slaughter of Saul and his sons on Mount Gilboa. Samuel's last-recorded words, describing the fate of "both Israel and you [Saul]," reprise the final words of his *apologia:* "Both you [Israel] and your king [Saul] will be swept away" (12:25). Apart from v.20, Samuel does not appear again in the two OT books named after him, though his importance and influence continue to leave their mark throughout the rest of the Bible.

20–25 His strength gone, King Saul falls on the ground "full length." Fearful earlier because of the Philistine threat (v.5), Saul is now "filled with fear" because of Samuel's words of doom. In addition he lacks physical strength because he has eaten no food "all that day and night" (19:24).

The medium, politely referring to herself as Saul's "(maid)servant" (GK 9148; see 1:11;

25:27), reminds him that she risked her own safety for him. The verb for "hear," "obey," "listen to" (GK 9048) plays a prominent role in this section: The medium "obeyed" Saul when she "did" (lit., "listened to") what he told her to do; she now wants him to "listen to" her and eat some food; although he at first refused, he finally "listened to" her when his men joined her in urging him. Having eaten, Saul and his men go out into the night—"that same night" (v.25) in which Samuel's words have sealed the fate of a doomed king.

2. The dismissal of David (29:1–11)

1–5 The chapter begins by recalling the muster of Philistine and Israelite armies described in 28:4. The Philistines gathered their "forces" at Aphek (mentioned only here and in 4:1)—the staging area for Philistine troop deployment in the first and last battles in 1 Samuel.

The personal involvement of the Philistine "rulers" demonstrates their perception that the present battle was crucial. David and his men, mercenaries in the Philistine army (cf. 28:1), fall in behind at the behest of Achish king of Gath. The commanders, understandably wary of David (cf. 18:30), question the wisdom of including "Hebrews" in the army. But Achish, who had earlier made David his "bodyguard for life" (28:2), rises to his defense: (1) Although David had at one time been an "officer" of Saul, he "left" Saul. (2) Having fled from Saul, David has now been with Achish for "over a year" and has therefore had sufficient time to demonstrate his loyalty. (3) During this entire period Achish has found "no fault" in David. Unconvinced, the Philistine commanders demand that Achish "send" David "back" to Ziklag (see 27:6), fearing that David might turn against them during the fighting. They want no fifth column in their ranks. The commanders conclude their critique by reminding Achish of the victory refrain—by now well known (see 18:7–8)—sung by the women of Israel in honor of (Saul and) David.

6–11 Achish, not willing to buck his peers on this point, tells David about the commanders' concern but without sharing any details with him. To assure David of the truth of what he is about to say, he takes a solemn oath in the name of David's God. As far as Achish is aware (but cf. 27:8–11), David has been "reliable" (GK 3838). He then advises David to "go in peace," a cordial expression of farewell (2Sa 15:9; cf. 2Sa 15:27).

David's response echoes in part some of Achish's own words (cf. v.6). In addition, David wants to know "what [he has] done" to deserve such suspicion, again playing the role of the innocent victim (cf. 17:29; 20:1; 26:18). He wants to fight (or pretends that he does) against the enemies of his "lord the king"—Achish, at least in this context.

For the third time (cf. vv.3, 6) Achish vindicates David's honor and dependability. In Achish's eyes David is like "an angel of God" (cf. 2Sa 14:17, 20; 19:27; Zec 12:8). But he goes on to request urgently that David return to Ziklag before he needlessly angers the Philistine rulers even further. David and his men leave early in the morning, doubtless relieved that they have avoided fighting against David's countrymen.

3. The defeat of the Amalekites (30:1–31)

1–3 Having been dismissed by Achish, David and his men begin the long trek from Aphek (29:1) to Ziklag (see 27:6) in "the land of the Philistines" (29:11) and arrive there on the "third day." In the meantime the Amalekites (Israel's agelong enemies, who inhabited large tracts of land southwest of the Dead Sea) had "raided [lit., stripped; GK 7320] the Negev and Ziklag" (see v.14 for more details). The Amalekites had taken advantage of David's absence from Ziklag and retaliated for David's earlier raid (27:8). They had also "taken captive" everyone who lived in the town, from the youngest to the oldest (vv.2, 19). The captured "women" receive pride of place in v.2, probably because David's two wives were included among them (v.5).

4–8 Weeping aloud is an understandable reaction when the situation seems hopeless. But the abject sorrow of David and his men would soon be replaced by confident expectation as a result of the Lord's assurance of victory. David mourns the apparent loss of his two wives, whom he had moved to Ziklag after Achish had assigned the town to him (cf. 27:3–6).

David is further grieved because his men blame him for their plight. They even consider "stoning him." Convinced that they will never see their children again, the men are "bitter in spirit" (cf. 1:10; 2Ki 4:27). While in 22:2 people who were "discontented" flocked to David's leadership, here his men are so distraught that they are ready to harm him.

David's spiritual discernment now comes to the fore: He "found strength" in the right Person (cf. Ezr 7:28; Dan 10:19). By using the expression "the LORD his God," the narrator emphasizes David's intimate relationship with the One who from the beginning has always been "with him" (see 16:18).

As at Keilah, so also at Ziklag David inquires of the Lord through Abiathar the priest. When the rejected Saul inquired of the Lord, no answer came (28:6); when the "man after [God's] own heart" (13:14) does the same, the Lord answers specifically and with precision (cf. also 23:2, 4). David is commanded to "pursue," he will "certainly overtake," and he will "succeed in the rescue." True to his promise, the Lord makes sure that David has "recovered" everything (vv.18, 22).

9–20 The staging area for the campaign against the Amalekites is the Besor Ravine. Of David's "six hundred men," two hundred are too "exhausted" (vv.10, 21) to continue the rigorous march. David and the four hundred others, however, press on. Finding a starving Egyptian in a field, whose cruel Amalekite master had left him for dead simply because he had become ill, they give him water and food. His enforced three-day fast has apparently weakened him, because after eating he is "revived."

The emphatic "we" at the beginning of v.14 suggests that the slave participated personally in the Amalekites' raids. Among the pillaged regions were the Negev of the Kerethites, an undefined portion of Judahite territory, and the Negev of Caleb (named after the clan that occupied it and of which Nabal was a member [25:3]). Last of all, says the Egyptian, "Ziklag we burned."

The Egyptian agrees to show David where the Amalekite raiding party has gone if David will swear not to kill him or "hand [him] over to" his master; the present text is silent concerning whether he does so. In any event, the Egyptian leads David down to the Amalekite bivouac. The raiders are not only "eating" and "drinking"—in contrast to the former plight of the Egyptian slave, who had considered himself one of their number—but also "reveling." After all, they had recently "taken" great quantities of plunder (cf. vv.18–20).

David and his men are more than a match for the Amalekites, who must have been much more numerous than the Israelites. Even after a full night and day of fighting, during which large numbers of Amalekites fell, "four hundred"—the same figure as David's original army (v.10)—are still able to get away on their camels.

Emphasizing the completeness of the rout and the scope of David's victory, the narrator reports that everything the Amalekites had taken, David "took" back, including (most important of all) "his two wives." Indeed, "nothing was missing." The success is attributed to David as the leader of his men; the plunder is "David's plunder."

21–25 David, however, understands that the plunder is ultimately not his but the Lord's, and he must therefore exercise the utmost care in its disposition. Returning to the Besor Ravine, he and his troops are met by the two hundred men who had remained behind (cf. vv.9–10). As was his custom on such occasions (17:22; 25:5–6), David "greeted" them.

As Saul had his "troublemakers" (10:27) at the beginning of his reign, so also David has his. They declare their unwillingness to share the plunder with men who had not participated in the campaign against the Amalekites. David, generously calling the troublemakers "my brothers," reminds them that the booty is not, as they think, "the plunder we recovered" but rather "what the LORD has given us." God has enabled them to defeat those who came against them. However exhausted the men who remained behind might have been, they deserve a reward for staying with and guarding the "supplies" (see 10:22). They are thus not to be considered inferior and are to share equally in the plunder. The magnanimous David, who knows full well that he has been divinely deputized to distribute the Lord's plunder as he wishes, makes sure that loyal service is suitably compensated. David makes the principle of equal sharing of plunder a "statute and ordinance."

26–31 The final section of ch. 30 begins as does the first: "David arrived in Ziklag." Representing Judah, the elders (cf. 2Sa 19:11) receive a "present" (lit., "blessing"; GK 1388) from David (see comment on 25:27). The Judahite elders, who are David's "friends," stand in contrast to the Amalekite raiders, who are "the LORD's"—and therefore David's—"enemies."

Concluding the chapter, vv.27–31 list the specific places where David's "present" was distributed and give additional information concerning the areas raided by the Amalekites. David thus ingratiates himself to the elders and other inhabitants of Judah. And even before David the king-elect has finished currying favor with Israelites living in the south, King Saul has died while fighting Philistines in the north, a story vividly and tersely related in the last chapter of 1 Samuel.

4. The death of Saul and Jonathan (31:1–13)

1–7 The Philistine threat has hung like a pall over Israel throughout 1 Samuel almost from the beginning (cf. 4:1–2), and the end is not yet. Even now, as Samuel promised, the Philistines fight Israel (cf. 28:19), and, as all too often under Saul's erratic leadership, "many" Israelites "fell slain." Symbolizing defeat for Israel, the verb "fell" (GK 5877) appears three times in this section (vv.1, 4–5).

Although Saul and Jonathan had earlier engaged "in hot pursuit" of the Philistines (14:22), now the tables are tragically turned: The Philistines "pressed hard" after Saul and his sons. Of the four sons of Saul, three (including Jonathan) are killed (vv.2, 6, 8) before Saul himself commits suicide. The other son, Ish-Baal/Ish-Bosheth, may not have been present on the battlefield (see 2Sa 2:8, where he enters the scene).

With Saul helpless and virtually alone, the Philistines moved in for the kill. As the fighting grew "fierce" around him, the archers "overtook him," and he was badly wounded. Saul does not want those "uncircumcised fellows" to finish him off. Relying on his armor-bearer to do as he is told, Saul tells him, "Draw your sword and run me through." But Saul's armor-bearer—like David before him (26:23)—"would not" kill the Lord's anointed. Since Saul is determined to die on his own terms, he has no alternative but to take his own sword and fall on it. Thus the man who had originally been introduced as the one who would "deliver [God's] people

from the hand of the Philistines" (9:16) meets his end by dying at their hands.

Seeing that his king is dead, the armor-bearer follows his example and falls on his own sword. As if to stress the camaraderie and mutual loyalty within the Israelite army, the narrator states that all the warriors—Saul, his sons, his armor-bearer, his men—die "together." The Philistines now occupy deserted Israelite towns in the valley of Jezreel and in Transjordan.

8–13 The following day the Philistines come back to the battlefield to "strip the dead." As David had earlier cut off the head of Goliath (see 17:51), they now cut off the head of Israel's king and put it on display in the temple of Dagon as a trophy of war (1Ch 10:10). They also strip Saul of his armor and display it in the temple of their goddesses. Messengers "proclaim the news" of the resounding victory and its aftermath.

The report is to be broadcast throughout Philistia but especially "in the temple of their idols." It is indeed ironic that a book that begins at the "house of the LORD at Shiloh" (1:24) ends at the "temple" of one or more pagan deities. As for the mutilated bodies of Saul and his sons (Saul's suicide did not prevent his body from being abused, v.4), the Philistines fasten them to Beth Shan's wall.

At the beginning of his reign, Saul's first military action had been to rescue the people of Jabesh Gilead from the Ammonites (11:1–11). At the end of his reign, after his final military action (which cost him his life), the grateful people of Jabesh pay tribute to Saul and his sons by retrieving their bodies from Beth Shan (doubtless at great personal risk), burning them, and giving them an honorable burial. Then, in honor of Saul, they fast for seven days (cf. also 2Sa 1:12).

At best, Saul remains a complex and enigmatic figure, at once hero and villain. Perhaps the fittest conclusion to the story of Saul, as well as the most appropriate transition from 1 Samuel to 2 Samuel, is the Chronicler's inspired coda: "Saul died because he was unfaithful to the LORD; he did not keep the word of the LORD and even consulted a medium for guidance, and did not inquire of the LORD. So the LORD put him to death and turned the kingdom over to David son of Jesse" (1Ch 10:13–14).

2 Samuel

INTRODUCTION

See the introduction to 1 Samuel.

EXPOSITION

I. Consolidation of Monarchy in Israel (1:1–20:26)

The overriding theme of the books of Samuel is the beginning of Israel's monarchy in the eleventh century B.C. Having discussed its prelude (1Sa 1:1–7:17), advent (1Sa 8:1–15:35), and establishment (1Sa 16:1–31:13), the author next turns to its consolidation under David, Israel's greatest king.

A. David's Accession to Kingship Over Judah (1:1–3:5)

The story of David's rise to the kingship begins with an account of the decimation of Saul's line (1:1–16) and ends with a summary of David's fecundity (3:2–5). Nestled in the center of this literary unit is the narrative of David's anointing as king over Judah (2:1–7), signaling the replacement of Saul and his house in southern Canaan.

1. The death of Saul and Jonathan (1:1–16)

Second Samuel begins as 1 Samuel ends—with an account of the death of King Saul and his son Jonathan, the heir apparent. But while 1Sa 31 describes the events as they occurred, 2Sa 1:1–16 consists of a report of the events filtered through the not disinterested words of an Amalekite.

1–5 Saul's defeat and death at the hands of the Philistines and David's victory over the Amalekites occurred at approximately the same time. The distance from Mount Gilboa to Ziklag is more than eighty miles, a three-day trip for the Amalekite fugitive. Torn clothes (cf. v.11) and dust on one's head are signs of anguish and distress, appropriate and understandable behavior in a man who has so recently witnessed a battlefield scene of suf-

fering and death. The man demonstrates his submission to David by prostrating himself.

David's desire to know where the man has come from is doubtless prompted by the man's appearance. His response—that he has escaped from the Israelite camp—makes David all the more curious; so he demands that the man tell him what has happened. His report reveals that the Israelites "fled" (GK 5674) from the battle against the Philistines and that many of them died. What is more, continues the man—who obviously thinks that he is bringing David good news (4:10)—"Saul and his son Jonathan are dead." David of course wants to know how the messenger can be so sure of this latter assertion; so the man tells his story.

6–10 The Amalekite's account deviates in several important respects from that in 1Sa 31. Most of the proposed solutions to the problem only serve to further complicate it. On Mount Gilboa (the scene of Saul's last battle, 1Sa 31:1), the Amalekite encountered the wounded Saul, who was supporting himself by "leaning on his spear." Seeing the Amalekite nearby, Saul called out to him. The man replied with the response commonly used by servants: "What can I do?" Perhaps to be sure that the man was not a Philistine, who might abuse the Israelite king if he had

These are the slopes of Mount Gilboa, where Saul and his son Jonathan were killed by the Philistines.

434

the chance (cf. 1Sa 31:4), Saul asked the man to identify himself.

Satisfied as to the general identity of the young man, Saul uttered words reminiscent of the earlier description of David's dispatching of Goliath: "Stand over me and kill me" (cf. 1Sa 17:51). Although in mortal agony and wanting to die, Saul seemed unable to take his own life. Apparently happy to oblige, the Amalekite claims to have fulfilled Saul's wish to the letter. He "knew" that the fallen king could not survive, and—since he himself had killed him—he could also "know" for certain that Saul was dead. After killing the king, the Amalekite took Saul's "crown," the primary symbol of his royal authority (cf. 2Ki 11:12), as well as a band that he was wearing on his arm.

11–12 Having once been a valued member of Saul's court, David undoubtedly recognizes the crown and armlet. But the messenger could scarcely have been prepared for the response of David and his men, who tear their clothes with heartfelt expressions of grief over Saul and Jonathan and mourn and weep. They also fast, but only "till evening," which was apparently David's usual practice in such situations (cf. 3:35). Their sorrow extends to the people as a whole, since all Israel has suffered tragic and irreparable loss in the death of their king.

13–14 Apparently after the period of mourning is over, David questions the messenger again. David wants to know something of the man's background. The man affirms that, in addition to being an Amalekite, he is the son of an "alien." David has now learned all that he needs to know concerning the man. Since his father was a resident alien, living in Saul's realm, the young man can be expected to have at least minimal knowledge about Israel's basic traditions, including the inviolability of "the Lord's anointed." By the Amalekite's own testimony, he had destroyed the Lord's anointed king, something David had never done (see 1Sa 24:6, 10; 26:9, 11).

15–16 Far from receiving the reward that he thinks David will surely give him because of the "good news" he thought he was bringing (cf. 4:10), the Amalekite's callous bravado has sealed his own doom. David has the young man executed with the words, "Your blood be on your own head" (cf. 1Ki 2:31–33). In the light of 1Sa 31, it is clear that the young man's claim to have killed Saul was false, however much the rest of his story may appear to have the ring of truth.

2. David's lament for Saul and Jonathan (1:17–27)

17–18 That David was the author of this remarkable poem about 1000 B.C. is universally recognized. The poem is strikingly secular, never once mentioning God's name or elements of Israel's faith. Like Joshua's poetic address to the sun and moon (Jos 10:12–13), this lament was eventually written down in the "Book of Jashar" (a poetic collection no longer extant).

19 "Mighty" is probably best understood as being parallel to "glory," and thus "slain" is parallel to "fallen." "Heights" here refers to Gilboa, located in "Israel," which was Saul's main realm and to whose people David's lament is addressed. Not yet king over all Israel, David orders that the lament be taught only to the men of "Judah" (v.18), where he has already gained considerable influence.

20 The verb translated "proclaim" (GK 1413) almost always implies good news—in this case, of course, only from the standpoint of the Philistines. "Gath," on the eastern edge of Philistine territory, and "Ashkelon," by the sea, represent all of Philistine territory. The "daughters of the Philistines/uncircumcised" will rejoice at this news, in contrast to the "daughters of Israel," who must "weep for Saul" (v.24).

21 This verse consists of a curse on the "mountains of Gilboa," the site of the Israelite defeat (cf. Ps 106:38; Hos 4:2–3). In Hebrew thought, "dew" was often a symbol of resurrection or the renewing of life (cf. Ps 110:3; Isa 26:19). Regarding Saul's shield being "defiled" (GK 1718), the text is unclear as to whether the Philistines treated Saul's shield as they wished or whether it was "rejected (with loathing)" in the sense that the shield is pictured as lying on the mountains, worthless and neglected, no longer oiled and ready for action.

22–23 Each verse refers to both Saul and Jonathan by name, the only verses in the lament to do so. They summarize the bravery, the determination, the comradeship, and the ability of the two men. Jonathan's "bow" did not turn back from "blood," and Saul's "sword" did not return (to its sheath) "unsatisfied" from "flesh" (cf. Dt 32:42; Isa 34:5–6).

The Hebrew word order of v.23 suggests that the king and his son, inseparable in life as in death, would continue to be honored in death as in life.

24 Verse 24 mirrors v.20 (see comment). Here David calls on the "daughters of Israel" to "weep" (GK 1134) for Saul, as he and all his men had done (v.12). Weeping for/over a person was a universal custom in ancient Israel (3:34; Job 30:25; et al.). The "daughters" are probably wealthy women of the land since Saul has lavished fine clothes and expensive jewelry on them.

25–26 "How the mighty have fallen" is a verbatim echo of v.19 and at first gives the impression that the lament concludes at this point. The addition of "in battle," however, signals that v.25 is a false ending. The two lines of v.25 reverse the elements of v.19, its mirror image.

David's grief is for Jonathan, his "brother" (GK 278)—not in the sense of "brother-in-law" (a true enough description; cf. 1Sa 18:27) but of "treaty/covenant brother." David's further statement that Jonathan's "love" (GK 173) for him was "more wonderful than that of women" should be understood to have covenantal connotations (i.e., covenantal/political loyalty; translated "friendship" in Ps 109:4–5).

27 The song ends as it began, with the central theme of "How the mighty have fallen!" David's lament for Saul and Jonathan is characterized by both passion and restraint. While giving full vent to his feelings on hearing the report of their death, David displays no bitterness toward his mortal enemy Saul. Since in v.18 David orders that the men of Judah be "taught" his lament, apparently the epic hymns of Israel's history were intended to be taught and applied from generation to generation. David's lament may well have been a favorite.

3. David anointed king over Judah (2:1–7)

1–4a Now that King Saul is dead and buried, the time has come for the private anointing of David (1Sa 16:13) to be reprised in public. David decides to leave Ziklag (1:1)—but not

without seeking divine guidance. Unlike Saul, David "inquired of the LORD," doubtless by asking his friend Abiathar the priest to consult the Urim and Thummim stored in the ephod that he had brought with him from Nob (1Sa 22:20; 23:6; cf. 23:1–4, 9–12; 30:7–8).

David wants to know whether he should "go up" to one of the towns in the hill country of Judah. By means of the sacred lots, the Lord responds affirmatively. When David then asks for a more precise destination, the lots pinpoint Hebron as the place. Located twenty-seven miles northeast of Ziklag, Hebron was the most important city David sent plunder to after defeating the Amalekites (1Sa 30:31) and looms large in chs. 2–5. Obedient to the divine command, David severs his ties with Philistine Ziklag, and, with his two wives Ahinoam and Abigail (27:3; 30:5), moves to Judahite Hebron. He also takes with him the army of men who have rallied to his leadership, and they together with their families settle in Hebron and its nearby villages. David is publicly anointed by the "men of Judah" as king over Judah. David's elevation to kingship, however, is fundamentally due to divine anointing (1Sa 16).

4b–7 Word eventually reaches David that the men of Jabesh Gilead had given Saul a decent burial. Since Jabesh is an Israelite (not Judahite) town and therefore presumably still loyal to Saul's house, David realizes that he must try to win them over to his side. He therefore sends messengers to them with overtures of peace and friendship, an approach that stands in sharp contrast to the tactics used by David's men in the rest of the chapter.

The Jabeshites are commended for "showing kindness" (in the sense of demonstrating loyalty) to Saul. "Kindness" (GK 2876) of this sort ultimately derives from God, as David himself recognizes (cf. 9:1, 3, 7). Indeed, he invokes the Lord's "kindness and faithfulness [GK 622]" on the Jabeshites. Both of these are part of all genuine covenant relationships, and David stresses his eagerness to transfer the Jabeshites' covenant loyalty from Saul to himself. He offers to show them the same favor that Saul had shown them. He reminds them that Saul their master is now dead and that the house of Judah has anointed him as king. He concludes his offer by encouraging them to "be strong and brave." But there is more than one fly in the ointment, as the rest of the chapter clearly suggests.

4. War between Saul's house and David's house (2:8–3:1)

2:8–11 Abner, Saul's cousin and the commander of Saul's army (cf. 1Sa 14:50; 17:55; 26:5), had either avoided or escaped from the battle on Mount Gilboa that had resulted in the death of Saul and his three sons (1Sa 31:8). Still ostensibly loyal to the dead king, he had taken a fourth son, Ish-Bosheth, and brought him to Mahanaim, far away from the continuing Philistine threat. Located just north of the Jabbok River in the tribal territory of Gad (Jos 13:26, 30; 21:38), it would later serve as a place of refuge for David during the rebellion of Absalom (17:24, 27; 19:32; 1Ki 2:8).

Ish-Bosheth ("Man of shame"), mentioned only in chs. 2–4, is perhaps to be identified with Ishvi in 1Sa 14:49. Not killed in Saul's last battle (cf. 1Sa 31:2), he may have been something of a coward. Scribal tradition often substituted the word *bosheth* ("shame"; cf. GK 1017) for the hated name of the Canaanite god Baal (cf. Jer 3:24). Thus Ish-Bosheth's real name was E/Ish-Baal, "Man of Baal" (cf. 1Ch 8:33), Mephibosheth's (4:4) was Merib-Baal (1Ch 8:34), and Jerub-Besheth's was Jerub-Baal (11:21; cf. Jdg 6:32). Since *baal* is also a common noun meaning "lord" or "master" and could therefore be used occasionally in reference to the one true God (cf. Hos 2:16), Saul presumably did not intend to honor the Canaanite god Baal when he named his son Ish-Baal (which would mean "The man of the Lord")—especially since the name of his firstborn son Jonathan means "The LORD has given."

Although David became king over "the house of Judah" by popular anointing (v.4), Abner single-handedly makes Ish-Bosheth king over "all Israel," thus demonstrating that he is the real power behind the throne of Israel now that Saul is dead. Gilead was located thirteen miles north of Mahanaim, indicating something of the difficulty David faced in attempting to win the Jabeshites over to his side. The territories of Ephraim and Benjamin are probably selected to represent those areas within Israel that could be reasonably considered to have been under Saul's control ("all Israel" is an obvious hyperbole

for the northern tribes). Ephraim was the largest tribal territory in the north, and Benjamin was the homeland of Saul (1Sa 9:1–2). It is this realm that Ish-Bosheth now inherits—with the ambitious Abner son of Ner pulling the strings.

While Ish-Bosheth was reigning over Israel, the tribe of Judah "followed David." Since David is the man after God's own heart, following David implies following the Lord.

David became king of all Israel shortly after Ish-Bosheth's death (4:12–5:3).Because David's reign in Hebron was more than five years longer than Ish-Bosheth's in Mahanaim (2:10–11; cf. 5:5), it must have been several years after Saul's death before Ish-Bosheth had gained enough support to become king over the northern tribes. Thus Ish-Bosheth's two-year reign would have coincided with the last two years of David's seven-and-one-half-year reign over Judah.

12–17 David and Ish-Bosheth each attempted to seize the other's kingdom. Full-scale warfare was not the only way to accomplish such a goal, however. It could be done between teams of champions. Saul's cousin Abner, together with Ish-Bosheth's men, meet David's nephew Joab, together with David's men, at the "pool of Gibeon." Once again the hand of God can be seen working on David's behalf.

Ish-Bosheth's men and David's men sit down on opposite sides of the pool of Gibeon, probably facing each other. Abner makes a proposal, which Joab accepts, that some of the young men in one group "fight hand to hand" with some in the other. Twelve from each group are "counted off." The number twelve here doubtless stands for the twelve tribes of "all Israel," whose fate hangs in the balance. The initial skirmish ends quickly. Each man "grabbed" his opponent by the head, thrusting a dagger into his side. Just as all the men had met at the pool "together," so also all the men now fall down "together." Following that was a fierce battle, ending in the defeat of Abner's men.

18–23 Asahel, one of the three "sons of Zeruiah," is compared to a gazelle, though his speed as a runner would eventually prove to be his undoing (cf. v.23). The initial combat between Ish-Bosheth's men and David's men broadens and becomes more dangerous. Abner, not spoiling for a fight and eager to get out of harm's way, flees the scene of the massacre. Asahel, however, is determined to overtake and kill Abner, nothing deterring him. After identifying his pursuer to his own satisfaction, Abner tells Asahel to give up the chase; he advises him to appease his desire for vengeance by killing one of the young men fleeing from Gibeon. The single-minded Asahel, however, is adamant.

Abner then issues a final warning: Unless he stops chasing Abner, Asahel will be the one who dies. Why would he want Abner to strike him "down"? And if Abner kills Asahel, how could he "look" Asahel's brother Joab "in the face"? Abner's fear of Joab proves to be not unfounded (cf. 3:27, 30). Asahel, however, refuses to listen. Continuing to run full speed ahead, he closes the gap between himself and Abner, and the latter suddenly turns to face his pursuer. Asahel's momentum hurls him onto the butt of the spear of Abner, who thrusts it through Asahel's "stomach" (cf. 3:27; 4:6; 20:10), killing him on the spot. As David's men began passing by that place, they stood transfixed in horror at the death of a fallen comrade.

Asahel, though dead because of his headlong pursuit of Abner, would be long remembered in Israel. He is listed first among the Thirty, David's military elite (23:24). It would only be a matter of time, however, before Asahel's brother Joab would avenge his great loss (3:30).

24–28 Although others came to a halt at the sight of their dead comrade, Joab and Abishai (Asahel's brothers) continue their pursuit of Abner. At sunset they come face to face with the Israelites ("the men of Benjamin," since they probably formed the largest number as the tribe of Saul), who take their stand "on top of a hill"—an ideal vantage point from which to direct or engage in battle if necessary (cf. Ex 17:9–10). Just as Abner had earlier proposed that hostilities begin (v.14), so he now proposes that they cease with the words: "Must the sword devour forever? . . . How long before you order your men to stop pursuing their brothers?"

"How long" commonly introduces questions implying a rebuke. Abner cleverly baits Joab by referring to the two groups of antagonists as "brothers"—and Joab bites by accepting the identification. When brothers fight brothers, the result can only be "bitter-

ness" and shame (Ob 10). Joab thus calls off the chase, and Abner's timely plea thus leads to results remarkably similar to those described in 1Sa 25:34.

29 It was customary for armies to travel at night, probably to be as inconspicuous as possible. Marching eastward across the Jordan, Abner and his men continue until they arrive at Mahanaim.

30–32 Including Asahel, a total of twenty of David's men are "missing" in action, presumably all dead. The body count of Ish-Bosheth's men, however, is "three hundred and sixty." The eighteen-to-one ratio in favor of David demonstrates how terrible was the cost of Abner's arrogance (v.14) and how thoroughly "Abner and the men of Israel were defeated by David's men" (v.17).

Joab's men took Asahel's body to Bethlehem, the hometown of David and his clan, where Asahel would be given a proper burial in "his father's tomb." During much of ancient Israelite history, multiple burials in family tombs cut into the underlying rock of the slopes of hills were commonplace. Having left the body of their fallen comrade in Bethlehem, Joab and his men continue on to Hebron, more than twenty miles southwest.

3:1 The "house of Saul" and the "house of David" figure prominently in the next several chapters (cf. esp. ch. 7). War—almost inevitable when rivals aspire to the same throne—continues between them "a long time" (at least for the two years of Ish-Bosheth's reign over Israel). But Ish-Bosheth's weakness is no match for David's strength, and the outcome is a foregone conclusion.

5. Sons born to David in Hebron (3:2–5)

2–5 Anointed king over Judah in Hebron, David settled down with his two wives Ahinoam and Abigail and began to build a substantial family during his seven-and-a-half-year rule there. His firstborn son Amnon ("Faithful"), the son of Ahinoam, would ultimately be killed by the men of Absalom (13:28–29), David's third son. His second son, Kileab, whose mother was Abigail, is mentioned only here and apparently died before he was able to enter the fray to determine who would be David's successor as king of Israel.

Absalom ("[Divine] Father of peace") was the son of Maacah, a Geshurite princess whom David may have married as part of a diplomatic agreement with Talmai, the Geshurite king. See chs. 13–18 for the story of Absalom.

Adonijah ("My Lord is the LORD") the son of Haggith would figure prominently in the struggle for David's throne (cf. 1Ki 1–2), eventually to be assassinated in favor of Solomon. David's polygamy, begun with Ahinoam and Abigail (1Sa 25:43), continues unabated—indeed, it increases—in Hebron.

B. David's Accession to Kingship Over Israel (3:6–5:16)

1. Abner's defection to David (3:6–21)

The devastating defeat of Ish-Bosheth's men by David's men (2:30–31) has made its impact on Saul's cousin Abner. Ruthless and ambitious, Abner is a canny politician who sees the handwriting on the wall. He therefore sets about to transfer Ish-Bosheth's kingdom over to David—and Ish-Bosheth can only sit by helplessly and watch the inevitable unfold (vv.9–11). Doubtless hoping for a prominent place in David's kingdom, Abner wants to be the divinely chosen agent in delivering Israel to David's rule.

6 Abner is not only well positioned to wrest Israel's kingdom from the hapless Ish-Bosheth but also to do with it whatever he pleases—including delivering it to David. While Abner was "strengthening his own position," it was characteristic of David that he "found strength" in the Lord his God (1Sa 30:6).

7–11 Ish-Bosheth's surprise question to Abner—"Why did you sleep with my father's concubine?" (i.e., Rizpah)—arrives like a bolt from the blue. This act by Abner is probably intended to assert his claim to Saul's throne (cf. vv.8–10; 16:20–22; 1Ki 1:1–4; 2:13–22). Abner responds indignantly to Ish-Bosheth: "Am I a dog's head—on Judah's side?" That is, how can Ish-Bosheth possibly think that Abner would defect to Judah? He protests that although he is loyal to Saul's house, Ish-Bosheth is accusing him "now." He has not, after all, handed Ish-Bosheth over to David. He therefore pretends not to be able to understand how Ish-Bosheth can "accuse" him of cohabiting with Rizpah.

Far from denying Ish-Bosheth's accusation, however, Abner takes a strong oath of self-imprecation, vowing that he will become God's instrument in bringing about what the Lord had promised to David—namely, transferring the entire kingdom of Israel to David. Cowardly and powerless, Ish-Bosheth can do nothing to stem the tide of Abner's ambitions.

12–16 The preliminary meeting between Abner and David takes place through messengers rather than face to face. Abner's rhetorical question, "Whose land is it?" is perhaps intentionally ambiguous. To Abner it means, "The land of Israel is mine to give" (and therefore David should make an agreement "with me")—though it could also mean, "The land of Israel is yours because of God's promise." In any case, the Lord is working behind the scenes to deliver the northern tribes into David's hands.

For his part, David is willing to accept Abner's proposal only on one condition: that he bring Michal, Saul's younger daughter, with him when he comes to Hebron. David is adamant, warning Abner not to come without bringing Michal.

David chooses his words carefully. When speaking to Abner he refers to Michal as "daughter of Saul," thus reminding Abner that if he agrees to bring her with him he has turned his back on Ish-Bosheth for good and has assented to David's succession to Saul's throne. When speaking to Ish-Bosheth, however, David calls Michal "my wife," thus reminding Ish-Bosheth that she is David's wife (cf. 1Sa 18:25–27) and that the responsibility for her being now with Paltiel is Ish-Bosheth's, since he is the son and heir of Saul, who wrongfully gave her to Paltiel in the first place (1Sa 25:44). Now that Saul's death has given him a free hand, David wants to strengthen his claim to Saul's throne by retrieving Michal.

The guardian and brother of Michal, Ish-Bosheth, powerless as ever, readily consents to David's demand and takes Michal away from her husband Paltiel. When Abner and Michal depart for Hebron, the heartsick and weeping Paltiel tags along as far as Bahurim, where Abner orders him to go back home. And so it is that Michal is added to David's roster of wives.

17–21 The time when Abner "conferred" with Israel's elders was probably before the events of vv.15–16. Abner's counsel to the elders is straightforward: There is no reason to delay any longer in making David king over all Israel. God had promised David that he would be divinely endowed to "rescue my people Israel from the hand of the Philistines," a word originally spoken concerning Saul (see 1Sa 9:16). In any event, God himself is the true Deliverer of his people (cf. esp. 1Sa 7:8) and thus sovereignly chooses whom and when he will.

On his way to Hebron, Abner pays special attention to the Benjamites, Ish-Bosheth's kinsmen, and tells them of his plans. He then went on and told David what Israel and Benjamin wanted to do. Though counted among the northern tribes and an indispensable part of the kingdom of Israel, the "house of Benjamin" would eventually become inextricably linked to the house of Judah (cf. 1Ki 12:21–23).

Arriving in Hebron with Michal, Abner and his twenty men sit down to a feast prepared for them by David. With his offer to bring "all Israel" into a covenant relationship with David, Abner's defection to the house of Judah is complete. The agreement between the two men in vv.12–13 was personal and is not to be confused with the national "compact" now being made between north and south. Abner assures David that the end result of the compact would be that "you may/will rule over all that your heart desires" (1Ki 11:37). Abner's mission now complete, David sends him away and he goes "in peace" (GK 8934).

2. The murder of Abner (3:22–39)

22–27 In the middle of this otherwise tranquil scene the narrator states that David's men and Joab return from a raid. Arriving in Hebron and learning that Abner has come and gone, Joab goes to David and demands to know why he released Abner—the only genuine obstacle to David's sitting on Israel's throne—when he had him firmly in his grasp. After all, Abner is a cousin of Saul, who must therefore be an opponent of David. Indeed, to Joab, Abner has doubtless come to Hebron for the sole purpose of learning everything that might well prove useful in the future. Joab's accusation that David allowed Abner to "deceive" him is ironic in light of his own subsequent treachery (cf. Pr 24:28–29).

David is realistic enough to recognize that he is still too weak to risk a showdown with the sons of Zeruiah (v.39). The brash Joab thus feels free to leave David without so much as waiting for a response to his rebuke; nor is David told that Joab's men pursue Abner and bring him back.

Pretending that he wants to discuss a private matter with him, Joab takes Abner into a relatively secluded area. Then, "to avenge" (GK 928) the blood of his brother Asahel, Joab kills Abner. The method used is the same used in Abner's killing of Asahel and thus illustrates the principle of retaliation in kind.

28 Upon hearing of Abner's murder, David declares himself and his kingdom "innocent" (GK 5929) of all personal responsibility for Abner's death. The motif of innocence is first recorded in the assessment of his friend Jonathan (1Sa 19:5; cf. also Pss 19:13; 26:6; 64:4). Needless to say, that opinion is not shared by disaffected Israelites, who hold David accountable for the massacre of the Saulides and continue to think of him as a "man of blood" (cf. 16:7–8).

29 David places the blame for Abner's death squarely where it belongs by cursing the "head of Joab" and devoutly hoping that Abner's blood will "fall" upon it—i.e., that Joab's bloodguilt will eventually bring about his own destruction through divine vengeance (cf. v.39). Just as David had absolved himself and his "kingdom" of all guilt in the matter (v.28), so also now he includes Joab's "father's house" in Joab's condemnation. In pronouncing this curse, David uses colorful language. He pleads that Joab's house will never be without people who would suffer in five categories: (1) has a "running sore"; (2) has "leprosy"; (3) "leans on a crutch"; (4) falls by the sword; and (5) lacks food. The first three curses relate to physical ailments, the fourth to war, and the fifth to famine.

30 Since the blood of a kinsman was to be avenged by the death of the one who had shed it, Joab and Abishai invoked the hoary custom of the blood feud as a rationale for murdering Abner. It is, however, questionable whether the blood vengeance of Joab and Abishai was justified, seeing that Abner had killed Asahel in battle. Indeed, David later excoriates Joab for having shed the blood of Abner "in peacetime as if in battle" (1Ki 2:5). Joab, of course, may have had an ulterior motive in wanting Abner out of the way, for Abner could supersede him as commander of David's army (8:16; 20:23; 1Ki 1:19; 11:15, 21).

31–35 David issues commands concerning Abner's funeral: The murderer Joab is required to attend, as are all his men. David's weeping and mourning over a slain family member, comrade, or friend is not only a concession to custom but also—and far more significantly—an indication of his tender heart (cf. 1:12; 13:36–37; 18:33; 19:1–4). Joab and his men walk in front of the funeral procession; David brings up the rear. Expressing his grief, the king "wept aloud" at Abner's tomb.

The rhetorical question that begins the lament requires a negative answer. With his hands not bound and his feet not fettered, Abner was surely not "lawless." Just as with Saul and Jonathan and their comrades in arms, David fasts till evening (see 1:12). Try as they might, Joab's men are unable to induce David to eat the customary funeral meal (cf. Jer 16:5, 7). Although David could not have been completely unhappy about the death of his most powerful rival for control, his grief is genuine.

36–37 David's magnanimity impresses Joab's men and is sure to draw them ever closer to his inner circle of advisors. Indeed, in their eyes he can do no wrong. David was not an accessory to Abner's death. His protestation of innocence, believable then to his own cohorts, is ratified now by the northern tribes.

38–39 The chapter concludes with David's final brief encomium for Abner and final imprecation against Joab and Abishai, both of which are directed to his own men. Just as it was important for all Israel to know that David was innocent of the death of Abner (v.37), so also David wants his men to "realize" that in Abner a great man has been lost to Israel.

David realizes that although he is "the anointed king," he is nevertheless "weak." By contrast Joab and Abishai are "strong"; and David, exercising commendable caution, realizes that he is not presently able to rebuke

them with any semblance of authority. In the hearing of his own men, however, he repeats the curse against Joab (cf. v.29), perhaps this time including Abishai.

3. The murder of Ish-Bosheth (4:1–12)

The only viable threat left to the throne is Saul's son Ish-Bosheth and Jonathan's son Mephibosheth. Chapter 4 removes them from the scene, one explicitly and the other implicitly.

1–3 When Ish-Bosheth heard that Abner had died, "he lost courage"—a typical and expected reaction. Abner's death left a power vacuum in the north, and it is therefore not surprising that all Israel became "alarmed."

Among the opportunists eager to take charge are two of Ish-Bosheth's men, Baanah and Recab, who are "leaders of raiding bands." Such groups functioned under David's authorization as well (3:22; 1Ch 12:18) and were not uncommon elsewhere during the early days of Israel's monarchy (cf. 1Sa 30:1, 8, 15). These two men were members of the tribe of Benjamin and thus loyal to Saul (and Ish-Bosheth).

4 Jonathan's son Mephibosheth is introduced parenthetically to demonstrate that his youth and physical handicap disqualify him for rule in the north. When the nurse of Jonathan's son learned that the boy's father had been killed (1Sa 31), she decided to flee with the boy to a safer location. In her headlong flight the boy fell from her grasp and became permanently crippled. Five years old when his father died, Mephibosheth was now twelve (cf. 2:11).

5–7 Baanah and Recab go to where Ish-Bosheth was staying (doubtless in Mahanaim) and arrive there at the time of siesta, knowing full well that Ish-Bosheth would be sleeping. They gain access to his sanctum through subterfuge and stab him "in the stomach"—a technique rapidly becoming the preferred method of killing.

Ish-Bosheth is assassinated while lying on "the bed in his bedroom," luxuries available only to the wealthy or to royalty in those days (Ex 8:3; 2Ki 6:12; Ecc 10:20). Recab and Baanah "cut off" (GK 6073) Ish-Bosheth's head and bring it to David as a trophy of their vile deed. To avoid easy detection they travel through the night a distance of almost thirty miles.

8 Presenting the head of Ish-Bosheth to David, Recab and Baanah remind him that Ish-Bosheth's father, Saul, had been David's "enemy." Indeed, Saul had "tried to take" David's "life" on many occasions. But now, say the assassins, the Lord himself—to whom belongs all vengeance (cf. Heb 10:30)—has "avenged" (GK 5935) David not only against Saul but also against Saul's "offspring."

9–11 David now takes an oath in the name of the Lord. To the assassins' reminder that Saul had tried to take David's "life," the king responds that the Lord delivers his "life" out of "all trouble" (including the difficulties he had faced when he was a fugitive from Saul's wrath). Like the Amalekite who claimed to have killed Saul (1:10), Recab and Baanah can hardly have expected David's blistering response to their murder of Saul's son Ish-Bosheth. The man who had "told" David that Saul was dead was of course the Amalekite (see comment on 1:4). Although he thought he was bringing "good news," he brought about only his own death at David's headquarters in Ziklag (cf. 1:1). Expecting a "reward" for his news (cf. 18:22), he received death instead.

If David condemned the Amalekite for delivering the finishing blow to the mortally wounded Saul on the battlefield, then a similar fate is self-evident in this context: (1) Recab and Baanah, "wicked men," have killed Ish-Bosheth, an "innocent" (lit., "righteous"; GK 7404) man. (2) Although Saul was killed in a context of danger and violence in battle, Ish-Bosheth was murdered in what should have been the secure and peaceful serenity of his own home and bed. David's outrage (whether real or pretended) over the circumstances of Recab and Baanah's assassination of Ish-Bosheth causes him to hold them accountable.

12 Death begets death: The Amalekite claimed to have killed Saul, and in retaliation David "put him to death" (v.10); Recab and Baanah have killed Ish-Bosheth (v.11), so David gives the order that they in turn be killed. David's men mutilate the dead bodies of Recab and Baanah by cutting off their hands and feet. Following the ancient custom

to expose to public view the entire corpse of the victim whenever possible (cf. 21:9–10; 1Sa 31:9–10; Dt 21:22–23; Jos 10:26–27), the bodies of Recab and Baanah are "hung" in Hebron. It is ironic indeed that the prolonged struggle between Ish-Bosheth's men and David's men begins and ends by the placid waters of a pool (see 2:13).

The contrast between the treatment of the remains of the assassins and of Ish-Bosheth could hardly be more striking. While the dead bodies of Recab and Baanah are impaled in a public setting to disgrace them and deter others, Ish-Bosheth's head is given an honorable burial in Abner's tomb at Hebron—the headquarters of David, their political rival.

With the death of Ish-Bosheth, no other viable candidate for king remains for the elders of the northern tribes. Meanwhile David sits in regal isolation, above the fray as always, innocent of the deaths of Saul, Jonathan, Abner, and now Ish-Bosheth. The way is open for his march to the throne of Israel.

4. David anointed king over Israel (5:1–5)

1–3 That the kingdom about to be established under King David is intended as a truly united monarchy is underscored by the use of the word "all" three times (vv.1, 3, 5). The "elders" of Israel, representing the "tribes," come to David at Hebron with the express purpose of submitting to his rule. Preliminary consultations with them had been initiated by Abner (3:17), but his death had postponed further discussion.

The elders give three reasons for their submission to David. (1) Their reference to themselves as "your own flesh and blood" signifies their sense of kinship with him. David is a "brother Israelite" (Dt 17:15). (2) During Saul's reign David was Israel's best army officer. (3) They understand that the Lord has chosen David (cf. 3:18) as Israel's new king. They sense that the Lord has invested David with the titles of "shepherd" (GK 8286) and "ruler" (GK 5592) as well as "king" (GK 4889). Apart from God himself (Ge 48:15; 49:24), David is the first example of a specific person being called a "shepherd" (cf. Nu 27:17). Moreover, the motif of David as shepherd was prefigured at his earliest anointing (see 1Sa 16:11).

In the ancient Near East, the figure of the shepherd was associated with gentleness, watchfulness, and concern. Since it is the shepherd's task to lead, feed, and heed his flock, the shepherd metaphor was a happy choice for benevolent rulers and grateful people alike. David thus becomes the paradigm of the shepherd-king (cf. Ps 78:70–72; Eze 34:23; 37:24), and it is not surprising that "great David's greater son," Jesus Christ, is introduced frequently as the "good shepherd" (Jn 10:11, 14), the "great Shepherd" (Heb 13:20), and the "Chief Shepherd" (1Pe 5:4).

David is also called a "ruler," a title that provided a convenient transition between judgeship on the one hand and kingship on the other. David's sovereignty is underscored by the threefold reference to him as "king" in v.3. He does not go to Israel's elders in Mahanaim; they come to him in Hebron. Their need for him is greater than his for them—although the stakes are enormous on both sides.

Abner had suggested earlier that Israel "make a compact" with David (3:21). But now that the moment for such an agreement has arrived, the king initiates "the compact" with his (future) subjects. At the same time, however, the covenant should not be understood as bestowing on David the role of all-powerful suzerain and dooming the Israelites to become his craven vassals. The covenant-making formalities take place "before the LORD," acknowledging that the proceedings are under his guidance and enjoy his blessing (v.12).

As David had earlier been anointed king over Judah (2:4), so now he is anointed king over Israel, "as the LORD had promised through Samuel" (1Ch 11:3). The news of the anointing would soon become well enough known to cause concern in the hearts of the Philistines (v.17).

4–5 David became king in Hebron when he was thirty years old. His overall reign of forty years matches that of Saul (cf. Ac 13:21) as well as that of his son and successor Solomon (1Ki 11:42). His reign consisted of seven and a half years in Hebron over Judah alone (2:11) and thirty-three years in Jerusalem over all Israel and Judah. Although Jerusalem had not been unknown to David before the elders of Israel anointed him (see 1Sa 17:54), he is now determined to make it his capital.

5. David's conquest of Jerusalem (5:6–12)

6–8 Far and away the most important city in the Bible, Jerusalem is mentioned there more often than any other. Geographically and theologically it is located "in the center of the nations" (Eze 5:5). Known also by its abbreviated name "Salem" (Ps 76:2), it makes only one appearance in the OT before the time of Joshua (Ge 14:18).

Soon after being anointed king over all Israel and Judah (v.5), David deploys his men for a march on Jerusalem "to attack the Jebusites, who lived in the land." Some of the Jebusites lived outside the fortress at Jerusalem (cf. 24:16), where the temple of Solomon would eventually be built (2Ch 3:1).

The interchange about the "blind" and the "lame" is an example of pre-battle verbal taunting. Thus in v.6 the Jebusites smugly claim that even disabled people can withstand any attack on their fortress, while in v.8 David retaliates in kind by characterizing his enemies as "lame and blind." The overconfident Jebusites, however, do not count on the skill and determination of David, who captures the fortress of Zion and renames it the "City of David." For more on the capture of Jerusalem, see 1Ch 11.

Up to this time Jerusalem had been on the border between Judah in the south (Jos 15:1, 5, 8) and Benjamin in the north (Jos 18:11, 16). Tied to no tribe, the City of David could champion its neutrality, central location, and virtual impregnability as qualities that made it and its environs the ideal capital for David's newly established, united kingdom.

9–10 David thus "took up residence" in Jerusalem where the Jebusites lived (v.6). He then set about to repair the surrounding areas "from the supporting terraces inward." Joab (David's commander-in-chief) "restored the rest of the city" (parts of which were doubtless damaged or destroyed as a result of Joab's attack to capture it; see 1Ch 11:8).

The assertion that David "became more and more powerful" is reminiscent of 3:1. Now as earlier, however, David himself is not the source of his strength; "the LORD God Almighty" (a title for God that is more royal than military), the true King of Israel, grants his power and, as always, is "with him."

11–12 The events described here occurred a long time after those recorded in vv.6–10.

Hiram did not become king of Tyre (a well-fortified island in the Mediterranean Sea) until about 980 B.C., more than twenty years after David was anointed king over Israel and conquered Jerusalem. Hiram continued his friendly relations with Israel's royal house well into the reign of David's son Solomon (1Ki 5:1–12; 9:10–14). Hiram traded building materials (which Israel lacked) for agricultural products (which Phoenicia lacked). Thus Hiram sends to David logs of "cedar," carpenters, and stonemasons. All this activity would eventuate in a "palace for David"—a palace that would fill him with a certain unease (7:1–2).

Witnessing God's evident blessing on his life, David once again acknowledges the Lord's role in establishing "him as king over Israel" (v.12). Indeed, David's throne and dynasty would be established forever (7:11b–16; 22:51; 1Sa 25:28), culminating in the eternal reign of great David's greater Son (Lk 1:30–33). As Israel's ideal ruler, David has the privilege of seeing his kingdom "exalted" (GK 5951) by the Lord himself. All this is not for his own sake alone but also, and primarily, for the sake of "his" (i.e., God's) people.

6. Children born to David in Jerusalem (5:13–16)

13–16 In violation of the divine decree to Israel's future kings not to "take many wives"

(Dt 17:17), David adds "more" concubines and wives to the wives he already has (see 3:5). This is the first time that concubines are mentioned in connection with David.

David fathered many children in Jerusalem. Although vv.14–16 list only sons born to him by his wives, the name of at least one of David's daughters has survived (Tamar, the sister of Absalom; cf. 13:1; 1Ch 3:9).

The first four names are of sons born to David by Bathsheba (1Ch 3:5), two of whom appear elsewhere in the biblical narratives. The two main claimants to David's throne in his later years were Absalom (his third-born, 3:3) and Solomon (his tenth-born). Solomon would eventually outlast his rivals for the throne and rule over the united kingdom (cf. 1Ki 1:28–39).

C. David's Powerful Reign (5:17–8:18)

1. The Philistines defeated (5:17–25)

17–21 As soon as the Philistines learn "that David had been anointed," they become concerned and go to "search" for him, an unnecessary task if David had already occupied the formidable fortress of Zion. So apparently this incident occurred after David's anointing and before the conquest of Jerusalem. The "stronghold" to which David retreats is therefore not the fortress of Zion. Also, David "went down" to the stronghold (a per-

This is Lloyd K. Townsend's painting of the way that the City of David must have looked during the time of David and Solomon (facing west). The only direction from which any enemy could attack and hope to conquer Jerusalem was from the north. Used by permission.

son went up to Jerusalem). Possibly the cave of Adullam is the place intended.

The locale of the two battles of vv.20–25 is the "Valley of Rephaim," on the border between Judah and Benjamin. A relatively flat area, its fertile land produced grain that not only provided food for Jerusalem but also attracted raiding parties.

To meet the Philistine threat David, as always, "inquired of the LORD" by consulting the Urim and Thummim through a priest: Should he attack the Philistines, and would the Lord hand them over to him? The divine answer is emphatically affirmative to both questions. In obedience to God's command, David goes to engage the Philistines in battle at Baal Perazim, where he defeats them and carries off their idols, which they had probably brought onto the battlefield as protective talismans. The purpose of carrying the Philistine idols away from the battlefield was so that, at David's command and in accordance with Mosaic prescription (Dt 7:5, 25), they could be burned up (1Ch 14:12).

22–25 On a subsequent occasion, the Philistines again came to attack David, again in the Valley of Rephaim. As before (v.19), David inquires of the Lord. Unlike earlier, however, this time David is told not to go straight up. Apparently the first confrontation was with a smaller contingent of Philistines, whereas now a flanking movement is strategically preferable. The Lord instructs David to "move quickly" as soon as he hears the sound of "marching" in the treetops, promising to go out in front of them. David, acting at God's command, defeats the Philistines and pursues them "all the way from" Gibeon to Gezer.

2. The ark brought to Jerusalem (6:1–23)

Apart from brief mention in 1Sa 14:18, the ark of the covenant has not been mentioned since 1Sa 7:2. David now adds to political centralization in Jerusalem a distinctly religious focus by bringing to the city the most venerated object of his people's past: the Lord's ark—repository of the covenant, locus of atonement, throne of Israel's invisible Lord.

1–5 For the third time (cf. 5:17–21, 22–25) David assembles his troops, here to serve as a military escort for the ark of the covenant. David's "chosen men" are reminiscent of

Saul's elite corps of soldiers (see 1Sa 24:2). For at least half a century the ark of the covenant had been sequestered in Kiriath Jearim, in the house of Abinadab—either inaccessible to the Israelites because of Philistine control of the region, or languishing in neglect (perhaps partially because King Saul had shown no interest in it; cf. 1Ch 13:3).

The solemnity of the scene that unfolds is enhanced by the grandiose description of the ark and the repeated references to it. It is depicted as the seat of authority of "the LORD Almighty, who is enthroned between the cherubim" (see 1Sa 4:4). It is also referred to as the "ark of God" and the "ark of the LORD." The ark "is called by the name/ Name," an idiom denoting ownership and thus here emphasizing that the ark is the Lord's property. The term "Name" (GK 9005) not only refers to the Lord's name but also stands for his presence.

David's intention to "bring up" the ark to the City of David is of course not only commendable but also entirely appropriate. At the same time, however, his first attempt to do so follows Philistine rather than Levitical procedure. David and his men transport it on a "new cart" (see 1Sa 6:7–8). Abinadab's sons (or perhaps grandsons), Uzzah and Ahio, were given the task of guiding the cart, Ahio walking in front and Uzzah presumably bringing up the rear.

With David taking the lead, the Israelites begin "celebrating." In this context "before the LORD" means "before the ark." "Songs" and "harps, lyres, tambourines, sistrums and cymbals" were staple elements on such joyful occasions.

6–11 At the threshing floor of Nacon (possibly a place of sanctity), Uzzah (whose name, ironically, means "Strength") sensed that the oxen pulling the cart were stumbling and that the ark might fall to the ground. Thus he "reached out" to steady the ark and "took hold of" it. Despite whatever good intentions he may have had, his doom was sealed.

The wrath of divine judgment fell on Uzzah for several reasons. (1) Most obvious was "his irreverent act" of putting his hand on the ark (cf. 1Ch 13:10). (2) Uzzah was transporting the ark in a cart rather than carrying it on his shoulders as prescribed in the law. (3) There is no evidence that he was a Kohathite Levite (cf. Nu 4:15). Just as God had "struck down" (GK 5782) and put to death some of the men of Beth Shemesh for looking into the ark (1Sa 6:19; cf. Nu 4:20), so also God "struck [Uzzah] down" for touching the ark. Ironically, he died "beside" the ark, which he had been attempting to rescue from real or imagined harm.

The Lord's anger causes David to react first with anger of his own and then with fear. He is understandably indignant that the divine "wrath" (GK 7288) has broken out against Uzzah and resulted in his death, a seemingly harsh penalty for so small an infraction. It is not surprising that David's anger against God should be mingled with fear of him; he questions whether the ark can "ever" come to him.

David decides that a cooling-off period is in order before he is willing to give further consideration to taking the ark to be "with him" in the "City of David." Instead, he gives the ark a temporary home in the house of Obed-Edom, a Levite (1Ch 15:17–18, 21, 24–25; 16:4–5, 38)—possibly a Kohathite Levite (cf. Jos 21:20, 24–26; 1Ch 6:66, 69). There the ark remained for three months, during which time the Lord blessed the house of Obed-Edom with numerous descendants (cf. 1Ch 26:8). This fact led to the confidence of David that the Lord would bless the house of David forever (7:29).

12–19 When David is told of the Lord's blessing on the house of Obed-Edom "because of the ark," he proceeds to bring the ark up to the fortress, accompanied by "the elders of Israel and the commanders of units of a thousand" (1Ch 15:25). If in the case of the first attempt there was celebration and singing (v.5), now there is "rejoicing."

"Those who were carrying the ark" were, of course, (Kohathite) Levites (1Ch 15:26). It seems likely that every six steps a bull and a fattened calf were sacrificed, after which the procession continued. Given the proximity of the house of Obed-Edom to the City of David, such a procedure would not have been needlessly cumbersome or time-consuming.

Prefiguring the priestly functions of King David, the prophet Samuel had earlier worn a "linen ephod" (see 1Sa 2:18) and most likely the linen robe normally worn under the ephod (cf. 1Ch 15:27; also Ex 28:31). During the time of the Israelite monarchy, kings occasionally officiated as priests (cf. 24:25; 1Ki 8:64; 9:25).

"With all his might" David "danced before the LORD"—i.e., before the ark, the symbol of the Divine Presence. He and the entire nation now "brought up" the ark from the house of Obed-Edom to Jerusalem. The scene is punctuated with shouts of excitement and triumph and with the sound of ram's-horn trumpets.

"Michal daughter of Saul" (so described because she is depicted here as being critical of David and is therefore acting like a true daughter of Saul) watched the proceedings from a window. Perhaps still smarting from her separation from her former husband Paltiel (cf. 3:13–16), Michal looks at David leaping and dancing with something less than the love she at one time had for him (see 1Sa 18:20), and she reacts with disgust. Once she had helped David escape through a window (1Sa 19:12); now, peering at him through a window, she despises him "in her heart."

The ark is brought in and set in its predetermined place "inside the tent David had pitched for it." Apparently at a somewhat later date, another tabernacle was constructed and installed at the high place in Gibeon (1Ki 3:4; 1Ch 16:39; 21:29; 2Ch 1:3, 5, 13), about six miles northwest of Jerusalem. Thus there were in effect two tabernacles: The one in Jerusalem served as the repository for the ark (1Ch 16:37), while the one in Gibeon housed the other tabernacle furnishings (1Ch 16:39–40).

During the time that the Mosaic tabernacle was not in use (for whatever reason), various offerings continued to be sacrificed without necessary benefit of the bronze altar of burnt offering. Now David sacrifices "burnt offerings and fellowship offerings" as an act of gratitude and consecration "before the LORD" (i.e., honoring the Divine Presence symbolized by the ark). In particular, the fellowship offering signified the desire of the worshipers to rededicate themselves to God in covenant allegiance and to reaffirm their king as God's covenanted temporal ruler.

After bringing an unspecified number of offerings, David blesses the people "in the name of the LORD Almighty," once again performing the role of a priest. David adds to his blessing the distribution of food.

20–23 Having blessed the Israelites who witnessed the procession of the ark (v.18), David returns home to "bless" (GK 1385) his own household. When a warrior returned victorious from battle, the women of his hometown would come out to meet him and would celebrate with music and dancing. David might have expected his wife Michal to celebrate his similar triumph in much the same way. If so, he is quickly disappointed.

Michal's words drip with the "How" of sarcasm: David, the "king of Israel" (an office once occupied by her father Saul), has "distinguished himself." To what extent David's state of undress was scandalous is impossible to say (see comment on v.14). Far from the kind of "vulgar fellow" who would be an exhibitionist, David makes it clear that he is most concerned about how the Lord evaluates his actions, insisting that he is celebrating "before the LORD," not before the "slave girls." In his rebuke of Michal, he clearly dissociates himself from Saul ("your father") and the Saulides by asserting that God had chosen him rather than them.

The chapter ends on a somber note: "Michal daughter of Saul" remains childless to her dying day. In ancient times childlessness, whether natural or enforced, was the ultimate tragedy for a woman.

3. The Lord's covenant with David (7:1–17)

1–3 Settled in his royal house and victor over his enemies, David's regal status is now beyond question. He can thus now be referred to as "the king."

David decides that the time has finally come for him to do what any self-respecting king worthy of the name should do: build a house for his God. The contrast between his own house and that of the Lord is stark: The human king is "living" in a sumptuous "palace" while the "ark of God remains" in a mere "tent." Constructed of the finest materials and with the best available workmanship (see 5:11), David's palace overwhelms in size and splendor the relatively simple tent. To David's credit he recognizes that the imbalance needs to be rectified.

Safe within his well-fortified palace and behind secure frontiers, the king doubtless had plenty of time for a major construction project. The Lord has "given him rest from all his enemies around him," fulfilling during David's reign a promise he had made to Israel

centuries earlier (cf. Dt 3:20; 12:10; 25:19; Jos 1:13, 15) and had already fulfilled during the lifetime of Joshua (Jos 21:44; 22:4; 23:1).

Just as Saul had been advised by Samuel the prophet (1Sa 3:20), so also David would be counseled by various prophets, the most important being Nathan. Agreeing that the king should fulfill his desire to build a house for God, Nathan understands that David will ultimately follow the path of obedient servanthood because "the LORD is with" him.

4–7 The messenger formula ("This is what the LORD says") pinpoints Nathan as the mediator of the divine oracle. David is now referred to by the Lord as "my servant David," a description that he willingly and humbly accepts (v.26).

The Lord's first question in v.5 expects a negative answer (cf. 1Ch 17:4). In the broader context, at least two reasons are given why David himself did not build the temple: (1) He was too busy waging war with his enemies (1Ki 5:3); (2) he was a warrior who had shed much blood (1Ch 22:8; 28:3). Neither reason dims David's vision, however, and before his death he makes extensive preparations for the temple (cf. 1Ch 22:2–5; 28:2).

The tabernacle will still suffice as the Lord's dwelling. He reminds Nathan that he has never "dwelt" in a permanent house, not from the day of the Exodus. He has been content with "moving from place to place," demonstrating his continuing desire to walk among his people. The irony in v.6 must not be missed: Although God condescends to accompany his people on their journey with a tent as his dwelling, a tent carried by them, all along they have in fact been carried by him.

The second question (v.7) also expects a negative answer. It implies that the Lord never required the Israelites nor any of their rulers to build him a "house of cedar." The word "people" (GK 6639) used with reference to Israel is an important theme in the chapter, employed four times in each half. "I will be your God, and you will be my people" or the equivalent is doubtless the most characteristic covenant expression in the entire OT (cf. v.24; Ex 6:7; Lev 26:12; Dt 26:17–18; et al.).

8–11a The repetition of the messenger formula (cf. v.4) marks the start of a new section of Nathan's oracle. Here, however, the word "LORD" has been augmented by "Almighty"

(GK 7372), a regal title that stresses the Lord's function as covenant Suzerain of David, his "servant" vassal.

The divine grant to David is divided into two parts: promises he will realize (vv.8–11a) and those to be fulfilled after his death (vv.11b–16). In vv.7b–8a the Lord reviews his earlier blessings on his servant David. He begins by reminding David of where he found him. Once a mere shepherd boy, David has been given a much weightier responsibility: to be "ruler" (GK 5592) over the Lord's people Israel.

As the Lord had been "moving from place to place" (v.6) with his people, so he has been with David wherever he has gone. He had promised to "cut off" (GK 4162) David's enemies from before him. Now the Lord promises three things.

(1) He will make David's "name great," a promise that is a clear echo of the Abrahamic covenant (cf. Ge 12:2). It is fulfilled in 8:13.

(2) The Lord will "provide a place" for Israel. This had been predicted long ago (Dt 11:24; cf. Jos 1:3–4). And far from being temporary, the "place" that God would provide would be the land where he would "plant" (GK 5749) them (cf. Ex 15:17; Pss 44:2; 80:8). Having a home of their own, David and his countrymen will be free from "wicked people" and their oppression. Although oppression had been virtually endemic in Israel during the entire period of the judges, such would no longer be the case.

(3) The Lord will give David "rest" (GK 5663) from all his enemies. The method he will use will be to "subdue" them (1Ch 17:10). As always, the ultimate Giver of the rest is God himself.

11b–16 "The LORD declares to you" introduces God's promises to David's descendants: a "house" (GK 1074; i.e., a dynasty); a throne and kingdom that will last forever; a "house" (GK 1074; i.e., a temple); and a Father-son relationship, including covenant love that will never be taken away. "House" is obviously used with two different meanings in these verses. All the promises will be fulfilled after David's death (i.e., his being laid to "rest" with his "fathers"; see comment on 2:30–32).

It is David's "offspring" who will build the Lord's temple. The emphasis that his offspring will "come from your own body"

forges yet another striking link to the Abrahamic covenant (cf. Ge 15:4). The possibility of understanding "offspring" (lit., "seed"; GK 2446) as either singular or plural is exploited by Paul in Gal 3:16 (see comments on that verse). The Lord goes on to promise that he will "establish" (GK 3922) the "kingdom" and "throne" of Solomon.

In v.13a, "house" means temple. David's offspring has been designated to build a temple for the Lord's "Name." As for v.13b, the Lord promises that the Davidic dynasty, throne, and kingdom will endure "forever" (a fact mentioned seven times in ch. 7).

The Lord's words in v.14a are doubtless the best known as well as the most solemn in the entire chapter: "I [emphatic] will be his father, and he [emphatic] will be my son." In its original setting the son is Solomon. The statement is therefore a formula of adoption. Because of its typological use in 2Co 6:18 and Heb 1:5, v.14a has long been considered messianic in a Christological sense.

A further aspect of the father-son metaphor is its covenant setting. The use of "father" for God and "son" for Solomon is thus entirely appropriate in what has justifiably come to be known as the Davidic covenant. Although the Davidic king was to enjoy the unique relationship of being the Lord's "son," the Lord would use "men" as agents of divine judgment on Solomon (and his dynastic successors) "when he does wrong." It is not an idle promise: "The rod" of divine wrath fell on Jerusalem and her citizens because of the sins of David's descendants (cf. La 3:1).

Finally, the Lord promises that although he "took away" (GK 6073) his love from Saul, the divine "love" (GK 2876) will never "be taken away" (GK 6073) from David's son Solomon and his descendants, through whom David's throne "will be established." That David's "house" will "endure" echoes Abigail's insight in 1Sa 25:28. That the throne of David will remain "forever" refers ultimately to Christ, because David's kingdom came to an end.

Taken together, vv.14b–15 have often been understood to mean that the Davidic covenant is unconditional: No matter what David's descendants do, the Lord's love will "never be taken away" from them. But that the Lord will punish the king for disobeying the law at least qualifies the promise if not making it conditional. Kings are not to use the Davidic promise as a justification for wicked behavior.

17 It was incumbent on a prophet to report "all the words" that the Lord commissioned him to proclaim, and Nathan keeps nothing back.

4. David's prayer to the Lord (7:18–29)

18–21 In response to the Lord's promises as mediated through Nathan, David "went in" (probably into the tent he had pitched for the ark) and sat "before the LORD." Beginning his prayer with appropriate humility and deference, David addresses God with a title found in the books of Samuel only here—"Sovereign LORD"—which he employs seven times in vv.18–29. And if God is sovereign to David, he recognizes his own status as vassal by referring to himself ten times as the Lord's "servant" in vv.19–29.

The central theme of the prayer is David's "house/dynasty," a word that occurs seven times (vv.18 ["family"], 19, 25, 26, 27, 29 [twice]). Though his household is insignificant at present, David is confident that it will become great in the future because of the proven reliability of God and his promises. That the Lord has brought him to this point in his experience would be sufficient for David, but he gratefully recognizes that in God's eyes it is "not enough." The Lord has even better things in store for him in the future.

The Lord has honored his servant beyond measure, and David asserts that there is scarcely anything more that he can say. He affirms that the Lord "know[s]" (GK 3359) his servant, which perhaps includes the fact that he has "chosen" him (cf. Ge 18:19; 2Sa 6:21).

If David earlier knew that the Lord had blessed him "for the sake of" his people Israel (5:12), he now confesses that the Lord has done a "great thing" (GK 1525) simply for the sake of his "word" (GK 1821) and according to his "will" (GK 4213). The greatness of God overwhelms David, for the Sovereign Lord is "great" (GK 1540), he has done "great" (GK 1525) wonders (v.23), and his name is "great" (GK 1540; v.26).

22–24 Verse 22 is only one among many OT texts describing God as unique. That there is "no one like" the Lord is a major theme in the Song of Hannah (1Sa 2:2; see also 10:24). Three times in v.23 Israel is referred to as God's "people," the one elect "nation" (GK 1580) out of all the "nations." Israel's powerful "God" is contrasted with the nations' impotent and ineffective "gods."

Israel's matchless Lord has gone out to do three things for his grateful people: "redeem" GK 7009) them, "make a name" for himself, and "perform great and awesome wonders" by driving out the enemy. The ancient establishment of Israel as God's own people "forever" is now to be channeled through David and his dynasty, which will continue "forever" (vv.25, 29). The OT manifestation of the kingdom of God is now to be mediated through the Davidic monarchy.

25–29 David is much concerned about the permanence of the promise the Lord has made concerning the Davidic dynasty. The covenanted establishment of David's house would be a visible sign of the greatness of God's name. Indeed, "LORD Almighty" would become widely known as the appropriate royal title of the Great King, the God of Israel.

David is grateful that God has "revealed" to him his plans and purposes: "I will build a house for you." He acknowledges that the Sovereign Lord alone is God and that his words are "trustworthy" (GK 622). Although 2Sa 7 never uses the term "covenant" (GK 1382) of God's promises to David, "good things" (GK 3208) is a technical term synonymous with "covenant" in contexts like this (cf. 2Ch 21:7; Ps 89:3; Isa 55:3).

David concludes his prayer with a request to the Lord to "be pleased" to bless the Davidic dynasty. Since it is the Sovereign Lord himself who has promised, David speaks with the calm assurance of a man who knows that his house will continue forever "in your sight." The prayer of David thus ends on a note of confident contentment.

5. David's enemies defeated (8:1–14)

1 It is impossible to know for certain whether the divine promises of ch. 7 preceded or followed the divine victories of ch. 8. In any event, the account of the Philistine defeat resumes the story told in 5:17–25. Exactly what David "took" from the Philistines cannot be determined with certainty. The importance of the conquest of Philistia by David can scarcely be overestimated.

2 As David defeated the Philistines, so also he defeated the Moabites. Why he fought against Moab is unknown, especially since the Moabitess Ruth was his ancestress (cf. Ru 4:10, 13, 16–17) and Moab had at one time sheltered his parents (see 1Sa 22:3–4). His method of executing a specified number of prisoners of war is not attested elsewhere. Only a third of its inhabitants are "allowed to live" (cf. 1Sa 27:9, 11).

The Moabites "became subject to" David, which included bringing "tribute" (GK 4966). This word often means "gift(s)/offering(s)" presented as sacrifices, which are thus understood as tribute brought into the throne room of the Great King. After David's death, nations conquered by him would continue to bring tribute to his son Solomon (1Ki 4:21) and his successors.

3–12 Despite the limited information available about Aram during David's reign, the space given to its conquest in this chapter testifies to its overall significance in the scheme of things. David "fought" and "defeated" the Arameans. His main adversary is "Hadadezer son of Rehob." Hadadezer ("[The God] Hadad is [my] help") is the Hebrew form of an Aramean dynastic royal title.

The pronoun "he" (v.3) most likely refers to Hadadezer, for David could not have extended his power to the Euphrates before the defeat of Hadadezer. Marking the eastern reaches of David's realm, the Euphrates was one of the fixed boundaries of the land promised to Abraham (Ge 15:18).

In driving back the forces of Hadadezer to the Euphrates, David obtained substantial numbers of chariots, charioteers, and foot soldiers. Most of the horses that pulled the chariots he "hamstrung" (i.e., severed the large tendon above and behind their hocks to disable them). Reinforcements from Damascus came to "help" Hadadezer, but David defeated them, and the Arameans became tributary to him.

Part of the tribute that David took from Hadadezer was his officers' "gold shields," ceremonial or decorative shields not used in battle (cf. SS 4:4; Eze 27:11). They were brought to Jerusalem and eventually placed in Solomon's temple, where they remained for well over a century (see 2Ki 11:10). Three towns that belonged to Hadadezer yielded a "great quantity of bronze" to King David. Solomon used the bronze in his construction of the articles of the temple (1Ch 18:8).

The news of David's defeat of the entire army of Hadadezer eventually reaches the ears of Tou king of Hamath, who had been at war with Aram. Tou wants to make peace with David, so he sends his son Joram to "congratulate" him on his victory over Hadadezer and to bring a voluntary gift of "articles of silver and gold and bronze" in order to gain David's goodwill.

In grateful acknowledgment of divine blessing, David dedicates all the articles—whether received as gifts, as tribute, or as plunder—to the Lord. After recording the defeat of Aram in the north, the narrator includes a summary of David's conquest of neighboring nations in every direction: south (Edom), east (Moab and Ammon), west (Philistia), and southwest (Amalek).

13–14 David's "striking down" the Edomites was accomplished through Abishai son of Zeruiah (see 1Ch 18:12), but David gets the credit because he is the supreme commander. At the same time, Abishai's brother Joab strikes down 12,000 Edomites (cf. the title of Ps 60). David then "put garrisons throughout Edom." In all his successes, however, the Lord was the One who "gave victory."

The regions added to David's realm through the defeat of all the nations more than doubled the territory of Israel, thus initiating the golden age of Israelite history. David's new boundaries correspond to those outlined in the divine promise to Abraham (Ge 15:18; cf. also Dt 11:24; Jos 1:4).

6. David's officials (8:15–18)

15 A mighty warrior, King David now reigns over "all" Israel and administers justice and equity to "all" his people. "Doing what was just and right" was the hallmark of a strong king in the ancient Near East and included such reforms as the elimination of oppression and exploitation (cf. esp. Ps 72).

16–18 As expected, the commander of David's army is Joab son of Zeruiah. Jehoshaphat is recorder and remains so into the reign of Solomon (1Ki 4:3). The function of the recorder was apparently either to have oversight of state records and documents or to serve as a royal herald. Though appearing

KINGDOM OF DAVID AND SOLOMON

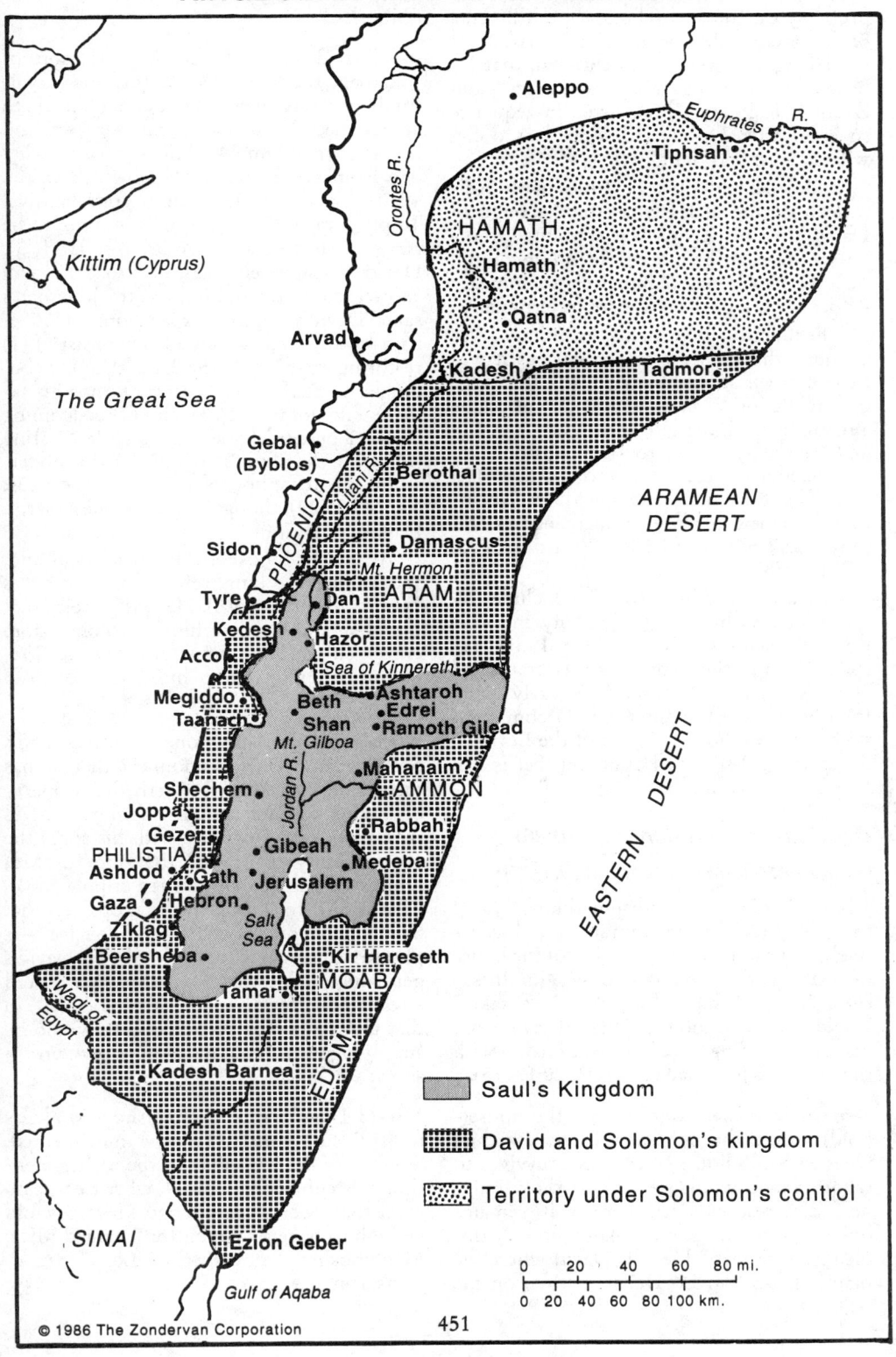

Aleppo

Euphrates   R.

Tiphsah

Orontes R.

HAMATH

Hamath

Kittim (Cyprus)

Qatna

Arvad

Kadesh   Tadmor

The Great Sea

Gebal
(Byblos)

Berothai

ARAMEAN
DESERT

Litani R.

PHOENICIA

Sidon   Damascus

Mt. Hermon

Tyre   Dan   ARAM

Kedesh

Acco   Hazor

Sea of Kinnereth

Megiddo   Beth   Ashtaroh
Taanach   Shan   Edrei
        Mt. Gilboa   Ramoth Gilead

EASTERN   DESERT

Jordan R.

Mahanaim
AMMON

Shechem

Joppa
Gezer   Gibeah   Rabbah

PHILISTIA
Ashdod   Gath   Medeba
        Jerusalem

Gaza   Hebron

Ziklag   *Salt
Sea*

Beersheba   Kir Hareseth

Tamar   MOAB

*Wadi of
Egypt*

EDOM

Kadesh Barnea

	Saul's Kingdom
	David and Solomon's kingdom
	Territory under Solomon's control

SINAI

Ezion Geber

Gulf of Aqaba

0   20   40   60   80 mi.

0 20 40 60 80 100 km.

451

here by name for the first time, Zadok was probably one of the preliminary fulfillments of the oracle of the man of God in 1Sa 2:35. It is striking, and perhaps intentional, that Jehoshaphat (meaning "The LORD judges") and Zadok ("Righteous") are listed in sequence so soon after David is described as doing what is "just and right" (v.15).

Zadok shared priestly duties with Ahimelech during at least part of the reign of David. Possibly Zadok was appointed to offer sacrifices at the tabernacle in Gibeon (cf. 1Ch 16:39–40) and Ahimelech to minister before the ark of the covenant in Jerusalem.

The function of Seraiah as "secretary" was as much that of secretary of state as it was that of royal scribe. Benaiah was in charge of David's bodyguard (23:22–23), became a royal executioner (cf. 1Ki 2:25, 34, 46), and eventually rose to the position of commander-in-chief of Israel's army (1Ki 4:4). The Kerethites and Pelethites constituted a corps of foreign mercenaries employed as David's bodyguard (for details see ZPEB, 1:787).

The list of David's officials concludes by reporting that his sons (how many and who they were is not stated) were "royal advisers" (GK 3913), the same word translated "priests" in v.17. Apparently in early Israel there were priests who were (1) connected with the royal house, (2) not of the Levitical order, and (3) serving a function that is still largely unknown to us.

D. David's Court History (9:1–20:26)

1. Kindness to Mephibosheth (9:1–13)

1 Now that he is the undisputed king, David can afford to be magnanimous. He thus actively seeks out anyone "still left of the house of Saul" so that he might show "kindness" (GK 2876) to him "for Jonathan's sake." David's desire to show kindness derives from his long-standing covenant relationship with the deceased Jonathan (1Sa 18:3; 20:12–15).

2–5 David makes contact with the house(-hold) of Saul through Ziba. David asks him whether Saul's house "still" has a survivor to whom David would be able to show kindness. Ziba responds that there "still" remains one of Jonathan's sons, a man who is "crippled in both feet." He tells David where the man is living—in Lo Debar, a town on the

other side of the Jordan. David sends for Mephibosheth.

6–8 David meets "Mephibosheth son of Jonathan, the son of Saul" (his ancestry is fundamental to the narrative). Mephibosheth approaches David with "your servant" and bows down to him. Doubtless knowing what had happened to his uncle Ish-Bosheth (cf. 4:5–8), he is understandably apprehensive. To put him at ease David tells him not to be afraid. True to his earlier promise (vv.1, 3), David declares emphatically that he will show Mephibosheth kindness for Jonathan's sake. David's specific expressions of covenant loyalty to Saul's grandson consist of (1) restoring to him all the land that had belonged to Saul (though certainly not his father's kingdom; cf. 16:3), and (2) welcoming him as a perennial guest at his table. "Eating (food) at the (king's) table" can be understood as a metaphor referring to house arrest (cf. 2Ki 25:29), though that is not necessarily David's intention.

Again Mephibosheth "bowed down" and, speaking to the king, referred to himself as "your servant" (cf. v.6). He was grateful that David should "notice" him. Becoming more craven still in his submission to David, Mephibosheth referred to himself as a "dead dog."

9–11a Ziba is "summoned" into David's presence, and David announces that he has turned over to Mephibosheth the property belonging to Saul and his "family." David then gives Ziba (together with his sons) the responsibility to "farm" the land for Mephibosheth, since the latter is a cripple (v.13). Ziba is also to "bring in the crops" so that Saul's grandson may "be provided for"—a phrase that seems to cast a cloud over David's generous pledge that Mephibosheth would always "eat [food] at [the king's] table," in that it appears that Mephibosheth would be supplying some if not most of his own provisions.

11b–13 David's intention to show kindness to Saul's survivors (v.1) is now implemented. Some time has passed since the earlier mention of Mephibosheth in 4:4, when he was no more than twelve years of age. He is now old enough to have a "young son" named Mica. Mephibosheth moves from Lo Debar to Jerusalem.

2. The Ammonites defeated (10:1–19)

1–5 The deceased king of the Ammonites was Nahash (1Sa 11:1–2). When political power is based on dynastic rule, a king about to die can reasonably expect his son to succeed him as king (cf. 2Ki 13:24). Thus Hanun becomes king of Ammon. Assuming that Nahash is the same Ammonite king defeated by Saul (1Sa 11:1–11), the kindness he showed to David may have been expressed during David's days as a fugitive from the Israelite royal court. David now wants to reciprocate by showing "kindness" (GK 2876) to Nahash's son, thereby cementing the alliance already existing between the two nations. Just as the events of ch. 9 promoted domestic harmony inside Israel, so this event helped maintain the viability of one of David's international agreements and strengthen his position outside Israel.

The means chosen by David to show kindness is sending a delegation to "express his sympathy" on the death of Nahash. The Ammonite "nobles," convinced that David's delegation are spies, share their suspicions with Hanun. Accepting the assessment of his men, Hanun decides to refuse David's cordial overtures and to humiliate David's messengers. He begins shaving off "half of each man's beard," no doubt vertically rather than horizontally to make them look as foolish as possible. He then cuts off their garments "in the middle at the buttocks" and sends them on their way. Forced exposure of the buttocks was a shameful practice inflicted on prisoners of war (cf. Isa 20:4).

Hanun's treatment of David's men was clearly a violation of the courtesies normally extended to the envoys of other states in ancient times. Indeed, the indignities heaped on them are a grotesque parody of the normal symbolic actions that accompanied mourning. When David was told about their humiliation, he sent messengers to tell them to stay at Jericho until their beards had grown back; only then could they return to Jerusalem. The regrowth of the beards of David's men would portend disaster for the Ammonites.

6–14 The Ammonites' perception of themselves is accurate: They have become a "stench" in David's nostrils, affirming that David would almost surely be expected to declare war against Ammon. In anticipation of that likelihood the Ammonites, at enormous cost, hire a large army of Arameans to supplement their own troops.

Upon learning that the Ammonite-Aramean coalition has been formed, David takes no chances. He sends out the entire army, under the leadership of his commander Joab, to engage them. While the Ammonites prepare to defend their city by amassing at its most vulnerable point, the "entrance to their city gate," the troops from the various Aramean districts are deployed in "the open country."

Before the battle is joined, Joab decides on a strategy and encourages his brother Abishai. He perceives enemy battle lines in front of him and behind him, thus recognizing that he must divide his army if he is to prevail. Sensing that the Arameans are the stronger of the two forces in the enemy coalition, he chooses some of the best troops and leads them personally to fight against the Arameans. The rest of the men he puts under the command of Abishai, who leads them against the Ammonites.

Failing to size up one's opponent adequately, for whatever reason, can prove disastrous. Joab therefore stresses vital communication between the two commanders so that either can come to the other's "rescue" if necessary—an outcome that the Ammonites and Arameans would be unable to accomplish with respect to each other.

Joab's "Be strong" is clearly reminiscent not only of the ringing words of encouragement of Moses and the Lord to Joshua and to all Israel (Dt 31:6–7, 23; Jos 1:6–7, 9) but also of those of the Transjordanian tribal leaders to Joshua (Jos 1:18). Joab senses that he is responsible not only for the people of Israel but also for "the cities of our God." Like Eli before him (see 1Sa 3:18), Joab resigns himself to divine sovereignty: "The LORD will do what is good in his sight."

Leading Israel's finest troops and convinced of the Lord's guidance, Joab marches into battle against the Arameans, who turn tail and flee. As soon as the Ammonites learn of Aram's headlong retreat, they scurry to the protection of the walls of Rabbah. Apparently unable to pursue his advantage against the Ammonites by besieging the city—for now, at least—Joab returns to Jerusalem.

15–19 Undeterred by what they consider a minor setback, the Arameans regroup their forces. Hadadezer sends for Aramean reinforcements from beyond the eastern side of the Euphrates River, and his army commander Shobach leads them to Helam. When David's intelligence network informs him of the exact location of the Aramean forces, he musters his entire army and crosses the Jordan River eastward to engage the Arameans in battle (see also comment on 11:1). The Israelites prove to be more than a match for them; David and his men press their advantage and inflict huge numbers of casualties on the enemy. The defeat of the Arameans leaves them no option; they sue for peace and become subject to the Israelites (cf. 8:6). The defeat of the Ammonites is reported in 12:26–31.

3. David's sin against Bathsheba (11:1–5)

1 The story, continuing the account begun in ch. 10, is set "in the spring, at the time when kings go off to war." Springtime, which marks the end of the rainy season in the Middle East, assures that roads will be in good condition (or at least passable), that there will be plenty of fodder for war horses and pack animals, and that an army on the march will be able to raid the fields for food.

David sends his commander Joab and his army to continue the battle against Ammon. The result is the mass slaughter of the Ammonites and the siege of Rabbah, their capital city, the reduction and capture of which is yet to come (cf. 12:26–29). Every able-bodied man in Israel goes to war—except the king himself. The contrast between David and his men could hardly be expressed in starker terms. Staying home in such situations was not his usual practice, of course (cf. 5:2; 8:1–14; 10:17). Indeed, leading one's troops into battle was expected to be the major external activity of an ancient Near Eastern ruler (see 1Sa 8:5–6, 20). Although therefore reprehensible in itself, David's conduct on this occasion opens the way for royal behavior that is more despicable still.

2–5 Perhaps because of the oppressive heat of a spring sirocco, David lengthens his afternoon siesta into the cooler part of the day. Getting up from his bed and taking a stroll, "from" the roof of his palace he sees a "very beautiful" woman bathing. The heat of the unusually warm spring day has forced the woman to bathe outside to escape the suffocatingly hot atmosphere of her house. Failing to heed the warning of texts such as Nu 15:39, David lusts after her and sends someone to find out who she is.

The woman is Bathsheba, the daughter of Eliam and the wife of Uriah the Hittite. Eliam was the son of Ahithophel (23:34), who was in turn David's counselor (see 15:12). Since Eliam was one of David's warriors and thus perhaps a foreign mercenary, and since Bathsheba is listed along with the pagan ancestresses of Jesus (Mt 1:3–6), she possibly was of non-Israelite origin. She was married to Uriah the Hittite, another of David's mercenary warriors (cf. 23:39). He was apparently a worshiper of the Lord (his name probably means "The LORD is my light"). Like Ahimelech the Hittite before him (see 1Sa 26:6), Uriah depends on his master David for sustenance and support. In return he gives total loyalty to the king.

It is thus the wife of a trusted servant that David is about to violate, and v.4 mercifully tells the story in the briefest possible compass. Master of all he surveys, David has everything—and yet does not have enough. David sends messengers to get her. She came to him, and David "slept with her." The scene is blatantly adulterous.

The parenthetic sentence—"She had purified herself from her uncleanness" (i.e., her ceremonial uncleanness from her menstrual period; cf. Lev 15:25–26, 30)—informs the reader that Bathsheba was clearly not pregnant when she came to David. Shortly thereafter she found out that she was, leaving no doubt that the child is David's. Of all the fateful conceptions recorded in the OT (cf. Ge 16:4–5; 19:36; 25:21; 38:18; Ex 2:2), Bathsheba's ranks near the top of the list in terms of future repercussions.

4. The murder of Uriah (11:6–27)

6–17 David hatches a three-phase scheme to cover up the serious problem of Bathsheba's pregnancy, each phase more ruthless than the preceding: a clean one (vv.6–11), a dirty one (vv.12–13), and a criminal one (vv.14–17).

As Bathsheba had sent word to David informing him of the problem, David now sends word to Joab to begin the process of seeking a solution. At David's command Joab sends him "Uriah the Hittite," the full description underscoring Uriah's mercenary status and therefore presumably also his loyalty to David. Uriah "came to him," just as Bathsheba had come under similar circumstances (v.4).

David begins his conversation with Uriah in an apparently cordial way by asking about the welfare of Joab, the soldiers, and the war. Ostensibly satisfied concerning how things are going on the battlefield, David tells Uriah to go down to his house and "wash" his "feet." Although usually an expression describing an act affording refreshment and relaxation in a land where dusty roads are the rule (see 1Sa 25:41), the phrase may well be intended here as a double entendre, given the euphemistic use of "feet" in the sense of "genitals" (cf. Ex 4:25; Dt 28:57). Thus Bathsheba's washing and Uriah's washing would both involve or eventuate in sexual cohabitation. So Uriah "left" the palace, and a royal gift "was sent" after him.

"But Uriah slept"—not with Bathsheba, as David had hoped, but "at the entrance to the palace" with all of David's servants. The next day, when David learns that Uriah did not sleep with his wife, he obviously wants to know why. Just as David and his men had always "kept themselves from women" whenever they set out to do battle (1Sa 21:4–5), so now Uriah refuses to sleep with his wife. How could Uriah in good conscience "eat" and "drink" and "lie" with his wife, while the rest of the army was on the battlefield? That he calls Bathsheba "my wife" could hardly have failed to rebuke David, who had callously violated the relationship between Uriah and the person most precious to him. Uriah concludes his statement to David by emphatically rejecting the king's offer. Taking a solemn oath, which translates literally as "By your life, and by the life of your soul," Uriah swears that he will not so much as think of doing the unthinkable.

Failing in his first attempt to cover up his sin, David tries again: "'Stay here one more day.' . . . So Uriah remained in Jerusalem" for two more days. Although he will not go to his own house to eat and drink, he has no such scruples in the king's house. When David gets him drunk, he assumes that Uriah's inhibitions will be overcome and that he will automatically go home, sleep with Bathsheba, and thus absolve David of any charge of her child's paternity. At first it appears that

David's plan will succeed: Indeed, "in the evening he went out to sleep on his mat." But on his bed at home? With his wife? No, on the bed where he had slept earlier: "among his master's servants. He did not go home."

His second attempt at covering up his affair with Bathsheba having failed, David senses that he has exhausted his options and so decides to have Uriah killed. David takes no chances: In the morning he "wrote a letter to Joab and sent it with Uriah." Doubtless unknown to him, Uriah carries to Joab his own death warrant.

David orders Joab to put Uriah in the front line of battle against the Ammonites where "the fighting is fiercest." Uriah is then to be abandoned to his fate: He will be "struck down and die." "Cursed is the man who kills his neighbor secretly," intones Dt 27:24. David "struck down" (GK 5782) Uriah and took his wife (12:9), and these things were done "in secret" (12:12). The implication is obvious: David's heinous actions are punishable under the divine curse.

At this point in the account, however, Uriah is still alive. When Joab receives David's letter, he recognizes that to isolate Uriah as the only fatality in the attack would cast suspicion on David's motives. Joab thus besieges Rabbah, the Ammonite capital, and puts Uriah at a "place" where its best troops are defending it. But he also sends other "men" in David's "army" to accompany Uriah into the heat of battle. And so it is that "some" of the mercenaries are sacrificed so that one, relatively unnoticed, might die. David's criminal purpose is finally accomplished: "Uriah the Hittite died."

18–27a Sending a complete "account of the battle" to David through a messenger, Joab warns the latter that the king's anger may "flare up"—presumably when he learns of the high casualty count. Indeed, says Joab, David may ask a series of questions designed to reveal the stupidity (in his opinion) of Joab's battle plans against Rabbah. To get too near a city wall in ancient times was to flirt with mortal danger, since arrows and other missiles rained down from protected positions. Joab thus senses that when David hears about the casualties he will want to know why his men needlessly risked their lives.

Arriving in Jerusalem, Joab's messenger tells David "everything" his master has sent him to communicate. He apparently elaborates somewhat on the words of Joab, however, by giving (or concocting) a few additional details. The powerful Ammonites, says the messenger, "came out" from Rabbah to engage the Israelites in "the open," but David's men were able to drive them back to "the entrance to the city gate."

As the messenger completes the fulfillment of his mission to David, his words remind us that the tragedy has come full circle: The archers' death volley has been fired "from" the wall. And it is not the guilty king, safe in his fortress palace in Jerusalem, who suffers; the enemy's arrows find their mark in his innocent "men," who are sacrificed so that David can inconspicuously dispose of his ultimate target, Uriah.

Temporarily oblivious to the divine displeasure, David resorts to a platitude: "The sword devours one as well as another." From his own selfish perspective the king is basically saying that what is done is done, that it cannot be helped, and that innocent people will often get caught in the crossfire when vital goals are pursued. What is more, David further masks his true concerns by telling the messenger to authorize Joab to "press" the attack against Rabbah as part of the royal message that will "encourage" him.

When the news of Uriah's death reaches Bathsheba, she mourns for him. David, however, apparently sheds no tears for Uriah (cf. 1:12). With the husband of Bathsheba now dead and the period of her mourning now over, the way is open for David to bring her to his house. The phrase emphasizes the abuse of royal power that David exercises. Bathsheba becomes David's wife, and in due course a son is born of their earlier adulterous act. Although short-lived and unnamed, the child would not be unloved during the days of his fatal illness (cf. 12:16–24).

27b This is the only reference to "the LORD" in the entire chapter. David would later confess that his sin with Bathsheba is known to God and is therefore deserving of divine judgment (Ps 51:4).

5. Nathan's rebuke (12:1–25)

1–10 In his prophetic role Nathan is sent by the Lord to proclaim his convicting word to the king. That Nathan's rebuke begins with a parable makes it none the less effective. Now

a rich man, David should have remembered what it was like to be "poor" because by his own admission he himself had once been a "poor man" (see 1Sa 18:23).

The parable is clear enough. David is the rich man, and Uriah is the poor man with only one "ewe lamb" (= Bathsheba). The verbs used of the ewe lamb indicate that it is prized as a genuine member of the poor man's family (cf. especially the references to eating, drinking, and sleeping, precisely the things Uriah refused to do with his wife in 11:11). "Food" is literally "piece (of bread)," meager fare at best. That the ewe lamb stands for Uriah's wife becomes clear at the end of v.3, where the status of the lamb is raised to that of a human being.

The word for "traveler" (lit., "walker"; GK 2144) reminds the reader that David's trouble began because he had earlier "walked around" on the roof of his palace (see 11:2). Bound by culture and tradition to provide hospitality for his guest, the rich man set about to prepare a meal for him. Instead of slaughtering one of his own animals, however, he took the poor man's one ewe lamb instead—just as David had sent messengers to get Bathsheba. That the rich man "refrained" from taking one of his own animals is a key element in understanding the main point of Nathan's parable.

Understandably, David's moral indignation against the rich man in Nathan's parable takes the form of burning anger that will not be assuaged until justice is done. David, using the Lord's name in a solemn oath, declares that the one who did this "deserves to die"— David of course being oblivious to the fact that he himself is "the man" (v.7a). David's actual sentence reflects Ex 22:1, where the penalty for a stolen lamb is "four times over." Nathan then delivers his terse incriminating word to David: "You are the man."

Nathan goes on, using an amplified variation of the messenger formula, to remind David that it was the Lord who had anointed him king and delivered him from Saul's clutches. Just as Saul, the Lord's anointed, had fallen from grace, so also would David— though not in the same way or to the same degree. Furthermore, the Lord "gave" Saul's "house" and wives (presumably including at least Ahinoam [1Sa 25:43] and perhaps his concubine Rizpah [cf. 3:7]) to David. That they are given into David's "arms" is an ironic allusion to Nathan's parable. And the God whose generosity knows no bounds would have "given" even more to David if he had considered it appropriate. But David's unbridled desire and willful murder have foreclosed that option.

If Saul lost the kingdom through having "rejected [GK 4415] the word of the LORD" (1Sa 15:23), David is judged because he has decided to "despise [GK 1022] the word of the LORD." To despise the Lord's word is to break his commands and thus to incur guilt and punishment (cf. Nu 15:31), and that without remedy (cf. 2Ch 36:16). It is to do what is evil in his eyes (cf. Ps 51:4). It is tantamount to despising the Lord himself. David thus finds himself in unsavory company (cf. 1Sa 2:29–30).

11–12 The second section of the Lord's oracle (vv.11–12) is relentless in the immediacy with which it threatens retaliation against the king. As David has done what is evil, so the Lord will bring "calamity" (GK 8288) upon him, "before your very eyes"—events such as Amnon's rape of Tamar (13:1–14), Absalom's murder of Amnon (13:28–29), Absalom's rebellion against David (15:1–12). David's punishment for his crimes against Bathsheba and Uriah is a clear example of a conditional element in the Davidic covenant (see comment on 7:15–16).

As David "took" Uriah's wife, so the Lord will "take" David's wives. As the Lord "gave" Saul's property and wives and Israel's kingdom to David, so he will now "give" David's wives to someone else, to "one who is close to you"—ironically, an expression earlier used of David himself in similar circumstances (see 1Sa 15:28; 28:17). The "one who is close" to David turns out to be his own son Absalom.

13–14 To his credit, David confesses to the prophet Nathan that he has broken God's law. Though he could have vacillated or indignantly denied Nathan's accusation or ridded himself of Nathan in one way or another, David accepts full responsibility for his actions. And, as might be expected, the prophet does not leave the king comfortless. Nathan comes to David with words of divine grace. In judging the rich man for his cruelty (v.5), David had unwittingly chosen his own death penalty (cf. Lev 20:10; Dt 22:22). But the Lord, through his prophet, announces the forgiveness of David's sin and preserves his life. That God does not hesitate to strike people down for what might be considered lesser infractions (see 6:7) makes his forbearance here all the more noteworthy.

At the same time, however, the Lord is not through with David, for David shows "utter contempt [GK 5540] for the LORD" (cf. 1Sa 2:17). While David will not "die," the son born to him will.

15–23 Having fulfilled his prophetic mission, Nathan leaves the palace and goes home. The Lord then strikes Bathsheba's newborn son with what proves to be a fatal illness. The phrase "the child that Uriah's wife has borne to David" underscores the fact that David's adultery and murder will claim yet another innocent victim.

Despite the prophet's pronouncement that the child's fate is sealed, David is not yet willing to resign himself to the death of his son. He therefore intercedes for the child's life. Ostensibly as a symbol of mourning, he "fasted." David's servants stand "beside" him, concerned about him and urging him to get up and take care of his personal needs. He refuses, however, and will not so much as eat any food with them.

The death of the child takes place on "the seventh day." David's servants are reluctant to tell him of the child's death for fear that their master may do something "desperate." Aware of the whispering of his servants and thus realizing that the child is dead, David gives verbal expression to his own worst nightmare. The servants finally affirm to him that the child is indeed dead. Having admitted to himself the inevitable, David gets up from the ground, washes, puts on lotions, and changes his clothes, no doubt exchanging mourning garb for normal clothing.

After entering the "house of the LORD" (the tabernacle; see comment on 1Sa 1:7) to worship him, David then goes to "his own house." There he breaks his fast (cf. v.16) and eats ordinary food. Understandably, David's servants are confused. While the child was alive, David—acting like a mourner—had "fasted and wept." Now that his son is dead, however, the king puts on garments befitting royalty and enjoys a good meal.

David readily admits that his conduct might appear peculiar, but he was counting on the open door of the divine "perhaps":

"Who knows?" But why should he fast now? Since the netherworld is the "Land of No Return," the child "will not return" to David, and nothing that David can do will "bring him back again." Indeed, David's only option for a reunion with his son is to "go to him."

24–25 At the beginning of the narrative, Bathsheba had been "the wife of Uriah the Hittite" (11:3), but as an outcome of the sin of King David she has become "his wife." David "comforted" Bathsheba (who doubtless mourned her son's death) when he "went to her and lay with her." In due course she gave birth to yet another son, named Solomon, which apparently means "(God is) his peace."

On the basis of his love for Solomon, the Lord "sent word through" the prophet Nathan, who was thereby instructed to call David's newborn son Jedidiah ("Loved by the LORD"), a name similar to that of David himself (see 1Sa 16:13). Why the boy was given two names is not known.

If at the beginning of ch. 12 Nathan rebuked the king (vv.7–14), at its end he comforts him. But Nathan's ministry with respect to David and Solomon is not yet finished. During David's last days Nathan plays a key role in the succession of Solomon as king (cf. 1Ki 1:11–14, 24–27).

6. The Ammonites defeated (12:26–31)

26–28 Intensifying the siege of Rabbah (the Ammonite capital city) begun in 11:1, Joab captures its "royal citadel," probably the major fortification either within the city or guarding the approaches to it. The city now rendered defenseless, Joab sends word to David that he has fought against Rabbah and taken its "water supply." Joab advises David to muster the "rest of the troops" and lead them in the final attack against the city. He warns the king that if he refuses to become personally involved, Joab himself will capture Rabbah, and it will be named after Joab rather than after David. Since it was vital that Rabbah become a part of David's domain, he must be credited with seizing it.

29–31 Thus David finishes what Joab has begun. Having "mustered" the necessary troops, he captures the city. Of the many trophies seized by David, one of the most spectacular was a gold crown that had rested on the Ammonite king's head and was now

transferred to David's. Set with "precious stones," the crown was of such enormous weight and value that it was probably used only on ceremonial occasions. The plunder was in "great quantity." Upon the people David heaped a number of atrocities (cf. 8:2), apparently forcing them to work on various building projects.

Only after David had extended the forced labor requirement to the other defeated Ammonite towns did he and his troops return to Jerusalem. The Israelite victory was thus both thoroughgoing and complete.

7. Amnon's sin against Tamar (13:1–22)

1–2 The events in this chapter occur some time later. A sister of Absalom, Tamar, is "beautiful" indeed (as were a number of the members of the family of David: cf. 1Sa 16:12; 17:42; 2Sa 14:25, 2). As a "virgin," Tamar is protected property, inaccessible to males, including her brother. Amnon is therefore "frustrated" to the extent that he becomes lovesick, because "it seemed impossible for him to do anything to her."

3–5 As the son of David's brother Shimeah, Jonadab is Amnon's cousin, and thus all the people mentioned by name in vv.1–22 are members of the same family circle. Jonadab is also Amnon's "friend." He wants to know why Amnon looks so "haggard" all the time. On hearing the reason, Jonadab advises Amnon to go to bed and "pretend to be ill." When David hears of his son Amnon's "illness," he will come to see him. At that point Amnon should tell his father that he wants Tamar to come and give him something to eat, preparing it in his room. As she does so, Amnon will "watch her"—but in what sense? Amnon's desire to "watch" reminds us of his father's earlier voyeurism.

6–9 Amnon readily accepts the advice of Jonadab, whom he perceives as acting in his best interests. But although on David's arrival Amnon at first quotes Jonadab's words verbatim, he chooses his own terminology in describing what he wants her to do after she actually comes: "make some special bread." The cakes/dumplings will strengthen his heart, but they will also reflect his amorous intentions.

Without hesitation Tamar obeys David's command to go to the house of her "brother Amnon." As might be expected, Amnon is "lying down," a posture devastating for Tamar. Amnon's response to Tamar's six acts of solicitude on his behalf leads to a climactic seventh act of the capricious sort so characteristic of spoiled royalty: He "refused" to eat. He asks everyone to leave the room so that he can be alone and ravish his sister unhindered.

10–14a Once they are alone, Amnon tells Tamar to bring the "food" to him so that he might "eat" from her hand. The language Amnon uses is designed to perpetuate the charade of his pretended illness (cf. vv.5–6). Unsuspecting, Tamar brings the "bread" to Amnon, her "brother," in the "bedroom"—a locale usually reserved for rest and bliss but where betrayal and violence all too often hold sway (cf. 4:7). As soon as the gullible Tamar was within arm's reach, Amnon "grabbed" her. His lustful demand is both ominous and insensitive: "Come to bed with me, my sister."

Tamar's immediate response to Amnon is indignant as well as frantic, in effect saying "No." She matches his "my sister" with "my brother," but in the sibling rather than in the amorous sense. One by one, her short sentences bespeak her terror: "Don't force me." She calls Amnon's intended act of rape a "wicked thing" (GK 5576).

As far as Tamar herself is concerned, she wants to know where she could possibly get rid of her "disgrace" (GK 3075). And as far as Amnon is concerned, Tamar warns him that if he gives vent to his lustful desires, he will be like one of Israel's "wicked fools."

Having asked and answered her own rhetorical questions, Tamar voices her final plea. She implores Amnon to speak to the king (referring to him not as their father but by his title, since she anticipates his acting in an official capacity rather than as a family member). She is sure that David will not keep her from "being married to" Amnon. After all, had not her ancestor Abraham married his half sister Sarah (cf. Ge 20:12)?

Tamar does not appear to be inherently opposed to the idea of marrying Amnon. What she is adamantly against is sexual intercourse with him outside the marriage relationship. Her most eloquent pleading, however, is to no avail. Amnon "refused to listen to her."

14b–15a Amnon had "grabbed" his half sister earlier (v.11), and he has apparently not released her throughout the entire dreary episode. He is, after all, "stronger" than she. So he "raped her." The immediate denouement of the rape is poignantly anticlimactic. A rapist's emotional response following the crime is unpredictable; Amnon "hated" Tamar (cf. the opposite reaction in Ge 34:2–3).

15b–16 Scarcely has Tamar had a chance to catch her breath after being ravished by Amnon before he tells her, "Get up and get out!" Before, consumed by lust, he had begun by begging Tamar to "come [in]"; now, repulsed by disgust, he concludes by banishing her.

Although Tamar's response here is much briefer than her earlier pleas (vv.12–13), she is no more ready to obey Amnon's commands now than she was earlier. She begins in the same way as she had before: "No!" (see v.12). Amnon's sending Tamar away would only add insult to injury by involving him in a greater "wrong" than the rape itself. For the third time, however, Amnon "refused" (vv.9, 14, 16).

17 In v.9b he wanted everyone else out of his bedroom so that, without the presence of witnesses, he could have his own way with Tamar; here he wants Tamar out of his bedroom so that, in her absence, he will not be reminded unduly of the awful sin he has committed. "This woman" here is best rendered simply "this thing," reflecting the contempt in which Amnon now holds Tamar.

Amnon's second command to his servant is to bolt the door. The purpose of securing doors is all too often to prevent or conceal an evil deed (see Ge 19:6; Jdg 3:21–24). Needless to say, a door keeps people not only in but also out.

18–19 Although Tamar's arrival into Amnon's presence was carefully orchestrated (vv.6–9a), her forced departure is abrupt indeed, being locked out by the servant. Once the man has satisfied his lustful desires, he discards the woman (cf. similarly Jdg 19:25) as though she were so much refuse.

But Tamar is one of "the virgin daughters of the king," a status that should have made her doubly untouchable. By no means trash, she wears a "richly ornamented robe" that befits her regal position. Now no longer a virgin, she tears her robe as a symbol of her ravished state. The act of tearing her garment also gives expression to her mourning over her irreparable loss (cf. v.31; 15:32), as do her putting ashes on her head and her weeping (cf. 19:4).

20 The advice of Absalom is both matter-of-fact and calculating. Choosing his words carefully, he asks Tamar whether Amnon has "been with" her—an expression that, though not sexually explicit, is at least suggestive of potential involvement (cf. Ge 39:10). He counsels her to be quiet about the matter for the time being; he, her brother, will solve the problem within the parameters of the family. Therefore Tamar should not pay undue attention to it or worry about it. For the foreseeable future Tamar lives in Absalom's house. There she remains "desolate" (GK 9037), which includes the meanings "unmarried" and "childless" (see Isa 54:1). For an Israelite woman it was a living death (cf. 2Sa 20:3).

21–22 When David hears about Amnon's rape of Tamar and its sequel, he is understandably "furious" (cf. 12:5). But even though he is king, he feels powerless to act because he himself is guilty of a similar sin: his adultery with Bathsheba. His guilt paralyzes him.

Meanwhile Absalom bides his time, saying nothing "either good or bad" to Amnon. Absalom's remarkable forbearance, which would last two years, along with his earlier immediate recognition of Tamar's situation (v.20), suggests the possibility that Absalom has been behind this event, advising Jonadab what to say to Amnon, in order that Absalom would have just cause to kill Amnon and remove him as David's oldest son from likely succession to the throne (see also comment on vv.32–33). Amnon's acquired hatred for his half sister Tamar (v.15) is reprised in Absalom's acquired hatred for his half brother Amnon.

8. The murder of Amnon (13:23–39)

23–24 Two full years having passed, Absalom determines that the time is ripe to avenge the rape of his sister Tamar. He chooses the season of sheepshearing as a suitable if macabre backdrop for the murder of his brother Amnon. As the sheep of Absalom would lose their wool, so David's firstborn, the potential shepherd of Israel, would lose his life.

Absalom invites the king, together with all his sons and officials, to join in celebrating their mutual prosperity at Baal Hazor. Absalom's words to his father are well chosen in terms of both politeness and protocol. In his invitation he refers to himself as "your servant."

25 David declines the invitation, knowing that if his entire retinue would accompany Absalom it would be "a burden to" him. Absalom's urging to the contrary notwithstanding, David refuses to go and gives him his "blessing" (or "farewell"; GK 1385).

26a After asking for the impossible, Absalom cannily requests that Amnon alone be allowed to come. He probably realizes that David, knowing that Absalom may intend to harm Amnon because of what he did to Tamar, will not accede to his latter request any more than he did to the former. On the other hand, perhaps Absalom hopes that the two years that have elapsed since the rape have dimmed the event in his father's mind. In addition, Absalom refers to Amnon as "my brother," apparently to assuage whatever lingering fears David may have.

26b–27 To Absalom's chagrin, David does not agree immediately. His "Why?" smacks more of the suspicious than of the incredulous. This time, however, Absalom's urging is successful—and perhaps beyond his wildest expectations: The indecisive king not only allows his son Amnon to go but also sends the rest of his sons along with him.

28–29 Emboldened by his increasing success, Absalom is now in command. To be "in high spirits from drinking wine" is often to invite mischief (cf. Est 1:10–11) or disaster (see 1Sa 25:36)—or, in this case, mayhem ("Kill him"). Absalom both encourages and reassures his men. At the designated time, the "men did to Amnon what Absalom had ordered." Panic-stricken, the rest of the king's sons decide against waiting to find out whether Absalom's execution order will extend to them. They flee for their lives.

Thus David's adultery with Bathsheba is mirrored in his son Amnon's rape of Tamar, and David's murder of Uriah is reprised in Absalom's execution of Amnon. Applicable to the present situation, a principle enunciated by Paul says it best: "A man reaps what he sows" (Gal 6:7).

30–31 Before the princes arrive in Jerusalem, a false "report" comes to David, claiming that Absalom has killed "all the king's sons." It would seem that David's usually reliable intelligence network (see 10:5) has failed him this time. Like far too many rumors, the one that reaches David is a gross exaggeration.

David's immediate reaction to the news is both predictable and understandable: He "stood up" in alarm, just as his sons had done (v.29). Echoing the behavior of his disgraced daughter Tamar, who tore her robe to bewail the loss of her virginity, David tears his clothes as a sign of mourning, and his servants dutifully follow suit. As a further symbol of his grief, the king lies "on the ground" (cf. 12:16).

32–33 The false "report" is quickly challenged by Jonadab. The fact that he knows that "only Amnon is dead" and that his murder has been Absalom's expressed "intention" for the past two years lends further credence to the theory that Absalom and Jonadab had long ago hatched a plot to do away with Amnon, David's heir apparent and thus an obstacle to Absalom's pretensions. Jonadab's confident assertion being the true state of affairs, David should not "be concerned about the [false] report."

34–35 Whereas the king's sons had "fled" to avoid Amnon's fate (v.29), Absalom has meanwhile also "fled," in this case to escape royal retribution. Although the other princes escape to the refuge of Jerusalem, Absalom flees across the Jordan, far from Jerusalem—a flight mentioned three times (vv.34, 37, 38). One of the watchmen atop the walls of Jerusalem sees a number of men (the king's other sons) on the road leading to the city from the west. As Jonadab had earlier assured the king that of all his sons only Amnon was dead (see vv.32–33), so he now advises David to see with his own eyes that "the king's sons are here." He then adds a statement that is doubtless intended to ingratiate himself to David: "It has happened just as your servant said."

36–39 David's servants and sons join him in weeping and wailing "loudly" and "bitterly" at the tragic loss of David's firstborn son.

For his part Absalom, David's third son, flees for his life to Geshur in Aram (cf. 15:8) to find protection in the household of Tal-mai, his grandfather on his mother's side (see 3:3). David continues to mourn for "his son"—doubtless Amnon, although the fact that the narrator does not name him leaves open the slight possibility that Absalom is intended (cf. 18:33–19:4). The depth of David's grief over Amnon's death is underscored in the statement that he mourned for his son "every day."

The narrator ends the section by briefly exploring David's attitude toward Absalom after the period of mourning for Amnon is over. The king has no desire to march out against Absalom. Instead, he is ready to be prodded toward a reconciliation.

9. The wise woman of Tekoa (14:1–20)

1 The full name "Joab son of Zeruiah" (1Sa 26:6) signals a new beginning in the narrative (Joab has not been mentioned since 12:27). Joab chooses a time when he knows that David is thinking about Absalom.

2–3 Determined to enlist an expert to help his cause, Joab sends for a "wise" (GK 2682) woman to be brought to Jerusalem. His choice of a woman rather than a man is perhaps related to the nature of his mission, and his decision to engage a stranger rather than an intimate (such as Jonadab) may be calculated to catch David off guard and therefore help him ultimately to view his relationship to Absalom more objectively.

Upon the woman's arrival, Joab tells her to pretend that she is in mourning and to act as if she is grieving for the dead. She is thus asked to play a fictitious role. By telling her to pretend that she has "spent many days grieving for the dead," Joab is intentionally

These are the ruins of Geshur at the northeastern end of the Sea of Galilee, where Absalom's mother and grandfather came from.

comparing her with David (see 13:37). Indeed, the woman from Tekoa and the king of Israel are twice bereaved: She has lost her husband and a son, and he has lost an illegitimate son born through Bathsheba as well as Amnon his firstborn.

Joab next orders the woman to go to the king and speak to him the specific words that he tells her (cf. v.19b). Joab is to be commended for choosing a messenger who is "wise" enough to use the words in the most persuasive way before the king.

4–5a Arriving at the royal court in Jerusalem, the woman of Tekoa gains an audience with David, as Joab had commissioned her to do. She pays due respect to the king by falling before him. In his role as judge and paramount, David in genuine concern asks the woman, "What is troubling you?" (cf. Jos 15:18; 1Ki 1:16; 2Ki 6:28).

5b–8 The woman begins her first appeal to David by identifying herself as a widow. As the sequel indicates, she is a consummate actress and spins a tale that is eminently believable.

Using the usual submissive language (referring to herself as David's "servant"), she states that her two sons got into a fight. The goal of one of the sons was apparently mayhem, and thus the battleground of choice was at some distance from their village—in a field with no witnesses and/or rescuers. There, says the Tekoite, one of the brothers killed the other.

The woman then states that, after the slaying of her son, clan loyalty took over and demanded retribution against the murderer. The Tekoite comes to David, not to dispute the general custom of blood vengeance, but to question its strict application to her only surviving son. Fabrication though it is, her story is persuasive enough to convince David that she is telling the truth. She claims that she has been ordered to hand over her other son to the clan. She concludes by hinting at the likelihood that their ulterior motive in putting her only surviving son to death was to get rid of the "heir" and thereby gain possession of the family property (cf. also v.16). She thus raises the issue of a conflict of interest.

In a final personal plea (v.7), the wise woman adds a note of pathos to her request. She accuses the clan members of wanting to extinguish the only "burning coal" remaining to her. He is all she has left, and when he is gone, her deceased husband will be without "descendant," and her husband's "name" (GK 9005) will be blotted out and thus forgotten.

The wise woman from Tekoa has spun an admirable tale. Plausible enough for David to believe it, the situation it describes differs enough from his own to keep him from becoming suspicious of her true purposes. Her story prepares the groundwork for what Joab wants her to accomplish.

Although David surely has the power and authority to reverse the decision of the woman's clan, he at first treads cautiously so as not to alienate a group that forms part of his own power base. Unlike his earlier forceful and decisive response to Abigail (1Sa 25:35), his statement to the Tekoite is uncharacteristically vague: "Go home, and I will issue an order in your behalf."

9–10 Undeterred, the woman is not to be dismissed quite so easily. Like Abigail before her, she makes a confession of guilt in the hope that doing so will force David to take action. Impressed by the woman's persistence, the king commits himself personally to make sure that no one who chose to interfere with the royal decision concerning her would ever "bother" her again.

11 Pleading that the king will pray to the Lord on her behalf, the Tekoite asks for divine help in preventing the "avenger of blood" from killing her only surviving son (cf. Nu 35:6–28; Dt 19:1–13; Jos 20).

Again using the Lord's name in a solemn oath (see 12:5; 1Sa 14:39), David promises her that not one hair of her son will "fall to the ground." David's reference to the "hair" of the woman's son is both ironic and poignant. The hair of his own son Absalom was not only an index of his handsome appearance (cf. vv.25–26) but would also contribute to his undoing (cf. 18:9–15).

12–17 Having received the assurance she needs, the woman is now ready to make her second appeal. When David gives her permission to say whatever she wishes, she addresses him in an open and forthright way. In the light of his firm determination to intervene on behalf of the murderous sibling for whose life she has just pleaded, why has the king "devised" (GK 3108) a thing like this? Unlike her own situation, which involves only a small clan, by allowing (or forcing) Absalom to remain in exile David has jeopardized the future welfare of all God's people.

To make sure that David understands the ramifications of what she is saying, the woman points out that his willingness to help her son convicts the king himself because he has not "brought back" Absalom, his own banished son. The woman of Tekoa demonstrates her expertise and wisdom by using a proverb about water spilled on the ground. Although its exact application is debatable (e.g., whether it means that life once lost cannot be recovered, or that death is inevitable, or that punishment for sin is irrevocable), the image of wasted water is suggestive and therefore appropriate in any event.

It is best to translate v.14b as a rhetorical question: "But will not God dedicate himself, and will he not devise [GK 3108] ways to make sure that a banished person does not remain estranged from him?" The Tekoite implies that God will effect Absalom's return from Aram to Israel. Although David has "devised" one thing, God "devises" another.

Having made her point, the woman concludes her second appeal by intermingling elements of it with those of her first appeal. She indicates that she had nothing to lose by seeking an audience with the king. She hopes that the king will "deliver" her from her avenger. She is afraid that her clan members will "cut off" her and her son from God's "inheritance" (either the land and people of Israel or an individual family's landed property in the Lord's land).

The Tekoite wants David's decision to bring her relief from a bad situation (v.17). Like Achish before her (see 1Sa 29:9) and Mephibosheth after her (cf. 19:27), she compares David to an "angel of God." David is capable of "discerning good and evil." The woman's stated desire that the Lord might be "with" the king not only expresses her hope that God will help him make the right decision(s) but also echoes a recurring theme with respect to David in the books of Samuel (see 1Sa 16:18).

18–19a Balancing the woman's request (cf. vv.4–5a), David makes a request of her—that she not keep the truth from him. He senses that she is not acting entirely on her own initiative and wants to know whether Joab's "hand" has been influencing her in what he now recognizes is her (= Joab's) effort to return Absalom to Jerusalem.

19b The woman takes a solemn oath that translates literally, "By the life of your soul." She implies that the king's words hit the mark precisely: Joab had engineered her deceptive gambit.

20 Ultimately, of course, David is not fooled by the fictitious story. Like an angel of God, he discerns good and evil (v.19) and knows "everything that happens in the land." If Joab has been able to "change" the present situation, his ploy is transparent to David. The woman may be "wise" (v.2), but the "wisdom" (GK 2682) of the king is like that of a divine messenger and, by implication, of God himself. At the same time, however, the Tekoite's compliment is not without its backlash. In its wider context, the narrative depicts the kind of royal power that Absalom will either try to undermine or seek to usurp.

10. Absalom's return to Jerusalem (14:21–33)

21 The name "Absalom" appears prominently in the section, but the key player is clearly Joab, who mediates between the king and his son and is eventually the catalyst that brings about their reconciliation. The king, impressed by the urgency and logic of the woman's arguments in her desire to save the life of her son, applies them to his own situation. He tells Joab that he will bring Absalom back from exile.

22–24 Like the Tekoite before him (cf. v.4) and Absalom after him (cf. v.33), Joab falls "face to the ground" before the king. The statement that Joab "blessed" (GK 1385) David surely implies a prayer directed to God that David would receive a divine blessing. Continuing in an attitude of humility mingled with courtesy, Joab expresses his gratitude that he has "found favor in [the king's] eyes."

Through the good offices and personal mission of Joab, Absalom's three-year exile in Aram comes to an end as he returns to Jerusalem. Not yet welcome in David's quarters or the royal court, however, Absalom must "go to his own house" within the palace precincts. Thus Joab's ultimate goal remains unfulfilled. David is still not ready to allow Absalom to have an audience with him.

25 Since he has a "handsome" father (1Sa 16:12; 17:42) and a "beautiful" sister (see 13:1), it is not surprising that Absalom himself should be "handsome." Like the most ideal of priests (cf. Lev 21:17–18, 21, 23) or the most desirable of women (cf. SS 4:7), Absalom is totally without "blemish" (GK 4583). Such uncommon good looks often attract fawning praise (cf. Ge 12:14–15), and so handsome is Absalom that in Israel he is the most "highly praised" of all.

26 Refraining from cutting one's hair was an emblem of the Nazirite (cf. Nu 6:5). For Absalom, however, it is a sign of vanity. Its weight is remarkable. What Absalom proudly considers his finest attribute will prove to be his downfall (cf. 18:9–15).

27 The narrator notes that three sons were born to Absalom, though they must have died in infancy (see 18:18). The name of his daughter has been preserved: Tamar, the same as that of her aunt, Absalom's sister, whose beauty his daughter reflects.

28–32 For two whole years, Absalom is not allowed to have an audience with the king. He finally decides to take drastic measures to get Joab's attention again and perhaps also to get even. He instructs his servants to torch a nearby field belonging to Joab. The loss of an entire crop of barley was a tragedy in ancient times (cf. Ex 9:28–31; Joel 1:11). On the basis of the Mosaic law (cf. Ex 22:6), Joab would have every right to demand adequate compensation.

If Joab's indignant reaction is understandable, Absalom has a ready answer. Joab has been unresponsive to Absalom's repeated pleas for his mediation, leaving Absalom with few alternatives. Unless the king grants him an audience soon, he might as well never have left Geshur in the first place. Absalom declares himself ready to be "put ... to death" (cf. the penalty for the Tekoite's son because of his alleged fratricide in v.7).

33 The three chief players in the chapter (the king, Joab, Absalom) come face-to-face at its end. Joab, suitably chastened by Absalom's rebuke, submits to his request and relays his desires to David. Summoned to the court, Absalom humbles himself by falling with his

"face to the ground." But perhaps Absalom also gets the last laugh, at least for a while: Although he has "bowed down" to King David and then has been "kissed" by the king (who acts according to royal protocol and not as Absalom's father; cf. 19:39), David's subjects would soon "bow down" before Absalom himself, who would then "kiss" them (15:5–6).

11. Absalom's conspiracy (15:1–12)

1–6 Absalom's providing himself with a "chariot and horses" and "men to run ahead of him" symbolizes his ambition to acquire the trappings of royalty (see 1Sa 8:11). His plan to ingratiate himself to the people of Israel is as simple as it is subtle. Early each morning he takes up a position alongside the main road leading to Jerusalem's city gate, the place where disaffected citizens would be expected to bring their complaints for royal adjudication. He then asks such a person what town he is from. If the plaintiff responds that he is from one of the tribes of Israel, Absalom then assures him—apparently without further ado or investigation—that his claims are valid and "proper." He proceeds to commiserate with the person by deploring the fact that the king has no representative on hand to hear the case.

Needless to say, a solution for the plaintiff's dilemma is ready at hand: Absalom suggests that he should be appointed judge. Everyone could come to him, and he would personally see to it that justice was served. Continuing his royal posturing, Absalom proceeds to "take hold of" and "kiss" anyone who approaches him to "bow down" to him. In everything he does Absalom implies that he himself, and not King David, is best suited to provide the people with the "justice" they deserve. Thus Absalom "stole the hearts" of the men of Israel. Something must have gone seriously awry with David's rule to explain the readiness with which the people were willing to abandon him and follow his son.

7–12 After he has lived in Jerusalem for four years, Absalom decides that the time has finally come for him to seize the kingdom. As a way of masking his true intentions, he asks David for permission to go to Hebron (the same place where David was first anointed king; cf. 5:3), where he intends to fulfill a vow that he had made to the Lord. David, apparently unsuspecting, tells his son to "go in peace."

Meanwhile Absalom sends "secret messengers" throughout Israel. Their mission is to alert the various tribal territories that a prearranged signal ("the sound of the trumpets") is their mandate to declare Absalom king of Israel. A large contingent of men from Jerusalem, unsuspecting of Absalom's true intentions, has accompanied him to Hebron.

Realizing that if his designs on Israel's throne are to have any chance of success he will need all the expert advice he can get, he sends for David's own counselor, Ahithophel, whose son Eliam (cf. 23:34) is doubtless Bathsheba's father (11:3). It is therefore understandable that as Bathsheba's grandfather Ahithophel was an enemy of David.

Years before, David had experienced the exhilaration of growing stronger, while the house of Saul grew weaker (3:1). Now, however, the shoe is on the other foot. The evil alliance of Absalom's ambition and Ahithophel's advice causes Absalom's following to increase.

12. David's flight (15:13–37)

13–18 A messenger comes to David with bad news: The hearts of Israel are now "with" Absalom, and they are following him. David sees no way out but to "flee," an activity that is not new to him (cf. 1Sa 19:12, 18; 22:17)— and a cruelly ironic twist on Absalom's earlier flight to escape his father (see 13:34, 37–38). To his officials David counsels the utmost speed since Absalom can be expected to move quickly. If Absalom succeeds in overtaking David and his men, they will be brought to ruin and Jerusalem will be "put . . . to the sword," a terrifying fate at best.

The king's loyal officials are ready to abide by whatever decision he "chooses." In addition to his numerous wives, David also had many concubines, ten of whom he leaves behind to take care of the palace (see 16:21–22). All the rest flee with the king. David pauses temporarily as all his officials, together with his crack mercenary corps (the Kerethites, Pelethites, and Gittites), march before the king. By any reckoning David has a sizable and dependable military force to protect him from whatever contingency

might arise from Absalom's delusions of grandeur.

19–23 The first high official in David's retinue to whom the king speaks is Ittai, the leader of the Gittite mercenaries, who is apparently considered trustworthy enough to share command of Israelite troops as well (see 18:2). David wants to know why he, of all people, would wish to accompany him in his flight, and he suggests that Ittai return to Jerusalem and stay with "King Absalom." It would seem that David considers Absalom's coup d'etat an accomplished fact. Ittai has nothing to gain and everything to lose by remaining with David. Because of Ittai's recent arrival on the scene, David is reluctant to make him "wander about" on a journey of uncertain destination.

Not to be dissuaded, however, Ittai takes the most solemn of oaths as he swears undying loyalty to David: He will never leave the king, whether in "life or death." David—however reluctantly—honors Ittai's determination and agrees to let him march on.

Whatever problems certain citizens of Jerusalem and other towns may have with David, people living in the countryside see him in a different light. He is their king, and they weep "aloud" in fear of an uncertain future as the entourage passes by. David crosses the Kidron Valley east of Jerusalem. Large numbers of his followers continue on toward the northern part of the Desert of Judah.

24–31 Sharing priestly duties during the reign of David, Zadok and Abiathar decide to accompany him on his flight from Jerusalem. Not wanting to leave the ark of the covenant in the city and perhaps trusting in its supposed powers as a military palladium if war should break out (cf. 1Sa 4:3–4), Levites carry it across the Kidron. As during another procession of the ark (see 6:13), they halt long enough for sacrifices to be offered.

Sensing no need for the ark to accompany him, David directs Zadok to take it back to the city. Hoping to "find favor in the LORD's eyes," he is prepared to resign himself to the will of God. David is confident that if the Lord so chooses, he will bring him back to Jerusalem to see again not only the ark in its proper setting but also the Lord's "dwelling place" (probably the city; cf. Isa 33:20). Even if the Lord is not "pleased" with David, he will accept "whatever seems good" to the Lord.

Zadok and Abiathar will be of more help to David back in Jerusalem than if they flee with him, so David tells them to return to the city with Ahimaaz and Jonathan. As for David himself, he will continue on his way and wait at the "fords in the desert" on the west bank of the Jordan. David expects the two priests to be involved together in gathering data about Absalom's plans. Following David's instructions (v.29), the two men took the ark back to Jerusalem with their sons and stayed there.

David and the people now ascend the Mount of Olives. As they do so, they express their sorrow and love by "weeping" and their despair and sense of foreboding by covering their heads. David walks barefoot to symbolize the shameful exile on which he is now embarking.

A harried king feels surrounded by conspirators, and David's intelligence network informs him that Ahithophel (his name means "My brother is foolishness") is among them. The news alarms David, and he turns to God for help: "O LORD, turn Ahithophel's counsel into foolishness [GK 6118]."

32–37 The summit of the Mount of Olives was a place "where people used to worship God." Upon arriving there David finds Hushai the Arkite waiting to "meet" him, his robe "torn" and dust on his head. As in the case of Zadok and Abiathar (cf. vv.24–29), David is convinced that Hushai will be of more value to him back in Jerusalem than as a fellow refugee. David therefore tells Hushai to return to the city and promise Absalom the same kind of faithful service that he had already given to David himself. By becoming a member of Absalom's inner council, Hushai would be able to assist David by "frustrating" (GK 7296) Ahithophel's advice, in answer to David's prayer (v.31).

Zadok and Abiathar are to be David's eyes and ears in the palace while the king is fleeing, and he wants Hushai to collaborate with them by telling them anything he hears there. The three men will then send the priests' two sons to David with whatever helpful information they have been able to gather. And so it is that Absalom, the king's treasonous son, and Hushai, the king's loyal "friend," arrive at Jerusalem simultaneously.

13. Kindness to Ziba (16:1–4)

1 Proceeding beyond the summit of the Mount of Olives, David is met by Ziba (see 9:2), the steward of Saul's grandson Mephibosheth. Ziba's entourage includes donkeys loaded with all kinds of provisions, items especially suited for men on the march. Apparently Ziba wants to demonstrate his loyalty to David.

2–4 Suspicious either of Ziba's motives or of the origin of the supplies, David inquires why he brought them. Ziba deftly dodges the question of whether he has a right to bring them and concentrates instead on their purposes, all of which are good and proper: The donkeys are for the king's household to ride on, and the foodstuffs are for nourishment and refreshment. People on an arduous journey quickly become "exhausted" and need special attention. Ziba, whatever his ulterior motives may be, declares his willingness to help.

Still skeptical, David wants to know where Mephibosheth is, perhaps to speak directly to him to find out whether Ziba is telling the truth. Ziba's response—later indignantly denied by Mephibosheth (cf. 19:26–28)—is that the latter has decided to stay in Jerusalem in the belief that the house of Israel will return the kingdom to the house of Saul and therefore to Mephibosheth himself. Apparently Ziba either did not know or did not care that the kingdom of Israel had long ago been torn from Saul by divine decree and given to David (see 1Sa 15:27–28).

For the moment at least, David chooses to believe Ziba. Without hearing the other side of the story, he punishes Mephibosheth in absentia by giving Ziba everything that formerly belonged to his master. Not unexpectedly, Ziba's response is servile: "I humbly bow." Mephibosheth has taught him well (cf. 9:6, 8).

14. Shimei's curse (16:5–14)

5–6 On the line of march of David and his party is Bahurim, the hometown of Shimei, a member of one of the Saulide clans. Shimei is in an ugly mood and curses David. Shimei's headstrong actions will not ultimately go unpunished (1Ki 2:8–9) in spite of his repenting of them (cf. 19:18–20). Not content with hurling curses at the king, Shimei pelts David and his officials with stones. Fortunately for

David, his armed escort is protecting him on all sides.

7–8 Shimei continues his curse by demanding that David get out of Benjamite territory. He refers to David not only as a "man of blood" but also as a "man of Belial" (NIV, "scoundrel"). He tells David that because of all the blood he has shed in Saul's family, his ruin is inevitable (cf. 3:28 for the truth of this accusation). In any event, Shimei and doubtless many of his compatriots are apparently ready to acknowledge David's son Absalom as their new king.

9 Abishai cannot understand why a "dead dog" (a term of reproach and insult) should be allowed to curse David with impunity. To get rid of a minor annoyance like Shimei, Abishai wants to kill him.

10–12 Knowing that the "sons of Zeruiah" usually work in concert with one another, David's rebuke to Abishai apparently includes his brother Joab. "Sons of Zeruiah" is probably used in a disparaging or contemptuous sense here. David's long experience with God's intimate presence has taught him that if the Lord has prompted Shimei's curse, no one should question Shimei's motivation, however vindictive or otherwise unworthy it might be.

Widening his audience, David now addresses not only Abishai but also all his officials. He acknowledges that Absalom, like Saul earlier, is trying to take his life. It is not surprising, then, that the Saulide Shimei—"this Benjamite" (cf. 1Sa 9:21; 1Ki 2:8)—should be bent on David's ruin. David's mandate concerning Shimei is clear and forthright: "Leave him alone." David hopes that the Lord will turn this curse to his own benefit. After all, it is not an "undesired curse" (Pr 26:2). Thus David, while still pleading for divine mercy, reckons with the punishment that God is inflicting on him.

13 Shimei's pelting David with stones and cursing him do not stop. His persistence in such dangerous activity bears eloquent witness to the depth of his anger and frustration. As David and his party continue slowly on their way, Shimei keeps pace along a hillside that parallels the road. In addition to his stone-throwing, Shimei begins throwing dirt.

14 The king arrives in Bahurim (v.5a) with his entire entourage. The physical and psychological stresses of the journey leave him and his company exhausted, and he thus takes the time to "refresh" himself.

15. Ahithophel's advice (16:15–17:29)

15–19 Resuming the narrative that ends in 15:37, v.15 describes Absalom's arrival in Jerusalem with the main Israelite army, together with Ahithophel, who had formerly been "David's counselor" but has now defected to Absalom—doubtless because he feels that the future lies with the son rather than with the father.

Enter Hushai, who will turn out to be the fly in Ahithophel's ointment, an integral member of David's fifth column in Absalom's fledgling court. He is again described as David's "friend" (see 15:37). A Davidic loyalist, Hushai speaks to Absalom in words that are an exercise in studied ambiguity. If Absalom understands Hushai's "Long live the king!" as a reference to himself, it is virtually certain that in his own mind Hushai is thinking of David.

Although the first part of Absalom's response to Hushai may be intended as a question, it is also possible to read it as a caustic comment: "So this is the love you show your friend!" He questions Hushai's "love" (GK 2876), his covenant fidelity, to David. He also wonders aloud why the supposedly faithful Hushai did not "go with" David.

Hushai counters by ostensibly declaring his loyalty to Absalom. Beginning with the emphatic "No," he affirms that he will remain with the one whom the Lord has "chosen" (GK 1047). By appearing to refer to the pretender Absalom, Hushai is engaging in flattery since nowhere is Absalom stated to be the Lord's choice. On the other hand, the OT fairly teems with references to David as the one whom God has chosen—and thus Hushai once again secretly has David in mind.

As Hushai concludes his assurances to Absalom, he becomes less ambiguous, although even here he avoids mentioning Absalom's name directly. David had earlier asked Hushai to offer the same service to Absalom that he had formerly performed for David (cf. 15:34), and Hushai now fulfills that request.

20–22 Having listened to Hushai's pledge of fealty, Absalom turns his attention to a counselor whom he feels confident he can trust. Ahithophel first suggests that Absalom preempt his father's harem and that he have sexual relations with the ten concubines whom David had left behind in Jerusalem to take care of the palace. David had illicitly slept with a woman who was not his wife (cf. 11:4), and now his son is counseled to follow in his father's footsteps. Doing so, Absalom would make himself a "stench" in David's nostrils—a fact not necessarily to be deplored, although not without its inherent dangers. In this case, however, Ahithophel clearly believes that the "hands" of Absalom's supporters would be "strengthened" by such a bold move on his part.

Having the utmost confidence in Ahithophel's advice, Absalom agrees to it. A tent is pitched on the roof of the palace (cf. 11:2). The "tent" may have been intended to symbolize the "pavilion" occupied by the bridegroom and bride on their wedding night (Ps 19:4–5; cf. Joel 2:16).

Thus with the full knowledge of the people of Israel, Absalom sleeps with his father's concubines—little remembering that to do so may well jeopardize his inheritance rights (cf. Ge 35:22; 49:3–4) and compel him to forfeit them to another (see 20:3 for the final stage of this episode).

23 In theory, of course, Ahithophel's advice concerning David's concubines was entirely appropriate, since a king's harem was expected to be passed on to his successor (cf. 12:8). It is therefore understandable that both David and Absalom should respect the "advice" of Ahithophel and regard it as equal to that of one who "inquires of God." The value of Ahithophel's advice was like that of a priestly oracle divinely sent.

17:1–4 Sensing that he has successfully shored up Absalom's claims to kingship over Israel, at least in the eyes of the citizens of Jerusalem, Ahithophel now suggests to Absalom a bold military expedition that he is convinced will result in David's death. The "twelve thousand" suggests one unit from each of the twelve tribes to demonstrate the involvement of all Israel in Absalom's rebellion. Ahithophel also advises an attack on David while he is "weary" and "weak." His strategy involves a lightninglike surgical strike that would result in David's company fleeing in terror and the death of only "the king." All the other people would then be brought back to Jerusalem unharmed.

Absalom seems just as impressed by Ahithophel's advice on this occasion as he was earlier (cf. 16:20–22), an opinion shared by the "elders of Israel"—upon whom, after all, the ultimate responsibility for entering into covenant with a new king devolves. Nevertheless Absalom, realizing that whatever plan he adopts must be as nearly foolproof as possible, decides to get a second opinion.

5–13 Absalom therefore summons Hushai, whom he knows to be a trusted confidant of David but who—like Ahithophel (cf. 15:12)—has offered his services. In his response, Hushai first of all denigrates Ahithophel's second piece of advice by asserting that it is "not good"—a judgment that reflects the Lord's determination to frustrate Ahithophel's counsel.

Hushai makes capital of David's longstanding reputation as a "fighter." Indeed, David and his men are as "fierce," and therefore as dangerous, as a "wild bear robbed of her cubs." Due caution must be exercised in trying to outsmart or overpower David, whose fame as an "experienced fighter" (GK 408 & 4878) is widely known. David is a past master at knowing how and where to hide from pursuers (see 1Sa 23:22–23).

Warning Absalom that David on the offensive would have the strategic advantage and would therefore draw first blood, Hushai points out that the exaggerated news of the initial defeat would cause uncontrollable panic among Absalom's troops. Absalom's "bravest soldier" is no match for David's "brave" men, who in this regard emulate their leader (see 1Sa 18:17). Though their hearts be like that of a lion, Absalom's troops will "melt" with fear. David, after all, is a "fighter" (GK 1475) who has not flinched in the presence of lions (cf. v.10) or bears (cf. v.8), among the most dangerous of animals (see 1Sa 17:34–37).

After eloquently belittling Ahithophel's counsel, Hushai gives some advice of his own. If followed, his plan is so elaborate that it will consume enough time for Hushai to send instructions to David concerning what to do in the light of Absalom's troop movements. Hushai suggests that Absalom needs a much larger force than the mere "twelve thousand" men proposed by Ahithophel. He must enlist every able-bodied Israelite, "from Dan to Beersheba"—an enormous army. The ultimate flattery: Absalom will personally lead them into battle. Neither David nor any of his men will be able to survive an onslaught of such magnitude. David cannot possibly escape—not even if he "withdraws" into the presumed safety of a city. Using a vivid hyperbole, Hushai envisions the entire Israelite army attaching ropes to that city in order to "drag" it down into the valley. David's supposed haven will be so thoroughly demolished that not a "piece" of it will be found.

14 Hushai's rhetoric wins the day, thus giving David and his troops time to escape across the Jordan and regroup. Absalom makes his fateful choice, and Hushai becomes the point man in the Lord's decision to "frustrate" Ahithophel's counsel. The admittedly "good advice of Ahithophel," described so glowingly in 16:23, and the forthcoming "disaster on Absalom," implied in and hastened by Ahithophel's suicide (v.23), thus flank the erroneous judgment of Absalom and his men.

15–16 Having given Absalom advice that, if implemented, would turn out well for David (vv.5–13), Hushai now gives similar advice to the priests Zadok and Abiathar, who are in a position to carry out Hushai's instructions through their sons Ahimaaz and Jonathan (see 15:35–36). He quickly rehearses the substance of Ahithophel's advice and then contrasts it with his own obviously superior counsel.

Since there is no time to lose, Hushai's advice and its execution (vv.17–22) are suffused with an atmosphere of urgency. His message for David is that it would be too dangerous to spend even one more night in the desert. The king's only option is to cross the Jordan immediately. If he refuses to do so, he and his entire party will be "swallowed up."

17–22 The messengers designated to bring word to David (cf. v.16) are Jonathan and Ahimaaz, sons of Abiathar and Zadok respectively (see 15:27–28, 36). So as not to be accused of attempting to subvert Absalom's plans originating in Jerusalem while at the same time wanting to be near enough to keep in touch with developments there, Jonathan

and Ahimaaz are staying at En Rogel, a spring in the Kidron Valley on the border between Benjamin and Judah close to Jerusalem.

A servant girl from Jerusalem relays the necessary information to the two men, who cannot risk "being seen" entering the city. But in spite of their caution a young man sees them and reports their whereabouts to Absalom. Knowing that they must act quickly, the two men leave En Rogel and go to Bahurim (cf. 16:5). There they climb down into a well in a residential courtyard, and the wife of the house's owner keeps their presence secret by spreading a covering over the mouth of the well. She then scatters "grain" over the covering, ostensibly to dry it out. The ruse works, and the men's hiding place is kept secret.

When Absalom's men arrive in Bahurim and ask the woman where Ahimaaz and Jonathan are, she says that they have already left. Apparently not believing her, they search the area, returning to Jerusalem only after failing to find the two fugitives. As soon as Absalom's men are gone, the two climb out of the well and go to deliver Hushai's instructions (cf. vv.15–16) to David, who is presumably still at the unspecified "destination" mentioned in 16:14. They advise him to cross the Jordan River and to do so "at once" in the light of Ahithophel's advice to Absalom to strike quickly and decisively. Sensing that there is no time to lose, David and his entire party cross over to the eastern side of the Jordan River under cover of darkness.

23 If 16:23 describes Ahithophel in glowing terms as being at the height of his power and influence because of the extraordinary brilliance and dependability of his "advice," 17:23 depicts him as realizing that his good "advice" has not been followed this time. Knowing that the implementation of Hushai's advice will not result in the death of David, who will thus return to Jerusalem seeking revenge on his enemies, Ahithophel therefore decides that the only course of action open to him is suicide. He returns to his hometown, puts "his house in order," and strangles himself. David's prayer of 15:31 is now answered.

24–26 The account of the crossing of the Jordan by Absalom parallels the similar narrative concerning David (vv.17–22), who stays one step ahead of his pursuers by continuing on to Mahanaim, the earlier headquarters of his rival Ish-Bosheth (see 2:8). Since Joab had apparently accompanied David on his flight from Jerusalem, Absalom had appointed Amasa to replace him as head of the army; he was most likely a relative not only of David but also of Joab. Although the exact location of Absalom's camp is not specified, the "land of Gilead" presumably encompassed Gad, and therefore Mahanaim, at this time—an ominous prospect for David and his men.

27–29 David is befriended upon his arrival in Mahanaim. Three staunch allies come to his aid: the Ammonite Shobi son of Nahash from Rabbah, Mephibosheth's patron Makir from Lo Debar, and the Gileadite Barzillai from Rogelim. They bring essential foodstuffs to supply his needs and those of the people with him. Knowing full well that the rigors of the desert flight have caused David and his party to become "tired" and that they are "hungry and thirsty," the allies give them the rest and provisions they need. Refreshed, David and his troops will engage Absalom and his army. The battle will be joined in Transjordan, and the outcome there will determine which of the two men will rule over all Israel.

16. Absalom's death (18:1–18)

1–5 David has formidable military strength at his disposal. He divides them into three divisions and sends them out under the command of Joab (the overall commander of David's army), his brother Abishai, and Ittai. Though a Philistine, Ittai the Gittite (see 15:19) is considered loyal enough to share command of David's regulars with Joab and Abishai.

David announces his intention to march out with them as well. The men point out that if they are forced to flee, or even if half of them are killed in battle, Absalom's soldiers "won't care about us." But "you," on the other hand, are "ten thousand" times as important as the troops (i.e., David is equal to all of them together). They are convinced that he will be of more help to them if he remains behind in Mahanaim.

Acquiescing to their wishes, David stands "beside the gate" of the city, a prominent and visible location from which to review the troops as they march off to battle. His final

order to his three commanders is that they be "gentle" (GK 351; i.e., that they not deal too hastily) with Absalom. David's reference to his son as "the young man" indicates something of his paternal affection in spite of Absalom's destructive ambition, arrogance, and treachery.

6–8 The locale of the initial confrontation is "the field," which provides ample room for large-scale troop movements. In spite of the fact that the "forested hill country" of Ephraim and Manasseh was west of the Jordan River, the location of the armies of David and Absalom in Transjordan demands an eastern site for the specific "forest of Ephraim" mentioned here.

If in v.6 "army" refers to David's troops, in v.7 it signifies Absalom's men. "Defeated" and "casualties" highlight not only the devastation that has befallen Absalom's troops but also the key role played by the Lord in their overthrow. That "the forest claimed more lives . . . than the sword" reminds us that natural phenomena are often more deadly than human enemies (cf. Jos 10:11). This is best explained by the superiority of David's more skilled, private army being at home in the uneven and dangerous terrain and thus having a decided advantage over the larger conscript army of Absalom.

9–18 These verses provide a macabre example of how a forest can claim victims. Riding his "mule," a suitably regal animal, Absalom gets his "head" (most likely through his thick hair, cf. 14:26) caught in a tangle of "thick branches growing out from a large oak" tree as the mule passes under them and leaves its owner behind.

One of David's men is the first to see Absalom hanging in the tree. In reporting to Joab what he has seen, the man is characterized as a messenger who ordinarily brings bad news. To Joab, however, the news is bad only in the sense that Absalom is still alive.

Joab's call for violence and vengeance is totally in character: "What! You saw him?" Joab cannot understand why the man did not kill Absalom on the spot. Had he done so, it would have been incumbent on Joab to give the man ten shekels of silver as well as a warrior's belt (cf. 1Ki 2:5).

Not nearly so insensitive and unscrupulous as Joab, the man affirms that even a hundred times as much silver could not induce him to "lift [his] hand against" Absalom, who is after all the "king's son." He had been among the troops who had heard David order his three commanders to be gentle with Absalom, and he now reminds Joab of that fact. If he had killed Absalom, Joab would not have defended him, since ultimately "nothing is hidden from" David, who, like an angel of God—indeed, like God himself—"knows everything that happens in the land" (14:20). The king would surely execute the murderer of his son (cf. 1:15; 4:5–12).

Petulant and impatient, Joab declared his unwillingness to wait for his man to kill Absalom and decided to take matters into his own hands. He "plunged" three sharp-pointed weapons into Absalom, which pierced his heart. Mortally wounded, Absalom was then surrounded by ten of Joab's men, who finished the grisly task of striking and killing Absalom. In so doing they performed one of the functions of "armor-bearers" (cf. 23:37), who were expected to be ready to fight and kill when the occasion arose (cf. 1Sa 14:13–14; 31:4). Absalom's death brings to three the number of sons that David has lost as a result of his sins against Bathsheba and her husband Uriah.

Israel's erstwhile leader now dead, Joab "sounded" the trumpet to recall his troops. Absalom's corpse is thrown into a large pit in the forest, and an enormous heap of rocks is then piled up over him. The survivors among Absalom's troops have meanwhile fled to their homes.

The account of Absalom's demise concludes with a brief flashback summary of his own self-serving attempt to perpetuate his name. There are thus two monuments commemorating Absalom (the "heap of rocks" and the "pillar"), each in its own way as pitiable as the other.

17. David's mourning for Absalom (18:19–19:8)

19–23 Jubilant over the fact that Absalom's army has been defeated by David's troops, Ahimaaz asks Joab for permission to report to the king. His desire to "take the news" is doubtless prompted by his feeling that David will be as happy about the outcome of the battle as he himself is. What could be better news for David than that the Lord has delivered him from the rebellious Israelite troops?

Joab, however, at first refuses to send Ahimaaz, perhaps because he does not want to endanger the life of a messenger who will in fact be bringing bad news to the king. Another more likely messenger comes to Joab's attention: "a Cushite" (a person born either in the upper Nile region or in central and southern Mesopotamia). In their relationships with the people of Israel, Cushites were alternately friendly (cf. Jer 38:7–13; 39:15–18) or hostile (cf. 2Ch 14:9–15). Thus Joab sends him on his way, instructing him simply to tell David what he has seen.

Undeterred and unafraid, Ahimaaz again requests permission to take the news to David. As before, however, Joab tries to deter him and attempts to convince Ahimaaz that none of the news can be expected to "bring . . . a reward." Persistent to the end, Ahimaaz pleads a third time—and Joab finally relents. So intent is Ahimaaz on performing his mission well that, even though the Cushite has a head start, Ahimaaz outruns him, following a route that is less direct and longer than that of the Cushite, but over smoother territory.

24–27 The scene shifts to Mahanaim, the temporary headquarters of David. There the king, waiting for news of the outcome of the battle, sits between "the inner and outer" gates of the city, perhaps in one of the guardrooms. A watchman, standing on the roof of the gateway complex that forms part of the city wall, looks out toward the horizon and catches sight of a lone runner approaching the city. When the watchman calls to the king below and reports what he has seen, the king assumes that if the runner is by himself "he must have good news." The watchman then sees another man running, and this time he calls the information down to the city gatekeeper, whose duties included the dissemination of news to interested parties. The king is thus duly notified, and his response is the same as before.

Ahimaaz's reputation as a superb athlete has preceded him, and the watchman recognizes his running style even before he has gotten close enough for his face to be visible. For the third time David responds favorably, characterizing Ahimaaz as a "good" man and the news he brings as "good." However, the news turns out to be anything but good.

28–33 Arriving in Mahanaim, Ahimaaz first reassures the king with the common greeting. Ahimaaz bows down before King David "with his face to the ground." Beginning with an outburst of praise, Ahimaaz informs David that the Lord has "delivered up" the king's enemies. Again referring to Absalom as "the young man," David insists on knowing whether he is "safe." For his part Ahimaaz, who perhaps does not know that Absalom is dead, responds simply that he saw great "confusion," and he does not "know what it was." His question unanswered, David tells Ahimaaz to step aside and wait for the next messenger.

The Cushite then arrives with essentially the same report as Ahimaaz. When the king asks him the same question about Absalom, the Cushite responds that Absalom is dead. In the light of his obvious concern about his son, David's reaction to this death is totally predictable: He is shaken. Seeking privacy to weep alone, he goes up to the room over the city gateway and laments. David's mournful cry is filled with the pathos of a father's grieving heart: "If only I had died instead of you."

19:1–4 Doubtless a beneficiary of David's intelligence network, Joab is eventually told of David's "weeping" and "mourning" for his son Absalom. It is not long before Joab's entire army hears of it as well, with the result that what should have been for them a great "victory" (brought about by the Lord) becomes a cause for "mourning." Far from capitalizing on their triumph as an occasion for celebration, the men slink into Mahanaim like those who sneak in because cowardice has forced them to flee the battlefield. Meanwhile David, with face "covered," continues to cry aloud in mourning for his dead son.

5–8 David's army commander begins by upbraiding him for humiliating the very men who are responsible for having saved the king's life as well as the lives of all who are near and dear to him, including his "wives and concubines." But the heart of Joab's complaint is that David loves those who hate him and hates those who love him. Whatever else it may involve, at the very least "love" (GK 170) in this context surely implies covenant loyalty.

Joab has received the clear impression that the "commanders" and their men mean nothing at all to the king. Indeed, in his present frame of mind David would trade Absalom's life for those of everyone else. He swears on oath to David that if the king does not immediately go out and "encourage" his men by nightfall, no one will remain loyal to him. The troops of Judah thus having deserted David, no greater calamity for him throughout his entire life could possibly be imagined.

However reluctantly, the king is prodded into action by Joab's harsh words. If David formerly sat in the gateway of Mahanaim awaiting news of the battle's outcome, he now takes his seat there in his official capacity as king and head of the army.

18. David's return to Jerusalem (19:9–43)

9–15a Animated discussion is the order of the day as some Israelites remind their countrymen that David, despite whatever flaws he may have, had in fact been their conquering hero in the past, who had rescued them from their perennial enemies, the Philistines. But now he was still outside the country. Absalom, however, is dead, so the Israelites insist on knowing why their fellow Israelites "say nothing" about returning David to his rightful place on the throne in Jerusalem.

Sending word to his friends Zadok and Abiathar, the priests, David tells them to ask the elders of Judah (whom he had counted as his friends many years before) why they should be the "last" to bring the king back to the city (the desire to do so was by no means unanimous throughout Israel). In the meantime David is privy to the substance of the ongoing discussions, the news of which has reached him at his "quarters" in Mahanaim. At least partly because of his ancestry David senses a special tie between himself and the Judahite elders; so he repeats his incredulous question: "Why should you be the last to bring back the king?"

In addition Zadok and Abiathar are to say to Amasa, Absalom's army commander and also a blood relative of David (see 17:25): "Are you not my own flesh and blood?" Although Joab was also related to David (see 1Sa 26:6), he was Absalom's chief executioner as well (cf. 18:14–15), and thus his position as David's army commander is in jeopardy. By means of a strong oath (cf. 3:35), David replaces Joab with Amasa as the commander of his army.

Although it is impossible to know for certain whether it was David who "won over the hearts of all the men of Judah" (some texts make Amasa the subject), the end result is that they send word to the king to return to Jerusalem with all his men. Happy to comply with their request, David leaves Mahanaim and arrives at the Jordan River. The question concerning whether Israel or Judah would "bring the king back" is resolved—at least temporarily—in favor of Judah.

15b–23 Various other significant constituencies, however, also vie for David's approval. Shimei the Benjamite, Mephibosheth the Saulide, and Barzillai the Gileadite are the three key figures that represent them. The men of Judah intend to bring the king across the Jordan, from which he will lead his followers to ultimate triumph over the land.

Accompanying the men of Judah is Shimei, the Benjamite from Bahurim. He who had earlier been quick to curse David and pelt him with stones (16:5–14) now hastens to beg for mercy. With him are not only a thousand of his countrymen but also "Ziba, the steward of Saul's household, and his fifteen sons and twenty servants" (cf. 9:10). Shimei and his companions have come to take the king and his household westward across the ford of the Jordan and are eager to "do whatever he wished."

The story of Shimei continues in v.18b. He meets David on the eastern side of the Jordan, fully admits that earlier he did wrong, and begs the king not to hold him guilty and punish him. A short time ago he had called David a "man of blood" and a "scoundrel" (16:7–8); now he addresses him respectfully as "my lord the king." Recognizing how inappropriate his earlier conduct was, he readily confesses his sin. His misdeeds are part of a past that he would just as soon forget.

But Abishai, one of David's army commanders, will hear none of it. He wants to put Shimei to death for his cursing of "the LORD's anointed," not only because such rashness is entirely in character for Abishai, but perhaps also because to curse the king was considered a capital offense.

David's reply to Abishai echoes verbatim his response to him in an identical context earlier (see 16:10). David is in full control of the situation and he alone will determine Shimei's fate. David's response is addressed to both Joab and Abishai, though primarily to the latter. They have become his "adversaries" (GK 8477), meaning here his "legal accusers." Wanting to know why Abishai thinks he has to stand up for the king's rights, David rhetorically asks whether anyone should be executed. Turning to Shimei, he promises him on oath that his life will be spared.

24–30 The second—and central—of the three key men who come to meet David is Mephibosheth, Saul's grandson. David's exile from Jerusalem has encompassed many days if not weeks, and during that entire time Mephibosheth has not cared for his feet, mustache, or clothes in a way befitting a guest of royalty (cf. 9:7, 10–12). His refusal to wash his clothes demonstrates his desire to remain ceremonially unclean during the king's absence (cf. Ex 19:10, 14). David wants to know why Mephibosheth decided not to go with him when he was forced to flee from Absalom (cf. 1Sa 30:22). Mephibosheth counters that he had indeed wanted to go along but that since he is lame (see 5:8; 9:13) he needed to have his donkey saddled. Probably the string of donkeys Ziba had earlier saddled and brought to David (16:1–2) included Mephibosheth's own private mount. He also accuses Ziba of having slandered him in David's presence.

Mephibosheth, however, consoles himself that David will not be deceived by Ziba's actions. After all, King David is "like an angel of God" and therefore not only "knows everything that happens in the land" (14:20) but also exercises divine wisdom "in discerning good and evil" (14:17). He readily admits that Saul's descendants—including himself—deserved death from David, whose life Saul had persistently and mercilessly tried to take from him. By contrast, Mephibosheth is grateful that David has given him the privilege of being among those who eat at his table (see 9:7).

David responds to Mephibosheth by ordering him and Ziba to divide the land that he had originally restored to Mephibosheth (9:7) but had later turned over to Ziba (cf. 16:4). David demands this division to discern whether Mephibosheth or Ziba is the liar (cf. 1Ki 3:16–28). Mephibosheth offers the entire estate to Ziba; presumably, therefore, he received the fields back.

31–39 The third and last of the three representatives to meet David at the Jordan is Barzillai the Gileadite. In some respects the presence of Barzillai at the Jordan is more significant than that of either Shimei or Mephibosheth. It is not only that he symbolizes the vast Transjordanian regions, the control of which was crucial to any Israelite king, but also that with respect to David he has the prestige (he is eighty years old; cf. Ps 90:10) and sufficient means to send him back to Jerusalem. It was, after all, who along with others "had provided for the king" during the royal exile in Mahanaim (see 17:27–29). David makes it clear, however, that he wants to repay Barzillai's kindness by inducing his friend to take up residence with him in Jerusalem so that the king can "provide" (GK 3920) for him as he had earlier "provided" for the king.

But Barzillai protests that the number of years left in his life is limited at best and that therefore it would make no sense for him to move to Jerusalem. Like Hushai (15:13–37), Barzillai does not want to be a burden to David, perhaps in the sense that he would require constant care and attention. He wants only to accompany the king across the Jordan for a short distance; he will then return to Rogelim, where he will die and be interred in the family burial site. If the king agrees, Kimham (probably one of Barzillai's sons) will be Barzillai's surrogate at the royal court. David agrees to this proposition, adding that he is prepared to do for Barzillai anything his friend desires.

Formalities concluded, the crossing of the Jordan by the king and his party takes place opposite Gilgal. Before Barzillai returns to his home, David kisses him and gives him his "blessing" (GK 1385).

40–43 David's escort had consisted of all the troops of Judah and half those of Israel. The acrimony between the two groups increases when the men of Israel complain to the king that the men of Judah might as well have kidnapped him and his men to keep as many as possible of them from sharing the privilege of accompanying the king to Jerusalem.

The men of Judah have a ready answer, of course. David is from their tribe; thus there is no need for the men of Israel to be angry over what seems to the men of Judah to be perfectly natural. Nor have the latter taken advantage of their relationship to the king. Indeed, they strongly deny that they have taken any of the king's provisions.

But the men of Israel reject all such explanations. Judah is only one tribe, while Israel has ten "shares" in the king—i.e., ten tribes in the overall kingdom. They conclude that it logically follows that they have a greater claim on David than Judah has. They want to know why the men of Judah treat them with such contempt, and they conclude their part of the debate by reminding the Judahites that they were the first to speak of returning David to his rightful place in Jerusalem (v.20).

The words of the men of Israel, however, cause the men of Judah to respond more "harshly" still, which not only echoes the earlier fears of David as he anticipated King Saul's wrath (cf. 1Sa 20:10) but also foreshadows the foolish attitude of Rehoboam as he—king of Judah and potentially king of all Israel—irrevocably alienates the northern tribes (cf. 1Ki 12:13).

19. Sheba's rebellion (20:1–22)

1–2 Sheba is introduced as a "troublemaker." Reference to him as a Benjamite marks him as a northerner and perhaps a Saulide partisan as well (cf. 1Sa 9:1). The way in which his story is introduced suggests that Sheba picks up the baton dropped by Absalom.

Sounding a ram's-horn trumpet, Sheba delivers a brief but powerful statement that would become a rallying cry for future secessionists (cf. 1Ki 12:16). He declares that he and his compatriots have "no share" in David's realm and no "part" in "Jesse's son." Having lost patience with David, he orders "every man to his tent." Despite the fact that David had been divinely anointed king over Israel, Sheba apparently suspects that David's loyalties basically lie in the south and therefore urges the representatives of the northern tribes to recommend secession. Although the men of Judah remained with their king, escorting him all the way to Jerusalem, the "men of Israel"—following Sheba's lead—deserted David. The time to secede is not yet ripe, however.

3–7 Before his flight from Jerusalem in the wake of Absalom's conspiracy, David had left ten concubines to take care of the palace. Upon his return he takes the concubines and puts them in a house under guard, virtually incarcerating them. He no longer sleeps with them, as Absalom had done (see 16:21–22). They are forced to remain as widows for the rest of their lives.

David's second step is to order Amasa, his new army commander, to summon the men of Judah (for military action) to come to Jerusalem within three days; Amasa is to be there personally as well. Amasa, however, takes longer than the time allotted. Apparently losing patience with him (and perhaps also fearing that he may have defected), David gives a command to Abishai, another of his generals. After describing the danger if Sheba is left to do as he wishes, David insists that Abishai muster David's men and pursue Sheba before he goes into a fortified city and so escapes from him.

That David ignores Joab in his planning is noteworthy (see 19:13). "Joab's men" now march out "under the command of Abishai," who is also over the Kerethites and Pelethites (David's mercenary troops) and all the "mighty warriors" (perhaps also mercenaries). The immediate task of Abishai's substantial army is to pursue Sheba.

8–13 The story of Amasa's death is eerily reminiscent of several other violent episodes recorded in chs. 2–4. Amasa belatedly joins Abishai's army at Gibeon. Joab is there, and he wears a "military tunic," which included a type of belt often used to hold a sheathed dagger. Not concealed, the dagger was fastened on over the tunic and was therefore in plain view.

Joab steps forward and contrives to allow his dagger to fall out of its sheath. With a natural movement in such circumstances, he picks it up with his left hand and continues to greet Amasa, referring to him as his brother. Joab then takes Amasa "by the beard" with his right hand, ostensibly to "kiss" him, but in reality to kill him. Amasa is not on his guard against the "accidentally" dropped dagger. Before he realizes what is happening, Joab has "plunged" the dagger into his "belly" (see 2:23; 3:27; 4:6), and Amasa dies. Joab and Abishai then continue the pursuit of Sheba.

One of Joab's men attempts to rally his comrades to the chase by linking loyalty to the discredited Joab with loyalty to David. The corpse of Amasa lies wallowing in its blood in the middle of the road, and it is an unacceptable distraction that slows their progress. Seeing this, the man drags the body into a field and covers it with a garment. All the men finally join Joab in pursuit of Sheba.

14–22 The account of Sheba's defeat, which parallels the attempt of David to foil him (vv.3–7), is divided into two unequal sections. The first episode (vv.14–15) describes the violent siege of Abel Beth Maacah by the ruthless Joab. The second episode (vv.16–22a) relates the story of the subtler and more nuanced approach of the wise woman of Abel and illustrates the truism that less is more.

Trying to drum up support for his secessionist cause, Sheba stays one step ahead of his pursuers as he passes throughout Israel, eventually arriving at Abel Beth Maacah. Since the city was at the northernmost end of the land, Sheba had to travel through all Israel to reach it. Apparently, however, he was able to enlist only the "Berites." Compared to those who were ready to follow Joab (v.11), the number of men following Sheba is pitiable indeed.

Lacking neither confidence nor desire when it comes to besieging cities (cf. 11:1), Joab leads his troops against Sheba in Abel Beth Maacah. He builds a "siege ramp" at Abel, which serves as a means of access for attackers to pull down the city wall itself.

At this point a "wise woman" (unnamed) makes her appearance. Calling out from the city (perhaps from the top of the wall), she pleads for patience and asks to speak to Joab. Having confirmed his identity and gained his attention, she submissively refers to herself as his "servant." He in turn indicates he is listening.

The wise woman establishes the credentials of her city, her fellow citizens, and herself—not only as purveyors of wisdom, but also as peacemakers. The woman therefore rebukes Joab for besieging the city and accuses him of trying to destroy a city that is a "mother in Israel" (cf. Jdg 5:7). She wishes to know why Joab would want to swallow up "the LORD's inheritance," a phrase referring either to the land and people of Israel or to the share of Abel Beth Maacah in that land.

Impressed by the logic of the woman's arguments as well as by her sincerity, Joab relents. He categorically denies that it is his intention to destroy the city. He assures her that he is interested only in apprehending Sheba, whom he characterizes as being from the "hill country of Ephraim" and who has rebelled against King David.

Joab tells the wise woman that if the citizens of Abel will release Sheba to him, he and his men will pull back. Promising Joab that Sheba's head will be thrown to him from the wall, the woman relays her proposal to the people of the city. Impressed by her wise advice, they proceed to cut off Sheba's head and toss it out to Joab. Thus the rebellion of Sheba comes to an inglorious end—all because of the calming advice of the wise woman of Abel. Joab calls off the siege of Abel and returns to Jerusalem. With this, the so-called Court History of David (9:1–20:26) reaches its conclusion for all practical purposes.

20. David's officials (20:23–26)

23–26 Since the roster of officials does not begin with the statement that David "reigned over all Israel" (cf. 8:15–18; 1Ki 4:2–6), this may reflect David's weakened position in the wake of the rebellions of Absalom and Sheba. All rivals for power now eliminated, Joab is commander of "Israel's entire army," while Benaiah (not Abishai, v.7) retains formal control over the Kerethite and Pelethite mercenaries.

A new and ominous figure, Adoniram, makes his appearance in the royal cabinet; he is in charge of the institution that put prisoners of war into "forced labor" on public works projects (cf. Dt 20:10–11).

Jehoshaphat is still David's recorder (see 8:16), but Sheva has replaced Seraiah as secretary. Ira the Jairite is probably "priest" in the sense of "royal adviser" (see comment on 8:18).

II. Epilogue (21:1–24:25)

The basic theme of 1 and 2 Samuel is the beginnings of Israel's monarchy in the eleventh century B.C. (its prelude, advent, establishment, and consolidation). The last four chapters of 2 Samuel, which conclude the magisterial history of the judgeship of Samuel, the reign of Saul, and the reign of David, function as an epilogue to the two books of Samuel as a whole.

A. The Lord's Wrath Against Israel (21:1–14)

1–4 Lengthy famines were common in the ancient world, and it is therefore not surprising that at least one famine of unusual severity should occur at some point during the forty-year reign of David. Since it is often only "in their misery" that God's people pray to him (Hos 5:15), perhaps David has not "sought the face of the LORD" (v.1) until the catastrophe is fully upon Israel. David thus makes his way to the divine throne room, perhaps entering the tabernacle itself, in order to receive mercy and help for his people.

The Lord's answer is not long in coming: Saul was to blame because of his bloody rule (cf. Nu 35:33; cf. Dt 19:10). He had killed the Gibeonites and thus violated the age-old treaty made with them by Joshua (Jos 9:16), one of the provisions of which was that the Israelites would "let them live" (Jos 9:15, 20–21). David is determined to right this wrong of Saul, so he summons them to discuss the matter with them.

Wanting to rectify the situation, David asks the Gibeonites whether there is anything he can do to "make amends." The Gibeonites begin by indicating to David that they are not asking either for money from the clan of Saul or for the execution of Israelites in general. Only when David expands his initial question to "What do you want me to do for you?" do the Gibeonites become more specific in their demand.

5–6 The Gibeonites' desire for vengeance concerns one "man" and, since he is now dead, focuses on his descendants. They therefore request that seven of Saul's male descendants be turned over to them—seven suggesting full retribution (see 1Sa 2:5). Saul's "bloodstained house" would now be completely avenged (cf. Nu 35:33). They are to be killed and exposed "before the LORD," perhaps so that his blessing might be sought. Ironically, the act is to take place at "Gibeah of Saul," the hometown of the one who had "put the Gibeonites to death" (v.1) in the first place. David acquiesces to their request.

7–9 Because of the "oath before the LORD" sworn long ago between David and Saul's son Jonathan (see 1Sa 20:42), the king spares Jonathan's son Mephibosheth, whose future is presumably now secure. Although he is

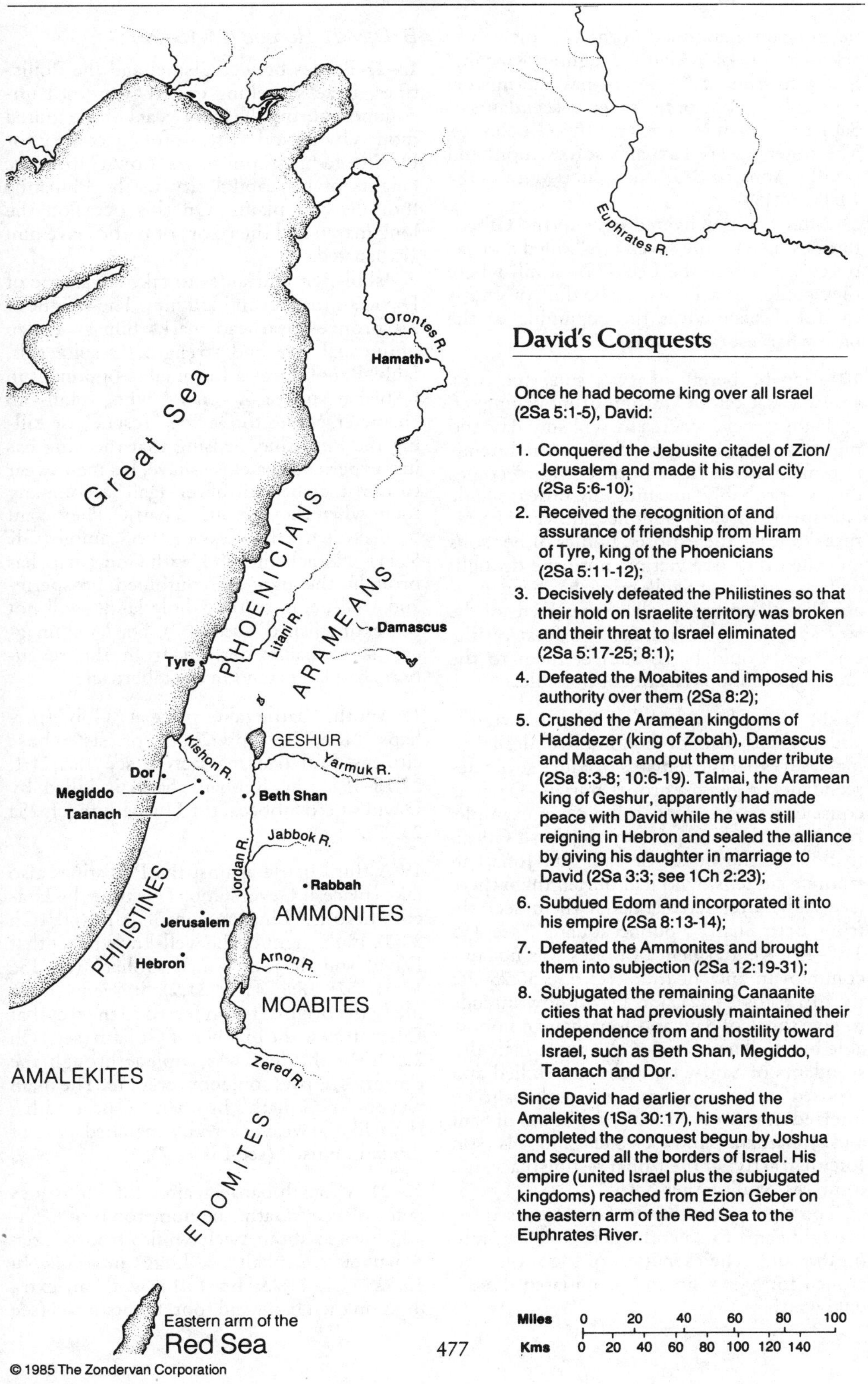

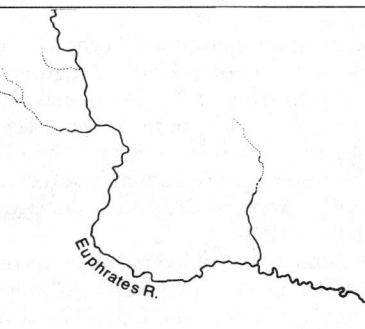

Euphrates R.

Orontes R.

Hamath•

Great Sea

PHOENICIANS

ARAMEANS

•Damascus

Litani R.

Tyre•

Kishon R.

GESHUR

Yarmuk R.

Dor•

Megiddo

Taanach

•Beth Shan

Jordan R.

Jabbok R.

PHILISTINES

•Rabbah

Jerusalem•

AMMONITES

Hebron•

Arnon R.

MOABITES

AMALEKITES

EDOMITES

Zered R.

David's Conquests

Once he had become king over all Israel (2Sa 5:1-5), David:

1. Conquered the Jebusite citadel of Zion/Jerusalem and made it his royal city (2Sa 5:6-10);

2. Received the recognition of and assurance of friendship from Hiram of Tyre, king of the Phoenicians (2Sa 5:11-12);

3. Decisively defeated the Philistines so that their hold on Israelite territory was broken and their threat to Israel eliminated (2Sa 5:17-25; 8:1);

4. Defeated the Moabites and imposed his authority over them (2Sa 8:2);

5. Crushed the Aramean kingdoms of Hadadezer (king of Zobah), Damascus and Maacah and put them under tribute (2Sa 8:3-8; 10:6-19). Talmai, the Aramean king of Geshur, apparently had made peace with David while he was still reigning in Hebron and sealed the alliance by giving his daughter in marriage to David (2Sa 3:3; see 1Ch 2:23);

6. Subdued Edom and incorporated it into his empire (2Sa 8:13-14);

7. Defeated the Ammonites and brought them into subjection (2Sa 12:19-31);

8. Subjugated the remaining Canaanite cities that had previously maintained their independence from and hostility toward Israel, such as Beth Shan, Megiddo, Taanach and Dor.

Since David had earlier crushed the Amalekites (1Sa 30:17), his wars thus completed the conquest begun by Joshua and secured all the borders of Israel. His empire (united Israel plus the subjugated kingdoms) reached from Ezion Geber on the eastern arm of the Red Sea to the Euphrates River.

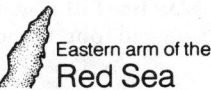

Eastern arm of the
Red Sea

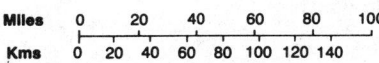

Miles	0		20		40		60		80		100
Kms	0	20	40	60	80	100	120	140			

never again mentioned in the OT, his namesake—a son of "Aiah's daughter Rizpah," Saul's concubine (see 3:7)—has the misfortune of being one of the seven descendants of Saul to be handed over to the Gibeonites. The other six are Rizpah's son Armoni and the five sons of Saul's daughter Merab (1Sa 14:49; 18:19).

After being delivered over to the Gibeonites by David, the seven are "killed and exposed . . . before the LORD" on a hill where they could be easily seen. The time of year is carefully specified as the beginning of the barley harvest (i.e., late April).

10 Rizpah, bereft of two sons (cf. v.8), spreads "sackcloth" (a sign of mourning; cf. 3:31) on a rock, where she will stay day and night for the foreseeable future. She intends to remain there at least until the "rain" comes down—probably meaning an unseasonable late-spring or early-summer shower. She refuses to leave the exposed bodies of her sons and the other five victims until the drought ends as a sign that Saul's crime has been expiated. Furthermore, to allow the "birds of the air" and the "wild animals" to feast on the carcasses would be to subject them to the most ignominious treatment possible.

11–14 Upon being told of Rizpah's vigil—and perhaps also of her implied desire to make sure that the remains of Saul's seven descendants be given a proper burial—David is conscience-stricken to follow her example. He makes the long journey to Jabesh Gilead to retrieve the bones of Saul and Jonathan from its citizens, who had buried them there (see 2:4b) after having taken them secretly from Beth Shan's "public square" (see 1Sa 31:8–13). Reinterment of bones was not uncommon in ancient times (cf. Ge 50:25–26; Ex 13:19; Jos 24:32), and David now intends to give those of Saul and Jonathan an honorable burial. The bones of the seven male descendants of Saul who had been "killed and exposed" are also gathered up, perhaps to be interred near (or even with) the bones of Saul and Jonathan. And so Saul and his son Jonathan arrive at their final resting place, the tomb of "Saul's father Kish."

The three-year "famine" (v.1) caused by drought came to an end when God sent rain on the land. The execution of the seven had atoned for Saul's sin and propitiated the divine wrath.

B. David's Heroes (21:15–22)

15–17 Battles between Israel and the Philistines, Israel's agelong enemy, were not uncommon during the early years of the united monarchy period. It was often necessary for David and his troops to go "down" from the heights of his capital city to the Philistine foothills and plains. On this occasion the long march and the rigors of battle leave him "exhausted."

Ishbi-Benob decides to take advantage of David's situation and kill him. The weight of his bronze spearhead marks him as a man of unusual size and strength. Despite this, Ishbi-Benob faces a formidable opponent in "Abishai son of Zeruiah," who, totally in character, comes to David's "rescue" by killing the Philistine. Sensing that the king has just experienced a close shave, his men swear to him that he will never again accompany them when they go out to battle. They want to make sure that David, the "lamp" (GK 5944) of Israel—he who, with God's help, has brought the light of continued prosperity and well-being to the whole land—will not be "extinguished" (see 14:7). The lamp imagery is probably derived from the seven-branched lampstand in the tabernacle.

18 Another battle takes place at "Gob" (perhaps "Nob," the "town of the priests" whose citizens Saul had massacred; see 1Sa 21:1; 22:18–19). The Rephaite Saph is killed by David's hero Sibbecai the Hushathite (cf. 2Sa 23:27).

19 A third battle against the Philistines also takes place at Gezer/Gob. This time the Israelite hero is "Elhanan son of Jair" (cf. 1Ch 20:5). In the light of the well-known fact that David son of Jesse killed Goliath (cf. 1Sa 17:51, 57; 18:6; 19:5; 21:9), it seems most likely the original text referred to the fact that Elhanan slew the brother of Goliath (see 1Ch 20:5). As the text was copied through the centuries, errors somehow crept in. The main weapon of Goliath's brother, "a spear with a shaft like a weaver's rod," matched that of Goliath himself (see 1Sa 17:7).

20–21 A fourth battle against the Philistines takes place at Gath, the hometown of Goliath, located about twelve miles from Gezer. A nameless Rephaite, a "huge" man (cf. Nu 13:32; 1Ch 11:23; Isa 45:14) with an extra digit on each hand and foot, taunts Israel (see

1Sa 17:10). He is soon dispatched, however, by David's nephew Jonathan.

22 Thus "four" Rephaite giants are killed by David's men. If there is no indication in the text that David personally did battle with them, he nevertheless shares the credit for their death because he is king and his men act under his command.

C. David's Song of Praise (22:1–51)

1 Ps 18 agrees with ch. 22 that the psalm recorded in both books originates with David. The Lord is the eminently worthy recipient of David's song.

If God's people tend to believe that the ark of the covenant (cf. 1Sa 4:3) or the king of Israel saves them from the hand of their enemies, David knows full well that the Lord is the one who has "delivered him" (GK 5911). Exactly when the psalm was first recited is uncertain, although it must have been after the prophet Nathan had announced God's covenant with him.

2–4 In his introductory words of praise, David affirms that the Lord is everything to him, that he is all he needs. Nine epithets underlining God's protecting presence are divided into three sets of three each: "my rock," "my fortress," "my deliverer"; "my rock," "my shield," "the horn of my salvation"; "my stronghold," "my refuge," "my savior."

The Lord as "shield" (GK 4482) not only protects David from his enemies but also ensures the safety of all who are godly (cf. v.31). "Stronghold" (GK 5369), a secure, lofty retreat that the enemy finds inaccessible, is a frequent metaphor for God in the Psalms (cf. e.g., Pss 9:9; 59:9, 16, 17). As such he is the "refuge" (GK 4960) of his chosen one. That the Lord is therefore eminently able to save him from "violent men" is a theme to which David returns at the end of the poem (v.49), and that God delights to "give victory to" his people, to "save" (GK 3828) them from all their enemies and from every calamity, is a prominent thread running throughout the books of Samuel.

Having described at length the God who is strong to save, David states for the record what has become his habitual exercise: "I call to the LORD"—a practice he shares with saints of all times and places. Such a God, supremely "worthy of praise," specializes in assuring his people that they will ultimately be saved from their enemies (cf. Nu 10:9).

5–7 Among the reasons David gives for praising the Lord is the fact that God has already delivered him from his enemies. Whether in images watery or terrestrial, "death" threatened to swallow David. The metaphor of "waves" as an instrument of divine judgment occurs elsewhere in psalmic literature as well (cf. Pss 42:7; 88:7). "Swirled about" and "coiled around" can be equally used with reference to the sea (Jnh 2:5) and the land (Pss 40:12; 116:3; cf. Pss 22:12, 16; 49:5; 118:10–12). "Overwhelmed" is used of divine visitants again and again in Job (cf. 3:5; 9:34; 13:11, 21; et al.); and just as the snares of death "confronted" David, so did days of suffering confront Job (cf. 30:27).

In v.6, death is pictured as a hunter setting traps for his victims. Just as calling to the Lord should be our lifelong response to an all-sufficient God (vv.2–3), so also calling to the Lord should be our immediate reaction when we are threatened by nameless dread or mortal danger. When in "distress" (GK 7639), David knew to whom to turn (cf. Pss 66:14; 102:2). From his "temple," his heavenly dwelling, God heard the plea of David, whose cry for help reached the ears of the Lord.

8–16 Situated at the center of David's paean of praise to God for having delivered him from his enemies is a magnificent theophany. The "foundations of the earth" answer to the "foundations of the heavens," reminding us of God's greatness through the vast reaches of his creation. If the opening section concentrates on God's majestic being, the theophany focuses on his mighty omnipotence.

The poetic description of the divine self-manifestation is cast in terms of natural phenomena related to earthquake and storm. An earth set to quaking and trembling by the power of God is a common motif. Serving as an appropriate counterpoise to the quaking earth is the shaking of the "foundations of the heavens." Earth and heaven alike tremble when the Lord is "angry" (cf. Isa 13:13) at the enemies of his people (cf. 1Sa 14:15). Unlike the altar smoke and fire in the Isaianic theophany (cf. Isa 6:4, 6), the present context seems to define the "smoke" as storm clouds and the "fire" and "burning coals" as flashes of lightning. "Smoke" in the Lord's "nostrils" depicts the judgment of divine wrath against his enemies (cf. Isa 65:5), and "burning coals" can metaphorically represent instruments of divine punishment (cf. Eze 10:2).

In theophanic splendor the Lord "parted the heavens and came down" (cf. Ps 144:5). When God descends from heaven, his appearance is awesome indeed (cf. Ex 19:11, 18, 20; Ne 9:13). Although on occasion he comes down to rescue, usually his descent is for the purpose of judgment (cf. Ge 11:5; 18:21; Isa 31:4; 64:1, 3; Mic 1:3). At such time his "feet" are planted on "dark clouds," which signal the ominous approach and destructive power of a violent thunderstorm (cf. Dt 4:11; Ps 97:2–4).

One or more "cherubim" are the means of transportation that the Lord "mounted." If above the ark of the covenant the cherubim (winged sphinxes) support the throne from which God reigns over his people (see 6:2; 1Sa 4:4), in storm theophanies the cherubim support (or pull) a chariot, pictured in the form of swift clouds that scud across the heavens (cf. Ps 68:4, 33).

Darkness shrouds the middle verse (v.12) of the theophany. The God of wind and rain is pictured as if dwelling in storm clouds, which form his "canopy" and from which he thunders. Interfacing with the darkness is the "brightness" of the Lord's presence, a "brilliant light" (Eze 1:4, 27) that surrounds him. Thunder, lightning, and their effects round out the theophany, the final three verses of which provide its only explicit references to the name of "the LORD."

"Arrows" as a figure of speech for "bolts of lightning" appear also in Hab 3:9 (cf. 3:11) and Zec 9:14. Together with thunder, lightning is a common accompaniment of theophanies (cf. Ex 19:16; Ps 77:18; Eze 1:13–14). And as thunder "routed" the Philistines in the days of Samuel (1Sa 7:10), so lightning has "routed" David's enemies.

With its emphasis on cosmic phenomena, the closing verse of the theophany (v.16) reprises its opening (v.8). If the heavens respond to the earth in v.8, the "earth" answers the "sea" in v.16. However firm and stable the foundation of the heavens and the earth may be in the normal course of events, the Lord of the universe can shake them and lay them bare in accordance with his sovereign

will (cf. Ps 82:5). Severe dislocation and exposure take place "at the blast of breath" from his nostrils, a display of divine wrath (cf. Ex 15:7–8; Job 4:9). The rebuke of the Lord as an index of his anger brings the theophany full circle.

17–20 David concludes his overall description of deliverance from his enemies (vv.5–20) by asserting that the self-revealing, all-powerful Sovereign of the universe reached down from heaven and saved him on earth. The Lord "drew" David out of "deep waters," a cosmic metaphor that symbolizes a threatening peril (cf. Pss 32:6; 144:7).

Although powerful, David's enemies were no match for God, who rescued him. In speaking of the "day of my disaster," David uses a common expression that elsewhere refers to an experience of divinely sent judgment, punishment, or vengeance (cf. Dt 32:35; Job 21:30). The background is perhaps the widespread practice of the "river ordeal," a form of legal trial in which a suspected criminal was thrown into a river and his success or failure in attempting to swim to shore was interpreted as a divinely sent index of his guilt or innocence. In the present context the case for such a relationship is strengthened by the proximity of "day of my disaster" to the "deep waters" that threatened David. Through every trial, the Lord himself was David's "support."

That the Lord safely brought David out of the ordeals through which he had gone (cf. Ps 66:12) implies that he is the God who "sets [his chosen ones] free" from the worst their enemies can do to them (v.49).

21–25 That the Lord "delighted" (GK 2911) in David (v.20) leads to his description of the two bases of God's saving deliverance: the righteousness of those who are rescued by God (vv.21–25) and the justice of God himself (vv.26–30). Is David saying that his "righteousness" (GK 7407) has earned God's favor? Hardly. Far from taking matters into his own hands, David had "kept the ways of the LORD" and had waited for divine vindication against his enemies.

"Cleanness" of hands, while intended here in a moral and spiritual sense (cf. Ps 24:4), is an idiom that derives ultimately from the practice of washing one's hands with "soda" (cf. Job 9:30). That the Lord was a God who "rewarded" people according to their righteousness was a principle David had embraced long before he became king (cf. 1Sa 26:23).

David is determined to keep God's laws before him so that he may not be tempted to turn away from the divine "decrees" (v.23; cf. 1Ki 11:11). His testimony that he has been "blameless" before the Lord is echoed later not only in the statement that God shows himself "blameless" to those who are "blameless" (v.26) but also in David's realization that the God whose way is "perfect" (v.31) makes "perfect" the way of his chosen one (v.33).

26–30 The second main factor that served as a basis of God's deliverance is the Lord's justice, which is evident in his actions. To the "faithful" (GK 2883), those who have appropriated the (covenant) love demonstrated to them by the Lord, God shows himself faithful. To the "blameless" (GK 9459), the one who has been made perfect in God's eyes, the Lord shows himself blameless. To the "pure" (GK 1405), God shows himself "pure." But to the "crooked" (GK 6826), the one whose words are "perverse" and whose paths are littered with traps for the unwary, the Lord shows himself "shrewd." At the hinge of the poem, David acknowledges himself (and his God) to be "faithful," "blameless," and "pure," whereas his enemies are "crooked."

The contrast established between the godly and the godless is summarized in v.28. Continuing to address God in the second person, David asserts that the Lord saves the "humble" but that his eyes bring low the "haughty." David as the "lamp" of Israel (see 21:17) merely reflects the blinding light of the glory of God, who is the "lamp" of David himself (cf. Ps 18:28).

With God on his side, David feels invincible. Since "scale a wall" is clearly the meaning of the second line of v.30 (cf. SS 2:8; Isa 35:6), the alternative NIV translation ("run through a barricade") provides a more suitable parallel in the first line than "advance against a troop."

31–37 The psalm's third major section (vv.31–46), which expounds the outworking of God's saving deliverance, begins by describing the Lord as the enabler of his servant David. God's name is placed front and center. The Lord, whose works and ways are "perfect" (GK 9459), makes David's way perfect by providing him with everything he needs to ensure victory over his enemies. The Lord, whose word is "flawless" in the sense that like precious metals in a refiner's furnace it has been "tested" to the point of proving its purity (Ps 119:140), is a "shield" (GK 4482) who protects all who "take refuge" in him.

The Lord's irresistible and omnipotent ability is linked to his absolute incomparability. David's two rhetorical questions demand the uncompromisingly negative answer "no one." There is no god "besides the LORD"; there is no "Rock" apart from our God. Uniquely beyond compare, the Lord brooks no rivals.

Next David glorifies the God who readies him for battle. The Lord "arms [him] with strength," making him physically, mentally, and spiritually powerful.

David is grateful to the Lord for giving him the surefootedness of a deer, enabling him even to stand on the perilous "heights" without fear of falling (cf. Dt 32:13; Isa 58:14; Hab 3:19). The Lord also "trains [David's] hands for battle" and strengthens his arms so that they are powerful enough to bend a bow of "bronze" (a hyperbole).

The last two verses of David's description of God as enabler address the Lord directly. He gives David a shield that guarantees victory, and he condescends to stoop down in order to make David great. He broadens the path beneath David's feet, so that his ankles do not turn.

38–43 Adequately strengthened and properly equipped by the Lord (vv.31–37), David was able to gain victory over his enemies with God's help. As he describes the thoroughness of his triumph, he virtually exhausts the lexicon of Hebrew verbs that have to do with annihilation.

God has "armed" David "with strength" and "made" his enemies "bow" before him in craven submission (cf. Ps 17:13). David's "adversaries" will "rise" no more. If the Lord has broadened David's path "beneath" him (v.37), and if his enemies have fallen "beneath" his feet (v.39), David joyfully confesses that the Lord has caused them to bow at his feet. The Lord has made David's enemies turn their backs in flight, and David has thus "destroyed" his "foes."

Although the enemy tried to find relief from David's onslaught, there was "no one to save them." Giving his enemies no quarter, David beat them as fine as the dust of the earth. He "trampled" them with his feet (cf. Eze 6:11; 25:6) as though they were "mud in the streets." Thus David's enemies are portrayed as objects of humiliation and contempt.

44–46 Again, David gives credit to God for enabling him to gain the victory over his enemies. He acknowledges that God has "delivered" (GK 7117) him from "attacks of my people" (better translated, "of the people," i.e., his enemies).

David's conquests resulted in large numbers of people he "did not know" becoming "subject to" him. Since the enemies of God can be expected to "cringe" before him, there is no reason why foreigners under David's control should not "come cringing" to the Lord's anointed. Indeed, "as soon as they hear" they obey him. David's power and reputation strike terror in subject and foreigner alike, and they all "lose heart." Their only recourse is to "come trembling" from their "strongholds." Utterly dejected, the peoples in and around David's realm cower before him and his God.

47–51 "The Lord lives!" echoes David's description of the Lord as "the living God" decades earlier (see 1Sa 17:26). From this fact springs the rest of his words of exultation. He begins with a common outburst of praise to which he is no stranger (see 1Sa 25:32), directing it to the omnipotent Lord who is his "Rock" (GK 7446). The God who is himself "exalted" (GK 8123) has "exalted" his servant David. "Rock" and the reference to God as "Savior" (GK 3829) remind his people that his mighty power works hand in hand with his redemptive grace. When the Lord "avenges" (GK 5935) his chosen king, he puts the nations under him and sets him free from his enemies. Indeed, David is exalted above his "foes" (cf. Ps 140:1, 4, 11).

Because of all that God has done for him, none of which he can possibly repay, David speaks to the Lord directly and announces he will "praise" him "among the nations"; he will praise the "name" of him who alone is worthy of praise (cf. Ps 8:1, 9). That the nations of the world would share in David's praise to the Lord was a firm belief of the apostle Paul, who in Ro 15:9 quotes 2Sa 22:50.

David ends with parallel references to the Lord's "king" and the Lord's "anointed." To his king the Lord gives great victories, and to his anointed—to David and his descendants—he shows "kindness" (GK 2876). God's covenant with David guarantees that the "kindness" here affirmed would continue to bring untold blessing to the Davidic line for all future generations (see 7:15). The "messenger of the covenant" (Mal 3:1), the Lord's representative and Messiah, would confirm and establish the Davidic covenant; the Lord's messianic servant, himself a "covenant for the people" (Isa 42:6; 49:8), would fulfill the Davidic covenant as king through unending days (cf. Isa 9:7; Luke 1:31–33). It is thus significant and satisfying that the Song of David, a psalm of impressive scope and exquisite beauty, should begin with "The Lord" (v.2), the Eternal One, and end with "forever" (v.51).

D. David's Last Words (23:1–7)

1 The phrase "last words" need not be understood in the sense of the last words David spoke during his lifetime but is doubtless used in a way analogous to "last will and testament" or the like. Verses 1b–7 summarize his final literary legacy to Israel.

David begins by identifying his poem as an "oracle" (GK 5536) and by providing us with a laudatory self-description. After calling himself the "son of Jesse," he awards himself three titles that appear grandiose, two of which give the Lord the glory for his success. David considers himself a man exalted by the Most High, anointed by the God of Jacob (cf. Pss 20:1; 24:6), and designated as "Israel's singer of songs."

2–4 David next ascribes divine origin to the revelation that comes to him. "The Spirit of the Lord spoke through" him and delivered to him the message that God wanted him to receive. David is conscious of the fact that the "word" of the Lord was on his "tongue" (cf. Ps 139:4) and that the mighty "Rock of Israel" had spoken to him.

"Qualities of an Ideal King" could well be the caption of the Lord's portrait of royalty mediated through David. "Fear [GK 3711] of God," the generic term for "religion, piety" in ancient Israel, was a common wisdom motif (see 1Sa 12:14). Thus he who rules in the fear of God rules "in righteousness" (GK

7407; lit., "as a righteous one," an epithet that has clear messianic connotations; cf. Jer 23:5; Zec 9:9).

The first half of v.4 compares the rule of the righteous king to the benefits of sunlight, the second half to the fertilizing effects of rain. It is remarkably similar to Ps 72, where the ideal ruler, characterized by "righteousness" (72:1–2), will endure as long as the "sun" (v.5) and will be like "rain" that waters the earth (v.6). The righteous king is like the first light of morning, just after dawn (cf. 17:22; 1Sa 14:36).

The image of "brightness" is continued into the latter half of v.4—now related to the lightning that accompanies thunderstorms. As the fructifying influence of rain helps the grass to grow (cf. Dt 32:2), so also the benevolent rule of a righteous king causes his people to flourish (cf. Ps 72:6–7). If the presence of the ideal king produces health and prosperity, the absence of royal rule guarantees famine and drought.

5 Encouraged by the possibilities for righteous leadership implied in the Lord's words, David speaks positively of his "house" (i.e., his family and dynasty), of the everlasting covenant that God had made with him, of the fruition of his salvation, and of the fulfillment of all his desires. He had been convinced that his "house" would be "established" in God's presence (7:26), and he is now sure that his "house" is "right with God."

6–7 David now describes the fate of "evil men." All of them are to be cast aside like "thorns" (GK 7764), whose sharp-pointed branches make them too dangerous to pick up with unprotected hands. Anyone touching them is well-advised to use a tool of "iron" or the "shaft of a spear"—both offensive weapons that can be used to kill an enemy. A parallel way of destroying thorns (or enemies) is to burn them up "where they lie." If evil men are "cast aside," the anointed of the Lord, God's Messiah, is "exalted" (v.1).

And thus David's "last words" (v.1) come to an end. Along with all his other poems, they represent a legacy and variety of hymns that are unparalleled elsewhere in Scripture. Israel's ideal king was indeed Israel's beloved singer.

E. David's Mighty Men (23:8–39)

8–12 The parallel in 1Ch 11:10–41 is introduced with the statement that David's mighty men and/or their chiefs "gave his kingship strong support to extend it over the whole land." Since the context is the anointing of David as king over Israel after his seven-year reign in Hebron (1Ch 11:1–3) followed by the conquest of Jerusalem (1Ch 11:4–9), vv.8–39 doubtless represent the organization of David's military command at a time relatively early in his reign over all Israel. "Mighty men" is a general term for unusually strong and courageous soldiers (cf. 1Sa 2:4).

First to be mentioned is Jashobeam (1Ch 11:11). Among others during David's long reign, he was "chief of the Three." In terms of David's military administration, the regular regiment of four hundred to six hundred men was divided into three units: Two fighting units and one unit to guard the weapons (see 1Sa 25:13; 30:9–10). Like Abishai (cf. v.18), the courageous Jashobeam "raised his spear against" a large number of men, whom he succeeded in killing in a single encounter.

Next to Jashobeam was Eleazar, the second of the "three mighty men." He was from a Benjamite clan. Unlike other Israelite troops, who retreated from a second epic battle against the Philistines near "Pas Dammim," Eleazar "stood his ground" and joined David as, tit for tat, they "taunted" the enemy. Eleazar struck down the Philistines with such fierceness that his hand "froze to the sword." But there was victory nonetheless—a "great victory" that was brought about by the Lord.

Third and last of the "three mighty men" was "Shammah son of Agee." As fear of the Philistines had struck panic in the hearts of Israel's troops on other occasions, so also the Israelites fled when the Philistines "banded" together (cf. v.13) in a field full of "lentils." Depending on divine help for victory, however, Shammah took his stand in the middle of the field and defeated the enemy.

13–17 The story of David and the three mighty men at the cave of Adullam is one of the most familiar and best loved in the entire corpus. An act of loyalty and unselfish bravery is matched by an act of gratitude and self-effacing chivalry, and the result is an account that highlights the most admirable qualities in all four men.

The "thirty chief men" are doubtless to be equated with the "Thirty" (vv.23–24) who were already a part of David's growing military force when he was at Ziklag (cf. 1Sa 27:6–12; 29:1–30:26). Early on, the Thirty had apparently formed a kind of supreme command under David. Three of them had now come to him at the "cave of Adullam" (1Sa 22:1), while a detachment of Philistines was camped in the "Valley of Rephaim" (see 5:18).

At David's hometown of Bethlehem in Judah (see 1Sa 16:1; 17:12), the Philistines had established a "garrison." His throat parched, David expressed aloud his wistful longing for a drink of water from the well near Bethlehem's gate, where as a boy he had doubtless slaked his thirst on many occasions. So loyal were David's three mighty men that his wish became their command: Heedless to the danger facing them, they marched the twelve miles from Adullam to Bethlehem, "broke through" the Philistine lines, drew water from the well, and carried it back to David.

Instead of drinking the water, David "poured it out" before the Lord as a libation offering (cf. Ge 35:14; Nu 28:7). Instead of quenching his thirst, he solemnly and emphatically denied that he would even think of doing such a thing as he declared that the water symbolized the very blood of his men, who had served him at the risk of their lives. The exploits of the courageous warriors would be remembered for all future generations.

18–23 "Abishai the brother of Joab son of Zeruiah" is well known as a brave if impetuous fighting man (see 1Sa 26:6; 2Sa 2:18; 3:30; 16:9; 18:2; 19:21; 21:17). Like Jashobeam (see v.8), Abishai was more likely chief of the "Three" than of the "Thirty." Also like Jashobeam, Abishai "killed" a large number of men. His prodigious feat of courage made him as "famous" as the Three themselves and doubtless contributed to his being "held in greater honor" than the Three. Indeed, although he was not included among them, he became their commander.

"Benaiah son of Jehoiada" was a "valiant" fighter who performed a number of exploits. He struck down "Moab's two best men" and, in the midst of adverse circumstances, killed a lion (see 1Sa 17:34–37). The most formidable of Benaiah's accomplishments was apparently his encounter with a huge Egyptian. Armed with only a club, Benaiah snatched the Egyptian's spear from him and killed him with it.

Since Benaiah was for a while "over the Thirty" (1Ch 27:6), it is not surprising that he should be held in greater honor than the Thirty were (v.13). King David rewarded Benaiah by putting him in charge of his "bodyguard," a position similar to that once occupied by David himself in the days of Saul (see 1Sa 22:14).

24–39 A roster of notable warriors is the second of the two main segments comprising the literary section that preserves the names and the exploits of David's mighty men. If the first segment (vv.8–23) focuses on the Three, the second concentrates on the Thirty.

The parallel list in 1Ch 11:26–41 often varies from that in Samuel, especially in the last few verses. Many of the differences consist of minor spelling or transcription errors.

Some of the names in vv.24–39 are very familiar, some are less so, and some are otherwise unknown. Joab's brother Asahel was killed by Abner (cf. 2:23), Saul's cousin (cf. 1Sa 14:50–51). Elhanan son of Dodo is not to be confused with the Elhanan who killed Goliath's brother (see 21:19). Likewise Shammah the Harodite is not to be confused with other leaders named Shammah (see v.11).

Especially interesting is the listing of "Eliam son of Ahithophel the Gilonite" (v.34). Father of Bathsheba (see 11:3), Eliam was also the son of Ahithophel, David's counselor who defected to Absalom (see 15:12)—perhaps inclined to do so because of David's sin against Ahithophel's granddaughter.

If Asahel the brother of Joab (v.24) came to an untimely end at the hands of Abner (cf. 2:23), Uriah the Hittite (v.39) met his tragic death because an adulterous king could find no other way to cover his sinful tracks (see 11:14–17). None would doubt that in virtually every other respect David, who often genuinely sought to do God's will, was an ideal king—"except in the case of Uriah the Hittite" (1Ki 15:5).

F. The Lord's Wrath Against Israel
(24:1–25)

The books of Samuel close with the account of a plague sent by God against Israel because of David's sin in ordering a census of his troops, providing a fitting conclusion to the story of David by calling attention, once more and finally, not only to his ambition and pride, but also to his humility and remorse.

1–9 The anger of the Lord "burned against" Israel because of an unspecified sin. If the subject of "incited" (GK 6077) in v.1 is surely the Lord, it is just as surely Satan in the parallel text of 1Ch 21:1. Thus the Lord through Satan "incited" David against Israel by commanding him to "take a census" of Israel and Judah. Since census-taking was not sinful in and of itself (cf. Ex 30:11–12; Nu 1:1–2), what was the nature of David's transgression? Apparently by taking a census David was impugning the faithfulness of God in the keeping of his promises—a kind of walking by sight instead of by faith.

David tells Joab and the army commanders with him to go throughout the entire land of Israel and count the "fighting men." He is also to "enroll" them, an act with purposes more military than statistical.

Joab, sensing David's hidden agenda, immediately expresses his reservations. His hope that the Lord will "multiply" the troops a hundred times over and that David's eyes will see it is doubtless voiced with reluctance since he wonders how the king could possibly "want" to do such a thing. Joab is positive that David's precipitous action will "bring guilt on Israel" (1Ch 21:3). But the king is adamant. "Overruled" by David's word, Joab proceeds to carry out his orders.

Territories conquered by David are not included in the census. As leader of his team, Joab transmits to David the results of their efforts. He reports the number of "able-bodied men" who can "handle a sword." The tally of fighting men recorded in Joab's report differs from that in 1Ch 21. According to v.9, the figures in Israel and Judah are 800,000 and 500,000 respectively, while in 1Ch 21:5 they are 1,100,000 and 470,000. Apparently v.9 refers simply to "Israel" whereas 1Ch 21:5 covers "all Israel" and therefore Chronicles' first sum is greater because the regular army of 288,000 (1Ch 27:1–15) is in-cluded. As for the difference between the 500,000 men of Judah in v.9, it is likely that the figure in Samuel is rounded off while that in Chronicles is more precise.

A second problem relates to the hugeness of the numbers themselves. For a discussion of this problem, see the introduction to the book of Numbers.

10–17 Eventually coming to the realization that his command to take a census of Israel's fighting men had been not only "repulsive" to Joab (1Ch 21:6) but also "evil in the sight of God" (1Ch 21:7), David is "conscience-stricken." He now confesses to the Lord: "I have sinned greatly" (see 12:13), having become sensitive to the enormity of willful rebellion against God (cf. Ps 19:13). Not waiting for a prophetic word of absolution this time, David begs the Lord to take away his guilt, realizing he has done a "very foolish thing."

Although David may not have needed a prophet to mediate the assurance of divine forgiveness to him, he apparently does need a prophet to outline for him his future options. As the "word of the LORD" had come to the prophets Samuel and Nathan in critical situations, so also it comes to the prophet Gad, who is David's "seer."

The Lord's "three options" turn out to be "three punishments": "three years of famine," "three months of fleeing," "three days of plague." As the suggested periods decrease in length, the specific punishment linked with each period increases in severity. The choice is David's to make, however. Before Gad can bring back to the Lord an answer from the king, David must "think it over and decide."

Since David is forced to choose among these three evils, he is in "deep distress" no matter what he does. But because the people of God have always confessed that his "mercy is great" (cf. Ne 9:19, 27, 31; Ps 119:156), David expresses his desire to fall into the hands of the Lord rather than of other people. David chooses the three-day plague.

Divine judgment in the form of a plague was not long in coming. Indeed, it began "that morning." In all, "seventy thousand . . . died." If David, bent on conquest, had planned the census as a military muster (see v.2), the Lord's response is not unexpected.

Who, precisely, are the hapless victims of the plague? The NIV considers them to have been ordinary Israelite "people" (GK 6639). But based on contextual reasons, the word should be translated "fighting men" (cf. v.9).

The "angel of the Lord" is the instrument of the divinely sent plague. Since the Hebrew word for "angel" (GK 4485) also means "messenger," most likely the angel of the Lord here is a special messenger from the court of heaven who bears all the credentials of the King of heaven and can therefore speak and act on his behalf. Thus when the angel of the Lord appears, the Lord himself is symbolically present. In any event, surely the angel and the Lord are not simply to be equated, for in v.16 they are clearly distinguished from each other.

Having already killed a large number of men throughout the rest of the country, the angel now stretches out his hand to destroy the capital city itself. At this juncture, however, the Lord is "grieved" because of the severity of the punishment, and thus he says, "Enough!"

Visible to David's eyes, the angel and his destructive actions in striking down the men repulse the king. He again confesses his sin and wrongdoing. The men who are being killed are merely "sheep," he says, who are not guilty and for whom David feels responsible. David's loving concern for and care of "sheep," whether literal or metaphorical, has characterized him from his first appearance in the books of Samuel to his last. Rather than witness the further destruction of his men, he calls the wrath of God down on himself and his own family.

Significantly, the angel of the Lord is at the threshing floor of Araunah the Jebusite. Threshing floors in ancient times were often places of sanctity.

18–25 In response to David's urgent prayer, the angel of the Lord (see 1Ch 21:18) orders the prophet Gad to tell David to "go up" to Araunah's threshing floor. There David is to build an altar to the Lord. Prompted by the divine command, David obeys.

Araunah leaves the threshing floor and pays homage to David, his acknowledged superior, by bowing down before him with his "face to the ground" and calling himself David's "servant."

To Araunah's query concerning the purpose of David's visit the king says that he wants to buy the threshing floor from him as a suitable place where he can "build" an altar to the Lord. "Burnt offerings and fellowship offerings" will propitiate the divine wrath and bring the plague to an end (cf. Nu 25:7–8; Ps 106:30).

Although they usually toiled as draft animals (cf. 6:6), "oxen" were also commonly sacrificed as burnt offerings and fellowship offerings. Although oxen, threshing sledges, and ox yokes constitute the material of his livelihood, Araunah is prepared to give them to David for a higher purpose and expresses his hope that the Lord will "accept" David.

To Araunah's gracious (though perhaps not totally disinterested) offer David replies in characteristic fashion, pointedly referring to the Lord as "my" God: "I will not sacrifice to the Lord my God burnt offerings that cost me nothing." His emphatic "No" resonates with the sound of authority as he insists on paying for the threshing floor. The transaction is finalized as David agrees to pay Araunah "fifty shekels of silver" for the threshing floor and the oxen, an amount that balloons in the Chronicler's parallel to "six hundred shekels of gold"—a price, however, that doubtless includes the entire "site."

And so David king of Israel and Judah buys a threshing floor and builds an altar on it. He then sacrifices his offerings as a means of seeking divine favor. The Lord "answered prayer in behalf of the land." The angel of death having "put his sword back into its sheath" (1Ch 21:27), divine judgment is "stopped."

Although David appears content simply to build an altar on the threshing floor of Araunah the Jebusite, his son Solomon would eventually build the temple there (cf. 1Ch 22:1) on the hill called Moriah (cf. 2Ch 3:1; also Ge 22:2).

The Old Testament in the New

OT Text	NT Text	Subject
2Sa 7:14	2Co 6:18; Heb 1:5; Rev 21:7	Father and son
2Sa 22:50	Ro 15:9	Praise among the nations

1, 2 Kings

INTRODUCTION

1. Historical Background

The events of Israel's history from the latter days of King David till the capture of Jerusalem are selectively recounted in the two books of Kings, to which two short footnotes are appended, one concerning an incident in the early days of the Exile (2Ki 25:22–26), the other concerning the release of the captured Judean king Jehoiachin after the death of Nebuchadnezzar (2Ki 25:27–30). The historical details span 971 to 562 B.C.

The involved period moves from the politically powerful and luxurious days at the close of the united kingdom under Solomon to the division of the kingdom under Rehoboam; it then traces the fortunes of the northern and southern kingdoms to their demise in 722 B.C. and 586 B.C., respectively. Numerous references to the external political powers and peoples of the times—e.g., the Egyptians, Philistines, Phoenicians, Arameans, Ammonites, Moabites, Edomites, Assyrians, and Chaldeans—are integrated into the inspired record. In particular the Israelites were to experience the Aramean threats and Assyrian pressures of the ninth century B.C., the great Assyrian invasions of the eighth century B.C., together with the resultant Assyrian peace in the seventh century B.C., and the fall of the Neo-Assyrian Empire at the hands of the rising power of the Chaldeans under their brilliant king Nebuchadnezzar II.

Kings is, however, more than an account of the political and social history of this period. It records Israel's spiritual response to their God, who had taken them into covenant relationship with himself (2Ki 17:7–23), and who had bestowed great privileges on them through the promise made to David (1Ki 2:2–4). Accordingly, within its pages is found a detailed summary of their spiritual experiences—particularly their kings, prophets, and priests, whose activities largely point to the need for the advent of the one who would combine the intended ideal of these three offices in himself.

2. Unity, Authorship, and Date

The inclusion of the material on but one scroll shows that the Hebrews considered the books of Kings to be one book. Thematically the continuity of the Elijah narrative (1Ki 17–2Ki 2), itself part of the prophetic section dominating 1Ki 16:29–2Ki 9:37, and the recurring phrase "to this day" (1Ki 9:13; 10:12 ["since that day"]; 2Ki 2:22; 10:27; 14:7; 16:6; 17:23, 34, 41; 21:15) clearly indicate that the two books of Kings form a single literary unit.

The author of the book mentions using several source documents, such as: (1) "the book of the annals of Solomon" (1Ki 11:41), drawn from biographical, annalistic, and archival material contemporary with the details of 1Ki 1–11; (2) "the book of the annals of the kings of Israel," mentioned some seventeen times in 1Ki 14:29–2Ki 15:31 and drawn largely from the official records of the northern kingdom that were kept by the court recorder (cf. 2Sa 8:16; 20:24; 1Ki 4:3; 2Ki 18:18, 37; 2Ch 34:8); and (3) "the book of the annals of the kings of Judah," mentioned fifteen times (1Ki 14:29–2Ki 24:5), being a record of the events of the reigns of the kings of the southern kingdom from Rehoboam to Jehoiakim.

Other unnamed sources may likewise have been drawn on for the book's final composition, such as the court memoirs of David (1Ki 1:1–2:11), a cycle involving the house of Ahab and the prophets Elijah and Elisha (1Ki 16:29–2Ki 9:37), the records of the prophet Isaiah (Isa 36–39), and two concluding historical abstracts (2Ki 25:22–26, 27–30).

At least the majority of the book bears the impress of being the product of one author, who, as an eyewitness of the Jewish nation's final demise, was concerned to show the divine reasons for that fall. In so doing he utilized many sources, weaving the details together into an integrated whole that graphically portrayed Israel's covenant failure. Despite the lack of dogmatic certainty, a reasonable case can be made for Jeremiah as the author. Since he was descended from the priestly line of Abiathar, and since in all probability his father, Hilkiah, was active in communicating both the traditional facts and the teaching of Israel's past, it is very likely that Jeremiah had access to historical and theological source materials. Furthermore, he would have had more ready entree to the royal annals than any other prophet. Certainly no other prophet was so intimately involved in the final stages of Judah's history. If so, Jeremiah may have been active in composing the greater part of the history of the book of Kings (1Ki 14–2Ki 23:30) during the so-called silent years of his prophetic ministry after his call in 627 B.C., during the long reign of the godly Josiah. Certainly the contents of all but the last appendix (2Ki 25:27–30) could have been written by Jeremiah. Perhaps the appendix was added by Baruch or one of the prophets within the Jeremianic tradition; 2Ki 25:22–26, which was drawn from Jer 40–44, possibly also was written by the same writer as a bridge to the later historical notice concerning Jehoiachin.

3. Origin, Occasion, and Purpose

The origin of the basic collection itself would clearly be Jerusalem. The book gives the impression of having been written by an eyewitness to those climactic events closing the checkered histories of Israel and Judah, those dramatic affairs providing the occasion and purpose of the book. Contemplating the tragedy taking place before his very eyes, the author sets forth an accurate record of the events of his own day and those that had transpired since the glorious days of the time of Solomon. As such, Kings forms a sequel to 1 and 2 Samuel.

Kings is, however, more than a chronicle of events. Selecting his sources and utilizing his own experiential knowledge in a masterly way, the author writes to demonstrate conclusively to his readers both the necessity of believers keeping their covenantal obligations before God and the history of those most responsible for leading God's people in their stewardship of the divine economy: Israel's kings and prophets. Hence Kings everywhere bears the twin marks of redemptive history and personal accountability.

4. Theological Values

The main theological interest is the relationship of a sovereign God to a responsible people, Israel. In striking such a balance, the author of Kings draws particular attention to the Mosaic and Davidic covenants. Indeed, the redemptive history and theological perspective of Kings are largely developed through David and Israel's appropriation of God's blessing in accordance with her compliance with the standards of the Law (cf. 1Ki 2:4–5).

From the first chapter to the last, God is seen in sovereign control of the world governments. He alone is the living God who is the Creator and Provider of life. Both transcendent and immanent, he is the omnipresent, omnipotent, and omniscient God to whom the angels minister and with whom all the world has to do. A God of love and goodness, he is also a God of justice and righteousness.

Although human beings are sinners, God is the author of redemption and graciously forgives those who humble themselves before him. Moreover, he hears and answers prayer and faithfully keeps his promises. We ought to worship him and follow him completely. Accordingly, great prominence is given to the temple and its institutions. Believers should make God's inviolable Word and standards the center of their lives and live so as to be concerned for God's sacred reputation.

God has revealed himself in many ways, but especially to Israel, that nation he had granted great covenant promises to, especially through David, his servant. Although God has redeemed Israel and patiently guided, cared for, and suffered with his people, they had rejected him despite his repeated warnings. Because of Israel's unique relationship to God, the sin of idolatry is severely denounced. On the positive side, great place is accorded to prophecy.

Thus Kings is not only history but redemptive history, built around the twin themes of divine sovereignty and human responsibility, particularly as they were operative through God's covenant people, Israel. In this regard comparison may be drawn between Kings, Samuel, and Chronicles. Whereas 1 and 2 Samuel feature human responsibility in the stewardship of the divine economy and 1 and 2 Chronicles emphasize the divine sovereignty, 1 and 2 Kings attempt to effect a balance between the two.

5. Chronology

Because the OT writers utilized only relative reference points in affixing their time-sequence structure, an absolute dating of a given event on the basis of OT data is largely impossible. Moreover, the complexity of methodology and lack of uniformity in determining dated events greatly hamper the quest for precision. Thus in some eras Israel began its new year in the fall; in others, in the spring. In some cases the nonaccession-year system, by which the remaining days of a calendar year in which a king was crowned were counted as that king's first year, was used; in others, the accession-year reckoning was employed, in which case the king's first year would begin with the first day of the calendar year following his inauguration. Furthermore, adding the reign of years of all Israelite kings yields too high a total for the period between Solomon and the fall of Jerusalem.

Accordingly, recourse must be made to secular dates in the ancient Near East that have been established with greater precision. The Canon of Ptolemy (the Greek geographer and astronomer of Egypt, c. A.D. 70–161) has been particularly helpful. Ptolemy made a list of the rulers of Babylon from 747 B.C. until his own day. Also the finding of the ancient Assyrian lists, by which a given year was named for the person who occupied the office of *limmu* (eponym), has been of great importance. These lists also often mention important historical or astronomical details, such as an eclipse of the moon or sun. One such solar eclipse has been scientifically computed to have occurred on 15 June 763 B.C. The dating of the whole list can therefore be affixed, resulting in a reliable series of dates for the period 892–648 B.C. Interestingly enough, the accession year of Sargon II of Assyria as king over Babylon in both the Assyrian lists and the Ptolemaic Canon comes out to 709 B.C., providing a cross-check on the reliability of these two external sources. Dates for the period before 892 B.C. must be sought from Mesopotamian data drawn from the various Assyrian and Babylonian lists, from synchronous histories, and from Egyptian sources. Dates for the period after 648 B.C. can be gleaned both from Ptolemy's Canon and from the annals of the later Babylonian kings. This latter source yields a series of precise dates within the period of 626–566 B.C.

These sources provide a fairly accurate time sequence for dating the events of the ancient Near East, particularly so for the period represented by Kings (971–566 B.C.). Therefore where OT events are actually mentioned in external records, they may be assigned precise dates. Since several events are common both to Kings and external sources, the general time framework of much of the period from Solomon to the fall of Jerusalem can be acknowledged as well established.

The position taken here follows basically that of J. Barton Payne ("Chronology of the Old Testament," ZPEB, 1:829–45), which, though a modification of the coregency theory, maintains a high regard for the Hebrew text. Payne affirms that the nonaccession-dating system was used in the northern kingdom (by which the year of a king's enthronement is considered as both his first year and the last year of his predecessor) and that the new year always began in the fall. The southern kingdom, however, began its year in the fall and used the accession-year system until 848 B.C., when, under the influence of Athaliah, Jotham changed Judah to the nonaccession system. However, both kingdoms utilized the accession-year system from the early eighth century B.C., probably under the influence of Assyria.

EXPOSITION

I. The United Kingdom (1Ki 1:11–11:43)

A. Solomon's Exaltation as King (1:1–2:11)

1. Adonijah's plot to seize the crown (1:1–10)

The book of Kings begins with the rather sad circumstances surrounding the accession of Solomon to the throne of his father, David. Two primary factors are involved: (1) David's feebleness and apparent laissez-faire attitude toward government in his later years, and (2) Adonijah's self-willed ambition to succeed his father, based on the fact that he was the oldest of David's surviving sons. In this ambition he was supported by some influential members of David's government, despite David's clearly expressed designation of Solomon.

a. David's feebleness (1:1–4)

1 This brief account of David's feebleness and apparent inability to act decisively is given as the backdrop to Adonijah's attempted coup. It is somewhat startling to see the once so vigorous king now, at scarcely seventy years of age (cf. 2Sa 5:4–5), in such a state of debilitation. One thing that did more than anything else to sap David's strength and will to govern decisively in his latter years was the series of disasters let loose on him and his family following his disgraceful act of adultery with Bathsheba and the indirect murder he committed in an attempt to cover up his sin. This shattering chain of events included Amnon's rape of his half-sister Tamar; Amnon's subsequent murder by Absalom, Tamar's full brother; Absalom's revolt with its severe disruptions, followed by his death, with its great emotional impact on David (2Sa 18:32–19:8); David's ill-judged census with the resultant plague; and then Shibni's brief revolt.

2–4 The suggestion made by David's ministers conforms to a type of diatherapy attested in later literature. A virgin was chosen because she had the status of a concubine, though in actual fact she served David as a nurse. The whole point of the paragraph is to show (1) how David's feebleness encouraged Adonijah to believe he could successfully force David's hand in his favor, and (2) why Adonijah's later request to Solomon brought about such severe consequences.

b. Adonijah's attempted coup d'état (1:5–10)

5–6 Adonijah, encouraged by David's feebleness and aided and abetted strongly by Joab, David's military chief of staff, and by Abiathar, one of the two high priests, thought he could force David's hand by presenting David and the people with the accomplished fact that he already was king. Adonijah no doubt felt justified in his claim to the throne in that he was probably the oldest surviving son, thus putting him in the line of succession. He surely knew that this attempt was in direct contravention of God's will and David's explicit wishes (2Sa 12:24–25; 1Ch 22:9–10; 28:4–7). Adonijah, however, was like Absalom, his brother, in being willful and self-centered, though a naturally attractive person and a born leader. Verse 6 notes David's failure in the matter of disciplining Adonijah as a boy. One wonders how much of this failure was due to the loss of his own moral credibility because of the Bathsheba affair. Amnon and Absalom showed a similar willfulness.

7 Joab, the most powerful of Adonijah's supporters, had always been fiercely loyal to David, but not to David's wishes (see comment on 2:5). In supporting Adonijah's pretensions to the throne, Joab was acting in keeping with his character. It is likely that the planning and execution of the attempted coup was as much Joab's doing as Adonijah's. He was not consciously disloyal to David, but he opposed David's (and God's) choice of Solomon as David's successor and did his best to frustrate David's will.

Abiathar, the other named active supporter of Adonijah, had been the only survivor of Saul's massacre of Ahimelech the high priest and his family. He fled to David at Keilah, bringing the ephod with him (1Sa 22:20–22; 23:6, 9). He served as high priest during David's reign and seems to have been senior to Zadok (1Ki 2:26–27; Mk 2:26). It seems, though, that at least from the time David returned the ark to Jerusalem, Zadok gained in prominence since he presided as priest in the tabernacle at Gibeon (1Ch 16:39). It is tragic to see one who had been with David in his difficult years, and who had, like Joab, remained faithful, now opposing what he knew to be David's—and, more important, God's—wishes.

8–10 There were those, however, who did not support Adonijah. Zadok was the son of Ahitub (2Sa 8:17), a descendant of Eleazar, the third son of Aaron. In 1Ch 12:26–28 he is listed as a warrior of the house of Levi and one of those who came to David at Hebron to offer him the rulership over all Israel. He is cited in eight passages as serving along with Abiathar as chief priest under David's rule (e.g., 1Ch 15:11). After the ark was restored to Jerusalem, Zadok is described in 1Ch 16:39 as serving at Gibeon, where the tabernacle was situated. Later, when David was forced to flee Jerusalem before his son Absalom, it was Zadok who had charge of the ark (2Sa 15:24–25). Both he and Abiathar were loyal supporters of David.

Benaiah of Kabzeel, son of Jehoiada, was renowned as one of the greatest of David's thirty mighty men (2Sa 23:20–23; 1Ch 11:22–25). David put him in charge of his body-guard, the Kerethites and Pelethites (2Sa 8:18; 20:23; 23:23).

Nathan was a "non-writing" prophet who played an important role in David's reign. David had gone to him to indicate his desire to build a temple for the Lord, and it was through Nathan that God responded with the Davidic covenant (2Sa 7). Later God sent Nathan to deal with David over the matter of his sin with Bathsheba (2Sa 12). Nathan was also sent by God to David on the occasion of Solomon's birth to declare God's special love for Solomon (2Sa 12:24–25). Solomon was there shown to be a symbol of God's forgiving grace (that David recognized this is seen in the choice of the name Solomon ["peace"; GK 8934]—i.e., the rift between God and David was healed—as well as in the appellation Jedidiah). But the passage also clearly implies God's choice of Solomon as David's successor. Nathan apparently had David's full confidence as God's spokesman, and he demonstrated here again his sensitivity to God's will as well as to David's wishes regarding the succession to the throne.

Shimei and Rei are otherwise unknown, though Shimei may well be the Shimei, son of Ela (4:18), who was appointed by Solomon as one of twelve district governors (4:7). Also absent was David's "special guard" (vv.8, 10).

Adonijah's attempted usurpation of the throne began with a ceremonial gathering of his supporters. Absalom had begun his coup in a similar manner (2Sa 15:11–12). The participation of Abiathar and Joab in the ritual sacrifice and communal meal lent an aura of legitimacy to the occasion.

En Rogel was located slightly southeast of Jerusalem, near the confluence of the Hinnom and Kidron valleys. This place was farther removed from the palace than Gihon, the normal place for such festivities. As such, it was ideally located for Adonijah's purpose of presenting David with an accomplished kingship, counting on David's illness to render him incapable of overturning Adonijah's plans.

2. The counterplan of Nathan and Bathsheba (1:11–31)

Nathan's prompt and decisive action foiled Adonijah's plot by rousing David to take the steps necessary to ensure the public proclamation of Solomon as king. By so doing Nathan not only worked out God's will but also saved Solomon's life. Despite the urgency of the situation, however, Nathan displayed once again the ability to act tactfully and judiciously, just as he had done when he brought to David's attention the enormity of his sin in connection with Bathsheba and Uriah.

11–31 Nathan proposed to send Bathsheba in first. Her status as favored wife would ensure a quick hearing, and immediate action was indeed necessary. Her role was to rouse David to action by asking him how he could allow Adonijah to become king when he had solemnly sworn that Solomon should reign after him. Nathan would then confirm her statements and tactfully urge David to act.

The validity of Solomon's claim to the throne was not in question here. Both Bathsheba and Nathan knew David's disposition in the matter. The danger was that Adonijah would succeed to the throne through David's inaction. Thus they made three points: (1) Adonijah was making a determined bid for the throne; (2) "The eyes of all Israel are on you, to learn from you who will sit on the throne of my lord the king after him" (v.20); and (3) if Adonijah should become king, the life of Solomon and Bathsheba would be in serious danger.

David responded vigorously and promised to carry out that very day the oath he had made with regard to Solomon.

3. Solomon's anointing (1:32–40)

32–40 The men that David called to carry out the public anointing of Solomon were Benaiah, the commander of David's special guard; Zadok, the priest; and Nathan, the prophet. The "servants" are identified in v.38 as the guard composed of Kerethites and Pelethites.

Gihon, the site of the anointing, was just outside the city in the Kidron Valley, on the east bank of Ophel. It was at that time Jerusalem's major source of water and was therefore a natural gathering place of the populace.

That Solomon was mounted on David's royal mule demonstrated to the populace that this anointing had David's blessing. Thus there could be no doubt whatever in the public mind as to David's wishes in the matter of the succession. Had David not acted with decision, the people might well have supported Adonijah's claims. As it was, they followed David and supported Solomon with great spontaneous rejoicing.

4. Adonijah's submission (1:41–53)

41–53 David's response to the coronation was both touching and typical of him. David saw in this event the beginning of the fulfillment of God's promise to him as described in 2Sa 7, and he was profoundly grateful to a gracious and loving God. The kingdom would not be removed from David at his death as was the case with Saul. Rather, in Solomon there began the long line of David's descendants that would ultimately lead to the promised Messiah, who was both the son of David and the Son of God.

The swelling sound of the public rejoicing and of the instruments reached the ears of Adonijah's supporters at En Rogel. Their initial puzzlement soon turned to alarm as they learned from Jonathan, son of Abiathar, that Solomon had been publicly proclaimed king and that this had been received with great enthusiasm. This effectively put an end to Adonijah's plot as the participants quickly scattered.

Adonijah's response was to seek asylum by grasping the horns of the altar. He expected Solomon to execute the rival claimant to the throne, as he himself would have done had he been successful in gaining the throne. Solomon was more gracious, however, guaranteeing Adonijah's safety as long as he conducted himself properly. To be a "worthy man" in this context simply meant that Adonijah would renounce any claims to the throne, that he would avoid seditious intrigue, and that he would support Solomon's rights with regard to the kingship over Israel. Solomon as coregent acted here with the full authority of kingship.

5. David's charge to Solomon (2:1–11)

1 David's last charge to Solomon has to do with Solomon's spiritual life; he also gives instruction concerning the disposition of matters pertaining to Joab, to the sons of Barzillai, and to Shimei. There can be no doubt that much of Solomon's early spiritual vitality and dedication to God may be attributed to David's deep personal relationship to his Lord and his desire to honor him. It is probable that since David knew from the time of Solomon's birth that he was to be his succes-

sor, he gave him special instructions to prepare him for kingship.

It is clear from 1Ch 22–29 that David did everything in his power to smooth the way for Solomon to follow him as king, not only in drawing up the plans (cf. 1Ch 28:11–19) for the temple, amassing the necessary materials and funds (cf. 1Ch 22:14–16) and soliciting the help and cooperation of Israel's leadership (cf. 1Ch 22:17–19), but also in admonishing and encouraging Solomon to carry out faithfully the task committed to him (cf. 1Ch 22:6–13; 28:9–20). In Solomon, David found a responsive and humble heart. Amnon, Absalom, and Adonijah, Solomon's three older brothers, were spiritually and morally deficient; but Solomon had a heart prepared by God, and he responded willingly to David's instruction.

David's legacy to Solomon was thus much more than a great kingdom with secure borders, tributary nations, and considerable wealth and prestige. Far more important, he instilled in Solomon a love for God and his Word. He gave to Solomon a proper orientation to life and leadership and was himself an outstanding role model, despite his failures, of a man whose heart truly beat for God.

2–3 David's final words of admonition echo those of God to Joshua (Jos 1:6–9) as the latter was about to begin in his role as commander of the hosts of Israel (cf. also Dt 31:6–8, 23). His basic injunction was that Solomon should conduct himself in his personal life, and in his role as leader of God's people, in accordance with God's law. Solomon was to be strong and to show himself to be a man (cf. 1Sa 4:9).

4 These words hark back to 2Sa 7:12–13 and point to Solomon's responsibilities in the matter of the Davidic covenant. This involves primarily a mental and spiritual attitude in which there is a wholehearted devotion to God. Though the covenant is unconditional with respect to its ultimate goal of bringing in the Messiah from the line of David, each individual king had to heed God's law from the heart if he wanted to experience the blessing of God.

5–6 The second part of David's last words left Solomon with some matters that he considered to be unfinished business. First was Joab, the commander of David's armies. Joab had been a mixed blessing to David—fiercely loyal, but not always faithful in carrying out his wishes. On the good side it can be said for Joab that he was an outstanding general, an example of his ability being the initial capture of Jerusalem for David (1Ch 11:6, 8). He never wavered in his loyalty to David's kingship. He also had occasional flashes of spiritual insight, opposing the census (1Ch 21:3–4) that brought grief to David.

On the other hand, there were many problems that Joab created for David. He had a repeated history of taking matters into his own hands, often creating embarrassing situations for David and even forcing his hand. Joab had killed Absalom against David's express command. In 2 Sa 3:22–27 he killed Abner in an act of treachery.

After the revolt of Absalom, David appointed Amasa (Absalom's field commander) to muster the men of Judah to track down Sheba who had led ten tribes in a secessionist move (2Sa 20). When Amasa failed to meet the appointed deadline, David turned to Abishai, Joab's brother, to lead the punitive expedition. But Joab took matters into his own hands and treacherously killed Amasa (who had come belatedly) and then took command of the armies. Now once again Joab was trying to force David's hand, supporting Adonijah's attempted usurpation of the succession to the throne.

Why had not David dealt with Joab before this? The answer is probably that David felt under obligation to Joab, and though David was certainly not lacking in courage, he was not able to cope with the mixture of Joab's loyalty and his misdeeds. Yet he realized that Joab's murder of Abner and Amasa, at least, must not go unpunished. Solomon was the natural one to deal with the matter, since Joab had been guilty of sedition in attempting to forestall the succession to the throne of the man of David's choice.

7 In the matter of the sons of Barzillai, David was simply asking Solomon to continue to carry out his own promise to Barzillai as a reward for his loyal support during David's brief exile during Absalom's revolt (2Sa 19:31–39).

8–9 The matter of Shimei was more difficult. He had clearly acted in a death-deserving way during David's flight from Absalom (2Sa 16:5–14). Yet on his return to Jerusalem, David had pardoned Shimei (2Sa 19:18–23). Perhaps David felt the pardon had been rash. At any rate he knew that Shimei's "repentance" was not a sincere one and that he was a potential troublemaker. David now left the matter in Solomon's hands, trusting in Solomon's wisdom to deal properly with the situation.

10–11 Having made all the preparations possible for a successful reign for his son, David died, having ruled a total of forty years, including the first seven years at Hebron over Judah alone. Just how long the coregency lasted cannot be stated with any degree of certainty. Estimates range from two to three months (because of the extreme senility described in 1:1–4) to several years.

B. Solomon's Establishment of the Kingdom (2:12–3:28)

1. The assumption of the throne (2:12)

12 However long or short the coregency was, v.12 states that when David died, Solomon's rule was firmly established. There was no question in anyone's mind who was king, and Solomon had firm control over the kingdom.

One matter that is usually lost sight of is that during Adonijah's attempt to preempt the throne, Solomon himself did not indulge in plotting to make the throne certain for himself. He exercised remarkable restraint. But once he was formally declared to be king, he acted firmly and with decision and dispatch.

2. Adonijah's further plot and execution (2:13–25)

13–17 That Adonijah was ambitious and not yet done with his hopes for securing the throne for himself is seen in this section. In asking for the hand of Abishag, he was almost certainly not pursuing romantic interests but trying to secure for himself a claim to the throne. Although 1:4 states clearly that David had no marital relations with Abishag, her function being a therapeutic one, she was officially regarded as being one of David's wives. As such, she would provide an additional argument for Adonijah's royal pretensions. He informed Bathsheba that the kingdom had been as good as his and that all Israel had regarded him as king, thus clearly indicating that his aspirations were not really dead.

18–22 Bathsheba, realizing Abishag's true status, saw no harm in the request and went to Solomon to intercede for Adonijah. But Solomon saw through the scheme and, probably startling his mother considerably, spoke rather vehemently: "You might as well request the kingdom for him!"

23–25 Solomon reacted swiftly to Adonijah's ploy and ordered Benaiah to execute him. Though this may seem harsh, it was clearly necessary since Adonijah was evidently still hoping to establish himself on the throne. To leave him alive with such ambitions would leave a festering sore in the kingdom.

3. The deposition of Abiathar (2:26–27)

26 Abiathar was banished to his home in Anathoth (a few miles north of Jerusalem). He deserved to die because he opposed not only David's will but also God's will in the matter of succession. But since he had served faithfully, having been loyal to David in his hard times and having borne the ark (2Sa 15:24, 29; 1Ch 15:11–15) in his capacity as high priest, Solomon allowed him to live. The reprieve from execution, however, was dependent on continued good behavior.

27 The removal of Abiathar from the active priesthood and the sole tenancy of Zadok as high priest werea fulfillment of God's word to Eli (1Sa 2:30–33).

4. The execution of Joab (2:28–34)

28–29 Solomon now began to carry out David's injunctions with regard to his own "unfinished business." Having heard of Solomon's actions with regard to Adonijah and Abiathar, Joab knew that judgment would not be long in coming. In seeking sanctuary by grasping the horns of the altar, he no doubt was thinking only of his involvement with Adonijah's plot. It would be in keeping with Joab's character to have dismissed from his mind any thought of blame, much less punishment, in regard to the two murders. In any case, Joab's act of seeking sanctuary would put Solomon's execution order in as bad a light as possible by making him appear to be violating a commonly accepted sanctuary. Solomon would have to contend with strong emotions on the part of many of the people.

30–33 Joab's refusal to leave frustrated Benaiah's mission since he hesitated to touch Joab while he clung to the altar. When Solomon sent Benaiah back to execute Joab at the altar, he justified the order as an act of justice to remove bloodguiltiness from David and his descendants. Solomon was carrying out his father's wishes. This matter was of great importance to David's conscience and the integrity of his reign because the murders were not a private matter. One might term Joab's murders as political assassinations. The national interest and conscience were involved.

34 Benaiah carried out Solomon's order. No public outcry is recorded. On the contrary, the last sentence in the chapter states that "the kingdom was now firmly established in Solomon's hands" (v.46).

5. The elevation of Benaiah and Zadok (2:35)

35 The two chief conspirators as well as Adonijah were now removed. It should be clearly understood that though Solomon's actions strengthened his hand and fixed him firmly in the rulership, his acts were not acts of personal vengeance or political expediency. These men had actively and with deliberate forethought opposed God's will. It must also be made clear to all the people that Joab's willful acts could not be condoned, even though they were perpetrated in the name of David's government. Joab and Abiathar were now replaced by Benaiah and Zadok.

6. The execution of Shimei (2:36–46)

36 Shimei was not one of the conspirators with Adonijah, but he had considerable potential for stirring up opposition to the house of David. His attitude toward the latter is seen in 2Sa 16:5–13. In a gesture of generosity, David forgave him for his cursings and acts of hatred. Yet David no doubt realized the insincerity of Shimei's repentance and the very real probability of a return on Shimei's part to active hostility at the earliest sign of weakness. But he also felt that justice had not been served. Shimei was a scoundrel and needed to be dealt with. David was powerless because of his promise. It was up to Solomon to see to it.

37 Solomon's wisdom and ability to govern are demonstrated at the very outset of his reign. By forbidding Shimei to cross the Kidron Valley on pain of death, Solomon kept him from his kinsmen, who had been the spearhead of the revolt against David under Sheba (2Sa 20).

38–40 For three years Shimei obeyed the restriction of the king; but when two of his slaves fled to Achish of Gath, he violated his parole and went after his slaves personally. Had Shimei taken the conditions of his confinement seriously and been an honest man, he should have gone to Solomon and requested either that the latter regain his slaves for him or else allow him to make the trip.

41–43 Solomon calls Shimei to account for his breach of an oath to God. He had already been the recipient of a gracious pardon from David. But now Solomon was going to mete out justice on the exact terms of the oath. Shimei had taken grace lightly and demonstrated his unrepentant heart. For this he would die in strict accord with the terms of their agreement. He was unworthy of another pardon.

44 With Shimei's execution justice was fully served; yet Solomon astutely allowed Shimei to condemn himself.

45–46 The last opponent of the Davidic dynasty was now gone, and David's throne had been securely established. David had his detractors; but God caused him to prevail, not only in his own rule, but in seeing his son Solomon sitting on his throne as God had promised. The Davidic covenant was now on its way toward fulfillment. Solomon—granted by God's grace a kingdom of peace and prosperity—is, in this and in his extraordinary insight, a type of the coming Son of David, the Messiah.

7. The spiritual condition of Solomon's kingdom (3:1–3)

1 Solomon's marriage to Pharaoh's daughter was the seal of a political alliance with Egypt. That such a marriage came about gives some indication of the importance of the kingdom Solomon inherited from his father as well as the decline of Egyptian power at this time. Formerly Egyptian Pharaohs consistently refused to allow their daughters to marry even the most important and powerful foreign kings. In this instance it appears that Pharaoh felt it to be advantageous to ally himself with Solomon, giving him not only his daughter but also Gezer as a wedding gift. This would give him clear trade routes through Palestine. Solomon, on the other hand, could by this means secure his southern border.

The rendering "made an alliance with Pharaoh" reflects accurately the Hebrew (lit., "became Pharaoh's son-in-law"), which stresses the relationship between father-in-law and bridegroom rather than that between the bride and the bridegroom. This was a rather common practice for cementing and maintaining international agreements and securing a nation's borders.

The city of David was located on the southern portion of the eastern ridge of Jerusalem. This lies between the Kidron Valley on the east and the (now nonexistent) Tyropoeon Valley on the west. It slopes down into the Valley of Hinnom at the point where it joins the Kidron Valley. This was the site of Jebusite Jerusalem and David's Jerusalem. Solomon extended the city to the north, where he also built the temple.

Solomon kept Pharaoh's daughter in the older city of David until he had completed his building projects. Then he built a palace for her (1Ki 7:8; 9:24; 2Ch 8:11), presumably as part of his palace complex. According to 2Ch 8:11, Pharaoh's daughter was not housed in David's palace. She was not to live in David's palace "because the places the ark of the LORD has entered are holy." Thus, though Pharaoh's daughter temporarily resided in the city of David, it would not have been in the palace itself.

2 The "however" is intended to point out that, though conditions generally were very good, there was one matter that needed correcting, the practice of sacrificing at the "high places" (GK 1195). These were open-air sanctuaries that were mostly found on hilltops (1Ki 11:7; 2Ki 16:4), but also in towns (1Ki 13:32) and in valleys (Jer 7:31; Eze 6:3).

The high places were a constant sore point in Israel, and the prophets of God frequently spoke out against them. There were two basic problems with them: (1) they detracted from the principle of the central sanctuary (Dt 12:1–14); and (2) since worship at high places was a Canaanite custom, syncretism was not only a very real danger but an all too common occurrence. Israel was specifically forbidden to utilize pagan high places and altars (Dt 12:2–4, 13), and as soon as God had established his people in the Promised Land, they were to worship at a sanctuary in the place appointed by God.

The latter half of the verse gives the reasons for the common use of various "high places" for worship: the temple had not yet been built. Before Eli's time the tabernacle had been at Shiloh; but with the Philistines' capture of the ark, Shiloh lost its significance as the place of God's presence among his people. Even after the ark was returned by the Philistines, it remained for years in the house of Abinadab (1Sa 7:1), until David removed it to Jerusalem (2Sa 6) to a tent he had prepared for it there (v.17). In the meantime, the tabernacle was removed from Shiloh after the capture of the ark.

The ark next appears at Nob (1Sa 21), where it remained until Saul massacred the priests there (1Sa 22). At some point after this event, it was moved to Gibeon, where it is mentioned in connection with Zadok's high priestly ministry (1Ch 16:39–40). There were then, in effect, two tabernacles during David's reign. The one in Gibeon was without the ark; the one in Jerusalem had the ark but not the original trappings of the tabernacle (2Ch 1:3–5). This state of affairs matched that of the double priesthood of Zadok and Abiathar.

3 High commendation is here given to Solomon. He loved the Lord and showed it in his walk. He truly feared the Lord and obeyed David's instruction with regard to his walk before God. David himself had loved God from the heart and was deeply aware of the grace of God at work in his life. Solomon, the son of Bathsheba, as the least likely candidate to be God's choice as David's successor, must have been conscious of God's gracious hand in his life.

8. Solomon's sacrifice at Gibeon (3:4)

4 According to 2Ch 1:2–3, the entire leadership of the nation went with Solomon to Gibeon to bring a great offering to God. One thousand burnt offerings were brought, indicating that this was an especially important occasion. The purpose was clearly to bring thanksgiving for establishing Solomon in the kingdom and also to seek God's blessing on his reign.

9. Solomon's dream and prayer for wisdom (3:5–15)

5 God's appearance to Solomon in a dream indicated clearly that God had not only graciously received the sacrifices but was prepared to do great things for Solomon and his people. Solomon was later once again favored with an appearance of God (1Ki 9:1–9). That God had in such a remarkable way declared himself willing to pour out his blessing on Solomon and his work makes the king all the more culpable in his later apostasy (cf. 1Ki 11:9). With great privilege comes great responsibility.

6 Solomon responded to God's gracious offer by a heartfelt expression of gratitude for God's great kindness demonstrated toward David during his lifetime and now also after his death in providing David a son as successor, the first in the line from which Messiah would come. God was able to exercise kindness and express his love toward David because of his responsiveness in seeking God and walking in his ways. The emphasis is on God's kindness rather than on David's righteousness.

7 Solomon's declaration here showed his true humility before God, as God's pleased response demonstrates. The term "little child," or young lad (GK 5853), relates both to his relative youth and to his inexperience in government.

8 The responsibilities facing Solomon were all the greater in that Israel was God's chosen nation. She had to be governed in accordance with God's precepts if the people were to experience his blessing. Thankfulness and praise are added for the faithfulness of God in respect to the Abrahamic covenant. The words "too numerous to count or number" reflect the words of God to Abraham in Ge 13:16. God had greatly blessed and increased Abraham's people in stature and numbers.

9 Solomon asked for an understanding or "discerning" (GK 9048) heart so that he might govern God's people justly. In seeing the need for these qualities and in seeking

them for himself, Solomon is a type of the Messiah, the Son of David par excellence.

10–13 Solomon bypassed the kind of request that most men would commonly make—prosperity, a long life, victory over enemies, etc. He sought the more essential thing, and because of this God promised him the wisdom that he sought in such measure that he would stand alone among men (cf. Mt 6:33). In addition God granted him what he had not requested—wealth and honor unequaled in his lifetime. In granting Solomon "a wise and discerning heart," God gave him the ability to judge and rule well. But God here also went beyond Solomon's request and opened up his understanding in areas beyond those having to do with rulership (see 1Ki 4:29–34; 10:1–25).

14 God reminds Solomon of his continued responsibility to walk righteously before him as David had done and as David had enjoined him to do. God's faithfulness to the Davidic covenant remained fixed; but if Solomon wished to enjoy God's fullest blessing, he must walk in accordance with God's will.

15 When Solomon awoke, very much aware that God had spoken to him in a dream, he returned to Jerusalem and brought burnt offerings and fellowship offerings. By so doing the king was expressing his thanks for God's goodness. He brought all his officials together for a feast so that they also might rejoice in thanksgiving at this renewed manifestation of God's grace toward Israel and the house of David.

10. Solomon's wisdom: the smothered baby (3:16–28)

16–27 Since there were no witnesses, it was impossible to prove by conventional means which litigant here had a just case. Solomon displayed his extraordinary insight into human nature as well as shocking boldness of action in exposing fraud. The mother of the dead baby wanted a baby of her own. This desire for a baby to mother was stronger than her grief and love for her dead baby. In trying to attach to herself the other woman's baby, she was motivated equally strongly by her envy of the other woman who still had her baby. It was this underlying motive that was the target of Solomon's startling edict: "Cut

the living child in two." Thus the Gordian knot was cut and true justice was done.

28 Solomon's verdict and the way it was achieved soon became common knowledge, and the people held him in great awe. Here was clear evidence to an unusual degree of a God-given ability to rule wisely and justly.

C. Solomon's Organization of the Kingdom (4:1–34)

1. His officials (4:1–19)

1 Considerable changes were made in Israel during the reigns of the previous two kings. When Saul became king, there was a loose confederacy among the tribes. Through his early victories he welded the nation into a kingdom. But his governmental style was modest and simple. He made no great demands on the people. There was no great central bureaucracy and no lavish court. There is no record of any system of taxation.

David developed a kingdom in a truer sense. His rule was much stronger than Saul's, and he had far greater and more lasting success in defeating Israel's enemies. By the time he died, he had established a great and powerful empire, extending Israel's borders and exercising control over vassal states from the Gulf of Aqaba and the River of Egypt to the northwestern part of the Euphrates. He captured Jerusalem from the Jebusites and made it a strong and permanent capital. His court, though not lavish, was far more extensive than Saul's. His chief officials were almost as numerous as Solomon's. David seems to have had some system of internal taxation, and he certainly received tribute from his various vassal states. One matter of organizational development that was particularly dear to David's heart was that of the temple ministry. He laid the groundwork for an elaborate worship service, including music, in preparation for the time when the temple would be built.

Solomon inherited a great kingdom. His role was one of consolidation and increased internal strengthening. He established a well-organized and strong central government, much stronger than ever before. He developed a system of taxation and forced labor to support a much admired and elaborate governmental structure and to pay for his great building projects, the foremost being the temple and the palace.

Verses 2–19 list Solomon's officials (vv.2–6 his chief administrators, vv.7–19 his district governors). Verses 11, 15 indicate this list was compiled at about the midpoint of Solomon's reign, since two of the officials are sons-in-law of Solomon. In addition, the names of especially prominent men who served in the earlier part of Solomon's reign are included. This is certainly true of Abiathar, who was deposed almost immediately, and probably of Zadok, who had already served at length under David and most likely didn't live long into Solomon's reign. In Abiathar's case, it is of course possible that he still carried the title of priest even though he was no longer permitted to function as such.

2–3 Various suggestions have been made with regard to Azariah and the office held by him. The best view appears to be that this Azariah was the grandson of Zadok (1Ch 6:8–9) and became the high priest after the death or incapacitation of Zadok. (The designation "son" for "grandson" is common OT usage.) Ahimaaz, Azariah's father, had apparently died or else could not serve for some reason.

The two "secretaries" served as private secretaries as well as secretary of state. Their father had served in the same office under David. The "recorder" (lit., "the one who calls, names, reminds, reports"; GK 4654) was also a high official. He was in charge of palace ceremonies, the chief of protocol. He reported public needs to the king and in turn was the king's spokesman.

4 Benaiah, formerly commander of David's special guard, now became the "commander-in-chief" of all the armies. As stated earlier, Zadok probably did not serve long under Solomon, being elderly at Solomon's succession to the throne. Abiathar was almost immediately deposed. They are listed here because of the outstanding roles they had played in the kingdom.

5 Azariah son of Nathan was in charge of the twelve district governors named in vv.7–19. Zabud was another son of Nathan. His function as priest may have been to assist the king in the exercise of his spiritual and ceremonial concerns. He was also called the "personal adviser" (GK 8291) of David. This seems to have been a title of honor and distinction and indicated one who was a close and trusted friend of the king (cf. 2Sa 15:37).

6 Ahishar was "in charge of the palace." Under Solomon his functions were apparently restricted to that of chief steward of the palace, but his office gradually gained in importance until it was comparable to the office of the Egyptian vizier, the first minister of state. A good example of the importance that this office took on is found in Isa 22:15–24, in which Shebna, the one "in charge of the palace," must be deposed because he had misused his power in self-aggrandizement. His replacement would "be a father . . . to the house of Judah." He would have the key of the house of David on his shoulder. "What he opens no one can shut, and what he shuts no one can open."

Adoniram was in charge of the forced labor or corvée. This system was widely practiced in the ancient Near East as a means of carrying out public building projects. Samuel (1Sa 8:12–17) warned that this would be one of the evils of instituting a monarchy. Its extensive use by Solomon, even though lighter demands seem to have been made on Israelites than on foreign subjects and vassals, eventually created great bitterness and dissatisfaction. This was one major reason given by the northern ten tribes for their secession from the kingdom.

7 The responsibility of these "governors" (GK 5893) was to supply provisions for the royal court. Each was responsible for these provisions for one month out of the year. The twelve divisions coincided only in part with the old tribal divisions. In only six instances are tribal names mentioned. The twelve officers were under the general supervision of Azariah (v.5).

8–19 The order of the districts is most likely the order in which supplies were to be sent. The territory of Judah is not explicitly mentioned. "The land" would refer to Judah, which had an unnamed governor, perhaps because he was part of the court itself (i.e., perhaps the Azariah of v.5). The NIV rendering—"he [i.e., Geber] was the only governor over the district"—reflects the interpretation that, despite the size of the district governed by Geber, there was only one governor. It would appear that Judah may have received special privileges, which would tend to foster resentment on the part of the other tribes.

2. His kingly splendor (4:20–28)

20 This and the following verse hark back to the Abrahamic covenant and give testimony to the faithfulness of God in carrying out his promises. The growth of the nation, numerically and territorially, the prosperity of the people, and their happiness all attest to the blessing of God. Solomon's kingdom in its broad outlines and at the acme of its greatness was a foretaste, a type, of the yet future and far greater fulfillment of God's promise in the millennial reign of Christ. Essential here is the rulership of both David and Solomon. David in his passionate love for the Lord, in his great victories over the enemies of God's people, and in his establishment of a great kingdom is a type of the coming Messiah. Solomon also is such a type, in his wisdom and reign of peace.

21 The countries that David had conquered remained subject to Solomon and brought him tribute throughout his reign. This was one noteworthy sign of God's blessing in keeping with the Davidic covenant. The usual experience of ancient empire builders was that when the old king died, the subject nations would withhold tribute and challenge the new king in rebellion. This necessitated repeated punitive expeditions to reinforce the former king's terms and to prove the ability of the new king to enforce his will. Solomon did not have to do this. God granted him a peaceful reign in which he could focus his energies on the temple and other building projects. He was also able to devote himself to administrative matters, to the building up of extensive and expanding foreign trade, and to his pursuit of wisdom and knowledge.

22 The magnificent court of Solomon as well as his fabled wisdom stirred great interest throughout the surrounding world (cf. v.34; 10:1–9). The provisions noted were daily requirements. The "cor" was a large measure of capacity. It was equivalent to the homer ("a donkey load"). Estimates vary considerably as to the exact amount involved—from forty to one hundred gallons. The daily requirement of fine flour amounted to between 150 and 280 bushels, that of coarse flour or meal, 300 to 560 bushels.

23 In addition to the large numbers of domesticated animals, game animals were also brought in. The exact identity of the "choice fowl" is not clear.

24–25 Solomon's kingdom was peaceful and prosperous. With control over all the kingdoms west of the Euphrates, Solomon was able to provide peace and security for his people. The statement that "each man [sat] under his own vine and fig tree" speaks of undisturbed prosperity and became a favorite catch phrase to indicate the ideal conditions prevailing in Messiah's kingdom (Mic 4:4; Zec 3:10). To enjoy the fruit of the vine and the fig tree meant there was a complete absence of warfare and economic disruption.

26–28 The reading "four thousand" reflects 2Ch 9:25. The Hebrew here reads "forty thousand" and is considered an old copyist's error. (Because of early systems of numerical abbreviation, transmission errors with numbers were more likely than in other portions of the text.) The twelve thousand horses may also indicate horsemen. Possibly the horse and rider as a unit is in view.

3. His superior wisdom (4:29–34)

The one attribute most characteristic of Solomon is "wisdom" (GK 2683). Interest in wisdom was widespread in the ancient world. In the Gentile world wisdom was primarily associated with the ability to be successful. It was not a speculative discipline but intensely practical. It pertained to all walks of life: priests (regarding proper practice in ritual), magicians (regarding skill in the practice of their arts), craftsmen of all sorts (regarding skillful workmanship), and administrators (regarding good management), etc. It did not usually deal with pure moral values. Though frequently associated with religious activity, its concern had to do with ritual and magical skills.

In the OT "wisdom" is frequently used in the broad sense of skill in craftsmanship or administration. An outstanding example is Ex 31:3, in which the two craftsmen appointed to make the tabernacle were given "skill" (lit., "wisdom") in carrying out their work. This kind of practical wisdom is applied to life as a whole—the art of being successful, i.e., how best to make one's way through life. Wise men were those who had unusual insight into human nature and in the problems of life in general. Thus they were sought as advisers to kings and rulers. At the very heart, however, of the concept of wisdom lies the recognition that God is the Author and End of life and that a meaningful or successful life is one that has its focus in him (cf. Job 28:28). True wisdom gives discernment in spiritual and moral matters.

29 The expression "breadth of understanding" means a comprehensive understanding and is illustrated by the numerous areas of knowledge in which Solomon was at home (vv.32–33).

30 The "East" here probably refers to Mesopotamia generally, which was commonly regarded as a major seat of culture and learning (cf. Isa 2:6). It produced a great body of literature, most of it mythological, but also much wisdom material.

31 Solomon's wisdom was recognized to be greater than that of any other man. He is compared in particular with four men noted for their wisdom as expressed in proverbs and songs. Ethan is the author of Ps 89, Heman of Ps 88. Calcol and Darda, apart from their appearance in 1Ch 2:6, are otherwise unknown. It seems likely that the expression "sons of Mahol" is a designation of membership in a guild or profession, i.e., "singers" (GK 4689; lit.,"dance," but sacred dance and song were closely related).

32 Many of Solomon's proverbs are preserved in the book of Proverbs. These were not only unusually sagacious but were inspired by the Holy Spirit. Besides the Song of Solomon, two songs or psalms are similarly preserved in Scripture (Pss 72; 127).

33 Solomon was skilled and learned in many areas. He was an astute observer of life and nature and from his careful observations was able to illustrate various facets of human nature and activity. God had granted Solomon great insight and a great thirst for knowledge.

34 The name Solomon soon became synonymous with a superior wisdom, so much so that kings of distant nations sent representatives to Jerusalem. This involved more than curiosity. It was a mark of respect and perhaps in many instances a desire to profit from his wisdom and learning (cf. ch. 10, which gives a concrete example in the visit of the queen of Sheba).

D. Solomon's Building Program (5:1–8:66)

1. Preparations for building the temple (5:1–18)

a. The league with Hiram of Tyre (5:1–12)

After he had firmly established himself and his administration, Solomon began laying the groundwork for carrying out what was perhaps the major achievement of his reign—building the temple and the palace complexes. The planning and oversight of the construction program of a project of such magnitude required considerable managerial skill, and Solomon demonstrated here again the unusual gifts granted him by God (cf. Da 1:30).

1 Hiram of Tyre, who had made peace with David and was his best friend, sent an embassy to extend his best wishes to Solomon on his accession to the throne. This king now offered Solomon a continuation of friendly relations.

2 Solomon responded in kind and in a preliminary to a trade agreement disclosed to Hiram his intentions with regard to the building project.

3 "You know" is a good indication that Hiram's relationship to David was more than one of peaceful coexistence or even of healthy commercial relations. David had let Hiram know what his intentions had been in regard to the building of the temple, a matter that had been very much on David's heart (2Sa 7:1–17; 1Ch 17:1–15). He felt it to be inappropriate that he should live in a fine palace when God's "house" was in reality a tent. Even after he was told that he would not be allowed to build the temple, he did all he could in the planning and preparation for the temple (1Ch 22; 29) to give Solomon as much help as possible.

4–5 God firmly established Solomon in the kingdom. There was peace within the kingdom, and there were no threats from the outside. The new king was prepared to carry out his father's wishes (cf. 1Ch 22:11–16; 28:9–21). Solomon could not help but be impressed by David's intensity and sense of purpose. He was very aware of his great responsibility, both toward God and toward his father. This is made quite clear by his quoting God's word to David.

6 Solomon asked Hiram for a trade agreement similar to the one that had existed between David and Hiram, but on a much larger scale (cf. 2Sa 5:11; 1Ch 22:4). The cedars of Lebanon were famed for their beauty and were greatly desired by rulers of Mesopotamia, Egypt, and Syro-Palestine for their building projects. Hiram's work force, skilled in felling and transporting timber, would be supplemented by labor sent by Solomon. The payment for goods and services was to be set by Hiram.

7 On receiving Solomon's message, Hiram acted enthusiastically. Solomon's request would initiate a major trade agreement beneficial to both parties.

8–9 Hiram agreed to Solomon's proposal and stated that he would be responsible for shipping the timbers by log rafts to the port that Solomon would designate. From that point they would be Solomon's responsibility. In return Solomon was to provide Hiram with provisions for his court.

10–11 There was an ample supply of timber for Solomon. In return he provided Hiram with wheat and olive oil, commodities not found in abundance in mountainous Phoenicia, whose economy was primarily based on an extensive shipping trade and export of timber.

12 The quality of wisdom is once again attributed to Solomon, seen here as a fulfillment of God's promise. The aspect of wisdom referred to is that of managerial and diplomatic prowess. Solomon in 1Ki 3 humbly recognized his deficiencies, and God granted him an abundant measure of wisdom so that he might be able to deal successfully with the various problems that might arise from his large undertaking.

b. The levy on the people (5:13–18)

13–14 The following verses give information on the labor force that Solomon raised to carry out the great task of gathering materials and then building the temple. The thirty thousand conscripted laborers were taken from all the tribes of Israel and sent in shifts of ten thousand to help the Phoenicians in the felling and transporting of the timbers from Lebanon. Each shift stayed one month at a time, so that each man worked for So-

lomon four months per year. The other eight months he worked on his own fields. This method of providing labor (called corvée) for large public projects was common in the ancient world but a fairly new innovation in Israel. In the list of David's officials, Adoniram is said to be over the forced labor. This would indicate that David used the corvée system to a limited degree, but nothing further is said about it. Solomon, however, used it extensively. The more splendid the royal court, the greater the demand on the people.

15–16 The 70,000 carriers and 80,000 stonecutters were non-Israelites (2Ch 2:17–18). They constituted a permanent "slave labor force" (1Ki 9:22), with the more onerous tasks to perform. The dressing of the stones was done by Israelite and Phoenician craftsmen. The stone was quarried in Israel, probably much of it in Jerusalem itself. The 3,300 foremen and overseers here were mostly Canaanites, with a smaller group of Israelites acting as higher supervisors.

17 The "large blocks of quality stone" for the foundation of the temple were squared off so that each stone would fit perfectly. According to 6:7 these large ashlar blocks were cut and squared at the quarry.

18 Other stones were prepared along with wood beams by skilled craftsmen, some from Israel, but most from Phoenicia. The city Gebal (Byblos) is particularly mentioned as providing a large part of these artisans. Again, according to 6:7, these men performed their craft at a place apart from the building site itself. This required careful planning and measuring and illustrates how well organized the whole program was and how skillfully the work was done.

2. The building of the temple (6:1–38)

a. Introduction (6:1)

The temple was in reality a permanent tabernacle as far as its symbolism and typology are concerned. It is basically the dwelling place of God with his people. There is a spiritual and symbolic continuity that transcends the structure itself. This is seen, for example, in the exchange between David and God in 2Sa 7, in which God is described as living among his people in a tent, moving with them from place to place. From God's perspective there is no essential difference, whether the house be a tent or a splendid structure of stone and cedar.

1 Solomon began the actual building of the temple in the fourth year of his reign. Since this event is linked to the Exodus of Israel from Egypt, this verse is one of the major pieces of internal evidence for the dating of the Exodus. The end of Solomon's reign is 931/930 B.C. This puts the beginning of his forty year reign at 971/970 and the fourth year at 967/966 and the date of the Exodus at 1447/1446. This date accords well with other biblical evidence (Jdg 11:26 and the length of the time of the Judges) as with external historical evidence.

The site of the building of the temple is not given here, but 2Ch 3:1 states that it was "on Mount Moriah, where the LORD had appeared to his father David. It was on the threshing floor of Araunah the Jebusite, the place provided by David." This was also the site of the (aborted) sacrifice of Isaac by Abraham (Ge 22:2). It lay on the rocky platform just to the north of the city of David on the eastern ridge of Jerusalem.

b. The outer structure (6:2–14)

2 Verses 2–10 give the general dimensions of the temple. These are inside measurements and do not include the thickness of the walls. The temple is here the main, central structure of the temple complex. Its dimensions were sixty cubits long by twenty wide by thirty high. (The cubit was approximately eighteen inches in length.) This was exactly twice the size of the tabernacle proper.

3 There was a portico (or porch, vestibule) attached to the front of the "main hall of the temple." It measured ten by twenty cubits, its long side going along the breadth of the temple proper.

4 The "clerestory windows" were probably on the side walls above the side chambers (cf. v.5). The exact nature of the windows is not known. Some have suggested slatted or latticed windows. Others suggest windows narrower outside than in.

5–6 Against the outside walls of the temple proper (main hall and inner sanctuary), Solomon built a three-tiered structure divided into an unspecified number of rooms (cf. Eze 41:5–11). Verse 10 gives the height of these rooms as five cubits each. At each level of the side rooms, the thickness of the wall was decreased by a half cubit on the outside wall and similarly on the inside wall so that the floor beam rested on the resulting offset ledge. Thus the width of each successive story increased by one cubit. By this means the beams had supports without being "inserted" or bonded into the inner temple wall. They were not structurally a part of the temple.

7 It is not necessary to see here a concession to the long-standing prohibition in Israel against using iron in the construction of the altar (Ex 20:25), since iron was indeed used at the quarries. It does indicate excellent organization and planning. The erection of the temple could go much faster and with far less confusion by utilizing precut and prefitted materials. In addition, the relative quiet

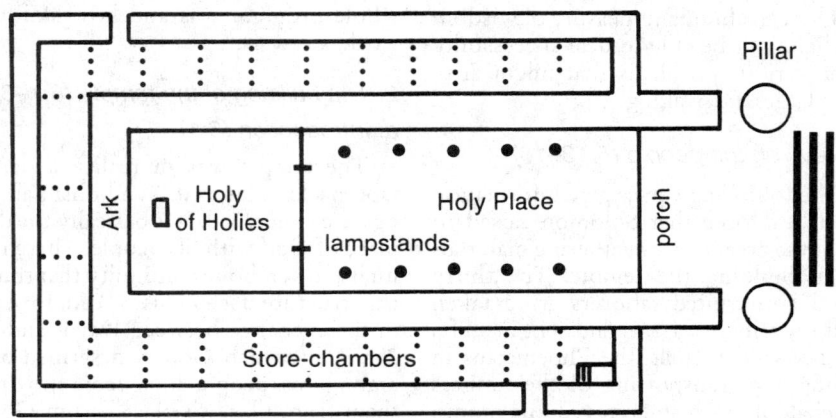

The floor plan of Solomon's temple

would be consistent with the sacredness of the undertaking.

8 The entrance to the side room was on the right (south) side, probably in the middle. Access to the second and third levels is most often understood to have been by means of a spiral staircase that led through the middle story to the third floor.

9–10 Apart from the statement that the roof was constructed of beams and cedar planks, no details are given. The use to which the "side rooms" were put is not mentioned, but they were undoubtedly intended for storage.

11 According to 9:2, after the dedication of the temple, the Lord appeared to Solomon a second time (the first time being at Gibeon, ch. 3), referring to direct personal appearances of the Lord. In the present passage God evidently spoke to Solomon through a prophet.

12–13 These are encouraging words, putting God's blessing on the building of the temple. God was with Solomon in this massive undertaking, and he would recognize the temple as his dwelling place among his people. This promise takes in two aspects of the Davidic covenant. (1) God established for David a lasting dynasty and declared that his son Solomon would be the one to build the house for the Name of the Lord that David had desired to build. (2) Solomon, in order to experience the blessings of the Davidic covenant, had to exhibit the faith and obedience of David toward the Word of God. The same holds true for each generation of Israelites. Thus the temple in all its splendor and ritual is by itself not sufficient. God requires obedient hearts.

14 This concludes the exterior structure. The next verses describe the work done in the interior.

c. The inner structure (6:15–35)

15 When the exterior structure was complete, Solomon lined the interior walls with cedar planks from floor to ceiling. The floors were also covered with wood, in this case pine or fir. Whatever the exact identity of this wood, it was often used together with cedar. The two were highly regarded and became a symbol of luxuriousness and stateliness. It is evident that Solomon was sparing no expense in

building the temple, using the finest and costliest materials available. His prayer in ch. 8 makes it clear that in doing this Solomon was giving expression to his sincere love for and devotion to God. Though God could not be enriched, Solomon was demonstrating in a practical way that nothing but the best is good enough for God.

16–18 The inner sanctuary or "Most Holy Place" was partitioned off from the main hall by cedar planks. The dimensions were twice those of the inner sanctuary of the tabernacle. This left forty cubits for the main hall, likewise twice as large as those of the Holy Place in the tabernacle. No stone was visible anywhere in the temple. Not only was everything lined with cedar, but the wood paneling was covered with fine, delicate carvings.

19 The inner sanctuary was the Most Holy Place or Holy of Holies because it housed the Ark of the Covenant, a symbol of the presence of God (cf. 1Sa 4:4; 2Sa 6:2). In Ex 25:21–22 God told Moses that he would meet with him there and give him all his commands for the Israelites. The top of the ark could be called "the mercy seat" or "atonement cover," in view of the annual sprinkling by the high priest of the blood of atonement. It was from between the cherubim that the glory of the Lord began his departure from the temple (Eze 10:4). Thus the ark in the Most Holy Place is the focal point of the temple and its ritual—not as an object of worship or superstitious awe, but as the place where God manifested his presence in his converse with his people.

20–22 This holy room was a perfect cube, overlaid in its entirety with gold, as was the cedar altar of incense. This altar was physically placed in the main hall or Holy Place directly before the entrance into the Most Holy Place (Ex 30:6), but functionally and symbolically it was associated with the Most Holy Place. Thus v.22 notes that it "belonged to the inner sanctuary" (cf. also Heb 9:4). By means of this altar, the priest could daily burn incense in the worship of God who was symbolically enthroned between the cherubim in the inner sanctuary.

Not only the inner sanctuary, but all the inside walls of the temple were overlaid with gold. The gold chains, stretched across the front of the inner sanctuary, served to strengthen the concept of the inaccessibility of this Most Holy Place.

23–28 Two cherubim made of olive wood and covered with gold were placed in the inner chamber. Each had a wingspan of ten cubits. They were so placed that they faced the door (2Ch 3:13). Thus their combined wingspan reached from one wall to the other. (By contrast, the two cherubim on the ark faced each other.) These composite figures (cf. Eze 1:4–14) represented the cherubim associated with the throne and government of God (Eze 1:22–28). They were also the guardians of the way to God (Ge 3:24). The impact to the beholder of these representations of the cherubim would be to impress on that person the awesomeness of God's holiness. Approaching God is not a light or frivolous matter and must be undertaken in the exact way he has prescribed—through the blood.

29–35 Doors of olive wood were made for the entry to the inner sanctuary and larger, double-leaved doors of pine or fir for the entry to the main hall. The jambs for both sets of doors were of olive wood. The doors as well as the walls (vv.20–22) and even the floors were covered with gold, with gold hammered into the carvings on the door. The covering of the floors with gold has often been scoffed at as being preposterous; yet it is in keeping with Solomon's desire to show forth in the temple, as much as humanly possible, the glory of God. It was his testimony to the greatness of God, and indeed the fame of this temple was spread far and wide so that honor and glory accrued to God as a result.

d. The court (6:36)

36 An inner court, called in 2Ch 4:9 the court of the priests, was built with three courses of dressed stone and then one layer of trimmed cedar beams (cf. Ezr 6:4). The author describes another court that enclosed the whole temple and palace complex (7:9–12).

e. Conclusion (6:37–38)

37–38 Seven years were required to complete the temple. An enormous amount of hours and a lavish expenditure of funds were involved. All the plans and specifications of David were carried out. It must have been a moment of great satisfaction to Solomon to see the fulfillment of his father's dream; and

when God acknowledged the temple by filling it with his glory, Solomon's joy knew no bounds.

3. Solomon's other buildings (7:1–12)

1 It took Solomon almost twice as long to build his palace complex as to build the temple. This was due to the numerous public and private building units that were constructed, six of which are briefly described in this passage. Also, in the case of the temple, there had been extensive advanced planning and acquisition of materials. This was not the case with the palace. The temple and the palace were included in one large complex and were enclosed within one courtyard (v.12), perhaps to give visual expression to the fact that the king was to act on behalf of God. He himself was to walk in God's ways and, as shepherd of the people, lead them and direct them to God. As such, he was a type of Christ.

2–5 The Palace of the Forest of Lebanon was a separate building, so named because of its cedar construction. It was an imposing structure one hundred cubits long, fifty cubits wide, and thirty cubits high. Its exact function is not perfectly clear, though it is referred to in 10:17 as the repository of three hundred shields of gold (cf. Isa 22:8). This latter passage is in a context of warfare, so real weapons, not ceremonial shields, are involved. This indicates that the building was at least in part an armory.

6–7 The five building units described in vv.6–9 may have been part of one grand structure. The colonnade was a magnificent porticoed entry hall, through which one entered the Hall of Justice. There was a throne hall or royal audience chamber where the king personally heard complaints and meted out justice in cases that could not be handled by lesser officials (cf. 3:16–28). The layout of this throne room was most likely similar to that of contemporaneous throne rooms in Syria and Assyria. Usually the throne was placed at the end of the hall left of the entry. The throne itself is described in 10:18–20.

8 As to the private residence of Solomon as well as the one for Pharaoh's daughter, nothing is said except that they were similar in design and set away from the public building.

9–12 The stones used in the palace complex were high quality, precisely cut, and trimmed on both inner and outer faces. The foundation stones were large, measuring twelve to fifteen feet in length. Similar ashlar stones have been found above the foundations of the southern "palace" in Megiddo. The large outer court enclosed both the temple and the palace works of Solomon. The construction, three layers of stone and one of cedar beams, was the same as for the wall of the inner court. This typically Phoenician construction style is represented at Megiddo in the Solomonic gate as well as in the gate of the court to the southern palace.

4. The vessels of the temple (7:13–51)

a. Hiram the craftsman (7:13–14)

13–14 Hiram ("Huram"; so also in 2Ch 2:13; 4:11) was an outstanding master craftsman brought in from Tyre. He is obviously to be ᵈ⸱stinguished from the king of the same ᵃᵃme. He was half Phoenician and half Israelite, his mother being from the tribe of Naphtali. He was skilled in bronze work; and 2Ch 2:14 adds that he was likewise skilled in working with gold, silver, iron, stone, wood, and various dyes and fine linen (cf. Ex 31:2–3; 35:30–31). Literally, Hiram was "filled with wisdom [GK 2683] and understanding [GK 9312] and knowledge [GK 1981] in doing every kind of bronze work." This illustrates the broad semantic range of the words "wisdom" and "understanding." Hiram's wisdom consisted in his practical skills. Solomon not only utilized the finest materials, but also spared no expense in hiring the finest workmen.

b. The two bronze pillars (7:15–22)

15 These two ornamented bronze pillars are the first of the objects made by Hiram for the temple. Every indication is that they were not structurally part of the temple but were freestanding. They were placed "at" or "near" the portico (v.21; cf. 2Ch 3:17). Numerous examples have been found of similar pairs of freestanding pillars in the ancient Near East. These pillars were quite large, eighteen cubits high with a circumference of twelve cubits. They were hollow, four fingerbreadths thick (Jer 52:21), and were cast in molds (v.46).

16–20 The "capitals," also bronze, were cast separately and were five cubits in length. They were bowl shaped (v.42; 2Ch 4:12–13) and were adorned with pomegranates, lily petals, and a network of interwoven chains.

21–22 The pillar placed on the right or south side of the entrance to the portico was named Jakin ("he established"). The other, on the left or north side, was named Boaz ("by him is he mighty"). These twin pillars may well have been a memorial in which David (the planner) and Solomon (the executor) give humble testimony to the grace of God in establishing for David a perpetual dynasty; the pillars also testified to the king's dependence on God for a successful reign. In practical terms the pillars were to be an ever-present reminder to each successive king of the fact that he was ruling by God's appointment and by his grace, and that in God lay his strength.

c. The bronze Sea (7:23–26)

23–26 The great Sea, made of cast bronze, was another marvelous example of the superb craftsmanship of Hiram. It was cast in one piece, including the lilylike rim and the two rows of gourds below the rim. The bronze bulls were cast separately, since they were later removed by Ahaz and replaced with a stone base (2Ki 16:17). The exact shape is not known. The Sea, together with the ten movable basins, served as the basin had in the tabernacle, for ceremonial cleansing. The Sea was used by the priests for their washing, while the basins were used for the rinsing of the burnt offerings (2Ch 4:6). The ceremonial stipulations for the priesthood with regard to the cleansing were intended to teach a truth that transcends mere ritualism, namely, that one who would approach God and serve him needs to be cleansed from the pollution of the world.

d. The ten bronze basins and their stands (7:27–39)

27–37 Ten mobile stands were constructed to carry the basins. They were four cubits square and three cubits high. There were lavishly engraved panels all around the stands, every available space being utilized in depicting cherubim, lions, and palm trees. The wheels were like chariot wheels. The word "handles" is probably better rendered "supports." The axles went through the bottom of

TEMPLE FURNISHINGS

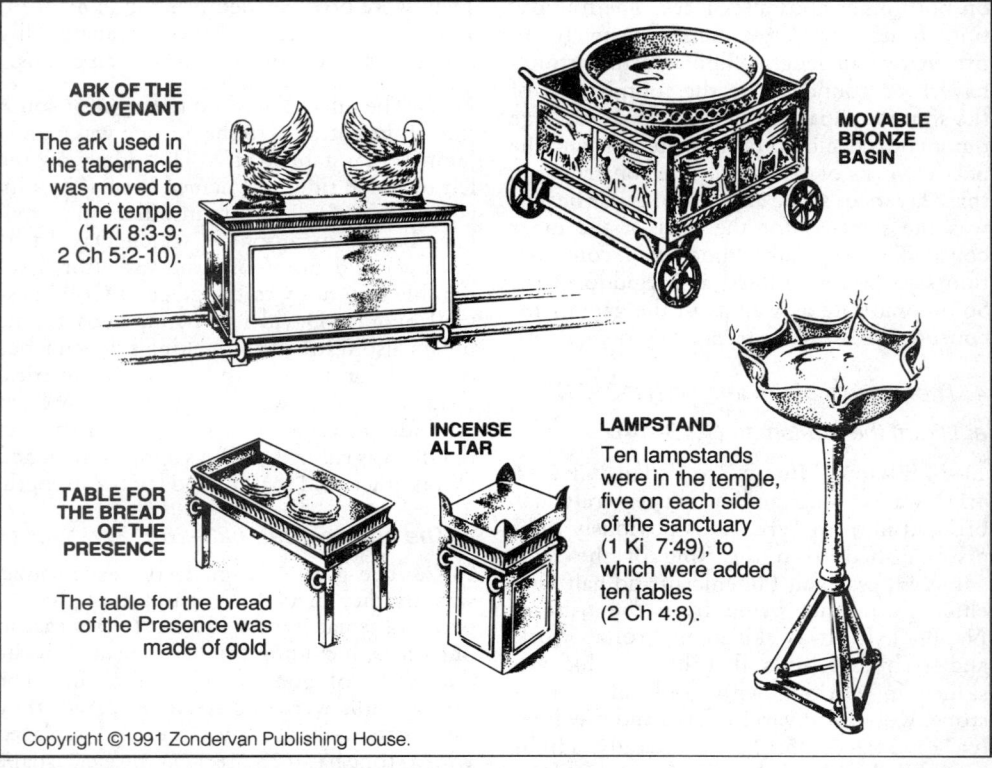

ARK OF THE COVENANT

The ark used in the tabernacle was moved to the temple (1 Ki 8:3-9; 2 Ch 5:2-10).

MOVABLE BRONZE BASIN

TABLE FOR THE BREAD OF THE PRESENCE

The table for the bread of the Presence was made of gold.

INCENSE ALTAR

LAMPSTAND

Ten lampstands were in the temple, five on each side of the sanctuary (1 Ki 7:49), to which were added ten tables (2 Ch 4:8).

these supports. These stands were mobile so that the basins could be moved to wherever they were needed.

38–39 The basins were also bronze, each holding forty baths (c. 230 gallons) and measuring four cubits (c. six feet). Though they were mobile, their normal placement was in the main hall of the temple, five on the right side and five on the left. Their purpose was to supply water for rinsing the burnt offerings (2Ch 4:6). The Sea was placed at the southeast corner of the temple (cf. Eze 47:1–2).

e. Summary of Hiram's bronze work (7:40–47)

40a The small bronze implements are listed, starting here. The basins are small vessels used for carrying away the ashes from the altar (cf. 2Ki 25:14; 2Ch 4:11). The shovels were for the actual removal of the ashes from the altar, and the sprinkling bowls were large bowls used at the altar of burnt offering, probably for catching blood.

40b–45 A summary of the items of bronze fashioned by Hiram begins at this point. Our account does not mention the bronze altar (2Ch 4:1).

46–47 The casting of the bronze was done in the lower Jordan Valley. Succoth was on the east side of the Jordan on the Jabbok River as it comes into the Jordan Valley. Zarethan is not as certainly located but is perhaps downstream on the Jabbok River, closer to the Jordan. This general area shows abundant evidence of having been an active center of metallurgy during the period of the Hebrew monarchy. There is an abundance of good clay; and with available wood for charcoal and a prevalent north wind, this area was an ideal center for metalsmiths.

The casting method used by Hiram was the lost-wax process, used from 2500 B.C. in Egypt until the Middle Ages. It is still often used for high quality sculptures. First a clay core is made, then covered with wax to the desired thickness. The wax is molded according to the intended design, then overlaid with specially prepared clay. The whole mold is then evenly baked for a period of time, possibly several days. During this time the wax is withdrawn through the outer mold through vents. Then molten bronze is poured into the same vents. Huge furnaces must have been used by Hiram, and great skill was required to ensure a uniform flow and distribution of molten metal and proper escape of gases. Only a master craftsman could have successfully carried out so huge an undertaking as was required here.

f. The furnishings of the temple (7:48–50)

48 A list of golden furnishings and implements begins here. On the golden altar, see comments on Ex 30:1–4. On the table of the bread of the Presence, see comments on Ex 25:23–30. The present passage does not mention the number of tables, but 2Ch 4:8 informs us that there were ten tables of the Presence. Later, in 2Ch 29:18, after Hezekiah had the temple purified, the priests reported to him that "the table for setting out the consecrated bread, with all its articles" had been purified. It would seem from these accounts that, though there were actually ten tables, they were often considered as a unit (one table in ten parts, so to speak), which they were as far as their function and symbolism were concerned.

49 On the golden lampstands, see comments on Ex 25:31–40. Here again, as with the table of the Presence, the one lampstand of the tabernacle became ten, yet so far as their function and symbolism were concerned, they were one unit. The symbolism of the earthly sanctuary as described in Heb 9 is based on the OT descriptions of the tabernacle, which served as the basic model for the temple.

50 It is noted that even the sockets of the doors of the Most Holy Place and of the main hall were of gold.

9. The treasures of the temple (7:51)

51 With the completion of the temple, Solomon brought into the treasury (possibly the side rooms of ch. 6) the great wealth of gifts David had dedicated to the Lord (1Ch 29). David had, in his great love for the Lord, given freely and gladly his "personal treasures of gold and silver for the temple" of his

God, "over and above everything" he had provided for the temple (1Ch 29:3). His love for God and his great enthusiasm encouraged his officials to give in a commensurate way. David's infectious joy affected the whole nation. His praying in 1Ch 29:10–20 is a model that is difficult to surpass, of joyous thanksgiving for the privilege of being allowed to give to the Lord. His prayer that God might give Solomon the wholehearted devotion to keep God's commands and to build the temple had now been answered. One cannot help but feel that, just as David's officials caught the joy of giving, so did Solomon catch the enthusiasm of carrying out the great program of building the temple. This is an excellent illustration of one of the great principles of leadership.

5. The dedication of the temple (8:1–66)

a. Moving the ark and the tabernacle to the temple (8:1–11)

1–2 With the completion of the temple and with all the furniture in place, the crowning event was about to take place, the placement of the ark into its permanent home. For Israel it marked the beginning of a new era. Now, more than ever before, there was a feeling of permanence. The ark was no longer housed in a temporary shelter in Jerusalem; the dichotomy in the sanctuary, with the ark in Jerusalem and the tabernacle at Gibeon, was ended.

To mark this great occasion with the dignity and solemnity it deserved, Solomon assembled all the elders of Israel with the tribal and family chiefs. As God's anointed shepherd, he involved all Israel through its elders and chiefs in the moving of the ark and the dedication of the temple. This involved more than mere pomp and ceremony. Solomon was serious about the spiritual significance of this occasion; and he desired that the heart of all Israel be knit together in the dedication of the temple and, more important, in the dedication of their hearts to God.

The Feast of Booths was the last in the series of yearly feasts and was also known as the Feast of Ingathering. It was a harvest feast, but, more important, it celebrated the end of the desert wanderings and God's bringing his people home into the Promised Land (Dt 12:8–11). Zechariah 14:16–21 singles out this feast as mandatory for surviving

Gentiles as well as redeemed Israel in the Messianic Age. This is consistent with the understanding that it celebrates the fulfillment of God's promise, the establishment of Israel in the land under God's Messiah.

For Solomon the completion of the temple symbolized the fulfillment of God's promise, not only to establish Israel, but also to live in their midst and be their God (cf. Rev 21:3). Without God's presence Israel's possession of the land would be an empty blessing (cf. Ex 33:12–16). It is God's presence that makes Israel uniquely blessed among all nations.

3–5 It was the priests who took up the ark in the prescribed manner. Before the ark was a great procession of the assembled chiefs and elders, led by Solomon. In keeping with the solemnity of the occasion, sheep and cattle were sacrificed in such numbers that no one could keep track. The participial form "sacrificing" indicates that the sacrifices were being made as the ark progressed the short distance from the city of David to the temple (cf. 2Sa 6:13). We should note that the Tent of Meeting (traditionally called the tabernacle) was also brought up. This was the original tent that had been at Gibeon. It, with its furnishings, was evidently stored somewhere in the temple.

6–8 The priests, who alone were permitted in the temple proper, placed the ark in its appointed place, under the outstretched wings of the golden cherubim, the representations of those highly exalted angelic beings associated with the throne of God and his rule (see 6:23–28). The ark was placed crosswise to the door, in a north-south alignment. The staves, which were extended lengthwise along the ark, were also aligned in the same direction, crosswise to the door. This accounts for the statement that the wings of the cherubim, which stretched north to south, overshadowed the ark and its staves. These staves, or carrying poles, were so long that the ends could only be seen if one were to look into the Most Holy Place from a place near the opening (i.e., the staves extended considerably beyond the doorway). The statement about the staves shows that Ex 25:15 was complied with, that the staves were not to be removed from the ark. Even though the ark was now in its permanent home, the staves remained in place, a reminder to God's people of their journeys in the desert. Though all the other furnishings had been newly made, the ark, representing the ruling presence of God, was still the same as that made while Israel was encamped at Sinai.

9 The ark had in it only the two stone tablets from Horeb, the witness of the covenant God had made with his people. It was for this reason that the ark was called the "ark of the covenant of the Lord" and also the "ark of the testimony." Here was the abiding witness to God's solemn purpose with regard to Israel, to make it a "kingdom of priests and a holy nation" (Ex 19:6). It was also a sobering reminder to Israel of her responsibilities before God. With regard to this latter aspect of the ark of the testimony or witness, it must be remembered that were it not for the blood of the atonement, the ark must of necessity be a throne of holy and terrible judgment, for "there is no one righteous, not even one" (Ro 3:10). But by God's gracious provision, the ark became a throne of mercy for the one who by faith approached in God's appointed way. Thus while the ark was too holy for even the priests to touch, and while it spoke of the awesome holiness and majesty of a sovereign God, it became through the atoning blood a witness to the forgiving, protecting, and comforting presence of God for the believer.

10–11 When the priests had placed the ark in the Most Holy Place and had withdrawn, the cloud of the glory of God descended and filled the temple, just as had been the case at the inauguration of the tabernacle (Ex 40:34–35). God was thereby graciously acknowledging Solomon's handiwork and indicating his intention of dwelling with his people. The glory cloud was the visible manifestation of the presence of God. The concept of the manifested glory of God (sometimes called his *"shekinah* glory") is a pervasive and important theme in the OT and extends into the NT (see comments on Joel 3:20–21).

b. Solomon's address (8:12–21)

12–13 Solomon recognized the glory cloud for what it was and saw in it God's approval and promised presence. God said that he would "dwell [GK 8905] in a dark cloud." This is not his normal, regular habitation, but he manifested himself in this form for Israel's sake. Solomon's response to this gracious manifestation was that he had built a "magnificent [lit., princely; GK 2292] temple" for the Lord so that he might sit enthroned in regal splendor as befits his majesty. Solomon was under no illusions, as though God needed the temple for his own sake. But just as God is enthroned in heaven, so he has seen fit to use Solomon's temple as his throne on earth.

14 Solomon had been speaking to God. He now turned to the people and blessed them. As king and shepherd, Solomon was to be both the civil leader and the spiritual leader. Solomon, having been graciously put on the throne by God, having been allowed to carry out the great task of building the temple, and having experienced the entering of the glory cloud into the temple, blessed the people. He did so on God's authority, as the representative of the Lord.

15–21 The blessing takes the form of praise to God for fulfilling his promise to David (cf. 2Sa 7). What God has promised he has also carried out. The "hand" (GK 3338) is the biblical symbol for sovereignty. Two aspects are mentioned by Solomon: (1) God has raised up Solomon to sit on David's throne, as he had promised, and (2) God has allowed Solomon to build the temple. Since the Davidic covenant implied benefit to Israel through God-appointed leadership and ultimately the coming Messiah, God had clearly begun the fulfillment of the covenant; and Israel could expect to receive the bounty of God's blessings if the people walked in his ways.

c. Solomon's sevenfold prayer of dedication (8:22–53)

The theme of the prayer (vv.22–30). The theme of Solomon's dedicatory prayer is that as God had seen fit to honor his word up to that time, he would continue to do so in accepting the prayers of his people and in granting forgiveness. These prayers are seen as being directed to God through the temple. Solomon was praying, in effect, that God might always recognize the temple as the way for sinful people to approach a holy God.

22 Solomon stood before the whole assembly, on a bronze platform, three cubits high (2Ch 6:13). He stood facing the assembly

with his hands outstretched in prayer, a common attitude in the ancient world (cf. Isa 1:15). Solomon stood as the representative and shepherd of his people, leading them in public worship and acting as intercessor. His prayer stands as one of the great public prayers of Scripture (cf. Ezr 9:5).

23–24 Solomon's opening great confession shows that he was greatly moved on this occasion. It was a day of fulfilled desires and prayers, a day in which God had graciously manifested himself in the glory cloud, a day of bright hope for Israel and the house of David in their covenant relationship with God. When Solomon extolled the greatness and uniqueness of the Lord, it was with a full and overflowing heart. What particularly moved Solomon was the faithfulness of God in carrying out his promise. In citing the faithfulness of God in maintaining his covenant and his love, Solomon did not lose sight of the human responsibility to respond to God and to love him wholeheartedly.

25 Solomon's confidence in praying was bolstered by previously answered prayer. A second ground of confidence was God's own promise. His servants had frequently claimed his promises when they prayed, and God honored these requests (cf. Ex 32:13; Da 9:1–18). In making this petition, Solomon recognized his own responsibility and tacitly rededicated himself to walking after God.

26 The major point, however, of these verses is a plea that God, who had so far been faithful in every way to his covenant with David (as evidenced in the completion of the temple and the rulership of Solomon), might always accept this temple and condescend to dwell there, receiving those who approach him by way of the temple.

27 Solomon made it clear that he was under no illusions as to the meaning of the temple, nor was it, properly speaking, a home for God. He acknowledged that it would be utterly impossible to build a house that could even begin to be commensurate with the majesty of the Lord. God does not need the temple, but the temple needs God! God does not need Israel, but Israel needs God!

28 Solomon realized that on the actual merits of the case, he would have no right to pray as he did, were it not for God's own promise given by his grace. The only claim Solomon had on the Lord was God's own word, freely given; but God's word is a bond that cannot be broken, so that Solomon was able to pray with assurance and confidence.

29 This verse forms the core of the entire prayer. God had condescended to allow a temple to be built for his name (5:5). He had by this means identified himself with his people. The temple provided a place of contact between human beings and God, a way for sinful people to approach a holy God, to have their sins forgiven, and to live in fellowship with him. Solomon prayed that God might continue to acknowledge the temple and the one who comes to him by way of the temple, as he had promised.

30 Solomon anticipated various situations in which a sinful people, suffering calamity because of God's judgment, would repent and pray. Solomon's earnest request was that God would not close his ears to repentant and believing prayer that was directed to God by way of the temple. God's own dwelling place, or place of enthronement, is in heaven. The temple, as the place on earth where his name is enthroned, is a type of the true heaven and at the same time the way of approach to God.

Seven specific requests (vv.31–53). The background to most of the various calamities described in the following verses is found in Lev 26 and Dt 28–30. Both passages begin with the description of the blessing that would be Israel's portion if God's people walked in his ways. The bulk of the material describes the curses in the form of various calamities that would befall the people if they did not obey God. Each calamity was designed to bring the people to repentance; but if they still would not repent, then worse would come. In both passages the final blow was exile from the Land of Promise. But in Lev 26:40–45 and Dt 30:1–10, God promised that when they were cast out of the land, if they would then take to heart what had befallen them and repent, God would listen to their prayer and restore them to the land.

31–32 Solomon's *first* request involves cases in which an oath was brought before the Lord in attesting to the truth of a claim (cf. Ex 22:11), cases in which there were no human witnesses (e.g., Ex 22:6–12; Lev 6:1–5).

These had to do with damage or loss of property entrusted to another, dispute over whether a piece of property has been found by another, or when fraud of some sort has been perpetrated. Solomon prayed that when an oath was brought before the Lord in such a case, he would judge between the guilty and the innocent, judging the one and establishing the innocence of the other. Solomon's concern was not only for upholding justice, but perhaps chiefly for the sanctity of an oath brought before God, so that his holiness might not be taken lightly.

33–34 Solomon's *second* request involved prayer for forgiveness after a defeat by the enemy (cf. Lev 26:17; Dt 28:25). This defeat was caused by sin and the repeated refusal to listen to God's admonitions. It entailed subjugation by the enemy with considerable hardship and the taking of prisoners (not here a mass removal of population). The conditions of restoration are here given as (1) turning back to God (repenting), (2) confessing God's name (i.e., acknowledging his lordship), and (3) prayer in the temple. This last element implied a coming to God in the way prescribed by him. The answer looked for is the forgiveness of sin and restoration of the captives to the land.

35–36 Solomon's *third* request concerned the drought brought on the land by the sin of the people (cf. Lev 26:19; Dt 28:23). Israel's crops depended on good and well-timed fall and spring rains. The Canaanites thought that they would ensure for themselves fertility for their land and abundant rains by worshiping Baal, the supposed god of the storm. The Israelites were prone to emulate their neighbors in the licentious worship of this idol. As a consequence God did withhold rain (cf. chs. 17–18) so that his people might realize that the Lord alone is the provider of all blessing. This passage gives the same three conditions of restoration as v.33. Restoration involved answered prayer in the forgiveness of sin and the restoration of rain. In addition, Solomon prayed that God might teach Israel how to walk before him so that they might enjoy the fullness of God's blessing.

37–40 Solomon's *fourth* request dealt with famine, various kinds of plagues, and enemy incursions that brought about severe economic disruptions (cf. Lev 26:16, 19–26; Dt

28:22–23, 38, 59–61). The emphasis was on individual recognition and acknowledgment of sin. It put the stress on personal and individual responsibility before God; first, in each person recognizing his or her own guilt and responsibility; and, second, in turning to God in sincere prayer. The emphasis here was on the heart, i.e., the inner person, rather than on ritual alone. God, who knows the heart, would respond to a person's prayer in accordance with the reality of one's repentance. The object was that people would fear God.

41–43 Solomon's *fifth* request recognized God's wider purpose in his dealings with Israel, namely, that as Gentiles saw God working in and through Israel, they might desire to know Israel's God. Solomon prayed that as the foreigners approached God through the temple, God might hear them so that they too would truly come to fear God.

44–45 Solomon's *sixth* request involved situations where the people did not have access to the temple because they were in a foreign country. In this instance it involved soldiers sent to battle in distant places. Under these circumstances they were to pray to the Lord, toward the temple. It was not the temple per se that rendered prayer effective; it was the Lord who saw fit to dwell there who answered prayer.

46–51 Solomon's *seventh* request dealt with the last in the series of calamities God promised to bring on Israel if the people persisted in disobedience (Lev 26:27–39; Dt 28:45–68). But just as God provided hope for a repentant Israel in Lev 26:40–45 and Dt 30:1–10, so did Solomon, on the basis of these passages, pray that God would continue to show himself a faithful and forgiving God. A mass deportation of the nation as a whole, with resultant scattering through many nations, would normally spell the end of the nation. In Israel's case, however, God would use calamity and distress to bring the people to an awareness of their sin so that they would turn to God, receive forgiveness, and be restored. The conditions of restoration were clearly outlined: a change of heart, i.e., a repentant spirit that led to confession of their sin; a turning back to God with all their heart and soul; and a praying toward the land of their fathers and the temple (trusting in God's promise; cf. Da 6:10). For those who responded as indicated, there would be complete restoration and vindication. God, who loved his people enough and was strong enough to bring them out of the iron-smelting furnace of Egypt, would also bring about his full and sovereign purposes with his people.

52–53 Though throughout his prayer Solomon put great stress on the centrality of the temple, this was not for reasons of vainglory, as being his special accomplishment. His basic concern was for his people. God had singled them out from all nations to be his special inheritance, and he had delivered them from Egypt. May he continue to care for his people until his complete purpose is fulfilled!

d. Solomon's benediction (8:54–61)

54–56 As Solomon stood before the people to bless them, his heart was filled with praise; and once again he spoke of God's faithfulness in fulfilling all his promises. The key word here is "rest" (GK 4957), which has important soteriological connotations. In Dt 12:9–10 "rest" was described as Israel's living in security in the Land of Promise. In the following verses, Israel is told to bring her sacrifices to the place (temple) where God would cause his name to dwell. Then would the people rejoice before the Lord (Dt 9:12). There can be no doubt that Solomon saw the temple as the completion of the picture of rest as portrayed in Dt 12. Not only was Israel living in peace and security, enjoying the fruitfulness of the land, but God was formally dwelling in their midst. This made everything complete.

The rest enjoyed by Solomon and his generation was not complete, nor was it final. Psalm 95:7b–11 gives sad expression to the fact that Israel had not entered God's true rest because of unbelief and rebellion (see Heb 3:7–4:11).

57–61 Solomon here expresses a twofold wish with a twofold purpose: (1) May the Lord always be with us and never forsake us so that he may turn our hearts to him! (2) May the Lord always remember to uphold our cause so that all peoples may know that the Lord is God! The first speaks of a continued internal working of God to make his people conformable to his will. The second speaks of a continued external working of God to bring about a change in the

Gentiles, that they too may come to a saving knowledge of God. These verses also illustrate the balance between God's work in the human heart and life on the one hand and man's responsibility on the other.

e. Solomon's dedicatory sacrifice (8:62–66)

62–63 All Israel joined Solomon in bringing sacrifices on this grand occasion. The large number was appropriate both to the occasion and to the number of people present to participate in the fellowship offerings. For these offerings the fat, blood, and entrails belonged to the Lord, while the flesh was eaten by the offerer. These offerings were brought over a period of fourteen days, since the normal period of seven days for the Feast of Tabernacles was extended by another seven days. The fellowship offering was a voluntary act of worship and was intended to testify to the fellowship between God and the one whose sins had been forgiven. After those portions belonging to God had been offered, a communal or fellowship meal was held for the offerer and his family and for the Levites.

64–66 To accommodate the large numbers of sacrifices, the whole middle part of the court in front of the temple was consecrated. The large number of sacrifices and the involvement of the people attest to the unity of purpose and the wholeheartedness of the devotion of people and king.

The Feast of Booths was in itself a grand occasion for rejoicing and for an enhanced spirit of community among all Israelites. The dedication of the temple made this occasion all the more joyful and memorable, and the time of celebration was suitably extended. When the people left, they went home rejoicing and with a great feeling of satisfaction in the realization that God's blessing was on the king and on the nation as a whole. This was indeed a memorable and significant occasion.

E. The Activities of the Solomonic Era (9:1–11:43)

1. The Lord's second appearance to Solomon (9:1–9)

1–2 God had already signally honored Solomon by appearing to him at Gibeon. Now once again God appeared to him to encourage him to remain faithful and to walk in God's ways. This made Solomon's later declension all the more reprehensible (cf. 11:9–

10). The time of this appearance was after the completion of Solomon's major building projects—the temple and palace complexes. Though it might seem strange that the Lord waited thirteen years after Solomon's prayer of dedication to reply, there are three considerations that make this entirely feasible.

(1) God did indeed respond immediately to Solomon's prayer. The Chronicler records the consuming of the sacrifices by fire sent from heaven immediately after Solomon's prayer, followed by the filling of the temple once again with the glory cloud (2Ch 7:1–7). This must certainly be considered as both an answer from God and a clear endorsement of the temple and of Solomon's dedicatory prayer. At this point no other answer was really necessary.

(2) There is no reason why there could not have been an unreported message through a prophet. This would have gone unrecorded because of the much more momentous appearance of God himself with essentially the same message. The recording of this appearance was important because of 11:9–10.

(3) The final consideration seeks to provide an answer to the question of the reason for the Lord's appearance to Solomon at this point in time if it was not in direct response to his dedicatory prayer. The answer may be that Solomon had come to a spiritual crossroads. It is significant that the year in which he completed the palace (his twenty-fourth year, twenty years after he began the temple) is mentioned three times (7:1; 9:1, 10). Apart from the notations on the year that he began building (6:1) and finished building the temple (6:38), this is the only event linked to his regnal calendar.

A second matter that points to a crossroads at this time is the remark in 11:4, that as Solomon grew older he began to follow after other gods, despite God's two appearances to him (11:9). This declension obviously began after his twenty-fourth year, since God did not condemn him in ch. 9. It was certainly a gradual thing that began in the heart and only slowly began to appear openly. It would be in keeping with the character of God to speak forcefully and urgently to Solomon, warning him against turning from his walk with God (cf. vv.6–9).

3 God acknowledged the temple, consecrating it by putting his name there. Neither the ritual nor the splendor of the building made it the dwelling place of God. Rather, it was God's sovereign and gracious choice to dwell among his people and to acknowledge them as his own. Solomon had asked (8:29) that God's eyes might be on the temple. God replied that not only his eyes but also his heart would be there. The following verses state the conditions.

4–5 These words reiterate the responsibilities of those who would come after David. Again it is emphasized that more than ritual observances were in view. It was the integrity of the heart that he demanded. Unfortunately, this was where Solomon failed later in life. It was not that he rejected God, but that his heart became divided in his loyalties (11:4) so that the passion for God that characterized his father and Solomon himself in his younger years was no longer there.

6–9 These verses give dire warning as to the disastrous consequences that resulted from apostasy. Solomon's history (ch. 11) shows that this warning was needed, particularly at this time in his life. This appearance of God was an act of grace and was intended as an urgent reminder to Solomon to guard his heart. A second thing to note here is that the consequences of disobedience were far-reaching. As kings, Solomon and his successors were responsible for the whole nation. Failure on the king's part affected all the people. Israel's subsequent history amply illustrates this principle. As the king went, so went the people.

There are two interrelated consequences that would result from disobedience. One was the exile of the people; the other was God's rejection of the temple, leading to its destruction. This state of affairs would lead in turn to a twofold reaction on the part of Gentile observers: (1) ridicule of Israel, and (2) questions as to the reasons for such a disaster.

Verses 8–9 describe the lesson to be learned from this by the Gentiles as they asked one another why this destruction had come about. The destroyed temple would become an object lesson in disobedience. In the answer given as to the reason for this destruction—namely, that it is because Israel has forsaken God and turned to idols—there is implied amazement that a people could be so foolish as to reject the God who had taken

them out of bondage and made them into a great nation, proving himself in the process with great and mighty deeds.

2. The business relation between Solomon and Hiram (9:10–14)

10–14 This paragraph relates a business transaction between Solomon and Hiram involving the transfer of twenty border towns. These towns were in Galilee in the western part of the territory of Asher. They lay generally east and southeast of the city of Acco. In the arrangements made in ch. 5, Solomon traded wheat and oil for timber. Hiram also sent 120 talents of gold (equivalent to about four and one-half tons) to Solomon. Apparently more payment was required than what Solomon could provide in grain and oil; so he ceded these border towns. Hiram, after inspecting the area, was not happy with the towns and, according to 2Ch 8:2, returned them to Solomon (presumably in favor of payment of a different kind), who then rebuilt the towns and settled Israelites in them.

3. The levy of forced labor and urban development (9:15–24)

15 "Supporting terraces" is traditionally and generally known by the name "Millo" (basically a transliteration from the Hebrew). The most widely held view is that this consisted of architectural terracing and buttressing along the northeastern slope of the east hill of Jerusalem, the city of David. Such buttressing would have filled a considerable depression between the city of David and the temple and palace complex to the north. The purpose would have been to allow the construction of more buildings in the area and, perhaps more important, adequate fortifications as near to the water supply as possible. Its construction was a major undertaking (cf. 11:27), ranking in importance with the fortification projects of Jerusalem, Hazor, Megiddo, and Gezer.

In addition to the expanding and strengthening of Jerusalem, three key cities were selected for rebuilding (Gezer) or for enlargement and strengthening of fortifications (Hazor and Megiddo). Recent work has demonstrated that these three cities had certain characteristics in common with regard to their fortifications attributable to the Solomonic era. Noteworthy are distinctive casemate walls with the outer wall measuring five feet and the inner wall four feet thick. The interior chambers are seven feet wide (similar walls from this era have been found in numerous cities throughout Israel).

Most distinctive are the gate complexes, which are identical in plan and virtually of the same dimensions in all three cities. These gates feature a four-entry, six-chamber inner gate, with twin towers at the first entry. Most of the gate extends inward from the casemate wall, with only the twin towers extending out from the wall. At both Megiddo and Gezer an outer double-entry gate has been found.

Hazor was strategically placed in the north (c. three miles north of the Sea of Galilee), being situated at the juncture of the two major highways approaching from the north. It became Israel's chief bulwark against northern invaders until it was destroyed in the eighth century by Tiglath-pileser III.

Megiddo was the great fortress that controlled one of the major passes from the Plain of Sharon on the coast into the Valley of Jezreel through the Carmel range. It figures in prophecy as the staging area for the last great battle (Armageddon) in which Christ will defeat the forces of the Antichrist.

16 Gezer, on the road from Joppa to Jerusalem, had been a powerful Canaanite city. Though it was included in the tribal territory of Ephraim, it was not occupied by the Israelites until the time of Solomon. Then it was given to Solomon as a wedding gift by Pharaoh to his daughter. He had burned the city and killed its inhabitants, giving it to Solomon to rebuild and inhabit with Israelites.

17 Upper and Lower Beth Horon were strategically placed, controlling the access to the highlands of Judea from the coastal plain through the Valley of Aijalon. The lower city, being about one and one-half miles farther west, was fortified by Solomon to guard against enemy approach from its vulnerable western side.

18 Baalath was the designation of several cities in Canaan. The one in question here is most likely the city also known as Kiriath Jearim, where the ark was kept for some time after its return from the Philistines. This assumes that the names Baalath and Baalah (by which name Kiriath Jearim was also known) are interchangeable. This would then be a fortress guarding another of the western approaches to Jerusalem.

19 Solomon built up an extensive network of supply centers and towns to house his chariotry. These places are not specified but certainly included the cities just mentioned in addition to other strategic locations throughout the kingdom. Though he was a man of peace, Solomon was well prepared militarily to defend his kingdom.

20–23 On the forced labor or corvée, see comments on 4:6 and 5:13–18.

24 On Pharaoh's daughter, see comment on 3:1. Since the work on the Millo (or "supporting terraces"; cf. v.15) was not begun until after the queen had been moved, likely the Millo had to be located near or in the city of David and the construction activities would have been at or near the site of her temporary home. It also appears likely that existing structures may have been razed to allow the construction over a large area of this buttressing work.

4. Solomon's religious activities (9:25)

25 This note is added to show that once the temple had been built, Solomon's practice of sacrificing at the various high places (3:2–4) ceased. Presumably the people followed him in this. As king he led the people, as on the day of dedication, in bringing before the Lord the burnt offerings and fellowship offerings on the three great feast days.

5. Solomon's commercial activities (9:26–28)

26–27 A completely new approach to international trade began here as far as Israel was concerned. Phoenicia was the major shipping power in the Mediterranean, while Israel controlled the major inland trade routes in the Levant. With Israel newly exercising control of the Negev as far as the Gulf of Aqaba, new possibilities opened up. Solomon made a treaty with Hiram of Tyre that was apparently mutually attractive. Both kings would be able to conduct extensive trade throughout the Red Sea area. In this venture Hiram supplied the seamen and shipping and shipbuilding skills, and Solomon gave Tyre access to the Red Sea and probably undertook a major share of the financing.

28 Ophir was fabled for its fine gold (Job 22:24) and as a center for the obtaining of exotic goods. It provided a rich source of revenue for Solomon and Hiram. Its location is still debated.

6. Solomon and the queen of Sheba (10:1–13)

The visit of the queen of Sheba is a graphic illustration of the fame of Solomon and of the awe that the reports of his wisdom and splendor inspired. The many legends and highly embellished accounts that have grown around this visit among Arabs, Jews, and Abyssinians attest to the widespread knowledge of the event and to the interest it created.

1 Sheba was in southwest Arabia, present-day Yemen. It is the best-watered and most fertile area of Arabia. By employing an extensive irrigation system, it developed a strong agricultural economy. But its chief strength lay in its being a center of trade. Its location kept it fairly secure from the power struggles in the Fertile Crescent and at the same time enabled it to be a convenient trade depot for traffic involving Africa, India, and the Mediterranean countries. It was famous for its trade in perfumes, incense, gold, and precious stones.

Solomon's fame reached the queen, probably through the caravan traders that regularly passed through Israel on their way to Damascus or to Gaza. His fame was associated with the name of the Lord. It was well known that he was an enthusiastic and faithful servant of the Lord and that he humbly attributed his wisdom and success to the

The upper picture is a model of Megiddo on location, showing what scholars for many years believed were Solomon's stables (more recent study suggests that the stables were from the time of Ahab, though Solomon's stables may be located underneath Ahab's. The picture to the right shows a portion of a Megiddo stable with a manger or feeding trough for the horses (located in Rockerfeller Museum).

Lord. Possibly the real reason for the queen's going to Solomon was for purposes of making trade agreements, but this is not stated. Undoubtedly business was transacted under the polite fiction of an exchange of gifts. Our passage makes it clear, however, that she did come to see for herself whether the glowing reports had been exaggerated or not.

"Hard questions" (GK 2648) is generally translated "riddles," which were enigmatic sayings or questions that cloaked a deeper philosophical, practical, or theological truth. They were a favorite sport and a way to test one's mettle. No doubt the "hard questions" posed by the queen were not mere frivolous tests of mental quickness but a genuine seeking for truths hidden in some of the enigmatic sayings known to her.

2 The queen came with a large caravan of camels carrying the trade goods for which Sheba was noted. Spices (Arabian balm) were native to South Arabia and were thus perhaps the most valued item in the whole inventory. Though v.10 mentions 120 talents of gold and many precious stones, the spices are singled out for special comment. Never again were so many spices brought in as on that occasion. When she arrived, she put before Solomon all the questions on her mind.

3–5 Solomon's wisdom was not exaggerated. The queen was not disappointed in his ability nor in the wisdom he displayed. Not only his wisdom, but the splendor of his court and the manner of the temple ceremonies overwhelmed her. She was totally undone.

6–7 The queen had thought the reports about Solomon to be exaggerated, that no person could be as great as he was reputed to be. Yet now she freely confessed that his fame had not even begun to do him justice.

8 "*How happy* your men must be!" is the word found so often in the Psalms (cf. Ps 1:1 et al.) translated "Blessed!" (GK 897). It stresses the subjective appreciation of a great favor or blessing, an experience to be enjoyed, savored, to its fullness. It is quite possible that Solomon's servants had begun to take for granted all that they were experiencing in Solomon's presence. But the queen, seeing all this for the first time, was overwhelmed with wonder.

9 A wise and good king is a blessing to his people, and God's choice of Solomon as king was a mark of his love and favor for Israel.

10–12 On v.10, see comments on v.2. The wealth of precious materials brought to Solomon from Sheba caused the writer to insert at this point the mention in particular of a very precious wood that was imported in unheard of quantities (just as with the spice or balsam that had just come from Sheba). The identity of this almugwood is not known today. Traditionally it has been thought to be a type of sandalwood, but there is no certainty on the matter. Solomon used it for "supports" (steps?) in the temple and his palace and for musical instruments.

13 Solomon gave the queen all she asked for (in trade for the items she had brought?). In addition he bestowed lavish gifts on her in keeping with his majesty.

7. The wonders of the Solomonic era (10:14–29)

14–15 The 666 talents (twenty-five tons) represent Solomon's yearly income in gold from all sources, including commerce and taxes. In addition there was an unspecified amount of income from tolls or tariffs from the various merchants and business agents that traveled through the land, as well as tribute from conquered kings. The "Arabian kings" were tribal chiefs of miscellaneous peoples living in the desert to the south and to the east. The governors were probably the district governors (4:7–19).

16–17 These verses describe the ceremonial shields that Solomon kept in the Palace of the Forest of Lebanon. They were wood or basket-work, covered with gold plate instead of leather. The large shield was either oval or rectangular to cover the whole body. The small shield was carried by archers (2Ch 14:8). The weights per shield were about seven and one-half and three and three-fourths pounds respectively.

18–21 The ivory throne, overlaid with finest gold, was a large and imposing object, in keeping with the symbolism of the seat of justice and rulership of a great kingdom. The armrests were flanked by lions, as were each of the six steps. Verse 21 well illustrates the wealth of Solomon's kingdom.

22 The "trading ships" (lit., "ships of Tarshish") most likely were large merchant ships designed to carry ore. They were seaworthy enough to travel long distances under difficult weather conditions. These ships came to be used for other types of cargo as well. It is likely that refined metals were shipped out of Ezion-geber in return for the exotic items listed in our passage (cf. Eze 27:12).

23–25 To the statement in 4:29–34 extolling the breadth of wisdom and knowledge of Solomon, this passage adds, first, that he was wealthier than any king on earth and, second, that "the whole world sought audience with Solomon to hear the wisdom God had put in his heart." This is in accordance with God's promise of 3:13.

26 This passage brings to mind the three prohibitions of Dt 17:16–17 for the anticipated kings—he must not acquire many horses, take numerous wives, or amass for himself great amounts of gold and silver. For his failure regarding the second prohibition, Solomon is taken to task in ch. 11. He is not taken to task, however, for the other two prohibitions. In the matter of horses, there seem to be two concerns: (1) the false reliance on chariotry (the most potent weaponry of the day) as a means of preserving and/or expanding the kingdom, and (2) making some of the Israelites go back to Egypt for the horses (cf. Isa 31:1–3).

On amassing personal wealth, one must remember that wealth was one of the bonuses God had promised Solomon (3:13). It was God's gift, and he should not be criticized for it. No doubt the prohibition in Deuteronomy has to do with motivation and priorities, in which personal gain is the issue.

27 That which is considered a "precious" metal, silver, became a "common" metal because of its abundance. Cedar, which had to be imported from Lebanon, became as common (in buildings) as the indigenous sycamore-fig trees.

28–29 Solomon not only acquired chariots and horses, he became a trader in these items. They were imported from Kue (probably Cilicia) and Egypt. The Cilicians had been known for some time as breeders of fine horses. Solomon's agents were active in seeking out the best horses and values available.

8. Solomon's many wives (11:1–13)

Considering the grand heights of Solomon's spiritual fervor and the great wisdom granted him by God, it seems impossible that he could have been so foolish as to succumb to idolatry. Yet it did happen, not overnight, but by slow degrees. First it was tolerated in his household. Once he became accustomed to it and comfortable with it, he also began to participate in idolatry with his wives. Solomon never renounced the Lord, but his heart was not entirely devoted to the Lord either. The syncretism that he began to display was a curse that plagued Israel through the years and ultimately led to the destruction of Jerusalem and the temple and to the exile of the people. Solomon's life stands as a solemn warning against ungodly alliances and relationships that can only destroy the believer's spiritual vitality (cf. Ne 13:26).

1–3 Solomon was a great man, but he had feet of clay. He was spiritually unable to survive his disobedience to God's prohibition in Dt 17:16–17 on taking more than one wife (see 10:26–29). In the Pentateuch God frequently warned Israel against intermingling and intermarrying with the Canaanites. Part of the reason was the extreme moral degeneracy of the Canaanites. Intermarriage inevitably led to toleration and finally observance of Canaanite religious practices (Ex 34:12–17; Dt 7:1–5). Another danger was that there was great similarity in some of the religious terminology; and though the theology behind the terms was radically different, it was very easy to adopt by degrees a comfortable syncretism and ultimately to forget the Lord and to serve idols.

If anyone should take these warnings seriously, it should be the king, who should lead by example. Yet Solomon apparently considered himself above the law and paid a bitter price. Though some of his many marriages may originally have been entered into for the cementing of diplomatic alliances and others merely for the purpose of increasing the royal harem to add to the splendor of the king, vv.1–2 point out that Solomon "loved" many foreign women and that he "held fast to them in love." This speaks of strong emotional attachment, which is normal and desirable in a husband. But because Solomon was attached to the wrong women, he was led astray. The seven hundred wives and three hundred concubines, though they added to the splendor of Solomon's kingdom, were his downfall.

4 As Solomon grew older, his resistance wore down, and he became increasingly vulnerable. His service to the Lord became more and more perfunctory. The writer here measures his love for the Lord by the standards of David, who, with all his faults, loved God with a passion throughout his lifetime.

5–8 "Ashtoreth" is a deliberate distortion of Ashtart, the Canaanite fertility goddess. The revocalization is based on the word for "shame." "Molech" (or "Milcom," as the text reads here) is a deliberate distortion of the word for "king." In not only allowing these practices in his own household but participating in them to some degree, Solomon sinned grievously against the Lord. Apparently Solomon showed no favoritism but treated all the gods alike, even to the honoring of "Chemosh," the Moabite equivalent of the Ammonite Molech or Milcom.

9–10 Solomon's sin was all the greater because of the special privileges he had enjoyed. God had singled Solomon out by appearing to him twice (see comments on 9:1–2). Solomon lacked neither proof nor evidence of God's love and power. He had abundantly tasted God's love (1) by being chosen, contrary to custom and expectation, as David's successor; (2) in being given the special, personal name "Jedidiah" (i.e., "loved by the Lord"); (3) in receiving every benefit imaginable; and (4) in being visited by God twice for encouragement and admonition. He had also abundantly seen the power of God in that (1) he was put on the throne in the face of the power and influence of Adonijah's followers (Joab in particular), (2) he was granted unchallenged power and prestige as king, and (3) he was given success in his endeavors beyond all expectation. This should have created in Solomon a lifelong love and devotion of the deepest kind.

11–13 The second special privilege that was Solomon's was his relationship to David and the covenant God had made with him. He had not earned it; he was born into it. He had also been thoroughly instructed and trained by David (and possibly Nathan) in preparation for the high calling that was his (see

comment on 2:2). As much as he could, David had poured into him his own love and passion for the Lord and his dreams for the house that would reflect the glory of the Lord. Solomon threw aside all these privileges when he followed after idols. He frittered away the continued joy and fellowship with God that could have been his for life. The punishment would be in accordance with the terms of the covenant with David. Yet even there God exercised mercy for David's sake. The kingdom was not taken from Solomon during his lifetime, nor was the kingdom to be totally removed from the line of David. God would keep the tribe of Judah for the descendants of David to rule and would eventually fulfill all his promises to David.

9. Solomon's adversaries (11:14–40)

a. Hadad the Edomite (11:14–22)

14–22 Hadad was the first of three men raised up by God to be adversaries against Solomon. It appears that as Solomon's reign drew to a close, these three men became increasingly worrisome to him. Hadad was of Edom's royal family, the only survivor of a severe slaughter when David's army under Abishai, son of Zeruiah, defeated the Edomites with a slaughter of eighteen thousand men (2Sa 8:13–14; 1Ch 18:12–13). This slaughter seems to have taken place over a period of six months when for some unknown reason Joab sought to destroy the Edomite army. Hadad managed to escape and found his way to Egypt with a number of servants. There he was given Pharaoh's sister-in-law as his wife. He continued in Pharaoh's favor, and Hadad's son was raised with the royal household. Hadad, however, continued to harbor strong bitterness against Israel; and the moment the news came that David and Joab had died, Hadad returned to Edom. There, in some unspecified way, he created trouble for Solomon, presumably not being very effective until Solomon's later years.

b. Rezon of Damascus (11:23–25)

23–25 The second adversary was Rezon, who had served under Hadadezer, king of Zobah. After David defeated Hadadezer (2Sa 8:3–9), Rezon, who had escaped, formed a group of raiders and bandits who ultimately gained control of Damascus. Since David had thoroughly defeated Zobah and Damascus, put garrisons in the latter city (2Sa 8:6), and reduced it to a tributary, it seems likely that Rezon's seizing of Damascus did not take place until later in Solomon's reign. At some point, probably after he had finished his palace, Solomon defeated Zobah and Hamath and went as far as Tadmor, making it a fortified outpost. Thus it is unlikely that Rezon made his move into Damascus until Solomon's declining years. However that may be, he was Solomon's troublemaker in the north while Hadad caused problems in the south.

c. Jeroboam (11:26–40)

26–28 The third and by far most serious problem for Solomon in his latter years was Jeroboam, an Ephraimite of considerable ability and energy. The story of his rebellion, or "lifting his hand against the king," starts with v.27. He was part of the Ephraimite labor force working on the Millo (see 9:15) and filling in a breach in the wall of the city of David. Jeroboam did his work so well that he attracted Solomon's attention and was put in charge of the contingent from Ephraim and Manasseh. He was evidently a charismatic leader.

29–32 About this time, while still overseeing this construction project (which took place sometime after Solomon's twenty-fourth year [9:10–15]), Jeroboam met Ahijah the prophet from Shiloh. This of course was a planned meeting on Ahijah's part. When they were alone in the open country, Ahijah symbolically told Jeroboam what God's plans were for him and Solomon. He tore his own new cloak into twelve pieces, told Jeroboam to take ten, and then explained the meaning of the prophecy.

33–36 On vv.33–35, see comments on vv.7–13. With the words "that David my servant may always have a lamp before me in Jerusalem" (v.36), God expressed the unconditional aspect of the Davidic covenant: He would at some future time reestablish the throne of David in full glory—in the person of the Messiah, the Anointed One. The symbolism is striking and beautiful. Not only would the line of David be perpetuated just as a light is kept burning, but this light was in Jerusalem, the city where God chose to put his name. There was in view, then, a future for God's city, Jerusalem.

37–38 God gave Jeroboam the grand opportunity of establishing a lasting dynasty. The conditions were the same as those imposed on the sons of David. The standard of the godly walk is once again David. Unfortunately, though Jeroboam was extremely able, he was an unworthy man. He proved to be an ambitious and greedy opportunist. Chapter 12 shows that he had the ability of playing on people's emotions to achieve his ends. All his subsequent actions demonstrate the mentality of a man who was determined to achieve his own ends, ignoring God and his ways in the process.

39 Here is both a reaffirmation of the enduring nature of God's promise to David and a clear statement to Jeroboam and his successors that the house of David would win in the end. Starting with Rehoboam's loss, first, of the ten tribes, then the deprivations of Shishak (ch. 14), Judah became both the smaller and generally the weaker kingdom. It was indeed a shock for Rehoboam and the tribe of Judah to be reduced overnight from the most powerful tribe in an illustrious and world-renowned kingdom to a small state that was soon stripped of what wealth it had left. But God said that it would not always be thus. There seems to be an implication here that in the future the tribes would all once again be under the leadership of Judah.

40 At some point after the prophecy of Ahijah, the attempt at rebellion spoken of in v.26 took place. No details are given. Presumably, Jeroboam was busily fanning the flames of dissatisfaction on the part of the northern tribes with the leadership of the house of David and, in particular, the oppressive requirements imposed on them to maintain the splendid style of Solomon's government. There is a contrast here between Jeroboam and David, both of whom became kings after a disobedient king. David waited on God, but Jeroboam took matters into his own hands. Solomon, also, was disappointing. Rather than bowing humbly before the will of God as David had done under God's chastening hand, Solomon reacted in the manner of Saul, causing Jeroboam to flee into exile.

10. Solomon's death (11:41–43)

41–43 The royal annals of Solomon contained a far more complete record of the events surrounding his administration, but the account recorded in Scripture is God's inspired message, given for the instruction and benefit of the reader. Solomon left a big mark in history. His memory and fame live on. He represents the first stage in the fulfillment of the Davidic covenant; and, despite his faults, he foreshadows the coming Christ, the true Son of David. In addition, his inspired words of wisdom as recorded in Scripture have challenged, taught, and inspired people throughout the ages.

II. The Divided Kingdom (1Ki 12:1–2Ki 17:41)

A. The Division and Early Kings (12:1–16:14)

1. The accession of Rehoboam and secession of the ten tribes (12:1–24)

1–2 "All the Israelites" manifestly refers to the representatives of the northern tribes. The basic differences between the northern and southern tribes had never been fully resolved even in the strong administrative periods of David and Solomon. That Rehoboam consented to go to Shechem for the inaugural ceremonies underscores the critical nature of the times and the insecurity of his position on the throne.

Jeroboam, mindful of his previous anointing (cf. 11:26–40) and confident that the time was ripe for him to make a move toward securing the throne, returned to lend his weight to the negotiations. Perhaps the ten tribes had actually gathered at Shechem expressly to make Jeroboam their king.

3–5 Jeroboam was well received by the delegation and accompanied them to the meeting with Rehoboam, where their demands for social reform were voiced. Particularly burdensome were the corvée, or compulsory service (over which, interestingly enough, Jeroboam had been appointed by Solomon [see 11:28; see also comments on 4:6; 6:14]), and the taxation that Rehoboam's father levied on the land. Both lay on the people like a heavy yoke. After hearing the northern tribes' demands, Rehoboam obtained a three-day period for considering the terms of their requests.

6–11 Calling in the elder counselors who had served through the difficult Solomonic years, Rehoboam was advised to grant the demands of the northern tribes so as to gain their loyalty. Next Rehoboam turned to his own contemporaries for advice. This group may have served as an administrative advisory body, perhaps concerned with national preparedness. The young men gave Rehoboam the counsel he wished to hear. They advised him to follow a harsh line. Was Solomon too hard on them? He would be tougher. His little finger would be thicker than Solomon's loins!

12–15 When the northern delegation returned on the prescribed day, Rehoboam followed the advice of the younger men implicitly, delivering the harsh ultimatum. The author of Kings interrupts the narrative to point out that the decision of Rehoboam and his counselors was in accordance with a turn of affairs arranged by God's sovereign disposition, as prophesied previously by Ahijah (cf. 2Ch 10:15).

16–17 After Rehoboam's unfavorable reply to their request, the delegation delivered its formal note of secession. That the delegates were prepared for the worst seems obvious from their carefully composed poetic reply. The reply itself is drawn largely from the traitorous words of Sheba, who led an unsuccessful rebellion in the days of David (2Sa 20). The long-standing jealousy between the tribes, coupled with the hostility of the northern tribes to the Davidic covenant (2Sa 7), comes to the surface in all its ugliness and fateful consequences. Consequently, the kingdom became divided. Rehoboam retained the rule only over Judah and Benjamin, which Rehoboam's forces managed to occupy as a much needed buffer zone between Jerusalem and the north.

18–24 Rehoboam quickly tested the decision of the delegates by sending Adoniram, his chief tax collector, to gather the taxes; he gathered only stones for his effort. With Adoniram dead and the people gathered into a bitter mob, Rehoboam fled for his life. There remained only the formal invitation to Jeroboam to become king of the northern tribes, followed by the coronation ceremony before the assembled multitude. The schism was complete and was to be permanent, despite a long period of incessant warfare between the two states. Having failed to acquire the north's willing subservience, Rehoboam decided on an outright invasion of the new kingdom; thus he gathered a large army (cf.

2Ch 11:1–4). However, Shemaiah the prophet warned Rehoboam not to attempt to undo what God had decreed; Rehoboam wisely abandoned the attack.

2. The reign of Jeroboam in the northern kingdom (12:25–14:20)

a. The condemnation of Jeroboam's religion (12:25–13:34)

25–30 Jeroboam's plans for the administration of the new kingdom are now detailed. It was imperative that he act wisely, lest the people become dissatisfied and return their allegiance to Rehoboam. No doubt much of the administrative machinery (minus the hated corvée established by David and Solomon) was utilized. His years serving Solomon in a responsible position probably aided Jeroboam's leadership in this area. Shechem was refurbished and made the capital. Peniel received his attention also and may have served subsequently as an alternate royal residence.

The people, however, had to be cared for not only administratively but also religiously. Here Jeroboam miscalculated and substituted human wisdom for divine direction. Although God may have allowed the kingdom to be divided politically, he intended no theological schism. Fearing that a continued adherence to the established faith with its center of worship in Jerusalem might bring about a return to the south in the people's affection, Jeroboam established an alternate and more convenient religious experience. Rather than making the long trip to Jerusalem, the people of the north could now select one of the two more accessible worship centers: Dan, in the northern sector of the northern kingdom, or Bethel, in the extreme south, both of which had long-standing traditions as religious cities. Bethel was to be especially prominent throughout the rest of the history of the northern kingdom (cf. Am 7:13).

At each cult center Jeroboam erected a temple, probably to house the sacred image and altar. The golden calves he caused to be erected were probably not intended to be construed as pagan images per se but representations of animals on whose back stood the invisible god, unseen by the eye of the worshiper. Similar practices involving the worship of the Canaanite god Baal Hadad are well documented in the literature and art of Ugarit. It was inevitable that religious confusion and apostasy would soon set in.

31–33 To further his religious goals, Jeroboam instituted a new religious order drawn from non-Levitical sources. Indeed, the Levitical priests refused to have any share in such unscriptural procedures, choosing rather to leave their homes and go over to Rehoboam and the southern kingdom where the true faith was retained (2Ch 11:13–17). In this they were followed by many other believers from the north. Completing his religious innovations, Jeroboam instituted an annual feast on the fifteenth day of the eighth month, no doubt rivaling the Feast of Tabernacles in the seventh month in Jerusalem.

13:1–3 God sent his prophet out of Judah to rebuke Jeroboam and his apostate religion. How tragic that no prophet could be found in the north who could speak for God's cause! The man of God came to the altar where Jeroboam was leading in the false sacrifices and prophesied by the authority and power of the word of the Lord that a coming prince of the house of David, Josiah by name, would one day burn the bones of Jeroboam's priests on that altar, thereby defiling it forever (cf. 2Ki 23:15–20). In confirmation of his prophecy, the prophet gave a sign: the altar would be split apart and its ashes poured out. According to the Levitical regulations, the ashes were to be carried off carefully to a clean place for disposal (Lev 1:16; 4:12; 6:10–11). Their pouring out, together with the destruction of the altar, would signify God's invalidating of the sacrificial service being held at Bethel.

4–6 Infuriated, Jeroboam pointed his hand at the prophet and gave orders that he be seized. But the very hand, stretched out in condemnation, was itself rebuked by being instantly withered. The king who would himself "take a hand" in the religious ceremony of his people found that strong hand totally impotent. Moreover, the prophesied sign descended on the altar with a lightninglike stroke. Terrified and humbled Jeroboam pled with the man of God that his hand be restored; whereupon the prophet interceded with God, and the king's hand was restored to its former condition. Another miracle had occurred!

7 Finally Jeroboam was convinced by the twin miracles of the altar's destruction and the restoration of his withered hand that the prophet was indeed from the Lord, hence a man whose authority and power were to be reckoned with; so he invited the prophet to dine with him. Whether Jeroboam intended the dining hall of the sanctuary or that of his own home in Bethel is not certain. Whether or not Jeroboam hoped to win such a holy man over to his side, he clearly intended to try both to mollify the prophet's stand and to save face before the multitude.

8–10 The man of God, however, would not be so easily manipulated. He refused most stringently. Nothing the king could offer enticed him. God had laid on him three rules of conduct for the road: he was neither to eat nor to drink nor even to return by the way he had come. So holy was his mission that the very way he had traveled had been rendered sacred (cf. Mt 2:12; Jas 2:25). Rejecting the king and his offer, he departed by another road.

11–22 Learning of the incident in Bethel from his sons and recognizing that the man of God must be a true prophet, an aged prophet of Bethel set out to overtake the man of God. Probably the old prophet hoped for fellowship and encouragement. When heat finally overcame Jeroboam's rebuker, the old prophet invited the man of God to dine with him, assuring him that his previous instructions against eating and drinking had been superseded by a subsequent revelation. Was not he also a prophet?

The prophet from Judah was too easily convinced by the old man's deception. Perhaps a fundamental flaw in his character can herein be detected: his carrying out of God's charge may have been sheerly from command, not conviction. At any rate, he went with the prophet of Bethel. While they were dining, the word of the Lord truly did come to the old prophet. Because the man of God had disobeyed the full counsel of God, he would not be buried in the tomb of his father; this meant that he would meet a violent death along the way home.

23–30 As soon as the meal had ended and the man of God had taken his leave, a lion met him on the road, killed him, and stood over his fallen body. Eventually the news of the tragedy reached the aged prophet. Surmising that the events were the fulfillment of the Lord's prophetic judgment, he went and found that all was as it had been reported: the body of the man of God lay on the road with the lion yet standing guard beside it. The body had not been eaten, nor had the prophet's donkey, which stood beside his fallen master. This could only be the judgment of God! Striding past the sentrylike lion, the prophet tenderly picked up the body of the man of God, brought it back to town, and after proper mourning, laid it to rest in his own tomb.

31–32 After the burial, the old prophet gave instructions that when he died he should be laid to rest beside the man of God. So powerful an effect had the whole series of events produced on him, and so assured was he that all the man of God had predicted would surely come to pass, that the old prophet longed, at least in death, to be united with this holy man. The prophecy that the man of God had made was fulfilled minutely in the reform of Josiah (2Ki 23:15–18).

33–34 One would think that the foregoing events would have influenced Jeroboam to turn to God. Such was not to be the case. Having had his hand restored and being rid of the irksome prophet from Judah, Jeroboam only intensified his apostate religious policy, a program that was to become the ruin of the northern kingdom and for which his name was to live in infamy. Thus it was to be repeatedly said of the wicked kings of the northern kingdom: "He walked in all the ways of Jeroboam son of Nebat and in his sin"(e.g., 16:26).

b. The consequences of Jeroboam's religion (14:1–20)

1–3 When Jeroboam's son fell critically ill, the king sent his wife in disguise to Ahijah to learn whether the prince would recover. Since Ahijah had successfully predicted his kingship (11:29–39), Jeroboam doubtless hoped that the old prophet might once again have good news. Perhaps he sent his wife because he himself felt convicted that he had not heeded Ahijah's admonitions (11:38).

4–16 Since Ahijah was now aged and blind, there was every hope that the subterfuge might succeed. But God had disclosed King

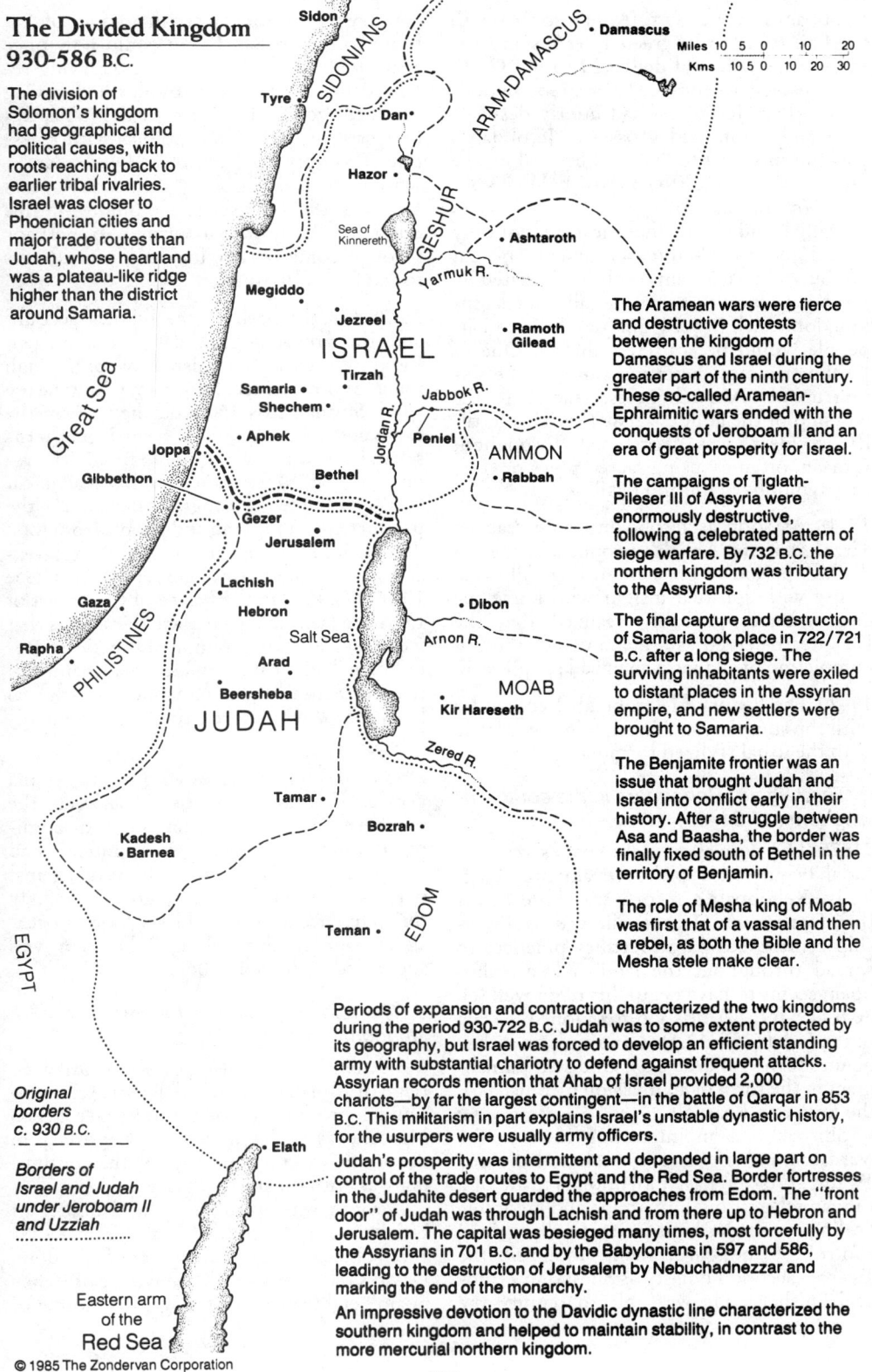

The Divided Kingdom
930-586 B.C.

The division of Solomon's kingdom had geographical and political causes, with roots reaching back to earlier tribal rivalries. Israel was closer to Phoenician cities and major trade routes than Judah, whose heartland was a plateau-like ridge higher than the district around Samaria.

Great Sea

Sidon

Tyre

SIDONIANS

Dan

Hazor

Sea of Kinnereth

GESHUR

ARAM-DAMASCUS

Damascus

Miles 10 5 0   10   20
Kms   10 5 0   10   20   30

Ashtaroth

Yarmuk R.

Megiddo

Jezreel

ISRAEL

Ramoth Gilead

Tirzah

Jabbok R.

Samaria

Shechem

Jordan R.

Peniel

AMMON

Aphek

Joppa

Bethel

Rabbah

Gibbethon

Gezer

Jerusalem

Lachish

Hebron

Gaza

Salt Sea

Dibon

Arnon R.

PHILISTINES

Rapha

Arad

Beersheba

JUDAH

MOAB

Kir Hareseth

Zered R.

Tamar

Bozrah

Kadesh Barnea

Teman

EDOM

EGYPT

Original borders c. 930 B.C.

Borders of Israel and Judah under Jeroboam II and Uzziah

Elath

Eastern arm of the Red Sea

© 1985 The Zondervan Corporation

The Aramean wars were fierce and destructive contests between the kingdom of Damascus and Israel during the greater part of the ninth century. These so-called Aramean-Ephraimitic wars ended with the conquests of Jeroboam II and an era of great prosperity for Israel.

The campaigns of Tiglath-Pileser III of Assyria were enormously destructive, following a celebrated pattern of siege warfare. By 732 B.C. the northern kingdom was tributary to the Assyrians.

The final capture and destruction of Samaria took place in 722/721 B.C. after a long siege. The surviving inhabitants were exiled to distant places in the Assyrian empire, and new settlers were brought to Samaria.

The Benjamite frontier was an issue that brought Judah and Israel into conflict early in their history. After a struggle between Asa and Baasha, the border was finally fixed south of Bethel in the territory of Benjamin.

The role of Mesha king of Moab was first that of a vassal and then a rebel, as both the Bible and the Mesha stele make clear.

Periods of expansion and contraction characterized the two kingdoms during the period 930-722 B.C. Judah was to some extent protected by its geography, but Israel was forced to develop an efficient standing army with substantial chariotry to defend against frequent attacks. Assyrian records mention that Ahab of Israel provided 2,000 chariots—by far the largest contingent—in the battle of Qarqar in 853 B.C. This militarism in part explains Israel's unstable dynastic history, for the usurpers were usually army officers.

Judah's prosperity was intermittent and depended in large part on control of the trade routes to Egypt and the Red Sea. Border fortresses in the Judahite desert guarded the approaches from Edom. The "front door" of Judah was through Lachish and from there up to Hebron and Jerusalem. The capital was besieged many times, most forcefully by the Assyrians in 701 B.C. and by the Babylonians in 597 and 586, leading to the destruction of Jerusalem by Nebuchadnezzar and marking the end of the monarchy.

An impressive devotion to the Davidic dynastic line characterized the southern kingdom and helped to maintain stability, in contrast to the more mercurial northern kingdom.

Jeroboam's hypocrisy to Ahijah so that with her first footstep he greeted her instantly as Jeroboam's wife and delivered to her God's dire message of rebuke. Despite God's goodness to him, Jeroboam had utterly despised God and committed gross sin. Jeroboam's contemptuous attitude is emphasized by the phrase "thrust me [the LORD] behind your back" (cf. Eze 23:35).

Ahijah added a further message: not only would Jeroboam's dynasty quickly be cut off, but because the sin condition initiated by Jeroboam would permeate all Israel, the kingdom itself would one day fail, and its people would be scattered abroad. One of Jeroboam's most besetting sins was the setting up of "Asherah poles," sacred to the worship of the goddess Asherah. This fertility goddess was worshiped throughout Canaan, often by using sacred poles or trees that symbolized life and fertility.

17–18 As soon as Jeroboam's wife reached Tirzah, true to Ahijah's prophecies, the lad died. A period of great mourning followed. Those with spiritual insight who knew the circumstances probably realized that the lad's death served as a guarantee of the full completion of all that Ahijah had prophesied.

19–20 The history of Jeroboam I concludes with the summary of his reign in accordance with the usual stylized formula.

3. The reign of Rehoboam in the southern kingdom (14:21–31)

21–25 The notices of Rehoboam's reign in Judah begin with a spiritual evaluation. Tragically, Rehoboam's record was little better than Jeroboam's. He, too, allowed rival worship centers and pagan fertility practices to spread throughout the land. While Rehoboam seems to have begun his reign well (cf. 2Ch 11:5–17, 23), he soon abandoned the law of the Lord (2Ch 12:1). As a result, in Rehoboam's fifth year (926 B.C.), God sent punishment in the form of an invasion by Shishak I, the Egyptian Pharaoh.

Shishak had an interesting history. Toward the end of Egypt's weak and divided Twenty-First Dynasty, mention is made of a Libyan who through marriage and favorable dealings with the high priest finally gained control of the government, founding the Twenty-Second Dynasty as Sheshonq I (biblical Shishak). He was able to reunify the

country and restore a certain amount of stability to the crown. Egypt could now once again look beyond her borders. Having renewed the old ties with Byblos and having regained economic supremacy in Nubia, this king saw an opportunity to deal with Palestine. Probably he had advised Jeroboam—whom he had harbored for many years awaiting the demise of Solomon—in his quest for the northern throne. So, perhaps through some border incident, pretext was found for a full invasion.

26–28 On the basis of the biblical account and the archaeological data from ancient Egypt, it is clear that Shishak swept through much of both Israel and Judah, taking heavy spoil. Shishak lists 150 cities he took in the campaign. The Chronicler records that Jerusalem itself was severely looted; only the repentance of Rehoboam and his leaders at God's rebuke through Shemaiah, the prophet, saved the land and people from total destruction. Significant among the spoil treasures were Solomon's golden shields (see 10:16–17), kept in the Palace of the Forest of Lebanon (see 7:2). To replace the shields that were used at state ceremonial functions, Rehoboam had bronze shields made and entrusted them to the commander of his royal bodyguard, who stored them in the guardhouse.

29–31 The chapter closes with the additional notice of strained relations between the northern and southern kingdoms throughout Rehoboam's reign. Since Rehoboam had complied with the divine prohibition against overt warfare (cf. 12:21–24), more than likely this reference is to a "cold war" or to occasional border skirmishes. Rehoboam was succeeded by his son Abijah.

4. The reign of Abijah in the southern kingdom (15:1–8)

1–5 Attention is focused on the short-lived reign of Abijah in but few details: (1) the continuing prominence of the dowager queen Maacah, (2) the continuance of apostasy in the southern kingdom, and (3) the continuing war with the north.

Maacah was apparently the daughter of Uriel of Gibeah (2Ch 13:2) and Tamar (2Sa 14:27), hence the granddaughter of Absalom, David's rebellious son. The favorite of Rehoboam's eighteen wives, she was the mother of

Abijah and the grandmother of Asa. Her continued prominence testifies to her strong personality.

Rehoboam's spiritual example was reflected in his son. Abijah's imitation of his father's religion stands in bold contrast to that of his forefather David, with whom God had entered into covenant relationship (2Sa 7:4–17). Although Abijah was a poor representative of the house of David (cf. 11:4), yet God, who remains faithful (2Ti 2:13), would honor the man after his own heart in preserving his heir (cf. 1Sa 13:14; Ps 89:19–29; Ac 13:22). Furthermore, God was to take a hand in turning the religious situation in Judah around—he would raise up a godly son to the throne of Judah.

6–8 Abijah inherited his father's continued friction with Jeroboam and the northern kingdom, only now it took the form of open warfare between the two Hebrew states. Fortunately for Judah, Abijah's underlying faith could rise to the surface in times of crisis. In a major battle between the two antagonists, Abijah and his few troops were delivered from certain defeat when the Lord intervened for them on behalf of Abijah's prayer (cf. 2Ch 13:3–22).

5. The reign of Asa in the southern kingdom (15:9–24)

9–15 When Asa assumed the kingly office in the twentieth year of Jeroboam's reign (910 B.C.), the influence of Maacah, his grandmother and the dowager queen, was still pronounced. Although Asa's long forty-one year reign was to be eventful, during his first ten years he enjoyed a time of peace (cf. 2Ch 14:1), perhaps the benefit of Abijah's victory over the north.

Asa used these ten years wisely, expunging idolatry and enforcing the observance of true religion, securing the defenses of the country and strengthening the armed forces (2Ch 14:2–8). In all this "he did what was right in the eyes of the LORD." His piety and wise preparations would put the country in good stead, for shortly after this period he faced and defeated an invasion led by Zerah the Ethiopian (2Ch 14:9–15), probably a commander of the Egyptian Pharaoh Osorkon I (914–874 B.C.).

In the third month of the fifteenth year of his reign, Asa, encouraged by the prophet Azariah (2Ch 15:1–7), convened an assembly in which all true Israelites were invited to renew the covenant with the Lord. The meeting was attended with great praise and joy (2Ch 15:9–15). At the same time Asa instituted stringent spiritual reforms, aimed at removing the remaining vestiges of idolatry and fertility rites (2Ch 15:8). Even the politically and religiously powerful Maacah was disposed of once and for all. No doubt she had used the outbreak of the war as an occasion to reintroduce the public worship of Asherah (cf. 2Ch 15:16). While Asa stopped short of a total cleansing of the land, he was a God-fearing man who led the way for his people in public dedication to God (cf. 2Ch 15:17–18).

16–17 Meanwhile in the northern kingdom Jeroboam had died and was succeeded by Nadab, his son (vv.25–32). Nadab reigned only two years before he was assassinated by Baasha, who instituted the short-lived second Israelite dynasty. Baasha's ascension year was the third year of Asa's reign. Throughout Asa's early years, Baasha had been occupied with securing the throne and other internal affairs. However, he had probably looked on disapprovingly at the turn of events in Judah. But with a victorious and strengthened Judah whose renewed vitality had succeeded even in drawing away many of his citizens, Baasha could no longer remain inactive. Moving swiftly into Judah, Baasha seized Ramah, only four miles north of Jerusalem itself. This action not only stopped the further drawing away of Baasha's subjects, but also cut off the main road north out of Jerusalem, thus shutting down all communications between Judah and Israel. This gave Baasha control of the trade routes.

18–19 Asa's reaction was singularly strange. Despite God's great deliverance from Zerah and Asa's own religious reforms, Asa turned suddenly to human devices to deal with the new crisis. Perhaps his own forces had suffered heavy losses in the past war. Perhaps the many years of success had encouraged him to rely on himself in political affairs while trusting God for spiritual matters. Asa did not even bother to pose the problem to God as Rehoboam had done (cf. 12:22–24). Stripping the temple and palace of treasures, Asa sent a delegation to the Aramean king Ben-Hadad, proposing that he break his treaty with the northern kingdom and put military pressure on it so that the Israelite incursion into Judah would be recalled.

A long-standing hostility had existed between the Arameans and the Hebrews. David had subdued the chief Aramean tribes, occupying the main area of Syria itself (cf. 2Sa 8:3–12; 1Ch 18:3–11); and although these regions largely remained subservient to Solomon, already in Solomon's day Rezon ben Eliada had managed to establish himself in Damascus, being "Israel's adversary as long as Solomon lived" (11:23–25).

Apparently a new dynasty had gained control in Damascus and, with the division of the united monarchy, had supported the northern kingdom. Ben-Hadad, who first appears here in history and was to play a major role in the affairs of the Near East in subsequent years, had a treaty alliance with Baasha. But seeing Asa's treasure and sensing the gain that was to be had from a new league with Judah and from a military venture against Israel, Ben-Hadad was only too happy to help. He may have followed Asa's suggestion of appealing to a prior treaty between Damascus and Jerusalem as a pretext for coming to Judah's aid against Baasha.

20–22 Moving swiftly, Ben-Hadad ravaged Baasha's northern sector, not only gaining for himself access to the international caravan routes that led from Egypt through Phoenicia and on to Damascus, but giving Asa the desired relief in Judah. For in order to meet the new emergency on his northern flank, Baasha was forced to abandon his operations at Ramah.

Asa, for his part, quickly mobilized Judah's forces and retook Ramah, dismantling Baasha's fortifications and using the building material to fortify Mizpah and Geba, thus providing strongholds for his reestablished control in Benjamin.

Needless to say, Asa's actions did not solve the relations with the north, but they did give him respite from further invasions throughout the rest of his reign. Although we hear of no more wars in Asa's day, it was a time of spiritual defeat. His self-assertedness took its toll. The Chronicler reports that when God sent his prophet Hanani to rebuke him for having forsaken God to trust in human beings in the war, Asa both threw that seer into prison and dealt harshly with any

who dissented with state policy. Thus began a long and checkered history of the persecution of God's prophets (2Ch 16:7–10; cf. 2Ki 17:13–14).

23–24 The parting notices concerning Asa deal with the loathsome disease in his feet that served only to harden his heart. For his funerary observance, Asa had the air filled with sweet spices (2Ch 16:12–14); but no amount of man-made perfume can hide the noxious stench of the life of a believer alienated from God! How far he had fallen and from what great spiritual heights! Asa's life remains as an exemplary admonition to believers to abide humbly in Christ, lest their lives become totally unproductive for God.

6. The reign of Nadab in the northern kingdom (15:25–31)

25–31 Jeroboam's son Nadab succeeded him, reigning in Tirzah. In his second year Nadab attempted to capture the important Philistine city of Gibbethon (cf. 16:15–17). However, in the midst of the siege he was assassinated by Baasha (probably one of his military officers), who seized the throne. Baasha immediately liquidated all the royal house, thus confirming Ahijah's prediction that God would judge the sins of the house of Jeroboam (cf. 14:9–16).

7. The second dynasty in Israel (15:32–16:14)

a. Baasha (15:32–16:7)

32–34 Political change did not signal a change in spiritual outlook. The founder of the second dynasty proved to be as wicked as Jeroboam and Nadab before him. Baasha compounded his murder of Nadab and the remainder of the first dynasty by walking in the spiritual prostitution that Jeroboam had introduced.

16:1–4 Accordingly, God sent Jehu the prophet to reprimand Baasha and announce his demise. Jehu told him that although God had exalted Baasha to be king (though not sanctioning Baasha's means of getting there), hoping for a change in the spiritual climate of Israel, Baasha had sought only his own ends and had perpetuated the persistent sins of his predecessors. Therefore he and his house would fall like that of Jeroboam, and beasts and birds of prey would feed on their fallen bodies.

5–7 Baasha had come from lowly origins. Except for his war with Asa (15:32), little is heard of him; and the scriptural account quickly passes on to Elah, his son. God's denunciation of Baasha adds further explanation to the subsequent condemnation of Asa for not leaving his war with Baasha in God's hands.

b. Elah (16:8–14)

8–14 As in the case of Jeroboam's son, so Baasha's son, Elah, reigned but two years and was also assassinated. Like Nadab, Elah was interested in Gibbethon and had sent his army commander, Omri, to put it under siege. He himself remained behind in Tirzah. During a drinking bout at the house of Arza, Elah's official, Zimri a military officer, killed him. Zimri thereupon assumed the kingship, subsequently murdered all Elah's descendants, and finished the second dynasty, as Jehu had prophesied. The Lord's judgment on the house of Baasha had come quickly.

B. The Era of the Third Dynasty (1Ki 16:15–2Ki 9:37)

1. Interregnum: Zimri and Tibni (16:15–22)

15–20 Zimri's fiery ambitions were to go up in flame. As soon as the encamped army at Gibbethon heard of the coup d'état, they proclaimed their commander, Omri, king and marched on Tirzah. Having retreated to the inner recesses of the palace citadel, Zimri set fire to it, burning himself to death. The author notes that Zimri's spiritual condition had been no different than those leaders who had preceded him.

21–22 In the wake of Zimri's unsuccessful rebellion, loyalties in Israel remained divided, half supporting Omri and half supporting a certain man named Tibni.

2. The reign of Omri in the northern kingdom (16:23–28)

23–24 After a four-year struggle Omri succeeded in gaining control of all the northern kingdom. He immediately undertook the building of a new capital that would lie in neutral ground (as David had done in selecting Jerusalem) and would be militarily defensible. He selected a strategic and centrally located hill site overlooking the chief commercial routes of the Esdraelon Plain. There he built his new capital city and named it Samaria, after Shemer, its former owner.

25–28 Despite Omri's forward-looking vision for restoring Israel's strength and his many accomplishments, spiritually he was more destitute than all his predecessors. Not only did he perpetuate the spiritual sins of Jeroboam, but his ties with Phoenicia were to unleash on Israel the common pagan social band religious practices known to the ancient world. Thus the scriptural record concerning Omri is both brief and condemnatory.

3. The reign of Ahab in the northern kingdom (16:29–22:40)

a. The accession of Ahab (16:29–34)

29–30 Ahab's twenty-two year reign marked the depths of spiritual decline in Israel. No more notorious husband and wife team is known in all the sacred Scriptures (cf. 21:25–26). Ahab built on his father's foundation, not only in bringing Israel into the arena of international conflict, but causing the people to serve and worship Baal.

31–33 Ahab was a man of complex character. The remainder of this chapter makes it clear that he was unconcerned with true, vital faith (cf. 21:20). Not only did he participate personally in the sins of Jeroboam, but having willingly married Jezebel, he followed her in the worship of Baal-Melqart, officially instituting and propagating Baal worship throughout his kingdom.

34 An example of his spiritual infidelity is seen as he granted to Hiel of Bethel the authority to rebuild Jericho as a fortified town, despite Joshua's long-standing curse. The undertaking was to cost Hiel the lives of his eldest and youngest sons, in accordance with Joshua's prophetic pronouncement (Jos 6:26).

The subsequent chapters of 1 Kings show that Ahab was selfish and sullen (20:43; 21:4–5), cruel (22:27), morally weak (21:1–16), and concerned with luxuries of this world (22:39). Though he could display real bravery (ch. 20; 22:1–39) and at times even heeded God's word (18:16–46; 20:13–17, 22, 28–30; 21:27–29; 22:30), nevertheless he was basically a compromiser as far as God's will was concerned (20:31–34, 42–43; 22:8, 18, 26–28).

The divine estimation of his character stands as a tragic epitaph: "There was never a man like Ahab, who sold himself to do evil in the eyes of the LORD" (21:25).

b. The prophetic ministry of Elijah (17:1–19:21)

(1) Elijah's call (17:1–6)

1 In those dark times God raised up a light, the prophet Elijah. Reared in rugged Gilead, Elijah was a rugged individualist, a man of stern character and countenance, zealous for the Lord. Elijah sought Ahab and delivered the Lord's pronouncement. In contrast to those who were not gods, whose idols Ahab ignorantly worshiped, the living Lord, who was truly Israel's God, would withhold both dew and rain for the next several years.

Already the drought had lasted some six months (cf. Lk 4:25; Jas 5:17 with 1Ki 18:1); now the reason for it all was to be revealed to Israel's apostate leadership. The message was clear: Israel had broken the pledge of its covenantal relationship with God (Dt 11:16–17; 28:23–24; cf. Lev 26:19; 1Ki 8:35). Therefore God was demonstrating his concern for both his people's infidelity and their folly in trusting in false fertility gods like Baal. No rain! There would not even be dew until God's authentic messenger would give the word! Unknown to Ahab, Elijah had agonized over the sin of his people and had prayed to the Lord for corrective measures to be levied on his people. Accordingly, Elijah was God's logical choice.

2–6 To impress the message and its deep spiritual implications further on Ahab and all Israel, God sent Elijah into seclusion. Not only would Ahab's frantic search for the prophet be thwarted, but Elijah's very absence would be living testimony of a divine displeasure (cf. Ps 74:1, 9). Moreover, Elijah himself had much to learn, and the time of solitude would furnish needed moments of divine instruction. Obeying God's directions implicitly, Elijah walked the fifteen miles from Jezreel eastward to the Jordan River. There in Kerith, one of the Jordan's many narrow gorges, Elijah took up his residence. Alone and relying solely on divine provision, Elijah was nourished by the available water of Kerith and by ravens sent from God.

(2) Elijah and the widow at Zarephath (17:7–24)

7–16 When the heavy rains of late autumn and early winter, which were needed to prepare the earth for cultivation, failed to materialize, God set the second stage of caring for his prophet into operation. He sent him to a certain widow of Zarephath in Phoenician Sidon, Jezebel's own homeland. On arriving there, Elijah was led to the widow whom God had mentioned. The prophet put a severe test before her. If she would first bake a small loaf for Elijah before seeing to her family's needs, God would honor her faith with a supply of flour and oil so long as the drought should last. Taking the prophet at his word, she obeyed; and all came to pass, even as he had promised.

The incident must have served not only as a source of great comfort for the simple, godly non-Jewish woman (cf. Dt 10:18–19), but also as a strengthening to Elijah's faith in God's providence (cf. Ps 37:3–4; Isa 41:10). This episode also stands impressed in the pages of history as a lasting memorial to the availability of God's full provision to all who believe, whether Jew or Gentile (Mt 10:41–42; Lk 4:25–26).

17–24 With the passing of time, the widow's little lad, who had been thus rescued from death through Elijah's miracle, fell fatally ill. Gently taking the lad from his mother's arms, the prophet carried him up to his own quarters. Elijah was puzzled as to the Lord's purpose in all this. Pleading with the Lord for the lad's life, he followed prayer with active faith, stretching himself out on the boy three times. Perhaps the widow had already experienced some hope in giving the body of the boy to the prophet. Elijah, too, was confident that God would yet do another miracle. Their expectation was rewarded. Life returned to the lad, and Elijah returned him to the widow's arms.

God's purpose was now evident. The widow's sin was not at issue, but the testing had come so that her newly found faith might be brought to settled maturity. The Lord was not only the God of the Jews but of all those who believe; he was not only the God of the living but the God of resurrection (cf. Lk 20:38; Jn 11:25–26) Furthermore, the Lord's word once again proved true in the mouth of the prophet.

(3) Elijah and Obadiah (18:1–15)

1–6 During the third year of Elijah's stay in Zarephath, God commanded Elijah to present himself before Ahab; he, not Baal, would send rain on the land. By now the effects of the drought were severe. A heavy famine lay on the land. Ahab then summoned Obadiah, the royal chamberlain, and revealed his plans for a sweeping survey of the land to see whether there would be any fodder available at all for the animals. Presumably Ahab would take one route and Obadiah another.

7 Obadiah was a believer. He had even risked his life to hide and sustain one hundred of the Lord's prophets from Jezebel's purge. As Obadiah proceeded on the king's commission, Elijah met him. Though he could scarcely believe his eyes, Obadiah recognized Elijah and bowed respectfully to God's great prophet.

8–15 Elijah gave Obadiah a higher commission: he was to inform Ahab that Elijah was back and wanted an audience with the king. Obadiah protested that such a mission might cost him his life. Since Ahab had scrupulously sought Elijah everywhere, and since God might conceivably send Elijah off at a moment's notice, should Obadiah report to Ahab that he had found Elijah? For if he should come and not find the prophet, Ahab's wrath might be vented on the faithful Obadiah. After Elijah had assured him that he would surely remain to meet Ahab, Obadiah sought the king.

(4) Elijah and the prophets of Baal (18:16–46)

16–19 Ahab, hoping to deal with Elijah from a position of strength, greeted him with the charge of being a troublemaker in Israel. Possibly the king was implying that the famine was all Elijah's fault; because of Elijah's hostile attitude, Baal had become angered and so had withheld rain for the past three years. Elijah's reply is particularly instructive. Not he, but Ahab and his family were the real troublers, because they had made Baal worship the state religion. Did Baal have the power to withhold and bring rain? Let the priests of Baal and Asherah (Baal's consort) be brought together at Mount Carmel, Baal's

stronghold. Let it be seen once and for all who truly is God!

20–21 When Ahab had assembled the priests of Baal on Mount Carmel to confront the Lord's prophet, Elijah addressed the many people who had gathered to see the contest. The choice Joshua had given the people (Jos 24:15) was now theirs to make: Serve God or serve another god (cf. Mt 6:24). But unlike the people at the time of Joshua, Elijah's audience held its peace.

22–24 To this hesitant multitude Elijah proposed a test in accordance with the scriptural precedent established by Aaron (Lev 9). The 450 prophets of Baal were to choose two bulls, one for their offering and the other for Elijah, who would oppose them by himself. After each contestant had prepared an altar, each would wait for his god to ignite the wood under the sacrifice. The multitude agreed to this.

25–29 Elijah deferred the first opportunity to Baal's prophets. Despite all their plaintive wailing and ecstatic dancing, when morning gave way to noon and still Baal had failed to provide the necessary fire, Elijah began to taunt his antagonists. Was Baal not a god? Perhaps he was lost in deep thought or preoccupied with his many cares or had gone to care for his many commercial interests. All these activities were characteristic of the duties attributed to the pagan gods. Perhaps, like many of the gods of the ancient Near East, he was asleep and needed to be awakened by cultic ritual.

The prophets of Baal became more frantic. In renewed frenzy they lacerated themselves with swords and spears, the blood flowing freely down their perspiration-soaked bodies. The ritual went on and on at an increasingly feverish pitch. As the time for the evening sacrifice came, there was still no response.

30–32 Turning from Baal's prophets, Elijah called the people to an altar of the Lord that was in ruins. Selecting twelve stones according to the number of the tribes of Israel (a fact that underscored the divine displeasure concerning Jeroboam's schism), Elijah rebuilt the altar and then dug a spacious trench around it.

33–35 When the wood had been arranged on the altar and the sacrifice cut and placed on the wood, Elijah amazed his audience by commanding that four large jars of water be filled and poured on the offering and wood. He had this done a second and a third time so that not only the altar but the sacrifice and the wood were thoroughly drenched, and water filled the surrounding trench.

36–38 At the precise moment when all hope of igniting the wood seemed totally lost, Elijah stepped forward and called on God. He pleaded with the covenant God of Israel to validate that he alone was still God in Israel and that this Elijah, who had prophesied the drought and was now calling for a miracle, was truly his servant. He asked God to answer him so that all would know that the Lord was ever anxious for their repentance and return to him. Striking with lightninglike power, God answered; and such an answer! Heavenly fire fell and consumed not only the wood and sacrifice but the stones, the soil, and even the surrounding water. What a contrast! The prophets of Baal had kept up their wailing and wild ritual for the better part of a day and met with dead silence. Elijah's petition had lasted less than a minute but produced spectacular results. The difference lay in the One addressed.

39–40 The people responded in true belief and worship. Falling to the ground, they confessed that truly the Lord alone was God! But Elijah wanted total commitment from those who were gathered there. He commanded that these prophets of Baal be seized and executed. Their wicked crimes against humankind and God demanded the death penalty. The people reacted instantaneously; they took Baal's prophets in charge to the Kishon Valley and executed them there. Elijah himself remained behind; the people would see to the execution.

41 Then Elijah sought a private audience with the king, for he had an important message to deliver. Ahab could break from the fast of the day and take nourishment, for God would soon send the long withheld rain.

42–46 While the king went away rejoicing to eat and drink, Elijah climbed farther up the mountain to pray and observe God's working. While Elijah buried his head between his knees in full and reverential concourse with God, he sent his servant to the mountain's peak to herald the approaching rain. The servant, however, quickly brought back the report: "No rain in sight." Again and again as Elijah persevered in heartfelt prayer, the servant was sent to the summit. On the seventh trip he returned with the good news. A small cloud, the size of a person's hand, could be seen on the distant horizon.

Elijah did not hesitate. He sent word to Ahab that he should leave now lest a torrential rain overtake him on the way. Nor did Ahab tarry. As he made haste for Jezreel and Jezebel, the sky grew black with heavy clouds, and strong winds began to blow. As he rode along, the downpour fell on him.

What a momentous day it had been for the king! How his head must have reeled with the thoughts of the contest: the pitiful screams of the helpless priests of Baal, the calm and yet awe-inspiring petition of Elijah, the terrifying and spectacular holocaust that followed, the repentance of the people, and the execution of the pagan prophets! As Ahab rode along through the gathering downpour, the Spirit-empowered prophet through whom God had effected his great triumph, ran ahead of the royal chariot like a specter.

(5) Elijah and Jezebel (19:1–9a)

1–3a On his arrival at Jezreel, Ahab recounted to Jezebel all that Elijah had done. The words are significant. Although Ahab had witnessed God's power in the famine and in the consuming of the sacrifice and the sending of the rain, before the imposing presence of Jezebel he attributed it all to Elijah, even blaming him for the death of the prophets of Baal. Her reaction was predictable. She sent a message to Elijah, giving him twenty-four hours to leave Jezreel or be killed. The threat was effective; Elijah ran for his life.

Probably Elijah had played into Jezebel's hands. Had she really wanted Elijah dead, she surely would have seized him without warning and would have killed him. What she desired was that Elijah and his God be discredited before the new converts who had aided Elijah by executing the prophets of Baal. Without a leader revolutionary movements usually stumble and fall away. Just when God needed him the most, the divinely trained prophet was to prove a notable failure.

It has often been asked how a man could experience such divine provision, perform such great miracles, single-handedly withstand 450 pagan prophets and the king himself, and yet cower before feminine threats. It must be remembered, of course, that Jezebel was anything but a "mere woman." She was of royal blood and every bit a queen. She could be ruthless in pursuing her goals. Her personality was so forceful that even Ahab feared her and was corrupted by her (16:31; 21:25). Both the northern kingdom (16:32–33) and the southern kingdom, through the marriage of her daughter Athaliah to the royal house of Judah (2Ki 8:16–19; 11:1–20; 2Ch 21:5–7; Ps 45), experienced moral degradation and spiritual degeneracy through her corrupting influence.

Yet Elijah was not without blame. God's subsequent tender dealings with his prophet were to bring his spiritual problem to light. His God-given successes had fostered an inordinate pride that had made him take his own importance too seriously. Moreover, Elijah had come to bask in the glow of the spectacular. He may have fully expected that because of what had been accomplished at Mount Carmel, Jezebel would capitulate and pagan worship would come to an end in Israel—all through his influence!

The great spectacle had failed to melt Jezebel's icy heart and, worse, she wanted to take his life. Thus, Elijah's pride was shattered, and he became a broken man. What Elijah needed to learn, God would soon show him. God does not always move in the realm of the extraordinary. To live always seeking one "high experience" after another is to have a misdirected zeal. The majority of life's service is in quiet, routine, humble obedience to God's will.

3b–9a When the fleeing prophet had reached Beersheba, some ninety miles to the south, he dismissed his servant. There was no need to jeopardize his life further. In his extreme dejection, Elijah wished only to be alone. Nor, for that matter, could he be safe in Beersheba, for Jezebel's influence could reach even this southernmost city. Accordingly, Elijah turned still farther southward, journeying out into the desert.

Taking refuge under the scant shade of a broom tree, Elijah prayed for death. He, the mighty prophet, had stood for God as boldly as any of those who had gone before him. Yet here he was, alone and seemingly deserted in this desert wasteland, the very symbol of a wasted life. Yet God would tenderly nourish and lead his prophet to a place where he would get some much needed instruction. After a forty-day trek, Elijah found that he had been drawn by divine providence to Mount Sinai, the sacred place of God's self-disclosure.

After arriving at Mount Sinai, Elijah located a cave and fell fast asleep. He may have been in a spot more sacred than he realized. The Hebrew text says, "He came there to *the* cave," possibly the very "cleft of the rock" where God had placed Moses as his glory passed by (Ex 33:21–23).

(6) Elijah and the Lord (19:9b–18)

9b–10 At length the word of the Lord aroused Elijah. The penetrating interrogation called for minute self-evaluation. Did Elijah yet understand his failure and God's gracious guidance in bringing him to this place? Elijah's reply indicated that he did not. Like Phinehas of old, he alone had been very zealous for the Lord in the midst of gross idolatry (cf. Nu 25:7–13). His soul was somewhat bitter at having served God so earnestly and spectacularly and yet having experienced rejection and solitary exile.

11–14 The Lord did not comment on Elijah's self-justification but offered instruction. He was to come out of the cave and stand before the Lord, for he would soon pass by. Suddenly a rock-shattering tempest smote the mountain around Elijah. Surely this would announce the divine Presence. But the Lord was not in the wind. There followed a fearful earthquake, but still God was not there. A sudden fire followed; yet God had not come. All these physical phenomena were known to be frequent precursors of God's coming (Ex 19:16, 18; Jdg 5:4–5; 2Sa 22:8–16; Pss 18:7–15; 68:8; Heb 12:18). There followed a faint whisper, a voice quiet, hushed, and low. Elijah knew it instantly. It was God! What a lesson for Elijah! Even God did not always operate in the realm of the spectacular!

Pulling his prophet's cloak over his face, Elijah made his way reverently out of the cave. Again came the divine question: "What are you doing here, Elijah?" Elijah's reply was the same (cf. v.10). How slow he was to learn! Yet much of what he said was true. Though he had failed, at the last he had been faithful; and truly persecution was rampant in Israel. It was understandable why he would feel quite alone.

15–18 God again dealt graciously with his prophet. He was to go back to the northern kingdom, the place where he had veered off the track with God in his spiritual life. Elijah still had work to accomplish for God. That task was threefold: (1) in the realm of international politics, he was to anoint Hazael to succeed Ben-Hadad, Israel's perennial adversary in Damascus; (2) in national affairs, Jehu was to be anointed as the next king; and (3) in the spiritual realm, Elisha was to be commissioned as his own successor.

The threefold commission was singularly interrelated. Jehu's work would supplement that of Hazael, that is, any who fell to Israel to escape Hazael's purge would be dealt with by Jehu. In turn those who survived Jehu's slaughter must face the spiritual judgment of Elisha. To encourage his restored prophet further, God set the record straight: there were still seven thousand true believers in Israel.

(7) Elijah and the call of Elisha (19:19–21)

19–20 Since the key figure in Elijah's three-fold commission was Elisha, Elijah sought him out first. He found Elisha busily engaged in plowing. Coming on him suddenly, Elijah threw his mantle over Elisha, a symbol of Elisha's call to the prophetic office. Elijah himself continued on without a word. When Elisha was able to collect his wits, he ran after Elijah, asking only that he be allowed to take leave of his family. Elijah's reply indicates that he himself had not called Elisha; it was God's call. Whether Elisha would follow that call was his own decision.

21 Elisha meant business for God. Taking his leave of Elijah, Elisha returned home to enjoy a farewell meal with his family and friends. The meat was cooked over Elisha's

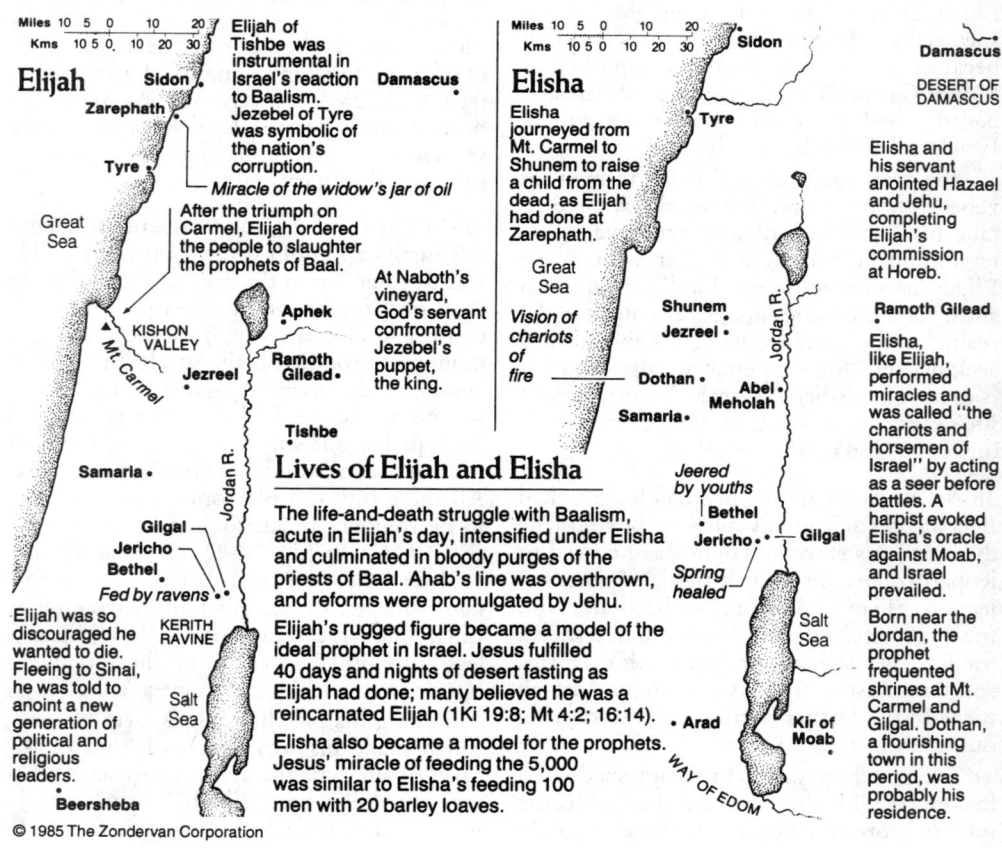

Elijah

Elijah of Tishbe was instrumental in Israel's reaction to Baalism. Jezebel of Tyre was symbolic of the nation's corruption.

— Miracle of the widow's jar of oil

After the triumph on Carmel, Elijah ordered the people to slaughter the prophets of Baal.

At Naboth's vineyard, God's servant confronted Jezebel's puppet, the king.

Elijah was so discouraged he wanted to die. Fleeing to Sinai, he was told to anoint a new generation of political and religious leaders.

Elisha

Elisha journeyed from Mt. Carmel to Shunem to raise a child from the dead, as Elijah had done at Zarephath.

Vision of chariots of fire

Jeered by youths

Spring healed

Elisha and his servant anointed Hazael and Jehu, completing Elijah's commission at Horeb.

Elisha, like Elijah, performed miracles and was called "the chariots and horsemen of Israel" by acting as a seer before battles. A harpist evoked Elisha's oracle against Moab, and Israel prevailed.

Born near the Jordan, the prophet frequented shrines at Mt. Carmel and Gilgal. Dothan, a flourishing town in this period, was probably his residence.

Lives of Elijah and Elisha

The life-and-death struggle with Baalism, acute in Elijah's day, intensified under Elisha and culminated in bloody purges of the priests of Baal. Ahab's line was overthrown, and reforms were promulgated by Jehu.

Elijah's rugged figure became a model of the ideal prophet in Israel. Jesus fulfilled 40 days and nights of desert fasting as Elijah had done; many believed he was a reincarnated Elijah (1Ki 19:8; Mt 4:2; 16:14).

Elisha also became a model for the prophets. Jesus' miracle of feeding the 5,000 was similar to Elisha's feeding 100 men with 20 barley loaves.

own plowing equipment. Thus he had burned his past behind him. Henceforth he would serve God. However, this first meant learning more of him through Elijah.

c. Ahab and the campaign for Samaria (20:1–43)

1–6 Ben-Hadad, the king of Israel's perennial enemy around Damascus, saw his opportunity to eliminate a famine-weakened Israel. Gathering a coalition of some thirty-two kings, he swept southward, quickly putting Samaria itself under siege. To humiliate Ahab further, he sent messengers demanding silver and gold and the choicest of his wives and children. When Ahab agreed to his terms readily, Ben-Hadad demanded the additional right to unlimited search of the palace and the houses of Ahab's officials so as to carry away anything of value.

7–12 Ahab was alarmed at this demand and convened his council of elders. Advised by the elders not to capitulate, Ahab sent back a refusal to Ben-Hadad. The Aramean king sent a third note to Ahab, threatening to destroy Samaria so thoroughly that there would not be enough left of it to make a handful of dust for each of his men. Ahab's proverbial reply is a classic illustration of Near Eastern colloquial wisdom: "One who puts on his armor should not boast like one who takes it off" (cf. v.11). Ben-Hadad "got the message." Infuriated, he gave orders to prepare for the attack.

13–14 While Ben-Hadad and his men reinforced their courage with strong drink, Ahab received a divine messenger. An unknown prophet of God advised the king that if he would call on the select officers of his provincial commanders to lead the attack, God would give him the victory.

15–21 Setting out at noon with the young officers in the lead, the Syrian (Aramean) forces were, in accordance with the prophecy, easily routed. The Arameans suffered heavy losses of men and material, Ben-Hadad himself barely escaping with his life. Surely such a divine deliverance against impossible odds should have convinced Ahab of God's continuing concern for him and the people of Israel. But this was not the case.

22–25 After Ahab's victory, the prophet returned to warn the king to strengthen his defenses, for Ben-Hadad would surely return next year. The warning was well-taken, for even then Ben-Hadad's counselors were advising him that since Israel's gods were mountain gods, Israel could be defeated in the plains. Ben-Hadad only needed to replace the defeated officers with new commanders, raise another army, and choose a battle site in the plains.

26–31 Following their respective counselors' advice, both kings faced each other in battle in the valley before Aphek. Although the Israelite forces were vastly outnumbered, God promised Ahab through his prophet that because the Arameans considered his power to be limited to the mountains, he would see to their defeat.

In the ensuing fray, Ben-Hadad's army suffered almost total annihilation. Even most of those who escaped the battlefield died under the collapsing walls of Aphek. Within the citadel of Aphek, where Ben-Hadad and his counselors had taken refuge, the Aramean king was advised of a new plan. Since the Israelite kings were reputed to be tender-hearted, if the royal party put on garments of repentance and approached Ahab, perhaps he would be merciful.

32–34 Accordingly, Ben-Hadad's counselors went to Ahab with pleas of mercy. They were not disappointed, for Ahab commanded that Ben-Hadad be summoned for conciliation. When Ben-Hadad offered to return the Israelite territory that his father had previously taken (cf. 15:20) and establish new trade concessions, Ahab effected a treaty with Ben-Hadad and released him. In so doing Ahab was trusting in his own appraisal of his needs and the world situation rather than in God, who had given him the miraculous victory. One reason for Ahab's leniency toward Ben-Hadad may lie in his appraisal of the troublesome political situation of those days. Aleady Assyria was on the move against the Aramean tribes. By joining in forces with Ben-Hadad, Ahab hoped to have a sufficiently large force of chariots and infantry to stand up to the Assyrians.

35–40a Ahab's leniency toward Ben-Hadad and self-trust were not to go without divine rebuke. God again raised up a prophet to deal with Ahab. This prophet, by divine command, asked one of his companions to smite him. Because the second prophet refused to obey the divine direction, he was immediately killed by a lion. The first prophet then got another man to strike him. Thus wounded he waited in a disguise for Ahab. When the king passed by, the prophet represented himself as a soldier who had been wounded in battle and had been assigned to watch a prisoner, on penalty of his life or the payment of a large sum of money. Unfortunately, he had inadvertently allowed his prisoner to escape.

40b–43 Merciless Ahab confirmed the sentence. At that point the prophet revealed himself to the king. The prophet's action had been symbolic. Ahab was that one who had allowed the prisoner to escape; therefore, as he himself had judged to be right, the king would pay with his life and Israel would suffer loss. It was a sullen and angry Ahab who returned in triumph from the battle to his palace in Samaria.

d. Ahab and the conscription of Naboth's vineyard (21:1–29)

1–5 Ahab's covetous eye became enamored with a choice vineyard that lay next to his palatial retreat in Jezreel. He desired to turn this vineyard into a vegetable garden; so he offered to buy it from its owner, Naboth, or give him another in exchange for it. When Naboth declined to part with his paternal inheritance because of his allegiance to God's law (cf, Lev 25:23–28; Nu 36:7–12), Ahab returned indignantly to the palace. There Jezebel found him, sulking in bed with his face turned to the wall and refusing to eat.

6–8 Jezebel's inquiry revealed Naboth's refusal to grant Ahab's wishes. Having assured him that she knew how to handle such situations, even if the king did not, Jezebel had letters sent in Ahab's name to the elders of Naboth's village, in a conspiracy against him.

9–10 On a given day the elders and nobles, who comprised a sort of local senate (cf. Dt 16:18), were to call an assembly for solemn fasting, as though the city had committed some great sin (cf. 1Sa 7:6) whose penalty needed averting (cf. Lev 4:13–21; Dt 21:1–9; 2Ch 20:2–4; Joel 1:14–15). Naboth was to be given a conspicuous place so that the two ac-

cusers could easily single him out. It may be that Naboth was an influential person anyway; so his prominent position at the meeting would not arouse suspicion.

The charge against Naboth was twofold: he had blasphemed both God and the king. The penalty for such action was death by stoning (Dt 13:10–11; 17:5), outside the city (Lev 24:14; Dt 22:24). Proper procedure called for the witnesses to lay their hands on the accused and cast the first stones. Since death by stoning was the responsibility of the whole community, the rest of the people were to take up the stoning.

11–16 The queen's directive was duly carried out. Naboth's sons were also put to death at this time (cf. 2Ki 9:26), so that no living heir could lay claim to that land. When word was taken to Jezebel that Naboth was dead, Ahab immediately took possession of the property. Tragically, the Scriptures do not indicate that Ahab was concerned enough to ask how Naboth had died or how the property was suddenly available for royal claim.

17–20a Once more Elijah was summoned by God to confront Ahab. Ahab no longer called Elijah "the troubler of Israel" but "my enemy." Doubtless his guilt weighed so heavily on his own conscience that he knew Elijah was there to condemn him.

20b–24 Elijah gave God's message plainly: because Ahab had sold himself to do only evil, God's sure judgment would come on him. In the very place where the dogs had licked up Naboth's blood, they would do likewise to Ahab. Yes, Ahab and his house would be cut off like those of the first two dynasties, his spiritual predecessors in idolatry. The divine sentence envisioned a terrible slaughter and carnage. Nor would Jezebel escape; the dogs would eat her flesh by the wall of Jezreel.

25–26 The divine estimation of Ahab is clearly rendered: Ahab was the vilest of all the Israelite kings. Completely under the domination of his wicked, pagan wife, he was unmatched in evil and spiritual prostitution in Israel.

27–29 Ahab reacted strongly to the Lord's rebuke by clothing himself in sackcloth and fasting. Therefore God again sent Elijah word concerning the king: because he had humbled himself, the threatened punishment would be delayed until the lifetime of his son. However, no stay of execution would be granted for the villainous Jezebel.

The king's remorse was sincere; paradoxically Ahab could be influenced for good by the divine message. Therefore the Lord in his longsuffering bore with the king yet further. There is little indication, however, that Ahab's basic character was altered so as to produce that godly repentance and genuine faith that lead to a real conversion experience. To the contrary, there is no indication that he changed his idolatrous ways, much less restored the ill-gotten vineyard. How gracious is an ever-loving God who deals in boundless mercy even with a thankless and thoughtless generation!

e. Ahab and the campaign for Ramoth Gilead (22:1–40)

1 Some three years after the last Syrian (Aramean) war (ch. 20), probably late in the same year that the combined Aramean and Hebrew forces had withstood Shalmaneser III at Qarqar (853 B.C.), Ahab became concerned for the recovery of Ramoth Gilead to the east of the Jordan. Although the territory had been ceded over to Israel by Ben-Hadad in his submission to Ahab, the affair with Assyria had probably kept the Israelites from reoccupying the territory. With the threat of hostilities somewhat relaxed, however, and with Ben-Hadad once again flexing his military muscles, the strategic importance of Ramoth Gilead became all too apparent.

2–5 When Jehoshaphat king of Judah arrived in the north to visit his brother-in-law Ahab, possibly to evaluate the international situation now that Qarqar was past, he found a concerned Ahab. Having shared his worries concerning Ramoth Gilead with his official staff, Ahab asked Jehoshaphat whether he would join him in a campaign to reoccupy the area. Jehoshaphat instantly put himself and his forces and supplies at Ahab's disposal, but quickly added that he would like to have the Lord's mind as to the venture.

6–14 Accordingly Ahab called in his prophets. He had gathered another four hundred prophets, probably belonging to the state religion established by Jeroboam. These all prophesied victory for Ahab in the projected campaign. One of them, a certain Zedekiah son of Kenaanah, had even cast a pair of iron horns to symbolize that the allied Israelite forces would surely gore the Arameans to death at Ramoth Gilead. Jehoshaphat, however, failed to be assured by these pseudo-prophets of an unlawful cult and asked whether a prophet of the Lord were available for consultation. Ahab could produce only one—a certain Micaiah son of Imlah, whom he hated because he seemed always to prophesy evil against the king. Nevertheless, at Jehoshaphat's insistence Micaiah was summoned. As he was brought to the waiting kings, he was informed that the "other prophets" had all given a favorable prognostication and so was warned to be agreeable. Micaiah, being a true prophet of the Lord, replied that he could speak only what the Lord told him to say.

15–23 At first Micaiah told Ahab to "attack and be victorious." Ahab sensed the sarcasm and demanded the truth. Micaiah answered with two parabolic visions. In the first Israel was likened to shepherdless sheep scattered on the mountains, which must find their own way home. In the second Micaiah described a heavenly scene in which the Lord and his hosts discussed the best way to get Ahab to Ramoth Gilead so that he might fall in battle. It was decided that false prophets, possessed by a lying spirit, would feed Ahab's ego by assuring him of victory in the projected battle.

24–25 Micaiah's message was clear: Ahab's prophets were wrong; Ahab would go up to defeat and death. At this point Zedekiah son of Kenaanah decided on a face-saving measure: he slapped Micaiah on the face, inquiring as to how the Spirit of the Lord had gone from himself to go to Micaiah. Micaiah had a prophecy for Zedekiah, also. Zedekiah would understand Micaiah's prophecy fully in that day when he would hide himself from the enemy in an inner room.

26–28 Ahab demanded that Micaiah be put in prison on minimum rations until the king should return. Micaiah had one last word for the king and all the assembled people: If Ahab returned at all, then the Lord had not spoken through Micaiah!

29–33 Despite Micaiah's warning, Jehoshaphat accompanied Ahab to the battle. Although he disdained Micaiah's prophecy,

Ahab obviously did not take it lightly; for though Jehoshaphat went into battle in full royal regalia, Ahab disguised himself. Jehoshaphat's compliance with Ahab's plan nearly cost him his life, for Ben-Hadad had given strict order to his commanders to search out the king of Israel. Thus he repaid Ahab's leniency (cf. 20:34, 42) with severity. Mistaking Jehoshaphat for Ahab, Ben-Hadad's men were on the verge of killing the Judean king when his cry convinced them that they were pursuing the wrong man.

34–36 Ahab was not to escape the prophecy, however. A "random" arrow found its mark, inflicting a mortal wound so that Ahab was wheeled out of the battle. Although he had many shortcomings, cowardice in battle was not one of them. So that the soldiers would not become discouraged by his death, Ahab had his dying body propped up in his chariot. As the sun set on the day's battle, Ahab's life blood gave out. When it was known that the king was dead, as Ahab had feared and as Micaiah had predicted, the army scattered.

37–40 The dead king's body was returned to Samaria and buried. While his blood-stained chariot was being washed at a pool frequented by prostitutes, true to the various prophecies (20:42; 21:19; 22:17, 20), dogs licked up his blood. Thus did the notorious Ahab leave his famed ivory palace behind him; he was succeeded by Ahaziah, his son.

4. The reign of Jehoshaphat in the southern kingdom (22:41–50)

41–42 Jehoshaphat, who had ruled three years as coregent with his father, Asa, came into independent rule in the fourth year of Ahab of Israel (874–853 B.C.) or 870 B.C. His total reign was some twenty-five years (873–848 B.C.). The record of Jehoshaphat's reign is greatly abbreviated by the author of Kings, containing only a short sketch of his lengthy reign, a brief evaluation of his spiritual condition and activities, and a few notices of international events before recording his death. A fuller discussion of the events of Jehoshaphat's reign can be found in 2Ch 17:1–21:1.

43–46 Jehoshaphat's spiritual condition was basically sound and largely commended by God (cf. 2Ch 17:3–4; 19:4–7; 20:3–13, 32). His concern for spiritual things (2Ch 17:7–9) manifested itself in religious and social reforms (cf. 2Ch 17:6; 19:3–11). Accordingly God blessed his reign (2Ch 17:1–6, 12–18:1) and gave him respite and respect with all the lands round about (2Ch 17:10–11; 20:28–30). He did, however, stop short of a full purging of idolatry (2Ch 20:33); and the marriage of his son Jehoram to Athaliah, Ahab's daughter, was to bring about a tragic condition in Judah (2Ki 8:18–19; 11:1–3; 2Ch 21:6–7, 11).

Three other tragic areas are singled out in the divine record: (1) Jehoshaphat went with Ahab to the battle of Ramoth Gilead, despite Micaiah's warning (cf. 2Ch 18:28–19:3); (2) he subsequently entered into an ill-fated commercial venture with Ahaziah (2Ch 20:35–37); and (3) still later he went with Jehoram on his Transjordanian expedition (2Ki 3:6–27).

47–49 The historical notice is probably intended to explain how it was that Jehoshaphat could have renewed commercial activities in Ezion Geber. The Edomite weakness may be attributable to Jehoshaphat's victory over the Transjordanian coalition, as detailed in 2Ch 20. Jehoshaphat's commercial alliance with Ahaziah was denounced by the Lord through his prophet Eliezer (2Ch 20:36–37). Because Ahaziah was an apostate, God had sent a storm to destroy the fleet before it could set sail. Evidently Jehoshaphat was wise enough to refuse a second trading proposal put forward by Ahaziah.

50 The notice of Jehoshaphat's passing is amplified by the fact that his further life and history were recorded in the historical records of Jehu son of Hanani (cf. 2Ch 20:34).

5. The reign of Ahaziah in the northern kingdom (1Ki 22:51–2Ki 1:18)

51–53 The chapter closes with a notice of the accession of Ahab's son, Ahaziah, and a note that he "provoked the LORD, the God of Israel, to anger, just as his father had done."

The Old Testament in the New

OT Text	NT Text	Subject
1Ki 19:10, 14, 18	Ro 11:3–4	A saved remnant

2 Kings 1:1–4 Ahab's son Ahaziah (853–852 B.C.) perpetuated his father's wickedness, incurring God's judicial anger (1Ki 22:51–53). The divine judgment took numerous forms: (1) politically, Moab found in the death of Ahab occasion to rebel against Israel; (2) economically, God thwarted Ahaziah's attempted commercial enterprise with Jehoshaphat (1Ki 22:47–48; 2Ch 20:36–37); (3) personally, the circumstances of Ahaziah's life were allowed to proceed in such a way that Israel's new king suffered a serious fall through the latticework of the upper chamber to the courtyard below.

Ahaziah was aware of the seriousness of his physical condition. In such circumstances a person's basic spiritual temperament will often surface. Immersed in the Baalism of his father, Ahaziah naturally sent messengers to inquire of the oracle at Ekron whether he would recover from his injuries. Scarcely had they begun their mission when suddenly an austere-appearing man, dressed in a rough animal-hide garment girded at the waist with a leather belt, interrupted them. Before they could gather their composure, this man sternly announced the answer to their message, together with a denunciation of the whole mission. The king had erred in seeking information from the false god of the Philistines; and he was wrong in hoping that he might recover, for surely he would die in his wickedness.

5–8 The fearful appearance and awful message caused the messengers to return instantly to the king, where they reported to Ahaziah the whole episode. The king recognized at once that the stern rebuke was from none other than Elijah the Tishbite. In at least this he was correct, for God had caused Elijah to meet the king's messengers and deliver the divine sentence. The secret mission and the hidden desires of the royal chambers were not unknown to the true King of the universe. What an awesome realization that must have been for Ahaziah! Yet there is no hint in the scriptural record that Ahaziah repented. Rather, all that follows speaks of an obdurately stubborn and sinful heart.

9–10 It seems that Ahaziah knew well the whereabouts of Elijah and immediately sent off a contingent of soldiers to bring him (by force if necessary) to the king. Ahaziah apparently picked a commander and squad that shared his insolent ungodliness; for on arriving where Elijah was located, they demanded the prophet's surrender. Elijah seized on the aptness of the prophetic title "man of God"; he was indeed God's man! Since that was so, such ungodliness—even in the line of duty— would be judged. Instantly, at Elijah's bidding, heavenly fire consumed the commander and all his men.

11–14 When the captain and his fifty men did not return, Ahaziah sent a still more arrogant commander together with his fifty-man squad, who met the same judgment. Doubtless word of the fate of those soldiers had by now become known to the king, so that he selected a third commander and his fifty; this selection was of a man of greater wisdom. As this commander and his men dutifully placed themselves before Elijah, they respectfully petitioned him both for their lives and for the prophet to kindly consent to accompany them back to Samaria and to the king.

15–18 In accordance with God's instructions, Elijah went with the commander to Ahaziah where he repeated clearly in the king's ear the divine sentence. Ahaziah's case was settled. Because of his stubborn disbelief and settled wickedness, the king would surely die. And so it happened, his brother Joram succeeding the childless Ahaziah in what was the second year of the reign of Jehoshaphat's son, also named Jehoram (852 B.C.), of the southern kingdom.

6. The eras of Jehoram of the northern kingdom and Jehoram and Ahaziah of the southern kingdom (2:1–9:37)

a. Prophetic transition: Elijah and Elisha (2:1–25)

1–2 The account of Elijah's last journey on earth begins with the aged prophet walking with his trusty aid, Elisha. The two departed from a certain Gilgal, probably not the well-known Gilgal of Joshua's day, but one located some eight miles north of Bethel in the hill country on the way to Shiloh. As they proceeded southward toward Bethel, Elijah indicated to Elisha that the Lord wanted him to go all the way to Bethel to visit his prophetic school there and so urged Elisha to stay on in Gilgal. The polite form of Elijah's command indicates that the prophet's words were permissive rather than prohibitive.

The reason for the command is not explicatively stated. Elijah no doubt knew that this was the day God would take him to be with himself (cf. vv.1, 10) and that he would leave his work to others—especially to Elisha (1Ki 19:16). Perhaps he sought an assurance of the Lord's will with regard to that succession by putting Elisha to the test. More likely the test was primarily for the strengthening of Elisha's faith. It would appear from the narrative that Elijah had disclosed to his various students that his ministry was nearing a close and that one day soon he would pass by for the last time.

Elisha either knew from separate divine communication or strongly suspected that this day might be Elijah's last. Strongly desirous of God's will for his life and concerned that he would indeed succeed Elijah as the Lord's prophet to Israel, Elisha was determined to be with his tutor until the end. Accordingly he would not be dissuaded; he would go where Elijah went.

Even though Elijah knew this was to be his last day on earth, his life was so ordered that he was humbly going about his normal duties when the Lord decided to take him. Moreover, his last concern was that the Lord's work would continue after his passing; so he wanted to assure himself of the progress of his "seminary students."

3 When Elijah and Elisha reached Bethel, the company of prophetic students perhaps wondered whether this would be the expected day. Not wishing to impose themselves on Elijah, they delicately drew Elisha aside to inquire of him whether this was that day. Elisha was convinced of it and indicated as much to them but commanded them strongly not to speak of it. Elijah would have no self-gratifying show of form toward himself. Whatever glory would occur on that day would be to God, not to his prophet. Nor would there be tears of sorrow, for it would be a day of joyous triumph for the Lord. Elijah's wish was for God's work to go on uninterrupted, with or without his presence.

4 As Elijah prepared to leave for the school at Jericho, about fourteen miles to the southeast, he again gave permission to Elisha to remain behind. Once more Elisha steadfastly refused.

5–7 The scene at Bethel was replayed at Jericho. Again the members of the prophetical school asked Elisha about Elijah's departure; again Elisha demanded their silence; again Elijah instructed Elisha to stay behind, this time as he headed for the Jordan River, some five miles away. Once more Elisha averred that he would not leave Elijah's side. Three times Elijah had tested his successor; thrice Elisha stood the test (cf. Mt 4:1–11; Lk 22:31–62; Jn 21:15–27). When the two prophets left for the Jordan, fifty of the prophetical students followed at a distance, anxiously awaiting the Lord's dealing with Elijah. What a contrast these fifty spiritually concerned young men formed with the squads of fifty that Ahaziah had recently sent to Elijah (cf. ch. 1)!

8 The two great prophets, master and successor, stood at the banks of the Jordan. Taking his prophet's mantle and rolling it up rodlike (cf. Ex 14:16–28), Elijah smote the river. Immediately the waters on one side piled up in a heap, the waters on the other side running off toward the Dead Sea. As long ago, the Jordan again parted; and the two passed through on dry ground. Only here the order is reversed. Whereas Israel had crossed into Canaan to take possession of her God-appointed earthly heritage and Elisha, too, must return there to the place of his appointment, Elijah passed out of Canaan through the boundary waters of Jordan to his heavenly service, there to await his future renewed earthly appearance (cf. Mal 4:5; Mt 17:4; Mk 9:5; Lk 9:33). In this regard his ministry anticipated that of his Messiah who came incarnate to an earthly service (Jn 1:12) and subsequently as resurrected Savior ascended again into heaven, there to await his triumphant, glorious second advent (cf. Zec 14:3, 9; Mt 24:30; Ac 1:9–11; 1Ti 3:16; Rev 19:11–17).

9 Elijah, sensing the imminency of his departure, asked what further thing he could do for his successor. To the very end he remained concerned for others and for the continuance of God's work.

Elisha's reply suggests that he caught the intent of his master's question. He asked for a double portion of Elijah's spirit. Undoubtedly Elisha did not ask this simply for the privilege of being Elijah's successor in terms of the Deuteronomic legislation concerning the eldest son's inheritance (Dt 21:17), for such both he and Elijah knew him to be (cf. 1Ki 19:16–21). Nor was this simply to give some confirmatory sign for Elisha's appearance, for this is scarcely a "difficult thing." Rather, the enormity of the loss of Elijah, that Spirit-filled and empowered prophet, must have so gripped the humble Elisha that, claiming his position as firstborn, he asked for the firstborn's "double portion"—i.e., for especially granted spiritual power far beyond his own capabilities to meet the responsibilities of the awesome task that lay before him. He wished, virtually, that Elijah's mighty prowess might continue to live through him.

10 All this lay beyond Elijah's power to grant. Nonetheless it was not beyond the divine prerogative. Indeed, doubtless by divine direction, Elijah told Elisha that if God so chose to allow Elisha to see Elijah's translation, then (and only then) would the full force of Elisha's request be granted. The sign would indicate to Elisha that God, who alone could grant such a request, had done so.

11–12 And so it would be! Suddenly, as the two walked and talked together, a fiery chariot swooped between them and took Elijah along in its terrific wind up into heaven. It was over in an instant. Elisha could but cry out in amazed tribute to his departed master. The translated prophet had been a spiritual father to Israel and as such, spiritually, her foremost defense. Elisha would doubtless be pleased at the same testimony given to him at his death (13:14). Elijah was now gone. One era had ended; another had begun.

13–14 In joy mixed with sorrow, Elisha turned from viewing the heavenly spectacle that had assured him of his request to Elijah and saw yet a further sign—Elijah's fallen mantle lay at Elisha's feet. The younger prophet had once had that mantle symbolically laid on his shoulders (1Ki 19:19); now it would rest there permanently. All he need do was pick it up. As he did so, "he picked up" as well the load of service that Elijah had left for him to do. With that very same mantle, he retraced his steps and reached the Jordan. Repeating Elijah's actions, he cried out for divine intervention on his behalf. Once again the Jordan parted, bringing not only full confirmation of his prophetic office to Elisha, but divine accreditation for him before the

eyes of the fifty students who had witnessed the entire event.

15–18 The fifty instantly recognized the transferral of prophetic prominence to Elisha and accepted his leadership. The maker of Elijah's actual translation to heaven without seeing death was more difficult to comprehend, as was the mysterious doings of the Spirit of God with humankind (cf. 1Ki 18:12). To their repeated insistence that they be allowed to search the existing countryside to be sure that Elijah was truly no longer in the vicinity, Elisha at last gave in. When they were fully satisfied that Elijah was nowhere to be found, they returned to Elisha, doubtless with greater resolve to listen to their new leader.

19–22 The chapter closes with two miracles of Elisha. These immediately established the character of his ministry—his would be a helping ministry to those in need, but one that would brook no disrespect for God and his earthly representatives. In the case of Jericho, though the city had been rebuilt (with difficulty) in the days of Ahab (1Ki 16:34), it had remained unproductive. Apparently the water still lay under Joshua's curse (cf. Jos 6:26), so that both citizenry and land suffered greatly. Elisha's miracle fully removed the age-old judgment, thus allowing a new era to dawn on this area. Interestingly, Elisha wrought the cure through means supplied by the people of Jericho so that their faith might be strengthened through submission and active participation in God's cleansing work.

23–25 Elisha's sweet memories of Jericho received a souring touch at Bethel. The public insult against Elisha was a mocking caricature of Elijah's going up into heaven, aimed ultimately at the God whom he represented. Indeed, Elisha's whole prophetic ministry was in jeopardy; therefore the youths' taunt had to be dealt with decisively. The sudden arrival of the two bears who mauled forty-two youths to death would serve as both an awful sentence on unbelievers—and thus, too, on Jeroboam's cult city—and a published reminder that blasphemy against the true God and his program would be met with swift and certain consequences. With these two miracles Elisha's position as successor to Elijah as God's chief prophet to Israel was assured.

b. Jehoram and the Moabite campaign (3:1–27)

1–5 The notice of Jehoram's (Joram's) accession over Israel is accompanied by a spiritual evaluation. Although he had torn down the stele to Baal that Ahab and Jezebel had erected, his perpetuation of the state cult of the golden calves that Jeroboam had established was condemnable. Thus he led Israel in continued apostasy. Within a few years of the beginning of Jehoram's twelve-year reign (852–841 B.C.), Mesha, the Moabite king, refused to send the required tribute of wool and rebelled against Israel.

6–9 Quickly mobilizing his forces, Jehoram also enlisted Jehoshaphat of Judah to join with him in the expedition against the Moabites. Jehoshaphat remained a relative of Jehoram of Israel; for his son (and coregent), also named Jehoram, was married to the Jehoram of Israel's aunt, Athaliah. Jehoshaphat quickly agreed. Moreover, he probably felt that he had a score to settle with Moab for the previous Moabite-Judean war (2Ch 20:1–29). In that campaign Judah had regained mastery over previously held Ezion Geber and apparently had control over Edom itself; for when Jehoram asked his advice in planning the expedition, Jehoshaphat immediately proposed a route through Edom. Not only would this have the element of surprise to commend it, but it would gain the allied help of the Edomite forces. Moreover, it would ensure the invaders not only protection for the rear, but the advantage of avoiding a head-on assault across the Arnon River and into the Moabite strength that a northern invasion would necessitate. Nevertheless a week's trek through the eastern Edomite watershed nearly accomplished what the Moabites desired: the wasting of the total armed forces of the allies together with their water supply. The allies seemed at the point of extinction.

10–14 The king of Israel was terrified, seeing only certain doom. Jehoshaphat, whatever his shortcomings, was concerned with spiritual things, and, as on another occasion (1Ki 22:7), he asked for a true prophet of the Lord. One of Jehoram's attendants reported that the prophet Elisha was available. Recognizing that God's presence was with Elisha, Jehoshaphat led the other two kings to God's prophet. At their approach Elisha addressed Jehoram—whose war with the Moabites the campaign really was—with words of strong rebuke. Why had Jehoram come to God's prophet and not to those of Baal, whom Israel's royal house served? But for King Jehoshaphat's sake, Elisha promised the kings that he would seek God's mind in this situation.

The ascension of Elijah into heaven in a fiery chariot has captured the hearts of artists throughout the centuries. The picture above is a depiction of this event that is found in the Roman catacombs (second to third century). To the right is a painting of the same event on the ceiling of the Carmelite monastery on Mount Carmel.

15–19 Having called for a harpist, Elisha went to prayer. God's answer came: there would be ample water for the physical needs; moreover the Lord would give them victory over the Moabites. The revelation included directions for human response. The kings' men were to dig ditches; for though they would see no storm, yet the Lord would send water in abundance.

20–25 At the time of the morning sacrifice, the area was filled to overflowing with water that ran down out of the mountains of Edom. God had sent necessary, life-giving water. Flash flooding in otherwise dry wadis is common enough in arid portions of the world. Not only the timing of the heaven-sent waters, but the total effect of their arrival bespeak the miraculous fulfillment of Elisha's prophetic message.

These waters were to spell death for the Moabites. Viewing that same water, reddened by the soil and gleaming all the redder in the rising eastern sun, the enemy mistook it for blood and, surmising that the three former antagonists had had a falling out that had led to their near mutual extermination, they rushed to the Israelite camp intent on plunder. Too late they realized their mistake. The disorganized Moabite soldiers were met by the well-stationed allies who not only turned them back but, in turn, invaded Moab, effecting a great destruction. The Moabites fell back in disarray as far as Kir Hareseth, where they determined to make a final stand.

26–27 As the desperate struggle of the siege of Kir Hareseth continued, the frenzied Moabite king sacrificed his firstborn son and the heir to the throne so that the anger of his gods might be appeased and the city delivered. While Moab's god could never deliver the king and the city, the act had the desired effect. Sickened by the maddened spectacle of senseless human sacrifice, the allies lifted the siege and returned to their homes.

c. Elisha's miracles (4:1–6:7)

(1) The replenishing of the widow's oil (4:1–7)

1 Chapters 4–7 make up the heart of what is frequently known as the Elisha cycle (chs. 2–13), being a collection of Elisha's miraculous deeds and ministry. The first of these records the special case of a widow who, because her husband had been a prophet, came to Elisha for aid. The death of her husband had brought on desperate circumstances: an outstanding indebtedness she was unable to meet had occasioned her creditor's insistence that her two children be taken as slaves to work off the debt. However inhumane this might seem, the creditor was within his rights; for Mosaic Law allowed him to enslave the debtor and his children until the Year of Jubilee in order to work off a debt (Ex 21:2–4; Lev 25:39; Ne 5:5; Isa 50:1; Am 2:6; 8:6; cf. Mt 18:25).

2–4 Having learned from the woman that she had nothing that could provide sustenance for the family except a small flask of oil (for anointing the body), Elisha instructed her to borrow utensils from her neighbors and, having done so, to shut herself up in her house and fill them with the oil that would come from the flask. She could thus repay her creditor and use the overabundance for her family's needs.

5–7 The woman responded in faith and, miraculously, all came to pass as Elisha had promised. The fact that she herself was to act in faith would enlarge her faith; the fact that Elisha would not be there when the miracle took place would display the power of God alone and thus encourage her to still greater faith. Devout obedience can produce brimful spiritual blessings!

(2) The revivification of the Shunammite's son (4:8–37)

8–14 The course of Elisha's ministry often took him through Shunem, where certain kind friends lived. Accordingly, at the wife's suggestion, the husband prepared special quarters for Elisha wherein he might rest. On one such journey Elisha wondered how he might repay the Shunammite woman's many kindnesses to him. When she indicated that she lived comfortably among her own people and had no special needs, Gehazi, Elisha's attendant, pointed out that the couple was childless; and, since the husband was old, the woman's longing for a child seemed hopeless. Jewish tradition asserts that Gehazi's motives were engendered by lust. Certainly the suggestion may have been innocent enough; but as the story unfolds, it does appear that the woman surely did not trust Gehazi.

15–28 Under divine direction Elisha acted at Gehazi's suggestion and informed the Shunammite woman that in the next year she would give birth to a son. So it came to pass, at the appointed time the child was born and in time grew into a young lad. One day as he helped his father in the field, the lad was taken suddenly critically ill and died. After placing the lad's body on the bed in the chamber of the prophet who had first announced his life, the Shunammite lady immediately set out for Mount Carmel where Elisha was ministering. Her faith convinced her that somehow Elisha could be instrumental in again doing the seemingly impossible. He had previously announced life for her who had no hope of producing life; perhaps he could once more give life to her son. Bypassing Gehazi whom Elisha had sent to meet her, she made directly for Elisha; and grasping tightly his feet, she poured out the details of the tragedy.

29–30 Elisha quickly sent Gehazi ahead with instructions to lay the prophet's staff on the dead lad. Although the author of Kings assigns no reason for Elisha's instructions and actions, Elisha surely did not send Gehazi on a hopeless mission. Because he was young, Gehazi could cover the distance to Shunem quickly; and it was imperative that a representative of God arrive there as soon as possible. Very likely Gehazi's task was preparatory and symbolic of the impending arrival of Elisha himself.

But the woman, who apparently had never trusted Gehazi, would entrust neither herself nor the final disposition of her son to him but rather stayed with Elisha until he could reach Shunem. Her faith and concern for her son's cure were totally centered in God's approved prophet.

31–37 As Elisha and the mother approached the city, Gehazi reported that, though he had carried out Elisha's bidding, nothing at all had happened. Perhaps Gehazi had expected something extraordinary. But the merely routine fulfilling of one's duties will never effect successful spiritual results. Elisha went straight to the dead lad and, putting all others out and shutting the door, besought the Lord for the lad's life. His prayers were followed with prophetic symbolic actions, doubtless learned from his teacher Elijah's experience with the widow of Zarephath (cf. 1Ki 17:17–

22). Elisha stretched his body on the lad's so that his mouth, eyes, and hands correspondingly met those of the lad; and the boy's body grew warm again. After rising and walking about in continued prayer, he repeated the symbolic action. This time the lad sneezed seven times and opened his eyes. Having sent Gehazi for the mother, Elisha delivered the recovered lad to her. The woman gratefully thanked the prophet, joyfully took up her son, and went out.

As in the case of Elijah and the widow of Zarephath, both Elisha and the Shunammite woman had seen their faith successfully tested; and they were rewarded with the desires of their hearts and corresponding increase in their faith.

(3) The rectification of dinner problems (4:38–44)

38–41 This chapter closes with two incidents relative to Elisha's miraculous help in food matters in the prophetic school at Gilgal. In the first instance, a student who had been sent to gather wild vegetables brought an unknown type to them and cut the gatherings into the stew. Its bitter taste convinced the diners that the stew was poisoned; so immediately they cried out to Elisha. He called for flour to be brought; and when he had stirred it into the pot, the stew was found to be both tasteful and safe. Elisha's faith effected a miraculous cure. As had been the case with Elijah his teacher, Elisha had used flour to demonstrate the concern of God for one's daily provisions (cf. 1Ki 17:14–16).

42–43 The second case involves the multiplication of a score of small loaves of fresh barley bread and some ears of new grain. These had been brought to Elisha as firstfruits. Normally these portions were reserved for God (Lev 23:20) and the Levitical priests (Nu 18:13; Dt 18:4–5). Because the religion in the northern kingdom was apostate, the loaves had been brought by their owner to one whom he considered to be the true repository of godly religion in Israel. Elisha did not hesitate. He ordered them distributed to the young prophets, despite the protest of his servant (probably Gehazi) who realized that, humanly speaking, the gift was insufficient to feed everyone. Nevertheless Elisha ordered their distribution, telling his servant that there would surely be sufficient for all—in fact, some would be left over.

44 As Elisha had promised, so it came to pass. Elisha's faith in the miracle-working God had again been rewarded; and he, on whom the believer is to wait for daily bread, had supplied richly (cf. Mt 6:21).

(4) The restoration of Naaman (5:1–27)

1–7 The latter days of the reign of Israel's king Jehoram were marked by hostilities with the Aramean king Ben-Hadad II. Probably due to Israel's failure to participate in the continued Syro(Aramean)-Assyrian confrontation that marked most of the sixth decade of the ninth century B.C., the Arameans continually chastened the northern kingdom with systematic raids (cf. 2Ki 6:8), culminating in an all-out military excursion into Israel (cf. 2Ki 6:24–7:20).

During the course of one such raid, an Israelite maiden had fallen into the hands of Ben-Hadad's field marshal, Naaman. Although Naaman was a brilliant commanding officer, he suffered from a serious and incurable skin disease. On one occasion when Naaman was home from fighting and relations were stabilized somewhat between Damascus and Israel, the Israelite servant girl informed her Aramean master that there was a prophet in Israel who could effect Naaman's cure. When Naaman was advised of such a hope, he spoke to Ben-Hadad who, in turn, sent Naaman with rich gifts and a letter of introduction to Jehoram so that the Syrian (Aramean) general might be healed. Jehoram, believing the situation to be impossible, thought that Ben-Hadad was seeking an occasion for renewed warfare. Evidently no mention was made of Israel's prophet in the correspondence, so that Jehoram was unaware of the context of the request.

8–14 News of the whole affair reached Elisha, who sent word to Jehoram that God was still at work in Israel and could work through his authoritative prophet. Accordingly Naaman was sent to Elisha, who, rather than receiving him, sent his servant to meet Naaman. He must understand that Elisha served a greater king than did the Syrian (Aramean) general. However Elisha's message through Gehazi was one of great hope. If he would but wash himself seven times in the Jordan, he would be cleansed. Naaman, angered by his poor reception and thinking Elisha was a quack, strode away angrily. Yet God was at work in the proud, self-reliant Gentile's life; he used Naaman's own Aramean aide, who suggested that since Elisha's instructions were simple enough, they ought to be tested. What did he have to lose? Naaman followed the advice and was instantly cured.

15–19 Gratefully Naaman returned to Elisha and offered him rich gifts. Although Naaman urged them on him insistently, the prophet refused. Naaman had become convinced that Israel's Lord alone was God. Naaman asked Elisha whether two mule loads of Israelite soil might be taken with him back to Syria so that whenever circumstances forced him to bow ceremonially to the Aramean gods with his king, he might in reality be placing his knees in the soil of the true God of Israel. Thus he might be a true, though secret, believer. His request granted, Naaman set out for home.

20–21 The story next focuses on Gehazi, who saw an opportunity to gain some of the proffered commodities for himself. Slipping away stealthily, he overtook the Syrian (Aramean) general. What a contrast can be seen in the meeting between Naaman and Gehazi! Naaman's descent from his chariot to meet Elisha's servant was a mark of his being a changed man. No longer a proud, arrogant person, the grateful, reverent, and humble Aramean came down from his honored place to meet a prophet's servant. He who had been a fallen, hopeless sinner displayed the true believer's grace. Contrariwise Gehazi, who had enjoyed all the privileges of his master's grace, was about to abuse them and fall from that favor.

22–26 Having convinced Naaman that Elisha had experienced an unexpected need, he extracted from the grateful Syrian (Aramean) commander a handsome sum of gifts, which he subsequently concealed until he could have opportunity to retrieve them. He then attempted to steal back to Elisha's house unnoticed—only to be confronted by the prophet. His master knew all that had transpired! Gehazi's lies only worsened the situation.

27 Accordingly, Elisha announced Gehazi's punishment: Naaman's leprosy would become Gehazi's. Elisha's privileged aide was banished in disgrace, for he had misused his favored position in an attempt to acquire wealth for himself. Gehazi needed to learn that the ministry has no place for those who would make merchandise of it. The moral and spiritual flaws in his character that one senses in the previous record have surfaced. His basic spiritual insensitivity had betrayed him in the time of testing so that rather than his character being refined, his work was refused.

(5) The recovery of the axhead (6:1–7)

1–7 In contrast to Gehazi who had received the reward of his unfaithfulness, the account unfolded here is a demonstration of the reward of faithful labor. During the evil days of Jehoram's reign and Elisha's prophetic ministry, a certain meeting place for the sons of the prophet's instruction proved too small for their assembly. This school apparently was located in Jericho near the Jordan, a known center of prophetic instruction (cf. ch. 2). Accordingly Elisha acceded to the request to build larger quarters and even went with them to the work. In the course of their labor, one student lost the iron axhead of his borrowed ax and cried out to Elisha. In the power of God, Elisha then caused the submerged axhead to surface and instructed the pupil to retrieve the ax; thus he would personally participate in the miracle. Attempts to explain fully or to explain away the miracle are fruitless.

Naaman was told by Elisha's servant to wash in the River Jordan seven times. This is a waterfall that is found on the river.

d. Elisha's ministry (6:8–8:15)

(1) Prelude to war: the Aramean incursion (6:8–23)

8–12 The account now returns to the intermittent warfare between the Arameans and Israelites. Time after time the Israelite king and his forces were delivered from ambush because of Elisha's warning, for by divine revelation Elisha was party to the Aramean king's secret plans. Elisha's aid to Jehoram became common knowledge and was duly reported to the Aramean king, who had suspected a traitor within his own court.

13–20 Accordingly, having learned that Elisha had gone to Dothan, the Arameans surrounded the city by night to take Elisha by force. Doubtless Elisha knew about all this, too, but allowed himself to be trapped so that the subsequent entrapment of the Arameans might work to God's glory and for his good. When Elisha's servant awakened and saw the great Aramean force, he cried out in dismay to Elisha. Elisha, however, assured him that the forces of God outnumbered the forces of the enemy. In accordance with Elisha's prayer, the servant's eyes were enabled to behold the company of an innumerable angelic host that stood ready to intervene for Elisha. However, this incident would not be one of protracted battle but another case of miraculous deliverance. In accordance with Elisha's prayer, the enemy army became totally blind and was led away by Elisha to Samaria, about ten miles away. Once inside the city, the army discovered that instead of taking Elisha captive, they were prisoners of Jehoram!

21–23 At Elisha's directions, rather than killing their enemies, the Israelites treated them to a sumptuous feast and, having given them provisions for the journey home to Syria (Aram) , sent them away. Elisha's intercession and instructions proved ultimately to be the divine remedy for the momentary ills of Israel: the Arameans reported Israel's kindness, and their guerrilla raids ceased.

(2) The siege of Samaria (6:24–7:20)

24 At a later date war broke out again between Ben-Hadad II and Jehoram. Perhaps the miraculously arranged temporary lull had been divinely designed to teach Israel God's abiding love and concern for his people, to whom he had sent his duly authenticated prophet, Elisha. But with no evidence of repentance by Israel, God withdrew his protective hand; and Israel faced a full-scale Syrian (Aramean) invasion. The Arameans were eminently successful, penetrating to the very gates of Samaria itself and putting the city under a dire siege.

25–29 The lengthy siege evoked a severe famine that, in turn, produced highly inflated prices for the humblest commodities. So scarce had food become that one day, as the king was on a tour about the embattled city's wall, he stumbled on a case of cannibalism. By agreement two women had eaten the son of one of them; but when it came time for the second woman to surrender her son to the fire, she had hidden him, thus occasioning the first woman's complaint to the king.

30–33 Jehoram's reaction was one of anguished horror. He tore his robes, revealing his sackcloth garments of grief underneath. Enraged and blaming Elisha for the whole affair, he dispatched a messenger to seize and behead Elisha. When he had come to himself, however, he ran after his messenger, hoping to stay his hand. By divine insight Elisha knew the details of the whole episode and instructed certain elders who were with him to bar the door of the house until Jehoram could overtake his executioners. When the king arrived, he was admitted into the house. Convinced that the Lord had pronounced the doom of the city, Jehoram had all but given up any hope of the Lord's deliverance. Yet perhaps his realization that all that had transpired was from the Lord carried with it the faintest hope that God would yet miraculously intervene. The restraint of the messenger and the king's words hint at the faint hope of divine consolation. Such comfort Elisha would proceed to give.

7:1–2 Elisha seized on the king's last glimmer of hope. By the next day conditions would so improve that products would be available again, even though at a substantial price. Jehoram's chief aide found such a statement preposterous. Even if the Lord should open the windows of heaven and pour down a flood of flour and grain, so dire had the famine been that even this would not suffice to effect Elisha's prediction.

The aide's words are filled with ridicule and heaped with sarcasm, as if to say, "Oh sure, The Lord is even now making windows in heaven! So what? Could this word of yours still come to pass?" Whether the aide thought of the biblical phrase (Ge 7:11) or of the heavenly windows of the Baal fertility cult is uncertain. In any case he was skeptical of the whole thing.

The prophet assured Jehoram's aide that not only would the prophecy come true, but the officer would see it with his own eyes. However, he would not eat any of it! His faithless incredulity would cause him to miss God's blessing on the people.

3–5 God moves mysteriously. His means of effecting the fulfillment of Elisha's prophecy were perhaps no less amazing than the aide's taunts. Four leprous men who lived outside the city gate knew that their situation was desperate. Accordingly, they resolved to surrender to the Arameans. Death already stared them in the face; they had nothing to lose by going over to the Syrians (Arameans). Slipping away at twilight they traveled circuitously to the far end of the besieger's encampment. As they moved cautiously into the camp, to their surprise they met not one man—the camp was totally deserted.

6–7 The author of Kings explains that the Lord had miraculously caused the Arameans to hear what seemed to them the approach of a great army to liberate the besieged Israelites. Throwing caution to the wind, they had abandoned the camp with its supplies, running for fear of their lives. Precisely how the Lord produced the desired effect is not stated; but whatever the method, the Lord had once again miraculously intervened for his undeserving people.

8–14 The four rushed about eating and drinking their fill, gathering and hiding their booty. When the exhilaration of the moment had worn off, they realized that as Israelites it was their duty to tell the good news to others. Accordingly they hurried on the shortest way to the city and informed the gatekeepers that the Arameans had suddenly left. The good news reverberated throughout the city, reaching even the ears of the sleeping king. A cautious Jehoram was not so certain of the state of affairs. Perhaps the Arameans had withdrawn a bit to lure the Israelites into the camp so as to fall on them unawares and thus gain entrance into Samaria. Acting on the advice of his officers, he sent two chariot teams to scout out the whereabouts of the Arameans. While Jehoram could scarcely spare them, yet if they were overtaken by the enemy, their plight would be little worse than what seemed inevitable should they remain in Samaria.

15 The scouting party soon returned with the staggering news. It was all true. For some reason the Arameans had fled in panic, leaving the road strewn with equipment and clothing as far as the Jordan River.

16–20 The king commanded the people to go to the Aramean camp and plunder it. By day's end Elisha's amazing prophecy stood fulfilled, including the portion that dealt with Jehoram's aide. For in their mad rush for spoil, the people trampled him to death in the gateway he had been assigned to guard.

(3) Postscript to war: the restitution of the Shunammite's land and the coup d'état of Hazael (8:1–15)

1–6 Chapter 8 opens with a last glimpse of Elisha's former servant, Gehazi. Apparently King Jehoram of Israel had summoned Gehazi to learn from a reliable source something of the great prophet whose miraculous prediction had just come to pass. The wise deployment of divine providence is also in evidence; for the Shunammite woman (probably widowed by this time) had just returned after the seven-year famine that she had fled from at Elisha's warning, only to find her property had been appropriated by someone else.

A woman of strong resolve, she immediately determined to take her case directly to the king, to whom she was going when she happened on Jehoram talking with Gehazi. God had so arranged the details of life that Gehazi could identify the woman and so aid in the verification of her claim; and she, in turn, would be living proof of Gehazi's account to the king of Elisha's mighty deeds. The king acceded to her request.

7–8 The next incident from the Elisha cycle both closes the wars with Ben-Hadad II and initiates the critical circumstances that would culminate in the crucial events of 841 B.C. Ben–Hadad II, the Aramean king (860-842 B.C.), lay ill. News reached him that his old antagonist, Elisha, was at that very moment traveling in the area. Feeling that Elisha's arrival might be fortuitous, he sent Hazael, one of his trusted officials, with an appropriate royal escort to inquire of Elisha whether or not he would recover from his sickness. He could not know, of course, that Elisha had come to carry out the Lord's instructions to Elijah relative to dynastic change, both in Damascus and in Samaria (1Ki 19:15–17).

9–11a Hazael dutifully carried out his master's instructions. Elisha's reply to Hazael was an enigmatic one: the answer to the king's question was both yes and no. Yes: if left to normal circumstances of healing, the king would recover; and no: Elisha, who was at that moment anointing Hazael as king, knew that this treacherous man would use the king's illness to effect his coup d'état. Accordingly Hazael could testify truthfully to the king. The illness was not a fatal one of itself. Elisha's reply and icy stare indicate that Hazael had already plotted the king's demise through the situation and that Elisha knew his secret thoughts. Hazael blushed in shame.

11b–13 Elisha's stares soon turned to weeping. In answer to Hazael's question, Elisha indicated that he wept for the great barbarity that Hazael, as Aram's next king, would inflict on Israel. Despite Hazael's protests to the contrary, such would indeed be the case (cf. 10:32–33; 13:3).

14–15 Doubtless Elisha's assurances to Hazael that he would be the next king of Damascus gave pretext to him that he had a mandate to be carried out. When he returned to the palace, he told his master the good news: the king would surely recover. However, the next day opportunity came to carry out the long-standing purpose. Having smothered the king, he assumed the throne.

e. The reign of Jehoram of the southern kingdom (8:16–24)

16–18 The author of Kings now shifts his attention to the southern kingdom and to the two sons of Jehoshaphat. The synchronism of v.16 records the year of Jehoram's assumption of full power of state. Jehoram's ungodly character is noted along with the primary factor in the spiritual apostasy: his marriage to Ahab's daughter. The Chronicler (2Ch 21:11) adds that Jehoram made the entire nation of Judah to sin according to the religion of the Canaanites.

19–24 The perverse nature of Jehoram is further evidenced in that after his father's death he slew all his brothers and any possible claimant to the throne (2Ch 21:2–4). Despite Jehoram's spiritual and moral bankruptcy, God honored the covenant with the house of David (cf. 2Ch 21:7) and did not destroy the kingdom. Nevertheless Jehoram and Judah did experience judgment in the form of three military engagements (cf. 2Ch 21:10): (1) Edom revolted successfully, a rebellion that nearly cost Jehoram his life in attempting to suppress it (cf. 2Ch 21:8–10a); (2) simultaneously Libnah revolted (cf. 2Ch 21:10b); and (3) the Philistines and Arabians launched a massive attack that reached Jerusalem itself and cost the king all his sons except Ahaziah (cf. 2Ch 21:16–17 with 2Ch 22:1). Judah and its kings were smitten with the plague (2Ch 21:12–15), Jehoram himself succumbing eventually to an incurable disease in the bowels (2Ch 21:15, 18–19). Thus an unfortunate period of Judah's history, in the form of a wicked and apostate son of the house of David, passed, wicked Jehoram himself being excluded from the royal sepulcher (2Ch 21:20b).

f. The reign of Ahaziah of the southern kingdom (8:25–29)

25–26a Ahaziah succeeded his father, Jehoram, in the critical year 841 B.C. He was not to survive the momentous waves of political events that were to inundate the ancient Near East in that year. Indeed, in 841 B.C. Shalmaneser III of Assyria (859–824 B.C.) at last was able to break the coalition of western allies with whom he had previously fought a long series of battles (853, 848, 845). While all these complex details were part of God's teleological processes in the government of the nations and his dealing with Israel, doubtless the long-standing controversy and the growing specter of Assyrian power could be felt in the political intrigues that brought about the death of Ben-Hadad II of Damascus and the downfall of the Omride Dynasty in Israel. Before 841 had ended, Hazael would be master of Damascus (where Shalmaneser had set him up after having defeated him in battle), the pro-Assyrian Jehu would initiate the fourth dynasty in Israel (chs. 9–10), and

the wicked Athaliah would sit as usurper on the throne of Judah (ch. 11).

26b–29 Ahaziah, too, was under the pagan spell of wicked Athaliah (cf. 2Ch 22:3–5) and perpetuated the Baalism that his father had fostered. Likewise, at the first opportunity he joined Ahab's son Jehoram in renewed hostilities with the Arameans in Ramoth Gilead (1Ki 22:1–40). Once more the battle went badly for Israel and Judah, for in that battle King Jehoram was sorely wounded and returned to Jezreel for rest and recovery from his wounds (cf. 9:11–16). The chapter ends with a concerned Ahaziah going to visit Jehoram in Jezreel. He would not return to Jerusalem alive (cf. 9:16, 24–29).

g. The reign of Jehoram of the northern kingdom (9:1–37)

1 In those critical days when King Jehoram remained at the royal retreat in Jezreel recuperating from his wounds suffered in the battle against the Arameans at Ramoth Gilead (8:28–29; 9:14), Elisha summoned his trusty attendant, who was one of the "company of the prophets," in order to send him with a commission to anoint the next king of Israel. The scene of this anointing would be that same Ramoth Gilead where the Israelite troops remained stationed in prolonged confrontation with the Damascene Arameans.

2–3 Once there the young prophet was to single out Jehu, the ranking army commander, take him aside privately into a room, pour a flask of oil on his head, and pronounce that God had anointed him as the next king of Israel. Having accomplished his task, the prophet was immediately to hasten from the house so as to avoid any diminishing of the act itself. God's work is often best done and left to have its own impact.

4–10 The young prophet duly did as he was instructed. Arriving in Ramoth Gilead, he sought out Jehu; and, having brought him into the house, he anointed his head and delivered God's solemn words to him. Jehu's divine commission was twofold: (1) he was to annihilate all the wicked and apostate house of Ahab and (2) thereby avenge the blood of God's own who had been martyred for their faithfulness. In this, Jehu was to be God's instrument of divine vengeance against Jezebel's bloody persecutions. When he had finished these words, in obedience to his orders, he literally ran from the house.

11–13 After the young prophet had fled, Jehu went out to the court where his fellow officers were sitting. They, of course, wanted to know what had occasioned the arrival of "this madman" (GK 8713). The term betrays the low spiritual condition of the soldiers and carries with it their contempt for God's prophets. When Jehu replied rather nonchalantly that this sort of character was liable to say anything, the officers, suspecting something important had occurred, pressed him all the harder. Jehu then revealed the gist of what had happened: God had sent the prophet to anoint him as king! Perhaps recalling the similar past anointings of Saul and David and assuredly sporting for insurrection, the officers responded immediately, spreading their cloaks under Jehu as a sign of submission. Having blown the trumpet, they proclaimed to all the army that Jehu was the next king of Israel.

14–16 The enthusiastic response to the prophet's pronouncement by his men prompted Jehu to take an active lead in a formal coup d'état. Having doubtless left a security force to continue the defense of Ramoth Gilead and having given instructions that none be allowed to slip out of the city and go with a warning to Jehoram in Jezreel, Jehu took a select group of troops and set out for Jezreel and the recuperating Jehoram. In God's providence (cf. 2Ch 22:7), Ahaziah of Judah was at Jezreel visiting his ailing relative (cf. 8:29).

17–21 The scene switches to Jezreel. As Jehu rode swiftly toward the city, the watchman announced the approach of troops. Jehoram sent a messenger on horseback to intercept the column and inquire as to its mission. When the horseman reached Jehu and asked him whether all was well, Jehu bid him to fall in with his troops, which he did. When the watchman reported all this to Jehoram, a second horseman was sent out—with the same result. When the watchman next reported that the approach of the chariot looked like the wild driving of Jehu, Jehoram and Ahaziah rode their chariots out to meet him. Significantly, they met Jehu at the plot of ground that Ahab had purloined from Naboth.

22–24 A third time Jehu was asked whether he had come in peace. The royal query was greeted in a still rougher manner than the preceding two. Jehoram's espousal of the idolatry and witchcraft instituted by Jezebel had rendered any talk of "peace" impossible. Jehoram realized that Jehu's reply meant that a coup d'etat was taking place. Having warned Ahaziah of the treachery, Jehoram attempted to flee but was struck dead in his chariot by Jehu's well-aimed arrow.

25–29 In fulfillment of Elijah's prophetic threat (cf. 1Ki 21:19–24), which apparently Jehu and his chariot officers had heard, Jehu instructed his aide to throw Jehoram's fallen body onto Naboth's field. Ahaziah's attempt to escape Jehu was also abortive. Taken at face value, this account seems to say that Ahaziah was wounded on the ascent to Gur and died in Megiddo, from which his body was taken to Jerusalem for burial. In 2Ch 22:8–9, Ahaziah was overtaken in Samaria where he had sought refuge with relatives and was brought to Jehu and executed, his body being interred with honor by Jehu's men. One possibility of reconciling the accounts is to suggest that although Ahaziah was wounded at the ascent to Gur, he was apprehended by Jehu's men in Samaria (where he lay recovering from his wounds) and then taken to Megiddo, where he was put to death, his body being given to his servants who took him to Jerusalem for burial (v.28; cf. 2Ch 22:9).

30–34a News of all this had no doubt reached Jezebel. Sensing her own imminent demise, she arranged herself in queenly fashion and went to the window to await Jehu's arrival. As Jehu entered the gate below, she called tauntingly to him with words calculated to cut Jehu down to size. Jehu is called a "Zimri," a name that had become synonymous with "traitor," the implication being that usurpers usually do not last too long themselves. Jehu was fully up to the occasion. Looking up to the window where Jezebel was, he called out for anyone who would stand with him. When some of the eunuchs responded to Jehu's bidding, Jezebel was thrown to the courtyard below. Jehu subsequently rode over the fallen body and went in to dine in the banquet hall of his predecessor.

34b–37 Later, on thinking over the events that had recently transpired, Jehu gave instructions that Jezebel's body be given a proper burial, since she had been a king's daughter. But his second thoughts were too late. The servant found precious little of Jezebel's remains. When this was reported to Jehu, he recognized immediately the full force of Elijah's awful prophecy (cf. 1Ki 21:23).

C. The Era of the Fourth Dynasty (10:1–15:12)

1. The reign of Jehu in the northern kingdom (10:1–36)

1–8 With the deaths of Jehoram (9:24–26), Ahaziah and his attendants (2Ch 22:8–9), and Jezebel (2Ki 9:32–33), Jehu next moved to eliminate any competitive threat to his newly won crown from the surviving members of the royal family who had taken refuge in Samaria, the capital city. He warned those officials who cared for them to prepare for battle. The heads of state in Samaria felt that resistance was futile and sent Jehu a letter of submission. With this concession in hand, Jehu sent a second letter, demanding that the heads of Jehoram's surviving heirs be brought to him in Jezreel. Again the officials complied and sent the severed heads to Jehu, who then had them placed in two piles before the gate of Jezreel. This gruesome deed was often practiced in the ancient Near East.

9–11 On the next day Jehu addressed the assembled people, absolved them of any guilt, and again proclaimed his divine mission. While it was true that he had slain his master, the heads of the slain sons of the house of Ahab had come there through other means and so were a further sign that all of Elijah's prophetic threats were coming to pass. Having said that, Jehu ordered the seizure and execution of any who might yet remain of Ahab's descendants in Jezreel, as well as any of Jehoram's officials, aides, and friends. Even the state priests who served them were put to death.

12–14 With affairs settled to his liking in Jezreel, acting on the favorable response of the leaders of Samaria, Jehu set out for Israel's capital city. As he traveled southward, he met a party of forty-two of Ahaziah's relatives who were coming to pay their respects to the royal family of Israel and Samaria. They would fare no better than the deceased Judean king. Jehu ordered their instant seizure and execution. As ordered, there were no survivors. Jehu's reason for this mass murder is not given. Perhaps it was intended to be further evidence of his goal to stamp out Baalism everywhere. Perhaps he even held wild hopes of someday being able to lay some claim against Judah as well. Jehu was taking no chances. Since the two royal houses were related (cf. 8:16–18), no possible claimant would be allowed to live. Furthermore, their demise might pose some question as to proper succession to the Judean throne.

15 On leaving yet another bloody scene, Jehu encountered a mysterious figure, one Jehonadab the Recabite, who, having heard of Jehu's anti-Baal crusade, had apparently come to meet the new Israelite king. Jeremiah (Jer 35) records that Jehonadab was the leader of an ascetic group that lived an austere, nomadic life in the desert, drinking no wine and depending solely on the Lord for their sustenance. Separatist to the core and strong patriots, they lived in protest to the materialism and religious compromise in Israel. Accordingly, Jehonadab was extremely interested in Jehu's reputed desire to purge the nation of its heathenism. Perhaps he hoped that in Jehu a sense of national repentance and longing for the Lord God of Israel would now take place.

16–17 Jehu recognized Jehonadab immediately and, having greeted him with the usual blessing, inquired whether he was in agreement with him. When Jehonadab replied that he was, Jehu gave him his hand, both in friendship and to receive him into his chariot so that he might witness Jehu's further zeal for the Lord. One wonders what Jehonadab must have felt when, on their entrance into Samaria, Jehu's first order of business was the execution of any who might be in any way related to the house of the preceding dynasty. Nevertheless he continued with Jehu in his further purgation. With the death of the "sons of Ahab," the divine sentence had been carried out to the fullest (1Ki 21:21).

18–24 Jehu's continued purge of Baalism in Israel next took the form of deception. Feigning that he himself was a devotee of Baal, he ordered a great assembly for sacrifice to be held in Samaria and ordered all the priests and ministers of Baal to come, on penalty of death. On the day set for the feast, the various ministers arrived. To readily identify them as Baal's faithful, each was given a special robe. With the temple of Baal crowded with Baal's priests, and with the temple guarded securely by eighty selected guards, Jehu and Jehonadab entered the temple to see the opening sacrifices.

25–27 When the ceremonies had begun, Jehu and Jehonadab stepped outside; then Jehu gave the prearranged signal for the guards to enter the temple and slay the worshipers. This they did, penetrating even into the ruined shrine of the temple. None escaped. After the execution had been accomplished, the wooden images and stone statues of Baal were carried outside and demolished; then the temple itself was torn down and burned. To desecrate the site and mark the contempt attendant to it, Jehu converted it into a place for public convenience.

28–36 Jehu had exterminated the worship of Baal in Israel. For this the Lord commended him and promised him a royal succession to the fourth generation. Yet Jehu was to prove a disappointment to God; for his reform was soon seen to be political and selfish rather than born of any deep concern for God. Not only did he not keep the law in his heart, but he perpetuated the state cult of the golden calf established by Jeroboam I. Despite his comet-like beginning, spiritually speaking, Jehu was a falling star; so his reign is largely passed over in silence.

Because of his idolatry, God allowed the Arameans to plunder and reduce systematically the size of Israel, beginning with the loss of Israel's Transjordanian holdings. Although defeated by the Assyrians, the Arameans had managed to retain independence. Hazael took advantage of Assyria's preoccupation with affairs in the east and with revolution at home to take over Israel's holding in Transjordan and to actually march into Israel and Judah. Only the emergence of a new strong Assyrian king in 841 B.C. checked Hazael's relentless surge.

2. The reign of Athaliah in the southern kingdom (11:1–16)

1 On the news of the death of her son Ahaziah, Athaliah, the dowager queen, took whatever measures were necessary to seize the throne for herself, including the murder of her own grandchildren and all that remained of the royal family. With all natural heirs put out of the way, she ascended the throne, inaugurating a seven-year reign.

2–3 As in other desperate times, a godly woman would be used of God to stem the tide of apostasy. This ninth-century "Jochebed" was named Jehosheba. A princess in her own right—being the daughter of Jehoram and sister of Ahaziah—she was also the wife of the high priest Jehoiada (2Ch 22:11). Conspiring with her nurse (and doubtless the high priest as well), Jehosheba hid the baby, at first in one of the palace chambers, then subsequently smuggled him into her temple quarters where she managed to conceal him for six full years.

4–12 In the seventh year, with the child now older, Jehoiada mustered his courage (2Ch 23:1) and laid plans to dislodge the usurping queen from her ill-gotten throne. First, he secured the allegiance of the military officials and temple personnel. Second, he summoned the Levites and heads of families throughout the southern kingdom to Jerusalem and swore them to loyalty to the true king (cf. 2Ch 23:2). Third, on a set day he had the temple personnel seal off the temple area at the changing of the guard and had trusted guards deployed in strategic fashion. Then, with everyone in place, Jehoiada led the king to the appointed spot, perhaps in the innermost court between the temple and the altar, and anointed him as king, to the shouts of acclamation of the gathered throng. By putting the crown on the young king's head and a copy of God's law in his hand, Jehoiada was acting in accordance with ancient scriptural precedent, a move calculated to strengthen the hand of the supporters of the rightful king of the people.

13–16 When the clamor of the people reached the ears of Athaliah, she made her way to the scene of jubilation. The sight that greeted her eyes doubtless made her heart sink. There, on the royal dais at the eastern gate of the inner court to the temple, stood a newly crowned king, surrounded by the high officials both in the religious order and in the military, amid great fanfare and the joyous shouts of the people. She shrieked out her condemnation: it was treason. But her cry was to have as little effect as that of Israel's Jehoram to Athaliah's son Ahaziah (9:23). At Jehoiada's command she was seized and escorted to the gate used for the palace horses and put to death by the sword. Thus Athaliah, the most infamous queen of Judah, died at the hands of her executioners, much as did her mother Jezebel, queen of Israel (9:27–37).

3. The reign of Joash in the southern kingdom (11:17–12:21)

17–21 After the departure of the deposed Athaliah, Jehoiada led the king and the people in a twofold ceremony of covenant renewal: on the one hand, the king and the people swore their unswerving allegiance to God; on the other, the people affirmed their unfailing support of the reconstituted Davidic line. In attestation to their vows, a thorough cleansing of the land followed. Baal's temple was torn down, his priest Mattan slain before the images, and the altar thoroughly pulverized (2Ch 23:17). Not only was the pagan worship of Baal put away, but a reorganization of the temple worship followed that was in accordance with the law of Moses and that followed the order instituted by David.

That day was capped with a thrilling scene. With Jehoiada in the lead, the royal bodyguard escorted the young king toward the palace, followed by the high officials representing the military, civil, and religious orders, with the joyous people bringing up the rear. From the eastern temple the ecstatic entourage swept majestically out the inner temple court and, moving southward through the middle court, entered through the upper gate into the palace. Eventually the throng reached the throne room, where the king was duly enthroned. It had been a memorable day—a day when Jerusalem and Judah ascended to the spiritual heights. Yet while the fire of spiritual reforms had been ignited and was to burn brightly for a time, in the very dependence of the king on others could be seen a flicker that would one day cause the fiery zeal for the Lord to sputter before the chilling winds of apostasy. This same Joash and many of the same officials would, on another day, bring Judah down to the dregs of the degraded Canaanite religion that they had just rendered dormant. Merely programmed religion is perilous; genuine faith must be personal.

12:1–6 Chapter 12 begins with a notice of Joash's matrilineage. Then follows a favorable evaluation of his earlier years as king, together with the notice that nevertheless worship at the various high places continued. Next is an account of the preparations for and repair of the temple. Joash's first edict in this regard (doubtless made early in his reign; cf. 2Ch 24:5) called for the setting aside of money collected as a result of the payment of special religious taxes and voluntary offerings. The Chronicler adds that the Levites were to gather such funds personally, collecting them from the cities of Judah. Although all haste was bidden in the matter, yet by the twenty-third year of Joash's reign the task was still not done (cf. 2Ch 24:5). No formal reasons are cited for this seeming lack of effort by the Levites. Whatever the problem was, the system was not working.

7–16 Accordingly Joash decided to take matters into his own hands and decreed that a chest be set outside the wall to the inner court at the southern gate on the right side of the entrance into the temple, so that all who passed through might cast their contributions in for the temple's repair (cf. 2Ch 24:8). Joash also had a proclamation read throughout Judah as to the need and intent of the box, urging all citizens to participate willingly in accordance with Moses' ancient institution (cf. Ex 25:2–3; 30:12–16; Lev 27:2–8 with 2Ch 24:9). The response was tremendous (cf. 2Ch 24:10). Soon there was ample money to begin the work and the workers were commissioned (cf. 2Ch 24:11–13). So successful had been the king's program and so well did all concerned carry out their duties that there was even money left over for the provision of sacred vessels for the sanctuary service (2Ch 24:14).

17–21 The narrative quickly shifts in time, noting that the Aramean king Hazael had renewed his pressure against Israel and Judah, penetrating down the coast as far as Philistia and turning then inland to make a direct attack against Jerusalem. A siege of Jerusalem was averted only when Joash stripped the royal treasury and the wealth of the temple as payment to Hazael.

The reason for this drastic turn of events can be gleaned from the supporting details in 2Ch 24:14–22. Regular temple worship had continued throughout the days of Jehoiada; but after the death of the godly high priest, Joash fell into the hands of godless advisors who turned his heart to Canaanite practices. Although the Lord continually warned the king and his confidants, his pleadings fell on deaf ears. Indeed, in one instance the king and his staff went so far as to stone Jehoiada's son Zechariah for delivering the Lord's pronouncement against them.

Accordingly, when God's patience had run full course, he delivered Joash and Judah into the hands of the Arameans. The plight of the northern kingdom (cf. 2Ki 13:1–3) also descended on the south. Hazael, though equipped with an inferior army, was under God's direction immediately successful, defeating Judah suddenly and sending much booty back to Damascus (2Ch 24:23–24). The campaign brought death to many in Judah. Even the king was sorely wounded (2Ch 24:25). The narrative in Kings joins the historical report at this point. With total defeat imminent, Joash bribed Hazael and so delivered Jerusalem. Nothing, however, is recorded of any repentance on Joash's part. So obdurate did he remain in his sin that he was to die in a palace intrigue. Even though he was interred in Jerusalem, he was excluded from burial in the royal sepulcher (2Ch 24:25).

4. The reign of Jehoahaz in the northern kingdom (13:1–9)

1–9 In the very year that Joash launched his campaign to repair the temple, Jehoahaz, son of Jehu (10:35), ascended the throne in the northern kingdom. He was to reign sixteen years (814–798 B.C.). Because Jehoahaz perpetuated the sins of his father in following the long-standing state religion instituted by Jeroboam I, God allowed the Aramean king Hazael (843–798 B.C.) to afflict the northern kingdom directly. Hazael's affliction of Israel was to trouble Jehoahaz throughout his reign, though, apparently, the earlier part of Jehoahaz's rule was most severely affected (cf. v.32). So sore had the Aramean encroachment been that the northern kingdom was at one point left with but fifty horses, ten chariots, and ten thousand infantry—a far cry from the time when Ahab alone could muster

two thousand chariots for the allied forces at Qarqar.

In such lowly circumstances Jehoahaz at last sought the Lord's favor. While his repentance was seemingly genuine, the state religion of the golden calves was allowed to remain, as was the cult connected with the Asherah pole in Samaria. Nevertheless God in his covenant mercy did so arrange the circumstances as to send relief to Israel (probably in the person of Adad-Nirari III, 811–783 B.C., of Assyria), with the result that the closing years of Jehoahaz's reign were free of Aramean intervention.

Little else is reported of Jehoahaz's reign, Jehu's son going to his reward in 798 B.C. and being succeeded by his son, Jehoash.

5. The reign of Jehoash in the northern kingdom (13:10–25)

10–13 The account of the sixteen-year reign of Jehoash of Israel begins with a typical notice of his evil character, a mention of the most important event in his reign (his war with Amaziah), and a statement as to his demise. A record of an incident in which Jehoash met with the dying Elisha follows.

14 Jehoash addressed Elisha with words reminiscent of the venerable prophet's own testimony at Elijah's translation (cf. 2:12). While they were full of respect, the words were less than full of faith. Yet because of the very fact that Jehoash had at least come to Elisha and had addressed him courteously, the Lord was to use the occasion to attempt to increase Jehoash's slim faith.

15–20a Elisha instructed Israel's king to pick up his bow. When he had done so, the prophet placed his own hands on those of the king, thereby indicating that what he was about to do would be full of spiritual symbolism. That act was the shooting of an arrow out the east window—toward Aram. Elisha explained the deed: Jehoash would win a total victory at Aphek against Arameans. But the divine promise was to be augmented by personal participation. Accordingly, Jehoash was told next to shoot arrows into the ground; obviously victory at Aphek was to be followed by subsequent victories over the hated Arameans. Jehoash obediently complied, but with his own reasoning powers. He struck the ground three times with his arrows rather than using the five or six arrows that he had with him. Elisha was justifiably angry with the king. Had he used all his arrows, the Arameans would have been completely vanquished. Now Jehoash would gain but three victories. With this pronouncement the aged prophet had finished his earthly course.

20b–21 One last miracle would attend God's faithful prophet. In those last dark days before stability was restored to the area by Adad-Nirari III, bands of Moabite marauders ravished the land at the beginning of the harvest season. Evidently Elisha had died at such a time. On one occasion, as a funeral procession made its way to the burial place, a looting party swooped down on them. In their need for swift flight, the members of the procession quickly halted and hastily placed the body of the dead man in the first available tomb—which happened to be Elisha's. When the burial party lowered the linen-wrapped body of the dead man into the tomb, it came into contact with the remains of Elisha. Instantly the man was revived. The juxtaposition of this event with the account that precedes makes it clear that herein was another divinely intended sign for Jehoash and Israel: God was the God of the living, not the dead, not only for Elisha and the man who had been restored to life, but for Israel as well. Israel could yet "live" if she would but appropriate the eternally living God as her own. The entire episode was, further, a corroborative sign that what Elisha had prophesied would certainly come to pass. Only a living God could guarantee such a thing (cf. Isa 44).

22–25 The chapter closes with some historical notices concerning the strained Aramean-Israelite relations during the reign of Jehoahaz and Jehoash. Conditions improved during Jehoash's reign in that the Israelite king, in accordance with Elisha's prophecy, defeated the Aramean king Ben-Hadad III, son of Hazael, three times. The growing preoccupation of Adad-Nirari III with the affairs in the east and Joash's treaty link with him, along with the growing weakness of Aram in the days of Ben-Hadad III, provided the historical framework for the outworking of Elisha's prophecy. This record is a further indication of the inviolability of God's word and God's continued faithfulness to the basic covenant made with the patriarchs.

6. The reign of Amaziah in the southern kingdom (14:1–22)

1–7 If those who conspired against Joash, Judah's eighth king, had hoped for a dramatic change in governmental leadership, they were to be disappointed. Amaziah did indeed carry out his office in accordance with the demands of orthodoxy, as witnessed by his stringent treatment of the sons of his father's assassin. Yet the Scriptures record that he did not serve God "wholeheartedly" (2Ch 25:2). Certainly he was no David; rather, he was another Joash; for he perpetuated the state policy of allowing sacrifice and offerings in the high places.

Two dramatic events were to mark Amaziah's reign: (1) his God-given victory over Edom and (2) his self-inflicted loss to Israel. The first is dismissed in a single verse but receives expanded treatment in 2Ch 25:5–15, where the basic weakness in Amaziah's character is readily shown.

According to the Chronicler, Amaziah laid careful plans for the reconquest of Edom (lost in the days of Jehoram [8:20–22]). He began with a general census and conscription of able-bodied men twenty years of age and upward (2Ch 25:5). He added to the three-thousand-man army by raising another one hundred thousand mercenaries from Israel (2Ch 25:6), which, however, he subsequently dismissed when rebuked by one of the Lord's prophets (2Ch 25:7–10, 13). Thus encouraged that his cause was just and that God would give him the victory, Amaziah invaded Edom and inflicted a crushing defeat.

Life's successes are not, however, always the victories they seem to be. A notable defeat for Amaziah occurred here (2Ch 25:14–16). Having vanquished Edom and carried off booty and captives, he foolishly worshiped their captive gods. For this the man of God again rebuked Amaziah. This time, however, Amaziah no longer "needed God," for he considered that he himself had won the battle. So he threatened the prophet and sent him away. Yet before he left that prophet announced Amaziah's doom for his spiritual callousness and self-will.

8–10 This knowledge of Amaziah's character and the information that the dismissed and disgruntled Israelite mercenaries had looted the northernmost Judean cities on their way back home to Israel (2Ch 25:13) set the background for the second major event of Amaziah's time—the contest with Jehoash of Israel (cf. 2Ch 25:17–24). Still irked by the strong prophetic rebuke, Amaziah sought the advice of those who would indulge his self-will (2Ch 25:17). Angry over the conduct of the Israelite mercenaries, he used their actions as a provocation for war. Moreover, having defeated Edom with ease, Amaziah overestimated his own abilities and reasoned that he would have little trouble with his northern brother (cf. 2Ch 25:19).

To Amaziah's arrogant battle challenge, Jehoash returned a reply couched in parabolic fable. For Amaziah to presume to challenge Jehoash was like a lowly thistle making pretentious demands against a great Lebanese cedar, only to be trampled under foot by a passing animal. How empty the boasting of such a puny antagonist! Similarly Amaziah ought not to let success over a tiny nation go to his head. In locking horns with Jehoash, the renowned victor over the Arameans, Amaziah was inviting personal and national disaster.

11–16 Amaziah's headstrong ambitions nevertheless knew no bounds. Throwing caution to the wind, he moved his troops to a confrontation with Jehoash at Judean Beth Shemesh. In that battle Jehoash emerged the victor, routing Amaziah's army (2Ch 25:22) and taking Judah's king captive. Jehoash followed up his triumph with a thrust against Jerusalem that resulted in the loss of some six hundred feet of city wall, the confiscation of the temple furnishings and palace treasures, and the taking of many prisoners of war. Amaziah's lesson in self-will had cost his nation dearly. The Chronicler (2Ch 25:20) reports that behind it all lay the wise hand of divine providence that arranged the details of the lives of all concerned, in order to teach Amaziah and Judah the folly of trusting in foreign gods.

17–22 The account of Amaziah's life closes with a further note that he outlived Jehoash of the northern kingdom by some fifteen years and apparently was then released to return home by Israel's next king, Jeroboam II. Such a move would cause an unsettling factionalism, for Judah would now have two kings: Azariah, whom Amaziah had made coregent before his battle with Jehoash, and the restored Amaziah. Amaziah's apostasy

had already brought him many adversaries; his return only aroused old antagonisms and, doubtless, new political enemies. The tension of having two kings was resolved in a conspiracy against Amaziah that first caused his flight and then ended with his death in Lachish.

7. The reign of Jeroboam II in the northern kingdom (14:23–29)

23–29 The chapter closes with a brief notice of the forty-one year reign of Jeroboam II (793–752 B.C.). The era of Jeroboam (northern kingdom) and Azariah (southern kingdom) would mark a significant change in the fortunes of God's people. These would be days of unparalleled prosperity for the twin kingdoms, both economically and politically. Indeed, together they would acquire nearly the same territorial dimensions as in the days of the united monarchy. However, God's blessings are too often taken for granted. And so it proved to be in Israel-Judah of the eighth century B.C. Spiritually the lives of God's people degenerated into open sin in the northern kingdom and into an empty formalism in the south. In such an era God therefore raised up the great writing prophets, one of whom, Jonah, is mentioned here.

Great responsibility for Israel's spiritual problem lay with her leadership. Jeroboam II, while a capable administrator and military leader, had no concern for vital religion (cf. 1Ch 5:11–17; Hos 4:6–5:7; 7:5). He simply carried out the ritual of the standard state religion begun by Jeroboam I. Nonetheless Jeroboam's external accomplishments were many. In accordance with an unrecorded prophecy of Jonah, Jeroboam restored fully the borders of Israel so that they extended from the entrance of Hamath (located in the great Beqa Valley amid the Lebanese Mountains south of Hamath) to the Sea of Arabah (or Dead Sea). Apparently even Hamath and Damascus came under Israelite control. Amos (Am 6:13–14) indicates that the Transjordanian territories were probably also recovered at this time.

In all this the faithfulness of God, despite Israel's unfaithfulness (cf. Hos 2:2–3:5; 11:1–14:8; Am 3:1–15), is evident. Because Israel had fallen into such desperate spiritual conditions, a merciful God had acted on behalf of his people. As he had granted them deliverance from external pressures by sending

Adad-Nirari III of Assyria against the Arameans (cf. 13:5, 22–23), initiating a period of recovery under Jehoash (13:25; 14:14–15), so now in a grander way he culminated that deliverance with full victory over the Arameans, one that included Israel's recovery of its former boundaries.

When Jeroboam II died in 752 B.C., he left behind a strong kingdom, but, unfortunately, one whose core foundation was so spiritually rotten that the edifice of state would not long withstand the rising tides of international intrigue and pressure.

8. The reign of Uzziah in the southern kingdom (15:1–7)

1–4 Judah's tenth king was Azariah ("The LORD has helped"), known also as Uzziah ("The LORD is my strength"), the latter name possibly being assumed on the occasion of his independent reign. Azariah had been made coregent at the time of Amaziah's ill-conceived campaign against Jehoash (14:8–14; 2Ch 25:17–24). After Amaziah's release at the death of Jehoash in 782 B.C. and subsequent assassination in 767, Azariah took the throne in his own right and ruled until 740. Thus, counting his coregencies, Azariah ruled some fifty-two years.

Several reasons may be found for such a lengthy reign besides the longevity of the king. First, Israel's perennial enemy, Assyria, was in a state of severe decline. After the death of the vigorous king Adad-Nirari III (810–783), Assyria was ruled by three weak kings—Shalmaneser IV (782–774), Assur Dan III (773–756), and Assur Nirari V (755–746)—who strove desperately to maintain themselves against the advance of their hostile northern neighbor, Urartu, and cam-

The time of Jeroboam II was one of great wealth in the northern kingdom of Israel. This ivory pendant found at Tell Gezer is a piece of jewelry that only the rich could afford. Courtesy Tell Gezer Excavations.

paigned mainly to the south and east. Moreover, Assyria was rocked internally by plagues in 765 and 759 and by internal revolts (763–759).

Second, relations between Jeroboam II of Israel and Azariah remained cordial so that together the two nations were able eventually to acquire nearly the same territorial dimension as in the days of the united monarchy. Indeed, the Chronicler makes it clear that the era of the early eighth century B.C. was one of great expansion militarily, administratively, commercially, and economically, a period whose prosperity was second only to that of Solomon (2Ch 26:1–15).

Third, and more basically, Azariah was noted as a man who utilized well the spiritual heritage that he had gained from his father (cf. 2Ch 26:4–5). Accordingly, God's abundant blessing was shed on him (2Ch 26:6–15) so that his fame spread throughout the Near Eastern world (2Ch 26:8, 15).

The mention of the continued worship at the "high places" indicates a state policy of noninterference with competing religious forms that had been in force since at least the time of Joash (cf. 12:3; 14:3–4). The apparent compromise is indicative of a basic spiritual shallowness in Israel and Judah that was to surface in the prophecies of the great writing prophets of the eighth century B.C.

Times of plenty and ease too often lead to spiritual lethargy. God's abundant blessings can all too readily be taken for granted and become commonplace. In such circumstances a people's religious experience can degenerate into an empty formalism or, worse, erupt into open apostasy and moral decadence. So it was in eighth-century Israel. Hosea (775–725 B.C.) warned of the misuse of wealth and the twin dangers of apostasy and loose morality. Joel (770–765) cried out against Judah's superficial religion. Amos (765–755) spoke a similar message, while also emphasizing Israel's moral and social corruption. The collective prophetic challenge to repent and return to making God primary in the believers' lives reflects the low spiritual tone of the times.

5–7 Great earthly success is seldom well-managed to spiritual benefit. As with Solomon before him, Azariah's successes proved to be his undoing. His great power fostered such pride and haughtiness that about 750 B.C. he sought to add to his vast power by usurping the prerogatives of the sacred priesthood. Challenged to his face by the priests as he attempted to make an offering at the altar of incense, he was also instantaneously judged by God, who smote him with leprosy. Driven from the temple forever, Azariah remained a leper thereafter, dwelling in isolation until his death (2Ch 26:16–21). During Azariah's last decade, due to his leprosy, his son Jotham was made coregent and public officiator, though doubtless Azariah remained the real power behind the throne.

9. The reign of Zechariah in the northern kingdom (15:8–12)

8–12 Little is recorded of Zechariah, the fourth descendant of Jehu to assume the throne of Israel, except the familiar evaluation that he did evil in perpetuating the idolatrous sins of Jeroboam I and that he died in an assassination plot. With the passing of Zechariah, the Lord's prophetic promise to Jehu (10:30) stood fulfilled (cf. Am 7:9).

The shortness of Zechariah's reign and that of Shallum, his murderous successor, doubtless points up the great contrast in their abilities with those of Jeroboam II and underscores the weakness of the northern kingdom. The openness of Shallum's deed was expressive of Israel's social degradation.

D. The Era of the Decline and Fall of the Northern Kingdom (15:13–17:41)

1. The reign of Shallum in the northern kingdom (15:13–15)

13–15 Shallum's designation "son of Jabesh" may mark either a clan name or indicate that he was the leader of a Gileadite reaction against the crown. His minimal reign of but one month was terminated by a retaliatory raid by Menahem, who, in turn, usurped the throne.

Menahem, who may have been a military commander under Zechariah, brought his forces against Shallum in Samaria from Tirzah, an ancient Canaanite city important for its strategic commercial location and noted for its surpassing beauty (SS 6:4). Tirzah had served as a royal retreat (1Ki 14:17) and as a national capital (16:8–10) and had remained an important city.

From Tirzah, Menahem launched a savage campaign against Tiphsah for its failure to open its gates to him. This latter city, whose exact location remains uncertain, may have withstood Menahem and Shallum or may have contested Menahem's attempt to reassert Israelite strength in the area. Although Tiphsah is otherwise insignificant in OT history, its importance to Menahem lay in its attitude toward him at a time when he could allow no rebellion to his authority if his quest for the throne was to be carried out smoothly. Menahem thus served notice that he would brook no resistance from any quarter.

2. The reign of Menahem in the northern kingdom (15:16–22)

16–22 Menahem's decade of rule is characterized as one of total sinfulness. In addition to further prostituting Israel's religious experience, he compromised her independence by becoming a vassal to Pul (or, more properly, Tiglath-pileser III, 745–727 B.C.) of Assyria. His motive in doing so was not one of patriotic concern for Israel's survival. Rather he hoped that the Assyrian alliance would solidify his hold on the throne of Israel. In order to gain the Assyrian king's backing, he levied a tax of fifty shekels of silver on the wealthy men of the realm so that the assessed levy of one thousand talents of silver might be gathered. Since a talent then weighed about seventy-five pounds, this was obviously a tremendous sum.

Nevertheless, the sum was fully met, and Tiglath-pileser "withdrew and stayed in the land no longer." While Menahem thus bought the crown for himself and respite from Assyria, the hard stipulations were to cause further internal friction that was to ignite the fires of insurrection soon after his son, Pekahiah, succeeded him. Although Menahem had thought to buy time, perhaps even Israel's independence, his policy was to spell out the beginning of the end. A totally apostate Israel was to reap the harvest of her spiritual wickedness at the hands of the very ones whom Menahem had trusted for deliverance.

To understand the complex events of the late eighth century B.C., a word must be said concerning the Assyrians. After nearly a half century of decline, Assyria reawakened with the usurpation of the throne by Tiglath-pileser III in 745 B.C. Indeed, he and his successors in the Neo-Assyrian Empire were to effect a drastic change in the balance of power in the ancient Near East. Having solidified the kingdom in the east, Tiglath-pileser turned his attention to the west in 743. Although the exact course of his western campaign is difficult to follow, it seems clear that all of Syro-Palestine submitted to the Assyrian yoke. Among those nations and kings whose tribute is recorded in his annals is the name Menahem of Israel, thus confirming the biblical account.

3. The reign of Pekahiah in the northern kingdom (15:23–26)

23–26 Few details are recorded of the two-year reign of Menahem's son Pekahiah except the notice of his evil spiritual condition and the coup d'état that took his life. The insurrection originated with the king's own personal bodyguard. While two of the chief officers (Argob and Arieh) remained loyal to the king, even laying down their lives for him, the third, Pekah (apparently an influential Gileadite), found an occasion to trap the king in the citadel of the royal palace. Having slain him, Pekah seized the throne.

The usurpation and troubled times that were to follow make it clear that there was an anti-Assyrian party that had remained submerged during the rule of the fiery Menahem. Indeed, the notice of a twenty-year reign for Pekah would seem to indicate that this Gileadite strong man had laid claim to the crown some twelve years earlier and had been prevented from taking the throne only by Menahem's swift action in those unsettled times during Shallum's conspiracy. Pekahiah's appointment of Pekah to be a chief officer among his bodyguards may thus have been an attempt to placate the rival party.

4. The reign of Pekah in the northern kingdom (15:27–31)

27–31 The chronology of Pekah's time is beset with serious problems. To Pekah is attributed a twenty-year reign, beginning with the end of the fifty-two-year reign of Azariah of Judah. Further, v.30 indicates that his reign was terminated by Hoshea's conspiracy in the twentieth year of Jotham's rule. Verse 33, however, indicates that Jotham reigned but sixteen years. Moreover v.32 notes that Jotham himself began to rule in Pekah's second year. Further synchronisms occur in v.8, where the thirty-eighth year of Azariah is

marked as Zechariah's accession year; in 16:1, where the seventeenth year of Pekah and the accession year of Ahaz are equated; and in 17:1, where the twelfth year of Ahaz is given as the first of Hoshea's nine years.

Because the fall of Samaria can be assigned confidently to 722 B.C. on the basis of both biblical and secular history, and because Azariah's fifty-second year can be shown to be 740 B.C., it would appear that there is no room for a twenty-year reign for Pekah, particularly in that due allowance must be made for the reigns of Zechariah (six months), Shallum (one month), Menahem (ten years), Pekahiah (two years), and Hoshea (nine years) in the same interval of time.

The resolution of these data, while difficult, is not impossible. Probably because Pekah carried out a consistent anti-Assyrian policy, the chronicles of the southern kingdom gave full credit to Pekah's regnal claims. It would seem that already at the death of Zechariah in 752 B.C., Pekah had claimed the kingship and was recognized as king in Transjordanian Gilead. However, the swift action of the Israelite military forces through Menahem prevented Pekah from furthering his aspirations for the next decade. In 742, when the powerful Menahem died, the problem of Pekah again surfaced, Pekahiah solving the problem by bringing Pekah into a position of prominence within his own bodyguard. After two years Pekah was able to find an opportunity to dispose of Pekahiah and rule in his own right over all Israel until the troublesome international events associated with Tiglath-pileser III's second western campaign (743–732) forced his demise at the hands of a pro-Assyrian faction led by Hoshea (732).

Pekah's stormy beginning was to characterize his short independent rule. In 734 Tiglath-pileser III swept out of Assyria on a second western campaign that was to break the anti-Assyrian coalition headed by the Aramean king Rezin and Pekah of Israel. By 732 the alliance was thoroughly broken and Damascus had fallen. All the western Fertile Crescent, from the Taurus Mountains on the north to the border of Egypt on the south, lay in Assyrian hands. The Syrian (Aramean) states were divided into five provinces, Israel into three.

The battle against Israel centered in Galilee: Ijon, Abel Beth Maacah, Janoah, Kedesh, and Hazor all being known Galilean cities. The text also adds significantly that Tiglath-pileser III swept into Pekah's center of power, Gilead (cf. 1Ch 5:25–26). Because the cities lay in a general north-south direction, the biblical account may well preserve the Assyrian king's line of march. The mention of Janoah may indicate that after the victory over Kedesh, Tiglath-pileser divided his forces, half proceeding southward against Hazor and on to Gilead, and the other half moving southwest to Janoah and then on to Phoenicia.

With the loss of Galilee and Gilead and with the presence of Assyrian troops all along Israel's western frontier, it seemed evident that Pekah's anti-Assyrian policy had brought Israel to the point of extinction. Accordingly, while Tiglath-pileser was concluding the siege of Damascus in 732, a pro-Assyrian party, led by Hoshea, succeeded in defeating and displacing Pekah, an insurrection that cost the controversial Gileadite his life. By dispatching Pekah and submitting to Tiglath-pileser, the ultimate demise of Israel was postponed for a decade. But her end was sure, for her corruption was total, permeating all levels of society. In vain God's prophets had pleaded with an unrepentant and apostate people (cf. Isa 1–5; Mic 1–3; 6–7).

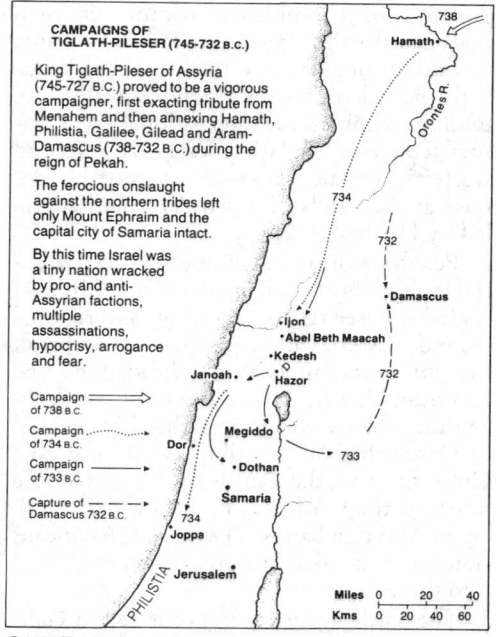

CAMPAIGNS OF
TIGLATH-PILESER (745-732 B.C.)

King Tiglath-Pileser of Assyria (745-727 B.C.) proved to be a vigorous campaigner, first exacting tribute from Menahem and then annexing Hamath, Philistia, Galilee, Gilead and Aram-Damascus (738-732 B.C.) during the reign of Pekah.

The ferocious onslaught against the northern tribes left only Mount Ephraim and the capital city of Samaria intact.

By this time Israel was a tiny nation wracked by pro- and anti-Assyrian factions, multiple assassinations, hypocrisy, arrogance and fear.

Campaign of 738 B.C.
Campaign of 734 B.C.
Campaign of 733 B.C.
Capture of Damascus 732 B.C.

Hamath
Orontes R.
738
734
732
Damascus
Ijon
Abel Beth Maacah
Kedesh
Janoah
Hazor
732
Megiddo
Dor
Dothan
733
Samaria
734
Joppa
Jerusalem
PHILISTIA

Miles 0 20 40
Kms 0 20 40 60

© 1985 The Zondervan Corporation

5. The reign of Jotham in the southern kingdom (15:32–38)

32–33 The reign of Jotham was a continuation of that of his father, Azariah (Uzziah). Already coregent for at least a decade, political and religious conditions remained largely as they were in Azariah's day; the country's prosperity continued as well (2Ch 27:1–4). Regrettably, that prosperity was to lead, as it so often does, to spiritual neglect (cf. Isa 1–5), a condition that was to make Judah ripe for open apostasy in Ahaz's day. Although the Chronicler (2Ch 27:6) gives Jotham a clear record, one cannot but wonder at the extent of the effect that Azariah's sin had had on Jotham and that, in turn, on the young Ahaz.

34–35 Jotham turned his attention to his country's internal needs. He rebuilt the Upper Gate at the northern entrance of the temple and did extensive work on the wall of Ophel (2Ch 27:3; cf. 2Ch 26:9). He also turned his attention to urban planning, constructing cities in the highlands of Judah that, together with a system of towers and fortification in the wooded areas, could serve the nation of Judah both economically and militarily.

At the onset of his reign, the Ammonites, from whom Azariah had exacted tribute (2Ch 26:8), refused to acknowledge Jotham's overlordship. This occasioned successful campaigns against the Ammonites so that they once again paid their tribute (2Ch 27:5). Jotham thus proved himself to be a mighty warrior. The notice that this tribute continued into the second and third year may correlate with the probability that Jotham had turned over the reigns of government to his coregent son, Ahaz, about the year 736, possibly because of some failure in health or rising international tensions.

36–38 Toward the end of Jotham's days, political storm clouds began to appear on the international horizon. The Chronicler speaks of "all his wars" (2Ch 27:7); and the author of Kings notes that Rezin, the Aramean king, and Pekah, Israel's king, began their incursions into Judah. The issue was designed by the Lord to test the young Ahaz in spiritual things, but there would be no repentance in this third generation.

6. The reign of Ahaz in the southern kingdom (16:1–20)

1–2 The account of Ahaz's wicked reign as given by the author of Kings centers around three main subjects: (1) his character (vv.1–4), (2) his war with Rezin and Pekah (vv.5–9), and (3) his further apostasy as consequence of his reliance on Tiglath-pileser III (vv.10–18). Other details concerning his life and times (cf. vv.19–20) can be found in 2Ch 28 and Isa 7–12.

Ahaz's reign forms a stark contrast with that of his father and grandfather, and yet they had sown the seeds of the apostasy that would fructify in Ahaz's day. The luxury and ease of the time of Uzziah and Jotham had produced a spiritual indolence in Judah that would allow Ahaz's open sin to flourish.

3–4 Not content to continue the standing state policies of limited religious compromise (see 15:5–7), Ahaz transgressed the bounds of propriety by imitating the idolatrous heathen practices of Israel. Most nefarious of all was his participation in the debased Molech rites, even going so far as to send his own son through the sacrificial fires (cf. Lev 18:21; 20:1–5; Dt 12:31; 2Ki 21:6). These rites took place at the confluence of the Hinnom and Kidron valleys in a sacred enclosure known as Topheth (cf. 23:10; Isa 30:33; Jer 7:31). The exact nature of the sacrifices and the divinities involved have been the subject of much discussion. The finding, however, of the same type of sacred place with the same name in the transplanted Phoenician colony of Carthage, where the sacrificial offering was called by a name made up of the same Semitic consonants (MLK) contained in the name "Molech," would seem to argue that there was no deity named Molech to whom the Judeans sacrificed. Rather, the real god involved was the old Canaanite deity Baal, with human sacrifice made to him called *mlk* (cf. Jer 19:5; 32:35). The rites were heinous and a total defilement of the God-given sacrificial service. The later spiritual reformation of Josiah was to bring an end to these sinister proceedings, a judgment Jeremiah utilized in picturing God's coming judgment on his sinful people (Jer 2:23; 7:30–33; 19:5–6).

The valley's reputation for extreme wickedness gave rise to the employment of its name as a term for the eschatological place for punishment of the wicked, a designation confirmed by Christ himself (Mt 5:22; 10:28; 13:42, 50; 18:9; 23:15, 33; 25:41).

5–6 The causes of Ahaz's war with Israel and Syria (Aram) were at least fourfold. (1) On the human level, Rezin of Syria and Pekah of Israel were doubtless desirous of Judah's support in their planned insurrection against Tiglath-pileser III of Assyria. (2) The two leaders may have had a personal dislike for Ahaz. (3) On the spiritual plane, the whole affair seems to be a concentrated satanic effort to put an end to the Davidic line on the throne in Jerusalem (cf. Isa 7:5–7). (4) God was superintending the whole complex undertaking. He would deal with an apostate Israel (cf. 17:5–18; 18:11–12), thwart the satanically inspired plans against the house of Israel by bringing defeat to Rezin and Pekah (Isa 7:5–16), and bring chastisement to a spiritually bankrupt Ahaz (2Ch 28:5, 19).

The full details of the complex international situation must be gleaned not only from ch. 16 but also from 15:37; 2Ch 28; and Isa 7:1–16. These sources show that the Syro (Aramean)-Israelite alliance had been operative against Judah already in Jotham's day (15:37). The allied attack against Judah was two-pronged. Rezin came along the eastern portion of Judah, driving down to the key seaport of Elath and taking it (2Ch 28:5). Pekah launched an effective general campaign against northern Judah that resulted in the death of thousands of Judeans and the capture of hundreds of others (though the captives were later granted their freedom and returned to Jericho through the intercession of the prophet Obed; cf. 2Ch 28:6–15). Moreover, the newly liberated Edom took the opportunity to strike back, carrying away some Judeans into captivity (2Ch 28:17). As well, the Philistines found the time ripe to make renewed incursions into the western Shephelah and take captive certain cities in southern Judah.

Then a new attack, aimed at taking Jerusalem itself and installing a client king on the throne, took place (Isa 7:2–6). Surrounded by hostile enemies on all sides Ahaz received God's prophet Isaiah. He assured Ahaz that the enemy would fall; God himself would see to that. Ahaz could ask any confirmatory sign that he wished, and it would be granted (Isa 7:7–11). Ahaz, with a flare of piety, refused Isaiah's words (Isa 7:12), preferring to rely on his own resourcefulness. (God nevertheless gave Ahaz a sign, the prophecy associated with the virgin birth of the Messiah, Isa 7:13–16; cf. Mt 1:22–23.)

7–9 Ahaz sent away to Tiglath-pileser III and hired his deliverance from what seemed certain defeat (cf. 2Ch 28:16, 21). Tiglath-pileser complied all too readily, eventually thoroughly subduing the Arameans, taking Damascus and deporting its inhabitants, and executing Rezin. Israel was spared only through Hoshea's coup d'état and swift submission to Assyria, a takeover that cost Pekah his life (15:29–30).

God's message through Isaiah (Isa 7:7–9, 16) had come true, though the total picture was not in accordance with God's desires for Ahaz. Accordingly, Judah, far from being actually delivered, would also soon feel the heel of the oppressor marching through her land and streets (cf. Isa 7:17–20). What had been an opportunity for spiritual victory had become a first step into a quicksand bog that would ultimately swallow Judah in defeat and deportation.

10–11 After Tiglath-pileser III had secured Damascus, he apparently summoned his new vassals there to receive their tokens of submission, among whom was Ahaz. While at Damascus Ahaz was much impressed with a type of altar in use there and sent back instructions to Uriah, the priest, for its construction, a task duly completed before the king's return.

12–13 When Ahaz returned he had his daily offerings presented on this new altar, thereby dedicating the altar's use to the Lord. The offerings that were made were all of the sweet savor type, expressing the maintenance of the believer's communion with God: the burnt and meal offerings symbolizing dedication and service, the fellowship (peace) offering symbolizing fellowship, and the drink offering emphasizing the joy of life poured out to God in Spirit-led obedience. What a parody of piety! He who knew nothing of genuine godliness would feign his devotion to God—and that via an alien altar!

14–16 The following verses catalog Ahaz's further religious innovations, all of which speak clearly of his deepening apostasy. The prescribed bronze altar was transferred from facing the sanctuary entrance to the north.

Accordingly, all future offerings would be made on the recently dedicated Damascene altar. The bronze altar would henceforth be used by Ahaz in connection with his divination practices, indicating Ahaz's involvement in Assyrian cultic rites.

17 Ahaz went even further. The high stands holding the altar were appropriated by him for their bronze. Likewise, he lowered the molten sea by taking away the bronze bulls that supported it and placed it on a low stone pedestal.

18 Not content with these "reforms" in the ceremonial furnishings, Ahaz went still further. The king's own covered stand that opened into the inner court, together with his private entrance to that place, were removed "in deference to the king of Assyria." The exact impact of these words is difficult to ascertain. Whether Tiglath-pileser wanted less prestige to be held by his new vassal or felt that such a special royal place might indicate too close a tie to an established religion that might later foster a spirit of independence against Assyria is uncertain. At any rate, the wholesale changes were either made at the Assyrian king's suggestion or were done to gain his pleasure.

19–20 Ahaz went yet further in his apostasy. According to 2Ch 28:24–25, he went so far as to mutilate the temple furniture and close the temple itself so that the services within the Holy Place were discontinued. "Worship services" would henceforth be held only in connection with the new altar or at one of the several altars erected throughout Jerusalem or at the high places dedicated to the various gods that were established throughout Judah by royal edict (v.4). All this not only speaks of Ahaz's depraved spiritual condition but was probably carried out as an expression of his goodwill toward Tiglath-pileser. Officially nothing offensive to the Assyrian king would henceforth be practiced. Thus did Ahaz go to his reward, clothed, spiritually speaking, in an Assyrian mantle.

7. The reign of Hoshea in the northern kingdom (17:1–23)

1–3 Hoshea had been granted the throne by the military in a purge that was largely a placating move toward Assyria. That such was the case can be seen in that when the opportunity presented itself, Hoshea quickly attempted to throw off the Assyrian yoke by entering into an anti-Assyrian coalition. That effort, however, failed, a failure that would seal the fate of the northern kingdom.

When Tiglath-pileser III died in 727 B.C. and was succeeded by his son Shalmaneser V (727–722), the time seemed ripe for certain western states to renounce their vassal status. Moreover, a seemingly important ally lay southward in the delta of Egypt, one Tefnekht, the Pharaoh of the Twenty-Fourth Dynasty. Tefnekht had succeeded in bringing the decadent Twenty-Second Dynasty to an end and was even then vying for prominence in Egypt with Piankhy, the Pharaoh of the Ethiopian-based Twenty-Fifth Dynasty (which had dispatched the Theban Twenty-Third Dynasty).

4 The mention of "So king of Egypt" has occasioned a good deal of controversy, for there is no known Egyptian king by that name. Attempts have been made to identify this "So" with Osorkon of the Twenty-Third Dynasty or with Shabako of the Twenty-Fifth Dynasty, or to assign to him merely a field commander's status. The simplest answer is that Sais, the Egyptian capital of the Twenty-Fourth Dynasty, would be pronounced *sa* in Akkadian (the lingua franca of the ancient Near East) but *so* in Hebrew. Thus understood, v.4 would read, "He had sent envoys to Sais, even to the king of Egypt" (see NIV note).

5–6 Hoshea (as well as Judah, 18:21) was to learn that Egypt was indeed "a splintered reed." Tefnekht could not even survive Egypt's internal struggle. Nor was Hoshea to succeed against Shalmaneser. The Assyrian monarch marched quickly into Israel, secured its submission, and imprisoned Hoshea himself. Subsequently he again invaded the land, devastating its length and breadth, and he placed Samaria under siege in the year 725 B.C.

Ultimately the Israelite capital fell (722), and its surviving inhabitants were deported to Mesopotamia and Media. The natural reading of the biblical record would seem to be that Shalmaneser is to be identified with "the king of Assyria." Sargon (Shalmaneser's successor), however, claimed that he had captured Samaria. The problem may possibly be resolved by holding that though Shalmaneser was still king, he was not personally present at Samaria's fall, the culmination of the campaign being accomplished by his general Sargon.

7–8 The author rehearses the causes that necessitated the divine punishment. His indictment of Israel begins with a reminder that God alone had released the Israelites from their oppression and bondage in Egypt and had brought them to the Promised Land. Their historical foundation was essentially a spiritual one. Having brought Israel from bondage to glorious freedom, God had every right to expect them to walk in newness of life, as befitting a redeemed people (cf. Dt 5–6; 10:12–11:32).

9–17 The opposite, however, had been the case. The shameful record of Israel's spiritual prostitution is catalogued (cf. Isa 5; Mic 6:3–5, 9–16). Against the clear prohibitions of God (Ex 20:2–6; Lev 18:4–5, 26; 20:22–23; Dt 5:6–10), the people had entered into the worship patterns of the pagan nations that God had driven out of the land. This apostasy had been formally initiated by Israel's own kings, and all Israel had followed their devious plan to pretend to worship God in the official state religion.

Matters had grown even worse. The external rites had become more openly false. Israel's worship included setting up sacred shrines and Asherah poles, the following of pagan incense customs, worshiping at cultic high places, and even open idolatry. Divination and deliberate sorcery had further corrupted their spiritual experience. Like the surrounding nations, they followed worthless idols and became useless to God. Most basic of all, they had not only denied God's covenant with them but had refused the God of the covenant, rejecting his rightful sovereignty over them. God had sent prophets to warn the people to turn from this wickedness, but they consistently refused to listen to them. Therefore, the Israelites appropriated the punishment that God had meted out against the Canaanites when he drove them out of the Promised Land: he drove Israel out (vv.18–20, 23) into exile (v.23).

18–23 Israel had aroused God's righteous wrath. In accordance with the set terms of the inviolable covenant, God must punish her. This he did, by allowing Israel to fall into the hands of the Assyrian invader. Judah had been left to ponder her own spiritual condition before God. Unfortunately, she would not learn from the lesson of Israel.

8. The repopulation of Samaria (17:24–41)

24 To the demise of Israel and her indictment, a historical note is appended. In accordance with the deportation system used so fully by Tiglath-pileser III and followed by his successors, a vast transplantation of populaces occurred. Israelites were sent to Mesopotamia and even beyond; Babylonians and Arameans were transferred to Israel. Not only did the Assyrian monarchs hope to make the repopulated and reconstituted districts more manageable, but they hoped to train and encourage the citizenry to transfer their loyalties to the Assyrian Empire.

25–27 The new settlers in Samaria, however, soon encountered difficulties. Perhaps because many unburied bodies still remained after the bloody warfare and due to the depopulating of the land, voracious lions began to roam freely through the area. When the immigrants arrived, they faced this menace, and many of them lost their lives. They immediately suspected that "the god of the land" was punishing them because of their failure to worship him. Therefore, they sent a report to the Assyrian king for some religious leadership. There was some truth to their evaluation of things. Although God had sent his people into exile because of their failure to live up to the stipulations of the covenant with God, he would not leave the land without any witness to himself. The lions were a reminder of the broken covenant and of God's claim on the land (Lev 18:24–30).

28 The Assyrian king granted the request. Accordingly, one of Israel's exiled priests returned to the land and reinstituted the worship of the Lord at Bethel, the traditional cult center of the northern kingdom. The religion, however, that such a priest taught was the false worship instituted by Jeroboam. The result was a mixture of truth combined with the corrupted experience of Israel (now deepened by two centuries of growing apostasy) and the pagan rites brought by the new settlers.

29–31 Moreover the various immigrants continued the worship of their own gods in the places where they settled. Those from Babylonia worshiped Succoth Benoth, probably a deliberate scribal pun on the Babylonian Sarpanitu, Marduk's wife. Those from Cuth continued their worship of Nergal, the god of pestilence.

Those from Syrian (Aramean) backgrounds worshiped the deities associated with their cults. The Syrian (Aramean) gods that are recorded here are likely all deliberate misspellings. Ashima is possibly an abbreviated form of the goddess Malkat Shemayin or the Canaanite Asherah (cf. Am 8:14, NIV note). Some have suggested a connection with the late Syrian (Aramean) goddess Sima or with the Phoenician god Eshmun. Nibhaz is otherwise unknown, the most usual conjecture being that it is a corruption of the word for altar, now deified. Tartak is possibly a miswriting of Atargatis, the familiar Syrian goddess. Adrammelech and Anammelech are similar corrupt names probably representing Canaanite forms of the important Phoenician deities Baal and Anat, known from Phoenician and Ugaritic names.

32–41 Thus this Samarian worship from the onset was syncretistic. While the various people observed the worship of the Lord (in its Jeroboamic corrupt form), they also continued their own religious practices. The author of Kings evaluates the situation as being one of total confusion. Above all he makes it clear that the new Samarian worship did not represent the true faith; not only was it syncretistic, but it violated the clear commands and stipulations contained in Israel's covenant with God.

With this summation the divine case against Israel has been made. Despite all that the great Redeemer had done for his people, their thankless, hardened, and apostate hearts had led them into spiritual, moral, and social corruption and thus to their own demise. Israel's checkered history should have provided a lesson for Judah; it remains an example for the church today (cf. 1Co 10:11–13).

III. The Southern Kingdom (18:1–25:30)

A. The Reign of Hezekiah (18:1–20:21)

1. Hezekiah's accession and early deeds (18:1–12)

1–2 Perhaps the knottiest of all scriptural chronological problems occurs in this chapter. The data are these: the third year of

Hoshea is the accession year of Hezekiah's twenty-nine-year reign (cf. v.1 with 2Ch 29:1); v.9 equates Hoshea's seventh year with Hezekiah's fourth year; and v.10 places Hoshea's ninth year in juxtaposition with Hezekiah's sixth year. Thus the dating of the early years of Hezekiah's reign is inextricably tied with Hoshea's rule. Since Hoshea came to the throne in 732/731 B.C., Hezekiah would appear to have begun his rule in 729/728.

Verse 12, however, records the invasion of Sennacherib that led to the famous Battle of El Tekeh as being in Hezekiah's fourteenth year. Since that date can be accurately determined as being 701 B.C., this verse would seem to place Hezekiah's accession date at 716/715 (cf. Isa 36:1). Adding to the difficulties is the scriptural notice in 16:1–2 that Ahaz reigned sixteen years after Pekah's seventeenth year (736/735), making Ahaz's final date to be 720/719.

Despite the many ingenious attempts to resolve these difficulties, the harmonization of these data remains a thorny problem. Obviously we are not yet able to grasp fully the details and principles that the Hebrew writers used in making these chronological correlations. While definite resolution of the details cannot be made at present, it may be simplest to view 729/728 as Hezekiah's first year as coregent with Ahaz, a joint rule that he was to share until 720/719. After Ahaz's death in 716, Hezekiah would then have ruled independently from 715 onward, or fourteen years before the Assyrian campaign of 701. Since the commencement of Hezekiah's independent rule began only in 715 and Ahaz's reign must have terminated in 720/719, the actual reins of government must have passed to Hezekiah some three or four years before Ahaz's death, just as Jotham lived on until 732 after committing governmental control to Ahaz in 736.

3–4 Hezekiah's godly character is sketched at the onset of things. He was concerned about the things of God, following in the footsteps of David his forefather in performing righteous deeds. This took the form early in his reign of a thorough reformation of the idolatrous practices of Ahaz. Not only did Hezekiah take away the high places and destroy the cultic stone pillars and Asherah poles, but his iconoclastic purge singled out Moses' bronze serpent (cf. Nu 21) that had lately become an object of veneration.

5–7 The divine evaluation is a favorable one: (1) there was none who equaled Hezekiah in his trust of the Lord; (2) he followed the Lord faithfully; and (3) he obeyed implicitly the law of God. Hence God was with him and blessed him with success. Hezekiah's character stands as a reminder that living for God's glory is for the believer's good also (cf. v.7 with 2Ch 31:20–21).

While the writer of Kings concentrates on the political events of Hezekiah's reign, the author of Chronicles gives supplemental information as to Hezekiah's continuing reformation. Hezekiah's spiritual concern brought about a cleansing of the temple, thus undoing the evil deeds of Ahaz (2Ch 29:3–19). This was followed by a reconstruction and rededication of the temple (2Ch 29:20–36), accomplished with proper sacrifices (vv.20–24), with sincere worship (vv.25–30), and with glad service to God (vv.31–36). Hezekiah's further reforms included the reinstituting of the Passover (2Ch 30), an observance performed with careful forethought (vv.1–12) and in accordance with the divine command, tempered with mercy (vv.13–22) and with protracted festivity (vv.23–27). The author of Chronicles tells of still later iconoclastic purges in which all the people of Israel participated (2Ch 31:1) and of Hezekiah's further attention to spiritual details and provisions (2Ch 31:2–19), closing with the notice that Hezekiah characteristically lived out his life in utter devotion to God and so was successful in all that he did (2Ch 31:20–21).

8–12 After the writer of Kings has familiarized his readers with Hezekiah's godly faculties, qualities undergirding him in the many crises of his life, he immediately turns his attention to one of the most critical episodes of Hezekiah's existence and of the southern kingdom as well. As an example of his godly concern and good success, he points out that Hezekiah rebelled against the king of Assyria. Not only that, but he turned against "the great king's" vassal, Philistia, defeating it from one end to the other. All Hezekiah's deeds, even his military accomplishments, thereby stand in stark contrast to the example of fearful Israel that perished because of unbelief and disobedience.

The time of Hezekiah's rebellion and occupation of Philistia must lie late in his reign, probably near the middle of the last quarter of the eighth century B.C. Hezekiah's early years were doubtless devoted to religion and internal affairs. Indeed, Sargon's western expeditions in 717/716 and again in 712, the latter of which was centered in Philistia and involved military action against Egypt and Transjordania, would make any military move by Hezekiah most unlikely until much later. However, Sargon's last half-decade (710–705) was occupied with troubles nearer home. Restless Arameans applied constant pressure in southern Mesopotamia; there was also the ever-present menace of Merodach-Baladan (cf. 20:12–13), the perennial king of Bit-Yakin and claimant to the throne of Babylon. Accordingly, Hezekiah's growing boldness and military operations had to fall within Sargon's last years, probably occurring at his death in 705, the usual occasion for such actions.

2. The Assyrian invasion (18:13–37)

13 The date of Sennacherib's campaign must be calculated from the time of Hezekiah's independent rule in 715, a date that harmonizes well with the data from Assyrian sources. Sennacherib (705–681 B.C.) was at first occupied with affairs close to home and so was not free to deal with Hezekiah. His first two campaigns were launched against the nearer menace, the continuing presence of Merodach-Baladan and the pesky Arameans, problems he inherited from his father. But having secured things in the south and east, Sennacherib was free to deal with the west, against which he launched his famous third campaign. His annals record the might of his all-out attack. Swooping down from the north, Sennacherib quickly dispatched the Phoenician cities and then unleashed his fury against Philistia. He notes that the citizens of Ekron had thrown in their lot with the Egyptians and Hezekiah of Judah, even going so far as to deliver their king (and Sennacherib's vassal) into the hands of Hezekiah for confinement. Apparently by-passing Ekron for the moment, Sennacherib marched down the Philistine coast as far as Ashkelon. Having secured the submission of that key city and having deported its king to Assyria, Sennacherib turned his attention inland in a thrust that would not only secure the key city of Judean Lachish but would effectively separate the remaining Philistines and Judeans from Egyptian help.

14–16 Verse 14 joins Sennacherib's campaign at this point. Sennacherib has taken Lachish and is busily engaged in mopping up the nearby fortified cities of Judah. With Phoenicia and most of Philistia laid waste, and with Sennacherib's forces already in the land, Hezekiah sensed the enormity of his impending doom. Overwhelmed by a sense of certain tragedy, he acted out of human propriety and sent a letter of submission to Sennacherib, indicating that he would agree to whatever terms of tribute Sennacherib would demand. In meeting Sennacherib's levy, Hezekiah went beyond the terms, emptying the coffers of both temple and palace and even stripping off the gold from the doors and door posts of the temple.

17–18 Hezekiah's generosity served only to whet Sennacherib's appetite. Doubtless he reasoned that these could only be a token payment; surely immense stores of wealth must lie hidden within the fortified walls of Jerusalem. Accordingly, as he continued operations in the Lachish area and laid plans for the capture of Ekron, Sennacherib sent a strong contingent under the direction of senior members of his staff to place Jerusalem under siege.

The Assyrian delegation came to the aqueduct of the Upper Pool, on the road to the Washerman's Field (cf. Isa 7:3). There they sent for Hezekiah, who, rather than appearing himself (probably considering it improper protocol to do so), sent three chief officials to deal with the three Assyrian delegates: Eliakim, son of Hilkiah, the palace administrator (cf. Isa 22:20–21); Shebna, the scribe; and Joash, son of Asaph, the king's herald.

The location of the meeting place of the two delegations has been much discussed. Similarly, the precise identification of the various pools mentioned in connection with the Assyrian menace (cf. 20:20; 2Ch 32:4, 30; Isa 22:9, 11; 36:2) and Hezekiah's plans for the defense of Jerusalem (2Ch 32:1–8; Isa 22:8–11) have been subjects of much controversy.

The available data seem to point to a northwest Jerusalem location for the meeting place, at a spot where the enemy might easily enjoy a commanding view of the city. If so, the Upper Pool of v.17 and the pool of 20:20 (cf. 2Ch 32:30; Isa 8:5–8) are to be differentiated. Certainly Hezekiah would have taken steps to ensure the security of both pools, as well as the cutting off of all the water sources available to Sennacherib's army (cf. 2Ch 32:3–4; Isa 22:9–12). Further evidence for differentiation between the pools comes from the scriptural indication that the Upper Pool was in existence before Hezekiah's siege preparations, being the scene of Isaiah's earlier meeting with Ahaz (Isa 7:3). What a contrast in circumstances this spot was witnessing! Here Isaiah had carried the encouraging message of the God of the universe to a godless king; now the emissaries of the great king of Assyria bore a distressing dispatch to the God-fearing Hezekiah.

19–25 The Assyrian message to Hezekiah was couched in terms of brilliant psychological warfare. Sennacherib's warning is given in two stages: in vv.19–22 he pointed out that Hezekiah's tactics and trust were ill conceived; in vv.23–25 he suggested that Hezekiah's supposed strengths were really weaknesses.

Thus Sennacherib cautioned Hezekiah that his military preparations and faith in Egypt's power to deliver Jerusalem were doomed to failure. Relying on Pharaoh, as a matter of fact, is like trusting one's weight to a splintered staff! Even Hezekiah's professed confidence in God was ill taken, since Hezekiah's iconoclastic purge had destroyed many opportunities of additional divine help. Surely the Judean king's insistence on worshiping only one God at one altar in Jerusalem was sheer bigotry!

Beginning with v.23 the Rab Shakeh ("field commander") reiterated the folly of Hezekiah's course of action. Did Hezekiah trust in military strength? What real strength did he have? Sennacherib had the resources to put two thousand horses at Jerusalem's disposal, but there would not be enough trained horsemen in Judah to ride them! The implication was that wars were won with chariotry, precisely the point where Hezekiah was lamentably weak. How, then, could Hezekiah have thought to repulse even the least of Sennacherib's officials? Any reliance on puny Egypt for chariots was nonsense. Further, as for Hezekiah's reputation

for trusting in the Lord for deliverance, this again was folly; for it was the Lord himself who had told Sennacherib to attack and destroy Judah!

26–27 The answer of Hezekiah's embassy was scarcely one of strength. Fearing the effect of the Assyrian official's words on the populace that lived on the wall, he requested that the field commander switch his speech to Aramaic. The Assyrian's haughty retort was that those on the wall had a stake in all this, as well as Hezekiah. After all, when the Assyrians really placed the city under heavy siege, the common Jerusalemites would take the brunt of the attack. So great would be the hunger and so scarce the provisions that Jerusalem's citizenry would be reduced to consuming their own bodily issues. They had a right to hear!

28–32 As the field commander continued his remarks, he shouted all the louder. He told the people that Hezekiah was not to be trusted. Hezekiah could not deliver them from the Assyrians, and the Lord would not do so. The Assyrian official lashed out at Hezekiah's previous words of encouragement and categorically denied their truthfulness (cf. 2Ch 32:7–8). Rather than believing their king, they should align themselves with the rising star of Sennacherib. They should conclude a peace treaty with "the great king"(v.28) by surrendering and coming out to him. Then they could enjoy the fine things of their own land in abundance. Furthermore, the Assyrian king would take them to a new and better life in another land, which he had especially set aside for them. Rather than the grim prospects that faced them, theirs could be a life of peace and plenty, of life and not death.

The field commander's words were carefully chosen and highly emotive. By their acquiescence to the Assyrian king's demands, the Judeans would thereby conclude an agreement with him that would effect blessed conditions for all concerned.

33–35 Having urged the people to reject Hezekiah's promises and choose those of Sennacherib, the field commander gave the people incentives for doing so by citing evidence of Sennacherib's victories. Hezekiah was only misleading them with his talk of deliverance by the Lord their God. None of the gods of the many leaders that had opposed Sennacherib had delivered his people. Could they expect more?

The Assyrian official viewed all gods alike. The proof of their capability was in their power to deliver their people. This they had not done, neither the gods of the Arameans nor those of Jerusalem's sister, Samaria. The implication was clear: The Lord, like the other gods, was unable to stop Sennacherib.

36–37 The field commander's words were not received in the way that he had hoped. Faithful to Hezekiah's instructions, his delegates remained stonily silent. They came back sadly to the king, however, and told him of the enemy's words.

3. The continued siege of Jerusalem (19:1–13)

1–2 When Hezekiah heard the report of his delegation, he was filled with grief. Tearing his clothes and donning sackcloth (traditional symbols of mourning), he went with heavy heart to the temple to pour out his soul before God. God's very name and reputation were at stake in this time of national crisis! Desiring to do all that was within his power to know God's will, he sent Eliakim, Shebna, and the leading priests, all dressed in sackcloth, to meet with Isaiah so that he might hear God's word through his prophet (cf. Dt 18:18).

3 In briefing Isaiah as to the present emergency, the king's delegation also explained Hezekiah's deep concern in the matter. This was a day of "distress" (GK 7650). This word connotes not only the idea of trouble because of the Assyrian menace, but the anguish of heart that every true Israelite must have felt. Furthermore, it was a day of "rebuke" (GK 9349) or correction; Hezekiah sensed that the Lord was even now chastising his people (Hos 5:9–15). As well, it was a day of "disgrace" (GK 5541) or contempt; perhaps God was even now about to reject and cast off his people completely (cf. Dt 32:18–43; Jer 14:12; La 2:6).

4 It is to Hezekiah's credit that he realized the deeper spiritual issues involved in the crisis. It was not enough to bring the stated services and religious practices up to standard; God must be a living reality in every believer's life.

Despite his zeal for holiness, perhaps he had erred in the way that he, as king, had led the people in the realm of international politics. Had he perpetuated the policies of Ahaz in depending on his own wisdom and the strength of others in dealing with national affairs rather than depending on God? Far greater than the danger of the Assyrian at the walls was divine displeasure.

Hezekiah realized that God was the living God, in contradistinction to any of the so-called gods that the field commander had mentioned. Moreover, Hezekiah knew that God was jealous for his own name and would intervene on behalf of a people whose heart was right toward him. Further, he was "your God"; that is, Isaiah was his personal spokesman. Hezekiah therefore urged Isaiah to join him in prayer for the remnant of God's people.

5–7 Hezekiah's trust in God and confidence in Isaiah were not misplaced. Isaiah indeed did have a message for the repentant Hezekiah. He was not to fear the blasphemous words of Sennacherib's underlings—nor of Sennacherib himself. Indeed, "the great king," rather than adding Jerusalem to his list of conquests, would himself be given a spirit of fearfulness, so that when distressing news came to him out of Assyria, he would give up the siege and head for home immediately. Once there he would be killed. God assured Hezekiah that he was in control of the entire situation, superintending the details in accordance with his purposes.

God did not disclose to Hezekiah how all this would come about. It was enough for him to know and to believe that God would deal with the Assyrian threat. Thus Hezekiah's faith could mature as he continued to pray and wait for God to effect his plan. What a wondrous experience awaits those who trust in God completely!

While the Scriptures do not say so, Hezekiah obviously returned a negative reply to Sennacherib's demands. Accordingly the field commander set out to deliver Hezekiah's refusal to his master.

8–9 Learning that Sennacherib had moved on to join his siege forces at Libnah, the field commander joined him there with his report. The reason for Sennacherib's removal follows in v.9: it had been reported to him that the Egyptian army under Tirhakah was even

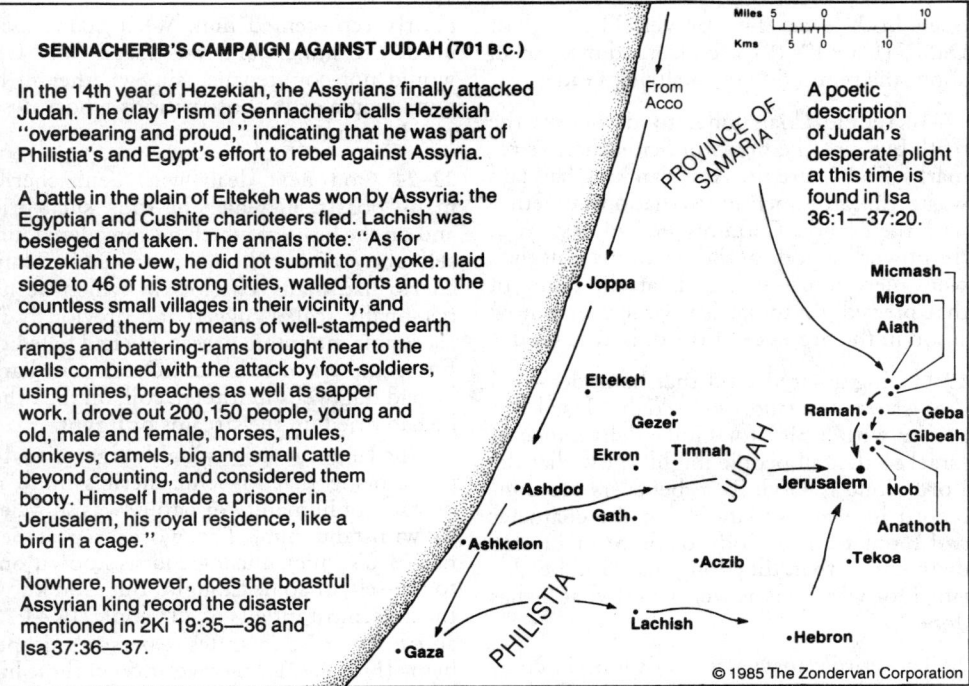

SENNACHERIB'S CAMPAIGN AGAINST JUDAH (701 B.C.)

In the 14th year of Hezekiah, the Assyrians finally attacked Judah. The clay Prism of Sennacherib calls Hezekiah "overbearing and proud," indicating that he was part of Philistia's and Egypt's effort to rebel against Assyria.

A battle in the plain of Eltekeh was won by Assyria; the Egyptian and Cushite charioteers fled. Lachish was besieged and taken. The annals note: "As for Hezekiah the Jew, he did not submit to my yoke. I laid siege to 46 of his strong cities, walled forts and to the countless small villages in their vicinity, and conquered them by means of well-stamped earth ramps and battering-rams brought near to the walls combined with the attack by foot-soldiers, using mines, breaches as well as sapper work. I drove out 200,150 people, young and old, male and female, horses, mules, donkeys, camels, big and small cattle beyond counting, and considered them booty. Himself I made a prisoner in Jerusalem, his royal residence, like a bird in a cage."

Nowhere, however, does the boastful Assyrian king record the disaster mentioned in 2Ki 19:35—36 and Isa 37:36—37.

A poetic description of Judah's desperate plight at this time is found in Isa 36:1—37:20.

© 1985 The Zondervan Corporation

now advancing through the Philistine coast to aid the Philistine city of Ekron. Apparently by-passing Ekron, the Assyrian king was able to bring his forces safely to El Tekeh, where he met and defeated the Egyptian troops. After the victory at El Tekeh, Sennacherib turned back inland to capture Timnah and then Ekron itself.

While Sennacherib was thus engaged in fighting, he sent a siege contingent to Jerusalem so that Hezekiah could not attack from the rear. He also sent his field commander back to Jerusalem with a message for Hezekiah designed to continue the psychological warfare.

10–13 Understanding clearly that Hezekiah's previous reply indicated a firm belief that the Lord would deliver Jerusalem and his people from the Assyrian king, Sennacherib concentrated his message on the absurdity of such a belief. Hezekiah certainly knew that Assyria had destroyed all those countries that had opposed him, and none of their gods had been able to deliver them. To make Hezekiah take even more notice and fear, he added that the kings of those countries had paid the price of oblivion. Hezekiah had better take care!

4. The deliverance of Jerusalem (19:14–37)

14–15 Sennacherib's letter was duly delivered and reached Hezekiah's hands. When he had read it, he took it along with him to the temple and spread it out before the Lord. Hezekiah's action was one of simple faith that God still planned to intervene even as he had promised. As a child bringing his broken toy to his father for repair, so Hezekiah laid the issues in God's sight for resolution. Hezekiah then poured out his soul's concern to his heavenly Father. He addressed God as the personal God of Israel who was his possession and the One who in infinite mercy meets with his people from his dwelling place between the cherubim above the ark of the covenant. While he is Israel's God, he is also the only true God who sovereignly controls the destinies of all nations. He is nothing less than the Creator—and Consummator—of all things.

16 Hezekiah next pleaded with God to take notice of the way Sennacherib had blasphemed him. The figures are full of intensity. A person who wishes to hear more distinctly turns one ear toward the source of the sound. Those who desire to see more clearly must open both eyes. The prayer, like that of Daniel (Da 9:17–19), is concerned most of all about the reputation of the living God.

17–18 Yet Hezekiah understood not only the truth but also the limits of Sennacherib's remarks. To be sure the Assyrian king had laid waste the aforementioned nations together with their lands. Certainly he had destroyed the powerless gods of those nations. But they were mere idols—not gods at all! None of that proved anything, for Sennacherib now stood in the presence of the only true God.

19 Having assured God that he understood the issues at hand, Hezekiah closed his prayer with a plea for God's deliverance of Israel so that all people might know that the Lord alone is God. True believers are concerned in every situation that the character and reputation of God not be brought into disrepute; rather, they long that God be glorified for who he is as well as for what he has done.

20 The Lord's answer was not long in coming. Isaiah sent a message from God to Hezekiah, assuring him that his prayer had been heard. The major portion of that message is composed within a threefold poetic utterance: (1) for Sennacherib there is a reply to his misguided boasting (vv.21–28); (2) for Hezekiah God gives a sign that he would deal with Sennacherib and deliver his people (vv.29–31); and (3) for all there is a prophetic declaration that Sennacherib would not even begin the battle of Jerusalem, let alone conquer it (vv.32–34).

21 The first of the utterances is given in the ancient taunt-song form, designed so as to humiliate Sennacherib by casting his own words in his teeth, thus showing him how ridiculous they sounded. Did Sennacherib despise and degrade all nations and their worship? Jerusalem, in turn, would disdain him, tossing her head at him as he fled in cowardice. The term "virgin" (GK 1435) emphasizes that Jerusalem would not be violated by Sennacherib. By the use of a rhetorical question, God pointed out that Sennacherib had not wisely considered his course of action. His pride and arrogance had caused him to insult the Holy One of Israel. God's own holiness had been manifested clearly through his chosen people Israel, however much they may have failed him or

poorly represented him. What Sennacherib needed to understand was that a holy God would not countenance sin, whether in his own people or in those nations whose destinies he controls.

22–24 God next dealt with Sennacherib's many boasts, in which he took such pride and on the basis of which he considered himself above other humans or God. Sennacherib had many chariots in which he had personally scaled rugged and previously inaccessible mountain passes. He had felled the finest timbers of Lebanon. On the one hand, he had dug wells in foreign soil; on the other, he had dried up the streams of Egypt.

The language here is highly figurative, the point being that in Sennacherib's mind no obstacle of humanity or nature was sufficient to withstand him. The words repeat Sennacherib's inner musings, ideas known only to himself, or so he thought. But God knows the innermost intents of all people (Ps 44:21), and his word penetrates a person's deepest being (Heb 4:12). The revelation of these hidden desires ought to have struck terror into Sennacherib's heart, convincing him that the Lord was truly God.

25–26 God then confronted Sennacherib with that which he had apparently not considered: Sennacherib's successes were foreordained by God. Moreover God's purposes had not been done in secret; he had proclaimed them through his prophets of all ages and even then was bringing them to pass. The result had been that Sennacherib had been able to wreak havoc on people who were totally powerless and as helpless as tender herbage and plants before the blasts of the sirocco. No, Sennacherib should not boast as though what he had done was either self-generated or self-accomplished. It was God's divine government that was at work; Sennacherib was but God's instrument of correction for Israel and the nations.

27–28 Having revealed to Sennacherib that he knew his innermost thoughts and desires and that in his sovereign administration of the flow of history he had ordained Sennacherib's past successes, God then informed Sennacherib that he was aware of his every action, including his blasphemous insolence. Sennacherib had enjoyed God-given success; now he would learn of defeat. He would be subdued like an animal and return to his own land.

29–31 God next turned to Hezekiah with a reassuring sign. God had similarly offered Hezekiah's father, Ahaz, a sign (Isa 7:11), which, when refused, was given to the people. The sign would be one of extreme importance to besieged Jerusalem. In what remained of the present year, there would be food enough from that which had been spilled accidentally in the sowing and had sprung up by itself as an aftergrowth. Since military campaigns were regularly planned to coincide with the harvest so that the armies might live off the land, and since Israel's year began in early fall, there would be little left of "this year." Accordingly, as the new year dawned, due to the extent of the devastation, they would again largely depend on grain that came up of its own accord in random fashion.

For the third year, however, there was a direct divine command: "Sow and reap, plant vineyards and eat fruit." Here was direct assurance that the people might resume normal agricultural activities with full expectation of eating the fruits of their labor. When in the harvest of the third year the people ate in abundance, they would know assuredly that God had been in the entire crisis. He had allowed the Assyrians to chastise his people for their own good. But because of Judah's godly leadership, he had delivered them, as a testimony both to the godless Sennacherib and to his spiritually slack nation. From this they should learn their lesson that God was dealing with a backsliding people. The experience should serve as a further sign of that future remnant that the Messiah will deliver at his coming.

32–34 God closed his utterance with a final message to the Assyrian king. Sennacherib would not only not enter Jerusalem but would not even lay a full-scale siege against it. No arrow would fall into the city; neither shield nor siege ramp would appear before it. Quite the contrary, Sennacherib would turn around and go home; for God himself was defending and would deliver Jerusalem, not only for his own name's sake (vv.4, 19), but on the basis of his standing promise to David (cf. 2Sa 7; 1Ki 11:13, 34–39; 2Ki 8:19).

That Sennacherib failed in his attempt to take Jerusalem is apparent from the annals of his third campaign. Although he claimed the capture and despoiling of some forty-six Judean cities, when it came to Jerusalem, he could only report that he had made Hezekiah a prisoner in his palace in Jerusalem. The only validity to Sennacherib's face-saving claim can be seen when he surrounded Jerusalem during his protracted campaigning in Judah and Philistia.

35–36 That very night the prophetic utterance was fulfilled. As the Assyrian army slept, the angel of the Lord slew 185,000 of the soldiers. When Sennacherib and those who survived arose the next morning, they were greeted by a veritable graveyard. All around them lay bodies, dead bodies! Having already just received alarming news from home (cf. v.7) and with his army now decisively depleted, Sennacherib broke camp and returned to Nineveh. Though he would yet fight another five campaigns, he would never again return to Judah. The Israelites' God was the living God!

37 Some twenty years later (681 B.C.), two of Sennacherib's own sons assassinated him and successfully escaped to Urartu. Another son, Esarhaddon (681–668), succeeded Sennacherib as king. The last vestige of the divine prophecy stood complete. While God's program may seem to tarry (cf. 2Pe 3:4–9), it will be accomplished.

5. Hezekiah's miraculous recovery (20:1–11)

1 Taken at face value, the opening phrase—"in those days"—seems to place the events of this chapter near the time of Sennacherib's invasion in 701 B.C. In the light of chronological difficulties, it seems best to take the phrase to be a general statement referring to some time in the reign of Hezekiah. Thus the events of ch. 20 (cf. Isa 38–39) probably belong chronologically before those of 18:7b–19:37, these latter verses being recorded beforehand simply as the example par excellence of Hezekiah's trust in God (cf. 18:7a). If Isaiah's prophecy in chs. 36–39 forms the basis for the text in Kings, and if the events of Isa 36–37 (cf. 2Ki 18:7b–19:37), though occurring later, are given first to round off his discussion dealing with the Assyrian period of his ministry before moving on to the Babylonian period (Isa 40–66), then the author of Kings may be following the thematic order of Isaiah.

In those critical days, then, when Sargon was moving toward Ashdod to deal with the western rebels (among whom Hezekiah himself had been somewhat implicated), Isaiah delivered God's message to a sick Hezekiah. It was time for Hezekiah to put his house in order; for as things stood, he would surely die. Hezekiah needed to be certain that not only were the affairs of state in order, but that he and his house were on proper terms with God.

2–3 Hezekiah was a man of faith. Turning his face to the wall, thereby both dismissing Isaiah and entering into solitary communion with God, Hezekiah poured out his heart to his Lord. Hezekiah reminded God of his faithfulness, both in his personal conduct and in his righteous deeds, and of his wholehearted devotion to God. Hezekiah then wept bitterly. In accordance with God's own promises, Hezekiah had a right to expect a longer life (cf. Ex 20:12; Dt 5:29; 30:16). But Hezekiah's concerns were deeper than any personal desire for added years. What would become of that nation? His reforms were barely yet in progress. What would become of Judah? There was so much more to be done. Deeper still, he would die without a male heir, for no son had yet been born to him. What, then, would become of the house of David? The program and person of God were at stake, and Hezekiah believed that somehow he was vitally involved in them. How could it end like this?

4–6 Isaiah had not yet cleared the palace when God sent him back with a message for Hezekiah: the Lord God of his father David had heard Hezekiah's righteous prayer and justifiable concern and had seen his tears. Therefore God would heal him and give him fifteen additional years of service. Moreover, for his own name's sake and because of the promise made to David, God would deliver Jerusalem throughout Hezekiah's lifetime. The mention of Hezekiah's going into the temple on the third day is both a recognition of his godly habit of life and a reminder of his obligations to render thanks to the Lord for his healing.

7 Not only did Isaiah have spiritual news and instructions for Hezekiah, he also had direc-tions for the king's physical recovery. In accordance with those orders, a poultice of figs was mixed and applied to Hezekiah's ulcerated sore, and he recovered. Although God chose to work through the accepted medical standards of the day, it is certain that ultimately the healing was effected by the divine word.

8–11 Hezekiah asked for a confirmatory sign that what Isaiah had said was true (cf. Isa 7:12). Isaiah asked Hezekiah whether the sun's shadow should go forward or return ten places. Hezekiah reasoned that going backward would be the greater sign, since that would contradict the natural processes. In accordance with Hezekiah's choice, Isaiah prayed to the Lord, and so it came to pass. By whatever means the deed was accomplished, it was a miracle effected by the sovereign power of God alone and intended to be a sign to Hezekiah that he would recover and serve his Redeemer yet another fifteen years. What a comfort this knowledge ought to have been to Hezekiah throughout his remaining years! Yet the author of Chronicles records that Hezekiah did not fully respond to God's kindness toward him. Rather, he became proud so that God's wrath came on him and his people, a judgment that was averted only when Hezekiah humbled himself and repented (2Ch 32:25–26; cf. 2Ki 18–19).

6. Hezekiah and Merodach-Baladan (20:12–21)

12 During his newly acquired years, God soon allowed Hezekiah's intentions to be put to the test (cf. 2Ch 32:31). The Babylonian king, Merodach-Baladan, hearing of Hezekiah's miraculous recovery together with the supernatural sign, sent an embassy to Hezekiah, ostensibly to deliver a message of congratulations and a gift to him. The checkered career of Merodach-Baladan, however, makes it clear that his motives were politically engendered, hoping to find in Hezekiah a new ally in his struggles against Assyria.

13 Hezekiah received the messengers warmly. Doubtless he told them the whole story of his healing and the remarkable incident of the retreating of the sun's shadow. But he went beyond this. To impress his guests still further, he showed them the vast store of riches contained in the palace complex.

14–18 When the Babylonian embassy had left, Isaiah immediately confronted Hezekiah, who was still dazzled by the fact that he could have been so well known in distant Babylon. He freely told Isaiah all that had transpired. Rather than earning the prophet's commendation, Hezekiah drew his condemnation. Hezekiah had been foolish. Not only would the extent of Jerusalem's wealth now be known and desired by all (cf. Sennacherib's demands in 18:13–16), but one day this same Babylon would invade the land and carry off its populace and all its treasures. Yes, even Hezekiah's own descendants would be taken captive and employed in the service of a Babylonian king (cf. 24:12–16; 2Ch 33:11; Da 1:3–5). Quite out of keeping with his righteous character, Hezekiah's folly would prove to be a contributing factor in the fulfillment of the ancient prophecies (Lev 26:33; Dt 28:64–67; 30:3). Hezekiah's experience remains a stern warning to all the perils of pride (cf. Pr 16:5, 18; 28:25–26; 29:23). At the same time, Hezekiah did receive one assurance through Isaiah's words: he would have a son to succeed him.

19 Hezekiah responded with humility and genuine godliness, acknowledging the propriety of Isaiah's God-given message. Hezekiah's last words contain a touch of pathos. While he was thankful that God would keep his promise not to surrender Judah and Jerusalem in his day (cf. v.6), yet he realized that his own actions had put his nation and his posterity in danger.

20 The chapter closes with a notice of Hezekiah's many achievements. The extent of his success is enlarged on by the author of Chronicles, from whom we also learn that the water conduit mentioned here dealt with the waters of Gihon (2Ch 32:27–31). These waters were directed within Jerusalem's walls via a specially constructed tunnel leading to a reservoir, known as the Pool of Siloam. The completion of this 1,777-foot tunnel made the waters of Gihon inaccessible to an enemy but were readily available to a besieged population.

21 Thus passed the king who was unsurpassed in his trust of the Lord (cf. 18:5). He was buried with full honors by the citizenry of Jerusalem in the upper section of the tombs of the sons of David (2Ch 32:33).

B. The Reign of Manasseh (21:1–18)

1–6 Manasseh came to the throne of Judah at the age of twelve, reigning for some fifty-five years (698/697–642 B.C.), the longest reign in Judah's history. Born soon after the crisis with Sargon, Manasseh must have seen God's great deliverance at Jerusalem. Nevertheless, with his father's death, he soon plunged into every manner of spiritual wickedness. The high places Hezekiah had destroyed were rebuilt, the Canaanite religious practices relative to Baal and Asherah were reintroduced, and he established and participated in a state astral cult. So far did his spiritual prostitution take him that Manasseh introduced pagan altars in both the outer and the priest's courts and even in the temple itself. Ultimately the hated Asherah pole was placed in the temple, the very abode of the sacred name. Moreover, he went so far as to involve his own son in the loathsome and detestable rites of infant sacrifice; he practiced sorcery and divination and consulted purveyors of demonic activity.

7–9 Manasseh's great evil provoked the Lord to anger; placing the Asherah pole within the temple was especially offensive. God had promised to dwell in peace among his people forever (cf. 2Sa 7:13; 1Ki 8:16; 9:3), if they would but serve him in righteousness (cf. 2Sa 7:10; 1Ki 9:6–9). But the people indulged themselves with the lustful Manasseh rather than harken to their Redeemer. Accordingly, Manasseh's Judah exceeded in spiritual degradation the original Canaanites whom God had driven out before Israel (cf. Am 2:9–10). What a tragedy! How superficial had been the nation's compliance with Hezekiah's reforms! Without a strong spiritual leader, the sinful people quickly turned to their own evil machinations. The judgment of God could not be far away.

10–11 Throughout Manasseh's wicked reign God warned of the grave consequences of the king's sin, sending repeated warnings to his prophets. Yet neither king nor people paid any attention to God's denunciations (cf. 2Ch 33:10).

12–13 God therefore set in motion those forces that would bring destruction on Jerusalem and Judah (cf. Jer 15:1–4). In rehearsing the coming judgment, God used three well-known literary figures: (1) the tingling ears, (2) the measuring and plumb lines, and

(3) the dish wiped clean. By the first he emphasized the severity of the judgment: it would be of such untold dimension that it would strike terror into the hearts of all who heard of its execution (cf. 1Sa 3:11; Jer 19:3–9). By the second God used a figure often associated with building (cf. Zec 1:16) but employed also of the measuring of destruction (Isa 34:11; Am 7:7–9). Just as God had taken the measure of Samaria so as to destroy it, so Jerusalem would fall. Even as the Lord had plumbed the house of Ahab in order to exterminate it, so the people of Jerusalem would be executed. By the third literary figure, the complete destruction of Jerusalem was emphasized. As one wipes a dish clean, turning it over so that no drop of water is left, so Jerusalem's destruction would be total. None would remain.

14–16 Because Israel had forsaken God and provoked him to wrath time without end since he had redeemed them from Egypt, he would forsake wicked Judah, the last vestige of his inheritance. He would give them over for a prey to be looted and plundered (cf. Dt 28:49–68; Isa 42:22; Jer 30:16; Hab 1:5–11). The wicked reign of Manasseh had become the capstone of the wall of sin that Israel had built between herself and God. God now hadtaken its measure and marked Judah for destruction.

17–18 The writer of Kings brings Manasseh's history to a close by indicating further source material for the details of his infamous life and by noting that at his death he was buried in his private garden called "The Garden of Uzza." The picture thus presented by our author is bleak, portraying the dominant themes of the vast majority of Manasseh's long reign. This critical evaluation is a proper one. Manasseh's personal example and leadership in sin were to have a permanent effect, bringing on Judah's demise despite the temporary reforms of Josiah.

The author of Chronicles records that the Lord humbled Manasseh by allowing him to fall into the hands of the king of Assyria, an event that brought about Manasseh's repentance and a short period of religious reformation (2Ch 33:11–17). Although the time of Manasseh's capture, release, and repentance is nowhere indicated in 2 Kings, the fact that this record presents such a uniform description of Manasseh's bad character suggests

that this experience must have occurred late in his reign.

The widespread revolts during the reign of Ashurbanipal, which occurred from 652–648 B.C., may have provided the occasion for Manasseh's summons to Babylon and imprisonment. If so, his subsequent release and reform were apparently far too late to have much of an effect on the obdurately backslidden populace.

C. The Reign of Amon (21:19–26)

19–22 The short reign of Amon was a replay of the earlier period of his father, Manasseh. The author of Kings notes simply that he was as evil as his father and so perpetuated all of Manasseh's earlier idolatry. The author of Chronicles (2Ch 33:21–23) adds that Amon failed to humble himself but rather "increased his guilt."

23–26 In 640 B.C., the wicked Amon was assassinated by his own officials who, in turn, were executed by the populace. Amon's son Josiah was established as the next king. Although the Scriptures give no reason for the conspiracy, its cause may lie within the tangled web of revolts that Ashurbanipal suppressed from 642–639 and that caused him to turn his attention to the west. Certainly his menacing advance took him as far as Phoenicia. At this time, too, he may have resettled newly deported elements in Samaria (cf. Ezr 4:9–10). Amon's death may thus reflect a power struggle between those who wished to remain loyal to the Assyrian crown and those who aspired to link Judah's fortunes to the rising star of Psammetik I (664–609) of Egypt's Twenty-Sixth Dynasty. At any rate, in 640 B.C. Amon's body was interred in the Garden of Uzza; and his eight-year-old son, Josiah, acceded to the Judean throne.

D. The Reign of Josiah (22:1–23:30)

1. Ascension and early reforms (22:1–7)

1–2 A mere lad of eight years of age when he came to the throne, Josiah probably owed much of his spiritual concern to his mother, Jedidah, and probably to the guidance of pious men in prominent positions. He quickly demonstrated himself to be one who followed his ancestor David in godliness, walking circumspectly before God and other people.

3–7 The author of Kings quickly moves to the most outstanding example of Josiah's godly fidelity: his repair of the temple in his eighteenth year (622 B.C.). According to 2Ch 34:3–7, however, this example of piety was preceded by a time of definite committal to the Lord at the age of sixteen and, beginning some four years later, by a thorough iconoclastic purge in which he not only attacked the idolatry of Judah but eventually took it on himself to extend his efforts to Israel. Accordingly, Josiah's action here in his eighteenth year was quite in keeping with his true spiritual character.

At this time Josiah sent his secretary Shaphan to Hilkiah the high priest with a royal command to utilize the freewill offerings of the people for the appropriation of supplies and the paying of the laborers so as to begin the repair of the temple.

2. The Book of the Law (22:8–13)

8–10 When the royal commission arrived, Hilkiah also had news for them: he had found a copy of the Book of the Law. Although scholars have often argued as to the contents of that manuscript, the king's later reaction when he heard the law read and the subsequent further reforms (23:4–20) and religious observances (2Ch 35:1–19) indicate that it included at least key portions, if not the whole, of Deuteronomy (e.g., Dt 28–30).

The royal commission stayed long enough to be assured that the king's wishes had been carried out (2Ch 34:10–13), during which time Shaphan had an opportunity to examine the new scroll. When the commission returned, Shaphan reported to the king. His orders had been carried out and the work begun. He also told the king about the exciting new discovery that he had brought back with him and proceeded to read selected portions of it to the king.

11–13 The king's reaction at the reading of the law was one of immediate contrition, as expressed in the sign of lamentation and grief—the tearing of his robes. The basis of his grief was twofold: Judah's guilt and her coming judgment. The nation had sinned grievously in breaking God's covenant in both its idolatry and its social injustices; therefore, in accordance with the terms of that violated covenant, judgment must come. With repentant and sorrowful heart, Josiah

sent a commission made up of trusted officials and the high priest Hilkiah to the prophetess Huldah, who lived in the second district of Jerusalem (cf. Zep 1:10), to inquire as to the Lord's present intention regarding Judah.

3. The advice of Huldah (22:14–20)

14–20 Huldah faithfully rendered the Lord's message for the people and Josiah. Because Judah had persisted in its idolatry and wickedness, the sentence of judgment recorded in God's Word, which the king had just heard, would surely come to pass. As for the king himself, because he had responded to God's Word and humbled himself, and because he had grieved over Judah's sinful conditions, he would be spared the anguish of seeing God's devastating judgment carried out.

At first sight the promise seems to be at variance with the fact that Josiah died in battle (23:29–30). However, though the words in v.20 might be construed as indicating peaceful death, such need not be the case. The phrase "be gathered to one's fathers" simply points to the fact that people die and are buried, not to the manner of their death. The point here is that Josiah would die at peace with God before his awful sentence would descend on the nation.

4. Further reforms (23:1–23)

1–3 On receiving Huldah's answer, the king convened his elders for consultation. As a result of that meeting, all levels of Judean society were called together in public assembly so that they might hear a reading from the newly found scroll. When that had been accomplished, the king led his people in a ceremony of covenant renewal wherein they pledged themselves to follow the Lord and his commands unswervingly. Like Moses and Joshua of old, Josiah took his place as a virtual mediator of the covenant between his people and their sovereign Lord.

4–7 The covenant renewal was followed by renewed religious reforms. In accordance with the royal command, the priests conducted a thorough search of the temple to remove anything that spoke of heathen worship. In accordance with the scriptural standards, the pagan cult articles were taken outside Jerusalem to the Kidron Valley and burned—their ashes being subsequently taken to Bethel, where paganism first had its official sanction in Israel. In taking the detested pagan abominations to the Kidron, Josiah followed the lead of the earlier royal reformers Asa (1Ki 15:13) and Hezekiah (2Ch 29:16; 30:14). The removal of the ashes to Bethel constituted a public denunciation of the place.

8–9 Josiah also recalled all the Levitical priests from their duties at the various high places throughout Judah. While those priests were admitted to the fellowship, their previous service had rendered them ineligible to officiate in the temple services; hence they were put on a status with those priests who had bodily defects (Lev 21:17–23). The high places were then desecrated so that those spurious centers of worship might no longer be maintained. Likewise, the altar at the high place that was situated at one of Jerusalem's own gates was torn down.

10–12 Josiah's reforms were thoroughgoing. Topheth, the sacred precinct in the Valley of Hinnom, sacred to the Molech rites, was desecrated. The horses dedicated to the sun, which were quartered at the very entrance to the temple, were disposed of and their chariots burned. His reforms likewise turned to the altars used in astral worship, located on the roof of the upper room built by Ahaz. These doubtless had been restored by Manasseh and Amon, along with the construction of the pagan altars (cf. 21:5). The pulverized debris from these objects was cast into the Kidron Valley.

13–18 Even those cult places that had enjoyed a long existence, having escaped the thoroughgoing reforms of Hezekiah, were now dismantled and desecrated. The pagan altars near Jerusalem had been built by Solomon himself. The altar at Bethel, which Josiah's reform also reached, had been established by Jeroboam at Solomon's death; but in the course of time a purely Canaanite worship had apparently replaced the earlier worship of the golden calf. In the former cases Josiah defiled those cult places by filling them with human bones (cf. Nu 19:16). In the latter instance, not content with destroying the high place and burning the Asherah pole, he exhumed the human bones from the graves situated on the mountain and burned them on the altar, thus defiling it forever. This action fulfilled the words of the unknown prophet of Judah of old (1Ki 13:26–32). The remains of that prophet, along with those of the misguided prophet of Bethel (1Ki 13:11ff.), however, were left undisturbed.

19–20 Indeed, not only Bethel, but all the high places of the former northern kingdom were to feel the wrath of Josiah's purge. The various high places were destroyed and the priests of those illicit rites were slaughtered on their altars, which were further desecrated by the burning of human bones on them (cf. 2Ch 34:6–7).

21–23 Josiah's attitude toward spiritual reform was not purely negative. He also gave instructions that the Passover be held as soon as it could be done in strict accordance with the law. Accordingly, in the eighteenth year of his reign, the Passover was celebrated in Jerusalem, the likes of which had not been seen since the days of Samuel. Not only was it observed as the law prescribed (2Ch 35:1–19), but it was celebrated by all Judah and Israel (2Ch 35:18).

5. Latter days (23:24–30)

24–25 The author of Kings approaches the end of Josiah's just reign. The thought of Josiah's strict piety in keeping the laws of the Passover leads to the further observation that he was ever consistent in his application of the law. As Josiah had meticulously fulfilled the requirements of the law relative to Israel's ceremonial worship with his many reforms, his repair of the temple, and his reinstituting of the Passover, so had he put away the evils of false personal religion. This included both those who dealt in spiritism and all sorts of objects of detestable idolatry. In summary it could be said of Josiah that none of the kings of Israel and Judah was his equal in zeal for the law. As Hezekiah had been unequaled in faith among the kings (18:5), so Josiah knew no rival in uncompromising adherence to the Law of Moses.

26–28 The account of Josiah's godly life ends on a note of sadness. Despite all that he had done to remove Judah's idolatry, Manasseh's gross spiritual wickedness had had a permanent effect. Although Judah's outward worship experience had been set in order, the people's confession had been a mere externality. With the passing of Josiah, the internal condition of their obdurately apostate heart quickly surfaced (cf. Jer 5). Accordingly, God's just wrath would yet reach his sinful people. If the prophets and righteous Josiah had not been able to turn the people from their wicked ways, only God's judgment could have the desired effect.

29–30 Josiah's death at Megiddo can be attributed to his part in the complex international events of the last quarter of the seventh century B.C. With the death of Ashurbanipal in 626, the already decaying Neo-Assyrian Empire began to crumble quickly away. By 625 the Chaldean king Nabopolassar had been able to achieve independence for Babylon. From that point onward throughout the course of the next two decades, the Assyrian territory was systematically reduced, especially as Nabopolassar found common cause against Assyria. In 614 the time-honored capital of Assyria, Asshur, fell to the Medes. In 612 Nineveh itself fell to the coalition of Chaldeans, Medes, and Ummanmande, the surviving Assyrian forces under Ashur-u-ballit fleeing to Haran.

In those critical times concerned with the rising power of the new Mesopotamian coalition, Egypt's Twenty-Sixth Dynasty Pharaoh, Neco, honored the previous diplomatic ties with Assyria. As Neco's predecessor, Psammetik I, had come to the aid of Assyria in 616 B.C., so Neco moved to join the surviving Assyrian forces under Ashur-u-ballit. It was to prevent this movement of Egyptian aid that Josiah deployed his forces in the Valley of Megiddo in 609. That action cost Josiah his life, though it did delay the Egyptian forces from linking with their Assyrian allies before Haran fell to the Chaldeans and Medes. A subsequent attempt to retake Haran failed completely; and the best Egypt could give the doomed Assyrians was a four-year standoff, the opposing armies facing each other at Carchemish, on the western Euphrates.

The Chronicler (2Ch 35:20–25) reports that Josiah had refused Neco's attempts to avoid the affair at Megiddo and rather, having disguised himself, had personally fought against the Egyptians until he was mortally wounded. At that point Josiah was rushed back to Jerusalem where he was buried in his own tomb. Quite understandably he was lamented by all the people, including the

prophet Jeremiah. Thus passed one of God's choicest saints and one of Judah's finest kings. Josiah's determined action had brought about his tragic death, but he was thereby spared the greater tragedy of seeing the ultimate death of his nation a scant twenty-three years later.

E. The Last Days of Judah (23:31–25:21)

1. The reign of Jehoahaz (23:31–33)

31 At the death of the courageous and pious Josiah, the people of the land selected his third surviving son, Shallum, who took the throne name Jehoahaz (cf. 1Ch 3:15 with Jer 22:11–12), to be the next king. The selection of Jehoahaz is beset with problems. According to 1Ch 3:15, Johanan, not Jehoahaz (or Shallum), was Josiah's eldest son. Because nothing further is known of Johanan, he had probably died much earlier. Jehoiakim, the next eldest son, was passed over, the kingship being conferred on Jehoahaz, who was two years younger (cf. v.36).

Just why Jehoahaz was selected instead of Jehoiakim is not certain, though the reason may lie in the fact that they had different mothers, Jehoahaz being Josiah's son by Hamutal, whereas Jehoiakim's mother was Zebudah. Perhaps Hamutal enjoyed a favored status.

32–33 Jehoahaz was no Josiah, however; nor, indeed, was any of his sons. His deposition was swift in coming. Within three months Pharaoh Neco summoned Jehoahaz to meet him in Riblah of Syria, his base of operations and staging area for the Assyrian campaigns.

2. The reign of Jehoiakim (23:34–24:7)

34–37 At Riblah, Neco replaced Jehoahaz with Eliakim, Josiah's second son, giving him the throne name Jehoiakim (cf. 2Ch 36:4). Neco then took Jehoahaz as a captive to Egypt, where he remained until his death (cf. Jer 22:10–12; Eze 19:1–4). Neco imposed a severe tribute on the new Judean king, a sum Jehoiakim raised by levying a heavy taxation on the citizenry. Judah had appeased her new overlord, and she had a new king. A far cry from his godly father, Jehoiakim was to lead Judah into still deeper trouble spiritually and politically.

Jehoiakim's rule was like that of the wicked kings who preceded Josiah. Jeremiah represents him as a monster who despoiled his own people (Jer 22:13–14); opposed the Lord's servants (Jer 26:20–23; 36:21–23); filled the land with violence, apostasy, and degradation (Jer 18:18–20; cf. 11:19); and led his people into open apostasy and degradation (Jer 8:4–12, 18–9:16; 10:1–9; 11:1–17; et al.).

24:1 Jehoiakim and Judah were soon to change masters. After the final defeat of the combined Assyrian and Egyptian forces at Carchemish, Nebuchadnezzar overtook the remaining Egyptian forces at Hamath. Those Egyptian troops that managed to escape fled to Egypt (cf. Jer 46:2ff.). Nebuchadnezzar boasted that he thus took "the whole land of Hatti" (i.e., Syro-Palestine); so doubtless our text is correct in reading that Judah and Jehoiakim became his vassal. This is further corroborated in Nebuchadnezzar's own chronicles when, after reporting his succession to the kingship in 605 B.C., he recorded for the following year the submission and tribute of "all the kings of Hatti."

Although Jehoiakim served Nebuchadnezzar for the next three years, he apparently awaited an opportunity to throw off the Babylonian yoke. When in 601 Neco turned back Nebuchadnezzar's forces at the Egyptian border, Jehoiakim assumed that his moment had arrived and so rebelled. Once again Judah would lean on the broken reed of Egypt.

2–7 War had cost both the Chaldeans (Babylonians) and the Egyptians so dearly that Nebuchadnezzar was unable to mobilize the troops and equipment to deal with impudent Judah, now newly allied to his Egyptian adversary, Neco. Accordingly, Nebuchadnezzar spent the next few years in rebuilding his armed might in anticipation of the time when he could deal with the insurgents. Meanwhile he moved against the Arameans and Arabians, thus strengthening his hold on Judah's Egyptian flank. This also put him in a position to utilize the Transjordanian tribes to send raiding parties into Judah. The author of Kings reports that that harassment found its ultimate origin in God's command to bring judgment to a wicked Judah that had followed in the train of Manasseh's wickedness, a judgment the prophets had repeatedly warned about (cf. Jer 15:1–9; Hab 1:2–6; Zep 1:4–13; 3:1–7).

In 598 B.C., Nebuchadnezzar was ready. Gathering his huge force, he set out for Jerusalem and the impenitent Jehoiakim. But Nebuchadnezzar was not to avenge himself on the Judean king personally; for even as he set out for Judah, Jehoiakim lay dead, succeeded by his son, Jehoiachin.

3. The reign of Jehoiachin (24:8–16)

8–9 With his father dead, young Jehoiachin was faced with the awesome specter of the advancing armies of Nebuchadnezzar. Certainly he would get no help from Egypt, for Neco was in no position to challenge Nebuchadnezzar again (cf. v.7). Nor did the lad have the spiritual maturity to be able to utilize godly wisdom.

10–16 The armies of Nebuchadnezzar soon arrived and placed Jerusalem under a siege. At the appropriate time, Nebuchadnezzar himself appeared before the beleaguered city, to whom Jehoiachin, the royal family, and the officials of state made their surrender. Having taken his hostages in charge, Nebuchadnezzar stripped the royal palace and the temple of their treasures as spoils of war. He had previously taken part of Jerusalem's smaller treasures (2Ch 36:7; Da 1:2). This time, his despoilment was a major one, with only a few smaller gold and silver items left behind (cf. 25:15), along with the larger brass vessels (cf. 25:13–17; Jer 27:18–22). Moreover, he perpetuated the deportation system made famous by the Assyrians, seizing ten thousand of Jerusalem's leaders from every walk of life (including the prophet Ezekiel; cf. Eze 1:2; 33:21). With only the poor and unskilled people of the land remaining, it might be assumed that Jerusalem would cause no further trouble.

4. The reign of Zedekiah (24:17–25:21)

17–20 Nebuchadnezzar left the city standing; installed Josiah's remaining son, Mattaniah (whom he renamed Zedekiah), on the throne; and in due time returned to Babylon. While Jerusalem had been spared momentarily, its demise was certain. Not only was Zedekiah no better than the other descendants of Josiah, but even this latest judgment of God through the Chaldeans had had no effect on an obdurately apostate people. All that God had done both previously and currently to Judah and Jerusalem had been because of his settled wrath against their sin. Yet nothing had helped. Twice wicked Judah fought on against the divine chastisement (cf. Jer 37:1–2). The final blow would not be long in coming.

25:1–4 Late in 588 B.C., Zedekiah, like other Judean kings, was lured into the foolish mistake of rebelling against Babylon. There seems little doubt that his decision to do so was related to a renewed confidence in Egypt, on whom Israel and Judah had relied mistakenly so many times before. Zedekiah's confidence was ill-placed, however, for the Egyptian king possessed neither the strength nor the sagacity to merit such trust. The Egyptian king's own life was marked by a series of political and military difficulties that ended in his death.

Nebuchadnezzar immediately responded, this time sending the full weight of his mighty army. After setting up headquarters in Riblah, Jerusalem was placed under total siege (cf. Jer 39:1; 52:4; Eze 24:2). With Jerusalem securely blockaded (cf. Jer 21:3–7), Nebuchadnezzar proceeded to reduce the Judean strongholds systematically (cf. Jer 34:7), thereby cutting off both military relief and economic replenishment. At one point Nebuchadnezzar's forces were forced to withdraw momentarily to deal with an Egyp-

tian relief column under Apries (Jer 37:5), much to the joy of the misguided Jerusalemites, who prematurely assumed that they had been delivered from the siege (Jer 37:6–10). Nonetheless Jerusalem's beleaguered defenders were kept enclosed by the Chaldeans almost continuously until July of 586 B.C. Finally, when strength and provisions were completely exhausted, the Neo-Babylonian troops breached the walls and poured into the city (cf. Jer 39:2–3). The prophesied tragedy had occurred (cf. Jer 19–20; 27–28; 37:8–10, 17; 38:17–23).

5–7 Still further prophetic details were to be realized; for when Zedekiah and the remaining Judean army attempted to gain their freedom by slipping through a secluded gate near the king's garden, they were soon overtaken by their Chaldean pursuers (cf. Jer 32:5; 34:3; Eze 12:12–13 with Jer 39:3–5; 52:7–8). Zedekiah was taken captive to Nebuchadnezzar at Riblah. There, being forced to witness the execution of his own children—so that the last thing he would remember seeing was the end result of his foolish disobedience—his eyes were put out. He was then led away in bronze fetters to Babylon, where he remained a prisoner until his death (cf. Jer 52:11).

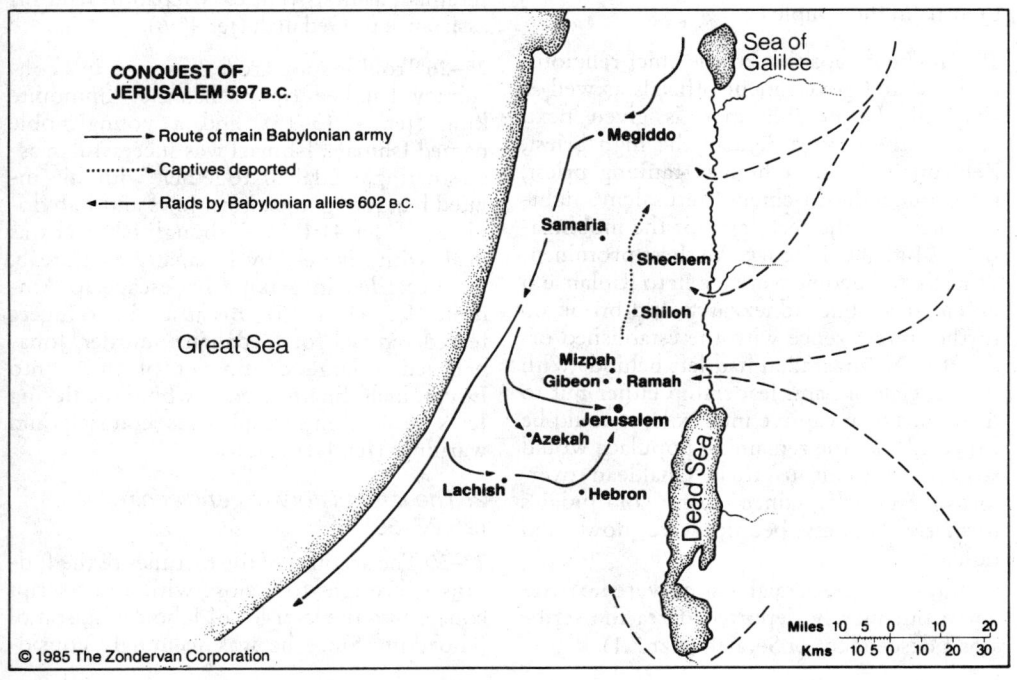

CONQUEST OF
JERUSALEM 597 B.C.

———► Route of main Babylonian army

············► Captives deported

◄— — — Raids by Babylonian allies 602 B.C.

Sea of Galilee

Great Sea

Megiddo

Samaria

Shechem

Shiloh

Mizpah
Gibeon • Ramah
Jerusalem
Azekah

Lachish • Hebron

Dead Sea

Miles 10 5 0   10   20
Kms 10 5 0 10 20 30

© 1985 The Zondervan Corporation

8–12 About one month later, Nebuzaradan, the commander of Nebuchadnezzar's own imperial guard, arrived in Jerusalem to oversee its despoliation and destruction. Having set fire to all of Jerusalem's permanent buildings, including the temple and palace (cf. Jer 52:13), the Chaldeans demolished the city's walls. Then they deported certain valued elements of the citizenry of Jerusalem and the populace of the surrounding countryside, some of whom apparently willingly defected to the invaders (cf. Jer 39:9; 52:15). Only the poorest of the people were left. These were to work the nearby fields and vineyards so that a stratum of inhabitants unlikely to cause further insurrection might be left to care for the basic needs of the remaining people of the land (cf. Jer 39:10; 52:16).

13–17 Particular notice is given to the temple furniture and furnishings that the Chaldeans carried away as spoils of war. Primary focus is on those heavy bronze items that had to be broken into smaller pieces to be removed: the pillars, the movable stands, and the Sea. Indeed, the bronze gained from those items—together with the bronze bulls under the bronze Sea (cf. Jer 52:20) was incalculable. A comparison of this account with the fuller inventory in Jer 52:17–23 reveals a thorough looting of all the gold, silver, and bronze utensils in the temple

18–21 The disposition of the chief religious, military, and government officials as well as sixty of the notable men is given next. Among these were Seraiah the high priest, Zephaniah the next highest ranking priest, the commander-in-chief of Jerusalem's fighting men, and the secretary for the mobilization of Judah's citizenry. All these prominent officials and people were taken to Riblah and executed. Nebuchadnezzar would brook no further interference with the established order that Nebuzaradan had left behind. With the officialdom and leadership either put to death or taken captive into exile, it could be expected that the remaining populace would passively submit to their Chaldean overlords, especially since many of Judah's formerly landless people were now land holders.

Interestingly, Seraiah's sons were not executed but merely deported. Ezra the scribe was a descendant of Seraiah (Ezr 7:1).

F. Historical Appendixes (25:22–30)

1. Judah in exile (25:22–26)

22–24 The captivity of God's disobedient people, begun in 605 B.C., was completed: Seventy years would go by until the exiled Judeans would again see their homeland (2Ch 36:15–21). To the history of the united and divided kingdoms is appended a note regarding the establishment of the new Judean vassal state. Fuller details are given in Jeremiah, from where these data are perhaps drawn. Of the prominent men of Jerusalem, only Jeremiah and Gedaliah were left behind (cf. Jer 39:11–14). Jeremiah's stand on the Babylonian issue was doubtless well known. Gedaliah's attitude was probably that of Ahikam, his father and a noted official (2Ch 34:20), who had supported Jeremiah (Jer 26:24). Accordingly Gedaliah, who probably had the needed training, seemed the logical choice to be Babylon's governor-designate over the newly formed district.

The choice was a popular one, and at first things went well (cf. Jer 40:1–12). Because of their confidence in Gedaliah, many of the surviving little guerrilla bands made their way back to Jerusalem to lay down their arms and take up residence there, as did many of the Judeans who had fled to the Transjordanian lands (cf. Jer 40:11–12). Even Jeremiah at first went to Mizpah to lend his assistance to Gedaliah (Jer 40:6).

25–26 Trouble soon arose, however, in a conspiracy hatched by Baalis, the Ammonite king (Jer 40:13–15), and a young noble named Ishmael. Ishmael was successful in assassinating Gedaliah together with his invited banquet guests, both Jews and Babylonians (cf. Jer 41:1–3). Although Ishmael was dealt with severely by Johanan ben Kareah, he succeeded in making his escape to Ammon (Jer 41:11–15). Because the refugees feared reprisal for Gedaliah's murder, Johanan led a large contingent of them into Egypt, including Jeremiah, whom the fleeing Jews took along despite his counsels and warnings (Jer 41:16–43:7).

2. The later history of Jehoiachin (25:27–30)

27–30 The account of the fortunes of the Judeans is brought to a close with a postscript concerning the later lot of Jehoiachin, son of Jehoiakim. Since he was seemingly considered by the Judeans as the last legitimate king, news of his later condition would be of great significance. After the death of Nebuchadnezzar in 561 B.C., his son and successor, Evil-Merodach (561–560), released the Judean king from prison and accorded him due royal recognition. This included a place at the king's table and a regular allowance for the rest of his life (cf. Jer 52:31–34).

Thus the final curtain falls on the drama of the divided monarchy. What had been a note of dark despair is illuminated by the light of God's gracious concern for his own. Although God's people had been judged as they must, yet God would be with them even in the midst of their sentence. Jehoiachin's release and renewed enjoyment of life thus stand as a harbinger of the further release and return of all the nation, in accordance with God's promises (cf. Jer 31:18; La 5:21). The spiritually minded believers perhaps would see in this incident an assurance of God's greater redemption from bondage of those who looked forward to him who gives release and eternal refreshment to all who love his appearing.

KINGS OF ISRAEL AND JUDAH

This chart depicts the reigns of the kings of Israel and Judah from Jeroboam of Israel and Rehoboam of Judah until the fall of Jerusalem. As best can be determined, the dates reflect the official reign of each king and not any years of his co-regency with another king. The center column is divided into increments of twenty years; the outside columns give the passages in 1 and 2 Kings and 2 Chronicles where the reign of each king is described. By using this chart, you can see at a glance both the length of each reign and the kings in Israel and Judah who were contemporaries. The final column depicts when the major prophets lived and ministered.

PASSAGES	KINGS OF ISRAEL	DATE B.C	KINGS OF JUDAH	PASSAGES		PROPHETS
I Kings				**I Kings**	**2 Chron.**	
12:25 –14:20	JEROBOAM I	**930**	REHOBOAM	12:1-24; 14:21-31	10:1 –12:16	
			ABIJAH	15:1-8	13:1-14:1	
15:25-31	NADAB	**910**	ASA	15:9-24	14:2 –16:14	
15:32 –16:7	BAASHA					
		890				
16:8-14	ELAH					
16:15-22	ZIMRI, TIBNI/OMRI					
16:23-28	OMRI					
16:29 –22:40	AHAB					Elijah
		870	JEHOSHAPHAT	22:41-50	17:1–21:3	
2 Kings						
1:1-18	AHAZIAH					
3:1–8:15	JORAM	**850**				Elisha

KINGS OF ISRAEL AND JUDAH

PASSAGES 2 Kings	KINGS OF ISRAEL	DATE B.C	KINGS OF JUDAH	PASSAGES 2 Kings	PASSAGES 2 Chron.	PROPHETS
		850				Elisha (cont.)
			JEHORAM	8:16-24	21:4-20	
9:30 −10:36	JEHU		AHAZIAH	8:25-29	22:1-9	
			ATHALIAH	11:1-21	22:10 −23:21	
			JOASH	12:1-21	24:1-27	
		830				
13:1-9	JEHOAHAZ	810				
13:10-25	JEHOASH		AMAZIAH	14:1-22	25:1-28	
		790				
14:23-29	JEROBOAM II		AZARIAH (UZZIAH)	15:1-7	26:1-23	Jonah
		770				Amos
						Hosea
15:8-15	ZECHARIAH, SHALLUM					
15:16-22	MENAHEM	750				

Copyright ©1991 Zondervan Publishing House

KINGS OF ISRAEL AND JUDAH

PASSAGES 2 Kings	KINGS OF ISRAEL	DATE B.C	KINGS OF JUDAH	PASSAGES 2 Kings	2 Chron.	PROPHETS
		750				Hosea (cont.)
15:23-26	PEKAHIAH					
15:27-31	PEKAH		JOTHAM	15:32-38	27:1-8	Isaiah Micah
17:1-6	HOSHEA	730	AHAZ	16:1-20	28:1-27	
	FALL OF SAMARIA	722				
			HEZEKIAH	18:1 –20:21	29:1 –32:33	
		710				
		690				
			MANASSEH	21:1-18	33:1-20	
		670				
		650				

582

KINGS OF ISRAEL AND JUDAH

PASSAGES	KINGS OF ISRAEL	DATE B.C	KINGS OF JUDAH	PASSAGES		PROPHETS
		650		**2 Kings**	**2 Chron.**	
			AMON	21:19-26	33:21-25	Zephaniah
			JOSIAH	22:1 −23:30	34:1 −35:27	Nahum
		630				Jeremiah
		610	JEHOAHAZ	23:31-33	36:1-4	Habakkuk
			JEHOIAKIM	23:36 −24:7	36:5-8	Daniel
			JEHOIACHIN	24:8-17	36:9-10	Ezekiel
			ZEDEKIAH	24:18 −25:21	36:11-21	
		590				
		586	FALL OF JERUSALEM	25:8-17	36:15-19	
		570				
		550				

1 Chronicles

INTRODUCTION

1. Background

God used the history of the ancient kingdom of Israel to reveal truths about himself and his relationship to humankind. But while he inspired the OT writers of the books of both Kings and Chronicles to interpret this history, their theological messages are distinct. If 1 and 2 Kings, composed after the final collapse of the kingdom in 586 B.C., concentrates on how sin leads to defeat (2Ki 17:15, 18), then 1 and 2 Chronicles, coming after the two returns from exile in 537 and 458 B.C., recounts, from the same record, how "faith is the victory" (2Ch 20:20, 22). Readers today may therefore find strength from God, knowing that his moral judgments (Kings) are balanced by his providential salvation (revealed in Chronicles).

2. Date and Authorship

While Chronicles contains no direct statement about the circumstances of its own composition, still a fairly clear picture does emerge from the biblical data. The last-recorded event in 2 Chronicles is the decree of Cyrus in 538 B.C., permitting the Jews to return from their exile in Babylon (36:22–23). One genealogy in 1 Chronicles (3:17–21) includes King Jehoiachin's grandson Zerubbabel, who led this return in the following year, and it goes on to name two of Zerubbabel's grandsons—Pelatiah and Jeshaiah—thus extending the time to about 500 B.C. The sons of four other men are then mentioned, but without indication of their place in the genealogy. The last of these is Shecaniah, whose line reaches down to seven great-great-grandchildren (3:24). So if Shecaniah belongs to the same general period as King Jehoiachin (born 616), these four additional generations would again suggest a time around 500 B.C. as the earliest possible date for Chronicles.

Recent discoveries have produced external evidence by which the latest possible date for the books may now be set. The discovery of fragments of an actual manuscript of Chronicles among the Dead Sea Scrolls makes a third-century date difficult to maintain; thus it is imperative to place the Chronicler's activity in the Persian period (c. 538–333 B.C.). More specifically, if we accept the tradition that the OT canon was finalized during the general period of the Persian monarch Artaxerxes I, who died 424 B.C. (cf. Ne 12:22, where the reference to Darius II—who was crowned in 423—is the last historical allusion to appear in the OT), then Chronicles would have to have been written before 420. If its composition, moreover, is associated with the work of Ezra, the Aramaic language found in the book that bears Ezra's name matches that of the Elephantine papyri, which likewise belongs to the fifth century B.C.

Relationships between the books of Chronicles and Ezra provide the most important single clue for fixing the date and also the authorship of the former volume. Since Chronicles appears to be the work of an individual writer, who was a Levitical leader, some identification with Ezra the priest and scribe (Ezr 7:1–6) appears possible from the outset. This conclusion is furthered, moreover, by the personal qualities that the writer displays. The literary styles of the books are similar, and their contents have much in common: the frequent lists and genealogies, their focus on ritual, and their joint devotion to the law of Moses. Most significant of all, the closing verses of 2 Chronicles (36:22–23) are repeated as the opening verses of Ezra (1:1–3a). Jewish tradition affirms that Ezra wrote Chronicles, along with the book that bears his name.

For those, therefore, who accept the historicity of the events recorded in Ezra—from the decree of Cyrus in 538 down to Ezra's reform in 458–457 B.C.—and the validity of Ezra's autobiographical writing within the next few years, the date of composition for both books as one consecutive history must be about 450 B.C., and the place, Jerusalem.

3. Sources

If Ezra the scribe is the man responsible for the present book of Chronicles, his "scribism" may well account for the careful acknowledgment of historical sources that appears through the volume. These fall into the following categories.

a. Genealogies

For the tribe of Simeon, the author of Chronicles explains, "They kept a genealogical record" (1Ch 4:33); and for Gad he identifies his sources even more closely: "These were entered in the genealogical records during the reigns of Jotham [751–736 B.C.] king of Judah and Jeroboam [II, 793–753] king of Israel" (5:17). He refers to similar official genealogical lists for Benjamin (7:9), Asher (7:40), "all Israel" (9:1), the Levitical gatekeepers (9:22), and the family of Rehoboam (2Ch 12:15); and the very nature of his book suggests numerous others that just did not happen to be so mentioned.

b. Documents

Since the Chronicler not only describes how the Assyrian king Sennacherib "wrote letters" against Judah but then goes on to cite excerpts from them (2Ch 32:17–20), these too seem to represent a literary source (cf. an immediately preceding message that is quoted as deriving from this same monarch, vv.10–15). The book also concludes with a proclamation made by the Persian king Cyrus, which he "put in writing" (36:22–23). Another kind of documentary source underlies the detailed descriptions of the Solomonic temple in Jerusalem, because references are made to the plans "of all that the Spirit had put in his [David's] mind" for it (1Ch 28:11–12)—and not just in his mind, but "'All this,' David said, 'I have in writing from the hand of the LORD upon me'" (v.19).

c. Poems

The author alludes to songs of praise in the words of David and Asaph in 2Ch 29:30 (cf. the titles to Pss 50; 73–83), and in 35:25 to laments for Josiah that were chanted by Jeremiah (not to be identified with his later, canonical Lamentations over Jerusalem). Neither is actually quoted, though the allusions suggest the author's use of poetic sources (cf. David's reemployment of Pss 95:1–5; 96; and

106:1, 47–48, which Ezra did quote in 1Ch 16:8–36).

d. Prophecies

Among its sources Chronicles refers to at least eleven different prophetic books: those by the earlier prophets Samuel, Gad (1Ch 29:29), Nathan (1Ch 29:29; 2Ch 9:29), Ahijah (2Ch 9:29), Shemaiah (12:15), and Iddo, including both the "visions of Iddo" (9:29) and his "annotations" (13:22); and those by the later prophets Jehu son of Hanani (20:34), Isaiah, including both his "vision" (the OT book, 32:32) and his last history of Uzziah (26:22), and Hozai (33:19, perhaps meaning simply a book of "the seers"). Second Chronicles alludes (36:22) to the fulfillment of Jer 29:10, and the author seems to quote from Jer 29:13–14 in 2Ch 15:4 (unless both are drawing on Dt 4:29).

e. Other histories

Ezra's major reference work was "the book of the kings of Israel and Judah" (2Ch 27:7; 35:27; 36:8; et al.). He also refers at one point to the "annals of King David" (1Ch 27:24, which may have been part of the same work) and to the "annotations on the book of the kings" (2Ch 24:27). But though much material from the canonical books of 1 and 2 Kings does reappear in Chronicles, these cannot be the source here cited, since passages such as 1Ch 9:1 and 2Ch 27:7 refer to "the book of the kings" for additional data on genealogies and wars, about which nothing further actually occurs in our canonical books. So while Ezra did use this major reference work directly, it must have been some larger court record—authentic but now lost—from which both Kings and Chronicles drew.

All in all, 57.8 percent of the text of Chronicles exhibits verbal parallels with other portions of the OT. These include especially the Pentateuch and Joshua for the genealogies and other such listings, and 2 Samuel and 1 and 2 Kings for the history.

4. Occasion and Purpose

When Ezra returned from Babylon in 458 B.C., his heart was set on enthroning God's law in the postexile community of Judah (Ezr 7:10). He took immediate steps to restore temple worship (7:19–23, 27; 8:33–34) and to eliminate a number of mixed marriages that had arisen between certain Jews and their pagan neighbors (chs. 9–10). Based on powers granted him by the Persian king (7:18–25), Ezra seems to have been the one who commenced the refortification of Jerusalem (4:16), though subsequently thwarted by bitter Samaritan opposition (vv.17–23; cf. Ne 1:3–4). Not until 444, when Ezra was joined by Nehemiah, were the walls actually finished (Ne 6:15–16) and the law of Moses formally recognized by the community (ch. 8). Yet if Ezra was the Chronicler, then the appearance of his book about 450 becomes explainable as a concrete literary means to aid in the achievement of his purpose of rebuilding the theocracy (i.e., the acknowledgment of God as their king).

5. Theology

Ezra honors the transcendent majesty of God (1Ch 29:11) and quotes statements from past history describing him as above all gods (2Ch 2:5), dwelling in heaven (6:18; 7:14), and ruling all earth (20:6). The Lord's presence must be mediated, therefore, by his "name" (which carries the force of his person, 12:13), especially in the temple (1Ch 22:7; 29:16), and by his Spirit, especially for communications (1Ch 12:18; 2Ch 15:1; 24:20). Angels occupy a greater place in Chronicles than in the corresponding parts of the other OT histories (1Ch 21:12 or 21:18, 20, 27), as does also the Lord's mediation through Satan (21:1).

Yet God can be immanent as well, intervening into history (1Ch 12:18; cf. 2Ch 20:13) in answer to human prayers and songs (2Ch 14:11; 18:31; 20:9–12). The continuity of his concern is emphasized by the phrase "God of [the] fathers," used in quotations (1Ch 29:20; 2Ch 20:6) and by the Chronicler himself (2Ch 13:18; 15:12); and his covenant love for Israel (6:14) is recognized even by foreigners (2:11; 9:8). The Lord is the God of revelation, who fulfills his predictions (10:15; 36:21) and keeps his promises (1Ch 17:26; 2Ch 1:9; 6:15). Prophets of God who appear in Chronicles (but not in Kings) include Iddo (2Ch 13:22), Azariah son of Oded (15:1, 8), Eliezer (20:37), and Jeremiah (35:25; 36:12, 21–22). Corresponding attention is given to the written Mosaic Law, which must be taught (17:9) and honored (31:4, 21).

6. Theological Themes and Interests

A careful reading of Chronicles shows that the author has certain recurring theological interests that he promotes throughout his work.

a. Promise of God

The Lord takes center stage and leaves no doubt as to who is in charge. Thus, rather than giving political, sociological, military, or economic explanations—or stating immediate causes for events—the author presents God as the Lord of history and the cause of its events.

The prominence of God may be seen in several incidents. God put Saul to death and gave the kingdom to David (1Ch 10:14); God routed the armies of Jeroboam when he attacked Abijah (2Ch 13:13–16); God destroyed the mighty army of Zerah when it battled Asa and his smaller forces (2Ch 14:12–13); the Lord established the kingdom of Jehoshaphat (2Ch 17:5) and defeated a military alliance of Moab, Ammon, and Mount Seir even before the Hebrew army began to fight (2Ch 20:22–23).

Perhaps the finest example of God's direct, divine intervention in history may be seen in the way he utterly destroyed the mighty army of Sennacherib when that proud Assyrian ruler dared to challenge the power of the Almighty and to compare him to the gods of the other nations (2Ch 32:16–22).

b. Retribution

The idea of sowing and reaping is hardly new to Chronicles, but it is modified in at least two ways. (1) The burden of obedience lies primarily on the shoulder of the king of the nation. (2) The principle does not work automatically or mechanically. The sovereign ruler is often warned by a prophetic word; hence the ruler can repent and avert a calamity or military defeat (cf. 2Ch 7:14).

c. Vocabulary

The author's third theological interest is his constant use of standard vocabulary and expressions like "seeking God," "pure heart," "faithfulness," and "forsaking the LORD." Because seeking God and being faithful to him bring about his blessings, it is not surprising to find many exhortations and injunctions to do so.

d. Things used in worship

A fourth interest is the ark, the temple, and the priesthood. Two chapters cover the transporting of the ark to Jerusalem; eight chapters deal with the preparation for building the temple. Three chapters describe the actual construction of the temple, and three more cover its dedication. Furthermore, three chapters cover Josiah's reforms, with special emphasis on the restoration of the central sanctuary and its functions.

e. Worship

A fifth interest is closely related to Israel's worship at the temple. The Chronicler is concerned about the nature of true worship as opposed to correct ceremony. This concern for the right attitude of the heart may be traced in two ways. First, the word "heart" (GK 4222) is used some thirty times in Chronicles. Thus the activity of seeking God should be accompanied with the right inner attitude. A second way of tracing the Chronicler's concern for true worship may be seen from his treatment of Hezekiah's reform. Hezekiah is portrayed as one of the godliest Judean kings.

f. Kingdom

A sixth interest is the kingship in Israel. The kingdom of God and the kingdom of Judah are often treated as if they are one and the same entity (cf. 1Ch 28:5; 29:23). The kingdom is important as the guardian of the temple. After the division of Solomon's kingdom, the Judean kings regularly expressed their commitment to God in terms of religious reforms (cf. reigns of Hezekiah and Josiah). True worship in Israel was not preserved by godly priesthood but by godly kingship.

g. History

A seventh interest is seen from the way the Chronicler records historical events. For example, it is not enough for him to describe the building of the temple; he must go beyond that and point out the striking resemblance of this event to the construction of the tabernacle in the desert.

h. Omissions

A final interest of Chronicles is in the material that he chose to omit from his discussion of Israel's history. From the reign of David, he deleted three main blocks of material. He left out the events found at 1Sa 15–31. Also deleted is the material found in 2Sa 1–4. The third block of omitted material involves David's sin with Bathsheba and the problems that followed it (2Sa 11–1Ki 2, with the exception of the census).

Concerning the reign of Solomon, Chronicles omitted the struggle between Solomon and Adonijah for the throne, the steps Solomon took to solidify his position, and the material dealing with Solomon's many foreign wives, with the resultant spread of idolatry and God's punishment of the king for this sin (1Ki 11).

After the division of Solomon's kingdom, the Chronicler did not deal with the northern kingdom on its own terms and for its own intrinsic interest. Instead he dealt with it only as it came into contact with the kingdom of Judah.

The Chronicler recorded a history of Israel in which he chose both to emphasize certain points and to delete some material. This was no plot or attempt to suppress the truth. In developing his theological commentary on the events of the past, he left out certain elements that did not contribute to the point he was emphasizing. Those who want another perspective on history can read the former prophets or recite the facts that were well known to Israel.

EXPOSITION

I. Genealogies (1:1–9:44)

A. Patriarchs (1:1–54)

Chronicles begins with nine chapters of genealogies. Their purpose was to show the place that the 450 B.C. postexilic community of Judah occupied within total history. They serve two practical functions. (1) For the immediate situation, genealogies were important in providing the framework within which true Hebrews could establish their genealogical roots and by which religious purity could be maintained against outside groups and influences.

(2) For the church's overall perspective, the genealogies reflect the providential design that marks the sweep of history from Eden onward. Particular names serve as reminders of God's dealings in the past; and the genealogies' focus on David and his dynasty embodies the OT hope for the future Messiah, with the meaningfulness that this provided for Ezra's generation.

1–4 Ezra's survey commences with Adam, not just Abraham, the father of the Hebrews. This points to the unity of the race (Ac 17:26) and to the universality of God's redemptive program within history (Ge 3:15). Verses 1–4 are compiled from Ge 5. Seth's brothers, Abel and Cain, with the latter's line (Ge 4:17–25), are omitted as irrelevant.

5–7 Verses 5–23 are drawn from the "table of nations" in Ge 10:2–29. The seven sons of Japheth founded the people of Europe and northern Asia (e.g., from Javan comes Greek Ionia; from Gomer, the ancient Cimmerians of the Russian plains; and from Madai, the Medes and Persians of Iran. Tubal and Meshech were ancestors of the eighth-century Tabali and Mushki, who inhabited the Turkish plateau, according to contemporary Assyrian inscriptions). Areas proposed for the first two Greek subgroups in v.7 include Elishah (in south Greece) and Sardinia; the latter two—"Kittim and Rodanim"—denote the islands of Cyprus and Rhodes.

8 The four sons of Ham founded ethnic groups in Africa and southwestern Asia (e.g., Put in Libya on the Mediterranean coast of Africa west of Egypt; and Cush, or "Ethiopia").

9–11 Yet the five listed sons of Cush founded tribes that extended eastward from the coast of the Red Sea, across southern Arabia, to the Kassites in the Tigris-Euphrates Valley. The second river of Eden can thus be said to border Cush (Ge 2:13), and Babylon and Assyria pertain to the Cushite leader Nimrod (10:8–11).

12–16 The Hamitic Philistines were "sea peoples" before settling in Palestine, coming from the Casluhim, who were of Egyptian origin but are related to the Minoan culture of Caphtor (Crete) and the southern coast of Asia Minor (Am 9:7).

17 The five sons of Shem produced the peoples who remained closest to humankind's original home in west-central Asia. Yet they ranged from Elam, north of the Persian Gulf, to Aram in Syria and Lud (Lydia) in central Turkey.

18 The name Eber forms the root of "Hebrew"; but this patriarch was ancestor not only of Abraham (v.27), but also of a number of other unsettled people, known in ancient history as Habiru or Apiru.

19–23 The only "dividing up" of the earth to which Genesis makes reference in its postdiluvian context is that which occurred at the confusion of languages at Babel (Ge 11:1–9). The name Peleg seems to have been derived from this event (see NIV note).

24–27 The list of names from Shem to Abram sums up the table of Ge 11:10–26. Both men constitute significant reminders of God's special relations with his people: the first, as the initial example of the Lord's association with a particular part of humanity, i.e., the Semites (Ge 9:26), and Abraham as a climactic witness to divine election (12:2; 17:7). The latter's change of name is explained in Ge 17:5.

28–34 The information on the families of Abraham and Isaac is identical with that found in Ge 25:1–4, 9, 13–16. Abraham's nomadic Arabian descendants through his two subordinate wives, Hagar and Keturah, are given first, before the biblical record focuses on Sarah's son, Isaac, who was the child of promise. Arabs became increasingly influential in Judah (cf. Ne 4:7–6:1) after occupying Ezion Geber at the northeast end of the Red Sea in 500 B.C.

35 The remainder of ch. 1 summarizes the "table of Edom" in Ge 36:4–5, 11–13, 20–28, 31–43—with few scribal corruptions in spelling. The subject of the rest of 1 and 2 Chronicles is Jacob (Israel) and the Twelve Tribes that descended from him; but before the record focuses on this younger of Isaac's twin sons, it lists the elder brother, Esau, and the Edomite tribes that he founded. They were Israel's closest "brothers" (Ob 10, 12) and near neighbors, after Arab pressure forced them into southern Judah fifty years prior to Ezra.

36–37 Timna, a daughter of Seir (v.39), became a subordinate wife of Esau's son Eliphaz (Ge 36:12) and was later honored by having her name bestowed on an Edomite chieftain and his district (36:40; cf. 1Ch 1:51).

38–41 Seir belonged to a group called "Horites" (Ge 36:20), the ancient Hurrians, a major people of Mesopotamia. Some had settled in Edom (= Seir) before the coming of Esau (Dt 2:12, 22).

42 Uz was the name of the home of the patriarch Job (Job 1:1), who may thus have been an early Edomite descendant of Esau (cf. La 4:21). Similarly, Esau's son Eliphaz, the father of Teman (v.36), seems to have been in the ancestry of Job's friend Eliphaz the Temanite (Job 2:11).

43–54 The death of King Hadad (v.51) is not mentioned in Ezra's biblical source (Ge 36:39), perhaps because Hadad II was still living when Moses wrote this part of the Pentateuch, a thousand years before the writing of Chronicles.

B. Judah (2:1–4:23)

1. The clan of Hezron (2:1–55)

Chapter 2 resumes the specific development of the nation of Israel. It continues from 1:34, where the two sons of Isaac had been introduced. Since the line of the elder, Esau, was summarized in 1:35–54, Ezra can now concentrate on the younger of the twins, Israel. But while our Chronicler lists all twelve of the sons of Israel-Jacob, his attention quickly focuses on Judah (v.3), the description of whose tribe occupies the next two and one-half chapters. Indeed, after a supplement on those portions of the tribe of Simeon that remained as neighbors to southern Judah (4:24–43), the genealogies of Chronicles devote themselves principally to Benjamin (chs. 8–9) and the priestly tribe of Levi (ch. 6). Only chs. 5 and 7 are left, for outlines, respectively, on the tribes of Transjordan and north Israel. The land that was occupied by the Jews who returned from the Babylonian exile consisted primarily of the tribal territories of Judah and Benjamin. Also, the people who made up Ezra's community were largely from these same two tribes (Ezr 1:5; 10:9), which had composed the former southern kingdom. In his effort to maintain national purity, it was therefore nat-

ural that the Chronicler should concentrate on these particular genealogies. Judah was especially prominent (Ezr 4:4, 6): from it the very name "Jew" is derived.

Among the ten-listed grandsons of Judah (1Ch 2:5–6; 4:21–22), the primary interest of this chapter (from 2:9 onward) rests on Hezron, the elder son of Perez, from whom were descended some of the leading elements of Judah's later population. Hezron's third son, Caleb, in his turn received major attention in two sections (vv.18–20 and 42–55; cf. 4:1–4), though Hezron's second son, Ram, is presented first, because he embodies the messianic hope of Israel: from him comes the family of David (2:10–17).

1 Verses 1–2 are drawn from Ge 35:22–26 and Ex 1:1–5. All the passages list in first place Jacob's six sons by his wife Leah (from Reuben through Zebulun), in the order of their birth; and the Pentateuchal sources place the four sons of the handmaids (Dan through Asher, in their order of birth) after Jacob's younger son by his wife Rachel, namely, Benjamin.

2 Chronicles, however, follows Genesis in placing Joseph before Benjamin; and before them both it puts Dan, following Zebulun, perhaps because these last two receive no further treatment in Chronicles.

3–4 These verses reflect the sordid dealings that Judah, his sons, and his Canaanite daughter-in-law Tamar had with each other (Ge 38; esp. vv.2–7, 29–30; cf. 46:12). Yet God in his grace used Tamar to be an ancestor of David and of Jesus Christ (Mt 1:3)!

5 Since Judah's first two sons died without issue, and since his third son is taken up in ch. 4 (vv.21–23), the present section focuses on the remaining two, as listed in Ge 46:12 and Nu 26:21.

6 Except for Zimri, these Zerahites can be identified from 1Ki 4:31 as later descendants, not immediate "sons," of Zerah. Ezra singled them out as examples of God-given wisdom (cf. v.20) during the Solomonic period. Heman and Ethan, moreover, became authors of inspired psalmody (Pss 88–89), with which Ezra's concern for proper worship caused him to be involved. These authors must not, however, be confused with David's musicians, Heman, Asaph, and Ethan (1Ch

15:19), who were from the tribe of Levi, not Judah (cf. 6:33–44).

7 Carmi is another Zerahite, identifiable from Jos 7:1 as an immediate son of Zimri. While the latter has been equated with Zerah's son Zimri, he really appears (in Jos 7:17–18) to belong to the time of his direct grandson Achan. The last named is here called Achar ("disaster") because he was a "bringer of disaster" on Israel. The name reminds us of his sin under Joshua at Jericho and how God's judgment may bring consequent disaster on his people (Jos 7:25; cf. 6:18 and the naming of the place as Achor in 7:26).

8–10 Verses 9–12 are drawn from Ru 4:19–22. This passage furnishes the chief links in the ancestry of David, but it is by no means complete: three centuries elapse between Ram son of Hezron and Nahshon son of Amminadab, whose leadership "of the people of Judah" dates to the days of Moses in the desert (Ex 6:23; Nu 1:7; 2:3) and whose son Salmon married Rahab the prostitute after the fall of Jericho (Mt 1:5).

11–12 Another three centuries elapse before we reach Boaz the husband of Ruth, who were the grandparents of Jesse the father of David.

13–15 These verses supplement 1Sa 16:6–9 on Jesse's family. Following his sixth son, Ozem, this source mentions another brother (1Sa 16:10; 17:12) before David, but he is not named; he may have died soon after these events.

16–17 The genealogies of these four warriors, made famous under their half-uncle David (cf. 2Sa 2:18–19; 19:13), are drawn from 2Sa 2:18 and 17:25; but apart from this latter passage, we would not have known that their mothers, Zeruiah and Abigail, were stepdaughters of Jesse, born to David's mother by her presumed earlier marriage to Nahash.

18–19 The remainder of ch. 2 (vv.28–55) tabulates the descendants of the other sons of Hezron, through lists that have not been preserved elsewhere in Scripture. Some of the names that follow designate whole communities that sprang from his line; e.g., Tekoa (v.24), Beth Zur (v.45), Kiriath Jearim, Bethlehem, or Beth Gader (vv.50–54). Hezron's son Caleb is not to be confused with Moses'

spy of the same name (1:15), who appeared three hundred years later.

20 Bezalel is recalled as the Calebite whose craftsmanship, given by the Spirit of God, equipped him to superintend construction for the Mosaic tabernacle (Ex 31:2–5; cf. 2Ch 1:5). An interval of centuries seems again to separate his father, Uri, from their ancestors, Caleb's son Hur. The last named should thus be distinguished from their contemporary, the leader Hur, who joined Aaron in upholding the hands of Moses (Ex 17:10, 12; cf. 24:14).

21–22 The Transjordanian conquests of Jair, a later descendant of Hezron's son Segub, also occurred under Moses. These are documented in Nu 32:41 and Dt 3:14, where Jair is called a son of Manasseh, through Segub's mother, the daughter of Makir (vv.21, 23), rather than through his father, Hezron.

23–24 The total of sixty towns includes Jair's twenty-three plus a remaining thirty-seven at Kenath (Nu 32:42); they may also be combined under Jair's name (Dt 3:4, 14; Jos 13:30). Their loss to the Arameans may have occurred in the early ninth century, since by King Ahab's day (853 B.C.) Ramoth Gilead lay on the frontier (1Ki 22:3).

25–40 The descendants of Jerahmeel (vv.25–41) came to occupy a broad area in the Negev of southern Judah. Some critics dismiss the Jerahmeelites as aliens; but while they can be mentioned with the Kenites (1Sa 30:29), who had a truly foreign origin, and can even be described in parallel with Judah (1Sa 27:10), Jerahmeel himself is stated to be the firstborn son of Hezron, into whose clan foreign elements may subsequently have come to be incorporated. Sheshan's daughter who married Jarha (v.35) is probably the Ahlai mentioned in v.31.

41 The Elishama here named represents the twenty–third generation after Judah. With a lapse of some eight hundred years, this would bring us to about 1100 B.C., or to the generation of Jesse the father of David. Proposed identifications of Elishama with the priest of that name (2Ch 17:8), in about 850 B.C., are thus unlikely chronologically and impossible because of the latter's tribe (Levi, not Judah).

42–46 The closing verses of the chapter revert to the family of Caleb. The line of descent shows that individuals are intended, though their associated groups did occupy such centers in Judah as Hebron, Mareshah, and Ziph.

47 The relationship of the six sons of Jahdai to Caleb is not given.

48–49 Caleb's "daughter" Acsah was only a distant descendant of Caleb the son of Hezron, though she was an immediate daughter of Caleb the son of Jephunneh, the faithful spy (listed in 4:15). She is remembered as the bride of Othniel, the first of the judges (Jdg 3:9–11), having been promised to him for his conquest of Debir (Jos 15:15–19; Jdg 1:11–15).

50–53 Ephrathah (v.50) is a variant form for the name of Caleb's wife Ephrath (v.19).

54–55 The Kenites were originally a foreign people (Ge 15:19), some of whom, by marriage or by adoption, became incorporated into the tribe of Judah (cf. the instance of the family of Hobab, the brother-in-law of Moses, Nu 10:29–32; Jdg 1:16, 4:11). There is always room among the people of God for those who come to him by faith (Ex 12:38, 48; Eph 2:19). The clan of Recab later included the reformer Jehonadab (2Ki 10:15, 23), who preserved the purity of his descendants by retaining their primitive forms of nomadic life (Jer 35:6–10).

2. The family of David (3:1–24)

This chapter chronologically follows ch. 2, which had traced several of the branches of the tribe of Judah down to the time of Israel's united kingdom. At this point, however, the record restricts itself to the royal line of David (2:15) and carries it through five centuries, to about 500 B.C. The prophecy of Jer 22:30 in 597 had made it clear that no purely human descendant of his line could ever legitimately again occupy the throne; and when the Persians authorized the restoration of the Jewish community from Babylon in 538, they permitted no kingship.

Yet the Davidic family maintained its importance. It was represented in the return to Palestine, it supplied civic leaders for Judah (including her first two governors, down through 515 [Ezr 5:2, 15]), and Zechariah prophesied that it would continue to do so

(Zec 12:7–10). This house held the ultimate hope of Israel. The Messiah would someday arise from it, that Son of David whom postexilic prophecy identified as more than human. He would be God's "fellow" (Zec 13:7, KJV), pierced as a man but acknowledged as deity (12:10). He would bring redemption from sin (13:1) and God's kingdom on earth (14:9).

1–9 This listing of David's children repeats and supplements 2Sa 3:2–5; 5:13–16; and 13:1. Daniel, his son by Abigail, is named, alternatively, Kileab in 2Sa 3:3.

The list of younger sons (vv.5–8) is repeated in 14:3–7. Solomon was chosen to succeed David (22:9) rather than one of his older brothers, at least three of whom were murdered in inner-family struggles. The third son listed in v.6 (omitted in 2 Samuel) is Elpelet (cf. 14:5); his early death may account for David's choice of a longer form of this same name for his younger brother, Eliphelet (v.8). The next to last son (v.8) was originally named Beeliada (14:7), meaning "The (divine) Master knows." But this was changed (both here and in 2Sa 5:16) to Eliada ("God knows"), to avoid the idolatrous implications of Baal. In 2Sa 13 is a report of the scandal of Tamar's rape by her half-brother Amnon and the vengeance by her brother Absalom.

10–16 The remainder of the chapter lists the Davidic line of succession, first to the throne (vv.10–16, following the order that is in 1 and 2 Kings), and then, during the Exile and

Both an Islamic mosque and a Jewish synagogue stand over the traditional site of the Cave of Machpelah in Hebron, where Abraham, Sarah, Isaac, Rebekah, Jacob, and Leah were all buried. Courtesy Bastiaan Van Elderen.

beyond, to such nonkingly leadership as they may have enjoyed (vv.17–24, which are new).

Azariah (v.12), as used here (and in 2 Kings), represents the throne name of Uzziah, as is used elsewhere in Chronicles (cf. Isa 6:1). Similar is the name Shallum (v.15; cf. Jer 22:11) for Jehoahaz (2Ch 36:1–4; 2Ki 23:31–34). Though younger than Jehoiakim, he was preferred to him for the throne, following Josiah's death in 609 B.C; and though older in fact than Zedekiah (2Ch 36:2, 11), he is here listed after him, probably because his reign was so much shorter. Josiah's firstborn son, Johanan, is not mentioned elsewhere and may have died young.

The name Jeconiah (v.16; shortened to Coniah in Jer 22:24, 28; 37:1; see NIV note) means "Establishes (does) the LORD"; it usually has its elements transposed into Jehoiachin (2Ch 36:9–10; 2Ki 24:8–17), which means "The LORD establishes."

17 Shealtiel was the physical son of Neri (Lk 3:27) but must have become the legal (adopted) son of Jeconiah soon after the latter's captivity in March 597 B.C., since five out of the seven sons are mentioned on a Babylonian ration receipt dated to 592.

18 Shenazzar has been equated with Sheshbazzar ("prince of Judah," at the return in 538–537, Ezr 1:8); both seem to be shortened forms of the Akkadian Sin-aba-usur.

19–20 Shenazzar was succeeded as the first Persian governor of Judah (Ezr 5:4, 16) by his nephew Zerubbabel (2:2), physically the son of his next older brother Pedaiah, but reckoned as the legal son of the oldest brother, Shealtiel (Ezr 3:2, 8; Hag 1:1, 12; Mt 1:12; Lk 3:27). Shealtiel may have died without having children, so that his brother would have raised up seed to his name according to the custom of the levirate (Dt 25:5–10). The authenticity of many of the names that follow is confirmed by archaeological evidence from sixth and fifth centuries seals and letters.

21 The Hebrew text does not have "and" to introduce "the sons of Rephaiah, of Arnan. . ." These are not stated to be further grandsons of Zerubbabel but are presumably contemporaries of Jeconiah the captive whose relationship to him has not been preserved.

22–24 Since only five names now appear in the list of Shemaiah's six sons (v.22), one must have fallen out.

3. Other clans of Judah (4:1–23)

None of the genealogies of Judah recorded here appears elsewhere in Scripture. Verses 1–8 supplement ch. 2 on the clan of Hezron, a son of Judah's fourth son Perez. In particular they concern four sons of Hur (cf. v.4), who were grandsons of Hezron's third son Caleb, and eight branches of his fifth son Ashhur. Verses 9–20 describe the situations of eight leaders in Judah: Jabez, Kelub, Kenaz, Jehallelel, Ezrah, Hodiah, Shimon, and Ishi. However, while they too might be classified under Hezron, their exact relationship to him remains unknown, either because of gaps in Ezra's own sources or because of a lack of care in subsequent scribal transmission. Verses 21–23 outline the clan of Judah's third son Shelah (cf. 2:3).

1 Author Ezra expected his readers to recognize (from 2:5, 18, 50) that the five descendants of Judah, from Perez to Shobal, were not brothers but successive generations. "Carmi" must therefore be a scribal error (caused by 2:7?) for Caleb (Kelubai; cf. NIV note on 2:9).

2 These data supplement 2:52 on Hur's first son Shobal, where Haroeh had appeared as a variant for Reaiah.

3–5 Similarly v.3 on Hur's fourth son and v.4 on his fifth and sixth sons supplement 2:19; and vv.5–8, on the family of his uncle Ashhur, supplement 2:24.

6–8 "Haahashtari" is not a proper noun but is adjectival and designates "one descended from A(ha)shtar."

9–10 Jabez's prayer of faith became an occasion of grace, so that God kept and blessed him, rather than causing him "pain" ("Jabez" means "he causes pain").

11–12 Ir Nahash (v.12; cf. NIV note, "city of copper," or "coppersmith") is Khirbet Nahas, on the west side of the Arabah, south of the Dead Sea.

13–14 Though originally a foreign Kenizzite (whether of Canaan, Ge 15:19, or of Edom, 36:42), Othniel was adopted into Israel's tribe of Judah and became the first of the judges (see 2:49, 55). He who is adopted into the people of God can even become a leader.

15 Caleb was Othniel's brother; but he was sufficiently older (Jdg 1:13; 3:9), having belonged to the previous desert generation, among whom he was honored as one of the two faithful spies (Nu 13–14).

16 The settlement of Jehallelel's descendants, with those of Calebite Mesha, at Ziph (cf. 2:18, 42) in the southeastern part of Judah (Jos 15:24), confirms the preexilic authenticity of Ezra's source, since in his own day Judah's southern border failed to reach even to Hebron.

17–20 The wife of Mered intended in v.17 is Bithiah (v.18). Her identification as a daughter of Pharaoh would locate this event during the early part of Israel's sojourn in Egypt (before 1800 B.C.), the union probably being made possible because of Joseph's prominence.

21–23 Mareshah, in southwest Judah, experienced dual settlement (cf. v.16), both from these descendants of Judah's third son, Shelah, and from his fourth, Perez (2:4).

Over long periods Israel's genealogical clans could be associated with particular places, be organized into particular guilds—whether of linen workers (here), of potters (v.23), or of scribes (2:55)—or be maintained by particular royal patronage (4:23), a situation that has been confirmed archaeologically by means of distinctive pottery marks.

C. Simeon (4:24–43)

Because of their massacre of Shechem (Ge 34:24–30), the patriarchs Simeon and Levi were condemned to have their tribes scattered among Israel (49:5–7). The subsequent faithfulness of the Levites (Ex 32:27–29) converted their situation into one of blessing and of priestly leadership (Dt 33:8–11). But the Simeonites remained accursed (omitted altogether in the tribal blessings of Dt 33). Simeon was granted lands in Palestine only within the arid southwestern portions of Judah (Jos 19:1–9; cf. 15:26, 28–32, where these appear among territories that Joshua had previously assigned to Simeon's more favored neighbor); and it campaigned cooperatively with Judah in their conquest (Jdg 1:3).

Chronicles records first the primary genealogy of Simeon (4:24–27), then its list of towns (vv.28–33), and finally a summary of two of its later migrations (vv.34–41, 42–43). For after the division of Solomon's kingdom in 930 B.C., elements of Simeon either moved to the north or at least adopted its religious practices (cf. the inclusion of Beersheba along with the shrines of Ephraim that are condemned in Am 5:5), so that they are counted among the northern tribes (2Ch 15:9; 34:6). Other Simeonites carried on in a semi-nomadic life in isolated areas that they could occupy, such as those noted at the close of this chapter (v.41 dates to Hezekiah, 726–697 B.C.).

24 This list of Simeon's sons comes from Nu 26:12–13, which reflects Ge 46:10 and Ex 6:15, though with variations in spelling and with the omission of a third son, Ohad. The next son's name, Jarib, has been corrected by the Syriac to read Jachin, as in the other lists.

25–37 These verses constitute a supplement preserved only in Chronicles. Mibsam and his son Mishma should not be confused with Ishmaelites of the same names (1:29–30).

Beth Biri (v.31) is the Chronicler's postexilic designation for Beth Lebaoth (Jos 19:6), and for Shaaraim we should read (with Jos 19:6) Sharuhen, a historically significant city located in this area.

38–40 The name Gedor has been emended, with the LXX, into Gerar, a city south of Gaza toward Philistia in the west (cf. 2Ch 14:13–14). Yet the presence of Meunites (see below on v.41) and the direction of Simeon's other recorded attack, toward Seir (vv.42–43), suggest a Gedor "overlooking the Dead Sea" to the east.

In v.40 the Canaanites, as a branch of the Hamites (1:8), seem to be intended here.

41–43 The Meunites constitute an Edomite tribe; see 2Ch 20:1 (cf. 26:7). The phrase "remaining Amalekites" (v.43) implies some previous avenging work, i.e., of Saul (1Sa 14:48; 15:7) and of David (1Sa 30:17; 2Sa 8:12), against these ancient enemies of God's people (cf. Ex 17:8–13; Dt 25:17–19). Yet the tribe of Simeon was motivated as well by economic factors of overpopulation (v.38) and shortage of pasture (vv.39, 41).

D. Transjordan Tribes (5:1–26)

Though the OT's postexilic restoration centered in Judah, the population included elements from all twelve tribes, whose identity the Chronicler was anxious to perpetuate (cf. Ezr 6:17; 8:35). Chapter 5 concerns those once settled east of the Jordan rift. Even prior to Joshua's conquest of Canaan in the west, Moses' people had suffered a series of unprovoked attacks from the kings in Transjordan (Nu 21:21–23, 33). But all this had been of God (Dt 2:30) and resulted in the Israelites' acquisition of the whole territory from the Arnon (midway on the east shore of the Dead Sea) northward, and on through Gilead and Bashan. Moses then granted these areas (Nu 32:33–42), respectively, and at their own request, to Reuben (the subject of 1Ch 5:1–10), Gad (vv.11–17), and half of the tribe of Manasseh (vv.23–24; cf. 7:14–19, on their western half).

The remaining verses of ch. 5 describe an early, joint military campaign (vv.18–22, elaborating v.10)—in which God rewarded their faith and their prayers with a great victory over the Ishmaelites—and their later deportation to Assyria (vv.25–26), as the result of collective apostasy.

1 Reuben's crime of incest with his father's subordinate wife Bilhah (Ge 35:22) cost him his rights of the firstborn (49:4), which involved a double portion of inheritance (Dt 21:17). This was transferred to Joseph, first son of Rachel, the wife whom Jacob-Israel loved (Ge 49:25–26; cf. 48:20–22, on Joseph's double-tribed status, through his sons Ephraim and Manasseh). Joseph's leadership was first exercised personally (Ge 50:21), then later through Joshua (an Ephraimite), and thus for three more centuries (cf. Jdg 8:1–2; 12:1–6).

2 Yet Judah eventually became strongest: Jacob's prophecy of this tribe's preeminence over the other (Ge 49:8), and even of a scepter (v.10), was fulfilled in David's kingship (2Sa 5:1–3; cf. 7:8), which entailed the effective rejection of Joseph (Ps 78:67–70), and was rendered eternal through David's Greater Son, who was also God's Son (2Sa 7:14), Jesus the Messiah (Mt 1:1).

3 Reuben's four sons are listed just as in the Pentateuch (Ge 46:9; Ex 6:14; Nu 26:5–6),

but Ezra's data in the rest of the chapter are unique to Chronicles.

4–5 The text does not say from which of Reuben's sons Joel was descended.

6 The Assyrians exiled the Israelite border tribes in 733 B.C. (vv.22, 26; 2Ki 15:29).

7–9 The settlement in the areas mentioned here (named also in Nu 32:38) preceded 850 B.C., since they are claimed as Moabite in Mesha's inscription, as well as subsequently (Jer 48:1, 22; Eze 25:9).

10 Saul himself fought in Transjordan (1Sa 11:1–11), but with the Ammonites instead of the Hagrites, and at Jabesh Gilead, not far east of the river.

11 The plains of Bashan, extending from the gorge of the Yarmuk and thence north and east of Galilee, pertained to Manasseh (v.23). By wide scattering Gad's outposts reached them; but its major settlements lay in Gilead, south of the Yarmuk (cf. v.16).

12–15 The Gadite Buz is not otherwise known and is not to be confused with Abraham's nephew, Buz, the son of Nahor (Ge 22:21).

16 Sharon refers here, not to the coastal plain north of Philistia (Jos 12:18), but to broad pasturelands somewhere in Transjordan.

17 The reigns of Jotham and Jeroboam II extended from 793 to 731 (to 753, for the latter, in Israel; and 750–731, for Jotham, in Judah).

18–19 Hagar was the mother of Ishmael, whose twelve sons, in turn, included Jetur (NT "Iturea," Lk 3:1) and Naphish (Ge 25:12, 15; cf. the presence of such Arab tribes with Moab in Ps 83:6). Though "the battle was God's" (v.22), his people still had to initiate it!

20–22 God's divine presence did not mean that his people would not have to cry out in the battle; but when they did, he vindicated the prayers of those who trusted in him. The great numbers taken, including one hundred thousand people, shows this to have been no mere raid but a total, permanent occupation.

23 Senir was the Amorite name for Mount Hermon (Dt 3:9).

24–26 Since Pul was the private name of Tiglath-pileser III prior to his accession in 745 B.C., the NIV has properly translated: "God stirred up the spirit of Pul ... that is, Tiglath-Pileser." The Lord used even Assyrians to accomplish his purposes (Isa 10:5–6).

E. Levi (6:1–81)

The tribe of Levi became Israel's hereditary religious leaders (see comments on 4:24–43). Ezra took special pains to ensure their presence within the second return, which he led back in 458 B.C. (Ezr 8:15–20); and from the very start, postexilic Judah depended on their proper service (1:5; 3:8; 6:18–20). Levi included the priesthood, so that Ezra himself was careful to present his Levitical credentials (7:1–5), going back to Aaron, Israel's initial high priest. Authentic genealogy, indeed, was essential for investiture (cf. 2:59–63)—hence the practical relevance of this chapter to the Chronicler's own day.

Yet a deeper and more abiding significance lies in the nature of Israel's priesthood as types. Their service in the sanctuary reflected a heavenly pattern (Ex 25:9, 40; Heb 8:2, 5); and the atoning acts performed by Aaron's descendants were but foreshadows of that ultimate sacrifice, accomplished by Jesus Christ, our Great High Priest, by the offering up of himself once and for all (Heb 9:14, 24–25). Chapter 6 commences with Pentateuchal citations and concludes with territorial lists taken from Joshua, but it consists primarily of materials not found outside Chronicles.

1–2 Levi's sons always appear in this order based on age (Ge 46:11; Ex 6:16; Nu 3:17; 26:57). Kohath is singled out (Ex 6:18; Nu 3:19) as the ancestor of the priestly group.

3 This Amram is a family ancestor, separated by some 250 years and nine generations from the father of Moses and Aaron (cf. Ex 6:20; Nu 26:59) and from about five thousand Amramites living in their day (cf. Nu 26:62). Of the sons of Aaron (derived from Ex 6:23; Lev 10:1; Nu 3:2; 26:60), the first two died for their sacrilege (Lev 10:2; Nu 26:61); and the succeeding line of priests is here traced only through Eleazar (cf. Ex 6:25; Nu 25:7).

4–7 Some links have been omitted from the priestly genealogy: the twenty-one generations after Eleazar, down through Jehozadak

at the Exile (v.15), span more than eight hundred years; and forty years per generation seems overly high. The list includes no descendants of Eleazar's younger brother, Ithamar, who held office during the last of the judges and the early kingdom—e.g., Eli, Phinehas III, Ahitub, Ahimelech I (= Ahijah?), Abiathar, and Ahimelech II (1Sa 14:3; 22:20; 2Sa 8:17). Other preexilic high priests are not listed either.

8 Serving under David in 1000 B.C. was Zadok (2Sa 8:17; 15:24), son of Ahitub II (not to be confused with Ahitub I, noted above as the grandfather of David's other priest, Abiathar, who was of the Ithamar branch). Some critics reject Zadok's Hebrew genealogy and label him a Jebusite, perhaps to be associated with Melchizedek (see Ge 14:18).

9 Zadok's grandson Azariah I became high priest under Solomon, 970 B.C. (1Ki 4:2).

10 Azariah II, "who served as priest in the temple Solomon built," would thus belong later and, allowing for gaps to include the long-lived Jehoiada (2Ch 24:15), could be the high priest who resisted Uzziah's trespass against the temple and its priesthood in 751 (26:17).

11–15 Hilkiah (v.13) discovered the Book of the Law of the Lord given through Moses (2Ch 34:14), the event that led to Josiah's reformation of 622. Seraiah (v.14) suffered martyrdom to the Babylonians in 586 (2Ki 25:18); but his son Jehozadak was father of Jeshua (or Joshua), Judah's famous high priest of the return from captivity fifty years later (Ezr 3:2; 5:2; 10:18; Hag 1:1; Zec 3:1; 6:11).

16–30 The divisions of the three Levitical clans are those found in Ex 6:17–19 and Nu 3:18–20 (cf. Nu 26:58). Since Korah (v.22) is known to have come from the clan-patriarch Kohath through the branch of Izhar (vv.37–38), Amminadab could possibly be an alternative name for it. Korah was the leader who rebelled against Moses and whom the earth swallowed (Nu 16:32). Assir, Elkanah I, and Ebiasaph were then his sons (Ex 6:24) and not successive generations.

Uriel (v.24) may be the Levite who led the entire Kohathite clan in David's day (15:5). Comparisons of v.25 with vv.35–36 show that this is not the Elkanah of v.23 but rather the great-great-great-great-grandson of his brother Ebiasaph, i.e., Elkanah II.

Zophai, Nahath, and Eliab (vv.26–27) appear to be variant names for Zuph, Toah, and Eliel (vv.34–35). The Levite Elkanah IV is the husband of Hannah and the father of Samuel, the judge and prophet.

31–32 In his zeal for the proper worship of God, Ezra makes affirmations about the Davidic musicians (cf. Ezr 2:41). The "Tent of Meeting" was for God's meeting Israel (Ex 29:42–43), not for the people with each other!

33–38 David's musician Heman, 1000 B.C., is eighteen generations removed from Moses' adversary Korah, in 1445.

39–43 The name of Asaph's ancestor Shimei (v.42), the immediate son of Gershon (v.17), seems here to have been transposed with that of Jahath. The similarity then of five out of the six names of his descendants—from Jahath through Ethni (v.41)—to those of his brother Libni—Jehath to Jeatherai (vv.20–21)—has led some interpreters to assume that this must be an erroneous doublet, drawn from a single tradition. Yet 23:10 confirms the existence of Jahath as a legitimate, parallel branch of Gershon's younger son Shimei; and a deliberate reuse of names among brothers' sons is not infrequent (cf. the name Mahli, vv.19, 47, or how the Mahli of v.19 took for his child the name of this same older son of Gershon, i.e., that of his cousin Libni, v.29).

44–53 Ethan and Kishi (v.44) appear also as Jeduthun and Kushaiah (15:17). Verses 50–53 repeat vv.4–8 on the priestly line from Aaron, down to Zadok and Ahimaaz. This confirms that the Zadokite priests, alone among the Levitical divisions in David's day, had the authority to make a sacrificial atonement (v.49). It also furnishes a transition to the subject of the priestly cities that follows.

54–55 The remainder of ch. 6 lists the forty-eight towns that were assigned to the various branches of the tribe of Levi. As Jacob had predicted, they did become scattered among Israel (Ge 49:7). The list is taken from Jos 21. Ezra's reference to "the first lot," which went to the Aaronic priests, confirms the record that when Joshua distributed the land in 1400 B.C. among the western nine and one-half

tribes and Levi, he accomplished it by means of a lottery (Jos 4:2; 21:10).

56–60 The lands of Hebron (v.56) had been promised to Caleb by both Moses and Joshua (Jos 14:6–15). On the six cities of refuge (v.57), see Nu 35; Dt 19:1–10; Jos 20. Hilen (v.58) is the Chronicler's postexilic name for Holon (Jos 15:51; 21:15).

61–81 The nonpriestly Kohathites (v.61) also received towns out of Ephraim (v.66) and Dan (Jos 21:5, specifically Elteketh and Gibbethon, 21:23). The latter are required in v.68 to make up the subtotal of ten, where they are missing due to textual corruption. Jokmeam (v.68) is the Chronicler's postexilic name of Kibzaim (Jos 21:22).

F. Benjamin and Five Other Tribes (7:1–9:44)

1. Summaries (7:1–40)

Just as in the case of the two and one-half tribes of Transjordan (cf. the introductory discussion to 5:1–26), Ezra was concerned to perpetuate clan frameworks for other members of the former northern kingdom. Some representatives had associated themselves with Judah at the Fall of Samaria in 722 B.C. (cf. 2Ch 30:1–2), or even previously (11:13–16); and Josiah's expansion a century later embraced many more (34:6; cf. 1Ch 9:1). Others regained their place among God's people during the Exile of 586–538 (cf. Eze 37:15–23) and were able to return to Judah under Zerubbabel or under Ezra himself (cf. the casual allusion in Lk 2:36 to Anna of the tribe of Asher, one of the "ten lost tribes"). In the buffer zone between north and south lay Benjamin, which could include even the northern religious center of Bethel (Jos 18:22). It is summarized in ch. 7, along with the Ephraimite tribes, but is treated in greater detail in chs. 8 and 9 as Judah's major ally, both in the preexilic kingdom and postexilic restoration (1Ki 12:21, or the "two-twelfths" implied in 11:30–31, and Ezr 4:1).

This chapter outlines the clan structure that characterized Benjamin and five other tribes. Its sources are Ge 46 and Nu 26, but most of the later genealogies and other data lack biblical parallels. No mention is made of either Dan or Zebulun. Possibly these tribes had little influence or relevance among the Jews who made up Ezra's community.

1 The sons of Issachar appear as listed in Nu 26:23–24, with Puah as a variation on Puvah. Issachar's sons are also listed in Ge 46:13 and Nu 26:24.

2 Among the valiant descendants of Tola may have been the later judge who bore that clan name (Jdg 10:1).

3–5 For Izrahiah and his four sons, even with "many wives," to have "36,000" warriors seems unlikely, as does the total of 145,600 for just one tribe of the twelve. This appears to be the first of nine passages in Chronicles where "thousand") might better be translated as "chief" (a similar Hebrew word). Hence we should read in v.2: 22 chiefs, 600 (men); in v.3: 36 chiefs; and in v.5: 87 chiefs.

6 Among the sons of Benjamin, Bela and Beker correspond to Ge 46:21 (cf. Nu 26:38). The third, Jediael, is not mentioned elsewhere. Other sons appear in 8:1–2.

7–12 The figures, as in v.3, should best be read: v.7, as 22 chiefs, 34 men; v.9, as 20 chiefs, 200 men; and v.11, as 17 chiefs, 200 men. Ir and Aher (v.12) may be shortened forms for the names of Bela's youngest son Iri (v.7) and younger brother Aharah (8:1; cf. Nu 26:38).

13 Naphtali's sons correspond to those listed in Ge 46:24 and Nu 26:48–49, with minor changes in spelling. Bilhah was the servant of Rachel and the mother of Naphtali (Ge 30:3–8).

14 That Manasseh had an Aramean concubine may have reminded Ezra's readers of the racially mixed Samaritans in their own day (2Ki 17:24, 29; Ezr 4:2–3). As appears from the more complete record of western Manasseh in Nu 26:29–33, Asriel and Shemida (v.19) were the immediate sons of his grandson Gilead (cf. Jos 17:2).

15–19 Zelophehad (v.15) came three centuries later. His was the case raised by his daughters that prompted Moses' laws about female inheritance rights (Nu 26:33; 27:1–11; 36:1–12).

20–24 Of Ephraim's four sons noted in vv.20–21, 23, only Shuthelah had been recorded previously (Nu 26:35); Ezer and Elead had probably joined the families of their grandfather Joseph's brothers, who had settled in Goshen, only to be slain there on the northeastern border of Egypt by Palestinian raiders who came down from their birthplace in Gath.

25–29 Joshua is listed eight generations after Rephah. Taking Rephah's father as Ephraim's fourth son Beriah (v.23), we perceive Joshua's birth (c. 1500 B.C.; cf. Jos 24:29) to have been eleven generations after Joseph's, corroborating the approximately four-century interval that separated these two leaders.

30–40 The list of Asher's children plus two grandsons reproduces Ge 46:17 (cf. Nu 26:44–46). Shomer's brother Helem (v.35) appears in v.32 as Hotham. Father-son sequences between verses suggest that Ulla (v.39) may be a variant name for Ara in v.38. In v.40 the numeral "thousand" should probably be read "chief"; hence, 26 chiefs (see comment on v.3).

2. Benjamin (8:1–40)

First Chronicles 8 forms a major supplement to the summary of Benjamin given in 7:6–12. Its opening verses, however, on his first generations in Egypt, are based on Nu 26:38–40 (rather than on Ge 46:21, as in ch. 7). Verses 6–28 are almost without biblical parallel; they outline the genealogy of two family groups as these developed after the Hebrew conquest and resettlement of Canaan: the Benjamite household of Ehud, Israel's second judge (vv.6–7), and that of Shaharaim, some of whose great-grandchildren lived in the neighborhood of Jerusalem (v.28). The remainder of the chapter concerns the relatives who lived near them and who formed the ancestry of Saul, part of whose descent had been given in 1 Samuel.

Chronicles elaborates on this material, not simply because of the significance of King Saul and his family, as it continued a dozen generations after him, but primarily because of the importance of Benjamin as a tribe, which ranked second only to Judah in postexilic society, and because of the status it provided for many within its clan framework (cf. introductory discussion on ch. 2, and Ne 11:4, 7, 31, 36).

1–2 The name of Benjamin's third son, Aharah (Aher, 7:12), corresponds to Ahiram in Nu 26:38 (Ehi, in Ge 46:21), as do also those of the grandsons Addar (= Ard) and Naaman (v.3).

3–5 The second name in the list of Bela's sons (Gera) reappears as the seventh name (v.5); the former may have died prematurely.

6–7 Some five hundred years separate the latter Gera from his descendant Ehud, the left-handed Benjamite judge (Jdg 3:15). The nature of the civil rivalry that led Ehud's son Gera to deport his own clansmen remains unknown.

8–13 Though Shaharaim's movement to Moab seems to locate him in Palestine in Ehud's general period (cf. the Benjamite towns mentioned in vv.12–13), his exact ancestry is lacking. The divorce of his first two wives demonstrates even further the moral deterioration of Israel during c. 1300 B.C. (cf. the previous Benjamite outrages condemned in Jdg 19:22–28; 20:12–14). The victory over the men of Gath (v.13) preceded their major Philistine reinforcement in 1200 B.C.

14–27 Meshullam, Heber (v.17), Ishmerai (v.18), and Shimei (v.21) seem to be variants for the names of Elpaal's sons Misham, Shemed, Eber, and Shema, as listed earlier (vv.12–13).

28 The phrase "all these" then identifies Beriah's and Shema's sons (vv.14–16, 19–21), brothers (vv.17–18), and grandsons (vv.22–27) as the ones living about Jerusalem.

29–32 When Mikloth and his son Shimeah (v.32) are said to live not only (following the lit. Heb.) "over against" their brothers (Mikloth's immediate family, in vv.30–31), but also "with" their relatives, we conclude that Mikloth's otherwise unidentified father Jeiel (cf. 1Sa 9:1 and the variant form, Abiel) should be grouped with the sons of Beriah and Shema.

33 Jeiel's fifth son, Ner, was the grandfather of Saul, the first king of Israel (1043–1010 B.C.), and also the father of Abner, Saul's military commander and uncle (1Sa 14:50–51). Abinadab (1Sa 31:2) appears elsewhere (1Sa 14:49) as Ishvi. Abinadab's brother's name, Esh–Baal (meaning "man of the [divine] Master"), is changed throughout 2Sa 2:8–4:12 to Ish-Bosheth ("man of shame"); for the Hebrew word *baal* could be treated as a proper noun designating the shameful idol of that name.

34 Similarly Merib-Baal ("warrior of the Master") appears in 2Sa 4:4–21:7 as Mephibosheth ("one who scatters [?] shame").

35–40 The warriors' "grandsons" (v.40) represent the thirteenth generation after Mephibosheth, who was five at the death of Saul and Jonathan in 1010 B.C., which brings us to the Exile of 586.

3. Jerusalem's inhabitants (9:1–44)

Chapter 9 continues the Chronicler's discussion of preexilic Benjamin (begun in 7:6) by cataloging the family groups that lived in Jerusalem just prior to its capture and destruction in 586 B.C. In addition to Benjamin (vv.7–9), these included clans from Judah (vv.4–6) and especially from Levi because of its key functioning in the temple services: whether from among the priests (vv.10–13), the nonpriestly Levites in general (vv.14–16), or the more specialized gatekeepers (vv.17–19). This in turn leads into a description of their duties (vv.20–34). Jerusalem did, however, lie within the tribal boundaries of Benjamin (Jos 18:16, 28), and it had already received some discussion in the preceding chapter (8:28, 32); hence its inclusion at this point. Such information about former population groups and activities, in what was still the nation's capital city, was of prime importance to Ezra and his colleagues in their efforts to restore legitimate theocracy to Judah in their own postexilic situation.

1 This transition verse shifts the reader's attention away from the tribal registers that have gone before. "The book of the kings" designates a court record now lost (see the introduction).

2 The NIV's phrase "the first to resettle" represents words that are, literally, "the dwellers, the first ones." In the present context the event that separates the Chronicler from "the first ones" is defined as the Babylonian captivity (v.1); hence the dwellers should probably be understood as the former, preexilic Jerusalemites (cf. the introduction to this chapter).

The "temple servants" (GK 5987) were literally "given ones." They might consist of captives who had been spared but enslaved to temple service. Early Hebrew examples include certain Midianite women (Nu 31:35, 47) or the people of Gibeon (Jos 9:22–23), but their organization as a class is credited to David (Ezr 8:20).

3 Individual Jerusalemites who had come from Ephraim or other northern tribes receive no further mention, since the list that follows cites only major clan leaders.

4–9 For "Shilonites" (v.5), read Shelanites, as in Nu 26:20, since Perez (v.4), Shelah, and Zerah (v.6) make up the divisions of Judah (2:3–4).

10–13 Jedaiah, Jehoiarib, and Jakin, with Malkijah and Immer (v.12), are the names of the second, first, twenty-first, fifth, and sixteenth of the twenty-four priestly courses established by David (24:7–18), rather than names of individuals. The fact that Azariah IV (v.22) is the son of Hilkiah (see 6:13) dates this listing to shortly after 622 B.C.

14–16 Shemaiah came from Merari, the third of the three Levitical clans. Mattaniah belonged to the first, Gershon, through Asaph, one of David's chief musicians. Obadiah was again of Merari, through the chief musician Jeduthun (= Ethan; cf. 6:44), while Berekiah's ancestor Elkanah bears a frequently reappearing Kohathite name.

17–18 Since the temple faced east, the "King's Gate" was the main gate (cf. Ac 3:2, in NT times), i.e., the king's entrance (Eze 46:1–2) and most honored station. Ezra's phrases "camp" of the Levites and God's "Tent" (v.19; cf. NIV note) recall how Levi once encamped on the four sides of the tabernacle (Nu 3:25–38).

19–20 Though Korah had been slain (see 6:22), his line continued. Coming from Kohath—the second clan but also that of Moses, Aaron, and the priests—the Korahites were even honored, by appointment as gatekeepers under Aaron's faithful grandson, Phinehas I, on whom God bestowed the Levitical covenant of peace (Nu 25:11–13). Their status continued, through Kore, whether denoting Korah's immediate grandson of this name (1Ch 26:1) or a later Kore in 725 B.C. (2Ch 31:14), down to this Shallum a century later.

21 Since both Meshelemiah and Zechariah served under David (26:8–11), this "Tent of Meeting" (cf. 6:32) would seem to refer to the curtained form of God's house (16:1; 17:1; cf. 22:1 and Ps 30 title) erected prior to Solomon's permanent temple (see v.19, NIV note).

22–24 It was appropriate that Samuel, himself a Korahite (6:27) and one of the doorkeepers in his youth (1Sa 3:15), should have anticipated David in their final organization (1Ch 26). The way Israel could commit to them "their positions of trust" indicates something of how the righteous live by faith, or trust, in God (Hab 2:4; Ro 1:17).

The number of their chiefs could vary: 94 under David (26:8–11); compare 139 among the first return (Ezr 2:42) and 172 under Nehemiah (Ne 11:19).

25–29 Twenty-four guard stations (26:17–18) and 216 chosen gatekeepers (212, v.22, plus the 4 leaders of vv.26–27, who stayed permanently in Jerusalem) works out exactly to nine people for each post. If we assume eight-hour shifts, this would require seventy-two men on duty, one week out of every three; twelve-hour shifts would require forty-eight on a week's duty, once every four or five weeks.

30 Reference seems to be to spices used for the holy anointing oil, for those who mixed it were a closely restricted group (Ex 30:33, 38).

31 "The offering bread" refers to the flat cakes that were used in the grain offerings (Lev 2;6:14–18; 7:9–10).

32 "The bread" refers to "the bread of the Presence" that was set out in rows on the golden table to symbolize the communion of the redeemed with God (Lev 24:5–6).

33 The musicians mentioned here are the leaders named in vv.14–16.

34 This verse then sums up all the Levitical inhabitants of Jerusalem (vv.10–33).

35–44 The rest of ch. 9 reverts to reproducing the lines of Benjamin that lived near Jerusalem. It virtually repeats 8:29–38 on the family of Saul; but its purpose here is to introduce the tragic conclusion to his reign (ch. 10).

II. The Reign of David (10:1–29:30)

A. Background: the Death of Saul (10:1–14)

Having established Israel's historical setting and ethnic bounds in the preceding genealogies (chs. 1–9), the Chronicler now enters his main subject, the history of the Hebrew kingdom, with its theological conclusions. His central character is David, on whom the remainder of 1 Chronicles focuses (chs. 10–29). David's devotion led him to set up the institutions of public worship that Ezra was so eager to maintain. David's heroic personality exemplifies the success that God bestows on those who trust in him. His posterity, moreover, constitutes the ruling dynasty of Judah throughout the rest of its independent history (the content of 2 Chronicles) and would bear its ultimate fruit in the eternal kingdom of Jesus the Messiah. Practical aims like these also explain why Ezra omitted the less edifying events of the reign of Saul; for he moves directly from the king's Benjamite genealogy (9:35–44) to his death (ch. 10), which precipitated David's rise to the throne (v.14). First Chronicles 10:1–12 derives directly from 1Sa 31, with slight differences in the choice of the details described; vv.13–14 then point up the chapter's negative doctrine: God condemns those who forsake him to failure.

1 The Philistines were a Hamitic people, but of Minoan background rather than Canaanite (see on 1:12). Before the year 2000, some had settled on the southern coast of Palestine (the very name of which means "Philistine land") and encountered Abraham (Ge 21:32; cf. 26:14). They remained after Joshua's conquest in 1400 (Jos 13:2–3) and only temporarily lost certain of their cities to Judah (Jdg 1:18). Shamgar's skirmish with them in 1250 (3:31) was successful but simultaneously demonstrates Israel's material disadvantage to their presence (cf. 1Sa 13:19–22). With the Fall of Crete to widespread barbarian movements in 1200, the "remnant . . . of Caphtor" (Jer 47:4) reinforced the earlier Philistines on Asia's Canaanite mainland.

For a century, following a crushing defeat of the Peleset (generally conceded to be the Philistines) by Pharaoh Rameses III, the Philistines seemed content to consolidate their city-states; but then in three waves they almost overwhelmed Israel. The first extended for forty years, including Samson's time (Jdg 10:7; 13:1; 1Sa 4), but was broken in 1063 B.C. by Samuel at the second battle of Ebenezer (1Sa 7:13); and the second wave, for perhaps ten years, by Saul at the battle of Micmash in 1041 (14:31). Now 1Ch 10, which dates to 1010 B.C., marks the onset of the Philistines' last major advance and period of oppression, which would be broken some seven years later by David (1Ch 14:10–16).

Mount Gilboa lay at the head of the great east-west Valley of Esdraelon, below Galilee, so that its loss by Israel enabled the Philistines to penetrate to the Jordan and even beyond (1Sa 31:7).

2 On Saul's sons, see 8:33.

3–4 Saul's fear of "abuse" (GK 6618), if the Philistines should take him alive (cf. Jdg 16:21), drove him to suicide, which was unprecedented in the OT (though cf. later occurrences in 2Sa 17:23; 1Ki 16:18). This testifies to the Philistines' cruelty despite material culture (cf. v.9 and today's use of "Philistine" as a byword for barbarism).

5 The context makes clear that Saul's death occurred at his own hands (see also comments on 2Sa 1:6–10, where an Amalekite reported to David that he had killed Saul, probably hoping for a reward).

6 Those of Saul's house who stood with him ("all his men," 1Sa 31:6) died together at Gilboa; others, however, both of his sons and troops, did survive (1Ch 8:34–40; 2Sa 2:8; 21:8). Alternatively, this may be the Chronicler's way of intimating the otherwise omitted data in 2Sa 1–4 on Ish-Bosheth.

7–10 According to 1Sa 31:10, the Philistines hung Saul's body on the walls of Beth Shan, a major city between Gilboa and the Jordan; the deity in whose temple they put his armor was Ashtoreth, goddess of sex and war. Saul's head was placed in another's temple, that of the vegetation god Dagon (cf. 1Sa 5:2–5). The validity of the two buildings has been attested archaeologically by the discovery of both temples in Beth Shan's ruins of this period.

11–12 The men of Jabesh Gilead in Transjordan remained faithful to Saul, their deliverer thirty years earlier (1Sa 11:1–11).

13–14 Saul's unfaithfulness consisted of disobeying God's words through Samuel (1Sa 13:8–9; 15:2–3) and of consulting the spiritist at Endor (28:7–13) instead of persevering— he had made some inquiry of him (v.6)—in prayer for divine grace.

B. David's Rise (11:1–20:8)

In this section, the author covers the period between 1003 and about 995 B.C., during which David rose to the zenith of his power. The seven and one-half years of disputed succession, civil war, and Philistine domination (2Sa 1–4) that followed Saul's death in 1010 (cf. 2Sa 5:5) are passed over. But they are not denied: Ezra's observation in the opening verse of the section (11:1), that Israel came to "Hebron" to anoint David, constitutes a tacit recognition of his initial installation there, but only by his own tribe of Judah (2Sa 2:4,10b); of the rejection of his appeal to the other tribes to the north and east (vv.5–6); and of their eventual choice of Saul's son Ish-Bosheth, 1005–1003 (vv.8–10a).

Instead, Chronicles amplifies the record of 2Sa 5–10, which includes David's capture of Jerusalem and its establishment as a new political capital for him and his supporters (1Ch 11–12); his achievement of independence from the Philistines (ch. 14); his return of the ark of the covenant, which made Jerusalem the religious capital of united Israel (chs. 13; 15–16); and the triumphant advance of his armies in every direction (chs. 18–20). Only the account of David's personal kindness to Jonathan's lame son Mephibosheth (2Sa 9) is omitted.

The heart of this section is found in God's prophecy to David through Nathan (ch. 17): "I have been with you wherever you have gone. . . . I will subdue all your enemies" (vv.8, 10). The Lord's "great promises" (v.19) applied not only to David, but to "my people Israel" as a whole (v.9)—not only in the early tenth century B.C., but for "the future of the house of your servant" (v.17). Its assurances are applicable to Ezra's struggling postexilic community; to the present church of Jesus, whom David predicted: "He will be my son" (v.13; cf. Ps 110:1; Mt 22:42–45); and to that yet future kingdom of the Messiah, whose "throne will be established forever" (v.14).

1. David established in Jerusalem; his heroes (11:1–12:40)

The section's initial subdivision documents David's ascendancy. Following his consecration as king over a reunited Israel (11:1–3), one of his first acts was to capture and then to strengthen Jerusalem (vv.4–9; cf. 2Sa 5:1–10). The Chronicler then proceeds to describe David's heroes: "the Three" (vv.10–19), two of the major commanders (vv.20–25), and "the Thirty" (vv.26–47; cf. 2Sa 23:8–39). The concluding list in ch. 12, however, is unique to 1 Chronicles. It describes the military leaders and tribal officers who came over to David before his final anointing and who played a primary role in his eventual elevation to the kingship (v.38). It suggests David's growing popular support beyond the four hundred men of 1Sa 22:2 (later six hundred, 27:2).

1 The phrase "all Israel" is characteristic of the Chronicler's concern for the unity of God's people. Emphasis here falls on the portions of Israel that had so far not recognized David's kingship.

2 The Lord's appointment of David dates back some twenty years to his first anointing, in the privacy of his family, by Samuel (1Sa 15:28; 16:1–13). As David then demonstrated his ability for leadership (18:5, 16), he was increasingly recognized as standing in line for the throne (23:17; 25:30), even by Saul

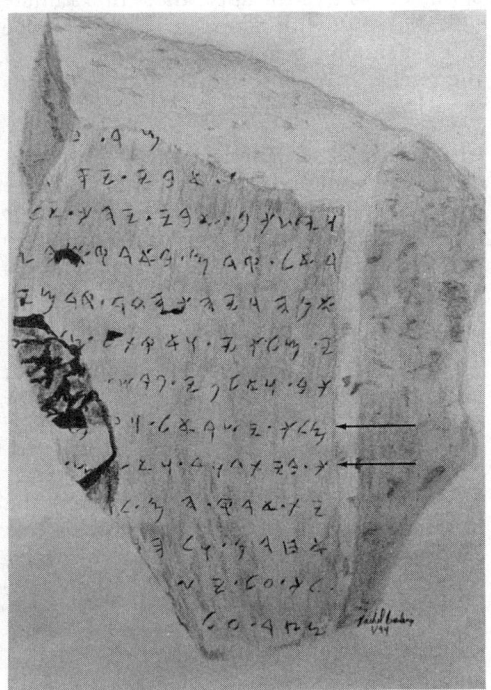

This is a drawing of the first clear reference in stone to the House of David (found in 1993 at Tel Dan). The lines with the arrows read: "the king of Israel . . . of the house of David." Drawing by Rachel Bierling.

himself (24:20; 26:25). At Saul's death David had received a second anointing, over Judah (2Sa 2:4); and Abner had started the preparation for his total rule (3:10).

3 This third anointing was preceded by a "compact" (lit., "covenant"; GK 1382) before the Lord, by which both king and people acknowledged their mutual obligations under God. Such a "constitutional monarchy" was unique in the ancient Near East, for the only effective curb against despotism is one's personal belief in God and commitment to his higher kingship. Contrast the reputation for clemency and the religious scruples of even a weak Hebrew monarch like Ahab (1Ki 20:31; 21:3–4, 27–29) with the natural (unrestrained) ruthlessness of his Canaanite wife, Jezebel (21:7–10).

4–5 Allusions to Jerusalem appear first in the Ebla tablets of 2400 B.C. The city is described as Salem in reference to Abraham in 2000 (Ge 14:18) and as Urusalim in the Egyptian Amarna letters, which may confirm the Hebrew conquest in 1400. Jerusalem had led a southern Canaanite alliance against Joshua (Jos 10:1–5), who defeated its army and executed its king (10:10, 26; 11:7, 10). The tribe of Judah overran the defenses of the city itself (Jdg 1:8), but the Jebusites soon reoccupied it. For almost four centuries Judah had been unable to win back Jerusalem and drive out its Canaanite inhabitants (Jos 15:63; Jdg 1:21; 19:10–11), which helps explain the latter's overconfidence against David (1Ch 11:5; 2Sa 5:6). David had posted notice long before of his intention against the haughty city (1Sa 17:54).

While 2Sa 5:6 identifies the attackers only as "David's men," Chronicles includes "all the Israelites" (cf. v.10 and 12:38, which concede the primary role exercised by David's particular followers).

6 The king's offer that whoever "leads the attack," i.e., first penetrated Jerusalem, would become commander over the armies of united Israel may represent an attempt on his part to replace his effective but self-willed nephew Joab, who had been leading the forces of Judah up to this point (cf. 2Sa 3:39). Joab nevertheless retained his post by bravely achieving the initial entrance, ascending a concealed watershaft from the Gihon spring so as to end up within the city walls.

7 David's relocation to Jerusalem was a strategic move. It provided him not only with an impregnable citadel militarily, but also with a neutral site politically as a capital, lying as it did on the border between Judah and the northern tribes (cf. Washington, D.C.). He called it "The City of David." Near Eastern conquerors not infrequently named cities after themselves.

8–9 "Terraces" (GK 4864; lit., "Millo"; cf. NIV note) means "filling." These "terraces" had been built so that the city's eastern walls could extend far enough down the steep Kidron slope to encompass the Gihon watershaft, and they suffered a continuing need for repair (1Ki 11:27; 2Ch 32:5).

10 The remainder of the chapter is a catalog of David's mighty men, introduced at this point because of the significant role they played in his rise to the kingship and in his establishment at Jerusalem. Their listing, down through Uriah the Hittite (v.41), corresponds to one of the appendices in 2 Samuel (2Sa 23:8–39), with minor variations. Twelve of their number reappear as commanders of the twelve corps into which David's troops were later organized (1Ch 27).

11 The hero's sensational victory was actually over eight hundred men (2Sa 23:8). Three hundred seems to be a scribal error, perhaps influenced by the number that appears in v.20 or by the nature of the numerical symbols employed.

12 David's greatest champions were "the Three," though the record of the third, Shammah (2Sa 23:11), has accidentally been dropped.

13–14 After the words "the Philistines gathered there for battle," we should insert the material supplied in 2Sa 23:9 (following this clause) and on into v.11 (through a similar clause).

15 Next to "the Three" ranked "the Thirty"—which was apparently the original number in this legion of honor among David's men. Second Samuel 23:24–39 actually lists thirty-seven, including the outstanding "Three" and the two commanders; and 1Ch 11:41b–47 adds sixteen more, as new heroes were added to the group. Which ones of the "Thirty" performed the deed that follows is not stated.

The Valley of Rephaim, where the Philistines encamped, lies southwest of Jerusalem. Its mention connects this event with their first campaign against David (14:8–9), even before his capture of the city. David had thus retreated to his old outlaw stronghold at Adullam (1Sa 22:1; 2Sa 5:17). Its citation constitutes another allusion to David's difficult rise to power, which the Chronicler never seeks to conceal.

16–18 David poured out the water he had longed for as a libation offering to the Lord (Lev 23:37), showing both how precious he considered his men, who had risked their lives to get it, and how centrally he placed God in his own life.

19 David called the water their "blood," since life does depend on its presence (cf. Ge 9:4; Lev 17:14; Dt 12:23).

20–21 Abishai was David's half-nephew. His heroism was demonstrated by his having volunteered to go down at night with David into Saul's camp (1Sa 26:6–7). He had also been a joint commander, with his brother Joab, against the forces of Ish-Bosheth and Abner (2Sa 2:24). He was later to lead divisions in the wars against the Ammonites (10:10), Absalom (18:2), and Sheba (20:6). The locale of this incident has not been preserved, but it may have occurred when Abishai commanded an expedition against Edom (1Ch 18:12).

22 The NIV phrase about Moab's "best men" reads in the Hebrew the *"'ari'el* [GK 738] of Moab." *'Ari'el* must here be used, not in its impersonal sense of "the altar-hearth of God" (Isa 29:1–2, 7), but in its personal sense (lit., "the lions of God)"; that is, Benaiah overcame "the mighty lions (of Moab)," with the superlative use of "God."

23–25 When the spear of Benaiah's Egyptian opponent is said to be like "a weaver's rod," the reference is to the heavy shaft of a loom that holds the threads taut; i.e., this was a massive weapon. For such heroism he became commander of David's professional Cretan and Philistine troops (1Ch 18:17) and later of Solomon's entire army (1Ki 4:4).

26 The roster of the Thirty begins at this point and must have been first formulated some time before David became king of all Israel; Asahel, the youngest of David's half-nephews, was killed pursuing Abner in his uncle's war against Ish-Bosheth (2Sa 2:18–23). Elhanan, son of Dodo, should not be confused with Elhanan son of Jair, the hero who slew the brother of Goliath (1Ch 20:5).

27 The phrase "the Harorite" has two scribal errors and should read "the Harodite," i.e., "a man from Harod," the pool near Mount Gilboa where Gideon tested his men (Jdg 7:1–7). But while the place names are subject to a measure of control, a number of the personal names (vv.27–38) differ from those found in the parallel list in 2Sa 23:25–36, perhaps partly because of later spelling patterns in Ezra's day, some 475 years after the writing of 2 Samuel.

28–31 Benaiah from Pirathon (v.31) is not to be confused with Benaiah the commander (vv.22–25) from Kabzeel, near Beer Sheba, in the south.

32–47 "Ahijah the Pelonite" (v.36) should read "Eliam [= Ammiel, 1Ch 3:5] the Gilonite" (cf. 2Sa 23:34), the father of Bathsheba and a son of David's counselor, Ahithophel (2Sa 11:3), who did come from Giloh (15:12).

12:1 Among those who supported David prior to his rise over all Israel (11:3), the first group listed in 12:1–7) is datable to the sixteen months just before Saul's death in 1010 B.C. They came to Ziklag, the town on the southwestern border of Judah, over which David had been appointed as a vassal ruler by Achish, the Philistine king of Gath (1Sa 27:5–7).

2 The warriors were from Benjamin and were significant both for their individual prowess and for the fact that even though they were Saul's fellow tribesmen, they recognized David as God's appointed sovereign.

3–7 Though Ishmaiah (v.4) is not listed among the Thirty, at one time he served as their commander (cf. also v.18 and 11:21). The five Korahites (v.6) were of Levi (see 6:22; 9:19) but probably lived in Benjamin.

8–15 Those listed from Gad joined David even earlier while he was still in Judah in his desert stronghold, presumably the cave of

Adullam (11:15; 12:16; cf. 1Sa 22:1). Jeremiah (v.13), the tenth Gadite leader, differs from the fifth (v.10) in that his Hebrew name has a longer form. During the first month (March/April), the Jordan is in its spring flood (cf. Jos 3:15; 4:18), which makes the Gadites' achievement in vv.14–15 all the more noteworthy.

16–18 The Holy Spirit literally "clothed himself with" Amasai (v.18). So inspired, his devotion to David as God's chosen servant is then expressed in Hebrew poetry.

19–22 The leaders from Manasseh arrived just before Saul's death at Gilboa, which lay in the western part of Manasseh's territory. David, however, was sent away from the actual battle, as explained in 1Sa 29. The Philistine commanders' mistrust and fear of David are stated clearly in 1Sa 29:4–5. The Manassites' help against the raiders is explained in 1Sa 30.

The NIV rendering "like the army of God" (v.22) reflects a Hebrew phrase that is literally "like the camp of God" (cf. 11:22). It may be connected to the idea expressed in the divine name "LORD of hosts [= armies]" in 11:9 (NIV, "LORD Almighty"), which can refer to the armies of Israel. Here, however, David's multitude may be compared, poetically, with the heavenly hosts, whether of stars (Dt 4:19; Ne 9:6; Ps 33:6) or of angels (Ge 32:1–2; Ps 103:20–21).

23 The chapter concludes by enumerating the officers who came to Hebron seven and one-half years later to turn over the entire nation to him (bringing us back to 11:1).

24–37 Although some have defended the accuracy of the large numbers given in these verses or have suggested that they are deliberate hyperbole, since these delegations are limited to specially equipped leaders "famous in their own clans" (v.30; cf. v.25), presumably the same that are cited at the beginning of the next chapter as "commanders of thousands and commanders of hundreds" (13:1)—the numbers given should probably not be read as bare totals but, in v.24, for example, as "six (commanders of) thousands, eight (commanders of) hundreds." There were, as we might say, 6 colonels and 8 captains, for a total of 14, not 6,800. Notice what would otherwise be the incongruously small totals in v.28 with Zadok and 22 officers, or

v.32, the apparently large delegation of 200 chiefs from Issachar. The number of officers assembled thus amounts to 398 (not 340,800 in Hebron at one time!).

Among the warriors from Levi (vv.27–28), Jehoiada the priest seems to have been father of Benaiah, the major commander (11:22; 27:5), while Zadok, still young at this time, may be the Aaronite who became the colleague of Abiathar and later, under Solomon, his successor as high priest (29:22; 1Ki 2:35; 4:4).

The men of Issachar (v.32) "understood the times" and thus cast their lot with David rather than Saul.

38–40 The three-day feast at David's accession was an immediate, historic celebration; but it points to the doctrine of the future, messianic feast (Ps 22:29; Isa 25:6; Rev 19:7).

2. The ark sought (13:1–14)

This chapter (esp. from v.6 onward) parallels the first part of 2Sa 6:1–11. Chronologically the events it describes followed David's wars with the Philistines (2Sa 5:18–25), and perhaps the construction of his palace as well (5:11–12; cf. 1Ch 14:1). But to the Chronicler the account of David's search for the ark of God takes precedence over these other matters, to which he turns in the next chapter (14:1–2, 8–17). Logically in his mind, piety has greater significance than civil action. Ezra's primary concern was to lead the members of his postexilic Jewish community into an enthusiastic commitment to the faith and the practices enjoined in the law of Moses (Ezr 7:10). He therefore describes next the king's attempt to bring the Ark of the Covenant to Jerusalem, which illustrates a renewed desire on Israel's part to seek God (1Ch 13:3) and to worship him (v.8). Even the temporary suspension of David's attempt (vv.9–13) became a demonstration of the necessity for exact conformity to the divine standards for worship, while the blessing that attended Obed-Edom's care for it (v.14) exemplified God's positive reward for one's devotion.

1 David consulted the military leaders, as in 2Sa 6:1.

2 But the Chronicler adds other details, whether of a more democratic character, i.e., calling in "the whole assembly" ("all the people," v.4), or of a more religious, including "priests and Levites," those consecrated to "the will of the LORD our God." The phrase "the rest of our brothers" is literally "our brothers that are left." This may reflect something of the seriousness of the third major Philistine oppression against Israel, 1010–1003 B.C. (see 10:1), which David had just broken (2Sa 5:20, 25).

3–4 The ark was a gold-covered chest, which contained among other items the stone tablets of the Decalogue (cf. Heb 9:4), which witnessed to God's covenant with his people. The ark was the most holy object in the whole system of Mosaic worship, for it served primarily as a sacramental symbol of the very presence of God, whose glory cloud was enthroned above it (v.6; Ex 25:22; cf. 1Sa 4:7). Israel, however, lapsed into a mechanical concept, that God was necessarily present with the ark. To overcome such superstitious notions about their having "God in a box," the Lord thus allowed his holy ark to be captured at the disastrous first battle of Ebenezer, about 1085 B.C. (1Sa 4:10–11). But once this lesson had been absorbed, he resumed his manifestations of power from over its golden cover, the mercy (atonement) seat.

Disrespect toward the holy object led to divine plagues, first against the pagan Philistines and then against the men of Judah at Beth Shemesh, who felt compelled to remove this fearful presence from their sight (1Sa 6). For eighty years, therefore, it rested in the house of Abinadab at Kiriath Jearim (1Sa 7:1), some eight miles west of Jerusalem on the border between Benjamin and Judah.

Characteristic of the religious insensitivity that marked the entire period of David's predecessor, the ark had not been sought in the days of Saul. One possible exception is noted in 1Sa 14:18; and even at this point the ark may not have been brought out but only asked for.

5 David assembled "all the Israelites," specified in 2Sa 6:1 as thirty thousand men. They gathered from Lebo Hamath in the north, in the valley between the Lebanons, to as far away as "the Shihor," traditionally understood as an Egyptian word meaning "pool [or stream] of Horus," perhaps here identifying a watercourse in Egypt's eastern delta.

6–9 "Baalah of Judah" (from 2Sa 6:2)—or here, lit., "Baalath ... that [belongs] to Judah"—is a Canaanite name for Kiriath Jearim (or Kiriath Baal, in Jos 18:14). Uzzah and Ahio were sons, or descendants, of Abinadab (2Sa 6:3). The locations of "the threshing floor of Kidon" (called by the variant name "Nacon," 2Sa 6:6) and of "Perez Uzzah" (v.11; cf. NIV note) remain unknown.

10 The severity of the divine judgment against Uzzah, even though his action had been well-intentioned, provided an illustration to all future generations of the necessity for reverence and for absolute conformity to God's directives concerning his holy objects. The transgression in this instance was twofold. (1) The ark should not have been placed on a cart but carried by hand, as David himself later acknowledged (15:13). True, the Philistines had previously transported it on a wagon (1Sa 6:11), but they had acted in heathen ignorance. (2) It should not have been touched. Even its authorized carriers, Levites of the clan of Kohath (cf. 15:2)—which Abinadab may or may not have been—had long ago been warned against this by Moses, on pain of death (Nu 4:15).

11–12 David's anger is psychologically explainable, if not ethically justifiable; for it was he who had the overall responsibility for the course of these events. But his anger rapidly turned to fear. His unwillingness, as he said, to "bring the ark of God to me," meant, in effect, that he did not want to bring it to his capital in Jerusalem, the city of David, that was so closely identified with himself.

13–14 Obed-Edom the Gittite (i.e., a resident of Gath) was indeed a Levite of the clan of Kohath, family of Korah (26:1, 4). As a Korahite gatekeeper (15:18, 24, and also a musician, v.21), he met the requirements of the law for service as a caretaker of the ark; and he was signally blessed.

3. Independence from the Philistines (14:1–17)

On the whole ch. 14 reflects its source in 2Sa 5:11–23, with a few additions. The events it describes do not seem to fit the three-month interval that elapsed between chs. 13 and 15, during which the ark remained with Obed-Edom (13:14; 15:25). They rather precede this (cf. introductory discussion to ch.

13). After summarizing certain aspects of his family (vv.1–7), Ezra delineates the king's first international crisis, that of his confrontation with the Philistines (vv.8–17). For when David had finally fled from Saul's kingdom (c. 1012 B.C.), he had become a Philistine vassal (1Sa 27:1–28:2); and during his years at Hebron, which parallel the period of their third major oppression of the Hebrews (1010–1003; see 10:1), the Philistines probably considered him as just another client king. Yet with his anointing as monarch over the reunited Israel, David became a threat they could no longer ignore (v.8). They attacked immediately, even before David had been able to occupy Jerusalem (11:7; see 11:15). But because he looked to the Lord for his strength and for his strategy, he was able to beat back two Philistine offenses, to secure the independence of God's people, and to terminate forever the threat of Philistine conquest and oppression. The teaching of ch. 14 has a valid principle for Christian believers: "God has gone out in front of you to strike the Philistine army [i.e., your enemies]" (v.15).

1–2 Some scholars have dated Hiram's kingship over Tyre to about 969–936 B.C., which is in the time of Solomon rather than of David (cf. 2Ch 2; cf. 8:18; 9:10, 21). But Chronicles (and 2Sa 5:12) associates the construction of David's palace with David's being "established . . . as king" before the ark came to Jerusalem (15:1); so it may not be out of place to think of earlier dealings with Hiram of Tyre (who would subsequently become king) or even that David had entered into some kind of relationship with Hiram's father Abibaal, which was renegotiated with Hiram and continued into the reign of Solomon. In any event, this palace witnesses to how a pagan monarch may be used to serve the people of God (cf. Isa 23:18).

3 David's taking "more wives" was a historical fact but a moral failure, directly contrary to the law (Dt 17:17). This sin led to a whole series of disasters later on (2Sa 11:27; cf. the implications of 13:4, 32, and even 1Ki 1:5–6).

4–7 The list of David's younger sons has appeared also in 3:5–8.

8 The statement that David "went out to meet" the enemy summarizes several preceding events, including raids by the Philistines

(v.9), his own initial retreat to the stronghold of Adullam (2Sa 5:17), and the exploit of his heroes at the well of Bethlehem (1Ch 11:15).

9 The Valley of Rephaim lay southwest of Jerusalem and formed part of the boundary between Judah and Benjamin (Jos 15:8). It may correspond to the "Valley of Baca" (Ps 84:6), due to the balsam trees that were there (vv.14–15). These are named, literally, "weepers" (*beka'im*) because of their drops of milky sap.

10–12 Trusting in God's promise of victory, David completely routed the Philistines at Baal Perazim (cf. NIV note), so that he and his men took away their idols (2Sa 5:21) and burned them, as required in the law (Dt 7:5, 25).

13–15 Against the Philistines' renewed invasion, the Lord guided David into an encircling movement. The signal for springing this ambush was a supernatural "sound of marching in the tops of the balsam trees," perhaps similar to the miracle recorded in 2Ki 7:6.

16–17 David's striking the Philistines down "all the way . . . to Gezer," on the Philistine border, signified their total expulsion from Israelite territory.

4. The ark brought to Jerusalem (15:1–16:43)

While the transfer of the ark from Kiriath Jearim to Jerusalem occupies but ch. 6 in 2 Samuel, it takes up three in this book: ch. 13, which carries the account up to its turning aside to the house of Obed-Edom, and chs. 15–16, on its final move into Jerusalem. This latter section parallels 2Sa 6:12–20, but with a number of additions. These include David's elaborate preparations, both to prevent any recurrence of the tragedy that had brought about Uzzah's death (15:1–15), and also to ensure an appropriate retinue of singers (vv.16–24); his provision of a model psalm of thanksgiving, that was used on the occasion of the ark's actual installation into its new tent-abode (16:7–36); and his establishment of a permanent Levitical organization to maintain the regular services of worship before the ark in its Jerusalem sanctuary (vv.4–6, 37–42).

By the time of Ezra, Jerusalem had become more important religiously than politically; and so it has remained, even up to the present. Our Chronicler therefore resumes the narrative, begun in ch. 13, on how the ark came to be brought inside the city; for it was this event that started the transformation of Jerusalem into the religious capital of Israel. It remained only for an angelic revelation to David—that Mount Moriah, on its north side, was to be the site for the altar of God (= "the house of God," 22:1; 2Ch 3:1)—to establish the Lord's ultimate centralization of Hebrew religion at this sanctuary. It became the fulfillment of what Moses had long before predicted, that the Lord God would choose a place out of all their tribes for his name to dwell; to his holy hill his people were to come for pilgrimage and sacrifice (Dt 12:5–7, 11–12).

1 It was the time needed for constructing these Davidic "buildings," clearly more than the three months during which the ark remained with Obed-Edom (13:14), that causes 14:1 to be dated before ch. 13 (cf. 14:1 and 2).

At this point David "prepared . . . a tent for the ark" (cf. v.12). His primary reasons are given later (16:1–4). For it was not simply that reports had reached him of God's blessing on the household of Obed-Edom (2Sa 6:12)—indicating both that the danger surrounding Uzzah had passed and that similar blessings might now be anticipated for Jerusalem as well (!)—but he had a religious motivation, seeking to establish a center of prayer and praise to the Lord (16:4).

2 Chapter 15 (here and in v.13) gives a further explanation for Uzzah's disaster (cf. 13:10): the Levites should have carried the ark, as prescribed in Dt 10:8.

3–4 So when David assembled Israel to bring the ark the rest of the way into Jerusalem, he was careful to ensure the presence of priests and Levites (named in v.11). The latter are then particularly enumerated in vv.5–10, along with the total number of their followers, some 862 in all.

5–10 In addition to the three major clans of Levi—Gershon, Kohath, Merari (vv.5–7)—there appear three subgroups within Kohath: those of his third and fourth sons, Hebron and Uzziel (vv.9–10), and of Elizaphan (here), who in particular was one of the three sons of Uzziel (Ex 6:22; Lev 10:4). With the passage of generations, these must

have gained sufficiently in numbers or in importance to warrant their separate representation.

11–15 David's order to the Levites to "consecrate themselves" (GK 7727) involved certain prescribed ritual washings and the avoidance of any form of ceremonial defilement (Ex 19:10, 14–15; Lev 11:44).

16 The worship of God frequently takes the appropriate form of joyful song; and this occasion, on which the ark of the covenant was conducted into Jerusalem with a glad procession, marked the historical beginning of the ministry of the Levitical singers in Israel. Concerning the musical instruments specified, the second, the "harp" (GK 4036), was more of a zither; the third, "cymbals" (GK 5199), literally means "those which cause [people] to hear" (cf. v.19). Their function seems to be that of marking time, by sounding clearly and loudly.

17–19 From the prominent clan of Kohath, Heman son of Joel, who was in turn a son of the prophet Samuel (6:28, 33; 1Sa 8:2), was in first place among the musicians appointed for the occasion by the Levites themselves (also in v.19, but contrast 16:5–7). With Heman were Asaph and Ethan, from the other two clans—all three of whom continued on, serving as the chief musicians under David's subsequent permanent arrangements (16:37, 41–42).

20 Aziel is a shortened form of the name Jaaziel (v.18). The phrase "according to *alamoth*" occurs also in the title to Ps 46. Since this noun means "maidens, virgins," such as are mentioned as beating tambourines in ceremonial processions of singers and other musicians (Ps 68:25), it may indicate music produced in a soprano register.

21 The phrase "according to *sheminith*" occurs also in the titles to Pss 6 and 12. The word is derived from the root for "eight" and is usually thought to indicate music in a lower octave, in contrast to the preceding verse, though it might indicate an instrument that had eight strings.

Obed-Edom the Gittite was, in his hereditary position, a gatekeeper (v.18; or "doorkeeper," v.24). But in recognition of his faithful care for the ark during the preceding three months (13:14; cf. also the attendant risk, v.12), he was honored with a place among the zither players; and his post was subsequently made permanent (16:5, 38). Berekiah and Elkanah then took over some of the "keeping," and carrying, duty en route.

22–23 The position of Kenaniah is uncertain. Though not listed in v.11 with the Levitical leaders, he is still designated "the head Levite." The NIV joins him with the preceding musicians as in charge of the singing. Yet the chief musicians have already been designated (v.17); and it seems better here to join Kenaniah with the following "keepers" (vv.23–24) and to translate the word rendered "singing" (GK 5362) in its more basic sense of "burden" or "load" (cf. v.27, "carrying the ark"). Verse 22 (and v.27) then says that Kenaniah was the head Levite in charge of the central task of transporting the ark. The thought of 26:29—where Kenaniah was "assigned duties away from the temple," over external and material affairs rather than directing in worship—corresponds to this.

24 Seven priests are singled out as trumpeters (cf. 16:6). Blowing on silver trumpets was the one aspect of ceremonial music that had been legislated through Moses and was a function reserved for them (Nu 10:8). Jehiah is probably the gatekeeper Jeiel of vv.18, 21, and 16:5, though why he should be singled out for honor along with Obed-Edom is not explained.

25–26 The whole assembly, including the elders and commanders, sacrificed seven bulls and seven rams; that is, David personally was responsible for the offering up of just one animal of each of these kinds (cf. 2Sa 6:13). God is said to have "helped the Levites," i.e., they were not struck down, as Uzzah had been (13:10).

27–29 The "ephod" (GK 680) was a surplice, or cape, worn in worship (Ex 28:6; 1Sa 2:18). Beneath it David wore a robe of white linen—as did also the Levites—but in his enthusiastic devotion, dancing, and celebrating with all his might before the Lord, he seems to have removed an outer garment and uncovered himself in a way that his wife Michal considered "unkingly" (2Sa 6:20). David's uninhibited love for God stands in stark contrast to the rigid, unsympathetic attitude of this daughter of Saul (cf. 2Sa 6:21–23).

An evidence preserved in writing of the "shouts" (GK 9558) with which the ark was brought up to Jerusalem may be found in Ps 24. Composed by David, it could hardly have had a more fitting occasion for those cries of praise: "Lift up your heads, O you gates . . . that the King of glory may come in" (v.7; cf. also Ps 132:8).

16:1 The statement that "they," i.e., the qualified Levites, "presented . . . offerings," just as "they" constituted the ones who "brought . . . and set" the ark in its place, provides background for clarifying the words in the next verse about "David . . . sacrificing" (see also in 2Sa 6:13, 17). While each OT worshiper, according to the law of Moses, was expected to lead his own sheep to the sanctuary and slay it (Lev 1:3–5a; 3:2a), only the Aaronic priests were entitled to offer up the blood or other portions on the altar (1:5b; 3:2b, 5).

In addition to burnt offerings, there were "fellowship offerings." The latter not only symbolized atonement, as choice parts were burned in sacrifice on the altar, but also depicted the restored fellowship with God that comes as a result of the reconciliation. Most flesh from the fellowship offerings was eaten by the people themselves, sitting down, as it were, as guests at God's table, celebrating the restoration of their peace (fellowship) with him (Lev 7:15).

2 Though David's sacrifice was accomplished through the mediation of qualified priests, he still invoked God's blessing on the people (cf. v.43 and Solomon's similar act in 1Ki 8:55–60). Some of those matters often associated with priests—such as praying for blessings (Nu 6:24–26) or wearing linen robes and ephods (cf. 15:27)—were not necessarily restricted to the sons of Aaron.

3 The king's gifts to the people consisted of bread, *eshpar* (GK 882), and raisins. *Eshpar* occurs only here and in 2Sa 6:19. It may mean "a cake of dates," but the present contextual reference to the flesh of animals, as used in Israel's feasting, could favor a "portion of meat."

4 David's appointment of Levites to minister in music and praise to God marks a significant advance in the history of Israel's worship (cf. 15:16). His previous arrangements for music (15:16–21, 24, 27–28) had been devised for just the one occasion; but now a continuing service is envisioned (cf. 16:37–42). The initial experiment must have proved to be eminently successful! But David acted on divine command, conveyed through the prophets Nathan and Gad (2Ch 29:25). For with the ark permanently enshrined in Jerusalem (though cf. 2Ch 35:3), those Levites who had formerly been charged with its transport could now be reassigned to other appropriate duties, such as gatekeepers; and in particular the "singers" came to assume a leading role in Judah's public devotion. Their presence constitutes a distinctive stress within Chronicles.

5 The king's elevation of Asaph to be the chief musician, confirmed in v.37, denotes a shift away from the Levites' own choice of Heman as the leader, up to this point (see 15:17). No reason is given, though Asaph did represent the senior Levitical clan of Gershon (6:39–43). Personal ability may also have been a contributing factor, for Asaph and his descendants are listed as composers for twelve of the inspired OT psalms (Pss 50, 73–83). The name "Jeiel" represents "Jaaziel" in 15:18, 20.

6 Of the seven priestly trumpeters who participated in the procession into Jerusalem (15:24), only the sixth, Benaiah, to whom was added a Jahaziel, was permanently assigned to service before the ark; the others probably returned to their duties at the tabernacle, which remained still at Gibeon (see v.39).

7 This verse introduces a model psalm of thanksgiving that has, with only slight modifications, been taken over from the OT Psalter of the period, as follows: vv.8–22 = Ps 105:1–15; vv.23–33 = Ps 96; and vv.34–36 = Ps 106:1, 47–48. That the king "committed" (GK 5989) his poem "to Asaph" sheds light on the phrase found in so many of the psalm titles: "For the chief musician." What David composed, the Levitical musicians were to perform in worship.

8–12 After four introductory verses exhorting God's people to praise him, the call to "remember" (GK 2349) his "wonders" of old summarizes the message of Ps 105. This psalm, one of the OT's great surveys of the Lord's faithfulness, is a reminder that was particularly appropriate at this turning point in Israel's history.

13 One of David's few changes in the text of Ps 105 (v.6) occurs here, where he substitutes the name Israel for that of the grandfather, Abraham. He may have felt that his reference to the immediate ancestor of the twelve Hebrew tribes was more fitting on this national occasion.

14–17 The "covenant" (GK 1382) was God's legal instrument for the redemption of his people. Through it he graciously bequeathed an inheritance of reconciliation with himself to those who were its qualified heirs, i.e., those who met its condition of sincere faith in his promise (Ge 15:6; Heb 11:6). Though the instrument of redemption was first revealed in Eden to fallen Adam (Ge 3:15), it was confirmed to Noah (9:9) and to Abraham (1Ch 16:16) and his chosen seed (Ge 17:7; Ex 19:5–6; Gal 3:29) for a "thousand generations." Its ultimate accomplishment depended on the death of Jesus Christ, the divine testator (Heb 9:15–17), an event symbolized under the anticipatory older testament by the shedding of sacrificial blood (Ex 24:6–8; Heb 9:18–22).

18–22 The Hebrew patriarchs wandered without a home of their own; for though they had been promised Palestine, it was in fact only their descendants who received it (Heb 11:9): David's contemporary audience. The titles by which the patriarchs are described possess, at this early period, more generalized meanings than those they came to have later. They are called "anointed" (GK 5431) in the sense of being set apart by God's Spirit—a phrase elsewhere used specifically for prophets (1Ki 19:16), priests (Ex 29:7), and kings (1Sa 2:35), with whom the presence of the Spirit was symbolized by a visible anointing with oil, and ultimately for Jesus (Christ = Messiah = "Anointed One"; 1Sa 2:10; Ps 2:2; Ac 10:38).

The patriarchs are also called "prophets" (GK 5566), in the sense of being recipients of God's special revelation—a title later used specifically for those who proclaimed God's revealed will (cf. Ex 7:1–2). Abraham was thus designated a "prophet," at the time of God's special protection against Abimelech, the Philistine king of Gerar (Ge 20:7); others of the patriarchs did, however, make specific predictions (e.g., Jacob, Ge 48:19; 49:1). Psalm 105:16–45 then continues Israel's history on into the career of Joseph, the descent into Egypt, and the Lord's deliverance of the Hebrews in the Exodus, on the desert journey, and right up to the conquest of Canaan; but David now turns to another source.

23–26 With its appeal for "all the earth" to honor the Lord, Ps 96 identifies itself as one of a series of six liturgical hymns (Pss 95–100) stressing the Creator's royal majesty. A recurring and key phrase, quoted in 1Ch 16:31, is this: "The LORD reigns" (Ps 96:10, but also 97:1; 99:1). Such a theme was of course particularly relevant on this occasion, during which "the King of glory" (Ps 24:7–10) entered Jerusalem—and David quoted the entire psalm.

27–28 David's expression "in his [God's] dwelling place" represents a change from the original phrase in Ps 96:6, "in his sanctuary," appropriate enough for use before the tabernacle at Gibeon (1Ch 16:39), but less so before the ark was in its new location in the city of Jerusalem.

29–32 The idea of people coming "before him" (v.29) took on fresh reality with the arrival of the ark, over which the cloud of God's presence rested (Nu 7:89). All people are told to worship the Lord in (lit.) "an adornment of holiness." The NIV's "his holiness" adds an unwarranted pronoun and shifts the phrase into a characteristic of God rather than of his worshipers (cf. NIV note).

33 While earlier messianic prophecies had foretold our Lord's universal, millennial reign (Ge 49:10; Nu 24:17; 1Sa 2:10), these words—"he comes"—may be the first in all of written Scripture (though Job 19:25 may well have been spoken earlier) to set forth the doctrine of the glorious second coming of Jesus Christ.

34–36 Having quoted all of Ps 96, David concluded his model hymn with the opening and closing verses of Ps 106. Like Ps 105, with which he began, Ps 106 too is a historical psalm. It has less emphasis, however, on God's faithfulness and Israel's waywardness and its results, up through the period of the judges (106:34–47), truths still very much needed by those who had witnessed the fate of Uzzah.

The prayer "gather us and deliver us from the nations" (v.35) was particularly fitting in light of the third Philistine oppression, just ended (cf. 10:1; 13:2; 14:8, 16); this release may in fact account for David saying, "O God our Savior," whereas the original in Ps 106:47 had been, rather, "O LORD our God."

Midway in v.36 the quoted model hymn ceases and Ezra's narrative resumes, with the response of "all the people," those who were present then at that time with David. Yet what they responded is itself a continuation of the quotation from Ps 106:48, demonstrating that the quoted material belongs to the time of David and not simply to that of Ezra (cf. v.7).

The people's first exclamation, "Amen" (lit.,"firm, steady"; GK 589) could be rendered "True indeed!" Their second, "Praise the LORD" represents the familiar plural contracted form of Ps 106's *halleluyah* (i.e., "Hallelu Yah)."

37 A daily ministry, now before the ark, was fitting, since this holy object represented the continuing presence of God with his people. It was "the ark of the covenant," with its testamentary promise, "I am the LORD [Yahweh, 'the One who is present'; GK 3378; cf. Ex 3:12, 14] your God" (v.4; cf. v.15, or Ge 17:7–8).

38 Hosah had not been mentioned previously. He was another doorkeeper, though of the clan of Merari (26:10–11), compared to Obed-Edom of Kohath (vv.1, 4). Obed-Edom's father is also named for the first time and is not to be confused with Jeduthun (alternate name for Ethan) the chief musician (vv.41–42), both because Ethan belonged to the clan of Merari, and because the name as given here in the consonantal text is really Jedithun. Obed-Edom continued in his double post of both musician (v.5) and doorkeeper (cf. 15:21).

39–40 Zadok (see comment on 6:8), however, was sent back (cf. 15:11) to Gibeon to serve as high priest at the tabernacle, which continued to exist as Israel's primary sanctuary for sacrifice (v.40) till Solomon's construction of the Jerusalem temple (2Ch 1:13; 5:5). Abiathar, on the other hand, seems to have remained at the capital (cf. 27:34), which may account for David's double high-priesthood (18:16).

41–43 God's "love" (GK 2876; also in v.34) refers to his loyalty to the provisions embodied in the covenantal relationship (see comment on 19:2; cf. Ge 21:23; Ps 136:10).

5. Nathan's prophecy (17:1–27)

As indicated in the introductory analysis of chs. 11–20, the heart of 1 Chronicles is to be found in ch. 17. Its substance is drawn from 2Sa 7 and largely corresponds to it, as it sets forth the abiding significance of the person and work of David. Chronologically ch. 17 came after the termination of the wars chronicled in ch. 18 (cf. 17:8, and as explicitly stated in 2Sa 7:1); and it should be dated about 995 B.C.

The chapter contains three major sections. (1) David desired to erect a permanent temple for the ark, which was not granted (vv.1–6). (2) God promised that even though David could not build a house for him, the Lord would still build a house for the king (vv.7–15). Just as God had prospered David up to this point, so he would continue to prosper his kingdom. The next member of the dynasty would construct the temple (vv.11–12). Then, in what was eschatological time for David (NT times for us), his ultimate successor in this human dynasty would also be acknowledged as the Son of God (v.13); and in time to come, the Son of David would establish God's kingdom on earth (v.14). (3) The king praised God for such incredible grace (vv.16–27).

1 By quoting David's full statement, "the ark of the covenant of the LORD" (cf. 2Sa 7:2, simply, "the ark of God"), the Chronicler calls initial attention to the significance of this chapter within the history of covenantal thought (cf. v.12). Nathan the prophet had already been God's agent to guide David in organizing the Levitical musicians (cf. 16:4), and he is best known for how he would later rebuke David for his sin with Bathsheba (2Sa 12). Nathan aided Solomon in the latter's rise (1Ki 1:10–11) and recorded some of the historical sources on which Ezra was able to draw for his own work (1Ch 29:29; 2Ch 9:29).

2–3 In reply to David's inquiry about building a temple, Nathan did tell him to "do it." But this was his immediate, human reaction: unofficial, noninspired (God's word did not come to him till that night), and, as it turned out, wrong.

4 While 2Sa 7:5 had been content to record God's question, "Are you the one to build me a house?" Chronicles includes his strong prohibition: "You are not the one to build me a house." The reason, given only later (in 22:8; 28:3), lay in David's ruthless warfare (cf. 2Sa 8:2). Yet Chronicles preserves another addition over 2 Samuel: the Hebrew text says literally, "build me the house." The idea of there being such a house was legitimate, just that David was not the one to build it.

5–6 Historical precedent shows that since the days of the Exodus, God had not "dwelt in a house," except briefly in Eli's building at Shiloh (1Sa 3:3); and this had been destroyed by the Philistines after the first battle at Ebenezer (Jer 7:12).

7–9 For v.9, the context (cf. 2Sa 7:1) suggests, and the Hebrew permits, a past rather than a future rendering: "I have provided ... and have planted them so that they have a home ... and are no longer disturbed." God's words that the wicked do not oppress Israel "as they did at the beginning" serve as a reminder of the sufferings of the Hebrews in Egypt (Ex 1:13–14).

10–11 God's promise to "build a house" for David is a play on words: the king could not build God a house, i.e., a structure "of cedar" (v.6); but God would build him one, i.e., a dynasty of descendants ("offspring").

12 While God did not here employ the term covenant, what he revealed was one; and it is so designated subsequently (2Sa 23:5; Pss 89:3, 34; 132:11–12). This Davidic covenant was the sixth, and last, to be established in OT times (see ZPEB, 1:1007–10), the new covenant of Jer 31 not being established until NT times. God's plan had moved onward from the Edenic (Ge 3:15), Noachian (9:9), Abrahamic (15:18), and Sinaitic covenants (Ex 19:5–6), through the Levitical (Nu 25:12–13; cf. 1Ch 9:19), down to this revelation; and it involves three stages.

(1) God promised David a successor, the "one who will build" the temple, i.e., Solomon, an identification confirmed by God's words in v.11: "one of your own sons." (2) God promised to "establish his throne" as a continuing dynasty. (3) That throne would be established "forever," a feature made possible by Jesus Christ, who, as God's Son (see the next verse), is the only one to possess a

rule that is endless (Lk 1:32–33); and in this lay David's own salvation (2Sa 23:5). As Messiah he would set up his kingdom, in human hearts, at his first coming (Da 2:44a; Lk 17:21), though its external realization over the world awaits his second coming (Da 2:44b; Lk 17:24).

13 This verse along with Ps 2:7, 12, is one of the major OT revelations on the deity of the Messiah. It foretells Jesus' being uniquely God's Son (Heb 1:5; cf. Ac 13:33; Heb 5:5), for it is not really applicable to Solomon (cf. 22:10) or to any other of David's more immediate successors (by some sort of "double fulfillment"). Jesus, however, combined in his own Person a perfect humanity and full deity (Mt 22:42–45; Php 2:9), so that he might, by the one, become an accredited substitute for sinful people in his death (Heb 2:17–18; 1Pe 2:24), and yet, by the other, be able to compensate infinitely for their sins and restore them to heaven and to God the Father by his resurrection (Jn 1:18; 14:6).

14–15 Unlike David's predecessor, Saul, whom God removed (v.13), Jesus would possess a permanent status over God's kingdom. Here again the Chronicler brings out more of the personal messianic character of God's words to Nathan (2Sa 7:16 had included only his speaking in the more impersonal terms of David's "kingdom" and "throne").

16 The king's sitting "before the LORD" suggests that he went to the tent that was enshrining the ark (16:1).

17–21 In the phrase "as . . . the most exalted of men" (v.17), the first word in the Hebrew is a rare noun meaning a "turn"; the correct rendering may be "the turn of mankind to come," i.e., "the generation to come." David was expressing his awe at God's favor, compared to his own lowly origin (v.7).

22–26 That Israel is the Lord's "people" and that he is "their God" (v.22) restates the central promise of the Lord's reconciling testament (cf. 16:15 and 37), found from Ge 17:7 to Rev 21:3.

27 David's conclusion is one of faith in God's words: claiming the immediate blessing and affirming its eternal outcome.

6. Conquests and administration (18:1–17)

The order of chapters in this part of Chronicles (cf. 18:1; 19:1) is based on the sequence found in 2Sa 8, which is topical rather than chronological. The subject of the chapter is twofold: David's wars of conquest—to the west, against Philistia (v.1); to the east, against Moab (v.2); to the north, against the Arameans of Syria (Aram; vv.3–11); and to the south, against Edom (vv.12–13)—followed by a descriptive survey of his administration (vv.14–17). The theme, twice repeated (vv.6, 13), is one of encouragement to all believers: that the Lord gave victory to David wherever he went.

1 The NIV's "In the course of time" actually indicates no more than a succession of topics. By strict chronology ch. 18 precedes ch. 17, and ch. 19 (introduced by the same phrase) likewise precedes ch. 18 (cf. v.3). David was now able to take the offensive and capture Gath, the most inland of the five Philistine cities (2Sa 8:1), which made it the one most threatening to Judah (20:6, 8; cf. 1Sa 5:8; 17:52).

2 Though the Chronicler does not seek to cover up David's acts of vengeance (cf. 20:3), he does omit the details about his harsh treatment of Moab (2Sa 8:2).

3 Zobah was an Aramean state of Syria lying northeast of Damascus and south of Hamath. The attempt of its king Hadadezer to "establish his control along the Euphrates" could refer to some early, eastward campaign but seems rather to be based on the situation in 19:16, his gathering of forces along this river, with the aim of recouping the losses that he suffered because of his first defeat by Israel (detailed in 19:6–15).

4 Seven thousand is probably the correct number for the "charioteers" (cf. 19:18) that David took captive (cf. 2Sa 8:4). To preserve the peace David took the strong measure of hamstringing most of the enemy's chariot horses.

5–8 The towns of Tebah (cf. NIV note to v.8) and Cun (called Berothai, 2Sa 8:8) lay in the Coele Syria valley between the Lebanons. The tribute that David gained (cf. v.11) contributed to the vast resources (outlined in 22:2–5, 14–15) that he furnished to Solomon

Major Covenants in the Old Testament

COVENANTS	REFERENCE	TYPE	PARTICIPANT	DESCRIPTION
Noahic	Ge 9:8-17	Royal Grant	Made with "righteous" (6:9) Noah (and his descendants and every living thing on earth—all life that is subject to man's jurisdiction)	An unconditional divine promise never to destroy all earthly life with some natural catastrophe; the covenant "sign" being the rainbow in the storm cloud
Abrahamic A	Ge 15:9-21	Royal (land) Grant	Made with "righteous" (his faith was "credited to him as righteousness," v. 6) Abram (and his descendants, v. 16)	An unconditional divine promise to fulfill the grant of the land; a self-maledictory oath symbolically enacted it (v. 17)
Abrahamic B	Ge 17	Suzerain-vassal	Made with Abraham as patriarchal head of his household	A conditional divine pledge to be Abraham's God and the God of his descendants (cf. "As for me," v. 4; "As for you," v. 9); the condition: total consecration to the Lord as symbolized by circumcision
Sinaitic	Ex 19-24	Suzerain-vassal	Made with Israel as the descendants of Abraham, Isaac and Jacob and as the people the Lord has redeemed from bondage to an earthly power	A conditional divine pledge to be Israel's God (as her Protector and the Guarantor of her blessed destiny); the condition: Israel's total consecration to the Lord as his people (his kingdom) who live by his rule and serve his purposes in history
Phinehas	Nu 25:10-13	Royal Grant	Made with the zealous priest Phinehas	An unconditional divine promise to maintain the family of Phinehas in a "lasting priesthood" (implicitly a pledge to Israel to provide her forever with a faithful priesthood)
Davidic	2Sa 7:5-16	Royal Grant	Made with faithful King David after his devotion to God as Israel's king and the Lord's anointed vassal had come to special expression (v. 2)	An unconditional divine promise to establish and maintain the Davidic dynasty on the throne of Israel (implicitly a pledge to Israel) to provide her forever with a godly king like David and through that dynasty to do for her what he had done through David—bring her into rest in the promised land (1Ki 4:20-21; 5:3-4).
New	Jer 31:31-34	Royal Grant	Promised to rebellious Israel as she is about to be expelled from the promised land in actualization of the most severe covenant curse (Lev 26:27-39; Dt 28:36-37, 45-68)	An unconditional divine promise to unfaithful Israel to forgive her sins and establish his relationship with her on a new basis by writing his law "on their hearts"—a covenant of pure grace

Major Types of Royal Covenants/Treaties in the Ancient Near East

Royal Grant (unconditional)
A king's grant (of land or some other benefit) to a loyal servant for faithful or exceptional service. The grant was normally perpetual and unconditional, but the servant's heirs benefited from it only as they continued their father's loyalty and service. (Cf. 1Sa 8:14; 22:7; 27:6; Est 8:1.)

Parity
A covenant between equals, binding them to mutual friendship or at least to mutual respect for each other's spheres and interests. Participants called each other "brothers." (Cf. Ge 21:27; 26:31; 31:44-54; 1Ki 5:12; 15:19; 20:32-34; Am 1:9.)

Suzerain-vassal (conditional)
A covenant regulating the relationship between a great king and one of his subject kings. The great king claimed absolute right of sovereignty, demanded total loyalty and service (the vassal must "love" his suzerain) and pledged protection of the subject's realm and dynasty, conditional on the vassal's faithfulness and loyalty to him. The vassal pledged absolute loyalty to his suzerain—whatever service his suzerain demanded—and exclusive reliance on the suzerain's protection. Participants called each other "lord" and "servant" or "father" and "son." (Cf. Jos 9:6,8; Eze 17:13-18; Hos 12:1.)

Commitments made in these covenants were accompanied by self-maledictory oaths (made orally, ceremonially or both). The gods were called upon to witness the covenants and implement the curses of the oaths if the covenants were violated.

for making "the bronze Sea," etc. (cf. 2Ch 4:2–5, 18).

9–13 Instead of Abishai (cf. 11:20) overcoming the eighteen thousand Edomites (v.12), 2Sa 8:13 speaks of David's supreme leadership; and the title to Ps 60 names Joab (the senior commander, v.15; cf. on 11:6) as a conqueror of twelve thousand.

14–15 Within David's "cabinet" some of the civil officers seem to have followed the pattern of Egyptian administration. The post of Jehoshaphat the "recorder" (lit., "one who reminds"; GK 4654) corresponds to the Egyptian "chief of protocol," whose responsibilities included audiences and communications.

16–17 Shavsha (Seraiah, 2Sa 8:17), with no father listed, seems himself to have been foreign; his office was "secretary [of state]" (GK 6221). Benaiah (cf. 11:23), in contrast to Joab (v.15), who led the general Israelite militia, commanded David's standing force of professional, foreign troops: the Kerethites, a people connected with the Philistines (1Sa 30:14; Eze 25:16), probably Cretans, and the Pelethites, seemingly a shortened name for the Philistines themselves.

7. Victories over Ammon (19:1–20:3)

The climax of David's international struggles came in 995 B.C. (before the birth of Solomon, 2Sa 12:24) and arose out of two campaigns against the Ammonites. These people were related to the Hebrews (cf. v.1) and lived directly east of them in the portion of Transjordan that lies east of the Jabbok River (Dt 3:16), as it flows northward before bending west to enter the Jordan. A major teaching value to be found in 19:1–20:3 is summarized by Joab's words of trust and encouragement in v.13: "The LORD will do what is good in his sight."

1 On "in the course of time," see comment on 18:1. "The Ammonites" were descendants, by incest, of Abraham's nephew Lot (Ge 19:36–38). During the chaotic days of the Hebrew judges, they had been guilty of repeated incursions against the Israelite tribes to their west (Jdg 3:13; 10:7–9, 17–11:33; 1Sa 11:1); but they had been first repelled and then subdued by Saul (1Sa 11:11; 14:47).

2 Their late king "Nahash" would hardly have been the same oppressor who had precipitated Saul's elevation half a century earlier (1Sa 11:1) but may have been his son. The latter's relationship to David had been one of *hesed* (GK 2875), meaning not so much "kindness" as "loyalty" to covenanted treaties and their obligations (cf. 16:41). These may have had their origin in the common threat that both men faced in Saul, perhaps when David had been fleeing from him some twenty years earlier. One might compare the help that David received from the neighboring king of Moab (1Sa 22:3).

3–5 Hanun's shaving of David's emissaries is explained in 2Sa 10:4 as involving half their beards. For an Oriental this was an insult of the worst sort, and particularly after David's expression of faithful concern (v.2; cf. the vengeance in which it resulted, 20:3).

6 The quantity of silver paid out by Hanun for mercenary support amounts to over thirty-seven tons. The value, however, represents a unique, once-and-for-all payment, sent in desperation. "Aram Naharaim" occupied land between the Tigris and Euphrates rivers; this was area that provided reinforcements for the second Syrian (Aramean) advance (v.16). The Chronicler uses its more general name to include the states of Beth Rehob and Tob, mentioned in 2Sa 10:6, 8 (cf. Ge 36:37).

7 In the light of 2Sa 10:6, the total of 32,000 mercenaries seems to include foot soldiers and horsemen (cf. v.18) as well as charioteers. The same verse has 1,000 in the contingent from Maacah. Their gathering point was near "Medeba" in north Reuben in Transjordan (Jos 13:16), though why they selected this location southwest of the Ammonite border is not known.

8–9 Joab's battle with Ammon was finally engaged before the gates of "their [capital] city," i.e., Rabbah (v.15; 20:1), the modern city of Amman.

10–13 After appealing to his men to do their utmost for their people and their God (cf. 1Co 16:13), Joab in faith committed the outcome to the will of the Lord (cf. the same sort of balance that is stresses in one's spiritual salvation (Php 2:12–13).

14–15 Joab did not at this time follow up the victory by laying siege to Rabbah; it may have been too late in the year (cf. 20:1).

16 This regathering of Aramean forces beyond the Euphrates seems to provide the setting for 18:3.

17–18 In the light of 18:4, the Chronicles figure of 7,000 charioteers seems to be the original that lies behind the seven hundred in 2Sa 10:18. Likewise, Chronicles' identification of 40,000 as "foot soldiers" is the correct reading, as opposed to Samuel's "horsemen" (see NIV note), because the figure approximates the total of 20,000 plus 22,000 foot soldiers given in 18:4–5.

19 The "vassals" of Hadadezer included his client kings (2Sa 10:19).

20:1 Springtime marked the end of the rainy season and permitted the resumption of warfare. The Chronicler's statement that "David remained in Jerusalem" suggests to his readers, without having to retrace all the sordid details, what 2 Sa 11:2–27 records on David's shameful adultery with Bathsheba and the murder of her incorruptible husband, the king's hero Uriah (1Ch 11:41).

2 –3 Joab did, however, summon David to Rabbah in time for its capitulation (2Sa 12:27–29), so that his ruler was present to take the crown from the head of Ammon's national idol, Milcom (NIV note; cf. 1Ki 11:5, 33; Zep 1:5)—its very weight in gold ("about 75 pounds," NIV note) precluded any wearing of it by a person. The author of 2Sa 12:31 adds "work at brickmaking" to the labor with saws, picks, and axes.

8. Philistine wars (20:4–8)

Ezra's treatment of David's ascendancy (1Ch 11–20) concludes with the record of three incidents that occurred during battles with the Philistines. Even as the preceding section (19:1–20:3) had elaborated on one aspect of the survey of David's conquest (ch. 18)—namely, the Ammonite struggle, as the basis for the Aramean wars that were introduced in 18:3—so the present, brief section elaborates on David's Philistine wars and capture of Gath, which had been mentioned in 18:1 (cf. the references to Gath in 20:6, 8). The first two incidents are not pinpointed historically but also seem to belong to the period between the two initial Philistine offenses against David in 1003 B.C. (14:8–17) and the rest that God granted him from his enemies about 995 (17:8; 2Sa 7:1).

4 On "in the course of time," see comment on 18:1. "Gezer" may indicate the general location of the otherwise obscure place-name Gob (2Sa 21:18); the former identifies the border city the Philistines had retreated to after David's victories in his war for independence (cf. 14:16).

The champion "Sibbecai," from the Judean town of Hushah (4:4), was one of David's "Thirty" heroes (11:29) and the commander of his eighth corps (27:11). The Philistine "Sippai" ("Saph," 2Sa 21:18), whom he overcame, is traced back to the "Rephaites," an ancient people (Ge 14:5) noted for their large size (Dt 2:21). Except for those remaining in the kingdom of Og in Bashan, the Rephaites had generally died out by the time of Moses (Dt 3:11).

5 This second battle too took place in Gob (2Sa 21:19). "Lahmi" was brother to Goliath, the well-known victim of David's heroism (1Sa 17). But perhaps because of his unfamiliar and indeed unique name, a later copyist of the parallel passage in 2Sa 21:19 introduced a small but far-reaching corruption, as if Elhanan had killed Goliath himself. On the "weaver's rod," see comment on 11:23.

6–8 The use of the article with "Rapha" (also in v.8) suggests that this is not a personal, individual name, except perhaps in the sense of an eponymous ancestor of "the Rephaites" (v.4).

C. David's Latter Days (21:1–29:30)

1. The census (21:1–30)

After 995 B.C., about twenty years elapsed between the concluding events in David's rise to power (chs. 11–20) and the resumed narrative of deeds performed in the latter part of his reign, which occupies the balance of the book (chs. 21–29). The intervening period was one of crisis and personal failure on David's part, triggered by his sin of adultery with Bathsheba (2Sa 11). This in turn set off a chain reaction of crime: the king's murder of Uriah (ch. 11) and a series of similarly wanton acts on the part of Amnon (ch.13), Absalom (chs. 14–19), and even such less obviously motivated rebels as Sheba (ch. 20).

Since Absalom's revolt occupied a total of eleven years (2Sa 13:23, 38; 14:28; 15:7, variant reading), or about 990–979, 1 Chronicles brings us down to about 975. Here our Chronicler takes up his account with David's census (see also 2Sa 24). His reasons for a gap of this length are not difficult to surmise: little of what transpired during those two decades would encourage a postexilic Judah, before whom Ezra was seeking to portray a piety that characterized David at his best.

With the census (1Ch 21), however, a chain reaction of a different caliber was inaugurated. Despite its sinful inception, it provided the immediate setting for God's revelation of the site of his temple and for the preparation that ensued (ch. 22). This in turn leads into David's administrative arrangements, whether in matters of religious (chs. 23–26) or civil organization (ch. 27). First Chronicles concludes with a final charge from David that both Solomon and all Israel would continue faithful to their God (chs. 28–29). Events like these definitely were germane to the purpose of the Chronicler. Beyond the opening chapter, however, there is no direct parallel elsewhere in the OT.

For the events of ch. 21, Scripture presents us with no less than four explanations (see vv.1, 3). Yet however complex the motivation for Israel's census and for the disaster that followed, Ezra's record now serves a double function. On the one hand, the various aspects of David's repentance remain exemplary for readers up to this moment (cf. vv.8, 13, 17, and 24). On the other hand, the decision of God to establish his altar and temple at Moriah in Jerusalem have affected all history (cf. Rev 11:1); for this mountain became the focus of the Holy City (v.2), where his Son was crucified (v.8). And it will continue to affect history; for from this "city he loves" (Rev 20:9), he will someday rule the nations of earth (v.4; cf. Isa 2:2–4) and then eternally heal the dwellers of his new earth (Isa 65:17–19; Rev 21:1–2; 22:2).

1 For the first time in Scripture, the word "Satan" (GK 8477) appears without the definite article as a proper noun. He is still "the adversary" (as in Job 1–2; Zec 3:1–2), with his changeless malice toward God and human beings; but Satan has now become his name. David's numbering of his people was thus brought about, in the first instance, by the devil's hatred of God's people and of God himself (cf. Job 1:11; 2:5).

Yet 2Sa 24:1 goes deeper and shows that Satan, the instrument (cf. 1Ki 22:22–23; Job 1:12; 2:6), was actually being used to accomplish "the anger of the LORD . . . against Israel." That is, the disaster that was brought on because of the census served to punish the nation (1Ch 21:7) for her sins, including repeated revolts against God's anointed king, David. The last revolt under Sheba had terminated only shortly before (cf. the introductory discussion to ch. 21. Furthermore, there were God's ultimate and positive goals, ensuring that the results of it all would mean the establishment of his altar and temple (cf. above).

2–3 There was also the immediate, human factor—meaning David's own motivation—that was evil (vv. 7–8, 17) and, as Joab dared point out to the king, contributed to "bring guilt on Israel." A census was not in itself wrong (cf. the God-directed census in Nu 1 and 26). But on this occasion David seems to have ordered this because he was placing his trust in "multiplied troops" rather than in the promises of God (contrast 27:23 with Ps 30:6, the title of which indicates its composition at this time; cf. 22:1).

4 The route of Joab and his officers "throughout Israel" is outlined in 2Sa 24:4–6; and v.8 adds that it took almost ten months.

5 The total figures that they gathered require clarification in two directions. (1) In comparison with those given in 2Sa 24:9, Ezra's sum of 1,100,000 for all Israel is larger than Samuel's 800,000, which probably did not include the regularly organized army (note the lack of an "all" before "Israel") of 288,000; but his sum of 470,000 for Judah is a bit smaller than Samuel's 500,000, which may here simply be a round number. (2) On the basis of the noun that means either "thousands" or "chiefs" (cf. 7:3–4; 12:24), we should probably think in terms of a muster of 1,570 outstanding military figures and not necessarily of over a million and a half "men . . . who could handle a sword."

6–7 Joab's exemption of Levi from this census (the tribe was numbered in 23:3) had precedent, because of that tribe's special religious status (Nu 1:49–50). This fact may also explain his deliberate exclusion of Benjamin, since both Jerusalem (with God's ark) and Gibeon (with the tabernacle, v.29) lay within its borders (Jos 18:25, 28). We do know that his work was interrupted by God's "wrath [that] came on Israel" (1Ch 27:24), in this very Benjamite area (21:15).

8 David's confession resulted from his troubled heart or conscience (2Sa 24:10), perhaps pricked by Joab's rebuke.

9 "Gad" the "seer" had already counseled David, both before he became king (1Sa 22:5) and after (2Ch 29:25), and was later to compose one of the source documents for his reign that was used by Ezra (29:29).

10–12 The alternate punishments set before David were of approximately equal severity. God's instrument for executing the plague would be "the angel of the LORD." Compare the similar situations both before (1Sa 6:3–6) and after (2Ki 19:35). But while those cases may have involved the divine angel of the covenant (cf. Ex 23:20–21; Mal 3:1), presumably preincarnate appearances of Christ, this one apparently did not; it was simply an ordinary "angel."

13 The king's submission to the word of the Lord through his prophet is both commendable and sets apart Hebrew religion from the lack of such ethical restraint within paganism generally (cf. 11:3). David wisely chose punishment from God (a plague) rather than that from other people (an invasion).

14 Punishment as such, however, remained inescapable; and "seventy thousand men of Israel fell"—a tragically appropriate sentence on a king whose sin had been that of trusting in the numbers of his troops (see v.3).

15–16 David and his civic officials, "the elders," were already in penitence ("sackcloth"), perhaps on their way to the tabernacle at Gibeon (vv.29–30), when they saw the destroying angel with his drawn sword facing Jerusalem. But his hand was withdrawn (2Sa 24:16).

17 David's second confession (cf. v.8) is recorded more fully here than in 2Sa 24:17. It illustrates his willingness to accept full responsibility and to sacrifice himself for his people's sake. The latter he calls "sheep," and Scripture frequently compares leader and people with a shepherd and his flock (11:2; cf.

Ps 23; Jer 23:1–4). But while the king was indeed to blame for having "sinned and done wrong," the plague in question was not entirely a case of an innocent nation suffering for the crimes of its leader.

18–22 The Chronicler omits Araunah's opening question (2Sa 24:21) and moves directly to David's words, which show his compliance with Gad's instructions to build an altar there on his threshing floor.

23 The "oxen" would have been present to pull the wooden "threshing sledges" over the wheat. The grain offering always had to accompany the sacrifices of flesh (Ex 29:40–41; Lev 23:18; Nu 15:4).

24 By refusing to present an "offering that costs me nothing," David confirmed the truth that God takes no pleasure in the man who yields only what involves no sacrifice. He requires of his followers a totally surrendered life (Ro 12:1; cf. Lk 21:1–3).

25 So David bought "the site"—which may have included the whole area of Mount Moriah—for 15 pounds of gold (cf. NIV note)—an enormous sum (cf. 2Sa 24:24, which notes a much smaller amount [20 ounces of silver] for the threshing floor itself).

26 God's answer of "fire from heaven on the altar" publicly attested his acceptance both of the king's repentance and of the altar site (cf. Lev 9:24).

27–30 Furthermore, the angel's sword was sheathed and the plague ceased (2Sa 24:25). On the tabernacle's contemporaneous location at Gibeon (v.29), see 16:39.

2. Temple preparations (22:1–19)

The Chronicler was vitally concerned to ensure support for the Jerusalem temple in his day (Ezr 7:15–17; 8:25–30, 33–34). No more fitting stimulus for dedication in this regard could then be found than in the example set by David when he made preparations for the construction of that temple; and this is the subject of 1Ch 22 (cf. also chs. 28–29). Ezra first summarized David's own efforts (vv.2–5) and then recounted the words of exhortation by which he privately encouraged Solomon to carry through in its building (vv.6–16); he publicly charged the leaders of Israel to assist his son in this task (vv.17–19).

Though no parallels to the chapter now appear in Scripture, Ezra must have been able to use sources that are no longer available for us today.

1 In view of the revelations of God's presence that occurred in the preceding chapter (cf. esp. 21:15, 26), David announced that his new altar on Araunah's threshing floor had become the designated place for Israel's burnt offerings, and that this site on Mount Moriah (2Ch 3:1) was in fact "the house of the LORD God," even though the building had yet to be erected. Such words therefore explain how the title to Ps 30 can simultaneously claim authorship by David and yet also be an occasion for its composition at "the dedication of the temple." That psalm does fit historically at this point (compare Ps 30:5–6 with David's attitudes and experiences in 1Ch 21).

2 The king began by drafting the resident "aliens" to work as stone cutters. This situation is attested by the existence of a cabinet post on corvée labor, held by Adoram (2Sa 20:24), and is confirmed by Solomon's similar arrangements later on (2Ch 2:17–18 and 8:7–9).

3 The king's provision of "a large amount of iron" reflects how conditions had changed during his time—known archaeologically as Iron Age I—because of the incorporation of iron-producing Philistines within the sphere of Hebrew control.

4 To handle the "cedar logs," Solomon was later forced to draft a considerable number of Israelites (1Ki 5:13–14), though foreigners were used for the stonework.

5 Nowhere does Scripture connect Solomon's age with some historically datable point. As a result we do not know exactly how young Solomon was about 975 B.C. After reigning forty years (2Ch 9:30), Solomon was succeeded by his son Rehoboam, then aged forty-one (12:13); and Solomon could well have had a one-year-old son at his accession in 970, if Solomon himself had been born about 990. This would make him twenty at the time. Furthermore, though David's relationship with Bathsheba dates from about 995 (cf. the introductory discussions to chs. 17 and 19), Solomon was apparently not the first son that she bore to David but the fourth

(1Ch 3:5), which brings us once again to about 990 for his birth.

6–7 That the temple was to be built "for the Name of the LORD" means more than his reputation or honor; ultimately, it means his Person. Specifically, God's "Name" stood for the glory-cloud of his presence in the tabernacle or the temple (Dt 12:11; 2Ch 6:20).

8 The "word of the LORD" David referred to had been brought to him by the prophet Nathan, before Solomon's birth (17:4). But the king here first revealed why God had refused him permission to build the temple: he had "fought many wars" (stated again in 28:3). The point was not simply that warfare had preempted his energies (cf. 1Ki 5:3), but that it had polluted his hands with undue bloodshed. David had become guilty of excessive violence (e.g., in 2Sa 8:2). His explanation carries serious ethical implications for us today (Mt 5:9).

9 Though Solomon's succession was later disputed by his older brother Adonijah (1Ki 1:5–13, 24–25), he had been divinely favored, even before birth (2Sa 12:24–25); and he is here designated to "reign" over Israel, as David himself proceeded to acknowledge to Bathsheba on oath (1Ki 1:13, 30). God moreover promised Solomon a reign "of peace" (*shalom*; GK 8934). Fulfillment came by his having to engage in only one known battle (vs. Hamath, 2Ch 8:3).

10 In this verse David directly quotes from Nathan's prophecy in 17:12–14 (cf. 28:6). As predicted in the first clause, Solomon did "build a house" for God's name; and, as in the last, "the throne of his kingdom" did come to be established "over Israel forever." The middle clause, however, where God prophesies, "He will be my son," must he read in the light of a condition that was attached and that demanded a faithfulness that Solomon failed to achieve; it was, however, accomplished in Jesus Christ. David seems to have quoted the entire passage, including its middle part, so as to identify the more immediately relevant promises that both preceded and followed it in context.

11–13 David's blessing on his son, in its various aspects, set a pattern for subsequent benedictions. In v.11 he particularly invoked success for Solomon as he should "build the house" (cf. 28:10). In vv.12–13 David (harking back to Jos 1:7–8) emphasized how he should keep "the laws . . . that the LORD gave Moses."

14–16 The tremendous quantities of gold and silver that David provided add up to over forty thousand tons, a fabulous amount, with a far greater ancient purchasing value. This, together with smaller but related amounts given in 29:4, 7, constitutes the one place in Chronicles where its figures are large enough to justify invoking God's special providence to account for them.

17–19 David's goal, expressed here to the leaders of Israel, of bringing "the ark of the covenant . . . into the temple" was in fact accomplished in 2Ch 5:7; this act would mark the achievement of all his various efforts on its behalf, and on God's behalf, as so far described throughout chs. 13; 15–17; 22.

3. Levitical organization (23:1–26:32)

David's concern for the worship of God in the temple went beyond the material preparations that he made for the construction of its building, just described (ch. 22). Of even more lasting significance were the arrangements that he made for the organization of its ministering personnel, the Levites (chs. 23–26). Guided by the Lord through his prophets (2Ch 29:25), the king exercised his administrative genius to establish a system of procedures that helped maintain legitimate worship under his successors, that provided the operational framework for promoting the revival of Mosaic theocracy in the days of Ezra the Chronicler (see the introductory discussion to ch. 6), and that continued to meet the needs of God's worshiping people on into NT times (cf. 24:10 as reflected in Lk 1:5, 8).

In 970 B.C. (26:31; cf. v.1), David took a census of the male Levites aged thirty and above; and he found that they numbered 38,000 at that time. His fundamental idea was to divide the men of the tribe into four operational units (23:1–5). The remainder of ch. 23 pauses to review the Levitical genealogies (cf. ch. 6) by outlining the main clans and family groups (vv.6–23), and this is followed by a brief survey of their duties (vv.24–32). The four units are then enumerated. A main body of 24,000 were assigned "to supervise the work of the temple of the LORD" (ch. 24;

cf. 23:4), and this chapter proceeds to describe how the priestly descendants of Aaron were organized into groups (23:6), as were also the nonpriestly Levites who assisted them (vv.20–31); 4,000 others were appointed as musicians (ch. 25); 4,000 worked as doorkeepers, under whom were incorporated a variety of positions such as the temple treasurers (26:1–28); and the remaining 6,000 "were assigned duties away from the temple, as officials and judges over Israel" (26:29–32). The priests, the musicians, and presumably the temple Levites as well, were specifically assigned to twenty-four different courses. These subdivisions provided a means for rotating them in service on a monthly basis.

1 David's full life is witnessed to by the fact that these events are dated in the fortieth, i.e., the last, year of his reign (26:31; 29:27); they are identified, indeed, as being his "last instructions" (23:27).

The process by which Solomon was then "made . . . king" is passed over in Chronicles. The unhappy details of his disputed succession (see 22:9; cf. 1Ki 1) and of the ruthless consolidation that followed on his recognition as ruler (1Ki 2) were common knowledge and contributed little to the purposes Ezra was seeking to achieve.

2–4 The Levites "thirty years old or more" were numbered, as in Moses' day (Nu 4:3, 23), but also those down to twenty years of age. The total of 38,000 has, like so many of the figures in Chronicles, been roundly criticized, but unnecessarily so. Under Moses in the desert, a more limited enumeration of the Levites—only those who were between the age of thirty and fifty, and who were able to do the work of transporting the tabernacle—had produced a sum of 8,580 (Nu 4:47–48); and the Hebrew tribes as a whole had averaged over 50,000 warriors each (1:46; 26:51). Under David the main Levitical body of 24,000 was divided into twenty-four monthly courses; and 1,000 on duty at any one time, considering the work, is not unreasonable.

5 The instruments the king "provided" exhibit another aspect of David's musical prowess, which was long remembered in Israel (Am 6:5).

6 The review of the genealogy of Levi, which extends from this point down through v.23, is paralleled by the listings in 6:16–30 and by those in 24:20–30. Minor variations exist in the spellings of some of the names and in other details.

7 The fact that the Gershonite "Ladan" is listed in first place connects him with Libni, which was the senior subclan of Gershon. No allusion is made to Libni's son Jahath (as in 6:20), since the purpose of ch. 23 is not that of providing a complete genealogy but rather of marking out those divisions within the clans of Levi on which the Davidic organization was based.

8 Jehiel, Zetham, and Joel were ancient Levitical patriarchs. They should not be confused with the division chiefs of David's day, as listed in 24:20–30 (cf. Jehdeiah, descended from the patriarch Shubael, v.20), though at certain points in ch. 24 only the patriarchal family-founders are listed, without the current chiefs (as in v.23).

9 Since the "Shimei" of this verse belongs to "the families of Ladan," he should probably be distinguished from the Shimei of vv.7 and 10, his great-uncle (after whom he seems to have been named), the brother of Libni (6:17).

10–11 By combining the senior Shimei's latter two families into "one assignment," or course, David secured nine Levitical courses organized out of the clan of Gershon: six from Ladan and three from Shimei.

12–14 As in Dt 33:1 and in the title to Ps 90, Moses is set apart as "the man of God." He ranks as perhaps the greatest human figure in the OT (Dt 34:10–12).

15–20 From the four sons of Kohath (not including the priestly descendants of Aaron, v.13), nine more courses are derived, though "the [Davidic division] chiefs" (NIV, "the first") are specified for only the first three.

21–22 The sons of Mahli's son Kish "married their cousins," the daughters of Eleazar. The property of the subclan of Mahli was thus preserved intact, according to Moses' regulation (Nu 36:6–9; cf. v.11); but this left it with only one course, of Kish.

23 The sons of Mahli's brother, Mushi, account for three more. So to bring Merari's courses up to six, and thus to gain a total for all Levi of twenty-four (nine, nine, and six), two more were probably derived from the four sons of the Merarite Jaaziah (24:27).

24–27 David's Levitical census actually extended to those "twenty years old or more" (cf. Moses' limit of thirty, v.3). Yet even Moses had later included in the tribe's assigned work force Levites down to the age of twenty-five (Nu 8:24); and David lowered it five years further. His reasoning may have been that with the permanent establishment of the tabernacle and the ark in Jerusalem, physical requirements for the service were no longer so demanding (v.26); or it may have been that he simply anticipated increasing needs in manpower for the construction and operation of the new temple.

28–30 "The bread set out on the table" was "the bread of the Presence" (cf. 9:32). On "the grain offerings," see 21:23. The daily services of praise by the Levites accompanied the regular sacrifices that were prescribed for every morning and evening and were offered up by the priests (Ex 29:38–39; Nu 28:3–8).

31 More elaborate sacrifices were required for the weekly sabbaths, for the beginnings of months, and for the annual feasts (Nu 28:9–29:39). The last named involved Israel's five set celebrations, the "appointed feasts" of Passover, Pentecost, and Tabernacles (which was preceded by Trumpets and the Day of Atonement; cf. Lev 23). The first three were also designated pilgrimage feasts, for which the presence of every adult Israelite male was expected at the central sanctuary (Ex 23:14–17; Dt 16:16).

32 The author, Ezra, made it clear that the main body of the Levites were "under their brothers the [priestly] descendants of Aaron." They were to be the priests' helpers (v.28) in such matters as preparing the sacrifices and other matters of service and in maintaining the sanctuary, just as Moses had prescribed (Nu 3:6–9; 4:23–33).

24:1 Ezra now takes up the priests. This followed logically on his presentation concerning the Levites as a whole (ch. 23), of which they formed a part (v.13). The primary subject of the first nineteen verses of ch. 24 is how David organized the priests of his time into "divisions" or courses (GK 4713). Ezra does, however, grant this a priority in treatment, before he describes the corresponding set of courses for the rest of the Levites in vv.20–31.

2 The deaths of Aaron's two older sons, together with the reasons involved, are recorded in Lev 10:1–2.

3 The men who advised David in establishing the courses were official representatives of the branches of Aaron's two surviving sons: for Eleazar it was the high priest Zadok; for Ithamar, however, it was no longer Abiathar (as in 15:11), who was too old to be bothered with administrative details, but (as in 18:16) his son Ahimelech II (24:6), grandson of that Ahimelech I who had served as high priest prior to David's own kingship (1Sa 22:9–20; 23:6).

4 By dividing the priests into "sixteen" courses taken from the descendants of Eleazar and "eight" from those of Ithamar, David secured a total of twenty-four. This made possible either a system of monthly shifts or a system of fortnightly shifts once each year.

5 The king's impartiality is significant. Even though Eleazar, as senior surviving son, had been designated leader of the Levites and of those who worked in the sanctuary (Nu 3:32), and even though he had eventually succeeded his father Aaron as high priest (20:28), it was only the physical fact of the "larger number" (v.4) of priests who traced their ancestry to him that gave Eleazar numerical superiority in courses; those of Ithamar received an equal standing (cf. the even-handedness of Ex 28:1, 40–43).

6 Assignment was objective, by lot (v.7); it was witnessed by the king, Zadok, and Ahimelech—all three; and it was recorded by an unbiased (and otherwise unknown) non-priestly Levite, Shemaiah. Indeed, while the Hebrew of this verse is not completely clear, it would appear that the lots alternated between Eleazar and Ithamar for the first sixteen courses, with half of Eleazar's descendants having to accept the remaining eight.

7–19 Listings of the actual divisions appear not simply here but also at three later points in the OT, in postexilic times (Ne 10:2–8; 12:1–7; 12:12–21); and there are several incomplete references as well. The eighth course is specifically cited in the NT (cf. Lk 1:5); the names of the first, second, fourth, ninth, and twenty-fourth have been found in a manuscript at Qumran.

With the passage of time, some of the Davidic courses died out or had to be consolidated with others, and new ones were formed to take their places. At the first return from exile in 537 B.C., only four courses were registered: David's second, third (Ezr 2:36–39; Ne 7:39–42), fifth (if Pashhur had come to represent the older Malkijah; cf. 9:12 and Ne 11:12), and sixteenth. By 520 twenty-two were again operative (Ne 12:1–7), but only half of them were the courses as originally organized by David.

Jehoiarib (v.7), who received the first assignment, headed the course that later produced the Maccabees (1Mc 2:1; 14:29). The seventh course, of Hakkoz (v.10), is documented down into the days of the Maccabees (1Mc 8:17). The eighth, Abijah, was the one under which Zechariah, the father of John the Baptist, performed his priestly ministry (Lk 1:5). The family of the seventeenth course, Hezir (v.15), was prominent in intertestamental times; and the name appears on one of the major tombs in the valley to the east of Jerusalem.

20 The phrase "the rest of the descendants of Levi" identifies the bulk of the Levites, who were not descended from Aaron and who served as temple assistants. Verses 20–31 proceed to describe their allocation into divisions that corresponded to the priestly courses, just listed. For some reason the nine divisions of the clan of Gershon (23:7–11) are not discussed. The next nine (24:20–25) correspond to the family groups that arose from Levi's second son Kohath, through his four sons, Amram, Izhar, Hebron, and Uzziel (23:12–20). For each of their courses, Ezra also listed the name of the man who served as division chief during the time of David—e.g., for "Shubael" the chief was Jehdeiah—except for the four courses of Hebron, the names of whose Davidic chiefs may simply not have been available to Ezra when he was writing.

21–30 For the clause "Isshiah was the first [GK 8031]," we should read, "Isshiah was the chief" or "leader." "Shelomoth" (v.22) is a variant of the name "Shelomith" (23:18). The last four courses listed for the clan of Merari (vv.29–30) correspond to the four Merarite family divisions as described in

23:21–23, though the only chief's name to appear is that of Jerahmeel, representing in David's day the Mahlite group of Eleazar and Kish, which had been consolidated into one (cf. 23:22). Two other courses, however, should probably be assigned to the groups descending from Jaaziah (cf. 23:23). Jaaziah is stated to have been a Merarite (24:27) and yet is distinguished from Mahli and Mushai, the actual sons of Merari (v.26). He may have been a later member of the clan, the numerical growth of whose offspring had reached such proportions that by the time of David they achieved separate recognition among the Levitical courses.

31 The subject of the clause "they also cast lots" must be the chiefs of the divisions of the nonpriestly Levites (cf. vv.20–30). The stated correspondence of their method of organization with that of "their brothers the descendants of Aaron" favors a similar division of their followers into twenty-four rotating courses, even though not spelled out, as it was for the latter.

25:1 Chapter 25 concerns David's organization of the four thousand Levitical musicians (23:5) into courses of service that correspond to those of the priests and temple Levites (ch. 24). Division heads for the musicians consisted of "the sons of Asaph, Heman and Jeduthun," the chief musicians who belonged, respectively, to the Levitical clans of Gershon, Kohath, and Merari. David had commissioned them some thirty years earlier to minister before the ark in Jerusalem (16:4–7, 37, 41–42). Their service, moreover, is identified as a form of "prophesying" (cf. Heman's description as "the king's seer," v.5). The association is legitimate. On the particular musical instruments, see comments on 15:16. It was with specific reference to the Levites who performed on these instruments that God, through Nathan and Gad, gave David his instructions for their designated stations (2Ch 29:25).

2 Asaph "prophesied" (GK 5547) to a degree beyond that of simply recreating the hymns of others, as directed "under the king's supervision." Asaph and his descendants were directly inspired to compose at least twelve of the canonical psalms (50; 73–83; cf. 1Ch 16:5).

In Jerusalem today entertainers dress in ancient garb and play replicas of ancient instruments, such as the harp.

3 Jeduthun (as in 9:16; 16:41–42), also called Ethan (see 6:44), was twice singled out in titles to the psalms as the chief musician responsible for the public presentation of King David's compositions (Pss 39; 62).

4 The name of the Kohathite musician Heman's fourth son, Shubael, of the subclan of Izhar, is not to be confused with the Kohathite course of the same name but drawn from the senior subclan of Amram (23:16; 24:20).

5 Heman's status as "seer" received further witness, if he was perhaps the inspired composer of some of twelve other psalms, which were written by "the sons of Korah" (Pss 42–49; 84–85;87–88), of whom he was one (1Ch 6:33, 37). God's blessing Heman with "fourteen sons" would be, to the Oriental mind, nothing short of a doubly perfect heritage of power. The mention of his "three daughters" reminds us that women shared in musical services (cf. Ps 68:25).

6–8 The singers "cast lots" to determine without prejudice the arrangement of the twenty-four courses, serving under the sons of Asaph, Heman, and Jeduthun. Yet all took part, whether "teacher" (GK 1067), probably referring to the 288 skilled musicians of v.7 (twelve per course), or "student" (GK 9441), which suggests that all 4,000 of the Levitical musicians were involved in the allocation.

9–31 As it worked out, the third, second, and fifth courses did go, respectively, to Asaph's three oldest sons.

26:1 The first twenty-eight verses of ch. 26 describe King David's third unit of Levites (cf. the introductory discussion to ch. 23), i.e., the 4,000 "gatekeepers" (23:5; cf. 9:19; 15:21; GK 8788). These were the temple guards (vv.1–19); and with them were included certain other officials, such as treasurers, who were responsible for the physical operation of the sanctuary (vv.20–28). The temple itself had not yet been built; but the king seems to have made these arrangements in anticipation, while the actual casting of lots "for each gate" (v.13) may have come later, after the structures were completed. God's assignment here to "businessmen" suggests something of the importance he attaches to each person's part in the kingdom, material and spiritual.

The Chronicler had already identified two groups of gatekeepers, appointed by David when the ark was first brought to Jerusalem (16:38); and a number of later listings occurred as well, either shortly before the Exile (9:17–29) or after (Ezr 2:42; Ne 11:19; 12:25). A remarkable persistence is exhibited in the names of some of the Levitical gate-keeping families. An example appears in the first and leading group, of (Me)shelemiah (vv.1, 14), though also cited simply as Shallum (9:17, 19 [though cf. v.21]; Ezr 2:42) or Meshullam (Ne 12:25).

The name "Asaph," father of Kore, is an abbreviation for Ebiasaph, who was a son of the rebellious Kohathite, Korah (cf. 6:22; 9:19). He should therefore not be confused with David's contemporary Asaph, the more famous chief musician, who belonged to the clan of Gershon.

2–8 Obed-Edom (v.4) was another Kohathite descendant of Korah, who is best known for the divine blessing that he received for having faithfully cared for the ark, following the death of Uzzah (13:13–14). Though he had

gained appointment as a Levitical musician, he continued also to maintain his status as a doorkeeper (cf. 15:21; 16:38). In the thirty years since the ark first came to Jerusalem, the number of those associated with Obed-Edom exhibited a net decrease of six, down to sixty-two (cf. 16:38).

9 Yet with the 18 "sons and relatives" of Meshelemiah, plus 13 more of Hosah (v.11), the total number of hereditary leaders for the sanctuary guards totals 93. By the time of Jerusalem's fall in 586 B.C., the figure had risen to 212 (cf. 9:22), though the number of Levites available to serve under them may have become much less than the 4,000 present in David's day (23:5).

10–11 The king had commissioned Hosah of Merari to be a gatekeeper along with Obed-Edom (16:38).

12–13 The purpose of the "lots" that "were cast" was to assign the gatekeepers to locations about the sanctuary, not, at this point, to determine periods for their rotation, as had been the case for the priests, temple Levites, and musicians (chs. 24–25).

14 "Shelemiah" (cf. NIV note) represents an abbreviated form of the name Meshelemiah (vv.1–2, 9). Together with his son Zechariah, he and his associated leaders received responsibility for two of the gates, east and north, leaving one each for Obed-Edom and Hosah.

15 Because the palace complex lay to the south of the Mount Moriah sanctuary, some have questioned the possibility of a south gate. Most of the palaces, however, were erected after David's time (1Ki 7:1–12); and even then their presence would seem to suggest the need for such a gate, for both the rulers and the people (Eze 46:9–10). Obed-Edom was honored with this assignment toward the south and its palaces (cf. 15:21).

16 The "Shalleketh Gate" is known only to have faced west and to have been located on the "upper [or ascending] road," probably one coming northward up through the Tyropoeon Valley from the lower city to the higher elevation of Mount Moriah. The word "Shalleketh" itself is a proper noun. "Shuppim" is not otherwise identified, but his association with Hosah suggests that he may have been another leading gatekeeper from the clan of Merari.

17 Because the east gate was the main one, six guards were assigned to it, as compared with four to the north (and to the other directions). This gave Meshelemiah ten guard posts.

18–19 With Hosah's four posts at the west gate and two at the "court" (a term of uncertain meaning, but probably denoting a colonnade or court), his group of six stations yields a total of twenty-four guard posts that were assigned by lot (cf. chs. 24–25).

20–21 The gatekeepers' positions of trust (see 9:22) included two major treasurerships: the one over the treasuries of the temple, with their offerings and valuable equipment (cf. 9:28–29), and the other over the treasuries of dedicated objects (vv.23–28). The former were placed in the charge of "Jehieli," which is an adjectival form meaning "Jehielites" (the group of Jehiel). This identifies the Gershonite course number 1 of temple Levites.

22 The treasurers chosen from "Zetham and . . . Joel," which are Gershonite courses numbers 2 and 3 (23:8), are then called "sons of Jehiel"; for the leadership was recognized as pertaining to the senior branch.

23–24 The latter treasuries were placed under the care of Levites chosen from the clan of Kohath and, particularly, from within its four listed subclans, from the "Amramite" sons of Moses. These belonged to the courses numbers 10 ("Shubael") and 11 ("Rehabiah").

25 In David's day the individual treasurer for the dedicated objects was from Rahabiah, i.e., "Shelomoth" (instead of "Shelomith," NIV). His name is not to be confused with Shelomoth, Gershonite course number 4 of the temple Levites (23:9), or with Shelomith, Kohathite course number 12, from the subclan of Izhar (23:18; cf. 24:22).

26–28 Examples of "the things dedicated by King David" (v.26) are cited in 18:11 and 2Ch 5:1.

29 The latter four verses of ch. 26 describe David's fourth and last major operational unit of Levi, the six thousand external officials and judges (23:4). Moses himself had

first directed that the Levites, who would be responsible to teach the Word of God (Dt 33:10), should perform the corresponding function of interpreting it in judgment (Dt 17:9; cf. 2Ch 19:8–11). These officers were then drawn primarily from the second and third subclans of Kohath, namely Izhar and Hebron. On the Izharite Kenaniah, King David's "head Levite," see 15:22.

30–31 Among the Hebronites, Hashabiah is probably that son of Kemuel who served as David's "officer over the tribe of Levi" (27:16–17); and Jeriah identifies the senior course number 13, belonging to the subclan of Hebron (23:19). These two, between them, accounted for 4,400 (1,700 plus 2,700, v.32) of the 6,000 Levitical judges.

32 The statistic that 2,700 Levites maintained the laws of "God and . . . the king" among the tribes west of the Jordan (v.30) seems strange but indicates the importance of the district of Gilead.

4. The civil organization (27:1–34)

Having outlined David's religious organization (chs. 23–26), the Chronicler adds ch. 27 on his civil arrangements. The year 970 B.C. had constituted a high-water mark in Israel's political experience; and its splendor was a far cry from the impoverished condition of the Jewish subprovince that existed in Ezra's day (cf. Hag 2:16–17; Zec 14:10). But even though it could have had little organizational relevance for the returned exiles in 450—and even less for us today—this rehearsal of past glories must have thrilled Ezra's discouraged people with the truth that tangible political results are included in God's decree for his faithful servants (cf. Rev 2:26).

This chapter surveys three aspects of the Davidic regime: its military system of twelve army corps, each with its own commanding general and twenty-four skilled chiefs (cf. v.1), who were committed to a term of active duty one month each year (vv.1–15); the ethnic organization of twelve listed Hebrew tribes (cf. v.17) in their various geographical regions, each with its responsible officer (vv.16–24); and the royal administration, including both the central "cabinet" executives and the overseers of the king's properties in the field (vv.25–34).

1 A significant key to our understanding of these first fifteen verses appears in the Chronicler's introductory emphasis on the "commanders of thousands." When the verse concludes by referring to each "division's 24,000 men" (there is no word for "men" in the original), the word for "thousand" (GK 547) may indicate "chief" (who could command a thousand troops) rather than numerical "thousands" (cf. 7:3–4, and the stress in 27:3 on leaders of "all the army officers for the first month"). For while the idea of a national militia of 288,000 organized into twelve corps of "24,000 men" each is reasonable enough (cf. over 600,000 in Moses' day, Ex 12:37; Nu 1:46; 2:32; 11:21; 26:51), the alternative rendering of "24 chief men" (throughout vv.1–15) has two advantages: negatively, it relieves the capital of the congestion of some 48,000 rotating troops, who, literally, "came in and went out month by month" (NASB); and positively, it would allow the king to keep in touch with his military leaders.

2 Each "lieutenant general" who commanded one of the twelve army corps was a distinguished military figure in his own right and is cited in the roster of David's heroes (11:11–47; cf. 2Sa 23:8–39), though with occasional variations in spelling and with facts of family information added here. "Jashobeam" was the first of "the Three" great champions (11:11).

3 Jashobeam's ancestor "Perez" was the fourth son of Judah and founder of its major clan.

4 "Dodai" was the father of Eleazar, the second of "the Three" (see 11:12). "Mikloth was the leader," or, as we might say, executive officer, for this second corps.

5–6 The exploits of "Benaiah" son of Jehoiada the priest (see 11:22–25; cf. 12:27–28) elevated him to the leadership of David's Cretan guard (see 18:17). This probably explains why "his son Ammizabad" exercised actual command over the third corps. On Benaiah's position in respect to "the Thirty," see 11:25 and the comments on 11:15 and 12:4.

7 Holding the title of commander of the fourth corps was Asahel, the first man to be named in David's legion of honor, which

made up "the Thirty." "His son Zebadiah was his successor," due to Asahel's untimely death at the hands of Abner (see 11:26).

8 Over the fifth corps was "Shamhuth the Izrahite." This defining adjective really means "of Zerah," the other leading clan of Judah (cf. v.3 and the equivalent term "Zerahite," vv.11, 13). His name appears third among the Thirty (11:27).

9–15 The remaining seven generals were selected from among the next nine members of the Thirty (11:27–31). "Heldai," commander of the twelfth (27:15), was a descendant of Othniel, the first Hebrew judge (Jdg 1:13; 3:9–11).

16–17 While most of the tribes of Israel had one outstanding individual chosen to be the ethnic "officer" (vv.16–25), two were appointed for Levi: the high priest "Zadok," to represent its Aaronic or priestly branch (cf. 6:8; 12:27–28; 16:39), and "Hashabiah," for the remainder (see 26:30–31). Manasseh also had two officers, corresponding to its two regional halves, west (v.20) and east (v.21) of the Jordan. The tribes of Gad and Asher remain unlisted, either because the names of their tribal officers were not available to Ezra, or because they were dropped from the text by later copyists' mistakes.

18–20 Judah's representative, Elihu, is called "a brother of David" (v.18). This could possibly identify the unnamed brother born between Ozen and David; but it then becomes difficult to explain why his name was not mentioned in 2:15, if he did survive (cf. 2:15). Elihu may actually have been a more distant "brother" (= relative); or the name might be a variant for Jesse's oldest son, Eliab (2:13).

21–22 The tribal officer for Benjamin was "Jaasiel," a "son of Abner," who had commanded the troops of his nephew King Saul and had been the power behind Saul's son Ish-bosheth (26:28; cf. 8:33 and 11:2).

23 The Lord's promise "to make Israel as numerous as the stars" dates back to Abraham (Ge 15:5; 22:17; cf. 12:2; 13:16), over a thousand years before David. The king, therefore, did not order a total numbering of Israel (including minors); for that might have seemed to cast doubt on the prophecy. He did, however, sinfully decree a census of the men of fighting age, apparently through a lack of faith in God's protection of his kingdom (cf. 21:3).

24 The Hebrew of this verse says simply that Joab "began to count but did not finish."

25–32 In the remainder of the chapter, with its list of royal administrators, Azmaveth must have had charge of the central stores in Jerusalem, which contrasts with Jonathan's similar post "in the outlying districts."

The "western foothills"(v.28) constituted the piedmont area between the Philistine coastal plain and the Judean hill country. The king depended on his personal properties in all the areas such as these, rather (as far as we can tell) than on taxes, to support his growing administration. A concluding list of major counselors (v.32) supplements the earlier outlines of David's cabinet as presented in 18:15–17 (cf. 2Sa 8:15–18; 20:23–26).

33 Hushai's post of "king's friend" (cf. 2Sa 15:37) may have begun on an informal and personal basis; but it became an official advisory position (cf. 1Ki 4:5). Ahithophel was the ill-fated "counselor" who deserted David for his son, the rebel Absalom (2Sa 15:12, 31; 16:20–23), but whose advice was subverted by Hushai (15:32–37; 17:1–16).

34 After his suicide (17:23), Ahithophel "was succeeded by Jehoiada," son of the commander Benaiah (cf. 27:5); he was also the grandson of his namesake, the militant priest (see 12:27–28).

5. Final words (28:1–29:30)

The occasion for the final chapters of 1 Chronicles is a continuation of what was introduced in ch. 23: the assembling by the king of the leaders of Israel (23:2 = 28:1 and 29:1). The date is still 970 B.C. (26:31), and the subject is a final portion of "the last instructions of David" (23:27). The king's purpose has been not simply to organize the Levites on a permanent basis (chs. 23–26), but also to arouse the whole nation to the momentous task of erecting God's temple in Jerusalem (cf. 22:6, 11, 19). Now David once again charged the people (28:2–8) and his son Solomon (vv.9–10) to consecrate themselves to this holy effort. David then presented his son with the inspired, written plans for the temple (vv.11–19) and encouraged him for the

work that lay ahead (vv.20–21). He turned also to the nation, represented by its assembled leaders, and urged on them an all-out campaign of giving for the building (29:1–5). They rose to the challenge (vv.6–9), and David praised the Lord for their devotion (vv.10–22). Solomon was then confirmed on the throne of Israel by a second ceremony of anointing (cf. v.22), and David passed on to his eternal reward (vv.22–30).

1–2 On the king's previous desire to build a temple, see 17:1–4. The structure is here identified as "a place of rest for the ark" (Ps 132:8, 14; i.e., a more permanent one than the tent in which it had been kept heretofore, 1Ch 16:1) and as God's "footstool" (Ps 132:7; La 2:1). The latter term points specifically to "the place of atonement" or "mercy seat" (v.11; i.e., the golden cover of the ark, over which the glory-cloud of God's presence was enthroned; Ex 25:20–22; 2Sa 6:2).

3 David's desire to build the temple, however, had been denied because of his excessive bloodshed (cf. 22:8). The king's public explanation here corresponds to what he had already told Solomon privately (22:7–16).

4 David's statement that God "chose me from my whole family to be king over Israel forever" must refer, not to him personally, but to his "family," i.e., his dynasty (cf. vv.5, 7), which would culminate in Jesus Christ, who would reign forever (17:14). The divine choice had been revealed through a process of progressive elimination: from the whole of national "Israel," through the tribe of "Judah," down to the Davidic "family" in particular (Ge 28:14; 35:10–11; 49:10; 1Sa 16:1–3; 1Ch 17:16–17, 23–27). Compare its earlier stages of clarification: from "the seed of woman," through Noah and Shem, to Abraham (Ge 3:15; 6:17–18; 9:26; 12:1–3).

5 Yet, in a deeper sense, what David acknowledged was not his own kingship but "the kingdom of the LORD over Israel." He, and all of earth's rulers, are but vice-regents, deputies who act as representatives of God to uphold his standards (29:23; 1Sa 12:14; Ro 13:1–6).

6–8 Solomon did build God's "house" (cf. 2Ch 5:1), but as far as being "established" (GK 3922) or being "chosen" (GK 1047) to be God's "son" is concerned, v.7 states an explicit condition: "if he is unswerving in carrying out my commands and laws"—which Solomon was not (1Ki 11:1–11). This brought about the admonition in v.8. Moreover, between God's words "Solomon . . . will build my house" and "I have chosen him to be my son," the full prophecy, through Nathan, had originally included an intervening statement that shifted the point of reference beyond Solomon to the more distant future, i.e., "and I will establish his throne forever" (1Ch 17:12). That is, the fulfillment of true sonship to God the "Father" was not achieved by Solomon (cf. 22:10); it was an ideal that was actualized only in Christ.

9–10 David's appeal to his son to serve God with his whole heart and a "willing mind" parallels his similar final admonition recorded in 1Ki 2:2–4.

11 The Hebrew phrase underlying the words "the place of atonement" is literally "the house of the atoning cover" (or of the "mercy seat"; cf. v.2). It denotes the room that housed the ark of the covenant, designated in the tabernacle as "the most holy place" and in the temple as the "inner sanctuary" (2Ch 5:7, 9).

12–18 "The plans of . . . the temple" were directly revealed to David by the inspiration of the Holy Spirit (cf. v.19), even as those for the tabernacle that preceded it had been given to Moses (Ex 25:9, 40; 27:8). The major pieces of its furnishings (vv.14–18) were symbolic of the great truths of God's salvation; and some—e.g., the altar, sea, ark, and even certain of the priestly garments—typified the atoning sacrifice, moral purity, incarnate presence, and holiness of Jesus Christ (Heb 8:5; 9:8–12, 23–24).

Ezra referred to "each table" (v.16) because, in contrast to the single table of bread of the Presence (9:32) made for the Mosaic sanctuary (Ex 37:10), the Solomonic would have ten of them (2Ch 4:8).

Since the Lord could poetically be said to ride on cherubim as on a chariot (Ps 18:10; Eze 1), they are here designated simply "the chariot" (v.18). The Chronicler's reference is probably not to the small golden cherubim that formed part of the ark's holy cover, which had been made long before, but rather to those larger wooden but gold-plated cherub-angels of the inner temple, which

were to "shelter the ark" as a whole (2Ch 3:10–13). They emphasized the real presence of God in the temple.

19 Because the words "he gave me understanding" have no "and" before them in the Hebrew but are connected with the first part of the verse rather than its latter part, we should preferably read: "the LORD gave me understanding in writing." David was saying that not only were the temple plans revealed by God (v.12), but that they were given to him in written form from God, to be handed to Solomon (v.11), an ultimate testimony to their divine character.

20–21 David's final charge to Solomon (cf. vv.9–10; 22:11–16; Pss 27:13–14; 31:23–24), that he should "be strong and courageous" because the Lord would "not fail . . . or forsake" him, reflects the stirring charges of Moses to Joshua (Dt 31:7–8, 23), and of the Lord himself (Jos 1:5–9,18; cf. 1Co 16:13).

29:1–3 David had expressed concern before about Solomon's youthful inexperience and about his own need to compensate for this by preparing materials for the temple (v.2; cf. 22:5 and 14). The "stones of various colors" (v.2) were probably mosaic pebbles. "Over and above" (v.3) the great amounts he had already prepared (cf. 22:14), David next contributed his personal treasures.

4 Israel's finest gold was imported from "Ophir" (cf. 2Ch 8:18). This amounted to about 110 tons of gold and 260 tons of silver.

5 The king's appeal for each giver to "consecrate himself" (lit., "to fill his hand"; GK 3338 & 4848) was a technical phrase used to describe ordination to the priesthood; and Scripture, significantly, places the act of giving on this same level of devotion.

6–7 The "daric" was a Persian gold coin, first issued by Darius I in the century before Ezra; in David's day this figure—the equivalent of about two and one-half talents—would have represented the corresponding weight in small pieces of the precious metal. The weight of gold contributed by David's leaders comes to about 190 tons, and there were about 375 tons of silver. David's example (v.4) thus incited a gift on the part of his officers that was half again as large as his own. Since it was a rarer commodity then than it is today, 3,750 tons of iron are also mentioned. The total of just the silver and gold adds up to an enormous sum by contemporary values. While the sum is only one twenty-fifth of the quantity tabulated in ch. 22, it still amounts to so much, particularly in ancient purchasing power, that it too should be recognized as the other large figures in Chronicles; it is to be accounted for through an act of divine providence. (cf. 22:14).

8–9 On "Jehiel" and course number 1 of "the Gershonite" temple-Levites, see 26:21. A "willing response" to the needs of the Lord's worship produced great rejoicing on the part of both the king and the people; and, still today, God loves cheerful givers (2Co 9:7).

10 David's reaction to his people's devotion was to praise the Lord (vv.10–20). The phrase "our father Israel" here signifies the patriarch Jacob (Ge 32:28); he too (cf. v.15) had had occasion to praise God for his goodness (Ge 32:10; 33:11). The Hebrew word order could suggest divine fatherhood—"The LORD, God of Israel, our Father"—rather than a patriarchal characteristic; but see v.18.

11 This verse supplies the conclusion to the Lord's Prayer: "For thine is the kingdom" (Mt 6:13, KJV).

12–19 The truth that "everything" we have "comes from" God is the foundation for the doctrine of stewardship. Its basis is this: since our property is his (Ps 24:1), and since we hold it only temporarily and in trust (1Ch 29:15–16), it should therefore be used for him (Lk 17:10).

20–21 When Ezra spoke of the "sacrifices in abundance for all Israel," he probably intended fellowship offerings, the one major category of sacrifice in which all the worshipers participated, feasting as guests around the table of the Lord (cf. v.22 and 16:1).

22 The "great joy" of those at this gathering, particularly in respect to Solomon's being "acknowledged" (GK 4887), is reflected also in 1Ki 1:40. By stating that David's son was acknowledged for "a second time," the Chronicler makes no attempt to conceal but rather recalls to his readers the well-known facts that he does not recount about Solomon's first induction to the throne. This had been precipitated by the attempt of his older half-brother Adonijah to displace him (1Ki 1:25, 39). Such confirmatory rites, even to the point of reanointing, had value, particularly in cases of disputed succession (cf. 1Sa 10:1, 24; 11:14–15; 16:13, 2Sa 2:4; 5:3).

The position Solomon acceded to is here defined as that of "ruler" (v.22; GK 5592) or "leader" (lit., "a conspicuous one"). It was a characteristic title among the early sovereigns of Israel (1Sa 9:16; 13:14; 25:30; 1Ch 5:2; 11:2; 17:7). Zadok too (cf. 6:8; 16:39) was reanointed, though for him it was to the position of sole high priest, his previous colleague Abiathar having been disqualified in connection with Adonijah's plot (1Ki 1:7; 2:26).

23–30 In his concluding summary of David's reign, the Chronicler itemizes those aspects of his success that had the greatest appeal to Oriental thought: "long life, wealth and honor" and a "son" who "succeeded him," which form a not inappropriate incentive for seeking the blessing of God in Occidental thought as well. First Kings, unhappily, adds specific features to David's final characterization that are of a less complimentary nature (1:1–4, 15; 2:5–6, 8–9).

Ezra's closing reference to his written sources, and particularly to the way Samuel, Nathan, and Gad recorded the circumstances of "Israel and the kingdoms of all the other lands," probably relates to those kingdoms that immediately surrounded Israel, so many of whom David had been enabled to incorporate within his own realm (cf. ch. 18).

The Old Testament in the New

OT Text	NT Text	Subject
1Ch 17:13	Heb 1:5; Rev 21:7	Father and son

2 Chronicles

INTRODUCTION

See introduction to 1 Chronicles.

Just as 1 Chronicles paralleled and drew on 1 and 2 Samuel (starting at 1Sa 31), so 2 Chronicles parallels 1 and 2 Kings. Its first nine chapters constitute the third out of the four major divisions into which the Chronicler's history naturally falls. These chapters are devoted to the reign of Solomon (970-930 B.C.), the son of David, and correspond to 1Ki 1–11. Even more so than in 1 Kings, the Solomonic record in 2 Chronicles shows a greater concern for Solomon's temple—six out of the opening nine chapters (chs. 2–7)—than it shows for Solomon's kingship (as compared to 1Ki 5:1–9:9). The third division of Chronicles does commence and conclude (chs. 1 and 8–9) with basic facts about Solomon's reign. The final division is about Judah's history down to the destruction of Jerusalem and the Exile.

II. The Reign of Solomon (2Ch 1:1–9:31)

A. Solomon's Inauguration (1:1–17)

Chapter 1 concerns the king's inauguration. Shortly before his death in 970 (1Ch 29:26), King David had seen his son Solomon safely seated on the throne of a united Israel (cf. 23:1); and, by means of a second anointing, he had ensured the allegiance of the nation's leaders to him (see 29:22). Solomon's personal career as monarch, however, was inaugurated when God appeared to him in a dream at Gibeon (2Ch 1:1–13, paralleling 1Ki 3:4–15). This event, perhaps more than any other in history, brings to mind the biblical principle of Jas 1:5.

1 The opening verse of 2 Chronicles draws together two other references: (1) that Solomon was "established firmly" recalls the struggle at his accession as this was recorded in 1Ki 1 (cf. 1Ch 29:22), and (2) that God made him "exceedingly great" picks up the thought of 1Ch 29:25.

2–4 Ezra, the author, clarifies 1Ki 3:4 by identifying the various elements that made up Solomon's "whole assembly," those who represented "all . . . Israel" and who accompanied him to Gibeon. At the time Moses' tabernacle, "God's Tent of Meeting," was located at this center, seven miles northwest of Jerusalem (see 1Ch 16:39). With the ark now at the Jerusalem capital, these two cities became the only legitimate places for divine atonement. First Kings 3:2 does recognize the reality of deviation in popular practice; but the principle of centralized worship, of services of sacrifice only where God revealed himself, had been established by Moses almost five hundred years earlier (Ex 20:24; Lev 17:3–9; Dt 12:5). Other "high places," even if used in the name of the Lord God of Israel, were necessarily excluded. This was because of their contamination through association with Canaanite Baal worship: they stood under God's ban (Nu 33:52; Dt 12:2). Indeed, Solomon's first drift toward sin became apparent by his recognition and use of such unauthorized high places.

5–6 The "bronze altar" made by Bezalel (see 1Ch 2:20) had a frame of acacia wood, but it was overlaid with bronze (Ex 38:1–2).

7–8 When that night God "appeared to Solomon," it was in the form of a dream (1Ki 3:5, 15; cf. 1Sa 28:6). The "kindness" that God showed Solomon was his *hesed* (GK 2875; lit., faithfulness to what he had previously covenanted; cf. 1Ch 16:41): in this instance, that Solomon should succeed David as king (see 22:9).

9 God's "promise to . . . David"—primarily as revealed in 1Ch 17:11–14—that Solomon prayed might "be confirmed" (GK 586) included the permanent establishment of David's seed on the throne of Israel and the erection of the temple at Jerusalem. The Lord had already fulfilled his promise to Abraham, that he should have descendants "as numerous as the dust of the earth" (Ge 13:16; 22:17; cf. 1Ki 4:20; 1Ch 27:23).

10 The central teaching of ch. 1 lies in Solomon's selfless prayer for wisdom, which was the precise characteristic that his father David had already invoked for him (1Ch 22:12). The newly inaugurated king's desire to have it so that he might "lead this people" Israel reads, literally, that he might "go out and come in before this people." Such words referred originally to military leadership (1Ch 11:2; cf. 1Sa 18:13) but are here broadened into representing good governmental administratorship in general.

11–13 God granted Solomon's request. His factual knowledge was to some extent limited by his cultural environment; but his "wisdom," in the sense of that divinely given ability that can apply knowledge to life situations (as shown by his authorship of Proverbs, Ecclesiastes, and Song of Songs; cf. 1Ki 4:29, 32), has never been surpassed (1Ki 3:12). God also granted him an unparalleled concentration of wealth (v.15; cf. 1Ch 22:14) and honor (1Ch 29:25; Mt 6:29), which illustrates Christ's teaching: "Seek first his kingdom and his righteousness, and all these things will be given to you as well" (Mt 6:33).

14 Chapter 1 concludes (vv.14–17) by adducing historical evidences for the fulfillment of God's promises. King Solomon's "chariot cities" and other urban constructions have been validated archaeologically by excavations at cities of his period from Hazor in the north to Gezer in the southwest. Megiddo too contains Solomonic structures, including an intricate gateway complex, a palace area, and perhaps even its well-known subterranean water system. Two huge, stone stables holding about 450 horses were formerly attributed to the wise king—and may still be based on his planning—but, at least to the level to which they have been so far recovered, they seem now to be datable to King Ahab in the next century. (Currently there is some doubt as to whether these were even stables, but perhaps were grain storage bins.)

15 Solomon's silver, "and [his] gold," too (which does not receive mention in the parallel passages: 9:27; 1Ki 10:27), were as common as "stones"—whose abundance are plainly evident to any tourist to the Holy Land. Solomon also made cedar as plentiful as the sycamore-fig trees, which abound in "the foothills" (cf. 1Ch 27:28).

16 Kue is probably Cilicia, in what is now southern Turkey, at the east end of the Mediterranean; it was a prime ancient supplier of horses.

17 The price for chariots and horses ran about fifteen pounds and three and three-fourths pounds of silver each, respectively. Each chariot cost four times as much as each horse, because of the craftsmanship required and because the wood itself had to be imported into Egypt. The law of Moses, significantly, forbade excess in these very matters (Dt 17:16); they were, in fact, the sorts of sins that Solomon's prosperity eventually precipitated.

B. Solomon's Temple (2:1–7:22)

1. Preparations (2:1–18)

Despite the greatness of King Solomon's armies, wealth, and material possessions (1:14–17), it is not these things that are the most important for us today; nor were they for Ezra in his day. It was Solomon's temple that captured the greatest concern. This building was, after all, the place where the people worshiped God (but see John 4:21; cf. Mt 27:51).

To the Jews of 450 B.C., the temple overshadowed every other aspect of the career of Solomon. Through the rites of atonement that were performed at its altar, God brought Israel into reconciliation with himself (cf. 2Co 5:18); and continuously these rites symbolized the presence of the Lord in the midst of his redeemed people (2Ch 7:1–2; Ex 29:45–46). Salvation was bound up in the temple, even if in a preliminary and anticipatory way. For even as its altar and priests were a figure that pointed forward to Christ's sacrifice on the cross (Heb 7:27; 8:4–5; 9:9–12), so the structure itself was a type, a material prophecy of that day when the Word of God would become flesh and "tabernacle" among us (cf. Jn 1:14). Still today it serves as a type of that future glorification that awaits us in the heavenly presence of God himself (Ex 24:18; Heb 9:24).

Solomon's preparations for the temple possessed considerable antecedents. King David had already prepared in many ways: providing the design for the whole complex, gathering supplies, and enlisting personnel (1Ch 22; 28–29). Solomon, however, still needed to organize the labor force (2Ch 2:2,

17–18). A further aspect, and perhaps the most significant of his preparations, lay in the young king's search for technical assistance from Hiram king of Tyre (cf. v.12). This way Solomon could gain an experienced superintendent of construction and also a supply of timber from the incomparable cedars of Lebanon (vv.3–10). A suitable contract was soon negotiated (vv.11–16).

1 In addition to the temple, Solomon is said to have constructed a palace for himself (cf. v.12). Though repeatedly mentioned, little is known about it except for the time involved in its building and for some of the costly wood used in its construction (8:1; 9:11; cf. 7:11). It seems to have lain south of the temple on Mount Moriah, but north of the older city of Jerusalem on Mount Zion (cf. 1Ch 26:15), in the space that existed between them.

2 The distribution of the king's "conscripted" laborers between "carriers and ... stone cutters" is based on the total of 153,600 given in v.17. These workers were drafted from the alien population that was resident in Israel, according to plans that had already been formulated by David (see 1Ch 22:2). The total figures are validated by 1Ki 5:15–16 (cf. 2Ch 2:18). Solomon also conscripted some 30,000 men out of Israel to labor in relays of 10,000 men each, one month out of every three (1Ki 5:13–14). Precedent for such monthly rotation appears in Egypt, where the system grew out of the three-month period for the annual inundation of the Nile.

3 The king then sent a communication, the text of which appears in vv.3b–10, to "Hiram [a shortened form of Ahiram] king of Tyre." This city was a Phoenician port, newer and lying to the south of its counterpart Sidon, and situated on an island off the Mediterranean coast. Tyre lies, indeed, just north of the white cliffs that marked the northern border of Israel and specifically the tribe of Asher. It possessed the finest harbor in the area, and its inhabitants were noted for their ship building and commerce.

The occasion for King Solomon's writing had been furnished by the arrival of a Phoenician delegation sent by Hiram to console Solomon over the death of his father, David, who had been Hiram's friend, and to congratulate him on his own accession (1Ki 5:1).

The new king's request that Hiram send him "cedar logs as you did for my father David" (cf. 1Ch 14:1) must not be misunderstood as implying either that the logs were to be used for a palace, as had been the case with David (cf. v.4), or that they were the first timber to be provided for the temple (cf. David's previous accumulations in this regard, 1Ch 22:4, 14).

4 Concerning the activities projected for accomplishment within the temple, the "burning [of] fragrant incense" before the Lord was an act that was performed twice daily on the altar of incense (Ex 30:6–8). In reference to the "consecrated bread," see 1Ch 9:32; on the daily "burnt offerings," 23:30; and on the "appointed feasts," 23:31.

5 Solomon's affirmation that "our God is greater than all other gods" testifies to his religious commitment, even when dealing with a powerful pagan king. The latter's response then indicates a corresponding willingness on Hiram's part to recognize the Lord.

6 Even though the temple was designed to house the glory cloud of God's presence (5:13–14), Solomon, from the very outset, acknowledged that it could not "contain him," in the sense of restricting or in any way confining his infinitude to this one location (cf. 6:18; Ac 7:48–49). God in his grace has seen fit, on various occasions, to manifest himself for purposes of revelation and redemption; the supreme demonstration of this fact lies in the incarnation of Jesus Christ (Jn 1:14). Yet in all such cases, significant qualifications are present that prevent any reduction in the Lord's glory or any manipulation of God on the part of men. Such localization is always voluntary on his part, undertaken on his initiative alone (6:5–6); it is paralleled by his continuing and simultaneous omnipresence (16:9); and it is revocable at his will, capable of termination whenever he may deem it to have become detrimental to his purposes.

In the light of the greatness of God, Solomon confessed his own inadequacy: "Who then am I?" His humility becomes all the more noteworthy in view of his own unsurpassed wealth, wisdom, and power (cf. 1:12, 14–15).

7 Solomon requested from Hiram a skilled workman and in fact hired a number of experienced Phoenicians (vv.8, 14) to work with his own men. For despite a growing number of "skilled craftsmen" in Israel, their techniques remained inferior to those of their northern neighbors, as is demonstrated archaeologically by less finely cut building stones and by the lower level of Israelite culture in general.

8–9 The materials that the king requested consisted preeminently of "cedar logs." The fragrant cedars of Lebanon were famed throughout the ancient world. They were resistant to decay and superior to any timber native to Palestine. This valuable resource was particularly squandered under Turkish rule, so that today only a few isolated groves of magnificent trees survive. The further product, rendered "pine," probably refers to the Phoenician juniper, while the "algum" (GK 454) or almug (not mentioned in the parallels that occur in 1Ki 5:6, 8, 10) was a foreign import. It has been traditionally translated as "sandalwood," because it was brought in from Ophir (9:10) and used for ornamental woodwork and for musical instruments (9:11). Sandalwood, however, does not grow in Lebanon; and the term seems here, as indicated by the NIV note, to represent another variety of juniper.

10 Solomon's payment to the Phoenicians was based on the charges that he had asked them to quote (1Ki 5:6). First Kings goes on to speak of his delivering an identical "twenty thousand cors of wheat" but of only twenty cors of "pressed" oil (5:11, NIV note; cf. the listing here of "twenty thousand baths of [ordinary] olive oil"). Ten baths are contained in one cor; but the Chronicles figure still represents 115,000 gallons (NIV note), as compared to 1,200 gallons in Kings. The latter makes no mention at all of the "barley" and "wine." Kings puts a limitation both on the product—in respect to the oil, it is speaking of a special, luxury kind—and on its recipients; for Kings refers only to the royal household of Hiram and not, as in Chronicles, to the larger group of Phoenician "servants, the woodsmen who cut timber." Furthermore, Kings concerns an annually repeated delivery, while in Chronicles it is a one-time payment. Seen in this light, the differing figures suggest no unreasonable proportions.

As to the actual amounts involved, the 125,000 bushels of the two different grains

and the 120,000 gallons of the two liquids (cf. NIV note) represent considerable quantities; but they are not beyond the magnitude either of Solomon's resources or of the temple project that he was financing. Such payments constituted a heavy drain on the economy of Israel. When they were prolonged, because of Solomon's private building projects (cf. v.1 and 1Ki 7:1–2), they exhausted the kingdom (1Ki 9:10–11).

11–12 Hiram's answer to Solomon includes words of praise to the Lord and of appreciation for his love to Israel, which are not recorded in 1Ki 5. This speech is appropriate, not simply theologically, but also practically, coming from the lips of an accomplished businessman, who was dealing with a promising prospective customer—whatever may have been Hiram's individual doctrinal commitments, or lack of same.

13 The name of the master craftsman whom Hiram sent to Solomon is "Huram-Abi." This may be rendered "Huram, my father," not in the sense of a physical relationship (Hiram's father is known to have been Abibaal), but of social status, meaning, "my (trusted) administrator," or "adviser" (as in Ge 15:8; Jdg 17:10).

14 Huram-Abi's mother was, by tribal descent, (lit.) "a woman from the daughters of Dan," but by immediate situation, "a widow from the tribe of Naphtali" (1Ki 7:14). Yet the fact that his father came "from Tyre" gave Huram-Abi a combined Phoenician-Hebrew endowment, which enabled him to deal both linguistically and culturally with the two nationalities of workmen who would be responsible to him.

This superintendent's diversified skills included the capacity to handle precious metals, wood, stone, and fabrics. He thus presents a parallel to the wide-ranging abilities of Bezalel, the master builder of the Mosaic tabernacle (Ex 31:2–5). The "purple" cloth that he could employ was produced from what was actually a deep red dye, obtained from the murex shellfish of the Phoenician coast. Such material was called "royal purple" because of its quality, scarcity, and cost.

15–16 Despite limited facilities, Joppa had a small projecting point of rocks that set it apart from the generally unprotected sands and beaches of southern Palestine. It is mentioned in Egyptian documents as early as the time of Thutmose III, who was probably the Pharaoh of the Hebrew oppression, dying just before the Exodus in 1446 B.C. (Ex 4:19). Joppa served as the port (cf. Jnh 1:3) for inland Judah and for the city of Jerusalem. Before one reached Solomon's capital, however, there were some thirty-five miles of flat, then hilly, and finally rugged terrain.

17–18 Ezra here itemizes "3,600 foremen" out of the total of 153,600 aliens. There were, in addition, 250 chief Israelite officers (8:10), making a total of 3,850. The parallel passages in 1 Kings list only 3,300 foremen (5:16) but then have a correspondingly larger number of chief officers, "550" (9:23), again making a total of 3,800. Since Kings does not distinguish the aliens from the Israelites, the differences in figures would seem to be due to the ways the respective authors distinguished the "chief" officers.

2. Construction (3:1–4:22)

Having explained something of Solomon's preparations for the temple (ch. 2), the Chronicler moves into a description of its actual construction (chs. 3–4). His material forms a parallel to and represents an abridgment of 1Ki 6–7.

1 "Mount Moriah" was the summit, in the area of that same name on which Abraham had shown his willingness to sacrifice his son Isaac (Ge 22:2), over one thousand years earlier. "The threshing floor" of Araunah, which was located on Mount Moriah, was then sanctified even further by David's encounter with God at that place (1Ch 21:18–22:1).

2 Construction on the site did not begin till "the fourth year" of Solomon's reign, probably because of the planning and preparation that had to precede it (2Ch 2). This particular regnal year extended from the fall of 967 B.C. to the fall of 966; but since "the second month" begins in April/May, the exact date must have fallen in the spring of 966.

3 Cubits "of the old standard" represented an earlier, sacred measure. These ran about three inches longer than the ordinary cubit, which was a trifle under eighteen inches (see Eze 40:5; 43:13). On this basis the temple building measured about 105 feet by 35 feet, rather than 90 by 30; and it had doubled the dimensions of the tabernacle.

4 Along the entire front of the temple stretched a porch, or portico, that was open on the front. Its depth was 10 cubits (1Ki 6:3; c. 15 feet); the present text tells how high its side walls rose, namely, 20 cubits (30 feet).

5 "The main hall" refers to the temple proper, and particularly to its outer room, which corresponded to the "Holy Place" in the tabernacle. Compare the reference in v.8 to the inner room as the "Most Holy Place," called elsewhere the "oracle" (v.16). As for the wood that the king used (i.e., pine), see 2:8; and cedar was employed as well (1Ki 6:9).

The paragraphing in the NIV connects Solomon's provision of a layer of "pure gold" for "the inside" (v.4) with this same main hall. The expenditure was enormous. But it was with these very projects in mind that David had proceeded with his earlier, massive preparations (cf. 1Ch 22:14; 29:4, 7).

6 The reference to "precious stones" may suggest mosaics, inlaid in the floor (cf. 1Ch 29:2). The gold "of Parvaim" seems to denote a place name, perhaps in southeastern Arabia; or it may be a variant name for Ophir.

7 The term rendered "doorframes" usually is limited to the "threshold" or "sill"; but the present context of beams overlaid with gold favors a broader meaning. The carved decorations included palm trees and flowers (1Ki 6:29) but especially "cherubim." The appropriateness of depicting these angelic creatures lay in their association with the holy and majestic presence of God (Ge 3:24; cf. their major function in vv.10–14, concerning the inner room). They appear normally in human form but with wings (Eze 1:5–6).

8 The "six hundred talents of fine gold" with which the interior of the oracle was overlaid are not mentioned in 1Ki 6. They consumed only a fraction of what David had provided (1Ch 22:14) but still constituted about twenty-three tons of gold.

9 The "nails" which fastened the gold sheets to the walls involved a much smaller amount of gold, totaling only twenty ounces (one and one-fourth pounds, NIV note).

10–13 The two large cherubim, when placed side by side, had a total wingspread of thirty-five feet. They are thus not to be confused with the small cherubim on the ark but were great gold-plated figures of olive wood (1Ki 6:23), which filled the Most Holy Place and overshadowed the whole ark.

14 The temple's "curtain" (GK 7267) corresponds to the curtain that separated the two rooms in the Mosaic tabernacle (Ex 26:31); it was supplementary to the wooden doors mentioned in 4:22 and 1Ki 6:31–32. It emphasized the fact that even though the awesome presence of God, represented by the glory cloud in the Most Holy Place, was present with human beings, it was at the same time separated from them. The curtain portrayed the spiritual truth that the way to God was not yet open (Heb 9:8) and that it would not be till Christ would perform the true atonement to reconcile God and humankind. This then would end the anticipatory forms of the older covenant, including the curtain (Mt 27:51).

15–17 The "two pillars" were freestanding, set up at the portico in front of the temple (1Ki 7:21). Their size, "thirty–five cubits long," seems to be the result of a copyist's error. The whole building was only twenty cubits high (cf. v.3); 1Ki 7:15 specifies that they were eighteen cubits each (twenty-seven feet), a figure confirmed by 2Ki 25:17 and Jer 52:21.

Each pillar had an ornamented capital, which added "five cubits" (c. nine feet) to its height. The existence of ornamental pillars has been repeatedly attested by archaeology; subbases for such pillars were found in front of the temple at Hazor, and obelisks constitute an Egyptian illustration of the same sort of thing. Their very names symbolized the sustaining power of God, concretely exhibited by the permanence of the temple.

4:1 Turning in ch. 4 to the furnishings of the temple, Ezra first describes its main "altar." It was large—about thirty feet square (NIV note)—made of "bronze," and apparently in stages, with connecting stairs, since it rose to a height of fifteen feet. Just as in the tabernacle, the altar was the first main object to be met as one entered the sanctuary court. It demonstrates that God may be approached only through sacrifices, i.e., through the substitutionary and testamentary death of Christ (Heb 8:2–3; 9:12).

2 The "Sea of cast metal" corresponded to the more modest bronze basin of the tabernacle (Ex 30:18). It was used by the priests for washing (v.6; cf. Ex 30:21) and taught the necessity for purity on the part of those approaching God. It pointed typically to the washing of regeneration and sanctification provided in Christ (Tit 3:5; Heb 9:10). The circumference of the Sea, given as forty-five feet, was only approximate; for its diameter was a full fifteen feet (ten cubits).

3 The "cast figures of bulls . . . in two rows," "below the rim," are called simply "gourds" in 1Ki 7:24. Unless this is a copyist's mistake due to the similarly sounding words, the explanation may lie in a more general description in Kings of these ornamental bands of round-shaped animal heads.

4 Distinct from these cattle were the "twelve bulls" that stood under the Sea and served as its base. They probably denoted the twelve tribes of Israel (cf. Ex 24:4), just as the tribes had once camped, three on each side of the tabernacle (Nu 2).

5 That the Sea was "a handbreadth" thick refers to a person's four fingers held together (i.e., a little over three inches). The capacity stated in the present Chronicles text of "three thousand baths" should be read with 1Ki 7:26 as "two thousand." Chronicles' larger number could have arisen through an unclear reading of the numerical symbols.

6 The large reservoir that constituted the Sea then supplied the "ten" smaller "basins" (holding 40 baths, or 230 gallons each) on their wheeled carts or bases (cf. 1Ki 7:27–39). Their function was for rinsing the offerings, a point not brought out in 1Ki 7:38–39.

7 As compared with the one golden lampstand in the tabernacle, the temple had "ten," and they were no doubt made "according to the specifications" as in Ex 25:31–40. Once again (cf. v.1) vv.7–10 find no corresponding, parallel passages in 1Ki 7, though Kings does mention the contents of vv.7–10 in its concluding summary (1Ki 7:48–49 = 2Ch 4:19–20). The lampstands, each one with its seven branches, continue to symbolize the perfection with which God's church must unceasingly shine for him (Lev 24:3–4; Mt 5:14), as supplied by the oil of God's powerful Holy Spirit (Zec 4:2–6).

8 Of the "ten tables" (only one was made for the tabernacle; cf. 1Ch 28:16), it seems that only one table at a time (13:11; 29:18) was used for displaying the bread, as it was set out fresh every Sabbath, to symbolize Israel's reestablished communion with God and their life in his Presence (v.19; Lev 24:5–8; cf. 1Ch 9:32; 28:16). The "sprinkling bowls" were not particularly associated with the tables but seem rather to have been used for collecting the blood of sacrifices, which was then sprinkled about the altar in the temple services of atonement (cf. Ex 24:6; 29:16; Lev 1:5; 3:2).

9–11 Moses' tabernacle had only a single court. The more developed ritual of the temple led to a division between the inner courtyard of the priests (1Ki 6:36; 7:12)—also called the upper court, because it was elevated, so that the priests would be more visible as they performed their sacred duties (Jer 36:10)—and the outer "larger court" for Israel's general worshipers. Yet this very division into two courts (2Ki 23:12) gave concrete expression to the fact that under the old covenant there had not yet been achieved that universal priesthood of believers that would come about through Jesus Christ. In him all the people of God have direct access to the Father (Jer 31:34; Gal 3:28; Heb 4:14–16). A later distinction of a separate "court of the women" arose only between the OT and NT.

12–15 In the summary of the work performed by Huram (cf. 2:14) for the temple, the first items to be mentioned are the two bronze pillars (cf. 3:15) with their "bowl-shaped capitals" (see 1Ki 7:17–20). Their bulbous lower capitals were covered by an ornamented network or grating, while the upper sections consisted of a flaring crown, like opened lilies.

16 The name "Huram-Abi" connotes "Huram my administrator" (see comment on 2:13).

17–18 The places at which Huram cast the bronze articles for the temple were located "in the plain east of the Jordan," about halfway between Galilee and the Dead Sea. The deep clay located at "Succoth" and "Zarethan" provided suitable molds for the great metal objects.

19–21 In the summary of the temple furnishings, the "gold floral work" refers to the ornamentation on the lampstands (Ex 25:33).

22 The "gold doors" were made of carved olive wood, which was in turn overlaid with gold (3:7; 1Ki 6:31–35). The "doors of the main hall" opened onto the portico and the courts and led from the "Holy Place," which was the outer room of the temple. The inner doors to the oracle provided protection additional to the curtain for sealing off this Most Holy Place (cf. 3:14).

3. Dedication (5:1–7:22)

After having described the construction of Solomon's temple in chs. 3–4, the Chronicler devotes his next three chapters to events connected with its dedication. The material makes up a single unit that extends from the king's summons to the men of Israel in 5:2 down through their dismissal in 7:10, together with an introductory verse and an appended but related answer of God to the dedicatory prayer (7:11–22). These three chapters present a close parallel to their source in 1Ki 8:1–9:9. Much of their theological importance lies in the light that Solomon's ceremonies of dedication throw on the significance of the temple concept as a whole.

When he had assembled the representative leaders of Israel, the king's first act was to conduct the ark of God's covenant into the temple and to enshrine it in the Most Holy Place (5:1–10). He thus constituted the structure on Mount Moriah as the successor to Israel's previous sanctuaries; and God confirmed the validity of Solomon's procedure by taking up his own, localized dwelling within the temple and filling it with the "*shekinah*," the cloud of his Presence (vv.11–14; see comment on 1Ki 8:10–11).

Chapter 6 consists primarily of two utterances by King Solomon: his blessing on the people, which is actually a testimony of praise to the Lord for his faithfulness in prospering the temple project up to this point (vv.3–11), and his long prayer to God, dedicating the building for his sanctuary and imploring his favorable response when Israel should submit their petitions toward his Presence within the structure (vv.12–42). This action too was visibly confirmed by the Lord, as he sent down fire from heaven on the new altar (7:1–3). Two weeks of extensive dedicatory sacrifices and feasting followed (vv.4–10).

A final section, sometime after Solomon had completed his own palace, describes how the Lord appeared to the king by night and verbally confirmed his agreement to the request that he would dwell in the temple and answer the prayers that were addressed to him there. His blessing, however, was conditioned on Israel's continued faithfulness; and he threatened exile and the temple's destruction if the nation should become apostate (7:11–22).

1 A preliminary action of Solomon was to bring into the temple "the things his father David had dedicated" (cf. 1Ch 18:10–11; 22:14; 26:26–27; 29:2–5). Some of David's treasures must have remained, even after the great outlays for erecting the temple. The "treasuries" themselves may have been located in the "upper parts" (3:9) of the building, in some of the rooms that surrounded the sanctuary proper (1Ki 6:5–10).

2 The first step in the activities of dedication was for the king and the assembled national leaders to bring the ark up from the old citadel of Zion to the temple area situated on the more northerly ridge of Moriah (cf. 3:1; Ps 48:2). For forty years the ark had remained in the tent that David had first pitched on its arrival in Jerusalem (cf. 1Ch 15:1; 16:1).

3 The assembly was delayed until "the festival in the seventh month," i.e., until the Feast of Tabernacles (cf. 7:8–10). The work on the temple structure as such had been finished (5:1) in the eighth month of Solomon's eleventh year (1Ki 6:38), i.e., in Sept./Oct. 960 B.C. (cf. 3:2). This entails a lapse of eleven months (until the fall of 959) for the official dedication ceremonies; but there were doubtless other matters that had to be arranged after the completion of the building.

4 In transporting the ark Solomon took the added precaution of employing the priests, taken from among the total group of Levi, to perform this work (vv.5, 7; 1Ki 8:3; cf. 1Ch 13:10; 15:4).

5 Also "brought up" was the "Tent of Meeting," or tabernacle (cf. 1:3), from its previous location at Gibeon (cf. 1Ch 16:39).

6 The large number of sheep and cattle sacrificed followed the more modest precedent set by David when he first brought the ark to Jerusalem (1Ch 15:26; 16:1–3).

7–8 The holy object was placed in the temple's "inner sanctuary." The name of this place derives from an Arabic word meaning "back," i.e., the shrine that was situated in the innermost, or back, portion of the temple, "the Most Holy Place" (cf. 3:5). On "the cherubim," under whose wings it rested, see comment on 3:11.

9 Though the curtain (cf. 3:14) concealed the ark itself from view, the poles by which the ark was carried must have projected on one or both of its sides, so as to be visible from the door. The statement that "they are still there today" must have been quoted by Ezra from his sources (9:29), particularly from 1Ki 8:8, out of those portions that were written before the destruction of Jerusalem in 586 B.C. The ark had been gone for over a century by Ezra's day.

10 The fact that by Solomon's time "there was nothing in the ark except the two tablets" of the Decalogue shows that the golden pot of manna (Ex 16:32–34) and Aaron's rod that budded (Nu 17:10–11; Heb 9:4) must have been lost during the intervening vicissitudes through which the ark passed. The Chronicler's reference at this point to the Lord's Sinaitic covenant may be attributed to the fact that the Ten Commandments, as engraved on Moses' two tablets of stone, expressed the basic response that God expected from his covenant people, whom he had already redeemed (Ex 20:2; cf. 19:4–6). The tablets could in a sense be called "the testimony" (25:16, 21) to his covenant.

11 In the ceremony during which God granted his confirmation to this new home for the ark, Ezra's word that the priests were present "regardless of their divisions" refers to the way they had been organized by David into their twenty–four hereditary courses (1Ch 24:3–19). But the normal rotations in service could be disregarded on an occasion as significant as this, in which all were present.

12 The Chronicler is the first OT writer to refer to the "fine linen" worn by the Levites (cf. 1Ch 15:27). The "120 priests sounding trumpets" (cf. 15:24) may suggest a figure of five drawn from each of the twenty-four priestly courses (cf. 1Ch 24:4).

13–14 The idea expressed by *hesed* (GK 2876), here rendered as God's "love," means more specifically his "faithfulness" (cf. 1Ch 16:41). The "cloud," which was in fact "the glory of the LORD," had first guided the people of Israel out of Egypt (Ex 13:21–22) and then through the desert (40:36–38); and it is associated with the angel of God (14:19; 23:20–23), presumably the preincarnate presence of Christ. At the dedication of the Mosaic tabernacle, almost five hundred years before Solomon, the cloud of God's glory had filled that earlier sanctuary (40:34–35). In the days just before the Exile, Ezekiel had envisioned the sin of Israel as driving the glory cloud out of the sanctuary (Eze 10:18–19; 11:23); and it had not returned to the second temple, of Ezra's day. The "*shekinah*," as it came to be called (see comment on 1Ki 8:10–11), meant God's "glorious dwelling." It appeared during Christ's first coming (Mt 17:5; Ac 1:9), and it will accompany his glorious second advent (Ac 1:11; Rev 1:7; 14:14).

6:1 The first two verses of ch. 6 reflect on the immediately preceding event, when God had demonstrated his approval of the king's relocation of the ark in the new temple. The Lord's words that he mentions, about dwelling "in a dark cloud," refer to God's presence on the top of Mount Sinai, shrouded in a cloud (Ex 19:9; 20:21), and also in the Mosaic tabernacle, as veiled off in its Most Holy Place (Lev 16:2).

2 Though the purpose of the temple was for the Lord "to dwell" there "forever," there was still the attached condition that Israel must continue faithful (7:19–20; Mt 23:37–38). They did not; and the temple was twice destroyed (586 B.C. and A.D. 70). But Christ has promised that he will yet reign on Mount Zion (Mt 23:39) and rule forever in the New Jerusalem (Rev 21:2).

3 While he was speaking with God, Solomon had been facing the temple and the cloud of the divine Presence that filled it. Now, for his address with its blessing on the people, Solomon turned around and faced east, toward the crowd that stood beyond the altar.

4 Solomon's blessing on Israel consisted of a recalling of God's verbal promises to David—that the temple would be built and David's dynasty established (v.10; cf. 1Ch 17)—and of God's material fulfillments of them "with his hands," i.e., in history.

5–6 These promises included God's choice of Jerusalem (cf. 1Ch 22:1), that his "Name" might be "there" (vv.8, 20; cf. v.33), which meant his very Presence (cf. 1Ch 22:7).

7–9 Solomon's thoughts on David's relationship to the temple repeat the latter's own words from 1Ch 28:2–3.

10–11 God's covenant could be said to be in the ark, insofar as the two tablets of the Decalogue that the ark contained did constitute "the testimony" to it (cf. on 5:10). This covenant is identified in 1Ki 8:21 as the Sinaitic covenant (cf. 1Ch 16:15 and 17:12), the one that God "made with our fathers when he brought them out of Egypt."

12 For making his major prayer to God in ch. 6 (vv.12–42), Solomon turned back from facing the people (cf. v.3) and, as he stood "before the altar," again faced west, toward the temple.

13 This verse forms an insertion made by Ezra and is not found in 1Ki 8, between v.22 and v.23. It seems to clarify that Solomon was not "before the altar" to perform a priestly function. He stood rather on an elevated "bronze platform" so that his prayer could be better seen and heard by the people. The term for "platform" (GK 2257) normally designates a "basin" but here denotes a "stage." The way that the king "then knelt down" (cf. 1Ki 8:54) gave public acknowledgment to the fact that he too was only God's servant, administering a kingdom that was not his own (cf. 1Ch 28:5).

14–17 The prayer itself through v.39 closely approximated 1Ki 8:23–50a. It consists of praise to the Lord for his faithfulness to his covenant and of petition for its preservation (vv.16–17). Then come more words of praise, for God's infinity in space (v.18), and yet of petition, for his attention to the king's and people's prayers when made toward the temple (vv.19–42). God keeps his "covenant" and the "love." These synonymous expressions are rightly rendered "covenant of love"

(NIV; cf. 5:13, 1Ch 16:41). In other words, God's covenantal love, made efficacious through the death of Christ, is the source of all blessings, both for believers today and for those who received "the promised eternal inheritance . . . under the first covenant" (Heb 9:15). He reserves these blessings, moreover, for those who are his "servants" (GK 6269; v.14), because faith must always be manifested by obedience (v.16; Jas 2:17–26).

18 In reference to Solomon's constant recognition that "even the highest heavens" cannot contain the infinite Person of the Lord, see 2:6.

19–21 It was because the king recognized God's infinity that he prayed concerning the requests people make toward "this place," toward the earthly temple, that they may be answered by God "from heaven, your dwelling place." He proceeded to identify *seven* concrete situations for which he requested the Lord's intervention from heaven, as follows:

22–23 (1) Swearing to an "oath . . . in this temple." Testimony in doubtful cases was confirmed by an oath at the sanctuary (Ex 22:10–11; Lev 6:3–5); so God is petitioned to intervene in order to "establish innocence."

24–25 (2) "Defeat" and exile "by an enemy." Prayer was needed in such calamities because both of them could be the result of God's punishing their sin (Lev 26:17, 23; Jos 7:11–12; cf. Dt 28:48).

26–27 (3) Lack of "rain." The phenomena of nature sometimes have moral causes; specifically, Israel could suffer drought in times of apostasy (Lev 26:19; Dt 11:10–15; 1Ki 17:1).

28–31 (4) "Disease" or other "disasters." "Plagues" of various sorts could likewise result from sin (Lev 26:16, 20, 25–26; cf. Dt 28 passim), because God "knows" what is in "the hearts of men" (cf. 1Sa 16:7).

32–33 (5) "Foreigners" coming to pray "toward this temple." From its outset Israel's sanctuary was thus designed to be "a house of prayer for all nations" (Isa 56:6–8). The goal of the nation's election was a universal knowledge of God (cf. Ge 12:3; Eph 2:11–13, 19); and even in OT times aliens who would come in faith to the Lord were assured of reception as proselytes into Israel (Ex 12:38, 48;

Ru 1:16; 2:12). They would be attracted by God's "great name," which involved his actual Presence in the temple (cf. v.6).

34–35 (6) In "war." God will fight for his own, who cry to him in the battle (14:11–12; Dt 28:7; 1Ch 5:20).

36–39 (7) In "captivity," caused by "sin." Solomon's confession that there is no one who does not sin emphasizes the consistent biblical teaching on humanity's total depravity (cf. Dt 28 passim; Jer 13:23; 17:9; Eph 2:3). The resulting exile to "a land far away," as well as Israel's subsequent restoration on repentance, had been predicted as early as Moses (Lev 26:33, 44–45); and it all came about (2Ch 36:16, 22–23), even as Solomon had prayed.

40 At this point Chronicles omits most of the king's prayer that is recorded in the parallel passage of 1Ki 8:50b–53, since it was less relevant for a Judah that was no longer in exile in Ezra's time.

41 Solomon drew his last two verses from Ps 132:8–10 (not included in the parallel passage in 1Ki 8, after v.53). This royal psalm, while anonymous, seems to have been written by David or by one of his associates, for that similar occasion forty years before when the ark was first installed in Jerusalem in its tent (cf. this verse and Ps 132:8 with Nu 10:35, and Ps 132:13–14 with 1Ch 16).

42 In his prayer "do not reject your anointed one," the king now meant himself, though in subsequent usage it would express Israel's hope in the coming Messiah, as the climax of Solomon's line. In Ps 132:10 it had referred to his father, David. Furthermore, to the original wording of the psalm, and as the basis for his own blessing, Solomon added the request for God to "remember the great love" promised to David (see comments on vv.14–17). This same basis was later validated when it was taken up by God himself in words given through the prophet Isaiah (Isa 45:3).

7:1–2 Divine approval that rested on the temple services (cf. vv.1–3) and on Solomon's prayer of dedication in particular (ch. 6) was shown by "fire" that "came down from heaven" on the altar. It was in this same way that God had inaugurated the sacrificial services at the Mosaic tabernacle (Lev 9:24) and at the Davidic altar on Moriah some forty years earlier (1Ch 21:26).

3 Now all the people also saw "the glory of the LORD above the temple," which constituted a greater manifestation of what had already been revealed to the priests inside (5:13–14). Thus they knelt on "the pavement," which was associated with the outer, lower court (Eze 40:17; 42:3), and repeated the familiar refrain about the Lord's faithfulness to his covenant promises (v.6; cf. 5:13). King Solomon then added a blessing of his own on the congregation (1Ki 8:55–61; omitted here, perhaps because by the time of Ezra the only priests did this).

4–5 In the festivities that followed, the large numbers of animals sacrificed—22,000 cattle and 120,000 sheep (cf. 35:7)—are confirmed by 1Ki 8:63. They are defined as "fellowship offerings" (v.7), to be eaten by the people (cf. 1Ch 16:1; 29:21). They provided the basis for fifteen full days of feasting (2Ch 7:9–10).

6 The Levitical musicians stood east of the altar (5:12) away from the temple (cf. 1Ch 6:31; 16:4; 25). The priestly trumpeters were stationed "opposite" them and were therefore west of the altar, between it and the temple.

7 "The fat" of the fellowship (= peace) offerings, along with certain other choice pieces, was presented as a token sacrifice to God, prior to the feasting on the part of the people (Lev 3). Concerning the "burnt offerings" (Lev 1) and "grain offerings" (Lev 2), see 1Ch 21:23.

8 Solomon had delayed the temple's dedication for a number of months (cf. comment on 5:3) so that it might be celebrated along with the harvest Feast of Tabernacles, when at the latter season all Israel would be coming in pilgrimage to Jerusalem (Ex 23:16–17). They therefore gathered "from Lebo Hamath" in Lebanon, toward the Euphrates River in the northeast (cf. on 1Ch 13:5), down "to the Wadi of Egypt," i.e., the Wadi el Arish, midway between Palestine and Egypt to the southwest (Jos 15:5, 47).

9 The "eighth day" marked the final convocation of the Feast of Tabernacles (Lev 23:36; Nu 29:35), on the twenty-second day of the seventh month. The special dedication feast, in other words, had lasted "for seven days," from the eighth of the month to the fourteenth, including the great Day of Atonement on the tenth (Lev 16), which was followed by the regular Feast of Tabernacles "for seven days more," from the fifteenth to the twenty-second.

10 The Chronicler's statement that "on the twenty-third day" Solomon "sent the people to their homes" constitutes a summary of the more detailed information of 1Ki 8:66, that on the eighth "day he sent the people away. They blessed the king and then went home, joyful."

11 Chapter 7 concludes with the Chronicler's description of the Lord's appearance to the king, so as to assure him personally that his prayers on behalf of the temple would be answered. But this event occurred only after the king had also completed his "royal palace" (cf. on 1Ch 14:1), some thirteen years later (1Ki 7:1; 9:10). The interval brings us down to Solomon's twenty-fourth year, or to 947/946 B.C.

12–13 This was the Lord's second appearance to Solomon (1Ki 9:2), the first having occurred at Gibeon at the start of his reign (2Ch 1:3–13). God's speaking of times when he would "shut up the heavens," etc., specifically recalls the wording of the petitions in Solomon's dedicatory prayer (e.g., 6:26, et al.), which the Lord here promised to answer.

14–15 For a comment on the expression "my people, who are called by my name," see comment on 6:32. The sentence, as it continues, forms what is probably the best known and most loved verse in all Chronicles. It expresses the stipulations that God lays down for a nation to experience his blessing, whether that nation be Solomon's, Ezra's, or our own. Those who have been chosen to be his people must cease from their sins, turn from living lives of proud self-centeredness, pray to the Lord, and yield their desires to his Word and his will. Then, and only then, will he grant heaven-sent revival.

16 Concerning the significance of God's "Name" being "there," see comments on 6:6; 1Ch 22:7.

17–18 The Lord's promise that the Davidic dynasty would "never fail to have a man to rule over Israel" emphasizes the messianic hope that characterizes the Chronicler's eschatology. This same wording reappears elsewhere (e.g., in Mic 5:2). God's covenant to "establish" (GK 7756) the throne of David harks back to 1Ch 17 (vv.12, 14); but in the remaining verses of the present revelation, the divinely imposed condition of faithful obedience, which was first revealed in 2Sa 7:14b, is made just as explicit as in the parallel passage of 1Ki 9:6–9.

19–22 The possibility that Solomon and his successors (cf. NIV note) might "go off to serve other gods" was what actually happened (1Ki 11:1–8; 2Ch 36:16); and it led to the very results (vv.20–22; 36:20) that the king had himself anticipated (6:36).

C. Solomon's Kingdom (8:1–9:31)

1. Its achievements (8:1–18)

The Spirit of God guided Ezra to encourage his people by rehearsing in 1 Chronicles the history of King David's God-given power (cf. introduction to 10:1–20:8). This book now contains a corresponding presentation of the results of serving God as these are exhibited by Solomon with all his glory. The Chronicler thus concludes his record about David's son by outlining the achievements of his kingdom (ch. 8), followed, in turn, by illustrations of the splendor that surrounded his rule (ch. 9). Ezra's account corresponds to the material found in 1 Kings, except that he omits the following sections about the king's enlarged but bureaucratic organization (1Ki 4), his extravagant palace complex (7:1–12), the idolatry that resulted from his gross polygamy (11:1–8), and the political deterioration that resulted during his latter years (vv.9–40)—probably because they would not have contributed to his goal of strengthening Judah's theocracy. The present chapter parallels 1Ki 9, with its catalog of Solomon's successful enterprises. These include his expansion, both civil and military (vv.1–6); his organization of manpower (vv.7–10); his guidance of public worship (vv.11–16); and his commercial achievements (vv.17–18).

1 The date, after "twenty years," was 946 B.C. (cf. comment on 7:11).

2 The reference to "villages that Hiram had given" to the king assumes without further comment the unhappy record preserved in 1Ki 9:11–13, about how Solomon had previously had to surrender twenty non-Israelite towns in Galilee to the Tyrian, apparently because of unpaid building debts (cf. 2Ch 2:10, 15). Hiram, moreover, found this collateral so poor that Solomon seems to have had to take back the territory. He did then alleviate the poverty of the towns by "settling Israelites in them" and thus succeeded in expanding his borders.

3 Solomon's only recorded military campaign resulted in his conquest of "Hamath" in Lebanon, perhaps for having abandoned its former friendship (1Ch 18:9–10) and breaking the peace. Hamath bordered on "Zobah," which had already been occupied by the Hebrews (see 18:3); and the two place names are combined, since by Ezra's day they had been joined into the one Persian province.

4 "Tadmor in the desert" lay 150 miles northeast of Damascus, midway on the caravan route to Mari on the Euphrates River. It thus controlled the trade on this desert "cut-off" to Babylon.

5 The two "Beth Horons" were located on the border between Ephraim and Benjamin and controlled a major pass, northwest of Jerusalem, that led down to the port of Joppa.

6 "Baalath" lay nearby in Dan (Jos 19:44; cf. 1Ch 13:6), and other cities rebuilt by Solomon are listed in 1Ki 9:15–18. Concerning his chariot cities, see comment on 1:14.

7–10 On Solomon's force of "conscripted" Canaanite labor, see comment on 1Ch 22:2.

11 Early in his reign (1Ki 3:1), Solomon had married a daughter of "Pharaoh." But despite the attendant prestige and political advantages, such marriages introduced foreign idolatries and, eventually, apostasy into Israel (11:1–4). At this point Solomon still retained enough spiritual sensitivity to keep her residence out of "places" made "holy."

12–13 Solomon "sacrificed," but only through priestly mediators (cf. comment on 1Ch 16:1). He would not have assumed the right to do so directly, any more than he personally would have "built the altar" (cf. vv.1–6). The "requirement for offerings" on special days had been spelled out by Moses (Lev 23:37–38).

14–16 Solomon was careful to maintain the organization of the priests, Levites, musicians, and others, in their twenty-four respective "divisions," as these had been developed by David (1Ch 23–25; cf. 26).

17 "Ezion Geber and Elath" were ports at the north end of the Gulf of Aqaba that provided a strategic commercial access southward into the Red Sea and beyond. While earlier archaeological judgments about the presence of copper smelters at the former site have had to be revised, some final refining may have indeed been performed here on metals that were mined farther north in the Arabah valley.

18 Solomon's refineries provided a product for export, to be exchanged for gold from "Ophir." Ophir (location uncertain) was thus reached via the Gulf of Aqaba and the Red Sea. The statement that "Hiram sent him ships commanded by his own officers" means that the Tyrians constructed ships from materials that had been sent overland to Ezion Geber. They then guided the less experienced Hebrews so they could navigate the ships, making an expedition in three years (9:21). The revenue from each trip amounted to about seventeen tons of gold.

2. Its splendor (9:1–31)

Jesus spoke of "Solomon in all his splendor" (Mt 6:29), and 2Ch 9 documents his glorious rule with a series of historical illustrations: the visit he enjoyed from the queen of Sheba (vv.1–12); the revenue he obtained, together with the shields, throne, and other luxury items that this produced (vv.13–21); and the extent of the fame and power

This island, south of Eliat in the Gulf of Aqaba, is one of the possible locations for Solomon's port of Ezion Geber.

that he achieved (vv.22–28). The chapter concludes with a summary of his reign as a whole. It closely parallels 1Ki 10.

1–3 The partly Semite and partly Hamite kingdom of "Sheba" (1Ch 1:9, 22) lay at the southwestern point of the Arabian peninsula and on across the Red Sea into eastern Ethiopia. Excavations at Marib, its capital at this time, and elsewhere have confirmed its cultural developments. Sheba was famed for its commerce in gold and spice, and it simply could not allow Israel's expanding trade from Ezion Geber (described in 8:18) to go unnoticed. Its queen, accordingly, visited Solomon, with commerce as an underlying issue, but also "to test" his God-given wisdom (1Ki 10:1; cf. 4:29–34) "with hard questions." Such verbal interchange remains a familiar Arabic custom up to the present.

4–6 The NIV reading—of the "burnt offerings [Solomon] made" (cf. 8:12)—is based on the ancient versions and on 1Ki 10:5; it is probably the preferred reading. The Hebrew of Chronicles seems to suggest a procession by the royal party for temple worship. On "the greatness" of the king's "wisdom," see v.23 and 1:12.

7–8 Even Solomon's pagan visitor was led to recognize that "the LORD" was the one by whom Solomon had been placed on Israel's throne and for whom he was ruling (cf. on 1Ch 28:5). The king's desire "to maintain justice and righteousness" had, indeed, been the purpose of his request for wisdom in the first place (cf. comment on 1:10).

9 The queen's gift, also recorded in 1Ki 10:10, amounted to over four and a half tons of gold.

10–11 On "Ophir" see 8:18. "Algumwood" is probably a variant for almugwood (see 2:8).

12 The Hebrew that underlies the NIV wording "he gave her more than she had brought" (to the king) is compressed and difficult; but it should probably be rendered either "every wish she desired, he gave her a return for," or, according to what "she had brought" (cf. 1Ki 10:13). The statement has usually been interpreted as describing the completion of a satisfactory commercial transaction or as an expression of Solomon's munificence. In Ethiopic and Jewish tradition, it is maintained that the queen of Sheba subsequently bore a son to Solomon.

13–14 Solomon's annual revenue in gold was approximating twenty-five tons, as had been previously mentioned in 1Ki 10:14.

15–16 The unit of weight, by which the gold that was applied to the king's "large" and "small shields" was counted, does not appear in the Hebrew text. The NIV assumes the "beka," or half-shekel, so that the figure of 300 for the smaller shields would approximate the amount recorded in 1Ki 10:17. Yet unstated weights in Hebrew usually assume the unit of "shekels." Furthermore, since Kings and Chronicles are in exact agreement on the amount of gold in the large shields, it is probable that they agree on the amount (half as much) in the smaller as well—though in Kings this is expressed in a differing unit of measure, i.e., the heavy mina, equaling 1000 shekels. Solomon's "Palace of the Forest of Lebanon," where the shields were placed, was located in Jerusalem but received its name from its rows of Lebanese cedar pillars (1Ki 7:2–5).

17–21 Solomon's fleet of "trading ships" (v.21) are designated in 1Ki 10:22 as "ships of Tarshish" (NIV note). Since, according to 1Ki 9:26–27 they actually navigated the Red Sea, it seems unlikely that they "went to Tarshish," in the western Mediterranean (perhaps referring to Sardinia). Perhaps they were "Tarshish-type" ships (cf. NIV note; see 20:36). As is usual in Semitic time-reckoning, the "three years" occupied by the expedition need include only the last part of the first year and the first part of the last year, so that the minimum trip time need have consumed only a little over one year.

22–24 Solomon was wealthy by anyone's standard. The term for "weapons" (v.24) describes "armor" as well.

25 Solomon's "four thousand stalls for horses" accords well with both the archaeological evidence (cf. 1:14) and the reference in 1Ki 10:26 to "fourteen hundred chariots" (cf. 1Ki 9:19). The parallel passage in 1Ki 4:26, however, which reads "forty thousand stalls," should probably be attributed to scribal corruption.

26 The observation that Solomon's rule extended as far as the Euphrates "River" (cf. NIV note; see comment on 1Ki 4:21, 24) corresponds to the limit that God had promised to Abraham over a millennium earlier (Ge 15:18).

27 Concerning the "foothills," see 1Ch 27:28.

28 On Solomon's imported horses, see 1:16.

29–31 The Chronicler's references to documents by Nathan, Ahijah, and Iddo are taken up in the introduction. In 1Ki 11:41, "The book of the annals of Solomon" is mentioned by the author.

IV. The Kingdom of Judah (10:1–36:23)

The work of the Chronicler falls into four major parts. The last of these, which makes up chs. 10–36, concerns the kingdom of Judah. After Solomon's death in 930 B.C., the southern area, Judah, became separated from the northern area, Israel. This section of Chronicles has three unequal sections: (1) on the division (chs. 10–11); (2) on the rulers, good and bad, of the people of Judah (13:1–36:16); and (3) on its ultimate fate of exile into Babylon (36:17–23).

The final editor of 1 and 2 Kings, writing midway in the Exile, recognized this tragedy as the outworking of the moral righteousness of the Lord, as he rendered to his faithless people exactly what their deeds deserved (2Ki 17:7–23; 24:1–4). But the Chronicler, writing after the restoration of 538–536, recognized how God had been at work throughout these four centuries of Judah's decline, sovereignly accomplishing his holy purposes. The Lord's faithfulness to David continued steadfast (1Ch 17:13; cf. 2Ch 7:18).

A. The Division of the Kingdom (10:1–11:23)

Even in chs. 10–11, on the initial division, Ezra could say of Rehoboam's refusal to grant reforms, and of the rebellion at Shechem that resulted: "This turn of events was from God" (10:15; cf. Ge 50:20; Ac 2:23); and on the young king's attempt to resubdue Israel, he could quote God's word through the prophet, by which he prevented any such reunion: "This is my doing" (11:4). The overriding divine purpose was to separate the godly in Judah from the apostate in Israel (vv.6–22) and to concentrate in the south those who remained faithful out of the northern tribes: thus "they strengthened the kingdom of Judah" (v.17). The two chapters of this section draw largely on 1Ki 12; but see the comments on 10:19, which calls attention to the omission of the history of the north. Furthermore, 11:5–12 and 18–23 utilized some different, and later lost, source; for they now stand without parallel in the OT.

1 Solomon's son "Rehoboam went to Shechem" to be crowned ruler of Israel. He had already succeeded his father in Judah (9:31); but even though the Davidic dynasty had been constituted by the Lord's appointment (1Ch 17:14), each king was still subject to popular confirmation (v.4, cf. 1Ch 11:3). Rehoboam could reign only as a "constitutional" monarch and servant of the people (cf. comment on v.7) under God (cf. comment on 9:8 and 1Ch 28:5). Shechem lay thirty miles north of Jerusalem in Ephraim, on the border of Manasseh (Jos 17:7). It formed a center for the northern tribes and after this event became their first capital (1Ki 12:25).

2 Some years before, Jeroboam I ("son of Nebat") had been divinely anointed to be ruler over ten-twelfths of the nation of Israel (1Ki 11:26–40). It was because of this that he was "in Egypt," having "fled from Solomon."

3–4 The "heavy yoke" to which the northerners objected had resulted from Solomon's extravagances (1:17) at the expense of his people (cf. Dt 17:17, 20).

5 Without acceding to their request, Rehoboam remained, so far, fair and prudent in his conduct.

6–7 The parallel passage in 1Ki 12:7 quotes even stronger advice by the elders to the king: not simply that he "be kind" and "favorable" to the people, but that he "be a servant" and "serve" them.

8 The "young men" to whom Rehoboam preferred to turn were probably some of Solomon's many sons, rendered callous by upbringing in the luxurious harem and court at Jerusalem.

9 By his words "How should *we* answer these people," Rehoboam already identified himself with autocracy.

10–15 The whole course of events "was from God" (v.15), who had, through his prophet "Ahijah the Shilonite," ordained the division of the kingdom of Israel as a punishment for Solomon's decline into idolatry (1Ki 11:29–33).

16–17 The rebellious spirit of the northern Israelites against the Davidic dynasty that God had established was equally sinful (13:5–7). Their cry, literally, of "Every man to your tents," had been employed before, against David (2Sa 20:1). The situations of life in Palestine are naturally those of geographical isolation; its broken terrain encourages political disruption.

18 In his position over the "forced labor," Adoniram hardly constituted a wise choice for quieting Israel. He was probably one of the most hated figures in the land, an embodiment of oppression.

19 After this verse that summarizes "Israel's rebellion" (paralleled by 1Ki 12:19), 1Ki 12:20 proceeds to describe how the northern tribes made Jeroboam their king. Chronicles, however, omits it. Ezra dismisses the history of Israel from this point onward and concentrates on the faithful remnant in Judah.

11:1 As had been prophesied by Ahijah (see 10:15; cf. 1Ki 11:31–32), only the two tribes of "Judah and Benjamin" remained loyal to the Davidic dynasty (vv.3, 12). Their muster of 180,000 men seems to be the largest troop total found in Chronicles (granting the possibility that at some points the term rendered "thousands" may mean "chiefs"; see comments on 1Ch 7:3–4; 12:27), and it corresponds to the sum given in 1Ki 12:21. The figure is a plausible one, in light of the carefully enumerated listing of over 600,000 for the whole nation in Nu 1:46; 26:51. That, of course, was in the days of Moses; but the population would hardly have been less under Solomon than then (cf. the similar expressions of populousness given in Dt 1:10; 10:22; 1Ki 3:8; 4:20).

2 "Shemaiah the man of God" was the same prophet who later confronted Rehoboam, after his unfaithfulness and defeat by Egypt (12:5–7). He also composed one of the source records for his reign (12:15).

3 Ezra's phrase "all the Israelites in Judah and Benjamin" includes what 1Ki 12:23 specifies as "the rest" of the other tribes, i.e., the godly survivors out of a larger, apostate group (Lev 26:39, 44; Isa 20–23).

4 On the Lord's word "This is my doing," see comment on 10:15.

5 Having been prohibited from retaking Israel, Rehoboam proceeded to refortify "towns" in the territory that he still had "in Judah." In light of the unsettled times that lay ahead for Rehoboam (cf. 12:2, 15), he acted wisely.

6–12 The fifteen cities that Ezra lists lie toward Judah's southern and western borders. Their choice seems to have been dictated by threat from Egypt (12:2–4).

13–14 Jeroboam had rejected the Levites (cf. 1Ki 12:31) as part of his total policy of separating Israel from religious dependence on Judah (1Ki 12:26–28). The expression "Jeroboam and his sons," i.e., his successors, indicates that migrations by the faithful to Judah was a process that continued down through the years.

15 In addition to his golden "calf idols" (1Ki 12:28–29), this Ephraimite also set up images of goats (cf. Isa 13:21; 34:14).

16–17 Jeroboam's idolatries, though they were sinful in their goal of seeking to supplant the true worship of God in Jerusalem, still accomplished a providential function by driving the godly southward, so that they "strengthened the kingdom of Judah." The reason their migrations to the south were limited to a period of "three years" may have been simply because the godly became depleted in the north, but it may also have been due to Rehoboam's own lapse in the south (12:1–2).

18–20 In a summary of the royal family, with which the chapter concludes, Rehoboam's wife "Maacah" seems to have been a granddaughter of Absalom, through his immediate daughter Tamar, the wife of Uriel (13:2; cf. 2Sa 14:27; 18:18). Mahalath was thus, simultaneously, Rehoboam's second cousin (via Eliab) and half-cousin (via her father Jerimoth's unnamed mother), while Maacah was the king's half-cousin once removed.

21 By taking "eighteen wives" Rehoboam willfully disregarded the law of God, in respect to both kingly abuse (Dt 17:17) and polygamous marriage (Lev 18:18), not to mention his disregard of the disastrous precedent set by his father, Solomon.

22 The king's appointment of Abijah (see comment on 12:16) "to be the chief prince" may imply some form of coregency; compare a similar elevation received by Abijah's grandfather Solomon, when threatened by a disputed succession (cf. 1Ch 23:1; 29:22).

23 Rehoboam "acted wisely," not simply by delegating to some of his other sons a measure of the authority for national defenses that the divided kingdom of Solomon now required—and by providing them with property and wives—but particularly by "dispersing" them. It was a step that helped ensure the smooth transfer of power to Abijah (v.22).

B. The Rulers of Judah (12:1–36:16)

In the three and one-half centuries between the division of Solomon's kingdom in 930 B.C. and the Babylonian exile in 586, Judah experienced twenty rulers. The nineteen men and one woman varied in their abilities, from the strongest and best to the weakest and worst. The destiny of any country depends to a great extent on the character of its leaders; and this was particularly the case among the Hebrews, into whose history God chose to intervene more directly than he has for other nations. The Chronicler could thus stimulate the people of his day to a greater devotion by pointing them back to his nation's more faithful monarchs and to those earlier miracles by which the Lord had delivered Judah.

Yet at the same time, and out of the same historical data, Ezra warns his people against compromise with the world, against disregard for the law of God, and against apostasy from the Lord himself. Judah's overall history was one of religious decline. Sin became so ingrained that even a ruler like Josiah could not reverse its downward courses. In respect to any particular generation, God "can" cast away his people whom he foreknew (cf. Ro 11:1–2).

By and large 2Ch 12:1–36:16 corresponds to 1Ki 14:22–2Ki 24:20; but significant differences remain. Much of the material found in

Kings is omitted from Chronicles, specifically the detailed lives of some of the prophets and, most obviously, the entire history of the northern kingdom (cf. 10:19). To the history, however, of Judah in the south, considerable material from other sources is added. Chronicles thus supplies us with inspiring (and inspired) examples of faith and deliverance that find no echo within the summaries provided by Kings.

1. Rehoboam (12:1–16)

The first ruler of the divided kingdom of Judah was Solomon's son Rehoboam, who reigned from 931 to 913 B.C. His kingship is the topic of 1Ki 14:21–31 and 2Ch 12. The latter chapter commences with his establishment (v.1a), after the division of Solomon's kingdom had become permanent (chs. 10–11). Chapter 12 then describes Rehoboam's punishment for abandoning the law of God (vv.1b–6) and the restoration that followed on his resubmission to him (vv.7–12). It concludes with a summary of the king's seventeen-year reign (vv.13–16).

1 The term "all Israel" now shifts from pointing to the entire nation (9:30) (1) to its northern half (in contrast to Judah, 11:1), (2) to "all the Israelites in Judah and Benjamin" (11:3), or, (3) as here (cf. NIV note), to Judah alone as constituting the true Israel. Rehoboam "abandoned" God's law by turning to the immoralities and polytheism of the surrounding Canaanites (1Ki 14:23–24; 15:12). Herein lay the ultimate cause for Egypt's invasion of Judah.

2 In the king's "fifth year" (925 B.C.), "Shishak attacked." Known in Egyptian history as Sheshonk I, he was the founder of the Twenty-Second Dynasty and its most energetic Pharaoh. This particular campaign is documented by a list of conquered Palestinian cities that stands to this day carved on the wall of his temple of Amon at Karnak, Thebes. An immediate cause lay in his desire for plunder, which was directed even more against his former protégé, Jeroboam, in the north (see 10:2) than against Judah.

3 The details preserved in vv.3–8 have no parallel in 1Ki 14. They would seem to derive from Ezra's special sources, particularly from the records of Shemaiah (v.15). Among Shi-

shak's troops, the "Sukkites" were likely foreign mercenaries.

4 Concerning Judah's "captured . . . fortified cities," the destruction of Lachish is particularly attested by archaeology.

5 On "Shemaiah" see comment on 11:2.

6–7 "When . . . they humbled themselves," deliverance came soon (v.12). This principle possesses permanent validity for Christian living (cf. 1Pe 5:6), though Rehoboam seems not to have taken his own experience to heart (v.14).

8 The point that God wanted them to grasp was "the difference" between what results from serving the Lord and from serving the world (Mt 11:28–30).

9–11 Rehoboam's "bronze shields," with which he was forced to replace the gold ones (cf. 9:15–16), dramatically illustrate how his faithlessness reduced his condition to a mere imitation of the glory that had once been his.

12–14 Concerning God's putting his Name in Jerusalem (v.13), see 1Ch 22:7 and 2Ch 6:32.

15–16 Of the two literary sources cited by the Chronicler for this reign, it was the "records . . . of Iddo" that particularly dealt "with genealogies." The son who succeeded Rehoboam, "Abijah" (cf. 11:22–23), appears in 1Ki 14:31; 15:1; et al., under the name "Abijam." The latter may have been his personal name, as contrasted with his throne name in Chronicles (cf. 1Ch 3:12, 15).

2. Abijah (13:1–14:1a)

Chapter 13 concerns the second man who ruled over post-Solomonic Judah, Rehoboam's son Abijah (cf. on 12:16). The one prominent event of his three-year reign (913 to 911 B.C.) was his war with Jeroboam (1Ki 15:6–7). But while the parallel record about Abijah that appears in 1Ki 15:1–8 contains only the briefest of summaries, Ezra's independent sources (cf. 2Ch 13:22 on Iddo) furnished him with the details unique to Chronicles. They describe the bravery against great odds of Judah's new king, which sprang from his trust in the God whose law he obeyed (vv.3–12), and the triumph over Israel that came as a result (vv.12–21): "The men of Judah were victorious because they relied on the LORD, the God of their fathers" (v.18). The book of Kings does, however, include a negative evaluation of Abijah (1Ki 15:3–5), not reflected in Chronicles, "that his heart was not fully devoted to the LORD."

1–4 The exact location of "Mount Zemaraim" (v.4) is uncertain. The town of Zemaraim lay within the territory of Benjamin (Jos 18:22); so the battle must have occurred on the border between the "country of Ephraim" (Israel) and Judah, perhaps near Bethel (v.19), on the northern boundary of Benjamin.

5 The Lord had indeed "given the kingship of Israel to David and his descendants" and this was to be "forever" (1Ch 17:14), which seems to be the meaning of the phrase "a covenant of salt." Salt is well known as a preservative, hence the idea of "everlastingness."

6–7 The term "scoundrels" represents "the sons of Belial" (GK 1175 & 1201). But even though Belial, by NT times, had come to refer specifically to Satan (2Co 6:15) or the Antichrist (2Th 2:3), this OT word should be taken simply as a common noun, in its literal meaning of "worthlessness." Abijah recounts how such men "opposed Rehoboam . . . when he was young." In point of fact his chronological age was forty-one (12:13); but he still was "indecisive," i.e., immature in his understanding and experience (cf. 10:8–15), so that he was not "strong enough to resist them."

8–9 Scripture says that Jeroboam made the golden calves to be gods; they were "other gods, idols made of metal" (1Ki 14:9). Jeroboam's own words in 1Ki 12:28—"Here are your gods, O Israel"—show his attitude toward them.

10 While at this point Abijah's affirmation "The LORD is our God" rings with sincerity, a longer view of his history requires some modification in evaluation; for "he committed all the sins his father had done before him" (1Ki 15:3, witness his polygamy, described in 2Ch 13:21; cf. Ezra's earlier evaluation of Rehoboam in 12:1). Also noteworthy is that the prophets of the northern and southern kingdoms had sanctioned the division. So Abijah used religious arguments for his own political ends. Yet since the northern

kingdom had acted in unbelief and apostasy, his words carried some conviction.

11 Concerning the king's loyalty to the ceremonial laws of Moses, see the following comments: on the daily "offerings," see 1Ch 23:30; 2Ch 4:1; on the "fragrant incense," 2Ch 2:4; on the "bread" and its "table," 1Ch 9:32; 2Ch 4:8; on the "gold lampstand," 2Ch 4:7. Actually, Solomon's temple contained ten such tables and lampstands (4:7–8); but one of each of these may have been the original article dating back to Moses, hence the singular terminology.

12–14 The "priests with their trumpets" were to "sound the battle cry," specifically to call the Lord to their rescue (as in fact it came about, vv.14–15; cf. Nu 10:9). The king's final appeal, "Men of Israel, do not fight against the LORD," was particularly appropriate for Ezra to include, in light of the opposition that the Jews of his day faced from the Samaritans, in this same area of northern Israel. Jeroboam then attacked.

15 So "God routed Jeroboam," though whether this was through direct supernatural intervention or through the courage of his embattled people as they saw themselves surrounded by the enemy is not stated.

16–18 The slaughter inflicted on Ephraim of "five hundred chiefs," even if this term is not rendered as "thousands" (cf. comment on v.3), still represented the loss of over half "among Israel's" particularly "able men," a staggering blow for the limited northern kingdom.

19 Abijah "took . . . Bethel," the actual center for Jeroboam's calf worship (1Ki 12:29, 33), though the idol itself had probably been removed for safe keeping to some place farther north before the city's capture. Significantly, some eighteen years later Bethel was reoccupied by the Ephraimites (cf. 16:1). "Jeshanah and Ephron" were located four miles north and northeast of Bethel respectively.

20 Judah's victory may have encouraged the Arameans of Damascus to enter into a treaty with Abijah (cf. 1Ki 15:19), which would further have impeded Jeroboam from "regaining power." The details on how "the LORD struck him down" are not elaborated elsewhere. His death occurred in 910 B.C., three years after Ahijah's own.

21–14:1a This particular volume of "the prophet Iddo" (cf. 9:29; 12:15) is called his "annotations" (GK 4535, meaning a "commentary," perhaps on the king's official court record).

3. Asa (14:1b–16:14)

This section concerns Asa son of Abijah (cf. 1Ki 15:9–24, the parallel section that has only sixteen verses and does not touch on major sections in 2Ch 14:3–15:15; 16:7–10). Out of the history of Asa's long reign, 911–870 B.C., Ezra selected four outstanding events for his record: (1) the king's first reform, dating to his initial ten years of peace (14:1b–8); (2) his victory over Zerah the Cushite in 897 (vv.9–15); (3) Judah's second reform that came as a result (ch. 15); and (4) the hostile moves made against Asa by Baasha of Israel in 895 and his series of religious deviations that followed (ch. 16). Asa, however, was still the most godly monarch to arise in Judah from the division of Solomon's kingdom up to this point (1Ki 15:11).

14:1b When Chronicles describes the country as being "at peace for ten years," this era would cover the first decade of Asa's rule, from 910 to 900 B.C., i.e., until the days before Zerah's invasion in 896 (cf. 15:19). Nine years of this period overlapped the reign of Baasha in Israel (909–886). In 1Ki 15:16 we read of war between these two rulers "throughout their reigns."But since 2Ch 4:1b explains that he built the cities "since the land was at peace," his actual conflict with Baasha must have broken out only subsequently. The peace, which may be traced back, in part, to Abijah's crushing defeat of Israel (13:17, 20), stemmed primarily from Asa's first reform (14:3–5) because, as he said, "We have sought the LORD our God . . . and he has given us rest" (v.7).

2–6 The king "removed . . . the high places," in obedience to Dt 12:2–3; but the people seem to have continued to resort to them, despite the royal purge (15:17). The "sacred stones" were Canaanite in origin and were thought quite literally to contain the local fertility gods, the Baalim. The "Asherah poles" were wooden and were associated with Baal's goddess-consort who bore this name. Both, when carved, became idols (cf. 1Ki 14:15).

7–8 As a conclusion to his description of Asa's initial reform and of the prosperity that resulted, the Chronicler enumerates Asa's army, with its three hundred specially trained men from Judah (the word "thousand," GK 547, should be translated "chief, officer, specially trained warrior") with "two hundred and eighty" special warriors "from Benjamin" (notice the contextual emphasis on their specialized weapons and their distinction as "brave fighting men").

9 Turning to the Cushite invasion (vv.9–15), Ezra enumerates the enemy as embracing, by contrast, "a thousand specialists" (cf. NIV note) "and three hundred chariots." "Cushites" (i.e., Nubians; cf. 1Ch 1:8) served as Egyptian mercenaries and, by the close of the next century, had come to rule all Egypt, as the Twenty-Fifth Dynasty (cf. on 2Ch 32:1). The name "Zerah" may be Osorkon I, second Pharaoh of the Twenty-Second Dynasty, who tried to duplicate the invasion and pillaging of his predecessor Sheshonk (cf. comment on 12:2). His forces may have attracted a mixed following of bedouin Arabs as well (cf. the reference to "camels" in v.15). But the results this time, against godly Asa, were quite the opposite of what had permitted the easy plundering of Rehoboam (12:9).

10 The "Valley of Zephathah" remains unidentifiable; but it did lie "near Mareshah," which was a town that marks the entrance into the Judean hills and was situated between Gaza and Jerusalem, lying twenty-five miles farther along to the northeast. It was one of the points that Rehoboam had fortified in anticipation of just such an attack as this (11:10).

11 This climactic verse may express the idea, as in the NIV, that "there is no one [person] like you" who can help the powerless but also the mighty. Yet fully as meaningful is the idea (so KJV) that it is no harder for God to help the powerless than the mighty (cf. 1Sa 14:6). The point is that for God the humanly impossible is as nothing (Ge 18:14); and Asa had the faith to commit himself to the Lord and to expect the impossible (cf. Mk 9:23).

12 Thus "the LORD struck down the Cushites," though again (cf. comment on 13:15) the detailed means that he employed are not stated.

13–14 Asa's army "pursued them as far as Gerar," located southeast of Gaza, on their presumed flight back to Egypt. History attests to the fact that "they could not recover": Israel experienced no more interference from the decadent Twenty-Second and Twenty-Third Egyptian dynasties. Not until 160 years later did Egypt reappear to trouble Israel (2Ki 17:4).

15 Judah also attacked "the camps of the herdsmen" (lit., "tents of cattle") that belonged to the Philistinized semi-nomadic cattle-tenders who were found in the area (cf. comment on v.9).

15:1 Asa's second great period of reform (cf. 14:2–8, on his earlier efforts) occupies 2Ch 15. His actions came as a result of the victory in 896 B.C. over the Cushites (14:12–15), and particularly because of the preaching of "Azariah son of Oded," a prophet who remains unknown apart from this passage.

2 The clause "If you seek him" recalls David's admonition to Solomon (1Ch 28:9); and Azariah went on to illustrate its truth from Israel's past history.

3 His words about the "long time" when "Israel was without the true God" probably refer to the lawless, and often faithless, days of the judges (Jdg 21:25). Their being "without the law" was closely connected with their being "without a priest," since one of the latter's major functions was "to teach" the law that God had given through Moses (Lev 10:11).

4–7 On God's being "found by them" when "they sought him" (v.4), see Jdg 2:18. On their situation being such that "it was not safe to travel about," see Jdg 5:6. The prophet concluded by appealing for resolute faith on their part, with the promise of reward from God.

8 Asa's renewed reformation involved the removal of Judah's "detestable idols," and also of the sexual immoralities that accompanied such originally Canaanite worship (1Ki 15:12). Much had already been accomplished earlier (14:3); but this second stage of reform took care of the yet remaining idolatrous abominations. It was also a more extensive

removal, "from the whole land"; for it included areas Asa "had captured in the hills of Ephraim" during the five years of hostility that had immediately preceded (v.10; cf. 14:1). This in turn implies the accomplishment of certain Judean victories, not otherwise recorded, even as there must have been defeats too (cf. on 13:19; 16:1).

9 The statement that "large numbers had come over to him from Israel" illustrates how God's purpose in dividing Solomon's kingdom was in fact being achieved (cf. introduction to chs. 10–11; comments on 11:3, 14): a faithful "remnant" was being gathered and preserved. It may also help to explain, however, why Baasha of Israel proceeded to his acts of reprisal soon thereafter (16:1). On the coming of "people from . . . Simeon," see comments on 1Ch 4:24–43.

10–11 The "third month of" Asa's "fifteenth year" was May/June 895 B.C. The people may have "assembled at Jerusalem" at that time so as to observe the Feast of Weeks (Pentecost), one of Israel's three annual pilgrimage celebrations (cf. 1Ch 23:31; also Lev 23:15–21). This assembly probably took place in the year following Zerah's attack (v.19), since the pursuit, the gathering of plunder (v.11), and the occupying of the surrounding territories by Asa's forces (14:13–15) must have consumed several months.

12 The "covenant" (GK 1382) referred to here is the one great, everlasting testament of the Lord (see comment on 1Ch 16:15) that he decreed for the redemption of his people. The succeeding verses on Asa's "covenant renewal" bring out some of its basic features. First, on the objective side God provided for the restoration of fallen people back into fellowship with himself. The reality of this restoration is indicated by the fact that he had become "the God of their fathers." God thus entered into a saving relationship with his elect (Ge 17:7; Jer 31:34; Jn 17:6).

13–14 Second, on the subjective side, the people were to respond to him in faith and obedience. They therefore swore to "seek the LORD, the God of their fathers, with all their heart and soul" (v.12). Conformity on this particular occasion was enforced on pain of "death" (cf. Dt 17:26). It is preferable for a person to be restrained in this life than for him or her to be lost for eternity (Dt 13:12–15; Mk 9:43–48).

15 Third, the result is an inheritance of peace: "the LORD gave them rest on every side." The immediate rest granted to Judah was one of relief from her enemies, but it was indicative of a more fundamental rest that comes to all who have been accepted by God. Covenant rest embraces all the joys of redeemed life in the present (Ps 103), of heavenly life beyond the grave (Ps 73:23–26; Heb 4:9–11), and of ultimate life in the kingdom of God on earth (Ps 96:12–13; Rev 20:6; 22:5).

16 For the remaining verses of ch. 15, the parallel in 1Ki 15:13–16 resumes, thereby attesting to the reality of Asa's reform. Rehoboam's second wife, "Maacah" (see 11:20), was not only still living but must have been an influential figure at the Jerusalem court. Asa, however, has left a significant example to us through the way he placed religious loyalty above family loyalties, when he "deposed her from her position." The Kidron Valley, in which he burned her Asherah pole, is the gorge that lies between the east wall of Jerusalem and the Mount of Olives.

17 That Asa "did not remove the high places from Israel" is a commentary, not on the commendable programs of reform as instituted by the king himself (see comment on 14:3), but on the sad facts of the people's spiritual condition.

18 The treasures Asa "brought into the temple" (see 5:1) included "articles that he and his father had dedicated," namely, Abijah's spoils from Jeroboam (13:19) and his own from Zerah and his allies (14:13–15).

19 The NIV translation of this verse is subject to criticism on two counts. (1) The Hebrew lacks the word "more" and says simply, "There had not been war." (2) It is known that the king was involved in a serious conflict with Baasha (ch. 16), who died in the twenty-sixth year of Asa's reign (1Ki 15:16, 33). Baasha had thus been dead for almost a decade before Asa's thirty-fifth year. Perhaps Ezra's reference is to the thirty-fifth year after the division of the Solomonic kingdom in 930 B.C. and this verse relates then to Zerah's invasion in 896. It could thus be rendered, "There had not been war until the thirty-fifth year," which had reference to Asa's reign.

However, the expression "the thirty-fifth year of Asa's reign" is exactly the same expression as in 16:1. Thus, it seems unlikely that 15:19 dates from the beginning of the kingdom and 16:1 from the beginning of his own reign. Another suggestion views the figures here and in 16:1 as twenty-fifth and twenty-sixth, respectively (cf. 1Ki 16:8).

16:1 Despite the king's two reforms and remarkable victory that are recorded in the two preceding chapters, ch. 16 proceeds to describe a series of religious deviations of which he became guilty in his later life: in relation to Israel (vv.1–9), to the prophet Hanani and others of his own people (v.10), and to his final illness (vv.11–14).

The "thirty–sixth year," which had reference to "Asa's reign" (see comment on 15:19), was 895 B.C.; and the event in question probably occurred after the assembly in May/June of that year (15:10). At this point Judah was confronted by "Baasha king of Israel." The latter had overthrown the dynasty of Jeroboam I, usurped the crown, and then reigned in Ephraim from 909 to 886 (1Ki 15:27–29, 33). He had been consistently hostile toward Asa (1Ki 15:16) and now became particularly aroused against him, probably because of the defection of many of his people south to Judah (2Ch 15:9). He advanced southward, apparently capturing Bethel at this time (cf. on 13:19). Baasha then "fortified Ramah," which lay on the main north-south highway along the Palestinian central ridge, only five miles north of Jerusalem. He thus effectively blockaded all movement into Judah.

2 Asa's response was to take "silver and gold"—all that he had (1Ki 15:18)—from the Jerusalem temple and palace to purchase help from the Aramean king, Ben Hadad I in Damascus. At one stroke Asa thereby sacrificed the results of his own piety (cf. 2Ch 15:18) and of God's blessing (14:13–14); he induced a pagan ruler to an act of perfidy (v.3) and precipitated a pattern of Syrian (Aramean) intervention into the affairs of Israel that would have disastrous results throughout the succeeding century (cf. 2Ki 10:32–33; 12:17–18); and, in the most serious deviation of all, he departed from the Lord by placing his primary dependence "on flesh" (Jer 17:5).

3 The earlier Syro-Judean treaty Asa referred to must have existed between Ben-Hadad's father Tabrimmon, the son of Hezion (1Ki 15:18), and Asa's father Abijah (cf. comment on 2Ch 13:20). This earlier ruler Hezion may perhaps be Rezon, the adversary of Solomon and the founder of the current kingdom in Damascus (1Ki 11:23–25); so the Arameans themselves had a history of switching allies at their convenience.

4 Ben-Hadad therefore conquered "Ijon," located east of the Leontes River, as it flows southward out of the Syrian Beka Valley between the Lebanon ranges, shortly before its course turns west into the Mediterranean; Ijon thus lay on a natural route south into Israel. Eight miles farther south, on the headwaters of the Jordan, was "Abel Maim"; and four miles east of it lay "Dan." The Arameans, indeed, took "all the store cities of Naphtali"—specified in 1 Kings as "all Kinnereth," meaning the plains on the northwest side of Galilee.

5 Faced with such losses in Israel's far north, "Baasha abandoned" his operation against the kingdom of Judah in the south, so that for the moment Asa's stratagem appeared to have succeeded.

6 The men of Judah reused the materials from Ramah to "build up Geba and Mizpah." Since we do not know the exact location of these cities, Asa was either counterattacking by pushing Judah's borders northward again or defensively drawing in his lines to the south.

7 Verses 7–10 are unique to Chronicles. "Hanani the seer" was father to Jehu the seer, who would later serve Asa's son Jehoshaphat (19:2; 20:34). He not only condemned Asa's loss of faith (see comment on v.2) but went on to speak of the success the king would have enjoyed had he not deviated from trusting God: the Aramean army would have been his. The point is that "Aram," as Baasha's ally (v.3), would presumably have joined with Israel in attacking Judah; and God would then have delivered over the entire enemy force to Asa.

8–9 Hanani also reminded the king of the fate of the "Cushites" (see NIV note) and of their accompanying Libyans (cf. 12:3; 14:9, 11). Hanani's reference to the "eyes of the LORD,"

as ranging "throughout the earth" was later repeated by God himself, speaking through a postexilic prophet Zechariah (Zec 4:10). The emphasis is that no problem can arise for God's people of which the Lord is not aware and from which he cannot deliver them (cf. Ro 8:32), provided their hearts are "fully committed" in respect to him.

But King Asa, from then on, would "be at war"—immediately with Baasha (1Ki 15:32), and, after the latter's death in 886, with his successors; for the state of constant belligerency between Israel and Judah seems to have terminated only in the reign of Asa's son Jehoshaphat (18:1), shortly before 865 (cf. comments on 18:2; 22:2).

10 Asa's reaction was to compound his sin by putting Hanani "in prison." This is the OT's first recorded royal persecution of a prophet, but many such instances were to follow (18:26; 24:21; Mk 6:17–18). One sin, moreover, leads to another; and he also "brutally oppressed some of the people."

11 Ezra here makes his first reference in 2 Chronicles (cf. 1Ch 9:1) to his primary literary source, "the book of the kings of Judah and Israel." This work cannot be our present 1, 2 Kings, which, instead of providing a fuller description of "the events of Asa's reign, from beginning to end," contain only a fraction of what appears in Chronicles (cf. introduction to chs. 14–16). This document seems to have been some extensive court chronicle that is now lost.

12 In his thirty-ninth year (871 B.C.), Asa deviated in still another direction, by seeking help for his foot disease "only from the physicians." While these may have been pagans, Scripture usually speaks positively of those who heal (Ex 21:19; Jer 8:22); medicine is God's gift (cf. 2Ki 20:7). The king's sin lay in having recourse to them *only* and not seeking "help from the LORD," who is the ultimate healer of diseases (2Ki 20:5; Ps 103:3).

13–14 Chronicles clarifies the general statement of 1Ki 10:24 that Asa "was buried with [his fathers] in the city of ... David" by speaking of "the tomb" that he had cut out for himself. The "huge fire," with "spices" and "perfumes," was not for cremation but "in his honor."

4. Jehoshaphat (17:1–20:37)

The regnal years of Asa's son Jehoshaphat reached from 873 to 848 B.C. (cf. comment on 17:7–9). Many of the features, moreover, that the Chronicler records of Asa's reign reappear in his description of the reign of his son. These parallels extend even to its organization under four major headings (cf. introduction to chs. 14–16), which, for the career of Jehoshaphat, correspond to the textual divisions found in chs. 17–20. The first of these (ch. 17) reminds one of the account of Asa's first reform, as it describes how his son in 866 B.C. removed idolatry from Judah, taught God's law, and strengthened the kingdom. But even as Asa had entered into an unholy alliance with an Aramean king, Ben-Hadad I, so Jehoshaphat allied himself with the Ephraimite ruler, Ahab, and was thereby drawn into a nearly fatal campaign against Ramoth Gilead in 853 (ch. 18).

Furthermore, even as the prophet Azariah had preached to Asa and inaugurated the earlier king's second reformation, so Jehu son of Hanani directed Jehoshaphat into a further reform in religion and into reorganization in the administration of justice (ch. 19). Finally, just as Asa had had to face the invading Cushites from the southwest, so Jehoshaphat met and overcame a vast army from the east (20:1–30), by trusting in the Lord. A concluding section then summarizes Jehoshaphat's reign and speaks to the failure of his commercial alliance with Israel (20:31–37). Out of these portions only ch. 18, together with the concluding remarks in 20:13–37, finds a parallel in 1Ki 22:2–49.

1 Jehoshaphat's strengthening of "himself against Israel" was directed specifically against Ahab (874–853), second king of the dynasty founded by the military leader Omri, infamous for the Baal worship advocated by his wife Jezebel. Asa's hostility with the northern kingdom thus continued, at least initially, under his son (see comments on 16:9; 18:1).

2 The Ephraimite "towns ... captured" by Asa included not simply the bastion of Ramah (cf. 16:1), but other communities as well (cf. 15:8).

3 The verse is perhaps better rendered "Jehoshaphat walked in the former ways" of his ancestor David, the Chronicler's implication being that David's latter ways were less exemplary (cf. 2Sa 11–21). Concretely Jehoshaphat disdained "the Baals"; each individual field had its own guiding master (*baal*; GK 1251), i.e., its own fertility spirit.

4–5 The practice of Israel, which Jehoshaphat also avoided, included Jeroboam's deviations in respect to the priesthood and the calendar, as well as his calf worship (cf. comment on 13:8; cf. 1Ki 12:28–33).

6 Concerning "the high places and the Asherah poles" that Jehoshaphat removed, see comment on 14:3. The introductory adverb "furthermore" is more normally rendered "and again he removed the high places." That is, Jehoshaphat renewed his father Asa's earlier opposition to local shrines (14:3; cf. 1Ki 22:46). Yet just as with Asa (see 2Ch 15:17), the king's official act was not sustained by his subjects: "The people continued to offer sacrifices and burn incense there" on the high places (1Ki 22:43).

7–9 Though Jehoshaphat's "reign" is said to have covered twenty-five years (20:31), i.e., 872–848 B.C., it can also be said to have terminated in only twenty-two years (eighteen, in 2Ki 3:1, plus four more, in 8:16), i.e., from the death of his father, Asa, in 869. Jehoshaphat must therefore have enjoyed an additional three-year coregency, commencing in 872, a procedure that was probably necessary because of Asa's illness, which became increasingly serious in the following year (see 16:12). Yet his dispatch of a religious teaching mission (17:7–9) seems sufficiently independent to suggest that what v.7 calls his "third

Jehoshaphat "stationed troops in all the fortified cities of Judah" (17:2). This is the ruins of one of Judah's fortresses in the 10–9th centuries B.C. They are only 25–70 meters in diameter, and most of the fortresses are on hills within eyesight of each other.

year" must have been that "of his" sole "reign," or 867.

The mission consisted of five government officials, nine Levites, and two priests, as named. For Jehoshaphat seems to have recognized how important it was for all the leaders of God's people (cf. Mt 28:20) "to teach" them "the Book of the Law of the LORD" (the Pentateuch, at least Deuteronomy, though it could by this time have included the historical books through 2 Samuel and much of Psalms and Proverbs as well). Teaching was not limited to the professional Levites (Dt 33:10) and priests (Lev 10:11). They "went around to all the towns . . . and taught" (cf. the traveling evangelists mentioned in NT times, 3Jn 7–8).

10–18 The king's "experienced fighting men" (v.13) that he "kept in Jerusalem" involved five groups, that consisted respectively of 300, 280, 200, 200, and 180 specially trained leaders (reading in each verse "leader," rather than "thousand"; see comments on 1Ch 7:3–4 and 12:27). The total was thus 1,160 (not 1,160,000).

19 Yet even here, "these . . . who served the king" in the city of Jerusalem were specifically the five commanders, as listed. Portions of their followers would then have been stationed "in the fortified cities throughout Judah."

18:1 Chapter 18 is taken from 1Ki 22:2–35 and is the only extract from the records of Israel used by Ezra. His reason seems to have been because it involved King Jehoshaphat almost as much as King Ahab of Israel, and also because the message of the prophet Micaiah, about which the chapter centers, had spiritual applications that extended far beyond the career of Ahab (cf. esp. vv.7, 13, 19–20, 27).

Jehoshaphat "allied himself with Ahab." This act is not only condemned (19:2), but it is also seen as the root of far-reaching consequences, made all too clear by a series of disasters that followed (18:31; 20:37; 21:6; 22:7, 10). Initially it entailed the "marriage" of Jehoshaphat's son Jehoram to Athaliah, the daughter of Ahab. Their marriage, in turn, furnishes an approximate date for the alliance (c. 865 B.C.), because a child of this union (Ahaziah) was twenty-two at his own accession in 841 (22:2). A major cause that led to

the alliance may be found in the growing threat of Assyria in the north. Its ruthless monarch Ashurnasirpal II (884–859) was already pressing into Lebanon; and his successor, Shalmaneser III, is known to have fought a drawn battle against a coalition of western states, including Damascus and Israel, at Qarqar on the Orontes River in 853.

2–3 Ahab urged Jehoshaphat to join him in a campaign to recover Ramoth Gilead. This was a key city on the eastern edge of Transjordanian Israel, south of the Yarmuk River, astride the Gilead trade route that went north to Damascus and beyond. It had been seized by the Aramean king of Damascus (16:4, or perhaps subsequently; cf. 1Ki 20:34); but Ahab may have felt that the Arameans had been sufficiently weakened by their losses at Qarqar to permit its recapture at this time, later in 853.

4 Though Jehoshaphat had already committed himself to the enterprise and he went on to disregard the divine guidance that was given him (v.28), he still retained the religion of the Lord to the extent that he insisted on seeking "the counsel of the LORD."

5 Jehoshaphat put little confidence in Ahab's four hundred court prophets (cf. v.6). These were men who confessedly spoke in the name of the Lord and not of Baal (vv.5, 10). But it was the Lord in the corrupted form of a golden calf (cf. 13:8); and their words were false (v.22), couched in terms that were calculated simply to please the hearers (v.12; cf. Mic 3:5, 11).

6–8 "Micaiah" remains unknown, apart from this incident. He never prophesied anything good about Ahab—because of the character of Ahab. The true prophets of Israel were, indeed, distinguished by the fact that they consistently warned their nation of the results of its sin (Jer 23:22; Mic 3:8).

9 The two kings sat on their thrones at "the gate of Samaria," the traditional place for rendering judgment (Ge 23:10; Ru 4:1).

10–11 The "iron horns" made by the false prophet Zedekiah were designed to symbolize victory for Ahab (Dt 33:17), but perhaps also to accomplish it, insofar as they were superstitiously believed to contain magical potency.

12–13 The true prophet Micaiah, by contrast, could tell the king "only what . . . God says." The revelations that he transmitted were objectively received and were distinguishable from the subjective thoughts and desires of his own heart (Jer 14:14; cf. 42:4, 7).

14–15 Micaiah's words "Attack and be victorious" were spoken in irony, as the tone of his voice must have immediately indicated to Ahab.

16–17 Micaiah's serious but figurative words "These people have no masters" continue the analogy of flocks and shepherds (cf. Nu 27:16–17); they were a prediction of Ahab's death in battle (2Ch 18:34). But the Hebrew troops would be free to "go home in peace," as brought about by the very orders of the Aramean king Ben-Hadad II, that his men were to fight only against Ahab (v.30).

18–19 As "Micaiah continued," with his vision of heaven itself, he spoke of "the host," or army, that was standing on either side of the Lord, which consisted of angelic spirits (cf. the "sons of God" in Job 1:6). The Lord's question in v.19, "Who will lure Ahab . . . to his death?" testifies to the truth that God can work through spirits to incite evil people like Ahab to manifest their sin and thus be led either to punishment or to repentance (cf. 1Sa 16:14–15; 18:10–11).

20–21 The Hebrew that underlies the phrase rendered "a spirit came forward" reads literally, "the [well-known] spirit came forward," i.e., Satan the tempter (as in Job 1:6–12). Apparently Micaiah seems to have assumed among his hearers a working knowledge of the book of Job, as already recorded in the days of Solomon.

22 The seer's emphatic phrase "these prophets of yours" underlines their differentiation from God's true prophets.

23 The way Zedekiah "slapped Micaiah on the face" indicates in itself that the Holy Spirit was not present with him (Jas 3:17; but cf. 2Ki 1:10–12). Yet his brazen claim to possess "the Spirit of the LORD" (NIV note) need not be watered down—though he may not have been personally aware that his optimistic message had in fact been supernaturally implanted in his mind, by Satan. Zedekiah's next words are difficult. He seems to be ac-knowledging Micaiah's claim that the Lord's Spirit had come "to speak to" him; but he asks, "Which way did the Spirit" actually "go when he went from me?" Not, presumably, to Micaiah!

24 Micaiah's rejoinder was to predict that Zedekiah would "go to hide in an inner room." Its fulfillment is unknown; but the prophecy seems to suggest an attempt on his part to escape pursuit, perhaps as Ahab's family would take vengeance on the false prophets, after the king's death.

25–26 Ahab's orders to send Micaiah back to the magistrate "Amon" imply that the prophet had already been put in custody at the time. A precedent for persecution of prophets had been set under Asa (cf. comment on 16:10).

27 The prophet's final statement, "Mark my words, all you people," was addressed to a plurality (lit., "peoples, nations"; GK 6639). He was calling all the world to serve as his witness (cf. Mic 1:2).

28–29 Ahab's plan to "enter the battle in disguise" was a futile attempt to escape the decree of God (v.16), and it failed (v.33).

30 Ben-Hadad's plan, in turn, to concentrate on no one "except the king of Israel" assumed that if Ahab could once be taken, the war would be won (cf. 2Sa 21:17)—and it was also the means for fulfilling Micaiah's prophetic vision.

31–32 The words "and the LORD helped [Jehoshaphat]. God drew them away from him" are an addition by Ezra, not found in 1Ki 22:32. However, they (1) show the seriousness of Jehoshaphat's deviation, how he would have reaped a fatal fruit from his sinful alliance with Ahab, had God not intervened; (2) suggest the reality of his faith, that when "Jehoshaphat cried out," this was not just an expression of fear on his part but apparently a prayer for divine help; and (3) demonstrate the greatness of the grace of God, rescuing people without a need for man-made alliances, or even, as in this case, in spite of them.

33–34 The arrow then struck King Ahab in a vulnerable spot—between the "scaly mail" armor and its "appendages," i.e., penetrating the abdomen. With his death, 2Ch 18 closes; 1Ki 22 has five more verses (vv.36–40) with further details, which Ezra omitted as less relevant for his particular audience.

19:1 Jehoshaphat's safe return from Ramoth Gilead fulfilled a final detail in Micaiah's prophecy (see comment on 18:16).

2 Hanani the seer had confronted King Asa half a century earlier (see comment on 16:7); and his son Jehu the seer had already condemned the dynasty of Baasha in Israel, some thirty-five years before this occasion in 853 B.C. (1Ki 16:1, 7). Jehu's message was once again a negative one, opposing Jehoshaphat's alliance with Israel (see comment on 18:1). But he went beyond the specific matter of this alliance and raised a more general ethical question, "Should you . . . love those who hate the LORD?" (cf. Mt 5:44).

Jehu therefore announced to the king, "The wrath of the LORD is upon you." In fact, it already had been (18:31), and it still would be (20:1, 37; 22:10). Unlike his father, Asa, however, who had refused to humble himself before God when confronted by Jehu's father Hanani (cf. 16:10), Jehoshaphat did submit to the judgment of God as conveyed by Jehu. This encounter, indeed, seems to have precipitated the king's second great reform, both in its religious aspect (v.4) and in its judicial implications (vv.5–11).

3 Jehu himself seems to have anticipated the king's positive response by his balanced acknowledgment, both of "some good" in him (cf. the approval soon to be granted Jehoshaphat by Elisha, 2Ki 3:14) and of some of the values that had emerged from his first reform, particularly the elimination of the "Asherah poles" (17:6; cf. 14:3).

4–7 Jehoshaphat's admonition to the newly appointed judges, that they were "not judging for man but for the LORD," is a standing reminder that good government springs from commitment to God.

8 "In Jerusalem . . . Jehoshaphat appointed some of the Levites" to serve on the central court of appeals and "to settle disputes." If the chronological order here is correct, Jehoshaphat's new judges were not appointed at the time the king had gone out (v.4) among the provinces (so as to be able to "return" with him); rather, they were already "in Jerusalem."

9–10 Israel's faithful judges were not simply to decide cases and render verdicts but were also to "warn" (GK 2302) their "brothers" against sin in the sight of God. They too were responsible to the Lord, and their ultimate motivation was to live so that divine "wrath" would not "come on" either them or their fellow Hebrews.

11 In the Pentateuch religious, civil, and moral law are juxtaposed, often without differentiation. Among the earlier prophets Samuel had begun to insist on certain priorities: that to obey was better than to sacrifice (1Sa 15:22), though Moses himself put love of God (Dt 6) and faith (Dt 7) before detailed legislation (Dt 12–26). Now, however, a distinction is explicitly made (though perhaps based on Dt 17:9, 12) between matters "concerning the LORD" and "matters concerning the king." Among the later prophets the difference between moral law and ceremonial law was sharply drawn (Isa 1:11–17; Am 5:21–24). Under Jehoshaphat's judges, Levites were to "serve as officials" (GK 8835).

20:1 Soon after 853 B.C. (see comments on 18:3; 20:35), Jehoshaphat faced an unexpected invasion by the combined forces of Moab, Ammon, and "the Meunites" (cf. 1Ch 4:41; 2Ch 26:7). These last were a people of Mount Seir in Edom (cf. vv.10, 22–23), perhaps from Maon, near Petra.

2 The enemy forces attacked by means of a little-used route, advancing around the south, or the Edomite end "of the [Dead] Sea," for they took "En Gedi," about midway on its western shore.

3–4 Jehoshaphat "proclaimed a fast" to emphasize in the presence of the "LORD" Judah's distress (cf. Jdg 20:26). Fasting did not exist as an official part of preexilic Hebrew religion (but cf. Lev 16:29–31); yet from the time of Samuel on, it had been employed to stress the sincerity of the prayers of God's people when they were facing special needs (1Sa 7:6; cf. Ac 13:2–3).

5 The "new courtyard" the king stood before was the temple's "large court" (see comment on 4:9); and it was probably called this because it was one of the innovations in Solomon's structure. Under him it had for the first time been separated from the "court of the priests." It is also possible that Jehoshaphat had recently restored it (cf. 17:12).

6–9 The king's plea, "If calamity comes upon us," was a quotation from Solomon's prayer that had been offered at the temple's dedication (6:28–30; cf. 7:13–15).

10–11 By referring also to Dt 2:5, which recorded how God would not "allow Israel to invade" the lands of Seir, Jehoshaphat was in effect calling on the Lord to honor Israel's obedience in this regard. He spoke also of God's specific bestowal on Israel of the very land that these enemies were in the process of invading.

12 Jehoshaphat's conclusion—"We have no power … but our eyes are upon you"— embodies a faith similar to that demonstrated by his father Asa (14:11).

13–15 Jahaziel's words, "The battle is not yours, but God's," reflect the spirit of David against Goliath (1Sa 17:47).

16–17 From a point seven miles north of En Gedi, "the Pass [ascent] of Ziz" wound inland, up to the Valley of Beracah (v.26), west of Tekoa, which was located south of Bethlehem toward Hebron. "Jeruel" lay on this same route, southeast of Tekoa. Jahaziel's further words, "Stand firm and see the deliverance the LORD will give you," reflect the speech of Moses at the Red Sea (Ex 14:13).

18–20 The "Desert of Tekoa" occupies a sharp drop-off, immediately to the east of the town. Jehoshaphat's words, "Have faith in the LORD your God and you will be upheld" were quoted a century later by Isaiah to King Ahaz (Isa 7:9; cf. 28:16; Mk 9:23).

21 At this point singers "went out at the head of the army," just as the ark of God and the priestly trumpeters had at Jericho (Jos 6:9). They praised the Lord "in [their] holy array" (cf. 1Ch 16:29), a rendering that seems preferable to that found in the NIV text.

22–30 The "ambushes" that the Lord then set against the invaders are not identified; but they may have consisted of some of the more rapacious Seirites (Edomites), since the men of Ammon and Moab proceeded to turn on the men of Mount Seir. The result was that "they helped to destroy one another," just as had occurred at the triumph of Gideon (Jdg

7:22). On the location of the Valley of "Beracah" ("blessing" or "praise"), see comment on v.16.

31–33 Here alone, for the concluding portion of ch. 20 (vv.31–37), information parallel to 1Ki 22 appears (vv.41–49). On the acknowledged failure to eliminate Judah's "high places," see comment on 17:6.

34 On "the annals of Jehu" being "recorded in the book of the kings," see comment on 32:32.

35 Jehoshaphat's "alliance with" Ahab's son "Ahaziah" belongs to the brief period of the latter's reign over Israel, 853–852 B.C.

36 On ships being "built at Ezion Geber," see 8:17. Archaeology indicates that after the demise of the original Solomonic settlement there, the site's second occupational level dates to the days of Jehoshaphat in the ninth century, though it seems soon to have fallen into Edomite hands (cf. 21:8). The phrase "trading ships" interprets a more literal rendering of the Hebrew, i.e., "ships that could go to Tarshish" (NIV note). The thought is that these vessels belonged to the class of ships that went to Tarshish (see comment on 9:21); their actual destination was Ophir (see comment on 8:18; cf. 1Ki 22:48).

37 The prophet "Eliezer … of Mareshah" is unknown apart from this passage. But because of Jehoshaphat's sin in allying himself with the wicked Ahaziah (v.35), which Eliezer condemned, the ships were wrecked; for God will not honor a compromising alliance. The NIV text says that they were therefore "not able to set sail to trade," which represents the general idea of the Hebrew; but it may be rendered more closely that they were "never fit to sail to Tarshish" or to anywhere else, including their particular goal of Ophir (cf. v.36). First Kings 22:49 adds that Jehoshaphat then refused Ahaziah's offer for a joint sailing endeavor.

5. Jehoram (21:1–20)

The sole reign of Jehoshaphat's son Jehoram extended from 848 to 841 B.C. and forms the subject of 2Ch 21. Dominating the chapter is the sad fact that Jehoram was married to Ahab's daughter and that he "walked in [their] ways" (v.6). It therefore describes, on the one hand, his viciousness and apostasy (vv.1–11) and, on the other, his condemnation, delivered through the prophet Elijah, and his overwhelming failures, both national and personal that came as a result (vv.12–20). Much of the first half of the chapter corresponds to the same information (though cf. v.2) found in 1Ki 22:50 and 2Ki 8:17–22, with some elaboration by the Chronicler; but the second half (except for a few words in the king's death notice; cf. 2Ki 8:24) is without biblical parallel.

1 "Jehoshaphat . . . was buried . . . and his son succeeded him" as sole monarch, in 848 B.C. But since Jehoshaphat's eighteenth year (2Ki 3:1), four years before his death (see comment on 17:7), can simultaneously be designated as his son Jehoram's second year (2Ki 1:17), it appears that the latter must have been associated with his father on Judah's throne since 853.

2 Because vv.3–4 have no parallel in Kings, their context would seem to have been drawn from the lost court chronicle mentioned elsewhere by Ezra (20:34; 25:26; cf. comment on 16:11) or from other literary sources.

3 Jehoshaphat's giving his six younger sons "many gifts," but also dispersing them throughout the "cities in Judah," shows that he was following the wise policy established by his great-grandfather Rehoboam (cf. 11:23).

4 When Jehoram, however, proceeded to massacre his brothers (cf. 22:10; Jdg 9:5), along with certain "princes" (or "prominent officials"), he was already demonstrating the unholy influence of his ruthless wife, Athaliah. The latter herself became the instigator of the crime of 22:10 (cf. 1Ki 18:4; 19:2; 21:7–15). The king's personality had thus become twisted to the point that he apparently suspected others of acting as he would have, if they were given the opportunity. Yet his brothers' principles were, in fact, much higher than his own (v.13).

5–7 God's unwillingness "to destroy" the dynasty of David was what had preserved Judah previously as a kingdom, despite Solomon's sin (1Ki 11:12–13). God had made a covenant with David.

8 At this time, and "because Jehoram had forsaken the LORD" (v.10), "Edom rebelled" against its Hebrew governors (1Ki 22:47); indeed Moab, to Edom's north, had already become independent (2Ki 1:1).

9 When the king attempted to use force to reimpose his authority, "the Edomites surrounded his chariot commanders," almost overwhelming the Judean army. Jehoram then not only "broke through"; he also "struck them down" at Zair (2Ki 8:21), a few miles south of the site of his father's victory at Beracah (2Ch 20:26).

10 Jehoram failed, however, to quell Edom's "rebellion." His campaign thus parallels Israel's failure shortly before, when it had attempted to resubdue Moab (2Ki 3:6–27). Also in revolt at this time was "Libnah," a semi-Philistine city in the vicinity of Gath.

11 Jehoram built up the "high places," the very shrines that his father and grandfather had tried to eradicate (cf. 14:3; 17:6), where the people "prostituted themselves." Though the Canaanite worship thus reintroduced did involve sexual immorality (cf. 1Ki 22:46), the emphasis here is on how the king "led Judah astray" into faithlessness with respect to the Lord, her divine husband.

12–15 That Jehoram "received a letter from Elijah" has been labeled a product of the imagination, on the basis that Elijah had nothing to do with the southern kingdom and clearly was not living at this time (2Ki 3:11 [i.e., before Jehoshaphat's death and Jehoram's installation in 848 B.C.]). However, Elijah's career did involve the south, specifically "Beersheba in Judah" (1Ki 19:3); his flight took him, indeed, as far south as Sinai (v.8). Also, though Elijah's last dated act occurred in 852 (2Ki 1:3, 17), his translation to heaven (2:11) still need not have occurred till after Jehoram's accession as sole monarch over Judah and his crimes of slaughtering his brothers and his officials, in the year 848 (8:16). Elijah may, however, have been gone by the time of the delivery of his letter, so that its sentence of doom could have had the force of a voice coming from the dead.

16–17 The land's fortunes suffered a complete reversal; for "the Philistines," who had rendered tribute to Jehoram's father (2Ch 17:11), now "invaded Judah." They were joined by "the Arabs who lived near the Cushites," i.e., by nomads from the borderlands between Philistia and Egypt. In the outworkings of God's justice, the man who began by massacring his own brothers (v.4) ended by suffering the loss of his sons and wives (cf. 22:1).

18–20 The king's "incurable disease of the bowels" seems to have been some extreme form of dysentery. In further contrast to his father (cf. 16:14), he died without "fire in his honor." Jehoram's death was unmourned, without even normal burial "in the tombs of the kings" (cf. 24:25).

6. Ahaziah (22:1–9)

The reign of Jehoram's son Ahaziah ran its course during the one year of 841 B.C. (cf. v.2). Its theme is once again that of retribution (cf. 21:17); and, in Ahaziah's case, it was his sinful alliance with the wicked house of Ahab in Israel that brought about its own punishment (22:4) in the form of premature death for the young monarch (v.9). The sequence of events is explained in more detail in the parallel passage of 2Ki 8:25–10:14, though 2Ch 22 adds unique details from its own special sources (vv.1, 9b), as well as certain observations by Ezra (vv.4b, 7a) that are not found in Kings.

1 The Chronicler's supplementary notice that Ahaziah was made king by "the people of Jerusalem" suggests that there was some uncertainty about the succession (cf. 23:13; 2Ki 23:30), perhaps because of the threat of Ahaziah's own mother, the ruthless Athaliah (cf. v.10). Concerning "the raiders who . . . had killed all" Jehoram's "older sons," see 21:17.

2 The reading found in the LXX and 2Ki 8:26 for Ahaziah's age (NIV note) of "twenty-two years" is to be adopted, rather than the Hebrew text's "forty-two," which would make him older than his father (cf. 21:20). His reign of "one year" fell entirely within the twelfth year of Joram of Israel (2Ki 8:25; cf. 3:1), whose death occurred at the same time as his own (9:24, 27), so that his rule must actually have been only a few months.

3–4 The way that Ahaziah's mother "encouraged him in doing wrong" is explained by this queen's patronizing of the Phoenician Baal worship of her stepmother Jezebel (cf. 23:17), and is a further testimony to the dominating influence of both these evil women

(21:6; cf. 21:4 and Dt 7:3). Ahaziah was not only encouraged to do evil by his mother, but he also followed the bad advice of the members of the house related to him through his mother. This was "to his undoing."

5 The Transjordanian Israelite city of "Ramoth Gilead" had been seized by the Arameans (18:2), and Ahab's attempt at its recovery in 853 had led instead to his own death (18:34). Yet with the murder of the Aramean king Ben Hadad II by Hazael some ten years later (2Ki 8:7–15), Ahab's son "Joram" recaptured the city, but only to be attacked in 841 by Hazael (2Ki 9:14), who wounded Joram there.

6 Joram returned from Ramoth to Jezreel, at the head of the Esdraelon Valley, where his father Ahab's palace was located (1Ki 21:1) and where his nephew Ahaziah "went down to see him."

7 The full record of how "the LORD had anointed Jehu to destroy the house of Ahab" is contained in 2Ki 9.

8 It was only after Ahaziah's own death (v.9) that Jehu killed the forty-two relatives of Ahaziah (2Ki 10:12–14).

9 This verse should probably begin "he also [not he then] went in search of Ahaziah." The final movements of Ahaziah are difficult to trace but may perhaps be reconstructed as follows: he fled south from Jezreel so as to hide "in Samaria. He was brought to Jehu," who fatally wounded him near Ibleam (between Jezreel and Samaria); he fled by chariot northwest to Megiddo, where he died (2Ki 9:27); and his body was carried by Ahaziah's servants to Jerusalem (9:28), where they buried him.

8. Athaliah (22:10–23:21)

This section draws on its canonical source in 2Ki 11 and follows it rather closely. It shows how Jehoshaphat's marriage alliance with the house of Ahab (18:1) eventually resulted in an attempt to exterminate the dynasty of David and in the official paganizing of Judah. For after the death of her last remaining son (22:1, 9), Athaliah proceeded to slaughter her own royal grandchildren—so as to ensure the throne for herself—and to establish the sort of Baal worship her mother Jezebel had been devoted to as the state religion of the southern kingdom. Under the protection, however, of the high priest Jehoiada, a single, one-year-old son of Ahaziah, named Joash, survived (22:10–12). Finally, when the lad had become seven, Jehoiada carried through a revolt that brought about the coronation of Joash (23:1–11), the execution of Athaliah (vv.12–15), and the extirpation of her false worship (vv.16–21).

10 The reign of Israel's only queen, Athaliah the mother of Ahaziah, extended for six full years, from 841 to 835 B.C. (cf. 22:12; 23:1).

11–12 "Jehosheba" (cf. 2Ki 11:2), a sister of the late king Ahaziah, rescued her infant nephew Joash by hiding him "in a bedroom," i.e., in one of the palace rooms where mattresses and bedding were stored. Chronicles reveals the fact, otherwise unrecorded, that she was also the "wife of the [high] priest Jehoiada," who must have been many years her senior (cf. 24:15). The two of them later removed Joash to "the temple of God" for safety.

23:1 As explained in 2Ki 11:4, the five "commanders of units of a hundred" were the officers of the Carites (cf. the Cherethites, 1Ch 18:17) and of other elements of the royal guard.

2 The gathering of "the Levites and [clan] heads" is not mentioned in 2Ki 11, but such an action is not thereby rendered suspect. It must have been accomplished with considerable secrecy, since the uprising caught Queen Athaliah wholly by surprise (v.13).

3 "The covenant with the king" was made specifically with Jehoiada as his protector (v.1; 2Ki 11:4). Once again we see the requirement of popular confirmation, which played so prominent a part in the history of the succession of Israel's "constitutional monarchs" (cf. 1Ch 11:3; 2Ch 10:1).

4–7 The situation of the "priests and Levites" as "going on duty on the Sabbath" was that which concerned the changing of the Levitical courses in their temple service (cf. 1Ch 24:4, 20). The sentence reads literally, "the third [of you priests . . .]"—with the definite article in the Hebrew—since, as 2Ki 11:5–7 makes clear, this group contrasts with the other two-thirds, who were going off duty. The former were "to keep watch at the doors," both of the palace (2Ki 11:5) and of the temple, to prevent any unauthorized, non-Levitical personnel from entering the sanctuary (2Ch 23:6).

Verse 5, as shown by 2Ki 11:5b–6, constitutes a parenthesis that identifies the three parts of the third who were coming on duty: (1) those "at the royal palace" (which might mean simply "the house of the king," i.e., his chamber in the temple, 22:12, for Athaliah's palace remained open, 23:12); (2) those "at the Foundation Gate" (called the Sur Gate in 2Ki 11:6, a temple gate of uncertain location); and (3) those "in the courtyards of the temple" (specified in Kings as stationed at the gate behind the guard).

8–9 Ezra here introduces the two companies of Levites "who were going off duty": they had not been released but instead were assigned to guard the temple for the king (2Ki 11:7) with the weapons that were being kept there.

10 When Jehoiada is said to have "stationed all the men," this company must have included the non-Levitical clan heads (v.2) and such of the royal guard as may have been considered faithful by the five commanders who had entered into the covenant with him (v.1).

11 The "copy of the covenant" that Joash was given (lit., "the testimony"; GK 6343) may have been simply the terms of the contract under which he was to rule but was more likely the required scroll of the law of Moses, which testified both to his royal position under God and to his responsibilities for godly conduct while in office (Dt 17:18–19). Chronicles adds to 2Ki 11:12 that it was the high priest "Jehoiada and his son" who "anointed" Joash.

12–13 In support of Joash there came "all the people of the land," who are here distinguished from the military officers. They did not form a party or a social class (though in postexilic times the expression did come to designate the non-Jewish inhabitants of Palestine, who hindered the work of restoration by the returning exiles).

14–16 Along with Jehoiada's political revolution came a corresponding religious revival— that king, priest, and citizenry would together "be the LORD's people" (v.16). This included their reaffirmation of the southern kingdom's limited monarchy, in which all its social elements pledged allegiance to God as their ultimate Sovereign (cf. vv.3, 11).

17 The execution of "Mattan the priest of Baal" carried out the requirement of God's Word directed against those who should lead others into false religion (Dt 13:5–10).

18–21 The priests then reestablished the true worship, according to the prescriptions of Moses and of David for the Levitical priests (1Ch 23) and for the singers (ch. 25).

8. Joash (24:1–27)

Joash, the young son of Ahaziah and grandson of Athaliah, reigned over Judah for forty years, from 835 to 796 B.C. His rule, moreover, serves as a characterization in miniature for the historical course of his entire nation. During the earlier years of his reign, Joash lived uprightly, honoring the Lord and providing for the temple, whose structure and sacrificial services depicted God's eternal plan of salvation (vv.1–14). But in later years he departed both from the Lord and from his sanctuary (vv.15–19; cf. Mt 21:13); he murdered the prophet who rebuked him, who was the son of the very priest who had preserved, enthroned, and guided him up to this point (vv.20–22; cf. Mt 21:38); he suffered a humiliating subjugation to the forces of Damascus (vv.23–24; cf. Lk 19:43–44); and he died incapacitated by battle wounds and slain by his own officials for his crimes (vv.25–27; cf. Mt 21:41). Just as Asa's rejection of the prophetic word resulted in God's judgment, military troubles, downfall, and, ultimately, death (presumably from his diseased foot), so was the fate of Joash. This chapter stands in general parallel to 2Ki 12, but with supplements of varying length—ranging from the one verse summary of Joash's family (v.3) to the four paragraphs concerning his lapse at the death of Jehoiada (vv.15–22)—which probably derived from Ezra's special source called the "annotations" (cf. v.27).

1–2 Joash began his career by doing "what was right in the eyes of the LORD," except that he had no success in removing Judah's high-place shrines (cf. 14:3; 2Ki 12:3); and he continued in his uprightness "all the years of Jehoiada" (cf. v.14), i.e., until some time after the twenty-third year of his reign, datable to

813 (2Ki 12:6). Following the death of his protector, however, he fell into serious sin (vv.17–18).

3 The fact he had "two wives" was censurable (cf. Dt 17:17), though Jehoiada may have felt that this was an improvement over the state of some of his royal predecessors (cf. 1Ch 14:3; 2Ch 11:21).

4–5 After the acts of vandalism and sacrilege committed under Athaliah (v.7), it had become necessary "to restore the temple." For this purpose he collected "money" (lit., "silver"; GK 4084); coinage entered the ancient world only during Israel's exilic period. "But the Levites did not act at once," both because of natural inertia (still true even of Christian workers) and because of the priestly demands that seem to have exhausted the normal revenues for current operations and for their own support (2Ki 12:7; cf. Nu 18:19). Yet the Chronicler, at least at this point, seems to view the priests in an overall better light than the Levites.

6 Concerning the "tax imposed by Moses," 2Ki 12:4 specifies three sources of revenue: "money collected in the census," a half-shekel per head (Ex 30:14; 38:26; Mt 17:24; cf. Ne 10:32); "money received from personal vows," in substitutionary redemption payments, varying from three to fifty shekels (Lev 27:1–8; Nu 18:15–16); and "money brought voluntarily to the temple."

7 On "the Baals," see comment on 17:3.

8 So Jehoiada (as stated in 2Ki 12:9) "made a chest," with an opening in its lid to receive the donations. The priests agreed to surrender responsibility, both for taking collections and for making repairs for the temple (12:8); their needs were henceforth to be met by "the money from the guilt offerings and sin offerings" (12:16; cf. Lev 5:16). The high priest then had it "placed outside, at the [south] gate of the temple," that is, to the right of the altar (2Ki 12:9).

9–12 A "proclamation was then issued" to publicize the new procedures (v.5) and to insure the payment of the Mosaic tax (v.6).

13–14 Thus "they rebuilt the temple"; for none of the precious metal that was received was converted into sacred equipment (2Ki 12:13), at least not till the repairs were finished. The author of 2Ki 12:15 brings out the commendable honesty and faithfulness of the workers.

15 The notice of the death of Jehoiada "at an age of a hundred and thirty" has led some to charge the Chronicler with a fictitious figure. But the literal count corresponds to actual history. The precise placement of this priest within the gap that occurs in the Aaronic genealogy (cf. 1Ch 6:10) between Ahimaaz's grandson Johanan (born c. 960 B.C.) and Azariah II (in 751, 2Ch 26:17) is unknown. If Jehoiada succeeded the high priest Amariah II (in 853, 2Ch 19:11; cf. 1Ch 6:4) at an age of 85, he would have expired in 808, some time before the death of his protégé Joash in 796. Jehoiada's span of life was unique at this period, but not impossible, particularly for a man specially blessed of God.

16 Jehoiada had become by marriage a brother-in-law to Joash's royal father Ahaziah (2Ch 22:11); but burial "with the kings" was still a marked honor, which stands in distinct contrast to Joash's own eventual fate (24:25).

17–18 The "officials of Judah," to whom Joash now listened, were of the class most attracted by the materialism of Baal worship (cf. Zep 1:8). They were also the first to suffer God's penalty for it (cf. v.23). Concerning "Asherah poles," see comment on 14:3.

19 Among the prophets sent to testify against Israel, some of the earlier ones, such as Shemaiah and Jehu, had been heeded (11:2; 12:5; 19:2); but the later ones—Hanani, Micaiah, and now Zechariah (16:7; 18:16; 24:20)—increasingly were not.

20 The expression that the Spirit "came upon" Zechariah means literally that he "clothed himself with" him (cf. 1Ch 12:18).

21–22 The expression that Joash did not remember Jehoiada's "kindness" (GK 2876) means the latter's "faithfulness." The king owed his power and position, and indeed his very life, to this priest's loyalty (ch. 23). Joash's murder of Jehoiada's son Zechariah has sometimes been interpreted as the event to which Jesus referred (Lk 11:51) as the last-recorded martyrdom in the OT canon; but this appears improbable. Our Lord's allusion most likely was to Zechariah the son of Be-

rekiah (Mt 23:35; cf. Zec 1:1), coming at the close of the minor prophets.

Zechariah's dying prayer, "May the LORD see this and call you to account," is one of imprecation rather than of forgiveness; but it is justified because of Zechariah's position as the Lord's prophet and because of the king's wickedness in going against the Lord.

23–24 The invading Arameans are first said to have killed Judah's "leader" (GK 8569). They then sent to Damascus "all the plunder" of Jerusalem. Joash had stripped from the temple all the treasures that had been accumulated since the days of Asa (cf. 2Ki 12:18), whose sin thus reaped its final reward (cf. comments on 2Ch 16:2, 9). "Only a few" Arameans overcame "a much larger" Judean army, just as Moses had threatened (Lev 26:17).

25 The king's "officials" then assassinated him "in his bed" at the house of Millo (2Ki 12:20), probably in Jerusalem (cf. 1Ch 11:8). Chronicles adds that the reason for the conspiracy was to avenge Zechariah. But their act was still murder and is condemned (cf. 25:3). In 2Ki 12:21 Joash's s burial is described as being "with his fathers in the City of David"; but while Chronicles confirms this as to its general location, Ezra also specifies that it was "not in the tombs of the kings" (contrast v.16).

26–27 The "many prophecies" about Joash probably refer to such prophetic threatenings as are noted in vv.19–20. The Chronicler's literary source for this reign, "the annotations on the book of the kings," suggests some interpretation of the more basic court chronicle (cf. 13:22).

9. Amaziah (25:1–28)

This chapter concerns the reign of Joash's son Amaziah (796–767 B.C.). Except for an introduction on Amaziah's succession (vv.1–4) and a conclusion on his death (vv.25–28), it concentrates on two wars that he undertook and on the lessons to be learned from them: (1) his reconquest of Edom, through obedience to the Lord (vv.5–16); and (2) his ensuing defeat by Israel, in punishment for engaging in a form of idolatry to which he succumbed after his earlier victory (vv.17–24). His demise repeats a familiar theme: Rejecting God's prophetic word results in di-

The Edomite capital city of Sela (later called Petra; see comment on 25:11–12) was cut out of sheer rock. The only entrance into that city was through a narrow passageway in the rocks, making it one of the most secure cities in the ancient world.

vine judgment, military defeat, downfall, and ultimately death. These data depend on and closely follow 2Ki 14:1–20. They are considerably augmented, however, by fresh material concerning the king's Ephraimite mercenaries (vv.5–10, 13) and his Edomite idolatry (vv.14–16, 20), presumably as drawn from the Chronicler's larger source cited in v.26.

1–2 Amaziah "did what was right" (cf. vv.4, 10), "but not wholeheartedly" (see vv.14, 16, 20). Notice also 2Ki 14:4, on how he allowed the high places to remain standing.

3–4 Though Amaziah executed his father's murderers, he spared "their sons," as had been prescribed by Moses (Dt 24:16).

5 Because of such losses as had been suffered under his father, Joash (24:23), Amaziah's muster of able men with "spear and shield" fell considerably short of the enumerations made under Asa and Jehoshaphat (see comment on 14:8; 17:14–18); but it still recorded the "three hundred" specially trained warriors (cf. comment on 1Ch 7:3–4; 12:37, that "thousand" should be rendered "chief").

6 Amaziah then "hired a hundred" more "from Israel," at the cost of an equal number of silver "talents." At twelve hundred ounces each, this sum meant something over three

and three-fourths tons. But no support that is purchased from the ungodly, such as these Ephraimites were, could enjoy the Lord's blessing.

7–10 A man of God confronted the king, reminding him that it is God who has the controlling "power to help or to overthrow." Amaziah then asked what he should do with his hired mercenaries. On the prophet's advice, Amaziah dismissed them, who, despite their payment, were furious over the loss of what they had anticipated as further plunder. But the king was placing his trust in God, just as his fathers had done (cf. 14:11; 20:12).

11–12 "Seir," or Edom, had now continued independent from Judah for half a century (21:8); and it was ruthlessly subjugated. The decisive battle occurred at "the Valley of Salt," which had been the scene of David's victory two hundred years before (1Ch 18:12). It probably lay at the southern end of the Dead Sea. Amaziah eventually occupied the Edomite capital of Sela (2Ki 14:7)—the later famed city of Petra.

13 The Ephraimite mercenaries "that Amaziah had sent back" proceeded to vent their rage by pillaging Judah's frontier towns in northwestern Benjamin. Thus Amaziah's initial reliance on human beings (vv.6–7) brought about its own punishment.

14–15 The futility of "gods, which could not save their own people" should have been obvious, but people still often tend to worship that which is demonstrably inadequate.

16 The king's silencing of the Lord's prophet at least involved no more than threats (contrast 16:10; 24:21).

17–19 Amaziah's pride over defeating Edom led him to challenge the far stronger kingdom of Jehoash (798–782) in Israel, the senselessness of which the latter proceeded to portray by his fable.

20–21 The battle was joined at "Beth Shemesh," fifteen miles west of Bethlehem, on Amaziah's own picked ground. This town lay "in Judah" on its Danite border (Jos 15:10).

22–24 The disaster that resulted for the king included the destruction of the least defensible portion of Jerusalem's wall, namely, the part facing north, "from the Ephraim Gate," on its west side, "to the Corner Gate," facing northeast. It also included the loss of the temple treasures that were "in the care of Obed-Edom," i.e., of the old Levitical family of gatekeepers and musicians that bore his name.

25–27 As a further divine punishment on Amaziah (cf. v.20), these losses led to a mounting conspiracy "against him in Jerusalem." At a preliminary stage his sixteen-year-old son Uzziah was elevated first to a twenty-three year coregency in 790 (26:1). A final stage was precipitated by Amaziah's flight to Lachish, twenty-five miles southwest of Jerusalem on the route to Egypt, in 767. If this represented an attempt by the ex-ruler to recover his throne, it failed; for his pursuers "killed him there."

28 Amaziah was buried in the "City of Judah" (i.e., Jerusalem), a later term for "the City of David" (2Ki 14:20).

10. Uzziah (26:1–23)

This chapter concerns Amaziah's son Uzziah, whose total reign extended from 790 to 739 B.C. His career runs parallel to those of his father, Amaziah, and grandfather, Joash: for the earlier portion of all three of these long reigns was marked by piety and by a corresponding prosperity (see vv.1–15). But the latter part of each introduced some more or less serious religious deviation, which in Uzziah's case resulted in his suffering a stroke of leprosy, a banishment from his own palace, and, eventually, death (vv. 16–23). Yet his failure was less far reaching than the outright idolatry practiced by his immediate predecessors, and his achievements mark him off as one of the half-dozen leading monarchs of Judah. The content of most of ch. 26 is unique to Chronicles, since 2Ki 14:21–22; 15:1–7 present little more than a summary of his reign.

1 The new king's designation, "Uzziah," was apparently his throne name. His personal name, Azariah (NIV note), appears in eight of the twelve references that are made to him in Kings, and also in the genealogical recapitulation found in 1Ch 3:12, perhaps because the use of his personal name may have been resumed after he became a leper. Since he was sixteen years old at his accession as coregent in 790 (see comment on 25:25–27), he must have been born when his father was fifteen (25:1). Early marriages were not uncommon in the ancient Near East.

2–3 The "Elath" that Uzziah "rebuilt" has been identified with Period III of Tell el Kheleifeh. The statement that this occurred only after Amaziah's death (in 767) confirms the reconstruction of Uzziah's accession, noted under 25:27, as occurring some time prior to the demise of his father.

4 "He did what was right," even though 2Ki 15:4 cautions that the high places still remained. Furthermore, below the surface prosperity that was enjoyed by both kingdoms at this time, the contemporaneous preaching of Hosea and Amos indicates the presence of serious moral and spiritual decay.

5 Uzziah's mentor, Zechariah, though apparently familiar to Ezra, can no longer be identified today. The God-given success that resulted for Uzziah is borne out historically. The four decades that marked his overlapping reign with Jeroboam II in the north, from 790 to 750 B.C., have been called Israel's "Indian summer" (cf. vv.8, 15): a time when the Assyrians, who had weakened Israel's Aramean enemies at Damascus on its northeastern border (cf. 2Ki 12:17–19; 13:3–5), had not yet begun their own destruction of the Hebrew states (cf. 15:19, 29). Yet by the time of Uzziah's death, the prophets were expressing forebodings about what lay ahead (Isa 6:1, 11–12).

6 In his western offensive, the king overpowered three Philistine centers: "Gath," the most inland city (and the most exposed to Hebrew attack), whose destruction left the Philistines with only four main cities thereafter (cf. Am 1:6–8; Zep 2:4); "Ashdod," near the Mediterranean, the one that lay almost directly west of Jerusalem; and the smaller town of "Jabneh," which stood about ten miles farther north, between Ekron and the Sea (Jos 15:11).

7–8 "The Arabs" from the unknown site of "Gur Baal" and "the Meunites" seem to have been nomadic enemies of Judah, inhabiting its southeastern border.

9 "The Corner Gate" (25:23), "the Valley Gate," and "the angle of the wall" were located at northeastern, southwestern, and eastern points, respectively, of Jerusalem's fortifications (Ne 3:13, 19, 31).

10 The reality of Uzziah's "towers in the desert" (of arid southern Judah) has been validated by the discovery of an eighth-century tower at Qumran. Concerning "the foothills," see comment on 1Ch 27:28. "The plain" then refers to the plateau of Transjordan; for though this area had formerly been under Ephraimite control, Uzziah seems to have regained it from the Ammonites, who had occupied it (v.8).

11–12 To muster Judah's troops, Maaseiah held the post of "officer" (GK 8853), a scribal or mustering official (Ex 5:6).

13–14 While a figure of 2,600 for the "family leaders" placed "over the fighting men" (v.12) seems appropriate for a strong kingdom like Uzziah's, the enumeration of his more professional soldiers should probably be taken to read 300 special warriors (the same number as Amaziah's; see comment on 25:5), together with 7,500 "men trained for war."

15 The description of his "machines . . . on the towers . . . to hurl stones" has been interpreted to mean devices from which to hurl stones; i.e., they were shielding mantles, used to cover defending troops as they repelled enemies seeking to scale the walls; for question exists about the use of catapult machines at this time.

16 In the chapter's latter section, on Uzziah's religious deviation, his sin in entering the temple to burn incense consisted not simply in usurping what was an exclusively priestly prerogative (v.18; Ex 30:7–8; cf. Nu 18:7), but perhaps also in arrogating to himself a Canaanite type of office, of semi-divine priest-king (see Ge 14:18; cf. Nu 12:10).

17–18 "Azariah the priest," who withstood the king, is probably Azariah II, as listed in 1Ch 6.

19–21 The "separate house" Uzziah as a leper had to stay in is literally "house of [the] freedom" (cf. NIV note). His son "Jotham" assumed coregency in the palace. The date of this transfer of power is 751 B.C., since Jotham's twentieth year (2Ki 15:30) was equivalent to his son Ahaz's twelfth (16:2), which is 732.

22 "The prophet Isaiah" recorded the other events of Uzziah's reign, though this work is now lost, even as Isaiah later did for those of Hezekiah's reign (see comment on 32:32).

23 Rather than suggesting that Uzziah was buried only "near" his fathers because "he had leprosy," one might more naturally render the Hebrew as that he was "buried with" them, and then conclude the thought either negatively—"in a field for burial . . . for" he was a leper—or more positively—"with them, although" he was a leper; that is, he was honored in death despite his malady.

11. Jotham (27:1–9)

The official sixteen-year kingship of Uzziah's son Jotham extended from 751 to 736 B.C., but it overlapped the reigns of his predecessor (cf. comment on 26:19–21) and successor (see comment on v.8) to such a degree that he himself is left with little independent notice in Scripture. The nine verses here furnish some elaboration on the even briefer notices that relate to this monarch in the parallel passage of 2Ki 15:32–38; and they most notably concern his victory over the Ammonites, together with its evaluation (vv.5–6). Jotham was a good king, and God rewarded his righteousness (vv.2, 6).

1 Since Jotham's reign lasted for a total of "sixteen years," the reference to its "twentieth year" in 2Ki 15:30 must be prophetic—for Jotham's successor had not yet been introduced in Kings at this point, or even Jotham himself.

2 The "corrupt practices" of his people are explained elsewhere in Scripture as consisting of sacrificial services carried out on Judah's high places, with accompanying immoralities, idolatries, and superstitions (2Ki 15:35; cf. Isa 1–6, which pertains to this period).

3–4 The temple's "Upper Gate" (cf. 23:20), which "Jotham rebuilt," was situated on its north side (Jer 20:2; Eze 9:2). The "hill of Ophel," on the other hand, lay to its south, in the upper part of the old city of David.

5 Included in the tribute that the king gained from Ammon was a considerable sum of silver.

6 A testimony to Jotham's "power" has been the discovery of his official seal at Ezion Geber, Judah's outpost that continued under Hebrew control throughout his reign.

7 The reference to "all" Jotham's wars suggests that prior to the Ammonite campaign (v.5), for which as king he had sole responsibility, he may have served as field commander for the alliance that was conceived by his quarantined father, Azariah-Uzziah (26:21), and which is mentioned in Assyrian annals (but not in the OT) as overcome by Tiglath-pileser III about 743 B.C.

8–9 Though "he reigned sixteen years" (cf. v.1), it was after only eight of these, in 743, that Jotham seems to have associated his son Ahaz with him on the throne (comment on 26:21), perhaps because of his defeat by Tiglath-pileser (see comment on 28:5; cf. 2Ki 15:37).

12. Ahaz (28:1–27)

The official reign of Jotham's apostate son Ahaz extended from 743 to 728 B.C. He was, indeed, one of the weakest and most corrupt of all the twenty rulers of Judah. His record in 2Ch 28 is illumined by the prophecies of Isaiah that belong to this period (chs. 7–12), and it runs parallel to the history in 2Ki 16. But apart from the opening four verses and

the concluding formula in vv.26–27 (cf. 2Ki 16:19–20), and a few words in v.16 (2Ki 16:7), the composition of these two historical chapters remains distinct. Both report the reign of Ahaz through two stages: (1) his apostasy from the Lord and the defeat that he suffered as a result, at the hands of Syro (Aramean)-Ephraimite attacks (2Ch 28:1–7); and (2) his subsequent appeal and capitulation to Assyria, which led him into even further corruption and idolatry (vv.16–25). Between these sections, however, the Chronicler inserts a discussion of how the prophet Oded succeeded in rescuing a group of Judean captives out of Ephraim (vv.8–15), though none of this has been preserved in 2 Kings.

1 Since "Ahaz was twenty years old" when he acceded to coregency in 743 (cf. on 26:21; 27:8), and since his father, Jotham, had been twenty-five at his own accession eight years previously (27:1), the time interval separating their births must have been only thirteen years. Jotham, and then Ahaz himself, have the lowest ages of paternity that are recorded for the Hebrew kings (cf. comments on 26:1; 29:1).

2–4 On the "Baals" see comment on 17:3. The "Valley of Ben Hinnom" descended eastward below the southern edge of the city of Jerusalem; and it became noted as the scene of Judah's most revolting pagan practices (33:6). It was later defiled by King Josiah and converted into a place of refuse for the city (2Ki 23:10); thus the perpetual fires of "Gehenna" became descriptive of hell itself (Mk 9:43). While 2Ki 16:3 had recorded that Ahaz "sacrificed his son [sing.] in the fire," Ezra adds that it was sons (pl.); that rendered his conduct even worse. The Canaanite practice of child sacrifice had been forbidden to Abraham (Ge 22:12), and under Moses it was made a capital offense (Lev 20:1–5). For the "high places" (v.4), see comment on 14:3.

5–7 The kings of "Aram" and of "Israel" to whom God handed Ahaz over were, respectively, Rezin and Pekah (752–732 B.C.). These two may have turned against Judah because of the failure of the alliance that Uzziah had directed against Assyria (see comment on 27:7) and because of the sufferings that had resulted for them and their people (2Ki 15:19; cf. v.37), but from which Judah had escaped unscathed. In what has been called the Syro (Aramean)-Ephraimite counteralliance, they besieged but could not capture Jerusalem (2Ki 16:5; Isa 7:1). Rezin did, however, take Elath (2Ki 16:6; cf. the comments on 2Ch 26:2; 27:6); and it was not regained by Israel till A.D. 1948.

8 Even as v.6 should probably be understood as recording that in one day Pekah killed 120 specially trained warriors (cf. comments on 1Ch 7:3–4; 12:27), so too v.8 should best be treated as stating that the Israelites took captive from their kinsmen 200 trained warriors, plus "wives, sons and daughters"—a more plausible rendering than to think of 200,000 women, etc.

9–11 The northern prophet "Oded" is otherwise unknown, but he was God's spokesman for warning the Ephraimites that those who serve as the Lord's instruments for punishment must not exceed their appointed mission (cf. Isa 10:5–19). Their own standing, he observed, was hardly guiltless (2Ch 28:10, 13).

12–14 The fact that Pekah's "soldiers gave up the prisoners and plunder" (v.14) testifies to the feelings of brotherhood that still existed between the two Hebrew kingdoms, to the authority of Israelite prophecy, and to the grace that God employed in his treatment of the nation of the worthless Ahaz.

15 Those who were "designated" to be responsible then "provided" for the prisoners, in accordance with the OT standard of showing love, even toward one's enemies (Ex 23:4; Pr 24:17; 25:21; cf. Mt 5:44).

16 In 734 B.C., in an act that amounted to a breach of faith with God (cf. comments on 16:2, 9; 25:6, 10), Ahaz threw himself at the feet of Assyria's rulers for rescue and help. Isaiah had opposed this ill-advised act as being both useless and faithless (Isa 7:4–7). What Ahaz really did was to place Judah under the iron heel of Tiglath-pileser, to cause the deportation of three and one-half of the tribes of Israel to Assyria in 733 (2Ki 15:29), followed by the remaining six and one-half tribes eleven years later (17:6), and eventually, in 701, to bring about Judah's own devastation by the armies of Sennacherib (18:13).

17 Again "the Edomites . . . attacked Judah," for they seemed ever on the alert to capitalize on Judah's calamities (cf. 20:10–11; 21:8). Their incursions of 735 B.C. and their seizure of prisoners may have been the occasion for the prophecies of Obadiah (v.11) and Joel (3:19).

18–21 "The Philistines" did not simply rebel from Judean control, but they also "raided towns in the foothills . . . of Judah." Even a gift to the Assyrians "did not help" Ahaz; for though the rebellions were put down, the states involved were not returned to Judah but organized into Assyrian provinces.

22–23 The reverence Ahaz paid "to the gods of Damascus" took a particular form; he sacrificed on an altar patterned after the one found there (2Ki 16:10–13). Since "the kings of Aram" were by this time Assyrian (16:10a), interpreters until recently had assumed that the price of a nation's submission to the empire of Assyria included their compulsory worship of its deities. Recent studies, however, have indicated that such was not necessarily the case.

24–25 The paganism of Ahaz was designed not simply to supplement the worship of the Lord, but to supplant it and close the Lord's temple.

27 The death of Ahaz occurred in the same year as that of "the rod that struck" the Philistines, i.e., of Tiglath-pileser III (Isa 14:28–29); and the official accession of "his son Hezekiah" is thus dated to 727/726 B.C. (cf. comment on 31:1). Yet since Ahaz's sixteen-year reign actually terminated in 728, it would appear that popular dissatisfaction must have forced his abdication and Hezekiah's assumption of de facto rule at least a year prior to the end of the king's life (cf. 2Ki 18:9–10). Correspondingly, even though Ahaz "rested with his fathers and was buried in . . . Jerusalem," his body "was not placed in the tombs of the kings" (see comment on 24:25).

13. Hezekiah (29:1–32:33)

The twenty-nine-year reign (see comment on 29:1) of Ahaz's son Hezekiah was counted officially from 726 to 697 B.C. (see comment on 28:27). Hezekiah's trust in the Lord (2Ki 18:5) and strength of character, moreover, formed an exact antithesis to the apostasy and surrender to expediency that had stigmatized his father's rule. In the area of religion, where Ahaz had converted Jerusalem into a center for idolatry and its accompanying immoralities and atrocities, Hezekiah's first official act was to cleanse the Lord's temple of its pollution (ch. 29). He celebrated an epoch-making Passover (ch. 30); and he campaigned far and wide to stamp out the idolatrous high places and to establish the pure religion of the OT (ch. 31). Then in the area of politics, where Ahaz had shortsightedly surrendered himself and his kingdom to the empire of Assyria, Hezekiah planned and fought for Judah's welfare and freedom—not always wisely, but with eventual success (ch. 32).

1 Hezekiah's "twenty-nine year" reign includes a divinely granted extension of fifteen years (2Ki 20:6), revealed to him in his fourteenth year (712 B.C., 18:13; 20:1), just before Merodach-Baladan's embassy, and embracing God's promise to deliver Jerusalem from Assyria (an event that occurred eleven years later, in 701). The king's recorded accession is thus placed at 726; for even though this specification leaves a technical interregnum (actually, a regency by Hezekiah; cf. 2Ki 18:1) that lasted over a year following the removal of Ahaz (see comment on 2Ch 28:27), it also allows for Hezekiah, whose age was then twenty-five, to have been born when his father was about thirteen (cf. comment on 28:1).

2 Hezekiah not only did "what was right," but he so trusted in the Lord (cf. Isa 26:3–4) that "there was no one like him among all the kings of Judah, either before him or after him" (2Ki 18:5).

3 "The first year of his reign" must refer to the one that followed his official accession in 726 rather than to the one at the time of his rise to power two years before (see comments on v.1; 28:27). "His first month" would then have been March/April 725. He then "opened the doors of the temple," which had been shut up by the apostate Ahaz (v.7; 28:24), "and repaired them," a project that included overlaying them with gold (2Ki 18:16).

4 After this initial act, the king's cleansing of the temple proceeded through four stages: (1)

reconsecrating the Levitical personnel (vv.4–14); (2) directing them to purify the temple itself (vv.15–19); (3) rededicating the sanctuary and altar (vv.20–30); and (4) encouraging the populace to renew their presentation of sacrifices (vv.31–36). To institute the first stage, he assembled the priests and Levites "in the square on the east side," presumably in the wide space in front of the temple (Ezr 10:9).

5 Concerning the Levites consecrating themselves (also in v.15), see comment on 1Ch 15:12.

6–11 The places to which Hezekiah could say that God had scattered the sons of Judah "in captivity" (v.9) included Damascus, Samaria, Edom, and Philistia (28:5, 8, 17–18). What the king desired is summed up as "a covenant" renewal (see comment on 15:12). Hezekiah proceeded to address the Levites and priests paternalistically as "my sons." He reminded the former that God had chosen them to serve him (Nu 3:7–8; Dt 10:8) and the latter that they possessed the special function of "burning incense" or, more properly rendering the Hebrew, of offering sacrifices (cf. v.21).

12–14 Kohath, Merari, and Gershon were the three clans that made up the tribe of Levi (1Ch 6:1). Separate mention, however, is given to "Elizaphan," a man who had been the leader of the Kohathites in the days of Moses (Nu 3:30) and whose family had subsequently developed to almost assume the status of a subclan (cf. 1Ch 15:8). "Asaph," "Heman," and "Jeduthun" were the founders of the three families of the Levitical musicians (1Ch 25).

15 Hezekiah's orders for cleansing the temple are said to have followed "the word of the LORD," for they were issued in conformity to the inspired Mosaic law (cf. Dt 12:2–4).

16–17 When the priests are said to have "brought out ... everything unclean" that they found in the temple, this included not simply accumulated rubbish, but specifically the filthy idols and their accompanying equipment that King Ahaz had introduced (2Ki 16:15). The Levites then "carried it out to the Kidron Valley," east of the temple. This was the same place where Asa had burned his queen-grandmother's repulsive

Asherah object over a century and a half before (cf. comment on 15:16).

18–19 The faithless "Ahaz" had "removed," and even partially destroyed, "the articles" used in the Lord's worship (28:24; 2Ki 16:17).

20–22 On the "sin offering" and its ritual that marked the temple's rededication, see Lev 4:1–5:13. On the sprinkling of the blood of the slain animals, see Lev 17:6; Nu 18:17.

23 For the assembly to lay their hands on the goats of the sin offering was to designate these as substitutes for their own lives and to transfer their sins to the animal victims (Nu 27:18–21; cf. 8:18–19). The goats thus served as types of Christ's death in the sinner's stead (2Co 5:21).

24 The blood of the slaughtered offerings was effective "to atone for all Israel" (as in Lev 4:13; 16:30). The verb Ezra used (GK 4105) means basically to "appease" or "pacify" (Ge 32:20; Pr 16:14), and hence to avert punishment by paying a ransom. Ultimately what saved the Israelites was their anticipation of Christ's death on the cross, who bore the wrath of God that had been incurred by all human beings as sinners (Mk 10:45; Ro 3:25).

25–26 On the "instruments" of David, see comment on 1Ch 23:5.

27–30 On the "burnt offering," see Lev 1. The Hebrew that lies behind the phrase "singing to the LORD" is literally "the song of the LORD," which suggests a specific writing, i.e., perhaps including the canonical Psalms that were then available for use in worship. By Hezekiah's day this would have included the Psalter's Davidic Books I and IV and its Solomonic Book II (Pss 42–72). Also mentioned are some of the compositions "of Asaph the seer" (whose name appears with Pss 50; 73–83).

31–33 Concerning the final resumption of sacrifice (cf. v.4 comment), the Chronicler observes that those who were particularly "willing brought burnt offerings" (v.31); for these were wholly consumed on the altar. In contrast were the more numerous "sacrifices" (the "consecrated" offerings of v.33, or "fellowship offerings" of v.35), which were largely eaten by the sacrificers in feasts that followed the services of presentation (cf.

comment on 1Ch 29:21). The "thank offerings" were a subcategory within the fellowship offerings (Lev 7:12–15).

34 The lower-ranked Levites, somewhat surprisingly (see 24:5; Eze 48:11), now showed themselves "more conscientious . . . than the priests" (but cf. 30:3 and the lack of principle evinced by the high priest Uriah only nine years before this, 2Ki 16:10–11). The truest faith is often found among the humble; and throughout history "professional" religious leaders have too often been among those least willing to submit to Christ and to the Word (cf. Jn 7:48).

35 The choice, and burnable, "fat of the fellowship offerings" was presented to God on the altar prior to the time of the people's feasting. On the "drink offerings," see Nu 15:5, 7, 10.

36 Thus Hezekiah and the people rejoiced at what the Lord had brought about, for in the last analysis all spiritual achievements find their origin in God's grace (30:12; 1Ki 18:37; Ac 11:18).

30:1 Chapter 30 concerns Hezekiah's epoch-making Passover Feast: first the preparations for it (vv.1–12) and then its observance (vv.13–27). The king "sent word" throughout Judah, but also sent letters inviting Ephraim and Manasseh, i.e., Israel, to come to Jerusalem for its celebration. Any such compliance had been prohibited during the two centuries that had followed Jeroboam's division of the Solomonic empire (vv.5, 26; 1Ki 12:27–28). But now King Hoshea's capital in Samaria was subject to Assyrian siege (v.6; 2Ki 17:5), and the northern ruler was powerless to interfere. The Assyrians, furthermore, would probably have encouraged anything that suggested defection from their rebelling vassal. The sincerity of Hezekiah's concern for Israel is suggested by his subsequent naming of his son and crown prince Manasseh.

2 A Passover celebrated in the second month would be a month late. But such a delay had been authorized by Moses himself when circumstances made it necessary (Nu 9:10–11), as was indeed the case here (cf. 2Ch 29:17).

3–5 The people were not able to celebrate the Passover during the first month (29:3), and particularly on its prescribed fourteenth day (cf. 29:17). Concerning the priests' not consecrating themselves, see comments on 29:34 and 1Ch 15:12. That the feast "had not been celebrated in large numbers" (v.5) meant, among other things, celebrated as a united kingdom (see v.1).

6–9 The ruler wrote, "Come to the sanctuary" (v.8); Passover was one of the three annual pilgrimage feasts that required the presence of every male at the temple (see comment on 1Ch 23:31). His word of assurance that their exiled brothers "will be shown compassion ... and will come back" was based on this same prediction, as made by Moses (Lev 26:40–42).

10–12 Many of the northerners—particularly those of Ephraim—still "scorned and ridiculed" the king's appeal (but see vv.11, 18): human depravity is so total that people will resist a gospel call even on the brink of disaster (cf. Am 4:10; Rev 9:20).

13 The "Feast of Unleavened Bread" continued for a full seven days beyond the actual date of the Passover (Lev 23:5–6). It served to remind the Israelites of their hasty departure from Egypt and of their perpetual need to maintain lives separated from sin (Ex 12:11, 34; 1Co 5:7).

14 Jerusalem's idolatrous "altars" (28:24) were thrown "into the Kidron Valley" (cf. comment on 15:16; 29:16).

15 The ceremony of the "slaughtered ... Passover lamb" functioned as (1) a memorial to God's past deliverance of Israel from the tenth plague in Egypt (Ex 12:27); (2) a symbol of his present and continuing claim over sinners, which was met by a rite of redemption (Ex 13:15); and (3) a type of his future, ultimate justification for his people procured through the substitutionary death of Christ, the Lamb of God (1Co 5:7). The religious leaders apparently were put to shame by the zeal of some of the people and responded accordingly.

16 "The priests sprinkled the blood" as it was "handed to them by the Levites," though normally it would have been presented to them directly by the head of each household (cf. Lev 1:11).

17 But here "the Levites had to kill the Passover lambs," because "many in the crowd had not consecrated themselves," so that they could not stand before God in ritual purity (cf. Nu 9:6). The value of the sacrificial service, as a propitiation of God, depended on its typifying the perfect ransom of Christ (Heb 9:14).

18–20 "Yet they [did eat] the Passover": because of Hezekiah's prayer of intercession, the people were to this extent enabled to share in the feast. If they really sought God in their hearts, their failures in regard to outward conformity—at least on this first occasion—could be "healed" (v.20; GK 8324), i.e., pardoned. The situation reflects the biblical principle that faith takes precedence over ritual (Jn 7:22–23; 9:14–16).

21–23 The extension of "the festival" for "seven more days" (v.23) parallels the way Solomon joined a special seven-day celebration for dedicating the temple with the regular week for the fall Feast of Tabernacles (see comment on 7:9).

24 The generous quantity of animals provided by the king and his officials for the fellowship offerings (see comment on 29:31) may even have contributed to the decision to extend the feast. The Chronicler's combined totals of two thousand bulls and seventeen thousand sheep, have been criticized as too big. Yet on a similar (but less hurried) occasion, King Josiah and his officials were able to provide twice this number (35:7–9).

25–27 The phrase "the priests and the Levites" (v.27) may here be rendered as "the Levitical priests," since these were the priests whom Moses had authorized "to bless the people" (Nu 6:23–27; cf. Lev 9:22).

31:1 Chapter 31 moves on to describe Hezekiah's campaign to eradicate Canaanite idolatry from Israel and to reestablish true OT religion. The majority of its contents (vv.4–19) concern the king's efforts to ensure material support for the Levites, who constituted the nation's religious personnel. Only the opening sentence (v.1a) finds a parallel in 2 Kings (18:4); but just as in the Chronicler's two previous chapters (cf. introduction to ch. 29), this lack furnishes no warrant for questioning its authenticity. In his reforms the king had the support of his contemporary Judean prophets, Micah and Isaiah (Isa 13–27 applies particularly to Hezekiah's reign between 728 and 712 B.C.). They were respected by the kings (32:20; cf. 2Ki 19:2; Jer 26:18–19), and their writings illumine the entire period (cf. Isa 22:1–14; 24:1–13).

The monarch's crusade in Judah against "the Asherah poles" and "the high places" is attested by the summary in 2Ki 18:4a. He was also compelled to destroy Nehushtan, the brazen serpent of Moses, which the people had perverted into an object of idolatry (18:4b). His campaign extended northward as well; for some of the Ephraimites had repented, after two centuries of apostasy (30:11, 18), and the presence of Assyrian troops rendered those who remained obdurate incapable of opposing Hezekiah.

2 The Hebrew for Hezekiah's assigning the priests to divisions is definite: he "appointed *the* divisions of the priests" (NASB, emphasis mine). He reestablished the twenty-four rotating courses (see comment on 8:14; 23:4) that had been set up by David (1Ch 25) to ensure orderly worship. The word used for the Lord's "dwelling" (lit., "camp"; GK 4722) reflects the desert situation under Moses (see comment on 1Ch 9:18).

3 Just as Solomon had done (see comment on 2:4), "the king contributed" the regular "burnt offerings" for the temple. Specifications in this regard had, indeed, been set forth by Moses (Nu 28–29). Concerning "the morning and evening burnt offerings" and those for the "appointed feasts," see comment on 1Ch 23:29–31.

4 Remuneration for "the priests" was derived primarily from certain designated parts of the sacrifices (cf. Lev 6–7) and from "the best of the firstfruits of your soil" (Ex 23:19; cf. Nu 18:12), while that for the "Levites" came from tithes that were contributed by the other tribes (Lev 27:30–33; Nu 18:21–24; cf. v.5). They "could devote themselves" to God's work, unhindered by secular pursuits, only if they received these portions regularly (cf. Ne 13:10).

5 Though the other commodities listed among the dedicated "firstfruits" could be used in Israel's offerings, the "honey" could not, even in the grain offerings that accompanied the other (animal) sacrifices (Lev 2:11). But it was still an acceptable gift for supporting the priests.

6 The "tithe of the holy things" may be a general term for these token portions of the offerings that became the property of the priests who presented them (cf. Nu 8:8–11).

7–8 The Israelites began bringing their contributions "in the third month" (May/June), the time of the Feast of Pentecost and of the grain harvest (Ex 23:16a), and they finished in the seventh month (Sept./Oct.), the time of the Feast of Tabernacles and of the ingathering of the fruit and vine harvests at the end of the agricultural year (Ex 23:16b).

9–10 The high priest Azariah III (also mentioned at the end of v.13; cf. 1Ch 6:4) is probably not the Azariah (II) who resisted Uzziah (2Ch 26:17) almost thirty years prior to this.

11–13 Conaniah's office (v.12) dated back to David, who had first organized some of the temple gatekeepers so as to have charge of the dedicated gifts (see 1Ch 26:20, 26).

14 The gatekeeper "Kore" (cf. 1Ch 9:19) was the Levite responsible for "distributing the contributions"—whether of the "consecrated gifts" (cf. v.4) or of the additional "freewill offerings"—to their legitimate priestly recipients (Lev 7:14).

15 Deputy administrators carried out a final distribution locally, "in the towns of the priests," as these had been determined by Joshua, throughout the tribes of Israel (Jos 21:9–19). A more precise rendering of the statement that they "assisted him faithfully" might be that they "assisted him in their positions of trust" (cf. 1Ch 9:22).

16 Portions were granted to "males three years old or more . . . who would enter the temple to perform the . . . various tasks." Assignments for work within the operational units of the Levites had originally been based on a minimum age of thirty (1Ch 23:3); but if there is not a copyist's error here, the priests' children as young as three must have accompanied their fathers in the service and so received their portions, directly, in the temple.

17 Such reestablished distributions obviously gave a renewed, practical significance to "the genealogical records." On the reasons for service by "Levites twenty years old or more," see comment on 1Ch 23:24.

18 Thus Kore and his associates consecrated themselves, and the Hebrew adds "in holiness" (GK 7731). It was no light responsibility, particularly in view of the numbers of women and children involved (cf. Ac 6:1), as they fulfilled "their positions of trust" (cf. comment on v.15).

19–21 "In everything" the king "worked wholeheartedly" (v.21), in obedience to the law of Moses; "so he prospered" (cf. 2Ki 18:6–7).

32:1–3 After recounting all of Hezekiah's religious reforms (chs. 29–31), the Chronicler summarizes his political activity, generally on the assumption of the reader's knowledge of the more detailed accounts that are found in 2Ki 18:7–20:21 and Isa 36–39. He records how in 701 B.C. Sennacherib king of Assyria "invaded Judah"; but behind this deed lay a whole sequence of events.

Assyrian domination had come about in 734, through the specific invitation of Hezekiah's father, Ahaz (28:20–21). In 715 Ashdod and certain other Palestinian states had rebelled, urged on by Egypt (cf. 2Ki 17:4) and by Babylon; for Ezra also records the latter's embassy to Hezekiah (2Ch 32:31). But in 711 the Assyrians resubdued Ashdod (Isa 14:28–31, 20:1); and Hezekiah yielded to the will of God (20:2–6) by submitting to Sargon II, who called himself the subjugator of Judah.

On Sargon's death in 705, Hezekiah disregarded the Lord's word through Isaiah and became involved in plots with Egypt (Isa 30:1–5; 31:1–3). He assumed leadership in a western revolt and even imprisoned the Philistine king of Ekron, who had refused cooperation (2Ki 18:8). The result was the invasion by Sargon's son Sennacherib. His "thinking to conquer" Judah's "fortified cities" did in fact succeed (2Ki 18:13; Isa 36:1), except in the case of Jerusalem.

4–5 To aid in their capital's defense, the Hebrews blocked all the springs, especially the Gihon (see v.30), directly east of city, "and the stream that flowed" from it into Jerusalem. Concerning the king's "reinforced supporting terraces," see NIV note; comment on 1Ch 11:8.

6–7 The Hebrew words for "he . . . encouraged them" are literally "he spoke to their heart." The king's statement that "there is

greater power with us than with" Sennacherib recalls an earlier assurance made by Elisha (2Ki 6:16); it reflects the basic meaning of the name of Israel's covenant God, Yahweh ("He is present [with us]," Ex 3:12, 14; cf. Isa 7:14; Mt 1:23).

8 Hezekiah's disparagement of the Assyrian, that "with him is only the arm of flesh," seems traceable to Isaiah (Isa 31:3), and was later quoted by Jeremiah (Jer 17:5). But Hezekiah's own "hard work" (v.5) had been criticized by Isaiah (Isa 22:9–10) because of the king's reliance on human beings rather than on the Lord (22:11; 30:15–16). In his annals for 701, Sennacherib was thus able to boast that he "shut up [the king] like a caged bird inside Jerusalem"; that Hezekiah was deserted by his Arabian mercenaries and compelled to release Sennacherib's pro-Assyrian Philistine vassal so as to be restored to his throne in Ekron; and finally that Hezekiah himself had to capitulate, paying a huge indemnity and surrendering over two hundred thousand captives to Assyria. These facts are assumed without comment in Chronicles, though the last two elements are elaborated by other Scriptures.

9–11 "Later," i.e., after Hezekiah's payment of the stipulated tribute (2Ki 18:14), the treacherous Assyrian proceeded to scrap the just negotiated peace treaty (cf. Isa 33:7–8), to lay "siege to Lachish," twenty-five miles southwest of Jerusalem, and to make further demands on the beleaguered Hezekiah. To enforce them Sennacherib "sent his officers," including his supreme commander (2Ki 18:17), with a large army "to Jerusalem." In view of the final results (v.21), it is not surprising that Sennacherib's annals say nothing further about this later aspect to his campaign. Indeed, the very insolence of his message that follows (cf. vv.10–15 with 2Ki 18:19–25, 28–35; Isa 36:4–10, 13–20) begins to provide justification for the stirring hopes expressed earlier by Hezekiah (vv.7–8; cf. v.11).

12 By his question, "Did not Hezekiah himself remove this god's high places?" Sennacherib must have been hoping to take advantage of any popular dissatisfaction that was felt against Hezekiah's reforms.

13–15 More straightforward was Sennacherib's blasphemy against the Lord—as if

God were no more "able to save his people" from Assyria than had been the false deities of those nations that the aggressor's ancestors had already destroyed (cf. v.19; Isa 10:15).

16–19 "Sennacherib's officers spoke further against the LORD," excerpts of which appear in vv.18–19 (cf. the fuller record in 2Ki 18:27–35). Sennacherib "also wrote letters," since he had had to withdraw his troops attacking Jerusalem (see comment on v.9) to meet an advance by an Egyptian force under Tirhakah, younger brother of the current Twenty-Fifth Dynasty ruler and himself later to become Pharaoh, from 690 to 664 B.C. (2Ki 19:8–9).

20 For details on the anguished pleas and yet ringing affirmations of faith with which Hezekiah and Isaiah "cried out in prayer," see 2Ki 19:1–7, 14–34. This verse, it should be noted, is the only reference in Chronicles to the deeds of the prophet Isaiah (26:22 and 32:32 refer to his writings about Uzziah and Hezekiah).

21–23 Then "an angel . . . annihilated all the fighting men . . . of the Assyrian king," specifically, 185,000 in one night (2Ki 19:35). The proposal has been advanced that a plague carried by rodents was what struck down the invaders. This is based on an Egyptian legend—which does confirm the general fact of a miraculous deliverance—that Tirhakah (and Hezekiah) owed victory to field mice that ate up the Assyrians' weapons.

But while God can indeed make use of natural means for delivering his elect (cf. Ex 14:21; 1Sa 6:4), the rapidity and intensity of this disaster render the plague proposal inadequate as an explanation for what happened in 701 B.C. The event ranks, in fact, with Israel's crossing of the Red Sea as one of the two greatest examples of the Lord's intervention to save his people. So Sennacherib "withdrew to his own" land and was slain (2Ki 19:36–37; Isa 37–38).

24 "In those days"—fifteen years before his actual death (2Ki 20:6), or in 712—Hezekiah, seriously ill, prayed. "The LORD . . . answered him," promising him recovery (2Ki 20:4–6), "and gave him a miraculous sign" of the shadow that moved backward (2Ki 20:8–11).

25–26 "But Hezekiah's heart was proud" (cf. v.31); and the result was "the LORD's wrath," as declared through Isaiah's threat of impending exile to Babylon (2Ki 20:16–18; Isa 39:6–7). But because "Hezekiah repented . . . the LORD's wrath did not come upon them" in his days (cf. 2Ki 20:19; Isa 39:8; Jer 26:19).

27–30 To ensure a permanent water supply within his capital's walls, "Hezekiah . . . channeled" the flow of "the Gihon spring" through a 1,700 foot tunnel cut into the rock beneath Jerusalem (v.30). Archaeological confirmation of this engineering feat came in 1880, with the discovery, at its lower portal, of the Siloam Inscription, written in old Hebrew by the very workers who accomplished it.

31 The envoys of Babylon, to which Ezra here refers, were those sent by Marduk-apaliddina, the Merodach-Baladan of 2Ki 20:12–13. Their mission appears to have been not simply to inquire about the king's illness and about its accompanying "miraculous sign" (v.24)—of understandable interest to astrologers such as the Babylonians—but also to

Water still flows through the tunnel that Hezekiah built to bring water from the Gihon Spring into the city of Jerusalem.

arrange practical measures against Sargon's aggression, which did overpower Ashdod and the West in the following year and drove Marduk-apal-iddina from his throne in the East two years after that. The experience served "to test" (GK 5814) Hezekiah, whether he would place his trust in human treaties or in God; and it was his eagerness for the treaties that incurred the Lord's wrath (v.25).

32 Ezra's description of his main literary source as being "the vision of the prophet Isaiah" (cf. Isa 1:1) "in the book of the kings" (cf. 20:34) indicates that at least chs. 36–39 of Isaiah (which are reproduced within 2Ki 18–20) must have been incorporated into that larger court chronicle from which both he and the writer of Kings, prior to him, were accustomed to draw.

33 The NIV translation that Hezekiah was buried "on the hill where the tombs . . . are" is literally, "in the going up [or ascent] of the tombs." But this expression could as well be rendered "in the upper section of the tombs," on the hypothesis of some additional excavation at a higher level, when the lower tombs had become occupied.

14. Manasseh (33:1–20)

Manasseh, evil son of the godly Hezekiah, had the longest reign of all the Hebrew monarchs, from 697 to 642 B.C.; and he more than any other single person was responsible for the final destruction of the kingdom of Judah (2Ki 23:26; 24:3; Jer 15:4). Most of his fifty-five-year reign was devoted to thoroughgoing paganism, religiously, and to a renewed subjection to Assyria, politically. This part of his record (vv.1–10) closely parallels its literary source in 2Ki 21:1–10. During his closing years, a personal crisis did bring back Manasseh to repentance; but it was too late to produce a significant national effect (2Ch 33:11–20). Most of this material, moreover, is unique to the Chronicler.

1–3 Concerning the "high places . . . Baals, and . . . Asherah" poles, see comments on 14:3; 17:3. The king's apostate worship of "the starry host" had evil precedents going as far back as the time of Moses (Dt 4:19; Ac 7:42), but such practices were a particular sin of Assyro-Babylonians, with their addiction to astrology. Whether the Assyrians made it a policy to force their religion on the nations that became subject to their empire is open to question (cf. 28:23), but it is a fact that when Sennacherib's son Esarhaddon advanced westward against Egypt, Manasseh did weakly submit himself to him, in 676, which must have provided some stimulus for the astral worship in Judah.

4–5 On the Lord's "Name" remaining in Jerusalem forever, see comments on 1Ch 22:7; 2Ch 6:2, 6; on the two temple "courts," see comment on 2Ch 4:9.

6 Manasseh "sacrificed his sons in the fire in the Valley of Ben Hinnom," just as his grandfather Ahaz had (28:3); and he "practiced sorcery," etc., attempting to communicate with the dead by using "mediums"—which Scripture uniformly condemns as contrary to faith in God (Ex 22:18; Dt 18:10–12). The Hebrew word for "spiritist" (GK 3362) is literally "a knowing one." It referred originally to ghosts, who were supposed to possess superhuman knowledge; but it came to be applied to those who claimed power to summon them forth, i.e., to witches. The king also engaged in tyranny, shedding "much innocent blood" (2Ki 21:16).

7–9 The Lord had promised not to remove the Israelites but stipulated: "if only they will . . . do everything I commanded them . . . through Moses" (see comment on 7:14, 19).

10 "The LORD spoke" to Judah by "his servants the prophets," threatening their destruction (2Ki 21:10–15); "but they paid no attention."

11 The occasion on which "the king of Assyria . . . took Manasseh prisoner . . . to Babylon" may have arisen in the year 648, when Ashurbanipal finally overcame a revolt that had been led in that city for four years by his own brother. Egypt, under a new dynasty (the twenty-sixth), had taken this opportunity to escape the Assyrian yoke; and Manasseh may have been tempted to try the same thing. But because Judah lay closer to Assyria, or because it lacked Egypt's greater resources, this attempt failed.

12–13 In any event, "in his distress he . . . humbled himself greatly before God"; for it sometimes takes a crisis to drive a person to God and to become converted (cf. Ac 9:3–5).

14 On "Gihon" and "Ophel," see comments on 32:30; 27:3. The king's rebuilt fortifications extended as far as "the Fish Gate," in Jerusalem's north wall (Ne 3:3).

15–17 In his remaining years, Manasseh did what he could to reverse his years of apostasy. Ezra explains that "the people, however, continued to sacrifice at the high places," because half a century of paganism could not be counteracted by a half dozen years of reform. It is true that Judah presented the offerings "only to the LORD their God," but the high places were still contrary to Moses' law for a central sanctuary (cf. comment on 1:2–4). In practice, moreover, worship on those sites meant little more than applying a new name to the old Baal worship, with all its debased rites.

18–20 The king's "prayer to his God" is no longer preserved. This text did, however, provide a basis on which someone shortly before the time of Christ composed the fifteen verses that make up the apocryphal Prayer of Manasseh, a book that appears in some manuscripts of the LXX.

15. Amon (33:21–25)

The remainder of ch. 33 deals with the brief reign of Manasseh's son Amon (642–640 B.C.). This man was the reflection of his father's essentially pagan life, not of his repentant last years and death. Under the new king, Judah quickly relapsed into the superstitious practices of Manasseh before his conversion. After only two years Amon died at the hands of his own courtiers. His record follows and somewhat abbreviates its earlier source in 2Ki 21:19–26.

21–23 When the Chronicler says that "Amon worshiped . . . all the idols Manasseh had made," this seems to suggest either that their removal (v.15a) had not involved their destruction, or that Manasseh's concentration on bringing about reform in Jerusalem (v.15b) had left intact those relics of his former paganism that characterized the local high places (v.17).

24–25 Concerning "the people of the land," who took vengeance on Amon's assassins and restored order to Judah, see comment on 23:13.

16. Josiah (34:1–35:27)

In contrast to his father, Amon, Josiah proved to be a good king over the people of Judah (640–609 B.C.). He was the last such, sad to say; but he was also in some respects their greatest (v.2). Josiah instituted the most thorough of all the OT reforms, dating to 622, and one that restored Israel's commitment to God's book. It was this faith in holy Scripture that was then able to keep the nation's hope alive during the Exile through most of the succeeding century (cf. Da 9:2), during the difficult century of restoration that followed (Ezr 7:10; Mal 4:4), and during the next four hundred, silent years until the appearance of John the Baptist (Mal 3:1; 4:5–6) and the kingdom of Jesus the Messiah, God's personal Word, who fulfilled the written Word (Mt 5:17–18).

Within 2 Chronicles Josiah's record occupies the two chapters that immediately precede the closing chapter of the book; and they deal with four primary topics: (1) the earlier stages of the king's reforms (34:1–7); (2) the great reformation that occurred in the eighteenth year of his reign, beginning with the repair of the Jerusalem temple and climaxing with the discovery of the Mosaic Book of the Law and with Judah's responses to it (34:8–33); (3) Josiah's unsurpassed Passover observance (35:1–19); and (4) his tragic death (35:20–27).

1–2 Josiah "did what was right," particularly in his devotion to "all the Law of Moses" (2Ki 23:25), so that in this respect (see comment on 29:2, on the "trust" that was Hezekiah's area of strength) "neither before nor after Josiah was there a king like him" (2Ki 23:25).

3 In the "eighth year" of his rule, in 632 B.C., when "he was still young," just sixteen, he began to seek the Lord personally; and in his "twelfth year," in 628, he began to purify Judah nationally of its high places and related paganisms (see 33:3). The latter date identifies a particular time of chaos that occurred throughout the ancient Near East, one that was precipitated by an invasion from the north of barbaric, nomadic horsemen known as the Scythians (628–626 B.C.). Their incursions wrought terror among complacent Jews (Jer 6:22–24; Zep 1:12); and, though they never actually raided much beyond the open plains of coastal Palestine—where they were eventually stopped by the Egyptians—they did produce two major effects that concerned Judah.

(1) In the area of religion, the Scythian presence seems to have conditioned the calls of the contemporary prophets Jeremiah (Jer 1:2, 14) and Zephaniah (Zep 1:2, which refers to local Judean threats, vv.3–4). It further correlates with the above noted second stage of Josiah's revival; but this latter went far beyond the momentary fear usually associated with superficial "fox-hole" type religion (cf. 2Ch 34:3–7).

(2) In the area of politics, the Scythian hordes succeeded in sweeping away the Assyrian imperial domination that had been Judah's nemesis throughout the preceding half century. Indeed, after Ashurbanipal's death about 631, and as a result of the barbarian tidal wave in 628, the way was cleared for Josiah to reestablish a united kingdom of Israel to the extent that it had occupied when it had first chosen David almost three centuries before. Whether the king's achievement of political freedom involved a corresponding religious repudiation of Assyrian idolatry is open to question; only Canaanite forms appear as the objects of Josiah's purge.

4 The term for "idols" means ones "cut out, carved," while the "images" were "cast."

5–7 Josiah's campaign against idolatry included not simply Judah and Jerusalem, but extended also into "Manasseh" and "Ephraim," just as Hezekiah's reform had a century earlier. On "Simeon" see the introductory discussion to 1Ch 4:24–43. That Josiah's endeavor "reached as far as Naphtali" in Galilee shows that he recovered most of the formerly Assyrian province of Israel (cf. v.9), a fact that is archaeologically attested by seventh-century inscriptions from the land itself.

8 On Joah's position as "recorder," see comment on 1Ch 18:15. "Shaphan" is identified in 2Ki 22:8 as "secretary" (see comment on 1Ch 18:16).

9–10 The officials gave Hilkiah the high priest the money the Levitical doorkeepers had collected from the people of Ephraim, etc. Presumably the people brought the silver as far as the temple gate (2Ki 22:4)—perhaps to deposit it in a chest similar to the one once provided by King Joash (see 2Ch 24:8); the Levites collected it from there.

11–13 The builders did the work so faithfully that no audit was required (2Ki 22:7), just as had been true under Joash (2Ki 12:15).

14–15 At this point in the year 622, Hilkiah found "the Book of the Law"—called the "Book of the Covenant" in v.30, which suggests Ex 19–24 (cf. 24:7). Yet the curses that the book contained (2Ch 34:24) suggests Lev 26 and Dt 28; and the ensuing stress on the central sanctuary (2Ki 23:8–9) implies Dt 12. "The Book" thus was at the least the book of Deuteronomy. It is called "the covenant" in Dt 29:1, for example. It contained the curses (Dt 28); it alone called for a central sanctuary that was stored at the temple, usually by the side of the ark (Dt 31:25–26). "The Book" seems to have become misplaced during the apostate administrations of the previous kings, Manasseh and Amon, under whom the ark had been moved about (2Ch 35:3).

The book is described as "the Law of the LORD that had been given through Moses" (lit., "by the hand of" Moses). For though all the passages in the Pentateuch do not claim to have been written down (cf. Ex 17:14; 24:4; 34:27; Lev 18:5 [Ro 10:5]; Nu 33:2; Dt 31:9, 22) or even spoken by Moses (compare Dt 33 with 34), Scripture is nevertheless clear that all its contents do belong to a historical period no later than his (Dt 4:2; 12:32), and that they were composed under the guidance of Moses. Indeed, our Lord declared that those who refuse to believe Moses' words cannot consistently accept his own either (Jn 5:47).

16–19 In response to hearing what was written in "the Book," the king "tore his robes," personally convicted by the immediate and terrifying relevance of threats such as those inscribed in Dt 28:36 (cf. Lev 26:32–33; 2Ch 34:21, 24, 27), prophecies that were "written there concerning us" (2Ki 22:13).

20–22 Ezra's almost casual reference to the "Huldah" prophetess indicates how foreign the idea of discrimination based on sex was to the spirit of the OT (cf. Jdg 4:4; 2Sa 20:16). Huldah's location in the second district can no longer be identified; but the name suggests one of the extensions to Jerusalem, either to the north or to the west.

23–25 The Lord confirmed that he would "bring disaster on . . . Judah," that he would "not turn away from the heat of his fierce anger . . . because of all that Manasseh had done to provoke him" (2Ki 23:26).

26–28 Josiah, however, was told that his eyes would "not see all the disaster" (v.28). Postponements of divine wrath had been granted previously to King Hezekiah (cf. on 32:26) and even to King Ahab of Israel (1Ki 21:29), when they too displayed humility and repentance. Josiah would "be buried in peace," i.e., before the disastrous fall of Judah that constitutes the point at issue here. Though the king was buried in honor, he did, in fact, die from battle wounds (35:23–24).

29–31 "The covenant" that Josiah "renewed" was the one contained in the Book of the Covenant, specifically the revelation of God's older testament—the pre-Christian revelation that was the Lord's eternal instrument for the redemption of his elect people. During this rite in the temple, the king stood "by his pillar," as in 23:13.

32–33 The Chronicler reports briefly that "Josiah removed all detestable idols." For more details on his thorough purging of the land of its high places—with their accompanying immoralities—of its astral worship, of its spiritism, and of its other paganisms, see 2Ki 23:4–14, 24. His field of action included "all the territory belonging to the Israelites" (cf. its enumeration by tribes in v.6). In particular the king destroyed the altar of Jeroboam I at Bethel, along with the other high places of Samaria, and he killed such of the priests as remained (2Ki 23:15–20, exactly as had been predicted in 1Ki 13:2, over three hundred years before).

In summary Ezra says of the Israelites under Josiah that "as long as he lived, they did not fail to follow the LORD." Yet the testimony of Jeremiah, who actively supported the king's reform (Jer 11:1–5), shows that for many this "following" may have consisted more in external compliance than in commitment from the heart (11:9–13).

35:1 The Chronicler's third major topic concerning the reign of Josiah (cf. introduction to chs. 34–35) describes how the king celebrated a great Passover (35:1–19). Its observance served to provide a public confirmation to his reform as a whole; it resulted, indeed, from Judah's obedience to that same rediscovered divine Law, "as it is written in the Book of the Covenant" (2Ki 23:21). "The first month," to which the celebration is dated, is March/April within Josiah's climactic eighteenth year (2Ch 35:18), namely 622 B.C.; contrast the way in which Hezekiah had had to postpone the keeping of his Passover to the second month (cf. 30:2).

2–3 On the teaching office of Judah's "Levites," see comment on 17:7. Josiah told them to "put the sacred ark in the temple," because during the dark days of Manasseh and Amon (33:7; cf. 28:24) it seems to have been removed by these faithful ministers and carried elsewhere for its protection (cf. comment on 34:14).

4 Concerning their "divisions, according to the directions written by David . . . and by . . . Solomon," see 1Ch 24:4, 20; 2Ch 8:14.

5–6 By directing the Levites to "slaughter the Passover lambs," the king continued the practice that had been worked out by Hezekiah (see comment on 30:17). Josiah's goal was to prevent the sort of confusion that had arisen during the more precipitous reform and Passover of his great-grandfather, some 103 years earlier (cf. 30:16–18).

7–9 The historicity of the quantities of animals provided by Josiah has been even more criticized than for those recorded in reference to Hezekiah's celebration (see comment on 30:24). Yet when one considers that Josiah had careful advanced planning, that the animals were prepared for "all Judah and Israel who were there," and that it was an unprecedented affair, which "none of the kings of Israel had ever celebrated . . . as did Josiah" (v.18), then his "thirty-thousand sheep and goats . . . and also three thousand cattle" appear to fall well within the category of the explainable. Furthermore, when compared with the numbers of sacrificial animals that the Chronicler quotes from other Scriptures (cf. 2Ch 7:5's citation of 1Ki 8:63, about Solomon's dedication of the temple as requiring 120,000 sheep and 22,000 cattle), his unique listing here for Josiah pales into relative insignificance.

While the flocks of sheep and goats provided for the paschal lambs, the cattle must have served for fellowship offerings, for the feasting throughout the days of Unleavened

Bread that followed the Passover (see comments 30:24; 1Ch 29:21).

10–15 Ezra's statement that "they set aside the burnt offerings" (v.12) suggests that the Levites saved certain choice parts of the Passover lambs "to offer to the LORD" (cf. v.14), somewhat after the pattern of the fellowship offerings (Lev 3). Then the people roasted and ate the Passover itself (as in Dt 16:7).

16–19 Concerning "the Feast of Unleavened Bread," see 30:13. To the time span of v.18, that "the Passover had not been observed like this . . . since the days of . . . Samuel," 2Ki 23:22 adds what could be an even longer interval, "since the days of the judges." The point is that Josiah's feast came up to the Bible's ceremonial standards as no others had since those in the era of Moses and Joshua.

20 The phrase "After all this" introduces Ezra's final topic on Josiah: the king's death, dated 609 B.C. The cause lay in a military advance by "Neco King of Egypt," a leading Pharaoh of the Twenty-Sixth Dynasty, as he made an active bid to succeed to the rule of the Assyrian Empire in the west. Nineveh had fallen three years before, in 612; and the Egyptians opposed the rival claims of Babylon by going up the Euphrates River "on behalf of" the king of Assyria (2Ki 23:29). Neco's immediate objective was to cross the river and retake the city of Haran. This town lay east of Carchemish, which constituted in its turn a key center on the westernmost bend of the Euphrates.

21 The Pharaoh addressed Josiah: "It is not you I am attacking"; for Neco desired, without further delay, to march along the Palestinian coast and so meet "the house with which I am at war," namely, the Babylonian army under the capable crown prince Nebuchadrezzar. His words for persuading Josiah, that "God has told me to hurry," would have had a special appeal for a godly king concerned about keeping God's word.

22 Josiah, like King Ahab at Ramoth Gilead, then "disguised himself" for protection against his fate (cf. 18:29). For though this next truth might have come as a surprise to the king, "what Neco had said" actually had come "at God's command." The Lord's consistent message to his people had been that they must rely on him and, correspondingly,

keep themselves from involvement in the international power politics of their day (cf. on 16:2, 9; 28:16; 32:1, 5).

The reality of the contest at "Megiddo" has received archaeological confirmation from the ruins of the site's Stratum II. This level belonged to an unwalled town during the time of Josiah, and it evidences a measure of contemporaneous destruction. Megiddo lies on the strategic pass through the ridge that separates Palestine's coastal plain from the Esdraelon Valley to its northeast. It has been the scene of key battles from the fifteenth century B.C. down to World War I. The conflict of the ages, against Christ at his second coming, will be joined at "Armageddon" (Rev 16:16)—lit. translated, "the mountain of Megiddo."

23–27 Josiah died in the conflict. "Jeremiah composed laments for Josiah," whom he highly esteemed (Jer 22:15–16). These dirges are then said to be "written in the Laments"—a book that is no longer extant and which must not be confused with the prophet's later laments over Josiah's sons (22:10, 20–30) or Jerusalem's fall (Lamentations).

17. Jehoahaz (36:1–4)

The reign of the godly king Josiah's son Jehoahaz lasted only three months (609 B.C.), following the death of his father in battle (35:24). But while the Chronicler includes no direct moral evaluation of Jehoahaz, the fuller account in 2Ki 23:30–35, which served as Ezra's source, makes it clear that the young sovereign "did evil in the eyes of the LORD" (v.32). He, in fact, established a pattern of wrongdoing that characterizes the rest of the kings who make up the subject of this concluding section of 2 Chronicles (12:1–36:16). As a mark of divine justice, it was the removal of Jehoahaz that marked the end of independent government in Israel.

1–2 At his accession in 609, Judah's new leader, Jehoahaz, "was twenty-three years old," which made him two years younger than King Jehoiakim, his brother, who succeeded him (v.5). The "people of the land"— its free citizens (see comment on 23:13)— apparently saw more hope in Jehoahaz than in his older brother. His three-month reign continued only till Pharaoh Neco (II) of Egypt could find opportunity to replace him (cf. 35:20–21).

3 Neco also "imposed on Judah" an indemnity of silver and gold (cf. similar amounts listed in 25:6; 27:5), amounting to about three and three-fourths tons and seventy-five pounds respectively.

4 The Egyptian changed the name of Jehoahaz's brother from "Eliakim," meaning "God raises up," to "Jehoiakim," which means "Jehovah (the LORD) raises up." This seems to indicate his willingness to continue the status of the religion of the Jews. More tangibly the Pharaoh's control over the king's name demonstrated his lordship over his person; indeed, it would be four and a half centuries before the Jews would again be able to exercise political freedom, under the Maccabees. Neco then carried Jehoahaz off to Egypt, where he died (2Ki 23:34; cf. Jer 22:10).

18. Jehoiakim (36:5–8)

The Chronicler's record about the kingship of Jehoahaz's older brother Jehoiakim (vv.5–8) again represents an abridgment of the previously written biblical history (2Ki 23:36–24:7). On this occasion Ezra does include a moral judgment against Judah's new ruler (v.5); and in the political sphere his reign (609–598 B.C.) marked the transference of the Hebrew kingdom from Egyptian control to its ultimately fatal Babylonian domination.

5 During his "eleven years" Jehoiakim "did evil." As explained in Ezra's more detailed sources, this king first taxed his land to provide tribute to the Pharaoh (2Ki 23:35)—though he himself lived in luxury (Jer 22:14–15). He perverted justice and oppressed the poor (Jer 22:13, 17); and he persecuted the prophets that God sent to reprove his sin (cf. 2Ch 36:8, 16; Jer 26:21–24; 32:36).

6 After four years the Babylonian leader "Nebuchadnezzar" (whose name is more accurately rendered as Nebuchadrezzar, see Jer 21:2 note) "attacked" westward. In the spring of 605, he and his forces won a decisive victory over Neco at Carchemish (cf. comment on 35:20; Jer 46:2). As a consequence the Egyptians were driven back to their own borders; and the whole western Fertile Crescent, including Palestine, was given into the hands of Nebuchadnezzar (2Ki 24:7). The victor proceeded to bind Jehoiakim "with bronze shackles" to carry him into captivity;

such a threat may, however, have been sufficiently effective to render unnecessary his actual removal to Babylon.

7 The fact that "Nebuchadnezzar took to Babylon articles from the temple," together with an initial captivity of selected Jewish hostages, including the prophet Daniel (cf. Da 1:1–3), marks the beginning of Israel's seventy-year Babylonian exile, 605–536 B.C. (Jer 29:10).

8 While Ezra refers only to his primary source (Israel's major court record) for "the other events of Jehoiakim's reign," it is known that these events included three years of serving Nebuchadnezzar (until 602), which were followed by a rebellion (2Ki 24:1–2). This presumably occurred in connection with a renewed rivalry between Egypt and Babylon, who fought a battle in the following year that resulted in a draw. Jehoiakim died on December 9, 598, just before his punishment could be meted out.

19. Jehoiachin (36:9–10)

In these two verses the Chronicler summarizes the more extensive data about the reign of Jehoiakim's young son, Jehoiachin, which is found in 2Ki 24:8–17. Like his uncle Jehoahaz of eleven years before (see 2Ch 36:1–4), the current world power permitted Jehoiachin to be king, but only for three months, at the close of 598 and at the beginning of 597 B.C. He thus reaped the bitter fruit of the rebellion that his father had instigated (see comment on v.8).

9 Since Jehoiachin had at least five children by the year 592 (see 1Ch 3:17), the variant reading (cf. NIV note) must be adopted, which says he "was eighteen years old when he became king"—not "eight." His reign of "three months and ten days" terminated on March 16, 597.

10 On April 22, 597, King Nebuchadnezzar had Jehoiachin deported from Jerusalem; he was "brought ... to Babylon" along with a second and more extensive deportation (see comment on v.7). This included the prophet Ezekiel and ten thousand of the leaders and skilled workers that made up the backbone of Jewish society (cf. 2Ki 24:10–16).

20. Zedekiah (36:11–16)

"Jehoiachin's uncle, Zedekiah" (v.10) was appointed to rule over the remnant of Judah by King Nebuchadnezzar of Babylon. As the last of the twenty monarchs of the southern kingdom, his eleven-year reign extended from 597 to 586 B.C. Through acts of infidelity toward his imperial master, he unwisely touched off the final revolt that brought down the vengeance of the Babylonians on Judah and Jerusalem; and thus both the state and the city were destroyed. Yet ultimately Nebuchadnezzar served only as an instrument for accomplishing the sentence of God against his guilty nation: "The wrath of the LORD was aroused against his people and there was no remedy" (v.16).

11 Being only "twenty-one" at the time of his appointment, Zedekiah was by far the youngest of Josiah's sons to occupy the throne (see 1Ch 3:15). Furthermore, though "he reigned in Jerusalem," the fact that seals have been discovered with the inscription "Eliakim steward of Yaukin" indicates that, at the least, his nephew Jehoiachin continued to wield influence as a recognized possessor, even if an absentee one, of royal property and, at the most, that Zedekiah may have ruled to some extent as a regent for his exiled predecessor.

12 The statement that Zedekiah "did not humble himself before Jeremiah" sums up a complex relationship that existed between the king and the prophet. Zedekiah first disregarded Jeremiah's messages (Jer 34:1–10); he came in time to direct his inquiries to this same prophet (Jer 21); and he finally pled with him for help (Jer 37). But at no point did he sincerely submit to the requirements of the Lord that Jeremiah transmitted to him. King Zedekiah was a weak man, largely controlled by a few vicious nobles who were left, along with the inferior remnant of Judah (Jer 38:1–5).

13–16 At the instigation of Hophra, a new Pharaoh (589–570 B.C.) of the Twenty-Sixth Dynasty in Egypt (cf. Jer 37:5; Eze 17:15), Zedekiah "rebelled against King Nebuchadnezzar, who had made him take an oath in God's name." Zedekiah had been bound as a vassal to the Babylonian monarch; and it was his faithlessness that became his own undoing (Eze 17:13–19).

C. The exile (36:17–23)

Unlike the book of Kings, with its central message of stern moral judgments, Chronicles exists essentially as a book of hope, grounded on the grace of our sovereign Lord. The chapters on Judah's rulers (12:1–36:16) describe some great military victories and reforms, which sprang out of faith in God, even in the midst of the nation's overall spiritual deterioration. Then after having demonstrated that the Lord could, and did, reject his people for their disobedience (36:17–21), the Chronicler moves on to identify the groundwork by which Judah's postexilic restoration was effectuated, through the Persian king Cyrus's decree of 538 B.C. (vv.22–23). Thus, in a repopulated land with a rebuilt temple—that still depicted God's changeless way of salvation—a nation refined by its trials could more adequately celebrate the Lord's continuing providence together with his anticipated triumph in the messianic kingdom that yet must come into being. History is a process, not of disintegration, but of sifting, selection, and of development. When decades of exile had removed the dross, a remnant of purer gold would respond to the appeal for return to the Promised Land: "The LORD his God be with him . . . let him go up" (2Ch 36:23)

17 On January 15, 588, the Lord "brought up" against Judah "the king of the Babylonians"; and on July 28, 586, Jerusalem fell. For greater detail on the city's capture and pillage, see 2Ki 25:1–21; Jer 39:1–10; 52:4–27. This destruction of Judah is also the subject of the biblical prediction that involves more verses than any other direct prophecy that is to be found within Scripture—608, distributed among seventeen different books of the Bible.

18–19 "The articles from the temple" were "carried to Babylon," and on August 14 the sanctuary itself was burned.

20 In describing "the remnant [GK 8636], who escaped from the sword," Ezra omitted, as less relevant to the restored, postexilic community, discussion about the regathering of refugees under Gedaliah and the flight of their remnant to Egypt (2Ki 25:22–26; Jer 40–44), about the small fourth deportation of 582 B.C. (Jer 52:30), and about "the poorest people of the land" who were left scattered in

Palestine (2Ki 25:12). He speaks rather of those "carried into exile" in the third and great deportation of 586 (cf. the first and second deportations in vv.7, 10). Correspondingly, archaeology has demonstrated the thorough depopulation of Judah at this time.

Thus the exiles came "to Babylon," where "they became servants"; and yet, after an initial period of discouragement (Ps 137) and oppressive service (cf. Isa 14:2–3), at least some Jews gained favor and status (2Ki 25:27–30; Da 1:19; 2:49; 6:3). Those who were among the more worldly grew indifferent and drifted away from their faith (Eze 33:31–32), but the more godly increased in their spiritual maturity (cf. Ne 1:4; Est 4:14–16; Da 1:8).

21 The statement that for "seventy years . . . in fulfillment of the word of the LORD spoken by Jeremiah" (see comment on v.7) "the land enjoyed its sabbath rests" seems to correlate the full span of the Exile with an equivalent number of sabbatical years (Lev 25:1–7; 26:34). This produces a total figure of 70 times 7 or 490 years; and the idea is that of making up for half a millennium of neglected sabbatical rests.

22 In October 539 Babylon fell to "Cyrus king of Persia," as he overthrew Nabonidus and his son Belshazzar, who were its last native rulers (Da 5). Cyrus's policy of cooperating with local religions and of encouraging the return of exiles has received explicit archaeological confirmation from the inscriptions of the king himself (cf. the famous Cyrus Cylinder).

23 The words authorized by Cyrus, "The LORD, the God of heaven, has given me all kingdoms," should be recognized, from the viewpoint of Scripture, as constituting inspired truth, though from the viewpoint of contemporary Persian government they were probably understood as diplomatic language. Cyrus could thus address a Babylonian audience, saying, "Marduk, king of the gods [confessedly, the leading deity of the pantheon of Babylon, but not of Persia!] . . . designated me to rule over all the lands" (Cyrus Cylinder; see comment on v.22). But this monarch was still God's instrument for the providential restoration of Israel (Isa 44:28–45:5). The next book of the Bible, Ezra, picks up the narrative at precisely this point.

Ezra

INTRODUCTION

1. Background

The Babylonian exile in the sixth century B.C. was preceded by earlier deportations beginning in the eighth century by the Assyrians from both Israel and Judah. Deportation began with Tiglath-pileser III, who attacked Damascus and Galilee in 732 (2Ki 15:29), carrying off at least 13,520 people to Assyria. Then Shalmaneser V and Sargon II besieged Samaria in 722 (2Ki 17:6; 18:10). Sargon boasted that he carried off 27,290 (or 27,280) persons from Israel, replacing them with various other peoples from Mesopotamia and Syria.

Whereas Israel's population in the late eighth century B.C. has been estimated at 500,000 to 700,000, Judah's population in the eighth-to-sixth centuries has been estimated at between 220,000 and 300,000. Jerusalem's population likely was swelled by refugees from the north when Samaria fell in 722. At the time of Nehemiah, however, the city had contracted to 6,000 persons. Judah had escaped the attacks of Tiglath-pileser III when Azariah (Uzziah) paid tribute to the king, though Gezer was captured. But when Sennacherib attacked Judah in 701 B.C., he deported numerous Jews, especially from Lachish. His annals claim that he deported 200,150 from Judah, but this may be an error for 2,150.

The biblical references to the numbers deported by the Babylonians under Nebuchadnezzar are incomplete and somewhat confusing, giving rise to conflicting interpretations as to the actual number of Judeans deported. Until 1956 we had no extrabiblical evidence to confirm the attack on Judah in Nebuchadnezzar's first year. Either in that year or soon after, Daniel and his companions were carried off to Babylon.

In 597 B.C. Nebuchadnezzar carried off "all the officers and fighting men, and all the craftsmen and artisans—a total of ten thousand" (2Ki 24:14). According to v.16, "the king of Babylon also deported to Babylon the entire force of seven thousand fighting men . . . and a thousand craftsmen and artisans." If these figures represent only the heads of households, the total may have been closer to thirty thousand. On the other hand, Jeremiah enumerates for 597 B.C. but 3,023 captives (Jer 52:28) and for 586 only 832 captives from Jerusalem (v.29). In 582, after the murder of Gedaliah, 745 were deported, for a grand total of 4,600 (v.30). The smaller figures of Jeremiah probably represent only men of the most important families. Depending on one's estimate of the numbers deported and the number of returning exiles, we have widely varying estimates for the population of postexilic Judah. An estimate of 150,000 is probably correct.

An important difference between the deportations by the Babylonians and by the Assyrians is that the Babylonians did not replace the deportees with pagan newcomers. Thus Judah, though devastated, was not contaminated with polytheism to the same degree as was Israel.

According to the biblical record, the Babylonian armies smashed Jerusalem's defenses (2Ki 25:10), destroyed the temple and palaces (2Ki 25:9, 13–17; Jer 52:13, 17–23), and devastated the countryside (Jer 32:43), killing many of the leaders and priests (2Ki 25:18–21). The severity of the Babylonian devastation has been amply confirmed by archaeology, evidences of which have been uncovered at such places as Beth-Shemesh, Eglon, En Gedi, Gibeah, and Jerusalem. Thousands must have died in battle or of starvation (La 2:11–22; 4:9–10). After the deportations only the poor of the land—the vine-growers and farmers—were left (2Ki 25:12; Jer 39:10; 40:7; 52:16), occupying the vacant lands (Jer 6:12; see comment on Ezr 4:4). A few refugees who fled to different areas drifted back (Jer 40:11–12). For the next fifty years these people eked out a precarious existence under the Babylonian yoke (La

5:2–5), subjected to ill treatment and forced labor (vv.11–13).

During this time some limited forms of worship were continued in the ruined area of the temple (Jer 41:5). The Scriptures themselves pass over developments in Palestine and stress the contribution of the returning exiles from Babylonia.

In light of the fact that the intellectual and spiritual leaders were the ones who were deported, the Scriptures must reflect the historical situation. Judging from earlier Assyrian reliefs and texts, the men were probably marched in chains, with women and children bearing sacks of their bare possessions on wagons as they made their way to Mesopotamia. The exiled Judean king, Jehoiachin, was maintained at the Babylonian court and provided with rations (2Ki 25:29–30).

After several years of hardship, the exiles made adjustments and even prospered (Jer 29:4–5). They were settled in various communities—e.g., on the river Kebar near Nippur, sixty miles southeast of Babylon (Eze 1:1–3; cf. Ezr 2:59–Ne 7:61). When the exiles returned, they brought with them numerous servants and animals and were able to make contributions for the sacred services (Ezr 2:65–69; 8:26; Ne 7:67–72).

With the birth of a second and a third generation, many Jews established roots in Mesopotamia and wanted to remain there. The spiritual life of the Jewish community in Mesopotamia is documented by Ezekiel, who was in exile either after 597 or 586. Ezekiel 8:1 refers to the prophet "sitting in my house and the elders of Judah were sitting before me" (cf. Eze 3:15; 14:1; 20:1; 24:18; 33:30–33). Deprived of the temple, the exiles laid great stress on the observation of the Sabbath, on the laws of purity, and on prayer and fasting. It has often been suggested that the development of synagogues began in Mesopotamia during the Exile (but see Ne 8:18). The trials of the Exile purified and strengthened the faith of the Jews and cured them of idolatry.

The exiles who chose to return to Judah found their territory much diminished. The tiny enclave of Judah was surrounded by antagonistic neighbors. North of Bethel was the province of Samaria. South of Beth-Zur, Judean territory had been overrun by Idumaeans (cf. on Ezr 2:22–35). The eastern boundary followed the Jordan River, and the western boundary the Shephelah (low hills).

The Philistine coast had been apportioned to Phoenician settlers. The Persians did make Judah an autonomous province with the right to mint its own coins.

2. Reign of Artaxerxes I

Nehemiah served as the royal cupbearer of Artaxerxes I (Ne 1:1; 2:1), the Achaemenid king who ruled from 464 to 424. The traditional view places Ezra before Nehemiah in the reign of Artaxerxes I, the third son of Xerxes and Amestris. His older brothers were named Darius and Hystaspes. Their father was assassinated in his bedchamber, between Aug and Dec 465, by Artabanus, a powerful courtier. In the ensuing months Artaxerxes, who was but eighteen years old, managed to kill Artabanus and his brother Darius. He went on to defeat his brother Hystaspes in Bactria. His first regnal year is reckoned from Apr 13, 464 B.C.

From 461 Artaxerxes I lived at Susa. He used the palace of Darius I till it burned down near the end of his reign. He then moved to Persepolis, where he lived in the former palace of Darius I. He completed the Great Throne Hall begun by Xerxes.

When Artaxerxes I came to the throne, he was faced with a major revolt in Egypt that was to last a decade. The Egyptian leaders defeated the Persian satrap Achaemenes, the brother of Xerxes, and gained control of much of the Delta region by 462. The Athenians, who had been at war with the Persians since the latter had invaded Greece in 490, helped the rebels capture Memphis, the capital of Lower Egypt, in 459. This situation may have led the Persians to support Ezra's return in 458 in order to secure a loyal buffer state in Palestine.

In 456 Megabyzus, the satrap of Syria, advanced against Egypt with a huge fleet and army. During eighteen months he was able to suppress the revolt. A fleet of forty Athenian ships with six thousand men sailed into a Persian trap. In spite of promises made by Megabyzus, the Egyptian leader was impaled in 454 at the instigation of Amestris, the mother of Artaxerxes I. Angered at this betrayal, Megabyzus revolted against the king from 449 to 446. If the events of Ezr 4:7–23 took place in this period, Artaxerxes I would have been suspicious of the building activities in Jerusalem. How then could the same king have commissioned Nehemiah to rebuild the walls of the city in 445? By then both the Egyptian revolt and the rebellion of Megabyzus had been resolved.

Artaxerxes I ended his long forty-year reign by dying from natural causes in the winter of 424 B.C.—a rarity in view of the frequent assassinations of Persian kings.

3. Authorship and Date

As in the closely related books of Chronicles, one notes the prominence of various lists in Ezra-Nehemiah. Evidently obtained from official sources, these comprise (1) the vessels of the temple (Ezr 1:9–11); (2) the returned exiles (Ezr 2:1–70; Ne 7:6–73); (3) the genealogy of Ezra (Ezr 7:1–5); (4) the heads of the clans (Ezr 8:1–14); (5) those involved in mixed marriages (Ezr 10:18–43); (6) those who helped rebuild the wall (Ne 3); (7) those who sealed the covenant (Ne 10:1–27); (8) residents of Jerusalem and other cities (Ne 11:3–36); and (9) priests and Levites (Ne 12:1–26).

Also included in Ezra are seven official documents or letters (all, except the first, in Aramaic; the first is in Hebrew): (1) the decree of Cyrus (Ezr 1:2–4); (2) the accusation of Rehum et al. against the Jews (4:11–16); (3) the reply of Artaxerxes I (4:17–22); (4) the report from Tattenai (5:7–17); (5) the memorandum of Cyrus's decree (6:2b–5); (6) Darius's reply to Tattenai (6:6–22); (7) the king's authorization to Ezra (7:12–26).

Certain characteristics common to both Chronicles and Ezra-Nehemiah have led many to hold that the author of Chronicles was also the author/compiler of Ezra-Nehemiah. The verses at the end of Chronicles and at the beginning of Ezra are identical (see comment on Ezr 1:1). Both Chronicles and Ezra-Nehemiah exhibit a fondness for lists, for the description of religious festivals, and for certain phrases. Especially striking in these books is the prominence of the Levites and of temple personnel. Because of his interest in the temple and the cult, it is assumed that the "Chronicler" was a Levite, or even a singer.

Though there are many complex relationships between Ezra-Nehemiah and Chronicles, we regard Nehemiah as the author of the Nehemiah memoirs and Ezra as the author of both the Ezra memoirs and the Ezra narrative, with a later follower of Ezra's circle as the Chronicler. We would date the composition of the Ezra materials about 440, the Nehemiah memoirs about 430, and 1 and 2 Chronicles about 400.

4. Purpose and Values

Ezra and Nehemiah record the return of the Jewish exiles from Babylonia and the rebuilding of the temple and the walls around Jerusalem. These accounts highlight the importance of the temple and its personnel. Of vital importance were the attempts to keep the community pure from the syncretistic influence of the neighbors who surrounded it. In some cases Jewish communities compromised and were assimilated out of existence, as at Elephantine in Egypt. The measures taken by Ezra and Nehemiah to safeguard the Jews from commingling with non-Jews may appear harsh to modern society, but in the light of history they were necessary.

a. The book of Ezra

The book of Ezra reveals the providential intervention of the God of heaven on behalf of his people. In ch. 1 the Lord is sovereign over all kingdoms (v.2) and moves even the heart of a pagan ruler to fulfill his will (v.1). He accomplishes the refining of his people through calamities like the Conquest and the Exile. He stirs the heart of his people to respond and raises men of God to lead his people (v.11). Ezra 3 shows that the service of God requires a united effort (v.1), leadership (v.2a), obedience to God's Word (v.2b), courage in the face of opposition (v.3), offerings and funds (vv.4–7), and an organized division of labor (vv.8–9). Meeting these requirements resulted in a sound foundation for later work (v.11), tears and joy (vv.11–12), and praise and thanksgiving to the Lord (v.11).

Ezra 4 teaches that doing the work of God brings opposition: in the guise of proffered cooperation from those who do not share our basic theological convictions (vv.1–2) to complete work that we alone are responsible for (v.3); and from various groups of opponents, such as those who would discourage and intimidate us (v.4), professional counselors who offer misleading advice (v.5), false accusers (vv.6, 13), and secular authorities (vv.7, 21–24). Far from being discouraged, however, we need to be alert and vigorous, knowing that by God's grace we can triumph over all opposition and accomplish his will with rejoicing (6:14–16).

Ezra experienced the good hand of God. As a scribe he was more than a scholar—he was an expounder of the Scriptures (7:6, 12). He believed that God could guide and protect from misfortune (8:20–22). As an inspired leader he enlisted others and assigned trustworthy men to their tasks (7:27–28; 8:15, 24). He regarded what he did as a sacred trust (8:21–28). Ezra was above all a man of fervent prayer (8:21; 10:1), deep piety, and humility (7:10, 27–28; 9:3; 10:6).

b. The book of Nehemiah

The book of Nehemiah, perhaps more than any other book of the OT, reflects the vibrant personality of its author. (1) Nehemiah was a man of responsibility; he served as the king's cupbearer (1:11–2:1). (2) Nehemiah was a man of vision. (3) He was a man of prayer (1:5–11; 2:4–5). (4) He was a man of action and cooperation (2:16–18; ch. 3). (5) He was a man of compassion (5:8, 18). (6) He was a man who triumphed over opposition. (7) Finally, Nehemiah was a man with right motivation who sought to please and serve his divine Sovereign.

EXPOSITION

I. The First Return From Exile and the Rebuilding of the Temple (1:1–6:22).

A. The First Return of the Exiles (1:1–11)

1. The edict of Cyrus (1:1–4)

It had been nearly seventy years since the first deportation of the Jews by the Babylonians to Mesopotamia. Though the initial years must have been difficult, the second and third generation of Jews born in the Exile had adjusted to their surroundings. Though some had become so comfortable that they refused to return to Judah when given the opportunity, still others, sustained by the examples and teachings of leaders like Daniel and Ezekiel, retained their faith in the Lord's promises and their allegiance to their homeland.

1 Ezra 1:1–3a is virtually identical with 2Ch 36:22–23. "In the first year" means the first regnal year of Cyrus, beginning in Nisan 538, after his capture of Babylon in October 539. Cyrus, the founder of the Persian Empire, reigned over the Persians from 559 till 530

B.C. He established Persian dominance over the Medes in 550, conquered Lydia and Anatolia in 547–546, and captured Babylon in 539. Isaiah 44:28 and 45:1 speak of Cyrus as the Lord's "shepherd" and his "anointed."

Daniel (Da 1:21; 6:28; 10:1) was in Babylon when Cyrus captured it. "The word of the LORD spoken by Jeremiah" was the prophet's prediction (Jer 25:1–12; 29:10) of a seventy-year Babylonian captivity. The first deportations had begun in 605, in the third year of Jehoiakim (see Da 1:1). The seventieth year would be 536.

"Proclamation" (GK 7754) was an oral announcement in the native language in contrast to the copy of the decree in 6:3–5, which was an Aramaic memorandum for the archives.

2 The phrase "the God of heaven" occurs primarily in the postexilic books (i.e., Ezra, Nehemiah, Daniel). The city of Jerusalem and the house of God are both prominent subjects in Ezra-Nehemiah. "A temple for him at Jerusalem in Judah" is literally "a house for him in Jerusalem that is in Judah." The formulation "Jerusalem that is in Judah" is characteristic of Persian bureaucratic style. Cyrus instituted the enlightened policy of placating the gods of his subject peoples rather than carrying off their cult statues as the Assyrians, Elamites, Hittites, and Babylonians had done before. His generosity to the Jews was also paralleled by his benevolence to the Babylonians. Ultimately, however, it was the Lord who had "moved" his heart.

3–4 The religious orientation of the Achaemenid kings—Cyrus and his successors—is a controversial issue. "Where survivors may now be living" (lit., "everyone who remains over") refers to survivors of the capture and deportation (cf. Ne 1:2). The Hebrew word for "living" (GK 1591) is cognate to the word for "resident alien." The deportees continued to be regarded as aliens, as were the Susians and Elamites who were "resident" in Samaria years after their deportation (4:10, 17). "The people of any place" probably designates the many Jews, especially of the second and the third generation, who did not wish to leave the land of their birth. "Freewill offerings" were voluntary gifts (vv.4,6; 2:68–69; 3:5; 7:13–16; 8:28) and voluntary service (v.5; 7:13), the keys to the restoration of God's temple and its service.

2. The Return under Sheshbazzar (1:5–11)

5–6 The Lord stirred not only the heart of the Persian king but also the hearts of many of the exiles who had maintained their faith in the Lord in spite of the devastation of their homeland. A vivid attestation to this faith is an inscription carved at Khirbet Beit Lei, five miles east of Lachish, which can be translated: "I am the Lord your God: I will accept the cities of Judah and will redeem Jerusalem," perhaps incised by a refugee to express his trust in God's faithfulness despite the desolation of the Holy City (cf. La 3:22–24).

7 Conquerors customarily carried off the statues of the gods of conquered cities. The Philistines took the ark of the Jews and placed it in the temple of Dagon (1Sa 5:2). The Hittites took the statue of Marduk when they conquered the city of Babylon. As the Jews did not have a statue of the Lord, Nebuchadnezzar carried off the temple goods instead (cf. 2Ki 25:13; Jer 52:17).

Jeremiah spoke of false prophets who prematurely predicted the return of these vessels (Jer 27:16–22; 28:6); he prophesied their ultimate return (27:22). Belshazzar had the audacity to drink from some of the temple vessels (Da 5:23).

8 The Persian name "Mithredath" means "given by Mithra." Mithra(s) was the Persian god whose mystery religion became popular in the Greco-Roman world. Another official with the same name appears in 4:7. Sheshbazzar, who had a Babylonian name, was probably a Jewish official who served as a deputy governor of Judah under the satrap in Samaria (cf. Ezr 5:14).

9–11 When the Assyrian and Babylonian conquerors carried off booty, their scribes made a careful inventory of it. The actual figures in the Hebrew text add up to 2,499 rather than 5,400, perhaps because only the larger and more valuable vessels were specified. The exact meanings of the Hebrew words for the objects are uncertain. We know nothing about the details of Sheshbazzar's journey, which probably took place in the spring of 537. Judging from Ezra's later journey (7:8–9), the trip probably took about four months. The caravan would have proceeded from Babylonia up the Euphrates River and then south through the Orontes Valley of Syria to Palestine.

B. The List of Returning Exiles (2:1–70)

1. Leaders of the return (2:1–2a)

1 The list of returning exiles in vv.1–70 almost exactly parallels the list in Ne 7:6–73. The list of localities indicates that people retained their memories of their homes and that exiles from a very wide background of tribes, villages, and towns returned. A comparison of Ezr 2 with Ne 7 reveals a number of differences in both the names and the numbers that are listed. Though the lists of temple personnel show few variations, there are differences in about half the cases of the lists of the laity. Many differences may be explained by assuming that a cipher notation was used with vertical strokes for units, horizontal strokes for tens, and stylized mems (Heb. letter "m") for hundreds.

2a The KJV's colon after Zerubbabel implies that all those who followed were among those returning with Zerubbabel in 537. The NIV, NRSV, et al., place a comma after Zerubbabel, leaving open the possibility that the list may include those who returned to Judah at a later date. The list of eleven leaders in Ezr 2 is increased by the addition of "Nahamani" inserted before the name of Mordecai in Ne 7:7.

On "Zerubbabel" see 5:2. "Jeshua" is a name similar to "Joshua" (Ne 8:17) and to the Greek "Jesus"; it means "The LORD [Yahweh] is salvation." If he is the same as the Joshua of Hag 1:1, he was the son of Jehozadak, the high priest carried into exile (1Ch 6:15) and the grandson of Seraiah, the high priest put to death by Nebuchadnezzar (2Ki 25:18–21). "Nehemiah" was not the same person as the king's cupbearer. "Seraiah" means "The LORD is Prince." "Reelaiah" is paralleled in Ne 7:7 by "Raamiah." "Mordecai" is based on the name of the god of Babylon, Marduk (Jer 50:2). It is the name borne by Esther's uncle. "Mispar" is paralleled in Ne 7:7 by "Mispereth." "Bigvai" is a Persian name meaning "happy."

2. Families (2:2b–20)

2b "The list of the men of the people of Israel" may have been of males only over the age of twelve.

3 "The descendants of Parosh" represented the largest family of priests returning from Babylon. Members of this family returned

CHRONOLOGY: EZRA-NEHEMIAH

Dates below are given according to a Nisan-to-Nisan Jewish calendar (see chart on Hebrew Calendar). Roman numerals represent months; Arabic numerals represent days.

YEAR	MONTH	DAY	EVENT	REFERENCE
539 B.C.	Oct.	12	Capture of Babylon	Da 5:30
538	Mar.	24	Cyrus's first year	Ezr 1:1-4
537	to Mar.	11		
537(?)			Return under Sheshbazzar	Ezr 1:11
537	VII		Building of altar	Ezr 3:1
536	II		Work on temple begun	Ezr 3:8
536-530			Opposition during Cyrus's reign	Ezr 4:1-5
530-520			Work on temple ceased	Ezr 4:24
520	VI =Sept.	24 21	Work on temple renewed under Darius	Ezr 5:2; Hag 1:14
516	XII =Mar.	3 12	Temple completed	Ezr 6:15
458	I =Apr.	1 8	Ezra departs from Babylon	Ezr 7:6-9
	V =Aug.	1 4	Ezra arrives in Jerusalem	Ezr 7:8-9
	IX =Dec.	20 19	People assemble	Ezr 10:9
	X =Dec.	1 29	Committee begins investigation	Ezr 10:16
457	I =Mar.	1 27	Committee ends investigation	Ezr 10:17
445 444	Apr. to Apr.	13 2	20th year of Artaxerxes I	Ne 1:1
445	I =Mar.-Apr.		Nehemiah approaches king	Ne 2:1
	Aug.(?)		Nehemiah arrives in Jerusalem	Ne 2:11
	VI =Oct.	25 2	Completion of wall	Ne 6:15
	VII =Oct. to Nov.	8 5	Public assembly	Ne 7:73-8:1
	VII =Oct.	15-22 22-28	Feast of Tabernacles	Ne 8:14
	VII =Oct.	24 30	Fast	Ne 9:1
433 432	Apr. to Apr.	1 19	32nd year of Artaxerxes; Nehemiah's recall and return	Ne 5:14; 13:6

540 B.C.
530
520
510
500
490
480
470
460
450
440
430 B.C.

with Ezra (8:3); some of them assisted in rebuilding the wall (Ne 3:25). "Parosh" (GK 7283) means "flea" (cf. GK 7282) and may connote insignificance (cf. 1Sa 24:14). Insect and animal names were common among the Hebrews.

4-12 "Shephatiah" means "The LORD has judged." Other members of the family returned with Ezra (8:8). "Arah" means "wild ox." "Pahath-Moab" means "governor of Moab" (cf. 8:4; 10:30; Ne 7:11; 10:14). These may be the descendants of the tribe of Reuben who were deported from the province of Moab by Tiglath-pileser III (cf. 1Ch 5:3–8). "Elam" was the name of the country in southwestern Iran in the area of Susa (cf. v.31; 8:7; 10:2, 26; Ne 7:12; 10:14).

"Zaccai" may mean "pure" or may be a shortened form of Zechariah ("The LORD has remembered"). "Bani" is a shortened form of Benaiah ("The LORD has built"); Ne 7:15 has Binnui. "Azgad" ("Gad is strong") is either a reference to Gad, the god of fortune, or to the Transjordanian tribe of Gad. The greatest numerical discrepancy occurs here: Ezra lists 1,222 whereas Nehemiah lists 2,322.

13–20 "Adonikam" means "my Lord has arisen." "Ater" means "Lefty" (cf. Jdg 3:15; 20:16). "Hezekiah" means "The LORD is my strength." "Bezai," a shorted form of Bezaleel, means "in the shadow of God."

3. Villagers (2:21–35)

Verses 21–35 list a series of villages and towns, most of them in Benjamite territory north of Jerusalem. Significantly, no references are to towns in the Negev south of Judah. When Nebuchadnezzar overran Judah (Jer 13:19), the Edomites (cf. Obadiah) opportunistically occupied the area. By the fifth century B.C., Nabataean Arabs (Mal 1:2–5) were pressing on the Edomites, who moved west and occupied the area south of Hebron, later known as Idumaea.

21–25 "Bethlehem"—among the returnees may have been the ancestors of Jesus (Mic 5:2). "Netophah," a city south of Jerusalem, was settled by Levites (1Ch 9:16). "Anathoth," a village named after the Canaanite goddess Anath, was located three miles north of Jerusalem and was the home of the prophet Jeremiah (Jer 1:1). "Azmaveth" was two miles farther north. "Kiriath Jearim" means "village of the woods," (cf. Ne 7:29). This was the site eight miles northwest of Jerusalem where the ark rested (1Sa 6:21; 7:1). "Beeroth" means "wells," a site located twelve miles north of Jerusalem.

26–28 "Ramah" ("the height") was five miles north of Jerusalem. "Geba" was located east of Ramah. "Micmash," eight miles northeast of Jerusalem, was the scene of Jonathan's exploit (1Sa 13:23). "Bethel" ("the house of God") was located twelve miles north of Jerusalem. As a border town, it probably became a part of Judah in Josiah's reign. Bethel, however, was destroyed in the transition between the Babylonian and Persian periods. Excavations have revealed a small town on the site in Ezra's day.

29–35 "Nebo" was perhaps the same as Nob, which has been located on Mount Scopus, just to the east of Jerusalem. "Harim" means "dedicated to God." "Lod," modern Lydda, ten miles southeast of Jaffa, is today the site of the Israeli International Airport. "Jericho" is the famous oasis city just north of the Dead Sea. "Senaah" means "the hated one." The largest number of returnees (3,630) is associated with Senaah, which is perhaps not a specific locality or family but a low-caste people.

4. Priests (2:36–39)

Four clans of priests are named with a total of 4,289, or about one-tenth the total. They may have been inspired by the hope of serving in a rebuilt temple.

36–39 "Jedaiah" ("The LORD has known") was a family of priests noted during the time of David (1Ch 24:7). "Immer" means "lamb" (cf. 1Ch 24:14). On "Harim" see comment on v.32

5. Levites and temple personnel (2:40–42)

40 The Levites, descendants of Levi (Ge 29:34), may have originally been regarded as priests (Dt 18:6–8); but they became subordinate to the priestly descendants of Aaron, brother of Moses (Nu 3:9–10; 1Ch 16:4–42; 23:26–32). The Levites were then prohibited from offering sacrifices on the altar (Nu 16:40; 18:7). As the Levites had no inheritance in land, they lived in forty-eight Levitical cities and were supported by tithes (Dt 12:12, 18; 14:29). They were butchers, doorkeepers, singers (1Ch 15:22; 16:4–7), scribes and teachers (2Ch 35:3; Ne 8:7, 9), and even temple beggars (2Ch 24:5–11).

41 On "the singers," see Ne 11:22–23; 12:29; 13:10. "Asaph" (lit., "he removed") was one of the three Levites appointed by David over the temple singers.

42 "Gatekeepers" (GK 8788) are mentioned thirteen times in Ezra-Nehemiah, nineteen times in Chronicles. They are usually regarded as Levites (1Ch 9:26; 2Ch 8:14; 23:4; Ne 12:25; 13:22) but are sometimes differentiated from them (2Ch 35:15). At times as many as four thousand gatekeepers were mentioned (1Ch 23:5). Their primary function was to tend the doors and gates of the temple (1Sa 3:15; 1Ch 9:17–32), though they were also expected to perform other menial tasks (2Ch 31:14). The psalmist said he would rather be a doorkeeper in the house of his God than to dwell in the tents of the wicked (Ps 84:10). The 139 gatekeepers listed here belonged to six small clans. "Shallum" means "complete"; "Talmon" means "brightness"; "Akkub" means "protected."

6. Temple servants (2:43–58)

43–45 A long list of names (thirty-five in Ezra, thirty-two in Nehemiah) follows the heading "temple servants"; but the clans must have been very small, averaging about nine members. The temple servants and the sons of Solomon's servants together numbered 392 (v.58)—more than the total of the Levites, gatekeepers, and singers (vv.40–42). Though of a very menial status, they must have served God with true devotion. The Hebrew word for "temple servants" ("Nethinim"; GK 5987) occurs only in 1Ch 9:2 and in Ezra-Nehemiah. They occupied a special quarter in Jerusalem (Ne 3:26, 31; 11:21) and enjoyed exemption from taxes (Ezr 7:24). They participated in the rebuilding of the wall (Ne 3:26) and signed Nehemiah's covenant (Ne 10:29).

46–54 "Hanan" ("[God] is gracious") is derived from the verb for "to be gracious." The name "Johanan" ("The LORD is gracious") has given us the name John. "Giddel," a shortened form of Geddeliah, means "The LORD has made great." "Rezin" is an Aramaic name that means "prince" (cf. Pr 14:28). "Meunim" seems to be related to the Maonites (Jdg 10:12), an Arab tribe south of the Dead Sea subdued by Uzziah (2Ch 26:7). A city near Petra is named Maan. "Nephussim" refers to a Bedouin tribe descended from Ishmael (Ge 25:15; 1Ch 1:31; 5:18–22). "Neziah" is "faithful"; "Hatipha" means "snatched," as a captive in childhood.

55–58 The phrase "the descendants of the servants of Solomon" occurs only in this passage and in Ne 7:60; 11:3. These may be the descendants of the Canaanites whom Solomon enslaved (1Ki 9:20–21). "Hassophereth" is a feminine form that means "the scribe"; women scribes were rare. An analysis of the figures in these lists yields the following percentages of the total (v.64): families, 53.2; villagers, 29.6; priests, 14.7; Levites, 0.2; singers, 0.4; gatekeepers, 0.5; temple servants and descendants of the servants of Solomon, 1.4.

7. Individuals lacking evidence of their genealogies (2:59–63)

59 The Hebrew word *tel* (GK 9424) designates hilllike mounds that cover the remains of ruined cities. "Tel Melah" ("mound of salt") is possibly a mound strewed with salt (cf. Jdg 9:45). "Tel Harsha" is "mound of potsherds." Tel-Abib (Eze 3:15) means the "mound of a flood," i.e., a place destroyed by a flood.

The Jewish exiles were settled along the Kebar River (Eze 1:1) near the city of Nippur, a city in southern Mesopotamia that was the stronghold of rebels. Of the exiles who returned, members of three lay families and three priestly families were unable at this time to prove their descent. Some may have derived from proselytes; others may have temporarily lost access to their genealogical records.

60 "Delaiah" is "The LORD has drawn." "Tobiah" ("The LORD is good") was the name also of one of Nehemiah's chief adversaries (Ne 2:10, 19). The total of 652 could not prove their genealogies.

61 "Hobaiah" means "The LORD has hidden." "Barzillai" ("man of iron") of Gilead in Transjordan helped David during his flight from his son Absalom (2Sa 17:27–29; 19:31–39; 1Ki 2:7). That the bridegroom took the name of his wife's father reflects a marriage arranged by a father who had only daughters. The children from this marriage belonged to the wife's family (cf. Ge 29–31; 1Ch 2:34–36).

62 Genealogies figure prominently in Chronicles, Ezra, and Nehemiah. The knowledge of relationships was highly regarded in ancient times.

63 "The governor" probably refers here to either Sheshbazzar or Zerubbabel. "The most sacred food" refers to the most holy part of the offering—the portion of the priests. "The Urim and Thummim," objects kept in the breastplate of the high priest, were used for divining God's will (cf. Ex 28:30; Lev 8:8; Nu 27:21; Dt 33:8). They were probably two small objects made of wood, bone, or stone, perhaps of different colors or with different inscriptions, that would give a yes or no answer.

8. Totals (2:64–67)

64 The given total of 42,360 is considerably more than the sum of the actual figures given from the figures in Ezr 2 and Ne 7. To account for the difference of about twelve thousand presents problems. Were these unspecified people women and/or children? If there were relatively few women among the returnees, the pressures for intermarriage would have been considerable.

65 The ratio of slaves—one to six—is relatively high; that so many would return with their masters speaks highly of the relatively benevolent treatment of slaves by the Jews. The male and female singers listed here may have been secular singers who sang at weddings, funerals, etc. (2Ch 35:25) as distinct from the male temple singers of v.41.

66 "Horses" in the OT are usually associated with royalty and the military. The horses listed here may have been a donation from Cyrus for the nobility. "Mules" are hybrid offspring of donkey stallions and mares. They combine the strength and size of the horse with the patience and sure-footedness of the donkey. They were not originally bred in Palestine; Solomon had to import them (1Ki 10:25; 2Ch 9:24). As precious animals they were used by the royalty and wealthy (1Ki 1:33; Isa 66:20).

67 The "camels" mentioned in the OT were the one-humped Arabian camels as distinct from the two-humped Bactrian camels. The camel can carry its rider and about four hundred pounds and can travel three or four days without drinking. "Donkeys" were surefooted and able to live on poor forage. They were used to carry loads, women, or children. Sheep, goats, and cattle are not mentioned. They would have slowed the caravan.

9. Offerings (2:68–69)

68 The caravan probably followed the Euphrates River north to a point east of Aleppo, crossed west to the Orontes River Valley, then traveled south to Hamath, Homs, and Riblah. They would then have either passed through the Beqah Valley in Lebanon (cf. Jer 39:5–7; 52:9–10, 26–27) or have proceeded east of the Anti-Lebanon Mountains to Damascus and then to Palestine. As the people were expending most of their savings, their giving demonstrated a true spirit of dedication to God's service (cf. Ex 36:5–7; 2Co 9:6–7).

69 The parallel passage in Ne 7:70–72 gives a fuller description than the account in Ezra. In Ezra the gifts come from the heads of the clans but in Nehemiah from three sources: the governor, the chiefs of the clans, and the rest of the people.

The "drachma" (GK 2007) was the Greek silver coin worth a day's wage in the late fifth century B.C. More likely the coin intended here was the Persian daric, which was a gold coin, named probably after Darius I, who began minting it. The coin was famed for its purity, which was guaranteed by the king. Its value equaled the price of an ox or a month's wages for a soldier. Since the coin was not in use until the time of Darius I (522–486 B.C.), its occurrence here in 537 B.C. has been labeled anachronistic. Its use is better viewed as a modernization by terms current at the time of the book's composition of earlier values, perhaps the Median shekel.

A "mina" equaled 1.26 pounds of silver; five thousand minas would be 6,300 pounds of silver. A mina equals five years' wages.

10. Settlement of the exiles (2:70)

70 Later Nehemiah would be compelled to move people by lot to reinforce the population of Jerusalem, as the capital city had suffered the severest loss of life at the time of the Babylonian attacks. The survivors, who came for the most part from towns in the countryside, naturally preferred to resettle in their hometowns.

C. The Revival of Temple Worship (3:1–13)

1. The rebuilding of the altar (3:1–3)

1 "The seventh month" is Tishri (Sept–Oct), about three months after the arrival of the exiles in Palestine. Tishri is one of the most sacred months of the Jewish year. The first day is the New Year's Day (Rosh Hashanah) of the civil calendar, proclaimed with the blowing of trumpets and a holy convocation (Lev 23:24). Ten days later the Day of Atonement (Yom Kippur) is observed (Lev 23:27). From the fifteenth to the twenty-second day, the Feast of Tabernacles (Succoth) is celebrated (Lev 23:34–36). "Assembled as one man" and similar expressions of the unity of Israel are found in Nu 14:15; Jdg 6:16; 20:1, 8, 11; 1Sa 11:7; 2Sa 19:14.

2 Jeshua, the high priest, took precedence over Zerubbabel, the civil leader, in view of the nature of the occasions (cf. v.8; 5:2; Hag 1:1). During their long stay in Babylon, the Jews were not able to offer any sacrifices, as this could only be done in Jerusalem. Instead they were surrounded by a myriad of pagan temples. Thus the exiles' first task in the midst of hostile neighbors was to erect once more an altar to sacrifice to the Lord.

The Jews' "enemies" did not have anything to fear from the rebuilding of the temple, as they did later from the rebuilding of the wall. Sincerely or not, they at first offered their help to rebuild the temple.

3 "Despite their fear" is literally "for with fear" or "for in fear." The Hebrew word means a terror inspired by people (Pr 20:2) or by animals (Job 39:20). "The peoples around them" is literally "peoples of the lands."

2. The Festival of Booths (3:4–6)

4 The original Hebrew word for "tabernacle" (GK 6109) refers to the "huts" constructed for this feast, which is sometimes simply called "the feast" or "the feast of the Lord." It was originally a joyous harvest celebration (Ex 23:14–16; 34:22–23; Lev 23:33–43; Nu 29:12–40; Dt 16:13–16; cf. 1Sa 1:1–3; 1Ki 12:32).

Jews today celebrate the feast by building a hut covered with an open roof of branches, decorated with fruits and vegetables. Following Lev 23:40, Jews also use the palm, the willow, and the myrtle as the "lulav" ("a shoot or young branch") and the "ethrog" (a yellow citron known in Israel only from Hellenistic times). During each of the nine days of the feast, the lulav and the ethrog are held in the hands and waved in all directions. The "burnt offerings" (GK 6592) were those sacrifices prescribed for morning (Lev 1:13) and evening (Nu 28:3–4).

5–6 The new moon marked the first day of the month and was a holy day (Nu 28:11–15; cf. Col 2:16). "The appointed sacred feasts" include such festivals as the Passover, Weeks (Pentecost), and the Day of Atonement (Lev 23). The renewal of the "freewill offerings" (cf. 1:4; GK 5607) fulfilled the promise of Jer 33:10–11. Notice that the revival of the services preceded the erection of the temple itself.

3. The beginning of temple reconstruction (3:7–13)

7 As with the first temple, the Phoenicians (of Tyre and Sidon) cooperated by sending

timbers and workmen (1Ki 5:7–12). The latter were paid in "money" (lit., "silver") that would have been weighed out in shekels (see comment on 2:69). Ancient Phoenicia (modern Lebanon) was renowned for its cedars and other coniferous trees. Both the Mesopotamians and the Egyptians sought to obtain its timbers either by trade or by conquest. Cedars, mentioned seventy-one times in the OT, can grow to a height of 120 feet with a girth of 30 to 40 feet. Their fragrant wood resists rot and insects. The wood was floated on rafts down the coast and unloaded at Joppa (cf. 1Ki 5:9; 2Ch 2:15–16).

Sidon, twenty-eight miles south of modern Beirut, was one of the greatest of all the Phoenician cities (Ge 10:19; 1Ki 5:6; 16:31; 1Ch 22:4). After the conquest of the island of Tyre by Nebuchadnezzar following a thirteen-year siege, Sidon became prominent. Renowned for its maritime trade (Eze 26:4–14), Tyre was later transformed into a peninsula by Alexander the Great.

8–9 The second month, Iyyar (Apr/May), was the same month when Solomon began his temple (1Ki 6:1). As the Jews probably returned to Palestine in the spring of 537, the second year would be the spring of 536. Previously the age limit for the Levites was thirty (Nu 4:3) or twenty-five years (Nu 8:24). It was reduced to twenty (1Ch 23:24, 27; 2Ch 31:17), no doubt because of the scarcity of Levites. Zerubbabel and Jeshua were involved in laying the foundation of the second temple, though 5:16 describes Sheshbazzar as also laying the foundation.

10 The "trumpets" (GK 2956) were made of beaten silver (Nu 10:2). Except perhaps for their use at the coronation of Joash (2Ki 11:14; 2Ch 23:13), trumpets were always blown by priests (Nu 10:8; 1Ch 15:24; 16:6). They were most often used on joyous occasions such as here and at the dedication of the rebuilt walls of Jerusalem (Ne 12:35; cf. 2Ch 5:13; Ps 98:6). "Cymbals" (GK 5199) were also played by priests and Levites.

11 "They sang" may be antiphonal singing by a choir divided into two groups, i.e., singing responsively (see Ne 12:8–9). "He is good," a constant refrain in Scriptures (1Ch 16:34; 2Ch 7:3; Pss 106:1; 136:1; Jer 33:10–11), implies the goodness of a covenant-keeping God. "Love" (GK 2876) means "steadfast love."

12–13 The loud shouting expressed the great jubilation of the people (cf. 10:12; cf. Jos 6:5, 20; 1Sa 4:5; Ps 95:1–2). The tears and outcries expressed the deep emotion of the occasion. Traditionally, Hebrews show their emotions by weeping out loud (cf. 10:1; Ne 1:4; 8:9). Whereas the elders were overcome with the memories of the splendors of Solomon's temple, the younger returnees shouted with great excitement at the prospect of a new temple. The God who had permitted judgment was also the God who had brought them back and would enable them to complete this project.

D. The Opposition to the Rebuilding (4:1–24)

1. Opposition during the reign of Cyrus (4:1–5)

This chapter summarizes various attempts to thwart the efforts of the Jews. In vv.1–5 the author describes events under Cyrus (539–530 B.C.), in v.6 under Xerxes (485–465), in vv.7–23 under Artaxerxes I (464–424). He then reverts in v.24 to the time of Darius I (522–486), when the temple was completed (cf. Hag 1–2). The author drew on Aramaic documents from v.8 to 6:18, with a further Aramaic section in 7:12–26.

1–2 As most of the exiles were from Judah, their descendants became known as Jews. Benjamin, the small tribe occupying the area immediately north of Judah, was the only tribe beside Judah that remained loyal to Rehoboam when the ten northern tribes rebelled. Saul, the first king of Israel, came from this tribe, as did Saul of Tarsus (Php 3:5).

The people who proffered their help were evidently from the area of Samaria, though they are not explicitly described as such. After the fall of Samaria in 722 B.C., the Assyrian kings kept importing inhabitants from Mesopotamia and Syria "who worshiped the LORD, but ... also served their own gods" (2Ki 17:24–33). The newcomers' influence doubtless diluted further the faith of the northerners, who had already apostasized from the sole worship of the Lord in the tenth century.

Even after the destruction of the temple, worshipers from Shiloh and Shechem in the north came to offer cereals and incense at the site of the ruined temple (Jer 41:5). Moreover, the northerners did not abandon faith in the Lord, as we see from the names given to Sanballat's sons, Delaiah and Shelemaiah (the "iah" refers to "Yah" or "Yahweh"). However, they retained Israel's Lord, not as the sole God, but as one god among many gods; Sanballat's name honors the moon god Sin.

3 The Jews tried tactfully to reject the aid proffered by the northerners by referring to the provisions of the king's decree. Nonetheless their response understandably aroused hostility and determined opposition.

4 "The peoples around them" (lit., "the people of the land") began "to discourage" (lit., "to weaken the hands of"; cf. Jer 38:4) the Jews. "Make them afraid" (GK 987) often describes the fear aroused in a battle situation (Jdg 20:41; 2Sa 4:1; 2Ch 32:18; Da 11:44; Zec 8:10).

5 On the hiring of counselors, compare the hiring of Balaam (Dt 23:4–5) and the hiring of the prophets to intimidate Nehemiah (Ne 13:2). "Down to the reign of Darius king of Persia" passes over the intervening reign of Cambyses (529–522), who conquered Egypt in 525 B.C., and that of the usurper, the Pseudo-Smerdis, who seized power in 522 for seven months.

2. Opposition during the reign of Xerxes (4:6)

6 "Xerxes" (Heb. "Ahasuerus"; cf. NIV note; the king mentioned in Esther) was the son of Darius. When Darius died at the end of 486, Egypt rebelled; and Xerxes had to march west to suppress the revolt. The Persians finally regained control by the end of 483. "Accusation" (lit., "hostility"; GK 8478) occurs only here and in Ge 26:21, where it is the name of a well the herdsmen of Isaac and Gerar quarreled over.

3. Opposition during the reign of Artaxerxes I (4:7–23)

a. The letter to the king (4:7–16)

7 There were three Persian kings named "Artaxerxes": Artaxerxes I (464–424), Artaxerxes II (403–359), and Artaxerxes III (358–337). The king in this passage is Artaxerxes I.

The author of the letter was Tabeel, writing with the approval of Mithredath (on "Mithredath," see comment on 1:8). "Tabeel" means "God is good" (cf Isa 7:6). Near-Eastern kings used an elaborate system of informers and spies. But God's people could take assurance in their conviction that God's intelligence system is not only more efficient than any king's espionage network but is omniscient (cf. 2Ch 16:9; Zec 4:10).

8 "Rehum" ("merciful") was an official with the role of a "chancellor" or a "commissioner." "Shimshai" means "my sun" (cf. Samson). Rehum dictated and Shimshai wrote the letter in Aramaic. It would then have been read in a Persian translation before the king (v.18).

9 "Associates" (GK 10360) were persons supported by the same fief, often children of the same parents. Persian bureaucracy reflected prominently the principle of collegiality; each responsibility was shared among colleagues. "Erech" was a great city (Ge 10:10) of the Sumerians, famed as the home of the legendary Gilgamesh. Excavations at the site have produced the earliest examples of writing. Susa was the major city of Elam in southwest Iran. Because of Susa's part in a major revolt against the last great Assyrian king (669–633 B.C.), Ashurbanipal, the city was brutally destroyed in 640. So thorough was the Assyrian destruction of Susa's ziggurat that only recently have excavators recognized its location.

10–11 Ashurbanipal was famed for his large library at Nineveh. He is not named elsewhere in the Bible but was probably the king who freed Manasseh from exile (2Ch 33:11–13). He may be the unnamed Assyrian king who deported people to Samaria according to 2Ki 17:24. The descendants of such deportees, removed from their homelands nearly two centuries before, still commonly stressed their origins. Probably the murder of the Israelite king Amon (640–642 B.C.) was the result of an anti-Assyrian movement inspired by the revolt in Elam and Babylonia. The Assyrians may then have deported the rebellious Samaritans and replaced them with the rebellious Elamites and Babylonians.

11 "Trans-Euphrates" (lit., "across the river") is a phrase that first appeared in the reign of Esarhaddon. Palestinians defined the "land across the River" as Mesopotamia (Jos 24:2–3, 14–15; 2Sa 10:16). Mesopotamians, on the other hand, saw it as including Syria, Phoenicia, and Palestine (1Ki 4:24). When Cyrus conquered Babylon in 539, he appointed Gubaru governor of Babylon and the "land beyond the River." This became the official title of the Fifth Satrapy (5:3; 6:6; Ne 2:7; et al.).

12–13 The Aramaic word for "repairing" (GK 10253) is from either the root "to repair" or the root "to lay." "Taxes" (GK 10402) designates a fixed annual tax paid by the provinces into the imperial treasuries. "Tribute" (GK 10107) was the rent tax in Babylonia. Estimates are that between twenty to thirty-five million dollars worth of taxes were collected annually by the Persian king. The Fifth Satrapy, which included Palestine, had to pay the smallest amount of the western satrapies. The Persians took much of the gold and silver coins and melted them down to be stored as bullion. Very little of the taxes returned to benefit the provinces.

14 "We are under obligation to the palace" is literally "we eat the salt of the palace." Salt was used in the ratification of covenants (Lev 2:13; Nu 18:19; 2Ch 13:5). The English word "salary" is derived from the Latin ration of salt given to soldiers (cf. the expression "a man who is not worth his salt").

15–16 "The archives" is literally "book of the records" (cf. 6:1–2; Est 2:23; 6:1). There were evidently several repositories of such documents at the major capitals.

b. The letter from the king (4:17–23)

17–20 "Greetings" is the Aramaic *shelam* (GK 10720; cf. Heb. *shalom*; GK 8934). As the king was probably illiterate, documents would be read to him (cf. Est 6:1); those written in Aramaic were "translated" into Persian (cf. comments on 4:8; Ne 8:8). There was some truth in the accusation mentioned here. Jerusalem had rebelled against the Assyrians and the Babylonians in 701, 597, and 587 B.C. (2Ki 18:7, 13; 24:1; etc.). According to the Hebrew text of 1Ki 9:18, Solomon rebuilt Tadmor, the important oasis in the Syrian desert that controlled much of the Trans-Euphrates area. His international prestige is reflected in that he was given a pharaoh's daughter in marriage (1Ki 3:1; 7:8).

21–23 After provincial authorities had intervened, the Persian king ordered a halt to the Jewish attempt to rebuild the walls of Jerusalem (see comment on Ne 1:3). Most scholars date the episode of vv.7–23 before 445 B.C. The forcible destruction of these recently rebuilt walls rather than the destruction by Nebuchadnezzar then becomes the basis of the report made to Nehemiah.

4. Resumption of work under Darius (4:24)

24 The writer, after a long digression detailing opposition to Jewish efforts, returns to his original subject—rebuilding the temple (vv.1–3). According to Persian reckoning the second regnal year of Darius I began on 1 Nisan (Apr 3), 520 B.C., and lasted till Feb 21, 519. In that year the prophet Haggai (Hag 1:1–5) exhorted Zerubbabel to begin rebuilding the temple on the first day of the sixth month (Aug 29). Work began on the temple on the twenty-fourth day of the month—Sept 21 (Hag 1:15). The date is significant. During his first two years, Darius fought numerous battles against nine rebels, as recounted in his famous Behistun Inscription. Only after the stabilization of the Persian Empire could efforts to rebuild the temple be permitted.

E. The Completion of the Temple (5:1–6:22)

1. A new beginning inspired by Haggai and Zechariah (5:1–2)

1 Beginning on Aug 29, 520 B.C. (Hag 1:1) and continuing till Dec 8 (Hag 2:1–9, 20–23), the prophet Haggai delivered a series of messages to stir the people to commence work on the temple. Two months after Haggai's first speech, Zechariah joined him (Zec 1:1). Haggai 1:6 describes the deplorable situation: housing shortages, disappointing harvests, lack of clothing and jobs, and inadequate funds—perhaps as a result of inflation (see on comments Ne 5). Haggai rebuked the people and proclaimed that because the Lord's house had remained "a ruin" (Hag 1:4, 9), the Lord would bring a drought (Hag 1:11) on the land. This implies that very little progress had been made in the sixteen years since the first foundation was laid.

2 "Zerubbabel" is a Babylonian name that means "seed of Babylon"; it refers to the man's birth in exile, probably before 570 B.C. Here and in Ezr 3:2, Ne 12:1, and Hag 1:1, he

is described as the son of Shealtiel—son of Jehoiachin, penultimate king of Judah (1Ch 3:17). Though Jehoiachin was replaced by Zedekiah, he was regarded as the last legitimate king of Judah. Zerubbabel was the last of the Davidic line to be entrusted with political authority by the occupying powers. In 1Ch 3:19, however, Zerubbabel is listed as a son of Pedaiah, another son of Jehoiachin and brother of Shealtiel. Pedaiah may have married the widow of his dead brother, Shealtiel, in a levirate marriage (Dt 25:5–6). On Jeshua and Jozadak, see comment on 2:2.

2. The intervention of the governor Tattenai (5:3–5)

3–5 A document that can be dated to June 5, 502 B.C., cites Ta-at-tan-ni as the "governor" who was subordinate to the satrap over Ebirnari. Shethar-Bozenai may have functioned as a Persian official known as the "inquisitor" or "investigator." "Structure" (GK 10082) suggests an advanced stage in the rebuilding of the temple. The Persian governor gave the Jews the benefit of the doubt by not stopping the work while the inquiry was proceeding. On the "elders" see v.9; 6:7–8, 14; Jer 29:1; Eze 8:1; 14:1.

3. The report to Darius (5:6–17)

6–7 That such inquiries were sent directly to the king has been vividly confirmed by the Elamite texts from Persepolis, where in 1933–34 several thousand tablets and fragments were found in the fortification wall. Dating from the thirteenth to the twenty-eighth year of Darius (509–494 B.C.), they deal with the transfer and payment of food products. In 1936–38 additional Elamite texts were discovered, dating from the thirtieth year of Darius to the seventh year of Artaxerxes I (492–458 B.C.).

8 The interpretation of the phrase "large stones" is uncertain. The LXX has "choice" or "splendid" stones (cf. 1Ki 7:9–11). The translation "large" (lit., "rolling"; GK 10146) is suggested because the size of the stones was such that they were likely placed on rollers to move them. "Placing the timbers in the walls" may refer to interior wainscoting (1Ki 6:15–18) or to logs alternating with the brick or stone layers in the walls (1Ki 6:36).

9–12 According to 1Ki 6:1, Solomon began building the temple in the fourth year of his reign, in 966 B.C. The project lasted seven years (1Ki 6:38). In response to the challenge of the Persian authorities, the Jewish elders declared that they were the servants of the God of heaven and earth and recounted the building of the first temple by Solomon, which must have been an object of national pride. They then confessed that because of their fathers' sins, God had been provoked into using the pagan Babylonians in chastising them, just as Jeremiah had warned.

The Chaldeans inhabited the southern regions of Mesopotamia and established the Neo-Babylonian Empire (626–539 B.C.). Their origins are obscure. There may have been some original kinship with the Arameans, though they were consistently distinguished from the Arameans in Assyrian documents (cf. 2Ki 24:2; Jer 35:11). In the late seventh century B.C., the Chaldeans with the Medes, led by Nabopolassar, the father of Nebuchadnezzar, overthrew the Assyrians. Of the fall of Jerusalem on March 16, 597, extant Chaldean chronicles laconically report: "He then captured its king [Jehoiachin] and appointed a king of his own choice [Zedekiah]" (cf. 2Ki 24:17).

13 For the title "king of Babylon," see comment on Ne 13:6. In cuneiform contracts in Mesopotamia and in Syria, Darius is also designated "king of Babylon."

14–15 Cyrus appointed Sheshbazzar "governor" (cf. 1:8, 11). Both Sheshbazzar and Zerubbabel (Hag 1:1; 2:2) were "governors." Both are said to have laid the foundation of the temple (v.16; 1:3; 3:2–8; Hag 1:1, 14–15; 2:2–4, 18). Probably Sheshbazzar was an elderly man about fifty-five to sixty at the time of the return, whereas Zerubbabel was a younger contemporary about forty. Sheshbazzar may have been viewed as the official Persian "governor" whereas Zerubbabel served as the popular leader (3:8–11). This may be why the Jews mentioned Sheshbazzar here when speaking to the Persian authorities. Whereas the high priest Joshua is associated with Zerubbabel, no priest is associated with Sheshbazzar.

With God all things are possible. Consider the fate of the temple and its vessels. How desperate and hopeless the situation of the Jews must have seemed from the destruc-

tion of Jerusalem by Nebuchadnezzar to the desecration of the temple vessels by Belshazzar in a feast the night Babylon fell to Cyrus (Da 5)! Prior to that night there was utter destruction, deportation, and desecration; after that night reconsecration, return, and rebuilding. For those who could lift their hearts above the dismal prospects of earth to the God of heaven, a promise of an anointed one by the name of Cyrus had been made (Isa 44:28–45:1) long before the capture of Babylon by the Persians. What mere human prognosticator could have guessed such a turn of events?

16–17 It was important that the temple be built on its original "site" (v.15). Though Sheshbazzar presided over the laying of its foundation in 536, so little actually was accomplished that Zerubbabel evidently had to preside over a second foundation some sixteen years later (cf. 6:3). The fate of Sheshbazzar is uncertain. In view of his advanced age, possibly he died soon after his return to Jerusalem.

4. The search for the decree of Cyrus (6:1–5)

1 "The archives" is literally "house of books." The phrase then reads "in the house of the books where the treasures were laid up." Many Elamite documents were found in the so-called treasury area of Persepolis, along with other artifacts.

2 Persian officials wrote on scrolls of papyrus and leather, as discoveries in Egypt show. "Citadel" is probably from the Akkadian word for "fortress." Media was the homeland of the Medes in northwestern Iran. After the rise of Cyrus in 550 B.C., this Indo-European tribe became subordinate to the Persians. "Ecbatana" was the capital of Media.

The Aramaic "memorandum" of the decree of Cyrus in vv.3–5 is comparable to the Hebrew version of the king's proclamation in 1:2–4. In contrast with the latter, the Aramaic is written in a more sober, administrative style without reference to the Lord.

3–5 "Ninety feet high and ninety feet wide" is literally "60 cubits its height and 60 cubits its width" (see NIV note). The cubit was the distance from the elbow to the finger tip, or slightly less than eighteen inches. No length

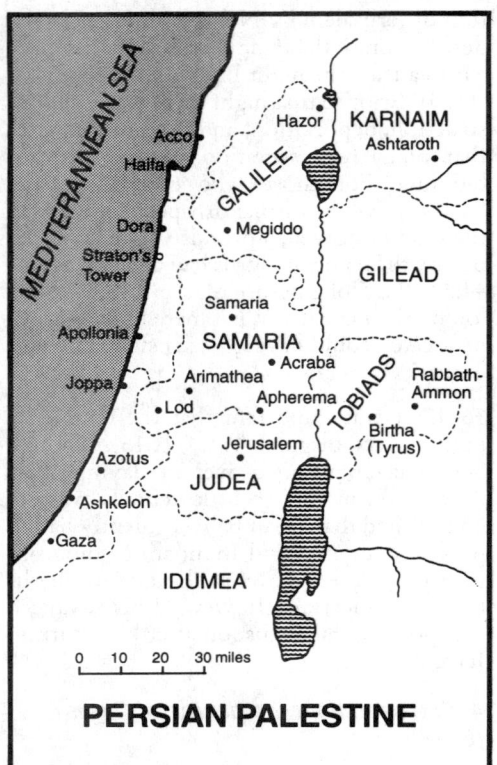

PERSIAN PALESTINE

meanings. Here it seems to mean royal "funds," which could mean that the rebuilding was to be done at government expense, with a hint of government subsidies for the offerings. Ancient documents indicate that the Persians paid for temple repairs out of royal funds.

9 A lamb was offered every morning and evening; two were offered on the Sabbath, seven each at great feasts and at the beginning of each month, and fourteen every day during the Feast of Tabernacles (Lev 1:3, 10; Nu 28). The "burnt offering" (GK 10545) was a sacrifice that was wholly consumed on the altar (in contrast to the fellowship offering; cf. Lev 3; 7:11–36). "Wheat" was offered as fine flour, either alone (Lev 5:11–13), mixed as dough (Lev 2:1–3), or as cakes (Lev 2:4). "Salt" was offered with all oblations (Lev 2:13; Mk 9:49). "Wine" was poured out as a libation (Ex 29:40–41; Lev 23:13, 18, 37). "Oil" was used in the meal offerings. Other ancient documents demonstrate that Persian monarchs were interested in foreign cults.

10 "Sacrifices pleasing" is literally "sacrifices of sweet smell" (cf. Ge 8:21; Da 2:46). In pagan religions the sacrifices were viewed literally as nourishment for the gods, but not in the worship of the Lord (Eze 44:7). Darius also commanded that the Jews be allowed to "pray for the well-being of the king and his sons."

11 Decrees and treaties customarily had appended a long list of curses against anyone who might disregard them. Anyone who would change Darius's decree would be "impaled" on a beam from his own house. The OT cites the hanging or fastening of criminals (Ge 40:22; 41:13; Nu 25:4; cf. Est 2:23; 5:14; 9:14; et al.). According to Dt 21:22–23, a criminal was stoned and his corpse hung on a "tree" (cf. 2Sa 21:6, 9).

12 At the end of his famous Behistun Inscription, Darius warned: "If thou shalt behold this inscription or these sculptures, (and) shalt destroy them and shalt not protect them as long as unto thee there is strength, may Ahuramazda be a smiter unto thee, and may family not be unto thee, and what thou shalt do, that for thee may Ahuramazda utterly destroy!"

is given here. These dimensions contrast with those of Solomon's temple, which was 20 cubits wide by 30 cubits high by 60 cubits long (1Ki 6:2). The dimensions here in v.3 are probably not descriptions of the temple as built, but specifications of the outer limits of a building the Persians would support. The second temple was manifestly not as grandiose as the first (3:12; Hag 2:3). On "large stones," see comment on 5:8 (cf. also 1Ki 6:36; 7:12). Such use of timber beams with masonry is attested at Ras Shamra and elsewhere. On the vessels of the temple, see comment on 5:14–15.

5. Darius's order for the rebuilding of the temple (6:6–12)

6–7 "Stay away from there" is literally "be distant from there." When Babylonian kings like Nebuchadnezzar and Nabonidus rebuilt temples, they searched carefully to discover the exact outlines of the former buildings.

8 "Treasury" (lit., "possessions," "properties"; GK 10479) occurs frequently in extrabiblical Aramaic with a wide variety of

6. The completion of the temple (6:13–15)

13–14 Work on the temple made little progress because of opposition and the preoccupation of the returnees with their own homes (Hag 1:2–3). Because they had placed their own interests first, God sent them famine as a judgment (Hag 1:5–6, 10–11). Spurred by the preaching of Haggai and Zechariah, and under the leadership of Zerubbabel and Joshua, a new effort was begun (Hag 1:12–15). The reference to "Artaxerxes" seems out of place because this king did not contribute to the rebuilding of the temple. His name may have been inserted here because he contributed to the work of the temple at a later date during the time of Ezra (7:21–26).

15 "Adar," the last Babylonian month, was February-March. The temple was finished on March 12, 515 B.C., a little over seventy years after its destruction. As the renewed work on the temple had begun Sept 21, 520 (Hag 1:4–15), sustained effort had continued for over four years. According to Hag 2:3, the older members who could remember the splendor of Solomon's temple were disappointed when they saw the smaller size of Zerubbabel's temple (cf. 3:12). Nonetheless the second temple, though not as grand as the first, lasted much longer.

The general plan of the second temple resembled the first. But "the Most Holy Place" was left empty as the ark of the covenant had been lost through the Babylonian conquest. The "Holy Place" was furnished with a table for the showbread, the incense altar, and one menorah instead of Solomon's ten.

7. The dedication of the temple (6:16–18)

16 For the dedication of Solomon's temple, see 1Ki 8. This verse and v.19 emphasize that the leadership of the returned exiles was responsible for the completion of the temple. This dedication of the temple was a joyous occasion. The Jewish holiday in December that celebrates the discovery of pure oil, its prolongation, and the rededication of the temple captured by the Jews by the Maccabees is known today as Hanukkah.

17 The number of victims sacrificed was small compared to the thousands in similar services under Solomon (1Ki 8:5, 63), Hezekiah (2Ch 30:24), and Josiah (2Ch 35:7).

Nonetheless, they represented a real sacrifice under the prevailing conditions.

18 This ends the Aramaic section that began in 4:8; another Aramaic section begins at 7:12. The priests were divided into twenty-four courses, each of which served at the temple for a week at a time (cf. Lk 1:5, 8).

8. The celebration of the Passover (6:19–22)

19 The date would have been about Apr 21, 515 B.C. Since the destruction of the temple in A.D. 70, Jews have not sacrificed Passover lambs but have substituted eggs and roasted meat. Only the Samaritans continue to slaughter lambs, for their place of worship is on Mount Gerizim (cf. Jn 4:20), though their temple has also been destroyed.

20 "Ceremonially clean" (GK 3196) is used almost exclusively of ritual or moral purity, especially in OT passages relating to the priests. Priests and Levites had to be cleansed in order to fulfill their ritual functions. In 2Ch 29:34, the Levites in the time of Hezekiah are described as more upright in heart in sanctifying themselves than the priests (2Ch 30:17–19).

21 The returning exiles were not uncompromising separatists; they were willing to accept any who would separate themselves from the syncretism of the foreigners introduced into the area by the Assyrians. "The unclean practices" are literally "uncleanness," "filthiness." Idolatry had defiled the land (Eze 36:18; cf. Ge 35:2), and the Israelites were unclean because of it (cf. Eze 22:4; 36:25).

22 The joy experienced here was more than a political celebration or a displaced person's gladness at his return home. This was a deeply religious joy "because the Lord had filled them with joy." "King of Assyria" is a surprising title for Darius, the Persian king. Assyria was originally in the area in northeastern Mesopotamia along the banks of the upper Tigris River, centering around its capital, Nineveh. After the fall of that city in 612 B.C., the term "Assyrian" was used for formerly occupied territories. Persian kings adopted a variety of titles, including "king of Babylon" (cf. 5:13; Ne 13:6). In Ne 9:32 "kings of Assyria" could signify, not only

Assyrian, but also Babylonian and Persian kings. The latter meaning may be intended here.

II. Ezra's Return and Reforms (7:1–10:44)

A. Ezra's Return to Palestine (7:1–8:36)

1. Preparations (7:1–10)

1 "After these things" refers to the completion and dedication of the temple in 515 B.C. (cf. ch. 6). The identity of the Artaxerxes mentioned here has been disputed. If this was Artaxerxes I, as the traditional view maintains and which we believe is correct, Ezra arrived in Palestine in about 458. This view assumes a gap of almost sixty years between the events of chs. 6 and 7. The only recorded event during this interval concerns opposition in Xerxes's reign (485–465 B.C.; cf. 4:6).

The genealogy of Ezra given in vv.1–5 is an extraordinary one that lists his ancestors back to Aaron, brother of Moses. "Ezra" is a shortened form of Azariah, a name that occurs twice in the list of his ancestors. "Seraiah" ("The LORD is Prince") was the high priest under Zedekiah who was killed in 587 B.C. by Nebuchadnezzar (2Ki 25:18–21; Jer 52:24), some 129 years before Ezra's arrival. "Azariah" ("The LORD has helped") is the name of about twenty-five OT individuals, including one of Daniel's companions (Da 1:6–7). "Hilkiah" ("My portion is the LORD") was the high priest under Josiah (2Ki 22:4).

2 On "Shallum" see comment on 2:42. "Zadok" ("righteous") was a priest under David whom Solomon appointed chief priest in place of Abiathar, who had supported the rebel Adonijah (1Ki 1:7–8; 2:35). Ezekiel regarded the Zadokites as free from idolatry (Eze 44:15–16). The Zadokites held the office of high priest till 171 B.C. The Sadducees were named after them, and the Qumran community looked for the restoration of the Zadokite priesthood.

3–4 "Amariah" means "The LORD has spoken"; "Zerahiah," "The LORD has shone forth"; "Uzzi," "[The LORD is] strength"; and "Bukki," "vessel [of the LORD]."

5 "Abishua" ("My father is salvation") was the great grandson of Aaron (1Ch 6:4–5); "Phinehas" ("the Nubian"), his grandson. "Eleazar" means "God has helped."

6 "A teacher" (lit., "scribe"; GK 6221) is a person who served as secretary, such as Shaphan under Josiah (2Ki 22:3). Others took dictation, as Baruch, who wrote down what Jeremiah spoke (Jer 36:32). From the exilic period the scribes were scholars who studied and taught the Scriptures. In the NT period they were addressed as "rabbis." "The hand of the LORD his God was on him" is a striking expression of God's favor.

7–9 Most scholars assume that the seventh year of Artaxerxes I should be reckoned according to the Persian custom of dating regnal years from spring to spring (Nisan to Nisan, which was also the Jewish religious calendar). Thus Ezra would have begun his journey on the first day of Nisan (Apr 8, 458) and arrived on the first day of Ab (Aug 4, 458). The journey took 119 days (including an eleven-day delay, cf. 8:31), or four months.

Spring was the most auspicious time for such journeys; most ancient armies went on campaigns at this season. Though the direct distance between Babylon and Jerusalem is about five hundred miles, the travelers would have had to traverse nine hundred miles, going northwest along the Euphrates River and then south. The relatively slow rate is explicable by the presence of children and the elderly. The full phrase "the gracious hand of his God was on him" occurs here, in 8:18, 22, and in Ne 2:8, 18. This phrase denotes God's permanent help and grace that rest on a person or a congregation.

10 Ezra was learned in the law of Moses (v.6), as a "teacher of the Law of the God of heaven" (v.12). He not only studied the Scriptures but taught and interpreted them (Ne 8). Bible study was not merely an intellectual discipline but it was also a personal study for his own life and for the instruction of his congregation.

2. The authorization by Artaxerxes (7:11–26)

11 Many scholars regard the letter of Artaxerxes I permitting Ezra's return in 458 (or 457) as the beginning point of Daniel's first 69 weeks (Da 9:24–27). If each week represented a solar year, then 69 times 7 years equals 483 years, added to 457 B.C. equals A.D. 26, i.e., the traditional date for the beginning of Christ's ministry. Others, however, regard

the commission of the same king to Nehemiah in 445 B.C. as the starting point (Ne 1:1, 11; 2:1–8). From this date, by computing according to a lunar year of 360 days, the same date of A.D. 26 is reached.

12 The text of the decree in vv.12–26 is in Aramaic. The phrase "king of kings" was used by Assyrian kings, as their empires incorporated many kingdoms. It was then adopted by Neo-Babylonian kings like Nebuchadnezzar (Eze 26:7; Da 2:37, 47). The rabbis applied to God the title "King of the king of kings."

13–14 The king used the term "Israelites" rather than "Judeans." Ezra's aim was to make a united Israel of those who returned. "Seven advisers" corresponds with known Persian tradition. Many scholars believe that "the Law" Ezra brought with him was the complete Pentateuch in its present form.

15–17 Critics ask whether the Persian king would be so generous. The Persian treasury had ample funds, and such benevolence was a well-attested policy. The custom of sending gifts to Jerusalem from the Jews in the Diaspora continued down through the Roman Empire till the Jewish-Roman War, when the Romans diverted these contributions to the temple of Jupiter instead.

18–19 See comments on 5:17 and 6:1.

20–21 There are over three-hundred travel texts from Persepolis, which report the daily operations of a highly developed system of travel, transport, and communication. Other Elamite texts from the treasury at Persepolis give examples of the royal disbursement of supplies and funds. Haggai 1:8–11 indicates that work on the temple was delayed because of a lack of contributions from the Jewish community. Perhaps the provincial officials did not cooperate in carrying out the royal commands.

22 A "talent" (lit., "circle"; GK 3970–71) in the Babylonian sexagesimal system was 60 minas, with a mina being 60 shekels. A talent weighed about 75 pounds. A hundred talents was an enormous sum, about 3 3/4 tons of silver. This amount, together with a talent of gold, was the tribute that Pharaoh Neco imposed on Judah (2Ki 23:33). A "cor" was a donkey load, about 6 1/2 bushels. The total

amount of wheat, 650 bushels, was relatively small. The grain would be used in meal offerings. A "bath" was a liquid measure of about 6 gallons; therefore, the amount of oil was 600 gallons. "Salt without limit" is literally "salt without prescribing [how much]" (see comments on 4:14; 6:9).

23 The Persian king expressed urgency in his command. "Wrath against the realm of the king" hints at Egypt's revolt against the Persians in 460 B.C. and Egypt's temporary expulsion of the Persians in 459 with the aid of the Athenians. In 458 (457) when Ezra returned to Palestine, the Persians were involved in suppressing the revolt. We do not know how many "sons" the king had at this time, but he ultimately had eighteen.

24 In the ancient world, priests and other temple personnel were often given exemptions from enforced labor or taxes.

25 Royal judges under the Persians had life tenure but were subject to capital punishment for misconduct in office. Ezra was told to administer justice according to Jewish (OT) laws.

26 The extensive powers given to Ezra—"must surely be punished by death"—are striking. Possibly the implementation of these provisions involved Ezra in much traveling, which would explain the Bible's silence about his activities between 458 and 445. Other documents show that it was Persian policy to encourage both moral and religious authority that would enhance public order.

3. Ezra's doxology (7:27–28)

27–28 Here is the first occurrence of the first person for Ezra, a trait that characterizes the "Ezra Memoirs" that continue to the end of ch. 9. "Praise" (lit., "blessed"; GK 1384) opens the prayers that Jews recite today: "Blessed art Thou, O Lord our God." Ezra recognized fully that the ultimate source of the favor granted by the king was the sovereign grace of God (cf. 6:22). "To bring honor" can mean "to glorify." Human beings can beautify, but only God can endow with true glory. Later passages show that Ezra was primarily a priest and scholar rather than an administrator. Yet the assurance that God had called him and had opened the doors gave Ezra the courage and strength to undertake this great task.

4. Returnees with Ezra (8:1–14)

1 Verses 1–14 list those who accompanied Ezra from Mesopotamia, including the descendants of 15 individuals. The figures of the men listed total 1,496, in addition to the individuals named. There were also a considerable number of women and children (v.21). An additional group of about 40 Levites (vv.18–19) and of 220 "temple servants" (v.20) are also listed.

2 On "Phinehas" see 7:5. "Gershom" ("sojourner") was also the name of the elder son of Moses and Zipporah (Ex 2:22). "Ithamar" ("isle of palms") was also the name of the fourth son of Aaron (Ex 6:23).

3 "Shecaniah" means "The LORD has taken up his abode." "Zechariah" ("The LORD has remembered") was the name of about thirty individuals in the Bible, including the prophet and the father of John the Baptist (Lk 1:5–67).

4–6 "Jahaziel" means "May God see!" "Ebed" (lit., "slave") is probably a shortened form of "Obadiah" ("slave of the LORD"). "Jonathan" ("The LORD has given") is the name of sixteen individuals in the OT.

7–9 On "Elam" see 2:7. "Jeshaiah" means "The LORD has saved." "Athaliah" ("The LORD is exalted") was also the name of a famous queen, daughter of Ahab and Jezebel (2Ki 11). On "Shephatiah" see 2:4. "Zebadiah" means "The LORD has given." "Michael" ("Who is like God?") is the name of ten OT individuals, including the archangel. "Joab" means "The LORD is father." "Jehiel" means "May God live!"

10–12 "Josiphiah" ("May the LORD add!") appears only here, but it is a name closely related to Joseph. On "Zechariah" see v.3. On "Azgad" see 2:12.

13–14 "The last ones" probably implies that these followed earlier members of the family who came with Zerubbabel. "Eliphelet" means "(my) God delivers." "Jeuel" is "The LORD has stored up." "Shemaiah" ("The LORD has heard") is the name of twenty-eight individuals in the Bible. On "Bigvai" see 2:2.

5. The search for Levites (8:15–20)

15 "The canal that flows toward Ahava" probably flowed into either the Euphrates or the Tigris. "Three days" would be from the ninth to the twelfth of Nisan, as the actual journey began on the twelfth (cf. v.31). The "Levites," who had been entrusted with many menial tasks, may have found a more comfortable way of life in exile.

16 "Eliezer" means "my God is help." "Ariel" ("Lion of God") appears only here as a personal name (cf. 2Sa 23:20; 1Ch 11:22); elsewhere it is a cryptic name for Jerusalem (Isa 29:1, 2, 7). "Meshullam" ("rewarded") is the name of nineteen OT individuals. He may be the same person who opposed the marriage reforms (10:15). "Men of learning" is literally "those who cause to understand" (cf. 1Ch 25:8; 2Ch 35:3; Ne 8:7–9).

17–18 "Iddo" means "strength." "Sherebiah" possibly means "The LORD has sent scorching heat." "A capable man" is literally "a man of insight." "Mahli" means "shrewd."

19 "Hashabiah" ("The LORD has taken account") is the name of eleven OT individuals, primarily Levites. "Merari" means "bitterness." Only about forty Levites from two families were willing to join Ezra's caravan. The service of God requires dedication and sometimes moving from a comfortable situation.

20 On "temple servants" see comment on 2:43. Humanly speaking, the dedication of this group is remarkable. Socially they were a caste of mixed origins and were inferior to the Levites in status. But God's Spirit had motivated them to respond in larger numbers than the Levites.

6. Prayer and fasting (8:21–23)

21 For the association of fasting and humbling oneself, see Ps 35:13. Ezra prayed for a journey unimpeded by obstacles and dangers (cf v.31). "Children" designates those younger than twenty, with a stress on the younger ages. Such "little ones" are most vulnerable in times of war (cf. Dt 20:14; Jdg 21:10; Eze 9:6). The vast treasures they were carrying—"our possessions"—offered a tempting bait for robbers.

22 Scripture speaks often of unholy shame (Jer 48:13; Mic 3:7) and sometimes of a sense of holy shame. Ezra was quick to blush with such a sense of holy shame (cf. 9:6). He had gone out on a limb by proclaiming his faith in God's ability to protect the caravan. Having done so, he was embarrassed to ask for human protection. Grave dangers faced travelers between Mesopotamia and Palestine. Some thirteen years later Nehemiah was accompanied by an armed escort (see comment on Ne 2:9). For the phrase "everyone who looks to him," see 1Ch 16:10–11; 2Ch 11:16; Pss 40:16; 69:6; 70:4; 105:3–4.

23 Fasting implies an earnestness that makes one oblivious to food. For the association of fasting and prayer, see Ne 1:4; Da 9:3; Mt 17:21 (NIV note); Ac 14:23.

7. The assignment of the precious objects (8:24–30)

24 This rendering implies that Sherebiah, Hashabiah, and ten others were the twelve leading priests. But according to vv.18–19, they were the leaders of the Levites at Casiphia. The verse can be rendered "I set apart twelve of the leading priests *besides* Sherebiah, Hashabiah, and ten of their brothers" (emphasis mine). According to v.30, both priests and Levites were entrusted with the sacred objects.

25 "Offering" literally means "what is lifted" (i.e., "dedicated" or "given for the cult"; cf. Ex 25:2; 35:5; Lev 7:14; Dt 12:6). The offerings came not only from the Jews but also from the king.

26–28 For comparison "650 talents" equals 49,000 pounds or close to 25 tons of silver (cf. 7:22). "100 talents" equals 7,500 pounds. These are enormous sums, worth millions of dollars. On "darics," see comment on 2:69 (cf. Ne 7:70–72). "Polished bronze" may have been orichalc, a bright yellow alloy of copper highly prized in ancient times.

29–30 Both people and objects were sacred and "consecrated" (GK 7731) to God. Ezra carefully weighed out the treasures and entrusted them to others. He instilled a sense of the holiness of the mission and the gravity of each individual's responsibility. Each was responsible to guard his deposit, his "talent." The data were carefully recorded and rechecked at the journey's end (v.34).

8. The journey and arrival in Jerusalem (8:31–36)

31–32 "We set out" means literally "to pull up stakes" (i.e., of tents). After an initial three-day encampment (v.15), another eight days elapsed while Levites for the caravan were gathered. The actual departure was on the twelfth day. The journey was to take four months (see comment on 7:9). Nehemiah also "rested three days" after his arrival in Palestine (Ne 2:11).

33 "Meremoth son of Uriah" later repaired two sections of the wall (Ne 3:4, 21) and signed the covenant established through Nehemiah (Ne 10:5). "Eleazar" is "God has helped." "Jozabad" means "The LORD has given." "Noadiah" means "The LORD has kept his appointment."

34 According to Babylonian tradition, almost every transaction, including sales and marriages, had to be recorded in writing. Ezra may have had to send back a signed certification of the delivery of the treasures.

35–36 The animal sacrifices were made as a thanksgiving to God for his mercies and as a sin offering to acknowledge their unworthiness for such mercies. Compared with the offerings of the returnees under Zerubbabel, when many more exiles were involved (6:17), the offerings on this occasion, except for the identical number of male goats, were far less.

B. Ezra's Reforms (9:1–10:44)

1. The offense of mixed marriages (9:1–6a)

1–2 Ezra had reached Jerusalem on the first day of the fifth month (7:9). The measures dealing with intermarriage were announced on the seventeenth day of the ninth month (cf. 10:8 with 10:9), or four and a half months after his arrival. Those who brought this problem to Ezra's attention were probably the ordinary members of the community rather than the leaders, who were themselves guilty. When those in positions of responsibility fall, they lead others astray. Humanly speaking there may have been reasons for such intermarriages, such as a disparity between the number of returning men and available Jewish women.

"The neighboring peoples" (lit., "peoples of the lands") included the pagan newcomers who had been brought into Samaria by the

Assyrians and had infiltrated south, and Edomites and others who had encroached on former Judean territories. The eight groups listed designate the original inhabitants of Canaan before the Hebrew conquest (Ex 3:8, 17; 13:5; 23:23, 28; Dt 7:1; 20:17; Jos 3:10; 9:1; 12:8; Jdg 3:5; 1Ki 9:20). Only the Ammonites, Moabites, and Egyptians were still extant in the postexilic period (cf. 2Ch 8:7; Ne 9:8). "Perizzites" is perhaps a designation for villagers. The "Jebusites" occupied the city of Jerusalem (Jos 15:8; 18:16, 28), which was known as the city of Jebus (Jdg 19:10; 1Ch 11:4–5) before its capture by David.

"Ammonites," the descendants of Lot by an incestuous union with his younger daughter (Ge 19:38), occupied the area around Rabbath Ammon, modern Amman in Transjordan. "Moabites," the descendants of Lot by his elder daughter (Ge 19:37), occupied the area east of the Dead Sea. Ruth was a Moabite woman (Ru 1:4). According to the Pentateuch intermarriage with Egyptians was legitimate.

On "mingled the holy race [lit., holy seed]," compare Ps 106:35. The "officials" probably served the Persian government as tax collectors. These leaders were indeed leading the people, but in the wrong direction (cf. 10:18; Ne 6:18). Marrying those who did not belong to the Lord was infidelity for the people of Israel, who were considered to be the bride of the Lord.

3 Ezra continues to write in the first person: "When I heard this, I tore my tunic and cloak." Rending one's garments commonly expressed distress or grief (cf. Ge 37:29, 34; Est 4:1; Job 1:20; Isa 36:22; Jer 41:5; Mt 26:65). Ezra's act of pulling out his own hair is unique in the Bible; elsewhere the head is shaved (Job 1:20; Eze 7:18; Am 8:10). Nehemiah's personality was significantly different from Ezra's: when confronted with the same problem of intermarriage, instead of pulling out his own hair, he pulled out the hair of the offenders (Ne 13:25)! Ezra's influence was not due to his official position but to the moral outrage he demonstrated.

4 Those with a proper perception of God's holiness will tremble at his word (see Heb 12:18–29, esp. v.21). The "evening sacrifice" took place about three P.M. (cf. Ex 12:6; Ac 3:1). The informants had probably visited Ezra in the morning, so that he must have sat in this position for many hours. The time of the evening sacrifice was also the appointed time for prayer and confession.

5–6a "Self-abasement" (GK 9504) means "mortification," "humiliation." "With my hands spread out" means with palms upwards (cf. Ex 9:29; 1Ki 8:22; Isa 1:15).

2. Ezra's confession and prayer (9:6b–15)

6b On "I am ashamed," see comment on 8:22. "Disgraced" (GK 4007) means "to be humiliated or confounded," connoting the pain that accompanies shame. Ezra felt both an inner shame before God and an outward humiliation before others for the sins of his people.

7 "From the days of our forefathers"—the Hebrews were conscious of their corporate solidarity, unlike the individualistic emphasis of modern Christianity. Ezekiel 21:16 vividly describes "the sword" (cf. Ne 4:13b) of the Lord at work as an instrument of his judgment; though the king of Babylon wielded the sword, it was actually the Lord himself who exercised divine judgment. After the conquest of Judah by the Babylonians in 605 B.C., the Jews—except for about a century from the Maccabean Revolt in 165 B.C. till Pompey's intervention in 63 B.C.—did not enjoy autonomy until the establishment of the state of Israel in 1948.

8 "Has been gracious" signifies the Lord's grace or mercy for the "remnant" of his people. "A firm place" is literally a "nail" or a "peg," as a nail driven into a wall (cf. Isa 22:23) or a tent peg into the ground (Isa 33:20; 54:2). An increase in light suggests vitality and joy (1Sa 14:27, 29; Pr 15:30; 29:13).

9 The Persian kings were favorably disposed to the Jews: Cyrus (539–530 B.C.) gave them permission to return (Ezr 1). Darius I (522–486) renewed the decree of Ezra (Ezr 6). His son Xerxes (485–465) granted Jews privileges and protection (Est 8–10). Artaxerxes I (464–424) gave authorizations to Ezra (Ezr 7) and Nehemiah (Ne 1–2).

"New life" (GK 4695) is the same word translated "relief" (v.8). "A wall of protection" is used of a low fence around a sheepfold (Nu 32:16) or of a wall bordering a path (Nu 22:24). The qualifying phrase "in Judah and Jerusalem" indicates a metaphorical reference in the sense of "protection."

10–11 On these two verses compare Lev 18:24–26; Dt 7:1–6; 2Ki 17; 23:8–16; Eze 5:11; Ro 3:19. "Polluted by the corruption" refers to both the corruption of Canaanite idolatry and the immoral practices associated with it (cf 2Ch 29:5; La 1:17, Eze 7:20; 36:17).

12 Verses 10–12 are not drawn from a single quotation but from many passages (Dt 11:8–9; Pr 10:27; Isa 1:19; Eze 37:25). In the NT era the problems of interfaith marriage were recognized by Christians as they had been by Jews. Marriages with unbelievers were condemned (2Co 6:14); widows were explicitly advised to marry within the faith (1Co 7:39).

13–14 "Angry" (GK 647) is related to the word that means both "nose" and "anger" (cf. Eze 38:18). When God's anger came on the Israelites, it was because they had failed to perform their covenant responsibilities (cf. Dt 7:4; 11:17; 29:25–28; Jos 23:16).

15 A proper sense of God's holiness sheds light on our unworthiness (cf. Isa 6:1–5; Lk 5:8). For comparable passages of national lament, see Pss 44, 60, 74, 79, 80, 83, et al.

3. The people's response (10:1–4)

Verse 9 indicates that the people assembled on the twentieth day of the ninth month (Kislev) of the first year (i.e., Dec 19, 458), in the cold, rainy season. The examining committee began its work ten days later (v.16). The committee completed its work in three months (v.17), on March 27, 457.

1 Hereafter Ezra is spoken of in the third person. "Weeping," not silently but aloud (cf. on 3:12; Ne 1:4; Joel 1:12–17), like laughing, is contagious. The people also "wept bitterly" (lit., "wept with a great weeping"). "Throwing himself down" implies that Ezra kept on throwing himself on the ground. The prophets and other leaders used object lessons, even bizarre actions, to attract people's attention (Isa 7:3; 8:1–4, 18; Jer 19; 27). The women and children are mentioned. Entire families were involved.

2 Ezra, the wise teacher, waited for his audience to draw their own conclusions about what should be done. Shecaniah (different from that of 8:3) led the way. His father is possibly the same Jehiel mentioned in vv.21 and 26, as he also was of the family of Elam (see 2:7). Perhaps Shecaniah was grieved that his father had married a non-Jewish mother. Six members of the clan of Elam were involved in intermarriages (v.26).

3 "Make a covenant" (lit., "to cut a covenant") derives from the practice of cutting a sacrificial animal. Originally it may have involved passing between the pieces with the implied curse that whoever did not keep the covenant should be cut up like the animals (Ge 15:9–18). "All these women and their children" reflects the fact that in ancient societies, as often in ours, mothers were given custody of their children when marriages were dissolved (cf. Ge 21:14). In "the counsel of my lord" is perhaps better rendered in "the counsel of the Lord" (cf. Ps 33:11; Pr 19:21; Isa 19:17; Jer 49:20; 50:45).

4 Shecaniah gave a clarion call to action. Weeping was not enough. Courageous and painful decisions had to be made. The people themselves had to respond.

4. The calling of a public assembly (10:5–15)

5 Ezra first enlisted the aid of the leaders of the priests, Levites, and laity and had them swear an oath. The oath, a solemn declaration made under divine sanction, could be assertive, exculpatory, or promissory. An assertive oath called God to witness the truth of a statement (1Ki 18:10; Ro 1:9; Php 1:8). An exculpatory oath sought to clear a person from an accusation. A promissory oath, like the one here, related to future undertakings. In biblical oaths the implied curse for nonfulfillment is often expressed in the vague statement, "May the LORD deal with me, be it ever so severely, if . . ." (Ru 1:17; 2Sa 3:35; 1Ki 2:23). On rare occasions the full implications of the curse are spelled out (Nu 5:19–31; Job 31; Pss 7:4–5; 137:5–6).

6 Complete fasting (i.e., abstaining from food and drink; cf. Ne 1:4) was twice observed by Moses (cf. Ex 34:28; Dt 9:18; cf. also Jnh 3:7). Ordinary fasts involved abstaining from eating only (1Sa 1:7; 2Sa 3:35). "He continued to mourn" describes the reaction of those who are aware of the threat of deserved judgment (Ex 33:4; Nu 14:39; 1Sa 15:35; 16:1). "The room" typifies certain chambers in the temple area that were used as storerooms (8:29; Ne 13:4–13).

7 While Ezra continued to fast and pray, the chiefs and elders ordered all the exiles to assemble in Jerusalem. Though Ezra had been vested with great authority (7:25–26), he used it sparingly and influenced the people by his example.

8 As the territory of Judah had been much reduced, the most distant inhabitants would not be more than fifty miles from Jerusalem. All could travel to Jerusalem "within three days." "Forfeit" means to ban from profane use and to devote, either to destruction (e.g., Ex 22:20; Dt 13:13–17) or for use in the temple, as here (cf. Lev 27:28–29; Jos 6:18–19; 7:1–26).

9 Usually Judah alone is mentioned, but a few passages also refer to the exiles who came from or who settled in the area of Benjamin north of Jerusalem (1:5; 4:1). The plaza or square where they assembled was either in the outer court of the temple or more probably in the open space before the Water Gate (Ne 3:26; 8:1). The trepidation of the people was caused by two separate reasons: their transgressions and the weather.

"The rain" indicates heavy torrential rains. The ninth month, Kislev (Nov.–Dec.), is in the middle of the rainy season, which begins with light showers in October and lasts to mid-April. December and January are also cold months in Jerusalem, with temperatures in the fifties and even forties; sometimes it even snows (2Sa 23:20; Ps 147:16–17; Pr 31:21). The assembly sensed a sign of divine displeasure in the abnormally heavy rains (cf. 1Sa 12:17–18; Eze 13:11, 13).

10 Ezra was not only a scribe (7:11–12, 21) but also a priest. The sins and failures of the exiles were great enough; they had added "to Israel's guilt" (cf. 2Ch 28:13) by marrying pagan women.

11 "Confession" (GK 9343) almost always means "thanksgiving," except here and in Jos 7:19. A better translation than "foreign wives" might be "pagan wives," implying not only a different nationality but also adherence to a different religion.

12–13 The Lord so convicted the hearers that what Ezra had said was right that they spon-

taneously and unitedly responded in an extraordinary manner, "with a loud voice" (cf. 3:12; 2Ch 15:14; Ne 9:4), acknowledging their need to do something about the situation. A spokesman for the people, however, pointed out the practical difficulties in view of the inclement weather. "Sinned" (GK 7321) connotes an act of revolt or rebellion (cf. 1Ki 12:19).

14 The "elders" were the older men of the community who formed a governing council in every village (cf. 1Sa 30:26–31). Those at the gate of a town served as magistrates (Dt 19:12; 21:3, 19; Ru 4:1–12). There were also "judges" (cf. Dt 16:18–20). "The fierce anger" is a phrase used only of God's wrath (cf. 9:14; cf. also Ex 32:12; Nu 25:4; Dt 13:17; Jos 7:26; Ne 13:18; et al.).

15 The truth of the narrative is indicated by the candor with which the opposition to the reform measures is recorded. Why these four men opposed the measure is unclear. Perhaps they were protecting themselves or their relatives, or they viewed the measures of separation as too harsh. On Meshullam, see comment on 8:16. If he is the son of Bani in v.29, he himself had married a pagan wife.

5. Investigation of the offenders (10:16–17)

16–17 The committee began its work ten days after the assembly had met in the rain. They completed their work three months later, on March 27, 457. The investigating elders and judges did their work carefully and thoroughly. They discovered that about a hundred couples were involved.

6. The list of offenders (10:18–43)

18–19 Among those involved were the descendants of Jeshua, the high priest (see comment on 2:2). For the symbolic handshake, see 2Ki 10:15; La 5:6; Eze 17:18. According to Lev 5:14–19, a "ram" was the guilt offering for a sin committed unwittingly. Though the offenders may not have fully realized the gravity of their offense, they had no excuse; the Scriptures plainly set forth God's standards on marriage.

20–24 The list continues of all those who had married pagan women. Only one singer and three gatekeepers were involved. There is no representative of the Nethinim (2:43–54) or of the descendants of Solomon's servants

(2:55–57). The lowest classes were the least involved in intermarriage; the pagan women were probably not attracted to them.

25–43 The names in this part of the list concern those who were not priests or who were not involved in any sort of priestly activity.

7. The dissolution of the mixed marriages (10:44)

44 Some of the marriages had produced children, but this was not accepted as a reason for halting the proceedings. As it was just under eight months from the time of Ezra's arrival to the committee's findings, the offspring mentioned here must be either the offspring of mixed marriages contracted in Mesopotamia or the offspring of mixed marriages contracted by those who had returned earlier to Palestine. The percentage of those who intermarried in that community of 30,00 people was 0.4 percent (ranging from 8.1 percent among the Levites, to 2.2 percent among the gatekeepers, to 0.3 percent among the laity).

Nehemiah

INTRODUCTION

See the introduction to Ezra for comments on the book of Nehemiah.

EXPOSITION

I. Nehemiah's First Administration (1:1–12:47)

A. Nehemiah's Response to the Situation in Jerusalem (1:1–11)

1. News of the plight of Jerusalem (1:1–4)

The walls of Jerusalem that had been destroyed by Nebuchadnezzar, despite abortive attempts to rebuild them (Ezr 4:6–23), remained in ruins for almost a century and a half. Such a lamentable situation obviously made Jerusalem vulnerable to her numerous enemies. Yet from a mixture of apathy and fear the Jews failed to rectify this glaring deficiency. They needed the dynamic catalyst of an inspired leader, a man named Nehemiah.

1 Though the books of Ezra and Nehemiah were bound together from the earliest times, "the words of" indicates the title of a separate composition (cf. Jer 1:1; Am 1:1). The name "Nehemiah" means "the comfort of the LORD" or "The LORD has comforted." "Hacaliah" is contracted from "wait for the LORD" (cf. Zep 3:8). The reference to his paternal sepulchers in Jerusalem (2:3, 5) may mean that Nehemiah came from a prominent family.

"Susa," a major city of Elam in southwestern Iran, was located in a fertile plain 150 miles north of the Persian Gulf. At this time it served as a winter palace for the kings, but the area became intolerably hot during the summer months. Daniel (Da 8:2) saw himself in a vision at Susa. It was the site of the story of Esther. Ezra 4:9–10 refers to the men of Susa who were deported to Samaria.

2 Hanani was a brother of Nehemiah. "Jews" became the name of the people of Israel after the Exile.

3 The lack of a city wall meant that the people were defenseless against their enemies. Most likely Nehemiah's distress was not caused by the condition of walls torn down 140 years before his time but by the episode of Ezr 4:7–23. According to this passage Jews had attempted to rebuild the walls earlier, in the reign of Artaxerxes I. But after the protest of Rehum and Shimshai, the king ordered the Jews to desist.

4 Nehemiah "sat down" (cf. Ezr 9:3), "mourned" (cf. Ezr 10:6; Da 10:2), and "fasted." During the Exile fasting became a common practice, including solemn fasts to commemorate the taking of Jerusalem and the murder of Gedaliah (Est 4:16; Da 9:3; 10:3; Zec 7:3–7). On "the God of heaven," see comment on Ezr 1:2.

2. Nehemiah's prayer (1:5–11)

5 God is the One to be feared (cf. Dt 7:21; Da 9:4). "Who keeps his covenant of love" is literally "who keeps covenant and steadfast love." The latter word (GK 2876) means the quality that honors a covenant through thick and thin (cf. Ezr 3:11).

6 Nehemiah did not exclude himself or members of his family in his confession of sins. A true sense of the awesomeness of God reveals the depths of our own sinfulness (Isa 6:1–5; Lk 5:8).

7 "Commands" (GK 5184) is the usual word for commandment, as in the Ten Commandments (Ex 24:12). "Decrees" (GK 2976) indicates something prescribed, such as the statute of Joshua (Jos 24:25) and the commandment to keep the Passover (Ex 12:24). "Laws" (GK 5477) indicates legal decisions or judgments (Zec 7:9).

8 "Remember" (GK 2349), a key word, recurs frequently in the book (4:14; 5:19; 6:14; 13:14, 22, 29, 31). After the Babylonian conquest, Jews were scattered farther and farther. In the NT period there were more Jews in the Diaspora than in Palestine (Jn 7:35; Ac 2:9–11; Jas 1:1; 1Pe 1:1).

9 "I will gather them" is a frequently made promise (Dt 30:1–5; Isa 11:12; Jer 23:3; et al.). The phrase "a dwelling for my Name" recalls Dt 12:5.

10 Though they had sinned and failed, they were still God's special people, by virtue of their redemption (cf. Dt 4:34; 9:29).

11 "Cupbearer" literally means "one who gives (someone) something to drink." An indefinite article here suggests that there were several. Often they had other responsibilities as well.

B. Nehemiah's Journey to Palestine (2:1–20)

1. The king's response (2:1–8)

1 On a Nisan calendar "the twentieth year" was Apr 13, 445, to Apr 1, 444. On the calculation of Daniel's seventy weeks (Da 9:25) from the decree of Artaxerxes I to Nehemiah, see comment on Ezr 7:11.

Four months passed from Kislev, when Nehemiah first heard the news (1:1), to Nisan, when he felt prepared to broach the subject to the king. Even though Nehemiah was a favorite of the king, he would not have rashly blurted out his request (cf. Ge 40:20; Est 5:6; Mk 6:21–25). He carefully bided his time, constantly praying to God to grant the proper opening. "When wine was brought for him, I took the wine"; i.e., it was now Nehemiah's turn to pour the wine.

2 Regardless of one's personal problems, the king's servants were expected to keep their feelings hidden and to display a cheerful countenance before him. So far Nehemiah had managed to do this; now his burden for Jerusalem betrayed itself, no doubt in his eyes. Artaxerxes seemed to trust Nehemiah to such a degree, however, that no suspicious thought crossed his mind. He was concerned to discover what was distressing his cupbearer. Anxiety must have gripped Nehemiah, not so much for the king's question, but in anticipation of the request that he was to make, knowing full well that the king himself had stopped the Jewish efforts at rebuilding the wall (Ezr 4:17–23).

3 "May the king live forever!" was a common form of address to kings (1Ki 1:31; Da 2:4;

3:9). Notice that Nehemiah did not mention Jerusalem by name, as he wished to arouse the king's sympathy by stressing first the desecration of ancestral tombs.

4 "Then I prayed to the God of heaven" is the most beautiful example of spontaneous prayer in the Scriptures. Before turning to answer the king, Nehemiah uttered a brief prayer to God. Despite his trepidation, he knew that he stood not only in the presence of an earthly monarch, but before the King of the heavens. One of the most striking characteristics of Nehemiah was his recourse to prayer (cf. 4:4, 9; 5:19; 6:9, 14; 13:14).

5 Fortified by his appeal to God and confident in the quality of his past service, Nehemiah was encouraged to make his bold request to the king. He still did not mention Jerusalem by name but referred to it as "the city in Judah."

6–7 Though the word for "queen" (GK 8712) may simply mean a concubine, the definite article indicates that she was the queen or the chief woman of the harem. According to Da 5:2, royal women could be present on a public occasion.

In addition to safe-conduct letters, Nehemiah probably asked for a brief leave of absence, which was later extended. Nehemiah spent twelve years on his first term as governor of Judah (5:14). He then returned to report to the king, and later returned to Judah for a second term (13:6).

8 The chief forester's name, "Asaph," means "The LORD has gathered." The location of the king's forest, where Nehemiah was to obtain timber for the gates, is unclear. Some place it in Lebanon, famed for its forests of cedars (cf. 1Ki 5:6, 9; 2Ch 2:8–9, 16; Ezr 3:7). Others believe it is Solomon's Garden at Etham, about six miles south of Jerusalem, well-known for its fine gardens (cf. 2Ki 25:4; Ecc 2:5–9; Jer 39:4; 52:7); this seems more probable. In the construction of city gates, indigenous oak, poplar, or terebinth (Ge 12:6; Jos 19:33; Jdg 4:11; Hos 4:13) would most likely be used, rather than costly imported cedars from Lebanon.

2. The journey to Palestine (2:9–10)

9 Nehemiah apparently set out immediately. Unlike Ezra (Ezr 8:22), he was accompanied by an armed escort, though not because his faith was weaker than Ezra's. Rather, because of his position as official governor of Judah, it was in accordance with custom that he should have an escort assigned him.

10 The identity of Sanballat as "the Horonite" most likely identifies him as coming from either upper or lower Beth-Horon, two cities twelve miles northwest of Jerusalem (Jos 10:10; 16:3, 5). Sanballat was the chief opponent of Nehemiah (v.19; 4:1, 7; 6:1–2, 5, 12, 14; 13:28). Although not called governor, he had that position over Samaria (cf. 4:2).

"Tobiah" means "The LORD is good." He may have been a Judaizing Ammonite, but more probably he was a believing Jew, as indicated by his name and that of his son, Jehohanan (6:18). "Official" (GK 6269) is literally "slave" or "servant" (cf. v.19; 13:1–3), a term often used for high officials (cf. 2Ki 22;12; Jer 36:24; Lam 5:8). Tobiah was married to the daughter of Shecaniah (cf. 3:29; 6:18); and his son Jehohanan married the daughter of Meshullam, son of Berekiah, leader of one of the groups repairing the wall (cf. 3:4, 30; 6:18). Tobiah also was closely related to the priest Eliashib (13:4–7). He was no doubt the governor of Ammon or Transjordan under the Persians. The reason Sanballat and Tobiah "were very much disturbed" was not basically religious but political. The authority of the Samaritan governor in particular was threatened by Nehemiah's arrival.

3. Nehemiah's nocturnal inspection of the walls (2:11–16)

11–12 After the long journey three days of rest were necessary (cf. Ezr 8:32). Nehemiah took only a few men into his confidence at first. He acted with great care, going out at night—no doubt by moonlight—to inspect the situation firsthand.

13 Nehemiah did not make a complete circuit of the walls but only of the southern area to see how much was preserved. Jerusalem was always attacked where she was most vulnerable, from the north; thus there was probably little preserved in that direction. According to 2Ch 26:9, Uzziah fortified towers in the west wall, on the Tyropoeon Valley. "Jackal Well" (lit., "spring of the dragons") may have been the major spring of Jerusalem, the Gihon, its name being derived from the serpentine course of the waters of the spring to the Pool of Siloam. "The Dung Gate" (cf 3:13–14; 12:31; 2Ki 23:10), situated near the Valley Gate, led to the rubbish dump in the Hinnom Valley (cf. 3:13).

14 "The Fountain Gate" was possibly in the southeast wall facing toward En-Rogel. According to 2Ki 20:20 (2Ch 32:30), Hezekiah diverted the overflow from his Siloam Tunnel to irrigate the royal gardens (2Ki 25:4).

15–16 Nehemiah retraced his steps and reentered the city at the Valley Gate on the west slope of Ophel. The "nobles" were the notable men who directed public affairs.

4. Nehemiah's exhortation to rebuild the walls (2:17–18)

17 The walls and gates of Jerusalem had lain in ruins since their destruction by Nebuchadnezzar some 140 years before, despite attempts to rebuild them. The leaders and people had evidently become reconciled to this sad state of affairs. It took an outsider to assess the situation and rally the people to renewed efforts.

18 Nehemiah could personally attest that God was alive and active on his behalf. He had come, moreover, with royal sanction and authority. What was required and what Nehemiah provided were a vision and decisive leadership. Nehemiah was clearly a shaker, a mover, and a doer.

5. The opposition of Sanballat, Tobiah, and Geshem (2:19–20)

19 Various documents indicate that Arabs became dominant in the Transjordanian area from the Assyrian to the Persian periods (cf. Ge 25:13; Isa 60:7; Jer 49:28–33). They enjoyed a favored status under the Persians. "Ridiculed" (GK 1022) means "showed contempt for" (cf. 2Sa 6:16; 2Ki 19:21; Est 3:6).

20 Nehemiah appealed to historical claims to reject the interference of the Samaritan, Ammonite, and Arabian leaders in the affairs of Jerusalem. By his great confidence and dependence on God for success, he inspired the leaders and the people to a task they had considered beyond their abilities.

C. List of the Builders of the Wall (3:1–32)

This chapter is one of the most important in the OT for determining the topography of

Jerusalem. Though some locations are clear, others are not. Opinions differ widely about whether the wall enclosed the southwest hill, today called "Mount Zion" (2 1/2 miles, enclosing 220 acres), or only the original settlement—including the temple area—of the southeast hill of Ophel (just under 2 miles, enclosing 90 acres).

The list, which was probably preserved in the temple, proceeds in a counterclockwise direction about the wall. Some forty-one parties are named as participating in the reconstruction of forty-two sections. The towns listed as the homes of the builders seem to have represented the administrative centers of the Judean province. Altogether, ten gates are listed. Most of the rebuilding was concerned with the gates as the enemy's assaults were concentrated on these structures. Certainly not all the sections of the walls or buildings in Jerusalem were in the same state of disrepair.

1. The northern section (3:1–7)

1 "Eliashib the high priest" was the son of Joiakim (see 12:10; Ezr 10:6). His house is mentioned in vv.20–21. It was fitting that the high priest should set the example. "The Sheep Gate" (cf. v.32; 12:39) was no doubt located in the northeast section of the wall near the Birah fortress; Jn 5:2 locates it near the Bethesda Pool. What "the Tower of the Hundred" (cf. 12:39) refers to is unclear: perhaps its height (one hundred cubits) or one hundred steps or a military unit (cf. Dt 1:15). "The Tower of Hananel" (see Jer 31:38; Zec 14:10) was the most northern part of the city. The towers were associated with "the citadel by the temple" (2:8) in protecting the vulnerable northern approaches to the city.

2 "Zaccur" (short for "Zechariah"), was a Levite who later signed the covenant (10:12).

3 "The Fish Gate" (cf. 12:39) was known in the days of the first temple (Zep 1:10) as one of Jerusalem's main entrances (2Ch 33:14). It may be the same as the Gate of Ephraim, which led out to the main road north from Jerusalem that then descended to the coastal plain through Beth-Horon, likely close to the site of the present-day Damascus Gate. It was called the Fish Gate because merchants brought fish from either Tyre or the Sea of Galilee through it to the fishmarket (13:16).

4 Meremoth repaired a second section (v.21) and later signed the covenant (10:5); likewise Meshullam (v.30; 10:20). Nehemiah complained that he had given his daughter to a son of Tobiah (6:18)—perhaps one of the men who accompanied Ezra (Ezr 8:16).

5 "Tekoa" was a small town five miles south of Bethlehem, famed as the home of the prophet Amos (Am 1:1). Tekoa does not appear in the list of those who returned with Zerubbabel (Ezr 2:21–35). The "nobles" (lit., "exalted ones"; GK 129) were aristocrats;

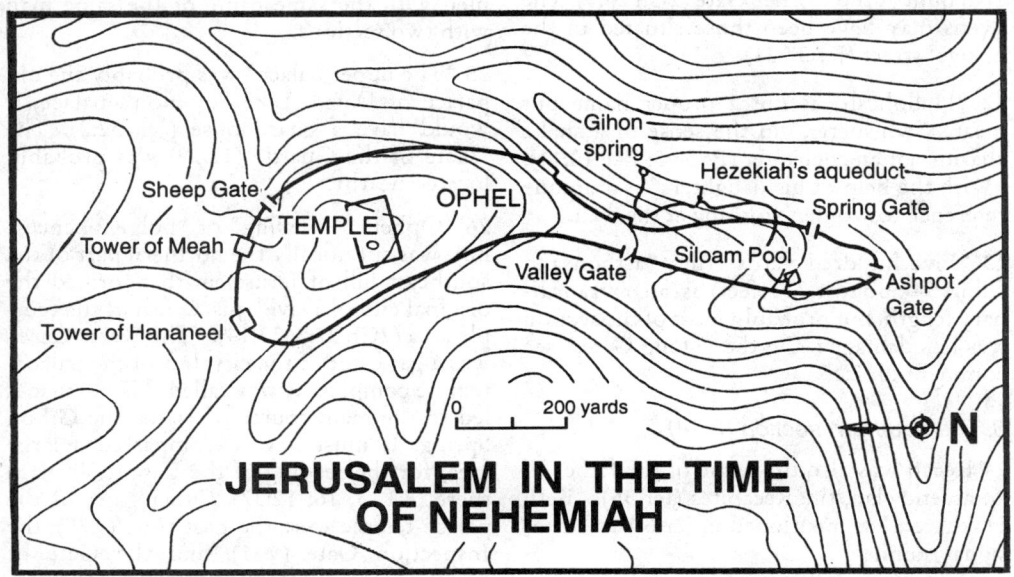

JERUSALEM IN THE TIME OF NEHEMIAH

they disdained manual labor and "would not put their shoulders to the work."

6 "The Jeshanah Gate" was situated in the northwest corner and is identified with the Corner Gate of 2Ki 14:13 and Jer 31:38. This gate probably led to the area of expansion of the city of Jerusalem (Zep 1:10).

7 "Mizpah" ("Lookout Point") is identified with Tell en-Nasbeh. Along with Gibeon, this town was under the jurisdiction of the governor of Trans-Euphrates.

2. The western section (3:8–13)

8 "One of the goldsmiths" means a member of a goldsmith guild. The industrial district of the goldsmiths and perfumers may have been located outside the walls (cf. vv.31–32). "The Broad Wall" is usually understood as a thick wall. Such a wall was discovered in 1971.

9–10 "Rephaiah" had charge of half the central district, one of the five districts of Judea. It made sense for Harumaph and others to repair the wall nearest their homes.

11 "Hasshub," short for "Hashabiah," was one who sealed the covenant (10:23). "Another section" clearly indicates that our list is only partial, as no first section is mentioned. "The Tower of the Ovens" is mentioned only here and was located on the western wall, perhaps in the same location as the one Uzziah built at the Corner Gate (2Ch 26:9). The ovens may have been those situated in the bakers' street (Jer 37:21).

12 "Hallohesh" is not a proper name but means "whisperer," in the sense of a snake charmer or an enchanter (Ps 58:5; Ecc 10:11). "With the help of his daughters" is a unique reference to women working at the wall.

13 "Five hundred yards" (lit., "a thousand cubits"—about 1,720 feet) is an extraordinary length, but probably most of the section was less damaged. On the "Dung Gate," see comment on 2:13.

3. The southern section (3:14)

14 Recab was also the name of the father of an ascetic clan, the Recabites (Jer 35). "Beth Hakkerem" is mentioned in Jer 6:1 as a fire-signal point.

4. The eastern section (3:15–32)

15 "The Fountain Gate" may also be translated "Spring Gate." This may have faced the En-Rogel spring (see comment on 2:13). "Col-Hozeh" (lit., "everyone a seer") may indicate that the family practiced divination. The "Pool of Siloam" was likely a water channel (cf. Jn 9:7), and "King's Garden" was located outside the walls where the Kidron and Hinnom valleys converge (2Ki 25:4).

16 "Beth Zur" was a district capital, twenty miles south of Jerusalem. On David's burial, see 1Ki 2:10; 2Ch 21:20; 32:33; Ac 2:29. "The House of the Heroes" may have been the house of David's mighty men, which served later as the barracks or the armory.

17–19 "Keilah" was a city southwest of Jerusalem and eight miles northwest of Hebron, situated near the border with the Philistines. It played an important role in David's early history (1Sa 23:1).

20 "Baruch" is literally "blessed." "Zealously" is from the root "to glow," "to burn," usually used of anger but also of zeal.

21 The residences of the high priest and his colleagues were located along the eastern wall of the city, corresponding with the retaining wall of the temple area above the Kidron Valley.

22–24 The name "Hasshub" also occurs in v.11, which means that we have either two men with the same name or the same man with two sections.

25 "The upper palace" was probably the old palace of David. Like Solomon's palace, it would have a guardhouse (Jer 32:2). The "Gate of the Guard" (12:39) was probably located nearby.

26 "Ophel" ("swelling" or "bulge," hence a hill) was specifically the northern part of the southeast hill of Jerusalem that formed the original city of David, just south of the temple area (2Ch 27:3; 33:14). "The Water Gate" was a gate, not of the city, but of the palace-temple complex. It was called this because it led to the main source of water, the Gihon Spring. It must have encompassed a large area, for the reading of the Law took place there (8:1, 3, 16; 12:37). Other gates of the palace-temple were the East Gate (v.29), the Inspection Gate (v.31), and the Gate of the Guard (12:39). "The projecting tower" was on the crest of the Ophel Hill.

27 The common people of Tekoa did double duty, whereas the nobles of Tekoa shirked their responsibility (see v.5).

28–30 Athaliah entered "the entrance of the Horse Gate on the palace grounds" (2Ch 23:15) and was slain there. This gate, in the easternmost part of the city, was one through which a person could reach the Kidron Valley (see Jer 31:40). The "East Gate" (see comment on v.26) may have been the predecessor of the present "Golden Gate."

31 Some of the goldsmiths apparently inhabited an area to the east of the walls of the temple area; others, however, worked on sections in the west (see v.8 above). "The Inspection Gate" was in the northern part of the temple (see comment on v.26).

32 This verse brings us to the northeast corner of Jerusalem, the point of departure near the Sheep Gate (v.1). We know from ch. 5 that there were deep economic differences in Judean society. With the exception of the nobles of Tekoa (v.5), everyone pitched in, from the high priest (v.1) to goldsmiths and perfume-makers (vv.8, 31) and even women (v.12), to accomplish a common task. Some, like the commoners of Tekoa, even did more than their share (v.27). What an inspiring example of what can be done when God's people work together under dynamic leadership!

D. Opposition to the Rebuilding of the Walls (4:1–23)

1. The derision of Sanballat and Tobiah (4:1–5)

1 Sanballat (see 2:10) "became angry" (lit., "became hot"; GK 3013) and mocked the Jews when he saw what was happening in Jerusalem (cf. his initial reaction in 2:19).

2 Disputes between rival Persian governors were quite frequent. Sanballat rapidly fired five derisive questions to taunt the Jews and discourage them from their efforts. Regarding his last one, fire had damaged the stones, which were probably limestone, and had caused much of the stone to crack and to disintegrate.

3 "Fox" (GK 8785) is also translated "jackal" (cf. Ps 63:10; La 5:18; Eze 13:4). The jackal

usually hunts in packs, whereas the fox is normally a nocturnal and solitary animal. The context therefore suggests that a fox is intended: the point of the sneer is that any wall the Jews built would be so flimsy that even the light footsteps of a solitary fox would collapse it.

4–5 Nehemiah did not personally take action against his opponents but called down the vengeance of God. His prayer uses the language of Jeremiah (Jer 12:3; 17:18; 18:21–23).

2. The threat of attack (4:6–15)

6 The people kept diligently working on the city wall, in spite of the mockery of their opponents.

7 On the Arabs, see comment on 2:19; on the Ammonites, see comment on Ezr 9:1. Ashdod was one of the five major Philistine cities (Jos 11:22; 13:3); it was overrun by the Assyrians in the eighth century B.C. (Isa 20:1). The numerous enemies of the Jews became even more angry (see comment on v.1) as they heard of the progress on the repair of Jerusalem's walls.

8–9 The mockery of the enemies now turned to their plotting together to fight against the Jews. Notice the balance between prayer and posting a guard as Nehemiah's answer to this threat.

10 "Is giving out" (lit., "to stumble, totter"; GK 4173) depicts a worker tottering under the weight of his load and ready to fall at any step. The complaint may reflect a song sung by the builders.

11–12 Nehemiah must have had good sources of information to learn of these plots. The vigilance of Nehemiah and his fellow Jews forestalled any attempt at violent attack. "Ten times over" is an idiomatic expression for "again and again" (Ge 31:41).

13 Nehemiah posted men conspicuously in those areas most vulnerable along the wall— "the lowest points." The "sword" is the most frequently mentioned weapon in the OT (see Ezr 9:7).

14–15 The best way to dispel fear—"Don't be afraid of them" (cf. Dt 3:22; 20:3; 31:6)—is to remember the Lord who alone is to be feared.

3. The rebuilding of the walls (4:16–23)

16 "Spears" (GK 8242) designates lances or spears with long shafts used as thrusting weapons (Nu 25:7–8; 1Ki 18:28). "Shields" (GK 4482) were small and round and were made of wood and wickerwork, for they were combustible (Eze 39:9). From 2Ch 18:33 it seems that "armor" (GK 9234) primarily designated breastplates of metal or more probably of mail, which were joined to a lower appendage. In some cases such cuirasses may have been made of leather (cf. 1Sa 17:38; 1Ki 22:34; 2Ch 26:14).

17 Each person bringing material for building carried his load with one hand and a "weapon"with the other.

18–20 The "sword" (GK 2995) was worn in a sheath (1Sa 17:51) hung on a girdle (1Sa 17:39; 18:4; 25:13; Ps 45:3). The trumpet is the *shofar* (GK 8795) or ram's horn (Jos 6:4, 6, 8, 13), used for signaling as in times of attack (Nu 10:5–10). A single trumpeter accompanied Nehemiah, though other sources imply that trumpeters were placed at varying intervals. For the concept of the "Holy War" in which God fights for his people, see Jos 10:14, 42; Jdg 4:14; 20:35; 2Sa 5:24.

21 Work usually stopped at sunset (Dt 24:15; Mt 20:1–12). To work "till the stars came out" (cf. Job 9:9) indicates the earnestness of the people's efforts.

22 Apparently each builder had a "helper" (lit., "young man, servant"; GK 5853). These people were probably young assigned assistants, not personal servants of the workers. Even those who lived outside Jerusalem stayed in the city at night so that some of them could serve as sentries.

23 The last three words of this verse are literally "each man his weapon the water." The NIV rendering suggests a pattern similar to the way in which Gideon's selected men drank their water with weapons in hand as an indication of their vigilance. Though the precise meaning is not clear, the implication is that constant preparedness was the rule.

E. Social and Economic Problems (5:1–19)

1. The complaints of the poor (5:1–5)

The economic crisis faced by Nehemiah is described in ch. 5, in the middle of his major effort to rebuild the walls of Jerusalem. Since the building of the wall lasted only fifty-two days (6:15), it seems unlikely that Nehemiah would have called a great assembly (v.7) in the midst of such a project. More likely the assembly was called only after the rebuilding of the wall, taking v.14 as retrospective. On the other hand, the economic pressure created by the rebuilding program may have brought to light problems long simmering that had to be solved before work could proceed.

Those affected by the economic crisis were (1) the landless who were short of food (v.2); (2) the landowners who were compelled to mortgage their properties (v.3); (3) those forced to borrow money at exorbitant rates because of oppressive taxation (v.4); and (4) those forced to sell their children into slavery (v.5).

1 The gravity of the situation is underscored in that the wives joined in the protest as the people ran short of funds and supplies to feed their families. Their complaints were not lodged against foreign authorities but against their own fellow countrymen who were exploiting the poor at a time when both were needed to defend the country. The cry of the oppressed people is a cry to God for justice (cf. Ex 3:7; 22:22–23; Ps 9:12; Isa 5:7).

2–3 Economic conditions forced even those with considerable property to mortgage to the aggrandizement of the wealthy few (cf. Isa 5:8). The rich got richer, the poor poorer. The economic situation was aggravated by conditions in nature that had produced a famine. Such hardships were expressions of God's judgment (Isa 51:19; Jer 14:13–18; Am 4:6). In times of dire need the wealthy usually have enough stored up to feed themselves. It is the poor who suffer because of the huge rise in prices caused by scarcities.

4 On taxes see Ezr 4:13, 20; 6:8; 7:24. It is estimated that the Persian king collected the equivalent of twenty million darics a year in taxes. Little of this was returned to the satrapies. Rather, it was the custom to melt down the gold and silver and to pour it into jars that were then broken and the bullion stored. At Susa alone Alexander found nine thousand talents of coined gold (about 270 tons) and forty thousand talents of silver (about 1,200 tons) stored up as bullion. As coined money was increasingly taken out of circulation, inflation became rampant. The acquisition of land by the Persians and its alienation from production helped produce a 50 percent rise in prices.

5 In times of economic distress, families would borrow funds, using members of the family as collateral. If a man could not repay the loan and its interest, his daughters, sons, wife, or even the man himself could be sold into bondage. A Hebrew who fell into debt would serve his creditor as "a hired servant" (Lev 25:39–40). He was to be released in the seventh year (Dt 15:12–18), unless he chose to stay voluntarily. The ironic tragedy of the situation for the exiles was that at least in Mesopotamia their families were together. Now because of dire economic necessities, their children were being sold into slavery.

2. The cancellation of debts (5:6–13)

6 Nehemiah "was very angry." There are times when we must speak out against social injustices (cf. Mt 21:18–19; Mk 11:12–18; Lk 19:45–48; Eph 4:26).

7 After reflecting on the issue, Nehemiah called a meeting with the "nobles and officials." "Usury" means to impose a burden or claim for repayment of debt. The OT passages prohibiting the giving of loans at interest (Ex 22:25–27; Lev 25:35–37; Dt 23:19–20; 24:10–13) were not intended to prohibit commercial loans but rather the charging of interest to the poor so as to make a profit from the helplessness of one's neighbors.

8 Though one could use a poor brother as a bond servant, one was not to be sold as a slave (Lev 25:39–42). The sale of fellow Hebrews as slaves to Gentiles was a particularly callous offense and was always forbidden (Ex 21:8)—though it was sometimes done (see Joel 3:6). The people's guilt was so obvious that "they kept quiet," having no rebuttal or excuse.

9 Failure to treat others, especially fellow believers, with compassion is an insult to our Maker and a blot on our testimony (cf. Pr 14:31; 1Pe 2:12–15).

10 The granting of loans is not condemned, nor is the making of profit. But the OT condemns the greed and avarice that seeks a profit at the expense of people (Ps 119:36; Isa 56:9–12; 57:17; Jer 6:13; 8:10; 22:13–19; Eze 22:12–14; 33:31). In view of the gravity of the situation, Nehemiah urged the creditors to relinquish their rights to repayment with interest.

11 The interest being charged was "the hundredth part," i.e., one percent per month.

12–13 "Amen" (GK 589) means "to believe or trust." It is used in passages that praise God (e.g., 1Ch 16:36; Ne 8:6; cf. 1Co 14:16), in doxologies (e.g., Pss 41, 72, 89, 106), and as an assent to an oath and its curse formula (Nu 5:22; Dt 27:15–26).

3. Nehemiah's unselfish example (5:14–19)

14 Nehemiah served his first term as governor for twelve years before being recalled to the king's court (13:6), after which he returned for a second term of indeterminate length. Provincial governors normally assessed the people in their provinces for their support, e.g., "food allotted to the governor." But Nehemiah bent over backwards and sacrificed even what was normally his due to serve as an example to the people (cf. 1Co 9; 2Th 3:8).

15 "Governors" is the plural of the word used of Sheshbazzar (Ezr 5:14), Zerubbabel (Hag 1:1, 14; 2:2), and various Persian officials (Ezr 5:3, 6; 6:6–7, 13; et al.), though Nehemiah was certainly not referring here to Ezra and Zerubbabel. Persian practice usually exempted temple personnel (cf. Ezr 7:24), which made the burden on the laity much heavier. If the governors themselves were extortionate, their "assistants" often proved even more oppressive (cf. Mt 18:21–35; 20:25–28).

16 Nehemiah's behavior as governor was guided by principles of service rather than by opportunism—unusual in the ancient world.

17–18 When Solomon became king, he sacrificed 22,000 oxen and 120,000 sheep and held a great seven–day feast for the assembly (1Ki 4:22–23; 8:62–65). As part of his social responsibility, a governor or ruler was expected to entertain lavishly. The people of Judah were afraid to present a defective sheep to Nehemiah's predecessor, but they were not above offering such an animal to the Lord (Mal 1:8). The meat listed here would perhaps be sufficient to provide one meal for up to 800 persons, including the 150 Jews and officials mentioned in v.17.

19 Some have suggested that Nehemiah's memoirs were inscribed as a memorial set up in the temple (cf. 13:14, 22, 31).

F. The Completion of the Walls Despite Opposition (6:1–19)

1. Attempts to snare Nehemiah (6:1–9)

1–4 "Ono" was located seven miles southeast of Joppa near Lod. It was in the westernmost area settled by the returning Jews (Ezr 2:33; Ne 7:37; 11:35). It may have been proposed as a kind of neutral territory, but Nehemiah recognized the invitation as a trap (cf. Jer 41:1–3). Nehemiah's sharp reply may seem like a haughty rebuff to a reasonable invitation, but he correctly discerned the insincerity of his enemies and their evil designs. His own utter dedication to the great enterprise of the wall made that his top priority. He refused to be distracted with lesser matters that would divert and dissipate his energies. Nehemiah's foes were persistent, but he was equally persistent in steadfastly resisting their blandishments.

5–7 Letters during this period were ordinarily written on a papyrus or leather sheet, rolled up, tied with a string, and sealed with a clay bulla (seal impression). The latter was intended to seal the letter and to guarantee its authenticity. Sanballat obviously intended that the contents should be made known also to the public at large. The Persian kings did not tolerate the claims of pretenders to kingship. Usurpers such as Jeroboam (1Ki 11:29–31) and Jehu (2Ki 9:1–3) hired false prophets. Such mercenary prophets were condemned by Amos (7:10–17).

8–9 Nehemiah did not mince words in his reply. He called the report a lie. He may well have sent his own messenger to the king to assure him of his loyalty. The Hebrew idiom "to cause the hands to drop" means to demoralize (cf. Ezr 4:4). Jeremiah was accused of "weakening the hands of the soldiers" (Jer 38:4; NIV, "discouraging the soldiers").

2. The hiring of false prophets (6:10–14)

10 Since he had access to the temple, Shemaiah was probably a priest, possibly one of those who were particularly friendly with Tobiah. He likely had shut himself up in the temple as a symbolic action to indicate that his own life was in danger and to suggest that both must flee to the temple. Most likely Shemaiah's words were a ruse in which he pretended to be in personal danger and tried to get Nehemiah to take refuge in the temple. Shemaiah could legitimately have proposed that Nehemiah should take refuge in the temple area at the altar of asylum (Ex 21:13; 1Ki 1:50–53; 2:28–34; 8:64; 2Ki 16:14), but not for him to take refuge in "the house of God," the temple building itself.

11–13 Even if his life was genuinely threatened, Nehemiah was not a coward who would run into hiding. Nor would he transgress the law to save his life. As a layman he was, of course, not permitted to enter the sanctuary (Ex 29:33; 33:20; Nu 18:7). That Shemaiah proposed a course of action contrary to God's word revealed him as a false prophet (Mt 24:3–10). Had Nehemiah wavered in the face of the threat, his leadership would have been discredited, and morale among the people would have plummeted.

14 In the OT only three other women are mentioned as being prophetesses: Miriam (Ex 15:20), Deborah (Jdg 4:4), and Huldah (2Ki 22:14; 2Ch 34:22). The prophets and prophetesses may have favored a policy of accommodation and objected to Nehemiah's work as divisive (cf. Isa 9:15; 28:7; Jer 2:26; 27:9–10; et al.).

3. The completion of the walls (6:15–19)

15 Most likely on Oct 27, 445 B.C., the walls of Jerusalem were completed. Remarkably, though neglected for nearly a century and a half, they were rebuilt in less than two months under Nehemiah's leadership. One might have expected a description of the celebration and the dedication of the wall immediately on its completion, but we do not encounter this until 12:27.

16 The rapid completion of the wall despite such overwhelming odds could only have been accomplished with God's aid, and knowledge of this fact thoroughly discomfited Nehemiah's enemies (cf. 1Ch 14:17).

17–18 Tobiah was doubly related to influential families in Judah. He was married to the daughter of Shecaniah, and his son Jehohanan was married to the daughter of Meshullam, who had helped repair the wall of Jerusalem (3:4, 30).

19 Tobiah's friends and relatives acted as a Fifth Column. They attempted both to propagandize on behalf of Tobiah and to act as an intelligence system for him. Tobiah himself kept on trying to frighten Nehemiah.

G. The List of Exiles (7:1–73a)

1. Provisions for the protection of Jerusalem (7:1–3)

1 The gatekeepers normally guarded the temple gates (1Ch 9:17–19; 26:12–19); but because of the danger in the city, they were appointed to stand guard at the city gates, along with the singers and the Levites (see comments on Ezr 2:40–42).

2 Hanani, Nehemiah's brother (cf. 1:2), is a shortened form of the name Hananiah. He was placed in charge of Jerusalem, i.e., over Rephaiah and Shallum who were over sections of the city (3:9, 12). The "Hananiah" mentioned here is likely another individual (cf. NIV note). "The citadel" (see 1:1) was a fortress located at the northwest corner of Jerusalem. Theoretically garrisons were directly controlled by the king, and their commanders were enrolled upon the king's list. In practice, however, governors like Nehemiah could appoint their own men.

3 Normally the gates were opened at dawn, but this was to be delayed until the sun was high in the heavens (Ge 18:1; Ex 16:21; 1Sa 11:9). The OT distinguishes the sun from the stars, not by its great light, but by its heat (Ex 16:21; 1Sa 11:9; Ps 121:6; Isa 49:10). Inhabitants of the Near East are conscious of the sun's heat, especially during the summer (Ps 32:4). The gates were to be shut and bolted before the guards went off duty.

2. Nehemiah's discovery of the list (7:4–5)

4 The enclosed area of the city of Jerusalem was "large and spacious" (lit., "wide of two hands and large," an expression that means extending to the right and left). As the actual circuit of the walls of the city had been contracted from the earlier dimensions of the city, this expression must be relative to the number of people who were to be housed, once the damaged houses were rebuilt.

5 On "registration by families," compare v.64; see Ezr 2:62 and 8:1, 3.

3. The list of exiles (7:6–69)
a. Families (7:6–25)

6–25 The following list of names is essentially the same as that found in Ezr 2:1–70. See also the commentary on that section for the nature of the list and for some of the variations in names and discrepancies in numbers. "Raamiah" (v.7) means "The LORD has thundered" (Ezr 2:2 has "Reelaiah"). "Nahamani" is a variant form for Nehemiah; it does not occur in Ezr 2:2. "Nehum" is probably an error for Rehum, which appears in the Ezra list. For "Gibeon" (v.25), Ezr 2:20 has Gibbar, probably a corruption of Gibeon.

b. Villagers (7:26–38)

26–38 There are variations in the numbers between this section and Ezr 2:21–35.

c. The priests (7:39–42)

39–42 The names and numbers are identical with the parallel passage in Ezr 2:36–69. Perhaps the lists of priests were kept more accurately than those of the laity.

d. Levites (7:43)

43 The small number of Levites who returned is striking. As Ezra was about to leave Mesopotamia, he found not one Levite in the company; so he delayed his departure until he could enlist some Levites (Ezr 8:15–20).

e. Temple staff (7:44–60)

44–60 Again there are variations in numbers and names between this section and Ezr 2:41–58. Ezra 2:50 includes Asnah, which is lacking here in v.52. Ezra 2:55 has Hassophereth and Peruda instead of Perida (v.57).

f. Individuals without evidence of genealogies (7:61–65)

61–65 On the towns in v.61, see Ezr 2:59.

g. Totals (7:66–69)

66–69 See also Ezr 2:64–67. Ezra 2:65 lists 200 men and women singers, rather than 245.

4. Offerings for the work (7:70–72)

70 "Drachmas" were Greek coins weighing about 3/10 of an ounce; "1,000 drachmas" would weigh about 19 pounds. As a drachma was ordinarily a silver coin, the Hebrew word may designate the Persian daric (see comment on Ezr 2:69).

71–72 The weight of "20,000 drachmas" would be about 375 pounds; "2,200 minas," about 2,550 pounds; and "2,000 minas," about 2,500 pounds.

5. Settlement of the exiles (7:73a)

73a Many returning exiles were not from Jerusalem, whose population no doubt suffered the greatest casualties in the Babylonian attacks. These naturally returned to their own hometowns, leaving Jerusalem underpopulated (cf. 11:1–24).

H. Ezra's Preaching and the Outbreak of Revival (7:73b–10:39)

1. The public proclamation of the Scriptures (7:73b–8:12)

Chapters 8–11 seem to interrupt the narrative of Nehemiah's work on the wall. The traditional view sees the reading of the Law by Ezra as the first reference to him in about thirteen years, since his arrival in 458 B.C. Since Ezra was commissioned to teach the Law (Ezr 7:14, 25–26), it seems strange that there was such a long delay in the proclamation of it.

7:73b–8:1 The phrase "all the people assembled as one man" is identical with Ezr 3:1, which also refers to an assembly called in the seventh month of the year. The object of that meeting, however, was to restore the altar of burnt offerings and sacrificial worship. Possibly Ezra had instituted the practice of holding such assemblies on the seventh month, Tishri, the beginning of the civil year.

"In the square before the Water Gate," which gate led to the Gihon Spring, may be the same as the broad place before the house of the Lord (Ezr 10:9). Assemblies were held by the city gates (Jdg 19:15; 2Ch 32:6). "The Book of the Law of Moses" was most likely the Pentateuch. Ezra could certainly have brought back with him the Torah (i.e., the Pentateuch).

2–3 "The first day of the seventh month" was the New Year's Day of the civil calendar (Lev 23:23–25; Nu 29:1–6), celebrated also as the Feast of Trumpets with a solemn assembly and cessation from labor. "Women" did not participate in ordinary meetings but were brought together with children on such solemn occasions (Dt 31:12; Jos 8:35; 2Ki 23:2). The people evidently stood for about five hours attentively listening to the exposition of the Scriptures.

4 The "platform" was capable of holding Ezra and thirteen others. "Shema" is a shortened form of Shemaiah (see Ezr 8:13). "Anaiah" ("The LORD has answered") was one of those who signed the covenant (10:22). "Mishael" ("Who is what God is?") was also the name of one of Daniel's friends (Da 1:6).

5 The "book" was actually a scroll rather than a codex or book, which did not become popular till the early Christian centuries. The rabbis concluded from "the people all stood up" that the congregation should stand at the reading of the Torah.

6 "Praised the LORD" is literally "blessed the LORD." In Jewish synagogues a benediction is pronounced before the reading of each scriptural section. On "the great God," cf. 9:32; Dt 10:17; Jer 32:18; Da 9:4. The Jews customarily "lifted their hands" in worship (cf. Ezr 9:5; Pss 28:2; 134:2; 1Ti 2:8). The repetition "Amen! Amen!" connotes the intensity of feeling behind the affirmation (2Ki 11:14; Lk 23:21). The Amen as a congregational response is known from the time of David (cf. 1Ch 16:36). It was later used in the synagogue and in the church (1Co 14:16).

"Bowed down" (GK 7702) is always followed by the verb "to worship"; it may mean "kneel down." Originally "to worship" (GK 2556) meant to prostrate oneself on the ground. The verb is used relatively rarely of an individual's worship of God (Ge 22:5; 24:26, 48). Such private acts often involved actual prostration "to the earth" as with Abraham's servant (Ge 24:52), Moses (Ex 34:8), Joshua (Jos 5:14), and Job (Job 1:20). There are also three cases of spontaneous communal worship in Exodus (4:31; 12:27; 33:10). In 2Ch 20:18 Jehoshaphat and the people "fell down in worship before the LORD" when they heard his promise of victory.

7–8 On "the Levites," see comment on Ezr 2:40. "Instructed" (GK 1067) literally means "causing to understand." Reading in the ancient world was normally done aloud (cf. Ex 24:7; Dt 17:19; 2Ki 5:7; Ac 8:28). "Making it clear" (GK 7300) has been understood, since the time of the rabbis, as referring to translation from Hebrew into an Aramaic Targum (cf. NIV note). Ezra wanted to make sure everyone understood God's law.

9 The powerful exposition of the Word of God can bring deep conviction of sin. But repentance must not degenerate into a self-centered remorse but must issue into joy in God's forgiving goodness (cf. 2Co 2:5–11).

10–11 "Choice food" means delicious, festive food prepared with much fat. The fat of sacrificial animals was offered to God as the tastiest element of the burnt offering (Lev 1:8, 12), the fellowship offering (Lev 3:8–10), and the guilt offering (Lev 7:3–4). "Send some to those who have nothing prepared" reflects the Jews' tradition of remembering the less fortunate on joyous occasions (2Sa 6:19; Est 9:22). This was one example of the social conscience and concern of the Jews (Ex 23:11; Lev 19:10; 23:22; Dt 14:28–29; 26:12–13; et al.). "The joy of the LORD" (i.e., joy in the Lord as they ate and worked before him) would sustain them.

12 Even today, the day after Sukkoth (Feast of Tabernacles), the Jews celebrate a festival called *Simhat Torah* ("rejoicing over the Torah"), in which they parade in a circle inside the synagogue seven or more rounds with a different person holding the scrolls of the Torah each time. Children carry flags with inscriptions extolling the Word of God.

2. The Festival of Booths (8:13–18)

13–14 The people in this revival had an insatiable appetite to learn more about the Scriptures. "Booths" (GK 6109) were made out of branches. This feast, celebrated from the fifteenth of Tishri (Sept-Oct) for seven days (Lev 23:39–43), was one of the three great feasts (along with Passover and Pentecost) during which all Jewish men were to assemble in Jerusalem. It was a joyous agricultural festival that celebrated the completion of the harvest (see Ex 23:16; Dt 16:13; Ezr 3:4; the feast of Jn 7 was probably the Feast of Booths).

15 With the exception of palm trees and other leafy trees, the trees mentioned here are not the same as those prescribed in Lev 23:40. The "olive" tree is widespread in Mediterra-

nean countries. According to Dt 8:8 it was growing in Canaan before the Conquest. It takes an olive tree thirty years to mature, so its cultivation requires peaceful conditions. The "wild olive tree" (lit., "tree of oil") is more likely a resinous tree like the fir. "Myrtles" are evergreen bushes with a pleasing odor. "Palms" are date palms; such trees were common around Jericho (Dt 34:3; 2Ch 28:15). "Shade trees" means literally "leafy trees." On present-day celebration of the Feast of Booths, see comment on Ezr 3:4.

16 "Roofs" in Palestine were flat so that one could walk on them (Jos 2:6; 1Sa 9:25–26; et al.). Near-Eastern houses were built around a court. "The Gate of Ephraim" was a gate of the oldest rampart of Jerusalem, four hundred cubits east of the Corner Gate (2Ki 14:13; 2Ch 25:23). It was restored by Nehemiah (12:39).

17 The statement "from the days of Joshua son of Nun" hardly means that no celebration of the Feast of Booths had taken place since then, as such celebrations are mentioned after the dedication of Solomon's temple (1Ki 8:65; 2Ch 7:9) and after the return of the exiles (Ezr 3:4). It must mean that the feast had not been celebrated before with such exceptional joyousness or strictness of observance. The great joy compares to that experienced at the renewal of the Passover under Hezekiah (2Ch 30:26) and at the revival under Josiah (2Ki 23:22; 2Ch 35:18).

18 "Assembly" is "a solemn or festal assembly" (cf. Lev 23:36; Nu 29:35; Dt 16:8; 2Ki 10:20; Joel 1:14).

3. A day of fasting, confession, and prayer (9:1–5a)

Interestingly, the ninth chapter of Ezra, of Nehemiah, and of Daniel are each devoted to confessions of national sin and prayers for God's grace.

1 Many scholars find it strange to have a day of penance following a festival of joy and consider the events of this chapter to have originally followed Ezr 10. There would thus have been a three-week interval between Ezr 10:17 and Ne 9:1. The text, however, refers to events that occurred two days after the end of the Feast of Booths, which took place from 15 to 22 Tishri. Five days after this feast began was Yom Kippur or the Day of Atonement (Lev 16:29), on which everyone searched his or her own heart. Though not held on the tenth day, this day of penance resembles the spirit of the Day of Atonement. The month of Tishri was particularly a month of "fasting" (Zec 7:5). "Sackcloth" was a goat-hair garment that covered the bare loins during times of mourning and penance. The placing of "ashes," often rendered "dust," on one's head as a sign of sorrow is mentioned in Jos 7:6, La 2:10, and Eze 27:30 (cf. also 2Sa 13:19; Job 2:12).

2–3 "Those of Israelite descent" is literally "the seed of Israel" (cf. Ezr 9:2). On "had separated themselves," see comments on Ezr 9:1; 10:8, 11, 16. On "confessed," see comment on 1:6. The congregation spent about three hours in the study of Scriptures and three hours in the worship of the Lord (see 8:6).

4 The "stairs" perhaps led to the platform mentioned in 8:4. On "loud voices" see comment on Ezr 10:12.

5a Five of the eight names are the same as five names in the previous verse. "Stand up and praise [lit., bless] the LORD." Jews begin their prayers with "Blessed" and stand for the benediction.

4. A recital of God's dealings with Israel (9:5b–31)

5b "Your glorious name" is literally "the name of your glory." The Hebrew word for "glory" (GK 3883) comes from a root that means "weighty," and then by extension "honored." The prayer reviews God's grace and power in creation (v.6), in Egypt and at the Red Sea (vv.9–11), in the desert and at Sinai (vv.12–21), at the conquest of Canaan (vv.22–25), through the judges (vv.26–28), through the prophets (vv.29–31), and in the present situation (vv.32–37). Ezra's prayer is a marvelous mosaic of Scriptures.

6 Ezra's prayer begins notably with the affirmation "You are alone the LORD," which, though not in the same words as the famous Shema of Dt 6:4, expresses the central monotheistic conviction of Israel's faith. "Starry host" (lit., "army," "warriors"; GK 7372) may mean stars, but seems more likely to mean angels (cf. 1Ki 22:19; Pss 103:20–21;

148:2). Not only people, but also "the multitudes of heaven" worship before the Lord. These include the "sons of gods" (Ps 29:1–2), which also probably means angels (cf. Ps 89:6). According to Ps 97:7 even "all gods" bow down before him.

7 "Ur of the Chaldeans" is found only here and in Ge 11:28, 31; 15:7. Ur is usually identified with the famous Sumerian city in southern Mesopotamia, occupied in the first millennium B.C. by the Chaldeans. "Abram" ("the father is exalted") was changed to "Abraham" ("the father of a multitude"), according to Ge 17:4–5.

8 "Faithful" (GK 586) is used only a few times of individuals (e.g., Moses in Nu 12:7). Whether the reference alludes to Abraham's faith in believing that God would grant him a son (Ge 15:6) or in being willing to sacrifice Isaac (Ge 22) is unclear. On the different people, see v.24 and Ezr 9:1; the latter lists surrounding populations and so includes also Ammonites, Moabites, and Egyptians. "Girgashites," a Canaanite tribe listed seven times in the OT, is of uncertain identity. On "because you are righteous," see Ezr 9:15; Ps 119:137; La 1:18.

9 The "Red Sea" ("Sea of Reeds") was probably one of the Bitter Lakes that the Suez Canal now passes through.

10 "Miraculous signs" (GK 253) is often coupled with "wonders," especially of events connected with the plagues of Exodus (Ex 7:3; Dt 4:34; 6:22; 7:19). On "you made a name," compare v.5, also 1:9, 11; Isa 63:12, 14.

11 On "you divided the sea . . . and they passed through it," see Ex 14:21–29; Ps 78:13; 1Co 10:1–2; Heb 11:29; and on "you hurled their pursuers," see Ex 15:4; Isa 43:16–17.

12–13 On "with a pillar of cloud you led them," see v.19 (cf. Ex 13:21–22; Nu 14:14; Dt 1:33; et al.). On regulations and laws, see comment on 1:7.

14–16 On "your holy Sabbath," compare Ex 20:8–11; 31:13–17; Dt 5:15; Eze 20:12. "Bread from heaven" (Ex 16:4, 10–35; Pss 78:24; 105:40; Jn 6:32, 51, 58), "water from the rock" (Ex 17:6; Nu 20:8; Ps 105:41), and "take possession" (see v.23; Dt 11:31; Jos 1:11) recall significant events from Israel's past. "Became arrogant and stiff-necked" is a figure borrowed from the driving of stubborn oxen who resist guidance.

17–18 The forefathers "refused to listen" (cf. 1Sa 8:19; Jer 11:10) and "failed to remember the miracles" (cf. Mk 6:52). Numbers 14:4 reports the proposal to "appoint a leader." God is "gracious" (cf. v.31) and "forgiving" (cf. Ps 130:4; Da 9:9). The "image of a calf" recalls Ex 32:4–8 and Dt 9:16.

19–21 "Compassion" (GK 8171) renders a word that is cognate with "womb," which connotes a deep and tender feeling toward those who are dear to us or need our help. The "good Spirit" and the "manna" recall Nu 11. On "their thirst" see v.15. In the desert wanderings the people "lacked nothing" (cf. Dt 2:7; 8:4), and their "clothes did not wear out" (cf. Dt 29:5). The absence of natural deterioration evidenced God's special guidance.

22 "The remotest frontiers" probably refers to Transjordan. Sihon refused the Israelites passage through his land, which was in Transjordan between the Jabbok and the Arnon (Nu 21:21–33; Dt 2–3; Jdg 11:19–21). "Og" was the Amorite king of Bashan with sixty cities (Dt 3:3–5; Jos 13:12). His defeat was one of the great victories of the Israelites (Jos 9:10). "Bashan" was the fertile area north of Gilead in Transjordan.

23–24 On God's promise to Abraham, see Ge 22:17; 26:4; et al. "Their sons went in and took possession" recalls Ge 22:17; 26:4; Ex 32:13; Dt 1:8; 10:22; et al. On "you subdued before them the Canaanites," see v.8; Dt 9:3; Jdg 1:4. On "along with their kings," see Dt 7:24; Jos 11:12, 17.

25 The list of land, cities, houses, etc., corresponds to the lists in the Sinai covenant and its renewal (Dt 6:10–11; Jos 24:13). "Fortified cities" designates such sites as Jericho, Lachish, and Hazor. The lack of rainfall during much of the year made it necessary for almost every house to have its own well or cistern to store water from the rainy seasons (2Ki 18:31; Pr 5:15). By 1200 B.C. the technique of waterproofing cisterns was developed, permitting the greater occupation of the central Judean hills. The chief cultivated trees of Palestine were the olive, fig, apple, almond, walnut, mulberry, sycamore, and pomegranate (cf. Dt 8:8; 2Ki 18:32). Date

palms grew in the Jordan Valley (see comment on 8:15). When they entered Canaan, God warned his people not to cut down any fruit trees (Dt 20:20). As to their physical needs, the Israelites had enough, and they enjoyed life.

26–27 Putting the law "behind their backs," the forefathers "killed [the] prophets" (see 1Ki 18:4; 19:10, 14; 2Ch 24:20–22; Jer 26:20–23), thus committing "awful blasphemies." When God "handed them over . . . they cried out to" him (cf. Jdg 4:3; Ps 107:6, 28); and "from heaven [he] heard" (see 2Ch 6:21, 23, 25, 30, 33). He gave them "deliverers," i.e., judges like Gideon and Samson, who were great military leaders.

28 The history of the "judges" is a cyclical story of deliverance, apostasy, and then deliverance again (Jdg 3:7, 12; 4:1; 6:1; 8:33–34; et al.).

29–31 The ordinances of God are such that "a man will live if he obeys them." The people "stubbornly . . . turned their backs" (lit., "they presented a stubborn shoulder"). By his "Spirit" (cf. Zec 7:12) and through his "prophets," God appealed to the people; but they "paid no attention." So he "handed them over." Yet God "did not put an end" to the erring people (see Jer 4:27, 30:11, 46:28). Nehemiah's long recital of Israelite history significantly excludes any reference to the reigns of Saul, David, and Solomon.

5. Confession of sins (9:32–37)

32 "Now" marks the transition from a survey of the past to a supplication for the present situation. God is "mighty," and he "keeps his covenant" (see 1:5; Dt 7:9; 1Ki 8:23; 2Ch 6:14). The nation had suffered "hardship" (cf. Ex 18:8; Nu 20:14; La 3:5).

The first of the "kings of Assyria" to affect Israel was Shalmaneser III (858–824 B.C.; not mentioned by name in the OT). He reported that he defeated Ahab at the important battle of Qarqar in 853. The great Tiglath-pileser III, also known as Pul, expanded the Assyrian empire to the Mediterranean. He attacked Phoenicia in 736, Philistia 734, and Damascus in 732. Early in his reign (752–742) Menahem of Israel paid tribute to him (2Ki 15:19–20). During his campaigns against Damascus, Pul also ravaged Gilead and Galilee and destroyed

Hazor and Megiddo (2Ki 15:29). King Shalmaneser V (727–722) laid siege to the city of Samaria—a task completed by Sargon II (721–705). Sargon's commander carried on operations against Ashdod (Isa 20:1). Sennacherib (704–681) failed to take Jerusalem in 701 (2Ki 18:13–17) but captured Lachish. Esarhaddon (681–669) conquered Egypt and extracted tribute from Manasseh of Judah (2Ki 19:37; Isa 37:38; Ezr 4:2). Ashurbanipal (669–633) was probably the king who freed Manasseh from exile and restored him as a puppet king (2Ch 33:13; Ezr 4:9).

33–34 In everything that happened God had "been just," but the people still "did not pay attention."

35–37 "Goodness" (GK 3206) is an attribute of God's covenant faithfulness, in a "spacious" (see 7:4; cf. Ex 3:8; Jdg 18:10; 1Ch 4:40) and "fertile" (see v.25) land. Yet the people did not turn from their "evil ways." They became "slaves" (see Ezr 9:9; Ne 5:5) in the fruitful land God had given their forefathers (see 10:35, 37). Persian rulers drafted their subjects into military service.

6. A binding agreement (9:38)

38 "Making" is literally "cutting"; see comment on Ezr 10:3. The word here rendered "a binding agreement" (GK 591) in 11:23 is "a royal prescription"; it is related to "Amen," and its root has the connotation of constancy. The usual word for "covenant" (*berith*; GK 1382) appears in 1:5; 9:8, 32; 13:29; and Ezr 10:3.

a. A list of those who sealed it (10:1–29)

1–8 This is a legal list, bearing the official seal and containing a roster of eighty-four names arranged according to the following categories: leaders, priests, Levites, and laymen. Verses 2–8 contain twenty-one names, most of which reoccur in 12:1–7. In Ezr 2:36–39 four priestly families are listed; in the later list of 1Ch 24:7–18, we have the arrangement of twenty-four courses that served as the basis of the rotation for priestly service (Lk 1:8).

9–13 Of the Levites seventeen are mentioned by name. "Associates" is literally "brothers."

14–27 Of the leaders of the people listed here, twenty are also found in the lists of Ezr 2 and

Ne 7. "Anathoth," a name derived from the Canaanite goddess Anath, is also the name of the city of Jeremiah (Jer 1:1); as a personal name, it occurs only here and in 1Ch 7:8. "Hezir" means "swine" (cf. 1Ch 24:15; on animal names as nicknames, see comment on Ezr 2:3).

28–29 On Levites, gatekeepers, singers, and temple servants, see comments on Ezr 2:40–43. On wives and children, see comment on Ne 8:2–3. Verse 29 recalls Dt 27–29 (see comments on 5:13; Ezr 10:5). "A curse" (GK 460) means an adjuration with an imprecation of grievous punishments in case of a failure to keep the oath.

b. Provisions of the agreement (10:30–39)

30 The first provision was not to contract any mixed marriages (see Ezr 9–10).

31a The provisions of vv.31–34 may have been a code drawn up by Nehemiah to correct the abuses listed in ch. 13 (e.g., vv.15–22). Though the Sabbath passages in the Torah (Ex 20:8–11; Dt 5:12–15) do not explicitly prohibit trading on the Sabbath, this is clearly understood in Jer 17:19–27 and Am 8:5.

31b According to the Mosaic legislation (Ex 23:10–11; Lev 25:2–7), in the seventh year the land was to lie fallow; and the collection of debts was not to take place (Dt 15:1–3).

32 The rest of the provisions of the contract dealt with offerings for the temple and its staff. According to Ex 30:13–14, a "half shekel is an offering to the LORD" from each man twenty years old and older as a symbolical ransom. Later Joash used the annual contributions to repair the temple (2Ch 24:4–14). In the NT period Jewish men everywhere sent an offering of a half-shekel (actually its equivalent) for the temple in Jerusalem (Mt 17:24). One explanation why the offering should be "a third of a shekel" rather than a half shekel is that the later shekel was based on a heavier standard; thus one-third of the later shekel was equal to one-half of the earlier shekel.

33 "The bread set out on the table" was the twelve cakes of fine flour arranged in two rows of six set out each Sabbath (Lev 24:6–7). On "regular grain offerings" see Ex 29:38–41; Nu 28:3–8. On "burnt offerings" compare

Ezr 8:35. "The Sabbaths, New Moon festivals and appointed feasts" recall Nu 28:9–16. "To make atonement" (GK 4105) means "to cover" or "to wipe away" one's sin; hence to expiate. It describes the effect of the sin and trespass offerings (Lev 4:20; Nu 5:8).

34 "Lots" were used among God's people to determine the will of the Lord (1) to apportion the land among the tribes (Nu 26:55; Jos 14:2; 18:10); (2) to detect a guilty person (Jos 7:14; 1Sa 14:42; Jnh 1:7); (3) to choose the first king, Saul (1Sa 10:19–21); (4) to settle disputes (Pr 18:18); (5) to determine the courses of the priests, singers, gatekeepers (1Ch 24:5; 25:8; 26:13; Lk 1:9); (6) to determine who should dwell in Jerusalem (Ne 11:1); and (7) to choose the replacement of Judas Iscariot (Ac 1:26). Though there is no specific reference to a wood offering in the Pentateuch, the perpetual burning of fires would have required a continual "contribution of wood" (cf. 13:31; Lev 6:12–13).

35 The offerings of the "firstfruits" were brought to the temple for the support of the priests and Levites (Ex 23:19; 34:26; Lev 19:23–24; Nu 18:13; Dt 26:1–11). Actually, the law stipulated only seven kinds of plants for the firstfruits. The promise to bring the firstfruits of "every tree" was an act of exceptional piety.

36 The firstborn of men and beasts and the firstfruits of field and garden (Lev 19:23–25) were to be given to God. They could be set free for secular use only by redemption (Ex 13:13, 15; 34:20; Lev 27:26–33; Nu 3:44–51; 18:15–17; Dt 14:23–26).

37 On "storerooms," see comments on Ezr 8:29; 10:6. On "offerings," see Ezr 8:25; Ne 10:39; 12:44; 13:5. These contributions were for the maintenance of the priests. "New wine" can refer to freshly pressed grape juice (Isa 65:8; Mic 6:15), but it can still be intoxicating (Hos 4:11). "A tithe of our crops" is literally "tithe of our land." The practice of giving a tenth was an ancient one (Ge 14:20; 28:22). The law decreed that a tenth of the plant crops was holy to the Lord (Lev 27:30; Nu 18:23–32). There is no reference here to a tithe of cattle (as in Lev 27:32–33). Tithes were meant for the support of the Levites (13:10–12; Nu 18:21–32). "Towns where we work" were perhaps agricultural towns.

38–39 The Levites were to give in their turn "a tenth of the tithes" they received (Nu 18:25–32). Chambers in the outer courts of the temple were used as "storerooms" for silver, gold, and other objects. The people pledged themselves to "not neglect" God's house. The prophet Haggai (1:4–9) had accused the people of neglecting the temple.

I. The New Residents of Judah and Jerusalem (11:1–36)

1. Selection of the new residents (11:1–2)

1 "Lots" (see comment on 10:34) were made out of small stones or small pieces of wood. They were shaken (Pr 16:33) and cast (Ob 11; Na 3:10) on the ground (1Ch 24:31; Eze 24:6; Jnh 1:7). "The holy city" (cf. v.18) is a rare use of the phrase in a historical narrative that is usually found in prophetic texts (e.g., Isa 48:2; 52:1; Da 9:24; Joel 3:17; cf. Mt 4:5; 27:53; Rev 11:2). The practice of redistributing populations often involved the forcible transfer from rural settlements to urban centers.

2 In addition to those chosen by lot, some people volunteered, from a sense of duty, to live in Jerusalem. Evidently most would have preferred to stay in their native towns and villages (cf. Ezr 2:1). "Commended" (lit., "blessed") is a word usually used of God but at times of people (cf. 1Ch 16:2; 2Ch 6:3; 30:27).

2. The provincial leaders (11:3–24)

a. A topical statement (11:3–4a)

3–4a These verses succinctly preview the specifics of vv.4b–36. Verses 3–19 are a census roster that can be compared with the list in 1Ch 9:2–21 of the first residents in Jerusalem after the return from Babylonia. About half the names in the two lists are identical.

b. From Judah (11:4b–6)

4b–6 For "Shelah" the Hebrew has Shilonite, i.e., an inhabitant of Shiloh, which belonged to the northern kingdom rather than to Judah. The word therefore probably indicates a descendant of Shelah, Judah's third son (Nu 26:20). "Able men" (lit., "men of valor") were originally valiant, free men whose later descendants became wealthy and served in the armed forces (cf. v.14; 2:9; 4:2; 2Ki 15:20; Ezr 8:22).

c. From Benjamin (11:7–9)

7–9 On the role of "Benjamin" in the returning exiles, see comment on Ezr 4:1. Benjamin provided twice as many men (928) as Judah (468) to protect the city of Jerusalem. "The Second District" was a new suburb to the west of the temple area.

d. From the priests (11:10–14)

10–14 "Seraiah" was the descendant of the high priest who was taken prisoner by Nebuchadnezzar (2Ki 25:18–21). "Supervisor" (GK 5592) denotes a chief or leader among the priests.

e. From the Levites (11:15–18)

15–18 "The outside work" refers to work that took place outside the temple (cf. 1Ch 26:29). Asaph and Jeduthun were two of the three leaders of the temple choirs (cf. 1Ch 16:42; 25:1–2; Pss 39; 50, 73–83). The relatively small number of Levites (284) compared to the priests (a total of 1,192 in vv.12–13) is striking.

f. From the temple staff (11:19–24)

19–24 On "the gatekeepers" see comment on Ezr 2:42. "Ancestral property" designates the inalienable hereditary possession including land, buildings, and movable goods acquired either by conquest or inheritance (Ge 31:14; Nu 18:21; 27:7; 34:2; 1Ki 21:3–4). In the OT it describes the land of Canaan as the possession of both the Lord and Israel, including the individual holdings of tribes and families. The Lord's inheritance is Israel herself (Dt 4:20; 9:26, 29; 1Ki 8:51–53). On "the temple servants" see comment on Ezr 2:43; on "Ophel" see comment on Ne 3:26. On "the singers" see comment on Ezr 2:41. David regulated the services of the Levites, including the singers (1Ch 25).

3. Places settled by those from Judah (11:25–30)

This is an important list, which corresponds to earlier lists of Judean cities. All these names also appear in Jos 15 except Dibon, Jeshua, and Meconah. The list, however, lacks a number of cities listed in Ezr 2:20–34 and Ne 3. The limits of the Judean settlement after the return from Babylon have been confirmed by archaeological evidence; none of the coins minted for Judah has been found outside the area demarcated by these verses.

25 "Kiriath Arba" ("city of four [giants]") was the archaic name of the city of Hebron (Ge 23:2; Jdg 1:20), the important city twenty miles south of Jerusalem. Hebron is the traditional site of the burial of Abraham, Sarah, and other patriarchs. "Its settlements" is literally "its daughters" (cf. Nu 21:25, 32; 32:42: Jos 15:45, 47; 1Ch 2:23; 2Ch 13:19).

26–27 "Jeshua," "Moladah," and "Beth Pelet" were all near Beersheba (cf. Jos 15:26), a city about forty miles southwest of Jerusalem. "Beersheba" means "well of the seven" or "well of the oath" (Ge 21:25–31). This city represented the southernmost limit of Israel's population (cf. Jdg 20:1; 1Ch 21:2).

28–29 "Ziklag" is celebrated as the town given to David by Achish, king of Gath (1Sa 27:6) and taken by the Amalekites (1Sa 30:1). "En Rimmon" was probably nine and a half miles north northeast of Beersheba (cf. Jos 15:32; 19:7; 1Ch 4:32). "Zorah" was the home of Manoah, Samson's father (Jdg 13:2). "Jarmuth" was one of five Canaanite cities in the south that attempted to halt Joshua's invasion (Jos 10:3–5).

30 "Zanoah" was a village in the Shephelah district of low hills between Judah and the area of Philistia (Jos 15:34). The men of this town repaired the Valley Gate (Ne 3:13). "Adullam" was the city between Jerusalem and Lachish where David hid in a cave from Saul (1Sa 22:1). "Lachish" was a great Judean city midway between Jerusalem and Gaza. The Assyrian king Sennacherib failed to take Jerusalem in 701 B.C. but did capture Lachish. Later the city was captured by Nebuchadnezzar (Jer 34:7); it was then resettled during Nehemiah's time. "Hinnom" is the valley southwest of Jerusalem.

4. Places settled by those from Benjamin (11:31–35)

31 "Geba" was six miles northeast of Jerusalem (cf. Jos 18:24; Ezr 2:26; Ne 7:30). The traditional northern limit of Judah (2Ki 23:8; Zec 14:10), Geba was fortified by Asa (1Ki 15:22). "Micmash," seven miles northeast of Jerusalem (cf. Ezr 2:27; Ne 7:31), was the location of the strategic pass to the Jordan Valley, where Saul and Jonathan fought the Philistines (1Sa 13–14). "Aija," an alternative name for "Ai," was just three miles southeast of Bethel (cf. Jos 7–8). "Bethel" ("house of God") was the northernmost town listed here for the Benjamites but was not listed among the people rebuilding the walls of Jerusalem.

32 "Anathoth," three miles north of Jerusalem, was the birthplace of Jeremiah (Jer 1:1). At "Nob" (probably Mount Scopus), just north of the Mount of Olives, the sanctuary was established after the destruction of Shiloh (Jer 7:14). "Ananiah" was probably Bethany, two miles east of Jerusalem.

33–35 "Hadid" was three to four miles northeast of Lydda, near the mouth of the Aijalon Valley (cf. Ezr 2:33; Ne 7:37). "Zeboim" was possibly north of Lydda and "Neballat" east. Lydda itself (here "Lod") is today the site of Israel's international airport, ten miles from the coast (cf. Ezr 2:33; Ne 7:37). Peter healed Aeneas in this town (Ac 9:32–38). "Ono" was five and a half miles northwest of Lydda. The enemies of Nehemiah tried to lure him to a conference there (Ne 6:2; cf. Ezr 2:33; Ne 7:37). "The Valley of the Craftsmen" may be the broad valley between Lod and Ono. The oak trees of the nearby Sharon plain were undoubtedly useful to artisans working in either wood or iron.

5. Transfer of Levites from Judah to Benjamin (11:36)

36 Certain divisions of Levites, who had been located in Judah, were now transferred to Benjamin to rectify the disproportion presumably discovered in Nehemiah's census.

J. Lists of Priests and the Dedication of the Wall (12:1–47)

1. Priests and Levites from the first return (12:1–9)

1–6 "Shealtiel" was the father of Zerubbabel according to verse 1 and Ezr 3:2, 8; Hag 1:1; but 1Ch 3:17–19 lists him as the uncle of Zerubbabel (see Ezra 5:2). "Jeshua" was the high priest about 560–490 B.C. (cf. Ezr 2:2; Ne 7:7, 12:10, 26). "Seraiah" (cf. 11:11; 12:12) is called Azariah in 1Ch 9:11 (cf. comment on Ezr 2:2). The "Ezra" listed in v.1 is, of course, not the same Ezra who returned eighty years later.

7 The rotation of twenty-four priestly houses may have been established at the time of David. There are twenty-two heads of priestly houses mentioned here in vv.1–7. Inscriptions listing the twenty-four courses of the priests presumably hung in hundreds of synagogues in Palestine.

8–9 The singing was in antiphonal fashion, with two sections of the choir standing opposite each other (cf. v.24; 2Ch 7:6, Ezr 3:11).

2. High priests and Levites since Joiakim (12:10–26)

10–21 All but one of the twenty-two priestly families listed in vv.1–7 are repeated in this later list that dates to the time of Joiakim, the high priest in the late sixth and early fifth century B.C.

22 "Darius the Persian" was either Darius II (423–404 B.C.) or, less probably, Darius III (335–331 B.C.), the king whose empire Alexander the Great conquered.

23 The "book of the annals" (cf. Ne 7:5) may have been the official temple chronicle containing various lists and records. Compare the annals of the Persian kings (Ezr 4:15; Est 2:23; 6:1; 10:2); "the book of the annals of the kings of Israel," mentioned eighteen times in 1 and 2 Kings; and "the book of the annals of the kings of Judah," mentioned fifteen times in 1 and 2 Kings.

24–26 On "who stood opposite," see comment on v.9. For "David's directions," see 1Ch 16:4; 23:27–31; 2Ch 8:14. From 11:17 we would have expected Mattaniah and Bakbukiah to be associated with the leaders of the choirs mentioned in v.24, rather than with the gatekeepers of v.25. On "gatekeepers," see comment on Ezr 2:42 (cf. Ne 3:1).

3. Dedication of the walls of Jerusalem (12:27–43)

27 Earlier, Solomon had dedicated the temple he built (1Ki 8), as had Zerubbabel (Ezr 6:16). The "dedication" (GK 2853) of the wall culminates the efforts of the people under Nehemiah's inspired leadership. Great enthusiasm must have characterized their march to the joyful music.

"Cymbals" (GK 5199) were used for religious ceremonies (2Sa 6:5; 1Ch 16:42; 25:1; 2Ch 5:12; 29:25; Ezr 3:10), as were "harps"

Extensive archaeological excavations continue in the City of David (part of present-day Jerusalem). In this picture, the wall labelled "1" is from the time of Nehemiah.

(GK 4036; e.g., 1Sa 10:5; 2Sa 6:5; 1Ch 15:16, 20, 28; Ps 150:3). The harp was an instrument with strings of varying lengths. The "lyre" (GK 5575) was an instrument with strings of the same length but of different diameters and tensions.

28–29 "Netophathites" were from Netophah, a town near Bethlehem (1Ch 2:54; 9:16; Ezr 2:22; Ne 7:26). "Beth-Gilgal" was perhaps the Gilgal near Jericho (Jos 4:19–20) or the Gilgal of Elijah (2Ki 2:1), some seven miles north of Bethel.

30 The verb "purified . . . ceremonially" (GK 3197; cf. 13:9, 22, 30; Ezr 6:20) is used most frequently of the purification necessary to restore someone who had contracted impurity to a state of purity so that that person might participate in ritual activities (Lev 22:4–7). The Levites are said to have cleansed all that was holy in the temple (1Ch 23:28) and the temple itself (2Ch 29:15) during the times of revival. Ritual purification was intended to teach God's holiness and moral purity (Lev 16:30).

31 There were two great processions, starting probably from the area of the Valley Gate (2:13, 15; 3:13) in the center of the western section of the wall. The first procession led by Ezra (v.36) and Hoshaiah (v.32) moved in a counterclockwise direction on the wall; the second with Nehemiah moved in a clockwise direction. They met between the Prison Gate and the Water Gate and then entered the temple area (cf. Ps 48:12–13). The literal rendering "to the right" is misleading, as this procession went left to the south. Since Semites oriented themselves facing east, the right hand often represented the south.

32–37 "Ezra" in v.33 is not Ezra the scribe (v.36). Each choir was composed of seven priests blowing "trumpets" (see comment on Ezr 3:10) and Levites playing on other musical instruments. "Asaph" was the founder of one of the three guilds of Levite musicians (1Ch 25:1–2). On the "Fountain Gate," see comment on 3:15; on the "Water Gate," see comment on 3:26. The procession went around the southern end of the walls, then turned north up the eastern wall to the Water Gate.

38 The second choir, led by Nehemiah, moved "in the opposite direction" from Ezra's choir (lit., "to the left," but meaning northward; see comment on Ne 12:31). That procession went in a clockwise direction around the northwestern sections of the wall. On the "Tower of the Ovens," see comment on 3:11; on "Broad Wall," see comment on 3:8.

39 On the "Ephraim Gate," see comment on 8:16. This gate is not mentioned as in need of repair in ch. 3. On the "Jeshanah Gate," see comment on 3:6; the "Fish Gate," 3:3; the "Tower of Hananel" and the "Tower of the Hundred," 3:1; the "Inspection Gate," 3:31.

40–43 "The choirs sang" (v.42) is literally "the singers made [themselves] heard." "Great sacrifices" were offered because "God made them rejoice with great joy" (cf. 1Ch 29:9; Jnh 4:6). "The women" (see comments on 8:2; 10:28) "could be heard far away" (see Ezr 3:13; cf. 1Ki 1:40; 2Ki 11:13).

4. Regulations of the temple offerings and services (12:44–47)

44–45 On "storerooms" and "contributions," see comments on 10:37, 39. The people of Judah were "pleased" (i.e., it gave them great joy) to contribute their offerings to support the priests and Levites (cf. 2Co 9:7).

46–47 Asaph, a founder of one of the three musical guilds, was a Gershonite Levite to whom David entrusted the "service of song" in the tabernacle (cf. 1Ch 6:39; 2Ch 29:30; 35:15; Pss 50, 73–83). On "Zerubbabel," see Ezr 2:2; 3:2, 8; 4:2–3; Ne 7:7; 12:1. "Contributed" (GK 5989) translates a participle implying continued giving. On "the Levites set aside," see comment on 10:38–39.

II. Nehemiah's Second Administration (13:1–31)

A. Abuses During His Absence (13:1–5)

1. Mixed marriages (13:1–3)

1 The reference to "the Book of Moses" is to Dt 23:3–6 (cf. Nu 22–24). On marriages to Ammonites and Moabites, see comment on Ezr 9:1.

2 "Balaam" was the seer summoned by Balak, the king of Moab, to curse Israel (Nu 22–24). He came from Pethor in northwestern Mesopotamia (Nu 22:5). An Aramaic inscription from Deir 'Alla in Transjordan refers to Balaam. Though hired to curse the Israelites, through the inspiration of the Lord

he blessed them instead. Later, however, he helped lead Israel to worship the Moabite god at Peor (Nu 25:1–3; 31:16; cf. Rev 2:14). In the NT his name is symbolic of avarice (2Pe 2:15; Jude 11). Curses had a power of their own; once uttered they could not simply be recalled. They could, however, be canceled by blessings (cf. Jdg 17:1–2).

3 The same term for "foreign descent" (GK 6850) is used in Ex 12:38 ("other people"). There, however, the mixed multitude was welcomed as they had agreed to the worship of the Lord, whereas it is implied that this was not the case here.

2. Tobiah's occupation of the temple quarters (13:4–5)

4 Some scholars identify "Eliashib" with the high priest of that name (cf. 3:1, 20; 13:28). Others argue that it is unlikely for a high priest to have been placed in charge of storerooms. The word rendered "closely associated" is used in Ru 2:20 to indicate that Boaz was related to Naomi and Ruth. We do not know Tobiah's exact (cf. 2:10) relationship with Eliashib.

5 During Nehemiah's absence from the city to return to the Persian king's court, Tobiah had used his influence with Eliashib to gain entrance into a chamber ordinarily set aside for the storage of tithes and other offerings (Nu 18:21–32; Dt 14:28–29; 26:12–15). These storerooms were evidently in the inner court of the temple (those mentioned in 10:38–39 and Zec 3:7 were parts of the outer court). Frankincense (NIV, "incense"), like myrrh, is a resin derived from trees that grow only in Somalia and Arabia.

B. Nehemiah's Return (13:6–7)

6–7 The thirty-second year of Artaxerxes I ran from Apr 1, 433, to Apr 19, 432 B.C. This verse and 5:14 indicate that Nehemiah's first term ran for about twelve years, until 433/432. We do not know the exact length of his second term, but it must have ended before 407 B.C., when other sources inform us that Bigvai was governor of Judah.

C. Nehemiah's Expulsion of Tobiah (13:8–9)

8–9 Nehemiah was a man of a volcanic temperament who expressed his indignation by taking quick action (vv.25–28; cf. 5:6–13; cf. contrast with Ezra in Ezr 9:3). On "to purify," see comment on 12:30 (cf. Lev 12; 14:4–32; 17:15–16). Though only a single chamber used by Tobiah has been mentioned before (vv.5, 7–8), the plural "rooms" here shows that other chambers were involved.

D. Reorganization and Reforms (13:10–31)

1. Offerings for the temple staff (13:10–14)

10 Nehemiah seems to be correcting an abuse of long standing. Strictly speaking the Levites had no holdings (Nu 18:20, 23–24; Dt 14:29; 18:1), though some may have had private income (Dt 18:8). The Levites were thus dependent on the faithful support of the people. This may explain the reluctance of many Levites to return from Exile (see comment on Ezr 8:15).

11–12 Nehemiah's rebuke of the officials here recalls his earlier rebuke of the selfish wealthy who exploited the less fortunate in granting them usurious loans. On tithes, see comment on 12:44.

13 On the nature of the profession "scribe," see comment on Ezr 7:6. Of the four treasurers put "in charge of the storerooms," one was a priest, one a Levite, one a scribe, and one a layman of rank. They all needed to be "trustworthy" (cf. 9:8, "faithful") in distributing the necessary supplies. This would ensure that supplies were distributed equitably.

14 Nehemiah was concerned that God would remember him (v.31; cf. 5:19) and "not blot out" (see Ex 17:14; 32:32) what he had done "faithfully," i.e., his good deeds inspired by steadfast love (cf. 1:5).

2. The abuse of the Sabbath (13:15–22)

15 Grapes were, of course, trodden by foot, but not normally on the "Sabbath." There was always the temptation on the part of merchants to violate the Sabbath rest (cf. Isa 58:13; Eze 20:13, 16; 22:8, 26; 23:38); this was especially true of non-Jewish merchants. The high regard for the ideal of the Sabbath was, however, expressed by those parents who called their children Shabbethai (cf. Ezr 10:15; Ne 8:7; 11:16).

16 Tyre (see comment on Ezr 3:7) was located only a dozen miles north of the border between Israel and Lebanon. The Tyrians supplied some of their famous cedars for the rebuilding of the temple (Ezr 3:7). It was renowned for its far-flung maritime trade (Eze 26:5, 14) and its export of fish (Eze 26:4–14). Most of the fish were either dried, smoked, or salted. Fish were an important part of the diet. They were sold at the market by the Fish Gate (2Ch 33:14; Ne 3:3; 12:39).

17–18 Nehemiah rebuked especially the nobles who were the leaders (cf. vv.11, 25; cf. 5:7). "Desecrating" (GK 2725) means to turn what is sacred into common use, to profane.

19 The gates began to cast long "evening shadows" even before sunset, when the Sabbath began. The Israelites counted their days from sunset to sunset. The precise moment the Sabbath began was heralded by the blowing of a trumpet by a priest.

20–21 When the gates were shut on the Sabbath eve, the persistent merchants carried on their activities outside the gates for two weeks until Nehemiah noticed them. Nehemiah was not a man of idle words. He meant what he said and was not averse to backing up his words by force (v.25).

22 The Sabbath was sanctified, not just by a negative cessation of ordinary labor, but by a consecration of that day to joyous gatherings. Fasting and mourning were not to be observed on the Sabbath. Once again, Nehemiah speaks a brief prayer to God.

3. Mixed marriages (13:23–29)

23–24 Ezra had dealt with the same problem of intermarriage some thirty years before. On "Ashdod" see comment on 4:7. Ammon was across the Jordan River (see comment on Ezr 9:1). Tobiah, Nehemiah's enemy, was influential in that area (cf. comment on Ne 2:10). The Ammonites worshiped the god Molech (Milcom) by sacrificing children in the fire (Lev 18:21; 2Ki 23:10, 13). The Moabites worshiped Chemosh, to whom they sacrificed their children (Nu 21:29; 2Ki 3:27). The Hebrews recognized other people as foreigners by their languages (cf. Ex 21:8; Dt 3:9; Jdg 12:6; Ps 114:1; Isa 33:4–19; Eze 3:5–6).

25 On Nehemiah's rebuke of others, see vv.11, 17 (see also comment on Ezr 9:3 for contrast between Ezra and Nehemiah). Plucking the hair from another's beard was an action designed to show anger, to express an insult, and to mark someone to scorn (2Sa 10:4; Isa 50:6). Nehemiah's action was designed to prevent future intermarriages, whereas Ezra dissolved the existing unions.

26–27 Solomon was Israel's outstanding king in wealth and political achievements (1Ki 3:12–13; 2Ch 1:12). He reigned for forty years (1Ki 11:42), built the magnificent temple (1Ki 6:1–38), and constructed an even more splendid palace for himself (1Ki 7:1). His fame spread beyond his borders so that the queen of Sheba in southwestern Arabia traveled fourteen hundred miles to test his fabled wisdom (1Ki 10:1–3). His international prestige is demonstrated in that he was given the daughter of a pharaoh in marriage (1Ki 3:1; 7:8; 9:16, 24; 11:1; 2Ch 8:11).

According to 1Ki 11:1–3, Solomon had seven hundred wives and three hundred concubines, among whom were Moabite, Ammonite, Edomite, Sidonian, and Hittite women. He began his reign humbly by asking for wisdom from the Lord (1Ki 3:3–15). In later years, however, his foreign wives led him to worship other gods, so that he built a high place for Chemosh, the god of the Moabites on the Mount of Olives (1Ki 11:7).

On the phrase "terrible wickedness," compare 2Sa 13:16; Jer 26:19.

28 We do not know the name of "one of the sons of Joiada son of Eliashib the high priest." The phrase "the high priest" could refer to either Joiada or Eliashib, though more likely it designates Joiada (cf. 12:10). The offending son would then have been a brother of Johanan, the man who succeeded Joiada as high priest (12:22–23). He was married to a daughter of Sanballat.

According to Lev 21:14, the high priest was not to marry a foreigner. The expulsion of Joiada's son may have followed this special ban or the general interdict against intermarriage. Such a union was especially rankling to Nehemiah in the light of Sanballat's enmity (see comment on 2:10).

29 Nehemiah's prayer to "remember them" implied a prayer that God would judge them accordingly (cf. 6:14).

4. Provisions of wood and firstfruits (13:30–31)

30 "Duties" (lit., "divisions"; GK 5466) refers to the assignment of particular duties to groups of priests and Levites, possibly on a rotating basis.

31 On the wood offering and firstfruits, see comments on 10:34–35. The last words of Nehemiah—"Remember me with favor."—recapitulate a repeated theme running through the final chapter (vv.14, 22). His motive throughout his ministry was to please and to serve his divine Sovereign.

Nehemiah provides us with one of the most vivid patterns of leadership in Scriptures:

1. *He was a man of responsibility*, as shown by his position as the royal cupbearer.

2. *He was a man of vision*, confident of who God was and what he could do through his servants. He was not, however, a visionary but a man who planned and then acted.

3. *He was a man of prayer*, who prayed spontaneously and constantly even in the presence of the king (2:4–5).

4. *He was a man of action and cooperation*, who realized what had to be done, explained it to others, and enlisted their aid. Nehemiah, a layman, was able to cooperate with his contemporary, Ezra the scribe and priest, in spite of the fact that these two leaders were of entirely different temperaments.

5. *He was a man of compassion*, who was moved by the plight of the poorer members of society so that he renounced even the rights he was entitled to (5:18) and denounced the greed of the wealthy (5:8).

6. *He was a man who triumphed over opposition*. His opponents tried ridicule (4:3), attempted slander (6:4–7), and spread misleading messages (6:10–14). But through God's favor Nehemiah triumphed over all difficulties.

The Old Testament in the New

OT Text	NT Text	Subject
Ne 9:15	Jn 6:31	Bread from heaven

Esther

INTRODUCTION

1. Background

Five books that are found together in the third division of the Hebrew Bible (Song of Songs, Ruth, Lamentations, Ecclesiastes, and Esther) collectively are called the five *Megilloth* ("Scrolls"). The book of Esther is generally the last of the five, probably because it is read during Purim, the last festival of the Jewish year. In our English Bibles it is found after Ezra and Nehemiah, probably because of the role of Persia in the three books.

The book of Esther has continued to be controversial. Reactions range from ecstatic delight for the victory of the Jews over their enemies to violent dislike and rejection because of what appears to be indefensible moral conduct and because of the absence of any reference to God.

Esther is one of two OT books named for a woman, the other being Ruth, and one of several not quoted in the NT. Like Song of Songs, it does not mention God; like Exodus, it deals specifically with persecution of the Hebrew people.

Esther contains the account of the origin of the Feast of Purim, one of two festivals adopted by the postexilic Jewish community that are not found in the Mosaic law; the other one is Hanukkah, a festival that began during the time of the Maccabees (i.e., between the OT and NT). The events of Esther are set in Susa during the reign of Xerxes, king of Persia (486–465 B.C.), whose empire reached from India to Ethiopia. Esther is the only OT book in which the entire narrative takes place in Persia.

Against a background of centuries of persecution, it is understandable why Purim has become such a favorite of the Jews. It recalls a time when they were able to turn the tables on those who wanted to destroy them. Purim is celebrated today amid a carnival-like atmosphere, with masquerade parties, noisemaking, and revelry. The story is reenacted in synagogues with the audience hissing Haman and cheering Mordecai.

This book is a profound statement about the heroic resistance necessary for survival in the face of violent anti-Semitism that continues to the present day.

2. Authorship and Date

The text of Esther nowhere names the author nor gives the date of its writing. Authorship of the book has often been attributed to Mordecai. However, it is unlikely that Mordecai would have penned the paean of praise about himself in 10:3. Augustine suggested Ezra as the author. But the most that can be said is that the identity of the author remains unknown.

Because of this, there can be no absolute certainty about the date of its composition. It cannot have been written earlier than the death of Xerxes (465 B.C.), as 10:2 suggests that his reign had ended, but that is the most that can be said for certain. Two principal periods have been proposed as the likely date: an early date (450–300 B.C.) and a late date (175–100 B.C.).

Arguments for the earlier date include the numerous Persian names and loanwords. It is unlikely that so many words of this type would have occurred in a composition written in the late Greek period without modification. Another argument for the early date is the author's intimate knowledge of Persian customs and the topography of Susa and the Persian royal palaces. Such familiarity with Persian life argues for a date in the Persian period and perhaps not long after Xerxes' reign, for this kind of knowledge would not likely have survived till the Maccabean period. If the earlier date is accepted, the author was probably a Persian Jew. If it was written in the second century, he was probably a Palestinian Jew.

3. Purpose

Many interpreters take the position that the major purpose of the book of Esther was to explain the origin of Purim, to justify its celebration (since it is not mentioned in the Torah), and to regulate its manner of observance. Some believe that the purpose of Esther was to record the remarkable deliverance of the Jewish people at a critical time in their history and to keep the memory of that deliverance alive through the annual observance of Purim, in order to kindle their nationalistic fervor. An immediate purpose served by the book was to assure the Jews who did not return to their homeland after the Exile that God still loved them and would protect them from unjust oppression.

Most commentaries overlook what may well be the actual intent of this book—to teach God's providential care of his people (see Theological Values). This oversight is understandable because the doctrine of providence is presented so subtly in Esther; God's name is not even mentioned. The possibility of another purpose is suggested under Special Problems—i.e., to show that God's displeasure may be manifested by his silence.

4. Special Problems

Three problems are especially associated with the book of Esther: lack of a single mention of God's name in the book; moral and ethical practices by Mordecai and Esther; and a number of what appear to be historical inaccuracies.

a. Absence of God's name

The book of Esther's failure to mention God is glaring. The explanation can best be seen in the providence of God and his hiddenness (see Theological Values). Many believe that there is an indirect reference to Esther's faith when she spoke of fasting (4:16; cf. 4:3; 9:31). The statement "relief and deliverance ... will arise from another place" (4:14) comes very close to being an acknowledgment of God and probably should be understood that way.

b. Moral and ethical practices

The nationalistic and vengeful spirit of the book of Esther caused many problems among early Jewish and Christian readers and continues to do so. The leading characters do not consistently exhibit noble qualities. Xerxes was cruel, sensual, and capricious. Esther was willing to hide her identity to become queen and did not appear reluctant to marry a Gentile. Mordecai advised her to conceal her identity in order to become queen. Esther showed no mercy when Haman pled for his life and even demanded that his sons be hanged. Not content with deliverance of her people, she and Mordecai with the king's permission wrote a decree authorizing their people to slaughter and plunder their enemies. Mordecai insolently refused to bow to Haman.

The author never explicitly condemns any of the moral shortcomings of Esther or Mordecai but seems to describe their triumph with approval. Perhaps only someone who has experienced severe persecution can understand, without necessarily approving, the unrestrained exultation evoked by victory over one's persecutors.

The best approach to the moral problems of Esther is neither blind defense nor blanket condemnation. If immoral practices among the Israelites are found in the preexilic period (idolatry, adultery, lying, etc.), why should anyone be surprised to find other expressions of ungodly conduct in the postexilic period?

There is an explanation that addresses both the omission of God's name and the moral problems of the book (and that at the same time reveals a link between the two). The entire book should perhaps be seen as a subtle but powerful reminder that God's people sometimes fail to consult him prior to acting, do things that are contrary to his will, and consequently experience his displeasure by his silence. The disturbing ethical practices of Esther and Mordecai resulted in the deliverance of the Jewish people from a terrible pogrom, but their success does not prove that the means used were pleasing to God. There are numerous examples in the Bible of great men and women of God committing immoral acts (e.g., Ge 12:10–20; 19:8, 30–38; 2Sa 11).

In these examples, there is no explicit rebuke by God—only his silence. However, the silence of God—the feeling that he is very distant—can express his disapproval just as powerfully as his open rebuke through the prophets. What is usually interpreted as the providence of God working silently but effectively on behalf of his people should be reexamined to see whether God's silence should be interpreted as evidence that the people were working out their own affairs without consulting him. There is no evidence that the Jewish people entered into a period of blessing after the events of Esther, a blessing that might have been expected if God were guiding their actions. His clear promise, after all, was that if they obeyed him, they would be blessed (Dt 28). Mordecai's elevation (10:3) may not have been God's stamp of approval on his actions; it may instead show that if we use human means to achieve our purposes, we will receive human rewards (cf. Mt 6:5).

The real message of Esther may well be that God's people are prone to use the same means as ungodly people for achieving their goals rather than taking a bold step of faith that God will work out his purposes without human initiative, least of all resorting to immoral acts in a crisis situation.

c. Alleged historical inaccuracies

Scholars have long debated the historicity of the events described in Esther. An unbiased examination of all the arguments, however, leads to the conclusion that there is no valid evidence for denying the historicity of any of the people or events found in the book. Admittedly, the lack of confirmation of Vashti or Esther is a difficult problem, but all the facts are still not in. There is nothing in Esther that could not have happened.

5. Theological Values

The omission of God's name does not detract from the theological worth of Esther. It could be interpreted as his hiddenness as he works out his purposes. This hiddenness can sometimes be explained as evidence of his displeasure, which may be the key to the ethical problems of Esther that disturb many sincere Christian exegetes. In the OT God sometimes spoke out to show his displeasure toward his people's sins (e.g., Isa 1:15; Jer 17:1; Am 6:8). Sometimes he expressed his displeasure by withdrawal and silence (e.g., Eze 11:23). The Jews in Esther's time did not deserve God's favor (no one ever does). Mordecai and Esther were not blameless.

Esther implicitly teaches God's providential care of his people. Vashti's deposition, Esther's selection as her successor, and Mordecai's discovery of the plot against the king and his subsequent reward are only a few of the many "chance" happenings that are better explained by God's way of effecting the deliverance of his people from their persecutors. The book implies that even when God's people are far from him and disobedient, they are still the object of his concern and love, and that he is working out his purposes through them (4:14). There is also a reminder that if one fails to carry out God's tasks, he will work out his purposes through another. The sovereignty of God is implicit in the events of the story. The fast-moving events that seem to be under the control of men such as Xerxes and Haman prove in the end to have been directed by God for the benefit of his people. Even the law of the Medes and Persians, which should have brought about the slaughter of the Jews, was overruled.

The book of Esther teaches (1) the law of retribution for sin by the hanging of Haman on his own gallows, (2) the reward for faithfulness, and (3) the value of standing for one's convictions even in the midst of a dangerous situation.

EXPOSITION

I. Esther Elevated to Queen of Persia (1:1–2:23)

A. The Great Banquets of Xerxes (1:1–9)

1 The story of Esther is said to have taken place during the reign of the Persian monarch Xerxes. The Hebrew word used throughout the book is transliterated as "Ahasuerus" (see NIV note on v.1), a variant of Xerxes' name. As grandson of Cyrus the Great (550–530 B.C.) by Atossa, Cyrus' daughter, Xerxes inherited an empire from his father, Darius I (520–486 B.C.), that stretched east to west from India (probably a reference to the northwestern part of the Indus River region) to Cush ("Ethiopia," i.e., the Upper Nile region). Xerxes was the Persian monarch who made an ambitious but disastrous attempt to conquer Greece in 480–479 B.C. He divided much of his energy during the remaining years of his reign to an ambitious building project at Susa and Persepolis. He was murdered by his vizier Artabanus, who then placed Artaxerxes I (cf. Ezr 7:1; Ne 2:1) on the throne.

For purposes of governing, Xerxes' empire was divided into 127 provinces and twenty satrapies (according to Herodotus) or as many as thirty-one (according to other sources). "Provinces" were political subdivisions of the "satrapies" (cf. 3:12).

2 "At the time King Xerxes reigned" suggests the beginning of his reign, but v.3 says it was in the third year. It may only mean that Xerxes took up his residence in Susa, the royal winter residence and capital of ancient Elam. In the summer Susa was unbearably hot. Susa was both the name of the city and the name of the royal fortress or citadel that occupied a separate part of the city. Fire destroyed the royal buildings during the reign of Artaxerxes I (465–424 B.C.), but they were rebuilt by Artaxerxes II (404–358). Susa's location made it a center of traffic on the roads to Persepolis, Sardis, and Ecbatana.

3 In the third year of his reign, Xerxes gave a great banquet to display his wealth and glory. Its purpose may have been to make plans for his Greek campaign. All his nobles and the military and political leaders of Persia and Media were present. Historical sources confirm huge numbers of guests (as many as 69,574) at banquets put on by the Persian kings.

4 For 180 days (six months) Xerxes displayed his vast wealth and royal regalia to his guests. A question has been raised as to whether the guests could have exercised their administrative duties and also all have been present during the entire 180 days or whether they might have come by rotation until all had experienced the king's hospitality. Possibly the king displayed his wealth for 180 days and then gave a feast that lasted seven days.

5 The context indicates that a seven-day banquet was given for all the men who were in the citadel of Susa, from the greatest to the least (i.e., both nobles and commoners were included). The banquet was held in the king's garden. Persian palaces usually stood in a park, surrounded by a fortified wall.

6 With eyewitness accuracy the author described the white-and-blue linen hangings in the garden that were fastened with cords to silver rings on marble pillars. He described couches of gold and silver placed on a mosaic pavement of porphyry, marble, mother-of-pearl, and other costly stones. Archaeologists have found the remains of Xerxes' palace and have verified the accuracy of the opulence described in this verse.

7 Wine was served in golden goblets, no two alike. The king's "liberality" assured an abundant supply of wine for all the guests.

8 The guests were served according to Persian law; the word for "command" (GK 2017) here may mean the special rule made for this feast. No one was compelled to drink; at the same time, no restrictions were placed on what a guest could consume. The king's wine stewards had been instructed to serve each man whatever he wanted, however much or little.

9 At the same time the men were being entertained by the king, Queen Vashti gave a banquet for the women in the royal palace, though such separation of the sexes at banquets was not required by Persian custom. The queen's name has raised a question about the historicity of the book of Esther, as the only known name of Xerxes' queen was Amestris, a cruel and imperious woman. But Amestris is probably a Greek version of the name Vashti.

B. Vashti's Dethronement (1:10–22)

1. Vashti's refusal to obey the king (1:10–12)

10–11 On the seventh and last day of the feast, when the king was in high spirits, he sent his seven eunuchs (seven was a sacred number to the Persians as well as to the Hebrews) to bring the queen before him, wearing the crown, so that he might display her beauty to the assembled guests. The name of the eunuchs are all Persian in origin. Eunuchs are usually associated with the king's harem, but they also played important roles in many

These are the ruins of the palace of King Xerxes at Persepolis. Courtesy Oriental Institute of the University of Chicago.

political and administrative affairs (cf. Jer 29:2; Da 1:7; Ac 8:27).

12 The queen refused to answer the king's summons, and he became enraged. His male ego had suffered a public affront. Though the motive for her refusal is not stated, she probably did not choose to degrade herself before the king's drunken guests.

2. The wise men's advice (1:13–22)

13–14 Angered by Vashti's disobedience, the king consulted his wise men, "who understood the times," to determine what should be done to her. Like their Babylonian counterparts, these wise men were astrologers and magicians who gave counsel according to their reading of celestial phenomena. The king normally consulted experts in matters of law and justice and heard their opinions before he acted on any matter. There were seven wise men, all with Persian names, called "the seven nobles of Persia and Media" (cf. the Council of Seven in Ezr 7:14). Their high rank allowed them "special access" into the king's presence.

15 The king wanted to know what could be done legally to the queen for disobeying his command. It seems strange that he would have to consult others before dealing with a rebellious wife, but apparently the law protected her from his caprice.

16 Memucan, one of the seven nobles and perhaps their spokesman after they had discussed the matter, advised the king that Vashti had not only done "wrong" to the king but also to all the nobles and all the people throughout all the provinces of the kingdom. Apparently there was no existing law to deal with the situation, hence the consultation between the king and his nobles.

17–18 More was involved than the queen's affront to the king. With keen perception Memucan saw that if left unpunished, Vashti's rebellious attitude toward her husband would influence other women in the kingdom to rebel against their husbands' authority. The nobles anticipated there would be no end of disobedience, disrespect, and discord in their own homes.

19–20 Memucan advised immediate and drastic action to deal with the situation. He advised Xerxes to issue a "royal decree" to be included among the laws of the Persians and Medes that could never be repealed, forbidding Vashti from ever again entering the presence of the king; her position should be given to someone better than she. The advisors wanted to be sure that Vashti could never again be restored to the king's favor, lest she take vengeance on them. Memucan further advised the king to proclaim the decree throughout the empire so that all women from the least to the greatest would respect their husbands.

21–22 Memucan's advice pleased the king and the other nobles. Xerxes ordered dispatches sent to every part of the kingdom, to each people in their own language. He wanted to be sure that all his subjects understood the decree. The decree proclaimed that every man should be ruler over his own household.

C. Choosing a New Queen (2:1–23)

1. The search (2:1–4)

1 After Xerxes' wrath "had subsided," he remembered the deeds of Vashti and his decree that deposed her. It is uncertain whether he now regretted his rash action and wished to reinstate her but was prevented because his decree was irrevocable (cf. Da 6:14–15), or whether his thoughts now turned to a replacement for the queen. The king divorced Vashti in the third year of his reign (1:3) and did not marry Esther till the seventh year (2:16). Between the events of 1:3 and 2:16, Xerxes made his disastrous expedition to Greece. Returning from his naval defeat at Salamis in 480 and his humiliating rout at Plataea in 479, he turned his thoughts to remarriage, through which he hoped to find solace.

2 The king's personal attendants proposed that the king choose another wife from among the beautiful young virgins. They may have seen and felt more than others the king's unhappiness that the putting away of Vashti had caused him.

3–4 In all the provinces officials were to be appointed to locate all the beautiful young virgins and bring them to the harem in Susa. There they would be placed under the care of Hegai, the king's eunuch. Beauty treatments of all kinds of ointments and cosmetics would be applied to each of the virgins for twelve months (cf. v.12) in preparation for her presentation to the king. The one who pleased the king would be made queen in the place of Vashti. The courtiers' suggestion pleased the king; so he ordered that the search begin. Fathers apparently did not voluntarily present their daughters as evidenced by the king's appointment of officials to search for the candidates.

2. Esther as a candidate (2:5–11)

5–6 At this juncture in the narrative, Mordecai is introduced for the first time. His name is the Hebraized form of the Babylonian god Marduk. Idolatrous names for devout Jews grew out of a practice during the Diaspora of giving both a Babylonian and a Hebrew name to the same person (cf. Da 1:6–7). He is called a "Jew" (GK 3374), a word derived from "Judah" that was used from the time of the Exile to refer to an Israelite. Possibly Mordecai was a eunuch because no wife or family is mentioned (v.7) and because he had access to the women's quarters (v.11). His ancestry is traced through his father and grandfather to his great-grandfather, Kish, of the tribe of Benjamin.

Verse 6 begins "who had been carried into exile from Jerusalem . . . with Jehoiachin." If the antecedent of "who" is, as seems likely, "Kish," this man was carried away into captivity with King Jehoiachin in 597 B.C.

7 Mordecai "brought up" his cousin (other sources say Mordecai was Esther's uncle), whose Hebrew name was Hadassah ("myrtle"). She is better known by her Persian name Esther, which is derived from the Persian word for "star," or from the name of the Babylonian deity Ishtar (known in Hebrew as Ashtoreth). Her age at the time of the death of her parents is not given, but Mordecai took her as his own daughter; he probably adopted her. The author describes her as "lovely in form and features."

8 After the king's edict had been proclaimed, girls from all over the empire were brought to Susa, including Esther. They were placed in the care of Hegai, who was in charge of the harem.

9 Hegai must have discerned that Esther had the qualities that would please the king, for she "won his favor." Immediately he began to provide her with beauty treatments and special food so that the required twelve months of preparation could be completed without delay. Esther apparently did not object to breaking the Jewish dietary laws. Hegai assigned seven maids from the king's palace to take care of her and transferred Esther and her maids to the best quarters of the harem.

10 Mordecai forbade Esther to reveal her Jewish nationality, and she dutifully obeyed him. Obviously she would have stood little chance to be selected queen if she were not Persian, but why would Mordecai want her to marry a Gentile? Such a marriage was a violation of Jewish laws (cf. Ezr 9:1–4, 14, 10:3, 11, 18–44; Ne 10:30; 13:23–27). Also, there was no threat by Haman or known antipathy to the Jews at the time to warrant his secrecy. Mordecai has been accused of ambition for political advancement that could be realized if his cousin were queen. The author expresses no disapproval of the subterfuge.

11 Mordecai was careful to keep close check on Esther. Every day he walked near the courtyard of the harem to try to gain information about his cousin.

3. The traditional procedure (2:12–14)

12 Further information is given about each candidate's beauty treatment. The treatment required twelve months before a candidate was allowed into the king's presence. For six months oil of myrrh was applied to her and for six months, perfumes and cosmetics.

13 When each candidate was ready to be presented to the king, whatever she desired to take with her from the harem to his palace was given to her (i.e., jewels, clothing, etc.).

14 The maiden chosen would go into the king's presence in the evening to spend the night with him. The next morning she would return to another part of the harem and be placed under the care of Shaashgaz, the king's eunuch who was in charge of the concubines. She never returned to the king again unless he was pleased with her and summoned her by name. Those rejected lived the rest of their lives like widows (cf. 2Sa 20:3).

4. Esther chosen as queen (2:15–18)

15 When Esther's turn came to be taken to the king, she did not request any of the usual ornaments or cosmetics to enhance her beauty. She only took the things that Hegai, the king's eunuch, had suggested. She trusted him to know what would please the king. Her modesty and humility impressed everyone who saw her. Her father's name is given in this verse as Abihail. This name occurs in the OT twice as a woman's name (1Ch 2:29; 2Ch 11:18).

16 It was the tenth month and the seventh year of Xerxes' reign when Esther was taken to the king; it was four years after Vashti had been deposed (cf. 1:3; see comment on 2:1).

17 None of the previous candidates had attracted the king sufficiently for him to make her his wife; but he immediately loved Esther and placed the royal crown on her head, thereby making her queen in place of Vashti. After seeing Esther the king had no desire to continue the search for a queen.

18 A great wedding feast was given by the king for all his nobles and officials. As a generous gesture to mark the occasion, he proclaimed a holiday, i.e., a release from work, throughout the provinces. He distributed "gifts" liberally, as befitted such a monarch.

5. An attempt on the king's life thwarted (2:19–23)

19–20 All the virgins were assembled again. At that time Mordecai was sitting at the king's gate. No reason is given for the assembly. Esther had been careful to keep her nationality secret, as Mordecai had instructed her. From the time she first came under his care, she had been obedient to his commands and continued to listen to him, even after being elevated to the position of queen. Her continued obedience to Mordecai becomes important to the plot. Mordecai's position at the gate was not that of an "idler" but represented some kind of duty or official position he occupied. He may have been appointed to this position by Esther to give him easier access to the royal quarters. Men who "sat at the gate" were frequently elders and leading men, respected citizens who settled disputes that were brought to them.

21–22 During the time he was sitting at the king's gate, Mordecai either overheard or was informed about a plot to kill Xerxes by two of the king's officers, Bigthana and Teresh (cf.

6:2). They were eunuchs, guards of the door—i.e., men who protected the king's private apartment—who had become angry with Xerxes. Mordecai got word to Esther about the plot; and she relayed the information to the king, giving credit to Mordecai, without mentioning their relationship. Plots against Persian monarchs were not uncommon. Xerxes was in fact assassinated in his bedroom in a similar situation in 465 B.C. in a conspiracy led by his chiliarch Artabanus.

23 When Mordecai's report was investigated and found to be true, the two men were hanged on a "gallows" (lit., "tree"; GK 6770). The entire event was recorded in the "book of the annals" (i.e., official court records of memorable events). It is hard to understand why Xerxes forgot to reward Mordecai at that time.

II. The Feud Between Haman and Mordecai (3:1–8:17)

A. Haman's Plot to Kill Mordecai (3:1–15)

1. Haman's anger with Mordecai (3:1–6)

1 Sometime later the king elevated Haman by giving him a place of honor above all the other nobles of the empire. It was probably the same office that was later given to Mordecai (cf. 10:2). This is the first mention of Haman. The text identifies him as the son of Hammedatha the Agagite (otherwise unknown). Jewish tradition considers him to have been a descendant of the Amalekite king Agag, an enemy of Israel during Saul's reign (cf. 1Sa 15:7–33). The Amalekites were ancient enemies of the Jews (cf. Ex 17:8–14; Nu 24:7; Dt 25:17–19). Saul failed to destroy the Amalekites completely as God had ordered him to do, and consequently the kingdom was taken from him (cf. 1Sa 15:23).

2–4 By command of the king, all the royal officials at the king's gate knelt down and paid honor to Haman. Mordecai, however, refused to kneel before Haman or to honor him. In spite of repeated appeals by the royal officials, Mordecai refused to obey the king's command. Apparently he had told them that as a Jew he could not bow before any human being. The officials informed Haman of Mordecai's insolence to see whether it would be "tolerated." There are many examples of God's people prostrating themselves before a king or other superiors (cf. Ge 23:7; 27:29;

1Sa 24:8; 2Sa 14:4; 1Ki 1:16). It is unlikely that Mordecai could have been elevated next to the king if he had refused to kneel before Xerxes. The most probable reason was Mordecai's pride; no self-respecting Benjamite would bow before a descendant of the ancient Amalekite enemy of the Jews.

5–6 On learning that Mordecai refused to kneel before him or to pay him honor, Haman was enraged. So great was his wrath and injured pride that he determined to destroy all the Jews in Xerxes' kingdom. Haman was not satisfied with killing only Mordecai but was determined to succeed where Saul had failed (cf. 1Sa 15:9); Haman would destroy all his enemies.

2. A day of revenge chosen by lot (3:7–15)

7 In the twelfth year of Xerxes' reign (474 B.C.), five years after Esther had become queen (2:16), "the *pur* (that is, the lot)" was cast in Haman's presence to determine the day for the slaughter of the Jews. The purpose of the lot may have been only to determine an auspicious day for Haman to go before the king to make his request to kill the Jews. The non-Hebraic word *pur* anticipates the institution of Purim (i.e., "lots") in ch. 9.

8 To gain the king's support for his plan, Haman described the Jews, who were scattered in all the provinces of Persia, as a people who kept themselves aloof, who had different customs, and who would not obey the king's laws. Haman reasoned that it was not in the king's best interest to "tolerate them." Haman did not mention Mordecai as the special object of his wrath.

9 To obtain the king's permission to destroy the Jews, Haman appealed to the monarch's greed, offering to put ten thousand talents of silver of his own private fortune into the royal treasury to pay the men who would carry out the pogrom. The value of the silver was a fabulous sum, estimated to weigh approximately 375 tons. It has also been estimated to represent the equivalent of two-thirds of the annual income of the Persian Empire. Perhaps Haman planned to acquire such a large sum by confiscating the Jews' property.

10–11 The proposal apparently was immediately acceptable to the king. He removed the signet ring from his finger and gave it to Haman with instructions to keep the money and to do whatever he pleased with the Jews. The signet ring was a symbol of royal authority and in ancient times was used instead of a written signature to seal official documents. Thus Haman was given unlimited authority to carry out his plan. The king was unaware that by giving blanket authority to Haman to execute the Jews, he had also placed his own wife under a death sentence. The king's rejection of Haman's silver may have been only an example of Oriental politeness that did not actually mean he rejected the payment (cf. 4:7, where it seems that the bribe was paid).

12 On the thirteenth of the first month (Nisan), the royal secretaries were summoned to write out in the script of each province and in the language of each people Haman's orders to the satraps, governors, and nobles. The orders were written in the king's name and sealed with his ring. Three echelons of officials are named—"satraps" (GK 346), who ruled over the twenty major divisions of the empire; "governors" (GK 7068), who ruled smaller subdivisions of the satrapies; and "nobles" (GK 8569), who served under the governors and were perhaps chiefs of the conquered peoples.

13 Dispatches were sent by "couriers" to all the provinces with orders to annihilate all the Jews, young and old, and to plunder their goods on the thirteenth day of the twelfth month (Adar). No reason is given for the lapse of almost a year from the time of the decree till its implementation. With so much advance notice, the Jews would have had time to escape. The piling up of verbs—"destroy, kill and annihilate"—expresses the idea of thoroughness.

14–15 The decree was to be made law in every province, and all were to know about it so they would be ready for the day. The couriers departed in haste for the provinces at the king's command. The edict was also circulated in the citadel of Susa. Then the king and Haman sat down to drink, unconcerned about the tragedy soon to be inflicted on the Jews. The people of Susa were bewildered by what was happening. Apparently they did not share Haman's passionate anti-Semitism.

B. Mordecai's Plan to Save His People (4:1–17)

1. Reaction to the edict (4:1–3)

1 On learning what Haman was plotting, Mordecai expressed his grief and humiliation in typical Oriental fashion. He tore his clothing, put on sackcloth, and sprinkled ashes on himself. Then he walked about the city wailing loudly.

2–3 Mordecai went no farther than the king's gate, as no one was permitted within the gate who was wearing sackcloth. Apparently a person in mourning was considered ceremonially unclean. Perhaps Mordecai hoped to attract Esther's attention (cf.4:4). Not only was Mordecai in mourning, but in every province where the edict was announced, it was greeted by the Jews with fasting, weeping, and wailing. Many of them lay down on sackcloth and ashes.

2. Mordecai's appeal to Esther (4:4–17)

4–5 Some of Esther's maids and eunuchs must have seen Mordecai at the king's gate; so they reported his behavior to Esther. No reason is given why they felt one Jew's grief should be reported to their queen since they apparently did not know about her relationship to Mordecai, though they did know the two were acquainted (cf. 2:11, 22). Esther was distressed to learn of Mordecai's sorrow. She sent clothes for him to wear in place of the sackcloth, probably so that he could enter the palace; but he refused to accept them. This may have indicated to Esther that his actions were not caused by personal sorrow but by a public calamity. Since Mordecai would not come to her, Esther sent Hathach, one of the king's eunuchs who had been assigned to attend her, to find out what was troubling Mordecai.

6–7 Hathach looked for Mordecai in the open square of the city in front of the king's gate, probably the marketplace. There Mordecai told the eunuch what had happened that caused him to be in mourning. He told Hathach how much money Haman had agreed to pay into the royal treasury for the privilege of destroying the Jews (cf. 3:11). We are not told how Mordecai learned about the transaction between the king and Haman.

8 Mordecai had a copy of the edict for the Jews' annihilation that was being circulated in Susa. He asked the eunuch to give it to Esther and to explain it to her. He told Hathach to urge Esther to go to the king to plead for mercy for the Jews. Mordecai's request would require that the queen reveal her Jewish identity.

9–11 After Hathach told the queen what Mordecai had said, she instructed him to return to her cousin to remind him that no one could approach the king in the inner court without a royal summons, upon penalty of death. On occasion the king had been known to extend his golden scepter to an uninvited person as a gesture of mercy. According to historical sources, a person could send a letter to the king asking for an audience. Why this procedure did not occur to Esther can only be surmised. Since she had not been summoned by the king for a month, Esther did not know whether he would forgive her if she approached him without a royal summons. She may have concluded that she had lost the king's favor. It appears that initially Esther was more concerned about her own welfare than about her people.

12–14 Mordecai responded by telling Esther that she would not escape Haman's edict against the Jews because she was in the king's house. If she remained silent, deliverance of the Jews would come from another source; but because of her cowardice, she and her father's family would perish. Not even royal status could protect her from the king's edict. Then Mordecai asked the question that has become the classic support of the doctrine of providence as a key to the understanding of the book of Esther: "Who knows but that you have come to royal position for such a time as this?" Her exaltation as a queen may have been God's way of obtaining a savior for his people. In the phrase "from another place," "place" may be a veiled reference to God.

15–16 Esther sent a reply to Mordecai, affirming her willingness to risk her life in behalf of her people. She asked him to assemble all the Jews who were in Susa to fast for her for three days and nights. She and her maids would also participate in the fast. Afterward she would go to the king, even though to do so was contrary to the law. In a final expression of courage and willing submission, she said, "If I perish, I perish." Prayer and fasting before God were customary concurrent practices in times of sorrow, anxiety, or penitence. The author makes no mention of God or prayers being made to him.

17 Mordecai departed from the open square in front of the king's gate and carried out Esther's instructions.

C. Esther's First Banquet (5:1–8)

1 "On the third day," i.e., when the fasting was completed (cf. 4:16), Esther dressed in her royal splendor and went to the inner court of the palace in front of the king's hall. Xerxes was sitting on his throne in the hall, facing the entrance. From this position he could see Esther standing in the court. She had waited to see what he would do, as she had already violated the law by entering the inner court (cf. 4:11).

2 Esther's beauty evidently pleased the king; so he did not rebuke her. Instead, he held out the golden scepter in his hand as a gesture of favor toward her. Esther approached the throne and touched the tip of the scepter.

3 The king wanted to know why she had come to him. He assured her that any request she might make, even up to half the kingdom, would be granted. He realized that only a pressing need could have caused Esther to risk coming to him unsummoned. The offer of half the kingdom was probably an example of Oriental courtesy that was not intended to be taken too literally (cf. Mk 6:23).

4 Instead of forthrightly pleading for her people, Esther invited the king and Haman to a banquet she had prepared that day. She undoubtedly realized that it was not a psychologically propitious moment to plead for her people. Perhaps Esther included Haman in the invitation so that he would be present when she made her accusations against him.

5–6 The king ordered Haman to be summoned at once. The two men then went to Esther's banquet. While they were drinking wine, the king again asked to know the nature of Esther's request.

7–8 For a second time Esther postponed giving a direct answer to the king. Instead she invited the king and Haman to a second ban-

quet the following day. She indicated that she would present her petition to the king at that time.

D. Haman's Plot Against Mordecai (5:9–14)

9–10 Haman left the banquet happy and in "high spirits" because of the honor that had been accorded him by the invitations to the queen's private banquets. When he encountered Mordecai at the king's gate, however, Haman was filled with rage against the Jew because Mordecai did not stand up or show fear in his presence (cf 3:2). But Haman controlled himself and went to his home and called his wife, Zeresh, and his friends together to tell them about the great honor accorded him by the king and the queen. Mordecai had apparently heard that Esther had been favorably received by the king and was encouraged by this turn of events; thus he had removed his sackcloth.

11–12 In an expansive mood Haman boasted about his wealth, his many sons, and the honor shown him by the king. He also exulted about the invitation to Esther's private banquet to which only he and the king had been invited. Haman's boasting only accentuated his later humiliation and fall from favor (cf. Pr 16:18). An early OT interpretation (in a Targum) records that Haman had 208 sons in addition to the ten who held government offices (cf. 9:10).

13 In spite of the things that should have brought him happiness, Haman had no satisfaction as long as he saw Mordecai sitting at the king's gate. Haman's wealth and honors could not satisfy him when he thought of one Jew who failed to show him the proper respect he felt he deserved!

14 Haman's wife and friends suggested a plan that would remove the source of his irritation. She told Haman to have a gallows erected seventy-five feet in height and then to ask the king to have Mordecai hanged on it. With that business out of the way, Haman could go with the king to Esther's banquet and be happy. His wife's suggestion delighted Haman, and he had the gallows built, confident that the king would approve his request. The height of the gallows was exorbitant, but it is consistent with what we know of Haman's vanity and obsessive desire for revenge.

E. Haman's Humiliation (6:1–13)

1. Discovery of an unrewarded deed (6:1–5)

1 The same night of Esther's first banquet, the king was unable to sleep; so he ordered the royal annals (see comment on 2:23) to be brought in and read to him. No doubt God was behind the king's sleeplessness. This entire chapter shows how circumstances fit together to overrule the evil intentions of Haman.

2–3 In the course of reading the annals, the record of Mordecai's exposure of the plot of Bigthana and Teresh against the king was found. On inquiring what "honor and recognition" had been bestowed on Mordecai, the king was told that nothing had been done to honor him. The oversight must have disturbed Xerxes, as it was a reflection on him for not rewarding one of his benefactors.

4–5 Though the hour was late, the king inquired if anyone was in the court. He intended to set the matter right without further delay. As if by chance, Haman had just entered the outer court to speak to the king about having Mordecai hanged on the gallows he had erected. The attendants advised the king of Haman's presence; so the king ordered that he be brought to his bedchamber at once. It seems strange that Haman came in the middle of the night to make his petition, but perhaps he knew the sleeping habits of the monarch.

2. Mordecai honored (6:6–11)

6 The text suggests that abruptly and without an exchange of greetings the king asked Haman what should be done for a person whom the king delighted to honor. Haman assumed the king meant to honor him. It is one of the great ironies of the story that Haman was to decide how the man he desired to hang would be honored.

7–9 The vain Haman, not needing additional wealth, suggested that the one to be honored be given a royal robe that had been worn by the king, along with a horse the king had ridden, and that a royal crest be placed on its head. Horses wearing crowns or head ornaments are depicted on both Assyrian and Persian reliefs. Haman further suggested that one of the king's most noble princes lead the "honoree," garbed in the king's robe, on the horse through the city streets. As he led horse and rider through the streets, the prince was to proclaim, "This is what is done for the man the king delights to honor!" Haman must have been ecstatic in anticipation of the high honor he thought was about to be accorded him before all the people of Susa.

10 The suggestion delighted the king. He ordered Haman to carry out the plan at once. Then for the first time the king named the man who was to be honored—Mordecai, Haman's adversary! The king warned Haman not to "neglect" any of the honors he had proposed. It seems strange that the king would knowingly honor a Jew so soon after enacting an edict to destroy all the Jews in his kingdom.

11 Haman had no choice but to carry out the king's orders. No writer, however gifted, could adequately describe the chagrin and mortification Haman must have experienced as he robed Mordecai and led him through the streets. One wonders what brought the greatest enjoyment to Mordecai—his being remembered by the king, the people's adulation, or Haman's humiliation!

3. Haman's wife affirms his downfall (6:12–13)

12 Afterward Mordecai returned to the king's gate, where he had been sitting before Haman had been forced to lead his foe through the streets of Susa mounted on the king's horse. The honor had not changed Mordecai's position before the king as a Jew awaiting the execution of Haman's edict. Haman, however, rushed home with his head covered, an expression of his grief and wretchedness. Covering the head was a way of expressing mourning (cf. 2Sa 15:30; Jer 14:3–4). Haman must have hoped to find solace from his wife and friends.

13 Haman told his wife and friends all the details of his humiliating experience. If he expected comfort from them, he did not receive it. Instead they, seeing the handwriting on the wall, warned Haman that the Jew had been responsible for the beginning of his downfall. They were convinced that he could not stand against Mordecai; Haman's ruin was already assured. They seem to have conveniently forgotten that his humiliation was largely the result of their suggestion (cf. 5:14).

F. Esther's Second Banquet (6:14–7:10)

1. Haman summoned to the banquet (6:14)

14 The conversation between Haman and his friends was interrupted by the appearance of eunuchs sent by the king to escort Haman to Esther's banquet. The fact that they "hurried" to bring him suggests that as the result of his humiliating experience with Mordecai (cf. 6:11), Haman had either forgotten about the queen's banquet or he did not want to attend it.

2. Haman exposed and executed (7:1–10)

1–2 The king and Haman went "to dine" with Esther at her invitation. At her second banquet, the king once again sought to discover the nature of Esther's petition (v.2). Again he assured her that it would be granted, "even up to half the kingdom" (cf. 5:3, 6). He made his inquiry while they were drinking wine, which was customarily served after the meal.

3 The queen no longer withheld her request from the king. She began courteously by asking whether she had "found favor" with the king. She dared not presume on the goodwill of Xerxes. She unmasked Haman, but by doing so she revealed her own identity without knowing what the king's reaction would be. The king must have looked at her in stunned silence when she asked for her life and also for the lives of her people. It probably took him some time to grasp the fact that she also was a Jew.

4 Without waiting for the king to speak, Esther hastened to explain that she and her people had been sold for destruction, slaughter, and annihilation. She added that if it had been a matter of selling them as slaves rather than killing them, she would not have troubled the king with such a petty problem. But their destruction would be an economic loss to the king.

5 The king's reaction was immediate and wrathful. He demanded to know who had dared to do such a thing. He must have felt that the plot to kill the Jews that also encompassed his wife was a personal affront. Either he ignored his complicity in the affair, or he felt that he had been duped into agreeing to the Jews' destruction. A careful reading of ch. 3 shows that Haman did not mention the Jews by name; so perhaps the king was unaware of the full contents of the decree he had signed.

6 Without hesitation Esther identified Haman as the enemy. Haman was struck with terror by the accusation, for he knew that his fate was automatically sealed by Esther's words.

7 The enraged king arose abruptly and went into the palace garden. The situation created a dilemma for the king because he could hardly condemn Haman for carrying out orders that bore his royal seal. Xerxes probably needed some time to collect his thoughts before acting. Haman, knowing that the king had already decided his fate, remained to beg Esther for his life.

8 Haman's timing could not have been worse. Just as he fell on the couch where Esther was reclining to plead for his life, the king walked in. Angrily he accused Haman of attempting to molest the queen even while she was with her husband. As soon as the words left the king's mouth, servants or court officials covered Haman's face. The king's angry words were a sentence of death. Although there is no evidence that it was a Persian custom to cover the face of a condemned criminal before he was led away to execution, that was probably its meaning here. Esther looked on in silence as her enemy was led away.

9 One of the king's eunuchs, Harbona, remembered the gallows that Haman had just erected for the execution of Mordecai and so informed the king. If the king had been considering mercy for Haman, the reminder that Haman had knowingly plotted the death of a man who had saved the king's life was sufficient to seal his fate. The king's immediate response was "Hang him on it!"

10 No mention is made of the time that elapsed between the pronouncement of the sentence and its execution, but Haman was probably carried away and hanged immediately. The king's wrath "subsided." As an act of poetic justice, Haman lost his life on the very gallows that he had anticipated would bring him such joy at Mordecai's execution.

G. Mordecai's Elevation (8:1–17)

1. Exaltation over the house of Haman (8:1–2)

1–2 On the same day that Haman was executed, King Xerxes gave Haman's entire "estate" to Esther, probably as compensation for all she had suffered. Persian law gave the state the power to confiscate the property of those who had been condemned as criminals. The queen revealed her relationship to Mordecai, whereupon the king invited him into his presence. Xerxes removed from his finger the signet ring that he had "reclaimed" from Haman and gave it to Mordecai, thereby making him prime minister with power to act in the king's name (cf. 3:10). Mordecai became one of the select group of courtiers who had the right of access into the king's presence. Esther placed her kinsman in charge of Haman's estate. Haman's wealth, title, and power now belonged to his enemy Mordecai.

2. Reversal of Haman's decree (8:3–14)

3 With a great show of emotion, Esther fell at the feet of the king and begged him to "put an end" to the evil plan Haman had devised against the Jews. Haman's overthrow and Mordecai's elevation could not give Esther comfort so long as Haman's decree against the Jews remained unrevoked.

4 The king extended his scepter after her emotional plea. His gesture was intended to encourage her to rise from her prostrate position before continuing to speak.

5–6 With proper deference to the king and an expressed hope that she enjoyed the king's favor, Esther petitioned him to issue an order "overruling" Haman's dispatches. She reminded him that Haman's orders had been sent with the explicit purpose of destroying the Jews in all the king's provinces. Esther expressed her grief in face of the impending disaster about to fall on her kin, thus revealing her true character—that she was not merely self-serving. Esther was careful to place the blame on Haman for the wicked plot and not on the king.

7–8 The king responded by first reminding Esther and Mordecai that he had executed Haman and given his estate to her. The king then told them to write another decree in his name in behalf of the Jews. He gave them permission to word the decree as seemed best to them. He reminded them that he could not write the new decree himself, as no prior document written in his name and sealed with his ring could be "revoked," even by the king himself. It could only be neutralized by another decree.

9 The royal secretaries were summoned "at once." It was the twenty-third day of the third month, two months and ten days after Haman had issued his order. They wrote out Mordecai's orders to the Jews and to the other government officials of the 127 provinces. The orders were written in every language spoken in the provinces. Therefore no one in the Persian Empire would be able to plead ignorance of Mordecai's orders.

10 Because of the authority granted him by Xerxes, Mordecai wrote the orders in the king's name and then sealed the dispatches with the king's signet ring. They were then sent throughout the empire by "mounted couriers." Fast horses were used to carry Mordecai's message throughout the empire without undue delay.

11–12 Mordecai's edict granted the Jews the right to "protect themselves" against anyone who might attack them, to slaughter women and children, and to plunder the property of their enemies. The day set apart for the Jews to take revenge on their enemies was the thirteenth day of the twelfth month (cf. 3:13). The decree was almost a paraphrase of Haman's edict. It is difficult to understand why the Persian ruler would allow a Jewish minority to massacre his subjects at will. Yet we have already observed Xerxes' indifference to the value of human life (cf. 3:11), and it was the only way to neutralize the preceding edict.

13 Mordecai's edict was to be issued as law in every province of the empire and made known to all the subjects, regardless of their nationality. Everyone would realize that the Jews would be ready on the designated day to take vengeance on their enemies.

14 Riding the royal horses, the couriers hastened to deliver the edict to all parts of the kingdom, knowing it was a royal decree. The decree was also circulated in the citadel of Susa.

These stone horses and rider are relics of the Persian period. Courtesy Jewish Institute of Religion.

3. Popular reaction (8:15–17)

15 Mordecai left the king's presence wearing royal garments of blue and white that befitted his new position. He also wore a large crown of gold and a purple robe of fine linen. The verse closes with the statement that the city of Susa had a "joyous celebration." As it is difficult to understand why the Persian residents of Susa would rejoice at a decree that could be used against them, the statement probably refers to the joy of the Jewish residents of Susa.

16–17 When the edict became known throughout the provinces, there was great joy among the Jewish people, accompanied by feasting and other celebrations. "People of other nationalities" became Jews out of fear of what the Jews might do to them. The statement that they "became Jews" may mean that they pretended to be Jews or took the side of the Jews. The tables had turned so completely that it was now dangerous not to be a Jew.

III. The Jews' Day of Vengeance (9:1–19)

A. A Great Slaughter (9:1–10)

1 The thirteenth day of the month Adar arrived for the carrying out of both edicts. The nine months that elapsed since the second decree was signed are passed over in silence. The Jews now had "the upper hand" over those who hated them. This chapter assumes a universal hatred of the Jews (cf. vv.2, 5, 16) that was not expressed previously.

2 The Jews gathered in their cities throughout the provinces to "attack" anyone who tried to destroy them. Fear seized the people of other nationalities; no one was able to stand against the Jews.

3–4 The nobles and other political leaders "helped" the Jews because of their fear of Mordecai and the influence he had with the king. Mordecai was not only prominent in the palace, but "his reputation spread" throughout the empire. He had become increasingly powerful during his brief months as prime minister.

5 The Jews showed no mercy to their enemies. They massacred those who hated them; there were no restraints imposed on them by the king. The Jews did not limit themselves to self-defense. They hunted out and destroyed those who might harm them. Their fury can only be understood by those who have experienced a long history of persecution.

6–10 In the citadel of Susa, the Jews killed five hundred men and also killed the ten sons of Haman, who shared in their father's guilt. The Jews did not, however, take any plunder in Susa, though the edict granted them this right (cf. 8:11); their restraint shows their motive was not personal enrichment.

B. Vengeance in Susa (9:11–15)

11–12 The king was informed of the slaughter taking place in the citadel of Susa. He reported the figures to Esther and asked whether she knew what the Jews were doing elsewhere in the provinces. He also encouraged her to make any other request of him that she desired, and it would be granted. Xerxes' only desire was to please his queen; he showed no concern for his subjects who were being killed.

13 Esther asked for a second day for the Jews in Susa to continue killing their enemies. She also asked that Haman's ten murdered sons be hanged on gallows as an additional act of degradation on Haman's house. She may have hoped the deed would serve as a deterrent against further Jewish persecution.

14–15 The king granted Esther's request for a second day and issued an order to hang Haman's ten sons. On the next day, the fourteenth of Adar, the Jews killed an additional three hundred of their enemies in Susa but did not take any plunder.

C. Celebration in the Provinces and in Susa (9:16–19)

16–17 Elsewhere in the Persian provinces, the Jews killed seventy-five thousand of their enemies on the thirteenth of Adar but took no plunder. On the fourteenth day they rested and celebrated their victory with feasting and rejoicing.

18–19 The author added these verses to explain why in his time Jews living in the city kept the Feast of Purim on the fifteenth of Adar whereas Jews living in the country observed it on the fourteenth. The Jews in Susa were permitted two days for killing their enemies and therefore celebrated their victory on the fifteenth. Jews elsewhere had only one day for slaughtering their enemies and therefore celebrated their victory on the fourteenth. In addition to feasting, they gave presents to one another.

IV. Institution of the Feast of Purim (9:20–10:3)

A. Mordecai's Letter (9:20–28)

20–21 When Mordecai learned that the Jews were celebrating their victory on two different days, he recorded what had happened and then sent letters to all the Jews in all the provinces of the kingdom. In the letter he authorized them to celebrate their victory over their enemies thereafter on both the fourteenth and fifteenth days of Adar.

22–23 The two-day celebration would be observed as a memorial to the time when the Jews "got relief" from their enemies. Their sorrow and mourning had been transformed into joy and celebration by the turn of events. Mordecai instructed them to observe the days by feasting and by giving food to one another and gifts to the poor. The Jews agreed to observe their celebration every year in the same way as they did that first time and in accordance with the instructions given them by Mordecai.

24–25 The narrator now begins a summary of the events that led to the establishment of the Jewish festival of Purim. Haman, the Jews' enemy, had cast the *pur* to determine on which day he would destroy the Jews (see comment on 3:7). When the plot was brought to the king's attention, "he issued written orders" that Haman's evil scheme should come back on his own head. He also ordered the death of Haman and his sons on the gallows (though not at the same time; cf. 7:10; 9:14).

26–27 In the first explicit reference to the Jewish festival of Purim, the author explains that the name finds its origin in the word *pur* (cf. 3:7; 9:24). As a result of the instructions given them in Mordecai's letter, the Jews took it on themselves to observe the fourteenth and fifteenth days of Adar every year in the way prescribed and at the time appointed. The festival would be observed by their descendants and "all who join them" (i.e., proselytes to the Jewish faith). Thus Purim became the first Jewish festival for which there is no basis in the Torah, but it is considered just as binding as the other festivals.

28 The author makes a final exhortation for the Jews to remember the days of Purim in every generation by every family wherever they may live. The days of Purim should never cease to be celebrated by the Jews nor forgotten by their "descendants."

B. Esther's Confirmation (9:29–32)

29–30 Esther, together with Mordecai, wrote with the full authority of her position to confirm "this second letter concerning Purim." This letter to all the Jews in the 127 Persian provinces is most likely the letter described in vv.29–31, which was intended to add authority to Mordecai's first letter (vv.20–22).

31–32 The purpose of the letter was to establish the days of Purim at the times decreed by Mordecai and Esther (i.e., the fourteenth and fifteenth days of Adar). Esther's decree confirmed the regulations about Purim. It was written down "in the records" to be available to future generations for verification.

C. The Greatness of Mordecai (10:1–3)

1 Even as it had begun, the book closes with a statement that reveals the imperial power and wealth of Xerxes. He was able to impose "tribute" (i.e., forced taxation or involuntary labor ; cf. Ex 1:11; 1Ki 5:13; ;9:21) to the most distant shores of his empire. It is unclear as to what the relevance of this verse is to the rest of the book. Perhaps Mordecai was a factor in augmenting the king's power over the other nations under his control (cf. Joseph in Ge 41).

2 The reader is told that the mighty acts of Xerxes as well as a full account of the greatness of Mordecai were recorded in the book of the official annals of the kings of Media and Persia (cf. 6:1; 1Ki 11:41; 2Ch 25:26). Media is mentioned first here, whereas it follows the mention of Persia in 1:3, 14, 19.

3 The book closes with a paean of praise to Mordecai, who rose to be second in rank to King Xerxes and "preeminent" among the Jews. He was held in "high esteem" by his fellow Jews because he worked for their good "and spoke up for the welfare of all the Jews" (cf. Ps 85:8; Zec 9:10).

Job

INTRODUCTION

1. Background

The uniqueness of the book of Job derives from its depth and thoroughness in dealing with the relationship of human suffering to divine justice, commonly called theodicy (from Gk. *theos* ["god"] and *dike* ["justice"]). Numerous documents, especially from ancient Mesopotamia and Egypt, demonstrate that this type of wisdom writing was well established in the OT world; but none touches on these matters so eloquently and fully as this OT book.

The book of Job cannot be forced into any single literary classification. It is generally called Wisdom literature, but that describes more the subject matter than the form. The book is largely poetry of various genres (lament, wisdom, proverbs, hymns, etc.), and in places it is more difficult to understand than any other part of the OT. Job abounds in words occurring only once. The grammar, syntax, and orthography (spelling) often stand outside the regular forms of classical Hebrew.

2. Authorship

It is quite possible that in the composition of the book of Job the author used source materials, and that the book went through some kind of literary development. But any attempt to know exactly what that was is sheer guesswork. We do not know who wrote the book, but his work has witnessed to the spirits of the faithful throughout the ages that he was divinely inspired.

Presumably the poet based the material on wisdom poetry passed down through the generations. The wisdom poetry of the speeches in Job includes poetic genres such as laments, hymns, proverbs, and oracles. As in all Semitic poetry, parallelism is foremost. This comes from an artistic urge toward symmetry through balanced lines and other units of composition. The poet, however, was a free spirit; so he created unique and intricate patterns of relationship between thought and form parallelism.

3. Date and Source

As is true with much Wisdom literature, the actual composition of the book of Job as we have it is hard to date with precision. It is possible that the book, or perhaps parts of the book, existed outside Israel for a long time as oral tradition or perhaps even in written form until an unknown Israelite author under divine inspiration gave it its present literary form. This would account for the non-Israelite flavor of the book as well as for its unquestioned place in the Hebrew canon.

It seems likely that Job himself lived in the second millennium B.C. (2000 to 1000 B.C.) and shared a tradition not far removed from that of the Hebrew patriarchs. Job's longevity of 140 years, his position as a man whose wealth was measured in cattle and who acted as priest for his family, and the picture of roving Sabean and Chaldean tribesmen fit the second millennium better than the first. The book, however, may not have reached its final form until the first millennium. Anywhere in the OT biblical period is a possible date, though attempts to place its time of writing as late as the second or first century B.C. have been dealt a decisive blow by the discovery of parts of a Targum of Job among the Dead Sea scrolls.

The exact place of origin is as difficult to determine as the exact date. The book shows considerable Aramaic flavor, suggesting that Job and his friends lived near centers of Aramaic influence. At the end of the second millennium, some Aramean tribes moved south and settled on the borders of Babylonia and Palestine, but they continued to control the caravan route through the Khabur River area. This was when Aleppo and Damascus became Aramean centers and when the Chaldean tribes invaded Babylonia.

Job himself lived in the land of Uz (1:1). Genesis 10:23 ties Uz with the Arameans, as does Ge 22:20–22. The latter passage also ties in Kesed (the Chaldeans) with the Arameans and the Uzites but does not make them identical. These passages refer to nations or tribes that were related, sometimes mainly by their proximity. The land of Uz was east of Palestine, but its precise location cannot be determined. Job had great influence in an unnamed town (29:7). According to La 4:21, Edom was in the land of Uz. It seems then that Uz was the name of a region east of Palestine, including the Edomites and adjacent tribes.

4. Purpose

The purpose of the book of Job cannot be reduced to a single simple statement. The author appears to have had a multifaceted purpose under the general theme of wisdom teaching about God and human suffering. The various parts of the book speak with somewhat different purposes in mind. The Prologue teaches the wisdom of one's total submission to the will of the Creator. The readers view the drama from the divine perspective where they learn of God's secret purpose to expose the falsehood of the Accuser and to prove Job's faith. The Dialogue, on the other hand, gives the human perspective. Job knows nothing of what transpired in the heavenly council. The author's purpose is to teach the believing community some profound lessons positively and negatively about honesty and reality in our relationship with God and about a person's limited knowledge of the divine purposes.

The author of Job intends to show how the theological position of Job's friends represents a shallow and only partial observation of life; i.e., human suffering is always in proportion to one's sins. Overall there is no studied attempt to justify God with regard to the suffering of the innocent. But the author finally demonstrates that God does not abandon the sufferer but communicates with him at the proper time.

Another subsidiary purpose of the book is to show that though human beings are often sinful, weak, and ignorant, they can, like Job, be relatively pure and upright even when in the midst of physical distress, emotional turmoil, and spiritual testing. The divine speeches demonstrate to Job that God is Creator and Sustainer of all things and yet is willing to communicate with Job as his friend and not his enemy, as Job had imagined him

to be. While this does not answer all Job's questions, it is really all Job needs to know.

Satan was permitted to afflict Job and then test him through the instrumentality of would-be helpers who used all the words of traditional piety. Job's major problem was this vexing question of theodicy (see above). How can God be both good and sovereign in the light of the suffering of the innocent and the prospering of the wicked? The book pursues a middle course between the concepts of an evil deity on the one hand and a limited deity on the other. But there is no attempt to give a rational or philosophical solution. The picture is the same as that given in Genesis where the Serpent (Satan), as a creature of God subject to his will, is also in rebellion. Here the Accuser bears the responsibility for Job's trouble, though he is permitted to do so by God. The problem of theodicy is left on the note that God in his omnipotence and omniscience can and does use secondary means to bring about his higher and perfect purposes. One such purpose in Job's suffering is to humiliate the Accuser, proving Job's devotion to God is pure.

Initially Job stands the test even when his wife says, "Curse God and die!" (2:9). But as his troubles multiply, Job has second thoughts; he wrestles with God, challenges God, and sinks into depths of despair, with moments of trust and confidence, only to fall again into despair. Throughout the book Job defends his own essential innocence (not sinlessness) against the view of his friends, who rarely move from the single theme that suffering is the immediate corollary of sin, and that because Job has grievously sinned, God has become his enemy. But Job's own view of why he is suffering is in a state of flux. So he says many unfortunate things; yet in it all he does not do what Satan said he would—he does not curse God to his face (2:5).

While the counselors make no progress in their arguments, Job gradually grows somewhat less belligerent. He appears to us to be self-righteous in his peroration (chs. 29–31), but this must be understood in its cultural context. He persistently calls for an audience with God to argue his case. He also calls for a friend in heaven to plead his cause at the divine tribunal. He is confident he will be vindicated (13:18; 19:26). The counselors consistently stand on God's side, sometimes uttering beautiful hymns; but they could not seem to move from their fallacious notion that the righteous always prosper and sinners always suffer and, conversely, that suffering proves sinfulness and prosperity proves righteousness.

Eliphaz is not quite so crass; but he still insists that though the righteous suffer a little and the unrighteous prosper a little, the righteous never come to an untimely end (4:7; 5:16–19), and the wicked—even when they prosper—are in dread of calamity (15:20–26). Bildad is convinced that Job's children died for their sins and warns Job that he will receive the same fate unless he gets right with God (8:4–6). Zophar is bent on denouncing Job as a mocker of God. Job's suffering is ample proof of his sinfulness, and repentance is his only hope (11:13–15).

Much of what Job's counselors said is theologically sound and true in the abstract, but it did not necessarily apply to Job. It is not so much what they say but what they leave out that makes their counsel so shallow. They all finally reach the conclusion that Job is obstinate and that his refusal to humble himself and repent proves he has committed sins of great enormity (but cf. Jn 9:3).

The book does not attempt to formulate a rational solution to the problem of evil, especially that aspect that tries to relate God's goodness and sovereignty to the suffering of the innocent. Although Job is exercised about God's justice, his ultimate concern is more practical than theoretical. His practical concern is not healing and restoration but his own vindication as an upright man. Job does not ask for rational answers; nor does God give such to him when he appears, though Job is finally vindicated (42:7–9). There were no heinous sins for which he was being punished. When God does rebuke Job, it is for his ignorance (38:2) and presumption while arguing his case (42:2), not for a profligate life. God is apparently telling Job in chs. 38–41 that human beings do not know enough about God's ways to make judgments concerning his justice.

In his appearance to Job, God ignores the problem of theodicy. He gives no rational explanation or excuse for Job's suffering, but Job is not crushed; he is only rebuked and then shown to be basically right while the friends are condemned for their presumptive and arrogant claim to a knowledge of God's ways (42:7). Job thus realizes that God does not need human advice to control the world and that no extreme of suffering gives one the right to question God's wisdom or justice, and of this he repents (42:2–6). On seeing the power and glory of God, Job's rebellious attitude dissolves and his resentment disappears. Job now gets what he sought for. His friends do not see him pronounced guilty; so their view of his suffering is refuted.

Job is not told why God tested him. He comes to accept God on God's own terms; and while we know the full story, Job had to walk by faith even after he was vindicated. That God never impugns Job's character proves that Satan has failed and that Job's testing has come to an end. Though he has not demanded restoration, God, having achieved his higher purpose through Job, now restores him. Job in his suffering, despite moments of weakness, surpassed in righteousness his detractors who had not suffered as he had. After all his doubts and bitterness, Job arrived at that point of spiritual maturity where he could pray for those who abused him (42:10).

The issues raised in the book are among the most profound and difficult of human existence. The answer was already on Job's lips in the Prologue when he said, "The LORD gave and the LORD has taken away; may the name of the LORD be praised" (1:21b); and "Shall we accept good from God, and not trouble?" (2:10). The truth Job learned was that God must be God and that of all values and all existence only God and his glory must ultimately prevail.

5. Major Characters

a. Job

Apart from the Bible nothing is known of Job. He was not an Israelite and showed no knowledge of the covenant between the Lord and his chosen people. Indeed, there is not in the book the slightest hint of any acquaintance with the history of the Hebrew people. There is, however, no good reason to question Job's historicity as a well-to-do patriarch who lived east of the Jordan at a time before the emergence of the Hebrews as a nation.

Job assumes two roles. The author presents him as a truly righteous man whose commitment to God is total, yet who can still struggle with God to the point of rage over the mystery of God's ways. Job does not know what the reader knows—that God honors him by testing, thus expressing his total confidence in Job. But Job must remain ignorant of this for it to be genuine. For the intended message of the book, the raging Job is just as important as the patient Job. In his suffering Job served God supremely, not as a stoic, but as a feeling man who had to come to terms with the mystery of the divine.

b. Eliphaz

Based on a variety of passages, we have good reason to believe Eliphaz was an Edomite. According to Ge 36:4, a man named Eliphaz was the firstborn of Esau, the progenitor of the Edomites, and Teman was his son (v.11). A number of prophets mention Teman as an Edomite city or district (Jer 49:7, 20; Eze 25:13; Am 1:12; Ob 8–9). Jeremiah assumes Teman was known for its wisdom. Apparently Eliphaz was the senior member since he spoke first. Throughout his speeches, at least until his final speech in ch. 22, he shows a broader spirit than the others, accepting Job as a pious man gone astray. Though failing in compassion, he alone of the three showed some consideration and respect.

c. Bildad

This non-Hebrew name is not mentioned in any other OT book. Bildad considers Job's struggle over the justice of God as blasphemy, and he uses his erudition and knowledge of ancient wisdom tradition to prove to Job that his family got what they deserved and warns him about a similar doom. Genesis 25:2, 6 provides some helpful information about his tribe, the Shuites. They were descendants of Abraham through Keturah and inhabitants of "the land of the east." Apart from a possible phonetic problem, Ge 25:3 suggests this tribe lived near Dedan, which Jeremiah locates near Tema and Buz (Jer 25:23), far from the Euphrates. Bildad's name is probably a combination of Bil (baal, "Lord") and Adad, a well-known storm god (cf. Ben-hadad, the Aramean royal name, and the names of the Edomite kings Hadad the son of Bedad (Ge 36:35) and Baal-Hanan.

d. Zophar

Zophar is from Naamah, but not the little Israelite town in the western foothills (Jos 15:41). Scholars cannot agree on either the derivation of Zophar's name or the location of the place. But it must have been somewhere in north Arabia or Edom. Zophar was the most caustic of the counselors. His message to Job was repent or die the horrible death the wicked deserve.

e. Elihu

Elihu appears only in chs. 32–37. He has the distinction of having his father's name recorded. "Barakel the Buzite" (32:2) seems to identify Elihu as one whose father was a leading figure in a clan more closely related to Job (Uz and Buz were brothers; cf. Ge 22:21). Elihu's name means "He is my God"; it is the only name of the five characters that was used by Israelites (cf. 1Sa 1:1; 1Ch 12:20; 26:7; 27:18). The Aramaisms in Elihu's speeches fit the statement that Buz was the son of Abraham's brother Nahor, whose son Laban spoke Aramaic (Ge 31:47). Elihu gives his youth as the reason he dared not speak while the older men held forth.

EXPOSITION

I. The Prologue (1:1–2:13)

The Prologue introduces us to Job as a man of faith and shows how his fortunes on earth were directed by heavenly forces beyond his control. But its full purpose lies even deeper. It is a deliberately planned foundation on which the spiritual message of the book is based. Without this prologue the Job of the dialogues and monologues might justly be considered a man with an insufferable self-righteousness, and the reader would be left without a heavenly perspective, much as in the other theodicies of the ancient Near East. With this Prologue the purpose of the book is clarified—to show that in a world where evil is a reality, good people may appear to suffer unjustly, but that such injustice is precipitated by the Accuser and, though permitted by God, it is an expression of God's total confidence that the faith of his servant will triumph.

A. Job's Felicity (1:1–5)

1–5 Job is presented as a man who worshiped ("feared"; GK 3710) God and "shunned" (GK 6073) evil and whose life was crowned with great prosperity. Fearing the Lord and shunning evil are the controlling principles of wisdom (28:28). Although the author does not use the term wisdom (*hokmah*; GK 2683) here, this repeated description of Job (1:1, 8; 2:3) labels him a truly wise man. That Job was "blameless" (GK 9447) and "upright" (GK 3838) should not be construed to imply he was sinless (cf. 13:26; 14:16–17). The former, from the root "be complete," usually refers to a person's spiritual maturity and the integrity of one's inner being. The latter, meaning "straight," "right," is used in many contexts dealing with human behavior that is in line with God's ways. Together they provided an idiomatic way to describe Job's high moral character.

Job was the owner of large flocks and herds of sheep, camels, oxen, and donkeys, cared for by a large number of servants (1:2–3).

Job lived in Uz, a land somewhere east of Canaan on the edge of the desert (vv.1, 19). He lived in an area where farming could be carried on (v.14) but also near a town (29:7). Job's wealth is described in terms similar to those used of the patriarchs, the stress being on animals and servants. Job was greater (richer) than any of the people of the East. This shows he was a well-known sage among the easterners. According to v.5, Job, like the patriarchs, functioned as a priest for his family. He took his sacrificial obligation seriously, viewing it as expiation for sin. To Job this included even sins of the heart, for he made special offerings just in case his sons had secretly cursed God. The matter of cursing God is to be a key theme in the development of this drama.

B. Job Tested (1:6–2:13)

1. Satan's accusations of Job (1:6–12)

6–12 There are two scenes in heaven, each depicting the divine council (cf. 2:1–6). Each is followed by a series of events that result from the encounter between the Lord and Satan. The divine council is made up of "the sons of God" (NIV, "angels"), supernatural beings who are above human beings but created by God (Ps 8:5). The Hebrews otherwise called them the Lord's messengers (Ge 19:1; 24:7; 48:16; Ps 104:4; Mal 3:1; et al.). The Accuser (lit., "the Satan"; GK 8477) is such a being, whose business is to roam the earth as the Accuser of those committed to serving God (1Pe 5:8; Rev 12:10). Here we find him questioning Job's motive for religious devotion: "Does Job fear God for nothing?" It is not the Accuser but the Lord who initiates the

testing of Job; for the Lord's statement that Job is his servant implies more than mere servitude; it means God and Job are in a covenant relationship based on solemn oaths.

As in Ge 3, God sets the stage and allows a person to be put to the test. Here the Lord uses secondary means to accomplish his purpose. That purpose is not just to test Job as an end in itself but to give him the opportunity to honor his Lord, to whom he has pledged his allegiance with a solemn oath. That allegiance becomes a significant part of the cosmic struggle between Job's adversary and the Lord. Will Job curse God or not?

Understanding this struggle is basic to understanding the book of Job as well as the whole historical-religious drama of the Bible (Ge 3:15; Ro 16:20). The Accuser insinuates that Job's allegiance is hypocritical. If only God would remove the protective hedge he has placed about Job, this "devout" servant would certainly curse God to his face. The attack is on God through Job, and the only way the Accuser can be proven false is through Job. So Satan is given limited but gradually increased access to Job—first to his possessions, then to his family, and finally to his physical well-being. But through it all, the primary purpose of Job's suffering, unknown to him, was that he should stand before other people and before angels as a trophy of the saving might of God.

2. Job's integrity in loss of family and property (1:13–22)

13–19 According to v.5 Job's custom was to make offerings for his family. The very day he made these offerings, this devastation took place. The coming of the messengers of misfortune, each on the heels of the other, all on that one fateful day, has its dramatic effect heightened by the narrator's style. We are informed, however, that it is really the work of the Accuser, this master of evil, who can and does use both the elements of nature and humankind to accomplish his purpose. Satan is a great juggler and has manifested himself as such in Paradise (Eden) and in the temptation of Jesus Christ.

20–22 Tearing one's outer garment and cropping one's hair were common gestures of violent grief in the biblical world. Such response to grief included weeping and wailing (Ps 42:3; Jn 11:33–35).

The wisdom quatrain (v.21) introduces us to the poetic parallelism found in all the speeches beginning in ch. 3. Here the attitude of Job, in contrast to that in the Dialogue, is one of supreme faith and total resignation to the sovereign will of God. Job did not understand why but believed that his trouble came from God. Job was ignorant of what had taken place in the divine council—that God allowed the Accuser to strike thus far. But Job was right, it was the Lord who had taken away. The use of secondary means does not solve the problem of evil, nor is it the purpose of the book of Job to solve this logical dilemma.

When Job said, "May the name of the LORD be praised [GK 1385]," he was using the same word that Satan used in v.11 as a euphemism with the opposite meaning ("curse"; GK 1385). The play on words stresses how the Accuser is foiled at this point. Instead of cursing God to his face, Job praised him.

Here the author, being a Hebrew, uses that special covenant name ("LORD"; GK 3378) for God. Job and his friends were not Hebrews; so they use other Hebrew epithets for God. Here in the Prologue the composer of the book carefully identifies the Job of faith and wisdom as the same Job with questions and defiance in the Dialogue and Monologue. But more important is his identification of the God of the Dialogue with the true God whom the Hebrews worshiped.

Up to this point, though deprived of family and possessions, Job did not sin with his lips (cf. 2:10) by accusing God of "wrongdoing" (GK 9524).

3. Satan's further accusations (2:1–6)

1–3 At a special time set aside for it, the Accuser again appeared with "the sons of God" and as a subordinate presented himself before the Lord. The Accuser continued to roam the earth, obviously looking for those he would take "captive to do his will" (2Ti 2:26). He lost the first round of this contest. For the third time the Lord triumphantly described Job as a unique servant (no one like him), a pure and devout man who has become even stronger as a result of the testing. "He still maintains his integrity."

As if to add a bit of irony, the Lord said to the Accuser, "You incited me against him to ruin him without any reason." The words should not be used to imply that God can somehow be stirred up to do things that are against his will. On the contrary, God suggested Job to the Accuser (1:8; 2:3) in the first place. All Job's suffering was part of the divine purpose, as God says in 38:2: "Who is this that darkens my counsel with words without knowledge?" But when God uses a secondary cause to affect the life of a human, even Satan can be said to stir him up.

The phrase "without any reason" (GK 2855, a word elsewhere translated "without cause") needs some clarification. Satan had a cause or reason for doing what he did—to discredit God; and certainly God was accomplishing his own cause or purpose. In 1:9 Satan used the same word to accuse Job of having an ulterior purpose for serving God. Now God taunts the Accuser with the counteraccusation that Satan himself is the one who wants to see injustice done. The translation of this key word as "without any reason" is good at this point. It means there was no immediate sinfulness in Job that called for punishment.

4–6 Satan did not consider his energy to have been wasted. His next move was to obtain permission to attack Job's body. With the adage "Skin for skin! A man will give all he has for his own life," Satan suggested that even Job's triumphant faith expressed in his doxology (1:21) was only a ploy by which he was purchasing his personal well-being. He was even willing to sacrifice the skin of his loved ones to save his own. If God would send his hand against Job's body (i.e., permit Satan to do so), Job's verbal piety would prove to be a sham; and he would curse God to his face. The contest was about to take on a new intensity. God placed Job in the hands of their mutual adversary but limited his power—"you must spare his life." The suffering of the innocent is a mystery that defies all human logic.

4. Job's integrity in personal suffering (2:7–10)

7–8 It is not important for us to know about Job's disease. The symptoms were many. The "painful sores" all over his body, from the soles of his feet to the tip of his head, were perhaps only the initial stage of the malady. Job speaks of other complications in 30:17, 27, 30. The Semitic root for "sores" (GK 8825) denotes fever and inflammation, but in the OT it describes diseases that have symptoms appearing on the skin (Ex 9:9; Lev 13; Dt 28:27, 35). The scratching Job did with the potsherd was because of the nature of his disease. He used this only as a counterirritant and not for the ancient practice of laceration as a sign of mourning for the dead (Dt 14:1).

9–10 Not knowing the limitation God had put on the Accuser, Job's wife at this point diagnosed the disease as incurable and recommended that he curse God and die. Job's mental anguish was certainly intensified by his wife's advice. Had he followed it, the contest would have ended with the Accuser as the victor.

Job's reply is remarkable in the compassion he showed toward his wife and in his total acceptance of God's will for his life. He might have accused his wife of blasphemy but chose to accept it as a statement of desperation. Her "talking like a foolish woman" does not refer to intellectual foolishness but to religious apostasy (as in Pss 14:1 and 53:1). To curse God was essentially a way of denying he is God. Job was willing to believe that his wife was only talking like a blasphemer. Job's wisdom, on the other hand, was to receive with meekness whatever prosperity or disaster God might send. Such wisdom was not rooted in his intellectual capacity but in his fear (worship) of God.

Now the author repeats practically the same testimony of Job's verbal innocence given in 1:21. Despite all that has happened to him, up to this point Job did not err with his lips. This section of the Prologue provides the basis of the NT description of Job as a man of perseverance (Jas 5:11).

5. The coming of the counselors (2:11–13)

11–13 It took time, possibly months, for the news to pass by word of mouth and for the three sages, friends of Job, to come (cf. 7:3). Teman, an Edomite city and a center of wisdom (Jer 49:7), is the only place of the three that can be definitely located. The friends arranged a meeting so they could join together to console Job. Shuah was the name of an eastern tribe (Ge 25:2, 6).

When the counselors join together near Job's home, they are stunned by what they see. Like the Suffering Servant of Isa 53, Job is disfigured beyond recognition, at least from a distance. The three friends had come to show grief and console Job; they may have come largely to go through the proper motions. It does not appear that they were ready for what they encountered.

The friends immediately went into a drastic form of mourning usually reserved for death or total disaster. They tore their robes of nobility, wailed, and threw dust into the air. Then they sat in silence before Job for seven days and nights. Like the elders of fallen Jerusalem in La 2:10, Job's friends sat on the ground with dust on their heads and kept silent. For one of them to speak prior to the sufferer would have been in bad taste.

II. The Dialogue–Dispute (3:1–27:23)

A. Job's Opening Lamentation (3:1–26)

The spiritual tone of Job's life changes dramatically here. The man of patience and faith sinks into a state of despondency and spiritual depression, so frequently a major problem to those who endure severe physical illness or impairment. In ch. 3 Job establishes an attitude that largely colors all that he says in the succeeding chapters. In all his many words of despair, nowhere will he come closer to cursing God to his face (cf. 2:5) than here in ch. 3. By cursing the day of his birth, he is questioning the sovereign wisdom of his Creator. At this point the drama is intense, for the Accuser, whom we will never see again, seems to have triumphed. Whether he has or not will be determined by what follows.

1–2 The words "After this" introduce the Dialogue, a major division of the book. In fact, the entire third chapter, though a part of the Dialogue, is transitional.

3–10 The way Job curses the day of his birth has two interesting features. First, he expresses a desire for the annihilation of that day, a would-be negation of God's creative act in bringing such a day into being. As God had said in Ge 1:3, "Let there be light," so Job, using the same terminology in v.4, says, "As for that day, let there be darkness" (lit. tr.). Job intends to give full vent to his feelings. He wishes that day could be so annihilated that even God would forget it. Job wants the day lost in total darkness, not even numbered anymore as a day in the calendar.

The second feature is Job's use of personification. He personifies both the night of his conception and the day he was born. That night speaks about what it has witnessed, the birth of a boy. It is more vivid to imagine the day perishing as a person than as a span of time. A barren night unable to conceive results in a literal night in which no shout of joy will be heard.

Contemporary mythology used the term "Leviathan" (GK 4293) for a monster of chaos who lived in the sea, and the Sea itself was a boisterous deity who could be aroused professionally. But to Job, a strict monotheist (31:26–28), this was simply vivid imagery, the use of proverbial language tailored to his call for the obliteration of that day. The figure may be of an awakened monster of chaos who could perhaps swallow that day or even usher in the end of days.

11–26 Job continues his pitiable complaint with a series of rhetorical questions. There is a progression in his thought. Since the day of his birth did happen (v.10), the next possibility was a stillbirth. But since he was alive, he longed for a premature death. In vv.13–19 Job conceives of death as falling into restful sleep (v.13). It is clear that he does not consider it annihilation. The dead are in a place where there is no activity, where everyone finds rest; even the wicked stop making trouble there.

In addition to the progression of thought, there is also a symmetry of ideas in these verses. Job wishes he had been a stillbirth and then imagines himself joining the great (kings, counselors, rulers) who rested in Sheol. Then in v.16 he repeats the issue and follows with a description of the small (the wicked, the weary, the captives) who also rested in Sheol. A concluding line wraps it up with the thought that the small and great are all alike in Sheol, where even the slave is freed from his master.

The last of Job's rhetorical questions comes in vv.20–23. To paraphrase: Why is light given to a man who is miserable? Why is life given to a man who has no future? His suffering is so intense both physically and mentally that death in comparison would be an exquisite pleasure, like finding hidden treasure. The very thing he dreads the most happened. It thus appears to him that the very God who had put a hedge of protection and blessing about him (1:10) subsequently hemmed him in with trouble and distress.

What does this chapter teach us? Job's attitude is certainly not normative—just the opposite. What we can see is how even a man of great faith can fall into the slough of despond. That one as great as Job should have such a struggle of faith is a source of support to those similarly afflicted, especially when viewed in the light of the rest of the book of Job. God prefers we speak with him honestly, even in our moments of deepest gloom.

B. The First Cycle of Speeches (4:1–14:22)

1. Eliphaz (4:1–5:27)

With artistic flare Eliphaz sounds the keynote for all else that he and his companions will say. Job in ch. 3 was so obviously wrong that it was not hard for Eliphaz to appear to be right. But we must keep in mind that the counselors were basically wrong, even though their words were often right (see 42:7–8).

1–11 Eliphaz, a man from Teman, an Edomite city noted as a center of wisdom (Jer 49:7), on the surface spoke as if he thought Job was basically righteous and that his sufferings were temporary. But in reality Eliphaz was not convinced of this. Later he openly agreed with the harder line against Job used by his friends (22:1–11). Eliphaz's opening statement sounds like he was truly concerned for Job's welfare but could not resist the temptation to give Job some "proper" instruction. Some compliments are offered. Job is called a "wisdom teacher"—like himself. But the compliment is followed by a warning to Job, who had instructed and strengthened those in trouble, that he must be careful lest he fail to apply to himself the lessons he taught others.

In v.6 Eliphaz affirmed that Job was basically an upright man who only needed the wisdom to see that all deserve some punishment for sin, for no one is completely pure (v.17).

According to Eliphaz, Job's faith in God and blameless conduct (1:8; 2:3) should have saved him. Verses 8–11 may be an excursus about the fate of the wicked without reference to Job, or they may reveal that he really was not all that certain about Job. Moreover, Job's experience did not support the idea that the innocent never perish. With the perspective of the Prologue, the reader has insight that proves Eliphaz's statement is shallow. But Eliphaz would also say things that were not so shallow. For example, he would admonish Job to be patient and see the disciplinary aspect of suffering (5:17–18).

12–21 At this point Eliphaz bolstered the authority of his words by an appeal to the supernatural—an eerie and hair-raising experience in which he received a divine oracle. Uncertain about what it was he saw, he claimed "a form" (GK 9454) spoke in the silence of the night.

Eliphaz went on to tell how inferior the angels are to God. More so a human being, whose body, like a house of clay, is as fragile as a moth. It is clear that Eliphaz saw mortals as almost zero in God's sight—hardly more than an insect that may perish unnoticed. Like collapsing tents people "die without wisdom." This is no mere statement about the death of the ignorant. Eliphaz is saying, "They die, and it is not by (of) wisdom." That is, there is no special purpose in it. To a God so transcendent that he does not even trust the angels, the death of a sinful person is of little consequence.

It hardly seems possible to stress too much that God is transcendent. Eliphaz, however, succeeds in taking this important truth and misapplying it. In fairness to Eliphaz, the verbs in vv.19–21 may only express possible consequences of human sinfulness, not what happens to every sinner. Eliphaz's point then is that since all deserve this, we should be patient when temporary suffering comes.

5:1–7 Eliphaz next directed his words more explicitly toward Job. There was no mediator among the holy servants of God (the angels) who would dare answer a plea from Job. Why? Because he was behaving like a fool. Fools pay no proper heed to God (Ps 14:1). Their houses are cursed, their children crushed, and their wealth depleted (cf. 1:13–19). Eliphaz was not quite explicit, but Job no doubt got the point. He was establishing a connection between moral and physical evil. Trouble does not sprout up like weeds in the field; one must sow and cultivate trouble.

The "sparks" that fly upward are literally "the sons of Resheph" (GK 1201 & 8404). This name is used seven times in the OT, mostly for flames or lightning (Dt 32:23–24; 1Ch 7:25 [proper name]; Pss 76:4; 78:48; SS 8:6; Hab 3:5). This imagery from the contemporary mythology need not imply anything about the theology of the speaker or author. Eliphaz was probably saying that human beings, like the sons of this colorful and pestering figure, stir up their own trouble or are the victims of uncontrollable natural forces such as disease, plague, and death.

8–16 Verses 9–16 are in the form a creedal hymn on the nature of God as the Lord of creation and salvation. So Eliphaz admonished Job to appeal to God who does only what is right. He punishes the unjust and delivers the lowly. This is of course exactly what Job believed, but such advice did not help him understand why he was suffering so intensely. On the contrary, since it implied he was getting just what he deserved, it only added to his confusion.

These lines are a fine example of hymn genre in OT poetry. That is why the apostle Paul could cite a line from v.13 in 1Co 3:19: "He catches the wise in their craftiness." But in Eliphaz's case, what is absolutely true is misapplied—the sick room is not the place for theological strictures that may turn out to do more harm than good. Eliphaz as a counselor is a supreme negative example. Great truths misapplied only hurt more those who are already hurting.

17–27 Eliphaz continued his lofty words with another unit of fine poetry. The purpose of his creedal poem in vv.9–16 was to show sinners (fools) how transcendent and holy God is. Sinners get what they deserve, and only the righteous have hope. It is a terrifying statement that God, because he is a holy God, hates sinners. But as a man dedicated to wisdom, Eliphaz balanced this with another poem addressed to anyone who understands God's "discipline" (GK 4592). Typical gnomic truth maintained that the correcting wounds of God were temporary—truly good people will always be rescued. The very God who injures them will heal them; they will be blessed and again enjoy the good things of life.

But in the light of Job's experiences—the loss of his family, his economic ruin, his sickness—there is a thoughtless cruelty inherent in applying the words of vv.19–26 to him. For example, if Job benefits from God's discipline, then "his children will be many"—but Job's children were dead. It is not what Eliphaz knew that is wrong; it is what he was ignorant of—God's hidden purpose—that made all his beautiful poetry and grand truth only a snare to Job. Moreover, while things he said are good even for a sufferer to contemplate—such as the disciplining aspect of suffering—even these words, we know from the Prologue, do not apply to the case in hand.

Eliphaz's patronizing attitude revealed in his closing sentence must have been galling to Job, his peer.

2. Job's reply (6:1–7:21)

1–7 The two themes of Job's speech are introduced here. In vv.1–4 Job complained against God and in vv.5–7 against the counselors. First he attempted to justify his own "impetuous" words with an appeal to his overwhelming misery brought on by the arrows of God. Then he claimed the right to bray like a donkey or bellow like an ox deprived of fodder and left to starve. Job starved for the right words that, like food (Am 8:11), could bring strength and nourishment. The food Eliphaz dished out was absolutely tasteless; worse, it turned Job's stomach. Despite his bodily misery, Job's major concern was for the needs of his spirit. If only he could hear words that would nourish his soul rather than sicken him more!

8–10 Again (cf. 3:21) Job earnestly asked God to bring an end to his suffering by bringing an end to his life—a mercy killing! He would then have some joy even in pain. He would have one consolation left before he died—

that he had not denied the words of the Holy One, though he emphatically rejected the words of Eliphaz. Verses 1–10 form a unit based on a theme about the use of words: Job's words (v.3), Eliphaz's words (vv.6–7), and God's words (v.10).

11–13 Job complained that he had no reason to be patient, for he had nothing to look forward to. As a vulnerable creature made of flesh, he had no human resources left. Even his natural ability, the gifts that contributed to his success, had been driven from him. This is a reply to Eliphaz's words in 4:2–6.

14–21 Turning in despair to his friends, Job pled for kindness ("devotion"; GK 2876), even though they may have thought that he no longer feared God. Instead he found them like wadis that run dry. Verse 21 is the climax of Job's reaction to his friends' counsel. They offered no help.

22–23 Job never asked his friends for anything tangible. It was not as if they were being asked to pay a ransom to save him. The thought goes back to v.14, where he asked only for what would cost them nothing—their faithful love and kindness, despite what they thought he had done.

24–27 Job's words are a challenge and an indictment. His friends needed to be specific about his sins and be sure they were right. He insisted that they speak the truth just as he affirmed a compelling desire to speak only the truth before God. His words may have been painful, but they were honest, even though his friends treated them as wind. In his mind it was their arguments that were specious. He labeled them as men of such severe cruelty that they could have cast lots for an orphan or bartered away a friend.

28–30 Here Job softened his tone and appealed to his friends as men of compassion. He pled for justice, for a reconsideration of their indictment of him. His integrity was at stake, and that was more important to him than life itself. In v.30 Job again employed the figure of words as morsels of food. He reaffirmed the honesty of his own words and claimed for himself a discriminating taste for the truth.

7:1–2 These verses form a complaint to God: The life of a human being, so full of toil and suffering, is like hard military service, like a toiling slave longing for the shade, or like a hired person working for mere pittance.

3–10 These are the words of a chronic sufferer. There had been months of futility and nights of tossing in misery, nights that seemed to drag on endlessly. Yet almost in the same breath Job described his purposeless life as passing with incredible speed, a complaint heard on the lips of the aging or any who feel their days are numbered. In v.5 Job described one of the symptoms of his disease—scabs that crack and fester. Worse than the disease itself, Job lost all hope of being healed. He believed his only release from pain was death.

Beginning in v.7 Job addressed God directly, and this continues throughout the chapter. His words are an empirical view of the human lot on this earth. Human life is only a breath. One goes down to the grave and never returns. Death is so final—a person disappears like a cloud, and his family sees him no more.

11–21 Again Job asserted his determination to cry out in agony of spirit over the apparent injustice of God who, it seems, would not leave him alone. Even when sleep did come, he blamed God for his terrifying dreams. This brings up several theological issues. First, does the book of Job teach a lesson about God's willingness to allow for Job's rage? Job's extreme language fits his cultural setting but was a source of great offense to postbiblical Jews who sometimes felt the need to theologically correct his words. That is exactly what was done in v.20. Both an ancient scribal tradition and the LXX show the original reading of the final line to be "Have I become a burden to you?" (cf. NIV note). The present MT reads "I have become a burden to myself"—an early attempt to remove what was thought blasphemous. If Job's raging attitude was reprehensible in the eyes of later interpreters, it was accepted by God (though not desired, cf. 38:2) as part of the struggle of a man who was determined to open himself wholly to God.

Second, was Job giving a parody of Ps 8? Like the psalmist, Job asked, "What is man that you make so much of him?" The biblical answer is, of course, that humanity is the work of God's hands, created in his own image. God's purpose for the world centers around the human race, his crowning creation, to whom he gave the world. God makes much of them, for they are meant to be God's surrogates on earth. But Job, in his current condition, believed God's interest in him was only negative—as if God's only interest were to torment him for his sin, not letting him alone long enough to swallow his spittle. God even used him as a target for his arrows.

Contrary to all this, the reader knows from the Prologue that a loving God waited for that moment when Job's test would be over and the hand of the tormentor (the Accuser) would be removed. But at this moment it appears to Job that God is the tormentor. The reader knows God was using a secondary means and that Job's conception of God as tormentor was askew. The reader also knows that because God is sovereign, the problem remains logically unresolved. This age-old dilemma between divine sovereignty and divine goodness is a permanent backdrop throughout the book of Job. The dilemma is there, but it is not the purpose of this book to attempt to solve the problem.

It would be a mistake to think that Job was wrestling with a purely intellectual problem. His concern was more experiential, though he was also seeking a way to make his experience (suffering) agree with his theology (the justice of God). Job's pathetic words at the end of this chapter show that he still entertained doubts about his own blameworthiness, but they also suggest that he felt God was being unjust. These are words he would eventually regret (40:4).

3. Bildad (8:1–22)

Bildad's speech contains an important negative lesson about human nature in general and about the qualities of a good counselor. He heard Job's words with his ears, but his heart heard nothing. This truth should be viewed in the light of Job's plea for compassion in ch. 6. All people under the most ordinary circumstances need compassion; how much more Job in his extremity! Repeatedly in ch. 6 Job called himself a helpless (v.13) and despairing man (vv.14, 26) in need of the devotion of his friends. It seems almost incredible that Bildad would reply so callously. There is not only steely indifference to Job's plight but an arrogant certainty that Job's children got just what they deserved and that

Job was well on his way to the same fate. The lesson we must learn is that there are such people in the world and that they do their heartless disservice to humankind under the guise of being the special friends of God.

As he appears in the Dialogue, Job becomes a man whose frame of mind is not totally conducive to loving relationships with others. Anyone who curses the day of his birth and looks on death as preferable to life is in need of help. His three friends were there for that purpose, but Job came to view them as part of his problem rather than as those who offered therapy. Their view that people do suffer for their sins and need to be brought face-to-face with that reality was not wholly wrong. The assumption that Job was one of these is what led them astray as counselors.

The lessons we learn from Job's friends about counseling are negative, but the three are not alike. The book presents three counselors instead of one because each had his own approach and message for Job. Eliphaz began somewhat sensitive to Job's needs but eventually lost patience (ch. 22). The other two were aloof and superior. None of them was able to accept Job unconditionally. It is true that Job was a stubborn patient, but they were unable or unwilling—or both—to become involved with him. Their advice was well-meant and often accurately and artistically stated, but it succeeded in making Job even more stubborn and resistive to them. No doubt a large part of the problem was their academic commitment to a viewpoint they refused to alter, namely, that sin brings suffering and suffering is evidence of sin.

Job forced his counselors to accept or reject his contention that he was not suffering for his sins. In 6:24 he had said, "Teach me, and I will be quiet; show me where I have been wrong." That they did not accept Job's contention made them unwilling to listen and hence miserable as counselors. Bildad could only reply, "God does not reject a blameless man" (v.20). However, had they accepted Job's contention, the book would have lost a major part of its message, a message that centers around the mystery of God's purposes in dealing with his creatures. An important lesson to be learned from the book is that counselors must be willing to listen, to become involved, and to have respect for the integrity of the human personality they are trying to

help. And they must always bear in mind that they may not fully understand the nature of the case.

1–10 Bildad was blunt. "Your words are blustering wind," he said as a preface to his one and only theological point: Job's suffering was the proof of his sinfulness. Since God cannot be unjust, there is only one conclusion—Job and his family had received the punishment they deserved. Job should plead for mercy. Then, if he deserved it, God would restore him. Bildad failed to see that mercy implies the forgiveness one receives even though one does not deserve it. Eliphaz had appealed to revelation; Bildad appealed to tradition. To Bildad nothing less than the teachings of the ancients proved the orthodoxy of his viewpoint. If Job would only take the time to consider ancient tradition, he would find that God only does right. Sinners get just punishment, and good men are blessed with health and prosperity.

11–19 This poem on the destruction of the wicked has a literary quality similar to that demonstrated by Eliphaz in his masterly poem on the good man in 5:17–26. Those who ignore God, Bildad called "godless" (GK 2868); the word means something like our word "hypocrite." The hope of these persons is unreliable. Like a spider's web (v.14), it provides no support. The godless are like papyrus plants without water (vv.11–12) or like vines with shallow roots clinging to rocks, destined to be pulled up or left to wither and die (vv.16–18).

20–22 Bildad thought he heard Job say that God perverts justice (v.3). Job did have problems about divine justice; but he had not yet blatantly accused God of being unjust, though he came close to it (6:20). Job found it difficult—if not impossible—to understand God's justice. Although Job did not claim perfection, he considered himself a blameless man. This was also God's view of him in the Prologue (1:8; 2:3), but Bildad was sure that God had rejected Job. Since God does not reject blameless people, Job could not be one. Therefore, he must be a hypocrite. The situation, however, could be remedied: if only he would turn to God, Job's lips might laugh again.

4. Job's reply (9:1–10:22)

In these chapters Job's words move from extolling God (9:1–13)—perhaps as a display of theological acumen to impress the counselors—to blaming God. Would God ever treat him justly? He doubted it (vv.14–31). Does God mock the innocent? Job thought probably so (vv.21–24): "If it is not he, then who is it?" (v.24). These are hard words, but his question instead of a statement implies doubt. These words are followed in vv.32–35 with a yearning for someone strong enough to take up his cause with God. But in ch. 10 Job decided to plead his own cause and direct all his words to God. How could God who created him want to destroy him—and that without any formal charges?

1–24 In vv.1–13 Job intended to show that his problems were not due to gross ignorance of God's ways. Those ways are past finding out, but he knew as much about them as they did. His opening remark—"Indeed I know that this is true"—is a grudging admission that what Bildad had said contained the right theology. But he had more than Bildad's words in mind. Job immediately called to mind Eliphaz's rhetorical question in 4:17: "Can a mortal be more righteous [GK 7405] than God?" Eliphaz and Job seem to use the word "righteous" in a slightly different sense. The former is thinking of ontological superiority, whereas Job is thinking of legal vindication (i.e., innocence).

Bildad's accusations in ch. 8 turned Job's mind to the subject of legal vindication. In 8:20 Bildad had said, "Surely God does not reject a blameless man." To Bildad God's justice required punishing the guilty and blessing the innocent (see also 8:3–6). Job fervently believed that he was innocent of any sin that would warrant the kind of punishment he was enduring. But he was frustrated in his attempt to vindicate himself. God's wisdom was too profound and his power too great for Job to debate in court.

Verses 4–13 constitute a hymn in which Job describes God's awesome power. God shakes the earth from its place and makes its pillars tremble; he speaks to the sun, and it does not shine, he stretches out the heavens and treads on the waves of the sea—the creation and control of all natural forces.

Job closed the hymn with the words that Eliphaz used in 5:9: "He performs wonders that cannot be fathomed, miracles that cannot be counted." But Job was applying these words in a way opposite to how Eliphaz used them. Eliphaz was trying to show how God does what is good and right. He lifts to safety those who mourn and delivers the poor from the clutches of the powerful. But Job saw God's power as if it were amoral, a sovereign freedom, an uncontrollable power that works mysteriously to do whatever he wills so that no one can stop him and ask, "What are you doing?" (v.12). Yes, God's anger makes even the armies of Rahab (the boisterous demonic power associated with the sea; cf. Isa 51:9) cower at his feet. Job thought such a God would overwhelm him in any attempt to show his innocence. Job could only plead for mercy; even worse, Job doubted God would give him a hearing.

In vv.21–24 this God of Job's imagination was worse than morally indifferent; he even mocked the despair of the innocent and blocked the administering of justice. Since everyone gets treated the same way—the blameless and the wicked—Job threw all caution to the wind: "I have no concern for myself; I despise my own life." He added, in effect, "If God is not responsible for this, then who is?" (cf v.24).

These are words of a sick and desperate man. They are a forceful reminder to anyone who has to counsel the sick, that people who face deep trials often say irresponsible things in their struggle to understand their suffering in the light of God's compassion. Not all Job's words are wrong, but it is a mistake to try to make them all represent valid theology rather than the half-truths of a person struggling to understand. They deal with the mystery at the very heart of the book of Job: the problem of evil for which no human being has a logical explanation. So Job reasoned, as many have, that if God is sovereign, truly sovereign, he is responsible for all evil.

Job did not mention the corollary: If there is evil beyond God's control, then he is not truly sovereign. Job stressed only God's irresistible might; and it appears to him that if God held him to be guilty, there was nothing that he could do to establish his innocence. Yet he believed he was innocent and was concerned with disproving the contention of his friends that God only destroys the wicked and always cares for the righteous. Job's experience told him that sometimes God crushes the innocent for no reason at all (v.17). We who are privileged to see the drama from the divine perspective know that Job was innocent and that God did have a cause, a cause beyond the purview of Job, a cause that could not be revealed to Job at that moment.

25–35 Verses 25–31 fall together as an expression of deep despair. Job was unable to suck sweetness from a single day; there was not a glimpse of joy, not a smile, only one unending blur of suffering. Since God arbitrarily chose to treat him as a criminal, what could he do to purge himself? Even if he were able to purge himself, God would plunge him again into a slime pit so that even his clothes would detest him.

In vv.32–35 Job went back to the theme of vv.14–20. He was frustrated over the immenseness of God! What Job did not realize was that in wrestling with God he was moving in the direction of a right relationship with his Maker. If he only understood what God was doing, that would have made his suffering bearable. But as it was then, he bore a burden that was even greater than his suffering—his apparent inability to stand in God's presence as an upright and blameless man.

In v.33 Job touched on the mystery through which God would eventually provide godliness for man. He yearned for a mediator ("someone to arbitrate"; GK 3519) between himself and God. Such a person does not have to be one who stands over both God and Job in order to judge between them. As "one who argues a case," he is a negotiator who is able to bring parties together. We should not infer from this that the book of Job here is directly predictive of the NT doctrine of Christ as mediator. For one thing Job was not looking for a mediator to forgive him of his sins so that he might be received by God; Job was yearning for a mediator who could prove that he was innocent and could somehow be effective with God despite his infinite power and wisdom. But having said that, we have here a rudimentary idea that is certainly evocative of that NT concept. This idea will move on to greater ramifications in 16:20–21 and 19:25–26.

10:1–22 In ch. 10 Job continued to bewail his sorrowful condition. Life had become an unbearable burden. In his bitter anguish he determined to speak out, once again directing his words to God. He called on God, though not for healing and restoration (which, incidentally, he nowhere ever asked for); but he wanted to know again why he was suffering: "Tell me what charges you have against me" (v.2). Job could not understand how God, the Creator, who looked on his original creation and considered it good (Ge 1:31), could turn his back on the work of his hands. Had not Job dedicated his life to God, in contrast to the wicked who received God's smile? Job knew that God was not limited like human beings who have mere eyes of flesh and a certain number of years. Did God have to search out Job's faults when he knew that he was innocent? Job put God on the witness stand and plied him with questions. Job could not understand how the God who so marvelously made him in the womb could be willing to destroy him.

The NIV takes v.13 with what follows; if this is correct, then in v.13 Job was saying that God brought him into being so that he might hound him over his sin and let no offense go unpunished. Apparently Job was saying that it did not make any difference whether he was innocent or guilty, because he was full of shame and drowned in affliction anyhow. No matter how much he tried to assert his integrity, it seems that God insisted on stalking Job like a lion, showing his awesome power in wave after wave of oppression.

Poor Job, the God whom he imagined was so angry with him was not angry with him at all; but in his current state of mind, he reverted back to his original wish to have died at birth, to have been carried straight from the womb to the tomb (vv.18–19). In ch. 3 Job saw Sheol as a place where he might have found some rest from his troubles; here in ch. 10 he longed for a few days of release on earth before he had to go to that place of no return, which he envisioned as a land of gloom and deepest night.

Job had reached about as far as a human being can go into the depths of depression and despair, but it would do us well to be reminded that even the apostle of hope said in 2Co 1:8–9: "We were under great pressure, far beyond our ability to endure, so that we despaired even of life. Indeed, in our hearts we felt the sentence of death. But this happened that we might not rely on ourselves but on God, who raises the dead." In his despair Job still wrestled with God, but it was still to the living God that his cry was lifted up. An important question yet to be faced is, Did Job have any hope that transcended this life?

5. Zophar (11:1–20)

Zophar was a severe man. Like Bildad he lacked compassion and was ruthlessly judgmental. He thought Job, who was suffering to the point of despair, was getting much less than he deserved.

1–12 Zophar considered Job's words pure mockery, for he thought Job was claiming flawless doctrine and sinless perfection. Job has steadfastly maintained his innocence or blamelessness in contrast with wickedness (9:22), but he did not claim to be perfect (7:21). Though he complained bitterly of the treatment God appeared to be giving him, to this point he has not been sarcastic, nor has he mocked God or even ridiculed his friends. He has accused them of being shallow in their arguments and callous in the way they have dealt with him (6:24–27).

Zophar spoke with eloquence about God's infinitude (vv.7–8), justice, and omniscience (vv.10–11). Job needed a stiff rebuke from God because God had favored him by forgetting some of his sin, or at least had allowed Job to forget some of his sin. Either way, the words were designed to suggest the enormity of Job's sin. Zophar's only reason to believe Job had sinned to such an extent was derived from the extent of Job's suffering, which he took to be God's way of exposing secret sin. That Job would not admit it was taken to be additional evidence of his pride and hardness of heart. So Job needed to be humbled. The best way to humble him was to bring him face-to-face with the immensity of God. If the limits of the created cosmos were beyond Job's understanding (vv.7–9), how much more the mysteries of God!

In vv.10–11 Zophar touched on the omnipotence and omniscience of God who sees through the deceit of people like Job and keeps a permanent record of it. All this was designed to humble Job, but Zophar apparently doubted that it would. He then attempted heavy-handed shock treatment to get through to Job. Sharply sarcastic, Zophar labeled Job a witless, empty-headed man with as much chance to become wise as a wild donkey has to be born tame.

13–20 Job's only hope was to stretch out his hands to God and repent. This is good advice for a person who has lived a life of sinful indulgence, but to Job's ears it was pious arrogance. It was arrogant for Zophar to assume he knew why Job was suffering; he had reduced the solution of this very complex human problem to a simplistic formula—every pain has a sin behind it. Zophar erroneously suggested that if one repents and gets right with God the struggles and troubles of life will dissolve. This common error is made by many well-meaning Christians who fail to distinguish between forensic forgiveness that cancels the guilt of sin and the immediate consequences of a profligate life, bringing trouble and distress. But we know from the Prologue that Job's troubles were not the result of a profligate life; so Zophar was wrong on both counts. Job's troubles did not come as a penalty from God; and even if they did, Job's repentance would not guarantee that life from then on would be "brighter than noonday" and that people would stop molesting him and instead "court his favor."

6. Job's reply (12:1–14:22)

There is good reason to question the chapter division in this long speech. The most natural break comes in 13:20. Job first answered his counselors (12:1–13:19), then addressed God (13:20–14:22). With patience running out, he chose to match Zophar's harshness with sarcasm—"Doubtless you are the people, and wisdom will die with you" (12:1). Job was sure he knew as much as they did and begged to differ with their view of suffering. Being comfortable themselves, they could afford to be contemptuous toward him. If only he were treated justly, Job would not be suffering the way he was. He repeated the unanswerable question: Why did God treat him so badly? Why should a man who is righteous and blameless be made a laughingstock (v.4) when sinners and idolaters go undisturbed (v.6)? This is the kind of question that made them brand Job as a man whose feet were slipping (v.5).

1–25 This poem breaks neatly into three stanzas. The first (vv.4–6) states Job's problem: "Why me, God, and not those who really deserve misfortune?" In the second (vv.7–12) Job complained that the whole world was afflicted with the same apparent injustice. Why should this be when all things, including the very breath of humankind, are in God's hands? Bildad had already accused Job of attributing evildoing to God (8:3) and had appealed to the authority of past generations to prove Job was wrong. Now Job appealed to the experience of humankind and all creation to support his view that it makes no difference whether people are good or bad. God does not use morality as the basis for granting freedom from affliction. Job's counselors were so superficial that they had not yet struggled with this difficult problem. Their thoughts on the subject were simplistic. Job considered their words bland and superficial, certainly not a worthy part of the wisdom of elders. He had already accused them of serving tasteless food (i.e., thoughts; cf. 6:6–7).

In the third stanza (vv.13–25), Job expounded on God's sovereign freedom—with his power and wisdom he does whatever he wishes. Job stressed the negative use God makes of his power. God tears down what humans build, sends drought and flood, makes fools out of judges, sends priests and nobles into captivity, and deprives kings of their reason.

What Job was saying may be a mockery of the lopsidedness of Eliphaz's creedal hymn in 5:18–26, where everything good happens to the righteous. It is hardly a parody on God's wisdom since in v.13 Job ascribed wisdom to God in conjunction with his purpose and understanding. In this context Job's problem is with the counselor's wisdom, not God's. He was attempting to answer Zophar's question: "Can you fathom the mysteries of God. . . ? What can you know?" (11:7–8). He was saying that God's actions were indeed mysterious and strange. Job could not figure them out, but he knew as much about them as the others.

In other words, Job believed the mystery was profound; and he was amazed that the "sages" would be so shallow. Job saw God as so wise and powerful that he cannot be put in a box. He has sovereign freedom. Job illustrated this by drawing a word picture of the mystery of God's acts in the history of the human race. God humbles great people and nations, showing himself to be the only truly sovereign being.

13:1–27 Job continued to show his irritation at Zophar's remark about his being an inane, witless person (11:12). His friends talked about God—Job maintained he could do that as skillfully as they. He was confident that given the opportunity he could prove his case before God, for he knew their accusations were false. Despite the unfortunate things he had said earlier about God—"He would [not] give me a hearing" (9:16) but "multiply my wounds for no reason" (9:17), and "he destroys both the blameless and the wicked" (9:22)—Job still believed all this could be reconciled if only he could argue his case directly with God (v.3). But his counselors smeared him with lies. They were quacks who could show their wisdom only if they kept quiet.

Job's argument in vv.6–12 has the following interesting twist. How dare his friends argue God's case deceitfully and use lies to flatter God? Job warned them about lying even while they uttered beautiful words in defense of God. If they were going to plead God's case, they had better do it honestly. God would judge them for their deceit even if they used it in his behalf. This proves what Job believed about God. We know from the Epilogue (42:7) that Job's assessment was right. Job's friends' words about God may have been true, but they were worthless because they were empty maxims, mere clichés. Moreover, their assessment of Job was wrong. If God would have examined their lives, they would not have been able to deceive him the way they deceived other people. For their hypocritical partiality toward God and their dishonest charges against Job, God would surely punish them.

On the other hand, Job was so sure he would be vindicated that he repeated his desire for a hearing before God (vv.13–19). He viewed this boldness on his part as one of the evidences that what they said about him was not true. If Job were a hypocrite, would he be willing to put his life in jeopardy in this way? Such a man would not dare come before God. Even if slain, Job would not wait but would remain in "hope" (v. 15; GK 3498) and would defend his ways before God; he was sure God would vindicate him. Although certain that his friends' charges were false,

Job did not claim sinless perfection. He admitted the sins of his youth for which he hoped he had been forgiven. Why, then, did God keep frightening him with his terrors and treating him as an enemy, indeed, as an enslaved prisoner of war whose feet were branded? He saw himself as helpless, as swirling chaff, or as a windblown leaf. If God would only stop tormenting him and communicate, Job felt all would end well.

13:28–14:22 Job's mercurial mood changed again. At the end of ch. 13 he again lost grip on his confidence and regressed to a hopeless feeling. From 13:28 to 14:6 Job mused on the misery of human beings in their pathetically brief life, uttering a brief but structured poem, designed to introduce the theme of the plight of the human race. People are impure; so they are worthy of punishment. Job, however, uttered a plea that the sovereign God, who gives to each a short span of numbered days, would let his poor creatures alone until their hard labor on earth was over. Again we must be reminded that a key factor remained a mystery to Job—the presence and power, albeit limited, of the Accuser who understandably is not mentioned at all in the dialogue.

In 14:7–22 Job turned again to death as the only way out of his impasse. A tree may be cut down and its stump appear to be dead; yet at the scent of water it springs to life and sends out new shoots. Such an observation cannot be asserted for human beings. They are more like a lake run dry. When one's lifetime runs out, it cannot be renewed. But Job suggested that God could provide a remedy by simply taking his life till his anger was over and then, by resurrection, call him back from Sheol.

This chapter proves that Job believed in the possibility of resurrection, though he saw humanity differently from the tree that can be cut down and immediately renewed. Human beings lie down and do not rise until the heavens are no more. But the assumption is that humankind will be raised. Job was saying that if God wanted to, he could hide Job in Sheol till his anger passed and then raise him. Job's pessimism arose, not from a skepticism about resurrection, but from God's apparent unwillingness to do anything immediately for him. Therefore his hopes were dashed; his life had become a nightmare of pain and mourning—with nothing to look for but death.

Job knew that eventually God would cover all his offenses, and he longed for him as the beneficent Creator who delights in those whom he has made. But despite his faith in God's power over death, Job was convinced that God would not even allow him the exquisite release of death. The waters of suffering continued to erode until his bright hope was a dim memory and nothing mattered anymore but the pain of his body and the continual mourning of his soul.

C. The Second Cycle of Speeches (15:1–21:34)

1. Eliphaz (15:1–35)

In vv.1–13, Eliphaz plied Job with questions designed to shame him into silence. Verses 14–16 form an apex about which his words hinge. They derive from his vision in 4:17–19 and here state his thesis: God's holiness versus human corruption. The remaining half of the chapter is a dramatic description of the dreadful fate of the wicked.

1–6 Eliphaz was angry. He had run out of patience. The time to be polite (4:2) and indirect was over. He considered Job's words not only valueless but deceitful and irreverent. In his opening lines he accused Job of belching out a hot wind of useless words. Worse, his mouth spoke as it did because of the sin in his heart. Job had condemned himself by his ungodly talk. Such irreligion made him a dangerous person, able to lead others astray (v.4).

7–13 Eliphaz now chided Job for arrogance. Was Job wise enough to sit in the council of God's angels? In reality he was not even wise enough to be in harmony with the elders and wise men on earth. "God's consolations" (v.11) are the gentle words Eliphaz tried to use with Job (see 4:1–6), only to receive a raging response.

14–16 Eliphaz repeated the thought that came to him by "revelation" (4:17–19)—that human beings are too vile to stand before God. The oracle had made a deep impression on him.

17–20 Eliphaz bolstered this "revelation" with wisdom that came from tradition—the wicked never escape the torment they deserve; and even if they do for a moment, trouble is just around the corner.

21–35 Eliphaz next presented a poetic discourse on the fate of the wicked. To the counselors Job's idea that the wicked prosper was a great heresy; his poem refutes this notion (cf. 4:17–26). He refused to believe that any wicked person prospers, except perhaps for the briefest moment. Eliphaz believed that wicked people always suffer distress and anguish. They know disaster is stored up for them. He pictured the wicked man as a quixotic figure who uselessly attacks God with full armor and thick shield. No doubt it is all a caricature of Job, whose "eyes flash" as he "vents [his] rage against God" (vv.11–12).

In vv.27–35 the caricature continues with a variety of figures—the fat, rich, wicked man who finally gets what he deserves. He is like a grapevine stripped before its fruit is ripe or an olive tree shedding its blossoms. As long as Eliphaz rejected the notion that the wicked prosper and its corollary that the innocent sometimes suffer, he would never have to wrestle over the disturbing mystery

of how this fits with the justice of God. Eliphaz viewed humankind as either all good or all bad. He allowed no room for a good man to have doubts and struggles, and those who are bad Eliphaz wanted to reduce to zero.

In his query "What is man, that he could be pure?" (vv.14–16), Eliphaz's view of humanity comes through clearly. There is nothing in his words that would lead one to the conclusion that God has any love for sinful human beings. Indeed, the deity Eliphaz worshiped was mechanical; he behaved like the laws of nature, so that sinners could expect no mercy. The sinner always gets paid in full—trouble and darkness, terror and distress, the flame and the sword. God will see to it.

In describing such a fate, Eliphaz made sure that all the things that had happened to Job were included—fire consumes (vv.30, 34; cf. 1:16), marauders attack (v.21; cf. 1:17), possessions are taken away (v.29; cf. 1:17), and houses crumble (v.28; cf. 1:19). Although the modern reader often misses the point that these barbs are all directed at Job, we can be sure that Job himself felt their sting.

2. Job's reply (16:1–17:16)

In these chapters we find a direct contradiction of what the counselors have said. Job's thoughts match, by means of contrast, those of Eliphaz in ch. 15; but his opening words are an answer to the opening words of all three (cf. 8:2; 11:9–3; 15:2–6). In 15:12–13, 25–26, Eliphaz accused Job of attacking God, but Job claimed the reverse was true; God assailed him (16:8–9, 12–14). Eliphaz saw all people as vile and corrupt in God's eyes (15:14–16), but Job believed he had been upright and would be vindicated (16:15–21). Eliphaz thought the words of the wise supported him (15:17–18), but Job was convinced that there was not a word of wisdom in what he had to say (17:10–12). Because God had closed their minds to understanding (17:4), they were incapable of doing anything but scold him (16:4–5; 17:2).

1–5 Job, with purpose, chose in the word "miserable" (GK 6662) the same word that Eliphaz used to suggest Job had conceived his own misery ("trouble" in 15:35; GK 6662), and he threw it back at him when he called them "miserable comforters." He affirmed how he would have given genuine

The olive tree is often used metaphorically in the Bible. Eliphaz uses it in his caricature of the wicked (15:33).

encouragement to them if the tables were turned, but all he got were arguments and scoldings. The opening words of ch. 16 are full of meaning for all who aspire to counsel others. It is a powerful negative example. The counselors had become gadflies, pestering Job who was certain that they had no understanding of his real problem.

6–14 In v.6 Job turned again to the enemy— the god his mind had created—the one who wore him out and tore him in his anger. He viewed himself as one whom God had seized by the scruff of the neck and thrown into the clutches of the wicked. God had made Job his target, an object of attack; like a warrior he pierced him without pity. The figure was no doubt suggested by Eliphaz's description of the wicked man (meaning Job) who shakes his fist at God, defiantly attacking the Almighty (15:25–26). Job saw the situation as just the reverse of that in vv.12–14. Job recognized that God could do whatever he wished, but Job was anguished by the thought that God acted like his enemy. So Job and Eliphaz were polarized in their respective views. Was God attacking Job or Job attacking God?

There was no question in Job's mind that God sent the pain—"you have devastated my entire household." So in vv.6–8 Job said that it did not make any difference whether he spoke or did not speak, his pain was still there. It wore him out and had become the major witness against him, for on it his detractors had based their arguments. To them it was proof of his sinfulness. As if that were not bad enough, he thought God had assailed him, crushed him, and turned him over to his detractors.

15–17 Here we see a pathetic figure in sackcloth, sitting with brow in the dust, eyes sunken and face bloated with tears, avowing innocence. From this sad figure arises a baneful cry, but one that has not totally lost hope, as vv.18–21 show.

16:18–17:2 Verses 18, 22, and 17:1 indicate that Job thought he would die before he could be vindicated before his peers; so he was concerned that the injustice done to him should never be forgotten. That is what he meant when he called on the earth never to cover his blood or bury his cry. In Ge 4:10–11 Abel's innocent blood was crying out to God as a witness against Cain. So Job was

consoled to think his cry would continue after his death. And there is one in heaven who would listen to it. He firmly believed that he had a friend, an advocate, an intercessor on high who would plead his cause.

There are indications that Job considered this advocate to be greater than a human being. He was in heaven. In 9:33 the one "to arbitrate" was a mere wish, but he was also described as one who could put his hand on both God and Job. In 19:25 the "Redeemer" who lives must also be a heavenly figure since Job made a special point of how he would eventually stand on the earth (dust). Certainly God gave Job this hope in the midst of his darkest hours to point to the one who would ultimately fulfill it. But Job probably understood only a limited part of its fullest meaning.

3–5 What "pledge" or guarantee was Job asking for? The translation of v.3 is difficult. The following paraphrase may help clarify the meaning: "Give attention (O God) to becoming my guarantor (that I am right) with you, for who else will shake my hand to prove it?" If God put up such a guarantee for Job, it would not only silence his mockers (the counselors) but would prove they were guilty of false accusation and deserving of the sanctions and punishment they had implied Job deserved. Verse 5 is a proverb. Job was reminding his counselors of the dire consequences of slander.

6–9 Unfortunately such a guarantee from God was not evident. On the contrary, Job saw God as the one who made him suffer humiliation. There were few who believed he was innocent. Most people thought they were doing God a favor by spitting in Job's face; at least that is how Job felt. But in vv.8–9 he was saying that truly good men can pity him in his suffering without turning away from what is right. This is what his counselors could not understand. To them every pain had a sin behind it, and God could not be doing this to Job unless he deserved it. Another interpretation of vv.8–9 is that Job was being sarcastic. He was saying, "You upright men are appalled at this." He had already accused them of having contempt for sufferers like him (12:5).

10 Job was outraged at his friends' attitude, which he considered completely devoid of wisdom. The verse lends added weight to the interpretation of vv.8–9 as sarcasm.

11–16 The counselors had said that night would be turned to day for Job if only he would get right with God (cf. 11:17). In vv.12–16 Job made a parody of their advice. It was like going to the grave with the notion that all you have to do is treat it like home where warmth and loved ones are and it will become so. No, Job's fondest desires were shattered; he had no hope but death. He closed this section as he opened it, with the despair of the grave (16:22–17:2). This despair was not quite as reprehensible as was their faulty advice.

3. Bildad (18:1–21)

Following the pattern of Eliphaz and Zophar, only Bildad's opening lines were directly addressed to Job (cf. 15:2–3 and 20:2–5 with vv.2–4 here). In the rest of the speech, with typical redundant and discursive rhetoric, he launched into a poem on the fate of the wicked. In this chapter Bildad made no attempt to admonish Job as he had done in 8:5–7, 20–22.

1–4 Bildad considered Job beside himself, a man no longer acting fully responsible. He resented Job's attitude toward them as belittling and accused Job of being irrationally self-centered. The world was going to remain the same no matter how much Job ranted against the order of things.

5–21 Bildad felt Job did not really understand the doctrine of retribution. He probably considered Job weak on this subject because Job kept harping on how the righteous suffer and the wicked prosper. Bildad's concern was to establish in Job's mind the absolute certainty that every wicked person gets paid in full, in this life, for his or her wicked deeds. He said nothing of a final judgment but was sure the lamp of the wicked would be snuffed out. As their step weakens, they are trapped and devoured. "Terrors startle him on every side and dog his every step." Death is part of the punishment, not a dividing line after which punishment comes. The only after-death retribution for Bildad was having one's memory (name) cut off, with no offspring or survivors. Death is personified in vv.13–14.

4. Job's reply (19:1–29)

The chapter divides into four logical stanzas. In the first Job shows increasing irritation over his counselors' shameless attacks and his impatience with their superior claims (vv.2–5). Then follow Job's feeling of abandonment by God and his perception that God's attack on him is wrong (vv.6–12). Then he blames God for alienating his kinsmen and household, even his wife (vv.13–20). In vv.21–27 he ends this lament, to our amazement, with a triumphant expression of faith in the one who will ultimately champion his cause and vindicate him (vv.23–27). This stanza is bracketed by words to his friends whom Job does not believe will ever have pity (v.21). So he warns them of the dire consequences of their false accusations (vv.28–29).

1–12 Verse 4 literally reads "my error lives [remains] with me." Job implied his friends had no right to interfere, no right to behave as if they were God (cf. v.22).

Job's words in v.6—"God has wronged me"—are the very thoughts that elicited Bildad's retort, "Does God pervert justice?" (8:3), and later Elihu's words, "It is unthinkable that God would do wrong, that the Almighty would pervert justice" (34:12). The only way to handle Job's words is that it was Job's faulty perception that caused him to perceive things in this way. He did not know God's plan (42:2). But even without heavenly knowledge, Job's perception was better than Bildad's, who also lacked the heavenly knowledge that it was God who was permitting the Accuser to strike Job.

In a sense the Accuser was acting as the hand of God, for he had said to God, "But stretch out your hand and strike his flesh" (2:5). And God had replied, "Very well, then, he is in your hands" (2:6). So Job was not totally wrong when he said, "The hand of God has struck me" (19:21). Bildad could not begin to appreciate Job's predicament. And because he had reduced God and his actions to an impersonal formula, Bildad was incapable of showing any mercy toward Job.

In Job's mind God was at war with him. God's troops laid siege as if Job were a fortified city; but, alas, he was only a tent. In a series of largely military images, the tension of Job's lament rises with each succeeding verse; but the chronological sequence is in reverse of the way it really happened. In v.8 his paths are blocked or walled up, that is, he is taken in captivity. In v.9 he suffers royal dethronement—stripped of his honor and crown as a defeated king (see his words in 29:14, where Job claimed righteousness and justice as his robe and turban). In v.10 he is torn down (like a wall) and uprooted (like a tree, more drastic than the figure in 14:7). And finally in vv.11–12 God's troops advance and build a siege ramp against him. Reverse this order and you have a step-by-step description of what happened in siege warfare.

13–19 Leaving this compelling figure, Job spoke quite literally of how his family and friends had turned against him. In any society nothing hurts more than rejection by one's family and friends, but what could be worse in a patriarchal society than to have children ridicule the patriarch?

20 What does escaping with only the skin of one's teeth mean? The NIV suggests that only Job's gums were left unaffected by his ailment. The KJV made a literal translation of it and thereby created an idiom for a narrow escape. But is Job talking about a narrow escape here?

Up to this point Job had come to the conclusion that he was soon to die (10:20; 16:22–17:1). His experience created in him a sense of amoral chaos in the world and in his life. His sense of being crushed caused him to look repeatedly toward death as a kind of hopeless release (14:18–22; 16:11–16). He knew he was innocent and sought above all else to be vindicated. His compassionless counselors had reiterated their impersonal theology that declared him guilty. He felt that God was angry with him and had become the enemy who attacked and crushed him. He perceived that he was alone in a cruel and amoral world. There was no one left who understood, no one to plead his cause or bear witness to his innocence. And this was what he wanted most of all, not release, not retribution, but only justice, someone to vindicate him.

In two earlier chapters (9; 16) where he expressed deep bitterness toward God, Job also touched on this same "Advocate" theme. In ch. 9 it was only a desire—"If only there were someone to arbitrate between us" (9:33). But in chs. 16 and 19 it becomes a firm conviction—"my witness is in heaven" (16:19) and

"I know that my Redeemer lives" (19:25). As in 13:15, here in ch. 19 this hope extends to include Job himself as a participant in the process of vindication—"I myself will see him on my side" (v.27).

21 Deserted by loved ones, Job needed radical friendship, not theological banter. This was not the first time Job called for pity (cf. 6:14). It is necessary to feel with Job his sense of total desertion if we are to understand the passage. It is within this context that he turned to God in vv.25–26.

22 Job's appeal failed. He thought his counselors had joined forces with God as "the hound of heaven" to sniff him out and to be in on the kill (cf. 16:9). Although Job's perception of God may have been wrong (not understanding the role of Satan, the Accuser), his perception of them was correct. They had presumed to take on themselves the role of divine judicial authority (e.g., see 15:11a, where Eliphaz assumed his words were God's words). As part of the "Chase" metaphor, in v.22b Job included a typical Semitic idiom for slander—they devour his flesh.

23–24 These words arise from Job's desire to defend his integrity. Believing that he was at the point of death, Job felt he had nothing to lose by speaking out (7:7–11; 10:1; 13:3, 13–28; 16:18). But they are also a direct response to Bildad's taunt in 18:17, suggesting Job would be permanently forgotten (cf. Pr 10:7). With no hope left of proving his righteousness, Job looked to the future, leaving his case with posterity (Ps 102:18). His wish to inscribe his words was uttered with poetic expansiveness that contemplated possible ways—in a scroll or on a rock. Whether the lead was to be used on the rock or was another medium is not clear. Permanency is the issue—inscribed forever.

25–29 Are these the only words Job wanted inscribed or did he mean all his words where he had over and over proclaimed his innocence? The conjunction that begins v.25 (not reflected in NIV) may be the word "but." This would mean that Job was leaving the thought of inscribing his words permanently to the even more favorable situation of having a living "Redeemer" who would champion his cause even after he was gone. Job's hope in the midst of despair reached a climax.

Slandered by his friends and with death imminent, Job looked to the future where his Defender waited. This time it seems as if the "Redeemer" is God himself, for there is no mention of his Defender pleading with God (as in 9:33–35; 16:19–21).

The meaning of the word *goel* ("Redeemer"; GK 1457) is fundamental to understanding this passage. The word had both a criminal and a civil aspect. As "blood avenger," a *goel* had a responsibility to avenge the blood of a slain kinsman (Nu 35:12–28). Such a person was not seeking revenge but justice. On the civil side he was a redeemer or vindicator (cf. "kinsman-redeemer" in Ru 3–4). Here such a person had the responsibility to "buy back" and so redeem the lost inheritance of a deceased relative. This might come by purchasing from slavery or marrying his relative's widow in order to provide an heir. As such he was the defender or champion of the oppressed. A *goel* also delivers individuals from death, as is testified of the Lord in Ps 103:4.

Here Job had something more in mind than one who would testify to his integrity. In 16:18 he cried, "O earth, do not cover my blood." Job saw himself a murder victim. He depended on his *goel* to testify for him but also to set the books straight. God, who had become his enemy, would become his friend, and those who had joined in the kill would be punished (vv.28–29).

In Hebrew the emphatic position of the pronoun "I" in v.25a shows Job had a settled conviction: "I, yes I know." The words "my Redeemer [Vindicator]" indicate a personal relationship, and the word "lives" (GK 3782) must mean more than merely "alive" but implies he would continue his work of vindicating Job's integrity and avenging Job's death, as Job implied in vv.28–29.

Does "upon the dust [GK 6760]" mean "upon the earth" (NIV) or does it mean "upon my grave" (cf. NIV note)? The term refers to the grave in 7:21; 17:16; 20:11; 21:26 (cf. Ps 22:29; Isa 26:19); but it can mean "the earth," as in Job 41:33. So Job may have meant merely that the human arena here on earth is where his Vindicator would testify; but since the context is about Job's decaying body, it may be a specific reference to his grave. Are, then, vv.26–27 a reference to Job's resurrection? In 14:10–14 Job said nothing about general eschatological resurrection;

but he believed in God's power to raise the dead and had a desire and hope that God would set a time and raise him. Similarly here in ch. 19, we may see a resurrection in which Job would see God with his own eyes and as his friend. While he was anticipating the doctrine of resurrection, he was not spelling out the teaching of a final resurrection for all the righteous.

Verse 26a is a most difficult line. Literally it reads "after my skin they have struck off—this!" The general meaning alludes to the ravages of Job's disease. Verse 26b is clearer. Job expected to see God. Job was convinced that even if he died, he would live again to witness his own vindication.

At the end of ch. 16 Job was obsessed with the notion that someone in heaven would stand up for him and plead his case. But here in ch. 19 he expected to witness his own vindication on earth. Indeed, his own eyes would gaze on his Vindicator. As it turned out, Job did not need the intermediary mentioned in ch. 16 because his idea that God was against him proved to be without foundation. The lesson that suffering does not show that God is alienated is one of the most enduring themes in the book. Job's feelings of alienation and the condemnation by his friends produced in him a consequent feeling of need for a Redeemer (Vindicator), which is strongly evocative of a sinner's basic need before a holy God (cf. 1Ti 2:5–6). But in Job's case, as an innocent sufferer, he finally realized that God himself would appear to him, whom he would see with his own eyes (cf. 19:27 with 42:5); then Job would learn that his God was not alienated or unconcerned but was both his Vindicator (*goel*) and his friend.

5. Zophar (20:1–29)

1–3 Zophar took Job's words, especially his closing words in 19:28–29, as a personal affront. Job had dared to assert that on Zophar's theory of retribution, Zophar himself was due for punishment. To him such could only happen to the wicked. Zophar was the most emotional of the three; and he was not about to let Job's rebuke go unanswered, though in ch. 19 Job had earnestly pled for a withdrawal of their charges. Here he had nothing new to say to Job but said it with passion. The speech is full of terrifying imagery.

4–11 Zophar could not abide the thought that the wicked prosper. Underneath the words lie the comfortable fact that he was a healthy and prosperous man, which, in his view, was itself proof of his goodness and righteousness. To him the joy and vigor of the wicked would always be brief and like a fantasy. Oppressing the poor is the mark of the truly wicked (vv.10, 19). On this subject Job had no quarrel with Zophar (see 31:16–23). But, of course, he denied being that kind of person.

12–19 The evil person's wicked deeds, especially robbing the poor, are tasty food that pleases the palate but turns sour in the stomach. God will force such a one to vomit up ill–gained riches. In his peroration (chs. 29–31) Job would stress his own social conscience and strongly deny Zophar's veiled accusation.

20–28 When a wicked person's belly is filled and there is nothing left for him to devour, God then vents his anger against him. The man flees from an iron weapon only to be shot in the back by a glittering bronze arrow that must be pulled out of his liver. Such attention to figurative detail is often overlooked as meaningless. On the contrary, the more eloquently it could be said, the more the ancient speaker was able to convey how deeply he felt and how sincerely he was trying to make his point. But Zophar, despite his eloquence and sincerity, had no compassion. He left no room for repentance and put all his stress on the importance of material possessions, while Job at this point was increasingly concerned over his relationship with God, no matter what happened to his body or possessions (19:23–27).

29 Like Bildad in 18:21, Zophar concluded his speech with a summary statement in which he claimed all he had said was in accord with God's judicial order for the wicked.

6. Job's reply (21:1–34)

In this closing speech of the second cycle, Job was determined to prove that he had listened to what his counselors had said. This he did by quoting or otherwise alluding to their words and then refuting them.

1–3 If the counselors could give Job no other consolation, they should have at least paid close attention to his words. Evidently he sensed that the dialogue was about to break up since he implied the other parties were not even listening.

4–6 Job was appalled at the counselors' failure to have any compassion; but if his complaint were only against them as human beings, he thought his bitterness would not be justified. His rage was based on the idea that God may be responsible. Job was terrified because he knew how awesome a task it is to complain against God. Yet in all honesty, he could find no other way out of his predicament. Job's anguish over not understanding what God was doing is proof that he was not indifferent or arrogant. It was the counselors who assumed they knew what was going on.

7–15 The counselors had elaborated on the horrible fate of the wicked (15:20–35; 18:5–21) against Job's claim that the wicked often prosper. Those who wish to know nothing of God's ways, who even consider prayer a useless exercise, flourish in all aspects of their lives. Far from dying prematurely, as Zophar said in 20:11, they live long and increase in strength. Bildad's claim that the wicked have no offspring or descendants to remember them (18:19–21) was flatly denied by Job. Job painted a word picture in vv.7–13, illustrating the domestic pleasantness and prosperity often enjoyed by godless people who dare to defy the Almighty.

16 The NIV has not caught fully the correct interpretation. The way Eliphaz used these same words in 22:17–18 helps interpret Job's words. What Job was saying was, in effect, "Look, the prosperity of the wicked is from God, despite the fact that their counsel is far from him" (cf. Ps 1:1). "Why *do* the wicked live on . . . increasing in power?" (v.7; emphasis mine).

17–21 Job alluded directly to Bildad's words in 18:5, with the retort "How often. . . ?" And if children have to pay for their father's sins as Eliphaz (5:4) and Zophar (20:10) said, then the wicked being evil are encouraged to say, "What do we care?" (cf. v.21). Job was disturbed at the apparent injustice of it all. He felt that immediate punishment for the wicked would be the only just procedure; but he found just the opposite in life. Again failure to understand fully God's ways had led both Job and the counselors astray; yet Job did not pretend to understand, but they did. Moreover, Job was suffering physically and emotionally, and they were not.

22–26 Job admitted that his knowledge of God's ways was defective, but it was precisely his high view of God that had created a problem. Those who do not believe in an absolutely sovereign God cannot possibly appreciate the depth of the problem Job presented. Even with all our additional revelation (Ro 8:28), we often stand in anguish over the apparent injustice and seeming cruelty of God's providence.

27–33 Job realized his counselors were going to repeat the same worn-out clichés that implied he was a wicked man. He called these clichés schemes by which they wronged him. He challenged them to investigate the total experience of people throughout the world to determine whether he was right. He was saying that it is impossible to derive a just law of retribution from what we observe in this present world. Their simplistic view was wrong, claimed Job, for all too often there is no one to denounce the wicked for what they have done, and there is no one to punish them. Contrary to the description of the wicked in chs. 8 and 20, the ungodly are often buried with the highest honors.

34 Job opened this discourse with a plea for a kind of consolation based on his counselors' quiet listening. He closed by returning to that thought with a blast at what they had offered as consolation, their answers riddled with falsehood and nonsense.

D. The Third Cycle of Speeches (22:1–26:14)

1. Eliphaz (22:1–30)

Eliphaz, the least vindictive, was provoked to agree with his friends that Job had been a very wicked man (vv.4–5). He did not even attempt to answer Job's shocking statements in ch. 21 but moved on to accuse Job of various social sins (vv.6–11) and of failing to appreciate the wonderful attributes of God, especially God's omniscience (vv.13–14) and his justice, goodness, and mercy (vv.16–18). All Eliphaz felt he could do for Job was to make a final plea for repentance (vv.21–30).

1–3 Eliphaz was here reacting to Job's notion that God allowed human wickedness to go unpunished (ch. 21), and in his reactionary mood he went to the opposite extreme of suggesting there is nothing that people can do to benefit God. This is the now familiar unbalanced stress on divine transcendence: the concept that human beings are nothing in God's eyes and that even their virtue is useless. God does not need us; it is we who need him. Since everything has its origin in God, our giving it back—even in service—does not enhance God in any way.

Verse 3 carries the thought a step further. A translation that fits well into the context might be: "Would it please the Almighty if you were vindicated? Would he gain anything if you did live a blameless life?" Two observations are in order. (1) Eliphaz did not know of God's contest with the Accuser over Job's former blameless life (chs. 1–2). The Almighty had especially chosen Job to be an instrument through whom he would gain glory and the Accuser be humiliated. (2) Eliphaz seemed so convinced of Job's wickedness—even to the point of exaggeration (v.5)—that he did not believe he could be vindicated. So in his mind Job's blamelessness was hypothetical nonsense. For Job to be vindicated would be a lie; so how could God take pleasure in that?

4–11 Verse 4 is pure irony. In 4:6 Eliphaz had been sincere about Job's "piety" (GK 3711), but here he spoke of it tongue-in-cheek. He no longer believed Job was basically a God-fearing man. Job's troubles were God's rebuke. That they were great testified to the extent of his sin. So Eliphaz felt free, perhaps obligated, to expound on the possible nature of those sins. Job's sins are described in terms of social oppression and neglect. In other words, Eliphaz felt Job had deceived himself by trusting in his ritual piety (what he had done for God) while his real sin was what he failed to do for his fellow human beings. For this God sent snares and peril, darkness and floods. These were not literal but commonly used figures of trouble and distress.

12–20 As noted, Eliphaz's tone had been more positive and sympathetic than the others, but here he threw the weight of his argument with Bildad and Zophar, though not completely. Having become convinced Job was a man who followed the path of the ungodly, Eliphaz used Job's own words to refute him. Had not Job complained that the blessing of the wicked was God's doing (21:13–16)? Eliphaz turned that around by saying that the wicked are destroyed before their time, i.e., before they can fully enjoy the good things God provides.

21–30 Eliphaz was, no doubt, sincere in this his last attempt to reach Job through a call to repentance. This call for Job to submit; to be at peace with God; to hear God's word and hide it in his heart; to return to the Almighty and forsake wickedness; to find delight in God rather than in gold; and to pray, obey, and become concerned about sinners could not be improved upon by any prophet or evangelist.

There are some problems, however, that beset these powerful words. They assume Job was an ungodly man and that his major desire was a return to health and prosperity. But Job was not ungodly, and he had already made clear his desire to see God and be his friend (19:25–27). Job's words have not always sounded friendly toward God, and Eliphaz did not have the capacity to understand the nature of Job's wrestling with God where Job expressed to God his deepest feelings of fear and his bafflement over what appeared to be an unjust and cruel providence. To Eliphaz's black-and-white mentality, those words (backed by Job's troubles) were sad proof of Job's need to repent and "get right" with God. His assumption that Job did not know how to pray aright would eventually be controverted by God himself, and Eliphaz would have to depend on Job's prayers (42:8).

2. Job's reply (23:1–24:25)

While the meaning of ch. 23 is quite clear, scholars have seen serious problems in ch. 24. In addition to the difficulties in making sense of the text, there is the issue of determining whose words these are. Since there is no agreement, it seems wiser to let the text stand and above all refuse to force modern categories of logic and rhetoric on it.

In the final verses of ch. 23, Job made his apology for his emotional language, which had been so misunderstood by his friends. He had been terrified by what he came to accept as God's plan for his life (vv. 14–16). The mystery, however, was still there. Job did not understand what God was doing. So in all honesty he still needed to speak out and call for the thick darkness to be removed (v.17).

1–2 Job was becoming less fractious. A play on words in v.2 leaves somewhat open the question of whether he was still rebellious or just bitter.

3–7 Job's spiritual movement during this dispute is evident again when we compare his attitude about a hearing with God in ch. 9 with his thoughts on the same subject here. Job still wanted a fair trial, for he was certain he was blameless, i.e., above the charges that had been made. He doubted in 9:14–20 that God would even give him a hearing and that even while pleading for mercy he would be crushed. At this point he admitted he was not totally innocent (9:15–20), though he still considered himself blameless (9:21). After Zophar's abuse in ch. 11, where he was flatly labeled a wretched sinner (11:5, 14), Job reacted with a bolder assertion of his blamelessness (13:13–15). In ch. 22 we noticed how Eliphaz, the least accusatory of the three, had moved closer to the others with his quip, "Are not your sins endless?" (22:5). So here Job reasserted his claim to be an upright man with renewed confidence that God agreed with him. This is why having an audience with God was very important to Job. He continued to be positive (13:18) about the outcome of such an encounter (23:6–7).

Our knowledge of the doctrine of justification by faith with its premise of human depravity (cf. Ro 1–3) makes it difficult for us to understand this part of the message of the book of Job. It is helpful to look on Job as illustrative of Christ, who also suffered unjustly to fulfill the purpose of God (cf. Joseph, Ge 37–50). We have seen how Job's upright life was so rooted in the fear of God that even God himself used Job as an example of godliness (1:8; 2:3). So Job was not wrong in calling for his own vindication (Pss 17:2–3; 26:1–3; et al.).

8–12 Job was still frustrated, however, over the matter of finding God (cf. v.3). He could not find him (but cf. 42:5). Though he wrestled with God verbally, he had no immediate sense of God's presence nor of God's voice communicating with him. Yet in reply to Eliphaz (22:21), Job claimed to have heard God's words and treasured them in his heart.

He rejected Eliphaz's call for him to return to God (22:23), for he felt he had never turned away from God in the first place. Job did not think God was testing him as a means to purge away his sinful dross. It was rather to prove he was pure gold. Job's words have to be the words either of a terrible hypocrite or of a deeply committed believer.

13–17 The literal Hebrew expression in v.13 is a monotheistic affirmation: "He [God] is the unique [one]." Job's God was the same as Israel's God—he is the only one; there is no other (Dt 6:4). As the all-powerful sovereign Deity, God did what he pleased. Job's fear (vv.15–16) was the necessary corollary to the truth that God was sovereign and therefore could not be put in a box and be told what he could and could not do by human beings. What might this God who does what he pleases have had in mind for Job? A real part of the living faith Job expressed in vv.8–12 was his determination not to be silenced despite the darkness he felt over the intention of God, who had no one to answer to for his behavior.

24:1 Job now expressed the mood that dominates in this chapter—a complaint on why God did not set straight the balance of justice. Job felt God should demonstrate his justice by openly punishing the wicked. In the divine speeches God would teach him a tremendous lesson about this, which he did not now understand: The principle of retribution does not operate mechanically in this world but according to the divine will.

In this chapter Job presented a picture of a world that was still a deep enigma to him. His courageous honesty led him to expound on the mystery of how the wicked get by unpunished while they perform their evil deeds against the innocent.

2–12 The wicked are so brazen they pasture stolen flocks on stolen land. Since the orphan is without inheritance, his donkey represents all he owns. Job appreciated those ancient civil laws that protected widows and the orphans (cf. Ex 22:22). Job cited the pitiful case of the destitute who had to carry food while they themselves went hungry and had to tread the winepress while they suffered thirst. The great enigma is that all this was going on and God did nothing (cf. Ps 73:2–3; Hab 1:13; Mal 3:15).

13–17 The murderer, the adulterer, and the thief share a characteristic that is self-condemning: they all love darkness rather than the light (cf. 38:12–15; Ps 82:5).

18–24 Although these words may not sound like Job's sentiments about the wicked, Job never claimed the wicked always prosper or never come to a bad end. His problem was that God treats the good and bad alike.

25 It is strange that Job spoke as if he had just made an argument against the views of his friends rather than partially agreeing with them. After developing a series of vignettes about the deeds of the wicked and the sufferings of their victims (vv.1–17), Job finally mouthed the view of his friends about God's judgment on the wicked. Job may have been either quoting them with irony or complaining that this judgment comes piecemeal, a little here and a little there (see esp. vv.23–24).

Eventually the wicked die and are forgotten; they lack security and have their day only for a little while (22:16–18)—but where are the great days of stored-up judgment so the righteous can be sure that justice for such horrors is meted out? Job was not convinced that piecemeal judgment was truly just, since the righteous often suffered the same. There is no direct teaching of final judgment to set right the balance of justice, but there is a concept here that anticipates the teaching that God must have his day.

3. Bildad (25:1–6)

This is the last we hear from Job's three counselors. Perhaps they had exhausted their arguments.

1–3 Bildad did not bother to answer Job's recent argument. He only repeated what had already been said by Eliphaz (4:17–21; 15:14–16). Bildad wanted to show how God's power established order in the heavenly realm and that his dominion extends to all created beings.

4–6 God's majesty palls everything (moon and stars), and it reaches everywhere. So how can any person be considered righteous or pure in God's eyes? Bildad's point was that human beings are maggots in God's eyes.

Eliphaz was the first to question the possibility of anyone's purity before God (4:17). In ch. 8 Bildad's words left the door open only for those who were truly blameless (8:20). Job, repeating the issue in 9:2, wanted to know how he could prove his blamelessness since God was so inaccessible. In 15:14–16 Eliphaz came very close to a nihilistic view of the human race—they are hopelessly "vile and corrupt, who drink up evil like water!" But in ch. 22 Eliphaz left the door open for Job to be restored, but not on the basis of mercy, for he must bear the penalty for whatever he has done. Then if there is repentance, Job could be restored (22:21–23). But Bildad repeated the old question of 9:2 with an implied negative answer. If God is inaccessible, it is because he is too pure; and a human being, like Job, is a hopeless worm.

4. Job's reply (26:1–14)

1–4 Bildad struck a most sensitive nerve. In all Job's speeches nothing had been more important to him than his determination to be vindicated, to be shown blameless in God's tribunal. Bildad has just labeled that impossible. Job could not restrain himself. He leveled a sarcastic reply directly at the speaker. He had nothing but contempt for Bildad's wisdom. In his colorful ironic exclamations, he considered himself powerless, feeble, and without wisdom, but not a maggot. If Bildad would only impute to him the dignity every human being deserves, he could have some compassion.

Job wanted to know who "wrote" Bildad's material. He certainly knew Bildad was mouthing Eliphaz's words (4:17). Job considered inane Bildad's argument that the majesty and power of God are the reasons why humanity cannot be righteous before him. It is proof of the poverty of his thought. It angered Job because he knew they all agreed that he was a reprobate sinner and so had given up the idea that he was an upright person temporarily suffering for sins. No, he was a worm whose case was hopeless. So Job dared to remind them that they too were hopeless as counselors.

5–6 The term translated "the dead" (GK 8327) means "shades or spirits of the dead." Here they tremble as God casts his eye on them in Sheol. But who are those that "live in the waters"? Job's earlier allusion to Sheol as "the land of gloom and deep shadow" (10:21) is like this passage. It is possible that those "beneath the waters" are those conceived of

as buried in "the lowest pit, in the darkest depths" (Ps 88:6). The thrust of these verses is that there is no place hidden from God. Job's remark was an emphatic rejoinder to Bildad's statement (25:3) that the light of God shines on everyone. Even "Sheol" (see NIV note; GK 8619) and "Abaddon" (see NIV note; GK 11) provide no hiding place from the searching eye of God (cf. Pr 15:11).

7–8 The word "skies" is a justifiable insertion in v.7. Although *saphon* means "north" (GK 7600), the verb "spreads out" is never used of the earth but is often used in reference to the heavens (cf. 9:8). This imagery is continued by the words "over empty space." It is difficult to postulate what "empty space" might be intended by Job if he were referring to a northern region of the earth where the majestic mountains rise.

Job was pointing to God's power as incomprehensible. The heavens are visible; yet they do not fall to earth; there is no visible means of support. Even the earth itself can be said to hang on nothing. That God can spread out the heavens over empty space, hang the earth on nothing, and fill the clouds with water without their bursting is intended to make us stand in awe. Job was boldly expressing in poetic terms the marvelous and majestic power of God.

9 God uses the clouds to enshroud him in his lofty abode (Ps 104:3–13; Am 9:6). He appears in heaven in golden splendor and awesome majesty. But people can no more look at him directly than they can look at the sun (37:21–22).

10 The NIV interprets the literal Hebrew "he draws a circle" as God's establishment of the horizon, which acts as the line of demarcation between light and darkness (day and night). Job was ascribing to God, and not to the incantations and rituals of the nature cults, the authority and dominion over night and day.

11 Here the mountains are called the "pillars of the heavens" while in 9:6 they are the "pillars of the earth." They are pillars because their foundations go beneath the waters of the sea (Jnh 2:6) and reach to the clouds as if supporting the vault of the sky. The thought was common that the earth would shake at its foundations when God expressed his anger (Ps 18:7, 15; Isa 2:19, 21; et al.). Such phenomenological language was based on volcanoes and earthquakes. The force exerted by a thunderclap (Ps 77:18) is perceived as "the blast of the breath from your [God's] nostrils" (Ps 18:15).

12–13 Job continued his exaltation of God as Creator and Ruler of all nature. In the process he demythologized the language of the popular myths that described creation as the overcoming of chaos. Job's intent to demythologize is quite evident. Here the sea that God subdues is not the pagan deity Yam. Job depersonalized Yam by using the definite article ("*the* sea"), thus expressing his innate monotheistic theology. The Akkadian hero god Marduk employed seven winds to overthrow Tiamat (the chaotic goddess of the Deep); here God's own breath clears the heavens. All the power of the wind is his breath. Further, by his own wisdom, skill, and power he "cut Rahab to pieces" and "pierced the gliding serpent," unlike the pagan Marduk who depended on the enablement of the father-gods.

A study of the OT names for the well-known Canaanite mythological sea monsters like Rahab shows how purposefully the OT authors used that language to enrich their own poetic conceptions of the supremacy of the one and only true God. This is especially true of poetry that deals with cosmological, historical, and eschatological themes (cf. Ps 89:9–10).

Making the heavens beautifully bright by his breath could be a reference to the creation account of Genesis, when God separated the light from the darkness of the initial chaos (Ge 1:2–4); but it more likely refers to the clearing of the skies after a storm. Job, then, demonstrated God's authority over the domain of Mot (the god of death) in vv.5–6 and over the domain of Baal (the cosmic storm god) in vv.7–10. And in vv.12–13 Job drew attention to God's awe-inspiring power over the domain of Yam (the stormy sea god; cf. Mt 8:23–27, where Jesus demonstrated his divine power over storms as the Son of Man).

14 For Job these manifestations and deeds are but mere shadows or whispers of the smallest part of God's might. How beautifully and humbly Job asserted the majestic omnipotence of God! But he ended the poem convinced of the mystery that surrounds that omnipotence.

The sea monster Rahab is often equated with Egypt. In Egyptian mythology, the serpent Apep (depicted here) is Ra/Re's most dangerous foe; Apep is also slain and cut up. Likewise in Job 26:12, Rahab is cut up by the Lord. Drawing by Rachel Bierling.

E. Job's Closing Disclosure (27:1–23)

The change from "Then Job replied" to "And Job continued his discourse" marks a separate discourse (ch. 27), probably as a concluding statement by Job to balance the introductory statement in ch. 3. This poem is mainly about God's just punishment of the wicked. Job opened by denying he was such, though his counselors had so labeled him.

1–6 An oath based on the existence of God was the most extreme measure available (the last resort) in Job's society for a condemned person to plead innocent. Either he was innocent, or he would suffer the divine sanctions; for if Job was a liar, he was blaspheming God. He was saying that his integrity (blamelessness, not sinlessness) was more important to him than life itself. But Job did not fear death because he spoke the truth. He knew he could swear before God without forfeiting his life. He felt God had denied him justice but inconsistently still knew that somehow God was just; so he could swear by his life.

We have little difficulty agreeing that God never does wrong—until tragedy comes into our lives. Then we may begin to ask ourselves what we have done wrong, or we may even question God's goodness. Deep down we know that neither question is right. So Job too emphatically denied either alternative. He was throwing the mystery into God's lap, as it were, and leaving it there. Here at the very heart of the problem of evil, the book of Job lays the theological foundation for an answer that Job's faith anticipates but which Job did not fully know. God, the

Sovereign and therefore responsible Creator, would himself in the person of his eternal Son solve this human dilemma by bearing the penalty of the sins of humankind, thus showing himself to be both just and the justifier (vindicator) of all who trust in him (Ro 3:26).

7–10 Job's oath is followed by an imprecation against his detractors. The imprecation had a juridical function and was frequently a hyperbolic means (cf. Pss 109:6–15; 139:7–9) of dealing with false accusation and oppression. Legally the false accusations and the very crimes committed are called down on the perpetrator's head. Since the counselors had falsely accused Job of being wicked, they deserved to be punished like the wicked. They knew nothing of mercy though Job pled for it (19:21). They spoke only of God's justice and power; yet they would soon become the objects of God's mercy despite Job's imprecation, which was later changed to prayer on their behalf (42:7–9). The imprecation was a dramatic means by which Job, as a blameless man, declared himself on God's side.

11–12 Here Job added a warning and made an application directly to his "friends." He was reminding them of an issue on which they all agreed—that the wicked deserve God's wrath. But they had put Job in that category falsely. He did not have to explain to them about God's ability to set things straight.

13–23 Job expounds here eloquently the subject the counselors know so much about—the fate of the wicked—to dramatize the punishment they deserved for their false and arrogant accusation. The reference is to God in v.23, not to the storm in the preceding verse. Also, "his place" at the end of v.23 means "heaven," God's place. The verse should read: "He claps his hands against them and hisses at them from his dwelling [heaven]."

III. Interlude on Wisdom (28:1–28)

This poem stresses a typical theme: the inaccessibility of wisdom except through piety. But it appears to be more than that. No speaker is identified at the beginning of the poem, though one might assume the author meant it to be Job. Job was frustrated and unable to find a wisdom solution to the mystery behind his suffering. The counselors had

been only a hindrance. The change in style and the irenic tone may be the Hebrew author giving his judgment on the previous speeches. So the theme—"Where can you find wisdom?"—is certainly not extraneous. The poem develops the theme with skill by first concentrating on the inquisitive nature and technological ability that enable a person to find the riches of the earth no matter how difficult they are to obtain (vv.1–11). The second stanza dwells on the value of wisdom and its scarcity compared with even the greatest treasure on earth (vv.13–19). The third stanza (vv.21–28) finally addresses the question asked in the refrain. Wisdom has a source, but it is so elusive that only God knows the way to it. We can find it only when we fear God and honor him as God (v.28).

1–11 Earth's material riches have a source. The first two verses accomplish a rhetorical purpose; they set the tone without explicitly stating the theme (see comment on vv.12–14).

Verses 3–11 illustrate ancient technological ability in mining. Searching in the blackest darkness required light. This could be accomplished by cutting a shaft and letting in sunlight or by torches. The ability to cut shafts through rock is seen in the elaborate "waterworks" in cities like Jerusalem and Megiddo, long before the tunnel of Hezekiah, whose Siloam Inscription tells of the rigors of boring through hard limestone. Copper was mined in Edom and the Sinai Peninsula.

While there was no gold in Palestine, Egypt controlled rich mines in Nubia. As for iron, it was not used widely in Palestine till shortly before 1200 B.C., but there is evidence of working terrestrial iron (as opposed to meteorite iron) back to about 6000 B.C. The OT reflects Israel's lack of technical knowledge in smelting and smithing iron before the time of David. The Philistine monopoly is mentioned in 1Sa 13:19–21. Iron mining was developed on the plateau east of the Jordan Valley, and clay in the floor of the valley was used in making large bronze castings for Solomon's temple (1Ki 7:46).

Apart from the translation difficulties at the beginning of v.4, we now have knowledge of miners being lowered down deep shafts in cages or baskets. Verse 5 could be a reference to volcanic action, but there is ancient evidence of shaft mining where fire was used to split rocks and to reach ore. In their search for treasure, human beings reach paths that even a falcon's eye (one of the best in nature) cannot see. Where beasts at the top of the food chain cannot set foot, human hands touch as they lay "bare the roots of the mountain."

12–14 These verses are a refrain that states the main theme and is followed by a response. The response in v.13 is clearer when the Hebrew translated "comprehend its worth" is rendered "know its abode." Observe how as a refrain, vv.12–14 are parallel in form and meaning with vv.20–22. In v.14 "the deep" and "the sea" give the same negative response as do "Destruction" and "Death" in v.22. The thrust is that even if one were able to probe these inaccessible places, wisdom could not be found.

15–19 Here wisdom is given substance and objectivity so that the author could compare the search for it with the human search for treasures of gold, etc. Human intelligence and determination may enable people to accomplish amazing feats of technical ingenuity, but left to themselves they cannot find wisdom. The author piles up words for precious metals and stones to lay stress on how exceedingly rare and costly wisdom is. Humans may be clever, even ingenious and wealthy, but they are rarely wise.

20–22 Verses 12 and 20 are clearly the same refrain. Verses 13 and 21 give the same answer to the questions, though in different terms: v.13 stresses human ignorance of wisdom and v.21 nature's blindness to wisdom. That Destruction and Death have a rumor about wisdom probably means those who reach that place have a belated understanding they missed in life (cf. Lk 16:19–31).

23–27 The poem reaches its climax. God alone knows where the wisdom is, for he is omniscient. Human beings must search for their treasure, but God sees everything without searching. When he brought order out of the primeval chaos, he used wisdom to do it. Wisdom is the summary of the genius God used to fashion the universe (cf. Pr 3:19–20).

28 We must look to God for wisdom. To acknowledge him as God and to live within the sphere of his life-giving precepts is wisdom

for us (Dt 4:5–6; Ps 111:10; Pr 8:4–9; 9:10). In the process of studying God's revelation, we will learn that the price of wisdom—perfect obedience to God—is still beyond our reach (cf. Ro 11:33). In the spirit of Job 28, the apostle Paul assures us this mystery is hidden in Christ (Eph 3:8–10; Col 2:2–3).

IV. The Monologues (29:1–42:6)

A. Job's Peroration (29:1–31:40)

Like a lawyer summing up his case, Job began his monologue with an emotional recall of his former happiness, wealth, and honor (ch. 29) and proceeded to lament, not the loss of wealth, but the loss of his dignity and God's friendship (ch. 30). He completed this trilogy with a final protestation of his innocence (ch. 31). This chapter is an oath of innocence that effectively concludes with Job's signature in 31:35. There is no more Job could say; the case rested in God's hands. Job had to be shown to be a liar and suffer the punishment he called upon himself or be vindicated.

1. His past honor and blessing (29:1–25)

Chapter 29 deals with both active and passive aspects of Job's former life. He was blessed by God and honored by other people. But he was also socially active, a benefactor and leader. His benevolence was an important part of the high position he held in his society where social righteousness was expected of every ruling elder. So a description of Job's benevolence is in the climactic position in this oration, with the key line (v.14) in the exact middle of the poem. Such benevolence established his right to the honor and blessing the surrounding verses describe. This chapter then sets the stage for ch. 30.

1–6 Job longed for the precious days when he had enjoyed God's watchful care and guidance. God had been his friend. Job had enjoyed the blessings of family and wealth. Verse 6 sums up the blessing in figurative language that reminds us of the words used to describe Israel's blessing in the land of promise—there it was "milk and honey," here "cream" and "olive oil." Job had such abundance that only hyperbole can describe it—"drenched with cream" and "streams of olive oil."

7–11 The public square was the business center, town hall, and courthouse combined. We have no idea what city this was, but any city that had a gate and public square was a major urban center. Job was a city father who occupied a prominent seat. The reaction to Job in the square is fully in keeping with his culture and times. This deference to Job from young and old, princes and nobles, shows he was a ruler (cf. 1:3). Correct protocol demanded silence until the most honored person had spoken. Hushed, with their tongues sticking to the roof of their mouths, all waited in silence for Job to speak. Verse 11 implies that he had spoken and registers the effect.

12–17 These verses are a stanza about Job's social benevolence. Verse 14 stands in its center, and the entire stanza is the climax because it presents the reason he was so honored and blessed. In these few verses Job covered a large area of the social responsibility of rulers who aspired to be godlike (Ps 68:5). Literally Job said, "I put on righteousness and it robed me," implying a veritable incarnation of righteousness.

This passage should be read as instruction, as a stimulus to our social conscience. Job responded to the poorest of the poor, gave comfort to the dying and joy to widows, assisted the blind and lame, and assumed the role of father and advocate for those who had no one else to look to. He was not just a protector but militantly opposed the wicked. Job did not concentrate on religious responsibilities but on that area where humans most often fail—in their response to the sufferings of others. Although this stanza is idealistic—Job no doubt failed in some ways—it is to be accepted, not as self-righteousness, but as an eloquent testimony to the tenor of Job's life as "a blameless and upright" man who "feared God and shunned evil" (1:1, 8; 2:3).

18–20 The man who had provided for others faced the prospect of a shortened life instead of the patriarchal ideal of 110 years with family gathered about (cf. Ge 50:22). He had hoped to flourish "like a tree planted by streams of water" (Ps 1:3) and to remain strong and virile. But was Job thinking of his family in v.18? Perhaps not. The verse reads literally: "I thought, 'With [in] my nest I will expire [die].'" Translating "nest" as "house" (GK 7860) impairs the poetic effect.

In v.20 Job reflected on his former "glory" as a warrior and hunter. His "glory remaining fresh" means his continued prowess, vehemence, and splendor with weapons.

21–25 To bring to a balanced conclusion this first of the three connected poems, Job now returned to the theme of vv.7–11. His effect on others was charismatic. People waited expectantly to drink in his words. Even his smile carried a blessing (cf. Nu 6:24–25; Ps 4:6). So in this way Job again was godlike, so much so that his counsel was valued, his approval sought, and his leadership accepted with gratitude.

2. His present dishonor and suffering (30:1–31)

The threefold use of "But now" in 30:1, 9, 16 stresses the contrast with ch. 29. Job now dwelt on the negative side of the three themes of ch. 29 in the following order: honor, blessing, and benevolence. The removal of God's blessing is far worse than affliction by other human beings; so it was put in the climactic central position.

1–10 The conceptual correspondence with 29:7–11 is striking. Notice the emphasis on the young and old (29:8) and on the chief men and nobles (29:9–10). The highest strata in society had stood hushed in respect (29:9–10) and then had spoken well (29:11) of Job. Here the lowest riffraff mocked him. Indeed, they could not be kept quiet, for he had become a byword among them. There people had commended him (29:11); here they detested him. There they had covered their mouths with their hands (29:9); here they spit in his face.

11–15 These verses begin by taking us right back to 29:20, where Job had mused on his former life as a hero with his bow ever new in his hand. But here God has unstrung his bow. Earlier Job's tribe had gathered about to hear every good word that fell from the lips of their benevolent leader. But here he was no longer leading the way like "a king among his troops" (29:25). Instead he saw himself like a city under siege (civil war?). Verses 12–14 use the terminology of siege warfare. Job thought of himself as a city with a wide, gaping breach in its wall. The stones come crashing down, and amid the rubble the instruments of siege warfare roll through. The tranquility and dignity he had so enjoyed have vanished like a cloud.

16–23 Job shifted from this sorry relationship with his fellow human beings to an even sorrier subject, the removal of God's blessing from his life. He cried out to God but got no answer. When God was his friend, it was like having a light over him in the midst of darkness (29:3). But at this time his days were full of suffering and his nights full of misery. These verses show us that Job's basic complaint still remained. It was not only God's silence but his violent treatment of Job that had become the sufferer's greatest problem. It would be no problem at all if Job's concept of God were limited. That not being the case, in Job's mind it must have been God who was responsible for all this.

The NIV translation of v.18 does not do justice to the key word it renders "becomes" (GK 2924). It can mean "to disguise oneself" ("let oneself be searched for"; cf. 1Sa 28:8). Since God is all powerful, he can do anything. He can even disguise himself as Job's clothing and bind Job's neck at the collar. But the use here is more like Ob 6, where Esau "is plundered" or "exposed." Here perhaps Job's clothing "is ripped off," and in the process he is choked by the collar of his tunic and hurled into the mud.

Job saw his problem with God as twofold: God would not answer him, and God actively afflicted him. Job's only prospect for the future was death. What was so devastating to him was not the fear of death, for he had already asked for it as a relief (6:8–10; 14:3), but that he should have to face it with God as his enemy (13:24). God's constant attack, his ruthless might, was so completely the opposite of Job's "intimate friendship" with God in those bygone days when he had still perceived that God was on his side (29:4–5).

24–31 Here Job was in the position of those poor wretches to whom his heart and strength went out in 29:12–17. As a summation of his case, he packed his argument with emotion and righteous indignation. Justice was all on his side. The very benevolence he so freely had dispensed he now looked for in vain. Verse 26 also reminds us of his expectations in 29:18–20. So here he presented himself to the court as he was, his body marred and burning with fever; he himself was ex-

hibit A. As he often did, Job closed the stanza with a strong figure of speech (cf. 29:6, 14, 17, 25; 30:15). His "path had been drenched with cream" (cf. 29:6), now his "harp is tuned to mourning and [his] flute to the sound of wailing."

3. His negative confession and final oath (31:1–40)

We now arrive at the climax of the peroration. This chapter is a negative testament by which Job closes the matter of whether he was being punished for his sins. After such a statement, in the jurisprudence of the ancient Near East, the burden of proof fell on the court. That is why v.40 says that "the words of Job are ended." Each disavowal had to be accompanied by an oath that called for the same punishment the offense deserved on the basis of the principle of "an eye for an eye and a tooth for a tooth." Since the charges against Job were wide and varied, he needed to give a similarly wide disavowal. Here he specified and called for condemnation and punishment from both God and other people if he was guilty of any of those sins.

1–4 The covenant ban on Job's eyes parallels God's all-seeing eye (v.4), and these verses enclose vv.2–3, which speak of God's judgment on the wicked whose sins he sees. The lines are an introduction to Job's catalog of oaths protesting his loyalty to God. So Job, by declaring a covenant ban on his own eyes, appropriately brought to the fore the covenant theme that underlies and gives meaning to the oaths he was about to make.

Job's making a covenant with his eyes was not merely a promise not to lust after "a girl" (GK 1435). The sin he had in mind was more fundamental, or it would not have commanded this position in the poem. Job was emphatically denying an especially insidious and widespread form of idolatry: devotion to "the maiden," i.e., the goddess of fertility. As the Venus of the Semitic world, she was variously known as the Maiden Anat in Ugaritic, Ashtoreth in preexilic Israel (Jdg 2:13; 10:6; 1Sa 7:3–4; 1Ki 11:5, 33), and Ishtar in Babylon. She is probably the Queen of Heaven in Jer 7:18 and 44:16–19. Even token worship of the sun and moon is disavowed in the middle of the poem (vv.24–34); so a disavowal of the temptation to even look at the sex goddess is rendered likely when we keep in mind that "the maiden" in Ugaritic is precisely the word used here. The Hebrews were constantly warned about this ubiquitous fertility cult (cf. Dt 16:21–22; Hos 4:14).

The covenant-ban language of v.1 was a forceful way for Job to stress his allegiance to God, and the divine sanction in vv.2–3 was equivalent to the self-imprecation in the oath format (vv.6, 8, 10, 14, 22). Indeed that is the force of the imprecations, as may be seen by the references to God's judgment in almost every case.

5–8 In Job's world there were no atheists or even secularists. Everyone believed in the validity of divine sanction. This made the oath the ultimate test of integrity. Job opened the series of oaths by clearing himself of being false and deceitful. In v.6 he mentioned commercial dishonesty and moved on to clear himself of avarice. Clearly v.7 is talking about any evil deed his hands may have done; the verb translated "defiled" (GK 1415) really means "cling to." With God's honest scales in mind, Job completed the oath with a self-imprecation that would balance the scales: May he not get any gain from what his hands may plant!

9–12 From here to v.23 Job cleared himself of social sins. The sin of adultery heads the list. Adultery was heinous because it struck at the roots of the family and clan. In the Mosaic Law it was a capital offense (Lev 20:10). Here Job's hypothetical sin calls for "eye for eye" justice—the same would happen to his wife. The moral observation that follows states that adultery was an offense punished both by human law and by the law of God. In v. 12 Job used a striking figure also found in Dt 32:22, in which fire kindled by God's wrath "burns to Sheol" and "devours the earth and its harvests." "It" refers to the sin but by metonymy means "God's wrath on the sinner."

13–15 We may truly stand amazed at Job's egalitarian spirit, for he took seriously the rights of his servants (slaves?). He did not just admit their right to have grievances but to openly express them and expect justice. Even more amazing in terms of what we know about slavery in the OT world, Job based this right on the principle that all human beings are equal in God's sight, because he who created them all is both their Master and his, and that this Master shows no favor-

itism. So Job considered any act of injustice to those under him as an affront to God.

16–23 Eliphaz had already accused Job of gross sins against the poor in 22:6–9, and in 29:12–17 Job had spoken positively about the depth of his social conscience. Here he closed the issue with a series of oaths of clearance enforced by a final fierce self-imprecation. In v.16 "the desires of the poor" parallel "the eyes of the widow" and present a touching picture suggesting sensitivity to their wants beyond merely meeting basic needs for survival. In v.20 "his heart" really means "his loins." The force of the parallelism is lost unless one can feel the pathos of a shivering body thankfully warmed by Job's fleece. In v.21 the verb "I have raised" means literally "cuffing" the fatherless with impunity because of one's political power.

The breaking off of the offending arm creates a dramatic imprecation (cf. Mt 5:29–30). Verse 23 is meant to be a statement that applies to all the oaths; for it contains an absolutely necessary ingredient for such clearance oaths to have meaning—the fear of God, i.e., complete faith in his power to effect the curses. Thus such terror of God set Job to trembling.

24–28 Job began again with another firm denial of idolatry. But here the temptations are different. Instead of the appeal of the ever popular sex goddess, it is the appeal of gold and the apparent luster of two of the most commonly worshiped astral deities, the sun and moon. Job denied even secret homage to them.

29–34 Verses 31–32 can best be understood as Job's oath that his servants never complained about his lack of generosity. He had freely shared food and home with all who came his way. Despite the inconvenience, Job's servants were of one mind with him.

Job denied hypocrisy (i.e., hiding one's sins) in vv.33–34. That he admitted to sin is important to see since one might easily assume he was claiming perfection in this chapter. Reading behind the lines, one can appreciate how important an issue general knowledge of his sins might be and how great the temptation would be to maintain his public image (cf. v.21).

35–37 Job strategically brought his oration to its climax with a sudden change in tone. In

13:14–16 he was not so certain about his innocence and thought he might even put his life in jeopardy by calling for a hearing. He was now sure of his innocence, so confident of the truthfulness of these oaths that he affixed his signature and presented them as his defense with a challenge to God for a corresponding written indictment.

How does this brash attitude toward "his accuser" fit the statements accompanying the oaths about Job's fear of God's terror? This strange paradox in Job's mind that God, to whom he appealed for support, was also his adversary is the main point of the chapter. Fearing the terror of God (v.23) is meant for those who break covenant with him. Job knew he had not done this. But he could not deny the existential reality that he stood outside the sphere of covenant blessing. Something was wrong.

There was only one way Job knew to make this absurd situation intelligible. That was to appeal to his just and sovereign Lord as a vassal prince who had been falsely accused. Even though he had repeated it often, he obstinately refused to accept as final that God was his enemy. Job wanted God to reply to his defense with a list of the charges against him, so that whatever doubts were left may be publicly answered.

The opening words of the theophany (God's answer to Job in chs. 38–41) throw some light on the posture of Job in these verses. God rebuked Job's brashness (38:2–3) as a darkening of his counsel. And as for the proud prince wearing the indictment like a badge of honor, God set aside his majesty and assumed a human stance calling on Job to brace himself and prepare to wrestle with the Almighty.

38–40 These verses are clearly anticlimactic, but that does not mean they belong in another place in this chapter (cf. 3:23–26; 14:18–22). Job denied avarice. He had not eaten of the produce of his land by not paying for the labor or by cheating the tenant farmers. The second line of v.39 might mean "causing the death of the owners." In that case it is something similar to Jezebel's illegal seizure of Naboth's vineyard in 1Ki 21. That the land personified as a witness cries out and weeps over the horrible deeds done there lends support that murder as well as avarice is in mind.

And that in turn is why the primeval curse on the land is invoked (cf. Ge 4:8–12).

B. Elihu Speeches (32:1–37:24)

The speeches of Elihu are skillfully woven into the fabric of the book and have a legitimate role. They give another human perspective in which we find a more balanced theology than that of the counselors. But we need not assume everything he said is normative even though he claimed a special inspiration (32:8, 18). Elihu's attack on Job was limited to his statements during the dialogue. He did not accuse Job of a wicked life for which he was being punished. So Elihu was not guilty of false accusation, and that may be the reason he was not rebuked by God (42:7).

Elihu tried to be sensitive to Job but deserves some criticism for a weakness common to many—his overconfidence in his ability to do what the others could not. This makes him sound sanctimonious; but once Elihu got into his message, he seemed to improve as he went along. His poems in chs. 36–37, while at points difficult to understand, have a masterly quality similar to other great poems in the book.

Another purpose behind Elihu's speeches was to deal with Job's extreme language. Job was extreme at times (cf. 9:14–24), but it was due to his determination to be honest. He was also inconsistent. He questioned God's justice on the basis of his experience but was deeply committed to it since he laid all his hope for vindication on it. Elihu sensed this inconsistency and scored Job for wanting vindication while also accusing God of indifference to human behavior (35:2–3). Elihu assured Job that God's wisdom coupled with his power to carry out his wise purposes guaranteed that his discipline would ultimately prove redemptive (36:11–16). Despite his anger (32:2–3) and wordy lecturing style, Elihu never got bitter as did Bildad and Zophar. Nor did he stoop to false accusation about Job's earlier life (cf. Eliphaz in 22:4–11). He presented God as a merciful teacher (33:23–28; 36:22–26). Suffering is disciplinary (33:19–22), not just judgmental. The counselors glorified God with their hymns but remained cold and detached. Elihu had a warmer personal response to the greatness of God (37:1–2). He included himself as one who should be hushed in awe before God. Elihu said God reveals both his justice and his covenant love in his sovereign control of his covenant love in his sovereign control of the world (37:13, 23); and this is the reason the wise of heart should worship him. That is a fitting note of introduction for the Lord's appearance.

1. Introduction (32:1–5)

1–5 Job had closed his peroration with a final flourish of bravado. He was so certain of his blameless life that he would be willing to march like a prince into the presence of God and give an account of his every step. The attempt of his friends to convince him of his sinfulness had failed. Job could have no more to say, having challenged God. The friends had no more to say because they considered him a hopeless hypocrite (22:4–5).

The book at this point introduces Elihu, a young man who in deference to age has waited with increasing impatience for the opportunity to speak. Four times in the Hebrew text we are told he was angry. First at Job for justifying himself rather than God and then at the friends because of their inability to refute Job. We are not told explicitly why or under what circumstances he was there. The Prologue says nothing of bystanders, though it implies Job sat in an open public place where the friends could see him at a distance (2:12). These verses simply imply that Elihu was among bystanders who listened to Job and his counselors.

Elihu's speeches are presented as a human reaction the apparent "self-righteousness" of Job and to the counselors' ineptitude. His concern was not that the latter falsely condemned Job but that in failing to disprove Job's claims about his blameless life they succeeded in condemning God. After all, they had claimed that God never afflicts the innocent and always punishes the wicked. Verses 4–5 reveal clearly that Elihu's major target was Job. He "waited before speaking to Job." Elihu's reply to the counselors was secondary, as is evident in his speeches.

2. The first speech: part 1 (32:6–22)

6–14 Elihu's reason for daring to intrude on ground usually reserved for sages was that wisdom comes from God—the old may lack it, the young may have it—if the Spirit of God grants it. Obviously Elihu believed he had been thus blessed. The counselors' reasoning had not impressed him. He caricatured them as groping for words and unable

to handle bombastic Job. In v.13 Elihu seemed to be accusing them of using a falsely pious appeal to let God handle Job as a way out of their responsibility to refute him. But they had not made any such statement. In v.14 Elihu avowed that he would have used a different set of arguments had he been in the Dialogue with Job.

15–22 Elihu launched out on a soliloquy all about words—his words. Words have failed Job's counselors, but here he was standing by with so many words inside him that he was fairly bursting at the seams. There was no way that he could hold them back. He promised himself (and anyone listening) that he would be absolutely impartial. In usual Semitic rhetoric, he carried the matter of impartiality to an extreme. He would not even use honorific titles, something he had never learned to do skillfully for fear of God's punishment.

To us Elihu is insufferably wordy. It takes him twenty-four verses to say, "Look out! I'm going to speak." Elihu meant to be eloquent; and in his culture, wordiness was the essence. He intended to present a human viewpoint free of the acrimony that ultimately bound the thoughts of the three friends. His intention was noble.

3. The first speech: part 2 (33:1–33)

1–7 Elihu spoke directly to Job, appealing to him by name (vv.1, 31). The counselors studiously avoided even mentioning Job's name, which indicates how formal their relationship was. From ch. 12 on Job had lost all confidence in the sincerity of his friends (cf. 12:2; 13:4–5; 16:2–5; 19:2–6, 28–29; 21:3, 34; 26:1–4). Elihu was aware of this; so he opened his speech stressing his own honest intent.

Having in mind Job's earlier words to God in 13:21—"Withdraw your hand far from me, and stop frightening me with your terrors"—Elihu said that he, like Job, was only a creature of God nipped from clay; so Job needed to have no fear in marshaling arguments against him. But the words "if you can" in v.5 belie an attitude of superiority despite his attempt to allay Job's fears.

8–22 Finally Elihu began his argument. He had already shown an awareness of Job's precise wording. Now with some freedom he quoted the sufferer, picking out lines from various speeches. In 9:21 Job had claimed to be "blameless." In 10:6–7 he had complained, asking why God had to probe for sin in him when God knew he was not guilty. In 13:19 he had challenged anyone to bring charges against him, and in 13:23 he had requested God to show him his sin. We can be sure ch. 13 is referred to because 33:10b–11 are virtually identical to 13:24b and 27a.

Some of Job's words, especially out of context, sound like a claim to sinlessness (e.g., 23:10–12). Eliphaz certainly had that impression from Job's words (15:14–16). But the precise words of v.9 were not uttered by Job, and on occasion Job admitted to being a sinner (7:21; 13:26). He claimed nothing more for himself than what (unknown to him) God had already pronounced him to be (1:8; 2:3). Elihu then did not understand what was happening from the divine perspective. His defense of God was like that of the counselors, especially in their earlier speeches, but without their rancor against Job's person.

In v.12 Elihu appealed to God's transcendence as the reason Job was wrong to dispute with him. His words sound banal, for hymns have already been uttered about God's greatness (4:8–16; 9:2–13; 11:7–9; 12:13–25; 25:2–6); but his purpose is commendable. God's thoughts and purposes are beyond human ability to comprehend; so how can anyone know what God is doing? But for the moment, beginning in v.13, Elihu set aside the issue of Job's guilt or innocence and of God's transcendence (both of which he would return to) to answer Job's frequent complaint, that God would not give him a hearing (cf. 9:16, 35; 13:22; 19:7; 23:2–7).

God did communicate with humankind in various ways and often. Elihu expounded on two of these—dreams and illness. Elihu tailored the possibility of this kind of revelation to Job's case. Job had already experienced dreams and visions from God, but they had only terrified him (7:14). This was, however, just the kind of revelation Elihu thought Job needed. And Job should have interpreted this as God's instruction to keep him from ultimate destruction. Unfortunately, Elihu overlooked the real question about which Job wanted an audience with God, namely: What are the sins I am accused of?

The second way Elihu found God revealing himself is even more tailored to Job's case: "Or a man may be chastened on a bed of pain" (v.19). God's purpose in suffering is to chasten people for their own good lest they find themselves face-to-face with death. But Elihu did not make the crude claim so often on the lips of the counselors—that Job's sufferings were the proof of a wicked life.

Elihu's message is not exactly new, for Eliphaz had touched on the disciplinary aspect of suffering in 5:17–18. The subject, however, has not been broached again till now. Its emphasis by Elihu is commendable, but it is not the kind of communication from God Job has had in mind. After each description of how God communicates with humankind, Elihu ended on the theme that God does so to redeem a person's life from the pit. Elihu depicted the sufferer at the edge of the pit—exactly where Job found himself—about to go on "the journey of no return" (16:18–22). There can be no question that Elihu had in mind ch. 16 as he picked up the subject of an interceding angel.

23–30 Eliphaz was convinced that there was no heavenly mediator who would listen to Job (5:1). In 16:18–21 Job had dared to suggest that he had such a witness, an advocate in heaven who would intercede for him, pleading "as a man pleads for his friend." The life of the "hypothetical" sufferer here hangs in the balance; no mere mortal can save him. Elihu considered such an event only a possibility, and even then this heavenly mediator would be "one out of a thousand"—a rare one indeed—who might do the job. His job was first "to tell a man what is right for him." So in a sense this "angel" became a third means of revelation from God to humankind. He also provided for mercy in behalf of the suffering and even provided a ransom to save their lives. All this would happen only if people listened to the revelation and turned to God for grace. Such redeemed persons would openly admit their sin and praise God for his grace.

So Elihu had both agreed and disagreed with Job and with the counselors. He had added the element of God's mercy, a subject avoided by the counselors who constantly appealed to God's justice. Elihu felt there was a place for grace. A ransom may have to be paid, but people are restored and only then come to make their public confession. Those who have truly had a conversion experience have joyous communion with God; they are thankful and contrite.

In vv.29–30 Elihu made a case for the patience of God who will favor a person even when he or she falls away two or even three times. This should encourage Job who had not yet even experienced it once.

31–33 Unfortunately, like so many well-meaning messengers of grace, Elihu was so completely convinced of his good intentions toward Job that he became insufferably overbearing.

4. The second speech (34:1–37)

Elihu claimed he wanted Job to be cleared. It seems Elihu had repentance in mind as he called on Job "to speak up" (33:32) or else listen and learn wisdom. He saw himself as a teacher of wisdom (33:33). As he proceeded to do that in ch. 34, he believed even the wise could benefit from his chosen words (vv.2–4). Once again his method was to quote Job (vv.5–6), and his purpose was to show that Job's words were theologically unsound. Like the counselors, Elihu picked out only those words of Job that he needed to prove his point.

Elihu, however, was not in all respects like the counselors. He did not express their view of suffering. He considered suffering to be one of the ways God communicates with humankind. Unlike the counselors, Elihu did not totally condemn Job. He thought Job, through association with the wicked, had picked up some of their views (vv.8–9). Elihu accused Job of talking like a wicked person (v.36) and of being rebellious rather than submissive (v.37). But in 33:23–28 he had shown some understanding of God's free grace in dealing with human waywardness.

Elihu had a compelling desire to uphold the truth that God always does what is right (vv.10–12). While the counselors saw this only in terms of black and white, Elihu presented the sovereign Creator as one who intentionally and momentarily exercised benevolence toward all humanity (vv.13–15). Elihu was zealous to counter Job's complaint that God treats the wicked and the righteous alike, for this would mean God does evil (vv.10–30). Elihu was convinced Job needed to repent over such a rebellious notion (vv.33–37). He, like Job and the counselors, revealed no knowledge of the events in the divine council. So it appears Elihu was not an angelic messenger from God, for he had a limited perspective and presented, therefore, only a human estimate of Job's spiritual condition.

1–4 In 12:11–12 Job was sarcastic about the bad "food" the counselors had been dishing up to him under the guise of "the wisdom of the aged." Elihu here was determined to show where real wisdom lay, where food may be found that was really good. He called for all who were wise to join him in his banquet of words to find out how good they were.

5–9 The quote in v.5 is accurate. Job had used these very words about himself (cf. 12:4; 13:18; 27:2, 6); but he never labeled himself as a person "without transgression" (i.e., "guiltless"). Despite Elihu's claim in 33:32 that it would please him if Job were shown to be in the right, Elihu had already made up his mind; he was angry at Job for justifying himself rather than God (32:2). Here his anger surfaces.

In v.7 Elihu drew again from the words of Eliphaz. The latter had said Job "drinks up evil like water" (15:16) and had censured Job for venting his rage against God and shaking his fist at the Almighty and defiantly attacking him (15:25–26). Elihu did not go as far as Eliphaz in accusing Job of this, but it is enough that Job kept company with such people. Verse 9 is not a direct quote from Job. Job had imagined the wicked saying this in 21:15 and then had complained that calamity did not come very often on them (21:17). So it is only by implication that Elihu could accuse Job. His accusation was based on Job's sentiment that the righteous get the same treatment as the wicked.

10–15 Intrinsic to v.9 is the accusation that God is not just. From this point on throughout the next twenty-one verses, Elihu expounded on the theme "God only does right." Job had wailed "that those who provoke God are secure" (12:6) while one who is "righteous and blameless" is made "a laughingstock" (12:4; cf. 10:3; 21:7–8; 24:1–12). To Elihu this could mean nothing else than an accusation that God does wrong, and it is unthinkable that God would do wrong. But that does not solve the mystery. Job was probing when he questioned, "Why do the innocent suffer?" Job saw that "the fatherless child is snatched from the breast, the infant of the poor is seized for a debt" (24:9), "the murderer . . . kills the poor and needy" (24:14), "but God charges no one with wrongdoing" (24:12). "No!" said Elihu, "God repays a man for what he has done." Whether Job saw it or not, Elihu insisted on that most basic truth. "It is unthinkable" that God would perpetrate evil.

Elihu's next words (v.13) get us deeper into the mystery. They infer that God is the Creator and therefore not accountable to Job. Further, in vv.14–15 he asserts a person's complete dependence on the continuing exercise of God's free grace to continue one's existence.

16–20 From all this Elihu maintains that human beings are not in a position to stand as God's judge. Without God's impartial judgment, especially on those who hold power, the world would dissolve into hopeless anarchy. Because of his omnipotence, no one can influence him as he actively governs.

21–30 Such impartial governance of the world is typified by God's punishment of the wicked rulers who disregard his ways. This justice lies behind all the order there is, and it is confirmed and guaranteed by God's omniscience as well as his omnipotence. Job had complained over the delay of justice (21:19–24:1). Elihu maintained that God does not have to set times for inquiry and judgment. His omniscience enables him to judge all the time. God hears the cry of the poor and needy and punishes the wicked openly, but it is his prerogative to remain silent if and when it pleases him. Even then he keeps his control over individuals and nations for the common good. And even then he may use the wicked to punish the wicked and so keep the godless from ruling.

31–37 Having closed his defense of God, Elihu resumed admonishing Job. He was apparently trying to show Job how untenable his position was by means of an illustration. If someone should repent after God has disciplined him, must God be subject to human wishes as he governs the world? The implied answer is "Of course not!" Elihu was certain that any wise person he might consult would agree that Job's behavior was like the wicked who multiply words against God. So Job deserved to be tested.

The illustration in vv.31–32 is probably given to shame Job for lack of contriteness. The question in v.33 could be meant to startle Job. Must God recompense him for unfair treatment? Obviously not. Again Job's sin was that he arrogantly made himself equal with God and played the part of a rebel.

5. The third speech (35:1–16)

Job had raised questions that really disturbed Elihu. In this speech he dealt with several very important issues that arose out of Job's problem about God's justice. Elihu began (vv.1–3) by showing Job how inconsistent he was to claim in one breath that God would vindicate him and then in another to complain he got no profit out of not sinning (cf. 34:9). In other words, if God is so unjust, why did Job want to be vindicated by him? Elihu had missed Job's point, that he wanted to be vindicated because he did believe God was just. Of course Job, in his struggle to understand what God was doing, had sent out two signals, one of which Elihu, like the others, had not been able to hear.

In answer to Job's inconsistency (vv.4–8), Elihu claimed it was God who got no benefit from Job whether he did right or not. God is far too transcendent for human beings to affect him by their little deeds. Job's righteousness or lack of it affected only people like himself (v.8).

Another issue grows out of that last statement and centers around Job's concern over God's apparent indifference to the cries of the oppressed (cf. 24:1–12). Elihu maintained that God is not indifferent to people, but people are indifferent to God. People want God to save them; but they are not interested in honoring him as their Creator, Deliverer, and Source of wisdom (vv.9–11). Human arrogance keeps God from responding to the empty cry for help (vv.12–13). That is why God had not answered Job. The deafness from God derived from Job's complaints, questions, and challenges that reveal the same kind of arrogance (vv.14–15). They are words without knowledge (v.16).

1–3 Job did not use these very words, but Elihu tried to reproduce two of Job's viewpoints. Job was sure he would be vindicated (cf. 13:13–19), but where did he say, "What do I gain by not sinning?" Job felt that, according to the principle of retribution, his suffering was not just. He was found guilty without charges. So to Job a desire to be cleared made sense. But Elihu could only see in Job's words the accusation that God is unjust.

4–8 The relationship between divine transcendence and human behavior was often on Job's mind. He saw God as too attentive— the Watcher of men (7:17–20)—and yet so transcendent that he could say to God, "If I have sinned, what have I done to you?" (7:20). To Elihu God was too transcendent to be either helped by righteousness or hurt by sin. This is further refined by alluding to two kinds of sin, omission and commission, which can neither deprive God nor hurt him in any way.

There was no place in Elihu's theology for doing God's will out of love for him. What we do affects our fellow human beings by being good or bad (v.9). And though God may punish or reward us as Judge, there is no place for him in the role of a Father who can be hurt or pleased by us.

9–16 Job had devoted an entire speech to the subject of God's apparent indifference to his plight (ch. 23) and the plight of all who suffer and are oppressed (ch. 24). Elihu stated the issue in v.9 and then set about to give an answer. He had already said that God's purpose in human suffering was to teach (discipline) and to warn (33:16–22). Or he may remain silent because he was using a tyrant as his instrument of punishment (34:29–30). Or he may only be restraining his wrath in hope for repentance (33:29–30). Elihu was not totally rigid in his moralistic justice since he allowed for the possibility of a mediating angel who could provide a ransom for the sinner and plead for grace (33:23–24). There is the possibility that those who cry for relief are also sinful and unwilling to bow before God as their Creator and Savior. They cry only because of physical pain and not out of spiritual hunger.

The "songs in the night" are most likely songs of praise as a result of deliverance (cf. Ps 42:8). Verse 11 refers to the capacity of the divine-image bearer (man and woman) to hear the voice of God in contrast to brute beasts. As Elihu saw it, God does not listen to the cry of people when it comes to him as the empty sound of a brute beast.

Elihu felt that failure of the suffering to see that their Maker is also the author of wisdom and joy is a sign of arrogance on their part. Job might not be wicked, but he shared this arrogance and so got no answer. Elihu seems to have been offended by the idea that Job should consider himself a litigant at God's court.

With his multiplicity of empty words, Job should not have expected to be heard. Even worse was Job's rebellious spirit—chiding God for hiding his face (13:24; 23:3; cf. v.14) and seeking to march into his presence as an impatient litigant (13:15; 31:35–37). Now, with his case before God, Job dared to complain about waiting for an answer and continued to accuse God of injustice.

6. The fourth speech (36:1–37:24)

Elihu needed a little more time to develop fully his defense of God's justice. First he presented his premise that God is mighty and firm of purpose (v.5), that he will not grant life to the wicked but always grants the rights of those who are wronged (v.6). He then proceeded to tell how that purpose is carried out (vv.6–10). No matter what life may bring, whether chains or affliction, God never takes his eyes off the righteous but uses their troubles for disciplinary instruction and to call them to repentance (vv.7–10). Responding to his call determines the course of a person's life and fate—obey and live under his blessing; disobey and die in bitter resentment (vv.11–14).

Having forsaken his condemnatory spirit (35:14–16), Elihu sought to comfort Job with the possibility of deliverance (v.15a). It was time Job saw the hand of God in his suffering. Job must understand that God was wooing him from the jaws of adversity, from slavery and oppression to freedom and comfort (vv.16–17). Verses 18–21 are a further warning to Job probably about the dangers of prosperity and of turning to evil.

In v.22 Elihu completed his theme on God's purpose in human suffering by returning to his original premise: the greatness of God's power and the uniqueness of his ways (vv.22–23). He is also the perfect teacher who makes no mistakes. Job would do well to sit at the Master's feet and learn that his hand never does wrong. Then Job would be prepared to extol God and his work (vv.24, 26). Elihu was so overwhelmed by the greatness of God that he burst forth into a hymn of praise. Its theme is the mystery of God's ways in nature. But Elihu's real purpose was to impress Job with the mystery of God's ways in providence. The two sometimes coincide (37:13).

The hymn extols the work of God in the autumnal rain. His hand distills the drops, pours out the moisture on earth, and thus provides for the needs of humankind (vv.27–28). With flashing lightning and the crash of his thunder, God ushers in the winter season with its drenching rain and driving winds, its ice and snow, so that human beings and all God's creatures see his power on display (vv.29–30).

After this hymn Elihu asked Job a series of humbling questions about the mysteries of nature (37:14–18). If Job could not understand how God performs these marvels much less assist him, how then could he understand the far less obvious mysteries of God's providence (vv.19–20)?

A final lesson from nature captured Elihu's imagination. When the winter is past and the skies are swept of clouds, the sun reigns supreme, and so does God in his golden splendor (vv.21–22). With this suggestion of divine theophany, Elihu returned again to his original premise about God's power and good purpose for man (v.23) as the reason for us to worship him (v.24). When all is said and done, therefore, Elihu's speech prepares for the appearance (theophany) of God that follows.

1–4 Elihu was apologetic over the fact that he had even more to say in defense of God. The words "one perfect in knowledge" likely refer to God (cf. 37:16). Elihu would hardly claim for himself the same perfection he attributes to God. Probably Elihu was claiming to be one "perfect of utterance" because his speech derived from God, who is the source of perfect words.

5–14 Everything Elihu said from here on rests on the affirmation in v.5. God's power assures the fulfillment of his purpose. He will never grant life to the wicked but will always see that those who are afflicted receive justice. Verses 6–7 reflect God's ultimate purpose since vv.8–12 are conditional. Elihu was making room for Job's complaints about the suffering of the righteous and the prosperity of the wicked. He was also answering Job's

frustration over God's surveillance. God never takes his eyes off the righteous. But to eventually enthrone them, he must discipline them for their own good.

God's unfainting purpose is to reach the hearts of people, if necessary by "cords of affliction." He makes them listen "to correction"; that is, he gets their attention and then calls for repentance. Once attention is gained, obedience leads to life and disobedience leads to death.

15–21 Elihu disapproved of Job's contention that the wicked prosper; and even though he agreed that the righteous suffer, it was only because of their waywardness, which needs correction. So there was hope for Job. He could be rescued by his suffering if he heard the voice of God wooing him away from the jaws of distress.

Verses 17–20 are a sharp rebuke of Job for being unjust and for misuse of his power and wealth. Elihu was admonishing Job to learn the lesson God was trying to teach him through his suffering. Job would someday realize his affliction was of more value to him than his wealth and all his efforts to justify himself. Verse 20 is difficult but seems to mean that Job should not long for the night when God's terrible justice will be meted out but should learn the lesson of submission, which God was teaching Job through his affliction.

22–26 In a real sense these verses are both the climax of the preceding section and the first stanza of a hymn of praise. Elihu returned to the theme he began with—the power of God. He considered God's power and wisdom as the themes Job should dwell on rather than on God's justice. The wisdom of the great Teacher assures the justice of his actions, and his power makes certain that his wise purposes will be fulfilled. God's ways derive from his sovereign freedom. This rules out one's right to question God's moral conduct. Because human beings see God's work at a great distance, they cannot understand it completely; so those who are wise will look on it with delight and praise. Elihu was here preparing the way for the theophany when Job would finally see his sovereign Lord and learn about his dominion.

27–33 The hymn continues by extolling God's great power in the elements. Having admonished Job about praising God for his work (v.24), Elihu here illustrated God's work in nature. Following the hymn Elihu closed his speech with admonitions to Job based on its contents (37:14–24).

God's greatness in his creation is demonstrated by the rain cycle. Rain was considered one of the most needed and obvious blessings of God. Condensation and precipitation, while not technically understood, were certainly observable. But evaporation is not. Elihu did not need a knowledge of physics since God is the one who does this.

The Hebrew word for "his pavilion" (v.29; GK 6109) is rendered "his canopy" in Ps 18:11, which the parallel line in the psalm clearly defines as "the dark rain clouds of the sky." "Bathing the depths of the sea" might be rendered "lights up the depths of the sea," since "to cover [bathe]" (GK 4059) with lightning is equivalent to lighting up. The NIV note on v.31 suggests "by them [the showers] he nourishes the nations" rather than "governs" (better rendered "to judge or punish"). Judging or punishing by the storm is conceivable in terms of God's use of lightning. So when the lightning performs God's purpose in striking its mark, it is against those he chooses to punish (37:13).

37:1–13 Elihu was impressed with God's voice as his word of dominion and power. By fiat he controls the snow and rain, and thunder is nothing less than the roar of his voice (cf. Ps 29). Elihu's heart pounded as God put on an awesome display of his power. The passage continues to reveal a keen observation of atmospheric conditions and their effects. The clouds are reservoirs of moisture and arenas of lightning. In their cyclonic movement they are subject to God's commands and perform his will. Elihu saw a direct relationship between God's rule over nature and his dominion over human affairs.

Verse 13 is a thematic climax that lists ways God may use the storm. Elihu wanted to do more than impress Job with God's power in nature. Thus he showed how the mystery of God's ways in nature coincides with the mystery of his ways in providence. When God's purpose is corrective, as punishment for the wicked, the storm is often connected with the deliverance of his people, thus demonstrating his covenant love (Jos 10:11; 1Sa 7:10–11; Ps 105:32–33). God may also, however, demonstrate his covenant love by sending the rain in season (Dt 11:13–17). Therefore, there appear to be three different purposes for the storm: to punish, to show his love, and for his own pleasure (cf. 38:26). Some things that God does have no other explanation than that they please him. Having arrived at this amazing point, Elihu was prepared to apply this truth to Job's situation.

14–20 The questioning format anticipates the divine method in the upcoming speeches. Job needed to stop and think of how absurd his position was. He was asked to supply knowledge he obviously did not have and was chided for his abysmal ignorance in the light of God's perfect knowledge. Sweltering in the heat of the dry season with the sky like a brazen mirror, Job sat helpless. He could do nothing about the weather but endure it. How then can a mere creature, so lacking in knowledge and strength, expect to understand God's justice? Had Job not drawn up his case, affixed his signature, and called for an audience with God?

21–24 Elihu shifted his attention from his moral application back to a contemplation of the elements. But it was only to make an even more forceful moral application. After the storm, with the clearing skies, comes the sun in its brilliance; likewise, in golden splendor and awesome majesty God comes from his heavenly abode. Elihu admonished Job that he needed to see God as God, almighty and morally perfect, and to prove he was wise in his heart by worshiping (fearing) him.

C. The Theophany (38:1–42:6)

God offers Job no theological explanation of the mystery of his suffering. The book, however, is teaching us through the divine theophany that there is something more fundamental than an intellectual solution to the mystery of innocent suffering. Job's greatest anguish was over the thought that he was separated from God. Normally sin is the reason, as the counselors perceived. But Job learned through the theophany that God had not abandoned him. And it gradually dawned on Job that without knowing why he was suffering he could face it, so long as he was assured that God was his friend. Job's past experience with God was nothing compared with the experience that he found through the theophany. Such an experience was like hearing about God compared with the joy of seeing him (42:5)—by which he meant something not literal but of the heart.

Job had the high privilege here of sitting at the feet of the Lord. He needed to learn something about the character of God by walking through all creation with him and contemplating his natural marvels. Job would be made wonderfully aware of who God is in a universe full of paradoxes for humankind and yet filled with joy and wonder. In this way Job learned to take God at his word without understanding hardly any of the mysteries of his universe, much less the reason why he was suffering.

One of the purposes of the Lord's speeches is to show that neither the counselors nor Job possessed complete knowledge. Indeed, the speeches show how very limited human knowledge is. On the surface it would appear that the speeches concentrate only on the natural world, but careful reading reveals something else. In the first speech (chs. 38–39) God's works in the natural creation are in view. Then follow two chapters of proof that Job—and we today—know little of God's world. Job then agreed that his words were based on ignorance: "I put my hand over my mouth. . . . I will say no more" (40:4–5).

The second speech begins on an entirely different note. The introduction (40:8–14) tells about God's power and ability to crush the wicked and to look on those who are proud and to humble them. The purpose goes beyond showing Job that God is creator and sustainer of the natural world. It is to convince Job that God is Lord also of the moral order, and appropriately Job's response this time was repentance (42:1–6).

1. God's first discourse (38:1–40:2)

38:1 Job saw no "golden splendor" or even the "awesome majesty" imagined by Elihu (37:22). Indeed, it seems he saw nothing but the storm from which he heard the voice of "the LORD" (GK 3378). This Israelite covenant name for God appears in the Prologue, in the Divine speeches, and in the Epilogue; but "the men of the east" (Job's friends) do not know God by this name. The reason, of course, is that those intervening chapters preserve the authentic vocabulary of that earlier generation or at least of a non-Israelite society.

2–3 How did Job "darken" (GK 3124) or obscure God's counsel? Undoubtedly this refers to the extreme language of Job during his moments of poetic rage when he struggled with concepts of a deity who was his enemy—a phantom deity, one his own mind created. Here he needed to brace himself and wrestle with God as he really was. God chose to ply Job with questions, but strangely he said nothing about Job's suffering; nor did he address the problem of theodicy. Job did not get the bill of indictment or verdict of innocence he wanted. But neither was he humiliated with a list of the sins he had committed for which he was being punished. So by implication Job's innocence was established, and later it was directly affirmed (42:7–8).

It was important for Job to know that God was not his enemy as he had imagined. This encounter with the Lord to learn the lesson that God is God was Job's assurance that all was well. Job did not learn why he was suffering; but he did learn to accept God by faith as his Creator, Sustainer, and Friend. To learn this lesson he needed to learn who God really was. This Job was about to do by walking with God through his created universe and being questioned about his limitations as a creature in comparison with God's power and wisdom in creating and sustaining the universe. The speeches succeeded in bringing Job to complete faith in God's goodness without receiving a direct answer to his questions concerning God's justice.

4–7 The irony in the Lord's words "Surely you know" is sharp and purposeful. Job had dared to criticize God's management of the universe. Had he been present at the Creation (an obvious absurdity), he might have known something about God's management of its vast expanses. But even the angels who were there could only shout for joy over the Creator's deeds. And here Job, an earthbound man, has lost sight of who this Creator is. As a man full of words and often questioning what the Lord was doing, he was told of the celestial chorus that celebrated God's creative activity, which was beyond any mere creature's ability to improve on by comment. That Job was learning this lesson we may infer from his response in 40:4–5.

For personification of the stars (v.7) in parallel with "the sons of God," see Ps 104:4, where the winds are God's messengers (angels) and the lightning bolts his servants (cf. Heb 1:7).

8–11 In the ancient Semitic world, control of the boisterous sea was a unique symbol of divine power and authority. The Lord controls the sea by his spoken word (cf. Lk 8:24–25). That message is conveyed by the "doors" being the bounds the Lord sets for the sea.

12–15 The morning and dawn are personified. Surely Job did not give orders that caused these servants of the Lord to rise and seize "the earth by its edges and shake the wicked out of it." The figure is based on the idea that daylight catches the wicked in the act and disperses them like one who shakes dirt from a blanket. The dawn flashes across the earth from east to west; and this, in the figure, is like seizing it by its edges and shaking it out. Verse 14 pictures the long, deep shadows of early morning when the earth reminds us of clay taking the shape of the seal pressed into it or of the folds of a garment. Daylight deprives the wicked of the kind of "light" they need. Here we have a subtle figure, for "the light" the wicked are denied is certainly "the darkness" that is their element, indeed, "deep darkness is their morning" (24:17). The wicked "put darkness for light and light for darkness" (Isa 5:20).

16–18 Here God turned to mysteries of created things not visible to the human eye. Note the progression: journeying, then seeing, and then understanding what you see. Each step is increasingly impossible for Job. The Lord's control over this unseen netherworld is just as real as his control over the sea or the land of the living (cf. 26:5–6). What did Job know about those realms where no living human being had ever been?

19–21 What did Job know about the mystery of light and darkness? Again personification creates a vivid figure of God's cosmic control. The irony that focuses on Job's creatural nature gives the clue to one of the purposes of the divine speeches—to show Job that God is God. To have been born before Creation in order to know all this is a patent absurdity.

22–30 Again the Lord questioned Job about his ability to journey to those inaccessible places (cf. vv.16–17) where he could see the sources of nature's rich supply. The term "storehouses" is used in Jer 50:25 as a place

for storing weapons (armory). In this case the arsenal figure carries out the thought that snow or hail are often God's weapons (Pss 78:47–48; 148:8; Isa 30:30). Sometimes with them he controls the destiny of nations.

After querying Job about these cosmic mysteries, the Lord made a statement that sounds trite on the surface but demands the attention of every human being. Elihu spoke of God's use of the elements to punish or bless (37:13), and there he hinted at the point that the Lord made here—that he has the right to display his power for no other reason than his own good pleasure. When he "waters a land where no man lives," God demonstrates that human beings are not the measure of all things. He waters the desert only because it pleases him to do so.

Could Job give the Lord realistic answers to questions Job's contemporaries had simplistically answered? Does the rain have a father or the ice a mother? The rhetorical question is to impress on Job that these apparent male and female aspects of nature are God's doing and his alone.

In v.30 the freezing of the surface of the deep was a phenomenon unknown by common experience in and around the lands of the Bible. Like other passages in Job (cf. 26:7–10), this text reveals an expanded knowledge of natural phenomena.

31–33 Job had moved with the Lord from the "recesses of the deep" and "gates of death" (vv.16–17) to heavenly constellations. The terminology draws on the interpretation of those fanciful figures the ancients saw in the celestial constellations. Our language in this space age still uses the same terms. The antithesis of binding and loosening the imagined fetters that hold together the cluster of stars called Pleiades or the belt of the hunter Orion rests on poetic license and literary convention. The message is about God's cosmic dominion of these stars as they seasonally move across the sky. Job understood neither the laws of the heavenly bodies nor God's "inscription [signature]" in the earth, and that is exactly what the Lord was talking to Job about.

34–38 These verses all refer to meteorological phenomena and related matters. The difference between them and vv.22–30 seems to be the time, place, and purpose of the weather. Verse 38 indicates that the seasonal rain is in view. After the long months of the dry season, the Lord is the one who orders the clouds to release their moisture. Job and all humanity can only raise their voices in prayer to him who controls the former and the latter rain, that extension of the rainy season that provides a greater harvest.

The language used here has a playful humor. Imagine Job, if he were able, giving the clouds an order and suddenly being inundated with water. Or Job might decide to dispatch the lightning bolts, if he could, and they would report like lackeys to him and say, "Here we are." So even these seasonal rains are the result of the Lord's bidding, who numbers every cloud and measures every jarful of rain.

39–41 These verses begin a new aspect of the Lord's control over nature. From 38:39 to 40:30 the focus is on creatures of the animal world that are objects of curiosity and wonder to people. The choice is somewhat random. It has never crossed Job's mind to hunt prey for lions or to stuff food into the outstretched gullets of the raven's nestlings. But are not their growls and squawks cries to God, on whom all these creatures ultimately depend?

39:1–4 Through the wild kingdom and its rich variety of creatures, God informs Job of his creative and sustaining activity. He provides for each species its own gestation period and ability to bear young in the field—without assistance and with a divinely ordered wisdom to provide for themselves and their young. The offspring of an ibex doe, unlike human infants that need years of care, can stand within minutes of birth and soon gambol off to thrive in the wild.

5–8 One of the most admired animals of the OT world was the wild donkey—admired for both its freedom and its ability to survive under the harshest conditions. While its relative the domesticated donkey suffers the noise pollution of the crowded cities and the abuse of animal drivers, the wild donkey can laugh at that and somehow find green morsels in places humans cannot survive, the salt flats and the barren leeward hills.

9–12 Here there is an explicit contrast between the "wild ox" (GK 8028) and the tame ox. This animal is believed to be the now-extinct aurochs. Next to the elephant and

The "mountain goats" of 39:1 may be the ibex, shown here.

rhino, it was the largest and most powerful land animal of the Bible world. Most of the nine OT occurrences of the word make reference to it as a symbol of strength (cf. Nu 23:22; 24:8; Dt 33:17; Ps 29:6; et al.). It was already rare in Palestine in the time of Moses. Once again it is a bit of divine humor to even mention the possibility of this fearsome creature harnessed to Job's plow, working his fields, or tethered in his barn.

13–18 The question format is dropped, and the stanza speaks of God in the third person. The question format was used to impress on Job his impotence in performing deeds that take divine power and wisdom. But since the ostrich appears to be ridiculous in its behavior, it simply was not appropriate to ask Job whether he could match God's strength or wisdom because neither is in view.

The ostrich has a tiny brain but is well programmed with instincts that assure its survival. It does not forsake its eggs. The seeming cruelty to her young (cf. La 4:3) derives from the practice of driving off the yearlings when mating season arrives. The ostrich has exceptional eyesight—the largest of any land animal with 360-degree vision. But the text concentrates on the bird's most incongruous feature: tremendous legs. One kick from this bird can tear open a lion or a human being.

The lesson is that God can and does make creatures that appear odd to us if that pleases him. Imagine a bird that can't fly. Though it has wings, it can run faster than a horse. Job could not understand what God was doing in his life, and God was telling him the created world is just as difficult to rationalize.

19–25 The horse is the only animal in this poem that is domestic. This unexpected feature still serves the Lord's purpose, for only one kind of horse is viewed—the charger, the war-horse. The creatures of the wild in their proud freedom and curious behavior are obviously beyond Job's control, but even a creature that people have tamed can display fearsome behavior that excites our imagination. The lines burst with the literary energy needed to do justice to the performance of this amazing creature during the height of the frenzy of battle.

26–30 In v.26 the marvel for Job to contemplate is one we still view with amazement—the migratory instincts of birds. Our knowledge that some birds fly thousands of miles each year (cf. the arctic tern) serves to validate this particular choice of God's faunal wonders. The two words used in vv.26–27 are the Hebrew generic names that include several species. The first appears to be the sparrow hawk, a bird not resident to the Holy Land but known because it stops off there each year in its migration. The griffon vulture is the largest bird of the area. The same word is used for the true eagle (NIV), but here a carrion eater is in mind. Several interesting characteristics of this bird are mentioned: its soaring ability, its aerie (nest) high on the crags, and its phenomenal eyesight.

40:1–2 These two verses conclude the first speech. Since Job has said nothing, a small problem arises because "the LORD answered Job and said" (lit. Heb.). This idiomatic expression announces a hortatory line (v.2). Here the Lord gets to the point. Job had set himself up arbitrarily as God's accuser. How could Job assume such a lofty position in the light of who God is? After this front-row seat surveying the marvels and mysteries of God's created universe, was Job still ready to make his proud insinuations and accusations about the nature of God's lordship over all things? It was Job's turn to speak again. But there would be no long speeches, no more rage, no more challenging his Creator.

2. Job's humbling (40:3–5)

3–5 Job, the challenger, in a hand-over-mouth posture, realized how complex and mysterious God's ways were. Job's reply was based not so much on his being "unworthy" (GK 7837) as on his insignificance. God had not crushed Job but had cured Job's presumption. The Hebrew verb translated "unworthy" means "to be light" or "lightly esteemed" and in that sense "contemptible."

Job had been so moved by this experience that he was released from his problem—his concern to be vindicated. And yet God had given him no explanation of his sufferings. Job had gone beyond it to see and trust God as his friend, to a full realization that he must reckon with God as God. And yet Job still did not know how God had put himself on trial when he allowed Job to be afflicted under Satan's instigation. So Job was humbled and thereby prepared for the Lord's second speech, which pulls together some important threads and brings the drama to a climax.

3. God's second discourse (40:6–41:34)

The prologue in vv.8–14 shows how the lengthy descriptions of the two creatures "Behemoth" (42:15; GK 990) and "Leviathan" (41:1; GK 4293) serve the purpose of the book in a subtle and yet forceful way. This time God would accomplish more than he had in the first speech, where he humbled Job by showing him how he was Creator and Sustainer of the natural world. Here God would convince Job that he was also Lord of the moral order, one whose justice Job could not discredit. And appropriately Job's response this time was repentance (42:1–6).

The concentration on these two awesome creatures, placed as they are after the assertion of the Lord's justice and maintenance of moral order, lends weight to the contention that they are symbolic, though their features are drawn from animals like the hippopotamus and crocodile. Both words are used often in the OT without symbolic significance. But Leviathan sometimes symbolizes evil political powers (cf. Ps 74:12–14; the monster here is Egypt). The same is true of Isa 27:1, where again Leviathan is historicized to represent the final evil power in the end time. Imagery similar to Job is found in Rev 12–13, where we see a beast (Behemoth) as well as a dragon (Leviathan), both of whom only God can subdue.

Those who regard these creatures as literal animals must admit that the description given here in Job is an exaggeration of the appearance and power of hippopotamuses and crocodiles. Both creatures share two qualities. First is the open (on the surface) quality of a beast with oversize bovine or crocodilian features. This meets the needs of the uninformed (as to events of the Prologue) Job, who was learning a lesson about the Lord's omnipotence. Second is the hidden quality of a cosmic creature (the Accuser of the Prologue), whose creation preceded (40:19) and whose power outranks (41:33) all earthly creatures.

6–14 Using the same formula of challenge (v.7), God presented to Job another barrage of questions designed to bring him back to reality. After all, Job's last words were a challenge (31:35–37) that threw into question God's integrity by suggesting that any indictment God might bring against Job would prove to be false. But all such was hypothetical nonsense. It came straight from Job's imagination. God had no such indictment of Job in the first place; but Job's attitude had to be corrected, for he wrongly assumed that he had to be vindicated by God. To do this the Lord reminded Job of who he (God) was. Did Job have an arm like God's? Was he almighty? And where were Job's majesty and glory? Job began to realize why God had in his first discourse taken him through his garden of natural wonders. Could Job by his power and glory create and sustain all that? Obviously not! So Job needed also to leave to his Creator supremacy in the moral realm: Job had no power to crush wickedness finally; so obviously he needed to leave that ultimate exercise of justice to God and trust him to do right.

These verses are presented as an aggressive challenge to Job. "Unleash your fury . . . crush the wicked . . . then I myself will admit that your own right hand can save you." But they are lovingly designed to shake Job's spirit into realizing that God is the only Creator and the only Savior there is. Job needed to learn to rest quietly and trustfully in that truth. To confirm this truth the Lord proceeded to paint the word pictures of these awesome creatures that defied God and humankind. Indeed, the second is so awesome nothing on earth is his equal (41:33).

15–24 Only one other place in the OT (Ps 73:22) uses the word *behemoth* as a singular. The *oth* ending normally marks the plural when the singular word simply means *beast*. Here the ending has an intensive force, meaning the beast par excellence; i.e., the beast becomes a monster. But if Behemoth is a mere beast in Job 40, the language, apart from hyperbole, is difficult to understand. In v.19a it is labeled the "first among the works of God." We suggest this is mythopoeic language (cf. Ps 74:13–14), intended as another way of referring to a unique cosmic creature such as the Accuser in the Prologue. He is beyond the pale of mere human strength, just as the Accuser was. But this information cannot be revealed to Job, and that explains the extravagant language. The use here of Behemoth and Leviathan is a poetic repetition, just as Ps 74 refers to the breaking of the heads of the monster and the heads of Leviathan, both referring to the power of Egypt at the Red Sea.

41:1–34 Verses 1–9 develop the thought that Leviathan is far too powerful for a human being to handle. The first eight verses are addressed to Job; and they assert that any relationship Job may attempt to have with the Leviathan will be doomed to failure— whether by treaty or by force. At this point God states that he alone has the power to control Leviathan; therefore he is the only Supreme Being. In these verses we reach the climax of the stanza. Before this climax the stress was on human impotence before the Leviathan. After the climax (vv.12–34) the poem becomes a masterly description of this creature that goes beyond anything ascribable to a mere crocodile or whale. Swords, javelins, arrows, clubs, slingshots— all are ineffective against him according to vv.26–29. Is this merely a crocodile or should it be understood in light of Isa 27:1, etc.?

By telling of his dominion over Behemoth and Leviathan, the Lord is illustrating what he has said in 40:8–14. He is celebrating his moral triumph over the forces of evil. Satan, the Accuser, has been proved wrong, though Job does not know it. The author and the reader see the entire picture that Job and his friends never knew. God permitted the Accuser to touch Job as part of his plan to humiliate Satan. But now that the contest is over, God still did not reveal his reason to Job. Because Job did not find out what the readers know, he could be restored without destroying the integrity of the account. To understand this is to understand why the forces of moral disorder are veiled underneath mythopoeic language about ferocious, uncontrollable creatures. Again we emphasize that if the specific and ultimate reason for his suffering had been revealed to Job—even at this point—the value of the account as a comfort to others who must suffer in ignorance would have been diminished if not cancelled.

D. Job's Closing Contrition (42:1–6)

1–2 Job's immediate response shows that he understood clearly the thrust of the second divine speech. Job opened his mouth to tell God that he had gotten the message: God's purpose is all that counts; and since he is God, he is able to bring it to pass. There is nothing else Job needed to know—only, perhaps, that this Sovereign of the universe was his friend (42:7–8).

3–4 There are two unannounced quotations in these verses. In v.3 Job appropriately agreed with the quote from 38:2. He admitted that he did, indeed, obscure God's counsel through ignorance. Chastened thus by the wonders of God, he quoted in v.4 the line God himself had seen fit to use twice on Job (38:3; 40:7, at the opening of each speech). The question is expressive of the nature of the divine discourses. God took the witness stand in his own behalf and cross-examined Job, who now records the final effect of this proceeding.

5–6 Job had heard about God. Finally his often-requested prayer to come into his presence has been answered—the result: withdrawal of his rash statements when he fantasied about God's failure to be just and loving. Concerning the phrase "and repent" (GK 5714), Job did not need to repent over sins that brought on his suffering since his suffering was not the result of his sin. But that is not to say that Job had nothing to be sorry for. His questioning of God's justice, for which God chided him in 38:2 (quoted in v.3), is enough to call forth a change of heart and mind. Besides, the word translated "repent" has a breadth of meaning that includes not only "to be sorry, repent" but also "to console oneself" or "be comforted." So it may be that Job was saying that because he had had this encounter with God—since he has really "seen" God—he now understood that God was his friend, not his enemy. So he was consoled and comforted though still suffering.

V. The Epilogue (42:7–17)

Job has learned that human beings, by themselves, cannot deduce the reason why anyone suffers. Still unknown to Job was the fact that his suffering had been used by God to vindicate God's trust in him over against the accusations of the Accuser. So without anger toward him, God allowed Job to suffer in order to humiliate the Accuser and provide support to countless sufferers who would follow in Job's footsteps. Once the purpose of the book had been fulfilled, Job's suffering could not continue without God's being capricious. We see here the heart of the difference between the suffering of the wicked as punishment and of the righteous to accomplish God's higher purpose. This lavish restoration (double all he had) is not based on Job's righteousness but on God's love for him as one who had suffered the loss of all things for God's sake and for no other reason.

A. The Verdict (42:7–9)

7–9 Why did God commend Job for "speaking of him what is right" and condemn the counselors, who had always taken God's side, often with beautiful creedal hymns? God had just rebuked Job for his many wrong words during his dispute with the counselors; in what sense, then, was he here commended for saying what was right? The counselors certainly lacked the right information about why Job was suffering. Job spoke without understanding (v.3) and was often fiery and emotional in his remarks (15:12–13; 18:4). His opinions and feelings were often wrong, but his facts were right. He was not being punished for sins he had committed. But the friends were claiming to know for a certainty things they did not know and so were falsely accusing Job while mouthing beautiful words about God. Job rightly accused them of lying about him and trying to flatter God (13:4, 7–11).

In v.8 the counselors, no longer with Job, are ordered by God to go back to Job with sacrificial animals sufficient to atone for their transgressions. The sacrifice performed by Job was an integral part of the worship in which Job prayed for them. Praying for your enemy was already taught and practiced in the OT (Ps 35:12–14; 109:4–5). And showing mercy to one's enemies was a faith principle clearly required in Ex 23:4–5. Since God had a high purpose for Job's suffering, the counselors had made themselves enemies of God by accusing Job. The large sacrifice shows how grave the Lord considered their sin; nevertheless, he accepted Job's intercession. Job did not fail to love those who had spitefully abused him when he was most helpless. This lofty and practical truth is a fitting theological finale to a book that calls forth a rigorous exercise of both soul and mind.

B. The Restoration (42:10–17)

10 When Job received again his prosperity, righteousness was rewarded and his whole case defeated. All things being equal, sin brings suffering and righteousness blessing. Since Job had successfully endured the test and proved that his righteousness was not rooted in his own selfishness, there was no reason for Job to continue to be tested; his sufferings needed to cease. God created humans so that he might bless them, not curse them. Job had been declared innocent of all those false accusations; so he could not continue to suffer as punishment. And God's higher purpose had been fulfilled; so there was no reason why Job should not be restored.

11 Job's relatives, who had kept their distance from the suffering spectacle (19:13–15), here proved themselves to be fair-weather friends.

Their comforting and consoling came a little late, but their presents were expensive: a "ring of gold" (for the nose [Ge 24:47; Isa 3:21] or the ears [Ge 35:4; Ex 32:2]) and a "piece of silver" (cf. Ge 33:19; Jos 24:32). The latter was not money in the sense of coinage but an early designation of weight like the shekel (Ge 23:16).

12–15 Verses 12–13 highlight the twofold increase of Job's possessions as compared to the Prologue (1:3). Everything is twofold except Job's sons and daughters. It is curious that the author ignores the sons and concentrates on Job's daughters. The daughters are named and granted an inheritance even when sons are available. The stress on the great beauty of Job's daughters is characteristic of the epic tradition. Their names are indicative of their beauty: Jemimah means "turtledove"; Keziah is probably an aromatic plant as in the name Cinnamon ("cassia" in Ps 45:8); and Keren-Happuch means "a jar (horn) of eye paint."

16–17 Job's longevity was in keeping with patriarchal tradition (possibly double the normal span of Ps 90:10). Certainly the wisdom ideal of seeing one's grandchildren is fulfilled twice over to the fourth generation (cf. Ge 50:23), and the patriarchal formula "old and full of years," expressive of a completely fulfilled life, is used (cf. Ge 25:8; 35:29).

The Old Testament in the New

OT Text	NT Text	Subject
Job 5:13	1Co 3:19	God and the crafty
Job 41:11	Ro 11:35	God owns all

Psalms

INTRODUCTION

1. Background

The English designation "psalm" comes from the Greek *psalmos* (GK *6011*; "songs sung with musical accompaniment"), a translation of the Hebrew *mizmor* (GK 4660; "a song accompanied by musical instruments"). The Hebrew title (*tehillim*) signifies the contents of the book: "songs of praise." In the 150 psalms the Holy Spirit has given us more than a book of Israel's prayer and praise. The book of Psalms is a cross section of God's revelation to Israel and of Israel's response in faith to the Lord. The Psalms invite us to experience how God's people in the past related to him. They witness to the glory of Zion, to the Davidic covenant, to the fidelity of God, to the Exodus and Conquest traditions, to God the Creator-Redeemer-King, and to the Lord as the Divine Warrior. The book of Psalms is God's prescription for a complacent church, because through it he reveals how great, wonderful, magnificent, wise, and utterly awe-inspiring he is. If God's people before the Incarnation could have such a faith in the Lord, witnessing to his greatness and readiness to help, how much more should this be true among twentieth-century Christians! The book of Psalms can revolutionize our devotional life, our family patterns, and the fellowship and the witness of the church of Jesus Christ.

The book of Psalms is first and foremost God's Word to his people. We hear the voice of God in each individual psalm. Its purpose is the same as that of any part of Scripture; the Psalms are "useful for teaching, rebuking, correcting and training in righteousness, so that the man of God may be thoroughly equipped for every good work" (2Ti 3:16–17). The Psalms are nevertheless unique. In them not only does God speak to his people, but the people speak to God. God encourages us to use the language of the Psalms in our individual and communal prayers and praise. By applying these ancient psalms to a new situation, the life of faith, hope, and love of the individual Christian, the Christian family, and the Christian church may be greatly enhanced.

The values of the Psalms to the individual and to the Christian community are many: (1) It is a book of *prayers,* of a human being's communion with God. (2) It expresses one's *praise* to God for acts fulfilled in the past. God's goodness in fulfilling his past promises becomes the occasion for a greater hope in the future. (3) The Psalms have a distinct place in Christian *liturgy,* having been sung by Christians throughout the centuries. (4) The Psalms inspire the believer with *hope* of the kingdom of God: the new state of justice, righteousness, and bliss. (5) The Psalms reflect the *faith* experience of the "community" of God's people. Their expressions of frustration, impatience, anger, and joy reflect the tension between promise and alienation. (6) In the Psalms God addresses both the *individual* and the *community*. (7) The value of the Psalms lies in their *connection* between the OT and the NT. Strictly speaking, they belong to the OT. Yet the psalmists longed for the day of redemption. From the early church we have inherited a new perspective of reading the Psalms in the light of Jesus' mission and work.

2. The Study of the Book of Psalms

The books of Psalms, Job, Proverbs, Ecclesiastes, Song of Songs, and Lamentations make up the poetical books in the English OT. However, poetic forms are found throughout the OT, especially in the books of the prophets.

The Psalms usually carry a heading. The heading or superscription may contain any or all of the following categories of information: identification with a person, association with a historical event, musical and liturgical details, and the type or genre of the psalm.

The psalms were gathered in separate collections that were eventually brought together into one book under the guidance of the Holy Spirit. Several collections arose over the centuries: smaller ones, such as the psalms associated with the sons of Korah (42–49; 84–85; 87–88) and with Asaph (50; 73–83), the second Davidic psalter (51–71), and the Hallelujah psalms (146–50). The larger collections consisted of the psalms associated with David (3–41; cf. 72:20) and the Elohistic psalter (42–83)—itself a collection of smaller collections: the Korahite (42–49) and Davidic (51–71) psalms; the Asaphite psalter (73–83); and the Songs of Ascent (120–34). The process of collection began with smaller collections, to which individual psalms or other collections were added, resulting in a final collection of 150 psalms.

Hebrew poetry does not have meter or "rhyme" as in English. Rather, Hebrew uses various literary devices. Distinctive of Hebrew literature is *parallelism.* Today we distinguish between synonymous, antithetic, synthetic, climactic, and emblematic parallelism. Parallelism is a most fundamental Hebrew literary device.

In *synonymous* (identical) parallelism the members of a line express the same basic idea in several different ways (1:1). *Emblematic* parallelism is a form of synonymous parallelism in which one member of the line contains a figurative (metaphor or simile) development of the same thought (44:19, 22). In *antithetic* parallelism the members of the line are set in contrast to one another (44:3). In *synthetic* parallelism the members of a line complement one another harmoniously to create the desired effect (12:1). *Climactic* (step or chain) parallelism is a further development of synthetic parallelism. Not only do the members of the line harmonize, they also develop the thought colon upon colon. The finest example of this type is Ps 44 (see the commentary).

Internal parallelism is parallelism treated in isolation from other verses. External parallelism denotes the kind of parallelism when two or more verses are compared with one another (Ps 30:8–10). Standardized phrases or paired synonyms are common in Hebrew poetry. Certain synonyms recur in the same or in a different order (cf. 44:24).

Hebrew poetry employs many literary devices. *Acrostic* refers to the poetic practice of opening each line, verse, or stanza with a different letter of the alphabet (e.g., 25; 34; 37; 111; 112; 119; 145). *Alliteration* is the phenomenon of repeating similar sounds at the beginning of words (e.g., 22:4). *Apostrophe* results from a development of personification (see below). For example, in Ps 68:15–16 the psalmist describes the mountains and addresses them rhetorically. *Assonance* is the phenomenon of repeating similar sounds within words (cf. 44:7). *Chiasm* changes the order of the members of a line. Its frequency is so great that the commentary cannot call attention to the many occurrences.

Ellipsis is the phenomenon of leaving something out of the text that must be read into the colon from the context. The resultant ambiguity forces readers to involve themselves with the text, as they have to choose between two or more options. *Hendiadys* is a figure of speech in which two expressions are intended to be understood as one. Hyperbole or exaggeration creates a picture in the mind that shuns literalism (cf. 40:12). *Inclusion* is a form of repetition in which the beginning and end of the section (verse, strophe, or psalm) *enclose* the unit by the restatement of the same motif or words or by a contrastive statement (cf. 70:1, 5). *Merismus* is a coordination of nominal phrases, expressive of totality (e.g., in 105:14, "man" and "kings" denote any and everybody). *Metonymy* refers to meaning by association. *Onomatopoeia* describes a word whose sound creates the effect intended by the speaker. *Paronomasia* is a play on words or, better, a use of two or more identical or similarly sounding words with different nuances in meaning.

Refrain is a form of repetition. *Repetition* is inherent in the concept of symmetry, according to which words and phrases are repeated in the same, synonymous, or antonymous ways. Repetition is the most important element in Hebrew poetry, for it conveys symmetry and asymmetry, harmony and dissonance. *Synecdoche* is a figure of speech in which the part stands for the whole or the whole for the part. For example, the "hand" of the Lord denotes all his being.

There are several categories of psalms. One is the *psalms of praise*, with two subcategories: descriptive and declarative praise. Additionally there are *lament psalms,* of which are the individual and the communal lament psalms. In the individual lament and

Types of Hebrew Parallelism

Type	Characteristic	Example
I. Synonymous	Repetition of same thought	
Identical	Each element is synonymous	Ps 24:1: The earth is the LORD's, and everything in it, the world, and all who live in it.
Similar	Each element is similar	Ps 19:2: Day after day they pour forth speech; night after night they display knowledge.
Incomplete	Second element of previous line is repeated	Jer 17:9: The heart is deceitful above all things and beyond cure. Who can understand it?
Continued	Second element is repeated and built upon	Ps 24:5: He will receive blessing from the LORD, and vindication from God his Savior.
II. Antithetic	Parallel by contrast (by use of the opposite)	Ps 1:6: For the LORD watches over the way of the righteous, but the way of the wicked will perish.
III. Synthetic—	Building on a thought	
Completion	Completes a thought	Ps 2:6: I have installed my king on Zion, my holy hill.
Comparison	Draws an analogy	Pr 15:17: Better is a meal of vegetables where there is love than a fattened calf with turmoil.
Reason	Gives a reason	Pr 26:4: Do not answer a fool according to his folly, or you will be like him yourself.
Conceptual	Use of theme element	Ps 1:1: Blessed is the man who does not walk in the counsel of the wicked or stand in the way of sinners or sit in the seat of mockers.
IV. Climactic	Builds on same word	Ps 29:1: Ascribe to the LORD, O mighty ones, Ascribe to the LORD glory and strength.
V. Emblematic	Use of simile or metaphor	Ps 42:1: As the deer pants for streams of water, so my soul pants for you, O God. Pr 25:25: Like cold water to a weary soul is good news from a distant land.

Taken from *Chronological and Background Charts of the Old Testament* by John Walton. Copyright© 1978 by The Zondervan Corporation. Used by permission.

amid difficulty. In this dialogical relationship the psalmist freely expresses his frustration with God's slowness in answering him.

Other types of psalms are *enthronement psalms*, which celebrate the Lord's kingship, and *wisdom psalms*, which show clear affinity with the wisdom literature. Other literary forms are *Zion Songs* (46; 48; 76; 84; 87), *Triumphal Hymn* (68), *Pilgrimage Songs* (120–34), and *Creation Praise* (8; 104; 139). Several other categories are not literary designations but have grown out of the liturgical use of the Psalms.

The *Hallel psalms* too are not to be confused with a literary genre. Instead they form three separate collections: the "Egyptian Hallel" (113–18); the "Great Hallel" (120–36 or 135–36 or 136; Jewish sources vary on extent); and the concluding Hallel psalms (146–50). The Hallel psalms had a significant part in the praise (*hallel*) of the Lord. The Egyptian Hallel and the Great Hallel (most of which are pilgrimage songs: 120–34) were sung during the annual feasts. The concluding Hallel psalms (146–50) constituted a part of the daily prayers in the synagogues after the destruction of the temple (A.D. 70).

EXPOSITION

Book I: Psalms 1–41

Psalm 1: God's Blessing on the Godly

The first psalm with its pronouncement of blessing on all who respond in fidelity to the God of the covenant appropriately introduces the book of Psalms. The placing of this psalm is significant because it both invites and encourages God's people to live godly lives. It also provides the assurance that the righteous will be rewarded and that, in the end, God "knows the way of the righteous." The first psalm sets the tone for the entire Psalter because of its concern for God, for godly living, and for the hope of the godly in the realization of the promises of the covenant.

Psalm 1 is a *wisdom* psalm and shares many features common to the book of Proverbs and to other psalms designated as wisdom psalms (34; 37; 49; 73; 111–12; 119; 127–28; 133). Psalm 1 holds forth the blessedness of godliness and encourages wisdom as the way of life.

I. The Discriminating Way of the Godly (1:1–2)

1 The opening phrase of the psalm is an appropriate introduction to the book of Psalms. The formula "Blessed is the man" evokes joy and gratitude, as man may live in fellowship with his God. The word "happy" is a good rendition of "blessed" (GK 897), provided one keeps in mind that the condition of "bliss" is not merely a feeling. Even when the righteous do not feel happy, they are still considered "blessed" from God's perspective. Such happiness is promoted by two kinds of activities: *dissociation* from the wicked and *association* with and devotion to God. The godly do *not* (1) walk in the counsel of the wicked, (2) stand in the way of sinners, or (3) sit in the seat of mockers. Rather, they reflect on the Lord in their walking, standing, and sitting (cf. Dt 6:7). The parallelism is synonymous and profoundly portrays the totality of evil.

In contrast, the "mockers" (GK 4370) have no regard for God and his commandments. They do not respond to instruction (9:7; 15:12) but stir up strife by their insults (22:10). Thus the way of folly entails a devotion to self and to the group in all areas of life.

2 The righteous are positively identified by their association with "the law of the LORD." The "law" (*torah*; GK 9368) signifies primarily instruction that comes from God for the purpose of helping us to live in harmony with God's will. The believer's delight is not only in knowing, studying, and memorizing the Word of God but especially in *doing* God's will.

"Delight" (GK 2914) expresses all that makes the child of God happy. The law is more than a delight; it is the believer's chief desire. The fear of the Lord, as the beginning of wisdom, is expressed as a delight in God's law (112:1). The delight of the godly in doing God's will on earth (Mt 6:10) is the result of a special relationship with the Lord.

The godly person "meditates" (GK 2047) on the law of God day and night. Since the Bible was generally not available to God's people, they memorized and meditated on the word (cf. 119:11), the perfections of the Lord (63:6), and his mighty acts (77:12;

143:5). The one who meditates *continually* reflects God's word in life.

II. The Future of the Godly and the Wicked Contrasted (1:3–5)

3 The happiness of the godly is likened to a tree. Unlike trees growing wild or planted in the fields, where the amount of rainfall varies, the tree the psalmist envisions has been planted purposely by irrigation canals.

The imagery of leaves and fruit assures the godly that they will receive God's blessing and will enjoy life as a gift of God (cf. Eze 47:12). The "prosperity" of the righteous is God's blessing on their words and works (cf. 90:14–17). The psalmist thus encourages the godly to pursue the way of wisdom. The prosperity of the righteous—guaranteed or limited to the godly—is a gift of God, a byproduct of wise living.

4–5 How different is the end of the wicked! The metaphor of chaff reveals both the uselessness of the wicked and the ease with which God will deal with them. Even as the winnower casts the chaff to the afternoon breeze, so the Lord will drive away the wicked.

The end of the wicked may not be clear while they are alive, but from God's perspective they have no future. They cannot withstand the judgment of God. They are judged by being alienated from the congregation of the righteous, i.e., those who have a relationship with God and enjoy his presence—both now and in the life to come.

III. The Discriminating Way of God (1:6)

6 The reason for the certainty of the judgment lies in God's knowledge of the affairs of humankind. God's "knowledge" is a deep commitment to, love for, and care of his own; hence the translation "the LORD watches over." The Lord offers no protection to those who are not reconciled to him; rather, their end is destruction (cf. Mt 7:23; cf. vv.15–27).

Psalm 2: The Messianic King

Since its subject concerns the anointing and coronation of a Davidic king (cf. 2Ki 11:12), Ps 2 is classified as a *royal* psalm. This psalm is one of the most quoted in the NT. It was favored by the apostles as scriptural confirmation of Jesus' messianic office and his expected glorious return with power and authority. The first-century church applied the second psalm to the Messiah as an explanation of the crucifixion of Christ by the rulers (Herod and Pontius Pilate), the nations, and Israel (the priests, scribes, and Pharisees), who had conspired together against the Messiah of God (Ac 4:25–28). Paul applied it to Jesus' ministry: his sonship, resurrection, and ascension to glory, which confirmed God's promises in Jesus as *the* Messiah (Ac 13:32–33; cf. also Heb 1:3, 5–6; Rev 12:5; 19:15).

The theological significance of Ps 2 lies in the hope that it entails. The anointed king rules by God's appointment. The wise response of repentance is a victory for the Messiah and a *token* of the final victory over his enemies, the opponents of God's kingdom (cf. Rev 19:19–21; 20:7–10). From the perspective of typology, Jesus is the fulfillment of the psalm. The psalm offers a special hope for the church as we look forward to the day of our redemption, to the era of peace and victory (Isa 65:20–25).

I. The Rebellious Nations (2:1–3)

1–2 "Why" expresses the irony of the tumultuous efforts against the Lord and his anointed. The psalmist expressed astonishment that the rulers of the earth even tried to counsel together against God, but it is clear that the nations' attempt is in vain.

The rebellion of "the kings" is an outright rejection of the Davidic king, constituting a threat to the universal rule of God. The rebellion is against the Lord and "his Anointed One" (GK 5431). The "Anointed One" refers to any anointed king who was seated on the throne of David.

3 The goal of the rebellion is lordship. The kings of earth are trying to break away from their required allegiance to the King of kings. "Chains" and "fetters" refer to the manner in which the yoke of a cart or plow is placed on the necks of animals. Thus the yoke of God's kingship is not merely rejected; it is insolently thrown off. The kingdoms of this earth are by nature opposed to the rule of God and his Messiah.

II. God's Rule in Heaven (2:4–6)

4 In this section the scene shifts from earth to heaven, where we catch a glimpse of God mocking the feeble attempts of the rulers. Above the turbulence of the nations, God sits and reacts to their rebellion against him with laughter. His laughter is an expression of ridicule, for he knows their end (cf. 37:13).

5 In his appointed time, God speaks with words as well as with acts so that the nations will be terrified by his anger. The "anger" (GK 678) of God is an expression of his "jealousy" (Na 1:2–6). He tolerates no opposition or competition but requires absolute loyalty (vv.11–12).

6 The emphatic "I" introduces the words of God's decree to appoint to the throne a Davidic ruler who will bring the nations to submission. God's reaction to the stirring on earth is the installation of an anointed king. The Davidic king ruled in Zion, God's chosen dwelling place. God had sanctified the city by his presence; therefore Zion was his "holy hill."

III. God's Decree (2:7–9)

7 The "decree" (GK 2976) of the Lord deals with the Davidic king and the establishment of God's kingdom on earth. The divinely appointed king speaks about the Lord's promise, publicly proclaiming his own relationship with God, the Great King. This decree determines his relationship to the king and to the nations. The Davidic king is by birth and by promise the "son of God," and God is the Davidic king's "father" (cf. 2Sa 7:14). In actuality this relationship is confirmed at the moment of the coronation. Therefore the theocratic king must respond to the interests and desires of his father and represent God's will to his people. Jesus is the Christ, the "Son" of God by the Father's proclamation (Mt 3:17; Mk 1:11; Lk 3:22).

8 The privilege of kingship lies in the relationship between God and the king. As the "son" of God he may freely ask for an extension of his rule, because it fits within God's planned universal rule. The father graciously grants to his son the promise of the worldwide rule as his "inheritance" (GK 5709). Since God is the Ruler of the world, he authorizes the Davidic king to extend his kingdom to "the ends of the earth."

9 The rule of God's messiah brings stability, even if he has to use force. His sovereignty may be expressed as an "iron rule" in which rebels are crushed like fragile clay vessels (cf.

Jer 19:11). The "scepter" (GK 8657) is a symbol of rule. It is the means of discipline and judgment. As the scepter of a monarch, it symbolizes here the authority granted by God to rule with great power over the nations.

IV. The Rule of the Messiah on Earth (2:10–12)

10–12 The universal rule of God is expressed by his patience, calling for kings and rulers to assess their situation. If they are wise, they will respond favorably. The wise response includes both a spirit willing to receive God's revelation about the anointed and his kingdom and a joyous spirit of submission to the Lord. Submission is expressed by the word "serve" (GK 6268). The "fear" (GK 3711) of the Lord in this situation is not a sign of emotional instability but a mark of wisdom. It is expressive of the day of his wrath on the nations. Because God requires submission to himself and to his son and blesses those who trust in him, "the LORD" may well be the subject of the verbs, "worship the LORD with reverence; tremble, and kiss the king, lest the LORD be angry with you ... for his anger flares up in a moment" (NEB). This would fit in with the conclusion of the first psalm. He will most surely bless those who find refuge in him, whereas the sinners will perish.

Psalm 3: Quietness Amid Troubles

This is the first psalm included in the collection of psalms ascribed to David (Pss 3–41, with the exclusion of Pss 10 and 33). The mood of the psalm is established by its genre. It is an *individual lament* psalm in which the main speaker expresses confidence in personal and individual deliverance by God (vv.3–8). The historical situation reflected in the psalm finds David at a low moment in his life. Because of his sin with Bathsheba (2Sa 11–12), his life was torn apart by family troubles (2Sa 12:15–14:33), and his kingdom was wrenched from his grasp by Absalom's rebellion (2Sa 15:1–19:43). The hearts of Israel were with Absalom (2Sa 15:13). The anointed of the Lord (cf. Ps 2:6) was forced to flee Jerusalem and wait out the crisis at an encampment across the Jordan (2Sa 17:24). Thus the psalm reflects the national situation as well as the personal feelings of David.

The theological significance is that the Lord will redeem his anointed one, establish his kingdom, and bless his people! Since Jesus is the Messiah, the Anointed One, the believer joins with Israel in the assurance of God's promise, the reception of the benefits of the people of God through the Messiah, the hope of the Messiah's complete victory, and the desire for the establishment of the age of blessing.

I. Lament Over the Enemies (3:1–2)

1–2 David laments over his many adversaries, who comprise a united front. They mock David and exclaim that his God will not take care of him! They curse the king (cf. 2Sa 16:7–8) and conclude that he has been abandoned by the God whom he has served so diligently and in whom he has put his trust.

In the midst of this tragedy, the king prays, "O LORD." The psalmist addresses God by his revealed covenant name, "Yahweh." In the language of prayer in the OT, this address has the same connotation as "Abba, Father" in the NT. For the people of God, the name of the Lord is the assurance that his promises to David will be fulfilled (cf. 2:7–9). He is the Father of Israel and particularly of David (and his sons) as the anointed king.

II. Prayer to the Lord (3:3–4)

3 God is so different from the "many" who oppose him. David is certain of God's promises confirmed in the covenant (cf. 2:6–9). Therefore, his confidence rests in the nature of God, described here as a "shield" (GK 4482). He is convinced that God's kingship is forever. And although the kingship has been forcibly removed from the Lord's anointed, he is still protected by God's kingship.

The power of the Great King is referred to by the word "glory" (GK 3883). Even as a king can be described as glorious because of his vast armies, so the Lord is glorious because he can marshal the angelic host to aid his children (34:7; 91:11). The king puts his confidence in the protection that God alone can provide, because his glory is greater than any human power. He has power to raise up the humble and abase the mighty (1Sa 2:7–8; Ps 103:7–9). He exalts whom he wills and when he wills.

4 Even when he was removed from the presence of God in Jerusalem, the king knew that the Lord would answer him when he called.

Leaving Jerusalem weeping, barefoot, and with his head covered (2Sa 15:30), he now raises up his "voice" to the Lord. The confidence that God will answer him is based on the father-son relationship that the Lord promised to his anointed (cf. 2:7). David's confidence in prayer lies, not in righteous deeds done in the flesh, but in the gracious promises of God.

III. Trust in the Lord (3:5–6)

5–6 Lying down to sleep expresses David's confidence in God's response to his plea. The psalmist knows that God "sustains" (GK 6164). He looks up to God while facing the "tens of thousands" who have surrounded him as a city under siege. David's commitment to God results in an abandonment of his problem to God. Though David has been moved by the "many enemies" (vv.1–2), prayer renews his confidence in the One who will be victorious over the many, and with this thought he consoles himself and goes to sleep.

IV. Prayer for Deliverance and Expression of Hope (3:7–8)

7 At this point the psalm moves with a quickening rhythm. The prayer's intensity is marked by the words "Arise, O LORD! / Deliver me, O my God!" The psalmist freely seeks to rouse the Lord to action. The skeptics have already concluded that "God will not deliver him" (v.1). Here he calls for deliverance and uses his enemies' word for God—but in a personalized way ("my God")—as he petitions God to prove his adversaries wrong.

Striking the enemies on the jaw is an expression of humiliation (cf. 1Ki 22:24; Isa 50:6). The metaphor of the breaking of teeth likens the enemies to wild animals whose strength is taken away when their teeth are crushed (cf. Ps 58:6). The psalmist has hope that regardless of what enemies may arise from within or from without the kingdom of God, God will be victorious (cf. 1Co 15:24–28; 2Th 1:5–10).

8 Victory belongs to the Lord, and he grants it to his beloved. That the psalmist is not only concerned for himself and the security of his kingship is evident by the conclusion. His prayer is that, through the victory granted to the Lord's anointed, God's blessing may return to his people. The spirit of the shepherd-king is revealed by his concern for the welfare of his people.

The blessing of God is the result of his gracious deliverance. He granted the "blessing" of his presence, protection, and prosperity to Abraham (Ge 12:2–3) and confirmed it to Israel (Dt 26, esp. vv.5–10). To David, God has promised the removal of wicked people and external enemies as well as the subsequent peace of his people (2Sa 7:10–11, 29). David looks forward to the time of full blessing. In his hope lies ours, for in Jesus' promises the victory and blessings of God are assured.

Psalm 4: An Evening Hymn (in Despondency)

The psalm is an evening hymn (v.8) and forms, together with the morning psalm (Ps 5; cf. 5:3), avenues for believers to come to their heavenly Father in prayer. As an expression of confidence in God, the psalm helps the reader to meditate on God's fatherly care and to leave the troubles and causes of anxiety in his hands.

The literary genre of the psalm fits the *individual psalms of lament,* with motifs characteristic of the subgenre, *psalms of confidence.* The mixture of the genres may account for the lack of consensus in determining the structure.

I. Prayer (4:1)

1 In his need the psalmist David turns to his "righteous God." He believes that regardless of his innocent suffering, God will act triumphantly on behalf of his servant. The word "righteous" (GK 7406) expresses the relation between God and his people. It signifies more than an absolute standard or norm. He has promised them his presence and victory over adverse circumstances.

Faith in God's righteousness is based on God's covenant promise that he will come to the rescue of his children in need (Ps 25:4–5; Isa 45:13). Calling boldly on God is a privilege that belongs to his children. It is to this end that the psalmist calls on God as "my righteous God." He calls on the Lord in his "distress," though the nature of this distress is not clear. Boldly, yet humbly, he casts himself on the "mercy" (GK 2858) of God, who has covenanted to be loving and faithful to his own. Prayer is a form of communication

in which children of God cast themselves on the mercy of God.

II. Call for Trust in the Lord (4:2–5)

2 The "men" belong to the class of prominent citizens. As a class they form the landowners, the wealthy, and the powerful in Israel's society. The leadership has gone astray. (1) They have scoffed at the Lord's "glory"; i.e., they have despised the position of the king. "Glory" (GK 3883) is bestowed by God on his anointed king (3:3). (2) They characterize themselves by a diligent pursuit of what is vain ("delusions") and deceptive ("false gods"). They have trodden the king's glory into the ground by betraying it for an unspecified worthless cause.

3–5 In a series of seven imperatives, the enemies are called on to respond in a more constructive way. (1) They should recognize that the Lord has chosen David to be his friend. He is "the godly" set apart by the Lord, who has bestowed on him his steadfast love, confirmed to him by covenant (cf. 2Sa 7:15a).

(2) The command to "[be] angry" (GK 8074) seems strange in light of Eph 4:26, 31. The verb can also be translated as "be disturbed" or "tremble." Though the enemies may have strong feelings of enmity, they must learn to submit themselves. The sense of the clause is "tremble with fear, and stop sinning."

(3) The prohibition "Do not sin" is an exhortation for the enemies to repent from their evil way of life. Hatred of God's people is always wrong (cf. Jas 3:9), but it is especially reprehensible when directed toward God's anointed.

(4) If the enemies persist in their way, David exhorts them to do so secretly, while they lie on their beds. "Search your hearts" signifies thinking and planning. The wicked may think their perverse thoughts to themselves, if they have to, but they should not be expressed publicly.

(5) The enemies should wail over their past hostility. "Be silent" (GK 1957) has the sense of keeping still like a stone (Ex 15:16). Since the verb is parallel with "tremble" (i.e., "in your anger"), it is preferable to assume that David calls on his opponents to "wail" over their sin against him and against the Lord.

(6) and (7) The last two imperatives call for *true* repentance: "Offer right sacrifices and trust in the LORD." The enemies are to present the sacrifices to the Lord in accordance with his ordinances and with the attitude of commitment, because he does not delight in mere sacrifice (1Sa 15:22; Ps 50:14). They must be "sincere" sacrifices, presented as an expression of submission to him.

III. Prayer (4:6–7)

6 As a true shepherd of Israel, David knows the hearts of the people. It is a time of turmoil and frustration because of unfulfilled expectations regarding the covenant blessings. It is not clear who the "many" are. Regardless, David prays for them and calls on God to make his covenant blessings evident both to the nation and to himself. He does this first by an allusion to the priestly benediction (Nu 6:24–26). They asked, "Who can show us any good?" David responds by pointing away from himself and to the Lord as the author of blessing.

7 David continues his prayer that the Lord may restore to the nation the fullness of his blessing. The disgrace of the king has brought an end to God's blessings. While the people lament, David prays, because the Lord had "filled [his] heart with greater joy." God-given joy is vastly more important than all the food the world can give.

IV. Expression of Trust (4:8)

8 The enemies diligently pursued vanity and deception in an attempt to frustrate the king and bring down his glory (cf. v.2). David is not worried about the outcome. He commits his way to the Lord as he goes to sleep. The enemies may have vexed themselves on their beds (v.4), but he experiences "peace" (GK 8934), the peace that comes as a blessing from God (Nu 6:26). His confidence in the Lord "alone" is the reason for his peaceful sleep. The expression "make me dwell in safety" connotes not only the absence of enemies and hostilities but also the presence of peace.

Psalm 5: A Morning Prayer (in Anticipation of God's Presence)

This psalm is generally categorized as an *individual lament* psalm. It shares elements of the psalms of *confidence* (vv.1–3; 8–12) and

also of a *community* lament (vv.11–12). There is no agreement on the original life situation.

I. Prayer for God's Justice (5:1–3)

1 The lament is an expression of a great need felt by the psalmist. He expresses himself with audible sounds. In his state of mind he does not think about the formalities of prayer, because he knows that the Lord hears both inner thoughts ("sighing") and audible "words." As an oppressed person, he is revealing his need to find someone who can redeem and deliver. The psalm presupposes that an injustice has been done.

2 Because of the apparent injustice, David prays to no one other than his "King." The phrase "my King and my God" recognizes that while God is the sovereign King and able to deliver, he is close enough to his children that they may call him "my God," the equivalent of "Abba."

3 With the dawn of each new day, prayer is renewed with the hope that the Lord will soon respond. The "morning" is symbolic of a renewal of God's acts of love (cf. La 3:23). The change from darkness to light brings with it the association of renewed hope. In the early morning hours the psalmist seeks the Lord in prayer because he knows that God will not forsake him. During the day he waits with "expectation" (GK 7595) to see what the Lord will do for him.

II. Affirmation of God's Hatred of Evil (5:4–6)

4–6 Whereas other religions bring together good and evil at the level of the gods, God has revealed that evil exists apart from him and yet is under his sovereign control. The psalmist shows a clear conviction that God hates in the most radical way any form of evil and denies lawless persons any right to his presence.

God's absolute hatred of evil is revealed in how he will quickly judge unfaithful people as well as those who oppress the poor (Mal 3:5). The negative statements "cannot dwell" and "cannot stand" are complemented by the phrase "you destroy."

God hates both the sin and those who sin against him. The particular sins are examples of a way of life. The liar is only a hairbreadth away from the murderer. Though a liar may claim that he only goes so far with his deception, when he is caught, the liar is a dangerous person, because he may attempt to cover his tracks. The "bloodthirsty" are not necessarily guilty of murder but no longer know the limits between "mine" and "thine" and thus twist and pervert justice, even at the cost of human lives or dignity. Instead of "taking pleasure" in evil, the Lord "abhors" all who practice wickedness.

III. Hope in Fellowship With God (5:7)

7 In contrast to the wicked who will not be able to "stand" or "dwell" in God's presence (vv.4–5), the psalmist prays with expectation that the Lord will permit him to enjoy his presence. The hope of fellowship with God is based, not on his own righteousness, but on God's sovereign "love" or "mercy" (GK 2876). For the psalmist the hope of entering into the temple is much more than the physical walking into the courts of the temple. He seeks the affirmation of God's love for him in an evil world and, hence, the assurance of God's presence with him. Because he knows that God is "holy," he prostrates himself in the direction of the temple with the prayer of hope that the Lord will answer him. His submission to his covenant God is further brought out by the manner of his approach: He bows down "in reverence."

IV. Prayer for and Hope in God's Righteousness (5:8–12)

8–9 The psalmist prays for the Lord to "make straight" (GK 3837) his path by leading the godly in his "righteousness" (GK 7407). This prayer has two components. On the one hand, he prays for the Lord's presence to guide him by leveling the obstacles from the way of life (cf. 27:11). On the other hand, he prays for the Lord to show himself righteous because his divine order is challenged by the ungodly.

The wicked are further described as instruments of destruction and death. By their reign of terror, they are opposed to the God of life and truth. The heart of the wicked is full of "destruction." Their mouths, filled with lies and deceit, are likened to "an open grave," because of their deadly words. With their slippery tongues they sow discord, hatred, and death.

10 At the root of the evildoers' actions is their rebellion against God. The chaos caused by the evildoers requires a response from the Lord. For this reason the psalmist prays for their demise. The phrase "declare them guilty" calls on the Lord both to declare a guilty verdict and to judge them with an appropriate sentence. That is, the psalmist prays that the Lord will hold the wicked culpable for their acts and will remove them from the covenant community. The seeds sown in unrighteousness and unfaithfulness must bear their fruits by bringing calamities on the wicked. God's justice must cause the schemes of the wicked to backfire on themselves.

11–12 The just acts of God leading to the conviction and the destruction of the wicked give the godly community a reason to rejoice in his righteousness. The righteous acts of God include the preservation of the godly, "who take refuge" in him, and their glorification, as they praise him for the establishment of his righteousness and justice on earth. The psalmist hopes that God's judgment of the wicked will provide the righteous with a greater reason to rejoice in the marvelous powers of salvation and victory, which he shares with his own. The "righteous" are the same as those "who love your name." The Lord protects his own under the cover of his wings (cf. 91:4).

The grand conclusion exalts the Lord as the God who deals graciously with the righteous. Their hope lies in the Lord, who will constantly guard his own "as with a shield." "You surround [GK 6496] them" may also be translated as "you crown them." On the one hand, the Lord extends his protection and favor, likened to a "shield." On the other hand, he bestows his royal glory on the godly.

Psalm 6: A Prayer (in Deep Anguish)

This psalm is one of seven penitential psalms (6; 32; 38; 51; 102; 130; 143) of the early church. In a strict sense, however, it is not a penitence psalm, for there is no confession of sin or prayer for forgiveness. The psalm can be categorized as an *individual lament* psalm. It is not possible to be certain of its original setting. Throughout the first part the psalmist speaks of personal suffering so intense that he may collapse. He prays that God may heal him and no longer be angry.

With a sudden twist he turns to the wicked and, in an assured voice, announces that they, instead, will be disgraced (v.8).

I. Prayer for God's Favor (6:1–3)

These first three verses express the perplexity of the psalmist during a period of depression. The tragedy is intensified by the semblance of God's anger; for the psalmist, his suffering is nearly more than he can bear, and there is no end in sight. He asks for God's grace to sustain him.

1 The verbs "rebuke" (GK 1722) and "discipline" (GK 3579) are often synonymous. The discipline of the Lord may seem so harsh that it seems he is angry. David prays that the Lord will not discipline him in wrath. His discipline is indeed there, but the psalmist does not understand why it has come or how long it is going to last. God's discipline is for the purpose of sanctification; however, in David's present experience it almost works the opposite result. God seems to have forsaken him (v.3).

2 In his suffering (cf. vv.8–10), David turns to the Lord as if to say, "Father, my covenant faithful God." He does not confess his sins but asks the Lord to demonstrate his covenant promises: restoration (v.2) and loyalty (v.4). In a manner characteristic of the OT, he identifies suffering with judgment and judgment with God's wrath (cf. 38:1–3)—a wrath that can have terrible effects (cf. Isa 66:15–16; Jer 10:10; Mic 1:2–4; et al.).

The verb "faint" (GK 583) is sometimes used to express the process of withering of leaves and crops; metaphorically it signifies the weakness of strong people and of fortifications (Isa 24:4; Jer 14:2; La 2:8). For this psalmist it shows how his vigor (spiritual, psychological, and physical) has been brought down. The word "bones" suggests the depth of his depression, which has affected his most inner being.

3 The "anguish" is even more intense because it seems that the discipline has no regard for the psalmist's frailty and has no apparent end in sight. He wants the Lord to "be merciful" (GK 2858; v.2) so as to restore him. If not now, when? Verse 3 is incomplete with its final cry "how long?" Because of the intensity of his emotions, he cannot complete his thought (cf. 31:1; 35:17; 74:10; et al.).

II. Prayer for God's Love (6:4–5)

4 David boldly calls on the Lord to "turn" (or "return"; GK 8740). At this moment, in the depth of his suffering, he needs his God—who has promised not to leave him— to extend his "unfailing love" (GK 2876) to him and thereby deliver him. Only the Lord can take a person out of deep depression so as to give a sense of personal well-being.

5 What is a human being when he is dead? This does not mean that the OT denies life after death, but it puts the emphasis on the present life, lived in relationship to God. There is still time for the psalmist to praise his Creator. The combination of "remembers" (GK 2352) and "praises" (GK 3344) suggests that "remember" is more than an intellectual act of mental representation. It is an intense spiritual act of bringing to mind what God has done as a basis for gratitude (cf. 111:4).

III. Need of God's Love (6:6–7)

6–7 Suffering produces tears. David does not know how much longer he can bear the anguish, insomnia, and tears. He is alone at night in his bed, but his foes are there too, in his thoughts. He cannot renew his strength by himself! The failing eyesight he refers to is not the result of old age but of deep sorrow.

IV. Prayer for God's Favor (6:8–10)

8–10 These verses mark a radical change in tone. Instead of the lament there is a renewal of strength by which the psalmist proclaims to the enemies that the Lord has been victorious in him and that, consequently, they need to prepare themselves for God's vindication of him. Such a transition from lament to victory occurs in other psalms (e.g., 20:6; 22:22; 28:6; 31:19; 69:30).

The Lord has come to the rescue of his servant. He has heard his child crying for favor. He will now deal with the enemies who "do evil" by bringing on their heads the terrible fate they brought on David: shame, agony, and sudden disgrace. Confidence springs up only from conditions changed by the Lord, not from a mere psychological lift or personal effort. When grace penetrates into the depth of an anguished soul, joy in the Lord anchors faith.

Psalm 7: The Righteous God Loves the Righteous

The specific genre of Psalm 7 has been difficult to determine because it contains elements of an individual lament (vv.1–2), an oath (vv.3–5), a psalm of the Lord's kingship (vv.6–12), and a thanksgiving hymn (v.17).

I. Prayer for Refuge (7:1–2)

1–2 The first phrase ("O LORD my God") expresses the confidence that the heavenly Father cares for his child on earth. "I take refuge in you" amplifies the closeness of the psalmist's relationship with God. In the deepest need, the anguished soul cries out to the Father, confident that only the Lord can deliver him from those who pursue him (cf. 1Sa 23:28; 24:14; 25:29; 26:18). David feels as if he is being mauled by a lion and torn to pieces. His predicament reveals the tension between knowing that he is innocent (vv.3–5) and experiencing the apparent judgment of God.

II. Oath of Innocence (7:3–5)

3–4 The psalmist appeals again to his heavenly Father using the same words as in v.1. The repetition of "if" (three times in Hebrew) together with his readiness to suffer for any wrong he may have done show that he is confused. He is astonished that the Lord permits him to be treated as an evildoer. He swears in the presence of God that he is innocent, though not perfect!

5 David argues that he has not done anything to friend or foe to deserve this treatment! If he were a man of treachery, he would gladly permit his enemy to trample him to death. He willingly suffers the curses of the covenant, knowing that the wicked do not deserve "life" and "glory" as do those who are blessed with the covenant promises.

III. God's Righteous Judgment (7:6–13)

6 The psalmist puts forth request after request as he pours out his heart before the Lord. He calls on God to act *now* in judgment and in wrath. He appeals to God's sense of justice and integrity (v.8). He believes that when God is provoked, "justice" (GK 5477) will be done. Hence the repetitive prayer requesting the Lord to act: "Arise . . . rise up . . . Awake."

7–8 When the Lord comes in his indignation, the nations can no longer escape their due. He calls them to account because he rules over them. He has searched his heart to see whether he has been disloyal to God or to any human being. In the depth of his heart, he knows that while he is not sinless, he is a man of "integrity" (GK 9448). Because of the gravity of his suffering and alienation from God, only God can graciously renew their relationship.

9–11 The affirmation of God as "righteous" (GK 7404) and as one who "searches" is no cause for the righteous to be afraid. They have taken "refuge" in his grace. Their faults are not hidden from his sight, because he tests "minds and hearts," i.e., a person's innermost being. The righteous depend on the gracious relationship initiated and confirmed by God.

God "expresses his wrath" against those who have been tested and are found wanting. He is the "righteous judge" who protects the godly with his saving shield, for they are "the upright in heart," and judges the wicked in his wrath. The "upright" (GK 3838) are full of integrity; in their loyalty to God they can ask him to judge them and search their hearts. But before the judgment occurs, the Lord takes the judgment seat and gathers the nations around him (vv.7–8a).

12–13 David's conviction that God will judge evil grows as he portrays the Lord as a righteous "warrior" (GK 1475) with sword, bow, and arrows. His lightnings are the "flaming arrows." The reference is to arrows dipped in flammable material, such as oil or pitch, and set aflame before being shot. If the wicked do not repent, their judgment is sure. The sharp sword, deadly weapons, and flaming arrows are metaphors of his inescapable judgment. God is *preparing* himself for judgment at his appointed time.

IV. Judgment of the Guilty (7:14–16)

14–16 Evil is metaphorically portrayed in these verses in the language of conception and birth. The wicked are filled with evil, as a pregnant woman about to give birth. Once wickedness is born, it grows into "trouble" and "violence" (cf. Mk 7:21–22; Jas 1:14–15). The certainty of judgment (vv.12–13) and the prevalence of evil find their point of contact

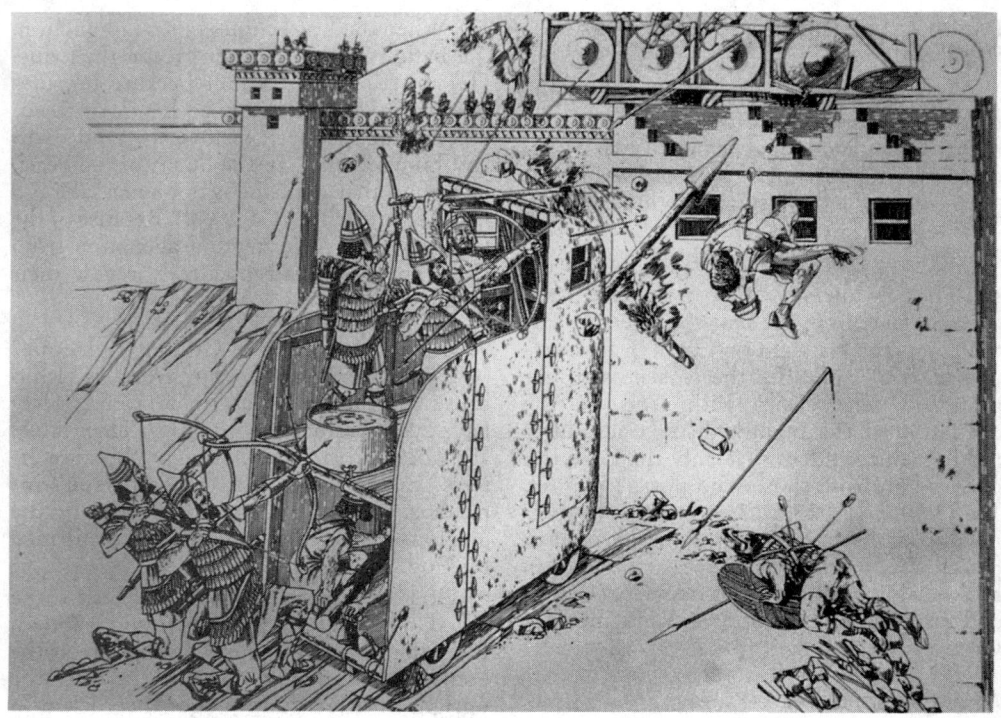

This is an artist's impression of an assault on the walls of a city, based on Assyrian reliefs. The psalmist in 7:12–13 compares God to a warrior with sword, bows, and arrows. Drawing by Gert LaGrange. Courtesy of the Lachish Excavations.

in the doctrine of the retribution of evil (cf. Pr 26:27; Mt 26:52).

V. Praise of God's Righteousness (7:17)

17 The righteous rejoice in the righteousness of God. His righteous judgment affects both the wicked and the righteous. The wicked fall, whereas the righteous experience deliverance in God's acts of judgment. The attribute of God's "righteousness" (GK 7406) is what he does or will do on behalf of his own. He is a victorious God who triumphs over evil and will avenge his children. Despair is thus transformed into hope, and hope is expressed in the singing of praise to the Lord.

The "name" of the God of Israel is Yahweh ("the LORD"; GK 3378). He alone is "God Most High." "Most High" is an epithet of deity and first occurs in the interaction between Melchizedek and Abraham, where it refers to the "Creator of heaven and earth" (cf. Ge 14:18–20, 22). Here the "Most High" describes the universal rule of God, to whom his subjects sing praise (cf. 9:2; 50:14; 92:16). The hope of the godly is in the final removal of evil. Therefore, their praise must include affirmations of God's righteousness and the victory of our Lord Jesus.

Psalm 8: The Glory of the Creator and of Humankind

The hymnic quality of this psalm has been observed by many. The difficulty of classification is due to the many elements woven together in a poetic blend. For our purpose we shall consider it as a *hymn of praise* and, more particularly, a hymn of *creation praise*. The Lord is the object of praise (vv.1, 9). Therefore the praise is not an expression of joy in creation apart from the Creator but looks at God as the good Creator, Ruler, and Sustainer of the world.

The significance of Ps 8 lies in its approach to Creation and its application to the Messiah. The biblical account of Creation was intended to help Israel praise the Lord as the sole Creator of everything in heaven, on earth, and in the sea. The NT applies the glory of humankind to the Messiah, as he has subjected everything to himself (Heb 2:6–9; cf. 1Co 15:27; Eph 1:22). In Jesus' victory the Christian has received the glorious renewal of which the psalmist speaks (Heb 2:10–11)!

I. Ascription of Praise (8:1a)

1a The introductory and concluding ascriptions of praise form an inclusion within which the glory of the Creator is the object of celebration. The Redeemer-God is Lord over his people. The name "our Lord" addresses God as king (cf. 97:5). The Redeemer-King of Israel is the Creator! His "name" ("LORD") is glorious over all the earth by virtue of his creative activities (cf. Ge 1:1–31). The word "majestic" (GK 129) is a royal attribute denoting his victories (Ex 15:6), his might in judgment (1Sa 4:8; Ps 76:4), his law (Isa 42:21), and his rule over creation (Pss 8:1, 9; 93:4). All creation reveals the power and glory of God's name (Ro 1:20).

II. The Glory of the Great King (8:1b–2)

1b–2 The Lord's glorious rule over heaven is no surprise from a theistic perspective (19:1). But the marvel is that his creation not only reveals but is glorious (cf. Isa 6:3). The discordant note sounded by the enemies in his creation is silenced by the praise of children (cf. Mt 21:15–16). Regardless of how the wicked assert themselves, they cannot outdo the evidence of God's glory on earth and in heaven. His glory is established ("ordained"; GK 3569), and no enemy can overcome his kingdom. The continuity of the human race is God's way of assuring the ultimate glorification of an earth populated with a new humanity (Hab 2:14).

III. God's Interest in Humanity (8:3–4)

3–4 The Creator has established two spheres of rule: heaven and earth. He has established the celestial bodies in the firmament and has given them the rule over day and night (Ge 1:17–18), whereas he appointed humankind to govern the earth (Ge 1:28). The heavenly bodies all have their appointed place. In relation to the vastness of space, the order and the importance of the heavenly bodies, "what is man"? The word "man" (GK 632) is a poetic word for a human being in his frail human existence (9:20; 90:3; 103:15), whereas

"son of man" (cf. 80:17; 144:3) is contrasted with "God" ("heavenly beings"). Human beings are by nature earthlings, and yet they are the particular objects of God's attention. The Creator has invested glory and honor on them. The verbs "mindful" (GK 2349) and "care for" (GK 7212) convey the care of God, who remembers positively by acting on behalf of the human race. Instead of "visiting" persons with judgment, as their sins deserve, God's goodness extends to all creatures in his care (Mt 5:45).

IV. Humanity's Derived Glory (8:5)

5 The significance of human beings is not to be limited to their existence before sin came into the world. They still are "crowned" with glory. The sequence of verbs expresses poetically the status that God, by his divine decree, has given to humankind. The verses could be rendered as "You made [perfect] him a little lower than the heavenly beings and crown [present] him with glory and honor. You make [present] him ruler over the works of your hands; you put [past] everything under his feet."

"Glory and honor" are attributes of God's kingship (29:1; 104:1) that are extended to a human being's royal status. Yet people are not divine; they are in "the image and likeness of God" (Ge 1:26–27). In this exalted status they may be said to be "less than God" (NIV note) or less than "the heavenly [angelic] beings" (the Hebrew allows for either translation).

V. Humanity's Glory as Ruler (8:6–8)

6–8 Humanity's position over creation was granted before the Fall (Ge 1:28), but it was not taken away after the Fall (Ge 9:1–3, 7). Human beings are God's appointed governors (vassals) over creation. Their function on earth is to maintain order, to shine God's light on creation, and to keep a beneficent relationship with all that God has created on earth and in the sea. The Great King has appointed the human race to maintain dominion over creation and not be controlled by creation.

VI. Concluding Ascription of Praise (8:9)

9 See verse 1 above.

Psalm 9: Prayer and Praise for God's Just Rule of the Nations

This psalm is an incomplete acrostic psalm (*aleph-kaph*) and seems to have formally belonged together with Ps 10 (*lamed-taw*). It is an *individual lament* psalm, combining prayer with praise and telling of God's just rule over the nations. The next psalm is an *individual lament* psalm in which prayer focuses on the enemies of the covenant, who have at one time belonged to the faithful.

I. Individual Praise (9:1–2)

1–2 In response to a distressing situation, the psalmist brings himself to praise God in anticipation of the hour of deliverance. He exhorts himself to such praise, not only as a therapy to forget his troubles for a moment, but also to deepen his trust in the Lord. The depth of gratitude and joy finds expression in five synonymous verbs expressive of praise: "I will praise . . . tell . . . be glad . . . rejoice . . . sing praise." He praises God with all his "heart," for he loves the Lord without reservation.

The various verbs for praise express the intensity of the psalmist's love for God. His God is none other than the God of "wonders" (GK 7098), i.e., God's marvelous acts of redemption and judgment. These acts were regularly rehearsed as a reminder of God's goodness and love, especially for comfort in time of need. The psalmist praises the "name" of God ("LORD"), who is also the "Most High," in hope that the name of God will protect his servant and that the Lord will manifest again a "wonder" on his behalf.

II. Judgment on the Wicked (9:3–6)

3 The psalmist now prays that the Lord will "turn back" (GK 8740) his enemies so that they will be no more. When God makes the enemies to flee, they will stumble and perish. "Before you" may be interpreted as "from your presence," "because of your presence," or "in your presence."

4–6 The prayer contains a request that the Lord will uphold his own, rule righteously, and rebuke the nations, so that ruin and destruction will overtake them and their memory may perish. The child of God may freely present his "right" or "cause" to his or her Redeemer-God. The "right" is the case lodged against the wicked. Belief in God's justice is liberating because God is both Advocate and Judge. Freedom from worry is God's gift to his child, because God judges "righteously."

The "righteous" judgment of God is guaranteed by his rule. He is the Great King over all and, thereby, has authority to judge effectively. To this end the psalmist prays that God will "rebuke the nations and destroy the wicked" (cf. v.5). The "rebuke" (GK 1721) of God is both his wrath against the enemy and his defense of the righteous. In the end it will seem as if the wicked have never existed. He will blot out their name.

III. Hope in God's Just Rule (9:7–10)

7–10 The ground of hope in prayer is the belief that the Lord rules! The hope of the godly during duress remains in the presence of God's kingdom. Though not always transparent, the Lord is King! Belief in his kingship affirms one's conviction of the difference between his rule and that of the nations and gives hope in the biblical teaching that he shall establish righteousness on earth. Because he reigns, there is hope. He is the "refuge" and "stronghold" for his children. God as a "refuge" (GK 5369) is a metaphor for the power and goodness of the Lord for the "oppressed," an OT equivalent of "poor in spirit" (cf. 10:17; 74:21). He will "never" forsake those who rely on him!

The psalmist is confident that God's rule is beneficial to the godly, i.e., to those who "know" the name of the Lord. He cares for them (1:6), and they trust in his "name" to deliver them from distress. They "seek" him with their whole being and are not like the nations that forget God (v.17).

IV. Communal Praise and Individual Prayer (9:11–14)

11–12 The praise of the godly rises out of their conviction that God cares. The psalmist calls on them to join with him in singing a hymn, the focus of which is God's just rule. He is "enthroned in Zion" (cf. 2:4, 6). Zion is his "footstool," or the earthly manifestation of his heavenly rule (cf. 2:4; 76:2; 132:13–14). This Great King serves his people, vindicating the needy. Even when they were in distress and it seemed as if God was not present, the nations were to understand that his nature will never tolerate injustice done to his elect. He does not forget the atrocities suffered by the poor; he cares for "the cry of the afflicted."

13–14 The enemy causes the affliction, and the gravity of the experience often gives rise to a prayerful cry for help (cf. v.12; 88:13) with the hope that God may "see" and "have mercy." The intensity of the suffering is comparable with death. David feels as if hell ("the gates of death") is here. Life has turned into a trial of alienation, affliction, and disaster, and he cannot dig his way out. Only in "Zion" may the godly find rest because God dispenses his righteousness to them where he is. The "Daughter of Zion" stands for God's people (Mic 4:8) or for Jerusalem, the city of God (Isa 1:8; 10:32).

The praise of God is a recounting of the "salvation" (GK 3802) of God. The psalmist looks forward to God's deliverance and to the end of the rule of the wicked. He also looks forward to the time when he will "declare" the "praises" of the Lord. The public proclamation involves a remembrance of God's "wonders" (v.1), of his "praises" (i.e., his praiseworthy acts), and of his glorious acts of "salvation."

V. Judgment of the Wicked (9:15–18)

15–18 These four verses are to be regarded as the hymn of praise the psalmist spoke of in v.14. The trust of the godly is grounded in their conviction that "the needy will not always be forgotten, nor the hope of the afflicted ever perish." Therefore they can anticipate the time when the principle of retribution takes effect and the afflicted find relief. The song includes hope pertaining to the end of the wicked, as if it already had taken place, much the same as the song "Fallen! Fallen is Babylon the Great!" (Rev 18:2). (*Higgaion* is a musical notation (cf. 92:4). Combined with *Selah*, it may indicate a meditative mood in which vv.17–18 are to be sung.)

VI. Hope in God's Just Rule (9:19–20)

19–20 The mood changes from pensive meditation on God's faithfulness to the elect (v.18) to a rousing cry for immediate deliverance. "Terror" is not an indication of complete alienation and doom; rather it is an act by which the nations may "fear" the Lord, recognizing their human frailty. The cry comes out of a broken spirit and shows no

evidence of enmity or a desire for revenge. The issue is God's justice and faithfulness to his own. If he does not judge the nations, they will never realize that they are revolutionaries against their Creator-King. They are but "men," i.e., weak and human. The "terror" of the acts of God strikes the ungodly with a sense of hopelessness, but God's vengeance on the wicked signifies hope and redemption for the godly!

Psalm 10: Human Rule and God's Kingship

The focus of Ps 10 lies on the problem of theodicy, i.e., the justice of God in face of the prosperity of the wicked Israelites. The psalm gives a moving picture of the development of evil within the covenant community.

I. Questions (10:1)

1 The assurance of God's kingship and justice is missing in the opening note of the psalm. The tone is set by the interrogative "Why?" The psalmist does not accuse God of having forsaken his own; rather it seems to him as if "the times of trouble" are too much a burden to carry. His prayers for deliverance are unheard. He needs God's help, but it is as if God keeps his distance by keeping himself well-hidden. The question also introduces the riddle of the prosperity of the wicked and the suffering of the righteous (cf. Ps 73). The riddle is not *resolved* but is *refocused* on the God who cares for his own (v.14).

II. The Rule of the Wicked (10:2–11)

2 In their pride the wicked act as "gods" in this world. Their vile words and despotic acts offend and hurt the people of God. But God does not always react swiftly to protect the honor of his name. The people whom the psalmist describes were familiar with God and his law, but they openly rejected the godly way of life in favor of freedom and power. The ways of evil and righteousness are inconsistent. Evil cannot tolerate godliness but pursues the godly with an unholy zeal. The righteous, whom the wicked attempt to trap, are not "weak" but "afflicted." The translation "hunts down" (GK 1944) brings out the "hot pursuit" of the wicked. But it is not clear whether the godly are actually "caught" by their crafty schemes or whether the psalmist prays that the wicked may be caught by their own plots.

3–4 The evil man's hatred of the godly expresses a total disregard for the Lord and his commandments. He is filled with self. The wicked "boasts" that whatever he desires, he can accomplish by his scheming. This greedy man has no regard for God or his commandments. He "praises" himself but spurns the covenant God. His goal in life is a purposeful avoidance of God. He is not an atheist, but instead he has conveniently chosen to live without God. The rejection of the Lord is evident from the greedy man's warped sense of justice and concern (v.5), his false confidence (v.6), his foul language (v.7), his perverse acts (vv.8–10), and his utter disregard of accountability to God (v.11).

5 Success may crown injustice. The prosperity of the godly (1:3) is guaranteed by God, but the wicked make every effort to take their share. They flaunt the "judgments" ("laws") of God. Because God has not yet come in judgment, the wicked become more brazen in their selfish, despotic rule. They have contempt for any who get in their way and count them as their "enemies" (cf. Mal 1:13).

6 In their prosperity the wicked presumptuously take to themselves the privileges of the righteous—those whom God has promised will not be moved. The wicked do not need God. Moreover, they are "happy" with themselves. In their pride they may live without a sense of accountability, for they do not expect retribution. Moreover, they take measures never to experience "trouble" as they autonomously attempt to avoid God's righteous judgment.

7–10 The wicked may appear not to be dangerous, but they use their tongues as a weapon. They intimidate with their curses and threats; their oath is worthless because it is a lie. But they are so powerful and persuasive in their speech that they always seem to get their way. Their speech reflects their scheming (vv.3–4, 6), and their intent is to work destruction. "Trouble and evil" are a way of life for them. They lie in wait like wild animals to ambush and gain control over innocent victims. Once the wicked have their victims, they carry them off like a "lion." The psalmist also compares the wicked to the hunter who pursues his prey and traps it in a net. Thus the victims are overpowered by brute force. They receive no justice or mercy.

11 The psalmist returns to his starting point (cf. vv.2–4). The arrogance of the wicked expresses itself in injustice, but their root problem is their utter disregard for the Lord. They have rejected the covenant God by speech and actions. They mistake God's patience with evil for God's lack of interest in justice and the innocent victims. Their boldness grows as they no longer sense any accountability to God for their actions.

III. Prayer for Deliverance (10:12–15)

12–15 Verses 12 and 15 together form the prayer for God's intervention. In between these two verses the psalmist reflects on the folly of the wicked. He asks with amazement "why" or "how" the wicked dare to revile God and imagine that God does not see evil (cf. v.11). He answers his own question, calming his feelings of disturbance and anxiety at the presence of evil. God does after all see their evil exploits.

The wicked may spurn God and his judgments (vv.3–5), while the innocent victims seek protection from their heavenly Father. The emphatic use of "But you" and "you" implies that the sole hope of the victims is in their abandonment to their God, who has promised to help the fatherless and all his children in need (cf. vv.17–18). God's patience explains the delay in justice.

IV. The Rule of God (10:16)

16 The hope of the righteous in a just world lies in the Lord. His kingship is established "for ever and ever." How can the wicked think that they will last "from generation to generation" (cf. v.6)? Together with the nations, they will perish from "his land," so as to leave God's people at rest. The concern of the psalmist here is with the "land" of Israel, where anarchy prevailed. The word "nations" refers to the wicked in Israel, who act like the nations.

V. Resolution (10:17–18)

17–18 God's kingship was revealed to Israel (Ex 15:18) and came to expression in Israel. Because God is faithful to the covenant, he has promised to judge the needy. "The fatherless and the oppressed" is a reference to the class of people who were most easily wronged but were protected by God's law (Ex 22:22–24; Dt 10:18; 16:11, 14). God gives the needy what they desire by stopping the reign of terror by those who act like gods. The idiom "who is of the earth" expresses the weakness of humankind.

Psalm 11: Refuge in the Righteous King

The psalm is an *individual lament* with an emphasis on confidence in the Lord. The lament is expressed in the words of the friends who despair of evil (vv.1c–3).

I. Refuge in God (11:1–3)

1–3 The wicked are fully intent on making anarchy their way of life. They haunt the "upright in heart," i.e., the godly, who know and love the Lord and therefore do his will. The wicked are bent on ridding themselves of those who do God's will on earth. There are two responses to the immediate threat: escape or refuge. Reason dictates *escape*. The godly seem to be powerless against such treachery. In view of this, the psalmist asks, "What can the righteous do?" The psalmist has already answered this counsel by his personal expression of trust: "In the LORD I take refuge." Trust and confidence in the Lord mark this psalm (cf. vv.4, 7).

"Flee like a bird" is an expression of quick escape in search of quietness (cf. 55:6; 124:7). The psalmist quickly dismisses escape. His advisors argue against him with facts. The wicked slander him as they stalk like predators for the kill. Their tongues are bent like bows; their words are "arrows" against the string. They lie in ambush and lurk in the dark, and their "tongues" hurl sudden abuse at the godly. The wicked are deceptive and filled with treachery. They seek to destroy the very "foundations" (GK 9268)—a metaphor for the order of society (75:3; 82:5; Eze 30:4). This order has been established by the Lord at creation and is being maintained. God's justice and law are being replaced by human autonomy and its resultant anarchy.

II. The Lord Is the Righteous King (11:4–6)

4–5 The psalmist looks beyond both his advisors and his enemies to the Lord, raising his eyes to heaven. The "holy temple" is God's palace in heaven (18:6; 29:9). God is "holy," and from his throne in heaven he sees all humankind. The "throne" is a symbol of his royal rule and authority to judge (cf. 9:7; 47:8). The Lord's eyes "test" humankind as he patiently observes their feverish activities. It may seem as if God, by his inactivity, does not care; but he sees and examines the wicked together with the righteous. "Examine" (GK 1043) denotes the activity of the smith in the process of purifying gold or silver (cf. Jer 6:27–30; 9:7). The holy God may not immediately judge the wicked, but his holiness excludes any love for those who "love violence."

6 In his own time God will judge the wicked with "fiery coals and burning sulfur," just as Sodom and Gomorrah were destroyed (cf. Ge 19:24). Another image of judgment is the "scorching wind." The hot desert wind blows over the Middle East during the changes in season from spring to summer and from summer to fall. Its effects are devastating, as the beauty of vegetation changes over night into parched, withered plants (cf. Isa 21:1; 40:7–8). The wicked will be like the flowers of the field, which are here today and gone tomorrow. Destruction will be their "lot" (GK 3926 & 4987; lit., "portion of their cup"). This term reminds one of the head of a household who gives each member a cupful to drink at a meal. Thus God gives the wicked a "cupful" of his wrath (cf. Isa 51:17, 22; Eze 23:31–33; cf. Mt 26:39).

III. God Is the Refuge of the Righteous (11:7)

7 God loves those who do righteous acts. He who sees and examines everyone promises that only the "upright" of heart will see him (cf. 17:15; 63:2). To see the face of God is an expression of deliverance from adversity, of close communion, and of the reality of God's blessed presence in this world and in the world to come.

Psalm 12: Lying Tongues and the Truthfulness of God's Word

This psalm, a *community lament,* is a prayer on behalf of or by the people of God for deliverance from the deceptions and scheming of the godless (vv.1–4). The Lord promises to protect his own (v.5), but he expects his children to live with the tensions resulting from a walk in faith. The psalm also includes a statement of confidence in God.

I. Prayer for Deliverance (12:1–4)

1 The description of the prevalence of evil is a connecting link with Ps 11:2–3. The intent of the wicked was to rid themselves of "the upright in heart" (11:2; cf. v.7). The psalmist observes that the godly, characterized by their faithfulness to the Lord, have vanished. Of course, this is hyperbolic language, but it is a manner of bringing before the covenant God his promise to free his people.

2–4 The wicked disobey God with their tongues. They pervert and twist truth. Their goal is to gain power by flattery, deception, and clever schemes. They do not tolerate authority but prefer autonomy and anarchy. The wicked are "double-hearted" (lit., "with deception") by the very way they speak (cf. Jas 3:10–12). Their aim is power, and that end justifies any means. They do not shrink from flattery, boasting, denying God's way, and exalting their own way. The psalmist cries out to God that perverse speech will cease and that righteousness thereby may be established.

II. Promise of the Lord (12:5)

5 The Lord answers the cry of the needy, even as he has promised. He hears their groaning (79:11; 102:20) and prepares himself to act on their behalf. The exaltation of God must bring the abasement and removal of the wicked (Isa 33:11–12); God protects the afflicted from their oppressors. The last clause in Hebrew is literally "he will blow at him." The NIV rendering describes the wicked as "those who malign them." It may also refer to the afflicted as those who "pant for" deliverance (cf. NEB).

III. Reflection on God's Promises (12:6)

6 The assurance of the godly ultimately lies in God's promises. His "words" are pure ("flawless"), refined like silver that has been subjected to a sevenfold process of purification (cf. 18:30; 119:140). Over against the lies, deceptions, treachery, perverse speech, and scheming of the wicked is God's word!

IV. Prayer for Deliverance (12:7–8)

7 In response to the assurance of God's word, the psalmist brings his lament to a peaceful conclusion. Regardless of the circumstances of life, God's children are assured of the special protection of their heavenly Father. The wicked may turn the world upside down, but God will guard his own. As he has promised (Nu 6:24–26), he keeps them "safe" from the wicked, "from such people" (lit., "from this generation"). The word "generation" (GK 1887) signifies here a group of people who live at the same time; i.e., contemporaries.

8 God's guarding his people is a reality even when the wicked walk around as kings. When vv.1, 7–8 are read together as an inclusion, the comfort lies in God's protection from an evil generation that is, after all, characterized by human frailty. Therefore the hope of the psalmist lies in the Lord, his covenant God. The psalm contains no resolution to the problem of evil, but it recognizes that evil is under the full sovereignty of the Lord.

Psalm 13: Waiting for God's Salvation

This psalm, a deeply moving picture of despair and trust, realistically depicts the anguish of the soul, yet a soul that also experiences a deep faith. The psalm is classified as an *individual lament*, but it is also expressive of the needs of the community of God's people. The situation that brings the psalmist to the point of despair may be illness.

I. Expression of Despair: How Long? (13:1–2)

1–2 The fourfold repetition "how long" emphasizes the intensity of emotions. David looks first at God as the source of his trouble, when he asks, "Will you forget me forever?" (here "forever" means "continually" or "utterly"). For some reason unknown to David, God has removed his covenant mercy from him (cf. 10:1, 11). The hiding of God's face is an expression for alienation and curse. The psalmist is alone, and suffering in loneliness aggravates the anguish. He searches his thoughts as to what has happened.

God is displeased, but why? When the psalmist turns to the people around him, he sees his enemy. The enemy is on the periphery of his concern, and yet he is always there. Is the enemy death, the presence of evil in the world, or oppressors who have nearly "overcome him" (v.4)? There seems not to be sufficient reason for limiting the situation to illness and death, because the clause "sleep in death" (v.3) may be a metaphor for deep depression and suffering. The psalmist is disturbed in his deepest being by God's lack of interest, by the adversaries (adversities), and by his own feelings.

II. Expression of Prayer: Give Me Light! (13:3–4)

3–4 The psalmist believes that God has hidden his face from him; therefore he asks, "Look on me." Divine abandonment and alienation made the psalmist experience despair, but God's "look" (GK 5564), expressive of favor, renews life. The psalmist asks for God to "answer" (GK 6699) him. The answer is a positive message of God's favor by which the Lord frees his servant from the causes of the anguish of soul. The psalmist believes that only by God's favor will he receive "light" for his eyes. Anyone who is relieved from troubles and blessed with God's protection, peace, and favor shows his or her inner spiritual condition in outward appearance (cf. 36:8–9). One's eyes sparkle with God's grace.

The psalmist's prayer here contains an urgent appeal for God's covenant favor. If he were to be vexed and overcome by "death," the enemies would have cause to gloat. Their joy expressed not only pleasure in the fall of the godly but also in God's failure to be faithful to his covenant promises. The "fall" (GK 4572) is a stumbling under a load too heavy to carry. Before more trouble comes, and before the godless have reason to rejoice over the defeat of the godly, God must act to protect his honor.

III. Expression of Hope and Trust: Let Me Sing! (13:5–6)

5–6 Though he has experienced deep despair, the psalmist does not give up. His feet did not slip. He held on to the promise of God's covenant love. He was not overwhelmed by his troubles. The emphatic "But I" is a surprising response from the heart of a depressed person. Because life may be so bitter for some, it is only by God's grace that the heart of faith may groan, "but I."

The effect of God's love for which the psalmist longs is the experience of salvation. "Salvation" (GK 3802) signifies the *whole* well-being of God's child. He needs the assurance that God cares (v.1), as well as the experience of victory over his enemy and over adverse circumstances (vv.2, 4). He also needs the healing in his thoughts of anguish and self-pity (v.2). God's "salvation" takes care of all his needs. He will therefore rejoice in the Lord when God shows his fatherly care.

Psalm 14: God Deals With Foolish Evildoers

This psalm is parallel to Psalm 53. The language is similar except on a few points, which may be explained by the context in which each was finalized. The genre has been disputed. Because of its affinity with the lament psalms against the wicked, it has been categorized as an *individual lament*. However, the contrast between the fool and the one with understanding is representative of the wisdom psalms. Another representative element is the *prophetic* motif, incorporated in a liturgical prayer.

I. The Fool (14:1)

1 The "fool" (GK 5572) is neither ignorant nor an atheist. The word is synonymous with the wicked, who aggressively and intentionally flouts his independence from God and his commandments (cf. 53:1; 74:18, 22). The "fool" in his heart denies the practical import of God's existence. He shuts off the affairs of this world from divine intervention and denies any personal accountability to God for his actions (cf. 10:4; 73:11). Within the congregation he may mimic the sounds of faith, but his true self shows disregard for God, his commandments, and his people. He is characterized by an absence of concern or love for others, but he is occupied with himself.

Three phrases describe the perniciousness of the wicked. (1) "They are corrupt." (2) "Their deeds are vile"; i.e., detestable acts are done out of complete disregard for God's majesty. (3) "There is no one who does good" is a summary statement about the absence of godliness.

II. The Lord's Perspective (14:2–3)

2 The Lord "looks down" as witness and judge on his creatures and observes the affliction of his children. The wise (in contrast to "the fool") are those "who understand [and who] seek after God." They love to do the will of their covenant God on earth.

3 As God observes humankind, he is overwhelmed by the evil he sees. It seems as if "all have turned aside" and have "become corrupt," as if no one "does good." The negative picture of the fool (v.1) is reinforced by the

totality of human evil. Humankind has become apostate because it has "turned aside" (cf. 53:3; cf. Ro 3:11–18).

III. The Prophetic Perspective (14:4–6)

4–6 The Lord is the "refuge" (GK 4726) of the wise—called "my people," "the company of the righteous," and "the poor." Fools are not numbered among them because they are "evildoers" who do not know the Lord intimately or care about his looking down from heaven. They busily pursue their self-interests and, in so doing, "devour" (GK 430) God's people. Their hatred of righteousness and the vulnerability of the righteous combine to make the wise easy prey. They "devour" the possessions of others and add them to their own, completely disregarding the rights of their subjects (cf. Isa 5:8).

Suddenly, God's judgment will come on the wicked. Their power and terrorizing will come to an end when the Lord intervenes on behalf of his "people." Then "dread" will overtake the fools, while the righteous will enjoy the presence of their covenant God. The wicked may for a time heap abuse on "the plans of the poor." But even in their persecution, God is "the refuge" of his children.

IV. The Hope of the Righteous (14:7)

7 The conclusion is a most appropriate prayer for "salvation" (GK 3802). The phraseology "restore the fortunes" is characteristic of the prophets as they describe the era of restoration when Israel, restored to the land, will again enjoy the blessings of God (cf. Eze 16:53; Zep 2:7). After the Exile God demonstrated his faithfulness by his renewed blessings, by restoring Israel to the land, and by permitting his temple to be rebuilt. The psalmist anticipates an era when God will vindicate his people and deliver them from the fools who oppress them. In Jesus' coming Jews and Gentiles are further assured of God's concern, vindication, and presence with his people (cf. Ro 11).

Psalm 15: Who May Live in God's Presence?

This psalm begins with a question and concludes with God's promise. The question-and-answer method, coupled with the concluding promise, suggests that it is a *wisdom* psalm.

I. The Question (15:1)

1 The repetition of the interrogative particle "who" is not so much a question of the *identity* of those entering into God's presence as it is of *what kind* of a person may enjoy his fellowship. The verbs "dwell" and "live" are metaphors for communion with God. The complementary usage of "sanctuary" and "your holy hill" suggests the background of a pilgrimage to Mount Zion, God's holy hill. As the pilgrims approached Jerusalem—the city of God, where his "sanctuary" was located on the "holy hill"—they had to examine themselves before entering the courts of God's sanctuary.

II. The Response (15:2–5a)

2–5a The wise are primarily characterized by the word "blameless" (GK 9459). It is not synonymous with "perfect" but with an attitude of the heart desirous of pleasing God. The blameless are people of integrity in relationship to God and others. In their personal relations, they express a righteous and faithful lifestyle. Regardless of what God requires, the blameless do God's will on earth.

The words "righteous" (GK 7406) and "truth" (GK 622) are synonymous with "blameless." The righteous *do* what is right, living in accordance with God's expectations. The phrase "truth from his heart" reveals the fidelity between one's "heart," as the seat of one's being, and one's speech, which expresses one's inner being.

The activities of walking, doing, and speaking are not to be isolated as separate expressions of the righteous path but express synthetically that everything the wise do is in harmony with the expectations of God and humankind. The three negative conditions in v.3 give examples of what a blameless person does not do. The word for "neighbor" (GK 8276) is somebody with whom one frequently associates. The wicked have no sense of loyalty and lay traps for anyone to fall into. The wise, on the other hand, do not purposely hurt their fellow human beings, let alone their friends.

The wise neither initiate nor rejoice in the reproach of their associates; they empathize in their hurt. The "vile man" is a "reprobate," known for his evil deeds. The godly, in other words, are not free to "despise" any sinner, only those who are hardened in their perversities. They ably distinguish between those who "fear the LORD" and those who are reprobates. In their self-respect they respect the rights, gifts, and status of others.

When they promise, make a vow, or swear to do something, the wise remain true to their word (cf. Ecc 5:1–7; Mt 5:33–37). They have a deep sense of integrity and must often make material sacrifices to be honest. Their honor is more important than their wallet.

The concern of the wise shows up also in their relationship to the poor and to those who need justice. The poor at times need a loan to keep themselves from being sold into slavery. "Usury" (GK 5968) was the practice of charging high interest. It was prohibited because of the need of the poor not to get *further* into debt. The law instructed Israelites not to take advantage of the adversities of a fellow Israelite who had fallen on hard times (Ex 22:25–27; Lev 25:35–36; Dt 23:19).

Often the poor were dragged into court and taken advantage of by the well-to-do, who could easily afford to pay a bribe to thwart justice. Bribery was strictly prohibited in the law (cf. Ex 23:8; Dt 16:19). The godly witness or judge should refuse any bribe as being a perversion of justice. Although the law clearly prohibited usury and bribery, it did not prohibit receiving equitable compensation. The godly person does not discriminate against the poor in favor of the rich, powerful, and influential.

III. The Promise (15:5b)

5b The reward of God ensures that the wise will "dwell" with the Lord (v.1; cf. 23:6). They may experience adversities, but they will never fall, as will the wicked. They will never be "shaken" (GK 4572; cf. 16:8). This is God's promise. Clearly the ethics of God's people are not a system of morality independent of the Lord but have a theological basis (cf. Mt 5–7).

Psalm 16: Refuge in the Lord

The confession of *confidence* in God exemplifies a deep trust in the Lord in both life and death. The life-setting of this psalm is difficult to determine. The psalm may at least be viewed as a composition made during a time of peace and quiet.

I. Confidence in the Lord (16:1–4)

1 The psalm opens with words of trust in God, who alone is able to give shelter. The expectation of safe-keeping is grounded in God's promise to keep and to guard the members of the covenant community who seek "refuge" in him (cf. 7:1; 11:1; 17:7).

2 The psalmist approaches God as "my Lord" (*Adonai*, GK 151) and as "my good" ("I have no good thing"). "My Lord" reveals the psalmist's submission to God as "Master" and "Ruler" (see 8:1) over against those who run after other gods (v.4). Hence his confidence is in God's care for him. He further describes his relationship to his God as the source of all his benefits. The sovereign God is "my good," i.e., the reason for his existence and joy (cf. 73:25).

3 Delight in God also finds expression in a joyful acceptance of "the saints" (GK 6221). The "saints who are in the land" are the godly on earth, not angelic beings; they are consecrated to the Lord (cf. Ex 19:6). The "saints" are also known as "the glorious ones" (GK 129), as the Lord himself bestows glory and majesty on his own (cf. 8:1, 9; 93:1, 4). The psalmist thus expresses the importance of the community of the saints.

4 The ungodly's idolatrous acts are described as pouring of "libations of blood" and swearing by the names of the idols. "Of blood" may refer to human sacrifices (Isa 57:5–6) or to guilt due to bloodshed (Isa 1:15; 66:3). The psalmist strongly states his antipathy to such idolatrous practices. Paganism is a way of life completely inconsistent with trust in God as the sovereign Master. The psalmist makes no mention of their idols, in keeping with his declaration that he will not "take up their names" on his lips (cf. Hos 2:17).

II. The Experience of Faith (16:5–6)

5–6 Having demonstrated his abhorrence of idolatry and his decision not to join in with those who poured out a drink offering, the psalmist now recognizes how good the Lord is to his own. Loyalty to the Lord is in response to his acts of beneficence. Using language reminiscent of the conquest of Canaan, the psalmist reflects on all that the Lord has done. However, he goes beyond the occupation of Canaan in considering God's benefits. The Lord promised the members of the priesthood to be their share and inheritance (Nu 18:20; Dt 10:9; 18:1). Israel as a whole was his inheritance (Jer 12:7–9). But the godly can join in with the experience of the psalmist, wherever and whenever they live. God deals kindly with his children in that he bestows on them his covenant blessings and promises.

The nature of God's benefits are described as "pleasant" (GK 5833) and "delightful" (GK 9182). Even as God gave his people a pleasant land as an inheritance, so the psalmist rejoices in the bounty of God's goodness to him. However, his joy is not first and foremost in God's gifts but in the Lord himself.

III. Confidence in the Lord (16:7–8)

7–8 The theocentric focus is further supported by the psalmist's response of praise. He shows his loyalty to the Lord in "praise" (lit., "bless"; GK 1385) and in obedience. In life situations the psalmist is not easily moved by the idolaters (v.4), because his chief goal in life is to love God and live for him. By day he can say that the Lord gives him counsel, which aids him to live wisely. At night God "instructs" him through the meditation with his inner self. God is always present at his "right hand." Therefore, his confidence in the Lord is the result of his experience of God's goodness, grace, and fatherly instruction. As a sage, the psalmist can claim God's promise that the wise and righteous "will not be shaken" (cf. 15:5; 21:7; 62:2, 6; 112:6).

IV. The Experience of Faith (16:9–11)

9–10 The basis for the psalmist's joy is twofold. (1) His God is the sovereign Master to whom he has fled for protection (vv.1–2). (2) The Lord has been good to him (vv.2b, 5–8). His conclusion to this psalm of confidence begins with "Therefore"; but the "therefore" introduces additional, though related, reasons for his confidence. The Lord cares for him in life and in death. In life the Lord gives him security (vv.5–6) and in death, protection. He may go into "the grave," but the Lord will not permit his beloved ("Holy One") to suffer eternal alienation; even in death his relationship with God continues. The phrase "see decay" is a metaphor for total isolation and abandonment from God's presence.

In the apostolic preaching this verse had a particular apologetic significance, as both Pe-

ter (Ac 2:27, 31) and Paul (Ac 13:35) quoted v.10 as proof of the resurrection of our Lord. They appropriately argued that since David died and did not rise from the grave, the psalm received a special significance in view of Jesus' death and resurrection. Jesus, as the Son of David, arose from the dead, "because it was impossible for death to keep its hold on him" (Ac 2:24). The resurrection of our Lord gives a ground for the confidence of all believers since they too will not suffer corruption. The Father will crown his beloved with life.

11 The psalmist develops further the nature of life with God. Its origin is with God, and its goal is the presence of God, even to be at "your right hand." It produces "joy" and "eternal pleasures." "The path of life" signifies the way that leads to life. It is a wisdom term for the fullness of life that only the wise can achieve (Pr 5:6; 6:23; 10:17; 15:24). The psalmist conceives of life in fellowship with God both in this world and in the hope of everlasting fellowship with God.

Psalm 17: A Prayer for God's Justice

The concern for righteousness dominates this psalm from beginning to end. It concludes with the hope that the psalmist will see God "in righteousness" (v.15). The prayer is a psalm of innocence under the general category of lament psalms.

I. Prayer of a Righteous Man (17:1–5)

1 The psalmist uses three intense expressions to call on the Lord ("Hear . . . listen . . . give ear"). Being in deep distress, he confidently approaches God in prayer. The psalmist's "cry" (GK 8262) is a desperate call for help and an intense form of prayer. His cry is "a righteous plea"; that is, the psalmist prays as an innocent man who is not to be charged with the deception of his contemporaries. He has lived in accordance with God's righteous law and can say that his prayer "does not rise from deceitful lips." Prayer requires an attitude of sincerity, without hypocrisy (cf. Jas 5:16–18).

2 The content of the prayer is twofold: for vindication and for investigation. In the belief that God is sovereign and faithful, David rests his case with God and looks forward to his goodness in this life and in the life to come (v.15). In his second petition, the psalmist prays that the Lord will examine his integrity ("what is right"). He is not claiming perfection but addresses God out of the sincerity of his heart and presses for a resolution to his difficulty.

3 The psalmist believes that he has done nothing to deserve his suffering and that he has not transgressed with his lips against God's commandments. His prayer is confident, but it is a godly confidence, expressive both of the deepest trust in and of a tender walk with God. Therefore he requests God to "test" (GK 7671) his heart, i.e., to put him through every conceivable examination to determine the purity and integrity of the heart. The psalmist wants the Lord to examine him especially at night, for at that time he is isolated from his occupation and social relations and is alone with God. That examination involves a self-examination, as one reflects on one's attitude, loyalty, and obedience to God's commandments.

4–5 The psalmist is confident of his integrity even when the Lord enlarges the scope of his examination to his actions and words. He has paid careful attention to wise living by not associating with the "violent" (GK 7265), i.e., with those who have no consideration of God or his commands. The violent were the gangsters of the OT, who robbed and murdered without blinking an eye (cf. Jer 7:11; 18:10). David had held onto the way of God, without slipping into the way of thieves. The "paths" (GK 5047) of the Lord refer to the ways of godliness, in opposition to the "ways" of the violent."

II. Prayer for Protection (17:6–9)

6–9 David appeals to God to respond to his petition. His urgency is based on the confidence that God will answer him. The boldness in his calling on God expresses the close relationship, further described by the metaphors "the apple of your eye" and "the shadow of your wings." These metaphors express the love of God in his acts of care and protection for those who are dear to him (cf. Dt 32:10–12). Since the enemies have become a real threat, intent on assailing him and destroying him, David calls on God to act again on behalf of his beloved.

However, God answers prayer, provides "refuge" to those who seek it, and delivers the godly with his "right hand," which signifies the strength by which he sustains and redeems his own from trouble. The psalmist looks to God to demonstrate his promised acts of love and loyalty. Because the need is *now,* he prays for God's deliverance with great intensity. God stoops down to deliver his children.

III. The Wicked (17:10–12)

10–12 The psalmist, overwhelmed by the thought of his foes, elaborates on their evil. The wicked are "like a lion" in their pursuit of the godly. The "lion," a symbol of brute strength and a ferocious appetite (cf. Jdg 14:14), presents a powerful picture. Their beastlike nature finds expression in their callous hearts, arrogance, pursuit to the death, and violence. They are greedy, self-loving, and insensitive to others (cf. 73:7; 119:70). The outward expression of the wicked is consistent with their inner being. They speak "with arrogance," which excludes God and concern for others. Without mercy they track down, surround, and finally destroy those weaker than themselves.

IV. Prayer for Deliverance (17:13)

13 The mood shifts as David gazes away from the threat of the wicked and looks to his God. He prays that God will act, not in the future, but *now.* The call to "rise up" (GK 7756) and act in deliverance and vindication is common to other psalms (3:7; 7:6; 9:19; et al.). Instead of directly confronting evil himself, he expects the Lord to "confront" it in his stead. The Lord will not tolerate their opposition; rather he will make the wicked bow down. This is not an act of worship but of total destruction by the "sword" of the Lord.

V. The Wicked (17:14)

14 The description of the wicked as "men of this world whose reward is in this life" interprets the enigmatic Hebrew "from a world their portion in life." Clearly the psalmist prays for God to act against the wicked and to rescue his own. The second part of this verse relates back to the metaphor of the wings under which the psalmist found refuge; God provides for the needs of his cherished ones.

VI. Hope in Righteousness (17:15)

15 God will confront the wicked in judgment, but the godly will see his "face." The wicked will be forced to bow down and will be destroyed, whereas the godly will enjoy God's presence "in righteousness." "Righteousness" (GK 7406) has the sense of victory and joy procured by the Lord and shared with his beloved. The wicked were self-satisfied (v.10) and shared their wealth with their descendants so that they too would "be satisfied." But the godly do not comfort themselves with the thought of transitory "blessings." They will be "satisfied" with the "likeness" of God! "When I awake" suggests that this prayer is an evening prayer (4:8). At the same time, however, the psalmist by inspiration is looking for a greater experience with God that can only be a part of the postresurrection world.

Psalm 18: Royal Thanksgiving

This psalm has been variously categorized. Some have divided the psalm into two units: an individual lament (vv.1–30) and a royal thanksgiving psalm (vv.31–50). However, based on a careful study of the parallel psalm in 2Sa 22, scholars today generally agree that the psalm is a psalm of thanksgiving.

I. The Lord, the Rock of Israel (18:1–3)

1 A unique verb expressive of "love" (GK 8163) for God opens the psalm. This verb is usually used to affirm God's compassion for humankind. It implies the need of the one who receives the compassion and is associated with the mother's care for her children. David thus expresses his commitment to the Lord who is his source of strength, comfort, and sustenance. The phrase "I love you" communicates an intimacy of his relationship based on experience. The further description of the Lord as "my strength" (GK 2619) supports this argument. David has seen the "strength" of God in his adversity.

2 The divine epithets used in this verse are derived from David's familiarity with battle and with the geographical scenery of Canaan. These metaphors convey the intensity of David's love for his God as the all-sufficient One. God is the Great King who is able to deliver those who call on him. He is the "rock" (GK 6152) of Israel (Dt 32:4, 15, 18, 31, 37), who is faithful from generation to generation. The Lord provides a "refuge" (GK 2879) for his own. The "refuge" was an isolated high place in a mountainous region, whose natural relief provided excellent strategic advantages (e.g., Jerusalem, Masada). Because God is the Redeemer of his people in physical and spiritual needs (cf. v.48), the psalmist knows that he can always find refuge in him.

The Lord protects his servant as with a "shield" (GK 4482) so that the adversities of life may not penetrate and destroy his child. Instead, he elevates him with "the horn of salvation." The word "horn" (GK 7967) is a symbol of strength; theologically it denotes the vertical intrusion of the Lord's power and victory over against the kingdoms of humanity. The imagery of a high place lies also behind the phrase "my stronghold" (GK 5369). It is a place of refuge in the rocks (cf. Isa 33:16).

3 The outburst of metaphors affirms David's confidence in the Lord's ability to deliver. Therefore, he is praiseworthy (48:1; 96:4). Whenever he calls on the Lord in prayer, David tastes the sweetness of his deliverance. This reminder of "the enemies" forms a transition to his reflections on God's deliverance in great adversity (vv.4–19).

II. Affliction (18:4–6)

4–6 The psalmist recalls the intensity of his anguish as if ropes were wrapped around him and as if death, personified as "cords of death" and "cords of the grave" (Sheol; GK 8619), were pulling him downward. Another metaphor is that of rushing streams ("torrents") that threaten to destroy him (cf. 30:1; cf. 2Sa 22:5). He cannot escape because he is trapped by "the snares of death." Paganism seems to triumph, as chaos rules and God's deliverance is not forthcoming. But at this point David turns to the Lord. After his prayer, he portrays the Lord's coming with great power and glory, in order to establish order and justice and to redeem his servant.

III. The Lord's Coming to Help (18:7–15)

7–15 God is concerned with the distress of his children. His reaction in his heavenly glory is couched in the language of theophany. The earthquake is an expression of his anger. The smoke and the fire represent his readiness to avenge his enemies. Thus he mounts the cherubim, soars as a bird on "the wings of the wind," and swoops quickly downward. The clouds are his chariot (cf. 68:33) and the wind makes up the wings (cf. 104:3–4) with which he flies downward on the rescue mission. The darkness of the clouds heightens his brightness. As the Divine Warrior moves closer to the enemies, he announces his coming with "hailstones," "bolts of lightning," and "thunder." Then he shoots forth "his arrows" in the form of lightning and thus rids himself of his enemies. No opposition can stand his presence because he penetrates even the sea (v.16) and "the foundations of the earth."

He is the glorious and victorious King over heaven, earth, and sea. His rule is established, and there is no question as to his sovereignty and supremacy. But because the rebellious forces are on earth, the earth "trembles and quakes" as it anticipates the fear of the guilty who are seized with "terror and dread" and tremble with anguish at the prospect of his judgment.

IV. The Lord's Deliverance (18:16–19)

16–19 The portrayal of God's indignation and readiness to vindicate gives comfort to the psalmist. He does not fear God's coming in anger, because his Father comes to his rescue. Though the enemy forces are strong (vv.4–5), the Lord prevails over their great strength. He delivers the psalmist from the adversity and provides a new dimension of life. Instead of "disaster," he experiences the Lord to be his "support." Instead of the enmity of his foes, he experiences the redemption of the God who delights in him.

V. God's Faithfulness to the Faithful (18:20–29)

The triumph of faith is expressed here in the realization that the Lord has been faithful, that he has kept his word, and that he rewards the faithful. The psalmist has argued that the love of God moves heaven and earth for the sake of his own. Now he instructs the hearers (readers) what God expects of his children.

A. Human Faithfulness to God (18:20–24)

20–24 Loyalty to the Lord shows itself in practical ways, but in essence it is an internal spiritual response. The psalmist's attitude to God is described as "righteousness" (GK 7406)—that response to God that adheres to his decrees and shuns evil. Righteousness is the joyous expression of love to God for all his mercies. Therefore he is devoted to "the ways of the LORD" (cf. Dt 8:6) and to "his laws." God's laws regulate all of life and help his servant to respond appropriately to the challenges of life. David's hands are clean and he has "integrity" before the Lord. He praises the goodness of God who has dealt with him faithfully.

B. God's Faithfulness to His Own (18:25–29)

25–26 The Lord helps his own, those who are concerned with being "faithful," "blameless," and "pure." Faith, loyalty, and sanctification are inseparable. God responds with deep concern to his covenant children, whereas he deals in kind with the "crooked." Even as God deals lovingly with those who love him, he lets the crooked acts of the wicked boomerang on their own heads. They receive their just deserts. Thus the psalmist rejoices in God's justice, as he deals with each in accordance with his works.

27–29 These affirmations of God's goodness and justice are the basis for hope. Even in adversity the "humble" hope in God; even in "darkness" the saints look to him for light. The "haughty" (GK 8123) are those who have little or no regard for the Lord (10:5–6). They often oppress or disregard the rights of the godly. But the Lord graciously turns the misfortunes of his saints and grants them the joy of life. Thus the psalmist expresses a spirit of confident joy. There is no barrier that the Lord cannot overcome, whether it be a "troop" or the wall of an enemy city. The presence of the Lord gives confidence of victory.

VI. The Lord's Goodness (18:30–45)

A. The Divine Perfections (18:30–36)

30–36 The Lord's ways are "perfect" (GK 9459). His perfections are those qualities by which he relates to his creation. He is full of "integrity" (cf. v.25b) to those who respond to him with "integrity." His word, likewise, is "tested" and found to be "flawless" (GK 7671; cf. 12:6; 119:140).

Because of God's commitment to protect his loyal children by word and work, he is their "shield" (cf. 3:3) and "Rock," with the result that they are victorious, strong, and free. They "take refuge in him." The ascriptions of goodness to God lead the psalmist to exclaim, "Who is God besides the LORD?" The answer is no one!

The Lord "arms" (GK 273) the psalmist with strength. The verb signifies giving support or strengthening at a time of need (cf. v.39). Since God is the Rock of Israel, he alone can give strength. The strength of the Lord results in success. David compares this strength to the sure-footedness of an ibex ("deer"), whose agility permits it to walk on narrow ledges in mountainous and rocky terrain. He also compares himself to a warrior with special strength. In God's strength he is free.

B. The King's Victory Over the Enemies (18:37–42)

37–42 With the help of the Great King, the messianic King need not be afraid of the enemies. The emphasis lies on his prowess in battle as he aggressively beats back his enemies. He expects nothing less than their total destruction. The enemy, being in dire straits, calls for help from allied forces, but none dare fight against the divinely anointed King! It is apparent that the Lord is with the psalmist, strengthening him and giving him complete victory. The enemies' strength is reduced so that they are no more than useless "dust."

C. The Glorious Deliverance (18:43–45)

43–45 With gratitude to the Lord, the psalmist summarizes the effects of his campaigns. First, he is victorious over the enemies. They have responded to him, just as the enemies of God did in earlier times to God's presence as the Divine Warrior (cf. Ex 15:14–16; Jos 2:11, 24). The nations submit themselves to his sovereignty (cf. Ps 2:8–12). Second, the nature of the messianic rule is glorious. The Lord has made his anointed king to be "the head" of nations in fulfillment of his word to Israel (Dt 28:13).

VII. The Lord, the Rock of Israel (18:46–50)

46–50 The psalmist returns to an affirmation of his confidence in "the Rock" of Israel (cf.

vv.1–3). The Rock is no other than the Divine Warrior who is the "Savior" (GK 3829) of the messianic King. The acts of deliverance involve complete subjugation of the enemies and exaltation above the nations as expressions of divine vindication. He is the God "who avenges" (94:1) and "who saves" (94:19–23).

The psalmist reflects on the acts of God to encourage God's people to look at the messianic King as the divinely chosen instrument of deliverance. The Divine Warrior has chosen the anointed King of David's lineage to establish his kingdom. Every Christian knows that this King is none other than Jesus the Messiah. In him we receive God's "love," and in him we are victorious.

Psalm 19: God's Perfections Revealed in Work and Word

This psalm reflects, more than any other, the beauty and splendor of the Hebrew poetry found in the Psalter. The psalm comprises three separate motifs brought together into a unified *wisdom hymn:* creation praise (vv.1–6), a wisdom psalm (vv.7–11), and a prayer for God's forgiveness and acceptance (vv.12–14).

I. The Revelation of Creation (19:1–6)

A. The Revelation of the Skies (19:1–4b)

1 The glory and wisdom of God are evident in the vastness of space. The psalmist calls attention to "the heavens" (GK 9028) as he begins the first verse and concludes with the synonym "the skies" (GK 8385). These words signify the place where God put the sun, moon, and stars for the purpose of giving light and for distinguishing "day" from "night" (Ge 1:14–19). The universe is a revelation of God's creation of the magnificent heavenly bodies, which are characterized by radiance and regularity. The verbs "declare" and "proclaim" express the continuous revelation of the heavens. The wars and disturbances on earth often camouflage God's glory, as they divert attention away from the created heavenly bodies. God alone is the Creator; the heavenly bodies are "the work of his hands" (cf. Dt 4:19; 17:3).

2 The alternation of "day" and "night" reveals the constancy of God's creation. The cycle of day and night contributes to the regularity of the seasons and thus to the regular-

Sunsets, such as this one over the Mediterranean Sea, remind us of the glory and power of our God (19:1–6).

ity of the agricultural calendar (Ge 8:22). They reveal "knowledge" (GK 1981) in their own distinct "speech." The "knowledge" is not only knowledge about God but also a special kind, best understood as God's wisdom, revealed in his creation (cf. Pr 8:22–31).

3–4b Being unrestricted by the division of languages, natural revelation transcends human communication without the use of speech, words, and sounds. To those who are inclined to hear, revelation comes with no regard for linguistic or geographical barriers.

B. The Revelation of the Sun (19:4c–6)

4c–6 Life on earth depends on the regularity of the sun. The psalmist did not know all that we know today about the solar system. His concern was to portray in a phenomenal way how the sun rises, as it were, from "a tent." The sun is metaphorically compared to a "bridegroom" and a "champion." The joy of the bridegroom, coming from the wedding canopy or the bridal chamber, represents the radiance of the sun. The "champion," rejoicing in his strength as he sets out to run his course, represents the power of the sun, as it seems to move through "its circuit." The sun also reveals God's glory, power, and wisdom. One does not have to listen for words, because the effect of the sun is evident, as "nothing is hidden from its heat."

II. The Revelation of God's Law (19:7–11)

7–11 The revelation of God's law is clearer than the revelation in nature. It is greater because it is given by the covenant God, whose name is Yahweh (tr. "LORD," vv.7, 8, 9); na-

ture reveals the glory of the Creator-God (see v.1). It is also greater because of the comprehensive nature of the revelation. This is brought out by the choice of the synonyms for God's revelation: "law" (GK 9459), "statutes" (GK 6343), "precepts" (GK 7218), "commands" (GK 5184), "fear" (GK 3711), and "ordinances" (GK 5477); for an extended treatment of these terms, see EBC, 5:184–87. The synonyms are not to be studied in abstraction but give a comprehensive emphasis that *all* the words of the Lord are beneficial. Although the benefits of natural revelation are with us on a daily basis, the comprehensive benefits of God's revelation in the law are so much greater.

The list of four benefits is given to encourage the godly to embrace the law of God as an expression of his wisdom. (1) God's word "revives" (GK 8740). Its restorative quality gives healing to the whole person by assuring forgiveness and cleansing and by giving life to the godly. (2) God's word is the source of "wisdom" to all who are ready to receive it. Both the inexperienced ("the simple") and the wise develop as they begin with "the fear of the LORD" and embrace the will of God in all aspects of life. (3) God's word gives "joy" (GK 8523). Heartfelt joy is equivalent to inner peace and tranquility, as one loves God with all one's heart, i.e., with one's innermost being. (4) God's word gives "light to the eyes." The internal joy radiates through the eyes. It expresses the joy of being alive and of receiving God's blessings. Thus the Lord has made the sun for light in creation and has given his word for light in redemption.

God's word reflects his own integrity, uprightness, and fidelity. It is "trustworthy" (GK 586) in the sense that his statutes are true in principle and are verifiable in the situations of life. It is "right" (GK 3838) in the sense of straightforward and just. God's word is not perverse or crooked but encourages the godly to be upright. It is "radiant" (i.e., "pure"; GK 1338), and its purity effects the clean and upright way of those who are "pure." It is "enduring forever," as it does not change with the times. It is "sure" (i.e., "faithful"; GK 622), as it reflects the fidelity and loyalty of God. It is "righteous" (GK 3838) as it reflects God's righteousness. It is sweet like the finest honey. These metaphors refer to the great value of God's word in terms of its effects on those who observe them. It causes integrity, loyalty, uprightness, purity, and growth in righteousness.

Because of its revelatory qualities and its transforming effects in the godly, the word of God is of greater value than the most valuable objects of human striving: money and fine food. It keeps the wise on the narrow path by forewarning them of possible pitfalls and by guiding them on to the benefits of godliness. The word "servant" (GK 6269) bears out the willingness of the psalmist in doing God's will. It applies to one who by appointment, office, or choice commits himself or herself to doing someone else's will—in this context, the will of the covenant Lord.

III. Prayerful Reflection (19:12–14)

12–13 The psalmist reflects on himself in relation to God and his revelation. In Ps 8 he looked at the dignity of humanity (8:4a). Now he reflects on humanity's sinfulness and limitations. Human beings are such insignificant parts in the vastness of space. Just as nothing is hidden from the heat of the sun (v.6), and even as the "voice" of the natural revelation penetrates to "the ends of the earth" (v.4), so God's word with all its perfections (vv.7–9) penetrates and examines a person. The godly stand, therefore, in fear before their Creator-Redeemer, knowing that they may have "hidden faults" or "errors" that he has not yet discovered.

The psalmist is concerned about these faults because he aims to live "blameless" before God. Therefore he asks for forgiveness and an ability to express humility and contrition. "Willful sins" are those often attributed to the "arrogant," who have no regard for God. "The great transgression" could be idolatry, adultery, or any other sin against the moral law of God.

14 The heavens "declare," "proclaim," "pour forth," and "display" without the benefit of human speech; yet they speak clearly of the glory, power, and wisdom of God. The Lord has revealed his word in speech and written forms accessible to people. In turn the psalmist, as a redeemed creature of God, prays that his expressed and unspoken words may be acceptable to his God, his Rock and his Redeemer; namely, the Lord, the covenant-loving God.

Psalm 20: Prayer for Victory

Concern for God's blessing on the king in facing national distress dominates this psalm. It contains a beautiful expression of solidarity between the people and their king, as all are involved in imploring the Lord's favor. It is a *royal psalm.*

I. Prayer in Need (20:1)

1 The people pray for God's covenant blessings on the king as their representative. God has promised to protect, to be gracious to, and to give peace to his people (Nu 6:24–26), thus placing his "name on the Israelites" (v.27). But now that the "distress" is here, they invoke the "name of the God of Jacob" to protect the king. "The God of Jacob" refers to the Redeemer who delivered Jacob (= Israel) from Egypt (Ex 19:3–4) and who promised to deal justly with his people (cf. Ps 146:5–10). The Lord has promised to bring about all the promises made to the patriarchs.

II. Prayer for God's Royal Help (20:2–4)

2 The word "sanctuary" (lit., "holy thing," "holiness"; GK 7731) is not the usual term. Apparently the psalmist has in mind Zion, God's holy hill, where the temple was located. God's holy place was localized at Jerusalem but was not limited there. Jerusalem was an earthly reflection of "his holy heaven" (v.6)—a phrase that denotes the universal rule of God. The "help" and "support" the people pray for are evidence of God's presence as the Great King. "Support" (GK 6184) may indicate provision of food and drink (104:15) or a demonstration of God's loving acts (94:18), by which God strengthens (18:35), restores (41:3), and delivers his people (119:117). The "support" of the Lord takes care of all the king's needs as he goes out to battle.

3 God's favor was sought by means of the "sacrifices" and "burnt offerings." The Israelite practice of presenting sacrifices and offerings before a military campaign was an act of devotion and submission to the Lord (1Sa 7:9–10; 13:9–12). Their purpose was not primarily to atone for sin but to seek God's favor and to consecrate oneself for war. As dedicatory offerings, they were burned on the altar so as to make "an aroma pleasing to the Lord" (Lev 1:13). The offerings did not inevitably guarantee the Lord's favor, be-

cause he delights in loyalty more than offerings (1Sa 15:22–23).

4 The prosperity of the king is dependent on God's presence and favor (vv.2–3). The king's "heart" had to show a walk of integrity with his God in order for "plans" to come to fruition. As the king received counsel before battle, it was important to discern God's will (cf. 2Sa 16:20; 1Ki 22:7).

III. Rejoicing in Anticipation (20:5)

5 When the Lord responds to the prayer, he will demonstrate his presence and favor by giving victory to the king. The people pledge loyalty to the king by affirming their joy in his victory. They also pledge loyalty to the Lord by raising their banners "in the name of our God." Moses raised a "banner" (GK 1838) to the Lord after the war with the Amalekites as a token of perpetual war as long as the Amalekites existed as a people (Ex 17:15–16). Here the raising of the banners signifies God's victory over the enemies. The people conclude their prayer with the petition for the Lord's blessing.

IV. Confidence in God's Royal Help (20:6–8)

6–8 The psalmist reflects on the nature of Israel's warfare in contrast to warfare in the ancient Near East. Kings multiplied for themselves horses and chariots to secure victory, power, and control. Israel's kings were prohibited to "acquire great numbers of horses" (Dt 17:16) but were required "to revere the LORD" (v.19). Underlying this contrast is the belief in God's sovereign kingship over the nations and his readiness to deliver his own people.

Israel's strength is in the name of their God rather than in the numbers of chariots and horses. The Lord is the source of power, because his name is "the LORD," because he is the Great King who dwells in "his holy heaven," and because he is able to deliver with "the saving power of his right hand."

The phrase "Now I know" is an emphatic expression of confidence in the Lord and in the victory that formed the substance of the prayer (vv.1–5). God's commitment is to "his anointed" by covenant (2Sa 7; cf. Ps 2:2b, 7–9), and therefore the "anointed" king is the divinely appointed means of the Lord's

deliverance. The outcome will be complete victory.

V. Prayer in Need (20:9)

9 The psalm begins and closes with a prayer for the king. "Answer us when we call!" forms a symmetrical relation with "May the LORD answer you when you are in distress" (v.1). People and king call on the Lord, await an answer, and are dependent on the Lord's act of salvation. The prayer "save the king" must be understood as a prayer for his victories.

Psalm 21: The Rule of God Through His King

This psalm, in contrast to Ps 20 which pleads for victory, celebrates the victory already achieved (cf. 20:4; 21:1–2). Psalm 21 contains elements of *thanksgiving* (vv.1–7) and *confidence* (vv.8–12).

I. The King's Joy in the Lord's Strength (21:1)

1 The theocratic king knows that the victories are God's gracious gifts and that they are the evidence of God's "strength" (GK 6437). In 20:5 God's people were looking forward to the time when they could "shout for joy." Here the king leads the people in praise, addressing God as the gracious and victorious King by whose strength the people have been delivered. Therefore the king "rejoices" and even expresses his exuberance.

II. God's Gifts to His King (21:2–6)

2 The king had prayed for victory, and his people had joined in imploring the Lord to give the king "the desire of his heart" (20:4). The king had counseled in his heart, formed his plans, and spoken about the execution of his plans before the Lord. The Lord has blessed those thoughts and spoken requests. The king's ways were aligned with God's plans; therefore he was successful.

3–6 The Lord of glory comes to welcome the king as if he were the sole victor. The king is treated as the commander-in-chief of God's army on earth. His victory was the Lord's doing, but the king receives his reward. In reward for his loyalty, the Lord bestows on his servant great gifts: his presence, rich blessings, a crown of pure gold, a long rule, great glory, and honor. These gifts are symbolic of the divinely decreed rule of David and his descendants, as promised in 2Sa 7:12–16. The Lord himself comes out to bless the king with his "presence" and to crown the victor with great joy.

The assurance of these promises lies in God's recognition of his anointed king. He bestows "life," i.e., the establishment of the Davidic dynasty (2Sa 7:16; cf. Ps 72:17). The Lord guarantees the continuation of the Davidic dynasty by the "crown of pure gold." Kingship is by divine right, and this right is symbolized by the placing of a beautiful crown on David's head.

III. The King's Response (21:7)

7 The king confirms his loyalty to the Lord. His commitment strengthens his relationship. The king declares his loyalty to the Lord as a "trust" or dependency, and the Lord assures him that his "love" will not depart. The "unfailing love" (GK 2876) is God's gratuitous expression of loyalty to the king who looks expectantly for his blessing. Therefore, "he will not be shaken."

IV. The People's Expectations of the King (21:8–12)

8–10 The people look for a demonstration of the royal power and glory bestowed on the king by the Lord. They view the anointed king as God's means of establishing God's kingdom on earth by ridding the earth of enemies. To him belong the blessings of the covenant (vv.3, 6). The Lord has given the king the keys to the kingdom, because it is through the "hand" of his anointed that the foes will be removed. The covenant curses pertain to the enemies of God's people (cf. Ge 12:3) and to the ungodly within the covenant community (cf. Ps 3:1, 7). The Lord will destroy the king's enemies "in his wrath." The execration will be so complete that their offspring will be no more.

11–12 All who do not submit to the rule of God's anointed king are included among those who "plot evil." The messianic kingship requires absolute loyalty to the Lord and his anointed King (Ps 2). All the adversaries of the king will be subjugated and annihilated. The rebellious people will not succeed with their "wicked schemes"; instead they will be routed because of the bow that is aimed at them. There is no enemy force that

can stand up against the king, because God has strengthened his "right hand" by which he delivers his people (v.8) into the victorious kingdom of Jesus Christ, by whom all enemy powers and forces—even death—will be "swallowed" (cf. Isa 25:8; 1Co 15:54–57). His kingdom will be forever!

V. The People's Joy in the Lord's Strength (21:13)

13 The psalm appropriately concludes with an ascription of praise to the Lord. He is the source of "strength" and "might." The king and his people rejoice in God's kingship and the blessings he has bestowed on them. The king led in praise (v.1), and now the people join in. We can experience even greater joy since the coming of our Lord. He is our King, and he will bring in the fullness of promise.

Psalm 22: Anguish and Joy

Psalm 22 is an *individual lament* psalm in which the assembly of the righteous is invited to participate both in giving thanks and in the communal meal, associated with the votive offering (vv.25–26). Because of the reference to Ps 22 in the Passion narrative of our Lord, it is tempting to treat this psalm as messianic, predicting our Lord's suffering (cf. Mt 27:39–46; Mk 15:29–34).

I. God's Abandonment, Rule, and Praise of Israel (22:1–5)

1 The prayer begins with a cry to "my God" with three questions. The psalmist pours out his heart. In the intensity of his suffering, there is no other recourse than to cast himself on God. But at the same time he shows his amazement by the three questions: Why has the Lord "forsaken" me, made no attempt at "saving" me, and not listened to my "groaning"? God's absence becomes unbearable.

Abandonment or alienation is the experience of suffering, when one hopes for deliverance but no help is forthcoming. Even though the psalmist feels abandoned, because he is a child of the covenant, he has great expectations that his covenant God, who has promised to hear and to deliver, will come to his aid.

2–3 The psalmist keeps on bringing his prayers before God "by day" and "by night." He is not silent, but God is! Then he reflects on who his God is. He is holy in his kingship ("enthroned") and is the object of Israel's constant praise. The psalmist's "Yet you" indicates a tension in his experience with God and in God's dealings with Israel. His God has abandoned him and is the object of questions (vv.1–2), whereas God has saved his people and is the object of their praise (vv.3–5).

4–5 The history of redemption reveals God as loyal and able to save. Israel's trust in him was not put to shame, because when they cried, they were delivered. The psalmist was familiar with the glorious acts of God in history. But it seems as if God does not care to deliver *him*, "yet" (v.3). Whereas the "fathers" and Israel had occasion for praise, the psalmist feels himself cut off. The faith of the ancestors and the faith of the psalmist are one, but their experience is far different. God delivered his people, but the psalmist is left abandoned.

It is in this light that we can more deeply appreciate our Lord's cry on the cross, "*Eloi, Eloi, lama sabachthani?*" ("My God, my God, why have you forsaken me," Mt 27:46; Mk 15:34). On the cross our Lord was forsaken by and alienated from the Father. In this experience, symbolized by darkness, he was cut off from God's mighty acts of deliverance done for his people. He was alone, separated from God the Father and from his people.

II. Public Spectacle (22:6–8)

6–7 As the psalmist reflects on his own situation, God's absence dwarfs his self-image. In contrast to the emphatic "you" (v.3), he refers to himself emphatically: "But I." God is enthroned, but he is "a worm and not a man." He feels less than human. God is holy and receives the praise of Israel, but the psalmist is the object of scorn and reviling. Unwanted, alone, and full of anguish, he cannot enjoy the presence of others. Out of disregard for his feelings, they apply their "theological" measuring sticks to his situation and conclude that if he truly were to trust God, he would not suffer. They mock him, shaking their heads—a sign of either rejection or astonishment.

8 The impious mock the psalmist with their argument against his kind of piety. They question his suffering in the light of their my-

opic view of God's love and his promises of deliverance. They conclude either that the psalmist had boasted of trusting in God but was hypocritical or that God does not love him. These ancient mockers pose the issue of the problem of evil and suffering in a most agonizing way. The hope of the godly was in God's "delight" (GK 2911) in his saints, especially during times of adversity (cf. 37:23). The support of the Lord's hand (37:24) is not there, and the mockers make the most of this occasion.

III. God's Covenantal Responsibilities (22:9–11)

9–11 In reflecting on his own desperate situation, the psalmist moves his eyes from the mockers around him to God with an emphatic "Yet you." The problem of suffering finds some focus in God's sovereignty and love for his own. From birth he has owed his life to God, and from birth the Lord has been his covenant God and has shown him his love. God is his father by the covenant and had taken it on himself to be his guardian and protector. How can God leave his child alone, now that he is in trouble and needs help? The psalmist prays for God not to be far away. In his past experience the Lord had been close to him, but now he is distant.

IV. Abandonment and Prayer for Covenantal Favor (22:12–21)

A. The Enemies (22:12–13)

12–13 The strength and ferocity of the enemies is compared to that of the "bulls of Bashan" and to "roaring lions." The bulls of Bashan were proverbial for their size because they were well fed on the lush vegetation of the Bashan (cf. Am 4:1; Mic 7:14)—the region known today as the Golan Heights. As they encircle the psalmist, their "horns" (v.21) are all too evident and inspire fear.

Similarly, the psalmist is unnerved by the enemies who "open their mouths wide against [him]." This action describes the activity of lions. The strength, pride, and deadly intent of the enemies are matched by their cruelty, abuse of power, and hatred of godliness.

B. Personal Anguish (22:14–15b)

14–15b The psalmist feels the impact of the alienation deep within his inner being. Great fear is likened to "water" (cf. Jos 7:5; Eze 7:17; 21:7) and to "wax" (2Sa 17:10). These express formlessness and bring out the inner feelings of an anguished man. He can no longer function as a human being. The "bones," "heart," "strength," and "tongue" fail him, not because of any serious disease, but because of a traumatic response to being hated and alienated. Lack of resilience and inability to cope any longer with the trauma of life are brought out in the image of the dried-out and useless "potsherd." Sherds are pieces of broken pottery. The psalmist is a "broken" man.

C. Severity of the Situation: Life Itself (22:15c)

15c Because of his deep suffering, the absence of hope, and the ever-present reality of evil around him, the psalmist prepares himself for death. Implicitly, he holds the Lord responsible for his suffering ("you lay me").

D. The Enemies (22:16a)

16a The psalmist briefly returns to consider his enemies. They are nothing but "dogs." Dogs in David's day came in many kinds and in great numbers to garbage dumps, ate whatever was thrown away, carried diseases, and transmitted them to humans. The dog was not a pet in the ancient Near East.

E. Personal Anguish (22:16b–17)

16b–17 Just as the imagery of the enemies as bulls and lions evokes feelings of fear and powerlessness, so also the imagery of the dogs creates a picture of a powerless, righteous sufferer on the heap of ashes. The dogs viciously attack him, gnawing at and biting into his feet and hands. He is but skin and bones and is unable to ward them off. His misery is the source of gloating and entertainment.

F. Severity of the Situation: Life Itself (22:18)

18 The division of the garments by lots continues the same picture as in v.15c. The psalmist feels as if he is about to die; therefore the wicked are waiting to swoop down on him like vultures. The "garments" ("clothing") are divided up like the spoils from battle.

G. Cry for Help (22:19)

19 The scene changes, as the psalmist again opens his prayer with an emphatic "But you" (cf. v.3). The sudden shift away from his terrifying condition leads him to confront his covenant God, as he prays, "But you, O Lord." This name for God evokes memory of God's promises to be near, to support his people, and to protect them from adversities. He, and he alone, is the psalmist's "Strength" (GK 394).

H. Severity of the Situation: Life Itself (22:20a)

20a The psalmist implores God to listen to his prayer, because of the utter despair and meaninglessness of his situation. There seems no way out. In view of the absence of any alternative, he prays that the Lord may spare his "life" (see comments on vv.14–15). But he is not ready to die. Only the Lord can deliver him and restore life.

I. Enemies and Cause of Anguish (22:20b–21)

20b–21 The psalmist concludes by returning to the imagery of the enemies as dogs, lions, and oxen, but now in reverse order. They had succeeded in terrorizing him so as to rob him of any desire to live. Yet, as he concludes with the petition, "save me," his hope rests in the Lord who has thus far not answered him (v.2).

V. Public Praise (22:22–24)

22–24 The mood changes after the cry for deliverance (vv.19–21). The psalmist declares "the name" of the Lord in the congregation of the faithful. The Lord has responded to his prayer and has removed the suffering from his servant. No longer need he ask why his God has forsaken him, because the Lord has blessed him by not hiding his face. The Lord has been faithful. The "brothers" may be the psalmist's relatives, friends, or, better, members of the congregation. The "congregation" [GK 7702] is here a technical term for the congregation of the righteous, which excludes the ungodly and mocking Israelites (cf. vv.7–8). They are further identified as "you who fear the Lord."

The taunts of the mockers are now drowned out by the songs of the faithful. The true sons of Jacob are those who fear the

Lord (cf. 24:6). They will honor him with devoted hearts. The verbs "praise," "honor," and "revere" form the outward expression of the fear of the Lord. Those who love the Lord will rejoice in the Lord. These words constitute an encouragement to all the godly: the Lord will rescue those who trust in him (v.8).

VI. God's Presence and Rule: The Praise of Israel and the Nations (22:25–31)

25 The psalmist affirms the importance of public worship in terms of praise and the presentation of freewill offerings. A vow was often made during a period of distress (cf. 50:14; 61:8; 66:13) and was fulfilled after God had shown his loyalty (65:1).

26 The psalmist shares his freewill offerings (cf. Lev 7:16–21) by a communal meal with the poor and afflicted so as to give them a sense of relief, which he has so recently experienced. He blesses them with the comfort that even as food has strengthened their bodies, so shall the Lord strengthen their hearts, enabling them to endure the period of their affliction with patience.

27–28 The psalmist now looks beyond the congregation of the righteous in Israel to "the ends of the earth." Here the theme of God's lordship over all people is emphasized. He has "dominion" (GK 4867) over all the earth (v.3) and those who live in it. Therefore the nations—included in the Abrahamic covenant as "all the families of the nations" (Ge 12:3; Ps 96:7)—will "remember" (GK 2349) the Lord. The act of remembrance is an act of obeisance and worship.

29 Among the worshiping community the psalmist sees the prosperous and "all who go down to the dust," i.e. those who are fainthearted, sickly, dying, and filled with anguish, even as the psalmist once lay "in the dust of death" (v.15). Both well-fed and poor people will join in the worship of God.

30–31 The praise of God will extend from generation to generation, throughout history. The object of the proclamation is God's "righteousness," i.e., his acts of deliverance whereby he demonstrates his sovereign, gracious, and victorious rule. Each generation will join in with the telling of the story of God's kingship (cf. vv.3–5) and will add what

God has done for them. This is the essence of redemptive history.

Psalm 23: The Goodness of God

Psalm 23 is a *psalm of trust and confidence.* It expresses confidence in God's goodness—in this life and in the life to come. The personal way in which the psalmist speaks of God, the imagery of God's soothing guidance, and the ensuing confidence in God have all been factors in making this one of the most charming and beloved of the Psalms.

I. The Lord Is My Shepherd (23:1–4)

1 The first word of the psalm, "The LORD," evokes rich images of the provision and protection of the covenant-God. The emphasis of the psalmist is on "my." The temptation in ancient Israel was to speak only about "our" God (cf. Dt 6:4), forgetting that the God of Israel is also the God of individuals. The metaphor of the shepherd is not only a designation or name of the Lord, but it points toward the relation between God and his covenant-children: "I shall not be in want."

2–4 The image of "shepherd" arouses emotions of care, provision, and protection. A good shepherd is personally concerned with the welfare of his sheep. Because of this the designation "my shepherd" is further described by various aspects of God's care: "he makes me lie down ... he leads ... he restores ... he guides"; and by the resulting tranquility, "I will fear no evil."

The shepherd's care is symbolized by the "rod" and the "staff." A shepherd carried a rod to club wild animals and a staff to keep

Bedouin still care for sheep on the hills of the Holy Land (cf. Ps 23). This flock is located south of Hebron near Beersheba.

the sheep in control. These two represent God's constant vigilance over his own and bring "comfort" (GK 5714) because of his personal presence and involvement with his sheep. The "green pastures" are the rich and verdant pastures, where the sheep need not move from place to place to be satisfied. The fields, even parts of the desert, would green during the winter and spring. But in summer and fall the sheep would be led to many places in search of food. God's care is not seasonal but constant and abundant. The sheep have time to rest, as the shepherd makes them to "lie down." The "quiet waters" are the wells and springs where the sheep can drink without being rushed. Through these means, God renews the sheep so that they feel life in his presence is good and worth living. The word "soul" in v.4 denotes the same as "me" in v.2, i.e., "he restores me."

The nature of the shepherd's care also lies in *guidance*. He leads his own in the "paths of righteousness." "Righteousness" (GK 7406) here signifies "right" in the sense of "straight," i.e., the paths that bring the sheep most directly to their destination. He does not unnecessarily tire out his sheep. Even when the "right paths" bring the sheep "through the valley of the shadow of death," there is no need to fear.

The idiom "shadow of death" portrays death as a deep shadow or as deep darkness. This imagery is consistent with the shepherd metaphor because the shepherd leads the flock through ravines and wadis where the steep and narrow slopes keep out the light. The darkness of the wadis represents the uncertainty of life. The "straight paths" at times need to go through the wadis, but God is still present. The shepherd who guides is always *with* the sheep. The presence and guidance of the Lord go together. He is bound by his name ("for his name's sake") to be present with his people (cf. the meaning of "LORD" in Ex 3:12).

II. The Lord Is My Host (23:5–6)

5 The Lord is the host at a banquet "table" laden with food and drink. Before entering the banquet hall, an ancient host would anoint the honored guests with oil made by adding perfumes to olive oil. The overflowing "cup" symbolizes the care and provisions of God, previously represented by "green pastures" and "quiet waters." Moreover, the

Lord vindicates his servant "in the presence of [his] enemies," expressing both the adversities of life and God's love toward his own. In the presence of God, the guests forget their troubles and tears.

6 The "goodness" (GK 3202) of God is demonstrated in his abundant care and promises, evidence of his blessing. The "love" (GK 2876) of God is his covenantal commitment to bless his people with his promises. Instead of being pursued by enemies who seek his destruction, God's "goodness and love" follow the psalmist. He need not fear, because God's loving care follows him throughout life. The psalmist's experience of God's "goodness and love" is equivalent to dwelling "in the house of the LORD," a phrase that signifies abiding in the environs of salvation. The believer gets a taste of everlasting fellowship with God.

Psalm 24: The King of Glory Is Our God

This psalm consists of three parts. Each part brings out a different consideration of God: (1) the Creator-God (vv.1–2), (2) the holy God (vv.3–6), (3) the glorious King (vv.7–10). The hymn celebrates *God's kingship* as it relates to his people. God is King by virtue of having created all things, but he desires to rule over the people who open themselves to him by living clean, pure lives in his presence.

I. The Great King (24:1–2)

1–2 The psalm first introduces us to the Creator-King, who rules over the earth. The Lord owns "the earth" and "everything" on it. His rule is established particularly because he has made the world habitable (Isa 45:18). "Seas" and "waters" may have reflected the forces of chaos in Canaanite cosmogony; but in Israelite usage they are not hostile, chaotic forces, but fully under the Lord's dominion (cf. 136:5–6). The earth is "established."

II. The Hill of the Lord (24:3–6)

3 The psalmist expresses the nature of fellowship with God as ascending "the hill of the LORD" (Mount Zion, cf. 2:6; cf. also 15:1; 24:3) and standing in "his holy place." Those who seek his favor need to prepare themselves, not only ceremonially, but also by sanctifying their lives.

4 The Lord expects purity and singleness of heart from all who seek his presence (cf. Mt 5:8). Purity of "hands" and "heart" is the condition of living before God in accordance with his precepts and out of the desire of his heart. *Singleness* of devotion is expressed by the godly person refusing to dishonor the Lord's name by idolatry or by hypocrisy.

5 The Lord rewards believers for their walk of integrity. The "blessing" (GK 1388) is the status of God's favor extended to his loyal servants, who enjoy the promises of the covenant. They also receive "vindication" (GK 7407) from their Savior-God. The Redeemer will help, provide justice, and grant the ultimate vindication only to those who are faithful to him.

6 The group of people ("generation") with whom God is pleased walks with integrity, not because of outward constraint, but by an internal desire to please him. To "seek [GK 2011] him" is an expression of a sincere desire to live in accordance with God's standards, in the presence of his "face." The "generation" of the upright are, thus, the true descendants of Jacob.

III. The Divine Warrior (24:7–10)

7 It is difficult to be sure of the original setting of the psalm. This difficulty raises the question of the referent of "heads," "gates," and "doors." "Lift up your heads" is possibly an idiom for rejoicing by the godly. Similarly, "gates" may be symbolic of the people collectively (cf. Isa 14:31). The sense then would be: "Rejoice greatly, O you people [who live within the gates]" (cf. Zec 9:9). On the other hand, the psalmist may be literally addressing the gates of the temple to open up. Or since the temple itself was not yet erected in David's time, the psalmist may be referring to the "ancient doors" of Jerusalem. Consequently, both the city and the people are called on to receive with joy and anticipation the Great King. The repetition in v.9 bears out the importance of proper preparation for "the King of glory."

8–10 "The King of glory" is "the LORD strong and mighty, the LORD mighty in battle," and "The LORD Almighty." He is the God of the covenant people, who brings blessing, victory, and vindication to his people (v.5). "Strong and mighty" and "mighty

in battle" portray him as the Warrior *for* his people. He is not coming to fight against them but for them. He is "LORD Almighty" (lit., "of hosts"; cf. GK 7372) as he commands both the heavenly beings and the host of stars and constellations.

Psalm 25: A Prayer for Deliverance, Guidance, and Forgiveness

This psalm is an *individual lament* with strong similarities to a prayer of confidence, especially vv.1–3, 8–15. The setting cannot be determined with certainty. As a psalm of David, it may fit in the period of his adversities after his sin of adultery. Forgiveness forms a motif throughout. The adversities the psalmist details classify the psalm as a *community lament*. The emphasis lies on the personal effect of adversity in the areas of self-examination, guidance, and submission to the Lord. The psalm is acrostic with a few irregularities.

I. Prayer for Deliverance and Guidance (25:1–3)

1–3 Distressed by his ever-present adversaries, the psalmist turns to the Lord in prayer. He sets forth his joyful confidence in the Lord, with an attitude of submission and anticipation. The close relationship between the Lord and the psalmist is set forth by the phrase "O my God" and "I lift up my soul." He prays that the wicked will not overpower him. From his perspective evil cannot be victorious, because it is an insult to those who trust in the Lord. Others have trusted in the Lord and have not been disappointed (cf. 21:7; 22:4–5; 26:1). He affirms the confident hope of the godly, that they will receive God's protection and never be "put to shame." However, "the treacherous," who have no regard for the Lord, receive their just reward for their faithlessness.

II. Prayer for Guidance and Forgiveness (25:4–7)

4–5 The psalmist needs guidance, because he desires to imitate God. He reveals an earnest desire to do God's will by praying to know "your ways," "your paths," and "your truth"—expressions that pertain to a manner of life consistent with God's law. The imitation of God requires a submissive spirit to divine instruction. True godliness is not outward conformity to God's law but a spiritual application of God's law to one's life. Thus the psalmist prays for the internalization of God's word. He does not submit to a set of principles or to a legal system but to the "Savior," in whom he has put his "hope."

6 The psalmist prays for God's covenant "mercy" and "love," which he has extended "from of old" to his covenant people: Abraham, Isaac, Jacob, et al. David reflects on the actual demonstrations of the Lord's mighty acts on behalf of Israel. An expression of God's mercy is his readiness to forgive sin (cf. Ex 34:7).

7 The psalmist now prays that the Lord will not remember his past sins, shortcomings, and rebellious spirit. He wants the Lord to deal with him, not in accordance with his lack of loyalty, but according to God's own commitment of loyalty. The ground of forgiveness is God's *goodness* toward his people. Forgiveness is that act of grace whereby God extends his love, as if the sin had never taken place!

III. Assurance of Guidance (25:8–10)

8–10 God's acts on behalf of his covenant people are characterized by several qualities: "good," "upright," "right" (or "just"), "loving," and "faithful." His divine perfections are revealed for the sake of sinners, so that they may learn the ways of the Lord. The Lord is the Master-Teacher who in a gracious and upright manner "instructs . . . guides . . . and teaches" sinners. The "humble" (GK 6705) are those sinners who have already submitted themselves to his covenant lordship in the fear of the Lord (vv.12, 14). They have learned "all the ways of the LORD." Because God deals with his children justly, lovingly, and faithfully, he expects them to keep the "demands of his covenant."

IV. Prayer for Forgiveness (25:11)

11 The petitioner rises to a new confidence as he reflects on the name "LORD." Great though his sin is, God's forgiveness "for the sake of [his] name" is greater.

V. Assurance of Guidance (25:12–14)

12–14 The "fear of the LORD" is an inner responsiveness and willingness to learn of the Lord. The humble (v.9) continually seek his mercy, forgiveness, and instruction. Maturity in godly wisdom leads to godliness, communion with God, and covenantal bliss. How great the benefits are! First, the Lord has a distinct way for the godly to walk, for he guides them on "the paths of righteousness." Second, the godly enjoy his fellowship. Those who do his will are his confidants, as was Abraham (Ge 18:17), and they receive full enjoyment of the covenantal relationship. Third, the covenantal blessedness is summarized by two promises: "prosperity" (cf. 34:10; 37:28–29) and continuity of "seed" and "land" (Ge 15:7; Dt 1:8, 21, 39; 4:1; 6:1–2; et al.). By these Israel was assured of the establishment of God's kingdom.

VI. Prayer for Deliverance and Protection (25:15–22)

15–22 The psalmist returns to the motif of the enemies as he prays with fervor that the Lord will deliver him from "the snare" of his adversities. He is entrapped and cannot untangle himself from his difficulties. He hopes longingly for help and, while waiting, has committed himself to "integrity and uprightness." As he receives God's instruction in humble fear of the Lord, the psalmist develops in godliness.

The psalmist's dependency is brought out by "lonely and afflicted" and "I take refuge in you." The exact nature of his suffering is not clear, but it seems to be related to his awareness of and sensitivity to his "sins." The effects of sin are great; and though the psalmist sees a correlation between sin and suffering, he casts himself on God for forgiveness and deliverance. The heart of God's saint shows "integrity and uprightness" by demonstrating a deep concern for Israel as a whole.

Psalm 26: The Innocent Plea for Redemption

In this psalm the psalmist casts himself on the Lord with the request that the Lord pay attention to his circumstances. His troubles are undeserved. Because of the strong pleading with God, it has characteristics similar to the *individual lament* psalms. However, the absence of the clear circumstances of his adversity and the emphasis on his innocence have led scholars to view it as a *protective psalm*.

I. Prayer for Vindication and Affirmation of Innocence (26:1–3)

1–3 For God to "Vindicate" (GK 9149) someone is for him to declare his servant to be innocent and to avenge himself of the wicked. In his own heart the psalmist knows that he has walked with God in integrity. Linked with this prayer for vindication is a petition for God to examine his deepest and innermost recesses, his "heart" and "mind." The psalmist offers himself *completely* for a total examination and desires divine approval. Thus vindication is not primarily an expression of God's righteous wrath and indignation against the wicked but a reassuring word from God.

The psalmist believes that God has motivated and enabled him to walk in God's truth with integrity of heart. God's presence is an authentic experience for him. He is not a man of self-confidence, for he has trusted "in the LORD." "Without wavering" and "continually" describe the kind of trust the psalmist has in his God.

II. Dissociation From Evil (26:4–5)

4–5 In his devotion to the Lord, the psalmist has demonstrated a hatred of evil in any shape or form. He does not "sit" (cf. 1:1) with wicked people—described as "deceitful men" (GK 8736; i.e., people who have given themselves to the pursuit of vanity), "hypocrites" (GK 6623; i.e., those whose ways and motives are hidden from others), and an "assembly of evildoers."

The assembly of evildoers is in stark contrast to the "great assembly" of v.12. The word "assembly" (GK 7736) often denotes Israel as the "congregation" of the Lord (cf. Ex 12:6; Lev 16:17; Nu 14:5; et al.). However, within God's people there was a segment who refused loyalty to the Lord. They established an "assembly" within an assembly, those who were really separate from the Lord. The psalmist affirms his hatred of evil and his complete dissociation from it.

III. Affirmation of Innocence and Love for the Lord (26:6–8)

6 The psalmist reflects on his joy in participating in the worship of God and affirms that in the integrity of his heart he is privileged to draw near to God. "Wash my hands in innocence" need not refer to the ritual of washing one's hands (cf. Ex 30:18–21) but may express purity of heart (cf. 73:13) or a declaration of innocence (cf. 24:4; Mt 27:24).

7 In spite of his troubles, the psalmist looks forward to bringing his offerings of devotion, while proclaiming to his fellow worshipers the acts of God's goodness. His "praise" (GK 9343) consists of words of thanksgiving for what the Lord has done. The reason for that thanksgiving is the history of salvation in which the psalmist shares.

8 The psalmist's concern with integrity, devotion, and praise flows out of a heart filled with "love" for the Lord and for God's house. "The house" consists of more than brick and mortar: the Holy One of Israel lives in the midst of his people. He made his "glory" to dwell among his people (Ex 40:34–35; 1Ki 8:11).

IV. Dissociation From Evil (26:9–10)

9–10 The psalmist sets himself off from sinners whose lot is in the hands of an angry God. His prayer "Do not take away" is a prayer for divine favor and a prayer that he may not be condemned by God's judgment together with the wicked. The sinners are those who have given themselves to a life of sin and rebellion against God. But the psalmist is not one of them. Therefore he has a reason to hope that the Lord, in his anger, will yet spare him.

V. Affirmation of Innocence and Prayer for Redemption (26:11–12)

11a In contrast to bloodthirsty and evil men, the psalmist affirms his determination to continue in his walk with the Lord. Evil presents no temptation for him. He knows the One in whom he believes and is determined to cling to him in devotion, regardless of external circumstances.

11b–12 The psalmist prays that the Lord's examination will turn into evidence of his mercy. He sees himself with the godly in Israel. Among them he will praise the Lord for the evidences of his goodness. Thus he will reassure other believers of what God can do in the lives of his children. The test of faith is public and so should be the celebration of God's sustaining grace. The psalmist knows that the One who loves him will not permit his feet to stumble. Therefore he says that his "feet stand on level ground." His confidence is in the Lord.

Psalm 27: Confidence in the Lord

This psalm is related to the previous psalm by a common concern for God's tabernacle (cf. 26:8; 27:6), by an expression of dependence on the Lord (cf. 26:1–2; 27:3–8), by a prayer for vindication (26:1, 9–10; 27:2–3, 12), and by the hope in divine deliverance (26:12; 27:13–14). There is no general agreement on the genre, but the heading ("of David"), the reference to war (v.3), and the concept of sonship (v.10) favor this as a *royal psalm*.

I. Confidence in God's Presence (27:1–3)

1–3 The confidence of the psalmist lies in the Lord. He has experienced the Lord's presence and describes it as "light" and a "stronghold." "Light" (GK 240) pertains to the experiences of "salvation" and the confidence of the joyous and glorious victory God has promised to his people. The Lord is "the light" of his people (cf. 4:6; 18:28; 43:3; Jn 1:4, 9; 8:12; 1Jn 1:5).

Moreover, God is likened to a "stronghold" (GK 5057). He is the strength of his people, providing a place of refuge for them. The intimate knowledge of God's protecting presence gives confidence and banishes fear. Regardless of how great his adversities, the psalmist looks at the greatness of the Lord in relation to the insignificance of his own problems. The "evil men" are individual enemies in contrast with the national enemies. Opposition and outright "war" do not touch him because his "heart" is strengthened by the Lord.

II. Prayer for God's Presence (27:4–6)

4 The psalmist's longing for God's temple expresses the intensity of his seeking after God himself (cf. v.8; Mt 6:33). He desires to dwell in the temple of God for the rest of his life and to "gaze" on the Lord's beauty and to "seek" (inquire after) him. The "beauty" of the Lord is his favor toward his own.

5 The psalmist seeks the Lord in his "day of trouble," whatever it may be. He anticipates finding protection for himself and his people in God's "dwelling," i.e., the "tabernacle." With the assurance that he is in God's protective hands, he further likens this protection

to being placed "high upon a rock." God is that rock for those who trust in him.

6 Confident of God's care and help in trouble, the psalmist anticipates victory over those who have troubled God's people. He vows to sacrifice to the Lord to express his devotion, while singing a hymn to his God. Doubtless he proclaims the mighty acts of God's redemption in his "shouts of joy" and song, in anticipation of victory. His expressions of loyalty result from a trusting heart.

III. Prayer for God's Presence (27:7–12)

7–10 The mood changes suddenly. The depth of anxiety is expressed in "hear my voice," "be merciful to me," "do not hide your face," and "do not turn. . . . Do not reject." The repetitious language communicates the intensity of the soul's searching and the greatness of his need. He is praying for immediate deliverance out of the adversity. The grounds for his prayer are the covenant name of the Lord, the devotion of the psalmist to his loving God, the acts of God's past loyalty as the "helper" and Savior, and the Father-son relationship.

Through his prayer the psalmist develops a deeper sense of dependence on the Lord. Adversity often masquerades as God's lack of interest or outright anger. When God hides his face, he removes his blessings. But the psalmist knows that the Lord is his heavenly Father. He looks for the intimacy of a relationship with his Father in heaven even in the experience of God's wrath; he expects the Lord to "receive" him.

11–12 Having prayed for God's mercy and in fellowship with the Lord, the psalmist hopes that he will again enjoy God's protection. The "straight path" signifies that all obstacles have been removed. Only the Lord can take the psalmist and God's people out of their distress and lead them into safety. The psalmist prays also for victory over the enemies. If God is with his people, no force is sufficiently powerful to oppose them. At issue is whose "desire" will be granted: the psalmist's or his enemies'? According to 41:2, the Lord protects his own and does not hand them over to "the desire of [his] foes." The submissiveness of the psalmist to God's guidance contrasts to the "violence" of the ungodly.

IV. Confidence in God's Presence (27:13–14)

13–14 The psalm concludes on a triumphant note. In spite of his difficulties, the psalmist is strongly convinced that the Lord will come to the rescue of his people. He believes that he will taste God's "goodness" (GK 3206) in fellowship, protection, guidance, and victory. "The land of the living" denotes "life" on earth over against the state of death. The words of encouragement are reminiscent of Moses' words to Joshua (Dt 31:7), of God's commission of Joshua (Jos 1:6, 7, 9, 18), and of Joshua's words to the people (10:25). Redemptive history did not conclude with the Conquest. It continues as long as God's people "wait for the LORD" and do his will.

Psalm 28: Prayer to the Lord, My Strength and My Shield

The psalmist begins with an urgent prayer in the form of an individual lament (vv.1–5) and concludes with an expression of confidence in the Lord, his strength (vv.6–9). The hymnic thanksgiving to the Lord contains both a blessing and a prayer. The psalm is associated with David and portrays the Lord as caring for his people through his "anointed one" (v.8). It is not clearly a messianic psalm, nor is it a royal psalm. However, it shares with the royal psalms the expectation that the Lord will rule victoriously over his people.

I. Personal Prayer (28:1–2)

1–2 The prayer is directed emphatically to the Lord—"to you." This phrase is symmetric with the last clause of v.2: "toward your Most Holy Place." Prayer is an expression of dependence on the Lord for help. He alone is the "Rock" who gives strength and sustenance to his people. Prayer is also a privilege that belongs to his covenant people—addressed to "the LORD." This prayer arose out of an urgent need whose specific nature is not important enough to be remembered.

In his prayer, the psalmist makes two petitions. (1) He calls on the Lord to act *now*. Though he may have suffered for some time, the psalmist calls on him to "not turn a deaf ear." The silence of God aggravates the psalmist's suffering to the point of becoming unbearable. It is as if he is ready to die. The "pit" is synonymous with "Sheol" (cf. 22:29; 30:3–4; 88:4; see GK 1014 & 8619). Instead of blessing, the psalmist experiences adversity. But before the testing becomes too severe, he petitions the Lord to be sensitive to his needs.

(2) The second petition, a "cry for mercy," underscores the first. The psalmist calls for God's grace to extend to him. As he cries out in his distress, he prays that the All-Merciful may come to his help. To this end he lifts up his hand in prayer, a symbolic expression of his utter dependence on the Lord. The psalmist conforms to an ancient practice of raising his hands to the Most Holy Place (cf. 63:4; 134:2; 141:2), the dwelling place of God on earth.

II. Prayer for Justice (28:3–5)

3 The psalmist's true concern is with God's honor. But the psalmist suffers from the apparent lack of justice. Therefore he prays that the Lord may lift him out of his troubles (cf. 26:9–12) so that he will not be likened to nor judged with the wicked. The wicked are those whose hearts persist in practicing evil and in speaking deceptively.

4–5 The psalmist goes on to pray for God's judgment on the wicked. His concern for retribution does not arise out of some morbid sense of joy in their suffering. He submits himself to the Lord who will requite (Mt 16:27; 2Ti 4:14; Rev 20:12–13; 22:12). The wicked have had their chance; but instead of accepting their responsibility to the Lord, they showed their disregard for him. They have not learned how to respond to God and to his mighty acts. Instead they have occupied themselves with the works of their own hands. Since the wicked do not show a proper regard for the "works" of the Lord or "what his hands have done," their due punishment is destruction.

III. Trust in God's Justice (28:6–8)

6–8 In anticipation of his righteous judgment and the experience of vindication, the psalmist bursts out in a hymn of praise to God. He knows that the Lord has heard his prayer for mercy and looks forward to an even greater deliverance. The psalmist calls the Lord "my Rock" (v.1), "my strength," and "my shield." No longer does he feel threatened to the point of despair; he is now overjoyed and jubilant. He trusted in the "rock" of his salvation, and that "Rock" proved to be a reliable, covenant-faithful God. His confidence in God's justice goes beyond his own experience. The Lord is the God of his people. Since the Lord takes care of the individual, he will most certainly prove himself to be the "strength of his people" and the "fortress" or "stronghold" of his anointed king. "Salvation," i.e., the victory, belongs to him.

IV. Personal Intercession (28:9)

9 In a truly theocratic fashion, the psalmist prays, not only for himself, but also for the people. People and king, nation and individual belong together. He closes his prayer of lament and thanksgiving with a prayer for deliverance from oppression, for the Lord's blessing on his own people, and for God's royal kingship over his own.

Psalm 29: The Victorious Kingship of the Lord

In a grand hymn of praise, the psalmist sets forth a portrait of the Lord as the victorious King. The hymn of praise focuses on a particular aspect of the rule of God. Because of the metaphorical significance of the thunder, the hymn evokes a response of awe at the revelation of God or at his demonstration of victory over the enemies.

I. In Praise of the Lord's Kingship (29:1–2)

1–2 Three times the "mighty ones" are called on to give praise to the Lord. The "mighty ones" (i.e., the divine assembly of heavenly beings who surround the throne of God) are to show due honor to his "glory and strength" and to his "name." The "name" of God is a respectful reference to "the LORD" in the demonstration of his "glory and strength"—a combination that stresses his powerful acts in creation and redemption. The psalmist praises the Lord for his rule, sovereignty, and majesty in relationship to his people and to all his works.

II. The Glorious Voice of the Lord (29:3–9)

3–4 The glory of God rests on all his creation: sky, sea, land, and wilderness. The thunderstorm is a powerful illustration of the majesty and power of God—even at sea. The Mediterranean Sea was a mighty force whose powerful waves could cause great destruction. But the Lord is sovereign over the terrible forces of the sea (cf. 93:3–4).

5–6 The glory of God is also evident in the mountains (114:4, 6). In his presence they are shaken like small objects. These mighty mountain ranges, rising to an altitude of ten thousand feet above sea level, are dramatically portrayed as skipping like a calf and like a wild ox. By the effect of God's power, the grand cedars on Mount Lebanon are felled and splintered to pieces.

7–9 The "voice of the LORD" resonates in heaven and on earth. The psalmist associates the thunder so intimately with the lightning that he reflects on the terrible effects of a lightning bolt. The glory of God reveals itself in the desert regions, over which the Lord also rules. The proper response of God's heavenly creatures is their ascription of glory to the Great King. Everyone in his heavenly temple cries out, "Glory!"

III. In Praise of the Lord's Kingship (29:10–11)

10–11 Though the storms rage and the mountains quake, the Lord is king. His enthronement over "the flood" assures his children that great as his power is, he is sovereign. As in the days of the Flood, so it is at any time that God's glory can be expressed in severe judgment. He rules over nations and peoples that inhabit and traverse land and sea. The demonstration of God's glory in nature gives a sense of tranquility and awe. The Lord, our God, is powerful in his glory. He can and does protect his people.

Psalm 30: Praise for God's Faithfulness in a Time of Need

Praise constitutes the key motif of this psalm. The manner of description of the psalmist's suffering and his exhortation to the "saints" (v.4) to praise the Lord suggest that it is an individual psalm of thanksgiving. If the psalm is Davidic, it may have been composed at the dedication of David's palace or of the building materials of the temple (cf. 1Ch 22:2–19).

However, the word used here for "dedication" connotes the completion of the temple (cf. 1Ki 8:63); so it is preferable to view the psalm as an *individual thanksgiving psalm* associated with David, and to consider the superscription a later addition.

I. Praise for God's Wonderful Acts (30:1–3)

1–3 The psalmist experienced a terrible sickness that brought him to the edge of life. Instead of feeling abandoned by the Lord, he witnessed God's goodness in answering his prayer and by healing him. He exalts God because he brought him up from near death, listened to his prayer, and did not allow the wicked to rejoice. The phrase "you lifted me" means "you saved me." The particular circumstances of the trouble are not relevant, but the experience of deliverance was important to the psalmist. The enemies had no occasion to "gloat."

The psalmist praises the Lord for answered prayer, calling God by his revealed name: "O LORD my God." In the intimacy of communion lies the secret of answered prayer. Since the Lord has brought him up from the "grave" (GK 8619) and saved him from descending into the "pit" (GK 1014, 1071), he praises him as the Exalted One.

III. God's Favor and Anger (30:4–7)

4–7 The praise of God goes from individual praise to a communal celebration. The "saints" (GK 2883) are all those who are loyal to the Lord. They praise "his holy name" for forgiveness and restoration. The psalmist confesses within the assembly that he has sinned against the Lord by a haughty, independent spirit. When everything was going well with him, he "felt secure," even to the point of self-confidence. Apparently he had come to a point of practical atheism.

In his "anger" the Lord had afflicted the psalmist, who in his despair cast himself on the Lord. The period of anguish was like "night" to him, because of the intense experience of weeping. His sorrow resulted both from the suffering and from repentance. The psalmist then returned to the Lord his God (cf. v.2) and experienced his forgiveness. The Lord then restored him—a restoration or healing that is compared to morning light. Such restoration changes weeping into joy. The psalmist knows that it was by the "favor" (GK 8356) of the Lord that he was restored—a word that signifies a renewal of love, forgiveness, restoration, and blessing. The psalmist now feels himself more secure and likens his renewed dependence on the Lord to a "mountain." In his own strength, he was weak; but in God's healing, he became like a mountain.

IV. Praise for God's Wonderful Acts (30:8–12)

8–10 How different is the psalmist's relationship with his God from the time that he felt himself secure within himself! He states emphatically that he looks toward the Lord "for mercy" (GK 2858). He then reflects again on the desperate situation in which he found himself (vv.9–10; cf. comments on vv.3–5).

11–12 The Lord was faithful in changing circumstances. He effectually changed wailing into dancing, mourning into joy, and a deathly cry into a song of joy. Such is the goodness of God. Because of the mercy of the Lord, the psalmist vows to continue in the praise of God. The NIV translates "glory" (GK 3883) as "heart." The word often occurs in parallelism with "soul" (7:5; NIV, "life") and so frequently refers to the whole human being or existence. He will glorify the Lord!

Psalm 31: How Great Is Your Goodness!

The tone of the psalm vacillates between lament and thanksgiving, but the nature of the troubles is unclear. The psalmist makes extensive use of repetition as a literary device.

I. Prayer (31:1–18)

A. Prayer for the Lord's Righteousness (31:1–5)

1–5 The prayer opens with an emphatic declaration of trust. The psalmist has taken refuge in "the LORD," i.e., the covenant-keeping God (cf. Ex 3:15; 6:3; Ps 20:1). In these words he pours out his heart before his Father, who has promised to take care of him. He trusts in the Lord because he knows that he will not be put to shame. The Lord will deliver for the sake of his name, and he is the "rock" (GK 7446) and "fortress" (GK 5181) of his covenant people. The Lord identifies with them; his honor is at stake when they hurt, collectively or individually.

As the Great Shepherd of his people, the Lord leads and guides (v.3; cf. 23:2–3). In his prayer the psalmist seeks a demonstration of the Lord's "righteousness" (v.1; GK 7407), a divine perfection by which the Lord assures his own that he cares for their well-being. The nature of his problem is not specified but involves the enemies who are waiting to "trap" him.

There is an urgency in the psalmist's request "come quickly." In spite of the travail of his soul, he submits himself to God's righteousness because he is "the God of truth." As such, he is "refuge" (GK 5057) for his people. Even in his great need, the psalmist has not lost heart. His trust in the Lord is an act of abandonment: "Into your hands I commit my spirit" (cf. Lk 23:46). God's expectation of his people, before and after Christ, remains the same.

B. Expression of Trust (31:6–8)

6–8 The phrase "worthless idols" can be rendered "vanities of vain," emphasizing the total worthlessness of idolatry. How different is the Lord, whose "love" (GK 2876) finds expression in his acts of deliverance from the enemies! That the Lord "saw" and "knew" is enough, because this is the first stage of his deliverance. The psalmist thus rejoices in anticipation of God's act of deliverance, who will guide him into "a spacious place," far away from his enemies.

C. Prayer for the Lord's Favor (31:9–13)

9–10 The feelings of confidence ebb away in a flood of tears as the psalmist details his troubles in the center part of his prayer. The enemies he has thus far alluded to take on a real shape. They create "distress" by their ridicule and shunning. They are agents of death. The psalmist casts himself on the mercy or favor of the Lord. He knows that by covenant he has a right to expect the Lord to act, but his situation is so desperate that he cannot wait. His cry for mercy is an expression of deep despair. His joy in life is gone; his mental anguish has sapped his physical strength to a point approaching death. The references to "soul," "body," "life," "years," "strength," and "bones" refer to the whole human being, physical and spiritual.

11–13 The psalmist's life ebbs away because of his enemies. He knows that the Lord has promised him life, but he is downcast and disgraced. The enemies have deeply affected him by their slanderous schemes and mockery. The phrase "I am forgotten by them" expresses the depth of despair. His enemies dread him like a disease and act as if he does not exist. He has become useless, "like broken pottery." "And plot to take my life" sums up his concern with life over against death, with justice in opposition to injustice, and with the Lord's fidelity in contrast to the treachery of others.

D. Expression of Trust (31:14–18)

14–18 In broad strokes the psalmist repeats the various elements already introduced as a transition to the hymn of thanksgiving (vv.19–24). The repetition reveals his heightened sense of confidence in his Redeemer. (1) He affirms his basic confidence in the Lord, his God. (2) He commits his circumstances to God's sovereign control. (3) He commits himself to the love of God. (4) He prays for a resolution to the drama: the end of his adversaries. The psalmist trusts that the Lord will honor his prayer so that he need no longer stand shamefaced in the presence of his enemies. When the Lord extends his *love* in his covenant blessing, the treachery and scheming of the wicked will end.

II. Thanksgiving (31:19–24)

19–22 The Lord is "good" by working things out righteously for those "who fear [him]." Even when they are oppressed like a "besieged city," they are kept safe in "the shelter of [his] presence." While he may "hide them," he nevertheless makes it clear "in the sight of men" that the godly are under his protection. In the context of injustice and adversity, he manifests his "wonderful love" in loneliness and abandonment. The formula of blessing "praise be to the LORD" expresses the joy of the redeemed after having experienced his salvation.

23–24 The psalmist confesses his frailty in having questioned God by despairing in his "alarm." But he was proven wrong, and the Lord triumphed. He did hear and did come to his rescue! The psalmist thus encourages the godly to learn from his experience. He exhorts them to hope and trust in the Lord regardless of their circumstances. Faith is not a one-time commitment but an abandonment to the living God, who has promised to "preserve" his own. The life of faith lets God be God—by responding to him in "love," by living in the strength of faith, by observing his word, and by waiting in the "hope" of redemption.

Psalm 32: The Blessing of Forgiveness and Wise Living

Psalm 32 has a special significance in the life of the church and the Christian. It is one of the seven penitential psalms (6; 32; 38; 51; 102; 130; 143), and its association with David encourages the Christian to use the psalm as an assurance of God's forgiveness. Yet this psalm is more than a penitential psalm. Because it includes elements of thanksgiving (vv.3–8) and wisdom (vv.1–2, 9–11), we conclude it is an adaptation of a *thanksgiving psalm* to the wisdom tradition.

I. Blessing of Forgiveness (32:1–2)

1–2 Forgiveness is freely and graciously given by God regardless of whether there be a "transgression," "sin," or "iniquity" (NIV, "sin"). "Transgression" (GK 7322) is an act of rebellion and disloyalty; "sin" (GK 2631) is an act that misses—often intentionally— God's expressed and revealed will; and "iniquity" (GK 6411) is a crooked or wrong act, often associated with a conscious and intentional intent to do wrong.

Three verbs express the absoluteness of divine forgiveness: (1) "are forgiven" (lit., "carried away"; GK 5951) is the act of removal of sin, guilt, and the remembrance of sin; (2) "are covered" (GK 4059) is the gracious act of atonement by which the sinner is reconciled and the sin is a matter of the past, so that the Lord does not bring it up anymore; (3) "does not count" (GK 3108 & 3110) expresses God's attitude toward those forgiven as "justified." The voice of wisdom is heard in the last phrase, where the blessedness of forgiveness is contingent on integrity.

II. Lesson From Experience (32:3–5)

3–5 The description of the anguish of suffering is compared to the wasting away of "bones" and the sapping of physical strength. God's discipline weighed so heavily that the psalmist nearly succumbs under its pressure. God's discipline, like the hot, dry Mediterranean summer climate, dries up the psalmist's vigor like a plant in the heat of summer. In a truly repentant spirit, the psalmist confesses his sin. The three synonyms for sin associated with three synonyms for forgiveness are now associated with three verbs for confession: (1) he "acknowledged" (GK 3359),

(2) he "did not cover up" (GK 4059), and (3) he did "confess" (GK 3344).

III. God's Protection (32:6–7)

6–7 The psalmist encourages the "godly" to draw near to God in his affirmation of God's ability to protect and to deliver from adversity. Even in great adversity, likened to the rush of water through the narrow confines of a wadi, the Lord will protect those who seek refuge in him; he is their "hiding place." Their joy in deliverance expresses itself in joyful shouts as a tribute to God's fidelity.

IV. Promise of Wisdom (32:8)

8 There is a sudden shift from the encouragement of God's protection to the exhortation to wise living (vv.9–11) as the psalmist quotes the Lord, who has promised to instruct his children, give them wisdom, and watch over them. The pattern of "three" is resumed in the promise of God to "instruct," "teach," and "counsel."

V. Lesson From Experience (32:9)

9 Some animals must be bridled to be useful. God gives the godly freedom on the highway of godliness. They draw near to him out of a personal desire for holiness. Those who do not draw near are like animals that have to be held in check.

VI. God's Protection (32:10)

10 This section repeats essentially the assurance of God's protection and love to those who trust in him. The requirement of "trust" (GK 1053) is equivalent to the expression of reliance on the Lord. The wicked may experience endless adversities, whereas the wise will experience the constancy of God's love and protection.

VII. Rejoicing in Forgiveness (32:11)

11 The encouragement to wise living concludes with an exhortation to rejoice. The godly who are mindful of all the benefits (forgiveness, protection, guidance) of the Lord will rejoice! The benefits are limited to the "righteous," who are "upright in heart."

Psalm 33: The Lord Is a Sovereign and Gracious Ruler

Although Ps 33 is commonly classified as a hymn of praise to the Lord "as Creator," the principal theme appears to be praise of God's creative activities in the realms of nature and human history. The structure reveals a cyclical pattern by which each generation is encouraged to praise the Lord for past and present evidences of his love. Consequently, each generation is to expect the Lord to give further reason for praise as the eyes of faith are fixed on him and on a renewal of his love.

I. Song of Praise (33:1–3)

1–3 Singing praises to the Lord was a joyous occasion. The community of worshipers consisted of the "righteous" and "upright." The call to praise assumes that the godly know the Lord, submit themselves to his lordship, and affirm a renewal of hope and trust in his love and deliverance (vv.20–22). Every time they meet together for the praise of the Lord, they have further reasons for singing to him. The renewal of his loving acts on behalf of his own gives rise to a response of gratitude in a "new song"—"new" in the sense that it celebrates a *new* act of God's redemption.

II. Perfections of the Lord (33:4–5)

4–5 The nature of the Lord is the major reason for the celebration. The word "right" (GK 3838) is the same as the word "upright" (v.1). An upright person is without deception, full of integrity of heart, and the opposite of the perverse (Pr 8:8). The Lord's verdicts, rule, and relationship with his people are all characterized by a working out of his plans. The rule of faith is that whatever God decrees is right, and whatever he brings to pass is faithful and true. The Lord's love is evident in his works on earth.

III. The Lord Is the Creator-Ruler (33:6–11)

6–8 By his word God established order on earth and in heaven. Space with its "starry host" is awe-inspiring; the Lord made it and rules over it. He contains the seas as easily as a farmer keeps the grain in a storehouse. Since the Lord made everything and rules over the universe, all nations should recognize that he alone is the Creator-Ruler.

9 The nations must also know that the order in the world is not the result of a harmonious coexistence of the gods. Everything reflects God's wise decree and sovereign rule. Whatever he spoke came into being.

10–11 The nations are fully under his control. Creation and providence are the timely operations of God's purposes. Nothing will "thwart" his plans, which he has purposed for the encouragement of the godly.

IV. The Lord Is the Ruler Over Humankind (33:12–17)

12–17 The Lord freely chose to be the God of his people and appointed them to be his "inheritance" (GK 5709). Israel received a special status out of all the nations (cf. Ex 19:5; Dt 4:20; 9:26, 29; 32:9; et al.). God sees everything that happens on earth. As he is seated on his throne, he not only knows what happens but also understands what humans are doing and planning because he has created them. Everyone is accountable to him. Moreover, people can never thwart God's purposes, because in and through all their planning and affairs, God works out his own goals. Human beings may look at military stratagems ("army," "warrior," "horse"), but the Lord is sovereign over them all. He alone can save, and he alone can bring to nothing.

V. The Lord's Love for His People (33:18–19)

18–19 God's favor rests on those who "fear him" and who "hope" in his "unfailing love" (GK 2876). Therefore, God's people have reason to celebrate. They alone are "blessed" by the very privilege of being a covenant people (v.12). The nations depend on military power. Regardless of how powerful or how threatening an enemy may be, the godly need not fear because "the eyes of the LORD are on those who fear him." They know that he will deal with them with "unfailing love" and will deliver them from any adversity.

VI. Hope in the Lord's Love (33:20–22)

20–22 Regardless of circumstances, each generation of God's people witnesses the new acts of his love. He is their "help" and "shield." They trust in his "holy name," with which they associate past acts of deliverance. Trust requires submission, a willingness to let God be God. The believing community looks expectantly to the Lord, who will work out his plans for the establishment of his kingdom and the renewal of the earth.

Psalm 34: Wise Counsel for the Poor of Heart

This psalm is an irregular acrostic. It is generally categorized as an *individual thanksgiving hymn*, but the wisdom element (vv.8–22) may well argue in favor of its being a *wisdom psalm*. Two basic themes unfold: thanksgiving and wisdom.

I. Thanksgiving for God's Goodness and Justice (34:1–7)

A. Individual and Communal Praise (34:1–3)

1–3 The psalmist opens with personal praise in the form of a hymn. His praise of God is continual, God-centered, and the product of a grateful heart. This is the kind of an offering the Lord will not reject. His own response to adversity and deliverance is to encourage the "afflicted" (GK6705), i.e., the people of God who seek him diligently (v.11). The great chorus of all God's saints joyfully celebrates what God has done on behalf of his own.

B. Individual and Communal Experiences (34:4–7)

4–5 The wise and experienced author teaches from his own experience. He knows what "fears" are, those horrid experiences in life as well as the dread of the unknown. He has also witnessed how God's saints radiate confidence and joy. They look for the light of his countenance and are blessed with the abundance of his goodness and blessing.

6–7 The psalmist may actually point to someone in the audience as he says, "this poor man" (or "humble"). God's people know that the Lord has delivered them from all adversities. The psalmist assures the godly that the "angel of the LORD" protects his beloved. This may indirectly refer to the Lord or allude to the host of angels God has charged with protecting his own. However, protection and deliverance are predicated on evidence of allegiance in the form of "fear of God."

II. In Praise of Wisdom (34:8–22)

A. Exhortation to Wisdom (34:8–14)

8–10 The wise "taste" (GK 3247) God's goodness for themselves by taking "refuge" in him and by submitting their way of life to his. "Blessed" (GK 897) are those who find refuge in the Lord, because they will taste and see that the Lord is good (cf. 1Pe 2:3). Blessed also are those who "fear" him, because they will lack nothing. The psalmist encourages godliness by contrasting the situation of the godly with young lions who may suffer want. The godly are encouraged to seek the Lord because he provides for all our needs (cf. Mt 6:33).

11–14 In wisdom literature the students of the sages are known as their "children" (cf. Pr 1:8; 4:1). The first lesson in that school is "the fear of the LORD," which expresses itself in submission to his way. The next lesson consists in doing the will of God: integrity of language versus deception, practice of good versus evil, and pursuit of peace versus trouble. The reward of wisdom is enjoyed in this life, because God is good to those who seek him. He looks on them with favor and is responsive to their needs.

B. The Rewards of Wisdom (34:15–22)

15–22 The "ears" of the Lord hear the cry of the righteous. His "face" is close to the "brokenhearted" and "crushed." They need not be overcome by their troubles. The way of wisdom assures those who walk by it that God is present, even when they suffer "many troubles." But they do not need to be afraid, because the Lord will deliver his own. The protection of "bones" symbolizes the Lord's care for his own. The wicked will perish, but the godly will find the Lord to be faithful. Those who trust in him will not perish.

Psalm 35: A Prayer for Vindication

With great emotion and urgency, David prays this prayer. The context in which the psalm arose is not certain as its language shifts between legal and military. It may be classified as an *individual lament*.

I. Call on the Divine Warrior (35:1–10)

1–3a The psalmist boldly opens his case with an appeal to God's justice. "Contend" (GK 8189) is a legal term. The legal imagery is further developed in the confession of God's justice in v.10. In need of help, the psalmist casts his burden on the Lord and asks him to represent his case as counselor and prosecutor. The metaphor of a lawsuit changes to that of warfare. The Lord is likened to a warrior who fights on behalf of his own. He comes with a small shield and a "buckler" (a large, possibly rectangular, shield often carried by a shield-bearer; cf. 1Sa 17:7, 41), together with a "spear and javelin."

3b The psalmist is in need of the reassuring words: "I am your salvation." The pronoun "I," when referring to the Lord, signifies the God who has promised to be the Deliverer of his own (Ex 6:6–8). The psalmist is not only looking for divine assurance but also for a new act of God: "salvation" (GK 3802). This word signifies more than reconciliation with God. The biblical view of life is that a threat to the well-being of soul or body requires a divine act of deliverance.

4–8 Prayer for God's deliverance is followed by a prayer for God's vengeance. The psalmist calls for God's judgments to fall on the enemies in the forms of "shame" (i.e., military defeat), "chaff" (i.e., worthlessness), "dark and slippery" paths (i.e., troubles and uncertainties), and "ruin." The psalmist affirms his innocence of any wrongdoing. The statement of unjust treatment is followed by three more imprecations and a climactic statement of the anticipated deliverance.

9–10 When the Lord's justice is expressed against the wicked and the righteous witness the Lord's salvation, they have cause for rejoicing. David's exclamation "Who is like you, O LORD?" arises out of anticipation of the divine deliverance; he knows that the Lord is his Helper and Savior. He may have to wait; but in the meantime he confesses that the Lord is just to the needy. When the Redeemer-Warrior comes to bring in righteousness, all the redeemed will join together in songs of praise because he has delivered them from their troubles and afflictions.

II. The Troubled Soul (35:11–18)

11–16 The psalmist feels himself betrayed by those he has done good to in the past. He had shown concern for their affliction by tokens of mourning and by intercessory prayer. In his own adversity the psalmist found out that his allies were unreliable friends, who brought him low. They used false witnesses to accuse him, to slander him, and to express their anger against him.

17–18 The psalmist also experienced that the Lord was far from him. He laments to his God, "O Lord, how long will you look on?" The "Lord" (GK 123; Master [of the universe]) must have seen all that the rogues have done, but how long will it be before he will act justly? This question of God's justice is an expression of hope in God's ultimate faithfulness. The psalmist has become an international spectacle, and the honor of his people and of his God is at stake. When the Lord has shown his mercy on the king, he will lead the congregation in proclaiming publicly the mighty works of the Lord.

III. Prayer for Vindication (35:19–25)

19–25 The psalmist returns with a final portrayal of injustice. He has been innocently betrayed by his allies. They have turned against him in their speech, betrayed their ill-feelings with their eyes, and rejoiced in his misfortunes. Their words sound harsh as they claim to have evidence against him. The

The face of this Israelite soldier, with a shield and a spear (cf. 35:2–3), is that of King Jehu of Israel. Drawing by Rachel Bierling.

witnesses have stood up and have testified, "with our own eyes we have seen it."

In view of the injustice of his former allies, who are filled with treachery and twist the truth to their advantage, the psalmist entrusts his case to the Lord. He too has seen what both the psalmist and his enemies have done, and he will not remain quiet. Thus the psalmist cries out to the Lord to vindicate him. The "righteousness" of God is at stake. The psalmist prays that the Lord will act on his behalf so that his enemies will not be overcome with feelings of victory. David is convinced that God's speedy trial will end their irritating joviality.

IV. Joy of Deliverance (35:26–28)

26–28 The psalmist prays that justice and righteousness may triumph. He contrasts the wicked and the godly by praying that the enemies of God may suffer the curses of the covenant. He also prays for the Lord's people, who suffered disgrace when their anointed king was disgraced. His ultimate hope is in the redemption of God's people.

When justice returns to earth, God's people will be filled with joy. They will pray for the enlargement of God's kingdom over the self-exaltation of the enemies. The triumph of the Lord's justice evidences his love for his servant David, his concern for his well-being, and—by means of the Lord's anointed—his loyalty to Israel's well-being (v.20). Then the "tongue," which has thus far been the instrument of petition and imprecation, will again praise the Lord for his "peace" ("well-being") and "righteousness."

Psalm 36: The Blessedness of the Wise

This psalm has a variety of genres: individual lament, wisdom, and hymn. The final product is best understood as a wisdom psalm, of which the first four verses set the mood.

I. The Nature of the Wicked (36:1–4)

1–4 The ungodly live with no concern for the fear of God (Pr 1:7). They deceive themselves into thinking that God neither knows nor cares about evil in the world. Evil is their companion, even when they are in bed. They think of getting ahead, of their own good, without concern for justice and righteousness. They take a firm stand (cf. 1:1) in their commitment to wrongdoing. Their speech reflects their inner being in that their words are "wicked and deceitful." Their thoughts, speech, and acts harmoniously mirror the inner "evil" of their being. By rejecting wisdom, they no longer reject "what is wrong."

II. The Wisdom of God (36:5–6)

5–6 The Lord's wisdom is reflected in his "love," "faithfulness," "righteousness," and "justice." His "faithfulness" (GK 575) guarantees the constancy of his "love" (GK 2876) for his own. God's "righteousness" (GK 7407) will effect "justice" (GK 5477) on earth so that the righteous will experience his salvation and the wicked his judgment. God's wisdom affects everything he has created, particularly his own creatures, "man and beast." By his love and justice they live and enjoy living.

III. The Joys of Wisdom (36:7–9)

7–9 God is truly concerned for all humankind (cf. the phrase "low among men"). The Creator protects, feeds, and gives drink. All exist by his goodness. Yet from the context we should limit the privilege of God's special protection to godly people. They alone have a right to find protection under the "shadow of his wings." They alone have access to his "house," enjoying the communal meals as a token of his goodness and provisions for them (Isa 65:13). They are given to drink, as it were, from the "river of delights" and the "fountain of life." The Lord, the source of wisdom, grants his children all their needs. "Life" and "light" speak of the fullness of salvation in the presence of God.

IV. Prayer of Protection From Evil (36:10–12)

10–11 Because the godly live by God's unfailing love and righteousness, the psalmist prays that the qualities of God's wisdom may continue toward the "upright in heart," i.e., those who "know" the Lord. He prays for them and exhorts them to persevere in the knowledge of God. This requires trust in and fidelity to the Lord. For their part, the godly desire to be like God. To this end they pray that they may be kept from evil (cf. Mt 6:13). If evil prevails, the "gifts" of life and home, material and spiritual blessings, may be taken away, allowing the "proud" to be victorious and drive them from their blessings.

12 The concluding prayer petitions the Lord to care for his children in the confidence that evil will cease. Evil cannot coexist with God's rule. It must fall. When that moment comes, the joy of God's blessed presence, protection, and provisions will be precious to the godly.

Psalm 37: Wise Living in a Crooked Generation

In a moving way the psalmist deals with the issues of life and death, wisdom and folly, and reward and punishment. At issue is the power, greed, and prosperity of the wicked and the suffering of the righteous. This issue and the manner of resolution provide sound reasons to approach Ps 37 as a *wisdom psalm*.

I. Exhortation to Hope in the Lord's Deliverance (37:1–6)

1–6 The wise must carefully watch their response to the wicked. It is all too easy to be adversely affected by their prosperity. Regardless of how well off the evil are, they are nothing but mortals who live on an earth under God's just and sovereign rule. The wicked may thrive like grass and plants, but they will not stand up under adversity. As the lush spring vegetation may quickly lose its beauty in the face of a hot, dry desert wind, so too the wicked will quickly fade away.

Instead of giving in to self-pity and envy, the wise trust in the Lord, submitting to his will in the resolution of the dilemma. In this spirit they delight themselves in the Lord. This "delight" (GK 6695) is a more positive reaction than "jealousy," as the wise learn to enjoy all their blessings with contentment. Those who "trust" (GK 1053) in the Lord (i.e., wait for him to act) will "dwell in the land" and do their work ("enjoy safe pasture") with the assurance that the Lord's blessing rests on them. He will grant the desires of those who put themselves completely under his fatherly care.

Because the Lord is righteous and just, the wise have the assurance that he will extend "righteousness" (GK 7406) and "justice" (GK 5477) to his own. These two words refer to the evidences of God's rule over this world, when he establishes the righteous order and glorifies his children. That glory will be unveiled like the rising sun at dawn and like the bright light at noon. The righteous may suffer from evildoers (v.1) but they live in the hope of the day when God will deal justly with evil.

II. The Comfort of Divine Retribution (37:7–11)

7–11 Wise living deals first with negative emotions—anger, fretting, and jealousy. These lead to sin against God, self, or others. Wise living resists evil by trusting in the Lord and doing good. A righteous person begins by being "still before the LORD" and by waiting for his deliverance. Living faith knows that God will act.

God's justice against the wicked is their premature end and ultimately the complete annihilation of evil. They will perish like grass on the day God has determined for them (v.13b). Then his own people will "inherit the land." This refers first to Canaan, but the promise extends to all God's people and to the whole earth (cf. Mt 5:5). The promises of God are only for the "meek" (GK 6705), who trust God "in hope" of justice and who actively do his will on earth. Theirs is the kingdom! They will "enjoy great peace." "Peace" (*shalom*; GK 8934) stands for the beneficence of the godly, in contrast with the life of suffering.

III. The Contrastive Ways of the Righteous and the Wicked (37:12–26)

12–17 The wicked "plot" to get the upper hand. Their godlessness is expressed in an obsession with evil and a hatred of good. They "gnash their teeth" in bitter jealousy. Like soldiers in a desperate battle, they use any trick to overcome the godly. They rule with "sword" and "bow," symbolic of their strength and abuse of power, and they eagerly await the destruction of the godly. Their victims are the "poor and needy," i.e., the destitute and those robbed of justice. Their goal is a chaotic autonomy, a world in which injustice is law. There is no place for those "whose ways are upright" in their world.

In contrast to the wicked, the wise man knows that a "little" with godliness is preferable to plenty with godlessness (cf. Pr 15:16; 16:8, 19). Above the wicked is a just God who does not act immediately but "laughs at the wicked." He sees the end from the beginning and assures the godly that "their day is coming." It will be that terrible "day of the Lord," when "the power of the wicked" (symbolized by the piercing swords and broken bows) will be broken. They will get their just deserts.

18–22 The Lord knows "the days of the blameless," i.e., the many days of their lives. Whereas he sees "the day" (sing.) of the wicked, he will bestow his covenant favors on his own in the days (pl.) to come. They will continue even in the "days of famine," but the wicked come to an end. The godly may suffer adversities, but, unlike the wicked who "wither," they will "enjoy plenty." The righteous are "blessed" by the Lord and are therefore guaranteed his covenant mercies: life and its full enjoyment. In contrast to the wicked, who hoard for themselves, the righteous are like God and "generously" help the poor.

The demise of the wicked comforts the righteous. They are like sacrifices going up in smoke or beautiful flowers that readily disappear. They certainly will "vanish" because of God's curse. They may even come to poverty in this life so that they have to borrow to stay alive, being unable to pay back; but ultimately they will be "cut off" from the presence of God and all his benefits.

23–26 The focus moves from the contrasts between the godly and the wicked to the various blessings of the godly. (1) The Lord establishes the godly, even in times of adversity. They may "stumble," but they will not fall, for the Lord keeps them from falling. (2) The Lord takes care of the physical needs of his children. He gives life to his people and supports the righteous with "bread." They are not "forsaken." They have God's promise that he will not completely forsake his own (Ge 17:7; 28:15; Mt 28:20). (3) God gives to his own because they, like him, are gracious stewards (v.26). God's blessing also extends to the next generation, as "their children will be blessed" (Ac 2:39).

IV. Call for Wise Living in View of the Belief in Divine Retribution (37:27–33)

27–31 The psalmist has given the godly much reason for encouragement as well as a wise perspective on life. However, the righteous must persevere in doing God's will. Thus they have a responsibility to their children, because God will protect their descendants

and will permit them to dwell in the land, whereas the offspring of the wicked will be cut off.

The ground for all the blessings is the love of God. He "loves [GK 170] the just" (Pr 2:8) and therefore will never forsake "his faithful ones" (i.e., "his saints"; GK 2921). The Lord loves the wise, who promote justice and are loving. They fear the Lord, revere God, and desire to do his will. The law is written on their heart. In harmony with their "heart" (GK 4213), they speak wisely and thus establish justice and do "not slip" by giving in to the evildoers or by envying them.

32–33 The ungodly cannot tolerate true piety. They can readily dismiss the hypocrite, the fake, and the enthusiast, but the living faith of the wise evokes furious reprisal. The wicked are pictured as thugs who lie in ambush to destroy the wise. The righteous, however, are not forsaken by the Lord. He will not suffer them to be tried unjustly by the unjust. Even when it seems that the wicked hold power and pervert justice, God promises to establish justice and to rid the earth of evil.

V. Exhortation to Hope in the Lord's Deliverance (37:34–40)

34–40 Facing evil in the world, the wise response of the godly comprises (1) hope in the Lord, (2) loyal obedience to him, and (3) faith in his justice. God exalts the righteous, gives them the land, gives them a future (or posterity), delivers them and protects them from troubles, and crowns them with victory ("salvation"). However, he brings down the wicked, even when it seems as if they would live forever. The godly will live to "see" that judgment of the wicked. The psalmist concludes the psalm by calling the godly to look to the Lord for protection, deliverance, and victory. Help is promised to those who "take refuge in him." He is their "stronghold."

Psalm 38: A Prayer for Reconciliation

In this *individual lament* the psalmist calls on the Lord for healing from a crippling disease. He is overwhelmed with guilt, abandonment, and a desire for renewed fellowship with God. Because of the themes of sin, guilt, judgment, and hope in God's salvation, Ps 38 has been used as a penitential psalm (cf. Pss 6; 32; 38; 51; 102; 130; 143).

I. Prayer for Reconciliation (38:1–4)

1–4 Not all disease results from individual sin. But the affliction of the psalmist is associated with "my guilt" / "my sin" and "your anger" / "your wrath" / "your wrath." The ferocity of the Lord's anger is so great that the psalmist feels himself to be the object of his attacks. It is as if he has been set up to be pierced by God's "arrows." The idiom "your hand has come down upon me" symbolizes the extent of alienation, resulting from a severe form of discipline. God's rebuke penetrates deep into the psalmist's being so as to bring him down. Suffering can be a form of God's discipline for the righteous.

The intensity of God's discipline has affected the psalmist's capacity to enjoy life. No part of his being has been left unaffected; there is no "soundness" (lit., "peace"; GK 8934) in his bones (i.e., his body; cf. 6:2). The psalmist does not question God's justice. Throughout the lament he recognizes his own sinfulness. He has come to the breaking point because the consequences of his sin and guilt have "overwhelmed" him like a flood. Therefore, he lifts himself up to the Lord with the prayer for relief, compassion, and reconciliation.

II. Pain of Anguish (38:5–12)

5–8 The experience of suffering is all around the psalmist. He sees and feels the pain of his wounds, his back aches, and he is "utterly crushed." The anguish results from his mental and spiritual pain as he reflects on the reason for his suffering—his sin. He calls sin "folly" (GK 222) because it has found him out. Sin is sin; but when it is done conscientiously, it is "folly." All joy of life is far from the psalmist. He is bowed down and mourns. He despairs within himself; all he can do is "groan" within himself.

9–10 In the state of depression, one's thoughts are not coherent. "Longings" here signifies "sighing" of the heart. The psalmist looks up to God with the hope that he will understand the meaning of his groans. Thus even in his state of depression, the psalmist does not doubt his relationship with the covenant Lord but calls on the One who heard Israel's groaning (Ex 2:25) to listen also to him. He desperately wants to do something about his situation. But he feels that he no longer has the proper perspective—"even the light has gone from my eyes."

11–12 The psalmist's personal sense of abandonment is aggravated by his being shunned. His friends are afraid of associating with a sick person or with a sinner. His enemies do not leave him at peace; they aggravate the situation by adding to his troubles and speaking lies.

III. Prayer for Vindication (38:13–16)

13–14 In his loneliness the psalmist feels himself isolated from the world like a deaf or mute person. He has no words or interest in defending his innocence. He is silently absorbed in his suffering, knowing that he has sinned; and he waits for God to initiate reconciliation.

15 In his total abandonment the psalmist cries out to God as his sole refuge. Because of his sin, guilt, and the consequences of sin, he has no argument against his foes. However, even in his darkest moments there is still the glimmer of light borne out of a living faith. He knows that God can answer, and he still addresses God as "Lord my God." The psalmist claims that the Ruler of the universe is his God.

16 The psalmist has no other hope left than waiting for the Lord. There is little time left. The foes are using every opportunity to remind him of their strength and power and of his weakness. Their self-exaltation increases at the cost of his life.

IV. Pain of Injustice (38:17–20)

17 The psalmist is concerned with the enemies who desire to glory over the death of one of the godly so that they may exalt themselves over God. And he is concerned with the promise of God that he would not permit the righteous to stumble (15:5; 37; 112:6). His "pain" in forms of physical suffering and anguish of mind is ever-present, inescapable.

18 The psalmist confesses his sins again (cf. vv.3–4). Troubled by guilt and the consequences of sin, he clings to the Lord for his assurance. But as long as he is suffering, there remains a lingering doubt about the efficacy of God's forgiveness, just as Christians who in their suffering from sin continue to plead with God for full pardon and restoration.

19–20 In his soul-searching experience, the psalmist has found himself to be innocent of wrongdoing against those who gloat over his adversities. Instead he has treated them well. Yet he is overwhelmed by the number and the enthusiasm of his opponents. It is possible that he is speaking hyperbolically or that in his distress a few troublers seem many.

V. Prayer for Reconciliation (38:21–22)

21–22 In conclusion the psalmist calls on the Lord as "Lord" (the covenant God), "my God" (equivalent to "my Father"), and "Lord my Savior" (Master of the universe, powerful and able to save). Since the Lord has promised to be near, he prays, "Do not forsake me." Since a child of God needs the presence of his heavenly Father, he prays, "Be not far from me, O my God." Since he submits himself to the sovereignty of God, he prays, "Come quickly to help me, / O Lord my Savior." Thus he commits his cause to this great God, his Father.

Psalm 39: A Stranger to Life and an Alien With God

In a moving way the author of this psalm draws us into the reality of life with its vexing problems and the unresolved quest for meaning. This psalm is in the form of an *individual lament*.

I. Silence Before the Lord (39:1–3)

1 In view of his internal and external circumstances, the sacred author has determined not to speak anymore. He has made a personal commitment to control himself. He intends to scrutinize his behavior, especially his speech, to see whether there is any unbecoming action. He has found it difficult to "muzzle" his mouth, but he has come to the point where it is necessary. The external circumstances that necessitate his determination are due to the ungodly.

2 The psalmist desires to speak forthrightly about his internal problems but fears that he may be misunderstood or that he may speak irreverently and give occasion to the enemy. For the sake of God, he vows to be silent in his suffering. He becomes intensely aware of his limitations; and in his self-awareness he is vexed with life.

3 In his silence the psalmist learns more about himself, especially how difficult it is to control himself. The metaphors "my heart grew hot" and "the fire burned" express anger. The more he reflects on his situation, the more he becomes exasperated. His whole being is aflame. He has to speak.

II. Prayer for Divine Illumination (39:4–6)

4 Unable to resolve his problem, the psalmist turns to the Lord for instruction. The purpose of knowing life's end is not that he may plan for every day of his life. In the greater awareness of the brevity of life, he hopes that the Lord will guide him in an understanding and acceptance of this brevity.

5–6 The psalmist compares his life to a "handbreadth" (about four inches). In his heart he feels that life is like a mile, but in reality it is a brief span of time. Even when a person seems strong and self-assured, from God's perspective he or she is little more than a "breath." Human existence and future are filled with uncertainties; a person is "a mere phantom." People may go about busily and gain status and wealth, but they are mortal and cannot control affairs after death.

III. Prayer for Deliverance (39:7–8)

7–8 The psalmist concludes that nothing in life is important or reliable unless one's hope is secured in God. In searching for the meaning of human life, he has come to a renewed commitment to God. He is also more aware of his own shortcomings in the presence of God. More than ever, he realizes his need for God's forgiveness, reconciliation, and healing. His hope is in the Lord, for whose deliverance he waits anxiously. When the Lord vindicates his servant, the foolish scoffers will have no more occasion to rejoice.

IV. Silence Before the Lord (39:9)

9 When he was silent (v.2), the psalmist was deeply disturbed and feared that he might say something disrespectful about or to his God. Now he realizes that his condition is the Lord's will. Thus he willingly accepts it from God's hand. He does not understand everything; but at least he knows that a personal God is in charge of his life, not an impersonal force.

V. Prayer for Divine Sustenance (39:10–11)

10–11 The psalmist is vexed by the discipline of the Lord in his life. Human frailty and God's discipline hedge him in. For the child of God, disappointments, adversity, and fatherly discipline are reminders of God's fatherly concern. While the discipline is like a "scourge," yet the psalmist learns through anguish the meaning and brevity of life. Human beings are not divine.

VI. Prayer for Deliverance (39:12–13)

12–13 In submission to God's will and in recognition of his humanity, the psalmist returns to the Lord with a renewed spirit, addressing him as "the LORD," the covenant God. Even though he feels himself a stranger in God's presence (as his fathers were), is a sinner, and suffers adversities, he has no doubts about belonging to God's community. He prays for the Lord to remove his judgment and to again renew his joy, so that he may have a foretaste of the Lord's covenant presence.

Psalm 40: The Joyful Experience and Expectation of Salvation

This psalm is composed of two themes: thanksgiving of the individual (vv.1–10), followed by an *individual lament* (vv.11–17). It may be a prayer based on God's past acts of deliverance, i.e., a royal prayer.

I. Personal Experience of Salvation (40:1–3)

1–2 The experience of salvation is the story of what God has done. The psalmist recounts what happens when one waits "patiently" for the Lord (cf. Ps 27). The allusions to death and dying in the words "slimy pit," "mud," and "mire" suggest that David was seriously sick, even to death. Healing was then a salvation from the netherworld (cf. 69:2, 14), out of which the Lord "lifted" him. But the metaphors may also express the threat to Israel's national existence by an enemy attack. The king personified the severity of the crisis by the imagery of his own suffering and the Lord's deliverance.

3 In proper response to God's help, David renewed his praise to him. The newness of the song lies in the event of salvation history. The recent victory was one additional chapter in a long series of God's involvements with his people, inspiring the people of God with the renewed sense of awe for their covenant God.

II. Blessedness of God's Protection (40:4–5)

4–5 David speaks of the blessedness of those who put their confidence in the covenant God, whose acts of protection are innumerable. Indirectly he exhorts people not to depend on human strength or idolatry. The mighty acts of the Lord are "wonders" (GK 7098), i.e., acts of supernatural and providential deliverance that are too numerous to recount (cf. 104:24; 106:2; 139:17–18; John 21:25); they are the manifestations of "the things you planned for us." The history of redemption shows an inner cohesiveness and movement, unfolding the "thoughts" of the Lord that will ultimately result in the restoration of heaven and earth.

III. Expression of Commitment (40:6–8)

6–8 David is aware that the Lord is not pleased with mere sacrifice (cf. 1Sa 15:22–23). He is opposed to mere formalism and declares his personal commitment to the Lord in the form of "open ears." He has heard the law of God—especially the requirements of kingship. Thus David, the Lord's anointed, presents *himself* as a dedicatory offering to the Lord. Commitment is a wholehearted desire to conform one's way of life to the will of God, as prescribed in the Word of God.

IV. Proclaiming God's Perfections (40:9–10)

9–10 David proclaims the good news of the Lord's perfections to the congregation assembled for worship. He must speak by an inner compulsion; he cannot be quiet. He explains that his commitment is correlative to the perfections of the Lord's rule: "righteousness ... faithfulness ... salvation ... love ... truth." The Lord's *righteousness* is expressed in any act ordered on behalf of his people's welfare and the execution of his kingdom purposes. The nature of God's righteous acts is that he is *faithful* to his covenant people, resulting in their *salvation*. That faithfulness is a corollary to his unfailing *love* and *truth*, i.e., fidelity.

V. Prayer for God's Perfections (40:11)

11 The psalmist then prays that the Lord will continue to bestow his covenant "love" (GK 2876) and fidelity or "truth" (GK 622) on his anointed servant and through him on the nation. Because of the great need (cf. v.12), he also implores God to have compassion or "mercy" (GK 8166, 8177) on him.

VI. Confession of Sin (40:12)

12 The king is troubled by the adversities caused by his enemies (cf. vv.14–15). Though he speaks of "my sins," as a theocratic leader he takes on himself the sin of the nation and pleads with the Lord to have compassion on the nation. The consequences of sin had a paralyzing effect on him and his ability to rule God's people. So great was the affliction that he felt overwhelmed like a flood (cf. 2Sa 22:5; Jnh 2:5).

VII. Prayer for God's Protection (40:13–16)

13–15 David prays that the Lord will "quickly" help him out of the crisis. He affirms that it must be God's will and his act of deliverance. He also prays that those who rejoiced in his and the nation's misery may be proven wrong in their assumption that the Lord lacked power to redeem his people. He prays for his enemies' fall and shame in accordance with the principles of justice and with the promise of God to curse those who cursed his own (Ge 12:3). The enemies liked taking potshots at God's people, shouting contemptibly, "Aha! Aha!" David prays that the Lord will change their fortunes so that they will know who is God.

16 When the Lord demonstrates anew his righteous act of deliverance, God's people will rejoice in his salvation. They are characterized by their "seeking" the Lord and "those who love your salvation." David prays here, not for himself, but for his people who have joined him in waiting for the salvation of the Lord.

VIII. Personal Need of Salvation (40:17)

17 The psalmist concludes on a note of urgency. The last three words express the need: "do not delay." He is in desperate need and humbly casts himself and his people before the Lord. The Lord remains "my help and my deliverer" and "my God" even in crises.

It is on this ground that David prays for speedy deliverance.

Psalm 41: God's Blessings in Adversity

This psalm has elements in common with an individual lament (vv.4–10). Yet the introductory (vv.1–3) and concluding (vv.11–12) verses set the mood of thanksgiving for the psalm in such a way that it is best treated as a *thanksgiving of the individual.*

I. Affirmation of God's Blessings (41:1–3)

1–3 The phrase "blessed is" begins (see comment on 1:1) and closes the first book of Psalms. God's children are blessed as they receive grace upon grace! But his blessings are not automatic. He looks for those who wisely conform to his heavenly kingdom on earth, who are concerned for those in need (cf. Mt 5:7; Jas 1:27). The Lord has promised to protect his people from harm and bless them with a long life of good health, prosperity in their promised land, and sustenance in time of need (cf. Ge 12:2–3; Ps 72; 2Co 1:20).

II. Prayer for Healing (41:4)

4 The psalmist's prayer for healing and restoration is based on God's promises. The emphatic use of "I" is for the purpose of contrasting the words of his prayer with the words of the foes (v.5). There is no note of despair. He is not depressed by the weight of his sin; he confesses his unwitting sins and asks for the Lord's mercy.

III. The Words of the Enemies (41:5–9)

5–6 The psalmist laments over the reaction to his sickness from his enemies. Their words were filled with hatred and were void of sympathy. They slandered, hoping that evil would triumph and the righteous and their seed would perish from the earth. They remain filled with deception, hypocrisy, and selfishness.

7–9 Even on his sickbed the psalmist imagines hearing the whisperings of his adversaries. They describe his sickness as "a vile disease." "Vile" (GK 1175) is a translation of "Belial" and can also be rendered as "a sickness from the devil." While the psalmist thinks of himself as innocent of known transgression (vv.11–12), his adversaries hope he will die! They think that his sins have found him out and that he is accursed. The rumors become so malicious that his "close friend," whom he regards as a member of the family, turns against him. The idiom "has lifted up his heel against me" signifies a treacherous act (cf. Ge 3:15; Ps 55:12–14). Thus both friend and adversary malign his name, believing that his death is justified (cf. Jn 13:18).

IV. Prayer for Healing (41:10)

10 The prayers of vv.4 and 10 frame the lies of the enemies. The psalmist cannot respond to their accusations but wholeheartedly trusts in the Lord and in his promise to protect him against his enemies. He prays that the Lord will be gracious to him and restore him and that he will "repay them." This prayer is not vindictive but shows a concern with the honor and justice of God, who has promised to sustain the godly in sickness and in health.

V. Confidence in God's Blessings (41:11–12)

11–12 Even in his adversity the psalmist is confident that the Lord will be true to his promises. Within his heart he knows himself to be a man of "integrity." He also claims the promise that the Lord supports those who love him—especially in their adversities. He longs for the moment when the Lord will deal kindly with him in the presence of his enemies and that he will enjoy God's presence and the experience of his blessings forevermore (cf. 23:5–6).

Concluding Doxology to Book I (41:13)

13 The Lord is "blessed" (GK 1385; translated here as "praise be to") in the sense that he is praiseworthy. The Lord, the God of Israel, has covenanted to be their God and the God of their children. Since he is blessed forever, God's people have assurance that he will continue in his care. To this Israel responds with a twofold "amen."

Book II: Psalms 42–72

Psalms 42–43: Hoping in the Lord's Salvation

The literary unity of Pss 42 and 43 is such that they should be treated as one psalm because of (1) the absence of a superscription above Ps 43; (2) the repetition of a refrain (42:5, 11; 43:5); (3) development of thought

from remembrance (42:4, 6) to a specific hope of restoration (43:3); and (4) the lament form. Each psalm is an *individual lament*. Even though the life-situation remains controversial, it is evident that the psalmist was isolated from the temple worship. He may have been a refugee, but it is more likely that he had been exiled to Aram, Assyria, or Babylon and was in the hands of taunting captors (vv.3, 10).

I. Lament (42:1–4)

1–3 The simile of the "deer" expresses the intense yearning of the psalmist for a taste of God's presence. As usual "soul" (GK 5883) does not denote the spiritual aspect of a person exclusively. The psalmist's longing is for "God," then "the living God," and finally "the face of God" (NIV, "meet with God"). He wants to "meet with God" in the temple on Mount Zion. He is hemmed in by his own question, by his longing for God's presence, and by his enemies who tauntingly ask, "Where is your God?" Down deep in his heart he asked the same question, "Where is my God?" The depth of his sorrow is expressed by "tears" as his "food." Not knowing where else to turn, he looks to God for the answer to his despairing feeling.

4 In adverse conditions the psalmist cannot do much more than to "remember" (GK 2349). He meditates on the pilgrimages to the temple, the festive celebrations, and God's triumphs in the history of salvation. During the three annual pilgrimage festivals (Passover, Firstfruits, and Tabernacles; cf. Lev 23:4–44; Dt 16:1–17; et al.), the pilgrims gathered in Jerusalem and presented their offerings and sacrifices with great rejoicing. The pouring out of the soul is an expression of the intensity of one's emotions.

II. Hope (42:5–6a)

5–6a The psalmist analyzes his feelings and asks questions of himself, expressing both despair and hope in God. In his alienation, faith is tried and triumphs! Faith and doubt are twins; and when doubt seems to triumph, true faith calms its questions. Hope leads the psalmist away from despair. His hope is focused on the glorious acts of salvation and victory. He anticipates the fulfillment of God's promises, even when help is far off.

III. Lament (42:6b–7)

6b–7 In spite of the psalmist's expression of hope, he is still "downcast." Therefore he returns in his memories to the Promised Land, symbolized by "the land of the Jordan, the heights of Hermon," and the water imagery with which the psalm began. But this time the memories of water are overshadowed by a deep sense of despair. The waterfalls with its rocks, breakers, waves, and awesome noise metaphorically portray his condition. Instead of enjoying the "living water" of the "living God," he is continually faced with an expression of God's judgment.

IV. Hope (42:8)

8 By day and night the psalmist experiences the evidences of God's care, protection, and blessing. The very experience of communion made the Lord as "real" to him as "the God of my life." In contrast to the past, his "love" (GK 2876) seems to be lost; and the psalmist's praise of God's love has changed into continual mourning for God's absence (cf. v.3).

V. Lament (42:9–10)

9–10 In his moments of doubt and reflection on God's absence, the psalmist remembers that his God is "my Rock." He is the place of refuge. He asks twice "why" God has forgotten him. In the present situation, he has no other recourse than to mourn because he has been abandoned to godless people, who taunt him continually. He is like a dying man, and his God is silent. His whole being ("my bones") is distressed.

VI. Hope (42:11)

11 These reflections bring the psalmist again to a point of despair, self-examination, and an affirmation of hope in the future saving acts of God (see comments on v.5).

VII. Lament (43:1–4)

1–2 The psalmist now intensifies his prayer for redemption and for the enjoyment of fellowship with the Lord. He has demonstrated his love (42:8) in the past, but the psalmist is not satisfied until he is fully restored to his God. In his distress he calls the Lord "God my stronghold." Not only is he the Rock of refuge (v.9), but also he is the Deliverer of his people in need. This God is powerful to "vindicate" him. The psalmist has gone around as

in "mourning" because of the absence of God and the antagonism of the ungodly. The questions are similar to those of 42:9.

3–4 In the darkness of the adversities, the psalmist asks God for his "light" and "truth." The "light" (GK 240) of God is the experience of the fullness of his redemption (36:9). The "truth" (GK 622) of God is the expression of his covenantal fidelity (40:10; 57:3). If only God will send these two personified expressions of his love to "guide" him back, then he will experience restoration. The psalmist's concern is for a return to Jerusalem, "your holy mountain," God's dwelling. The anticipation to return to "the altar of God" and the temple relates back to the pilgrimage festivals (42:4). Redemption will result in great joy. The God who is "my stronghold" becomes "God, my joy and my delight."

VIII. Hope (43:5)

5 The refrain returns to the conflict between faith and doubt, to the contrast between the present and the future, and to the hope that "I will yet praise him" (see comments on 42:5).

Psalm 44: Redeem Us Because of Your Unfailing Love

The mood of the two previous psalms also dominates Ps 44. These three are examples of the lament genre and reflect a period of God's rejection of his people (42:9; 43:2; 44:9, 24). They also express the hardship experienced by the reproach of the nations (42:3, 10; 43:2; 44:13–16). Psalm 44 is a *national lament* reflecting defeat in battle.

I. God's Past Acts of Deliverance (44:1–3)

1–3 God's people had heard the story of what he had done for their ancestors "in days long ago," including the era of the Conquest. Against all odds Israel inherited the land, because God fought on their behalf. Israel's victories were not their own. Though they used their swords and were valiant in battle, they realized that the fulfillment of the land-promise was God's. He had "planted" them and had let them "flourish" like the branches of a tree. They were the recipients of his favor—"the light of [his] face," by which they had been victorious in the past.

II. Confidence in God (44:4–8)

4–8 This section begins with an emphatic confession of God as the Great "King" and also the Commander of Israel's "victories." Only when the Israelites had put aside their confidence in weaponry and bravery could they become instruments in God's hands. They had cause to "boast" in the "name" of the Lord, when they had fought in his "name." Each participant in this prayer confesses his personal reliance on the Lord in v.6.

III. Suffering and Disgrace (44:9–16)

9–16 These reflections on the traditions of God's past victories and on the national and personal confidence in God's triumphant kingship are shattered by the reality of the present. From the evidence presented in the charges, seemingly the Lord had "rejected" and humiliated his people. They have been allowed to be conquered, plundered, scattered like sheep, and enslaved by their enemies. Consequently the name of Israel has been disgraced among the nations. At the heart of the charges is the feeling that the Lord cares little for his people. Why else did he sell them out so easily and cheaply to the enemy? The consternation of the people is an expression of their concern with the present reality. Faith in God, the Divine Warrior-King, was being tested in the current crisis.

To this situation each godly person joins in a personal expression of agony. The disgrace of the nation affects each citizen; each one speaks of "my disgrace." The sounds of the "taunts" of enemies and neighboring nations are heard "all day long."

IV. Claim of Innocence (44:17–22)

17–22 In spite of all their suffering, the hearts of the people are right with God. They cling close to him with a strong determination to remain faithful by keeping his covenant, by remaining completely devoted to his way, and by not giving themselves over to idolatry. Yet God continues to permit devastation and darkness to oppress them. The adversities are likened to a place made desolate by war, i.e., "a haunt for jackals." "Deep darkness" is a metaphor for adversities, often resulting in despair.

The people's suffering is not because of their sins. Rather, they suffer "vicariously" like "sheep to be slaughtered." In their fidelity to the Lord, they receive greater abuse than if they had conformed to the pagan world. In suffering for the honor of God, they need reassurance of his love (cf. Ro 8:36–39).

V. Prayer for Deliverance (44:23–26)

23 The questions of faith express the conviction that a chasm exists between the promises of God and reality. Out of their deeply felt need, the people of God ask, "Why do you sleep?" Not that they believe God is asleep, but because they seek his immediate attention to their plight, they plead with him to "awake" (GK 6424).

24–26 The present adversity has created a darkness, because "the light" of God's face, which their forefathers had experienced (v.3), is hidden. In dependency on God's favor, they prostrate themselves to the ground. They do not have the power to rise up, but in prayer they implore God to rise up on behalf of them. Redemption pertains to the welfare of God's people in body and soul, who petition him to look again at their low estate. In conclusion they submit themselves to the love of God. He covenanted himself to the people and promises them his "unfailing love" [GK 2876].

Psalm 45: The Wedding of a Son of David

The psalm is a *royal psalm* and functioned as a *wedding song* at the occasion of the wedding of a royal couple. Because of the theological significance of the wedding and the function of the Davidic king within God's order, the wedding song in a special way applies to our Lord, who rules as the Son of David (cf. Heb 1:8). This psalm extols the privileged position of God's people and sets forth God's expectations of the king, his appointed vassal on earth (cf. Pss 2; 110).

I. Introduction (45:1)

1 Having been moved by "a noble theme," the sacred composer adds his own word of tribute to the king. It may be that he has received a word from the Lord and writes or recites the psalm to bless the royal couple. As an artist in his own right, he speaks the words of a "skillful writer."

II. The Royal Groom (45:2–9)

A. Address to the King (45:2–5)

2 The description of the Davidic king is idealized, as the poet projects a conception based on theocratic expectations. He is the one blessed by the Lord because of the promise given to David (2Sa 7:11–16). The king's "excellence" (GK 3636) lies in God's presence with him. It is God's divine blessing manifested in his speech, his royal valor, his concern for establishing God's kingdom on earth, and the continuity of his dynasty. The king's speech is wise, as his words are "anointed with grace."

3–5 The poet wishes the king success in his military pursuits. When he goes out with sword on his side, he confidently leads his troops to victory. The "splendor and majesty" speak of his past victories and the confident expectation of additional victories every time he marches at the head of his troops. He does not rest until his enemies recognize his authority. The success of the king is due to his concern for what is important to the Lord and his covenant people—"truth, humility and righteousness." His concern for "truth" keeps him loyal to God and to his people. His concern for "humility" keeps him continually dependent on his covenant. His concern for "righteousness" is demonstrated in his ordering the affairs of state to correspond with God's plans. The kingdom of the son of David is an expression of the kingdom of God on earth.

B. The Glory of the Bridegroom (45:6–9)

6–7 The throne of David is assured by covenant. Each king on that throne is reminded that he is king by "divine right." The "scepter of justice" is a royal symbol of his authority to establish a rule of integrity based on the laws of God. In his deep love for "righteousness," he opposes all forms of "wickedness." God's rule will be established on earth. Our Lord is the descendant of David inherited the royal throne (cf. Heb 1:8–9). As the "Son" of God, his kingdom is everlasting.

8–9 The inspired poet turns his attention to the preparations for the wedding ceremony. The descriptions and references to the robes, spices, music, the royal daughters, and the royal bride all reinforce the rightness of the moment and of the anointing of this son of David. The evident blessing of God on the king assures the continuity of the dynasty (cf. 2Sa 7:16).

III. The Royal Bride (45:10–15)

A. Address to the Bride (45:10–12)

10 The bride is seated to the right of the king and is adorned with the valuable gold of Ophir, a proverbially fine gold. The queen is of foreign descent, having left her father's house (cf. Ge 12:1). The psalmist encourages her to be loyal to the people of God by forgetting her own loyalty to her native land. He also encourages her to submit herself fully to her husband, the king, to show that she belongs to the people of God (cf. Ru 1:16).

11 The king is God's anointed representative. Submission to him implies submission to the God of Israel. So while the king delights in the physical beauty of his wife, she respects him as her "lord" (GK 123). It would be wrong for her to compare him to the kings of the nations with their powers of state, cultural refinements, and idolatrous ways.

12 The people of Tyre are personified as "the Daughter of Tyre." They, as well as other rich nations, will bring tribute to Jerusalem. During Solomon's regime precious gifts were brought to Jerusalem because of his international reputation. The prophets envision the era of restoration as a time when the nations will bring gifts to signify the special position God's people have among the nations (Isa 60; Zec 14:14; cf. also Rev 21:24, 26). So the young bride is comforted with words that bring out the advantages and the honor of being a member of God's people, especially of the royal household.

B. The Glory of the Bride (45:13–15)

13–15 The scene suddenly shifts from the throne room to the beautiful bride as she prepares herself for the wedding and enters the royal palace with her maids of honor. She is adorned in a magnificent gown made of gold-embroidered fabric. She and her wedding party are carried into the palace as if on floats of "joy and gladness."

IV. Conclusion (45:16–17)

16–17 The poet moves from the queen to the king as the most prominent member of the wedding party (vv.2–9). The bride is most blessed by marrying into a family blessed by God's promise of continuity of leadership. If the king will fulfill God's expectations, then the Lord himself will "perpetuate" the memory of the king for generations. Moreover, the nations will sing his praise as an expression of their continued respect (cf. 1Co 15:24–26; Heb 10:12–13).

Psalm 46: The God of Jacob Is Our Fortress

This psalm has been popularized by Martin Luther's rendition in "A Mighty Fortress Is Our God." As a *song of Zion* (cf. 48; 76; 84; 87; 122), it celebrates the presence of God. The combination of the hymnic and the oracular genres has made it virtually impossible to identify the original life situation. The change from a hymn to a prophetic oracle (vv.8–10) suggests that the original *psalm of confidence* was transformed into an eschatological psalm.

I. Confession (46:1, 7, 11)

1, 7, 11 The threefold confessional statement presents Israel's great God in a personal way. They call him "God," "the LORD Almighty," and "the God of Jacob." The Lord is the Great King over the world, but he is particularly and fondly confessed as "the God of Jacob" because he has covenanted himself to be the God of Israel. God's people need not fear his presence, because the "for us" and "with us" assure them of the meaning of his covenant name, Yahweh ("LORD"; cf. Ex 3:13–17). He is Immanuel, "God with us."

This great God is "ever-present" with his people. He is the source and effectiveness of Israel's "strength." He is like a "refuge" (GK 4726) where one finds rest and asylum (cf. 14:6; 61:3; 91:2, 9). He is like a "fortress" (GK 5369) in an isolated, elevated place (cf. Isa 33:16), where people built a stronghold against the enemy. When the people are in distress, they need his special protection. Then he is close to them.

II. Theophany (46:2–6)

2–3 Israel's confession is that they will not fear even when God's coming in judgment is preceded by radical cosmic phenomena: earthquakes and floods. The world catastrophes are the "woes" of the Day of the Lord heralding the messianic age. Nations and kingdoms may cause great consternation and create havoc on earth (v.6), but they will fall quickly when the Lord speaks his word of judgment (cf. Rev 11:18).

4–6 Surrounded by a world aflame, the people of God are "the city of God." They need not fear but have reason to be glad because God, the "Most High," has identified himself with them and now dwells with them. They will always be assured of his readiness to help them. The "river" is a metaphor of blessing and restoration. The help of God "at break of dawn" suggests that in the darkness of distress the people of God know that the Lord will not let them suffer unduly long. His acts of unfailing love are renewed each morning (La 3:22–23).

III. Prophetic Oracle (46:8–10)

8–9 In this oracle, the psalmist first exhorts the godly to be wise and discerning by considering the works of God. The recitation of the mighty acts of God plants deep in the memory of his people the evidences of his care, protection, and providential rule. Those who are wise enough to remember and look at the world around them have tokens of God's faithfulness toward his people. They know that the Lord's plan for humankind includes the cessation of wars and the era of peace. Since God's people have reason to be glad in distress because of God's presence (vv.4–6), how much greater will be their joy when the causes of distress are no more!

10 The psalmist then encourages the godly to "be still" (GK 8332) and to "know" (GK 3359) that the Lord is God. Though it was tempting to ally themselves with foreign powers, to rely on military strength, or to give themselves over to idolatry and pagan ways, the godly must learn to persevere to the end. The "knowledge" of God includes a factual knowledge about him, his past acts, and his promises. The life of faith is lived in commitment to God's sovereignty, rule, and ultimate exaltation over all the nations.

Psalm 47: The Lord Is the Victorious King

This psalm celebrates the kingship of God (cf. Pss 93–100). Within the present context it provides a connection with the two hymns of

Zion (Pss 46; 48), as it adumbrates the victorious rule of the Lord over all the earth. Its genre conforms to the psalms celebrating the Lord's kingship. It also has a prophetic, eschatological dimension as the psalmist longs for the full establishment of God's rule on earth.

I. Praise of the Lord's Mighty Acts (47:1–2)

1 In anticipation of God's kingship, the nations must joyfully acclaim the Lord as the Great King by clapping their hands. The heavenly beings already sing praises to him (cf. 29:1). The kingdom of God will only be established when the "nations" on earth join with the heavenly choirs, celebrating his universal and everlasting kingship. While clapping the people "shout" joyously a victory cheer.

2 The people are struck with awe on account of the mighty works of the Great King. Here the emphasis is on God, who is "the LORD Most High, the great King over all the earth." Kings in the ancient Near East loved to designate themselves by this title since with it were associated superiority, suzerainty, and the power to grant vassal treaties. Any king assuming this title could not tolerate competition. So it is with the Lord. He alone is the Great King over all the earth!

II. The Lord's Mighty Acts (47:3–4)

3–4 The psalmist reflects on the Lord's mighty acts in salvation history. He has subdued the nations (cf. 135:8–11; 136:10–20) and given their land to his people as an "inheritance" (GK 5709; cf. 28:9; 105:11; 135:12; 136:21–22) because of his deep love for them. The term "the pride of Jacob" denotes here the reasons for Israel's joy in the Lord.

III. The Lord's Victorious Kingship (47:5–6)

5–6 The Lord is victorious! He has "ascended" to his heavenly palace with "shouts of joy" and "the sounding of trumpets." His victory march is acknowledged by his subjects on earth. They could rebel because of the return of the Great King to his heavenly abode. But instead they are encouraged to continue doing homage to him by singing his praises. The psalmist stresses the urgency of responding to the Lord's heavenly reception with earthy songs of praise.

IV. The Lord Is King (47:7–8)

7–8 The psalm returns to the reflection of God's kingship on earth. His ascension into his heavenly palace and his rule over earth emphasize his universal dominion. The Lord is King over "the nations"; they too must acclaim his sovereignty and discern that he is different from all other gods, as he is "seated on his holy throne." Although his throne is in heaven (103:19; Isa 66:1), his footstool extends to earth (99:5; 132:7). Since he is "holy," those who approach him consecrate themselves (cf. Rev 4:9–10; 5:1, 7, 13; 6:16; 7:10, 15; 19:4).

V. Universal Acknowledgment of the Lord's Kingship (47:9)

9 At this point the prophetic, eschatological element distinguishes itself. The psalmist prays that all the "nobles" and "kings" of the earth may acknowledge the Lord's kingship. They are accounted as one with "the people of the God of Abraham." That is, the Gentiles join together with Israel in the worship of God (cf. Ge 12:3; Jn 12:32; Ro 4:11; Gal 3:7–9). The psalmist further explains that all nations are the subjects of God's rule, whether they recognize it or not. God is "exalted"; truly he is "the LORD Most High."

Psalm 48: The Beautiful City of God

In Ps 47 the Lord receives praise as "the great King." In Ps 48 the greatness of God is shared with his people, who are likened to "the city of God." Whereas Ps 46 could be categorized as either a song of Zion or a psalm of confidence, Ps 48 is more clearly a *song of Zion*. The stress is on proclamation of the good news of God's presence that results in the joy of God's people.

I. Our God Is the Great King (48:1–3)

1–3 The hymn begins with an ascription of praise to God because of his accommodation to humankind. God is the Lord ("the LORD") of his covenant people and the Great King of the universe. He is sovereign, powerful, and glorious; and he alone is worthy of human praise. However, God's people, who are citizens of "the city of our God," have additional reasons for praising him: his presence, protection, love, and righteousness.

The Great King has chosen to reside among his own people in "the city" on "the holy mountain"—a reference to Jerusalem and Mount Zion. Only because God condescends to dwell there may she be called "beautiful" in her elevation and "the joy of the whole earth." The beauty and joy are not inherent in Mount Zion, because it is surrounded by higher mountains offering a better panoramic view. The godly looked on the city, mountain, and temple as symbols of God's presence with his people.

II. The Perfections of Our God (48:4–11)

4–7 The description of the hostile forces is reminiscent of Ps 2. The kings of the nations have united together in their warfare against God. Their united effort gave them confidence. The description of God's response inspires his people. The bold, confident, and strong opposition was broken miraculously. It is likened to the destruction of the "ships of Tarshish" that were the pride and glory of seafaring nations such as Phoenicia. Although strong and majestic, a strong wind could easily toss them about on the open sea and destroy the vessels, people, and cargo!

The ease with which the Lord destroys the opposition terrifies the nations. They were overcome with fear, and their strength melted away (cf. Ex 15:14; Jos 2:11). It was as if they had seen a theophany (cf. 46:2–3). Their anguish is likened to a woman in labor. Great is the power of our God.

8–11 When God shows himself to be the fortress of the godly, they "see" what he has done and are even more convinced that God makes his city "secure forever." The mighty acts of God evidence the presence of "the LORD Almighty," the Ruler of heaven and earth. The identification with the history of redemption is expressed by the verbs "hearing" and "seeing." God's people have witnessed his presence in ordering the events of the world and in working out the redemption of his people.

In response, the godly "meditate" on God's mighty acts and reflect on the long history of God's involvement with Israel and of the evidences of his "unfailing love." Their reaction of "praise" is a positive response in contrast to the dread that fell on the nations. They declare God's "righteousness" (GK 7406), the benefits of his victorious and glorious rule in which they share. The "right hand" of God includes power, justice, righteousness, and love. The people also "rejoice" in his "judgments," the ways he establishes his kingdom by bringing defeat to the opposing forces.

III. The Great King Is Our Shepherd (48:12–14)

12–13 The psalm concludes with an invitation to walk around in Jerusalem and to observe her defense system: "her towers," "her ramparts," and "her citadels." It is possible that the pilgrims made a procession around Jerusalem as part of a sacred rite. The kings of Judah received their significance on two counts: their loyalty to the Lord and their concern with the security of Jerusalem and Judah. Because the temple was in Jerusalem, the defense of Jerusalem was an expression of loyalty to the Lord.

14 Those who had seen the defense system of Jerusalem had a picture of a greater truth: the protection of God. They could tell their children and grandchildren about the beauty, strength, and history of Jerusalem, reminding them that the Lord is "our God for ever" and that he, like a good shepherd, will continue to "guide" (or "protect"; GK 5627) his own "to the end."

Psalm 49: The Folly of Riches Without Wisdom

The problem of the prosperity of the wicked is difficult, but the psalmist gives us a ray of light on resolving this problem in this *wisdom* psalm.

The image of the citadel (cf. 48:13) was a familiar one in Bible times, and it still is today. This fortress is that of Montfort, built in medieval times.

I. Introduction (49:1–4)

1–2 The introduction reflects the combination of two traditions: the tradition of the prophets (cf. Mic 1:2) and the tradition of wisdom (cf. Pr 1:8). The psalmist invites everybody from all nations in the "world" to listen to his lesson in godly wisdom. The voice of wisdom goes out to all people: "low" (people without a sizable estate) and "high" (people with a substantial estate); that is, "rich and poor alike."

3–4 The psalmist draws the interest of his hearers, impressing on them the importance of the discussion by using four words for wisdom: "wisdom" (GK 2684), "understanding" (GK 9312), "proverb" (GK 5442), and "riddle" (GK 2648; cf. Pr 1:1–6). The first two words are plural and may be used to intensify the ideas: "great wisdom" and "great understanding." The second pair of words may express the means by which wisdom is to be communicated: by "proverb," i.e., more particularly by a reflection on the "riddle" of life and death, accompanied by the music of a "harp."

II. Question (49:5–6)

5–6 The inspired teacher of wisdom begins his lesson on wisdom by asking a relevant question. Why should one not fear old age and the uncertainty of the future? People try to cushion themselves by heaping up wealth with the hope that this will continually provide an income and keep them from harm and abandonment. But the response to fear is not found in the fleeting sense of well-being that wealth may provide. Those who put their confidence in wealth are all too often those who trouble and deceive the poor, aged, and lonely. There is a certain sense of assurance here, as if he is saying, Do not be afraid of those who take advantage of adversities for selfish gains!

III. The Certainty of Death (49:7–12)

7–9 Because "death" is the common experience of humankind, the rich cannot boast of any advantages over the poor. They cannot use their money to redeem themselves from death or to send a substitute for themselves. They may live on a grandiose scale so as to give the impression that they will live forever; but they too must ultimately face death for what it is: a separation from the land of the living, from the comforts of life, and from social and economic distinctions.

10–11 A careful study of life confirms his conclusion that death is a leveler. All people die, whether wise or foolish. The "foolish and the senseless" have hoarded up wealth for themselves. Those who have made any attempt to perpetuate their own memory by naming property after themselves may only be remembered by the names engraved on their tombs. Their end is in death, and they are forever cast out from their wealth and real properties.

12 The inevitable conclusion is presented in the form of a "proverb." Human beings cannot use wealth to their advantage in death. One end overtakes all people and animals alike, namely, "death" (cf. Ecc 3:19). The very nature of "life" is that it has a built-in obsolescence.

IV. The Folly of Riches (49:13–14)

13 The Bible is not against riches as such but the attitude of self-sufficiency and self-confidence so often associated with riches. The rich come under condemnation for their insensitivity, scheming, deception, and attitude that they rule the world (cf. Jas 5:1–6). Those who agree with their words, often benefiting from their power and prestige, will also die.

14 Death is personified as a shepherd who leads the rich as sheep to the slaughter. Those who have cared for themselves in life will waste away in death. But the righteous will be victorious. When their night of darkness is over, there will be "morning," and their lot will be changed.

V. Resolution of the Question (49:15–20)

15 The confidence of hope breaks through with the affirmation of the resurrection and of fellowship with God. The Lord will intervene on behalf of the godly and redeem them from the clutches of "death." No money can buy these privileges (v.7).

16–19 The triumph of faith gives no ground to fear what is transitory. Riches, splendor, or praise of self makes no difference in the grave. The tragedy of riches is that they give a false sense of security. Yet the godless rich will die like animals without the hope of the dawning light. Death is described as a place of absolute darkness, where not a single ray of light (hope) penetrates—ever (cf. 88:11–12).

20 The purpose of the psalm was to instruct everyone, including the rich, in the path of wisdom. The psalmist did not intend to disparage the godly rich who received their wealth as a blessing from God. The difference between humans and animals lies in the degree of "understanding." If one has no understanding of himself as a human being, of his mortality, and of his God, he lives and dies "like the beasts that perish."

Psalm 50: A Heart of Gratitude

This psalm is concerned with true loyalty to God. Loyalty is antithetical to formalism and hypocrisy, as the Lord requires a heart of gratitude. The psalm encompasses features of theophany, accusation, warning, and an invitation to repent. The references to the covenant and to the laws suggest a setting around the Feast of Tabernacles.

I. The Righteous Judgment of God (50:1–6)

1 None other than God himself summons the inhabitants of the earth to prepare themselves for the great judgment to come. The great Creator-Redeemer-Covenant God has made a covenant with creation (Ge 9:8–17; cf. Hos 2:18) and with the nation Israel. His rule extends far beyond Israel to the whole earth, poetically described as "from the rising of the sun to the place where it sets."

2 God's relationship with his people, however, is special to him, as expressed in the portrayal of Zion: "perfect in beauty." The God who at one time revealed himself at Mount Sinai "shines forth" from Jerusalem, where he had made his name dwell. The light of God's presence was evident in the glory-cloud in the desert (Ex 13:21–22; Nu 9:15–23); the same God repeatedly showed Israel the light of his presence (cf. 4:6; 18:28; 27:1; 36:9; 43:3).

3–4 This great Ruler of the universe appears, attended by phenomena designed to inspire "fear" in people. He is like "a consuming fire" (cf. Heb 12:29) and an angry "tempest" when he comes in judgment. His message is not consoling to Israel, because he summons "the heaven above and the earth" as witnesses against his own people. In their presence, the Lord commands all his covenant people to be gathered for judgment.

5–6 The covenant people were consecrated by covenant (Ex 19:5–6; 24:5–8) and sealed by "the blood of the covenant" (24:8). The earth gathers up all the members of the covenant community while the heavens declare that God is the Righteous Judge. It was a great temptation of God's covenant people to believe mistakenly that everything was in order between them and God. The proclamation of "righteousness" affirms that God, the Righteous Judge, will order everything on earth in accordance with his will. He does not tolerate anything that does not satisfactorily meet his requirements.

II. Warning to the Godly (50:7–15)

7–8 The people used to present their sacrifices and offerings to the Lord in Jerusalem. They imagined God as being in need of food, and they complied with his requirements (cf. Lev 1–7). But, unlike pagan religions, God needs nothing from his subjects. The God who spoke to Israel through Moses and the prophets in the words "Hear, O Israel" (Dt 5:1; 6:3–4; 9:1; Isa 39:5; Jer 22:2; Am 7:16) again speaks to his people of his covenantal rights. The words are a prophetic indictment against his own people.

9–11 God does not need offerings—not even dedicatory ones—if they do not express true gratitude and joy from the givers. Everything belongs to him! What are the tens of thousands of animals from Israel's stalls and pens compared with the millions of animals in the forests and fields, on the hills and mountains, that already belong to him?

There is a note of sarcasm in the use of "your" in "your stall" and in "your pens." It is as if God has heard them proudly say, "This is my bull / goat from my stall / pen!" To this boastful claim God responds with an emphatic "mine" and concludes his claim with a restatement of his ownership. His rule extends to all creation.

12–13 The next step in the argument presents Israel with the inescapable folly of their thinking. Many thought that they were feeding God and that God needed them to keep him well fed and therefore content. To this he responds that if he were in need, he could take care of himself, because he is the Ruler of the world and of every living creature. He did not reveal his laws on offerings and sacrifice in order to be "fed." The "flesh" and "blood" of animals had another significance, which had escaped the people.

14 The "thank offerings" and "vows" (i.e., votive offerings) belong to the category of voluntary offerings in which the offerers shared by eating from the offering (cf. Lev 7:12; 22:29). God desired communion with his people. Instead of presenting "dedicatory offerings" in a spirit of pride, they had to learn that the "Most High" invites them for a banquet to enjoy his presence. Of course, the offering must reflect the true intent: "thankfulness."

15 The Lord will graciously move his people to gratitude if they humble themselves and call on him in their need. When the spirit of pride is broken and their trust in God restored, they will again enjoy the benefits of answered prayer and experience the Lord's deliverance of those who call on him. In response they are expected to give "honor" (GK 3877) to him.

III. Warning to the Wicked (50:16–21)

16–17 The renewal of the promise of deliverance (v.15) is not without obligation. Those who really want to be his "consecrated ones" (v.5) will wisely respond, whereas the wicked will foolishly cast away God's requirements of faith and repentance. God hates the hypocrites who parrot the law yet abandon it at any opportunity to promote their self-interests. Those who do reject the divine instruction are called "wicked" or "foolish." To the psalmist, one either keeps the covenant or rejects it.

18–20 The particular charges are representative of the whole Decalogue. It is true that those who have broken the seventh, eighth, and ninth commandments have broken the whole covenant. But those who associate with covenant breakers fall under the same condemnation!

21 Too often God's silence is taken as his approval. The people mistook God's patience for an inability to do anything about the evil on earth. They did not understand that the Lord is the Wholly Other One who cannot

be boxed in by humans. In his own time God will judge his people openly.

IV. The Righteous Judgment of God (50:22–23)

22–23 The grace of God is manifest in his patience. Though his people continue to have problems, he is still patient with them. He invites them to repent and to devote themselves to a life of godliness. He will reject those who do not repent, treat them as noncovenant people, and judge them severely. But the remnant that heed the word of prophecy and honor God will witness the fullness of his "salvation" (GK 3829).

Psalm 51: Forgiveness and the Community

This psalm is classified as one of the seven penitential psalms (Pss 6; 32; 38; 51; 102; 130; 143), a subdivision of the psalms of *individual lament*. The superscription relates the context of this psalm to David's heinous sin with Bathsheba (2Sa 11:1–12:25), after he had been rebuked by the prophet Nathan. The lament form suitably fits the spirit of contrition and prayer for restoration.

I. Prayer for Individual Restoration (51:1–2)

1 In desperate need of divine forgiveness, the sinner can do nothing but cast himself on God's mercy. The verb "have mercy" (GK 2858 & 2859) occurs frequently in psalms of lament (cf. 4:1; 6:2; 31:9; 41:4, 10; 56:1; 86:3). When sin disrupts fellowship with the covenant-Lord, the sinner has no right to divine blessings. However, the Lord has promised to forgive, a forgiveness based solely on his "unfailing love" (GK 2876) and "great compassion."

2 Forgiveness is an act of divine grace whereby sin is blotted out and the sinner is "cleansed" by the washing away of sins (vv.2, 7, 9; cf. Ex 32:32; Nu 5:23; Ps 32:2). The OT sacrifices and ritual washing symbolized the removal of sin and the renewal of fellowship with the Lord.

II. Confession and Contrition (51:3–6)

3–4 In his search for forgiveness, the psalmist opens his sinful heart. The variety of words he uses for sin expresses its seriousness (see comments on 32:1–2). He knows himself intimately and sees how rebellious he has been.

His confession is more than introspection, as he knows that he has sinned *against the Lord*. The psalmist does not reject or argue with divine justice (Ro 3:4), because the Lord's verdict is "right."

5–6 Confronted by God's righteous verdict, the psalmist is more deeply pricked by his own sinfulness. His confession of depravity is not an excuse for his treachery but serves to heighten the distance between the Lord and himself. God is just, whereas human beings are so corrupt that their whole being cries out for help. In their sinfulness they cannot respond in confession unless the Lord sends "wisdom" from on high, which alone can bring a remedy to the sinful heart. Only by receiving revelation from the outside ("you teach me") can the inside become whole.

III. Prayer for Restoration (51:7–12)

7–12 In his prayer for forgiveness, the author employs two verbs, used in vv.1–2, in reverse order: "wash" and "blot out." He prays that the Lord, like a priest, cleanse him from his defilement. The Israelites were to present themselves before the priest on the occasion of their purification. The priest, satisfied that the unclean person had met the requirements for purification, would take a bunch of "hyssop" and sprinkle the person with water, symbolic of ritual cleansing. Here the psalmist petitions the Lord to be his priest by taking the hyssop and by declaring him cleansed from all sin. The metaphor "whiter than snow" was applied to clean garments and by extension signifies forgiveness, cleansing, and newness.

Even as God's displeasure with sin brings judgment, metaphorically described as broken bones, so his pleasure brings joy of heart. The joy is more than an emotional expression; it is a contented resting in God. Hence it is known as "the joy of your salvation."

Forgiveness and cleansing are prerequisites for communion with God. Wisdom maintains communion. For this reason the psalmist renews his prayer for divine wisdom and sustenance. In the spirit of true contrition, the psalmist prays for a "pure heart," a "steadfast spirit," the "Holy Spirit," and a "willing spirit." Without the internal renewal, the psalmist fears the possibility of divine rejection (cf. 1Sa 16:14). Spiritual renewal always leads to godliness and wisdom.

IV. Thanksgiving (51:13–17)

13 Sinners who have experienced a deep sense of their own sinfulness, the forgiveness of God, and the sweetness of restored joy show concern for others. The psalmist who prayed "restore to me" also prays that he may be instrumental in restoring sinners to the "ways" of the Lord.

14–15 "Praise" is an appropriate response to divine deliverance. Deliverance from "bloodguilt" (GK 1947) signifies either the judgment resulting from a grave sin requiring the death penalty (cf. Eze 18:13) or the sin that led to the death of an innocent person. One who has tasted the grace of God in life cannot but praise him for a new lease on life. God's "righteousness" (GK 7407) manifests itself, not only in judgment (v.4), but also in forgiveness (cf. 1Jn 1:9), when he sets aside the just penalty for sin. The psalmist looks to the Lord for renewed favor, so that he may freely praise him for his grace ("open my lips").

16–17 A deeper commitment results from a heart of gratitude. The Lord "delights in" truth rather than "sacrifice." The psalmist is not opposed to sacrifices per se (see v.19), but he senses God's concern for inner loyalty as a prerequisite for the presentation of animals for sacrifice. He commits himself unreservedly to the Lord by presenting "a broken and a contrite heart." The prerequisite for spiritual renewal (vv.10–12) is humility—which is also the prerequisite for a walk with God (cf. Mic 6:8).

V. Prayer for National Restoration (51:18–19)

18–19 The canonical significance of these verses lies in the community identification with David's sin, the need for grace, and the anticipation of divinely bestowed joy. The people of God pray for another manifestation of God's love (these verses may have come from the exile). Jerusalem's walls have been breached and the sacrifices have ceased. The Lord's "good pleasure" ("favor"; GK 8356) made Zion prosper under the postexilic leadership of Zerubbabel and Nehemiah. In the days of Nehemiah, when these prayers had been answered (cf. Ne 12:43), the people were again filled with joy.

Psalm 52: An Uprooted and a Sprawling Tree

This psalm contrasts the godless and the godly. The superscription relates it to an episode in David's life, when Doeg had betrayed and executed the priests of Nob who had helped David (1Sa 22:17–23). The genre of the psalm is complex, with elements of lament (vv.1–7), thanksgiving (v.9), wisdom (vv.6–7), an oracle of judgment (vv.1–7), and a mocking saying (v.7). On the whole, the positive tone at the end sets the tone of the psalm as a *psalm of trust*. The righteous will prevail, regardless of the opposition.

I. The Folly of Evil (52:1–4)

1–2 By means of a question followed by a series of accusations, the folly of evil is shown for what it is. In life the wicked may act as a "mighty man" (GK 1475), who autonomously "boasts" of his power, exploits, and accomplishments. Evil appears in acts but also in words, both expressing the internal plotting of an evil heart. The wicked are con artists. Deception is their trademark, and they are bent on destruction of the godly.

3–4 The values of the wicked are completely distorted. They love anything that is twisted, perverted, and corrupt. Falsehood and aggressive words aim at the undoing of others. They stand for whatever is against God's standards of goodness and "righteousness." In the end the psalmist rebukes the wicked with "O you deceitful tongue!" (cf. James's discussion in Jas 3:1–12).

II. God's Complete Judgment (52:5)

5 The righteous God cannot forever tolerate evil. The wicked will be demolished like a structure. They will be castaways and vagabonds, homeless and without family. Moreover, they will be like an uprooted tree. In the end they will be cut off from "the land of the living" (cf. 27:13).

III. Wisdom Derived From God's Judgment (52:6–7)

6–7 The reaction of the godly to God's judgment is first characterized by awe and terror. They "see" and "fear" the acts of God. Gradually they realize that his judgment was for their encouragement, and their fear changes into joy. They are filled with a triumphant derision for their former oppressors. Righ-

teousness triumphs over evil! Furthermore, they learn a lesson from this judgment. Those who live and act independently from God and trust in themselves will be brought down. The wicked may turn away from the Lord as their stronghold and turn to the fleeting security of power, riches, and ill-gotten gains. But when these are taken away, their lives fall apart.

IV. The Blessing of Righteousness (52:8–9)

8–9 In contrast to the "mighty" (v.1), whom the Lord uproots like a tree and destroys like a building (v.5), are the godly. They are likened to a tree flourishing within the house of the Lord. The imagery of the tree brings out the blessedness of the godly (cf. 1:3; 92:12–13; Jer 11:16). They are like a luxuriant, productive olive tree. The olive tree may last for hundreds of years, and a productive olive tree supplies about six gallons of oil per year.

The godly prosper to the extent that they depend on the "unfailing love" (GK 2876) of God for their nourishment and fellowship. Their response to God's righteousness is praise, and they boast in the Lord. As long as they trust in his love "forever and ever," they have many reasons to praise the Lord "forever." The "name" of the Lord assures the godly that God is righteous and loving.

Psalm 53: God Deals With Foolish Evildoers (53:1–6)

1–6 This psalm parallels Ps 14 (see comments on that psalm). Psalm 53's position favors an ancient tradition relating to the life of David. Psalm 52 relates to the story of Doeg (cf. 1Sa 22) and Ps 54 to the incident of the Ziphites (cf. 1Sa 23; 26). The term "fool" (*nabal*; GK 5572) is suggestive of Nabal, who acted foolishly to David and his men (cf. 1Sa 25). This psalm encourages God's people to pray for restoration on the basis of God's historic acts.

Psalm 54: Surely God Is My Help!

As in Ps 52, the superscription connects the psalm with David's flight from Saul. The spirit of the psalm reflects that of an *individual lament*.

I. Prayer for Deliverance (54:1–2)

1–2 "Save [GK 3828] me" and "vindicate [GK 1906] me" express the source and the nature of David's deliverance. "God" alone can deliver him from the troubles stated in v.3. He must come to protect and rescue his child from evil. David's confidence lies in his reliance on the Lord's revelation of himself in the past. He has revealed his "name" (cf. v.6; 20:1) and his "might" to Israel (cf. 21:13; 66:7). The "name" (GK 9005) of the Lord signifies his covenant protection and his blessing.

II. Occasion of the Prayer (54:3)

3 This verse is nearly identical to 86:14. David's opponents are called "strangers" and "ruthless men," who have no "regard for God." "Strangers" (GK 2424) may denote those who had become estranged from God and the covenant community (cf. Isa 1:4) or non-Israelites (1Sa 23:11–12). They had little regard for God or other people, as they were "ruthless" individuals who insisted on their rights and desires.

III. Affirmation of Trust (54:4)

4 In a hymnic manner, the psalm shifts from worry over the arrogant to a confident trust in the Lord. Triumphantly the psalmist exclaims, "Surely God is my help," acknowledging that the Lord is the only one who grants support to his people. He looks forward to enjoying his God-given life (cf. 51:12).

IV. Resolution of the Prayer (54:5)

5 The resolution of David's prayer lies in the conviction that God is just. He will not permit his children to suffer without vindication. Evil must and will be repaid. The Lord is faithful in his relationship to his people; therefore the psalmist is calm, trusting that his God will protect him from his adversary.

V. Thanksgiving for Deliverance (54:6–7)

6–7 The resolution of the psalm shines forth in a victory hymn of thanksgiving. A votive offering is presented before the Lord but enjoyed in the fellowship of family and friends. The godly will hear all the Lord has done for his child, and his praise will resound. His "name" will be exalted, because he has brought deliverance and will continue to bring deliverance. The Lord is "good." He is our Helper and Sustainer.

Psalm 55: The Lord Sustains the Righteous!

This psalm is an *individual lament*. It moves from despair, to complaint, to a note of confidence in the Lord.

I. Despairing Prayer (55:1–3)

1–3 The injustices heaped on our psalmist cry out for divine retribution. This battered victim turns to the Lord, asking him to "listen" to and "answer" his "prayer." God's silence is surprising because the Lord had decreed to Israel that he would not "ignore" their problems (Dt 22:1, 3–4). The psalmist is full of inner turmoil. Instead of the roaring of the sea, he hears the "voice" (lit., "noise"; GK 7754) of his enemies threatening his existence. They cause him to suffer grievously.

II. Personal Reflections (55:4–8)

4–5 How the psalmist yearns to escape his situation! His .heart is palpitating like a woman in labor ("in anguish" is elsewhere translated "in labor"; GK 2655). He is full of "fear" and "horror." The fear of death overtakes him as he reflects on his present condition.

6–8 Another manner of expressing the psalmist's deep despair is in the escape imagery, as he wishes to be like a dove, free to fly to a high and far-away place! He wishes to find quiet serenity in the desert or protective shelter as in a sudden storm.

III. Prayer for Justice (55:9–15)

9–11 Injustice, unrighteousness, and deception in word and deed are prevalent in the city of the human race. The psalmist sees no righteousness wherever he turns; rather, evil is king. "Confound" (GK 7103) may contain an allusion to the Tower of Babel (Ge 11:1–9; cf. 10:24). Even as the wicked cause harm with their words, the psalmist prays that the Lord will bring "harm" ("confuse") on the ungodly.

12–14 The adversary is not "an enemy" or "a foe" from whom he could expect trouble and from whom he could hide. "But it is you" identifies the betrayer as one equal in status, "a man like myself," a "companion," a "close friend." He has been betrayed by one with whom he has enjoyed "sweet fellowship" within a circle of like-minded people. He reflects on the pleasant memories of spiritual unity they had among the throngs of pilgrims in the temple.

15 The magnitude of the friends' treachery and apostasy explains the severity and impetuosity of this prayer. The former friends can no longer be dissociated from the adversaries; they must come to an end, together with the evil perpetrated by them. The psalmist prays that the Lord will remove them from the land of the living and bring them down in their physical vigor ("alive") into Sheol ("the grave"; GK 8619).

IV. Assurance of Justice (55:16–21)

16–18 The perversity of evil by "day and night" (v.10) evokes regular prayer three times a day (i.e., throughout the day). The salvation of the Lord contrasts with his judgment on the wicked (v.15) and is in response to the psalmist's prayer. The answer brings the wicked to their doom and the godly to their experience of triumph and freedom. The net result will be peace ("unharmed"; GK 8934), even though the opposition has been great.

19 The basis for hope lies in the confessional statement. God, "enthroned forever" as the Great Judge, will bring judgment on those who trouble his people and do not respond to him in godly fear.

20–21 In contrast to the Lord's fidelity is the treachery of the wicked. They stab their friends in the back. They have no regard for commitments and promises. They are hypocrites in that they know how to win friends but in their heart have no loyalty, loving "war" rather than peace.

V. Reflection on the Lord (55:22–23b)

22–23b Confident that the Lord is enthroned (v.19), the psalmist encourages the godly to reflect on his justice. In contrast to the treachery of human beings, the Lord will "sustain" the righteous so that they will not be overcome. The oracle of salvation encourages the godly to "cast [their] cares" on the Lord. On the other hand, the justice of God requires vindication on the evildoers. After all, they have no respect for life and veracity. They shall die in the vigor of life.

VI. Hopeful Trust (55:23c)

23c The psalm concludes on a note of confidence in the Lord. "But as for me" expresses the psalmist's submission to the will of God regarding the current circumstances and the future of the ungodly. His trust is in the Lord, the Redeemer-Divine Warrior (cf. 26:1; 37:5).

Psalm 56: Walking in Darkness With God's Light

This psalm expresses the lament of an individual. The psalmist cries to the Lord on account of his opponents who twist his words against him. He himself trusts in the Lord.

I. Lament (56:1–2)

1–2 The lament begins with a characteristic prayer for "mercy" (GK 2858 & 2859). The psalmist pours out his heart as he paints his adversity in rapid strokes: it is continual ("all day long"; cf. v.5) and varied (cf. "pursue"; "attack"; "slanderers"). The opposition is fierce and will not be satisfied until its goals are achieved. The opponents are only "men" (GK 632), but their strength and violence are not to be underestimated.

II. Trust in God (56:3–4)

3–4 Difficult as life is, the psalmist has learned to "trust" (GK 1053) in the Lord. Fear is there, but he neither feels it nor stares at his problems but looks to his Redeemer who will deliver him. He knows that his attackers are only "mortal man" (lit., "flesh"; GK 1414) and that the Lord is God. His promise is secure and will come true.

III. Affliction and Imprecation (56:5–9a)

5–6 With confidence in the Lord's justice as promised in his Word, the psalmist presents his case more clearly before the Lord. His adversaries "twist [his] words" by distorting his intentions in order to ruin him. They plot so as to undo whatever he has planned to do right. Moreover, they set him up like an enemy-at-war. They continually gather together ("conspire"), wait ("lurk"), and prepare for the kill.

7 The psalmist turns to the Lord in a petition for justice. How could the Lord let them get by ("escape")? The psalmist invokes God's judgment on all who may consider themselves members of the covenant community together with "the nations."

8–9a The reason for hope in God's justice lies in his divine nature and in his promise to vindicate his children. Thus the psalmist adds a personal note about the extent of his suffering. His "lament" is known to the Lord, recorded in his "record" (lit., "book"; GK 6225). He has also put the "tears" into a "wineskin" (cf. NIV note), to bring to remembrance all the occasions of suffering. The psalmist rests his case. When the Lord comes to the rescue of his people, the enemies will be routed.

IV. Trust in God (56:9b–11)

9b–11 The emphatic "by this" summarizes the psalmist's confidence in God's acts of vindication, compelling proof of the covenant relationship. The psalmist looks for the demonstration of God's love for him so that he may "know" again how much God cares for him. He rests on the promises ("word") of the Lord, as he praises the Lord of promise. With this certainty of relationship, fear of other human beings has no place.

V. Thanksgiving (56:12–13)

12 Instead of ending with lament and petition, the psalmist concludes with ringing thanksgiving and victory. In anticipation of the deliverance, the suffering saint has made a vow to present a "thank offering" to the Lord as an expression of his devotion.

13 The Lord receives praise because he is true to his promises, especially his promises to not let his beloved stumble on account of the wicked, to avenge himself on the wicked, and to give "the light of life" to his children. In response to God's goodness, the psalmist desires to walk "before" the Lord (cf. Ge 17:1). Only life in God's presence gives meaning to his children. It is as if "the light of life" is shining brightly like the sun!

Psalm 57: The Exaltation of the Lord in the Midst of Alienation

Psalms 56 and 57 portray confidence in the Lord during adversity. Psalm 57 is an *individual lament* psalm that, like the previous one, ends in thanksgiving.

I. Lament and Refrain (57:1–5)

1–5 The phrase "have mercy on me" is common to psalms of lament (cf. 6:2; 56:1). Because his need is great, the psalmist seeks asylum with the Lord. He goes from a general reference ("disaster") to a specific expression of his need ("those who hotly pursue me"). Though his enemies persecute him unjustly, he seeks God's protection. The "disaster" is like a violent storm, but the Lord can give him "wings"—a metaphor for protection and refuge.

The name "Most High" (GK 6610) signifies that the Lord is exalted in his rule over all that he has created (cf. Ge 14:22; Pss 46:4; 47:2). The Israelites believed that there was no one like their God (cf. Ex 15:11) and that he was the only One who could help people. This God brings judgment on his enemies and deliverance to his own. He "fulfills" his plan by bestowing "his love and his faithfulness" as a positive grace and by delivering the psalmist from oppression. The need is great. The enemies "hotly pursue," like "lions" greedy to devour. They are on a war path: "spears and arrows . . . sharp swords."

II. Thanksgiving (57:6–11)

6 The Lord is true to his word. The wicked receive their due punishment, and the righteous draw comfort from God's rule over the earth. The wicked, like hunters who catch their prey with a net or by digging a pit or hole, use any scheme to exhaust the righteous. The psalmist readily admits that they had nearly succeeded. He trusted in the Lord's promise to lift up those who are bowed down and to keep the godly from slipping. He rejoices in God's goodness to him because the wicked are entrapped in their own scheming.

7–11 The wicked did not rely on the Lord and were found out, whereas the psalmist experienced inner transformation. Out of a grateful heart, he sings songs of praise and makes a joyful noise. He will "awaken the dawn" with the song of the redeemed, signifying a new era of the Lord's salvation. So great is his gratitude that he prays that all the nations may know and fear the Lord. The psalmist articulates his marvel at the vastness of the "love" (GK 2617) and "faithfulness" (GK 622) of the Lord.

Psalm 58: Surely the Righteous Still Are Rewarded

One of the seven imprecatory psalms (cf. Pss 6; 35; 58; 69; 83; 109; 137), this is a *lament* psalm; but it is unclear whether it belongs to the individual or the communal type of laments. It may well be classified as a prophetic type of lament in which David speaks prophetically of God's judgment on evil (cf. Ps 14).

I. Concern for Justice (58:1–2)

1 David confronts the rulers with their lack of sensitivity to justice. They do not render a judgment characterized by "righteousness" (GK 7406) and "equity" (GK 4797; NIV, "uprightly"). The rule of the wicked seldom reflects God's standards of governance and justice.

2 The reason for the unjust rule lies in the nature ("heart") of the wicked judges. They are evil in the very core of their being, as they act out the "injustice" of their hearts and continually cause "violence" wherever they go.

II. The Lies of the Wicked (58:3–5)

3 The nature of the wicked is amplified in two ways. First, they are wicked from birth and begin to devise evil from their very youth. They "go astray" from what is right; they are deceptive, selfish, and bend the rules in their favor.

4–5 Second, the wicked are likened to "the venom of a snake." The snake had been trained by a charmer but has since become unresponsive to the "tune" of the charmer, who is highly skilled as an "enchanter." The wicked are as dangerous as the venomous cobra that bites his trainer when touched and handled by him. They are insensitive to God, justice, and the cries of the poor and needy (cf. 36:1–4; 140:3).

III. Prayer for Justice (58:6–8)

6 Even in his prayer for justice, David illustrates the aggressiveness of the wicked by the metaphor of "the lions" (cf. 10:9; 22:13, 21). The radical nature of evil requires a response from the God of justice. True to the analogy, the psalmist prays that the Lord will smash the teeth of the lions and knock out their "fangs."

7–8 The author changes his analogy to an inanimate object: "water." Fear inspired by God causes the courage of his opponents to "vanish" like water that ebbs away. David further prays that the arrows of the wicked may be "blunted" and that they themselves may be "like a slug," whose trail is nothing but a slimy track, or like a "stillborn child." Neither ever sees the sun. So the psalmist prays that the wicked may perish.

IV. Expectation of Justice (58:9)

9 This verse is problematic. The mood changes from a prayer to an expectation of justice (introduced by "before"); something is surely going to happen (cf. Isa 7:16; 8:4). But exactly what is unclear because of the present ambiguity of the Hebrew text (see the NIV note).

V. The Joy of the Righteous (58:10)

10 The joy of the righteous comes to full expression when they see evidences of God's justice. The imagery of feet in blood portrays the victory (cf. Isa 63:1–6; Rev 14:19–20; 19:13–14). It is not so much that they are bloodthirsty but rather that they delight in justice. The reign of terror must come to an end! It is better to understand the word "avenged" (GK 5934) as "victorious."

VI. Affirmation of Justice (58:11)

11 With the triumph of God, the righteous are vindicated and God and his kingdom are being established. "Men" (GK 132), who have experienced the oppressiveness of evil, will testify that God rules ("judges") with righteousness and equity (cf. v.1). God is concerned with the "righteous" (GK 7404), who will "be rewarded" for their loyalty (cf. 2Ti 4:8).

Psalm 59: My God Is My Champion

Because of style and vocabulary, this psalm's categorization has been difficult to define. It is a *lament* psalm, but what sort? The motifs of God's rule, the nations, and God's judgment of the nations may argue in favor of a national lament—or it may even be classed as a royal lament.

I. Prayer for Deliverance (59:1–3)

1–3 Common to the language of the lament is the repeated call on the Lord to "deliver," "protect," and "save" the godly from the wicked. The prayer for deliverance discloses both hope in the Lord's ability to fully deliver and the urgent need for deliverance. The occasion for the lament is the presence of adversaries, who are evil through and through, having no regard for human life. They thrive on alienation and enjoy bringing calamity on others. Like soldiers in ambush, they secretly wait to catch the godly.

II. Innocence and Protestation (59:4–5)

4–5 The psalmist protests that this trouble is unjust. He has not provoked his enemies; yet they have come out against him as public enemy number one. They prepare for a public assault. The psalmist's protestation of innocence serves to intensify his reliance on God's intervention. Though evildoers may plan evil and create chaos on earth, God has promised to protect his covenant people. The Divine Warrior is "LORD God Almighty [GK 7372]."

III. The Wicked and God (59:6–8)

6–8 The wicked are like "dogs" that terrorize the streets of the city. They bring anarchy, enjoy chaos, and speak arrogantly. Their mouths are like "swords" as they mock and scoff, challenge God's sovereignty, and belligerently ask, "Who can hear us?" In spite of the commotion on earth, the Lord is not moved. From his perspective evil is ridiculous; it is self-destructive. He will see to it that the rule of oppression will end and that his own will be vindicated (cf. Ps 2).

IV. Hope in God (59:9–10a)

9–10a The Lord is stronger than the enemy. They are "fierce men" (v.3), but he is the "Strength" (GK 6437) of his people. Though evildoers may prowl the streets of the city and promote anarchy, the Lord is the "fortress" (cf. v.1). In the face of the hatred shown by the enemies, the Lord is the "loving God" by whose love his people thrive.

V. Imprecation on the Wicked (59:10b–13)

10b–13 Evildoers must be held accountable for their sins. They are utterly deceptive and crooked; hence the evil they have plotted must come on their own heads. Whatever lot befalls the wicked comes to them as an ex-

pression of God's "wrath" for their many sins.

Purposefully the psalmist prays that the judgment of the wicked will be gradual so that the power of the Lord may become more evident. On the one hand, the mighty acts of God encourage the godly, as they rejoice that the Lord goes "before" them in combat with evil. The assurance renews the spirit of God's servant, as the humiliation of the wicked gives him reason to hope. On the other hand, the just judgments of the Lord are instructive to the nations, who must know that they cannot taunt the God of Israel. Any time God acts on behalf of his people, his acts witness to his sovereignty and his care for "Jacob," even "to the ends of the earth." He is the "shield" (GK 4482) who provides protection for those who submit to his lordship.

VI. Confidence in God's Response (59:14–17)

14–17 The wicked are terrorizing like a pack of dogs (cf. v.6). But the godly, encouraged by the vision of God's laughter and by the assurance of his love, "praise" the Lord instead, who is the "Strength," "love," and "fortress" of his own during times of adversity. Since the Lord's love is new every morning (cf. La 3:23), his servants can renew their song "in the morning." Thus the noise of evil "at evening," a metaphor of affliction, will be exchanged for the song of the redeemed in the morning. Such a vision of God's rule over the world, of his love for Israel, and of the protection of his people transforms the lament into a song of confidence.

Psalm 60: Has God Forgotten Us?

There are sad moments in the history of the people of God. This psalm raises the issue of apparent divine abandonment and challenges the godly to abandon themselves to the love and compassion of a wise God. The psalm is a *national lament,* composed of two laments (vv.1–5, 9–12) and an oracle (vv.6–8).

I. Rejection (60:1–3)

1–3 It is evident that adversity has strained the covenant relationship between God and his people. They feel that his temporary abandonment of them has brought nothing but trouble. Rejection is serious because it results from God's anger. God's people live a meaningless existence without his presence. The psalmist likens abandonment to a state of war ("burst forth"), to an earthquake ("you have shaken ... it is quaking"), and to a state of intoxication ("wine that makes us stagger").

The lament is occasionally interrupted by brief prayers for relief and restoration: "restore us!" and "mend its fractures."

II. Confidence of Victory (60:4)

4 The Lord has raised a "banner" (GK 5812), designating a place where the godly may find refuge under the protection of the Divine Warrior. Those who "fear" him will find protection from the attacks of the enemy, who is symbolized by the "bow."

III. Prayer (60:5)

5 The familiar cry of the lament songs is "save us" (or "me"). The people pray to be saved out of their desperate situation. The petitioner asks for nothing less than divine intervention in avenging the enemy and vindicating the godly. The ground of the petition is God's promise to his people, who are "those you love."

IV. Oracle: God's Response (60:6–8)

6–8 Answering the prayers of his people, the Lord gives an oracle of hope. He thunders "from his sanctuary" and reminds his people of his promise that the earth is his and that no enemy will survive against him! God is sovereign over Israel, as he alone "parcel[s] out" the portions: Shechem, Succoth, Gilead, Manasseh, Ephraim, and Judah. The geographical references represent all the regions that make up the heritage of Israel in Palestine and Transjordan. He is also sovereign over the nations: Moab, Edom, and Philistia.

Ephraim is called a "helmet" (lit., "the strength of my head"), symbolic of force; Judah is a "scepter" (cf. Ge 49:10), symbolic of dominion and governance. The Lord's authority over the nations is symbolized by Moab coming with a washbasin to have his feet washed, by Edom being tossed the sandal of the victorious Warrior, and by a victory "shout" over Philistia. All nations must submit themselves to his rule (cf. 46:8–9; 72:8).

V. Rejection (60:9–11)

9–11 The lament resumes in the light of the oracle of hope. The pain of the defeat and hence of God's apparent rejection is still real. The questions evoke a strong positive response, as the Lord alone will lead the armies into battle and victory. The king is not looking for a human solution to his problems, because he knows that such "help ... is worthless." He looks to the Lord in hope that he will bring about the victory over the enemy.

VI. Confidence of Victory (60:12)

12 Here the confidence of divine protection flows over into confidence in victory. The oracle of God (vv.6–8) was sufficient to inspire the people not to fear the enemy or to be troubled by the setback. The Lord is still with them, and he will bring them through this adversity with renewed strength, joy, and victory. The psalm opens with God's treatment of his people as his enemies (vv.1–3) and closes with his enmity against the enemies of his people. Truly the Lord is just in his rule!

Psalm 61: A Prayer From a Fainting Heart

The psalmist's longing for God is a familiar motif in the Psalms. The genre of this psalm is debatable. It may be categorized as an *individual lament* or a *royal lament*.

I. Prayer for Protection (61:1–2)

1–2 The psalmist hopes to find divine protection from adversity. The nature of the misery is not spelled out, but it wears him out so that he becomes weary of life to the point of despair. It seems that he is so far from God that he speaks to him from a great distance. "From the ends of the earth" here is most likely a metaphor for despair, alienation, and spiritual separation from the Lord. "The rock" (GK 7446) is a metaphor for protection, denoting a fortified or strategic place where one can find refuge (27:5). The confession "the rock that is higher than I" expresses faith in the Lord's exalted position and his ability to deliver.

II. Expression of Confidence (61:3–5)

3 In the past the psalmist has found the Lord to be a "refuge" (GK 4726) from trouble and

"strong" (GK 6437) like a "tower." "Towers" were used for military purposes; in the case of a siege, people could find protection in them (cf. Jdg 9:51–52). Even in the present affliction caused by "the foe," the psalmist encounters the protection of the Almighty.

4 The psalmist longs for the moment when the Lord will invite his suffering saint to fellowship with him. The imagery of the tent goes back to the desert experience (cf. Ex 33:7–11; Nu 11:16–17) when the Lord resided among the tribes of Israel in a tent. The psalmist longs to be a welcome guest with the Lord "forever." Another metaphor for divine protection and recognition is "the shelter of your wings" (cf. 36:7; 57:1; 91:4).

5 The psalmist has learned to face the future with confidence, knowing that the Lord will answer and already has answered his vows, made during times of duress as a part of a prayer for deliverance (cf. 50:14–15). The Lord will be true to his covenant promises in response to the cry of those who fear his name (cf. 34:7, 9; 103:11, 13, 17). The "heritage" (GK 3772) refers both to the land (cf. Dt 2:19; 3:18) and to the enjoyment of the benefits of covenant life (cf. Ps 37:9, 11, 22, 29, 34; cf. Mt 5:5).

III. Prayer for Protection (61:6–7)

6 The prayer for a long life suggests the prosperity of the reigning monarch as well as the preservation of his dynasty (cf. 2Ki 20:6; Ps 45:6). The latter thought is amplified in the second part of this verse.

7 The monarchy in ancient Israel was established and maintained by the promise of God's "love and faithfulness" (2Sa 7:28; 15:20; Pss 40:11; 89:14). The Lord had promised that David's dynasty would be "enthroned . . . forever" (cf. 89:36). These promises of the Lord have found their focus in Jesus (Eph 4:7–13).

IV. Expression of Confidence (61:8)

8 The prayer vacillates between lament and confidence. The vows were to be fulfilled as an expression of gratitude as soon as the prayers were answered (cf. v.5). The "praise" of the Lord would be continual ("day after day").

Psalm 62: Rest and Reward

While facing calamity, the psalmist shows a strong reliance on the Lord, for rest is found in him. This psalm arises out of a context of great adversity and may be categorized as a *psalm of confidence*.

I. Confidence in the Lord (62:1–2)

1–2 The psalmist's whole being receives consolation from the conviction that the Lord is sufficient. He can give "rest" (GK 1957) to all who seek quietness of heart. Resting in God requires waiting and patience. The Lord is the strength of his people ("rock," "fortress") and the source of "salvation" (GK 3802); the latter signifies the whole process of redemption extending to vindication and to the enjoyment of covenant privileges. The psalmist's faith rises to a new height in believing the promise of God that the righteous "will never be shaken."

II. Human Beings Are Unreliable (62:3–4)

3–4 In contrast to his great confidence in the Lord, the psalmist has little faith in human beings, who are destructive, selfish, and deceitful. Yet faith in the Lord overcomes the strongest opposition, as is borne out in the question "How long?" which is an indignant challenge of the confidence of the ungodly. These devise many forms of evil. They attack with words and deeds and will not rest until those who were seated on a "lofty place" are toppled. They intend to bring ruin and destruction by anarchy and insurrection, by delighting in deception, and by hypocritical speech.

III. The Lord of My Salvation (62:5–7)

5–7 Facing this enmity, the psalmist finds his strength in the Lord alone. He explains that his "hope" for "salvation" lies in the Divine Warrior who fights for him. Faith is the antidote to despair (cf. 37:7). Silence in the presence of the Lord will speed the deliverance he offers.

IV. Exhortation to Trust in the Lord (62:8–10)

8–10 The emphatic confession of trust in the Lord (vv.5–7) transforms into an even bolder proclamation, calling on all the godly to put their trust in God. Human beings are unreliable; they are but "breath," lacking in lasting perfections. Their riches and power are all too often the result of "extortion," deception, and theft. But even when riches are gained legitimately, there is an inherent danger in self-reliance. The godly know that their hope lies only in the Lord. Though they may have to wait for salvation, they know that God provides a "refuge" (GK 4726).

V. Confidence in the Lord (62:11–12)

11–12 The psalmist's confidence probes further into the promises of God to his people. He is reminded of two divine promises that he has heard—that God is "strong" and that he is "loving." That is, he is able to deliver his people, and his deliverance is an act of love. The covenant God will richly reward the godly who trust in him and who shun human deceptive power. The wicked will also receive their deserts.

Psalm 63: The Excellence of God's Love

This psalm reflects the genre of *individual lament* with its characteristic complaint, expression of confidence in the Lord's ability to help, and anticipation of public praise.

I. Longing for the Lord (63:1)

1 The emphatic "O God" signifies the same as "LORD" (GK 3378), the covenant-faithful God. The psalmist yearns for fellowship with the Lord like one who thirsts for water in the desert.

II. Vision of God's Beneficence (63:2–3)

2–3 The psalmist changes metaphors from desert to a prophetic vision of God's beneficence: holiness ("in the sanctuary"), "power," "glory," and "love." The God he worships is the Great King who promised to dwell among his people in the ark of the covenant (cf. 1Sa 4:21; Pss 78:61; 132:8). His yearning for God is heightened by the past experience of fellowship and by the evidences of his covenantal love. Hence he seeks to "glorify" the Lord.

III. In Praise of the Lord (63:4–5)

4–5 Even if the psalmist were to endure adversity throughout the rest of his life, he commits himself to the "praise" (GK 1385 & 2146) of God and to a life of trust in his deliverance. His praise is the response of faith to God's perfections and anticipates the deliverance. The "name" of the Lord is the ground of hope and trust, because he has signed and sealed his covenant with his "name." The psalmist expects the Lord to come through to provide abundantly for his needs. He expresses the bounty of deliverance in the metaphor of a banquet.

IV. Longing for the Lord (63:6–8)

6 The psalmist reflects on the Lord during the "watches" of the night. According to OT practice, the night was divided into three watches of four hours each (cf. Jdg 7:19; 1Sa 11:11). He remembers the Lord's past acts and draws comfort during the night when the shadows of adversity haunt him.

7–8 "In the shadow of your wings" expresses God's acts of fellowship and protection. The Lord has promised to be close to his own, but he also expects his children to draw close to him as they seek his help and support. "My soul clings to you" is a human response to God's invitation to "hold fast to" him. The psalmist has learned to "sing" while awaiting the Lord's "help" and a new demonstration of the strength of his "right hand."

V. Vision of God's Judgment (63:9–10)

9–10 His newly gained perspective of the Lord's power to deliver inspires the psalmist by the hope of the Lord's vindication. The Divine Warrior will triumphantly subdue the enemies. They had planned to destroy the righteous, but the Lord will bring them down to the lowest parts of the earth. The psalmist expresses his hope in the final triumph of God's justice.

VI. In Praise of the Lord (63:11)

11 The vision of divine vengeance and justice causes the king-psalmist to rejoice. In his present suffering (vv.1, 6–8), he longed for God to come through in triumph. He will then be happy ("rejoice") and "praise" (lit., "boast"; GK 2146) with all those who swear by the divine "name." The deception of the adversaries will cease and the praise of the Lord alone will be heard!

Psalm 64: Prayer for Protection

The psalm is an *individual lament*, expressive of an unwavering belief in divine retribution (lex talionis).

I. Petition (64:1)

1 The prayer begins with an emphatic "hear" (GK 9048). "God" has promised to be near to his people (Dt 4:7), but the psalmist experiences that God's presence is elusive. Hence he prays for God's preservation from "the threat [lit., fear; GK 7065] of the enemies." He greatly fears that his adversary has the power to take his life. But he also knows that the Lord has the power to preserve the physical life of his people.

II. Prayer for Protection From the Enemies (64:2–6)

2–3 The "conspiracy" results from the enemies banding together in their council of war (cf. 2:1). They have no regard for God. In their secret assembly and noisy provocations, they are like an army preparing for war. Their speech is as lethal as a sharpened sword and as "deadly arrows."

4 The wicked, intent on exterminating the godly, lie in "ambush" and wait for the opportune moment to make a kill. They "shoot . . . without fear" of God or other people. The unprovoked extermination of the "innocent man" (i.e., one blameless in character) must come to the attention of God.

5–6 The wicked are rebels who, like gangsters, undermine the establishment. They "encourage" one another with their "evil plans," scheming together to lay snares for the righteous. They foolishly believe that they are not accountable to anyone (see their confident question, "Who will see?"). They believe the plans they have made will be successful. In spite of their boldness and invincible spirit, the psalmist trusts in the Lord, who knows the thoroughly evil "mind and heart of man."

III. God's Protection and Vengeance (64:7–9)

7–8 Just as the wicked suddenly ambush the godly (v.4), so the Lord will "suddenly" bring his judgment. Their punishment will be based on the "law of retaliation" (lex talionis), i.e., their sins will boomerang on them (cf. 62:12). The Lord will shoot them down, as it were, with "arrows." The shame they had planned to bring on the godly will come on them.

9 The bold challenge of autonomy and anarchy (vv.3–6) has its counterpart in the fear imposed by God's judgment on humankind. The wicked asked, "Who will see us?" and were unafraid. But God did see them, and when all "mankind" sees the power of God, they will "fear." Then justice will triumph! The psalmist encourages all to "proclaim" and to "ponder" (lit., "learn from"; GK 8505) the acts of God.

IV. Rejoicing and Encouragement (64:10)

10 The psalmist encourages the godly to hope in the Lord during adversity. God will vindicate his servants, who are "upright in heart." The sound of their lament will give way to the sound of praise in honor of the Lord. He alone establishes justice on earth!

Psalm 65: The Bounty of Our Savior

The psalmist ascribes praise to the Lord in this *hymn of thanksgiving.*

I. In Praise of God's Presence (65:1–3)

1 In an august way this psalm calls on the community of God's people to join together in order to praise the Lord. They have come to "Zion," the city of God, to fulfill their vows and to present their offerings. The vows express gratitude to God for fulfilling his promises.

2–3 Praise is appropriate because of the Lord's many beneficent acts and because of his unmerited favor to his people. They had sinned grievously against him. Their guilt and acts of rebellion ("transgressions"; GK 7322) weighed heavily on them. Yet the Lord "forgave" (lit., "atoned," "covered"; GK 4105) their sins so as to remove both the sin and its consequences. Though undeserved, the Lord does answer prayer. The evidences of his gracious rule witness to "all men" and lead them to seek God's favor.

II. The Blessedness of God's Presence (65:4)

4 The Lord hears particularly the prayers of those whom he "chose" (GK 1034) and whom he has brought "near" to enjoy his presence. Whoever is loyal to the Lord is blessed with "good things." God's gifts include spiritual benefits both in this life and in the life to come.

III. In Praise of God's Rule (65:5–8)

5–7 God has revealed his "awesome deeds" in delivering his people from adversity, enemies, and famine. But the demonstration of his power is not arbitrary. He is righteous and he acts with "righteousness" (GK 7406), which guarantees the establishment of his rule. He is the God of our salvation ("O God our Savior"). But more than that, he is also "the hope" (GK 4440) of all humanity! The universality of the gospel finds expression in the phrases "all the ends of the earth" and "of the farthest seas." This God is the Creator, the One who formed the mountains. The great Creator-God is still "armed . . . with strength," protecting his people (symbolized by his stilling the seas with their roaring waves). The "nations" represent a challenge to God's sovereignty, but he rules over them as well.

8 Great and majestic are God's "wonders" in nature and in history. People everywhere must recognize God's power and respond in "fear" (GK 3707). His rule extends from east ("where morning dawns") to west ("evening fades"). The nations will rejoice with "songs of joy" when the Lord brings justice and peace to earth.

IV. The Blessedness of God's Rule (65:9–13)

9–11 All the covenantal benefits are blessings of God to his people. Water is one such blessing. People prepare the land before the fall rains by making "furrows" and "ridges." They rejoice when after the gentle rains vegetation grows. They rejoice even more when they see the latter rains in the spring, which permit the crops to mature and to produce abundant harvests. It is as if God's "carts" (i.e., clouds) overflow.

12–13 God's blessings extend to uncultivated land and to the flocks. He blesses the "desert," the "hills," and the "valleys." So abundant is his goodness that creation rejoices together with God's people in the beneficence of his redemption. Truly the Lord is Creator and Redeemer!

Psalm 66: Come and See What God Has Done

This psalm is composed of two independent but related units. The first unit (vv.1–12) is a hymn, which may be further divided into two separate hymns. The second unit (vv.13–20) contains an individual thanksgiving psalm.

I. Universal Praise of God's Kingship (66:1–7)

1–4 The psalmist calls on the whole earth to respond with acclamation to God's royal majesty. The occasion of the universal praise is the revelation of his "glory" (GK 3883). His glory and his "power" attend his mighty "deeds." The works of the Great King evoke "awe" (GK 3707) among the worshiping community. But God's "enemies" too will bring homage ("cringe"), though not from the heart. All peoples of the earth, willingly or unwillingly, will "bow down" before the Lord, singing praise to his holy name.

5–7 When the Israelites came out of Egypt, they crossed through the Red Sea as on "dry ground" (cf. Ex 14:21–15:18). They had witnessed God's mighty deeds and, with Moses, responded in acclamation, "The LORD will reign for ever and ever" (Ex 15:18). Having witnessed his "awesome" acts, they were assured that the Lord's "eyes watch the nations." Israel's praise also contains a warning. If the enemies of the Lord continue to oppose and ignore the past, they too will be the object of his terror. God will not tolerate any obstacle to the full revelation of his glorious rule on earth (cf. Isa 2:6–22).

II. Community Praise of God's Kingship (66:8–12)

8 The goodness of God in the history of redemption occasions a renewed outburst of praise. The community of God's people invokes the "peoples" to listen to the good news of what the Lord has done and to "praise" his name for his new acts of redemption together with Israel.

9–12 God's people confess that the Lord is sovereign in testing and refining his people like silver. The trials are likened to "prison," a metaphor for alienation and duress. They endured great affliction, as if "burdens" had been placed on their "backs." The Lord, nevertheless, had permitted all these things to take place. It seemed as if mortal "men" (GK 632) were prevailing. But its purpose was for trial. During their testing God's people looked for his grace with greater zeal. He was faithful, and he "preserved" them and brought them into "a place of abundance."

III. Individual Thanksgiving (66:13–20)

13–16 As a personal expression of gratitude, the last portion of this psalm leads the individual worshiper to personalize the experience of God's people throughout the history of redemption. The psalmist speaks of himself, as he comes to the temple to present burnt offerings of "fat animals" in fulfillment of his "vows," as he praises the Lord before "all . . . who fear God," and as he tells the story of the personal acts of deliverance from trouble ("what he has done for me").

A "vow" (GK 5624) often arose in a period of adversity, promising an action to be accomplished as soon as God had answered one's prayer. The nature of the sacrifice was carefully specified (Lev 22:18–21).

17–20 The celebration of deliverance from trouble includes (1) lament ("I cried out"); (2) a declaration of commitment or fidelity ("his praise was on my tongue"); (3) a declaration of innocence in suffering ("if I had cherished sin"); and (4) praise ("God has surely listened").

Psalm 67: Grant Your Blessing on All Your Creation

This psalm contains elements characteristic of the psalms of *blessing* and of the psalms ascribing kingship to the Lord.

I. Prayer for God's Blessing and for the Inclusion of the Nations (67:1–3)

The blessing, reminiscent of the priestly benediction (Nu 6:24–26), pertains to three aspects of blessing: (1) protection (Nu 6:24); (2) favor (grace, v.25); and (3) peace (v.26). The allusion to the benediction was sufficient to remind Israel of God's blessings in their totality.

1 God's grace is the basis of his blessing, making life on earth not only possible but even enjoyable. He removes the curse and judgment of the created world since the Fall. He delights in his own, assuring them that he receives them and cares for them with joy.

2 The purpose of God's blessing is so that the nations may "know" (GK 1977) his way. From observing God's blessing on his peo-

ple, they should be able to deduce his royal sovereignty and acknowledge Israel's God as God. Thus they too may enjoy the fullness of his "salvation" (GK 3802), which pertains to all the benefits of God: his kingship, rule, blessings, and promises.

3 The blessing of God gives rise to "praise." Israel's praise lies in the expectation that the nations too will join in the praise of God. When salvation is extended to the nations, they too will join in praising God.

II. Prayer for the Rule of God (67:4)

4 As he rules the nations, God does not exclude them from sharing in the joy of his presence. They must acknowledge him as the Giver of all good things. To Israel he granted his oracles (Ro 3:2; 9:4–5); and through the Jews came the Savior as the final revelation of the "way" of God (Ro 9:5; cf. Ac 4:12; 9:2). As the gospel goes out to the nations, they must come to the Father through the Son.

III. Prayer for Inclusion of the Nations (67:5)

5 For v.5 see the comment on v.3 above.

IV. Prayer for God's Blessing (67:6–7)

6–7 The psalm concludes with a prayer for God's blessings. The prayer reiterates the element of hope in God's universal rule. Without pointing to the Messiah, the psalm anticipates a glorious messianic era in which Jews and Gentiles share in the glorious presence of God. When God blesses his people, it is with the goal of provoking the nations to jealousy so that they too might come to know him, share in his blessings, and have reason to praise him.

Psalm 68: God Is a Father to the Oppressed

The psalm includes prayers, hymnic praise, thanksgiving, and oracles. If there is one unifying theme, it is centered around the Lord as the Divine Warrior, who comes to deliver his people in Mount Zion.

I. Prayer for God's Coming as the Divine Warrior (68:1–3)

1–3 In God's presence no foe can stand. The impotence of the opposition is likened to "smoke" and to "wax." The "wind," "smoke," and "fire" are manifestations of God's presence (theophany). The theophany does not instill "the righteous" (GK 7404) with dread. Instead, the perishing of the "wicked" is an answer to their repeated prayers, and God's people will rejoice greatly in that hour of vindication (cf. 2Th 1:5).

II. In Praise of Divine Vindication (68:4–6)

4 The community is convoked to celebrate the acts of divine vindication. To this end they remember what "God"—the one "who rides on the clouds," whose name is "the LORD" (GK 3378)—has done for his people. The focus is on the "name" that God revealed to Israel (Ex 3:15), signifying his fidelity to fulfilling his covenant promises (cf. Ex 6:6–8). This God is all that Israel needs. The ascription "who rides on the clouds" contrasts the God of Israel with Baal, whom the Canaanites worshiped as "the rider on the clouds." Here the "clouds" signify the chariot of God racing through the sky bringing blessing and curse, vindication and vengeance.

5–6 From "his holy dwelling" in heaven, the Lord watches all humankind. His eyes focus on the destitute and the oppressed, whose rights are trampled by the powerful and the rich. In hymnic language the psalm refers to the Lord as "father," "defender" (GK 1908), "restorer" (NIV, "sets"), and redeemer ("he leads forth"). He acts on behalf of those who look for protection and vindication: the fatherless, the widows, the lonely, and the exiles ("prisoners"). Wherever there are oppressed people, whether they belong to the people of God or not, the Lord's rule brings transformation from injustice to justice and from oppression to vindication. He changes their sorrow to "singing" by judging the rebellious.

III. A Reflection of the Divine Warrior (68:7–18)

A. Exodus, Desert Wandering, Mount Sinai, and Settlement (68:7–10)

7–8 As the Divine Warrior, the Lord led Israel out of Egypt and through the desert. He appeared at Mount Sinai in a theophany, attended by earthquake and storm (cf. Ex 19:16–17). Awesome was his coming. The Lord is the God of Mount Sinai by revelation and the God of Israel by covenant.

9–10 As Israel's covenant King, the Lord also provided the "abundant showers" of water, manna, and meat in the desert and continued to shower the land of Canaan with his blessed rains. The "weary inheritance" seems to be the people whom the psalmist calls "your people" (cf. 2Sa 23:13). The Lord provided abundantly for his people; he established them in the land and provided bountifully for all "the poor," i.e., those who had been afflicted in Egypt.

B. Conquest of Canaan and Subjugation of the Nations (68:11–14)

11 The Lord is the Divine Warrior. He spoke and his oracle was realized in the conquest of the land. The women celebrated his great acts in song and dance (cf. Ex 15:20–21; Jdg 5; 11:34; 1Sa 18:6–7).

12–13 In the Hebrew text, the women sang of how the kings of Canaan fled with their armies, leaving their spoils behind. The men who stayed behind did not share in the spoils, whereas their wives shared in the booty.

14 The victory of "the Almighty" (GK 8724) was so great that it resembled "snow" on Mount Zalmon (one of the mountains by Shechem; cf. Jdg 9:48). The psalmist is metaphorically highlighting the power of the Lord, who is victorious in destroying the opposition. The corpses of the victims and their weaponry are lying like scattered snowflakes on the mountains.

C. The Establishment of the Theocracy in Jerusalem (68:15–18)

15–16 The psalmist adumbrates the glory of Mount Bashan, but stresses that its glory is dwarfed by the majesty and holiness of Mount Zion. Mount Bashan looks with "envy" at Mount Zion, because the Lord has chosen to establish his "reign" there.

17 The Lord who went ahead of his people (v.7) is portrayed as surrounded by an entourage of thousands of "chariots," representative of his heavenly servants. He who revealed his "holiness" (GK 7731; NIV, "his sanctuary") on Mount Sinai is "the Lord" (GK 151; cf. v.11), who also went ahead of his people to protect and to bless them (vv.7–10).

18 On the victorious completion of the Exodus, the Desert Wanderings, and the Conquest, the Lord returned as it were to heaven ("on high") to celebrate his kingship on earth. The Divine Warrior had successfully subjugated his enemies, having made them "captives" and having received tribute from the conquered nations. In commemoration of his mighty acts, he chose Jerusalem among the mountains to establish his abode, where the "LORD . . . might dwell forever" (cf. 2Co 2:14; Eph 4:8).

IV. In Praise of Divine Vindication (68:19–20)

19–20 The comfort of God's presence occasions a renewal of praise. He is "the Lord" (GK 151), who promised deliverance and victory (v.11) and now cares deeply for his people and leads them out of "death." He is "God our Savior" and his nature sets in motion the history of redemption, because "our God is a God who saves." His rule extends over all angels in heaven and to all the earth. He is known to the believing community as "Sovereign LORD."

V. An Oracle From the Divine Warrior (68:21–23)

21–23 The community also rejoices in having received an oracle from the Lord, the thrust of which is comfort in adversity and an assurance of God's vindication. The godly believe that the Lord will avenge the enemy— expressed poetically by reference to "the heads of the enemies" and to "the hairy crowns." Though the enemies trouble Israel on land or at sea, though they escape to the escarpments of the rocks or try to hide at sea, the Lord will bring them down and share his victory with his people.

VI. Joyful Anticipation of God's Coming as the Divine Warrior (68:24–35)

A. Processional Hymn (68:24–27)

24–27 The oracle inspires the people with greater hope as they await the Lord's "procession." Ahead of everybody is the Lord, whom the psalmist addresses personally as "my God and King." Previously the whole community was involved in thanksgiving (vv.19–20). This time the personal pronoun ("my") involves each worshiper as he or she anticipates the coming of the procession. The Lord is viewed returning victoriously from battle to his "sanctuary." This processional language reflects the customs of battle. The princes and leaders of the tribes join in singing the victory hymn. For purposes of brevity and representation, the poet has selected the southern tribes (Judah and Benjamin) and the northern tribes (Zebulun and Naphtali). Together they form one people, "the great congregation."

B. Prayer (68:28–31)

28–29 With renewed enthusiasm the people of God call on the Lord to demonstrate his "power" and "strength." He has revealed the terror and majesty of his strength in his past victorious acts; but by his own decree, and by his nature as the Redeemer-God, the community expects him to act again. The Lord has established his majesty in his temple in Jerusalem. The subject nations, led by their kings, bring him homage (cf. 76:11; Isa 18:7; 60:3–7; 66:20; et al.).

30–31 The prayer contains a petition to strike those nations that will not submit to the Lord. They are likened to "the beast among the reeds" and a "herd of bulls," both of which denote oppressors and troublers of the nations. They must come to an end, as the same nations that have loved warfare and tribute are "humbled" and despoiled. Even mighty Egypt and Cush, who often formed a power base with Egypt, will submit to the Lord.

C. Triumphal Hymn (68:32–35)

32–33 Since the kingdom of the Lord extends to all nations, and since the nations must one day submit to him, the Lord calls on the "kingdoms of the earth" to respond appropriately to his sovereignty. The phrase "the ancient skies above" suggests the excellency of the Lord whose rule extends to the highest heaven. The thunder reveals the majesty and power of his rule.

34–35 The praise of the subject nations must include an ascription of his sovereignty ("the power of God"). He has shown his dominion ("majesty") over Israel. This God is "awesome" in his deeds but still present with his people. He alone is their source of strength. This God is "blessed" (GK 1385; NIV "praise be") and is to be praised.

Psalm 69: The Zeal for Your House and God's Love for His Own

This is an *imprecatory* psalm of the *individual lament* genre. Because of its many NT references, this psalm has been interpreted messianically.

I. Lament (69:1–28)

A. Prayer Out of Personal Need (69:1–4)

1–3 The adversity of the wicked is like deep "waters," coming up to the psalmist's "neck," so that he is losing his "foothold." The psalmist is "worn out" and his "throat" seems to be burning ("parched") from repeatedly calling, "Save me"; for the Lord has not yet responded to his cry. He can go no farther, because his eyes also "fail" him.

4 The psalmist is the object of fierce hatred—but "without reason." His enemies deal in "treachery," accusing him of stealing and requiring him to restore what he has not taken. They are out to destroy him (cf. Jn 15:25).

B. Affirmation of God's Knowledge (69:5)

5 God knows that the psalmist has acted without wisdom, i.e., foolishly, and that he has committed "acts of wrongdoing" ("guilt"; GK 873). Thus he humbly admits his humanness in the presence of the Lord.

C. Disgrace for the Sake of God (69:6–12)

6 The psalmist speaks on behalf of all the godly as he addresses the Lord as "Lord, the LORD Almighty." This phrase includes three designations for God: He is the "Lord" (GK 151) of the universe, the "LORD" (GK 3378) of the covenant, and the Divine Warrior ("Almighty," GK 7372). This is the "God of Israel," the Great King of the whole world.

7 Because God must be true to his promises, David prays that God's people will never be overtaken by calumny. As David turns to the particular, himself, the problem gains a new perspective. For God's sake he is being disgraced with "shame."

8–12 For the sake of God, David has become like a "stranger" and an "alien" to his own kin. While he prays and fasts on account of his adversity and the prevalent godlessness, people respond with laughter, mocking, and drinking songs. Dear to his heart is the "house" of the Lord. He was so desirous of pleasing God in the face of ignominy that his "zeal" consumed him, like "a devouring flame."

D. Deliverance for the Sake of God's Servant (69:13–18)

13 The psalmist casts himself even more forcefully on the mercy of the Lord. The phrase "time of your favor" is a technical phrase for God's restorative graces: full forgiveness, deliverance, and restoration to the full benefits of God's relationship with his people. David further specifies what he understands by "favor": deliverance (vv.14–18); God's love and blessings ("the goodness of your love," v.16); "sure salvation"; and "your great mercy" (v.16; cf. 103:8, 17–18).

14–18 The "mire" and the "floodwaters" are about to overtake the psalmist. As he prays, he becomes more intense: "Rescue me.... Do not let the floodwaters engulf me ... or the pit close its mouth over me." In his misery he renews his petition for God's love and mercy as expressions of God's presence. The time for deliverance is now; hence urgency is expressed in staccato-like terseness: "Do not hide ... answer me quickly, for I am in trouble. Come near." Because of the numerous enemies and their deceptiveness and mocking, he prays that his redemption be near.

E. Affirmation of God's Knowledge (69:19–21)

19–21 Again David quiets himself with the thought that God knows everything about him—including his scorn, disgrace, and shame. He looks for those who identify with him, but there is no sympathy or comfort. Instead, they make things worse for him. They do their best to aggravate his troubles (cf. the metaphors "gall" and "vinegar").

F. Prayer for God's Judgment on the Wicked (69:22–28)

22 Characteristic of the imprecatory psalms, the psalmist hurls God's curses on the enemies. They have made life intolerable for him. As a matter of justice and concern, David prays that the Lord may deal equitably with his enemies. The wicked who had ruined his table will find that their table will be "a snare ... and a trap."

23–28 The psalmist's eyes and strength have been failing because of his long wait for God's redemption. He prays that his enemies may suffer divine wrath and may lose courage and strength. Since he is forsaken by family and friends, he prays that the wicked may be homeless, childless, and without a future. They have enjoyed their lives and are guilty. In the end they should have no part in the community of God's people on earth nor in the hereafter. To this end he prays that their names be removed from "the book of life," i.e., God's record of the "righteous" (cf. 56:8; 87:6; Ex 32:32–33; Isa 4:3; Da 12:1; Mal 3:16; Rev 3:5; 13:8; et al.). "Salvation" in v.27 is literally "righteousness" (GK 7407), paralleling v.28b.

II. Hymn (69:29–36)

A. Personal and Communal Praise (69:29–32)

29 This verse forms a transition between the lament and the hymn. The "salvation" (GK 3802) of the Lord extends to the complete protection of his own, both body and soul. "Salvation" is a synonym of "righteousness" (GK 7407). Both denote a complete vindication of the godly by their righteous God, who will "protect" his own.

30–32 David looks forward to the time when he can record his deliverance by praising his God in a song of thanksgiving. The sacrifice of the lips in such thanksgiving is better than the sacrifice of a bull. Thus the "poor" and those "who seek God" will take heart, join with him in gladness, and be satisfied.

B. Affirmation of God's Present Care (69:33)

33 Literally translated this verse reads: "Surely, the LORD hears the needy." The "needy" (GK 36; i.e., "his captive people") will be assured that the God of the covenant listens to and answers their prayers.

C. Cosmic Praise (69:34)

34 All creation joins with the salvation of God's people (see also Isa 44:23; 55:12; cf. Ro 8:18–22). The interrelationship of the welfare God's covenant people and nature is also found in Isaiah (e.g., 44:23; 55:12; cf. Ro 8:18–23).

D. Affirmation of God's Eschatological Deliverance (69:35–36)

35–36 The psalmist prays for the speedy deliverance of Zion, her cities, and her people. The attack of the enemies on God's people is an attack on God's kingdom. Whether Judah was under attack or had just come out of a period of war and desolation, the Lord promises to restore his people, strengthen them, and permit them and their children to enjoy his benefits.

Psalm 70

This psalm is virtually identical with the prayer in 40:13–17. The main differences lie in the absence of the divine name and in the addition of "hasten" at the very beginning of the psalm. Possibly this psalm was adapted from Ps 40 for a special occasion.

Psalm 71: Longing for the Lord's Righteous Acts

The combination of lament and thanksgiving indicates that this is an *individual lament* psalm.

I. Prayer of Confidence (71:1–4)

1–4 The psalmist repeatedly prays for deliverance from his present affliction. The ground for hope lies both in his trust in God and in his belief that the Lord is "righteous" (GK 7407). This conviction that God rules and acts righteously upholds him in his faith that the Lord will deliver him from the wicked, from those who are devoted to evil and unrighteous acts. The Lord is his "rock," his "refuge," and his "fortress."

II. Affirmation of Confidence (71:5–8)

5–8 The Lord has been the psalmist's "hope," "confidence," "praise," "strong refuge," and "splendor" from his "birth." His God is no other than Yahweh (LORD; GK 3378), the covenant-redeemer God. Although he has become a "portent" (GK 4603; i.e., a sign of trouble and divine retribution) to his contemporaries, he nevertheless throws himself on God as his refuge. The Lord has been close to him in deliverance and protection throughout his life. Based on this affirmation of trust, he has had reasons to declare the Lord's royal praise in the past and looks forward to ascribing the powers of royalty to the Lord in the future.

III. Prayer in Old Age (71:9–13)

9–11 Lament shapes the petition. The psalmist prays that the Lord will not abandon him in old age. "Cast away" and "forsake" signify a state of condemnation and curse. The vile enemies are all too ready to condemn him to death, to accuse him as a sinner worse than they are, and to justify their evil course of action.

12–13 The prayer calls on the Lord to vindicate his servant speedily by giving him "help" and by bringing retribution on God's enemies. His enemies are "evil and cruel" (v.4) "accusers." The psalmist awaits the Lord's judgment.

IV. Hope in Old Age (71:14–18)

14–16 In response to his lament, the psalmist affirms that his "hope" (GK 3498) is in the Lord. He expects the Lord to vindicate him, resulting in a new declaration of "praise." The nature of vindication will be nothing less than an expression of his "righteousness" (GK 7407). His "mighty acts" and "marvelous deeds" (v.17) establish his "righteous" kingdom. These are the acts of the psalmist's "Sovereign LORD."

17–18 The psalmist has devoted himself to God since his youth. He has praised him and anticipates proclaiming his praise to another generation. The "power" of God is the demonstration of his "might" and an expression of his fidelity. All who "come" will hear this gray-haired saint retell the story of the Lord's mighty deeds.

V. Affirmation of Confidence (71:19–21)

19 Faith triumphs as the psalmist leads to a grand vision of the Lord's "righteousness," reaching to "the skies." It is nothing less than his perfection as evidenced in the "great things." There is no God in heaven above or being on earth who is like the Lord!

20–21 Great have been the psalmist's troubles. Yet the Lord's power is so great that he can extend his love into the deepest depths. He alone has the power over life and death. Instead of shame (v.1), the psalmist will receive "honor" (lit., "greatness"; GK 1525; i.e., the Lord's saving acts). Instead of "troubles" (v.20), he receives "comfort" from the Lord God.

VI. Thanksgiving With Confidence (71:22–24)

22–24 The psalm concludes with a vow to praise the Lord publicly for his "faithfulness," as expressed in his "righteous acts" of deliverance. The Lord delivers his children and avenges those who harm them. He is "the Holy One of Israel" in his acts of redemption.

Psalm 72: The Glory of the Davidic Kingdom

This psalm is a *royal psalm,* wherein petition is made for the prosperity of the Lord's anointed. The psalm begins with a prayer for the messianic kingship of David's dynasty and ends on an ascription of praise to the universal kingship of the Lord.

I. Prayer for Davidic Kingship (72:1)

1 Petition and praise well up from the heart of faith, as the psalmist invokes God's blessing on the Davidic dynasty. To be an instrument of God's kingship on earth, the monarch must conform to the divine standards of "justice" (GK 5477) and "righteousness" (GK 7406). The king, talented as he may have been, had to live in accordance with the revelation from God.

II. Hope for Righteousness and Justice (72:2–4)

2–4 The king is an instrument of God's blessing to his people. He must "judge" the cases before him in accordance with "righteousness" and "justice." Thereby the people will share in the benefits of theocratic rule, knowing that their king is working for them. The "afflicted," "the children of the needy," and the people at large will benefit from his upholding their rights and avenging the "oppressor." Vindication ("the fruit of righteousness") brings "prosperity" as a sense of well-being to the people.

III. Prayer for Longevity and Universal Rule (72:5–11)

5–6 The hope is that the wise king will remain a blessing for a long time. The duration probably refers to the length of the royal dynasty rather than the individual ruler. The prosperity is likened to rain showers on "a mown field" and on "the earth"—a picture of new growth.

Concern in the Old Testament for the Poor and Oppressed

A. The Basis	
1. Theological	
a. The land belongs to the Lord, not to his people	Ex 9:29; 19:5–6; Lev 25:23:23–24; Job 41:11; Pss 24:1; 50:12
b. The Lord loves justice	Job 34:19; Pss 11:7; 33:5; Isa 30:18; 61:8; Jer 9:24
c. The Lord watches over the poor	Ps 146:9
d. The Lord protects the poor	Pss 12:5; 34:6; 35:10
e. The Lord defends the cause of the poor	Dt 10:18; Pss 10:17–18; 68:5; Pr 23:10–11
f. The Lord is the refuge of the poor	Pss 9:9; 14:6; Isa 25:4
g. The Lord delivers the poor	1Sa 2:8; Pss 34:6, 18; 35:10; 107:41; 113:7
h The Lord helps the poor	Pss 40:17; 70:5; Isa 41:17
i. The Lord provides for the poor and oppressed	Ps 132:15; Isa 61:1–3
2. Historical	
a. The Israelites were oppressed slaves in Egypt	Dt 15:15; 16:12; 24:22
b. The Lord redeemed his people from slavery	Dt 24:17–18, 22; Jer 34:13–14

B. Laws in the Old Testament	
1. General principles	
a. There must be no poor in the land	Dt 15:4
b. The underprivileged must not be taken advantage of	Ex 22:21–23; Dt 24:14
c. The underprivileged must not be denied justice	Ex 23:6; Dt 24:17; Isa 1:17; Jer 7:5–6; 21:12; 22:3; Zec 7:9–10
d. Equal justice pertains to all	Ex 23:2–3; Lev 19:15; Dt 1:17; Pr 28:21; Mic 6:8
e. Rulers must defend the poor, the afflicted, and the oppressed	Ps 72:4, 12–14; 82:3–4; Jer 22:2–3, 15–16
2. Specific laws	
a. The poor were allowed to glean in the fields	Lev 19:10; 23:22; Dt 23:24–25; 24:19–21; Ru 2:2–3, 15–17
b. No interested was to be charged on loans to the poor	Ex 22:25; Lev 25:35–37; Dt 15:7–11; 23:19–20; Ne 5:7, 9–13; Ps 15:5
c. A cloak taken as pledge had to be returned by sunset	Ex 22:26–27; Dt 24:12–13, 17

B. Laws in the Old Testament	
2. Specific laws (cont)	
d. Millstones could not be taken as security for debts	Dt 24:6
e. Wages must be paid daily	Lev 19:13; Dt 24:15; Jer 22:13
f. Israelites were not to be sold in permanent slavery	Ex 21:2–11; Dt 15:12–18
g. Every seven years, all debts were to be canceled	Dt 15:1–3; 31:10; Ne 10:31
h. Every seventh year land was not to be tilled, so that the poor could get food	Ex 23:10–11; Lev 25:1–7
h. Every fifty years all land must be returned to its original assigned owner (the Year of Jubilee)	Lev 25:8–54

C. Judgment Pronounced on Those Who Oppressed the Poor	
1. In the historical books	
a. Against Rehoboam	1Ki 12:3–15 (cf. 11:29–31)
b. Against Ahab after stealing Naboth's vineyard	1Ki 21:17–22 (cf. vv. 1–14)
c. Against leaders in Nehemiah's day	Ne 5:1–13
2. In the prophets	
a. From Isaiah	Isa 1:23–25; 3:13–15; 5:22–25; 10:1–2; 29:21; 32:6–7; 58:6–7; 59:4–15
b. From Jeremiah	Jer 2:34–35; 5:26–29; 7:4–8; 17:11; 21:11–14; 22:13
c. From Ezekiel	Eze 16:49–50; 18:10–13; 22:6–7, 29; 33:31; 34:1–5, 18–22
d. From Hosea	Hos 12:6–8
e. From Amos	Am 2:2–8; 3:14–4:2; 5:7, 10–12; 6:3–7; 8:4–7
f. From Obadiah	Ob 8–14
g. From Micah	Mic 2:1–5, 8–9; 3:1–4, 9–12
h. From Habakkuk	Hab 2:6–11
i. From Zechariah	Zec 7:8–14; 10:2–3
j. From Malachi	Mal 3:5

7–8 As long as the Davidic dynasty is responsive to divine wisdom, the Lord guarantees that righteousness and peace will flourish. The effects of his administration will last, and its benefits on the population will long be enjoyed. The rule of the Davidic dynasty will not only extend in time but also in space. The Lord's messianic government spreads out over seas, rivers, and land. The world belongs to God.

9–11 Kings and nations will submit to the divinely appointed ruler. The nations will present their tribute as acts of submission. The nearby nations are represented by "the desert tribes" and the "enemies," the distant nations by kings of "distant shores": Tarshish, Sheba (modern Yemen), and Seba (in Africa). The imagery reflects the Solomonic era of peace, righteousness, and international diplomacy (cf. 1Ki 4:21, 34; 10:1–29).

IV. Hope for Righteousness and Justice (72:12–14)

12–14 The psalmist returns to the theme of hope in an era of righteousness and justice. The divinely appointed king represents God's concern for the oppressed. The destitute, disadvantaged, and social outcasts are his subjects; but more than that, they are also his concern. Those against whom others discriminated are the very people whose concerns the king takes to heart. His "pity" (GK 2571) is the ground for action, transforming sympathy to empathy. The king loves them and values their very lives as his own. He will "rescue" (GK 1457) the destitute from their adversaries and from their prosecutors. He will grant them life by taking away the pangs of death.

V. Prayer for Longevity and Universality (72:15–17)

15–17 This prayer includes a petition for the longevity of the king and the perpetuity of the dynasty. The concern for the "name" of the king relates to the continuity of his regime as well as to the continuation of the blessings of his regime. The security and perpetuity of his kingship are advanced by the subject nations who bring him tribute and pray for his welfare. The prosperity of the king blessed by the Lord extends to all realms, represented here by "grain" and "fruit." The psalmist petitions the extension

of blessing to all the subject nations. They too will be "blessed" (GK 1385; cf. Ge 12:2–3; 22:18; 26:4).

VI. Praise of God's Kingship (72:18–20)

18–20 The concluding doxology closes Book II of Psalms. The Lord is to be praised. He is God, "the LORD," "the God of Israel," who has done and will continue to do "marvelous deeds" on behalf of his people. Through them he has demonstrated his "glorious name" in all the earth (cf. Isa 6:3; cf. Lk 1:68).

The congregational response to the doxology is a twofold "Amen" (GK 589; cf. 41:13; 106:48; Ne 8:6). They confess that these words are true. The final verse separates the psalms associated with David from those of Asaph (73–83).

Book III: Psalms 73–89

Psalm 73: The Suffering of God's Children and the Goodness of God

The psalmist struggles within himself as to the appropriate response to evil and injustice in the world. This psalm is best categorized as a *wisdom psalm* in which lament is the vehicle of communication.

I. Experience and Belief (73:1–3)

1 The psalmist has learned from his own experience that God is good. The "pure" (GK 2342) are not perfect but live in loyalty to God in speech and action, thus evidencing their "pure" motives. They are without hypocrisy. The word "heart" occurs six times in vv.1–26.

2–3 The psalmist readily and publicly admits that he "envied the arrogant" and ungodly in their "prosperity." Engaged in self-pity and questioning God's justice, he was filled with resentment and could easily have joined those he envied. He nearly failed, but God sustained him and kept him.

II. Prosperity of the Wicked (73:4–12)

4–12 The wicked seem to be carefree and unconcerned about tomorrow. They are doing well, as their wealth and power increase. They seem like "gods" who do not suffer from the frailties, adversities, diseases, and toilsome labor common to most people.

Their eyes sparkle because everything is going well for them. They do not regard God and his commandments. Instead, they are puffed up with "pride." They leave behind a trail of violence, living at the expense of others. The wicked rule with their tongues. By intimidation they instill fear in others, and they act as if they can get by without responsibility to God. They decree how things are to be done on earth and what God can do in heaven. Most distressing to the psalmist is that it seems as if God lets the wicked get by with their wickedness.

III. Personal Reaction (73:13–17)

13–14 The psalmist confesses that he doubted the value of his own concern with sanctification. Keeping his heart "pure" and his hands "washed . . . in innocence" expresses his concern for justice and righteousness. The psalmist confesses his self-doubt and envy. Being "plagued" and "punished" probably refers to his mental turmoil.

15–17 The psalmist confesses a deep concern for the people of God. He had thought about removing himself for the sake of the prosperity and peace of his soul, but he could not sever ties with God's people. He further confesses that though he cannot understand the ways of God, he did experience God's peace when he entered into the sanctuary. Overwhelmed by the greatness, glory, and majesty of God, the psalmist rediscovers that the Lord is just! In the end evil is not and never will be victorious.

IV. Affirmation of God's Justice (73:18–20)

18–19 Whereas the Lord had not permitted the psalmist to slip into sin, the wicked are doomed to fall. It may take several generations before they are brought down to God's judgment, but the assurance of Scripture is that they will be judged "suddenly" and "completely."

20 The wicked are like "a dream," which has a sense of reality when one is asleep but is gone at the moment of awakening. God's righteous judgment brings all things into perspective. The psalmist's experiences of anguish of mind will turn out to be little more than a nightmare, a bad dream.

V. Evaluation of the Psalmist's Reaction (73:21–22)

21–22 The psalmist was deeply affected by envy and anguish. Deep inside he was grieved and embittered, resulting in a state of depression. In this state he was irrational (cf. 94:8), not ruled by wisdom.

VI. The Desire of the Godly (73:23–26)

23–26 Because of God's presence, the psalmist is assured of his protection and guidance. God protects him by holding his "right hand," by giving him internal fortitude, and by providing for all his needs. God guides his servant by giving him wisdom and insight as he travels on to everlasting glory. The "glory" (GK 3883) of God is his blessed presence, which affects one's whole way of life. There is no one but God, his Sustainer in heaven, with whom the psalmist longingly desires to fellowship. Therefore he is more prepared to face his present existence with all its problems. He is prepared to grow older and experience failing health and even adversity because God is his "strength," "portion," and "refuge" (v.28). "The Rock" (GK 7445; NIV, "strength") of Israel is present with him.

VII. Experience and Hope (73:27–28)

27–28 In anticipation of God's just acts of vindication, the psalmist declares his hope in his God. The wicked must perish in the end because they are "unfaithful" to God. These verses are a fitting conclusion to the psalm. Envy has turned to hope, and God's goodness to Israel is also experienced at the individual level. "It is good to be near God."

Psalm 74: The Destruction of the Temple

God's people in exile weep over the destruction of the temple (586 B.C.), the symbol of the presence and the protection of God. In this *community lament* the godly nevertheless affirm the creative and redemptive powers of their covenant God as the ground for their petition to be redeemed.

I. Prayer for Remembrance (74:1–3)

1–3 With God's sanctuary in ruins, the psalmist calls on the Lord to investigate the fate of Jerusalem. It seems as if the ruins are everlasting, because every moment of God's anger is like an eternity. The "why" arises because of the present alienation of God's "sheep" in the context of their past relationship with him. How can God be angry with his own people forever? With "turn your steps" (GK 3727; lit., "lift up"), the psalmist petitions the Lord to look with pity on the ruins of the city of God and to remember when he redeemed his people from Egypt, formed them to be his "inheritance," and maintained a relationship of grace with them.

II. Destruction of the Temple (74:4–8)

4 The presentation of Jerusalem's destruction is given in moving detail, focusing on the desecration of the temple by hostile forces. The enemies "roared" like lions as they captured the temple area itself. Instead of witnessing the "signs" of God's presence and forgiveness (sacrifices, priestly rituals), the people had seen the pagan "standards" that symbolized their victory.

5–7a The enemy behaved like mad men as they used their axes on the woodwork of the temple. The beautiful carved work (cf. 1Ki 6:23–35) was destroyed by pagan implements of destruction. The gold overlay (1Ki 6:19–22) was stripped (2Ki 25:13–17) off the wood. Then they burned the temple to the ground (cf. 2Ki 25:9).

7b–8 The lament focuses on the act of defiling the temple, emphasizing that the symbolic place of God's covenant and his mercies was desecrated by hostile Babylonians. Their evil intent is clearly expressed by the words "They said in their hearts." Their goal was to destroy the meeting place of God with his people and thus change Israel's destiny and remove any reminder of God's past loyalty and worship.

III. Feeling of Abandonment (74:9–11)

9–11 This section concludes the lament and forms a transition to the confession of God's kingship. God's people are disturbed at his apparent absence. They no longer witness any "miraculous signs" (GK 253), see the symbols of Israel's worship, or hear the oracles of God. Instead they hear the scoffing of the enemies. In their abandonment the godly show a deep concern for the honor of God's name, reviled by the pagans. Thus, on behalf of the community of God's people, the psalmist asks, "How long?" and "Why?"

IV. God's Past Involvements (74:12–17)

12–13a The laments give way to a hymn in which the psalmist represents the community in its worship of the great "king." He has shown himself to be Israel's king "from of old," i.e., since he redeemed them from Egypt. He has done acts of "salvation," being victorious over Israel's enemies. As King, God has led his people heroically from victory to victory.

13b–17 The current victory of the pagans and the seeming power of their deities require a powerful demonstration of the Lord's sovereignty. The psalmist chooses the language of Canaanite mythology to celebrate the Lord's victory over the nations. His absolute power is vividly expressed in the language of crushing the heads of Leviathan and of feeding them to the wild animals. The "monster" symbolizes the wild, uncontrolled forces of the sea. The Creator-God has made and now sovereignly rules over the waters, the earth, day and night, the heavenly bodies, and the seasons of the year. The Lord, the covenant Redeemer, had also demonstrated his sovereignty in history by redeeming his people from Egypt.

V. Prayer for Remembrance (74:18–21)

18–21 The confessional hymn, celebrating God's creative and redemptive powers, revitalizes the godly with hope. They petition the Lord to "remember" (GK 2349) the conduct of the enemies ("wild beasts") and the afflictions of his covenant people ("your dove"). The enemies have mocked and reviled the Lord's name, "the LORD." While they thought they had autonomy over God's people and therefore over the God of Israel, they are nothing but "foolish people" for denying the power of the Lord.

VI. Destruction of God's Enemies (74:22–23)

22–23 In conclusion the lament renews a bold appeal for the Lord to act. As long as the foolish mocking continues, the enemies have reason to boast in their strength. As long as their loud noise "rises continually," it seems that the Lord has rejected his people "forever." But their power is nothing compared to the Lord's, when he rises to defend his cause.

Psalm 75: Justice Is the Lord's

In view of the strong opposition of the arrogant, the godly community looks to God for deliverance. The genre of the psalm appears to have characteristics of a communal *thanksgiving hymn.*

I. Thanksgiving (75:1)

1 The community of God's people bursts out in a song of thanksgiving. The godly recall the "wonderful deeds" (GK 7098) of the Lord, his acts in creation and in the salvation of his people.

II. Oracle of the Lord (75:2–5)

2–3 Though God may let wicked individuals and nations go unpunished and even the godly may pray for their deliverance for long periods of time, the Lord will suddenly introduce "the appointed time" for judgment. The "upright" (GK 4797) judgment of God pertains to both aspects of his righteous rule: vengeance on the enemies and vindication of the godly. The Lord is in control, even when it seems that everything is falling to pieces. The "pillars" shore up the moral order, preventing his creation from collapsing.

4–5 The Lord's word comes directly to those who cause chaos, anarchy, and immorality on the earth. The "arrogant" (GK 2147) live without regard for God and his commandments. They speak insolently and are impatient with the distinction between the divine and the human. They are no different from the "wicked," who boast in their power and autonomy—expressed by the word "horns" (GK 7967), which they lift up "against heaven."

III. Prophetic Oracle (75:6–8)

6–8 God's judgment will be universal. Since his rule extends "from the east or the west" and includes deserts and mountains, no one can escape it. Those who exalt themselves against the Lord will be brought down. Like a cup of spiced wine, the Lord pours out his judgment on the wicked (cf. Rev 15:7; 16:19).

IV. Thanksgiving (75:9–10)

9–10 The psalmist takes it on himself to perpetuate the story of God's mighty acts. In retelling the story of salvation in song, the redeemed will forever remember what the Lord, the "God of Jacob," has done. He is committed to protect and help his people. Since God is opposed to the "horns" of the wicked, he vows to bring them to destruction. He will vindicate the righteous, however, by raising their "horns."

Psalm 76: The Lord Is the God of Jacob

The adoration of the Divine Warrior by his own people includes both a reflection on past victories and a hope for the full establishment of his kingdom on earth. The psalm is in the form of a victory hymn.

I. God's Relationship With His People (76:1–3)

1–2 God had graciously established a relationship with his people, who had come to "know" (GK 3359) him by his gracious condescension to dwell in the temple of Solomon ("the tent"). The Lord has chosen "Salem" (cf. Ge 14:18) as his royal city so that both Judah (the southern kingdom) and Israel (the northern kingdom) may comfort each other with the assurance that the Divine Warrior is in their midst.

3 Jacob and Israel experienced the triumphs of the Lord. He is the Warrior who goes ahead of his people. Nothing can stop him. The collection of weapons taken from the enemy witnesses to his power.

II. The Divine Warrior (76:4–7a)

4 The Divine Warrior is "resplendent" (i.e., enveloped by light) as he shoots forth the thunderbolts. He is the "majestic" One.

5–7a The kings and rulers of the nations are the "valiant men" who rebel against God and against his anointed king (cf. 2:1–2). They rely on "horse and chariot," i.e, political power and military strength. But human warriors pass away into "their last sleep" and are powerless to raise their strong "hands." The enemies are felled by the "rebuke" of the Lord. The God of Jacob is "awe-inspiring" (NIV, "to be feared"; GK 3707).

III. The Divine Judge (76:7b–9)

7b–9 The rhetorical question "Who can stand?" should shock the reader! No one can stand before him in his anger! The Lord rules over the nations. He is the Great Judge of the universe speaking "from heave purpose of the "judgment" is twofold. First, it lets the nations know that the Lord is the sovereign King. Second, it gives comfort to the people of God in that he rises to help "all the afflicted of the land." The "afflicted" (GK 6705) are those who await the deliverance of the Lord.

IV. The Relationship of the Nations With God (76:10–12)

10 All acts are under God's sovereign control. Even the most hostile acts against his rule will bring him "praise." The Lord turns a person's rebellious expression of anger to his glory. When he goes out as a man of war (Isa 59:17–18), his opponents must submit to his lordship.

11–12 In view of the dreaded judgment of the sovereign Lord over all people, all must respond wisely, being careful to pay their vows to the Lord. God's people must be examples to the nations of loyalty to him, but the nations too have an opportunity to respond to the awe-inspiring nature of the Lord. He will crush the hostile opposition of the nations to his rule.

Psalm 77: A Remembrance of God's Greatness

The mood of the psalm changes from lamentation to reflection and ultimately gives way to a joyful hymn celebrating the greatness of the God of Israel. The psalm may be read as an *individual lament* psalm.

I. Cry for Help (77:1–2)

1–2 The psalmist repeats the words "I cried out to God" by way of emphasis; his prayer is intense because of his "distress." He longs for a renewal of communion with the Lord, inaugurated by new acts of God. To this end he "sought the Lord." He "stretched out" his hands in prayer and continued to lift up his hands "at night." Yet even in his laments he remains restless on account of the distance between him and God. He looks to God as the sole comforter of his soul.

II. Remembrance of God in Hymns of the Night (77:3–6)

3–6 In his remembrance the psalmist recalls the acts of God. But such remembrance gives him groaning and spiritual exhaustion rather than comfort. He reflects on "the former days," when the songs sung at night were comforting, permitting him to sleep quietly even in great adversity. But these night hymns comfort no longer, for his eyes are kept "from closing." The psalmist troubles himself further as he "muses" and "inquires."

III. Questions (77:7–9)

7–9 Doubts and questions are expressed by the greatest saints of God (cf. Ps 22:1; Mt 27:46). The psalmist asks whether God will "reject" (GK 2396) his people forever by not extending to them his "favor" (GK 8354). The "favor" is his willingness to be reconciled with his people by forgiving their sins and by blessing them with his grace. The psalmist continues with the questions as to why the "unfailing love" (GK 2876) of God is gone and why "his promise" has become ineffective. He further ponders the question why God does not forgive and show mercy on his people.

IV. Remembrance of God's Mighty Deeds (77:10–12)

10–12 The remembrance of the age-old acts of God is the basis for faith. The name of God "Most High" (GK 6609) goes back to Abraham (Ge 14:22). This God, the Creator and Protector of creation, is none other than "the LORD," the covenant God. The psalmist remembers his "mighty deeds," "miracles," and "works."

V. Confidence in God's Help (77:13–20)

13–15 The hymn ascribes power to God. His holy "ways" pertain to what he has done on behalf of his people. They exclaim with the psalmist, "What god is so great as our God?" Only the Lord demonstrates his holy power "among the peoples" on behalf of his people, "the descendants of Jacob and Joseph." The nations witnessed his mighty "miracles," performed by his "mighty arm," and they trembled (cf. Ex 15:14–16; Ps 66:8).

16–20 The drama of creation and redemption is depicted with great literary imagination. The powers of the waters and the mysterious forces of the depths of the seas tremble in the presence of God. The Lord's power was displayed in clouds, rain, thunder, and lightning. God led his people through the Red Sea. Though his presence ("footprints") was not "visible" to them, it was apparent in his awesome power by which Israel passed to Sinai. They were led "like a flock by the hand of Moses and Aaron" through the desert.

Psalm 78: Lessons From Israel's History

The wisdom motif of vv.1–4 introduces a didactic psalm. The psalmist is concerned to show how Ephraim lost its special status of blessing and prominence in favor of Judah.

I. Call to Wisdom (78:1–4)

1–4 The importance of the "teaching" lies in the insights gleaned from Israel's history. "The words of my mouth" are words of wisdom, expressed in "parables" (GK 5442; proverbial forms of teaching) and in "hidden things" (GK 2648)—"hidden" in the sense that humans cannot comprehend that God continues to be merciful and patient with a "rebellious people" (cf. Mt 13:35). The wisdom communicated from the fathers to each new generation pertains to the Lord's "praiseworthy deeds" and the demonstration of his "power" and "wonders." The history of redemption is revelatory.

II. Lessons From Israel's History (78:5–64)

A. Past and Future Generations (78:5–8)

5–8 Each generation must remember that the Lord revealed the divine oracles to Israel as an expression of the covenant relationship that he had sovereignly and graciously established between himself and Israel. Israel was expected to teach this revelation from generation to generation so that each generation might "put their trust in God" by remembering "his deeds" and by keeping "his commands." The "hearts" of the desert generation were "not loyal" (i.e., not established: GK 3922), and their "spirits were not faithful" to God. Instead, they were thoroughly rebellious.

B. Israel in Egypt and in the Wilderness (78:9–16)

9 The spirit of "the men of Ephraim" represents the spirit of Israel as a whole. They were richly blessed with an extensive patrimony among the tribes of Israel (cf. Ge 48:15–20; 49:22–26; Dt 33:13–17). "Armed with bows" fits well with their aggressiveness (cf. Jdg 8:1–3; 12:1–6). However, they also lost because they had to flee in war, perhaps

referring to the Philistine incursion and victory at Ebenezer (1Sa 4:1–11).

10–12 The people were defeated because of flagrant disobedience and disregard of God's covenant and law. They were no longer moved by the history of redemption, because they had forgotten God's expressions of loving concern, the "wonders" and "miracles" performed in Egypt and in the desert.

13–16 The Lord had led Israel through the Red Sea, whose waters congealed like a wall (cf. Ex 15:8; Jos 3:13, 16). Throughout their desert sojourning, he showed his presence with them in the pillars of "cloud" and "fire." Moreover, he supplied them miraculously and abundantly with water (cf. Ex 17:6; Nu 20:8–11).

C. Israel in the Desert (78:17–31)

17–31 In response to the evidences of God, the people rebelled. They refused to believe, even in the face of the evidence. They were skeptical about God's ability to provide food in the desert. He demonstrated his powers by giving Israel manna and meat, but the unbelieving generation was condemned because the people were not overwhelmed by God's ability to deliver. They were not concerned with God or the wonders of God but were fleshly in their basic orientation to life. They "craved" food and died in their lust. True faith looks beyond the gifts to the giver, the Lord of Glory.

D. God's Mercy on a Rebellious People (78:32–39)

32–33 The people had seen God's "wonders" (GK 7098), but "they did not believe" in them. They rejected the very evidences that should have led them to faith in God. Consequently he abandoned the generation of the desert to "futility" and "terror." Life became nothing but "futility" (GK 2039; cf. Ecc 1:2), filled with sudden catastrophes. At the end the desert generation passed away (Nu 14:22–23).

34–35 God punished the people for their sins. They did respond on that particular occasion with all the evidences of true repentance by returning to him "eagerly." They wanted to get the discipline over with and return to normal life. In their return they made mention of God as "their Rock" and of "God

Most High . . . their Redeemer." All too often their sole purpose of recognizing God is to derive benefits such as victory in war and provision of food.

36–39 The people's repentance was true contrition but was intentionally deceptive. They may have worshiped the Lord outwardly but not with their hearts. They "would flatter" (GK 7331) him, thinking they could lure God into their schemes, but every prayer was deceptive. In "their hearts" they had determined not to be loyal to the Lord. But the Lord was true to his character; his compassion found expression in his forgiveness of their sins, in his forbearance with their stubborn spirits, and in his empathy with the human condition, so that his full anger did not destroy them. He remembered that they were, after all, "flesh" (GK 1414; i.e., mortal).

E. Israel in Egypt and in the Wilderness (78:40–55)

40–41 Israel's history of frequent rebellion stands in stark contrast to all the evidences of God's goodness. Humanly speaking, the Israelites as his children caused great grief to their heavenly Father in the desert. They "rebelled," tried his patience, and "vexed the Holy One of Israel."

42–51 The Lord had shown his fatherly care in Egypt and in the desert. In turn he had expected his people to sanctify his holy name by remembering him (Ex 3:15). But "they did not remember" all the evidences of his power, such as his turning the rivers of Egypt into blood and troubling the Egyptians with the ten plagues. Death in Egypt was an expression of God's "hot anger, his wrath, indignation and hostility." He was sovereign over Egypt's adversities by sending the messengers ("angels") of adversity, resulting in the death of the "firstborn" of all the males in Egypt.

52–55 Instead of adversity, God brought great blessings to his own people like "a flock"/"like sheep," a metaphor for Israel. He drowned the Egyptians in the Red Sea, while guiding his own people so they needed not be afraid; he brought them safely to the Promised Land; he drove out the Canaanites; and he gave each tribe its allotted patrimony.

F. Judgment on a Rebellious Generation (78:56–64)

56–58 The psalmist returns to the refrain of Israel's rebelliousness. The people in the land were essentially no different from the desert generation. Though the Lord had given them his statutes to live by, they provoked him with cultic "high places" and with "idols." In this they were unreliable, like a "faulty bow" that springs wrongly when needed.

59–64 Because of Israel's treachery, God removed his glorious presence from them. Ephraim could have been a leader among the tribes but turned out to be self-serving, bellicose, and idolatrous. God's anger came to concrete expression in the destruction of the tabernacle at Shiloh and in the capture of the ark (1Sa 4–5), symbolic of his might and "his splendor." Young men and priests were killed in battle, leaving behind unmarried maidens and widows, who were too greatly afflicted to "weep" over the dead.

III. Good News: God Has Chosen David (78:65–72)

65–72 While the Philistines prevailed over Israel, it seemed as if the Lord was asleep. The renewal of his acts of mercy to Israel was so overwhelming that the psalmist likens God to a "hero" (GK 1475; NIV, "man"), who feels himself more heroic when intoxicated with wine. In his valor he overcame the enemies of his people and gave the honor of victory and peace to David, from the tribe of Judah, thus rejecting the supremacy of Ephraim. The favored position of Judah was further symbolized by the choice of Jerusalem (Mount Zion) as the place for his temple.

The temple on earth was "like the heights," which may denote the high mountains or the heavenly temple. God's presence on earth is connected with the Lord Jesus, who himself said that he is the temple of God (Jn 2:19–21). David was taken from shepherding the flocks to take care of God's flock, "his inheritance." He proved himself wise by being upright in the midst of a stubborn people. He guided their national, political, and religious interests with "understanding." The promises pertaining to God's kingdom, messianic rule, and presence find their focus in Jesus the Messiah. All who receive him as the Messiah of God find in him the "bread . . .

from heaven" (Jn 6:41), the water of life (Jn 7:37–39), and life everlasting (Jn 11:25–26)!

Psalm 79: Lord, Remember the Sheep of Your Pasture

This lament was written probably on the occasion of Jerusalem's fall and the subsequent exile of Judah. Its structure reflects the characteristic elements of the *national lament*: questions, prayer, and hope.

I. Lament (79:1–4)

1–2 The lament focuses on the grief caused by the enemies. They showed no respect for the land and people of God or for the city of God. The psalmist laments over the unburied bodies of those who fell by the ravages of warfare. Because their relatives were too busy trying to survive the siege or were in exile, the dead were left to the wild animals and the birds of prey. The lack of burial was considered a terrible fate.

3–4 The enemies of Judah had no regard for God or for his people. Blood, i.e., human lives, was like run-off water. Those who were left had no reason to rejoice. They carried the reproach and scorn of their oppressors.

II. Question (79:5)

5 The heart-rending "how long" is a cry from a wounded people. Having received a severe blow, they ask not why but how long they must suffer. God is angry because of their sins. His jealous anger is so great that it is likened to a consuming fire.

III. Prayer for Vindication and Forgiveness (79:6–9)

6–7 Justice must be done because of the conduct of the heathen. They had no regard for God, nor did they call on his name (cf. 75:1). Instead they desecrated and destroyed God's land and people.

8 The remnant in exile believed that they had been spared for a reason. The prayer "Do not hold against us" is a humble petition for forgiveness, a request for God to blot out any memory of the accumulation of iniquities of the past generations. They were in "desperate need" of God's mercy, which brings reconciliation, forgiveness, and restoration.

9 Hope looks to God as "our Savior" (GK 3829). He is the Deliverer of his children, but

they have to submit themselves to him as they await his salvation. They appeal to his glorious name, which he has revealed to Israel. The idea of redemption means deliverance from the enemies and forgiveness for sins "for [his] name's sake" (i.e., by his grace). The sins are not only those of their ancestors but also those of the present generation.

IV. Question (79:10a)

10a The psalmist renews his reflection on the reproach and the scorn caused by the heathen nations. In view of their atrocities and the glory of the Lord's name, why should their taunt be tolerated any longer?

V. Prayer for Vindication and Restoration (79:10b–13)

10b The prayer of the godly is that the Lord will deal justly and speedily with those who have disgraced his people. Those who have witnessed the spilling of the innocent blood around Jerusalem (v.3) are not filled with hatred and bitterness. Rather, their words express the cry of a needy and suffering people who look toward their heavenly Father for deliverance.

11 At the time of the Exodus, God had seen the affliction of his people and had heard their groanings (Ex 2:24; 6:5). The people in exile, feeling like prisoners "condemned to die," are not unlike those in Egypt. They too groan for the moment of their deliverance and pray that the Lord will rise up and deliver them with his strong "arm."

12–13 The sevenfold restitution expresses a concern for full justice. The judgment must be equal to the severity of the reproach of God's name! The psalm concludes on a note of hope, as God's people are still "the sheep" of his pasture. They anticipate praising God for their redemption from the oppressors and for their forgiveness.

Psalm 80: Make Your Face to Shine on Us

The psalm is a *community lament*. Its origin may be associated with the last days of Israel (c. 732–722 B.C.).

I. Prayer for Deliverance (80:1–3)

1–2 God's judgment on Israel ("Joseph") is not because he has not shown his regard or love for them. He cared for the northern tribes as much as he cared for the southern tribes. He is the Great Shepherd who dwelt in the midst of his people. The psalmist prays that the Lord may open his ear and "shine forth" in his glorious array as the Divine Warrior. The Lord has the "might" to show his "salvation" (GK 3802; NIV, "save") to his people.

3 God's people are the objects of his wrath. Only he can "restore" (GK 8740) them by forgiveness of their sins, by renewal of the covenant, and by driving out the enemies. When the face of the Lord shines on his people, they are blessed with his presence and favor and will be "saved."

II. The Lord's Present Anger (80:4–7)

4–7 The "LORD God Almighty" (GK 7372; lit., "of hosts") can marshal all the hosts of heaven to the aid of his people. However, he can also use the hosts on earth to judge the nations, including Israel. God is angry with his people; though they pray for his grace and blessing, it is without avail. Instead, they suffer from oppression and ridicule. Their food and drink are nothing but "tears" in great abundance. Their enemies "mock" them. The godly ask how long the Lord's anger will linger, as they long for divine salvation.

III. The Lord's Past Mercy (80:8–14a)

8–11 Israel is frequently likened to a vine (cf. Isa 5:1–7; 27:2–6; et al.). The Lord brought them out of Egypt and into the land of Canaan. He cared for them like a vinedresser as he cleared the ground, planted the vine, and nurtured it. Israel occupied the land, subdued the people, and controlled the nations from the Euphrates ("the River") in the east and "the mighty cedars" of the Lebanon mountains in the north to the Mediterranean on the west. The people had enjoyed the full possession of the land during the days of David and Solomon (2Sa 8:3; 1Ki 4:21).

12–14a Though God had extended much care to Israel in fulfillment of his promises, he had permitted his vineyard to be taken over by "boars" and by wild creatures. The people pray that "God Almighty" may look again with kindness on his vine with his mighty acts of salvation and rule.

IV. Prayer for Deliverance (80:14b–19)

14b–19 Israel is like a "root." However, the people have become a useless vine. They perished by the "rebuke" of God's anger. They pray that the Lord will sustain them in their hour of need so that the renewal of his favor will lead to a new commitment for Israel. The ground of hope in restoration lies in "the man at your right hand," also called "the son of man." These allusions to the Davidic dynasty focus the hope of the godly in the continuity of God's redemptive purposes.

Psalm 81: If My People Would But Listen to Me

The psalm is associated with a feast appointed by the Lord. The feast is a part of a complex of festivals beginning with the New Year's festival on the first day of the seventh month (Tishri), followed by the Day of Atonement on the tenth day and the Feast of Tabernacles on the fifteenth. This psalm was an appropriate "invitation" to covenant renewal during the feast, when God's people reflected on all his acts in the past and on their hope for the future.

I. Festal Hymn (81:1–5)

1–5 In hymnic form the covenant community is called on to celebrate the festivals corporately. Together they sing joyously to the accompaniment of musical instruments. The "full moon" fell on the fifteenth of the lunar month and coincided in the seventh month with the Feast of Tabernacles. This festival was of the greatest import in the OT and was also known as "the feast" (here "our Feast"). Its purpose was to proclaim aloud the mighty acts of the Lord in the history of salvation, beginning with the Exodus. The Lord ordained his people to observe this Feast, together with the other festivals, as his "decree," "ordinance," and "statute."

II. Oracle of the Lord (81:6–16)

A. God's Past Care (81:6–7)

6–7 The Lord had freed Israel from the oppressive tasks in Egypt, where they had carried "baskets" with clay and bricks in various building projects (cf. Ex 1:11). Israel had groaned under the burdens and prayed for deliverance (Ex 2:23–24; 6:5), and the Lord had saved them. In addition, he had also spoken to them at Mount Sinai "out of a thundercloud" (cf.18:7–15; also Ex 19:18–19; 20:18). Without comment, the Lord reminds his people of the tragic incident at Meribah (Ex 17:1–7; Nu 20:1–13).

B. Exhortation to Listen (81:8–10)

8–10 The Lord expected his redeemed and consecrated people to conform to his likeness by listening to and obeying his commandments. Throughout the wilderness experiences he had supplied all their needs and had promised rich blessings for those who would respond wholeheartedly to him. The Lord is always ready to "fill" the needs of his people.

C. God's Judgment on Rebellious Israel (81:11–12)

11–12 Instead of loyalty to the Lord, born out of gratitude for their redemption and for the promises of the future, the Israelites continued in rebellion. They did not listen or submit to the Lord. Therefore God abandoned his own people. They were treated as "stubborn" children.

D. Exhortation to Listen (81:13)

13 The grace of God is so great that he cannot abandon his people completely. He again laments his people's obdurateness. Their problems can be resolved only by the direct intervention of the Lord. To this end he holds out the glorious future before them as a real possibility (vv.14–16).

E. God's Future Care (81:14–16)

14–16 The Lord is able to deliver his people. If they commit themselves to him, he will protect them and subjugate their "foes." His deliverance will be quick and lasting because his "hand" will press hard on their enemies and cause them to suffer punishment "forever." The Lord will richly supply the needs of his repentant people. He will lavish on them the best care ("the finest of wheat" and "honey from the rock").

Psalm 82: The Judgment of God in the Great Assembly

The psalm declares that all powers, real and imagined, are subject to God.

I. God's Judgment Over the Gods (82:1)

1 God is ready to judge, "presiding" (GK 2205) as the Great Judge. For Israel there is

no other God than the Lord. He embodies within himself all the epithets and powers attributed to pagan deities. There are three options for explaining "the great assembly" of the "gods." The gods are: (1) human judges who are condemned by the Great Judge for being unjust; (2) the principalities and the powers of other nations that oppress Israel; (3) pagan deities judged by God, who rule the darkness of the world.

II. Judicial Questioning (82:2)

2 God calls "the gods" of the nations to account, indicting them on two counts: they are unjust, and they are evil.

III. God's Expectations of Justice (82:3–4)

3–4 The Lord accuses the gods of irresponsibility to his just rule, for they do not show concern for justice. The gods of the nations have failed. Failure to observe God's decrees inevitably leads to his condemnation.

IV. God's Condemnation of Evil (82:5)

5 The "gods" stand condemned by their folly, moral darkness, and destruction of God's order. Their rule is nothing but "darkness," i.e., "evil." The "gods" further their own powers by destroying the "foundations of the earth," a metaphor for God's rule on earth. Even in pagan nations the Lord has established some order by common grace, and he holds the ungodly accountable for their reign of terror and self-aggrandizement at the expense of his order.

V. Judicial Sentence (82:6–7)

6–7 Though the gods were known as "the sons of the Most High" in Canaanite mythology, they cannot be! They do not reflect the concerns of God with justice, morality, and order. In this pretend trial the Lord declares the "gods" to be nothing more than "mortals," i.e., "mere men" (GK 132). Hence, God implicitly condemns all humans who adopt the pagan way of life.

VI. God's Judgment Over the Earth (82:8)

8 The godly respond by anticipating that one day the God who judged the nongods to extinction will advance his judgment on earth. Our Lord's prayer ("your kingdom come") is most appropriate whenever we experience injustice. The Lord alone is God; there is no other!

Psalm 83: A Lament Concerning the Presence of Evil

This psalm is a *national lament* in which the psalmist prays for the Lord's intervention against many enemies. This is the last psalm in the collection of psalms attributed to Asaph (50; 73–83).

I. Prayer for God's Action (83:1)

1 The psalmist addresses the only true God, who is none other than "the LORD," the "Most High" (v.18). With this in mind, he prays that God may act on behalf of his people.

II. Plottings of the Enemies (83:2–4)

2–4 The enemies "are astir" like armies preparing for an attack. They "rear their heads" as an expression of overt hostility and confidence. Their enmity is against God and his people, wanting nothing less than their total annihilation.

III. Greatness of the Opposition (83:5–8)

5 The psalmist rephrases the intent and the manner of the opposition. The nations are "against" the Lord himself and not just against God's people. They have made an "alliance" against him as an expression of solidarity.

6–8 The psalmist further specifies ten nations who "hate" the Lord: (1) Edomites (the descendants of Esau); (2) Ishmaelites (descendants of Ishmael; cf. Ge 16:15–16; 25:12–18); (3) Moabites (descendants of Lot); (4) "Hagrites" (a nomadic tribe living east of the Jordan); (5) the people of Gebal (uncertain); (6) Ammonites (also descendants of Lot); (7) Amalekites (a nomadic tribe descended from Esau; cf. Ex 17:8–13; Jdg 6:3); (8) Philistines; (9) the people of Tyre; (10) Assyrians (Israel's enemy to the north).

IV. Great Acts of God in Israel's History (83:9–12)

9–12 The future judgment of God is mirrored in the great acts of the Lord in Israel's history. The psalmist selects events from the period of the judges (cf. Jdg 4–8). The omission of the names of the judges indicates that the primary deliverer was the Lord himself!

The victory over the Midianites and their rulers was a reason for the Israelites to rejoice.

V. Shaming of the Enemies (83:13–16)

13–15 The psalmist likens the enemies' lot to that of "tumbleweed," "chaff," and "forest." The psalmist prays that the Lord will destroy their enemies as "fire" destroys forests and the vegetation on the mountains. He also prays that the Lord will confound the plotting of the wicked as by a "tempest" and "storm."

16 The confidence of the nations will be shaken by God's sovereign presence. The psalmist prays for the Lord to change their pride and boasting to "shame" (GK 7830). However, he shows a deep awareness of God's gracious nature as he opens a door to those among the nations who will seek the "name" of the Lord.

VI. Prayer for God's Action (83:17–18)

17–18 The psalmist trusts that the Lord will confound the wicked who scheme against him and the chosen people of God. He also prays that the nations may come to "know" the Lord as sovereign Ruler and as the covenant Lord. "Name" (GK 9005) signifies not only the benefits of forgiveness, grace, and mercy to those who love him but also his powerful acts of judgment.

Psalm 84: A Deep Longing for the Presence of God

This psalm contains a collage of diverse genres: hymn, prayer, lament, and a song of Zion. Its setting may reflect a festive procession to Jerusalem during one of the festivals.

The psalmist longs to be a doorkeeper in the house of the Lord, i.e., in the temple courts (84:10).

I. Longing for the Courts of the Lord Almighty (84:1–4)

1–4 The love for the "dwelling place" (GK 5438) of the Lord is foremost in the heart of the psalmist as he reflects on the temple proper as the place of God's symbolic presence, together with "the courts," where the worshipers and pilgrims assembled. He physically longs for the experience of God's presence. His total attention is on the "LORD Almighty," the Great King, who is the "living God."

Reflecting on the temple courts, the psalmist pictures the birds that make their nests in the temple eaves. The common birds have their nests and raise their young close to the "altar" of the Lord Almighty. The thought of these lowly birds in such a glorious place overwhelms the psalmist, who expresses his awe in the form of a blessing. As God's blessing was not limited to the temple courts, the blessing on those "who dwell" (GK 3782) in the house of the Lord may well be extended to all who do the will of God.

II. The Blessing on the Pilgrims (84:5–7)

5–7 The psalmist blesses all who have put their confidence ("strength") in the Lord. They trust the Lord for refuge, especially in times of need. The second part of the description is far from clear; as the NIV interprets it, it suggests a pilgrimage to Jerusalem.

The blessedness of God's presence and help finds expression in the processional imagery of a road, a desert, and the abundance of water as the people of God pass from adversity (exile) to the blessedness of his presence in "Zion" (v.7). Faith in God is the ultimate goal, transforming weak people into those who "go from strength to strength" and the Valley of Baca into springs and pools (both images of God's blessings).

III. Prayer for God's Blessing on the King (84:8–9)

8–9 The psalmist turns to the Lord in a prayer for the king ("your anointed one"; GK 5431), who is the "shield" (i.e., protector) of his people. Since he too is dependent on the Lord's blessing, the psalmist prays that the Great King may extend his goodness to the earthly ruler.

IV. Hymnic Praise (84:10–11)

10–11 The psalmist esteems one day of fellowship with God in service as a temple guard a thousand times better than receiving public recognition and wealth. The "sun" is symbolic of the era of restoration, often referred to by the words "light" and "brightness." "Favor" (GK 8354) is God's expression of grace by which he draws near to his own and shares his "glory" with them. As a result of this fellowship, he will shower all his "goodness" on those who walk in a "blameless" manner.

V. The Blessing of God (84:12)

12 The psalm ends by encouraging everybody to seek the Lord by putting their trust in him. "Blessed" (GK 897) are those who submit to the Great King, who grants his blessings to those who find their refuge in him.

Psalm 85: Surely His Salvation Is Near!

In the context of some national catastrophe, the people of God cry out for deliverance from adversity. This psalm is a *national lament.*

I. Proclamation of God's Past Acts (85:1–3)

1–3 Restoration for Israel resulted from God's sovereign acts of grace: removal of wrath and his forgiving of sin. The "wrath" and "fierce anger" of God occurred when his holiness had been offended by the sin and transgression of his people. They had been dispossessed of their lands, bereft of children and loved ones, and despoiled by the enemies. But the Lord graciously forgave the sins of his people. His forgiveness implies the removal of both sins and the consequences of sin. God exchanged his wrath for his "favor" (GK 8354). The "land" is his land and the people his people!

II. Laments and Prayer for Restoration (85:4–7)

4–7 The psalmist laments the recent problems that have deprived God's people of enjoyment of God's favor. He interprets them as expressions of God's "displeasure" (GK 4088). The lamenting community prays that the Lord will "restore" (GK 8740) them by extending the benefits of his "unfailing love" (GK 2876)—which is synonymous with the enjoyment of God's "salvation" (GK 3829), because salvation extends the benefits of God to his people: victory, peace, and enjoyment of this life and the life to come.

III. Anticipation of God's Salvation (85:8)

8 In submission to the Lord, the people await his response. They receive assurance that the Lord "promises peace" and will thus grant them relief from their grief. After all, they are "his people, his saints."

IV. The Oracle of Hope (85:9–13)

9 God's "salvation" is "near," but only those "who fear him" in the spirit of wisdom will inherit his benefits. The fullness of salvation brings his people "glory" (GK 3883), as they share in the benefits of God's victory. God shares his glory with his own.

10–11 God alone can send "love" (GK 2876), "faithfulness" (GK 622), "righteousness" (GK 7406), and "peace" (GK 8934) as his messengers to accomplish his purpose. The four divine attributes are portrayed here as meeting and kissing one another. The Lord is the source of unfailing love. His love is faithful and his faithfulness is expressed in love. The new era establishes his "righteousness," expressive of the evident kingship of God in and over his people. The extent of these benefits is further guaranteed by the contrastive complementary usage of "earth" and "heaven" in the sense of "everything."

12 The promises of God extend to the enjoyment of the land. His blessings result in the enjoyment of "what is good," i.e., the "harvest."

13 The psalm began by reflecting on God's past acts of salvation, and it ends by looking forward to final redemption. "Righteousness" (GK 7406), personified as a messenger, denotes God's final victory and salvation. Those who fear him will enjoy the benefits of his kingdom of "righteousness."

Psalm 86: Give Me a Sign of Your Goodness

This is the only psalm associated with David in the third book of Psalms. It is an *individual lament* psalm. His plea for mercy is based on his own needs, the lordship of God, his unique status as God's servant, and the nature of God.

I. Prayer for Mercy and Confession of Confidence (86:1–5)

1–5 In his confession of need, David humbles himself in the presence of his God as a needy creature. He prays that the Lord will "hear" and answer his prayer by guarding his "life" (lit., "soul"; GK 5883, a word signifying the whole person). Hope begins with submitting oneself fully to the protection of God and is demonstrated by absolute loyalty to him. The psalmist trusts in the Lord and waits for his gracious response. He alone can transform adversity into "joy." The Lord has promised to extend his benefits to all who call on him: his goodness, forgiveness, and love.

II. Prayer for Mercy (86:6–7)

6–7 The prayer is for God's "mercy." The phrase "cry for mercy" (GK 7754 & 9384) is a prayer from a needy heart. The prayer exudes confidence in the Lord's help in the "day of my trouble."

III. Hymn of Confidence in the Lord (86:8–10)

8–10 The anticipation for God's favorable response leads into a hymnic expression of the greatness of God. There is no other God like the Lord, whose "deeds" are "marvelous" and "great." David affirms his confidence in his God by proclaiming his great acts, by affirming his wholehearted commitment to the God who "alone" can do these wonders, and by expressing his belief that all people will one day submit themselves to the Lord and join with Israel in worshiping the Lord. They too will "bring glory" by bringing him their offerings and by obeying him. The Lord alone is God, and the gods of the nations are worthless.

IV. Anticipation of Deliverance (86:11–13)

11–12 In the confidence that the Lord will have mercy on him, the psalmist looks beyond the present troubles to his own renewed commitment to the Lord. In his desire to walk wisely in the presence of God, he asks for guidance and a new heart—an "undivided heart." He longs for inner renewal so that he may walk "in your truth" and "fear your name" (i.e., gain a heart of wisdom; cf. Pr 1:7). This renewed commitment finds expression in words of praise to the Lord and glorious acts of obeisance to him.

13 The affirmation of confidence presupposes that this great God will and does deliver those who call on him. He remains true to his nature (vv.5, 13, 15), i.e., his "love" (GK 2876). Adversity is like "the depths of the grave" (or better "of Sheol"). Though "Sheol" (GK 8619) may denote the realm of the dead, it also connotes the experience of adversity that ultimately may be likened to death.

V. Prayer for Deliverance (86:14–17)

14–15 The "arrogant" and "ruthless men" may be a personification of adversity. In this world of alienation, the godly are often the object of persecution. Confidence is in the covenant God, who is known by his qualities of compassion, grace, patience, love, and fidelity.

16–17 The psalmist repeats the prayer for divine "mercy" (cf. vv.3, 6). He looks as a "servant" for the "strength" of the Lord. He is "the son of your maidservant" (or "your faithful son"; see NIV note). The "sign" (GK 253) of God's goodness is some evidence of the Lord's care for his servant. He has cast himself on the promises of God, on his past great and marvelous acts, and on his attributes. He prays that his faith will triumph and that the enemies of God may witness the evidences of the Lord's fidelity so as to shame them.

Psalm 87: Glorious Things of Thee Are Spoken

As rich as the theology of this psalm is, its exegesis has raised many issues. It is usually associated with the Zion Psalms (48; 76; 84; 122; 137).

I. Hymn in Praise of Zion (87:1–2)

1–2 Zion, the city of God, symbolizes God's kingdom presence. He has established it on earth (cf. Heb 11:10) by entering into a covenant relationship with Israel (cf. 114:2). Jerusalem was located on a mountain, often designated as Mount Zion or God's "holy mountain" (99:9; cf. 3:4; 15:1; Isa 11:9; 65:25). The special quality of Jerusalem did not reside in her natural holiness but in the "love" of God. The phrase "the gates of Zion" is a poetic reference to "Zion." "Dwellings of Jacob" may denote the Israelite cities that have not been chosen as *the* religious center.

II. God's Register in Heaven (87:3–6)

3–6 The psalmist suddenly changes his focus from the earthly Jerusalem to the glorious future of the "city of God," about which he is ecstatic. The Lord himself has revealed the glories of Zion through his prophets. Among the nations he records are Rahab (meaning Egypt), Babylon, Philistia, Tyre, and Cush. These nations represent the various powers that dominated much of Israel's history as oppressors, troublers, and enticers. Regardless of the past, individuals from these nations may still participate in God's "city." The participants are "those who acknowledge" (GK 3359) him, i.e., who worship the Lord as the living God. On this confession their names are recorded as having been "born in Zion." Thus Zion here goes beyond the city on earth to the city of God, where all the names of the godly are recorded.

III. The Joy in Zion (87:7)

7 The psalmist concludes with a scene on earth. The crowds in the earthly Jerusalem are celebrating the glory of Zion: "All my fountains are found in you." Zion is associated with "the fountain of life," of "salvation" (Isa 12:3), "a river whose streams make glad the city of God" (Ps 46:4).

Psalm 88: A Prayer in the Darkness of Despair

This is an *individual lament* psalm in which the psalmist knows nothing but sorrow. However, even in the darkness of his grief, he turns to the Lord for deliverance.

I. Prayer for Help (88:1–2)

1–2 In the midst of tribulation, faith holds on to the God who has promised to deliver. In his suffering and perpetual anguish, the psalmist prays day and night with the hope that the Lord will respond to his prayer. This prayer is a deeply piercing shout for divine help.

II. The Experience of Dying in Life (88:3–5)

3–5 The psalmist's adversity has been with him for so long that he is satiated, but not with God's blessings. He is so deeply galled that he feels his life ebbing away from him. He exists like a shade, "a man without strength." He further compares himself with an unknown soldier who together with "the slain" was buried in a mass grave. He experiences the absence of God, like those who are dead. He does not deny God's remembrance and care but is speaking the way adversity often appears to people.

III. It Is the Lord's Doing (88:6–9a)

6–9a The lament turns into an accusation. He feels like a dead man, having been placed by God in "the lowest pit" and in "the darkest depths." God has treated him like the wicked. Therefore he indicts God with oppressing him unjustly and with removing even his "closest friends." God's "wrath" has overpowered him like "waves," leaving him utterly helpless. His situation is like that of Job.

IV. Prayer for Help (88:9b–12)

9b–12 In his "grief" the psalmist continually entreats the Lord. The Lord had shown to his people his "wonders," "faithfulness," "love," and "righteous deeds"; the psalmist, however, feels far removed from God's righteous deeds. If he were to go to "the grave," he would be unable to praise God. He speaks about death as a place where there is nothing but "darkness." He longs for the Lord's full deliverance and his covenant mercy.

V. It Is the Lord's Doing (88:13–14)

13–14 In his torment the psalmist has called on the Lord "every day" (v.9), and he keeps on bringing his petitions before him "in the morning." His persistent prayers mark him as a godly man who believes in the Lord's righteousness and fidelity, but he still feels rejected. The depth of despair is most acutely experienced by those who have tasted the goodness of God and the closeness of communion with him.

VI. The Experience of Dying in Life (88:15–18)

15–18 The lament concludes by tying together the major themes. (1) The psalmist has suffered for a long time. (2) He is completely engulfed by adversity and sees no way of escape. (3) He is exhausted to the point of "despair" (GK 7041) because of his inability to cope with the Lord's "terrors." (4) He knows that the Lord is sovereign even in calamity. (5) He is abandoned to himself and to his God. He prays for deliverance all alone, separated even from his "closest friend." Though the psalm ends on a lament, faith triumphs, because in everything the psalmist has learned to look to "the God who saves" (v.1).

Psalm 89: Will You Reject Us Forever?

There is little agreement on the type or genre of the psalm.

I. A Hymn of the Lord's Kingship (89:1–18)

A. Individual Praise of the Lord's Kingship (89:1–2)

1–2 The theme of this portion of the psalm is in praise of the Lord's "great love" (GK 2876). That love is constant, as promised and confirmed in the covenant. His commitment to David is guaranteed by God's rule over "heaven." The Lord has established his "faithfulness" to David far from the changes of this earthly scene.

B. the Lord's Fidelity to David (89:3–4)

3–4 The Lord is committed to David, his "chosen one" and "servant." "Chosen one" (GK 1040) emphasizes the special "covenant" (GK 1382) relationship as the king is elected by the Lord himself to serve in his behalf. "Servant" (GK 6269) emphasizes the special role of being the Lord's representative to the people. Even when the party with whom the Lord makes his covenant breaks it, its binding nature obligates the Lord to fulfill its terms. He himself will "establish" (GK 3922) the rule of Davidic dynasty.

C. Heavenly Praise of the Lord's Kingship (89:5–8)

5–8 The Lord has established his love in heaven. Rather than being jealous of David's special privileges on earth, heaven rejoices in God's kingship. His rule is unquestioned by "the holy ones" (the "heavenly beings"). They praise God for his "wonders" and "faithfulness." He is "greatly feared," "awesome," and "mighty." The heavenly hosts serve him willingly as "God Almighty." They constantly stand in awe of the splendor of the Lord.

D. The Lord's Universal Rule (89:9–13)

9–13 The Lord's rule is also found on earth, extending even to the wild and foaming sea. Rahab, possibly identical with Leviathan (cf. 74:14; 104:26), represents any overt expression of hostility, such as that of the Egyptians (cf. 87:4; Isa 30:7; Eze 29:3; 32:2), who were defeated at the Red Sea (cf. Ex 14:15). The Lord's sovereignty over the earth was established when he created everything. Mounts Tabor and Hermon join together with all creation in praising the Lord. All creation witnesses to his dominion, strength, and victorious rule, symbolized by "your arm" and "your hand."

E. The Lord's Fidelity and Congregational Praise (89:14–18)

14 The Lord's rule is full of "righteousness and justice." More than that, he is also full of "love and faithfulness."

15–18 The subjects of his rule are "blessed" under his administration, joining with creation in praise of their Redeemer. Unlike creation God's people benefit from his personal presence, "righteousness," exaltation, and protection. The true subjects have learned to exult in his name, rely on his favor, acknowledge his sovereignty, and respond to his holy presence.

II. The Covenant With David (89:19–37)

These verses share words and thoughts with 2Sa 7:4–17. The covenant with David was a further development of the Abrahamic and Sinaitic covenants.

A. Word of Promise (89:19–29)

1. Choice of David (89:19–23)

19–20 The Lord revealed through the prophet Nathan "in a vision" (cf. 2Sa 7:4) that he had chosen David to be his "servant . . . anointed" with "sacred oil." The Lord "exalted" him, bestowing on him "strength."

21–23 The real source of David's power and authority lay in the Lord's presence and purpose. The mighty "hand" and "arm" of the Lord strengthened David in all his exploits. No one could say that David was strong by himself. The goal of the Lord's succor was to extend his dominion over earth. Since his purposes stand, no power on earth can thwart him.

2. Promise of universal reign (89:24–25)

24–25 The Lord himself will increase David's regime and cause it to flourish. His love and fidelity will surround David. In his name all the Lord's promises toward David will be fulfilled. The glory bestowed on David will ultimately be recognized by all nations.

3. Promise of messianic reign (89:26–27)

26–27 The messianic ruler will be treated as a son rather than as a vassal or servant. In this relationship he will more fully experience God's power of deliverance as "the Rock my Savior." The primacy over the nations is given to the Davidic king. He is recognized as "my firstborn," even as Israel is the "firstborn" of the Lord (Ex 4:22; cf. Jer 31:9; Rev 1:5). Furthermore, he is "the most exalted" king among the nations.

4. Choice of descendants (89:28–29)

28–29 The Lord renews his commitment to David in affirming his "covenant" of "love" and "faithfulness," which extend "forever," as long "as the heavens endure."

B. Word of Warning (89:30–37)

In assuring the Davidic dynasty glory, divine support, and continuity, these promises are conditional. The responsibility lies on each king to fulfill his role as a representative of God's rule on earth.

1. Warning (89:30–32)

30–32 The Lord expects the Davidic king to be loyal to him by keeping his law, statutes, decrees, and commands. "Sin" and "iniquity" are expressions of rebellion against the Lord. The penalty for disobedience was severe: The Lord would not withhold "the rod" (GK 8657), a symbol of authority and an instrument of inflicting wounds.

2. Affirmation of love (89:33–34)

33–34 Yet the "love" (GK 2876) of God outweighs his judgment. Though he may discipline severely, he will still extend his love to David's offspring. The Lord will never "violate" his own covenant; what he has promised by oath stands.

3. Affirmation of promised word (89:35–37)

35–37 The emphasis here lies on the fidelity of God. His commitment to David's place in the history of redemption is such that it is on a par with the heavens (cf. v.29). The covenant with David is so important to the Lord that he has sworn by himself that David's lineage will be seated on the "throne" (GK 4058), symbol of divinely granted authority over the earth.

III. A Lament (89:38–51)

A. Complaints Against God (89:38–45)

38–40 The God who decreed the Davidic covenant (v.19) has "rejected" (GK 2396) his "anointed one" (GK 5431). In his anger he seems completely unconcerned with his covenant. The acts of casting the crown into the dust, spurning the covenant, and destroying the fortifications are usually associated with the activities of Israel's enemies. Here, however, God is the perpetrator of the hostile acts. The Lord has abandoned his people and rejected the covenant of "love," i.e., the covenant with David.

41–45 Instead of coming to the support of his own people, the Lord has given victory to Israel's enemies because the Lord raised their "right hand." With Israel's defeat David's crown and honor are cast to the ground. It appears that the Lord has flouted every promise made to David, including the perpetuity of his dynasty. The image of the "mantle of shame" denotes the disgrace of the Davidic dynasty.

B. Questions and Petitions (89:46–51)

46–51 The questions here bring out the intensity of the psalmist's agony. If the Lord continues to hide his face and to maintain his "wrath," faith and hope may yield to despair. Hence the psalmist prays to the Lord to remember that his people are human. The phrase "how fleeting is my life" underscores that need, as the psalmist pleads with the Lord to renew his "love" during his lifetime. Instead of enjoying God's acts of his "former great love" sworn to David, the people are perishing and the "anointed one" is mocked. The psalm ends on a note of disorientation, a paradox with the opening affirmation of God's love. What a shocking contrast!

IV. Doxology (89:52)

52 The third book of Psalms concludes with a doxology. In spite of the concluding questions raised by Ps 89, the doxology affirms the necessity to praise the Lord as an appropriate response to all circumstances in life.

Book IV: Psalms 90–106

Psalm 90: Teach Us to Number Our Days

This psalm is a reflection on the transience of life. The superscription attributes it to Moses.

I. The Lord Is God (90:1–2)

1 The psalm begins with and ends on an affirmation of God as "the Lord" (GK 151), the Creator and Ruler of the universe. The Lord himself has been Israel's "dwelling place" (GK 5061), the oasis of refreshment and encampment for his people for many generations. The metaphor is related to the imagery of God's protection.

2 The psalmist expresses the greatness of God's fatherly care in the imagery of birth. It is not entirely clear who is giving birth: God or the earth? More likely it is the earth giving rise to mountains, but not apart from the creative role of the Lord in the process of the formation of the earth (cf. Ge 1:11, 20). The confessional statement "you are God" affirms both God's kingship over creation and his otherness.

II. God's Authority Over Humanity (90:3–6)

3–6 In comparison with God, humanity is nothing but "dust." In comparison with God's eternity, a person's brief span of life is likened to "new grass," which shoots up only shortly to be parched. "Morning" and "evening" depict the brevity of life. Even if someone were to live to a thousand years, in God's reckoning it would be but "a day" or, even less, "a watch in the night" (i.e., a four-hour period). We may look at our fellow beings as strong; but as far as God is concerned, they may be swept away as by the waters of the flood.

III. God's Wrath (90:7–10)

7–10 The psalmist explains that human frailty and anxiety are an expression of God's judgment. The Lord's "anger" and "wrath" create a barrier between the Lord and us, as we become more aware of our "iniquities" and "secret sins." "Iniquity" (GK 6411) denotes our awareness of sin, and "secret" (GK 6623) sins are those hidden from the public eye but seen by the Lord. Since the Lord sees every sin we commit, his wrath is always there. Our lives are therefore marked by brevity and by vexation.

IV. Proper Response to God's Wrath (90:11–12)

11–12 Human beings generally do not pay attention to the divine law of sin and retribution. The question "Who knows. . . ?" is to be understood as a strong affirmation: "Nobody knows. . . !" But those who fear the Lord are fully aware of the fierceness of his anger. To "number" (GK 4948) one's days is an act of recognition of the vast difference between God and finite humanity. The wise reckon continually with God's existence and human accountability. They pray for "a heart of wisdom" and are receptive to divine revelation/instruction: "teach us." Wisdom begins and ends with the fear of the Lord (cf. 111:10; Pr 1:7).

V. Prayer for God's Mercy (90:13–16)

13–16 The psalmist's prayer consists of three elements. (1) He prays for restoration to God's favor. Though they are suffering, they are still his "servants," and they are waiting patiently for a new beginning (cf. "in the morning") of the "compassion" of their Master. The favor of God is particularly known as his "unfailing love" (GK 2876). (2) The psalmist prays that the Lord will restore the joy of his people's salvation. They have sung and will continue to sing of God's "deeds," longing for a renewed demonstration of them. (3) God's people long for the continuity of divine blessings rather than an occasional evidence of his love.

VI. May the Lord Be Our God (90:17)

17 In conclusion the psalmist prays that God's "favor" may rest on his people and "establish" (GK 3922) them as having value. The Lord's acceptance of his own assures a certain permanence of their work. Life under the sun may be vain; those under God's judgment can accomplish no ultimate good. But frail and sinful as human beings are, the love of God can transform what is weak to his own glory.

Psalm 91: In the Shelter of the Most High

Psalm 91 contains both a *wisdom psalm* (vv.1–13) and a *divine oracle* (vv.14–16).

I. Invitation to the Protection of God (91:1–2)

1–2 The blessings of godliness and the pursuit of wisdom are for all who seek God as their highest good in life. To this end the psalmist employs several names for God: "Most High" (GK 6609), "the Almighty" (GK 8724), "the LORD" (GK 3378), and "my God" (GK 466). These names evoke confidence in the power of the Creator God and in the endearing love of the covenant Lord.

The description of God's protection contained in this psalm is couched in metaphorical language. "Shelter" and "shadow" suggest the imagery of a mother bird under whose wings baby birds find safety. "Refuge" and "fortress" suggest a military installation. Thus, those who trust in the Lord enjoy his hospitality and protection.

II. Forms of Protection (91:3–8)

3–4 The Lord protects his people from any adversity by evil people, likened to "the fowler's snare" and "the deadly pestilence." He protects them as with feathers (cf. "his wings"). The "shield" and "rampart" develop the imagery of "refuge" and "fortress." The Lord's care is both tender and sufficient because he is faithful to his people.

5–7 The protection of God extends to both day and night. He gives security from all natural and supernatural causes of "fear." Afflictions come on the wicked as just expressions of God's provocation, but those who fear him need not be afraid of the "arrow" that brings diseases. There is no limit to his protection because he has full authority over all things that happen on earth. The greatness of God's protection is further amplified by the ratio of "a thousand" or even "ten thousand" to one.

8 Seeing God's salvation with the eye of faith further encourages the godly, whom the Lord has promised to protect and bless. The godly will witness the justice and fidelity of the Lord as well as the punishment of the wicked.

III. Invitation to the Protection of God (91:9–10)

9–10 The psalmist's personal experience encourages people to embrace the way of wisdom by making "the Most High" one's "dwelling" (GK 5061). In him they find "refuge," and they can be confident that whatever happens on earth is with his knowledge. Nothing happens outside his will, whether "harm" or "disaster."

IV. Forms of Protection (91:11–13)

11–13 The Lord charges "his angels" with the protection of the godly, wherever they may be. They have been charged with lifting the godly out of danger and delivering them. The Lord may permit many things to happen to his children, but they know that no power is outside God's control.

V. The Oracle of Salvation (91:14–16)

14–16 The Lord announces his salvation oracle to all who "love" him and "acknowledge" (GK 3359) his name. "Love" (GK 3137) signifies a deep longing or desire for the Lord. The fullness of his redemption becomes real in those who long for it. The relationship finds expression in communion, in answered prayers, and in the rewards due to wise living. The Lord assures his own that they will enjoy themselves in this life and in the life to come. They will see his "salvation" (GK 3802).

Psalm 92: In Praise of the Lord

Psalm 92 embodies a *hymn* (vv.1–3) and an individual thanksgiving (vv.4–15).

I. Hymn in Praise of the Most High (92:1–3)

1–3 "Praise," "make music," and "proclaim" all accent the place of praise as an external response to the acts of God. The Lord expects his people to respond in exclamation of his "name" (GK 9005) with which all of his beneficent acts are associated. As always, the occasion for praise is the evidence of the Lord's "love" (GK 2876) and "faithfulness" (GK 575). As the priests and Levites prepared the morning and evening sacrifice (cf. Ex 29:39–41), the Levitical singers led God's people in worship, using a "ten-stringed" instrument, a "harp," and a "lyre."

II. Hymn of Thanksgiving (92:4–14)
A. Joy in God's Works (92:4–5)

4–5 The acts of God must not be separated from his "love" and "faithfulness," because his "deeds" are expressive of his inner nature. The "deeds" are his mighty acts of deliverance. He abases the wicked and exalts the righteous.

B. Judgment on Folly and Exaltation (92:6–8)

6–8 There are two responses to God's works in redemptive history. The wicked respond like wild animals (the word "senseless" [GK 1280] is expressive of animal-like behavior). They begin and end with themselves, with no respect for God. Even when they increase in power and prestige, they are nothing but grass, which quickly perishes in the heat.

In contrast, the psalmist leads the people of God in a response of faith. "Exalted" (GK 5294) connotes the Lord's authority as the supreme Judge. Because the Lord rules and judges, the psalmist sings praise to him for bringing down the wicked and for sharing his exalted glory with his saints.

C. Judgment and Exaltation (92:9–11)

9–10 The Lord's exaltation will vindicate his people, removing completely and suddenly any opposition to his sovereignty. In contrast to his judgment on evildoers, the Lord bestows his favor on the godly. "Exalted" (GK 8123) expresses how God's people are rewarded richly by the supreme Judge. It is uncertain what kind of an animal the "wild ox" is, but its power and ferocity are proverbial. The imagery of "horn" evokes the metaphor of "oil," as oil was poured from a horn (cf. 1Sa 16:13).

11 God's justice in life is one aspect of the hope of the godly. Another aspect is the complete cessation of evil. Evil and God cannot coexist. In the affirmation of God's past acts lies hope for a greater future!

D. The Prosperity of the Righteous (92:12–14)

12–14 The wicked are easily swept away whereas the "righteous" are likened to a "palm tree" and to "a cedar of Lebanon." Both symbolize strength, longevity, and desirability. The representation of trees growing and bearing fruit "in the courts" of the Lord suggests the closeness of the righteous to their God. Whereas the wicked perish prematurely, the godly rejoice in the promise that the Lord's favor rests on them even in old age.

III. Praise of the Lord (92:15)

15 The godly "proclaim" in hymns of praise and thanksgiving the mighty deeds of the "upright" Lord. They exclaim that he is their "Rock" (GK 7446), on whom they rely for sustenance and stability. He does not disappoint his children, because "there is no wickedness in him."

Psalm 93: The Lord Reigns Gloriously

This psalm belongs to a group of psalms (47; 93–100) that affirm the Lord's rule over the earth.

I. The Lord's Glorious Kingship (93:1a–b)

1a–b God's reign is evident in his creation. His rule is visible, as his glorious mantle spreads out all over his kingdom. His works reveal the nature of the Great King: his glory and strength.

II. The Lord's Kingship on Earth (93:1c–2)

1c–2 The Lord established his kingship on earth when he created the "world." The nations may rage against his rule, but it will not fall. The Lord is "from all eternity."

III. The Lord's Kingship Over the Seas (93:3–4)

3–4 The "seas" is a metaphor of the nations (cf. Ps 89:9–10). Though the waters rise up and "pound" with great force, the Lord is "mightier." He has also established his kingship over the seas.

IV. The Lord's Glorious Kingship in Jerusalem (93:5)

5 God's "statutes" are symbolic of the covenant relationship, as they testify to the people of Israel of the revelation entrusted to them. God's glory radiates throughout the created order, as the revelation of his hiddenness (i.e., his "holiness"). God's covenant is "firm," as are his presence and promises, "for endless days."

Psalm 94: The Lord Is the Judge of the Earth

Psalm 94 is made up of two parts: a *national lament* (vv.1–15) and an *individual lament* (vv.16–23), which bring together the individual and the community in their common concern.

I. The God of Vengeance (94:1–2)

1–2 The Lord, the covenant God, is "the God who avenges"! His vengeance is not vindictive but a response to the evil perpetrated by the wicked. Evil has its own rewards, namely, "what they deserve." The prayer for the Lord to "shine forth" is a prayer for a theophany, when the Lord appears in his royal splendor to bring justice into a world of anarchy. When he appears, he will "rise up" in judgment as the "Judge of the earth."

II. The Arrogant Words of the Wicked (94:3–7)

3–7 The questions bubble forth as the psalmist reflects on the arrogance of the wicked. They excel in boastful rejoicing in their power. Their speech is like a spring, gushing forth nothing but insolent words. When the ungodly harass God's children, they brazenly affront the Lord. Any deprivation, prejudice, injustice, or trampling on the rights of God's people is a throwback on the Lord, who has promised to care for his people.

III. Rebuke of the Wicked (94:8–11)

8–11 The psalmist addresses the folly of evil by a rebuke. The wicked foolishly establish their little kingdoms on earth, believing that there is no God who will call them to account. They need to know that the Lord knows what is in the hearts of all humans. His hearing and seeing may result in judgment and in deliverance (cf. Ex 2:24–25).

IV. Blessing of the Wise (94:12–15)

12–15 All wisdom comes from God, even the wisdom found among the nations. However, the Lord has given his own people a clearer form of revelation, and those who respond wisely to his instruction are "blessed" (GK 897). They receive his protection from whatever disasters others may plot against them. God's commitment extends to "his people" by covenant. Theirs is the promise of the kingdom, characterized by the order of God, which "all the upright in heart" seek (cf. Mt 5:6; 6:33).

V. The Lament on Account of the Wicked (94:16–21)

16–19 The psalmist returns to the prayer for divine vindication. He knows that the Lord alone will "rise up" and "take a stand" as the royal Judge. He admits that he nearly slipped away into the netherworld. Yet he experienced the presence of the Lord by the support of his "love" (GK 2876). He further confesses that he was nearly overwhelmed with despair, but the Lord came to his rescue.

20–21 It seems as if the reign of corruption, unjust decrees, and oppression of the righteous live side by side with the reign of God. But the psalmist knows that human autonomy can never exist together with God's purpose of establishing his kingdom on earth. A human kingdom is destructive, whereas the kingdom of God is restorative.

VI. Confidence in the Vengeance of the Lord (94:22–23)

22–23 The psalmist closes by calling on the godly to cast their lot with his God. He is the "fortress" and "rock" for all who "take refuge" in him. He will repay the wicked for their boastful words and oppressive acts. The godly hold firm that the kingdom is the Lord's and that he will vindicate them by destroying the wicked and by removing all forms of evil from this world.

Psalm 95: Let Us Kneel Before Our Maker

Though this psalm is not explicitly a psalm ascribing kingship to the Lord, its theme is nevertheless in harmony with the spirit of these psalms.

I. Call to Worship (95:1–2)

1–2 The community is summoned to come together for the purpose of celebration. The object of the joyous ceremony is no other than "the LORD" (GK 3378), and the occasion is an act of deliverance. "The Rock of our salvation" defends and delivers his people, and the people respond with "thanksgiving." The community worships the Lord in word and music.

II. Hymn to the Lord the Creator-King (95:3–5)

3–5 The exaltation of the Lord is due him because he is "the great King" who alone rules over all his creation. The nations may have their deities, but the God of Israel is exalted over all the "gods" of the nations. The Lord's creative acts constitute the ground of his kingship.

III. Call to Worship (95:6)

6 "Worship" (GK 2556) is a concrete act of obeisance, expressive of one's devotion to the Lord. The reason for worship is placed within the context of God's universal kingship and his covenant love.

IV. Hymn to the Lord, the God of the Covenant (95:7a–c)

7a–c The people of God approach him with a hymn celebrating God's commitment. As their "Maker" he is also their shepherd, and they are "the people of his pasture," i.e., "the flock under his care."

V. Response and Reflection on the Lord's Judgment (95:7d–11)

7d–9 God's relationship with his people has been marred by apathy and outright disobedience. "Today" is still the moment of grace. At "Meribah" ("contending") and "Massah" ("testing") Israel had acted wantonly against the Lord. These places symbolize a whole generation of faithless Israelites who dared to challenge the Lord, even though they had witnessed all the mighty works in Egypt, by the Red Sea, and in the desert.

10–11 The Lord cared for the generation of the desert for "forty years," though their "hearts" were corrupt and they repeatedly proved that they did not love the ways of God. The psalmist reminds his audience of the Lord's anger with his people. He loathed them as a righteous person loathes sin. Thus they could not and did not enter into the "rest" of God (see Heb 3:7–4:11).

Psalm 96: The Lord Will Judge the World in Righteousness

This psalm belongs to a group of psalms (93–100) that affirm the Lord's rule over the earth and form a subcategory of the descriptive praise psalms.

I. Proclamation of Universal Praise (96:1–3)

1–3 The content of the praise is "the new song," i.e., a fresh outburst of praise to God, occasioned by a new act of "salvation" (also known as "his marvelous deeds"). The exact nature of the salvation may include all acts in redemptive history: creation and redemption. The people of God must give leadership by giving "praise" to his name every day.

II. The Majesty of the Lord (96:4–6)

4–5 The hymn exclaims the Lord's greatness, his being "worthy of praise," and his awe-inspiring nature. The Lord alone is God. The pagans may claim that their gods have power over the heavenly realms, but this is excluded by virtue of the Lord's sole claim to having created "the heavens."

6 God's royal glory is evident in creation. We are surrounded by the evidences of his royal presence: "splendor and majesty . . . strength and glory."

III. Proclamation of Universal Praise (96:7–9)

7–9 The ascription of "glory" (GK 3883) to God may be in the form of the praise in worship or the presentation of an offering in the temple. The combination of "glory" and "strength" brings out the nature of his powerful acts. They reveal his royal "splendor." The entire earth is invited to participate. The Lord expects reverence, submission, holiness, and awe of his divine majesty and presence.

IV. The Rule of the Lord (96:10–13)

10–12 The second hymn ascribes dominion to the Lord. He has established his rule on earth by his creation and his rule with "equity." The coming of God as Judge is a cause for all nature to rejoice and be glad.

13 The Lord comes to establish "righteousness" and "truth" on earth. The hymn closes on the same motif that it began with: the affirmation of God's rule—both his vengeance on the ungodly and deliverance for the godly.

Psalm 97: The Joys of Zion

This psalm belongs to a group of psalms (93–100) that celebrate the Lord's kingship and form a subcategory of the descriptive praise psalms.

I. The Revelation of the Lord's Glory (97:1–6)

1 The psalm opens on a positive affirmation of the reign of the Lord, which extends to all "the distant shores" of the earth. The nature of the Lord's reign is much more important than the fact that he reigns.

2–6 The magnificent portrayal of the Lord's coming in "clouds and thick darkness" is reminiscent of Israel's experience at Mount Sinai; it also designates the awesome nature of the Day of the Lord (cf. Joel 2:2; Zep 1:15; Rev 11:5). His coming is so great that it "lights up the world," shakes the earth, and melts the mountains. The revelation of God's glory is overwhelming.

II. Exhortation to Worship (97:7)

7 The nations must come to the true worship of the Lord. If they persist in idolatry, they will be put to shame. Idols are be proven worthless on the day of the Lord's coming.

III. Zion's Worship (97:8–9)

8–9 The people of God rejoice in his rule. They confess that "truly" the Lord is "the Most High" over the earth and above all angels.

IV. The Effects of the Lord's Glorious Rule (97:10–12)

10–12 The godly "love the LORD"; they are wise in that they hate anything tainted by evil. They need not fear the day of the Lord's appearance, because he will protect them from the wicked. They will enjoy the benefits of the rule of God. "Light" (GK 240) signifies the blessed state of redemption and victory. The "righteous" and "upright in heart" will enjoy the new age of restoration as the dawning of light. The exhortation to rejoice anticipates the Lord's coming with his blessings.

Psalm 98: A New Song to the Lord

This psalm reflects on the reasons for God's universal praise. This psalm also anticipates the universal restoration of all things, when God's kingdom will be established on earth.

I. Joyful Celebration of Past Acts of Deliverance (98:1–3)

1–2 The "new song" celebrates the Lord's victory. The worshiper moves from a reflection of one specific event to the worship of the Redeemer-God. The "marvelous things" (GK 7098) are the acts of the Lord done in his own power. The nations witness that the Lord is victorious as he blesses his people.

3 The motivating factors for the demonstration of God's power are his "love" (GK 2876) and his "faithfulness" (GK 575) to his covenant people. They who asked to be "remembered" in love and compassion at the time of the Exile have experienced that the Lord does remember. Though the primary focus is on Israel, the Lord provokes the "ends of the earth" to jealousy.

II. Worship of the Great King (98:4–6)

4–6 All the inhabitants on earth must prepare themselves for God's coming by an open welcome, shouting "for joy," bursting "into jubilant song," and making "music." This praise is in response to the expectation that his salvific acts will benefit all who rejoice.

III. Joyful Anticipation of God's Coming (98:7–9)

7–9 Nature echoes and reverberates the joy of God's people as they anticipate the coming of the Great King. The rejoicing of animal and plant life in the sea and on earth constitutes the totality of all of created life. The "groaning" of nature (Ro 8:19–21) will give way to rejoicing. At his coming, the Great King will fully establish his victorious dominion over the created world in "righteousness" and "equity."

Psalm 99: The Lord Is the Revealer-King

This psalm belongs to a group of psalms variously designated as the enthronement psalms or the psalms celebrating the Lord's kingship (93–100).

I. The Exaltation of the Lord in Israel (99:1–5)

1–5 The Lord is highly exalted in heaven, as he "sits enthroned between the cherubim." The imagery of the cherubim derives from the ark of the covenant, whose lid was a gold slab on which two cherubs with spread wings

stood (Ex 25:17–22). The ark of the covenant signified the establishment of God's kingdom on earth and as such became known as his "footstool." The sovereign and glorious rule of the Lord should inspire all inhabitants of the world to "tremble" and "shake." The nations must praise the "name" with which the acts of redemptive history are associated—the name "LORD" (GK 3378).

The nature of the King's rule is like his character: "holy" (GK 7705), "mighty" (GK 6437), and "just" (GK 5477). He has "established equity" and done what is "right" for the sake of his people ("Jacob"). Because the Lord is "exalted" over the nations, the people of God must lead the nations in "exalting" the Lord.

II. The Revelation of the Lord to Israel (99:6–7)

6–7 The word "priests" (GK 3913) should not be taken too narrowly, because in the strict sense Moses was not a priest. The noun is here loosely used for "servants" or "intercessors." Moses, Aaron, and Samuel interceded on Israel's behalf. They "called" on his "name" in intercessory prayer, and he responded to their prayers. He performed mighty wonders on behalf of his people and he also revealed himself as "he spoke to them from the pillar of cloud."

III. The Exaltation of the Lord in Israel (99:8–9)

8 The psalmist restates that the Lord has been good to Israel, as he "answered them." He is a consuming fire to those who deprive him of his rights, but he is gracious in that he readily forgives the people.

9 Because of the Lord's greatness, holiness, and justice, the people of God must submit themselves to his lordship by exalting him. Thus they may give leadership to the nations. Worship is an act of submission to his kingship and a proper response to his awe-inspiring presence.

Psalm 100: The Lord Is God and He Is Good

In hymnic form the worshipers sing about the Lord and his covenant relationship with his people.

I. Call to Give Thanks (100:1–2)

1–2 The psalmist calls on "all the earth" to come before the Great King. The nations must recognize that the Lord is God, by whose grace and blessings his people exist. Submission to his rule comes out of a response of joy and gratitude for his covenant promises. The "gladness" (GK 8525) reflects the joy in living in harmony with the Creator, Redeemer, and King.

II. Celebration of the Covenant (100:3)

3 The imperative "know" (GK 3359) signifies acknowledgment or confession. The people confess him as covenant Lord, their only true God. They also confess their accountability to him and their privileged position. The Lord, in turn, cares for them (cf. the shepherd imagery used here).

III. Call to Give Thanks (100:4)

4 The communal confession arouses another invocation to give thanks to the Lord. The worshiping community enters the temple courts through the gates. They come "with thanksgiving" and "with praise," appropriate sacrifices for all the benefits they have received.

IV. Celebration of the Covenant (100:5)

5 God's people adumbrate God's name on account of his goodness to them. He is "good," full of "love" (GK 2876) and "faithfulness" (GK 575). He remains faithful to his people because he has covenanted to do so.

Psalm 101: Commitment to Excellence

Clearly the psalm belongs to the *royal psalms,* and further it is in the form of a declaration of commitment.

I. The King's Commitment to God's Kingdom (101:1–3a)

1–3a Because of the Lord's constancy in his "love" (GK 2876) and his administration of "justice" (GK 5477), the psalmist breaks forth into thanksgiving and is motivated to lead "a blameless life" before God. His loyalty is to the Lord and not to the ways of this world. The brief prayer "when will you come to me" suggests a need, either personal or for the people, though there is no indication of the original situation.

II. Hatred of Evil (101:3b–5)

3b–5 The godly leader shuns evil in any form. In his law, the Lord required his covenant people to put him before their eyes, to cling to him with all their heart, and to know him (cf. Dt 11:18, 22; 30:20). Slander, gossip, and false witness bring out the heart condition of people. A false testimony may injure someone's reputation or even bring a wrong verdict. A royal judgment will rest on those who are not acting rightly within the covenant community.

III. Love for God's People (101:6)

6 The king recognizes all those who are "faithful" and "blameless." He invites only people of integrity to "dwell" with him and serve in his presence as appointed courtiers.

IV. Hatred of Evil (101:7)

7 The king excludes from dwelling in his house and joining his administration all who do not conform to God's high standards of integrity.

V. The King's Commitment to Justice (101:8)

8 The king further vows that in his daily routine of dispensing justice he will further advance the theocratic goals. The "wicked" and the "evildoer" have no place in Jerusalem, "the city of the LORD." He will bring an end to their reign of terror.

Psalm 102: You Remain, but I....

This psalm is classified as one of the seven penitential psalms (Pss 6; 32; 38; 51; 102; 130; 143). In an individual lament, the psalmist emphasizes the suffering and discipline often associated with sin.

I. Introductory Prayer (102:1–2)

1–2 The psalmist roots his introductory prayer in the vocabulary of the liturgical traditions of his time.

II. Lament (102:3–11)

3–11 The psalmist compares his life to "smoke," "glowing embers," withered "grass," birds, and "an evening shadow," which all express the transitoriness of life. In the tension of being and not-being, the psalmist despairs. He is full of feverish anxiety, experiences adversity, and is alone in his suffering. In his depressed condition, he forgets to eat and drink. Consequently he wastes away to mere "skin and bones." His enemies look at him as having been abandoned by his God. Yet the psalmist knows that the Lord has not rejected him because of his sin. He suffers from the full brunt of God's "great wrath."

III. Promises (102:12–22)

12 The psalmist has been reduced to little more than a fleeting existence. On the other hand, the Lord's fame remains from generation to generation. As long as his rule lasts, his fame will be told and retold.

13–14 The Lord's sovereignty extends over all creation and time. In his freedom he will rise from his throne and show mercy to his people. The Lord had decreed seventy years for Judah's exile in Babylon, and thereafter it would fall. Then would come the "time" of God's favor, a new era marked by forgiveness, renewal of the covenant, and the restoration of the people to the land. "Zion" symbolizes the covenant relationship and all the privileges entailed by it, material and spiritual. God's people are the "servants," who yearn for the reestablishment of Jerusalem.

15–17 The city's future is completely dependent on the Lord, who has promised to "rebuild" it and to endow it with the glory of his personal and royal presence. The new era will mark a renewal of his covenant love as evidenced in answered prayers of his servants, "the destitute," and the universal reverence for and worship of the Lord.

18–22 The promises of vv.12–17 must be recorded for the sake of all generations to come. When those promises are realized in God's acts of redemption and the restoration of Zion, there will be greater confidence on the part of "a people not yet created," as they will "praise the LORD."

The Lord's response to the suffering of his servants is that he "looked down from his sanctuary on high" to respond to their needs. Those who were oppressed are likened to "prisoners" and "those condemned to death." Out of the ruins of Zion/Jerusalem and the "groans" of the exiled population, the Lord promised to raise up a new people and resettle them in Zion. The nations too would join in the worship of "the name of the LORD," in fulfillment of the many prophetic oracles.

IV. Lament (102:23–27)

23–27 Occupied with the brevity, vanity, and anguish of life, the psalmist laments that his vitality is cut off "in the course of my life." He contrasts his transitory existence with the great work of creation and with the Lord himself. He believes that only God has the power to cut short his ordeal rather than to take his life. The eternal God is the Creator of heaven and earth; he will remain forever, whereas they will some day "perish" (cf. 2Pe 3:8). He is the "first and last," and he does not change.

V. Concluding Perspective (102:28)

28 The future of the godly is tied up with God himself and with his promises. The psalmist praises the Lord in that he will be true to "the children of your servants." They and their descendants will "dwell" and be "established" in the Lord's presence.

Psalm 103: His Compassions Fail Not!

In hymnic fashion the psalmist praises the Lord for the many benefits bestowed on him, characteristic of the *individual thanksgiving* psalm.

I. Individual Praise (103:1–2)

1–2 Praise of God begins with the self. As the psalmist exhorts himself to praise the Lord with his "soul" (GK 5883) and "inmost being" (i.e., his whole person), he has nothing else in mind than a full commitment to the act of giving thanks. The "name" (GK 9005) of the Lord calls to remembrance all his perfections and acts of deliverance. "Praise" (GK 1385) is the response of awe for God, while reflecting on what the Lord has done for his people. The opposite of "praise" is forgetfulness. To "forget" (GK 8894) the "benefits" of the Lord is to disregard his covenantal lordship.

II. Praise for the Lord's Goodness to Individuals (103:3–5)

3 The forgiveness of "sins" is God's gracious act of removing the consequences of sin as well as the sin itself. The "diseases" (GK 9377) may be sicknesses, but are more likely a metaphor for adversities or setbacks.

4 Instead of letting his beloved be taken by adversity, the Lord redeems by exalting him to royalty with his "love and compassion." "Love" (GK 2876)) is the assurance of the constancy of his fidelity toward his own. The complement of "love" is divine "compassion" (GK 8171), that quality by which God as the heavenly Father empathizes with human frailty.

5 The Lord forgives, redeems, sustains, and fully restores all the covenantal benefits, even though sin has breached the covenant. The Lord "satisfies" his children with all the blessings of the covenant so as to "renew" them like an "eagle." The "eagle" symbolizes vigor and freedom.

III. Praise for the Lord's Kingship Over Israel (103:6–19)

6 The Lord does not tolerate injustice in the world. His rule is characterized by "righteousness" (GK 7407), his righting what is wrong. This word relates to God's deliverance of his people from evil and oppression and to his punishment of oppressors.

7–10 The psalmist reflects on God's "ways" and "deeds," revealed to Moses (cf. Ex 34:6–7). Though the Lord may be justly angry because of sin, he does not maintain his anger for long. Great as his wrath may be, his mercy is greater. God's rule is characterized by grace.

11–14 The love of God is not indiscriminate. He loves those "who fear him." He will forgive them, have compassion for them, and treat them as his children. Though he expects godliness, he is also understanding of their frailty. All of them are but "dust."

15–18 From the perspective of God's universal rule, "man" is nothing more than human. His existence is "like grass" or "like a flower of the field." Over against the brevity and weakness of human existence is the greatness of God's love for those who fear him. His "love" (GK 2876) and "righteousness" (GK 7407) last forever. Those who respond to the Lord in "fear" will enjoy the fullness of the covenant relationship, and their children will see the salvation of the Lord (cf. 102:28).

19 The psalmist calls on the community to recognize the Lord's kingdom. His "throne" may be in heaven but his kingdom extends to all creation. This affirmation is both the conclusion of the hymn and the transition to a universal call to worship the Lord.

IV. Universal and Individual Praise (103:20–22)

20–22 The psalm concludes with the psalmist calling on all heavenly creatures ("angels," "mighty ones," "heavenly hosts," and "servants"), serving the Lord on high, to join together with all creation in the praise of God. Those heavenly hosts are always loyal to the Lord, and he expects the same from his creatures on earth.

Psalm 104: Great Is Your Faithfulness to All Creation

Psalm 104 is a *psalm of praise* describing God's greatness in ruling and sustaining his vast creation. It is complementary to the prose account of creation in Ge 1.

I. In Praise of God's Royal Splendor (104:1–4)

1 The exclamation "praise the LORD" arises out of the heart of those who consider themselves blessed to know the covenant Redeemer-God, whose name is Yahweh ("the LORD"). Praise is expressed in two ways: direct ("you"; v.1) and indirect ("he"; vv.2ff.). The nouns "splendor and majesty" amplify the royal nature of his rule.

2 Light is vital to life. The psalmist portrays God as covered with light. The light reveals something of his glory, because God is light (1Jn 1:5). God's second creative act is "the firmament" or "the heavens" (Ge 1:6–8), described here as a "tent" stretched out over the earth. As a camper pitches a tent, so God prepared the earth for habitation.

3–4 The imagery of the firmament gives occasion to reflect on the divine glory above the firmament. The "beams" on the water above the firmament provide the support for his royal palace. The "chambers," built above the first story of a house for the purpose of privacy and seclusion, represent God's involvement with and separation from his world. The Lord sovereignly controls the elements, as if he "rides" on a "chariot," using the wind, clouds, and lightning ("flames of fire") for his purposes. The Lord is surrounded by his servants, whether they be created like the angels or be powers inherent in his created order (winds, lightning).

II. The Material Formation of the Earth (104:5–9)

5–6 These verses focus on the third day of Creation: the formation of the land (cf. Ge 1:9–10). The waters covered the whole earth, forming a vast "deep" and covering both mountains and valleys as if with "a garment." The "foundations" were already there by divine creation, awaiting God's act of separating the waters so as to make the dry land appear.

7 The word God spoke at creation is poetically transformed to a "rebuke" and "the sound of your thunder." The Lord limited the power of the water by a show of his power. He is sovereign over all powers.

8–9 "The waters" (v.7) flee over the mountains, down the valleys, into their allotted place. Since the Flood the Lord determined that water should never again cover the earth.

III. The Glory of the Animal Creation (104:10–18)

10–12 Through the bountiful rain the Lord provides richly for his creation. God is the source and sustainer of life! Water provides drink for the wild animals, of which "the wild donkeys" are representatives. It also provides for growth of trees and shrubs, in whose branches the birds nest and sing.

13–15 Water also provides for domesticated animals and especially for humankind. The Lord satisfies all the needs of his creation, for he has the power and wisdom to water mountains and to sustain plant and animal life. He supplies human needs indirectly through providing fodder for "the cattle" and directly through supplying people with "food." In his free grace, the Lord richly blesses "man" with ample provision. "Wine" is given for the uplifting of one's spirit and oil for one's appearance.

16–18 The Lord waters the mountains so that the lofty trees have their needs fully provided for. Lebanon was proverbial for its cedars. The birds find nesting places in the trees. Even as the cedar and pine are selectively chosen as samples of majestic trees, so the "stork" is a stately bird. The mountains are also a hideout for "the wild goats"—a kind of ibex—and the "coneys"—a Syrian coney or rock badger.

IV. The Regularity in the Created World (104:19–23)

19–23 The moon and sun are also in God's hands. The "moon" represents the lunar calendar by which the "seasons," the festival days of Israel, were determined. Sun and moon denote the regular order of day and night, when animals and humans have an opportunity to provide for themselves.

V. The Glory of the Animal Creation (104:24–26)

24–26 The world of creation reveals the power, wisdom, and creative diversity of the Lord. He has multiple "works" all over his world. All of life belongs to him, on "the earth" and in "the sea." The Lord provides for the great number of sea creatures that inhabit the seas; the "leviathan" is here only a large sea animal, one of God's creatures.

VI. The Spiritual Sustenance of the Earth (104:27–30)

27–30 The very source of the well-being of God's creation is in the providence of the Lord. All creatures, including human beings, have their being in God. He gives and sustains life by his life-giving Spirit. But he also takes away the life-spirit from his creatures.

VII. In Praise of God's Royal Splendor (104:31–35)

31–35 The Lord has bestowed his "glory" (GK 3883) on his creation. His handiwork will flourish as long as he sustains it. One's response to the Lord's presence should be praise, devotion, and concern with pleasing the Lord. Those who do not join in with a grateful response are outside the covenant of grace. They have no place on God's earth. The psalmist longs for a world that is fully established and maintained by the Lord. The hymn concludes on the same note of thanksgiving and praise with which it began: Hallelujah!

Psalm 105: The Lord's Acts in Salvation History

The hymnic celebration of the history of redemption from Israel's sojourn in Egypt to the Conquest is the theme of this psalm. Its motif complements the creation hymn (104) and the hymn of God's faithfulness (106).

I. Invocation to Praise (105:1–6)

1–6 The Lord is the *object* of worship. From the phraseology we learn about "what he has done," "all his wonderful acts," and "the wonders ... his miracles, and the judgments." He acts marvelously on behalf of his people, so as to pass "judgments" on their enemies. His acts reveal the Divine Warrior in his holiness and "strength." The name of this God is none other than Yahweh ("the LORD"; GK 3378), on whose "name" the people call with shouts of joy and with gratitude.

The *subjects* of worship are the people for whom the Lord has done his wonderful and mighty acts: the descendants of Abraham and Jacob. Through Abraham his descendants have become God's "chosen ones" (GK 1040). They are expected to "seek the LORD" in his holy temple with a true spirit of devotion. In the acts of praise, public rejoicing, and remembrance of God's acts in redemptive history, the people of God express a unity as heirs of the Abrahamic covenant and of Jacob's election over against Esau.

The goal of *praise* is threefold. (1) Praise magnifies the Lord. (2) Praise intensifies Israel's appreciation of the history of their redemption. (3) Praise witnesses to those outside the covenant community.

II. The Covenant of Promise (105:7–11)

7–11 In hymnic language the psalmist ascribes covenant fidelity to "the LORD." He is the "God" of Israel by covenant, but his authority extends to "all the earth." He made an eternal "covenant" (which is equivalent to "the oath" and to "a decree") with Abraham, Isaac, and Jacob. The covenant is a sovereign administration of grace and promise.

III. The Protection of the Lord (105:12–15)

12–13 God's protection is transparent in the patriarchal narratives. The psalmist begins describing Israel's beginnings at the stage when there were few members of the covenant and when the covenant community was not stable. They were continually vulnerable to the jealousy of the kings, subject to pagan immorality, and contingent on the ever-changing political environment (Ge 12–35).

14–15 Abraham's descendants did not succumb to political and moral pressures. Their strength did not lie in numbers but in the Lord's protection. He had promised to curse all those who curse Abraham and his seed, for they were the Lord's "anointed ones" (cf. Ge 12:2–3). They are also designated as "my prophets." By plagues and dreams the Lord "rebuked" kings.

IV. The Providence of the Lord (105:16–23)

16–19 The episodes of famine, Joseph's enslavement and exaltation in Egypt, and migration to Egypt evidence divine providence. The Lord was as much involved in Israel's protection as he was in bringing the adversity of famine on the land. To this end he led Joseph into enslavement in Egypt. He was humiliated in his unjust imprisonment, but he was finally greatly exalted through his God-given ability to interpret dreams (Ge 40–41).

20–23 Through the order of Pharaoh, Joseph was released from prison and elevated to the high office of "master of his household" (cf. Ge 41:14, 40) and administrator over all Pharaoh's possessions (cf. Ac 7:10). The king became an instrument of God's plan. This again is providence. All recognized the "wisdom" given to Joseph so that he, a Hebrew, was given full liberty to instruct leaders and elders. Then through divine providence Israel (Jacob) entered Egypt (here called "the land of Ham") as "an alien."

V. The Protection of the Lord (105:24–36)

24–27 The first two verses summarize Ex 1: Israel's multiplication and Pharaoh's jealousy and hatred. The Lord blessed, providentially created Israel's adversity, and was all too ready to protect his people. He then chose Moses ("his servant"; GK 6269) and Aaron (his "chosen" one; GK 1047)—both men instruments of redemption and of demonstrating his power in the form of "miraculous signs" and "wonders."

28–36 The psalmist selects eight out of the ten plagues. The omission of two plagues and the variation in order have no bearing on the historicity of what happened in Egypt. The plagues are framed between the ninth and the tenth affliction on the Egyptians: darkness

(Ex 10:21–28) and the death of the firstborn (Ex 11:4–8; 12:29).

VI. The Fulfillment of Promise (105:37–45b)

37–41 The Lord then brought his people out of Egypt (vv.37, 43). He took marvelous care of them, sustaining them by his presence, protecting them, and providing for them in fulfillment of his covenant with Abraham. The people left Egypt with supplies of silver and gold to provide for their needs in the Promised Land. As they exited Egypt, the Israelites were glad and sang songs of victory. Egypt too was happy when Israel left, because with the departure of Israel came the end of the plagues. In the desert, the Lord continued to provide them with food and drink.

42–44 The exodus from Egypt and God's presence, protection, and provision reveal his concern for the covenant. Abraham is God's

Miracles of the Old Testament

Miracle	Reference
Burning bush	Ex 3:1–14
Rod becoming a snake	Ex 4:1–5; 7:8–13
Leprous hand	Ex 4:6–12
Ten plagues	Ex 8:14–12:30
Dividing of the Red Sea	Ex 14:21–31
Water from the rock	Ex 17:1–9
Destruction of Korah	Nu 16:31–35
Aaron's staff budding	Nu 17:1–19
Water from the rock in Kadesh	Nu 20:9–11
Bronze snake	Nu 21:4–9
Balaam's donkey	Nu 22:20–35
Jordan divided	Jos 3:7–17
Fall of Jericho	Jos 6:1–20
Sun standing still	Jos 10:1–14
Slain lion	Jdg 14:5–10
Dagon's temple pulled down	Jdg 16:23–30
Thunder and rain	1Sa 12:16–18
Jeroboam's hand withered and restored	1Ki 13:16
Elijah fed by ravens	1Ki 17:1–6
Widow's flour and oil	1Ki 17:8–16
Widow's son raised from the dead	1Ki 17:17–24
Sacrifice consumed by fire	1Ki 18:30–39
Rain in answer to prayer	1Ki 18:41–45
Jordan divided	2Ki 2:1–8
Waters sweetened	2Ki 2:19–22
Widow's oil multiplied	2Ki 4:1–7
Shunammite's son restored to life	2Ki 4:8–37
Poison stew rendered harmless	2Ki 4:38–41
Feeding of one hundred men	2Ki 4:42–44
Naaman healed of leprosy	2Ki 5:1–19
Floating axhead	2Ki 6:1–7
Blinded eyes	2Ki 6:8–23
Dead man restored to life	2Ki 13:21
Hezekiah healed	2Ki 20:1–7
Three men delivered from blazing furnace	Da 3:23–27
Daniel delivered from the den of lions	Da 6:10–23
Sea stilled when Jonah cast in	Jnh 1:15
Jonah delivered from fish's mouth	Jnh 2:10
Withering of the vine	Jnh 4:6–7

"servant" (GK 6269) and his descendants are God's "chosen ones" (GK 1040). He brought them with great joy out of Egypt into the Promised Land. By right of conquest they freely inherited all the benefits of the Promised Land of Canaan.

45a–b The emphasis throughout the psalm lies on God's goodness. However, God's purpose for his people was nothing less than to have a responsive people. The author reminds God's people of their responsibility: keeping the precepts of the Lord. In doing so they express joyous gratitude for all the benefits the Lord has provided for his people.

VII. Concluding Praise (105:45c)

45c The psalm begins with a call to praise and ends on a fitting conclusion: "Hallelujah."

Psalm 106: Remember the Lord's Love and Israel's Disobedience

This psalm favors the hymnic genre in its thematic approach to Israel's history, revealing Israel's unresponsiveness to all of the Lord's mighty acts.

I. Invocation to Praise (106:1–2)

1–2 The doctrine of God shines through significantly even in the complaint, prayer, and history of rebellion. The doxology and invocation extol the Lord for his goodness and for his enduring "love." Praise is linked to the revelation of God in history, given for "his mighty acts." This God is none other than the powerful Divine Warrior.

II. Prayer for God's Salvation (106:3–5)

3 In view of the goodness, love, and mighty acts of the Lord, "blessed" (GK 897) are all those who enjoy his benefits. As in Ps 1, the blessing is conditioned on pleasing the Lord and doing what is right.

4–5 In desperation and in a spirit of contrition, the author prays that the Lord may again bestow his blessing on the godly and "remember" (GK 2349) his covenant; the synonym for "remember" is "come to my aid." The effect of God's remembrance is salvation and restoration for individual members of the covenant people. They look to the change from alienation to salvation and from wrath to "favor" (GK 8356). God's salvation results in renewal of his blessing, "joy," and participation in the worship of the Lord.

III. Acts of God's Love: Salvation (106:6–12)

6–7 The Divine Warrior is known to Israel for his mighty acts, as from the beginning of Israel's history he displayed his power to deliver and fulfill by "miracles." But Israel often went astray and acted corruptly. God delivered a people who resisted his authority and kingship, for "they rebelled" against him immediately after their deliverance from Egypt.

8–12 The Lord's deliverance from Egypt discloses his fidelity to his covenant, his rule over the nations, and his "mighty power." His power extends to his word, because by his "rebuke" (GK 1721) he brought the sea to submission. The Red Sea became an instrument of deliverance and judgment. (1) The Lord led his people to freedom, when the sea bed was dry, "as through a desert." The Divine Warrior freed them from their foe, who vanished from sight. (2) The Lord judged the Egyptians as none of them survived. Israel saw the hand of the Lord in the great wonders and praised him for "his promises."

IV. History of Israel's Unbelief and God's Judgment (106:13–43)

A. Impatience: Wasting Disease (106:13–15)

13–15 Israel's faith faltered quickly. They readily gave in to impatience when he did not anticipate their needs. Their refusal to submit to his counsel signified an independence that would develop into their becoming stiffnecked and stubborn. They "put God to the test" with their selfish spirit. He gave them what they wanted; but the consequences were severe.

B. Jealousy: Death and Fire (106:16–18)

16–18 Korah (a Levite), Dathan and Abiram (Danites), and 250 leading men of Israel challenged Moses and Aaron in a most insolent manner. They were "envious" of their closeness to the Lord and argued in favor of the sanctity (priesthood) of all believers. The three leaders went down into the earth, whereas the company of 250 wicked men were destroyed by fire.

C. Idolatry: Near Destruction (106:19–23)

19–20 At Horeb Israel made the golden calf as a symbolic representation of deity, in violation of the second commandment. They worshiped the material rather than the resplendent "glory" of God. "Their Glory" is none other than their Savior-God.

21–23 Idolatry denies the nature of the God of revelation and the God of salvation. Too easily did the people overlook the manifestation of his mighty acts in Egypt (i.e., "the land of Ham") and by the Red Sea. Thus the Lord was ready to "destroy them." But Moses, their leader, interceded for Israel. "Stood in the breach" pictures the bravery of a soldier who stands in the breach of the wall, willing to give his life in warding off the enemy. The Lord responded to Moses' intercession by not destroying the people.

D. Unbelief: Death (106:24–27)

24–25 At Kadesh Barnea the people rebelled again. This time they did not believe that the Lord could lead them into the Promised Land. "His promises" no longer seemed valid. Instead of praising him, they "grumbled" and "despised" his promise of the land.

26–27 The oath of God pertained both to that generation and to the generation of the Exile. In the desert the Israelites died without entering the Promised Land; in the Exile they were scattered "throughout the lands."

E. Idolatry: Plague (106:28–31)

28–29 In their idolatrous practices the Israelites even devoted themselves to "the Baal of Peor," a local Moabite god. They participated in the communion sacrifices devoted to "lifeless gods." Thus they made God jealous and provoked his wrath, resulting in his immediate judgment.

30–31 Phinehas, the grandson of Aaron, killed an Israelite who had joined with a Midianite woman (Nu 25:7–8). This heroic act of devotion checked the plague. His faith was richly rewarded with a covenant promising a perpetual priesthood.

F. Rebellion: Trouble (106:32–33)

32–33 Less than a year before Israel was to enter the Promised Land, Moses too provoked the Lord. At Meribah he was to speak to the rock. Instead, he hit it, having been thoroughly provoked by Israel in their rebellion "against the Spirit of God." But Moses' "rash words" against Israel were not justifiable. Consequently he was punished in not being permitted to enter the land. This is what the psalmist calls "trouble."

G. Idolatry and Acculturation: Exile (106:34–43)

34–38 Because of their commitment through marriages to the indigenous Canaanite population, the Israelites could not be faithful to doing what "the LORD had commanded." The Canaanite "customs"—idolatry, sacrificial rites, human sacrifice, murder—entrapped them away from the revealed religion of Sinai. They "worshiped" the gods of the nations by the sacrifices of Israelite children, thus shedding "innocent blood."

39 These various practices "defiled" (GK 3237) the people, rendering them ritually unclean for the worship of God. The pagan way of life was a form of religious prostitution. The people were unclean, and the land was equally defiled by the sinful practices.

40–43 Consequently Israel suffered the greatest humiliation in her history: Exile. God had sworn to scatter the rebellious people among the nations but had patiently waited. He had helped them many times. But their ancestors had not waited for his counsel in the desert, and the generation of the Exile rebelled by following their own counsel. Yet even in his anger the Lord still considered Israel as his own people!

V. Acts of God's Love: Restraint (106:44–46)

44–46 The Lord permitted nations to invade, control, and oppress his people from time to time. On the other hand, he still heard their "cry" of "distress" and acted on their behalf. His "great love" is grounded in his "covenant" with the patriarchs. His anger is tempered by his great love.

VI. Prayer for God's Salvation (106:47)

47 The whole community has sinned (v.6). Thus no one can fully enjoy God's benefits until he restores his favor to his "chosen ones . . . [his] nation" (v.5). To this end the psalmist prays, "Save us." God alone is able to restore his people from adversity and affliction, because he is "LORD our God," i.e., he has covenanted himself to be the God of Abraham and his descendants. His salvation will result in thanksgiving and praise.

VII. Invocation to Praise (106:48)

48 The last verse forms an appropriate conclusion to the fourth book of the Psalms (90–106). The doxology declares the praise of God as "the God of Israel." As his "love endures forever" (106:1), so will his praise from his people be "from everlasting to everlasting." In hope of deliverance and prosperity, the people of God respond with an "Amen!"

Book V: Psalms 107–150

Psalm 107: Lessons From the Experience of the Saints

This psalm is the first of the fifth book of psalms, a *thanksgiving-wisdom* psalm, and complements the confession of sin and prayer for divine favor and restoration (Ps 106).

I. Invocation to Give Thanks (107:1–3)

1–3 The congregation is called on to confess God's covenant faithfulness, affirming his goodness and love toward the redeemed. This is a common liturgical formula, much like a confession of faith. "The redeemed of the LORD" have experienced adversity in exile and have been delivered by the Lord. He has delivered them from "adversity" (NIV "foe," but preferably "trouble"; GK 7640). The Lord gathers his people, as it were, from all directions, wherever they are found.

II. Reasons for Thanksgiving (107:4–32)

A. Wanderers in the Desert (107:4–9)

4–5 The reference to the "desert wastelands" could be an allusion to the wandering of Israel in the desert or to the experience of the Exile (though "wandered" can also denote profligate living; GK 9494). The desert is a place to cross through, not to aimlessly wander in. There is no city for protection, and one's supplies of food and water may readily be depleted. Life loses its meaning as one experiences purposelessness.

6–9 God heard the prayer of people in "trouble" (GK 7639). His deliverance was full of surprises, as he supplied all the needs of his people. He straightened the way; led them into the city; and provided for their shelter, food, and drink. This God is the object of the thanksgiving hymn, because he manifests his "unfailing love" (GK 2876) in his "wonderful deeds" (GK 7098). His mercy is not limited to the covenant people, because the Creator-God is kind to "men."

B. Prisoners (107:10–16)

10–12 Suffering also comes in the form of captivity. The language of "darkness," "gloom," and "iron chains" connotes despair, deprivation of rights, and the judgment of God. Their misfortune was not accidental but resulted from an intentional breach of faith with the Lord. They "rebelled" against his revelation and despised his royal authority. "God . . . Most High" denotes the Creator-God, who sovereignly rules over his creation. Israel defied his authority, but he broke their rebellious spirit, forcing them to submit to his sovereignty by "bitter labor." When they could not endure their lot, they "stumbled" like people without God.

13–16 Yet the Lord cannot forget his own people. He delivered them, regardless of their rebellious spirit, from every adverse condition. For this the "redeemed" may give thanks.

C. Sick People (107:17–22)

17–18 This is another description of God's judgment on those who were "rebellious" against him. They were "fools" (GK 211) because they went astray in their love of wrong. Their "affliction" was sickness to death. They "loathed" their "food," as they felt that death was nearby.

19–20 What the people deserved they did not get. The Lord "saved" them too when they cried to him in their "distress." The "word" against which they rebelled became the word of promise, comfort, and restoration. The "word" (GK 1821) is personified here as God's messenger of healing and deliverance from "the grave."

21–22 The people must render thanks to the Lord. Thanksgiving is not an empty platitude but consists of a concrete expression of loyalty to the Lord by the giving of "thank offerings," accompanied by "songs of joy."

D. Sailors on the Sea (107:23–32)

23–24 Merchants who crossed the seas in search of fortune witnessed the marvels of God's creation at sea. The Lord's power is so great that he can easily stir up "mighty waters" and then calm them.

25–27 By the word of the Lord, he lifted up the waves of the sea, which frightened the merchants as they rose "up to the heavens" and "went down to the depths." As the ship was being tossed about as a plaything, the seafarers, unable to do anything about their lot, became dispirited and terrified. They tried to hold on to something solid, like "drunken men" who stagger and try to find stability. All their skills at navigation were ineffective so that they became desperate.

28–32 The sailors too prayed in their distress, and the Lord responded to their prayer. He silenced the sea and brought the sailors safely to their destination, thus making them "glad." Their joy brought them to expressions of devotion to the Lord. The proper response of thanksgiving finds its fullest development here. The merchants must publicly declare what God has done in communal worship and in places of leadership.

III. Reasons for Praise (107:33–42)

33–34 The hymn of praise ascribes to the Lord the power to change things. His authority is limitless. He can reverse the condition of anything and therefore the way of life of everybody! The wicked who prosper in their God-given land may find their land useless, parched, and "a salt waste," as happened to the area of Sodom and Gomorrah.

35–38 The Lord can also transform the desert into a well-populated area. The "desert" was "parched ground" that, when supplied by the abundance of the Lord's "pools of water" and "flowing springs," blossomed into fields of harvest. Where there are water and good land, people may come and benefit from God's good land. Their bounty is by the blessing of God, even as is their increase in number.

39–40 The people whom the Lord has blessed with fields, homes, and families are not dependable. In their prosperity they may exalt themselves. But in time God's judgment will find them out. The people may suffer from "oppression, calamity, and sorrow." Their "nobles" will be abased.

41–42 "The needy" (GK 36), i.e., the "upright" who wait for the Lord, draw comfort from seeing the justice of God. In his power he blesses them and silences the ruthless power and great evil of "the wicked."

IV. Invocation to Gain Wisdom (107:43)

43 The conclusion to this psalm transforms the hymn of thanksgiving to a wisdom psalm. The righteous will become "wise" by studying the acts of "the great love of the LORD" in the affairs of humankind.

Psalm 108: Praise and Prayer

This psalm consists of two parts (vv.1–5, 6–13), each of which has its duplicate in another psalm. Verses 1–5 derive from Ps 57:7–11 and vv.6–13 are parallel with Ps 60:5–12. See these psalms.

Psalm 109: The Lord Loves the Needy

This is one of the imprecatory psalms. Its genre reflects the *individual lament* type.

I. Invocation to the God of Praise (109:1)

1 The noun "praise" (GK 9335) is not an attribute of the Lord but serves as a catch-all for all the reasons God is worthy of the praise of his people. The psalmist prays that the God who has responded in the past will act again on behalf of his covenant child by not remaining silent.

II. The Words and Acts of the Ungodly (109:2–5)

2 David charges his enemies because their words are untrustworthy. The threefold description of the speech of the wicked seems to be uppermost in his mind: it is "wicked," "deceitful," and "lying."

3–5 The deceptiveness of the wicked comes out of a heart of "hatred." In his friendship the psalmist had done acts of kindness, but the wicked had returned "evil for good." During his friendship and even in his adversities he remained "a man of prayer," in constant communion with God.

III. Imprecation (109:6–15)

A. Guilty on Earth (109:6–8)

6–8 The psalmist hopes that an evil person may be found guilty by "an evil man," whom he also calls "an accuser" (lit., *satan*; GK 8477). Through the instrumentality of human institutions and by means of wicked people, other wicked people are condemned, and in this process God's righteousness is vindicated. The "accuser" stands "at his right hand" (cf. Zec 3:1, but cf. v.31) for the purpose of bringing accusations against one of their kind. The verdict must be "guilty" (GK 8401; the same word as "evil man"). When oppression, evil, and godlessness are cut short, the Lord establishes his rule over the earth by a built-in obsolescence of human structures.

B. Family (109:9–10)

9–10 The psalmist further prays that the family of the wicked man may be without support and comfort. The reduction of his wife to widowhood and his children to being orphans is a disgrace to the family name, as they would be at the mercy of others. The guilt of the father would thus affect his whole family. Out of destitution they would have to be "wandering beggars" and homeless.

C. Possessions (109:11)

11 The psalmist also prays that the family of the guilty man may never enjoy "the fruits of his labor." The forfeiture of the family fortune by equally ruthless men ("strangers") would further reduce the survivors to dependency and indebtedness.

D. Family (109:12–13)

12–13 In their destitute state, the widow and orphan had legal rights and claims on expressions of "kindness" (GK 2876). The psalmist's imprecation extends to any who extend a helping hand to the survivors of the guilty. No "kindness" or "pity" was to be shown. The disgrace should even be greater, as the psalmist prays that the family name will be removed from the face of the earth. Sin does have consequences!

E. Guilty Before God (109:14–15)

14–15 The psalmist asks God to be just by always remembering the guilt of the whole family. Even when "their names" are "blot-ted out," the psalmist prays that the Lord will never permit the memory of their sins to be "cut off." While forgiveness is possible for repentant sinners, hardened sinners are beyond salvation. Unforgiven sins are viewed as "memorials" that "remain before the LORD."

IV. The Acts and Words of the Ungodly (109:16–20)

16 The harshness of the psalmist's attitude to the wicked was because they hated, cursed, oppressed, and harassed "the poor and the needy and the brokenhearted." The psalmist himself is "poor," "needy," and "brokenhearted" (v.22) and is the object of the attack! The purpose of the hounding is the "death" of the righteous.

17–20 The wicked reject "friendship" (vv.4–5) and love in favor of "curse" (GK 7839), which was intended to destroy a human being, his position, his family, and the remembrance of his name. Their love for cursing became so much a part of them that it was as if they "wore cursing as [their] garment." The wicked are evil through and through. It is "wrapped" about them and "tied forever" around them. The psalmist repeats the need for justice and vindication on the principle of lex talionis (retaliation).

V. Prayer for God's Love and Judgment (109:21–29)

21 David, in his desperate need, attempts to move the Lord on the basis of the Lord's nature, his own need, and a reminder of the wicked. The Lord, unlike the wicked, is good and full of "love" (GK 2876). His "name" is "LORD," and he is the "Sovereign" over all of life. To this covenantal God he prays: "deal well with me" and "deliver me."

22–24 David reminds the Lord that he is "poor and needy" and his "heart is wounded within" him (see comments on v.16). It is as if life flows out of him, like the disappearance of "an evening shadow." He is shaken "like a locust," as farmers would shake locusts off trees and shrubs and destroy them. Psychologically and physically the psalmist falters. His body no longer sustains him.

25–29 The psalmist reminds the Lord of the adversaries, who seek his downfall by heaping "scorn" on him and by rejecting him. His principle is clearly that of just retribution: shame and disgrace. He wants them to be "wrapped in shame as in a cloak." They must know that the deliverance of God's "servant" is the Lord's doing and that their judgment is also his work!

VI. Benediction of the God of Praise (109:30–31)

30–31 David concludes his prayer for deliverance and judgment with a fervent expectation of standing among the throngs of worshipers, filled with praise for the Lord. The Lord stands "at the right hand of the needy" as a protector. To this end the psalmist concludes on the note with which he began: the praise of God.

Psalm 110: The Kingdom of the Lord

This psalm may be classed with the royal psalms. Apostolic usage reveals a strongly messianic motif (cf. Mt 22:44; 26:64; Ac 2:34–35; Ro 8:34; et al.).

I. Promise (110:1)

1 The psalmist speaks of the promise of God pertaining to David and his dynasty. The Davidic king is a theocratic ruler in the sense that he rules over God's people under the Lord and yet is very close to him, at his right hand. The Lord promises to extend his dominion by subjugating the enemies. To make the enemies a "footstool" signifies absolute control, as when a victorious king placed his feet on the necks of his vanquished foes.

II. Victory (110:2–3)

2 The Lord will give strength to his king, symbolized by the "scepter from Zion." He has decreed that the Davidic king shall "rule" over the enemies.

3 We may infer from the military language that the royal troops are young, numerous, and valiant. The people come voluntarily on the day of battle. They consecrate themselves, are fully prepared, and place themselves at the service of the king. They will be as abundant as "dew" at dawn.

III. Promise (110:4)

4 From the priestly laws it appears that there is a clear distinction between Israel's three theocratic officers: king, prophet, and priest. However, David was dressed as a priest (2Sa

6:14), was in charge of the sacrifices (2Sa 6:17–18), and gave a priestly blessing to the people (2Sa 6:18). This was also true of Solomon (1Ki 8:14, 55, 62–64).

The irrevocable oath is none other than what the Lord promised to David pertaining to his dynasty (2Sa 7:13). Here the Davidic king serves as God's priest "in the order of Melchizedek." Melchizedek was a priest-king over Jerusalem (cf. Ge 14:18), who worshiped the Creator-God as supreme. The Davidic king is charged with responsibility over the true worship of the Lord.

IV. Victory (110:5–7)

5–6 When the king goes out to war, "the Lord," as the Master of the universe, supports him by being at his right hand. He furthers the king's power by crushing the resistance of kings. A day of accountability has been appointed, and on that day the Lord will "judge the nations," causing a great defeat for his enemies, symbolized by their "corpses" and "heads."

7 The theocratic king enjoys victory because of the God who fights for him. The king will tire himself out in battle but will be refreshed by a brook along the way of pursuit. The reason for the king's lifting up of his head in triumph is because of God's help.

Psalm 111: Celebration of God's Faithfulness

Psalms 111 and 112 form a unit. Psalm 111, celebrating the wonders of the Lord, is in the form of a hymn but has a clearly defined concern with wisdom.

I. Public Praise for God's Mighty Acts (111:1–3)

1 The psalmist calls on the community to praise the Lord. His praise is from the "heart," and he encourages the people of God to join in. The people of God belong to the "upright" (GK 3838) only because they do not belong to the category of "the wicked" (112:10). The "assembly" is the gathering of Jacob's descendants who fear the Lord.

2–3 The acts of God are marvelous and awe-inspiring. They bear further investigation, not to be fully comprehended, but to "ponder" and "delight in." His works are also "glorious and majestic." His royal splendor is particularly evident in his great acts of redemption on behalf of his people. They reveal his "righteousness," which is unfailing.

II. The Works of the Lord in Redemption (111:4–9)

4–9 The Lord has ordained the remembrance and proclamation of his redemptive acts—particularly the Exodus, the desert wanderings, the Conquest, and the revelation at Sinai—in the calendar of Israel. His name is "holy" and "awesome." The Lord has shown himself to be "gracious and compassionate" in his providential care of his people. His acts reveal his commitment to the "covenant" made with the patriarchs and confirmed at Mount Sinai. They also reveal that he is "faithful" and "just."

The "precepts" of God were to give order to God's people, that they might reflect the nature of their King in their national existence. God's word is "trustworthy" (GK 586) in that all of his promises come to pass. They reflect his "faithfulness" (GK 622) to his people. Thus the inspired author brings out the coherence between the Lord's acts and words. They all reflect his divine nature.

III. Response to God's Mighty Acts (111:10)

10 The revelation of the Lord's character and his fidelity to the covenant call for a response of wisdom in which God's people will "fear" (GK 3711) him, submitting to his rule and following his precepts. The fear of the Lord is "the beginning of wisdom." The wise have "good understanding." Another response is perpetual praise to the Great King.

Psalm 112: The Triumph of Faith

Psalm 112 is a *wisdom psalm*. It is an acrostic; it uses the "blessed is the man" formula, the vocabulary and concerns of wisdom literature, the contrast between the righteous and the wicked, and the blessings of wisdom.

I. Blessedness of Those Who Delight in Wisdom (112:1)

1 Those "blessed" (GK 897) by the Lord show themselves to be in active pursuit of godly wisdom. They begin with the fear of God and end with finding "great delight in his commands." These commands reflect

"grace and truth" as exemplified by Jesus (Jn 1:14).

II. Blessings of Righteousness (112:2–3)

2–3 The blessed are righteous, and they make every effort to establish God's righteous kingdom on earth, for their way of life shows a concern for God's majesty, glory, and greatness (111:2–3). The Lord rewards them with many and blessed descendants, wealth, and honor. They enjoy success in life, and their children share in the blessing of their godly parents. Thus godliness has its rewards in this life, in future generations, and in the life to come.

III. Blessing in Adversity (112:4)

4 The realism of the psalm breaks through. Adversity also comes on the path of the godly. When it does, however, they receive light. Their godly character is a "light" in darkness. They are "gracious and compassionate" like God.

IV. Blessings of Being Gracious and Compassionate (112:5)

5 Here "good" (GK 3202) is the quality of the righteous. They are "good" in that they are concerned about those in need and generously lend out money. They do not give their money away but invest it in the unfortunate, expecting to get it back only without interest. They show themselves a people of "justice" (GK 5477). They know God's revealed will.

V. Blessing in Adversity (112:6–8)

6–8 Because the wise hold to the precepts of God, they are "steadfast" in that they "will never be shaken," they "will have no fear," and their "heart is steadfast" and "secure." The wise may experience all kinds of surprises in life, but they will persevere in doing good. In all situations of life, they trust in the Lord, knowing that "in the end" God will turn the gloatings and fortunes of the wicked. Godliness has its rewards in this life and in the life to come.

VI. Blessings of Righteousness (112:9)

9 The psalmist has singled out generosity and compassion as the hallmarks of wise living. Such living leads to lasting success. The work of the godly endures; their reward is in the exaltation and honor of their children.

VII. The Curse on the "Longings" of the Wicked (112:10)

10 The wicked, as they see God's reward on the righteous (vv.6, 9), are filled with anger, bitterness, and jealousy. However, such anger will not last, for they will destroy themselves in their resentment. The wicked will not succeed. All their schemings and plans "will come to nothing."

The Egyptian Hallel: Psalms 113–118

The *Hallel* psalms are found in three separate collections: the "Egyptian Hallel" (113–118), the "Great Hallel" (120–136), and the concluding Hallel psalms (146–150). The Hallel psalms had a significant part in the "praise" (Heb. *hallel*; GK 2146) of the Lord. The Egyptian Hallel and the Great Hallel were sung during the annual feasts (Lev 23; Nu 10:10). The Egyptian Hallel psalms received a special place in the Passover liturgy, as 113–114 were recited or sung before and 115–118 after the festive meal (cf. Mt 26:30; Mk 14:26). The concluding Hallel psalms (146–150) were incorporated in the daily prayers in the synagogue after the destruction of the temple (A.D. 70).

Psalm 113: The Lord Is Exalted in His Saving Acts

Psalms 113 and 114 are both in the form of *descriptive praise* psalms.

I. Call to Praise the Lord (113:1–3)

1–3 The "servants of the LORD"—i.e., his loyal people together with the priests and the Levites—comprise all those who know the Lord. The threefold repetition of the "name of the LORD" calls attention to the acts and the self-revelation of the Lord. The praise of the Lord, who acted and revealed himself in creation and in redemption, is to be a lasting "praise" (GK 2146). Furthermore, the worship of the Lord is to be universal. With the coming of our Lord Jesus Christ, the true worship of God has been extended to all the globe.

II. The Sovereignty of the Lord (113:4–6)

4–6 The Lord is sovereign over everything. This bold statement evokes a rhetorical question: "Who is like the LORD our God?" The Lord is exalted in his rule, "enthroned on high." Yet he has also accommodated himself

to the needs of his people; he "stoops down" to his needy children! What a marvellous God—high and mighty, and yet deeply caring about people.

III. Call to Praise for His Acts of Deliverance (113:7–9)

7–9 The Lord takes care of the needs of the "poor" and "needy" by moving them from being outcasts of society to having a position of prominence. A barren woman in ancient society was a social outcast. However, the goodness of the Lord extends to blessing his people with children. The psalm concludes on the note it began with: "Praise the LORD."

Psalm 114: We Are the People of God!

Psalm 114 is one of the Egyptian Hallel Psalms (see Ps 113). By genre it is a hymn of descriptive praise.

I. The Covenant People (114:1–2)

1–2 Israel was marvelously delivered out of a foreign land, from a people who spoke a different language. It was this nation that the Lord chose for his "sanctuary" (GK 7731; often translated "holy") and "dominion" (GK 4939). These two words echo God's promises to all the Twelve Tribes. In Ex 19:5–6 he promised Israel that they would become his "treasured possession," a "kingdom of priests and a holy nation." The whole people became "holy" to the Lord; Israel had become his "sacred dominion." The references to "Judah" and to "Israel" in v.2 are not contrastive but parallel. All Twelve Tribes had become the "sacred dominion" of the Lord by covenant at Mount Sinai.

II. The Witness of Nature (114:3–6)

3–6 The wonder of Israel's election as the covenant people has its effect on the world of nature. The psalmist chooses the motif of Israel passing through the Red Sea and the Jordan River as a background for a celebration of the wonder of God's revelation to Israel. The mountains and hills "skipped" upon hearing about the victorious power of the Lord in these redemptive events (first stated positively, then by a series of rhetorical questions). It is as if the psalmist calls on nature to bear witness to that great event, when God established his kingdom on earth.

III. The Covenant God (114:7–8)

7–8 The repetition of "at the presence of" introduces the answer to the questions and the climactic conclusion. The God of Israel is "Lord" (GK 123), and the Master of the universe is no other than "the God of Jacob." His powerful and marvelous way has not ceased, for he *continues to turn* (lit. tr.) "the rock into a pool, the hard rock into springs of water."

Psalm 115: We Are the Servants of God!

Psalm 115 may be classified as a psalm of *communal confidence*. These psalms are closely related to communal thanksgiving songs and to communal laments.

I. Community Prayer for Help (115:1–3)

1 The community has suffered. With the adversity of God's people, the glory of the Lord is at stake. Consequently, they are concerned about the honor and glory of the name of the Lord. Only after making their protest with an appeal to his glory do the godly remind the Lord of his promised "love and faithfulness."

2–3 Because of the present adversity, the "nations" were quick in casting aspersions on the honor of Israel's God. The godly firmly believe that God is "in heaven" and that he can do whatever "pleases him"; but out of concern for his reputation among the nations, they raise this argument.

II. Impotence of Idols (115:4–8)

4–8 Whereas the Lord has the creative powers, the idols are "made" by human beings. They are limited in power because they are human artifacts, share in human limitations, and are made of materials that come out of the earth. They have human anatomical features, but they are powerless. Ultimately divine revelation is the difference between human religions and the true religion of the Lord. Not only are idols worthless, those who worship them are also vain. False worship is not innocent but demoralizing, and ultimately the worshipers will perish together with their perishable idols.

III. Confidence in the Lord (115:9–11)

9–11 How different is the religion of revelation! The people of God, led in worship by the priests, do not come to him with images. He comes to them with the promise of blessing ("help") and protection ("shield"). In response to his covenant, he expects nothing but loyalty from his people. The threefold call "trust in the LORD" has a corresponding threefold assurance of God's protection.

It is unclear whether those "who fear him" are a separate class from the house of Israel (i.e., the "God-fearers" or proselytes), or a synonym for "house of Israel," or a euphemism for all Israel (i.e., laity as well as priests). But the conclusion is the same, as the psalmist calls on everyone to "trust in the LORD" by abandoning false worship.

IV. Blessing of the Lord (115:12–15)

12–13 The godly are assured that the Lord will always "bless" (GK 1385) his own. Though they may experience affliction and testing, he "remembers" (GK 2349) those with whom he has made a covenant. The Lord does not discriminate between the tribes of Israel, between the laity and priesthood, or between the important and the social outcasts. He is the God of his people, and all his own will be the recipients of his blessing.

14–15 The blessing as a word of promise holds out a great future for God's people. In accordance with his promise to Abraham (Ge 12:2), the Lord will bless his people with fruitfulness in descendants. During periods of adversity, the people were concerned with their future. The Lord renews the promise through these words of benediction.

V. Power of the Lord (115:16)

16 The certainty of blessing, increase, and protection (vv.9–15) lies in Israel's belief in who God is: He is "the Maker of heaven and earth" (v.15), who sovereignly rules over everything he has created. He is enthroned in "the highest heavens," though he has graciously given the dominion of the created earth to humans—in the service of the Lord.

VI. Community Praise (115:17–18)

17 Humans must be submissive to the Lord alone. However, if the adversities of God's people persist, more and more may die. They will go down to "silence" in the grave and can no longer join in the processions, annual feasts, and liturgies.

18 Those singing this psalm pray for the opportunity to fulfill their calling to praise the Lord. Regardless of the outcome of their present dilemma, they know that their God will deliver them, because he has elected them to praise him on his earth. They affirm their commitment to "extol" him "both now and forevermore." The concluding exhortation "Praise the LORD" is the usual conclusion of each of the Egyptian Hallel psalms.

Psalm 116: Be at Rest, for the Lord Is Good

This psalm is the fourth of the Egyptian Hallel psalms (see Ps 113). By genre the psalm belongs to the classification of *individual thanksgiving* hymns.

I. Thanksgiving (116:1–2)

1–2 An emphatically placed "I love" opens the psalm. The psalmist's reason for the expression of endearment is motivated by answered prayer. The Lord has heard the "cry for mercy." God's attentiveness to prayer is restated in v.2, and the psalmist is encouraged to call on him "as long as I live."

II. The Need for Deliverance (116:3)

3 "Death" and the "grave" (GK 8619) are personified as hunters lying in wait with "cords" to entangle the godly. The psalmist had been in great distress; life had become like "hell."

III. God the Deliverer (116:4–6a)

4–6a In this terrible situation the psalmist resorted to his only hope: the "name" of the Lord, which signifies everything a human needs in life and death. He is fully aware that the Lord is "gracious" in his forgiveness and in sustaining his children, "righteous" in keeping the covenant, and "full of compassion" in his understanding of the limits of his children. This affirmation of the character of God is why he gives thanks.

IV. Thanksgiving (116:6b–7)

6b–7 The description of the character of the Lord evokes from the psalmist an affirmation of how the Lord "saved" him. The psalmist called on the Lord, "Save me" (v.4), and the Lord was true to his promise. Then reflecting on his past misery, he can speak words of comfort to himself because of God's goodness. He can be "at rest" because he knows his God.

V. God the Deliverer (116:8–11)

8–9 Only the Lord can change "death," "tears," and "stumbling" into a "walk before the LORD" and a joyful celebration of life "in the land of the living."

10–11 Especially in his distress, the psalmist learned the lesson of true faith: "I believed *even when* I said . . ." (see NIV note). He admits that in his "dismay" he became more aware of human limitations as he saw "men" (GK 132) for what they really are: "vain" (i.e., "liars").

VI. Vows of Thanksgiving (116:12–14)

12 The Lord was faithful, and the psalmist responds to his acts of goodness with a question that has only one answer. There is no way to "repay" the Lord.

13–14 As a token of his thanksgiving, the psalmist brings "a thank offering" (v.17), together with a drink offering, which he calls "the cup of salvation." At that time he called again "on the name of the LORD," this time to thank him and praise his holy name for his fidelity to his promises. The thank offering was a fulfillment of the "vows" made during the distress.

VII. God the Deliverer (116:15–16)

15–16 The psalmist confesses the great love of the Lord for his "saints" in that he does not lightly permit adversity or an early death. They are "precious" to him. The psalmist is God's "servant," born within the household of faith. Again he affirms the Lord's faithfulness to him.

VIII. Vows of Thanksgiving (116:17–19)

17–19 In the presence of the godly, the psalmist will show his gratitude to the Lord for his deliverance. He will present a "thank offering" (see comment on vv.13–14). As prescribed in the priestly laws, he had to present his offering in the courts of the temple in Jerusalem.

Psalm 117: Great Is His Love Toward Us

Psalm 117 is the fifth of the Egyptian Hallel psalms (113–118; see Ps 113). It is the shortest psalm, consisting of only two verses.

Its genre resembles that of the hymns of descriptive praise.

1–2 The usual "praise the LORD" in the Egyptian Hallel psalms is directed to the covenant community. However, this time the psalmist calls on the Gentiles ("nations"; GK 1580) to praise the Lord. The reason for the universal praise lies in the Lord's relationship to Israel: he reveals a constancy of "love" and "faithfulness." These two perfections are often paired, as God's love is always faithful.

Psalm 118: Open the Gates of Righteousness

Psalm 118 is the last of the Egyptian Hallel psalms (see comments on Ps 113). The psalm exhibits features of *communal* and *individual thanksgiving*.

I. Call to Communal Thanksgiving (118:1–4)

1–4 All Israel had enjoyed the benefits of God's "goodness" and his unfailing "love": the congregation of Israel, the priests, and "those who fear the LORD."

II. Thanksgiving (118:5–21)

5 Apparently here an individual worshiper represents the people in giving testimony to the Lord's goodness. Originally the worship leader may have been the king or a priest, but anyone of God's people may recite God's acts in response to the prayers of God's people. The worshiper thanks the Lord because he has heard his cry of "anguish." He was without perspective and in dire straits, but the Lord answered him by "setting [him] free."

6–7 The psalmist knew that the Lord was with him in all circumstances of life; based on that conviction he was not afraid of troubles caused by his fellow human beings. The presence of the Lord is personal. He comforts with his support and gives a new perspective on the future.

8–9 In a hymnic celebration, the individual worshiper confesses his confidence in the Lord. Such confidence is far superior to relying on flesh and blood. The mention of "man" in parallelism with "princes" is a literary manner of including all of humanity, both lowly and exalted.

10–12 The language of the troubles may be interpreted literally or metaphorically. If a king is the speaker, the reference to "all the nations," the repetition of "surrounded me" and "I cut them off," as well as the metaphorical comparison ("bees," "burning thorns") may be interpreted as a great victory over the enemies. On the other hand, this can also be interpreted as a hyperbole of great adversity. Great as the adversity was, the psalmist overcame his feeling of anguish "in the name of the LORD," which is powerful indeed.

13–14 The adversity was so great that the psalmist felt himself pushed and was "about to fall." However, the Lord was faithful to his promise to keep his own from falling or stumbling (121:3). The word "strength" (GK 6437) denotes his power in saving while "salvation" (GK 3802) suggests the whole process of his mighty acts, his judgment on the adversaries, and his help to his children. "Song" may mean "victory song."

15–16 The victory of the Lord provides the occasion for communal rejoicing. The godly join in the celebration of God's mighty acts. They sing a chorus or refrain whose subject is the Lord's "right hand."

17–18 The psalmist has individually experienced the Lord's power to restore and sustain life. The troubles are likened to death, but the Lord's favor is life. "Live" (GK 2649) signifies here the joyful proclamation of "what the LORD has done": his acts of discipline (cf. Heb 12:5–11).

19–20 In the festal procession only the "righteous" (GK 7404) are permitted entrance to the presence of the Lord, symbolically guarded by "the gates of righteousness." The psalmist strongly confesses his unswerving loyalty to and trust in the Lord. Those who enter into the Lord's presence must meet this requirement of covenant loyalty and trust.

21 In this company of the righteous, the psalmist shares his testimony of "thanks" for the Lord's victory. The emphasis is on the Lord's "salvation," which is consistent with the emphasis in this psalm on the Lord's gracious and complete deliverance of his people. The Lord has been with the individual as he was with Israel of old, in the days of Moses.

III. Thanksgiving Liturgy (118:22–29)

22–23 The Lord has given prominence to his suffering servant like a "capstone." This was an important stone that held two rows of stones together in a corner ("cornerstone") or stabilized the stones at the foundation. The Lord changed the speaker's adversity, likened to the throwing away of a capstone, into a "marvelous" demonstration of himself.

24–25 The day of thanksgiving is the day of salvation. The songs of rejoicing encourage the godly to renew their prayers for God's help. The phrase "save us" (*Hosanna*; GK 3828) is related to the noun rendered "salvation." The congregation requests the Lord to continue to do his wonderful acts so that they will "prosper."

26–27 In response to the people's trust in the Lord, the king or priest blesses all who come to the Lord in his "name." The people respond to this blessing with a confession that "the LORD is God," by whose "light" they exist and are protected from the darkness of famine, war, and exile. They also renew their thanksgiving to the Lord in making a procession to the temple in Jerusalem. They demonstrate their commitment in concrete acts, whether they come with "boughs in hand" during the Feast of Tabernacles (Lev 23:40) or with "festal sacrifices" (see NIV note).

28–29 The worship leader leads the community in the affirmation that the Lord alone is God. Israel must give thanks to him, because "he is good; his love endures forever" (cf. v.1).

The most significant stone in a doorway was the capstone, the top stone that was shaped like the letter "V." If that stone were removed, the entire archway would collapse. Jesus is the capstone of our lives (118:22).

Psalm 119: The Joy of God's Law in Distress

This longest psalm in the Psalter is well known for its teaching on God's law. Yet the beauty of this psalm lies in the psalmist's absolute devotion to the Lord. The genre corresponds most closely to that of the *wisdom psalms*. Yet the psalm also reflects elements of lament, thanksgiving, innocence, praise, and confidence. Psalm 119 is an alphabetic acrostic psalm, consisting of twenty-two stanzas of eight verses each.

The psalmist uses eight words for God's law:

1. "Law" (*torah*; GK 9368) occurs twenty-five times. In the broad sense it refers to any "instruction" flowing from the revelation of God as the basis for life and action. In the narrow sense it denotes the Law of Moses, whether the Pentateuch, the priestly law, or the Deuteronomic law.

2. "Word" (*dabar*; GK 1821) is any word that proceeds from the mouth of the Lord. It is a general designation for divine revelation.

3. "Laws" (*mishpatim*; GK 5477) pertain to particular legal issues ("case laws") that form the basis for Israel's legal system. God himself is the Great Judge.

4. "Statute(s)" (*eduth/edoth*; GK 6339) derives from the word that means "witness," "testify"; "testimony" is often synonymous with "covenant" (cf. 25:10; 132:12). The observance of the "statutes" of the Lord signifies loyalty to the terms of the covenant between God and Israel.

5. "Command(s)" (*mitswah/mitswoth*; GK 5184) is a frequent designation for anything that the Lord, the covenant God, has ordered.

6. "Decrees" (*huqqim*; GK 2976) is derived from the root for "engrave," "inscribe." God reveals his royal sovereignty by establishing his divine will in nature and in the covenant community.

7. "Precepts" (*piqqudim*; GK 7218) occurs only in the book of Psalms and appears to be synonymous with "covenant" (103:18) and with the revelation of God (111:7). Its root connotes the authority to determine the relationship between the speaker and the object.

8. "Word" or "promise" (*imrah*; GK 614) may denote anything God has spoken, commanded, or promised.

I. The Aleph Strophe (119:1–8)

1–8 The blessing of God (see 1:1) rests on those who give themselves to wise living. They are people of integrity ("blameless"), whose walk follows the path set out in God's revelation, "the law" (*torah*). In his "statutes" (*edoth*) God sets down how he is to be loved, and his loving children respond to his wishes. The "decrees" (*huqqim*) of the Lord give order to human lives, even as they uphold order in the created world. Negatively, the people of integrity "do nothing wrong."

The hope of the godly lies in the Lord. The psalmist prays that his response to God's revelation may be acceptable and that no "shame" or ultimate disgrace may overtake him. "Shame" (GK1017) connotes a state of being abandoned by the Lord and condemned to utter ruin. Thus he prays that the Lord will have mercy on his servant and "not utterly forsake" him.

The psalmist looks for God's favor by which he may again praise his God "with an upright heart." The "laws" (*mishpatim*) of God are "righteous" in that they establish divine order in this world, granting the godly a sense of deliverance and freedom. As a final expression of commitment, the psalmist stresses that he will "obey" the "decrees" of God.

II. The Beth Strophe (119:9–16)

9 The young man may keep his way "pure" (GK 2342) by the practice of godliness by living according to God's "word" (*dabar*).

10–16 The teacher exemplifies the wise response to God's revelation in vv.10–16. He demonstrates his sincere love for God by treasuring his "word" of promise (*imrah*) in his "heart." The act of "hiding" (GK 7621) God's word is not only memorization but extends to living in devotion to the Lord.

The teachable spirit begins with a proper regard for God. Little instruction in godliness takes place unless the heart is full of praise. The psalmist declares repeatedly that his inner "delight" and joy are in God and his revelation, not material acquisition. The external expression of this inner loyalty to the Lord is joyful obedience. Part of his practice of godliness is to speak positively about God's "laws" (*mishpatim*), which he treasures as having come out of the "mouth" of the Lord.

III. The Gimel Strophe (119:17–24)

17–20 In difficulty and distress, the Lord and his word are a comfort to the godly. The prayer for help presupposes a close relationship between the Lord and the psalmist. As a "stranger," his yearning for God and his word is so strong that he feels as if crushed in his alienation from God. He prays that he may "live" a life of fellowship with God and in obedience to his "word" (*dabar*), and he longs to see the "wonderful things in [God's] law."

21–24 God's blessing rests on those who submit themselves to the law of God, whereas his curse comes on all those who "stray" deliberately from it. The "arrogant" despise God and godliness with their "scorn and contempt." By contrast, God's "servant" shows his loyalty to God's "statutes" (*edoth*) by observing them and by "meditating" on his "decrees" (*huqqim*). In spite of opposition from the community and her "rulers," the psalmist receives joy and guidance from God's "statutes" (*edoth*) as his "counselors."

IV. The Daleth Strophe (119:25–32)

25–27 The psalmist's experience of mortality forces him even closer to the Lord. Only God can deliver him and through his "word" (*dabar*) give him a new lease on "life." In his adversities he becomes more teachable. He opens his life to God, believing that the Lord answers prayer. In his devotion to God, he desires to understand and apply God's word and thus deepen his dependence on the Lord. The word opens up the greatness of God's acts in creation and in redemption.

28–32 The word of God has the power to "strengthen" those overwhelmed with "sorrow." The word of God also keeps one from the ways of the world, as it renews an inner, burning desire to live a life of devotion to God. Such devotion focuses on doing God's will. On the one hand, the psalmist fully depends on the Lord for life, sustaining grace, and illumination (vv.25–29); on the other hand, he is fully responsible in "seeking" the kingdom of God by choosing and living a life of loyalty to God and his word.

The psalmist further prays that his lifestyle will keep him from anxiety and adversity ("shame"). He will not only "walk" (vv.1, 3) in the "path of your commands," but he will "run." The Lord has given him a sense of freedom from anxiety and care.

V. The He Strophe (119:33–40)

33–37 The purpose of God's positive direction and protection from evil is to encourage the psalmist to keep the law. Keeping the law was not a matter of external conformity in the OT but required "a heart" of absolute devotion to God. By God's help he will "follow" his "decrees" (*huqqim*) and receive God's reward. His "delight" of radical loyalty from the heart is a work of grace. He prays that the Lord may "preserve" him as he walks in the way of God.

38–40 The mood of the prayer changes abruptly to a call for action. The psalmist asks the Lord to "fulfill" his "word" or "promise" (*imrah*) of "righteousness" (GK 614) to his servant. In his righteousness God delivers, frees, preserves life, and removes a dreaded "disgrace." The delight in God's laws is in direct relationship to his prayer that the Lord's righteousness be established for him and for all of God's servants.

VI. The Waw Strophe (119:41–48)

41–42 This strophe continues the elements of prayer and commitment. The words "unfailing love" and "salvation" explicate the prayer for renewal "in your righteousness" (v.40). The "righteousness" of God extends to deliverance and vindication from one's adversaries. The dreaded "disgrace" will be removed, and the psalmist will rebuke the one who "taunts" him. Hope in salvation is grounded in God's word of "promise," and his promise calls for "trust."

43–45 The psalmist pleads with the Lord to be true to his promises. The psalmist promises to remain loyal to the Lord throughout life. His devotion is a free expression of his love for God, and in this walk he experiences the Lord's blessing and bounty.

46–48 The psalmist vows to speak about God's "statutes" (*edoth*) unashamedly, even in the presence of "kings." He is so full of love for God and so filled with joy in the prospect of salvation that he strongly asserts his "love" and "delight" as he prays and meditates.

VII. The Zayin Strophe (119:49–56)

49–56 The psalmist knows that the Lord's promises are sure; therefore he has "hope" and "comfort" even in suffering. The "arrogant mock" him, but he gets more provoked at their apostasy from God than at the suffering they cause him. They drive him to greater loyalty. The word of the Lord sustains and restores life. He can therefore sing the praises of God's "decrees" (*huqqim*) day and night. This lifestyle does not develop overnight but comes from habitual practice.

VIII. The Heth Strophe (119:57–64)

57–64 The strophe begins with a familiar formula of trust and ends on an exclamation of God's cosmic and unfailing "love" (GK 2876). The psalmist promises a deeper commitment "to obey" God's words. His petition for God's grace is urgent and corresponds to his diligence toward God's law. Even if the Lord delays his redemption, permitting the wicked to triumph for a while, the psalmist affirms his loyalty as being of primary importance. Faith in God's "righteous" laws triumphs and brings out a song of thanksgiving, freeing him from the "ropes" of the wicked (a metaphor for their reign of terror). The psalmist shows his love by his attentiveness to the word of God and by associating with the godly, who "fear" the Lord and "who follow [his] precepts." The world of creation witnesses to his love.

IX. The Teth Strophe (119:65–72)

65–72 The Lord is "good" because he is faithful to his word. "Knowledge" (GK 1981) primarily denotes the knowledge of God in one's communion with him and secondarily the response to the life of fellowship with the Lord. The psalmist's experience of humiliation and affliction, caused by "the arrogant," was good. Because of it he has given himself more to "learning," applying, and loving of God's "precepts" (*piqqudim*), "law" (*torah*), and "decrees" (*huqqim*). The discipline of the Lord has changed his life; he used to "go astray," but now he obeys God's word and is restored in fellowship.

X. The Yodh Strophe (119:73–80)

73–74 The psalmist believes that God has "made" him for the purpose of having "understanding" to fulfill his "commands" (*mitswoth*). Since he has initiated the relationship, the psalmist is confident that the righteous may soon rejoice.

75–80 The psalmist can say, "I know" that God's "laws" (*mishpatim*) are "righteous" and faithful, because he has an experiential knowledge of God, of his "unfailing love," and of his "compassion." God's purpose for affliction is to refine the relationship with his children. When he looks at humans, the psalmist sees the "arrogant," who have wrongfully dealt with him and must get their just deserts. While waiting he continues to "delight" in God's "law" (*torah*), to "meditate" on the Lord's "precepts" (*piqqudim*, v.78), and to walk in a "blameless" way before God. The psalmist also prays that they who "fear" the Lord may be encouraged and rejoice at God's vindication.

XI. The Kaph Strophe (119:81–88)

81–88 In his despair the psalmist looks only to the Lord for his "salvation," as promised in his "word." He is being persecuted "without cause," and his endurance is wearing down. His soul "faints," his "eyes fail," and he feels as if he is near the end of his strength. He feels himself to be "like a wineskin in the smoke," i.e., useless, shriveled, and unattractive because of being blackened with soot. In his loneliness he wonders when God will comfort him, and he asks the Lord to execute "justice" (*mishpat*). In contrast to the "arrogant," he loves God and his word. Thus he also submits himself to the Lord's "help" for preservation of life.

XII. The Lamedh Strophe (119:89–96)

89–93 The nature of the Lord is reflected in everything he has created, and "all things serve" him. The psalmist found "delight" in the "law" (*torah*) of the Lord. Had he not found meaning in his "affliction," he feels that he would have perished like a falling star. Therefore he will not forget the "precepts" (*piqqudim*) of the Lord, for they give order and preservation of life.

94–96 The psalmist knows that he belongs to God. Therefore he prays that the Lord will continue to sustain his life, in spite of the opposition of "the wicked." As their violence increases, he seeks refuge in a diligent study of the "statutes" (*edoth*) of the Lord. The

"commands" (*mitswoth*) of the Lord liberate him and give him a new lease on life.

XIII. The Mem Strophe (119:97–104)

97–104 The love of God's law derives from love for God. "Meditation" (GK 8491) is a form of devotion. The psalmist delights in his understanding of God's law. He reflects on his devotion in relation to the "enemies," "teachers," and "elders," and he rejects the way of the wicked. He was obedient to the Lord and did not "depart" from his laws. The "words" of promise (*imrah*) are likened to "honey"; God's instructions are sweet, and they lead to understanding and obedience.

XIV. The Nun Strophe (119:105–12)

105–12 The psalmist who hates "every wrong path" thanks the Lord that he has given him his "word" (*dabar*) as a guide and life-sustaining source ("light") as he walks on the "path" of life. The "laws" (*mishpatim*) of God are "righteous" and are comforting even in adversity. The psalmist affirms that the Lord alone can "preserve" life. Even in affliction he has learned to give the Lord "willing praise."

The wicked attempt to hunt down the psalmist and catch him. But he is determined to be loyal to the Lord. Thus far he has not yet strayed. His joy and determination to please the Lord are much greater than the affliction with which he lives constantly.

XV. The Samekh Strophe (119:113–20)

113–20 The ways of the righteous and the wicked are clearly divergent. The wicked are "double-minded," "evildoers," disobedient to God's word, and deceptive. The psalmist "hates" that lifestyle, but he "loves" the law of the Lord. He draws near to God for "refuge," for he is the psalmist's "shield" or protection. He thus prays that the Lord will "sustain" and "uphold" him so that he may "live." He also believes that the Lord's righteous judgment will come on the wicked. The Lord will "discard" them like "dross," the scum that forms when a precious metal is being refined. How different are the godly! They have hope. They draw near to God and find delight in his word.

The psalmist concludes with a final affirmation of godly fear. He stands in "awe" of the Lord and "trembles."

XVI. The Ayin Strophe (119:121–28)

121–28 The psalmist has done what is "righteous and just." Now he expects the Lord to conform to his "righteous promise," according to which the godly will be delivered from all adversities. God's "salvation" extends to all the needs of his people, as they look for a renewal of God's "love" (GK 2876) and deliverance from the "arrogant." The godly psalmist also reveals that he has a teachable spirit.

The psalmist affirms his love for the Lord's "commands" (*mitswoth*) and compares them favorably with "gold, more than pure gold." He also affirms his commitment to the Lord by expressing loyalty to his "precepts" (*piqqudim*). Together with the psalmist's affirmation of devotion is a righteous indignation at the way the ungodly have broken God's "law" (*torah*).

XVII. The Pe Strophe (119:129–36)

129–31 The psalmist considers the many benefits of God's word. His "statutes" (*edoth*) are "wonderful"; through them he gains insight into God's revelation. The psalmist uses the metaphor of "mouth" to suggest that he has a great appetite for the "commands" (*mitswoth*) of the Lord. He "pants" for them as he waits with great anticipation.

132–36 The Lord's blessing brings "mercy," directs and protects from sin and adversities, and extends God's favor to all of life. The psalmist's prayer for God's blessing is in accordance with God's own promises. He gives himself with greater commitment to do God's will and weeps over the continuation of rebellion and transgression. "Streams of tears" is a hyperbole for deep sorrow and anguish of soul.

XVIII. The Tsadhe Strophe (119:137–44)

137–44 The conviction that the Lord is "righteous" and "trustworthy" evokes a response of "zeal," which increases as the psalmist's adversities increase. His adversaries "ignore" God's laws, whereas he does not "forget" them. Instead, he "loves" them and finds his "delight" in them. Yet he feels that his loyalty to the Lord and his devotion to godliness have been unrewarded. Instead, troubles have come his way. But he holds on to faith in the Lord, praying humbly that he may

"understand" so as to be revived in his inner being.

XIX. The Qoph Strophe (119:145–52)

145–49 Out of the conviction of God's righteousness, the psalmist cries out for God's help. He feverishly presents his lament before the Lord that he may "answer" him in delivering him from adversity. While waiting for God's deliverance, he faithfully holds to God's expectations. His longing for God is so intense that he prays "for help" throughout the night. At that time he also "meditates" on God's "promises" (*imrah*). He waits for the Lord to come through, having put his "hope" in God's word and in renewal of God's "love" (GK 2876).

150–52 Though the wicked hunt the psalmist down, the Lord is nearby. Moreover, his relationship with the Lord has been well established. His "statutes" (*edoth*) are constant.

XX. The Resh Strophe (119:153–60)

153–60 The psalmist again affirms his loyalty to the Lord as the godless haunt him and flaunt the commandments of the Lord. As he looks at them, he also affirms his innocence in that he has purposefully avoided their influence (cf. 1:1). They are "the faithless" (GK 953), i.e., they have broken the covenant relationship with the Lord and their words and acts are unreliable.

There is the deep cognizance that only the Lord can "deliver" and "redeem." Therefore the psalmist prays for the Lord to "defend my cause." The very nature of his existence is in jeopardy. His adversaries are many, but God's "compassion" (GK 8171) is "great." The expression "all your words" means that from the beginning God's word is true, even as his "laws" (*mishpat*) are forever "righteous" (GK 7406). The fidelity and righteousness of his word sustain the psalmist.

XXI. The Sin and Shin Strophe (119:161–68)

161–65 The context of adversity is unchanged, as the "rulers" of the people continually "persecute . . . without cause." But the psalmist rejoices in the "promise" of the Lord and in God's instruction, like a warrior returning with "great spoil." He praises the Lord many times a day for his "righteous laws." The godly magnify God's name because they know he will vindicate them. Therefore they have "peace." Though surrounded by adversity, they are confident that with the Lord's help they will not "stumble."

166–68 In anticipation of that great day of "salvation," the psalmist gives himself to hopeful waiting and to the practice of godliness. He obeys God's precepts from a committed heart. He keeps God's laws out of "love," for God discerns all his activities, emotions, hopes, and fears.

XXII. The Taw Strophe (119:169–76)

The last strophe of this lengthy psalm contains a prayer for the Lord's salvation. The issues have not been resolved, but the design of the psalm is such that it raises the spirit of expectation in those who love God's word.

169–72 The psalmist comes before the Lord with a broken spirit, crying out for mercy. He appeals for "understanding" to discern how best to respond to his adversities with hope in the promises. He also asks for deliverance. In anticipation of that moment of redemption, he contemplates the joyful expressions of thanksgiving. Then he will bubble forth with "praise" and will respond in song to God's fulfilled "word."

173–76 Verses 173–75 repeat the motifs of prayer, a commitment to God's word, and an anticipation to praise the Lord for his redemption. "Hand" is a metaphor for God's powerful deliverance, for which the psalmist "longs," because God's deliverance preserves life. The last verse of the psalm is a cry from a broken spirit, not a confession of apostasy. The psalmist feels helpless, like a "lost sheep," and cries to his Good Shepherd to "seek" him, for he has not neglected God or his word.

Psalm 120: The Lord, I, and They

Psalms 120–134 form a collection known as the "Songs of Ascents," which in turn is a major part of the Great Hallel psalms (120–36; see comment on Ps 113). The meaning of the designation "song of ascents" is not clear. Likely the songs were sung in the three annual festival processions, as the pilgrims "ascended" to Jerusalem (cf. Ex 23:14–17; Dt 16:16). Though not beyond dispute, Ps 120 is an *individual lament.*

I. Assurance of Answered Prayer (120:1)

1 "On the LORD" expresses the sole dependence on God in the hour of distress. It is more natural to understand v.1 as having taken place in the past. The psalmist has already received assurance from the Lord that he will deal with his problem.

II. Prayer for Help (120:2–4)

2–4 The psalmist prays for relief and deliverance from false accusations and treachery. As the wicked have spoken deceptively, he prays that God will bring on them the fulfillment of their own words. The "deceitful" tongue is compared to a bow whose arrows are the words. The wicked must be uprooted for the sake of God's honor.

III. Expression of Desperation (120:5)

5 The psalmist laments his present condition, as he still dwells like a stranger "in Meshech," "among the tents of Kedar." Meshech is located in Asia Minor by the Black Sea; Kedar denotes the Arab tribesmen who lived in the Arabian Desert. In essence the psalmist is saying that his enemies are no better than hostile barbarians. He himself does not feel at home among an ungodly people.

IV. Longing for Peace (120:6–7)

6–7 The psalmist reminds the Lord that he has suffered long enough in his present situation. He has "lived" among apostates who "hate peace." They malign, slander, and make every aspect of life difficult for the godly. Tired of his affliction, he asks the Lord to establish peace.

Psalm 121: The Lord Is My Guardian

Psalm 121 is one of the fifteen "Songs of Ascents" (120–134; see Ps 120).

I. The Lord Is the Creator (121:1–2)

1–2 The psalmist is looking with great anxiety or longing to the hills. Perhaps he expected robbers to be hiding there. Or he may have looked with great anticipation if he were on a pilgrimage to Jerusalem (125:2). The "help" (GK 6469) the psalmist is concerned with pertains to protection, guidance, and blessing, which can only come from the Lord. He comforts himself with the thought that the Lord is "the Maker of heaven and earth." The creedal statement originally signified an apologetic statement on the Lord's sovereignty over all realms, thereby excluding any claims by pagan deities.

II. The Lord, the Guardian of Israel, Is "Your" Guardian (121:3–6)

3–6 The ground for the psalmist's confidence lies in the further development of the doctrine of God: the guardian ("he who watches") of Israel is the guardian of every believer. He protects, guides, and blesses his own. He will be their "shade" as he protects them day and night. The intensity of his care is further amplified as he never sleeps nor slumbers. The Lord is always there to help and to protect his people.

III. Blessing (121:7–8)

7–8 The Lord's care extends to all adversities, as he is sovereign over all affairs of life, especially the "life" (lit., "soul"; GK 5883) of his own child. Whatever his children do—whether they arrive at Jerusalem, go on a far journey, or return home—the Lord will "watch" over their affairs, "now and forevermore."

Psalm 122: May There Be Peace in Zion

This is one of the "Songs of Ascents" (120–134; see Ps 120). It is a Song of Zion by genre (46; 48; 76; 84; 87; 132), psalms that have much in common with the royal psalms as they celebrate the glories associated with Jerusalem: temple and kingship.

I. The Pilgrim's Joy (122:1–2)

1–2 The psalmist is reflecting on the many times that he has heard the call to go to the house of the Lord. At this point he is standing in Jerusalem and rejoicing—with the thousands of other pilgrims during one of the three pilgrimage feats, Passover, Firstfruits, and Booths. These held a special redemptive-historical significance, as they commemorated God's goodness in the Exodus, the Conquest, and his continual care (cf. Dt 16:16).

II. The Pilgrim's Praise (122:3–5)

3–4 In praise of Jerusalem the psalmist looks above the heads of the throngs, where the walls and buildings of the city rise, giving the sense of being joined together. The Israelite tribes came together to praise "the name of the Lord" as an act of loyalty to his command (cf. Dt 12:5–6; Ps 81:3–5).

5 Jerusalem was not only the religious center, symbolized by the "house of the Lord" (v.1), but also the political center, symbolized by "the thrones for judgment." The kings of Judah upheld God's kingship to the extent that they were faithful in dispensing justice.

III. The Pilgrim's Prayer (122:6–9)

6–9 The psalmist longs for "the peace [shalom; GK 8934] of Jerusalem." The city whose name means "city of peace" did not always experience peace; nor did she provide "security" (GK 8932) and "prosperity" (GK 3202) to her population. The psalmist thus prays that Jerusalem may truly be a city of peace to all who love her, i.e., for "my brothers and my friends." In his reflective prayer on the peace of Jerusalem, the psalmist mentions her "walls" and "citadels," as well as "the house of the Lord."

Psalm 123: Have Mercy, O Lord

This is one of the "Songs of Ascents" (see Ps 120). It is a combination of *individual lament* and *community lament*.

I. Dependence on the Lord (123:1–2)

1–2 The Lord, to whom the psalmist looks dependently, rules sovereignly. He is exalted on the throne. This God is faithful to his people. They are threatened by the "arrogant" (v.4), and they look to the Lord for his intervention and mercy.

II. Prayer for Mercy (123:3–4)

3–4 The need for "mercy" arises out of a deep awareness of injustice done to God's children. They have unjustly "endured" great "contempt" and "ridicule" from the "proud" and "arrogant" of the world.

Psalm 124: Our Helper Is the Maker of Heaven and Earth!

This is one of the "Songs of Ascents" (see Ps 120). Its genre reflects that of the *communal thanksgiving songs*.

I. The Presence of the Lord (124:1–2a)

1–2a The repetition here is for the purpose of emphasis. Because the Lord has been with his people, they have not perished. The OT saints had a grateful awareness of God's presence in their midst.

II. Protection From Dangers (124:2b–5)

2b–3 The presence of God results in his blessings, which include protection from enemies and dangers. Throughout her short history Israel was attacked from all sides. It often seemed as if enemies vented their anger with the living God against his people. The nations intended to destroy "life," which God had given to his people. However, life granted by the Lord cannot be smothered to death.

4–5 The violent acts that threatened to overwhelm God's people are likened to "the flood," "the torrent," and "the raging waters." The metaphor of water as a destructive force is common because of the torrential rains known to that part of the world. God's people nearly succumbed to its power, but the Lord was on their side (vv.1–2).

III. Praise to the Lord for Protection From Dangers (124:6–7)

6–7 The praise of the Lord is a transition between the confession of God's past acts of protection (vv.1–5) and the confession of confidence in the Lord. The song of thanksgiving praises God for delivering his own from the wicked, who, like wild animals, devour their prey. This is the Lord's doing; therefore he is to be praised!

IV. The Presence of the Lord (124:8)

8 The motif of God's presence begins and concludes this magnificent psalm. He is our "help," and he protects us by his "name." We need not fear, for the Maker of heaven and earth is in full control.

Psalm 125: Peace Be on Israel

This is one of the "Songs of Ascents" (see Ps 120). It is a mixture of confidence and lament, hence it could be either a *communal psalm of confidence* or a *communal lament*.

I. Internal Strength (125:1)

1 Mount Zion symbolizes God's power and help, his presence in blessing and protecting his people, and the privileges of the covenantal relationship. Because of their unshakable confidence in the Lord, the people are strong like Mount Zion.

II. Confidence in the Lord's Help (125:2)

2 Surrounded by mountains, Jerusalem was secure by its natural defensibility. So the psalmist compares the Lord to the hills around the city and the people to Mount Zion. The hills connote endurance and a sense of assurance and protection. God is "around" and present with his people.

III. Confidence in the Triumph Over Evil (125:3)

3 The "scepter [a symbol of rule] of the wicked" cannot coexist with the presence of God. Israel knew that the Lord had promised never to permit the wicked to prevail over the righteous, and this promise included the promise of "the land" of Canaan. If evil were to prevail, it might be an occasion for some of the godly to be tempted, to lose heart, and to fall away. For the sake of God's people, wickedness must come to an absolute end!

IV. Prayer for the Lord's Help (125:4–5b)

4–5b The people ask the Lord to remember them by doing good. He delivers "those who are good," i.e., "those who are upright in heart." Good works are expressions of an "upright heart." The "evildoers" are apostates who have turned "to crooked ways."

V. Peace (125:5c)

5c The benediction of God rests only on those who trust in him. They will receive God's "peace" (*shalom*; GK 8934).

Psalm 126: The Restoration Is Here!

This is one of the "Songs of Ascents" (see Ps 120). Its form reflects the genre of the *community laments*.

I. Joy of God's People (126:1–2a)

1–2a The restoration of "the captives to Zion" took place in 538 B.C. The people knew about the promises of restoration; but when the actual moment came, it was an overwhelming experience—they were like those "who dreamed." Great had been the sorrow of God's people in exile; but the restoration from exile filled their hearts with happiness, and they proclaimed with "laughter" and "shouts of joy" what God had done for them.

II. Proclamation Among the Nations (126:2b)

2b So great was the act of restoration that the "nations" (GK 1580) heard about it, too. Whenever the Lord "has done great things," his mighty works witness to his glorious ability to deliver his own.

III. Thanksgiving (126:3)

3 The wonder of deliverance is precious to God's people. First, they are in shock (v.1), but then they are overwhelmed with "joy."

IV. Prayer (126:4)

4 The returnees' prayer reflects on the harshness of their existence. Though they were restored, "nature" was not smiling kindly on the people. They pray for a restoration of their well-being in the land, like "streams in the Negev." The wadis in Canaan are generally dry; but when it rains, the water runs down its "streams" with great rapidity.

V. Assurance of Answered Prayer (126:5–6)

5–6 The short but intensive prayer of v.4 is answered. The Lord will turn their "tears" into "songs of joy." That assurance of blessing also encourages them to be responsible. The people are to go out and sow whatever little they have left, because the Lord will bless them. They must "lose" their seed before they can gain. The psalm concludes on the expectation of another divine miracle to take place: the people will "return" singing "songs of joy," because of the plentiful harvest.

Psalm 127: The Blessing of the Lord

In this song of ascent (see Ps 120), a *wisdom* psalm, the futility of life and the blessing of God are two contrastive themes.

I. Futility and Blessing (127:1–2)

1 The building of the house may refer to construction of a house or the raising of a family. In the OT it is usual to speak of a family as a "house" (cf. Ge 16:2; Ex 1:21; Ru 4:11; et al.). A second concern is the protection of the city—the Lord himself guards it. Thus the psalmist suggests that human efforts in the construction of one's house and involvement in the community's welfare are useless unless one trusts in the Lord.

2 The psalmist does not depreciate the importance of hard work. But he decries this as an inferior way of life if the hard work is only to provide daily food and clothing for oneself and the family. The higher way of life begins with trusting the Lord in one's work. With his blessing on their labor, the godly can rest without anguish.

II. God's Blessing on the Family (127:3–5)

3–5 The blessings of the Lord on the godly family are many. He gives children as an inheritance, and he also gives them a sense of security and protection. The psalmist likens the children of one's youth to "arrows." As the arrows protect the warrior, so the godly need not be afraid, when blessed with "sons." A house full of children, born before one becomes old, serves as a protection against loneliness and abandonment in society. These children have received a godly example at home; and when they come together in the city gate (the place where court was held), they will speak on behalf of their aging father in the presence of their enemies.

Psalm 128: The Family Blessed by the Lord

This psalm of ascent (see Ps 120) is a *wisdom psalm* (see Ps 127).

I. The Blessing of a God-Fearing Family (128:1–4)

1–2 The wise man is primarily concerned with walking in the ways of the Lord. The one who fears the Lord is a man of integrity; he receives a blessing from the Lord in all his labors.

3–4 The blessing mentioned in this psalm extends to the man's home. He will enjoy the warmth of wife and family around his table as he eats the fruit of his labors. His wife is compared to a fruitful vine, a plant that expresses tranquility, peace, and prosperity. His children are likened to olive shoots; the olive tree is a symbol of longevity and productivity. These images remind one of the eras of David and Solomon and of the messianic era. The blessedness of the godly man will extend to other generations.

II. The Benediction (128:5–6)

5–6 Blessing is not to be limited to a few days or years but to one's entire life. God's blessing goes with his people everywhere, even when they are not in Jerusalem. For the NT people of God, the blessing of God is on all those who are indwelt by his Holy Spirit.

The godly in the OT were concerned about the worship of God, the defense of Jerusalem, and the welfare of the Davidic dynasty. They knew that if a godly king were ruling over Jerusalem and if godly priests were serving in the temple, God's blessing would extend to his people. To see one's children's children is equivalent to "all the days of your life." The final blessing, "Peace be upon Israel," is equivalent to the prayer that the godly may see "the prosperity of Jerusalem" (cf. 122:9).

Psalm 129: The Lord Is Righteous

This is one of the "Songs of Ascents" (see Ps 120). The psalm reflects the genre of a *communal confidence psalm*.

I. Prayer for Divine Deliverance (129:1–4)

1–2 The psalmist has effectively brought together the individual in relation to the people of God. Difficult as certain moments in Israel's history have been, the people have been miraculously spared.

3–4 The psalmist likens the enemies to a farmer who plows the fields with long rows. The "plowmen" are the warriors, the long furrows are the wounds and adversities, and the field is "the back" of Israel. In spite of all their troubles, the Lord has delivered his own. The "cords" denote the yoke whereby the plow was attached to the neck of an animal.

II. Prayer for Divine Judgment (129:5–8)

5–8 The enemies who "hate Zion" are those who have no regard for God and his promises. "Zion" denotes the Lord's presence among his people, his covenant and blessing, and the hope in the victorious establishment of God's kingdom. The people pray that the wicked may wither like "grass on the roof," which is soon forgotten.

The enemies of Zion include not only the wicked of the world but also the Israelites who do not fear the Lord (cf. 125:5). They may feign piety, but in reality they are against God. The psalmist particularly singles out the godless Israelites who enjoyed hearing the greetings "The blessing of the LORD be upon you" and "we bless you in the name of the LORD" but whose lives were far from the Lord.

Psalm 130: May the Blessing of the Lord Be on You!

This psalm is classified as one of the seven penitential psalms (6; 32; 38; 51; 102; 130; 143). It also belongs to the "Songs of Ascents" (see Ps 120). Its genre reflects some features of the *individual lament*.

I. Lament (130:1–2)

1 To the godly, sin, guilt, and God's fatherly discipline are like being cast into "the depths" of the sea, a metaphor of adversity and trouble (cf. Jnh 2:2, 5), connoting a feeling of alienation from God. In his dire situation the psalmist calls on the "LORD," his covenant God.

2 The psalmist prays that the Lord may "be attentive" to his petition for "mercy" (GK 9384). This presupposes a servant-master relationship in which the "servant" petitions his "master" ("Lord") for a particular favor.

II. Confession of Sin (130:3–4)

3–4 The mercy of the Lord is found in forgiveness. He does not "keep" our "sins" in mind. If he did, even the most godly could not "stand" (GK 6641) in his presence, i.e., pass through his judgment and enjoy the benefits of his presence. God is feared, not only because of his great judgment and harshness, but also because of his great love in forgiving.

III. Waiting for the Lord (130:5–6)

5–6 The psalmist hopes in the Lord. He has learned to be submissive to God, the fountain of grace. From his concern with waiting like a watchman, who waits to be released from guard duty at the dawning of a new day, and from the concluding assurance that the Lord will redeem his people from their sins, we deduce that the anticipated "word" (GK 1821) denotes a new act of salvation by which the godly are upheld. The repetition in v.6 creates a deep sense of longing, dependence, and assurance.

IV. Confidence in Redemption (130:7–8)

7–8 Confidence in the Lord inspired the psalmist to call on all Israel to renew their submission to the Lord. The call "put your hope in the LORD" flows out of his own experiences (v.5). God's "unfailing love" (GK 2876) and "redemption" (GK 7014) are unmerited favors, which he sovereignly bestows on his children. His "full redemption" is so great that he can even forgive all his people from all their sin and free them from its consequences.

Psalm 131: Contentment With God

This is one of the "Songs of Ascents" (see Ps 120). In form it is an *individual psalm of confidence.*

1 The psalmist has experienced how wonderful complete submission to God is. The godly know that true godliness begins in a "heart" that is not proud, with eyes that do not envy, and with a walk of life that is humble rather than being preoccupied with "great matters."

2–3 David has enjoyed his walk with God in which he "stilled" himself and "quieted" his soul. He was like "a weaned child." This is a picture of contentment. Based on his wonderful relationship and walk with the Lord, David calls on Israel to trust in the Lord forevermore.

Psalm 132: The Tabernacling of the Lord

This psalm is one of the "Songs of Ascents" (see Ps 120). It is a tenth-century composition, celebrating the bringing of the ark of the covenant into Jerusalem (cf. 2Sa 6:12–19; Ps 132:6–10). The literary genre seems closest to a Song of Zion, especially because of its emphasis on the temple and on God's election of Zion.

I. Prayer for David (132:1, 10)

1, 10 The psalmist or a grateful congregation prays that the Lord will kindly remember all the acts of David's devotion. David had endured great "hardships" in the conquest of Jerusalem (2Sa 5:6–12) and in bringing the ark to Jerusalem. Verse 10 completes the thought of v.1. The prayer upholds David by the special designations "your servant" and "your anointed one" (GK 5431). These designations apply to David and to all his descendants who were anointed as kings over Israel or Judah.

II. David's Devotion (132:2–5)

2 Though the "oath" and "vow" to the God who had protected, guided, and blessed Jacob are not recorded in 2 Samuel, David was determined to bring the ark to Jerusalem and to have a temple built. When he heard that God had blessed Obed-Edom, the guardian of the ark (2Sa 6:12), he immediately made efforts to bring the ark to Jerusalem.

3–5 David strongly desired to build a temple for the Lord, a "place" for God's "dwelling." He made a temporary structure for the tabernacle and later desired to build a more permanent structure. That latter one had to wait until Solomon's reign to be constructed.

III. David's Concern for God's Presence (132:6–9)

6–8 David and his men heard of the whereabouts of the ark when they were at Ephrathah, "in the fields of Jaar." The people joined in the festal procession as the ark was led from Obed-Edom's house to Jerusalem, "his dwelling place," also known as God's "resting place." The placement of the ark in Jerusalem ushered in a new era in God's rule over Israel: the Davidic era.

9 The priests who served in the presence of the Lord were his instruments for dispensing "righteousness" This word (GK 7407) is synonymous here with "salvation," signifying victory, blessing, and deliverance. This blessedness resulted in great joy to God's loyal servants.

IV. Prayer for David (132:10)

10 See the comments on v.1.

V. God's Reward to David (132:11–12)

11–12 The Lord responded to David's "oath" (v.2) with his own "oath." David's concern and effort in establishing a "dwelling" (v.5) for the Lord were symmetric with the Lord's concern to establish the throne of David. The promises to Abraham (Ge 17:6) came to fulfillment during that grand era of David's and Solomon's kingship. David was the divinely appointed "seed" by whom the promises of the covenants were fulfilled.

God's promises must be balanced by responsibility. The king by his unique office must keep the "covenant," i.e., "the statutes" of the Lord. Only if the kings remained loyal to the covenant God would the dynasty of David rule.

VI. God's Presence in Zion (132:13–18)

13–14 The presence of the Lord on earth is related to his choice of Zion. In Zion, the earthly city of the Great King, God made his "dwelling" and "resting place." David prayed that the Lord might establish a "place" for "his footstool" in Jerusalem (vv.5, 7); and the Lord assured him that he "has chosen" and "desired" to establish his kingdom there.

15–16 The presence of the Lord guarantees his beneficence in "salvation," "abundant provisions," and "joy." The "poor" and the "priests" will share in this new age.

17–18 The "horn" (GK 7967) denotes the great vigor of the Davidic dynasty, by whom the Lord planned to rule over the earth (89:24–29; cf. Lk 1:69–75). David was further assured that his "lamp" (cf. 2Sa 21:17) had been "set up" and would be kept burning by the Lord. Through his dynasty ("crown") God's kingship was established, because God subdued his enemies. God's word of promise contains the Christian hope in the majesty, rule, and dominion of our Lord Jesus Christ, who as David's son will put down all of God's enemies (cf. Rev 19:17–21).

Psalm 133: The Communion of the Saints

This is one of the "Songs of Ascents" (see Ps 120). The metaphors, images, and blessing formula favor the classification of *wisdom psalms*.

I. Blessing (133:1)

1 The psalmist pronounces a blessing on those who "live together in unity." During the pilgrimages, the pilgrims came to Jerusalem from many different walks of life, regions, and tribes. Their unity was in conformity with the regulations for the three annual feasts (Ex 23:14–17; Lev 23:4–22, 33–43; Nu 28:16–31; 29:12–39; Dt 16:1–17). During these feasts the Jews celebrated their common heritage: redemption from Egypt and encampment around the tabernacle in the desert (cf. Nu 2).

II. Comparison With Oil and the Aaronic Ministry (133:2)

2 Fellowship of God's people on earth is an expression of the priesthood of all believers (cf. Ex 19:6; cf. 1Pe 2:9–10). The psalmist compares the expression of harmonious unity to the special, fragrant oil used by the priests (cf. Ex 30:22–33). Only the high priest and the other priests could be anointed with this oil. Aaron as the "head" of the priestly clan is representative of all the priests. Through the priestly institution the Lord assured his people of forgiveness and blessing.

III. Comparison With Dew (133:3a)

3a Because of its high altitude and abundant precipitation of rain, snow, and dew, Mount Hermon was proverbial for lush greenery even during the summer months (cf. 89:12) and for its dew that sustained the vegetation. The experience of the pilgrims is like that of the refreshing dew of Hermon. During the summer months virtually no precipitation falls on Jerusalem. During these months at least two pilgrimages were held: the Feast of Firstfruits in May/June and the Feast of Booths in September. Regardless of how harsh the conditions of the pilgrimage, the fellowship of the brotherhood of God's people was refreshing.

IV. Blessing (133:3b)

3b Where God's people live together "in unity," "there" the Lord sends blessing— "even life forevermore." "Life" (GK 2644) is a gift of God, not as an end in itself, but for communion with the people of God.

Psalm 134: May the Lord Bless You From Zion!

This is the last of the "Songs of Ascents" (see Ps 120). It is a liturgical hymn.

I. Call to Worship (134:1–2)

1–2 The psalmist calls on the priests to lead the people in worship. The priests are "the servants of the LORD," who "minister" (lit., "stand"; GK 6641) in the temple ("the house of the LORD"). They praise the Lord in song and with musical instruments both day and night. They also offer up prayers with hands lifted up "toward" the sanctuary, i.e., toward the Most Holy Place (cf. 1Ki 8:30).

II. Priestly Benediction (134:3)

3 These words are reminiscent of the priestly blessing (cf. Nu 6:24–25). The blessing extends to all of life, wherever the people of God may go or live, because the Lord is "the Maker of heaven and earth."

Psalm 135: The Lord Is Free in His Marvelous Acts

This psalm is a hymn of descriptive praise of God the Creator and Lord of history.

I. Israel's Praise (135:1–4)

1–2 Verse 1 is practically identical to 113:1 and together with v.2 is a continuation of 134:1–2 (see comment on 134:1–2). The "praise" (GK 2146) of God included a recitation of his mighty acts in creation and in redemptive history as an expression of devotion to the covenant God.

3–4 The praise of the Lord celebrates that he is "good" (GK 3202) to his covenant people and "pleasant" (GK 5833) to those who have experienced his electing love. The joyous proclamation of the name of the Lord evolves out of a relationship initiated (cf. "chosen") and maintained by him.

II. The Lord's Greatness as Creator (135:5–7)

5–7 The confession of God's greatness is expressed in the personal language of faith—"I know." His greatness pertains to his rule over all creation, to the exclusion of any other deities. The Lord is God over all realms because he is the Creator of all; his authority is unlimited. His greatness even extends to the elements of nature. Only the Lord has powers to "the ends of the earth."

III. The Lord's Acts in Redemptive History (135:8–14)

8–12 The power of the Lord is displayed in nature and in Israel's history. His greatness in the Exodus and Conquest motif is portrayed in climactic strokes: the tenth plague (Ex 12:29) as the last of his "signs and wonders" in Egypt and the victory over the "many nations" and "mighty kings" in Transjordan and the Promised Land. These lands he sovereignly gave to his people Israel as their "inheritance."

13–14 The psalmist celebrates the name and the remembrance of the Lord in this liturgical conclusion. The "name" of the God of Israel is Yahweh ("the LORD"; GK 3378), as revealed to Moses (Ex 3:15; 6:3, 6–8). That name increased in significance as the Lord increased his activities throughout the history of redemption and revealed more and more of himself. God promises to "vindicate his people" from their adversaries and thus to "have compassion on his servants."

IV. The Inability of Idols (135:15–18)

15–18 The affirmations of God's acts in creation and in redemption—together with his promise to continue to act in history—are set in the polemical context of the exclusive powers of the Lord. The psalmist illustrates the vanity of idolatry by an extensive quotation from Ps 115:4–8.

V. Israel's Praise (135:19–21)

19–21 The only appropriate response to the message of this psalm is to "praise the LORD," for he is the source of Israel's blessing. As a part of the liturgical significance of this psalm, the psalmist celebrates the promise of the Lord to be present in Zion (= Jerusalem).

Psalm 136: The Lord Is Good!

This is the last of the Great Hallel psalms (see Ps 120) or, according to some Jewish authorities, the only Hallel psalm. It was asso-

These two dagger-like objects, made out of gold, represent the idol Asherah (cf. 135:15–18). Courtesy of Tell Gezer Excavations.

ciated with the Feast of Passover. The literary form is that of an antiphonal hymn.

I. Hymnic Introit (136:1–3)

1–3 The hymn opens on a note of thanksgiving familiar from other psalms. However, this psalm is different in that it repeats the liturgical formula "His love [GK 2876] endures forever" after every colon. The reason for praising the Lord lies in his beneficent acts. Since he is "the God of gods" and "the Lord [GK 123] of lords," he alone is to be thanked for all the acts in creation and in redemption.

II. Creation Hymn (136:4–9)

4–6 Since the Lord alone is God and King, he alone is to be praised for his "great wonders" (GK 7098). His work of creation reveals his great "understanding." In his wisdom he made the heavens and "spread out" the earth on the waters of creation like a tent or curtain.

7–9 Though God's creation on earth reflects great glory, his work in space has always seemed overwhelming. Heaven, with the sun and moon, affects life on earth and hence is evidence of God's goodness to all on earth.

III. Redemption Hymn (136:10–22)

10–15 Of the many wonders in Egypt, the tenth plague receives particular mention. The Lord brought Israel out of Egypt "with a mighty hand and an outstretched arm," a metaphor for God's great and personal strength on behalf of his people. In Egypt and at the Red Sea, the Lord showed up Pharaoh and his forces by judging them, while he delivered the Israelites.

16–20 The Lord guided his people through the desert. Not only did the Lord strike down the firstborn in Egypt, he also struck down the great and mighty kings, beginning with Sihon and Og. The psalmist is selective in his choice of events, for he makes no mention of the giving of the law and the covenant at Mount Sinai, nor does he mention Israel's many rebellions.

21–22 The conquered land became Israel's "inheritance" (GK 5709). In 135:12 Israel is called "his people Israel," whereas here the term is "his servant Israel" (cf. especially Isa 41:8; 44:1–2).

IV. Redemption Hymn (136:23–24)

23–24 The mighty acts of God in Egypt, in the desert, and in the conquest of the land are a sampling of his power and his purpose. Israel hereby confesses that the Lord is a Redeemer-King, who alone is able to deliver them from their enemies. He remembers his people in their distress.

V. Creation Hymn (136:25)

25 The hymn returns to a reflection of God's goodness as the Creator. His love is evident in that he continually cares for his creatures.

VI. Hymnic Conclusion (136:26)

26 The hymn concludes on a note of thanksgiving. In vv.2–3 the psalmist referred to the Lord as "the God of gods" and "the Lord of lords." Here he adds a related concept: "the God of heaven."

Psalm 137: If I Forget You, O Jerusalem

This psalm has a mixed classification: communal lament (vv.1–4), a song of Zion (vv.5–6), and a curse (vv.7–9). Strictly speaking, it is a *communal lament*, the genre being determined by the opening of the psalm.

I. The Lament (137:1–4)

1–2 For many Judeans life in Babylon was good. They lived by the Tigris and Euphrates rivers and enjoyed regular harvests because of a complex system of irrigation canals. But that does not mean that the godly were happy in Babylon, being far removed from Jerusalem. In the midst of plenty, they "wept," mourning the loss of Zion.

3–4 The dainties of Babylon were tainted with the taunts of the captors, who "demanded songs of joy." These taunts may have focused on the magnificent "songs of Zion," celebrating the majesty and protection of the Lord over his people. The Israelites could not sing of the glories of Zion and the strength and protection of their God, because the city lay in ruins and the people were captive in a "foreign land."

II. The Confession of Confidence (137:5–6)

5–6 For the exiles the love for God and for Jerusalem was intertwined because of the temple. Loyalty lies in remembering instead of forgetting. The godly vowed never to forget God's promises and to persevere, waiting for the moment of redemption. As part of the vow, the godly took on themselves a formula of self-cursing.

III. Prayer for Divine Intervention (137:7–9)

7 As the psalmist reflects on the moments of Judah's fall, he remembers the Edomite involvement. They had done everything to disgrace Judah and to keep the Judeans from escaping (cf. La 4:21; Eze 25:12–14; 35:5–15; Ob 11–14). They also encouraged the Babylonians to "tear [Jerusalem] down to its foundations!" The word "foundations" (GK 3572) also pertains to the God-established order in creation, in his rule, and in the election of his people. The Edomites hoped for the destruction of the Lord's rule on earth.

8 The psalmist prays that Babylon, personified as the "Daughter of Babylon," will come to an end. A blessing ("happy"; GK 897) will lie on anyone who helps bring down Babylon. That is, the idiom of blessing is used here for the purpose of imprecation ("curse").

9 The psalmist prays that the Lord will bring on Babylon's head the atrocities they had committed in Judah and elsewhere. Wars were very cruel in the OT, and the Babylonians were famed for their cruelties. The psalmist relishes the thought that some day the proud Babylonian will be rendered so defenseless that they are unable to defend even their infants.

Psalm 138: The Lord Delivers the Humble

This psalm has the distinctive features of the *individual thanksgiving* psalms.

I. Individual Thanksgiving (138:1–3)

1–3 The praise of the Lord is both an expression of devotion and a witness against the impotence of idols. Praise of the "name" of the Lord involves a personal experience of God's covenant perfections: his "love" (GK 2876) and "faithfulness" (GK 622). The Lord is constant in his love toward his children, and so great is his faithfulness that the psalmist exclaims that whatever the Lord has done in the past is dwarfed by what he is still doing! His praise ends with a confession as to what the Lord has done. He not only answers

prayer but strongly encourages the psalmist, revitalizing his life.

II. Communal Thanksgiving (138:4–6)

4–6 The nations together with their gods and kings will some day pay homage to the Lord. The psalmist's confidence lies in his conviction of the Lord's faithfulness to "the words" of promise to his people. The fulfillment is evident in "the ways of the LORD" at the sound of which the nations will respond with song. Exalted as the Lord is in his kingship, he deals favorably with "the lowly" so as to deliver them out of their affliction. Pride is offensive to him because he alone is the Exalted One.

III. Confidence in the Lord's Presence (138:7–8)

7–8 Confident of his God, the believer confesses his indubitable faith in the Savior-King. He anticipates "trouble" because the life of a believer is not immune from adversities. However, he rests assured. The Lord will keep him alive, delivering him from his "foes." The psalmist portrays the Lord as reaching out his "hand" as an expression of help, while dealing in judgment with those who cause his adversity.

The psalmist's confidence also comes from a recognition that the Lord has a purpose that includes individuals. His concern is of the most profound and lasting kind, as it is nothing less than his enduring "love" (GK 2876).

Psalm 139: The Lord Knows Me!

The various components of this psalm expose us to the intensely personal relationship between the psalmist and his God. The psalm defies the canons of genre criticism.

I. The Lord's Discernment of Individuals (139:1–6)

1–6 The Lord "knows" (GK 3359) his own—a word that means complete divine discernment. In his prayer (vv.23–24), the psalmist prayed for the Lord to examine him as in a judicial case and to declare him to be innocent of all charges. Now that the ordeal is over and he has been justified by the Lord, the psalmist testifies that the Lord is a righteous judge. The Lord knows him through and through.

The accused is not afraid of his judge, for the Judge is more than an arbiter; he is the one in whom the psalmist has found protection. The knowledge of God referred to here is a knowledge that graciously discerns in favor of those who are loyal to the Lord. By grace humans are blessed. The psalmist exclaims that God's favorable acts toward him are "too wonderful" and "too lofty" to apprehend.

II. The Lord's Perception of Individuals (139:7–12)

7–12 The "presence" (parallel with "Spirit") of God is everywhere; hence he perceives all things in all places. We cannot hide from the all-seeing eye of the Lord. Unlike pagan deities, the Lord's authority extends to "the heavens ... the depths ... the wings of the dawn ... the sea." The Lord's hand protects his children wherever they are, even in "darkness." There is only light with God, and his light brightens up the darkness so that the psalmist can say affirmatively, "The night will shine like the day, for darkness is as light to you" (v.12).

III. The Lord's Purpose for Individuals (139:13–18)

13–14 Confidence in the Lord's ability to discern the nature and needs of his people comes from a belief in God's purpose. He is the Creator, and his creative concerns include individuals! All of God's "works" are "wonderful," but the believer senses more than any other part of God's creation that he personally is "fearfully and wonderfully made." He lives with a personal awareness of God's gracious purpose. The psalmist reveals a unique awareness of God's grace toward him and responds with thanksgiving.

15–16 Even in the early stages of formation in the womb, the Lord had a purpose for the undeveloped embryo. God's writing in the book refers to his knowledge and blessing of his child "all the days" of his life. His life was written in the book of life, and each of his days was numbered.

17–18 The "thoughts" of God are too magnificent, too numerous, and too exalted for a human being to comprehend, whose "thoughts" are fully known to the Lord. But the Lord's love is real. When awake the psalmist knows that he still enjoys God's presence.

IV. Prayer for Vindication (139:19–24)

19–20 Overwhelmed as he is with gratitude for God's purpose in him, the psalmist sees no purpose in the existence of the wicked. They foil God's purposes by their rebellious ways. They are destructive, scheming, and rebellious to the rule of God. The ascription "bloodthirsty" (GK 1947) denotes a lack of respect for life and a disregard for justice and righteousness. The psalmist commits the wicked into God's just hands.

21–22 Devotion to the Lord excludes any loyalty to those who hate him and rebel against him. The psalmist hates, abhors, and shuns the enemies of God. In doing so, he affirms his own devotion to the Lord.

23–24 The psalmist asks for God to discern his motives and his actions, especially in the context of vv.21–22. This prayer comes out of a situation when evil people had accused him. Instead of directing himself to his adversaries, he raises up his voice in lament to God, who alone as the righteous Judge can discern his "heart" and "thoughts." He desires nothing less than conformity to God's will. He closes by acknowledging that there are only two ways that a person can follow: one leading to destruction and the other to life and fellowship with God.

Psalm 140: You Are My God!

The psalmist has been falsely accused and turns to the Lord for deliverance, because he is the righteous Judge. The psalm exemplifies the spirit of the *individual lament*.

I. Prayer for Deliverance From Evil (140:1–5)

1–5 The psalmist's lament arises out of a real situation, in which wicked people perpetrate their evil. They are "evil men" because of their violent acts. They also sow discord with their speech ("their tongues"). They devise wicked schemes in their evil hearts, leading to intentional anarchy and perpetual agitation.

The psalmist prays for God's deliverance, lest the wicked control him. Because of the intensity of evil, he casts himself wholly on the Lord. Those who are violent scheme maliciously and act viciously. They are intent on entrapping and destroying the righteous, just as a fowler ensnares animals with the "snare," the "net," and the "traps."

II. Confidence in God's Deliverance (140:6–8)

6–8 In contrast to the lying speech of the wicked, the psalmist declares, "I say to you, 'You are my God.'" He seeks protection from no other than the "LORD," the covenant God and Master of the world. This God will avenge and deliver his people. He is "strong" in his salvation. In v.8, the psalmist renews his lament, pleading for God to act, lest evil succeed and wickedness be lifted up arrogantly.

III. Prayer for Divine Justice (140:9–11)

9–11 This imprecation is an expression of concern for God's just rule. The psalmist prays that the Lord will boomerang on the heads of the wicked what they have spoken with their lips. The "burning coals," "fire," and "miry pits" are metaphors for divine judgment. As long as there are "slanderers," justice is not established. Hence the psalmist prays that the wicked may not have a place among the people of God. The "men of violence" should find no rest.

IV. Confidence in God's Deliverance (140:12–13)

12–13 The psalmist's lament changes to a victory cry: "I know." In v.6 the psalmist speaks confidently, "You are my God," being fully persuaded in his whole being that the Lord is the just Judge who will interpose for his people. His people are "the poor" (or "the humble"; GK 6714), as they are dependent on him for deliverance. At the time of the divine intervention, "the righteous" will alter their prayers for deliverance to songs of triumph, sung in the presence of the Lord.

Psalm 141: May My Prayer Be Like Incense!

The spirit of this lament resembles that of Ps 140.

I. Prayer for Deliverance (141:1–2)

1–2 With great urgency the psalmist raises his hands in prayer to God—an act symbolizing dependence on and praise to the Lord. The repetition of "call" and the different verbs for God's intervention express the frequency of prayer and the urgency of the situation. Though David is in a precarious situation, his "prayer" is like a sweet-smelling offering to the Lord. Incense was presented on the altar of incense every day to the Lord as a pleasing offering (cf. Ex 30:7–8). Gradually incense became associated with prayer (cf. Rev 5:8).

II. Prayer for Wisdom (141:3–5c)

3–4 Evil comes in many forms: the sins of speech, of the heart, and of action. The psalmist asks the Lord to help him in his struggle with any form of temptation. Speech especially indicates one's relationship to the Lord. The wise trust in him to guard "over the door" of their lips.

The word "men" (GK 408) denotes men of land, rank, and status within the community. However, these members of the aristocracy are "evildoers" who practiced "wicked deeds." Their riches permit them the enjoyment of the "delicacies" in life.

5a–c Instead of receiving encouragement and privilege from the well-to-do but godless members of the community, the righteous receive joy from the discipline and words of rebuke by the wise. A wise person responds to wisdom as an expression of "kindness" (or "love"; GK 2876) and welcomes it like "oil," a symbol of honor extended to a welcome guest (cf. Pr 27:9).

III. Prayer for Vindication (141:5d–7)

5d–7 This prayer is an imprecation against the godless aristocracy. The psalmist prays that they may die a cruel death, being thrown down the cliffs. The shock of God's judgment on their despotic regime will affect their followers and may bring them to their senses.

IV. Prayer for Deliverance and Vindication (141:8–10)

8–10 The psalmist's "eyes" of faith are toward the "Sovereign LORD," who provides "refuge." He prays for deliverance on the one hand and for vindication on the other. God's deliverance brings life. The wicked destroy life, as they set "traps" and "snares" for the righteous. God's vindication comes in the form of retribution on them.

Psalm 142: The Lord Alone Is My Portion in the Land of the Living

This psalm is an *individual lament.*

I. Lament of the Individual (142:1–2)

1–2 In two parallel expressions the psalmist makes his lament known to the Lord. These phrases illustrate the tension between anguish of soul and dependence on the Lord.

II. Loneliness in Suffering (142:3–7a)

3–4 The psalmist's adversity and prayers have brought him to the point of total exhaustion. Nevertheless, he relies on his God, who knows his situation. At the present time, he is walking on a "path" that is repressive and full of entanglements. Regardless of where he looks, the Lord is not at his "right" hand. He has no one to defend him against his adversaries. He yearns for the path of the Lord, which leads to salvation.

5–7a The psalmist cries from his heart for relief. At the same time he confesses that the Lord is his "refuge" and his hope. He then remembers his present situation, his "desperate need." "Prison" may denote actual imprisonment or may be a metaphor for his desperate condition. The psalmist further prays that the Lord's deliverance will give him a renewed opportunity to praise his name.

IV. Public Thanksgiving (142:7b)

7b The resolution to his despair will not only bring him to thanksgiving but will serve as an encouragement to the righteous community. They too will hear the psalmist's thanksgiving and will be edified. God's acts of deliverance are acts of "goodness" (GK 1694).

Psalm 143: Lead Me on Level Ground

This psalm is classified as one of the seven penitential psalms (6; 32; 38; 51; 102; 130; 143). It is an *individual lament.*

I. Prayer for God's Righteousness (143:1–2)

1 In an urgent appeal David throws himself on the "faithfulness and righteousness" of the Lord. Both qualities connote the absolute fidelity and perfection of God in keeping his promise with his covenant children.

2 Another reason for the urgency of God's response lies in the psalmist's awareness of his own unrighteousness. He knows that God's judgment could find him guilty and thus condemn him to remain in his troubles.

II. Lament (143:3–6)

3–4 The adversity is described in general terms. The enemy hunts the psalmist down so that he feels as if he lives "in darkness," like those who have been "dead" for a long time. Having no apparent reason for living, the psalmist is discouraged to the point of despair.

5–6 David's alienation and despair grow as he reflects on what God has done in the past. He does "remember," "meditate," and "consider" the acts of God in creation and in the history of redemption. He turns to the Lord for help with outspread hands. His need for God is so great that he likens himself to "a parched land."

III. Petitions and Prayer (143:7–12)

A. Petitions for Deliverance (143:7–8a, 9a)

7–8a, 9a Out of his deep despair the psalmist calls on the Lord to renew his "unfailing love" (GK 2876) and to "rescue" him speedily. He waits for God's deliverance as a watchman waits for dawn. As long as God hides his face, he feels cut off from God's favor and is like "those who go down to the pit," i.e., as good as dead.

B. Expressions of Confidence (143:8b–c, 9b, 10b)

8b–c Even in the depth of his despair, the psalmist is confident of the Lord. He has put his trust in him ("for to you I lift up my soul").

9b, 10b The reason for the psalmist's trust is that the Lord is his refuge and his covenant God. He is sustained by the Lord's promise to be the God of his people (Ex 6:7).

C. Petitions for Guidance (143:8b, 10a, c)

8b, 10a As an expression of humility and hope in the future, the psalmist desires to know "the way" he should go, i.e., the way of the Lord's "will." Doing that will as revealed in God's word implies complete submission, so that what we do is acceptable in his sight.

10c The psalmist believes that if the Lord instructs him and guides him on a level path, he will experience divine illumination by the Spirit of God. The presence of the Spirit will further guarantee God's protection.

D. Concluding Prayers (143:11–12)

11–12 These verses form a proper conclusion. (1) The psalmist petitions the Lord for deliverance for his "name's sake," returning to the promises of his "faithfulness and righteousness" (v.1). (2) All of "life" is before the Lord, but the psalmist feels as if he is dead. Therefore, he prays that the Lord will preserve his "life" by delivering him from "trouble." (3) He prays that the Lord may deal righteously with his adversaries by silencing them. (4) He himself vows to remain God's "servant."

Psalm 144: The Lord Is My Warrior

In this psalm the king prays for the Lord's help for himself and for God's blessing on his people.

I. Hymn of Praise (144:1–2)

1–2 The king praises the Lord his God in the language of Ps 18: "my Rock"; "my fortress, my stronghold and deliverer"; and "my shield." According to his promises to David, the Lord gives military success so that the nations will be subject to him. The jubilant praise motivates the king to boldly petition the Divine Warrior to act on his behalf.

II. Human Need (144:3–4)

3–4 David knows his God and is convinced that the Lord does "care for him" and "think of him." In his praise of God, he exclaims that human beings, finite and unreliable, are unworthy of the love of the Lord. They are unstable and short-lived. The "care" of the Lord is nothing less than his commitment to be gracious and to fulfill his promises.

III. A Prayer for God's Involvement (144:5–8)

5–8 The psalmist calls on the Lord to appear as he did at Mount Sinai, where in the midst of smoke, lightning, and earthquake he came down to his people (cf. Ex 19:11, 18–19). The enemies are the object of the "lightning," also called "arrows," so that their power will be effectively eliminated. Their words and inti-

mating actions are nothing but "lies." The people of God are the object of his deliverance, as he puts forth his right hand to "deliver . . . and rescue." The marvel of grace is that the exalted God condescends to "come down" to the aid of his own!

IV. Hymn of Praise (144:9–10)

9–10 Despite the calamity the king confidently sings praise to the Lord. He expects God to be faithful in giving "victory" to him and the "kings" that follow. Subsequent to the victory, "a new song" will be raised to the Lord, celebrating the new acts of God.

V. Prayer for God's Involvement (144:11)

11 This verse is a repetition of vv.7–8 and appears to be here for the purpose of symmetry.

VI. Prayer for Blessing on God's People (144:12–15)

12–15 David prays unselfishly for the blessing of the Lord on his nation. He prays that their "sons" may grow to be strong like verdant plants, that their "daughters" may become pleasing maidens, like richly decorated "pillars" adorning a Near-Eastern palace, and that the Lord may lavish riches on them by increasing the fields, flocks, and herds without fear of foreign invaders. Blessed are the people that experience the Lord's ability to save, protect, and bless.

Psalm 145: Great Is the Lord's Universal Kingdom!

This psalm is an alphabetic acrostic, except for the letter *nun*.

I. In Praise of the Lord's Kingship (145:1–3)

1–3 Synonyms for "praise" set the mood for the psalm. The object of the praise is "my God the King." The psalmist calls on the community to praise God unceasingly. The reason for praise lies in God's greatness. As the "great" King he deserves human "praise." In his presence, we must admit our limitations, for no one can fully understand God's purposes and his ways.

II. In Praise of the Lord's Faithfulness to the Covenant (145:4–9)

4–9 The unceasing praise of the Lord comes from the grateful instruction of the new generation by the older generation. The process of transmission of salvation history from one generation to another is by the telling of God's "mighty acts" of deliverance. The "works" of the Lord reveal his "might," his "glorious splendor," his "power," his awe-inspiring nature, his greatness, his "abundant goodness," his "righteousness," and his relational perfections (i.e., that he is "gracious and compassionate, slow to anger and rich in love"). God's kingship is magnificent, his sovereignty beneficent, and his redemptive acts manifold. His is the kingdom, the power, and the glory!

III. In Praise of the Lord's Kingship (145:10–13a)

10–13a The meditation on the mighty acts of God occasions a renewed praise of the Lord's kingship. All his works, including the "saints," praise the Lord and give thanks for the expressions of his "glory," "might," and "kingdom." The marvel of divine condescension lies in his magnificence and eternal dominion.

IV. In Praise of the Lord's Covenant Fidelity (145:13b–21)

13b–16 The Lord is "faithful" (GK 586) and "loving" (GK 2883) to "all he has made," including his creation. His love evidences itself in his acts of restoration and in acts of provision. He satisfies the needs of every living creature as the master of a house opens his hand to all who are dependent on him.

17 These observations lead the psalmist to a renewed reflection on the nature of God. He is "righteous" (GK 7404) and "loving." His acts of restoration, redemption, and vindication extend to his whole creation.

18–20 Members of the Lord's fellowship are special because they "call on him," "fear him," and "love him." He hears the prayers of those who submit to his will "in truth"; i.e., they respond to his faithfulness with faithfulness. The Lord delivers his own in their time of need. He preserves those who love him, but he will avenge the "wicked."

21 The psalmist appropriately concludes this section with a vow to praise the Lord. Because the kingdom of God extends to all creation and because the Lord's acts are to all his creation, it is only appropriate that all humankind should respond to his "holy name."

Psalm 146: The Lord Reigns Forever and Ever

Psalms 146–150 constitute the last Hallel ("praise") collection (see comment on Ps 113). These five psalms are in the characteristic genre of the *hymn of descriptive praise*.

I. Call to Praise (146:1–4)

1–2 The communal call (v.1a) serves as the basis for the psalmist's determination to join in. He speaks to his own soul, "Praise the LORD, O my soul." His personal commitment to praise the Lord issues from the understanding that life is to be lived for the purpose of praising God.

3–4 The commitment to praise the Lord requires a dissociation from dependency on other people. The negative exhortation here is a positive way of renouncing humanism and of affirming a God-centered way of life. Humankind is unable to "save" because a person may die at any time, whenever God removes the "spirit" of life. A "man" (*adam*; GK 132) is mortal and to the "ground" (*adamah*; GK 141) he must return (cf. Ge 3:19). At death, all of his "plans" for help go down with him.

II. God the Creator (146:5–6)

5 The blessing of "the God of Jacob" rests on those who look to him for "help" (GK 6469). The psalmist may be alluding to the Songs of Zion, reminding God's people that the Lord, whose dwelling is in "Zion" (cf. v.10), is their "help" (cf. Ps 46:7, 11; 76:6). His kingship is established.

6 The "God of Jacob" is "the Maker of heaven and earth." He uses his power and control over all of his created universe, including the sea, to bless every creature. He is "faithful" (GK 622) to his people "forever."

III. God the Sustainer (146:7–9)

7–9 In hymnic style the psalmist celebrates the many acts of God. The Maker of heaven and earth "upholds . . . gives . . . sets free . . . gives sight . . . lifts up . . . loves . . . watches . . . sustains." The psalmist does not introduce anything new in this description of the Lord's mighty acts, but the manner in which he brings the various ways of divine sustenance together is most creative, including the conclusion.

IV. God the Great King (146:10a)

10a The reference to the Lord's rule in Zion has already been anticipated by the allusions to the Songs of Zion (cf. v.5). God's people expect him to be faithful, so that he will sustain them "forever."

V. Call to Praise (146:10b)

10b The hymn appropriately concludes with a renewed call to "praise the LORD" (cf. v.1).

Psalm 147: The Blessedness of the People of God

See the introduction to Ps 146.

I. In Praise of God's Restoration, Creation, and Redemption (147:1–6)

1–3 God's people praise God because of his fatherly goodness to his children, as well as to all his creation. First, the Lord is good in bringing restoration to his people. He restores "Jerusalem" by permitting its walls and institutions to be rebuilt after they had been lying in ruins. He will see to it that his people, the scattered "exiles" (GK 5615), who are further described as those who are "brokenhearted" and "wounded," will prosper within the walls of Jerusalem (cf. Isa 65:18). The Lord also "heals" the wounds of his grief-stricken children.

4–5 Second, the Lord is good to his creation. The Great Creator "determines" (GK 4948; i.e., takes an interest in and knows) the number of the stars. The psalmist exclaims how "great" God's royal sovereignty is in "power" and wisdom!

6 Third, the Lord is a good judge in the vindication of his people. He "sustains" the needy but judges the wicked.

II. In Praise of God's Creation and Love for His People (147:7–11)

7 The psalmist renews the imperatival call to praise with the emphasis on "thanksgiving" and the instrumental accompaniment. The verb for "sing" (GK 6702) belongs to the semantic field of praise.

8–9 Praise is due God because he is the good King. He sustains everything he has created: the "cattle" and "ravens"—representatives of two realms of the animal kingdom. The Lord is sovereign over and concerned with not only the magnificent stars but also the lowly creatures on earth.

10–11 The Lord rewards those who "fear [GK 3710] him," i.e., those "who put their hope in his unfailing love" (GK 2876). They know the vanity of military, logistical, or human power, because the "strength of the horse" or "a man" is nothing in comparison with the Lord's "power" (v.5).

III. In Praise of God's Restoration, Sovereignty, and Revelation (147:12–20)

12–14 The praise of the Lord begins with Zion, because the Lord has promised to be her God, to dwell in her, and to rule over her. He "builds up Jerusalem" (v.2) by fortifying her, by blessing her population with secure borders, and with prosperity.

15–18 The praise of God is evoked by a further reflection on his power in the world of nature. He orders and ordains everything in his created order, whether it be "snow," "frost," "ice," "hail," or "water." His "word" (GK 1821) is true and constant in nature.

19–20 Therefore God's people have hope! They too have received his "word" (GK 1821). Therefore they praise him. This word is first and foremost "his laws" by which Israel had to order their ways. God's word is to have the same effect on his people as it has on nature—order and constancy. The psalm closes with a call to communal praise of the Lord.

Psalm 148: Praise to the Lord, the Wise Creator

See the introduction to Ps 146.

I. Call on Heaven to Praise the Lord (148:1–6)

1 The psalm begins and ends on the familiar call, "Praise the LORD." The very "heights above," where God rules, together with outer space and the atmosphere of the earth, are invoked to join in Israel's praise.

2–4 In their order of closeness to the Lord, the psalmist addresses rhetorically the "angels," the starry hosts, and the elements to praise God. "His heavenly hosts" most likely refers to the angelic hosts that surround the throne of God. The "shining stars" could well be "the morning stars"; these are the planets visible at dawn. The "waters above the skies" refers to various forms of precipitation, which join in God's praise.

5–6 Praise of the Lord is due him because he is the Creator. The creative acts of God are marked by three characteristics. (1) The Lord created everything by his word. (2) He permanently ordered and regulated the world of nature. (3) The order and regularity of the heavenly bodies and of the forms of precipitation are due to his creative involvement.

II. Call on Earth to Praise the Lord (148:7–12)

7–8 By poetic license the psalmist put the "sea creatures" at the beginning of this list. The "sea" and its mysterious depths were associated in the Canaanite religion with the powers of Baal. Thus the psalmist is demonstrating the supremacy of the Lord over all objects of pagan worship, whether they be the starry hosts above or the "depths" of the sea.

9–10 The Lord has also fashioned the relief of the earth (mountains and hills). On it he has planted trees good for food, for building materials, and for nesting. He has made the animals that may find refuge and food on the mountains and hills.

11–12 The psalmist now portrays the world of people, consisting of kings and nations, old and young, male and female. The Lord created them all, all are subject to his bidding, and all owe him praise.

III. Rationale for Praising the Lord (148:13–14)

13–14 The psalmist restates the universal obligation of all creation to demonstrate their allegiance to God by praising him. The praise is to be given in the "name of the LORD." He is the exalted Ruler, sovereign over all. His kingship is endowed with "splendor." He is also to be praised because of his unique concern for his own people, who do his bidding on earth. This is the climax of the psalm. God loves and cares for all his creation, but he has a special affinity for "his people," "his saints," "Israel," also known as "the people close to his heart." He has endowed them with glory, symbolized by "a horn." He has raised them up for the purpose of giving him "the praise."

Psalm 149: The Lord Delights in His People

See the introduction to Ps 146. Psalm 149 celebrates a victory. Since it also shares the language and hope of the imprecatory psalms, it seems best to take it as an eschatological hymn.

I. The Present Joy of the Saints (149:1–5)

1–5 This psalm opens with the characteristic ascription of praise. This song is "new" because of the present occasions for praising the Lord: restoration and eschatological expectation of the Lord's full victory over evil (vv.6–9). The beneficiaries are the "assembly of the saints," a designation for the godly within the larger covenant fellowship.

The object of praise is "the LORD." He is their "Maker" (GK 6913), for he has elected, redeemed, and fashioned the descendants of Jacob into a community characterized by holiness and royalty. He is also their "King"; he has established his residence among his people, symbolized by "Zion." The "delight" (GK 8354) of the Lord guarantees his forgiveness, blessing, and restoration. He "crowns" his people with glory and splendor, thus sharing the benefits of his victory. "Salvation" and "honor" are synonymous.

The resultant expression on the part of the godly can only be joy. They are portrayed as "dancing." The people of God regularly celebrated the Lord's victory and blessing in dance (cf. Ex 15:20; Jdg 11:34). Also at home "on their beds," they rejoice in the glory bestowed on them by the Lord.

II. The Hope of the Saints (149:6–9)

6–9 "The praise of God" goes together with "a double-edged sword," as the one denotes a spirit of trust and confidence and the other a spirit of watchfulness. The Lord will grant victory to his people. He will avenge, punish, and bind in accordance with his "sentence written against them." The "sentence" (GK 5477) decrees that on the Day of the Lord, the wicked (individuals, nations, and kings) will be fully judged for the deeds done against God and against his people (cf. Isa 24:21–22; 41:15–16; Eze 38–39; Joel 3:9–16; Mic 4:13; et al.). The Lord will "inflict vengeance" by punishing the nations, by defeating their kings, and by dishonoring the nobles of the nations.

The psalmist returns to the motif of "glory" (GK 2077) as a reminder of the occasion for rejoicing. All the acts of God in judgment are to assure his own of his love and must evoke a response of divine "praise."

Psalm 150: Praise the Lord

See the introduction to Ps 146. In contrast to other hymns, Ps 150 is an enlarged introit, lacking the descriptive praise. It functions as a final doxology, bringing the Psalter to a solemn and joyful conclusion.

I. Praise the Lord in Heaven (150:1)

1 The psalm begins and concludes with "Praise the LORD" (Hallelujah), like so many other Hallel psalms (113–118; 120–136; 146–150). The angels in his heavenly "sanctuary" and in the heavenly bodies together with the waters "above the skies" are summoned to praise "God." The "mighty heavens" have been made by him and assure the order and well-being of humankind on earth.

II. Praise the Greatness of God (150:2)

2 The voices in heaven and on earth join together in the praise of the Lord's mighty acts. His "firmament" (NIV "heavens") together with "his acts of power" reveal how great he is.

III. Praise the Lord With Great Intensity (150:3–5)

3–5 The greatness of the Lord is celebrated with a corresponding devotion to him by wind, string, and percussion instruments, as well as by dancing.

IV. Praise the Lord on Earth (150:6)

6 All of God's creation that "has breath"—particularly humankind—is summoned to praise the Lord. The word "breath" (GK 5972) denotes all living creatures endowed with life by the Creator (Ge 1:24–25; 7:21–22), but always in distinction from the Creator (cf. Isa 2:22).

The Old Testament in the New

OT Text	NT Text	Subject
Ps 2:1–2	Ac 4:25–26	Kings against the Lord
Ps 2:7	Ac 13:33; Heb 1:5; 5:5	You are my Son
Ps 2:9	Rev 2:27; 19:15	Ruling the nations
Ps 4:4	Eph 4:26	Anger and sin
Ps 5:9	Ro 3:13	Sin of humanity
Ps 8:2	Mt 21:16	Children praising God
Ps 8:4–6	Heb 2:6–8	Lower than the angels
Ps 8:6	1Co 15:27; Eph 1:22	Everything subject to Christ
Ps 10:7	Ro 3:14	Sin of humanity
Ps 14:1–3	Ro 3:10–12	Sin of humanity
Ps 16:8–11	Ac 2:25–28, 31; 13:35	Resurrection of Christ
Ps 18:49	Ro 15:9	Praise among the nations
Ps 19:4	Ro 10:18	General revelation
Ps 22:1	Mt 27:46; Mk 15:34	God-forsaken cry
Ps 2:18	Mt 27:35; Jn 19:24	Dividing garments by lot
Ps 22:22	Heb 2:12	Declaring God's name
Ps 24:1	1Co 10:26	The earth is the Lord's
Ps 31:5	Lk 23:46	I commit my spirit
Ps 32:1–2	Ro 4:7–8	Blessings of forgiveness
Ps 34:12–16	1Pe 3:10–12	Turn from evil
Ps 34:20	Jn 19:36	No broken bones
Ps 35:19	Jn 15:25	Hated without a cause

The Old Testament in the New (Continued)

OT Text	NT Text	Subject
Ps 36:1	Ro 3:18	Sin of humanity
Ps 40:6–8	Heb 10:5–9	Offerings and obedience
Ps 41:9	Jn 13:18	A double-crossing friend
Ps 44:22	Ro 8:36	Sheep for the slaughter
Ps 45:6–7	Heb 1:8	God's eternal throne
Ps 51:4	Ro 3:4	God's righteous judgment
Ps 53:1–3	Ro 3:10–12	Sin of humanity
Ps 62:12	Ro 2:6	God's fair judgment
Ps 68:18	Eph 4:8	Ascension and gifts
Ps 69:4	Jn 15:25	Hated without a cause
Ps 69:9	Jn 2:17	Zeal for God's house
Ps 69:9	Ro 15:3	Insults on Christ
Ps 69:22–23	Ro 11:9–10	Judgment on enemies
Ps 69:25	Ac 1:20	Judgment on Judas
Ps 78:2	Mt 13:35	Speaking in parables
Ps 78:24–25	Jn 6:31	Bread from heaven
Ps 82:6	Jn 10:34	You are gods
Ps 91:11–12	Mt 4:6; Lk 4:10–11	Protecting angels
Ps 94:11	1Co 3:20	God knows human thoughts
Ps 95:7–11	Heb 3:7–11, 15; 4:3, 5, 7	No rest for the wicked
Ps 102:25–27	Heb 1:10–12	The unchangeable God
Ps 104:4	Heb 1:7	Angels and winds
Ps 109:8	Ac 1:20	Replacement for Judas
Ps 110:1	Mt 22:44; Mk 12:36; Lk 20:42–43; Ac 34–35; Heb 1:13	At God's right hand
Ps 110:4	Heb 5:6; 7:17, 21	Melchizedek
Ps 112:9	2Co 9:9	Gifts for the poor
Ps 116:10	2Cor 4:13	Faith and speech
Ps 117:1	Ro 15:11	Nations praising God
Ps 118:6–7	Heb 13:6	The Lord is my helper
Ps 118:22–23	Mt 21:42; Mk 12:10–11; Lk 20:17; Ac 4:11; 1Pe 2:7	Rejected cornerstone
Ps 118:26	Mt 21:9; 23:39; Mk 11:9; Lk 13:35; 19:38; Jn 12:13	Blessed is he who comes
Ps 135:14	Heb 10:30	God judges his people
Ps 140:3	Ro 3:13	Sin of humanity
Ps 146:6	Ac 4:24; 14:15	God the creator

Proverbs

INTRODUCTION

1. Background

The book of Proverbs is a marvelous collection of wise sayings and instructions for living a useful and effective life. The collection forms part of the larger group of biblical writings known as "wisdom literature"—literature that gives instructions for living while pondering the difficulties of life. Proverbial wisdom is characterized by short, pithy statements; but the speculative wisdom, such as Ecclesiastes or Job, uses lengthy monologues and dialogues to probe the meaning of life, the problem of good and evil, and the relationship between God and people. This type of literature was common throughout the ancient Near East.

2. Authorship and Date

The traditional view that Solomon wrote the entire book of Proverbs is supported by the titles in 1:1; 10:1; and 25:1. Moreover, Solomon was a wise man, writing proverbs and collecting sayings from other wise men (see 22:17–24:34). Proponents of this view have usually assumed that Agur (30:1) and Lemuel (31:1) were pseudonyms of Solomon.

This general view, however, stands in need of some revision. It is now recognized that Agur and Lemuel were probably not pseudonyms for Solomon and that 22:17–24:34 forms a separate collection of proverbs because it has a distinct form, separate title and purpose, and seems to be directly related to the "Instruction of Amenemope," an Egyptian document written between 1580 and 1100 B.C. It is impossible to determine who added this material to the collection of Proverbs. Furthermore, the title of 1:1, which has generally been taken to head up 1:1–9:18, may not actually refer to these chapters; it may simply be the heading of the whole book in its final form and may not necessarily indicate that the first nine chapters are from Solomon.

An examination of the titles in the book is important to the study of its authorship. The heading in 10:1 clearly credits Solomon for the subsequent material. In 10:1–22:16 there may be two collections (chs. 10–15; 16:1–22:16) due to the difference in style. The heading in 25:1 also affirms that Solomon was the author (or editor) of a larger collection from which the scribes of Hezekiah's court excerpted the proverbs in chs. 25–29. Once again there are differences of style between chs. 25–27 and 28–29.

In conclusion, then, Solomon is responsible for 10:1–22:16 and perhaps all or part of chs. 25–29. Most scholars, including many conservatives, see some dependence of 22:17–24:34 on the "Instruction of Amenemope." Presumably Israel knew these sayings by the time of Solomon. Most scholars also see chs. 30–31 as non-Solomonic and from a later date, perhaps from a contemporary of Hezekiah. The prologue to the book (1:8–9:18) would have been added to form an introduction, certainly by the time of Hezekiah, and possibly in Solomon's time. Finally, 1:1–7 headed up the final collection as a title.

3. Literary Forms

A casual reading of the Proverbs reveals the general form of a proverb. It is a short, pregnant sentence or phrase whose meaning is applicable in many situations. A thorough analysis of the proverbs reveals that these short sayings follow many patterns and constructions that have bearing on the meanings.

As with all Hebrew poetic discourse, the proverbs use different types of parallelism. *Synonymous* parallelism expresses one idea in parallel but slightly different expressions: "A fool's mouth is his undoing, / and his lips are a snare to his soul" (18:7). In *antithetical* parallelism the second line contrasts with the first: "The plans of the righteous are just, / but the advice of the wicked is deceitful" (12:5). *Emblematic* parallelism uses a figurative illustration as one of the parallel units:

"As vinegar to the teeth and smoke to the eyes, / so is a sluggard to those who send him" (10:26). Another helpful category is the general one of *synthetic* parallelism, in which the second line amplifies the first in some way: "The LORD works out everything for his own ends— / even the wicked for a day of disaster" (16:4). Lastly, proverbs whose second line simply completes the idea begun in the first are said to exhibit *formal* parallelism. One part may contain the subject and the second the predicate (15:31); the first line may state a condition and the second its consequences (16:7), its cause (16:12), or its purpose (15:24); and one part may state a preferred value or course over the other: "Better a little with the fear of the LORD / than great wealth with turmoil" (15:16).

Proverbs are essentially didactic, whether they follow the pattern of a formal instruction using imperatives or prohibitions (16:3; 23:9), are expressed in didactic sayings that observe traits and acts that are to be followed or avoided (14:31), tell an example story (7:6–23), make a wisdom speech (8:1–36), or develop numerical sayings (6:16–19).

Instructions often use motivations—reasons for complying. The most common form of motivation is a subordinate clause stating the purpose, result, or reason for the instruction: "Listen to advice and accept instruction, / and in the end you will be wise" (19:20). Sometimes the motivation is implied in a general observation: "My son, do not despise the LORD's discipline / and do not resent his rebuke, / because the LORD disciplines those he loves, / as a father the son he delights in" (3:11–12).

4. Theological Values

This collection of wise sayings is not exclusively religious; its teachings apply to human problems in general and not primarily to the problems of the religious community or to major theological themes such as election, redemption, and covenant. Rather, the teacher concerns himself with plain, ordinary individuals who live in the world. Accordingly, the sayings exhibit several distinctive characteristics. (1) They focus attention on individuals rather than on the nation, setting forth the qualities needed and the dangers to be avoided by people seeking to find success with God. (2) They are applicable to all people at any period in history who face the same types of perils and have the same characteristics and abilities (1:20; 8:1–5). (3) They are based on respect for authority, traditional values, and the wisdom of mature teachers (24:21). (4) They are immensely practical, giving sound advice for developing personal qualities that are necessary to achieve success in this life and to avoid failure or shame, and warning that virtue is rewarded by prosperity and well-being but that vice leads to poverty and disaster.

It would be wrong, however, to conclude that Proverbs is a secular book; its teachings are solidly based on "the fear of the LORD" (1:7), making compliance with them a moral and spiritual matter. In fact, the book teaches that this fear of the Lord is the evidence of faith; for the wise teacher enjoins people to trust in the Lord whose counsel stands (19:21) and not their own understanding (3:5–7). The purpose of proverbial teaching, then, is to inspire faith in the Lord (22:19). Such reverential fear requires a personal knowledge of the Lord ("fear" and "knowledge" are parallel in 9:10)—to find this fear is to find knowledge (2:5), a knowledge that comes by revelation (3:6). Ultimately, however, the fear of the Lord is manifested in a life of obedience, confessing and forsaking sin (28:18), and doing what is right (21:3), which is the believer's task before God (17:3). Since the motivation for faith and obedience comes from the Scripture, Proverbs relates the way of wisdom to the law (28:4; 29:18). In the final analysis we must conclude there are no *secular* proverbs that can be contrasted with *religious* ones; everything on earth serves the purposes of God and is potentially holy.

5. Content

Proverbs 1:8–9:18 is an organized introduction to the book with many admonitions and prohibitions as well as example stories and personified wisdom-speech. This section runs in cycles: the purpose of Proverbs is to give wisdom (1:1–7), but folly may interrupt this purpose (1:8–33); there are advantages to seeking wisdom (2:1–4:27), but folly may prevent one from seeking it (5:1–6:19); there are likewise advantages to finding wisdom (6:20–9:12), but folly may prevent this too (9:13–18).

Proverbs 10:1–22:16 is a collection of some 375 unrelated proverbs. Then, after the sayings patterned after the "Instruction of Amenemope" (22:17–24:22), another collection of proverbs is included (chs. 25–29). The last two sections include among other things the numerical sayings of the wise (30:10–33) and the acrostic poem on wisdom (31:10–31).

The book of Proverbs covers a wide variety of topics, most of them connected with daily living. Topics include such areas as wisdom in general, personal conduct, human attitudes (dangers of negative ones and value of positive ones), child-rearing, marital relationships, business tactics, use of money, friendship, instructions for rulers and judges, and use of alcohol. For a topical index on this book, see EBC 5:897–903.

EXPOSITION

I. Introduction to the Book of Proverbs (1:1–7)

A. Title: The Proverbs of Solomon (1:1)

1 This verse provides the general heading for the entire book, even though the proverbs of Solomon probably do not begin until ch. 10. What is a "proverb" (GK 5442)? A proverb may be described as an object lesson based on or using some comparison or analogy. It may be a short saying that provides a general truth (Eze 16:44), a lesson drawn from experience (Ps 78:2–6), a common example (Dt 28:37), or a pattern of future blessing or cursing (Eze 21:1–5). Its purpose is to help one choose the best course of action among those available— the foolish way is to be avoided and the wise way followed.

B. Purposes: To Develop Moral Skill and Mental Acumen (1:2–6)

2 The book of Proverbs has two purposes: to give moral skillfulness (developed in vv.3–4) and to give mental discernment (developed in v.6).

The first purpose is that the disciple will develop skillfulness and discipline in holy living (v.2a). "Attaining" (lit., "to know"; GK 3359) encompasses an intellectual and an experiential acquisition of wisdom and discipline.

"Wisdom" (GK 2683) basically means "skill." This word describes the "skill" of the craftsmen who worked in the tabernacle (Ex 31:6), the "wits" of seasoned mariners (Ps 107:27), administrative abilities (1Ki 3:28), and the "wise advice" of a counselor (2Sa 20:22). In Proverbs "wisdom" signifies skillful living—the ability to make wise choices and live successfully according to the moral standards of the covenant community. The one who lives skillfully produces things of lasting value to God and to the community.

The other object to be acquired is "discipline" (GK 4592; cf. 3:5), the necessary companion of wisdom. This word denotes the training of the moral nature, involving the correcting of waywardness toward folly and the development of reverence to the Lord and personal integrity.

The second major purpose of the book of Proverbs is for the disciple to acquire discernment (v.2b). "To understand" (or "discern"; GK 1067) means to distinguish *between* things, to compare concepts, form evaluations, or make analogies. Proverbs will train people to discern lessons about life, such as distinguishing permanent values from immediate gratifications.

3 The first purpose statement is now developed. The disciple will receive something worth having: a "disciplined" (GK 4592) and "prudent" (GK 8505) life. Discipline produces prudent living. To act prudently means "to act circumspectly." The three terms that follow express how prudent acts manifest themselves. (1) "What is right" ("rightness" or "righteousness"; GK 7406) means basically conformity to a standard (cf. Dt 25:15)—in this case, the standard of God's law (see Dt 16:18–20). (2) "What is . . . just" (GK 5477) signifies a "decision" like that of an arbiter (see Dt 16:18). It is applied to litigation (2Sa 15:2) and the precedent established by such (Ex 21:9). The term also connotes that which is fitting or proper (Jdg 13:12). Proverbs will develop a life that has a sense of propriety in making decisions. (3) "What is . . . fair" ("equity"; GK 4797) can describe what is pleasing (cf. Jdg 14:3). The book will instruct a lifestyle that is equitable, one that incorporates the most pleasing aspects.

4 The first purpose statement is now developed from the teacher's point of view—he will give shrewdness to the naive or "simple" (GK 7343). This naive person is one who is gullible (14:15), easily enticed (9:4, 16), and falls into traps (22:3). The instructor wants to give such a one a sense of "prudence" (GK 6893), the ability to foresee evil and prepare for it (13:16; 22:3).

The second half of the verse parallels "simple" (or "naive") with "[immature] youth," and "prudence" (or "shrewdness") with "knowledge" and "discretion." This latter expression refers to devising plans or perceiving the best course of action for gaining a goal. Such ability is crucial for the immature youth in this world.

5 Before elaborating on the second purpose statement for the book, the writer digresses to make an exhortation. The first verb advises the wise to hear and the second gives the purpose—"[to] add to their learning." Parallel to this advice is the counsel for the "discerning" to get guidance. This person has the capacity of one who is discerning. The "guidance" (GK 9374) to be obtained may be illustrated by the rope-pulling done by sailors to steer or guide a ship; it is the discernment to steer a right course through life. Proverbs is not simply for the naive and the gullible; everyone can grow by its teachings and learn how to conduct themselves in life.

6 The second major purpose of the book is to give mental acumen to the student (see comment on v.2). The teachings will develop one's ability in discerning "proverbs" and "parables" (GK 4886). This latter term may refer to a saying that has another sense to it that needs uncovering.

The disciple must understand also the "sayings" of the wise—the words that come from the sages. Their teachings at times take the form of "riddles" (GK 2648). This word may refer to what is obscure or indirect, such as the riddles of Samson (Jdg 14:13–14) or of the queen of Sheba (1Ki 10:1).

C. Motto: The Fear of the Lord (1:7)

7 Reverential "fear" (GK 3711) of the Lord is the prerequisite of knowledge. This term can describe dread (Dt 1:29), being terrified (Jnh 1:10), standing in awe (1Ki 3:28), or having reverence (Lev 19:3). With the Lord as the object, this word captures both aspects of shrinking back in fear and of drawing close in awe. It is not a trembling dread that paralyzes action, but neither is it a polite reverence. "The fear of the LORD" ultimately expresses reverential submission to the Lord's will and thus characterizes a true worshiper. In this context it is the first and controlling principle of knowledge. Elsewhere in Proverbs the fear of the Lord is the foundation for wisdom (9:10) or the discipline leading to wisdom (15:33); it is expressed in hatred of evil (8:13), and it results in a prolonged life (10:27).

On the other hand, fools disdain wisdom and discipline. The term "fools" (GK 211) describes those who lack understanding (10:21), do not store up knowledge (10:14),

Parables of the Old Testament

Parable	Reference
The trees	Jdg 9:7–15
The ewe lamb	2Sa 12:1–4
Two sons	2Sa 14:1–24
Thistle and cedar	2Ki 14:8–14
The vineyard	Isa 5:1–7
Almond rod and boiling pot	Jer 1:11–19
Linen belt	Jer 13:1–11
Wineskins	Jer 13:12–14
Potter and clay	Jer 18:1–10
Two baskets of figs	Jer 24:1–10
Cup of God's wrath	Jer 25:15–38
Useless vine	Eze 15:1–8
Cooking pot	Eze 24:1–4
Valley of dry bones	Eze 37:1–14
Measuring line	Zec 2:1–13
Golden lampstand and two olive trees	Zec 4:1–14
Flying scroll	Zec 5:1–4

fail to attain wisdom (24:7), talk loosely (14:3), are filled with pride (26:5), and are contentious (20:3). They are morally unskilled and refuse any correction (15:5; 27:22). Fools are people who "despise" (GK 1022) wisdom and discipline; they treat these virtues as worthless and contemptible (cf. Ge 25:34; Ne 4:4).

II. A Father's Admonition to Acquire Wisdom (1:8–9:18)

A. Introductory Exhortation (1:8–9)

8 The disciple is exhorted to heed parental guidance. "My son," the customary form of address for a disciple, derives from the idea that parents are primarily responsible for moral instruction (Dt 6:7; Pr 4:3–4). Here the disciple is to respond to ("Listen," with the attitude of "taking heed to"; GK 9048) "instruction" (GK 4592) that is normally the father's responsibility (except in 31:1, where it is the warning of the mother).

The son is also to follow his mother's "teaching" (GK 9368). This word may be cognate to a verb meaning "to point or direct," so that the idea of teaching might be illustrated as pointing in the right direction (see Ge 46:28). In Proverbs this instruction is for ordering the life (see also 6:20; 31:26).

9 For heeding the instruction of the law, the disciple is promised an attractiveness of life. "Grace" (GK 2834), the charm that teaching brings to the disciple, refers to those qualities that make him agreeable. The metaphor compares these qualities to an attractive wreath worn round the head. Obedience will thus improve the disciple. The one who loses the rough edges through disciplined training will present a pleasing presence to the world.

B. Admonition to Avoid Easy But Unjust Riches (1:10–19)

10–11 The summary statement warns the son not to consent to the enticement of moral misfits. The term for "entice" (GK 7331), related to the root of "simple" or "naive," means "to allure, persuade, entice, or seduce." Here the enticement is to do evil because it comes from "sinners" (in this context professional criminals, a gang of robbers). That is, the young man is being offered a part in a life of crime. He is being asked to join a vicious ambush; the verb for "to lie in wait" (GK 741) is used elsewhere of hostile pur-

poses such as murder (Dt 19:11), kidnapping (Jdg 21:20), or seduction (Pr 23:28). Here the aim is bloodshed. The attack is also evil. The wicked lie in wait for the innocent, and their attack is without a cause.

12–14 The criminals assure the novice of swift success: they will swallow up victims who are in the vitality of life as surely and swiftly as death opens and swallows its victims (cf. Nu 16:32–33). By sharing the stolen wealth, they will fill their houses with "plunder" (GK 8965; a word used elsewhere for spoils from war). So the offer made to the youth is to pursue with the roustabouts a life of easy but ill-gotten gain.

15–16 The young man's parents strongly advise him to avoid such evil companions because their lifestyle, though it may appear prosperous, leads to destruction. The advice "do not go" counters the allurement of the wicked—"Come along with us" (v.11). The primary reason for not going is that the sinners' purpose is bloodthirsty; therefore their retribution is sure (cf. v.18). In the final analysis, then, the trap the wicked lay for others in reality will catch them.

17–19 There are two ways to interpret v.17 within the context. One is to see a comparison with the folly of birds who fall into a snare even though forewarned—likewise the wicked fall into the snare God lays because they are driven by lust. The other is to see a contrast between the natural behavior of birds when forewarned and the irrational greed of robbers. In other words, it is futile to spread out a net for birds that are watching, but these men are so blinded by evil that they fail to recognize the trap. The blind folly of greed leads to their doom—retribution is the law that will take away their lives.

C. Warning Against Disregarding or Despising Wisdom (1:20–33)

20–21 Wisdom personified stands in the public space, exhorting the ignorant and the scornful to listen, warning of destruction if they refuse. The book has three such personifications—in 1:20–33; 8:1–36; and 9:1–6. Here the term "wisdom" is in the plural to signify the intensity and comprehensiveness of it all. In addition, the verb "call aloud" (GK 8264) expresses an excited exhortation.

The location of this exhortation is in the public places—"the street . . . the public squares . . . the gateways"—suggesting that wisdom is readily available for the business of living: it is for the common person, not the scholar exclusively. These places were the centers for all activities: daily affairs (2Ki 7:1), justice (Ru 4:1), employment (Mt 20:3), and even playing (Zec 8:5; et al.). Since wisdom touches all aspects of life, the setting is appropriate. In this setting wisdom, like a prophet, calls out.

22 Wisdom offers a complaint—"How long . . . ?" Three types of people are addressed by this: the "simple" (GK 7343), the scoffers or "mockers" (GK 4370), and the "fools" (GK 4067). The first is the naive person or the simpleton, the second the defiant and cynical freethinker, and the third the morally insensitive fool. Each is satisfied with one's ways and does not listen to reason.

23 The invitation takes the form of a conditional clause—"If only you would respond." Wisdom is firmly resolved to pour out her spirit, her active power, on those who respond. Like a copious spring she will gush forth to them.

24–28 There is grave danger, however, in disregarding the invitation given by wisdom. If the call has been extended for some time— "How long?" (v.22)—then this warning is given for a prolonged refusal. Because wisdom has been continually rejected, wisdom will laugh at the calamity of those who have rejected it. This retributive justice is expressed figuratively as wisdom's mocking at their distress. But then v.28 explains the meaning of the mocking—wisdom will not be there to help when the fools cry out from their distress. The figure of laughing reveals the absurdity of choosing a foolish way of life and being totally unprepared for disaster.

29–33 This section closes with a denunciation for despising wisdom. Not only had these foolish ones preferred their folly, but they had also despised the knowledge of ethical and religious principles for life. Moreover, they continually spurned wisdom's reproofs. The punishment for such indifference and antagonism takes the form of retribution. The term "fruit" is used metaphorically for the consequence of actions—likened to growth that culminates in produce. Their

way—their life and what it produces—stands in contrast to the way of wisdom that they had spurned.

The teaching of retribution is confirmed in v.32. The "turning away" ("waywardness") and the "complacency" will be the ruin of these people. But those who heed the teachings of wisdom will live in safety and security. The expressions used suggest a permanent, settled condition free from the sense of danger or dread. Such is the contrast between the false security of the wicked and the true and lasting peace of the righteous.

D. The Benefits of Seeking Wisdom (2:1–22)

1. The admonition to receive wisdom (2:1–4)

1–4 This chapter is a long poem in six parts: the appeal for wisdom followed by a fivefold blessing.

The teacher again makes the appeal: To attain wisdom requires constant meditation and a rigid discipline. The requirement of meditation begins with receiving the teaching. "Accept" is paralleled with "store up," a figure that implies that most teaching cannot be used immediately but that some time will pass before education's effects are felt. In the meantime the teachings will develop attitudes in their pupils that will influence their future actions. Such a perspective calls for patience by the students, making both heart and mind attentive ("ear" and "heart" represent the mental faculties).

The other requirement is the diligent search for wisdom. On their own initiative disciples are to summon or "call out . . . for" understanding. The elevation in the lines from "call out" to "cry aloud" suggests that, if understanding does not come immediately, one should put forth greater efforts. So the ear hears the teaching, the mind understands what is said, and the voice is used to inquire for true knowledge. This search for wisdom and understanding should be as diligent as the search for precious metal ("silver"), suggesting both the value of the treasure and the diligence of the search. The starting point is revelation—specific words and commandments—and the method is not one of free speculation but of exploring and treasuring the teachings.

2. Consequences of receiving wisdom (2:5–22)

a. Knowledge of God and his protection (2:5–8)

5 The point of this first consequence is direct: When you seek wisdom, you find God. The "knowledge of God" refers to more than intellectual opinion; it also encompasses religion and ethics. Coupled with the fear of the Lord, this knowledge means that the disciple will follow God's moral code; for to know God is to react ethically to his will, to follow his principles.

6–8 The reason the one who seeks knowledge will find God is that God is the source of wisdom and knowledge. Moreover, God has stored wisdom up as a protection for his saints. The word translated "victory" means "sound wisdom"; it includes the ideas of its effect: abiding success, achievement, and deliverance. So the verse states that God holds in store sound wisdom that is powerful for his saints.

b. Discernment for living (2:9–11)

9–11 The disciple will develop the intellectual capacity and moral insight to discern the path of what is "right," "just," and "fair" (cf. 1:3). "Path" (GK 5047) is used metaphorically for the course of a person's actions. The word is related to the verb for "to roll" and the noun for "cart"; so the noun literally means "the track of a wagon wheel." Thus "every good path" is a lifestyle that regularly leads in the direction of what is morally good.

Wisdom will take up its abode in the inner life, and knowledge will be pleasant to the soul. "Pleasant" (GK 5838) describes a quality that attracts one to an object—so knowledge is attractive and attracting. For those who assimilate wisdom, doing right becomes attractive and delightful; for they see its advantage. In addition, this assimilated wisdom will manifest itself in discretion and discernment that protect from evil or save the good man from the consequences of naiveté.

c. Protection from evil men (9:12–15)

12–15 These verses present the first of two specific examples of protection from evil—from the "wicked men." The adjective "wicked" (GK 8273) describes what is unpleasant, bringing pain and misery. Evil ways bring harm to others by speaking perverse things, i.e., things contrary to what is right and proper.

Verses 13–15 describe the wicked's purpose, pleasure, and perverted paths. Their purpose is to walk in the ways of darkness; they abandon the straight way to follow an evil way that can only be described as "dark"; it is devoid of ethical illumination. Their "delight" is in doing what is morally evil. This activity may not be due to an abnormal or sadistic delight but rather to dullness of conscience. Verse 15 then describes their perverted ways, using a variation of the expressions of the preceding verses—evil men are twisted and devious in the path they follow, constantly turning aside to the wrong ways. The disciple needs wisdom for protection from those who turn the Lord's ways upside down and try to draw others in by creating ethical chaos.

d. Protection from evil women (2:16–19)

16–19 Another class of evil persons from whom wisdom delivers is the licentious woman. Whereas the evil man brings pain and perversion, the evil woman brings moral ruin through a more subtle temptation. Prostitutes and adulteresses existed in Israel from the earliest times (Jdg 11:1; 1Ki 3:16; Hos 3:1). In this passage the licentious woman is first described; then her ruin and that of those who submit to her are presented as a warning.

The word "adulteress" literally means "strange [GK 2424] woman"; it describes this woman as outside the framework of the covenant community (though she is an Israelite woman, for her marriage is called a "covenant," and she offers communion sacrifices; cf. 7:5, 14). She is estranged from the corporate life of the community with its social and religious conventions. She is acting outside the legal bounds of marriage within the covenant.

The subtlety of the appeal comes from flattering speech—the adulteress talks smoothly (see 5:3). An example of such talk is found in 7:14–20. Acquiring discernment will protect the disciple from the smooth, seductive speech of a temptress. Seductive talk is evil, not only because it reveals a brazen character, but also because the adulteress is guilty of marital infidelity: she leaves the companion of her youth (here and in Jer 3:4

944

for the husband) and is unmindful of the covenant.

"Covenant" (GK 1382) probably refers to the temptress's marriage vows (Mal 2:14) but could mean the covenant law that prohibited adultery (Ex 20:14). If the marriage vows are meant, such a covenant was entered into at betrothal, when the dowry was established. The adulteress violates her pledge of fidelity.

The effective warning against this type of evil derives from understanding the result of such infidelity—it leads to destruction, the very opposite of the happy and prosperous life. "Her house" could be taken as "she *with her house* sinks down to death," but "she sinks down to death, *which is her house,*" may have better support; for 9:18 states that the dead are in her house and that her guests are in the nether world. Her paths lead to the "shades" (NIV, "the spirits of the dead"). The "shades" are the inhabitants of Sheol; the term describes the shadowy continuation of those who have lost their vitality and strength. So the inevitable fate of her course of life is to be among the departed in the realm of the dead. The expressions may carry a figurative rather than a literal meaning: Get entangled with her, and you may find only estrangement from the living community, among outcasts, moral lepers who have taken a journey into the land of no return.

e. Enablement for righteous living (2:20–22)

20–22 The passage ends on the more positive note that wisdom will enable people to do what is right and to enjoy God's blessing. Here the text brings in the Deuteronomic emphasis on the land—God's supreme gift being the fulfillment of the promises. The upright will enjoy security and prosperity in it, but the wicked will be rooted out in divine judgment.

E. Admonition to Follow the Way of Wisdom in Relationships With God and People (3:1–35)

1. Introductory exhortation (3:1–4)

1–2 The first exhortation is to follow the father's "teaching" (lit., "law"; GK 9368), because it will bring a long and peaceful life. Here the verbs "do not forget" and "keep" remind the disciple of general educational

discipline. The result is a life worth living, free from danger and trouble.

3 The second exhortation is to be faithful and trustworthy because it brings honor with God and man. "Love" (GK 2876) and "faithfulness" (GK 622) are the two basic covenant terms in Israel. The former is essentially fidelity to obligations arising from a relationship; the latter is essentially that which can be relied on, that which is stable. The two words together form a hendiadys, meaning "faithful love." These words, coupled with the allusion to Dt 6:8 and even Jer 31:3, show that the content of this disciplined life is faith in the Lord. By "binding" and "writing" the teacher is stressing that the teachings become a part of the disciple's nature. The ramifications of this terminology are that the disciple is actually subject to the Lord, not the teacher, and that the requisite "discipline" is respect and obedience for the Lord and his teaching, not merely for a human instructor.

4 Verse 4 provides the final motivation: favor and a good name. Parallel to 13:15, this difficult line probably signifies that the disciple will have a reputation for good understanding, meaning that he will be respected by God and other people.

2. Admonition to be faithful to the Lord (3:5–12)

5–6 Several specific instructions compose this general admonition to be faithful. The first is to trust in the Lord and not in oneself, because he grants success. "Trust" (GK 1053) carries the force of relying on someone for security; the confidence is to be in the Lord and not in human understanding. Such trust must be characterized by total commitment—"with *all* your heart," "in *all* your ways." "Understanding" (GK 1069) is now cast in a sinful mode (cf. 1:2, 6); so there is to be a difference between the understanding that wisdom brings and the natural understanding that undermines faith. When obedient faith is present, the Lord will guide the believer along life's paths in spite of difficulties and hindrances. The idea of "straight" contrasts to the crooked and perverse ways of the wicked.

7–8 The second instruction is to revere the Lord and avoid evil. Here too there is a difference between human wisdom and the new wisdom from above (cf. Isa 5:21). There must be a higher source—"fear the Lord and shun evil." Compliance with this is therapeutic: it will be health to the body and nourishment for the frame. The healing that the fear of the Lord and avoidance of evil bring is first and foremost spiritual. Scripture often uses the physical body to describe inner spiritual or psychical feelings.

9–10 The third piece of advice is to give back to God some of one's wealth as a sacrifice in recognition that God gave it (cf. Ex 23:19; Nu 28:26–27; Dt 18:4; 26:1–2). The admonition reminds the faithful of their religious duties to God. Then follows the promise of blessing in the "barns" and the "vats."

11–12 The final specific instruction warns the disciple not to rebel against the Lord's discipline, because it is an evidence of his love. Wisdom literature knows that the righteous do not receive uninterrupted blessing; suffering remains a problem for everyone, and this text records one of their solutions. This motivation recalls the language of the Davidic covenant (2Sa 7:14; Ps 89:32–33), which mentions discipline in love. Indeed, it is the father-son relationship that provides insight into the nature of that discipline (cf. Heb 12:5–6).

3. Commendation of the way of wisdom (3:13–26)

a. Wisdom the most valuable possession (3:13–18)

13 Verses 13–18 appear to be following a hymnic style, for "blessed" (GK 897) replaces the imperative. The statement "Blessed is the man," which begins the section, is followed by a series of motive clauses giving the reasons for this happy estate. "Blessed" describes heavenly bliss stemming from being right with God; it depicts the human condition of well-being that comes with God's blessing or as a divine reward for righteousness.

14–18 The statement concerning the blessedness of finding wisdom is now validated. Wisdom is better than wealth and riches; for her yield is power, influence, and respect—the gifts of life. She is compared to "a tree of life," the symbol of vitality and fullness of life. This figure, drawing on Ge 2–3 (cf. Ge

3:22), signifies that wisdom is the source of a long and beneficial life.

b. Wisdom essential to creation (3:19–20)

19–20 Wisdom, understanding, and knowledge are also valuable to God; for by them he created the universe. How wisdom was used in Creation and how it pictures Christ, the Wisdom of God, is discussed in the comments on 8:22–23. This section shows that the wisdom that directs life is the same wisdom that created the universe (see 8:20–31); to surrender to God's wisdom is to put oneself in harmony with creation, the world around one. The two verses concentrate first on the foundation of heaven and earth and then on the provision of waters on earth and from heaven, making a fine parallel to the nature of wisdom as the foundation and blessing of life.

c. Wisdom and a long and safe life (3:21–26)

21–26 This section forms an admonition to keep on the way of wisdom along with promises for such compliance. If disciples diligently preserve sound judgment and discernment, they can be confident that the Lord will guide and protect them. But they cannot let them out of sight for a moment. Whoever trusts and follows sound judgment in their life of righteousness will find not only strength and beauty in wisdom but also preservation in action and repose—in normal life and in times of disaster. In other words, their lives will be enriched, safe, secure, and without fear. True spiritual discernment that places its confidence in the Lord will not be disappointed.

4. Warning to avoid unneighborliness (3:27–30)

27–30 A succession of instructions now follows with regard to neighborliness. These ideas, expressed in the negative, follow naturally from the emphasis on love and faithfulness in v.3. Verses 27–28 exhort doing acts of kindness to those in need; for it is wrong to withhold help from a needy neighbor—people ought to be good neighbors. The father also prohibits plotting maliciously against an unsuspecting neighbor. Malice is a crime; it ruins community. Neither should anyone bring a groundless litigation against an innocent neighbor.

5. Warning against emulating the wicked (3:31–35)

31–35 In dealing with neighbors, one should avoid envying or emulating a violent person (cf. Ps 73:3–5). This warning is followed by the reasons, expressed in a series of contrasts. On the one side, the Lord detests the perverse, curses the house of the wicked, mocks proud mockers, and holds fools up to shame. But with the upright he is pleased, blesses their home, gives grace to the humble, and bequeaths honor to the wise. So wise and upright behavior pleases God and results in his blessing.

F. Admonition to Follow Righteousness and Avoid Wickedness (4:1–27)

1. Traditional teaching and its benefits (4:1–9)

a. Exhortation to acquire traditional wisdom (4:1–4a)

This chapter is comprised of three discourses on the value of wisdom, each including the motifs of instruction, exhortation, command, and motivation.

1 The first discourse begins with a double call, stressing the importance of receiving the teaching. This "instruction" is the moral instruction introduced previously (cf. 1:2); it adds self-control and guidance to the wisdom.

The significant feature of this first discourse is that the teaching is traditional. The plural "sons" suggests that disciples are in view and that the father is a teacher. However, the use of "mother" in v.3 and the fact that the teacher-pupil relationship was modeled on the parent-child relationship suggest that this is a father-children relationship.

2 The tradition being passed on is "sound" (GK 3202)—it is the voice of experience. But it must be received, the word "learning" (GK 4375) implying that it requires taking. Accordingly, this teaching is designated better as tradition.

3–4a The concern that these traditional teachings be received is reinforced by personal experience—they were lovingly handed down by the child's parents. They

were ingrained in his soul; he has seen them shape his life and prove reliable. So the home continues to be the prominent arena of learning as the parents in turn pass on the traditions (see Dt 6:6–9). In this section, then, the one teaching strengthens his credibility by informing his sons that it is a shared experience.

b. Benefits of acquired wisdom (4:4b–9)

4b Receiving this traditional wisdom wholeheartedly will bring life. "You will live" must mean experiencing life with all its blessings, life as opposed to the whole realm of death with which it is in conflict. Deuteronomy 30 captures the contrast forcefully—people are in a life-and-death struggle; choosing life means obeying the commandments in order to enjoy God's bounty. This theme of life appears in each of the discourses (4:4, 10, 22–23). Of course, the sage uses this motivation in the general sense, for there are always exceptions like Job.

5–6 A second benefit of traditional wisdom is security. After reiterating the exhortation to acquire wisdom and understanding, the teacher uses feminine verbs to promise protection and safety. Wisdom is personified as a woman, like a bride that is to be loved and embraced (v.8), but also having the qualities of an influential patron who can protect. Wisdom personified as a virtuous woman contrasts to the strange woman. If those being instructed give her wholehearted devotion, she will watch over them.

7–9 A third benefit is "honor." Using an implied comparison with a valuable object (cf. 3:14–15), the teacher implores the disciple to obtain this wisdom at all costs; for it is of supreme value. The personification continues in these verses, showing that embracing wisdom will bring honor like a wreath on the head. This honor essentially has to do with the character that wisdom produces; such virtue is readily recognized in the community (11:10–11).

2. Admonition to live righteously (4:10–19)

a. Pursuit of a righteous lifestyle (4:10–13)

10 The section begins with the repeated admonition to listen carefully to the instruction so that the life might be extended. The parallelism explains that the disciple must appropriate ("accept") wisdom's life principles.

11–12 That this teaching must be appropriated is underscored by the use of "I guide you." The figure of a road is now used. Living according to wisdom is like walking or running on a safe road, a course that will be free of obstacles, so that progress will be certain (see on 3:5–6). Verse 12 uses two synonymous, temporal clauses to fill out the image: when one lives by this teaching (walking and running), nothing will impede progress.

13 Not only is wisdom the means of making progress in life, it is life itself. Anything so essential must be enthusiastically maintained.

b. Avoidance of a wicked lifestyle (4:14–19)

14–15 The warning is to avoid evil ways and evil men by not even starting on the wicked path of life. Don't take the first step! The rapid sequence of imperatives in these verses stresses the urgency of the matter. And the expressions used continue the comparison of lifestyle with a path that can be traveled—only now the lifestyle is evil.

16–17 The first reason that one should avoid such a lifestyle is that it is enslaving. By using hyperboles the teacher portrays the character of the wicked as those who are addicted to evil (cf. Ps 36:4). They are so completely devoted to evil conduct that they cannot sleep until they find expression for it. Moreover, evil is their diet. This hyperbole stresses how powerful the influence of evil is in their life—it is like food and wine to the wicked.

18–19 In addition to being enslaved by evil, one should realize that becoming involved with evil is dangerous. Similes are now used to make the contrast vivid. The path of righteousness is secure and clear like the bright light of the daytime that shines brighter and brighter. On the other hand, the way of the wicked is insecure and dangerous, like darkness in which people stumble.

3. Admonition to concentrate on righteous living (4:20–27)

a. Exhortation to the father's teaching (4:20–22)

20–21 The exhortation in this third discourse uses several terms for parts of the body: the disciple must use ears to listen closely to the teacher's words, eyes to watch them closely, and the heart to determine to do them. By using ears, eyes, and heart, the teacher is exhorting the whole person to receive the traditions.

22 The reason for giving heed to instruction once again is that the words of wisdom provide life—a life of health. The health that is promised here is physical, emotional, and spiritual—the whole person. It is made possible because of God's words that bring deliverance from the evils that harm and hinder life.

b. Concentration on righteousness (4:23–27)

23 In this instruction for righteousness, the parts of the body that are used are those involved with expression or action. First, the "heart" (i.e., the mind; GK 4213) must be guarded diligently. Verse 21 instructed the disciple to guard wisdom in the heart. Now the heart must be guarded; for it is "the wellspring of life." The heart is the starting point of the activities of life (16:9; 23:19); it determines the course of life.

24 Righteousness will control the tongue, avoiding twisted and crooked speech. This is the next logical step; for words flow out of the heart. Wisdom produces truthful speech (8:13; 10:32; et al.).

25 Next, the eyes must be focused on proper goals. The wise person will have an unswerving directness, but the fool is easily distracted (17:24).

26–27 The imagery of the level, firm, and straight path is used again in these final verses to advise the disciple to avoid evil actions.

G. Admonition to Avoid Seduction to Evil (5:1–23)

1. A father's warning about deadly seduction (5:1–6)

a. Exhortation for discretion (5:1–2)

1–2 In this chapter we have a man-to-man warning to avoid liaisons with loose women, a theme that is fairly common in the wisdom literature of the ancient Near East. The initial exhortation is for the son to listen carefully to this warning that he may keep "discretion" (GK 4659) and knowledge, which will be basic for avoiding temptation to such disastrous folly.

b. Motivation: With wisdom seduction may be avoided (5:3–6)

3 The reason that the disciple should guard discretion is that the adulteress is seductive. "Adulteress" (lit., "strange woman"; see comment on 2:16) is here a married woman. But the main point the text makes is that her words are flattering. The images of dripping honey and smooth oil refer to her words, not her kisses (cf. SS 4:11).

4 The teacher uncovers corruption under the adulteress's charm. Afterward she is "bitter" as "gall" (Heb. word is "wormwood," an aromatic plant in sharp contrast to the sweetness of honey; GK 4360). The image of the two-edged sword (lit., a sword with more than one mouth) signifies that a liaison with this woman brings pain and destruction. The flattery conceals for a time the harmful side of this sin.

5–6 In fact, the wayward woman's lifestyle is the pathway to death. *Sheol* ("grave"; GK 8619) is not just the realm of the unblessed; for it is paralleled with "death." Although these terms could be hyperbolic for a ruined life, they probably convey a note of the real consequences that exist for a life of debauchery. The sadder part of this description is that she does not know how unstable her life is.

2. A father's warning to avoid ruin and regret (5:7–14)

a. Exhortation for prevention (5:7–8)

7–8 The second discourse begins with a warning not to turn aside from one's father's teaching. Going to the adulteress would be such a turning aside, and so the writer clearly warns against that—"Keep clear"; do not even go near her door.

b. Motivation: Obedience will avoid ruin and regret (5:9–14)

9–10 The writer warns that consorting with an adulteress will rob a person of health and prosperity. One's hard-earned substance could pass over to "strangers." The "strength" may refer to health and vigor that might be relinquished to a cruel enemy, perhaps an offended husband as in ch. 7 (although husband is not mentioned here). The

"years," the best years in the prime of life, would signify what those years produced, what he had worked for. Likewise the "wealth" would refer to the produce that laborious toiling had gained. The point of these verses is clear: The price of infidelity may be high; for everything one works for—position, power, prosperity—could be lost either through the avaricious demands of the woman or the outcry for restitution by the community.

11–14 When the foolish participant is ruined in such a way, there will be regret for not heeding the warnings. This theme is introduced with "You will groan" (GK 5637), a term used elsewhere for the loud groaning of the poor and distressed (Eze 24:23). Here the verb conveys an elemental cry of anguish when the guilty finds himself destitute. The use of both "flesh" and "body" underscores the fact that the whole body is exhausted.

3. Advice to find satisfaction at home (5:15–23)

a. Avoiding sharing love with strangers (5:15–17)

15–17 By using high figures the wise teacher instructs the son to find sexual satisfaction with his own wife and not strange women. These figures are not common in instruction material. But what is at issue is private versus common property. The images of a cistern, well, or fountain are used of a wife (see SS 4:15) because she, like water, satisfies desires. Channels of water in the street would then mean sexual contact with a lewd woman. According to 7:12, she never stays at home but is in the streets and the property of many. So the young man is advised to spend his sexual energy at home, producing children, rather than giving himself to "strangers."

b. Finding satisfaction with one's wife (5:18–19)

18 The advice is now plainly given—the proper course of action is to find pleasure in a fulfilling marriage. The first line, calling for the "fountain" to be blessed, indicates that sexual delight is God-given. Therefore one should rejoice in the wife who has from the vigor of youth shared the excitement and satisfaction, the joy and the contentment of a divinely blessed, monogamous relationship (see Mal 2:15).

19 The imagery for intimate love in marriage is now drawn from the animal world. The "doe" and the "deer" illustrate the exquisite gracefulness of a loving wife. Women frequently were named after pretty and graceful animals, such as the corresponding Tabitha and Dorcas (cf. Ac 9:36). The husband should be "captivated" (GK 8706) by the love of his wife. The word signifies a staggering gait and so here expresses the ecstatic joy of a "captivated" lover. It may even suggest "be intoxicated always with her love."

c. Motivation: Adultery is sinful folly (5:20–23)

20 Now the teacher shows the folly of adultery by raising rhetorical questions. Here he repeats the verb "captivated," but with the connotation of foolish delirium: "Why be captivated, my son, by an adulteress?" Common sense would say that such brief liaisons with strangers give no time for intimacy—that requires a lifelong bonding with the wife of one's youth.

21 Moreover, a person's ways are in clear view of the Lord who examines them. No matter how careful someone might be to conceal sin, one cannot conceal anything from God. Anyone who does not reckon on God's omniscience will get entangled in sin.

22–23 In sum, the lack of discipline and control in the area of sexual gratification is destructive. The one who plays with this kind of sin will become ensnared by it and led off to ruin. Verse 23 uses "led astray" this time to underscore that the crime spawns the punishment: "in the greatness of his folly he will *reel*" (pers. tr.). In other words, if the young man is not *captivated* by his wife but becomes *captivated* with a stranger in sinful acts, then his own iniquities will *captivate* him; and he will be led to ruin.

H. Admonition to Seek Release From a Foolish Indebtedness (6:1–5)

1. Conditions of indebtedness (6:1–2)

1–2 It was fairly common for someone to put up security for someone else—i.e., to underwrite another's debts. Here the guarantee of surety is graphically represented by the image of striking hands (cf. 11:15; 17:18; 22:26). But the pledge is foolish because the debtor is a neighbor who is a misfit. He would be un-

der no obligation to do this—it was merely an impulsive act of generosity. A gullible young man might lack judgment and be easily swept in, only to realize too late that he was "trapped" and "ensnared." Such a rash act of generosity might take a lifetime to pay.

2. Exhortation to obtain release (6:3–5)

3–4 The advice for an indebted person is to try to get released from the pledge as soon as possible. Freeing oneself may be a humiliating process, but it is far better than the debt. The verb "humble yourself" (GK 8346) may have behind it the literal idea of allowing oneself to be trampled on (perhaps, "prostrate yourself"). The pledge can be released if one begs the creditor, and one should lose no time in pressing the appeal.

5 The exhortation is then repeated and enhanced by two similes that suggest the motif of the person's being entrapped by the pledge.

I. Admonition to Avoid Laziness (6:6–11)

1. Lesson in diligence (6:6–8)

6 The teacher next directs a lesson to the sluggard, using the activities of the ant to make the point (cf. 24:30–34). Since the ant is a lowly creature, this comparison is somewhat degrading. But the sluggard can learn diligence from its ways.

7–8 The description of the ant's activities shows that although it appears to have no leader (even though it actually does have or-

The author of Proverbs frequently uses illustrations from nature, such as this gazelle (6:5).

ganization and cooperation), it provides for the future with great industry. The classic example of such foresight and industry is Joseph in Ge 41.

2. Danger of poverty (6:9–11)

9–11 These verses provide the motivation for the admonition—there is the danger of poverty. The rhetorical question—"How long will you lie there, you sluggard?"—is designed to rebuke the laziness in a forceful manner. Then, using effective irony, the instructor mimics the lazy person's speech. His point is that too much sleep will lead to poverty—it will rob the lazy person of potential increase.

Two similes illustrate the onslaught of poverty. The first—"like a bandit"—uses a difficult term that has been interpreted as a "dangerous assailant" or a "highwayman," i.e., a bandit that robs. The term "an armed man" is probably connected to the military ideas of "shield" and "deliver." It is perhaps to be connected with the Arabic word for "bold," "insolent," and interpreted here as "beggar" or "insolent man."

J. Warning Against Deviousness (6:12–15)

1. Description (6:12–14)

12–14 The subject matter is now the "scoundrel" (GK 1175) and the "villain" (GK 224). These terms describe one who is both wicked and worthless. A survey of use shows the word to describe people who violate the law (Dt 15:9; Jdg 19:22; 1Ki 21:10, 13; Pr 16:27; et al.) or act in a contemptuous and foolish manner against cultic observance or social institutions (1Sa 10:27; 25:17; 30:22). The instruction focuses on the devious activities of this type of person.

The description moves from the scoundrel's perverse sayings to his sinister sign language to his disruptive plots developed through deceit. The expressions in v.13 seem to refer to any look or gesture that is put on and therefore a form of deception if not a way of making insinuations.

2. Destruction (6:15)

15 Disaster will befall the troublemaker suddenly. It is uncertain whether "he will be . . . destroyed" refers to death or not. Probably the line means that a character like this will be ruined when exposed.

K. Conduct the Lord Hates (6:16–19)

1. Introductory statement (6:16)

16 The verses that follow condemn certain characteristics and activities; the terms "hate" and "detestable" show that these are taboo, for they deny the divine element in humanity. Verse 16 uses what is known as a numerical ladder, paralleling "six things" with "seven things" (see also 30:15, 18, 21, 24, 29; Job 5:19; Ecc 11:2; Am 1:6, 9, 13; 2:1, 4, 6; Mic 5:5). The point of such a poetic arrangement is that the present enumeration does not exhaust the list.

2. Delineation (6:17–19)

17–19 The seven things that the Lord hates are specific personal attitudes and actions. There is something of a contrasting parallel arrangement with the Beatitudes in Mt 5, which has seven blessed things to answer these seven hated things; moreover, the first beatitude ("Blessed are the poor in spirit," Mt 5:5) contrasts with the first hated thing ("haughty eyes," v.17; i.e., "a proud look") and the seventh ("peacemakers," Mt 5:7) with the seventh abomination ("stirs up dissension," v.19).

The first in the list, "haughty eyes," refers to a proud look suggesting arrogant ambition. This term "high" is similarly used in Nu 15:30 for the sin of the high hand, i.e., willful rebellion or defiant sin. Usage of "haughty eyes" in the OT is telling: it describes the pompous Assyrian invader in Isa 10:12–14 as well as the proud king in Da 11:12 (NIV, "pride"). God will not tolerate anyone who thinks so highly of oneself (see Pr 21:4; Isa 2:11–17).

The second description is "a lying tongue." The term is used in Jer 14:14 to portray false prophets who deceive people and in Ps 109:2 to describe the deceiver who betrays—a passage that the disciples applied to Judas in Ac 1:20. Deception in speech is harmful (Pr 26:28), but in the end truth will prevail (Pr 12:19).

The third description focuses on hands as the instruments of murder. Genesis 9:6 prohibited shedding human blood because people are made in the image of God—no matter what one might think of them. But shedding "innocent blood" was an even greater crime. King Manasseh had filled the streets with innocent blood (2Ki 21:16; 24:4). Princes did it for gain according to Ezekiel (22:27). Even King David was prohibited from building the temple because he had shed much blood (1Ch 22:8).

The fourth phrase concerns the heart that "devises wicked schemes." The "heart" (GK 4213) represents the will most often. Here it plots evil. God early on declared that the human heart was capable of this (Ge 6:5); and Proverbs elaborates on the theme, showing that the heart that schemes wickedness is also deceitful (12:20; 14:22).

The fifth description uses the figure of "feet that are quick to rush into evil." This captures the enthusiastic and complete involvement in activities that bring pain to all concerned.

The sixth abomination returns to the theme of deception. Here the focus is on perjury ("a false witness"), a direct violation of the Decalogue. This character pours out "lies" (GK 3942; cf. Ps 40:4; Am 2:4; Mic 1:14).

The final description is general—God hates one "who stirs up dissension." "Dissension" (GK 4506) is attributed in Proverbs to contentious, quarreling people (21:9; 26:21; 25:24) who have a short fuse (15:18). Paul, on the other hand, warns against envy, malice, and strife (1Ti 6:4). These things, then, God will not tolerate. If he hates these things, then conversely he must love and desire (1) humility, (2) truthful speech, (3) preservation of life, (4) pure thoughts, (5) the eagerness to do good things, (6) honest witnesses, and (7) peaceful harmony.

L. Warning About Immorality (6:20–35)

1. Reminder to heed instruction (6:20–24)

20–21 Youth are now exhorted to cling fast to the teachings of their parents. Implicit in these verses is the basic understanding that a good home life—i.e., father and mother sharing the rearing of the children together—will go a long way to prevent youth from falling into immorality.

22–24 The motivation for keeping these commands is that they will bring protection from the adulteress. Verse 22 strengthens the instruction by using language similar to Dt 6:7, and v.23 uses metaphors that are also used of the law (see Ps 119:105). But beside the general ideas of protection and direction, the specific benefit of the teaching will be in keeping the youth from the loose woman. She is described as an "immoral woman" and a "wayward wife." The context shows that this immoral woman is another man's wife.

2. Warning to avoid seduction (6:25–35)

25 The admonition warns against lusting in one's heart for the immoral woman's beauty or charm. The verb for "to lust" (GK 2773) is used in the Decalogue to warn against coveting. Lust, according to Jesus, is a sin of the same kind as the act, not just the first step toward sin (Mt 5:28). Playing with temptation is only the heart reaching out after sin. So one should not dwell on the woman's seductive charms in one's heart. "Eyes" are singled out here because the painted eyes and the luring glances are symptoms of seduction (see 2Ki 9:30).

26 The summary motivation for the admonition is that such sin has a high price—it may even ruin one's life. The parallelism in this verse is difficult. It is not meant to say that prostitution is better than adultery because it only impoverishes whereas adultery preys on the very life. Both are costly sins to be avoided.

27–35 The motivation now elaborates on the motif that punishment is inevitable. Playing on the word *ish* ("man"; GK 408) and *ishshah* ("woman"; GK 851), the instructor introduces the figure of "fire" (*esh*; GK 836). Scooping coals into one's lap would represent holding the adulteress, and walking on coals would signify further sexual contact with her. The self-evident answer to the questions is that the adulterer will "get burned"; he will not go "unpunished" ("touches her" is probably a euphemism as in Ge 20:6). The rest of the passage reasons that no restitution is acceptable for adultery as there might be with thievery. A thief, when caught, pays dearly. But the adulterer will be humiliated and ruined. Nothing will satisfy the husband but revenge.

The expression "destroys himself" stresses that the guilty one destroys his own life. He could be given the death penalty (Dt 22:22); but he apparently continues to live in ignominy, destroyed spiritually and socially (see 2:18; 1Ti 5:6). In a morally healthy society the adulterer would be a social outcast.

M. Admonition to Avoid the Wiles of the Adulteress (7:1–27)

1. Important teaching of the father (7:1–5)

Once again the theme of seduction surfaces in the instruction of the father (see 2:16–19; 5:1–23; 6:20–35). Here it takes the form of a narrative about an individual woman who draws a youth into adultery. It is a didactic narrative that serves to make an earnest warning. The adulteress is probably not a personification of evil in this chapter; that is fully developed in ch. 9. However, referring to wisdom as a sister certainly prepares for the personifications of chs. 8 and 9. Wisdom will obviate temptations, the greatest being the sexual urge.

1–4 The section begins by repeating the instruction for the son to preserve and practice the authoritative teachings in order to "live." The expression "the apple of your eye" is literally "the little man" in the eye, having reference to the pupil, where the object focused on is reflected. The point is that the teaching is so precious it must be guarded that closely. Verse 3 strengthens the admonition by alluding to the instruction for heeding the law given in Dt 6:8.

5 The reason for following these teachings carefully is to give protection from the wiles of the loose woman. She is called an "adulteress" and a "wayward wife," who has "seductive words" (lit., "smooth words").

2. Description of seduction (7:6–23)

a. The victim (7:6–9)

6–9 The narrative unfolds with the observation of an unwary youth strolling along the streets at night. He is described as "a youth who lacked judgment" (lit., "a youth lacking of heart," i.e., one void of common sense or understanding). He is young, inexperienced, and featherbrained. His evening stroll takes him intentionally down the street to her house. And then, if all this activity of the naive young man takes place under the cover of night, only trouble can follow.

b. The temptress (7:10–12)

10 The narrative next introduces the seductress who comes out to meet the innocent youth. She is "dressed like a prostitute" and has "crafty intent." This latter expression is difficult; the ancient versions took it with the meaning of causing the youth's heart to flutter or of bewildering or capturing his heart. The expression literally means "guarded in heart." She has locked up her plans and gives nothing away. This, interestingly, contrasts with her attire, which gives her away.

11–12 The text further describes this wayward woman as "loud and defiant," with a roving desire. "She lurks" at every street corner, waiting for the gullible young man to pass her way.

c. The seduction (7:13–20)

13–15 The steps in the seduction are carefully calculated to ensnare the inexperienced youth. First, she boldly grabs him and kisses him. This is followed by her flattering invitation, in which she explains that she has "fellowship offerings" at home and came out especially looking for him (only a fool would believe that she was that interested in him). These offerings refer to the meat left over from votive offerings made in the sanctuary (see Lev 7:11–21). Apparently the sacrificial worship meant as little to her spiritually as does Christmas to modern hypocrites. Her reference to these fellowship offerings may mean nothing more than that she has fresh meat for a meal or else that she is ceremonially clean, perhaps after her period. At any rate, it is all probably a ruse for winning a customer.

16–17 The third step is the report of her careful preparation. She is not poor; for she has a bed, and it is ready.

18 The fourth step is the direct proposition: "Come, let's drink deep of love." Her invitation speaks of complete satiety and sheer enjoyment in physical love.

19–20 The final step is the adulteress's disarming reassurance. She explains that "my husband" is not at home. He conveniently is gone on a journey; and judging from his taking a money bag and staying till the next full moon, they would be perfectly safe in their escapade (he might even be gone for a fortnight, if a comparison of v.9 and v.20 can give clues to the chronology). At any rate, her appeal is bold, exciting, and apparently safe. It would take someone with the wisdom and integrity of a Joseph to resist such an appeal (cf. the important motifs in Ge 39, esp. v.8).

d. The capitulation (7:21–23)

21–23 The fall of the simpleton, after a brief pondering, is sudden, because she seduces him with her enticing speech. Using the similes of an ox for the slaughter and a deer for the noose, the teacher warns of the complete ruin that can come to one guilty of allowing himself to be seduced. This sin could "cost him his life"—he needs to know this. The meaning of the verse may refer to moral corruption rather than a literal death. The arrow piercing the liver may refer to the pangs of a guilty conscience that the guilty must reap along with spiritual and physical ruin.

3. Deadly results of consorting (7:24–27)

24–27 With a final flurry of exhortations, the teacher warns his sons to stay away from the seductress's paths because consorting with her leads to death. The language is startling in its force; but the ruin that such evil brings is as devastating as death and may, of course, end in actual punishment. He stresses that she has been the death of many and that her house is the way that leads to the "chambers of death." Her house is not the grave. It is, however, surely the way to it, and the one who takes that way is pathetic indeed. A man's life is not destroyed in one instant; it is taken from him gradually as he enters into a course of life that will leave him as another victim of the wages of sin.

N. The Appeal of Wisdom (8:1–36)

In this chapter wisdom continues to be represented as a person (cf. ch. 7). The material combines 1:20–33, in which wisdom proclaims her value, and 3:19–26, in which wisdom is the agent of Creation. This personification of wisdom does have affinities with other ancient Near Eastern wisdom literature. But wisdom here is not presented as a god; rather, it is presented as a self-conscious divine being distinct from but subordinate to the Lord. It personifies the attribute of wisdom displayed by God.

Many have equated wisdom in this chapter with Jesus Christ. This connection works only so far as Jesus reveals the nature of God the Father, including his wisdom, just as Proverbs presents the personification of the attribute. Jesus' claims included wisdom (Mt 12:42) and a unique knowledge of God (Mt 11:25–27). He even personified wisdom in a way that was similar to Proverbs (Mt 11:19; Lk 11:49). Paul saw the fulfillment of wisdom in Christ (Col 1:15–20; 2:3) and affirmed that Christ became our wisdom in the Crucifixion (1Co 1:24, 30). So the bold personification of wisdom in Proverbs certainly provides a solid foundation for the revelation of divine wisdom in Christ. But because wisdom appears to be a creation of God in 8:22–31, it cannot be identified with Jesus Christ.

1. Introduction (8:1–3)

1–3 It is now wisdom's turn to exhibit her attractions—in the open, not lurking in secret. Wisdom continually attests to her value: the rhetorical questions show that she is ready to call out. But this crying out is in the high roads, at the doors of the city where people gather.

2. First cycle (8:4–9)

a. Invitation: Listen and gain understanding (8:4–5)

4–5 The invitation from wisdom embraces all classes of people: v.4 includes "men" and "mankind"; v.5 uses "simple" and "foolish." The invitation for the "simple" and the "foolish" is to gain "prudence" and "understanding."

b. Motivation: Wisdom is noble, true, and just (8:6–9)

6 Wisdom begins her motivation by declaring that she has noble things to say. The term "worthy" (GK 5592) means excellent things. When wisdom opens her mouth, she speaks what is upright. So what she has to say is excellent and right.

7 The things that wisdom says are also reliable ("true"; GK 622), i.e., firm and dependable; it is the reflection within the heart before the speech. This speaking truth is derived from detesting wickedness (e.g., wickedness is taboo for wisdom).

8–9 The motivation further indicates that wisdom's appeal is "just" and "right," which is contrasted with "crooked or perverse" and faulty. There is no hidden agenda and no deception in wisdom's teachings. Its teachings are in plain view, intelligible to all who have some discernment or who find knowledge (the theme of "to find" is introduced here; NIV, "have").

3. Second cycle (8:10–21)

a. Invitation: Receive instruction and knowledge (8:10)

10 The second cycle begins with the invitation to "take" (NIV, "choose"; GK 4374) "instruction" and "knowledge" over silver and gold. True wealth derives from the former, not the latter.

b. Motivation: Wisdom is valuable (8:11–21)

11 The reason one should choose wisdom over wealth is because wisdom is more "precious," more desirable than anything else. The goodness of wisdom is based on its incomparable value in life.

12–16 The value of wisdom may be found in its practical use, especially by those in power. Wisdom claims now to dwell with "prudence" (GK 6893), i.e., right knowledge in special cases. She also has knowledge and discretion. Parallel to this quality is the fear of the Lord, which leads to rejection of evil, pride, and perverse speech. Counsel, judgment, and understanding belong to wisdom; and that is power. Power naturally forms the transition to the practical side of these qualities—people in power use wisdom to govern the earth (see Isa 11:1–4, which prophesies how the Messiah will use wisdom in governing the world). Their government must be "just" and must derive from godly wisdom.

17–21 Wisdom rewards those who love her. The emphasis of this section is that wisdom is accessible only to those who seek it. Loving and seeking point up the means of finding wisdom. Those who find it obtain honor and wealth. This honor and wealth come along the way of righteousness.

4. Third cycle (8:22–36)

a. Motivation: Wisdom preceded and delights in Creation (8:22–31)

22–23 In this third cycle, the motivation for receiving wisdom precedes the invitation. The first two verses provide a summary: the Lord possessed wisdom before the creation of the world. The verb *qanah* (GK 7865) can mean either "possess" or "create." The older versions chose "possess"; otherwise it might sound as if God lacked wisdom and so created it before the world began. They wanted to avoid saying that wisdom was not eternal. The verb *qanah* occurs twelve times in Proverbs with the idea of "acquire"; the LXX and Syriac, however, have the idea of "create." Although the idea is that wisdom existed before Creation, the parallel ideas in these verses ("brought me forth," v.22; "I was appointed," v.23; and "I was given birth," v.24) argue for "create/establish" here.

24–31 The summary statement is now developed in a lengthy treatment of wisdom as the agent (or "craftsman"; GK 570) of Creation. Verses 24–26 reiterate that wisdom was established before Creation ("oceans" [v.24] or "deeps," recalling Creation); vv.27–29 declare that wisdom was present when God created (notice the same progress of preexistence to world-creating acts for the Logos ["Word"] in the NT [Jn 1:1–3; Col 1:15–16]); and vv.30–31 tell how wisdom rejoiced in God's creation ("delight day after day" [v.30] recalls that "God saw that it was good" in Ge 1).

b. Invitation: Listen to wisdom and be blessed (8:32–36)

32–36 Verses 32–33 offer the explanation to the sons to listen, for a blessing is in store for all who live by wisdom's teachings. The explanation of this follows in vv.34–36. The alternatives could not be more striking—it is a choice between life and favor and harm and danger. This contrast is further marked out by the verb "finds me" and "fails to find me" (lit., "misses me").

O. Consequences of Accepting the Invitations of Wisdom or Folly (9:1–18)

Chapter 9 forms the conclusion of the lengthy nine-chapter introduction to the book. Both wisdom and folly will make their final appeals; and both appeal to the simpletons, those who need to live by wisdom but who are most easily influenced by folly. Wisdom offers life with no mention of pleasure; folly offers pleasure with no mention of death.

1. Accepting wisdom (9:1–12)

a. Invitation to wisdom (9:1–6)

1 The text makes a transition now from the previous passage; wisdom was last seen as the director of work on the cosmic level (8:30–31), but now wisdom is portrayed among humans. She has prepared a house and established it on seven pillars (probably a reference to the habitable world, which is spacious and enduring; cf. 8:29–31; Job 38:6; Ps 104:5). The "seven pillars" seem to be part of the imagery of the house but may have cosmic references. The phrase has given rise to expressions like "the seven pillars of wisdom" or "the house that wisdom builds." Since seven is a sacred or ominous concept, the point seems to be that wisdom produces a perfect world.

2–3 Wisdom has prepared a sumptuous banquet in this house and sends out her maids to call the simple to come and eat. The figures of meat and wine represent the good teaching of wisdom that will be palatable and profitable (cf. Isa 55:1–2; Jn 6:51, 55). It is uncertain whether the mixing of wine here refers to the practice of mixing wine with spices or mixing it with water as the Greeks did. So just as one would prepare a banquet and invite guests, wisdom prepares to press her appeal. All this imagery lets the simpleton know that what wisdom has to offer is marvelous.

4–6 The call goes out to the simple, to those "who lack judgment," to turn aside to wisdom. Carrying the figure of eating forward, the writer invites people to eat the food and drink the wine, i.e., to appropriate the teaching of wisdom. This acceptance would necessarily prompt the simpleton to abandon the "simple ways" (or perhaps "simpletons") and "live." The proper direction is on the way of understanding.

b. Description of responses (9:7–11)

7–8a The "mocker" (GK 4370) has been met before in the book (1:22; 3:34). Mockers are those who will not live by wise and moral teachings and are not content to let others do so without their cynical mocking. The author warns that anyone who tries to rebuke and correct a mocker is asking for trouble; "insult," "abuse," and "hatred" are second nature to this cynical heckler. Thus the warning is put forth: "Do not rebuke."

8b–11 The authentically parallel idea forms the contrast—the wise person will love the one trying to correct him. "Love" (GK 170) has the idea of choosing and embracing; so this is the profitable response to corrective teaching. The parallelism of "wise" and

"righteous" underscores the interrelationship between these qualities and shows the predisposition of those who are teachable. Moreover, the theme of the fear of the Lord is brought forward here, because this is the foundation of all wisdom and all righteousness (see comment on 1:7). The epithet "Holy One" is plural, suggesting the majestic nature of the Lord—he is "All-holy." In the final analysis those who fear the Lord, add to their learning, and receive discipline will look forward to a long and productive life.

c. Consequence: Reward (9:12)

12 The conclusion of the matter is expressed by the antithetically parallel ideas: Wisdom rewards the wise, but mockery suffers alone. "Your wisdom will reward you" is literally "you are wise to yourself," meaning that wisdom brings its own reward; it is sufficiently satisfying to be worth pursuing. Conversely, "if you are a mocker, you alone must bear it [NIV, 'you alone will suffer']." These words anticipate the teachings of James (cf. Jas 3:1–12), that words we speak will haunt us through life.

2. Accepting the invitation of folly (9:13–18)

a. Invitation (9:13–17)

13 Now the rival "woman Folly" (GK 4070) presses her appeal for the naive to come and eat from her provision. She is the counterpart of the personification of wisdom. Her character is described as "loud," "undisciplined," and "without knowledge." "Loud" suggests riotous and portrays her as foolish and simplistic. To these troubling qualities is added the idea of ignorance, which must mean moral ignorance in Proverbs.

14–15 Folly's position is prominent in the city streets. We should note how she often imitates wisdom (cf. v.3), so that only the cautious and discerning are able to make the right choice. Her invitation, likewise, is to the passersby, here described as those "who go straight" on their ways. This would identify them as quiet and unwary.

16–17 Folly's invitation parrots wisdom's (see v.4). This competing voice, albeit louder and more appealing to those who "lack judgment," likewise invites people to eat. "Stolen water" is now offered to passersby instead of mixed wine from wisdom. The "water" is only sweeter than "wine" because it is stolen, much as food that is unjustly gained seems more delicious. The figures here are similar to those in the section on wisdom: the words and ways of folly are compared to food and drink. Compare 5:15–16 (water) and 30:20 (bread) to see the specification as sexual folly.

b. Consequence: death (9:18)

18 The contrast with Wisdom's banquet continues, but now the consequence for Folly's "guests" is startling. The naive who enter her banquet hall do not know that the "dead" (GK 8327; often translated "shades") are there. This word refers to the dead who lead a shadowy existence in Sheol (see comment on 2:18–19; cf. Job 3:13–19; Ps 88:5; Isa 14:9–11). The verse approximates the "as if" motif of wisdom literature—those ensnared by folly are as good as in hell, for that house is a throat to hell. Many "eat" on earth what they "digest" in hell. The point is that the life of folly—a lifestyle of undisciplined, immoral, riotous living—runs counter to God's plan of life and inevitably leads to death. Jesus warns people to avoid this broad way and follow the straight and narrow path of righteous, wise living (Mt 7:13–14).

III. The First Collection of Solomonic Proverbs (10:1–22:16)

Beginning with ch. 10 there is a notable change in the form of the material. No longer do we find the forceful admonitions to seek wisdom, the lengthy poems, or the developed pictures and personifications. Instead we find what more closely corresponds to the title "Proverbs"—a collection of independent, miscellaneous aphorisms, dealing mostly with the consequences of right or wrong actions on various topics.

The proverbs in chs. 10:1–22:16 seem to defy an orderly arrangement or outline, but they are indeed a collection of proverbs. With this in mind, yet still endeavoring to make this section as accessible and usable as possible to the reader, I give a topical heading to each of the proverbs in boldface type.

Chapter 10

1 **Effect of wisdom on others.** This antithetical saying declares that the consequences of wisdom or folly in the child affects the parents accordingly (cf. 17:21, 25; 23:24–25; 28:7; 29:3).

2 **Value of righteousness.** The sage asserts that "righteousness" (GK 7407) has far greater value than ill-gotten wealth. This word takes on the meaning of honesty in this contrast. Wealth in general can only be enjoyed for a while, but righteousness delivers from mortal danger ("death").

3 **Rewards, satisfaction of needs.** In another antithetical saying, the general observation is that the Lord rewards the righteous with the satisfaction of their needs. The text literally says that he will not leave unsatisfied "the appetite [lit., soul] of the righteous," which here includes the inner urge toward success.

4 **Wealth through diligence.** This saying attributes wealth to diligence. "Lazy hands" refers to the careless work that such hands produce.

5 **Diligence, opposite of idleness.** Once again idleness, which leads to ruin, is contrasted with diligence. The wise son seizes the opportunities with keen insight into the importance of the season.

6 **Rewards, words of blessing.** The focus of this contrast is on rewards. We would expect a curse to be the antithesis of "blessings." But the point is rather that behind the speech of the wicked is aggressive "violence," so he cannot be trusted.

7 **Good reputation.** Likewise, a reputation is determined by righteousness or wickedness. "Name" and "memorial" are often paired as synonyms. "Name" refers to fame; the name of the wicked will eventually disappear, and it will leave a bad memory that excites abhorrence.

8–10 **Conduct of wise and foolish.** These sayings contrast the wise person with the fool. The first exhorts compliance with "commands" from superiors—a fool talks too much to be attentive to them. The second holds out the promise that security goes with those who have "integrity," but the insecurity of retribution awaits the perverse. Verse 10 departs from the normal antithetical pattern to form a comparison: shifty signs, although grievous, are not as ruinous as foolish talk. Both are to be avoided.

11–12 Good and evil conduct. What the righteous say is beneficial to life, unlike the aggressive violence of the fool (cf. v.8b). The idea of the "fountain of life" may come from Ps 36:9 (see also Pr 13:14; 14:27; 16:22; Eze 47:1–12; Jn 7:38). As to attitudes, the wicked are motivated by hatred that brings dissension but the righteous by love that is harmonious. Love's covering wrongs is harmonious with forgiveness (see 1Pe 4:8).

13–14 Wise and foolish speech. Attention now turns to wisdom and folly. The critically perceptive person speaks wisdom, unlike the fool who constantly needs correction (cf. Ps 32:8–9). The second proverb extols the wisdom of silently storing knowledge rather than foolishly talking prematurely (see Jas 3:13–18).

15 Wealth and security. A contrast is provided here between rich and poor: Security comes with wealth. The image used is of a "fortified city," protecting its inhabitants against all adversity.

16 Rewards of life. Rewards are determined by moral choices—righteousness bringing life, wickedness, punishment (see Ro 6:23). The point seems to be that what one receives in life depends on a wise use of gifts and a righteous character. Don't blame poverty for the quality of life. The point again is to live righteously.

17 On discipline. Learning to accept ("heed"; GK 9068) discipline is wise because it will benefit others. This word means holding fast to discipline as a path of life. Unfortunately, abandoning correction influences others too.

18–21 On speech. In v.18 two errors are given, the second being climactic: hypocrisy is bad enough, slander is worse. At least in the first one—the "lying lips"—one keeps hatred to himself. In the ancient world much wisdom literature condemns lying and slander. Controlling the tongue (v.19) helps avoid sin (see Jas 3:1–12).

What the righteous say is infinitely more valuable than what the wicked intend (v.20). The contrast is between the tongue (i.e., what is said) and the mind ("heart," i.e., what is determined). Righteous speech, like silver, is valuable and treasured. Moreover, what the righteous say is edifying—it enhances ("nourishes") common life. "Fools," charac-

terized by a lack of discipline and little wit, ruin their lives and others as well.

22 Wealth as a blessing. God brings wealth to those whom he blesses—and without anxiety ("trouble"). In Ps 127:1–3, the psalmist stresses how the Lord gives to his beloved prosperity and safety as well as peace of mind. The proverb is also a warning against self-sufficiency.

23 On pleasure. One's character is revealed in what one enjoys. Evil conduct to the fool is "like sport" ("pleasure"); like child's play, it is so easy. This evil conduct is contrasted with wisdom, the delight of those who have understanding.

24 Hopes and fears for the future. This little contrast declares the working out of the fear of the wicked and the desire of the righteous. What the wicked fear will come on them, so that there is no security for them; the "desire" of the righteous, i.e., what they long for in their righteous lifestyle, will be given to them.

25 Confidence in calamity. Survival in catastrophes of life is reserved for the righteous, for they are properly prepared to meet the real tests of life. Matthew 7:24–27 addresses the same point: If people base their lives on temporal values, they must know that they can be quickly swept away.

26 Lazy servants. Vinegar to the teeth is an irritant that is unpleasant to experience, and smoke to the eyes is a hindrance to progress. This little proverb portrays the aggravation in sending a lazy servant on a mission—it could be a confusing, unpleasant ordeal.

27 The fear of the Lord. The fear of the Lord, which is the beginning of wisdom (1:7), contributes to a long and prosperous life. This is a saying that is generally true. Why the righteous suffer and even die young is a problem that perplexed Israel's sages (cf. Job; Pss 49; 73).

28 Hopes and fears for the future. This is a contrast of expectations: the righteous will experience the joyful fulfillment of their hopes, but what the wicked hope for will be dashed. The proverb is a general maxim based on God's justice.

29 Security in the way of the Lord. The "way of the LORD" refers to God's providential administration of life. Thus divine justice will be security for the righteous and disaster for the wicked.

30 Security of the righteous. This proverb concerns the enjoyment of covenantal promises, i.e., living in the land of Israel. It is promised to the righteous (see Lev 26; Ps 92). If the people lived in righteousness, they would enjoy the land; if not, they would be exiled.

31–32 Wise and perverse speech. Righteous speech can be beneficial to others and pleasing to God; good people use few words and choose them well. No one wants to listen to perverse words—words that the wicked say, generally without prior consideration and beyond prudent limits. The bold image of cutting out the tongue is hyperbolic.

Chapter 11

1 Honesty in business. Honesty pleases the Lord. This contrast between what the Lord abhors and delights in elaborates on the point. The Scriptures throughout condemn dishonesty in business (see Lev 19:35–36; Dt 25:13–16; Am 8:5; et al.). Whatever the Lord "abhors" must be avoided. Thus to be accepted by God in one's transactions, one must deal honestly (see 16:11; 20:10, 23).

2 Pride and Humility. "Humility" (GK 7560) describes those who know their place; the humble avoid disgrace and find wisdom. "Pride" (Gk 2295) is literally a boiling up; thus an overstepping of the boundaries and insubordination is meant. The proud are inflated to the level of self-bestowed divinity; they will have their egos deflated.

3 Integrity. Here is another proverb affirming the value of integrity. The contrast is between the upright and the unfaithful; those who use treachery (lit., "the crookedness of the unfaithful") are destroyed rather than guided by it.

4 Righteousness better than wealth. Righteousness is pleasing to God and more valuable than wealth when the "day of wrath" (i.e., divine punishment in this life; see Job 21:30; Eze 7:19; Zep 1:18) strikes.

5–6 Righteous and wicked conduct. These two proverbs contrast the righteous with the wicked. The first teaches that the righteous enjoy security and serenity through life; the second, that the sins of the wicked catch up with them.

7 The hope of the wicked. The expectations of the wicked perish with them (see Ps 49). Any hope for long life or success borne of wickedness will be disappointed.

8 Just retribution. Here is an expression of confidence in God's justice in bringing recompense into the world. The antithesis shows the consequences of actions with an unusual twist—the "trouble" the righteous escape falls on the wicked.

9 Safety from slander. This antithetical verse stresses that a righteous person can escape devastating slander through knowledge. The "godless" (i.e., the hypocrite or flatterer) is the one who "destroys" a neighbor. The righteous have sufficient knowledge and experience to identify and end the slander.

10 On joy. The common theme of this verse is joy; it comes from either the success of the righteous or the ruin of the wicked (cf. 2Ki 11:20; Est 8:15).

11 Helpful or harmful speech. The "blessing of the upright" is the beneficent words and deeds that bring enrichment to a community. But the words of the wicked have a disastrous effect on society, endangering, weakening, and ruining it with demoralizing, slanderous, and malicious criticism.

12–15 On speech. One should hold one's tongue rather than deride a neighbor. The wise man is a "man of discernment"; the other one "lacks judgment." How one treats a neighbor is significant in Proverbs—one was expected to be a good neighbor.

Verse 13 is a contrast between the gossip and the "trustworthy man." Talebearers go from one to another and speak disparagingly about someone in a malicious manner (see Lev 19:16; Jer 9:3). Such people are despised in society because they cannot be trusted.

In v.14, advice is essential for the stability of a nation. The term for "guidance" is comparable to steering a ship, here a ship of state; without it the nation is in danger. This saying assumes that the counselors are wise and intelligent, if "victory" is sure.

Verse 15 instructs people to avoid pledges with strangers if they want to remain financially solid. It focuses on the consequences of the action. The "stranger" (NIV, "another") refers to any unknown person, someone from another clan or family or even from another nation.

16–17 On kindness. Two contrasts are here juxtaposed: "a kindhearted woman" and "ruthless men," and "respect" (or "honor") and "wealth." The idea seems to be that one can seize wealth by any means, but "honor" is the natural reward for the gracious person.

Verse 17 contrasts the consequences of dispositions: "kindness" (GK 2876) is healthy, but anger brings trouble. One's well-being is at risk if the personality is volatile. "Trouble" (GK 6579) may recall Jos 7:25–26, where Achan troubled Israel.

18 Rewards justly earned. Ultimately, rewards are appropriate for different character traits. The second line extols the benefits for one "who sows righteousness," i.e., one who inspires righteousness in others while practicing it himself. What is sown will yield fruit (1Co 9:11; 2Co 9:6; Jas 3:18).

19 Conduct bringing life or death. Since life and death result from moral choices, righteousness must be pursued. "Life" and "death" describe the vicissitudes of this life but can also refer to beyond the grave.

20 Conduct pleasing to God. This contrast records certain things that the Lord either detests or delights in. The "perverse heart" is a twisted mind, i.e., the whole spiritual being is influenced toward evil; it is an abomination to the Lord. Conversely, to please God one should follow a blameless course of life (see 2:21; 17:20).

21 Certainty of retribution. God's just retribution is certain; one can depend on it. Those who escape it are the "righteous" (lit., the "seed of the righteous"; i.e., the righteous as a class of people, cf. Isa 1:4; 65:23).

22 Beauty without discretion. This proverb uses emblematic parallelism to describe a beautiful woman without "discretion." The description is probably of a woman with no moral sensibility or propriety—unchaste.

She is compared to a pig with an ornament. Why join a beautiful ornament and an unworthy body? The pig will not know its value.

23 Prospect for life. The consequences of hope are determined by moral character. God rewards the righteous with prosperity; wrath eventually comes on the wicked.

24–25 Rewards for generosity. The paradox presented here does not refer to financial investments. Rather, in God's economy generosity often determines prosperity: one must give in order to gain (see Ps 112:9; 2Co 9:6–9). In v.25, those who are generous toward others will be provided for themselves. The first description, "a generous man," is literally "the soul of blessing." "Blessing" (GK 1388) describes a "present" (Ge 33:11) or "special favor" (Jos 15:19). The verb "made rich" (NIV, "prosper"; GK 2014) means "to be made fat," drawing on the standard comparison between fatness and abundance or prosperity (Dt 32:15). The second line makes a comparison between providing water for the thirsty and generously providing for those in need (see Jer 31:25; cf. La 3:15). The kind act will be reciprocated.

26 Socially responsible business. This proverb reveals how a merchant's response to supply and demand will influence the customer's opinion of him. Some merchants hoard up the produce to raise the prices when there is a great need for the produce. Merchants must have a social conscience, too.

27 Prospect for life. One generally receives the consequences of the kind of life one pursues, whether good or evil. There is a divine justice. The expression "seeks [NIV, finds] goodwill" may refer to seeking God's favor (see Ps 5:12; Isa 49:8): Whoever diligently seeks good is seeking divine favor.

28 Security. Security and prosperity are determined by the object of faith. The righteous trust in the Lord and flourish. The image of the "green leaf" is a figure of prosperity and fertility throughout the ancient Near East. The image of falling uses the analogy of the physical act to portray coming to ruin in life.

29 Laziness. An avaricious man deprives his family of livelihood and brings them to nothing but distress. He gains nothing for his efforts, "wind" signifying that which cannot be grasped (27:16; Ecc 1:14, 17). The second line suggests that those who foolishly mismanage their accounts may have to sell themselves into slavery to the wise. So the ideas in the verse are complementary.

30 Righteousness brings life. Both "fruit" and "tree of life" are metaphorical, the first image signifying what the righteous produce and the second identifying that as a healthy, long life. The idea of "winning souls" means capturing or laying hold of people with ideas or influence (2Sa 15:6).

31 Certainty of retribution. Retribution for sin is certain, for the righteous and especially for the sinner. The proverb uses a "how much more" argument—argument from the lesser to the greater. Divine justice deals with all sin; and if the righteous suffer for their sins, certainly the wicked will.

Chapter 12

1 On discipline. Those who wish to improve themselves must learn to accept correction and learn from it. This proverb adds the contrast that to refuse it is brutish ("stupid" [GK 1280] is descriptive of a dumb animal). It is as if one distinction between humans and animals is this feature of receiving discipline.

2 Conduct pleasing to God. Obtaining the Lord's favor is the result of virtue. A "good man" is contrasted with a "crafty man."

3 Righteousness brings stability. Only righteousness brings stability in life—true of both society and individuals. Society cannot long endure if established on evil principles (see 10:25).

4 Character of a noble wife. The moral character of a woman affects her husband's enjoyment of life. "A wife of noble character" is a "crown," a symbol of honor and renown. A "disgraceful wife" (lit., "one who puts to shame," i.e., lowers one's standing in the community) will eat away her husband's strength and destroy his happiness.

5 Just and unjust plans. Righteous people are fair and honest. The thoughts (i.e., intentions) of good people are directed toward what is right. The wicked give deceitful advice, which can lead only to evil.

6 Skillful defense. The righteous are able to make a skillful defense against false accusations. The vivid picture of "lying in wait for blood" conveys that the wicked make a trap by their false accusations. The righteous, who through discipline and instruction have gained knowledge and perception, are able to avoid this danger.

7 Security of the righteous. The righteous are stable in times of trouble (cf. Mt 7:24–27). The image of the fate of the wicked being "overthrown" is forceful and may allude to Ge 19:21—they will be destroyed completely, like Sodom and Gomorrah.,

8 Appreciation of wisdom. This saying makes a point about the appreciation of clear thinking. In proportion to wisdom a person receives praise. "Wisdom" here (lit., "intelligent," as in 1Sa 25:3; GK 8507) refers to the capacity to think straight. The "warped mind" lacks the ability to see things as they really are and so makes wrong choices. No praise exists for this.

9 On humility. One should be satisfied with comfort at the expense of pretension. The point seems to be that some people live beyond their means in a vain show ("pretend to be somebody"), whereas, if they lived modestly, they could have some of the conveniences of life, e.g., a servant. Another way to read v.9a is "Better is the lowly that serves himself."

10 Compassion for animals. Compassion for animals is an indication of one's character. The righteous are kind to all God's creation (see Dt 25:4) because they have received his bounty.

11 Diligence prospers. One ensures income through diligent work and not through unfounded speculation.

12 Prosperity for righteous pursuits. This proverb is difficult to interpret. The verse seems to be saying that there are good rewards for the righteous, but the wicked are dangerous and perhaps get caught in their own devices.

13 Dangerous speech. Righteous people avoid evil talk because it is dangerous. The point of the parallel expression is that the "evil man" catches himself in his words (lit., "the transgression of his lips"). People who

Character Traits in Proverbs

Traits to be promoted		Traits to be avoided	
avoiding strife	20:3	anger	29:22
compassion for animals	12:10	antisocial behavior	18:1
contentment	13:25; 14:30; 15:27	beauty without discretion	11:22
diligence	6:6–13; 12:24, 27; 13:4	blaming God	19:3
faithful love	20:6	dishonesty	24:28
faithfulness	3:5–6; 5:15–17; 25:13; 28:20	distasteful	14:17
generosity	21:26; 22:9	greed	28:25
honesty	16:11; 24:26	hatred	29:27
humility	11:2; 16:19; 25:6–7; 29:23	hot temper	19:19
integrity	11:3; 25:26; 28:18	immorality	6:20-35
kindness to others	11:16–17	inappropriate desire	27:7
kindness to enemies	25:21–22	inappropriate positions	19:10
leadership	30:19–31	injustice	22:16
loyalty	19:22	jealousy	27:4
noble wife	12:4	laziness	6:6-11; 18:9; 19:15; 20:4; 24:30—34; 26:13–15
patience	15:18; 16:32	maliciousness	6:27
peaceful	16:7	meddling	26:17; 30:10
praiseworthy	27:21	pride	15:5; 16:18; 21:4, 24; 29:23; 30:13
righteousness	4:26–27; 11:5–6, 30; 12:28; 13:6; 29:2	quarrelsomeness	26:21
self-control	17:27; 25:28; 29:11	self-conceit	26:12, 16
strength and honor	20:29	self-deceit	28:11
strength in adversity	24:10	self-glory	25:27
teachable	15:31	self-righteousness	30:12
truthfulness	12:19, 22; 23:23	stubbornness	29:1
		unfaithfulness	25:19
		unneighborliness	3:27–30
		unmerciful	21:13
		vengeance	24:28–29
		wickedness	21:10
		wicked expressions	16:30

are righteous will not get themselves into a bind by what they say.

14 Prosperity through words and work. Proper speech and diligent work result in good things. If one's conversation is wise, intelligent, and honoring to God, it will result in blessing.

15 Wisdom takes advice. People demonstrate their maturity by how well they respond to sound advice. Reasonable (i.e., "wise") people will recognize and accept good advice, even if they themselves often give advice to others. "Advice" (GK 6783) is an application of wisdom and knowledge to a specific situation, either by astute observation or well thought-out opinion. Fools, on the other hand, are set in their own way and will not listen to advice.

16 Wisdom overlooks insults. Mature people are able to handle criticism without responding instinctively and irrationally. The wise do not give the enemy that satisfaction. It is not so much that the wise repress anger or feelings but that they are more shrewd in dealing with it.

17 True and false witnesses. The true witness is reliable because he tells the truth, always uttering what is right. The contrast is with the false witness and his lies.

18 Healing speech. Those who are wise do not cause harm by speaking hastily and inadvisably (see Lev 5:4; Nu 30:7). Such talk is like a piercing sword—it wounds. Conversely, the tongue of the wise brings "healing." Their words heal because they are faithful and true, gentle and kind, and uplifting and encouraging.

19 Truth outlasts lies. Truthfulness will outlive lies—forever. The little expression "only a moment" is literally "till I wink again."

20 Plans for evil or peace. The contrast here is between plotting evil and promoting peace with a view to the consequences. Plotting evil produces only sorrow and trouble, because "evil" (GK 8273) has the idea of pain in it. "Peace" (GK 8934), on the other hand, refers to social wholeness and well-being (see Pss 34:14; 37:37). The "counselors of peace," as the text literally reads, will reap both inner contentment from doing what is right and the pleasure of seeing positive results.

21 Security of the righteous. Here is a relative truth about the contrast between the righteous and the wicked with respect to calamity. "No harm befalls the righteous" means that decent people do not have frequent trouble of their own making.

22 Truth pleases God. Truthfulness rather than falsehood pleases the Lord. The contrast in consequences is strong: "pleasure" or "delight" versus "abomination." To speak falsehood is a misuse of a God-given faculty. We must act in good faith.

23 Discretion in speech. Wisdom is distinguishable from folly in speech. The "prudent" (lit., "a shrewd man") restrain themselves from displaying knowledge. The verb "keeps" (or "conceals") does not mean that they never speak; rather, it means they use discretion. Conversely, the intent of "fools" is to call out "folly."

24 Diligence. Diligence at work determines success and advancement. To put it bluntly, the diligent rise to the top and the lazy sink to the bottom, where they may be forced to work as if slaves (see also 6:6–11; 10:4; 12:27; 13:4; 19:15; and 21:5).

25 Encouraging speech. Words of encouragement will lift the spirits of someone who is depressed through anxious fear. Anxiety in the heart bows the person down—bowing in the sense of physical mourning (Pss 35:14; 38:6). The "kind word" probably includes encouragement, kindness, and insight—saying that which the person needs to gain the proper perspective and renew hope and confidence. One should seek to turn depression into rejoicing by saying the right things.

26 Dangerous associations. The righteous cautiously avoid dangerous friendships. There is a great variety of ways this verse has been translated and interpreted. The verb "is cautious" can be taken to mean "spy out" or "examine," which makes a fine contrast to the "leading astray" of the "way of the wicked." The proverb is advising correct action in friendships.

27 Success through diligence. Diligence leads to success. The negative image in the antithetical line is of the lazy person who cannot bring a project to completion. Just as a hunter may never cook what he finds, so the lazy person never completes a project.

28 Righteousness leads to immortality. Those who enter righteousness by faith and seek to live righteously are on the way to eternal life. "No death" may be taken to mean "immortality"; but it could also mean permanence and stability in this life.

Chapter 13

1 Accepting discipline. Those who are wise will respond properly to discipline. The "mocker" is the highest level of a fool. He has no respect for authority, reviles religion, and, because he thinks that he knows what is best, is not teachable. The change to a stronger word in the second line—"rebuke"—shows that he does not respond to any level of discipline.

2 Helpful or harmful speech. Words and wishes find their just rewards. This saying concerns the outcome of conduct. The clauses in this verse do not fit well. Most likely the second line is saying that the desire of the "unfaithful" (or "treacherous") is to obtain what does not belong to them. The "violence" that is their appetite refers to the violence that is done to others.

3 Wisdom of discretion. It is safest to hold one's tongue; a tight control over what one says prevents trouble (see also 10:10; 17:28; Jas 3:1–12). The old Arab proverb is appropriate: "Take heed that your tongue does not cut your throat."

4 On diligence. By contrasting "the sluggard" and "the diligent," the author makes the point that the fulfillment of dreams demands diligence. Rather than spend all day hoping for things that they do not have, the diligent will work toward realizing their dreams.

5 Hating falsehood or acting shamefully. Here is another contrast between the moral conduct of the righteous and the wicked: the righteous hate the way that is "false," but the wicked act vilely and shamefully. The words "shame" and "disgrace" can be taken as a hendiadys: "spread the smell of scandal."

6 Righteousness brings security. Righteousness, like a fortress, protects the person of integrity (see 2:11; 4:6). This may work through divine intervention or natural causes. "Righteousness" (GK 7407) refers to what conforms to law and order; so it is natural to expect that the perfect walk is safe. On the other side, perverse and malicious activity plunges one into sinful activity.

7 Honesty better than pretension. People may not be what they seem to be. Some who are poor pretend to be rich, perhaps to save face; some who are rich pretend to be poor, perhaps to conceal wealth and avoid responsibilities. Although there are times when such pretending may not be wrong, this proverb instructs people to be honest and unpretentious. An empty display or a concealing of means can come to no good.

8 Disadvantages of wealth. There are disadvantages to having possessions. The rich are exposed to legal and powerful assaults and may have to use their wealth as ransom. The poor persons are free from blackmail and so ignore the attack and endure the consequences of difficulties.

9 Prospect for long life. The righteous can anticipate a long and prosperous life. The images of light and dark are used effectively: "light" represents life, joy, and prosperity; darkness signifies adversity and death. The figure of the light may very well be drawn from the enduring flame of the temple light.

10 Wisdom takes advice. Those who are wise listen to advice rather than argue out of stubborn pride. The idea of "pride" (GK 2295) here describes contempt for other opinions, a clash of competing and unyielding personalities. This kind of conceited person creates strife, inflames passions, and wounds the feelings of others.

11 Prosperity through honest investment. Steady and wise investment produces prosperity. This is a warning against wild speculation. "Little by little" (lit., "hand by hand") stresses the diligent activity and the gradual growth of one's investment. But if the riches come quickly through some unfounded or dishonest means, one could lose them just as easily.

12 Encouragement and discouragement. It is invigorating to realize hopes; to fail to do so can be discouraging or depressing. This is a general saying, applicable to believers or unbelievers. Perhaps believers should make it part of their task to help others realize their hopes whenever possible.

13 Reward for heeding instruction. Safety lies in obedience to proper "instruction" and commands (a "command" [GK 5184] is more forceful than an instruction). The use of these two terms has religious significance: they usually refer to Scripture. The vivid point made in "will pay" (GK 2472) is that whoever despises the teaching will be treated as a debtor—he will pay for it if he offends against the law.

14 Benefits of instruction. The teaching of wisdom is life giving. The second line is the consequence of the first: not only does it give life, it turns one from the snares of death (a metaphor that suggests death as a hunter). On the "fountain of life," see also 10:11 and 14:27.

15 Discernment brings favor. Wisdom and intelligence add to one's social esteem. "Good understanding" describes the capacity for good sense, sound judgment, and wise opinions. The second line suggests that the way of treachery passes away (see NIV note).

16 Knowledge as basis of prudent acts. Actions either display wisdom or expose folly. The wise will study the facts and then make decisions. The "prudent" (GK 6874) here is one who knows the circumstances, the dangers, and the pitfalls; this makes him cautious. A fool will eventually make a fool of himself because it is his nature.

17 On servants. The faithfulness of a messenger determines the success of the mission. Here a "trustworthy envoy" (an expression suggesting government service—see Isa 18:2; Jer 49:14) ensures success (lit., "brings healing"). The "wicked messenger" falls into trouble, perhaps as a punishment.

18 Benefit of discipline. Responding correctly to discipline brings honor and success; "poverty and shame" come to those who refuse correction. The point seems to refer to commercial success: control and caution bring results.

19 Fulfilled desires. The lines here are difficult. One can surely say that Proverbs teaches people to make their desires good so that fulfilling them is cause for joy.

20 Associating with wise people or fools. Proper company contributes to safety and growth. One should associate with the wise and not with the fools. A wordplay in the second line stresses the power of association: "a companion of fools suffers harm." The point is clear: Examine who is influencing you.

21 Prosperity as reward of righteous. Here is teaching on recompense in absolute terms. It is this idea that Job's friends applied (incorrectly) to his situation. "Prosperity" comes to the righteous, calamity to the wicked.

22 Restitution by divine intervention. Divine justice determines the final disposition of one's inheritance. In Israel the idea of bequeathing an inheritance was a sign of God's blessing; blessings extended to the righteous and not to the sinners. See Ps 49:10, 17 for the idea of the wicked leaving their estates for others.

23 Poor, susceptible to injustice. Injustice can take away what hard labor produces. The verse may also be saying that anything produced through unjust means will not endure. The lesson concerns the proper way to deal with produce, not the size of one's resources.

24 Discipline as evidence of love. Parental love is displayed in disciplining the children responsibly. The powerful verbs "hates" and "loves" stress the point—hating a son probably means, in effect, abandoning or rejecting him. Too much lenience and too much harsh discipline are equally problematic. The balance comes when the child has room to grow while learning the limits.

25 Contentment as reward for righteous. Righteousness is rewarded by the satisfaction of one's physical needs (cf. the principles in Lev 26). This verse may also imply that what the righteous acquire will prove satisfying to them because they are righteous.

Chapter 14

1 Prosperity in the household. A woman's wisdom enables the household to thrive. The contrast is between wisdom and folly; wisdom builds the house, but folly tears it down (cf. 9:1a). To see these ideas worked out, contrast the wise woman (31:10–31) with the foolish one (7:10–23).

2 Fear of the Lord brings uprightness. Here is a contrast between those who fear the Lord and those who despise him—the distinction is in the conduct produced: uprightness versus perversion (see 2:15; 3:32; 10:19).

3 Effects of speech. What people say has a great bearing on how they are received. The fool's conversation brings punishment; his talk harms him and he brings trouble on himself. But the speech of the righteous brings them safety.

4 Prosperity in business. To be productive one must use the appropriate means. For the farmer, oxen are indispensable; so the wise farmer will see to it that his oxen are numerous and in good condition.

5 True and false witnesses. A faithful witness does not lie, while a false witness pours out lies. The saying addresses the age-old problem of false witnesses in court that slow down the quest for the truth (see 12:17 and 16:10).

6 Acquiring wisdom. Those who are serious and discerning acquire wisdom. The contrast is between the "mocker" and the "discerning" person. The former is intellectually arrogant; he lacks any serious interest in knowledge or religion. He pursues wisdom only in a superficial way so that he might have the appearance of being wise.

7 Unprofitable associations. One cannot increase in knowledge by associating with a fool—nothing comes from nothing, as many can affirm. The verse is teaching people to get away from fools because they did not receive knowledge from what the fools said. If you want to learn, seek out the wise.

8 Considering one's conduct. Biblical wisdom is practical theology. While the wise give careful consideration to their conduct, the way of the fool is "deception."

9 Reparation. This verse is concerned with offending others. The parallelism suggests that the idea is that fools ridicule reparation whereas the upright show goodwill.

10 Personal emotions. There are joys and sorrows that cannot be shared. In their deepest emotional feelings of "bitterness" or "joy" people alone can understand those feelings. This proverb forewarns against any forced attempts to express empathy.

11 Prosperity ensured. Personal integrity ensures domestic stability and prosperity. The contrast is a simple one and the sentiment general. For comparison see 12:7 and Job 18:15.

12 Destructive nature of worldliness. One should be warned that any evil activity that seems successful and safe can take any number of turns to destruction. The proverb recalls the ways of the adulterous woman in chs. 1–9. The first half of the verse does not state that the way that seems right is a vice, but the second half clarifies that. The image used is of a traveler on a straight road; it seems safe, but it is fatal, because the destination is wrong. "Death" signifies mortal ruin (see 7:27; 16:25; also Mt 7:13–14). Evil, in other words, is often deceptive.

13 Mixed emotions. Life is filled with bittersweet things—no joy is completely free of grief. At first reading this proverb sounds pessimistic. The point must be the alternating emotions of life. Or it is suggesting that in some superficial joy there is underlying pain, and that once the joy leaves, the "grief" is still present.

14 On retribution. One's deeds determine one's rewards. The faithless are those whose heart turns aside; they will partake of their own evil ways ("be fully repaid"). The good man will be satisfied from his ways—his deeds are rewarding.

15 Discernment, opposite of gullibility. Wisdom prevents gullibility. This verse contrasts the simpleton with the prudent, i.e., the youth who is untrained intellectually and morally with the wise one who has the ability to make critical discriminations. The simpleton believes every word, probably because he hears what he wants to hear. The prudent person, however, discerns every step.

16 Avoidance of evil. Wise people are cautious and not reckless. The first line of the verse simply says that "a wise man fears and turns from evil." Since the holy name is not used, the verse probably does not mean that he fears the Lord (as in NIV) but fears the consequences of his actions—the wise person is thus cautious. On the other hand, the fool is reckless, self-assured, and overconfident.

17 Distasteful character traits. Two character traits that are distasteful to others are the quick temper and craftiness. The quick-tempered person acts foolishly and loses people's respect, but the malicious plotter is hated.

18 Knowledge and prudence. The kind of honor one receives in life is based on the amount of wisdom used. The contrast is between the simple who "inherit" folly and the prudent who are crowned with knowledge. "Crowned" may mean "embrace."

19 Victory over the wicked. Ultimately the wicked will acknowledge and serve the righteous. The figure used here is of a conquered people kneeling before their victors awaiting their commands. While this proverb has its primary focus on triumphs in this life, one cannot help but think of the ultimate fulfillment of the thought in Php 2:10.

20 Popularity of wealth. Possessions determine popularity. This is just a statement of the reality of life. The poor are avoided and "shunned" (lit., "hated") as useless by their neighbors, but "the lovers of the rich are many."

21 Proper treatment of neighbors. One cannot sin against a neighbor and hope to enjoy God's blessings. The line contrasts the sin of despising a neighbor (assumed to be poor or at least in need) with showing favor to the needy. "Despises" (GK 996) means to treat with contempt or to discard one as worthless. To ignore a neighbor in this cold-hearted fashion is just as much a sin as showing favor to the poor is an act of righteousness.

22 Good and evil conduct. One's moral behavior is usually the result of planning. The contrast is between "those who plot evil" and "those who plan good." The result of the first is going astray and of the second showing faithful love (NIV note, "*show* love and faithfulness"; these words usually describe the Lord's intervention, but here they refer to the kind dealings of the righteous).

23 Diligence profitable. Profits come from hard work and not idle talk. The "hard work" is a term introduced in Ge 3:19. Empty talk leads to poverty (see Job 11:2;

15:3; Isa 36:5). People should be more afraid of idle talk than of hard work. Or, to put it another way, do not just talk about it—Do it!

24 Wealth as a benefit for the wise. Wisdom has its own rewards—here, riches. The second line seems to be saying that fools only have their folly. The point is that fools can only expect greater exposure of their folly.

25 True and false witnesses. Telling the truth in court effects swift justice in the outcome of the trial. The person who tells the truth "saves lives"—he is a true witness. The point is that this person will deliver someone else from death in a false charge by coming forward with the truth. On the other hand, a false testimony deceives the court and brings ruin. Nothing good is gained by perjury.

26–27 Security in the fear of the Lord. The reverential fear of the Lord leads to family security and to life (cf. 13:14). The "fear" finds expression in obedience to the law with all its rewards and punishments, and this ensures the safety. The children mentioned here are the God-fearer's children. Exodus 20:5–6 declares that children will reap the benefits of the righteous parents if they love the Lord too; so if fear gives the parents security in the Lord, it will be a refuge for their children.

28 Political power. A prince's power varies with the size of his empire. From a human viewpoint political power is based on the number of people in the party.

29 Patience and a quick temper. Patience is the evidence of "great understanding." Those with quick tempers (lit., "hasty of spirit") exalt folly, i.e., they bring it to a full measure. So one should cultivate understanding.

30 Benefit of contentment. It is healthy to find contentment, for envy brings constant turmoil. That is, a healthy spirit is the life of the body—it soothes. On the other hand, envy brings pain and problems. The word for "envy" (GK 7863) describes passionate zeal, a violent excitement that is never satisfied. The one who is "consumed with envy" has no peace.

31 Treatment of the poor. How people treat the poor displays their faith in the Creator. Here is the doctrine of the Creation in its practical outworking. Those who oppress the "poor" show contempt for their Maker, for that poor person also is the image of God. Showing favor for the poor honors God because God commanded this to be done (see Mt 25:31–46; cf. Pr 14:21; 17:5; 19:17).

32 Confidence in calamity. Those who trust and obey the Lord have a sense of security in catastrophe. The contrast is with the wicked who are cast down in the time of calamity; the righteous even in death have a "refuge." That is, the righteous hope in a just retribution. A problem often raised is that nowhere in the book of Proverbs is hope for immortality found. Rather death is seen as a misfortune. Nevertheless, this verse may be a shadowy forerunner of that truth.

33 Possession of wisdom. The greatest amount of wisdom resides with those who have discernment. The second line is difficult. It is usually translated "even among fools she lets herself be known." This may be ironic or sarcastic: fools, anxious to appear wise, blurt out what they think is wisdom but in the process turn it to folly.

34 National righteousness. The prosperity and the power of a nation depend on its righteousness. The verb "exalt" (GK 8123) means that the people's condition in that nation is elevated. On the other hand, widespread sin is a disgrace.

35 Clever and incompetent servants. A servant's competence will affect the king's attitude toward him: the wise servant is a delight, for he is the skillful, clever one. But the incompetent one is the bungler who botches the king's business and whose indiscretions and incapacity expose his master to scandal and criticism.

Chapter 15

1 Conciliatory speech. The way one answers another person will have an effect on the response. This antithetical proverb stresses that it is wise to use a gentle answer to turn away wrath. More than merely gentle or soft, the idea seems to be conciliatory, i.e., an answer that restores good temper and reasonableness. To use a "harsh" word is to cause "pain" (same Heb. word; GK 6776) and will bring an angry response. Gideon in Jdg 8:1–3 is a classic example of the soft answer that brings peace, whereas Jephthah illustrates the harsh answer that leads to war (Jdg 12:1–6).

2 Wise or foolish speech. How wise people are can often be determined by what they say: knowledge comes from the wise and folly from the fools. "Commends" (GK 3512) means literally "makes good" or "treats in a good or excellent way."

3 Divine omniscience. The Lord knows everyone completely. This verse is not meant as a statement of theology but as an incentive for conduct. For the righteous divine omniscience is a great comfort (cf. 2Ch 16:9; Ps 11:4; Heb 4:13).

4 Helpful or harmful speech. What a person says can bring either healing or harm. Healing words bring life and vitality to the spirit, but perverse, twisted, or "deceitful" words crush the spirit (cf. Isa 65:14).

5 Heeding discipline. How well one responds to discipline reveals one's character. The fool spurns it while the prudent individual heeds it, showing good sense (cf. v.20; 13:1, 18).

6 Reward for righteousness. Prosperity is one reward for righteousness. The Hebrew of the second line says that the income of the wicked is "a thing troubled." The word "trouble" (GK 6579) is usually calamity that one man brings on another (as illustrated by Achan).

7 Spreading knowledge. Wise people will spread knowledge when they speak—their words are profitable. This verse is concerned with teaching. The idea of the second part of the verse is simply that the fool has no comprehension of knowledge.

8 Acceptable and unacceptable worship. The spiritual condition of the worshiper will determine the acceptability of the worship. Sacrifices from wicked people are unacceptable because they are insincere and blasphemous (cf. v.29; 21:3, 27; 28:9, et al.; see also 1Sa 15:22; Ps 40:6–8; Isa 1:10–17). On the other hand, prayer from the righteous pleases God. Sacrifice is an outward ritual and easily performed by the wicked, but prayer is a private and inward act and not usually fabricated by unbelievers.

9 Conduct acceptable to God. Parallel to the preceding verse, this verse uses "detests" (GK 9359) to describe God's reaction to the life of the wicked, in contrast to "loves" (GK

170), which describes his approval of the righteous. God hates the way of the wicked, i.e., the sin but not the sinner; and God loves those who follow after righteousness.

10 Necessity of discipline. Discipline must be used for those who go astray, but in this discipline they may die prematurely. The word "path" (GK 784) is used for the life of righteousness stressed throughout the book. The relationship of the two lines is probably synonymous: the "stern discipline" of the first line is parallel to the death in the second. That is, it is one thing to sin and find forgiveness but another altogether to refuse correction and receive such stern discipline (cf. Ro 8:13).

11 Divine omniscience. The Lord knows every intent of every individual. The argument here goes from the lesser to the greater ("how much more"). Sheol and Abaddon represent the remote underworld and all the mighty powers that reside there (see 27:20; Job 26:6; Ps 139:8; Am 9:2; Rev 9:11). If that remote region with its inhabitants is open before the Lord, how much more the motives and thoughts of people (cf. Ps 44:21).

12 Discipline rejected. Mockers resist all efforts to reform them. They are fixed in their ways and will not change to live according to the advice of the wise (cf. 1Ki 22:8).

13 Joy and sorrow. The emotional condition of a person has an obvious effect on body and soul. Joy is inspiring and is expressed by a cheerful face, but "heartache" is depressing, i.e., "crushes the spirit." The words used here stress the pain and the depression with a note of despair (cf. 17:22; 18:14; Ge 40:6; Isa 66:2).

14 Knowledge sought by the discerning. Those who are wise and discerning desire knowledge (cf. v.7). Throughout Proverbs knowledge is linked with righteousness, and ignorance goes with sinfulness. "Feeds on folly" signifies the acquisition of folly.

15 Joy and sorrow. Life can be delightful or difficult, depending on one's circumstances and disposition. The contrast is between someone inwardly "oppressed" and a "cheerful" person. The proverb recommends the cheerful frame of mind; the image of the feast signifies enjoyment of life's offerings.

This is far better than the evil days (see Ru 1:20–21; Hab 3:17–18).

16–17 Spiritual things better than physical wealth. These two verses stress that spiritual things are far better than material wealth. The fear of the Lord brings more satisfaction than wealth with discontentment. "Turmoil" is anxiety; the reverential fear of the Lord alleviates such anxiety. Not all wealth has this disadvantage, but when it does, it is undesirable. Second, happy, loving relationships are more desirable than a great meal where there is hatred. All too often wealth replaces love in a family. The ideal is to have a loving family, friends, and great food; but short of that, a humble meal with love is preferable.

18 Effect of patience on strife. It takes great patience and calmness to maintain peaceful relationships. The contrast is with the "hot-tempered man" who stirs up dissension, and the person who is slow to anger (i.e., "patient"). See also 14:29 and 15:1.

19 Progress of diligence. Diligence normally determines progress in life. The slothful seem to find obstacles along the way—their way is like a hedge of thorns. By contrast, the way of the upright is like a well-made road; i.e., a "highway"—they have no reason to detour or swerve (see also 6:10; 10:26; 28:19).

20 Effect of wisdom on others. Wise children affect their parents' joy (see also 10:1). This verse describes the callousness of the one who inflicts grief on his mother.

21 Proper course of life. A valuable lifestyle must be maintained by wise decisions. This proverb shows the importance of good judgment and "understanding." The fool follows any whim of fancy, and it is a delight to him because he lacks "judgment" to see the folly in it. The one who has insight follows in a "straight course." Knowledge is the foundation of character.

22 Value of advice. The success of plans requires using good advice (see 11:14). This general observation has value on the personal and national level.

23 Appropriate speech. It is most satisfying to be able to give timely and fitting advice. To say the right thing at the right time is satisfying; it requires knowledge and wisdom.

24 Conduct beneficial for life. A life of wisdom preserves life. The righteous expect to live long and healthy lives (2:20–22; 3:18; 5:6; 10:17; 13:14). The second part of this verse clarifies the first: wisdom prevents a person from going to "the grave" (Heb. *Sheol*; GK 8619). "Upward" probably refers to physical life, while "going down to the grave" refers to physical death.

25 Divine justice. The Lord administers his justice through righteousness. He brings down the proud but protects the needy. Scripture amply confirms that the Lord champions the cause of the widow, the orphan, the poor, and the needy, who were often the prey of the proud (cf. 1Ki 21; cf. also Pr 16:19; Isa 5:8–10).

26 Plans pleasing to God. The Lord is pleased with plans that have righteous intentions. The "thoughts of the wicked" will harm other people, and these are an abomination to the Lord.

27 Greed and contentment. Those who are secure in their circumstances will not succumb to the evil devices of greed. The "greedy" are those who want a big cut, who are in a hurry to get rich, and who are not particular how it happens. The verse is actually a warning against taking bribes. "Gifts" could be innocent enough, but they may alter one's values. So hating bribes is the safest path to follow (see Ge 14:22–24; 2Ki 5:16, 20, 27).

28 Carefully planned speech. Those who are wise are cautious in how they answer, in contrast to the wicked who blurt out vicious things. The mind of the righteous "meditates on" or "studies" how to answer. This verse advises one to say less but better things.

29 God's response to prayer. God's response to prayer is determined by the righteousness of the one who prays. The wicked keep a distance from him, and God is inaccessible or deaf to their appeal (see the motif repeated in Ps 22). Of course, a prayer of repentance by the wicked is the exception, for by it they become the righteous.

30 Good news. It is uplifting to hear good news. The "cheerful look" (lit., "light of the eyes") may indicate the gleam in the eyes of the one who tells good news. The idea of

"health to the bones" comes from a Hebrew expression that is literally "makes the bones fat," a symbol of health and prosperity (see also 17:22; 25:25; Ge 45:27–28; Isa 52:7–8).

31 A teachable person. A teachable person will become wise. This proverb shows how the one who listens to reproof that is beneficial to life will be at home with the wise.

32 Benefit of discipline. Accepting discipline is important to personal development. Those who despise discipline, slight or despise themselves (i.e., they reject themselves as if they are of little value and so fail to grow). One must acquire understanding, especially about oneself, to grow spiritually, intellectually, and emotionally.

33 Fear of the Lord, wisdom, and honor. Humble submission in faith to the Lord brings wisdom and honor. The idea of the first clause is similar to 1:7 and 9:10. Here it may mean that "the discipline of wisdom [teaches] the fear of the Lord." The second clause has its contrast in 18:12, where pride leads to destruction. Here humility brings honor (see also 22:4).

Chapter 16

1 Divine enablement. The verse is in the form of a contrast—"the plans of the heart" and the "reply of the tongue" are contrasted by the prepositions "belong" and "from." The verse can be taken in one of two ways: (1) the thoughts and the speech are the same, or (2) the speech differs from what the person had intended to say. The second view fits the contrast better. God sovereignly enables people to put their thoughts into words. The word "reply" seems to refer to a verbal answer to another person (15:1, 23; Job 32:3, 5); so when someone is trying to speak before others, the Lord directs the words according to his sovereign will.

2 Divine omniscience. The Lord alone, by his Spirit and Word, can evaluate our behavior because he penetrates our hearts and knows our motives. People might seem "innocent" in their own estimation, but self-deception and rationalization make this estimation unreliable. The word translated "innocent" (GK 2341) is used for pure oils, undiluted liquids; here it signifies unmixed actions. The person may be far from pure when the Lord weighs the motives. The figure of "weighing" signifies evaluation (see Ex 5:8 ["require"]; 1Sa 2:3; Pr 21:2; 24:12; cf. 1Sa 16:7).

3 Plans committed to God. The verb "commit" (GK 1670) is literally "roll" (the figure of rolling, as in rolling one's burdens onto the Lord, is found also in Pss 22:8; 37:5; 55:22). This word portrays complete dependence on God, accomplished with a spirit of humility and by means of a diligent season of prayer. For our plans to succeed, we must also have God's approval. Not every plan we have is pleasing to him; but for those plan that are, this verse is a great comfort.

4 Divine retribution. Our sovereign God ensures that everything in life receives its appropriate retribution: all his acts are part of his plan. Since the wicked are punished in the end, this proverb adds that that is his plan for them. In God's order, every act includes its answer or consequence.

5 The fall of the proud. The Lord will surely bring down the "proud of heart," i.e., those who arrogantly set themselves presumptuously against God (see 2Ch 26:16; Ps 131:1; Pr 18:12). The second phrase explains what the Lord hating the proud means. One can be absolutely "sure" (lit., "hand to hand," as in a confirming handshake; cf. 11:21) that such people will not go free.

6 Freedom from sin. Faithfulness to the Lord brings freedom from sin. The first half of this verse speaks of atonement for sin, and the second of avoidance of sin—so from both sides the stress is on complete freedom from sin. The couplet "love and faithfulness" often characterizes the Lord, but here, in parallel to the fear of the Lord (as in 3:3–7), it refers to the faithfulness of the believer. Such faithfulness brings atonement for sin. The word "evil" can mean calamity or disaster, but it probably means sin or evil doing (see also v.17; 3:7; 4:27; 13:19). Thus, reverential fear of the Lord prompts the believer to turn from evil doing.

7 Peaceful conduct. The subject matter of the verse is "a man's ways" that are "pleasing" to the Lord. The question is: who is the subject of the second clause? The appropriate choice is the "man" and his "ways"—it is his godly lifestyle that disarms the enemies. A

life that pleases God will be above reproach and find favor with others. This is part of God's plan for rewards. But we must remember that like many proverbs, this one must not be pressed to universal applications (cf. 2Ti 3:12 for a contrasting statement).

8 Righteousness better than unjust wealth. Few possessions with righteousness is better than much gain with dishonesty. The form follows the "better" sayings and so presents a contrast. There are of course other options (such as wealth with justice), but this line does not consider them. The "little" is not necessarily abject poverty; it could refer to modest income. The main contrast is between "righteousness" and "injustice." Unethical conduct tarnishes great gain and will be judged by God.

9 Sovereignty of God. The Lord sovereignly determines the outworking of our plans. The Bible in general teaches that only those plans that are approved by God will succeed. The point of contrast in this verse is between what we plan and what actually happens— God determines the latter (cf. Eph 3:20).

10 Responsible speech. Next is a series of proverbs about kings. This first one teaches that kings must speak righteously in their official capacities. The first part states that when the king speaks officially, it is as if it were "an oracle." His words form an oracular sentence, as if he speaks for God (see Nu 22:7; 23:23; 2Sa 14:20). The effect of this is that his mouth "should not betray" justice. For a portrayal of the ideal king, see Ps 72 and Isa 11:1–5.

11 Honesty in business. The Lord is the source of honesty and justice in all human enterprises. This proverb concerns weights and balances; the law of the Lord prescribed that they be just (see Lev 19:36; Dt 25:13; Am 8:5; Mic 6:11). Shrewd people kept light and heavy weights to make dishonest transactions—as a modern individual might keep two sets of books. But the verse, using synonymous parallelism to stress the point, affirms that righteous and just measures are from the Lord.

12 Stability in government. A righteous administration determines the stability of a government. Kings detest criminal acts because their thrones are "established" in righteousness. This saying stresses the ideal that righteousness characterizes the administration in God's theocracy (see Dt 17:19–20; 2Sa 7:13–16; Isa 32:1). If this proverb had been written after the monarchy had disintegrated, there would have been a great variance between the ideal and the real. But coming from the golden age of Solomon, the ideal was still credible.

13 Honesty approved. People who are honest and candid are valuable to governments. Political leaders know that without such their domains would become anarchic. Those who speak uprightly please kings. Ideal rulers love righteousness and not flattery.

14 Wisdom appeases wrath. The wise person knows how to pacify the unexpected or irrational anger of leaders. This proverb, with its dictum and consequence, introduces the danger of becoming a victim of such caprice. The first part describes the "wrath" of the king as "messengers of death" (cf. Solomon's assassinations of Adonijah, Joab, and Shimei in 1Ki 2:25, 29–34, 46). When the kings's wrath so threatens, a wise person will try to pacify or "appease it."

15 Encouragement from rulers. This proverb is the antithesis of v.14. By using two figures it describes the benefits of having a king who is pleased with his subjects. The king's brightened face signifies his delight and thus means life for those around him. His favor is symbolized by the "rain cloud"—the latter rain or harvest rain, which is necessary for a successful harvest. Some of the ideas here are similar to Ps 72:15–17, which portrays the prosperity of the land as a blessing on account of the ideal king, whose righteous reign seems to ensure prosperity.

16 Wisdom better than wealth. Wisdom is more valuable than money. These two are not incompatible; but the comparison here is between wealth without wisdom and wisdom without wealth. The point of the verse is to encourage people to acquire wisdom and understanding (cf. 3:14).

17 Righteousness prevents evil. Righteous living is a safeguard against calamity. The first line asserts that integrity avoids evil, and the second explains further that the person who guards his way protects his life. Righteous living is like a "highway," a raised and well-graded road. This well-cared-for life, this integrity, turns from evil. The metaphor of the "way" means that the person "guards" his way and thereby safeguards his life.

18 Consequences of pride. Pride leads inevitably to a downfall. Arrogance is the first step down. The lines are synonymous. Many similar sayings have appeared to warn against pride.

19 Humility better than plunder. It is better to be oppressed than to oppress. One should cultivate a humble spirit regardless of economic status; but one should never share the loot of those antagonistic to God. The "lowly" and the "proud" are here ethical and religious descriptions for the haughty, who rebel against God and are overbearing and oppressive, and for the humble, who submit to God and are unassuming and inoffensive.

20 Blessing of faithfulness. Faithfulness to the Lord brings his blessing. This simple proverb stresses that those who trust in the Lord and "heed ... instruction" will be blessed by him; they will find earthly prosperity and heavenly bliss from living a life that is right with God.

21 Competent speech. Wise speech builds a reputation for competence and enhances influence. It leads to the reputation of being "discerning," and its influence coming from sweet or "pleasant words" is to "promote instruction"—namely, the teaching will be well received because it is persuasive.

22 Prospect for life. An individual's prospects in life are determined by one's wisdom. Here is another antithetical saying. "Understanding" is a "fountain of life" (see 10:11; 13:14; 14:27; 18:4), but "folly" brings "punishment" to fools. Again Proverbs affirms that little can be done for or with the fool.

23 Wise speech. Those who are wise ensure that they say wise things. The first part asserts that the wise heart "guides" the mouth; the second one adds that such a heart increases the reception of what one says (see v.21).

24 Beneficial speech. Pleasant words are comforting and encouraging. "Pleasant words" are described as "a honeycomb" (see Ps 19:10); added to this are the predicates "sweet" and "healing." One might recall how

Jonathan's eyes brightened when he ate the honeycomb (1Sa 14:27); such is the uplifting effect of pleasant words.

25 Consequence of conduct. This proverb is identical to 14:12. Conduct that seems to be right may end in disaster. The contrast is with the "way" that seems right and the "ways of death," which in the end provide the reality for the short-sighted evaluation.

26 On diligence. Hunger drives people to work diligently. Motivations are necessary for a person to continue working, especially if the labor is drudgery; hunger is the most frequent motivation. "Appetite" (lit., "soul"; GK 5883) means that part of human nature that craves food; for the "life" is a bundle of appetites. The second clause adds an explanatory idea: his "mouth" (NIV, "his hunger") presses him on.

27 Malicious conduct. Scoundrels plan ways to slander people. The "scoundrel" is literally a "man of Belial [GK 1175]"—a term describing deep depravity and wickedness. He is a wicked person, for "he digs up evil." The meaning of "plots" (GK 4125) is that of bringing evil to the surface (cf. 26:27; Jer 18:20). What he finds he spreads; his speech is like scorching fire—the simile speaks of the devastating effect of his words.

28 Divisive speech. Slanderers and gossips cause divisions. The wicked is described as "a perverse man" ("a man of falsehoods," "a liar") and a "gossip," namely, one who whispers and murmurs (18:8; 26:20, 22). This kind of person will destroy close friendships by what he says.

29 Evil associations. Violent people influence others toward violence. The word for "violent" (GK 2805) often refers to sins against society, social injustices, and crimes. The "path that is not good" must refer to habits of crime. The author warns people to keep away from such villains.

30 Wicked character traits. Often people who plan wicked things betray themselves with malicious expressions. Two such expressions are depicted here: winking the eye and pursing the lips. Facial expressions often reveal whether someone is plotting something evil (see 6:13–14).

31 Reward of a long life. Righteousness is rewarded with longevity in life. This proverb presents the ideal, of course, for it does not include evil old men. The equity envisioned in Proverbs is that the wicked come to an early end but the righteous endure. "Gray hair" is the "crown of splendor"; it can only be attained through righteousness. While the proverb presents a simplified observation, there is something commendable about old age that can remember a long walk with God through life and can anticipate unbroken fellowship with him in glory.

32 Patience more effective than power. Patience is preferable to physical power. Normally patience is an attribute of God (see Ex 34:6); here it describes a human being who has his emotions under control. This saying would have significant meaning in the times when military prowess was held in high regard.

33 Sovereignty of God. The Lord controls the decisions that are submitted to him. The verse concerns the practice of seeking divine leading through casting lots, which God controls. This chapter ends as it began, with a word about God's sovereignty.

Chapter 17

1 Value of peace. Poverty with peace is better than prosperity with strife. This contrast makes a preference for the better of two

This broken piece of pottery, with a name scribbled on it (called an ostracon), was likely used to cast lots (cf. 16:33).

circumstances. On one side is the "dry crust" with quietness, like bread without butter or a morsel of bread not dipped in vinegar. In this humble setting there is "peace and quiet," which is better than a house of "feasting" (lit., "sacrifices"; GK 2285) and "strife." The use of "sacrifice" suggests a connection with the temple in which the people may have made their sacrifices and had abundant meat to eat. Rarely would the Israelites have meat apart from sacrificial occasions. The contrast formed, however, is not between the morsel and the meat but between peace and strife. Abundance often brings a deterioration of moral and ethical standards as well as an increase in envy and strife.

2 Ability is better than privilege. Faithful and prudent servants are more highly honored than disgraceful sons. The setting is the ancient world where servants only occasionally advanced beyond their station in life. This proverb focuses on the prudent or "wise servant" who uses all his abilities effectively. This one rules over the "disgraceful son," becoming a joint heir with the brothers. The meaning is that the worthless son will be disinherited.

3 Divine omniscience. The Lord examines every thought and every motive. One side in the imagery used here is silver and gold being purified; the other is the Lord "testing" human hearts. Such examinations are always constructive; they are designed to improve the value of the one being purified.

4 Malicious speech. The wicked find malicious talk appealing. Those who listen to it are in fact malicious themselves. The metonymies "lips" and "tongue" signify speech, and the qualifications "evil" and "malicious" show this speech to be destructive. Leviticus 19:17 warns people to rebuke those with such malicious words and not to bear evil with them.

5 Speech that mocks the poor. Anyone who mocks the misfortune of the poor holds the Creator in contempt and will be punished. The first part of each unit identifies the subject matter: "mocking the poor" and "gloating over disaster" ("disaster" is meant to explain the poverty). The second part of each unit diverges: the first explains that those who do this reproach or "show contempt for" their Maker; the second line affirms that

they will be punished. The idea of reproaching the Creator may be mistaking and blaming God's providential control of the world.

6 Honor in family relationships. People treasure their family heritage. The synonymous parallelism here focuses on this point from two sides—grandchildren are a crown to the aged, and parents are an honor to children. This idea comes from a culture that places great importance on the family in society; older people have the preeminence and receive appropriate respect.

7 Dishonest speech. A dishonest leader is worse than an arrogant fool. A comparison shows which of two things is worse. The word for "arrogant" (GK 3856) can also be rendered "excellent" (see NIV note). It describes lofty speech, and this does not suit the fool. "Fool" (GK 5572) describes someone who is godless and immoral in an overbearing way (see 1Sa 25:25; Ps 14:1). The second line makes the point: "how much worse lying lips to a ruler!" This "ruler" is a gentleman with a code of honor, to whom truthfulness is almost second nature. Lies simply are not suited to him. So the lesson is that if fools should not speak lofty things, then certainly honorable people should not lie.

8 Success of bribery. Those who use bribery meet with widespread success. The word for "bribe" (GK 8816) may simply refer to "a gift" that opens doors, the explanation being that it was the custom to offer a gift for most occasions. This would not be as problematic as a bribe and would fit well in this positive statement. The Law clearly prohibited taking bribes (Ex 23:8); true bribery is described in v.23. This proverb is expressing a reality from the viewpoint of the one giving the bribe—it works. It is a "stone" that brings "favor," a "lucky" stone.

9 Love shown by discretion. How people respond to the faults of others reveals whether or not they have compassion. The contrast here is between "he who covers over an offense" of a friend and the one who "repeats" the news about it; the former promotes love and the latter alienates friends. Friendship requires the ability to forget. The true friend buries the wrong done for the sake of love.

10 Value of discipline. Discipline in the form of "rebuke" will benefit the wise but not the foolish. The wise will be humbled by a rebuke and learn from it; but not even a hundred lashes will make such an impression on the "fool." The proverb may also be saying that in general physical punishment is less effective than criticism.

11 Certainty of retribution. Those bent on rebellion will surely meet with severe retribution in the form of a "merciless official." This latter expression may refer to a pitiless messenger that the king would send; but it may also refer to storms, pestilence, or any misfortune that was God's messenger of retribution.

12 Dangerous associations. It is dangerous to encounter a fool engaged in folly. The first clause literally says, "Let a bear robbed of her whelps meet a man" (see 2Sa 17:8; Hos 13:8). The contrast explains that this would be less dangerous than meeting a "fool" engaged in "his [wicked] folly." The human, who is supposed to be intelligent and rational, in such folly becomes more dangerous than the beast that in this case acts with good reason.

13 Justice for ingratitude. Acts of ingratitude will be punished accordingly. This saying presents a condition and its consequences: the condition is when "a man" repays "evil for good"; and the consequences are that the punishment fits the crime—"evil will never leave his house." The verse does not explain whether God will turn evil back on him directly or whether people will begin to treat him as he treated others.

14 Strife controlled. Conflicts must be stopped before they get out of control. Starting a "quarrel" is like "letting out water" (NIV, "breaching a dam"). The image is of a small leak, perhaps in a dam, that starts slowly to spurt water. The problem will only get worse. One should stop a quarrel before strife breaks out.

15 Justice corrupted. The Lord hates any miscarriage of justice. This proverb uses effective wordplays to express the two things the Lord hates—declaring "righteous" (NIV, "acquitting") the person who is a "guilty [criminal]" and "declaring guilty" (NIV, "condemning") the person who is "righteous" ("innocent"). Such reversals are detestable to the righteous Judge of the whole earth.

16 Wisdom inaccessible to fools. This proverb asks a rhetorical question: What good is money, for what one really needs (i.e., wisdom) cannot be bought. The person under consideration here is the "fool" (GK 4067), the one who lacks the intellect to gain wisdom in the first place. He may desire the reputation of the wise, but he will not live up to its demands.

17 Friends are loyal in adversity. The love of a true friend is strong and constant. In this verse, the "friend" and the "brother" are equated. Faithful "love" is always present in a true friend, even in times of "adversity," when it might be severely tested.

18 Wisdom in business. It is foolish to pledge security for someone else's loans. The lack of judgment is introduced with the idea of striking hands and then clarified by "puts up security." The point is similar to 6:1–5.

19 Arrogant and contentious speech. Arrogant and contentious speech ends in destruction. The words used here are figurative: the "gate" is the mouth, and so to make it "high" is to say lofty things—the person in question brags too much (see 1Sa 2:3; Pr 18:12; 29:23). The figure would be comparable to the use of "trap" for mouth in American English. Thus the proverb is about a quarrelsome and arrogant individual who loves "sin" and invites "destruction." The destruction could be what he inflicts on others but may also mean what he brings on himself.

20 Wicked conduct. Wicked ways and words lead to trouble. The wicked person has a "perverse" heart, meaning he is morally crooked, and a "deceitful tongue," meaning he has turned away from the truth. All who are wicked in their plans and speech can expect only trouble ahead. The idea of "trouble" refers to calamity or adversity in this life.

21 Folly, a grief to others. Parents experience grief if their children become fools. It is not always a completely joyous experience to have children, not with the world and human nature as they are. "Fool" (GK 5572) portrays a slow-witted dullard, whether it be in spiritual, intellectual, or moral matters. A father who hoped for a son who would be a credit to the family and the faith may find only disappointment.

22 Emotions affect health. One's psychological condition affects one's physical condition: a healthy attitude fosters good health but a depressed spirit ruins health. The "heart," as with the spirit, refers to the mind. The positive and healthy outlook on life brings healing. On the other hand, a "crushed spirit," i.e., one that is depressed or dejected, has an adverse effect on the health of the body. "Bones" figuratively represents the body (encased in the bony frame): fat bones mean a healthy body (see 3:8; 15:30; 16:24), but dry bones signify unhealthiness (cf. Eze 37:1–14).

23 Justice perverted by bribes. Bribery perverts justice. The "wicked man" who accepts the gift is a corrupt judge or some other official. The fact that he accepts it "in secret" (lit., "from the bosom") indicates it is not proper. The purpose of accepting the bribe is "to pervert the course of justice."

24 Concentration on one's plans. The wise persist in following a course of wisdom. They understand the true issues of life and concentrate on the path of wisdom. "Fools," however, lack any serious concentration and are unable to fix their attention on anything—so they drift in the limitless sea of uncertainty.

25 Effect of folly on parents. It is a bitter grief to have a child turn out to be a fool. See v.21; 10:1; and 15:20.

26 Unjust punishment. It is a mistake to punish people who are innocent. The second part of this proverb is perhaps showing how wrong the first part is: namely, punishing the righteous makes about as much sense as flogging an official for his integrity. In any case, this verse clearly affirms that punishing the righteous is improper.

27 Self-control. The wise restrain their speaking and control their actions. They are "sparing" of words and "even-tempered" (lit., "cool of spirit"). The intent of this proverb is to teach that in order to gain composure and restraint one must develop knowledge and understanding.

28 The wisdom of silence. Silence is one evidence of wisdom. Even fools appear wise in silence—at least they conceal their folly by keeping silent. Fools who do this do not, of course, become wise; they just hide their folly.

Chapter 18

1 Antisocial character traits. An antisocial person is self-centered and unreasonable. This verse does not describe someone who is merely unfriendly or unsociable but one who is an enemy of society; its message is a warning against being a schismatic. The proverb goes on to describe the antisocial person as one who contends against all "sound judgment"; "defies" means "burst out in contention" (lit., "snarl," "show the teeth"; GK 1679). He opposes society and its decisions (see also 17:14; 20:3).

2 Fools and speaking. Fools prefer to give their opinion rather than acquire wisdom. They find "no pleasure in understanding" (i.e., they detest understanding). Instead, they love telling what is on their mind (cf. 20:19; Ps 98:2). This is the kind of person who asks questions to show how clever one is rather than to learn.

3 Effects of sin. Wickedness leads to "contempt," and shame (parallel to contempt) leads on to "disgrace" or reproach. The point is that punishment for wickedness comes naturally from the community. One possible disgrace might be the critical rebukes of the community against the wicked person (for an example of the Lord doing this, see Mal 2:9).

4 Profound speech. The words of the wise are an inexhaustible supply of blessing and counsel. The figure of "deep waters" suggests an inexhaustible supply of words or, more likely, the idea that their words are profound. The figures of "fountain of wisdom" and "bubbling brook" describe the speech of the wise as a continuous source of refreshing and beneficial ideas.

5 Injustice denounced. It is reprehensible to pervert justice by showing partiality in judgments (cf. Dt 10:17; Mal 2:9). The predicate "not good" is an understatement—it is vile and wrong. The second clause reinforces the first clause: the innocent should not be "turned aside" (deprived) of their rights (cf.17:26; 28:21).

6–7 Speech that invites trouble. Foolish people get themselves into trouble by what they say. The reference here may be to legal controversies; since they are wrong, they are punished. The "beating" is probably physical, given either by a father or by society (see 19:25; Ps 141:5). Verse 7 continues the point of v.6. What fools say is their "undoing"; it is a "snare" to them.

8 On gossip. People delight in listening to gossip. This sad observation simply affirms the common trait of human nature. The words of the "gossip" are like "choice morsels." When such tasty bits are taken into the innermost being, they stimulate the desire for more.

9 Effects of laziness. Laziness is destructive. The lines form a comparison to express that the lazy person and the destructive person are equally detrimental to society. The first is "slack" in work; the other is a "possessor [= dealer] in/of destruction" (NIV, "one who destroys"). The link between these two is the term "brother"; it signifies that they belong to the same classification. For example, the one who is slack may look for shortcuts and may make things that fall apart. His destruction may be indirect and slow in coming, but it is just as problematic.

10 Security in the Lord's name. The Lord is fully able to protect those who trust in him. The first line establishes this truth, and the second focuses on the trust of the righteous. This is the only place in Proverbs where the phrase "the name of the LORD" is found; it signifies the attributes of God, here the power to protect (cf. Ex 34:5–7). The metaphor of "strong tower" sets up the imagery of the second clause: "run" metaphorically describes a wholehearted trust in God's protection (see Isa 40:31), and "safe" (a military term; GK 8435) stresses the effect. Other Scriptures delineate how God protects his people in different circumstances.

11 Security in wealth. Wealthy people often assume that their wealth brings security. The imagery of safety (NIV, "unscalable"; GK 8435) links this proverb to the preceding; and since security is from God, this proverb is simply reporting a common assumption

without commenting on it. Any protection that wealth may bring is limited; for, as Ps 49 teaches, money cannot bring ultimate security.

12 The reward of humility. The way to honor is through humility (see also 11:2; 15:33; 16:18). The humility and exaltation of Jesus provide the classic example of this truth (see Isa 52:13–53:12; Php 2:1–10). An antithesis makes the point: pride in the heart is the way to a downfall, but "humility" is the prelude to "honor."

13 Premature speech. Speaking too hastily is foolish and leads to shame. Poor listening reveals that the person has a low regard for what the other is saying or is too absorbed in self-importance.

14 A healthy spirit. This proverb contrasts a healthy spirit with a "crushed spirit": a healthy attitude sustains a person, but depression is unbearable. In physical sickness one can fall back on the will to live; but in depression the will to live may be gone, and there is no reserve for physical strength. The figure of a "crushed" spirit suggests a broken will, loss of vitality, despair, and emotional pain. Few things in the human experience are as difficult to cope with as this.

15 Knowledge sought. Those who are wise eagerly search for knowledge. By paralleling "heart" and "ears," the verse stresses the full acquisition of knowledge: the ear of the wise listens to instruction, and the heart of the wise discerns what is heard to acquire knowledge.

16 Influence of gifts. One may gain influence with important people through gifts. "Gift" (GK 5508) is more general than "bribe" (as in 17:8, 23). Thus this proverb is simply saying that a gift can expedite matters. But offering gifts is risky (see 15:27; 21:14), for by doing so one may learn how influential they are and start to make bribes (see Ge 43:11 for an example).

17 Necessity of cross-examination. The first half of this verse affirms that the one side in a dispute may seem right, but it must be challenged by the other. The proverb reminds us that there are two sides in any dispute (legal, domestic, or religious) and that all sides in a dispute must be given a hearing.

18 Disputes divinely arbitrated. Serious disputes may be prevented through divinely inspired arbitration. The assumption behind this saying is that providence played the determining role in the casting of lots. If both parties recognized this, the matter can be resolved, no matter how strong the "opponents." Today God's word and spiritual leaders figure prominently in divine arbitration (1Co 6:1–8).

19 Effect of disputes. Serious disputes create insurmountable barriers among friends. The Hebrew suggests that "an offended brother is [more isolated] than a strong city, and disputes are like the barred gates of the city." The proverb is talking about changing a friend into an enemy by abuse.

20 Productive speech. Productive speech is satisfying. In Proverbs words can bring either good or evil; "fruit" and "harvest" have good connotations, and so constructive and beneficial speech is in view here. Such speech has the power to make people happy.

21 Consequences of speech. What people say can lead to life or death. This proverb affirms this point and then explains it: "those who love it will eat its fruit." The referent of "it" must be "the tongue," i.e., what the tongue says. So those who enjoy talking must bear its fruit, whether good or bad. We should be warned by this proverb, especially if we love to talk.

22 The blessing of a wife. Although this verse does not say it, what it has in mind is clearly a "good" wife. Whoever finds a good wife—or, as it could be broadened, a good marriage—finds "good" (GK 3202, meaning "fortune" or "favor," not a "good thing"). This word describes that which is pleasing to God, beneficial to life, and abundantly enjoyable. The second line explains the first: finding a good mate is the sign of "favor" (GK 8356) from God. That is, a good marriage is a gift from God. Proverbs 31:10–31 develops this idea more fully, whereas other passages lament a bad wife (e.g., 12:4; Ecc 7:26). The background of the saying may be Ge 2:18, which affirms that it was "not good for the man to be alone."

23 Humble or harsh speech. One's social status determines the tone of one's voice. The contrast is between the poor man and the rich man. The poor man "pleads for mercy" because he has no choice—he has to ask. The rich man, however, often speaks "harshly"; he has hardened himself against such appeals because of relentless demands. It is a general view of the way of the world.

24 Loyal friendship. It is better to have one good, faithful friend than numerous unreliable ones. The idea of the first line may be that too many friends can become one's undoing, especially if these friends use him. The second line is clearer: "there is a friend who sticks closer than a brother." This indeed is a rare treasure!

Chapter 19

1 Poverty better than folly. Personal integrity, even with poverty, is far better than foolish perversion. This proverb provides a contrast between two selected situations. One is poverty with integrity ("blameless") and the other is "perverse [speech]" of a "fool." The verse teaches people to follow honesty, even if it leads to poverty (see also 18:23; 19:22).

2 Zeal without knowledge. Ill-advised and thoughtless "zeal" (GK 5883) leads to failure. This word means "vitality," "drive"; it describes the eager person. Without knowledge such zeal will be unsuccessful. Neither is there success for those who are "hasty" (lit., "hasty with the feet") and "miss the way" (see Jdg 20:16; Job 5:24). The passage reminds us that we must know the time and the direction for action, or zealous effort will be a futile activity.

3 Blaming God. Fools are not willing to accept failure as their own; they try to blame God. The first line establishes the fact that it is "a man's . . . folly" that ruins his life; the second adds that he "rages" against God. Of course, to blame God is folly.

4 Effects of wealth. People run after the wealthy. Like 18:23–24, this proverb simply makes an observation on the reality of life by contrasting the rich and the poor; wealth adds many friends, but the poor are deserted by their friends. People will run after the rich, hoping to gain something; but they will avoid the poor, fearing that the poor might try to gain something from them.

5 False witnesses. A person who bears false witness, i.e., who "pours out lies," will be punished. The saying is general, because sometimes a perjurer gets away with the crime (see also v.9; 6:19; 14:5, 25).

6 Friendship with the influential. People seek the friendship of influential people. The verse's two ideas are loosely synonymous. The first uses the image of "stroking the face"; this means "to make the face soft" or "to curry favor" (cf. Ps 45:12). The second line introduces "gifts" again. As in 18:23, this proverb simply acknowledges the value of gifts, especially in business and politics.

7 Effects of poverty. People avoid those who are poor. The first two lines are loosely synonymous. But the third line adds, "He pursues them with pleading." The last line of the verse is open to various translations, none of which is completely satisfactory. The basic meaning of the passage is fairly clear, however: superficial friends and relatives will abandon a poor person. The plight of Job captures such an abandonment.

8 Wisdom is profitable. One who chooses wisdom and understanding "loves his own soul" (i.e., has regard for his own interests) and "prospers" (lit., "finds good").

9 On perjury. Those who bear false witness will be punished. This proverb is the same as v.5, except that the last line changes to "will perish."

10 Inappropriate positions in life. Two thoughts here present unbearable conditions, the second being worse than the first. "It is not fitting for a fool to live in luxury." Of course, if the fool changed and earned it, that is a different story, but this verse is about a misfit. The second thought is a slave who takes command over princes (see 12:24; 17:2). In these reversals the fool only makes worse his bad qualities—boorishness, insensitivity, and lack of discipline—and the slave becomes arrogant and cruel. For other unbearable things, see 11:22; 17:7; 26:1; 30:21–23.

11 Nature of patience. The first line refers to a person who prudently avoids anger and patiently passes over an offense. Patience like this is "his glory" (lit., "his honor," signifying more the idea of beauty or adornment).

12 Emotions of a king. This proverb observes that a king has the power to terrify or to refresh. By the use of two similes, it contrasts the king's "rage" with his "pleasure" or "favor." The first simile, the roar of a lion, presents him at his most dangerous attitude (see 20:2; Am 3:4); the second portrays him as benevolent. For similar teachings see 16:14–15; 20:2; 28:15. For a picture of the ideal king, see 2Sa 23:3–4.

13 How to ruin a family. Folly and strife destroy a home. Two problems bring chaos to a family. The first is a foolish son (lit., "son of a fool," meaning a son who is a fool), and the second is a "quarrelsome wife." The foolish son brings "ruin" to the father (cf. 10:1; 17:21, 25), but the quarrelsome wife is merely annoying (cf. 27:15–16).

14 A prudent wife. A prudent wife, unlike property, is God's special gift. The verse contrasts wealth that can be inherited from a father with a "prudent" wife who is from the Lord. When a marriage turns out well, one should credit God (see also 18:22; 31:10–31).

15 Consequences of laziness. Those who are lazy waste time and lose money. "Laziness" brings on a "deep sleep" (GK 9554). The Hebrew word describes complete inactivity (see Ge 2:21; Jnh 1:5); here it probably signifies lethargy. This individual wastes time that is needed to provide for himself and his family. Parallel is the "shiftless man," who goes hungry.

16 Obeying instruction. Obedience to instruction is a safeguard of life. These "instructions" (GK 5184) may refer to the teaching of the sages or to God's law. If it refers to God's commandments, then there is a stronger guarantee of safety for life. The second line announces that the one who holds in contempt "his ways" will die. "His ways" can refer to the conduct of the individual or to the divine instruction. If the latter is the case, then the punishment is more certain (even if through the courts).

17 Rewards for charity. The Lord rewards those who are charitable. Those who are "kind" to the poor are actually lending to the Lord, and the Lord will repay or "reward" them for their deed. This promise of reward does not necessarily signify that they will get their money back; the rewards in Proverbs involve life and prosperity in general (cf. Mt 19:27–28).

18 Benefit of discipline. It is necessary to "discipline" (GK 3579) children to prevent their premature death. This verb includes both chastisement and instruction. Proverbs here and elsewhere teaches that refraining from discipline allows a child to grow up stupid or wicked and thereby may result in his or her death. The motivation for discipline is "hope," an excellent reason to keep at it. The clause in the second half of the verse literally reads, "Do not lift up your life to kill him," meaning not to make the kind of decisions that will lead to the child's death (allowing him or her to go astray through neglect).

19 Hot temper. The second line of this proverb presents the consequence of the action of the first. A hot-tempered person is constantly in trouble. "Pay the penalty" suggests paying a fine; so the trouble could be legal. In the second line the warning is given that if you save such people from their legal troubles, you will have to do it again and again. Unless they change, they will always need bailing out.

20 Acceptance of instruction. By accepting advice and discipline, one becomes wise. The vocabulary of this verse reminds the reader of the first nine chapters of Proverbs: "Listen to advice and accept instruction [lit., discipline]." This advice is in all probability the teachings of the sages that will make one wise. "In the end" there will be maturity from all the discipline, and there will be a steadfast perseverance in the path of life.

21 Sovereignty of God. The success of our "plans" depends on the will of God. Only those that God approves will succeed (see 16:1, 9); his counsel or "purpose" will stand. Humans are diverse and uncertain; God is absolutely wise and sure.

22 Loyalty. Loyal love is better than wealth. What is desired is "unfailing love" (GK 2876), that bond between members of the covenant. Covenanters were expected to be faithful in their words and deeds of kindness. The second line may present a logical inference from this: "a liar" would be without "unfailing love" entirely, and so poverty would be better than that character trait.

23 Safety and contentment in the fear of the Lord. Piety brings a life of contentment and safety. "Life" (GK 2644) is probably a

metonymy for all the blessings and prosperity in life. Its essential features are resting "content" and not being visited by calamity or "trouble." When one lives a life of piety, the Lord provides a quality of life that cannot be disrupted by such evil.

24 Nature of laziness. Some people are too lazy to eat. This humorous portrayal is certainly an exaggeration. It probably was meant more widely for anyone who starts a project but lacks the energy to complete it. The sluggard "buries" his hand in the dish and is too lazy to pull it out—even to feed himself (see also 26:15)!

25 Results of discipline. Discipline affects people differently. Three types of people are mentioned here: the "mocker" with a closed mind, the "simple" or simpleton with an empty mind, and the "discerning" with an open mind. The simpleton learns by observing punishment given to the mocker. Although the punishment will have no effect on the mocker, it should still be given; for the simpleton will learn what the mocker does not. But the discerning person will learn from verbal rebuke, even if it is painful truth. This is the more rational way.

26 Mistreatment of parents. One who abuses one's parents is a disgrace. The saying portrays this ingrate as a person who "robs his father" and "drives out his mother." Father/mother may be taken as a poetic word pair rather than as two ideas separating what is done to the father and then to the mother (see 10:1; 17:21; 23:24).

27 Rejection of discipline. The verse includes an admonition and its motivation (a result). The admonition uses irony: "Stop listening to instruction, my son." Of course, it means "Do not cease." The result of ceasing to listen is that the son "will stray from the words of knowledge."

28 Corrupt witnesses. When the wicked witness in court, they wilfully distort the facts. Such activity certainly "mocks" justice. The second line carries the thought further by saying that the "mouth of the wicked" (what they use to witness) "gulps down evil."

29 Certainty of retribution. Fools will be punished. "Judgments" may be rendered "penalties"; this parallels "beatings" closely.

Chapter 20

1 Effects of alcohol. The formal parallelism shows first the effects of intoxication and then makes an evaluation. The drinks are "wine" and "beer," made from grapes and grains (see Lev 10:9; Dt 14:26; Isa 28:7). These terms may be metonymies for those who drink them, or they may be personifications. In either case, the point is the conduct of the inebriated person—mocking and brawling. The excessive use of intoxicants excites drinkers to boisterous behavior and aggressive and belligerent attitudes; it confuses the senses so that they are out of control. The only evaluation possible is that whoever imbibes is unwise—it just is not sensible to drink to excess. Moreover, given the ease with which one may make a habit of this, it is wise to avoid alcohol entirely. In the OT the use of alcohol was not prohibited; in fact, it was regularly used at festivals and celebrations. But intoxication was considered out of bounds for a member of the covenant community (see 23:20–21, 29–35; 31:4–7).

2 Emotions of a king. It is unsafe to provoke the anger of a king, who cannot be treated like other people. The "wrath" of a king is compared to a lion's roar, indicating imminent judgment. Anyone who angers a king "forfeits" (lit., "misses" or "sins against"; GK 2627) his life. The simple idea is that one would do well to stay away from any angry person (see also 16:14; 19:12).

3 Avoiding strife. Honorable people find ways to avoid strife. A contrast is presented here between avoiding "strife" and jumping at a chance for a "quarrel" (includes the idea of snarling like a dog). The former is the way of honor and dignity; the latter, the manner of a "fool." One cannot avoid strife entirely but should avoid every unnecessary confrontation (see also 17:14, 28; 18:2).

4 Results of laziness. A farmer who is too lazy to plant at the right time will find no harvest. The first line describes the lazy man or "sluggard" who does not plant in the autumn. The right time for planting was the rainy season (see Ge 8:22). It was cold, wet, and unpleasant. Perhaps such discomfort was his excuse. The effect is that at harvest time, when he "looks" (lit., "asks"), there is "nothing." Since he actually looks for some harvest, the verse suggests that he did plant but

perhaps at the wrong time or halfheartedly (contrast Ps 126:5–6). This character is typical of all who want excellence without putting forth the effort.

5 Discerning motives. Those who are wise can discern the motives of the heart. "Deep waters" probably means that one's motives are difficult to "fathom"—it takes a counselor with "understanding" to "draw them out." The line shows how important good counseling is.

6 Faithful love. It is rare to find a truly faithful friend. A contrast is offered here between many who claim to have faithful love and the rarity of one who actually has it. Many people profess "unfailing love" (GK 2987), but such professions are often hollow. The shift to "faithful" (GK 574) in the second clause makes this clear and captures the truth—it is rare to find one on whom you can actually depend.

7 Heritage of integrity. The integrity of parents extends to the lives of their children. Two terms portray this integrity: "righteous" (GK 7404) introduces the person as a member of the believing community who strives to live according to God's standards, and "blameless" (GK 9448) describes that person's lifestyle. In other words, this proverb describes a parent who believes in the Lord and lives out the claims of his or her faith. The second clause anticipates a blessing on the children. In God's economy the nature and actions of parents have an effect on children (Ex 20:4–6); they reap the benefits (see 14:26).

8 Justice necessary for a king. The righteous king discerns right from wrong. The king in the ancient world was a judge, whose counsel stood (see 2Sa 15:2–4; 1Ki 3:28; Ps 72:4; Isa 11:3–4). Justice is to be the basis of his administration; the image of winnowing shows that he removes evil from his realm (see Ps 101). The verse applies to any person in authority, but certainly the principle stands that a just government roots out the evils of society. Unfortunately, no government has ever lived up to this ideal.

9 Sinless conduct. No one can claim to be "pure" in thought and deed. There is a development in the second part of this verse. To claim to have kept the heart "pure" is to say that all decisions and motives are faultless; to claim "I am clean" is to say that moral perfection has been attained and that one is therefore acceptable to God ("clean" in the Levitical laws of purification means "purged of all sin"). Many passages affirm the inevitability of our sinfulness (Ge 6:5; 1Ki 8:46; Ps 143:2), and Ps 51:7 teaches that one can claim to be pure only if made pure by divine forgiveness. This proverb should bring us to personal humility and engender in us an understanding of the failures of others.

10 Honesty in business. The Lord detests dishonesty in business. See v.23 and 11:1, which are based on Dt 25:13–16.

11 Righteousness, displayed in actions. Righteous conduct reveals righteous character. The character of a "child" (GK 5853, a younger boy) can be recognized by his actions. Parents can recognize certain traits in a child's conduct. If they are pure and upright, they can cultivate this; if they are not, they must try to develop it through teaching, disciplining, and personal example.

12 Creation of human nature. The Lord has prepared people with the capacity to see and hear. By usage hearing also means obeying (see 1Sa 15:22; Pr 15:31; 25:12) and seeing also means perceiving or understanding (see Isa 6:9–10). The verse not only credits the Lord with creating these senses but reminds everyone of their spiritual use in God's service.

13 Diligence rewarded. Diligence leads to prosperity. The verse contrasts the ideas of loving sleep and staying awake, as well as their results of growing poor and being satisfied. Just as "sleep" can represent slothfulness, so opening the eyes and staying awake can represent vigorous, active conduct (see also 6:9–11; 19:15).

14 Honesty in business. Some people falsely appraise a deal to gain a bargain. This humorous but realistic proverb presents a buyer who complains about how bad the deal is for him, and then goes away bragging about it. This may simply reflect normal procedure in a world where haggling for prices was common, but it may also be a warning to the inexperienced on how things are done; it possibly also evaluates this procedure as a questionable business practice. Shrewdness is

one thing, but deceitful misrepresentation in order to buy under value becomes unethical.

15 Wise words. It is rare to find someone who speaks knowledgeably; "gold" and "rubies" are far more common. "Lips that speak knowledge" means "lips that impart knowledge," i.e., wise speech.

16 Fulfilled obligations. People should be held to their obligations. A person who foolishly becomes responsible for another person's debts should have to keep his word. Taking the garment was the way of holding someone responsible to pay debts. The "one" for whom this person took responsibility is called "a stranger"—probably meaning other members of society.

17 Effects of dishonesty. Good things acquired dishonestly will not bring satisfaction. "Food gained by fraud" means anything obtained through dishonest means; it appears to "taste sweet." The imagery is advanced in the second line: "he ends up with a mouth full of gravel" (i.e., a mass of small particles; see Job 20:14–15; La 3:16).

18 Accepting sound advice. Effective plans incorporate sound advice. This verse presents a continuous idea of first making plans and then waging the war. Sound "advice" and "guidance" are indispensable to the success of the mission. Many have offered figurative interpretations of "war" as life struggles, litigation, or even evil inclinations; but there is no justification for this—it likely describes preparation for going to war, and in that there is wisdom in the consensus of leaders (see 24:6).

19 On gossip. The first line pictures the gossip as one who goes about revealing secrets, and the second line warns against associating with those who are always ready to talk. If they are willing to talk to you about others, they will be willing to talk to others about you. The less contact you have with a gossip, the better off you will be.

20 Cursing parents. Under the law (Ex 21:17; Lev 20:9; Dt 27:16), whoever cursed one's parents was cursed with death. That judgment seems to be caught poetically in this single sentence proverb. Cursing (GK 7837) means treating one's parents lightly or contemptuously. The punishment is that "his lamp will be snuffed out," and he will be left in pitch darkness. The lamp is metaphorical for the life; for the lamp to go out means death (13:9) and possibly also removal of posterity. In actual practice this may have been a social punishment only, that such a person be considered as one who is dead.

21 Prosperity unsatisfying. The statement that prosperity gained suddenly will not be blessed seems rather general. The implication is that what is "quickly gained" (GK 987) is either unlawful or unrighteous. This verb describes a hurried or hastened activity; perhaps a wayward son seized the inheritance (cf. Lk 15:12) or even drove out his parents (cf. Pr 19:26). In either case divine justice is at work—this enterprise "will not be blessed"; rather than prosper, it will probably be wasted.

22 Retribution is God's work. Leave retribution to the Lord; he will bring about a just deliverance. The verse uses two imperatives to make its point. The righteous should not take vengeance on evil, for only God can repay evil justly (cf. Ro 12:19–20). Rather, the righteous must "wait" on the Lord; this involves belief in and reliance on him. The work of the Lord here focuses on the positive side—he is a deliverer rather than an avenger, although to "deliver" the righteous involves judgment on the wicked.

23 Honesty in business. The Lord detests dishonesty in business (see also v.10; 11:1).

24 Divine providence. God's control of our lives is beyond human comprehension. This proverb asks a rhetorical question regarding

Honesty in business required standard weights (20:10. 23), such as these stones. Courtesy Ilan Sztulman of the Tel Miqne-Ekron Excavations.

this topic: since the steps of a mighty person are from the Lord—how, then, can anyone discern or "understand" his way? How can we delude ourselves into thinking that we do not need the Lord when even a strong person's activities are divinely prepared? As an example, see Ge 50:20; see also Pr 3:6 for the proper advice in view of this truth.

25 Rash vows. This warning about making a rash vow addresses what was a common problem. Declaring something sacred (as in Mk 7:11) can lead a person into financial difficulties (Lev 27 explains that Israelites could buy themselves out of rash vows—it was expensive). After making a vow, one must consider to fulfill it. Too many people make promises under the inspiration of the hour, only later to realize that they have strapped themselves; they then try to go back on their word.

26 Removing wickedness through justice. A wise king discerns evil and purges his kingdom of the wicked. This proverb draws on the image of winnowing to explain how the king removes evil from his empire. The metaphor implies that the king can identify and rightly judge evildoers. The figure of driving the wheel over them represents a threshing process; the sharp iron wheels of the threshing cart easily serve the purpose (cf. Isa 28:27–28).

27 Conscience that searches motives. God provides everyone with a spirit that can evaluate actions and motives. The Hebrew literally says that the "breath" is the lamp of the Lord (see NIV note—the NIV interprets it differently and supplies "searches"). The "breath" (or "spirit"; GK 5972) is that inner spiritual part of human life that was inbreathed at Creation (Ge 2:7) and that constitutes humans as spiritual beings with moral, intellectual, and spiritual capacities. This spiritual nature includes the capacity to know and please God—it serves as the functioning conscience (the metaphor of "lamp"). This point is further developed in the second part; the searching makes it possible for people to know themselves. If one's spiritual life is functioning properly (i.e., yielded to God through salvation and controlled by his word [Heb 4:12]), then there should be increasingly less self-deception or indifference to righteousness.

28 Stability in government. Faithful covenant-love brings stability in society. The parallel ideas stress the security of the king's administration. The first line uses "love and faithfulness [lit., truth]," two terms that often form a hendiadys to express reliable love. "Love" (GK 2876) is singled out of this couplet to form the parallel idea that the throne is secure. These are covenant terms. In the Davidic covenant (cf. 2Sa 7:11–16) God promised not to take his covenant love from the king (cf. v.15) but to make his house stable and secure ("will endure," v.16). The two ideas are reiterated in Ps 89:19–37, which expresses the covenant in poetry. It is the Lord and his faithfulness to his covenant that ultimately makes the empire secure, though the enjoyment of divine protection requires the king to rule with loyalty to the covenant.

29 Strength and honor. Both youth and old age have their glory. This little observation reminds us that there are different commendations in life. For young men it is strength; for old men it is gray hair, which symbolizes dignity, wisdom, and honor. This verse must be taken in the context of ancient Israel and not modern civilization, which often has little respect for the elderly. In Israelite society, the elderly were the sages who offered their wisdom of experience to the people.

30 Spiritual value of discipline. Physical punishment may prove spiritually valuable. Loosely synonymous, the two clauses focus on corporal punishment. These "cleanse" the soul of evil. Though other proverbs have explained that certain people will never learn from such discipline, in general this saying is true.

Chapter 21

1 Sovereignty of God. A king's decisions are controlled by God. The first line affirms that the decisions ("heart") of the king are under the Lord's control ("in the hand"), and the second explains that he directs the king as he pleases. As a farmer channels the water where he wants and regulates its flow, so does the Lord with the king. No human ruler, then, is supreme; or, to put it another way, the Lord is truly the King of kings. Scripture offers many examples (Ezr 7:21; Isa 10:6–7; 41:2–4; Da 2:21; Jn 19:11).

2 Divine knowledge. The Lord evaluates our motives and not merely our actions. This verse reiterates the point that we may think we know ourselves; but the Lord knows our hearts, and his knowledge is evaluative (see also 16:2).

3 Priority of righteousness. The Lord requires righteousness before religious service. Doing "what is right and just" is more acceptable to the Lord than sacrifice (see 15:8; 21:29; 1Sa 15:22; Ps 40:6–8; Isa 1:11–17; et al.). It does not teach that ritual acts of worship are to be avoided; rather, it stresses that religious acts are valueless without righteous living.

4 On pride. Arrogant pride is sin. The Hebrew reads literally, "Haughty eyes and a proud heart, the tillage of the wicked is sin." What is "tillage"? This figure indicates that the product of the wicked is sin. Thus also pride and arrogance are products of the wicked. This verse portrays pride as sin.

5 Patient planning brings prosperity. This verse exhorts industriousness. Patience and planning lead to prosperity. The "plans of the diligent" lead to profit, while "haste" often leads to poverty. The text here warns about the danger of hasty shortcuts (see also 10:4 and 28:20).

6 Prosperity by fraud. A fortune gained by fraudulent means will be a fleeting treasure. The subject of this proverb concerns a "fortune" made by a "lying" tongue. Two ideas comprise the predicate: "fleeting vapor" and "deadly snare." It is as if the treasure disappears into thin air. The second idea, "deadly snare" (lit., "snares of death"; see also Ps 18:5), suggests a crime. In other words, ill-gotten gain is a fleeting pleasure and a crime for which punishment is prepared.

7 Just retribution. The wicked will be destroyed in their own devices. It is their "violence" that destroys them—it "drags them away," probably to more sin, but ultimately to their punishment. But they are not passive victims of their crimes—"they refuse" to do justice. In the final analysis they can blame only themselves, for they have chosen to persist in evil rather than do what is right.

8 Righteousness revealed in works. Righteous behavior reveals righteous character.

The first clause asserts that it is also true that sinful acts betray the wicked.

9 Peaceful family relationships. Simplicity with peace is better than prosperity with strife. The specific situation presented is sharing a house with a quarrelsome wife; it would be better to live on the corner of the roof. The reference is probably to a little guest room built on the roof (see 1Ki 17:19; 2Ki 4:10). It may be cramped and lonely—but peaceful in avoiding strife.

10 Wicked character traits. The wicked pursue evil, not mercy (see also 4:16; 10:23; 12:10; Isa 1:16–17). Those who live to satisfy their craving for evil think only of themselves. It is the propensity for evil that constitutes them as "wicked."

11 Effect of discipline. How mature one is determines how easily one learns. The contrast is between the wise and the simple; the former learns by instruction, the latter by example. This instruction of the wise not only causes them to know but gives insight into the issues of life; they never stop learning. By contrast the "mocker" is unteachable. Nevertheless, he should be punished, because the "simple" will "gain wisdom" through seeing that punishment (see also 19:25).

12 Certainty of judgment. Righteousness will be satisfied when the wicked are punished. There are two ways that this proverb can be taken. The easiest interpretation is to take "righteousness" to refer to God, "The Righteous One." God observes the house of the wicked and then hurls them to ruin (see 22:12). But Proverbs nowhere else refers to God in this way. The other interpretation takes "righteousness" to refer to a "righteous man" (cf. NIV note), presumably a judge or ruler, who, although he may be kindly disposed to the family of the wicked, is obliged to condemn them.

13 Unmerciful people. Those who show no mercy will not obtain mercy. Measure for measure, justice is expressed by this cause and effect statement: Those who shut their ears from the cry of the poor (i.e., refuse to help) will not be listened to when they cry out for help. So justice is meted out for the omission of a commandment as well as for evil acts (see the story of the rich man and Lazarus in Lk 16:19–31).

14 Injustice through bribery. Bribes can effectively pacify an angry person. The two clauses are synonymous; the first uses the more neutral word "gift" and the second the word "bribe." This proverb does not condemn or condone; it merely observes the effectiveness of the practice.

15 Effects of justice. How people respond to justice reveals their character. The occasion—"When justice is done"—can refer specifically to a legal decision or to doing right in general. The point is that people who are law-abiding citizens are pleased with justice; those who are not are terrified by it, tend to ridicule it, and try to get around it in some way. But by means of "terror" the wicked may be shaken into reality when justice is carried out.

16 Importance of wisdom. Those who abandon the way of wisdom inevitably ruin their lives. The subject matter is one who wanders away from the "path of understanding" or prudence, i.e., one who does not live according to the knowledge, discipline, and insight of wisdom. This person "comes to rest" (better, "to dwell") in the "company of the shades" (NIV, "dead"). Physical death is once again presented as the punishment for folly, which is sin. The wicked who follow the broad way that leads to destruction find themselves among the dead (Mt 7:13–14).

17 Cost of pleasure. Living a life of self-indulgent pleasure leads to poverty. "Joy" (NIV, "pleasure"; GK 5833) represents the effect of the good life; "wine and oil" represent the cause for joy. "Oil" signifies the anointing that goes with the luxurious life (see Pss 23:5; 104:15; Am 6:6). There is nothing wrong with joy or with enjoying the finer things in life. The "love" portrayed here must be excessive or uncontrolled, because it brings one to poverty. Perhaps other responsibilities are being neglected or the people are trying to live above their means.

18 Just judgment. In what way are the wicked a "ransom" for the righteous? "Ransom" (GK 4111) normally refers to the price paid to free a prisoner. The saying is either a general statement or an ideal that in calamity the righteous escape but the wicked perish in their stead (e.g., Haman in the book of Esther). We must think that when God punishes a community, it is the bad, not the good, that he is directing his anger against. Believers have a wholehearted trust in the justice of God (see Ge 18:23–25).

19 Peaceful family relations. Being alone is preferable to enduring domestic strife. This verse reiterates the theme of v.9 (see also 25:24), with one change—"a desert," which would be sparsely settled and quiet. These verses surely advise one to be careful in choosing a marriage partner and then to be diligent in cultivating the proper graces to make the marriage enjoyable.

20 Frugality of wisdom. This verse contrasts the wise person and the fool. With keen foresight and appropriate frugality, the wise prepare for the future. In their houses are "precious treasure and oil" (NIV, "choice food and oil"), but the fool "devours" it. In other words, the wise gain wealth but fools squander it.

21 Rewards of righteousness. Virtue will be rewarded. In fact, the idea may be that virtue has its own rewards. "Righteousness" and "love" (GK 2876) depict the lifestyle of the faithful covenant-believer who is pleasing to God and a blessing to others. Whoever pursues righteousness will be filled with "life, prosperity and honor" (cf. Mt 5:6; 6:33).

22 Wisdom greater than strength. This proverb uses a military scene to describe the superiority of wisdom. It tells how the wise can scale the walls of the city of the "mighty" and pull down their trusted stronghold. In a war victory is credited not so much to the infantry as to the tactician, the general who plans the attack. Brilliant strategy wins wars, even over apparently insuperable odds (see also Pr 24:5–6; Ecc 9:13–16; cf. 2Co 10:4, which explains that wisdom from above is necessary for spiritual victory).

23 Controlled speech. People who control what they say are more likely to avoid trouble than those who speak freely. The "calamity" may refer to social and legal difficulties into which careless talk might bring someone (see 13:3; 18:21). Therefore one should say only what is true, helpful, pleasant, and kind and avoid what is false, destructive, painful, and damaging to others.

24 On pride. These two lines portray the godless attitude and the scornful arrogance of

the "mocker." He is "proud" and "arrogant," acting with "overweening pride." Pride may refer to the refusal to submit to the Lord or describe the refusal to learn from wisdom. While the latter may be in view here, the two are not unrelated.

25 Result of laziness. The lazy come to ruin because they want the easy way out. The "sluggard's craving" must be coupled with "his hands refuse to work" to understand the point. Living in a world of wishful thinking and not working will bring ruin ("will be the death of him" is used hyperbolically).

26 Generosity reveals righteousness. This verse has been placed with the preceding because of the literary connection of the word "crave"—"he craves for more." The one who craves is contrasted with the righteous who give generously. One thinks of the contrast between Abram and Lot in Ge 13; Lot chose the more desirable land for himself, but Abram gave Lot his preference. To be generous in that way requires walking by faith and not by sight.

27 Unacceptable worship. God abhors worship without righteousness. The verse affirms that the "sacrifice" of the wicked is an abomination to the Lord and then intensifies the idea ("how much more") by referring to "evil intent" with the sacrifice. Hypocritical worship is bad enough; worship with evil intent is deplorable. God does not want acts of worship without repentance; he detests them from someone still bent on wickedness, who thinks a sacrifice will buy continued acceptance with God. God first requires of the worshiper true repentance and resolution to live righteously.

28 True and false speech. False witnesses will be discredited and destroyed. The first line affirms that a "false witness will perish," meaning either that his testimony will be destroyed or that he will be punished. The second line literally says, "A man who listens shall speak forever." "A man who listens" contrasts with the false witness of the preceding line and likely describes a witness who knows and understands what the truth is.

29 Genuine righteousness. Those who are truly righteous cultivate a consistent lifestyle that pleases God, in contrast to the wicked, who put up a "bold front." The image of the hardened face (i.e., "bold front") reflects a hardened heart; it portrays one who holds the opinions and views of others in contempt (see Isa 48:4; Jer 5:3; Eze 3:7).

30–31 Sovereignty of God. Human "wisdom," "insight," and "counsel" (NIV, "plan") must conform to God's will to be successful. If these qualities are in defiance of God, they cannot succeed; for human wisdom is nothing in comparison to the wisdom of God (see Job 5:12–13; also Isa 40:13–14). The contrast in v.31 is between the plans and efforts for the battle and the true acknowledgment of the source of victory—the Lord (see Pss 20:7; 33:17).

Chapter 22

1 Good reputation. The verse is not disparaging wealth; it is merely noting that a good reputation is worth more than silver or gold. Only a good name is to be desired, for it brings praise, influence, and prosperity. "To be esteemed" (GK 2834) means "good favor," i.e., one well thought of. A good reputation excels other blessings in life.

2 Sovereignty of God. Regardless of status in life, all are equally God's creation. The rich and the poor live side by side in this life, and both are part of the order of God's creation. People often forget this and make value judgments; they would do well to treat all people with respect, for God can as easily reduce the rich as raise the poor.

3 Avoiding trouble. Those who are "prudent" (GK 6874) avoid the dangers of life. They know where the pitfalls are, and they are wary. They are the product of training in wisdom and discipline, for one of the purposes of this book was to make the naive wary (see 1:4). The simple are unwary, uncritical, and credulous; they are not equipped to survive in this world and so "suffer" (GK 6740; this word describes a fine in 17:26 and 19:19; here it is more general; see 27:12).

4 Reward of piety. God rewards reverential piety. This verse lists two spiritual qualifications (humility and fear) and three rewards (wealth, honor, and life). "Humility" (GK 6708) here has the religious sense of piety and so fits well with "the fear of the LORD." For the idea of life as the product of piety, see 21:21; for the reward, see 3:2, 16.

5 Security through wisdom. Those who have the discipline of wisdom avoid life's dangers. The "wicked" are on a dangerous path, covered with "thorns and snares." In contrast, the wise and prudent guard their lives and avoid the trap.

6 Child training. Proper training of children will endure throughout their lives. The second clause here provides the result of the first. The imperative, "train" (GK 2852), includes the idea of "dedicate," and so the training should be with purpose. The NEB captures the point of early instruction: "Start a boy on the right road," i.e., "in the way he should go." There is a standard of life to which children should adhere. Of course, they would have to be young enough when change for the better is still possible. The consequence is that when they are old, they will not depart from it.

In recent years it has become popular to interpret this verse to mean that the training should be according to the child's way. That is, the wise parent will discern the natural bent of the individual child and train him or her accordingly. This may be a practical and useful idea, but it is not likely what this proverb had in mind. In Proverbs there are only two "ways" a child can go, the way of the wise and the righteous or the way of the fool and the wicked.

7 Effects of poverty. Poverty makes people dependent on others. The poor and borrowers become subservient to the rich. The verse may be referring to the apparently common practice of Israelites selling themselves into slavery to pay off debts (see Ex 21:2–7). It is not appreciably different from the modern debtor who is working to pay off bills.

8 Certainty of punishment. God will surely destroy the power of the wicked. The second clause carries the idea further, revealing how it works: "The rod of his fury will be destroyed." The rod represents the wicked person's power to do evil. In reaping trouble, this fellow will no longer be able to unleash his fury.

9 Nature of generosity. There is a reward for being generous to the poor. Such people have a benevolent disposition, keen social conscience, and deep concern for the poor. The irony is that because they are not prisoners of their selfish desires, they achieve the highest degree of self-fulfillment.

10 Source of strife. Mockers cause quarrels and strife. This proverb advises us to expel them. One can think of hecklers who are present only to disrupt a meeting; before serious discussions can begin, they should be removed.

11 Honest and graceful speech. Honest and gracious speech is highly respected. This verse is not easy to understand. The simplest interpretation is that someone who is honest and gracious will be welcomed in the courts of the palace (cf. 16:13).

12 Sovereignty of God. This proverb contrasts how God deals with truth and error. He "frustrates" the words of the "traitor" (NIV, "unfaithful"); but he keeps "watch over knowledge." The point is clear enough—the Lord acts to vindicate the truth.

13 Excuses of laziness. Lazy people make absurd excuses for not working. The verse humorously portrays them as not going out because they might be eaten by a lion in the streets (cf. 26:13)!

14 Divine judgment. Divine judgment brings ruin on the adulterer. The topic is the "mouth of an adulteress," perhaps a reference to her seductive speech (see 2:16–22; 5; 7). It is described as a "deep pit" where the guilty fall under God's judgment. The pit is like the hunter's snare, difficult to escape. So to succumb to the adulteress—or to any such folly—is both a sin and its punishment.

15 Parental discipline. Discipline will remove a child's bent to folly. A general contrast first explains that "folly" (GK 222) is in the child and then instructs how to get rid of it—"the rod of discipline." The child is morally immature; the training must suppress folly and develop potential (cf. 13:24; 23:13, 16; 29:15).

16 On extortion and bribery. Both oppressing the lowly by extortion and giving to the rich as bribery are folly and result in poverty. The first is an immoral act that God will punish and the second is a waste of money. Perhaps the verse is simply observing that it is easy to oppress the poor for gain, but it is a waste of money to try to buy a patron.

IV. The Sayings of the Wise (22:17–24:34)

A. Thirty Precepts of the Sages (22:17–24:22)

Introductory call to attention (22:17–21)

A new collection of sayings begins here, forming the fourth section of the book. This collection is not like that of 1:1–9:18; here the introductory material is more personal than 1:1–7 and the style differs, showing great similarity to the Instructions of Amenemope in Egypt (see the introduction).

17–21 In the introductory call to attention, the sage urges greater trust in the Lord and promises solid teachings that will prove reliable. This extended introduction reminds us that the wise sayings are not curiosity pieces; they are revelation, and revelation demands a response. The call is laid out with the exhortation to learn and to pass on the teaching, followed by three motivations: (1) there will be a pleasing store of wisdom; (2) there will be a deeper trust in the Lord—a distinctively Israelite aspect of wisdom literature; and (3) it will build reliability—the readers will grasp the truth and see themselves as special envoys to keep wisdom in their heart and on their lips.

1. Treatment of the poor (22:22–23)

22–23 This passage warns people not to oppress the poor; they are not to be exploited or crushed. The oppression pictured here may be in bounds legally, but it is out of bounds morally (e.g., similar to modern business ethics). The motivation is that the Lord will plead or "take up their case" and turn the plundering back on the guilty. The Lord will champion the defenseless.

2. Dangerous associations (22:24–25)

24–25 The warning is to avoid associating with a hothead because his influence could prove fatal (see also 1:10–19; 14:17, 29; 15:1). The "one easily angered" (lit., "a man of heat," i.e., "a hot-tempered man") is denounced primarily because such conduct is injurious, although the implication is also that it is morally bad.

3. Rash vows (22:26–27)

26–27 If people foolishly pledge what they have, they could lose it all (see 6:1–5; 11:15;

17:18; 20:16). The risk is that if someone lacks the means to pay, his creditors may take his bed, i.e., his last possession (cf. our expressions "the shirt off his back" or "the kitchen sink"). "Bed" may be a metonymy for the garment that covers the bed (cf. Ex 22:26).

4. Respect for property (22:28)

28 The sage warns against appropriating someone else's property. Removing an "ancient boundary" was always an issue; the general teaching is that ancient traditions, if right, were to be preserved. But violations were frequent (see Dt 19:14; 27:17; 1Ki 21:16–19; Isa 5:8; Hos 5:10). The boundaries were sacred because God owned the land and had given it to the fathers as their inheritance; to extend one's land at another's expense was a major violation of covenant and oath.

5. Benefits of skill (22:29)

29 Skill earns recognition and reward of advancement. The saying anticipates that persons "skilled" in their work will serve kings. These people might be scribes or officials; but the description would apply to all craftsmen. Such will find the proper setting where their skill will be appreciated and not be wasted on an ignoramus.

6. Caution before rulers (23:1–3)

1–3 This passage warns against overindulging in the ruler's food, because that could ruin one's chances for advancement. The expression "put a knife to your throat" means "curb your appetite" or "control yourself" (like "bite your tongue"). The reason is that the ruler's food may be "deceptive" (GK 3942)—it is not what it seems. Thus one should not indulge in his impressive feast— the ruler wants something from you or is observing you.

7. Fleeting wealth (23:4–5)

4–5 People should not wear themselves out trying to get rich, because riches disappear quickly. In the ancient world the figure of a bird flying off symbolized fleeting wealth. It is therefore folly to be a slave to it (see also Lk 12:20; 1Ti 6:7–10).

8. Unpleasant hospitality (23:6–8)

6–8 It would be a mistake to accept hospitality from "a stingy person" (lit., "an evil eye"), for his lack of sincerity will make the evening unpleasant. This miser (see 28:22) is ill-mannered and inhospitable; he is up to no good (contrast the "bountiful eye" in 22:9 [NIV, "generous man"]). Eating and drinking with him will be irritating and disgusting.

9. Wisdom wasted on a fool (23:9)

9 A "fool" despises wisdom; so it is a waste of time to try to teach him. A fool rejects discipline and instruction, often scorning the teacher who tries to change him.

10. Respect property (23:10–11)

10–11 Once again the instruction warns against removing a boundary stone and encroaching on the property of the defenseless (see 22:22–23, 28). Their "Defender" is strong and will plead their cause. The Redeemer/Avenger was usually a powerful relative who would champion the rights of the defenseless; but if there was no human defender, God would take up their cause (see Ge 48:16; Ex 6:6; Job 19:25; Isa 41–63).

Renewed call to attention (23:12)

12 The disciple is to apply his heart to discipline and listen carefully to knowledge. This introductory verse may have been added later, based on 22:17.

11. Necessity of discipline (23:13–14)

13–14 The sage instructs the continued use of "discipline" (GK 4592), for the one punished will not die. Discipline helps children to live a full life; if they die (prematurely), it would be a consequence of not being trained. In Proverbs such a death might be moral and social as well as physical.

12. Wise and joyful speech (23:15–16)

15–16 Children bring joy to their parents when they make wise choices. The wise "heart" means one makes wise choices; the "right" speech refers to direct and honest speech—there is no discrepancy between the speech and the intentions. One does not use deception or speak ambiguously to darken counsel.

13. Fear the Lord (23:17–18)

17–18 We must always be "zealous" for the fear of the Lord and not be envious of sinners. The contrast is between right and wrong envy; the one is spiritual exercise, the other a disease. The difficulty is that the sinful world seems more attractive. Thus the motivation provided is that the future belongs to the righteous.

Renewed call to attention (23:19)

19 The disciple is to listen, be wise, and keep his decisions right (cf. 22:17; 23:12). For a fuller treatment, see 4:25–27.

14. Poor associations (23:20–21)

20–21 Those who associate with "drunkards" and "gluttons" will become poor. These two represent the epitome of the lack of discipline. Excessive eating and drinking are usually symptoms of deeper problems; today, we usually focus more on the drinking because it is a dangerous social problem with far-reaching consequences.

15. Honoring parents (23:22)

22 Because of our parents' position and experience, their wise counsel should be heeded. The idea of honoring them (cf. Ex 20:12) takes on the precise nuance of listening to instructions.

16. Wisdom's estimation (23:23–25)

23–25 We should acquire truth and gain wisdom, discipline, and understanding—this sort of life pleases God and brings joy to parents. Getting truth means acquiring training in the truth, and gaining understanding means developing the perception and practical knowledge of the truth.

17. Following advice (23:26–28)

26–28 It is imperative to follow the teacher's warnings about temptation because Dame Folly is lurking. The teacher calls for the pupil to imitate him and shun the temptress. The passage portrays two types of loose women: unmarried ("prostitute") and married ("wayward wife"). In either case there is danger, for their way is a "pit" (GK 8757), the gateway to Sheol; and those who enter are as good as dead. But the danger is active—"like a bandit she lies in wait" (see 7:12) and multiplies the unfaithful among men.

18. Excessive drinking (23:29–35)

29–35 One should avoid the temptation to excessive drinking, for it leads to trouble when the senses are dulled. The sage gives a vivid picture of the one who drinks too much: he raves on and on, picks quarrels and fights, poisons his system with alcohol, gets bloodshot eyes, loses control, is confused, is unable to speak clearly, imagines things, and is insensitive to pain. While alcoholism is a medical problem, it is also a moral problem because it involves choices and brings danger to other people.

19. Evil associations (24:1–2)

1–2 One should not envy or desire the company of evil people, for they are obsessed with violence (see also 1:10–19; 3:31; 23:17).

20. Practicality of wisdom (24:3–4)

3–4 The use of wisdom is essential for domestic enterprises. In 9:1 wisdom is personified as a woman who builds a house, but here the emphasis is primarily on the building—it is a sign of security and prosperity. One can make a secondary application to building a family (cf. Ps 127). After all, if it takes wisdom to build a house, it also takes wisdom to build a household.

21. Wisdom is greater than strength (24:5–6)

5–6 Wise counsel is necessary for war. The point is that for victory strategy is more important than strength—but that strategy must be wise (see also 11:14; 20:18; 21:22).

22. Fools (24:7)

7 Fools cannot obtain wisdom. The verse portrays a fool out of his element: in a serious moment in the gathering of the community, he does not even open his mouth. Wisdom is beyond the ability of the "fool."

23. Disapproval of evil people (24:8–9)

8–9 The general public disapproves of wicked people who plot evil things. The picture of the wicked is graphic: they devise evil and are schemers, sinners, and scorners. The word translated "schemes" (GK 2365) elsewhere describes outrageous and lewd schemes (see Lev 18:17; Jdg 20:6). The "schemer" is a cold, calculating person. This type of person flouts all morality, and sooner or later the public will have had enough of them. The only way out for such wickedness is repentance and forgiveness.

24. Test of adversity (24:10)

10 How well one does under adverse conditions reveals how strong that person is. You never know your strength until you are put into situations that demand much from you. Of course, a weak person will plead adverse conditions in order to quit.

25. Preservation of life (24:11–12)

11–12 God holds us responsible for rescuing those who are in mortal danger. The use of "death" and "slaughter" seems rather strong in this passage; one might expect the verse to stress the need to rescue through teaching those who by their vice or imprudence are hastening toward destruction. The references may be general (i.e., to any who are in mortal danger) or specific (i.e., to those who are convicted). If the latter is meant, the sage is saying not to abandon the convicted in prison, for they need all the help they can get. The general application includes any who are in mortal danger, through disease, hunger, war—we cannot dodge responsibility, even by ignorance.

26. Future of wisdom (24:13–14)

13–14 One should develop wisdom because it has a profitable future. This proverb draws on the image of honey; its health-giving properties make a good analogy to wisdom. While the literal instruction is to eat and enjoy honey, the point is to know wisdom, for wisdom will have a long future to it.

27. Treatment of the righteous (24:15–16)

15–16 It is futile and self-defeating to mistreat God's people, for they triumph—the wicked do not! The warning is against attacking the righteous; to attack them is to attack God and his program, and that will fail (see Mt 16:18). The consequence, and thus the motivation, is that if the righteous suffer misfortune any number of times (= "seven times"), they will rise again; for virtue triumphs in the end. Conversely, the wicked will not survive—without God they have no power to rise from misfortune.

28. Misfortune of enemy (24:17–18)

17–18 It is dishonoring to God for us to rejoice over the misfortune of our enemies (these are personal enemies; the imprecatory psalms for the enemies of God and his program provide a different set of circumstances). The prohibitions "Do not gloat" and "do not . . . rejoice" extend even to the inner satisfaction (the "heart") at the calamity of the wicked; such people are still the image of God. The motivation for this instruction is the fear of the Lord's displeasure: God might even take pity on them! It is the property of God to judge, and it must not be taken lightly or personalized. God's judgment should strike a note of fear in the hearts of everyone (see Lev 19:17–18; Mt 5:44). So if we want God to continue his anger on the wicked, we better not gloat.

29. Envying the wicked (24:19–20)

19–20 It is foolish to envy the wicked, because they are doomed (see 3:31; 23:17–18; 24:1–2). Their lives ("lamp") will be suddenly "snuffed out."

30. Fearing God and the king (24:21–22)

21–22 People should fear both God and the government, for both punish rebels. The positive instruction is followed by the warning not to join (lit., "not get mixed-up with") "the rebellious" (lit., "people who change," i.e., political agitators; GK 9101). Verse 21a is used in 1Pe 2:17, and v.22 is used in Ro 13:4. The reward for living in peace under God in the world is to escape the calamities that will fall on the rebellious.

B. Further Sayings of the Wise (24:23–34)

23–25 Partiality in judgment. These verses contain several ethical teachings for judges: "To show partiality" is not right; calling the "guilty" (lit., "the wicked") "innocent" (lit., "righteous") will bring strong denunciation; but "those who convict the guilty" will be richly blessed. All these sayings set the standard that righteousness and evil be clearly distinguished by the courts (see 18:5; Lev 19:15; Dt 16:19).

26 Truthfulness. A truthful answer is the mark of friendship. The symbol of specifically kissing on the lips is mentioned only here in the Bible; it signifies that friendship is characterized by truth (cf. Ro 16:16; 1Co 16:20; et al.).

27 Financial stability. A man should be financially secure before he starts a family. Before entering marriage one should have a well-ordered life. In general we are to keep first things first.

28 False witness. This saying may be directed to the false accuser—an actual friend says the right thing. There should be solid reasons before one ever goes to testify against a friend.

29 Vengeance. Rather than give in to the spirit of vengeance, one should avoid retaliation (see also 20:22; Mt 5:43–45; Ro 12:9).

30–34 On laziness. The teacher makes several observations of the state of the sluggard that reveal that continued laziness will result in poverty. The reminiscence used here may be a literary device to draw a fictional but characteristically true picture of the lazy person (see also 6:9–11).

V. Proverbs of Solomon Collected by Hezekiah (25:1–29:27)

Chapter 25

1 This section of the book contains additional proverbs attributed to Solomon that were collected by the men of King Hezekiah (715–687 B.C.). These scribes or scholars "copied out" the sayings, i.e., transcribed them from one book to another. The proverbs in these chapters differ in that there are more multiple line sayings and more similes; chs. 28–29 are similar to chs. 10–16, but chs. 25–27 differ in having few references to God.

2 Providence searched out. This first saying expresses a contrast between God and kings. On the one hand, it is the glorious nature of God to "conceal" things. God's government of the universe and his providence are beyond human understanding—humans cannot fathom the divine intentions. Kings have to investigate everything; then they must make things open and intelligible to their subjects, especially judicial matters. Kings who rule as God's representatives must also try to represent his will in human affairs— they must inquire after God to reveal his will.

3 King's counsel. The king's decisions are beyond the knowledge of the people—this is a simple political fact. While a king ought to make judicial matters clear to the people (v.2), many things cannot be made known, being "unsearchable" because, perhaps, of his superior wisdom, his caprice, or the necessity of maintaining confidentiality. But the comparison with the heavens being high and the earth deep captures the nature of the king—he must be resourceful, inscrutable, always one step ahead, to keep a firm grip on power and to enhance his perception by the people.

4–5 Stability through righteousness. These two verses offer first an illustration and then its application. The lines are written with imperatives, forming instructive lessons. Just as a silversmith removes dross from silver so that he can have material to work with, so if the wicked are removed from the nation, the government will be left with righteous counselors and therefore "will be established through righteousness."

6–7b Wisdom of humility. It is wiser to wait to be promoted than to risk demotion by self-promotion. The lesson is straightforward: Promoting oneself in court may risk a public humiliation; but it would be an honor to have everyone in court hear the promotion from the king himself (see Lk 14:8–11).

7c–8 Cautious testimony. One must not be too eager to testify, lest one be put to shame publicly. "What you have seen with your eyes" (v.7c) fits well here, referring to a neighbor's private affairs. When this information is known, it is risky to go "hastily" to court; for if the case has no valid claim, then one will be in public disgrace. We should be cautious in divulging information.

9–10 Private quarrels. It is best to keep personal quarrels private to avoid public shame. Why? If in an argument with your neighbor you reveal another person's confidence, the one who hears you will shame you, and you will always have a "bad reputation." To put it more directly, do not divulge secrets in order to clear yourself in an argument. The point involves damaging a friendship by involving others in a private quarrel.

11 Profound speech. This proverb uses the simile of "apples of gold in settings of silver." The meaning is not entirely certain; but it does speak of beauty, value, and artistry. The "apples of gold" (possibly apricots, citrons, quinces, or oranges) may refer to carvings of fruit in gold on columns. The main point is obviously the immense value and memorable beauty of words used skillfully. A balanced and beautifully constructed saying, such as a proverb (cf. 8:19; 15:23), has lasting value.

12 Rebuke. A wise rebuke that is properly received is of lasting value. It is comparable to ornamental jewelry—pleasing and complimentary. The verse presents the ideal combination of the wise teacher and the willing student ("listening ear" means that the disciple is obedient to the rebuke).

13 Appreciation of faithfulness. A faithful messenger lifts up the spirits of those who sent him on the mission. The comparison in this verse is the "coolness of snow at harvest." Various attempts have been made to explain this idea: snow at harvest is rare, so it may refer to snow brought down from the mountains and kept in an ice hole; it may be the cool air with the snow, i.e., a refreshing breeze from snow-capped mountains; it may be a snow-cooled drink or an application of ice water to foreheads; or perhaps it is an imagined pleasure—snow at harvest. The lesson itself is clear enough: a faithful messenger is refreshing.

14 On bragging. The promises of a boaster are empty. The illustration here is clouds and wind that lead one to expect rain but do not produce it—they gain attention but prove to be disappointing and hence deceitful. Similar is the windbag who brags of gifts to be bestowed, but the promise is deceitful: "he does not give." One should not make false promises.

15 Patient and mild speech. Calm and patient speech can break down insurmountable opposition. By patience one can persuade a ruler; by soft speech stiff opposition ("a bone") can be broken down. The verse recommends conciliatory and persuasive advocacy, which succeeds in the end (see also 14:29; 15:1, 18).

16–17 Moderation. Anything that is over indulged can become distasteful. Verse 16 teaches that moderation ("just enough") is necessary in the pleasures of life (see 16:24). Verse 17 advises moderation in visiting others. We should not wear out our welcome with frequent visits. The motivation for the warning is that familiarity breeds contempt.

18 False witnesses. False witnesses are deadly in society. They are compared to a club, a sword, and a sharp arrow—all deadly weapons. Such people can cause the death of innocent people (see 14:5; Ex 20:16; Dt 5:20).

19 Unfaithfulness. An unfaithful person is useless and painful. Such a person is like a bad tooth and a lame foot. Both are incapable of performing—they are painful and ineffective. The second line has been taken two ways, with "reliance" (GK 4440) referring either to reliance on an unfaithful person or to what the unfaithful person relies on. In the first case, trusting a faithless person is like depending on a decaying tooth or lame foot. In the second, "reliance" refers to the basis of an unfaithful person's hope, e.g., wealth or power (as in 14:26).

20 Inappropriate conduct. Irresponsible attempts to cheer people up only make matters worse. The first line refers to one who takes away a garment on a cold day, an action that is inappropriate. The second simile mentions pouring vinegar on soda. The reference is to sodium carbonate, natural in Egypt (see also Jer 2:22), which is neutralized with vinegar; this is counterproductive. Thus it is inappropriate and counterproductive to "sing songs" to a "heavy heart." One needs to develop sensitivity to others; songs may only irritate the grief.

21–22 Kindness to enemies. People who treat their enemies with kindness will bring remorse to them and blessing from God. The imagery of the "burning coals" represents pangs of conscience, more readily effected by kindness than by violence. These burning coals produce the sharp pain of contrition through regret (see 18:19; 20:22; 24:17; Ge 42–45; 1Sa 24:18–20). Paul uses this expression in Ro 12:20. Furthermore, the Lord "will reward you." This last phrase shows that this instruction belongs to the religious traditions of Israel.

23 Sly words. The north wind that brings the rain is compared with a "sly tongue" that brings angry looks and infuriates people.

24 Peaceful family relationship. It is better to have peaceful solitude than companionship with strife (this verse is the same as 21:9).

25 Good news. Good news refreshes the wearied soul. The point of the verse is transparent (see also 15:30). It is true of love; it is true of spiritual realms. See Ge 45:27 for an illustration.

26 **Integrity**. The righteous who lose their position are useless. The images of the "muddied spring" (fouled perhaps by crossing animals) and the "polluted well" suggest an action that is unforgivable. The comparison is with the righteous person who "gives way" (lit., "is moved"; GK 4572) before the wicked. This verse has often been interpreted to refer to the integrity of the righteous being lost. But the line may refer to the loss of social standing and position by plots of the wicked. For the righteous to so fall indicates that the world is out of joint.

27 **Self-glory**. To seek one's own glory is dishonorable. The second line of this verse is problematic; it should make an analogy to honey—glory is good, like honey, but not to excess. Perhaps a line or two was dropped out as the text was copied.

28 **Self-control**. Without self-control a person is vulnerable. The point of the comparison to a broken-down city is that one who lacks self-control has no defenses.

Chapter 26

1 **Honor inappropriate to fools**. Honor is out of place with a fool. Verse 1 draws a comparison with snow in summer and rain in harvest to show that honor does not "belong" to the fool. The "fool" (GK 4067) is the stupid person who is worthless and vain—just the kind of person popular culture seems to honor. "Honor" (GK 3883) probably refers to the external recognition of worth, i.e., respect, advancement to high position, accolades, but could also include intrinsic worth. All the incongruities mentioned would mean that life was topsy-turvy.

2 **Undeserved curse**. An "undeserved curse" is ineffective. Like a fluttering sparrow or darting swallow, it does not settle down; it does not reach its destination (see 1Ki 4:33 for Solomon's interest in animals). It was commonly believed that blessings and curses had objective existence—that once uttered, the word was effectual. Scriptures make it clear that the power of a blessing or a curse depends on the power of the one behind it (e.g., Balaam could not curse what God had blessed; cf. Nu 22:38; 23:8). This proverb underscores the correction of superstition. The Word of the Lord is powerful because it is his word—he will fulfill it.

3 **Physical discipline**. A fool must be controlled by physical force. The point of this verse is that the "fool" is as difficult to manage as a donkey or horse. None of these respond to reason but must be driven by whip, halter, or rod.

4–5 **Responding to fools**. The one who responds to a fool appears like a fool. One should not descend to that level of thought. To get into an argument with a fool makes one look like a fool as well ("or you will be like him"). On the other hand, the one who rebukes a fool discourages him from thinking too highly of himself; there are times when it is wrong to be silent (cf. 2Co 11:16–17; 12:11). How can these proverbs both be true? In negligible issues one should just ignore stupid persons; but in issues that matter, they must be dealt with lest credence be given to what they say.

6 **Fools are useless as messengers**. To use a fool as a messenger is to invite trouble. Sending a messenger is like having another pair of feet; sending a fool on the mission is not only no help, it is like cutting off the pair of feet one has—it is a setback! "Violence" (GK 2805) means injustice or violent social wrongs; "drinking violence" is metaphorical for suffering violence. That is, sending a fool on a mission will have injurious consequences. It is better not to send a message at all than to use a fool.

7 **Fools are dense**. Proverbs are useless to fools—as useless as a lame man's legs, which hang down, preventing him from going too far. The fool does not understand the "proverb," has not implemented it, and cannot use it correctly and profitably.

8 **Honor is inappropriate to fools**. Honoring a fool is not only counterproductive, it is absurd. It is like "tying a stone" in a sling. If you honor a fool, what is intended cannot be accomplished—he would still be a fool.

9 **Fools' use of proverbs**. It is painful to hear fools use proverbs. The illustration is that of a "thornbush in a drunkard's hand." The drunkard does not know how to handle the thornbush because he cannot control his movements and so gets hurt. A fool can read or speak a proverb but will be intellectually and spiritually unfit to handle it; he will mis-

use it and misapply it. It is at just such a time as this that he should be answered (see v.5).

10 Fools are dangerous. Hiring a fool or a stranger is dangerous. The one who hires such a person is compared to "an archer who wounds at random." This line is difficult because it can be translated in different ways, but it does express something negative. Anyone who hires a fool or a stranger gives them ample opportunity to do great damage. The undisciplined hireling will have the same effect as an archer's shooting at random.

11 Fools persist in folly. Fools repeat their disgusting mistakes. No matter how many times they are warned, they never learn, not even from experience, but repeat their "folly." The simile of a dog returning to his vomit is graphic and debasing (cf. 2Pe 2:22).

12 Self-conceit. Those who think they are wise are almost impossible to help. The saying uses a comparison to stress how difficult it is to curb self-conceit—a fool has more hope. Self-conceit is actually a part of the folly the book decries, because for someone to think that he is wise when he is not makes him a "conceited ignoramus."

13–16 On laziness. These verses can be termed the "Book of Sluggards." The sluggard uses absurd excuses to get out of work (v.13; cf. 22:13). Sluggards do not think they are lazy and so are self-deceived: they would say that they are realists and not shirkers (v.13), that they are below their best in the morning and not self-indulgent (v.14; humor is used here; cf. 6:9–10; 24:33), that their inertia is an objection to being hustled (v.15; cf. 19:24), and that they are sticking to their guns and not mentally indolent (v.16), even though they are filled with self-conceit.

17 Meddling in a quarrel. Anyone who interferes in someone else's quarrel or fight is asking for trouble. The comparison is with grabbing a dog by the ears. This was dangerous, for dogs in the ancient world were not domesticated but wild, like jackals.

18–19 Deceptive speech. It is dangerous to deceive someone out of jest. Anyone who does this is like a "madman" shooting deadly arrows. By comparing the joker to a madman, the sage describes him as irresponsible

and dangerous—he may hurt people while thinking it is all good fun.

20–22 On gossipers and quarrelsome people. One good way to prevent a "quarrel" is to restrict "gossip," just as one can end a fire by withholding wood (v.20). But gossip is appealing (v.22); it is like "choice morsels" that are eagerly and thoroughly devoured by those who hear them (see 18:8 for more on gossip). Quarrelsome people start fights (v.21). Their quarreling is like piling fuel on the fire—strife flares up again and again.

23–25 Deceptive speech. The sage compares hypocritical speech to the glazing over of an earthen pot. Glaze makes it look dazzling and certainly different from the clay that it actually is. In the same way, "fervent" (lit., "burning," "glowing"; GK 1944) lips conceal an evil heart. On the surface what a person says fervently may be pleasing, perhaps speaking "charming" words of affection; but they merely cover one's true nature as one plotting evil. Thus the sage warns the disciple: "Do not believe" such people, for there are countless (seven) abominations they have planned. It takes great shrewdness and wisdom to discern who can be believed.

26–27 On retribution. Concealed malice will inevitably be made known. Verse 26 is concerned with how and where evil will be exposed; the sage assumes that righteousness will ultimately be victorious. Verse 27 suggests that whatever people sow they reap. It gives two illustrations—digging a pit and rolling a stone. The digging refers to laying a trap for someone, and rolling a stone is probably rolling it on someone. Measure for measure justice is in view—he will fall into his own pit, or the stone will roll on him. For examples consider Haman (Est 7:10) and Daniel's enemies (Da 6:24–28).

28 Deceptive speech. Deceptive speech brings ruin without regard for those it may hurt. The two lines portray the evil person who deceives as one who ruthlessly ruins people. The "ruin" could be on himself (an idea that fits the context of v.27) or on others (which seems to be the point of the verse).

Chapter 27

1 Plans in an uncertain future. Presumption about the future is dangerous because the future is uncertain. The verse is not ruling out wise planning for the future, only one's overconfident sense of ability to control the future—no one can presume on God's future (cf. Jas 4:13–16; cf. also Mt 6:34; Lk 12:20). Rather, humility is required; one must live from day to day, grateful for the life one has from God, with the awareness that it may be withdrawn at any time. A second application of the verse would be not to postpone to an uncertain future what is in one's power to do at once.

2 On humility and praise. It is best to let other people praise you, for your reputation comes from what others think of you, not from what you say about yourself. Self-praise is a form of pride, even if it begins with little things (such as who you know, where you have been, etc.), and it does not establish a reputation. "Someone else" in this proverb is literally "stranger" (GK 5799)—a person who can speak more objectively about your accomplishments and abilities.

3 Provocation by fools. Stone and sand are heavy, and whoever carries them knows the work is exhausting and painful. But more tiring is a fool's provocation, for the mental effort it takes to deal with it is more wearying than physical work—the fool brings a spiritual malaise for others to endure.

4 Jealousy. The sage focuses attention first on anger that is ruthless and destructive (lit., "a flood of anger"; see Job 38:25; Ps 32:6; Na 1:8 for the imagery used for destruction). In contrast "jealousy" (GK 7863), here in the negative sense (as opposed to the positive sense of "zeal" to defend a threatened institution for the right reasons), is a raging emotion that defies reason at times and takes the form of destructive violence, like a consuming fire (see Pr 6:32–35; SS 8:6–7).

5 Reproof as a part of love. Direct reproof is better than unexpressed love. "Open rebuke" is a frank, direct word of honest criticism or disapproval (from either a friend or foe). "Hidden love" is a love that is too timid, too afraid, or not trusting enough to admit that reproof is a part of genuine love; such love is morally useless. In fact, one might question whether or not it is sincere (see also 28:23; 29:3).

6 Value of reproof. Reproof given in love is superior to insincere expressions of affection. The wounds of a friend "can be trusted" because they are meant to correct (see 25:12; Dt 7:9; Job 12:20). But an enemy's kisses are deceptive (e.g., the deceitful kiss of Judas [Mk 14:43–45]), in spite of their profusion.

7 Need versus desire. Those who have great needs are more appreciative than those who are satisfied. Most agree that this proverb is capable of wider application than eating; it can apply to possessions, experiences, education, etc.

8 Security abandoned. To stray from home is to lose security. The parallelism compares a bird that "strays" from a nest with the man who "strays" from home. The reason for his straying is not given, but it could be because of exile, eviction, business, or irresponsible actions. The saying may be more general, simply asserting that those who wander lack the security of their home and can no longer contribute to their community life.

9 Advice from a friend. Advice from a friend is pleasant—just as perfume and incense bring joy to people. The second line is difficult. Many interpreters take it to mean the advice or counsel of a friend sweetening the soul.

10 Helpful friends. A friend who is available is better than a relative who is not. The conflict between 17:17 and 27:10b may be another example of presenting two sides of the issue, showing that such a matter cannot be resolved with one simple teaching. We should maintain relationships with family and friends but also realize that a neighbor who lives close to us will be more help than a relative who lives at some distance.

11 Teaching vindicated. A wise son (i.e., disciple) enables a father (i.e., teacher) to defend himself against his critics. The expression "treats me with contempt" refers to the taunting or criticizing of the instructor as a poor teacher. Teachers are usually held responsible for the faults and weaknesses of their pupils; but any teacher criticized that way takes pleasure in pointing to those who have learned as proof that he has not labored in vain (see also 1Th 2:19–20; 3:8).

12 Wisdom wary of evil. Avoiding the pitfalls in life requires wisdom (see 22:3). The contrast is between the "prudent" (GK 6874) and the "simple" (GK 7343); the first is the mature person who has developed a wariness (1:4), while the latter is the inexperienced youth who stumbles into things. The verse is a motivation for the naive to be trained; for life would be far less painful for them if they knew how to avoid life's dangers.

13 Obligations fulfilled. People must be held to their obligations, no matter how foolishly they were made (see also 20:16).

14 Inappropriate greeting. How, when, and why we say what we say is important. On the surface this verse appears to be describing one who comes in early and loud with a blessing or greeting; such a one is considered a nuisance ("it will be taken as a curse"). But "blesses" and "curse" may also refer to the loud adulation of a hypocrite, the person who goes to great length to create the impression of piety and friendship but is considered a curse by the one who hears him.

15–16 A quarrelsome wife. A quarrelsome mate is an unbearable irritant (see 19:13). Verse 16 adds the idea that the quarrelsome wife is also uncontrollable, like elusive winds that can gust at any moment, or like oil that one cannot control with the hand.

17 Helpful criticism. Constructive criticism between friends develops character and personality. The Talmud applied this proverb to two students sharpening each other in the study of the Torah.

18 Rewards for service. Those who faithfully serve will be rewarded in kind, just as one who takes care of a fig tree will eat its fruit. The fig tree needed closer attention than other plants; thus the analogy implies that the servant performs meticulous service for his master, anticipating the needs and watching over his charge. Such a servant will not go unrecognized and unrewarded (see also 22:29; 2Ti 2:6, 15).

19 Character traits reflected in thoughts. The verse literally says, "As water face to face / so a man's heart to a man." The simplest way to take it is to say that as clear water gives a reflection of the face, so the heart reflects the true nature of the man. Through looking at our heart attitudes we come to true self-awareness.

20 Desires are insatiable. The desires of human beings are as insatiable as "Death" and "Destruction," expressions for the underworld (see 15:11). Generations of people have gone headlong into the world below; yet it is never satisfied. In the same way, what a person desires is "never satisfied."

21 Praise as a test. Public opinion, or the praise of others, is normally a good barometer of the qualities and contributions of a person. The comparison of the point is with the crucible for silver and the furnace for gold—they refine and reveal the pure metals. Public praise certainly did form a test for Saul and David (1Sa 18:7), David coming out the better for it. But there is the other side of the matter as well, that righteousness will be denounced (Mt 5:11).

22 Folly is unalterable. Folly cannot be removed by force. The proverb uses the imagery of grinding grain in a mortar with a pestle, i.e., pulverizing, to discuss physical punishment for the fool. Since folly is his nature, it will not be removed from him.

23–27 Wealth is transitory. People should preserve what income they have because it does not long endure. Verse 23 provides the main instruction—take care of your livelihood. The motivation for this is that riches do not last long. The reasoning for wise care of income continues in the second half of the poem—the protasis is in v.25 and the apodosis in vv.26–27—if the growth is removed, then they can sell and use their livestock. The poem shows the proper interplay between human labor and divine provision.

Chapter 28

1 Confidence of the righteous. In contrast to the fear of the wicked who flee when "no one pursues," the faith of the righteous builds confidence. This proverb implies that the wicked, prompted by a guilty conscience or a fear of judgment, become fearful and suspicious of everyone. But the righteous, who seek to find favor with God and others, have a clear conscience and thus no need to look over their shoulders.

2 Stability in government. A nation's stability comes with ruler who is discerning and

This Bedouin girl must know the condition of her family's herd of camels and care for them (cf. 27:23–27).

knowledgeable. The reference to "many rulers" indicates that during rebellious times a nation has many changes of power or many people vying for power (cf. the period of the judges and the days of the northern kingdom of Israel with its nine dynasties as examples of political instability due to sin).

3 Oppressive rulers. A ruler who oppresses the poor destroys his own dominion. The first line introduces the subject matter—one who oppresses the poor—and the second line tells of the effect—like a driving rain he destroys and leaves nothing in the land (i.e., only the hardiest survive). The Hebrew text has "a poor man oppresses the poor" (see NIV note); if retained, it means that one would expect a poor man to have sympathy for others who are impoverished, but in fact that is not the case.

4 Respect for law. Obedience to the law determines one's attitude toward law-breakers. The contrast is between "those who forsake the law" and "those who keep the law." The former "praise the wicked," while the latter "resist them." Praising the wicked may mean calling them good, i.e., no longer able to discern good from evil (cf. Ro 1:18–32).

5 Perceiving justice. The contrast here between those who are evil and those who seek the Lord concerns the perception of justice. "Justice" (GK 1907) refers to the legal rights of people; but there are always those who believe justice is that which benefits them—otherwise it is not justice. To "seek the

Lord" originally meant trying to obtain an oracle from God (see 2Sa 21:1) but then came to refer to devotion to God (i.e., seeking to learn and to do his will). Only people attuned to the divine will can fully perceive what justice is. Without that standard, legal activity can easily become self-serving.

6 Righteousness better than unjust wealth. Honest poverty is better than dishonest wealth. The verse only contrasts a poor man with integrity and a perverse rich man (cf. vv. 8, 11, 20, 22, 25, 27; also 19:1), without recognizing that there are rich people with integrity and poor people who are perverse. The word for "ways" suggests that the person has double ways, i.e., he is hypocritical, a double dealer.

7 On the obedient. One who is obedient to the law will be discerning enough to lead an untarnished life. "Law" (GK 9368) may mean instruction, perhaps originally for this verse a father's instructions; but in this chapter that stresses religious piety, it probably refers to the law (though in Proverbs a father's instruction harmonizes with the law). The son who becomes a "companion of gluttons" has not kept the law; he shames his father because such profligacy brings disrespect on the family.

8 Wealth unjustly gained. Wealth amassed by unjust means will eventually go to the poor. The law prohibited making a commission or charging interest (see Ex 22:25; Lev 25:36–37; Dt 23:20; Ps 15:5). These laws were concerned with the necessities of life; if the poor needed help, the wealthy should give it to them as charity—they were not to take advantage of another Israelite's plight.

9 Prayer of the lawless unanswered. God will not listen to the prayers of those who will not listen to him. The prayer certainly will not be a proper prayer; someone who refuses to obey God cannot pray according to God's will—he will pray for some physical thing, perhaps even making demands on God. Of course, a prayer of repentance would not be an abomination to the Lord. But in general, God's favor is enjoyed by the righteous, and his abomination is incurred by the wicked.

10 Just rewards. Destruction awaits those who corrupt others; rewards await those who have integrity. The line shows that the wicked will be caught in their own devices; but it also shows that the righteous are corruptible—they can be led into morally bad conduct (see 26:27; see also Mt 23:15).

11 Self-deceit. Here is another contrast between the rich and the poor. In this one the rich man is filled with self-conceit, but the discerning poor man "sees through" the pretension.

12 Righteousness in government. People flourish under righteous administrations. The contrast is between the situation when the wicked come to power and when the righteous triumph.

13 Effectual repentance. Repentance and renunciation of sin bring God's mercy and blessing. This verse, unique in Proverbs, captures the theology of forgiveness found in passages such as Ps 32:1–5 and 1Jn 1:6–9. The contrast is between the one who "conceals" personal sins and the one who "confesses and renounces them." The former will not prosper; the latter will find God's "mercy."

14 Fear of the Lord. One's prospects in this life depend on reverential fear. The verse contrasts the one who "always fears" with the one who "hardens his heart." The first is blessed, while the second falls into trouble. The verse gives no object for "fear": various translations have assumed that it would be the Lord (so NIV), especially in the book of Proverbs. But it may be that the verse means fear of sin. In other words, the one who is always apprehensive about sin and its results will be more successful at avoiding it and finding God's blessing.

15 Wicked rulers. Political tyrants are dangerous and destructive. A wicked leader who rules over "helpless people" is compared to a "roaring lion" and a "charging bear"—beastly, powerful, insensitive, and in search of victims (cf. the animal imagery used in Da 7:1–8 for ruthless world rulers). The poor crumple under such tyrants because they cannot meet their demands.

16 Good versus bad rulers. The righteous ruler, not the tyrant, will remain in power. A tyrant will inevitably face the danger of rebellion and even assassination. A righteous administration, on the other hand, pleases the people and God, who preserves it.

17 Effects of guilt. The guilty fugitive will be isolated. This verse has some difficulties for the interpreter. The second line is either saying that it is futile to try to support a murderer on the run or that one should not interfere.

18 Security based on integrity. Integrity brings security; perversion brings insecurity. That is, the result of a righteous lifestyle is being "kept safe," whereas the wicked will fall.

19 Results of diligence. Prosperity depends on diligent work (see 12:11). There is a meaningful repetition here: the diligent person will have "plenty of bread," but the lazy person will have "plenty of poverty" (cf. NRSV).

20 Faithfulness. The "faithful man" is contrasted with the one who is "eager to get rich." The idea is that the first is faithful to his obligations to God and to other people; but the one who hastens to make riches is at the least doing it without an honest day's work and at the worst dishonestly. In a hurry to acquire wealth, he falls into dishonest schemes and bears the guilt of it—he will not be unpunished.

21 Injustice through bribery. Partiality in judgment is wrong, even though easily acquired. To show partiality destroys justice (see 18:5; 24:23; Lev 19:15; Dt 1:17; 16:19). The second line probably means that a man can be bribed for a very small price (i.e., piece of bread).

22 Effects of avarice. Avarice inevitably leads to poverty. Here we meet the man with the "evil eye" again (cf. 23:6, where this expression was used for the selfish, "stingy man"). The presumption is that this person's greed involves sin, for which he will be punished with poverty.

23 Reproof preferable to flattery. In the final analysis rebuke will be better received than flattery. The flattering tongue may be pleasing for the moment, but it will offer no constructive help like the "rebuke" (see also 15:5, 12; 25:12; 27:5–6; 29:5).

24 Robbing parents. Whoever robs one's parents, no matter how one seeks to justify it, is a destroyer. The point seems to be that of prematurely trying to gain control of the family property through some form of pressure and in the process reduce the parents' possessions and standing in the community. He could say, "It's not wrong," because he could reason that it would be his someday anyway.

25 Greed versus trust. The "greedy man" is pitted against the one "who trusts" the Lord. The first one is completely selfish and usually ruthless. His attitudes and actions stir up strife because people do not long tolerate him. He pushes so hard for the things he wants that his zeal becomes a hindrance to obtaining them. Conversely, the true believer, who is blessed by God, will be made abundantly prosperous.

26 On self-sufficiency. Security comes from a life of wisdom, not from self-sufficiency. One who trusts in oneself stands in stark contrast to one who follows the wisdom from above that this book has been teaching.

27 Generosity versus indifference. Generosity is rewarded but indifference is cursed (see also 11:24–26; 22:9). The generous do not miss what they give away, but those indifferent to the needs of the poor will be cursed often—by the poor, no doubt.

28 Stability in righteous government. The righteous flourish when wickedness is removed from government (see also 11:10; 28:12; 29:2, 16).

Chapter 29

1 Stubbornness. The verse is a warning about the peril of persisting in sin; it uses the image of the "stiff neck" to portray the obstinate person who disregards all rebukes (see Ex 32:9). The opposite of the stiff neck is a bending neck, i.e., submission. The stubborn person does not foresee misfortune and so will suddenly "be destroyed" without any healing. For similar proverbs see 6:15; 13:18; and 15:10.

2 Effect of righteousness on morale. Good people can enjoy life when righteousness predominates in government. There is rejoicing then, but people always suffer under wicked regimes (see 11:10–11; 28:12, 28).

3 Effect of wisdom on the family. Wisdom ensures joy and prosperity for the family. In contrast to the wise person who brings "joy" to his father is the son who brings grief by squandering his wealth on "prostitutes." For the financial consequences of vice, see chs. 1–9 (esp. 5:10; 6:31).

4 Security through justice. This verse contrasts a king who makes the nation secure with one who "tears it down." The former brings prosperity by championing "justice"; the latter is "greedy for bribes." The idea of "bribes" (GK 9556) is not the point; this king breaks the backs of the people with demands for monetary gifts (see 1Sa 8:11–18), and this causes divisions and strife.

5 Deceptive speech. The subject of this verse is one who "flatters his neighbor." Such flattering works by deception and guile. There is some uncertainty of the referent in the second line: "he spreads a net for his steps." This could refer to a net spread for the one flattered or for the flatterer himself. The latter would make the verse more powerful (see also 2:16; 7:5; 26:28; 28:23).

6 Security of the righteous. Only the righteous can enjoy a sense of security. The sage observes that the "evil man" is caught in his own sin (cf. v.5), but the righteous sing and are glad—two expressions that signify their confidence; they have no fear of snares and so can sing.

7 Justice for the poor. Only the righteous champion justice for the poor; they care about (lit., "know," i.e., "have sympathetic knowledge of") justice for the poor (see 20:8; 31:5, 8). But the wicked do not "discern knowledge"—they have no such interest or insight into the problems of the people (see Job 29:12–17).

8 Wisdom in averting anger. The wise maintain peace and harmony in society. They "turn away anger" rather than stir up strife. The "mockers" are those who laugh at moral obligations and stir up the baser passions of their fellow citizen, like kindling a fire. Such scoffers make dangerous situations worse, whereas the wise calm things down and ensure peace in the community.

9 Strife exacerbated. It is a waste of time to try to settle a dispute calmly or rationally with a fool. To go into court with a fool, you have to reckon with unreasonable and objectionable behavior. Whether this "fool" is angry or laughing, there is no possible resolution to the matter (cf. Pr 26:4 and its warning not to answer a fool).

10 Righteousness hated by the wicked. Bloodthirsty people loathe the integrity of the upright. Because they despise all sense of decency, they seek to destroy it. The second line forms a contrast; literally it reads, "as for the upright, they seek his life." "Seeking a life" was usually a hostile act, but here the contrast requires the idea of "seek to preserve a life" (NIV interprets this verse differently).

11 Self-control. It takes wisdom to restrain anger. This proverb contrasts "fools," who let out all their anger and are at the mercy of any moment when they happen to feel irritation, and the wise, who control their anger (see also 16:32; 25:28).

12 On lies. Once a ruler begins to listen to lies, his court will be corrupted. The point is that courtiers adjust themselves to the prince—when they see that deception and court flattery win the day, they learn how the game is played (see 16:10; 20:8; 25:2).

13 Life from God. Regardless of status or circumstances, all people receive their life from God. The imagery of giving sight means that God gives the light of life (see Job 33:30; Ps 13:3). God creates and controls them all (see 22:2).

14 Treatment of the poor. The duration of an administration depends on its moral character. It is important to guarantee fair and just treatment for all, especially the poor. To fail to do so is immoral (see 16:12; 20:28; 25:5; 31:5).

15 Effect of discipline. Discipline makes a child's behavior enjoyable ("a rod of correction" means "a correcting rod"). The focus on the mother in the last part is probably a rhetorical variation for the parent (see 17:21; 23:24–25) and not meant to assume that she will do the training (see also 13:24; 23:13).

16 Certainty of judgment. No matter how much wickedness spreads in the land, righteousness will live to see it destroyed (though this verse does not say when or how).

17 Effect of discipline. A disciplined child will bring contentment to parents (see also 19:18).

18 Obedience to revelation. A nation's well-being depends on obedience to divine revelation. This popular verse refers to two forms of divine revelation, vision and law. The first line is worded negatively—if there is "no revelation" (or "vision"; GK 2606), the people "throw off restraint" (cf. Ex 32:35). "Vision" refers to divine communication to prophets (as in 1Sa 3:1). The prophetic ministry was usually in response to the calamitous periods, calling the people back to God. If revelation is absent, people can expect spiritual and political anarchy. The second line provides the positive wording: there is a blessing for the one who keeps the law.

19 Method of discipline. It is not sufficient to train slaves by words alone. That is, slaves must be treated like sons (i.e., they frequently had to be corrected). This verse is probably a general observation on the times; doubtless there were slaves who did better (e.g., Joseph in Egypt; Daniel in Babylon).

20 Rash speech. It is easier to train a fool than to correct rash speech. The focus in this verse is on the one who speaks before thinking something through. The prospects of the fool are better, for rash speech cannot easily be remedied (see 26:12; Jas 3:8).

21 Lack of discipline. If someone pampers a servant from youth, in the end (of this procedure) such a person will have "grief." The idea of "grief" comes from the LXX (cf. NIV note).

22 Anger. Anger brings strife. The lines focus on the "angry man"—one who is given to anger and not merely temporarily angry. Not only does such a one stir up "dissension," but in so doing he also causes sin in himself and in others (see also 14:17, 29; 15:18; 16:32; 22:24).

23 Pride and humility. A humble spirit brings honor and respect, whereas pride leads to abasement (see Lk 14:11; 18:14).

24 Entanglements of sin. An accomplice in crime will find no easy way out of his dilemma. This verse is a little confusing; it describes the accomplice of a thief as his own enemy (lit., "he hates himself")—he hears a curse and will not speak up. According to Lev 5:1, if a witness does not speak up, he is held accountable for the crime. The case here might be where the guilty person is unknown; and when a curse is pronounced on that unknown culprit, the accomplice hears it but cannot speak up. So the curse attaches itself to him as well.

25 Security via faith in the Lord. True security is the result of trusting God and not other humans. Fear of others becomes a snare when it gets to the point of letting others control your life—their opinions and attitudes put subtle pressure on you, even hindering you from speaking the truth or doing what is right. Release from such bondage comes when people put their faith in the Lord alone (see 10:27; 12:2; Ac 5:29).

26 Justice from God. True justice ultimately comes from God. The great miscalculation is to assume that true justice depends on some ruler and that supplication must be directed first to him.

27 Hatred. The righteous and the wicked mutually detest the lifestyles of each other.

VI. The Words of Agur (30:1–33)

A. The Title (30:1)

1 The heading for this section identifies the words that follow as those of Agur, the son of Jakeh, for Ithiel and Ucal. There have been many attempts to interpret these names. It is most likely that someone other than Solomon wrote these sayings; they have a different, almost nonproverbial, tone to them.

The section is also entitled an "oracle" (Heb., *massa*; GK 5363). This word usually describes a prophetic oracle of some kind, though it is possible that Massa might be a place.

B. Agur's Confession and Petition (30:2–9)

1. Confession of ignorance (30:2–4)

2–3 Agur confesses that he is ignorant of the ways of God. He begins by lamenting that he has not learned wisdom, i.e., that he is not one of those who profess to understand the Holy One. "Ignorant" (GK 1280) refers to his intellectual dullness; he is like the lower animals (Pss 49:10–12; 73:22). The "Holy One" in this section is in the plural as in 9:10.

4 To make his point Agur includes five questions. These, like Job 38–41 or Pr 8:24–29, focus on divine acts to show that it is absurd for mortals to think that they can explain God's works or to compare themselves with God. These questions display human limitations; they may have a sarcastic tone, implying that some people think they understand the phenomena of the universe. The first question, accordingly, could refer to a human ("Who has gone up to heaven?") but may simply refer to God as the other questions do. The final question seeks to identify this sovereign God. To know a person's "name" is to exhibit power over and closeness to that person. The parallel reference to "son" has been identified as Israel, as a simple poetic parallelism for "his name," and (by Christian interpreters) as a reference to the Son of God.

2. Affirmation of the reliability of God's word (30:5–6)

5 Agur affirms that God's word is pure (NIV, "flawless"; GK 7671); this word, used elsewhere of purifying metal, is that God's word is trustworthy: there is nothing deceitful or false in it. The second half of the verse explains this meaning: it is safe to take refuge in the Lord (see Pss 12:6; 18:31).

6 This confidence is followed by a warning not to add to the Lord's words (see Dt 4:2), a tendency that is all too common.

3. Prayer (30:7–9)

7–9 Agur prays that God will prevent him from becoming deceitful and self-sufficient. He wants to be honest in all his dealings, and he wants a life of balanced material blessings. He reasons that if he has too much, he might become independent of God (see Dt 8:11–14); and if he has too little, he might steal and thus profane God's name. So acknowledging his own ignorance, relying on God's word for security in life, and praying that God will keep him from falling into temptation, Agur is ready to offer his words.

C. The Admonition of Agur (30:10–33)

1. Noninterference in domestic situations (30:10)

10 The advice here is not very clear on first reading. The warning could be taken literally: Do not slander a servant to his master; for if it is not true, then he will make you look

small, and you will be found guilty. Another view is that the verse refers to the delivery of a fugitive slave to his master. "Slander" in this case would refer to denouncing, i.e., accusing to authorities (see Dt 23:15–16). The advice then would be not to meddle in the affairs of someone else.

2. Four evil things (30:11–14)

Possibly there was a heading for this section at one time ("Three things, yea four. . . ."). All the things listed here begin with the word *dor* ("generation," meaning a class or group of people; see also Mt 11:16).

a. Disrespect for parents (30:11)

11 The first observation is that there is a segment of society that lacks respect for parents, in spite of the law (cf. Ex 21:17; Pr 20:20). The negative statement ("do not bless") follows the positive ("who curse"); "cursing" a parent could refer to defaming, treating lightly, or showing disrespect in general.

b. Self-righteousness (30:12)

12 "Filth" (GK 7363) often refers to physical uncleanness, but here it is moral defilement (cf. Isa 36:12; Zec 3:3–4). There is a generation, a group of people, who may observe all outer ritual but pay no attention to inner cleansing (see Isa 1:16; Mt 23:27). Such hypocrisy is harmful in every walk of life.

c. Pride (30:13)

13 The eyes of the proud are "high" (NIV, "haughty"; GK 8123) and their eyelids "disdainful" (GK 5951). These expressions refer to their arrogant attitude—the lofty view of themselves and the corresponding contempt for others (see also 6:17; Ps 131:1).

d. Oppressing the poor (30:14)

14 The imagery of the first half of the verse captures the rapacity of their power—their teeth and their jaws are swords and knives. The second part explains that they devour, like a ravenous and insensitive beast, the poor and the needy (see 31:8–9). Those who exploit and destroy other people are beasts.

3. Insatiable things (30:15–16)

15a Things that seem never to be satisfied are problematic for the normal enjoyment of life. The meaning of v.15a and its relationship to vv.15b–16 have been debated for some time. The "leech" is the symbol of greed because it sucks blood through its two suckers (here called its "two daughters" who cry "Give! Give!").

15b–16 There probably is a relationship in the numbering between v.15a and vv.15b–16: two daughters, three insatiable things, and four things that never say enough. The four insatiable things are then listed: "Sheol" (NIV "grave"; GK 8619), the abode of the dead (see also 27:20); the barren womb of one whose desire for children is all consuming (see Ge 16:2; 30:1); land that is not satisfied with water; and fire that continues until stopped.

There is no clearly stated ethical lesson; these are basic observations of life. But one point that could be made is that greed, symbolized by the leech, is as insatiable as these other things.

4. Punishment for parental disrespect (30:17)

17 Severe punishment awaits those who show disrespect for their parents. The sentence focuses on the "eye" that "mocks" a father and despises obedience to a mother. The eye manifests the inner heart attitude—so the contemptuous look runs deep. The punishment is talionic—the eye that mocks will be pecked out by the birds. By these images the sternest punishment is held out for those who hold their parents in such contempt.

5. Amazing things in nature (30:18–19)

18–19 Many things in nature are amazing but incomprehensible. This little observation also begins with the numerical formula "There are three things that are too amazing for me, four that I do not understand." The verb "amazing" (GK 7098) basically describes what is wonderful, surpassing, incomprehensible (cf. Ge 18:14; Jdg 13:18; Ps 139:6; Isa 9:6). The sage can only admire the wonders of nature—he is at a loss to explain it all.

It is not easy to discover what the four things have in common. They all are linked by the word "way" (GK 2006, meaning a course of action) and by a sense of mystery in each area. Suggestions for a common theme include the following: (1) all four things are hidden from continued observation, for they are there in majestic form and then are gone, not leaving a trace; (2) they all have a mysterious means of propulsion or motivation; (3) they all describe the movement of one thing within the sphere or domain of another; (4) the first three serve as illustrations of the fourth and greatest wonder, which concerns human relations and is slightly different than the first three.

The first entry is the way of the eagle in the sky, a marvelous creature soaring with apparent ease but certain determination and purpose, all hidden from the observer. Next is the way of the serpent on a rock. Here is the mysterious but smooth and efficient movement of a reptile without feet. The way of a ship in the sea portrays the magnificent movement of a vessel through a trackless sea. All these are marvelous to observe; they focus our attention on the majestic and mysterious movements in the sky, on the land, and on the sea.

The fourth mystery is "the way of a man with a maiden." The word for "maiden" (*almah*; GK 6625) does not in and of itself mean "virgin" but rather describes a young woman who is sexually ready for marriage. What is in view here is the wonder of human sexuality. This mystery might begin with the manner of obtaining the love of the woman but focuses on the most intimate part of human relationships, which the sage considers to be wonderful. All of it is part of God's marvelous plan for his creation and therefore can be fully enjoyed and appreciated without fully comprehending it.

6. The brazen woman (30:20)

20 Equally amazing is the insensitivity of the adulteress to sin. That this verse was placed here lends support to the idea that the previous verse is focusing on sexual intimacy in marriage; for just as that is incomprehensible (filling one with wonder), so is the way that human nature has distorted and ruined it. Carrying forward the use of the word "way," this verse describes "the way of an adulteress." It portrays an amoral woman more than an immoral one. The act of adultery is as unremarkable to her as a meal (the imagery of eating and wiping her mouth is euphemistic for sexual activity; see 9:17). It is incredible that human beings can engage in sin and then so easily dismiss any sense of guilt or responsibility, perhaps by rationalizing the deeds or perhaps through a calloused indifference to what the will of the Lord is for sexuality.

7. Abuse of position (30:21–23)

21–23 Certain people who are suddenly elevated in their status in life can be unbearable. The sage says that under these things the earth trembles and cannot bear it—obviously using humorous or satirical hyperbole to say that these changes shake up the order of life. This assumes that the elevated status was not accompanied by a change of nature. For example, it was not uncommon for a servant to become a king in the ancient Near East. It would be possible that once he became king, he would develop the mentality and disposition of a king and perhaps be better than the preceding ruler. But the "earth trembles" when a servant is king; unaccustomed to such dignity, he might become a power-hungry tyrant and oppressive ruler (e.g., Hitler). The second, a fool who is full of food, describes a fool who becomes prosperous but continues to be boorish and irreligious; but now he is overbearing and, worse yet, finds time hanging heavy on his hands. The third is the unloved woman who is married. Perhaps she is unattractive or odious, but also perhaps she is married to someone incapable of showing love. Being unloved, not sought or wooed, she is actually hated (see Ge 29:31, 33). The fourth is the maid who displaces her mistress. The tension from the threat of Hagar in Ge 16:5 and 21:10 shows how unbearable this could be. Such upheavals in the proper order of things make life intolerable.

8. Wisdom the key to success (30:24–28)

24–28 These verses focus on four things that are small but "extremely wise": ants, rock badgers, locusts, and lizards. The wisdom exhibited in the ants concerns their forethought and organization to make provision for food; the wisdom of the rock badgers (NIV, "coneys"; cf. NIV note) is found in their ingenuity to find a place of security; the wisdom of the locust consists in its cooperation and order, which when massed in military division becomes a force for human beings to reckon with; and the wisdom of the lizard is in its elusiveness and boldness. In God's creation wisdom manifests itself in a variety of ways, and humans can learn the value of wisdom over size and numerical strength.

9. Leadership qualities (30:29–31)

29–31 Leaders exhibit majestic qualities. There is a simple point to this observation: three things are "stately in their stride," four move with "stately being." Three examples come from the animal world, leading up to the fourth, the king, who has his army about him to defend against revolt.

10. A final admonition (30:32–33)

32–33 The sage advises those who have "exalted" themselves and "played the fool" and those who have "planned evil" to cease their efforts and control what they say; namely, "clap your hand over your mouth!" (cf. Job 40:4–5). The explanation for this warning is that it only causes strife. Two similes are used in the last verse, churning the milk and twisting the nose—both involve a pressing, the first producing butter from milk and the second drawing blood from the nose. In the same way stirring up anger (through pride and evil planning) produces "strife." There is also a subtle wordplay here, for "nose" is related to "anger." So the intent of this concluding advice is to strive for peace and harmony through humility and righteousness.

VII. The Words of Lemuel (31:1–9)

A. Title: The Words Taught to Lemuel by His Mother (31:1)

1 Nothing is known about King Lemuel. Jewish legend identifies him as Solomon and the advice as from Bathsheba from a time when Solomon indulged in magic with his Egyptian wife and delayed the morning sacrifices. But there is no evidence for this. The same question of translation for "oracle" (GK 5363) occurs here as in 30:1 (see comment on 30:1). This section is the only direct address to a king in the book—something that was the norm in the wisdom literature of the other countries. The instruction includes two warnings and then sound advice.

B. First Warning (31:2–3)

2–3 The king is warned not to spend his strength on sensual lust. The repetition of "son" shows the seriousness of the warning; and the twofold motivation adds to this impact—he is her son, and she has vowed him (cf. 1Sa 1:11). She advises him not to spend "his strength" or "his ways" on women. The term "vigor" (GK 2006) may allude to sexual

intercourse (see 30:19) or in general refer to the heart's affection or attention. "Women" in this passage are qualified as those who "ruin" (GK 4681) kings. Commentators note that this difficult term is close to an Aramaic word for concubine and an Arabic word that is an indelicate description of women. Whatever the precise meaning, the point of the verse is that while it would be easy for a king to spend his time and energy enjoying women, that would be unwise.

C. Second Warning (31:4–7)

4–7 Drinking wine and craving beer is not for kings. If this literally prohibits any use of such drinks, it would be unheard of in the ancient courts. Either excessive use of alcohol or troubling need for it (reflecting deeper problems) is what is meant. The danger, of course, would be to cloud the mind and deprive the oppressed of true justice. Verses 6–7 explain that a better use for strong drink is to relieve bodily suffering and mental distress. People in those conditions need to forget.

D. Instruction: Defend the Defenseless (31:8–9)

8–9 The king is to open his mouth (i.e., "speak up for") for "those who cannot speak for themselves." It is his responsibility to champion the rights of the poor and the needy, those who are left desolate by the cruelties of life (see 2Sa 14:4–11; 1Ki 3:16–28; Pss 45:3–5; 72:4; Isa 9:6–7).

VIII. The Wife of Noble Character (31:10–31)

The book of Proverbs comes to a close with the addition of this poem about the woman of valor. A careful reading of the passage will show that her value is derived from her character of godly wisdom that is beneficial to her family and to the community as a whole. Traditionally this poem was recited by husbands and children at the Sabbath table on Friday night. Christians too have seen it as a paradigm for godly women.

The theme of the poem, the wife of noble character, captures the ideals of wisdom that have filled the book. It may well be that this is more the point of the composition than merely a portrayal of the ideal wife. The woman here presented is a wealthy aristocrat who runs a household estate with servants and conducts business affairs—real estate, vineyards, and merchandise—domestic affairs, and charity. It would be quite a task for any woman to emulate this pattern. Some see this woman as an idealized wife, in an ideal home, in an ideal society—she is not just some man's dream woman but represents a universal type of woman. Others have also recognized that more is going on here than a description of the ideal wife. After all, the work says nothing about the woman's personal relationship with her husband, her intellectual or emotional strengths, or her religious activities. In general it appears that the woman of ch. 31 is a symbol of wisdom. If this is so, then the poem plays an important part in the personification of wisdom in the ancient Near Eastern literature. Indeed, many commentators rightly invite a contrast to the earlier portrayals of Dame Folly lurking dangerously in the streets—she was to be avoided—and Lady Wisdom, who is to be embraced. The Lady Wisdom in this chapter stands in the strongest contrast to the adulterous woman in the earlier chapters.

Several characteristics of this poem should be noted in order to appreciate its impact on the teaching of wisdom. First, the entire poem is arranged alphabetically (a pattern known as an acrostic). This means the first word of each line begins with a letter of the Hebrew alphabet in sequence. Most commentators recognize that such a pattern makes the work uneven and somewhat random in its organization. Nevertheless, the arrangement made memorization easier and perhaps also served to organize the thoughts. We may say, then, that the poem is an organized arrangement of the virtues of the wise wife—the ABC's of wisdom.

Second, the passage has striking similarities with hymns. Usually a hymn is written to God, but here apparently it was written to the wife of noble character. A comparison with Ps 111, a hymn to God, illustrates some of the similarities. The psalm begins with "Praise the LORD"; this is reflected in Pr 31:31, which says, "Her works bring her praise." Psalm 111:2 speaks of God's works; Pr 31:13 speaks of her works. Psalm 111:2 says that the works of the Lord are searched or "pondered"; Pr 31:13 says that she "selects" wool and flax. Psalm 111:3 says that the Lord's work is honorable (NIV, "majes-

tic"); Pr 31:25 ascribes strength and "dignity" to the woman. Psalm 111:4 says that the Lord is gracious and full of compassion; Pr 31:26 ascribes the law of compassion to the woman. Psalm 111:5 says that the Lord gives "food"; Pr 31:15 says that the woman provides "food" for her house. Psalm 111:10 says that the fear of the Lord is the beginning of wisdom—the motto of Proverbs; Pr 31:30 describes the woman as fearing the Lord. Psalm 111:10 says that the Lord's praise will endure; Pr 31:31 says that the woman will be praised for her works. It is clear that Pr 31 is patterned after the hymn to extol the works of wisdom.

Third, the passage has similarities with heroic literature. The vocabulary and the expressions in general have the ring of an ode to a champion. For example, "woman of valor" (v.10; NIV, "woman of noble character") is the same expression one would find in Judges for the "mighty man of valor" (Jdg 6:12; NIV, "mighty warrior"); "strength" (vv.17 [NIV, "vigorously"], 25) is elsewhere used for powerful deeds and heroics (e.g., Ex 15:2, 13; 1Sa 2:10); "food" (v.15) is actually "prey"; "surpass them all" (v.29) is an expression that signifies victory.

Putting these observations together, one would conclude that Pr 31:10–31 is a hymn to Lady Wisdom, written in the heroic mode. Wisdom is personified as a woman because the word "wisdom" is a feminine noun and naturally suggests it (cf. ch. 8), and because the woman is an excellent example of wisdom by virtue of the variety of applications it receives—at home, in the market, with charity, in business. A personification of wisdom allows the writer to make all the lessons concrete and not abstract (we can see them in action in everyday life); it provides a polemic against the literature of the ancient world that saw women as decorative—charm and beauty without substance; and it depicts the greater heroism as moral and domestic rather than as exploits in battle.

The poem certainly presents a pattern for women who want to develop a life of wisdom; but since it is essentially about wisdom, its lessons are for both men and women to develop. The fear of the Lord will inspire people to be faithful stewards of the time and talents that God has given; wisdom is productive and beneficial for others, requiring great industry in life's endeavors; wisdom is best taught and lived in the home—indeed, the success of the home demands wisdom; and wisdom is balanced living, giving attention to domestic responsibilities as well as business enterprises and charitable service.

A. Praise in General (31:10–12)

10 The introductory rhetorical question establishes the point that the wife of noble character is not easily found; but when she is, she is a treasure. Her description as "a wife of noble character" signifies that she possesses all the virtues, honor, and strength to do the things that the poem will set forth. This woman, like wisdom, is worth more than rubies (cf. 3:15; 8:11).

11–12 The noble woman's husband lacks nothing of value. The term "value" (GK 8965) usually means "plunder"; the point may be that the gain will be as rich and bountiful as the spoils of war. The capable woman inspires the confidence of her husband because in her business and domestic enterprises she proves able (cf. 1Sa 24:2). In any marriage, but especially when a large household is involved, such trust in the wife's abilities is essential.

B. Industrial Pursuits of the Household (31:13–15)

13–15 Now the cataloging of activities begins. The picture presented is of a large household that requires supervision. All indicators suggest that it is a wealthy and honorable household. This noble woman takes the responsibility to see that food and clothing are provided, making the choices, working with her hands, and ensuring that the food for the day will be there. The simile with the merchant ships suggests that she brings a continual supply of abundance.

C. Financial Enterprise (31:16–18)

16–18 This part of the account portrays the noble wife as a shrewd business woman, making wise investments from her earnings. There is no foolish purchasing nor indebtedness here. Verse 17 literally says that she "girds her loins with strength"—she is a vigorous and tireless worker, for girding is an expression for preparation for serious work. Consequently, she learns by experience that her efforts are profitable. The last line of v.18 may simply mean that she burns the midnight oil in following through a business opportunity, although it may signify that her house was flourishing without calamity (cf. Job 18:6; Jer 25:10).

D. Provision for the Family and the Poor (31:19–21)

19 Verse 19 focuses on the domestic activity of spinning: the "distaff" is the straight rod, and the "spindle" is the round or circular part. She "stretches out" (NIV, "holds") her hand to the work to provide clothing.

20 The noble wife also provides for the poor. The text literally says that she "opens her palm" to the poor; i.e, she gives to the poor with liberality (Ps 112:9). This was the hand that was diligently at work in the previous verse with an acquired skill; it is not the hand of a lazy, wealthy woman.

21 Moreover, the noble wife is well prepared for the future. When faced with cold, her family has warm clothes to wear. The word "scarlet" could be read also as "two cloaks," suggesting double garments for warmth.

E. Distinction by Industry (31:22–24)

22 The noble woman's clothing is "fine linen and purple," i.e., costly and luxurious. Garments dyed with purple indicated wealth and high rank (cf. Ex 25–37, passim; SS 3:10). One is reminded of the rich man in Lk 16:19, who also was clothed in purple and fine linen. The problem was not with the clothing he wore but that he was not charitable.

23 The woman's husband was important. The "gate" was the place of the assembly of the elders who had judicial responsibilities (Ru 4:1–12). The man was a prominent, well-known leader.

24 The woman's industry finds expression in business. The poet did not think it strange or unworthy for a woman to engage in honest trade. In fact, weaving of fine linens was a common trade for women in Palestine from antiquity.

F. Wisdom and Prosperity (31:25–27)

25 The noble wife is diligent and prudent in her work; her strength and honor come from her solid financial and economic position, as v.25b shows; so the result is that she is confident in facing the future.

26–27 She is wise and gracious in her speech. She uses good, practical common sense in her discussions; and her instruction is reliable. The last phrase of v.26 literally says "law of kindness": kind and faithful instruction comes from her. Finally, the wife's supervision of the household is alert, as a watchman.

G. Merits Recognized (31:28–29)

28 The wisdom of the noble woman inspires praise from her family—from those who know her the best. Unfortunately, praise often comes from outside the home, from those who do not know the person very well. This woman is of such worth that her children "rise up" to praise her.

29 This woman surpasses all other women. These words are probably the praise of the husband who speaks for the rest of the family.

H. Laudatory Summation (31:30–31)

30 These words could be the husband's but may better form the poet's summation of the matter. In any case, what is valued in the wife is her domestic efficiency and her piety rather than charm and beauty. Physical appearance is not necessarily dismissed—it simply does not endure as do those qualities that the fear of the Lord produces. Beauty is deceitful, and one who pursues beauty may very well be disappointed by the character of the "beautiful" person. The reference to the fear of the Lord brings the book full circle: it began with a reference to it (1:7) and ends with a similar reference.

31 As in v.23, there is a reference to the city gate, where all manner of business was conducted. The woman's works bring her praise in her own rights and not merely as an appendage of her husband.

The Old Testament in the New

OT Text	NT Text	Subject
Pr 3:11–12	Heb 12:5–6	Love and discipline
Pr 3:34	Jas 4:6; 1Pe 5:5	Grace for the humble
Pr 4:26	Heb 12:13	Level paths for your feet
Pr 10:12	1Pe 4:8	Love covers sin
Pr 11:31	1Pe 4:18	Receiving due reward
Pr 24:12	Mt 16:27; Ro 2:6	God's fair judgment
Pr 25:21–22	Ro 12:20–21	Treating one's enemies
Pr 26:11	2Pe 2:22	Dog returns to vomit

Ecclesiastes

INTRODUCTION

1. Background

Ecclesiastes is one of the most puzzling books of the Bible. Its apparently unorthodox statements and extreme pessimism caused its inclusion in the canon of Scripture to be questioned. However, because historically it was thought to have been the work of Solomon (see Authorship), its place in the canon of Scripture was generally secure.

2. Authorship and Date

Traditionally, the authorship of the book has been ascribed to Solomon. This is implied in the opening verse, where the author, "the Teacher" (Heb., *Qoheleth*; GK 7738), is described as the "son of David, king in Jerusalem." Again at 1:12 he states, "I, the Teacher, was king over Israel in Jerusalem." The tradition of David as singer and psalmist is borne out by an early reference at Am 6:5 and is taken seriously in the light of the lament for Saul and Jonathan (2Sa 1:17–27). We ought to take Solomon's reputation for wisdom equally seriously and see his court as the center that drew the wise from all quarters to discuss problems of living in a difficult world (1Ki 4:34).

Solomon was on the high road of trade and culture. He had important contacts with Egypt, including an Egyptian wife, and Egypt had a wealth of wisdom literature. This literature includes poems that reason about the problems of life. Other known writings of a similar type come from Babylon. Presumably, Solomon too listened, collected, and added to the literature by facing the realities of life and showing the way through for the God-fearing person. A close examination of the book of Ecclesiastes reveals that there are no passages that conclusively rule out the possibility that Solomon was the author (though to view someone other than him as the author is a defensible position for evangelicals to hold).

If Solomon was the author, then this book was written sometime during his time, presumably in his latter years. Because some of the expressions in the book seem to require a later date than the time of Solomon, it is plausible that his words, preserved by wise men over several centuries, were eventually recorded by a new Teacher in his own dialect or in the Hebrew of his time.

3. Purpose

The theme of the book appears in the prologue: "Meaningless! Meaningless! ... Everything is meaningless." The general conclusion comes in the epilogue, which speaks of fearing God and keeping his commandments because we must one day give account to him. The meaning and purpose of the book must be discovered within this framework. Life in the world is subject to frustration; but human beings can still accept their circumstances, even enjoy them, and find strength to live life as it comes.

The book tells us to begin where we are, with the assumption that God has his purpose for today. To fulfill this purpose we must use our God-given sense as well as our own experience of ourselves and that of others. God has a proper time for each thing to be done (3:1–8), and recognizing this allows us to accept life as it comes (3:11a), even though we know that we have fitted no more than one piece in the great puzzle. Thus we are directed from speculation (e.g., 8:16–17) to observation. It is right to meditate on the total work of God, but we are to glorify God in the common things of life; i.e., we are to make the fullest use of the present moment.

There may be times of stress and strain and special calling; but the norm is to eat, drink, and live our daily lives as those who gladly rejoice in God's good gifts and intend to use them to his glory. This is the theme of the refrains (2:24–26; 3:12–13, 22; 5:18–19; 8:15; 9:7–9). In fact, it tallies with the NT teaching that we are to eat and drink and do all our actions to the glory of God (1Co

10:31; Col 3:17), since he has generously given us everything for our enjoyment (1Ti 6:17). In all this there is nothing unworthy.

4. Theological Values

Ecclesiastes encourages the reader to a God-centered worldview rather than falling victim to frustrations and unanswered questions. None of its contents has to be rejected in the light of the NT. Although the NT revelation is vastly greater than that in Ecclesiastes, the two are not devoid of similarities (e.g., Jas 4:13–17). Like the people of God in Solomon's time, believers today are subject to the unexpected changes and chances common to humankind. Yet they know that God works through every vicissitude of life. Respecting the future, which for Solomon was shrouded in a shadow land, Christians have the glorious hope of being in the presence of Christ himself (2Co 5:6; Php 1:23).

The writer of Ecclesiastes was no humanist. He named God some forty times, and six times he spoke of the fear of God (3:14; 5:7; 7:18; 8:12–13; 12:13). He used the general name *Elohim* (GK 466) and not *Yahweh* ("the LORD"; GK 3378), the covenant name of God. This may be because he was writing about God in relation to the whole of humankind. Another possibility may be that as the OT period drew to its close, there was a growing reluctance to use the sacred covenant name in daily speech. Hence, when Ecclesiastes reached its final form—even if Solomon had been the author and had used the covenant name—reverence would have required the use of *Elohim*.

So far as a person's state before God is concerned, the book contrasts two classes of humanity. One comprises the God-fearing (3:14; 5:7; 7:18; 8:12–13; 12:13), righteous (3:17; 7:15–16, 20; 8:14; 9:2), good (9:2), and wise (frequently mentioned, e.g., 10:2). The other comprises the sinners (2:26; 7:26; 8:11; 9:2, 18) and the wicked (3:17; 7:15; 8:10, 12–14; 9:2). There is also frequent mention of fools (e.g., 5:4), a term that does not mean a jester or merely unwise person, but one who is godless and wicked (cf. Pss 14:1; 53:1). It is especially descriptive of those who act wrongly because they do not make any effort to discover the will of God. At the same time the book recognizes that there is no such thing as sinless perfection (7:20).

Strangely, there is no reference to repentance and forgiveness. There are, however, two references to sacrifices (5:1; 9:2), the second of which is linked to moral evil and uncleanness. Lest we downgrade Ecclesiastes because of its silence about repentance and forgiveness, we should take into account that a book on godly morals need not necessarily deal with these things. Rather, it assumes that the reader knows about these teachings.

EXPOSITION

I. The Meaninglessness of Nature, Wisdom, and Wealth (1:1–2:23)

1. The Theme: All Is Frustration (1:1–3)

1–3 "The Teacher" (GK 7738), writing as a wise and observant king of David's line, sets out his theme. He lives in a world riddled through with vanity, futility, and frustration. Human beings, struggling to live, meet frustration at every turn. One looks back to the record of sin's entry into human life (7:29; Ge 3). The human race chose to become self-centered and self-guided rather than remaining God-centered and God-guided. Thus they became earthbound and frustrated, and this book demonstrates that there is no firm foundation under the sun for earthbound people to build on so as to find meaning, satisfaction, and the key to existence.

2. The Frustration in Nature and History (1:4–11)

4–11 The Teacher plunges straight into the search for ultimate truth and stability in nature and in human history. He cites examples of research into repetitive phenomena, choosing first four basic facts of the created order: (1) the solid earth, (2) the rising and setting of the heavenly bodies, (3) air currents, and (4) the flow and evaporation of water. South and north are selected as a balance to the east and west of the sun. Solomon was interested in nature generally (cf. 1Ki 4:33).

Scientists define physical laws that have always operated; but if we ask them about origins or some ultimate purpose, there is nothing they can tell us from nature that will give us the meaning of life. The biblical view of nature, however, is that it testifies to a Creator, though it does not compel belief in him (e.g., Ps 19; Ro 1:20). But the Teacher is concerned with proof rather than testimony and rightly maintains that meaning and security cannot be found in nature alone. If everything is endlessly cyclical, how can we break out of the temporal circle into a state that leads somewhere? We may also ask, What is the true meaning to be found in nature—if there is a meaning, is it found in the beauty of spring or in the violence of the storm and the earthquake?

There is a similar impasse in the study of history. What help is there in an endless succession of birth and death? History shows men and women struggling to find meaning in their experiences, but all in vain. Every generation looks for some satisfying novelty, but each novelty can be analyzed as only a variant on the past. Obviously, there have been many inventions; but in the context the Teacher probably has in mind any invention that enables human beings to break out of nature and the succession of history into meaning, which transcends the sense of futility. They have not found it; and each generation, regarding itself as the greatest, still reaches no conclusion.

3. The Frustration of Wisdom (1:12–18)

12–13 The Teacher has confronted us with a situation that today might be called "existential." The human race exists in a series of experiences and cannot discover any onward meaning in them. All people can do is exist and make the best of what comes—or drop out altogether. Yet most people still believe that life has some meaning if only they could find it. In his first mention of God, the Teacher stated what comes out again later (e.g., 3:11)—namely, that God has given something to humankind that he has denied to the rest of the animal world: the constant, though often worrying, urge to make sense of life and to work toward a transcendent ideal. Human beings, in the likeness of God, look for meanings so that they can control and direct their instinctive desires.

14–15 There is so much people cannot understand. Not only are people aiming at unsubstantial ideals, which blow away like the wind, but their efforts to straighten things out and supply what seems to be lacking are continually disappointed. Today we have straightened out many of the twists of the past and added many comforts to life; but as many of us have seen in our lifetime, in one moment a whole generation or some dominant group of rulers can revive the horrors of the past and destroy what is truly good and meaningful in life.

16–18 The Teacher was remorseless in his effort to make us think, but even the wisdom of Solomon could not break through on the basis of human reason. We observe that those who have struggled to wrest the secret of the universe and those who have abandoned any attempt to understand it both find frustration. Those who take life seriously can never take it lightly. At the end of this section, the Teacher is frustrated because his thinking is earthbound under heaven, for he depends wholly on his own great wisdom and increased knowledge.

4. The Frustration of Unlimited Wealth (2:1–11)

1–2 We notice that this description of Solomon omits mention of immorality but is concerned with the joys of luxury. No serious thinker supposes that a Casanova is on the way to discover the purpose of living (cf. 7:26). The Teacher set his sights on those pleasures that many people considered worthwhile in themselves. He surrounded himself with happy people who kept him amused, but even the jokes and laughter grew stale (cf. 7:1–6).

3 The Teacher then turned to sensual pleasures. Yet he still kept a hold of himself so that he could analyze his experiences and see whether they proved to be the answer to all human desires.

4–8 A sensible use of money may be a form of creativity; so Solomon expressed himself in extensive buildings and planted things. Naturally Solomon did no more than supervise the work. He had only to give the word, and slaves did his bidding (cf. 1Ki 9:17–22). The service of others is something that money can buy.

Solomon also determined to be the largest owner of cattle and sheep. He did not lose sight of the need for an ever-increasing income; and his position of holding the trading bridge between Egypt and Asia made him one of the wealthiest monarchs of the day (1Ki 10:21–29). As a connoisseur of music, he collected at court the finest soloists and choirs. The final item in the list (translated "harem"; GK 8721) may well refer to Solomon's wives and concubines, but the Hebrew word does not occur elsewhere in the Bible.

9–11 More than any other man, Solomon was able to buy every single thing he imagined could satisfy him. He kept his sense of discernment intact (vv.3, 9). Solomon wanted to determine to what extent one could find the key to life in a varied use of great wealth. In the end money and the pleasures it can buy do not lift us out of the realm of earthbound frustration. The Teacher will later amplify this conclusion in terms of death and the handling of one's possessions (see 5:8–17). Despite riches we may still be empty shells and our gains only as substantial as the wind.

5. The Ultimate Frustration: Death (2:12–23)

12–16 A critic may object that the pursuit of luxury is the aim of a fool, but what of wisdom as a proper guide to life? Nobody who follows in Solomon's steps will ever have greater opportunities than he had for combining wisdom and wealth. Granted that wisdom is more worthwhile than folly and gives light in the darkness of life; yet both wise and foolish have to face the ultimate fate of dying, and death is the ultimate frustration. The Teacher did not go back on his conclusion that wisdom is better than folly but asked how much better it is in the light of the fact

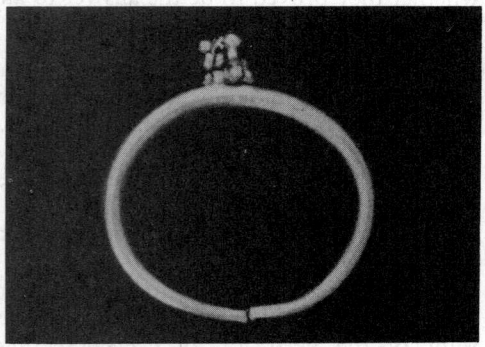

Gold rings were common luxuries among upper classes in times of prosperity. Courtesy of the Tell Gezer Excavations, 1972.

that both the wise and fools will be forgotten in future ages.

17–23 The Teacher found no security and purpose in the rewards of his labor. A person may not be so rich as Solomon but may live wisely and accumulate wealth in a perfectly legitimate way. Such people may wear themselves out in the process. Then comes death and the sharing of the estate. What sort of persons will the heirs be? They too may be wise; but they may also be fools, especially if they have imbibed their father's materialistic values without having had to struggle for a living.

II. Divine Order of Life (2:24–3:22)

1. Daily Life to Be Enjoyed (2:24–26)

24–26 This is the first of similar refrains that, if taken out of their context, might seem to advocate a life of mere pleasure seeking. The Teacher was clearly speaking to normal people in normal circumstances. He was not discussing physical and social evils that needed to be put right. Up to now he had considered life from the angle of the person who tried to have a knowledge of good and evil (cf. Ge 2:16–17) without being accountable to God for one's standards of thought or behavior. The alternative is the life of faith, which does not understand everything (see ch. 3) but looks for the hand of God in the events of daily life.

The walk with God means that we can ask for his wisdom to use life rightly and his knowledge to understand such of his ways as he may disclose to us, and thus experience the joy of fulfillment despite life's difficulties. The Wisdom writings of Scripture speak of life in a stable society where individuals and authorities should be carrying out the will of God. Normally such a society prospers. It is God's will that sinners who are here something more than fools and who, because they are sinners, do not mind what means they use for "gathering and storing up," should hand over their ill-gotten gains. The final sentence at v.26 obviously refers to the frustration for sinners.

2. God's Plan for Living (3:1–8)

1 Human beings are to take their lives day by day from the hand of God (2:24–26; 3:12–13), realizing that God has a fitting time for each thing to be done. The significance of this section is that human beings are responsible to discern the right times for the right actions; and when they do the right action according to God's time, the result is "beautiful" (v.11). The Teacher did not say that everything was imposed on them against their will, even though some events go beyond their understanding.

2 Birth and death, the boundaries of life under the sun, are mentioned first. Children have always been looked upon as a blessing from God (cf. Ps 127:3–5), whereas barrenness has been considered a judgment from him (Ge 30:22–23; 1Sa 1:6–7; 2:1–11; Isa 4:1; Lk 1:25). On the other hand, increased medical knowledge enables life to be extended far beyond the limits of threescore years and ten. So we look for God's plan, not for euthanasia, to determine when and whether to resuscitate lives that are ready to slip away. Planting and uprooting have both a natural and a metaphorical sense. The natural is taken up at 11:6, the metaphorical in Jeremiah's call to break up the fallow ground and uproot the thorns (Jer 4:3; cf. Mt 13:24–30).

3 Killing and healing involve the question of a so-called just war and capital punishment. What is God's plan for our time and for the specific situations that confront us? When should aggression be met by resistance and when should there be some healing compromise? When does an offender need a life sentence, and when does he need psychiatric treatment?

Tearing down and building up, while involving plans for building development, also have a metaphorical meaning. The Christian life has its negative and positive sides (1Co 3:10–15; Gal 2:18).

4–5 There are appropriate occasions for tears and laughter (Ro 12:15). Biblical society had a healthier attitude toward the use of weeping and mourning as a meaningful and healing part of life (cf. Ps 6:6–7; Jn 11:35). There is a time to clear the ground of loose stones before collecting other stones for building. There are also times for expressing or refraining from love, a relevant reminder for many people today that there are standards of sex.

6–8 Acquisition and sacrifice form part of life, as do tearing up and repairing, silence and speech. Love and hate are both needed, provided we love and hate the proper things

(Ro 12:9; 1Jn 4:20). When must we war against those who promote evil? With whom are we to be in happy agreement?

3. The Pieces and the Whole (3:9–15)

9–11 Admittedly, God has his proper time for every event, but we naturally want to grasp the whole plan he has for our lives. What is the point of it all? (1) We have to take steps to discover and fulfill the duties to be done each day. Doing the right thing at the right time yields a beautiful sense of fulfillment. (2) However much we see things as units of knowledge and experience, we must try to bring these units into a meaningful whole. This is an aspect of our likeness to God, who alone embraces the whole. The Fall occurred when our original progenitors chose to have their own knowledge of good and evil and to be in charge of their own lives. By cutting themselves off from God, they were without clear direction, no longer living in the light of God's whole plan.

In this fallen world the believer must ask, "Lord, what would you have me do now? I know my life has an eternal purpose, and I desire to understand how all things work together for good. But I realize that I am not as you and cannot say just why such-and-such a thing has come to me" (cf. v.11).

12–14 There is much to be enjoyed, especially as one goes through life doing good. It requires faith to declare that there is a permanency about all God-inspired good deeds. Therefore, one must walk in humble fear lest one miss the will of God in life. The fuller Christian revelation enriches these principles. Treasure may be laid up in heaven (Mt 6:20), works of gold and silver will survive the fire test (1Co 3:10–15), and a Christian's works in the Lord follow him or her (Rev 14:13). But unbelieving humanists, however earnest, cannot plan their lives in the light of eternity.

15 If we look for further guidance as to the will of God, we may find it in his working in history. History does repeat itself. We may discard the lessons of history, but God confronts us with them again and again (cf. 1:10). We have no basis for complaining that he has not warned us that he will call the past to account.

4. The Consequences of Mortality (3:16–22)

16–17 One of the greatest problems in understanding the total plan of God is that reward and punishment sometimes seem conspicuously absent. People in positions of power have a tendency to grab for themselves. Hence believers by faith hold that God will redress the wrong assessments made on earth (Mal 3:16–4:3; Rev 22:11–12).

18–22 Meanwhile, the Teacher centers his thoughts on the inevitability of death. God makes all sensible people realize that they are as much subject to death as is the animal world. Both are animated by a similar breath of life that sustains them while living and is withdrawn at death. People and animals also resemble each other in having bodies made of vegetable and mineral substances that revert to dust at death. There is no reference here to any personal spirit or soul, but the spirit or breath is the sustaining life that comes from God (Ge 6:17; Ps 104:29–30).

Most people behave as though they have endless time and close their eyes to the fact of death. God wants us to face that fact. The Teacher challenges those who live as though they are immortal and are never to be accountable to God (vv.16–17). We shall not be brought back for a second chance to cooperate with God in doing his will on this side of eternity. We must make the most of the present in order to please God. We cannot count on the future, since we do not know what it is.

The conclusion is a further summary of the refrain that God has his day-by-day plan for our lives and that we can find the joy of fulfillment in it.

III. The Frustration of Politics (4:1–16)

1–3 The Teacher had seen that God must inevitably redress the wrong judgments of unjust rulers (3:17) and that high and low must face the fact that they are but mortals (3:18–22). The Teacher met the valid objection that some people find it hard to take their lives each day from the hand of God and enjoy them (3:22). Granted that average persons in settled circumstances may not find much difficulty in aiming at this, but observation shows that the simple ways of life may be wrecked by leaders who misuse their power.

There are times when we thank God for delivering some poor tortured sufferer through death. Anyone who feels deeply, like the Teacher, may wish on occasion that he or she had never been born into all the sufferings of the world (cf. Mt 18:1–9).

4 This verse gives a profound diagnosis when it says that all achievement comes through a drive toward superiority. The desire for achievement is good in itself, since God never intended humankind to be static or simply passive. The challenge to be the best and to be breaking fresh ground always involves some rivalry of ideas and has led to notable scientific progress; but rivalry between individuals and nations may divert healthy competition into bitter envy. In industry, moreover, where the average worker has little scope for creativity, there is envy for another person's money or status. So a healthy drive becomes yet another frustration and a chasing after the wind.

5–6 Two proverbs follow. To ignore the drive for achievement and become a dropout is foolish self-destructiveness. But the drive must be harnessed to what is compatible with inner peace.

7–8 The drive may turn into miserliness—the overaccumulation of money or other possessions. Collecting possessions can become an obsession, which kills sane thinking and prevents a person from following the advice of 3:22. Here is another form of the power complex—wherein one's success gives that person a feeling of triumphant superiority.

9–12 The drive to succeed is mature when it has its interplay with the whole of society. Two acting together are better than one selfish individual; they can support each other when there is need for support. This proverb applies to all relationships. Individualism and divisions make for weakness. There is a proper complex of power in a three-strand rope, provided the strands are good and support one another.

13–16 Finally, the power complex is seen in the struggle between tradition and revolution. Political leaders or business executives may fight to keep their position when they are no longer capable of making wise decisions; yet they will not take advice. Young revolutionaries who have been imprisoned or kept down may indeed be wiser. But if they come to power, they too may succumb to the desire to lord it over everyone else; and those under them will be glad to be rid of them. So the Teacher concludes that power all too often brings only frustration. It does not hold the key to life.

IV. The Frustration of Life (5:1–7:29)

1. Quiet Before God (5:1–7)

1–2 In contrast to the power complexes of the previous chapter, we are brought quietly into the presence of God. Here is a keen analysis of motives in prayer and worship. We come before God in humility, recognizing his majesty and his right to our lives. We seek his guidance and listen to his words.

The alternative is to suppose that offerings can be a substitute for a God-ordered life. Sometimes extreme concern over one issue is an unconscious screen against facing other issues. It is as though we call God's attention to the sacrifice we are making while being blind to some essential command that he makes.

Yet we are meant to speak to God in prayer. The emphasis in v.2 is on rashness and haste. Prayer is not reciting a list as quickly as possible so as to rush once more into the round of daily life (cf. Mt 6:7–8).

3 As personal and business cares produce dreams, which are unsubstantial things, so many words produce foolish and empty prayer. When we come before God, our minds are full of our own business rather than with the worship of God. When we talk too much, we usually talk like fools. This can be especially bad in the house of God.

4–6 There is, however, a place for making resolutions (vows) before God. The challenge that comes through a sermon or a book and, above all, from Scripture itself should be clinched by definite commitment. The same follow-up is vital if in time of trouble we make a promise to do something if only God will deliver us. If we do not carry it through, it would be better to have made no commitment at all. We must not draw back and make an excuse about not having understood what we were required to do. This can only arouse God's displeasure, and he may well take away what we were hoping to keep for ourselves.

7 The section concludes with the reminder that our approach to God must be a realistic response to what he has shown us to be his will—not a wordy presentation of our dreams for ourselves. In other words, we should try to put ourselves in a position to discover God's way to use what he has given us in our daily lives.

2. Money and Mortality (5:8–20)

8–9 The Teacher again speaks of the use and abuse of money in daily life. Too often the struggle for power brings suffering for the underdog. Each shows servility toward those above and waits to take their place while lording it over those below him or her. The Teacher on the whole sees an advantage in a supreme ruler truly concerned for the welfare of the land. One hopes for a wise person at the head of the country or a business or an institution—one who has both ability and humility.

10 Struggle for power comes from the desire for more and more money. It is not wrong to have a proper concern for a living wage, but the prestige of perquisites and greed for luxuries make this verse as relevant as ever. These insatiable desires also bring frustration. Not money itself, but a love of money is "a root of all kinds of evil" (1Ti 6:10).

11–12 The person who has an abundance of material possessions may become a miser (4:7–8) or may never know real friendship because of the numbers of acquaintances who want to share in the wealth. On the other hand, assuming that one has a living wage, the honest worker can sleep peacefully at night. But the anxieties of money-grubbers drive them to sleeping pills and tranquilizers.

13–17 A note of even deeper sadness is that people may accumulate money, even to the extent of warping their character. Then a miscalculation or an unfortunate turn of events destroys everything. What they had hoped to leave to their children is gone. Perhaps the children have been counting on inheriting that money and have done nothing for themselves (cf. 2:18–21). So the parents have wasted the driving desire of their lives. They have measured success by wrong standards; and when their long struggle for money came to nothing, they died poor and frustrated (cf. Mt 6:19–21).

18–19 So the refrain comes again. The Teacher has described those who aim for money and lose real life. Can we then have life first and secondarily find a place for money? The refrain says yes, if we take life day by day from God and seek to know his plan, so far as it may be known. We must be willing to work. Once most work was constructive and often creative. Today many are involved in monotonous activity, another example of frustration. We must also look for constructive uses of leisure—activity that may not bring much money but will bring the added enjoyment that the Teacher has in mind. Therefore, it is right to pray and to look for work that will produce enough to live on and possessions we can enjoy with a good conscience, because they are things God has given us to enjoy (1Ti 6:17).

20 In summary, the ideal for those devoted to God is that they not brood over the past or worry about the future; for God fills their hearts with joy (cf. Mt 6:25–34; Php 4:4–7).

Again we remember that the Teacher in this section has in mind the average person with a living wage. Elsewhere, as we have seen, he takes up the frustration of the suffering and despised.

3. The Unfulfilled Life (6:1–9)

1–2 There is an obvious contrast between the wording of 5:19 and 6:2. It seems that 5:19 describes those who accept a standard of living for which they have worked, without continually craving for more (cf. 5:10; 6:9). The "man" described in 6:2 is more concerned with having everything he wants, and his God-given status in life allows this. But his tragedy comes when God allows this wealth to be taken over by a stranger. This may happen when the man has no children or when he loses his property through war, violence, or some other act of injustice. Many have been broken by such calamities. Others have refused to succumb to what the Teacher sees as vanity but have rebuilt a new life, often with less regard for the intrinsic value of possessions (Heb 10:34).

3–6 Many children and long life were looked upon by the Hebrews as a mark of God's blessing, but neither guarantees a satisfying life. Some parents think they have to decide how many children they ought to have, in view of the population explosion (see 3:2).

The exaggeration here may suggest that the large number of children keeps the whole family in poverty so that life cannot be enjoyed properly and so that at the end there is not enough to pay for the funeral. Or possibly, since children are considered in the Scriptures a blessing from the Lord, this verse may mean that a person may have double blessings—children and wealth—and yet not have the capacity to enjoy them and at the end die either in poverty or unloved or both. A life of total misery, which might have been avoided, is worse than natural abortion, by which a life never sees the light of day and never has to struggle in the arena of life (cf. Job 3:16). The death of the fetus reminds the Teacher of the death that awaits every person, even though they live to more than twice the age of the patriarchs.

7–9 This section speaks of another possible frustration. A human being has to work to live but has an insatiable appetite for more. This is common to both wise and foolish. Today the business world contains many clever people who work hard because they are obsessed with piling up money, while on the other side there are those who are ever alert for a quick profit—honest or dishonest. In between come the average people who, though poor in material things, have come to terms with life. They also work for their living but are content with what they have.

4. What Is Good? (6:10–12)

10–12 The Teacher was prepared to listen to objections. He said that human beings should do the will of God by being content to take their daily life from God's hand. But are they really free to choose? Since God is supreme, he has predestined everything and has made humanity too weak to resist. Reasoning, complaining, and arguing bring no answer and lead to further frustration. What value are categories such as "good"? Life is too short to worry about behavior. Even if moral standards have some bearing on the future, no one knows what the future will bring.

5. Practical Advice For Daily Living (7:1–14)

Ultimately the Teacher will return to the theme that obedience is possible even though we cannot discover the whole plan of God for us. So we now have some practical proverbs for daily living, showing that God's will for humanity is not a set of meaningless rules but a walk that brings a sense of fulfillment.

1–6 The first group of proverbs speaks of a serious view of life. The Teacher says that a good and well-deserved reputation is better than a mask of perfumed cosmetics. Preserve your good name until the day of your death and you achieve the potentiality of your birth inheritance (cf. v.8a).

If we are looking for signposts for living, we are more likely to gain insight when face-to-face with eternal things than in noisy company where the deeper realities of life are drowned in food, drink, and levity. Remembering that life on earth does not go on forever, we are moved to look below its surface. A sorrow shared may bring more inner happiness than an evening with back-slapping jokers.

Moreover, if we are in earnest about God's good plan (cf. 6:10–12), we must be ready for serious conversation with men and women who are experienced in life and be open to criticism from them. They may not answer all our problems, but their advice will be worth far more than popular songs devoid of serious moral content and the shallow humor of comedians.

7 The next proverbs are not so closely linked, though each relates to the question of how to live an acceptable life. If we hold an influential position, we must not use it for personal advantage. A reputation can be destroyed in a moment.

8–9 Patience is needed to see our resolutions and enterprises through to the end. How often we embark on something with pride in our ability to carry it through but abandon it because of a few discouragements! Then we may become angry and lash out at other people as an excuse for our own incompetence.

10–12 People have always looked back to the good old days. Even Christians sometimes overestimate the early church, the Reformation, or periods of revival. Wise people certainly learn from the past, but they live in the present with all its opportunities. Overmuch dwelling on the past can prevent us from overcoming the world, which often seems so much more wicked today than ever before. Many suppose that sudden wealth, which would relieve them of having to earn their living, would solve all problems. If money comes like this, one needs wisdom to use it properly. The security wisdom gives can be compared with the security associated with money; in fact, wisdom is a better guarantee of the good life.

13–14 God's name so far has not been mentioned in this section. The Teacher has set out advice that commends itself to any sensible person, even a humanist. But he is looking for the God-guided life that does not contradict the true wisdom of the ages but rather goes beyond it. The believer must look for the hand of the personal God.

The reference to God's "making crooked" (GK 6430) stresses his sovereign control over all events. There are some things that we cannot alter. As children of God, we commonly experience both good and bad and may even thank God for allowing hardships rather than giving us an entirely smooth passage (cf. Mt 8:20; Lk 10:38; 2Co 1:4–7). Part of the life of faith is accepting prosperity and adversity from God's hand without being able to explain just how everything will be worked out for the future (Ro 8:28).

6. Moderation Commended (7:15–22)

15 We have been told to live the good life. But if goodness is not rewarded in this life, why be good? The Teacher's life, like everyone else's, is lived in a world subject to frustration. It is all very well to talk of accepting prosperity and adversity (v.14); yet it is strange when righteous people die while they have still much to offer while villains survive to carry on their misdeeds.

16 This verse is not intended as an answer. In fact, its continuation at v.17 says that being a fool may bring on an early death, whereas the problem of v.15 is that a fool may live beyond his proper time. There may be unknown factors in the length of life of the good person and the bad, but there are some factors that are controllable. Being "overrighteous" is an obvious synonym for that type of Pharisaism that Christ warned against (Mt 5:20; 23:1–36). "Overwise" may be the subtle casuistry that such righteousness needs to support it (Mt 23:16–22), or it may be the substitute of a vast knowledge of facts for the knowledge needed for practical living (cf. 12:12).

17–19 We need not suppose that the Teacher means that we may be a little wicked so long as we do not plunge headlong into folly. We are not to model ourselves after either the prig or the villain. Neither can lead us to the full life. We need to take both pieces of advice to heart and to act on them. The way of victory is to keep God in the forefront of life. Wisdom is not the knowledge of accumulated facts but the inner strength that comes from a God-instructed conscience. There is a link between the fear of God and the true wisdom that gives inner strength (v.10; cf. Pr 9:10), which is here contrasted with mere power.

20–22 The good life has to be lived with the awareness that there is no such thing as sinless perfection. Righteousness is the settled way, though sins certainly occur and need to be repented of. The godly should be genuine and sincere. They should not listen to gossip, especially if they are hoping to hear themselves criticized or cursed especially by those who can observe them closely, such as their servants. The criticism may not be deserved, but again it may be.

7. Bad Relationships (7:23–29)

23–29 From a discussion of the good life, the Teacher passes to the intense depression he has felt when seeing men and women at their worst. Wise people admit that the problem of evil is insoluble, but practical evil is a horrible reality for which human beings can be held responsible. As in modern times, the Teacher faced the evil of unrestrained sex (cf. Pr 7). As an example of human folly, he warned against women of easy morals. Verse 28 is not about "upright" men and women but about "wise" men and women (NIV's "upright" is not in the MT). He found that an absolutely wise man is exceedingly rare, one in a thousand; but so far he had not found even this tiny percentage among women. One cannot blame God for this; so the fault lies in our misuse of our freedom.

Verse 26 may reflect Solomon's experiences with his hundreds of wives and concubines (1Ki 11:3–4). Though Solomon's desire to compete with other Oriental potentates may in large measure account for his building up a royal harem, he found that a harem did not provide the appropriate companion for a man. How much better he would have been with one good wife, such as he speaks of in 9:9 and Pr 31!

V. Life in View of Death (8:1–9:18)

1. The Inevitability of Death (8:1–14)

1 Chapter 7 concluded with a pessimistic view of human attainment of wisdom. Great teachers sometimes use exaggerated language to make their point (cf. Mt 19:24). Here the Teacher shakes himself out of his depression. There are truly wise people; and while true wisdom must be realistic, it need not make a person perpetually gloomy.

2–7 If you aim to please God, you are like a courtier who tries to please his king. Obey the king's commands, recognizing that you are pledged to serve him. If you displease him, you must accept the fact that there will be a rift between you. He is not accountable to you for what he does. When you know his will, you will be wise to do it at the right time and in the right way, even though you cannot see his full purpose.

8 The analogy of the king illustrates the concept of God's total plan. Like the king, God has the power of life and death; and, when the time comes for a person to die, he or she cannot insist on retaining the breath of life. Meanwhile, one must press on until the end. There is no escape from the battle by treacherously joining the enemies of the king.

9–13 Powerful oppressors who made a show of religious observances have had magnificent funerals and public orations in their honor. This has had its effect on society by creating an attitude of "If I can get away with it, I will do it." The only crime is in being found out. Servants of God know that they live in a fallen world, where bad people often escape punishment. Nevertheless, they look for the enduring approval of their Lord, for this is the purpose of living.

Up to the time when Ecclesiastes was written, God had revealed little about the future life. The superficial contradiction between v.12 and v.13 can best be resolved by the Teacher's realization that living a long time is not necessarily the same as prolonging one's days—a concept made meaningful by the revelation of eternal life in Christ. Such life is both qualitatively and quantitatively beyond any number of years on earth. The Teacher obviously believes in a future judgment (11:9). The day of the wicked, however long it lasts, will not be the normal day that closes with the lengthening of the evening shadows.

14 Yet the sense of frustration is not wholly removed so long as good and evil do not meet their just reward on earth. The Teacher does not hint again at the thought of the final assessment, because he intends to concentrate on life as it is meant to be lived now. The entire section should be compared with Mal 3:13–4:3.

2. Life to Be Enjoyed (8:15–9:10)

15 Once more the Teacher advocates the joy of life. As in 2:24–25, the gifts that God has given can be properly enjoyed only if they are accepted as God's gifts for use, not misuse. Both passages speak of the toil, or work, that God has given us to do to provide for our food and drink (cf. Ge 3:19; Ps 104:23). The verses say much the same as Jesus said in the Sermon on the Mount. Do not let your life be burdened with anxiety; relaxed enjoyment comes through seeking first the kingdom of God and taking food, drink, and clothing from the hands of your Father (Mt 6:25–34). So the Teacher refers to God-given work, God-given food and drink, and God-given joy. It is the realization of this that he commends.

16–17 The Teacher recognizes the tendency toward worry of people who want to know what lies ahead (cf. Mt 6:34). To some this worry is more acute than it is to others. The more capacity one has for thinking things out, the more one is puzzled by the apparent meaninglessness of life. So we must be content to take the pieces one by one, without being able to fit them into the plan that we know must be there (3:11).

9:1 The Teacher returns to the theme of the inevitability of death. The righteous and the wise try to act according to the plan of God, as far as they can determine it. But they have to accept both the good and the bad. Some things, of course, can and should be changed; others must be taken as they are and made stepping stones to higher things. The vital thing is to realize that there is a purpose beyond happiness and sorrow. In fact, you cannot use good and bad events as criteria to decide whether God loves you or hates you.

Your future may be a mixture of the two. When trouble comes, it is easy to ask, "What have I done to deserve this?" It is less easy to ask the same question when happiness comes.

2–4 When people try to estimate the quantity of God's love by what happens to them, they have to face the final fact of death and its significance. Death is the final "reward" that God gives to good and bad persons alike. It almost seems as though God does not care whether people are good or bad. So why be good? If evil pays in this life, why should they not fling themselves into whatever they want to do? The end is only death, after all, and good people die just as others do. The contrast is between a person who is ready to speak the truth on oath and a guilty person who refuses to be put on oath. The Teacher will not accept this. He is leading up to the way we ought to live in view of the finality of death. Instead of living the rotten life of drifting self-indulgence, we should ask the further question, "What is the real purpose of life?" While there is life, there is hope—but hope for what? Surely, in the light of this book, there is hope for using life to the full. A dog that is alive can respond in a way that is impossible for the king of beasts when he is dead.

5–6 The contrast between the dead lion and the living dog supplies the meaning for v.5. The Teacher believes in a future judgment (12:14); so here he cannot be teaching the nonexistence of the departed. The context concerns the ability to plan and work. The living at least know that death must come, but from a human perspective the dead have not had it revealed to them what future there may be for them. The Teacher is not teaching soul-sleep here. Rather his emphasis is on the contrast between the carnal knowledge of the living and the dead.

To fully understand this passage, it is important to realize that our knowledge of the hereafter depends on how much God reveals to us. Attempts to discover the state of the departed through mediums is forbidden in Scripture (e.g., Isa 8:19–20). The OT speaks of the patriarchs being "gathered to [their] people" (Ge 25:8; 49:33). The significance of this expression is shown in Christ's answer to the Sadducees concerning God as the continuing God of Abraham, Isaac, and Jacob:

"He is not the God of the dead but of the living" (Mt 22:32). The spirits in Sheol can be roused to address the king of Babylon when he dies and joins them (Isa 14:9). Yet they clearly do not have the capacities that they once had on earth. There is, for example, nothing corresponding to the temple worship in which they can join in singing the praises of God (Ps 115:17). Occasionally God speaks of a future resurrection, but this is linked to the coming of the Messiah (e.g., Ps 16:9–11; cf. Isa 25:7–8; 26:19; Da 12:2–3; Ac 2:24–35).

So the dead at that time did not know what future they could expect. They had to wait for this until after the resurrection of Jesus Christ. They are soon forgotten on earth, and memorial inscriptions are obliterated with time. "For them love, hate, ambition, all are now over" (NEB), and they cannot return to this life to do or undo.

7–9 The Teacher is not afraid to speak of God as concerned with our present life. We should start with the assumption that our circumstances have come to us with God's approval. Let us make the most of life. Let each day be a festal day, such as when we put on our best clothes. Our hair must not be unkempt like that of mourners (cf. Ezr 9:3) but should be neat (cf. Ps 23:5; Am 6:6). God's approval is not inconsistent with life in a world of frustration. If God has given us the blessings of a wife and, presumably, a family, we are to find happiness in the precious gift of love. This is what Solomon himself failed to find (see 7:23–29).

Food, drink, clothing, and family union form a God-given basis for the good life; and governments today regard them as human rights. But the breadwinner is to be indeed the breadwinner and is to live the good life with an honest day's work. One knows the degrading feelings that come through continued unemployment and the dangers that surround the son who can become a playboy through his father's money (2:19). The Bible has a firm doctrine of work, summed up in 2Th 3:6–13.

10 Now comes the climax. Perhaps Jesus was paraphrasing v.10 in Jn 9:4. The Teacher is not saying anything sub-Christian here. The Bible knows nothing of a purgatory where one can pick up the things neglected in this life. The NT agrees that it is deeds done in the body that count (e.g., 2Co 5:10).

3. Uncertainty and Inequity (9:11–18)

11–12 It may seem strange that the Teacher can maintain faith in God's plan while accepting the factor of "chance" (GK 7004). His theme, however, is that we live in a world where we cannot calculate the future precisely but must share the day-by-day events that come to good and bad alike (cf. Mt 5:45). What we must look for is the plan of God for us today, whatever factors have brought us to this day and will affect us for the future. But the mere possession of speed, strength, wisdom, cleverness, and skill does not in itself guarantee success. We cannot bulldoze our way through life. These capacities must be used against a background of intelligent anticipation and a sense of uncertainty. All of us have to face life as it is; and we cannot foresee the future when it transcends what can reasonably be expected. There is certainly a proper time for each action (3:1–11), and we naturally try now to use our gifts in the light of what we think the future will bring. Yet we cannot foresee every threat or obstacle. We need not give up, but we must continue to ask, In what respect are we to accept God's plan and go forward from here?

13–15 The Teacher gives an interesting example, perhaps from his own experience. Time and chance struck a peaceful city when a powerful king came against it. Time and chance also ensured that the battle was not won by the strong (v.11) but by a poor man who happened to have a wiser plan than anyone else in the city. But then the poor man encountered something unexpected: the people just forgot him. It was all part of the vanity and frustration of a self-centered world. Moreover, it was undoubtedly humiliating for the people to admit that they had been saved by a nobody.

16 What are we to conclude from this illustration? Certainly not that in view of the changes and chances of life we are better off not to use our gifts. It was right for the poor man to come forward and use his wisdom to thwart the king; it would have been right for him to do so even if he had known that his fellow citizens would not ask his advice in the future.

17–18 The citizens were the real losers. The wise man's quiet words in their councils would have been worth more than the chairman's shouting for order in a meeting of people who had nothing to say but insisted on saying it. Yet, though the poor man's wisdom proved more effective than the king's armies, some loud-mouthed counselor was afterwards allowed to undo much of the good that had been gained.

VI. Proverbs (10:1–20)

1. Wise Relationships (10:1–7)

1 The Teacher has returned to the subject of wisdom being superior to folly, even when it fails to gain the recognition it deserves (9:13–18). Since few of us are wholly wise or wholly foolish, we must be careful that such wisdom as we have is not spoiled by apparently insignificant, unwise behavior, just as dead flies in a pot of ointment may turn it into a foul-smelling mass (cf. SS 2:15).

2–3 "Right" is a natural symbol for the strong and good, while "left" signifies the weak and bad. Thus the wise gravitate toward the good, the foolish toward the bad. Even when the foolish try to keep in the middle of the road, their encounters with normal people show them up for what they are. Again, this may be taken as metaphorical.

4 Sometimes our encounters are with authorities. If we clash with them, we should not walk out in a temper. Nor if we are at cross purposes with our supervisor should we resign at once. We should rather take an objective look at ourselves, and maybe we will find that we should apologize.

5–7 Unfortunately, those at the top are not always right. They too may lack wisdom and enjoy manipulating people and situations. They find jobs for their supporters and enjoy humiliating anyone of influence. There are also many little manipulators in the world of business who have undeservedly risen to the top.

2. Wise Planning (10:8–11)

8–11 Despite difficulties and risks, you cannot sit back to avoid facing them in daily life. If you dig a hole in your garden, remember it is there when you go out at night. If you have to pull down an old wall, watch out for snakes. Whenever you decide to do a certain piece of work, your task will be easier if you make proper preparations. Don't blame the class for not listening if you haven't sharpened your wits with proper preparation. Finally, you may find yourself having to undertake a really dangerous task involving life or death. Do not keep putting it off. There is nothing for the snake charmer to do once the victim is dead.

3. Wise Speech and Thought (10:12–20)

12–14 Our ignorance of what will happen in the future should not eliminate common sense. Sensible talk meets with approval in a stable society, but destructive talk degrades. Unfortunately, much of the mass media is dominated by those who pull down moral standards rather than build them up. Again, there are clever arguments that try to interpret the significance—or nonsignificance—of human existence, with concepts that can only be uncertain. The multiplication of arguments that ignore the revelation of God in Jesus Christ can end only in foolishness (1Co 1:18–25).

15 In the context "work" may relate to the many arguments of v.14 (cf. 12:12). In a fine note of sarcasm, this proverb says that a person may be so involved in arguing about the universe that he misses what the ordinary person is concerned about, namely, finding the way home (cf. Isa 35:8–10).

16 It is hard to decide what sort of a king is described here. The word translated "servant" (GK 5853) can also mean "child" (cf. NIV note); it certainly designates an inexperienced person. "Servant" suggests that the king is someone who has suddenly come to the top by others and who keeps his power by letting his deputies do what they want." Child" suggests that the real power is that of the deputies. Those under the influence of such leaders manifest a lack of self-control, shown by feasting at breakfast (cf. Isa 5:11; Ac 2:15); such actions set an example that lesser men and women soon follow.

17 The king here described is born to rule and has been trained for his task since his youth. His close associates have the self-control that gives their lives strength and not dissipation.

18–19 Lazy rulers bring down the great house of the nation, just as a lazy householder lets the beams of his house collapse so that the roof sags and lets in the rain. In v.19 the Teacher apparently returns to the thought of extravagant feasting (cf. v.16). Food and wine occupy the minds of lazy rulers, and they behave as though money can buy everything.

20 When all is said and done, the average citizen must respect authority. The Teacher does not distinguish between good and bad leaders; he has spoken of both, and probably his advice here includes both. Since this verse speaks of wishing someone ill in the privacy of one's own home, it is a warning that malice toward the powers that be may lead to ultimate confrontation with them. If there is something wrong in your town or in the place where you work, you must either keep totally silent or be prepared for your proper criticisms to come to the ears of those at the top.

VII. Wisdom for the Future and the Present (11:1–10)

1. The Uncertain Future and Present Behavior (11:1–6)

The Teacher is approaching the climax of his book. We must fulfill God's purpose by accepting our daily lot in life as from him and by pleasing him make each day a good day. This section gives further wise advice in the light of an uncertain future.

1–2 A common interpretation of this passage is that of charity. The Eastern flat bread is light enough to float, and what you give in charitable gifts will be washed back to you as a reward. But this idea of investment in charity does not belong to the Teacher's thought elsewhere. An alternative view links the meaning with vv.4, 6. "Nothing ventured, nothing gained," as a proverb says. Be like the merchant who uses his capital for trade, including trade across the seas. But be sensible, and do not gamble everything on one venture.

3–4 We are bound to recognize the God-given laws of nature, but we cannot always forecast how they will operate. We often have to act before we can foresee all we would like to know about the future. The farmer who waits until he is completely certain of perfect weather conditions will never reap anything.

5 Life begins in mystery with the baby's conception and prenatal growth and continues with the mystery of the working of God's total plan. Few parents understand precisely how a baby is formed, but most follow the rules of common sense for the welfare of the mother and the unborn child. This is exactly the whole theme of the book. We cannot understand all the ways God works to fulfill his plan, but we can follow God's rules for daily living and thus help bring God's purpose to birth.

6 Because the future is unknown, we must accept calculated risks and believe that though some of our ventures may fail, a sufficient number of them will succeed. The Teacher has been drawing his illustrations from trade and agriculture. They are intended to be practical. One thinks of making an unwise investment in a single project that promises large profits or of the restlessness that risks the family's welfare by moving to some distant field that looks greener.

2. The Certain Future and Present Behavior (11:7–10)

The Teacher has discussed how we should act in view of the uncertainties of life. Now he speaks of the certainty of growing up and growing old.

7–8 First there is the happiness of life when vitality is high, when all things seem possible and the sun shines all the time (cf. 12:2). Yet one must face the inevitable restrictions (ch. 12) that old age brings just as one sees the sun going down toward evening and eventually setting. Life is lived in a world of vanity, and part of the vanity is the process of aging. On the day Adam and Eve disobeyed God, their bodies began to die (Ge 2:17; 3:19).

9 So youth have vitality at its fullest; and if they cannot feel the sense of fulfillment in it, something is wrong. To older people it may seem risky to advise a young person to walk in the ways of one's heart and the sight of one's eyes. Yet the advice is coupled with a reminder of responsibility before God, who is the Supreme Assessor. Taken by themselves, the words could present a picture of God as a grim, condemning judge, but this would be out of keeping with what the Teacher says elsewhere of God's approval of our enjoyment (e.g., 9:7).

10 Obviously, young people face strong temptations, and anxiety and frustration are as much a part of adolescence as vitality is. So youth must say no as well as yes and must discard whatever damages mind or body (cf. Col 3:8–14). The context and the general purport of the book suggest that the Teacher is referring to indulgences that bring guilt to the mind and damage to the body; he is not advocating hedonism here.

VIII. The Frustration of Old Age (12:1–8)

Remembering one's Creator in the time of one's youth, the theme at the end of the previous chapter, is especially important in view of the gradual loss of vitality as age takes its toll of the body and brain. Old age and death are the supreme frustration and meaninglessness that we experience.

1 The passage begins with a general, nonmetaphorical statement. Some today suffer from blindness, deafness, and other physical disabilities described in this chapter. However, as we grow older, we all have some traces of these marks of age, even if they do not develop to the extremes that this chapter describes. So the Teacher is justified in reminding young people that they cannot afford to put off faith in God their Creator until they are older. God wants the best of their lives.

2 The rhythm of life is like the rhythm of the year. Spring and summer give place to the clouds of autumn and winter. The showers that so quickly come and go in youth are succeeded by rain and clouds and then more rain. It becomes progressively harder to throw off troubles and anxieties.

3 The arms and hands that minister to the body begin to tremble, and the legs that once carried the body so strongly weaken and sag at the knee. The loss of teeth makes it hard to grind solid food, and the eyes are dimmed.

4 The organs of hearing gradually close, marooning the owner within the cramped house of the human body. The next picture is difficult to interpret; but, since the grinders must be the teeth (cf. v.3), "grinding" here is likely the voice that comes out softly and often indistinguishably through the toothless gums.

The next phrase is also variously rendered. "Men rise up at the sound of birds" possibly means that in spite of deafness the old person sleeps badly and wakes at the first bird call. An alternative is "he shall rise up to the voice of a bird"; i.e., the voice rises in pitch and grows thin like the twitter of a bird.

The final clause also refers to sounds. It may be a straightforward statement that singing women no longer move him, since their voices do not come to him with any clarity. Or just as he wakes early at the first song of the birds, so he dozes off in the evening as the voices of the singers fade in his ears. But if the whole verse is symbolic, the meaning could be that while the old man's voice is squeaky in conversation, when he tries to sing he can make only a dreary, low, moaning noise.

5 This verse mentions two concrete experiences that frighten old people: the fear of heights and of the traffic in the streets. The latter is specially applicable today; but the narrow streets of an Eastern town, with camels, donkeys, and bustling traders, were doubtless almost as terrifying to a slow-moving pedestrian.

The almond tree pictures the white hair of age. In Palestine, the tree begins to blossom in midwinter; and although the petals are pink at their base, they are white towards the tip. The general impression of the tree in flower is of a white mass. But the old man has no spring to follow so as to enjoy the fruit.

Now the lively, leaping grasshopper can only drag itself along, as happens when the days grow cold, an obvious picture of old age. "Desire" (GK 37) is literally the "caperberry" plant, which apparently was used as a sexual stimulant. One would expect some reference to declining sexual potency in these descriptions.

The Teacher has exhausted his description of the failing faculties, omitting little. It only remains to speak of the inevitable grave, inaugurated with the wailing of the professional mourners.

6 The young person must remember his Creator before the end draws near. The pictures in this verse describe total collapse. The silver chain from which the lamp hangs is snapped. The golden lamp bowl is crushed. The clay pitcher is broken to pieces so that no water

This is the caperberry flower along with several buds (see comment on 12:5). These buds were pickled and then eaten. It was thought that doing so would increase one's sexual desire and power.

can be brought from the well. The wooden wheel that lowers the bucket into the well has itself been broken. Another interpretation links the pictures here with parts of the body. The silver cord could be the spine, the golden bowl the head, the pitcher the heart, and the wheel the organs of digestion.

7 Whatever the interpretation of the details, the fixed fact is death. The body returns to its component parts (cf. Ge 2:7; 3:19). The OT consistently teaches that at death the life principle in humans and animals alike (3:19–21; Ps 104:29–30) returns to God, the Giver of life, to whom we must give account (11:9).

8 So having warned youth to make the most of life while they have the faculties to enjoy it, remembering that they must give account to God for the use of God's gifts, the Teacher reminds them that these gifts and life itself are fleeting. At the moment their faculties are flexible, but as old age sets in, they will harden and decay. One day all will cease in death, the supreme frustration and apparent meaningless end to life.

IX. Epilogue (12:9–14)

1. The Credibility of the Author (12:9–12)

Although it is usual to treat these words as the comment of a disciple, they could be by the Teacher himself, even by Solomon, who, in spite of personal failings, must have retained the gift of wisdom, which he had asked for and obtained (2:9; cf. 1Ki 3:9–12; 4:29–34). The claim here is no more boastful than are the words of the prophets who claim to be speaking the words of the Lord. So, whether written by the Teacher or by a disciple, these verses show that the book is not to be read as the chronicles of skepticism or advocating hedonism.

9–10 The Teacher taught others with full regard for his responsibility as one in a position of authority. He took great care in sifting wise sayings (cf. Lk 1:1–4). He did not confuse truth with dullness. On the other hand, he did not let his brilliance run away with him so as to cause him to write less than the truth—the danger of all popular speakers and writers.

11 Verse 11 claims God's inspiration for the Wisdom writers and hence is very important. It is their equivalent of "This is what the LORD says." The wise draw their wisdom from the Shepherd of Israel, the one true God (Ge 49:24; Pss 23:1; 80:1). Their wise teachings are to goad their readers to action and are to be seen as wholly dependable and worthy to be collected as Scripture.

12 Next comes a warning against the vast amount of literature that is a waste of time for the reader who is really concerned to find the truth. If we take the first sentence of v.12 as warning the disciple against going beyond the inspired words of the wise, this incorporates the theme of the book. In this world there will always be mystery, and human beings can fall into all sorts of error if they try to prove what cannot be proved (e.g., 3:11, 14; 7:14). There will always be books pouring off the presses. Students who have to study them for examinations, and those mature Christians who need to understand modern trends, know how wearisome they can be—and yet at times how attractive. This verse is certainly not intended to discourage Christian writers if they can write constructively and expound in modern terms those truths of life that are there in the Scriptures. Nor should we forget the great Christian classics that expounded the same truths.

2. The Conclusion of the Matter (12:13–14)

13–14 A good author usually summarizes the main points of his book when he comes to the end. The summary here is especially important.

Obviously, the Teacher is sometimes skeptical; but God is real to him, and he be-

lieves that God has revealed his will to humankind. If God had not done so, we could not be held accountable for our actions. Thus, although we may like to know more of the total plan of God, we know enough to be held responsible for what we do or fail to do. Our lives day by day must be lived as in the sight of God, who has given us the opportunity to fulfill his purpose for that day. Our actions, as well as the secret intentions of our hearts, are open to God, and one day they will be rewarded or punished (cf. 3:17; 11:9b).

The Old Testament in the New

OT Text	NT Text	Subject
Ecc 7:20	Ro 3:10	Sin of humanity

Song of Songs

INTRODUCTION

The introduction to Song of Songs is perhaps more important than that of any other book in the Bible because of the problem that the church has had in interpreting its meaning. Song of Songs is patently a collection of ancient Hebrew love poems celebrating the experiences of a lover and his beloved as they taste the beauty, power, agony, and joys of human sexual love. Is that appropriate, however, for a book that is part of the Scriptures?

1. Background

Why is the Song of Songs included in the Scriptures? Its few references to a historically identifiable person (Solomon) and to known places (Jerusalem, En Gedi, Tirzah) show its Jewish provenance. But the usual marks of biblical literature—religious themes, institutions, and practices—are absent. There are no references to law, grace, sin, salvation, or prayer. In fact, there is not a single, indisputable reference to the Lord God in the text.

Yet Song of Songs has held a significant place in the affections of the synagogue and the church. In Israel the book came to be associated with the greatest Hebrew festival, being read on the eighth day of Passover. During the first fifteen centuries of the Christian church, most major Christian writers turned their attention to this little work. Neither Jews nor Christians have been able to ignore it.

2. Interpretation

Since the Song of Songs is in the sacred canon, how is it to be interpreted? No book in Scripture has had such varied treatment. One medieval Jewish commentator said that it is like a lock for which the key has been lost.

a. Allegorical

The oldest documented interpretation of the Song of Songs sees it as an allegory. An allegory is an extended metaphor and normally is not rooted in history or the real world but is drawn from the mind and imagination of the author. Its purpose is not to present real events related to identifiable places and persons, but rather to communicate spiritual truth of an abstract nature. Allegory is an old device in which there is a divorce between the obvious literal meaning and the "high" spiritual message. As an allegory, the Jews saw this book as a depiction of the relationship of the Lord to his chosen people, Israel. Many Christians have seen the Song primarily as a statement of the love relationship between Christ and the church, his bride.

There are problems, however, in accepting the Song of Songs as an allegory. First, nothing in the text indicates that the intention of the author was to allegorize. Second, the people, places, and experiences recorded seem to be real, not literary devices. Third, this little book does not have the narrative character—the clear progressive story-line—that we usually expect in allegory. The result of the use of the allegorical approach is that the Song of Songs has become to an unusual degree a field for fertile imaginations.

b. Natural

Occasionally through history someone has become unhappy with the allegorical treatment and has raised a voice for a more natural approach to the plain sense of the text. Until the modern era a price was usually exacted for such bravery. In the first century apparently some Jewish readers understood the Song of Songs literally. Some were even singing portions of it in their drinking houses. This evoked the wrath of Rabbi Aqiba who pronounced an anathema on such practices.

In the eighteenth century, an Anglican bishop suggested that the book actually tells us about the marriage feast of Solomon. The bride may well have been the daughter of Pharaoh. He accepted the Song as historical but was willing to see something typological here. Solomon, the king of Israel, took a Gentile bride and made her a part of the people of God. In this way he foreshadows that other King, the Prince of Peace, who would take from among the Gentiles a bride, the church. This approach helped prepare the way for the almost universal rejection of the allegorical approach in favor of the stance most commonly taken among biblical expositors in our own time (see next section).

3. Purpose and Message

Why is this seemingly erotic little book included in the sacred canon? The Bible does not see marriage as an inferior state, a concession to human weakness. Nor does it see the normal physical love within that relationship as impure. Marriage was instituted before the Fall by God with the command that the first couple become one flesh (Ge 2:24). Therefore physical love within that conjugal union is good, is God's will, and should be a delight to both partners (Pr 5:15–19; 1Co 7:3).

The prospect of children is not necessary to justify sexual love in marriage. Significantly, the Song of Songs makes no reference to procreation. It must be remembered that the book was written in a world where a high premium was placed on offspring and a woman's worth was often measured in terms of the number of her children. Sex was often seen with reference to procreation; yet there is no trace of that here. The Song is a song in praise of love for love's sake and for love's sake alone. This relationship needs no justification beyond itself.

Song of Songs, however, is more than a declaration that human sexual love in itself is good. The use of the marriage metaphor to describe the relationship of God to his people is almost universal in Scripture. From the time that God chose Israel to be his own, the covenant was pictured in terms of a marriage. Idolatry was equated with adultery (Ex 34:10–17). The Lord is a jealous God. Monogamous marriage is the norm for depicting the covenant relationship throughout Scripture, climaxing with the Marriage Supper of the Lamb.

4. Authorship

Traditionally authorship of the Song of Songs was attributed to Solomon, due in part to the title, the six other explicit references to Solomon (1:5; 3:7, 9, 11; 8:11, 12), and the three references to an unnamed king (1:4, 12; 7:5). The case for Solomon's authorship is not definitive, but the case against it is equally far from being sure. Fortunately, a knowledge of who wrote this little book is essential neither to its interpretation nor to an appreciation of its content. As a work of literature of singular beauty and power, it stands on its own feet. Like other works in the Bible, it is enough to know that it is part of our sacred canon.

EXPOSITION

I. The Title (1:1)

1 The title for this little book, "Solomon's Song of Songs," is taken from the literal translation of the first two words of the Hebrew text. It means "the greatest of all songs." A comparable expression is found in the term "the Holy of Holies" (cf. Ex 26:33; et al.). The NIV correctly translates this "the Most Holy Place." Similar superlatives are found in the expressions "King of kings" and "Lord of lords." This immediately reveals the significance the author attached to his subject.

II. Courtship (1:2–3:5)

A. A Maiden's Amorous Musings (1:2–4b)

2 The book begins with the girl expressing her deep desire for physical expressions of love by her lover. There is a fascinating shift of persons from the third person to second person in the first two verses. Such a change is not unusual in Hebrew poetry. It is as if the beloved begins with the wish in her own mind and then shifts unwittingly to speaking directly to him.

Significantly, the girl speaks first. She is not extremely diffident but seems to see herself as of equal stature with the male. She longs to express her love to him, and she wants him to reciprocate. There is a sense in which she is the major character in this poem. This is one of the aspects of this work that makes it unique in its day. Much more of the text comes from her mouth and mind than from his. It is more her love story than his, though there is no failure on his part to declare his love and admiration for her.

3 We are quickly introduced to the association of love with the most pleasant tastes and smells. Love is so delightful that it should be accompanied with all that is pleasant, like perfumes. The lover's name is like "perfume poured out." "Name" (GK 9005) speaks of her lover as a well-known person. The maidens love him. Our lover is obviously the object of wide-scale affection.

4a The beloved longs for her lover to take her away with him, and speedily. Her emotion is intense, and she longs to be able to act on it.

4b The second part of v.4 can be significant to the story-line in the Song. It may be a declared intention (as translated here, following the Hebrew) or an address: "Bring me into your chamber, O King." The reference to "the king" suggests that we are really dealing here with a royal romance.

B. The Friends' Praise (1:4c)

4c The third part of v.4 confronts us with an annoying change of persons. Who are the "we" here? The women of Jerusalem? The girl? Two things are clear: the love of these two merits praise, and the lover merits the popular affection in which he is held. Most likely the speakers here are the daughters of Jerusalem, i.e., the friends of the maiden.

C. The Maiden's Self-Consciousness (1:4d–7)

4d The NIV is helpful here in including the last line of v.4 with this segment. Our maiden turns her attention to his public again: "How right they are to adore you!" The consciousness of these "daughters of Jerusalem" (v.5) and their affection for the maiden's lover makes her apprehensive. Her question is not about his attractiveness. It is about hers.

5–6 The maiden is self-conscious about her darkness. Kedar was a territory southeast of Damascus where the Bedouin roamed. Their tents were made of the skins of black goats. She explains that her color is due to her exposure to the sun as she worked the vineyards for her brothers. She obviously is from a family where the girls had to work. Mention is made in the text of her brothers, a sister (see on 8:8–10), and her mother. She was compelled to care for her brothers' concerns whether she cared for her own or not.

We notice a confidence in her about her own loveliness. There is an appealing modesty in our heroine; yet she is not overly diffident. Several times the separate emphatic first personal pronoun "I" is used (1:5–6; 2:1,

5; 5:2, 5–6, 8; 6:3; 7:10; 8:10). In every case it is the girl who is speaking. She is very much the appropriate match for the lover pictured here. The fullness with which the text presents her and the strength that she portrays make this little book most remarkable for its age and place in human history. The two lovers meet as equals.

7 The maiden next turns her attention to her lover and addresses him. The phrase "whom I love" is literally "whom my soul loves." "Soul" (GK 5883) can be used as an equivalent for the personal pronoun "I [love]." This word always carries with it a deep sense of personal emotional involvement.

The maiden wants to know where her lover grazes his flock so that she can be near him. Yet she does not want to unduly expose herself. She does not want to be like "a veiled woman" beside the flocks of his friends. That is, she does not want to be mistaken for a cult prostitute (cf. Ge 38:13–15). She is not looking for any lover. She has made a commitment to one, and she wants to know where she can find him.

D. The Friends' Admonition (1:8)

8 Next follows a response to the maiden: first, by the daughters of Jerusalem, to whom the maiden has spoken in the preceding segment (v.5); then by her lover (vv.9–11). Her uncertainty is met by the assurance that she is the "most beautiful" of all women (cf. 5:9; 6:1). The pronouns "you" and "your" are feminine singular; so we know there has been a shift in speaker, for the maiden would hardly be speaking to herself.

E. The Lover's Praise (1:9–11)

9–11 In v.9 we confront for the first time the Hebrew word *ra'yah* (GK 8299), translated by the NIV as "darling," the NEB as "dearest," and the NRSV as "love." This word occurs nine times in the Song, used each time by the lover of his beloved. The root idea in the word is associate, companion, or friend. It develops a strong connotation of commitment and delight.

Modern Western readers understand "most beautiful" and "darling." The next figure, though, is unexpected to us. The lover likens his loved one to a mare harnessed to one of Pharaoh's chariots. We have forgotten how beautiful horses can be when compared to other animals. We are also unaware what valuable creatures they were in that ancient world. The ancient royal courts insisted on brilliantly caparisoning the horses that pulled the king's chariot. The beloved's jewelry, earrings, and necklaces make him think of such.

After the middle of the second millennium B.C., mares were never used to draw chariots. Pairs of stallions were used for the royal vehicles. The presence of a mare among such stallions could be the ultimate distraction. So our lover pays his beloved the ultimate compliment to her sexual attractiveness. That he relishes this thought is clear. He will provide her with the jewelry of silver and gold to match her natural charms.

F. The Fragrances of Love (1:12–14)

12 The maiden now muses in response to her lover's affection and praise. The context up to now has been pastoral: flocks, herds, shepherds, and vineyards. Now it is of a table, expensive and exotic perfumes, spices from faraway places, and a king. The context is royal. This may be confusing to us because we do not usually associate shepherds and kings. But the Hebrew term for the rulers is "shepherds."

The maiden ponders the impact of the presence or the memory of the one lover on the other and describes it in aromatic terms. She is like nard ("perfume"; GK 5948) to him. It is as if his table is surrounded by the most delightful fragrance—herself. Nard, an ointment derived from a plant that grew in northern and eastern India, was used as a love charm in the ancient Near East (cf. Lk 7:36–50). Her presence as a reality in his life surrounded him like a choice perfume.

13–14 The beloved's impact on her lover was no greater than his on her. The consciousness of him brought sensations as real and as delightful as the smell of myrrh and henna blossoms. Myrrh, a resinous gum, came from trees in Arabia, Abyssinia, and India. It was highly prized in international trade and was used for incense (Ex 30:23), for perfuming garments of special people, for special occasions (Ps 45:8), for lover's beds (Pr 7:17), for preparing girls for visits with Oriental kings (Est 2:12), and for embalming corpses (Jn 19:39). Henna was a Palestinian shrub, whose leaves were used to produce a bright orangered cosmetic dye. It has been used in the

Near East to color the hair, hands, and feet. Its blossoms were fragrant, and it is the smell of the blossoms the maiden refers to here.

The maiden's consciousness of her lover sweetens her life the way the aroma of a sachet of perfume placed between the breasts makes a girl move in a cloud of fragrance. The thought or sight of him is as pleasant as the aroma wafted from a field of henna blossoms. Love has its own hallowing touch on all of life.

In this section the maiden's pet name for her lover—*dodi* ("my lover"; GK 1856)—appears for the first time. Apparently this word best expressed her joy in him. She uses it twenty-seven times as she speaks to him or about him. Five times it is used by the women of Jerusalem as they speak of him. Four additional occurrences are in the plural (1:2, 4; 4:10; 7:12). In each case it seems best to translate the plural form as "love making."

G. Love's Exchanges (1:15–2:2)

1:15–2:2 Now the dialogue between the lovers quickens. Three times he speaks, and twice she responds. They are becoming more direct in their expressions of love. A common language is developing to show the mutuality of their love. He calls her "beautiful" (GK 3637); she responds with the masculine form of the same word: "handsome."

The lover compares his beloved's eyes to doves. She speaks of his manner as charming and delightful. These lovers live in a different milieu from ours. It is pastoral; so their metaphors are drawn from nature. Notice the extensive references to animals, birds, trees, flowers, and mountains. The site of their love making is among the cedars and firs, in all of their greenery. It hints of a return to Eden (Ge 2:18–25), with its simplicity, naiveté, equality, and purity. It is as if this were the original couple.

H. Faint With Love (2:3–7)

3–7 The maiden now responds with a longer speech. Her senses are being stirred by his presence and the affirmations of his love. She finds herself feasting on it all. It is as if he is a tree that provides relief from the sun and delicious fruit for her hunger. Her satisfaction lies in him. And yet his nearness and his offering of love only intensify her desire. She is faint from it all. Her solution is not the removal of the desire that torments her. It is more food—raisins and apples—that will intensify that desire. She began with a desire for his kisses. Now she longs for his embrace. The beloved is being carried away by her passions. She relishes the joy. Yet she knows that love should have its own rhythm and its proper progression. Too fast too soon would spoil it all. So she adjures the women of Jerusalem not to encourage love beyond its right and proper pace. With the attention turned to the world beyond the two of them, the spell is for the moment broken and the first section (1:2–2:7) ends.

I. Love's Rhythm (2:8–3:5)

1. A lover's call (2:8–17)

8–17 We have seen thus far the beginnings of a free expression of love between a maiden and a man. The courtship has begun, and the desire for each other has been intense. She is weak with passion. At that point the protagonist, the maiden, appealed to the daughters of Jerusalem in her concern that the emotions of her and her lover not take them beyond the proper pace of pure love. So we now see them separated but longing for each other. Two poems (2:8–17; 3:1–5) make up this section. Again we find at the close of this division a plea for restraint.

This section is a good example of how tantalizing the Song can be for the interpreter. The maiden seems clearly to be in her own home in the city. She hears her lover's voice as he comes to visit her. He is like a gazelle or a young stag in his energy and in his passionate desire to be with her. He stands outside and calls her to go into the country with him to enjoy the beauty of spring as nature erupts with the passing of winter.

But is it an actual visit by her lover? Or is this a poetic projection of the maiden's own consuming desires for his presence? Regardless of how we interpret it, there is no way we can miss the trauma of true love with its ecstasy of longing and fear. The thought of his coming delights her. Her distance, like a dove in the clefts of the rocks, distresses him. He wants to see her form and hear her voice; for her voice is sweet, and her appearance is comely. Yet caution is called for.

Verse 15 raises questions over who is speaking and to whom. It seems that here we find a characteristic common to the moments of passion in these early chapters. Just as the

two lovers are about to surrender themselves to each other and forget the world, attention is turned to the larger world; hence the addresses to "the daughters of Jerusalem" throughout the Song. The appeal is made here to outsiders to prevent "the foxes," those forces that could destroy the purity of their love, from defiling their vineyards, which are blossoming. In 1:6 the maiden uses "vineyard" as a metaphor for her own person. So they plead for protection for the love that blossoms between them that nothing will spoil it.

The lovers may accept restraint on the pace of love's development, but there is no denying that they belong to each other. Here we are tantalized by the questions of whether we are to understand the text literally or figuratively. There seems clearly to be a double entendre character that pulls a cloak over the details of the lovers' love making—a metaphor in the service of the mystery and sanctity of sex! In 5:13 his lips are called "lilies." Thus it seems that she may be ready for him to graze on her lips as sheep "browse" in lush grasses. Here it certainly seems fair to look for more than one level of meaning. Perhaps this is to be related to the opening wish of our young lady (1:2).

2. A lover's seeking (3:1–5)

1–5 Our next poetic unit seems clearly to be a dream sequence. The lover is the maiden's obsession night and day. So in a dream she seeks him. She goes about the city in the night asking those whom she meets about her beloved. She finds him and will not let him go until she has brought him into her mother's home, into the very room where she was conceived. She is not looking for illicit consummation of their love. Consummation she wants, but even in her dream she wants that consummation to be right.

It may be that the reference to the maiden's bringing her lover to her mother's home reflects Ge 2:24, where the husband is to leave father and mother, but no like command is given to the woman. This passage may also reflect ancient Israelite marital customs now unknown to us (cf. Ge 24:67).

III. The Bridal Procession (3:6–11)

6–11 This unit is one of the most intriguing of all in the Song. It obviously is a wedding procession. The first problem has to do with who rides in the procession. The Hebrew suggests that it is the bride. There are indications that our hero comes from northern Israel, from Lebanon (cf. 4:8); the other geographical references support this. So our picture is of the groom and his men bringing his bride from her home to his city for the wedding.

The wedding "carriage" is identified as belonging to Solomon. In fact, it appears that he oversaw its building. His name has occurred only once before (1:5). It occurs three times in this brief section. It will not reappear until 8:11–12.

For the fourth time the daughters of Jerusalem are addressed. This time they are called "daughters of Zion," an expression occurring only here in the Song (cf. Isa 3:16–17; 4:4). The singular "daughter of Zion" is used twenty-three times in the OT. It normally refers to Israel as a nation. This is the passage that most definitively attaches the Song to Israel. In fact, this is the only passage where the name "Israel" occurs.

In v.11 we are told that Solomon wears "the crown" with which his mother crowned him for his wedding day. This obviously is not a reference to his coronation, since the high priest presided at that (cf. 1Ki 1:32–48; 2Ki 11:11–20). This may suggest that, if the Song did come from Solomon, it originated before his crowning in his most innocent period.

IV. The Wedding (4:1–5:1)

A. The Beauty and the Purity of the Bride (4:1–15)

1–7 The bride has now come to the groom. The time for consummation has arrived. The bride in biblical fashion is veiled (cf. Ge 24:65; 29:23–25; 38:14), but her lover is now free to enjoy her physical charms. The result is an erotic physical inventory of the details of her beauty. The description of her is given in metaphors that may seem alien to moderns. But even then the power of this bit of love poetry is moving. Her sense of modesty is protected. His freedom is uninhibited. She is his, and what he sees is perfection. To him there is no flaw in her.

Eyes luminous as doves, hair glossy black, perfectly matched white teeth with none missing, lips scarlet, and cheeks touched with color like a sliced pomegranate make her an object of beauty that brings ecstasy touched

with mystery. All this was veiled, but now it is his.

A long neck, which made her stately in appearance, like a prominent nose, seems to have been a mark of beauty in this ancient world. As was the custom, her neck was ornamented with layers of jewelry. Often these contained row upon row of beads or platelets like shields covering a tower. Her breasts had the grace and beauty that evoked tenderness like that produced by two fawns at play.

The lover's metaphors permit a chasteness and a modesty that less poetic speech would preclude. So when he says that he will go to his mountain of myrrh and to his hill of incense, he is most probably referring to the breasts he has just described and the body that awaits him. The night gives covering for their love.

8–15 The beloved has come to her lover. Her beauty is overwhelming. She has captured his heart. He wants her to be his forever. The invitation "come with me" is literally in Hebrew "with me," twice repeated. His desire is to have her with him.

For the first time the lover calls the maiden his "bride" (GK 3987). In ten verses (4:8–5:1) he uses this term of her six times. The focus of the word is on the married status of the woman, particularly on the sexual element presupposed in that status. The lover also calls his beloved his "sister" four times (vv.9–10, 12; 5:1). This is not uncommon in ancient Near Eastern love poetry as a love epithet.

The geographical references here are significant. They all speak of places in northern Israel. The indications are that the bride was originally from that area. Senir is the Amorite name of the Hebrew Hermon, the tallest peak (over 9,200 ft.) in the anti-Lebanon range.

B. Love's Consummation (4:16–5:1)

1. Invitation (4:16)

16 The maiden now responds to her lover's praise and his cry for her to cast her lot with him. The language is figurative; she picks up the metaphor that he has used of the locked garden (4:12). She invites her lover to enter her garden, make it his own, and enjoy its fruits. She calls for the north wind and the south wind to make her fragrances the more enticing.

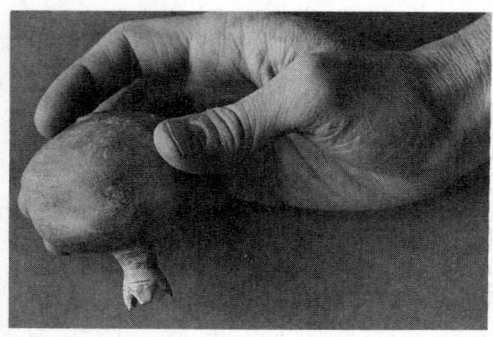

This pomegranate-shaped bottle at one time contained perfume. Fragrance is a common theme in Song of Songs (e.g., 1:1; 4:10–11).

2. Response (5:1a–d)

1a–d The language used here of love's consummation is classic in its chasteness, a character possible only through use of symbolic language. The beauty of expression fits the holiest of all human relationships. Metaphor plays the same role here as the veil in the temple. Sinful people need such to protect the mystery.

3. Joy (5:1e–f)

1e–f This brief unit is a problem to most commentators. Who is speaking? And to whom? The NIV takes these words to be those of onlookers or guests encouraging the couple to enjoy their love. The kind of relationship that our two lovers now have is more than a private affair. What one does with one's sexuality is from a biblical perspective always more than a private, personal thing. It has widespread social implications. Biblically, when a lover gives himself to his beloved as these two have done, the relationship of each has changed to all the rest of the human race. That is why traditionally in our culture a wedding cannot be performed without witnesses who represent broader society. The woman now belongs to the man and the man to the woman. This changes all other personal relationships. Furthermore, what one does with one's sexuality is of concern to God (Ex 20:14).

The public aspect of marriage helps explain the presence of "the daughters of Jerusalem" (2:7; 3:5; 5:8, 16; 8:4). It also explains the role of the "friends" as seen in the NIV (1:4b, 8; 5:1c, 9; 6:1, 10, 13; 8:5, 8–9). Self-giving love between the sexes is of social sig-

nificance. Society must know. How else can marriage be a witness and testimony to the relationship of Christ and the church? One Savior, one spouse! Again, one almost feels that the Song is a commentary on Ge 2:18–25 (see on 1:15–2:2).

This little unit bears witness also to the appropriateness of the festive character of weddings. Such joy demands that others rejoice.

V. The Life of Love (5:2–8:7)

A. Its Hesitancies (5:2–8)

2–8 The ecstasy of the preceding section is replaced by deep apprehension. What has been won seems now to be lost. This section most probably is to be taken like 3:1–5, as a dream sequence. Love brings its joys, but those joys are seldom unalloyed for long. We are such flawed and fragile creatures, and interpersonal relationships contain such subtleties. With our joys come fears. Often they surface in our dreams, arising from some sense of failure or fear of inadequacy.

So our maiden dreams that her lover comes for her. He comes knocking and calling. It is inconvenient for her to respond. She has already undressed, washed her feet, and is now in bed. She is slow to acknowledge his overture. Her hesitancy reflects a paralysis that we often experience both in dreams and in real life. Then the opportunity is gone. She finally rises to open to him, but he has departed. Love's chance is lost.

This is a remarkable picture of the kind of adjustments that are necessary in lifestyle in marriage. Our natural sloth, the differences between a man and a woman, our uncertainty about the other's thinking, the variations in our life rhythms, our unwillingness to alter our preferred patterns for the other, our own self-consciousness—all contribute to the problem of reading each other's advances. The lover misunderstands and departs. She is sick now with longing for him.

The bride's remorse and her love drive her out into the darkened city to seek her groom. The watchmen find her just as they did in 3:1–5. This time they are hostile. They beat, wound, and shame her. Does this treatment reflect the girl's guilt and sense of failure at the slowness of her response to her husband? There is a realism in the Song that merits our respect. The course of true love seldom runs smoothly for long. For every moment of ecstasy, there seems to be the moment of hurt and pain. The openness that lovers experience with each other makes possible both extremes. Not even love can guarantee perfect performance in personal relationships. Time and humility help. Our poet is dealing with such in this passage.

The bride's consciousness of loss and perhaps her feeling of blameworthiness drive her to call for her friends, the daughters of Jerusalem, to help. She urges them that if they find her lover, they are to let him know of her love for him.

B. The Friends' Concern (5:9)

9 The request of our hurting bride to the daughters of Jerusalem evokes a query. They want to know what is so remarkable about her lover, how he differs from other grooms.

Our questions here are numerous. Does this report an actual conversation, or is this part of the dream? The probability of such a midnight conversation seems unlikely enough. Or are we dealing with a master poet who uses this literary device to give the maiden a chance to recount the attractions and charms of the groom?

C. Love's Affirmations (5:10–6:10)

1. The beloved's praise (5:10–16)

10–16 This is one of the few poems that has come down to us from the ancient world in which the female gives an inventory of the male's features. Obviously it is her response to his description of her in 4:1–7. Her description witnesses to the uniqueness of this little book in its world in that it illustrates in its own way the equality of position and freedom that she enjoys. It is really her book (cf. Ge 2:18–25).

The bride sings. She sings of the handsomeness of her lover. Beginning with his complexion, ruddy and golden, and his hair, black and wavy, she descends from his eyes to his cheeks to his lips to his arms to his torso to his legs. The import is clear: he is one in ten thousand. She returns then to his mouth, which she finds to be a source of "sweetness" (cf. 1:2). In 2:3 she spoke of his fruit as sweet to her palate. He has spoken of her lips as dropping sweetness and honey. So she counters with the delights of his kisses (cf. Pr 5:3). His conclusion about her was

that she was beauty without flaw (4:7) and sweetness itself. She counters with the fact that he is altogether desirable.

All this is addressed to the daughters of Jerusalem. She is speaking of her lover, her "friend" (v.16). The word "friend" (GK 8276) is the masculine counterpart of his regular designation of her (cf. 1:9, 15; 2:2, 10; 4:1, 7; 5:2). Its root meaning is "to associate with," and it came to mean "friend" or "companion." The Song is unabashedly erotic. Yet it is never satisfied to be content with the physical alone. A normal person finds the erotic ultimately meaningful only if there is trust and commitment, delight in the other's person as well as in the body. The writer of the Song understands this. Our hero is her lover, but he is more: he is her friend.

2. The friends' inquiry (6:1)

1 Now the daughters of Jerusalem inquire of the bride as to where her lover is. They want to assist her in finding him.

3. The beloved's praise (6:2–3)

2–3 The bride's response to the friends' inquiry assures them that she has not really lost him. The anxiety in her dream was without foundation in reality. She is her lover's, but he is also hers. And he now is browsing in his garden of spices among the lilies. In 5:13 she has described his lips as lilies that drip with myrrh. The erotic implications in this language seem clear. Her fears were unwarranted. As he possesses her, she possesses him.

4. The lover's praise (6:4–10)

4–10 The lover speaks again in poetic ode about his beloved's beauty. She is like a great city to be taken. Tirzah was an ancient Canaanite center that served as the capital of the northern kingdom before Omri (c. 879 B.C.) established Samaria as the capital. This reference is a strong indication of an early date for the origin of the Song.

The reference to Jerusalem is the only time the name occurs except in the phrase "daughters of Jerusalem." It may seem strange at first for a lover to think of his bride as a great city. This figure is not unique, however, to the Song. The author of Revelation uses Babylon as a figure of a great prostitute and Jerusalem as the bride of Christ (Rev

18:2–19:3; 19:7–9; 21:1–2). Do we perhaps have in this metaphor an anticipation of the outcome of history for every believer?

The beloved is regal to the point of awesomeness. She appears like the dawn in its glory, fair as the moon, bright as the sun, terrible as an army with banners. She is more impressive than queens or royal concubines or virgins without number. The reference to queens, concubines, and virgins may well be a reference to the royal harem. She is without equal among women. Even the ladies of the royal harem acknowledge her superiority.

D. Love's Questions (6:11–13)

11–13 This is a tantalizing section. The words are familiar. The meaning is another matter. Does this represent a momentary separation of the maiden from her lover as she or he goes to investigate the flowering of springtime? Or are we to look for a deeper, more erotic meaning here?

If v.11 is difficult to interpret, v.12 is more so. Perhaps the best approach is to see a momentary separation that leaves the bride yearning again for her lover. So the daughters of Jerusalem call for her to return. Whoever is speaking calls the girl "the Shulammite." This verse with its two occurrences is the only place where this term is found in the OT.

In v.13 the bride responds to the guests who want to see her. She is modestly reluctant. She questions their desire. If she wonders why anyone would want to see her, she is to get an answer from her lover. The next unit is his description of her charms. It is a response to her description of him in 5:10–16.

E. Love's Repetitions (7:1–9a)

1–9a The groom's description of his bride begins with her sandals and feet and proceeds upward to the flowing locks of hair on her head. It should be compared with previous descriptions in 4:1–7; 5:10–16; and 6:4–10. This is the fullest detailing of her physical charms found in the Song.

Although the Song is really the bride's song, there are three occasions when the groom describes her beauty in detail and only one where she reciprocates. If the Song has any allegorical significance, it should indicate that God finds us much more delightful than we find him. If this seems strange, it should be remembered that his love is pure

and eternal. His capacity for love and joy is greater than ours even though the object of our affection is greater and infinitely more worthy.

This poem reflects the perpetual charm of the female form to the male. This song has been sung an almost infinite number of times. There is repetition here. Some of his figures are the same as those used in 4:1–15 and 6:4–10. But that is the nature of love. Our language has its limits. Our love pushes those limits and falls back in frustration at the inability of our words to communicate our ecstasy.

Even the beloved's feet are beautiful. Her rounded thighs, like the work of some more-than-human artist, capture him. Her navel has its own allure. He would like to fill it with spiced wine and drink from it. Her belly is round and wheat colored. The reference to the lilies that encircle the stomach reminds us that we are dealing with figures whose very ambiguity enriches the eroticism of the passage. Her breasts are symmetrical objects of grace and beauty that evoke tender and solicitous response. Her neck gives her stature and impressiveness. Her eyes are like pools—luminous, clear, and deep. The nose adds to her stateliness. Her head and hair crown her. She is awesome and majestic as Mount Carmel. A king is held captive by her tresses. She is an object of beauty and loveliness, a treasure of delights.

In v.7 the groom sees his bride as a palm tree loaded with luscious fruits. He turns again to her breasts and lips to enjoy his possession. We should not miss the element of near-adoration in our lover's depiction of his beloved nor be unmindful of the high value placed on the flesh in Scripture. The body is not an unworthy shell to be shucked in death. It is destined for resurrection. It may be the occasion for sin, but it can also be the very clothing of Deity, as in the Incarnation. If the devotion of our two lovers is but an imaging of the relationship of the true Bridegroom and his bride, it is fitting that there should be an almost noumenal air in the poetry.

F. Love's Belonging and Giving (7:9b–13)

9b–13 Now the maiden responds. There is no holding back. She belongs to him. There is a primeval Edenic purity about all of this. Once again we are reminded of that first couple that God gave to each other and commanded to be one flesh. We cannot keep from thinking of that context when she speaks of "his desire" (GK 9592) for her. This word is found in Ge 3:16 in reference to Eve's desire for her husband. It is as if we are observing the Fall momentarily reversed. It obviously is a strong, almost overpowering, urge. His desire for her easily equals hers for him. She is at no disadvantage. She relishes the security of her relationship to her husband.

The bride's joy and fulfillment are such that she is ready to get out into the fields and vineyards to let the common nature that flows in lovers and the cosmos rejoice together. "Mandrakes" were prized for their aphrodisiac properties. The joys the two now are experiencing in each other are but the beginning of raptures that she is prepared to bring to him.

G. Love's Longing and Liberty (8:1–4)

1–2 The bride continues to speak about leaving the security of their bed chamber and going into the fields and villages with him. Yet she is reluctant to leave the freedom that they have behind closed doors to express their love for each other. The proprieties demanded in public seem limiting. She would like the liberty in public that the brother and sister in that day had. So she wishes she could freely kiss him in public. She would like to take him to the house of her own mother, to the very chamber where she was conceived, and there give herself to him.

There is no sense of wrongness about their love. She is reminded of her mother, who in a similar relationship gave to her the life that she now enjoys with her groom. Her joy in him strengthens her identification with her own mother who taught her. With all the strength of the union with her husband, there is still the consciousness that she is a woman. She longs for a woman with whom she can share, and the appropriate one is her mother. This is no indication of withdrawal from her spouse.

3–4 The bride yearns for her lover's embrace. Apparently that yearning once more evokes the bride's remark to the daughters of Jerusalem. Again we are reminded that we are social creatures inextricably bound up in a web of human relations. In this moment of deepest intimacy, when no prying eyes are wanted, she thinks of her mother and her friend. Her ecstasy she would share with her mother and her wisdom with the daughters of Jerusalem. Love has its ecstasy when it is right, but it also has its pain when it cannot freely express itself. It is the better part of wisdom, she informs her friends, not to permit love to be awakened until the time is right. Love like this should have no shadows or constraints.

H. Love's Seal and Strength (8:5–7)

5–7 The drama is now almost over. The couple have followed her desire and now return from the trip into the fields and the villages. The friends, daughters of Jerusalem, spot the couple and call attention to them as they return. The bride leans on her lover.

The bride pays no attention to the call of the friends. She speaks only to her lover. She has not taken him to her mother's home. He has apparently taken her to the site of his conception. There they have sealed more deeply their love. She speaks of the depth of that sealing. An engraved stone or metal seal was a mark of ownership in the ancient world. Possession of another's seal indicated mutual access and possession. Her love is so total and so strong that she wants their mutual possession of each other to be as lasting as life. It is a strongly poetic demand for "until death do us part." Better to die than to experience the failure of love that produces jealousy. Love's demands are all-consuming. External forces cannot quench or drown it. Its value is greater than all the possessions one might ever possess. In all of human literature there are few passages on the power of love compared with this unit.

VI. Conclusion (8:8–14)

8–10 There is no consensus on the division of these final verses, nor is there agreement as to who is speaking and who is being spoken about. It seems most plausible to see vv.8–10 as coming from our heroine. She has now consummated her relationship with her beloved. She has tasted the mysteries of sexual love with her spouse. She is looking back with joy that she came to those sacred moments as a virgin. She thinks of her younger sister and longs for her to know the same joys that she now experiences. So she expresses her concern for the protection of her sibling.

This interpretation takes the expressions "wall" and "door" as antithetical rather than parallel. It sees "towers of silver" and "panels of cedar" as protective rather than as primarily ornamental. She with her groom commit themselves to guard her sister from the loss of something precious. She affirms vigorously that she kept herself chaste for her husband. Thus by keeping herself a virgin, she was as one "bringing contentment."

11–12 Verses 11–12 are among the more tantalizing in the whole Song. Solomon is referred to again. This time, however, it seems clear that he is not the hero of the piece. The speaker, whether it is the bride or the groom, is contrasting his or her vineyard with that of Solomon's. Solomon's vineyard is large and fruitful, very impressive. It contains a thousand vines. Solomon must let it out to tenants to keep. They share in the produce. It is a very extensive operation.

Our hero or heroine is in a very different position. But he/she is not unhappy. His/her vineyard is his/hers alone. And that is enough to satisfy our spokesman. To possess one's beloved is enough. It is to be wealthy beyond measure.

Is this passage a reference to Solomon's harem with his 700 wives and 300 concubines? If so, the question then is as to the pay of the vineyard keepers. Or is the reference here to an actual vineyard? Because of previous references to a vineyard, which seems clearly to have a symbolical meaning, one is tempted to see this as a reference to the sexual personage of the maiden. Vineyard and garden seem clearly to be used to speak of herself in previous passages (see 1:6; 2:15; 4:12; 5:1).

There is always the possibility, though difficult for us, that the reference to Solomon's vineyard is to be taken literally while the reference to the spouse's vineyard is metaphorical (cf. Jn 2:19). That would be consistent with the double entendres of the book. However we interpret this text, it is clear that the lover's concern is not for material wealth.

13–14 The closing two verses come from our groom and his bride. She seems to be in a garden with her friends. He calls to her. He wants to hear her voice. She who began the Song wishing for the kisses of his mouth answers. That response is in language used previously (cf.2:9, 17). She urges him to make haste and resume the delights of love. The figures of the deer and the mountain of spices symbolize for us for the last time the lover and his beloved. Restraints are gone. He is hers and she is his. They are free to pursue those delights of love that image a love to come for every believer.

The bride's call to her groom to hasten may find an interesting echo in Rev 22:17. The heavenly call has always been that of the Divine Groom for a human bride. In the Song she invites him to come. In human history he invites her to come. Love, Divine Love, calls to love, and love responds.

"Amen. Come, Lord Jesus!"

Old Testament Prophecies Fulfilled in Christ

OT Text	NT Text	Subject
Ge 3:15	Lk 22:53	Satan against Jesus
Ge 3:15	Heb 2:14; 1Jn 3:8	Jesus' victory over Satan
Ge 12:3	Ac 3:25; Gal 3:8	Gentiles blessed through Christ as the offspring of Abraham
Ge 13:15	Gal 3:15–16, 19	Messiah as the seed of Abraham
Ge 14:18–20	Heb 7	Jesus' priesthood according to the likeness of Melchizedek
Ge 18:18	Ac 3:25; Gal 3:8	Gentiles blessed through Christ as the offspring of Abraham
Ge 22:18	Ac 3:25; Gal 3:8	Gentiles blessed through Christ as the offspring of Abraham
Ge 49:10	Lk 1:32–33	Coming ruler from Judah
Ex 12:1–14, 46	Jn 19:31–36; 1Co 5:7; 1Pe 1:19	The Messiah as the Passover Lamb
Ex 16:4	Jn 6:31–33	Messiah to give true bread from heaven
Ex 24:8	Heb 9:11–28	The Messiah's blood to be shed as sacrifice
Lev 15:15–17	Ro 3:25; Heb 9:1–14, 24; 1Jn 2:2	Atoning sacrifice of blood
Nu 21:8–9	Jn 3:14–15	Life through looking at one on a cross
Nu 24:17	Lk 1:32–33	Coming ruler from Jacob
Nu 24:17	Rev 22:16	Coming star out of Jacob
Dt 18:17	Jn 6:14; 12:49–50; Ac 3:22–23	Coming prophet sent from God
Dt 21:23	Gal 3:13	Messiah cursed for hanging on a tree
Dt 30:12–14	Ro 10:6–8	Jesus is God's word near to us
2Sa 7:14	Heb 1:5	Messiah to be God's Son
2Sa 7:16	Lk 1:32–33; Rev 19:11–16	David's Son as eternal king
1Ch 17:13	Heb 1:5	Messiah to be God's Son
1Ch 17:14	Lk 1:32–33; Rev 19:11–16	David's Son as eternal king
Ps 2:7	Mt 3:17; 17:5; Mk 1:11; 9:7; Lk 3:22; 9:35; Ac 13:33; Heb 1:5	God's address to his Son
Ps 2:9	Rev 2:27	Messiah to rule the nations with power
Ps 8:2	Mt 21:16	Children to praise God's Son
Ps 8:4–5	Heb 2:6-9	Jesus lower than the angels
Ps 8:6	1 Co 15:27–28; Eph 1:22	Everything subject to God's Son
Ps 16:8–11	Ac 2:25–32; 13:35–37	David's Son to be raised from the dead
Ps 22:1	Mt 27:46; Mk 15:34	God-forsaken cry by the Messiah
Ps 22:7–8	Mt 27:29, 41–44; Mk 15:18, 29–32 Lk 23:35–39	Messiah mocked by a crowd
Ps 22:18	Mt 27:35; Mk 15:24; Lk 23:34; Jn 19:24	Casting lots for Jesus' clothes
Ps 22:22	Heb 2:12	Jesus to declare his name in the church
Ps 31:5	Lk 23:46	Messiah to commit his spirit to God
Ps 34:20	Jn 19:31–36	Messiah to have no broken bones

Old Testament Prophecies Fulfilled in Christ (Continued)

OT Text	NT Text	Subject
Ps 35:19	Jn 15:25	Messiah experiencing hatred for no reason
Ps 40:6–8	Jn 6:38; Heb 10:5–9	Messiah to do God's perfect will
Ps 41:9	Jn 13:18	The Messiah's betrayal by a friend
Ps 45:6–7	Heb 1:8–9	Characteristics of the coming King
Ps 68:18	Eph 4:7–11	Ascension and giving gifts to humans
Ps 69:4	Jn 15:25	Messiah experiencing hatred for no reason
Ps 69:9	Jn 2:14–22	The Messiah's zeal for God's house
Ps 69:21	Jn 19:29	The thirst of the suffering Messiah
Ps 69:25	Ac 1:20	Judgment on the Messiah's persecutor
Ps 78:2	Mt 13:34–35	Messiah to speak in parables
Ps 102:25–27	Heb 1:10–12	Characteristics of the coming King
Ps 110:1	Ac 2:34-35; 1Co 15:25; Eph 1:20–22; Heb 1:13; 10:12–13	Jesus exalted in power at God's right hand
Ps 110:1	Mt 22:41–45; Mk 12:35–37; Lk 20:41–44	Jesus as Son and Lord of David
Ps 110:4	Heb 5:6; 7:11–22	Jesus' priesthood after Melchizedek
Ps 118:22–23	Mt 21:42–44; Mk 12:10; Lk 20:17–19; Ac 4:10–11; 1Pe 2:7-8	Rejected stone to become capstone
Ps 118:26	Mt 21:9; Mk 11:9; Lk 19:38; Jn 12:13	Messiah to come in the name of the Lord
Isa 6:9–10	Mt 13:14–15; Mk 4:12; Lk 8:10; Jn 12:37–41	Hearts to be closed to the gospel
Isa 7:14	Mt 1:18–23; Lk 1:26–35	Virgin birth of the Messiah
Isa 8:14	Ro 9:32–33; 1 Pe 2:7–8	A stone over which people stumble
Isa 9:1–2	Mt 4:13–16; Mk 1:14–15; Lk 4:14–15	Ministry to begin in Galilee
Isa 9:6–7	Lk 1:32–33	David's Son as eternal king
Isa 9:7	Jn 1:1, 18	The Messiah to be God
Isa 9:7	Eph 2:14–17	The Messiah to be a man of peace
Isa 11:1–2	Mt 3:16; Mk 1:16; Lk 3:21–22	Branch of Jesse (David) to receive the Spirit)
Isa 11:10	Lk 1:32–33	Root of Jesse (David) as coming ruler
Isa 11:10	Ro 15:12	Salvation to be available for Gentiles
Isa 22:22	Rev 3:7	Jesus to receive the key of David
Isa 25:8	1Co 15:54	Death to be swallowed up in victory
Isa 28:16	Ro 9:32–33; 1Pe 2:6	Messiah to be the chief cornerstone
Isa 35:5–6	Mt 11:4–6; Lk 7:22	Messiah to be a mighty worker of miracles
Isa 40:3–5	Mt 3:3; Mk 1:3; Lk 3:4; Jn 1:23	Jesus' forerunner, a voice in the desert
Isa 42:1–4	Mt 12:15–21	Messiah as the chosen servant of the Lord
Isa 45:23	Ro 14:11; Php 2:10	Every knee to bow before the Messiah
Isa 49:6	Ac 13:46–47	Messiah as a light to the Gentiles
Isa 50:6	Mt 27:26–30; Mk 14:65; 15:15, 19; Lk 22:63; Jn 19:1, 3	Beating God's servant

Old Testament Prophecies Fulfilled in Christ (Continued)

OT Text	NT Text	Subject
Isa 50:6	Mt 26:67; Mk 14:65	Spitting on God's servant
Isa 53:1	Jn 12:38; Ro 10:16	Israel not to believe in the Messiah
Isa 53:3	Jn 1:11	Messiah to be rejected by his own people
Isa 53:4–5	Mt 8:16–17; Mk 1:32–34; Lk 4:40–41; 1Pe 2:24	Healing ministry of God's servant
Isa 53:7–8	Jn 1:29, 36; Ac 8:30–35; 1Pe 1:19; Rev 5:6, 12	Suffering Lamb of God
Isa 53:9	Heb 4:15; 1Pe 2:22	The sinless servant of God
Isa 53:9	Mt 27:57–60	Messiah to be buried in a rich man's grave
Isa 53:12	Mt 27:38; Mk 15:27–28; Lk 22:37; 23:33; Jn 19:18	God's servant numbered with transgressors
Isa 55:3	Lk 22:20; 1Co 11:25	Everlasting covenant through the Messiah
Isa 55:3	Ac 13:33	Blessings of David given to the Messiah
Isa 59:20–21	Ro 11:26–27	Israel's Deliverer to come from Zion
Isa 60:1–3	Mt 2:11; Ro 15:8–12	Gentiles coming to worship the Messiah
Isa 61:1–2	Mt 4:16; Mk 1:10; Lk 4:18–21	The Messiah anointed by the Holy Spirit
Isa 65:1	Ro 10:20	Gentiles would believe in the Messiah
Isa 65:2	Ro 10:21	Israel would reject the Messiah
Jer 23:5	Lk 1:32–33	David's Son to be a great King
Jer 23:6	Mt 1:21	David's Son to be Savior
Jer 23:6	1Co 1:30	Messiah to be named "Our Righteousness"
Jer 31:5	Mt 2:16–18	Rachel weeping when God's Son is born
Jer 31:31–34	Lk 22:20; 1Co 11:25; Heb 8:8–12; 10:15–18	Jesus and the new covenant
Jer 32:40	Lk 22:20; 1Co 11:25	Everlasting covenant through the Messiah
Jer 33:15	Lk 1:32–33	David's Son to be a great King
Jer 33:16	Mt 1:21	David's Son to be Savior
Jer 33:16	1Co 1:30	Messiah to be named "Our Righteousness"
Eze 21:26-27	Lk 1:32–33	A rightful crown for the Messiah
Eze 34:23–24	Jn 10:11, 14, 16; Heb 13:20; 1Pe 5:4	The coming good shepherd
Eze 37:24–25	Lk 1:32–33	Messiah to be David's son and a king
Eze 37:24–25	Jn 10:11, 14, 16; Heb 13:20; 1Pe 5:4	The coming good shepherd
Eze 37:26	Lk 22:20; 1Co 11:25	Messiah's everlasting covenant of peace
Da 7:13–14	Mt 24:30; 26:64; Mk 13:26; 14:62; Lk 21:27; Rev 1:13; 14:14	The coming of the Son of Man
Da 7:27	Rev 11:15	The coming everlasting kingdom of the Messiah
Da 9:24–26	Gal 4:4	Timetable for the Messiah's coming
Hos 11:1	Mt 2:14–15	Jesus to return from Egypt
Joel 2:28–32	Ac 2:14–21	God's Spirit to be poured out
Am 9:11–12	Ac 15:13–18	Gentiles would believe in the Messiah
Jnh 1:17	Mt 12:39–40	Messiah to be three days and nights in grave
Mic 5:2	Mt 2:1–6	The Messiah to be born in Bethlehem

Old Testament Prophecies Fulfilled in Christ (Continued)

OT Text	NT Text	Subject
Mic 5:2	Lk 1:32–33	The Messiah as an eternal king
Mic 5:4	Jn 10:11, 14	The coming shepherd of God's flock
Mic 5:5	Eph 2:14–17	The Messiah to be a man of peace
Zec 9:9	Mt 21:1–9; Mk 11:1–10; Lk 19:28–38; Jn 12:12–16	The coming ruler on a donkey
Zec 11:12–13	Mt 27:1–10	Thirty pieces of silver for a potter's field
Zec 12:10	Jn 19:37; Rev 1:7	Looking on the pierced Messiah
Zec 13:7	Mt 26:31; 26:55-56; Mk 14:27; 14:48-50	Striking the coming shepherd; the sheep flee
Mal 3:1	Mt 11:7–10; Mk 1:2–4; Lk 7:24–27	The forerunner to the Messiah
Mal 4:5–6	Mt 11:14; 17:11–13; Mk 9:11–13; Mk 9:11–13; Lk 1:16–17	The forerunner as Elijah returned

Isaiah

INTRODUCTION

The prophecy of Isaiah is the third longest, complete literary entity in the Bible, being exceeded in length only by Jeremiah and Psalms. Psalms is in a special category as a collection of separate literary units.

1. Background

a. Sources of information

The book of Isaiah itself is the major source of information. Additional and supporting material is contained in 2Ki 15–21 and in 2Ch 26–33. Other contemporary or near-contemporary prophets were Amos and Hosea, both of whom prophesied to the northern kingdom, and Micah, who, like Isaiah, was a vehicle of God's word to Judah. Assyrian clay tablets are a leading source of material outside the OT.

b. The life of Isaiah

The opening heading of the book (1:1) places the ministry of Isaiah in the reigns of Uzziah (or Azariah, as he is called in 2 Kings), Jotham, Ahaz, and Hezekiah. Likely his ministry continued into the reign of Manasseh. Nothing is known about Isaiah's father, Amoz. Jewish tradition declared him to be of royal stock. While this cannot be substantiated, Isaiah may have been an aristocrat, for he seemed to have easy access to kings (7:3; 37:21–22; et al.). His wife is called "the prophetess" (8:3), which may simply mean she was a prophet's wife. She was, however, the mother of his two known children, both of whom had names with symbolic meanings (7:3; 8:3, 18). Isaiah seems to have prophesied largely—if not exclusively—in Jerusalem and its environs. Isaiah 8:16–17 suggests that the rejection of his warning to Ahaz led to a temporary withdrawal from public ministry and concentration on his disciples. His last datable oracles were in 701 B.C. The noncanonical *Ascension of Isaiah* states that he was martyred (cf. Heb 11:37) in the reign of Manasseh (who came to the throne in 687 B.C.).

c. The international scene

Israel and Judah—under Jeroboam II and Uzziah respectively—enjoyed a period of prosperity during Isaiah's childhood, with little interference from foreign powers. Egypt was weak, while Assyria was occupied with problems elsewhere. The aggressive empire-builder Tiglath-pileser III (known in Babylon as Pul) came to the Assyrian throne in 745 B.C., and the situation quickly changed. Egypt reckoned the small kingdoms in Palestine and Syria to be within her sphere of influence, but Assyria began to carve out a western extension to its empire in that region. Damascus (732 B.C.) and much of Galilee fell to Tiglath-pileser; then Shalmaneser V (727–722 B.C.) and Sargon II (722–705 B.C.) attacked Samaria, the latter taking it in 722 or 721 B.C. In the last decade or so of the century, Egypt began to revive somewhat, and Assyria encountered trouble from Babylon. Because of this, Judah and other neighboring states rebelled against Assyria. Sennacherib (705–681) invaded Judah in 701 and subdued it; but God saved Jerusalem, which was to fall over a century later to a resurgent Babylon.

d. The reigns of Uzziah and Jotham

There are some problems in dating the reigns of the kings of Judah from Uzziah to Hezekiah. Uzziah's death has been variously placed between 747 and 735, the most likely date being around 740. Jotham seems to have been regent for some years before this; and, apparently, several years before his own death (731), he handed over the reins of effective government to his son, Ahaz. Apart from the inaugural vision recorded in ch. 6, nothing in the book can be dated with certainty from the reigns of either Uzziah or Jotham. Uzziah had been a godly man until the pride of his latter days (2Ch 26:16–21), but neither he nor Jotham removed the idolatrous high places.

e. The Syro-Ephraimite war

The threat from Tiglath-pileser brought Syria and Israel into coalition around 734 B.C., and they tried to force Judah to join them. Ahaz was on the throne at the time. Isaiah challenged him to trust in the Lord (ch. 7); instead, Ahaz called on Assyria to come to his aid. Damascus, the capital of Syria, was taken by the Assyrians in 732 and much of Galilee was subjugated (2Ki 15:25–29). Pekah, king of Israel, was murdered by Hoshea, who replaced him and reigned as a virtual Assyrian puppet. Pekah, king of Israel, and Rezin, king of Syria, had inflicted some harm on Judah before the Assyrians brought relief to Ahaz (2Ki 16:5–9), but more serious still were the religious consequences of the latter's appeal to Assyria (2Ki 16:10–20).

f. The fall of Samaria

The death of Tiglath-pileser in 727 B.C. raised false hopes of freedom for the little kingdoms on the Mediterranean seaboard. When Ahaz died about a year later, Isaiah uttered a prophecy warning Philistia of the consequences of revolt, and, by implication, counseled Judah against joining her (14:28–32). It was some time later that Hoshea withheld tribute from Shalmaneser V, who for three years besieged Samaria, which was later taken by his successor, Sargon. According to the Assyrians, over twenty-seven thousand Israelites were deported at this time, being settled in the northern parts of the Assyrian empire. For about a decade the area was fairly quiet, Sargon being occupied with wars elsewhere; but then Egypt began to encourage the Philistines and others to form a new coalition against Assyria. This coalition was crushed by Sargon in 711 in a battle on the Egyptian border. Judah under Hezekiah stayed out of this, heeding Isaiah's warning (20:1–6).

g. Hezekiah and Sennacherib

Sargon died around 705 B.C. and was replaced by Sennacherib. Immediately there was trouble in different parts of the Assyrian Empire, encouraged by the Ethiopian monarchs who were imparting new vigor to Egypt, and also by Merodach-Baladan of Babylon. This time, despite Isaiah's warnings (chs. 30–31), Hezekiah became involved and prepared Jerusalem for a siege (22:8–11). The Assyrian army invaded Judah, taking forty-six walled cities and devastating much of the countryside. It besieged Jerusalem, but Isaiah encouraged Hezekiah to trust in the Lord; and the city was delivered (37:36).

h. Babylon

Merodach-Baladan, a Chaldean prince, took power in Babylon in 721 B.C., declaring it independent of Assyria. Sargon entered Babylon in 711 or 710 without a fight. After Sargon's death, however, Merodach-Baladan became a leader of movements of rebellion against Sennacherib and sought to involve Hezekiah (39:1–2). Sennacherib defeated and deposed Merodach-Baladan; but Babylon revived again during the seventh century, becoming the dominant Mesopotamian power toward the end of that century. This led ultimately to the subjection of Judah to Babylon and to the fall of Jerusalem in 587. The ensuing Exile fulfilled God's warning to Hezekiah delivered through Isaiah (ch. 39) and forms the background to the following prophecies. However, at least part of chs. 56–66 seems to assume the passage of still more time, with the Exile a thing of the past and the people back in Judah again. Cyrus the Persian, the human instrument of the return, is referred to in chs. 44–45.

2. Authorship, Unity, and Date

a. The history of criticism

The book of Isaiah has come down to us as a unity, and the name Isaiah son of Amoz is the only one linked with it in any of the Hebrew manuscripts or ancient versions. Until late in the eighteenth century, only one extant writer questioned whether Isaiah wrote the whole book. This writer maintained that chs. 40–66 were the work of a prophet who lived late in the Babylonian captivity. In the late eighteenth century, soon after Pentateuchal criticism began to get into its stride, the new critical school took an interest in Isaiah, and chs. 40–66 were attributed to a prophet of the Exile, who soon was known as "Deutero-Isaiah." This view came to be held widely in scholarly circles. Subsequently, chs. 56–66 were attributed to yet another writer, "Trito-Isaiah," and some critics have divided the book still further, virtually fragmenting it.

b. The case for its unity

It is clear that the Jews accepted Isaiah's authorship of the later chapters of the book well before the coming of Christ. Ecclesiasticus, written early in the second century B.C., in 48:24 clearly refers to Isa 61:3. The pre-Christian Isaiah scroll from Qumran known as 1QIsa^a has the complete text of the book. More important, however, is the testimony of the NT, which quotes Isaiah—and from different parts (e.g., Jn 12:37–41)—by name more often than all the other writing prophets combined.

The case for the unity of the book is strong. While it would be too much to say that its rejection is invariably due to a rejection of supernatural prophetic prediction (e.g., the naming of Cyrus in 44:28 and 45:1), there is no doubt that this lies behind a great deal of the opposition to it. It seems likely that Isaiah lived on into the reign of Manasseh, that during this reign he was unable to function openly as a prophet, but that he committed to writing the revelations he received about the future of his people. No doubt the people in Babylonia, chastened by the hand of their God—and with a new awareness of his sovereignty—would watch events with a deep sense of anticipation, and these prophecies would themselves be instrumental in the hands of God in helping to create that atmosphere of faith and obedience that led to the return.

Only a realization that the whole book records the prophecies of Isaiah the son of Amoz can place the authority of its teaching as an important part of the OT preparation for Christ on the securest basis.

3. Theology

Isaiah's temple vision (ch. 6) of the thrice-holy God deeply influenced his whole prophetic career and his theology. Isaiah learned some things about God's holiness, transcendent separateness, and incomparable majesty and character. Isaiah's distinctive title for God is "the Holy One of Israel," used twenty-five times in all.

Isaiah learned that God is King, enthroned above all, eternal and deathless, unlike Uzziah and other earthly monarchs. He is also the Lord Almighty, so that the authority of the supreme King is wedded to an omnipotence that enables him to carry out his every purpose. As such, he could use Assyria and Babylon as instruments of his punitive purpose and yet include them also in the great judgments on all the nations (chs. 13–23). In fact, the entire world would come under his judgment (ch. 24). Isaiah is also given a wonderful disclosure of a great King for God's people, who himself bears the name "Mighty God" (9:6).

Isaiah saw that "the whole earth is full of his glory" (6:3); accordingly, he speaks of God as Creator both of the universe (40:26; 42:5; 48:12–13) and of his people, Israel (43:1, 15). He has a vision of the whole earth full of the knowledge of the Lord (11:9) and even of new heavens and a new earth (65:17; 66:22).

Because this great God is holy, Isaiah's encounter with him gives the prophet a smarting sense of sin. He is to be the mouthpiece of God, but Isaiah's lips are unclean. The people too have unclean lips; for, though worshiping their God with ritual (1:10–17), fasting (58:1–5), and words (29:13), they were in fact rebellious (1:2–6; 30:1–5; et al.). The prophet's scathing denunciations of idolatry (chs. 40–48) reflect not only his own conviction that there is only one God but also his holy intolerance of the sin of idolatry. Two sins that are singled out for special condemnation are pride and unbelief (e.g., in 2:6–22; 7:1–9). Isaiah also condemned injustice (1:16–17; 58:6–12; et al.).

But Isaiah also brings hope. His very name (meaning "The LORD Is Salvation") suggests that we should expect a positive note. The assurance of forgiveness for the penitent is constantly reiterated (1:18–19; 12:1; 30:18–19; 33:24; et al.); and, just as the ultimate sacrificial basis of forgiveness is suggested in 6:6–7, so it is shown to be grounded in the sacrificial sufferings of God's great Servant (52:13–53:12). But God's purpose is concerned not only with the individual but also with the nation, and the doctrine of the remnant is the guarantee of God's truth. In Isaiah's teaching about the remnant lies the seed of all that he declares about the future glory of Zion (see next section).

4. Eschatology

The message of Isaiah is strongly eschatological. The prophet frequently deals with the future destiny of Israel and the Gentiles. This book, like other OT prophetic Scriptures, has been understood in more than one way as far as its eschatology is concerned.

Clearly, a high doctrine of Scripture requires us to take the teaching of its every part seriously; it also requires that we consider the way the NT writers understood it.

The interpretation of the nature of Isaiah's prophecy ranges from very literal (i.e., every prophecy that can be taken literally should be so taken) to primarily spiritual (i.e., that the promises made to Israel are to be fulfilled in the church). Both of these extreme positions have difficulties in the light of the NT. A good case can be made for the fulfillment of many of the "Israel" prophecies in the church (e.g., Ac 13:46–48; 26:19–23 interpret Isa 42:6–7; 49:6–7 spiritually). But there is an important group of NT passages that can hardly be understood in any other way than in relation to literal Israel and geographical Jerusalem (e.g., Mt 19:28; Lk 21:24; Ro 11:26–27; cf. Isa 27:9; 59:20–21).

There may be passages that present us with continuing problems of interpretation and where it is not plain whether we should understand them literally or spiritually. Perhaps this is what we should expect. We are never promised complete understanding of biblical prophecies before their fulfillment. Their main purpose is to keep us expectant, obedient, and trustful and to provide, in their fulfillment, evidence of the faithfulness of God to his Word. In the fulfilled events themselves, God will be seen to be true.

5. Messianism and the Servant Songs

Each part of the OT presents its own witness to the Christ who was to come. There is no OT book—with the possible exception of the Psalter—that is so full and varied in its testimony, and certainly none is so beautifully integrated. Many themes enter this prophetic literature that are messianic in the broad sense; that is, they witness to the Christ presented in the pages of the NT. The themes of the *Branch* (cf. 4:2; 11:1; et al.), the *Stone* (cf. 8:14; 28:16–17; et al.), and *Light* (9:2; 42:6; et al.) are important concepts in Isaiah. These all move beyond their normal subpersonal uses to provide analogies of the coming One and his work. In the use of the terms *Child* (e.g., 9:6) and *King* (e.g., 9:6–7), however, we begin at the personal level (see 7:13–17).

The so-called Servant Songs, though clearly forming an identifiable series, have not been arbitrarily introduced to their context; for the servant theme is an important one in Isaiah from ch. 41 onward, with Israel often so-named (41:8–9; 43:10; 44:1–2, 21). Cyrus too, though not called God's servant, functions for him (44:28–45:7), with the prediction of God's prophetic servants (44:26) and the good of his servant Israel (45:4) as the background and the purpose of his work.

The Christian, guided by the use made of the Servant Songs in the NT (e.g., Mt 8:17; 12:17–21; Jn 12:38; et al.) can immediately say that they are fulfilled in Jesus. There is not a word of the songs that cannot be applied to him, even when the servant is called "Israel" (49:3); for, as Matthew clearly saw, Jesus was the perfect expression of what God intended Israel to be (cf. Mt 2:15 with Hos 11:1–2).

The prophet not only introduces a series of themes that prove eventually to be messianic, but he relates them in a kind of theological counterpoint. For instance, in chs. 8–9 we have the sanctuary (8:14; cf. Jn 2:19), the stone (8:14), the light (9:2), and the child King (9:7). The kingly theme is interwoven with that of the servant (e.g., 42:4; 52:13; 53:12), while both the king and the servant are endowed with the Spirit of God (11:1–3; 42:1; 61:1). This all gives the impression that some great person is in view, in whom all this material will find its ultimate focus.

EXPOSITION

I. Oracles Concerning Judah and Jerusalem (1:1–12:6)

A. God's Charge Against His People (1:1–31)

This chapter fitly opens the book. It vigorously sums up the teaching, not only of the prophet Isaiah, but of the whole prophetic movement.

1 The prophet's name means "The LORD Is Salvation." Nothing is known about Isaiah's father, and the Jewish tradition of Isaiah's royal birth is groundless. But he certainly had an extensive experience of kings! His knowledge of their imperfections fitted him to be a major channel of God's disclosure of the perfect king. "Vision" (GK 2606) suggests to us a mode of revelation, but it could be a technical term for an oracle of God, however received.

2–3 These two verses appear to introduce a trial scene. Here nature serves the purposes of prophecy. The heavens and earth witness God's complaint against his people, and the ox and the donkey dumbly rebuke Israel's ingratitude. Unreasoning beasts exhibit more sense and appreciation than unthinking Israel (cf. Jer 8:7). The words "children" and "they" are both emphatic in the Hebrew, underlining the unthinkable character of such filial rebellion.

4 The prophet's language suggests that guilt is an awful burden; that if paternity is truly revealed in character, then something has gone sadly wrong; and that the people have added insult to ingratitude.

5–6 The sinful people are addressed directly here. Their continuance in sin, like all rebellion against God, is utterly irrational. The whole surface of the body politic (i.e., the nation personified) testifies to the divine punishment, but the heart remains unchanged.

7–9 As Isaiah uttered these words, he may well have recalled the divine disclosure of things to come that had been given him at the time of his call (6:11–13). God's word had proved true. City and country were both suffering, for their inhabitants were powerless against the invaders. Isaiah likens the situation in the land to the roughly made shelters of the farmer's watchmen, standing desolate against the skyline once harvest was over. It was the restraining hand of the Lord Almighty that alone saved Jerusalem from sharing the fate of its environs, and the prophet stresses this by placing the names of the two destroyed cities in a position of emphasis.

10–15 Sodom and Gomorrah—shocking and deeply insulting names to Isaiah's hearers—suggest not only devastation but Gentile sin at its worst; yet the words "LORD" and "our God" have overtones of a covenant relationship unknown to the cities of the plain. The prophet presses home his point. Rulers and people have a Sodomlike offensiveness to God, and their ostentatious religious observances only aggravate the situation.

These verses highlight many features of Israel's system of worship. Verse 11 implies an abundance of sacrifices well beyond the divine requirements (cf. Mic 6:6–8). God was nauseated by such a surfeit, and the words "to me" and "more than enough" suggest the same kind of blasphemous, pagan idea of a god who needs to be fed with sacrifices that Ps 50 rejects with biting irony.

The temple courts felt the heavy tread of the worshiping throng, probably swollen at such times of national crisis; but "trampling" also suggests desecration. This puts the question "Who has asked this of you?" in its true perspective. God rejected "offerings" rendered "meaningless" by hypocrisy (cf. Jer 7:21–23; Hos 6:6; et al.). The people have been shown as burdened with guilt (v.4); but here God is shown as burdened with their sacrifices.

16–17 God's true way is announced and the moral note sounded. People are accountable, but the grace and power of fulfillment are God's alone. The prophet's words imply that the reclaimed sinner needs a course of instruction in the ways of God. This teaching process begins in the call for social justice and defense of the fatherless. Isaiah's rapid-fire style in these two verses underscores the authority and urgency of God's commands to his people.

18–20 Many see the words of v.18 as an offer of total forgiveness, for which vv.19–20 supply the divine conditions. Others understand the language to be ironic and render the second part of the verse, "If your sins are as scarlet, shall they be white as snow? If they are red like crimson, shall they be as wool?" The language permits either possibility. Verses 19–20 summarize the Deuteronomic theology of divine blessing (cf. Dt 28), which underlies much prophetic teaching. They contain a striking play on words. In effect God was saying, "Eat . . . or be eaten!"

21–23 The rhythm of Isaiah's poetry changes suddenly as he introduces the characteristic "limp" of a Hebrew lament, opening with the exclamation "how!" (cf. 14:4; 2Sa 1:19; Ps 137:4; et al.). Even though there is no explicit threat of judgment till v.24, the sensitive listener would hear the drumbeats of doom in the very sound of the poetic measure. Words like "justice" and "rulers" show that Isaiah was thinking primarily of the people's leaders; so the past he had in mind was perhaps the time of David, when Jerusalem first came under Israelite control. Silver and choice wine are probably metaphors for the rulers (cf. Jer 6:28, 30; Eze 22:18), who had become utterly decadent.

24–26 First was the ominous rhythm of the dirge (v.21), then came the vivid description of moral corruption (v.23), and here we have a terrifying catena of majestic divine titles. The first of them—"Lord" (GK 123), meaning "master"—is used of God by Isaiah more than by any other OT writer. In its absolute form, as here, it always introduces a note of judgment (cf. 3:1; 10:16, 33; et al.). The second—"the LORD Almighty" (GK 3378 & 7372)—often linked with it, indicates supreme power, while the third—"the Mighty One [GK 51] of Israel"—is a somewhat uncommon term suggestive of bulllike strength (Ge 49:24; Isa 49:26; 60:16). Still there was no respite. To complete the verbal buildup, God's message is prefixed by the agitated exclamation "Ah" (cf. v.4).

The burden God bears as the result of the meaningless offerings of his "foes" demands relief in judgment. His hand, so often stretched out against Israel's enemies, has turned against his own people (cf. Zec 13:7). His threat of vengeance has taken an unexpected turn, however, for it issues in cleansing rather than destruction. Although so sinful, they were still his people, and his judgments were directed to the removal of their impurities.

27–31 The theme of restoration continues for another verse (anticipating the great vision of ch. 2), until the threatening tone returns (v.28). Is Zion's redemption here physical or moral? Redemption terminology is normally used in the OT with a physical connotation and is often so applied to Jerusalem/Zion (e.g., 35:9–10; 51:10–11; 52:9; 59:20).

Sacred trees played an important part in the Canaanite fertility cult (cf. Dt 12:23; 2Ki 16:4; Hos 4:13), for deciduous trees like the oak or terebinth may well have symbolized the death and rebirth of the god. The "gardens" may be groves of these trees, or, alternatively, places of sacred springs or wells.

Verses 29–30 teach the lesson that a people under judgment may be instructed from the very symbols of their apostasy as to the folly of such departure from the true God, while v.31 imparts the even more important lesson that destruction may come on us from the very thing our sin has brought into being.

B. The Exaltation of God's House and the Extension of His Dominion (2:1–5)

1 This heading virtually repeats that with which the book opens, apart from the reference there to the kings. Isaiah literally saw "the word" (cf. KJV, RSV, et al.), which suggests that the revelation contained both visionary and verbal elements.

2–4 This glorious vision is found, with small variations, in Mic 4:1–3. Joel 3:10 contains language clearly parallel with Isa 2:4 and Mic 4:3. Apart from its use in Mic 4:4, the statement "for the mouth of the LORD has spoken" is found only in Isaiah (1:20; 40:5; 58:14).

"In the last days" relates the vision to the period when God's purposes will find fulfillment. The NT, making explicit that the Messiah comes twice, applies the phrase both to the period of his first advent (e.g., Ac 2:17; Heb 1:2) and to his second (e.g., Jas 5:3; 1Pe 1:5). The context of the oracle in Micah suggests that the first stage of its fulfillment took place in the return from Babylonia (Mic 4:1–10), when ruined Jerusalem (Mic 3:12) would be rebuilt and her temple raised again.

The whole of ch. 2 makes extensive use of the language of elevation and abasement to convey dignity and pride on the one hand and lowliness and humiliation on the other. There is clearly a figurative element here, picturing nations as streams (cf. Jer 51:44)—flowing upwards! The promised elevation of Mount Zion underlines its spiritual preeminence as the source of divine teaching for the nations. The word "established" reminds us of Ps 2:6 ("I have installed my King on Zion, my holy hill"). Both the hill and the King are secure because they are in the center of God's purpose for his people.

In Isaiah's day "the house of the God of Jacob" was at Jerusalem, not at the original Bethel ("house of God" [Ge 28:16–22]), for Bethel was the site of an apostate shrine (1Ki 12:28–29). The phrase "God of Jacob" underlines the special relationship of the true God with historical Israel, while "Zion"/ "Jerusalem" represents divinely ordained worship and divinely authorized government. So this passage weds together normal OT particularism with the vision of universal worship and peace.

The issues that set nations against one another do not disappear automatically but are settled by the supreme Judge, whose decisions are accepted. Thus there is no uneasy calm but peace based on righteousness (cf. 11:1–9; Ps 72). In the abolition of every cause of conflict, war itself disappears; and peace, with its economic consequences, takes its place.

5 Isaiah views the future obedience of the nations to the true God as a challenge to the house of Jacob to walk in his ways. The nations are not yet coming to Jerusalem to be taught by the Lord, but Israel already has his word. How unthinkable then that she should continue to walk in darkness!

C. The Day of the Lord (2:6–22)

6–9 The sore trials the people are to pass through will provide evidence that God has abandoned them to their enemies (not absolutely, or forever, as 4:2–6 will show), and this itself is the start of the great day of judgment on them. The causes of this judgment remind us of the divinely given constitution for the kingdom laid down in Dt 17:14–20, set in a context (Dt 16:18–18:22) of much reference not only to the leadership of the people but also to the need for separation from the abominable practices of the nations. The kings of Judah have been native-born, but this did not prevent the people from being contaminated by foreign religious and semireligious practices.

To "clasp hands" may refer to a gesture symbolizing the striking of a bargain. The people were seeking economic and military self-sufficiency, so that they need not depend on their God; yet at the same time they were groveling to man-made objects of worship.

10–11 The people had been abasing themselves, though in the presence of dumb idols and not the true and only God. Their action was appropriate, but their object of worship was wrong. The proud are eager to avoid the gaze of God, for his majestic presence drives every rival underground in the frantic and, of course, utterly unavailing search for cover. This picture of the people—enjoying the affluence of the land but turning aside to idols till the Lord establishes his sole right to worship by an act of judgment—is a reminder of Dt 6:10–15.

12–18 When God acts in judgment, it is often to upset human values so that everything can be seen from the divine perspective. Jerusalem's hill is to be exalted above other greater mountains (v.2), but all that is reckoned great by people will be brought low.

Much of the imagery of this passage can be viewed as Phoenician. It was in the hinterland of Tyre and Sidon that the cedars grew; it was there too that the highest mountains were found, and the grand designs of stonemasons and shipwrights were to be seen in its ports. "Every trading ship" was based in Phoenicia. This land was notorious for its religious influence on both Israel and Judah, for Jezebel's family became part of the dynastic stock of both kingdoms for a while (cf. 2Ki 8:16–18). It was from this quarter that religious syncretism had come during the previous century, and its features could still stand for alien religion. The main point, of course, is that God's act of judgment would humble every manifestation of human pride.

19–21 The terrifying revelation of the glory, power, and judgment of the one true God will give human beings—but too late—a proper sense of values. The silver and gold used to make idols are at last recognized as worthless in the light of his glory.

22 After the idols have been cut down to size by the revelation of the true God in his judicial majesty, the spotlight of the divine contempt focuses on human beings, whose dignity as creatures made in God's image had been cast away by their groveling before idols made by their own hands, and whose pride would be abased before God's disclosure (vv.11, 17–21). The reference to "breath" not only suggests frailty but also may be intended to allude to Ge 2:7. So, implies the prophet, you are worshiping gods you have made instead of the God who made you!

D. God's Judgment on Jerusalem and Judah (3:1–4:1)

1–7 The divine titles in v.1, with their stress on power (see comment on 1:24), anticipate a strong threat of judgment. The reference to famine is brief but ominous (cf. v.7); the prophet concentrates on the removal of responsible and trusted leaders. The people were showing too great a tendency to put their trust in human beings (2:22). The prophet warns them that the objects of their trust are to be removed. Those traditionally respected—"the old," "the honorable"—will be violently replaced by the manifestly inadequate and by the base oppressor. The situation would in fact reach such a pitch that the mere possession of some outward semblance of wealth or rank would attract the attention of those desperately seeking for someone to bring a measure of order to a situation of chaos. The phrase "this heap of ruins" anticipates the later picture of a destitute and defeated city (v.26).

8–12 The prophet reminds his readers of the spiritual and moral causes of this anarchy. Judah and its capital city are to reach the brink of total collapse, with disaster to follow, because of insolent and blatant rebellion against the Lord. "His glorious presence" is another reminder of 2:10. By his use of the phrase "my people," Isaiah is reminding them of their covenant relationship. Walking in the counsel of the wicked is especially influential and dangerous when done by national leadership (v.12).

13–15 The law-court scene here is reminiscent of ch. 1, while the reference to the vineyard anticipates ch. 5. Many passages show the responsibility of leadership among God's people and the exacting nature of his judgment of the shepherds of his people (e.g., Jer 25; Eze 34; Zec 10–11; Jn 10; Jas 3:1). Not only may leaders take people aside from the right path; but positions of privilege and responsibility may be used to foster self-interest rather than social good. This forms God's major accusation in this dramatic judgment scene. The great titles that close this section are a fearsome reminder that God not only has the right to judge his people but also the power to carry out his judgment.

3:16–4:1 If there is still some moral fiber in the women of a deteriorating society, the situation is not without hope; for they have the most formative influence on the younger generation. The arrogant pride seen in the rulers of Judah was, however, just as evident in its women. Those depicted here are clearly the wealthy, whose rich stores of finery had probably been bought by the plunder taken by their husbands from the poor (cf. v.14).

In v.9, the prophet linked the look on the face with a Sodomlike parade of sin, suggesting that all was not right in the sexual life of the community. This language moves swiftly from the ostentatious posturing of these women as they parade in the streets of Jerusalem to far from seemly attempts to attract male attention. The judgment formula "in that day" provides a further link with ch. 2 and introduces a catalog of their adornments and other luxurious paraphernalia. This stands in stark contrast to the repeated phrase "the poor" in vv.14–15.

The judgment would come through enemies who would take the Israelites captive, giving them the rough garb of prisoners of war. The removal of locks of hair suggests that the city would be taken by the Babylonians, who did this to those taken in war. "Branding" is also consistent with an enslavement due to capture.

By a swift and yet appropriate movement of thought, Isaiah turned from the daughters of Zion (v.16) to the city herself (vv.25–26), referred to in 1:8 as "the Daughter of Zion." The city and her gates are graphically personified. Isaiah boldly transports us from his confident predictions to their fulfillment.

Just as swiftly we return to the women of Jerusalem (4:1), perhaps those widowed through the violent overthrow of the city. The judgment on the city drastically altered the normal male-female proportions in the population. These concerned women are prepared to forego the normal perquisites of marriage to secure its status—or, at least, to gain the protection of a name. The interesting links with 3:7 suggest that the same judgment is in view, or at least one with the same kind of effects on the economy of the country. God's judgments do not always follow the same pattern—though they always proceed from the same principles, for his nature is unchanging.

E. Zion's Glorious Future (4:2–6)

2 The great contrast between this section and the preceding one is accentuated by the fact that both v.1 and v.2 commence with the phrase "in that day." This section itself (4:2–6) contains a note of judgment in v.4; but clearly the Day of the Lord, though basically judgmental, introduces also the salvation that is the sequel and consequence of God's cleansing act.

This verse contains a major question concerning the phrases "the Branch of the LORD" and "the fruit of the land." An ancient and pre-Christian interpretation applies both phrases to the Messiah. The Targum renders "the Branch" as "the Messiah." Most conservative commentators have taken at least the first of the two phrases to be messianic. "Branch" (GK 7542) occurs in four verses (Jer 23:5; 33:15; Zec 3:8; 6:12) as a technical messianic designation. It is more difficult, however, to take "the fruit of the land" in a messianic sense, for nothing like it is so used elsewhere in the OT.

The Bible's use of technical language reveals a tendency for words and phrases to begin quite lowly but, through their use in various contexts, to gather more connotations as time goes by. "Branch" is a good example (cf. also "servant" in chs. 42–53). In this way the depth of God's purpose is progressively revealed. The concept of the "branch" begins in Isaiah at the botanical level, which is in view here. The famine and devastation wreaked on the land by their enemies showed the Israelites their dire need of literal fruitfulness. The God of new life therefore promised that the future would be marked by such God-given fruitfulness.

The people's need of life, however, was far greater, embracing the nation's very existence—which was being threatened by its foes. There was need of reassurance that the God of new life would make the remnant of his people fruitful, too. But their deepest need was for the Messiah; thus, he appears as the ultimate "Branch of the LORD" in ch. 11. The reader familiar with this development will see v.2 in terms both of its meaning in this context and of the deeper significance that this language was destined to have in the rest of Isaiah.

3 This verse finds its explanation in v.4, for the holiness of Jerusalem is due to the Lord's action described there. The recording of the names of Jerusalem's inhabitants may seem at first to be simply a record that they are still alive after the judgments have taken place (cf. 1:9), but the eschatological context suggests that eternal life is in view.

4 Both the women of Jerusalem (3:16–23) and her people generally (1:16–20) needed cleansing, and the Lord promises to do this. What does *ruah* (GK 8120) really convey here? The NIV renders it "spirit," while the marginal note has "the Spirit." The word is also rendered "breath" or "wind" in the OT and is the regular word used for the Spirit of God. It is used in a context of judgment also in

30:28 (cf. 40:7), where the NIV does not take it as a reference to the divine Spirit. On the other hand, *ruah* is linked with judgment—though in a much milder context—in connection with the Messiah's ministry in ch. 11. Perhaps we should understand it as "a blast of judgment and a blast of fire" and see it as another example of a term destined for enrichment as the book proceeds.

5–6 In 2:1–4 Mount Zion is elevated above the surrounding hills; here it is protected by divine symbols reminiscent of the journey out of Egypt (Ex 13:21; 14:19–20). The protective symbols would not move, as they did during the Exodus; for the future Mount Zion is journey's end. The word "create" (GK 1343), used in Ge 1, occurs later in Isaiah to denote realities brought into being by the Creator in his new and final purpose (cf. 41:20; 45:8; 48:7; 65:17–18). The glory thus seen over all Jerusalem will itself be protected by a canopy, normally used for weddings and royal occasions. The bridal implications of 5:1 suggest that this was in view here. It will protect the city from the natural elements (cf. 32:2).

The picture in these verses is glorious and certainly has not been completely fulfilled as yet. The returning exiles did not experience such idyllic conditions, though this disappointment is traced by Haggai not so much to the purpose of God as to their own sin (Hag 1:5–9).

F. The Parable of the Vineyard (5:1–7)

1–2 Role-play was used from time to time by the OT prophets (cf. Zec 11:4–17). Here Isaiah assumes the guise of a folk singer. Possibly he was really singing—at least at first—a

In this restored winepress at Avdat in southern Judea, the grapes were trampled by foot and juice flowed through the hole at the end.

love song and was identifying with the friend of the bridegroom (the "best man"; cf. Jn 3:29–30). If so, of course, the bride and groom are depicted figuratively in terms of a vineyard and its owner. The use of "vineyard" for a bride is often found in the Song of Solomon (2:15; 4:16–5:1; 6:1–2; 8:12). Not until the last clause of v.2 can we see that this was to be a sad, not a glad, story.

3–4 What a dramatic change! The scene shifts to a courtroom (cf. 1:2–17; 3:13–15), and this time the human hearers are to act as assessors as the owner of the vineyard speaks. This suggests that the "vineyard" has moral responsibility. The discerning listeners have the first intimation that this parable is not for their comfort.

5–6 The abandonment of such an unprofitable venture was only to be expected; for who would waste further energy, time, and money? But there was more than this. Definite action—the removal of its hedges and wall—would be taken against it. The hidden meaning comes closer to complete unveiling when the last statement of v.6 is uttered. What human owner can control the weather? This is God!

7 The hearers fell into a trap skillfully laid for them. The figurative form is cast off, and God's people stand exposed as the guilty objects of his disappointment and judgment. They have condemned themselves, for the tacit agreement of the hearers to the criticism of the vineyard can be assumed.

G. Condemnation of Judah's Sins (5:8–30)

The eighth-century prophets were united in their condemnation of the social sins of the affluent society of their day (cf. Am 5:18; 6:1). Moreover, just as in Am 1–2 the threat of divine judgment came nearer and nearer home—so that it pointed eventually at Israel herself—so the "woe" (GK 2098) oracles here came to rest eventually on the prophet himself (6:5).

8–10 In an affluent society all do not always profit from increased wealth (cf. Mic 2:1). The horror of the prophets in response to the sin of covetousness in its application to land (cf. 1Ki 21:17–24) was almost certainly due to their recognition of the principle that the land really belonged to God and that he had

made the various tribes and families stewards of it in perpetuity.

The rich have coveted and appropriated both house and land, and the judgment of God would descend on each. Whatever the measures intended, the main point is clear: there will be a minimal return for a large outlay (cf. Hag 1:5–6).

11–17 Most societies consider early morning drinking a mark of moral degeneracy, for anyone who thinks first of drink when he or she awakes is in its grip. Wealth dubiously gathered may well be dissolutely spent. The day that starts with drink ends in musical banquets when wine is drunk well into the night. As in the previous "woe," the penalty is appropriate to the offense, for exile removes them from the land on which they had set their affections, and feasting and drinking come to an abrupt end. "Lack of understanding" (v.13) relates to the outlook described in v.12b.

"The grave" (*sheol*; GK 8619) is the place of the dead. The midnight revelers, their mouths open for more food and drink, will suddenly find that they have become the food of that hungriest of all monsters—death. Solidarity in punishment means that both "men of rank" and "masses" will suffer the consequences of the sins of the wealthy.

Verse 16 sums up the connection between holiness and righteousness. God's separateness is not simply ontological but moral; his holiness is not a simple synonym for his majesty but the basis in his eternal character of his righteous judgments on sinners. The moral nature of divine holiness finds one of its most awesome expressions in ch. 6.

Verse 17 continues the theme, for it shows the affluent agricultural society of the day (cf. vv.9–10) reverting to a more thoroughly pastoral one, with the animals taking over the ruins. This suggests that the various woes of this section are directed against the same people.

18–19 Isaiah was fond of the picture of the burden-bearer (cf. 53:6; 57:10). Here he pictures sinful Judah, not now "loaded with guilt" (1:4), as if it was on their backs, but drawing it as a heavy load behind them. The pictures are different, but their import the same. Acceptance of deceit, the big lie (cf. v.20), sets their feet on sin's wearying treadmill (cf. Ro 6:23).

Verse 19 sums up the people's sin and exhibits its true nature as cynical rejection of the living God and all his ways. They imply that nothing is happening (cf. 41:21–24). But the "woe" this section begins with is the prophet's witness to his faith that God will act in judgment on sin—in his own time. The phrase "the Holy One of Israel" here was probably uttered by them with a curl of the lip, in contemptuous reference to a distinctive note of Isaiah's prophetic message (cf. 30:11–12).

20 This "woe" has a link with the previous one (v.18), for "deceit" is there expounded as skepticism about the ways of God. Unhappily, it is an easy journey from such skepticism to the total reversal of values that this verse demonstrates, for God is the source of all values; and if we are wrong about him, we can soon be wrong about everything.

21 This verse too may have a link with the previous "woe," for the reversal of values expressed there may form the basis for the new "wisdom" of the godless, which is antagonistic to the divine wisdom (cf. 1Co 1:17–2:16; 3:18–23).

22–23 Verse 21 condemned the outlook of those who thought themselves wise while v.22 exposes the folly of that "wisdom." These men assessed themselves as heroes and champions. But these were not sober judgments, for their drink was talking through them. The situation was even more scandalous when we learn that they occupied positions of great responsibility, needing a clear head and an unweakened moral sense. In the place of justice, they acted corruptly (cf. 1:23; 10:1–2).

24–25 The series of "woes" is over. The last was pronounced against evil judges; now the supreme Judge begins to declare sentence. The fire of God will burn them; the hand of God will smite them. In 40:6–8 the prophet likens human life to grass and flowers, doomed to wither and die. Here he uses them as figures of judgment because they are so vulnerable to fire. To those familiar with grassland fires, the illustration suggests comprehensiveness and swiftness as well as the inexorable character of the judgment. The cause spelled out in detail in the preceding woes is summarily expressed as rejection of God's word. The word "law" (*torah*; GK 9368) is technical enough to suggest a reference to the Mosaic Law—the basis of Israel's God-given moral standard—and at the same time general enough to include Isaiah's own authoritative teaching.

Verse 25 seems to refer to a specific judgment not to be regarded as an isolated event but as a manifestation of that divine anger that continued to burn against the people. The mention of mountains shaking and dead bodies lying in the streets is appropriate if Isaiah has in mind the great earthquake in the days of Uzziah (Am 1:1; Zec 14:5).

26–30 What a gift of vivid description was given to this great prophet! The picture makes such an immediate appeal to the imagination that it requires little exposition. The great judgment, anticipated by the earthquake, is to come through a great army from afar, swift, single-minded, effective, ferocious, and altogether terrifying. A "banner" is raised by God as a rallying point for his punitive army. He will whistle to them like a beekeeper. The phrase "the ends of the earth" is hyperbole, since the Assyrians were in view. Regarding the references to the sea and land, the former occurs in a simile while the latter is literal. The prophet moves from the figure of the roaring lion to that of the roaring sea; and then, perhaps, calling to mind the literal sea—which might have been a means of escape from the foe if it had been less turbulent—he declares that there is no hope landward either. The cloud of Assyrian judgment has blotted out any light that may have indicated an escape route.

H. The Vision and Call of the Holy One (6:1–13)

1 The date of Uzziah's death has been much disputed. Isaiah 14:28–32 is an oracle from the year of the death of King Ahaz, and it is clearly appropriate to the political situation of that time. We are not surprised, therefore, to find something similar here; and we can well imagine the spiritual value to the prophet himself of a vision of the almighty King when an earthly reign of over fifty years had come—or was coming—to its end. The vision of the Lord's transcendence never left Isaiah: the exaltation of Israel's great God is a frequent theme in his oracles (cf. 2:10–22; 37:16; 40:12–26; 57:15).

2 This is the only biblical passage where heavenly beings are called "seraphs" (GK 8597). They are part of the great variety of heavenly beings created by God (along with others such as angels, archangels, principalities, powers, and cherubim). The seraphs are bright creatures, for the word means "burning ones"; yet they hide their faces from the greater brightness and the glory of the Lord. Covering the feet suggests humility.

3 There is no indication of the number of seraphs seen by Isaiah. Possibly he was present at an act of worship in the temple, perhaps at the New Year, and the antiphonal singing of the Levitical choir was echoed by the heavenly seraphs of his vision. The apostle Paul evidently believed that angels are present at Christian worship (cf. 1Co 11:2–16, which likewise deals with veiling and unveiling in the presence of God).

The threefold ascription of holiness to God (cf. Rev 4:8) has been interpreted in reference to the Trinity since the early Church Fathers. It is best for us simply to say that— in the fuller light of the NT—we can see the appropriateness of this threefold expression. The theme of divine holiness is of towering importance in Isaiah. This man of God could never forget the disclosure of transcendent purity he encountered when he was called to prophetic service (cf. Eze 1).

The language of fullness occurs three times in these verses (vv.1, 3, 4), twice in reference to the temple and once to the whole earth. So this passage, insisting as it does on the awesome transcendence of the sovereign God, also emphatically teaches his immanence. His transcendence is not remoteness or aloofness but is known through his presence in his created world and temple. Divine transcendence and immanence are always held in balance in the Bible's view of God (cf. 12:6).

The word "glory" (GK 3883) is used of God in his manifestation to his creatures. The essence of deity is inscrutable, but something of his glory can be seen if God is pleased to disclose it (Ex 33:17–23; Eze 1:28). In Jn 12:41, after quoting Isa 6:10, John said that Isaiah "saw [Jesus'] glory and spoke about him." This amazing statement is in fact altogether consistent with the high Christology of the NT writers, for Jesus is God incarnate, and the same God is revealed in both OT and NT. This might in fact suggest that John understood the threefold use of "holy" in trinitarian terms.

4 God's power is sometimes manifested in a physical tremor (cf. Ex 19:18; Ac 4:31) and his presence in a cloud of smoke (cf. Isa 4:5; Ex 33:9). So the God who normally hides himself from the senses occasionally made himself known in a form accessible to them, and he ultimately did so in the consummate unveiling of himself in his Son (1Jn 1:1–4).

5 The word translated "woe" (GK 208) here is different from that used several times in ch. 5. They are, in fact, synonyms, each possessing various nuances ranging from the threat to the sigh. This verse teaches us that to be an effective channel for God's penetrating word, the power of that word must be felt in the person's own conscience. It is true that the lips of the prophet were destined to proclaim God's truth; but if he was in the temple at worship, the primary reference may be to the defiled lips of the worshiper (cf. 1:15; 29:13). The people of the OT always felt a deep apprehension at the prospect of seeing God. This must have been underlined still more for Isaiah as he saw even the unfallen seraphs covering their faces in the presence of the Most High.

6–7 To serve God, Isaiah needed to be a clean instrument. The God of burning holiness himself (cf. 33:13–16) provides this cleansing from the sacrificial altar (cf. Nu 31:22–23; Mal 3:2). Significantly, one of the seraphs (see comment on v.2) is the instrument of purification administered to the prophet. Isaiah may well have learned from this experience that sinful human beings can join in the worship of the "burning ones" only when purified by the fire of God (cf. 4:4).

8 Isaiah is not coerced into service; rather, his will makes its ready response as a grateful reaction to God's forgiving grace. No doubt Isaiah's very response was itself the product of divine grace, but this is not where the stress falls here. Instead, we see him faced with the challenge to personal commitment.

The plural "us" is often taken to be either a reference to the Trinity (cf. v.3; Ge 1:26; 11:7) or to a council of heavenly beings. Many passages picture God surrounded by the heavenly hosts; but none suggests that God called on them for advice or even identified them with him in some way in his utterance. In a context that speaks both of waters and mountains (nature) and of nations (history), the Lord refutes the notion that he consulted others (40:13–14). The plural, therefore, suggests either the divine majesty or that fullness of his being that was to find its ultimate theological expression in the doctrine of the Trinity.

9–10 Isaiah was apprised of the people's hardness of heart by the Lord Almighty, who not only knew what would occur but had planned it; for he is King (vv.1, 5). The words of God to Isaiah are quoted in each of the Gospels (Mt 13:14–15; Mk 4:10–12; Lk 8:10; Jn 12:39–41) and twice by Paul (Ac 28:26–27; Ro 11:8). Each quotation is given as a comment on the rejection of God's word in Christ. The synoptic references all occur in connection with the parable of the sower, which, like here, anticipates widespread failure to make proper response to God's word, but which also, as here (v.13), shows cause for hope. The holy seed of the vision finds its NT counterpart in the good soil of the parable.

11–12 The tone of Isaiah's question is one of lament. The prophets did not find God's message of judgment easy to utter (cf. Jer 1:6 8, 17; Eze 2:3–8; et al.). They belonged to the nation they addressed and must often have wept for its sins and its certain judgment (Jer 9:1; 14:17). The opening chapters of the book (as well as later passages), recording material from the events of the prophet's day (1:7–9) and from oracles of future judgment (e.g., 3:25–26; 5:8–9, 13, 17), illustrate these verses.

13 The devastation, great as it was to be, would not be total; but even its survivors would have to submit to further judgment. The illustration from nature introduces an element of hope. God has so ordered nature that almost total destruction does not always extinguish life. He has a continuing purpose of life for the remnant of his people (see comment on 4:2). The word "seed" (GK 2446) suggests a link with the promise given to Abraham that his seed ("offspring"; GK 2446) would continue and be blessed by God (Ge 17:1–8; cf. Isa 51:2). That God should use the word "holy" (GK 7731) of the remnant of his people when it has been used already in v.3 in relation to his own transcendent being is condescending grace indeed!

I. The Sign of Shear-Jashub (7:1–9)

Isaiah 7:1–9:7 has a certain unity, not only in its historical background, but also on account of the children with symbolic names. The "day of Midian's defeat" (9:4), which occurs near its close, perhaps reveals the significance of the whole section. The day of Midian was God's great victory over a mighty horde through a weak human leader commanding a tiny force of soldiers without proper weapons (Jdg 6–7). Through things that are not, God brings to nothing the things that are, so that no flesh may glory in his presence (cf. 1Co 1:25–31).

1 For the historical background, see the introduction. It is clear from 2Ki 15:37 that the alliance of the two northern kings against Judah began before Jotham died. The challenge to the faith of Ahaz, therefore, came early in his reign and, given a different response from him, could have established him in a relationship of dependent trust on the Lord from the very beginning. The reference to Uzziah could form a studied link with 6:1, hinting at the undoubted spiritual connection between the two chapters. God's supreme kingship exalts him as sovereign, not only over Judah in the days of its earthly king's demise, but over Rezin, Pekah, and the great Assyrian monarch himself. Chapter 6 predicts unbelief; ch. 7 records its historical manifestation.

2 The designation of Ahaz as "the house of David" (cf. v.13) is most unusual. This phrase perhaps underlines the sin inherent in his fear and his failure to believe; for the security of David's house, to which he belonged, was guaranteed by the divine word (2Sa 7).

3 The name Shear-Jashub is, of course, symbolic (i.e., "a remnant will return"). If this name was given to him at birth, its choice may have been determined by the disclosure of the future given to the prophet at his call (6:13). There is a double ambiguity in it. It can suggest either warning or hope, and also either physical return from exile or spiritual return to God. Without doubt the element of warning is prominent in the present context.

The meeting place of prophet and king is precisely located, though we cannot now place it with certainty. An adequate water supply was imperative for a city under siege. The king was probably satisfying himself as to this or making arrangements for its improvement. He was therefore engaged in an activity directly related to the situation described in v.1, one that provided the setting for God's test of his faith and obedience.

4 How emphatic is Isaiah's exhortation! A verb commanding attention—"be careful"— is followed by three others counseling trust instead of fear. This is reinforced by the description of the two kings. Their anger may have been fierce, but there was little real fire left in them—they were virtually impotent.

5–6 There is a touch of contempt in the way the personal name of the usurper-elect is omitted (cf. "son of Remaliah"). "The son of Tabeel" cannot be identified with certainty, though, in view of the reference to "the house of David" (v.2), it seems most unlikely that he belonged to the authentic royal line of Judah.

7–9 The message of reassurance is clear. The rulers of the two small kingdoms to the north were but human beings; they could not stand against the decree of the sovereign Lord. Verse 8b is probably best viewed as a prophecy fulfilled in a series of events that included Tiglath-pileser's imminent invasion, the fall of Samaria to Sargon II, and eventually the racial mixture introduced to Ephraim by yet another Assyrian emperor, Esar-haddon, about sixty-five years after this oracle.

The verbs translated "stand firm in your faith" and "stand" are closely related in Hebrew. They would have stayed in the mind of Ahaz as a somber summary of the message he had received and rejected (cf. vv. 12–13, 17).

J. The Sign of Immanuel (7:10–25)

10–11 This oracle probably followed closely on the previous one, for it is related to the same situation. It implies that the earlier prophecy has been rejected or at least treated with noncommittal evasion by the king. If there had been even a spark of faith in Ahaz, God was willing to give it an opportunity of expression. He responded to Gideon's repeated request for a sign, even though it followed a clear revelation of his saving will (Jdg 6:14, 17–18, 38–40). Once again (cf. 9:4) a superior foe was threatening the nation. God went even further this time in his patience with human weakness, for he actually offered Ahaz the unrestricted choice of a sign. Rein-

forcement of such an overflowing gesture of grace hardly seems conceivable, and yet it is secured by the possessive pronoun "your," reminding him of his special relationship to God as the chosen king (cf. 2Sa 7:11–16).

12 Ahaz made his plans, but they did not include God or his will. His reply was a monumental piece of hypocrisy; he probably had Dt 6:16 in mind. It would be good to think that this reveals at least some small attempt earlier in his life to come to grips with this book, which the king was obliged to know and follow (cf. Dt 17:14–20).

13 Isaiah still addresses Ahaz as "house of David" (cf. v.2), with its implication of special promises and also of a continuing dynasty; but here he speaks of "my God" instead of "your God" (cf. v.11). The king may have been the current occupant of the divinely secured throne of David; but it was incumbent on him to hear the divine word through the prophet who, unlike him, was in a sensitive and responsive relationship with God. It was that relationship that made the king's rejection of the prophetic word a trial of God's patience and not simply a man's patience. God was weary of his unbelief.

14–17 This great passage is both important and difficult. Before suggesting a solution, it will be helpful to set out the main facts and problems that a satisfactory interpretation must come to grips with: (1) The mother and child must be seen as a sign to Ahaz. In fact, the reference to the house of David may suggest that the sign will be significant for the whole dynasty. (2) Why did Isaiah use the word *almah* ("virgin" NIV; "young woman," RSV; GK 6625), and what is its exact significance here? (3) Does the Hebrew verbal adjective in v.14 mean "will be" (see NIV) or "is" or "has been"? (4) Does Immanuel mean "God is with us" or "God with us"? (5) What is the significance of curds and honey (cf. v.22)? (6) What does v.15 mean? Is the discrimination in view dietary or moral? What age is in view? (7) Verses 16–17 appear to relate to historical events that actually took place in the comparatively near future. If this is so, how can the child be simply equated with the Messiah? (8) The chapters that form the context of this passage contain a number of other references to children. Do any of these shed light on the Immanuel prophecy? (9) Why did the LXX translators use the unambiguous word *parthenos* ("virgin"; cf. Mt 1:23; GK *4221*) to translate *almah*? (10) Can we gain any light from a study of the way Matthew handles other quotations from the OT?

Expressed briefly, the main question is: Can we find a solution that does full justice to the language of Isaiah and at the same time to Matthew's application of the prophecy to Christ? Most suggested solutions are inadequate. Neither the queen nor Isaiah's wife was a virgin, and there is no clear OT example of the use of *almah* for a married woman. It seems to be used consistently to designate a sexually mature but unmarried woman. There are considerable chronological difficulties that stand in the way of identifying the child with Hezekiah. It seems unlikely that Isaiah's wife would be designated "the prophetess" in 8:3 and yet be indicated so anonymously here. It also seems unlikely that mothers in general would be referred to by a singular noun with the definite article. Moreover, one would normally expect a sign to be more objective and specific than a general return to faith and hope among the people. If v.14 were not followed by vv.15–17, we could make a straightforward equation of Immanuel with the Messiah; but this context raises major problems. These verses certainly imply a close historical relationship between the child and the political situation of Isaiah's day.

The best view seems to be that the mother is a royal contemporary of the prophet, whose child's name would symbolize the presence of God with his people and who would foreshadow the Messiah in whom God would be incarnate. An unmarried young woman within the royal house would shortly marry and conceive. Her son would be called Immanuel ("God is with us"), probably in ignorance of the prophecy (which may have been given in the presence only of Ahaz) and possibly even as a presumptuous gesture to give the support of a complacent piety to the king's pro-Assyrian policy. Before the child is old enough to eat the characteristic solid food of the Land of Promise (and so well before the age of moral discretion), the Assyrians would lay waste the lands of Aram and Israel, which they did in 733–732 B.C., only a year or two after the prophecy was given.

The "sign" (GK 253) of the child, therefore, constitutes an indication that the all-sovereign and all-knowing God has the situation completely in hand, and it rebukes the king's lack of faith in him. It is true that the instrument of this devastation was to be Assyria, the very power Ahaz was courting instead of relying wholly on God. But in fact the events of 733–732 not only heralded the downfall in 722 of Samaria—the capital city of the northern kingdom that was a large part of the domain of the house of David in its earlier days—but within a generation led to the devastation of Judah itself (cf. 1:7).

This prophecy was given to the house of David and not simply to Ahaz ("you" in v.14 is plural). In the fullness of time, the messianic Child would be born of that house. He was to be a symbol of God's salvation of his people, not simply from physical foes like Rezin and Pekah, but ultimately from sin (cf. Mt 1:21). He represents the final purpose of God in his person as well as his work. For he is, in fullness of meaning, God with us; and his mother was a virgin at the time of her conception and not simply, as in the case of the earlier royal mother, at the time of the prophecy. Matthew's concept of fulfillment is wide-ranging and flexible and embraces many different kinds of correspondence between an OT passage and a NT event.

It is characteristic of Isaiah to introduce a messianic theme at a somewhat general level before spelling it out in unambiguously messianic terms (cf. 4:2; 42:1). This interpretation, therefore, enables us to see the passage as part of a wider pattern in the book. So Isaiah predicted the coming of a boy who would be a sign from God to his contemporaries and who would foreshadow Christ, in whom the terms of the prophecy would be fulfilled in fullest measure. In terms of his heavenly origin and his destiny of suffering, death, and burial—as well as his exaltation to the highest place, where he fills the whole universe (Eph 4:9–10)—the ultimate fulfillment in Christ of the sign given to Ahaz embraces the whole range of options presented to that king (Isa 7:11).

18–19 The phrase that v.17 ends with—"the king of Assyria"—should have struck terror in the heart of Ahaz. History has known few races equal to the Assyrians for sheer cruelty. An international scene dominated by this-ferocious nation was a sure recipe for sleepless nights in the Fertile Crescent, and the prospect of invasion from that quarter presented the mind with an intolerable thought. Yet such was the fate that Ahaz was risking by his course of action! The prophet spelled out the consequences in graphic language.

Whistling for insects finds mention in a number of classical texts. To create a universe, God had only to speak; to gather his instruments of punishment, he had only to whistle. In the years that lay ahead, rulers in Judah would look to the Valley of the Euphrates and to Egypt for military help, but God warned Ahaz that both areas were to be viewed as sources, not of support, but of great danger for his people. Lest his reference to bees might make Ahaz think the invasion is to be somewhat selective and limited in its effect, the prophet pictured them settling in places that were not their normal habitat. Not since the day of Midian (cf. 9:4) had an invading force been so comprehensively and graphically pictured (cf. Jdg 6:1–6).

20 Isaiah passes with ease from one vivid picture to another. The old enemy Egypt recedes from the picture so that the spotlight may be turned on Assyria, the new and even more terrible oppressor that appears on the northeastern political horizon. Shaving, particularly of the beard, was a way of inflicting shame on a defeated foe (cf. 2Sa 10:4–5). The word "hired" seems peculiar till we realize that the Assyrians were well paid—in land and booty—for their trouble. It could also be an allusion to the king's own inducement to Assyria to come west, though not against him but against his northern enemies (2Ki 16:7–8).

21–22 In a passage otherwise dark with judgment, this picture incorporates some element of hope for the future. Judgment will devastate the land, but the survivors will find that small resources will yield adequate provisions (cf. 2Ki 4:1–7). In this way (cf. 6:13) the purpose of God for his people will continue—if only in a remnant. That "curds and honey" are spoken of in connection with a remnant and with a child who foreshadows the Messiah (see comments on 7:1–17) reinforces other evidence of a divinely purposed link between the two in the prophecies of Isaiah (see comments on 4:2; 42:1).

23–25 The devastation of the country—caused by human foes as instruments of God's judgment—will affect the whole economy of the land and will set civilization back a stage or two. The agricultural economy, symbolized by the vine, will be replaced by the pastoral, symbolized by cattle and sheep, and even by the regime of the hunter, symbolized by the bow and arrow. If the king carried away in his imagination a picture of a land covered with briers and thorns, then the message was getting through.

K. The Sign of Maher-Shalal-Hash-Baz (8:1–10)

1–2 A large writing surface is in view, though its form or material is unspecified. Its size strongly suggests it was intended for public display, so that it conveyed a message and could be cited later as evidence when its prophecy was fulfilled. Its somber message of doom was to be interpreted a little later (cf. v.4). "Maher-Shalal-Hash-Baz" probably means "quick to plunder, swift to the spoil" (NIV note). This particular Zechariah is unknown (the name was extremely common), but Uriah the priest is probably the king's ally and instrument in apostasy who is named in 2Ki 16:11. "Reliable witnesses" need not describe their character so much as their position as people of standing in the community.

3–4 Isaiah's wife is called "the prophetess" because she was his wife or because, as the one who bore children with prophetic names, she became involved in the communication of the message of God. It is less likely that she was a prophetess in her own right. If, as seems probable, the events of vv.1–4 are in chronological order, the time involved—including both the pregnancy and the inarticulate babyhood of the child—would be between eighteen months and two years. This would place the inscribed prophecy in 734 B.C., for Damascus was occupied and Samaria plundered (cf. 2Ki 15:29) by Tiglath-pileser III in 732 B.C.

5–8 Here, as he so often did, Isaiah moves from literal statement to vivid picture-language, setting contrasting metaphors side by side; then he suddenly changes the second metaphor to another to bring out a further aspect of the full truth. Naaman had contrasted Jordan with Abana and Pharpar, the rivers of Damascus (2Ki 5:12), and so had justified his initial rejection of God's way of giving him deliverance from his leprosy. The nation of Judah was more culpable than Naaman, for he had been a Gentile; and the contrast Isaiah used is much more impressive than that used by the Syrian general.

"The gently flowing waters of Shiloah" certainly refers to Jerusalem's means of water supply and probably to the channel that conveyed a slow-moving stream of water from the spring Gihon. It is not impossible that the location of Isaiah's encounter with Ahaz in 7:3 has determined the language here. The challenge to the faith of the king may have been delivered to him at a place that here symbolized the very confidence in God (cf. Ps 46:4–5) that he had rejected. Verse 6 shows in fact that the die was cast and the king and his people were committed to a course of trust in Assyria, not in God.

The NIV's "rejoices over," though a little free, brings out the almost certain meaning of the language. The people were whooping with delight at the prospect of the downfall of the two northern kings.

"The River" without further explanation in the OT is always the Euphrates (cf. Jos 24:15). The metaphor is immediately explained as "the king of Assyria with all his pomp," a genuine Isaianic touch (cf. 10:16; 16:14; 17:3–4). Rivers in flood are viewed ambivalently in areas where this natural phenomenon is important. Normal flooding benefits the ground and its produce; abnormal flooding threatens crops and, if extreme, the lives of the people. This exceptional inundation of foreign troops would move inexorably southward, not respecting the border between Israel and Judah. The deluge would almost—but not quite—submerge the whole nation, for above the neck was the head, Judah's capital, Jerusalem (cf. 1:7–9). Here again, then, in the midst of a terrifying threat of judgment, the remnant theme reminds us of God's continuing grace (cf. also 7:21–22).

The metaphor suddenly changes. It seems that the Assyrian army is no longer a river in flood but a predator of the sky (cf. Eze 17; Hos 8:1). But is this really what the prophet meant to convey? The outspread wings could belong to the Lord, so that the image is one of protection and not judgment, amplifying in this way the promise implicit in "reaching up to the neck." God's protection of the cap-

ital was the down payment of his ultimate purpose for the whole land. So the assurance contained in the name Immanuel (7:14; cf. 8:10) would be justified by events.

9–10 The rebellious confidence of v.6b and the confident taunt of vv.9–10 occupy different worlds. The former belongs to the world of trust in human alliances and weapons, the latter is the exultant cry of faith in God. God's purpose is proof against all that people or nations—any person or nation—can do. Not only human power but also human wisdom must fall before the power and wisdom of God (cf. 9:4–6; 1Co 1:24–27).

L. Isaiah and His Children as Signs and Wonders (8:11–18)

11 In some way related to the normal process of prophetic inspiration, the hand of the Lord was on the prophet. He was under a special, divine constraint. He may have been troubled at his increasing isolation from the people he was called to address with the word and who persisted in rejecting it (cf. 6:9–10; 8:8).

12–15 The word translated "conspiracy" (GK 8004) can mean "treaty" (cf. NIV note), but more likely means "conspiracy" here. But if God was speaking here of a conspiracy, who was under criticism? Isaiah and those who welcomed his message ("you" in v.13a is plural) were to epitomize the response all the people should have made to his message, for a deep reverence for God banishes fear of other human beings. The word for "sanctuary" (GK 5219) comes from the same root as "you are to regard as holy." God will himself be a holy place in the midst of his people (cf. Ex 40:34–38; Jn 1:14; Rev 21:3).

The prophet has already shown in his language that he regarded the division of the kingdom as a tragedy of divine judgment (7:17). Both houses will face further judgment from God because of their attitude in the present crisis, though the mention of Jerusalem suggests he has Judah chiefly in mind. Perhaps he takes the judgment of apostate Israel for granted.

Isaiah uses two analogies to picture this judgment. God is often described in the OT as a Rock (e.g., Dt 32:4, 15, 18; Pss 18:2; 71:3), normally with implications of shelter and refuge. Here the prophet turns this familiar figure against the people. God the Rock is for his people who trust him, but he is against those who refuse to believe. To them he will be either a boulder over which a person falls in the darkness or loose rock at the edge of a ravine. Isaiah has already pictured people under the divine hand of judgment having to become hunters again (7:24); now he speaks of God as the hunter, who uses bird-snares and spring-traps as foils for his victims.

It is impossible in English to convey the terrifying force of the seven Hebrew words that constitute v.15. We suggest the following: "They will stumble, many of them, they will fall, be smashed, snared, seized." The NT writers saw the ultimate object of faith to be Christ. Human beings reveal their attitude to God by their faith in Christ or by their rejection of him; so the NT writers applied this prophecy to him (Mt 21:44; Lk 2:34; Ro 9:33; 1Pe 2:8).

16–17 These verses are often taken to mean that the prophet turned from public ministry to concentrate on those gathered around him who had accepted his message. In this way God's face would be hidden in judgment from the mass of the people. In substance this interpretation iscorrect, but it should be recognized that "testimony" and "law" may refer to an actual document, the written record of the prophet's message. This record was sealed—possibly in the presence of witnesses (cf. 8:1–2)—so that it could not be altered.

God's hiding of his face implies judgment (see Hab 1:13). Although persistent rejection of God's word leads to its withdrawal (cf. 1Sa 28:6; Am 8:11–13), the prophet, who had welcomed that word and became its channel, reposed confidence in God and in the fulfillment of it. Presumably his prophetic activity ceased for a while, perhaps until after the overthrow of Rezin and Pekah, which would then confirm the word of God through him.

18 Meanwhile, Isaiah and his children, with their symbolic names, were an eloquent visible message from God. Like Immanuel (cf. 7:14), they were signs pointing beyond themselves to the Lord and his word. Perhaps it is best to view Isaiah and his disciples here as foreshadowing Christ and his church, especially as Christ himself was a prophet and his disciples, who formed the nucleus of the church, were themselves a remnant of Israel, committed to God's word in him whom others had rejected. Literally, Isaiah had only

two children; figuratively, they included his disciples. This would make this passage somewhat uniform with 7:14–17, for in both Christ is presented in type. This means, then, that both the child Immanuel and Isaiah and his children constituted the same kind of sign (cf. 7:11, 14; 8:18).

M. The Light and the Child (8:19–9:7)

19–20 The law strictly forbade necromancy and other occult practices (cf. Lev 19:31; 20:6–7; Dt 18:9–14). The words "whisper and mutter" not only describe the low tones in which the occult practitioners gave their alleged messages but invite a contrast with the clear and distinct word of prophecy.

Verse 20 introduces the theme of divine light, which is important later in the passage. The true source of light is God's word, for God is himself light (10:17). The dawning light of God within a person provides its own evidence in the way God's word governs one's speech, if one professes to be God's mouthpiece.

21–22 The Assyrian invasions would bring an acute food shortage (cf. 3:1; 7:23–25). Hunger would foster anger, which the Israelites would blame, in part correctly, on their apostate king and, quite wrongly, on their God (cf. Rev 16:11, 21). As there is none from higher authority, they seek around them alleviation of their distress. The picture of total darkness here goes even beyond that in 5:30 and is comparable to 60:2, in a context that, like this, also promises new light from the God of grace.

9:1–2 Despite Israel's rejection of God's word through Isaiah (8:11, 17, 19–20), God plans to give his people light again. The humbling of the lands of Zebulun and Naphtali refers to the invasion and annexation of the northern parts of Israel by Tiglath-pileser III in 733/732 B.C. (see Introduction). "The way of the sea" almost certainly refers to Sharon or Philistia, while "Galilee of the Gentiles" is probably Gilead and southeast Syria. The Assyrians carved out three provinces for themselves from these areas. These lands, the first to feel the ominous tread of the warrior's boot (v.5), would be the first to see the new and great light God would focus on Israel (cf. 60:1–3; cf. Mt 4:15–16; Lk 1:79; Jn 8:12).

3–5 At this point the atmosphere of great joy that entered the prophecy at v.1 turns into exultant praise as the prophet, anticipating the people's own future joy in their God (cf. ch. 12), turns to address him. National enlargement probably presupposes conditions of peace and prosperity under the blessing of God. Both the farmer and the soldier have their times of joy at the climax of their work, and these provide illustrations of the joy that is to come to God's people.

"The day of Midian" has been rightly interpreted as the day of Midian's defeat. The Bible is full of pregnant phrases that contain great power of suggestion. The appropriateness of this phrase can be clearly seen when we recall the historical situation: a vast multitude of the enemy swarming all over the land (Jdg 6:1–6; cf. Isa 8:7–8); the giving of a sign (Jdg 6:17–22; cf. Isa 7:11–14); the emphasis on faith in God and not dependence on human beings (Jdg 7; cf. Isa 7:9; 8:12); and, perhaps, the defeat of great forces through apparently insignificant means (three hundred men in the case of Gideon, and the child of promise here). Most of all the passage promises total redemption by the Lord. Israel is to be utterly delivered from the oppressor (cf. 10:5; 14:25; and esp. 10:24–27).

Isaiah pictures the resultant peace in vivid pictures. The boot of the soldier that had tramped across Israel's territory and his garment impregnated with the blood of the dead when he lay down to sleep would be as obsolete as the sword (2:4).

6–7 The word "child" is in a position of emphasis. The first person plural "us" suggests a link with 7:14. Just as the theme of the Branch of the Lord (see comment on 4:2) becomes more and more explicitly messianic, so it is with the motif of the child. If the child of Isa 7:14–16 typifies the ultimate divine Christ, the child of these verses *is* that Christ. It is true that monarchs of the Near East often received exaggerated adulation from their subjects, especially at their enthronement and at subsequent kingdom renewal ceremonies. This is not Mesopotamia, however, but Judah, and Hebrew prophecy was founded on truth, not flattery. The prophets did not hesitate to speak stern words of judgment to their political overlords.

This passage does not necessarily imply that the child is to be a boy-king. In fact, Isa-

iah may not have regarded that as a blessing (cf. 3:4, 12). The context says much about children, so the child is spoken of in terms of his birth. The tenderness of the child also suggests a comparison with the defeat of Midian's army by Gideon's small band of men (Jdg 6–7), a comparison reinforced by the dual reference to the shoulder (cf. v.4).

The KJV has a comma after "Wonderful," but it seems likely that the prophet intends us to understand that the child has four names, not five. The first two suggest divine wisdom and power, for the word translated "wonderful" (GK 7099) has overtones of deity. The last two set forth the ends he accomplished by the exercise of these attributes—his fatherly care of his people and the bringing of peace with all its attendant blessings. In the context this quartet of names comes to its climax with "Prince of Peace." Its implications are spelled out in v.7.

The word "increase" (GK 5269) combined with the phrase "his [i.e., David's] kingdom" suggest that the prophecy has in view much more than a particularly great king of Judah (cf. 2Sa 7:12–16). David's kingdom went well beyond this; in fact, its boundary extended far beyond the traditional "Dan to Beersheba" limits of Canaan proper (2Sa 8). The language here is reminiscent of that pre-Davidic ruler of Jerusalem, Melchizedek (Ge 14:18). The harmonious linking of peace and righteousness occurs again, with more detail, in 11:1–9.

Since the beginning of ch. 7, the prophet has been making the most amazing disclosures in the name of the Lord; and these have come to a great climax in these two verses. Both the advent of the Messiah and the blessing of his people, the remnant of Israel, are guaranteed by "the zeal of the LORD" (cf. 37:32).

N. The Judgment of Ephraim (9:8–10:4)

The threat of Syria and Ephraim/Israel against Judah and the associated Assyrian move against the petty states of the Mediterranean seaboard form the background to everything from the beginning of ch. 7; so an oracle against Israel is not out of place here. Moreover, the prophecy of the child's universal reign on the throne of David (v.7) would remind the reader of the defection of the northern tribes (cf. 7:17; 11:13). This oracle stresses God's coming judgment because the northern kingdom was continuing its impenitent rebellion against the Lord.

8–12 The word of God has great power. Isaiah views its painful descent on Israel. National pride is usually most arrogant in a capital city. From the heart of the country, Samaria's citizens refused to take the fall of the northern provinces to the Assyrians (cf. 9:1) as more than a temporary setback in the building of a greater and a richer land. In city and garden, the merely adequate that had succumbed to judgment through foreign armies were to be replaced by the superior.

Ephraim may well have discovered that in a foreign alliance a nation shares not only its ally's resources but also its foes. The word "Aramean" is applicable more widely than to the citizens of Aram proper, the country over which Rezin reigned; and it may here designate enemies on his borders. The specific events referred to in vv.11–12 cannot be fully identified. Isaiah was fond of conveying the concept of judgment by using figurative language for eating (cf. 5:14; 9:20). The refrain in v.12b presents the fearful thought that the judgment already described does not exhaust the manifestation of God's wrath against his sinful people.

13–17 The Lord's judgment is both retributive and restorative in purpose when directed against his people. Isaiah's two illustrations here embrace the whole nation, both the honored and the insignificant. The prophet makes it clear that although the nation was being led astray by its leaders and its false prophets, and the guilt of these was therefore great, nobody was without blame. Even the fatherless and widows, the socially disadvantaged, must share in the judgment; for the contagion of godlessness had spread throughout the whole nation. The order of "ungodly" and "wicked" suggests that the first was the cause of the second (cf. Ro 1:18).

18–21 Both the Bible and experience teach that wickedness unchecked spreads like wildfire, and this is precisely what Isaiah indicates here. The reference to "a column of smoke" (v.18) suggests that the acrid stench of wickedness reaches the nostrils of God, which provides a transition to the different use of the same analogy in v.19. Here it is not wickedness but divine wrath that causes the blaze. In both cases the undergrowth and the

forest trees represent the people. The spreading flame of sin is followed in its turn by the fire of God's judgment, with perhaps just a suggestion of the punishment fitting the crime. "Briers" and "thorns" give us the impression that in the prophet's mind they stood for the consequences of sin (cf. Ge 3:18).

In vv.11–12 the prophet describes the attacks made on Israel by her external enemies. From the end of v.19, the more terrible picture of civil war takes over. The tribes of Manasseh and Ephraim should have been particularly close to each other, for they were both descendants of the sons of Joseph (Ge 48). The first civil war in Israel, however, was fought between the Gileadites of Manasseh and the men of Ephraim in the days of Jephthah (Jdg 12:1–6). Those who would not unite through a common sympathy sometimes did join together to pour out their hatred and jealousy against Judah. Both the earlier and later contexts (i.e., vv.18–19, 21b) suggest that this civil strife was to be viewed as a judgment from God.

10:1–4 Verse 1 suggests that the ruling class in Israel had devised a legal system that departed significantly from the Mosaic standard. The phrase "the oppressed of my people" expresses the affront to God's special relationship with the whole people that this evil legislation constituted. It may well have consisted largely in oppressive land laws (cf. 5:8–10). This phrase suggests the coming of a day of divine reckoning when possession of ill-gotten wealth would make some Israelites the sure objects of wrath.

The picture of cringing prisoners is so true to life, for there are few who can walk erect on their way to prison camp after defeat in war. It is possible, too, that Isaiah suggested that they were trying to avoid notice (cf. 2:10, 21) in order to escape death. The refrain that has occurred at various points in this oracle is truly terrifying in its climactic position. If even physical death does not satisfy the fierce anger of this holy God, what dread punishment lies beyond the grave?

O. The Judgment of Assyria (10:5–19)

The date of this oracle is not easy to determine, but Carchemish (v.9) was not captured till 717 B.C. This was about two years before the death of Ahaz; so the oracle could have been delivered within his reign, like most of the other oracles in chs. 7–12. A date in Hezekiah's reign is also possible, of course.

5–11 The emotional interjection "woe," with which v.1 also began, prepares us for the disclosure of Assyria's judgment in vv.12–19. Isaiah tends from time to time to anticipate a God-honoring denouement in this way. This oracle clearly relates in its theme to the preceding one (cf. 9:12, 17, 21; 10:4). God uses instruments to manifest his wrath in the judgment of his people. Assyria was the chief instrument God used in Isaiah's day. The word "godless" (GK 2868) must have been as shocking as the names "Sodom" and "Gomorrah" to those who were fastidious and even excessive in their observance of religious ritual (1:10–17). In fact, the lack of a specific reference to Judah may even have led Isaiah's hearers to think that he was speaking of some other nation, till the context put his meaning beyond doubt. The simile "like mud" (v.6) may be due to Isaiah's conviction that Judah has become spiritually and morally worthless (cf. Mt 5:13).

We have been given a glimpse into the mind of God; now we see the mind of Assyria. The two minds are at one only as to the acts of war themselves, not as to the ultimate purpose of those acts. Assyria and its boastful monarchs certainly had no intention of serving the punitive ends of the God of Israel; rather, they sought conquest and territorial expansion for their own glory. Verses 8–11 anticipate v.12, with its reference to the king of Assyria, though in fact the cities mentioned in v.9 were overcome by a series of Assyrian monarchs. Calno and Arpad, both in northern Syria, were taken in 738, Damascus in 732, Samaria in 722, and Hamath on the Orontes in 720 B.C. The ancient Hittite city of Carchemish on the upper Euphrates was vanquished in 717 B.C.

The king of Assyria's boastful rhetoric (vv.10–11) must have seemed quite irrefutable to the people of his day. In fact, Samaria had not withstood the might of his armies any more than the pagan cities, and Jerusalem ruled over an even smaller kingdom. It was a sad fact that neither the northern nor southern kingdom was without idols (cf. 2:8, 20). What the Assyrian had not realized was the special purpose of God for his people, especially his determination to deliver Jerusalem.

This drawing by Gert LaGrance, based on Assyrian reliefs, depicts an Assyrian attack on a town in Judah. A seige ramp was constructed against the wall and the infantry stormed the wall, while archers kept shooting arrows at the defenders. Courtesy Lachish Excavations.

The gods of the pagans were mere vanities, but the Lord was the living God (37:4).

12 This verse sums up the theology of this great oracle. God has two ends to fulfill in relation to Assyria. He will punish one nation through her and punish her through another, though the latter nation is not specified nor even hinted at here. The phrase "his work" (GK 5126) stands in strong contrast to the expression "my hand" in v.10. This may be God's "strange work" (cf. 28:21–22), but it is his work nevertheless; and Assyria is his agent for its accomplishment. Isaiah's special stress on the holiness and majesty of God made it inevitable that he would launch constant attacks on human pride.

13–14 Strength and wisdom were widely recognized as vital qualities for anyone in authority, especially for a king. The messianic King has them through the endowment of God's Spirit (11:2; cf. 9:6), but the Assyrian monarch boasted of them as his own. The removal of national boundaries and the consequent mixing of peoples was an Assyrian policy in the lands that they conquered (cf. 2Ki 17:6, 24). The picture of absolute power and total helplessness in v.14 may have been somewhat exaggerated, but there is no doubt that the might and ferocity of the Assyrians won them many overwhelming victories.

15–19 Assyria is pictured as a tool in the hand of the forester to be used for felling the trees. Isaiah uses logic to expose and to ridicule human sin. The tool or instrument breaking loose from the control of its master and exulting in its liberty is held by the Lord Almighty.

Two new pictures come into view to convey the judgment of God on the pride of his punitive instruments. The image of a sick person gradually wasting away under a consumptive disease and that of vegetation and forest trees destroyed by fire present different aspects of the demise of Assyria. Her enemies wore down her resistance over a period of some years, but the decisive moment came with the downfall of her capital, Nineveh, which is celebrated as an act of God in the prophecy of Nahum.

The picture of the destroying fire contains two notable features. (1) Isaiah uses the word *kabod* ("pomp," v.16; "splendor," v.18 [GK 3883]). God's own unique "glory" (see 6:3) has been revealed to Isaiah. None other may boast of his own splendor in the light of that. (2) The prophet does not tell us simply that the Lord will light the fire of judgment; instead, he declares that the Light of Israel will *become* a fire (v.17). God remains eternally the same, but humans may experience now one consequence of a particular divine attribute, now another. He is the Light of his people, and one day he will be the source of light for all the nations (cf. 2:1–5; 60:1–3); but here that Holy Light is felt by an arrogant conqueror as a fire of judgment. A torch was an agent of both light and heat.

Yet even in the midst of such judgment, there is a hint of hope, so characteristic of Isaiah's prophecies. God planned a devastating judgment for Assyria but, amazingly—for this is not Israel but a Gentile nation—not total obliteration. If Israel was to be left a remnant for the fulfillment of God's purposes for her, so too was Assyria! In this way we are prepared for the astounding revelation in 19:23–25.

P. The Deliverance of the Lord's Remnant (10:20–34)

20–23 The eschatological phrase "in that day" introduces some verses dominated by the doctrine of the "remnant" (GK 8637). That phrase also connects these verses with the previous passage. The words "him who struck them down" here denote the human instrument of God's wrath rather than God himself (cf. 9:13). How incredible that they should put their trust—as Ahaz had done (cf. 2Ki 16:7–9)—in a nation whose known character could guarantee nothing but rapine and almost inhuman cruelty and refuse to rely on the God who had lavished blessing on them throughout their history!

Verse 21 opens with the phrase *shear yashub* ("a remnant will return"), which is identical with the name of Isaiah's son (Shear-Jashub, 7:3). The emphasis here is positive. God will not utterly destroy his people. There are in fact two symbolic names in the verse, for "Mighty God" is evocative of the description of the messianic King in 9:6. The doctrine of the incarnation enables us to understand how relying on the Lord, the Holy One of Israel, can be equated with returning to the messianic King, whose name was "Mighty God." Here then the two great Isaianic doctrines of the remnant and the Messiah come together.

Verse 22 links the remnant doctrine with that which it appears to negate but which in fact in the purpose of God it guarantees—the promise to the patriarchs that their seed would be many (cf. Ge 22:17; 32:12). The reader has been prepared for this reminder of the promise by the name Jacob in vv.20–21. The promise could and sometimes did induce complacency (cf. Mt 3:9–10; Jn 8:33–40), for Satan takes even the Scriptures God gave as a blessing and interprets them to serve his purposes of error and damnation (cf. Mt 4:6; 2Pe 3:15–16).

Verses 22b–23 are particularly somber in their tone. God is described by titles of power; this fact—in combination with the reiterated word "decreed"—makes the threatened destruction truly terrifying, for it is sovereign and irrevocable. The great Euphrates produced one "overwhelming" (same word translated "swirling over" in 8:8) flood of judgment through the Assyrians, who overcame Israel, and another in the Babylonians, who brought Judah's kingdom to its end. These nations were wicked, but God used them as instruments of his righteous judgment.

24–27 The emphasis on God's power continues as the prophet uses the same divine titles as in v.23. This time, however, his power was to be directed to the salvation rather than the judgment of his people. Other parts of the country may feel the tread of Assyria's fearful host (cf. 9:1; 10:28–32), but Zion will be secure (cf. Ps 46).

The references to the "rod," the "club," and the "yoke" remind us of 9:4–7, with its promises of defeat for the strong enemy and of the peaceful government of the Child born to be king. The King is not here, but the deliverance is. Historical parallels are drawn with the vanquishing of Midian. The death of the two Midianite leaders at Oreb (cf. Jdg 7:25) was perhaps the decisive moment in the later stages of the battle, for an army in flight without leaders cannot regroup and counterattack. On both occasions Israel was greatly outnumbered, but her trust in God was shown by him to be well-founded. So would it again!

Verse 25 may be compared with 40:1–2. God's wrath against his people was real; but because they were his people, the foreign scourge would be used against them only for a limited time. God would call a halt and would then punish his unwitting instrument for its sin (cf. 10:12–19). Once again we encounter one of Isaiah's favorite figures, the bearing of a heavy burden (see at 1:4, 14). Israel was like a slave carrying a heavy burden or like a domestic animal yoked and laden. So there would be an Assyrian captivity, but it would be ended by divine action. "The yoke will be broken because you have grown so fat" may picture Israel as an animal so large that the yoke will not fit it. So she cannot be fully subdued by the enemy.

28–32 The processes by which the OT prophets were given their messages are known to us only in part, but we are aware that the vision was one important medium used by the inspiring Spirit. The superbly dramatic appeal to the imagination in these verses suggests a visionary provenance. Perhaps the prophet in his imagination was standing on the city walls looking northward and seeing the inexorable advance of the Assyrian army through places within and just beyond his normal range of sight. For sheer drama these verses have little to equal them in the prophets, except in Nahum.

Isaiah 36:2 tells us that the Assyrian army actually came to Jerusalem from Lachish, from almost exactly the opposite direction. Possibly some tactical situation arose that caused the Assyrian army to make a circuit around the city from Lachish, finally approaching it from the north. The history of warfare contains many parallel examples.

33–34 After the advance, the counterattack! The divine title of power, "the LORD Almighty," occurs no less than five times in this chapter. This is striking in a section of the prophecy where the mighty and ferocious Assyrian enemy is never far from sight, for it underlines the infinite superiority of the true God over even the greatest of nations.

The Assyrian hosts appear like an advancing forest. Suddenly the divine Forester begins to attack undergrowth, boughs, whole trees, and even the mighty cedars of Lebanon. The pride of Assyria (cf. v.13) caused it to become an example of the general principle laid down by God (cf. ch. 2): those who have great pride are always riding for a fall (cf. Pr 16:18).

Q. The Davidic King and His Peaceful Reign (11:1–9)

The messianic theme reappears, having been out of sight since 9:7; it is taken up at precisely the point where it was left before, because the Davidic throne is implied in the reference to Jesse, David's father, and the effective zeal of the Lord Almighty in the richly empowering Spirit of the Lord.

1–3a At the end of ch. 10 the axe of divine judgment fell on the forestlike army of Assyria; at the opening of ch. 11 the purpose of divine grace is seen in the growth of a shoot from the stump of Jesse. The reduction of the Davidic dynasty to a mere stump is a true metaphor for its condition when Christ was born; for, though still in existence, that dynasty had been without royal power for nearly six hundred years. The reference to Jesse—who was of course never king—rather than to David may point to the total absence of royal dignity in the house of David when the Messiah would come. But there was still life in the house, for God's purpose (cf. 2Sa 7:16) had not been set aside (cf. Eze 21:27). The Branch (see 4:2; 6:13) is now fully messianic. God's people need more than the promise of fertile land or of continued national life through the remnant. They need the very incarnation of God's life in the Messiah.

The Assyrian monarch had boasted of his own power and wisdom (10:8–14; cf. 14:12–14), but the supreme King will be equipped for his work by the Spirit of the Lord. There are links between this passage and 9:6. The earlier passage shows the King to be divine, while this exhibits his dependence, a combination that requires the Incarnation for its explanation. Solomon, Jesse's grandson—who might have seemed to be the fulfillment of the hope of "great David's greater son" and who was endowed with wisdom by God—might have seemed at first to be an expression of this hope in the earlier history of the people; but he fell far short of the divine ideal expressed in Dt 17:14–20, because he did not fear the Lord with an undivided heart (cf. 1Ki 11:1–13).

It may be that the basic description "the Spirit of the LORD" followed by three pairs of qualities attributed to the Spirit is intended to add up to a symbolical seven (cf. the seven "woes" of 5:8, 11, 18, 20, 21, 22; 6:5). If so, the symbolism would suggest that the Messiah was to be perfectly endowed by the Spirit with everything requisite to his kingly task (cf. Rev 5:6).

3b–5 The act of pronouncing judgment in the court is often treated in the OT as the acid test of a wise and incorruptible use of authority (cf. 5:21–23; Ps 72:1–4). Verse 3b does not mean that right judgment ignores evidence available to the senses but rather that it requires inner qualities of character (cf. Jn 2:25; 7:24). The word "judge" (GK 9149) has an ominous ring to us; but when used of the poor, it is almost synonymous with salvation (Pss 72:2; 82:2–4). Where there is corruption in the law courts, it is the poor who long for a righteous judge. The reiterated word "earth" also signifies "land." The rule of the messianic King is to be over Israel but also over the whole world (9:7; cf. 11:10).

In the divine economy, the word is active and powerful (cf. Ge 1:3; Isa 55:10–11), and the Messiah's word of judgment will be utterly effective (cf. Jn 12:48). He judges as "the Word of God" (Rev 19:13–15). This testifies to his great power (cf. v.2), because he is well able to execute the judgments he pronounces. In him word and consequent action are virtually one.

In the Near Eastern dress styles, the belt or sash was the garment that gave stability to the whole ensemble; and to dress oneself with the belt was to prepare for work. The Messiah would be prepared in character for his work of judgment.

6–9 Biblical eschatology may involve more than the simple restoration of conditions as they were in the unfallen world, but it certainly includes this (cf. Ge 1:26–28; Ps 8; 1Co 15:25–28; Heb 2:5–9). It is not now Adam who is to be king of the world but the messianic King. In his reign nature will be at peace with itself and with human kings. We know something of the effects of the Fall on human kings and on plant life (Ge 3:17–18); no doubt animal life—bound with the human race and the plants in the unity of a worldwide ecosystem—must have been affected also.

The normal prey of the fierce predators need have no fear of them under the Messiah's reign. Significantly, the calf is the most vulnerable to the lion and the fatted yearling the most desirable; yet the prophecy puts them together. The predators will so respect the lordship of humans, given to them before the Fall (Ge 1:28), that even the little child will command respect and, perhaps, will act responsibly and with benevolence toward the predators like a shepherd leading his flock.

The ecological issues are touched on in v.7, with its implied reference to Ge 1:30. Any adaptation of the ecosystem involved will presumably be a restoration of the world to its unfallen condition (cf. Isa 65:25).

Genesis 3 presents the serpent as human beings' first enemy within the animal kingdom. Thus, v.8 moves beyond vv.6–7. Venomous snakes will not harm children even when their play temporarily robs the snakes of their access to the world outside their homes. The instinct of self-preservation is deep in every creature; so this scene exhibits peace, trust, and harmony.

As a result of the taming of nature, Mount Zion, the holy mountain of God (v.9), will know a comprehensive peace and security that remind us of the comprehensive promises in 4:5–6. The breadth of the Messiah's reign (cf. 9:7) means, however, that the peace and security of Jerusalem will be a microcosm of a much wider blessing, because of the references to the sea here and to the nations in v.10. The restoration of human beings to God that is implied in "the knowledge of God" reverses the alienation introduced by the Fall, so making possible the restoration of their environment to its unfallen condition.

R. The Nation and the Nations (11:10–16)

10–11 In 5:26 God raised a banner to summon a nation as one of his instruments of judgment on his people, while here the messianic King has an attractive power that brings the peoples of the world together, just as the Lord himself attracts the nations in darkness to his marvelous light in 60:1–3. In 2:1–4 it was the word of God that had drawing power; here it is the Christ.

The eschatological phrase "in that day" relates this messianic teaching to the end times. Like most OT writers, Isaiah had a lively sense of the special importance of the Exodus from Egypt, when God had stretched out his hand to deliver his people. Isaiah looks forward to a time that will see an event comparable with it in redemptive significance. This will contrast with the Exodus,

for those who return will be the remnant of a larger people, while it was the greatly enlarged family of Jacob that left Egypt under Moses. The events will also differ because this time the people will not move together as a body from one point of departure but will come together from many lands and various points of the compass. Instead of going forth under a great leader, they will come together seeking a greater leader still.

The places referred to, with one exception, are located near the two great river-systems that have acted as mothers of civilization in the Near East: the Tigris-Euphrates and the Nile. The addition, however, of the phrase "the islands of the sea" is surprising. The word "island" occurs frequently in Isa 40–66 and appears to designate the Mediterranean maritime areas. The only reference to a dispersion of Jews in this area is in Joel 3:6. The considerable western dispersion in NT times is anticipated here by the Holy Spirit.

12–14 After a brief prose interlude (vv.10–11), the exalted poetry of the prophet is resumed. Isaiah first summarizes the thought of the two prose verses in poetic form, making it clear that by "his people" (v.11) he has Judah primarily in mind, even though "Assyria" may have suggested an application also to Ephraim. The Davidic dynasty had of course been associated exclusively with Judah for many centuries, ever since the division of the kingdom (cf. 7:17). The reference to Assyria (v.11) finds its explanation in v.13. Northern Israelites will also return, and the once-divided nation will be united. It had been torn apart through the sin of one of David's sons (1Ki 11:11); it would be reunited under David's Greater Son.

David's rule had extended well beyond the bounds of the territory of the Twelve Tribes (2Sa 8). Ephraim and Judah would make common cause against the Philistines, taking advantage of their location in the hill country to move down the slopes of the Shephelah, west of the Judean mountains, against the Philistines on the coastal plain. The three neighboring nations to the east and southeast would come under subjection again to Judah.

15–16 The nations mentioned in v.14 were small and insignificant when compared with the great militarist regimes of Egypt and Mesopotamia. God's hand of power would be stretched forth in fulfillment of his purposes for his people in both areas. He had dried up the water of the Red Sea before; he would act again to dry it up. He had used a great wind (Ex 14:21) at the Exodus; he would do so again to bring the people back from Mesopotamia, for the wind would produce there a delta not unlike that at the mouth of the Nile. The highway promised may contain an allusion to Ex 14:26–29, the dry road through the Red Sea; or it may mean that God will bring them back safely across the desert that stretched between Mesopotamia and the Mediterranean seaboard (cf. 35:8).

S. A Song of Joyous Praise (12:1–6)

Chapter 12 forms a fitting climax for this whole section. The preceding chapters have said much about the sins of God's people, warning them of the divine wrath and judgment that was sure to follow. They have also recorded God's declaration of forgiving grace for the penitent, the challenge to believe, and predictions of a glorious future for God's people. God's great name would be exalted, and his king would reign. Nothing could be more appropriate than a heartfelt psalm of praise to round off this section of the prophecy.

1–3 In ch. 11, the expression "in that day" introduces two verses (11:10–11) that focus on the Messiah and the remnant—and thus on the great final purposes of God for his people. This psalm of praise anticipates the feelings of his people when that great day comes. Isaiah pictures the nation like someone suffering under God's wrath because of rebellion against God (1:5–6). Though once united in sin and its divinely imposed consequences, the nation here engages as a body in one great act of thanksgiving (cf. Isaiah's proclamation of God's forgiveness to the people in the Babylonian exile in 40:1–5; 43:25, anticipating the sweet comfort of pardon they were to know at the end of their history).

The prophet's language here takes up words from the Song of Moses in Ex 15, so that Israel's first and final expressions of corporate praise are here brought together. The words "The LORD is my strength and my song; he has become my salvation" are almost identical in the Hebrew to two other verses (Ex 15:2; Ps 118:14). Isaiah's double use of "the LORD" is appropriate because the

people's trust in the Lord stands in strong contrast to the unbelief of Ahaz and his trust in Assyria (cf. 7:1–9; 2Ki 16:7–18).

The assertion that God is or has become the salvation of his people goes perhaps a little further than a simple statement that he has effected deliverance for them. It is as if his person has taken color from his work; the person and the work belong together so that the one can hardly be conceived without the other (cf. 1Co 1:30). To "the song of Moses, the servant of God" is added "the song of the Lamb" (Rev 15:3–4), for salvation receives its deeper meaning through him.

When it is said that he is "my strength and my song," the reader is made aware that this God is now everything to his people. Not only do they rely on him for strength, but they have abandoned all other trust. The prophet had been warned that the people would be spiritually unresponsive (6:9–10). In the future day that Isaiah visualizes, however, trust in God the Savior will be so complete as to banish all fear. Not only will the Lord receive all their faith; he will be the sole object of their praise. The redeemed have nothing else to sing about and yet everything to sing about when their song is of him.

Isaiah has already used the imagery of water to symbolize divine supplies that are totally reliable and can be trusted (8:6). The waters of Shiloah flowing gently and yet constantly into the city are replaced by wells of salvation from which the believing people may keep on drawing with joy. The figure suggests constant recourse on their part and constant provision on his.

4–6 The proclamation to all the nations that the Lord's name is exalted is typical of Isaiah (cf. 2:2–3, 11, 17; cf. Ac 2:21, 33; 3:13–16). With v.5, we find ourselves back in Ex 15:2, but without the references to horses, horsemen, and the sea. The truth is that the Exodus will be eclipsed by an even greater disclosure of God's power (Isa 53:1). It will therefore take its place at the beginning of a whole sequence of divine saving acts that may now be celebrated retrospectively in their totality. It will not be enough now that the people praise his name simply in the presence of one another. The whole world must know what he has done so that his name may be exalted in all the earth.

The universalism of these verses is now modified by a form of particularism. The song being sung celebrates God's forgiving grace and saving deeds for his own people, Zion. The pardoning grace of God is the source of many blessings, but none is more wonderful than his presence with his people. That presence was promised and sealed in the child Immanuel (cf. 7:14; 8:10, 18). Here its realization is celebrated and extolled by his people. The presence of God among his people is no contradiction of his transcendent uniqueness and separateness, expressed in the phrase "the Holy One of Israel." He is distinct but not aloof, for in him holiness and grace find their perfect union.

II. God and the Nations (13:1–23:18)

The Israelites were separated from the nations by God to be his own special people. They did not, however, live in isolation but were placed at the most strategic crossroads of the world. Here they were brought into contact with many other peoples—especially the world powers of Mesopotamia and the Nile, who could only engage each other in trade or in conflict by taking a route through or very near Israel's territory.

In the time of Isaiah, the international scene was dominated by the cruel and aggressive Assyrians, who were ruled by a succession of ambitious monarchs. Such a situation left a buffer state with only two options: submission or a protective alliance. This formed the general political context for Isaiah's prophetic ministry. Chapters 1–12 relate the kind of message he brought to Judah from the Lord. Foreign foes were instruments of God's judgment on his people for their sins. They were not to seek relief in alliances but were to trust in the Lord himself.

The international situation brought Judah into contact with virtually all the other states of the Fertile Crescent; and it is most appropriate that oracles declaring the destiny of each should be grouped together at this point. Every state lived under the threat of Assyria and sought its own way of handling it. Each would have to face judgment. If Judah and Jerusalem, God's own people, faced judgment—but not extinction— through Assyria (so chs. 1–12), it is inconceivable that these pagan nations should escape. These judgments were in effect anticipations of those universal judgments

that, along with the ultimate deliverance of the sons of Jacob, are set forth in chs. 24–27 as a climax to the oracles against the nations. Thus the divine holiness revealed to Isaiah in his temple vision in ch. 6 was to be expressed in judgment on Judah, her neighbors, and the whole universe.

A. Prophecy Against Babylon (13:1–14:23)

This "oracle concerning Babylon," has been the focus of much scholarly attention. Many modern scholars have been reluctant to accept it as an authentic utterance of Isaiah, assigning it to the sixth century B.C., shortly before the taking of Babylon by Cyrus the Great of Persia. However, the only historical context that is fully appropriate for it is 701 B.C., when the various peoples mentioned in chs. 13–23 were all involved in anti-Assyrian coalitions. The attempt of Babylon to get Judah involved in such a coalition almost certainly lies behind ch. 39.

Jeremiah 50–51 makes use of phraseology and ideas from Isa 13–14 and applies them to the fall of the Neo-Babylonian empire. In Jer 50:17–18, the prophet declared that the kings of Assyria and Babylon, having a common guilt in relation to Israel, would share a common punishment. There are really only two principles of organization for a society: the Babylonian principle (antagonism toward God) and the Jerusalem principle (submission to his purposes). The Babylonian principle is to be seen right through 13:1–14:27.

It is really unnecessary to transfer almost all of these two chapters to Assyria, as some have suggested. The events of 701 B.C. may have provided the historical conditions for this oracle, yet this does not require that all or most of it was fulfilled in the downfall of Assyria. If we accept supernatural foreknowledge in a prophet, Isaiah's prophecy may have been given in one historical era and fulfilled in another. We will therefore expound the oracle as a prediction of the downfall of the Neo-Babylonian empire and its monarch, uttered by Isaiah at the close of the eighth century, and so intended as a warning to Hezekiah and Judah not to put their trust in coalitions against Assyria inspired by Babylon (cf. ch. 39).

1 The use of a surname or a patronymic may serve the end of designating a person with some precision. In view of the denial by most

modern scholars that Isaiah, son of Amoz, had any part in prophecies concerning Babylon, we may see a special evidential purpose in its use here.

2–5 Imagination's curtain is drawn aside and a bare hilltop is disclosed, surmounted by a banner (cf. 5:26; 11:12; 18:3; et al.). A shout and a gesture are added so that the army will be mustered with urgency. The phrases "a bare hilltop" and "the gates of the nobles" suggest a contrast between the remote areas from which the army comes and the sophisticated urban civilization that it will destroy. Like the Assyrians (cf. 10:5), this army is the Lord's instrument. "Holy" here implies only that the persons so designated have been set apart by the Lord for his purpose—in this instance, punitive destruction.

The single shout of command is replaced by a tumultuous roar. It is the sound of human voices in such numbers and such volume that words are indistinguishable. The references to kingdoms, nations, and faraway lands would fit the armies of each of the successive world powers from Assyria through Babylon to Persia; but the mention of the Medes in v.17 plus the use of words like "hilltop" and "mountains" suggest that the army was being massed on the great Iranian plateau. "The ends of the heavens" probably refers to the distant horizons and so to the "faraway lands" from which the Medes came. The appropriateness of Isaiah's selection of designations for God can be seen in his use of "Lord Almighty" here.

The opening verses of the oracle have made it clear that the armies are the instruments of the Lord and that they are coming to execute his wrathful judgment on the whole land.

6–8 The "day of the Lord" is a frequent prophetic theme that emphasizes the certainty and decisiveness of the Lord's historical judgment in the future. It may be conceived in local or in universal terms. The Lord will expound his great name of power in terms of destruction when the day of his judgment dawns.

In vv.7–8 the prophet piles up expression after expression to convey the sense of fear that would overwhelm the objects of God's judgment. The phrase "their faces aflame" comes as something of a surprise, for shock normally pales the face. Perhaps the judgment would be recognized by those who suffer it not simply as a visitation of pain but as a punishment for wrongdoing, bringing a blush to their cheeks.

9–13 At this point this oracle of judgment about a great, coming world-power begins to expand to cover the whole world, though the NIV translation suggests that it is still local. The cosmic dimensions of vv.10–13, however, strongly suggest that v.9 needs to be understood universally also. Local judgments should stir in human beings a recognition of final accountability (cf. Mt 24).

God created the natural order as an environment for humans (Ge 1). The Fall disturbed this order, and some indication of this is given in the penalties prescribed by God (Ge 3:14–19). In v.10 we see God's hand of judgment falling on the great heavenly bodies, whose regular motions provide strong support for one's belief in an ordered universe. Their light-giving function (cf. Ge 1:14–19) will be hindered (cf. Mt 24:29; Mk 13:24–25; cf. esp. Mt 27:45; Mk 15:33; Lk 23:44–45).

Isaiah characteristically mentions arrogance and pride as prime targets of God's judgment on the wicked (cf. 2:11–18; 3:16–24; 10:8–16). Human pride is a blatant insult to the God who is highly exalted and to whom all his moral creatures should submit in obedient worship. Verse 12 makes it clear that the judgment pictured is universal. Verse 13 goes beyond v.10 by depicting the effects of divine judgment on the natural universe. There is to be a general convulsion of the whole created order (cf. 34:4). Thus the instability of the order of things since the Fall will be disclosed (cf. Mk 13), revealing the need for the eternally stable order of the kingdom of God that Christ's coming will establish.

14–16 The prophet has made no reference to the human agents of God's punitive justice since v.5; and at least since v.10 it has been clear that a universal judgment is in view. By definition such a judgment cannot be humanly executed, for everyone is to come under it. The prophet here returns, however, to the more local judgment on Babylon, for it is clear that human agencies of punishment are now being used again. A prediction of the Day of the Lord may expand and then contract again in this way, because each particular judgment foreshadows the great ultimate punishment to fall on the human race as a whole.

Beginning with Tiglath-pileser III, each great empire of Mesopotamia followed a policy of transportation and intermingling of peoples. As Babylonia is entered by its conquerors, those living there who have been exiled from their own homelands feel their isolation; and, like hunted or neglected animals, they try to make for home. Such attempts at survival will be quite fruitless. The bitter enemies of their overlords will make no distinction between the native-born and the unwilling incomer. This part of the prophecy shows that the downfall of Babylon will mean the deaths of many from other nations who find themselves within its borders when the blow falls.

17–22 Verse 17 is of special interest because of its reference to the Medes. These Iranian people, who—along with other Aryan tribes—came onto the Iranian plateau about the beginning of the first millennium B.C., were a constant thorn in the flesh of the Assyrian kings; and in 612 B.C. they captured the Assyrian capital, Nineveh. Thus in Isaiah's day they were a significant factor on the international scene. At this time the Babylonians were their allies in the eventual sack of Nineveh. By the middle of the sixth century B.C., however, the situation had altered considerably. After a period when there was enmity between the Medes and the Persians (their fellow Aryans), the Medes put their fierce fighting force at the disposal of Cyrus the Persian and were involved with him in the overthrow of Babylonia in 539 B.C. The Medes are probably mentioned here rather than the Persians because of their greater ferocity and also because they were better known to the people of Isaiah's day. Historical sources confirm that the Medes served Cyrus without thought of monetary reward.

Babylon, a very ancient city (cf. Ge 10:10; 11:1–9), seems to have had even in times of decline a special prestige among the peoples of the Near East. This was shared also by its leading deity, Marduk, and is well expressed in the phrase "the jewel of kingdoms," which Isaiah gave to it. Already Babylon was a sure candidate for divine judgment, but the cup of its sin was to become full in the days of its new empire, when it would oppress many nations and destroy Jerusalem and its temple.

It is interesting that Isaiah uses the analogy of the overthrow of Sodom and Gomorrah that we find also in 1:9–10. This suggests not only complete destruction but also its moral cause. The Assyrian king Sennacherib, who detested Babylon, utterly devastated it in 689 B.C. This was, perhaps, a partial fulfillment of the prophecy given here. Babylon was quickly rebuilt, and no comparable destruction took place by the Medes and Persians in 539 B.C. The prophecy did eventually find fulfillment, but over a considerable period of time. Darius the Great and Xerxes both issued important decrees of demolition. Alexander the Great apparently had great plans for the city, but they did not survive his death; and by the close of the first century B.C., Babylon was utterly desolate. So it is today. The last sentence of the chapter refers to Sennacherib's act of vengeance that stood at the beginning of the whole process and that, at the time of this prophecy, was to be accomplished within twelve years.

14:1–4a These verses are saturated with allusions to the Exodus from Egypt and the entry into Canaan. The New Exodus theme, which is so important later in the book, is the controlling motif here. The clue to this is given in the words "once again he will choose Israel." The expulsion of Israel from Canaan at the Exile would certainly make it look as if the covenant, so often flagrantly broken by the people, had finally been set aside by God. In fact, however, such was the depth and persistence of his steadfast love that his covenant purpose was never eclipsed by their unfaithfulness. His new choice was a reaffirmation of the old in the return from Babylonia.

The repeated name "Jacob" is a reminder that it is the God of the patriarchs who is setting his love on the people (cf. Ex 3:6–9). The patriarchs had been given the land by divine promise; therefore, it was already "their own land."

When Israel left Egypt, many other people left with them. There were also many aliens within their gates (Ex 20:10; 22:21; et al.). Jethro, Rahab, and other believing Gentiles found a place within the covenant of God with Israel. So it would be again (cf. 56:3–8). Furthermore, the nations in the land would become servants to them (60:9–14; 61:5), just as the Gibeonites had (Jos 9). We can find parallels to much of this in the actual events of the return from exile, for it was a decree of the Gentile Cyrus that was its immediate human cause (Ezr 1–4; cf. 6:1–12). There are, however, elements of the prophecy that were not fulfilled at this time, especially in the picture of God's people governing their oppressors. No doubt these are properly eschatological, so that the fulfillment at the return from Babylon itself foreshadows God's ultimate purpose for the people.

4b–11 At this point, one of the greatest poems in the whole prophetic corpus commences, running through v.21. Its form is really that of the funeral dirge, with the characteristic limping rhythm of a Hebrew lament, so plaintive and yet ominous to the sensitive ear. The form is appropriate, for it speaks of death (vv.9–11, 15). It is not sung at a funeral, however, for the subject of the song is a tyrant who will be denied proper burial, and the song lacks the pomp a great king would expect as his right at death (vv.18–20). There is a considerable element of irony, so that the whole song becomes a "taunt" (v.4a) in the guise of a lament.

The subject of this lament is the king of Babylon, the oppressor; but the reference to the Lord in v.5 is important. Apart from the less direct references of vv.13–14, it is the only place where he is mentioned in the poem; yet it dominates it just as much as he does the book of Esther. His action is implied in all the passive verbs of the poem. If the oppressor has ceased, it is because God has taken action to bring him low.

The "unceasing blows" and "relentless aggression" conjure up an atmosphere of terror. When a great tyrant reigns in Mesopotamia, all the little nations cower in constant fear. How impressive then is the great change intimated in v.7! The glorious peace that follows the downfall of the Babylonian oppressor becomes the setting for the glad sound of rejoicing.

The pine trees and cedars of v.8 may be literal, figurative, or both. The monarchs of Assyria and Babylon were greedy for wood, and their woodcutters stripped whole districts of their trees. Lebanon, with its magnificent trees, suffered more than most conquered territories at their hands. Understood both literally and symbolically, these trees may refer also to human rulers (cf. 2:13;

Jer 22:7; Eze 17:3; 31:3; Mk 13:24–25), who are also safe now.

"The grave" is the NIV's translation of the Hebrew word *sheol* (GK 8619), the place of the dead. The Babylonian king, though dead, still exists, but now in a different sphere. The picture of the petty kings rising from their thrones to accord a mocking welcome to their oppressor powerfully appeals to the imagination and clearly contains some elements that were intended to be taken seriously but not literally.

To rise from one's seat is a token of respect in many cultures. Therefore, it probably indicates not only surprise but also mock homage on the part of those whose submission had been all too real, though unwilling, during their lifetime. They had heard the sound of the Babylonian harpers making music for the king as they were brought trembling into his court. All his pomp and circumstance have disappeared. His soft couches and lush carpets have been replaced by maggots and decomposition.

12–17 The taunt song continues. Isaiah's prophecies make some use of what has been called "dead mythology," and this may well be an example of this. The language of the myth—known but not, of course, accepted as true by the prophet and his hearers—becomes a vehicle for his thought by supplying the basis of an analogy. Moreover, this passage itself seems to be echoed by the Lord Jesus in Luke 10:18, where language applied here to the king of Babylon is used of Satan. Nothing could be more appropriate, for the pride of the king of Babylon was truly satanic. When Satan works his malign will through rulers of this world, he reproduces his own wicked qualities in them, so that they become virtual shadows of which he is the substance.

To interpret v.12 and the following verses in this way means that the passage points to Satan, not directly, but indirectly, much like the way the kings of the line of David point to Christ. All rulers of international significance whose overweening pride and arrogance bring them to ruin under the hand of God's judgment illustrate both the satanic and the antichrist principles.

Verse 13 reminds us of the Tower of Babel (Ge 11:1–9), though the endeavor to be like God takes us right back to Ge 3. Here Satan first sought to reproduce in human life his own proud aspirations for equal status with God. The possession of power can, of course, prove disastrous in creating a desire for utter supremacy. One who is fitted for high authority must be aware that he faces grave spiritual danger.

The dominant feature of vv.13–14 is undoubtedly the repetition of the word "I." Only God himself has a right to speak in this fashion (13:11–12; 14:24–25; 41:9–10, 17–19; et al.). The analogy from Canaanite mythology probably extends to the reference to the sacred mountain. Like the proud figure in the myth, the king of Babylon sought for absolute sovereignty. It is a strange paradox that nothing makes a being less like God than the urge to be his equal, for in Christ, he who was equal with God stepped down from his glorious throne to display to the wondering eyes of humankind the humility of God (Php 2:5–8).

The leveling power of death is again underlined (vv.15–16; cf. vv.9–10). The death of such a great one in worldly terms causes people to think hard. There are more lessons to be learned about the meaning of existence at the place of death than at the place of birth (cf. Ecc 7:1–4). Only God really has the right to make the earth tremble (cf. 13:13; 24:1–4). Human tyranny can go too far, and God acts against it from his all-sovereign throne (cf. 40:23–24).

18–21 We know from the Egyptian pyramids and other royal tombs how much stress was put on proper burial in the Fertile Crescent in OT times. How horrifying to a great king of Babylon and to his contemporaries would be the prospect of his lying out in the open, unburied, his royal body indistinguishable from those of his soldiers, to be thrown into a common burial pit! What is the cause of such a fate? The great king—like Napoleon, Hitler, and many others—led many of his people into death on the battlefield to gratify his lust for power. God therefore makes the punishment fit the crime.

The principle of group solidarity in punishment is seen throughout the OT (cf. Ex 20:5–6; Nu 16:31–35; Jos 7:24–26). The reference to the conqueror covering the earth with cities (v.21) is perhaps a reminder of Ge 10:8–11, possibly implying that this Babylonian dynasty was following the ways of its great predecessor, Nimrod. Many rulers have sought to perpetuate their names through great city-building enterprises (cf. also Ge 11:4). No throne, no tomb, no progeny, no cities—in all these ways the Lord abases those who seek self-exaltation.

22–23 These verses constitute a kind of appendix to the taunt song. The all-powerful divine King asserts his own intention to act against Babylon. Clearly the language reflects vv.20b–21, but it also goes back to v.20a. The king of Babylon's sin would bring destruction, not only to his people, but also to his land. He wanted to possess the earth, but in fact the very reverse would take place; for his own land would be possessed—not even by human beings, but by owls—and it would be covered with pools of stagnant water. The analogy the passage closes with has an eloquence all its own. The reader can almost hear the woman of the house breathing a sigh of relief as she sweeps the rubbish out her door, knowing that her house is at last clean and fit for human habitation. Rubbish fit only for the broom of judgment—this was God's verdict on mighty Babylon!

B. Prophecy Against Assyria (14:24–27)

There was an emotional link between the names "Babylon" and "Assyria" for those who were under threat from Mesopotamia; this is enough to account for placing this brief oracle at this point.

24–25 Sometimes in Isaiah a divine statement is underlined in some particularly emphatic way (cf. 5:9; 9:7; 37:32), and so it is here. The name of God used here and the statement of his settled purpose (cf. 5:19) combine to assure us that the Assyrian cannot survive. If such a mighty God has designed to crush him, he is doomed indeed. As if to reinforce this certainty still more, God speaks of "my land" and "my mountains."

26–27 God is sovereign over human history. All nations will have to submit to his judgment. This principle will be seen in relation to other nations—both small and great—in the oracles that follow. God is not like a man who makes plans and finds he has no power to put them into effect. Perfect wisdom and absolute power find their unity in God.

C. Prophecy Against Philistia (14:28–32)

28 The heading of this oracle does not in fact establish the year of this prophecy, for there is much uncertainty about the date of the death of Ahaz. The Assyrian monarch whose death is implied in vv.29–30 is Tiglath-pileser III, Shalmaneser V, or Sargon II.

29–30 The death of a cruel, oppressive monarch is a cause of rejoicing for his subjects, but such celebration is often premature; for that monarch's aggressiveness often characterizes his whole dynasty. The prophet's inspired imagination combined two sets of images here. The Assyrian monarchs are likened to a series of reptiles, which is then likened to the succession of root, shoot, and fruit in a plant. In this way the Spirit used the natural gift of a deeply poetic imagination to vividly and powerfully convey prophetic truth.

In the light of v.32, the focus of attention has moved briefly in v.30a from Philistia to Zion. The godliness of the poor and needy and the certainty that God is their helper are often presupposed in the OT, for the integrity of the godly is rarely profitable in worldly terms. Here God assumes the role of a shepherd to his people (cf. 40:11). The destiny of Philistia is portrayed in stark contrast to this, for famine instead of fresh pasture will be its lot. Leaf, branch, or stem may wither and yet the plant survive, but what hope is there when the root has been destroyed?

31–32 The prophet vividly depicts the fear induced by the terror from the north. No doubt the "envoys" were Philistine diplomats sent to Jerusalem to encourage solidarity against the common Assyrian foe. As elsewhere, Isaiah's message encourages trust in God, not in alliances (cf. 7:1–9; 8:11–15).

D. Prophecy Against Moab (15:1–16:14)

There are special features of this oracle that make it at once one of the most moving and yet most enigmatic of Isaiah's prophecies. The inspired poet-prophet presents us with graphic pictures of judgment on Moab. Through its verses the anguished wailing of the bereaved and the fugitives touches the heart of the readers. And to our utter astonishment, we discover that the inspired page is wet too with the tears of the prophet himself!

Jeremiah wept for Judah (Jer 9:1), but Isaiah for Moab!

1–4 The small Moabite nation is often mentioned in the OT, sometimes on its own, sometimes with its near neighbor, Ammon. The origin of both nations is traced to Lot's incest (Ge 19:30–38). It is impossible to determine the exact historical circumstances of this oracle or even to identify the enemy with any certainty; it could have been Assyria or some incursive force of hungry and rapacious nomads from the desert—perhaps Israel (cf. 2Ki 14:25) or even Judah, though this last seems unlikely.

All the places mentioned in these verses were in Moab. The enemies no doubt had come unheralded. Their predatory purpose fulfilled, they had probably departed as suddenly as they had come. Behind them was a trail of death and destruction. The land was full of weeping people, some gathering at religious shrines to cry to their gods, others in public places to join in corporate displays of weeping. The sounds of such agonized wail-

The Mesha Stele of Moab relates their successful attacks on Israel. Isaiah prophesies the eventual destruction of Moab.

ing would strike the men of Moab's fighting force with a demoralizing terror.

5–9 None of the place names in these verses can be identified with certainty, apart from Zoar, at the southeastern tip of the Dead Sea. Apparently the general direction of flight for most of the fugitives was southward to Edom. The reference to "the waters of Nimrim" suggests that they were in a normally fertile area. Perhaps they passed it during the dry season and saw its withered vegetation as a symbol of their own condition. The Moabites were warned that there was no hope of alleviation. The reference to the enemy as a lion reminds us of the reference to Assyria in Am 3:12, where the ultimate lion of judgment is God himself (cf. Am 3:4, 8).

16:1–5 The prophetic searchlight, having exposed to view the whole land of Moab with its ruined cities and fleeing, homeless people, becomes a spotlight. It concentrates first on the city of Sela, the source of the message of vv.3–4a, and then on the fords of Arnon, where the Moabite refugees, who are the subjects of the message, gather. Sela, normally Edomite, appears to have been in Moabite hands at this time and may even have been the seat of its government. Moab was famous for its great flocks of sheep. The Moabite rulers sent lambs in recognition of the king of Judah's overlordship to support their appeal for asylum for their refugees, many of whom would be women with children.

The "shadow" (v.3; GK 7498) may well picture Judah as affording protection, like a great rock from the merciless midday sun (cf. 32:2); but it is also possible that it further develops the analogy of the fluttering young birds. These would be easy prey for a predator on the ground, unless the large shadow of the parent bird fell protectingly across them as they moved toward the earth.

Verses 4b–5 are probably the reply sent from Jerusalem to Sela. This passage resembles 14:32 in its triumphant assertion that Jerusalem is a place of security in the purpose of God. If the words are addressed from Judah to Moab, they are most naturally understood along messianic lines (cf. 55:3). The love and faithfulness referred to are in the heart of God and come to his people on the basis of his promise (cf. 2Sa 7:12–16). At one time Moab and Midian were allied against Israel (Nu 22:4; 25:1–18). Interest-

ingly, the prophet presents the Messiah's rule as extending over both Midian (9:4–7) and Moab.

6–7 These verses contain the only clear references to the sin of Moab. A true prophet would be expected to penetrate beyond the misery that results from God's judgment to the offenses against him that caused it, and this Isaiah does here. Because of pride the Moabites were brought to this sorry pass.

8–12 The prophet visualizes the land of Moab as a vast vineyard, with vines spreading to its farthest corners but now trampled underfoot by its enemies (cf. 5:1–7). In an agricultural community, harvest is a season of great joy (cf. 9:3). In Moab, however, the vineyards will be silent. The ripened fruit will not be trodden under foot in the winepresses, for judgment through foreign rulers will stalk the land.

Again (cf. 15:5) the prophet's heart is deeply moved by the undoubtedly deserved sufferings of the Moabites (v.11). The skilled and sensitive musician knows what instrument will best carry the feelings of his song to the heart of his hearers, and Isaiah's deep emotions come with all the pathos of a lament played on a harp. Unhappily, Moab's sufferings had not driven her to the true and living God but to the idol shrines of her god, Chemosh. There could be no help from such a source.

13–14 There had been earlier prophecies against Moab with the same general import as the oracle just given by the prophet here (cf. Am 2:1–3). Isaiah has a specific disclosure from the Lord as to the time of Moab's judgment. It most likely relates to Sargon's campaign against the tribal peoples of northwest Arabia, for the Assyrian army's route would naturally go through Moab. This would date the two closing verses of ch. 16 to 718 B.C.

Verse 14 refers either to the contract of a laborer with his master (cf. Ge 29:18; Lev 25:50, 53) or that of a mercenary soldier with his superior. In either case the point is the same, for the exact calculation of the period is important to the transaaction. The prophetic ministry did not require many such timed predictions (but cf. 7:8). Their fulfillment would, of course, provide additional clear evidence of their authenticity.

E. Prophecy Against Damascus (and Ephraim) (17:1–14)

Ephraim's devotion to the apostate shrines at Bethel and Dan had made her a perpetual rebel against the Lord, but now she became unequally yoked with a pagan nation in an endeavor to coerce Judah into an unholy league against Assyria. This oracle, therefore, certainly appears to belong to the period 735–732 B.C.

1–3 The oracle opens with a call to visualize what God would make of a once-proud city. The downfall of Damascus would not be an isolated event, for other cities too would be deserted. The double conjunction of Ephraim and Damascus and of Aram and the Israelites is striking. Israel had chosen to accept a close link with Damascus; so she had to accept the consequences of that relationship. A shared purpose involves a shared judgment. The basis of the league between the two nations was chiefly military; and, ironically, it was in military terms that she would suffer, in the loss of her "fortified city." This is no doubt a reference to Damascus, as the fortress that Ephraim herself hoped would protect her from the Assyrians.

The prophet's reference to the "remnant of Aram" likely relates to that kingdom itself. Damascus, in fact, fell to the Assyrians in 732 B.C., and Samaria, the capital of Israel, fell a decade later. The instrument of these judgments was to be Assyria, but the judgments were ultimately the great power of "the LORD Almighty."

4–6 The repeated phrase "in that day" underlines the decisiveness of the Lord's judgment on Ephraim. It has an eschatological quality in the sense that the great principles of that period cast their shadows before them. In other words, in such judgments God is making an emphatic point about sin and his attitude toward it.

The judgment on Ephraim was to be devastating, leaving the people decimated. The "glory of Jacob" suggests Ephraim's honor, the respect in which others would hold him. He would become subject to a wasting disease, making him perhaps as sorry a sight as if he just had a terrible beating (cf. 1:5–6; 52:14).

Isaiah develops the picture of a body politic suffering the consequences of sin in terms of the grain harvest. The reaper's arm encircles and makes taut many stalks of grain so that he can remove their heads by one sweep of his sickle. Fruit trees also will be climbed as far as possible and beaten to gather the great bulk of their fruit. In each case the farmer endeavors to leave as little as possible for the gleaners, who are allowed by law to gather anything edible that had been missed (Dt 24:19–22). So thorough would judgment be, and yet the destruction would not be total. The phrases "the glory of Jacob" and "the God of Israel" at the beginning and the end of this section are a reminder that the God of the patriarchal promises has an ongoing purpose beyond temporal judgment (cf. 6:11–13).

7–8 The judgment on Ephraim would bring a spirit of penitence to at least some of the survivors. The contrast between "their Maker" and "the work of their hands" shows that nothing is more misguided or pathetic than the human attempt to mend the relationship between oneself and deity by the work of one's own hands. The altars mentioned here may be the apostate shrines with their forbidden bull-images at Bethel and Dan. It may be, however, that we should read v.8a in the light of v.8b, for "the Asherah poles" (i.e., "symbols of the goddess Asherah"; see NIV note) reflect the naked paganism of Canaan. The presence of northern Israelites at Hezekiah's celebration of the Passover (2Ch 30) shows the fulfillment of this prediction.

9–11 The theme of judgment returns. When the Israelites came into the land of Canaan many years before, the strong cities of the land were abandoned to them. The Lord was at work for his people, giving them the Land of Promise. However, the situation has changed, and the same cities will be abandoned by the Israelites themselves as they are under the judging hand of God. Here again we see "the Light of Israel" becoming a fire (cf. 10:17).

The NIV treats vv.10b–11 as a further development of the illustrations of judgment given in vv.4–6. Judgment can be pictured as a thorough harvest that leaves only scattered gleanings, but it can also be pictured as disappointing in itself; for even the finest plants, which the grower has searched out in foreign lands and planted in ideal conditions, may come to nothing. Some kind of pestilence is implied here.

12–14 Mauchline points out that the thunder of many peoples amassing reminds us of the opening of Ps 2: nations mustering their armies and trying to carry out their plans and ambitions. The general nature of the picture is underlined by the implied comparison with God's creation ordinance restricting the flow of the waters across the face of the earth (cf. Ge 1:9; Ps 104:5–9). The God who rules both nature and history employs language taken from his control of the one to represent graphically his control of the other.

The imagery changes again. The foes are like great rushing torrents, but God opposes their waters by his wind; they become like chaff blown from the hilltop threshing floor (cf. Ps 1:4; 83:13; Isa 29:5) or like mere dust (cf. Isa 40:15), driven in its blinding grittiness before an advancing storm. God's judgment of the enemies of his people will be both decisive and swift.

The view at dusk is presented simply in terms of the overpowering emotion of terror, with countless hosts of pagan soldiers, eager for their prey. In the morning, however, it all seemed like a nightmare, for there was not an enemy to be seen! Doubtless God's action against Sennacherib's great army (37:36) is chiefly in view here.

The prophet closes with a general comment based on this singular example of God's care for his people and his city. The oracle opened with Damascus, moved on to deal with Ephraim, but at the end it appears clearly that all these events are part of God's plan to keep in safety those who were in Jerusalem and in the center of his purpose because they were trusting in him.

F. Prophecy Against Cush (18:1–7)

This oracle is unique in Isa 13–23 (except for ch. 20) in that it does not open with the word "oracle." Chapters 18–20 deal with Egypt and Cush, which were one at this time. The content of the passage hardly seems to warrant the use of the doom-exclamation ("Woe") with which it begins; for the doom is really pictured as falling on Assyria rather than on Cush, but perhaps it anticipates ch. 20. Biblical Cush is usually translated "Ethiopia," but the transliteration designates a much larger area than present-day Ethiopia—an area including the Sudan and Somalia. This mysterious area was normally in Egypt's area of influence and control; but for a period during the eighth century, Egypt was ruled by an Ethiopian dynasty. The visit of the ambassadors could be placed either during the Philistine revolt against Assyria (around 712 B.C.) or in the period of restlessness after Sargon's death in 705.

1–3 The phrase "the land of whirring wings" is highly evocative for anyone who has been in the Nile valley, with its swarms of insects. Ambassadors in OT days were not permanent officials placed by nations in the capital cities of other states but were emissaries sent out on special commissions. The purpose here was to foment rebellion against Assyria, which was very much in the interests of the rival power that straddled the Nile valley. The lightness of their papyrus vessels made it possible for them to be carried past rapids and other unnavigable stretches of rivers. The word "sea" (v.1; GK 3542) could be interpreted as the Nile, because the word can be applied to a great river.

The ambassadors were to return with all speed to the land they had come from; for their mission, though politically expedient, was spiritually inappropriate and irrelevant. The military reputation of the tall, handsome Nubians of Cush had been much enhanced by their recent conquest of mighty Egypt. Israel, remembering its own captivity in Egypt, might well have been particularly impressed. The message given to the messengers had universal application, for the whole world would reverberate at the trumpet blast heralding mighty Assyria's fall. The banner and the trumpet represent the call to rally for battle.

4–6 Isaiah often urged his contemporaries to adopt an attitude of quiet faith in their God instead of trusting in alliances with other powers (e.g., 7:4; 30:15). Here God himself is quiet, contemplating the frenzied scene of diplomatic and military activity. When Isaiah commends quiet trust, therefore, he is really calling his hearers to view things from a divine viewpoint.

The second simile in v.4 serves not only to reinforce the first but prepares for the disclosure of God's judgment described in v.5. The divine harvester is dealing with branches that reveal their barrenness by their emptiness (cf.

Jn 15:2, 5). The branches that are valueless to humans are left to the local birds and animals, who put them to their own use. This suggests that the fierce Assyrians would themselves become the prey of others.

7 The very people who from their position of strength had sent word to Judah to secure her cooperation in a military venture would come again with gifts for the true God in Zion. This picture is a specific illustration of the general vision of Zion as the religious center of the whole world.

G. Prophecy Against Egypt (19:1–25)

This oracle is of exceptional interest because of its amazing climax: the judgment of God on the Egyptians is followed by their repentance and conversion, by manifestations of God's grace to them, and by their incorporation in the people of God, along with their bitter enemy, Assyria, and the chosen people, Israel, who had suffered so grievously at the hands of both.

1–4 The Lord is pictured as riding on a swift cloud to Egypt. Here imagery is employed in connection with his interventions in history. Once before this, the God of Israel had judged the gods of Egypt (Ex 12:12; Nu 33:4) as well as its people. His appearance on the heavenly horizon fills them both with dread. Their power to resist him is still further diminished by internal division and internecine conflict. According to the Greek historian Herodotus, Egyptian unity—secured by the power of the Cushite dynasty—was destroyed by civil war.

The idols and human agents of paganism can be of no avail to the Egyptians in their predicament, because this oracle declares that they and their objects of worship will both be overcome by fear. There is little point in the demoralized turning to the demoralized!

The "fierce king" of v.4 most surely is Esar-haddon, king of Assyria, who subdued Egypt in 670 B.C. Ferocity was a general characteristic of all the Assyrian monarchs. The Egyptians were not to know this, of course; but their downfall before this monarch would mean the virtual end, not only of their greatness, but even of their independence, for millennia. Who is this whose power is so great that he can hand over one mighty nation to another? Why, of course, "the LORD," the Lord Almighty!

5–10 This passage graphically portrays Egyptian economics, with its total dependence on the Nile. Dry up the Nile and the whole Egyptian economy will grind to a halt. Who can—and will—dry up the Nile, which was a great deity to the Egyptians as well as a great river? The same God Almighty whose plans to intervene in the history of Egypt had been declared in vv.1–4!

Again we are reminded of the events associated with the Exodus, for several of the plagues had involved the judgment of the Nile. Fishing and linen industries were important; both were completely dependent on the fauna and flora of the Nile.

11–15 Constructive, progressive, and stable rule necessitates the marriage of power and wisdom, characteristics of God's great King (11:1–5) and qualities of God himself. Every great monarch feels the need of advice from wise counselors, but what if the wisest in the land have nothing but lunacy to offer? No matter how ancient nor how exalted their lore, it makes no difference to their ineptness. Zoan and Memphis were the two most important cities in Lower Egypt. They are mentioned together because of their administrative importance.

The quaint architectural analogy implicit in the language of v.13b is found in a number of OT passages (e.g., Ps 118:22; Zec 10:4). Its use in Isa 28:16 is particularly interesting in the light of its use here, for here the leaders who should have given stability to Egypt led her astray, while in the later passage the God of Israel promises a leader who will give true stability to his people. In Isa 28 the folly of the leaders is due to drink, while their confusion here is pictured as if it were the result of drunkenness.

When the prophet says, "The LORD has poured into them a spirit of dizziness," he is of course thinking of a personal spirit (cf. 1Sa 16:14; 18:10; 19:9; 1Ki 22:19–23). It is clear that this spirit comes for moral reasons and as a judgment from God. If we accept that God may use an evil human power in judgment (cf. 10:5), then there is really no difference in principle if he uses an evil spiritual being, as here. Foolish confidence in one's own wisdom leads not only to failure to produce appropriate counsel but also to walking and causing others to walk along a pathway that leads to disaster.

16–17 Isaiah uses the expression "in that day" forty-two times. Verses 16–17 bridge the first part of the oracle (dominated by judgment) and the remainder of it (centered in salvation and grace). They place emphasis on the fear induced in the Egyptians by God's acts of judgment (cf. v.1), which was a prelude to their repentance. The Exodus account frequently refers to the hand of the Lord and its activities against Egypt (e.g., Ex 8:19; 9:15; 13:3; 9, 16; et al.). Because God was on Israel's side, her very name became a terror to the Egyptians (cf. Ex 12:33; 15:16; Ps 105:38); so too the mention of Judah would terrorize the Egyptians.

18 The verse as it stands may mean that Jews were then living in Egypt, occupying five of its cities and so instituting a colony of worshipers of the Lord in this pagan land (cf. Jer 44:1, 15). On the other hand, it could refer to the conversion of Egypt to the worship of the true God. The five cities may be an allusion to the original conquest of Canaan by the Israelites. After the capture of Jericho and Ai by Joshua's forces, their first great victory was over the kings of five important Canaanite cities: Jerusalem, Hebron, Jarmuth, Lachish, and Eglon (Jos 10). This victory led to the conquest of the whole country. So the spiritual conquest of Egypt outlined in vv.19–22 starts with the conversion of five cities promised in v.18. This not only fits the context perfectly but would also furnish a further example of allusion to the Exodus-Conquest period that is such a feature of this oracle.

What then is "the City of Destruction"? The Hebrew seems like a play on "the city of the sun" (the Hebrew equivalent of Heliopolis). If so, then the conversion of the people of this stronghold of sun worship is perhaps treated as a major victory, decisive enough and significant enough as a great act of destruction at the time of the Conquest.

19–21 These verses spell out in detail the circumstances and results of the conversion of the Egyptians. The "altar" has sometimes been identified with the Jewish temple built at Elephantine in the sixth or fifth century. It is evident, however, that the final fulfillment of vv.16–25 has not yet come, unless it is all to be viewed as fulfilled spiritually in the triumphs of the gospel in Egypt.

Another echo of the conquest of Canaan is found in the reference to the monument or pillar. Pillars were associated with pagan worship in Canaan and so were prohibited to the Israelites (cf. Dt 7:5; 12:3), but it is clear from v.20 that something different is in view. Just as the altars constructed by the patriarchs were witnesses for the true God and his self-disclosure at these places, so various stones and pillars of witness were erected in the days of Joshua (see Jos 4:3, 20–22; 7:26; 8:29; 10:27). The pillar-monument here, situated on the border of Egypt, probably symbolizes the claiming of the land for the true and living God.

The analogy of the Conquest continues with a promise that could have come straight out of Judges (cf., Jdg 3:9, 15). The promise appears to be an assurance of deliverance from physical oppressors. Interestingly, the savior and defender is singular, while the oppressors are plural. The language is well fitted to refer to the supreme Savior, the Lord Jesus Christ.

A major theme of the Exodus story is the knowledge of the Lord that is given in its events. There is, however, an important distinction drawn between the form that knowledge took for the Israelites and for the Egyptians. The former knew the Lord in the context of his grace to them (e.g., Ex 6:7), the latter knew him as a God of judgment (e.g., Ex 7:5). It is more frequently declared that the events will bring the knowledge of God to the Egyptians than that they will bring it to Israel. The Lord will reveal himself to Egypt again, but this time in an entirely different way, much more after the pattern of his self-disclosure to Israel; for he will deal with them also on the basis of grace.

The references to sacrifices, grain offerings, and vows suggest a comparison with the Mosaic Law, perhaps to make it clear that the Egyptians are to be on equal footing with their erstwhile slaves who had been so gloriously redeemed from their midst. There is an implied rebuke of Israel in the assertion that "they will make vows to the Lord and keep them," which suggests that the basis of their relationship with him is the new covenant (cf. Jer 31:31–34), fulfilled in Christ's death as the ultimate sacrifice (cf. esp. Heb 8:7–9:15).

22 This verse is a virtual summary of most of the oracle. The reference to a plague is another clear echo of Exodus. In the time of Moses, the pleas of the Egyptians for the lifting of the plagues were heard through the intercession of Moses, though there was no true penitence in the hearts of Pharaoh and his servants. In terms of this prophecy, however, the plague will bring them to repentance, and God will hear their own cries for deliverance.

23 Astonishment reaches a new height here, for the revelation of God's amazing grace to the Gentiles embraces not only the old enemy, Egypt, but the new one, Assyria. In Isaiah's day, Assyria was feared by every little nation in the Fertile Crescent. Their brutality made them more of an object of general hatred than any other nation of antiquity. The Egyptians, Babylonians, and Persians were all capable of inhuman acts, but the Assyrian record for callous cruelty is difficult to parallel. This amazing verse assures Isaiah's hearers that Egypt and Assyria will drop their long-standing antagonism toward each other and cooperate, not only in a great road-building project that will further international communication, commerce, and peace, but they will come together in the worship of the true God, the God of the little Israelite nation whom they had both afflicted so sorely!

24–25 Israel, which seems for a time to have been out of the picture, now takes her place as one member of a trio of godly states. Some of Israel's own titles (cf. 1:3; 45:11) are applied to her former enemies. This suggests that the Lord has established a covenant relationship with these nations, perhaps extending to them the new covenant that he promised in Jeremiah to make with his people of Israel and Judah (cf. Jer 31:31–34).

H. Prophecy Against Egypt and Cush (20:1–6)

This passage gives not only an oracle but the circumstances in which it was delivered. This is understandable, because it was associated with an acted prophecy and so demanded a setting.

1–2 The five Philistine cities were united in a federation, and this union was dominated first by one and then by another of them. The rebellion against Assyria at this time centered in Ashdod. This revolt occurred 713–711 and probably developed in response to events further south. Egypt had been taken over by the Ethiopian dynasty in 715 B.C., and the petty states of Palestine seem to have felt there might be more hope of securing assistance against Assyria. The demise of Ashdod is mentioned in the Assyrian inscriptions and can be accurately dated in 711 B.C.

The way Isaiah was clothed suggests that the prophet was in mourning at this time, either because of personal bereavement or because of his concern about the nation. At least from the time of Elijah, however, such rough clothing was associated with the office of the prophet (2Ki 1:8; Zec 13:4; Mk 1:6). The wording does not preclude the possibility that he was wearing a loincloth (cf. v.4), for strict nakedness would have been religiously and socially unacceptable (cf. Ge 9:20–27).

3–6 The sign is given first and then its significance is clarified in a spoken prophecy. Acted prophecy occurs frequently in the OT (e.g., 1Ki 11:29–32; Jer 13:1–11; Eze 4). The act normally requires verbal interpretation before it becomes a true prophecy with a specific meaning. The sign was a message to those in Judah who were inclined to put their trust in Egypt (cf. 30:1–5; 31:1–3), especially in its revived strength under its new Ethiopian rulers. In fact, the Egyptian army sent to the help of Judah in 701 was defeated at Eltekeh; this was the first of a series of disastrous defeats by Assyria in the next few decades.

Verses 5–6 probably refer to different people, those in v.5 being chiefly the leaders of Judah, while v.6 refers to the inhabitants of the Palestinian coastal strip. This makes it clear that not only Ashdod but the whole Philistine federation would suffer; and it may even imply that Phoenicia, further north, would be smitten by the Assyrians.

I. Prophecy Against Babylon (21:1–10)

This passage has two main schools of interpretation. Some feel that the occasion depicted in the prophet's vision is the downfall of Babylon in 539, when Cyrus entered the city with his triumphant forces. Cyrus was originally king of Persian lands that were formerly part of Elam, and he had conquered Media a decade or so before his assault on Babylonia. So "Elam" and "Media" in v.2 refer to the multinational army of Cyrus.

The other interpretation relates the passage to the time of Merodach-Baladan, a prince of southern Babylonia. He revolted against Assyria and had himself crowned king of Babylon in 722 B.C., with the support of the Elamites. He reigned during several periods, and after his death Babylon had further times of independence from Assyria before Sennacherib's ferocious destruction in 689. There had, however, been earlier sackings of the city under Sargon II and Sennacherib, while Merodach-Baladan was alive. This puts not only the prophecy but also its fulfillment in Isaiah's day.

1a "The Desert by the Sea" could refer to the desert lands southeast of Babylonia, where Merodach-Baladan's home territory lay. Possibly it was the great plain that Babylon stood on. This plain was so divided by lakes and marshy stretches of country that it was appropriate to call it "the sea."

1b–2 The prophet saw in his vision an invader approaching Babylon from the desert lands, through which the invading armies would pass on their way to it. His strongly imaginative mind discerned a similarity between these and the whirlwinds that were liable to move up toward Judah through the Negeb. The prophet then told his hearers that he had been shown a dire vision. If this oracle refers to Cyrus and his attack on Babylon, it might have seemed dreadful at first, because the Jews in Babylon could well have perished in the overthrow of the city. In fact, however, this did not happen. Thus an application to the time of Merodach-Baladan is certainly feasible. News of his revolt against Assyria would encourage the Jews in the thought that Assyria might be weakened or perhaps even overthrown by him. The fall of Babylon would represent a severe setback to such hopes.

Most commentators take the words of v.2b as utterances of the Lord, in which he calls on Elam and Media to attack Babylonia. However, in the time of Isaiah it was more natural to see Elam and Media as enemies of Assyria and allies of Babylonia. Thus, as has been suggested, the cries are probably the battle cries of Babylon's allies against Assyria.

3–4 The oracle against Moab (15:5; 16:9, 11) showed the deep distress Isaiah felt when he contemplated the slaughter of human beings, even when these belonged to a nation that was often an enemy of his own people. But Isaiah's horror may have come from his own identification with his people so that he felt the deep dismay that came over them with the downfall of their hope in Merodach-Baladan. The latter is perhaps the more likely, because Isaiah speaks of fear as well as horror.

5 This verse paints a scene of feasting, but where was it enacted? Herodotus says that the taking of Babylon by the Persians in 539 B.C. was so swift that many who were at their wine in the city center did not even know that the outlying parts of the city were in enemy hands. On the other hand, if this is the leaders of Judah who are feasting (cf. 22:1–2, 13), the second half of the verse does not in this case depict a sudden change of mood, with agitated preparation for battle, but rather underlines the atmosphere of leisured ease. Arrangements are made for sentry duty, and the officers detailed for this use their time on guard to apply oil to their leather shields to prevent them from cracking when they are struck by the weapons of the foe.

6–10 The prophet had seen a vision; then he hears the word of the Lord. Isaiah is to have a man posted on the lookout. Any group of riders is to be reported, for they could be bringing news of what was happening in the far country. The lookout was at his post for many days. His tour of duty wearied him, but his patience was at last rewarded as a lone charioteer appeared on the horizon. The message he brought was that Babylon, from which the people have been expecting so much, had fallen, presumably to the Assyrians. The reference to the images of Babylon's gods and their shattering is perhaps an implied rebuke to Judah's leaders. How could they hope for the blessing of God on an alliance with pagans?

The people of Judah, who had already suffered much at the hands of the Assyrians, are depicted as prostrate but still alive, like grain that has fallen—bruised and yet safe—on the threshing floor after the thresher has battered it severely with his flail. The image underlining their helpless condition was also perhaps intended to convey a note of hope. Judah was not chaff but grain, and the Lord Almighty who had used Assyria to bring the downfall of Babylon was also the God of Israel who would protect his people and fulfill his purposes for them.

J. Prophecy Against Edom (21:11–12)

11–12 "Dumah" means silence or stillness and is a wordplay on Edom (see NIV note). As part of the Word of God, this short oracle must have both meaning and relevance. Its meaning is perhaps secured if we understand it through the wordplay in its title. God gives light to his people in the midst of perplexing historical circumstances; the very ministry of Isaiah is evidence of this. It is otherwise, however, with Judah's pagan neighbors. The reply of the watchman is so vague and enigmatic that it is tantamount to no reply at all. The one certainty is that the night will end in morning, but also that this will be followed by another night. Perhaps this refers to the lifting of the oppressive Assyrian overlordship, which would be replaced by another black night, the rule of Babylon.

K. Prophecy Against Arabia (21:13–17)

13–17 This oracle has often been thought to have close ties with the brief one that precedes it. It is noteworthy that Edom was really on the edge of Arabia. Dumah, Tema, and Kedar all occur in Ge 25:13–16, in the list of Ishmael's descendants. The Dumah referred to there, of course, would be the Arabian one, as Edom was the people of Esau (Ge 25:30).

Sargon II conducted a campaign against the northern Arabian tribes in 715 B.C., which could well provide an appropriate setting for this oracle. Armed men are drawn from various Arabian tribes, but they are no match for the Assyrians and are put to flight. They flee exhausted, parched with thirst, and in need of food. The caravans plying their trade and camping out in the wastelands and the settled town-dwellers of the oases are both urged to provide sustenance for the fugitives. The resistance of the Arab tribes will be short-lived, for their armies will be reduced to a meager remnant within twelve months. The closing oracle formula probably underlines the fact that this is the judgment of the God of Israel.

L. Prophecy Against Jerusalem (22:1–25)

This chapter divides into two sections: vv.1–14 show us Isaiah's strong denunciation

of Jerusalem's people because of their attitude on the occasion of a deliverance of the city from enemies outside its walls, while vv.15–25 focuses attention on two of the leaders of the people. If we read the first part in the light of chs. 36–37, we may well conclude that the occasion is the deliverance of the city from Sennacherib. Chapters 36–37 emphasize the divine deliverance that took place in response to the faith of Hezekiah and his people, while this present oracle makes it clear how shallow this faith really was. In a similar manner, the joyful attitude to Josiah's reformation taken by the writers of Kings and Chronicles stands in contrast with Jeremiah's recognition of the people's superficiality and shallow penitence. These perspectives were complementary.

1a The expression "Valley of Vision" has been variously understood by commentators, though always in reference to Jerusalem. We do not think of this city as situated in a valley because of the hills of Zion and Moriah on which it was built; but in fact it is comparatively low, being surrounded by hills (cf. Ps 125:2; Jer 21:13). The phrase may refer to the fact that it was the very place where so many prophetic visions had been received and then given to the people. This would, therefore, intensify the responsibility of her people for their reprehensible attitude.

The exceptional sharpness of the prophet's language indicates that he was deeply disturbed. If we have rightly located the prophecy during the deliverance from Sennacherib, this was late in Isaiah's public ministry; and he poured into this prophecy all the disappointment he had with his own people that must have accumulated throughout the decades that he had been prophesying. He had been warned that there would be little response (cf. 6:9–10), and he had certainly found this to be true in the days of Ahaz (ch. 7). Perhaps he had hoped for better things under Hezekiah, who was more godly than his predecessor. In this way, Isaiah identified with the feelings of the Servant of the Lord as the latter looked back on his own ministry (cf. 49:4).

1b–2a A noisy spirit of excitement came on the whole city, and the flat roofs were thronged with revelers. The people probably went up originally to survey the Assyrians outside the city; but finding them dead (cf. 37:36), they stayed to celebrate (cf. vv.12–13).

2b–3 Sennacherib, in his inscriptions, spoke of inflicting a defeat on Hezekiah; and this probably took place during the earlier stages of the Assyrian campaign in Judah (cf. 2Ki 18:13–16; Isa 1:5–9). Is the reference to the "slain" in v.2b an ironic comment on the revelers lying in drunken stupor who, only a short time before, had feared that they would be killed in battle? Possibly, though the prophet may be thinking of those captured and put to death in the early stages of the campaign. Isaiah's main point is that the people could not glory in themselves, as if they had won a mighty victory. In fact, they were so demoralized at the approach of the enemy that they simply fled.

4–8a Isaiah knew that Jerusalem, delivered by a wonderful act of God's grace, would one day perish at his hand. The people had learned nothing from what had happened. The spiritual sorrow of the prophet for his people was so deep that he was inconsolable. As a man of God, of course, he could accept what, as a Judean, he could not welcome; for the destruction of the people that had been revealed to him was the judgment of God.

The Day of the Lord, prophesied in 2:6–22, would fall on Jerusalem. The NIV has brought out the terrifying alliteration and assonance of three consecutive Hebrew words with its translation of "a day of tumult and trampling and terror." The people were looking down over the walls, gloating over the slain Assyrians. On God's great day those same walls would be battered down by the enemy, and the mountains surrounding the Valley of Vision would echo with the wails of Jerusalem's inhabitants.

This prophecy was fulfilled when Nebuchadnezzar took the city in 586 B.C., though history was destined to repeat itself in A.D. 70, when the Romans overcame Jewish resistance and entered Jerusalem to wreak havoc on its people and its buildings. There may have been Elamites and Syrians (from Kir) serving in the army of the Babylonian king. The mention of them imparts an extra dimension of terror to the oracle, because it pictures the besieging army as an international one.

8b–11 The prophet returns to the situation in Jerusalem when the Assyrian army appeared on the horizon. By their actions the people had made it clear to Isaiah that their trust was in human beings rather than in God. A city facing a long siege has many needs. Its defenders need adequate weapons. Jerusalem had, in the Palace of the Forest, its own royal armory (cf. 1Ki 7:2–5); and no doubt its staff undertook an urgent check on their supply of swords and spears that day. The walls of the city and especially its defensive towers were in need of repair, and some of its houses had to be destroyed to obtain stones for this, for there was neither time nor liberty of access to get stone from the Judean quarries. Any house that was not really needed would have to go. Ahaz, also in unbelief, had busied himself with the water supply of the city (cf. 7:1–3), and the men of Hezekiah's Jerusalem had the same outlook (cf. 2Ch 32:1–5). A special reservoir was built, probably to retain surplus water from the Pool of Siloam.

God is the maker of history as well as of nature. History, with its series of world empires and successive judgments (cf. 10:23–24), is all under his almighty hand; he is the God of Israel, for this people is in special relationship with him. Because of this situation, they should have looked to him with faith. Instead, they were busy trying to find ways of evading the challenge to believe.

12–14 There is something ominous about using a title of power—"the LORD Almighty"—instead of one of relationship, like "the God of Israel." If the people would not seek his grace in repentance, they would feel his power in a terrifying act of his judgment on their city. The prophet is outraged by the scene that presents itself to him as he walks through Jerusalem's streets. They should have been thronging with people, contrite in spirit, making their way to the temple in a corporate act of penitence.

Verse 14 contains one of the Bible's most terrifying sentences, comparable perhaps to the words of Rev 22:11. The revelers had probably slaughtered the animals used by them for their feasts at Jerusalem's temple. Let them not think, though, that any sacrifice could be offered to atone for this sin. At the very time when God's promises to protect Jerusalem were being so wonderfully fulfilled, the threat was given that the city would most certainly fall one day before its enemies and that nothing—just *nothing*—could avert the judgment of God on it.

15–16 Terrifying as this threat of judgment undoubtedly was, it might seem to some to lose something of its horror because it was so general. After all, Jerusalem was a community; and when an act of judgment strikes a group of people, any individual may seek to assure himself that he has simply been caught up in the consequences of other people's sins, whereas he himself is without specific blame. Isaiah allows no such escape route for the hardened conscience. God's people are dealing with "the Lord, the LORD Almighty."

The spotlight of judgment is now directed toward one man, Shebna, the steward of the king's palace (cf. 36:3, 11, 22; 37:2). The pyramid tombs of the Pharaohs epitomize the desire of prominent people in the ancient Near East to have a grandiose burying place so that they would be the objects of adulation for centuries after their death.

17–19 "Beware" forebodes for Shebna a future scene different from the one he had planned. The words "O you mighty man" take him at his own estimate of himself. God will show him who it is that has real power, for God will project him ignominiously out of his office and into another land—surely a reference to Assyria. The splendid tomb, hewn out at his order in some place of prominence, will not then be a witness to his greatness but to his overweening ambition; for he would lie dead in an alien land. He perhaps had paraded through Jerusalem's streets in ceremonial chariots (cf. 2Sa 15:1; 1Ki 1:5); but he would now be seen to be, not the glory of his master, the king, but his disgrace.

The contempt felt for Shebna is summed up in the scornful expression "this steward" (v.15). Perhaps this oracle does not tell us the whole reason for this contempt, that allied to the official's ambition and pride was a political policy (probably pro-Egyptian) that ran counter to Isaiah's message for the king and the people to trust only in the Lord. This would certainly explain why this oracle is associated here with the one in vv.1–14.

20–23 Shebna had been riding ostentatiously in his chariots and building a splendid grave for himself, seeking in all this the praise of other people. How much better to have

God's smile of approval and to be described, in a simple but eloquent phrase, as "my servant." Eliakim, who is also—like Shebna—mentioned in 36:3, 11, 22, and 37:2, is to take over Shebna's office and so to be given his ceremonial robes (cf. comment on 36:3). The word "father" suggests both his authority over the people of Jerusalem and the provision he would make for them in virtue of his office. Verse 22 is to be understood literally, for the steward would have the large master key of the palace fastened to the shoulder of his tunic (but cf. Rev 3:7; see also Mt 16:19; 18:18).

The simile of a "tent peg" symbolizes the stability of the kingdom (cf. 33:20). Through Eliakim his whole family would advance in social dignity, promoted, as it were, to a seat closer to the throne at the royal table. Apparently Eliakim had a different policy from that of Shebna, more in line with Isaiah's counsel to trust in God. If so, his advice to the king would help to secure a real and not just an apparent strength to the nation in a time of international insecurity.

24–25 The mood of the oracle changes dramatically. The true honor of "my servant" (v.20) is replaced by a satirical picture that reveals almost as much contempt as that shown toward Shebna in vv.15–19. Shebna's great sin was pride, but Eliakim's was nepotism. There is a legitimate honor that comes to those related to a family head with a high position in the land. Eliakim had, however, been chosen for office because of his own qualities, not theirs. The peg is not now seen giving strength to the tent but rather fastened to the wall of the palace kitchen with a motley assortment of kitchen vessels hanging from it (cf. Zec 14:21). The temptations of high office are many, and those who occupy them need the prayers of God's people.

M. Prophecy Against Tyre (23:1–18)

Phoenicia, with its two important ports of Tyre and Sidon, was the maritime commercial state contemporary with much of OT history. Until the time of the Assyrians, who had designs on the whole Mediterranean seaboard and its hinterland, this small state and its important commercial cities had been left relatively undisturbed by conflict. It certainly merited judgment, however, and would experience this at the hands of the Assyrians, just as other states in the area were to face. During the period 705–701 B.C., Sennacherib turned his attention to Phoenicia, which had been a nominal part of the Assyrian Empire for some time. The country was devastated, and Tyre itself was subjected to a long and bitter siege. It was later also besieged by the Babylonians, the Persians, and the Greeks under Alexander the Great, who virtually destroyed it in 333 B.C. after one of the greatest sieges in history. It may be that the prophecy, in terms of its fulfillment, incorporates elements from some of these later times as well as the time of the Assyrian onslaught.

1–5 The Phoenicians had a number of colonies and dependent trading-stations in the Mediterranean. Tarshish, probably in Spain, and some of the cities of Cyprus were among these. Ships making their way back eastward from Tarshish would call at Cyprus before completing their journey to Tyre. At Cyprus they would hear that their harbor had been destroyed; so they could not complete their journey. Sidon (v.2) was the other port that alternated with Tyre as the chief port of the land. The Phoenicians had special commercial links with Egypt, and no doubt many a Tyrian or Sidonian vessel would carry large quantities of grain from the fields of Shihor, in the Nile Valley. These commercial ties would be viewed with considerable suspicion by the Assyrians and other rulers of various world-empires, for Egypt was usually the final major enemy to be overcome before complete mastery of the Fertile Crescent and the eastern Mediterranean could be achieved.

The sea is personified as the mother of the Phoenicians, and nothing could be more appropriate. With so many Sidonians slaughtered by Assyria, Sidon was bereft of her children and left as if she had never had them. The sadness of the sea is matched by that of Egypt, whose trading links with Tyre and Sidon gave her sympathy.

6–9 The prophet next turns to the people of the nearest Phoenician colony, Cyprus. They would take the news farther west to Tarshish or even, perhaps, flee there. The prophet points to the contrast between Tyre's past gaiety and wide-flung colonization and commercialism and its current humbling under the mighty hand of God. No doubt all the rulers of world empires from Assyria onward

would plan to deal with Tyre on their way to other victories; but her downfall was really the work of the Lord, whose counsels ultimately prevail in the affairs of humankind. Isaiah never tires of saying that God is absolutely opposed to human pride in its every form.

10–12a Isaiah warns the Phoenicians that their trading links with Tarshish and Egypt should not induce complacency in them in the face of the threat of divine judgment (cf. Jnh 1:3–4). The hand that had been stretched out over the Red Sea in judgment on the Egyptians in the time of Moses was stretched out now even over the Mediterranean. No kingdom on its coasts could reckon itself immune from God's righteous wrath.

12b–14 If this prophecy comes from the year 703 or a little after, then it refers to the ferocious attack of Sennacherib, who had an almost pathological loathing of the Babylonians. If it is be dated a few years earlier, it could refer to the campaign of Sargon II against the Chaldeans in 710. Both events predate Sennacherib's attack on Tyre in 701. Neither Tyre nor even Cyprus, across the sea, could be regarded as a haven of safety when Assyria, the instrument of God's wrath (cf. 10:5–11), was on the rampage.

15–18 Many of Isaiah's oracles contain a note of surprise at their end, and so often it is a word of grace (cf. 8:16–9:7; 19:1–25; 42:18–43:13). Here, however, there is to be a partial

Siege towers became a common method of protecting soldiers while attacking a city (cf. 23:13). Drawing courtesy Carta, Jerusalem.

reprieve, with a new period of commercial success for Tyre, but with a view not so much to the blessing of her people as to supply the needs of the house of God in Jerusalem.

The period of seventy years is familiar to readers of Jeremiah (cf. Jer 25:11–12; 29:10), where it refers to the captivity of the Jews in Babylon; here, however, it applies to Tyre.

A careful study of the symbolic picture of Babylon in the book of Revelation reveals that not only did "Babylon" prophecies in the OT go into the construction of this picture but other oracles as well, and especially those against Tyre. The description of the great city as a harlot (Rev 17) probably owes something to this present passage. The comparison is appropriate, for the harlot bedecks herself in gaudy finery and enters into a commercial transaction with her clients. Seaports have always been particularly notorious in connection with prostitution. Tyre was an old, old city and so would need to attract her clients now by singing some song associated with her trade.

There is an important link here between the oracles against the nations (which come to their conclusion with this prophecy against Phoenicia) and the range of prophecies that occur later in the book. All three major parts of the book contain the notion that people from the Gentile nations will come up to Jerusalem, not only to worship (cf. 2:1–5; 49:6–7; 60:1), but also to make their treasures available for the use of the chosen people and in the temple of God (cf. 18:7; 45:14; 49:22–23; 60:9–14). This motif, therefore, gives a further change of tone to the final verse of the oracle. God's ultimate plan for Tyre—as for Ethiopia, Egypt, and Assyria (cf. 18:7; 19:18–25)—was to bring her into line with his central purpose for Israel. As in the days of Solomon, material from Israel's northern neighbor would again be used in the service of the temple (cf. 1Ki 5:1–12).

III. God and the Whole World (24:1–27:13)

A. The Judgment of the World (24:1–23)

This chapter is fundamental to the three that follow it. It speaks of a universal judgment. Not only does it make no reference to particular nations or specific historical events, it does not even restrict the judgment to the earth. This means that it sums up all the

judgments on particular nations, as predicted in chs. 13–23, and goes beyond them.

1–3 These verses are a fitting introduction to the chapter. They call for inner vision in the opening word "see" (GK 2180), so that the prophet is eager for his hearers to share what he has been given. A universal judgment on the earth is proclaimed, affecting all its inhabitants. What kind of disaster does the prophet have in mind here? "Lay waste" (GK 1327) signifies emptying. This emptying is amplified when the prophet says, "He will ruin its face." Perhaps the prophet is thinking of an earthquake, so that the inhabitants are scattered by the violence of the tremor. Or perhaps he is contemplating an extreme drought (cf. v.7), so that the earth's surface is dried up and cracked (cf. Mk 13:8).

Isaiah seems to have had the early chapters of Genesis in mind as he uttered the prophecies of this chapter. At the Tower of Babel judgment, the people were scattered (cf. Ge 11:9); and this was to happen again. God's judgment would be completely indiscriminate, for it would affect all strata of society. The religious, social, and economic relationships of human life would not restrain it. The affirmation that God has spoken underlines the certainty of the judgments predicted. They are so terrifying and so universal that some such assurance is needed.

4–6 These verses are characterized by a strong moral tone. The true and living God carries out his judgments on moral principles, not as the expression of an arbitrary will. If human kings experience his righteous wrath, it is because their actions and their way of life are contrary to his will.

Modern society is concerned about the physical pollution of our environment. Isaiah deals with the even more tragic and urgent matter of moral pollution, which is as widespread and serious today as it was in the eighth century B.C. While v.5 might seem especially appropriate to Israel, because of her possession of the Mosaic Law, the context makes it plain that the whole world is in view. The world did not possess the moral commandments of God in written form as in the Mosaic Law; but those laws nevertheless represent the will of God for humankind, and the human race is under judgment for their violation. The word "disobeyed" (GK 6296) implies at least some awareness of these moral requirements in the human conscience (cf. Ro 1:18–32; 2:11–16), thus an element of deliberateness in sin.

The judgment on original sin has already been passed, of course, and what is before us here is an eschatological judgment executed on the whole human race after centuries of disobedience to God. The earth—at the beginning placed under the dominion of the human race—has already been cursed and bears the scars of human folly. Bearing guilt means suffering its consequences and so experiencing punishment at the hand of God.

7–9 Although this judgment is universal, it appears to be carried out on earth, like many of the judgments in the book of Revelation; and there will be a remnant of humankind surviving it. The Genesis curse had affected the plant world, and thus the man whose daily work took him into the fields (Ge 3:17–19). Here the further curse of judgment affects the vines and those who use them to make drink. The prophet seems to be presenting a scene in which the vineyards are under judgment, so that little wine is available and that which is produced is bitter to the taste. The instrumental music and singing that often accompany bouts of drinking are heard no more. All the joy seems to have gone out of life, for the God of judgment is abroad.

10–13 Much has been written about the various references to "the city" in chs. 24–27. There have been many attempts to identify it with some particular city, especially Jerusalem or Babylon or an unnamed Moabite city. These attempts are probably all on the wrong track. As Clement has noted, it can best be understood as a pictorial description of organized human society, a type of "Vanity Fair." "When God asserts his will in judgment, he will bring to an end the existing human order, so that in a sense every city will be brought to chaos." These passages, therefore, help to prepare the way for the symbolic use of Babylon in the book of Revelation.

The city is in ruins; the entrances to all its standing houses are blocked, perhaps because of much rubble in the streets or because of a spirit of fear that has gripped the hearts of its remaining inhabitants. They lock themselves within their houses, hoping they will be safe from judgment (cf. 2:19, 21). Those still out in the streets are overtaken by a spirit

of gloom, symbolized by the lack of wine (cf. vv.7–9). Earlier Isaiah had spoken about the judgment of Ephraim, in league with Damascus, and likened the tiny remnant left after judgment to a few olive berries left on the remotest branches of a tree that had been beaten during harvest, to secure the maximum yield (cf. 17:6). Isaiah uses the same image here, but now in relation to the whole world.

14–16a Like Revelation, chs. 24–27 have the declarations of coming judgment interspersed with songs of thanksgiving. There has been a great judgment, but God has not made a full end to the earth's population. Those who remain lift up their voices in grateful praise to him. But who are they? Jews? Gentiles? or both? The book of Isaiah provides examples both of Jews (12:3–6) and of Gentiles (42:10–13) giving praise to God from the ends of the earth. What favors Gentiles is the reference to "the islands of the sea," for these are not normally associated with Jews. In fact, later in the book the phrase often refers to Gentiles considered collectively (cf. 41:5; 42:4, 10; et al.). That the Lord is described as "the God of Israel" must be regarded as neutral or perhaps even as slightly in favor of a reference to the Gentiles.

What begins as a purely factual statement becomes an exhortation before emerging again as an affirmation, implying that the exhortation has been heeded. The prophet heard the song first of all in the west. He called on those in the east to blend their voices also in harmony of praise to the Lord. As a result, the praises of the God of Israel ascend on all sides.

16b–20 The welcome interlude of praise is over. A balanced picture of the future in the Bible contains notes of judgment and salvation. The solemn fact, however, is that more space is given in Scripture to future judgment than to future salvation.

In face of the threats in v.17, the prophet lifts his voice in great sadness. Perhaps he saw his present attitude of sorrow as continuous with the future song of praise to be sung at the ends of the earth, because both were motivated by a desire for the glory of the Lord. To express one's gratitude to God for his grace and to reveal a sorrowful concern about the treacherous acts of humankind is to manifest the character of a godly person.

In Isaiah's day the international scene was dominated by the Assyrians. We think of international law as a comparatively modern phenomenon, but there were conventions and treaties in the ancient Near East. Aggression was never welcome; but when it was married to treachery, it was to be doubly feared. The prophet felt a deep horror as he thought about this, and he identified with his people's fear.

If vv.17–18 describe the effects of Assyrian aggression on the nations, there is a thematic unity to the present and the future, for the prophet may well be saying that the present Assyrian scourge is to be replaced ultimately by an even greater and more widespread judgment from God. God is the divine Hunter who pursues his guilty prey inexorably to a kill. There is no escape from the judgment of God (cf. Heb 2:1–3).

The language of the hunt is replaced by that of a flood, with allusion to the judgment of the Flood (cf. Ge 7:11). Isaiah does not seem to be thinking of an actual worldwide flood here, for God had promised that such a flood would never happen again (Ge 9:11–17). But the language of the Flood was appropriate to represent pictorially other great acts of judgment.

The whole earthly order is proved to be unstable (v.19), just as if some colossal earthquake had taken hold of it. Evidently all that can be shaken is being shaken. The drunken man and the swaying hut (v.20) convey an impression of total instability. Earlier the prophet had used the image of a hut (1:2, 8) to describe the divinely ordained effects of rebellion against God.

21–23 The vision of judgment that has already included the whole earth becomes yet wider, for it is seen to encompass "the powers in the heavens" as well as "the kings on the earth." The term "powers" (GK 7372) is sometimes used of the heavenly bodies (34:4; 40:26; 45:12) and sometimes of the angelic armies (1Ki 22:19; 2Ch 18:18). Since the prophet is speaking about punishment—despite the reference to other heavenly bodies in v.23—we take "powers" to apply to fallen angels (cf. Eph 6:12). The two sets of powers—in heaven and on earth—are at one in the fact of their rebellion but also in the possession of authority. Rebellion by a subordinate authority is serious, for such a being may well drag others down with him. Isaiah 14 pictures the great king of Babylon descending to Sheol. Here it seems that both the heavenly and the earthly rebels are confined in some kind of prison (cf. 2Pe 2:4; Jude 6; Rev 20:1–3).

Some suggest that "after many days" (v.22) refers to the Millennium, which harmonizes with a premillennial interpretation of Revelation, in which the spiritual powers of evil are bound in prison during the reign of Christ on earth, after which they—along with the unsaved dead—suffer eternal punishment in the lake of fire. "After many days" suggests that the imprisonment referred to in v.22 is an anticipation of God's final punishment.

The sun and the moon were created by God "to govern" (GK 4939) the day and the night (Ge 1:16–17). This expression, with its implication of authority, suggests that the term "host" can apply to both heavenly bodies and angelic beings (see comment on v.21) because there is in fact a relationship between them, with parts of the visible universe representing the spheres of authority of unseen heavenly beings. Whether or not this is true, the prophet pictures the two great heavenly bodies hiding their lights in shame when the Lord exercises direct rule in Jerusalem. All other glory is simply a reflection of his glory, and one day it will be seen that it can be no rival to him (cf. Rev 21:23).

The language of locality in v.23 may be literal or symbolic, in the latter case forming a link with the New Jerusalem of Revelation. The vision of Revelation also shows twenty-four elders, probably representing the redeemed under the old and new covenants, before the throne of God (Rev 4:4).

B. Psalms and Predictions of Judgment and Salvation (25:1–12)

The typical OT prophet is characteristically thought of as being a descending rather than an ascending mediator; that is, he functions for God toward humanity rather than for the human race toward God. This is, of course, only broadly true, for the prophet Amos prayed for the people to whom his stern messages of judgment were addressed (Am 7:2, 5), and Micah was virtually uttering the praises of the God of mercy in the last three verses of his book. Yet none of the prophets includes so much praise among their oracles as did Isaiah. He was a psalmist as well as a prophet.

1–5 Isaiah's call came to him in the temple (ch. 6), and he must often have joined the worshipers in songs of praise. The language of Psalms was in his heart. The prophet's song of praise is so worded that it may apply almost equally well to his own day or to the eschatological future he has portrayed so vividly in the previous chapter. There is a fitness about this, for God's activities at the End are all of a piece with what he does throughout history; and they provide a climax to the story of his dealings with humankind. What had been done was yet to be done.

The prophet displays a sense of personal relationship with God that is reminiscent of the psalmists of Israel. The focus of his praise is not simply the acts of God but his faithfulness. Each act of God reveals his attributes and makes us aware of what he is in his perfect character. The word translated "marvelous" occurs in one of the names of the messianic Child in 9:6. In the present context Isaiah is giving praise to God after describing his coming judgment on all the earth. The maleficent schemes and actions of people can never overturn God's own sovereign purpose, eternal in conception, declared in his Word, and executed in due time.

In our comment at 24:10–13, we accepted the view that references to a city of destruction in chs. 24–27 do not have any particular city in view but are general designations of society organized apart from any reference to God. Each specific city is a manifestation in a particular place and time of the general city-spirit, the determination that life is organized for human ends and not for the purposes of God. Such cities have often been brought down, and many will suffer such an overthrow in the future (cf. 40:23–24). The logical word "therefore" in v.3 should be especially noted. God's judgment of these cities leads the strong and ruthless nations to honor and revere the Lord.

The Psalms often extol the God of Israel as the Refuge and Shelter of his people. Verse 4 uses three different words, the first of them—"refuge"—repeated, to stress the same thought. The "poor" and "needy" stand in strong contrast to the "strong" and "ruthless nations" of v.3. Judah had faced the current representative of the spirit of ruthless militarism and imperial aggrandizement. She was, of course, utterly powerless, but she had found that her God had placed his wall of protection around her (see esp. chs. 36–37). He had been her refuge ever since the Exodus from Egypt (Dt 33:27). Contrasting weather conditions provide further illustrations of God's protecting care.

Isaiah has a most sensitive awareness of the power of words and the various ways one word may be used to convey somewhat different ideas. He moves easily here from the figure of the shady place to that of the shadow cast by a cloud, both giving protection from the fierce summer heat, yet in different ways. The raucous battle cries of the foreign armies become a triumph song when God intervenes on behalf of his people, and all is changed.

6–8 There is a close connection between v.6 and 24:23. We must not forget that chs. 24–27 constitute a special section within the book and that all the diverse parts of it are bound together into one. As the Lord's eschatological purposes unfold, he will reign in glory on Mount Zion. The prophet has already pictured the Gentile nations coming up to that mountain for worship (2:1–4); v.6 gives us a view of the great feast God will prepare for them.

Verse 7 may refer to the blindness of the nations, which in the past caused them to worship false gods. The theme of light from God is important in Isaiah, and in ch. 60 the prophet pictures the shining of a great light over God's people and all the nations moving out of the darkness that covers them and into that light. On the other hand, the prophet may have mourning veils or even a shroud of death in his mind. If this is so, then vv.7–8 are concerned with God's victory over death.

Paul quotes v.8a at 1Co 15:54 in application to the doctrine of resurrection. If God is going to deal finally with death and so with the tears occasioned by it, and if vv.6–8 are intended to continue and develop the thought that ch. 24 closes with, this raises an important issue of prophetic interpretation. The banishment of death belongs to the final stage of God's great plan and is associated with the descent from heaven of the New Jerusalem (Rev 21:1–4). This suggests that

Mount Zion and Jerusalem in 24:23 are not geographical terms but symbols for the ultimate society. This raises, therefore, the question of the relationship between the Millennium and the final state. It is most unlikely, of course—especially if v.7 is understood as a reference to the removal of spiritual blindness—that vv.6–7 (as well as 24:23) refer to the Millennium but that the prophecy moves on to the final state in v.8.

The disgrace of God's people can be best understood in the light of the later prophecy given in Eze 5:13–17. It lies in the fact that those who are destined by him for salvation must suffer judgment at his hands because of their sins. This too will pass away when that Day comes. God now stresses that these are his own promises, and so they cannot fail.

9 Once more we hear a song of praise to the Lord (cf. 24:14–16; 25:1–5). It wonderfully expresses the joy in God that comes when patient trust finds its reward in a consummated salvation. Its ideas and language are thoroughly characteristic of this prophet.

10–12 The destinies of Jerusalem and of Moab are here contrasted. The physical proximity of Mount Zion and the mountains of Moab should not be forgotten. The Moabite plateau can be clearly seen from Jerusalem, and this might even be included in the prophet's vision of this mountain exalted above all the surrounding hills (2:1–4). Moab, so easily visible, may therefore represent the surrounding pagan nations. If the purposes of the Lord are to triumph, so that all the nations will find their reconciliation with him and with one another at Mount Zion, it follows that their own pagan and aggressive purposes must be thwarted.

In a powerful anthropomorphic figure, the prophet pictures the Lord's hand resting in blessing on Mount Zion and his feet trampling on Moab in judgment (cf. 40:11; 63:3). The following similes are intentionally unpleasant and probably suggest that sin in its vileness reaps a harvest of judgment that is appropriate to it.

The pride of Moab is symbolized by the high fortified walls that surrounded its cities, making the people think them impregnable. The fall of the cities despite their protective battlement is just another reminder of the physical symbols of pride that are crowded together in 2:1–18. It is also an example of the general judgment threatened in v.2 on strong fortified towns.

C. Praise, Prayer, and Prophecy (26:1–21)

The movement of thought is beautiful. The prophet begins by uttering a song of praise, sung by Judah of the future. Its theme is the trustworthiness of God who protects the city of his oppressed people and destroys that of their oppressors (vv.1–6). Next Isaiah meditates on the ways of the righteous and of the wicked (vv.7–11). The Lord has blessed his people, despite their former acknowledgment of the lordship of other deities (vv.12–15). The people had been through a lot but accomplished little blessing for the world, and they confess this (vv.16–18). The God of grace then promises them a joyful resurrection to new life (v.19) after the revelation of his wrath against sin (vv.20–21).

1–6 The way chs. 24–27 are punctuated with songs of praise affects this whole section of the prophecy, for even the threats of judgment are seen in the perspective of thanksgiving that God is bringing his own purposes to fruition and that human arrogance and tyranny will not prevail in the end. The theme of the two cities links this passage with chs. 24 and 25. God here gives strength to the city by making salvation its walls and ramparts.

Every year large numbers of people from all parts of the land made pilgrimages to Jerusalem (cf. Dt 16) to take part in the great feasts. Many of the Psalms (e.g., Pss 120–34) were connected with these pilgrimages (cf. Ac 2:5–11). Isaiah may have had some such pilgrimage in mind here, or he may have had permanent settlement in view, the city being part physical expression and part symbol for the whole people of God, "the nation that keeps faith" (v.2). The latter seems more likely.

This righteous nation is made up of individuals who trust in the Lord, for the new covenant purpose of God provides for a gracious personal knowledge of him for every person included within that covenant (Jer 31:31–34). The gates of the city admit the returning members of the dispersed nation, and its walls symbolize divine protection; the Lord is himself the protecting Rock in whom believers trust. Just as there is a place of peace within the city for those who dwell in it with

God (cf. Ps 46), so the Lord gives "peace" to those who repose confidence in him.

Verses 5–6 take up again the theme of God's judgment on the worldly city. Once again the language of physical elevation is used to suggest pride (cf. 2:12–18). So often an ancient city was built on raised ground so as to gain the maximum military advantage from its physical elevation, which then became the basis for walls, battlements, and other means of defense. This stress on the vertical dimension became part of the typical image of the city for most people. When God judges the pride of the city, he lays it low. Here presumably the people of God who have suffered oppression from it tread it under foot. This suggests that they share in his victory (cf. Ps 110:2–3; 2Co 2:14).

7–11 The prophet describes the way of the righteous and contrasts this with the outlook of the wicked in a fashion reminiscent of Ps 1. The God of the righteous is himself righteous, and he is described here as "upright" (GK 3838)—a term used of God's word (Ps 33:4), his judgments (Ps 119:137), and his ways (Dt 32:4). Physical uprightness is often the linguistic basis for the moral concept of righteousness. The words also suggest appropriateness of destiny. Those who are straight or "on the level" have their path smoothed by the God who is upright.

"Laws" (GK 5477) is a better translation than "judgments" in v.8 (see NIV note), as this fits the context much better. Just as the NT believer looks forward "to a new heaven and a new earth, the home of righteousness" (2Pe 3:13), so the OT saint, represented here by Isaiah, longed for the coming of a day when God's name would be honored fittingly. The words "we wait for you" show Isaiah's conviction that such a day would come—and come by the activity of God himself. This passionate longing is not just a deep desire for a better order, a kind of moral Utopia. The whole expectation is personal; the prophet longs for God, day and night.

Sin blinds the mind of sinners so that they see nothing from a divine perspective, least of all their own sin. It is a function of judgment to teach humans the seriousness of sin and to show them that God cares deeply about righteousness (cf. Ac 5:1–14). In this respect, the prophet assures us, judgment is more effective than grace. Isaiah stresses that the wicked may receive undeservedly many blessings from the hand of God and yet show no regard for the righteousness that so greatly concerns him. Not only so, but even where general moral conditions are favorable to righteousness (i.e., in a time of spiritual revival), the wicked are determined to go their own way. Even now, God's hand is uplifted, ready to strike them in judgment; but they are totally unaware of it. The prophet identifies himself completely with the judgment of God on the wicked (cf. Rev 19:1–5). We must compassionately seek to bring the gospel to others, but on the day of judgment we must accept his every verdict; for as the Judge of all the earth, he does only what is right.

12–15 In v.11 Isaiah spoke about God's zeal for his people. It is as if Isaiah became suddenly aware of the contrast between God's dealing with Israel and with the nations and is moved to make this confession of the great unworthiness of those who have received such rich blessings from God. Verse 12 was probably written after the divine protection of Jerusalem in 701 B.C., expressing a profound truth that is destructive of spiritual pride.

The name "LORD" (GK 3378) is the distinctive name of the God of Israel by which he is set apart from every false god. Obviously this does not suggest that the "other lords [GK 123]" had real existence as deities but simply that they were believed to have and that their rule was sinfully acknowledged by the people in past times. It is possible to regard these "other lords" as the various nations that had exercised sovereignty over God's people, and certainly v.14 must refer to human beings. Perhaps it is best to think in terms of both false deities and the foreign rulers who regarded themselves as their representatives, the first being emphasized in v.13 and the second in v.14.

The rise and fall of nations and of great empires is a fact of history, and Isaiah sees it to be due to the activity of God in the story of humankind (cf. 40:23–24). Isaiah has already vividly pictured the descent of the king of Babylon into the world of departed spirits in 14:12–21, and now he makes it clear that this is the way all Israel's past oppressors have gone.

In 54:1–3 Isaiah foretells the expansion of the nation (cf. 9:3). We should, therefore, treat v.15 as predictive, expressing the prophet's certainty that what God has promised is as sure as if it has taken place already. Isaiah 9:7 contains the intriguing promise "of the *increase* of his government and peace there will be no end" (emphasis mine). All this will bring glory to God because it is his act, not theirs (cf. v.12), and because it will result in the showing forth of his glory in areas where paganism formerly held sway.

16–18 The prophet looks into the future as if it has all ready occurred. The people would come to the Lord in distress but with great earnestness. That "they could barely whisper a prayer" reminds us that fervor and noise are not necessarily spiritual companions. The phrase "when you discipline them" suggests that the prayer was motivated not only by distress because of foreign oppression but also by sorrow for sin.

The experience of childbirth forms the basis for a forceful analogy. The nation tried to achieve her own salvation, when, in fact, God alone could bring his own purposes for her to birth. Israel was like a woman in labor because of the pains she had suffered, yet unlike her in not giving birth to a child. All the suffering had been in vain. It was, in fact, to be only through the Servant of the Lord (52:13–53:12), not through Israel's suffering without him, that salvation would be brought to the earth. Birth into God's kingdom for the nations (Ps 87:4–7) is God's work alone—through his Messiah-Servant—and beyond the capacity of Israel herself. Only through him who is the true seed of Abraham (Gal 3:16, 28–29) can the nations become his children and so inherit the promise made to him (Ge 12:1–3; et al.).

19 This verse presents a glorious contrast for Israel not only with the dead and impotent tyrants who have lorded over her in the past (v.14) but with the strenuous and yet ineffective endeavors of Israel herself to bring forth spiritual fruit (vv.17–18). Certainly there are metaphors here, for the prophet calls the dead to awake and asserts that the earth will give birth to her dead. The metaphorical, however, must always rest on the literal; and it is with the literal that this verse commences: "But your dead will live; their bodies will rise." This verse itself prepares the way for Da 12:2, which fills out more fully the destinies of the righteous and the wicked beyond death and subsequent resurrection.

20–21 A time will come when God's wrath will have passed by. This "wrath" may be his wrath with Israel herself, and during the Exile the people are to encourage themselves with the assurance that this judgment on them will come to an end in God's good time. On the other hand, the wrath may be that expressed in God's punishment of the nations, which v.21 relates to. The latter is more likely because there is an allusion to the Passover in v.20. Just as the people of Israel found refuge within the blood-sprinkled doors of their homes (Ex 12), until the wrath of God against Egypt spent itself, so Israel is told to hide for a while, perhaps in Babylonian exile. Shutting the doors suggests safety and separation from the surrounding pagans, who were under judgment. Israel in exile was called to be a holy people.

While the people are hidden away in their places, God comes forth from his place for a punitive purpose. Verse 21 is a reminder of the general context and of the disclosure of the cosmic judgment given in ch. 24. The earth is not only the burial place of many who will desert her at the Resurrection; she has also admitted the blood and bodies of many whose deaths have been due to the sins of others, the terrible consequences of the acts of violent people. Places where great human tragedies and horrifying sins have taken place may disclose no evidence of their history to the casual passer-by, but on the day of the Lord's judgment on sin that evidence will appear to the terrified eyes of the perpetrators. Such secrets belong to time, not to eternity.

D. The Restoration of Israel (27:1–13)

The eschatological-apocalyptic section of Isa 24–27 is concerned with God's final purposes in the world. The prophecies recorded here concern the whole world, but they also relate to Israel and her place in the universal purposes of God.

1 This fascinating verse presents a graphic picture of God the great Warrior, going into battle against fearsome and monstrous enemies and utterly defeating them. The language draws on mythology; but this need cause us no serious problems. Writers frequently use illustrative material from a wide variety of sources. The use of mythology here simply shows that Isaiah and his readers knew these stories, not that they believed them.

The succession of adjectives describing the sword of the Lord stresses the fearsomeness of this weapon and so emphasizes that judgment will be completely effective. Some commentators suggest that if "his fierce, great and powerful sword" is in apposition to "his sword," then "Leviathan the coiling serpent" is in apposition to "Leviathan the gliding serpent." This would mean that the prophet had only two enemies in mind, not three. But if there are two Leviathans here, the first being perhaps a reference to the fast-flowing Tigris where the Assyrian heartland was and the second to the more sluggish and therefore more twisting Euphrates, the great river of the Babylonians, then the monster of the sea becomes Egypt, to complete the trio of Israel's great oppressors. But we can hold the latter interpretation and still think of the two phrases as being in apposition, so that the two Mesopotamian enemies are thought of as different manifestations of the same evil power centered in the Tigris-Euphrates basin.

2–6 One of the most memorable passages in Isaiah occurs in 5:1–7. Isaiah's parable of the vineyard there demonstrates that beauty of language and solemnity of theme are not inconsistent with each other. Moreover, his use there of the vineyard for Israel established this word as a symbol, used also here.

The phrase "in that day" (repeated from v.1) suggests that both the judgment on the enemies of God's people and Israel's own blessing belong to the same general eschatological era. In ch. 5, the vineyard is barren, unproductive, and threatened with judgment. Here, however, it is fruitful. There the parable began as a happy song to lull the hearers into a complacent mood and so take them unawares with the message of judgment. Here the opening mood is similar, but this time the atmosphere is sustained throughout.

"A fruitful vineyard" is literally "a vineyard of wine." This suggests both comparison and contrast with ch. 5. In v.3 the thought of 5:2 is carried through but expressed quite differently. There is even more emphasis on the loving concern of the Lord for this vineyard, and it is made clear that never for one moment does he forget its needs or relax his vigilance, lest it should become a prey to its enemies. The constant watering reminds us of Jeremiah's repeated assertion (Jer 7:25; et al.) that the Lord repeatedly sent his servants the prophets to speak to his people.

The wonderful statement that opens v.4 can be understood only in the light of the expression "in that day." The prophet is not describing Israel that then was but the Israel that was to be, when the wrath of God was past (cf. 40:2). "Briers and thorns" (likely meant to represent internal rather than external enemies, i.e., paganizers, not pagans) appear in ch. 5 both as part of the judgment of God on the vineyard and as the final evidence of its lack of real fruit. Here God pledges himself to destroy them should any such appear again to threaten his vineyard. Indeed, he appears eager to do this, perhaps as evidence of his covenant faithfulness to his people and his determination to do them good in every possible way.

Verse 5 is a neglected OT promise of forgiveness to the penitent. In v.4 the God of battles is marching against the briers and thorns with a flaming torch in his hand, about to set fire to this rank undergrowth. But before doing so, he proclaims the alternative of peace. His action against the briers and thorns is for the protection of his people, but in v.5 the enemies themselves are offered refuge (cf. 25:4), if they will accept his terms of peace.

Verse 6 brings the parable to a beautiful climax. The prophet does not speak of Judah but of Israel, for he has the whole people in view, represented now by a plant rather than a vineyard. The picture is at first perfectly normal. The root, the bud, and the blossom depict strong and healthy growth, everything happening in its season. The unexpected comes at the end. This plant will become extraordinarily extensive (cf. 16:8), filling the whole world with its fruit. Perhaps this is an allusion to the fruitfulness and extensive influence of Joseph promised in Ge 49:22. We can certainly see a spiritual fulfillment of this in the progress of the gospel throughout the world, for the Messiah is himself the true Vine (Jn 15:1–8) and his disciples the fruit-bearing branches. In this way God's purpose for Israel finds its expression in those who are joined by faith to him.

7–11 The word "Jacob" is used both within this immediate passage (v.9) and in its context (v.6), which suggests that Israel (the northern kingdom) rather than Judah is in mind. The fortified city could be Samaria, and the exile of v.8 would then follow its fall. A reference to Judah is not, of course, impossible. In this case the city would be Jerusalem and the exile in Babylon.

A third possibility takes into account that many of the references to cities in chs. 24–27 are general. The reference to Israel (i.e., Jacob) may be taken as the designation, not of Israel apart from Judah (the northern kingdom), but of Israel including Judah. The whole people and their judgment are in view. The fortified city stands for each stronghold overcome by the Mesopotamian enemies, and the Exile is the common experience of the whole people. A section of the book whose general subject is so comprehensive might be expected to treat the chosen nation as a whole in its concluding chapter. This is the standpoint from which we will view these verses.

The subject of v.7 is clearly the Lord. The questions are like those of the imaginary Jewish objector in Ro 3:1–8. There is no doubt that the new parable of the vineyard in vv.2–6 does not tell the whole story of Israel's relationship with God; for he has taken punitive action against his own people, not only against their adversaries. Despite the undoubted fact that God had often to beat his people very severely (e.g., 1:4–9), the implied answer to the question is no. God does make a distinction between his own people and their oppressors. All the chastisement is for a good end, to bring them to repentance.

Characteristically, Isaiah refers to judgment as a fierce wind (cf. 4:4; 41:16). The scorching east wind, driving the hot desert sand before it, was much dreaded (Ge 41:6; Job 27:21–22; Jer 18:17; et al.). Both the Assyrian and the Babylonian enemies came from the east and moved captives from Israel and Judah into exile. But exile, unlike destruction, is punishment tempered by mercy; for there is still life and therefore still hope.

It may seem strange that the language of atonement is used in v.9 in application to the penitence induced by exile rather than in reference to sacrifice. Through exile the nation would come to a penitent awareness of its guilt. The actual objective basis of its reconciliation with God is not so much in view as the practical cause of that reconciliation. The people were removed so that their sins might be removed. This becomes clear when we read the whole of v.9, for it is about a new attitude to the will of God, the product of a penitent heart. Isaiah is in line here with Jer 31:31–34 and Eze 36:24–31.

Israel's penitence would show itself especially in the destruction of pagan altars and symbols (cf. Ex 34:13; Dt 12:2–3). After God had purified Israel through banishment from the land and the experience of exile, she would return much chastened to carry out this commandment that she failed to do thoroughly enough at the beginning of her sojourn in the land.

In northern Israel, Samaria and other cities had been devastated by the Assyrians, who had also desolated many cities of Judah (1:7). Jerusalem too would eventually go the same way, through the Babylonians. Isaiah often represents the effects of judgment through war as the virtual reversal of civilization (e.g., 3:4–6; 5:17; 7:23–25). This language is quite literal. When a city is reduced to rubble, the domestic animals normally pastured outside the city are free to cross the broken walls and roam in the city. Soon vegetation emerges through cracks in the streets and between the fallen stones. The ghost town eventually has trees growing in it, and these will feed animals with their bark and supply firewood for the women of the surrounding villages.

In some respects Isaiah stood in the wisdom as well as in the prophetic tradition. His prophecies place emphasis from time to time on the importance of wisdom and discernment and the seriousness of inner blindness. This note is struck at the very beginning of the book (cf. 1:2). It was this culpable blindness that caused Israel's exile. The statement that God does not show "compassion" or "favor" to them is not, of course, absolute. It is perhaps a partial yes answer to the questions of v.7, the main answer to which is no. When the appointed time of their judgment came, God did not show compassion; but later, of course, he would and did.

12–13 These two verses conclude the great eschatological-apocalyptic section of Isaiah, but they do not teach the same truth; they are complementary rather than repetitive. In v.12

the prophet refers to the traditional boundaries of the Promised Land. God will treat this whole large area as one huge grain field. Never throughout its history did a pure Israel exist. There were always foreign and unbelieving elements in it. God's judgment would therefore begin at the land of his own people. If his threshing-floor yields much grain, there will be chaff, too. The nation is to be purified (cf. Eze 36:24–32).

The figure of the threshing floor is replaced by that of a trumpet. Beyond the Euphrates is the land of the Assyrians, and beyond the Wadi of Egypt is Egypt itself. In 2:1–4 and in 60:1–14, Isaiah describes Jerusalem as the focal point to which penitent Gentiles would come, both to hear God's word and to worship him. But not even Israel is there yet, and the prophet declares that the traditional lands of her captivity must yield up her lost and scattered ones so that they may join the worshiping throng at Zion's temple. Like v.6, this is capable of being interpreted at different levels.

IV. God and His People (28:1–33:24)

When the book of Isaiah was divided into chapters, clearly it was noted that at several significant points in this part the Hebrew word for "woe" (GK 2098) occurred; this was adopted as the clue to the appropriate division of chs. 28–33, except for the division between chs. 31 and 32. The material in those chapters seems to belong to the period of Hezekiah's reign.

A. Woe to Samaria (28:1–29)

1–4 Isaiah here seems to have had a vision of the alleged spiritual leaders of Ephraim, the northern kingdom (cf. v.7), staggering in their inebriation and wearing some kind of floral wreath on their heads, probably tilted at a jaunty angle. This suggested to him another crowned head, that of the hill on which their capital city, Samaria, was situated. This hill stands in a commanding position at the head of a "fertile valley." Amos also castigated Samaria for its drunken decadence (Am 4:1; 6:1, 6).

The Assyrian threat appeared on the eastern horizon at a time when the northern kingdom was relatively prosperous. It might seem to have been cut off in its prime; but, as this passage shows, the telltale signs of a de-

scent into decay were already present. There may have been flowers, but they were fading.

A strategically situated city may also be exposed to the elements. A destructive wind from the east (cf. 27:8) was no stranger to Israel, though this time it was not the hot "sirocco" coming in from the desert but a strong hail and rain-bearing wind that normally came from another direction. The prophet piles up words and phrases to convey the ferocity of the storm.

The "powerful and strong" one is undefined, and the object of its attack is unexpressed; but they are obviously Assyria and Samaria respectively. The Assyrians will tramp through Samaria's streets, and Samaria itself will be trampled on by the great foreign foe. Outside the city walls, figs would be growing. Sometimes a fig ripens before the normal season. Isaiah pictures a traveler—perhaps an Assyrian soldier on his way into the city—quickly picking and eating it. So sudden would Samaria's destruction be (v.4).

5–8 The prophet, changing the word "pride" in v.1 to "glory" (in the phrase translated "glorious crown") because of the possibly unfavorable connotation of the former, asserts that this is what the Lord will be to "the remnant of his people." Their glorying had had a physical focus, but this would be replaced by a spiritual one. Perhaps he had in mind the southern kingdom—so small in comparison with the northern, but with God in her midst—or else the remnant left behind in Israel by the receding Assyrian conquerors, or perhaps both. "In that day" should perhaps be understood eschatologically, so that the prophet's thought overleaped many intervening centuries to the last days.

The drunkards of v.1 are the leaders of the people, such as priests, prophets (cf. v.7), and probably also judges. The administration of justice requires great wisdom and clearheadedness. The prophet promises that God will himself be a spirit of justice giving wisdom to the judge, and that the people's arms will have success against the foe (cf. 11:1–5). The remnant would have God as their crown when Samaria, the crown of Ephraim, had been taken by Assyria.

Isaiah then turns his attention to the leaders of Jerusalem (cf. v.14). The vivid picture of spiritual guides lacking not only supernatural insight but even common reason ("befuddled") is horrifying. The realistic de-scrip-tion of the environment bears all the marks of eyewitness reporting.

9–10 As the prophet declares the word of God in this drink-dominated setting, his hearers make their response. The drunkards feel insulted. Are they not themselves spiritual leaders, well able to teach others? What right has this man to teach them the spiritual "milk"? Isaiah's words have hardly penetrated the alcohol-impregnated atmosphere that surrounds his hearers. What they have picked up are simply a few stray syllables, some of them repeated, like the baby-talk that delights the child but insults the adult. They mouth this gibberish back at the prophet. Their judgment lies in their failure to hear the word that could have led them back to God; but there is another judgment on its way, most appropriate in its form. Their sin has turned the word of God through Isaiah into a meaningless noise that may just as well have been a foreign language.

11–13 Very well, then, the next message will come through foreigners. The Assyrian devastation of Judah (cf. 1:5–9) is surely in view. Just as the drunkards picked up a few familiar sounds but no connected meaning, so the people of Judah would detect similarities between the Akkadian of the Assyrians and their own Hebrew (both Semitic tongues), without being able to understand what was being said. In reality it was through the Assyrians' swords that God would speak his message to Israel.

More serious still was the people's failure to hear God's word offering rest to those who insisted on rejecting it. The prophet was clearly speaking of the call to faith. Their disobedient refusal of the way of faith in God was therefore a continuing condition preventing the word from getting through to them. The effects of drink may pass off, but unbelief can be a permanent barrier to God's word.

On an earlier occasion, in the days of Ahaz, God had pointed out the way of faith and had warned the people against the consequences of rejecting this. Times may have changed, but not the principles of God's dealings with his people. The call to faith then had been accompanied by a warning of the consequences of walking in another way, and those consequences were the same now.

The drunkards' fall is thought of first of all as a result of their drunken staggering, but the range of analogies is then extended to the picture of the hunter's snare.

14–15 People may have lost their capacity to hear God's word, but this does not modify its character. We are commanded to hear it simply because it is his, and we are culpable if we do not hear. Rejection of God's word and confidence in our own selves often go hand in hand. Isaiah is not really quoting the "scoffers" in v.15 but ironically combining their words with his interpretation of their consequences. There can be little doubt that Isaiah has in mind the growing link between Judah and Egypt and the attempt in this way to warn off the Assyrians.

The "overwhelming scourge" contains a mixture of figures: for how can a scourge be said to overflow? The separate elements are from 10:26 and 10:22 respectively. Perhaps the leaders of Judah had the circumstances of the original Passover in mind. They thought themselves immune, like Israel sheltered beneath sacrificial blood in Egypt (cf. 1:10–17), but there could be no such refuge in that land for them now.

The reference to lies and falsehood may be an attack on that trust in expediency rather than in principle. It seems more likely, however, that the prophet was not charging them directly with a lack of integrity but rather that his words were still ironic. The assertion that Egypt would effectively come to their aid, which they believed to be sober truth, was in fact a lie.

16–19 In 8:14 the Lord had declared that he would be both a sanctuary—and Judah's sanctuary at Jerusalem was made of stone—and a stumbling stone for the people of Israel. Faith would make the difference. Here the stone illustration is presented in an eminently positive fashion.

Without doubt this passage is of great importance in the messianic teaching of the prophecies of Isaiah (cf. Ro 9:33; 10:11; 1Pe 2:4–6). In 8:14 the prophet used the stone analogy in a significant way. The Lord himself was calling people to faith. If they responded, he would be a sanctuary, a holy place, to them. As the altar of God in the temple was treated as a place of refuge (Ex 21:14; 1Ki 1:50), so God himself would be a holy place of refuge for them (cf. Eze 11:16).

If, however, they refused belief, he would be a stone of stumbling they would fall over. The altar of stone was, of course, set within a temple of stone, so that both the promise and the threat rest on the spiritualizing of the stone.

The stone-built temple is once again a picture of the God the people are to trust in. Instead of reapplying the stone illustration in a threat (but see v.13b), Isaiah declares God's condemnation of the poor Egyptian makeshift that the unbelieving people had constructed as a substitute for faith in God. A comparison of the language of 8:14 and the present passage shows us that there the sanctuary and stone were God himself whereas here the stone is laid by God. If this passage is a development of the former, then who in Isaiah's prophecies is both God and distinct from him? The clear answer is "the Messiah" (cf. 7:14; 9:6).

If then the stone is the Messiah, what messianic qualities or functions emerge from the prophet's words? Zion was itself, of course, the place of the temple and also the place where the leaders of the people lived. The stone is first of all a "tested" (GK 1046) stone. As a foundation stone it has been tested for strength and shape. However, it may be taken as a "testing" or capstone, shaped by the master mason for placing at the end of the whole building process, so forming a test of trueness of line for the whole edifice (cf. Ps 118:22; Mk 12:10). The Messiah comes as the consummation of the divine building project (Mk 12:6); and, although rejected by the religious leaders of his day—the spiritual counterparts of the unbelieving leaders here—he was God's proof of the soundness of the whole structure of messianic promise. If the prophecy is truly messianic, then it is eschatological; and if eschatological, then the idea of a capstone is most apt.

The testing stone is also "a precious cornerstone for a sure foundation." This clearly points to the stone that is placed on the living rock and that is of special importance also because it is at the junction of two walls. He is "precious" (GK 3701) because of his superlative value in the divine plan. The ultimate spiritual sanctuary will find its foundation in him. In the NT God's great "building" is the church, built on Christ as confessed and proclaimed by his people (Mt 16:13–19). Here too there is a call for faith.

In architecture the same stone cannot fulfill both purposes, i.e., both capstone and

The cornerstone was always the most important stone in a building or wall. The picture on the left shows part of the wall of old Jerusalem, with the cornerstone to the right. The picture above gives a closeup of that massive cornerstone. It is not known why there are holes in this stone; perhaps it was for drainage.

foundation stone; but God gives one great answer to the totality of human need: Christ.

The architectural language continues into v.17. Divine justice and righteousness may govern the entire building operation, from foundation to capstone, so that the entire edifice of promise and fulfillment is just and true. On the other hand, it may show up as unrighteous and false the flimsy human structures represented by the refuge or hiding place that the storms of God's judgment will demolish. A similar contrast between two buildings, where relationship to Christ and his teaching is the test of true construction, is found in Lk 6:46–49.

Verse 18 takes up language from earlier verses, chiefly from v.15, but also from v.2. Water will overflow the hiding place and carry the people away. The judgment will not pass quickly. Verse 19 clearly suggests that wave after wave of the enemy will come into Judah, so that the people's hearts will be dominated by fear throughout the whole period. Through hordes of cruel Assyrian warriors, then, God would speak his message of judgment to his people, who would not hear the prophet's message.

20–22 God's people had made their bed; now they must lie on it, and they would discover its inadequacy to provide true rest. Earlier the prophet used historical allusion for the comfort of his hearers (cf. 9:6; 10:26). Now such allusions become the vehicle of threats rather than promises. Earlier, at Mount Perazim and in the Valley of Gibeon, God came to his people's aid against their enemies (Jos 10:1–10; 2Sa 5:17–25). God's anger against the Philistines, dammed up so long by his people's sin, broke forth and overwhelmed them through David; now that anger, held back again through many a year of grace, would finally burst in a "strange work" of judgment against his own people.

Isaiah's reference to mocking should be compared with v.14. Those destined for judgment are bound with chains, suggesting that there will be no escape from that destiny. Isaiah's auditory experience of God makes him aware of a terrible judgment to come, in which the whole land will be involved. The devastating Assyrian invasions, culminating in the terrible siege and overthrow of Jerusalem by the Babylonians at a later period, progressively fulfilled this prophecy in line with the terms of v.19.

23–29 Isaiah knew how obtuse and spiritually hard of hearing his listeners were and so calls on them to pay close attention. Nature, as God has created it, contains so many illustrations of spiritual truth that the sensitive and godly observer is forced to conclude that there is divine design in this.

Agriculture requires the farmer to change his activity from time to time. Plowing is needed, but it is not a year-round activity. So God's purposes require him to act differently at different seasons, perhaps sparing Jerusalem in 701 B.C. and destroying it in 586 B.C. Then, too, a farmer does not normally sow all his fields with only one plant variety. In a mixed farming economy, space is found for a variety of crops. Once again, the variety of God's ways with people is being underlined. The farmer learns such things from God, by a study perhaps of nature. Why then is humankind so reluctant to learn from God in spiritual things?

Verses 27–29 take the illustration further. When it comes to harvest time, threshing takes different forms, each dictated by the type of crop harvested. More than this, threshing time comes to an end, for the ultimate aim of all this activity is to produce edible food. Plowing, sowing, threshing, and grinding are all means to this end. So God has his purposes in history, and through a sequence of events he brings them to pass. God's power ("the LORD Almighty") and wisdom, united in his nature, bring forth a pattern of events in the story of the human race. The agricultural processes here suggest pain, implying that it is possible to find oneself on the wrong side of God's purposes in history and so to experience his judgment.

B. Woe to Ariel (29:1–24)

This chapter presents the second of the "woe" oracles in this section of Isaiah's prophecies (see introduction to chs. 28–35). Despite the double use of the word in vv.1 and 15, the atmosphere—though solemn—is not one of unrelieved gloom. Not only is judgment promised for Jerusalem but also salvation.

1–4 What does the reiterated word "Ariel" (GK 790) mean? The connection of the city with David (v.1) and the reference to Mount

Zion in v.8 established its identification with Jerusalem. The NIV note ("The Hebrew for *altar hearth* sounds like the Hebrew for *Ariel*") does not make it clear that the word translated "altar hearth" (GK 789) in v.2 is exactly the same word "Ariel" and not simply like it in sound. In other words, "Ariel" is not simply a name but actually means something, "altar hearth." That name possesses a certain naturalness, derived from the fact that Jerusalem was a place of sacrifice, with an altar hearth in the temple where sacrifices were always burning.

David besieged Jerusalem when it was a Jebusite stronghold. When he took it, it became his capital city. Through many a difficult century in its history, it had never been taken again. The true poignancy of the "woe" here lies in the fact that the God who had enabled David to take it would now besiege this city himself, through its enemies, and cause its destruction by fire just as if the whole city had become an extension of the altar hearth within its temple.

The popular religion in the eighth century B.C. gave sacrifice too great a place in the relationship between God and his people, so that it was conceived to be almost purely external and ritualistic (cf. 1:10–17; 29:13). The point of v.1b is that it was at the festivals of the religious calendar that the Jerusalem altar was busiest. The people became more and more confirmed in their false assurance that all was well between themselves and God. What a shock awaited them! Verse 3—with its three-fold statement that God would become their enemy—is more forceful.

The penitence of spirit that was so conspicuously absent from the sacrifices that the people were making would at last come about through divine chastisement. Instead of pompous boasting (cf. 28:15), their speech would come as a mere ghostlike whisper from the ground where they lay prostrate.

5–8 The whole mood of the oracle changes as suddenly and dramatically as the events it depicts. God would judge his people by sending their enemies against their capital city, but he did not intend that city to be taken. The ominous towers and siege works are replaced by fine dust and blown chaff. Those sent in judgment would themselves experience it (cf. 10:5–19). Appearing to be so formidable, they would be cut down to size.

The "many enemies" are further described as "the hordes of all the nations." Moreover, the coming of the Lord Almighty is described as an awe-inspiring intervention. The language (esp. v.6), so reminiscent of Ex 19, suggests that the God of judgment is also the God of the law, his judgments expressing his concern for righteousness.

Isaiah's illustrations are appropriate and true to the common experience of humanity. We all know something of the dream that seems as vivid and compelling as reality itself. The city of Jerusalem, which seemed so real a prize to its attackers, would suddenly be seen to belong to the dream world of military ambition. The phrase "Mount Zion" itself has overtones of stability and divine protection (cf. Ps 48).

9–12 The inaugural vision of Isaiah's prophetic ministry made him aware that as he declared the word of God, many of his hearers would simply shut their eyes to the truth (cf. 6:9–10). The spiritual blindness of the drunken religious leaders was emphasized in ch. 28. The professional prophets, whether literally drunk or not, are pictured here as stumbling unsteadily through life, unable even to plot their own course, let alone point the way to others. Blindness, drunkenness, and sleep build a picture of total inadequacy in the realm of spiritual leadership.

The whole point of vv.11–12 is that Isaiah's own God-given vision was a closed book to the people of Jerusalem. To those who could read—perhaps the professional prophets—the vision contained mysteries to which their eyes were closed. Those who could not read—perhaps the ordinary inhabitants of Jerusalem—were removed further still from understanding. The seeming advantage of the professional prophets did not really place them ahead of the common people, for neither understood the vision.

13–16 Spiritual blindness (vv.9–12) is an appropriate partner of externalism and traditionalism. Here the spiritual condition is diagnosed and found to be malign indeed. Wrong teaching was based on mishandling God's true revelation, the sacrificial regulations, and the Mosaic Law as a whole respectively (cf. Mt 15:9). "Rules taught by men" applies not to the Levitical teaching itself but to the way it was applied by the priests. Human nature does not change but finds different expressions of its fundamental rebellion against God. So often the prophet says in effect that the God of Israel, who had shown himself to his people in one of his great attributes for their blessing, would demonstrate that same quality in an act of judgment (10:17; 28:20–22). He is "wonderful" and had done wonderful things for his people (Ex 15:11; Ps 77:2, 15), but his power to astound them would be turned against them. The prophet seems still to have in mind the judgments God had decreed against his people in vv.1–3. Isaiah shows great interest in the distinction between worldly and godly wisdom (e.g., 5:21; 11:2; 26:7–10).

Negotiations with Egypt to form an anti-Assyrian alliance were probably carried on in secret. If so, then Isaiah was implying that the negotiators thought their actions were so clandestine that even the Lord himself was denied access to them. When human minds are not controlled by the revelation of God, their thoughts of him easily become unworthy of who he really is. The prophet suggests that such people have a completely illogical view of God. Without doubt total depravity so affects the mind that people can no longer think God's thoughts after him in any adequate way.

Isaiah anticipates Jeremiah in his use of the illustration of the potter and the clay (cf. 45:9; 64:8; Jer 18:1–6; cf. also Ro 9:19–21). Each writer made somewhat different points; yet each argued for the sovereignty of God from this analogy.

17–21 Significantly, even when the human mind retreats from logic in its conception of God, God still addresses that mind. "In a very short time, will not Lebanon be turned into a fertile field and the fertile field seem like a forest?" appears to be a promise of blessing for the land. This transformation of the physical world becomes the introduction to the eschatological picture presented in the remainder of the chapter. The former spiritual insensitivity of the people will be a thing of the past (cf. 35:5–6).

Isaiah shows a concern for the godly poor (cf. 3:14; 11:4; 25:4). That the reference to them in v.19 is followed by a promise that those who "have an eye for evil" (cf. Pr 1:11–14; 12:6) will be cut down certainly suggests that it is the restoration of justice to the oppressed in the messianic kingdom that is in view. For the "mockers" (GK 4370), see 28:14, where the same Hebrew word is translated "scoffers."

The general picture of malignity rampant in v.20 becomes more specific in v.21, where the reader is transported to the court of law. Each of the three lines relates to a verbal sin, the clever and specious use of words that perverts justice. The prophets stressed the Lord's hatred of oppression furthered by the manipulation of the courts of justice (see 10:1–4).

22–24 Joshua 24:14 links the region "beyond the River" with Egypt as places where the people had served other gods. The language of redemption was regularly applied to the deliverance from Egypt, and there is no good reason why it cannot be applied to the exit of Abraham from Ur at the call of God. There may not have been the same human bondage, but in both cases they were under a regime acknowledging other gods. The passage makes much of the people's relationship to their ancestor Jacob, and the mention of Abraham further reinforces this emphasis on the past.

In v.23, the prophet has both the patriarch Jacob and his descendants in mind. There is such a solidarity between a people and their ancestor that they can be closely identified in this way. The shame of Jacob here certainly seems to be the dispersion of many of the people of Israel from their land because of their sin (see Dt 28:36–37, 63–64). God will bring his scattered children back to the land.

Isaiah's characteristic title for God is "the Holy One of Israel [Jacob]." This holiness sets him apart from all other beings, not least the false gods worshiped in the great civilizations of the Fertile Crescent. Thus there is probably a subtle connection between the reference to the redemption of Abraham (from idolatrous Ur and Haran) and the assertion that when scattered Israel will be brought back from the pagan lands of their dispersion they will keep God's name holy.

The emphasis on God's holiness is strong. It is as if this is his final vindication of his great name at the climax of Israel's history, inspiring awe and wondering gratitude in his people. It is their deep awareness of God's goodness to them as a nation that will produce a penitent and receptive spirit in those formerly wayward and complaining. God's own light will have dispersed the spiritual darkness that the prophet was so conscious of in the people he ministered to (cf. vv.9–16).

C. Woe to the Rebellious Children (30:1–33)

This chapter, like the two that precede it, commences with the word "woe," and, also like them, contains promises as well as threats. The people of Jerusalem will have judgments to face, but these will not annul the ultimate purpose of their God to bless them with his salvation.

1 The occasion is still the proposal to enter into alliance with Egypt as a defense against Assyria, whose dark shadow looms menacingly on the eastern horizon. The rebellion against Assyria was at the same time a revolt against God. The accumulation of sin by the people is probably an allusion to the alliance with Assyria in the days of Ahaz, a device to secure aid against Israel and Syria, which is the background to the oracles in chs. 7–9. The political alignment was now different but expressed the same sin—refusal to trust in the Lord and him alone.

2–5 The Ethiopian rulers of Egypt had sent ambassadors to the land of Judah either in 712 or 705 B.C. (see comments on 18:1–7). Now the ambassage moved in the opposite direction, perhaps during the period of Hezekiah's revolt against Sennacherib in the years 703–701 B.C. Zoan and Hanes were both in lower Egypt, though Hanes was a good deal farther south.

6–7 Isaiah not only visualizes Hezekiah's emissaries arriving at Egypt's court but also pictures the terrain and the animals of the environment and the Judean caravans. At the end of the journey, too, was an "animal"—Rahab, the Egyptian dragon. The Negev was inhospitable to travelers, which may have been the reason the messengers went this way, avoiding the more public route across the southern Mediterranean Sea. The large number of words for "lion" in Semitic languages gives some impression of the wildness and danger of much of the Near East in biblical times. "Darting snakes" renders the same Hebrew word as "darting, venomous serpent" in 14:29.

The journey was not only dangerous but costly, for it was expedient to carry a sub-

stantial bribe to this powerful potential ally. Egypt's reputation was undoubtedly great. And the advent of a new and vigorous regime may well have enhanced it, but Hezekiah was in for a shock. Great powers have chosen fearsome animal symbols for themselves, like the lion, the eagle, and the bear. Egypt, however, was identified by others with the mythological Rahab (see on 27:1). "Rahab the Do-Nothing" may be an ironic suggestion that the Judean messengers to Egypt were in more danger from the beasts of the desert than Assyria would be from that notorious supermonster, Egypt! If Assyria was to be shattered, it would be done by God (v.31), not Egypt.

8–11 The command to write has brought untold blessing and challenge to countless numbers. It may just be the ironic name for Egypt (v.7) that Isaiah is to write (cf. 8:1). On the other hand, the whole oracle may be in view. The purpose of writing is to secure a witness to God's solemn warning; vv.9–11 expound the necessity for this written warning.

The prophet repeats his accusation that the people were rebellious (cf. v.1; 1:2). An apostate priesthood and a rebellious people rejected the warnings that came through the true prophet of God. Isaiah's listeners would listen to him, but only if the content of his message was trimmed to their own desires. But the preacher was to bring a message to his listeners, not to find it among them. The words "way" and "path" in v.11, with their moral overtones (cf. Ps 1), may be a sarcastic echoing of Isaiah's own message to them, indicating that prophetic morality was unacceptable to such hearers.

The people's closing command to Isaiah is striking. His title for God was "the Holy One of Israel." This title—implying as it did the great demands that the relationship to such a God entailed—filled their hearts with loathing. Their ears could no longer tolerate its sound.

12–14 Isaiah's use of the "Holy One of Israel" is particularly significant. The people had resisted his use of it, but he was not their servant but the Lord's. Nothing would be trimmed to suit their taste. The people's reliance on "oppression" and "deceit" is probably a reference to Egypt, the oppressor par eminence. At this time her promises of aid were worthless. Judah's trust in a foreign power rather than in God would bring about her demise. A small fault in a wall may spread, and the onlooker may become so accustomed to the bulging wall that he does not detect the worsening of the problem till the collapse comes, and it is too late.

The prophet had to convey not only the suddenness of the judgment but also its completeness. He did this by likening the destruction of the wall to the breaking of pottery; the disintegration is so complete that nothing of value remains. This prophecy was not fulfilled in 701 but rather in 586, when Nebuchadnezzar took Jerusalem, and perhaps even more in the destruction of Jerusalem in A.D. 70 (cf. Mk 13:2).

15–18 "The Sovereign LORD" translates *Adonai* (GK 151) followed by *Yahweh* (GK 3378), thus combining God's sovereign authority with his redemptive name. Sovereignty and holiness find expression in vv.16–17 while redeeming grace is seen in vv.15 and 18. The word of God cuts right across ordinary human thinking (cf. 55:8–9). Those who have learned from God will turn to him in repentant faith, but continued rebellion against him produces panic when the foe appears in all his might. "Repentance" (GK 8746) here is literally "returning." In the contemporary political situation, to turn away from trust in Egypt and to return to the Lord were two sides of the same fact.

God had promised overwhelming victory to his people if they obeyed him but overwhelming defeat if they were rebellious (Lev 26:7–8; Dt 32:30). The lonely hill signal—which had served in a promise of God to suggest a fresh rallying of the scattered nation (11:10, 12)—here stands for shattering defeat. The whole army has gone into battle and met its death; the flag-bearer, kept back at the hilltop base in case he was needed for rallying purposes, discovers that he alone is left and so is without function.

The threatening tone of vv.16–17 gives place to an assurance that God is ready and willing to show mercy to his foolish and obstinate people. It is because God's justice must be expressed—and therefore punishment must fall on this rebellious people—that the manifestation of his mercy is delayed. As so often in the prophets, God's judgment falls first of all; but a remnant preserved through the judgment experiences the blessings of his grace and the fulfillment of his positive purpose for them. Those who wait for him will be identical with this remnant. The Babylonian exile and the return from it are chiefly in view here.

19–26 The God of Israel speaks to his people as if addressing the heart of one person, for singular forms are used most of the time. There is a solidarity among the people of Jerusalem that allows that city to be viewed as a single entity, a kind of corporate person, whom God addresses in grace. The people had been so dull of hearing when he spoke to them, but at their cry he comes immediately to meet them in their need. "The bread of adversity and the water of affliction" probably relate to the Exile, beyond which God would exhibit his grace to them.

The people's penitence would be accompanied by a new responsiveness to God's word through the prophetic teachers. Rejection of God's word always brings hardness of heart, so that the word cannot be heard as before. That word possesses ethical content, keeping God's people to the right path. It also possesses religious content, for their response to it will lead them to purge their land of idolatry. The idols, so splendid in appearance, were really worthless. The illustration stresses the repugnance with which they will now be viewed.

Isaiah had a deep attachment to the soil of his own land. It was not simply the natural affection of the patriot for his native land; for it was God's land, given by him to his people and from which he threatened to remove them as a consequence of their persistent sin (cf. Dt 1:8, 21–25, 34–40; 3:25–29; et al.). The prophet often saw God's blessing therefore in terms of good agricultural weather, increased fruitfulness, and fat cattle (cf. 4:2; 35:1–2; et al.). In the day of God's blessing on the land, even the working animals will live well above subsistence level.

The reference to the day of great slaughter and the fall of towers seems strange in this context. The Bible is realistic and shows that God's plan includes judgment for the rebel as well as blessing for the penitent. The choice of the word "tower" is doubly appropriate, for it has military connotations but also suggests haughty pride (cf. 2:15).

In keeping with the general context, the prophet declares that there will be abundant supplies of water from the mountains. The modern town-dweller views the hill country quite differently from the country farmer. The one sees its beauty, the other its agricultural barrenness. The language suggests that the mountains themselves will enjoy the refreshing waters with all their potential for fruitfulness.

This picture of nature, released from its present limiting conditions, is expanded further. Both the moon and the sun will be much brighter. The number "seven" is not chosen arbitrarily. It is as if the fullness of the divine creative energies is channeled to secure the greater radiance of the sun. The people had known severe chastisement from God through the Assyrians (cf. 1:5–9). Now his powers will secure healing.

27–33 With strong visual appeal, Isaiah describes God, not so much as the Redeemer of his people, but as the Judge of his enemies. The condemned foe is identified in v.31 as Assyria. The name of the Lord is, of course, a revelation of himself (Ex 3:13–15; 6:2–3). That his name is said to come from afar in judgment may be an allusion to Mount Sinai, where, in circumstances of awesome splendor (Ex 19), God showed himself in all his holiness to his people.

Verses 27–28 employ four illustrations of the wrath of God: (1) fire, with all its power to terrify and to destroy (cf. 33:14; Heb 12:29); (2) water (in 8:7–8 the prophet pictured the waters of the great Euphrates [i.e., Assyria] overflowing and reaching even to the neck of Judah; now he would similarly chastise Assyria); (3) the sieve of judgment, revealing the spiritual inadequacy of the unrighteous; and (4) the horse with a bit, suggesting that God will take the arrogant sinner down the road that leads to destruction.

God's judgments are often his means of salvation. Because Assyria was to be judged, Judah would enjoy God's deliverance. The great "festival" (v.29) in which there was a celebration night was the Passover (Ex 12:42). The prophet may have expected his hearers to draw the parallel between these two acts of salvation.

At certain times the heavens are loud with noise and are the source of God's many demonstrations of his power in nature (cf. Ps 29). This figuratively and vigorously presents the judgment of God. Amid all the noise of the storm, the Lord's arm strikes with many a forceful blow at his adversaries. Judah had been smitten through Assyria, but now God would punish Assyria. In v.32 God's people are portrayed rejoicing at his judgment on sin; this is because they must take his point of view on everything, and because this judgment is at the same time their salvation.

Some places have become symbols of spiritual realities. Zion-Jerusalem is the people of God, Babylon the world in arrogant opposition to God, and Tophet God's judgment on sin. Tophet was in the Valley of Hinnom to the south of Jerusalem (Jer 7:31–32), where apostate Jews offered their children by fire to the pagan deity, Molech. Perhaps the prophet is saying here that the king of Assyria himself must pay. He had dedicated himself to paganism, and now he would suffer for this in terrible judgment.

D. Woe to Those Who Seek Help From Egypt (31:1–9)

1–3 Hezekiah had repeated the sin of Ahaz in seeking an alliance with an alien power instead of encouraging his people to put their trust in the Lord. In so doing he showed he had failed to learn from history (for Egypt had proved to be anything but an ally to Israel in the past), from Scripture (since attempting to secure horses for cavalry units was against the divine constitution for the king; see Dt 17:1–20), or even from the experience of his father, Ahaz, which could have provided him with a salutary warning.

The decision to call for help from a particular source is in fact a value judgment, particularly when there are a number of options open. Judah was showing that it set greater value on Egypt ("Rahab the Do-Nothing," 30:7) than on the living God. The statement "yet he too is wise" is pregnant with sarcasm. False political wisdom ruled in the courts of Judah. The so-called wise men had themselves used sarcasm when speaking about the Lord's wisdom (5:19; 29:15). The prophet was convinced that divine wisdom would prove all vaunted human sagacity to be wrong (cf. 1Co 1:18–3:23).

"Disaster" (v.2) is literally "evil" (GK 8273) and is, of course, a reference to war (cf. Am 3:6). This is made the more terrifying by the assertion that God does not retract such threats of judgment (cf. Nu 23:19).

Comparisons are particularly odious when made between things or people differing in quality. The greatest distinction exists between the all-sovereign Creator and the universe he originated and rules. To us "flesh" seems so substantial, because it is visible and tangible, while "spirit" may seem ethereal. Nothing can be further from biblical thinking (cf. Zec 4:6; Jn 3:5–8). The invisible source of supernatural, almighty power in God is in an altogether superior class from the apparently strong but actually almost infinitely weak human beings and horses.

"When the LORD stretches out his hand" is ominous in reference to Egypt; for it has overtones of the Exodus, when all the power of that land was overcome by the Lord. Putting Isaiah's thought into a figure, the unequal yoke Judah was seeking with Egypt would mean that the fall of the one would bring disaster to the other also.

4–5 Is the lion, as Mauchline suggests, the Assyrians who have devastated Judah and are ready to devour Jerusalem, and are the shepherds the Egyptians who have come to aid Judah and have succeeded only in making an ineffectual noise that has not deterred or troubled the Assyrians? Or does the lion's behavior depict the Lord's descent from heaven to fight upon the hill of Zion (cf. 10:32), not allowing anyone to steal from him what belongs to him, as O. Kaiser thinks? Amos uses the lion figure of both God (Am 3:8) and Assyria (Am 3:12). The way the sentence is structured strongly suggests that the figure is intended to be understood in terms of God.

Verse 5 changes the figure but not the message, though it clarifies the peaceful intent of God's activity in relation to Jerusalem. Egypt could give no guarantee of that city's protection from the Assyrians, but God would make it his special care. In the closing line we are reminded of the Exodus. The God of the Exodus would protect his people in Jerusalem as he protected them in Egypt on the night of the Passover.

6–7 The Lord's deliverance of Jerusalem from Sennacherib was a singular demonstration of his reality and power, setting him apart from other deities (see chs. 36–37). The gods of many nations had failed to protect their devotees from the Assyrians, but now the true God showed he was supreme. Isaiah

called his people to repentance in anticipation of that day when, because of God's singular act of deliverance, the worthlessness of the idols would be recognized. Clearly idolatry was the deep revolt that the prophet called them to return from.

8–9 Isaiah makes it clear that the "sword" was not literal and that the Lord secured a great victory over Assyria by nonmilitary means (cf. 37:36–37). "Their stronghold" (lit., "their rock") conveys the picture of a fortress city, perhaps one in Assyria's heartland, approached by its enemies with their battle standards clearly visible. The sight was so unfamiliar to those who were used to constant victory for their armies that the task of the enemy would be made easy by their demoralization. The description of God, however, takes us back swiftly to Jerusalem, for whose sake Assyria was being judged, and whose temple and its ever-burning altar fire symbolized the presence of God with it.

E. God's Kingdom and the Triumph of Righteousness (32:1–20)

1–2 Are these verses messianic or do they picture an ideal government in which the whole administrative system of the country is in the hands of the righteous? The reader inevitably makes a link with the picture of the righteous messianic King given in ch. 11. The book of Isaiah presents its messianic theme in such a way that there is development from one passage to the next, and this passage certainly figures as a development of ch. 11, the new emphasis being on the association of others with the king in his righteous reign.

At the opening of ch. 31, the prophet had criticized those at the court who looked to Egypt for help against the Assyrian menace. No doubt the king would have to bear a special responsibility, but clearly the prophet had others at the court in mind as well. The whole sinful scene of government will pass away, and its place will be taken by a righteous king supported by subordinates who share his concern for righteousness and justice. Government, when it is righteous, affords protection from oppression. In the Messiah's kingdom, righteousness will reign and fear of the oppressor will belong to the past.

3–8 Isaiah was warned that he would see people shutting their eyes and ears to the truth he proclaimed (6:9–10). When the messianic kingdom comes, this spiritual insensitivity will be no more. Those who should have had minds made clear by the bright shining of divine truth in them had in fact been befuddled by drink (28:7–10) and had stammered out rash things instead of prophetic truth. This situation too is to be rectified. If leaders are blind, their people often share this blindness. A nation gets the leaders it deserves (cf. 3:4–7). The moral sense had been so warped in Judah (5:20) that there was failure to recognize the true nature of those who were in positions of leadership. This too would change in the Messiah's kingdom.

In v.5 the prophet speaks of the "fool" (GK 5572) and the "scoundrel" (GK 3964); in vv.6–7 he gives a description of each. In the OT folly often has overtones of godlessness (e.g., Ps 14). If the fear of the Lord is the beginning of wisdom (Ps 111:10; cf. Pr 1:7), then the godless man must be pursuing the wrong way.

Verse 6 presents an appalling picture of the fool, whose mind is controlled by evil, so that both his own life and his influence with others are evil. The messianic King demonstrates his godly righteousness by his concern for the poor and needy (11:4). The godless fool is utterly unconcerned for their most elementary needs (cf. 58:7). Scoundrels (v.7) are even worse. They stoop to lies and deceit to deprive the poor of their legal rights. In fact, scoundrels are precisely those from whom the messianic King will protect the poor (11:4–5). Conduct reveals character; and this is true of both the noble man, whose day will come in the messianic kingdom, and the scoundrel, who will face God's judgment.

9–14 In ch. 3, Isaiah had moved from condemnation of Judah's leaders to strong criticism of the women. Apparently certain aristocratic women were exercising unhelpful influence over their husbands and so had to share in judgment. The stress falls on their complacency, probably meaning the court's pro-Egyptian policy. The women too were relying on Egyptian help for the security of Jerusalem, and so of their homes.

This present prophecy was probably uttered a year or so prior to Sennacherib's invasion of Judah, which led to the situation depicted in ch. 1. It is probably the effects of such an invasion that the prophet had in view here, rather than a simple harvest failure. In this case, its failure is due to the inability of the people—because of enemy occupation—to gather the vintage and other ripe fruit. The women are called to mourning. It is not their husbands or sons who are dead but their land, but this in itself will produce some of the effects of widowhood; for poverty and malnutrition must surely be their lot.

Isaiah often speaks of "thorns and briers." This also points in the direction of enemy occupation rather than mere harvest failure, for the latter would not account for the generally unkempt condition of the countryside. There is a certain emotional quality attached to the phrase "my people." How sad that the land of God's people, a chosen land for a chosen people, should be reduced to such a lamentable condition! It was, of course, their sin that had caused this.

The word rendered "yes" (v.13) is intensive, suggesting that what follows goes beyond the Assyrian judgment to the Babylonian capture of Jerusalem and its results. This language, employing the singular, indicates that Jerusalem rather than the cities of Judah is in view. The devastation caused by Sennacherib's wind would be completed by Nebuchadnezzar's whirlwind.

15–20 The description of judgment suddenly changes to one of blessing. The contrast becomes particularly impressive considering the intentionally illogical words "a wasteland forever, . . . till" (vv.14–15)! Such a decisive assertion of judgment can only be canceled by an equally decisive manifestation of grace. The condemnation humans live their lives under is undoubtedly "forever," because death ushers in their judgment and its eternal consequences; but this condemnation can be canceled by the marvel of justifying grace through faith in Christ.

The reference to the Spirit is most appropriate. If ch. 32 amplifies certain aspects of the messianic prophecy in ch. 11 (see at vv.1–2), we might expect some reference to the Spirit, who has such a place of importance in that earlier chapter. The idyllic picture described there is echoed here, but it is particularly significant that the righteous king in v.1 is accompanied by righteous subordinates. This sug-gests a wider ministry of the Spirit, not confined simply to the Messiah himself. The NT brings together the OT teaching that both the Messiah and his people would know the endowment of the Spirit of God. Here we see an implicit link in Isaiah's own thought. The language of outpouring was destined to be far-reaching (Joel 2:28; Ac 2:17–21).

In v.13 we noted the emotional quality of the phrase "my people," as God's people experience his hand of judgment on them. But now God is able to bestow on them the blessing that is in his heart for them as his own beloved people. Verse 18, with its sequence of prepositional phrases, gives emphatic expression to God's promise that he will bring them, through righteousness, into a condition of "quietness and confidence forever" (v.17).

Verses 19–20 form a fitting conclusion to the oracle, because they sum up the two elements of coming judgment and ultimate blessing. Verse 20 picks up from 30:23–26 the picture of a plentiful economy based on abundant supplies of water, but it presents it in an even more desirable form. The amount of produce given by the soil will be so great that the farmer can actually allow his working animals to browse in the fields.

F. Woe to the Destroyer (33:1–24)

This oracle is the final one in a series of five, interrupted only by the messianic oracle in ch. 32 (see introduction to chs. 28–33). It is the only one of the series in which the introductory "woe" is directed against a foreign power.

1 Seemingly the first half of this verse takes up the boasts of the Assyrians, who had been all-victorious for so many years. The second half declares they will be caught in their own trap.

2–4 The people in the city had at last been brought to realize their total dependence on the Lord. These words are best understood as their prayer when the Assyrian army was at the gate. In 30:18–19, the prophet stated that their God would hear them when they called out to him. Here we see his words beginning to bear fruit. This must have been encouraging to Isaiah after so many years of unresponsiveness to his preaching. Verse 3 is an expression of general confidence in the Lord, with a possible echo of Ps 68:1. Joel 1:1–2:10

This cylinder records Sennacherib's campaign against Judah and against Jerusalem in particular. Indirectly, the Assyrian king admits he was not able to take Jerusalem, only shut up Hezekiah "like a bird in a cage." Courtesy Oriental Institute of Chicago.

points up the appropriateness of the image used here.

5–6 Isaiah believed that the Lord alone is fit to be exalted to the highest place; in ch. 2 he depicted this great God as finally given his rightful place when everything contrary to his supremacy has been debased. Here, he presents the complementary truth that the Lord is exalted already. Eschatological judgment is therefore simply the demonstration in history of that exaltation.

The major issue in recent chapters (esp. chs. 30–31) has been political security. If the Assyrian officers were below the city walls at the time of this oracle, with all hope of relief from Egypt gone, the words of the prophet are particularly significant. That "a rich store of salvation and wisdom and knowledge" is in apposition to "the sure foundation" shows that to the prophet the Lord was all the people needed (cf. 1Co 1:30; Col 2:2–3). The Lord himself was more than enough to give them protection from their enemies and wisdom in living as his people in the world.

The assertion that this "rich store" becomes available through the fear of the Lord reminds us of the association of "the fear of the LORD" with the messianic King (11:2–3). The word "fear" may also have been chosen because of the historical situation. The people trusted Egypt and feared Assyria; in fact, God was to be their fear just as the reference to a sure foundation suggests that he too should be their trust.

7–9 The prophet focuses attention on the sorry condition of Jerusalem, which led the people eventually to call on their God in penitent faith. Terror grips the hearts of the warriors within the city gates. Those who have been sent out to parley with the enemy return weeping, for their words would not penetrate the Assyrians' hard heart. All normal commerce between communities comes to a halt, and the treaty that apparently existed between Sennacherib and Hezekiah is treated as null and void.

The whole land was in mourning. The northern kingdom had already felt the heavy tread of the conqueror's feet; and the places named suggest that Judah would go the same way. If the withering of Lebanon refers to its trees, then this is clearly an indication that what happened was a divine judgment; for its slopes were covered mostly by evergreens, whose leaves do not normally wither. Sharon was one of the most fertile parts of Palestine while the Arabah was dry and arid. The prophet surveyed places farther north and saw the devastation, a hint of what faced Jerusalem if the Assyrians gained entrance.

10–12 The threefold assertion of God's exaltation reminds us of the thrice-exalted Servant of the Lord in 52:13. The enemy's plan to take Jerusalem will come to nothing, and the prophet uses the figure of a pregnancy to bring home its futility. Their destruction will in fact be self-induced, for it is the result of their sinful antagonism to God's people. In v.12 the prophet moves briefly from the particular to the general, making a point about the comprehensiveness of judgment, when it falls on all nations.

13–16 God speaks to the whole world, calling on people to learn from the object lesson provided by his judgment of Assyria. The terms "far away" and "near" describe the Gentile nations and Judah respectively (cf. 49:1; 57:19; Ac 2:39; Eph 2:13, 17).

The phrase "the sinners in Zion" jars the spirit, for such a situation should not exist. Zion was God's city. This was surely no place for the godless, and yet in every age the godless have lived cheek by jowl with the godly, contemptuous of the things of God that made their presence felt every day.

The effects of great judgments may have some kinship with those of spiritual revival, for a new sense of God—his power and his holiness—overtakes the sinners in Zion. Like those who heard Peter at Pentecost, these people, cut to the heart, cry out in their conviction of sin (cf. Ac 2:37). The "consuming fire" is not hell; it is God (cf. Heb 12:29)! Yet, in a sense, those who mistakenly interpret it as hell are not really so wide of the mark (see 10:17).

The cry of the convicted seems to require a negative answer. No human being can dwell in God's holy presence. Yet the prophet goes on to give his hearers a wonderfully positive reply. Time and again he had called his people to faith in God. To find security through the fear of the Lord is to have the key to great spiritual treasure, including that practical wisdom that indicates the way for the individual to walk as well as the right approach to international politics for the leaders (cf. 58:6–12; cf. also 32:3–8).

The book of Isaiah shows a deep concern about sins of speech (cf. esp. 6:5–7). The man of God will neither speak evil nor listen to it from the lips of others. The final line of v.15 underlines the importance of fleeing from temptation. Verse 16 promises security and provision to the one who thus dwells with God and walks in righteousness.

17–20 If this prophecy was uttered as the Assyrian army threatened Jerusalem, then these words would have been immensely reassuring to the beleaguered people. The "king" is either the Messiah or God himself; considerations of poetic structure support the former view. Viewing the land is presented as somehow complementary to seeing the king, and the greatness of the Messiah's earthly dominion has been asserted in passages like 9:7; 11:9–10 (cf. 26:15). In contrast to this embattled city, the only free territory left to God's people, the future king would appear as ruler over a wide empire.

Isaiah graphically pictures the people in the days of the Messiah reflecting on the past and contrasting their lot then with the blessings they now have. They had been the people of a king who had paid tribute to Sennacherib in attempting to buy him off (2Ki 18:13–16); and Assyrian officials had been seen in the streets of Jerusalem, the financial agents of an avaricious tyrant. The earlier prophecy had proved true. God had spoken to this people, in judgment, through men of strange speech (cf. 28:11).

At the time the prophet contemplates, however, all this is a thing of the past, subject still to vivid mental recall, but no longer experienced. The emphasis on sight—whether physical or mental—that characterizes the last few verses continues. Those who have been exhorted to see the king and the wide land of his domain are now called to view his capital city, the cultic center of the nation, where its joy in God finds its corporate expression at festival time. The enemies will be gone, and "peace" will reign (the meaning of "Jerusalem" includes "peace"). It possessed many fine buildings, but we are reminded that its people belonged to a race formerly nomadic (cf. the "tent" firmly fixed).

21–22 This chapter presents a picture of Jerusalem as a kind of Near Eastern Venice or Amsterdam. Most great civilizations have grown up around important rivers. Israel and Jerusalem were exceptions. Indeed, Isaiah remembers the concern for adequate water supplies that had been in the mind of Ahaz when he confronted him in the past (7:3). The city would now be amply supplied. Just as the prophet hastened to guard against a possible misconception of his imagery once before (see 31:8), so now he makes it clear that such broad rivers would be an unmitigated blessing. Many a city, formerly glad of all the advantages brought to it by its situation on a great river, has cursed its location when that same river brought an enemy armada into the very heart of it. Gates may keep out an enemy that a waterway may admit.

Verse 21 began with an assertion about the Lord before moving on to statements about Jerusalem. What Jerusalem is depends entirely on what Jerusalem's God is. Each of the three brief but impressive statements about God is structured so as to place emphasis on the divine name. All three recall different periods in Israel's history, for the period of the judges was preceded by that of Moses the lawgiver and succeeded by that of the king. All three were savior figures, acting as agents of God to bring deliverance to his people. Their God now sums up all these functions in himself.

23–24 It is clear that v.23 takes up again the imagery of the ship from v.21, but who is being addressed by the prophet? Assyria seems to fit the context. If a "mighty ship" was feared in Isaiah's day, it was Assyria. Let this

ship sail belligerently in the direction of Jerusalem, and its essential instability—making it vulnerable to its foes—will stand revealed. Assyria appeared to be anything but vulnerable, so that the prophet is speaking with God-given insight. Only God and God's prophet can penetrate the military facade to the true condition of Assyria. When it falls, its empire will be evenly divided; and even apparently impotent states will find themselves enriched from its plunder.

Verse 24 reminds us that the whole passage is really a description of the future blessedness of Jerusalem. The blessings of God will take both physical and spiritual forms. In Ps 103:3, the greater blessing of forgiveness is placed first; here it is placed at the end, to provide a climax for the whole chapter. No blessing is greater, none more urgently needed.

V. God's Purposes of Judgment and Salvation (34:1–35:10)

Despite what is said in ch. 34 about Edom, there is a universality about the references to the judgment to come.

A. Judgment on the World—and Edom (34:1–17)

1–4 Isaiah dramatically addresses the nations of the world here. They cannot hear him, for, presumably, he is speaking in Jerusalem; but his message concerns them all. He accumulates words and phrases—"you nations," "you peoples," "earth," "world"—to emphasize this universal scope. This makes the later particular reference to one small state all the more striking.

A great judgment will someday manifest the anger of God with the nations. It is significant that the prophet refers to the armies of the nations, for national arrogance and cruelty have so often found their focus in aggressive acts by military forces. Israel had in fact been on the receiving end of many such attacks, but divine retribution was coming. The fearsome description in v.3 drives home the point that God's wrath will lead to the death of his enemies.

Verse 4 transports us suddenly from earth to the heavens. The ultimate character of this judgment encompasses the entire cosmos (cf. 24:21–23; Mt 24:29; 2Pe 3:10; and esp. Rev 6:13–14). The way Isaiah illustrates this truth of cosmic judgment from situations familiar to his readers heightens the impression of God's absolute control over all things (cf. 40:12).

5–7 God is here the universal Judge, his judgments including even the very heavens. Then, with great suddenness, the sword of judgment falls on one of the smallest states in the biblical world: Edom. Edom was a traditional enemy of Israel, so this probably represents God's judgment on all Israel's foes. Edom had appropriated territory from Judah during the reign of Ahaz (2Ki 16:6). The prophecies against the nations recorded in chs. 13–23 do not contain an oracle against Edom, though many of Judah's neighbors are mentioned. Edom has not, however, been overlooked (cf. 11:14). Indeed, its fall was so certain that it was described as "the people I have totally destroyed."

In some respects cities, persons, and articles given over in destruction to the Lord were like sacrifices, for they were holy to the Lord (Lev 27:28–29; cf. Jos 6:17–19). This is probably why v.6 goes on to speak of sacrificial animals. The inhabitants of Edom, under divine judgment, were like sacrificial animals. The fate of both was death. Yet it seems inappropriate to liken the antagonistic Edomites to the docile domestic animals employed in ritual; so the prophet looks to the herds of wild oxen that no doubt roamed parts of Edom's territory; they too would die.

8–10 The word "judgment" (GK 5477) in v.5 sets the slaughter in Edom in a moral context, which is emphasized in v.8. This act of vengeance is to further God's purposes for Jerusalem, which, in times of weakness in Judah, might well have cause to fear a threat from the south. There is an implied comparison with the destruction of Sodom and Gomorrah. Edom's judgment will be so complete, so permanent, that it will be utterly desolate. The final line of v.10 may mean that, not only will Edom be unable to harass Zion herself, but she will not even witness the passage of armies from beyond her borders on their way to attack Judah.

11–15 Precise identification of these creatures matters little, for the general thrust of the prophet's thought is clear. Edom will become a desolate place, fit only for creatures of the wild. Just as nomads rejoice to find terrain that has been abandoned by its inhabitants, so the birds and beasts of the desert will move into the land whose people have suffered God's judgment.

What looks at first like a suggestion that Edom, now destroyed, may be reconstructed becomes, in the prophet's paradoxical language, a warning that God is in fact measuring it up rather for destruction. The references to "chaos" and "desolation," Clement notes, recall the formless void of the world before God imposed the created order upon it (Ge 1:2).

"Nothing there to be called a kingdom" in v.12 provides a kind of parallel to the description of Egypt in 30:7 as "Rahab the Do-Nothing." Just as a measuring line suggests architectural order, so a kingdom suggests social order; but there will be none.

16–17 Most likely "the scroll of the LORD" is the prophecy just given. Thus the communication of prophetic oracles to writing has importance because it makes possible later recognition of the veracity of God. What the Lord has said comes to pass because he is the God of truth. Scripture is God's witness to his own faithfulness. The Spirit of God puts into effect what his word has promised, and the birds and animals gathering in Edom are mute testimony to the truth of what he has said. God will order the new homes of these creatures in Edom so that each is given his proper place (cf. Dt 32:8). Even in his judgments God is concerned that everything should be done in an orderly way (cf. 1Co 14:40).

B. Blessing for God's People (35:1–10)

1–2 The prophet speaks of the desert but does not indicate its location. Verses 8–10 suggest that he is thinking about the exiles returning from Babylon and crossing the many miles of desert lying between Mesopotamia and the Promised Land. In view of the promise that the messianic King will be seen "in his beauty" as governing a far-stretching land (33:17), it is probably best to think in terms of all the terrain occupied or traversed by God's people, but with Zion (v.10) as the center of the kingdom and the end goal of the returning exiles.

Nature bursts not only into bloom but into song. The very environment of God's people reflects their mood of joy at what

God has done. The prophet does not say that the desert will burst into bloom *with* the crocus but *like* it. Probably he has in mind the transformation that comes over a land when winter ends and spring, with its characteristic flowers, suddenly comes with the advent of a few warm days.

The whole face of the earth is changed. So will it be with the desert. Lebanon's glory is found, of course, in its wonderful cedars, while Carmel and the plain of Sharon that runs south from it are covered with trees and other plant life. The beauty and splendor of transformed nature will be seen as a reflection of the beauty and splendor of the Creator and Redeemer (cf. 40:5).

3–4 The prophet returns briefly to his age and the fear that gripped the hearts of so many of his people in the face of the external threat (see esp. 7:2–9). Fear in the heart affects the ability of hands to work for God and of feet to walk in his ways. This could mean, then, that the returning exiles of v.10 are in view, needing divine encouragement to make the journey.

The link between ch. 34 and ch. 35 is emphasized by the contrasting pictures of topographical desolation and blessing and by the use of "vengeance" (GK 5934) in 34:8 and here. Biblical realism requires that peace be the result of righteousness, and righteousness demands the punishment of sin. Only when God has judged the enemies of his people can his salvation in all its fullness be theirs.

5–7 In view of the frequent references to spiritual blindness and deafness (e.g., 6:9–10; 29:9–12) and the promise that one day spiritual sight and hearing will be restored to the people (29:18), we are at once inclined to interpret v.5—and in harmony with it v.6—in spiritual terms. However, Jesus appears to allude to this chapter in Lk 7:18–23, and he takes the language literally and physically. But physical and spiritual sight and hearing have a symbolic relationship; and in God's ultimate kingdom his people will have glorified bodies and a perfected spirituality.

Renewed nature comes into view once again. The transformed desert is alive with the sound of living streams and gushing springs. The only sign of life before the water's advent was the jackal or wolf. But their place will be taken by the characteristic vegetation and population of lands with abundant water supplies.

8–10 In ancient times people did not build roads across stretches of desert. But this land is desert no longer, so roads are appropriate. The prophet concentrates on one highway, with a most exalted name. It is called "the Way of Holiness" because its goal is the Holy City of Zion, but also because it is intended for holy persons. Israel's highways were all intended for pilgrimage, of course, as people went up them at the feasts to meet the Lord in his holy temple. In the light of 26:7–8, the statement "It will be for those who walk in that Way" is probably to be understood morally, not simply ceremonially. Hazardous conditions faced desert travelers in that part of the world (30:6). This road will be free of predators, for it will be restricted to the redeemed.

Verse 10 brings the whole oracle to a glorious conclusion (cf. 51:11; 61:7). The most joyous periods of the year for the people of Judah had been the three annual pilgrim feasts, when they went up the highways to Zion singing pilgrim songs. The word "return" (GK 8740) makes it clear that they are in fact now coming from farther afield, probably not from Babylonia alone, but from all the lands of the Dispersion (see 49:8–26). The note of joy with which the oracle opens and which can be discerned through the language of its every part now takes over completely. Sorrow and sighing are denied any place in this revelation of God's purpose of joy for his people (cf. Rev 21:1–4).

VI. Isaiah and Hezekiah, Assyria and Babylon (36:1–39:8)

The narrative character of these chapters makes them somewhat different from other parts of the book. There are oracles of Isaiah here, but they are set in a historical framework. In the overall pattern of the book, they fulfill an important function. Chapters 1–35 have the Assyrian menace as their main historical setting; and, though many other nations are touched, the reader is never allowed for long to forget the dark shadow of that threat in the background. From the beginning of ch. 40, however, exile in Babylon forms the setting of his oracles. These four chapters therefore provide a historical transition, chs. 36–37 looking back to Assyria and chs. 38–39 on to Babylon. These chapters are practically identical with 2Ki 18–20, except for the poem of Hezekiah (Isa 38:9–20).

A. The Deliverance of Jerusalem from Sennacherib (36:1–37:38)

1–3 These events can be dated in the year 701 B.C., which raises a problem about the reference to the fourteenth year of Hezekiah's reign. Quite possibly a scribe made a slip when he should have written "twenty-fourth year," which harmonizes better with the historical facts. The NIV translates the familiar "Rabshakeh" (KJV, RSV) as "field commander" (GK 8072); he was probably second only to the supreme commander (KJV "Tartan"; GK 9580) of 20:1. Lachish, an important fortress city of Judah guarding the road to Egypt, was captured by Sennacherib. The location of the main Assyrian army at this point, because of its strategic position, precluded any possible hope of Egyptian help to Hezekiah.

Once again, as in the days of Ahaz (ch. 7), Jerusalem is being threatened by her foes. On that earlier occasion the aqueduct had been the place of decision for Ahaz. Much had happened over the more than three decades that separated that event from this one. Now the Assyrian himself is the threat, which in itself underlines the folly of Ahaz on that earlier occasion. This foe is much more powerful than the two allies of the earlier event. While there may have been some differences in the circumstances, the spiritual issue has not altered. Now at precisely the same spot, the son of Ahaz faces the same spiritual issue. How will he react?

The king of Assyria did not come personally but sent three of his leading men (2Ki 18:17), and Hezekiah did the same. In this way he preserved something of his dignity as the monarch.

4–7 The grandiose designation of the field commander's master ("the great king, the king of Assyria") contrasts sharply with the absence even of the word "king" in his reference to Judah's monarch. The tone of the speech is insolent, and the opening question shows that it is essentially an attempt to undermine any confidence the people might have. In a sense Hezekiah was the contemporary custodian of the messianic promises, as the dynastic expression "house of David" in

7:13 reminds us. The words of the field commander relayed to Hezekiah may even have encouraged him to trust in the God whose messianic promises were an implicit assurance that his line would continue.

Unknown, no doubt, to the field commander, his words in v.6 tallied exactly with what Isaiah had been saying about the futility of trusting in Egypt (30:3–7; 31:3). His use of a vivid illustration too may have reminded them of the prophet's words. No doubt the Assyrians were well aware of Hezekiah's religious reformation (2Ki 18:3–7). The field commander refers to Hezekiah here as if he is not addressing him. The speech, though ostensibly intended for Hezekiah, is so phrased that those who are to relay it to him will ponder its import.

8–10 The field commander's offer is sarcastic. Judah was indeed painfully weak in cavalry and looked to the Egyptian army to supply this lack (cf. 31:1, 3). The field commander does not at this stage attack the Lord's ability to save his people, but he does imply the anger of the Lord against his people. This coincides with what Isaiah constantly taught, that the Assyrian armies, wicked as they were, were accomplishing God's purposes of judgment (cf. esp. 10:5–11). The field commander could hardly have known about the prophecies of Isaiah.

11–12 Aramaic, ultimately the common language of Palestine, was at this time the diplomatic language of the Fertile Crescent, but unintelligible to the common people. The comment by Hezekiah's officials suggests that any confidence they themselves had left was fast ebbing away as a result of this speech (cf. v.22), and they feared its effect on the people. The vulgarity of the field commander's reply attests its authenticity.

13–15 Far from changing the language of his speech, the field commander raises his voice to enable the wider audience to hear more clearly. He gives at this stage no arguments against faith in the Lord's power to deliver his city.

16–17 The appeal suggests that many from the surrounding villages had taken refuge within Jerusalem at this time. The threat of exile was hardly likely to prove an extra inducement to the commander's hearers. The people were actually at the city walls at this time. In the foreground was the Assyrian detachment, including the arrogant speaker himself. Beyond, however, the people could see the devastation these Assyrians had wrought.

18–20 The reference to exile in v.17 would make the people think about Samaria's fate twenty years before. The commander gives a list of some of the main places conquered by Assyria, concluding with Samaria. Each had its distinctive gods, but all had proved ineffective against Assyria. The field commander concludes his speech with what must have seemed to him to be his punch line. But a frontal attack like this on such faith as they had may well have roused his hearers to a greater trust. The Lord had such a wonderful record of delivering his people that this man was in fact beginning now to tread on thin ice.

21–22 The silence on the wall had apparently been broken only by the request of v.11 (cf. Ecc 3:7).

37:1–4 Hezekiah presents a great contrast with both Ahaz (ch. 7) and his own former attitude (2Ki 18:14–16). The account in 2Ki 18 places the visit of the field commander after Hezekiah's first payment of tribute to the king of Assyria at Lachish. That the king of Assyria should demand tribute and then absolute surrender is not without historical parallel, nor is the change in Hezekiah's attitude inconceivable.

Hezekiah went into God's temple and sent for God's servant, the prophet. Hezekiah probably hoped for a reassuring word from the Lord as well as a promise that the prophet would pray. The reference to childbirth was probably proverbial. The words "it may be" do not betoken lack of faith but rather a realization on the king's part that the people, through their sins, had forfeited any right to expect divine deliverance. Their only hope was in his unmerited favor.

In one sense God would "hear" (GK 9048) the words of the field commander, for he hears everything. But the king was using the verb in that pregnant sense that implies that action will be taken as a result of what has been heard. There is a sense of sin implicit also in his reference to the Lord as "the LORD *your* God," for Isaiah had shown a faithfulness that rebuked both people and king. On the other hand, the reference to "ridicule [of] the living God" and "the remnant" are expressions of hope in God, because of his nature and his purpose for the remnant of his people, so often expressed through Isaiah himself (e.g., 10:20–27).

5–8 Isaiah had once before counseled a king not to be afraid (7:4), but Ahaz had proved unresponsive to the reassuring word of God. The expression "the underlings" (GK 5853) could be an insulting reference to the field commander and the other high officers who had formed the Assyrian delegation. More likely, however, the field commander's words were not the only insults to Judah's God from the Assyrians outside the walls that had assaulted the ears of the inhabitants of Jerusalem.

The reference to "a certain report" could apply to the report about Tirhakah (v.9). But this report did not send Sennacherib back to Assyria; rather, it gave him greater concern to reduce Hezekiah to submission.

At first v.7 seems irreconcilable with v.36. In fact, v.37 records two events: the withdrawal of the threat to Jerusalem and the return to Nineveh. The first may have been caused by the miracle recorded in v.36 and the second by a report of trouble elsewhere, perhaps in Babylon. For the manner of Sennacherib's death, compare v.38. Verse 8 is an incidental testimony to the concern for truth of fact that motivates the author.

9–13 The report of the approach of an Egyptian army gave greater urgency to the bid to gain Jerusalem. No military leader welcomes a war on two fronts. The message—sent by letter as v.14 makes clear—repeats much that the field commander had said (cf. 36:13–20), except that he attributes deception now to the Lord rather than to Hezekiah himself. The reader gets a shock when he sees the God of Hezekiah designated as "god," till he recalls that the words come from a pagan and represent his valuation of the God of Israel. Sennacherib's reference to his forefathers shows his pride in being a member of an all-conquering dynasty. The list of names is longer, and therefore even more impressive, than that given in 36:19.

14–20 Hezekiah prays in similar fashion to the early church in Ac 4 (esp. v.24). His address is theological in the best sense. As "LORD Almighty," his God has all power; and as the sovereign Creator, the Assyrians are subject to that power. The word "alone" is a critical glance at their paganism. On the other hand, the God of Israel has a special relationship with his people and therefore a concern to protect them from their enemies. The act of salvation Hezekiah prays for is to be a revelation of God to all the kingdoms on earth that the Lord alone was God.

21–25 Again God speaks to Hezekiah through Isaiah. Verses 21–22 clearly imply that, even though it was God's purpose to deliver his people, it was important that Hezekiah prayed. The oracle is a taunt song with the characteristic "limping" rhythm in Hebrew. Jerusalem is represented as a young girl rebuffing with contempt the unwelcome advances of a churl. Perhaps there is a suggestion that she is betrothed to the Holy One of Israel, a title for God characteristic of Isaiah's prophecies.

Characteristic too is Isaiah's emphasis on pride, especially the quotation of arrogant words by a foreign monarch (cf. 10:12–14; 14:4, 13–15). The annals of Sennacherib are dominated by the occurrences of the first person singular. It looks as though the course of his boasting follows that of his conquering marches. The emphasis here is on the king's ability to overcome any natural obstacle that lay in his path. The mountainous, tree-covered terrain of Lebanon could not hold him back, neither could the waterless lands of southern Palestine and Sinai. The streams of the Nile Delta were equally powerless to stop him, for he had but to tread on them. This final claim, of course, went beyond the facts but was perhaps made in anticipation of a great victory over Tirhakah (cf. v.9).

26–29 The question "Have you not heard?" anticipates the great rhetorical questions of 40:21, 28 and draws attention to Israel's God. All the great conquests of the Assyrians are to be ascribed to God, whose instruments they were. Many of Isaiah's oracles up to this point have spoken of judgment on the nations of the Fertile Crescent, including Israel and Judah; and a great many of them were in fact executed through Assyria. Everything had been preordained, and Assyria can boast of nothing. Without doubt the conquests of this nation were devastating. There was a fe-rocity and ruthlessness that the eastern Mediterranean had never seen before, and which has probably not been surpassed since, at least on the grand scale.

God knows all there is to know about the Assyrians, and Isaiah expresses this in language that had become standard (cf. Dt 28:6; Ps 121:8; et al.). The Assyrians often treated their prisoners like animals, with the use of the rope and the nose-hook. God would do the same.

30–32 Though Scripture does not encourage us to ask for signs, God's word is sometimes followed by a given sign (e.g., 1Sa 10:1–7). The Assyrian occupation of Judah had devastated its fields (1:7–8), and it would take years to recover. If this oracle was given at the close of one season, that just about to start would probably not be normal, for the people would have building as well as agricultural tasks to perform (32:13–14). The prophecy is therefore consistent with the departure of the Assyrians.

In characteristic fashion Isaiah moves from the literal to the figurative. The remnant is pictured as a vine or fruit tree. This prophecy relates specifically to the deliverance from Sennacherib. God underlines this prophecy and the certainty of its fulfillment in a most impressive manner. The word and sign become a threefold cord when the great affirmation that ends this oracle is spoken. This puts this prophecy on a par with the great messianic oracle of ch. 9, which also closes in the same way (9:7). In fact, the two are linked, for it was of David's line (represented now by Hezekiah) that the Messiah would come and on David's throne (in threatened Jerusalem) that he would reign.

33–35 This brief oracle puts the matter clearly and painfully. Far from entering Jerusalem, the Assyrian king would not even subject it to a normal siege. Sennacherib himself said in his famous "Sennacherib Cylinder" (see picture of this cylinder at Isaiah 33) that he shut up Hezekiah in the city like a caged bird. The phrase "for my sake" shows that the Lord answers prayer, and the phrase that follows it shows that he keeps his promises (cf. 2Sa 7).

36–37 "Went out" is often used of going forward to battle. "The angel of the LORD" is a divine figure, at once distinguished from

God and yet identified with him. Herodotus, the Greek historian, records that one night Sennacherib's army camp was infested by mice (or rats) that destroyed the arrows and shield-thongs of the soldiers. The rat, quite appropriately, symbolized plague (cf. 1Sa 6:4), which could well have been the means used by the angel of the Lord. The unexpected and shocking carnage seen by the living next morning is most vividly described.

38 An interval of twenty years passes, but we get the impression that Sennacherib's death is a further manifestation of divine judgment. His death at the hands of his own progeny is confirmed from Assyrian sources. His death when at worship in a pagan shrine should be seen as further evidence of the main thesis of these two chapters, that the God of Israel is the living and true God while all other deities are powerless.

B. Hezekiah's Illness (38:1–22)

1 The phrase "in those days" is similar to 39:1. In fact, all these events probably occurred within about two years. Thus the time reference is to be taken generally. The nature of Hezekiah's illness is not mentioned, nor is it stated that it is punishment for sin. God's command suggests that Hezekiah had a duty to his family and kingdom to arrange their future administration.

2–3 Hezekiah's prayer may have been a direct result of putting his house in order, or at least this may have intensified it; for, as a comparison of v.5 with 2Ki 21:1 shows, he would have been without heir if he had died within three years. He probably turned to the wall to shut out the faces of others while he prayed. Second Kings 18:5–6 confirms Hezekiah's statements about himself and shows that his manner of life was grounded in faith in God.

4–6 God's description of himself as "the God of your father David" implies that he keeps faith with his word, especially his promises to David in 2Sa 7. God is even more concerned about the continuance of David's dynasty than Hezekiah is.

7–8 Here is another sign of messianic significance (cf. 7:10–17), for Hezekiah's dynasty was the line of the Messiah. The sun had been about to set on the life of Hezekiah but now

it would return somewhat, prolonging the day. Attempts to explain this scientifically or to relate it to some calendrical adjustment have not been convincing. It is best to admit that we do not yet know the explanation but to accept this Scriptural testimony to the fact that a miracle took place.

9–14 Verses 10–14 are retrospective, the king recalling his thoughts during his illness by the device of self-quotation. Verse 10 assumes that a person can normally look forward to a certain probable life span. The reference to "gates of death" conveys an image of *Sheol* ("death"; GK 8619) as a city of the dead. To "see the LORD" probably refers to appearing in his presence in the temple. The king shows a right sense of priorities when he places this before the continuance of human fellowship. After the tent illustration, he alludes to the weaver rolling up and cutting a finished length of cloth from his loom. The recurrent statement "day to night" conveys the same idea of suddenness—in the morning perfect health, in the evening, death. Verse 13 seems to refer to a night spent in prayer, only to be ended in the morning when God suddenly falls on Hezekiah like a lion. The varied cries of Palestine's birds express the varied nature of Hezekiah's many cries to God, now quiet, now shrill, now mournful. The reference to Hezekiah's eyes conveys a picture of concentrated appeal to God and to him alone.

15–20 At this point the tone of the psalm changes dramatically. The opening question implies that the king feels that no words of his can do justice to his sense of gratitude to God for his great deliverance. The king has learned humility from this experience, for through it he has come to recognize that someone else controls the course of his life and the day of his death. The words "by such things men live" probably refer to the words and deeds of God mentioned in v.15. God the Creator is also God the Healer. The "benefit" of v.17 is his new understanding of God's gracious, forgiving love, expressed in his deliverance from death.

Verse 18 reflects Hezekiah's sense of forgiveness of sins. The deeper significance of death cries out for the forgiveness of sin, which Hezekiah has himself now experienced. His restoration to health has this as its crowning blessing: he can give thanks to

God. Rendered literally, v.19b says, "Father tells children about your faithfulness." If he is speaking in anticipation about his literal children rather than Israel as the children of God, this strengthens the view that part of Hezekiah's concern lay in his lack of a son at that time to succeed him. Verse 20 reminds us that Hezekiah encouraged the singing of the songs of David and Asaph in the temple worship (2Ch 29:25–30; cf. Rev 5:9–10).

21–22 These verses occur in 2Ki 20 immediately after the promise that the city would be delivered from the king of Assyria. The words of Isaiah and Hezekiah may have been recorded here to satisfy the reader's natural queries about the means of healing and the reason for the sign. Hezekiah is not criticized for asking for a sign. After all, Isaiah's two prophecies in v.1 and v.5 may have puzzled him by their contradictoriness. He sought not so much confirmation as clarification.

C. Envoys From and Exile to Babylonia (39:1–8)

This brief chapter sets the scene for the chapters that follow (chs. 40–66). These chapters—enigmatic prior to the reference to Babylon in ch. 43 and perhaps even before the dramatic mention of Cyrus at the close of ch. 44—become clear as to setting when seen to presuppose the fulfillment of the prophecy given in this chapter, which therefore fulfills an indispensable function.

1–2 Merodach-Baladan, known to secular history as Marduk-aplu-idinna, was king of Babylon 721–709 B.C. and again for nine months in 703 B.C. (see ZPEB, 4:191–92). Babylon had known years of greatness in the past and was to be great again. Merodach-Baladan's brief success in throwing off the Assyrian yoke was an earnest of this. There was, of course, a political motive for sending a deputation to Hezekiah. It could have taken place during the closing years of his first period of rule; but, in view of the time references in 38:1 and here, more likely it was in 703, two years before Jerusalem was delivered from Sennacherib.

The envoys were taken on a grand tour of the palace and the kingdom. Hezekiah's glad reception of them may have been due to a desire to be involved in concerted action against Assyria, and the display of his wealth would show he had something to offer as a potential ally.

3–4 Isaiah's inquiry may have been preliminary to the coming of a message from God to him, so that he would himself understand its significance. More likely its purpose was to emphasize to the king the reason for the prophecy. Hezekiah's conduct had been unbelieving, and there may have been pride in it also. These were the two sins most often condemned by the prophet.

5–7 "The LORD Almighty," the title of God used by Isaiah in v.5, lays emphasis on the infinite resources used by the Lord in his acts of power. Hezekiah's own resources may have seemed great to him, but those of the Lord were far greater; and they would be used in judgment against Hezekiah's people through the Babylonians. The reference to his "fathers" was perhaps a rebuke to his lack of a sense of stewardship. Through his folly, what his predecessors had gathered would be lost. Furthermore, his descendants would suffer in the judgment to come. It was not until Jeremiah's day that Judah's dynasty was to take its history of sin beyond the point of no return. Yet even in the midst of this declaration of a coming judgment, there may have been a hint of a continuing purpose of grace. Almost certainly Hezekiah did not have a son at this time to succeed him. The phrase "some of your descendants" would leave room for hope.

8 Hezekiah's acknowledgment that God's word was good probably includes a recognition that the judgment was appropriate—because deserved—and that it was not altogether unmixed with grace. His final statement was not selfish and unfeeling; more likely, it was a thankful recognition that God had not dealt with him personally to the measure of what he deserved.

VII. The Sole Sovereignty and Sure Promises of the Lord (40:1–48:22)

To move from ch. 39 to ch. 40 is to enter a part of the book (chs. 40–66) that has produced more scholarly literature than any other part of the OT. The number of different views as to authorship, structure, and other related matters is bewildering; and the debate as to the nature of the Servant Songs (see comments at 42:1–4) and the identity of the servant shows no sign of abating. The view taken here is that the whole book is the work of Isaiah of Jerusalem and that chs. 40–66 consist of oracles given to him by the Spirit of inspiration, thus enabling Isaiah to live in spirit in a future day, so that he might be the vehicle of God's message to the people of that day.

A. Good News for Jerusalem (40:1–11)

This passage sets the mood for chs. 40–48. The prophet responds to the command of God to bring a message of comfort to his people.

1–2 Such a command must have been a great joy to hear, for the prophet had been fulfilling such a discouraging commission as given in 6:9–13. Imperative or vocatival repetition is a characteristic of emotional speech and occurs frequently in Isaiah. The phrase "my people" itself suggests either comfort or rebuke rather than a message of judgment. In close connection with "your God," as here, it is really a covenant term.

Jerusalem is addressed, for God's saving deeds in Babylon were to make possible a new Jerusalem that would emerge from the ashes of the old. The "hard service" is the Babylonian exile. "Double" appears to be hyperbole used to impress on the people that the chastisement of the exile was really over.

3–5 Like other prophets, Isaiah was given visions (1:1), but he also heard words. An unidentified voice calls. John the Baptist, to whom the words are applied in the NT, was prepared to be such an unidentified voice (Jn 1:19–23). Isaiah 35:8–10 had spoken of a highway for the returning exiles, implying

As people in ancient times traversed the desert (cf. 40:3), camels were often used for riding and for bearing burdens.

perhaps that it would traverse the desert (35:1). This is made clear now; and, because it represents God's purpose for his people, it is called his highway.

"Prepare" (GK 7155) introduces the idea of the removal of obstructions. The whole concept is figurative, declaring in dramatic fashion that the Lord will let nothing stand in the way of the exiles' return. Coming back often has dual significance in Isaiah, combining the physical and the spiritual (see 7:3). John the Baptist's call to repentance does not settle the matter, for the NT fulfillment of an OT passage often moves the concept from the physical to the spiritual. It seems best to consider it physical here but with possible spiritual overtones. What is in prospect is an amazing new revelation of the glory of the Lord, not now for Israel only (as in her temple), but for all humanity (cf. 60:1–3).

6–8 The prophet hears a voice again; and, in response to his request, he hears the message he is to give. The self-sufficient do not respond eagerly to good news from God. The Exile itself must have made the people aware of their frailty. God is the only enduring reality in a constantly changing world, and he has himself designed it so. The following chapters lay great stress on the enduring word of God.

9–11 Zion is the first to hear the good news of her God's return and is commanded to climb, like a herald, to some elevated place to proclaim the news to her satellite towns (cf. Ac 1:8, "all Judea"). From vv.3–8 the reader has anticipated the coming of the Lord; and he is now described, with the reiterated call to attention—"see." There is a perfect balance of strength and tenderness here. "His arm" suggests his power manifested in the Exodus (Dt 4:34), appropriate in relation to a return from exile and due to be most wonderfully expounded later (see 53:1).

"His reward" and "his recompense," Whybray suggests, perhaps refer to the spoils of victory, in this case the rescued exiles, who are in a sense God's "captives." All this power is employed with great tenderness on behalf of his people, leading them back from Babylon to the fold in Jerusalem. "Sovereign LORD" in v.10 underscores the idea of a strong and tender Shepherd-King.

B. God the Incomparable (40:12–31)

These verses develop the "Here is your God!" in v.9 and describe more fully the all-powerful yet tender Shepherd-King.

12–17 The use of the magnificent anthropomorphisms in v.12 is so natural after the picture of God as a shepherd (v.11). These do not reduce God to a human level but simply give vividness to the theological truth of his personality.

"Mind" (GK 8120) can also be translated "Spirit" (see NIV note). This passage is about God's creative power, and Ge 1:2 gives the Spirit a place in this work.

Near Eastern marketplace commerce would take no account of the minute water drop in the measuring bucket or a little dust on the scales when meat or fruit was weighed. This passage implies the consummate ease of the Lord's control of history as well as of nature. He had given a sacrificial system but was not, like Babylonia's deities, tied to it, for the most impressive forest land known to the Near East was quite inadequate to furnish fuel or sacrificial animals for a worthy offering to him.

18–20 The reference to animal sacrifice—visible offerings made to an invisible God—leads Isaiah to speak of the spectacular folly of idolatry. Later (see esp. 44:12–20) he stresses the selection of the best materials and the finest human skills; but there is a touch of prophetic irony about the stated purpose of all this: "to set up an idol that will not topple."

21–24 God is like a father here, gently yet firmly chiding his children for their failure to see the relevance to their situation of God's disclosure in history and nature of the fact that he is sovereign. He is supreme over all; he utilizes the majestic heavens he has created to suggest, through their overarching form, that the universe is a home for him; and he allows no one to further his ambitions without limit. His absolute control over all human life is quite unchallenged.

25–26 Verses 18–20 had contrasted God with the idols that were all too common in Babylonia. Now the same question introduces an implicit contrast with the astral deities that dominated their religion. This passage asserts that, far from being deities in their own right,

the heavenly bodies have simply been created by the one Creator-God, who is also Israel's "Holy One." He orders their pattern, knows each in its distinctiveness, and upholds them all in their being (cf. Col 1:17; Heb 1:3).

27–31 The prophet's majestic view of God, stemming in part from the inaugural vision of ch. 6, is now brought to bear on the people's despondency. The name "Jacob" suggests the unworthiness of the chosen people but also brings to mind the ancestor's experience in the story of his descendants (cf. Mal 3:6); for Jacob too had been in exile in Mesopotamia as a result of his own folly. As God had said to Jacob (Ge 31:13), so he was now telling his progeny: Return to the Land of Promise. The language used here suggests that the people were bringing God down to their own level, thinking him either forgetful or tired—perhaps because their long history of folly seemed to be never-ending.

The closing verses assert that the God who upholds the stars (v.26) also supports his weary people. Those who found the journey to Jerusalem from other parts of the land tiring were given strength for it by God (Ps 84:5, 7). The people in Babylon could exchange their little strength for his omnipotence. The verb "renew" (GK 2736) suggests an exchange of strength. The threefold description in v.31 forms a climax, not its opposite; for the exceptional flying and the occasional running do not require, as does the constant walking, an ever-flowing stream of grace.

C. God the Lord of History for His People (41:1–29)

1 Most commentators dub this the beginning of a trial-speech, in which—as in 1:2—the scene is a courtroom. In his dealings with us, God sustains a multiplicity of legal roles; he is plaintiff, injured party, judge, lawgiver, and creator, each role finding its place within his many-sided relationship with sinners. In ch. 40, Isaiah spoke of God in the third person; here God himself speaks.

Although this verse is an address to the nations, the message of the chapter is intended for Israel. The discomfiture of the nations and the demonstration that their gods are impotent are intended to encourage God's people to trust in him. The repetition of "renew their strength" (cf. 40:31) may well be ironic. As the exiles renew their strength in the true God, so the nations are ironically exhorted to do the same—but in their man-made deities!

2–4 The Lord directs attention to himself as the true author of great historical events. But who is the mysterious "one from the east"? Most commentators have taken this and v.25 to be references to Cyrus, who is dramatically named at the close of ch. 44. If this prophecy comes from Isaiah of Jerusalem and not from an unknown prophet of the Exile, and if (see comments on 44:24–28) the revelation of the name of Cyrus is a moment of great prophetic drama, then we should expect some material at an earlier stage to stimulate the expectations of the reader. The references here and in v.25 are fully appropriate when applied to Cyrus. Every historical conqueror raised up by God is, despite his faults, a faint shadow of the great ultimate Victor, God's Messiah; and in him Israel is triumphant and her kingdom enlarged (9:2–7).

Cyrus, king of Persia, crossed the Tigris from the east and so entered the Babylonian Empire. He marched swiftly and victoriously against Croesus, king of Lydia, and took his capital, Sardis, in western Asia Minor, having already subdued the Medes in the north (cf. v.25). He could therefore be described as being both from the east and from the north. The references to "dust" and "chaff" recall 17:13; 29:5; and 40:24. In fact, this reference to Cyrus is an example of the general principle stated in 40:23–24. The conquests of Cyrus took him into areas quite unfamiliar to the people of his land (v.3). The past tenses of these verses should be interpreted as prophetic perfects, describing with vividness what is yet to be. The great conqueror does not hold the center of the prophetic stage for long, for he exists only to exalt the name of the Lord. Verse 4 declares the absolute sovereignty of God over history—from its beginning, through all its generations, and to its end. No wonder he can predict and raise up Cyrus!

5–7 Places remote from Cyrus's route get to hear of what he has done. These verses contain clear allusions to 40:18–20. In the cooperative effort of idol-making, the terrified peoples try to find strength. The atmosphere of panic in v.5 seems to disappear, for the more gods, the more security—or so they think; but v.29 shows how vain is such trust.

8–10 In Cyrus's day the people of Israel would be in exile in Babylon, itself under threat and eventually to fall to Cyrus. The remote islands may have been feeling fear (v.5), but these verses are God's answer to his people's fears.

Verses 8–10 describe Israel in several encouraging ways. The name "Israel" suggests what God is determined to make of his people (Ge 32:28), while the name "Jacob" indicates that God loves them and has chosen them despite their demerit. Taking them "from the ends of the earth" is hyperbole that stresses the distance of Abraham's journey from Ur to Canaan. God chose his people for a purpose of service; thus they cannot perish without that purpose being fulfilled. These people are loved for the sake of beloved Abraham (cf. Dt 7:7–8), to whom God gave great promises (Ge 12:1–3; 17:1–8; et al.). The strength already promised (40:31) would indeed be given to them. The threefold affirmation of strength (v.10) comes to its consummation in a reference to the "righteous right hand" of God, a reminder of the tender strength of the Shepherd-King in 40:9–11.

11–16 Those who are put to shame sometimes do not feel it as they ought, because of moral insensitivity. The call to leave their fear (cf. vv.8–10) comes yet again, with encouragements to trust in their God. The assertion "I am the LORD, your God" is a reminder of the opening of the Decalogue (Ex 20:2) and so suggests a new Exodus. This is reinforced by the use of "Redeemer" (cf. Ex 6:6; 15:13) and made even more emphatic by the phrase "the Holy One of Israel," which stresses God's special relationship with Israel as well as his own distinctive nature.

The description of Israel in v.14 represents the people's self-valuation, while v.15 shows what God's amazing purpose will make them (cf. 2Co 2:16; 3:5–6). Threshing with a heavy wooden sledge was preliminary to winnowing, which was carried out on hilltops where the wind could carry away the chaff. The hills are not now the location of the threshing floor but are themselves threshed! In this way the prophet stresses the powerful instrument God would make of this apparently insignificant people. Every hindrance to God's ultimate purposes in the international scene is overcome through a judgment executed through Israel.

17–20 The provision here described is an answer to prayer. The need for water dominates the passage (cf. 32:6–7). Through the difficult conditions that would beset the returning exiles, God expresses his total provision for their deepest needs. In the most unlikely places, plentiful supplies will be found, making the whole environment fertile and beautiful. God would supply all that his people needed by his power and grace.

21–24 The trial scene of v.1 resumes; but it is now the gods of the nations, not the nations themselves, who are called on for evidence. The concept of deity is, in some ways, simple, combining superhuman power and the claim to human worship. It has many implications, however, and ability to predict is one of these. This is the basis of the argument here. If the gods of Babylonia and other nations have objective reality as deities, they should be able to predict the future and also to so interpret history that past and future are seen to be linked in one divinely controlled plan. If prediction is beyond them, let them produce at least some evidence that they exist! They cannot respond; they and their worshipers are beneath contempt.

25–29 Cyrus was to emerge on the international scene at least a century and a half later. Here then is evidence indeed that what the gods of paganism could not do, the God of Israel could and did do. Here is prediction indeed! North and east ("the rising sun") are combined, for, considered from the standpoint of Palestine, Cyrus originated in the east and carried out major conquests in the north. The Babylonian idols might have been expected to predict Cyrus's coming, for his activities would greatly concern the people who worshiped them; but they were silent.

The prophet presses home his point with quite exceptional emphasis, for vv.26–29 are given over entirely to different ways of underlining the great contrast between the true God who predicts and the false gods who cannot. The coming of Cyrus was, of course, a message of good tidings for Israel (cf. 40:9), because through him would come the release of the exiles.

D. The Lord's Servant—the Perfect and the Defective (42:1–25)

In this part of the book, it is not easy, or perhaps even appropriate, to distinguish separate oracles. Certainly this whole chapter exhibits a point of unity in the servant theme.

1–4 The term "Servant Songs" is something of a misnomer, for there is no evidence they were ever sung. Through the prophetic word the reader's eye is directed away from the pagan gods to God's servant (cf. 41:8–10), in whom the servant mission of Israel finds perfect expression. There can be little doubt that we are intended initially to identify the servant with Israel, that we might be gently led to him who is the incarnation of God's mind for Israel (cf. Mt 12:15–21).

The words "in whom I delight" immediately suggest that the servant is either Israel idealized or Israel represented by the ideal Israelite (cf. Mt 3:17). If the baptism of Jesus was his official initiation into the messianic office, with the descent of the Spirit representing his anointing for the work, the present passage too presents Jesus' ministry in prospect from the perspective of his baptismal inauguration. There are, however, more personal links with the earlier messianic prophecies, in which the king, anointed by the Spirit, promotes justice (cf. 11:1–5; 32:1). Verses 1 and 4 suggest that even if we cannot completely identify the servant with a king, there is a regal aspect to his work.

Already the element of suffering in the servant's experience, which finds fuller and fuller expression until it achieves dominance in the fourth song (52:13–53:12), is gently suggested in v.4. Others, faced with what he would have to experience, would falter; but his faithfulness sustains him in the pathway of obedient service.

5–7 Just as Ps 2 presents the divine address to the messianic King or to Israel's king as foreshadowing him, almost certainly in the context of his kingly enthronement, so here, with the ministry of the servant in prospect, God assures him of divine support in the execution of his mission. As Genesis sets redemption in a context of creation, so the picture of God as Creator and Lord (cf. ch. 40) is summarily expressed here. His relationship to the universe is suggestive of almighty power. This power is now channeled for the support of his servant in the doing of his will. If we interpret this passage in terms of its ultimate fulfillment in Jesus, then it was through his earthly ministry with its climax in death that he was "made" a covenant and a light, just as through his sufferings he was perfected in experience for his priestly work (Heb 5:4–10).

Verse 6, with its reference to "a covenant for the people," makes us aware that the servant cannot be simply identified with Israel. He at least represents a group within it, perhaps the faithful remnant, if not an individual. Thus the reader is being gradually educated as to the identity of the true Servant of God. The "covenant for the people" implies a structured relationship between God and those already possessing his revelation, while "a light for the Gentiles" suggests the widening of the scope of this revelation. The covenant reference may be to the new covenant (Jer 31:31–34), presumably confirming the Abrahamic covenant (cf. Ge 12:1–3; et al.).

Verse 7 can apply both to the people and the Gentiles, but in fact it looks like an exposition of the light-imparting work of the servant. Ancient Near-Eastern prisons were extremely dark; but this verse teaches that the servant gives liberty as well as light (cf. 61:1–2). Freeing captives suggests the conquest of the captors and so kingship, while the opening of blind eyes and the enlightenment of the Gentiles introduce a prophetic feature into the work of this Spirit-anointed Servant of God.

8–9 The great assertion "I am the LORD" recalls 41:13 and so makes another link between the servant and Israel. Therefore, although the servant may not simply be Israel, he is closely associated with that people. God acts in the servant's work for his own glory. That work does not detract from his unique glory but rather ministers to it. "The former things" refers either to earlier prophecies given through Isaiah and already fulfilled or to the entire Israelite prophetic movement and its already fulfilled predictions. The point is that the God who has already proved his word true is able to make known new things. Perhaps he is speaking here of the predicted work of the Servant.

10–13 If we take this chapter as a unity, it is natural to see the chief cause of praise to be the work of the Servant. If his ministry is to reach to the islands of the sea, then it is not surprising that the whole earth joins in the song. The sea and the desert probably find special mention because they are great areas with few people. Even in such places there are islands and oases, and the people who live there are encouraged to join the universal song of praise. The Bedouin, represented by Kedar, and the inhabitants of rocky Sela will also be involved in this vocal worship. Even from the mountaintops, where perhaps only a wandering shepherd is to be found, singing voices are to be heard.

The song is a new one. Before there can be a new, however, there must be an old, and v.13 (recalling perhaps Ex 15:3–12) suggests that the old song was sung by Israel at its release from Egyptian bondage. If the song is occasioned by the work of the Servant, then he is to achieve a new Exodus, a great victory over the enemies of God. What an amazing paradox, when the gentleness of the Servant (vv.2–3) is pondered! This paradox is even more strikingly expressed in Isa 53:1, for "the arm of the LORD" denotes power (cf. also 52:13; 53:12). The nature of the enemies is not indicated here.

14–17 God presents himself as a pregnant woman. The long period of gestation—perhaps representing the Babylonian exile—is over; and God, who has seemed inactive, will be at pains to bring forth his people.

Verse 15 means that the Lord will remove obstacles to his people's deliverance (cf. 40:3–4), and the reference to the drying up of the waters may be an intentional allusion to the Exodus. The unfamiliar paths recall Abraham, who went out (from Babylonia) not knowing where God would take him (cf. Heb 11:8–9). Both the Gentiles and the Israelites need light from God. People worship idols because they promise more immediate satisfaction than does the worship of an unseen God. But here all such apparent promise that cannot in fact produce results will retreat before the deliverance effected by the true God.

18–20 This passage, depicting Israel as blind and deaf in her sin, stands in stark contrast to vv.1–7, where the perfect Servant of the Lord is depicted. Clearly we have been brought back with a jolt from the future's perfection to the present's lamentable failure. A blind and deaf person can hardly function as a servant. Verse 20 makes it clear that this condition is culpable; the faculties are in fact still present, but there is failure to attend. That is, the blindness is of the mind or heart rather than of the eye.

21–25 "Law" (GK 9368) here probably means "teaching" and includes the prophetic word. Whether Israel, as God's now useless servant, hears that word or not, God has determined to magnify it. By contrast, Israel in Babylon is anything but great and glorious. Her lot is a sorry one. Not only have the people been plundered, but they are themselves plunder for their enemies. In the perspective of history, the words "with no one to say, 'Send them back'" remind us that before long Cyrus would say just that.

Israel had failed to learn the spiritual and moral lessons of the Exile, tracing the calamity of it to their own rebellion against God. Herein lay their obtuseness. The occurrence of "we" in v.24 shows that the prophet himself has spiritual perception and moral sensitivity even if they have not. In this way he anticipates in his own person the Servant of the Lord whom he has so beautifully portrayed at the start of the chapter.

E. Grace Abounding and Despised (43:1–28)

This whole chapter expounds the redemptive grace of the Lord toward his people, grace that is highlighted at the end by reference to the people's sin.

1–7 The words "but now" link this chapter with ch. 42, where the prophet declared the consequences of Israel's refusal to obey the law of their God. Here Isaiah declares they will experience God as their Redeemer (cf. 44:1). The names "Jacob" and "Israel" together suggest God's grace to an unworthy people and his great purpose for them. His names and titles are reassuring, for those in v.3 imply a special relationship between God and his people, while his activities on their behalf—such as creation (out of "nothing" in Egypt), redemption, and protection—demonstrate his loving concern.

God promises his people that he will gather them from every quarter, the passage making many allusions to the Exodus. The waters and the rivers look back to the Red Sea and the Jordan, and the fire perhaps

points to Da 3. The nation's preciousness to him suggests a filial relationship, which becomes individualized in v.7. As the firstborn of Israel were ransomed by substitution at the Passover (Ex 13:14–16), so God would ransom Israel as his own firstborn (Ex 4:22–23). The statement "I am the LORD, your God" (v.3) recalls Ex 20, where the divine description is followed by the words "who brought you out of Egypt, out of the land of slavery" (Ex 20:2). So, learning from this significant past event, they could rest in his promise to bring them again into their own land, this time from every point of the globe. Fear is banished as God's nature, activities, and promises to his people are considered.

8–13 The atmosphere of the prophecy changes from comfort to challenge. Once again we are transported to a courtroom (cf. 1:2; 41:1, 21). Israel and the nations are in court together. What is being examined is the Lord's claim to uniqueness, to sole deity. First of all, only he can foretell. He alone is divine; this always has been and always will be the truth. From his dealings with Israel in the past—as Revealer and Savior of his people and Judge of others, at a time (presumably the Exodus) when the people's trust was in him alone—it is clear that he alone is God and Savior.

Israel appears in these verses as God's "witnesses" (vv.10, 12). Other nations can give no witness for their own impotent deities, but the Israelites have so much to declare; for the Lord's wonderful works have been done in their presence and on their behalf. Yet, sadly, though they are God's chosen servant, they are blind, deaf, and a failure. To make matters worse, their choice by him was with a view to intelligent faith in him, which should have made them most articulate and effective as witnesses for him.

14–15 The comforting tone of the opening verses of this chapter is now resumed, along with some reassuring titles and descriptions of Israel's Lord. The generalized promise of vv.5–7 gives place to a specific reference to Babylon, the first express mention of it since ch. 39. It is clear that Babylon is to be judged.

16–21 The fundamental principles of the divine activity are changeless, but the outward shape of that activity alters with the changing needs of God's people. God affirms—in detail and with emphasis on the deadly efficiency of his deeds—that he was the God of the Exodus, but he also asserts the wonderful freshness of his new act in prospect. He had made a way through the waters; now he would make a new way—through the desert! Water, formerly a barrier, would now be a blessing, with God as its source. The abundant provision for people would be enjoyed by the wild creatures also. This would perhaps be a foreshadowing of the regeneration of creation promised in Isa 11:6–9; 65:25.

22–28 Once again the mood changes, and comfort gives place to accusation. The Lord's past acts of grace should have evoked gratitude from his people, but they have offered him sins instead of sacrifices. Both ritualistic excess of sacrifices (cf. 1:2–17) and shameful neglect of them testify to their deep spiritual malaise.

Both here and in ch. 1 the assurance of forgiveness of sins is given in the context of sacrifice. The ultimate in sacrificial—and therefore priestly—teaching is given in 52:13–53:12, where there is full forgiveness through the Servant's sacrifice. Much in vv.22–25 recalls ch. 1, esp. the double use of the word "burdened" (GK 6268; see comments on 1:4, 14, 24). The appropriate has been doubly replaced by the unexpected—on God's side by his incredible grace, and on Israel's by her unthinkable ingratitude.

Verse 26 evokes memories of 1:18, where the divine urge to forgive is expressed in courtroom language, with a call for settlement of the issue. Here God speaks to establish the guilt of his people, for without a recognition of this they would never come for forgiveness. The first father could be Adam, Abraham, or Jacob; from their beginning and throughout their history the nation has been characterized by sin, even on the part of its spiritual elite. Not only would that elite be disgraced, but the whole people would suffer destruction at God's hands.

The word "destruction" (v.28; GK 3051) refers to "the irrevocable giving over of things or persons to the LORD, often by totally destroying them" (see NIV note and comment on Jos 6:17). In other words, God will treat his people as if they are pagan. Isaiah's opening vision, however, assured him that even devastating judgment for Israel would leave a remnant in whom God's purposes would find ultimate fulfillment (cf. 6:11–13).

F. Israel's Great God and the Folly of Idolatry (44:1–23)

1–5 Once again, as in 43:1, after a strong affirmation of divine judgment, God says, "But now." The name "Jeshurun" (see Dt 32:15; 33:5, 26), like Israel, provides a contrast in meaning with Jacob (i.e., "Deceiver"), as there can be little doubt that it means "the Upright One." This fact may suggest that the Jacob-Israel name combination, so common in chs. 41–49, is used to designate the people as sinful and yet as the object of the Lord's gracious purpose of redemption.

Whybray points out that the promises of abundant rain seem not to refer to miracles that will occur during the journey through the desert but denote the conferring of a blessing. Numerous progeny are often treated in the OT as a sign of God's blessing (e.g., Ge 15:5; 17:3–5), and spiritual progeny are evidence of God's blessing on his suffering Servant (53:10).

Isaiah is almost Pauline at this point, for the Gentile converts seem like an (adopted?) extension of the children of Israel. The statement "I will pour out my Spirit" reminds us of Joel 2:29, with its fulfillment at Pentecost and the Gentile evangelization that followed it. Verse 5 probably refers to the mark of a master on the hand of a slave (cf. 49:16).

6–8 The expression "This is what the LORD says" (v.6) is most apt as introducing verses in which God's perceptive word is proclaimed. Although the Lord is the God of his own special people, he is also sovereign over all history and so holds sole title to the designation "God." He is incomparable, especially in his power to interpret the past and predict the future. The statement "I established my ancient people," the phrases "the first" and "long ago" and the use of the title "Rock" from Dt 32 all evoke memories of the Exodus, assuring the people that the first Exodus was the guarantee of the second.

9–20 These verses commence with theological statements (vv.9–11) that introduce the imaginative scene in the idol-maker's shop. The workers share the worthlessness of their images. They are nothing and must suffer discrediting and judgment. Pagan religions have attempted to provide an intellectual framework and justification for idolatry. Isaiah will have none of this, because he is jealous for the glory of the God of Israel. Whether the medium be iron or wood, the enterprise deserves nothing but ridicule. God-given strength and skill are being misused, and sin has deprived the idolater of any sense of what is fitting. He uses a tree that is dependent on God's rain for its growth and uses it for two purposes—to make a fire for warmth and a god for worship! Here is the absurdity of idolatry, for sin has blinded the mind. Right from his call Isaiah in ch. 6 was aware of the blinding effects of sin. The words "he feeds on ashes" suggest that the idolater collects the ashes remaining after his fire has burned out—unbelievably foolish!

21–23 The call to "remember" probably embraces both the vast contrast between the true God and the idols and also the earlier reminders of his activity and power to predict revealed in the past history of his people. The promise of forgiveness in 43:25 is repeated, but now the people's sins are likened to passing phenomena of the sky, blotting out the sun for a while. This does not mean that their sins are not serious, but it does mean that God has determined to forgive them. The command to "return" implies the objectivity of God's redemptive provision, to which the people are called to react in penitence. This objective work is so wonderful that the whole universe is called on to share their exuberant joy at his redemption. Clearly the glory he displays is the glory of his grace.

G. God's Actions Through Cyrus (44:24–45:25)

This great passage, with its two explicit references to Cyrus, has attracted much scholarly discussion. Some modern scholars cannot conceive of supernatural predictive prophecy of such detail. Yet it cannot be denied that the context for such predictions is the most appropriate in the whole Bible; for Isa 40–48 says more about the Lord's power to predict than any other passage.

God assures his people that he plans to rebuild Judah, Jerusalem, and his temple, that this will become possible through the pagan Cyrus, and that the ultimate issue of the divine acts through Cyrus is that people everywhere will acknowledge God's uniqueness (44:24–45:8). His sovereign choice of such a vehicle is unchallengeable and the coming of Cyrus absolutely certain (45:9–13). God will vindicate Israel as his people in the eyes of pagan peoples subdued by Cyrus (45:14–17). This will herald a final challenge to paganism, the offer of salvation to people everywhere, and the ultimate submission of the whole world to his sovereign rule (45:18–25).

24–28 The assertion "This is what the LORD says" punctuates this section of the prophecy (cf. 45:1, 11, 18). The Lord is first designated as his people's Redeemer. The phrase "who formed you in the womb" links this passage with 44:1, confirming the integrity of Isa 40–48. The simple yet important affirmation "I am the LORD" recalls Ex 20:2 (cf. 43:11; see comment on 43:1–7).

With a series of prepositional phrases, Isaiah builds a powerful doctrine of the past activities of the God of Israel. He is the sole creator, the sole revealer of the future, and the sole guarantor of a new day for Jerusalem and Judah. The meaning of v.27 is disputed, but it most likely refers to the Exodus.

There have already been allusions to Cyrus (see comments on 41:2–4, 25–29), but his name has been held back for this great moment of poetic and prophetic climax. Only in 1Ki 13:2 do we find anything quite comparable in the OT, though Isa 52:13–53:12 could hardly be made more wonderfully specific if the name Jesus had been mentioned. Only a little less dramatic than the name is the description of Cyrus as "my shepherd," for this was a pagan foreigner. The term would remind the people of the shepherd role of their own kings, especially David (cf. 2Sa 5:2), and of the description of God in Isa 40:11. The lost sheep were to be rounded up and returned to their true fold in Judah by this foreigner, who would make possible the rebuilding of Jerusalem and the temple of Israel's God. This oracle gives the first explicit reference in Isaiah to God's plans to rebuild the city.

45:1–7 The last five verses of ch. 44, for all their majesty, contain only one main statement: "I am the LORD" (v.24). All else leads into or amplifies this great affirmation. It is repeated in vv.3, 5, and 6. This is surely significant in an address to a pagan king. "His anointed" and "my shepherd" (44:28) explain each other, for both meet in the concept of a divinely chosen and divinely employed king. There is precedent for the divine anointing of a non-Israelite king, though in one passage only (1Ki 19:15–16). Although the living God normally employed Israelites for such purposes, he is sovereign and may use whom he will.

Because in God's purpose Cyrus functions for Israel, he comes into the good of some of God's promises to that people. He would enjoy great triumphs over his enemies and would find their fortified cities no obstacle to his advance. The reference to great "riches" could refer to the treasures of Lydia—the riches of whose ruler, Croesus, were proverbial—or to those of Babylon; Cyrus overcame both. That all these victories were for the sake of little Israel is one of the ironies of God's control of history.

The prophet declares that Cyrus would call on the Lord's name (41:25) and that God's support of Cyrus has as its purpose that he might know that Israel's God is the Lord. Yet twice over it is denied that Cyrus acknowledges him (vv.4–5). In the Cyrus Cylinder (see EBC, 1:238), the king attributes his victories to Marduk, god of Babylon, though in Ezr 1 he is quoted as asserting that the Lord had given him dominion. Clearly Cyrus used the names of deities without any sense of exclusiveness.

The general assertions of absolute monotheism in vv.5–6 are underlined by the specific affirmations of v.7. There are three in all, the first related to the universe, the second to human society, and the third summing up. Genesis seems to imply the creation of darkness as well as light by God (Ge 1:1–5). Although it is said in Genesis that the light is good, there is no suggestion that the darkness is evil, for it too has its function (cf. Ps 104:19–24). The words shalom (GK 8934) and ra' (GK 8273), rendered "prosperity" and "disaster," are, literally, "peace" and "evil" (cf. Am 3:6). So the God who created darkness, which is not itself evil—though it is sometimes used to symbolize it—and who brings disaster as a punishment for sin, is supreme over all.

8 This verse suggests that the prophet had Ge 1 in mind. The heavens and the earth, called on first to witness the rebellion of God's people (1:2) and then to praise God for redeeming them (44:23), are now addressed in ecstatic apostrophe. The poetic imagination of the prophet sees the processes by which vegetation grows on the earth as symbols of God's saving work (cf. Heb 6:7). The God of creation and the God of redemption are one.

"Righteousness" and "salvation" are closely linked here. God's righteous order of the future is to include the manifestation of his salvation. In Pauline theology the righteousness of God is seen in the gospel (cf. Ro 1:16–17; 3:21–22; et al.); for through the bearing of sin by Christ, God's righteous wrath against sin has been fully manifested and sinners are given, by his grace, a righteous standing with God (Ro 3:25–26).

9–10 The point at issue in the quarrel is probably God's disclosure to his people that he would deliver them through pagan Cyrus. We cannot accuse God of using inappropriate means to achieve his ends. Isaiah was particularly gifted in portraying sin as ridiculous and illogical, as he does here with the illustrations of the discarded scraps of pottery and the lump of clay in the hands of the potter (cf. Jer 18:1–6). Verse 10 applies ultimately to God the Creator (cf. Ro 9:20–21).

11–13 In v.13 Isaiah again clearly refers to Cyrus (cf. NIV note). "My children" and "the work of my hands" allude to vv.9–10. The coming of Cyrus, though still future, is as certain as the existence of God's created universe. Not only is Jerusalem to be rebuilt (cf. 44:26–28), but its people will be freed from their exile, and that without any financial inducement to Cyrus.

14 This verse anticipates ch. 60. The people of Egypt, Cush, and Seba are seen here submitting to Israel. Despite their chains, the language suggests the people will voluntarily submit, and that for the best of reasons—recognition of Israel's God and him alone.

15–17 The startling disclosures just made prompt this prophetic exclamation of wonderment. The conversion of the Gentiles involves the discrediting of idolatry and the salvation and vindication of God's ancient people. The final phrase of v.17 makes it clear that this is no momentary thing but a permanent vindication of them by their God.

18–19 The introductory "This is what the LORD says" introduces some utterances of grandeur about God himself. He created the universe as an environment for humankind;

thus his work is to be discerned in history as well as in nature. Perhaps he does hide himself, for revelation is his sole prerogative; but when he does speak, his word is clear and true, enabling his people to find him.

20–21 After the disclosure about Egypt, Cush, and Seba in v.14, the prophet calls on the remnant of humanity left after all history's wars and upheavals. There is to be one last challenge to paganism. Only the Lord predicted the coming of Cyrus and the righteous salvation of Israel. He has established forever his claim to be recognized as the only God there is.

22–25 Amazingly, the God whose actions discredit paganism calls the discomfited idolaters, not for the judgment they so richly deserve, but for salvation—if only they will turn to him! God's great decree has been announced that all humanity will come to acknowledge his sovereignty. All will not be saved, but all must acknowledge the Lord as God alone. Under his ultimate sovereignty there will be both judgment for the rebel and salvation for God's people (cf. Php 2:10–11).

H. Babylon's Ineffectual Idols and the Lord Almighty (46:1–13)

1–2 All references so far made in the prophecy to pagan deities or idols have been general. Here, appropriately, where Cyrus and his victories are much in view, Isaiah named the two great gods of Babylon; Bel (also called Marduk) and Nebo, familiar to us from the compound names Belshazzar and Nebuchadnezzar. In ch. 45 Isaiah declared that every knee will bow to the Lord, and here he pictures the gods of great Babylon stooping low in humiliation. Isaiah applies the imagery of burden-bearing first to the gods of Babylon and then, in vv.3–4, to the Lord. The idols are taken from their places of honor and placed on the backs of animals, bundled off perhaps first in flight and then to captivity. It is true (see at 45:1–7) that Cyrus attributed his victories to Marduk, but there can be little doubt that those who heard of the downfall of Babylon would see in this a colossal defeat for her gods. The tiredness of the animals underscores the impotence of the gods. They have become a liability to both people and animals.

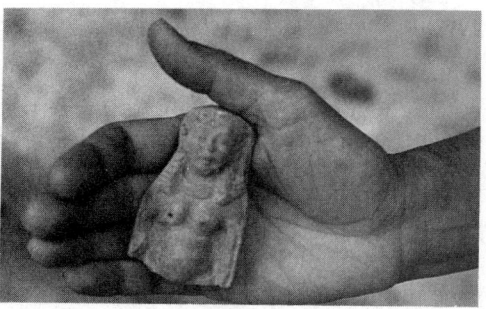

This small Egyptian god was broken during a Babylonian assault. How weak idols are! Courtesy Ilan Sztulman of the Tel Miqne-Ekron Excavations.

3–4 How different is the Lord's relationship to his people! His people do not carry him; rather, he bears them. Moreover, he always has done so and always will. The repetition of the fact that he is the God who carries his people gives place suddenly and dramatically to a new fact: he promises to rescue them. The work of Cyrus will be viewed as God's great work of deliverance.

5–7 The Lord's uniqueness (cf. 40:18, 25) has been singularly demonstrated in the overthrow of Babylon's gods. Not in their downfall alone, but at every point in their history, the idols' paltry character vividly contrasts with the Lord's unique majesty. The whole process of making idols, from the preparation through the commissioning of the workers and the transportation of the idols to their eventual worship is quite unavailing; for they are powerless to hear, to speak, or to save.

8–13 Isaiah concentrates here largely on consolation and encouragement, but he is a realist, knowing from experience that there was much unbelief among the people. They approached the prophecies of Cyrus and his work with skepticism. The Lord calls them to consider the history of his relationship with them. This illustrates that faith has objective reference and so is a response to revelation, to truth about God declared by God himself. The people's history had demonstrated his sole deity and especially his power to predict. Isaiah asserts it again: from the east Cyrus will swoop on his victims, as suddenly as the descent of an eagle from the sky. Whether they believe it or not, it will happen; for in this way the Lord will fulfill his saving purpose for Israel. The term "Zion" is a reminder of the promises of 44:26–28.

I. The Fall of Proud Babylon (47:1–15)

There is a sense of fitness to the downfall of Babylon's gods being followed immediately by a proclamation of the fall of Babylon herself, for there was solidarity between them.

1–4 The prophet's inspired imagination continues to overleap the years separating his own day from the close of the Babylonian exile. He addresses the proud capital city with irony as "Virgin Daughter of Babylon." She is to be dethroned and made to sit in the dust. Three analogies follow one another in swift succession: (1) she is a beggar, sitting in the dust; (2) she is a slave, divesting herself of the gentlewoman's veil and accepting the hard grind of manual labor; and (3) she is a fugitive, needing to tuck in her skirts to enable her to cross streams. The Lord declares all this to be an expression of his impartial punitive justice, and the prophet follows this by asserting that the judgment is to be understood in the context of his holy and redemptive purpose for Israel.

5–7 The prophet's interjection in v.4 is parenthetical, for the direct address from God is now resumed. Babylon will go from the blare of world publicity and the glare of the palace lights to the silence of obscurity! Babylon's dominion was not only over the southern Mesopotamian heartland of her empire but also over many petty kingdoms she had vanquished. The prophecy recognizes that the destruction of Judah and the exile of its people were to be understood as a divine punishment. Babylon, however, went too far, and the condition of the exiles may have worsened toward the close of their captivity. Characteristically, Isaiah underlines not only man's inhumanity to man, but also pride as a major cause of Babylon's judgment.

8–11 The accusation of self-sufficient pride already leveled at Babylonia is further expounded. This pleasure-loving lady of leisure will soon find herself a childless widow, her widowhood robbing her of the possibility of further family. Isaiah has already made it plain that sorcery and other ways of trafficking with the forbidden supernatural realm were a cause of God's judgment on his own

people (2:6; 8:19). For the Babylonians, sorcery also induced a mood of complacency, because the people relied on their magicians to predict the coming of the enemy and to defeat him. For them, the intellectual and the magical were intertwined.

12–15 The prophet taunts Babylonia sarcastically. Such a rag bag of spells and magic arts she has accumulated! Could it be that there is an outside chance of success? "Not a hope!" the prophet implies. Then he exhorts the experts with the horoscopes to provide deliverance. Babylonia, with its astral deities, was the natural home of the astrologer and his kin. The prophet identifies for a moment with the people, besieged with advice from such people and yet with no hope of a remedy for future calamity. In v.13 he says, "Let them save you"; and in v.14 he boldly asserts, "They cannot even save themselves."

The coming of the great judgment is likened to a consuming fire, and the tone of sarcasm returns in the second half of v.14. They should not mistake the meaning. This is fire as an enemy, not as a friend. The whole history of Babylon's long flirtation with astrology is bluntly dismissed in v.15. All this effort, all this expenditure, and at the end—nothing!

J. Israel's Stubbornness and God's Purpose of Grace (48:1–22)

1–6a The call to "listen" introduces God's charge that his people are stubborn skeptics. They are untrue both to their national names and to their religious profession. The name "Israel" means "he struggles with God" (Ge 32:28 [cf. NIV note]; cf. Ro 9:6) and "Judah" means "praise" (Ge 49:8; cf. Ro 2:28–29). The people were proud too of their citizenship in the place God had set apart for himself (cf. 52:1). God's own name was used in solemn religious vows and in prayer, not in true faith manifested in righteousness, but in presumptuous reliance on mere profession. Let them recall that he is also the Lord Almighty, implying that he may use this great power to bring judgment on them.

Not only were the people stiff-necked and brazen in their attitude toward God's word, but they had a chronic tendency to attribute his acts to other gods. The adjectives "wooden" and "metal" reflect the prophet's contempt for idols (cf. 44:19). Let them admit that he is the God of prophecy and fulfillment and therefore true to his word.

6b–11 From things foretold "long ago," the divine word proceeds to reveal new things: the work of Cyrus (vv.14–16) and the Servant of the Lord (v.16; 49:1–7). The word "create" (GK 1343), used in Ge 1 of God's creative word, is used in v.7 to emphasize that what God has declared is as certain as if it is already fulfilled (cf. Heb 1:1).

Israel was rebellious. God did not reveal these things earlier, for he knew how cynically his people would react. Their ears were shut to his glad tidings, while, as Isaiah will show, the Servant's would be open to accept his destiny of suffering (50:4). They were untrue to their own name, but God would vindicate his own. Rebellious and treacherous they might be, but they would always find him true, upholding the honor of his great name and therefore restraining the full outpouring of his wrath on the people of the promises.

12–16 The renewed call to "listen" apparently underlines the importance of the three great facts here declared. (1) God speaks of himself, his self-existence, his lordship over all history from its beginning to its consummation, and his creation and present control of all that is. (2) He speaks a word about Cyrus, whom he calls "the LORD's chosen ally." This makes explicit for the first time that Cyrus's work would bring down Babylonia (cf. 14:13–23).

(3) Another speaker mysteriously enters the prophecy. Numerous conservative commentators have argued that the new speaker introduced here is in fact God's Servant, the Servant of the songs. He is clearly not simply the Lord, and the phrase "Sovereign LORD" recurs in 50:4–5, 7, 9, in the context of the third Servant Song. Unlike the first and fourth songs, where it is God who speaks about him, here, as in the second and third, he himself speaks. Perhaps he is introduced here because Cyrus's work is simply a harbinger of the much greater deliverance he would bring to God's people (see comment on 53:1).

Grammatically "the Spirit" could be either a second subject (with "LORD") or a second object (with "me"), but it is almost certainly the latter. The NIV's rather free rendering is probably intended to leave both options of interpretation open.

17–19 Every sensitive teacher knows the pain of heart that comes when one pours oneself out for one's students who prove to be unteachable. Israel proved to be like that (cf. v.8); and God expresses his deep concern for them, because they are themselves the losers. The language used does not exclude all possibility of penitent amendment, as if all hope had gone. The similes speak of abundance; and the whole passage stresses the contingent nature of God's blessings, even some of these that have been the subject of his own promises. Divine grace can, of course, so work within the heart that promises seemingly uncertain of fulfillment are made sure by the regenerative work of the Spirit.

20–22 This most dramatic passage anticipates the call given in 52:11–12. The military-style command is explicit and urgent and is associated with a call to all the earth to praise God for his redeeming grace to Israel. The "shouts of joy" were perfectly natural, as those who have suffered internment in prison camps well know. Verse 21 suddenly moves from the future to the past, for the people's confidence in God as their Redeemer from Babylonia was to be based on his redeeming love demonstrated at the Exodus and his care of his people during their journey through the desert. In such a context v.22 may seem harsh, but the prophet was a realist, knowing the unbelief with which many of the people would view this vision. Acts of salvation are not for the stubbornly wicked and unbelieving but for those who have faith (cf. Rev 22:14–15).

VIII. The Gospel of the Servant of the Lord (49:1–57:21)

A. The Lord's Servant and the Restoration of Israel (49:1–26)

This is the second of the so-called Servant Songs, though, as we have suggested at 48:16, this passage is anticipated not only by ch. 42 but also by that verse.

1–7 Although a collective interpretation of this passage is not impossible and is naturally suggested by a consideration of v.3, a straightforward application to Israel is ruled out by vv.5–7. The reader is therefore forced by the material itself to face the question: Who is this?

If the first song can be viewed as contemplating the ministry of Jesus the Servant in prospect from the perspective of his baptism, this second song seems to be looking back on that ministry from its close. The distant nations are to benefit from his work; so he calls them to "listen" (v.1). This harmonizes with the prophetic ministry to which he was predestined (cf. Jer 1:4–5). In v.2 the penetrating character of the Servant's message is likened to two sharp weapons, and the implications of the second weapon are developed to bring out a further point. Concealment in the quiver suggests an eternal purpose manifest at the appropriate time (cf. 1Pe 1:20).

Isaiah 42:18–20 presents Israel as the deaf and blind servant of the Lord, and 44:21–23 assures us that nevertheless God intends to display his glory in Israel his servant. Here (v.3) that promise is reiterated. Matthew saw Jesus as the expression of God's mind for Israel (cf. Hos 11:1; Mt 2:15); and the Gospel of John asserts that God's glory is revealed in him (Jn 1:14; 2:11). Jesus, even more than Nathanael, is "a true Israelite, in whom there is nothing false" (Jn 1:47).

The close of the ministry of Jesus saw the great crowds of Galilean days no longer thronging him, the official religious leaders plotting his death, and the disciples forsaking him in the face of danger; but God would reward him (v.4; cf. Heb 12:2).

Verse 5 makes it clear that the Servant is not Israel per se, for he has a ministry to Israel. The people may despise him, but God honors him. Honor is shown in the range of his ministry, for through it he will in fact be brought to great honor before the world's kings and princes. The initial phrase "and now" suggests the transition from the limited ministry of the Gospels to the more extensive proclamation of his gospel through the apostles in Acts. The words "it is too small a thing" suggest an estimate of his person or of his work or of perhaps both. Israel has light but needs restoration, while the Gentiles need both light and salvation. The church's mission to the Gentiles is to be viewed in the context of the mission of Jesus himself (cf. Jn 20:21) and is to the uttermost parts of the earth (e.g., Mt 28:19).

Accordingly Paul and Barnabas could apply the words of v.6 to themselves (Ac 13:46–

47). The song of Simeon, however, applies this verse to Jesus (Lk 2:32). In other words, we have NT warrant for interpreting this second song both individually and collectively, with the second emerging out of the first.

Verse 7 prepares for the third and fourth songs. The unique servant's ministry was in fact rejected by the nation (cf. Ro 9–11). Great as he was, he came as a subject of God and of earthly rulers. As a result of his work, the highest of men and women would not only stand in respect and amazement but also would bow low in worship and submission.

8–12 Often in the NT it is said that the Messiah (Christ) rejected and crucified by humanity was raised and vindicated by God (e.g., Ac 2:23). The favor of God to the unique Servant is of course merited, but 2Co 6:2 shows that in Christ we share not only his service but also his acceptance (cf. Eph 1:6).

The background to "the time of my favor" is probably the Year of Jubilee in Lev 25:8–55 (cf. 61:1–2). The context here suggests that part of the Servant's work is to establish the aspects of the Abrahamic and possibly the Mosaic covenants that relate to the land of Canaan. Children and a land were major blessings of the covenant with Abraham (Ge 12:2–3); the first is mentioned in 48:19 and the second here. The Servant would be a kind of second Joshua (the Hebrew equivalent of "Jesus"). The land would be repopulated by freed captives.

The new conditions of the people are beautifully described. They are first pictured like sheep finding abundant pasture in a formerly barren land. In this land they will find food, water, and shelter. They will be guided by a compassionate shepherd (cf. Ps 23). These verses are echoed and applied to Christ in Rev 7:16–17. The pastoral imagery now disappears and is replaced by assurances of suitable road conditions and of a return from every quarter (cf. 35:8; 40:3–4; et al.).

13–21 The news of deliverance from Babylonia was to be proclaimed with joy to the ends of the earth (48:20); now the heavens and the earth are called to praise the Lord. The note of "comfort" with which ch. 40 opened returns, but now the prophet confronts the people's discouragement. Verse 14, like 40:9 (cf. 44:26–28), speaks not of Israel but of Zion. At the time of the return from the Exile, the Holy City would be in ruins, its walls reduced to rubble. The Lord assures her that he has not forgotten her. He uses two telling illustrations. Mother love is proverbial in every culture; God's love for this city and its people went well beyond this (v.15). The walls of Jerusalem would not even exist at the time of the return, but those people had been and were yet to be engraved on the hands of God (v.16).

Zion was to look up to see her restored citizens coming from every quarter (cf. Ge 13:14). God pictures Zion as proudly putting on her citizens, like a bride her jewels. The numbers coming would be so great that the city could not house them all. Zion regarded herself as a widow; but her husband, the Lord, had not forsaken or forgotten her. The children who would one day crowd to her are legitimate children, begotten through a living faith.

22–23 In v.7 the Servant was told that kings and princes would give him respect and submission. His people will also have their share, for not only will the nations rally to God's banner, tenderly bringing the exiled Israelites with them (cf. 11:10–12), but their exalted monarchs, with all the gentle care of parents, will also do obeisance before them. They will recognize the special place of Israel. God will not fail his people who trust in him (cf. 28:16).

24–26 Echoes of the Exodus constantly appear in this part of Isaiah. The question of v.24 recalls that this is exactly what God did when he delivered his people from Egypt (Ex 12:35–36). Moreover, not only did God make himself known to Israel but also to the Egyptians, and the greater redemption from oppression promised here will also lead to a wider recognition by all peoples of who God is. Verse 26a is a graphic and gruesome way of indicating the utter desperation of the enemies of Israel, overcome with hunger and thirst, in contrast to Israel's promised condition (vv.9–11).

B. Israel's Sin and the Servant's Obedience (50:1–11)

Here, as in ch. 42, the true Servant of God appears in a context speaking of rebellious Israel, named also as God's servant in 42:19. Here, as in 49:3, 6, the Servant is the perfect expression of God's mind for Israel. The imperfect servant, though not so named, appears in vv.1–3 and 11, and the perfect in vv.4–10.

1–3 The figures of divorce and debt set forth Israel's conception of the Lord's relationship to her. Exiled, she assumes that he has cast her off (cf. 40:27); but God her husband (cf. Jer 31:32) has not divorced her nor sold her to pay off his debts; for he, the Creator, has none. The cause of the Exile was simply sin on Israel's part; and if she returns to God, he will restore her.

Verse 2 rebukes Israel's unbelief. Through the prophets God called to the people but found no answering response (cf. 48:8). Their unbelief had closed the book of redemptive history to them. The end of this verse refers to the Exodus (cf. Ex 15:16; Dt 26:8; Ps 77:15). "A mere rebuke" suggests how simple an act of deliverance is for him. The argument from history is reinforced from nature, itself affected by the events associated with the Exodus. The judgment on the Nile and the clothing of the sky's brightness with darkness are fit symbols of God's power to judge Israel's enemies.

4–9 Although there is no explicit reference to the Servant here, there are many links with the other songs, as well as to 48:16. This divine title "the Sovereign LORD" also binds this third song together, occurring in four of six verses.

There is a contrast with vv.1–3. Here is response to God's word (cf. v.2; 42:18–20). The second song stressed the penetrating power of the word that the Servant transmits (49:2), while this one shows its pastoral effectiveness (cf. Isa 40:27–3; Mt 11:28–30). God's Servant waits on God in the morning watch (cf. Mk 1:35), the word he speaks comes from the God who sent him (cf. Jn 7:16–18).

Israel is rebellious, but God's Servant is responsive even when a destiny of suffering and shame is the subject of God's word to him. He does not draw back but "offers" his body to the tormentors. A combination of pain and shame introduces the Servant's conviction that this disgrace must yield place to a glorious vindication (cf. 52:13; 53:12). His face, cruelly assaulted, will not flinch before suffering (cf. Lk 9:51). Even in this, however, though the individualization reaches a high point, we are reminded of the picture of afflicted Israel in Ps 129. The Servant is the innocent sufferer par eminence.

God helps Israel (43:2, 5; 44:2) and Cyrus (45:1, 5); he will also help his unique Servant (cf. 43:1). The NT emphasizes the vindication by God through the resurrection of the despised and suffering Jesus (Ac 2:23–24; 3:15; et al.). Here in Isaiah there is no indication of the form the divine vindication takes. The setting is clearly forensic, and the trials of Jesus make this peculiarly appropriate. He too could confront his enemies with the challenge, "Can any of you prove me guilty of sin?" (Jn 8:46).

10–11 The people who obey identify themselves with the Servant's own attitude and so express their reverential fear of God. This fear is not one that makes people hide but draws them to God in faith. Verse 10b perhaps calls for repentance, for it speaks of walking in darkness and offers, by implication, light from God through the word of the Servant (cf. Jn 12:44–45). Before the advent of modern science, a source of light was also a source of heat, so the analogy of v.11 develops that which brings v.10 to its close. It reminds us of 1:29–31, teaching that the wicked will be caught in their own trap.

C. Listen! Awake! Depart! (51:1–52:12)

The climax of the servant theme and, indeed, of the Christological theme generally in this book is being prepared for in this passage. The many statements about God and the promises of what he will do, along with allusions to earlier parts of Isaiah, anticipate a great climax.

1–3 The prophet calls for maximum attention, the concentration of both the literal ear and the eye of the imagination (cf. Mk 4:3). His call is to those who fear the Lord (50:10). The people are to reflect on their origins, for this will encourage them as they await his deliverance from Babylonia. The Lord had brought this nation into being from such small beginnings, in fulfillment of his promises; and he is able still to translate his word into events.

God's promise to Abraham included both a land and a people (cf. Ge 17:1–8). The capital city of that land is now in ruins and its environs a wasteland, but God will comfort her by transforming her land and giving her a voice to praise him. Genesis has been in view in the reference to Abraham and Sarah; and it

is again when the prophet alludes to the Garden of Eden.

4–6 The repeated use of "my" presents a vivid impression of the personal activity of God on behalf of his people. The Lord will manifest his own righteousness to those who pursue it. The first Servant Song shows that the Servant is the mediator of this divine justice (42:1). Here we see that the law, justice, righteousness, and salvation are all to be widely disseminated throughout the nations. This combination suggests that there is going to be a thorough reordering of human life on the basis of God's own character, revealed in his law, expressed in his righteousness, and taking the form of salvation. Salvation and righteousness are closely parallel ideas here, providing a background for the Pauline doctrine of salvation as righteousness (e.g., Ro 1:16–17).

The prophet calls on Israel to consider the universe. The heavens and the earth that seem to be so stable are in fact less enduring than the salvation God has promised (cf. Mk 13:31).

7–8 Isaiah draws a close link between righteousness and the law of God, for the law publishes God's right way for the human race. The heart is where God's law should be (cf. Dt 30:14), and the new covenant pledges that it will be written there (Jer 31:31–34). The prophet assumes that the righteous in the land will experience antagonism from the wicked. Like the visible universe, the wicked will perish. The only abiding realities in God's new order are his own righteousness and salvation.

9–11 Characteristically, prophets stand facing the people, addressing them for God. They must often have prayed, however, for those to whom they were sent (cf. 1Sa 7:8; Am 7:1–6). Here Isaiah prays wonderfully, with great urgency expressed in the threefold cry, "Awake!" The prophet, who had been the inspired channel of the wonderful promises God had given to his people, now cries to God for their fulfillment. A new revelation of the power of his arm had been promised (cf. v.5). This had already been manifested in the destruction of Egypt's power, for Rahab and the monster are symbols of that land (see comment on 30:7). Here is praying indeed, in which God's great deeds in the past are made the basis of prayerful confidence in his power to act again for his people. Once before the people had entered the Land of Promise with joy, and so they would again.

12–16 God begins to answer his people's cry. He rebukes them for their lack of faith. As he had been telling them since ch. 40, he is going to make himself known to them as their Divine Comforter. The repeated "I" heightens the contrast between "the LORD [their] Maker" and the "mortal men" of whom they were afraid (cf. 40:6–8). Presumably the oppressors mentioned here are the Babylonians, though there is of course an important general principle here as well.

The "cowering prisoners" are either the people as a whole or a group of hostages imprisoned as surety of the good behavior of the remainder. If the Exile did become more severe toward its close, v.14 may reflect the fears of the people that death or extreme starvation would overcome them before their release.

Verse 16 is apparently an allusion to the Servant of the Lord, another indication that he is to be found outside the Servant Songs (cf. 48:16). The verse closes with references to God's creative work, in which he established the cosmos, and that special work he had pledged himself to on Zion's behalf.

17–20 The repeated "awake" of v.17 must surely be the divine call to Jerusalem that answers the call of the prophet to God (cf. v.9). The illustration of a cup, containing the awful wrath of God and so potent in its effects that those who drink it would be totally overcome by it, is a bold one (cf. Mk 10:38). Such a drunk person is, of course, unable to walk steadily without a guide; Jerusalem's sons, sharing her drunkenness, lie prostrate in the streets. The "double calamities" remind us of 40:2. The figure of inebriation gives way first to the general ("ruin and destruction") and then to the specific ("famine and sword," which probably represents the two calamities intended). God thus metes out his judgment through nature and people.

21–23 The question asked in v.19—"Who can comfort you?"—is answered here. The cup of God's wrath, justly placed by him in Israel's hand, is to be removed in mercy and transferred to her oppressors. The barbaric practice referred to in v.23 is well docu-

mented in the ancient Near East, especially in Assyrian inscriptions.

52:1–2 The cry "Awake, awake!" addressed first to God (51:9) and then to Jerusalem (51:17), comes again as a clarion call to that city. Babylon is to be debased and Jerusalem exalted. The strength that Jerusalem is to put on is the power of her God. Her garments typify armored might and perhaps priestly beauty, fitting in view of her new God-given holiness, having now a reality formerly lacking (cf. 48:2). The exclusion of the uncircumcised and the defiled should not be read as the product of a harsh nationalism but as a reminder that the alien had so often entered Jerusalem either to conquer or to pollute its worship or both (cf. Ps 79:1). Verse 2 especially reminds us of ch. 47; instead of Babylon, Zion is now to be enthroned in queenly splendor, a gloriously free city.

3–6 Verse 3 preserves in brief compass three important truths. Jerusalem was, in fact, handed over to Babylonia by God himself—as a punishment, of course. Yet those who were given to her paid nothing and so were owed nothing. Thus God would act again, but this time in redemption. So the word "redeemed," normally implying cost, does not have this connotation here.

Verse 4 traces a history of oppression and a sequence of oppressors, with v.5 showing that Babylonia is now to be added to Egypt and Assyria. The divine soliloquy in v.5 dramatically presents the question of the appropriate divine action in this new situation faced by his people. All three tyrant nations scoffed at the God of Israel with constant blasphemy. The expression "in that day" (v.6) points to a period in which God will act decisively for his people in vindication of his name. The prediction would be called to mind when it was fulfilled, thus establishing the true and exclusive deity of the God of Israel (cf. 45:21).

7–10 This exultant passage contains echoes of 40:1–11. Here the prophet brings together a number of important themes, virtually identifying peace, salvation, and the kingdom of God, reminding us that Christ's work secures these and every other blessing for God's people. How fitting this is just prior to the fourth Servant Song (52:13–53:12), in which the sufferings of God's Servant are described and their significance expounded!

Verse 9 reminds us that Zion is the ruined city of the future. Faith can claim the promises with joyous songs, rejoicing in God's comfort and redemption. The reference to God's "holy arm" takes us back to 51:9, and it is part of God's answer to his prophet's prayer. This powerful act of salvation will be as public as the deliverance from Egypt.

11–12 Urgent as the call to "depart" is, the departure from Babylonia will not be a pressured flight, unlike that from Egypt (Ex 12:33, 39). Interestingly, Babylonia is described, not as "here," but as "there," indicating that the prophet is in Judah and not Babylonia.

Ceremonial purity is important, especially for the priests who transported the holy temple-vessels (cf. 2Ki 25:14–15; Ezr 1:5–11). It is clear that the purpose of God includes the rebuilding of the temple. The most comforting word comes at the end, for God promises that he will protect this holy procession from both the front and the rear (cf. Ex 13:21–22; 14:19–20).

D. The Man of Sorrows and His Vindication (52:13–53:12)

The interpreter who has meditated on the third Servant Song in 50:4–9 and then moves on to this fourth song feels somewhat as the high priest must have felt when he moved from the Holy Place into the Most Holy Place on the Day of Atonement. This "song" is to be seen in its full glory, not only in the light of the NT interpretation of it, but also in terms of the context in which it comes to us. We have already commented (see 51:1–52:12) that this earlier passage anticipates a great climax. It should also be noted that the important phrase "the arm of the LORD" in 53:1 is anticipated in 51:9 and 52:10.

A great deal has been written on the interpretation of the songs in general and the fourth song in particular. Whatever may be said about the earlier songs, we take this one to be understood exclusively in individual terms, fulfilled in Jesus. It is readily granted that the principles of obedience to God's will whatever the cost, in which the cross is taken up by the disciple of Jesus, apply to individual Christians and to the church as a whole. The atoning significance of the sufferings of the Servant, outlined in this passage, is, however, peculiar to Jesus the unique Servant.

13–15 Once again, as in 42:1, God draws attention to his Servant. The Servant's wisdom was deeply self-denying, for it meant accepting ends determined by God and willingly shouldering a burden of untold suffering to make them possible. Here God's wisdom and human wisdom decisively part company. The threefold assertion of the Servant's exaltation is most emphatic, whether or not we spell it out in terms of resurrection, ascension and session, or second advent. The predicted exaltation is most reassuring as we approach predictions of shame and suffering.

The observers of the Servant have a double experience of astonishment, the first mingled with horror and the second, at least for those responding in faith, with joy. The theme of suffering and subsequent glory is here presented from the standpoint of the impression made on the onlookers. The strong word translated "appalled" (GK 9037) finds its justification in the words that follow, for the sight disclosed is of such exquisite suffering that the Servant's bodily appearance seems hardly human. We need not assume from this that the experience being described is purely physical, for deep inner experiences of anguish demonstrate their presence by their effects on the face and form of the sufferer.

The word "sprinkle" (GK 5684) has priestly-sacrificial overtones, preparing us for further sacrificial language later in the passage. In common with everything else in these three verses, "sprinkle" relates to the consequences of the Servant's sufferings rather than to the sufferings themselves. It also relates his sacrificial work to the world in general, not simply to Israel. His exaltation gives him complete supremacy over all; and kings will fall silent in his presence, overawed and eager to see and hear rather than to speak themselves in the presence of such an unprecedented revelation. Notice the striking reversal here of the discouraging words of Isaiah's commission (6:9–10).

53:1–3 The intimate link between v.1 and the closing verse of ch. 52 can hardly be missed and poses a difficulty for those who divorce the end of ch. 52 from this chapter. The two astonishing events of 52:14–15—the suffering of God's own wise Servant who deserved none of it and the subsequent elevation of one so dishonored by people—produce incredulity in many who hear the report of these things. God's way of doing things often does not seem to make sense to human beings (cf. 55:8–9; 1Co 1:18–31). The Cross is, however, where God's power resides, and here is the ultimate answer to the prophet's prayer of 51:9, anticipated by its foreshadowing in the new Exodus of 52:10.

Are the speakers in v.1 Gentiles or Israelites (the latter possibly speaking through the prophet as their representative)? The Servant's work was to have wide-ranging application (cf. 42:6; 49:6). In the context it would seem natural that the nations and kings (52:15), at first struck dumb by the astounding revelation, should then speak in response to it. The "arm of the LORD" is the disclosure of his power. So this revelation answers the prophet's representative prayer in 51:9.

Verse 2 echoes and contrasts with 4:2. The whole verse suggests that the Servant would be confronted with adverse conditions from his youth. In fact, Jesus could not be explained in terms of his human environment, which in his day was dominated by a legalistic Judaism almost devoid of the refreshing moisture of God's word truly understood and applied. Verse 2b implies that his true intrinsic beauty was hidden from people because they looked at him entirely from a human standpoint. The principle that human appearance is irrelevant to God's choice is more radically applied here than in the choice of David (cf. 1Sa 16:5–13). It is possible, however, that these words apply to the Servant's appearance produced by his sufferings (cf. 52:14).

In v.3 the onlookers move from failure to desire the Servant to despising and rejecting him, refusing even to look at him. The words translated "sorrows" and "suffering" really mean "pains" and "sickness." These might suggest either a sick person or one sick at heart (Jer 15:18). Another possibility, as Derek Kidner points out, is that of the physician's voluntary involvement; for he is also a man of pain and sickness in the sense that he gives himself to these things and their relief (cf. Mt 8:17).

There is another possibility. The concept of punishment finds many analogies in Isaiah's prophecies, from the whipping of the body politic in 1:5–6 to the inebriated helplessness of 51:17–20. In this case the punitive nature of the Servant's sufferings is indicated before the vicarious nature of them is made clear in v.4.

4–6 This central stanza of the fourth Servant song has a number of general characteristics. The first is the frequency of the first person plural. Who are the speakers here? Probably the amazed onlookers of the first stanza, who appear from 52:15 to be predominantly Gentiles. Then there is the frequency of words suggesting pain and punishment. The passage also emphasizes the sins of the onlookers, with one of the most vivid analogies given in v.6. Here is a picture of the willful and yet purposeless waywardness of sin, with a suggestion that this is an offense against love as well as holiness, for the divine Shepherd is a tender, loving image in the Bible (cf. 40:11).

The costly atonement provides the dominant theme of this stanza. Verse 4a views our punishment figuratively in terms of the visitation of disease, while v.4b shows the onlookers coming to the grievously wrong conclusion that the Servant was suffering for his own sins at the hand of God. Verse 5 shows that they have now accepted for themselves the objective fact declared in v.4a. Piercing and crushing are both appropriate terms for the Crucifixion, the first literal and the second figurative; and both are aptly summed up as "wounds" later in the verse. Peace and healing view sin in terms of the estrangement from God and the marring of sinners themselves that it causes. Verse 6 may well derive its language from the Day of Atonement ritual (cf. Lev 16:21–22); for as God was the Author of the ritual (cf. Lev 17:11), the high priest was simply his agent for transferring the sins of the people symbolically to the scapegoat.

Finally, we should note the element of conversion in vv.4–5. The onlookers put aside their premature judgment on the matter and accept that the sufferings of the Servant are not only penal but also substitutionary.

7–9 The term "oppressed" (GK 5601) was appropriate in relation to the trials and death of Jesus; for all those who tried him had a measure of human authority and misused it when they condemned him, or, washing their hands of him, allowed others to take him to the place of death. In it all, he was quiet and uncomplaining (cf. 1Pe 2:23), which suggests not only comparison but also contrast with Jeremiah (cf. Jer 11:18–20; 12:1–3).

The phrase "by oppression and judgment" is two nouns presenting concomitant aspects of the same fact. The judgment was in fact employed as an instrument of oppression. It seemed as though the Servant must die without descendants, which was regarded as a great misfortune in that society. The phrase "cut off" (GK 1615) strongly suggests not only a violent, premature death but also the just judgment of God (cf. Ge 9:11; Ex 12:15).

Verse 9 presents an enigma, forming a striking prediction fulfilled in due time and a transition to the final stanza, which describes the Servant's vindication. This enigma consists in the apparent juxtaposition of "the wicked" and "the rich," the former more appropriate to his rejection and the latter to his ultimate vindication. We are forced to conclude that the parallelism in this verse is not synonymous but antithetical, the first line indicating the human intention in his death and the second the divinely ordained intervention and transference. This in fact was strikingly fulfilled in the burial of Jesus (Mt 27:57–60). The Servant's gentle ingenuousness is asserted at the close of the stanza.

10–12 Verse 10a is almost shocking in its apparent presentation of arbitrary disregard for personal righteousness, until we recall the substitutionary nature of those sufferings (already declared in vv.4–6 and to be referred to again in v.12b). God is therefore not seen as harsh but as astonishingly gracious.

Verses 10b–11 remind us of 52:14–15; for after suffering comes vindication, suggesting the completion of the Servant's atoning work in his death and the opening of a new life beyond that death. The "guilt offering" may have special overtones of completeness, for it involved restitution as well as an offering to God. Nothing then remained to be done; the work was complete.

Verse 11a, with its contrast of "suffering" and "light," points to the Resurrection, which is still more clearly suggested by the earlier words "prolong his days" (v.10). In fact, the words "he will see his offspring and prolong his days" seem to stand in intended contrast with the second and third lines of v.8. There is a parallel here with Ps 22, where a sufferer now vindicated declares, "Posterity

will serve him" (Ps 22:30). In this context the Servant appears, not as a teacher, but as a savior.

Not "by his knowledge" does he justify us, but by bearing our iniquities. That is, we are saved by redemptive suffering, not simply by revelation. In this case, then, it is the experimental knowledge of faith that is in view; and we have here an important background for Paul's doctrine of justification through Christ's blood, appropriated by faith.

Christ's righteousness and therefore his innocence of sin furnished a basis for his substitution. The final clause of v.11 states the objective grounds of this justification, which is a new position before God, the righteous Judge, on the basis of what the Servant has achieved in his sufferings, not of what we have ourselves done or will do.

The opening statement of v.12 shows God honoring the Servant for his faithful work and the Servant in turn distributing the spoils of battle to others. In fact, it introduces a new note into the passage, for nowhere else is there military language. Christ's work is presented as a victory over spiritual foes, resulting in a distribution of spoils to those made strong in him (cf. Eph 4:8; 6:10–17). Some argue that the words "made himself nothing" in Php 2:7 translate a Semitic phrase meaning "he poured himself out" and are based on this verse. Both passages contain the ultimate in self-abnegation in dedication to the will of God.

The last three clauses of v.12 sum up the matter. The Servant was numbered with the transgressors, not only in the outward circumstances of his death (cf. NIV note on Mk 15:27), but as a general description of the meaning of his sufferings (Lk 22:37). Innocent, he was charged with human sins and so bore their penalty. Beyond this, he has an intercessory ministry, based on the finality of his sufferings. This means that even when vindicated by God, he is still concerned to minister to his people.

In 44:28 the name "Cyrus" is solemnly and dramatically revealed long before his coming. Our present passage speaks so eloquently of the work of Christ that even the inclusion of his name could add but little more to the extent of its disclosure of him.

E. God's Glorious Future for Jerusalem (54:1–17)

The change of mood between Isa 53 and 54 is abrupt. The Servant's task is seen to be fulfilled. But the incredible triumph of Isa 53:10–12 issues into the hymn of praise in 54:1–10, welcoming the dawn of the New Age.

1–3 The only appropriate response to a great work of God is joyous praise, which is exactly what we find here (cf. 12:5; 26:1; 35:10; 42:10–11; 61:10–11). In the OT culture childlessness was a deeply shameful state. The prophet has already indicated in 50:1–3 that there has been no divorce between God and his people. After the temporary separation of the Exile, Israel would bear more children than in earlier days.

A figure is taken from nomadic life, suggesting that the promises to Abraham and his family (Ge 12:1–3; 28:13–14) are in the prophet's mind. The family tent must be enlarged and thus will need to be strengthened. The probable allusion to Ge 28 finds confirmation when we find that the verb translated "spread out" (GK 7287) is used there also. The phrase "dispossess the nations" occurs elsewhere in the OT only in Deuteronomy and always in reference to the conquest of Canaan by Israel. This suggests that the primary reference is to the gradual expansion of the little postexilic community in Judea; however, it is possible to interpret it more broadly.

4–8 The figure of the restored wife continues to dominate the passage. People often fear disgrace more than physical danger. The shame of their youth is either Egyptian bondage (cf. Hos 11:1) or, less likely, affliction under the Assyrians; the widowhood is the Exile. In v.5 the prophet encourages them to think of the one who is the husband of his people. No less than six titles and descriptions are brought together here, all building up a picture of a God of immense power and overflowing grace. He is both able and willing to restore them to himself and to their land.

Illustrations have their limitations. God is no more to be thought of as a deserting husband than as an unjust judge (Lk 18:1–8), though both figures teach spiritual lessons. The repeated phrase "for a (brief) moment"

contemplates the Exile—which must have seemed so long to the people themselves—as a mere episode in contrast to God's everlasting kindness.

9–10 Illustrating his theme from both history and nature, Isaiah compares God's oath to the great postdiluvial promise of Ge 8:22, which itself related to the natural environment of the human race and so suggested the reference to the mountains. Even the visible universe, dominated for the Jews by the hills of their native land, would prove less enduring than God's love, guaranteed by his word (cf. Mk 13:31). A relationship between persons is given added strength by its formalizing in covenant terms. The beautiful Hebrew word *hesed* (GK 2876) is here translated as "unfailing love."

11–15 The expression "covenant of peace" (cf. Eze 34:25–31) in v.10 is expounded here (see esp. v.13). God's covenant with his people implies that he will protect them, as a husband does his wife. In fact, the marriage analogy is still present; and, as Eaton suggests, the adornment of Zion with jewels may relate to her preparation as a royal bride of the Lord. Certainly Rev 21:10–27 presents the New Jerusalem in the context of v.2.

This covenant of peace may not be identified with the new covenant of Jer 31:31–34, but it has important links with it; for in it the people will know God through his personal instruction. Thus v.13 can be quoted and applied to Christ and his disciples (cf. Jn 6:45). The city that has for so long known iniquity and judgment through enemies whom God visited on her will then be true to its name Jerusalem, a place of peace, resulting from its new righteousness. There is no reference to the Messiah, but the juxtaposition of righteousness and peace reminds us of 9:7; 11:1–9. All this will be under God's new regime. Yet perfect and effectively protected as the city is, there will still be evil intent on its destruction, suggesting the Satan-inspired antagonism faced by the church.

16–17 In v.15 God promised that he would not send attackers against his people; here he declares that destructive nations are created by him. They are in his power and so are restrained under his sovereign hand. Not only physical assault but moral accusation will be repulsed, for Israel's righteousness (v.14) is from him. The people then enter their heritage (Dt 4:21). "Servant" (GK 6269) in the singular occurs twenty times from chs. 41–53; but in chs. 54–66, since the supreme Servant and his unique act of divine service have been revealed, and he has made the singular use of the word forever his own, it never occurs again in the singular in this book.

F. The Generosity, Urgency, and Effectiveness of God's Word of Grace (55:1–13)

1–5 The voice may be that of the Near Eastern water vendor or the accents of personified wisdom (Pr 9:1–6). Either would be appropriate, for Isaiah was a master of illustrations from nature and culture. We may in fact discern overtones of both. The water carrier is also a wise counselor.

The water vendor is part of the normal commercial scene in the Near East; but God through the prophet offers the people in Babylon not only water but more costly drinks and invites them to a banquet (Lk 14:15–24). Verse 2 probably alludes to the people's preoccupation with settling down in Babylon. As Thexton puts it, "The prophet does not plead or argue but throws into the quiet pool of their complacency a disturbing pebble as he asks: 'Does all this really satisfy you? Is this what you are for?'" He speaks with urgency, "Listen, listen."

This passage, which constitutes an important link with the promises of a Davidic Messiah given earlier, is quoted by Paul in Ac 13:34 with reference to the resurrection of Christ, through whose risen kingship the promises of this passage receive their eternal and therefore their final fulfillment.

During the reign of David, Israel's kingdom reached its greatest extent. David, as a faithful worshiper of the Lord, was therefore a witness to God's truth to all the peoples in his empire, as well as being their leader. He anticipated in himself the prophetic and kingly functions of the Messiah. In God's future for his people here depicted, the empire will be wider still. The far parts of the earth will come up to Zion (cf. 2:1–5; 60:1–14), because she will attract them by the beauty her God has given her (cf. 54:11–12).

6–7 The call of vv.1–3 is echoed here but with a stronger moral emphasis. Earlier the folly of self-willed waywardness was stressed,

while here it is its wickedness. Verse 6 implies both a promise and a warning. There is urgency in this call, for the time is not unlimited. Both in lifestyle and in the attitudes that lie behind it, the sinner is wrong; and so repentance must touch the inner person as well as the outward deeds. The call here is not simply uttered to the people as such but to the individual. The promise of God's pardon is assured.

8–13 God's thoughts and ways are governed by righteousness—his righteousness—and his effective word therefore accomplishes a moral purpose, the reclamation of sinners from the error and wickedness of their ways. Verse 10 shows an awareness of the ceaseless round of nature but also of the purpose of it, which was hidden, at least for a time, from the Preacher (Ecc 1:5–7). The whole food-producing process is encapsulated within v.10, only the actual sowing of the seed being excluded (Mk 4:1–20; Heb 6:7–8). The passage teaches the efficacious nature of God's word and of the grace that works through it.

With God's conditions of repentance having been fulfilled and the people's return to the Lord having made possible a return to the land, the prophet can speak of their joyous and peaceful journey. He moves from the literal joy and peace to the metaphorical mountains and hills and then back again to the literal, for v.13 probably refers to the regeneration of the land (though this in turn may symbolize spiritual fruitfulness). All this will serve to bring glory to God.

G. Salvation Extended to the Disadvantaged (56:1–8)

Clearly there is a change in geographical perspective here. The people addressed in chs. 40–55 are being encouraged to return from the Babylonian captivity, whereas in chs. 56–66 they are in the land of Canaan. That land was a place of corruption (56:9–59:15a) and devastation (63:7–64:12), so that neither the moral standards of God nor the great hopes of the people found true realization in it. Everything cried out for something more; and, of course, it was never intended that the great promises given earlier in the book should find perfect fulfillment in the postexilic community but in an altogether new order. They are therefore confronted with their own failures and stimulated afresh both to turn to God and to hope in him.

1–2 Earlier (46:13) God chastised his people for their unbelief and failure to accept his word promising them an imminent salvation. Here, however, their general lifestyle and their failure to keep his law (cf. v.1 with 51:4), symbolized by the Sabbath, are under attack. But righteousness by works is not being taught here. The ideal here presented is negative only if the Sabbath itself is viewed in terms simply of the prohibition of work and not positively, in terms of opportunities of worship and of spiritual, mental, and physical renewal. The negative that brings v.2 to its close is balanced by the positive exhortations in v.1: "Maintain justice and do what is right." So, from now on, whether one trusts in the Lord or not is a matter for the individual to decide, and the most conspicuous sign of decision is observance of the Sabbath.

3–8 The worship system of Israel was centered in the temple and emphasized the particularism of the Jewish faith. Inevitably some who lived in the land would feel excluded, for passages like Dt 23:1–8 banned eunuchs and some foreigners from participation in the worship system. The prophet has a word of comfort for them, showing that the blessing pronounced in v.2 did not contain built-in racial or physical limitations.

Verse 3 speaks of the proselyte and the eunuch. The prophet engages with the sense of insecurity that must often have plagued proselytes. If even native-born Israelites could still have guilty consciences despite the offering of sacrifices (cf. Heb 9:9), how much more the "incomer"! The eunuch would have felt even more insecure, for his very place in the ongoing life of God's people was simply an episode. The family had great importance in Israel. A dry tree bears no fruit; a eunuch begets no children.

For each group God has an authoritative word of consolation through the prophet. This word is eschatological and so belongs to the new order of the future. Faithfulness to the Lord—expressed in keeping the Sabbath law—will give the eunuch a secure place in God's temple. (It should be noted that the Sabbath is treated in Ex 31:12–17 as a sign of the covenant, as here.) We can hardly imagine that the prophet is speaking literally when he refers to a memorial in the temple. There may

even be a suggestion of eternal life in the closing affirmation of v.5. The six marks of the foreigner (v.6) provide a beautiful description of true godliness, with love as its great dynamic, the very antithesis of Pharisaic legalism.

In one of Isaiah's greatest visions (2:1–4), the people of the nations come up to Jerusalem to worship in the house of the Lord. There their eagerness is highlighted, while here it is the divine initiative. The very one whose purpose involves gathering his own scattered people will include the foreigners too in the great pilgrimage to Jerusalem. The Court of the Gentiles was a kind of symbol and foreshadowing of this, and it is from this that Christ expelled the traders, using the words of v.7 (see Mk 11:17; cf. Jn 2:16). These Gentiles would not come simply on sufferance or as mere observers but as full participants, offering sacrifices alongside the Jews.

H. God's Message to the Wicked (56:9–57:21)

9–12 The people are viewed, implicitly, as the flock of God. The prophet, as God's mouthpiece, likens the enemies of Israel to wild beasts lurking in field and forest and ironically calls them to feast on the sheep. The watchmen—who almost certainly include false prophets (cf. Jer 6:17; Eze 3:17; 33:2–7) and perhaps other leaders of the people—belong properly to a different picture, that of a city in danger; but they are soon translated into the dominant scene as dogs, set to watch the sheep. Blindness, muteness, indolence, and self-seeking greed describe different aspects of their culpable ineffectiveness. When the analogy moves from the dogs to the shepherds, the same characteristics can be seen. Verse 12 graphically represents the drunkard's careless abandon (cf. 22:13) and inebriated optimism.

57:1–2 Verse 1 has an unexpected twist to its thought at the end, suggesting the rewarding of the righteous after death and leading into v.2. A man lying dead may seem to a distant observer to be resting. He is, indeed, if he is righteous.

3–10 The words of v.3 and v.4b are intentionally insulting, not to the parents, but to the children. This was a conventional way of indicating undesirable qualities. Sorcery (cf. 2:6) and adultery in combination point to pagan fertility rites. Those who practiced them apparently did so blatantly and with a mocking gesture against the true prophet of God sent to chastise them in his name.

The pagan rites of Canaan, featuring sacred trees (cf. 1:29–30), pandered to the sexual appetites of the worshipers. During the reign of Ahaz (cf. 2Ki 16:3–4) and of Manasseh (2Ki 21:2–9), Isaiah must have been deeply grieved by the pagan child-sacrifices practiced in the land. The references to ravines, crags, and stones are obscure but no doubt reflect aspects of paganism.

At v.6 the people are pictured collectively as adulterers or prostitutes. The place where adultery was committed was "a high and lofty hill" (cf. Jer 2:20), referring to the pagan high places. The analogy could refer either to the temple or to domestic houses, but there may be an implied comparison with the prostitute's sign of her trade. The sensitive Israelite reader would also remember that it was the word of God—and, most aptly, the assertion that there is only one God—that was to be inscribed on the doors (cf. Dt 6:4–9).

Molech (v.9), god of the Ammonites, is associated with child-sacrifice (Lev 18:21; 2Ki 23:10) in the OT. The olive oil and perfumes either are offerings or belong to the picture of the prostitute. The apostate people did not pursue their paganism as a kind of leisure activity but went to great lengths. They had courted the gods of nations far away and indulged too in necromancy. Weariness had not however induced them to give up. Verse 10 might represent an ironic comparison with 40:27–31 and perhaps suggest that there was a wicked, supernatural source from which this strength was derived.

11–13 The section closes with a message of comfort for those who had faith. The people had forgotten who God was (cf. v.15), for otherwise how could they fear the petty deities of the pagans more than their great and holy God? The references to righteousness and works are ironic. Verse 13 reminds us of the prophet's onslaught on idolatry in chs. 40–48 (cf. also 40:6–8, 24).

14–21 The urgent imperatives of v.14 echo 40:3, the second allusion to that chapter in this passage (see above). The great call for repentance in 55:6–7 finds expression in this picture of spiritual road-building requiring the removal of obstacles.

The wearied but unrepentant sinner somehow finds renewal of his strength to continue in sin (v.10); but here the "contrite and lowly" (lit., "those crushed [GK 1918] and bowed down [GK 9166]") are revived in the presence of the exalted, living, and holy God. The urgent call to bustling activity in v.11 contrasts strikingly with the eternal calm of v.15. The Lord is pictured as active in reviving the spirits of his dispirited people.

Verses 16–18 seem to allude to ch. 40 (cf. 40:1–2, 27; cf. also Ge 6:3). These verses reveal the righteous anger and the amazing grace of God and also the awful persistence of human rebellion against him. The unmerited nature of God's favor has rarely been expressed more beautifully than in v.18. The passage does not suggest that there is to be grace for the determinedly impenitent, for the "mourners" (GK 63) are probably identical with the dispirited of v.16, properly chastened and restored to God, but hardly daring to hope for comfort from him (cf. Mt 5:4). Once more the prophet employs a reiterated word—"Peace, peace"—to make a point. Possibly he uses the familiar conventional word of greeting (*shalom*) to emphasize that there is a welcome home for the wayward. The "far and near" here may simply be home-dwelling and dispersed Israelites respectively (cf. 11:11–12; 43:5–7; 56:8), or may include also the foreigners (cf. Eph 2:17).

This passage ends with the same warning to the recalcitrant as the prophet gave in 48:22, but with the addition of a telling illustration. In a book so well structured as this, it may mark the end of a particular section of prophecies.

IX. God as Judge and Savior (58:1–66:24)

These chapters, while confronting realistically the fact of human sin, present God's final purposes of both judgment and salvation and thus make us aware of both his justice and his grace.

A. The True Fast (58:1–14)

Although this oracle may have been intended especially for the postexilic community, there are a number of features that remind us of the eighth-century prophets. There is the emphasis on social righteousness and also particular phrases (cf. v.1 with Hos

8:1; Mic 3:8). An eighth-or early seventh-century provenance is therefore perfectly feasible. Its teaching also has links with the Sermon on the Mount (Mt 5–7).

1–3a The prophet has already exposed the empty ritualism of the people in ch. 1. Here he concentrates on one religious activity—fasting. A trumpet call is intended to rouse the hearers to action, but it must be clear and unambiguous (cf. 1Co 14:8). There is no mistaking the message here. The people showed outward evidence of wanting to do God's will, probably by consulting priests and prophets. They were prepared too to show their earnestness by enduring the minor inconvenience of fasting. A little abstinence did not matter if they could retain their basic lifestyle of disobedient rebellion against the moral demands of their God. Such empty externalism reappears in every age and culture.

3b–5 Through his prophet God exposes the people's hypocrisy (v.3b); their fasting was not spiritually motivated. Apparently they made the fast easier by idleness and made up for lost time by getting their laborers to work all the harder. Fasting undertaken as a duty can produce an edgy, irritable community, especially in difficult climatic conditions. Prayers offered with this kind of background would never reach the heavens (v.4b). The humbling seems to be a synonym for fasting. Sackcloth and ashes also suggest the extravagant expression of humiliation.

6–9a The questions of vv.6–7 point up the people's separation of religious observance and social righteousness. There were oppression (cf. Jer 34:8–22) and poverty in the land. The prophet even has to appeal to the claims of blood relationship, for their insular selfishness was leading some to neglect relatives.

The first two clauses of v.8 emphasize speed. Elsewhere Isaiah uses the verb "break forth" (GK 1324) of the hatching of eggs (59:5) and of water gushing forth (35:6). The word suggests suddenness and swiftness. God also pledges restoration of health, protection, and access to himself in prayer. "Light" perhaps encapsulates all this, for in these chapters it suggests fullness of divine blessing (cf. 59:9; 60:1).

9b–12 Isaiah develops the same basic theme again but with some variations. Oppression is emphasized by repetition, and there is also

a reference to character assassination. Verse 10 suggests that social concern is not just to be seen in an isolated episode but should be a way of life for God's people. We must spend not just our money but ourselves. The promise of v.8 is taken still further. The glorious dawn will issue in an even more glorious midday. In this light a full life can flourish under God's blessing. An intended postexilic readership seems in view in v.12.

13–14 The Sabbath here may represent the entire Mosaic covenant and the blessings to be enjoyed in following it (see 56:3–8). As Kidner says, "These verses describe the strictness and the gladness of the sabbath-keeping God desires. If fasting is to be an opportunity to show love to our neighbour, the sabbath should express first of all our love of God. . . . It will mean self-forgetfulness and the self-discipline of rising above the trivial. But to people of this spirit God can safely give great things."

B. Sin, Sorrow, and Salvation (59:1–21)

The prophet who could speak words of great comfort and encouragement could also confront his hearers with their sins and make them face unpleasant spiritual and moral facts. In ch. 57 he condemned adulterous paganism, in ch. 58 hypocritical fasting, and in the present chapter, injustice. Each of these chapters speaks about prayer. In ch. 57 it was not answered because it was not addressed to the true God (57:13); in ch. 58 because the petitioners are hypocrites (58:4); while here it is because of their sins and particularly their injustice.

1–8 The vivid anthropomorphisms of vv.1–2 remind us of ch. 40. Here, however, they stress condemnation rather than comfort. God is addressing people who have anticipated some kind of divine intervention and have prayed for it, but whose lifestyle reveals all too clearly that their desires and prayers are not directed toward the establishment of God's rule on earth; for they are themselves rebels against that rule.

The people are guilty particularly of social injustice. In words reminiscent of 1:15, the prophet moves from the worst effects of legal oppression (unjust condemnation to death) to the false witness that produced such a verdict, and ultimately to the state of deep social and moral apathy that was causing such a situation. He then employs two figures taken from the basic human needs of food and clothing. The metaphors suggest that what these evil people produce seems at first wholesome, only to be revealed for what it really is later. In fact, the illustration of the cobweb that is useless for clothing implies that evil is ultimately counterproductive, not only for its victims, but for its perpetrators.

The prophet is not condemning any particular class among the people, though perhaps he has chiefly in mind those in whose hands the administration of justice is placed (cf. 5:22–23). Because his words are not only strong but general, Paul was able to quote them in his general indictment of human sin in Ro 3:15–17. The image of the moral life as a walk dominates vv.7–8. "The way of peace" finds its definition at the end of v.8, making it clear that the prophet is speaking about the results of their conduct for themselves (cf. 57:20–21), not for others.

9–11 The people, accused and condemned in the earlier verses, now begin to face their own sins, or, at least, the consequences of them. The justice and righteousness referred to in v.9 belong to God, to be manifested on behalf of his people. The "darkness" mentioned here is caused by disobedience to God (see Dt 28:15, 29).

12–15a A much deeper note is now sounded. Hatred of the consequences of sin and its destructive effects on one's own life is not necessarily evidence of true repentance. Only when we face sin as rebellion against a holy God who loves us do we begin to see it as he sees it. The prophet seems to be identifying with the people, expressing what he knew should be their own penitence. He confesses on their behalf that all was being done against the Lord. Social justice is excluded from their society, along with truth—again probably truth of witness (cf. vv.3–4). The situation is so serious that the good person was at risk.

15b–18 Paul's quotation of vv.7–8 in Ro 3:15–17 is in a context that presents sin against the background of the wrath of God (Ro 3:18–20). Here that wrath manifests itself. The intervention probably applies to those who are willing to take the part of the oppressed. The salvation reference made here is God's saving activity on behalf of those unjustly treated (cf. 49:24–26). God goes to war against sin,

and this passage becomes a model for Paul's description of the Christian armor employed by God's people in their struggle against the devil, master of the realm of sin (Eph 6:10–17). In the final line of v.18, it becomes clear that God will do battle against evil in Gentile lands as well as in Israel.

19–21 The chapter that began with a picture of a nation utterly depraved by its sin moves now to a glorious climax in the grace of God. Verse 19 means that God's acts of judgment will cause people over all the world to reverence him, while the second part of the verse presents a further statement of the overflowing wrath of God against his foes. As he comes in judgment to the world, the Lord will come in quite a different character to Zion—but only when she repents. The NT shows that God has given two covenant gifts to his church—the Word made flesh in Christ and the Holy Spirit (cf. Gal 4:4–7). These two gifts are here pledged—at least in anticipatory forms—as eternal gifts. The words "in your mouth" may be personal reading, or it may be that the word given and appropriated is now to be proclaimed.

C. The Future Glory of Zion (60:1–22)

In 2:1–5 Jerusalem was distinguished by its elevation; it was the center from which the divine message would go out to all the world. In 42:6; 49:6–7, the servant of the Lord had a ministry to the nations, who in 52:14–15 were astonished by both his sufferings and his subsequent exaltation. Now the prophet depicts the future glory of Zion, a glory that is but the reflection of the glory of the Lord God himself.

1–3 In 52:1–2 God called Zion to awake and to sit on her throne. This passage calls her to shine with the divine glory. Impenetrable darkness covers the whole earth, and it once enveloped Israel when she was not walking in the light with her God (cf. 8:19–22; 59:9–10). The wonderful spotlight now shining on Zion's hill is really the divine glory that is situated above Jerusalem, whereas in the desert journeys it preceded and followed God's people (see Ex 14:19–20; Isa 52:12; 58:8, but esp. 4:5–6). His glory, so situated, would act like the sun, not only giving light, but causing the city itself to radiate it (cf. v.5). This light of God would have great power of attraction. The combination of "nations" and "kings" recalls 52:15; and this, along with the use of ch. 60 in Rev 21 and the linking of the glory of God and the Lamb in Rev 21:22, prompts us to think of the divine glory here as that of the risen Christ-Servant-Lamb.

4–9 God told Abraham to lift up his eyes and look at Canaan, which he and his seed were to possess (Ge 13:14–17). Here Zion is told to look and see her dispersed children coming from other lands. She glows with the radiance of God's glory and with the joy of a fulfilled hope. There are also streams of pilgrims from the far parts: wealthy sea-faring peoples like the Phoenicians and merchants from the deserts of Arabia. They all come with appropriate gifts: gold, incense, and lambs all finding their place in the worship of the temple. This passage, unfulfilled before the coming of Christ, can hardly teach literal sacrifice, for his sacrifice has fulfilled the entire OT system of offerings.

Psalm 87 predicts that foreigners will be registered among the citizens of Zion. Isaiah 19:23–25 places Egypt and Assyria alongside Israel as God's people. Do the "sons" (v.9) of Zion include foreigners or are they simply the dispersed of Israel returning on Gentile ships? Probably the latter, though the former is not impossible in the context.

10–12 Throughout much of her history, Jerusalem had been subject to assault from foreign enemies. The Babylonians destroyed her walls, and the Romans would do so again. Like other Near Eastern cities, Jerusalem's gates were shut every night as a protection against sudden attack. All this reflected the judgment of her God that was so often on her. Now she would be the object of his grace. Jerusalem would receive both the service and the wealth of the nations and their monarchs, and no opposition to her would be tolerated by her God. Any fulfillment of this after the Exile was only partial. The Persians made possible the rebuilding of the walls but did not do it themselves. Its true fulfillment lay beyond the OT era altogether.

13–14 Although these verses go beyond anything realized in history, they take up elements from the past. Just as Lebanon supplied wood for the building of Solomon's temple (1Ki 5), so it would again (cf. Eze 40–42). The nations that had come against Jeru-salem in such a scornful spirit would now do obeisance to her as the city of her God.

15–22 The exultant tone of this chapter is sustained right to its end. The city so oppressed by some had been avoided by others. Perhaps her smaller near neighbors are in view. Now foreigners and their monarchs will love and cherish her, delighting to supply her needs. This is because the Lord will be revealing himself to her in all the glory of his grace, as indicated by the titles used in v.16, each of which has covenant implications. "The Mighty One of Jacob" reminds the people both of the sinfulness and guile of Israel's ancestor and of God's unmerited favor.

In v.17 the merely adequate is replaced by the valuable. Once again peace and righteousness, those heavenly twins, are found together (cf. 54:13–14). The beautiful description leads first of all to literal statements about the absence of violence (v.18), and then to further abstractions, symbolizing God's action on Zion's behalf and her own reaction to this. There may be an implicit reference to the meaning of the name "Judah" (i.e., "praise").

Verses 19–20 supply important background for Rev 21–22. Genesis 1:14–19 describes the sun and the moon as mere lamps made by God for lighting the earth. The Lord himself, whose glory set over the city gives the latter its special glory in this chapter, is in fact replacing his creatures—the sun and the moon—with himself. This symbolizes the fact that God's people, in his community, will always know his presence and the revelation and joy that come from him. This constant fullness of divine light will transform everything, including all the imperfections of life.

Verse 21 foreshadows the declarations in Rev 21–22 that only those cleansed of sin may have any part in God's city. His promise to Abraham (Ge 17:8) will be fulfilled. The "shoot" illustration is found again (4:1; 6:13; 11:1; 53:2). God's splendor is displayed in the growth and fruitage of this despised shoot, which symbolizes Israel. Verse 22 develops it, for the tiny shoot is seen here in its fullest development. The second half of v.22 grounds these promises in God's great name—"the LORD." It is hinted that the fulfillment of this prophecy will be remote in time.

D. The Year of the Lord's Favor (61:1–11)

1–3 These verses present a picture of a man anointed by the Spirit of God, especially for the task of preaching (cf. 1Ki 19:15–16). He proclaims glad tidings (cf. 40:9; 41:27; 52:7). His anointing with the Spirit of God provides a link with both the kingly and the servant prophecies of this book (11:1; 42:1). If he is both King and Servant, then already within the book of Isaiah that union of the two in Jesus Christ is anticipated.

Those benefiting from the preacher's message are described as the poor, the brokenhearted (cf. Ps 147:3), the captives, and the prisoners. The "poor" (GK 6705) may be literal, but the word probably has overtones of piety as well. The "brokenhearted" appear again as those who mourn and grieve. They could be mourning for sin or over the destruction of Jerusalem, though this was itself punishment for sin. The poor and the mourners reappear in the Beatitudes (Mt 5:3–4). The captives and the prisoners are likely to be the Exiles (cf. 42:22; 49:9; 51:14), so that the overtones of a new Exodus are still present.

The first two lines of v.2 are important. The term *goel* ("Redeemer"; GK 1457) does not appear in this passage, but in the OT the Year of Jubilee—when slaves were set free and all land was returned to its original owners—was closely linked with the legislation providing for the kinsman-redeemer (Lev 25); and the same word was used of the avenger of blood (Nu 35:12). Moreover, the Hebrew word translated "freedom" in v.1 is *deror* (GK 2002), a technical term for the Jubilee release in the OT (cf. Lev 25:10, 13; 27:24; Jer 34:8–10; Eze 46:17). God presents himself here then both as Savior and Judge. Significantly, Jesus, in quoting these verses in Lk 4:18–19, stopped before the reference to "the day of vengeance."

The threefold bestowal in v.3 expresses the same basic idea in different ways. Ashes symbolize deep sorrow; and the crown, oil, and garment all suggest preparations for joyous festival. The "oaks of righteousness" allude to 60:21, but with the thought now individualized.

4–9 At Sinai God described his people as "a kingdom of priests" (Ex 19:6). This ideal would now come to pass. As the Levitical priests were for them, so is Israel's place among the nations to be, which implies that her priestly ministry is for their benefit.

The laws of inheritance, so closely linked to the Jubilee regulations, provided for a double inheritance for the firstborn (Dt 21:17). Previously, perhaps because privilege brings greater responsibility, Israel had received double punishment (40:2); now, as God's "firstborn" among the nations (Ex 4:22–23; cf. Ps 89:27), she has a "double portion" in her land. Perhaps the "land flowing with milk and honey" (Ex 3:8, 17; et al.) was itself reckoned to be of double value.

The land will be restored to God's people because those who had taken it had no right to it, and the Lord is a God of justice. The "everlasting covenant" (v.8), preceded by a reference to the divine faithfulness, probably undergirds the existing covenants; so it is evidence of God's integrity. The reference to their blessing among the nations suggests the Abrahamic covenant (cf. Ge 12:1–3) rather than the Davidic (cf. Isa 55:3).

10–11 The speaker in these verses is probably personified Zion, who expresses her unbounded joy in God. The analogy of clothing appears again (cf. v.3). Clothing often expresses either status or mood—or both (cf. Ro 13:14; Eph 4:22–24).

The final verse reminds us of 55:10–11, supporting the theme of God's faithfulness. God's faithful word will secure the growth of righteousness and praise in his people, which will be publicly displayed, as at a bridal feast, before all the nations.

E. Assured Prayer for Zion's Future (62:1–12)

1–7 Here the prophet takes his place among the great men of prayer in the OT. He has received a vision of Jerusalem, living in the good of all God's promises and shining with the glory of her God (ch. 60), and he now prays with persistence and deep feeling for that day to come. Assured praying rests on the promises of God (cf. Ge 32:9–12). Jerusalem will be a spectacle for the whole world to see. So often in the OT a "new name" is the pledge of divine action to change the status or character of a person (e.g., Ge 17:5, 15). Zion's new name will emerge in vv.4, 12 and will reflect the grace of God to her, for "the mouth of the LORD" in Isaiah is associated with utterances of grace (cf. 40:5; 58:14).

Once again Zion will enjoy an intimate relationship with her God.

The theme of the wife separated from her husband because of her sin and yearning for reconciliation and home often appears in this book from ch. 49 onward. It emerges again in vv.4–5. The promise that she would be a "crown" for her God (v.3) may reflect the idea that a wife, especially a queen, should be an adornment to her husband. The Servant of the Lord is a delight to him (42:1); so is she to be. Verse 5 suggests the analogy that loyal citizens may be said to be married to their city. The analogy of the bride and groom reminds us of Rev 21:2, 9; 22:17.

Verse 6 reminds us that the vision of vv.1b–5 inspires the prophet in his praying, and that prayer continues here. If the speaker is the prophet, the watchmen here may be his fellow prophets (cf. Eze 3:17) or the godly in general, protecting the city from the ravaging forces of evil by their prayers. If the speaker is God, the watchmen could still be the godly at prayer. True prayer begins and ends at the throne of God. God graciously involves others, through prayer, in the fulfillment of his great purposes.

8–9 These words are particularly assuring to Zion's prayer-watchmen. The solemn oath of God underlines his faithfulness, and that he has sworn "by his mighty arm" stresses his ability to carry out his word; for his arm is the executor of the divine will, its power in salvation already wonderfully demonstrated (cf. 53:1). Zion repeatedly had been subject to assault from enemies and had been robbed of food supplies, either by marauding armies or as the payment of taxes to foreign overlords. God had warned her that disobedience would bring this about; but now, through his gracious action, she is righteous (62:1), and the Lord promises that this will never occur again. The temple courts would throng with worshipers offering the harvest firstfruits to the Lord and rejoicing before him.

10–11a There is to be a massive pilgrimage to the city. A road-building and road-clearing project is to be undertaken, with the banner and a proclamation providing visible and audible signals to the nations of its completion; for, as ch. 60 shows, they will be instrumental in enabling the dispersed to return.

11b–12 Here is salvation in its final stage, the fulfillment of all that has gone before. Verse 12 furthers the theme of v.4. All these names bring out different aspects of God's grace to his people (cf. Hos 1). The first goes back to the beginning of their history as a nation (Ex 19:6). At that time they also knew what it was to be the Lord's redeemed people, but before the end this experience will have been filled out with other wonders of redeeming grace. Jerusalem's destiny as the wife of the Lord will find complete fulfillment because he has sought to win her from her sin and restore her to everlasting married fellowship with himself.

F. The Lord the Avenger (63:1–6)

1–6 The oracle is most dramatic. The only OT passage that in any way resembles it is the account of Joshua's encounter with the angelic captain of the Lord's host (Jos 5:13–6:5). The city watchman or sentry peers anxiously out at a solitary and majestic figure who appears on the scene, his garment spattered with crimson. When he first comes into view, it is clear that he is coming from the direction of Bozrah, Edom's capital. That Edom means "red" (cf. Ge 25:30) is particularly apt in this context. Is this fearsome figure who has been executing judgment on Edom now coming to judge Jerusalem? The answer makes it clear that this is the Lord himself, and that he is coming to his people, not as their judge, but as their righteous Savior.

As the figure draws nearer, the watchman directs a question to him, perhaps still with a measure of apprehension. The winepress metaphor has relevance only to judgment (cf. Rev 14:19–20; 19:11–16), though atonement involves the bearing of the wrath of God. The book of Revelation takes this passage to be fulfilled in Christ as the Judge of the world, and his title "the Word of God" there probably relates to the speech at the close of v.1. The Lord declares that he has executed the judgment alone. This suggests that this passage looks beyond historical judgments—in which God uses one nation to punish another nation—to the eschatological day of God's wrath.

The "day of vengeance" and "the year of my redemption" belong to the same complex of ideas, involving the *goel* ("redeemer"; see comment on 61:1–3). God's act of judgment against Edom is conceived to be a putting right of the wrongs done to Zion (see 34:8–15), especially when the Edomites took advantage of Judah's weakness after the fall of Jerusalem (La 4:21–22; Eze 25:12–14; 35:1–15). Thus, as at the Exodus from Egypt and also at the return from Exile—preceded as it was by the judgment on Babylon through the Persians—judgment and redemption would be effected by the same events.

Verse 5 recalls Rev 5 and the search for someone to open the Book of Destiny, with its revelation of ultimate judgments. This testifies to the universality of sin. Verse 6 widens the judgment, making it clear that Edom is simply an appropriate example of the judgment of God on the nations. In many prophetic passages, Edom appears to represent Gentiles under divine judgment. For drunkenness as a picture of the divine wrath, see 51:22–23.

G. A Psalm of Praise and Lamentation (63:7–64:12)

Since the start of ch. 60, Isaiah's prophecies have majored on Zion's exaltation, the final fulfillment of all God's purposes for her. No doubt the man who received such visions would be filled with a deep longing for their fulfillment, especially if he was passing through a period of intense, God-given awareness that Judah's sin was going to bring devastating judgment through the Babylonians. Just as the Spirit of God used such moods in the psalmists to produce many an impassioned lamentation, so he did also with Isaiah. Indeed, this passage is really a psalm of communal lamentation, wherein the prophet's identification with the nation becomes the means by which he expresses the deep longing of the most spiritually sensitive in it. Such prayers were part of the prophetic ministry.

7–10 The repeated word "kindnesses" (GK 2876) represents God's faithful covenant love. It is fitting that the prophet should begin with praise, for God has never failed to honor his covenant promises even though his people have so often proved untrue to him. In the Lord's saving deeds his faithfulness has revealed itself. Verses 8–10 present a picture of God as a disappointed Father, facing the fact that his children have rebelled against him. This does not deny his omniscience or

even the sovereignty of his purpose but expresses the fact that Israel's rebellion ought never to have been and was an offense against love as well as holiness.

God, declaring himself to be his people's Father, promised to save them from Egypt, declaring that he knew their afflictions (Ex 3:7–10). Verse 9 is one of the most moving expressions of the compassionate love of God in the OT. There are Trinitarian overtones in the passage, for "the angel of his presence"—in whom the Lord is personally present—is apparently a reference to Ex 23:20–23, in combination with Ex 33:12–14; and "his Holy Spirit" (cf. Nu 11:17, 25–29)—who can be grieved (cf. Eph 4:30)—is clearly personal. The people's rebellion brought God into conflict with them, as he had threatened (Ex 23:21; cf. ch. 32).

11–14 The prophet, still dwelling on the past deeds of God for his people, suggests that things have changed since "the days of old." The focus of attention is still the events of the Exodus period, when the nation came into being. Moses, like David, was taken from pastoring the flock to leadership of Israel, thus symbolizing the self-forgetful care God expects in those in authority over his people. The right arm of Moses symbolized and was accompanied by the right arm of God, for the Exodus was an act of divine power (see 51:9; 52:10; 53:1).

The two analogies of vv.13–14 point to the conditions of the crossing of the Red Sea and the Jordan respectively. The people found the sea bed—and perhaps the desert as well—easy to negotiate; and, descending from the plateau of Moab to the Jordan and across it, they were like a herd of cattle being led into green pasture. The word "rest" (GK 5663) recalls Dt 12:10 and Jos 21:44, though Heb 3–4 teaches that there is a deeper rest available in Christ.

15–19 The wistful note that was sounded in the last few verses now becomes explicit, and the characteristics of a communal lamentation appear clearly. In his prayer at the consecration of the temple, Solomon had called on God to hear his people's cry from his heavenly dwelling place (1Ki 8:44–53), and Isaiah has shown a personal awareness of God as exalted in his holiness (ch. 6; 57:15). This exalted God has pledged his zeal in the cause of his people (9:7; 37:32); but now, as he foresees the temple and its ruin, the prophet identifies with the people's cry for mercy.

In v.16 we have the first two of three references to God as "Father" (cf. also 64:8). This repeated plea gives the prayer special intensity. The sense of relationship with God goes deeper than national solidarity; it is the deepest fact of the people's life.

Verse 17 recalls Isaiah's commission and the warning he had then (cf. 6:9–13), that through his verbal ministry the people would become hardened in sin. The prayer perhaps alludes to the hardening of Pharaoh's heart in the Exodus story, which provides much background to the thought here. It recognizes that God has established that moral law in which sin hardens the heart, and does so by divine design (cf. Ro 1:18–32). The word "return" (GK 8740) may suggest the return of the shekinah glory to the temple as the symbol of God's dwelling among his people (cf. Eze 43:6–12). Certainly v.18 implies that their sense of alienation from him is not unconnected with the destruction of their sanctuary. There is a deep sense of special election in v.19.

64:1–7 The longing for renewed blessing expressed in the closing verses of the previous chapter is now poured out in a passionate outburst. The Exodus had been followed by the great revelation at Sinai, when the mountain trembled at the presence of God (Ex 19:16–19). On that occasion God descended on the mount (Ex 19:18). Here the prophet graphically conceives of the very heavens being rent by Israel's God in his eagerness to be once more in the midst of his people. The illustration of v.2 sets forth the judgment of God. Pharaoh and the Egyptians had learned the power of God's name at the Exodus (Ex 13:3, 18). The Sinai revelation had made God's people tremble; this new disclosure of him would terrify the nations of the world.

The God of the Exodus and Sinai who revealed himself to his people was the God of the unexpected, for in so many of the plagues the ordinary course of nature was interrupted. He was a unique God, for all other so-called deities are impotent. He was also a God of righteousness, caring about the obedience of his people to his laws. It is this ethical quality in him that is revealed over against the sins of his people.

Verses 5–7 present a many-sided doctrine of sin, remarkably full for an OT passage. Sin is a continual practice; it is defiling, it is destructive, and it creates a barrier between God and humankind—both from our side, for we do not want to pray, and from God's, because he will not hear us. God himself has determined that it will have these results. No wonder the people cry out, "How then can we be saved?"

8–12 Verse 8 quite suddenly moves from the thought of God as the moral governor to whom his people are responsible to the Father who brought them into being. Both Jeremiah (Jer 18:1–6) and Paul (Ro 9:19–21) develop the analogy of the potter and the clay and present God as sovereign in the realm of sin and judgment. The people cast themselves on the mercy of God, calling on him to remember their standing as his people. Because the land is itself holy, so are all its cities, though the prophet lays special emphasis on the desolation of Jerusalem. He appeals to the fact that the land is the Lord's; it was to him that the praises of earlier generations had been offered in the temple which he had set apart for that purpose but which now lay in ruins.

Verse 12 implores God to intervene and bring to his people that forgiveness and salvation that have been promised over and over again in this book, especially since ch. 40. What response did God make to this prayer? The two closing chapters will show us.

H. The Great Final Issues (65:1–66:24)

These two chapters are not only the end of the book but also its climax. Here eschatology reaches its zenith, for the promise of new heavens and a new earth (65:17; 66:22) not only goes beyond anything else in the book but even the speculative imagination could not conceive any greater reality. At the same time, the spiritual challenge to the reader and the ultimate issues of destiny are presented with great power.

Chapter 64 was an impassioned prayer in which the people, represented by the prophet, stated their sense of relationship to God but also made frank confession of their sins, crying to him for mercy. A man of deep spiritual sensitivity may—like Daniel (Da 9) or Ezra (Ezr 9)—take the burden of a whole community's sins on his heart and confess those sins with a depth of feeling that may be shared, in fact, by very few of his compatriots. Isaiah, at his call, had confessed not only his personal sin but that of his people generally (6:5). We will then treat these chapters as God's answer to the prayer of ch. 64.

1–5 Paul applies vv.1–2 to the Gentiles in Ro 10:20–21. The Hebrew for v.1a, translated literally, is "I permitted myself to be sought." The NIV is somewhat disappointing when it translates v.1b "to a nation that did not call on my name," following the LXX and the Targum but not the Hebrew text, which reads, "to a nation that was not called by my name." We therefore understand that v.1 applies to the Gentiles and v.2 to the Jews. This reminds us of the work of the Messiah, through whom the knowledge of the Lord will fill the earth (11:9), and especially of the Servant of the Lord, whose work will savingly enlighten the nations (42:6) through his sufferings and exaltation (52:15).

Verse 2 presents God's hands held out in love "all day long" (meaning perhaps all throughout Israel's history), but finding obstinate rejection of his ways (cf. 64:5). "Imaginations" may refer to the sinful product of the unsanctified imagination in idols. "Continually" seems to answer to "all day long," with the thought that the people's sinful insults to God were as constant and longstanding as his own gracious overtures to them. The catalog of sins in vv.3–4 suggests Rev 21:8; 22:15, which lead to the second death and thus exclude those from the Holy City who practice them. "Burning incense on altars of brick" must, because of its context, be pagan, though its exact significance is unknown. The first half of v.4 refers to the forbidden practice of necromancy (cf. 57:9; Dt 18:9–13), while v.4b probably refers to flagrant disregard of the laws about unclean meats that show a rebellious outlook.

There is a tone of irony in v.5a. Paganism has its "holy" men; and these instill fear in others lest they should come too close to them and be harmed. These descriptions of sin begin to give place to the assurance of punishment at the close of the verse (cf. Dt 32:22; Jer 17:4).

6–7 The introductory "see" is a call to attention. God has those sins written before him (cf. Rev 20:12). The people's prayer (64:12) is answered, but not in the way they would hope for. In responding to our prayers, God always keeps within the spiritual and moral structure he has established. His judgment on a nation often awaits the full term of its sin (Ge 15:16; Da 8:23; Mt 23:32; cf. Rev 14:15). The mountain shrines were centers of idolatrous worship (cf. 57:7; Jer 3:6; et al.).

8–10 Here again is the important doctrine of the remnant. The vineyard of Israel, so unproductive (5:1–4), has nevertheless produced some genuine grapes. They are the servants of God. In them the promises to "the chosen people" find their fulfillment, for this remnant is "my people who seek me." Those who had received the great OT revelation had a responsibility to seek the Lord on the basis of it, while those who had never known its light would receive it through a new divine initiative (v.1).

Sharon was beautiful and fertile; but Achor had an ominous sound, for it symbolized God's judgment on his people (Jos 7:24–26). Hosea had, however, presented the God's promise (Hos 2:15).

11–12 Here God turns to the rebels among his people. The reference to the holy mountain refers to the forsaking of the worship of the Lord at his temple. This worship involved the offering of items connected with the people's food and drink. Instead, these were being presented to pagan gods (cf. 1Co 10:21–22). Verse 12 recalls v.2 (cf. 55:1–7).

13–16 The term "Sovereign Lord" was characteristic of two passages picturing the Servant of the Lord (48:16; 50:4–5, 7, 9). Here the term occurs again, providing a link between the Servant and the servants. Those addressed in these verses as "you" are the same rebels God speaks to in vv.11–12.

God's people are promised food, drink, and table fellowship (cf. Rev 2:7, 17; 3:20; 21:6; 22:2, 17). Those still in their sins will be excluded, and their name will be a byword among God's people for the curse of God. The true servants of God will have a new name (cf. Rev 2;17), perhaps the name of their God (Rev 3:12), the "God of truth" (cf. Rev 3:14). The final promise of v.16 takes its significance from the fact that the nation's troubles had been the result of its sins. This full and free forgiveness would be achieved through the sacrifice of God's Servant (ch. 53).

17-25 The great promise, with its introductory call to special attention—"Behold, I will create new heavens and a new earth" (cf. Rev 21:1)—is staggering. The whole created order is to be renewed. Great and new as this promise is, the reader does not come to it completely unprepared, for it builds on passages like 11:1-9 and ch. 24. For those whose imagination cannot cope with the macrocosm, the prophet indicates that Jerusalem too is to be created anew. The God who had identified with his people in their affliction would now do so in their joy also. The former sorrows will be over (cf. Rev 21:4).

The picture in v.20 promises greatly extended but not infinite life; yet v.19 declares that weeping will be banished! Advisedly, we are to dwell on the positive blessings in v.20 and not on their negative implications. If we take the references to death seriously, we have here a blessed but not ideal state, not quite parallel therefore to the whole of Rev 21:4.

The people's blessedness is portrayed largely in terms reminiscent of the "godly materialism" of Deuteronomy (cf. Isa 62:8-9). The greatest blessing they will know, however, will be a relationship with God in which there is complete harmony between their prayer and his will, between his desire to provide and their dependence on him to give. Verse 25 (cf. 11:6-9) is a reminder that these blessings come only through the Messiah, while the words "dust will be the serpent's food" (cf. Ge 3:14) remind us that the overthrow of Satan, the great serpent (Rev 20:2), is the result of the work of the woman's offspring (Ge 3:15).

66:1-2a There was a reference to Jerusalem in 65:18-19 and to its holy mountain (65:11) but no express mention of the temple. These verses could mean that this great God, who could not be contained in the whole of the old created order (cf. 1Ki 8:27), could have no appropriate temple at all. But the postexilic temple was built at his command; so the passage must mean rather that no edifice made by human hands could be more than a symbol; and the symbol could, as Stephen made clear, come to be cherished above the reality (Ac 7:44-54).

2b-4 In 57:15, Isaiah refers to God's heavenly dwelling and the fellowship he offers the contrite and lowly in spirit. At Sinai, where the sacrificial system was given but before its details were made known, God's people trembled when the Ten Commandments were heard (Ex 20:18-21). Here a humble reverence for God's word is in view. This thought governs v.3, where the teaching is even stronger than in 1:10-20. The most sacred exercises of true God-given religion are like the worst sins when they are divorced from humility of spirit. Verse 4 repeats too the thought of 65:12. This is all the more striking in the light of the context of ch. 65, for there it is paganism that forsakes the holy mountain of God that is being condemned. Paganism that sets aside God's word and ritualism that obeys it in the letter only and not the spirit are both abominations to the Lord.

5-6 Once again the word of God passes from his enemies within Israel (vv.3-4) to his servants. The words in the second half of v.5 are uttered in irony. Verse 6 certainly implies that in some sense God accepted the Jerusalem temple as his, for from there he revealed his wrath against his enemies (see comment on 56:7).

7-11 In 54:1-3, just after the fourth Servant Song, Zion was told to rejoice and to prepare her tent for a great influx of inhabitants. This is emphasized again, with special stress on the suddenness of it. The questions of v.9 are really making the point that God promises not only a speedy but a complete work, with Zion's family deeply satisfied in their mother.

12-16 In 8:6-8 Isaiah pictured Assyria—the cruelest enemy Israel and Judah ever had to face—flooding the whole country like an immensely spreading inundation from the Euphrates. He went on to promise endlessly increasing peace as the result of the Messiah's reign (9:7). Now the analogy of the overflowing river is applied to that peace, the nations coming up, not in devastating conquest, but in peace and with their wealth (cf. 48:18; 60:11).

From the thought of Zion's children as nursed by her, the thought moves to God as the "mother" of his people. This is surprising because in earlier chapters God was represented as the husband and Zion as the wife (e.g., 54:5). Here the purpose is to make it clear that the Lord is the real source of those blessings mediated to Zion's children through her. The same flexibility is shown in

In the western wall of Jerusalem, someone has etched, in Hebrew, these words of hope from Isa 66:14: "When you see this, your heart will rejoice and you will flourish like grass."

v.14, where grass is not a symbol of human frailty (cf. 40:8) but rather of nourishment under the blessing of God. In this way God's power will be shown in grace to his servants but in wrath to his enemies. The manifestation of his wrath is expressed especially in terms of fire, which, like the whirlwind and the sword, has great destructive potential.

17–21 The book that has been largely poetical throughout ends in prose. To understand v.17 it should be remembered that it is possible to consecrate oneself to a false god. The prophet clearly has in view those described in 65:3–5. In v.18 "their actions and imaginations" refers to the Jews and their departure from the true God (cf. 65:2). Isaiah had seen the glory of the Lord in the temple (ch. 6), where it had also been revealed to him that the people of Israel would not accept his message. Frequently, during the course of his prophecy, he has seen the light of God going forth and the Gentiles being attracted to it (2:1–4; 42:6; 49:6; 60:1–3). Now he expresses their promised knowledge of God in terms reminiscent of his own inaugural vision.

"Those who survive" are the Jewish remnant, and they go out to many a foreign country to proclaim the glory of the true God. The beautiful picture in v.20 is based on the Levitical system of offerings. The Gentiles will bring the dispersed remnant to the temple, just as if the Gentiles themselves were Israelites and the members of the Dispersion were the offerings they would bring to present to the Lord. Grammatically it is possible that the words of v.21 apply to the Gentiles, which anticipates Paul's teaching that there is no barrier to blessing or to privilege in Christ (Gal 3:28–29). More likely, however, they apply to priests and Levites selected from among the regathered brothers mentioned in v.20.

22–24 God here makes the greatest and most comprehensive of all his promises: the guarantee of his pledges to his people. He further affirms that the wider vision of the worship of all humankind will also find its fulfillment. This is expressed in terms of the old God-given Jewish system of special days and Sabbaths for worship and, with many other aspects of these two final chapters, raises important questions of interpretation (see the section "Eschatology" in the introduction to Isaiah). The prophecy ends on a note of the starkest realism. It pictures vividly the lessons to be learned from the eternal judgment of God on sinners for their rebellion against him. Notice that this judgment will have the approval of human beings. This reminds us of the awesome "Hallelujah!" of Rev 19:1. God's people must agree with all he says, for he is God.

The Old Testament in the New

OT Text	NT Text	Subject
Isa 1:9	Ro 9:29	The remnant
Isa 6:3	Rev 4:8	Holy, holy, holy
Isa 6:9–10	Mt 13:14–15; Mk 4:12; Lk 8:10; Ac 28:26–27	Seeing but not perceiving
Isa 6:10	Jn 12:40	God binds the eyes
Isa 7:14	Mt 1:23	The virgin birth
Isa 8:12–13	1Pe 3:14–15	Do not fear
Isa 8:14	Ro 9:32–33; 1Pe 2:8	A stone on which people stumble
Isa 8:17	Heb 2:13	Trust in God
Isa 8:18	Heb 2:13	God's children
Isa 9:1–2	Mt 4:15–16	Galilee of the Gentiles
Isa 10:22–23	Ro 9:27–28	The remnant
Isa 11:10	Ro 15:12	The root of Jesse
Isa 13:10	Mt 24:29; Mk 13:24–25	The end times
Isa 22:13	1Co 15:32	Tomorrow we die
Isa 25:8	1Co 15:54	Death is swallowed up
Isa 25:8	Rev 7:17; 21:4	God wipes away tears
Isa 27:9	Ro 11:27	Full removal of sin
Isa 28:11–12	1Co 14:21	Through strange tongues
Isa 28:16	Ro 9:33; 10:11; 1Pe 2:6	Trust in the cornerstone
Isa 29:10	Ro 11:8	God seals the eyes
Isa 29:13	Mt 15:8–9; Mk 7:6–7	Hypocritical worship
Isa 29:14	1Co 1:19	Worldly wisdom perishes
Isa 29:16	Ro 9:20	Potter and clay
Isa 34:4	Mt 24:29; Mk 13:24–25	The end times
Isa 40:3–5	Mt 3:3; Mk 1:3; Lk 3:4–6; Jn 1:23	Voice in the wilderness
Isa 40:6–8	1Pe 1:24–25	Eternity of the word
Isa 40:13	Rp 11:34; 1Co 2:16	The mind of the Lord
Isa 42:1–4	Mt 12:18–21	The servant of the Lord
Isa 43:21	1Pe 2:9	Declaring God's praise
Isa 45:9	Ro 9:20	Potter and clay
Isa 45:23	Ro 14:11	Every knee shall bow
Isa 49:6	Ac 13:47	Salvation of the Gentiles
Isa 49:8	2Co 6:2	God's day of salvation
Isa 49:10	Rev 7:16	Eternal blessings
Isa 52:5	Ro 2:24	God's name cursed among Gentiles
Isa 52:7	Ro 10:15	Beautiful feet
Isa 52:11	2Co 6:17	Touch no unclean thing
Isa 52:15	Ro 15:21	Gentiles hear the gospel
Isa 53:1	Jn 12:38; Ro 10:16	Unbelief of Israel
Isa 53:4	Mt 8:17; 1Pe 2:24	Taking our infirmities
Isa 53:6	1Pe 2:25	Like sheep gone astray
Isa 53:7–8	Ac 8:32–33	Jesus as the dying lamb

The Old Testament in the New

OT Text	NT Text	Subject
Isa 53:9	1Pe 2:22	Sinless servant
Isa 53:12	Lk 22:37	Numbered with transgressors
Isa 54:1	Gal 4:27	Joy of the barren woman
Isa 54:13	Jn 6:45	All are taught by God
Isa 55:3	Ac 13:34	Blessings of David
Isa 56:7	Mt 21:13; Mk 11:17; Lk 19:46	God's house of prayer
Isa 59:7–8	Ro 3:15–17	Sin of humanity
Isa 59:20–21	Ro 11:26–27	Deliverer from Zion
Isa 61:1–2	Lk 4:18–19	God's Spirit on me
Isa 64:4	1Co 2:9	What no eye has seen
Isa 65:1	Ro 10:20	Salvation of the Gentiles
Isa 65:2	Ro 10:21	Obstinate Israel
Isa 65:17	2Pe 3:13	New heavens and new earth
Isa 66:1–2	Ac 7:49–50	No temple contains God
Isa 66:24	Mk 9:48	Unquenchable fire of hell

Jeremiah

INTRODUCTION

1. General

Jeremiah is the most autobiographical of all the prophets. He has been credited with the survival of his people after the fall of Jerusalem in 586 B.C., a veritable savior of the Jews. Nonetheless, this man of God is one of the most misunderstood of the great OT leaders.

The book of Jeremiah is longer than Isaiah or Ezekiel, and the Minor Prophets combined are about a third shorter. It is the longest book in the Bible if 1 and 2 Samuel, 1 and 2 Kings, and 1 and 2 Chronicles are reckoned as separate books. The book sheds valuable light on the subject of the decline and fall of the Judean kingdom and influenced theological thinking in subsequent ages.

2. The Person of Jeremiah

a. His background

Jeremiah's name, not uncommon in Israel, is of disputed meaning. His name may well reflect his parents' hopes for him and the nation, in which case the meaning "the LORD exalts" is preferable to "the LORD hurls" or "the LORD establishes." Jeremiah's relation to so many political events makes it strange that his name appears nowhere in Kings or Chronicles. He was born in 646 B.C. in the Levitical town of Anathoth in the territory of Benjamin; he died, probably in Egypt, not long after 586.

In his day Jeremiah was unquestionably the greatest spiritual personality in Israel. His was not a happy life; his expressions of sorrow are classic. Only he among the prophets showed his personal feelings as he proclaimed God's message. By birth, Jeremiah was a priest; by grace, a prophet; by the trials of life, a bulwark for God's truth; by daily spiritual experience, one of the greatest exponents of prophetic faith in his unique relation to God; by temperament, gentle and timid, yet constantly contending against the forces of sin; and by natural desire, a seeker after the love of a companion, his family, friends, and, above all, his people—which were all denied him.

Jeremiah's life—private and public—is openly displayed in his book: his brave actions, his tenderheartedness toward his coreligionists, and his deep emotional and spiritual struggles before God. His disappointments and sufferings were undeniably as poignant as those of any other Jewish prophet. His life may be characterized as being one long martyrdom.

Jeremiah the son of Hilkiah was of a priestly family, but nothing indicates that he ever exercised a priestly ministry. Possibly his father was the Hilkiah who found the "Book of the Law" in the temple (2Ki 22:8). Jeremiah's father was probably a descendant of Abiathar, the sole survivor of the priests of Nob (1Sa 22:20). After ministering under David, Abiathar was exiled by Solomon to Anathoth, where he had property (1Ki 2:26). That he was from Anathoth further accounts for the fact that in Josiah's day Jeremiah was not as well known as Huldah the prophetess (2Ki 22:14–20). That Jeremiah was a man of means may be inferred from his purchase of a field in 32:6–15.

Jeremiah was called to the prophetic office in the thirteenth year of Josiah's reign (1:2; i.e., 626 B.C.); he was about twenty years old at the time and served in that office for more than forty years. The Lord did not permit him to marry (16:2). Though his public ministry was long and checkered, there is no indication that he ever had any disciples; and his closest companion was his faithful secretary and scribe, Baruch the son of Neriah.

Jeremiah preached in Jerusalem until the fall of the kingdom of Judah in 586 (cf. 7:2; 22:1; 27:1–2; 32:1). After that, he labored for some time among the survivors in Judah and later among the Jews who had fled to Egypt (chs. 40–44). His call included both Israel and the other nations of his time (1:10). The call was both simple and direct (1:4–5), but the prophet's reaction differed markedly from Isaiah's (Isa 6) and Ezekiel's (Eze 1).

b. His public ministry

Jeremiah's ministry was carried on in a politically, socially, morally, and spiritually chaotic era. The glorious days of reformation under Hezekiah in the eighth century were eclipsed by the long, ungodly reign of Manasseh, who along with his fealty to the Assyrian monarchs maintained a syncretistic worship for his people. Jeremiah did not hide his hatred for the apostasy and social injustices of Manasseh. In this spiritual decline priests and prophets alike were implicated.

When Jeremiah began to preach, the godly Josiah had begun his reforms to wipe out idolatry from his kingdom. The content of the prophet's preaching confirms his full support of Josiah's reforms and calls for a truly repentant return to the Lord. Tragically, the people of Judah had already become so ungodly that they were no longer responsive to calls to return to God. But in grace the Lord continued to plead with Judah through Jeremiah. From the beginning of his ministry, Jeremiah never deviated from the position that Judah and Jerusalem were to be destroyed by a nation from the north and the people carried into captivity (4:5–9; 6:22–26). The threatening invasion of the northern enemy gave urgency to his warnings.

With Jehoiakim's rule (608 B.C.), Jeremiah again began a public ministry. In the famous temple address (chs. 7; 26), he indicated that only faithfulness to God could guarantee the nation's security; otherwise the temple would be destroyed. He aroused bitter opposition to himself and his message from all segments of the nation, including his own family. Sad and despairing because of the rejection of his message, he yet loved, prayed for, and agonized over his people. No greater and truer Jewish patriot ever preached the truth to them. Even when the Lord forbade him to pray for them, he continued to intercede. At times he felt that God himself had forsaken him. He even cursed the day of his birth.

Jehoiakim was so enraged with Jeremiah's denunciatory messages that he cut the scroll of his prophecy to pieces and burned it. So Jeremiah became a fugitive from the king's wrath. In the fourth year of Jehoiakim's reign (according to Hebrew reckoning [25:1], or in the third year according to Babylonian computation [Da 1:1]), Nebuchadnezzar of Babylon first invaded Judah. He had defeated Pharaoh Neco of Egypt at the Battle of Carchemish (605 B.C.), an event of unsurpassed importance because it settled the question of world supremacy in that day. After Egypt's defeat, Jeremiah counseled that it was futile and contrary to God's will to resist Nebuchadnezzar. One can imagine the unpopular nature of this message. Thereafter Jeremiah's life was one of uninterrupted misunderstanding and persecution.

Under Zedekiah's rule, Jeremiah fared no better, though this king was not so violently opposed to him as Jehoiakim had been. But Zedekiah was weak and vacillating, constantly fearing his powerful nobles. Jeremiah had some ministry to the king, but it bore little if any fruit. When the kingdom of Judea fell to Nebuchadnezzar in the eleventh year of Zedekiah's reign, the Babylonian king appointed Gedaliah as governor of Judah (40:1–6). Soon after his appointment the governor was assassinated by a descendant of the Davidic house (41:1–2), Ishmael son of Nethaniah. The remnant in Mizpah, against Jeremiah's protests, fled to Egypt from the wrath of Babylon (vv.16–18), and Jeremiah and Baruch were compelled to accompany them (42:1–43:7). At the end of his ministry, Jeremiah was at Tahpanhes in Egypt, where he both predicted Nebuchadnezzar's conquest of Egypt (43:8–13) and denounced the idolatry of the Jews there (ch. 44). Beyond this nothing is known of Jeremiah's life.

Jeremiah encountered more opposition from more enemies than any other OT prophet. Much of it stemmed from the fact that he continually preached one theme: unconditional surrender. Had not the Lord protected him, he would have been martyred.

Nothing certain is known of the time, place, or manner of Jeremiah's death. According to 44:29–30, Jeremiah was still alive around 570 B.C. (Pharaoh Hophra [Apries] reigned 588–569). By an unusual providence the prophet who fought his entire life against Egypt was forced to end his days there as a captive. A late, unattested tradition claims that the men of Tahpanhes stoned Jeremiah to death. There is a rabbinical account of his deportation with Baruch to Babylon by Nebuchadnezzar at the time of the conquest of Egypt and of his death there, but this is unconfirmed.

Singularly, this great man of God, so little heeded by his own people, has been accorded great respect after death. Alexandrian Jews especially have held him in profound regard (cf. 2Mc 2:1–8; 15:12–16; see also Mt 16:14). That later Jews saw in him their intercessor partially explains this.

3. Date and Authorship

Scholars have extensively discussed the origin of this book and have held differing opinions about it. Broadly speaking, they are divided into two groups: (1) those who think Jeremiah wrote very little of it, assigning the major part of it to other writers; (2) those who assign the entire book to Jeremiah (ch. 52 is treated separately) through the secretarial aid of Baruch (i.e., he was to Jeremiah what Luke was to Paul). The first group favors a division of the book into three sources: (1) messages dictated by Jeremiah; (2) a biography of Jeremiah, probably by Baruch; and (3) various contributions from redactors and later authors. The second school, which this commentary accepts, holds that the prophet dictated his messages to Baruch, his secretary (36:17–18; 45:1).

The passages in Jeremiah on the enemy from the north fit what is known of the Babylonians. Internal evidence indicates that the first written material of the book was done in the fourth year of Jehoiakim's reign (605 B.C.; cf. 36:1–2). In addition, passages like 29:1; 30:2; and 51:60 compel the conclusion that prophecies, apart from those contained in Baruch's scroll, were immediately recorded. The scroll burned by Jehoiakim was replaced with additions (36:32). Apparently through the first score of years of his ministry, Jeremiah had kept notes of his messages, which were put into writing at God's command (36:2). The burned scroll was replaced and the material gradually added to a replacement scroll. It seems reasonable that Jeremiah edited his work during the Captivity. The entire book was probably gathered together shortly after his death. The conclusion appears inescapable that Baruch's rewritten scroll was the basis for Jeremiah's written prophecies. The book bears marks of having been gathered together by one person at one time.

4. Historical Setting

a. Prophetic background

Just as the eighth century B.C. saw a galaxy of prophets in Israel, so did the end of the seventh and the first half of the sixth centuries. The contemporary prophets were Zephaniah (Zep 1:1), Obadiah (Ob 11–14), the prophetess Huldah (2Ki 22:11; 2Ch 34:22)—all in Judah—and Ezekiel (Eze 1:1–3) and Daniel (Da 1:1) in Babylon. Especially close is the relationship between Jeremiah and Ezekiel. Probably Nahum and Habakkuk were also contemporaries of Jeremiah. Three of the four major prophets were related to captivities: (1) Daniel in Jehoiakim's time (Da 1:1), (2) Ezekiel in Jehoiachin's time (Eze 1:1–3), and (3) Jeremiah in Zedekiah's time (1:1–3).

b. Historical background

Events. To understand Jeremiah's prophecy requires close scrutiny of his times because of (1) the critical events in the political world of his day—events in which Judah was directly affected—and (2) the number of kings in Judah who reigned during his career and with whom he had close contact. Jeremiah was a national and international figure. A general chronological table helps visualize the historical background of his book.

639–609 B.C.—the reign of Josiah
609 B.C. (3 months)—the reign of Jehoahaz
609–597 B.C.—the reign of Jehoiakim
597 B.C. (3 months)—the reign of Jehoiachin
597–586 B.C.—the reign of Zedekiah
586 B.C.—the fall of Jerusalem
586(?) B.C.—the assassination of Gedaliah

The times of Jeremiah are among the most important in OT history. Because of their significance, they are the best-documented times in all Israel's history. The book of Jeremiah is so filled with historical, biographical, and autobiographical material that his life can be synchronized with dates and known events to a degree unparalleled in the writings of other prophets. Events of significance during this period are as follows:

669–c. 630 B.C.—the dissolution of the Assyrian Empire after the death of Ashurbanipal
626 B.C.—the call of Jeremiah

612 B.C.—the fall of Nineveh and the Assyrian empire

609 B.C.—the death of Josiah at Megiddo

605 B.C.—the battle between Egypt and Babylonia at Carchemish, with Babylonia emerging victorious

605 B.C.—the first siege of Jerusalem by Nebuchadnezzar (Daniel exiled to Babylon)

597 B.C.—the second siege of Jerusalem (Ezekiel exiled to Babylon)

588–586 B.C.—the final siege of Jerusalem, beginning the Babylonian captivity

Nabopolassar, the father of Nebuchadnezzar and conqueror of Assyria, came from Chaldea, a province in the southern part of Babylonia, and reigned from 625 to 605 B.C. Nebuchadnezzar (more properly Nebuchadrezzar), the most famous of the Babylonian monarchs, ruled from 605 to 562 B.C.

Geographically and politically Judah was in a vulnerable position between the power politics of Egypt and Assyria. In the eighth century B.C., Isaiah had warned against trusting Egypt (Isa 30:1–7) and had keenly evaluated the threat of Assyria (Isa 37). By God's protection the kingdom of Judah had escaped Sennacherib's forces. But from the godly reign of Hezekiah, the nation declined to the lowest spiritual depths under the godless rule of Manasseh (2Ki 21:9–15; 24:3–4). If Jeremiah was called in his early twenties, he lived in the reigns of Manasseh and Amon. Under Manasseh's long, apostate reign of fifty-five years, the reforms of his godly father, Hezekiah, were forgotten. Judah was then under Assyrian power; so to please his overlords, Manasseh introduced syncretistic elements into the temple worship at Jerusalem. The northern kingdom (Israel) was already exiled (722 B.C.), and the remnant residing there had embraced mixed elements in their faith (2Ki 17:28). During the reigns of Esarhaddon and Ashurbanipal, the Assyrian power conquered Egypt; but the latter regained strength under Psammetik I (664–609 B.C.), so that Judah found herself balancing off one great power against the other.

Rulers. *(a) Josiah.* Josiah came to the throne when he was eight years old. Politically, Assyria was under strong opposition from Babylon, fighting to survive. This gave Judah more freedom to throw off Assyrian elements in her worship. In 633 B.C., Josiah sought the Lord (2Ch 34:3); his reforms began in 629 B.C. (2Ch 24:36); in 623–622 B.C., the Book of the Law was found in the temple (2Ki 22:3–8; 2Ch 34:8–15); and Jerusalem was made the only authorized center for worship. The reforms are detailed in 2Ki 22–23; though widespread and well inaugurated, they did not last, as is evident from Jeremiah's ceaseless condemnation of the nation's sins.

In 609 B.C., Pharaoh Neco of Egypt joined Assyria to strengthen them. Josiah, though he had been warned by Neco, interfered and lost his life at the Battle of Megiddo (2Ki 23:29; 2Ch 35:20–24). But Babylon, stronger than Egypt, dominated the world scene under Nabopolassar of Chaldea, ruler of Babylonia by 625 B.C. and the destroyer of Nineveh in 612 B.C. His son, Nebuchadnezzar II, succeeded him and reigned for forty-three years, having defeated Egypt at the Battle of Carchemish on the Euphrates River in 605 B.C. (46:2; 2Ch 35:20). Thereafter Babylon was master of the world. For years Jeremiah steadily counseled against Judah's involvement in world politics. When the people refused his counsel, he repeatedly entreated them to surrender to the superior forces of Babylon, who at that time were an instrument for carrying out God's will.

(b) Jehoahaz. Distraught over the calamitous death of godly Josiah, the people took matters into their own hands and set Jehoahaz (Shallum [22:11]), son of Josiah, on the throne. In three months of rule he manifested an anti-Egypt and pro-Babylon policy, for which he was summarily deposed by Pharaoh Neco (2Ki 23:31–33), who took him to Egypt and imposed tribute on the country. In his place Neco set on the throne Eliakim, oldest son of Josiah and half-brother of Jehoahaz (2Ki 23:34, 36), changing his name to Jehoiakim (2Ki 23:30–35; 2Ch 36:1–4).

(c) Jehoiakim. The reign of this king was the time of Jeremiah's greatest trial and opposition. Politically, king and prophet were diametrically opposed, the king favoring Egypt and Jeremiah counseling submission to Babylon. Spiritually, the two were even farther apart. Jehoiakim has been characterized as the worst and most ungodly of all Judah's kings. He has been labeled a bloodthirsty tyrant, an inveterate enemy of the truth. He cared nothing for the worship of the God of Israel, exacted exorbitant taxes, used forced

labor without pay, and had no regard for the word or prophet of God (22:13–14; ch. 36).

In Jehoiakim's eleven-year reign, the Battle of Carchemish took place (cf. 46:2). It was an event of permanent significance, for. it marked the transfer of power over the Middle East from Egypt to Babylon. This defeat was the final blow to Egypt's aspirations and guaranteed the Chaldeans the supremacy of the West. It was the turning point of the period and had important consequences for Israel's future. The Babylonians made Jehoiakim their vassal and exiled a number of Jewish nobles (2Ki 24:1), among them Daniel (Da 1:1). Some scholars consider this first taking of Jerusalem by Nebuchadnezzar the beginning of the seventy years of Judah's exile in Babylon (25:11); with it the dissolution of the Davidic kingdom had begun.

Jehoiakim sponsored idolatry and had no concern for the widespread social injustice in his realm (22:13–19; 2Ki 23:37). Of all the kings under whom Jeremiah prophesied, Jehoiakim was the most inveterate foe of the message and messenger of God (cf. 26:20–23; 36:20–26). In 598–597 B.C., he revolted against Babylon but was unsuccessful, thus adding to Judah's problems (2Ki 24:1–5). In Jehoiakim's time, Jeremiah was persecuted, plotted against, maligned, and imprisoned. The king destroyed his written prophecies, but the prophet did not swerve from his divine commission (cf. 11:18–23; 12:6; 15:15–18; 18:18; 20:2; 26:10–11, 24; 36:23). Jehoiakim died violently in Jerusalem in 598–597 B.C., in the eleventh year of his rule, as Jeremiah had predicted (22:18–19). The Chronicler records Jehoiakim's deportation to Babylon under Nebuchadnezzar (2Ch 36:6–7; see also Da 1:1).

(d) Jehoiachin. Jehoiakim was succeeded by his son Jehoiachin (also called Jeconiah and Coniah [see NIV notes on 22:24; 24:1]), who reigned only three months (cf. 2Ki 24:8). But this teenage king ruled long enough to reveal himself as a wicked monarch, whom Jeremiah strenuously denounced (22:24–30). Jehoiachin's father's rebellion against Babylon forced Nebuchadnezzar to besiege Jerusalem in 597 B.C., when Jehoiachin capitulated (2Ki 24:12). He was exiled to Babylon with many of Judah's upper class (among them the prophet Ezekiel [Eze 1:2]), and the temple was plundered (2Ki 24:10–16). Jehoiachin was a prisoner in Babylon for thirty-seven

years (52:31–34). He was released by Evil-Merodach, son and successor of Nebuchadnezzar (2Ki 25:27–30). Strangely, the Jews long held a hope of his restoration to the Davidic throne; and Ezekiel refers to him, not to Zedekiah his successor, as king.

(e) Zedekiah. Among the many accomplishments of the great Nebuchadnezzar were king-making and name-changing. After the exile of Jehoiachin, Nebuchadnezzar set on the Judean throne Mattaniah, a son of Josiah, full brother of Eliakim and uncle of Jehoiachin, and changed his name to Zedekiah (2Ki 23:34; 24:17; 2Ch 36:10; Jer 1:3), a fact confirmed by the Babylonian Chronicle. The situation in Judah at the outset of Zedekiah's reign was that a series of sieges and deportations with changes in rulers had depleted the small kingdom of some of its best minds. Zedekiah, weak, vacillating, deficient in personality, found it beyond him to exert effective governing leadership. A puppet of Babylon, to whose king he had sworn fealty in the name of the God of Israel, he was checkmated in every decision by the pro-Egyptian policy of his officials.

Zedekiah's relationship with Jeremiah was closer than any previous Judean king, with the probable exception of the godly Josiah. But he was powerless to protect Jeremiah from the vicious designs of the nobles and to follow the God-given counsel that Jeremiah ceaselessly reiterated about submitting to Nebuchadnezzar. In the fourth year of his reign, Zedekiah plotted rebellion against Babylon with a confederacy of the kings of Edom, Moab, Ammon, Tyre, and Sidon (27:3–11). This was their object in sending representatives to Jerusalem. The plot was denounced by Jeremiah and ultimately came to nothing. Perhaps Zedekiah's visit to Babylon that same year was intended to assure Nebuchadnezzar of his loyalty (51:59).

The end, however, was not far off. In the ninth year of his reign (588 B.C.), Zedekiah conspired with Pharaoh Hophra against Nebuchadnezzar. Babylon responded with an invasion of Judah, which ended when the city fell in the summer of 586 B.C. (2Ki 24:20–25:7; 2Ch 36:17; Jer 38:28–39:10). Throughout the siege, Jeremiah urged Zedekiah to surrender (21:1–10; 34:1–5, 17–22; 37:3–10, 16–17; 38:14–23). At one point the approach of the Egyptian army compelled the withdrawal of Babylon's forces, but the siege was

---

Chronological Order of Chapters in Jeremiah

Note: The following chart gives a proposed chronological order for the material in the book of Jeremiah. For those sections that have no dates cited in the text of Jeremiah, the dates suggested are tentative, though supported by evangelical scholarship (such passages are listed in italics). Jeremiah 52 is a historical supplement, virtually identical to 2 Kings 24:18–25:21 and probably not from the pen of Jeremiah. All dates are B.C.

Under King Josiah (640–609)

626	1:1–19
625–622	2:1–6:30
621–620	11:1–12:17

**Under King Jehoahaz
(three months in 609)**

Nothing (but cf. 22:10–12)

Under King Jehoiakim (609–598)

609	7:1–10:25; 26:1–24
608–606	18:1–20:18
606	35:1–19
605	*13:1–17; 13:20–17:27;* 25:1–38; 36:1–32
604	*45:1–46:12; 47:1–49:39*
599	22:1–23:40

**Under King Jehoiachin
(three months in 597)**

597	13:18–19

Under King Zedekiah (597–586)

597	24:1–10
594–593	27:1–29:32; *50:1–51:64*
588	21:1–14
587	30:1–33:26
587–586	34:1–22; 37:1–38:28
586	39:1–18

Under Gedaliah the Governor (586–585)

585	40:1–41:3

After Gedaliah's Assassination (585–580)

585	41:4–43:13
580	44:1–30

---

resumed (37:1–10). Meanwhile, because of the cowardly attitude of Zedekiah, Jeremiah was mistreated by his enemies in Judah (37:11–21; ch. 38). The destruction of Jerusalem at this time, annually observed in mourning among Jews the world over on the ninth of the month Ab, was the greatest judgment of God on Israel in the OT. Zedekiah, captured as he tried to escape, his sons slain before him, and his eyes blinded, was carried to Babylon with a company of his subjects.

After the destruction of the city and temple, the king of Babylon appointed Gedaliah governor of Judah. After a brief period (which, in the absence of evidence, could be three months or a few years), Gedaliah was murdered by a scion of the Davidic house, possibly at the instigation of pro-Egyptian sympathizers. Fearing reprisal from Babylon, the survivors of this tragedy fled to Egypt, taking Jeremiah and Baruch by force with them. So was completed a cycle begun with deliverance from Pharaoh by Moses centuries before. Strange, too, that Jeremiah, who counseled throughout his ministry against confidence in Egypt, should end his earthly days there against his will. Thus an important era in the theocracy in Israel was ended. The destruction of the sanctuary at Shiloh had closed the age of the Judges. The destruction of Solomon's temple marked the end of the period of the monarchy in Israel. The fall of the second temple by Titus (A.D. 70) was the catastrophic close of Israel's occupation of her land until modern times.

5. Theological Emphases

The dominant elements of Jeremiah's message are of paramount significance for his day and ours. What sustained him throughout a lifetime of grief and opposition was that he had an undying confidence in God and his promises (18:7; 29:14; 32:1–15). The two foci of his life and ministry were God—his goodness, his claims on humankind, his requirements of repentance and faith—and his wayward people—their welfare, both physically and spiritually.

Jeremiah enjoyed a high concept of God as Lord of all creation (27:5). The gods of the nation are nonentities (10:11 [the only verse in the book in Aramaic], 14; 14:22). God knows the malady of the human heart (17:9–10); yet he loves his people deeply (31:1–3), longing to bless those who trust him (17:7). Idolatrous worship and heartless, impenitent service are alike an abomination to him (19:4–6; 14:12). No greater insult can be offered God than to represent him under the form of dead idols. Idolatry was the special sin Jeremiah tirelessly preached against. Three kinds of falsehood stirred him: (1) false security that refused all calls for repentance, (2) false prophets who lulled the people into dangerous complacency, and (3) the false worship of idols. Worship was tendered to Baal, Molech, and the Queen of Heaven (Ishtar). Images of these deities were even placed in the temple (32:34; cf. 7:31; 19:5; 32:35; 44:18–19).

Immorality always accompanies idolatry. In Jeremiah's time moral corruption was widespread and social injustices abounded (5:1–9; 7:1–11; 23:10–14). Priests and prophets were as culpable as the rest of Judah (6:13–15). Yet the nation carried out its religious rites. But God was not to be placated with these merely external services. Jeremiah preached that judgment was inescapable. God had already used drought, famine, and foreign invaders (14:1–6; 4:11–22); he would yet bring the culminating visitation through Nebuchadnezzar (25:9). But God's love and faithfulness to his covenants would not permit the judgment to be fatal or final. There was a future hope. Jeremiah foretold the return from captivity in Babylon (25:11; 29:10) as well as the doom of Babylon itself (chs. 50–51). He did not hesitate to give Israel's hope tangible manifestation (32:1–15).

Jeremiah also had a ministry to the nations (1:5, 10). He saw Nebuchadnezzar as God's agent in the events of that day (27:6). He warned the other nations against resisting Nebuchadnezzar (27:1–11). In God's name he demanded righteousness of all nations (chs. 46–51). He voiced God's concern for the welfare of all peoples (29:1–14, esp. v.7).

Probably the outstanding emphasis in Jeremiah's ministry was the priority of the spiritual over everything else. He saw how secondary the temporal features of Judah's faith were. He saw his coreligionists trusting (1) an outward acceptance of the covenant of the Lord (11:1–5), (2) circumcision (9:25–26), (3) the temple (7:1–15), (4) the sacrificial system (6:20; 7:21–23), (5) outward possession of the law of Moses (8:8), (6) false prophecy (23:9–40), (7) prayer (11:14; 15:1), (8) the

throne (22:1–9), and (9) the ark (3:16). Jeremiah preached more about repentance than any other prophet. His overarching concern at all times was the condition of the individual heart. His exposition of the new covenant is outstanding in Scripture (31:31–34). The NT shows us how deeply this truth entered into the work of our Lord.

As for Jeremiah's predictions of the distant future, Israel will return in penitence to the Lord (32:37–40). The Messiah will rule over her in justice and righteousness (23:5–8). The remnant of the nations will enjoy blessing at that time (3:17; 16:19).

As for messianic prophecy, Jeremiah does not describe messianic times in detail. The person of the Messiah is not so prominent in his book. But Jeremiah does give some significant messianic passages: (1) the proclamation of a revelation of God that will outshine the ark of the covenant (3:14–17); (2) the disclosure of a new covenant (31:31–34); (3) the realization of the Mosaic ideal (Ex 19:6) with the fulfillment of the Davidic covenant (33:14–26).

The lasting value of Jeremiah's book lies not only in the allusions (between forty and fifty of them) in the NT (over half are in Revelation) but also in its being a wonderful handbook for learning the art of having fellowship with God. Here is personal faith at its highest in the OT, a veritable gateway to understanding the deeper meaning of the priesthood and the monarchy under the Davidic dynasty (23:1–8; 33:14–18). Indeed, the abundance of bright promises for the nation in chs. 30–33 has led commentators to designate this portion "The Book of Consolation." The most famous passage in Jeremiah's prophecy deals with the new covenant (31:31–34). He does not speak of personal resurrection but of the restoration of Israel.

Because Jeremiah is so unlike any other OT prophet, and because his writings are so inextricably bound up with his life and thought, the student of his prophecy must consider in depth the inner life and characteristics of this man of God, some elements of which have already been lightly touched on. Besides the features of his natural abilities, his emotions, his motivation, and his personal relationship to the Lord, there are the so-called Confessions of Jeremiah, his dialogues with the Lord, his imprecations on his enemies, and especially his prayer life. No

OT prophet has disclosed more of his heart and spiritual yearnings than he. Though he was gentle and timid (but never effeminate, as some have charged), because of the call and commission of God he adamantly held to his duty. He could not be swayed. No one in Judah was more patriotic; yet he never allowed himself to gloss over Judah's sin. His was a lonely and isolated life; though he longed for human fellowship and love, all his life he was denied a family and close friends. In spite of his deep love for his people, he was divinely compelled to proclaim almost monotonously their suffering and national doom. His fellowship with God was particularly deep and intimate. At times this was so frank that many modern students of his book feel he borders on the blasphemous, or at least on the irreverent.

We often forget that Jeremiah was a man of exceptional courage, unwaveringly determined to proclaim God's truth though the entire nation opposed him. Such a stance he maintained at great mental and physical cost. Imagine his agony of heart and mind when he saw his people undeviatingly headed for catastrophe, felt himself powerless to avert it, and was all the while experiencing the relentless opposition of those for whose benefit he was prophesying. These trials and temptations molded him into one of the greatest spiritual giants of all time. Because of his timidity, he was prone to discouragement and despair. The Lord gave him no signs or miracles to confirm the validity of his predictions. At one period of his life, Jeremiah had decided to resign his commission (20:8–9), but the divine compulsion would not let him do it. God had promised to make him an iron pillar and a bronze wall and did not default on his word.

It was apparently natural for Jeremiah to carry on extended dialogues with the Lord. These dialogues are valuable principally because they show how Jeremiah (and other prophets under similar conditions) kept separate his personal consciousness and the message of God (cf. 12:1–6; 14:7–15:21).

Some expositors have expressed their horror at Jeremiah's calls for revenge on his enemies; for them this is the chief blot on his life. But these imprecations are explicable on the same basis as those in the Psalms and should be understood as involving no feeling of personal vindictiveness. Jeremiah knew he was God's messenger; therefore, those who attacked him were arraying themselves against God. Jeremiah's intense fidelity to his God and his longing for the triumph of divine righteousness show that his curses were not so much personal as uttered for the vindication of the glory of the Lord. The OT saints, moreover, had no clear revelation of future retribution.

Nothing is more revealing of a man of God than his prayer life. Jeremiah lived, worked, and wept in an atmosphere of prayer and openness before the Lord. He was so committed to prayer for his wayward people that God had to proscribe such activity by him (7:16; 11:14; 14:11). And he included himself in his prayers: 11:18–20; 12:1–4; 15:10, 15–18; 17:14–18; 18:19–23; 20:7–11, 14–18—passages known as the Confessions of Jeremiah. In them are the most unreserved statements of any prophet in Israel. Other prophets narrate their experiences, but the OT has few parallels to these self-disclosures. In them Jeremiah stands in all his human frailty, his love for his people, and his utter devotion to the will and call of God.

Jeremiah had faith in the Lord and in his ultimate purpose for Israel and the nations. In spite of impending disaster on Judah, he found solid ground for confidence. Through all his denunciations he saw God's final aim to bless his people, whether the remnant in the land or the exiles in Babylon (29:1–14; 32:1–15). His prophecies of Israel's restoration are among the most glowing in the Bible (3:14–18; 30:18–22; 31:1–14; 33:10–13).

Jeremiah manifested a complete frankness with God, concealing from him no emotional reaction or fear. He even questioned the Lord's dealings with him and others (12:1; 15:10–18; 20:7). Moreover, he was able to love everyone (17:7–8). He enjoyed the devotion of Baruch (36:32), the friendship of the high priest Zephaniah (29:24–32), merciful deliverance at the hands of Ebed-Melech the Ethiopian (38:7–13), and the respect of King Zedekiah (38:14–28).

Jeremiah had an intense and unrelenting hatred of sin, rebuking it in scathing words. He scrutinized the political, social, moral, and spiritual life of the people. Prophets, priests, kings, nobles—even relatives—could expect no favoritism from him (cf. 5:1–5; 13:1–14; 23:1–4; 22:13–19).

Jeremiah displayed faith in the indestructibility of Judah, though in his day the nation was headed for judgment. Babylon was irresistible because of the purpose of God, but this never meant extinction of the nation (30:11, 18–22; 31:35–37; 33:19–26). Though considered a traitor by his contemporaries, he had more faith in the nation's future existence than his accusers did (chs. 32 and 37; see also 25:11; 29:7–14).

EXPOSITION

I. Prophecies From the Reign of Josiah (1:1–20:18)

A. The Call and Commission of Jeremiah (1:1–19)

1. The title (1:1–3)

1–2 These verses serve as the title for the entire book. They name the man through whom God gave the prophecies and refer to his home, the period of his main labors, and the chief national event of his times. The more usual formula for the title of a prophecy is "the word of the LORD." Here the term "words" (GK 1821) has a connotation broad enough to include both the prophecies and the events of Jeremiah's life. Jeremiah was a priest by birth but a prophet by calling. The "territory of Benjamin" bordered Judah on the south and Ephraim on the north. The date indicated is not that of Jeremiah's birth but of his call to service, namely, 626 B.C. (cf. 25:3). The call of God came five years before the important reforms of Josiah (2Ki 22–23).

3 The end of Jeremiah's ministry omits the events after the fall of Jerusalem because most of his ministry had already been completed. The reason why Jehoahaz and Jehoiachin are omitted is probably that their reigns lasted so short a time (three months each). Here, then, in Jeremiah's ministry was a service for God of more than two decades and possibly half a century. The Exile to Babylon occurred in the fifth month of 586 B.C. (2Ki 25:4–10).

2. The call of Jeremiah (1:4–10)

4 This verse is the heart of the prophetic experience. Jeremiah's call came not in a vision but by hearing the divine word. Unless the verse denotes inspiration by God, words are meaningless.

5 For Jeremiah to know that his commission was by divine decree, the Lord explained his motivation in accomplishing his purpose through him. Observe the four actions of God toward his prophet. That God "knew" (GK 3359) Jeremiah means not mere cognition but a sense of relationship (Am 3:2) and approval (Ps 1:6). God's claim on his life was prior to all other relationships (cf. Ps 139:13–16; Isa 49:1–5; Gal 1:15). Jeremiah's consecration was his being set apart for a definite spiritual purpose. He was appointed a prophet for a worldwide ministry.

6 Jeremiah, struck with terror over the magnitude of the task, pled his youth and inexperience (cf. Ex 4:10). The Hebrew word for "child" (GK 5853) does not connote a precise definition of age, but we may infer from the length of his ministry that Jeremiah must have been about twenty at the time of his call. Realizing that ability in public speaking was essential to the prophetic office, he stated his lack of eloquence. But what God required for Jeremiah's ministry, which was to be so sad and denunciatory, was a tender heart able to sympathize with the condemned. Little could the young man know how difficult and heartbreaking his task would be.

7–8 God never makes a mistake in choosing his servants. He empowers all he calls and provides the encouragement and help they need. Moreover, God's promise of his presence would dispel Jeremiah's fear, another source of his hesitation. He would be mercilessly opposed and persecuted, but the Lord would preserve him from the attacks of his enemies and give him the moral courage he would so greatly need.

9 As tangible evidence that he had empowered Jeremiah, in a spiritual experience God touched Jeremiah's mouth. Thus he was inspired to speak God's truth. From then on Jeremiah's words would be truly God's, and he would actually become a mouthpiece for God (cf. Isa 6:7).

10 The purposes of God in Jeremiah's ministry are twofold: destructive and constructive. God's word is accompanied with power so that the prophet will accomplish these objectives (Isa 55:10–11). For Jeremiah's ministry, the emphasis is undoubtedly on its destructive element. God's appointment brings with it his commitment of authority to carry out his goals for his prophet.

3. The vision of the almond rod (1:11–12)

11–12 Two visions were granted Jeremiah, evidently to authenticate his call. The first vision was that of an almond tree, which blossoms in January when other trees are still dormant. It is a harbinger of spring, as though it watches over the beginning of the season. So the Lord was watching to bring judgment on Israel's sins. What former prophets had said would come was about to happen. God was prepared to act because of world conditions. The "branch" (GK 5234) symbolizes judgment here, which would soon overtake Israel (cf. Mic 6:9). God keeps his word promptly and works toward an early fulfillment.

4. The vision of the boiling caldron (1:13–19)

13–14 The word "again" shows that the visions are closely related. The first deals with the time of the judgment; the second, with the direction and nature of the coming disaster. A "boiling pot" can only signify calamity. The pot was "tilting away from the north," i.e., facing toward the south, where its contents would be poured out. It would strike from Babylon. Though Babylon is located east of Judah, her armies—and all invading armies from Asia—would invade Palestine from the north because of the impassable Arabian desert. The disaster would engulf the entire land of Judah. The invasion would issue in victory for the enemy.

15–16 The "northern kingdoms" mentioned suit a Babylonian invasion under Nebuchadnezzar. The setting up of the thrones at the gates of Jerusalem, the place of public business, implies complete subjugation (cf. 39:3). Thus from the outset, Jeremiah is a preacher of judgment. As Isaiah speaks of the salvation of the Lord, Ezekiel of the glory of the Lord, and Daniel of the kingdom of the Lord, so Jeremiah incessantly proclaims the judgment of the Lord. The cause of Judah's punishment is stated in three clauses, which describe her idolatry. In a sense Jeremiah's entire book is an elaboration of what 1:16 says about this sin.

17–19 In the remainder of ch. 1, Jeremiah is given strong encouragement for his hard task, because his message would be neither welcome nor popular with his people. To fulfill his duties nothing less than utter commitment to God and to his strength would suffice. With God, Jeremiah would be invincible. In his darkest hours these words sustained him mentally, emotionally, and spiritually. He is commanded to prepare vigorously for action. He would need to rely on a triple defense against his fourfold enemy: kings, officials, priests, and people. The secret of spiritual victory is that Jeremiah is assured success on the condition of faith in God. He ultimately prevailed over all his enemies; and his prophecies were verified, attesting him to be a true prophet of the Lord.

B. Warnings of Judgment on Judah's Sins (2:1–6:30)

Chapters 2–6 form a connected message, coming probably from Josiah's reign, in the early years of Jeremiah's ministry (3:6). They show how little it was in Jeremiah's mind to excuse Judah's sin. The major themes in these five chapters are (1) God's indignation against moral and social sin, (2) his love for his people and land, (3) the certainty of doom on the unrepentant nation, and (4) salvation for the believing.

1. God's controversy with Judah (2:1–37)

No sooner had Jeremiah been appointed to the prophetic office than the Lord's message of condemnation began to sound out in Judah. The foci in this chapter are (1) the sacred love of God for his people and (2) their love of idols.

a. Israel's ingratitude (2:1–8)

1–2 To show the nation how far it had departed from the Lord, Jeremiah recalls their deliverance from Egypt. Like a devoted bridegroom, the Lord says that he still remembers their love as his true bride (cf. Hos 1–3). Proof that Jeremiah is speaking of Israel's love for God is shown by her following him in the desert at the time of their marriage, the period of her faithfulness and devotion to the Lord. Warmth, love, and purity marked her first relationship with the Lord. Apart from the golden-calf incident (Ex 32:1–29),

Israel's failures in the desert came from lack of faith rather than outright apostasy.

3 The earliest bond between God and Israel was not only a fragrant remembrance to him but also a sad contrast to her present apostasy. In those early favored days, Israel was set apart as sacred to God, his very firstfruits, because she was the first nation to worship the true God (cf. Ex 19:5–6; Am 6:1). No nation was to trouble Israel because she was dedicated to the Lord. To disobey this prohibition was to incur the wrath of God as in the unauthorized eating of firstfruits (cf. Lev 22:10, 16).

4–5 Because of the covenant relationship, Israel was still under divine protection (cf. Ge 12:1–3). But the strange question in v.5 is intended to awaken the people's consciences. The change in their relationship to God was not his fault but theirs. They had broken the marriage covenant by their infidelity in going after impure lovers. A play on words reveals how worshipers become like the objects they worship. The word "worthless" (GK 2038 & 2039) correctly conveys the idea that the Lord regards idols as without substance or reality (cf. 1Ki 16:13; 1Co 8:4). Jeremiah levels as scathing denunciations against idols as any prophet; idolatry was Israel's chief and besetting sin (see comment on 1:16).

6–7 Israel's attention is directed to the multiplicity of benefits the nation enjoyed at God's hand; yet the people were unmindful of his presence in their midst. They had forgotten their experiences in the desert and the dangers the Lord had graciously brought them through. They were brought to a "fertile land" (lit., "a land of Carmel"), one well cultivated and productive. But the people defiled God's land by their idolatry and immoral practices. Although God gave Israel the land, he had never relinquished his own ultimate ownership of it. In the truest sense, the land was a stewardship to Israel from the Lord.

8 The leaders of the nation, who possibly could have stemmed the tide, are included in the prophet's indictment. They were misleading the people. Jeremiah singles out several groups of leaders. The "priests" were wholly indifferent to God and to his will. Because they dealt with the law, the priests and Levites had well-prescribed regulations for the life of the nation. But in Jeremiah's time they acted as if they did not know the Lord at all. The civil authorities were no better. The "leaders" (Heb., "shepherds"; GK 8286)—i.e., temporal rulers, kings—were adept in violating the law of God. The "prophets" were probably the most culpable. Their high duty was to proclaim the will of God and bring the sinful people back to the Lord.

The priests and prophets were a particular grief to Jeremiah because he was a priest by birth and a prophet by calling. It was his lifelong trial to incur the persistent enmity of both groups. The false prophets, instead of speaking by God's empowerment, spoke for Baal. The reference to Baal here and elsewhere in the prophecy is to idols in general. Properly speaking, Baal (meaning "lord" or "master"), whose personal name was Hadad, was the chief male object of Canaanite (Phoenician) worship. As a nature god, he was the master of storm and fertility; his worship was cruel, degenerate, and unconcerned for human life. Idolatry is always worthless, devoid of any objective reality.

b. Israel's idolatry (2:9–19)

9–12 "Bring charges" (GK 8189) is a legal term for a plaintiff's (in this instance, God) introducing his case in court. The subject of the controversy is Judah's unparalleled idolatry. The people and their children are both included in the indictment. The heart of the contention is clearly stated. God's people have forsaken their living and true God, whereas even nations with false gods stay loyal to their worthless deities. So Judah is exhorted to investigate from Kittim to Kedar to verify the indictment.

Kittim, the Phoenician town Kition in Cyprus, gave its name to the whole island; then, by extension, the name was used for the islands and coasts of the west (see Ge 10:4; NIV note on Eze 27:6). Kedar was the name of an Arab desert tribe, which came to represent people of the eastern desert (Ge 25:13). Thus the nation is urged to observe conditions everywhere.

Mark the horror and amazement of the prophet at the enormity of Judah's apostasy! The people have acted more faithlessly than the pagans. God has not changed, but Judah has—and for what? The Lord himself was her glory. So incredible has this apostasy been that nature is called on to react to it. The heavens themselves are summoned as a witness in the Lord's litigation against his people. Because inanimate nature so consistently obeys God's commands, it is pictured as astounded at Judah's actions.

13 Like a lawyer, Jeremiah summarizes his charges: Judah's sin was compounded by rejection of truth and reception of error. The pagan nations had committed the one sin of idolatry, often exchanging one superstition for another. But Judah had exceeded them in disobedience in renouncing her own real God to serve nobodies. Jeremiah's figures are singularly vivid and apt. His nation's God is called the "spring of living water," the source of life, a metaphor often used in Scripture of God, salvation, and Christ (cf. Isa 12:3; 55:1; Jn 4:10–14; 7:37–39). Water was a rare luxury in Palestine, and water from perennial sources was cherished. On the other hand, cisterns could only store rain water. At best, they often yielded stagnant water; at worst, they cracked and allowed the water to seep out. Dead gods cannot impart life.

14 Sin inevitably brings its own punishment. By two forceful questions the Lord points out the consequences of disobedience. A slave or homeborn servant was the master's permanent property (Ex 21:1–6). Since that is so, why, then, has Israel become "plunder" to her enemies, as though her Lord could not protect her? Freed from Egyptian bondage, Israel has enslaved herself by her sins, this time to Assyria and Egypt.

Jeremiah compares the nation of Judah to a broken cistern that cannot hold water—like this one at Susita.

15 To specify how Israel became plunder, Jeremiah reminds the people of the depredations of Assyria and Egypt. The lion, a symbol of Babylon, was also a figure of Assyria; so the reference here could well be to the Assyrian conquest of the Ten Tribes in 722–721 B.C. (2Ki 15:19–20, 29; 17:4–26) and to Assyria's hostility to Judah also (Isa 10:24–32). But Egypt would not stop at exploiting Judah as well; for as Egypt was no help to the northern kingdom against the Assyrians, so it would be no help in Jeremiah's day against the threat of Chaldean power (37:7).

16 The Egyptian cities were Judah's allies on whom she depended. Memphis was the ancient capital of Lower Egypt; Tahpanhes was a fortified city on the northeast border of Egypt, southwest of Pelusium. They "shaved" the crown or scalp of the nation's head; this is probably a reference to Josiah's death at the hands of the Egyptians under Neco (2Ki 23:29). Thus both Assyria and Egypt were detrimental to Judah because they led not only to political slavery but religious disobedience as well.

17–19 With great courage Jeremiah states the cause of the impending judgment. The responsibility for it rests solely on the nation. The people would have to live with the fruit of their evil ways. God's leading was forsaken, so doom would come. Remonstrating with them further, Jeremiah asked whether they had learned nothing from the useless and dangerous game of power politics. Courting Egypt or Assyria was never in Judah's best interests. "Shihor" (meaning "Black River") is the Nile, so called because of its muddy appearance from the black deposit of soil after the annual inundations (cf. Isa 23:3). "The River" is the Euphrates, standing for the nations of Mesopotamia—here the Assyrians.

In Jeremiah's day there were two chief political parties, a pro-Egyptian one and a pro-Assyrian one. Of what help would godless nations be to Judah? Ultimately, her doom would be sealed, not by the presence or absence of treaties with allies, but by her defection from the Lord. The final cause of her calamity would be the hand of God, not the nations he used to punish her. Her great lack was the reverential fear of the Lord.

c. Israel's immorality (2:20–28)

20 Along with Israel's idolatry went unbridled immorality of long standing. "Broke off" indicates that long ago they had thrown off all restraint. In a powerful metaphor, Jeremiah pictures idolatry as adultery. Canaanite worship chose high hills and luxuriant trees to carry out its licentious rites. Judah rebelled against God's service and became a spiritual harlot. Although Jeremiah is speaking primarily of spiritual uncleanness, it must not be forgotten that sexual immorality of the lowest order was always a part of this so-called worship (cf. Hos 4:10–14).

21 Jeremiah changes to the figure of viniculture. God had planted Israel a choice vine, of completely reliable stock (cf. Isa 5:1–7; Eze 17:1–10; Hos 10:1; see also Jn 15:1–8). It was literally a "Sorek Vine," bearing a high-quality red grape. Though planted correctly, the result was corrupt, rotten branches alien to the genuine stock.

22–25 Judah's sins were so deeply ingrained that they were ineradicable. "Soda" is natron, a mineral alkali; "soap" is a vegetable alkali. Outer cleanliness could not hide the people's inner defilement. No amount of outward reform could please God. In spite of their record, the people defended themselves by brazenly denying wrongdoing. How could they claim innocence when they were carrying on their vile worship of Baal in the Valley of Hinnom with their child sacrifices? Shamelessly, like a young she-camel impelled by uncontrolled instinct to find satisfaction, so Judah went to extremes of idolatry, chasing after ever-new objects of worship. Modesty and self-control were gone. As a wild donkey in heat sniffs at the wind to find a male, so the people sought out idols; the idols did not need to woo them. Jeremiah pleads with them not to run their feet bare nor their throats dry in their lust for strange gods. But they reply that they are determined to do so in spite of God's warnings.

26–28 These verses underscore the senselessness of idolatry. The nation is warned that the people are doomed to shame in their idolatry, like a thief caught in the act. The condemnation rests on the same leaders as in v.8. Jeremiah quotes words of idolatrous adoration. What a disgrace that they should give idols the glory that is God's as Creator! The reference in v.27 could be to the ritual use of standing stones and wooden pillars or to primitive rites of worship of trees and stones. Having turned completely from the Lord, the people have descended to these depths. But in the hour of their trouble, they find out the worthlessness of their idols and appeal to God for deliverance. In time of trial, people somehow feel that they have a claim on God's help. The bitter irony of v.28 is meant to lead the people to realize the senselessness of trusting nonentities. Their false gods were as numerous as their towns (cf. 11:13).

d. Israel's irrationality (2:29–37)

29–31 In spite of all she has done, Judah thinks she has a case against God. She found fault with him because she could not manipulate him to her pleasure. She murmured at his judgments and chastisement, though the fault was hers. God's visitations were unavailing. Those who sought to lead her back to godliness were slain, as in Manasseh's reign and also in Jehoiakim's (2Ki 21:16; Jer 26:20–23). In seeking to turn Judah from her irrational ways, Jeremiah thunders, "You of this generation." Do the people think God is like a wilderness to them, unable to sustain and nourish their needs? A land of thick darkness with all kinds of imagined dangers? What has moved them to rebel against him, to wander at will? With this as their intention, all moral control and decency are lost.

32–33 The rhetorical question in v.32 focuses attention on the fact that although God is Judah's great adornment, she had forgotten him, though no bride would forget her wedding attire. The number of different Hebrew words in the OT (cf. Isa 3:18–22) used for ornaments shows they were in common use. Judah was without gratitude for God's gifts to her. So abandoned was she that she could even teach wicked women new methods of seduction. She used all kinds of artifices to make herself desirable to her lovers and cared nothing for God's love.

34–37 Social sins, such as the oppression of the poor, inevitably follow spiritual decline. The historic reference could be to Manasseh's reign, but not exclusively so (cf. Am 2:6–8; 4:1; 5:10–12). The victims were "the innocent poor." In spite of all these wicked actions, the nation considered itself innocent—the height of irrationality. Judah's argumentative self-justification will do nothing to avert the visitation of God. It is always easy to justify oneself, no matter how sinful one's life has become.

Jeremiah returns to Judah's determination to make allies to bolster her position in the political world. In the long run, both Egypt and Assyria will disappoint her; no alliance will work out to the nation's benefit. The omnipotent God will overrule all her overtures to her shame, disappointment, and grief.

2. A call to repentance (3:1–25)

The prophecies through ch. 6 are in all probability a condensation of those Jeremiah gave during Josiah's reign. The theme (ch. 2) of the faithless wife of the faithful God is continued in ch. 3, which contains repeated invitations for Judah to repent of her ways.

a. Judah, the faithless wife (3:1–5)

1 The chapter has an unusual beginning because the first word in the Hebrew text is "and saying." Probably the words "The word of the LORD came to me" were inadvertently omitted by an early copyist. The Lord is questioning the nation on the basis of the law of Moses. The law forbade the remarriage of a man with his divorced wife, even if her second husband had died or divorced her (Dt 24:1–4). The purpose of the law was to curb the husband's arbitrary use of his right to divorce his wife. But with the Lord's people, the case was different on more than one count. They had not been divorced at all but had played the harlot. Furthermore, they had sought out not one lover (god) but many. It is perhaps too much to say that the Lord did not recognize the claim of both Egypt and Assyria on Israel as their wife; but since Israel had left God for pagan lovers, God would abide by the law of divorce, relinquishing his right to receive her back.

The verb "return" (GK 8740) in the last line of v.1 may allow for more than one rendering. If it is taken as an imperative, then the Lord is calling the nation to penitence in spite of the gravity of her sins. If the clause is interpreted as a question, then the sense is "Would you now return to me [in spite of all you have done]?" (so NIV). The second view emphasizes the legal prohibition of the restoration of the union. Judah, unfaithful in the marriage relationship, had no right to return to

the Lord. Her pollution because of idolatry would make a reconciliation all but impossible. The broken bond was irreparable.

It is hard to see, however, how the Lord would be declaring a reconciliation impossible when, throughout the remainder of the chapter, he is pleading for that very thing in urging Judah to repent. Even the question form of the last clause can be understood to impress Judah that it would be no light thing, considering her many offenses, for God to reclaim her. God is not indignantly rejecting the possibility of her return. We must never forget that God, as he wills, exercises grace beyond the law. Ruth was a Moabite woman and was excluded from Israel (cf. Dt 23:3); how then does she become the ancestress of David and of the Lord Jesus? God operated by grace beyond the law. So God was ready to forgive Judah in spite of all her past failures. Legal claims to the contrary, God calls Judah to the solution to her predicament—namely, repentance.

2 But God's people must see that their return to the Lord does not permit continuance in sin. Their abandonment to idolatry was notorious. They had waited for lovers by the way as marauding Bedouin bandits of the desert waited for passersby to plunder. Their desire for idolatry was insatiable. Again, immoral practices were an integral part of the pagan fertility cult. Since God could not tolerate such disobedience, he chastised his people. As Moses had warned, sin would cause the withdrawal of God's prosperity of the land.

3 The rains are vital in a dry land. The early rains fell about October/November and the latter rain (for the maturing of the crops) fell in March/April (cf. Dt 11:10–17). But because of the nation's impudence, the discipline was ineffective. Natural providences that were meant to bring the nation to repentance were without success.

4–5 Instead of truly turning to the Lord, the people felt that a mere avowal of allegiance to him would suffice. The nation claimed that from then on—i.e., in the days of Josiah's reform—the Lord would be their sole guide and companion. The term "father" (GK 3) was sometimes used by a young wife of her husband. The Hebrew word denotes a husband and companion ("friend"). But the reformation was more apparent than genuine. The people's crying to God was empty lip service because they continued in their wickedness. Moreover, they were building on false hopes that God's anger would not last; so they persisted in wickedness to the limit of their power, evidently convinced that God's wrath would subside regardless of what they did.

b. Judah worse than Israel (3:6–10)

6 To show the gravity of Judah's spiritual condition, Jeremiah compares it with that of exiled Israel, the northern kingdom. The captivity of that nation should have been a warning to Judah, but the example had been lost on her. In spite of her sins, Judah considered herself favored beyond the possibility of judgment on her. How vividly this shows that Josiah's reformation was superficial and short-lived! Jeremiah uses strong language, calling the northern kingdom "faithless Israel." She had become apostasy personified. Thus Judah had learned nothing from the tragic fate of Israel, whose apostasies had led her into exile.

7–10 Furthermore, it was not as though the Lord had not shown patience with the northern kingdom, for he had waited for her to repent. But she did not. And Judah, called in v.10 "unfaithful," witnessed these dealings and their consequences but remained unmoved. The Lord used the metaphor of divorce to describe the captivity for Israel (cf. Dt 24:1–3). If anything, Judah tried to outdo her sister, Israel. Idolatry and immorality seemed trivial to her; she gave herself to idols of stone and wood, with all their base fertility rites. In Canaanite religion the main emphasis was on fertility and sex. Worship was entered into to ensure the fertility of the land, the animals, and the people. Sacred prostitution was practiced widely. Among the sacred objects were stone altars and the sacred tree or grove.

The Hebrew word underlying NIV's "mattered so little" can mean either "light" or "sound." In view of the context, the latter seems preferable, i.e., that Judah's immorality only sounded before God but went unnoticed by Judah herself. To make matters worse, Judah pretended repentance under the reforms of Josiah (cf. 2Ki 23; 2Ch 34–35). Such falsity could not hoodwink God. Apos-

tasy Israel and Treachery Judah were spiritual sisters, and the latter was worse than the former.

c. The call to return (3:11–14a)

11 In this section and the next, Jeremiah proclaims to the northern kingdom of Israel both a call to repent and a promise of restoration. First he gives a summary statement that, in view of what has been said, has only one logical conclusion: Apostate Israel was more righteous than treacherous Judah (cf. Eze 23:11). The northern kingdom did not have the example of judgment before her as Judah did; therefore Israel was less guilty. Also, only one of Israel's kings (Jehoahaz) is said to have sought the Lord, and that only when in distress because of the Syrian invasion (2Ki 13:1–5). Furthermore, Judah had greater privileges with a divinely appointed king and a revealed priestly service, together with the example of the kingdom of Israel.

12–13 The Lord calls Israel to return, for there was still hope for her. This call is directed toward the north, toward Assyria, where the Ten Tribes had been for about a century. Not all of the northern kingdom had been carried away; a remnant was left that mingled with the expatriated Assyrians to form the Samaritans. God promises not to retain his anger toward them, for though less guilty than Judah, they had no claim on restoration. It was all of grace. Such a call to return was meant to provoke Judah to jealousy. Mark well that Israel, contrary to many erroneous views, had not assimilated into the surrounding nations (cf. Jas 1:1).

Judah must recognize that the prerequisite for pardon and blessing was acknowledgment of her sins. There must be no palliation of them but a confession that she had scattered her favors among foreign gods, all the while heedless of God's voice.

14a Again the Lord summons Israel to return. The context is one of tenderness and regard for the intimate relationship between the Lord and his people. The ground of the plea is still the indissoluble marriage bond entered into at Sinai with the nation. Actually, a double figure is employed: Israel is both son and wife. Restatement of the marriage bond indicates acceptance with God.

d. Future blessing (3:14b–18)

14b The Lord promises that even if those who return to him are few, he will bring them back to Zion. The paucity of their numbers will not hinder the Lord's purpose for them. The word "clan" is not to be understood in the restricted sense of a "family" but of a people or tribe. No matter how small, a remnant will return; God's message of pardon is ultimately on the basis of individual response to him.

15 Once back in the land, the nation will need godly rulers; and this the Lord promises them. These "shepherds" (GK 8286; cf. "leaders" in 2:8; 23:4) will govern with knowledge, i.e., in the fear of the Lord. In contrast to the corrupt leaders of Jeremiah's day, they will conform to the mind and will of God.

16 In the time of their restoration to the land, the Lord's people will increase greatly (cf. 23:3). The phrase "in those days" (vv.16, 18) clearly refers to messianic times (cf. 30:24; 21:27, 29, 31, 33, 38). In that era of blessing, no one will even mention the ark of the covenant of the Lord. The worship of God will need no visible aids, for God will dwell among his people. The ark was the center of the religious life of God's people and the place where the high priest offered the blood of the sacrifice on the Day of Atonement. The old economy is to be dissolved. The old covenant, of which the ark was a central feature, is to give way to another—a preview of 31:31–34.

17 In the same vein, Jeremiah predicts that Jerusalem will be known as "The throne of the LORD." The ark of the tabernacle and temple represented God's throne on earth (Ex 25:22; 1Sa 4:4). Neither Israel nor the nations will then be misled into idolatry. Israel purged of idolatry will be a witness and blessing to all the nations (Ps 67).

18 United to God in holiness of life, Jeremiah predicts that the two long-divided parts of the nations will finally be reunited to dwell in the land promised to the patriarchs (cf. Eze 37). In summary, the elements of the promise are godly leaders, absence of outward elements of worship, the dwelling of God's presence with them, a godly life, a successful witness to the nations, and a unified nation.

e. Israel's disobedience (3:19–20)

19–20 From this point to the end of the chapter, there is an extended dialogue between God and Israel. God's love and favor met with Israel's ingratitude and disobedience. His intention was to give them a place as if they were sons. As a daughter, Israel was to receive an inheritance like that of sons, an event that was contrary to Hebrew practice (cf. Nu 27:1–8). Their legacy was the land of Palestine. But they had to match their words with their deeds. They would enter into the promise only when they practiced what they professed. But again they disappointed all expectations and committed treachery. What a contrast between God's hopes for them and what happened! From the rosy prospects of the future, Israel must be called back to the present.

f. Exhortation to repentance (3:21–25)

21 The prophet turns to the nation's avowal of repentance. Where they had so flagrantly carried on their idolatries, the people now lamented for their transgressions. Since their sin was public and prominent, so would their cries of penitence be (cf. 31:15).

22–23 In response to their genuine repentance, the Lord promised to heal the wounds his people had acquired in their apostasy (cf. 30:17; 33:6; Hos 14:4). Their answer showed the depth and reality of their penitence; they accepted the Lord's offer of pardon. Once more the way to ruin and the way of deliverance are stated. Idolatry with its wild and clamorous excesses is the way of death (cf. 1Ki 18:21–29), but the way of salvation and life is in the Lord (Ps 3:8; Jnh 2:9).

24–25 At last the people were convinced that idolatry has been their undoing. The "shameful" thing is Baal, the god of shame (cf. 11:13). How costly their idolatry was in terms of property and even more in terms of the sacrifices of their sons and daughters! And the malady was of long standing. So at the end of the chapter, we see the nation totally cast down by her sin and willing to endure the grief it had caused, lying prostrate on the ground.

3. The invasion from the north (4:1–31)

The preceding chapter closed on a note of confession on the part of the people. But vv.1–4 here show that the reform under Josiah was only superficial. More, much more, was needed.

a. The call to genuine repentance (4:1–4)

1–2 The people's cry of anguish (3:24–25) is answered by the Lord with an assurance of blessing when they do return to him. There is a vast difference between perfunctory repentance and heartfelt restoration to God. If Judah would truly repent, it must be to God alone. Furthermore, they must rid themselves of their detestable things, their idols. Evidently they had not yet done this. Moreover, if the people would remain steadfast (on their oath in the name of the Lord) in the essential qualities of truth, justice, and righteousness, then their example would profoundly affect the nations. Judah's conversion would herald blessing for the nations. To swear by God's name involves recognition of him as Lord. When the nations are being blessed, the Abrahamic blessing is being realized (cf. Ge 12:3; 18:18; 22:18; 26:4; 28:14).

3–4 Jeremiah uses two figures to show the nation's need of spiritual renewal: one from agriculture and the other from physiology. He exhorts the people of Judah to break up their neglected and untilled hearts. No farmer will sow seed on unplowed ground. So the plow of repentance and obedience was needed to remove the outer layer of weeds and thorns that had resulted from idolatry.

Again, Jeremiah calls for repentance—this time under the figure of circumcision. The hard encrustation on their hearts must be cut away. Outward ritual must be replaced by inward reality. The only alternative to obedience was the wrath of God. Jeremiah everywhere underscores the necessity for the new heart (cf. ch. 31).

b. The enemy on the way (4:5–18)

5–6 The remainder of this chapter concerns vivid portrayals of the invasion of the land, the siege of Jerusalem, the devastation of the land, and the decimation of the population. So certain is the judgment that Jeremiah sees the imminent invasion as already present. From v.5 on, the prophet is explicit in his warnings to the nation of calamity coming from the north. Since the siege is imminent, the people are warned to take refuge. The trumpet signals the danger. The fortified cities served as refuge for the fleeing rural population. The signal to point the way to Zion was well advised because the city was so strongly fortified. The "disaster from the north" tallies with what is known of the Babylonian invasion under Nebuchadnezzar.

7–9 Jeremiah compares the invaders to a "lion," a "scorching wind" or sirocco (v.11), and watchers or besiegers (v.16). The lion represented the Assyrians and Babylonians (here the latter; see comment on 2:15). So great was the Babylonian military prowess that the other nations feared it. For Judah Babylon's power would mean disaster to the land, its cities, and its citizenry (cf. 43:5–7).

The prophet encourages the people to lament, for there is no possibility of escaping the visitation. Unrepentant, the nation could only expect doom. Until their sins received their merited punishment, the blow could not be deflected from them. In the hour of distress, the very ones who should encourage the nation—king, princes, priests, and prophets—would be devoid of courage. The reference to their "losing heart" is not to a failure in understanding but rather to failure in stamina and valor.

10 At first reading, it appears that Jeremiah is blaming God for deceiving the nation. In the light of Jas 1:13, such action is impossible. The difficulty is not resolved by attributing the deception to the prophet's attempt to mislead the people by speaking God's message to them, for at no time had Jeremiah prophesied that Jerusalem would have peace. His message was always the opposite. The solution lies in the way the Jews spoke of evil in a world ruled by a righteous and holy God. God is said to do what he permits. Scripture often omits second causes and relates everything to God as the First Cause (cf. Ex 9:12; 1Ki 22:21–23; Eph 1:11; 2Th 2:11). The false prophets had spoken deceptively to the people; they had misled the people into false hopes; and God had permitted it all. Instead of peace, destruction faced Judah.

11–18 In a sense v.10 is parenthetical, for the prophet continues his portrayal of the invading army. With the approach of the enemy, the news will be carried by messengers in the way shown here. The foe is likened to the "scorching wind" from the desert that withers vegetation and brings discomfort to humankind. For winnowing and cleansing, a much less vehement wind is needed. Its purpose is not to sift but to judge; it does not separate good from bad but takes everything away. All would happen at God's command. Vivid metaphors—"clouds," "whirlwind," "eagles"—depict the Babylonian army with its chariots and war horses. No wonder the people cried out that they were ruined.

Even at that late hour there was still opportunity for repentance. Prophecies of judgment are conditional; obedience to God reverses the threat of judgment. But there must be inner cleansing, even of the thought life, if disaster was to be averted. The Lord's patience was wearied with Judah's continued unfaithfulness; so he asked how long their minds would be centered on wickedness. The need for repentance was urgent. The foe was near; there was little time left to return to God. Dan was the northern boundary of the land; Mount Ephraim was the northern border of Judah, not far from Jerusalem. The invaders were making rapid progress.

So unprecedented was the fate that would overtake God's people that the nations are called on to witness the judgment soon to fall on Judah. Resistance had not availed against the invaders; so they are finally seen besieging the capital, Jerusalem. As watchmen guard their fields from predatory animals, so Jerusalem would be surrounded to cut off any who would escape. All has come on her because of her own wickedness and rebellion. The calamity is bitter to bear because the people now realize that they have brought it on themselves. Their wounds are serious, reaching to the heart.

c. The agony of Jeremiah (4:19–22)

19–22 These verses express Jeremiah's personal involvement with the calamity of his people. The scene is so real to him that he cries out in physical pain. His profound emotion affects him physically. His personal anguish over the impending destruction is inescapable. So wholesale is the destruction that Jeremiah cannot suppress his deep sympathy with those he must denounce in obedience to the Lord's commission. Though he was accused of treason later, how can anyone reasonably deny the patriotism and love of Jeremiah for his people? Fellowship with God and obedience to his service always sharpen

the sensibilities of his servants. Thus the prophet agonizes in soul and can scarcely endure the scene of judgment on his people. He longs to know the end of the travail; so the Lord answers that the trial will continue as long as they persist in disobeying him. Their trouble is that they have no fellowship with the Lord in doing his will. Their moral values are completely reversed: they major in evil and minor in good.

d. The cosmic catastrophe (4:23–26)

23–26 This beautiful vignette has been acclaimed one of the most forceful passages in all prophetic literature. For vividness, simplicity, directness, breadth of reference, and gravity of subject matter, the verses are unique in Scripture. From a contemplation of Israel's calamity, the prophet is led by the Spirit who inspired him to witness cosmic catastrophe. Chaos engulfs the physical world. It is the story of Ge 1 in reverse. It may describe the coming Day of the Lord. All nature is in upheaval, and no area of life is left untouched. The apocalyptic overtone is unmistakable.

e. The desolation of the land (4:27–31)

27 Again, Jeremiah must impress his hearers with the actuality of the coming doom. The thrust of the passage is that the die is cast, and nothing can reverse the decree. Jeremiah puts in prophetic discourse what he saw in spirit. A ray of hope is held out: though the calamity will be real enough, the Lord will not allow it to accomplish the complete dissolution of the nation. There will be no reenactment of Sodom and Gomorrah's destruction (cf. Lev 26:44; Isa 6:13; Am 9:8; Mic 5:6–7). God is committed to preserving a remnant of his people.

28–31 Because God purposes grace toward the nation, none of the people should presume that judgment would not fall. The decision was irrevocable; the fulfillment came in 586 B.C. For this destruction of the land, the very heavens and earth would mourn. The Babylonians took over the military strategy of the Assyrians, becoming adept bowmen. Before such an adversary the only course would be to escape to the rocky hills; the whole city of Jerusalem would be deserted. The desperate condition of Israel is finally pictured under the figure of a harlot who even in her desperate hour still tries to allure the enemy by her wiles. Her "lovers" (lit., "paramours") are unimpressed and despise her. Jeremiah depicts her final agonies under the figure of a miscarriage of a first child with the mother in her final gasps for breath. Though undeserving, the nation will not find Jeremiah deaf to her agonizing cries. The courtesan will be murdered by her lovers, but the prophet enters completely into her plight.

4. Judah's total corruption (5:1–31)

This chapter reveals Jerusalem under moral investigation. A superficial reading of the earlier chapters of the prophecy might lead one to conclude that the nation has been charged with all it has been guilty of. But the depths of her sin against the Lord must be reviewed at length. The nation must come to a much fuller realization of her ingrained sin. The desperately low spiritual state of the nation must be brought under the searchlight of God's scrutiny. Moreover, her sin must be judged in view of her continued refusal to heed the Lord's gracious calls to repent and so avert disaster. What a telling portrayal of unrelieved apostasy!

a. The bill of particulars (5:1–9)

1–3 Investigation, full and impartial, must always precede indictment on a legal bill of particulars. The object of the search was to find one righteous person. For such a person who practiced justice and made truth (faithfulness) the goal of his life, the Lord promised to pardon Jerusalem. There may be an allusion here to Abraham's intercession for Sodom (Ge 18:23 33). Although Jeremiah's statement was justified, obviously some godly people like Josiah, Baruch, Zephaniah, and Jeremiah himself were living in Jerusalem. But the words certainly applied to the mass of the populace. In short, corruption was so widespread that exceptions were not significant (cf. Ps 14). The reference to those who said, "As surely as the LORD lives," does not mitigate the severity of Jeremiah's statement. Their oath was a spurious profession of piety. They used the most binding and the right form of oath, but their conduct showed it to be perjury. Even God's severe chastisements made no difference in their lives.

4–5 Jeremiah thought of extenuating circumstances for the plight of his people. The population was generally poor; their poverty kept them from opportunities of learning the way of the Lord. In his disappointment, the prophet had thought that the situation might be different among the nation's leaders. But a higher station in life did not mean greater piety. The great had thrown off all restraint, placing themselves above the law. The great and learned were no more open than the poor and ignorant. All classes were alike implicated. Judgment must follow.

6 Jeremiah uses three predators—"a lion," "a wolf," and "a leopard"—to portray the imminent judgment. Probably the beasts symbolize the Babylonians. The lion represents strength, the wolf ravenousness, and the leopard swiftness—all traits of Babylonians.

7–9 God reasons with his people to convince them of the justice of his judgments. His bounty to the people evoked not gratitude but a greater desire for idolatry. Material blessings only made them feel secure in their sins. Idolatry is always accompanied by immorality. Apostasy and adultery are a horrendous pair. Publicly and unashamedly the people thronged to the prostitutes' house, i.e., the idol temple; but their actions were not confined to apostasy but included physical immorality. Orgiastic rites accompanied the idolatry of Jeremiah's times. Notice how largely this chapter is concerned with the social sins of the people. In v.9 the Lord asks the nation whether he is not punishing them justly.

b. Denial of the Lord's activity (5:10–13)

10 The result of such ungodliness must be the outpouring of the divine wrath. Thus the Lord gives the people over to the attacks of their foes. The call is from God to Israel's enemies (cf. v.15). The Lord is prepared to have his vineyard destroyed. The branches are to be stripped off because they are fruitless and no longer belong to the Lord. But because God has not forgotten that he promised Abraham an eternal nation, he will not allow the complete destruction of his people. The stripping away of the branches is a full pruning, not a complete desolation. Only the branches are involved, not the root or stock. God always intended a remnant of his people to survive.

11–12 In presenting the reason for the punishment he has just announced, Jeremiah includes both parts of the nation—Israel and Judah. Although the destruction would not be absolute, it was amply warranted. Treacherously, the people tried to minimize the Lord's warnings. First, they brazenly lied about him. They scornfully said, "He will do nothing!" God, they thought, would not bring calamity on them. The Lord was not, they assumed, responsible for either their blessing or their trials; so they claimed to have nothing to fear. When told that disaster was impending, their response was that God would do no such thing (cf. Zep 1:12). So they denied God's intervention and even his interest in their ways. They were practical atheists.

13 In the second place, the people rejected the validity of God's word given through his prophets. They claimed that the Spirit in the prophets of the Lord was only wind. There is a play here on the Hebrew word *ruah*, which can mean "wind" or "spirit" (GK 8120). The prophets believed they had the Spirit of the Lord; the people claimed the prophets had only wind. Thus the people denied the inspiration of the message of God through Jeremiah. To label a prophet of God "wind" is the ultimate in irreverence. And the people had the effrontery to say that the judgment the prophets threatened would descend on the prophets themselves.

c. The judgment described (5:14–19)

14 Because the people denied the validity of the Lord's word to his prophets, the Lord determined to make that word a fire in Jeremiah's mouth to consume them. What they considered to be nothing more than wind, God would energize like fire. Though spoken by Jeremiah, they were still God's words. To make this pronouncement, the solemn, august name of God is used ("the Lord God Almighty"). God is the self-existent One, Commander of all the armies of heaven and earth. Here is expressed God's power over all created intelligences in the universe, a reference to the armies of Israel (Ex 7:4), the heavenly hosts (Ps 103:21), and the stars (Isa 40:26). God's word is never to be trifled with.

15–16 Jeremiah addresses the whole nation as he begins to describe the invading enemy. The description of the foe is both accurate and detailed; they were distant, ancient, enduring, unintelligible in speech, and deadly in war. The description points to the Babylonians. Distance would be no obstacle to the invaders because of their persevering and determined nature. The invaders would be an enduring, hardy people, used to war. The foe would be an ancient nation, for the national entity (to which the Chaldeans were later joined) was founded by Nimrod (cf. Ge 10:10; 11:31). Jeremiah emphasizes that the enemy would speak a language Israel did not understand. Thus the invaders would be the more fearful and unfeeling because they would not respond to cries for mercy. Finally, they would be invincible because their quivers would be filled with death-dealing arrows, always bringing more destruction. Every arrow could be depended on to slay someone.

17–18 Having so explicitly described the invaders' power, Jeremiah paints a vivid picture of the devastation they would wreak on the land. He adds a final blow to loss of harvest, children, flocks, herds, vines, and trees—the impoverishment and demolition of the fortified cities. Yet, in accord with v.10, the destruction would not be total. God's punishments are not vindictive but are meant to be restorative of the sinner. God must, and does, preserve a remnant according to his pledged word.

19 There is a direct relation between the nation's sin and its punishment—recompense in kind (Dt 28:47–48). The Exile is foretold. Because the people worshiped foreign gods in the Lord's land, they would have to serve foreign overlords in a foreign land. It was useless for them to inquire, as if they were blameless, why judgment had descended on them. The root of their difficulties was their slip into idolatry.

d. Israel's willful ignorance and rebellion (5:20–31)

20–21 This double exhortation is addressed to hearers concerned for their nation. Such a call to "announce" and "proclaim" the word of God occurs nowhere else in the book. They are to proclaim that moral blindness and deafness have kept the people from realizing their perilous state. The words Jeremiah uses refer to the people who had become like the idols they worshiped. The language is purposely blunt to awaken them to their dangerous condition.

22 God is to be adored and served because he controls the raging sea, the mightiest force in creation. Moreover, he does so by the most unlikely of restraining forces, the sand. Though small, sand can and does set a bound to the violence of the sea. If God can restrain the sea, surely he can restrain the invader. Israel is senseless to rebel against him.

23–25 Although the sea remains within its appointed limits, Israel has revolted against the Lord. The people have overstepped God's moral limits. Furthermore, they are blind to their dependence on God's providence. They do not see the hand of the Lord even in the balance of rain for harvest and his withholding it in times of his displeasure. The "regular weeks of harvest" are the seven weeks between the Feast of Passover and the Feast of Weeks (Lev 23:15–16). As Creator, God has control over the rain as he does over the sea. The withholding of seasonal rains was attributable to their sinfulness.

26–29 Three classes of people are arraigned before the divine justice: the rich oppressors of the poor, the lying prophets, and the time-serving priests (v.31). The wicked rich have acquired their wealth by deceit and heartless oppression of the poor and helpless. As a fowler snares birds by devices, so the people accumulate wealth by deceit. The trap was probably a clapnet as represented on Egyptian monuments. In those days fowlers would place several tame birds in a cage; when the wild birds saw them, they lighted on the cage, falling into the snare. The heartless aristocracy had wealth enough, but they were not satisfied. Prosperity did not bring piety. In fact, they excused their wicked deeds on the flimsiest grounds. They could not have troubled themselves less over whether the cause of the orphan was maintained. Jeremiah asked whether for sins like theirs, the people could possibly believe God would overlook inevitable judgment.

30–31 Jeremiah, viewing the moral wreckage, exclaims over the astonishing and horrible things transpiring in the land. Those who should have been the chief moral backbone of the nation had treacherously denied the Lord's commitment to them. Foremost among the guilty were the false prophets,

whose rosy predictions led the nation to its final doom in 586 B.C. Next to them were the spineless priests, who ruled "by their own authority." So the chapter closes with the tragic statement that those entrusted with the spiritual welfare of the nation were unworthy of their positions. Worse yet, the people were so unaware of the issues that they acquiesced in all that their leaders did. The people had lost all sense of moral values and did not realize they were being duped. They cherished their false security. But the final question is, In the time of retribution, when the calamity would strike, then what would they do?

5. The siege and fall of Jerusalem foretold (6:1–30)

The striking feature of this chapter is its rapidity of movement, leading to the gathering storm of invasion soon to engulf the capital and the land. It has been called a chapter of alarms; it begins on a note of impending doom and concludes with the utter rejection of the people.

a. The approach of the invaders (6:1–5)

1–3 The doom is so near that Jeremiah sees the invasion as already in progress. The attack comes from the north. Jeremiah calls the people to flee for safety. The city is no longer safe; it is soon to undergo a siege. The way to safety is only by flight. The people could never plead that they had not been fully warned. Benjamin is mentioned because geographically Jerusalem belonged to that territory. It was settled by Judeans and Benjamites (cf. 1Ch 9:3), separated by the Valley of Hinnom. Moreover, Jeremiah was a Benjamite and had strong ties with his own tribesmen.

Two means of warning were the trumpet call and the fire signal. Tekoa, twelve miles south of Jerusalem, was the home of the prophet Amos (cf. 2Sa 14:2; Am 1:1). Tekoa was the last town in Judah on the edge of the desert. The "signal" or "beacon" was to show the way. Such fire signals were used in military communication. Beth Hakkerem (lit., "house of the vineyard") is mentioned only here and at Ne 3:14. The people are to flee south because invasion threatens from the north. The disaster is personified: it "looms" or looks down on its prey.

Destruction is to fall on Zion, pictured as a beautiful and delicate woman. By a sudden change of figure, the invaders are portrayed as shepherds and their armies as flocks. They denude the land, everyone "tending [i.e., devastating] his own portion" (lit., "what has been assigned him"). This is not a picture of a horde of nomads trying to starve the city.

4–5 Jeremiah next presents a consultation of the enemies of Judah. Their speech reveals haste, impatience, and thirst for destruction. The army will brook no delay in taking the city. The call to prepare for battle included offering sacrifices and performing religious ceremonies because Israel had a religious view of war and considered it a sacred service undertaken in the Lord's name (cf. 1Sa 25:28). Though the enemy here is the Babylonian army, the Babylonians too had a religious concept of war. So eager is the enemy to destroy Jerusalem that they decide to make a surprise attack at noon, when soldiers would normally be resting. But the light is fading; so they must make a night attack. They will be satisfied with nothing less than the destruction of Jerusalem's fortresses.

b. The siege of Jerusalem (6:6–8)

6–8 The Lord appears to be leading the assault against Jerusalem by using the enemy as his agent of judgment. The early preparations for the siege include felling trees for bulwarks and building siege works. Mounds of earth were also heaped up to make them level with the walls to facilitate entry into the city. Again, the Lord reminds the people that the cause of judgment lay in Judah. Jerusalem, blessed of God for some four centuries, is now characterized as oppressive. As a well keeps its water cool and fresh, so Judah seems incapable of anything but sin. The cry of the oppressed is regularly heard in Jerusalem. All her troubles come from her persistence in sin. The Lord sees the people's spiritual sickness as unchanged. But in his infinite grace he warns them before it is too late. While there is still a ray of hope, he warns the people of the doom awaiting their continued defiance in their sin. Reluctant to part from his people, the Lord must issue another call to repent.

c. The fall of the city (6:9–15)

9 Once more Israel is viewed in the figure of a vineyard (cf. 5:10). A thorough gleaning, a complete devastation, awaits them. The Lord authorizes the enemy even to search out the remnant to take them captive—the enemy will not be satisfied with one invasion but will repeat it. The northern tribes may be implied by the main gathering of grapes. Judah, left as a remnant, is now also to be gleaned. The enemy leader is exhorted to pass over the branches repeatedly, lest any grapes be overlooked.

10 Responding to the nation's unbelief, Jeremiah identifies himself with the Lord in speaking of the people's obtuseness to his word. In fact, they regard it with contempt. To warn them further is useless; their ears are "closed." They resolutely refuse to listen to God. Here is the first hint of the lack of response of the nation to Jeremiah's message.

The picture above is Gert LaGrange's drawing of siege ramps built by the Assyrians in assaulting a city. The photo on the right shows the remains of an actual siege ramp. Note all the rock debris. The remains of the city wall are at the top. Courtesy Lachish Excavations.

11 Regardless of success or failure, Jeremiah's duty was to preach the Lord's message. Whether the people listened or not, he was divinely compelled to voice the Lord's indignation. Full of the divine wrath, he was commanded to pour it out on everybody—children, young men, married couples, the elderly—all were involved in the city's doom. Even the children and the aged were to be shown no mercy. The wrath was evoked by the sins now set forth: greed (v.13), deceitful prophecy (vv.13–14), loathsome deeds and shamelessness (v.15), obduracy (vv.16–17), rejection of the law (vv.18–19), and worthless sacrifices (v.20).

12–13 With the conquest of Jerusalem, houses, fields, and wives also would be violently given away to others. This is exactly what Moses had warned about. (Verses 12–15 are repeated in 8:10–12.) The entire gamut of society coveted gain. Because of their greed the people would lose everything. The blame lay largely with the priests and prophets who held out false hopes to the people regardless of the way they lived. Those whose integrity should have been exemplary practiced deceit.

14–15 Another sin was false optimism, listening to baseless promises of peace when there was no ground for it. The priests and prophets, physicians of no value ("they dress the wound of my people as though it were not serious"), misled the people. Only superficially did they heal the wound (lit., "the breach") between God and Judah. Their stock in trade was constant babbling that all was well (cf. Mic 3:5), making nothing of the people's heinous sin.

Lulled into complacency, the people lost all sense of shame for their abominable deeds. Insensitive to wrong, they were so hardened in sin that their hearts were no longer open to the message of truth. As for those who misled them, they were to share the fate of the nation they duped.

d. The cause for judgment (6:16–21)

16–17 The people's judgment was for their straying from the ways of the patriarchs into the ways of idolatry. Jeremiah pictures travelers who have lost their way; when they arrive at crossroads, the moment calls for clear decision. To go one way can mean death; to go another, life. "The ancient paths" and "the good way" are the same; they are the way of repentance, reconciliation, fear, and love of God. They were the ways of the Mosaic tradition. The result of walking in the way of obedience was peace and rest of soul (cf. Mt 11:28–29). But the people refused to walk in the ancient paths. The Lord even sent prophets as watchmen to warn them of impending danger (cf. Eze 3:17; 33:7). The nation obeyed neither the admonition nor the message of the prophets. God always gives ample warning of coming judgment. The people's disobedience was threefold: (1) they were unfaithful to the covenant bond with God; (2) they were unheeding of the warnings of the true prophets; and (3) they rejected the law (v.19).

18–20 God calls on the nations and all the earth to see how fully his people deserve their punishment. The Gentiles are being alerted to what is to happen to Judah. They will witness the righteous consequences of Judah's wicked deeds—her public humiliation. When sin is not forsaken, sacrifices are useless. This does not mean that Jeremiah was against sacrifices; he was only against unethical sacrifices. Incense came from Sheba, southwest of Arabia. Cane or calamus probably came from India and was used in making the holy anointing oil (Ex 30:23). These ingredients of worship were costly because they were brought from a great distance. But they were of no value when they were part of heartless, godless offerings. In themselves, sacrifices were never efficacious; all the prophets who speak of them as used in heartless worship deny them validity. Jeremiah's statement is all the more remarkable since he was a priest by birth.

21 The last verse of this section has been erroneously understood as saying that God placed stumbling blocks in the nation's way to bring about her eternal doom. But this is not at all the meaning. The "obstacles" refer to the Babylonians, who were the instruments to bring about Judah's physical destruction; they were not agents to effect her moral fall. The stress is on the general operation of God's moral law. In contrast to the rest promised in v.16, which they rejected, the people will meet with destruction that will engulf them all—from father to son and neighbor to friend. All will suffer the consequences of their wicked acts.

e. The terror of the enemy forces (6:22–30)

22–23 The direction "the north," from which the enemy will come, is again given. They will come from the remote parts of the then-known earth. The prophet describes their weaponry, cruelty, vigor, speed, and readiness for war against Zion. In their cruelty the Babylonians remind us of the Assyrians (Jnh 3:8). To burn prisoners in a furnace, impale them, and flay them alive were common occurrences in Babylonian wars. Their shouts in battle were like the roaring sea. The war horses seem to have been new to the nation, which was used to the war chariots of the Egyptians rather than to cavalry.

24–26 Jeremiah goes on to describe Judah's response to the news of the invading Babylonians. As one of the people, he expresses his emotions and theirs at the report that the enemy is actually attacking. There is no power in the people to resist; they are limp. Because "there is terror on every side," the people are warned not to go in undefended places, for to do so would mean death. Their trials are likened to the pain of childbirth and the death of an only son, leaving no one to carry on the family name. Among Jews death is always viewed as a calamity; and when an only son dies, it means the end of "immortality" for the parents, and the blow is unbearable. The destroyer will come suddenly on Judah; though they had been repeatedly warned, the people will find themselves unprepared because of their faith in false hopes.

27–30 The last verses of this chapter focus on the nation's incorrigibility. So that no one may think God has not given the people every chance, he is willing to have them tested for any merit or worth that may be in them. Therefore he informs Jeremiah that he is to act as a tester and assayer of the moral worth of Judah. Jeremiah evaluates them as the rebellious of the rebellious, i.e., "hardened rebels." They are entirely of inferior metal—bronze and iron, not silver and gold. And though the refining process is thoroughly carried out, there is no valuable residue to reward the labors of the refiner. In antiquity lead was put with silver in a crucible; when heated, the lead, acting as a flux, oxidized and carried off the alloy. But here the ore is so impure that the alloys are not removed. The labors of Jeremiah are in vain. As refuse silver, they are rejected by the Lord. There is a play on words: rejected silver, they are rejected of the Lord. So judgment is inevitable.

C. Jeremiah's Temple Address (7:1–10:25)

1. No refuge in the temple (7:1–34)

Chapters 7–10, known as the temple address(es), were not necessarily delivered on a single occasion. Jeremiah's address, which he delivered standing at the gate of the temple, has been called one of the majestic scenes of history. One crucial event in his ministry, it undoubtedly initiated the unrelenting opposition he experienced during the remainder of his life. According to 26:1, Jeremiah delivered it early in Jehoiakim's reign (c. 609–605 B.C.); and ch. 26 records the consequences of the address. The time was not long after the death of Josiah.

The entire discourse runs counter to Josiah's attempt to centralize worship at the temple in Jerusalem and appears to blast hopes inculcated by the earlier prophets, Isaiah among them. Josiah's reform promised a restoration of God's blessing, not the calamity of the temple and the dissolution of the commonwealth. In Isaiah's day the repentance of godly Hezekiah and the people issued in God's removal of the Assyrian threat in one night (Isa 37:36). But the spiritual decline of the nation proved irreversible in Jeremiah's time. The temple-gate address is an eloquent attack on the people's confidence in the temple as ensuring Jerusalem's inviolability from all enemies. The emphasis on ethical issues is paramount.

a. Misplaced confidence (7:1–7)

1 Jeremiah spoke at a critical time. The nation was shocked by Josiah's death, the removal of Jehoahaz, and the imposition of Jehoiakim as king by Pharaoh Neco. With Jehoiakim a religious reversal took place in the nation. Canaanite rites reappeared in Judah. The temple address was Jeremiah's first public sermon and the source of all his later opposition in the nation. Through it he made lasting enemies and may have been excluded from the temple because of it (36:5). It was a thoroughgoing denunciation of the worship of the day. The deliverance of Jerusalem in 701 B.C. in Hezekiah's reign had become almost legendary and led to the idea that Jerusalem was inviolable because of the sanctuary (cf.

2Ki 18:13–19:37). Jeremiah spoke during a lull in hostile political activity. Doubtless, many were ready to attribute the respite to the glory of the temple.

2–3 The immediate occasion of Jeremiah's address may have been one of the three pilgrimage festivals (Dt 16:16). The "gate" was the one that connected the outer and inner courts. The place suggested is the Eastern Gate. Jeremiah's position guaranteed him a wide hearing. It was doubly significant that Jeremiah's attack on the superstitious attitude toward the temple was uttered at that very place. Verse 3 states the theme of the sermon: Repent, if you expect to remain in your native land.

4 With great courage Jeremiah warned the people against believing the deceptive words of false prophets ascribing talismanic power to the temple. The threefold repetition of the false prophets' words expresses emphasis to the superlative degree. In effect they were saying, "These buildings are assuredly the temple of the Lord!" And they were saying this at a time when the temple was made central by Josiah's reforms in 621 B.C. The people were using these words like a magical incantation. The words were true, but what the people inferred from them was entirely erroneous. The temple had become a kind of fetish and object of faith. The basis for this was (1) the promise of an eternal dynasty to David (cf. 2Sa 7:11–14) and (2) the choice of Zion as God's earthly abode (cf Ps 132:13–16). Therefore no harm could come to the temple. The false prophets continually assured the people of the personal intervention of God in case of any danger to the temple and Zion. But Jeremiah thundered that the temple without godliness was a delusion.

5–7 Jeremiah had called for the people to repent; now he turns to the prescription for their remaining in the land. Profession and conduct must be in accord or all their efforts will be unavailing. The way of blessing must give spiritual and moral principles the first place in life. Four things are stressed: (1) justice; (2) concern for the alien, fatherless, and widow; (3) avoidance of judicial murders; and (4) abandonment of idolatry. Idolatry, the root of their problems and their first national sin at Mount Sinai, comes last for emphasis. Nothing less than spiritual renewal

would ensure continuance in the land God had given their fathers in perpetuity. As always, acceptance with God depends on true piety.

b. Indifference to godly living (7:8–11)

8–10 In their woeful spiritual state, the people were trusting in deceptive words that veneered their sins. They were guilty of violating five of the Ten Commandments; the Decalogue was still valid and binding on them all. All these violations were going on at the same time they were expressing confidence in the temple. Jeremiah's description may even be understood as expressing great indignation at the evil practices that their attendance at the temple was meant to atone for. The people felt that going to the temple granted them release from guilt, as though they had an indulgence to go on sinning. Ignoring God's ethical demands, they rested in ceremonial rites.

11 Ultimately the people were treating the temple, the house of God, as robbers do their dens. It was a temporary refuge till they sallied forth on another foray. Limestone caves in Palestine were used as robbers' dens; so Jeremiah's metaphor was clear to his hearers. Here was nothing less than corruption of the best and the holiest. The Lord, having seen the situation, would deal with it accordingly.

c. The example of Shiloh (7:12–15)

12 Shiloh was on the main highway between Jerusalem and Shechem. The Mosaic tabernacle was set up there after the conquest of Canaan (cf. Jos 18:1; 72:12; Jdg 21:19; 1Sa 1:9, 24). It was the abode of the ark and tabernacle during the era of the judges. At Shiloh, Israel went into idolatry (1Sa 4:1–11); so the ark was captured by the Philistines at the Battle of Ebenezer. Jeremiah's references to its destruction have been confirmed by excavations of the site, which revealed a city destroyed by the Philistines about 1050 B.C. Shiloh was to the judges what Jerusalem was to the kings. Jeremiah was a descendant of the Eli family; so the tragedy had personal implications for him. The sanctuary at Shiloh proved the falsity of the claim that the Lord was unalterably committed to an earthly temple and its preservation regardless of the moral state of the people.

13–15 Because they had committed the sins mentioned in v.9, the Lord had earnestly and continuously entreated the people through his prophets, but without response. By a strong anthropomorphism, Jeremiah portrays the Lord as "rising up early and speaking" (lit. Heb.). Again Jeremiah makes it plain that the people trusted the temple of God instead of the God of the temple. God is never dependent on any particular place of worship. For Jeremiah's hearers, this was unheard-of heresy. The outcome of Judah's ways would soon be exile. This was the message that inflamed Jeremiah's hearers and earned him their lasting hatred and opposition almost to the point of martyrdom.

d. Worship of the Queen of Heaven
(7:16–20)

16–18 Now the Lord explicitly forbids the prophet to intercede for his people. They were so obdurately sinful that praying for them was futile. What was particularly abominable to the Lord was the worship of the Queen of Heaven by the entire populace. This goddess was probably the Assyro-Babylonian Ishtar, the goddess of love and fertility. It appears she was worshiped mainly by women (cf. ch. 44, esp. vv.15–19). A female deity is foreign to OT theology; so the implication is that this cult was of non-Hebraic origin. Such worship was probably initiated by Manasseh (2Ki 21:1–9) and reintroduced into Judah by Jehoiakim. This obscene idolatry was practiced not only privately but also by whole families—including the children. The "cakes" have been described as round and flat, resembling the moon. Also, the people offered libations to other gods.

19–20 If they thought they were spiting God, the people were grossly insensate. They would bear both spite and shame as consequences of their sins. Moreover, sin affects all realms of nature. Devastation would fall on humans, beasts, trees, and produce of the soil.

e. Obedience better than sacrifice
(7:21–26)

21 Having been prohibited from interceding for the nation, Jeremiah had revealed the punishment awaiting Judah's idolatry. Undoubtedly he spoke the words of this verse

ironically and contemptuously. The purpose is to show how totally erroneous was Judah's concept of sacrifices. Because they have missed the true meaning of the Lord's worship, they might as well eat the sacrifices intended only for the Lord, for he cares for none of them. In other words, they could multiply their offerings as much as they liked because all of them were worthless.

22 The verse appears to invalidate the whole sacrificial system. The Hebrew text uses a rhetorical negation to point up antithesis between v.22 and v.23. Moreover, the negative in Hebrew often supplies the lack of the comparative. In short, the Hebrew idiom permits denial of one thing in order to emphasize another (cf. Lk 14:26). Sacrifices were always meant to be of secondary importance to obedience and godliness. Neither Jeremiah nor any other prophet decried sacrifices as such. They meant that moral law is always paramount to the ritual law. Significantly, when Lev 6–8 is read in the synagogue, this passage in Jeremiah is read as the concluding portion, called the Haphtorah.

23–26 Actually, God had not spoken at Sinai of sacrifices but only of obedience, and this even before the law was given (Ex 19:3–6). Jeremiah's words show that he had in mind the giving of the Ten Commandments. Among these there were no directions for sacrifices; they dealt solely with spiritual and moral matters. In Judah the whole sacrificial system was invalidated on the ground that it was not carried out in true faith. Obedience always was and would be the dominant consideration. And this very element was the one so conspicuously absent in the nation. Indeed, in spite of Jeremiah's consistent warnings, Judah did worse than her fathers.

f. Reception of Jeremiah's message
(7:27–28)

27–28 Just as the Lord had said at Jeremiah's call (ch. 1) that he would experience opposition, so now he informs Jeremiah that the nation would not listen to him. He would have no greater success in his ministry than did his predecessors. The nation was preeminent in this respect: the people continually disobeyed the voice of the Lord, their very own God. That faith must be joined with works was lost to them; so the time of Jeremiah was a sad epilogue to Judah's history.

g. Lament over Judah's desolation (7:29–34)

29 The prophet's attention now turns to the Valley of Hinnom, the center of the cult of infant sacrifice, introduced by Ahaz and Manasseh (2Ki 16:3; 21:6), abolished by Josiah (2Ki 23:10), but later revived under Jehoiakim. The command to cut off the "hair" is feminine in Hebrew, showing that the city (cf. 6:23) is meant. The charge stems from the fact that the Nazirite's hair was the mark of his separation to God (Nu 6:5). When he was ceremonially defiled, he had to shave his head. So Jerusalem because of her corruption must do likewise. Her mourning is because the Lord has cast her off. Because of her sin, the chief mark of her beauty must be cast away as polluted and no longer consecrated to the Lord.

When Israel encountered bereavement, defeat in war, or awareness of God's displeasure, the people would lament, lying on the ground, pouring dust on their heads, tearing their clothes, beating their breasts, and cutting off their hair. Now they were to lament on the "barren heights," for the place of their idolatries was to be the place of their mourning. Their lament would be heard at a distance, for that generation was the one on which God's wrath would be poured out.

30–32 The people had brazenly introduced their idols in the temple, as though to defy God to his face. Furthermore, they had set up high places (altars) in Topheth, near the eastern end of the southern part of the Valley of Hinnom.

The Hinnom Valley was a place of idolatrous sacrifices as well as the area for the debris and rubbish of the city. The rabbis saw it as a symbol of the place of future punishment, calling it Gehenna (see comment on Mk 9:43–48). Here the idolatrous nation burned their children to appease the fire god, Molech. This passage reveals that the children were not merely made to pass through an ordeal by fire; they were actually burned up. God disclaims any connection with this hideous practice (Lev 18:21; 20:2–5). Now their pagan sanctuary was to become their cemetery. Since they so flagrantly disobeyed God, they themselves would be slaughtered where their children were slaughtered. The slaughter of the coming doom of the city would be so great that Topheth would have

to be used for burial, thus changing the name of the place to The Valley of the Slaughter.

33–34 So complete would the desolation of the land be that no one would be there to drive the birds of prey from the carcasses. The highest indignity for the dead was to leave a body unburied (Dt 28:26; Isa 18:6). The chapter closes on the tragic note that all joy—even that of marriage—would be removed from Judah.

2. Remonstrance with Israel (8:1–22)

a. Desecration of the graves (8:1–3)

1–3 Even the remains of the long dead would be desecrated. The invaders would not be satisfied until the bones of the leaders as well as of the people of Jerusalem were exhumed. This would be the ultimate insult, signifying that the people of Judah were incapable of guarding the remains of their ancestors from desecration. This practice of violating the dead was not unknown in ancient warfare (cf. Am 2:1). The dead, especially kings and prominent leaders, were buried with treasures, so the graves may have been vandalized also for plunder.

Jeremiah elaborates on the fate of the dead. Their bones would be scattered in the open air under the sun to hasten their disintegration and would be exposed like refuse. All the stages of Judah's worship of idols are detailed in five verbs ("loved," "served," "followed," "consulted," "worshiped") to reveal the people's great zeal in doing so. The heavenly bodies that the people worshiped would be helpless to hinder the desecration heaped on their dead followers. The statement exposes the worthlessness of astrology.

In spite of the violation heaped on their dead compatriots, the survivors would prefer death to life because of the many trials they were yet to suffer at the hands of their captors. The banished are the whole nation of Israel (cf. 3:14), and the places where they have been driven are the countries outside Palestine (cf. Lev 26:36–39; Dt 28:65–67).

b. Obduracy of Israel in idolatry (8:4–7)

4–5 In a series of questions throughout this eighth chapter, God remonstrates with his people. First, he shows how contrary to nature is their apostasy. If a man falls down, he instinctively tries to rise as soon as possible. If he turns from the right way, he returns to it at the earliest opportunity. But Judah is different from others; her misconduct is unique. Having fallen into idolatry and having strayed from the path of obedience, she manifests no desire to either rise or return. It is too late to repent. The nation is incorrigible in her apostasy. Judah shows no desire to correct her ways but holds tenaciously to her deceitful idolatry.

6–7 God waited for the people to amend their ways; he listened in vain for some word of repentance and confession of guilt. They acted mindlessly. As a war horse rushes into battle, they impetuously followed their own way regardless of consequences. The figure stresses their determination to continue sinning. Even subhuman creatures know how to follow their instincts better than Judah follows the way of the Lord. Migratory birds recognize and follow the seasons of their migration instinctively. The stork, dove, swift, and thrush regularly return to Palestine every spring. They know more about God's appointed way for them than Judah knows about God's appointed way for her.

c. Penalty for Judah's falsity (8:8–13)

8–9 In spite of her willful ignorance of the law of God, the nation boasts of her wisdom. The chief offenders were the priests and false prophets. Apparently they thought that having the law meant they had all the wisdom they needed. Denying God's word by their deeds, they still boasted of its presence with them. To make matters worse, the "scribes" so manipulated the law of God as to falsify its message. They interpreted so as to assure the people that they could sin with impunity. In v.8 there is an appeal to reason, as there is an appeal to conscience in v.12. As a result of the people's delusion about their wisdom, they would not heed the word of the Lord. The answer to the question in v.9 is that there is no wisdom when God's word is rejected (cf. Pr 1:7).

10–12 Since God is a God of righteousness and holiness, he must visit on Judah the punishment he has warned them of. These three verses repeat what has already been stated in 6:12–15. God ordered Jeremiah to repeat the truth to impress it on the minds of the people. But the people, refusing to listen to God's word, were misled by false prophets and deceitful priests.

13 The failure of the vintage and the harvest is a frequent OT metaphor of complete devastation. When God's judgment struck, nothing would be left; the desolation of the land and the people would be complete. God would withdraw all his gifts. Since the nation bore no fruit morally, the dissolution of its commonwealth was imminent.

d. The invading army (8:14–17)

14–15 Jeremiah sees the invasion by the northern enemy occurring. Those in the rural areas ask themselves why they should stay where they live, exposing themselves to the enemy's cruelties. They exhort one another to flee to the fortified cities for greater protection and longer survival. Alas, even if they flee to the fortified cities, these, like "poisoned water," will be their ruin. The people find to their dismay that the opposite of what they looked for has come on them. The false prophets had purveyed only false hopes.

16–17 Jeremiah graphically describes the invasion of the enemy, who had already come from the north. Dan, in the far north of the land and bordering on Phoenicia, would feel the invasion first. So many would be the enemy's horses that their sound would shake the earth and they would desolate the land. Suddenly the figure for the invader changes to that of serpents that cannot be charmed away. The invader will be irresistible.

e. The sorrow of Jeremiah (8:18–22)

18–19 Though Jeremiah's predictions are coming true, he does not gloat over those who opposed him. Rather, he is thoroughly heartbroken. He agonizes over the fall of Jerusalem. He had lived in a state of tension between his love for his land and countrymen and his fidelity to God's commission for him. Now he foresees Judah's captivity and the distress of her exile. Forlorn and distraught, the exiles wonder why they have been conquered and degraded. How could this happen when the Lord their King was surely in Zion? They are trying to harmonize their theology with their deplorable condition. Why have they not been delivered? The King referred to is not the Davidic ruler but God. God answers their question with one of his. Why have they gone on defying him with their idolatries when they were constantly warned of his judgment on them?

20 Jeremiah drives home another truth by using the figure of the harvest. Harvest of barley, wheat, and spelt came in April, May, and June; harvest of summer fruits like figs, grapes, and pomegranates came in August and September, and of olives in October. If these were not provided, no fruit was garnered for the winter. The people had lost every opportunity given them by God, and now they were entirely without hope. One favorable time after another went unheeded. The time is past, of course, when either Egypt or other allies could come to their aid.

21–22 In spite of his denunciations, Jeremiah does not hesitate to identify himself with his people. Their hurt ("crushed") hurts him so deeply that he is filled with mourning and dismay. In a final metaphor Jeremiah asks why, since there is balm in Gilead and physicians to apply it, the nation's malady has not been healed. The balm referred to is the resin or gum of the storax tree, which was used medicinally. The prophet is distressed because he knows that though there is a remedy for the people, they have not availed themselves of it. Gilead is a mountainous region of Palestine east of Jordan and north of Moab; so the remedy is not far away. But Judah's sickness is not healed. The plaintive question "Is there no balm in Gilead?" has become proverbial.

3. Sin and punishment (9:1–26)

a. The prophet's lament (9:1–2a)

1–2a Jeremiah's metaphors show the depths of his grief. The destruction to be visited on the nation would be so thoroughgoing that he would weep day and night. The "fountain" is a reservoir or well rather than a spring. The "slain" of this verse are those in need of a physician in 8:22. Their sickness has ended in death.

Two strong emotions gripped Jeremiah: great sympathy for his people and utter revulsion against their many sins. The life of the people was so corrupt as to make it impossible for Jeremiah to live among them. Even a lonely lodging in the desert was preferable to the soul anguish he experienced in the midst of his people (cf. Ps 55:6–8).

b. The glaring sins of the day (9:2b–9)

2b The blatant sins Jeremiah describes are literal. Society was shot through and through with wickedness. The first sin in this bill of indictment was universal adultery. As the prophet has already shown, the reference is to their spiritual adultery of idolatry, with which gross immoralities were carried out. In toto the people were a treacherous assembly. The Hebrew word for "crowd" (GK 6809) is used for solemn assemblies on pilgrimage feasts. They had fallen far short of that concept. The sins of the tongue are noteworthy.

3 The picture is vivid: the tongue is the bow and the lying the arrow. The people are consummate liars. To "make ready" is literally "to tread" because one placed his foot on the bow to fit it with an arrow. Unwearied, the people went from one sin to another. They were valiant, but not for truth. They used their power and influence, not for helping their countrymen, but for oppressing the poor and needy. They had completely abandoned moral and social standards. The inner cohesiveness of the nation had broken down. Judah was laden with deceit. At the same time as Jeremiah was in anguish over the people's sufferings, he was appalled at the depth of their departure from the Lord. Willful ignorance of God was the root of their sin. They did not care to know or recognize him.

4–5a When a nation lacks spiritual dedication, human relations become insecure. Even the godly succumb to suspicion. Society is threatened when mutual confidence is lost. Even homes and families in Judah were split by mistrust. The unity of the nation was threatened from within. The covenant of God with his people required brotherly love, but their conduct violated this. They went to great pains to deceive one another.

5b–6 To show the unnaturalness of their wickedness, the people trained their tongues contrary to their proper function. Lying takes more effort than speaking the truth, but they were willing to endure the drudgery of sin. They persisted in their wrongdoing. Their desire to do evil exceeded their power and strength. The words of v.6 are addressed to the whole nation. Deceit was the very atmosphere of their life. They lived in it and would rather cling to their deceptive ways than recognize God and abandon their godless deeds. Verse 3 stated that they did not know God; now we are told that they flatly refused to know him. In a world ruled by a

Moral Governor, their woes inevitably stemmed from this recalcitrance.

7–9 The prophet returns to the metaphor of refining metals (cf. 6:28–30). But now the process would go on in the fiery furnace of affliction and would aim to remove the dross by suffering. The Lord was still seeking to purge, not exterminate, his people. Reasoning with them, the Lord asks how else he could deal with their sinful ways. No other choice was left him. What other action was open to him? The passage underscores the inevitability of judgment in view of God's righteousness. He still yearns over Judah, for he addresses the nation as literally "the daughter of my people." Again, the prophet emphasizes their deceitful dealings. Their tongues are death dealing; deceit is second nature to them. Even when their conversation appears to be cordial, in their hearts they are scheming to ensnare their neighbors.

c. The judgment threatened (9:10–16)

10–11 This section details Judah's punishment. Jeremiah prepares for mourning in the hour of disaster. The pastures in the Judean wilderness will be burned up because there will be no one to water and care for them. The land will be devastated and its inhabitants exiled. All will be so desolate that the cattle will disappear, and even the birds will abandon the land. So complete will the devastation be that only scavengers will remain.

12–16 Once more the Lord tries to show the people the cause of their ruin. The Lord challenges any of the wise of the nation to state the cause of their calamities. The wise will see by God's enlightenment that departure from God must always lead to punishment. In v.13 God himself answers the question in v.12. The nation had violated the law given at Sinai and constantly proclaimed by the true prophets; the people repeatedly ignored God's call to walk in conformity with his revealed will. Instead, they had followed a path to destruction. It was their defection from God that had brought along with it their flagrant social injustices.

The cause of the nation's problems was an insubordinate spirit that led the people into idolatry—their undoing from the wilderness period to that hour. Their sinful practices were handed down from one generation to another. In the metaphor "bitter food" and "poisoned water," the first is a plant with bitter juice, the second a poisonous bitter herb. They represent the bitter suffering in the fall of the kingdom and the Babylonian exile. The annihilation does not include the whole nation but only its ungodly members. Repeatedly, Jeremiah shows there will be no complete decimation of the people (cf. 4:27; 5:18; 30:11).

d. The universal lamentation (9:17–22)

17–18 This section describes the people's expulsion from their land. The "wailing women" were professionals employed to arouse relatives and others at funerals to outward display of their grief. They used plaintive cries, baring their breasts, flailing their arms, throwing dust on their heads, and disheveling their hair (2Ch 35:25; Ecc 12:5; Am 5:16).

19–21 As the people go into captivity, their wailing sounds out from Jerusalem (Zion). Jeremiah gives the words of the women's dirge. The demand for their services will be so great that they will have to teach others how to mourn, particularly their daughters and neighbors. Death will penetrate into the homes of poor and rich alike. Even children and young men will die in public places. A number of interpreters believe that the death referred to is the result of pestilence. But the passage need not be limited to this. The invading army could do the killing.

22 Here we see Death as the Grim Reaper. The custom was for a reaper to hold in his arm what a few strokes of his sickle had cut. Then he put it down, and behind him another laborer then gathered it into bundles and bound it into a sheaf. So death was to cover the ground with corpses, but the carcasses would lie there unburied because of the paucity of survivors and the great number of dead. The wages of sin is always death (Ro 6:23).

e. The ultimate good (9:23–24)

23–24 Jeremiah speaks of three things people of the world trust in: wisdom, strength, and riches. These three cannot help the worldly. If these fall short in the time of need, what will avail? Our highest good is to know God, not just intellectually or philosophically, but in spirit and in his true character. This is the true and lasting wisdom. The path of God's approval is clear. Ethical qualities follow a true knowledge of God. God manifests "kindness"—a readiness to manifest grace and mercy; "justice"—a proper evaluation of the rights of men; and "righteousness"—the absolute essential of all faith and worship.

f. Not privilege but morality (9:25–26)

25–26 These verses condemn faith in religious privileges. The paradox shows that circumcision is in itself as valueless as sacrifice, temple, or any other outward form of religious practice. If Judah has the rite of circumcision only in the flesh, she is no different from the pagans who have only an external sign and no inward faith. Judah cannot plead the virtue of her covenant sign when she does not possess what it stands for. The nations enumerated practiced circumcision but not of the heart. Outward rites are unavailing; the condition of the heart is paramount. Judah is placed among these nations—what degradation! Egypt is mentioned first because Israel was so prone to confide in them. Edom seems to have abandoned the practice until it was imposed on them by John Hyrcanus. The Arab tribes, recognized by their peculiar tonsure, were, along with those already mentioned, the objects of Nebuchadnezzar's attack (cf. 49:28–33).

4. Denunciation of idolatry (10:1–25)

The greater portion of this section is devoted to a condemnation of idolatry. Jeremiah shows his firsthand knowledge of idol worship, both Canaanite and Babylonian. Although people lose their awareness of the true God, they do not thereby lose their need of God. So they substitute the false worship for the true. Idolatry is the result.

a. The folly of idolatry (10:1–5)

1–2 This message is addressed to the whole nation of Israel, not just the Ten Tribes already in exile for more than a century. Those who remained in the land still retained the customs of their heathen neighbors before them. Jeremiah warns the people against being influenced to fall in with the cultic customs of the pagan nations in worshiping their gods. Idol worship was attended by elaborate ritual, motivated by demonic power, and accompanied by moral looseness. Thus it was a constant temptation. The signs of the heavens referred to are not the sun, moon, and stars, or signs of the zodiac, meant by God to be signs (Ge 1:14), but unusual phenomena like eclipses, comets, and meteors, which were supposed to portend extraordinary events. They struck terror into the hearts of those who worshiped the superhuman power in the stars. Both the Egyptians and the Babylonians were addicted to astrology. Idolatry that involves the heavenly bodies displeases God as much as the worship of man-made idols.

3–5 All idols are vanity. The worthlessness of worshiping them is proved by the worthlessness of the pagan gods. Jeremiah details every stage of the making of these worthless images. The first stage is the cutting down of a tree from the forest; the second stage, its shaping with an axe; the third, adorning the idol with precious metals; the fourth, fastening the idol in place. The final stage is dressing the idol in royal apparel. There is an exquisite touch of sarcasm in the mention of fastening the idol with nails. The mighty god has to be kept from tottering. Even after the image is secured, it has no more value than a scarecrow. Immovable, it has no power of speech to comfort the needy soul; it cannot walk to come to the aid of the harassed; instead, it is a burden to be carried. Incapable of moral decisions, it cannot counsel troubled souls.

b. The majesty of God (10:6–16)

6–8 Here the prophet contrasts the majesty of God with the uselessness of idols. Man-made idols cannot walk or stand unaided, but the true God is great in himself and in his power. To attempt to compare him with other gods or creatures shows woeful ignorance of his true character and attributes. In ancient times pagan nations had their own nationally restricted deities; but the Lord God of Israel is King, sovereignly ruling and wisely administering the affairs of the nations. Worship is due him by right and due no one else. Human beings at the highest point of their reasoning can never approximate, let alone comprehend, the blessed God of the universe (1Co 1:21). From a wooden idol no spiritual benefit or instruction can be expected. Instruction from idols is no more valuable than the idol itself. No human skill can turn wood into an intelligent creature. All the wise men among the pagans are foolish because their gods from which they receive instruction are no more than wood. Idolatry has no redeeming feature whatever.

9 At this point Jeremiah speaks of the origin of idols. Silver was obtained from Tarshish—either southern Spain or the island of Sardinia. Spain was rich in silver, iron, tin, and lead—all of which were sent to Tyre. Gold was brought from Uphaz (location unknown). Blue (violet) and purple were obtained from the murex, a Mediterranean shellfish. These pigments were costly and were used in the curtains of the tabernacle (Ex 25:4). In spite of all the workmanship lavished on them, idols are still the work of human hands.

10 In a telling contrast, Jeremiah presents the distinctive attributes of the God of the universe. He is the true God, i.e., God in truth. He is alive, the everlasting King, whose power is manifest in the earthquake and whose wrath the nations endure. This verse contains a threefold contrast with idols: (1) they are false, he is true; (2) they are dead, he is living; (3) they are transitory and subject to destruction, he is eternal.

11 This is the only verse in the book in Aramaic, the lingua franca of the day, so that the pagan idolaters would be able to read the judgment of God on their idolatry. The truths enunciated thus far are that (1) Israel is not to imitate the nations around her, (2) idols are powerless, and (3) God's power is infinite.

12–16 This section, repeated in 51:15–19, dwells on the theme of the might of the true God, especially in nature, and his relationship to Israel, particularly in his covenant promises. Both the power and the wisdom of God are clearly manifested in the creation of the heavens and the earth. Indeed, every thunderstorm witnesses to the omnipotence of God. Before these wonders of nature, people unenlightened by revelation are without knowledge. Every idolater will ultimately be ashamed when the nothingness of idols is revealed. For a thinking person to engage in idol making and worship is no less than a degrading of his or her God-given endowments. The prophet's final word on idols is that they are not only worthless but also a

God "makes the clouds rise from the ends of the earth" (10:13). These clouds are over the Jezreel Valley at Jezereel.

work of mockery, worthy only of being ridiculed.

In essence, instead of helping their devotees in time of need, idols will themselves be destroyed. On the other hand, Israel's God is totally distinct from idols; instead of being made, he is the Maker and Creator of all the universe. Moreover, he is still faithful to his covenant promises, though his people have rejected him (cf. 51:19). Though he is Lord of all, yet he has a special portion or inheritance in Israel. As we come to the end of this classic passage, we should remember this: The Babylonian exile accomplished what everything else failed to do. It cured the nation Israel of idolatry, making the people witnesses of the one true God in every country where they were scattered.

c. Exile for sinning Israel (10:17–22)

17–18 In respect to continuity of thought, vv.1–16 are parenthetical. In vv.17–25 the subject that was interrupted at 9:22 is resumed, thus concluding the temple sermon. The suggested date for the passage is 598–597 B.C., during the siege under Jeconiah. The present portion is a dialogue between Jeremiah and personified Jerusalem. The people of Judah are addressed as they are told of impending exile. Now the doom of the city is at the very gates, so they had better gather up their bundles from the ground because they are to be cast out of the land. Only distress awaits them.

19–22 A new era was to begin for the nation! On other occasions when the nation was invaded, the enemy took spoils and imposed tribute. But this time invasion would result in expatriation. This means for Jeremiah an almost unbearable burden; so on behalf of the nation he laments the catastrophe. The people now recognize and admit that they have merited divine judgment. They are resigned to God's punishment. Jerusalem is next seen as a tent-dwelling mother, deprived of her children and home. No one is left to rebuild the destroyed land. The blame is placed on the leadership of the nation. Doom is near; the report has it that the army of the enemy is approaching.

d. Prayer for the nation (10:23–25)

23–25 Jeremiah pleads the constitutional mental and moral weakness of humanity in extenuation of his predicament. We can never direct our lives so as to achieve blessing without God's help. We cannot decide the course of our lives. God is in ultimate control. True to his office, Jeremiah as the prophet of God acts as an advocate for his people. He prays that Judah will not be called on to suffer more than she can endure. He admits her merited punishment but pleads for it to be kept within limits. God should show a measure of mercy so that destruction will not come. It is in this context that the last petition is to be understood. The nations had been moved by a spirit of vindictiveness and out of proportion to what God had intended. They wanted to destroy Israel utterly.

Verse 25 is recited annually at the Passover service of the Jews. The enemies of Israel and the executors of God's wrath will one day experience his scourge also. This was fulfilled within a century. Nebuchadnezzar was punished with insanity. His grandson Belshazzar was slain in his revelry, and the empire was conquered by the Medo-Persians. Jeremiah's prayer is not that of a nationalistic Jew against hated Gentiles. It is a plea for God to destroy Judah's enemies before they are able to carry out their wicked aim to destroy his people. Thus closes this whole great section (chs. 7–10). Its undying message is that God seeks reality in life and worship, and no kind of ritual can ever be a substitute for piety.

D. Signs to Awaken Repentance (11:1–20:18)

1. The broken covenant (11:1–23)

Chapters 11 and 12 form a unit because there is no break between them. Since this section is not dated, scholars differ as to the historical setting. Most likely the historical setting was the reign of Josiah with his reformation, which proved to be only superficial. The date may even have been soon after the discovery of the Book of the Law, before the reform became widespread (v.6; cf. 2Ki 23). Chapters 11–20 contain material that is more autobiographical and more narrative than that in the previous chapters. In this section we find the prophet's "confessions," in a sense a private diary. The main emphasis of ch. 11 is an admonition to be faithful to the covenant.

a. The violation of the covenant (11:1–13)

1–3 The initial charges were not directed to Jeremiah alone because the imperatives are in the plural. The commands are not to the people, nor to the priests as the teachers of the law, but to the prophets of the time. The account in 2Ki 22–23 makes it clear that the godly king Josiah was not introducing a new covenant but only calling for a reaffirmation of the old Mosaic covenant, as did other of the prophets aside from Jeremiah. Jeremiah even repeats the very curse pronounced on those who violate the Lord's covenant with Moses (cf. Dt 11:28; 27:26; 28:15–19; 29:20–21). Ancient Near Eastern treaties contained both benedictions and curses for adherence or nonconformity to them.

4–5 Verses 3–5 contain a summary of the spiritual essence of the covenant (cf. 7:23). The time of the promulgation of the Mosaic covenant is seen as being the whole Exodus period. The iron-smelting furnace refers to the hardships the Israelites underwent in Egypt (cf. Dt 4:20). What the Lord was seeking was an obedient people for his very own, a people who would rejoice in their intimate relationship and fellowship with him. The Lord also had in mind his gracious promises to the patriarchs, which he wished to fulfill. "A land flowing with milk and honey" symbolizes the fertility of the land. Jeremiah reminds the people that they were still in possession of the Promised Land. His own answer to the pronouncement of the curse was "Amen," indicating his acquiescence in God's arrangement.

6–8 Verse 6 does not mean that the prophet must take a preaching tour "in the towns of Judah," for the expression is proverbial for the length and breadth of the country (just as the Lord's command to Jeremiah in 25:15–29 did not require him to itinerate among the nations). Judah's response to the Lord's command reveals faithlessness and breach of the covenant. In spite of the Lord's loving exhortation through his prophets, the people followed their own ways in violating the law of God. In fact, the nation had already suffered, in the exile of the ten northern tribes to Assyria, some of the penalty for their infractions of the covenant; the remainder of the judgment was soon to be realized in the coming visitation on Judah (cf. Lev 18:28; 20:22; Dt 29:28).

9–13 Jeremiah divulges an existing conspiracy against the covenant of God. It was not the outcome of hasty impulse but of settled policy. The conspiracy need not have been a formal one, though the people willed to assent to it. There was general though secret resistance to Josiah's policy of reform. The people had determined not to follow in the way of the Lord but in the wicked ways of their fathers. The "forefathers" were probably those who lived during the desert wanderings and during the time of the judges. Josiah's heart was right with the Lord, but true piety never comes by osmosis. People must submit individually to God and his ways. Of their own accord, Josiah's generation broke the covenant the Lord made with the nation. The only possible result was inescapable judgment. Not only would their worthless gods be impotent to help them, but the Lord also refused to help them. The hour of his patience was over.

Once more Jeremiah stresses the impotence of the people's idols. The people's appeals to the idols will, as always, go unheeded. Not that they had a paucity of idols, for their gods were as numerous as their towns; every city had its own special god. The "shameful god" is Baal. In spite of and contrary to Josiah's reforms, these secret practices were continuing.

b. Inadequacy of sacrifices (11:14–17)

14–15 Because the nation's wickedness had passed the limit of God's patience, Jeremiah is again forbidden (cf. 7:16) to intercede for his people. Their guilt had come to a climax. Their cries for help would go unanswered because they were not repentant. The text of v.15 is obscure. Apparently the people had

gone to the temple to pray and offer sacrifices. "My beloved" refers to Judah. The prophet is repeating the worthlessness of sacrifices without godliness and concern for social righteousness. Sacrifices will not avert the doom. Actually, all the people have is defiled meat (cf. Hag 2:12). In their hypocrisy they have tried to hide their apostasy by their temple sacrifices. How, then, can the people think they have a right to rejoice? They cannot, because God cannot be deceived.

16–17 Jeremiah goes on to compare the nation to a beautiful green olive tree—the way the Lord saw it and wanted it to be. Olive trees are common in Palestine, as elsewhere in the Near East. But Judah had become so barren that she must suffer the flames of judgment. The same figure is the basis of Paul's key passage about the relation of Jew and Gentile in Ro 11:17–24. God's ideal for the nation was for it to remain green and beautiful; but, because of the barrenness of sin, it must be destroyed. The judgment is clearly determined for both parts of the nation. Baalism has been their spiritual and political ruin.

c. Plot against Jeremiah's life (11:18–23)

18–20 Here is the first of Jeremiah's personal crises. Its context is the portion called "The Confessions of Jeremiah." In them are disclosed deep spiritual agonies. In this instance the plot against his life by his fellow citizens of Anathoth could well have been an aftermath of his temple address (ch. 7). Moreover, they may have resented his support of Josiah's reforms, with its abolition of local sanctuaries—something that would have been hard for the priests of Anathoth to swallow. It appeared to them that in exalting the Jerusalem priesthood, Jeremiah was further degrading that of Anathoth.

The plot was hatched in secret; so Jeremiah suspected nothing. The Lord had to reveal it to him. Rejecting God and his message, the nation was not afraid to reject his messenger. That his family, friends, and fellow citizens in his native town could conspire to assassinate him was something difficult to bear. God disclosed not only the plot to Jeremiah but also the very words the conspirators said. Unsuspecting and trusting, he was to be murdered in the full vigor of his life. Because he was unmarried (16:2) and thus had no progeny, even his memory would be eradicated. Both he and his work ("fruit") were to be obliterated. Destroying a tree with its fruit was proverbial of total destruction.

In v.19 the people speak, in v.20 the prophet speaks, and in vv.21–23 the Lord speaks. To understand v.20 we must realize Jeremiah was praying for God's vengeance on the plotters. Jeremiah was utterly open to the Lord and had entrusted his case to him who knows perfectly all human emotions, thoughts, and desires. This kind of prayer came from the conviction that his enemies were God's enemies. He was depending on the Lord to deal with them.

21–23 The Lord answered Jeremiah's request by indicating his intention to vindicate him. The people had threatened Jeremiah with death if he continued to preach in the Lord's name. That note of authority galled them. They tried to suppress God's message. Anathothites resented Jeremiah's favoring the deposition of the sanctuaries other than Jerusalem. (Anathoth was the home of the priestly house of Abiathar, a friend of David, who was deposed by Solomon, who in turn supplanted it with the house of Zadok.) It seemed to them that Jeremiah was siding with Zadok against their own ancestor. Furthermore, being priests, they doubtless hated his castigation of empty priestly ritual. Their punishment would come at the siege of Jerusalem. Death would prevail inside and outside the city. The young men of military age would die in battle, the rest by famine. The threat of "not even a remnant" must be understood only of Jeremiah's enemies, for some men of Anathoth did return to postexilic Judah (see Ezr 2:23). The year of their visitation was that of Nebuchadnezzar's conquest of the land. Anathoth was near the beleaguering armies and was thus more exposed to the carnage of war than Jerusalem.

2. Punishment and promise (12:1–17)

Out of the context of the opposition to his ministry he suffered in his hometown of Anathoth, Jeremiah deals with the question of the prosperity of the wicked. Jeremiah's perplexity is understandable because the OT does not offer full information on life after death.

a. The prosperity of the wicked (12:1–6)

1–2 The problem of the prosperity of the wicked in the light of God's righteousness is not directly solved here or elsewhere in Scripture. The only final answer is faith in the sovereign wisdom and righteousness of God. Jeremiah is still deeply troubled by the treachery of his fellow citizens of Anathoth. He acknowledges at the outset that God is righteous. Jeremiah refuses in principle to question the justice of God, but he still has questions about the success of the wicked in the light of his own trials. In a spirit of holy familiarity, Jeremiah would reason or argue the case with the Lord. The wicked he refers to are not just those of Anathoth but the wicked in general. With true discernment Jeremiah realizes that prosperity is not accidental but goes back to God's general grace in providing human needs. He uses the figure of a fruit-bearing tree. The wicked, instead of thanking the Lord for his goodness and worshiping him, are actually hypocrites, mouthing pious phrases without reality in their hearts.

3 Jeremiah now contrasts the state of his heart and life with that of the wicked. Their hatred of him was uncalled for. He speaks of his intimate fellowship with the Lord, who knows he is not speaking hypocritically. In strong language Jeremiah asks the Lord to deal with his enemies as they deserve. In asking him to "set them apart for the day of slaughter," Jeremiah is comparing the wicked to animal sacrifices. Though the wicked have been "planted" in the land, they will be utterly destroyed.

4 Jeremiah is describing some consequences of the prosperity of the wicked in Judah. The ungodly are a curse to the nation. God sends punishment, and the righteous suffer with the wicked. The drought does not negate what Jeremiah said in v.1 about the Lord's righteousness, because calamities like those he is describing affect the godly more than the wicked. The ungodly rich usually escape them. The land, beasts, and even birds suffer along with human beings. If the "he" near the end of v.4 refers to God, then it is the height of wickedness to claim that he is morally indifferent to the sin of the rich. This is practical atheism. Or perhaps the people are mocking Jeremiah's predictions and claiming they will never be realized. At least, "he" will perish before they do.

5–6 The Lord's answer to Jeremiah's complaint is meant to teach him that he is too impatient. He would have to suffer even more. What he had endured in Anathoth would be insignificant compared with the trials he had yet to undergo. His confrontation with the men of his own town has made him realize the magnitude of the task he had undertaken. He could not turn to his family for help because they were part of his difficulty. God now challenges him to greater courage and faith for greater trials in the future.

In spite of his problems, up to this point his situation has been like that of a dweller in a peaceful land. The language in v.5 is proverbial. "The flooding of the Jordan" (cf. NIV note) refers to the annual overflow of the Jordan in time of harvest (Jos 3:15) and earlier (April and May) that filled the Ghor (cf. ZPEB, 2:710). With the flooding of the valley, the beasts of prey were driven from their haunts along the river bank. The reference here is probably to the jungle of the Jordan, the land adjacent to the river covered with bushes and heavy undergrowth and inhabited by wild beasts (cf. 2Ki 6:2).

To give Jeremiah a glimpse of how serious matters would become, the Lord grants him a new disclosure. Even his own family cannot be trusted, for they will raise a hue and cry after him as though he were a criminal fleeing from justice. Nor will they be open and aboveboard; they will use threats to obscure their true intentions toward him.

b. Punishment on the ungodly (12:7–13)

7–8 The Lord, not Jeremiah, is still speaking, viewing future events as though already fulfilled. Judgment for breaking the covenant is in view. The historical background of this passage is probably the events recorded in 2Ki 24:1–2, when Jehoiakim revolted against Babylon after three years of submission. Nebuchadnezzar dispatched Chaldean, Syrian, Moabite, and Ammonite soldiers against Judah. The Lord's lament over the nation's devastation contains an abundance of figures: "house," "inheritance," "the one I love" (v.7); "a lion" (v.8); "a speckled bird of prey" (v.9); "vineyard," "field" (v.10). Having warned Judah of the consequences of disobe-

dience, the Lord now abandons her utterly to her enemies.

It was difficult for the Lord to punish his own guilty but beloved people. As ever, his judgment was tempered with love. Thus abandoned by their Lord, the people were incapable of resisting their foes. They surrendered to the enemy because they as fiercely as a lion had opposed the Lord. They had become his declared enemy, raising their voices against him. In saying that he hated his people, the Lord was declaring that he had withdrawn his love and protection from them. He forsook them as though he hated them; this was a greater agony for him than for them.

9 The question requires an affirmative answer. Speckled birds are unusually colored birds, which are attacked by other birds, who will not allow a strange bird among them. So the Lord's people, different from other nations, will be attacked by them. The Lord invites the wild beasts (Babylon and her allies) to devour the land.

10–13 The Lord's great love for his land is reflected in his three endearing designations of it ("vineyard," "field," "pleasant field"). The shepherds who have devastated his vineyard (Israel; cf. Isa 5:1) are the heads of the invading army. They have done what they wished, heedlessly breaking through and trampling the well-tended area. Though the desolation has been thoroughgoing, no one considers the causes that have brought such judgment. The "sword of the LORD" in the hand of the Lord's agents will do its work throughout the country. Apparently the enemies will invade from the east. As far as Judah is concerned, nothing has turned out successfully for her people. In spite of all their labors in the field, they gain nothing. They reap the opposite of what they expect. Their crops are a failure (cf. 14:3–4). In fact, the harvests are so poor that even the farmers are ashamed of them. The Lord had not prospered them at all.

c. Promise for the repentant nations (12:14–17)

14–17 In this section we have an anticipation of the prophecies in chs. 47–49. In prophesying to the nations, Jeremiah was fulfilling his commission (1:10). The nations (Syria, Moab, Ammon) were to be punished by the same enemy that punished Judah, namely, Babylon. The Lord identifies himself with

Judah when he calls the surrounding peoples "my wicked neighbors." They too will experience deportation from their lands. This is part of the answer to the prophet's complaint concerning the prosperity of the wicked. But this is not the end of the matter; these nations are promised future blessing after the Lord has chastened them.

A millennial setting is in view in vv.15–16. Repatriation is promised for Israel and the nations, who have learned about God from his people, just as Israel formerly learned the worship of idols through these nations. The basis of the predicted blessing is repentance and faith. If the pagans adopt the worship of God in truth, they will be incorporated into God's people. Israel will lead in godliness. There will be a remnant among the nations (cf. Ge 12:1–3; Ro 11:15). But the members of the remnant will have to make a genuine avowal of God as their own. Then the nations with Israel will know peace in the Messianic Age. When they were in the midst of the nations (vv.7, 9), it was to God's people's detriment; when the nations are in the midst of God's people, it will be to the nations' spiritual blessing.

The chapter closes with the alternative to faith and is a warning to all. For unbelief there will be doom.

3. Corruption of the nation's life (13:1–27)

a. The marred linen belt (13:1–11)

1–7 Was this act a real one or was it a vision? The chief problem with the literal view is that the distance to the Euphrates (Perath)—and two round trips were made—would require Jeremiah to walk hundreds of miles. The literal view is preferred because (1) the act would have to be witnessed to be of value as a message to the people; (2) the language supports the literal sense; (3) Jeremiah was away from Jerusalem for part of Jehoiakim's reign, and his absence could account for Nebuchadnezzar's kind feeling toward him because of previous personal acquaintance (39:11–12); (4) "Perath" should perhaps be understood as an abbreviation of Ephrata, the original name of Bethlehem, about six miles south of Jerusalem. Then it would be easy for Jeremiah to carry out the command literally.

Jeremiah was charged to buy a linen belt, place it around his loins or waist, but not to put it in water. It was to be of linen for two reasons: (1) Linen would easily rot, skin or leather would not; (2) the original cleanliness spoke of Israel's purity when first in fellowship with the Lord. Also, the linen belt would recall Israel's priestly calling (priests wore only linen) and character (cf. Ex 19:6). After wearing it for a while, Jeremiah was commanded to hide it in a crevice of the rock at the Euphrates, and he did so. After many days, he was ordered to go to the rock and retrieve the belt he had buried. It was ruined and worthless because it had been close to the moisture of the river. Why the Euphrates? The purpose of the trip may have been to underscore the influence of Mesopotamia in corrupting the nation religiously, beginning with ungodly Manasseh (2Ki 21). Also, there may be an allusion to the coming Babylonian exile.

8–11 A linen belt was used because just as it is placed closely about the body, so the nation Israel was brought into intimate relationship with her gracious Lord. The ruin of the garment teaches that idolatry corrupts anyone who engages in it. Idolatry had corrupted Israel from her loyalty to God and made her worthless. Instead of clinging to her God in faith and love, she destroyed herself.

b. The wine of God's wrath (13:12–14)

12–14 Possibly at a drinking feast, Jeremiah took occasion to utter a proverbial saying about jars ("wineskins"; GK 5574) and wine, which was probably a platitude concerning the hope of continued prosperity. The jar was the largest earthenware container for storing wine (Isa 30:14). The largest found in excavations hold almost ten gallons. When Jeremiah used the pun of filling, the wine drinkers mocked his banal remark, which he immediately gave a serious turn. Jeremiah pointed out that the people were the jars and were to be filled with the wine of God's wrath against their sin. He had turned their saying into a prediction of disaster.

Four groups are singled out for the judgment: the kings, the priests, the false prophets, and the people. Jeremiah had several kings in mind; all would be the objects of God's judgment. His mention of David's throne perhaps stresses how far they had fallen from the standard of worship in

David's day. All the people will be filled with mental intoxication, a symbol of helplessness and confusion. In the nation's drunkenness, the male portion of the population, who should have defended the land against the invaders, will be colliding one against another. Jeremiah anticipates the truth elaborated in 25:15–28; 51:7. Three times the Lord declares that he will show no pity on the nation.

c. Warning against pride (13:15–17)

15–17 Pride, the sin of Satan, infected the human family before the Tower of Babel and ever since. Jeremiah warns the people against pride in their spiritual privilege. Proud of their favored position before God as his chosen people, they refused to heed his message through his prophets. The scene in this section is that of a weary traveler on a mountain caught in the dark night. The statement "Give glory to the LORD your God" is an OT idiom for "Confess your sin" (cf. Jos 7:19). To do so would avert the evil about to come on the nation. But Jeremiah knew their obstinate ways; they would not listen. Firm in declaring the truth of God without fear or favor, he was nonetheless tender in his grief and compassion over their obduracy, which would yet lead them into captivity. He took no delight in the prospect of their misery.

d. Tragedy in the royal house (13:18–19)

18 The Lord commands Jeremiah to address the king and queen mother—King Jehoiachin and his mother, Queen Nehushta, who were carried away to Babylon in the second deportation under Nebuchadnezzar in 597 B.C. (cf. 2Ki 24:8, 12, 15). The address is an exhortation to humility in view of their impending loss of sovereignty. Because kings practiced polygamy, their mothers were highly influential (cf. 1Ki 2:19; 15:13; 2Ki 10:13). This was all the more true of Jehoiachin and his mother; because he was only eighteen when he began his short reign of three months, she probably had much influence over him. She is mentioned again—but not by name—in 22:26 and 29:2. Both the king and his mother were unreceptive to the message of God.

19 Unlike the invasion of Sennacherib (2Ki 18:13), Nebuchadnezzar would strike the cities of the South, the Negev (the barren area in the south of Judah; Jos 15:21–32). Though

the Negev is farthest from Jerusalem, it too would feel Nebuchadnezzar's might—an evidence of the total extent of Judah's captivity. The cities would be in ruins with no one to clear them. The statement that "all Judah" would be exiled is rhetorical exaggeration, since only some leaders and skilled workmen were taken to Babylon at that time (597 B.C.). Yet they represented the whole nation.

e. Captivity and shame of Judah (13:20–27)

20–21 Jerusalem is addressed under the figure of a shepherdess who has abandoned her flock. She has been derelict in duty and has misled her flock. Those "coming from the north" are again the Babylonians. Jerusalem was responsible for protecting the entire nation. For her unfaithfulness to the Lord's flock, Jerusalem would have to endure subjection to the very powers she had helped to gain control. There may be reference here to the foreign policy that courted Egypt and Babylon, especially the latter, when Judah was tributary to Neco of Egypt. Though she toadied to both, Judah would be dominated by them. Judah had tried to make binding alliances with Babylon on more than one occasion (cf. 4:30). Ultimately, she was the one who made the Babylonians her masters by invoking their aid against Egypt instead of trusting the Lord.

22 When Judah is in agony as a mother in childbirth, she will ask why she is suffering. Continuance in sin has deadened the nation's conscience. She does not feel she is suffering justly. The shameful way the conquerors treat the people will be like the shaming of a prostitute. Exposure of the secret parts was the public disgrace heaped on prostitutes.

23 Using a famous proverb, Jeremiah points out that Judah is so far beyond change that her repentance would be like a suspension of nature's laws. Yet God still invites people to repent. But with Judah sin was so ingrained that there was no hope of repentance. Here is a classic example of loss of freedom of the will through persistent sinning. Sin becomes natural. Jeremiah is speaking of the force of habit, not denying freedom of choice (cf. Jn 8:34). Obviously Jeremiah is stating the case radically. He does not mean to rule out any response to the working of God in people's

hearts to bring them to repentance, as v.27 shows.

24–27 Because of the nation's persistent sin, the Lord will subject the people to a process of winnowing—a familiar scene to them, for they had often seen the strong wind from the Arabian desert carry off the useless stubble. None of the things described is accidental; they are God's judgment on Judah for forgetting him and trusting in "the lie" (NIV, "false gods")—specifically, Baal. Judah's retribution will be to know the full measure of disgrace. The "neighings" are a bestial figure for illicit love (cf. 5:8; 50:11). The last question—"How long will you be unclean?"—shows that there is still opportunity for Judah to repent. The Lord does not close the door on a future return from idolatry. He still wants the nation to repent in time and so escape punishment. Two strong emotions struggled in Jeremiah: (1) the certainty of disaster for the nation and (2) the hope that it might yet be averted.

4. Drought and impending exile (14:1–22)

Chapters 14 and 15 are full of Jeremiah's grief for the future of his people. The references to invasions and exile cannot help to date the material before us because there were three invasions of Judah and as many deportations. Nor can one identify the material with a particular crisis in the life of the nation. The drought here is probably later than that mentioned in 3:3 and 12:4 because this one is connected with war (vv.17–18).

a. The critical drought (14:1–6)

1 The word for "drought" (GK 1314) is plural here, which may indicate a series of droughts. Rainfall in Palestine is never over-abundant. A year of drought can cause suffering. Unlike Egypt and Mesopotamia, Palestine depends on seasonal rainfall. In Israel a drought was never viewed as a chance occurrence. Drought had been threatened for disobedience (Dt 28:23–24) and was part of the covenant curses. The Lord's purpose in sending the drought was to bring the nation to repentance.

2–3 The entire country was suffering anguish from lack of water. The drought extended to the city. The nation was clothed in black to express its mourning. The capital cried out

for help. Nor were the nobles immune! When they sent their servants to the cisterns for water, they returned with empty vessels. Rain water, stored for time of need, had long been exhausted. In their mourning the people covered their heads, as though to shut out the painful sight. The famine afflicted city, country, human beings, and animals. The ground was "cracked." The farmers could not work the soil and, hence, could not expect a harvest. They too were in deep mourning.

5–6 It is sad for irrational creatures to have to suffer because the people have incurred God's displeasure. The doe, known for her care for her fawns, no longer was able to care for her offspring. The wild donkeys, known for their hardiness and ability to survive on very little, were greatly debilitated. Even on the bare heights they gasped for breath. Also, instead of the usual sharpness of sight, they lost the power of vision in their agony.

b. The confession of the nation (14:7–9)

7 The people acknowledge their apostasy and sin, which deserve only death. But they plead on solid ground—namely, that the Lord's honor may be exhibited to the pagan nations. Because there is no merit in Judah, the Lord's work in the people's behalf will reveal his nature as a God of compassion.

8–9 Thus Jeremiah entreats the Lord not to disappoint his people's hope in him ("Hope of Israel" is a favorite expression of Jeremiah; cf. 17:7, 13; 50:7). The people ask the Lord why he is as a stranger or traveler with no interest in the country he is only passing through. If he is their Hope and Deliverer in times of distress, why does he not now act as such in their behalf? The Lord is not powerless; so why should he hesitate like one paralyzed by fright? His presence is still among his people in the ark, the temple, and the sacred worship. Furthermore, the people plead the covenant, for they are called by the Lord's name. So they pray that the Lord will not forsake them.

c. The Lord's answer in judgment (14:10–12)

10–12 The Lord's reply explains his chastisements. Because his people have kept on in their wickedness, they were being punished for their ungodliness. Apparently the Lord considered the nation lacking in true penitence. They were constantly wandering after foreign gods; because the people rejected him, he was rejecting them. For the third time Jeremiah is forbidden to pray for the people (cf. 7:16; 11:14). They were beyond help because of their determined disobedience. Intercession was an important prophetic function, but Jeremiah was not permitted to intercede at that fateful time. Worse visitations than the drought would overtake the people—i.e., the sword, famine, and pestilence (the combination of these three appears seven times in the book). Neither fasting nor sacrifices would avail to recover God's favor, as long as the people were bent on idolatry. External marks of repentance were useless, since the Lord sought above all else reality, truth in the heart.

d. The doom of the false prophets (14:13–16)

13 The false prophets are blamed for the plight of the nation. As a mitigation of the nation's sin, Jeremiah, the unpopular true prophet, pleads that the false prophets have misled the people. False prophets are self-seeking, profiteering, and zealous for popularity, but with no authoritative word from God. In those desperate times they preached deliverance and peace, lulling the people into unwarranted complacency so that they would not believe in the imminence of judgment. They promised "lasting peace," the very opposite of Jeremiah's true message. Imagine the confusion in the minds of the people with the babel of bright promises over against Jeremiah's thundering message of doom.

14–16 Verse 14 points out the four methods by which the false prophets practiced their deception. The Lord's retribution on the lying prophets will be their endurance of the very punishment they would not predict. The people should have known that the Lord punishes sin, and they should not have believed the false prophets. The judgment of the nation is spoken of here because the people were willing to be deceived.

e. The grief of Jeremiah (14:17–18)

17–18 Jeremiah shows the hardened nation his grief in seeing their coming ruin. He grieves over both war and famine. He cannot view the people's distress dispassionately (cf. 9:18; 13:17). He calls Judah "the virgin daughter—my people" because she had been jealously kept from the idolatrous nations, as virgins are guarded in Oriental households. Now the prophet describes the conditions in the land after the fall of Jerusalem. The blame still falls on the false prophets and godless priests, who must be exiled to a foreign land.

f. Prayer of confession and plea for help (14:19–22)

19–22 The nation now pleads its own case with the Lord. The questions are more intense. The people cannot believe that the Lord has irretrievably cast them off. Now they freely admit that all their hopes and prospects have been blasted. They also admit the basis of their woes: their wickedness. They acknowledge the sinfulness of their ancestors. In desperation they plead three reasons for the Lord to help them in spite of their sins: (1) his reputation in the earth, (2) his temple, and (3) his covenant. The throne of God's glory is Zion, especially the temple (cf. 2Ki 19:15; Ps 99:1). Still haunted by the drought, they declare their belief that neither idols nor the heavens by themselves can give rain. Only God can end their trials, and they expect him to help them out of their difficulties.

5. Impending judgment and Jeremiah's complaints (15:1–21)

The break between chs. 14 and 15 should be disregarded. The mood in this chapter intensifies as Jeremiah elaborates on the Exile. In fact, he plumbs the depths of despair so deeply as to lead him to say some things the Lord rebukes.

a. Prayer unavailing for Judah (15:1)

1 The Lord refuses to avert judgment from his people; his decision to punish them is irreversible. Therefore the continued intercession of Jeremiah or of any others cannot succeed. The people's incorrigibility has placed them beyond the power of prayer. Moses and Samuel would have been unable to move the Lord from his decision (cf. Ex 32:11–14, 30–34; Nu 14:13–23; Dt 9:1–20, 25–29; 1Sa 7:5–9; 12:19–25). The Lord commands that the nation be sent from his presence. No longer can he tolerate them, nor does he want Jeremiah to keep reminding him of them. Nevertheless, the command is not absolute and final but conditional.

b. The punishment determined (15:2–9)

2–4 Should the nation ask where the people are going, the answer is that each will proceed to the punishment allotted him or her by the Lord. If they think they are only going to be banished, they are tragically mistaken. Their destination will be death by disease (cf. 14:12), warfare, or famine. It will also be exile. Then, as if these judgments were insufficient, the Lord speaks of "four kinds of destroyers against" the people. The first will destroy the living; the other three will mutilate and consume the dead. For a corpse to be dragged on the ground and then become carrion for bird and beast was the ultimate desecration of the dead (cf. Rev 6:1–8). When the Lord refers to making the people an object of horror to all kingdoms of the earth, he apparently has in view more than the generation of Jeremiah's time. Manasseh's sin is presented as a root cause of Judah's captivity. He had contributed to the moral decline of the nation, but the people had imitated his ways when he brazenly led Judah into idolatry (cf. 2Ki 21:3–7, 10–15; 23:26–27; 24:3–4).

5–7 No one will pity Jerusalem when the Lord forsakes her. She will be left desolate without anyone caring. Because the people repeatedly rejected the Lord and his worship by slipping back into apostasy, he will no longer be merciful to them. As a farmer winnows the wheat to remove the chaff, so the Lord will disperse the people from their cities—"the city gates" standing for the whole country. The population will be decimated. The cause of all this is the refusal of Judah to be truly repentant.

8–9 To the Lord's grief, Judah's widows will be more numerous than the sand of the seas, an amazing comparison. Even the mothers of warriors will not escape the destroyer, because Judah will be defenseless through the loss of her valiant sons in battle. Likely the reference to "mothers" is figurative of Jerusalem. The enemy will strike at noonday—suddenly and unexpectedly. To have seven sons is a Hebrew picture of complete happiness, but the mother has had her happiness pass all too soon. Because of the blessing of abundant offspring, she might have considered herself secure. But she is seen breathing out her soul or gasping for breath. Any survivors of the fall of Jerusalem will suffer the same end as those already slain.

c. Jeremiah's complaint (15:10–11)

10–11 In his overwhelming despondency the prophet laments his life's work and lot. Jeremiah's greatness lay in his sensitive nature that felt acute pain for his people and their doom. The hopelessness of the nation's situation and his own difficulties of his position weighed on him. He is lapsing here into self-pity. This is one of the saddest cries in the book. It must have been uttered at a time when he was experiencing great opposition, probably during Jehoiakim's reign. He feels deeply his alienation from the nation he loves. He wishes he had not been born. His tenderness in addressing his mother stands out. He is like one constantly in a lawsuit with his people. Borrowing and lending are proverbial reasons for disagreement and tense relations among people. The populace are cursing him because he attacked their sins so unsparingly. Passages such as this show that the prophets were not supermen but fully human.

The Lord responds to Jeremiah's complaint and gives him personal assurance. The force of v.11 is that God promises vindication for Jeremiah against his enemies as well as strength for his ministry, the objective of which is only good. In times of distress, even his enemies will ask for his intercession (cf. 21:1–6; 37:3; 42:1–6).

d. The inevitable judgment (15:12–14)

12–14 This passage clearly predicts the Exile. Bronze is an alloy of copper and tin. Unusually hard iron was available from the region of the Black Sea, famous for being harder than all other iron. The sense is that as little as people can break iron, Judah would not be able to sustain an attack from the power in the north, i.e., the Chaldeans. The question of v.12 demands a negative answer. Because Judah would not be able to withstand the northern enemy, her wealth and treasures would be freely carried off by the adversary. God's wrath against their sin would not be satisfied until all was plundered and taken to Babylon.

e. Jeremiah's charge against the Lord (15:15–18)

15–16 On the basis of his loyalty to the will of the Lord, Jeremiah pleads for divine help. He wants vengeance to be meted out by the Lord on those who have opposed his prophet. Jeremiah does not want the Lord to be patient with his enemies and withhold vengeance on them until he is gone. Jeremiah wants vindication in this life. In effect Jeremiah is pleading that God will not be so lenient with his persecutors as to give them time to destroy him. In a striking figure he recalls his first reception of God's message and how he made it his own. It symbolizes the assimilation of God's revealed truth. Jeremiah was every inch a chosen servant of the Lord. His chief delight was in God's word.

17–18 Jeremiah describes his solitariness in the midst of his people. Because he sided with God, he was cut off from the joys of those around him. He was filled with God's indignation against their sin. It greatly pained him to be out of step with his contemporaries. The hand of God was on him; the constraint of God's truth weighed on his spirit. The rhetorical questions in v.18 imply that for the moment Jeremiah gave way to despair. He was so deeply and continuously wounded that he wanted to know whether God had abandoned him and had proved unreliable. After all, his own family had betrayed him. The "deceptive brook" was a familiar figure. In Palestine many brooks have water only after a downpour. At other times a traveler may be disappointed if he looks for water in them. In his distraught state, Jeremiah charged the Lord with failure to fulfill his promises to strengthen him in his resistance against his enemies.

f. God's rebuke and encouragement (15:19–21)

19–21 The Lord tells Jeremiah that if he gives up his doubts and reproaches, avoids worthless statements, and holds to worthy ones, he may continue to be his prophet and mouthpiece. Jeremiah himself will have to undergo the refining process so that he can cleave to precious words, not worthless ones. He must lift his people and not let them drag him down to their level. His only hope is to trust more fully in God and be faithful to the message, whatever response it brings; God promises assurance and victory. These verses are practically a recommissioning of Jeremiah, in which God promises to keep him from the power of the violent wicked. There were such men in Judah, who finally assassinated Gedaliah, the governor of Judah, after the fall of Jerusalem. This word of encouragement was sufficient for the prophet's need; though opposition to his message mounted perilously, he never again complained to the Lord as he did in vv.10, 15–18.

6. Bane and blessing (16:1–21)

Again, the chapter division is illogical. The date for this passage is probably the fourth year of King Jehoiakim (2Ki 24:1–2). Jeremiah had complained of his loneliness in ch. 15, but the Lord promises him no relief. Two sections of the passage deal with doom and two with bright promises for the future.

a. The loneliness of Jeremiah (16:1–9)

1–2 Undoubtedly the Lord's command for Jeremiah not to marry was an emotional shock for him. Celibacy was unusual, not only in Israel, but throughout the Near East. Among the Jews marriage was viewed as a natural state for a man. The desire to perpetuate the family name led to almost universal marriage in Israel. But Jeremiah's dedication to his prophetic service allowed him no time for family life or for participation in the usual joys and sorrows of his countrymen. His compliance with the Lord's command not to marry shows his complete submission to the divine will and underscores the woes predicted for the nation. His being denied a wife and children would be a warning that the family life of the nation was to be disrupted. "This place" was Jerusalem and Judah. Jeremiah had already paid a price for his ministry: isolation from his countrymen (15:10), loneliness (15:17), no marriage, and no participation in funerals (v.5) or times of joy (v.8).

3–4 The Lord tells Jeremiah that the sorrows of parents will be increased. Children will die of "deadly diseases"—epidemic diseases. The number of deaths will be so great that there will be no time for mourning or burial.

5–9 Jeremiah must not mourn over the carnage in the land, for private sorrow would be exceeded by the national doom and mourn-

The vulture was considered a god of Upper Egypt. Egypt was one of Judah's enemies; Jeremiah prophesies that the Judeans would be food "for the birds of the air" (cf. 16:4)

ing. Abstinence from mourning would be a sign of universal disease and death on a universal scale. The rituals for the bereaved—even for those who lost a father or mother—would not be permitted. So Jeremiah would have to refrain from mourning because the Lord would no longer prosper his people or bestow his grace on them. Death would overtake nobles as well as common people. There would be no time to perform the pagan practices of mourning the people.

In time of death, fasting was usual. In the evening, however, food and drink were provided by friends, since the food and drink in the home of the mourner had become ceremonially unclean because of the dead body (Hos 9:4). In later Judaism the cup of consolation was a special cup of wine for the chief mourner (cf. Pr 31:6). Moreover, the prophet was also commanded to abstain from the joys of the people. This was to show the imminence of the calamity that awaited them. He could have little joy at marriage festivities when he remembered the threat hanging over them all. Nor were they to think that the doom was far off; it would happen in their lifetime.

b. The cause of the judgment (16:10–13)

10–13 Jeremiah's withdrawnness would mystify his people, so he would have to explain it. He was prepared to spell out the cause of their miseries and the reason for the Babylonian exile. Aided by the false prophets, the people had become complacent in their sinning. The prophet explains that they would be exiled for their lapses into idolatry, and he indicts the nation—first its ancestors, then the present generation—for forsaking the

Lord. In fact, the latter outdid the former in evil. With great force the Lord was going to "throw" them out of their land into an unknown land. While they may have known about the land, it was unknown to them by the actual experience of living. There Jeremiah ironically assures them that they would have the opportunity of indulging their desire for pagan worship day and night. And the Lord would completely withdraw his favor from them.

c. Restoration to the land (16:14–15)

14–15 Judgment is never God's last word. After exile will be repatriation. The Exodus from Egypt will pale in significance before the people's deliverance from Babylon and from worldwide dispersion. The future Exodus will be greater than the past one. The regathering mentioned here is the final one in the consummation of Israel's national history in the last days. The reference to "all the countries" shows that the prophet was predicting a restoration from a general dispersion. The return will be through God's gracious faithfulness to the covenant he made with the patriarchs regarding the land (Ge 12:1–3,7).

d. Complete retribution (16:16–18)

16–17 There would be no escape from the coming judgment of the Lord. The hunters and fishermen are the pagan conquerors who were to be God's instruments for chastising Israel. No one would escape the invaders. To seek to hide from God would be futile. Jeremiah was not speaking of two periods of divine visitation. Rather, he was simply indicating that in the day of reckoning there would be no place to find refuge anywhere. The Lord knows all the nation's acts; none of the people's deeds has escaped his notice. But first, before they can be restored, the people must undergo retribution for their iniquity.

18 The "double" penalty cannot be understood outside the context of the Hebrew viewpoint, which used the term to express ample, full, complete punishment (cf. Isa 40:2). So the punishment would be commensurate in full with the offense. Nothing is more defiling than idolatry. As corpses pollute, so do idols. The "lifeless forms" may refer to either the animals offered to idols or the idols themselves (cf. Lev 26:30; Nu 19:11).

e. The nations in blessing (16:19–20)

19–20 Jeremiah next worships the Lord for restoring Israel and drawing the Gentiles to him. He expresses the hope that the nations will finally turn from idolatry and confess the emptiness of such worship. The threefold "my" expresses the Lord's sustaining of Jeremiah in his loneliness. So unprecedented will the divine retribution be that even idolatrous nations will respect the name of the Lord. The nations will come to the Lord, not by human persuasion, but spontaneously and voluntarily (cf. Isa 2:1–4; 45:14; Zec 8:20–23). Without doubt the picture is messianic. It is best to take v.20 as a continuation of the declaration of the enlightened nations. Even they will see the folly of idolatry.

f. The goal of the punishment (16:21)

21 Once and for all, the Lord will manifest his hand and might—namely, by the severe trials incurred by disobedience to his word and his will. What is said will apply to both Jews and Gentiles; there is no need to exclude either one (cf. Eze 36:23; 37:14). All will vindicate God's unique glory. God is who he claims to be.

7. The deceitful heart of humankind (17:1–27)

As a whole, ch. 17 has no central theme but gathers together important aphoristic or proverbial sayings on the issues of life, sin, and the way of the curse and blessing.

a. Israel's ineradicable sin (17:1–4)

1 When Jeremiah says that Judah's sin is "engraved" (GK 4180) on the people's hearts and on their altars with "an iron tool" or "a flint point," he means that their sin is indelible. Thus God's judgment is inescapable. Sin, especially idolatry, had become an integral part of Judah's life. It had been etched on their very natures and on their temple worship (cf. Ex 27:2). Iron tools were used in cutting inscriptions on stone (cf. Job 19:24). The "horns of the altars" were the metal projections from the four corners. In the temple rituals sacrificial blood was sprinkled for expiation on the four horns of the altar (Lev 16:18). What a perversion to have sin inerad-

icably engraved on "their hearts" where the new covenant belongs (31:31–34) and on the very places where solemn expiation was made for the sins of the people!

2–4 The children in Judah would be so steeped in idolatry by their parents that the desire for it would emerge at the slightest provocation. Asherim were poles placed beside the altars in Canaanite worship; they were proscribed in the Mosaic Law (Dt 16:21). They represented the sacred tree (*asherah*), part of the Baal cult and a symbol of the Canaanite goddess Astarte. Thus long continuance in idolatry is implied. For such iniquities the nation would lose all its wealth to its enemies. "Mountain in the land" is an obvious reference to Zion or Jerusalem. It is addressed this way because of its eminent position as the center of the country. Moreover, Jerusalem is called "rocky plateau" in 21:13. In this case "plateau" does not have to denote level land but the surrounding countryside.

Jeremiah further elaborates on the loss of the nation's inheritance. The people have outraged the Lord's patience; so "through [their] own fault" they would be separated from their land.

b. The way of cursing and blessing (17:5–8)

5–8 The main concept of the broader context (vv.5–13) appears to be that of permanence. Verses 5–8 emphasize the need of reliance on God alone in all life's circumstances. Those who trust in human beings are referred to in vv.5–6; those who rely on God in vv.7–8. The results of choices are clearly spelled out: a curse on the former, a blessing on the latter. Where people depend on humankind, spiritual life cannot thrive; such persons are like the dwarf juniper of the desert, whose leaves are not refreshed by rain; so it is both stunted and starved. On the contrary, those who trust in the Lord are blessed indeed. They need fear no circumstance in life. Again, the figure of a tree is used. The blessed are firmly "planted" where there is abundance of water. Growth and fruitfulness, therefore, are assured.

c. Humanity's desperate heart condition (17:9–13)

9 If there is such blessing in trusting God, then why do people so generally depend on their fellow humans? The answer lies in the innate depravity of the human heart. The source of all human difficulty is the human "heart" (GK 4213; cf. Pr 4:23), which stands for the total inner being, including reason. From the heart come action and will. The human heart is more deceptive than anything else. It is desperately corrupt and, humanly speaking, incurable. Who on earth can plumb the depths of the heart's corruption and sickness? Even its owner does not know it.

10–11 The Lord knows the whole truth about the heart, and he will deal with all of us justly, according to our deeds. The noun translated "partridge" (GK 7926) may mean some type of sand grouse rather than a "partridge," because the partridge does not hatch the eggs of other birds. At any rate, the meaning of the passage is clear: ill-gotten gain is, like a bird with young from eggs that she has not laid, soon lost (cf. Pr 23:5). The brood forsake their foster mother. Those who weary themselves to accumulate wealth unjustly are moral and spiritual fools.

12–13 In these verses Jeremiah extols the majesty of God. True permanence is found only in the Lord. His sanctuary and throne refer to Jerusalem. Unlike riches soon lost is the eternal throne of God. That throne demands both reward and punishment. It is the fixed center of the universe and an endless source of comfort to the believer. In God's purpose it has been so from time immemorial. Those who forsake the Lord will suffer shame, for a life "written in the dust" instead of in the Book of Life (cf. Ex 32:32; Lk 10:20; Rev 20:12; 21:27) results from having forsaken "the spring of living water" (cf. 2:13). Those who do so are as unenduring as names written on the dust.

d. Jeremiah's plea for vindication (17:14–18)

14–15 From time to time the unwelcome nature of Jeremiah's prophecies drove him to plead for divine help. The Lord was his only hope and cure (cf. v.9). So Jeremiah prayed on the basis of his Lord's known faithfulness. Only the Lord can heal and save. The prophet's desire for healing and salvation undoubtedly included moral and spiritual ills as well as deliverance from his enemies. Jeremiah's coreligionists taunted him and scoffed at him daily because his predictions were not fulfilled. They criticized him for being a false

prophet (Dt 18:22). This was doubly difficult for him to bear because he had prayed the Lord to refrain from meting out his judgment on Judah. Scoffing, the mockers declared, "Let it [the word of the LORD] now be fulfilled." This passage indicates that the fall of Jerusalem had not yet occurred; if Jeremiah's prophecies had already been fulfilled, the people would not have asked their derisive question. God's continued long-suffering led the prophet's enemies to demand a visible confirmation of the word he preached.

16 So Jeremiah sets forth a threefold vindication of his ministry: (1) He has not refused to follow God's will; (2) he has not hoped for their doom; and (3) all his utterances were finally known to God. Moreover, he had not tried to relinquish his ministry because of the suffering it involved. The word "shepherd" (GK 8286) usually refers to a king, but here it refers to Jeremiah as a leader of the people. His enemies accused him of wanting disaster to overtake the nation. But he never wanted his threatenings in proclaiming the Lord's message to be fulfilled. He took no delight in predicting doom (cf. ch. 40). "The day of despair" is the day of the fall of the city, when the predicted woes would come on it. Furthermore, the Lord knew everything Jeremiah preached, including his prayers that the doom might be averted.

17–18 The "terror" Jeremiah feared was that the Lord might confound him and desert him before his enemies. He wanted the Lord's protection and prayed that his loyalty to him might not be the cause of his ruin. If the Lord would not encourage him, then he would be doubly bereft of comfort. For the vindication of God's truth, he needed to be proved right. It was this that pervaded his prayers for vengeance. There is no contradiction between v.18 and v.16 because the people in view are not the same. By "double destruction" is meant full, complete destruction (cf. comment on 16:18).

e. Sabbath observance (17:19–27)

19–23 Prophecies of doom were always ethically conditioned. The way of blessing was still open for Judah. The Sabbath was a vital part of the Decalogue and was the touchstone of Israel's contractual, covenant relationship with God. Because Jeremiah was against insincere worship, we have no against insincere worship, we have no ground for thinking he would oppose sincere religious practices.

The "gate" where the Lord commanded Jeremiah to deliver his message was one where a number of the people could be found, no doubt one of Jerusalem's gates. It was distinct from the gate of the priests and Levites. Obviously it was one of the temple gates. In v.19 "the kings" are successive kings of Judah; those in v.20 appear to be the king and his princes, i.e., his royal house.

This passage makes sense only if we understand that the people habitually violated the Sabbath. They used it to conclude the work of the week and to prepare for the coming week's work. Contrary to the word of Moses, the Sabbath had been chosen by the people to bring their produce in from the country, since they worked the fields during the week. This must not continue. The people carried burdens out of their homes in exchange for the produce brought into the city. The people's response to Jeremiah's preaching was highly negative.

24–27 Now the blessings on obedience follow. In summary, the Sabbath recognizes God as Creator, which is a witness against idolatry, and it marks the special covenant relationship between God and Israel. If obedience is forthcoming, the blessings are distinctive: (1) the continuance of the Davidic dynasty, (2) the settling and continuance of Jerusalem, and (3) the temple as once again the center of worship for the nation. Thus Judah is assured the promise of peace, prosperity, and permanence through her native dynasty and the authorized priesthood.

The several regions of Judah mentioned were still possessed by Judah and Benjamin. The land of Benjamin was north of Judah. The lowland or Shephelah ("western foothills") was the low hills stretching toward the Philistine maritime plain, west and southwest of Judah, and was the center of agriculture. The "hill country" was the central region, with the desert of Judah stretching down to the Dead Sea. The "Negev" was the arid South (cf. Jos 15:21–32). The offerings the people were to bring are divided into blood offerings (two) and bloodless offerings (two). The "incense" mentioned here was one of the ingredients added to the offerings. The list concludes with the "thank offerings," which

were the principal class of the fellowship offerings (cf. Lev 7:11).

The passage concludes with the price of disobedience, though God's yearning heart would yet keep his people from destruction. Fire is a symbol of destruction throughout the Bible (cf. Am 1:3–2:5).

8. The parable of the potter (18:1–23)

The potter's house is the most familiar of Jeremiah's figures and is found elsewhere in Scripture (cf. Job 10:9; 33:6; Ps 2:9; Isa 29:16; 45:9; 64:8; Ro 9:20–21; Rev 2:27). In this passage we have a true but mysterious blending of divine sovereignty and human responsibility. The Lord used the potter to illustrate how he deals with humanity.

a. The message of the potter (18:1–12)

1–4 God is not to be seen here as an arbitrary sovereign; the deeper level of meaning speaks of his grace that underlay the coming disaster on Judah. The command came to Jeremiah to go down to the pottery, where it was the Lord's intention to give him a message for the people. So he went there from the temple that was in the upper part of the city. The potter's house was probably on the slopes of the Valley of Hinnom (south of Jerusalem), where water and clay were found. Here the prophet was to be taught the principles of the divine government. At the pottery Jeremiah saw what was already familiar to him. The potter was making a vessel on the wheels, the upper and lower discs made of stone or wood. The lower one was worked by the foot of the potter and was attached by an axle to the upper one, on which the clay was worked. The discs were in a horizontal position.

As happened frequently in the daily life of a potter, the clay did not turn out right. Often in throwing the clay, some defect would become evident. The potter then rolled the clay into a lump to begin his task again to make a more suitable product. The chief point here is the power the potter had over the clay. The clay was in his hand and under his control. The defects were in the clay, not the hand of the potter. The potter's perseverance is to be noted.

5–10 Now Jeremiah is taught the meaning of the figure. The infinite power of the Lord is compared with that of the potter over his clay. Just as the potter remade the clay to

Jeremiah received a message from the Lord at the potter's house. On the left is a potter's oven, in which the clay pots were baked. Above are various kinds of pottery found at archaological sites.

conform to his purpose, so the Lord's will and power continue to mold the nation until it is conformed to his plan. The Lord will never be defeated even if Judah turns from his way for them. There is a conditional element in his dealings with his people. Repentance can always change the Lord's decree of judgment, for his threatenings are never unconditional. But the parallel between humanity and the clay must not be carried too far. Human "clay" is not passive. Upon a person's repentance God can rework him or her into a vessel of honor. The position is not one of absolute fatalism (blotting out human freedom), nor is it one where God's sovereignty is wholly dependent on a person's choice. Ultimately, no human being is completely free. But God in his mysterious working in human life has ordered it so that humanity may freely choose.

God does not exercise his omnipotence arbitrarily or capriciously but conditions everything ethically. Though the parable is meant principally for Judah, God deals similarly with all nations. All people are given the opportunity to repent and conform to God's purpose. When the Scriptures speak of his "relenting" (GK 5714) or repenting, we must understand this in the light of Nu 23:19. When used of God, repentance never means what it does for a human being, for God has never done anything wrong. But he does act differently toward men and women when they turn from disobeying him to obeying him (26:3). With God repentance is not a change of mind but his consistent response according to his changeless nature to the change in the nation's conduct. So in this parable the prophet is holding out the opportunity for Judah to repent.

11–12 Jeremiah now applies the parable of the potter to his nation. Responsibility clearly rests on them. When the Lord says he is "preparing" (GK 3670) calamity for Judah, the Hebrew verb is the same as the word for potter; so there is a play on words. The threatened calamity is the Exile. What was the nation's reaction? The people claim it was hopeless to try to dissuade them from their ways. Having gone too far to turn back, they condemned themselves. Their obduracy showed how deep-seated their love of idolatry was. What a disheartening response for Jeremiah to receive after all his pleading!

b. The fickleness of Judah (18:13–17)

13 Even the nations around Judah would have to attest to the revolting nature of her acts. Her willfulness in forsaking the Lord was without parallel in the ancient world. The horror is heightened by calling her a virgin. She had been hedged about by the Lord to preserve her sanctity.

14 The snow from Lebanon and cold running water are dependable, but Judah has proved herself fickle in the extreme. Her conduct has been wholly unnatural. Lebanon (lit., "white mountain") has permanent snow cover and so regularly provides moisture. Nature does not change its course, but Judah has. Nature's reliability puts to shame Judah's instability.

15–17 The appalling sin the people committed was idolatry in spite of a clearly defined path for their blessing. They forgot their Lord; they were misled by their false prophets, false priests, and false gods. The nation had lost its way. The "ancient paths" were those of blessing through obeying the Lord (cf. 6:16). The contrast is between a rough track in the country and an elevated causeway. The result of the nation's apostasy will be the desolation of her land. This condition will be so shocking that the land will be "an object of lasting scorn." People will shake their heads at the nation's uncommon stupidity. The Lord himself will scatter the people as the east wind, the sirocco from the desert east-southeast of Palestine. When the Lord says he will show them his back and not his face, he means that his face will be hidden from them. But this is the very treatment Judah has given him (cf. 2:27). God's "face" indicates his favor (Nu 6:24–26).

c. The plot against Jeremiah (18:18–23)

18–19 Unable to tolerate Jeremiah's drastic preaching, the leaders of Judah decided to hound him to death. Their opposition is spelled out: (1) slandering him and turning a deaf ear to his words (v.18), (2) digging a pit for his soul (vv.20, 22), (3) setting snares for his feet (v.22), and (4) planning to slay him (v.23). The very three groups he condemned were in the forefront of the plot against him. They boasted that because they had priests to instruct them in the law, wise elders to counsel them in the affairs of daily living, and (false) prophets to give them the word (supposedly from God), they had no need for Jeremiah. They could not conceive of a time when such ungodly leaders would be unable to fulfill their functions. So their aim now was to silence Jeremiah after they had rejected his message. They were certain that his words would not be fulfilled.

By a charge of treason, the leaders of Judah hoped to effect Jeremiah's downfall. His messages against Judah's policies provided ample basis for accusing him of treason. So he pleaded with the Lord to pay attention to him and to hear his enemies' plots. In so doing, he was using the same words as his foes but now in the affirmative sense. He wanted his prayers answered.

20–23 These verses give Jeremiah's reaction to his enemies' conspiracies against him. His imprecations are best understood in the light of the following: (1) Jeremiah's enemies were not merely personal ones but enemies of God and his truth, and his was not a vindictive cry for personal revenge; (2) life after death and retribution in the afterlife were not clearly revealed in OT times; and (3) Jeremiah delivers the people judicially to the course they have chosen for themselves. What hurt the prophet most was the manner in which his countrymen repaid good with evil. He had only sought their good and had even interceded for them when the Lord forbade him to do so (cf. 14:7–9, 21). Their response is described by the metaphor of digging a pit to trap wild beasts.

Jeremiah's words are admittedly strong, but that is because the leaders of the people had incited them against him, the Lord's prophet. Invaders will do their deadly work, in the wake of which other forms of death will come. Not only will calamity strike people outside the city, but even their own houses will provide them no security. Here is the outcry of the prophet's wounded heart. He realized the depth of the resentment and hatred toward him. Their plans had been concealed, but the Lord knew every secret plot against him.

9. The destruction of Jerusalem (19:1–15)

In ch. 19 we have another of Jeremiah's symbolic acts (cf. 13:1–11). He delivers his message in two places: in the Valley of Hinnom and in the court of the Lord's house; and its theme is the destruction of Judah in that generation.

a. The clay jar at Hinnom (19:1–5a)

1 The Lord commanded Jeremiah to buy a clay jar, one used as a receptacle for water. Because of the jar's narrow neck, it could never be repaired. Jeremiah was to take with him the elders of the people and of the priests to lend solemnity to the occasion. They were probably chosen to go with Jeremiah because they had lived under Josiah's reformation. The prophet was about to act out the final stage of Judah's spiritual hardness. A time inevitably comes when constant opposition to God will result in the people's overthrow. Whereas ch. 18 taught the sovereignty and patience of God, this passage treats the irreversible judgment about to fall on Judah.

2 The prophet was told to go to the Valley of Hinnom by way of the Potsherd Gate. Because of its proximity to the potter's house (18:1) and the dumping of potters' waste outside it, one gate of Jerusalem became known as the Potsherd Gate. It led to the Valley of

Hinnom, which was connected with child sacrifice. Josiah had made the valley a garbage dump for Jerusalem, whose fires constantly smoldered (see comment on 7:30–32).

3–5a Jeremiah's denunciatory words are addressed to the kings and the people. He uses the plural "kings" because the message is not only to the reigning king but to the whole dynasty that was responsible for the apostasy. The place of the calamity is Jerusalem; the disaster will be such that all who hear of it will be stunned. The sins that will bring on the Lord's judgment are then enumerated. By forsaking the Lord and cleaving to idolatry, the people "made this a place of foreign gods." They were making it an alien place by "denationalizing" it so that it appeared no longer Israelite. They had brought many innovations into their idolatry. Moreover, this kind of worship desensitized their moral nature, for they shed the blood of innocent people. One of the most debased forms of idolatry involved child sacrifice. It was practiced in the worship of Baal and Molech (cf. 32:35).

b. The imminent calamity (19:5b–9)

5b–7a By a strong anthropopathism, the Lord indicates that the enormities the nation committed in sacrificing children had never been enjoined on them or spoken of and had never even entered into his mind. It was totally alien to and opposed to his will. For these terrible violations of his law, the Lord would bring down such drastic destruction that the place called "Topheth," or the "Valley of Ben [the Son of] Hinnom," would have its name changed to the "Valley of Slaughter." Because the valley had water, an invading force would besiege it first; and its defenders would suffer casualties in trying to hold it. The Lord would make their plans fall to the earth. He would empty them of wisdom that could shield them and their country from the enemy.

7b–9 The tragic prospect facing the nation included death for the people at the hands of their enemies and consumption of their carcasses by birds and beasts. After the horrors and carnage of war had been perpetrated on the nation, passersby would "scoff" in scorn at the havoc. The word rendered "wounds" is used elsewhere of pestilences and literally means "blows," thus referring to the people's

calamities. The calamity will be so great that the people will be reduced to cannibalism; their distress will overcome natural affection. This prediction was literally fulfilled in 586 B.C., in the Babylonian invasion under Nebuchadnezzar, and again in A.D. 70, when Titus destroyed Jerusalem (cf. Lev 26:29; Dt 28:53–57; 2Ki 6:28–29; La 2:20; 4:10).

c. The destruction of Judah (19:10–13)

10–13 After this message of doom, Jeremiah was commanded to break the jar in the sight of the elders who accompanied him. In the Near East, it is still the practice to break a jar near a person who has done wrong to one and voice the hope that he will be similarly broken. Such an action is intended to bring about the downfall of one's enemies. So Jeremiah was vividly portraying the fate of the nation. The gravity of this act lay in that it not only illustrated the Lord's acts but actually inaugurated them. This was more than dramatization; it was seen as activating the Lord's word of destruction. This explains Pashhur's violent reaction and persecution in 20:1–6. The thrust of Jeremiah's acted oracle was to show the irrevocability of the nation's ruin. They knew of no way to mend a broken jar, which could only be thrown away. So Judah would be rejected because she failed to repent.

In Judah's downfall, the dead would be so numerous that even unclean Topheth would have to be used for their burial. Topheth was a place of uncleanness (cf. 7:31), made such by the detestable idolatry practiced there. So the homes in Jerusalem would be defiled by corpses just as their idolatries had made Topheth even more a place of defilement. Even the roofs of their houses had become places of religious corruption. On their roofs the people worshiped the starry host of heaven, a form of idolatry brought from Mesopotamia, where it had flourished.

d. The message summarized (19:14–15)

14–15 In the court of the temple area, to which the prophet had returned from Hinnom, Jeremiah repeated his message of doom. Its summary gave the meaning of the act he had just carried out. The crisis is pictured as rapidly approaching. The reference to "the villages around it" is probably to Jerusalem and the cities of Judah. The cause of the nation's calamity was the people's stubborn refusal to listen to the Lord's warnings. "Stiff-necked" is a figure taken from unruly oxen who resist the yoke (cf. Ac 7:51).

10. The lament of Jeremiah (20:1–18)

The prophet's symbolic actions in the Valley of Hinnom and his words in the temple court could not have gone unnoticed. This section carries the narrative forward and shows the consequence of what Jeremiah did and said.

a. Pashhur's persecution of Jeremiah (20:1–6)

1 Among the listeners to Jeremiah's words in the temple court was Pashhur, son of Immer, the deputy or executive priest entrusted with the responsibility for maintaining order through the temple police under his charge (he was not the Pashhur referred to in 21:1 and 38:1; cf. 1Ch 9:12). The mention in 29:25–26 of another person in the same position suggests that Pashhur was taken captive to Babylon in 597 B.C. (cf. 2Ki 24:15). The date of the prophecy of ch. 19 might have been the occasion of the Babylonian victory over Egypt at the Battle of Carchemish (605 B.C.). That prophecy may have been the reason Jeremiah was denied access to the temple (cf. 36:1–3). Immer was the sixteenth priestly family that returned to Jerusalem after the Exile (1Ch 24:14). Jeremiah was a threat to the authority of the overseer priest, especially since this priest added prophecy to his duties.

2 Angered beyond control, Pashhur "struck" Jeremiah ("had Jeremiah beaten") with his open hand. This is the first recorded instance of violence done to Jeremiah. Notice that "the prophet" stands in apposition to "Jeremiah," as if to indicate the sacrilege of Pashhur's act. For him Jeremiah's words were intolerable. His ministry was becoming a political threat to those who were supposedly concerned for the nation's security. The "stocks," where the prophet was confined, were intended both for restraint and torture. They held the feet, hands, and neck so that the body was almost doubled up. Jeremiah was put in the stocks at the Upper Benjamin Gate, one of the city's most conspicuous places.

3 The next morning Pashhur released Jeremiah only to find that he had not changed his message; instead he heard words of judgment for the indignity done Jeremiah. While "Pashhur" probably means "ease" or "tranquillity," Jeremiah now gave Pashhur a new name—"Magor-Missabib," meaning "terror on every side." From that time he would be "Mr. Terror All-around." The new name symbolized the terror Pashhur would be to himself and to those about him as a consequence of what the Babylonians would instill in the people of Judah.

4 Jeremiah here interprets the new name. For his opposition to the word of God through his prophet, Pashhur would be exiled to Babylon and die there. This was God's punishment for the calamity he had helped bring on the land by opposing the truth of God. This is the first time in the book that the king of Babylon is specifically mentioned as the conqueror of Judah. That is why some date this prophecy after the Battle of Carchemish (605 B.C.), where Nebuchadnezzar was victorious. When the Exile happened, it would be evident how Pashhur, in misleading the people, was responsible for the disaster. Pashhur's policy would bring judgment on him and on all he had persuaded to follow it.

5–6 Furthermore, Babylonians would plunder the land of its wealth and all its products. Both Pashhur and his family would suffer in the fall of Jerusalem and would die in exile. Apparently Pashhur had not only given the false prophets license to lie but, though a priest, had falsely assumed the prophetic office. For this he was worthy of death. He was probably exiled in 597 B.C. (the captivity of Jehoiachin) because later (29:25–26) Zephaniah had taken over Pashhur's position.

b. Jeremiah's inescapable call (20:7–10)

The remaining verses of this chapter are the last of Jeremiah's so-called confessions and are possibly his saddest and most bitter complaints. At the same time, the passage is one of his most significant self-disclosures. It reveals not only much about the prophet but also about the whole range of canonical prophecy. Nowhere else in Scripture is a prophet's sense of divine compulsion to his mission so clearly expressed. Jeremiah never doubted the reality of his call and never lost his identity under God.

7 The verb "deceived" (GK 7331) is bold and offensive to religious sensibilities. To be sure, Jeremiah is not accusing God of lying or misrepresentation; but what he calls seduction is the divine compulsion on his spirit. He is claiming that the Lord overpersuaded him to be a prophet. He pleads that, though the Lord overcame his resistance to his call (1:4–10) and he believed the Lord's promises, he has now been abandoned to shame. But the Lord had clearly informed Jeremiah of the difficulties he would face (1:18). Understandably, he could not have conceived of the magnitude and viciousness of the opposition, but the Lord had not lied to him. He complains that God had seized and "overpowered" him. This statement shows that God's prophets did not speak by their own will. Jeremiah's message was so unpopular that he was continually being mocked and laughed at—a mockery so blatant because Jeremiah's prophecies were so long in being fulfilled. As the doom of the nation approached, he felt the Lord had overpersuaded him in calling him to the prophetic office when he did not realize all it involved.

8–9 In summary form Jeremiah sets forth the gist of his messages: "violence and destruction." Jeremiah's prophecies were about coming disaster. The burden became so heavy that he finally decided he would no longer serve as a prophet. But he found out the impossibility of denying his call. He learned that it was irreversible and that God's word was irrepressible. Though he aroused opposition from his enemies, he could find no other satisfaction than in preaching God's truth. For Jeremiah the word of God was a reality, not the product of his thinking. It demanded expression in spite of opposition and derision. So great was this compelling force of the revelation that he never doubted its reality.

10 Jeremiah amplifies the reason he was so determined to resign his prophetic office. He includes some of the sayings he has overheard his enemies using. They mimicked him with the phrase "Terror on every side!" Because he had used it so many times, they made it into a nickname. Their plots were intolerable to his sensitive soul. They plotted to report him for treason by beguiling him into unguarded words that could be construed as treasonable. Even his trusted friends waited

for him to make a misstep. During the fourth year of Jehoiakim the die was cast. All Jeremiah could do from this time forward was to seek to alleviate something of the judgment that was certain to come on the nation.

c. Prayer for God's vindication (20:11–13)

11–13 This is Jeremiah's prayer and hymn of praise for the Lord's protection and vindication. This was the hope that encouraged him. A new calm enabled him to withstand all criticism and physical sufferings. His ultimate confidence was the Lord's presence as a warrior striking his foes with dread. Their defeat—never to be forgotten—was as certain as if it had already happened. The Lord, who tests his own and knows all their innermost thoughts, was Jeremiah's champion. Praise bursts forth from his grateful heart as the prophet contemplates the prospect of his ultimate vindication. His circumstances had not changed, but now he could sing for joy.

d. Jeremiah's curse on the day of his birth (20:14–18)

14 This passage is enveloped in gloom and despair, but sudden transitions are frequent in Jeremiah. The transition and contrast are psychologically understandable in view of the constant pressures on Jeremiah. Feeling an utter failure after being in the stocks, he wished he had never been born. The passage is emotionally authentic because he was being prepared for the greatest blow of all—the destruction of the beloved city of Jerusalem. The experience of Jeremiah at this time shows how difficult the task of God's servants can be and how readily available the grace of God is to sustain them in their darkest hours. Jeremiah's response is normal for one caught between two inescapable contrarieties: faithfulness to the message of God and love for one's sinful countrymen.

15–17 Jeremiah's wish that he never had been born is reminiscent of Elijah's cry when pursued by Jezebel after his victory at Mount Carmel (1Ki 19:1–3). But Jeremiah held no real animosity against the man who brought news of his birth; his cry is strictly rhetorical. In the East, the messenger who brings news of a son's birth is usually rewarded. The prophet did not curse his parents, for the law of Moses condemned this (Ex 21:17). The "towns" overthrown by the Lord are Sodom and Gomorrah. The outcry in the morning represents a call for help when under attack—either a shout of alarm or a trumpet blast. Jeremiah goes on to wish his mother's womb had been at once his birthplace and his grave.

18 As the last of Jeremiah's "confessions," this verse portrays the burden he had to bear without interruption. In his outward ministry he never wavered, but his ministry required him to spend himself totally. The "shame" he refers to is that of his inability to avert the catastrophe threatening his people. It is clear that Jeremiah had no revelation of life after death or of the resurrection of the dead. Later, the truth of his predictions was all too evident; so the ridicule against him ceased.

II. Prophecies From the Reigns of Jehoiakim and Zedekiah (21:1–39:18)

A. The Trials and Conflicts of Jeremiah (21:1–29:32)

1. Zedekiah's dilemma (21:1–14)

Chapter 21 moves on to the reign of Zedekiah (597–586 B.C.) and begins a new division of the book. Chapters 21–45 abound in references to time, place, and persons. In particular, chs. 21–23 contain a series of messages Jeremiah delivered during the reigns of Jehoahaz, Jehoiakim, Jehoiachin, and Zedekiah. Likely ch. 21 should be dated 588 B.C., when the Babylonians were advancing against Jerusalem but not yet besieging it at close range. This was the ninth year of Zedekiah's eleven-year rule. The siege lasted one and a half years (cf. 52:1, 4–7).

Chronologically, this chapter should come between chs. 37 and 38. Zedekiah was a vassal king elevated by Nebuchadnezzar (cf. 2Ki 24:17). The uncle of Jehoiachin, Zedekiah respected Jeremiah but did not have the moral courage to do what he knew was right. He was weak and vacillating, and his reign was made all the more difficult because the Jews still considered Jehoiachin (taken captive in 597 B.C.) as their true king and looked for his early return from exile. The personal interplay between Jeremiah and Zedekiah in the years before the fall of Jerusalem is one of the most remarkable features in the book (cf. 37:3–10; 38:14–18). In the unfolding of God's plan, chs. 21–29 are of vital importance be-

cause they foretell "the times of the Gentiles" (Lk 21:24).

a. The embassy from Zedekiah (21:1–7)

1–2 At the approach of the siege of Jerusalem after the Battle of Carchemish between Egypt and Babylon, Zedekiah sent a deputation to Jeremiah. Depending on Pharaoh Hophra of Egypt, Zedekiah had foolishly rebelled against Nebuchadnezzar. Now he was terrified at the desperate situation that his breach of fealty to Nebuchadnezzar had brought on him, and he wanted both Jeremiah's intercession and the Lord's intervention. Zedekiah had more respect for the prophet than Jehoiakim ever had. The members of the deputation were high officials. Pashhur is not the Pashhur referred to at 20:1 but the important official of that name in 38:1. Zephaniah succeeded Jehoiada the priest (29:25–26; 37:3; 52:24) and was second in rank to the high priest. He was slain by Nebuchadnezzar at Riblah; he and Pashhur opposed Jeremiah's views of the political prospects of the nation. Verses 1–2 are a fulfillment of 15:11.

The embassy hoped that Jeremiah would pray for the Lord's intervention by lifting the siege of Nebuchadnezzar. Zedekiah wanted an oracle that would reveal the future, showing, perhaps, that the invader and his army would withdraw from the city and the land. He was evidently thinking of the times of Hezekiah (2Ki 18–19), Jehoshaphat (2Ch 20), and the judges. Zedekiah fully expected deliverance from God, though he uttered no syllable of repentance or desire to do God's will.

3–4 In answer to Zedekiah's request, Jeremiah did not equivocate. Instead of the one oracle Zedekiah desired, God gave him three: one to King Zedekiah (vv.3–7), one to the people (vv.8–10), and one to the royal Davidic house (vv.11–14). For the nation there was no word of hope. The people could expect no help from God in averting the fall of Jerusalem; in fact, the Lord himself would also fight against them. The Babylonians were to conquer them as the instruments of God's judgment; since this is what the invading Babylonians were, it would be impossible to turn them back. All Judah's resistance and all their stratagems would prove useless. The reference to turning the weapons of war against them means that their defense of Jerusalem would fail.

The Babylonians (Chaldeans; see NIV note) were originally a seminomadic tribe living between northern Arabia and the Persian Gulf. In the tenth century B.C., the Assyrians gave the name Kaldu to the area. Later, "Chaldea" was used to include Babylonia as a whole (cf. Eze 23:23; Da 3:8). When the text indicates that the Babylonians were "besieging" them, the meaning is "closing in on you" or "blockading you," because the actual siege had not yet begun. But the defenders would be driven inside the city when they could no longer fight outside it.

5 To compound Judah's misery, the Lord himself was to fight against her; thus it was too late for the request for Jeremiah's intercession. The metaphor of the outstretched hand and mighty arm had been used many times of God's miraculous intervention on Israel's behalf in Egypt. But now it is used to express God's opposition to his people. Their doom was inevitable and their defeat total. Jerusalem would be crowded with refugees who, with their cattle, would have fled from the surrounding areas.

6–7 During a siege, an epidemic is always a threat. A fearful plague would weaken the people. Then the Lord would deliver Zedekiah into the invaders' hands. Slaughter awaited Judah. The prediction about Zedekiah and his court was literally fulfilled in 586 B.C. (cf. 52:9–11, 24–27). The idiom "put them to the sword" means to slay ruthlessly, mercilessly, without quarter. The fate of Zedekiah, his sons, and many Jewish nobles is clear in the OT. Though Zedekiah was not slain, he died of grief in exile as a blinded, deposed monarch.

b. The choice of ways (21:8–10)

8–10 This section is not part of Jeremiah's answer to the king's deputation. It is difficult to determine the time of this message. The setting of "the way of life and the way of death" before the people is reminiscent of the words of Moses (cf. Dt 30:19). Here, however, it refers to escape from physical death in the fall of Jerusalem. Jeremiah's counsel was for the people to submit to Babylon. Total warfare called for unconditional surrender if they were to be spared. To speak of his nation in this way was a difficult duty for Jeremiah,

and it was the reason they called him a traitor. But his motive was more than patriotism; it was the declared will of God. In 38:17–18 Jeremiah also advised giving in to the Babylonians. Again he was charged with treachery, a charge that proved false after the capture of the city when he chose to remain in the devastated land (cf. 40:6).

Though Jeremiah was actually counseling desertion (a form of treason), as a prophet of God he spoke with an authority higher than even that of a king. This made him most unpopular with the nation as a whole, which was in a life-and-death struggle with a powerful invader. Yet some people did take his advice (cf. 39:9; 52:15). All that was promised the nation was bare survival. Those who surrendered would have to realize they would lose everything but their lives. As for Jerusalem itself, it was doomed; the Babylonians, tired of repeated rebellions, would burn it.

c. Exhortation to the Davidic dynasty (21:11–14)

11–12 This message, directed to the royal house, relates to a time when there was still a possibility of escape through repentance and righteous living. The monarch and his court officials were to administer justice in the morning promptly and expeditiously. In the narrower sense, the call was to the king and his family; in the wider sense, to the entire court. It was fitting for Jeremiah to address the royal family because administering justice was the prerogative of the king and not of all. To avoid the heat of the day, court was held in the morning. Even at that late hour deliverance on these godly conditions was not impossible. It is possible that the Lord was not urging righteousness as if the people could escape punishment entirely but as the prerequisite for its mitigation.

13–14 Because of past deliverances (the city had been spared from capture for about two centuries), the people were caught up in a wholly unwarranted confidence in Jerusalem's invincibility. Complacent in their sins, the people asked, "Who can come against us?" The answer was that God would do so in judgment. They could not claim immunity from punishment on any other ground than obedience to God's will. Figuratively, "forests" was used of the royal palace (1Ki 7:2; 10:21). The prophets had a keen eye for natural beauty, and a forest connoted grandeur and stateliness. Thus this reference to forests has been equated with the entire city of Jerusalem.

2. Messages to the Davidic kings (22:1–30)

Once more Jeremiah gives us a cluster of prophecies (chs. 22–23), linked not by chronology but by similar themes. Both the temporal leaders (the kings) and the spiritual leaders (the prophets, apart from Jeremiah) were responsible for the national calamity. In the light of vv.13–18, this chapter, with its oracles about four kings of Judah, appears to belong to Jehoiakim's reign.

a. Exhortation to justice (22:1–9)

1–5 The Lord commanded Jeremiah to go down, evidently from Mount Zion, to the palace south of it. The words were directed to the ruling king and his court and are a strong exhortation to practice justice. The Lord demanded that the Davidic throne make justice its primary responsibility. The king was to be addressed publicly in the midst of his court. There was no question that the sins mentioned were present in the reigns of most Judean kings, but in Jehoiakim's time they were especially rife (cf. 2Ki 23:35). Since God never desires the death of the wicked but wants them to repent and live, the prophet held out blessing for obedience, a blessing that means nothing less than the continued prosperity of the Davidic dynasty, with the people settled securely in the land. On the other hand, the penalty was also specified; namely, desolation of the house of David and of the land. To emphasize the truth and solemnity of the occasion, the Lord swore by himself. There could be no stronger ratification of a declaration from God.

6–9 These four verses give a clear picture of desolation. Gilead and Lebanon in the north are mentioned because they were regions famous for their beautiful forests. Moreover, the cedars of Lebanon were largely used in the construction of Solomon's palace. The cedar columns were like trees of Gilead and Lebanon in their loftiness and magnificence. Those who destroyed this grandeur would be God's instruments of judgment. Even the surrounding nations would realize that the fall of Jerusalem and its palace were the work of the Lord. Furthermore, they would also

know the cause of the judgment. The covenant they violated would not be the Davidic covenant of 2Sa 7 but the initial covenant at Sinai referred to over and over in the earlier portion of the book. The extensive devastation would be a lesson to the nations on the perils of idolatry.

b. The fate of Shallum (Jehoahaz) (22:10–12)

10–12 Jeremiah tells the nation at large that they need not mourn the death of the godly king Josiah, who had been slain at the Battle of Megiddo in 609 B.C. (cf. 2Ki 23:29–35; 2Ch 35:75; Zec 12:11). It had become customary among God's people to sing dirges for departed rulers. But now they were to reserve their weeping for Josiah's son Shallum-Jehoahaz, who was to be forever exiled from the land. The fate of the slain Josiah was better than that of his son who was exiled to Egypt and died there (cf. 2Ki 23:34). Jehoahaz was the first ruler of Judah to die in exile. He took the throne following the tragic death of his father (cf. 1Ch 3:15). This arrangement did not meet the pleasure of Pharaoh Neco, who after three months deposed him and exiled him to Egypt. His older brother Eliakim, whose name Neco changed to Jehoiakim, was chosen by Neco to succeed Jehoahaz. Jehoahaz is contrasted with his father Josiah to highlight the tragic condition of the young king. Mourning would be more in place for him than for his departed father, Josiah.

c. The condemnation of Jehoiakim (22:13–23)

13–14 The prophecy against Jehoiakim is the most scathing of all Jeremiah's messages against kings. Though a son of the godly Josiah, Jehoiakim was the opposite of his father in temperament, action, and attitude toward God. There was constant conflict between the prophet and the king (609–597 B.C.). Jeremiah does not mince matters in stating the enormity of Jehoiakim's injustice and oppression. He mixed injustice with luxury. The building mania, common among Oriental monarchs, had seized him. What aggravated the condition of the nation was that, while he was paying heavy tribute to Neco, Jehoiakim decided to build and beautify his palace by forced, unpaid labor (cf. 2Ki 23:34–35), in direct violation of the law of Moses (cf. Lev 19:13; Dt 24:14–15). The appointments of his palace were sumptuous indeed. Jeremiah's reference to the people as the neighbors of the king shows how God regarded the sovereign-subject relationship in Israel.

15–16 Jehoiakim is contrasted with his father, Josiah. Scathingly, Jeremiah asks Jehoiakim whether building palaces of cedar made him a king. He had mistaken fine buildings as the mark of a true king. A splendid commendation of Josiah, who held to true values, follows. He enjoyed the normal comforts of life but never made ostentation his goal. He knew how to enjoy life without extortion or oppression. He was no ascetic but did not make it his ambition to rival Solomon in building. For Josiah to do justice and righteousness was food and drink. Therefore, he received the blessing and commendation of God. His deeds reflected true kingly piety, namely, to love God so much that he would not allow any of his subjects to be neglected in their hour of need. Fellowship with God is evidenced in social justice.

17 But Jehoiakim had a contrary spirit, and with splendid irony Jeremiah points out what Jehoiakim excelled in. His motivation was covetousness. This led him to practice oppression and extortion in order to pile up dishonest gain. Finally, he did not stop at "shedding innocent blood," which may mean that Jehoiakim persecuted innocent persons after rendering unjust decisions on them or that he had them slain (see 26:20–23).

18–19 Following this exposure of Jehoiakim's evil ways, the intrepid prophet tells him of the disgraceful death that awaited him; there would be no mourning for Jehoiakim. The references to brother and sister show by parallelism that his kin would not grieve for him, nor would he be lamented by subjects or friends. He would be buried without any royal funeral ceremonies (cf. 2Ch 35:24–25). But most shocking of all, Jehoiakim would be buried with a donkey's burial; his body would be left to the beasts and birds (cf. 36:30). He would be thrown outside the gates of Jerusalem, as though to ensure that he would no longer pollute the city in death as he had done in life. He died in 597 B.C.

20 This section probably is to be dated 597 B.C. Jeremiah calls on his contemporaries to mourn the disastrous results brought on the land by the foolish international policy of Jehoiakim. The occasion was probably the eve of Nebuchadnezzar's expedition against Judah. The regions mentioned—Lebanon, Bashan, and Abarim—represent the land in its entirety, from north to northeast to southeast. The invaders would overrun the whole land. Abarim refers to the regions beyond the Jordan, i.e., the mountains of Moab, east of the Dead Sea (cf. Nu 27:12; Dt 32:49). Likely the "allies" (lit., "lovers," "paramours"; GK 170) were Egypt and the other nations Jehoiakim relied on for aid against the Babylonians, because of the contrast with the nation's leaders—"your shepherds."

21–23 Jeremiah emphasizes the nation's practice of disobedience. The people all persisted in their willfulness in spite of God's blessing on them in times of prosperity ("when you felt secure"). The winds of adversity and invasion would carry off their leaders and allies alike. "You who live in Lebanon" refers to the king and his nobles in their cedar palaces. Jerusalem considered herself secure, like the eagles nesting in the cedars of Lebanon (cf. 21:13).

d. The rejection of Coniah (Jehoiachin) (22:24–30)

24–27 Coniah is the abbreviated form of Jeconiah, an alternate form of Jehoiachin. The son and successor of Jehoiakim, Jehoiachin was exiled in Babylon in 597 B.C. (cf. 2Ki 24:8–17; 25:27–30), after a reign of three months. Coniah's full name (Jeconiah) means "the LORD will establish," but permanence and stability were not his portion because of his wickedness. His punishment was mitigated after thirty-seven years (52:31–34).

The signet of a king was very valuable because it was used to authenticate official correspondence and documents. Jeremiah declared that even if Jehoiachin was as dear to God as a signet ring on God's right hand (and he was not), he would be torn off for his misdeeds. Jehoiachin and his mother (Nehushta [2Ki 24:8]) would suffer exile and die in Babylon, despite the promises of the false prophets (cf. 52:31–34). Both were taken to Babylon and never returned.

28–29 As though this fate was not enough, Jeremiah predicts severe judgment into the distant future. The questions show Jehoiachin's rejection by the Lord. They expected affirmative answers, but Jeremiah's concern was for the Davidic line rather than for Jehoiachin personally. He is likened to a broken earthenware pot, undesirable and worthless. His descendants are mentioned because children were born to him in captivity. There was apparently a desire to restore Jehoiachin from Babylon to replace Zedekiah (cf. 28:11; 29:1–32). Before he makes a final pronouncement on Jehoiachin, Jeremiah calls three times on the "land" to hear the word of the Lord. The whole nation was to be impressed by the fate of Jehoiachin.

30 The command to "record" (GK 4180) relates to a register of citizens (cf. Isa 4:3), i.e, a census list. Jehoiachin had seven sons (cf. 1Ch 3:17), but none succeeded him on the throne. Matthew's genealogy (1:12) includes Jehoiachin but shows only who Jesus' legal father was, not his natural one. Zerubbabel, grandson of Jehoiachin, though governor of Judah in 520 B.C., never ruled as king, nor did any other descendant of his. Jehoiachin's uncle, Zedekiah, reigned after him but died before him (cf. 52:10–11). Jehoiachin was thus the last of the Judean kings. In him the royal line became extinct. So ch. 23 goes on to speak of the new King to be raised up by the Lord (cf. 23:5–6).

3. Messiah the King (23:1–40)

This chapter is linked to Jeremiah's denunciation of the godless kings of Judah. The three already mentioned in ch. 22 are included along with Zedekiah. The date is probably in the time of Zedekiah's reign, which may also account for the fact that of the five monarchs (including godly Josiah) he is not mentioned by name (cf. Eze 34:1–6).

a. Godless leaders versus David's Righteous Branch (23:1–8)

1–2 The "shepherds" (GK 8286) on whom Jeremiah pronounced woe were not only kings but all the leaders of Judah—the civil leaders and the spiritual leaders (the prophets and priests). In Zedekiah's reign the court officials exercised inordinate influence on policy because of his weakness (cf. 38:5). The leaders were guilty of gross dereliction of duty. By oppression and shedding innocent blood, they destroyed the flock; those who were not destroyed were scattered to wander without protection. So the leaders were guilty of the very things the shepherds were charged with preventing. By leading the nation into idolatry, and so into the Babylonian captivity, the leaders had scattered the people. Moreover, contrary to the duty of shepherds to lead and feed the flock, they had driven the flock away. The doom on the people would not leave their leaders unscathed.

3–4 Just as the scattering of the people was literal, so also would the regathering be. The promise of restoration presupposes the Exile. The return from dispersion had already been announced in 3:15–18. Now it is God himself who does the work of the true shepherd, regathering his sheep from all countries. A world-wide dispersion is in view, not just in Assyria and Babylon. What the shepherds did in driving the people away is now attributed to the Lord because he ultimately carried out the penalty brought on them by their own sins and by the sins of their leaders (shepherds). The people would be returned to their own pasture. Moreover, God would replace the faithless shepherds with faithful ones. They would rule in godliness under the ideal King. The fulfillment of this prophecy awaits eschatological times (cf. Mt 19:28). The hour when assured peace will be Israel's and none will be missing or lost has not yet come.

5 The reference to good shepherds leads on to a prediction of the Messiah, the Davidic King par excellence. Though Jeremiah has few direct references to the messianic King, this is surely such an instance. The formula "days are coming" is a messianic formula; Jeremiah uses it to direct special attention to what is stated. In contrast to the troublous times of Jeremiah's day, there will be a time of blessing ahead. The promise is centered in David in view of the covenant in 2Sa 7:8–16.

After Jeremiah has denounced the faithless shepherds of the nation and has predicted the coming of good shepherds, he describes as a climax the incomparable rule of the King Messiah, the "Branch" (GK 7542). This designation has much in common semantically with "seed" (Ge 3:15), the Davidic "son" (2Sa 7), and the "servant of the LORD" (Isa 42–53). In each case there is a general reference to a number of individuals; but by a process of strict selection and narrowing down, the seed, the son, and the servant ultimately find highest fulfillment in the Lord Jesus, the Messiah, "the Seed of the Woman," "the Son of David," and "the Servant of the LORD." The Lord was thus superintending the historical process in such a way that his ultimate choice unmistakably was Jesus of Nazareth.

It is clear that the term "Branch" is symbolic of the Messiah because the adjective modifying it is a quality of persons and not plants. The shoot or sprout is a scion of the stock of David. "Branch" has a collective meaning when used horticulturally but not when used symbolically. Furthermore, the collective sense cannot be permitted here because (1) "a King who will reign" cannot refer to a number of kings; (2) "The LORD Our Righteousness" cannot speak of a series of monarchs; and (3) the parallel passages refer to one person (cf. 30:9; Eze 31:23–24; 37:24; for the use of Branch for the Messiah, cf. Isa 4:2; Jer 33:15; Zec 3:8; 6:12). Moreover, he will reign as a true king, not as a puppet like Zedekiah and his immediate predecessors. He will execute justice and righteousness like his ancestor David (cf. 2Sa 8:15). In contrast to the inequities and injustices common to the Davidic kings, the Messiah's reign will be the opposite.

6 Now Jeremiah dilates on the benefits that will come to Messiah's people from his reign. First, he will rule over a reunited nation; both Judah and Israel will be restored (cf. Eze 37:19). Second, he will bring salvation to his people. The verb "saved" (GK 3828) denotes spiritual deliverance. Third, peace and security will characterize Messiah's righteous rule.

Much diversity of opinion surrounds the interpretation of the last half of v.6. Does it refer to the nation as a whole (cf. 33:16)? That it is a symbolic surname (not for actual use but as an ideal inscription or objective characterization) seems apparent. This King who is "The LORD Our Righteousness" will be righteousness in actuality. Some see here the name of the Messiah and that of none other. It would, they believe, be totally out of keeping with the context for Jeremiah to be speaking of a Davidic descendant and then without warning or preparation to turn to a name for Jerusalem. The Jews also understood the name to be that of the Messiah.

7–8 That which is directly and inseparably related to the messianic hope is the national restoration of Israel (cf. 16:14–15). The future restoration of the people will exceed anything in the past. It will surpass the deliverance from Egypt. The Exodus will pale into insignificance in comparison with the future ingathering of the nation from worldwide dispersion. The inauguration of the new Exodus cannot be equated with the return of Israel under Cyrus in the last part of the sixth century B.C. (cf. Isa 11:11–12).

b. Condemnation of the false prophets (23:9–12)

9 The remainder of this chapter gives Jeremiah's classic denunciation of the false prophets. Because the tension between Jeremiah and the false prophets was greatest during Zedekiah's reign, this section may well be dated from that reign. The false prophets' characteristics were that (1) they used God's name without authorization, (2) they were of low moral character, (3) they spread false hopes and promises among the people, (4) the source of their messages was their own minds or those of other false prophets, and (5) they were never called of God. Other prophets also denounced these misleaders of the people (cf. Isa 28:7–13; Eze 13:1–16; Mic 3:5–12). Jeremiah did not take his condemnation of the false prophets lightly. It cost him tremendous emotional and physical stress. Next to the ungodly kings, they were those most responsible for bringing about the nation's ruin. He was disturbed and shocked at the enormity of their offenses and was so overcome with the trauma of it that he could only liken himself to a drunken man. Jeremiah showed no vindictiveness against those who tried to nullify his life's work, only heartbrokenness. When he contrasted their evil ways and words with the holy words of God, it was more than he could contemplate without deep agony of soul.

10 As always, immorality directly leads to godlessness. The influence of the false prophets on the nation was totally evil; the people followed the evil ways of their leaders. The adultery referred to is not just the spiritual unfaithfulness of breaking the covenant with God but the gross immorality of these

godless men, whose ways could never lead to repentance. The curse on violation of the laws of God was manifest in a drought. Their use of their power was perverted. Only in doing wrong were they strong.

11–12 Furthermore, the false prophets had accomplices—the priests. Instead of drawing the people to God, the priests were part of the national corruption. Their wickedness reached into the house of God itself; it was either greed like that of Eli's sons or idolatry as in Manasseh's day (cf. 1Sa 2:12–17, 22; 2Ki 21:5; 23:12; Eze 8:6, 10, 14, 16). The penalty for such sin would be spiritual blindness. "Slippery paths" symbolizes the punishment of falling into perilous life situations. The imagery of darkness parallels 13:16.

c. False prophecy in Samaria and Jerusalem (23:13–15)

13–15 The prophets of the northern kingdom (Samaria) were devoted to Baal and seduced the people from worshiping God. The prophets of the southern kingdom were worse, having learned nothing from the sinful deeds and tragic consequences of their counterparts in the north. The Samaritan prophets prophesied by a false god, but the Jerusalem prophets were misusing God's name and committing moral outrages. Polluted by adultery, advocating idolatry, living in immorality, and being indifferent to good and encouraging evil, they hardened the nation against repentance. The Jerusalem prophets had no influence for godliness. In God's sight all the people of Jerusalem had become as bad as those of Sodom and Gomorrah, and the prophets were the instigators. God's only recourse was to punish the prophets, and this he declares in unequivocal terms. Because they had poisoned the nation's spiritual springs, the Lord would inflict drastic judgment on them—portrayed by "bitter food" ("wormwood"; i.e., strong smelling and bitter tasting) and "poisoned water."

d. Characteristics of lying prophecy (23:16–22)

16–17 The false prophets' messages originated with them and thus lacked any real authority (cf. v.18). When they deceived the people with empty hopes by self-devised messages, they showed that their words had

not come from the mouth of the Lord. The heart of false prophecy was that it always held out false hope. Therefore the false prophets led the sinning nation into false security that prevented moral transformation. Because they continually denied any future evil or calamity, they could be called "success prophets." Their messages of peace and prosperity at any price marked them out as false. True prophets were burdened by necessary messages of doom (cf. 28:8–9).

18 According to Eastern custom, ministers or royal servants remained standing during deliberations. Standing in the council of the Lord pictures a group of friends in close consultation (cf. Ps 25:14). The council concept was an integral part of monotheism and was based on the Lord's desire to share his truth with his trusted servants. The reason for the false prophets' corruption was that they had not gone to the fountainhead for their message. Anyone who had had intimate dealings with the Lord could not follow the ways of the lying prophets (cf. v.22).

19–20 The tempest of the divine wrath was soon to burst upon the impenitent wicked. When that judgment finally fell, there would be no mistaking the Lord's intention. The force of the phrase "in days to come" is that when the judgment finally came, events would show the nation the truth of Jeremiah's words and warnings.

21–22 Because Jeremiah's message was relentlessly opposed by the false prophets, he had to express God's displeasure against them and their deceitful works. He showed clearly that no prophet of God can ever derive his message from observing the times he lives in. Graphically, Jeremiah points out how the words of the lying prophets were wholly unauthorized. Their call was merely from themselves. They never received a divine commission (cf. v.32); yet they ran, with their false messages, eagerly and energetically trying to accomplish their own objectives. No words could more emphatically state the falsity of their lives and ministry. On the other hand, if they had been in the intimate circle where God divulges his plans to his faithful followers, i.e., in his council, they would have uttered God's truth to his needy people. The result would have been the repentance of the nation and their restoration to godliness. A proof of the true prophet was his desire to win others to the way of godliness in which he himself was walking. The results of his ministry were indicators of the genuineness of his call and message.

e. Lying versus true prophets (23:23–32)

23–24 The questions in this section are meant to point out that the Lord cannot be circumscribed as though the false prophets could escape his notice. God is not a localized deity whom it is easy to avoid; he is inescapable (cf. Ps 139:7–10). God is both immanent and transcendent, omniscient and omnipresent. The false prophets cannot hide from God's judgment. An omnipresent and omniscient God cannot be deceived and has surely heard the lies of the false prophets.

25–26 This section contains a strong contrast between dreams and the word of God. Jeremiah is not denying that dreams were a legitimate method of divine revelation. But some of the false prophets relied on their dreams as the origin of their inspiration, a channel of revelation easily abused and counterfeited. The deceivers knew just how to trick the gullible, but the omniscient Lord was aware of their lies.

27–29 The impunity of the falsifiers would not last. They were having the same baneful effect on the contemporaries of Jeremiah as Baal worship had had on an earlier generation. When the lying prophets prophesied, the Lord was banished from the hearts of the nation. The truth of God and mere dreams were so different in essence that they had to be kept separate. If a prophet had a dream, he was to relate it as a dream and nothing more. Words of the false prophets have no value; those of the true messengers of God are as wheat, as food for believers. So Jeremiah then presents the qualities of the true word. In contrast to the useless, powerless words of the false prophets, God's truth is like fire. It is penetrating and purifying, and it consumes evil (cf. 5:14; 20:9). Moreover, God's word is full of power like a hammer strongly wielded. His message does not lull people in their sins; it crushes the heart to bring it to repentance. The true word convicts and converts; it neither amuses nor entertains.

30–32 Jeremiah describes three classes of false prophets. Three times he declares that

the Lord is against the false prophets (each verse begins with a statement of the opposition of God to the godless seers). The first group misappropriate the prophecies of the true prophets, giving them out as their own. To their lies they add plagiarism; their words were not original but stolen from others. A second group are accused of using their tongues as the main weapon in their deceptions. They "wag" them to introduce their lies by the formula of the true prophets: "The LORD declares." They did this to give their words a ring of authenticity. The last group held national interests paramount. Their word—true or not—must lift national morale. No wonder the prophet refers to their speech as empty talk.

f. The burden of the Lord (23:33–40)

33–34 There is here a play on the word "oracle" (*massa*; GK 5363). In its main meaning, *massa* comes from the verb "to lift, lift up"; thus it denotes a "burden" in the physical sense. By usage, however, the word came to mean that which was placed as a burden on the heart of a prophet, having already been such on the heart of God. Thus it referred to a threatening prediction or "oracle." Jeremiah indicates that the people, the priests, and the prophets had begun to use this important word mockingly and derisively. They would ask Jeremiah, "What is the oracle [burden] now?" The answer to the question in KJV and NASB is stated either as "What burden?" or "What burden!" NIV has "What oracle?" The LXX, Vulgate, and NRSV translate it, "You are the burden!" Not only were the lying prophets the burden, but the Lord immediately indicated that he would unburden himself of them. The word of God is ultimately not the burden on them, but they are a burden to the Lord.

35–37 Moreover, because the false prophets derisively called the word of the Lord a burden, when they themselves were a constant burden to him, the word "oracle" ("burden") was forbidden them. Since they misused the word, they were no longer to use it in their prophecies. So Jeremiah's contention was that, since all the prophets of his day were using this phrase in their oracles, such frequent and overdone usage destroyed the force of the words. Their use showed irreverence and impenitence. Interestingly, though the term "oracle" was used by canonical prophets, Jeremiah never used it of his own prophecies because it had become the hallmark of the lying prophets. Punishment would now follow their use of the word. Jeremiah even points out how they should inquire about a message from God. There were clear alternatives to "oracle" ("burden") they could use. What lying prophets spoke in jest would be found to be heavy indeed. Their mockery of the word would weigh them down and crush them. This was the penalty for misusing that word for their own purposes.

38–40 The last three verses of the chapter deal with the penalty for ignoring the Lord's admonition. The result of the false prophets' pointless mockery of God's oracles against them would be that they would live to fulfill them. False prophecy had assumed such proportions that drastic measures had to be taken to eliminate it. The horrifying prospect of being utterly forgotten of God loomed before the lying prophets.

4. The good and the bad figs (24:1–10)

This chapter belongs to the same period as chs. 22 and 23, namely, in the reign of Zedekiah. Its date is fairly well indicated by the chronological reference in v.1. The time was after Nebuchadnezzar had deported Jeconiah and his skilled laborers to Babylon in 597 B.C. Ezekiel was included in this captivity, which carried off the better element of the nation, those who would be useful to Nebuchadnezzar in his building projects and would not participate in a siege against his invading forces (cf. 2Ki 24:14–16).

a. The vision of the baskets of figs (24:1–3)

1–3 The purpose of the vision was to declare that those who went into exile with Jehoiachin would be better off than those left behind in Jerusalem; those who escaped the deportation would naturally think just the opposite. The emphasis is on the poor caliber of leadership left in Judah in contrast to the able men now in Babylon (cf. 52:28). Fig trees in Palestine produce fruit three times a year. The first-ripe figs are especially juicy and are considered a delicacy; they ripen in June (cf. Isa 28:4; Hos 9:10). The question the Lord asked Jeremiah was meant to focus attention on the vision and its explanation.

One of the most common trees in ancient Palestine was the fig tree, bearing its fruit.

b. The explanation of the good figs (24:4–7)

4–7 This passage identifies the good figs and holds out some comprehensive promises of future blessing: (1) constant prosperity from the Lord, (2) restoration to their own land, (3) permanent establishment in that land, and (4) spiritual turning to the Lord in genuine conversion. The passage says that the good figs are the exiles of 597 B.C. under Jehoiachin. The word "good" refers to the exiles' circumstances (they were not taken to Babylon for their piety and goodness). But the Lord promised that he would look with favor on them, which was manifested in their exemption from the horrors of the fall of Jerusalem in 586 B.C. and in their being cured of idolatry. These exiles prospered in Babylon (cf. 2Ki 25:27–30; Jer 29:4–7), and the influence of men like Daniel must have helped them. Jeremiah's evaluation of them was the exact opposite of the opinion prevalent among the people of the land. To them, the very fact that they had escaped exile was an evident token of God's favor to them.

After purification in Babylon, the exiles would return, whereas those left in Jerusalem would be slain at the destruction of the city. What appeared in 597 B.C. to be all disaster, the Lord would overrule for good. Jeremiah was right: the future of the nation lay with its exiled portion. Physical restoration to the land would be followed by spiritual renewal. God foretold their reinstatement into the original covenant (cf. 31:31–34)—an event in the distant future.

c. The meaning of the bad figs (24:8–10)

8 The bad figs represent Zedekiah and his courtiers, and for them a bleak future is prophesied. Those who remained with Zedekiah were yet to be scattered in disgrace. The reference to those living in Egypt could be the Jews who were deported with Jehoahaz to Egypt by Pharaoh Neco (cf. 2Ki 23:31–34). Or perhaps they were emigrants who were opposed to the Babylonian domination of Judah or who fled to Egypt at the first approach of Nebuchadnezzar. Archaeological research reveals that those who remained in Egypt set up a rival temple; the Elephantine Papyri confirm a Jewish colony with a temple in Egypt before 525 B.C.

9–10 The doom awaiting the Jews in Judah and Egypt is detailed. The new exiles would witness the same privations as the previous ones had. The people had failed to repent. Those left behind became more hardened in their wickedness. The broad prediction in v.9 surely looks beyond the imminent Babylonian exile to a worldwide dispersion. The prophecy of v.10 was fulfilled in part in the fall of Jerusalem in Nebuchadnezzar's day (cf. Dt 28:25, 37) but more so in the siege of Jerusalem by the Roman emperor Titus in A.D. 70 (cf. Mt 23:38).

5. Prophecy of the Babylonian captivity (25:1–38)

In 605 B.C., the Babylonians defeated the Egyptians at the Battle of Carchemish, thus bringing to an end the domination of Palestine by Pharaoh Neco of Egypt. This decisive battle affected the course of history in western Asia. Through it Jeremiah was enabled by the Lord to see the working out of the divine purposes of judgment on Judah. Not only is ch. 25 important historically, geographically, and prophetically; it is also remarkable for the abundance of its ideas, the variety of its figures, and the diversity of its style in treating the same theme of sin, repentance, and judgment.

a. Israel's rejection of the prophetic ministry (25:1–7)

1 This prophecy is precisely dated to show its extraordinary significance. The fourth year of Jehoiakim synchronizes with the first year of Nebuchadnezzar (cf. 36:1; 45:1; 46:2), i.e., 605 B.C. This verse and Da 1:1 are not in con-

flict. Archaeology has shown that there were two methods of chronological reckoning in the Near East—by accession year and by nonaccession year. Judah used the first method; Babylon, the second.

The first year of Nebuchadnezzar marked his first invasion of Judah with his allies (cf. 2Ki 24:1–2). It also began an important era in redemption history—"the times of the Gentiles" (cf. Lk 21:24)—because his reign began the succession of the four great kingdoms that exercised world dominion (cf. Da 2; 7). The emphasis in vv.1–7 rests on Israel's continued disobedience. Jeremiah's purpose was to lead the nation to reconsider her past sinful ways and to alert her to the future. The Lord's patience with Israel had at last been exhausted.

2–7 That Jeremiah could address "all" in Jerusalem and Judah shows that he was still able to move about freely and speak publicly (cf. 36:1, 5, 26). It must have been sad for him to look back on twenty-three years of faithful ministry for the Lord and then to have to pronounce it a failure as far as Judah was concerned. Nineteen years under Josiah and four under Jehoiakim (Jehoahaz and Jehoiachin ruled only three months each) did not suffice to turn Judah to repentance; she would not hear. It was now about the middle of Jeremiah's career (cf. 1:2–3), and more difficult days lay ahead. Moreover, in his grace the Lord had sent other godly prophets contemporary with Jeremiah to warn Judah of the impending disaster (Uriah, Zephaniah, and Habakkuk). The heart of the message of all true prophets was the appeal to God, lest the nation jeopardize the blessings of God and the privilege of living in the Promised Land. Above all, the people were repeatedly exhorted to forsake the senseless worship of idols; but their response was always the same—persistent obstinacy.

b. Prediction of the Exile (25:8–11)

8–9 Because of Israel's determined disobedience, the Lord had his agent of judgment ready to inflict the merited judgment. That agent was Nebuchadnezzar and his followers. The reference to "peoples of the north" is probably to the Babylonians in general. Nebuchadnezzar is designated three times as the Lord's "servant" (here; 27:6; 43:10), which shows the magnitude of the work committed to him (cf. Isa 44:28; 45:1). As the Lord's instrument, he was to execute the divine plan for Judah and the nations. He was unconsciously doing God's will by devoting whole populations to destruction.

10–11 Specifically, Jeremiah points out the domestic effects of invasion. Normal life would be totally disrupted, and the land would be shorn of its inhabitants. All joy and domestic work would go. Sounds of normal human activity would cease. In v.11, Jeremiah for the first time indicates the duration of the captivity in Babylon—seventy years (cf. 29:10). Most who take the number of years to be precise—namely, from the fourth year of Jehoiakim (the first year of Nebuchadnezzar) to the end of the Babylonian dynasty with the coming of Cyrus (cf. 2Ch 36:21–22; Ezr 1:1–3)—hold that the reckoning must be precise because Daniel (cf. 9:1–2) went to Babylon with the first deportation and knew that he had been there seventy years. Furthermore, the number of years involved in the period of the seventy heptads of years in Da 9:24–27 is based on the years of the Captivity.

Defenders of the precise period of seventy years offer a choice between 605 B.C. (or 606) and 536 B.C., when resettlement took place under Zerubbabel and Joshua; or 586 B.C., the beginning of the Babylonian captivity, and 516 B.C., the year of the completion of Zerubbabel's temple. The former appears more tenable in view of the period of the three deportations, dating from Jehoiakim's reign to Jehoiachin's to Zedekiah's.

c. Judgment on Babylon (25:12–14)

12–14 The same divine principles that worked against Judah's sin would also be effective against Babylon. Its rule was terminated by the Medes and Persians under Cyrus (c. 536–535 B.C.). The threat of everlasting desolation probably looks beyond the near future to a far-distant day. Babylon was not to be punished for carrying out God's will but for her own sins (cf. 50:11–13; Isa 13:19). God used Babylon, not because of her merit, but because of Israel's sin. Verse 14 indicates that Babylon would receive retribution in kind (cf. 50:29; 51:24). The "many nations" and "great kings" refer to the Medes and Persians with their many allies or tributary kings under Cyrus the Great. They

would impose forced labor on the once-invincible Babylonians.

d. The cup of God's wrath (25:15–29)

15–16 This powerful passage records a message about God's wrath on Judah and the nations. It is not that the nations would be given a potion to help them endure the force of God's fury but that the cup symbolizes his wrath. As the agent of God's fury, Nebuchadnezzar would be victorious over the nations. There is no need to believe that Jeremiah actually took a cup and went to these nations, because stupefying judgments are figured here. The cup is a common figure in Scripture to signify God's wrath (cf. 49:12; 51:7; Jn 18:11; Rev 14:8, 10; 16:19; 18:6; et al.). With the mention of the sword, fact replaces the figure. The horrors of war would drive the nations mad.

17–18 But how did Jeremiah take the cup and make all the nations drink it? The cup is not a physical cup but the wrath of God, and the drinking is not physical. Jeremiah declared the Lord's judgment on the nations through Babylon as his instrument. The roster of the nations that would suffer judgment began with Jerusalem and Judah. All the nations named in chs. 46–51 except Damascus are included. The list runs from south to north, from Egypt to Persia. The kings of Judah include Jehoiakim, Jehoiachin, and Zedekiah. The sins of Judah and her kings had been most offensive to God because Judah was so highly privileged. So they are the first to be mentioned. The words "as they are today" may have been inserted by Jeremiah after the fulfillment of the prophecy.

19–22 Egypt is listed after Judah because Pharaoh Neco instigated the alliance against the Babylonians. "All the foreign people" have been understood as being the mercenaries who joined the Egyptian forces, or foreigners in general, or some of the Egyptians of mixed blood. Uz (cf. Job 1:1) was east or northeast of Edom. The Philistine pentapolis, except for Gath, is mentioned next; by this time it had lost its importance (cf. 2Ch 26:6; Am 6:2). Jeremiah speaks of the remnant of Ashdod because that city was destroyed by Psammetik I (663–609 B.C.) after a siege of twenty-nine years. Ashdod was rebuilt in Nehemiah's day (Ne 13:23). Edom, Moab, and Ammon, all blood relations of Israel, were in Transjordania. The main Phoenician cities, Tyre and Sidon, are named as objects of Babylon's wrath. The coastlands were the Phoenician colonies in the Mediterranean, which some have identified with Cyprus.

23–25 The Lord's judgment moves on to other nations. Now northern Arabian tribes are mentioned. Dedan, a son of Abraham by Keturah, lived southeast of Edom (cf. Ge 25:3). Tema was a son of Ishmael (cf. Ge 25:15; Job 6:19). Buz represents a tribe descended from Nahor, brother of Abraham (cf. Ge 22:21). "All who are in distant places" are the Bedouins of the Arabian desert (cf. 9:26; 49:23). They are followed by the inhabitants of the portion of Arabia contiguous to Palestine. The "foreign people" may refer to many tribes of Arabia that had intermarried with Cushite elements. The location of Zimri is unknown. Perhaps Zimri is to be connected with Zimran, a son of Abraham by Keturah (cf. Ge 25:2). He lived in a region between Arabia and Persia. Elam and Media were lands east of the Tigris River. The first was northeast of the Persian Gulf, about 200 miles east of Babylon, and is here representative of all Persia. It was known as Elymais by the Greeks. Media was north and west of Persia. The arm of Babylon was to reach afar to the Caspian Sea, ultimately encompassing a worldwide dominion (cf. Da 2:38; 4:22).

26 Finally Jeremiah reaches the culminating point of the prophecy—the judgment of "Sheshach." This name occurs only in Jeremiah. Following Jerome, many hold that the name is a cryptogram (code) that stands for Babylon (see NIV note). The technical name for this type of cipher is Atbash, a system of secret writing that substituted the last letter of the Hebrew alphabet for the first, the next to the last for the second, and so through all the Hebrew consonants (cf. v.12; 51:1, 41, where the Chaldeans are meant under "Leb Kamai"). Sheshach has three consonants in Hebrew. By substituting *sh* = *b* (twice) and *ch* (or *k*) = *l*, we get *bbl*, the Hebrew consonants for Babylon (GK 951). The phrase "after all of them" indicates that Babylon's judgment too will come finally. Jeremiah may have resorted to the code name while Nebuchadnezzar was at the gates of Jerusalem.

27–29 This passage underscores the inevitability of the judgment Jeremiah has been describing. The same divine governmental principles apply to the other nations just as they do to Israel. The meaning of the cup metaphor is set forth. In a series of staccato commands, the Lord addresses all the aforementioned nations. They must be reduced to utter helplessness. Should any nation be so foolish as to seek to resist the will of God through Babylon, it will be futile. With irresistible logic God asks, as it were, "If Israel suffers, will you nations escape?" It will be impossible for any people to escape destruction for their sins (cf. Eze 9:6; 1Pe 4:17).

e. Judgment on all the world (25:30–38)

30–33 Turning from the metaphor of the cup, Jeremiah uses the metaphor of the lion. Like a lion's roar, the Lord's voice sounds from heaven against his own fold—the Holy Land and its people. Again, judgment begins with Judah. Suddenly the imagery shifts to a vintage scene, which was always attended with shouts of rejoicing. The shouting symbolizes a war cry; here it becomes the shout of the Lord treading down the nations (cf. Isa 63:3; Rev 14:19–20; 19:15). The noise is like the trampling of an army; it is the crash of war. Again changing the figure, Jeremiah portrays a lawsuit in which God is both prosecutor and judge of all the nations. Then he takes another metaphor of judgment from nature, namely, that of a tempest (i.e., Nebuchadnezzar). Nation after nation will fall under the domination of Babylon. Then in plain prose Jeremiah describes the appalling scene of the multitudes of unburied dead.

34–38 Jeremiah returns three times to the shepherd metaphor for the leaders of the nation. In each instance the shepherds are called "leaders of the flock," in short, the elite of the nation. They are to weep, wail, and cover themselves as thickly with dust as though they had rolled in it. The hour of reckoning has come so that only slaughter and dispersion remain for them. Jeremiah, great writer that he is, moves from the figure of a flock of sheep to that of "fine pottery" smashed by a fall. Flight from the calamity will be out of the question. The leaders will be inconsolable because with the decimation of the flock their pastures will be destroyed. Even the peaceful land will suffer the ravages of the

Lord's anger. As a lion abandons a den that has been destroyed, so the Lord will abandon his own land after he has devastated it with the sword of the oppressive invader.

6. Consequences of the temple address (26:1–24)

Chapters 26–45 combine incidents in the life of Jeremiah. Some are autobiographical; others are biographical. This chapter gives us the setting of the temple address (7:1–20). The affinities between chs. 7 and 26 are too many and too minute for them not to relate to the same address. Here the emphasis is on the results of the temple address and on a brief summary of it. The heart of the temple address was that unless Judah repented, Jerusalem would be as Shiloh. By his specific warnings, Jeremiah had incurred the wrath of the false prophets and their followers. And later on when he predicted the seventy years' captivity, they tried to bring about his death.

a. The temple address (26:1–6)

1–3 The Lord gave the prophet specific orders as to where and when he would address the nation and what he would say to them. The date is chronologically earlier than that of 25:1, most likely being the beginning of Jehoiakim's reign with his accession year (609–608 B.C.).

To give the greatest publicity to his message, Jeremiah was charged to stand in the outer court, where the people assembled. It was doubtless a feast day when the people from the towns of Judah came together for worship. Furthermore, Jeremiah was not to omit a word of his message for fear of the consequences of his preaching. Nor was he to trim it to suit the feelings of his hearers. Notice how the words "perhaps ... each will turn from his evil way" show that repentance is always an individual matter. Predictions of divine judgment are conditional. True repentance on the part of the people of Judah before the hour of doom would have been met by God's willingness to relent from his threatened punishment.

4–6 Here we have a kind of summary of the longer address in ch. 7. Three things stand out: the necessity of obeying God's law if the coming punishment was to be averted; Jeremiah's alignment with other prophets in Judah who had preached repentance or judg-

ment; and the unrelieved gravity of the sentence on the temple and on the city of Jerusalem. Shiloh was not far from Jerusalem; the people could see the evidences of its destruction (c. 1050 B.C.), even though it had been the first resting place of the ark of the covenant in the land. Even worse, Jerusalem and Judah would become notorious among the nations as examples of God's execration. Debased before the nations, Jerusalem would be an object lesson of the consequences of incurring God's wrath. What a contrast to the promise in Ge 12:3!

b. The arrest, trial, and condemnation of Jeremiah (26:7–11)

7–9 The people listened in hushed respect until Jeremiah had finished speaking, shocking though his words were. Even the priests and false prophets did not interrupt him. But once Jeremiah had concluded, the pent-up fury of the crowd broke loose. He was arrested and the death penalty pronounced on him. The priests, prophets, and people refused to believe his seemingly incredible prediction. For them it was blasphemy and false prophecy—both of which were crimes punishable by death (cf. Dt 18:20). The priests and false prophets were at the forefront of the opposition to Jeremiah. They were angered because they had consistently promised immunity to the city and sanctuary, relying on God's past deliverances (cf. Isa 37:36–37).

10–11 So great was the tumult around Jeremiah that the court officials, hearing of the mob's fury, hurried from the palace to the temple. It was indeed a timely move because the tumult could easily have led to Jeremiah's death. So the officials took their places where trials were held—at the "New Gate." The priests and false prophets, with their vested interest in the situation, were the leaders of the opposition against Jeremiah. Acting as the prosecution, they announced the verdict beforehand: "A judgment of death belongs to this man!" (lit. Heb.). Although Jeremiah had spoken against both the temple and the city, his accusers referred only to his words against the city. This gave their charge a political slant and appealed to those who heard the message.

c. Jeremiah's defense (26:12–15)

12–13 The prophet defended the message directly, courageously, and appropriately. Nowhere does he appear in a better light than here. He did not trim his message, cower, or beg for mercy. His defense was always the same: God had sent him to deliver the controversial message. Jeremiah stated the source of his message. He did not deny the truth he had preached; instead, he stressed its origin and authority. Their contention would have to be with God, for it was solely his message. Then Jeremiah called them to repentance. He was not to be diverted from the central issue but stuck to it with unswerving fidelity. There was still time for repentance. Though from the death of Josiah till the fall of Jerusalem conditions in Judah varied little, yet Jeremiah held out the only hope God offered his sinful people.

14–15 In the hour of trial, Jeremiah's courage and fidelity to God shone brightly. He did not plead for his life. He recognized the ability of his enemies to carry out the death sentence against him but warned them of the consequence of killing him. He knew that he faced imminent death; but he also knew that he had done no wrong, let alone committed any capital crime.

d. The release of Jeremiah (26:16–19)

16–19 The prophet's honesty and conviction by the Spirit gripped the hearts of the civil officials and the people. They sided with Jeremiah against the priests and false prophets. The judges and people were freer of prejudice than the religious leaders. They saw in Jeremiah what he claimed to be: God's spokesman. To the shame of the priests, the laymen alone realized the prophet was bound to preach what the Lord had committed to him. At this point the elders added their confirmation to what had been expressed. "Elders" here (GK 2418) expresses only that they were men of advanced age. They cited as a precedent the case of Micah in the days of Hezekiah (eighth century B.C.). Micah had lived more than a century before; he also prophesied about the destruction of the temple. As in law cases, citing a precedent carried weight. The reference to this prophecy turned the tide for Jeremiah.

Micah was a native of Moresheth, about twenty-three miles southwest of Jerusalem.

Possibly he was as influential in the reforms of Hezekiah as Isaiah was (cf. 2Ki 18:3–6). Micah's warning message bore fruit. Hezekiah and his people heeded the Lord's words and turned to him instead of threatening Micah's life. Thus the calamity was averted from Judah in that day. The people saw the possibility of averting judgment by repenting. The argument from precedent was successful. Though not explicitly stated, Jeremiah was acquitted by the civil leaders. They saw the enormity of the guilt that would be incurred by mistreating the Lord's messenger.

e. The murder of Uriah (26:20–24)

20–24 These can scarcely be the words of Jeremiah's opponents because there is no introductory formula. We do not know when the events narrated took place. Not all faithful preaching had the same results as Jeremiah's. Uriah's situation turned out differently, and he paid for his preaching with his life. Except for the Lord's intervention, this could have been Jeremiah's fate also (cf. 36:26). Jeremiah did not, however, run from his mission.

God does not always grant immunity to his servants. Uriah (mentioned only here) was a true prophet from Kiriath Jearim. His message agreed with Jeremiah's preaching. When Jehoiakim and his military leaders heard Uriah's words, their intense hatred of the truth sought an outlet in slaying Uriah; but he escaped to Egypt, the natural refuge for fugitives from Palestine. At this time rights of extradition prevailed between Egypt and Judah because Jehoiakim was a vassal of Egypt. Extradition was part of vassalage terms imposed by Egypt. The head of the embassy to implement it was Elnathan (perhaps the Elnathan of 2Ki 24:8, grandfather of Jehoiachin and father-in-law of Jehoiakim; cf. 36:12, 25). If so, his father, Acbor, was one of the deputation in 2Ki 22:12.

Once extradited Uriah was slain and dishonored by burial in a common cemetery, not in a family sepulcher. He was denied due process of law and the elementary right of burial with his ancestors. That Jehoiakim had no part in Jeremiah's case may mean it occurred early in his reign, before he gained influence over the civil leaders. Even though Jeremiah had been acquitted, he was still in danger. Ahikam, an official under Josiah (cf.

2Ki 22:12, 14) and father of Gedaliah, governor of Judah under Nebuchadnezzar after the fall of Jerusalem in 586 B.C. (cf. 39:14; 40:13–41:3; 2Ki 25:22), espoused his cause. And Ahikam's prominence helped secure Jeremiah's release.

7. The yoke of Babylon (27:1–22)

Chapters 27–28 attack the false optimism of the prophets of Judah and are dated by most scholars in the fourth year of Zedekiah (594–593 B.C.). Foreign envoys were coming to Jerusalem to promote a confederacy against Nebuchadnezzar. Neighboring countries were apparently trying to involve Judah in a rebellion against Babylon, an enterprise encouraged by the false prophets at Jerusalem. The contemplated rebellion failed because of Nebuchadnezzar's forthright action. Chapters 27–29 dispel the erroneous view that Babylon was just a passing power, not to be reckoned with. From 51:59 we may infer that Zedekiah was called to Babylon to explain what part he had in the unsuccessful plot against Nebuchadnezzar.

a. The message to the ambassadors (27:1–11)

1–2 With Judah on the verge of revolt against Babylon, God spoke to Jeremiah and commanded him to make a yoke and place it on his neck. The yoke, similar to that used for oxen, was made of wooden bars held together by leather thongs (see also 28:10). A yoke symbolized submission, servitude, and captivity.

3 Jeremiah did not make duplicate yokes to be sent to the kings represented in the conclave. He did, however, convey to the kings the message of the yoke. Their envoys had assembled to plan how to shake off the yoke of Babylon; so the yoke symbol was highly appropriate. Jeremiah required great courage to stand against these envoys as well as his own countrymen, but he was exercising his commission as a prophet to the nations (cf. 1:10). Smaller nations often revolted against their Mesopotamian conquerors, but seldom with success. Through Jeremiah the Lord is charging them all that it is his will for them to submit to Nebuchadnezzar for their own good. The enumeration of the kings is from south (Edom, Moab, Ammon) to north (the Phoenician cities of Tyre and Sidon). The rebellion of the smaller nations may have been activated by the accession of Psammetik II as the pharaoh of Egypt.

4–7 The message the envoys took back to their kings was that the sovereign Creator of the universe had the right to give the dominion of earth to whomever he pleased. Revolt was futile and wrong because God had appointed Babylon to execute his purpose of judgment. Resistance was useless because Nebuchadnezzar was God's instrument. To resist the known will of God is always spiritual suicide. Nebuchadnezzar's dominion was vast, extending even to the animals of the field. As to its duration, Babylonian rule would extend from Nebuchadnezzar to the third generation. It passed from him to Evil-Merodach and Belshazzar (52:31; Da 5:1, 30). Thus the Babylonian threat was not to be temporary, as the false prophets glibly promised. When the appointed time came for the termination of Babylonian supremacy, the rulers of Persia, Media, and contiguous areas finally overthrew it. God is Creator of the universe and Administrator in the affairs of the nations.

8–11 The meaning of the yoke is explained. Those resisting the Babylonian power would be punished by the threefold stroke of sword, famine, and plague. Above all, the prophecies of the false prophets were not to be trusted, for they were dealing in lies that would only lead the nation to disaster. Moved by the knowledge of God's message and its authority, Jeremiah did not shrink from opposing the whole array of false leaders in all the countries. The five kinds of soothsayers mentioned in v.9 all helped forward the policy of rebellion. They represented various pagan methods of predicting the future. The result for Judah would be deportation, a policy the Assyrians had used for Israel and one the Babylonians would use for Judah. But nations that obey God would remain in peace in their lands and would prosper.

b. The address to King Zedekiah (27:12–15)

12–15 The warning already extended to the envoys of the nations is now directed toward Zedekiah. Here we have the meaning of the yoke for the Davidic king. The thrust of the message is Zedekiah's submission to the

Babylonians. He was a weak and ambivalent ruler who could never carry through a resolve to follow the Lord wholly. Zedekiah is exhorted not to choose the way of resistance and disobedience, which would only bring disaster with it. So powerful was the influence of the false prophets at this time that the king had to be counseled to ignore their lying pronouncements. God never sent them; they predicted lies; the result of their advice could only be exile for the nation. To underestimate the power of a lie in times of national distress is sheer folly.

c. The warning to the priests and people (27:16–22)

16–18 So vital was the message of Jeremiah at this time that it had to be repeated to the priests and people. The false prophets were holding out baseless hopes that the temple vessels taken to Babylon were soon to be returned. This was a powerful incentive for Judah to revolt against the Babylonians, but Jeremiah reiterated the necessity of submitting to Nebuchadnezzar. The prophets of "peace" thought that their words would be more effective if they referred to details like the temple objects. Some were carried away in the deportation of Jehoiakim (cf. 2Ch 36:5–7), and even more were carried away in 597 B.C. (cf. 2Ki 24:13). Instead of these vessels being returned "shortly," as the lying prophets claimed, the vessels remaining in the temple would be carried off too (cf. 2Ki 25:13). In fact—and here Jeremiah places the false prophets under a severe test—if the prophets who were predicting a speedy return of the vessels taken to Babylon were indeed what they claimed to be, they could serve the nation best by praying that the vessels still in the temple would not be taken to Babylon. History reveals that the temple vessels were taken to the land of exile.

19–22 Of all the temple appointments, three are mentioned here (see also 52:17). The pillars were made of bronze and were placed in front of the temple; their names were Jakin and Boaz (cf. 1Ki 7:15–22). Before being taken away to Babylon, they were actually broken into pieces because they were too large to take intact. The Sea was a large cast basin, supported on the backs of twelve cast oxen and used for the washings of the priests (cf. 1Ki 7:23–26). There were also stands to support the lavers (cf. 1Ki 7:27–37; 2Ch 4:6), and the stands were on wheels. All these remaining vessels would be taken to Babylon also, Jeremiah prophesied. The hope the false prophets held out was impossible of fulfillment and hence not from God. To the prediction of the carrying away of all these things, the Lord added a promise that they would be restored in the day that he would execute judgment on Babylon. The vessels were returned to Jerusalem by Cyrus at the beginning of his reign (c. 536 B.C.; cf. Ezr 1:7–11).

8. Hananiah against Jeremiah (28:1–17)

Chapter 28 continues without a break in the narrative of ch. 27, which shows that Jeremiah was still wearing the yoke.

a. Hananiah's contradiction of Jeremiah (28:1–4)

1 The mention of the fourth year of Zedekiah as the "beginning of his reign" (lit. Heb.; NIV, "early in the reign"), which lasted eleven years, reflects Jewish usage. The date was indeed the beginning of his rule, for the Jews divided periods of time into halves: beginning and end. It means simply "in the first half of his reign."

Hananiah the prophet seized an opportunity when the temple was frequented by the people, either at the celebration of the new moon or a Sabbath, to contradict what Jeremiah had just said (cf. ch. 27). Apart from this chapter, we know nothing of Hananiah. He has been characterized as a fanatical nationalist prophet who was sincerely wrong. He was a native of Gibeon, five miles northwest of Jerusalem. It was one of the priestly cities; so Hananiah may have been a priest. The year was 594–593 B.C., and the fifth month places the episode in the summer.

2–3 Hananiah had the temerity to use the same introductory formula as Jeremiah, implying a claim for inspiration similar to his. The yoke refers to the one Jeremiah had just made. Flatly contradicting Jeremiah's God-given counsel of submission, Hananiah predicted a return of the captives and the temple vessels within two years, emphasizing the time element by putting it first. This mention of two years was meant to bolster the credibility of his false prophecy. He paid no attention to the warning in 23:31. That the prophecy was never fulfilled showed its falsity. The

Babylonian Chronicle indicates that Nebuchadnezzar was quelling a revolt in Babylon at the time. This may have acted as a spur to Hananiah's optimism.

4 Perhaps Hananiah saw approval on the faces of his hearers because he went even further. He predicted that Jeconiah would be restored from exile, a contradiction of Jeremiah's prophecy in 22:24–27 (fulfilled in 52:31–34). Hananiah's prediction showed he favored Jeconiah over the vacillating Zedekiah because he may have thought that the former would resist Nebuchadnezzar better. To make his message more uplifting, he made a sweeping prediction of the return of all the Judean exiles. One can well imagine the confusion created in the minds of the populace by the spectacle of the false prophet's denying the central elements in the message of the true prophet of God.

b. Jeremiah's appeal to the past (28:5–9)

5–9 Jeremiah's response to Hananiah was immediate. His "Amen" revealed how deeply he desired Judah's good. He was just as concerned for the nation as Hananiah was. As a man of God, he sincerely desired the captives' return. He reminded Hananiah of the words of the true prophets who had preceded both Hananiah and him. Hananiah's words contradicted their predictions just as much as they contradicted those of Jeremiah. The former prophets also spoke in warning messages because of the sinful condition of the people they ministered to. In view of the nation's long spiritual decline, prophecies of disaster were not new. He made it clear that the fulfillment of a prophecy remained the best proof of its truthfulness.

The scope of the prophetic activity was comprehensive, reaching to many lands and many kingdoms, small and great. In the contest between Hananiah and Jeremiah, antecedent probability was in favor of a prophet who spoke in agreement with the true prophets of the past. The trouble with the false prophets was that they always predicted prosperity unconditionally and without need of repentance. It is always less popular to predict calamity rather than prosperity; so the presumption of truth rests with the prophet of calamity. At this time Jeremiah evidently had no specific message from God against Hananiah.

c. Hananiah's response (28:10–11)

10–11 Because of Jeremiah's incontrovertible argument, Hananiah resorted to force. He took the yoke from Jeremiah's neck and smashed it, to show that Nebuchadnezzar's power would be shattered in two years. Once more Hananiah presumed to use the introductory formula of the true prophets. Instead of waiting for the fulfillment of his prediction, he acted violently to capture the people's attention and mask his own confusion. In doing so, he may have hoped to reverse the impact made by Jeremiah's making and wearing the yoke. Jeremiah left without replying. He could have been waiting for a time when emotions had cooled off. Also, he was doubtless waiting for further instructions from the Lord. There was no need for haste anyway, because it would take two years to see whether Hananiah's prediction came true. And Jeremiah may have left without answering Hananiah so as not to confuse the people.

d. Jeremiah's stronger pronouncement (28:12–14)

12–14 The Lord's answer through Jeremiah did come a short time later. To one who had falsified the Lord's reiterated intentions for Israel, it was an emphatic rebuttal. By breaking the yoke, Hananiah had raised false hopes of successfully resisting the invaders—hopes that were only to make their lot harder. By breaking it, Hananiah had alleviated the pain of the yoke. But Jeremiah replied that the people were exchanging the wooden yoke of submission for the inflexible iron yoke of servitude in Babylon. Not only were the people to suffer more, but, as 38:17–23 shows, Zedekiah's fate was more severe than that of Jehoiakim or Jehoiachin. Whereas for Hezekiah to resist Assyria in 701 B.C. was an act of faith, for Judah to rebel against Babylon in Jeremiah's time was an act of disobedience. Not only would all the nations serve Nebuchadnezzar, but his dominion would extend over all the wild animals.

e. Prediction of Hananiah's death (28:15–17)

15–17 Perhaps after an interval of only a few days, Jeremiah received a word from the Lord against Hananiah. First, the Lord said that he had not sent Hananiah. Second, Hananiah had misled Judah into believing lies. Hananiah had set a time limit of two years for the realization of his prediction, but the Lord did not choose to wait that long. He decreed that Hananiah was to die that very year, and he died in two months after his wicked prophecy. He had to die because in opposing Jeremiah he instigated rebellion against the Lord. The Jews knew the penalty for apostasy (cf. Dt 13:1–5; cf. Eze 11:13; Ac 5:1–11). Jeremiah's prophecy was authenticated in the death of Hananiah, which discredited him as a fraud. Thus the authority of the true prophet was vindicated.

9. Jeremiah's letters to the exiles (29:1–32)

This chapter may be placed a few years after the exile of 597 B.C. More important than the precise date are the contents of the chapter—a letter to the three thousand Jews who had been exiled with Jehoiachin to Babylon, among them a number of priests and prophets. In Jerusalem, Jeremiah heard that some exiled false prophets were predicting an early fall of Babylon and an early restoration of the exiles to Judah. Jeremiah's letters warned the exiles against this deception and urged them to wait patiently for God's time.

a. Introduction (29:1–3)

1–2 Jeremiah rightly felt he still had a God-given responsibility for the "surviving elders," those who had not died through the rigors of the deportation. Clearly some form of community organization like that in Judah

This is Herbert Anger's drawing of what the ancient city of Babylon looked like, based on excavations. The Ishtar Gate is in the foreground. In the background on the right are the famouns Hanging Gardens. Courtesy of the Oriental Institute of the University of Chicago.

had been continued in the Exile. The letter was directed not only to the elders but to all the exiles. The "queen mother" was Nehushta (cf. 13:18; 2Ki 24:8). The craftsmen and artisans were deported to help King Nebuchadnezzar beautify Babylon.

3 Jeremiah gave his letter to an embassy whom Zedekiah sent to Nebuchadnezzar. The embassy's purpose is not stated, but it likely was sent with tribute and assurance of Zedekiah's loyalty to Nebuchadnezzar. Elasah son of Shaphan was probably a brother of Ahikam (cf. 26:24); he agreed with Jeremiah and would have been welcome in Babylon. Gemariah son of Hilkiah was probably a son of Josiah's high priest Hilkiah (cf. 2Ki 22:3–4). Babylon probably permitted communication between Judah and the exiles. The exiles were just as subject to false prophets as the people in Jerusalem. They might have been expected to heed Jeremiah's words (cf. 24:5–7). The false hope of a quick end to the Exile would only have nullified the disciplinary effects of the Exile.

b. The letter of Jeremiah (29:4–19)

1) Warning against false prophets (29:4–9)

4–7 Rather than a word-for-word record of Jeremiah's main letter and the other subsidiary letters, we probably have the gist of what was written. Underlying the main letter is the assumption that Nebuchadnezzar was the agent of the Lord. Ultimately the Lord himself had brought about the Exile. Since the Lord's will was behind it, the part of wisdom was submission. The exiles were to settle in Babylon and live normal lives there, even praying for their captors (cf. Mt 5:43) and working for peace and prosperity. Otherwise, their influence would be negligible and their exile all the more galling.

What unusual advice for Jeremiah to give his exiled countrymen! History shows that in all the centuries of their worldwide dispersion, the Jews have tried to follow this pattern. They have identified themselves with the country of their residence, while at the same time looking toward eventual restoration to their native land.

Jeremiah's exhortations show that the Babylonian stay would be an extended one. His advice to build homes there implies they had not yet been in Babylon a long time. The freedom allowed them implies they were nei-

ther slaves nor prisoners in their new land. Any feeling that they should not build homes in a foreign, unclean land was thus dispelled. The wives Jeremiah encouraged them to marry were Jewish, not foreign (cf. Dt 7:3). The seed of Abraham must continue according to the divine promise (cf. Ge 12:1–3).

8–9 Again Jeremiah warned the exiles not to trust false prophets. In Babylon, as in Judah, false prophecy was flourishing (cf. vv.15, 21). The theme was always the same: a speedy return to the homeland. Rosy predictions were the stock in trade of such people. Such deceptive dreams could only work havoc among the exiles. The deceivers must not be trusted because they had never been commissioned by the Lord.

2) The seventy-year exile (29:10–14)

10–11 Jeremiah now presents a beautiful prophecy of encouragement to the exiles. The Lord's ultimate purpose for his people called for blessing. The length of the Exile is again given as seventy years (cf. 25:11). The seventy years were "for Babylon" because Jeremiah linked the duration of Nebuchadnezzar's kingdom with the termination of the Exile. The "gracious promise" is that of the exiles' restoration to Judah (cf. 27:22). Moreover, the Lord assured them that despite their surmise as to his lack of concern for their plight, he had not forgotten them. The Lord was not denying them hope for the future; it would not be realized immediately or in the near future. Jeremiah's words "hope and a future" are literally "an end and a hope," which means "a hopeful end." This word from the Lord was surely more heartening to the exiles' spirits than the false prophets' promises of quick deliverance.

12–14 The remainder of this section stresses the nature of the hopeful future. The Lord says that he could and would be entreated of the exiles. The promises, however, were contingent on their wholehearted repentance. Then the Lord would listen to them and make himself accessible to them. The declaration "I will gather you from all the nations and places where I have banished you" looks far beyond the Jews' return from Babylon to their future restoration from worldwide dispersion.

3) A "second letter" of Jeremiah (29:15–19)

15–19 Conceivably vv.15–19 form a second letter written at a subsequent time and inserted parenthetically here. The situation was doubtless something like this: The exiles asked why Jeremiah insisted on an exile of seventy years when their prophets in Babylon were telling them the very opposite. Jeremiah replied that the false prophecies would be shown to be lies and their perpetrators would perish. For the Jews to depend on the pronouncements of the deceivers was the highest folly. Actually, the Jews still in Jerusalem were soon to experience grievous judgments for their persistence in disobeying the Lord.

Again, it must be emphasized that vv.15–19 were probably part of a second letter not sent by the king's embassy (v.3) because the king in v.16 is Zedekiah, who was yet destined for exile. "This city" was Jerusalem. The false prophets made much of the fact that in Jerusalem a Davidic king still ruled, and they argued from this that the Exile would soon end. But those still in Judah were to undergo the calamities of war and were likened to vile figs of the worst sort (cf. 24:1–10). And even in exile, the grace of God was seen in raising up Ezekiel in 592 B.C. (cf. Eze 1:2–3). Once more the Lord states that he is the Author of the Exile.

c. Denunciation of the false prophets Ahab and Zedekiah (29:20–23)

20–23 Jeremiah was well informed about conditions in Babylon. Two false prophets, Ahab and Zedekiah—of whom nothing more is known than that they had famous names and were deceitful and grossly immoral—are singled out as examples of the heinousness of false prophesying. They were probably condemned as guilty of treason against the Babylonian crown. Like Hananiah, these false prophets would become object lessons of the Lord's wrath. Babylon used burning as a punishment (cf. Da 3:6, 20, 23).

d. Condemnation of Shemaiah (29:24–32)

24–28 After castigating the two false prophets for their deceit and profligacy (v.23), Jeremiah pronounces the Lord's condemnation on Shemaiah the Nehelamite, a false prophet who presumed to order a member of the priesthood in Jerusalem to silence Jeremiah.

Of Shemaiah nothing more is known than what we have in this passage. The background of his letter is clear. Jeremiah's letter understandably angered the false prophets in Babylon. Shemaiah, who was one of them, wrote the deputy priest Zephaniah to silence Jeremiah. Instead, Zephaniah read Shemaiah's letter to Jeremiah, who replied in a message predicting the doom of Shemaiah for denying Jeremiah's authority. The false prophets had apparently overlooked the promises Jeremiah had given (vv.10–14).

Zephaniah was the chief warden in charge of police regulations of the temple (cf. 21:1; 37:3; 52:24). Apparently Shemaiah, on his own initiative, had displaced Jehoiada the priest (cf. 2Ki 11:4) with Zephaniah. Although in that day insanity ("madman") may have been considered as an aberrant gift of prophecy (cf. 1Sa 19:20–24; 2Ki 9:11), this charge was an insult to Jeremiah. The "neck-irons" were an iron collar that held the head immovable while the prisoner was in the stocks (cf. 20:2). Knowing nothing of Jeremiah's divine call, Shemaiah had accused him of usurping authority as a spokesman for God.

29–32 After Zephaniah had read the letter to Jeremiah, the Lord told him to send a letter to all the exiles, unmasking Shemaiah's hypocrisy and announcing a twofold punishment: He would have no descendants, and he would not see the blessings on the Lord's people that Jeremiah had been predicting. Shemaiah had forfeited the privilege of participating in the restoration to the homeland.

B. The Book of Consolation (30:1–33:26)

1. Trial and triumph for Israel (30:1–24)

Chapters 30–33 constitute a group of prophecies that has been called "The Book of Consolation." Verse 1 of chapter 32 gives us the historical background of these prophecies (cf. 33:1). Jerusalem was in the final period of an eighteen-month siege by the Babylonians. Other Judean cities had already capitulated to them. The temporary intervention of Egypt (cf. 37:4–5) had failed to stem the tide of events, and Jerusalem remained disillusioned and helpless. Though written during a time of deep distress for Jerusalem, chs. 30–33 foretell a glorious future for the nation (cf. the latter part of 1:10).

Up to this point in the book, Jeremiah's prophecies have mostly been threatening and gloomy. Now the prophetic outlook changes. This is all the more striking since chs. 32–33 (probably chs. 30–31 also) were given in the tenth year of Zedekiah, when the final blow was about to fall. The overall theme is that Israel would not perish as a nation. Jeremiah was in prison, the city in dire straits by famine and disease; yet it was then that he spoke words of greatest comfort. He predicted the permanence of the nation, the coming of the Gentiles to the truth, the institution of God's new covenant of redemption, and the rule of the Davidic King over cleansed Zion.

a. Return from captivity (30:1–3)

1–3 These verses strike the hopeful theme of the nation's restoration. The Lord commanded Jeremiah to write these prophecies in a book to ensure their permanence at a time when so many in the nation were being exiled. Also, his activities may have been restricted at this time. Obviously "the book" was not to contain all we now have in the book of Jeremiah, not even all he spoke to this time.

The words "the days are coming" look to eschatological times (cf. 3:16; 16:14; 23:5; 31:27, 31). Jeremiah is contemplating the distant, not near, future of the nation. This statement restricts the material involved to "The Book of Consolation." To bring back any people from captivity indicates a restoration of their fortunes, which is the emphasis of this section. The good news was the promise of the people's restoration to and their possession of their homeland, a message of glorious hope in that gloomy hour. Moreover, we must not forget that this hope relates to Israel and Judah, not to one without the other (cf. v.10).

b. "A time of trouble for Jacob" (30:4–7)

4–6 Here the prophet speaks of the whole nation over which David and Solomon ruled. Jeremiah is stating that before the just-mentioned promise of restoration can be fulfilled, the nation must be severely disciplined, though t not to the extent of final calamity. "Fear" and "terror" point to war. The awful terror that will come can be compared only with the travail of a mother in childbirth, a figure of extreme distress.

7 It is not clear whether this passage is referring to (1) the immediate situation, (2) the whole period of the Captivity, or (3) the time of tribulation in the end time before Israel's final restoration. If the first, then "that day" may mean the day of the capture of Babylon, with emphasis on the terror caused by the approach of Cyrus. Cyrus was the Jews' liberator from those who took them captive.

However, in the light of the immediate context and what follows, it seems preferable to assume that the reference is to the Day of the Lord. "That day" was not one immediately at hand. It is not the day of the destruction of Jerusalem but the day of God's comprehensive judgment. The present is not to be excluded, but it is swallowed up in the future. That day is to be marked by great calamities. It is vitally important to remember that v.7 speaks of *Jacob's* trouble, not Babylon's. The prophetic Scriptures are replete with references to this unique time of Jacob's distress; e.g., "There is none like it" (cf. Mt 24:21 with Da 12:1; cf. also Jer 46:10; Isa 2:12–21; 13:6; 34:1–8; et al.). Notice that the travail will issue in both physical and spiritual deliverance (cf. Zec 12:1–13:1) and that liberation will be such that never again will Israel be enslaved by any nation. This can never be said of any deliverance to this present hour; it must refer to eschatological times.

c. Freedom from bondage to oppressors (30:8–11)

8–9 Only in the most preliminary way may "the yoke" refer to bondage to Nebuchadnezzar; what is meant is total liberation from all foreign oppressors. This can be effected only by the glorious intervention of Israel's messianic King (cf. Eze 34:23; Hos 3:5). After the yoke of foreign rule has been broken, the benevolent yoke of their King will be gladly assumed by the godly in Israel and Judah (cf. Mt 11:28–30). Notice the pairing of "the LORD their God" with "David their kin." It is significant that in the prophetic Scriptures a resurrection of David himself is not predicted as antecedent to the rule of his Son, the Lord Jesus Christ, on the Davidic throne (cf. Eze 37:24–25). The person indicated here is the future ideal King, the so-called second David (cf. "last Adam" and "second man" in 1Co 15:45–47). The Targum is correct in identifying this ideal King as "Messiah, the son of David." Among the Jews the name David came to be used of any royalty, much as Pharaoh, Caesar, or Czar, but only in the highest and final sense.

10–11 Jeremiah closes this section with promises of return, peace, freedom, and permanence. He refers to the nation as Jacob, God's "servant"—a title of honor. God's people are to be regathered from all the lands of their dispersion. Jeremiah makes a telling distinction between the fate of God's people and that of their oppressors: the oppressors may be removed finally from the scene of history, but God's people never will (cf. 4:27; 5:10, 18; 46:28). This is not partiality on God's part, for he will not overlook his people's sins. They can no more sin with impunity than any other persons or nation. The Lord must chasten them, and he will do so with justice, not capriciously. It is no wonder that Isaiah refers to Israel (i.e., Israel and Judah) as an eternal nation; for whereas Ammon, Assyria, Edom, Moab, and others no longer exist, Israel is present throughout the world today, even though in the divine chastening of dispersion.

d. Israel's wounds healed (30:12–17)

12–15 In turning to the serious condition of Israel, Jeremiah wants to show that her punishment was well deserved. Her wounds were, apart from God, incurable. Doubtless, the wounds are those she has received from her enemies because of her flagrant sins. Because God's people have transgressed so grievously, no one can defend them; moreover, there is no hope of their recovery. Jeremiah mingles his figures of speech: he sees Israel as a defendant in a lawsuit and as one suffering from a fatal wound. All her antagonists have the upper hand as they accuse her before God. What made her trial harder to bear was that Israel's allies had left her in the lurch. Her punishment clearly stemmed from the Lord because sin was at the root of all her calamities. Furthermore, she had no right to complain of her punishment since she amply deserved it.

16–17 The prophet contrasts Israel's mistreatment by her supposed lovers with the Lord's actions on her behalf. Because his people have undergone judgment and have acknowledged their guilt, God pronounces retaliation in kind on their enemies. The fu-

ture blessings begin with judgments on Israel's oppressors. God will heal her and afflict her enemies. The Babylonians who devoured the nation will in turn be devoured by the Medes and Persians. Those who treat God's people ill have to reckon with God as avenger (cf. Ge 12:1–3). Again, the promise of restored health precedes any action the Lord may take against Israel's foes. In their contempt, the enemies of God's nation called her an outcast, for whom no one cared. The figure is that of a woman put away by her husband (cf. Isa 62:4). The Lord considered this treatment of his nation a great offense because their words and actions revealed their disregard of God and his expressed purpose for his people. Ultimately, calling them an outcast impugned God's faithfulness to his elect people.

e. Rebuilt Jerusalem and her ruler (30:18–22)

18–20 Days of rich blessing are ahead. These verses deal with Jerusalem rebuilt, repopulated, and governed by a native prince responsive to the Lord. It also shows the nation experiencing the blessings of renewed fellowship with the Lord. The "tents" and "dwellings," now desolate, refer to the wretched condition of their houses in their homeland. Jerusalem will be rebuilt on its original location. The word "ruins" is the well-known term *tel* (GK 9424), now used by Arabs for the ruined mounds of Palestine that contain the remains of ancient cities. Jerusalem and its buildings are probably intended. The meaning is that the city will be settled by a king, with all that pertains to such a residence.

Furthermore, along with material prosperity will come joy and honor so long denied the people. Out of the city and palace will flow praise and merriment. Instead of degradation and insignificance, the people will grow in numbers and in the esteem of the nations as the Lord honors them. The children of Jacob will enjoy prosperity like that in the heyday of the monarchy under David and Solomon. The congregation—the people as a whole—will be established under God's oversight.

21–22 Embedded in this passage so full of promise is one of the most beautiful of the messianic predictions in the OT. First, the nation will be blessed by a native, not a foreign, ruler. This was surely a prophecy of strong consolation in view of the nation's imminent subservience to a foreign power. Second, this ruler will have the privilege of approach to God, i.e., priestly position and ministry (cf. Ps 110:4; Zec 6:13); he will need no mediator. Thus he will be greater than David and Solomon. Like Melchizedek he will have a dual role. No man can take to himself the office of priesthood (cf. Heb 5:1). In fact, it was dangerous for even a king to do so (cf. 1Ki 12:26–33; 13:1–6; 2Ch 26:16–20). This was permitted only to the priests and, on the Day of Atonement, only to the high priest. Here is a reiteration of the promise to restore the Davidic line. And no one would "devote himself to be so close" to God on his own initiative.

Immediately Jeremiah turns to the result of Messiah's ministry—the old covenant is renewed. The nation will be restored to the position of fellowship and worship that God intended for her. The people will be seen to be God's people.

f. Judgment, then blessing (30:23–24)

23–24 Before there can be blessing, judgment must be meted out to the guilty. This passage is inserted here lest the careless be given false security in their sins. In spite of promises of hope, God's moral purposes always remain the same. God is behind the judgment to be executed by Nebuchadnezzar. Jeremiah uses the figure of a sudden storm to describe it. The Lord does his work of redemption by his power displayed in judgment. The blessings Jeremiah has been speaking of are only for the godly. The reference to "the days to come" appears to point to a time after the judgment has passed.

2. The new covenant (31:1–40)

In ch. 30 the restoration of Judah is foretold; here that of the nation of Israel is predicted. The dominant themes in this chapter are the restoration of God's people and the new covenant.

a. God's mercy for Ephraim (31:1–6)

1–2 The time reference is the "days to come" of 30:24, i.e., the Messianic Age. Although vv.1–6 deal primarily with the northern kingdom, "clans of Israel" must be allowed to comprehend the Twelve Tribes in light of the promise to the whole nation in 30:22. Jeremiah dilates on the grace of God revealed to the northern tribes. "The people who survive the sword" could refer to those who survived the Exodus and the wilderness wanderings; more likely, however, it refers to the return of the Ten Tribes from Assyrian captivity, perhaps also including the later captives from Babylon. The Lord is continuing the grace he showed his people in the desert wanderings (cf. 2:1–3). The desert is thus a figure for the land of the Exile in contrast to their homeland. As of old, the Lord in his infinite grace is concerned about finding "rest" (GK 8089) for his troubled, weary people. What he did by the pillar of cloud and the pillar of fire in the desert, he was willing to do for the returning exiles.

3–4 In one of the most beautiful poems in his book, Jeremiah cites the declaration of the people: "The LORD appeared to us." Again the people recall the unparalleled love, grace, and comfort God had extended to them "in the past." What comfort was theirs in the recognition of such perpetual love! Addressing Israel as a virgin, unsullied before God, Jeremiah implies that the Lord sees her just as appealing as in the time of her departure from Egypt (cf. 2:1–3; Hos 2:14–23). Grace blots out the past. Both rebuilding and joy are promised the northern kingdom. Contrasted with the sorrow of the Exile (Ps 137:1) is the use of tambourines at dances in times of rejoicing. In ancient times dancing was often a religious exercise (cf. 2Sa 6:14).

5 Amplifying the thought of restoration, Jeremiah says that the hills of Samaria will be planted with vineyards. Essentially an occupation in time of peace, viniculture is often interrupted by war. But in the time Jeremiah is looking forward to, those who plant grapes will enjoy the fruit of their labors. The law of Moses did not permit the Hebrews to eat the fruit of the first three years. Fruit of the fourth year was given to God, but it could be redeemed and eaten (cf. Lev 19:23–25). Thus Jeremiah's reference to the vineyards implies that Israel will be settled in her land and enjoying it under normal conditions.

6 Even more glorious is Jeremiah's prediction that watchmen will direct those of Ephraim (the northern kingdom) to go up to Zion to

worship the Lord there. In the OT the temple in Zion was always considered the only authorized sanctuary. According to Jewish tradition watchmen were appointed for the appearance of the moon, from which their months were counted. Here the watchmen on the hills of Samaria are to show the northern kingdom how to go up to Jerusalem to keep the feasts, as the pilgrimage feasts were annually observed in ancient times (cf. Dt 16:16). This will mark the end of the disruption of the kingdom of Solomon in 930 B.C. Ephraim's condition in blessing will be permanent because Jeroboam's misleading them from the Lord's sanctuary will be a thing of the past. The breach of many centuries will at last be healed.

b. The restoration of Israel in joy (31:7–14)

7–9 Verses 7–14 emphasize joy at the end of the Exile. With exuberance Jeremiah celebrates the great salvation provided for Israel. Israel will be restored to her rightful position. Moreover, in his answer the Lord promises a return, not only from the north country, but ultimately from all parts of the earth. And from that restoration none will be excluded. The blind, the lame, the pregnant women—even those in labor, for whom the journey would be especially burdensome—will be included. The picture is of universal participation. Furthermore, the return will be accompanied by weeping and tears of repentance. Weeping for their sin and rebellion will then be overshadowed by the joy of return. Repentance, as always, issues in salvation. As the people give themselves to prayer, the Lord will lead them by streams of water, a metaphor of refreshment.

All this tenderness and concern for Ephraim (Israel) stem from the original elective purpose of God declared in Ex 4:22 (cf. Dt 32:6). The designation of "firstborn" in Ex 4:22 included the whole nation, whereas here it is transferred to Ephraim, the head of the Ten Tribes. Ephraim is mentioned before Judah (vv.23–26) because the Ten Tribes were in exile much longer and, humanly considered, were less likely to be delivered. The prophet could with warrant call Ephraim the firstborn, for Joseph actually received the birthright of the firstborn, which was forfeited by the sin of Reuben (cf. 1Ch 5:1–2). Sonship in the OT includes the concept of paternal love and care on a national scale,

rather than the NT concept of personal membership in the family of God by the Spirit.

10–14 The word is to be spread afar that the Lord has regathered Israel. The nations will be told that it was the Lord who exiled his people and that it is he who restores them. The figure of shepherd and flock portrays the dual concepts of tenderness and concern. Just as the Lord alone was responsible for Israel's chastisement, so now he alone will regather them. The Lord will ransom Israel, delivering the people from foreign bondage under the power of a pagan world ruler. Promises are heaped one upon another—predictions of joy, return to Jerusalem, nature transformed, and a new prosperity. Israel will be ransomed, redeemed, rejoicing, and restored. When the people come to Zion, they will find every need supplied. God's "bounty" (GK 3206) includes material blessings. Never again will God's people sorrow as they did in the time of their Exile. So great will be the prosperity bestowed on them that the priests will be satiated because of the many sacrifices brought by the worshipers. With abundant harvests, the portions of the priests will increase.

c. Israel's lamentable present (31:15–22)

15 From glowing predictions of tenderness and joy, Jeremiah turns back to the sad conditions of his day. He pictures Rachel at Ramah weeping disconsolately for the loss of her children. She was an ancestress of the northern tribes of Ephraim and Manasseh (through Joseph), as well as of Benjamin in the south. Undoubtedly, she is lamenting the exile of her children in 722–721 B.C. Ramah was five miles north of Jerusalem, the very place where exiles were gathered before deportation to Babylon (cf. 40:1). Jeremiah himself was in a camp for exiles in Ramah. She who had so longed for children (cf. Ge 30:1) is cruelly bereaved of them, but God purposes to restore them.

16–17 The Lord bids Rachel to stop mourning because now she can comfort herself by the promise of her children's return (spoken twice). The "work" to be "rewarded" includes bearing, rearing, sorrowing over, and praying for her children. As they were a source of grief to her, now they will be a joy on their return from exile.

A question arises as to how this prophecy of Rachel can be fulfilled in Herod's slaughter of the innocents recorded in Mt 2:17–18. First, it must be stressed that Matthew's method of quoting an OT reference does not automatically imply a direct fulfillment (cf. "The Old Testament in the New Testament," EBC, 1:617–27). For proof, see the immediate context in Mt 2:15, where Hos 11:1 in its original context unmistakably speaks of the nation Israel but by analogy and higher fulfillment refers to Christ. Similarly, that which related to Israel in original revelation is by analogy used in speaking of Herod's atrocities. In both cases God will overrule the nation's sorrow for her ultimate joy.

18–20 It is one thing to hear of Rachel's concern for Ephraim, but what was the latter's attitude? Ephraim expressed godly sorrow for his sins. He prayed for the Lord to restore him. He at last recognized the need to repent before restoration. He was formerly like an untrained calf, in need of training. Through the Lord's judgments he learned discipline. Once he was chastened and became submissive to the providences of the Lord, Ephraim smote his thigh (NIV, "breast") in grief and sorrow. The Spirit of God had done his effective work so that Ephraim recognized the shame his earlier sinful life brought on him. Finally we have the Lord's answer to Ephraim's confession of need. His fatherly concern for the prodigal Ephraim is beautifully expressed. Divine love will not be denied him in spite of his sin. Fatherly tenderness prevails over childish recalcitrance. Ephraim is forgiven.

21 Jeremiah now addresses the returning exiles of the northern kingdom. They are to make ample preparation for their homeward journey. The succession of imperatives shows the urgency of their preparation for return. It was the custom of caravans to set up pillars, poles, and heaps of stones to guide them. So the exiles are told to mark out the old route, to set up signs to help them find their way back. They are to pay heed to the way they went into exile in order to be able to retrace their steps. The imperatives admonish them not to delay their return by wavering.

22 This verse is difficult because the background is lacking. One view sees here a prophecy of the Virgin Birth of the Lord Jesus Christ. This ancient interpretation comes from the Church Fathers, but this interpretation is ill suited to the context. Granted that the word "virgin" occurs in v.21 and earlier in v.4, it is plain that these references are to Israel, not to an individual. Other solutions do not fare much better (see EBC, 6:571). It is foolhardy to be dogmatic about the meaning of these puzzling words. On the whole, it seems best to take them as a proverbial saying about something amazing and hard to believe.

d. Judah's bright future (31:23–26)

23–25 Jeremiah, after painting a magnificent picture of Ephraim's return and blessing, addresses Judah with words of strong assurance and with promises similar to those given Ephraim. When the southern kingdom and her cities are restored, the old greeting of those visiting Jerusalem will be heard once more. "O sacred mountain" refers to the temple mount and Jerusalem as a whole (cf. Ps 2:6; Isa 66:20). The city will again be characterized by her righteousness (cf. Isa 1:21). Once spiritual things are cared for, temporal things will be provided. Judah's cities will not be abandoned by their inhabitants, and those settled in them will enjoy tranquillity and prosperity without fear of marauders or invading armies. Indeed, every individual need will be amply met.

26 Jeremiah gives his own response to the bright promises of the millennial time under Messiah. The truths he had been communicating had been given him in a supernatural dream during a sleep that may have been ecstatic. Jeremiah's sleep was sweet because the truths he received in them were comforting predictions of future glory for God's people.

e. National increase under Messiah (31:27–30)

27–30 Because invasions and deportations had taken humans and animals from the land, the Lord used Jeremiah to portray a dramatic renewal of the land through resowing the country with both. That messianic times are in view is clear from the formula "The days are coming" (cf. 30:3). What a contrast to the condition of the land with its population and cattle decimated by the captivities! Once their chastisement and suffering are over, the

Lord will refashion his people and his land; he prefers to build rather than destroy. Verses 29–30 reflect the bitterness of the exiles who traced their predicament to the sins of their parents and ancestors. They felt that God was judging them unjustly for circumstances they were not responsible for (the popular proverb mentioned in v.29 is also used by Ezekiel in Eze 18:2–4). One would think that in light of Dt 24:16 no one would claim that children had to pay for the sins of their parents. The altogether sufficient answer to the fatalistic despair voiced by the proverb is that in the suffering of Israel individual responsibility is clear. Each man and woman was personally responsible; so none could claim exculpation.

f. God's new covenant (31:31–34)

This portion of the book has been acclaimed as one of the most important passages in the entire OT. It is beyond dispute that the passage has had tremendous influence on NT doctrine. Likely the concept of the new covenant is Jeremiah's greatest contribution to biblical truth.

At this point an outline of the remainder of the chapter, detailing the fullness of Jeremiah's revelation, will be useful:

1. The time of the covenant (v.31)—"The time is coming";

2. The Maker of the covenant (v.31)—the LORD (vv.3, 20, 32, 35);

3. The name of the covenant (v.31)—new (Ro 11:27; Heb 8:6–13; 10:14–18; also Mt 26:26–28; Mk 14:22–24; Lk 22:19–20; 1Co 11:23–25);

4. The parties of the covenant (v.31)—"house of Israel" and "house of Judah" (cf. Eze 37:15–19; Ro 9:4–5);

5. The contrasted covenant (v.32)—not like the old covenant: based on merit and works, susceptible of infraction, no enablement, did not give life (Gal 3:21);

6. The nature of the covenant (vv.33–34)—not dependent on external law nor human interpretation; law written on the heart; gives intimate knowledge of and fellowship with God, forgiveness of sins, and peace of heart;

7. The immutability of the covenant (vv.35–37)—the unchanging purpose of God reflected in the fixed order of nature;

8. The physical aspects of the covenant (vv.38–40)—rebuilt Jerusalem in holiness and permanence;

9. The Guarantor of the covenant (vv.31–40)—"declares the LORD" or "the LORD says" (nine times), as though to swear by himself (cf. Heb 6:17–18).

31 This mountain-peak OT passage stands in a real sense as the climax of Jeremiah's teaching. Jeremiah wrote the passage while he was shut up in the court of the guard. The words "the time is coming" have already been used by Jeremiah; they are an eschatological formula that places the prophecy in messianic times in the Day of the Lord, the consummation period of the nation's history (cf. v.27). The promise relates to a "new covenant" and is a prediction of a radical change in God's economy (i.e., his dealing with humanity). Thus when Jeremiah foretold a new covenant, by implication the Mosaic covenant became the old one (cf. Heb 8:13). Moreover, the new covenant is an eternal one. National covenants do not die because of old age. The old covenant spoke of a great physical deliverance from Egypt through the blood of lambs and the power of God; the new covenant proclaims a great spiritual deliverance from sin and death through the efficacious blood of the Lamb of God and the power of God. The Passover Feast memorialized the first; the Lord's Supper memorializes the second.

Jeremiah explicitly presents the parties to the covenant: the Lord, the house of Israel, and the house of Judah. Notice that the covenant brings to mind the cleavage of the nation into two kingdoms, but notice also that both parts of the nation are included. The whole covenant is for the whole nation. Significantly, the new covenant will be with God's chosen people, as was the old. It could not be made with the church because no former (old) covenant had been made with her.

Does this mean that believers today have no part in this new covenant? Surely not, for the same death of Christ that implemented the new covenant for Israel does so for all sinners for all time. The testimony of the entire NT is too clear on this point to be misunderstood. Because Israel rejected the covenant in the first advent, Gentiles availed themselves of its provisions (cf. Ro 9:30–33); and Israel will yet ratify it at the climax of her history (cf. Zec 12:10–13:1). Thus it is correct to say that all believers in Christ are by virtue of this covenant grafted into the stock of Abraham (cf. Ro 11:16–24).

Does this mean that another covenant needs to be made for either Israel or Gentiles? Obviously not, since both share redemption by faith in the blood of the new covenant. Writing to Hebrews of his time, including believing Hebrews, the writer of the letter to the Hebrews makes clear how the new covenant now avails for both (cf. Heb 8; see also Eph 3:1–7).

Some ask how the new covenant can apply to the church when it was to be negotiated with Israel and Judah. The historical argument is insurmountable: when the new covenant was inaugurated (see the gospel accounts), there was no church, nor could there be until the resurrection of Christ (cf. Eph 1:22–23). Furthermore, although Jer 31 does not state it, the making of the new covenant was inextricably bound up with the crucifixion of Christ for all humankind. When Israel refused to enter into the covenant (cf. Isa 53; Mt 22:1–10; Lk 14:15–23), God having but one way of salvation for all ages of history, the offer of redemption (the procuring means of the covenant) went out to all people. Although the church is not explicitly seen in the OT, the salvation of non-Jews is predicted more than once (cf. Isa 49:1–7, esp. v.6). It is the new truth of the NT that redeemed Jews and Gentiles constitute the church of this age. Salvation is possible only through the death of Christ, and this is the basis of the new covenant. All sinful humanity is thus in view in this covenant. Finally, Israel as a nation will ratify the covenant after the "full number of the Gentiles has come in" (Ro 11:25–27).

32 Jeremiah points out in this verse that the new covenant is built on the fact of Israel's failure under the old covenant. Because the old covenant was a legal one ("If you do . . . I will do"), it was incumbent on both parties to maintain its provisions. Israel did not, for the people broke the first commandment before Moses descended from Sinai. The fault lay with the people and their sin; they broke the covenant. Thus the new covenant must supersede the old. If the old covenant had not been broken, then what need was there for the ministry of Jeremiah or any of the OT prophets?

The day when the covenant was "made with their forefathers" refers to the whole period of the Exodus (cf. 7:22). "I took them by the hand" is a tender nuance of paternal love and concern. The blame for breaking the covenant rested wholly on Israel and Judah, for there was no fault in God; he had ever been as faithful to them as a faithful husband to his wife. This marriage relationship was the very basis on which God expected obedience to and fidelity in the covenant.

33 Once more Jeremiah stresses the nature of the covenant as a national covenant. The parties are the same as in v.31. The time factor is after the return from exile. Instead of changing his covenant relationship to his people because they broke the old covenant, in his grace God finds a way whereby they will not break the new covenant. God will write the law on their hearts. The old covenant had been engraved in stone; the new covenant will include a revolutionary change in will, heart, and conscience. It will be an internal covenant. The law now becomes a principle of life (cf. Ro 8:1–4), a part of the nature of God's people. The core of the new covenant is God's gift of a new heart (cf. Eze 36:25–27). The motivation for obeying God's law is inner knowledge of his will, coupled with an enablement to perform it—all founded on the assurance that sins are forgiven.

Permanence is also a feature of this covenant (cf. vv.35–37). Since the inward dynamic was absent in the old covenant, it could not be effective. There must be an inner force, a new power. The entire transaction implies the new birth set forth in the gospel. The regenerate spirit is the source of all godly action. The "heart" (GK 4213) includes one's emotional, ethical, and intellectual life. The goal of the covenant is that relation between God and his people that was emphasized from Abraham's time on (cf. Eze 11:19; 18:31; 36:26; Jn 1:10–13; 3:1–16).

Is it not strange that many believers today yearn for laws and rules, putting themselves under the economy of the old covenant, which Jeremiah, Christ, and the apostles warned was not capable of fulfillment? No wonder the new covenant is a missionary message for the world! Its nature is individual, internal, and universal. The reason Jeremiah emphasized the national factor (cf. vv.31–33) was that he wanted to stress the origin of the covenant and to sharpen the contrast between the new covenant and the old covenant, which was made with Israel only at Sinai.

34 One grand feature of the new covenant is that it affords a clear apprehension of God and his will by believers without human mediation. God will be known instinctively and his will performed spontaneously (cf. Isa 54:13; Jn 6:45). The knowledge spoken of is not theoretical knowledge transmitted by religious instruction. It is rather knowledge of God based on a heart experience of divine grace and imparted by the Holy Spirit, with assurance that the believer has been received into the family of God through the forgiveness of sins.

This knowledge does not militate against or render unnecessary religious instruction (cf. 1Co 12:28–29; Eph 4:11–12). There will be direct access to God for both Jew and Gentile through Christ, our High Priest (cf. Heb 4:16; 10:19–22). This does not mean that every believer will be self-sufficient and independent of others. But it does indicate that all will have their own experience of God without resort to others. "The least of them" is broad in meaning and includes "the least" in intellectual ability, in influence or position, in moral capacity—all are included in the comprehensive scope of the phrase.

The climax of this wonderful section comes in the revelation that the basis of the new covenant is forgiveness of sin. Thus gratitude for forgiveness will issue in spontaneous obedience. The new covenant does not envision sinlessness but forgiveness of sin, resulting in restoration of fellowship with God. Its foundation is the absolute and complete forgiveness of all sins. The covenant shows no dependence on law, temple, sacrifices, ark, human priesthood, nation, or country. The old covenant did not, could not, and was never intended to save anyone. The last clause of v.34 states that what grace forgives, divine omniscience forgets.

In summary, the enunciation of the new covenant, which differs so much from the old, focuses on its permanence and its sustaining principle that evokes gratitude for the forgiveness of sin. The overarching emotion is love, not fear. The goal in both covenants is the same: "I will be their God, and they will be my people" (cf.Ex 29:45; Lev 26:12).

g. The perpetuity of Israel (31:35–40)

35–37 The value of the new covenant is that it is an eternal covenant made with an eternal people. The permanence of the nation is illustrated from the fixed arrangements in nature. The survival of Israel through the centuries can be explained only on supernatural grounds (cf. 33:20, 25). As unchangeable as the laws of nature is God's covenant with the deathless nation. The concept of "nation" (GK 1580) carries with it geographical location, government, and other ethnic features to be fully realized in the end time. In short, it is utterly impossible that Israel should cease to be a nation before God. National existence is assured, regardless of how God may have to deal with individuals in the nation. God regards his promises rather than their demerits.

38–40 Since a literal nation must have an actual geographical location, it is revealed that the capital, Jerusalem, will be rebuilt and expanded—the very city that Jeremiah was before long to see destroyed by the Chaldean army. A renewed covenant demands a renewed Jerusalem. It will be greatly enlarged and permanently settled. The rebuilding is not for the people themselves or for secular purposes but for the glory of the Lord. It will be dedicated and separated to him.

The rebuilding of the city will encompass the four corners of the capital (cf. Zec 14:10). The Tower of Hananel was the northeast corner of the city (cf. Ne 3:1; 12:39; Zec 14:10). The Corner Gate probably refers to the one at the northwest corner of the city wall (cf. 2Ki 11:13; 2Ch 26:9). The locations of Gareb and Goah are unknown. The valley of the corpses and ashes is generally understood to be the Valley of Hinnom (cf. 7:31). The Kidron flows east of Jerusalem (cf. 2Sa 15:23). The Horse Gate is apparently at the southeast corner of the temple courts (cf. Ne 3:28 with 2Ki 11:16; 2Ch 23:15). Thus even the polluted areas would be sanctified to the Lord.

In strong language this section closes with the affirmation that the city will be invincible forever. A permanent nation calls for a permanent capital. The rebuilding of the city envisioned here cannot be that effected in Nehemiah's day because the contextual considerations demand the end time for Israel (cf. "days are coming" [vv.27, 31]) and the temple rebuilt by Zerubbabel was again thrown down and destroyed (cf. Mt 24:1–2; Lk 21:2–4). Finally, in the broader context of prophecy, this passage will not permit an interpretation that applies it to a spiritual, heavenly, or symbolic Jerusalem.

3. The manifestation of faith (32:1–44)

This chapter shows the reality of Jeremiah's faith in the Lord's promises of the nation's restoration. The time was the second year of the siege of Jerusalem (588–587 B.C.). The siege had begun in Zedekiah's ninth year (cf. 39:1), but the Babylonians had withdrawn on hearing of the approach of the Egyptian army (cf. 37:5). Jerusalem fell in August of the following year, 586 B.C. On "the eighteenth year of Nebuchadnezzar," see comment on 25:1.

Chapter 32 deals with what happened during the years before the capture of Jerusalem, the destruction of the city, and the incidents that immediately followed. What Jeremiah did at that time showed his faith in the nation's restoration to the land after the Captivity. It was indeed a dark time. Jerusalem was undergoing its final siege, and Jeremiah himself was in prison. But it was also just the time for a heroic example of faith.

a. The setting for Jeremiah's act of faith (32:1–5)

1–2 This entire chapter moves within the framework of the OT law of redemption. The tenth year of Zedekiah was 587 B.C. (cf. 2Ki 25:8). The siege of Jerusalem was at an advanced state. The outlook was dark, the situation desperate. Verse 2 tells of Jeremiah's imprisonment; vv.3–5 give the reason for this.

Chapter 37 shows us that Jeremiah had not yet been imprisoned during the Babylonian siege of Jerusalem and the raising of that siege by the approach of the Egyptian army (cf. 37:4–12). During the temporary raising of the Babylonian siege, when he tried to leave the city to go to the land of Benjamin, Jeremiah was taken and thrown into a dungeon on the pretense that he was defecting to the Babylonians (37:11, 16). He remained there until Zedekiah ordered him to appear before him to be questioned about the outcome of the war. When he told Zedekiah that he would be captured by Nebuchadnezzar (37:17), Jeremiah then lamented about the difficulty of his own imprisonment (37:20)

and begged not to be put back into the dungeon. So Zedekiah ordered him (37:21) to be moved to the "courtyard of the guard," where he stayed until the city fell (38:13, 28; 39:14). He was shut up at the request of the officials (38:4–6) and at Zedekiah's command. The courtyard of the guard, probably a stockade (cf. Ne 3:25), was the part of the palace area set apart for prisoners. The soldiers who guarded the palace were quartered there.

3–5 There is no contradiction between v.3 and 37:15. Verse 3 is a general account without details. The officers had confined Jeremiah in Jonathan's house (37:15), but Zedekiah had moved him into the palace (37:21). Even though Zedekiah witnessed the fulfillment of Jeremiah's predictions, he was angry enough to imprison him, as if this could alter what was happening. Zedekiah, then, is ultimately responsible for Jeremiah's imprisonment. Zedekiah should have known by this time that Jeremiah's message was not his own. In plain, unequivocal terms Jeremiah foretold Zedekiah's fate. Most scholars believe that v.4 speaks of the Lord's punishment of Zedekiah. All that is intended by the passage, however, appears to be Zedekiah's death, because he was never released from Babylon.

b. The Lord's command (32:6–8)

6–7 Throughout this chapter Jeremiah is giving his own report of events. His purchase of the field from Hanamel, his cousin, was meant to encourage the people regarding their return from captivity and to show Jeremiah's firm faith in their future despite their desperate situation. The situation is all the more dramatic since the field Jeremiah was to buy had already been captured by the invading Babylonians.

The Lord told Jeremiah in advance that his cousin Hanamel would come to him. That Hanamel did so was in accordance with the law in Lev 25:23–28 (cf. Ru 4:1–6). Family property must not pass into the hands of an outsider. The purpose of this law was to keep property in the family. For the seller this was duty; for the relative or kinsman-redeemer it was a right. Thus such a transaction is spoken of as the duty of redemption and the right of preemption. Hanamel was evidently childless. The passage reveals that the ancient laws of land tenure were still followed in Judah in spite of its apostasy. In addition to the general law for all Israel, these land-tenure laws would in Jeremiah's time have special relevance to alienation of property belonging to priestly families—property that should not pass into nonpriestly hands.

8 Here was a public test of Jeremiah's prophecies about the future blessing of the land. Hanamel was able to visit Jeremiah because the siege was not yet a tight one. His request for his cousin to buy the field seemed preposterous with the enemy at the gates of Jerusalem and exile certain. When Hanamel came, Jeremiah knew that the Lord was behind the offer. He had not doubted the Lord's word and had its confirmation in vv.6–7. Now he realized all the meaning of the purchase in relation to the nation's future.

c. The purchase (32:9–15)

9–11 Jeremiah's faith sustained him in what appeared to be the inevitable loss of his money. We do not know the source of his income, nor can we speculate about the adequacy or inadequacy of the price or about the size of the field. The transaction was carried out with legal precision. This is the only account in the Bible of a purchase of this kind. Before the introduction of coinage about the sixth century B.C., payment in financial transactions was made by weighing out quantities of gold or silver. Signing, sealing, and the presence of witnesses were necessary for legalizing a transaction like the one between Hanamel and Jeremiah. Two copies of the deed were made, one for security and the other for future reference in proving that the agreed-on terms had not been tampered with. All the conditions of the sale were carefully specified. The title deeds went to the buyer. The practice of sealing deeds throws light on the metaphor of the seven-sealed scroll (Rev 5:1), which was the title deed to the world purchased by Christ.

12–14 The deed (in duplicate) was given Baruch, the trusted confidant and secretary of Jeremiah, for preservation from loss or mutilation. Up to this point, Baruch had kept himself in the background; this is the first mention of him in the book. The sale was made as public as possible; secret transactions were avoided. Moreover, the publicity stressed and disseminated the message im-

Jeremiah purchased a title deed to property in Anathoth and put it in a sealed jar. This jar and scroll are like those found at Qumran.

plicit in Jeremiah's purchase of the field. The documents were stored in clay jars to ensure their permanence (the Dead Sea Scrolls, written on leather, have survived in earthenware jars for over two thousand years). Usually the jars were sealed with pitch. As for Jeremiah's transaction, it is obvious that after the Exile the deeds would be of great value to the owners. Here, then, is an instance of ancient title insurance.

15 Finally, Jeremiah stated that his purchase of the field symbolized the restoration of Israel to her land after the Captivity. This afforded comfort to the beleaguered people of Judah. Jeremiah had availed himself of the opportunity the Lord had given him of showing his full confidence in the prophecy that had been revealed to him by the Lord.

d. Jeremiah's doubts and prayer (32:16–25)

16 Jeremiah may have longed for some reconciliation of his purchase with his prophecies of Jerusalem's destruction. There was the possibility that his hearers would accuse him of changing his position on the fate of Judah. He could hardly believe the promises the Lord had commanded him to proclaim. So he had misgivings when he thought it over later on. Although he had explained the meaning of the episode (v.15), he was still troubled by its improbabilities; furthermore, he also longed for reassurance for the people.

17–25 In his prayer Jeremiah deals with the Lord's grace to Israel throughout her long history. He begins at the place where all theology should begin—the person and works of God. He acknowledges the power of God in creation. Then Jeremiah speaks of the boundless grace of God to humankind and the truth of divine retribution for sin. Grace does not disregard the righteousness of God. Divine retribution is likened to a harvest laborer's putting his pay into the folds of his children's garments.

Next Jeremiah magnifies the wisdom of God, who in his omniscience surveys all the deeds of humanity in order to dispense absolute justice. Jeremiah sees the wonderful works the Lord did on behalf of Israel in Egypt as harbingers of mercies he continued to show them "to this day." After that Jeremiah summarizes the Lord's gracious dealings from the Exodus through the Conquest and Israel's settlement in the land. Finally, in spite of this outpouring of God's love to them, Jeremiah acknowledges that Israel decided to live in disobedience to God's will, thus bringing on themselves their present calamities.

The "siege ramps" (GK 6149) were earthworks used in capturing a city. The Babylonians had already reached the city walls. As the Lord had foretold, the enemy had ample weaponry. The siege was successful, the city was doomed, and there was no hope of escape. The Lord's long and patient warnings were coming true. The fall of the city and the divine command for Jeremiah's purchase of land seemed irreconcilable. The incongruity was plain. Why buy the field when it would soon be lost to the Babylonians? Yet God had commanded Jeremiah to buy the field and to do it publicly. It was a situation calling for faith in and obedience to the word the Lord had given him to proclaim. So Jeremiah prayed for illumination rather than for confirmation of his understanding of the purpose of God.

e. The Lord's answer (32:26–35)

26–29 The Lord's reply to Jeremiah's prayer was reassuring. As impossible as a bright future for Jeremiah and his people might seem, it was not outside the range of the Lord's power. The omnipotent God is the source of confidence for believers in all ages. So the Lord's assurance came to Jeremiah in the very words he had used (cf. v.17). A divine summary of the nation's punishment follows. The people's sins had made judgment inescapable, and Nebuchadnezzar's capture of Jerusalem was the inevitable retribution for persistent idolatry. The homes the Lord had given his people had been used for the degenerate worship of Baal. That the people practiced their idolatry on the rooftops shows their brazen defiance of the Lord's repeated warnings.

30–33 The nation's stubborn resistance to the Lord's will had characterized the people from the beginnings of their national existence, which 2:2 places at the Exodus (cf. Ex 32). The reference to the work of their hands probably includes not only their idols but also their deeds in general. This was what aroused God's wrath in punishing them. In sweeping condemnation Jeremiah declares the long-standing character of their idolatry "from the day [the city] was built." Solomon had completed the building of the city, and he was the first of all Israel's kings to fall into idolatry. All the inhabitants of the city, from the highest to the lowest, were implicated in the sin, unwilling to be taught and to be turned from their wicked practices.

34–35 The height of the nation's impiety was reached when the people set up their idols in the temple of God himself. Their obscene symbols had been removed during Josiah's reforms, but they were reintroduced in the years of apostasy after Josiah's reign (cf. 7:30; 2Ki 23:4, 6). Molech worship included human sacrifice; so along with gross idolatry went child sacrifice (cf. 19:1–13). So abhorrent was this practice that the Lord by a strong anthropomorphism says that it had never entered his mind that his favored people would stoop so low.

f. Promises of restoration (32:36–44)

36–42 The Lord views the "city" as representing the whole kingdom. In their ultimate condition, the people would be restored to their land, and the country would again be prosperous. After the punishment, a godly remnant would return from exile to normal activity. "All the lands" presupposes a worldwide dispersion.

The new covenant is reiterated because the prophets looked forward to more than just a physical return of the people (cf. 31:32). The covenant bond between God and his people will be renewed, and they will walk in righteousness. This relationship is at the heart of the covenant in the past and in the future. Material and spiritual blessings go hand in hand. Moreover, the nation will be characterized by unity of purpose and life. They will show singleness of purpose in both thoughts and acts devoted to the Lord. The reference to inner disposition and outward expression again points to the new covenant with its promise of a new heart. Unity always characterizes the Messianic Era (cf. Zep 3:9; Zec 14:9; Jn 10:16). The covenant will never again be broken (cf. Isa 55:3; Eze 37:26). Moreover, the promise of restoration ("assuredly plant them") is just as certain as the predictions of punishment. Whatever God foretells, he makes good.

43–44 Finally, Jeremiah returns to the main theme of this chapter. His transaction was an example to be universally followed in the future restoration. What he did will be repeated by many others in that coming day. A population increase after the decimation of warfare and exile is implied. Jeremiah mentions several specific places in the land to show that the Lord's promise covers the whole country (cf. 17:26). Benjamin is mentioned first perhaps because of the property of Jeremiah at Anathoth.

4. The righteous reign of the Davidic Ruler (33:1–26)

This chapter concludes the Book of Consolation (chs. 30–33). The remainder of Jeremiah deals with Jerusalem's final siege and destruction and with the ultimate results of the prophecies against the nations. It also contains additional promises of future blessing. The theme of ch. 33 is the restoration of Jerusalem and the reestablishment of its worship. The date and occasion are the same as in ch. 32. Once more the Lord gives Judah light in her darkest hours.

a. The exhortation to call on the Lord (33:1–3)

1–3 This new message probably came to Jeremiah soon after the Lord spoke to him about the field (ch. 32). He was still impris-

oned in the courtyard of the guard, where the elders and officers of the king could consult him. But the word of God is not bound. The pronouncements now to be given Jeremiah are weighty; so the Lord underscores their veracity by affixing his eternal name to them. He himself is surety for the program he is unfolding. So he invites Jeremiah to ask him for remarkable disclosures. The things to be revealed are "unsearchable" (GK 1290) because they are beyond the grasp of human knowledge. The things under consideration are the truths concerning the restoration of the nation and Jerusalem.

b. The certainty of the fall of Jerusalem (33:4–5)

4–5 All the efforts of the king and his people to save Jerusalem would be futile. Theirs was a lost cause. "The houses . . . and the royal palaces of Judah" were not demolished by the enemy but by the besieged people of Jerusalem who used them for defense against the Babylonians. But whatever measures were taken to defend the city would be useless. "The dead bodies" refers to the defenders of Jerusalem, not to the Babylonians. Opposing the invaders could not change the situation, for God had withdrawn his favor from his people because of their wickedness.

c. Days of return and rejoicing (33:6–13)

6–9 Past trials will yet be turned into blessings. So Jeremiah sets forth promises of prosperity: health, restoration, joy, and peace. The word "health" (GK 776) is literally "new flesh." The Exile will have a healing effect. The wounds of the nation will be bound up in peace and security. God will repair the losses and rebuild the land that had been destroyed. The restoration of Judah and Israel must refer to the latter days (i.e., the Messianic era) because the captivity of Israel did not end after seventy years. Judah and Israel will be restored as one kingdom, just as they were before the division of the kingdom under Rehoboam. Far more important than any territorial restitution will be the pardon and cleansing from the Lord. The future for the Jews will be so glorious that the nations will stand in awe of them and tremble at their greatness. Thus Jerusalem, with its former state reversed, will be made holy.

10–11 Jeremiah sees Judah and Jerusalem as already desolate and fallen. But they will arise; there will be joy in worship in the temple. Joy and gladness will not only mark the relationships of God's people but will also mark their worship in his temple. The liturgical words are those used by the Levitical singers in the temple service (Ps 106:1) and show that the temple will be rebuilt and the ministry restored as in preexilic days. Joy will be accompanied by security.

12–13 The reference to shepherds with their flocks points to a future time of peace, tranquillity, and prosperity. In ancient Israel and Judah, shepherds counted their sheep as they came to the fold at night. So in the restored and united kingdom, the shepherds will count their sheep in peace.

d. Restoration of royalty and priesthood (33:14–22)

14 Jeremiah declares that monarchy and priesthood, interrupted by the Exile, will coexist permanently. He proclaims the perpetuity of the Davidic dynasty and the Levitical priesthood without equivocation. The predicted restoration ("the days are coming") is not, however, to be looked for in the immediate time of the return from the Exile. Only in a limited and preliminary way were these promises fulfilled in Zerubbabel and Sheshbazzar after the Exile (cf. Ezr 1:8; 2:2; also 2:40–54; 8:15–20). Ultimately, they are combined in the highest sense in Christ (cf. Ps 110:4) and are yet to be fulfilled in his reign on earth.

15 The good word the prophets announced comprises the entire panorama of glorious promises made to both parts of the nation. "Those days" are the messianic times (cf. the parallel prophecy in 23:1–8). It is through the Lord Messiah, the righteous One, that the restoration and attendant blessings will be realized. Jeremiah's picture of the coming Messiah is varied and unique. He pictures the coming Messiah as (1) "the spring of living water" (2:13); (2) the good "shepherd" (23:4; 31:10); (3) the "righteous Branch" (here and 23:5); (4) the "Redeemer" (50:34); (5) "The LORD Our Righteousness" (23:6); (6) "David their king" (30:9); and (7) the agent of "the new covenant" (31:31–34).

16 Salvation and safety are in store for Judah and Jerusalem because of the presence of justice and righteousness personified. The name given the Messiah in 23:6 is here given to Jerusalem. The holy city can have the same name as the Messiah because she reflects that righteousness the Messiah bestows on her. Jerusalem will then be the embodiment of the nation's ideal in the Messiah. The city will be marked by righteousness.

17–18 If one sees in these verses a constant presence and succession of Davidic rulers and Levitical priests, then history does not validate this interpretation. But the passage claims no such thing. It says only that David's dynasty will never cease. Temporary interruption is only apparent; there is no true cessation. David's Scion still lives in the Messiah. To Jeremiah, David will never lack a descendant to occupy his throne. His dynasty will never be permanently cut off (see Lk 1:32–33 and comments). The permanence of the royal and priestly lines is thus forcefully stated. In the highest sense Christ as King-Priest, of course, fulfills these promises (cf. Ps 110:4).

But in the priestly realm the primary emphasis is on Levi's line, which must not be confused with Christ's priesthood after the order of Melchizedek. Monarchy and priesthood were the two bases of the OT theocracy. When these appeared to be in danger of extinction in Jeremiah's day, we find their continuance couched in sure and irrevocable terms. What is affirmed of the monarchy in v.17 is promised the priesthood in v.18. The Levitical priesthood is assured a permanent ministry (cf. Nu 25:13). As legitimate priests, they will serve the Lord.

19–22 What has been stated in 31:35–37 as a guarantee of the new covenant is now used to illustrate the certainty of the continuance of the monarchy and priesthood. The greater the promises, the stronger the assurances that they will be fulfilled. The certainty of the prophecies is riveted in God's order in nature, and the prophecies themselves are linked with the unfailing regularity of the natural order. A nullification of the covenant is an impossibility. Just as the covenant with Noah (cf. Ge 8:22) is kept, so the covenant with David (cf. 2Sa 7) and that with Levi (Nu 17) will also be kept. Moreover, the Lord adds a promise of a great increase in the descendants of David and the Levites; what was originally stated of the entire nation is here specifically applied to them (cf. Ge 15:5; 22:17).

e. Confirmation of the promises (33:23–26)

23–24 The reproach that the nation had suffered from her neighbors and even the unbelievers in her midst will be removed. The two kingdoms are Israel and Judah. This points to a time when the nation will still be divided as in Rehoboam's time. Certain Jews, discouraged by the times, thought that without freedom and a government of their own they were no longer a nation (cf. Ro 11:1). The fear and lament of the people shows that they considered that God had forsaken them utterly and finally.

25–26 Of what use would the greatest national promises be if the nation did not exist to enjoy them? The Lord guarantees his people that he will make good every promise. They will certainly return from exile. They are undeniably the eternal nation. The Lord will allow no one to impugn his covenant promises to Israel. The threefold mention of the patriarchs points to the whole chain of promises repeatedly given them. Nature will utterly collapse before God goes back on the slightest promise to his people.

C. Messages and Events Before the Fall of Jerusalem (34:1–39:18)

1. Zedekiah and the mistreated slaves (34:1–22)

Chapters 34–38 are largely occupied with Jeremiah's experiences during the siege of Jerusalem. Like other portions of the book, they are not in strict chronological order. Most of the events they narrate took place in the reigns of Jehoiakim and Zedekiah, shortly before the fall of Jerusalem in 586 B.C.

a. The warning to Zedekiah (34:1–7)

1–2 This section stresses the certainty of the Babylonian capture of Jerusalem. In view of this it would have been wise for Zedekiah to surrender. Jeremiah's faithfulness in delivering this warning led to his imprisonment. He set clear choices and their consequences before the king.

This passage must be dated before the actual siege began (i.e., 589–588 B.C.; cf. 39:1–2; 2Ki 24:20–25:1), because the Judean cities were only being threatened by Nebuchadnezzar at this time, and Jeremiah was not yet in prison. Cities like Lachish and Azekah (v.7) were not yet captured and Jerusalem was still free. The siege itself lasted from 588–586 B.C. Soldiers came from subject countries to join in the siege (cf. 2Ki 24:2). As v.22 shows, the Babylonians, who had temporarily retired from the siege (37:5), would return to finish the destruction of Jerusalem.

3 This verse discloses the fate of Zedekiah in the siege. The Lord's message to him was that he should not be led astray by the temporary respite in the siege; the situation was actually hopeless. Zedekiah himself would have to face the invader (32:4). The mention of a face-to-face confrontation with Nebuchadnezzar shows something of the fear he inspired. Zedekiah could not escape the consequences of his treason in breaking his covenant with Nebuchadnezzar. He would have to answer personally for it. After his confrontation with Nebuchadnezzar, Zedekiah was blinded and taken to Babylon (52:11; cf. Eze 12:13).

4–5 Through Jeremiah the Lord counseled Zedekiah to surrender. The Lord promised him that he would not be slain but would die in captivity. Unlike Jehoiakim (cf. 22:18–19), Zedekiah would die a natural death. The "funeral fire" does not refer to cremation, which was not practiced by the Hebrews, but to the custom of burning spices at royal funerals (cf. 2Ch 16:14; 21:19). The lamentation "Alas, O master!" was normally used of mourning for a king (cf. 22:18).

6–7 Speaking so boldly to the king was hazardous, but Jeremiah feared only God. At the time of this prophecy the only cities that remained uncaptured were Jerusalem, Lachish, and Azekah. The latter two had been fortified by Rehoboam (2Ch 11:5, 9); both were southwest of Jerusalem—Lachish, thirty-five miles, Azekah, fifteen miles, not far from the Philistine border. Since their fall was necessary to the capture of Jerusalem, they marked the southern limit of Nebuchadnezzar's invasion. The Lachish Letters give a vivid picture of these events. Letter 4 reads: "We are watching for the smoke signals of Lachish . . . because we do not see Azekah." That is, Azekah had already fallen. Lachish capitulated soon after this.

b. The perfidy against the slaves (34:8–11)

8–10 When the siege became more severe, Zedekiah made a covenant with the people to liberate their Hebrew slaves. The Hebrew law concerning slavery (cf. Ex 21:1–11; Lev 25:39–55; Dt 15:12–18) apparently had fallen into disuse. The covenant did not follow the letter of the law because it liberated all the slaves no matter how long they had served. It was ratified most solemnly in the temple (cf. vv.18–20). The covenant probably was made with the thought that the liberated slaves would join in defending the city.

11 When the siege was temporarily lifted through the intervention of their Egyptian allies, the Jews forced the liberated slaves back into former bondage. This was not only a shameful repudiation of their solemn covenant but a flagrant violation of Dt 15:12; it also profaned the Lord's name, in which they had made the covenant. To reimpose slavery on those who had been freed showed that the covenant had not been motivated by compassion, justice, and obedience to the Lord's command.

c. The sin of the nation (34:12–16)

12–14 The Lord reminds the people that their ancestors had been slaves in Egypt. Who, then, should have more compassion on slaves than those who were obligated to keep the Passover, the annual celebration of Israel's release from Egyptian slavery? Part of the law given at Sinai dealt with Hebrew slaves, and this the people had disobeyed. The words "sold himself" reflect the Near Eastern custom of voluntary slavery for economic reasons. The covenant Zedekiah made did not exactly fit the law in Dt 15:1, 12, because it required the immediate liberation of all slaves, not just those who had served six years. Thus the law did not cover this case. The "seventh year" is the year of liberation; the Hebrews counted both the first and the last years in calculating time periods.

15–16 The sin of Zedekiah and his people was especially serious because they had made the covenant of freedom in the house and name of the Lord. In contrast to earlier generations, they had decided to obey the law of releasing Hebrew slaves. Their covenant was not only a civil and economic act but a religious one as well. Their perfidy had profaned

the Lord's name, in which they had sworn this covenant. Zedekiah was already notorious for breaking his pledged word (cf. Eze 17:11–21) to Nebuchadnezzar on ascending the throne of Judah.

d. The Lord's retribution for the perfidy (34:17–22)

17–22 Since they had not actually given the slaves freedom, God ironically declares that the people themselves would be freed—freed from his protecting hand. The guilty would be freed for doom and destruction. Because they had enslaved their brothers and sisters, they were to be subjected to their enemies. The ancient method of making a covenant is indicated in v.18 (cf. Ge 15:9–17). The intention was that as they passed through the pieces of the divided sacrifice they invoked on themselves a curse that, if they broke the covenant, they would be cut in pieces like the sacrificial calf. Notice how large a number of the people had contracted to release slaves. The heinousness of their sin is underlined by the punishment decreed for them. The Babylonians had only temporarily lifted the siege to meet Pharaoh Hophra (cf. 37:5, 7–10). The Lord assured Zedekiah and the people that the destruction would finally be consummated. The Babylonians did return and destroyed the city.

2. The faithfulness of the Recabites (35:1–19)

The events of this chapter (which, along with ch. 36, precede chs. 32–34 chronologically) occurred at the close of Jehoiakim's reign, some seventeen years earlier (i.e., about 606 B.C.). The Babylonians and Arameans were ravaging the land (cf. v.11; 2Ki 24:2) and had driven many in Judah, the Recabites among them, to take refuge in Jerusalem.

a. Jeremiah's test of the Recabites (35:1–5)

1–2 The episode is a rebuke to the nation for their unfaithfulness to God. "The Recabite family" refers to their clan. They were a separatist group, stemming from Jonadab (or Jehonadab, c. 840 B.C.; cf. 2Ki 10:15–23). Desiring to return to the simplicity of the nomadic life, they had banned all sedentary occupations. As relations of the Kenites, they were kindred of Jethro, Moses' father-in-law (cf. Jdg 1:16; 1Ch 2:55). Their ancestor Jonadab was prominent in purging the northern kingdom of Baal worship in the time of Jehu (c. 840 B.C.). The Recabites lived in the southern deserts (1Sa 15:6) and in Israelite territory (Jdg 4:17; 5:24). With the fall of the northern kingdom, they moved south into Judah. The "side rooms" were probably anterooms of the temple used for storage and available to the Levites (cf. 1Ch 28:12). This chapter must not be interpreted in such a way as to imply that God necessarily approved of the restriction Jonadab placed on his descendants, the Recabites. What God commended was the fidelity of the Recabites to their convictions.

3–5 Jeremiah's testing of the Recabites was commanded by the Lord. We know essentially nothing of the persons mentioned in vv.3–4, except for Maaseiah, who was probably the father of Zephaniah the priest (cf. 21:1; 29:25; 37:3). He was in charge of the money given for the temple repair (cf. 2Ki 12:10). Jaazaniah was probably the leader of the group. The leaders were brought into the house of the Lord in order to publicize the message that was to follow. "The sons of Hanan" (a prophet of God) were probably his disciples. He appears to have been in sympathy with Jeremiah. The three leaders (cf. 52:24; 2Ki 25:18) probably had charge of the inner and outer court of the temple and the entrance door. They ranked next to the high priest and his deputy. Jeremiah put wine before the Recabites and invited them to drink.

b. The Recabites' loyalty to Jonadab (35:6–11)

6–11 The Recabites could not be tempted to disregard the commands of their ancestor, called "father" (GK 3) in the broad Semitic sense of ancestor. This prohibition was apparently meant to help them escape the defiling Baal worship, which was accompanied by wine drinking and carousing. Viniculture could not be carried on under nomadic conditions, so it too was banned. The restrictions imposed by Jonadab, however, went far beyond abstinence from wine and grape growing; they led to an austere and nomadic lifestyle, reminiscent of the Nazirites (cf. Nu 6:1–21). For over two hundred years this clan had obeyed their forefather's command. Again, Jeremiah's commendation was not the asceticism of the Recabites but their fidelity to Jonadab. With the invasion of Nebuchadnezzar and the Arameans, the Recabites could no longer live in tents in the open country but were forced to seek refuge in Jerusalem; but this did not compel them to drink wine.

c. The rebuke to Judah (35:12–17)

12–17 These verses drive home the purpose of the Recabite episode. Jeremiah probably spoke these words in one of the temple courts. They were meant to shame the people of Judah and Jerusalem for the way they had treated the Lord.

1. The Recabites obeyed a fallible leader; Judah's leader was the eternal God (cf. Mal 1:6).

2. Jonadab gave his commands to the Recabites only once; God repeatedly sent his messages to his people through his prophets.

3. The restrictions that bound the Recabites did not deal with eternal issues; God's messages to his people had eternal as well as temporal implications.

4. The Recabites obeyed the commands of Jonadab for about three hundred years; the Lord's people constantly disobeyed.

5. The loyalty of the Recabites would be rewarded; for their disloyalty God's people would be punished.

d. The Recabites' reward (35:18–19)

18–19 In promising to bless the Recabites for their fidelity, God did not commend all aspects of their lifestyle (cf. 32:1–15 on land tenure). The expression "serve me" (lit., "stand in my presence") has been variously understood. It is a technical term for the privilege of service, used of prophets (1Ki 17:1), priests (Nu 16:9), and kings (1Ki 10:8). The term usually involves service in the temple but may not connote that here. Some think the promise in v.18 was literally fulfilled in the Recabites' being in some way incorporated into the tribe of Levi. But the promise may be a general one because the expression was used of patriarchs (Ge 19:27), of Moses and Samuel (Jer 15:1), and of the nation worshiping the Lord (7:10).

3. Jehoiakim's penknife and God's Word (36:1–32)

This chapter contains a unique description of the writing of a substantial portion of God's Word. We learn from it how Jeremiah's prophecies were written down after he had spoken them. In those days dictating to a secretary was common. Taking dictation was then, as now, a specialized skill. Jeremiah dictated his book in Jehoiakim's fourth year (605 B.C.); when the first copy was destroyed (cf. vv.23, 32), a new one with additions was produced. This was a year of highly significant events: the Battle of Carchemish, the defeat of Pharaoh Neco, and the subjugation of Jehoiakim to Nebuchadnezzar. Events before and after the siege of Jerusalem are covered in chs. 36–44.

a. The dictation of the scroll (36:1–8)

1–3 The year is the same as in 25:1 (see comments). The way the events are narrated implies the presence of an eyewitness—doubtless Baruch, Jeremiah's secretary. The Lord commanded Jeremiah to write on a scroll all the messages he had received from the Lord from the beginning of his ministry under Josiah "till now," i.e., the fourth year of Jehoiakim (cf. 25:1–3; 30:2). (These were undoubtedly the messages Jeremiah had spoken to the people.) The contents of the scroll probably included a summary of Jeremiah's messages from 626–605 B.C. The written word might be more successful than the preached word. The impending capture of Jerusalem added weight to the hope that the Lord's warnings through his prophet might yet be effective. The purpose of all Jeremiah's prophecies of judgment was to spur the nation to repentance, hence the conditional nature of the warnings (cf. 18:8; 26:3).

4–8 Baruch, the prophet's secretary, came from a prominent family (cf. 45:1; 51:59). Jeremiah was inspired by the Lord to dictate to Baruch from memory. The dates in this chapter (vv.1, 9, 22) show that a number of months passed between the dictation and public reading of what was written. Jeremiah was "restricted" from going to the temple. The authorities had probably forbidden him to speak there because of his unpopular temple address (cf. 7:1–15; 26:1–7). With Nebuchadnezzar on the march against Jerusalem, Jeremiah's message could no longer be considered harmless. Because he could not go to the temple, he had Baruch act as his agent. To guarantee a good hearing of his written messages, Jeremiah chose a fast day when the people would be assembled in the temple. After the Exile, fast days were specified (cf.

Zec 7:3, 5; 8:19), but earlier they were called in times of emergency (cf. Joel 2:12, 15). Some public calamity had occasioned this fast. Internationally, it was a most opportune time for a fast because Jeremiah saw the significance of Egypt's defeat by the Babylonians at Carchemish in 605 B.C. There was a feeling that turning to the Lord in a public fast might avert the judgment that had been conditionally predicted.

b. The public reading (36:9–10)

9 The "fifth" year was 604 B.C., and the "ninth" month was about December. The fast (proclaimed by the people, not the king) was not that of the seventh month stated in the Law (cf. Lev 16:29; 23:27) but possibly one specially designated because of the first capture of Jerusalem in 605 B.C. (Jerusalem would again be invaded in 597 and 586 B.C.). The ninth month was the one in which the Babylonians sacked the Philistine city of Ashkelon. These events may have decided Jehoiakim's shift of allegiance from Egypt to Babylon. The public reading was the first of three readings that day (cf. vv.10, 15, 21). Because of the repeated readings, it is probable that only certain portions were read.

10 Gemariah was the son of Shaphan, Josiah's secretary of state (cf. 2Ki 22:3, 8, 12). This Gemariah was the brother of Ahikam, a friend of Jeremiah (cf. 26:24); he was not the Gemariah mentioned in 29:3. Shaphan's family was evidently a noble, godly one. Gemariah permitted Baruch to use his room in the temple's inner court. Evidently Baruch stationed himself at the door to Gemariah's room so that what he read could be heard by the assembled people.

c. The reading to the officials (36:11–19)

11–15 It was in Micaiah's father's chambers that Baruch read the scroll for the first time (cf. v.10). Micaiah doubtless felt that what Baruch had read affected the public interest; so he told the officials about it. When they had heard what was in the scroll, their response was immediate; and they asked that it be read to them. Of the officials mentioned, Jehudi, otherwise unknown, must have been an important person, since his ancestry is traced back to the third generation. Cushi (lit., "Ethiopian") does not necessarily imply Ethiopian descent, because the prophet

Zephaniah (cf. Zep 1:1) was a son of Cushi and of Hebrew descent. Observe the interest and respect the officials had for the message of the scroll. The way they addressed Baruch (vv.15, 19) implies that they favored him and Jeremiah. Baruch assumed the sitting position of an Oriental teacher (cf. Lk 4:20).

16–19 The reading showed the officials truths so opposed to the hopes of the king that they were stricken with fear. They believed the prophecies and may have feared for the lives of Baruch and Jeremiah as well as their own. Jehoiakim was no champion of the truth. Not in the sense of informers, but because of the terrifying contents of the book, they felt that the king should hear the message. The scroll contained such bold announcements at a time of crisis and struggle for the nation's existence that they felt it imposed a solemn responsibility on them. Not wishing to appear before the king as uninformed, they asked Baruch how the scroll had come to be written. Artlessly, he told them precisely how he had written down what Jeremiah had dictated. He had only put down the words; in no sense was he a collaborator or an editor. Realizing the potential danger involved and knowing the king's character, the officials showed their concern for the safety of Jeremiah and Baruch. Later on (cf. v.25) they even risked the king's displeasure. Their concern for safety was a wise precaution (cf. 26:20–23).

d. The reading to Jehoiakim (36:20–26)

20–21 King Jehoiakim's reception of the message was openly hostile. Unlike Josiah, his godly father (cf. 2Ki 22:1–23:25), Jehoiakim was not interested in spiritual reform but in an alliance with Egypt and, hence, was not favorable to Babylon (cf. 2Ki 23:34–35). Before the officials came into the inner courtyard where the king's chambers were, they deposited the scroll in the room of Elishama for safekeeping. They may have surmised what Jehoiakim's response to it would be; so they tried to keep it out of his reach. But the king ordered the scroll read in his presence.

22–26 So startling are the events that follow that Jeremiah describes them in detail. The king was in the winter house, a warm apartment in a sheltered part of the palace facing the winter sun (cf. Am 3:15). It was December, 604 B.C. A brazier ("firepot") with burning charcoal was placed in a low place in the middle of the room. Jehoiakim reacted violently to the reading. In an appalling act of blasphemy and contempt for God's written Word, Jehoiakim took a scribe's knife and cut off consecutive strips of the scroll as Jehudi read them and tossed them into the fire. Most of the court officials stood by indifferently. They shared the king's contempt for God's truth. Three men who opposed the king's actions are mentioned. Elnathan (cf. 26:22) was now on Jeremiah's side. In a further act, Jehoiakim compounded his sin by ordering the arrest of Baruch and Jeremiah. But the Lord intervened and used faithful friends to hide them.

e. The prophecies rewritten (36:27–28)

27–28 Soon after the king's destruction of the scroll, the Lord ordered Jeremiah to write a duplicate of it. God's message was not to be lost but rewritten *in toto*—with more added to it.

f. The condemnation of Jehoiakim (36:29–31)

29–31 The king's anger at Babylon may show that Jehoiakim had already decided on rebellion against Babylon (cf. 2Ki 24:1), a rebellion that resulted in the captivity during the reign of Jehoiachin. The three-month reign of Jehoiachin (cf. 2Ki 24:6, 8) does not contradict the prediction of v.30. Jehoiachin's succession was not a valid one but only a token one because he was immediately besieged by Nebuchadnezzar, surrendered in three months, and then went into exile, where he died after many years. No other descendant of Jehoiakim ever ascended the throne (Zedekiah was the uncle of Jehoiachin). Possibly Jehoiakim died either in a palace uprising or in an uprising of the people (cf. 22:18–19).

g. The prophecies recorded again (36:32)

32 Jehoiakim's destruction of the scroll was one of many attempts through the centuries to destroy God's Word. It is certain that our present text of the book of Jeremiah is longer than the original portions that had brief abstracts of Jeremiah's earlier prophecies. The additions doubtless included the doom of the godless king.

4. Resolute Jeremiah and weak Zedekiah (37:1–21)

Chapters 37–44 are a continuous record of the later work and experiences of Jeremiah, beginning with the accession of Zedekiah. They include the incidents from the fall of the city and from Jeremiah's sojourn in Egypt. In ch. 37 we have the captivity of the prophet, in ch. 39 that of Zedekiah.

a. Zedekiah's request (37:1–5)

1 This verse shows the fulfillment of the judgment Jeremiah pronounced against the godless Jehoiakim in 36:30. Instead of Jehoiakim's son Jehoiachin, Nebuchadnezzar put on the throne Zedekiah, Jehoiakim's brother and thus the uncle of Jehoiachin. The latter was deported to Babylon after three months' reign. Zedekiah had solemnly pledged his loyalty to Nebuchadnezzar in the name of the Lord. Because of Egyptian influence at his court, which he could not resist, Zedekiah decided to break his pledge. This was the immediate cause of the final siege of Jerusalem. This chapter appears to be the beginning of Zedekiah's reign, but earlier chapters have already spoken of him (cf. chs. 21, 27–79, 32, 34). He reigned for eleven years (597–586 B.C.).

2–3 The root of Judah's trouble was spiritual; the people were disobedient to God. In spite of his refusal to heed the word of God, Zedekiah sent messengers to Jeremiah (cf. 21:1–2). The approach of the Egyptian forces (vv.5, 9) seemed to contradict the message of 34:2–7; moreover, with the withdrawal of the Babylonian army, Zedekiah may have thought that Jeremiah's predictions of doom were wrong after all. Also, Zedekiah may have been encouraged by his alliance with Pharaoh Hophra (c. 590–570 B.C.). At any rate, he revolted against Babylon. Perhaps wanting a message from Jeremiah that would please him, he asked the prophet to pray for him (i.e., to support his actions). What Zedekiah wanted was for the Lord to make the temporary withdrawal of the Babylonians permanent. He may somehow have felt that the presence of Jeremiah, though he predicted doom, would ensure God's protection against Jerusalem's capture. As for his regard for Jeremiah, it was with superstition. Jehucal (cf. 38:1), one of the messengers sent to Jeremiah, later became an enemy of the prophet.

4–5 Jeremiah was not yet imprisoned (see also v.13). To help understand the narrative, there is a historical note in v.5 (see 34:8–11). At the approach of Egyptian troops, led by Hophra (cf. 44:30), Babylon temporarily raised her siege of Jerusalem. Soon after this, the Babylonians defeated the Egyptians and resumed the siege of Jerusalem.

b. Jeremiah's reply (37:6–10)

6–10 Jeremiah did not waver in his fidelity to the truth. The relief of Jerusalem was, he said, only temporary and would ultimately change nothing. This was only a passing incident. Circumstances and appearances to the contrary, God's ultimate word about Jerusalem was that it would be taken and burned. There was no basis for a false hope. Then the prophet stated in the strongest terms God's unchanging purpose to destroy Jerusalem. This was unquestionably his will. Escape was out of the question. Even the "wounded" would be able to carry out the doom threatening God's people.

c. The charge of treason against Jeremiah (37:11–15)

11–12 This section deals with Jeremiah's imprisonment after he was charged with treason. There was no proof whatever that he meant to defect to the Babylonians when the siege was temporarily lifted. His enemies misinterpreted his leaving the city and threw him into a dungeon. Apparently he left the city to care for certain of his property affairs in his native Anathoth. Jeremiah's intention is clear; the time was opportune for settling his affairs. But he planned to remain in Judah in spite of his divinely given warnings of impending disaster.

13–15 The Benjamin Gate was north of the city and led to the territory of that tribe. Irijah accused Jeremiah, who was already suspect because of his exhortations to surrender to the invaders (cf. 21:8–10), of defecting to the enemy. But Jeremiah could hardly have been deserting to the enemy, because they were already gone. The charge was vicious and nonsensical. Perhaps revenge for Jeremiah's prediction of the death of Irijah's grandfather Hananiah (cf. 28:16) motivated the charge. Many who heard Jeremiah followed his advice and deserted to the Babylonians (cf. 38:2, 19; 39:9; 52:15). The officials involved in beating and arresting him were surely not those of Josiah's time (cf. 26:16; 36:19), for they were probably captives in Babylon with Jehoiachin. Beating Jeremiah was an indignity his sensitive spirit felt deeply.

The home of Jonathan the secretary was made the prophet's prison, perhaps because he was just one of many deserters and political prisoners. It was not uncommon in the ancient East to use part of an officer's home as a prison. The treatment Jeremiah received is understandable, not excusable, on the grounds of the desperate plight of the city. Jonathan's house turned out to be a place where Jeremiah's life was endangered.

d. Jeremiah in the dungeon (37:16–21)

16–17 The prophet was put in "a vaulted cell in a dungeon" (lit., "the house of the cistern-pit"). The cell was a subterranean room adjoining the dungeon. The "long time" refers to the period when the Babylonians renewed their siege. So desperate was the situation for Jerusalem that Zedekiah felt he must have another message from Jeremiah even if he had to speak to him in secret. The nature of this meeting shows Jeremiah's unpopularity as well as Zedekiah's weakness in confronting his officials face to face. By this time he realized that Jeremiah was a true prophet of God. Evidently he was hoping Jeremiah would give him a more encouraging word about the Babylonian menace. But Jeremiah did not change his message; it was God's word, and the condition of Judah remained the same. Though without confidence in his advisers, Zedekiah was too weak to take a firm stand.

18–20 Jeremiah asked for justice, not pity. He wanted a valid accusation because he knew he was innocent of any treasonable actions. Since his words had proved to be true, why should he be imprisoned? If he was imprisoned for telling the truth, why were the false prophets, whose predictions were unfulfilled, not given the same treatment? They were the real traitors. Jeremiah's questions were uncomfortably fair because events had unmasked the false prophets (cf. Dt 13:1–5; 18:20–22). The situation was ironic: the false prophets who lied to the king and the nation were free; Jeremiah who told them the truth was in prison! The prophet then asks not to

be sent back to the house of Jonathan the secretary, lest he die there.

21 Solicitous for the welfare of the prophet, Zedekiah reversed the decision of his officials and transferred Jeremiah to the guardroom, a move that doubtless gave him more security and saved him other indignities. The king also gave him a daily allotment from the rapidly failing food supply. But he did not liberate the prophet, because he still feared his officials.

5. Confined in a cistern (38:1–13)

The events recorded in this chapter took place near the end of the siege of Jerusalem. As tensions mounted in Judah, the anti-Babylonian group at court wanted to do away with their chief opponent, Jeremiah.

a. The accusation against Jeremiah (38:1–4)

1–3 The officials' opposition to Jeremiah kept up to the fall of Jerusalem. They hated him for his condemnation of their godless policies. The four mentioned doubtless represented a larger group. Jeremiah's confinement in the courtyard of the guard (cf. 37:21) still permitted him to make his message known. With the security of the guardroom as a base, he could have had access to a good many people. Gedaliah was probably the son of the Pashhur who beat Jeremiah and placed him in the stocks (cf. 20:1–6). Jehucal is mentioned in 37:3. All were in the Egyptian party. They naturally quoted Jeremiah's words in their accusation. They considered his messages treasonable, and even to ordinary listeners they sounded that way. Clearly, Jeremiah spoke as one constrained by the Lord. His counsel was either to surrender or suffer ruin.

4 Jeremiah was officially charged with working against the war effort and with weakening the will of the people to resist the invaders. Since he was speaking during the final months of the siege, no wonder his message was judged dangerous. By weakening the morale of the soldiers with whom he was in contact in the guardroom, he infuriated his enemies. There was probably truth in the statement of Jeremiah's opposition (cf. v.19) because some would have believed his words. The officials on whom the burden of the defense of the city rested saw him only as a traitor and called for his death. Judah's leaders never saw that the Exile was God's way of using the Babylonians to purge the nation of idolatry.

b. Jeremiah in the cistern (38:5–6)

5–6 Zedekiah was too weak to withstand his officials. His capitulation to them was a clear giveaway of his lack of moral fiber. While he did not actually sign Jeremiah's death warrant, neither did he do anything to prevent it. The intention of Jeremiah's enemies was plain enough: they wanted to silence him for good. To throw Jeremiah into the miry cistern would have surely resulted in his death had he not been rescued. This was his third and harshest imprisonment. The cistern was deep, because ropes were used to lower Jeremiah into it. By this punishment his enemies tried to salve their consciences from the burden of having actually slain him. Restrained by the Lord, they stopped just short of executing his prophet. "Malkijah, the king's

son" was not one of Zedekiah's sons but a royal prince (cf.36:26).

c. The rescue of Jeremiah (38:7–13)

7–9 As "a eunuch," Ebed-Melech was excluded by divine law from the congregation of God's people (cf. Dt 23:1). In ancient courts eunuchs were employed as keepers of the royal harem. Thus they had private access to the king (cf. 2Ki 24:15). It must, however, be recognized that "eunuch" did not always mean a castrated person but had a broader meaning, such as "officer" or "court official." The times were surely out of joint. Only a foreigner cared enough about Jeremiah to rescue him. Evidently Zedekiah did not know how his officials had used his capitulation to them, and he was too cowardly to ask them about it. But one official, Ebed-Melech, took pity on Jeremiah and told the king of his plight. It took courage for him to oppose the prophet's enemies. Ebed-Melech did not mince matters in speaking to Zedekiah but told him that Jeremiah was in deadly peril.

These two photos show a huge cistern at Avdat. The picture on the right shows the small opening that leads into the cistern; through it water could be removed. The picture above shows the enormous cavern that was used to store water. The opening into the cistern is the ray of light on the right side of the picture. The square light at the end of the cistern is not original; that is, the cistern was sealed watertight. One can imagine Jeremiah's being confined in some such cistern.

He boldly accused the officials and pled with the king for the prophet's life. Under the famine condition of the siege, it was unlikely that Jeremiah would get food.

10 Zedekiah was concerned and provided a rescue team of thirty men. Thirty men would not have been needed to lift Jeremiah from the cistern, but they would have been a sufficient guard to discourage the officials from intervening.

11–13 Godly Ebed-Melech knew where to get the needed manpower. He knew what the wardrobe storeroom contained, and he understood how weak Jeremiah was. There is a fine touch of compassion in v.12. So Jeremiah was transferred to the guardroom. His fourth imprisonment, this was a lifesaving move from the noxious cistern.

6. Counsel to the king (38:14–28)

a. Zedekiah's secret interview with Jeremiah (38:14–23)

14–16 This was Zedekiah's last meeting with Jeremiah. The king realized that only through Jeremiah could he get the truth. Again he questioned (cf. 37:17) the prophet and received essentially the same answer. The king still hoped for a change in the Lord's message, but it remained the same. The meeting took place privately, probably in a room connecting the palace to the temple. Apparently Jeremiah believed that Zedekiah had approved the brutal treatment he had received. He was no longer eager to warn a king who would neither protect him nor believe his message—a king who could never be trusted to keep his word. Jeremiah was under no illusions as to how his message would be received. In a highly secret oath, the king promised Jeremiah that no harm would come to him for disclosing the Lord's message.

17–19 The alternatives for Zedekiah were still the same: surrender and live or resist and suffer the worst. Though Nebuchadnezzar himself was not at the siege, he had his headquarters at Riblah (cf. 39:5; 2Ki 25:6). Zedekiah was afraid of both the officials in Judah and the Jews who had defected to Babylon (cf. 39:9; 52:15)—a fear that affected his political decisions and showed his weakness of character and lack of faith. He was afraid the Babylonians would turn him over for torture to the Jewish defectors. They had always ad-

vised submission to Babylon and would have dealt harshly with him for not doing as they had done—a course of action that might have spared Jerusalem the agony of a long siege.

20–23 As for Zedekiah's refusal to obey God, the Lord showed Jeremiah in the vision of the two baskets of figs some of its consequences (24:1–10). The Babylonians usually treated rebel kings ruthlessly and often mutilated them and put them to death. So certain was the coming doom that Jeremiah even predicted what the women of the royal harem would say on being taken into captivity. More cutting than the ridicule of the defectors would be their ridicule on him for his gullibility in trusting faithless allies. Desiring to gain favor with their Babylonian masters, the women would point out that Zedekiah's friends had impelled him to a suicidal opposition. In his hour of deepest distress, Zedekiah's so-called friends would leave him in the lurch. Out of his own experience, Jeremiah could understand all this. But the Lord would not protect Zedekiah as he had protected the prophet. What had happened to Jeremiah physically (cf. v.6) would be the lot of the king politically and spiritually. So the blame rested where it belonged—on the shoulders of Zedekiah, who would bring indignity and defeat on himself, ruin to the nation and its capital, and lasting shame on his own family.

b. The officials' inquiry (38:24–28)

24–26 Again Zedekiah did not heed the Lord's advice that came to him through Jeremiah. Until the last moment the king remained weak and afraid. He was fearful that if news of his secret talk with Jeremiah leaked out, it would be seriously misunderstood by the officials. So he warned the prophet that the officials might kill him. This precaution was needed (v.27). Just as suspicious of the king as he was of them, the officials had been spying on him. So Zedekiah told the prophet to reveal only his plea not to be sent back to Jonathan's house (cf. 37:15, 20).

27 Jeremiah's compliance with the king's request has been severely criticized on ethical grounds. Jeremiah's answer has been called a "half-truth" or "a white lie" for the king's sake. But we must be extremely reluctant to fault a true prophet of God like Jeremiah—a man of courage, brotherly love, patriotism, tremendous spiritual stature, and unparalleled devotion. In Jeremiah's defense, the following points need to be considered. (1) The precarious position of the king must be taken into account. (2) To allay suspicion was as much in the king's interest as in his own. (3) Jeremiah's answer was not a falsehood because the petition was implied in vv.15–16. (4) At this critical time, the king did not want to occasion a break between himself and his generals. (5) The officials themselves had no authority to question either the king or the prophet. (6) Jeremiah told only what was necessary and no more.

28 This verse shows that the capture of Jerusalem verified Jeremiah's forty years of ministry to the nation of Judah.

7. The Fall of Jerusalem (39:1–18)

Without doubt, the fall of Jerusalem dramatically authenticated Jeremiah's prophecies. This account generally agrees with those in ch. 52 and 2Ki 25.

a. The capture of the city (39:1–3)

1–3 After the long siege, the city walls were finally breached and Jerusalem fell. The dates span the beginning and end of the siege, which lasted about eighteen months. The fall of the city, which had been weakened by the siege without and by famine within (cf. 52:4–16; 2Ki 25:1–12), is described more fully in ch. 52. Jeremiah gives the Babylonian names of the Babylonian high officials (it is unclear how many individuals are actually listed here). Nergal-Sharezer was Nebuchadnezzar's son-in-law, who succeeded him under the name Neriglissar. The "chief officer" was head of the eunuchs who served as chamberlains. "A high official is literally "chief magi." When these officials sat in the gate of the city, the prediction of 1:15 was fulfilled. The "Middle Gate" was probably between the upper and lower divisions of the city. The purpose of the officials' session at the Middle Gate was either to plan their military strategy or to establish their quarters there.

b. The fate of Zedekiah (39:4–8)

4–5 This passage describes the flight, capture, torture, and imprisonment of Zedekiah. The flight was at night; thus the verb "saw" is to be taken in the sense of hearing or learning that the Babylonians had taken the gate of the

citadel of Zion. Zedekiah, realizing the end of Jerusalem had come, still hoped to save his life. He and his company tried to escape by way of the Jordan Valley ("Arabah"). The position of "the two walls" can only be conjectured; there may have been a gate in a double wall between Zion and Ophel. Zedekiah aimed to escape to the eastern side of the Jordan. The "king's garden" was near the Pool of Siloam (cf. Ne 3:15). Zedekiah was captured and taken to Riblah, where Nebuchadnezzar had his headquarters. It was a strategic site, which had been the military headquarters of Pharaoh Neco in his campaign against Assyria (cf. 2Ki 23:33). Riblah, on the Orontes River fifty miles south of Hamath, some sixty-five miles north of Damascus, was a good vantage point for gaining control of both Aram and Palestine.

6–8 At Riblah, Nebuchadnezzar began slaying all the resisters, starting with the king's sons and going on to the nobles of Judah. Only Zedekiah was spared for captivity after he saw with his own eyes the slaughter and then was blinded. "The nobles of Judah" were those who had been so persistently and perniciously opposed to Jeremiah. By modern standards what Nebuchadnezzar did was unusually harsh, but it was in accord with ancient pagan practices and is understandable in view of the trouble that Judah and especially Zedekiah had given Babylon. Thus two prophecies were fulfilled: Zedekiah would see the king of Babylon and be taken there (cf. 32:3–4), and he would die in Babylon without ever seeing it (cf. Eze 12:13). To add to his torture, Zedekiah had to witness the slaughter of his sons and the nobles, so that the last memory of this world's light might remain a grief. Verse 8 adds the finishing touches to the gruesome scene. The fall of Jerusalem was so important that Scripture relates it four times—here, in ch. 52, in 2Ki 25, and in 2Ch 36.

c. The release of Jeremiah (39:9–14)

9–10 After Nebuchadnezzar had dealt with the leadership of Judah, he took the people of Judah into exile in Babylon. This final deportation of the nation (586 B.C.) came some eleven years after that in Jehoiachin's time. Nebuzaradan, "commander of the imperial guard" (lit., "chief of the executioners"), was the man who had this assignment. To make a new beginning and not leave the land utterly desolate, Nebuzaradan placed some of the poorest people in charge of fields and vineyards as their own, though with reclamation rights by the conqueror (cf. 52:16; 2Ki 25:12). The Babylonians doubtless felt that gratitude would prevent the settlers from rebelling.

11–14 More interesting than the land grant to the poor were the instructions of Nebuchadnezzar about Jeremiah. Undoubtedly the Babylonians had favorable information about Jeremiah and probably considered him a sympathizer. Besides, those who had deserted Judah in the siege gave a report of him. Jeremiah's advice about submitting to Babylon even during the siege had been proclaimed over so long a time that it could not have escaped the attention of the Babylonian authorities. They realized that he was no threat to them. Paradoxically, he was treated better by foreign invaders than by his own countrymen whom he so dearly loved. So word was passed along to release Jeremiah from the courtyard of the guard and to entrust him to Gedaliah, the appointed governor, with whom he was to remain. Gedaliah was the son of Ahikam, who had been active in saving Jeremiah's life (cf. 26:24). For three generations his family had been true to the word of the Lord that came through his prophets.

d. The commendation of Ebed-Melech (39:15–18)

15–18 Verses 11–14 show how the Lord preserved his prophet; vv.15–18 show the Lord's concern for Jeremiah's rescuer. The scene goes back to Jeremiah's imprisonment in the cistern (38:1–13). This message must have come to Jeremiah soon after Ebed-Melech had rescued him. It is included here so as not to break into the chain of events (cf. 38:14–39:14). Ebed-Melech needed this message of hope, for he had doubtless incurred the wrath of Jeremiah's enemies for lifting him out of the cistern and so feared reprisals. Ebed-Melech was assured that he would escape death because his compassionate acts were motivated by his trust in the Lord.

III. Ministry of Jeremiah After the Fall of Jerusalem (40:1–45:5)

Chapters 40–44 contain prophecies and a record of events after the fall of Jerusalem.

Chapters 40–42 deal with prophecies and events in Judah; chs. 43–44 with those in Egypt.

A. Ministry to the Survivors in Judah (40:1–42:22)

1. Gedaliah the governor (40:1–16)

a. The release of Jeremiah (40:1–6)

1 Since there is no prophetic word till 42:9, "word" is to be taken in the sense of history as well as prophecy. The two are related. Ramah is about five miles north of Jerusalem. This Benjamite town was the place where the captives were questioned before being deported to Babylon. In the confusion when Jerusalem fell, Jeremiah was at first taken and placed in chains—manacles for the hands only (cf. v.4). When Jeremiah arrived at Ramah, he was released at the command of Nebuzaradan, who had evidently been told who Jeremiah was and what Nebuchadnezzar had ordered to be done with him.

2–3 Some doubt whether Nebuzaradan could or would have said the words quoted in vv.2–3. The Assyrians, however, paid attention to the beliefs of the people whom they fought, for use in psychological warfare (cf. 2Ki 18:22, 33–35). The Babylonians may have been aware of certain supernatural reasons for Judah's fall; Jeremiah's reputation as a prophet was evidently known to them. Unquestionably the words sound like those of Jeremiah himself, and this may show that Nebuzaradan had some acquaintance with the prophet's teaching.

4–5 Nebuzaradan first freed Jeremiah from his manacles and then gave him a choice of where he would live. These actions were wholly within his authority as an official representative of Nebuchadnezzar, who was then in Riblah. Jeremiah was given the option of either going to Babylon or remaining in Judah. Nebuzaradan promised to care for him in Babylon: "I will look after you." Recognizing that Jeremiah was not sure about where he would go, Nebuzaradan sent him back to Gedaliah. The book says nothing about any relationship between Jeremiah and Gedaliah, who was made puppet governor of Judea by the Babylonians. It is obvious that Nebuchadnezzar had lost all faith in the house of David. His dealings with the last three kings of Judah were disappointing in the extreme.

6 Nebuzaradan sent Jeremiah off with some food and a gift. The way he treated the prophet stands in striking contrast with what his own countrymen did to him, particularly in the last days of Jerusalem (cf. Mt 13:57). Apparently the Babylonians did not care to have the Jews remaining in Jerusalem, their former capital; so they made Mizpah the administrative center of the remnant in the land. Jeremiah chose to stay in the land he loved. This does not mean that he doubted his own message in 24:4–10. He loved his people in spite of their mistreatment, hatred, and threats on his life. Now he would at least be free of ungodly priests and false prophets. His devotion to the land and his conviction that it would be the scene of future blessing influenced his decision to remain in it at this critical time.

b. Gedaliah's assurances (40:7–10)

7–8 Gedaliah's appointment by Nebuchadnezzar as governor encouraged some of the surviving Jews who had fled to neighboring areas to return to Judah. Just as Nebuchadnezzar had confidence in Gedaliah, so did his countrymen. The land had been deprived of its leaders; so chiefs of guerrilla bands, who remained hidden while the Babylonian army was besieging, waited the turn of events after the fall of the capital. They showed their trust in Gedaliah's ability to govern by joining him at Mizpah. He was a good ruler and was doubtless supported by Jeremiah. Ishmael was a grandson of Elishama, of the house of David (cf. 41:1). Netophah was a place in Judah between Bethlehem and Tekoa, about twelve miles west of Bethlehem.

9–10 Gedaliah tried to quiet the fears of the survivors and advocated submission to the conquering power. He sought to reestablish normal living in the land and promised to represent them before the Babylonians. To some, however, he appeared to be a collaborator with the destroyer of their nation. Since Jerusalem fell in the middle of summer (cf. 39:2), the people had time to gather the late fruits of summer to sustain them during their first bleak winter in the land. Moreover, they would need the harvests to pay tribute to the Babylonians. Everything was being done to hasten the return to normal peaceful condi-

tions. Notice that the invaders had shown great enlightenment in refraining from any defoliation or "scorched-earth" policy. The clause "the towns you have taken over" indicates that the captains of the roaming bands took what towns or cities pleased them.

c. The return of the fugitives (40:11–12)

11–12 With his forthright honesty, Gedaliah inspired confidence; and his orders were obeyed. Many of those returning to Judah had fled from the Babylonians and had taken refuge in a number of neighboring countries. In God's mercy these refugees constituted a remnant. That one of their own nation was made governor gave them confidence; thus they felt that the Babylonians were not wholly without compassion for them in their time of tragic need.

d. The warning of Gedaliah (40:13–16)

13–14 Judah was still in a state of much unrest. Now a plot to assassinate Gedaliah comes to light, instigated by Baalis, king of Ammon, who used as his agent Ishmael son of Nethaniah. The man who told Gedaliah of the plot was the loyal Johanan son of Kareah. Gedaliah had apparently forgotten that Ishmael was of the house of David and thus did not appreciate being passed by in Gedaliah's favor. Or Ishmael may have considered Gedaliah a traitor for agreeing to govern under the Babylonians. Baalis may have felt that eliminating Gedaliah would make it easier to carry out his own plans to conquer Judah. The king of Ammon may have feared that Gedaliah might again make Judah a formidable nation and a potential threat to him. Also, Baalis, an ally of Zedekiah and an enemy of the Babylonians (cf. 27:3), was angry that the family of Ahikam opposed the league referred to in ch. 27.

15–16 A man of ability but lacking in knowledge of people and their devices, Gedaliah was too trusting and naive to believe Johanan's warning. The least he could have done was to have protected himself against the assassination of which he had been warned. What Johanan feared, actually happened (41:1–3); and the remnant was scattered because of Gedaliah's death. Though Johanan tried earnestly to impress Gedaliah that his life was essential for the welfare of the remnant in Judah, he apparently failed to inspire confidence. Moreover, Gedaliah may have been overconfident. At any rate, he was not convinced of Johanan's veracity. Gedaliah was right in forbidding Johanan to assassinate Ishmael but wrong in his estimate of Ishmael.

2. The atrocities of Ishmael and the flight into Egypt (41:1–18)

a. The assassination of Gedaliah (41:1–3)

1 The narrative in ch. 40 goes on without a break in ch. 41. Because v.1 gives only the month and not the year, two dates have been proposed for the assassination of Gedaliah: 586 B.C. and 583–582 B.C. Those who support the first date believe that only three months elapsed from the fall of the city to the events now recorded (cf. 39:2). But others think the text does not require that the events in ch. 41 occurred in the same year as the fall of Jerusalem. On the basis of 52:30, they hold that the reaction of Babylon to the assassination took place after five years, so that 41:1 gives the end of Gedaliah's governorship only. The Jews still keep the Fast of Gedaliah in the seventh month (Sept/Oct), on the third day of the month, the first and second days being the New Year (cf. Zec 7:5; 8:19; see also 2Ki 25:8, 25). Ishmael came from a collateral line of the Davidic family through Elishama, son of David (cf. 2Sa 5:16). Moreover, he was prominent in affairs of state with Zedekiah.

2–3 The "ten men" should not be thought of as being alone, for they may have brought a retinue of attendants with them. Ishmael, being violently anti-Babylonian, may have been motivated by deep resentment at the cruel treatment of Zedekiah (cf. 39:6–7). Ishmael carried out his dastardly plot while enjoying the hospitality of Gedaliah. Pretending friendship for him, he violated the sacred law of Eastern hospitality. In spite of having been warned of an assassination plot, Gedaliah had taken no precautions. Ishmael made no distinction between Jews or Babylonians; he killed all the fighting men, including Gedaliah's Babylonian bodyguard. For eleven men to kill so large a group indicates how unsuspecting the victims were. The reference to "all the Jews" includes only those who were in the house with Gedaliah. The number of Babylonian troops was apparently small.

b. The massacre of the pilgrims (41:4–10)

4–5 For Ishmael human life was so cheap that he had no compunction in slaughtering seventy pilgrims. Such a deed could not be concealed indefinitely. A group of men from the northern kingdom were on the way to Jerusalem to lament its desolation. Josiah had destroyed the altar at Bethel (one of the lasting effects of Josiah's reform), so they were bringing offerings to the Jerusalem temple. They had even gashed themselves—a relapse into heathen custom forbidden in Dt 14:1. In spite of the destruction of the temple itself, they came to the temple site, which was still used for worship by those who survived the fall of the city. Even the ruins were held to be sacred.

Though living among heathen colonists (cf. 2Ki 17:24–41), the men from the northern kingdom had continued to worship the Lord in Jerusalem and to celebrate the feasts (cf. 2Ch 34:9). Their offerings were bloodless sacrifices because no facilities were available for animal sacrifices (cf. Dt 12:13–14, 17–18).

6–8 Ishmael went out to meet the men, weeping hypocritically as though for the loss of the temple. Courteously he invited them to pay their respects to Gedaliah the governor before going on to Jerusalem. So he lured them into Mizpah, where he had them trapped. Just as in the assassination of Gedaliah, Ishmael used the element of surprise. Here it enabled eleven men to slaughter seventy of the eighty pilgrims. The massacre may have been done for plunder and to intimidate the remnant in Judah. Casting them into a cistern was senseless, for it made Mizpah's water supply ceremonially unclean and unfit to drink. Ishmael's greed led him to spare ten of the eighty men because of their cache of food, which was probably concealed in a cistern in a field.

9–10 At this point Jeremiah inserts a historical notation, showing that King Asa of Judah (913–873 B.C.) had ordered this cistern to be made to ensure ample water for Mizpah when he fortified it against King Baasha of Israel (910–887 B.C.; cf. 1Ki 15:22; 2Ch 16:6). Ishmael's next stop was to transport the remnant of the people from Mizpah to Ammon (according to 40:14, Ishmael was in alliance with Baalis the Ammonite king). Ishmael's motive in transporting the remnant may have been threefold: (1) to escape punishment, (2) to find refuge with Baalis, who had instigated the assassination of Gedaliah (40:14), and (3) to sell the remnant as slaves to the Ammonites. The king's daughters, spared through Babylonian clemency, were royal princesses—not necessarily Zedekiah's own daughters, but women related to Ishmael. Included among this remnant were probably Jeremiah and Baruch (cf. 42:2).

c. The escape of Ishmael (41:11–15)

11–15 Johanan, having had prior knowledge of the plot, was quick to follow Ishmael's tracks. Now Johanan acted responsibly, not as he had previously wanted to do (40:15). He and those with him overtook the assassin before he had gone far—Gibeon is about a mile from Mizpah. Gibeon was the city of priests in the tribe of Benjamin (cf. Jos 18:25; 21:17). Possibly "the great pool" is the same as "the pool of Gibeon" (cf. 2Sa 2:13). Ishmael may have taken a circuitous route to confuse his pursuers. When the people saw Johanan and his companions, they rejoiced; for they had followed Ishmael only because they had been compelled to do so. And because of the popularity of Gedaliah, they were glad to see his murder avenged. Ishmael lost only two of his men and drops out of the narrative after fleeing to Ammon.

d. The flight to Egypt (41:16–18)

16–18 Johanan now decided to go as quickly as possible to Egypt. He and the army officers with him feared reprisals when the news of Gedaliah's assassination reached Babylon. Ishmael had completely frustrated any plans for peaceful settlement in the land. Geruth means "lodging place." Kimham was the son of Barzillai, the wealthy Gileadite and faithful partisan of David during the revolt of Absalom (cf. 2Sa 9:38, 41). Johanan, able in military matters (he had given advice to Gedaliah), was wrong in thinking flight to Egypt was the only solution to the problems of the remnant. Actually, it created other problems, and certainly it did not place them beyond the reach of Nebuchadnezzar.

3. Warning against going to Egypt (42:1–22)

Johanan overtook and routed Ishmael and his forces, the residue of which escaped to Ammon. At this point the remnant of people were afraid to remain in Judah, but they were equally afraid to seek safety in a foreign country. Johanan and the remnant were anxious not to make a mistake that would incur the wrath of God, which had already been poured out on Jerusalem and Judah; hence they inquired of Jeremiah. They did not recognize that by deciding to go to Egypt they had already decided on a certain course of action (cf. 41:17).

a. The inquiry of the remnant (42:1–6)

1–3 There was an unusual unity among the remnant, all of whom were without exception concerned about what they should do and where they should go. Jezaniah is the Azariah of 43:2 (cf. NIV note). The remnant came to Jeremiah, who had apparently been a captive of Ishmael. The esteem in which they still held Jeremiah is evident in their recognition of him as a prophet of the Lord. The inquirers hoped that God would answer according to their desires. They earnestly wanted confirmation of their decision, not guidance from the Lord (cf. v.17). According to their thinking, the unrest and absence of security in Judah made resettlement there an impossibility.

4–6 Jeremiah gently reminded the remnant that the Lord was their God as well as his. Since he was no longer restrained from praying for them, he would gladly agree to ask the Lord for guidance. Realizing the gravity of their situation, he promised not to hold back any part of the Lord's answer. At this, the people solemnly pledged to obey everything the Lord would tell Jeremiah; that is, they promised to obey the Lord regardless of the nature of his answer. Later on the record shows that they actually wanted approval to settle in Egypt (cf. 43:2). Even more, their request for the Lord to be "a true and faithful witness against us" implies their acceptance of his punishment for disobeying his express will.

b. The Lord's answer to Jeremiah's question (42:7–17)

7 For ten days Jeremiah awaited the Lord's message. We may imagine the suspense and tension of this time. The prophet wanted to be certain of the Lord's will. Here was a matter on which the entire future of the nation might depend and one that at the least was crucial for the remnant. Perhaps God wanted to give the Jews an opportunity to show the sincerity of their claim that they would obey his leading and to allow time for their anxiety that bordered on panic to be dispelled.

8–12 Once more Jeremiah had to deliver an unpopular message. In strong anthropopathic language the Lord implied that the penalty given Judah would be canceled. In other words, the Lord would change his dealings with the nation. God's dealings with us are according to our obeying or disobeying his will. At this point God promised he would deal with Judah in a different way since the people were now in a different category from before the fall of Jerusalem. During Nebuchadnezzar's siege of Jerusalem, the people had cause to fear him; now there was no occasion for them to do this. In fact, God would see that Nebuchadnezzar would show them compassion, and God would turn to their favor every action of this king.

13–17 In unsparing words, Jeremiah warned of the terrifying consequences if the remnant insisted on leaving the land. Trust in human beings would neither avail them nor bless them. They would find no safety in Egypt. In fact, going there would bring on them the very disasters they were trying to escape. For their part, the people hoped that the farther they were from Babylon, the less they would be in danger of invasion. Although Egypt had lost the Battle of Carchemish (605 B.C.), it had not been the scene of other military actions. Thus the remaining Jews could not fail to be impressed by the contrast between peaceful Egypt and war-torn Judah. Actually, however, Judah's trials were past; Egypt's were soon to begin. Jeremiah was quick to see that his listeners were already determined on a different course of action than the one the Lord had for them. Fleeing to Egypt would bring terrible trials. (Nebuchadnezzar was yet to invade Egypt; cf. 43:8–13.)

c. Further penalties for settling in Egypt (42:18–22)

18–22 The survivors of the fall of Jerusalem and Judah would suffer the same fate in Egypt that had overtaken them because of their disobedience. Egypt would be the place of their undoing, without a glimmer of hope of their returning to their native country. In

an epilogue after the Lord's reply, Jeremiah adds to the admonition in vv.13–18. The Lord's message remained unchanged—stay in the land and do not settle in Egypt. He rebukes them for asking his will with no intention of following it.

Jeremiah shows the remnant their duplicity in asking for a message from God when they had no intention of following it. All the time they were intent on doing their own will, in the hope that God's will would coincide with theirs. So they were victims of self-deception and self-delusion. How little did they realize that in Egypt the temptation for them to worship idols—the very sin that had led to the nation's fall—would be even stronger than before! Jeremiah also reminds them it was not he that had instituted the inquiry; they themselves were responsible for provoking the Lord's severe answer. The passage closes with the threefold judgment of sword, famine, and plague ringing in their ears. The issue was clear, the warning was faithfully transmitted; but the remnant were set on having their own way.

B. Ministry in Egypt (43:1–44:30)

Chapters 43–44 relate to the remnant in Egypt. Johanan and the people disregarded the Lord's warning and went there, taking Jeremiah and Baruch, probably by force. The prophet doubtless died in Egypt.

1. The flight to Egypt (43:1–13)

a. The warning flouted (43:1–7)

1–3 The response to Jeremiah's message from the Lord was both immediate and negative. In no uncertain terms, Azariah and Johanan and "all the arrogant men" who dominated the frightened remnant accused Jeremiah of lying. To divert attention from breaking their promise to obey the Lord's message, they tried to save face, not only by giving Jeremiah the lie, but also by accusing Baruch of conniving to get Jeremiah to deliver the remnant to the Babylonians. Because Jeremiah was an old man and might conceivably have been under the influence of his secretary and companion, the charge against Baruch had a superficial plausibility. But there was not a scintilla of evidence for it. The prophet who would not trim his message for the king would never have been manipulated by his secretary.

4–6 At the death of Gedaliah, Johanan, who appears in a bad light ever since his determined opposition to Jeremiah, became the rallying center for the people. His action cannot be divorced from an element of self-promotion. The remnant was made up of the many Jews who had fled to nearby countries after the fall of Jerusalem. Unfortunately they all agreed to follow Johanan and their other leaders instead of the Lord. Such is the perversity of fallen human nature; when people reach unanimity, too often they rebel against God's will. Jeremiah and Baruch were doubtless taken to Egypt against their will; for them to have gone there voluntarily would have violated Jeremiah's prophecies (cf. 32:6–15; 40:1–6; 42:13–18).

7 This verse shows the full extent of the people's disobedience. They arrived in Egypt at Tahpanhes, a fortress city on the northern border of Lower Egypt guarding the road to Aram. Pharaoh had a palace here. Located on the Pelusian branch of the Nile, Tahpanhes was known to the Greeks as Daphne (cf. 2:16). Think of it! Abraham's descendants returned to Egypt long after their liberation from it. With great suffering they had been delivered from their bondage in Egypt, only to return there a defeated and hopeless remnant nearly nine hundred years later.

b. Jeremiah's prophecy in Egypt (43:8–13)

The fugitives probably stopped at Tahpanhes to obtain permission from Pharaoh to enter the country and to assure themselves of some means of livelihood during their stay in it. We are not told how Jeremiah and Baruch fared in Egypt. Jeremiah's first message to the remnant in Egypt foretold the certainty of Nebuchadnezzar's victory over Egypt; thus the flight of the remnant was useless. Because of the tenor of his message, Jeremiah's stay in Egypt was not a happy one; when his political position became known, the government could hardly have favored him. There is no evidence of Nebuchadnezzar's conquest of Egypt, though there is evidence that he invaded it.

8–9 In Tahpanhes the Lord told Jeremiah to act out a message for the people. He was to hide some large stones in the mortar of the brick pavement at the entrance to Pharaoh's house. This was the place where Nebuchadnezzar would set up his throne on his invasion that would bring death and destruction to Egypt.

10–11 The Jews' flight to Egypt to escape the Babylonians was futile because the Lord was going to send Nebuchadnezzar to invade it (ch. 44). The royal "canopy" has been understood as a covering over the throne or perhaps as a gorgeous carpet on which the throne stood. A fragmentary text in the British museum indicates that Nebuchadnezzar's invasion of Egypt occurred in the thirty-seventh year of his reign (568–567 B.C.). It was a punitive expedition; after it Babylonia and Egypt had amicable relations. The Lord calls Nebuchadnezzar "my servant" (cf. 27:6)—the executor of death, captivity, and destruction for Egypt.

12–13 These verses show the Lord's unalterable opposition to the idolatry of Egypt. Nebuchadnezzar would burn the wooden images and the temples with them and carry off the idols of gold to Babylon. In ancient times idols of defeated foes were carried in the triumphal processions of conquering kings. Not only would the temples be destroyed, but the sacred pillars—i.e., the obelisks, monuments of Egypt's idolatrous pride (cf. Dt 16:21–22; 2Ki 23:14)—would be broken. Jeremiah likens the ease with which Nebuchadnezzar would do these things to the casual way in which a shepherd wraps himself in his garment. In fact, the conqueror would return unscathed from Egypt. The sacred pillars were the finest representations of Egyptian idolatry. The king of Egypt at this time was Pharaoh Hophra (cf. 44:30).

"The temple of the sun" (Heliopolis; modern Tell Husn) was about six miles northeast of Cairo. The sun god was elaborately worshiped there in antiquity. The reference to "Egypt" distinguishes the Egyptian city from the Palestinian one with the same name ("Beth Shemesh"; cf. 2Ki 14:11). But the prophet has not spoken his last word on Egypt; more follows in chs. 44 and 46.

2. Condemnation of Ishtar worship (44:1–30)

This chapter contains Jeremiah's last message. It has been dated 580 B.C. because the dispersion implied in v.1 would have taken some years. The message reviews the Lord's dealings with Judah and emphatically reminds the Jews in Egypt that their sins have brought on them the wrath of God that had been foretold by Jeremiah.

a. Exhortation to heed past experience (44:1–10)

1–6 This section rebukes the Jews dispersed in Egypt. It is surprising that the Jews were practicing idolatry in Egypt; they had not yet learned from their past sins. Jeremiah mentions four places, three in Lower (northern) Egypt—Migdol, Tahpanhes, and Memphis—and one in Upper (southern) Egypt. The mention of these places shows how rapidly the Jews had spread out in Egypt. The reason for Jeremiah's prophecy was the continued idolatry of the exiles in spite of their captivity. If ever a prophecy had immediacy, it was this one; for in it Jeremiah brought the light of history to bear on the very day in which he spoke.

7–10 Moving to the current hour, Jeremiah remonstrated with the people regarding the sins in which they were still steeped. Once more the nation was committing national suicide. All his warnings previously made no difference in their thinking or in their acts. The Jews in Egypt had become ensnared in the idolatry of that land—a sin that the Lord had foreseen and that was one of the reasons God had forbidden them to go there. This must have been disheartening for Jeremiah, who had spent a lifetime preaching against idolatry in Judah; the Jews were practicing in Egypt the very sins that had brought about the fall of Jerusalem. The remnant showed they were neither repentant nor contrite.

b. Warning of punishment (44:11–14)

11–14 Now judgment is announced. It is the same for the Jews in Egypt as it had been for those in Judah. The reference to "all Judah" covers all the Jews there in Egypt—with the exception of permanent Jewish settlers there and the few mentioned in vv.14b, 28. First of all, Jeremiah roundly rebukes them for coming to Egypt. Then he dramatically specifies the troubles the remnant can expect in Egypt. He makes it clear that he is not referring to any permanent Jewish settlers in Egypt (cf. v.14) but only to those who had sought refuge there in the hope of returning to the land of Judah at the earliest opportunity. Only casual fugitives will survive.

c. The stubborn persistence in idolatry (44:15–19)

15–19 This passage is one of the strangest in the book. How stubborn the resistance to Jeremiah's message was! The people openly and unashamedly refused to forsake their idolatry; indeed, they found pragmatic justification for it. They brazenly declared that they would keep on in their idolatry. The occasion here may have been an idolatrous feast in which the women had a major part, probably because Astarte, "the Queen of Heaven" (vv.17, 18, 19, 25), was the goddess of fertility.

The remnant—women as well as men—admitted that they were not engaging in any new worship. They affirmed a causal relationship between their idolatry and the abundance of food. They also affirmed that when they stopped their idolatrous practices, food shortages and war were the result. They doubtless ascribed their troubles to the reforms of Josiah, to which they senselessly attributed the downfall of Judah. In short, the remnant claimed that idolatry had done more for them than the Lord whom Jeremiah represented. Nothing is more blinding than unbelief. Not once did they connect their trials with their sins.

Finally, in an insolent rhetorical question that implied an affirmative reply, the women acknowledged to Jeremiah that they had carried on their worship of the Queen of Heaven with the full knowledge and approval of their husbands (cf. Nu 30:3, 6–7, 12). Why then should Jeremiah complain about their actions? The "cakes" had an image of Astarte on them, said to be the image of the full moon.

d. Condemnation of the remnant's stubbornness (44:20–30)

20–22 Verses 20–30 constitute the very last message of Jeremiah recorded in the book (the remaining chapters contain prophecies dating from earlier years). The message abounds in contrast and confrontation. Jeremiah flatly denies the women's twisted defense of their idolatry. How obtuse they were not to realize that all the while they were engaged in their detestable practices, God knew all about what they were doing! The plain fact was that God, now as before, could no longer abide their idolatries. This statement

On this silver pendant is etched the goddess Ishtar, the "Queen of Heaven" (cf. 44:17–19). Drawing by Rachel Bierling.

stands in marked contrast to their claim that prosperity attended them as long as they were idolatrous.

23–25 Since the people were going ahead with their idolatrous worship, Jeremiah announces their punishment. It was tragic that corrupt rulers had so influenced the nation's women. In a powerful expression of irony and revulsion, Jeremiah tells the remnant to proceed with fulfilling their godless vows. He may have been pointing to their incense and libations and to the very cakes they were carrying.

26–28 The severe prediction could be taken to mean that God was saying that he would no longer be their covenant God; thus they would forfeit the privilege of calling on his name. Or perhaps v.26 means that the remnant would not be able to name God's name because they would perish in Egypt. The death penalty is perhaps best understood with the qualification that "the remnant" (cf. v.14) are excluded from this threat. Only they will survive to know the truth of Jeremiah's prophecy; they will be easily numbered be-

cause they are so few. The outcome of events will demonstrate whose word stands; God is always willing to have his word tested alongside human words.

29–30 The last verses of the chapter give the sign of the truth of God's words—the fall of Pharaoh Hophra (588–568 B.C.), the ally of Zedekiah, who had sent an army to help him when Jerusalem was besieged (cf. 37:5). Even this Pharaoh whose protection the Jews had sought would succumb to his enemies. The text does not compel the interpretation that Pharaoh Hophra was killed in the invasion of Egypt by Babylon. The facts are otherwise. Hophra was overthrown by Amasis, one of his officers, who revolted against him and then shared rule with him. Amasis rebelled against Nebuchadnezzar in 570 B.C. and was defeated in 568 B.C. So sixteen years after the fall of Jerusalem, Hophra was dethroned and strangled by some of his subjects. Again Jeremiah was vindicated.

Scripture is silent on what happened to Jeremiah after the events of this chapter, though tradition has been overly active. There are many legends concerning his death. One states that he was killed at Tahpanhes. Another claims he carried away the tabernacle, hiding it in the mountain where Moses died (2Mc 2:4–8). Yet another indicates he was alive with Enoch and Elijah, expected to return as a forerunner of the Messiah.

C. The Message to Baruch (45:1–5)

This brief chapter contains the message the Lord gave to Baruch. Historically it supplements 36:1–8 and can be precisely dated at 604 B.C. (cf. 36:1). This antedates sections about the remnant and Egypt. The message was meant to encourage Baruch, who had become disheartened, just as Jeremiah had been. Jeremiah may have had other secretaries, but Baruch is the only one mentioned in the book.

1. Baruch's complaint (45:1–3)

1–3 Baruch came from an influential family of noble birth. He was the grandson of Mahseiah (cf. 32:12), governor of Jerusalem in Josiah's reign (cf. 2Ch 34:8). His brother had been chief chamberlain in the court of Zedekiah (cf. 51:59). He may have had hopes of attaining a high office or even of receiving the gift of prophecy. But such expectations were not to be realized. Rather, he was to spend his life in a secondary role. So he may have been depressed. "The words" refer to the scroll (ch. 36; cf. "the fourth year of Jehoiakim"). Baruch shared Jeremiah's burdens. He grieved over what he had to record about the people's sin and their coming punishment. His sorrow, pain, and groaning wore him out, and his emotional involvement in what he wrote gave him no rest.

2. The response of the Lord (45:4–5)

4–5 These verses imply that the Lord's concern for his people is greater than any human being's. The destruction of Judah is in view in v.4. On the other hand, it has been proposed that "throughout the land" actually refers to the whole earth (cf. "on all people" in v.5). The reply to Baruch's complaint was simple: Do not expect to be more than you are. Why should Baruch be so concerned about his own welfare and position? He should not be self-seeking. When the nation was suffering drastic judgment, instead of making demands, he should be satisfied that his life was spared. With this he must be content. The last clause of v.5 implies that Baruch would have to flee for his life. Short though the chapter is, it has a timeless message for the Lord's servant.

IV. Prophecies Concerning the Nations (46:1–51:64)

Except for ch. 52, the remainder of Jeremiah is made up of prophecies against foreign nations. The prophecies against Egypt (ch. 46) and Babylon (chs. 50–51) contain promises of Israel's restoration (cf. 46:27–28; 50:19–20). Some messages were sent to Babylon; others were delivered in Egypt. The battle between Egypt and Babylon at Carchemish forms the background for 46:2–6.

Jeremiah was a man of world vision. He was a contemporary of five kings of Judah, of the greatest monarch of the neo–Chaldean empire, and of four kings of Egypt: Psammetik I (664–609 B.C.), Neco II (609–594 B.C.), Psammetik II (594–588 B.C.), and Hophra (588–568 B.C.). The prophecies concern ten nations: Egypt, Philistia, Moab, Ammon, Edom, Syria (Damascus), Kedar, Hazor, Elam, and Babylon. They were doubtless given to Jeremiah at different times, though collected here under a common theme: judg-

ment. The prophecies move from west to east. Unlike the judgments pronounced against foreign nations by other OT prophets, the nations' sins are not identified.

At this point it is important to consider certain basic principles that underlie all biblical prophecies that threaten world powers. (1) God is the God of all the nations. As the Sovereign over everything, he has the authority to speak to all peoples. (2) God is first and foremost the God of holiness and righteousness (cf. Isa 6:3). (3) God's judgments are never vindictive (revengeful) but vindicative (justifying). (4) Judgment is God's strange work (cf. Isa 28:21; Eze 33:11). He does not delight in it; he rejoices in salvation (cf. Mt 1:21). (5) God is impartial. He judges among the nations just as he judges Israel's sin.

Caption for the Prophecies Against the Nations (46:1)

1 This verse serves as the introduction and title for all the chapters that follow, except ch. 52.

A. Concerning Egypt (46:2–28)

1. The defeat of the Egyptian army (46:2–6)

2 This chapter gives a prophecy against Egypt. The Pharaoh Neco referred to is the one who slew Josiah at Megiddo (609 B.C.) and placed Jehoahaz on the Judean throne. In three months he removed him, imprisoned him at Riblah, and set up Jehoiakim as king. In Jehoiakim's fourth year (605 B.C.), Neco was defeated at Carchemish. Carchemish is north of the junction of the Chebar and Euphrates rivers. The name "Carchemish" means "the fort of Chemosh," god of the Moabites (cf. 2Ki 23:13). The only great city in that region, it was the key to Syria on the east and commanded the passage of the Euphrates. It had been under the rule of the Hittites and Assyrians.

After the fall of the Assyrian Empire, at the Battle of Carchemish, the military ambitions of Egypt were blocked by the Babylonians. Thus it was one of the decisive battles in history. It proved that Assyrian power could not restrain the rising might of Babylon, which Egypt opposed in favor of Assyria. Nebuchadnezzar pursued Neco toward Egypt but was halted by the news of the death of his father, Nabopolassar. On returning to Babylon, Nebuchadnezzar was crowned king. Babylon now dominated Mesopotamia and the near eastern Mediterranean area. The times of the Gentiles had begun (cf. Lk 21:24; also Da 2:36–38). The fourth year of Jehoiakim was the first year of Nebuchadnezzar (see comment on 25:1).

3–6 In words tinged with sarcasm, Jeremiah vividly describes the preparation of the Egyptians for the battle, their march to it, and their defeat. The "shields, both large and small" were the large shield protecting the whole body of the heavily armed soldier and the small round buckler protecting the lightly armed soldier. Horses were always an important element of Egyptian warfare. Their helmets on, the Egyptians are told to put themselves in battle formation. Coats of mail ("armor") were worn by light troops. An army as well accoutered as the one described here would naturally be victorious. But events took an unexpected turn. Panic supernaturally induced brought defeat to such a force. The Egyptians were conquered and destined not to return home but to fall on foreign soil. History has fully confirmed Jeremiah's predictions: Egypt's advance was halted at the Euphrates.

2. The humbling of Egypt's pride (46:7–12)

7–9 Now the name of the nation whose army has been defeated is mentioned. The approach of the Egyptian army is compared to the annual flooding of the Nile. The rivers referred to are the branches of the Nile in the Delta region in Lower Egypt. Egypt's boast of world conquest and her defeat (vv.5–6) are described, and both descriptions lead to a climax. Her chariots and infantry are summoned to sally forth, implying that with them will be the mercenary troops which, from the time of Psammetik, formed the main part of the Egyptian forces. Cush and Put are Ethiopia and Libya (or Somaliland—both descended from Ham; cf. Ge 10:6; Eze 30:5). The Lydians (cf. Ludites, Ge 10:13) were not from the coast of Asia Minor but an African people living west of Egypt. They were the lightly armed part of the army.

10 There is more to military campaigns than international conflicts. Verse 10 presents the theological interpretation of the defeat of the Egyptians. Jeremiah does not speak of the Day of the Lord but of a day that is peculiarly God's—in short, the time of God's judgment on a nation.

11–12 Jeremiah advises Egypt to seek a remedy for her wounds. Her defeat dealt her an irrecoverable blow; she could not heal herself. From antiquity Egypt was famous for her medical arts. It was from Egypt and India that the knowledge of medicine came to Europe. The defeat will be publicized among the nations. In their rout, the warriors will get in each other's way.

3. The coming of Nebuchadnezzar (46:13–19)

13–14 Nebuchadnezzar's conquest of Egypt left it vulnerable to future attack. Not only at Carchemish but in Egypt itself the victory would be Babylon's (cf. 43:8–13). Nebuchadnezzar's invasion of Egypt came long after the Battle of Carchemish, which had prepared the way for it. Verse 14 announces that the foe has already reached the Egyptian borders. The surrounding nations had been subdued, perhaps even Tyre, so Nebuchadnezzar moved on Egypt. The news of the death of his father prevented Nebuchadnezzar from moving deeper into Egypt. He had to return to Babylon to take up his duties as king.

15–17 In v.16 the speech of the soldiers is overheard, as mercenary troops decide to return to their own countries. They call Pharaoh "a noise" (i.e., a braggart), blaming him for ruining his chances of victory by his procrastination—probably an allusion to his inaction when Nebuchadnezzar returned to Babylon after Carchemish.

18–19 Nebuchadnezzar's return to Egypt is likened to the majesty of Tabor and Carmel, mountains in northern Palestine on the road to Egypt. The Babylonian invasion of Egypt will be as outstanding as is Tabor among the mountains and as irresistible as impregnable Carmel. The defeated Egyptians are exhorted to provide themselves with what they will need for exile.

4. The fall of Egypt (46:20–26)

20–24 Jeremiah describes Egypt's doom in highly figurative language. The "beautiful heifer" is Egypt; the "gadfly" from the north is Nebuchadnezzar. Egypt's mercenaries are like calves fattened for slaughter. The fleeing

Egyptians will sound like a serpent escaping from woodsmen by slithering through underbrush. The Babylonians carried axes—a novelty to the Jews. The serpent figure is an ironic reference to one of the most noted of Egyptian deities, prominent even in royal insignia—the coiled uraeus. The devastating power of the enemy is likened to a locust plague (cf. Joel 1:1–2:27). To Jeremiah, Egypt will be at the mercy of the Babylonians.

25–26 Jeremiah now predicts judgment on the gods and kings of Egypt. Amon (Amun) was the chief god of No (Thebes), the capital of Upper Egypt. The judgment will overtake all the people of Israel who looked to the pharaoh for help against Babylon. Yet the desolation of Egypt will not be perpetual; the Lord promises her future restoration (cf. Isa 19:24–25; Eze 29:8–14).

5. Blessing on Jacob (46:27–28)

27–28 In striking contrast with the vivid portrayal of Egypt's fall and destruction is the salvation here promised to the people of Israel in words that will encourage them in captivity (cf. 30:10–11). Looking, as they do, beyond the captivity, vv.27–28 are indeed consoling. If Egypt's woes are but temporary, those of Israel are even more so.

B. Concerning Philistia (47:1–7)

The Philistines settled in the coastal region known as the Philistine plain. Their pentapolis consisted of Ekron, Ashdod, Gaza, Ashkelon, and Gath. The Philistines were greatly reduced in power by the campaigns of David against them, but during the divided kingdom they asserted their independence from Judah. Military actions against them from the Assyrian Age down through the time of Alexander the Great weakened them; finally they were conquered by the Maccabees (second century B.C.) and merged into Israel.

1 The somewhat indefinite historical reference makes it difficult to date this prophecy. One view identifies the Pharaoh as Neco, who conquered Gaza about the time he defeated Josiah at Megiddo (cf. 2Ki 23:29–30); another view sees the Pharaoh as Neco capturing Gaza on his return from his defeat at Carchemish; still another identifies the Pha-

raoh as Hophra, who took Gaza in his campaign against Tyre and Sidon.

2–3 Jeremiah uses a flood to describe the Babylonian threat to Philistia, Tyre, and Sidon. The word "waters" is an OT figure for an army (46:8; cf. Isa 8:7). The distress from the invading Babylonians will be so great that fathers will leave their children defenseless; limpness of hands indicates the paralyzing effect of fear. "The day" is not the Day of the Lord. In her distress, Philistia will find no help in her former allies, Tyre and Sidon. These two cities were flourishing commercial centers on the coast of what is now Lebanon. Jeremiah sees Philistia as the remnant of the ancient Aegean civilization headed by Caphtor (Crete; cf. Am 9:7). Crete was probably the original home of the Philistines before their entrance to Palestine (cf. Dt 2:23).

5–7 Shaving the head is a sign of deep mourning (cf. 16:6; 41:5; 48:37). To cut oneself was forbidden to the Jews (Dt 14:1). The "remnant on the plain" is difficult to explain. It is in apposition to Ashkelon (the RSV follows the reading of the LXX, translating "plain" as "Anakim," i.e., a tall nation). Connected with the Philistines (cf. Jos 11:22), the Anakim lived near Hebron in prehistoric times. The "cry" is that of the Philistines—their appeal is for the divine judgments to cease. That "the sword of the LORD" must first accomplish its judgment on the seacoast, the Philistine plain, is Jeremiah's answer.

C. Concerning Moab (48:1–47)

The Moabites were descendants of Lot (cf. Ge 19:37). They lived east of the Dead Sea and were often in conflict with Israel. Moab joined in the marauding bands Nebuchadnezzar sent against Judah in 602 B.C., after Jehoiakim's revolt (cf. 2Ki 24:2; Jer 12:7–13). They joined in a plot to revolt against Babylon early in Zedekiah's reign (cf. 27:1–11). The Moabites were conquered by Nebuchadnezzar and disappeared as a nation.

There is no way to determine with certainty the date of the prophecy in this chapter. Its historical setting may be the Moabite invasion into Judah during Jehoiakim's reign. This prophecy against Moab is longer than any other prophecy in chs. 46–49. It is the most thorough of all the OT prophecies about Moab.

1. Desolation of the Moabite cities (48:1–10)

1–2 More than a score of cities are mentioned in this chapter. "Nebo" is not the mountain (cf. Dt 32:49) but the city of Reuben (cf. Nu 32:38). According to the Moabite Stone, it was taken by King Mesha of Moab (c. 895 B.C.). Kiriathaim is ten miles west of Medeba. The towns of Moab will be plundered. Moab will have no more basis for boasting. Originally Moab extended from Heshbon to Bozrah. At Heshbon the Babylonians planned their attack on Moab. Once the capital of the Amorite kingdom of Sihon (cf. Nu 21:26; Dt 2:24), this city was given to Reuben (cf. Jos 13:17), then passed to the Gadites, becoming a Levitical city (cf. Jos 21:39). It was ten miles east of Jordan, opposite Jericho, almost midway between the Arnon and the Jabbok rivers. Its enemies decided on conquest and destruction.

3–6 Only destruction is decreed for Horonaim (the name is evidently used for the two Beth-horons; cf. 2Sa 13:34). The "little ones" may mean the "abject ones," made so by distress. Whether ascending or descending, the fugitives will go weeping as they flee from the enemy. Their condition is likened to a desert bush (juniper)—a picture of destruction and forsakenness.

7 Pride was the root of Moab's trouble. Her idolatry was centered in the worship of Chemosh, a name occurring several times on the Moabite Stone. Chemosh was the national deity of Moab (cf. Nu 21:29; 1Ki 11:7, 33). The reference to trust in "deeds and riches" implies that the reason for Moab's fall was her materialism. When Chemosh went into exile, his followers accompanied him. Idols were usually taken captive with their worshipers (43:12; Isa 46:1–2).

8–10 The "valley" is the Jordan Valley, which touched Moab on the west. All the Moabite cities will be involved in the doom. The "plateau" is the extensive region where most of the Moabite cities were located. With the towns doomed for destruction, flight would be the only hope for Moab; but she would need wings (v.9; see NIV note) to escape the sudden onslaught of the enemy. Since the Lord has commissioned Moab's enemies to punish her, they must be diligent in performing their duty.

2. The proud complacency of Moab (48:11–19)

11–13 Moab had enjoyed a more settled life than Judah, but now she will know upheaval and disturbances. The Moabites had been made tributary but not exiled. Now their rest will be changed to unrest. Moab had experienced a certain insulation from judgment, for she had not undergone frequent invasions and deportations. As in the figure of "wine," her flavor had continued unchanged. But no longer will Moab rest quietly. Unlike an earthenware jar that is carefully tilted so as not to lose the sediment of the wine, Moab will be roughly dealt with ("pour her out") and emptied like jars and smashed like jugs. Moab's hope will be unrealized; Chemosh will be powerless to aid her. Jeremiah compares Moab's hope to the useless confidence that the northern kingdom had in the Bethel sanctuary, where the bull was worshiped (cf. 1Ki 12:26–33). In the hour of trial, the bull did not protect the Israelites from Shalmaneser and deportation. Whether in Moab or Israel, God is interested only in genuine faith in him.

14–17 Moreover, Moab will no longer boast of her valor. When the enemy forces march on her cities, slaughter will abound. "The LORD Almighty" vouches for the prediction; in spite of what the Moabites think, the Lord is still their Lord also, not Chemosh. And the hour of reckoning is not far off. The blow will be so great that the neighboring lands will sympathize with the Moabites and mourn with them. The emblems of their rule and authority, "the scepter" and "the glorious staff," will be broken, showing that their power and national glory will pass.

18–19 Dibon stood on two hills, thirteen miles east of the Dead Sea near the Arnon River. Her people are commanded to come down and sit on the ground. The Moabite Stone was found here in 1868. Her residents are about to be deported, but in their hunger and thirst they must await the pleasure of the enemy. Aroer is the southernmost city of Reuben on the northern side of the Arnon River.

3. The downfall of Moab (48:20–28)

20–28 If anyone in Aroer should ask why the fugitives were streaming from Moab, the answer would be that the land of Moab was devastated. So Jeremiah issues the call to proclaim by the River Arnon the destruction of Moab. The Arnon is the perennial stream that flows into the Dead Sea. Thus the news that the Babylonians have utterly destroyed Moab will reach its very border. The towns involved in the destruction are named to show its extent. In Joshua's time they were in the portion allotted to the Reubenites and later reconquered by the Moabites. These towns are listed from north to south (most of the places are unknown). The "horn" (i.e., an animal horn) and the "arm" (i.e., a human one) are metaphors of strength and military power, which Moab will lose. The main reason for her fall was the sin of pride. Judgment will come on the Moabites because of their derisive, arrogant treatment of the Lord's people. Drunkenness from the wrath of God is the same metaphor that appears in 25:27–29. The Moabites are exhorted to leave their settlements and live precariously.

4. The pride of Moab (48:29–39)

29–35 Jeremiah has already referred to Moab's pride (cf. vv.7, 11), but not in the strong terms of v.29. Those who have heard of the sin are Jeremiah and his countrymen (cf. Isa 16:6). With pride always go boastings, but they are futile. Because of the impending judgment, the Lord expresses his compassion and sorrow for his creatures, the Moabites. "Kir Hareseth" was the chief fortified city of Moab (cf. Isa 16:7, 11). Moab's ruin is likened to that of a vineyard because Moab was noted for its vineyards. The joy usually accompanying the vintage will be replaced by lamentations. The bitter cry of mourning will be carried from one place to another so as to cover the whole land. Furthermore, God will cut off all the idolatrous worship of the Moabites.

36–39 Jeremiah will lament for Moab the way her people do. Flutes were used at funerals; so they denote mourning. The usual signs of mourning—shaved heads and beards, lacerated hands, and sackcloth—will be visible. Moab is no longer a useful vessel but a shattered one. She will be a sad spectacle to all: mourning, shame, ridicule, and terror will mark her.

5. The terror caused by the invader (48:40–47)

40–47 Finally, Jeremiah proclaims that God's judgment still hangs over Moab. He likens the swiftness of the enemy's approach to the flight of an eagle (vulture)—a reference to Nebuchadnezzar (cf. 49:22; Eze 17:3). The strongest cities in Moab will be utterly helpless, because of Moab's defiant pride toward God. There will be no escape from the calamity; it is everywhere (cf. Am 5:19). Even fleeing for refuge to Heshbon will not avert the destruction. Balaam's prediction will be fulfilled (cf. Nu 21:28; 24:17). Historically, the name Moab appears to have been submerged after her exile by that of the Arabians. But God's pity knows no end. Wrath is always his strange work in which he does not delight. The Moabites will not utterly perish (cf. 46:26; 49:6, 39); they too will have a remnant. So the restoration of Moab is predicted, though without details. "Days to come" refers here to messianic times.

D. Concerning Ammon (49:1–6)

Chapter 49 deals with prophecies against five (or six) nations. All had incurred God's wrath for their idolatry and their treatment of Israel.

The Ammonites were descended from Ben-Ammi, son of Lot (cf. Ge 19:38). Their territory was north of Moab. A more migratory people than the Moabites, it seems that the Ammonites originally occupied the land in which the tribe of Gad was settled after the fall of Sihon, who had probably captured it from Ammon. Their important city was Rabbah. The conquest of the Transjordanian tribes by Tiglath-pileser III of Assyria in 733 B.C. (cf. 2Ki 15:29) led the Ammonites to encroach on Gad's territory, which was east of the Jordan from Heshbon to the Jabbok (cf. Nu 32:34–36; Jos 13:24–28), and to settle between the Arnon and Jabbok rivers toward the desert.

The Ammonites were often in conflict with Israel; they opposed Judah during Jehoiakim's reign (cf. 2Ki 24:2) and helped the downfall of the remnant after the fall of Jerusalem (cf. 40:11–14). They joined in the invasion of Judah in 602 B.C. (cf. 2Ki 24:2) and were among the conspirators against Babylon (cf. 27:3). They were condemned because they confiscated land from Gad during the

Assyrian invasion in 733–732 B.C. The destroyer of Ammon, though not named, was probably Nebuchadnezzar.

1–3 Jeremiah asks whether the tribe of Gad had no heirs since the god of the Ammonites was inheriting their land and his people were living in Gad's cities. Although the northern tribes had been carried away by the Assyrian Tiglath-pileser III, their land still belonged to them and was to be inherited by their sons. Molech was the national god of Ammon (cf. 1Ki 11:5, 7, 33). Jeremiah prophesies that war and destruction will overtake Rabbah, the chief city of the Ammonites (now Amman, the capital of Jordan). Her nearby villages will be engulfed in the catastrophe. Jeremiah names two of the more prominent towns that the Babylonians will devastate.

Five or six miles from the Ammonite border, Heshbon had been under the Amorite king Sihon (cf. Nu 21:25 30, 34). Later it came under Moabite control. Ai is not the Ai captured by Joshua (cf. Jos 8:1–29) but the Ammonite Ai.

4–6 Living in an inaccessible country with mountains on three sides, Ammon considered herself beyond invasion. She was proud of her valleys made fertile by the Arnon waters. Everyone will flee precipitately by the shortest route with no one to rally the fugitives. Josephus says that Nebuchadnezzar defeated Ammon in the fifth year after the destruction of Jerusalem. The Ammonites opposed Israel even after the Exile (cf. Ne 4:1–15; cf. also 1Mc 5:6, 30–43). As with Moab (cf. 48:47), the Lord graciously promises restoration.

E. Concerning Edom (49:7–22)

This prophecy is closely related to that of Obadiah, which was written after 587–586 B.C. The Edomites, whose relations with Israel were always poor, were descendants of Esau (cf. Ge 36:1–19) who lived in the mountainous region south of the Dead Sea toward the Gulf of Aqaba until the Nabateans displaced them. Later on the Maccabees forced them to become Jews. The severity in all the prophecies about Edom reflects the close and stormy relationship between Esau (progenitor of the Edomites) and his twin, Jacob (progenitor of Israel). Edom's cardinal sin was its pride manifested in its unrelenting and violent hatred of Israel and its rejoicing in her misfortunes (Ob 3, 10–14). No future restoration is prophesied for Edom.

7–12 Teman was in northern Edom, the home of Eliphaz (Job 2:11); it was renowned for wisdom (Eze 25:13). The rhetorical questions show how suddenly calamity overwhelmed the wisest in Edom. Could they not see that destruction was imminent? Dedan, a tribe living south of Edom, was known for its commerce (25:23; Eze 25:13). The people of Dedan are warned to flee from their usual contacts with Edom, lest they be overtaken in its destruction. Contrary to the practice of grape gatherers, who left something for the poor, the enemies of Edom will leave nothing but will plunder everything.

The compassionate tone of v.11 is in keeping with the Lord's character. The sense is that when the men of Edom have been slain in war, their widows and orphans may look to the Lord for protection. But the nation will have to drink the cup of God's wrath (cf. 25:28). If Israel had to drink of this cup, how could Edom escape? Because of the Edomites' complicity in Jerusalem's fall, they are especially guilty (cf. Ob 10–14).

13–22 Here the desolation of Edom is underscored. Bozrah is referred to because it was the capital of Edom in Jeremiah's time. It was midway between Petra and the Dead Sea, and here it represents all the Edomite cities (cf. Isa 63:1). The completeness of Edom's overthrow is left beyond doubt. The cause of her downfall is her inveterate pride (cf. 48:7, 29; 49:4; Ob 3, 10–14).

The nations are summoned to war against Edom. Because of her fortifications and topography, Edom had convinced herself that she was impregnable. The "rock" referred to was later called Sela (Petra, a name that means "rock")—the capital city and chief fortress of the Edomites. The ruin of Edom will be irreversible (cf. Ge 14:2, 8). Edom's foe will pounce like a lion scattering a flock. Dispersion, destruction, and devastation will be her lot. Her doom shows how fearful it is to fall into the hands of the living God (Heb 10:31).

F. Concerning Damascus (49:23–27)

23–27 It is difficult to fit this prophecy into any recorded event relating to Damascus. The important cities in Aram were Hamath, Zobah, and Damascus—the last being the seat of a powerful dynasty. Hamath and Arpad had their own local kings and gods (cf. Sennacherib's boast, 2Ki 18:34; 19:13). Word of the enemies' approach terrifies one city after another. Hamath on the Orontes is about 110 miles north of Damascus, and Arpad is about 95 miles north of Hamath. Damascus was in southern Aram. All three Aramean cities had been conquered by Assyria (Isa 10:9). Damascus was also defeated by Nebuchadnezzar in 605 B.C. The reference to the "sea" must be figurative because Aram had no seacoast in ancient times. Damascus was famous in antiquity because of its location in a large oasis and because of its commerce (cf. Eze 27:18). It ought to have been abandoned before its conquest. The young men, soldiers, the walls, and fortresses of the city are all to be destroyed. Fire will ruin its walls and defenses. Ben-Hadad was the name of a dynasty that ruled Damascus in the ninth and eighth centuries B.C. as well as the name of individual kings (cf. 1Ki 15:18, 20; 2Ki 13:24). In conquering Damascus, Nebuchadnezzar vindicated Babylon's surge toward the west.

G. Concerning Kedar and Hazor (49:28–33)

28–33 Nebuchadnezzar also moved against some of the eastern tribes. Their secluded position in the Arabian desert will not ensure them of safety, for they too will feel the might of Babylon. Kedar was an Ishmaelite desert tribe (cf. Ge 25:13; Isa 21:13, 16; Eze 27:21). Although these nomads, who were rich in livestock, were good at archery (Isa 21:16–17), Nebuchadnezzar conquered them. Hazor is not the fortress Hazor in northern Palestine (cf. Jos 11:1–13) because this Hazor was in a desert region. The areas controlled by Hazor may have included Kedar and those named in 25:23. Little is known of the early history of the Arabs. Kedar (cf. 2:10) is mentioned often in Assyrian inscriptions. Terror and destruction will strike the people of Hazor and Kedar as they have other people (cf. 6:25; 20:4; 46:5). The Lord calls the Babylonian forces to attack Hazor. Behind judgment scenes the Lord is at work, carrying out his plan. As did so many others, Kedar and Hazor lived in careless self-complacency.

H. Concerning Elam (49:34–39)

34–39 This prophecy dates from the beginning of Zedekiah's reign (i.e., 598 B.C.). Elam was an ancient kingdom (cf. Ge 14:1), two hundred miles east of Babylon and west of the Tigris River. It had been an important power but was conquered about 640 B.C., in the time of Ashurbanipal of Assyria. Later it was united with Media, then Persia. Its capital, Susa, was the residence of Darius Hystaspes and became the nucleus of the Persian Empire (Ne 1:1, Da 8:2). The purpose of this prophecy may have been to show that Elam would not and could not curb the Babylonian power. The reference to breaking the bow is a pointed one because the Elamites were famous for their skill in archery (Isa 22:6); the bow was their main weapon. Nevertheless, invaders will overwhelm them from every direction. When compared with other prophecies of Jeremiah against foreign nations, this one against Elam does not mention Nebuchadnezzar but refers only to enemies in general. Verse 38 indicates that the Lord himself will sit in judgment on Elam (cf. 1:15). "In days to come" Elam is to be restored. Some have seen the fulfillment of this prophecy when Elam, with Susa as her capital, became the center of the Persian Empire. But the phrase shows the eschatological dimension of the prophecy.

I. Concerning Babylon (50:1–51:64)

The prophecy against Babylon is by far the longest of those against foreign nations. These two chapters emphatically stress the truth of Mt 25:31–46, that the criterion by which God judges the nations is their treatment of his chosen people whom he has made the vehicle of salvation (cf. Jn 4:22) and placed at the center of the consummation of human history (cf. Isa 2:1–4). The only clue to the date of chs. 50–51 is 51:59–60, which mentions the fourth year of Zedekiah—i.e., 594–593 B.C.

Two main emphases run throughout these chapters: the fall of Babylon and the return of the Jewish exiles to their home. This does not mean that Jeremiah was pro-Babylon or pro-Judah. He had declared that Judah must be punished for her sins, and Babylon was God's agent for it. Then Babylon is to be judged for her own sins.

1. Babylon's doom announced (50:1–10)

1–10 The references to Babylon are not, as a rule, to the city but to the nation. First of all, the idols of Babylon are discredited. Bel and

Marduk are alternate names for the same great Babylonian deity. Jeremiah sees the future doom as already completed. The idols are contemptuously referred to as "dung pellets" (NIV, "her idols"). "A nation from the north" (i.e., the Medes and Persians) will execute judgment on Babylon. The Lord exhorts his people to flee from Babylon because of the impending invasion. Scattered and penitent Israel is given a chance to escape. Flight alone will enable her to escape Babylon's doom. The reunited nation will return to Jerusalem to join herself to the Lord, never to forget the eternal covenant.

2. Babylon's sin and judgment (50:11–16)

11–16 Judgment on Babylon will be in retaliation for her treatment of Israel. Babylon herself is addressed so that she may realize the issues involved in her visitation. No nation in ancient times influenced the fortunes of Israel in a more devastating way than Babylon did. Her desolation is expressed in numerous ways. Babylon's enemies are summoned to wreak destruction on her. Babylon was in a fertile agricultural area. With the decline of her political power, the irrigation canals were silted up so that the country became desolate. Cyrus, who unified the Medo-Persian Empire and then overwhelmed Babylon (ZPEB, 1:1054–56), was careful to spare the country; so the references must be to a later attack. Babylon will learn the agony the law of retaliation entails.

3. Consolation to Israel (50:17–20)

17–20 This short portion summarizes the biblical interpretation of Israel's history. The sufferings of Israel are stated, then the judgment God will bring on those who inflicted such sufferings on Israel, next her return to her land in peace and plenty, and, finally, the greatest blessing of all—the pardon of Israel's iniquity. All these will be realized in messianic times.

4. God's vengeance on Babylon (50:21–28)

21–28 Once more God calls on the foes of Babylon to execute his wrath on her. "Merathaim" ("double rebellion") signifies Babylon; "Pekod" means "visitation" or "punishment." Cause and effect are thus indicated in the play on the place names—i.e., "double rebellion" and "visitation." The unexpected

nature of the visitation is pointed out. Babylon, who hammered so many nations to pieces, will know the armory of God opened against her through her foes. There will be wholesale slaughter of Babylon's finest men. Clearly God is reckoning with Babylon for having burned his temple in the capture of Jerusalem. The escapees from Babylon will announce in Zion that the Lord has avenged the destruction of his temple.

5. Babylon's arrogance (50:29–32)

29–32 The stress here is on Babylon's insufferable arrogance against the Lord. The fall of the proud will be complete. The exiles, as they summon archers, are seen exulting over God's retribution on Babylon. The call is to complete the extinction of the haughty empire. Verse 30 is practically a verbatim repetition of 49:26, where Jeremiah pronounced judgment on Damascus. It is equally appropriate. Babylon is viewed as the epitome of arrogance—pride personified! The message originally addressed to Jerusalem (cf. 21:13–14) is directed against Babylon here with the necessary changes. For godless Babylon the consequences can only be fall, fire, and final consumption.

6. Israel's Kinsman-Redeemer (50:33–40)

33–40 Few nations have ever realized that God is the "Redeemer" (GK 1457) of Israel. The OT concept of kinsman-redeemer includes the protection of a relative's person and property. It involves avenging the murder of a relative, the purchase of his alienated property, and/or the marriage to his widow (cf. Lev 25:25; Nu 35:21; Ru 4). God as Redeemer is voluntarily committed to champion Israel's cause. He will bring peace to his own but unrest to his oppressors. In a sense, Israel is the epitome of all that Babylon enslaved.

7. The permanence of Babylon's doom (50:41–46)

41–46 This section should be compared with 6:22–24 and 49:19–21. The lion now is Cyrus, whereas in 49:19 it was Nebuchadnezzar. The desolation of Babylon will be permanent, as was that of Sodom and Gomorrah. The doom of Babylon will indeed terrify the nations who witness it. In 6:22–24 Judah was warned of an unnamed northern invader; the same language is now directed against Babylon, with appropriate changes. The "many kings" are those who were allied with Persia (e.g., the Medes) to bring about the defeat of Babylon. The executors of Babylon's judgment are described as to their war paraphernalia, their vast cavalry, the deafening tumult, their military formation, and their merciless attitude toward their enemy. It is clear why the "king of Babylon" is overcome with fear. Verses 44–46 are practically a verbatim repetition of the condemnation of Edom in 49:19–21. The reason is clear: since Edom's sins resemble Babylon's, God in righteousness must judge them similarly. The phrase "among the nations" indicates a wider audience than the one in view in 49:21 because of the greater prominence of the Babylonian power.

8. The Lord's vengeance on Babylon (51:1–14)

1–4 Chapter 51, the longest in the book, continues the message of condemnation and ruin for Babylon and concludes with a word concerning an important mission sent to Babylon by Jeremiah. A northern enemy is dispatched against Babylon, which is to be destroyed as chaff is winnowed from grain. "Leb Kamai" is Hebrew for "the heart of those who rise against me"; it is a cipher for Chaldea (see comment on 25:26; cf. 51:41). Why Jeremiah used these ciphers is not known, because he generally used the name Babylon. An obvious reason would be to hide the identity of the nation prophesied against. It is the enemies of Babylon who are called on to perform the will of God regarding her. Though the Babylonians with their weapons guard the walls, yet they are to be attacked and none spared.

5–10 The judgment is the vengeance of the Lord on Babylon for her treatment of Judah. She that was as a cup of wrath to the nations will now be shattered herself (cf. 25:15–16). The cup was a golden one because she intoxicated the nations with her wealth and power. And there is no healing for her mortal wound. Thus will God vindicate his cause in Judah.

11–14 The aggressor (Media) is now identified and the work of judgment described. The Medes were allied with Babylon in the destruction of Nineveh in 612 B.C. Later they joined the Persians to defeat Babylon in 539 B.C. (cf. Da 5:28, 31; 8:20). Again Jeremiah specifies that this judgment is for the destruction of the temple. All Babylon's strength cannot avert her fall that has been determined by the Lord. The invaders will swarm over her like locusts.

9. The omnipotent Lord and impotent idols (51:15–26)

15–23 In ch. 10 Jeremiah showed how the house of Israel had no cause to fear the impotent idols of the pagans. Here he demonstrates to the Babylonians the uselessness of their idols, which will all be destroyed before the mighty Creator and Ruler of the universe. The biblical doctrine of the requital is predicated on the basis of God's control over the affairs of all the nations on the ground of his creative activity (27:5) and his zeal for righteousness (Ge 18:25). In vv.20–23, Jeremiah prophesies that Cyrus of Persia, the Lord's "war club," will shatter Babylon. This passage underscores the great power of Persia. Ten times the phrase "with you" falls like hammer blows.

24–26 Babylon was situated on a plain; so "O destroying mountain" is a metaphor for a powerful kingdom (cf. Da 2:35, 14–15). But Babylon will become as an extinct volcano—"a burned-out mountain." She will never be rebuilt.

10. The nations summoned (51:27–33)

27–33 A call summons the nations to fight against Babylon. As God's avenger, Cyrus will harvest her. The people north of Babylon, who were conquered by the Medes early in the sixth century B.C., are named: Ararat, Minni, and Ashkenaz. These three are called to aid the Medes against Babylon.

11. Babylon's defenses useless (51:34–44)

34–44 The Lord in his judgment will answer Zion's complaint against Babylon. This will mean the end of Babylon. Babylon is compared to lions' cubs. She will be given a feast, followed not by drunken sleep, but by the perpetual sleep of death. In v.41 "Sheshach" is mentioned again (see comment on 25:26; cf. 51:1). Two things Babylon was famous for were the god Bel and the great wall of the city. Bel will be compelled to disgorge the nations he has swallowed, and the great wall will collapse.

12. Warning to Israel to flee Babylon (51:45–48)

45–48 Again, the Lord's people are warned to flee the doomed city before disaster strikes. They will need faith and courage until Babylon falls. But they are not to be terrified by the rumors that will be rife, for each year will have its own rumors of tyrants against tyrants. Heaven and earth will rejoice over Babylon's fall (cf. Rev 19).

13. The certainty of Babylon's fall (51:49–53)

49–53 Retribution will overtake Babylon. The remnant of Israel is ashamed when they think of Jerusalem, for they have been the cause of the temple's having been defiled by strangers. And Babylon's idolatry will not escape judgment.

14. The completeness of Babylon's destruction (51:54–58)

54–58 Jeremiah sees the destroyers of Babylon as already present. The enemy overruns the land as tidal waves sweep over a country. When most needed, Babylon's men are made drunk by God's wrath. The slave labor of many nations expended in building the wall will have been for naught.

15. The mission of Seraiah (51:59–64)

59–64 This is Jeremiah's word to Seraiah, the staff officer who was responsible for looking after the comfort of the king of Judah whenever he stopped for the night. He was probably the brother of Baruch (cf. 32:12). In lieu of Jeremiah, Seraiah was to perform a symbolic act. The fourth year of Zedekiah (594–593 B.C.) was possibly the year when Zedekiah attempted to clear himself of complicity in a revolt against Babylon. Seraiah's symbolic act was a visual enactment of the fall of Babylon. This passage is an appendix to this prophecy against Babylon that shows how it was taken to Babylon. It is remarkable that at the very time Jeremiah was advising submission to that city, he was also foretelling its final overthrow. Verse 64b is commonly understood to be a compiler's note, added to separate ch. 51 from ch. 52.

V. Historical Supplement (52:1–34)

This chapter is a historical supplement to the book of Jeremiah. It deals with the fall of Jerusalem; tells what the Babylonians did to the temple and its vessels; describes how Nebuchadnezzar treated Zedekiah, Jehoiachin, and other officials; and lists the number of Jews taken into exile. The purpose of the chapter is to show how Jeremiah's prophecies were fulfilled in contrast to those of the false prophets. The chapter is almost identical with 2Ki 24:18–25:30.

A. The Fall of Jerusalem (52:1–11)

1–11 Verses 1–3 give a brief summary of the reign of Zedekiah and show the proximate cause of the fall of Jerusalem. The narrative goes on to give a vivid account of how the city fell. So crucial was this event that the OT records it four times—in 2Ki 25; 2Ch 36:11–21; Jer 39:1–14; and in this passage.

B. Results of the Fall (52:12–27a)

12–27a Here the narrative goes into detail about what happened in Jerusalem after it fell. There is no contradiction between v.12 and v.29. In the former the accession year of Nebuchadnezzar has been included; in the second it has not. The account of the taking of the sacred vessels to Babylon (cf. 1Ki 6–8) is more elaborate here than that in 2 Kings. Zedekiah's revolt surely had an effect opposite from what the priests and false prophets had wanted. Solomon's magnificent temple, one of the wonders of the ancient world, was plundered and ruined. In v.24 the three orders of the priests are referred to. Apparently the priests and false prophets had been

When the people of Judah fled from the Babylonian army, they headed toward the Arabah (52:7), a desolate area south of the city of Jerusalem.

largely responsible for inciting Zedekiah's revolt against Nebuchadnezzar. They and the chief officers of the city were captured because of their responsibility for the calamity.

C. Nebuchadnezzar's Captives (52:27b–30)

27b–30 The three deportations to Babylon listed here occurred (1) in 598–597 B.C., (2) in 587–586 B.C., and (3) in 582–581 B.C. Under Judean kings there were three deportations: (1) under Jehoiakim (606 B.C.), which marked the beginning of the seventy years of exile; (2) under Jehoiachin (597 B.C.); and (3) under

Zedekiah (586 B.C.). If only Jews are numbered or only males reckoned in vv.28–30, the ultimate total of exiles was doubtless much higher.

D. Evil-Merodach's Kindness to Jehoiachin (52:31–34)

31–34 This passage agrees with 2Ki 25:27–30. The humane treatment accorded Jehoiachin (c. 561 B.C.) is confirmed by cuneiform tablets. These verses conclude Jeremiah's somberly beautiful book with a comforting thought—namely, that the Lord did not forget the Davidic line, even in exile.

The Old Testament in the New

OT Text	NT Text	Subject
Jer 7:11	Mt 21:13; Mk 11:17; Lk 19:46	A den of robbers
Jer 9:24	1Co 1:31; 2Co 10:17	Boasting in the Lord
Jer 31:15	Mt 2:18	Crying in Ramah
Jer 31:31–34	Heb 8:8–12; 10:16–17	The new covenant
Jer 32:38	2Co 6:16	God and his people

Lamentations

INTRODUCTION

1. Background

The book of Lamentations consists of five laments, all but the third based on the destruction of Jerusalem by the Chaldeans in 587 B.C. and its aftermath. The vividness of the pictures points clearly to the work of an eyewitness. Though the author was conscious of the suffering elsewhere in Judah, he concentrated on the situation in Jerusalem.

2. Authorship

In Hebrew the book is anonymous (the LXX has an introductory verse that ascribes authorship to Jeremiah). Arguments for and against authorship by Jeremiah are evenly balanced. We do well, then, to respect the seal of anonymity impressed on the book by the Holy Spirit. The claim for authorship by Jeremiah appears mainly sentimental. Theological similarities with Jeremiah can expected from anyone who accepted his teaching and that of the great prophets in general.

3. Date

Few commentators seriously suggest that any of the five laments fall outside the period 586–538 B.C. Indeed, the lack of national hope points to completion before 562 B.C., when the release of Jehoiachin from prison (2Ki 25:27–30) must have awakened some expectation that Jeremiah's promises would be fulfilled. Such hope as is expressed in ch.3 is for the individual rather than the nation; elsewhere national hope scarcely rises above anticipation that hostile nations will share the judgment that has befallen Zion.

4. Purpose

Already in Zec 7:3, 5; 8:19, we find that the destruction of the temple on the seventh day of the fifth month (2Ki 25:8–9) was remembered by an annual fast. (This was transferred in the second century A.D. to the ninth day of the month and has since then commemorated the two destructions of the tem-

ple as well as the crushing of Bar Kochba's revolt in A.D. 135.) We may be certain that this fast was observed from the beginning, almost certainly with ceremonies in the ruins of the temple (cf. Jer 41:5, where pilgrimage to the temple area was a goal for pious people). For as far back as tradition reaches, Lamentations has been read on the ninth day of the fifth month; it is reasonable to assume that it was intended for this purpose from the first.

The immediate purpose of the book of Lamentations, however, does not fully explain its presence in the canon, because, at least for the Christian, it would now have little more than historical and antiquarian interest. The Bible finds room for every element of human experience, including overwhelming human sorrow. This can come to the individual (e.g., Job) or to the nation as a whole. In such a position even the comfortable words of Scripture do not always bring solace and a ray of light. Though Jeremiah had set a limit to Babylonian rule (25:11–12) and had promised national restoration (chs. 30–31), the hearts of the survivors were too stunned to appreciate these promises. Even in the era of the Gospel, the same thing occasionally happens; then the brokenhearted who turn to these laments discover that they are not the first to pass through thick darkness before emerging into the sunlight again. Thus they realize that their God is the one who puts their tears onto his scroll (Ps 56:8).

The modern reader may wonder at the extremes of sorrow expressed in the book and may be puzzled that the Jews should have continued to mourn the destruction by Nebuchadnezzar. It is in fact hard for us to realize how complete the destruction was.

The old "City of David" lies outside the present city walls. This is only partially due to the effects of the destruction by the Romans. The Chaldeans so broke down the Jebusite and Davidic walls and terraces that restoration was impossible; and Nehemiah had to build his wall much higher up the slope, greatly reducing the area of what had been the center of the city. At the return from exile, a completely new beginning was needed. Lamentations, in this sense, is a funeral dirge over an irrecoverable past.

5. Literary Form

Chapter 5 is a normal Hebrew poem of twenty-two verses. It consists of a long line, normally of five beats, dividing unevenly (3 + 2) and showing much less parallelism than normal Hebrew poetry. It would certainly have suited impromptu eulogizing of the dead. In chs. 1–4 a high proportion of the lines fall into this pattern, but there are sufficient exceptions to show that it was used in no mere mechanical manner.

In addition, these chapters are built on the basis of an alphabetic acrostic. Chapters 1–2 each contain twenty-two verses, each verse having three lines; the first word of each verse begins with one of the twenty-two letters of the Hebrew alphabet in order. Chapter 4 is on the same pattern but has only two lines to a verse. Chapter 3, with sixty-six verses, has three verses for each letter of the alphabet, thus reminding us of Ps 119 (though there the groups are of eight verses each). A further peculiarity is that in chs. 2–4 *pe* comes before *ayin*, contrary to the usual order of the Hebrew alphabet.

Various explanations have been offered for the use of such an acrostic structure. In Ps 119 it aids the memory, but that can hardly have been the motive here. One likely suggestion is that such a literary convention kept a control on the expression of profound grief. Another suggestion is that the use of the alphabet symbolizes that the completeness—"the A to Z"—of grief is being expressed.

6. Theological Values

The problem of suffering presented itself to Israel on two levels—national and personal. Jeremiah best shows that the two must be kept separate; for while he anticipated and justified the downfall of Jerusalem and the Davidic monarchy, he could not understand his personal suffering, which he as a righteous man should, according to popular theology, have avoided. The classical work on the suffering of the righteous is Job. Lamentations deals with national suffering.

While there is no effort to minimize Judah's sin, the writer is clearly overwhelmed by the greatness of her doom. There is a clear

recognition that the disaster was caused by God, not his enemies. Even the mockery of Judah's enemies was caused by God (2:17). Hence, the laments are shot through with prayer; and prayer leads to hope in a situation in which hope appears meaningless.

Ultimately there are depths in God's actions that finite human beings cannot grasp. God's revelation in word and act consistently shows his justice and covenant love; yet there is always a residue of human experience that demands our bowing to a wisdom too high for our understanding. This finds its supreme example in the Cross and in the cry of Jesus in Mk 15:34 (cf. Ps 22:1). This is why every facile theory of the Atonement has failed to satisfy for long, for there are depths concealed in Golgotha that pass human understanding. Only when in glory we see free will and predestination reconciled will we also grasp how God's sovereign will is compatible with his justice and covenant love.

EXPOSITION

I. The Desolation and Misery of Jerusalem (1:1–22)

This lament is evidently later than chs. 2, 4, and 5 (ch. 3 is undatable). The writer was no longer stunned by the utter brutality of defeat and destruction but was able to see what had happened in perspective. Jerusalem mourned by this time less for what she had suffered than for what she had become. The lament could be interpreted as a dialogue between poet and city; but we should rather see the poet's description moving the mourning, widowed city to burst out into a plea both to God and to those strangers who would pass by and see her misery and desolation.

1. The Poet's Description (1:1–11b)

1 The poet first looks at Jerusalem, the capital and representative of Judah, and contrasts what she once had been with what she now is. Even in the great days of David and Solomon, the territories of Israel never compared with those of Egypt, Assyria, and Babylonia at their height; as to buildings, riches (except perhaps in the days of Solomon), and population, Jerusalem never rivaled the great cities of the Near East. Yet we are not to take the poet's language as either nationalistic or sentimental. Israel as God's land and Jerusalem as the city of God's sanctuary always held the hope of seeing the Lord's universal kingship. So the poet is describing her potential in God's purposes. But what hope is there since the city is lying in ruins and the land a vassal or slave?

2 In the "night" of her desolation, Jerusalem is pictured as weeping, not merely because of her sufferings, but even more because she had been betrayed by her "lovers" and "friends." These terms (cf. Jer 4:30; 30:14) are best explained by Eze 23 and Hos 8:9-10. The suggestion is that once the monarchy was firmly established, Israel was always faced with an inescapable choice. She could rely on God for her safety against external aggression, or she could turn to allies great and small (cf. 1Ki 15:16–20). The prophets warned Israel that such alliances involved apostasy (cf. Hos 5:13; 8:8, 11; 14:3), but both the northern and the southern leaders would not listen. Judah had learned that such friends were a broken reed (Eze 29:6–7).

3 From Jerusalem the poet turns to the people of Judah who have gone into exile, leaving the city deserted. This does not mean that the afflictions and deportations have been completely effective. To "live among the nations" is used in 4:20 of national existence under the monarchy; hence "dwells among the nations" need not refer to the Exile. The lack of a "resting place" refers to Judah's inability to guarantee peace under the monarchy.

4 Not even pilgrims come to the sanctuary. Ezra 3:2–6 shows that the temple building was not necessary for sacrifices to be brought, and Jer 41:5 indicates that pilgrims came to the site even after the destruction of the temple. Apparently even that practice ceased, which suggests that this may be the latest of the laments. "Her priests" are any surviving priests who have escaped deportation and remain as near the sacred site as possible. The linking of the "maidens" with the priests is also found in Jer 31:13–14 and Joel 1:8–9, though it is unclear whether this had any part in the temple cultus (Ps 68:25).

5 All this had been foreseen in the covenant (cf. Dt 28:44); thus there is the frank and open confession that this was the Lord's doing "because of her many sins." Going into exile was one of the punishments foretold for

a breach of the covenant (cf. Dt 28:36, 63–68). A touch of added pathos is given by "her children" paying the penalty for the sins of their parents.

6 Zion's majesty has collapsed. Her "princes" have fled like famished stags before the hunters, caring nothing for the herd. Twice Jerusalem yielded without a fight (2Ki 24:1, 17; Da 1:2); and at the last Zedekiah and his captains fled for their lives, abandoning the doomed city (2Ki 25:4).

7 Jerusalem is seen as participating in the sufferings of her inhabitants. She remembers the days of "affliction and wandering," i.e., banishment in misery, when her people became the helpless prey of the conquerors. This supports the view that this lament was composed some time after the fall of the city. Worst of all is the mocking laughter of her enemies. In the vast majority of cases, laughter is linked with scorn (cf. Ge 17:17; 18:12; Job 8:21; Ps 126:2). The glee of Jerusalem's enemies comes doubtless from a human reaction to Israel's claim to be God's elect.

8–9 Jerusalem is compared to a debased prostitute, shamelessly exposing her nakedness and indifferent to the marks of menstrual blood on her garments. Since prostitution is repeatedly used for Israel's idolatry and Baal worship, it is obviously implied here. The completeness of Israel's collapse has finally brought her to her senses. She knows she has no grounds for begging for a reversal of fortune, but the insolent triumphing of the enemy calls for divine retribution (cf. Isa 10:12). "The enemy has triumphed" is literally correct but misleading. It is not the victory but the insolent boasting after it that is meant.

10 The worst feature of all is that Jerusalem has lost what she held most dear. Later sentiment had enveloped Jerusalem in a haze of earthly glory and beauty; but her outstanding glory then, as later, was the temple—and even the temple derived its chief glory from its sanctity. This has been brutally violated by the conquerors. Since the Ammonites and the Moabites, who were descended from Lot and thus distantly related to Israel, had been forbidden to enter the Lord's congregation (Dt 23:3), how much more the completely unrelated Chaldeans!

11a–b The poet brings his lament to a climax. In proportion to what Jerusalem has suffered, to say, "They barter their treasures for food," does not seem to be particularly serious. In addition, it is hard to believe that when the Chaldeans had finished plundering the city, there was much treasure left. Already Theodoret (c. 450) suggested that the true meaning of the statement was, "They gave their darlings for food to keep alive." It is unimportant whether we think of them eating their children (cf. 2:20; 4:10 [prophesied in Dt 28:53–57; cf. 2Ki 6:28–29]) or selling them into slavery. Probably both are intended.

2. The City's Plea (1:11c–16)

11c We are to think of Jerusalem's being so moved by the poet's words that she breaks out in a prayer, which forms a suitable halfway stage in the poem. It is not the fact of being despised but the extent to which she is looked down on that she hopes may move God to pity.

12 From God Jerusalem turns with a plea for pity to the nations round about, pictured as travelers passing along the roads of devastated Judah. "The day of his fierce anger" is the Day of the Lord. Just as in Mk 13 and parallels the fall of Jerusalem is linked with the sufferings of the end time, so it is here (cf. also Jer 4:23–28).

13–14 The fire from on high continues the picture of God's burning anger, acting like a high fever with its racking pains, which brings death. Not Jerusalem's enemies, but God himself had entrapped the city, bringing it to an inescapable and ignominious end (cf. Eze 12:13; 17:20). The result has been an example of desolation and weakness, as though from a fatal disease. "They have come upon my neck" implies that Jerusalem just could not withstand her enemies when they came against her. For a city that had Jerusalem's strength, the siege, which lasted only a year and a half, was surprisingly short (2Ki 25:1–2; cf. 17:5–6).

15–16 Nothing but despair is left. There is likely a climax here, and instead of "an army" (GK 4595) we should understand the Hebrew here as a joyful "harvest festival" to which, not Jerusalem, but her enemies are invited. So bitter is the experience that Jerus-

alem does not use the name "LORD" (yahweh; GK 3378), with its covenant associations (cf. Ex 3:14), but "Lord" (adonay; GK 151). Thus the poet is saying: "The Lord has rejected all the warriors in my midst," treating them like chaff: "he has summoned [a festival] against me to crush my young men," not merely to thresh them; and "in his winepress the Lord has trampled the Virgin Daughter of Judah," to provide the wine of rejoicing. Jerusalem's heartbroken sob is that "the enemy has prevailed." Defeat is bitter, but doubly so when the victors are God's enemies.

3. The Poet's Lament (1:17)

17 To prepare us for Jerusalem's final confession, the poet records that though Zion "stretches out her hands" in prayer, there is no comfort; for the destruction is the Lord's command. Abandoned by him, Jerusalem has become a filthy (menstruous) thing scorned by all.

4. The City's Confession (1:18–22)

18–22 While the poet has been speaking, Jerusalem has had time to consider her position once more. She immediately confesses that her plight has been caused by her own rebellion. Jerusalem's one hope is the Lord's judgment on her enemies, though she does not expect restoration as a result. She tells them that they will not suffer less than she has, the more so as "I called to my allies but they betrayed me." The very fact that Jerusalem's one hope and comfort is the similar fate awaiting her enemies is an almost irrefutable argument against Jeremiah's authorship, for he had foretold not only the downfall of the Chaldeans after seventy years but also the restoration of Jerusalem (Jer 25:12). This hopelessness is the best testimony to the utter shock the fall of Jerusalem caused even among the godly. It also helps explain Jeremiah's isolation, the optimism of many after Jehoiachin's deportation (Jer 28:1–4; 29:8–9), and the madness of Zedekiah's revolt.

II. The Lord's Anger With His People (2:1–22)

The main notes in the first lament were desertion, desolation, and shame; here the stress is on destruction. It seems to have been composed between the capture of the city in the fourth month (2Ki 25:3–4) and the coming of Nebuzaradan to mete out Nebuchadnezzar's vengeance (2Ki 25:8–12) a month later; for the dead still lay on the streets unburied. This would explain why the first lament, though the latest in time, is placed first. Initially the sheer impact of physical disaster is overwhelming; it is only later that the shame of it all is seen as even worse.

1. The Casting Off of People and Sanctuary (2:1–9)

1 The storm has passed over the poet's head. As he picks himself up and gazes on the desolation around him, he declares with the voice of faith that this has been the work of the "Lord" (GK 151), the All-Sovereign. The sun of Jerusalem has been hidden; "the splendor of Israel" (i.e., the temple) has been hurled from its high eminence ("from heaven"); and it has been spurned. "His footstool" can hardly mean the ark; for Jer 3:16, which must date from before the destruction of the temple, is evidence that it had vanished earlier.

2–3 All Judah has been devastated, and the kingdom has lost its sacred character. Both actively ("he has cut off every horn," i.e., all strength) and passively ("he has withdrawn his right hand"), the Lord God has destroyed his people.

4–5 God is then depicted as a mighty, hostile warrior, armed with bow to slay at a distance and with sword for close fighting (taking "on the tent of the Daughter of Zion" with "all who were pleasing to the eye"), and finally burning up all that is left. He has behaved like an enemy.

6–7 Like an enemy, the Lord "has destroyed his place of meeting" (the temple). "King and priest" are here linked; for, as the history of the monarchy clearly shows, the king was the supervisor of the temple cultus, even if he was excluded from many of the priestly functions. "The walls of her palaces" are fortified residences. Under the monarchy, too, the temple formed part of a grandiose complex, including the royal palace and state buildings. The enemies' shouts of triumph are compared to the festal shouts of joy (cf. Pss 66:1; 81:1; 95:1; et al.).

8–9 From the temple the lament passes briefly to the city and then to the king (surely Jehoiachin) and his ministers in exile. "The law is no more, and her prophets no longer find visions from the LORD" should be regarded as a unitary statement. There is no indication of God's will, either through priestly interpretation of the law or through prophetic vision.

2. The Agony of the People (2:10–17)

10 From the bitter past the lament turns to the even more bitter present. The mention of the "elders" and "young women" is probably intended to include the whole surviving population. Sitting on the ground in sackcloth, with dust on the head, in silence, and with the head bowed to the ground speak strongly of mourning.

11–12 The poet joins in the mourning in language that shows his physical participation. The fall of the city and the execution of the desperate men who have defended it do not bring the starvation to an end. During the first stage of military occupation, foraging in the surrounding countryside would not have been permitted. "Bread and wine" probably refers to essentials and semiluxuries.

13 So great is the suffering that words fail. It is probable that the extent of the sea is not intended; rather, the devastation of the city is reminiscent of the chaotic sea.

14 The best commentaries on this verse are Jer 23:18–22 and Eze 13:10–16. Just as many preachers are so obsessed with the holiness of the church that they have not been able to take its shortcomings seriously, so it was in Israel. It took the shock of the Babylonian

Visiters to Jerusalem today are shown Jeremiah's grotto, where he is believed to have wept deeply over the coming fate of the city.

exile to break the power and influence of the popular prophets and to discredit them finally.

15–17 In ancient times when each pagan city or group of cities had its own deity or deities, there was a degree of mutual toleration in spite of rivalries. However, Israel's claim that their Lord is the only God, that Israel is his people, and that Jerusalem is his capital causes bitter jealousy and joy at their downfall. "The Lord . . . has fulfilled his word, which he decreed long ago" refers presumably to passages like Lev 26:14–46 and Dt 28:15–68.

3. A Call to Prayer (2:18–19c)

18–19b Despair should drive people to God; so the poet calls Zion to prayer. The first phrase here should be translated, "Cry out from the heart, O wall of the Daughter of Zion." Though the expression may seem strange, it is a call for everything, including the ruins, to join in the prayer of anguish.

19c This line bears out the interpretation that the lament describes the situation after the capture of the city, not the sufferings during the siege.

4. The Response (2:20–22)

20–22 Whether the poet was composing a prayer for the survivors, whether it was meant as an ideal prayer, or whether it was a poetic expression of what was being prayed is immaterial. The prayer is a desperate recounting of utmost woe. Verse 20a is a reminder that there is a covenant relationship. Since the prophets had stressed the inviolability of the temple (cf. Jer 7:4), it is natural that they should gather there in its last hour. For the "solemn assembly" or "feast day," see comment on 1:15.

III. An Israelite's Complaint (3:1–66)

Were this lament in the Psalter, it is improbable that it would have been definitely linked with the fall of Jerusalem; for most of its language has no particular applicability to it, and that which has could come from any situation of major distress. The traditional view has seen in it Jeremiah's personal lament.

1. His Personal Sufferings (3:1–20)

1 In the OT "to see" (GK 8011) frequently goes beyond the obtaining of a visual image and involves a sharing in it. The omission of the name of God in vv.1–21—except in v.18— is intended to underline the poet's feelings of abandonment and separation. For "the rod of his wrath," see Job 9:34; 21:9; Ps 89:32; and Isa 10:5.

2–3 The Hebrew word for "driven" (GK 5627) is used of driving animals, never of God's gracious leading. It was done by the rod of his anger. "Indeed, he has turned his hand against me again and again, all day long" is a complaint of exceptional suffering.

4 The force of the Hebrew for "grow old" is not to make old but to produce the effect of aging, i.e., to wear out. "Has broken my bones" refers to fever pains, a meaning that suits Isa 38:13.

5–9 "Bitterness" speaks of one's ultimate poverty—the loss of all hope. "Darkness" is one of the traditional features of Sheol. The force of "those long dead" is that they are also forgotten. The mention of "chains" suggests that we should think of the poet's being "walled in" in some dungeon from which his cries for help cannot be heard. The poet is like a man trapped in a maze. The walls are so well built—"with blocks of stone"—that he cannot glimpse the right way through any cracks in them, while side paths lead to dead ends or away from escape.

10–12 Even worse, the poet finds the path beset with danger (for the bear and the lion, see Am 5:9 and Hos 13:8). If somehow he manages to escape his deadly foes and God's leading astray, he finds God, the grim hunter, there to shoot him, not his assailants.

13–15 "He pierced my heart with arrows" shows the power of the archer's arm. "Heart" is a valid equivalent for the metaphorical meaning but misses the literal picture of "kidneys," apparently intended here. It is easy to see Jeremiah as the butt of popular ballads. "Gall," which is traditionally rendered "wormwood," is the name given to certain plants used for imparting a bitter flavor to some drinks.

16–18 "He has broken my teeth with gravel; he has trampled me in the dust" suggests the violent grinding of the face in the ground by others. In the parallelism of "deprived of peace [*shalom*; GK 8934]" and "forgotten what prosperity is," *shalom* must carry its nuance of "success" or "prosperity." In "my splendor is gone," "splendor" (GK 5905) indicates "glory" rather than strength. Both for the prophet and for Israel, hope in the Lord was their glory; when that is gone, they are on the level of the pagans round about. The poet's mention of "the LORD" breaks the spell of misery that has bound him.

19–20 The Hebrew text at the beginning of v.19 can also be translated "Remember my affliction." The writer must first recall the character of the Lord (vv.22–23) before he calls out to him.

2. Consolation and Hope of Grace (3:21–39)

21–24 The "hope" (GK 3498) that the writer expresses here is not created by denying or minimizing suffering and misery. Rather, these are transformed when the mind is turned to God. The vital word in v.22 is "great love" (GK 2876), the covenant love and loyalty of the Lord that leads to "compassion." The covenant called Israel into existence, and the Lord's loving mercy to what he has created will not end. The very fact of awakening to a new day is in itself a renewal of God's mercy. Humankind has passed safely through the night, a foreshadowing of death. So the verse ends with "faithfulness," the counterpart of "great love." The poet has had so little of this world's goods and pleasures because his share has been the Lord (cf. Pss 16:5; 73:26; 119:57; 142:5).

25–27 In the Hebrew these three verses begin with "good" (GK 3202). It means above all that which expresses God's will and purpose. There is the acceptance of God's time and God's will, faith expressing itself in quiet hope and the learning of discipline.

28–30 This group of verses states how the principles of vv.25–27 will be worked out, especially that of bearing the yoke. God's yoke of service will separate one from ordinary human life and lead that person to be an outcast (cf. Job 2:8). Silence implies both acceptance of God's will and refusal to complain to other people. With this should go the complete submission to God pictured in v.29 by

the Oriental obeisance. It leads too to the willingness to be treated like a slave, for the yoke was a symbol of servitude. The principles formulated here will, of course, apply equally to the person called to be a prophet and to the people called to be God's private treasure (Ex 19:5–6).

31–33 These verses give reasons that will make the bearing of the yoke easier. God's rejection is temporary. Even if he afflicts, compassion and covenant love will again be shown; his infliction of pain and punishment is never arbitrary.

34–36 A contrast to God's gracious and loving dealing is offered in three pictures of man's inhumanity. There is the ill-treating of the prisoner just because he is a prisoner. There is the denial of justice. God is here called the Most High to stress that since he is the God of heaven, he is all-seeing; hence the denial of justice is a deliberate flouting of his will. There is the deliberate twisting of a human being's right, as though God does not see.

37–39 This section of the lament stresses the almighty power of God, which makes the acceptance of his will necessary. He is behind both good and calamity (cf. Isa 45:7); so why should people complain when they suffer for their sins? So long as they are alive, things can change.

3. A Call to Penitence (3:40–51)

This section divides into two parts. In vv.40–47 the poet puts a prayer into the mouth of the people. Then in vv.48–51 he adds his tears to the people's plea.

40–41 The people agree that complaint (cf. v.39) is out of place. They must examine their ways, i.e., what they have done. They lift up not merely their hands, the normal position for petition, but the whole inner person ("our hearts") to God; no mere formal prayer is involved.

42–43 There is a contrast between "we" and "you"; rebellion and disobedience are on Israel's side, a refusal to forgive on God's, with the implication that his attitude is just. The thought continues: "You have covered yourself with anger," and so pursuit and slaying have been merciless.

44–46 That God is veiled from a human being's gaze by cloud and darkness is commonplace in the OT (cf. Ex 20:21; 40:34–35; Lev 16:2; 1Ki 8:10, 12; et al.). But this veiling is never considered an obstacle to prayer. The confession of complete worthlessness follows. As a result of God's action, his people's enemies despise them openly (cf. 2:16; Ps 35:21). Judah cannot defend her honor and has no friends to do it for her.

47–48 The word translated "pitfall" probably means a hunter's trap (cf. Isa 24:17–18; Jer 48:43–44). The people's confession reminds Jeremiah of their sufferings and then even more of his own (cf. 9:1; 14:17).

49–51 Jeremiah's tears, i.e., his pleading for Israel, will continue until God responds. The Hebrew of v.51 is literally, "My eye has dealt with my soul from the daughters of my city." Scribal confusion may have resulted in the word for "my eye" instead of "suffering." The sense would be then, "Till the LORD looks down from heaven and sees the suffering done to me because of the daughters of my people," or something similar.

4. The Growth of Hope (3:52–57)

52–56 Agony over the fate of his people reminds the poet of his own fate. For the picture of the hunted bird, see Pss 11:1–2; 124:7; 140:5. Jeremiah 18:18 is an example of what is meant. "They tried to end my life in a pit" no doubt refers to the incident in Jer 38:6. "Waters closed over my head" is a common picture for distress (cf. Job 27:20; Pss 42:7; 66:12; 69:12; 88:7; 124:4; et al.). There is no real justification for taking *eben* ("stone"; GK 74) as a collective, i.e., "stones." A cistern was normally closed with a stone over its mouth. It is not easy to be sure of the exact force of the words in v.56. "Do not close your ears" refers to the remainder of the verse, which is his prayer ("my cry for relief").

5. An Appeal for Vengeance (3:58–66)

58–66 The rendering of these verses is straightforward. God's protection over Jeremiah in the past is an adequate basis for confidence in the future. We might think that the prophet has surely grown beyond such imprecations, and that in the destruction of Jerusalem he has seen God's punishment of his enemies. But we must remember that for the sake of his people, Jeremiah has abandoned everything, even the consolations of family life and children (Jer 16:1–4). In addition, though God gave him some of the most glowing pictures of Israel's restoration, including the promise of the new covenant, there is no indication that God gave him a glimpse of life beyond the grave. How heavy then must have been the burden of rejection and ingratitude that followed him even into Egypt!

IV. Zion, Past and Present (4:1–22)

We may reasonably date this lament not very long after ch.2. Sufficient time had elapsed for the first shock to wear off, and the poet is able to bring what has happened to a focus and so supplements ch. 2.

1. The Contrast (4:1–11)

1–2 Since gold does not tarnish and the second line refers to the destroyed temple, we can easily see a reference to its gold-covered panels and golden vessels so covered with dust that their value is no longer discernible. Similarly, it is no longer possible to discern the value of the enslaved survivors.

3–5 The "jackal" is a mammal whose maternal care might not be expected. The ostrich was proverbial because of its apparent neglect of its eggs (Job 39:13–18), and "my people" have become like it in their neglect of their babes. Money has ceased to have meaning; so the rich women have no helpers and only such food as they can find among the garbage.

6–9 Whether the lament says that "the punishment" or "the iniquity" of Judah is worse than that of Sodom (cf. Eze 16:44–52) is uncertain. Ultimately it is unimportant, for the measure of iniquity and its punishment are held to be linked. *Nazir* (GK 5687) is normally rendered Nazirite, but in Ge 49:26 and Dt 33:16 it is used of one separated by rank and qualities from his contemporaries. This is obviously the sense here, and so "princes" is a satisfactory rendering. The description is of men who are able to devote themselves to their physical appearance. An ignominious fate falls to these once fair nobles. So bad is their situation that death is preferable to life.

10–11 Hunger drives humans to inhuman action (cf. 2Ki 6:25–29). All this falls on the people because they have provoked the Lord to wrath.

2. The Sin of Priests and Prophets (4:12–16)

12 There is an obvious element of exaggeration here. Essentially it means that Jerusalem's deliverance in the time of Sennacherib showed people that, so long as the Lord's hand was over it, the city was impregnable.

13 This protection has been withdrawn because of the bloodguilt of the priests and prophets. We are here dealing with one of the fundamental concepts of prophetic ethics. Ezekiel 22:1–12 shows that the concept of "bloodshed" was far wider than murder or homicide; all that cut at the roots of society or that deprived people of their land and livelihood shortened their lives and so was bloodshed. Priest and prophet contributed positively and negatively—positively by advocating or condoning such behavior, negatively by failing to condemn those who wronged their fellow Israelites.

14–16 Usually these verses are taken as the direct continuation of v.13, giving the fate of the bloodguilty priests and prophets; bearing the mark of Cain, moral lepers, they are rejected wherever they go. However, Jer 29:15–23 and the earlier chapters of Ezekiel do not support such a picture for those who were deported with Jehoiachin, and the poet would hardly know the fate of those who survived the fall of Jerusalem. It may well be intended as a picture of the miserable survivors as a whole, as they are scattered abroad. This is supported by the mention of elders rather than prophets in v.16. It should be remembered that Judah is almost completely bereft of people of standing.

3. Vain Hopes (4:17–20)

17–20 The blindness of those who have gone into exile is matched only by that of those who are left at home. Hoping against hope, they have looked for Egypt's help almost to the last moment (Jer 37:3–10). The use of "we" suggests that the poet has shared in these hopes. This and the manner in which Zedekiah is spoken of are irreconcilable with authorship by Jeremiah. (For v.19, see Lev 26:8; Dt 32:30; Isa 30:16–17.) It is reasonably likely that the vivid memory of Zedekiah's

last, desperate attempt to escape (Jer 52:6–9) lies behind vv.19–20. Judah's madness and blindness are due not only to faith in the inviolability of the temple but also of the Davidic dynasty. This is the obvious explanation why Jeremiah has so little to say about the messianic hope. "Our very life breath" and "under his shadow" are taken from the ancient court-language of the Near East.

4. The Reversal of Doom (4:21–22)

21–22 The vain hopes are gone, and only the stark reality remains. To Edom, who stands for all the enemies of Judah (cf. Isa 34; Eze 35), the poet says, in effect, "Rejoice while you can, for judgment is coming to you also." Their nakedness involves shame and revelation of sins, but it also implies slavery (cf. Isa 47:2–3). The consolation for Zion is that she has received all the punishment she can (cf. Isa 40:2); there can be no more exile.

V. An Appeal to the Lord (5:1–22)

The absence of an alphabetic acrostic and "lament" meter suggest that this lament may be by another hand. Though there are some references to incidents during the siege, the lament deals mainly with the sequel, which suggests some lapse of time.

1. The Affliction of the Lord's People (5:1–18)

1–3 Remembrance in the Bible always involves resultant action; so this is a call to God to act. The word traditionally rendered "inheritance" (GK 5709) normally means "possessions," however obtained. In the poet's society the fatherless orphan and the widow without grown sons are the weakest, unless they have powerful patrons. There is an implied plea to God to act.

4 From 2Ki 24:14; 25:12 and Jer 39:10 we learn that most of those left in Judah were the very poor, who were expected to keep the fields and vineyards in order. No foreign settlers were brought in, though there is little doubt that this was Nebuchadnezzar's intention, overruled by God. So this verse probably refers to the heavy taxation that has to be paid if the survivors are to live.

5 The same idea underlies this verse. The author is not alluding to slave masters, though many people have been dragged away as slaves; rather, it is the need to live that drives them on, and they have forfeited God's promise of rest from their enemies (cf. Dt 12:10; 25:19; 2Sa 7:1, 11).

6–7 It is true that Nebuchadnezzar claimed to be continuing the Assyrian power, as did Cyrus later (cf. Ezr 6:22); but that can hardly be the force of "Assyria" here. The poet is referring to something "our fathers" did. The answer is suggested by Hos 2:5, 8, which shows Israel worshiping the Baalim, the fertility gods of nature. This reduced the Lord for them to a god among gods, and so they sought alliances with Egypt and Assyria (Hos 5:13; 7:11; 12:1). Now their descendants have reaped the bitter harvest, as Samaria had done a century and a half earlier.

8–10 Instead of their own king and ministers, the people are ruled by Babylonian officials, most of relatively low standing, who are proud of the title "slaves of the king"; there is no court of appeal against their arbitrary brutality. This shows itself in the difficulty experienced in obtaining food, which involves risk to life and limb and extreme exposure; "hot" skin is literally "scorched" or "black- .ened" skin, showing general starvation.

11–13 The brutality the people are experiencing is only a continuation of what they have experienced earlier, when the Chaldeans captured the city. "Princes have been hung up by their hands" suggests torture to make the rich reveal where they have hidden their treasures. This meaning is elaborated by the second element concerning elders; their being "shown no respect" manifestly refers to a deliberate shaming. Hence the hanging, perhaps impaling, is of the dead to dishonor their corpses. Since Nebuchadnezzar did not torture those whom he regarded as most guilty (Jer 52:10–11, 24–27), it is not likely that any were hung up or impaled while still alive. Now "young men toil at the millstones," doing women's work, whereas in happier days they would have been soldiers. "Boys stagger under loads of wood"; i.e., they are treated as serfs.

14–18 Old and young had found the course of life disjointed, and all joy is gone because of past sin. The supreme sign of God's anger is that the temple mount has become the abode of wild animals. No great lapse of time is suggested. The temple mount remains sa- cred ground (cf. Jer 41:5). We cannot affirm with any certainty whether sacrifices were continued on the sacred site; but if they were (note that there is no suggestion of this in Lamentations), it would have been only on special occasions. At other times even the surviving priests would have avoided the site in their consciousness of sin and defilement. Even today most strictly orthodox Jews will not enter the temple area. The West (Wailing) Wall is outside the holy area. And jackals rapidly occupy ruins.

2. The Lord's Abiding Power (5:19–22)

19–20 The "throne" is the visible symbol of kingly rule. The poet returns to the plea with which the lament began. "Remember" (v.1) is taken up by "forget"; "look and see" by "forsake."

21 Suddenly there is the overwhelming realization that true repentance is possible only as initiated by an act of God (cf. Jer 31:18, 33–34; Eze 36:26–27). This is a foreshadowing of the NT doctrine of regeneration. Unfortunately, it was grasped by few at the time. Judaism tends to lay great stress on the importance of repentance but always regards it as something essentially within human control.

22 The "unless" of NIV and others would normally lead us to expect a negative expression in the preceding verse. Probably the best rendering is the NEB: "For if thou hast utterly rejected us, / then great indeed has been thy anger against us." Whatever the cost in loss of dramatic effect, it is understandable that when Lamentations is read in the synagogue, v.21 is repeated at this point so that the reading will not end on such a sad note.

Just as it is difficult for us to grasp why Jeremiah should have had to suffer more than his contemporaries, so it seems strange to many that one who could so pour out his heart to God should receive so little consolation. There is not even the burning hope of return and restoration that Jeremiah and Ezekiel voiced. The simple fact is that the people of Israel—with few exceptions—had so failed to grasp God's revelation that an experience parallel to the bondage in Egypt and a new Exodus were needed to prepare Israel for the appearance of her Messiah and the world's Savior.

Ezekiel

INTRODUCTION

1. Background

Israel's idolatrous abominations caused the ten northern tribes of that nation to be taken into captivity by Assyria in 722 B.C. At that time the southern kingdom of Judah was spared through the influence of righteous men like Isaiah. Judah soon experienced a revival and spiritual refreshment under the leadership of young King Hezekiah. He had learned the spiritual lessons from the downfall of Israel and was encouraged by the ministry of the prophet Isaiah (2Ki 18–19). However, Hezekiah's faith in the Lord and zeal for the Mosaic covenant were forgotten when his son Manasseh and his grandson Amon rejected the ways of the Lord. For fifty–five years (2Ki 21:1–18) they turned the people to all kinds of idolatry and wickedness. This so perverted the people that they repudiated the law of God and forgot that it existed.

Josiah, Amon's righteous son, brought renewed hope to Judah; but it came too late. As he was having the temple repaired, a copy of the Law of Moses was discovered (2Ki 22). On reading it, Josiah was moved to obey it fully (2Ki 23). He purified the temple and officially cleansed the land of the abominations of Manasseh and Amon. But among the people this reformation was only perfunctory. The idolatry of Manasseh's long reign had so corrupted their hearts that there was little genuine repentance (cf. Jer 3:10). The Mosaic covenant declared that the nation of Israel would be taken captive and dispersed among the nations if the people continually disobeyed the stipulations of that covenant (Lev 26; Dt 28–29). That curse was now certain. It was the only thing that would remove the wickedness of Israel and cause the people to return to the Lord their God.

Meanwhile, on the international scene there was a new power struggle. Assyria, the dominant nation in the ancient Near East for more than 250 years, was declining, while the Neo-Babylonian Empire was rising under the leadership of Nabopolassar. In 612 B.C. the Babylonians defeated the Assyrians; and Nineveh, their capital city, fell. The remnants of the Assyrian army under Ashuruballit II retreated westward to Haran, where, with their backs to the Egyptians, they endeavored to keep resistance alive.

In 609 B.C. Pharaoh Neco of Egypt marched to the aid of Assyria with a large force. At Megiddo, Josiah, the reformer king of Judah, tried to stop the advance of Neco, only to be killed in the ensuing battle. Neco continued on to Haran to support Ashuruballit in his attempt to retain Haran, but the strength of the Babylonians gave them a decisive victory.

Though Neco failed in his effort to aid Assyria at Haran, he did begin to consolidate Palestine and Aram. He removed Jehoahaz, the pro-Babylonian son of Josiah whom the people of Judah crowned as their new king, and established Jehoiakim, Josiah's eldest pro-Egyptian son, as his vassal king in Judah. Throughout this international turmoil, Jeremiah the prophet warned the people of Judah to submit to the Babylonians and not to follow the enticements of Egypt. But they would not listen.

In 605 B.C. Nebuchadnezzar, the crown prince of Babylonia, attacked the combined Assyrian and Egyptian forces at Carchemish on the Euphrates in one of the most important battles of history. In Nebuchadnezzar's overwhelming victory, two great powers of the ancient Near East fell, never again to rise to international significance. As the Babylonians pushed their conquest southward, they invaded Judah and deported a group of young nobles from there (2Ki 24:1; 2Ch 36:6; Da 1:1–3, 6). This began the great Babylonian captivity of Judah that would ultimately affect every Israelite.

Jehoiakim was both a reluctant vassal of Babylon and a greedy ruler over his people, despising the Mosaic covenant and the reforms of his father, Josiah (Jer 22:13–17). After three years of unwilling submission to Nebuchadnezzar, Jehoiakim refused to heed the warnings of Jeremiah and revolted against Babylon in favor of Egypt (2Ki 24:1). The stalemate in battle between Babylon and Egypt on the frontier of Egypt in 601 B.C. encouraged him. His revolt was a mistake, for as soon as Nebuchadnezzar reorganized his army, he retaliated against those nations that had revolted and had refused to pay tribute to him.

In December 598 B.C., during the month that the Babylonians began to attack Judah, Jehoiakim died. His eighteen-year-old son, Jehoiachin, succeeded him (2Ki 24:8), only to surrender the city of Jerusalem to Nebuchadnezzar three months later. Jehoiachin, his mother, his wives, his officials, and the leading men of the land (2Ki 24:12–16), including Ezekiel (a priest; Eze 1:1–3), were led away into exile. Zedekiah, Jehoiachin's uncle, was established by Nebuchadnezzar as a regent vassal over Judah. Though in exile, Jehoiachin remained the recognized king of Judah by Babylon, as demonstrated from administrative documents found in the excavations at Babylonia.

Buoyed by false prophets' messages that Nebuchadnezzar's power was soon to be broken and the exiles would triumphantly return, and seduced by the seemingly renewed strength of Pharaohs Psammetik II (594–588 B.C.) and Apries (588–568 B.C.), on whom the vacillating Zedekiah pinned his hopes of restored national independence, the king was persuaded to rebel once more against Nebuchadnezzar. The response of Babylon was immediate. Early in 588 the Babylonian army laid siege to Jerusalem (2Ki 25:1; Jer 32:1–2), having already destroyed the fortress cities of the Judean hill country (vividly described in the Lachish Letters). In the fall of 586, Jerusalem was destroyed; Zedekiah was captured and blinded after witnessing the execution of his sons; many inhabitants of Jerusalem were murdered by the Babylonians; and others were deported to Babylon (2Ki 25:2–21; Jer 52:5–27). Judah had fallen.

During this period of international turmoil and unrest, combined with the immorality and apostasy of Judah, Ezekiel ministered. Having grown up during the reform of Josiah and having been taken captive in the deportation of Jehoiachin in 597 B.C., Ezekiel

proclaimed to the exiled Jews the Lord's judgment and ultimate blessing.

The following outline will clarify the chronological relationship between the Judean, Egyptian, and Babylonian kings.

1. Judean kings

Josiah (640–609 B.C.)
Jehoahaz (Josiah's second son) (609 B.C.)
Jehoiakim (Josiah's eldest son) (609–597 B.C.)
Jehoiachin (Jehoiakim's son) (597 B.C.)
Zedekiah (Josiah's youngest son; a regent) (597–586 B.C.)
Jerusalem destroyed (586 B.C.)

2. Egyptian kings

Psammetik I (664–609 B.C.)
Neco (609–594 B.C.)
Psammetik II (594–588 B.C.)
Apries (Hophra) (588–568 B.C.)

3. Neo-Babylonian kings

Nabopolasser (626–605 B.C.)
Nebuchadnezzar (605–562 B.C.)

2. Authorship and Date

Ezekiel's authorship of the entire book was never seriously questioned before the second quarter of the twentieth century. Recent objections to the book's unity have been based on critical literary analysis. Though Ezekiel's visions caused him to see events in Jerusalem while living in Babylon, there are fewer difficulties in accepting the traditional unity than in altering the text and devising stylistic, geographical, and historical objections. The style and content of Ezekiel are remarkably consistent. Some hold to a Palestinian locale for the composition.

Few books in the OT place as much emphasis on chronology as Ezekiel does. The first three verses of ch. 1 mark the chronological setting, dating the book by Jehoiachin's deportation to Babylon in 597 B.C. The first prophetic message is dated in "the fifth year of the exile of King Jehoiachin" (1:2; i.e., 593 B.C.), and the last-dated message (29:17–30:19) was given in "the twenty-seventh year" (571 B.C.). The book contains thirteen chronological notices. Chapters 1–24, which announce both the judgment on Jerusalem and Judah and the basis for it, are dated 593–589 B.C. (1:1–3; 8:1; 20:1; 24:1). The prophecies against the foreign nations in chs. 25–32 are dated 587–585 B.C. (26:1; 29:1; 30:20; 31:1; 32:1, 17), with the exception of 29:17–30:19. The messages of blessing and hope in chs. 33–48 were delivered between 585 and 573 B.C. (33:21; 40:1).

3. Place of Origin and Destination

Ezekiel 1:1–3 and 3:15 clearly define the place of origin of Ezekiel's ministry as Babylonia, specifically at the site of Tel Abib located near the Kebar River and the ancient site of Nippur. Many identify this "River" as a canal making a southeasterly loop, connecting at both ends with the Euphrates River.

The conditions of the Jews in the Babylonian exile were not severe. Though placed at the specific site of Tel Abib, it seems that they had freedom of movement within the country and the opportunity to engage in commerce. They were regarded more as colonists than slaves.

Ezekiel's messages were primarily for these exiles. He condemned the abominations that were leading Jerusalem and Judah to ultimate destruction. The exiles questioned the prophecies of Ezekiel; and he, in turn, answered them carefully. He played the role of a watchman to warn them of the impending judgment on Judah and to proclaim the hope of their ultimate restoration to the land of Israel. Though in some of Ezekiel's visions (chs. 8 and 11) he was carried to Jerusalem, his messages were not directly given for the benefit of the Jews in Palestine. The distance between Babylon and Jerusalem would preclude these messages being directed to Jerusalem, though certainly some of the concepts of Ezekiel may have filtered back to Palestine. Jeremiah, Ezekiel's contemporary, however, was simultaneously proclaiming a similar message of warning and judgment to those remaining in Jerusalem and Judah.

4. Occasion and Purpose

When God created the nation of Israel, he gave the people the Mosaic covenant (Ex 20–Nu 9; Dt) as their constitution, which told them how to live for the Lord. The law was not given to burden the Hebrews; it was given for their own good (Dt 10:12–13), so that they might be blessed (Dt 5:28–33).

Yet the history of Israel was marked by disobedience to this covenant. Often the nation followed the gods of the peoples around them. As the above historical sketch shows, the kingdoms of Israel and Judah became increasingly corrupt and ultimately forgot their constitution. The covenant itself had warned the Israelites that if they strayed from the Lord's ways revealed in the statutes and commandments of the law, the Lord would discipline them through dispersion in order to bring them back to himself.

Ezekiel spoke to his contemporaries, declaring to them the faithfulness, holiness, and glory of God. Their God would bring judgment, cleansing, and ultimate blessing through which all peoples might come to know that he, the God of Israel, was the one true God. The Lord desired to turn the exiles of Israel away from their sinful ways and restore them to himself. His judgment, therefore, was exercised as an instrument of love to cause them to see their abominations and to recognize the Lord's faithfulness to his covenants. He was indeed faithful to his promises, both to judge and to bless his people. The destruction of the city of Jerusalem demonstrated God's faithfulness to his holy character (cf. Lev 26; Dt 28–30) as revealed in his covenants. On the other hand, Ezekiel gave hope that one day the true Shepherd, the Messiah, would come to lead God's people. Though their contemporary rulers had exploited them and led them away from the Lord, in the future the people would be restored to the Promised Land (Ge 12:7) by a righteous leader. In that day all the covenants of the Lord would be fulfilled to his people (Eze 37:24–28).

Ezekiel, as a watchman for Israel, warned the people of the judgment that was imminent and stressed the need for individual responsibility as well as national accountability before God. Each Israelite was personally to turn to the Lord. Likewise, the whole nation must ultimately return to him.

5. Theological Values

Five prominent theological concepts pervade these prophetic pages: (1) the nature of God; (2) the purpose and nature of God's judgment; (3) individual responsibility; (4) the ethical, religious, and moral history of Israel; and (5) the nature of Israel's restoration and the millennial worship.

(1) God's attributes most strongly emphasized are those relating to his covenant promises. A righteous and holy God had

established a righteous way of life for the well-being of his people. If they followed the stipulations of that covenant, they would be blessed in every spiritual and physical way (Lev 26:3–13; Dt 28:1–14). If they rebelled against the Lord's righteous ordinances and disobeyed them, the Lord—being holy, just, and righteous—would discipline his people and withhold blessing (Lev 26:14–39; Dt 28:15–68). Ezekiel demonstrated the Lord's faithfulness to these promises. He was judging Israel and Judah because they had broken the law, but he would also faithfully restore the people to the land of blessing and confer on them messianic blessings of the Abrahamic, Davidic, and new covenants (Lev 26:40–45; Dt 30; cf. Ge 12:1–3; 2Sa 7:12–17; Jer 31:31–34).

(2) God's character logically reflects judgment. The Lord loved the Israelites and chose them as his very own people to bless the world (Ge 12:2–3; Ex 19:4–6; Dt 7:6–11). Since they strayed from his righteous ways, the Lord brought judgment on them to make them conscious of their wickedness so that they would return to him. Ezekiel continually declared that the purpose of the Lord's judgment was to cause Israel, or the nations, to "know that I am the LORD," a phrase repeated over sixty-five times in this book. Judgment was for Israel's good because it would result in their return to the Lord and their recognition that he was the only true God.

(3) Though the Lord often dealt with Israel nationally, Ezekiel balanced this with an emphasis on individual responsibility (cf. Dt 24:16; 29:17–21). A person was not delivered from God's curse by the righteousness of the majority of the nation or some other person's spirituality. Each person was accountable individually to God. Each person needed to obey the statutes of God's word in order to live righteously before him. Everyone was equally responsible for his or her own disobedience and unrighteousness. Therefore Ezekiel exhorted the exiles to turn from their sinful ways and live righteously, according to the Mosaic covenant (chs. 18; 23).

(4) Along with God's judgment announced in this prophecy, Ezekiel vindicated the Lord's righteous justice by recounting Israel's ethical, moral, and religious history. This was most vividly accomplished through the imagery of Israel as a spiritual prostitute who, having been wooed and married by God, had prostituted herself by going after the gods of other nations throughout her entire history. This idolatry and unfaithfulness had characterized her from her birth in Egypt.

(5) In spite of Israel's consistent idolatry, the Lord gave a message of hope through his prophet. One of the most complete descriptions of Israel's restoration to the land of Palestine in the end times was given in the hope messages (33:21–39:29), which enunciated the basis, manner, and results of Israel's restoration to the Promised Land. Likewise, the most exhaustive delineation of the worship system in the Millennium is set forth in chs. 40–48. Anyone studying eschatology must know these sections of Ezekiel.

EXPOSITION

I. Ezekiel's Commission (1:1–3:27)

A. The Vision of God's Glory (1:1–28)

1. The setting of the vision (1:1–3)

1–3 The setting of the Mesopotamian dream-visions, which occurred in both the Assyrian period and the Babylonian period, consisted of four elements: the date, the place of reception, the recipient, and the circumstances. Ezekiel included all four aspects in his vision.

The date of this vision is stated in two different ways: "in the thirtieth year, in the fourth month on the fifth day," and "on the fifth of the month—it was the fifth year of the exile of King Jehoiachin." The "thirtieth year" most likely relates to the age of Ezekiel. It was not uncommon that dates were given according to a man's age when personal reminiscences were being reported (cf. Ge 8:13). Additionally, Ezekiel was a priest, and a man entered his priestly ministry at the age of thirty (Nu 4:3, 23, 30, 39, 43; 1Ch 23:3). Therefore, Ezekiel apparently received this vision and his commission in the very year he would have begun his priestly service.

The "thirtieth year" of Ezekiel is related to the fifth year of King Jehoiachin's exile. The month is understood in v.2 from the explicit statement in v.1 (i.e., the fourth month). Since Jehoiachin was deported to Babylonia in 597 B.C., Ezekiel's commission must have been received in 593 B.C. Jehoiachin's year of deportation is the focal point of all dating within the book.

Ezekiel saw this vision "by the Kebar River in the land of the Babylonians." The river Kebar, a navigable canal, flowed southeast from the city of Babylon.

Ezekiel was the stated recipient of the vision. He was a priest and the son of Buzi. Nothing is known about Buzi, though as Ezekiel's father he would also have been a priest. The notation of Ezekiel's priesthood is significant. He would have been well acquainted with the Mosaic covenant and the priestly functions of the temple, both of which pervade the entire message of this book. Ezekiel was able to describe clearly the glory of God in the temple and the temple functions. He also was prepared to evaluate accurately the rebellion of his people against the explicit commands of the law, which was the basis for the Lord's judgments that Ezekiel announced. Moreover, this priestly background enabled Ezekiel to understand the millennial temple vision that concludes the entire prophecy.

The only circumstances set forth in this introduction to the subsequent vision were that "the word of the LORD came to Ezekiel" and "the hand of the LORD was upon him." These phrases occur whenever Ezekiel was about to receive or proclaim a revelation from God (3:22; 8:1; 33:22; 37:1; 40:1). "The hand of the LORD was upon him" connotes the idea of God's strength on behalf of the person involved (3:14), a concept inherent in the name "Ezekiel" (which means "God strengthens"). God was preparing Ezekiel to receive a vision that would provide the necessary framework for understanding the rest of the prophecy. It is important to the interpretation of this book to notice the phrase "I saw visions of God," for this immediately declared the nature of the following vision.

2. The description of the vision (1:4–28)

a. The living beings (1:4–14)

There appears to be a general pattern to the commission narratives of the prophets. First is the divine confrontation—an introductory word that forms the basis and background for the succeeding commission. Then the commission itself enumerates the task the prophet is called to and its importance. Third, the objections the prophet may offer

are stated, after which the "call" narrative closes with reassurances from the Lord that answer these objections and assure the prophet that the Lord is with him. All four elements are found in Ezekiel's commission.

The Lord confronted Ezekiel with this glorious vision to impress on him the majesty, holiness, and wonder of the God who was about to execute judgment on the people of Israel. Ezekiel was awestruck by God's holiness. The indelible impression of this theophany served as a constant encouragement to Ezekiel in his difficult ministry of announcing God's judgments on his own contemporaries. Against the backdrop of the awesome holiness of God visualized here, Ezekiel saw the wickedness of Israel and thereby understood why God had to judge his sinful people. When the nations profaned the Lord by claiming that Judah was in captivity because their God was weak, Ezekiel knew that his God was greater than Babylonia's gods. Though the Lord had chosen to discipline his people then, he would be victorious over all the nations when he restored Israel to the Promised Land.

This was the same glorious, covenant-keeping God who first revealed himself to Israel in a similar vision of splendor on Mount Sinai (Ex 19). He reappeared as the glory inhabiting the Most Holy Place in the dedication of the tabernacle (Ex 24:15–18; 29:42–46; 40:34–38). This theophany led the children of Israel through the desert (Nu 9:15–23; 14:10; 16:19; 20:6), filled Solomon's temple (1Ki 8:10–11; 2Ch 5:14), and appeared at Isaiah's commission (Isa 6:3). Though some may be disturbed that the manifestation of God's glory is not always the same, variation in details is to be expected when one considers the limitlessness of God. However, the consistency of the manifestation of God's glory was such that Ezekiel, a priest and a student of the Scriptures, immediately recognized that this was a vision of the glory of the Lord (v.28).

4–14 This vision began with a common introductory formula to visions: "I looked, and I saw." Ezekiel suddenly saw what appeared to be a raging electrical storm—dark clouds, lightning, and thunder—coming from the north. Within this storm he saw four figures resembling living beings (cf. Rev 4), which he describes. Though the beings looked like people, each one had four faces and four wings. The human face was dominant, being on the front of each creature, while the lion's face was on the right, the ox's (or cherub's; cf. 10:14, 22) face on the left, and the eagle's face on the back.

The wings were joined together (vv.9, 23), with two covering each side of each being and the other two spread for movement, touching the wings of the other living beings (vv.11, 23). When the wings fluttered, they sounded like a great thunder of rushing water, a violent rainstorm, or a noisy military encampment—like the voice of the "Almighty" God. The sides of the living being had hands like a human being's under its wing, straight legs, and feet like a calf.

The rapid movement of these living beings was like flashes of lightning. Their forward movement was in the direction in which the human face looked. When they moved, they did not turn around. These creatures moved only under the control of the "spirit" (v. 12; GK 8120), which, in this context of God's glory, is most likely the Holy Spirit of God.

In addition to the general appearance of brightness, these creatures contained in their midst that which looked like coals of fire, from which lightning issued. These living beings are identified in 10:15, 20 as cherubim. Certainly Ezekiel was acquainted with cherubim from his training in the temple, with its many representations of these creatures (Ex 25–26; 36–37; 1Ki 6; 2Ch 3), as well as his knowledge of the "cherubim" imagery from Mesopotamian culture with its guardian genii before temples. Cherubim often accompanied references to God's glory in the OT; yet their specific functions are nowhere clearly delineated.

b. The wheels and their movement (1:15–21)

15–18 There was one high and awesome wheel beside each of the four living creatures (cf. 10:9) that had the general appearance of a sparkling precious stone—"chrysolite"— with a rim full of eyes (cf. Rev 4:6).

19–21 When these wheels were functioning, they gave the impression of a wheel being in the midst of another wheel. The wheels moved in conjunction with the living beings, going in any direction, lifting up off the earth, and standing still. All the movement was under the direction of "the spirit."

Chapters 3 and 10 further describe the wheels as making rumbling sounds when they whirled (3:12–13; 10:5, 13).

c. The expanse (1:22–28)

22–28 An awesome expanse resembling sparkling ice appeared like a platform over the heads of the four living creatures (cf. Rev 4:6). The likeness of a throne made from precious lapis lazuli ("sapphire"; see NIV note on v.26) was above this expanse, and the likeness of a human being was on the throne (cf. Ex 24:10; Rev 4:2). This person appeared surrounded by fire, giving him a radiance similar to a rainbow (cf. 8:2; Da 10:6; Rev 4:3, 5).

The most significant phrase of the entire chapter is in the last verse: "This was the appearance of the likeness of the glory of the LORD." This reference would relate more directly to the likeness of the man on the throne, but Ex 19, 1Ki 6, Isa 6, Da 10, and Rev 4 confirm that the entire vision is a manifestation of God's "glory" (GK 3883; cf. v.1). The Lord revealed his magnificent person to Ezekiel to prepare him for ministry. He continued to appear to Ezekiel in this same fashion throughout the book to encourage him that he was a servant of Almighty God. When one genuinely sees God's glory, one cannot help but fall prostrate in worship before the Almighty God, as Ezekiel did.

This manifestation of the Lord's glory forms a backdrop for the announcements of judgment that Ezekiel would make. Since the glorious, holy God who gave the Mosaic covenant (Ex 19) could not tolerate disobedience to that covenant because of his righteous character, he had to execute judgment on the iniquity that his holy nature could not tolerate. Therefore, when God brought judgment on Jerusalem, his glory had to leave its residence in the temple (10:1–20; 11:22–23). However, Ezekiel saw the Lord's glory returning (cf. ch. 43) after the cleansing of God's people was completed. Thus the revelation of God's glory becomes a significant theme throughout the prophecy, showing a unity of purpose within the book.

B. The Lord's Charge to Ezekiel (2:1–3:27)

1. The recipients of Ezekiel's ministry (2:1–5)

1–2 The voice of God speaking from the theophany addressed Ezekiel with the title "son of man" (GK 1201 & 132). This became Ezekiel's normal designation throughout the remainder of the book (used over ninety times); this expression is found nowhere else in the OT except in Da 7:13; 8:17. This title indicates the frailty and weakness of a human being humbled before the mighty and majestic God. By this title Ezekiel was reminded continually of his dependence on the Spirit's power, which enabled him to receive God's message and to deliver it in the power and authority of the Lord—"This is what the Sovereign LORD says" (v.4). This same name—"Son of Man"—was given Christ in the Gospels (Lk 19:10) to emphasize his relation to humanity and his voluntary dependence on the Spirit of God (see comments on Da 7:13–14; Mk 8:31).

3–4 The commission side of Ezekiel's call narrative encompasses the majority of chs. 2–3. God was about to commission Ezekiel for a most difficult task. He was to go to his own people in exile, the people God described as rebellious against himself, his law, and his messengers, the prophets. This was not a new condition, for this nation had transgressed the Mosaic covenant throughout her history. God's chosen people were "obstinate" and "stubborn" (lit., "hard-hearted" and "hard-faced"), demonstrating a strong-willed determination to resist God and his ways. Undoubtedly a major contribution to Judah's current rebellion were the abominations of Manasseh that had stained the hearts of the people.

5 Ezekiel's message was not to be conditioned on his listeners' response. Even if the people closed their ears to his words, he was to speak in God's authority and not his own. Only then would the people know that a prophet had been among them.

2. Ezekiel's encouragement in the ministry (2:6–7)

6–7 In light of the difficult ministry Ezekiel was being called to, the Lord reassures him. Regardless of how frightful the opposition may be—pricking him as thorns or stinging him as scorpions—Ezekiel was not to be afraid or become dismayed and give up. On the contrary, he was to be faithful in proclaiming God's message, for his recipients were rebels who needed his warnings. This truth is still a source of encouragement to

those called to proclaim the truth of God's Word in the midst of a perverse and wicked generation.

3. The nature of Ezekiel's ministry (2:8–3:11)

2:8–3:3 The Lord's charge to Ezekiel emphasizes the absolute necessity of hearing, understanding, and assimilating God's message prior to going forth as a spokesman for the Lord. Ezekiel was to listen to God (2:8a) and not rebel against him, as did the people of Israel, who failed to listen to his word.

Before beginning his ministry, Ezekiel was to symbolize his complete acceptance of the Lord's message by eating the scroll. The nature of the message he would proclaim was written on the scroll: funeral dirges, mournings, and lamentations. Certainly this was not a joyous note on which to begin. But even when the ministry would seem difficult and distasteful, the Lord would cause his word to be as sweet as honey.

4–9 The recipients' response to Ezekiel's messages was not to govern the nature or manner of his ministry. The people rejected the divine messenger because they had been alienated from God. Though Israel was obstinate, and though it would have been easier to preach to foreign people in a foreign language, Ezekiel was to be strong and not respond in fear and dismay. The Lord fully prepared Ezekiel for his task by making him more determined than the people of Israel—as sharp and hard as flint. The Lord always

The Lord gave Ezekiel a scroll to eat, and then told him to go to speak the Lord's message to the house of Israel.

prepares and reassures his messengers with the needed equipment.

10–11 The word of the Lord had to become part of Ezekiel (cf. Jer 1:9) before he could "go" and "speak" (Eze 3:1). Thus the prophet was to meditate on the Lord's message, giving continual attention to it throughout his ministry. Only then would he be able to speak repeatedly with God's authority— even to audiences who did not care to listen to him.

4. The conclusion of the vision (3:12–15)

12–13 The vision concludes with Ezekiel's being raised up by the Spirit and hearing a final benediction that assured him that he had witnessed a revelation of God's glory. Ezekiel's transportation was not a case of hypnotism, autosuggestion, or the parapsychic phenomenon of bodily levitation. Rather, his transportation was in a vision, experienced under the compulsion of the Holy Spirit.

14–15 These verses recount Ezekiel's objection to his commission (the third element of the normal prophetic-call narrative; see comment on 1:1–14). As Ezekiel was brought back in the Spirit to the exiles at Tel Abib, he struggled with the distasteful ministry he had been called to. He was anguished and angry that he had to deliver a displeasing message to an unreceptive audience.

It took Ezekiel seven days to sort out his thoughts and feelings after having seen this vision. The Lord's hand was on him to control him as he sat appalled at the wonder and horror he had experienced. Ezekiel's condition and the period of seven days were instructive to the exiles: mourning for the dead normally took seven days (Ge 50:10; Nu 19:11; Job 2:13), as did the length of time for a priest's consecration (Lev 8:33). Ezekiel was being consecrated for the priesthood on his thirtieth birthday and commissioned to proclaim Judah's funeral dirge.

5. Ezekiel: a watchman to Israel (3:16–21)

16–17 Ezekiel's basic prophetic role was to be a watchman to the house of Israel (cf. chs. 18; 33). A watchman in OT times stood on the wall of the city as a sentry, watching for any threat to the city from without or within. If he saw an invading army on the horizon or any dangers within the city like fire or riots,

he would immediately sound the alarm to warn the people (2Sa 18:24–27; 2Ki 9:17–20).

18–21 Ezekiel was to listen to the Lord and then warn the people of Judah concerning judgment on the horizon. His warning was based on the Mosaic covenant (Ex 20–Nu 9; Deuteronomy), which showed those in a relationship with the Lord how to live life in the best way. The covenant's righteous stipulations, lovingly given for the good of the people (Dt 5:28–33; 6:25; 10:12–13), enabled them to enter into all the blessings God desired to pour out on them (Lev 26:1–13; Dt 16:20; 28:1–14; Mal 3:10–12). If they disobeyed these ordinances and wandered from God's way of living, the Lord promised that he would lovingly discipline his people to cause them to return to the righteous life he prepared for their good (Lev 26:14–39; Dt 28:15–68). Ezekiel, therefore, was to warn Israel that God's inescapable discipline was coming.

Ezekiel's role as a watchman (cf. Isa 56:10; Jer 6:17; Hos 9:8) was not reprobative and injurious but corrective and beneficial. He was to warn the wicked that if they did not turn from their wickedness, they would die in unrighteousness. Likewise, Ezekiel admonished the righteous not to turn from their righteous ways—loyalty to the Mosaic code—and disobey God's commands; if they did, they would surely die. These warnings were directed to individuals.

When a righteous person turned from righteousness and did evil, God placed a "stumbling block" before him. That person had already turned from God's ways and done evil; so this stumbling block was not placed by God deliberately to cause him to fall into sin. Rather, it was an obstacle set into the path of this person to see how he would continue to respond. If he fell, then physical death came.

If a watchman saw a potential danger to a city and failed to warn its inhabitants, he was held responsible for the following destruction. So God warned Ezekiel that if he failed to warn the people of God's curse on disobedience, Ezekiel would be responsible for their death; Ezekiel himself would have to die for his negligence. Those charged with declaring God's word have a weighty responsibility to be faithful.

"Life" (GK 2649) and "death" (GK 4637) in this context must be understood as physical, not eternal. The concept of life and death in the Mosaic covenant is primarily physical. That covenant was given to guide those who had already entered into a relationship with God by faith. The Hebrews could live righteously and freely by keeping these commands (Lev 18:5; Dt 16:20). But if they disobeyed, physical death, resulting in a shortened life, was the normal result (Dt 30:15–20). The emphasis was on living a righteous life. This covenant pointed the people on to faith in the Messiah, whose work for salvation is pictured in the festive and sacrificial system (cf. Heb 9:6–10:18); but the keeping of the commandments of the law never provided salvation. Throughout the Scriptures, eternal salvation is always by faith, never by works of any kind.

6. Ezekiel's muteness (3:22–27)

22–23 Ezekiel's commission concluded with a second glimpse of God's glory. Ezekiel, obedient to the Lord's command, went out to the plain where God's glory appeared to him, as it did in the vision of ch. 1.

24–27 As Ezekiel fell down before God in true humility and reverence, the Spirit prepared him to receive the message that he was to deliver to the exiles (cf. 4:1–7:27). Ezekiel was directed to return home and shut himself up in his house. The exiles would tie him up with rope. Then the Lord would make Ezekiel mute so that he could not reprove the people unless God opened his mouth. Whenever God did so, Ezekiel would speak only in the Lord's authority, regardless of the people's response. The phrase "Whoever will listen let him listen" (a favorite saying of Christ) stresses individual responsibility to respond to the message.

Ezekiel's muteness would last approximately seven and one-half years, until the fall of Jerusalem (cf. dates in 1:1–3 with 33:21–22). Yet he would deliver several oral messages in the intervening period (cf. 11:25; 14:1; 20:1). The concept of muteness, therefore, was not one of total speechlessness throughout these years. Rather, Ezekiel was restrained from speaking *publicly* among the people, in contrast to the normal vocal ministry of the prophets. The prophets usually moved among their people, speaking God's message as they observed the contemporary situation. But Ezekiel would remain in his home, except to dramatize God's messages (cf. 4:1–5:17). He would remain silent, except when God opened his mouth to deliver a message. Then his mouth would be closed until the next time that the Lord chose for him to speak. Instead of Ezekiel's going to the people, the people had to come to him. Though this rebellious people initially rejected Ezekiel's ministry, the elders started sneaking away to seek the Lord's message from Ezekiel as contemporary world events began vindicating his divine warnings.

II. Judah's Iniquity and the Resulting Judgment (4:1–24:27)

Chapters 4–24 combine a series of oral messages and symbolic acts designed to warn the people of Judah that judgment was coming and to explain the reason for this imminent discipline. In chs. 4–7 Ezekiel dramatized the coming siege of Jerusalem (ch. 4) and the subsequent dispersion of the people in exile (ch. 5). He concluded the drama by declaring that this imminent judgment would destroy pagan idolatry. The exile could not be escaped through human efforts (chs. 6–7). The vision of God's glory reappeared to Ezekiel (ch. 8) to expose, by contrast, the defilement of Judah resulting from her current participation in idolatrous heathen rituals. Subsequently God's glory left Jerusalem and Judah, enabling God to pour out his wrath on Israel in accord with the Mosaic covenant (chs. 9–11). The exiles objected to this, but Ezekiel effectively answered their complaints (chs. 12–19). They were reminded that their history, characterized by unfaithfulness to their Lord and spiritual prostitution promulgated by corrupt leadership (chs. 20–23), condemned them. Chapter 24 concludes by vividly describing the fall of Jerusalem.

A. The Initial Warnings of the Watchman (4:1–7:27)

1. Monodramas of the siege of Jerusalem (4:1–5:17)

a. The brick and the plate (4:1–17)

1–3 The Lord showed Ezekiel the methods he was to use in warning of the impending siege of Jerusalem and the resulting exile. Though Ezekiel was mute, God directed him to act out the warnings (probably just outside Ezekiel's house; cf. 3:24–25). The exiles had observed Ezekiel's unique seven-day consecration (3:15–16). Now they would wonder what strange thing he would do next. The parables Ezekiel acted out demanded an audience.

Ezekiel took a clay brick and scratched on it a diagram of Jerusalem. Then he simulated a siege of the city with "siege works," "ramp" (or "mounds"), battering rams, and military encampments. With an iron plate between him and the city, Ezekiel played this war game with determination for 430 days while prophesying against Jerusalem (vv.6–7). All this was "a sign to the house of Israel" of the coming siege of Jerusalem.

The "iron pan" was the kind used only by the priests for certain offerings (Lev 2:5; 6:21; 7:9). It was placed between Ezekiel and the city inscribed on the clay brick. The "pan" was declared to be a "wall." Normally walls provided protection. The Lord had warned Ezekiel of the hostile reception of his ministry (cf. 2:6). Therefore, the imagery portrays either Ezekiel's protection as he acted out the siege or the siege wall around Jerusalem erected by the Babylonians.

4–8 After acting out Jerusalem's siege, Ezekiel was directed to dramatize the length of time that God's people would undergo punishment for their iniquity. He faced north first (symbolically toward Israel), lying on his left side for 390 days to represent the time for bearing the punishment for Israel's sins. When the 390 days were "finished," then Ezekiel would "lie down again," this time for forty days on his right side, facing south (symbolically toward Judah), to portray the punishment for Judah's wickedness. He would be bound in each of these positions so that he could not change sides until he had completed the allotted days to portray the siege for each nation respectively. Ezekiel need not have been on his side twenty–four hours each day. The rest of ch. 4 has him fixing meals, while in ch. 8 he sat in his house with the exilic elders during the final days of lying on his right side. Apparently a portion of each day sufficed to fulfill the symbolism.

Though the basic meaning of this section is clear, the numbers have given rise to many explanations. Certain things are plain: each day represents a year (vv.5–6; cf. Nu 14:34),

and the years signify a period during which the people sinned. The numbers should be taken as literal periods of time, separated into two distinct and successive intervals of 390 and 40 years. Ezekiel's reference point for chronological determination is Jehoiachin's deportation of 597 B.C. This, therefore, suggests the starting point for measuring the time periods in these verses. The 430 years then denote the punishment inflicted by conquering foreign powers on the children of Israel and Judah from the deportation of Jehoiachin, their recognized king, to the inception of the Maccabean rebellion in 167 B.C. During the Maccabean period the Jews once again exercised dominion over Judah. Though this is a possible solution, we cannot be dogmatic about these numbers.

9–17 During the 390 days Ezekiel lay on his side acting out a "siege" of Jerusalem, God placed him on a strict diet. Ezekiel was to eat bread made from a mixture of several different grains. He would be rationed to two pints of water and one-half pound of bread for his daily food for over a year. This meager diet was to communicate the reality of the famine during the siege of Jerusalem. The Lord would "cut off the supply of food" in Jerusalem (as he promised in Lev 26:16, 20, 26, 29). There would be a scarcity of any one kind of grain for bread and also lack of water. The inhabitants of Jerusalem would rot away and look on one another in horror (cf. Lev 26:19, 35; 2Ki 25:3; Jer 34:17–22).

In addition to his beggarly sustenance, Ezekiel was to bake his rationed bread over a fire made unclean from human dung (cf. Dt 23:12–14). Though eating combined grains was acceptable, using human dung was defiling, for eating unclean food was forbidden by the Mosaic covenant (Lev 22:8; Dt 12:15–19; 14:21). Since Ezekiel, a faithful priest, had never eaten defiled food, he cried out to the Lord, requesting not to have to eat unclean food. God graciously permitted him to use the common fuel of cow's dung instead of human excrement. This unclean manner of preparing food described the Captivity that would follow the imminent siege and fall of Jerusalem. The captives would eat the defiled foods of the foreign nations they would be banished to.

God was not changing his law when he told Ezekiel to do all this. God temporarily caused Ezekiel to disregard the principle of eating unclean food to dramatize in an extreme way how abhorrent the Captivity would be. God used an acted parable to convey this truth in a way that would surely be understood; the eating of unclean food as a normal practice was not being condoned here. God sovereignly protected Ezekiel against any ill effects of eating defiled food.

b. The division of hair (5:1–4)

1 Ezekiel completed the drama begun in ch. 4 by shaving his head and beard, weighing the hair, and dividing it equally into three groups. This final act also pictured defilement. Shaving the head and beard was a pagan ritual for the dead (27:31; cf. Isa 22:12; Jer 16:16; Am 8:10), which the law forbade (Dt 14:1), and a sign of humiliation and disgrace (7:18; cf. 2Sa 10:4). If an Israelite priest shaved his head, he was defiled and no longer holy to the Lord (Lev 21:5). Ezekiel defiled and humiliated himself as a symbol of the humiliation of the people of Judah who were defiled and no longer holy to the Lord. Nothing was left to do but to mourn their death as a nation.

2–4 The hair symbolized the inhabitants of Jerusalem. One-third of them would be burned when Jerusalem was burned after the siege (2Ki 25:9). Part of these people would have already died through famine and distress during the siege (v.12a). The second third of the inhabitants would die by the sword when Jerusalem fell (v.12b; 2Ki 25:18–21a; 2Ch 36:17). The final third would be scattered to the wind in exile (v.12c; 2Ki 25:11, 21b). A portion from this last group would be judged by fire as they left Jerusalem, while some would die by the sword in captivity. Out of this final third, the Lord would deliver a remnant of Jerusalem's citizens—depicted by Ezekiel's placing a few hairs from this group securely into the hem of his garment.

c. The significance of the symbolic acts (5:5–17)

5 The Lord emphasizes the recipient of the siege and the coming judgments by the statement, "This is Jerusalem." Immediately one's attention was brought back to the city etched on the clay brick in 4:1. Jerusalem was the object of God's love. However, all these sym-bolic actions demonstrated what would happen to her.

6–7 A judgment speech—with accusations against Jerusalem enumerated and a verdict pronounced—reinforced the monodrama. The basic accusation was that Jerusalem, this blessed city, had responded to God's blessing by rebelling against his commandments, refusing his ways, and failing to live life according to the Mosaic covenant. She had become so wicked that she did not even adhere to the common laws of the nations around her. Some of Jerusalem's inhabitants would resort to cannibalism during the coming siege (v.10a; cf. Lev 26:29; Dt 28:53; 2Ki 6:28–29; Jer 19:9; La 4:10). They had already defiled his holy sanctuary with detestable idolatry (v.11a; ch. 8).

8–17 God would execute the judgments pronounced in the Mosaic covenant on Jerusalem in the sight of the nations. Never again would he execute a judgment like this. He would withdraw himself from the sanctuary (cf. 10:4; 11:22–23) to pour out his judgment without pity. One-third of the inhabitants of Jerusalem would die in the city through disease and famine; one-third would die by the sword; and a remnant would be scattered in every direction among the nations. Famine, wild beasts, plagues, and bloodshed would all be part of Jerusalem's judgment (cf. Lev 26:21–26). The land of Judah would become a desolation, causing the nations to ridicule her because of what God had done to her. At the same time these nations would be struck with fear and terror at God's justice and wrath even on his very own people. Judah's judgment served to warn these nations of the judgments God would bring on them if they cursed Israel (cf. Ge 12:3). As a result of this judgment, God's justice would be satisfied and the people of Jerusalem would know that the Lord had executed his wrath. The punishment was certain. The Lord had spoken!

2. The coming judgment on the land of Judah (6:1–7:27)

a. Destruction of pagan religious shrines (6:1–14)

1–7 God interrupted Ezekiel's muteness to announce judgment on Judah's mountains, hills, ravines, and valleys. Ezekiel set his face against these four geographical features of the land, for it was in them that the pagans normally established their religious shrines (cf. 2Ki 23:10). Canaanite religion—with its perverted emphasis on sex, war, cults of the dead, snake worship, and idolatry—preferred high places and groves of trees for its place of worship. Manasseh, king of Judah (695–642 B.C.), had led in the resurgence of these pagan cults.

The Lord next pronounced judgment on the heathen shrines and their cultic practices that had been adopted by his people. He would remove the temptation facing them by destroying all the "high places," "altars," "incense altars," and "idols." These shrines would become desecrated by the scattering of bones of the dead around them. The "scattering of bones" is a phrase used for judgment in which uncleanness and shame are conveyed (cf. Pss 53:5; 141:7). The bones would be those of the Israelites who had become engrossed in these pagan practices (cf. 2Ki 23:20; Jer 8:1–2). The Lord was faithful to his promise in Lev 26:30; he refused to allow anything to take his rightful place. Through this discipline Judah would know that he was the only God.

8–10 God always accompanies his pronouncements of judgment with the proclamation of a way to escape—by turning to the Lord and following his ways (cf. Jer 18:7–10). Thus within Ezekiel's judicial sentence was the Lord's assurance that some of the exiles would see the wickedness of their ways and be ashamed. They would remember the Lord and recognize that he did not speak in vain when he instructed his people to live righteously or they would suffer the threatened discipline. This remnant would respond to God's discipline and repent of the spiritual fornication that had grieved the Lord. They would come to know that their God truly is the Lord. The whole purpose of God's judgment was to bring his people back to him.

11–14 Reverting to his theme of impending judgment, the Lord instructs Ezekiel to demonstrate joy because of the coming judgment. Clapping the hands and stamping the feet signify either joyful praise or derision over sin and judgment (21:14–17; 22:13; 25:6; cf. La 2:15; Na 3:19). Ezekiel exhibits God's delight over the comprehensive eradication of pagan shrines and practices from the land. The entire land would become as desolate as

the desert toward Diblah. Everyone would be touched by the judgment: the distant ones by disease, the near ones by the sword, the remainder outside and inside Jerusalem by famine. Four times God directed Ezekiel to remind the exiles that the purpose for God's judgment was to restore his hearers to an experiential knowledge of God (vv.7, 10, 13, 14). This major thrust of the book called for an intimate relationship with the Lord rather than a destructive allegiance to impotent idols.

In every generation God's judgment and discipline are misunderstood by most people. God's chief desire is to bring people to himself—or back to himself. When humankind willfully refuses to turn to him, God mercifully uses discipline and judgment to cause the people to recognize that he is the only true God, always faithful to what he has said in his word!

b. The imminency and comprehensiveness of the curse (7:1–13)

1–4 God now gives a second message to Ezekiel, containing four brief, intensive prophetic speeches in poetic form that emphasize the imminency and comprehensiveness of the coming judgment on all Judah. Numerous short sentences and the repetition of words and phrases express the intensity of the message. The recurrence of the word "end" (GK 7891) stresses the finality of the judgment. Judgment had come! Imminency was heightened by the reiteration of the verb "coming," the repetition of "now," and the use of terms like "time," "day," and "is near."

The first prophetic speech (vv.1–4) emphasizes the extent—"the four corners of the land"—of the judgment and its basis; two main points summarize the reasons for judgment. Judah would be judged according to her wicked ways. Her abominations would be brought on her. The Exile would bring the Judeans into countries where the same abominable practices they had taken part in were a daily occurrence. The expectation was that this would cause them to detest such wicked rituals. Furthermore, the Lord would have pity on no one. He would not spare them. Though his forbearance and compassion had withheld discipline, such restraint would no longer continue. God's judgment genuinely manifested his love, for its purpose was to cause Judah to know that he is God.

5–9 The second oracle emphasizes the horror and surprise of the judgment as well as the person of the judge. The terror that would fill the land is stressed by the repetition of the words "disaster" and "end," in addition to the announcement that the judgment would be a time of panic, not joy like that experienced at harvest festivals (cf. Isa 16:10; Jer 25:30). The unexpectedness (chs. 12–19) of judgment is reflected by a play on words in "the end has come" and "roused itself," as well as by phrases such as "Doom has come," "time has come," and "the day is near." Verses 8–9 give the basis for the judgment stated in vv.3–4. The message closed by stunning the exiles with a new name for God: "The LORD who strikes the blow"—the one who would now judge Judah.

10–11 The third oracle focuses on the imminency, comprehensiveness, and readiness of judgment. The dawn of the judgment day had arrived; it had suddenly "budded" and "blossomed." The "rod" is either Nebuchadnezzar as the instrument of judgment or the insolence of the kings of Israel. The only passage in Scripture referring to a "budded rod" is Nu 17, where God used such a rod to denote his choice. But since judgment on Judah is described here, it would seem best to understand the "rod" as an instrument of judgment that had been divinely chosen and was ready for use. The concept of the budding rod stands in parallelism with the previous line of the poem (indicating imminency) and the following line (describing the nature of the rod God would use to discipline Judah—a rod of "arrogance"). Nebuchadnezzar fits the description of this rod as an instrument of judgment. God would use this weapon to devastate the land until nothing of value was left.

12–13 The last oracle emphasizes the permanency and quickness of the judgment. Its suddenness is illustrated by the inability one had to regain what one had sold because of the rapidity of the coming discipline. Most likely this example was given with the law of the sabbatical year (Dt 15:1–2) or the Year of Jubilee in mind (Lev 25:13–16). According to that law, if one sold land to pay for a debt, that land reverted to him on the sabbatical year or the Year of Jubilee, whichever came first. Ezekiel maintained that if one sold land under this arrangement, he would not realize its return since neither he nor the buyer would be in the land of Judah seven years hence. Though the buyer might rejoice over the fact that he would never have to return the land, it would not be a time of rejoicing for either party. When judgment came, neither would own the property. Babylon would possess it!

The vision of judgment was certain! God would not repeal it! No one would be able to continue to live in iniquity, for all wickedness would be judged.

c. The response to the curse (7:14–27)

14–18 The last half of this chapter vividly describes the reactions of the Judeans to this swift and violent judgment. Moral dissipation, famine, and disease had so decimated the nation that they would be unable to muster an army when the trumpet sounded for battle. Therefore the Babylonians would easily approach Jerusalem for the siege (cf. Lev 26:7).

Disease and hunger would slay those within Jerusalem, and the sword would catch by surprise those working outside the walls. Any fortunate enough to escape the initial invasion would flee to the hills. There, shuddering in fear, weak and dismayed, they would be ashamed of and humiliated by their sins that brought this destruction. They would put on sackcloth in mourning, shave their heads in humiliation, and moan like doves.

19 Nothing could deliver the Israelites from God's awesome wrath demonstrated in Jerusalem and Judah's destruction in 586 B.C. Many of the inhabitants had lived for wealth so long that material gain had become an obsession to them. Yet in the judgment these riches would mean nothing. Idolatry, wickedness, and materialism had robbed them of everything and led them into judgment. Money would be thrown away like something sexually unclean.

20–22 Judah had profaned her sanctuary. The "beautiful jewelry" refers to Jerusalem and her temple; "my treasured place" likewise refers to the temple when connected with the full discussion of Jerusalem's fall (see 24:21, 25). The people had taken ornaments and treasures from the temple and defiled God's temple by using them to make idols. Ironically, God would now allow foreigners to profane the temple, plundering its treasures. Everything would become spoil for Babylon.

23–24 "Chains" were prepared to bind the captives for deportation to Babylonia. This was their due for the violent crimes they had committed. As the Judeans were leaving, the worst foreigners among the nations would enter and possess the land, profaning their holy places. The land would come under Babylonian dominion.

25–27 The last response for some was to seek help. People would run to the prophet in hope of a visionary revelation of deliverance, to the priest for messages from the law that might help, or to the elders for counsel in this time of distress. None could offer help. They had no answers at all! The leadership had failed in its responsibility to lead the people in God's ways. It was too late! The anguish of judgment had come! If the people had sought peace earlier, it would have been available; but now there was no peace. Kings and princes would be horrified and mourn. God had judged Israel by her own judgments—by the Mosaic covenant they should have known and followed. The only redeeming factor was that they would learn that the Lord truly was God and that his covenants were to be obeyed!

B. The Vision of the Exodus of God's Glory (8:1–11:25)

1. The idolatry of the house of Israel (8:1–18)

a. The image of jealousy (8:1–6)

1–6 Verse 1 describes the single vision of chs. 8–11. The date was "in the sixth year, in the sixth month on the fifth day" (August/ September), 592 B.C. The recipient was Ezekiel. He received the vision while sitting in his house with the elders of Judah sitting before him. God's hand came on Ezekiel, causing him to be caught up into the vision. From the chronological notices of 1:1–3 and 8:1, it appears that he received his vision about fourteen months into his symbolic siege of Jerusalem. He was still lying daily on his right side, bearing the iniquity of Judah (cf. 4:6). Most likely the elders had been watching this performance, wondering whether anything new would happen. It was fitting for Ezekiel to be on his right side when this vision of Judah's judgment appeared to him.

In light of the distance and time involved, these elders were not contemporary elders in Judah who had come from Judah to Babylonia to seek counsel from Ezekiel. Moreover, the depraved character of the Judean elders revealed in this vision would not have led them to take such an arduous journey to Babylonia for genuine spiritual reasons. Rather, the elders sitting before Ezekiel were the leaders of the Judean exiles in Babylonia who had already been deported from Judah in the captivities of Daniel (605 B.C.) and Jehoiachin (597 B.C.).

The vision's primary thrust was to make known the cause of the coming judgment on Jerusalem. The political rulers, the prophets, and the priests were expected to lead Judah in her holy ways. In this vision Ezekiel saw the contrast between God's glory in the sanctuary and the extreme moral and spiritual corruption of the nation's leadership. The latter was the main cause for God's judgment on Jerusalem. In ch. 8 the abominable idolatry as practiced by Judah's leaders in the temple precinct was exposed. Chapters 9–11 depict the judgment of a holy God on the unholy perversion described in ch. 8. Progressively God's glory is removed from Jerusalem and Judah. Appointed men are sent to pour out fiery judgment on this wicked idolatry and its proponents. The Judean leaders are singled out for special condemnation in 11:14– 21, but the faithful remnant who repented of their sinful ways are marked for protection (9:4) and reassured of their ultimate restoration and cleansing (11:14–21).

The vision begins in vv.1–6 with Ezekiel seeing the same manifestation of God's glory that he had seen on the river Kebar in chs. 1– 3. In the vision of ch. 8, the likeness of a man of the same appearance as the one in the vision of ch. 1 (cf. 1:27) caught Ezekiel by his hair and transported him by the Spirit to Jerusalem in the vision. In Jerusalem Ezekiel saw God's glory in the temple. Such glorious splendor stood in stark contrast to the religious perversion being practiced in the temple area.

Ezekiel found himself standing at the entrance of the inner court's north gate, known also as the altar gate, because the altar of sacrifice was located just inside that gate (cf. Lev 1:11). He stood in the outer court at the gate's entrance, not in the inner court. As he looked northward into the outer court, he saw the "idol of jealousy." This idol provoked the Lord to jealousy, for he had declared in the Mosaic covenant that he alone was God (Ex 20:1–3) and that all idolatry was forbidden (Dt 4:16; 32:16, 21). The idol's description is vague; thus it cannot be identified with certainty. Possibly it is a reestablishment of the idol of Asherah, the mother-goddess of the Canaanite pantheon, which Manasseh had erected in the temple (2Ki 21:7; 2Ch 33:7) but later removed (2Ch 33:15). This image certainly had its attraction in Israelite history, for Josiah had also had to remove it in his reformation (2Ki 23:6). Jeremiah's denunciation of the worship of the Queen of Heaven may also relate to this image (Jer 7:18; 44:17–30).

The statement "But you will see things that are even more detestable" concludes this brief examination of the "idol of jealousy." This conclusion emphasizes the progressive severity of Judah's idolatry (vv.6, 13, 15).

b. Idol worship of the elders (8:7–13)

7–9 Ezekiel was brought into the north entry gate. There he saw a hole in the wall and was told to dig through the wall, enter, and observe what the elders of Israel were doing secretly in the inner court. These seventy elders were most likely the leaders of the nation who based their traditional position on Moses' appointment of the seventy elders to assist him in governing God's people (Ex 24:1, 9; Nu 11:16–25).

10–11 Jaazaniah, the son of Shaphan (possibly the son of Josiah's secretary of state; see 2Ki 22:8–14; 2Ch 34:15–21; Jer 26:24; 29:3; et al.), was leading these men in burning incense to all sorts of sculptured animals, reptiles, and detestable things. Perhaps the detestable things were the animals declared unclean in Lev 11.

12–13 The Judean leaders were practicing their corrupt worship of these idols in the dark, each in his own room. These individual chambers are difficult to explain. Were they built into the wall that separated the inner and outer courts, or were they rooms in the private homes of each elder, indicating that each was engaged in this perverse ritual privately as well as publicly? Contextually, the former is preferable, though no such chambers were known to have existed within the inner court of Solomon's temple.

These leaders rationalized their activities by declaring that God did not see them nor was he present anymore. He had forsaken the land, as demonstrated by the deportations of 605 B.C. and 597 B.C. They denied the existence of God in direct opposition to his name: "the one who always is." They negated his omnipresence and omniscience, choosing to exchange "the glory of the immortal God for images made to look like … birds and animals and reptiles" (Ro 1:23). In saying that God had forsaken the land, the elders repudiated his faithfulness to the Abrahamic covenant, his love for his chosen people, and his immutability. With this kind of rationalization, they permitted themselves to do anything they desired. If God did not exist, then no one need care about him.

c. Tammuz worship of the women (8:14–15)

14–15 Leaving the inner court and the iniquity of the elders, Ezekiel returned to the entry way of the inner court's north gate, where he observed women worshiping Tammuz, an ancient Akkadian deity, the husband and brother of Ishtar. Tammuz, later linked to Adonis and Aphrodite by name, was a god of fertility and rain, similar to Hadad and Baal. In the seasonal mythological cycle, he died early in the fall when vegetation withered. His revival, by the wailing of Ishtar, was marked by the buds of spring and the fertility of the land. Such renewal was encouraged and celebrated by licentious fertility festivals.

The date of this vision was in the months of August/September, when this god Tammuz "died." At the time of this vision, the land of Palestine would have been parched from the summer sun, and the women would have been lamenting Tammuz's death. They perhaps were also following the ritual of Ishtar, wailing for the revival of Tammuz. But there were still greater abominations for Ezekiel to see (cf. vv.6, 13).

d. Sun worship (8:16–18)

16 Ezekiel returned to the temple's inner court, where he noticed twenty-five men with their backs to the temple, facing east in sun worship. The identity of these men is unsure. Possibly they were part of the seventy elders just mentioned. But it would seem strange that only a portion of the seventy would have been engaged in the sun worship. Moreover, since this was the inner court and

only priests were permitted access into that court (2Ch 4:9; Joel 2:17), they may have been priests (though, to be sure, the seventy elders of Israel had just been seen practicing their idolatry within the inner court). The specific numbers of seventy (v.11) and twenty-five are probably given to aid in distinguishing the two groups. Therefore, it is more likely that these "twenty-five men" are priests. If so, the number twenty-five suggests that there was one representative of each of the twenty-four courses of the priests plus the high priest (cf. 1Ch 23). Regardless of their identity, sun worship was strictly forbidden by the Mosaic covenant (Dt 4:19); and both Hezekiah and Josiah had had to remove this pagan practice from Judah during their reigns (2Ki 23:5, 11; 2Ch 29:6–7).

17–18 These verses summarize this chapter of perverse idolatry by declaring that this wickedness of Judah's leaders had allowed violence to fill the land. All this had repeatedly provoked God. They were even "putting the branch [GK 2367] to their nose." This phrase is problematic. The word's normal reading is "twig." Possibly putting the twig to the nose was part of the ritual practice of sun worship, a concept that fits this context well. Regardless, the context implies that the act was offensive to God.

All these abominable, idolatrous rituals brought the wrath of a holy God. He would judge without compassion. He would refuse to listen to the people's cries for mercy, even though they shouted with a very loud voice. Judgment would come! The remainder of the vision continues to emphasize that point.

2. Judgment on Jerusalem and the departure of God's glory (9:1–11:23)

a. The man with the writing kit (9:1–4)

1–2 As Ezekiel stood in the temple's inner courtyard, aghast by the abominations being practiced, the Lord announced the coming of the city's executioners. Ezekiel saw them enter the "upper gate," equivalent to the inner court's north gate (cf. 2Ki 15:35; 2Ch 27:3; Jer 20:2; 36:10). Each executioner carried a lethal weapon in his hand. They gathered together and stood beside the bronze altar. Among them was a man clothed in linen and carrying a writing kit.

Ezekiel 8:18 provides a transition in the vision, where God announced judgment on Jerusalem. He would execute it through these seven men (six executioners and the man in linen). A holy and righteous God would not allow idolatry to rob him of his rightful place as Israel's true God. The basis of the judgment was God's glory and holiness as seen in the theophany of glory and the linen clothing of the man with the writing kit. Linen was often worn by divine messengers (cf. Da 10:5; Rev 15:6) and was used for priestly garments (Ex 28:42); thus linen portrays the purity and holiness of God. On the other hand, judgment was stressed by these men gathering at the bronze altar, the altar of sacrificial judgment, ready to execute their assigned task.

3 The glorious God prepared to delegate the execution of this judgment to these men as he arose from above the cherubim and proceeded to the temple's threshold. Most likely God's glory, envisioned in the man of 8:2, had separated from the cherubim throne-chariot in the vision and moved from the Most Holy Place (cf. 8:4) to the temple threshold. From there the picture of God's departure from his people in preparation for judgment began. With judgment imminent, God's glory could not be present over the ark of the covenant in the Most Holy Place or in the presence of the divine Judge. Therefore, the Lord vividly demonstrated his readiness to judge the people by withdrawing his glory from the Most Holy Place to the entry of the temple, in order to assign the tasks of judgment.

4 The Lord commanded the man clothed with linen and carrying the scribal implements to go throughout Jerusalem and mark everyone who had genuine remorse and concern for the sins of the city, who saw that the heathen ways of Jerusalem were contrary to the Mosaic covenant, and who desired to see that covenant properly instituted in the city. This man marked them on their forehead with a mark of protection as the impending judgment drew near (cf. Rev 7:3; 9:4; 14:1). These people had a righteous heart attitude.

b. The executioners' judgment (9:5–8)

5–7 God commanded the six men to follow the man with the scribal kit throughout Jerusalem and to exercise individual judgment on everyone who did not have the mark of protection, regardless of sex or age. They were to spare none. They began with the seventy elders polluting the temple with their secret worship of sculptured animals in the inner court. Judgment started in the temple (cf. 1Pe 4:17), the center from which religious leadership should come. However, Judah's leadership had become corrupt. Therefore, the temple courtyards would be defiled by the blood of these worshipers of heathen deities (cf. Nu 19:11; 2Ki 23:16).

8 As Ezekiel found himself the only inner-court survivor of the judgment, he became alarmed at the mass of people destroyed by these executioners. Although he could appear hard, his heart throbbed with love for God and his people. He pleaded with God not to eradicate the entire remnant of Judah. She was the only tribe left, and some of that tribe had gone into exile to Babylonia already (605 B.C. and 597 B.C.). The present judgment, illustrated by these six men, looked as if it would consume the remainder of Judah.

c. Vindication of God's judgment (9:9–11)

9–10 The Lord's response to Ezekiel's concern for the nation was to remind him that the iniquity of Judah was extremely great. Violence and spiritual perversion had filled the land because the people had forgotten God's character, assuming that he did not see what they were doing because he had deserted them. They denied God's omniscience, omnipresence, and faithfulness. The Lord had not left, because he presently was judging Judah for her iniquity and would not spare anyone. He did know the wickedness of the people, for he would recompense them for it.

11 As an encouragement to Ezekiel that all Judah had not strayed from God, the man with the writing kit reported, "I have done as you commanded." In other words, the righteous ones had been marked.

d. Coals of fire on Jerusalem (10:1–7)

1–2 God instructed the man clothed in linen to take fire coals from the center of the cherubim chariot (cf. ch. 1) and to pour them out in judgment on the city to purify it (cf. Isa 6).

4–5 This parenthesis clarifies the setting. The cherubim throne-chariot was in the inner courtyard to the south of the temple. The temple precinct had been cleansed by the six

men, and God's glory had moved to the temple door. From there it filled the temple and the courts.

6–7 The man in linen faithfully responded to the Lord's command to take coals from the cherubim. The cherub was probably the living being with a face like a "cherub." He handed the live coals to the man in linen.

e. Cherubim and Ichabod (10:8–22)

8–17, 20–22 The living beings of ch. 1 are identified as "cherubim" (GK 4131) in this passage. Cherubim appear elsewhere in the Scriptures, though they were new to the discussion in Ezekiel. In the ancient Near East, a winged sphinx with a human head and a lion's or bull's body was often identified as a "cherub." The OT cherubim are primarily represented as guardians and protectors (cf. Ge 3:24), though they also performed worship on the mercy seat of the ark of the covenant (Ex 25:18–20). Perhaps as a throne-chariot (cf. 1Sa 4:4; 2Sa 6:2; 2Ki 19:15; 1Ch 13:6; 1Ch 28:18; Pss 18:10; 80:1; 99:1), they were protectors and guardians of God's glory.

18–19 A principal theme in this vision and in the book of Ezekiel is the departure and return of God's glory. It departed from the temple because of the corruption within Jerusalem and Judah, but it would return in the end time when the nation had been fully cleansed (cf. 43:1–9). The gradual departure of God's glory began in 9:3 and 10:4, when the glory of God left the Most Holy Place and moved to the temple's entrance. God's glory departed from the temple's threshold and assumed its place on the cherubim throne-chariot. Together they went to the temple's east gate, from where they finally departed (cf. 11:22–23). Scripture declares (Dt 31:17; Hos 9:12) that this departure would occur if the people strayed from God's ways. In 1Sa 4 a similar example of the departure of God's glory at a time of judgment was memorialized by the name of Eli's grandson "Ichabod" (v.21), which means "inglorious." Once again, in Ezekiel's day God was writing "Ichabod" over Jerusalem and Judah.

f. Judgment on Jerusalem's leaders (11:1–13)

1 As Ezekiel watched God's glory move to the east gate of the temple complex, the Spirit brought him to that gate. Here God showed Ezekiel more of the perversion of the nation's leadership. Twenty-five men were gathered together, led by Jaazaniah, the son of Azzur, and Pelatiah, the son of Benaiah, leaders of the people (these twenty-five political leaders were different from the twenty-five sun worshipers of 8:16).

2–3 These leaders had given the people false and evil counsel. They had planned evil things, deceiving the inhabitants of Jerusalem and Judah by encouraging them to build homes at a time when the prophets were continually warning of the impending Babylonian destruction. These leaders were complacent and apathetic, believing that there was no imminent danger. They declared that Jerusalem's inhabitants were secure inside Jerusalem's walls by promulgating the proverb: "This city is a cooking pot, and we are the meat." Jerusalem, "the pot," provided security to its inhabitants, "the meat," just as a pot protects the meat within it. Prophets like Ezekiel were declared to be misguided men using scare tactics.

4–6 Ezekiel prophesies to these twenty-five men with a judgment oracle; the accusation is stated in vv.5–6 and the verdict in vv.7–12. He reminds these leaders that their actions were not hidden from God; he knew exactly what they were thinking, saying, and doing. He knew they had rejected the prophets' warnings, exchanged the righteous statutes of law for idolatry, and murdered the inhabitants of Jerusalem with their devious schemes.

7–12 The verdict was expressed in the same imagery as the people's proverbial statements in v.3. The "pot" of Jerusalem would protect only the righteous whom these wicked leaders had already slain. These corrupt leaders and their followers would be brought outside the "pot" of Jerusalem and struck down by the dreaded sword of foreigners. Babylonia would execute this judgment, slaying the Judeans throughout the land (cf. 2Ki 25:18–21). With the fall of Jerusalem to Nebuchadnezzar in 586 B.C., the Judean leaders and their subjects would know that the Lord was truly the Lord. They would observe that he faithfully executed the righteous judgment he had declared would come on those who failed to live according to his statutes. If Israel would obey, she would live (Lev 18:5).

Large cooking pots, some of them completely intact, are often found while excavating biblical sites.

But she had chosen rather to live by the idolatrous ways of the nations around her and to receive the law's curse instead of its blessing.

13 While Ezekiel was prophesying this message to the leaders, Pelatiah died. He did not actually hear Ezekiel's prophecy, but news of Pelatiah's death helped confirm Ezekiel as a prophet. This stunning result of his prophecy caused Ezekiel to fear once again that God would destroy all the remnant of Israel.

g. The future of the remnant (11:14–21)

14–15 Ezekiel's great concern for the remnant of Judah had not gone unnoticed by the Lord. God encouraged him in this message that he and a remnant, his kindred, were purposely being kept by God through the Captivity. The citizens of Judah had looked on the exiles as the unclean and sinful part of the nation. Was not God judging them by their deportation? The Judeans encouraged the exiles to get as far away from the land of Israel as possible, because God had given it to those still in Judah, not to the sinful exiles.

16–20 On the contrary, God now shows that it was the deported remnant that he cared for; and he shows his care by promising to regather the exiles to the Promised Land. This is the first mention of a future restoration in Ezekiel. Many of the prophets held out restoration as a continual hope to the righteous. On the basis of the Mosaic covenant, judgment was all the prophets could offer Judah for her sins. The promise of restoration to the land, though declared in the blessings of the Mosaic covenant (Lev 26:40–45; Dt 30:1–10), was based on the eternal covenants to Abraham (Ge 12:1–3), David (2Sa 7:12–16), and Jeremiah (Jer 31:31–34).

In exile the Lord would continue to be an ever-present sanctuary for his people, making provisions for them no matter where they were scattered. This is the same ever-present God who today meets the needs of those who trust him, regardless of their circumstances. God then promises that when he finished disciplining the remnant of Israel, he would (1) regather them, (2) restore them to the land of Israel, (3) cleanse the land of its abominations, and (4) fulfill the new covenant with them.

The new covenant promised in Jer 31:31–34 provided for a change of heart and a new spirit. This new spirit would be the outpouring of the Spirit promised by the prophets (Dt 30:6; Jer 31:33; Joel 2:28–29), further developed in Eze 36:26–27, and initially instituted in Ac 2. The new heart and spirit would replace Israel's old heart of stone (Zec 7:12), which had become so hardened against the Lord and his ways. The people would be empowered to live in the godly manner set forth in the stipulations of the Mosaic covenant. Finally they would truly reflect the Mosaic covenant formula: they would be God's people, and he would be their God.

Through his death for sin once for all, Christ, the Mediator of the new covenant (Heb 8:6), has made it possible for all believers to receive the Spirit's divine enablement so that they too may live according to God's righteous standards. This is available to all who place their faith in the resurrected Messiah, Jesus Christ.

21 However, God warns those who do not repent and follow him that they will be held accountable and will be judged.

h. The departure of the Lord's glory from Jerusalem (11:22–25)

22–25 After God had encouraged Ezekiel about the future restoration of the Judean remnant, his glory departed east from Jerusalem to the Mount of Olives. His presence among Israel is hereafter pictured as removed (until his return in 43:1–4). Judgment was now certain! Ezekiel was brought back to Babylonia in the vision, and the vision stopped. He then recounted the entire vision to the exiles who had been observing his symbolic siege and had seen him caught up in the vision.

C. The Lord's Reply to the Exiles' Invalid Rationalizations of Hope (12:1–19:14)

1. The dramatic tragedy of exile (12:1–20)

a. Introduction (12:1–2)

1–2 The introductory phrase indicates the beginning of a new series of messages. Ezekiel always gives specific dates for new visions or oracles. Since no new chronological notice is given, and since the speeches of chs. 12–19 are closely related thematically to the foregoing vision, presumedly these messages were uttered shortly after Ezekiel's explanation of the vision in chs. 8–11.

God immediately reminded Ezekiel that he lived among "a rebellious people." Ezekiel had been warned of this in his commission (2:3–8), but now he would experience that reality. The exiles had been watching his symbolic acts and hearing his judgment oracles for over a year. He had communicated the imminency of the judgment, its severity, and its basis (chs. 4–11) through every possible means. Though the elders had ears and eyes, they had neither heard his messages nor seen his visual signs in chs. 8–11 (cf. Isa 6:9–10; Jer 5:21). Ezekiel had to speak to this rebellion.

The exiles had not grasped the serious consequences of Ezekiel's warnings. They still hoped for an early return to Palestine, for they viewed the continued preservation of Jerusalem and Judah as signs of security. After all, Jerusalem was the eternal city. They presented several reasons for their hope and security—as well as their objections to Ezekiel's warning—in chs. 12–19.

First, if judgment was to come, it would not be in their lifetime, as Ezekiel had declared (ch. 12). Second, Ezekiel was only one of many prophets. Most prophets and prophetesses announced hope and reasons for optimism. Why should the people listen to Ezekiel (ch. 13)? Third, the leaders in Judah were ultimately responsible. If there was to be any judgment, it would be on them, not the exiles (ch. 14). Fourth, if real danger of judgment should exist, then they would only have to find some righteous man to intercede for them before God, and they would be delivered (ch. 14). Fifth, how could Ezekiel possibly believe that God would judge his own chosen people? He would not do that (chs. 15–16). Sixth, it would not be fair for God to judge anyone for his forefathers' sins. The people thought Ezekiel was saying just the opposite (ch. 17). Seventh, if judgment was really coming, then there was nothing they could do to stop it; for they would be paying for their fathers' sins. It would not make any difference if they repented (ch. 18). Eighth, Zedekiah, the contemporary ruler of Judah, could be trusted. He would throw off the yoke of Babylonia (ch. 19).

Ezekiel patiently, systematically, and adamantly challenged the naive reasoning of the exiles, undermining each source of their optimistic rejection to his warnings of judgment. When Ezekiel had finished his challenges, no excuses remained.

A basic pattern is noticeable in the structure of Ezekiel's prophecy: each vision is followed by a message that expands and develops the concepts in the vision. The vision of Ezekiel's commission (chs. 1–3), for example, was followed by the announcements of judgment on Jerusalem. The vision of Jerusalem's religious corruption in the temple and judgment in chs. 8–11 is now elaborated in chs. 12–19, which develops the wickedness of all leaders in Judah (kings, prophets, and priests) as the core of the nation's iniquity. These chapters emphasize corrupt leadership and reasons for the coming judgment.

b. A picture of deportation (12:3–16)

3–7 Ezekiel's symbolic acts undoubtedly drew curious spectators. Even though the exiles had failed to grasp the significance of Ezekiel's previous messages, once again God graciously sought to convey his warnings to them. Maybe they would understand this time. The Lord repeatedly encouraged Ezekiel to perform new dramas for everyone to see. Ezekiel would be a "sign" to them.

Therefore, Ezekiel is told to act out something familiar to everyone watching: the process of deportation. During the day he gathered the small amount of belongings a deportee could take with him and brought them out where everyone could see them. In the evening he dug a hole through the mudbrick wall of his house. Leaving through the hole, Ezekiel carried his bag like an exile. Next he covered his face and went to another place while all the people watched. Ezekiel's

act was a "sign" (GK 4603) that God would bring additional exiles to Babylon.

8–16 Since all the exiles had participated in a deportation themselves (either in 605 B.C. or 597 B.C.), they should have understood clearly Ezekiel's picture of deportation. God reminded Ezekiel that many had not understood the drama, for they were asking, "What are you doing?" Therefore, Ezekiel explained his dramatization so none would miss its meaning.

Ezekiel prophesied deportation of a remnant from Jerusalem in 586 B.C., especially as it related to Zedekiah, the current Judean ruler. Ezekiel told the captives that he was a "sign" to them of the exile that the current inhabitants of Jerusalem would soon experience. His message probably shattered any hope that they might have had that he was portraying their imminent departure from Babylonia back to the Promised Land.

Zedekiah was called "the prince" because he was not the legitimate king. That right belonged to Jehoiachin who was in Babylonia. Zedekiah would load his bags at night (2Ki 25:4; Jer 39:4; 52:7), escape with difficulty through the gates of the king's garden in southeast Jerusalem, and flee toward the Jordan, where he would be caught by Nebuchadnezzar's army like an animal on the hunt. The figure of a conqueror catching enemies in a net is from the imagery of the fowler or hunter in the ancient Near East. Zedekiah's troops would be scattered, and he would be brought before Nebuchadnezzar at Riblah. There his sons and the nobles would be slaughtered before his eyes, after which he would be blinded. Therefore Zedekiah would never see the land of Babylonia, though he would die there as a captive (cf. 2Ki 25:5, 7; Jer 39:6–7; 52:8, 10–11). Ezekiel's covering of his face in the dramatization likely indicated that Zedekiah would seek to disguise himself in his flight from the city. That in fleeing he "will not see" the land with his eyes would correlate with Zedekiah's blinding and deportation.

Moreover, God wanted to make clear the purpose of the Exile. The deportations were designed to show the deportees that the Lord was the faithful, loving, and powerful God over Israel, to which they would return. Lest the foreign nations misunderstand Judah's dispersion, God had the exiles testify that their abominations precipitated the deportations. In this way the nations would realize that the Lord was holy and righteous, and that he cared for his people. This would correct the common notion in the ancient Near East that a nation that was conquered was serving gods who were either powerless or no longer cared about their people. To prevent such a misconception, the Lord would send a remnant of Jews among the nations to witness that they were in exile only because of their own iniquity, not because of the Lord's failure. Then perhaps the nations too would come to know that the Lord was the only true God.

c. A drama of fear (12:17–20)

17–20 In another brief act Ezekiel was to quiver and tremble while he ate and drank. This displayed the fear and horror that would come on the citizens of Jerusalem and all the cities of Judah when their towns were destroyed and lay in ruins. The land would be emptied of its fruitfulness because of the violence that had been done in it. The violence they had done to others would return on their own heads. Thus the Judeans would know that the Lord was real and that he was faithful to his promises. Those things they had refused to learn in times of blessing, God would teach them through the horrors of judgment. But his judgment was still a manifestation of his love; for if he had not cared for them, he would never have disciplined them.

2. The faithfulness of God: the present judgment (12:21–28)

21–25 Ezekiel confronted the exiles' rationalizations of his messages. It had become obvious that the apathy of the Jewish exiles had blunted their understanding of his symbolic acts and oracles (12:2). They did not think that Ezekiel's prophecies were valid. Through a contemporary proverb the captives asserted that they believed all the previous judgments proclaimed by Isaiah, Micah, and others were not true, for they had not come to pass. Why should they now accept Ezekiel's prophecies as valid? Their outlook presumed on God's grace, long-suffering, and forbearance. It showed an unbelief in God's immutability and the trustworthiness of his word as revealed in the Scriptures. It was only because of his grace that God had

not disciplined Israel sooner. He had waited so Israel might change her mind and return to him. Instead, the people had strayed further, living in the fantasy of security when judgment was imminent.

God declared that the exiles' proverb would be heard no more, for judgment was imminent. On the contrary, the Lord would create a new proverb: "The days are near when every vision will be fulfilled." The judgments that the Lord had promised in the Law and the Prophets would soon be executed. Judgment on Jerusalem would bring the false visions and deceptive divinations, by which the false prophets continually sought to encourage unscriptural ways, to an abrupt halt.

26–28 Others had believed Ezekiel's warning of judgment yet thought it would come, not in their lifetime, but in the distant future. God's response to Judah was brief and to the point: Judgment would no longer be delayed! What God had said, he would do— and he would do it soon!

3. The condemnation of contemporary false prophets (13:1–23)

a. Judgment on the prophets (13:1–16)

1–7 In 12:21–28 Ezekiel spoke against the exiles' false security that led them to think that judgment was not imminent. They had received encouragement in this position by the visions and divinations of the many false prophets. Now Ezekiel would deliver God's denunciation on these prophets. Ezekiel was instructed to charge the prophets to listen to the Lord's word, not to their own hearts, for judgment ("woe") was about to be delivered against them for their foolish ways.

Before the judgment verdict was delivered (vv.8–16), God clearly delineated the characteristics of the prophets that had brought this judgment on them. The prophets were summarized as "foolish" (GK 5572). This word is a broad term that encompasses spiritual and moral insensitivity contrary to the nature of a wise man. Ezekiel described the basic cause of their foolishness as their reliance on their own hearts and their failure to seek God's revelation.

The prophets followed their own desires, failing to care for the people and seeing the perversions of their own hearts as God's revelation. Their visions were false and full of lies because they had really not seen anything at all. They were using pagan practices of divination to seek messages from God: watching the movement of stars, studying animals' internal organs, casting lots, etc. This only resulted in counterfeit statements that were deceitfully prefaced with the prophetic formula of divine authority: "The LORD declares." Yet the Lord had not spoken, nor had he sent them. They were only speaking from their own perverse hearts, hoping for a word of confirmation that never came. God emphatically denied that he had spoken through them.

These prophets followed their own spirit, not the Spirit of God. The desires of their fleshly spirits caused them to behave like "jackals among ruins." Jackals love to play among rubble, seeking dens for themselves. They do not care about the ruins. Similarly, these prophets did not care about the people of Judah but made dens in their own self-interest. They played their own games of false prophecy that destroyed the people and the land. So they failed to prepare the people for the difficult times ahead or for the intense times in which they lived. Judah faced judgment and deportation unless the people turned to the Lord.

The prophets were to step in and repair the "breaks in the wall" caused by violations of the Mosaic covenant. They were to exhort the people concerning the truths of that covenant in order to repair the breaks and protect the people from judgment. But they were negligent of their responsibilities. No one could be found to repair the "breaks" for God's people (22:30). Moreover, they failed to secure the sanctuary with holiness so that it might stand in the battles of the "day of the LORD"—not the future eschatological judgment but the immediate judgment of Nebuchadnezzar's invasion and siege of Jerusalem in which the temple would fall. Sinful abominations had been permitted in the temple due in part to the failure of these prophets to speak the truth and warn the people of the statutes and ordinances of the Mosaic covenant.

8–16 The false prophets had failed as "watchmen" over the nation of Judah, crying "peace" when judgment was on the horizon. These prophets had an empty word to speak and had seen lies. God's verdict was simple

and clear: "I am against you." Ezekiel repeated the reasons for the judgment.

These false prophets would be cut off from the people and have no part with the nation of Israel because they had misled the people. As prophets they had been in the hierarchy of the nation and in influential places, but they would no longer be in the council of God's people (cf. Jer 23:22). Instead, their names would be eliminated from the citizenry of Israel. They would not reenter the land of Israel at the time of their restoration from the Babylonian captivity (c. 539 B.C.). This judgment would cause the prophets to turn to the Lord and know that he existed as the only true God. The implication was that they still had an opportunity to repent and come to the Messiah in eternal salvation.

The judgment of the prophets is described in terms of their participation in "whitewashing." Since the prophets were declaring a time of peace and prosperity, it was not out of line for them to encourage home building. Consequently, they had gone around plastering walls and helping people decorate the thin partitions of their homes. It was the confirmation of a "settle down and live" philosophy. However, God declared that these walls and their decorative plaster would fall beneath the raging rains of his anger and the hail and violent wind of his wrath. When the walls were destroyed, so also would the prophets be consumed in the destruction. No one would be concerned about house decorations then. God would establish another new proverb: "The wall is gone and so are those who whitewashed it."

b. Judgment on the prophetesses (13:17–23)

17–19 The Lord exhorted Ezekiel to turn and prophesy against the prophetesses who, like the false prophets, also had prophesied from their own hearts. These women were involved in divination and sorcery. Their practice of witchcraft was common in the ancient Near East—especially Babylonia and Egypt. But witchcraft was forbidden in the Mosaic covenant (Lev 19:26). The practice of the false prophetesses was to tie bands of cloth to their wrists and place veils over their heads as they cast spells over people's lives in order to bind them and hunt them down. These women caused the righteous to die and kept the wicked alive.

Barley and bread were also instruments of sorcery. Hittite practices and later Aramean rituals demonstrate that divination was carried out with barley bread either as part of the pagan sacrificial ritual or as a means of determining whether the victim would live or die. The prophetesses, therefore, profaned God by misrepresentation. Though appearing to be God's prophetesses, they polluted his name when they used these occult practices.

These women not only had the power to kill people through their incantations, but they also lied to God's people. Because the Judeans listened to these lies, many died unnecessarily. This is not to say that the ultimate authority over life and death rested with these prophetesses, for that authority rests only with almighty God.

20–23 Ezekiel announces that God would tear off the cloth bands of these prophetesses, along with their veils with which they hunted people and bound them, thus freeing the righteous in Judah from their grip. The Lord then reasserted the reasons for this punishment. These sorceresses had used deceptive and counterfeit means to dishearten the righteous, pulling them into their cultic snare and influence. At the same time they encouraged the wicked to disobey God's ways. Therefore, God would cause their false visions and cultic divinations to cease, delivering his people from their wicked hands. When he would do that, then these prophetesses would know that he was the ever-present one, faithful and immutable Lord.

4. The effect of the false prophets on the leaders (14:1–11)

1–2 Some of the Judean elders in the exile came before Ezekiel. These "responsible" leaders came to seek clarification from him about his denunciation of the prophets and to inquire from him what God's ways for them should be. Their lives and attitudes showed they had followed the false prophets and prophetesses.

3 These leaders outwardly sought God's will by coming to Ezekiel, a true spokesman for the Lord. At the same time, however, they inwardly were exalting idols on the throne of their hearts as the real gods of their lives.

Theirs was a fickle, twofold allegiance. Their lust for idols led to the elders' stumbling into sin. Their outward rebellion against God, their practice of pagan rituals, and their refusal to keep the Mosaic covenant showed their inward worship of these false gods. No true direction can be given to those who have erected idols in their hearts.

4–11 The Lord broadened his answer to include any person in Israel who may have harbored this dual allegiance; phrases like "any Israelite" and "house of Israel" unmasked this hypocrisy. The elders represented the entire nation that had followed their leadership.

The Lord's reply was threefold: two portions related to the elders and the nation at large, while one was directed at the false prophets. The Lord first declared that he would give the elders over to the many idols in their hearts. God knew that satiation with idolatry was the only way for Israel to repent of her sin. The people would become nauseated with the emptiness and perversion of idolatry. God wanted to "recapture" their hearts that had become alienated from him through lust for these idolatrous practices. He wanted to convict them of sin so that they would heed his invitation to repent.

God purposes not only to convict sinners of their sin but also to bring them to his Messiah. Therefore he lovingly exhorted these double-minded elders and their followers to "repent" and to turn from their idols and abominations to him. Instead of heart allegiance to idols, a heart allegiance to God was necessary.

The Lord's second response was directed toward those who had refused his invitation to repent. If they did not heed this, God himself would answer their empty inquiry with action, not words. In fulfillment of the "curse" stipulations of the Mosaic covenant, God would set his face against these people, cut them off as citizens of Israel (cf. 13:9; Lev 70:3, 5–6), and make them "examples" and "bywords" for all nations to see his faithfulness in executing his covenant judgments (Dt 28:37). Then they would know that he truly was the ever-present God of Israel.

Finally, the Lord turned to the prophets whose false visions and deceptive proclamations had misled the elders and people. If these false prophets were enticed to prophesy in any way other than that which God had given through Ezekiel, it would only be because God had permitted it. God ultimately controls all things, even false prophets. These prophets would receive the same punishment God would mete out to the fickle inquirers, for the iniquity of each was the same: idolatry. The Lord consistently brought judgment on the idol worshipers in order to restore them to himself. Likewise, this judgment on the prophets was given so that the Israelites might no longer wander away from their Lord and defile themselves but that they might come into the relationship God had always desired them to have with him as his people. This relationship was expressed through the covenant formula: "They will be my people, and I will be their God" (cf. Ex 19:5–6; Lev 26:12; Jer 7:23; et. al.). God would remove the false prophets and leaders so that his people might be those who truly followed his ways as revealed in the Mosaic covenant.

5. No deliverance apart from personal righteousness (14:12–23)

12–14 As the elders listened to Ezekiel's call to repentance (vv.1–11), some no doubt wondered whether the impending judgment on Jerusalem might be diverted if some well-known righteous man or men could be found (cf. Ge 18). Ezekiel responds by saying that even Daniel, their contemporary, who was ministering before Nebuchadnezzar in the city of Babylon, if he teamed up with the likes of Noah and Job, could not save the nation. God reminded the elders that any nation that was unfaithful to him and turned to other gods would be punished, for God remains faithful to both his covenant curses and his covenant promises (Lev 26:22–26). Each individual and each land was responsible for its own standing before God.

15–20 Ezekiel illustrates his point through four common vehicles of judgment: beasts, the sword, disease, and famine. If any of these judgments were to come on the land, not even the personal righteousness of a Noah, a Daniel, or a Job would be able to deliver another person from judgment—even a member of his own family. These three righteous men were delivered respectively out of the dangers they faced, but each had little effect on his contemporary situation.

21–23 Judah's current situation was no exception. God would send his four severe judgments against Jerusalem. But to vindicate his justice before the exiles, the Lord would spare a small remnant of unrepentant Hebrews and send them into exile in Babylonia. This was strictly a manifestation of God's grace. When these unrighteous people would go into exile in Babylonia, the exiles already there would observe their deeds and see how wicked the Judeans had become. Through this the exiles would be consoled that God was perfectly just in his judgment on Jerusalem. As the exiles saw the Judge of all the earth doing right (Ge 18:25), they would be comforted in their sorrow over what had happened to Jerusalem.

6. Jerusalem, an unprofitable vine (15:1–8)

1–5 This parable implies that the exiles had asked about God's consistency. They understood that they were his chosen people, his choice vine, and did not believe that God's judgments would destroy Judah as Ezekiel had proclaimed. The parable shows the worthlessness of a vine except for bearing fruit. Its wood was too soft, weak, and crooked for building. It was not even fit for making a peg to hang some utensil or clothing on. If a vine was naturally of so little value, it certainly could not be expected to be useful when charred by fire.

6–8 In the parable the inhabitants of Jerusalem were likened to the vine. Just as the vine was profitable only for fruit-bearing, so Judah and Jerusalem were to be fruitful. The nation never was like other nations (trees) in military strength and riches except when they were trusting in the Lord (cf. David's reign). God had chosen Israel to be a blessing to the nations (Ge 12:1–3), though throughout her history she never had been very fruitful in this respect. Israel had been as unproductive as an uncultivated vine. Now, having experienced the fire of God's judgment through the Babylonian invasions and deportations, her value was entirely gone. She was worthless as a fruit-bearer (a blessing to the nations). She was fit only as fuel for fire. The Lord would return her to the fire of his discipline. The inhabitants of Jerusalem would be devoured, and the land would then lie desolate.

The reason for this fiery judgment was once more made clear: Judah had been unfaithful to the Lord and his covenant. They had failed to be a blessing to the world. They had disobeyed God's ordinances and had sinned. They were worthless and useless because of their idolatry. Graciously, the exiles could still be useful and fruitful for God, but only if they remained faithful to him. To cause them to return to himself, the Lord brought this ruin on those living in Jerusalem. Through this judgment the exiles would know that he was their ever-present God. So he disciplined his chosen people to make them fruitful instead of unproductive (cf. Jn 15:1–16).

7. Jerusalem's history as a prostitute (16:1–63)

a. The birth of Jerusalem (16:1–5)

1–2 The exiles were unconvinced by the parable of the vine (ch. 15). Certainly, they thought, the vine of Israel may have done a few things wrong in her past; but she was chosen of God and could not be as worthy of judgment as Ezekiel implied. Therefore, the Lord instructed him to "confront Jerusalem with her detestable practices." Ezekiel would show just how corrupt Israel's history was by tracing the history of Jerusalem, which became the capital of Israel and the symbol of the nation. Likewise, the purpose of this allegory was to show to the exilic leaders all the terrible abominations that had brought the impending judgment on Jerusalem. Needless to say, the abominations of Jerusalem pervaded the nation, and the judgments she would experience would likewise affect all Judah.

3 Jerusalem was conceived by the Amorites and the Hittites in the land of Canaan. The city was not founded by the Hebrews but by the heathen peoples of Canaan. The reference to Jerusalem's father as an Amorite and her mother as a Hittite shows how the city came into being. Jerusalem was a Jebusite city when the children of Israel entered the land under Joshua (Jos 15:8, 63) and a member of the Amorite league that joined together against the Hebrews at Gibeon (Jos 5:1).

4–5 Jerusalem had been treated in a manner similar to a child left to exposure on birth. It was the custom in the ancient Near East to wash a newborn child, rub it with salt for antiseptic reasons, and wrap it in cloths, changing these twice by the fortieth day after the umbilical cord was cut. Such common treatment was not given to Jerusalem, by analogy, in her beginning. She was a foundering city, uncared for by the people of Canaan or by Israel in the conquest of the land, for the Hebrews failed to conquer the city of Jebus (Jos 15:63). In fact, they allowed this city to lie exposed as an unwanted child throughout the period of the judges, a widespread custom in the ancient Near East that was used to eliminate unwanted children.

b. The Lord's courtship and marriage to Jerusalem (16:6–14)

6 The Lord saw Jerusalem in her ignoble condition and sent David, the newly anointed king over Israel (2Sa 5:6–10), to rescue her from the Jebusites and her maltreatment. God determined Jerusalem's destiny when he found her and stressed that she would live!

7 Once delivered, Jerusalem received the blessings and benefits of the Lord, her lover. He promised to increase her population like the plants of the field. Under his gracious care Jerusalem grew to full maturity as a city. Though she had reached marriageable age, she was still "naked and bare."

8–14 The Lord visited Jerusalem and claimed her in marriage by spreading his garment over her (cf. Ru 3:9). He entered into a marriage covenant with Jerusalem (cf. Ps 132:13–17). She became the Lord's city, where he dwelt when David brought the ark of the covenant to Jerusalem and purchased the threshing floor of Araunah, the Jebusite (2Sa 6; 24), in preparation for the temple's construction. As a groom to his bride, God lavished marriage gifts on Jerusalem: ornaments, cleansing, anointing, costly garments, jewelry, a crown, and fine foods. She was made exceedingly beautiful and advanced to royalty under the reigns of David and Solomon. Her fame and beauty became renowned throughout the ancient Near East as the capital of the leading nation of that day (1Ki 10; La 2:15).

c. Jerusalem's prostitution with other lands and gods (16:15–34)

15 No sooner had the Lord crowned Jerusalem with beauty and fame as his bride than she began to trust in her beauty rather than in God who gave it to her. She began to commit spiritual adultery with every nation. So-lomon led Israel contrary to God's way of faith by making treaties with many nations (cf. Dt 17:1–20; 1Ki 11:1–13). It was custom-ary to seal international treaties with a mar-riage. Solomon's many foreign wives attested to his reliance on these treaties rather than on the Lord. This led to his worship of the for-eign gods of his wives. The emphasis came to be on externals and material objects. The very gifts God had given to Jerusalem had become the means of her downfall, for she loved the gifts rather than the giver.

16–22 From rebellion under Solomon Jeru-salem, as the capital of Israel, gradually led the nation down the path of corruption. While the gifts of God were not inherently evil, Jerusalem became married to the gifts rather than to the Lord. She constructed pa-gan high places for worship and decorated them with her garments and committed adul-tery against God on them (2Ki 23:7). She formed male images from her precious metals and clothed them with her exquisite textiles. She fornicated by worshiping them with in-cense, libations, and offerings.

Worst of all, Jerusalem offered her children in sacrifice to these idols (cf. 2Ki 16:3; 21:6; 23:10; Jer 32:35). She entered into every kind of religious abomination practiced among the heathen peoples. She had forgotten what God had done for her in her youth when she had nothing and deserved nothing. She forgot that he rescued her from a despicable state and el-evated her to royalty and beauty.

23–25 It would have been enough if Jerusa-lem had simply entered into the abomina-tions of the pagan religions, but she became a militant advocate of these heathen practices. Jerusalem established pagan high places and mounds for abominable worship in every street. She offered herself lewdly as a prosti-tute by inviting every false religious ritual to come and have an intimate part of her syncre-tistic spiritual adultery. In doing so she made her God-given beauty detestable. So God be-gan to declare his "woe" on Jerusalem as she broke his heart with her prostitution.

26–29 Jerusalem also began to play the pros-titute with Egypt. Egypt had lusted after Is-rael throughout the united kingdom period. Then Jeroboam I and others prostituted themselves with Egypt (2Ki 17:4; 18:21; Isa

30:7; 36:2), though prophets like Hosea and Isaiah condemned this spiritual and political adultery. Jerusalem sought security through political relations with foreign nations rather than in her God. Thus the Lord delivered Jerusalem into the hands of the Philistines and caused the city to lose portions of the ter-ritory she had ruled over (cf. 2Ch 21:16–17; 28:18; Isa 1:7–8). Though this should have caused Jerusalem to reevaluate her sinful ways, she blatantly continued her harlotry, having political "relations" with Assyria and Babylonia. Yet her desires were never satis-fied. Ahaz sought relations with Assyria (2Ki 15:19–20; 16:7–18); and overtures to Babylo-nia were made even during the reign of Hezekiah (2Ki 20:12–19), though Isaiah re-buked the leaders for these political desires (Isa 20:5–6; 30:1–5; 31:1). Political relations with Assyria and Babylonia normally brought the demand to worship their gods.

30–34 The Lord cried out to Jerusalem, con-demning their weakness in soliciting suitors in his place. Because of the weakness of her heart relationship with God, she, as an un-faithful wife, had sought out nations with whom she could have her "relations" instead of with the Lord, her husband. Instead of the normal practice of receiving gifts or pay for her services as a prostitute, Jerusalem actually solicited these strangers (nations). She bribed or paid them to secure intimate relationships with them (cf. Hos 8:9). God summarized: Jerusalem has a rebellious and disobedient heart of infidelity. She is without excuse!

d. Jerusalem: judged a prostitute (16:35–43)

35–41 Judgment was declared on Jerusalem. She had indulged in obscene, spiritual adul-tery with the nations and their perverse idols. The Lord would now use these very nations as instruments to discipline her. Those na-tions Jerusalem had loved in fornication and those she had hated, God would use to strip her bare of all her riches and blessings so that all might see the barrenness and nakedness of Jerusalem and Judah without God's blessing. These foreign nations would judge her and make her pay the penalty for adultery and in-fanticide as set forth in the Mosaic covenant: death (Ex 21:12; Lev 20:10). They would mockingly destroy her brothels (places of idolatry), tear off her clothes (cf. Hos 2:12;

Na 3:5), and spoil her garments so that she would stand naked for all to see. Then she would be tried, stoned, and cut in pieces. Her houses would be burned as these nations executed God's judgment on her as one who practiced idolatry in contradiction to the law (Dt 13:12–18).

42–43 This punishment was ultimately accomplished by the Babylonian invasion of 586 B.C. under Nebuchadnezzar, whereby Jerusalem's idolatrous abominations ceased. She lay in burned ruins. The remnant of her population was taken captive into Babylonia. There the Israelites turned from idolatry to monotheism, learning the lesson God's judgment was designed to teach. At that time God's wrath also ceased against Jerusalem, for his justice was satisfied. So that Jerusalem might remember him once again, God brought this discipline on her. Though we may forget God, his love prevents him from forgetting his own. God takes his commitments in personal relationships seriously.

e. The perversion of Jerusalem (16:44–58)

44–48 Ezekiel changes the figure slightly at this point to make a comparison between Jerusalem, Sodom, and Samaria. These three cities are likened to three sisters, all the offspring of their Hittite mother and Amorite father. In what manner their mother, the Hittites, despised her husband and children is not clear. Perhaps she too had rejected the Lord and had sacrificed her children to idols. However, the emphasis of the allegory is to demonstrate the abominable degradation of sin that characterized the land of Canaan, for Canaan was renowned for her religious syncretism in which she experimented with every kind of idolatry and religious perversion.

A common proverb applied to these three cities: "Like mother, like daughter." Jerusalem, Sodom, and Samaria had all been nourished in the perverted religious systems of the land of Canaan, and now they were characterized by their parents' wickedness. However, Jerusalem had become the preeminent sister in spiritual abominations and wickedness. Though Samaria was Jerusalem's "older" sister to the north, greater in strength and military might, and Sodom (Ge 10:19) was Jerusalem's "younger" sister to the south, smaller in prestige and strength, Jerusalem had outstripped both in her depravity

and rebellion against God. Though both sisters were known for their extreme sin, Jerusalem had become more corrupt than either of them.

49–50 Sodom's chief sin had been pride and self-exaltation, stemming from her abundant materialism (food), given to her from God (Ge 13:10), which had resulted in false security, apathy, and disdain and neglect of the poor and needy. This material ease fostered sexual perversion (Ge 13:13; 18:20; 19:4–5). As evil as Sodom was, she did not begin to do evil like Jerusalem. Since God removed Sodom in judgment, certainly Jerusalem would receive greater punishment (La 4:6; cf. Mt 11:23).

51–52 Jerusalem had sinned twice as much as Samaria, the wicked capital of the northern kingdom, which had already gone into captivity because of her abominations before God (1Ki 12:25–33; 15:30; 16:20, 26, 31–34). Jerusalem's wickedness was so perverse that she caused Sodom and Samaria with all their evil to appear righteous by comparison.

53–58 Judgment would come on Jerusalem. Just as haughty Jerusalem abhorred Sodom when she was a byword among the nations because of her corruption, so Jerusalem would be a similar byword in her day to Edom and Philistia. The nations would despise her. Jerusalem's only hope was the promise that God would restore her from her captivity in the future. God would not only restore Jerusalem but would also restore Sodom and Samaria in that day when he brings restoration to the land of Canaan (cf. ch. 36). That restoration would humble Jerusalem and humiliate her for all her wickedness.

f. Restoration: the promise of love (16:59–63)

59 The Lord concludes this allegory by affirming his immutable faithfulness to his covenants. He would discipline Jerusalem (and Israel) as the Mosaic covenant promised, because they had failed to be faithful to him and had broken their covenant with him. The covenant broken by their spiritual adultery was the Mosaic covenant, the only one Israel entered through an oath (Ex 24:7–8; Dt 29:10–21). But Judah/Jerusalem had broken that covenant exactly as described in Dt 29.

Thus God would faithfully execute the justice of that covenant on them—the curses.

The word "oath" (GK 460) can also mean "curse" and was used both ways throughout the OT. God purposely used this term to communicate both the idea of Jerusalem's despising of the oath of Ex 24 and Dt 29 and the concept of her disregard for the promise of the curse.

60 Nevertheless, after the Lord completed his judgments on Jerusalem, he would continue to be faithful by remembering the everlasting covenant that he made with the nation in her youth. In the Mosaic covenant (Lev 26:40–45), the Lord promised that after his future and final judgment on Israel he would remember the covenant that he had made with Abraham, in which he promised to give the land of Canaan to Israel as an eternal possession (cf. Ge 17:7–8; Lev 26:42). This was an everlasting covenant, and God would graciously and lovingly remember to do what he had promised. The unfaithfulness of humankind does not alter the faithfulness of God (cf. 2Ti 2:13).

61–63 When God would remember his covenant with Abraham and restore Jerusalem and Judah to the land of Canaan, then Jerusalem would remember her evil ways that forced her into exile and would be ashamed. Jerusalem would be reestablished in the future kingdom (cf. ch. 48) in a place of preeminence. Though she had been more wicked than either Sodom or Samaria and would receive greater judgment, the Lord would sovereignly exalt her over them by giving them to her as "daughters" (20:43; 36:31). Thus these cities would no longer be thought of as "sisters" (city/nation) but as cities with their suburbs under the jurisdiction of Jerusalem (cf. v.46; Jdg 1:27). The Lord's return of Sodom and Samaria to Jerusalem as daughters is not based on the Mosaic covenant, however, but on the grace of God.

This restoration would cause Jerusalem to know that the Lord was her ever-present, always faithful God, who had chosen her of his own accord in the past and would save her in the future. Never again would Jerusalem and Judah mention their past sins; God would make atonement for their sins and forget all their iniquity. This, of course, was accomplished by Jesus Christ's death on the cross.

8. The riddle and the parable of the two eagles (17:1–24)

1–10 As the exiles listened to Ezekiel's long allegory of Jerusalem's history of spiritual infidelity to the Lord, some began to wonder why they were being judged for all the past sins of their nation. Ezekiel responds that they would be judged for their own contemporary lack of trust in the Lord, which they had shown by their tendency to rely on Egypt for security and by the corruption of their regent, Zedekiah.

Ezekiel uses a riddle to communicate this message. In it, the two kings are God and Zedekiah. The historical background for this riddle is found in 2Ki 24:6–20; 2Ch 36:8–16; and Jer 37; 52:1–7. Judah's kings were fickle in failing to follow the prophets' warnings and in yielding to the Babylonians, God's instrument of discipline. On the contrary, the kings continued to seek security and aid from Egypt. This issue was at the heart of this chapter.

The riddle is set forth in two parts. Verses 1–6 describe an eagle that was extremely glorious and multicolored. This bird flew to Lebanon (the land of Canaan; cf. Jos 1:4; 2Ki 14:9) and took the top of a cedar and the topmost young twigs and brought them to the land of merchants (Babylonia; cf. 16:29). Then the eagle took some seeds from Canaan and planted them in a land of fertile soil (cf. Dt 8:7; 11:11). The seed grew into a low spreading vine that sent out shoots and branches toward the eagle.

The second part of the riddle (vv.7–10) portrays another great eagle—not quite as glorious as the first—which caused the transplanted vine to turn its branches and roots toward it. Though the vine was initially planted in good soil so that it yielded abundant produce, it no longer thrived; it was uprooted and its fruit cut off by the east wind. No one was able to restore it.

11–14 For the interpretation vv.11–12a give the summons to listen; vv.12b–18 give the charges; and vv.19–21 announce God's intervention in judgment with the word "therefore." Each eagle represented a conquering king whom, in part, God used as an instrument of his punitive wrath on Judah. The first eagle was Nebuchadnezzar, the king of Babylonia, who had taken King Jehoiachin (crest of the cedar) and his young princes and nobles (topmost young twigs) into exile in Babylonia, a land of merchants (cf. 1Ki 10:27; 2Ki 24:10–12; Jer 22:15, 23). The cedar has messianic overtones (cf. Isa 10:33–11:1). It represents the line of David that culminates in the Messiah, Jesus Christ.

Jehoiachin was of the Davidic line. The "seed" was defined as one from the royal seed whom Nebuchadnezzar took and placed in the field of Canaan. This member of the royal seed was Zedekiah (or Mattaniah; cf. 2Ki 24:17; Jer 37:1), Jehoiachin's uncle, whom Nebuchadnezzar established as regent over the remnant in Judah by entering into a binding covenant with Zedekiah. Jehoiachin still remained the legitimate king though he was in exile in Babylonia. Zedekiah and the Hebrews remaining in the land with him should have become a flourishing vine, but instead they became a worthless and useless vine like the one already described in ch. 15. It was low and spreading because Nebuchadnezzar never allowed it to exalt itself.

15–21 The second eagle represented the king of Egypt to whom Zedekiah sent for military aid when he rebelled against Nebuchadnezzar in 588 B.C. and broke the covenant he had made with Nebuchadnezzar (cf. 2Ch 36:13). This act of trust in Egypt had been opposed rigorously by both Isaiah (Isa 30:1–2) and Jeremiah (Jer 37:1). God rhetorically asked whether the vine (Zedekiah and the small nation of Judah) would prosper. The emphatic answer was no! They would suffer God's judgment through Nebuchadnezzar when he attacked Judah, because Zedekiah had despised the covenant with him and had broken it by turning to Egypt (2Ch 36:13; cf. Eze 5:7).

Because of his disobedience both to his covenant with Nebuchadnezzar (sworn in God's name; cf. 2Ch 36:13) and to his covenant with God, Zedekiah would experience the judgments promised in the Mosaic covenant he had also broken. God would spread a net and seize him with the Babylonian army and bring him to Babylonia in exile. Egypt would be of no help when Jerusalem was besieged by Nebuchadnezzar, for Zedekiah's army would fall by the sword, the remaining population would be scattered throughout the land, and Zedekiah would ultimately die in Babylonia (cf. 12:13–14). Yet all this was a manifestation of God's grace, for he was

faithfully executing his justice so that Zedekiah might come to know that the Lord, the only true God, had spoken in these judgments.

22–24 This epilogue provides an oracle of salvation. Wherever God pronounces judgment, he normally declares hope as well. Judah had failed to remain "planted" and "fruitful." In the future, however, after God had cleansed Judah through his discipline, he would take a "tender sprig" from the topmost shoots of the cedar and "plant it on a high and lofty mountain." This cutting of the cedar was not from the first cutting made by Nebuchadnezzar in vv.4, 12, for Jer 22:28–30 declared that the physical line of Jehoiachin (Coniah) would not continue to sit on the Davidic throne. Rather, the line would continue through other descendants of David. This new cutting was, however, from the "cedar," the messianic line. It was the "tender one," a concept that had messianic implications (Isa 11:1; Jer 23:5–6; 33:14–16; Zec 3:8; 6:12–13). This was the Messiah whom God would establish as King over Israel in the messianic kingdom.

The high and lofty mountain may have reference to Mount Zion and the temple complex (cf. 20:40; Ps 2:6; Mic 4:1). This messianic kingdom would be as great and fruitful as a stately cedar tree. All the birds would nest in its branches—perhaps a figure of the nations of the world (cf. Da 4:17, 32, 34–37; Mt 13:31–32). They would submit to the Messiah and his rule.

9. Individual responsibility for righteousness (18:1–31)

a. Proverb versus principle (18:1–4)

1–4 In 16:44 Ezekiel set forth a proverb to show that Israel had taken on herself the heathen character of her environment. Ezekiel's hearers misapplied that proverbial concept. They reasoned that they were being judged because of the wickedness of their forefathers. This principle of the Decalogue teaches that children would be affected by their father's sin (Ex 20:5; Dt 5:9). Parents model for their children. Regrettably, children frequently practice the same sinful acts as their parents. Likewise, they must accept the same just punishment for such actions. Each child is individually responsible. A child can abort the "sin-punishment-inheritance" progression at any time, but he or she must repent and do what is right.

The misunderstanding of the exiles was expressed in the contemporary proverb, "The fathers eat sour grapes, and the children's teeth are set on edge"; i.e., what the father does affects his children. The people believed that righteousness and wickedness were hereditary; therefore, there was no reason to change one's ways.

The Lord's response to this new proverb was that the hereditary principle would cease immediately, for it had been erroneously applied to righteousness and unrighteousness. Each person lives or dies according to his or her own actions. God solemnly declares that "every living soul belongs to me"; he is the Creator of everyone, and all have equality before him. They are free to make a decision to walk in his ways or not. The principle of individual responsibility has always been true (cf. Ge 2:17; 4:7; Dt 24:16; 2Ki 14:6; et al.). A son is not bound to be like his father.

A basic principle is set forth at the conclusion of v.4: "The soul who sins is the one who will die." Life and death in this context are not eternal but physical. One enters into eternal life by faith in the Messiah, Jesus Christ, whether by looking forward in faith to his work on the cross, as did the OT saint, or in looking back in faith, as we do today. Eternal salvation is by faith alone (cf. Ge 15:6; Ro 4:5; Eph 2:8–9). The stipulations of the Mosaic covenant were given to a people who already had a trusting relationship with God, providing a concrete, practical outworking of faith in the God who redeemed Israel from Egypt and revealed his law. Trust in him entailed the ritual of blood sacrifice as well as obedience to his commands. If the people obeyed these commands, they would show their righteousness, receive God's blessings, and live. But if they failed to live according to God's ways as revealed in the law, the Mosaic covenant declared that even those who had believed in the Messiah would die physically (cf. Dt 28:58–66; 30:15–20). If, however, they had never trusted in their Messiah, portrayed in the sacrifices, then they would also die eternally.

b. Three illustrations of the principle (18:5–18)

5–9 The principle of individual responsibility shows that a righteous person in a trusting relationship with the Lord will live physically and eternally. First, however, the Lord must define righteousness according to the Mosaic covenant. Five legal areas differentiate righteous acts from unrighteous deeds. First, the righteous person refrains from pagan sacrificial meals at the heathen high mountain shrines and from the prevalent idolatry found in the northern kingdom of Israel (cf. Dt 12:21). Second, such a one refuses to defile his neighbor's wife or to have relations with a woman during her menstrual period (Ex 20:14; Lev 15:24; 18:19; 20:10, 18; Dt 22:22). Third, he does not oppress people through maltreatment and extortion but rather restores the pledge of a poor person's debt (Ex 22:26–27; Dt 24:6; Am 2:8). The wealthy take advantage of the poor, especially finding orphans, widows, and strangers easy prey for their extortion schemes. Fourth, the righteous person does not steal (Ex 20:15; Lev 19:13) but feeds and clothes the destitute (Dt 15:11; 24:19–22; Isa 58:7).

Finally, refusing to take interest from his fellow Israelites (Ex 22:25; Dt 23:19–20; Ps 15:5; Isa 24:2), the righteous individual practices only justice (Lev 19:15–16, 35–36; Dt 25:13–16). Interest could be charged foreigners in commercial relations, but it was contrary to the principle of love and concern for one of the covenant people to profit from a poor fellow Hebrew by extorting interest on charitable loans. Verse 9 sums up the definition of a righteous person: one who lives by the Mosaic statutes is righteous and will surely live physically and eternally to enjoy the blessings of life as God has planned (cf. Lev 18:1–5; Dt 11; 26:16–19; 30:15–20). This list clearly demonstrates that a person's attitude and acts toward others provide a true index of his or her faith and attitude toward God.

10–13 The second example deals with the unrighteous son of the righteous son. The son demonstrates his unrighteousness and lack of faith by a lifestyle opposite that of his father. Whatever his father did in righteousness, the son does not do; and whatever his father refrained from in righteousness, that the unrighteous son does. He also commits murder. Verse 18 summarizes his wicked deeds as extortion, robbery, and wrongdoing. Since he fails to live according to the righteous stipulations of the law, he will not live physically or eternally at all. This type of man was certainly manifested by the life of Manasseh.

14–18 The third illustration shows that an unrighteous man will not necessarily have an unrighteous son. If the grandson does all the righteous deeds of the Mosaic covenant, like his godly grandfather, and refuses to follow his wicked father's unrighteous acts, then he will not die because of his father's wickedness, but will surely live. But his father will die because of his own iniquity.

c. The explanation of the principle (18:19–32)

19–24 Having stated the basic principle of individual responsibility in vv.1–4 and illustrated it in vv.5–18, Ezekiel then elaborates aspects of this principle. The discussion was initiated by the exiles' rhetorical question: "Why does the son not share the guilt of his father?" God answers the question by a series of subprinciples.

First, whenever anyone—even the son of an unrighteous man—lives righteously, he lives physically and ultimately eternally. Second, the unrighteous sinner who disobeys God's righteous way for living will die physically and ultimately eternally. Third, a son will not bear the penalty for a father's sins, nor will a father bear the punishment for his son's sins. Fourth, the righteous live because of their righteousness (cf. Lev 18:5), but the wicked die because of their sin (Dt 30:17–18). Fifth, a wicked person can live physically and ultimately eternally if he or she turns from sinful rebellion, obeys the righteous commandment, and trusts in the Messiah. Past sins of such people will not be remembered because of their righteous acts by which they now live. Only God's marvelous grace has kept that wicked person from dying previously. Sixth, God does not rejoice when a wicked person dies. Rather, he is delighted when a wicked person turns to him in obedience and lives. Sinful humankind normally sees judgment as God's delight. Nothing could be further from God's desire; else he would not have sent his only Son to be judged on the cross for the sin of the whole world.

Finally, there is never a time or place where the righteous, who have trusted in the Messiah, can feel free to sin; for if they turn away from living by God's righteous stipulations and sin, then they too will surely die physically (but not eternally). They will die because of their unfaithfulness to God and their unrighteous acts. God never condones sin or grants anyone a license to disobey his holy commands.

25–29 Ezekiel again raises a rhetorical statement that expressed the mind of the exiles: "The way of the Lord is not just." God replies that it was Israel's ways, not his, that were inequitable and unrighteous. They sought to apply the principle of heredity incorrectly to righteousness and unrighteousness. The principle is repeated that the righteous are righteous only because they have practiced righteousness and justice according to the Mosaic covenant, and the wicked are unrighteous because they have turned from the righteous demands of the law. God's grace, in harmony with his law, always allows the wicked to become righteous by turning from their wickedness and practicing the righteous ordinances of the Mosaic covenant. Likewise, the righteous will die physically if they fail to walk in God's holy ways. Righteousness or unrighteousness is not inherited. Righteousness is reckoned to the individual when he or she does righteous acts of God revealed in the Scriptures. Likewise, unrighteousness is credited to the individual who fails to practice God's righteous ways. The decision is up to the individual, not heredity.

30–32 The Lord concludes this message by pleading with the people to repent individually from their sins. This was a strong invitation to live. Repentance was available to the people of Israel in Ezekiel's day. The Lord does not delight in the death of one person who dies because of his or her sin. Therefore the Lord exhorts the people to "repent and live!"

10. A lament for the princes of Israel (19:1–14)

1–9 The final question raised by the recipients of Ezekiel's messages concerns the trustworthiness of the contemporary rulers of Judah to lead the nation back to prominence. Ezekiel responds with a funeral dirge for Judah's princes. The contemporary rulers were not worthy of anyone's trust. They were examples of the wicked person in ch. 18. These rulers had been responsible for Judah's present condition. They would die. No true rulers would be left in Judah.

Ezekiel's lament centers first around the imagery of a lioness and her whelps. The figurative use of a lion normally had royal overtones, especially in reference to the Davidic line (cf. Ge 49:9). Contextually the lioness here must be identified as the nation of Israel. Israel had taken her place among the nations. The young whelps represented given kings of Israel, and in historical and biblical context they signified certain latter rulers in Judah.

The first whelp was Jehoahaz, who had been placed on the throne by the Judeans following the death of his father, Josiah (2Ki 23:31). Jehoahaz learned, as a young lion, to tear and devour humankind, doing evil in the sight of the Lord (2Ki 23:32). Becoming world renowned for the violence in his reign of three months, he was seized in 609 B.C. like a hunted lion and brought bound to Egypt, where he ultimately died (2Ki 23:33–34; 2Ch 36:1–4; Jer 22:10–12).

The second whelp was Jehoiakim's son, Jehoiachin (cf. 2Ki 24:8–17; 2Ch 36:8–10)—Jehoiakim himself is bypassed. Judah's hope had perished with the nation's decline under Jehoiakim's pro-Egyptian leadership. Hope was renewed as the young eighteen-year-old prince Jehoiachin became king. However, his reign was not substantially different from his father's, for Jehoiachin too learned to devour humankind.

Jehoiachin destroyed cities and desolated the land. He did not escape the snare of the "lion-hunting" nations that trapped him in their "pit" and brought him to Nebuchadnezzar in a "cage" in 597 B.C. Later he was released (2Ki 25:27–30; 2Ch 36:9–11). No longer would he "roar" in Judah.

10–14 The imagery changes to that of a "vine." This figure often typifies the nation of Israel as a whole (15:1–6; 17:1–10; cf. Ps 80:8–16; Isa 5:1–7; 27:2–6). The imagery used by Ezekiel probably changes since Zedekiah was not the legitimate legal king of Judah, as were Jehoahaz and Jehoiachin.

The vine referred to the historic nation of Israel. It had been planted beside abundant water in the land of Canaan (Dt 8:7–8), where it had grown large and fruitful during the kingdom period, with many branches for ruling scepters (or kings). Yet this vine was finally plucked up and cast to the ground,

where its exposed roots withered under the blasts of the east wind (Babylonia; cf. 17:6–10, 15). The vine (or nation) was transplanted into a desert place—into captivity. The "fire" that "spread from one of its main branches" was the destruction that Zedekiah, Judah's current ruler, had brought on Judah. Judah's current condition was the responsibility, in part, of Zedekiah. Ezekiel had answered the exiles' earlier question by demonstrating the foolishness of trusting in Zedekiah, for he was partially responsible for the imminent judgment. In fact, there was not a "strong branch" in Judah at all—no one "fit for a ruler's scepter," not even Zedekiah, who would be deported in 586 B.C. There was no hope! Judgment was coming!

D. The Defective Leadership of Israel (20:1–23:49)

1. The history of Israel's rebellion and the Lord's grace (20:1–44)

a. Rebellion in Egypt (20:1–9)

1 The chronological notice (July/August 591 B.C.) indicates the beginning of a new segment of the book and a new series of messages. Eleven months had passed since Ezekiel had delivered the previous revelations from God (cf. 8:1). During this time, however, the Jewish leaders in Babylonia had given thought to Ezekiel's response to their arguments against his prophecies. Apparently they still had some hope that Judah would be able to find deliverance from her present state.

The news of Egypt's victory in the Sudan had reached the remnant of Judeans at Tel Abib. Rumors also indicated that Psammetik II would make a triumphal conquest of Palestine. The exiles' expectations were most certainly heightened as they hoped that Egypt would prove to be the redeemer to free them from Nebuchadnezzar. Zedekiah had foolishly shared the same dream when he revolted from Babylonian rule and placed his confidence in Egypt's strength somewhere between the end of 591 and 589 B.C. Such a move was ill-timed; for the Pharaoh soon became ill, and the potential might of Egypt never materialized.

Ezekiel's messages in chs. 20–23 set forth the Lord's response to the unspoken query of the elders. God would not even listen to such a foolish question. Israel's history had been one of persistent rebellion against her God.

In spite of such rebellion, God had demonstrated unending grace toward his people with great long-suffering. The time had come for the nation to prepare herself for judgment, for the Lord was soon going to bring Nebuchadnezzar against Jerusalem to destroy the city and to take more captives to Babylonia (20:45–21:32). The wickedness of Judah—especially that of her leaders—was full (chs. 22–23).

2–6 The Lord summarized his response to the inquiry of the elders of Israel, probably concerning the outcome of Zedekiah's overtures to Egypt. (1) He refused to give them an audience for such a question; (2) he refused because of the abominations of Judah; and (3) the nation of Judah must be judged for her iniquity. These aspects would be enlarged as Ezekiel recounted the history of Israel's rebellion against God and God's undying forbearance and grace toward his wicked people.

Israel's history as a nation began in Egypt where God chose her. He made himself known to Israel and swore that he would be her God (Dt 7:6–11). He took an oath to bring his people into the fruitful and glorious land he had promised Abraham (Ge 12:7; Ex 3:8, 13–18; 6:1–8; Jer 3:19; Da 8:9; 11:16, 42, 45). To bring a nation into being, three elements were essential: (1) a people, (2) a government, and (3) a homeland. The people of Israel came into being in Egypt, the government was received at Mount Sinai, and the homeland was acquired through Joshua's conquest of Canaan (see introductory comments on 33:21–48:35).

7–9 Ezekiel declares that the reason Jacob's descendants had to undergo the prolonged discipline in Egypt lay in their detestable worship of Egyptian idols. God's benevolent love was not only shown to Israel in her special calling and promises but also in his warning to remove her pagan deities so that he alone would be her God (cf. 23:3, 8). The Lord did not want his people to develop incorrect worship patterns.

However, as Israel's history continued, she did not heed God's gracious warnings. She rebelled against him by continuing to worship the Egyptian idols. Therefore, the Lord determined to pour out his wrath on Israel in the 430-year captivity in Egypt. Yet when the captivity was completed, God graciously brought his people out of Egypt (cf. Ge 15:13–16) so that his name would not be profaned among the nations. The Lord's name embodied all he was. He did not want the Egyptian bondage to be misconstrued as a demonstration of his inadequacies. Though Israel had failed to sanctify the name of the Lord among the nations, the Lord himself would do so by delivering Israel from Egypt. Then all the nations would know that he was the Lord, the true, faithful, and powerful God of Israel (Ex 7:5; Ps 106:8–12).

b. Rebellion in the wilderness (20:10–26)

10–12 Ezekiel turned from Israel's corrupt beginning to the generation that God brought out of Egypt by his great power (Ex 12–15). God's kindness and grace were manifested in the Exodus and in his giving of the covenant. This covenant explained the godly principles that enabled one to live life at its best. Therefore, the Israelites were to observe all the commandments of the law, practicing them in daily life (Lev 18:5; Dt 10:12–13).

God revealed Israel's constitution in the pattern of the international suzerain-vassal treaties of the second millennium B.C., in which a great king entered into a covenant with a lesser power to provide blessings and protection to that vassal. The subject nation would, in turn, follow the stipulations laid down by the great king. God was the great king, and Israel had become his vassal. The Lord had been benevolent to Israel by bringing her out of Egyptian servitude. Israel, in turn, was to be a witness for God in the world, living according to God's righteous stipulations of the Mosaic covenant. The great king would seal this covenant by placing his "sign" in the midst of the legal policy. The Lord represented himself as the Creator in the sign of the Sabbath (Ex 20:8–11; 31:13, 17). By observing the weekly Sabbath, Israel would be reminded that God graciously set her apart as an instrument of blessing to the world and as a witness against the pagans who had exchanged the worship of the Creator for that of creation (Ne 9:14; Ro 1:25).

13–17 The phrase "the man who obeys them will live by them" (cf. Lev 18:5) is not a reference to salvation by works. Obeying God's laws demonstrated Israel's faith in the Lord; disobedience showed Israel's unbelief. In spite of the gracious blessings of God, this generation of Israelites rebelled against their Lord in the wilderness by rejecting the commands of the Mosaic covenant and profaning the Sabbaths (cf. Nu 11–14). Therefore, the Lord resolved to destroy Israel (Nu 14:11–12); yet he would not, because his name would be profaned before the nations if he destroyed his people. The nations would think that he was unable to protect Israel in the desert once he brought them forth from Egypt. Moses interceded on behalf of God's people (Nu 14:13–19; Dt 1:26–40) so that the Lord spared them. Instead, God declared that he would not bring that generation into the Promised Land because they had rejected his ways in their idolatrous hearts (cf. Nu 14:32). It was only because of the Lord's holy name that he graciously spared the nation from destruction.

18–26 All members of Israel twenty years and under had the prospect of entering the land of Canaan. God warned this new generation not to follow their fathers' idolatrous and rebellious ways. However, as in the cycle of their fathers, this generation also rebelled against the Lord, failing to live by the law and profaning the Sabbaths. Once again God resolved to destroy his people. Yet, as before, God's holiness restrained his wrath so that his name might not be desecrated among the nations (cf. Nu 16:21–22; 25:1–9). Instead, God swore that he would disperse his people among the nations (Lev 26:33; Dt 28:64; Ps 106:26–27), give them over to statutes they could not live by, and pronounce their sacrifices unclean. Then he would make them desolate and thereby cause them to know that he was the Lord their God. That God would give Israel "statutes that were not good" means that Israel would choose to live according to the world's ordinances that brought misery and death. The "gift" in v.26 referred to religious sacrifices (cf. Ex 28:38; Lev 23:38). The specific offerings were the child-sacrifices of their firstborn to their pagan deities (Ex 13:12; Lev 18:21; Dt 18:10)—a practice especially common in the worship of Molech (2Ki 21:6; 2Ch 28:3).

c. Rebellion in the conquest and settlement of the land (20:27–29)

27–29 The Lord describes the sin of Israel's first generations as blasphemy and unfaithfulness (Nu 15:30–31). When a person de-

spises God's word, that person slanders (or blasphemes) God. Israel had not learned by the mistakes of their forefathers. The generation of Hebrews who entered Canaan began practicing the Canaanites' heathen rituals they saw.

d. Rebellion of Judah in Ezekiel's day (20:30–44)

30–31 God suddenly brought the cyclic pattern of his benevolence, Israel's rebellion, his judgment, and his grace to bear on the contemporary scene. He challenged the current elders, as representatives of the exiles and Judah, with a question: Are you not rebelling like your fathers? Contemporary Israel was as rebellious as her ancestors had been. So the Lord turned to the immediate issue of the people's inquiry. He emphatically replied that he would not give an audience to anyone who disobeyed his ways and yet said that they wanted to know his will.

32–37 Because he loved them, God rejected Israel's desire to be like other idolatrous nations. In doing so he carried the cycle of judgment and grace into Israel's future history. In his judgment he would rule over her now; yet he would restore Judah at the end of the Babylonian captivity. However, there would be a second dispersion of the Israelites in which God would judge Israel and bring the people "into the desert of the nations" as he had done during Israel's Egyptian sojourn. This dispersion is most likely the one that happened in the first century A.D.

Yet, as God's grace follows judgment, so he would ultimately bring Israel into the bond of the covenant as his special possession. When a sheep passes under his shepherd's rod, it indicates that that sheep belongs to the shepherd. "Shepherd" was a common ancient metaphor for king. A rod could also have the connotation of wrath and discipline (Ps 89:32; La 3:1).

38 The covenant was described in terms of a cleansing that would result in the knowledge of God. This is the heart issue of the new covenant promise (36:25–38; Jer 31:31–34). Israel would ultimately become a cleansed flock of the Lord through the new covenant. The process of cleansing would purge out sinners from Israel in that they would not return to the land of blessing when the Lord ultimately restored his people to that land (cf. Da 12:10; Jer 31:34).

39–44 This brief summary of Israel's history of rebellion concludes with an application to Ezekiel's contemporaries. God had delivered them over to their idols since they too had refused to listen to him. The Lord also encourages them by reminding them of his ultimate grace to Israel at the end time. Once Israel was cleansed through the final judgment, God would make sure that she did not allow his holy name to be profaned among the nations again. God would accomplish this by bringing back all Israel of that day to worship on his holy mountain. There he would accept them and their sacrificial worship. The Israelites would have a contrite heart that loathed their past sins. They would come to see that God's grace had been poured out on them throughout the millennia, because the Lord refused to allow his holy name to be defiled. God had continually been dealing with them on the basis of his grace rather than of what they deserved.

2. Judgment on Judah's contemporary leaders (20:45–21:32)

a. The burning of the southern forest (20:45–21:7)

45–49 Having surveyed the history of Israel's rebellion and found the nation deserving of judgment in Ezekiel's day, God announced and described the judgment that he was about to bring on Judah. Four messages described God's judgment by Babylonia (cf. v.45; 21:1, 8, 18). The first message consists of a parable and its explicit interpretation (21:1–7). The parable describes a forest fire in the southern forest (the southern kingdom of Judah, a forested area in biblical times) that burned every tree, whether green or dry. Everyone would see that God had kindled the unquenchable fire.

Verse 49 provides a transition between the parable and its interpretation. Ezekiel's hearers were frustrated. Ezekiel, the old parabolic speaker, was at it again with another of his parables they did not understand. Therefore, God would give the interpretation.

21:1–5 The parable's interpretation is revealed in these verses. Ezekiel was instructed to "set [his] face toward the south" (20:46), defined as Jerusalem, its sanctuaries, and all

the land of Israel (i.e., Judah). The fire in the parable (20:47) represented a sword of judgment, i.e., the sword of Nebuchadnezzar and his armies (cf. vv.18–27). The green and dry trees symbolize the righteous and the wicked, respectively. God's judgment would be comprehensive. When God poured out his wrath on the sinners, the effects would cover the entire land from north to south. Each person would be touched by the sword of his fury. Both the righteous and the wicked would experience the land's devastation. Everyone would know that the Lord was the one who brought the judgment.

6–7 The effects of God's wrath on Judah would also be devastating. The people would lose strength. Ezekiel communicated these emotional responses to the people by groaning as one who was in emotional distress and in bitter anguish. When the exiles inquired as to the cause of his grief, he told them that he was a sign of the emotional distress they would have when God's judgment would come. At that time their hearts would melt, their spirits would faint, and their hands and knees would become weak like water.

b. The slaughter of the sword (21:8–17)

8–13 Ezekiel was instructed to sing a song (poem) about a sword, sharpened, polished, and ready for the slaughter, with the speed of lightning. The sword is pictured as ready to be taken by the hand of the slayer (identified as Nebuchadnezzar in vv.18–23).

Therefore, Ezekiel was to weep and wail, for the Babylonian sword of judgment was against Judah, God's people, especially her leaders. Ezekiel would strike his breast (or, better, "thigh"), a gesture of remorse, grief, and despair over this heartbreaking verdict (cf. Jer 31:19). The people of Judah had been tested and found wanting. Since the nation had failed the testing, the solemn question was whether Judah and her ruler ("the scepter," cf. v.10) would continue to exist. Would God's judgment be final?

Judah and the exiles were rejoicing and still hoping in the promise of the royal messianic line through the tribe of Judah. In Ge 49:10 both "scepter" and "my son" are used to describe the promise. The messianic overtones of Ge 49:9–10, together with the promises of the Davidic covenant (2Sa 7), were foundational to Judah's hope. The people were certain that God's messianic promises ("scepter of my son") would preserve them as a nation forever. They need not fear Ezekiel's pronouncements of judgment. However, they had forgotten the stipulation of discipline both in the Davidic covenant (2Sa 7:14) and in the cursing formula of the Mosaic covenant (Dt 28–29).

There was no immediate hope for contemporary Judah in the promises of Ge 49 (cf. v.27), for God would be faithful to exercise his justice in discipline on Judah and her current ruler in order to purify her. But the ultimate "scepter of Judah," the Messiah, would not be extinguished (cf. v.13). This was Judah's only hope in the midst of their current judgment. When Judah would ultimately be purified, then the "scepter" (Messiah) would rule over his people (cf. v.27).

14–17 Ezekiel clapped his hands in approval of the judgment but with scorn and contempt for the iniquity that had precipitated God's wrath. By this act Ezekiel demonstrated the Lord's attitude of justice toward Judah's sin and encouraged the sword's greater effectiveness. The intensity of the judgment was emphasized by the doubling and tripling of the sword; it became three times more effective than it normally would be. The sword totally encompassed the people; their hearts melted, and many fell in their gates in the lightning-fast invasion. Ultimately the sword seemed to be in God's hand. The judgment was comprehensive.

The song (poem) builds to a climax. The sword's devastation covered the entire country from right (or south) to left (or north), a play on words depicting the sharpening of the sword blade back and forth as well as the comprehensiveness of the judgment from north to south. The Lord gave his approval by clapping. But he also declared that his wrath would cease when this judgment was complete.

c. The imminent judgment by Babylonia (21:18–27)

18–21 The prophetic "sword song" is now integrated and reinforced by symbolic action. Ezekiel drew a map, perhaps in the dirt or on a brick, on which he made a road from Babylonia toward Canaan. He placed a signpost in the road where it forked, one branch leading toward Rabbath-Ammon, the capital

of Ammon, and the other branch descending to Jerusalem. Damascus was the normal junction where the road divided. The king of Babylonia, Nebuchadnezzar, was shown standing at the fork in the road, using all manner of magic and divination to determine which nation he should attack first. The combined conspiracy of Judah and Ammon against Babylonia in 589 B.C. undoubtedly precipitated this coming of the Babylonian army.

Shaking arrows inscribed with personal or place names was a form of casting lots. Each arrow was marked with a name, the arrows placed in the quiver, the quiver whirled about, and the first arrow to fall out was the gods' decision. Household idols were intimately related to ancestral inheritance; perhaps also they were consulted as mediums, who were supposed to give guidance. The liver, being the seat of the life, was commonly examined with a decision being determined from its color or markings. Nebuchadnezzar used all three means of divination with the same result. Though God did not condone divination in any form, he as the sovereign God controlled all things. He controlled these pagan practices to accomplish his will (cf. Jer 27:6).

22–23 The unanimous decision of this divining was to pursue the path to Jerusalem and to lay siege to that city (cf. 4:2). The inhabitants of Judah responded in unbelief. They were convinced that this was false divination and continued to place confidence in their covenant treaties with Nebuchadnezzar or their Mosaic covenant with God. The phrase "sworn allegiance" likely refers to the treaty-oaths made with Babylonia, for contextually the two participants are Babylonia and Judah. Judah was placing unfounded confidence in treaties she had broken. This provided no security at all. On the contrary, Nebuchadnezzar ("he") would bring Judah's iniquity to remembrance when he, as God's instrument of wrath, destroyed the nation.

24–27 This message was concluded with a judicial sentence. Since Judah's sins had become manifest, Jerusalem would be seized; and the wicked prince of Israel, Zedekiah, would be cut off in this time of final punishment (in 586 B.C.). The removals of the priesthood and the kingship from Judah are pictured in the removal of the high priest's turban (Ex 28:4, 37, 39; 29:6; et al.) and the king's crown. These would not be rightly worn again "until he comes to whom it rightfully belongs," a clear reference to Ge 49:10 and the king-priest Messiah (cf. Heb 5–7). Ezekiel uses this reference with its messianic overtones to stress that the kingship (and priesthood) would be removed in judgment but returned ultimately in the Messiah's coming in accord with Ge 49:10. God's judgment would be so complete that everything would be "topsy-turvy" socially. The threefold repetition of "ruin" stresses the intensity of God's wrath and its destruction administered by Babylonia.

d. Postponement of judgment on Ammon (21:28–32)

28–32 The other route that Nebuchadnezzar could have taken at the fork in the road was the road to Ammon (cf. v.20). Since Ammon would mock and mistreat Judah in her collapse before Babylonia, Ezekiel sings the same "sword song" to Ammon. The Ammonites had seen empty visions and divined lies that would lead them to fall on Judah, "on the necks of the wicked who are to be slain," at their time of punishment for iniquity.

God, however, stayed Ammon's terrorizing of Judah by calling for the sword to be placed back into the sheath. Why this was done, we do not know. God would judge Ammon by the sword in their own land, where he would pour out indignation on them with the fire of his wrath, delivering them to men skilled in destruction who would devour them. This judgment on Ammon was not forgotten just because Babylonia chose to attack Jerusalem first. It was certain! The time element of this judgment is not certain, though it seems related to the judgment soon to be executed by Babylonia. Ammon would be remembered no more.

3. The cause of judgment: Judah's idolatrous rulers (22:1–31)

a. Deliberate disobedience to the Mosaic covenant (22:1–16)

1–2 Though Israel's history of wickedness demanded discipline, it was the abominations of contemporary Israel and her rulers that had ignited the punishment. Since the people had failed to see this fact, God directed Ezekiel to deliver three judgment messages to make this clear once more. The first detailed the manner in which the nation, led by her leaders in the capital city, Jerusalem, had broken the Mosaic covenant. The second emphasized God's burning judgment that would display the people's impurity. The third message stressed the failure of every aspect of Judah's society—especially her leadership—to follow God's ways.

Ezekiel would act as a prosecutor of the nation, thus causing the "city of bloodshed" to become conscious of all her sins that were the bases of the coming judgment. Jerusalem's chief characteristic was her bloodguiltiness, the taking of lives. This perversion resulted from her disobedience to God's law.

3–5 The accusation is stated in two parts: the abominations of Jerusalem (vv.3–5) and the abominations of Judah's rulers (vv.6–12). Jerusalem had committed murder in various ways; these are itemized in the elaboration of the leaders' wickedness (vv.6–12; cf. 18:15–17). But the underlying cause of this bloodshed was the idolatry in the capital city. Her inhabitants had covered the city with idols contrary to her divine calling, which, in turn, defiled her (Ex 20:3–7). Since pagan religious practices did not restrict human sacrifice and wicked ways, the influence of idolatry had fostered indiscriminate murder that brought God's judgment near. Jerusalem would become a reproach to the surrounding nations. They would laugh at her miserable state and her infamous reputation.

6 The chief cause of Jerusalem's wickedness had been her evil rulers, especially her recent kings (Manasseh and Jehoiakim) and prince (Zedekiah). Each had acted in his own strength to shed blood through the misuse of power (cf. 2Ki 21:16; 24:4). Each went as far as his power enabled him. Each broke the explicit prohibitions of the Mosaic covenant (Ex 20:13).

7–12 The rulers ignored the rightful place and authority of parents, thus destroying the home (cf. Ex 20:12; Lev 19:3). Socially these leaders were taking advantage of the helpless (cf. Ex 22:21–24; 23:9; Lev 19:33; Dt 24:17). The indifference of the rulers to those they ruled over was directly related to their indifference to the holy things of God. They profaned the Sabbaths, thereby demonstrating their rejection of the Mosaic covenant and their great God (cf. Ex 20:8; Lev 19:3).

On the contrary, the rulers engaged in heathen rituals (cf. Dt 12:1–2; 16:21–22). Using informers ("slanderous men") these leaders carried out premeditated murders (cf. Lev 19:16; 1Ki 21; Jer 6:28; 9:3). These same officials engaged in sexual sins (cf. Lev 18:6–23; 20:10–21). They prospered through illegitimate gain (cf. Ex 23:8; Dt 24:6, 10–12; 23:19–20; 27:25). But the main cause was, "You have forgotten me, declares the Sovereign LORD."

13–16 Ezekiel concludes this judgment speech with God's verdict of scorn for Jerusalem's dishonest gain and murder. God struck his hands in a gesture of disapproval. He even questioned Jerusalem concerning her ability to stand through the days of judgment. Would her heart and hands be able to stand God's discipline? The judgment would be threefold: dispersion among the nations, cleansing of Jerusalem's impurity, and Jerusalem's desecration before all the nations by the Babylonians. God's primary purpose in judgment, however, was to cause his people to know that he was the Lord, the only true God.

b. The purification of judgment (22:17–22)

17–22 The imagery of the smelting process is at the heart of this second judgment speech.

Israel was shown to be worthless as dross already, as if from a previous smelting. Now she would once again be melted by the heat of God's wrath in the furnace of Jerusalem. This fire of God's wrath would literally be executed by the Babylonians when they burned and sacked Jerusalem. With this fiery trial, God desired to make himself and his justice known.

c. The void of righteous leaders (22:23–31)

23–29 The land of Judah was unclean and would therefore receive no "rain" of blessing in the day of judgment ("day of wrath"). Judah was an impure nation mainly because the people had failed in their responsibilities, especially those appointed as leaders. The "princes" (prophets?; see NIV note) had conspired against the people for the purpose of personal prosperity. They had led the people into situations (battle, rebellion, etc.) that had brought death to many, increasing the number of widows in the nation. These leaders were devouring lives like vicious lions.

The "priests" had done violence to that covenant by polluting God's holy statutes. They had failed to observe or to teach the distinction between the holy and profane, the clean and the unclean. They disregarded the observance of the Sabbath and profaned God through their pagan ritual practices.

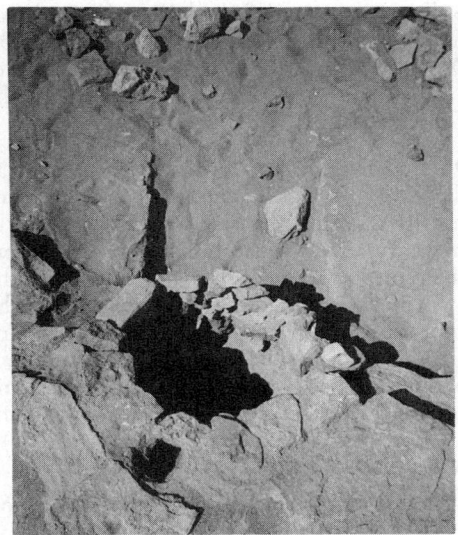

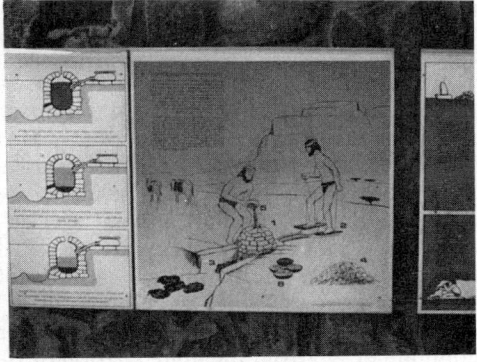

After ore was extracted from the earth, it was placed in a smelter and heated, in order to melt out the metal. The picture to the left shows the actual remains of a smelter at the Philistine city of Timnah. The photo above is a diagram at that site explaining to visitors how ancient smelting was done.

The political "officials" in the land had acted like ravenous wolves, using violence to destroy people for personal gain. Through their false visions and lying divinations, the prophets had whitewashed their own impure motives and led the people astray by falsely claiming to have God's authority.

Finally, God condemned the people for following this corrupt leadership and maltreating one another. They had practiced extortion, robbery, and oppression of the poor, needy, and stranger through unjust avenues. It was everyone for himself, each doing what was for his own profit (cf. Jdg 21:25).

30–31 The Lord was unable to find anyone who would stand defensively, through spiritual leadership and intercession, for the nation against the impending judgment. Moses had stood in the breach of the wall before the Lord in his day, to intercede for his people and to instruct them in the ways of the Lord as a leader. But now God could find no one to step to the front and to lead Judah to repentance and to a godly walk according to the stipulations of the Mosaic covenant. There was no ruler who would intercede for them. They were all corrupt! Therefore, the Lord concluded this last message with a judgment verdict. He would consume the people with the fire of his wrath. They were responsible for the coming judgment!

4. An allegorical summary of Israel's political prostitution (23:1–49)

a. Israel's sordid youth (23:1–4)

1–4 Ezekiel concludes his discussion of Israel's defective leadership with a summary allegory of the political adultery into which Israel's corrupt rulers had led the people. Several distinct speeches comprise the whole allegory. Before specific oracles are addressed to Samaria and Jerusalem, Ezekiel briefly discusses the family background of these "two sisters." They were both "born" of the same "mother," an emphasis on their common origin from the united nation of Israel that existed from the time of Egypt to Solomon. It was during their stay in Egypt as youths that they had learned the trade of prostitution (cf. 16:26; 20:7–8; Nu 25:3–9). God did not hedge in describing clearly and concisely the crudeness and perversion of wickedness and sin.

The two sisters are named. Samaria, the older in the sense of initiating perverted relations with other nations and in receiving her punishment first, was named Oholah, which means "her tent." The significance of this name is not clear, unless it refers to her propensity for heathen tent-shrines. Jerusalem, the younger of the two sisters, was called Oholibah, meaning "my tent is in her." Perhaps this name refers to God's temple ("tent" or "tabernacle") that dwelt in the city of Jerusalem (cf. 2Sa 6:17; 1Ki 8:4; et al.). Both cities belonged to the Lord as his possession, specifically as his nations. Whether this statement of possession was meant to convey "marriage" or "parenthood" is not indicated within the text. Both cities bore children. These children are most likely their inhabitants and satellite towns.

b. Samaria's prostitution (23:5–10)

5–8 The older sister was the first to be accused of being unfaithful to the Lord by seeking security in the strength of other nations. Samaria, the capital of the northern kingdom of Israel, had particularly sought "relations" with Assyria as her "lover." She had seduced the governors, officials, and military leaders of Assyria to enter into relations with her, which they willingly did (cf. 2Ki 15:19–20; 17:3–4; et al.). Not only did Israel submit to political alliances with Assyria, but she likewise defiled herself by going after the idols and gods of Assyria. This spiritual and political prostitution had characterized this nation since she began to practice it in Egypt. What she had learned in her youth had created a habit pattern that was increasingly difficult to break.

9–10 Therefore, the Lord announced his verdict. He would give Samaria into the hands of her lovers, the Assyrians, who would strip her bare of her inhabitants by either taking them into captivity or slaying them with the sword. This occurred in 722 B.C. Assyria, the object of Israel's sinful lusts, became the instrument of Israel's judgment. Samaria's prostitution was so perverse that her name became a "byword" for an immoral woman.

c. Jerusalem's prostitution (23:11–35)

11–21 God turned to deliver his accusation against Samaria's younger sister, Jerusalem. Though Jerusalem, the capital of the southern kingdom of Judah, observed the consequences of Samaria's prostitution in her fall to Assyria in 722 B.C., she did not learn from Samaria's experience. Instead, Jerusalem proceeded to engage in more lustful and corrupt fornication than that of Samaria. Rather than seeing her mission to be a servant of the Lord bringing salvation to the nations, like a prostitute Jerusalem cleverly used the nations for her own advantage.

Like Samaria, Jerusalem's first major "lover" was also Assyria (cf. v.5; 2Ki 16:8; Isa 7:7–9). Judah then extended her prostitution to the Babylonians. She had inordinate affections for the Babylonian rulers (cf. Jer 22:21), seeing images of them on walls. Perhaps this was an allusion to some Judean envoys who were sent to Babylonia and saw the witness of her great power demonstrated on walls. Judah did send messengers to woo Babylonia into "relations" with her, and Babylonia complied by entering into such "relations" with Jerusalem (cf. 2Ki 23:32, 37). Judah became defiled through this political alliance. She had trusted in the world powers rather than in God's perfect security. Jerusalem, however, realized her error in part after she became a vassal of Babylonia. She became disgusted with the Babylonians after she was debased. But it was too late! God announced that he also had become disgusted with Jerusalem, which would be demonstrated by her fall in 586 B.C. to Nebuchadnezzar.

As if Jerusalem had not learned her lesson, she turned away from Babylonia only to turn to Egypt for aid (cf. Jer 2:18; 6:8; 37:5–7; La 1:17). Jerusalem still failed to learn that security lay in the Lord. Egypt was extremely anxious to enter into "relations" with Judah; for the pharaohs were planning intervention in Asia. Such desire on Egypt's part was portrayed by lustful donkeys and horses, while Jerusalem equally desired to renew the sexual perversion of her youth with Egypt.

22–27 Having accused Jerusalem of crass prostitution with the nations, the Lord announces his judgment verdict in four short speeches. The first speech stresses that he would use Jerusalem's "lovers" to execute judgment on her. The Babylonians whom Jerusalem then hated would be commissioned by God to judge Jerusalem through military aggression. Babylonia with all her entourage of vassal nations would assault

Jerusalem with a hatred stirred by God's jealousy against Jerusalem.

The word "Chaldeans" (GK 4169) initially referred to the people living immediately north of the Persian Gulf. With the rise of the Neo-Babylonian Empire, however, the term was used for the entire Babylonian Empire.

Jerusalem's judgment is described in terms of ancient Near Eastern punishment for an adulteress: her "nose" and "ears" would be cut off. This was symbolized by the deportation of Judah's sons and daughters to Babylon (cf. 2Ki 24:10–16; 25:11; Da 1:1). The remainder of Jerusalem's inhabitants would die by the sword and fire (cf. 2Ki 25:18–21). Babylonia would strip Jerusalem of all her garments, leaving her disgraced as a prostitute. Jerusalem's "clothes" were her beautiful jewels, most likely a reference to her wealth and possessions (cf. v.46). The severity of Babylonian judgment and deportation would terminate Jerusalem's adulterous relationship with Egypt. Judah would forget Egypt and never seek aid from her again. Such has been the case ever since the Babylonian captivity in 586 B.C.

28–31 Babylonia's judgment on Jerusalem would demonstrate before all the nations the severity of Jerusalem's wicked adulterous ways. The desolation of Jerusalem would cause the nations to understand that Judah had erred greatly to receive such punishment. Jerusalem had committed political and spiritual adultery with the nations and their idols rather than trusting in the Lord for security and remaining faithful to him and his ways (cf. Ex 20:1–7; Dt 17:14–20). Since Jerusalem had followed Samaria's example and walked in her adulterous ways, she would share in the "cup" of Samaria's punishment.

32–34 The term "cup" (GK 3926) was often used by the prophets to refer to God's wrath. This "cup song" concentrates on the theme of judgment like the "sword song" (21:8–17). Jerusalem's "cup" of judgment would include ridicule and mocking. She would be drunken, sorrowful, horrified, and devastated. Jerusalem would drain the entire contents of God's wrath, shatter the pottery cup by casting it down, and tear her breasts in utter agony. The horror of her punishment was sobering.

35 The final message of these four judgment oracles is perhaps the most significant of all. The chief reason for Jerusalem's impending judgment was that she had forgotten the Lord. When a nation (or an individual) discards God, there is no other road to follow but that which leads to perversion and utter degradation.

d. Judgment for prostitution (23:36–49)

36–39 Though each city was treated separately in the immediately preceding messages, now the two sisters are combined. Ezekiel is exhorted to "judge" (GK 9146) both women—to prosecute them, exposing their abominations. They had committed spiritual adultery by worshiping idols rather than the Lord (cf. Ex 22:20; 23:13; Dt 4:15–24; 12:24–32). Part of this worship had involved child sacrifice, i.e., murder (cf. Ex 20:13; Lev 18:21; 20:1–5). The combination of idolatry and child sacrifice was performed in the Lord's sanctuary and thereby defiled it (cf. Ex 20:24–26). The implication was that these perversions were also performed on Sabbaths; thus they were profaned (cf. Ex 20:8–11; Lev 19:3, 30). In addition, the prophets had asserted that the Sabbath was neglected during most of the period of the divided kingdoms.

Samaria was equally condemned for defiling the temple. Perhaps she defiled the temple by her absence from proper worship in it and by her construction of heathen shrines.

40–42 These two "cities" were condemned for their adulterous political desires because they had sought out relationships with foreign nations for security alliances (cf. Dt 17:14–20). These two cities seduced foreign nations as a harlot lures lovers with her cosmetics and clothing, even offering them incense and oil of the Lord's sanctuary. All sorts of sordid "men" responded to the wooing, even drunkards from the desert— likely a reference to the Arabians, Moabites, Edomites, or Sabeans. These "lovers" gave Judah the hire of harlots—bracelets, crowns, etc.

43–47 God's indictment culminates in a summary verdict on "the one worn out by adultery." It was tragic that Jerusalem and/or Samaria would be known by this epithet. Those whom Jerusalem and Samaria lured into "relations" would now judge these two cities. Contextually the nations who would judge

Jerusalem and Samaria (essentially Assyria and Babylonia) are called "righteous men." This implies that they were acting righteously in judging Samaria and Jerusalem (cf. Cyrus in Isa 41).

Assyria and Babylonia would judge Samaria and Jerusalem with the judgment prescribed for an adulteress and murderer in the Mosaic covenant: death, normally by stoning (cf. Ex 21:2; Lev 20:10; Dt 22:22). The "sisters" would be tossed about, robbed, stoned, and cut down with the sword; and their children would be murdered and their houses burned.

48–49 God's purpose in this judgment is fourfold. (1) Such discipline would put an end to wickedness in the Promised Land. (2) This judgment would instruct all other nations ("women") in the fruitlessness of following the same sort of unrighteousness. (3) It was necessary, however, that these two cities and their respective nations bear the punishment for the sin of their idolatry. (4) God must execute this punishment to bring Israel and Judah into a correct and proper knowledge of himself.

E. The Execution of Jerusalem's Judgment (24:1–27)

Until now Ezekiel had variously proclaimed the Lord's coming judgment on Jerusalem and Judah. He had systematically answered each argument against the impending judgment. Nothing remained except for the enactment of that discipline (ch. 24). The beginning of Babylonia's siege of Jerusalem is described. Then Ezekiel prophesies against the foreign nations who had abused Judah and mocked her during her judgments (25:1–33:20). These foreign nations would be judged for their wicked attitude and actions toward Judah. However, the hope of future restoration and blessing would be promised to Judah.

1. The parable of the cooking pot (24:1–14)

1–2 The date was the very day Nebuchadnezzar's siege of Jerusalem began: December/January 589/588 B.C. Through divine revelation Ezekiel understood that the fulfillment of his prophecies had begun, two years and five months from the date of his last series of messages (cf. 20:1). This chronological notice, based on the years of Jehoiachin's exile, is corroborated by similar notices in 2Ki 25:1 and Jer 39:1; 52:4, which were based on Zedekiah's regnal years. The years of Zedekiah's reign and the years of Jehoiachin's captivity were synchronous.

The Lord commanded Ezekiel to "record the date" in the sense of permanently noting it. This affirmed the validity of his prophecies so that the exiles would surely know that a prophet had been in their midst. This specific day became a memorial day in Israel's history, remembered by an annual fast (cf. Zec 8:19).

Chapters 24–25 contain three messages delivered on the date given in 24:1. The first two (in ch. 24) stress the beginning of the siege of Jerusalem. Verses 3–4 describe the siege with a parable and its interpretation. The features of God's judgment are renewed. The second message emphasizes the response that the exiles and the Judeans should have had to this siege (vv.15–27). Ezekiel is instructed to restrain his emotions after the death of his wife to show the people that they should not mourn over Jerusalem's destruction. After all, they had continually defiled God's sanctuary and had been warned of the imminent judgment, which came as no surprise. Finally, Ezekiel declares that the scorn of Judah's neighbors would not go unnoticed. Judah was reminded of the Lord's perfect justice in executing judgment on these nations as well as Judah.

3–8 Ezekiel's parable of the boiling pot was given to "the rebellious house," the people of Israel. The key to interpreting the parable is given in v.2: "The king of Babylon has laid siege to Jerusalem this very day." The parable was given in light of this siege of Jerusalem.

Ezekiel once again concentrates his message in a song, here in the "cooking pot song" (cf. 21:8–17; 23:32–34). The parable describes a pot being placed on burning bones. Water would be poured into the pot and pieces of choice mutton boiled vigorously.

Two interpretative speeches follow the parable, each interpreting and expanding the parable and then announcing a verdict. The first verdict-speech (vv.6–8) identifies the pot and stresses the reasons for Jerusalem's present judgment. The "pot" represents Jerusalem, "the city of bloodshed." The pieces of meat, choice members of the flock, are nowhere explicitly identified. Since the

"pot" is Jerusalem, the context is one of a "siege" judgment; and the term "flock" was used elsewhere by Ezekiel almost entirely to represent the people of Israel (cf. ch. 34). Thus, the pieces of meat most likely picture Jerusalem's inhabitants, who would be "boiled" in the judgment fire of Nebuchadnezzar's siege. The parable portrays the siege of Jerusalem as her people boiling in the pot of God's wrath.

This first interpretative speech adds a new dimension of encrusted deposits on the pot. Verses 7–8 imply that these "deposits" represent the violent bloodshed of this "bloody city," which is like blood poured on a bare rock and not covered with dirt. Jerusalem had done nothing to cover (or to atone) for her bloodshed as required by the Mosaic covenant (Lev 17:13). Uncovered blood evoked God's vengeance (cf. Ge 4:10; Isa 26:21). The Lord declares that he has put Jerusalem's blood on the bare rock and would not allow it to be covered, so that his wrath might be poured out on her.

Another new feature is that after the cooking the pieces would be removed from the pot without favoritism. The concept of "casting lots" is that a "lot" would not fall on any person (piece of flesh), so that he would be granted favor to be removed to exile over against someone else. From a human perspective it is arbitrary and at random, but God is sovereign in all his doings.

9–14 The second verdict-speech continues the interpretation and expansion by emphasizing Jerusalem's purification through the judgment. Through the intense heat of the fire, the meat boiled until only the bones remained and were charred. On completion of this intense boiling (the siege), the contents were removed (deportation into exile) and the empty "pot" placed on the fire until it became red hot and "its heavy deposits" (filthiness of bloodshed) were melted and consumed. God would cleanse his holy city, Jerusalem. He had previously cleansed her (the deportations of 605 B.C. and 597 B.C.), but she was still unclean. She had become dirty and rusty again with the filthiness of her bloodshed. But the Lord's fire of judgment would now accomplish a complete work so that Jerusalem would be purified, but not till God caused his wrath on Jerusalem to cease. Ezekiel's entire prophecy implies that God's wrath would cease and that Israel will be cleansed completely when God begins to restore Israel to the land of Canaan in the end time (cf. 36:22–32).

This message is certain. God has spoken; he will do what he has said. He will not neglect this righteous judgment, for he is just. He spares no one in pity nor will he be sorry for anyone, for Jerusalem will receive the just due of her wicked deeds.

2. Signs to the exiles (24:15–27)

a. The death of Ezekiel's wife (24:15–24)

15–17 The Lord informs Ezekiel that shortly he would take Ezekiel's wife from him "with one blow," a phrase that normally refers to a plague or disease (cf. Ex 9:14). This predicted death of Ezekiel's wife is heightened when it is emphasized that she was "the delight of [his] eyes."

In the funeral rites of the ancient Near East, the mourner normally tears his garments and puts on sackcloth (2Sa 3:31). He removes his shoes and headdress (2Sa 15:30; Mic 1:8), shaves his head, and puts earth on his head (1Sa 4:12). The lower part of the face (from the mustache down) is covered with a veil of some sort (2Sa 15:30; 19:4). The mourner rolls his head or his whole body in dust and then lies, or sits, among a heap of ashes (Isa 58:5; Mic 1:10). He fasts for a day (2Sa 1:12; 3:35), after which friends bring "mourning bread" (Jer 16:7). Funeral lamentations are made by the family, relatives, and professional mourners (2Sa 1:17; 11:26; Mic 1:8).

In vv.16b–17 the Lord instructs Ezekiel *not* to use these normal procedures to mourn the loss of his wife. In fact, he was not to mourn at all, not even to shed a tear. He was only to groan silently. This was certainly an unnatural response to death, especially in the culture of Ezekiel's day. Priests mourned the death of a family member (Lev 21:1–3), but Ezekiel would not even be allowed that privilege.

18–19 Ezekiel probably shared this message with the people in the morning; in that evening his wife died. He faithfully responded to her death according to God's command, though undoubtedly this was one of the most difficult things he ever did. Only through the Lord's strength was he able to obey. Such an unnatural response to death immediately arrested the attention of his audience, and they readily inquired as to the meaning of his actions. Ezekiel's entire life was a testimony to the exiles.

20–24 The "delight" of the exiled people's eyes was the pride (2Ch 36:19; La 1:10–11) and affection that they had in the temple at Jerusalem (cf. v.25). However, the Lord would defile the temple and slay the Judean children in the Babylonian siege of Jerusalem. Ezekiel was to be a sign to them. They were to respond to the destruction of the temple and the death of their children in the same manner that Ezekiel responded to the death of his wife. Just as the delight of his eyes (his wife) was taken, so the delight of their eyes (the temple and their children) would be taken. They were not to mourn because Jerusalem's fall had been foretold by the prophets. Judgment should have been expected!

b. The removal of Ezekiel's muteness (24:25–27)

25–27 The Lord announces that Ezekiel's muteness (cf. 3:25–27) would be removed when the siege of Jerusalem was completed. On the day Jerusalem fell, a fugitive would escape to bring the news of Jerusalem's collapse to Ezekiel in Babylon. On the day that the fugitive arrived in Babylon, Ezekiel's mouth would be opened; he would have the freedom to move among his people and proclaim the message of hope for the future. He would once again intercede before the Lord on their behalf. This fulfillment is described in 33:21–22 (cf. 2Ki 25:8), in the very night on which Ezekiel delivered his great message of hope for Israel (33:31–39:29). The removal of his muteness would be another affirmation of Ezekiel's prophetic gift to the exiles. When they saw the fulfillment of the Lord's messages through his prophets, then the exiles would know that the Lord was the God of Israel.

III. Judgment on the Foreign Nations (25:1–33:20)

A. Judgment on Judah's Closest Neighbors (25:1–17)

1. Judgment on Ammon (25:1–7)

1–7 In 25:1–33:20 the prophet thematically groups all the oracles against foreign nations that he received from the Lord (cf. Isa 13–23; Jer 46–51). Though delivered at different times, topically they form a singular unit, significantly placed at this point in the book. Ezekiel had warned Judah of judgment in the first twenty-three chapters. Chapter 24 climaxed these warnings with the announcement of the beginning of Judah's foretold punishment. With the fall of Judah and Jerusalem, Ezekiel turns to announce judgment on the foreign nations that had in some manner cursed Israel (cf. 25:1–33:20; cf. Ge 12:3). By inserting these judgment oracles against the nations here, he concludes the book decisively and constructively with promise. Receiving a renewed commission in 33:1–20, Ezekiel closes his prophecy with the encouraging announcement that Israel would be brought back safely to the Promised Land (33:21–48:35).

Chapter 25 does not start a new series of messages. The four short oracles against Judah's immediate neighbors continue Ezekiel's dated judgment message begun at 24:1. The messages in this series announce judgment on Judah and then turn to denounce the surrounding nations that had rejoiced over Judah's downfall and had hoped for personal spoil and gain. God announces judgment on these nations lest their gleeful taunts continue and the exiles question his faithfulness to his promises.

The judgment announced on these nations had already been predicted several times by Jeremiah (Jer 9:25–26; 25:1–26; 27:1–11; 48:1–49:22). Nebuchadnezzar and his Babylonian armies would be the instrument of judgment on these nations as well as on Judah. They too would experience captivity in Babylonia for seventy years (Jer 25:11). Long ago God had promised that those who cursed Israel would be cursed (Ge 12:3). Now he would bring that "cursing" on these nations. Judgment would continue until the second coming of Christ, when the Lord will reign over them (cf. Isa 11:14; Da 11:41; Joel 3:1–4). Thus God's perspective of judgment extends from the immediate judgment by Babylonia to the end times.

Ezekiel was to prophesy against the children of Ammon, exhorting them to listen to God's word and not the message of their own gods. Judgment on Ammon has already been briefly discussed in 21:20, 28–32; but at that point in Ezekiel's argument Ammon's judgment was deferred until the prior discipline of Jerusalem was executed. The accusation and verdict against Ammon are stated in vv.3–5 and 6–7: Ammon is accused of expressing satisfaction over the misfortune of Judah, her enemy and rival. This was clearly shown by the interjection "Aha!" The Ammonites had clapped their hands and stamped their feet in joyous contempt over the temple's defilement (cf. 24:21), the desolation of the land of Judah, and the captivity of the Judean people by Babylonia.

God was ready to give the Ammonites as a possession to the "people of the East," who would exploit the land of Ammon by settling down in it and eating the produce of that country. The desolation of the land would be symbolized by the use of Rabbah, their capital, as a pasture for camels and the use of their land as a resting place for flocks. The "people of the East" are not identified here; but the immediate context, parallel passages, and ancient history all argue for the designation of "Babylonia." Ezekiel's proclamation of God's continuing purpose for judgment did not change in his announcement of judgment on Ammon. God desired that this discipline would cause the Ammonites to know that he was the Lord, the God of Israel, the only true God.

2. Judgment on Moab (25:8–11)

8–11 Moab had cursed the people of Israel, being disrespectful of Judah's divine election as an instrument of blessing to the world. Moab had likened Judah to all other nations because she had fallen to Babylonia. Such a defeat indicated to Moab and other nations that Judah's God was weak. Therefore, any special calling of Judah by that God was considered a joke. So Moab laughed at Judah's defeat in light of her professed election (Jer 48:27; Zep 2:8–9). Edom, known elsewhere in the OT as "Seir" (cf. Ge 32:3; 36:30; Eze 35), shared with Moab this same disdain of Judah. A more complete accusation of Edom follows in the next judgment speech.

The verdict on Moab manifested God's promise to curse those who curse Israel (cf. Ge 12:3). The Lord would expose Moab's northwest flank (the mountain plateau overlooking the Jordan rift) to the invasion of "the people of the East" (the Babylonians attacked Moab in 583/582 B.C.). The attack would begin on this shoulder of the land of

Moab, along a line drawn from north to south between the cities of Beth Jeshimoth (in the Jordan Valley), Baal Meon (about five miles southwest of Madebah), and Kiriathaim (location uncertain), "the glory of the land" (the best part). The people of Moab would be given as a possession to these "people of the East," along with the children of Ammon, implying that the same invasion was involved. Moab would be exiled and laid desolate (Jer 48:7–9). Neither Moab nor Ammon would "be remembered among the nations" until the end times. This judgment was to begin with Nebuchadnezzar and conclude with the second coming of the Lord. God's consistent purpose in judgment is stated again: that Moab would come to know that he is the Lord, the only true God.

3. Judgment on Edom (25:12–14)

12–14 The accusation against Edom centered on her perpetual attitude of vengeance against Judah, an attitude that began with the conflict between Jacob (Israel) and Esau (Edom; cf. Ge 25:30; 27:41–46; 32:4). Edom had desired to possess Israel and Judah (35:10) and had joined Ammon and Moab in degrading Judah (cf. v.8; 36:5; Ps 137:1, 7–9). She had committed grievous acts against Judah. Edom's behavior was inexcusable because he was a twin brother! Israel respected this solidarity, but Edom spurned it.

Therefore, God announces his verdict on Edom, a judgment that is expanded in 35:1–36:15. Edom would become a desolation as the Lord cut off both humankind and cattle from that land. This devastation would be comprehensive from Teman to Dedan. Other passages indicate that this punishment would be executed by Nebuchadnezzar (Jer 9:26; 25:21; 27:1–11; cf. Eze 32:29; Mal 1:2–5). However, God also declares that he would execute his vengeance on Edom in return for its vengeance on Judah, and that he would do so through the instrumentality of Israel. The historical context of Ezekiel's day precludes this event from happening at that time. However, Ezekiel and other prophets declared that Israel would possess Edom in the end time (cf. 35:1–36:15; Isa 11:14; Da 11:41; Am 9:12; Ob 18).

The purpose of God's judgment on Edom is stated differently than the norm: Edom would know God's vengeance in his judgment. They would understand that he was the faithful God of Israel who would curse those who cursed his people. In turn Edom would observe that he was the only true God.

4. Judgment on Philistia (25:15–17)

15–17 Ezekiel moves geographically clockwise as he announced judgment on Judah's closest neighbors. The Philistines also were accused of responding with vengeance against Judah, especially with contempt and perpetual enmity. Their goal was to destroy Judah. Such continual hostility against Israel by Philistia had been demonstrated in its interaction with Samson (Jdg 13–16), Eli (1Sa 4), Saul (1Sa 13; 31), David (2Sa 5), Hezekiah (2Ki 18:8), Jehoram (2Ch 21:16–17), and Ahaz (2Ch 28:18). God's judgment verdict declares that he would "cut off the Kerethites," a synecdoche for "Philistines" or a portion of them (1Sa 30:14; Zep 2:5). God's great vengeance against them was a judgment "in kind" for their revengeful attitude and actions against Judah. His destruction of Philistia would be complete, even consuming the remnant of those who were on the coast. His wrath, however, was for correction, so that Philistia would come to know through this act against them that he was the only true God.

Though the time of this punishment on Philistia was not stated, the context assumes the same time as the three verdicts executed on Ammon, Moab, and Edom by Babylon (cf. Jer 25:20; 47:1–7). The ultimate fruition of this judgment will be realized when Israel possesses Philistia in the end time (cf. Isa 11:14; Joel 3:1–4; Ob 19; Zep 2:4–7).

B. Judgment on Tyre (26:1–28:19)

1. Judgment by Babylon (26:1–21)

a. A judgment oracle against Tyre (26:1–14)

1–6 Ezekiel turns toward the north to announce judgment on the city of Tyre and its environs. The length of this oracle suggests the political and religious significance of this city. His indictment of Tyre is set forth in a series of four messages: a judgment speech with explanatory appendixes (26:1–21); a funeral dirge over the fall of the city (27:1–36); a judgment speech against the prince of Tyre (28:1–10); and a funeral dirge over the fall of the king of Tyre (28:11–19).

The date for these four oracles is given as "the eleventh year, on the first day of the month." The specific month was not stated. It seems that these oracles were pronounced against Tyre while the siege of Jerusalem was in process in the "eleventh" year.

Tyre is first mentioned as a strong, fortified town that formed part of the boundary of the inheritance of the tribe of Asher (Jos 19:29). Tyre had been prominent in the days of David and Solomon. Hiram, Solomon's contemporary, enlarged and beautified the city. It became an important maritime city of the ancient Near East. With the rise of Assyria to power, Tyre periodically submitted to Assyria's lordship, paying tribute out of the abundance of her wealth. Whenever possible, however, Tyre rebelled against the Assyrian power and withstood the Assyrian retribution in the security of its island fortress (as in the case of Sennacherib). As Assyria began to decline in strength, Tyre exerted her complete independence. Tyre was in this latter condition when these oracles were delivered.

Verses 1b–6 compose the basic judgment speech against Tyre with the accusation stated in v.2 and the verdict delivered in vv.3–6. Tyre was accused of delighting in the prospects of Jerusalem's downfall so that she might obtain the spoils of the city and the advantages of its fall (e.g., Jerusalem controlled the trade routes connecting Egypt and Arabia with the north). "Aha!" expresses Tyre's satisfaction over Jerusalem's misfortune. Tyre looked forward to the "gate to the nations" being broken down. The term "doors" refers to the gates of Jerusalem, which would be broken for the access to the nations. Jerusalem's gates would be broken by Babylonia and opened to Tyre.

Tyre's major desire was to be filled with the spoils of Jerusalem and with the opportunities, since Jerusalem lay "in ruins," that would then be hers in western Asia. The Babylonians had taken Jerusalem, leaving it open for Tyre to take advantage of the spoils of Jerusalem. It was this incessant desire for wealth and riches that brought God's wrath on Tyre in fulfillment of his promise in Ge 12:3.

God, who was personally against Tyre, would bring many nations successively, like the waves of the sea, to destroy Tyre and make her like a bare rock, useful only for drying nets. "Out in the sea" describes Tyre's almost impregnable situation. The cliffs of Moab, the heights of Edom, and the island fortress of Tyre were no defense against the sovereign Lord. Tyre would become spoil for all nations, just as she sought to spoil Jerusalem. Even Tyre's outlying coastal settlements would be destroyed. But even through this prolonged judgment, God's purpose would be that Tyre would too come to know that he was the Lord, the only true God.

The siege of Tyre by Nebuchadnezzar lasted for thirteen years (c. 586–573 B.C.). However, when Babylonia declined in power, Tyre regained her independence once again. This brief freedom lasted till the second "wave" of destruction brought her into submission to the Persians around 525 B.C. Tyre's remaining history demonstrated the continuing "waves" of conquerors. God was faithful to bring the "many nations" against Tyre in successive "waves" of conquest. The Lord Jesus did bring his preaching and healing ministry to this heathen city (Mt 15:21; Mk 7:24–31; Lk 6:17). Her responsibility and judgment would be less than that of the Galileans who rejected Christ's constant ministry to them (Mt 11:21–22; Lk 10:13–14).

7–14 Nebuchadnezzar and his great army are identified in v.7. The process of his siege of Tyre is fully described. The city's destruction and the slaying of its inhabitants are described, followed by the taking of spoils and the demolition of the remaining glories of Tyre. The change from "he" to "they" in v.12 may demonstrate a broadening of the instrument of judgment from Babylonia to the many future nations that would plunder Tyre. Alexander the Great literally threw Tyre's "stones, timber and rubble into the sea" when he built a one-half mile causeway out to the island fortress to conquer the city.

Tyre's desolation is emphasized by the lack of any song in the city (an indication of cessation of normal social activities) and by the town's bareness portrayed by the figure of a bare rock used only for spreading fishing nets to dry.

b. The response of vassal nations to Tyre's fall (26:15–18)

15–18 Tyre had many vassals who had depended on her as their protector. Ezekiel prophesies that when the news of Tyre's fall to Babylonia is received by these peoples, they would be terribly frightened. Their princes would abdicate their thrones, perhaps in an act of surrender and submission to Babylonia before she attacked them. As mourners they would not sing a lament song in luxurious dress. They would be stunned and stand amazed as to how Tyre could fall. These vassal rulers would sing a funeral dirge over the deceased Tyre. Ironically, Tyre had the poor sense to rejoice over Jerusalem's fall. These cities, however, had the good sense to realize that Tyre's fall spelled the same for them.

c. The Lord's concluding verdict (26:19–21)

19–21 A prophecy of Tyre's eternal death was certainly an appropriate response to the funeral dirge of the nations. Ezekiel refers to the imagery of vv.3–6 to pinpoint the aspect of the previous message that he wants to expand. At the time that Tyre would be made a ruin by the great waves of nations (v.3) and left as a barren rock (v.4), God would make sure that she never again regained her place of prominence on this earth. Tyre would die. She would "go down to the pit," as had those in the past who had already died. In her ruined state she would be as if she dwelt in Sheol in the earth below. Also, Tyre would never again exist and play an important role in history as she had in the past. Though some might look for her, she would not be found.

2. Ezekiel's funeral dirge over Tyre (27:1–36)

a. The building of Tyre's ship of pride (27:1–11)

1–3 A previous dirge had been sung by neighboring kings (26:15–18). This new message is another funeral lament, but one that Ezekiel himself sings at Tyre's death. The chief cause for this major maritime power's collapse was her pride. Tyre became full of self-conceit, presuming herself to be "perfect" in all she had acquired through trade with the nations. The Lord hates pride (Pr 8:13; 16:18).

4–11 The destruction of Tyre would be lamented like the wreck of a magnificent ship. The imagery is sustained through the poem and climaxes in the wreckage. In typical dirge style the deceased's former splendor is first accented. Ezekiel uses the imagery of a ship being constructed and equipped to show

Tyre's pride and development of prominence and dominion as a maritime empire.

Tyre's domain was in the heart of the sea. Her sea traffic extended throughout the ancient Near East. She obtained the finest materials through maritime trade. She used her dominion over other nations to build and beautify her own "ship" (Tyre). The wood for the frame (pine or fir) came from the district of Mount Hermon (Senir), while her "mast" was made from choice cedars of Lebanon. The ship's "oars" were from the oaks of Bashan; and her "deck," inlaid with ivory, was made of cypress wood from Cyprus. Her "sail" and "banner" were made of Egypt's fine linen, while her "awnings" were made of purple and blue textiles of Elishah. These verses convey the idea that Tyre's development into a beautiful and great maritime city-state came through acquiring the finest materials of her day from the areas that produced them. She obtained these materials through the prominence and power of her sea merchants.

Those who engineered the development and expansion of Tyre's merchant activity were native Phoenicians. Tyre secured the best-trained veteran sea merchants from the Phoenician cities of Sidon, Arvad, and Gebal (Byblos) to be her "crew" and "shipwrights." However, the intelligentsia of Tyre actually "sailed" the ship. She was so adept at sea trade that soon everyone traded with her. In turn this necessitated armed protection of her city and ships. She was then able to attract military mercenaries from far-off Persia, Lydia, and Put (in Africa), as well as more local soldiers from Arvad, Helech, and Gammad. Tyre's ability to allure these mercenaries came undoubtedly from her splendor, wealth, and power. In turn, the presence of these foreigners enhanced Tyre's significance. Truly Tyre became a magnificent maritime empire that attracted nations from all over the ancient Near East to trade with her and to come and experience her greatness as a city. In light of this Tyre could say, "I am perfect in beauty."

b. Tyre's vast commercial relations (27:12–24)

12–24 The nations desired to trade with Tyre because of the abundance of goods she had to trade. The list of geographic locations and the major items that each nation had to trade show the extent, abundance, and variety of Tyre's trade. Tyre traded with almost every region: from Tarshish (Spain) to northeast Anatolia (Tubal, Beth Togarmah) on an east-west axis (through the Aegean), and from Arabia through Syria and Palestine on a north-south axis.

c. The sinking of the ship of Tyre (27:25–36)

25–27 This last section of Ezekiel's funeral lament over Tyre gives God's verdict and the nation's response. The imagery of a sinking ship continues the metaphor and portrays Tyre's demise. Laden with all the wealth of the nations and her resulting pride in materialism, the "ship" became extremely vulnerable to the "seas." Led out on the high seas of commercial adventure by her obsession for more wealth, Tyre quickly succumbed to the strong "east wind" of Babylonia. All Tyre's "cargo" of wealth, materialism, and pride, along with those serving her, sank suddenly into the sea.

28–36 Those who had traded with Tyre quickly "abandoned their ships," i.e., their work for Tyre, and they stood stunned and shocked on the shore. They bitterly mourned for Tyre's death by putting on sackcloth, shaving their heads, placing dust on their heads, and rolling in ashes. They had never seen anyone collapse as quickly as Tyre. She had been supreme in the maritime world, constantly satisfying others with her wares, but now nothing was left. It had all sunk into the sea. Tyre was nonexistent.

The nations and kings who had traded with Tyre became afraid that they too would have the same thing happen to them (cf. 26:17–18). In fear and self-protection, they quickly turned from being ones who adored Tyre to ones who totally disowned her. They hissed at her in a derogatory manner. How quickly the proud fall! Tyre found this out. She would exist no more!

3. A judgment speech against the ruler of Tyre (28:1–10)

1–5 God commands Ezekiel to deliver a final judgment speech against the ruler of Tyre. Tyre's king is described as a very wise man. But he was so impressed with himself that he actually began to think that he was a god. He was sitting on the "throne of a god [Melkart, Tyre's patron deity] in the heart of the seas."

This arrogant pride and self-exaltation as a god brought God's accusation against Tyre's ruler. God charged that Tyre's ruler was not a god but merely a man. God questioned whether Tyre's ruler was as wise as Daniel, the prophet who had revealed secrets to Nebuchadnezzar. Did Tyre's ruler know all secrets? No! Tyre's ruler was only a man.

6–10 Ezekiel announces the verdict against Tyre's ruler. God would humble him by bringing him to a horrible, disgraceful death, the death of the uncircumcised at the hand of ruthless foreigners. Phoenicians practiced circumcision; so to be slain as an uncircumcised male would be to die a barbarian's death. No longer would he have beauty and splendor. Strangers' swords would cut off his wealth and grandeur. God mocked the ruler's claim to divinity by declaring that the ruler would not claim deity before his slayers but would be a mere mortal in their hands.

4. A funeral dirge for the king of Tyre (28:11–19)

This is one of the more difficult passages in the book of Ezekiel–if not in the whole Bible! The most logical and expected understanding of this section is to see it as Ezekiel's funeral lament for Tyre's king. The progression of the prophecies against Tyre have alternated judgment speeches with funeral laments. Since 28:1–10 set forth a judgment speech against Tyre's ruler, one would expect 28:11–19 to be the corresponding funeral dirge for this king. Many, however, have understood the king of Tyre to be Satan. But this interpretation has its difficulties, as will be noted below. Therefore, the most natural and logical understanding of these verses is that the human king of Tyre is the person under discussion.

11–12 The main difficulty in this passage lies in explaining the description given for this king. He is said here to be full of wisdom and perfect in beauty, concepts already conveyed about Tyre's ruler and his city. He is also "the model of perfection [lit., the one sealing a plan]." As Tyre's king and the mastermind of the city's commercial sea traffic, it is easy to understand how he would be known as the one whose plan enabled the city to become the maritime leader of its day.

13a This individual was also declared to have been in "Eden, the garden of God." The word "God" could refer either to the true God or to a god. "Eden" may refer to the Paradise described in Ge 1–3. It probably is a simile to portray the splendor of a given geographical area, its most common use (cf. Ge 13:10; Eze 31:9). It is impossible that Tyre's contemporary king was in the Garden of Eden at the time of creation; thus many argue that Tyre's king is Satan (see Ge 3). However, several conjectures about Satan need to be made if one chooses this interpretation.

If Tyre's literal king is in view, then a possible solution may be found in understanding ancient Near Eastern temples. These temples normally encompassed a large enclosure with a garden. If the term for "God" is understood as "god," then perhaps "Eden, a garden of a god" metaphorically describes the splendor of the temple complex of Melkart ("king of the city"), with whom Tyre's human king sought identity. Admittedly the phrase "you were in Eden, the garden of God" is a difficult obstacle to the interpretation, though plausible solutions do exist.

13b–14a In the ancient Near East a "cherub" (GK 4131) was understood to be a sphinxlike creature with an animal body (normally a bull or lion), wings, and a human head. These statutory creatures normally guarded the entrances to pagan temples. The cherubim of God guarded the ark of the covenant and the Garden of Eden, and they formed the throne-chariot of God. It seems that Tyre's king was identifying himself with the patron deity of Tyre, Melkart, directly or symbolically, as the god's guardian sphinx. The Phoenician male-sphinx (or cherub) was normally bejeweled and sometimes had the head of the priest-king. The sphinx was considered to be all-wise. Such a description fits well, for the king is called a guardian cherub (sphinx), and the many jewels listed as his covering befit the many jewels that adorned the Phoenician sphinx (cherub). The passage would then be declaring that the king of Tyre had become as the guardian cherub for the god Melkart and was bejeweled with his riches as a cherub-sphinx normally was. The term "created" is used in the sense of bringing the king to the throne. God is always the Creator; so this would demonstrate that it was the true God who had sovereignly placed this king on the throne of Tyre.

To assume that the stones were the garment of Satan in the Garden of Eden and that Satan was a guardian cherub of Eden are purely hypotheses. In fact, neither Michael nor Gabriel (archangels) is described as a cherub, and Satan was no doubt on the same level as these before his fall.

14b The phrase "holy mount" is consistently used to describe Jerusalem and/or Zion as the central place of worship and the dwelling place of the Lord (Ps 99:9; Isa 56:56:7). It is to "my holy mountain" that the children of Israel will be regathered in the millennial kingdom (Isa 11:9; 65:25). If "the holy mount of God" refers to Jerusalem, then this means that the king of Tyre was *in* (not *on*) the city of Jerusalem walking amid fiery stones after Babylonia destroyed Jerusalem. However, the ritual of burning a god has been discovered on a bowl from Sidon and is recorded in the cult of Melkart at Tyre. Melkart's resurrection was celebrated by a "burning in effigy," from which he would then be revitalized through the fire and the smelling of the burnt offering. Therefore, in keeping with the Phoenician religious-cultural background, perhaps the explanation of walking among the fiery stones is a reference to the king's self-exaltation of himself even as the god Melkart, to the extent of his claiming resurrection after burning by fire.

The "holy mount of God" is never used in Scripture to mean heaven, which would have to be its interpretation if the king of Tyre is identified with Satan. Likewise, walking among the fiery stones would be an enigma if Satan is the person described here.

15–19 Last, this king is declared to be perfect in his ways from the day he was created till he sinned. "Perfect" (GK 4003) does not mean "sinless perfection" but implies that one was blameless or unobjectionable in a given area. The king of Tyre was a good king against whom objections were not raised from the moment of his coronation until pride possessed him and he sinned.

The king of Tyre's sin of pride arose from the splendor he achieved through his vast commercial traffic. His obsession for material gain opened the city to all the evils prevalent in commercial traffic. He became filled with violence. His wisdom was dulled by the glitter of wealth and splendor. He also profaned his sanctuaries—likely a reference to the idolatries practiced in the temple of Melkart. Such a description is totally unfitting for Satan. Only by seeing Satan as the force behind Tyre's king and the spirit working in him can one even begin to relate these verses to Satan.

This funeral lament concludes with a description of the fall of this king under God's judgment. God would bring him down in disgrace from his self-deification, from "the mount of god." As a cherub he would be eliminated from the area of the fiery stones, i.e., his professed immortality by fiery resurrection would be destroyed when he died (or he would be removed from taking spoils from Jerusalem). God would cast him to the ground before all the world's kings and cause fire to come forth from him to devour him. Just what is meant by fire coming out from the king is not clear. His death would be sudden and horrible, and he would exist no more. Certainly this description is befitting a human but does not coincide with what we know of Satan's fall and ultimate destruction.

Thus Tyre's king is best understood as the literal human contemporary king of that city in Ezekiel's day. Each characteristic can be explained in light of the cultural and religious context of that day. Contrarily, to identify the king as Satan requires far too much presupposition. Most of these descriptions—if they do in fact relate to Satan—are revealed nowhere else in Scripture.

C. Judgment on Sidon (28:20–24)

20–24 Sidon, a sister city of Tyre, lay in the shadow of Tyre's maritime leadership in Ezekiel's day. God's judgment on Sidon would consist of a plague and death by the sword. Bloodshed would be rampant, but God's judgment was a manifestation of his grace, for therein the Lord was glorified when the Sidonians realized that he is truly the Lord and God. God's holiness demands that he be just and execute judgment on sin. This holiness was demonstrated in his judgment on sinful Sidon.

Verse 24 summarizes the previous judgment oracles against the nations (chs. 25–28). When these judgments are completed, Israel would be free from these despising and harassing nations' constant pain that she had received for so long. Israel would then recognize and know that the Lord truly is her God.

D. Israel's Restoration From the Nations (28:25–26)

25–26 By the judgment of the nations around Israel, Ezekiel encourages the exiles that God faithfully exercises his righteousness against other nations as well as against Judah. He encourages them further with a reminder that the Lord will regather them from among all the nations where they have been scattered. This restoration will take place when God executes his judgments on the nations, judgments that will not be completed until the end times. By regathering Israel God will demonstrate that he is the holy God, unique and distinct.

When the Lord restores Israel to Canaan, he will show his immutable character of faithfulness. He promised this land to Abraham (Ge 12:7), Isaac (Ge 26:3), and Jacob (Ge 35:12) in the Abrahamic covenant. The Lord will cause his people to live in that land in security and prosperity. At that time they will know without doubt that he is the Lord their God.

E. Judgment on Egypt (29:1–32:32)

Ezekiel concludes his prophecies against the nations with six judgment messages against Egypt. Egypt had played a significant role in the final days of the Judean kingdom. From 609 B.C. until her fall to Babylonia in 605 B.C., Egypt had dominated Judah. With the momentous victory over Egypt at Carchemish, Babylonia began to rule Judah. Nevertheless Egypt continued to try to regain the Judean allegiance, frequently encouraging Judah to rebel against Babylonia. The Egyptian Pharaoh Hophra tried unsuccessfully to interrupt the Babylonians' siege of Jerusalem.

Ezekiel's prophecies reflect this historical and chronological orientation. The advancement of Egyptian forces into Palestine under Hophra during Nebuchadnezzar's siege of Jerusalem seems to have precipitated this series of oracles. Ezekiel's first message is a general prophecy of Egypt's complete desolation because of her pride and her unreliable support of Judah (29:1–16). In his third prophecy (30:20–26), Ezekiel refers to the defeats of Pharaoh Hophra by the Babylonian forces; this was only the beginning of

God's judgments on Egypt. The entire nation would be destroyed because of Egypt's arrogant pride, a haughtiness that Ezekiel likens to that of Assyria at her height of power. But as Assyria was brought down by God, so also Egypt would fall (see Ezekiel's fourth message, 31:1–18). The prophet follows his judgment messages with a lament over Egypt's demise (32:1–16). A summary of his oracles of judgment against Egypt and a warning to the Judean exiles to turn to the Lord and live while there was still opportunity conclude Ezekiel's prophecies (32:17–33:20).

The second prophecy (29:17–30:19) is chronologically out of place; Ezekiel's thematic concern overweighs his chronological concern. By placing this chronologically final message immediately after the introductory prophecy of December/January 588/587 B.C. (29:1–16), Ezekiel provides an immediate and a full understanding that Egypt's ultimate and complete destruction, as foretold in that first message, would come through the Babylonians after 571 B.C. Likewise, the placement of the 571 B.C. message (29:17–30:19) after the introductory prophecy against Egypt provides a transition from the judgments on Tyre to those on Egypt. Nebuchadnezzar was the instrument of judgment on Tyre; but since he did not secure the spoils of war from that city because of Egypt's intervention, God said he would give Egypt as spoils to Babylonia instead. Finally, with the knowledge of ultimate judgment on Egypt acquired, each succeeding prophecy in this series of six messages can be better understood.

1. The introductory prophecy of judgment on Egypt (29:1–16)

1–7 Pharaoh is likened to a crocodile ("monster"; GK 9490) in the midst of the Nile that the Lord would catch, pull from the Nile, and leave on the dry land to die. Though the word used here may be translated either "monster" or "crocodile," it seems best in light of Egyptian culture and religion to use the imagery most fitting to the Egyptians. The "crocodile" was a fearful creature of the Nile. It was normally caught with hooks in the jaws and then pulled on dry land where it would be slaughtered. The crocodile god was considered Egypt's protector.

In the imagery the crocodile represented the pharaoh, the protector of Egypt, who dominated the Nile (i.e., all Egypt). This was Hophra's arrogant self-image. In his reign he sent an expedition against Cyprus, besieged and took Gaza (cf. Jer 47:1) and the city of Sidon, was victorious against Tyre by sea, and considered himself master over Palestine and Phoenicia. Such pride was consistent with the denunciation in this message, for the pharaoh felt that the Nile (Egypt) belonged to him and that he had created it for himself. This arrogance had also shown itself in an attempt to interrupt Babylonia's siege of Jerusalem—an attempt thwarted by God.

The imagery of catching a crocodile beautifully expresses God's judgment on the pharaoh. He would be pulled from his position of dominance and pride and left as carnage for the birds and animals. He would not even be afforded the royal burial so important to the pharaohs, a horrible fate. The indictment was broadened to include all Egyptians ("fish"?), for as a nation they had failed to be of political support to Israel. Rather, they were as a staff made of reeds that shattered when Israel leaned on it, seriously wounding her (cf. Isa 36:6).

8–16 Both the pharaoh and all Egypt would perish, and the land would become desolate when God brought the sword against that land because of their pride. The desolation would affect the entire country from Migdol in the northeast delta to Seveneh (located at modern Aswan opposite Elephantine Island on the east bank near the first cataract). These sites were ancient Egypt's northern and southern boundaries. The judgment would also extend into Cush (modern Ethiopia), between the Nile's second and third cataracts. The streams or canals in the Nile's delta would be affected also (cf. 30:12; 32:13–14).

While Egypt was desolate for forty years, her inhabitants would be scattered among the nations at the hands of the Babylonians. Egypt's fate was like a repetition of Judah's (cf. the forty years parallel in 4:6). If Egypt fell to the Babylonians about 568 B.C., as implied in the chronicles of the Babylonian kings, then a forty-year "captivity" of Egypt would end under the Persians. Since the Persians returned many of the peoples displaced by the Babylonians, this very well may be the case. Just because there is no direct statement in ancient history concerning this dispersion does not mean that it did not occur. God's word is more valid than our conjectures or ignorance.

When Egypt would be restored to her land after forty years, she would inhabit the area of Pathros or "Upper Egypt," the land area essentially between modern Cairo and Aswan. Never again would Egypt be a great kingdom. It would always be lowly and weak. No longer would Israel look with confidence toward Egypt. Every time she would look to Egypt in the future, Israel would be reminded of her sin in turning to Egypt for help in the past.

The purpose of God's judgment messages is always the same. He desires that those judged recognize that he is the Lord, the only true God, the God of Israel.

2. A day of the Lord: the consummation of Egypt's judgment (29:17–30:19)

a. Babylonia's compensation of Egypt for the spoilless siege of Tyre (29:17–21)

17–21 As a fulfillment of God's judgment on Tyre, Nebuchadnezzar and the Babylonian army laid siege to Tyre for thirteen years. The scant historical data indicate that Egypt and Tyre became allies under Pharaoh Hophra (Apries). The extended siege of Tyre was perhaps due to the aid Tyre received from the Egyptians. In such an act Hophra was going contrary to God's purposes. Not only was the siege prolonged by Egyptian support, but possibly Egypt's maritime aid enabled Tyre to send away her wealth for security during the siege. When Tyre surrendered about 573 B.C., Babylonia gained almost no spoils from the long siege. Therefore God promised in this latest-dated oracle of Ezekiel on Egypt that Nebuchadnezzar would receive Egypt as compensation for the spoils he failed to receive from Tyre. "Every head was rubbed bare and every shoulder made raw" indicates that they were carrying heavy loads on their heads and shoulders during the siege. Nebuchadnezzar would carry off Egypt's superior wealth as pay for his army and as a belated "reward" for his execution of God's judgment against Tyre.

For the first time the instrument of God's judgment on Egypt is revealed to be Babylonia under Nebuchadnezzar's leadership (cf. Jer 43:8–13). Since Nebuchadnezzar died in 562 B.C., this predicted desolation of Egypt by Nebuchadnezzar's army would have to have occurred before then. Historical notices imply that Babylonia invaded Egypt about 568/567 B.C.

God used Babylonia's conquest of Egypt to strengthen and encourage Israel in exile. The passage treats the judgment on Egypt and states that at the time of Nebuchadnezzar's invasion "a horn" will grow for Israel. The symbol must refer to the strength (cf. NIV note) and encouragement that Israel was to receive when she observed God's faithfulness in executing his judgment on her enemy, Egypt, in accord with these prophecies and the Abrahamic covenant (Ge 12:3). At this time Ezekiel's mouth would be opened among the exiles to proclaim God's purposes and workings more freely, since the exiles would be more ready to listen. Through these events the Israelites would perceive that the God who was accomplishing these mighty acts in faithfulness was the Lord their God.

b. Nebuchadnezzar's invasion of Egypt (30:1–19)

1–19 A "day of the LORD" may be any specific time period when God does a special work. The context demonstrates that this "day of the LORD" relates specifically to God's judgment on Egypt through Babylonia, with Nebuchadnezzar being the agent of judgment. In addition, the event is called a "day of Egypt," limiting the judgment to Egypt and her satellites alone. It would occur during the "time of doom for the nations," when Babylonia would bring God's wrath on those nations that had in some manner "cursed" Israel (cf. 25:32; Jer 25, 27, 45–48).

Egypt's day of the Lord, a day of doom, would be a dark day in her history ("a day of clouds"). The masses would fear as Egypt's proud strength ceased before Nebuchadnezzar's sword. Many would be slain. Egypt's great riches would be carried off to Babylonia along with many people. Not even a prince (leader) would be left in the country. Many idolatrous statues of the Egyptian gods would be destroyed in the Babylonian quest for complete victory and wealth.

The entire land would lie desolate from Migdol in the north to Syene in the south. Pathros, the major portion of Upper Egypt between modern Cairo and Aswan, would be

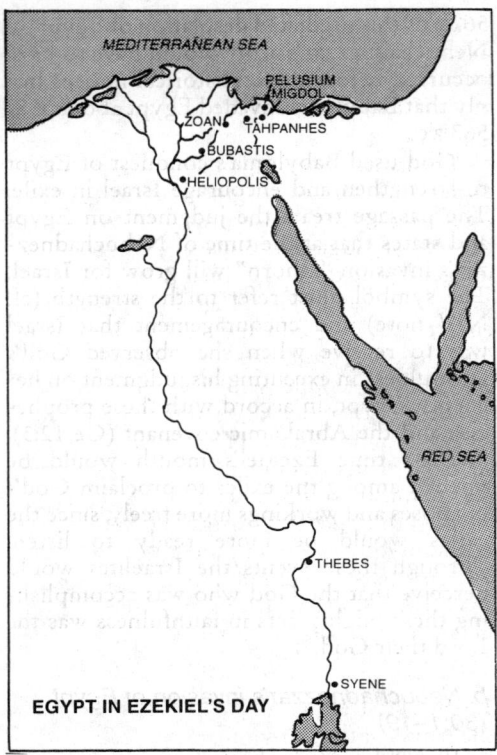

EGYPT IN EZEKIEL'S DAY

had sought to interrupt Babylonia's siege of Jerusalem at some point during the year 588 B.C. (Jer 34:1, 21–22; 37:5, 9). The Judeans' hopes were raised in expectation of deliverance from the siege. However, Hophra was not successful. The Babylonians defeated him and his army and sent them back to Egypt, after which Nebuchadnezzar renewed his siege of Jerusalem. The prophetic message in these verses follows Hophra's abortive intervention by a few months (March/April 587 B.C.). God declares that he had shattered Hophra's arm. The flexed arm was a common Egyptian symbol for the pharaoh's strength. Therefore Hophra's defeat was suitably represented by "breaking his arm." Ezekiel takes the imagery further by declaring that Hophra's arm had not been splinted so that it might heal.

This initial defeat of the Egyptian pharaoh was only a prelude of the complete devastation that God would bring on Egypt by Babylonia. In contrast God would strengthen Nebuchadnezzar's arms and place the Lord's sword in his hand to enable him to bring complete disability to Egypt. Nebuchadnezzar would symbolically break both arms of the pharaoh, so that Hophra would be unable to hold a sword at all. This occurred about 568 B.C. Again God reminds Egypt of her dispersion among the nations at that final destruction (cf. 29:12; 30:17–18). The result is equally reinforced: the Egyptians would realize that it was the Lord who brought this judgment.

laid waste. Egypt's major cities would bear the punishment of Babylon: Zoan in the northeastern delta; Thebes, Egypt's perennial southern capital; Pelusium, the residence of the ruling Twenty-Sixth Dynasty of Ezekiel's day located on the northeast border; Heliopolis, a major religious center; Bubastis; and Tahpanhes (cf. Jer 43:7–9). The Nile's streams would be dried up (cf. 32:13–14).

Egypt's allies would fall also to Babylonia's sword: Cush (Ethiopia), Lydia in western Anatolia (modern Turkey), Arabia, and Libya. Even the Judeans ("people of the covenant land"), who probably had fled to Egypt following Gedaliah's assassination (2Ki 25:23–26; Jer 43), would suffer under the Babylonian invasion. The judgment would be comprehensive and awful, though God's purpose would be accomplished. This judgment was a manifestation of God's grace; for through it he would finally cause the Egyptians to understand that he, the Lord God of Israel, is the only true God.

3. Pharaoh's broken arms (30:20–26)

20–26 Ezekiel returns to his chronological sequence of messages (v.1). Pharaoh Hophra

4. Egypt's fall compared with Assyria's fall (31:1–18)

1–9 This beautiful poetic message was delivered two months after the previous prophecy concerning the shattering of Egypt's strength (May/June 587 B.C.). The implication is that Egypt was still proud. Ezekiel uses the imagery of a great cedar of Lebanon, the tallest of the known trees, to represent Assyria, which had recently fallen (612 B.C.). Egypt, in turn, is compared with Assyria. The great cedar (Assyria) was well-watered—an indirect reference to her great water sources in the Tigris and Euphrates rivers. Egypt, of course, equally prided herself in her unending supply of Nile water. The cedar (Assyria) had been higher than all other trees (or nations); and she was more beautiful than any other tree, even every original variety of beautiful tree in the Garden of Eden. Every bird nested in her boughs, and every beast bore its young and was shaded under her branches. These birds and beasts represented the nations under Assyria's control and in her service (cf. Da 4:10–12, 19–22; Mt 13:31–32). Assyria was perhaps the greatest nation known to that point in history.

10–17 Assyria became proud of her greatness ("height"). For this cause the cedar (Assyria) was handed over to the ruler of nations (Nebuchadnezzar) to treat her as she had treated other nations—ruthlessly. She was cut down and cast aside by the most ruthless of foreign nations. God restrained Assyria's water source. She was worthless after her fall. All nations (other trees, birds, and beasts) mourned and trembled at the cedar's demise. No other nation of that day would ever reach the height that Assyria had reached.

18 If Egypt thought she was more majestic and had greater splendor than other nations of her day, the Lord reminds her that she too would "be brought down." She would "die" disgracefully as an uncircumcised foreigner without a decent burial—a horrible thought for proud Egyptian royalty that cherished its royal burial and despised foreigners. If God brought Assyria down, Egypt could be certain that she, who had never come close to Assyria's greatness, would also fall.

5. A funeral dirge for Egypt (32:1–16)

1–10 Two months had passed since the exiles in Babylonia had learned of Jerusalem's fall seven months earlier. As they began to comprehend that the Lord did exist and had been faithful to destroy Jerusalem even as he had said, they perhaps wondered whether God would be faithful to punish the heathen nations as he had declared. Conversely, Egypt had seen the collapse of Jerusalem and Judah, and Egypt may have begun to gloat in pride over her own survival and power. Lest the Egyptians think that God would not follow through to judge them, and lest the exiles begin questioning their new understanding of God's faithfulness to his word, Ezekiel delivers this funeral dirge for Egypt in March 585 B.C.

In the previous judgment prophecies against nations, Ezekiel often followed a judgment message with a lament over that nation. So, having delivered three oracles of condemnation, Ezekiel composes a funeral dirge. He portrays Egypt as dead, and so the funeral dirge was to be sung by the "daughters of the nations" as they watched Egypt expire.

The lament over Egypt is principally a recapitulation of the judgment messages, emphasizing Egypt's false pride and bewailing the fate of judgment. Once again the double imagery portrays the pharaoh's energetic pride but ineffective strength. Hophra is likened to a young lion and a thrashing crocodile that only muddies the streams of the Nile. The crocodile would be captured with a net and hurled on the open field as food for the birds and animals. The carnage would be so great that it would fill every ravine and mountain. It would be as if a great darkness covered the land, demonstrating that Egypt's great sun gods were impotent to help. Cosmic collapse is a common image with earth-shaking events. The nations who sang this funeral dirge would be stunned and horrified that Egypt had fallen in their midst.

11–16 The slaughter of Egypt would occur at the hands of the Babylonians, the most ruthless of all peoples. Everyone and every place would be touched, including the great Nile. When all life had disappeared, then the Nile would cease to be stirred up and would flow as smoothly as oil. Only then would Egypt's pride be shattered. So much did God care for Egypt that in his grace he brought this severe judgment so that they might finally realize that the Lord was the only true God and they would turn to him.

6. Ezekiel's summary lament over Egypt (32:17–32)

17–32 This is Ezekiel's final prophecy against Egypt, and it concludes his oracles against the nations (chs. 25–32). It was given in April 585 B.C. Ezekiel must wail for the Egyptians because they too would descend into the pit of death, as had all other mighty nations that had preceded them. Egypt would not be favored over the uncircumcised nations she had proudly disdained. She too would die a shameful, barbarian's death like all the other countries. God had wrought his terror on them, and he would continue to bring his terror on any nation that dealt violently with others in this world. That is the reason God quickly brought his terror through the Babylonians against Egypt.

F. Ezekiel's Warning to the Exiles (33:1–20)

1–20 This latter half of Ezekiel's concluding prophecy against Egypt echoes two previous messages: Ezekiel's commission as a watchman (v.7; ch. 3) and his exhortation to individual responsibility (v.8; chs. 3; 18). He had faithfully performed his watchman duty for Israel (v.9), warning her of God's impending judgment on the horizon (chs. 4–24). Three to four months prior to this present message, Ezekiel had also encouraged the people with messages of hope concerning their ultimate restoration to the land (33:21–39:29). They had not heeded his warning concerning judgment and consequently found themselves in captivity, with Jerusalem and Judah in ashes. Ezekiel was exonerated from guilt for the destruction and captivity because he had been God's responsible watchman. The Judeans could only blame themselves for failing to heed the warning. Therefore, Ezekiel gives one final warning to the exiles: Turn *now* to the Lord! At least the exiles had come to recognize that God's judgment had come because of their sin, not their parents' sin (cf. ch. 18).

Ezekiel seeks to encourage the exiles. God does not find pleasure in death because of wickedness. Conversely, God delights in those who turn from sin, follow his ways in the Mosaic covenant, and live! Each individual is personally responsible for his or her righteousness or wickedness. If one is declared righteous, it was because he or she has decided personally to follow the Lord. If one is judged wicked, it was because he or she personally has decided to reject the Lord and to live according to his or her own desires. To some Judeans it did not seem that God's ways were fair and just. However, God's ways are always fair and just, for he does not blame one person for another's sin. The Lord fairly judges every person according to his or her own actions.

IV. The Future Blessings of a Faithful Covenant God (33:21–48:35)

The majority of evangelical interpreters claim to use a "literal" grammatical-historical hermeneutic. However, that hermeneutic is viewed differently by different groups within evangelicalism. Some hold "literal" to mean "literalistic," meaning a straightforward reading of the text (usually excluding figures of speech). Others understand that "literal" interpretation allows for figures of speech, historical perspective, contextual study, progressive revelation, analogy of faith, etc. Still others understand "literal" as reading Scripture in a normal literal manner with most prophetic material seen as symbolic and figurative. Since most evangelicals maintain that they consistently use a literal hermeneutic and that others do not, the approach taken in this commentary will be briefly outlined.

This commentary approaches chs. 33–48 with a straightforward reading of the text in the light of history, context, figures of speech, the analogy of faith, progressive revelation, etc. The flow of the argument of the book is emphasized within the context of the entire canon of Scripture and its themes. Apocalyptic visions are viewed as containing considerable symbolism as well as much reality. The interpretations of divine interpreters within visions are followed. These interpreters interpret symbols (cf. ch. 37) but allow to be taken as reality what may be understood in a straightforward reading of the text (e.g., the temple in chs. 40–42). Spiritual lessons may be learned from the realities, even as the future temple of chs. 40–48, with its sacrifices, conveys spiritual lessons as described by the divine interpreter (e.g., the importance of holiness).

This commentary presents a view of Israel's future restoration to the land after which she will be cleansed, receive a new heart, and live in security and prosperity under the Messiah's rule in his future millennial kingdom. A literal temple will be constructed according to detailed plans in order to display God's holiness. Sacrifices will be instituted as memorials of the soteriological work of Christ on the cross. A real river will flow from the temple to heal the land. A completely new geographical setting will be established.

A. Restoration to the Promised Land (33:21–39:29)

God desires to bless; he does not delight in cursing. However, both blessing and cursing are very much a part of God's covenant program. Ezekiel's entire prophecy is given in light of God's covenants with Israel. In order to perceive the unity and development of

Ezekiel, it is necessary to understand God's covenants (see chart at 1Ch 17).

The *Abrahamic covenant* is God's basic program for blessing the world (Ge 12:1–3). In this covenant God declared that he would choose one man, Abram; from that one man he would create the nation Israel; and through that nation he would bless the world. For a nation to exist three elements are needed: a people, a government, and a homeland. The people of Israel came into being in Egypt from the twelve sons of Jacob (Israel). Israel's government was received on Mount Sinai in the form of the Mosaic covenant; the land was acquired through the conquest of Canaan under Joshua.

The *Mosaic covenant* (Ex 20–Nu 9, Deuteronomy) provided Israel's constitution, which governed all aspects of life. As Israel kept the Mosaic covenant, she would appropriate the blessings of the Abrahamic covenant; e.g., being in the land of blessing and being a blessing to the nations. However, at any point in history when Israel disobeyed the Mosaic covenant, she would find also that she did not benefit from Abrahamic covenant blessings and, in turn, would not be a blessing to the nations. Israel's failure to follow the Mosaic covenant was what caused her to be exiled in Babylonia. Israel found that her God was faithful to bring the judgments of Dt 27–28 on her.

In the *Davidic covenant* (2Sa 7:12–16) God promised that David's descendants would always sit on his throne: an eternal throne over an eternal kingdom. The concept of the Messiah is based on this covenant, for each king of Israel was a messiah, an "anointed one." This covenant promised that someday the final son of David would rule on David's throne.

Jeremiah announced a *new covenant* that God would make with his people, a covenant that would replace the functions of the Mosaic covenant. It would incorporate the Mosaic covenant in that its laws would be written on the hearts of those who believed in the Messiah. Under its provisions, all sin would be forgiven once and for all (by the Messiah), and the Spirit of God would be poured out on all who believed (cf. ch. 36; 2Co 3).

All these covenants provide the backdrop for Ezekiel's messages. After receiving his commission (chs. 1–3), Ezekiel warned Israel that the Lord would judge (curse) her in accord with the Mosaic covenant: she would be dispersed among the nations, and Jerusalem and Judah would become desolate (chs. 4–23). In ch. 24 Ezekiel declared that in the siege of Jerusalem, the execution of God's prophesied judgment on his people had begun. Then, as a reminder of God's faithfulness to the Abrahamic covenant, Ezekiel announced judgment on those nations that had oppressed Israel (25:1–33:20).

The fall of Jerusalem forms the pivotal point of Ezekiel's prophecy. The warnings against God's people had been consummated with that fall. But now there was the need to encourage the exiles that the Lord was as faithful to his promises to bless as he was to those to curse. The remainder of Ezekiel (33:21–48:35) emphasizes the blessings of the covenants. God promises to restore Israel to her land (Mosaic covenant, specifically Dt 30) and place within her a new heart and a new Spirit (new covenant). She will dwell in peace and security as her Lord, the Messiah, reigns over her (Davidic covenant). All God's promises of blessing will be consummated in the fulfillment of each covenant, including the *peace covenant*. The Messiah will reign over Israel forever, and no one will ever again dispossess Israel from her land.

The concept of the land is particularly significant to the six messages delivered in that one night before the news of Jerusalem's fall reached the exiles in Babylonia. Since Jerusalem had fallen, would the land be lost to Israel (33:21–33)? It was the false "shepherds" of Israel who had lost the land for Israel by leading the people astray from the truth. But the true "shepherd," the Messiah, would ultimately restore the land to Israel (ch. 34). Those foreigners who had possessed the land of Israel and had oppressed her people would be judged and removed so that Israel might again possess her own land (35:1–36:15). Then God would restore Israel to the Promised Land, an action described in 36:16–38 and beautifully illustrated in the apocalyptic vision of 37:1–14. Israel would return united with the Messiah as her singular ruler, and the Lord would inaugurate his peace covenant with her (37:15–28). Never again would a foreign power have dominion over Israel in her land (chs. 38–39).

1. Israel and the Promised Land (33:21–33)

21–22 The date and setting of the six messages in 33:21–39:29 are given in these two verses. Ezekiel had closed ch. 24 by prophesying that a fugitive would escape Jerusalem's destruction and come and report the city's fall to the Babylonian exiles. The fulfillment of that prophecy is in these verses. The siege of Jerusalem had begun in December/January 589/588 B.C. (24:1; 2Ki 25:1). Two years and seven months later, Jerusalem fell (September 586 B.C.; 2Ki 25:8). As the city fell, an unknown fugitive escaped—or was brought by the Babylonians—and came to report Jerusalem's destruction to the exiles. Five months later (December/January 586/585 B.C.), on the morning after Ezekiel delivered these six messages, that anticipated report came. Ezekiel's muteness, which had lasted for seven and one-half years (3:24–27), ended as God opened Ezekiel's mouth to speak these six messages of encouragement to the exiles immediately prior to their reception of the news of Jerusalem's fall (cf. 3:24–27).

23–29 The first of Ezekiel's six messages has two aspects: a question by the Judean remnant concerning the land (vv.23–29) and the manner in which the Israelites in Canaan and in Babylonia had responded to Ezekiel's ministry (vv.30–33). Jerusalem had fallen! Would Israel lose the land? The remnant in the ruins of Jerusalem were questioning the fate of the land promised to Abraham. Why were they, Abraham's descendants, now to be separated from the land given to their forefathers? Was not the Abrahamic covenant still valid? Did not the Abrahamic promises pertain to them as survivors of the destruction?

The Lord answers that the hope of keeping the Promised Land lay in a correct understanding of the covenants. For their disobedience of the Mosaic covenant stipulations, the Israelites failed to receive the Abrahamic covenant blessings, one of which was being in the Promised Land. The people had violated the Mosaic covenant statutes: they had eaten blood (cf. Lev 17:10–14; 19:26), worshiped idols (18:6; cf. Ex 20:4–5), made detestable things, shed blood with the sword (18:10; cf. Ex 20:13), and defiled one another's wife (18:6; 22:11; cf. Ex 20:14). In light of such violations, did they really think they should possess the land?

God's verdict was no! The judgments of the Mosaic covenant (Dt 27:28; 29:25–29) were being executed: those left in Judah would die by the sword or disease, or fall prey to animals. Their arrogant pride would cease. The land would become a desolation and waste. Most important, God's purpose for judgment on his people would be accomplished: they would come to know that he was their God when these judgments were executed.

30–33 The Israelites in exile and the remnant in Palestine had looked on Ezekiel's ministry in mockery. They had gossiped that they should go and hear God's word. Yet when they came to Ezekiel to listen to his messages, they had not acted in accord with his warnings. They orally expressed devotion, but their hearts were greedy for material gain. They were "playing games" with God. To them Ezekiel was no more than a good entertainer. He was amusing to listen to and to watch, with all his symbolic acts and prophecies. But just as an entertainer demands no response, so they did not sense a need to respond to Ezekiel's messages. However, as Ezekiel's prophecies became reality—and such had already begun in the fall of Jerusalem—then Israel would realize that a true prophet had been among them.

2. Shepherds false and true (34:1–31)

a. The accusation against the false shepherds (34:1–6)

1–6 In the previous message Ezekiel explained that Palestine had been lost to Israel because she had violated the Mosaic covenant. Therefore she would not now experience the blessing of being in the Promised Land, a blessing of the Abrahamic covenant only experienced when the nation obeyed the Mosaic covenant stipulations. But the more severe indictment belonged to Israel's leaders, depicted as "shepherds."

This judgment speech sets forth the reason for God's judgment on Israel's past "shepherds." Israel's leaders had thought only of themselves and material gain. They had not cared for the "flock." Instead of feeding the flock, they fed on the flock, taking food and clothing for themselves instead of providing for the people. They had failed to provide for the needy—those weak and sick. They had not sought for sheep that had been lost. They did not care what happened to the people as long as they had all their own personal needs met. They were harsh and brutal in their rule. God makes it clear that a leader has a primary responsibility to care for those he leads, even at the sacrifice of his own desires.

Because of the de facto lack of a shepherd to lead them, the flock of Israel was led astray and ended up being scattered among the nations (cf. Jer 23:9–10). Since they no longer had a shepherd's protection, they became as food for wild beasts. There was no shepherd to search them out and care for them (cf. Mt 9:36). Lack of leadership always leads to the disintegration of God's people and to personal and corporate heartache and injury.

b. God's verdict concerning the leadership of Israel (34:7–31)

7–10 Normal judicial procedure required repeating the accusation immediately before announcing the verdict. Israel's "shepherds" had been selfish, insensitive leaders who had plundered the flock for personal gain and had allowed the people to become prey for other nations. On this basis, God promises to remove the leaders from their position so that the flock of Israel might no longer be devoured by these wolves in shepherds' clothes. The Lord would hold each "false shepherd" accountable for his shepherding.

11–16b Though the people of Israel were responsible for their own actions, they had been led astray by brutal leaders. The Lord encourages the flock of Israel by declaring that he would personally assume the responsibility for "shepherding" them. The Lord promises to search, rescue, and regather the scattered flock from the nations, and to care for them as a loving shepherd. He would restore Israel to her own land and feed her on the lush pastures of her own mountains and ravines. Individual needs would finally be met; those lost would be sought and found. The injured would be healed; the weak would be strengthened. The Lord would care for every need of his flock.

16c–24 God would shepherd his people in justice. Those who had taken advantage of the flock would be treated like all other sheep or goats. Previous shepherds were likened to fat, sleek, and strong sheep because they had

fed on the best pasture and drunk the clear water. Out of lack of concern for the flock's other members, they arrogantly had trampled the rest of the pasture and muddied the clear drinking water. They had abused their positions of strength and "bullied" the other sheep, driving them away. These "shepherds" would be judged and destroyed, for there was no place for such irresponsible behavior among leaders.

The Lord would deliver Israel from all distress, whether from poor leadership or from the predatory nations. He would do so by appointing one true and responsible Shepherd for his people: the Messiah, his servant David. The Lord would be Israel's God; his servant David, the Messiah, would be Israel's Ruler on earth after he restored Israel to her land. Two members of the Godhead are clearly discerned with varying functions. The phrase "my servant David" regularly referred to the Messiah. Jeremiah equated the Messiah with the true Shepherd from the line of David, calling him "a righteous Branch," "the LORD Our Righteousness" (Jer 23:5–6). The identity is also implied elsewhere in the Prophets (Jer 30:9; Eze 37:24–25; Hos 3:5).

25–31 Finally, the Lord encourages Israel with the establishment of another covenant with them: the "covenant of peace" (cf. 37:26–28; 38:11–13; 39:25–29). This is *not* the new covenant. This peace covenant will be inaugurated when the Lord has fulfilled all his other covenants with Israel. (1) This covenant guarantees the ultimate removal of all foreign nations ("wild beasts") from Israel's land, so that she may live securely. (2) God will bless Israel and her land with "showers of blessings." The result will be full satisfaction from the land's abundant produce. (3) Israel will live in complete security. No longer will she be plundered or scorned by the nations; never again will she experience famine. (4) When God delivers Israel from all her captors and restores her safely to her land, then she will have realized that he truly is the Lord her God. (5) The Mosaic formula of relationship between Israel and the Lord will become a reality. The Lord will truly become their God, and they will finally be his people, following his ways at every turn. According to Jeremiah, this relationship will be entered when Israel accepts the new covenant

(Jer 31:31–34) instituted by the Mediator of that covenant, the Messiah (cf. Heb 8:6).

This announcement of the peace covenant provides a transition to the following messages delivered in this series of six oracles. Each elaborates an aspect of the peace covenant. Ezekiel 35:1–36:15 describes how the foreign plundering nations will be removed and judged in preparation for Israel's return to her own land. The message in 36:16–37:14 provides a beautiful and descriptive account of God's restoration of Israel to her land. Ezekiel 37:15–28 stresses the full reunion of the nation and the fulfillment of her covenants when this peace covenant is established. Finally, Ezekiel 38–39 develops the concept of Israel's complete security in the Lord, for he will thwart the final attempt by a foreign power (Gog) to possess Israel's land and to plunder God's people.

Israel could rejoice; for though she had experienced the cruel leadership of recent rulers, she is now assured that God will provide perfect leadership through the Good Shepherd, the Messiah, who will care for her as a shepherd should. There was hope!

3. Preparation of the land (35:1–36:15)

a. Removal of oppressors (35:1–15)

1–9 Ezekiel had encouraged the Babylonian exiles that they would no longer be governed by predatory rulers. Instead the Lord would establish his Messiah as their "shepherd." But what about the land of Israel? Did it not lie desolate? Were there not foreign oppressors presently ruling that country? How would the Messiah govern his people in a land ravaged by foreigners? These questions likely came to the captives' minds as they listened to Ezekiel. The Lord understood these concerns and desired to ease their fears by announcing that he would personally remove all foreign oppressors from Israel and prepare that land to receive her people.

Edom (Mount Seir; cf. v.15) was most likely chosen as a representative of those nations that had sought to occupy Israel's land and exert dominion over her. Edom, perhaps more than any other nation, had continually detested and resented Israel. It started with the conflict between Jacob (Israel) and Esau (Edom) (Ge 25:22–34; 27; 36:1). Edom had sought to block Israel's first entrance into the Promised Land (Nu 20:14–21; 24:15–19).

There were conflicts during the times of Saul (1Sa 14:47), Solomon (1Ki 11:14–22), Jehoshaphat (2Ch 20:1–23), Jehoram (2Ki 8:21), and Ahaz (2Ch 28:17). The prophets regularly made reference to Edom's antagonism toward Israel and the resulting judgment they would receive (Isa 11:11–16; Da 11:41; Am 2:1). Malachi demonstrated that the hatred between these nations was still common in his day (Mal 1:2–5). Therefore, it was fitting that Ezekiel used Edom as the epitome of nations that sought to overrun and acquire Israel's land for themselves.

Two brief accusations (vv.5, 10) against Edom are followed by respective verdicts (vv.6, 9, 11–15). First, Edom is indicted on two charges: she had harbored hostility against Israel throughout her history (cf. 25:12), and she was the accomplice of other nations and had delivered Israel over to them whenever possible. Psalm 137:7 and La 4:21–22 imply that Edom gladly aided the Babylonian invasion of Judah in 589–586 B.C. Obadiah 10–14 also denounces Edom for her betrayal of Israel in time of need. The implication of Ezekiel's accusation is that Edom would someday be Israel's antagonist again.

God would punish Edom. Since Edom had not refrained from bloodshed in her hatred of Israel, the Lord would bring unbridled bloodshed on Edom. Edom's land would be filled with inhabitants slain by the sword. As Edom had been continually hostile toward Israel, so God would bring an unending desolation throughout Mount Seir (cf. 25:12–14; Jer 49:13, 17; Ob 18). Cities would be uninhabited. No one would carry on normal relations with Edom, for she would not

Edomite towns east of Beersheba and west of the Dea Sea flourished in the seventh century B.C., until the Babylonian destruction of Judah in 586. This hill, like many hills in Palestine, contains the remains of a town.

exist. As a result of this judgment, however, Edom would know that the one who brought this discipline was the God of Israel, the only true God.

10–15 The second reason for judgment on Edom was threefold: Edom desired to control Israel and Judah; Edom, in her desire to devour Israel, had defamed her with contempt and had spoken boastfully against the Lord; and Edom had failed to recognize the God of Israel as the only true God. Edom felt that the Lord did not care what she did or hear what she said.

As Edom had done to Israel out of her anger, jealousy, and hatred, so God would do to Edom. Such a display of God's vindication against Edom would cause Israel to recognize that truly this was her God who was intervening on her behalf. Likewise, since Edom had rejoiced when Israel became desolate, so the Lord would make Edom desolate when all the earth is happy. This implies that Edom will not exist in the end time when God brings unparalleled joy to this earth. Through this judgment Edom will recognize that the God of Israel does exist and is the only true God.

b. A prophecy of encouragement (36:1–15)

1–12 This prophecy of encouragement takes the form of a judgment speech. The land of Israel could make the following charges against foreign nations: many nations had claimed the right of ownership of Israel, including her ancient religious sites; the nations surrounding Israel had brought desolation to Palestine as they trampled through the land in conquest. The land of Israel had become a mockery of evil rumors and gossip among the nations.

The Lord vindicates his righteousness and his people. He had declared in the Abrahamic covenant that he would bless those who bless Israel, but he also would curse those who curse his people (Ge 12:3). Therefore God declares that Israel has had enough scorn and shame from the nations. His fiery jealousy will come against those who had joyously and scornfully invaded Israel for spoils. As the nations had brought shame on Israel, so the Lord will cause them to bear shame and disgrace. He will emphatically lift up his hand against the nations in a symbol of strength and wrath. He will exonerate his people.

Blessing normally follows judgment in God's scheme. So, having pronounced judgment on the scornful nations, the Lord turns to encourage Israel by describing his preparation of her land for her return in the end time. This will be his work.

The mountains of Israel are contrasted with Mount Seir. After Israel's destruction one might have expected Mount Seir to triumph over the mountains of Israel. Though the land of Israel lay desolate in Ezekiel's day, God looks with favor on it and promises that he will prepare that land for Israel's return by making it productive and fruitful once again. The land will be encouraged by receiving its own people back. All Israel will return. The people and the cattle will be more plentiful than ever before. Her cities will again be inhabited and every waste place rebuilt. In demonstration of God's faithfulness to the Abrahamic covenant, Israel will finally possess her land as the inheritance promised by God but never before fully realized. When God restores his people, the condition of the land will surpass any previous state of the land. But will the land be deprived of its children (the Israelites) again and become desolate? The Lord reassures Israel that when God regathers his people to the Promised Land in that last regathering of the end times, the land will never again be deprived of its children. All will recognize that the Lord has done this great thing.

13–15 The second charge brought against the land is that she has devoured people and, in turn, has become "childless" among the nations. This conclusion arises from observing the many horrible misfortunes Israel had experienced. God refutes this false charge, for he will restore his people to that land. Then Israel will no longer hear taunts of scorn and shame from the nations. She will never again bear such reproach and will never again cease to be a nation. God encourages the exiles by declaring that he will give them the Messiah as their ruler and will remove the oppressive nations from the land of Israel to prepare the way for the restoration of his people.

4. The restoration to the land (36:16–37:14)

Ezekiel's previous message concluded with a description of the Lord's preparation of the land of Canaan for the return of his people (36:1–15). This provides the natural transition from God's removal of foreign oppressors from the land (35:1–15) to the subject of this new message: Israel's restoration to her land. This prophecy emphasizes the people's return and contains four distinct parts. So that the Lord's grace and mercy in regathering his people may be fully understood, the reason for their scattering among the nations is outlined by contrast (36:16–21). This is followed by a beautifully detailed portrayal of how the Lord will restore the people to the land (36:22–32), followed by the effective results of that return (36:33–38). As an encouragement to the Babylonian exiles, Ezekiel concludes this oracle with an apocalyptic vision, illustrating the return of God's nation to the land promised to their forefathers (37:1–14).

a. The basis for Israel's dispersion (36:16–21)

16–21 To highlight the importance of Israel's reestablishment on the land of their forefathers, Ezekiel summarizes Israel's past history that had brought her dispersion among the nations. By her disobedience to the Mosaic covenant stipulations, Israel had defiled her sacred land. Israel's two major crimes were (1) bloodshed, which was brought among her own people through infanticide, intrigue, violence, and selfishness, and (2) idolatry, which pervaded the people's lives and drew them continually away from the Lord. Their actions were so abominable that the Lord regarded their defilement as impure as that of a woman during her menstrual cycle. God had set forth in Israel's constitution, the Mosaic covenant, that if she persisted in disobeying the lifestyle given to her in that covenant, he would scatter her people among the nations in discipline (cf. Dt 29:1–30:10). The Lord had been faithful to his word and had sown Israel like seed throughout the countries of that day.

God was so concerned that Israel be restored to a proper relationship with him that he sent his people out of the Promised Land so that they might learn the importance of following his ways. God's ways are always best, for as the Creator of life he knows how life can best be lived. But in disciplining Israel in this manner, the Lord risked his own reputation in the world. A nation was uniquely tied to its land in the ancient Near East. If a people were forced off their land, whether by conquest, famine, disease, or any other reason, this was a demonstration that their god was not sufficiently strong to protect and care for them. Therefore, when God scattered Israel among the nations, they perceived that Israel's God was weak; thereby the name of the Lord was profaned among them.

But the Lord would not allow his name to be defiled forever. Israel's return to her land would be based on the Lord's compassion for his own holy name that had been profaned (cf. Mt 6:9; Lk 11:2). Through Israel's restoration, God would demonstrate to the nations that he was the only true God. His name would be set apart in holiness, as it should be. Therefore, so that his name might be vindicated, the Lord would restore Israel to her land, and not because of any great thing she had done. What a contrast between God's holiness and grace and human sin! Sin never deserves mercy; yet the Lord always deals graciously and mercifully as well as justly.

b. A description of the final restoration (36:22–32)

22–23 In OT times one's "name" (GK 9005) represents the person. Through Israel's rebellion against God, the people had defamed God's person. Therefore, not only would his covenant faithfulness be displayed when he restored Israel to her land, but he would also bring honor and sanctity to his name and person throughout the nations, through his supernatural regathering of Israel. Then the nations would know that the righteous and loving God of Israel was the only true God.

24–32 The reestablishment of Israel on her land is wonderfully described in these verses. God had already foretold Israel's restoration after the Exile when Moses restated the Mosaic covenant on the plains of Moab (Dt 29:1–30:10). The pattern of restoration defined here is return, cleansing from sin, enablement of the Spirit, and prosperity.

(1) The Lord will remove his people from the nations where they have been scattered. He will gather them and bring them back to the land of Canaan, which had been promised to their forefathers in the Abrahamic covenant.

(2) The Lord will cleanse Israel in her land from all sin and idolatry that has defiled her. "Sprinkling with clean water" symbolizes cleansing through divine forgiveness by blood (cf. Ex 12:22; Lev 14:4–7; 49:53; Ps 51:7; 1Co 6:11). For ceremonial cleansing to be more than a ritual, it was essential that the people repent and acknowledge their past iniquity about which God would remind them. As they would loathe their former transgressions with their shame and disgrace, they would understand how gracious was their cleansing. Likewise, if ceremonial cleansing were to be meaningful, actual cleansing and forgiveness of sin must be made. This will be through the new covenant (Jer 31:31–34); for Israel's return to the land, the people will accept the Messiah as their Savior, through whose death all sin has been once and for all forgiven. Iniquity will be remembered no more. They will exchange their old rebellious hearts of stone for sensitive hearts of flesh.

(3) In the new covenant the people will also receive a new spirit, God's Holy Spirit (cf. 11:19–20; 18:31; 37:14; 39:29; Joel 2:28–29; Ac 2:17–18; 2Co 3:6–18), who will enable them to live God's way (cf. Ro 7:7–8:4; Heb 8:6–10:39). The old Mosaic covenant will be written on the hearts of those living under the new covenant (Jer 31:33). Therefore, the new covenant replaces the Mosaic covenant by adding those things that made it better, but not by eliminating the good, righteous, and godly stipulations that described how to live a godly life. The new covenant provides forgiveness of sin once and for all and the Holy Spirit's indwelling.

(4) A cleansed Israel will return permanently to a productive and plentiful land that will be more than "flowing with milk and honey" (vv. 1–15). Never again will the land allow Israel to be disgraced among the nations through famine. Likewise, the epitome of the Mosaic covenant for Israel and the Lord is expressed in a formula that now will become a reality: Israel will be God's people and he will be her God. The nations will observe this marvelous transformation and see the Lord as the only gracious and loving God, for Israel will not deserve restoration.

This context, along with the historical perspective, make it clear that the return mentioned in this passage does not refer to the return to Canaan under Zerubbabel, Ezra, and Nehemiah, but to a final and complete restoration under the Messiah in the end times. The details of Israel's reestablishment on her land set forth here simply did not occur in the return begun in 538 B.C.

c. The effects of the restoration (36:33–38)

33–38 The effects of Israel's restoration will be great. The land will produce like the Garden of Eden. It will be Paradise regained (cf. Isa 51:3; Ro 8:19–22; 2Pe 3:13; Rev 21:1–4, 23–27). Ruined cities will be rebuilt and fortified for the many inhabitants. The people of Israel will increase so much that they will constitute a large flock for the Shepherd, the Messiah. They will be numerous like the flocks kept for the many offerings in Jerusalem during Israel's appointed feasts. The most important consequence of Israel's restoration will be the spread of the knowledge of the Lord throughout the world. The nations will unequivocally know that Israel's God has accomplished this great restoration. They will know that he is not a weak god but the only God who does exactly what he says. Israel herself will humbly acknowledge that the one who restored her is the Lord her God.

d. A vision of restoration (37:1–14)

1–2 Chapter 37 begins by simply revealing the apocalyptic vision that concludes Ezekiel's message on Israel's future restoration. Apocalyptic literature is not familiar to most people. This type of literature is symbolic visionary-prophetic, consisting of visions recorded exactly as they are seen by the author and explained through a divine interpreter. The theological content is primarily eschatological, normally being composed during times of oppression. Apocalyptic literature has a simple twofold form: the setting of the vision, in which the recipient and the geographical location are identified, and the vision per se, with its divine interpretation.

Ezekiel is brought by the Lord into a valley (or plain), perhaps the same valley mentioned in ch. 1 where Ezekiel saw the visions of God. Ezekiel sees the valley filled with innumerable bones that are extremely dry. The Spirit of the Lord leads him around the valley, and he passes among these bones.

3–10 This apocalyptic vision has two distinct sections: (1) Ezekiel recounts what he sees and does and (2) the vision is interpreted (vv.11–14). The Lord asks Ezekiel whether these bones will live. Ezekiel replies that only the Lord knows. A prophecy is then given to Ezekiel for the dry bones. The Lord will cause them to live. Tendons, flesh, skin, and breath will come on the bones so that live people will be formed. Then this "resurrected" people will know that God is the Lord. So Ezekiel does exactly as the Lord commands and proclaims the Lord's words to the dead, dry bones. While he is speaking, all the bones come together and take on themselves tendons, flesh, and skin. But no breath is found in them.

Ezekiel is instructed to prophesy again, this time to the breath to come from the four winds—probably indicating the full power of the entering breath (i.e., from every direction) to renew the bodies—and to breathe on these slain ones so that they might live. On doing so, Ezekiel sees this army of people come alive! The recovery of the bones to form bodies pictures Israel's ultimate national restoration. "Breath" (also "wind" or "Spirit"; GK 8120) entering these restored bodies portrays spiritual renewal. This imitated the sequence in ch. 36.

11–14 Apocalyptic visions were never meant to have every detail interpreted; only the major thrust of the vision was to be grasped. The bones are identified as the whole house of Israel, the slain ones of v.9 (cf. 36:10). These bones will declare three things about themselves. (1) They were dry, an obvious condition of bones from people who have been dead for a very long time. Though duration of time may be implied by the dryness of the bones, the emphasis is on spiritual deadness. (2) The bones declare that their hope has perished. The people of Israel have lost all hope of becoming a nation again or of seeing God's covenants fulfilled. (3) The bones say that they were separated from one another, i.e., the people had been separated and dispersed; that was their current condition.

The vision itself is rather self-evident and needs no interpretation once the bones are identified. The vision clearly demonstrates the restoration to life of a people who have been dead for some time. It is in two stages: first physical (or national) restoration and then spiritual renewal. The creation of humankind followed a similar pattern: the body

formed first, then the breath received (cf. Ge 2:7).

This national and spiritual restoration is elaborated in the interpretation section through another figure, that of a resurrection from graves. Both the imagery of dry bones becoming live people and the figure of resurrection from a grave illustrate the same truth. Israel, nonexistent as a people on their own land and scattered throughout the nations, will be brought back to life physically as a nation in their own land. Just as the events in the vision were miraculous, so will be Israel's restoration. Once in the land they will be renewed spiritually when God places his Spirit within them in keeping with the new covenant and the message just delivered in ch. 36.

The entire context of these six messages is future. Israel's national restoration in the end time is in view (cf. the chapters surrounding chs. 36–37). It is not to be just a physical restoration or merely a spiritual restoration. A national regathering of Israel from among the nations in the end time, a spiritual conversion of Israel, and a reestablishment of the nation in the land of promise are all in view in 36:16–38 and in this apocalyptic vision.

This can genuinely be termed a "rebirth" of the nation. God will provide all three essentials—a people, a government, and a land—once again in this rebirth of Israel in the future. The people of that day are brought together through restoration in 36:16–37:28. The land is provided in the prophecy of 35:1–36:15. The government of renewed Israel will be given in chs. 40–48. When Israel is restored and becomes a nation once again, then the people will definitely know that the Lord did it and that he and no one else is their God.

5. Israel's reunion amid fulfilled covenants (37:15–28)

15–17 Ezekiel uses a symbolic act to demonstrate that the two previously divided kingdoms of Israel and Judah will once again be reunited when God brings his people back into their land. Israel will then be complete with all her covenants fulfilled. Ezekiel took two sticks. He wrote the names of Judah and her companions on one and those of Ephraim and her companions on the other—one stick representing the former kingdom of Judah, the other the previous kingdom of Israel. When Ezekiel put these two sticks together in his hand, they became one stick.

18–28 The union of the two sticks into one portrays the reunion of the nations of Judah and Israel into a united kingdom in the land promised in the Abrahamic covenant. Never again will the nation be divided. The Messiah, David's Greater Son, will be the only King, Shepherd, and Prince that reunited Israel will ever have, in accord with the Davidic covenant. This united people of God will be cleansed from their former idolatry and transgressions through the complete forgiveness provided by the Messiah's death and the ministry of the Spirit promised in the new covenant. By accepting the new covenant Israel will be enabled through the Holy Spirit to follow the righteous stipulations of the Mosaic covenant and to live by them. Then Israel will finally be the unique, choice people that God had created for himself; and he will be their God—finally fulfilling the ideal of the Mosaic covenant.

The Lord will enact his peace covenant (cf. 34:25–29) with Israel at the time of her restoration to the land, when all her other covenants with God will be fulfilled. Under this peace covenant Israel will be established in her land, her numbers will increase (cf. Ge 22:17–18), and the Lord will place his sanctuary among his people forever. Then all nations will see that it was the Lord who made Israel holy. She will be set apart from all nations as God's special possession. No other nation will have the Lord dwelling in its sanctuary uniquely in its midst as Israel.

When all Israel's covenants have been consummated, then the Lord will enact his peace covenant with Israel. She will dwell in peace forever under the rule of her king, the Messiah.

6. The Promised Land and foreign possession (38:1–39:29)

These two chapters may be viewed as isolated from the previous messages that were delivered on the night prior to the arrival of the fugitive from Jerusalem to announce Jerusalem's fall (cf. 33:21–22). The message in chs. 38–39, however, should be seen as the sixth and last in Ezekiel's series of messages delivered that night before the news came of Jerusalem's destruction.

A major subject of the five previous messages had been the land of Israel; it concluded with God's peace covenant with his people (see introductory comments on 33:21–39:29 for a summary of these messages). The message in chs. 38–39 initially describes the entire nation of Israel peacefully dwelling in their land in security. They were living without walls, bars, or doors (38:7). The remainder of the message describes a final attempt by foreigners to possess the land of Israel. The endeavor would fail because God, faithful to the peace covenant and his name, would defend Israel. He would not permit his holy name to be profaned again by a conquest and dispersal of Israel (36:20; 39:7).

The events and details of chs. 38–39 are relatively easy to understand. The major interpretative difficulties are the identity of characters and places, and the time when these events occur.

a. The initial judgment speech against Gog (38:1–23)

1–3 Ezekiel prophesied against Gog of the land of Magog, the chief prince of Meshech and Tubal. The exact identity of each proper name has spawned many interpretations of this text. None of the proposed solutions have sufficient support to warrant their acceptance as the identity of the term "Gog." It does seem that Gog was a person, whether mentioned in this context by name or by title. Fortunately the specific identity of Gog is unnecessary to interpret the significance of this passage. Further discussion of the time of these events will aid in a more general identification of the person of Gog. Magog, a Japhetic descendant (Ge 10:7), is identified by Josephus as the land of the Scythians, a mountainous region around the Black and Caspian Seas.

The phrase "chief [*rosh*; GK 8031] prince of Meshech and Tubal" has been interpreted variously. *Rosh* presents the major difficulty in the phrase. Its normal meaning was "head" or "chief." Some understand it as a proper noun, a geographical area named "Rosh," but there is no evidence that a country named Rosh ever existed. Some would understand *rosh* as modern Russia, but the word "Russia" is a late eleventh-century A.D. term.

In the Hebrew both "prince" and "chief" are related equally to the geographical words Meshech and Tubal. Grammatically it would seem best to render the phrase as "the prince, the chief [head *or* ruler] of Meshech and Tubal." Meshech is the name of a son of Japheth in Ge 10:2 and 1Ch 1:5; the name is normally connected with the word Tubal (cf. 27:13; 32:26). The sparse data imply that Meshech and Tubal refer to geographical areas or countries in eastern modern Turkey, southwest of Russia and northwest of Iran. This, however, gives no basis for identifying these place names with any modern country. There are no data to support the contention of some that Meshech and Tubal refer to the modern Russian cities of Moscow and Tobolsk.

It can be concluded that Gog is a person from the region of Magog and that he is the prince, the chief ruler, over the geographical areas of Meshech and Tubal. These land areas or countries appear to be located generally toward the south of the Black and Caspian Seas, in the modern countries of Turkey, Russia, and Iran.

4–16 This section portrays Israel lying peacefully and securely in her land following her restoration by God. God had fulfilled his covenants with his people, and they were basking in the land's fruitfulness and the unquestioned security that they possessed in the strength of God's faithfulness to his word. Unexpectedly their safety came to be in grave jeopardy. Like a storm cloud's sudden darkness, disaster loomed on the northern horizon as an awesome horde of nations from every corner of the earth appeared. Gog, the chief prince of Meshech and Tubal, was their mastermind and commander. Peoples had joined him from every direction of the compass; Persia from the east, Cush (Ethiopia or Nubia) from the southwest, Put (normally identified as Libya) from the west or southwest, and Gomer (probably the ancient Cimmerians) and Beth Togarmah (possibly the ancient Til-garimmu southeast of the Black Sea) from the north. They were ready to invade Israel.

Gog had devised an evil plan. He intended to attack defenseless Israel who so naively trusted in her God. She had not protected herself; there were no city walls and no gates with doors and bars. Gog would plunder their land and gather all their possessions for his spoils. Other nations like Sheba and Dedan, along with merchants from Tarshish, would be shocked and question Gog's design to plunder and loot Israel.

God, however, made it perfectly clear that he sovereignly brought Gog on the land of Israel, though Gog thought it was his own idea. God would cause Gog to come on Israel by figuratively putting hooks in his jaws and leading him there. Though this may seem incongruous with God's restoration of his people and the security promised in the peace covenant, God would cause this invasion to be initiated by Gog so that all the world might know once and for all that the Lord was a faithful God. He would defeat Gog before Gog brought any harm to Israel and her land, even as God had promised (cf. 34:22, 28–29; 36:1–15). All would see that God was holy, right, and immutably faithful; and he would not permit his name to be profaned again.

The time of this invasion is indicated by temporal statements in these verses and the context of this message—the time of Israel's golden age in the end times. The phrase "after many days" (v.8) normally expresses an indefinite time period. It is sometimes used, however, to reach as far as the end times (cf. Jer 32:14; Da 8:26). The expression "in future years" is found only in this verse in the OT; one should understand its meaning in light of its context. The phrase "in days to come" tends to fix this invasion at the end times, for this phrase normally refers to Israel's final restoration to the messianic kingdom and Messiah's reign (cf. Ge 49:1; Isa 2:2; Jer 23:20; 30:24; Hos 3:5; Mic 4:1).

Verses 8 and 12 indicate that this invasion was planned at a time when Israel had been restored from the sword, having been regathered from among the nations. This regathering was followed by a peace and security that Israel would know in the restoration to her land (36:22–37:14). She felt so safe that she did not even seek to fortify herself. Israel has never enjoyed such an idyllic situation since she returned from Babylon in 539 B.C. The phrase "live in safety" describes messianic security after Israel's restoration. This oracle relates to other prophetic oracles concerning the end times and the Davidic, messianic kingdom (28:26; cf. Jer 23:6; 33:16; Zec 14:11). Finally, the entire context of these six messages of Ezekiel deals with the future restoration of Israel to her homeland by the Messiah. Thus the time of this invasion is the end times, after the people of Israel have been restored to the Promised Land and are living securely under Messiah's protection.

17–23 In his judgment God reminded Gog that the Lord's servants, the prophets, had formerly foretold this end-time invasion. Though there are no specific references to Gog in any of the other prophets, there are general references to the final destruction of the enemies of God's people (cf. Dt 30:7; Isa 26:20–21; Jer 30:1–21).

Israel's dependence on God was not in vain. At the very moment that Gog came against the land of Israel, God's burning wrath would arise against Gog. The Lord was a jealous God and would faithfully protect his own. God's fiery fury would break forth suddenly against Gog and his horde. The entire earth would be jolted with an enormous earthquake that would topple mountains, cliffs, and every wall. Every creature on the earth, within the sea and within the air, would shudder in awe and fear at the presence of almighty God who had come to annihilate Gog and his followers. Gog's armies and the nations following him would become so confused that they would slay one another in suicidal strife, while the Lord supernaturally destroyed them with diseases, bloodshed, and catastrophic torrents of rain, hailstones, and burning sulphur. God would vindicate his holy name and magnify himself as the only true God in the eyes of all nations with this annihilation of Gog. The purpose of all God's judgments is only to make himself known in all his greatness and holiness to those who can come to know him in no other way.

b. Reiteration and expansion of God's judgment speech against Gog (39:1–29)

1–2 These verses give a summary restatement of 38:1–16. God would sovereignly coerce Gog to invade Israel, but at the same time he would defeat Gog to display his faithfulness to Israel.

3–8 Ezekiel 38:17–23 described God supernaturally using the elements of nature to destroy Gog and his hordes: earthquakes, disease, and hailstones. Gog would be completely disarmed; his armies would fall throughout the land—on the mountains and in the open field. The slaughter of Gog's hordes would provide food for every bird of

prey and wild beast (cf. vv.17–20). In addition God would bring a fiery judgment on the territory of Magog and on her allies who felt secure in their coastlands and/or islands. God would use Gog's defeat as a demonstration to the nations that he, the Holy One of Israel, was the only true God. He was faithful to his covenant people to whom he had promised eternal peace and security in the peace covenant. He would not permit his holy name to be profaned again through the conquest and dispersion of Israel. Israel, in turn, would make the Lord's name holy in her midst; for she would see his immutable faithfulness through his protection of her in this final attempt to invade Israel's land. As encouragement to the Jewish exiles, the Lord stressed again that Gog's destruction would most certainly occur. The phrase "Holy One in Israel" expresses God's absolute separation from evil. He maintains his holiness and that of his land by judging Gog and by his keeping his promises.

9–10 God totally disarmed Gog's armies. So great was the resulting assemblage of weapons that it would take the Israelites seven years to burn them all. These weapons would provide fuel for Israel during these seven years so that she would not need to use any of her own fuel resources. Likewise, though Gog and his entourage had sought to take spoils from Israel, it would be Israel who would take spoils from them.

11–16 The magnitude of Gog's armies created a staggering problem with their death. All of them needed to be buried to cleanse the land of Israel. A specific valley known as the "valley of those who travel east toward [*or* of] the Sea" was designated as the burial place. Whether the proper rendering is "toward" or "of" could make a distinct difference as to which sea is involved. If the sea is the Dead Sea, then the valley would either be east of that sea—and therefore out of the normal boundaries of Israel—or a valley that led travelers east toward the Dead Sea. The only valley to fit remotely this description is the Esdraelon Valley in lower Galilee. If the sea is understood as the Mediterranean, then the specific valley could be any valley in the land of Israel east "of" that sea. None of the theories of identification of this valley can be substantiated without question because of the sparse data. The text does make it clear that the massive burial of Gog and his hordes in this valley would cause a major obstacle to travel. For this reason the valley would be named "the Valley of Hamon Gog" ("the hordes of Gog").

The multitude of carcasses would require more than seven months to bury to cleanse the land (cf. Lev 5:2; 21:1; Dt 21:1–9). Every person in Israel would be involved. For seven months they would bury the easily observed bodies lying on the ground. After seven months overseers would designate two groups to carry out a "mopping-up" operation (v.14). One group would search to find any remnant of a body—even a bone—and mark it. These would be collected and taken to the Valley of Hamon Gog for burial by the second group. A city named Hamonah ("horde") would be located in the Valley of Hamon Gog, perhaps viewed as a city of the dead. The city's exact nature is unclear. Gog's burial would be a memorable day for the Lord, for the death of this enemy demonstrates God's faithfulness to protect his people forever and brings glory to the Lord's name.

17–20 The search throughout the land for bones of the deceased enemy may have arisen due to the great feast on the dead by the carrion-eating birds and animals of prey invited to feed on the carnage of Gog and his followers. This great slaughter is called a "sacrifice" that the Lord prepared for these birds and animals on Israel's mountains (cf. Isa 34:6; Jer 46:10). The flesh and fat of princes, warriors, and their animals would be consumed; and their blood would be drunk until these fowls and beasts were glutted and drunk. "Rams and lambs, goats and bulls" of Bashan were always well-fed and strong. The parallel of this imagery to the defeated princes emphasizes that these were not weaklings but the strong and mighty of the earth.

Some observations on the relationship of these two chapters to the book of Revelation are in order. There is a clear allusion to the great feast of Eze 39:17–20 in Rev 19–21. Revelation 19:11–16 presents a heavenly scene of the Second Advent. The Lord comes on a white horse with his armies to judge and make war in righteousness. The sword that proceeds out of his mouth smites the nations as he treads out the winepress of his great wrath. Revelation 19:17–21 is a distinctly dif-

ferent section, in which an angel invites all the birds to a "great supper of God," a feast on the mighty leaders of the nations who have gathered against the Lord and who is slain by the sword of his mouth. The beast and the false prophet are seized and cast into the lake of fire. The birds fill themselves on the carnage of the others.

In his "great supper of God," John appears to allude explicitly to the feast on the carnage of Gog's hordes in Eze 39:17–20. Why would John directly link Eze 39 to Rev 19 in his argument? The restoration and messianic context of Ezekiel's message is also that of John. Revelation 19:11–16 presents a heavenly glimpse of the Messiah at his second coming after Israel has been restored to her land (cf. Rev 7). The beast and the kings of the earth with their armies (Rev 19:19) are certainly similar to the nations assembled with Gog in Ezekiel (Eze 38:4–7, 9, 15, 22; 39:4, 11; Rev 19:15, 18–19, 21). The Lord's judgment in Eze 38–39 finds parallel features in the Messiah's treading out God's winepress of wrath in Rev 19. The Lord calls for a sword against Gog, and the sword out of the Lord's mouth smites the nations that come against him in Revelation (cf. Eze 38:21; Rev 19:15, 20).

An explicit chronology is not set forth in Revelation. Therefore it is difficult to know the exact time of Rev 19, though the second coming of the Messiah is in view. It appears that Messiah comes to defeat all nations and perhaps conclude the Battle of Armageddon. Yet the context of Eze 38–39 sees Israel already at peace, dwelling in security, having been restored from the sword. Such would not be in harmony with the Battle of Armageddon. Since this battle is not mentioned in Rev 19 explicitly, perhaps the events of Rev 19 do not relate to Armageddon but specifically to the demise of the beast as foretold in Eze 38–39. Armageddon had already been treated in Rev 14 and 16. Therefore, though the Messiah may conclude the events of Armageddon with his return, the next event in a possible transition period between the conclusion of the Tribulation and the beginning of the Millennium would be this defeat of the beast who sought to make one final attempt to secure Israel's land.

Why would John not mention Gog in Rev 19 if this passage is a fulfillment of Eze 38–39? The last mention of the beast by John had been in Rev 17. If John used the name Gog in Rev 19, the readers would have been unaware of who he was in the Rev 19 context. By using the name "beast" and at the same time making explicit allusion to Ezekiel's Gog invasion in the unique feast of the birds, John apparently sought to equate the beast with Gog for his readers. Then his readers would see the events of Rev 19:17–21 as a fulfillment of the Gog prophecy, which helps establish the exact time when Eze 38–39 will occur.

Significantly, in addition to the specific allusion between Rev 19 and Eze 39 found in the "bird supper," none of the details of Eze 38–39 is violated in the Rev 19 context. Though the Rev 19 passage aids in determining the fulfillment and the time of Gog's invasion and defeat in Eze 38–39, other factors are involved in seeking to gain a complete perspective of these issues. Interpreting the time of these events in the prophetic program of the end times is a most difficult issue, which has resulted in several different positions. (For a more complete treatment, see EBC, 6:937–40.)

The majority of expositors see the events of Eze 38–39 taking place after the Millennium as described in Rev 20:7–10. The strong argument for this position is the explicit reference to Gog and Magog in Rev 20:8. The context of the Millennium would surely satisfy Israel's peaceful, prosperous, and safe dwelling. Restoration would have already been accomplished. Nations would be present to observe "Gog's" rebellion. Time would surely be available for the burial of bodies and the burning of weapons.

Objections, however, have been raised against this view.

1. It is argued that Gog is a northern coalition while in Revelation the armies come from the four corners of the earth. But it should be noticed that Gog brings with him nations from every point of the compass (38:5–6).

2. It is maintained that Ezekiel says nothing of Jerusalem, whereas John states that the nations encompassed the beloved city. In answer it should be observed that John's mention of the "beloved city" does not conflict with Ezekiel, for he states that Gog comes on the mountains of Israel, which most certainly include Jerusalem.

3. It is believed that the burning of the weapons and the disposal of the bodies mili-

tate against these events at the end of the Millennium, since the Great White Throne Judgment immediately follows. However, the chronology of Revelation does not demand immediate sequence of events, especially in Rev 19–20. A transition period here is plausible.

Therefore, it seems that Rev 20:7–10 is also a fulfillment of Eze 38–39. The fulfillment can be seen in two far moments: one in Rev 19:17–21 and one in Rev 20:7–10. The connection between Eze 38–39 and Rev 19:17–21 lies in the singular concept of God's defeat of the great final attempt of the Evil One to once again possess the land of Israel. Revelation 19 finds the attempt thwarted in the destruction of the beast and his armies (Satan's major representative on earth), whereas Rev 20 sets forth Satan's fall as the completion of this theme. Both are the last and greatest enemies of Israel. John only summarized the events in each case, since the full description had been recounted in Eze 38–39. The allusion to the great feast in Rev 19 was used by John to bring to his readers' attention the events of Eze 38–39, with which they would have been familiar. The term "Gog" was not used so as *not* to confuse the identity of the beast. On the contrary, in Rev 20 the explicit equation is made between Satan and Gog so that the readers also would identify Satan's rebellion with the events of Eze 38–39. Both passages describe attempts by Israel's greatest enemies, the beast and Satan, to possess the land of Israel and to nullify God's promise.

c. The summary of the six night messages (39:21–29)

21–29 Gog's destruction provides the climax of Ezekiel's six messages of encouragement delivered to the exiles the night prior to the fugitive's arrival with the news that Jerusalem had fallen. Gog's defeat would be the Lord's final display of his glory among the nations as he restored Israel to the Promised Land. All other nations would stand in awe at God's punishment on Gog.

These six messages have stressed God's covenant promises to Israel, especially those concerning the land. When Israel experienced God's marvelous faithfulness in restoration and protection against Gog, she would know without question from that day forward that the Lord was her God, the only true God, and that there was none other. In turn the nations would know that the Lord had not been a weak God when he sent Israel into exile; rather they would observe that he cared enough to set his face against Israel because of her sin of unfaithfulness to him. Likewise, the nations would observe that it was God's grace and faithfulness that brought Israel back from among the nations, gave her the Promised Land, and enabled her to live safely on that land without fear of oppression. In this way the Lord would show himself holy in the eyes of the nations. He was jealous for his name not to be profaned, as when the nations construed him to be as other gods. The Lord would never again turn his face from Israel and allow someone to oppress her! No one would bring terror on Israel again! God would cleanse Israel, removing her shame and sin and then pouring out his Spirit on her in accord with the new covenant. All Israel's covenants would be fulfilled. She would live securely forever under the peace covenant administered by her king, the Messiah!

B. God's Glory Returns (40:1–48:35)

The description in these nine chapters of a temple, the filling of that temple with God's glory, a sacrificial system for worship in that temple, priestly functions, and the tribal and priestly allotment of land is rather clear to the reader. But what does it all mean? Should these chapters be interpreted literally or figuratively? Since this portion of the book contains some very puzzling and difficult concepts that cannot be ignored, it is wise to examine some basic issues to determine as accurate an understanding of the text as possible.

Is Ezekiel 40–48 Historical or Future? These chapters have been interpreted as referring to the temple of Solomon, Zerubbabel, or Herod, or to a future temple in the Millennium or in the eternal state. Some interpret the section allegorically as teaching about the church and its earthly blessings and glories, while others understand the passage to symbolize the reality of the heavenly temple where Christ ministers today.

The historical fulfillments do not fit the details of the passage. The temples of Solomon, Zerubbabel, or Herod do not share the design and dimensions of the temple described in chs. 40–42. The worship procedure set forth in chs. 43–46, though Mosaic in nature, has not been followed in history in exactly the manner described in these chapters. The river that flows forth from the temple in 47:1–12 has never flowed from any of the three historical temples mentioned above. The only comparisons to this river are seen in Ge 2:8–14 and Rev 22:1–2 (cf. Isa 35:6–7; Joel 3:18; Zec 14:8). The geographical dimensions and tribal allotments of the land are certainly not feasible today, nor have they ever been followed in times past. Geographical changes will be necessary prior to the fulfillment of chs. 45, 47–48. Therefore, one should not look to historical (past or present) fulfillments of these chapters but to the future.

The figurative or "spiritualizing" approach does not seem to solve any of the problems of these chapters; rather, it tends to create new ones. When one abandons a literal interpretation, different aspects of a passage mean whatever the interpreter desires. Even apocalyptic visions such as those found in these chapters require a normal grammatical-historical hermeneutic. To interpret them in any other manner contradicts the interpretative guide in the vision who warns Ezekiel that he must write down all the minute details concerning the plan for the temple and its regulations so that these details might be considered carefully and followed in every aspect (40:4; 43:10–11; 44:5). Therefore a figurative approach does not suit the issues of Eze 40–48.

The general time frame of these chapters can perhaps be best understood in light of the development and flow of Ezekiel's argument in the entire book. He has shown the presence of God's glory in the historical Jerusalem temple and its departure from that temple because of Israel's sin of breaking the Mosaic covenant. The fall of Jerusalem and the captivity in Babylon were the consequence (chs. 4–24). After declaring how the nations would also be judged (25:1–33:20), Ezekiel encouraged the Jewish captives through six night messages of hope (33:21–39:29). In these he informed them that the Messiah would restore them to their Promised Land in the future and become a true shepherd to them. They would be cleansed and all their covenants would be fulfilled. Even in the end times, after the land prospers and Israel dwells securely in it, some will try to take the Promised Land away from Israel and profane the Lord's name; but the Lord will not permit it (chs. 38–39). It would seem logical, therefore, for Ezekiel to conclude the logical and chronological development of his prophecy by describing the messianic kingdom and the return of God's glory to govern his people (chs. 40–48) rather than suddenly reverting back to some historical period, whether immediately following the Exile or during Herod's temple, or to some undefined idealistic temple.

Ezekiel appears to have been contrasting the past and contemporary desecration of the temple and its regulations with the future holiness and righteousness of the temple and its functions—a format Ezekiel also used in chs. 33–39. The correct future procedure would bring shame and conviction on Ezekiel's contemporaries (43:6–12; 44:5–16; 45:9–12). This again points to a future fulfillment of these chapters.

God's glory is a most important feature of Ezekiel's prophecy. Its return to the new temple in 43:1–12 is the climax of the book. The context implies that this can only occur after Israel has been restored to the Promised Land and cleansed. The stress is on holiness. Holiness had not characterized Israel as a people heretofore; and Israel would not be a holy people in accord with God's standard until after they had been restored to the Promised Land and cleansed in the Messianic Age (ch. 36). When God's glory returns, it will remain in Israel's midst forever (43:6–7). The development of this unifying factor in Ezekiel's prophecy argues strongly for a future fulfillment of chs. 40–48.

Finally, the entire context and argument of the Scriptures concerning God's outworking of his redemptive plan in history place these chapters and the aspects mentioned above in the time of the consummation of all history. This is perhaps best seen in the river of life that flows from the temple to bring healing to the land (47:1–12). This concept is first seen in Ge 2:8–14 in the Garden of Eden, the perfect environment of God's holiness. With sin, this garden and its river were removed. But when God concludes his redemptive program and brings full salvation to humankind with eternal life through Jesus Christ, his Son, it is appropriate that the river of eternal life will again flow to demonstrate full healing on the earth. This conclusion to

the full circle of God's redemptive program is also shown in Rev 22:1–6 (cf. Isa 35:5–6; Joel 3:18; Zec 14:8).

Therefore, the context and argument of the book of Ezekiel as well as the development of God's redemptive program all argue strongly for a future fulfillment of the events of Eze 40–48 in the end times.

Does Ezekiel 40–48 Relate to the Millennium or to the Eternal State? It is first necessary to understand the prophetic perspective of the OT prophets. Their predictive revelations concerned two main issues: the time of the judgment and discipline that were to come on Israel because of her perennial sin and breaking of the Mosaic covenant; and the ultimate period of blessing, following Israel's judgment, when Israel would be restored to the Promised Land, cleansed of her sin, and brought into the messianic kingdom. At that time all of Israel's covenants would be fulfilled, and she would live in perfect security under the divine rule of the Messiah.

The OT prophets tended not to make distinctions within the period of discipline and judgment. Rather they portrayed near and far aspects of this time in the same passage. The discipline would begin with the Babylonian captivity and would continue till the end time. Some distinctions were observed, but chronological relations were seldom delineated.

Similarly, the prophets did not make distinctions between the Millennium and the eternal state when describing the period of messianic blessing. Further distinctions are primarily the result of progressive revelation disclosed in the NT, especially in the book of Revelation, though some distinctions are implied in the OT prophets (e.g., Da 9–12). Ezekiel, like his contemporaries, intermixed these various elements in his prophecies of judgment and the future kingdom. Undoubtedly this contributes to the difficulty in distinguishing the Millennium and the eternal state in these chapters.

In light of the whole Scripture, it appears that the Millennium is like a preview or "firstfruits" of the eternal state. Therefore, because the two are alike, they share distinct similarities. Yet because they are both different revealed time periods, they likewise reflect some dissimilarities. Since the OT prophets, like Ezekiel, frequently failed to see distinctions, one should be careful about stating that Eze 40–48 is describing only the Millennium or only the eternal state. One must look to the NT for any further clues for delineation, whenever such are given.

John uses many OT prophetic concepts and images in Revelation, as observed above in his allusion to the "bird supper" of Eze 38–39. Revelation 21–22 speaks of the eternal state, and there are definite allusions to Eze 40–48 in this portion of Revelation, with striking similarities. Both writers receive apocalyptic visions on a high mountain with an intercepting messenger present, holding a measuring rod to measure various structures (Eze 40:2–5; Rev 21:2, 10, 15). Both visions portray waters flowing forth toward the east, with trees alongside and leaves for healing (Eze 47:1–7, 12; Rev 22:1–2). The names of Israel's twelve tribes are written on the city's twelve gates in both visions (Eze 48:31–33: Rev 21:12), and three gates each are found on the east, south, north, and west sides of the city respectively (Eze 48:30–34; Rev 21:13).

In addition, however, there are equally clear dissimilarities between the two passages. The city's dimensions are different (Eze 48:30–35; Rev 21:15–17). The waters that flow toward the east have different sources: the temple in Ezekiel (43:7; 47:1–5) and God's throne in Revelation (22:1, 3). It might appear that these sources are really similar since Ezekiel maintains that God's throne is the temple; but John, in his vision, declares that God's throne is in Jerusalem. The temple and the city of Jerusalem are distinctly different entities in Ezekiel (45:2–4; 48:10, 15–17), and in the Revelation vision there is no temple (21:22; 22:3). Since a major aspect of Eze 40–48 is the temple and its regulations, perhaps this would argue for Ezekiel's discussion to reflect the Millennium more than the eternal state. The tribal allotments of Ezekiel include the sea as the western boundary (47:15–20), whereas in Revelation John declares that the sea no longer exists (Rev 21:1). That is, Ezekiel's tribal boundaries could not exist in the eternal state if the sea no longer existed. These dissimilarities suggest that Ezekiel's vision is more concerned with millennial concepts than the eternal state, whereas the Revelation vision is focused on the eternal state.

The river flowing east from the temple likewise appears to be millennial since the source is different from Revelation. But here the similar nature of the two passages is perhaps best observed. Ezekiel may very well be giving a glimpse of the eternal state with this similar facet. Perhaps what is seen in the Millennium will also be seen in the eternal state, though with slight modification. Since the Lord will take the place of the temple in the eternal state, the river could flow out of the millennial temple as the throne of God in Eze 47 and out of the throne of God, distinct from a temple, in Rev 22.

It seems, therefore, that Ezekiel 40–48 is primarily describing the millennial temple, its regulations for worship, and the tribal allotments. The Millennium is only a beginning, sort of a microcosm, of the eternal state and a transition into it. Consequently, to observe reflections of Eze 40–48 in the picture of the eternal state revealed in Rev 21–22 should be expected and should not surprise the reader.

Is Not the Existence of a Temple, Priests, and a Sacrificial System a Retrogression to OT Modes of Worship? A grammatical-historical hermeneutic will see a real temple, real sacrifices, and real priests functioning in the millennial context. When these are closely examined, it becomes evident that they are Mosaic in nature, though omissions and modifications are present. But the NT states that Jesus Christ died once and for all on the cross for all sin. There is no need for a further sacrifice for sin. Likewise, the Lord's Table is designed to bring remembrance of the Lord's death to the worshipers. Why go back to OT modes of worship set forth under the old covenant when the new covenant has been instituted?

An examination of Ezekiel's purpose, especially in this section, combined with a comparison of the Levitical worship concepts with those of Ezekiel and of the NT will help us solve some of these dilemmas. Ezekiel was a priest; thus he frequently looked on issues in his prophecy from a priestly perspective. He would be expected to view the new worship principles from his vantage point with a temple, sacrifices, and priests involved. Likewise, God normally reveals himself in terms of the culture and perspective of those receiving his revelation. Such could be expected here.

The recipients of this vision are described as "the house of Israel." This terminology is used by Ezekiel to describe Israel at any time in her existence—past, present, or future. Apocalyptic literature of the OT was to be a source of hope and encouragement in a time of discouragement. Revelation that a temple would be rebuilt in the messianic kingdom to which God's glory would return and in which the nation would worship the Lord as he had commanded would surely be an encouragement. Should not the description of worship in the messianic kingdom be in terms both understandable to Israel as well as in keeping with the covenant worship of her God?

In Eze 37:15–28 all the covenants given to Israel would be fulfilled at the time of her restoration to the Promised Land and the institution of the messianic kingdom. This includes the Abrahamic, Davidic, new, peace, and Mosaic covenants. The covenant formula of the Mosaic covenant—"they will be my people, and I will be their God"—will be operative as Israel walks in the stipulations of the Mosaic covenant, cleansed under the new covenant and experiencing the eternal reign of her king, the Messiah, under the Davidic covenant (37:23–26; cf. Ex 19:5–6; Lev 26:12; Dt 26:18–19; Jer 30:18–22; 31:33; 32:36–40). Because Israel was in a relationship with God through the Abrahamic and Mosaic covenants, she had always been expected to worship the Lord in holiness. Her entire worship procedure was designed to point her to God's holiness and to her need to be holy before him (cf. Leviticus). The basic emphasis throughout Eze 40–48 is on God's holiness. The holiness of the Lord's temple and the worship of him are contrasted with the profaning of his name and his temple in Israel's past worship. Israel would have a final opportunity to worship God correctly—in the purity of holiness. Such worship would demonstrate that Israel had truly been redeemed and cleansed.

Ezekiel 40–48 presents only the Hebrew perspective of millennial worship. This does not preclude other worship forms from also existing and being carried out (cf. Lk 22:18). The manifestations and functions of all God's covenants do not contradict but rather complement one another. Israel will finally be a people of God, living and worshiping in the holiness revealed in the Mosaic stipulations.

The omissions and modifications from the Mosaic system observed in Eze 40–48 are undoubtedly present to enable the various aspects of the covenants to harmonize.

But is not the presence of a temple anachronistic? In answer, the existence of a temple as a place of worship is the normal concept from an OT perspective. Likewise, without a temple complex sacrifices cannot be offered properly. Therefore, the temple will be necessary for worship (Eze 43–46).

Ezekiel sets forth two major purposes for the millennial temple. First, the temple will provide a throne for God among his people (43:6–7), the residency of his glory (43:1–12) from which he will rule over his people. Second, the temple complex will reflect God's holiness by its walls of separation, various courts, and temple divisions (40:5; 42:14–20). The design of the structure will cause the people of that day to be ashamed of their iniquities. Therefore, a temple structure should not prevent or hinder other worship forms that may exist in the Millennium (e.g., the Lord's Table), unless one divides the periods of God's working so that only certain architectural forms can be used for the worship of God at a given time. There have been a variety of structures in which Christians have worshiped in the church age. There seems to be no scriptural concept that forbids a Christian from worshiping in a temple built to almighty God. A temple, in and of itself, does not appear to be anachronistic.

A second major difficulty is the relationship between Ezekiel's sacrificial system and the NT teaching of Christ's death as a finished and complete work for sin. To understand the issues, we must describe Ezekiel's millennial sacrificial system. In doing so, we will compare it to the Mosaic system. Almost all aspects of the Ezekiel system are identical with Mosaic procedure. It is primarily the omissions, with some modifications in keeping with the purpose of Ezekiel's worship, that compose the differences.

Although the general phrase "all the appointed feasts of the house of Israel" is used in 45:17, only three festivals are explicitly mentioned in these chapters: Passover and the Feast of Unleavened Bread, the Feast of Tabernacles, and, by implication, the Feast of Firstfruits. Passover (45:21–24) began on the fourteenth day of the first month (Nisan), and the people were to eat unleavened bread for seven days (cf. Ex 12:1–30; Nu 28:16–35). The "leader" offered a sin offering each day along with a grain offering for himself and for the people of the land (cf. Nu 28:22–24). Daily the leader also offered a burnt offering with its grain offering (cf. Nu 28:19–21, 23–24). These items parallel those in the Levitical system. Likewise, Ezekiel declares that the same offerings as those made for Passover will be made for the Feast of Tabernacles for a similar length of time (Eze 45:25). Numbers 29:12–38 only differs by adding a daily drink offering. This festival began on the fifteenth day of the seventh month and lasted for seven days, as prescribed in the Mosaic system. In addition, Eze 44:30 states that "the best of all of the firstfruits ... will belong to the priests." This does not necessarily imply a Feast of Firstfruits but is the only mention of the idea of firstfruits in the Ezekiel system.

The offerings and sacrifices to be used in worship and consecration of the temple make up most of the Ezekiel system. In addition to the offerings of the various festivals, the Israelites will be required to offer daily to God burnt offerings with their accompanying grain offering in the morning (cf. Ex 29:38–42; Lev 6:12; Nu 28:3–7). The Mosaic procedure required this offering daily, both in the morning and in the evening, along with a drink offering. Offerings on the Sabbaths, new moons, and all appointed festivals will include the burnt offering, grain offering, and drink offering in Ezekiel's worship (45:17; cf. Lev 23:37; Nu 28:9–15). Only on the observance of new moons did the Mosaic list add the sin offering. Ezekiel also declares that the priests are to sacrifice for the leader a burnt offering and a fellowship offering on both the Sabbath and the new moon (46:2–7; Nu 29:39). The leader may also offer a freewill burnt offering and fellowship offerings on the Sabbath (46:12).

Ezekiel's temple is purified ("atoned for") on the first and seventh days of the first month (of each year?) with a sin offering (45:18–20). Similar procedures are outlined in the Mosaic system but with the addition of burnt offerings and fellowship offerings (cf. Nu 7:87–89; 2Ch 7:1–10; 29:20–24). When the altar of burnt sacrifice is built, it will be cleansed, consecrated, and dedicated for seven days with both burnt offerings and sin offerings (43:18–25; cf. Ex 29:36–37; Lev 7:14). After the seven days, the altar may be used for regular offerings (43:27). This passage is silent concerning whether the altar's cleansing and consecration are to be repeated. Finally, Israel will make a special contribution of grains, oil, and animals for the leader to use in the regular atonement for the house of Israel (45:15–17; cf. Lev 9:17–21). The atonement offerings are the sin offering, grain offering, burnt offering, and fellowship offering. No time is specified as to how often or when such atonement is to be made.

The priesthood in Ezekiel is composed of the Levites as helpers in the maintenance, administration, and function of temple worship; but those of the Zadok line will be the only ones permitted to minister before the Lord with the most holy things (44:5–16). The other Levites are denied this privilege due to their past unfaithfulness in carrying out the duties of the sanctuary. There is no high priest. The only stated priestly functions are the slaughter, washing, cooking, and eating of various sacrifices (40:38–42; 42:13; 44:29; 46:20; cf. Lev 7:7; Nu 18:8–10).

Therefore, most stated aspects of the worship procedure in Ezekiel are like those of the Mosaic system. The major omissions include the absence of a Day of Atonement, an ark of the covenant, the Feast of Weeks (or Pentecost), a high priest, and a full, ministering Levitical priesthood. The absence of the Day of Atonement and of the ark of the covenant where the atoning blood was sprinkled suggests that the work of propitiation has already been accomplished. One would think these items would have been included in the millennial system of Ezekiel, since they were extremely important factors in the Mosaic system. Being an argument from silence, however, it is difficult to be certain or to make any significant argument. The lack of a high priest may point to the high priesthood of Jesus Christ, who will be ruling in the Millennium (Heb 4:14–5:10; 7:11–8:13).

In other words, the millennial worship system is distinctly different from the Mosaic system only in that certain Mosaic elements are omitted or modified, most likely because of Christ's finished work on the cross. Millennial sacrifices are also discussed elsewhere by the OT prophets (Isa 56:6–7; 60:7, 13; 66:20–23; Jer 33:15–22; Zec 14:16–21).

The question whether these sacrifices are efficacious is crucial. The Mosaic covenant was given to a people who had already entered into a relationship with the Lord in the Abrahamic covenant. The Mosaic covenant was not given to bring one into a relationship with God but to demonstrate how one in that relationship was to live holy before him. True worship grows out of a personal relationship with God.

The Mosaic worship system, therefore, was to be used by those in a relationship with God. Never did the sacrifices and offerings deliver one from sin. They were never efficacious for the Israelite or anyone else. Rather, the sacrifices were picture lessons and types of the Messiah's work, whereby he would atone for all sin in a propitious manner through the sacrifice of his own blood once and for all. The sin and guilt offerings were reminders of one's personal inherent sin and the need for cleansing from that sinfulness by the shedding of innocent blood. These offerings were observed in much the sense in which a believer today confesses sin (1Jn 1:9) in light of the finished work of Christ for sin. The believer's confession itself is not efficacious; it is only Christ's finished work that provides forgiveness of sin. Confession, however, reminds a believer that he or she sinned and that the sin has been forgiven by Christ's blood. The sin and guilt offerings, therefore, reminded the Israelites that they were sinful and that they needed the Messiah's innocent blood, typified in the animal, to cleanse them of their sin and to bring forgiveness from God.

The burnt offering pictured the offerers' commitment to the Lord. It was voluntary, even as commitment is today. The burnt offerings required daily and at other festivals were constant reminders that the Israelites needed to be totally committed to their Lord. The fellowship offerings reflected the offerers' thanksgiving to God and the peace that existed between them and God. Certainly believers today are to express their thankfulness to God for the various blessings bestowed on them because of their relationship with the Lord.

The concept of atonement creates a major problem for many with the sacrificial system in Ezekiel. The Hebrew verb means "to atone by offering a substitute" (GK 4105), which is always used in connection with the removal of sin or defilement. When a sacrifice for atonement was brought in the Mosaic

system, it was brought because God required it, not because of the initiative of the offerer (Lev 10). God alone gave forgiveness and cleansing, not the sacrifice. Ultimately, the basis for forgiveness and cleansing was the work of the Messiah's innocent blood as the ransom for the penalty of death. The sacrificial animal could not offer an efficacious ransom; rather, the atonement sacrifice was only a picture lesson of Christ's finished work.

All mentions of "atonement" in Eze 40–48 relate to the concept of purification or consecration of the temple or altar with the exception of two references. The atonement of the people is mentioned only in 45:15–17. There the concept is the same as that in the Mosaic system: a picture lesson of the ultimate atoning work of Christ when he would pay the ransom price of his blood to atone for sin and provide forgiveness of sin once and for all.

The Mosaic Day of Atonement for sin (cf. Lev 16:21–22, 30, 31) occurred annually in OT times, but it will not be observed in the Millennium. But sin will still occur in the Millennium among the house of Israel. Therefore the atonement offerings for the leader and the people will be a marvelous reminder of the work that the Messiah accomplished on the cross to enable their sin to be forgiven. It will also remind them that they are sinful people who need that redemption provided through the innocent blood of Christ. The sacrifices in Ezekiel are memorials of Christ's work even as the Mosaic sacrifices were picture lessons and types of the work he would do. Neither is efficacious.

The writer of Hebrews in chs. 7–10 discusses the relationship between the Mosaic sacrifices and the work of Christ. It is instructive to examine these chapters, for they confirm the argument stated above. The law required that nearly everything be cleansed with blood, and without the shedding of blood there was no forgiveness (Heb 9:21–22). This is observed in both the Mosaic and the Ezekiel systems of atonement. But the elements of the tabernacle (temple) and its furnishings were only copies of heavenly things (9:23); and though they needed to be purified with sacrifices, the real need of purification would be made by Christ's sacrifice, of which these things were only copies (9:24–28). These aspects of the Mosaic covenant were only a "shadow" (i.e., a picture) of the things that were coming; they were not the reality itself (10:1). Because the Mosaic covenant dealt here in shadows, the Mosaic system could never make its worshipers perfect through the repeated sacrifices that never could take away sin (10:2–4, 11). The sacrifices cleansed only outwardly as a picture (9:11–14); Jesus inwardly cleanses our consciences from the sinful acts that lead to death (10:8–14). If the Mosaic sacrifices could have cleansed its worshipers and made them perfect, those sacrifices would have stopped once and for all, but they could not (10:2). Therefore they were continued as regular reminders of sin, because it was impossible for the blood of animals to take away sin. Jesus offered himself once for the sins of humankind. The reality of the pictures had come, even as promised in the new covenant (7:27).

The writer of Hebrews goes on to say that where sins have been forgiven, there is no longer any sacrifice for sin. Understood in the context of Hebrews described above, there is no longer the need for the picture lessons and reminders, now that the reality of Christ's efficacious blood sacrifice has been offered once and for all. However, the writer of Hebrews does not declare that pictorial sacrifices and festivals absolutely can no longer be observed as reminders and picture lessons of what Christ did after his singularly efficacious sacrifice has been completed. Since the sacrifices and festivals in the OT system were only pictures themselves, they never conflict with the sacrifice of the Messiah. They never were and never could be efficacious.

Likewise, the sacrifices in the millennial system described by Ezekiel are only picture lessons and reminders of the sin of humankind and of the only efficacious sacrifice for sin once and for all made by Christ. The millennial sacrifices will be both reminders to believers in millennial worship and picture lessons to unbelievers born in the Millennium. That is their purpose. On the basis of the OT role of the sacrifices and the argument of the writer of Hebrews, it does not appear that the pictorial sacrifices of the Mosaic system or the memorial sacrifices of the millennial worship conflict with the completed work of Jesus' sacrifice for all sins once and for all on the cross.

In addition, the very observance of the Lord's Table is an argument in favor of this memorial view. The observance of the Lord's Table is not a substitute for Christ's death and does not in that sense conflict with the finished work of Christ. As a memorial, the Lord's Table will apparently be celebrated with Christ present in the messianic kingdom (Millennium) when Christ returns (Mt 26:29; Mk 14:25; Lk 22:18). If the Lord's Table is a memorial and the sacrifices of the Ezekiel system are memorials, the two should not in any way conflict with each other but should be able to coexist. One, of course, may ask why both need to be observed if they perform the same role. Perhaps the Lord's Table is the primary memorial to those believers of the church age while the sacrifices in Ezekiel will be the primary commemoration of the Jews in the Millennium, though nothing certainly prohibits any of the singular people of God—Jews or Gentiles—from participating in the worship of either memorial.

In summary, the sacrificial system in Ezekiel's worship will be used as picture lessons to demonstrate the need for holiness in the consecration and purifying of the temple and the altar. They will be visual reminders of human sinfulness and one's need for redemption, as well as pictorial memorials of the finished and completed sacrifice of the Messiah who provided atonement for humankind once and for all. Thanksgiving to God will be visually expressed in the fellowship offerings. In addition, the sacrifices will provide food for the millennial priests (44:29–31), even as they did for the Mosaic priests. Priests will be necessary in the millennial worship system to conduct the sacrifices for the leader and the people. Priests will also carry out all the necessary ministries of the temple. Their main role, however, will be to demonstrate to everyone in the Millennium the distinction between the holy and the profane (Eze 44).

A Summary of the Argument of Ezekiel 40–48. Thirteen years have passed since Ezekiel had encouraged the exiles with the six messages of restoration hope (33:21–39:29). Then, through an apocalyptic vision, Ezekiel gives a final encouragement by describing the nature of the messianic kingdom. This vision is the culmination of the book, revealing the climax of God's working with Israel throughout history. God establishes Israel as a holy nation to worship him and demonstrate his person. When God originally created Israel, three elements were essential for her existence: a people, a government, and a homeland. When God reestablishes Israel as a nation in the messianic kingdom, these same three elements must exist. God will regather the people through the great restoration described in chs. 34–37. He will then give Israel her new government (guidelines for living) and establish her in the Promised Land forever (chs. 40–48).

The reestablishment of Israel's government is described in chs. 40–46. The center of her new life will be the Lord himself, who will return in glory to rule in her midst (43:1–9). The need for a residence for God's glory will be fulfilled in the construction of the millennial temple described in detail in chs. 40–42. Here God will reign with the temple as his throne (43:7), just as he had done previously in the tabernacle and then the temple. The regulations in 43:13–46:24 describe how the priests, leaders, and the people are to live holy lives. Requirements and functions are outlined; and Israel is charged to perform these regulations in an unerring manner, thereby demonstrating God's holiness (43:10–11; 44:5–8).

The description of Israel's restoration to the Promised Land is given in ch. 36. Then in chs. 47–48 the Lord demonstrates how he will continually heal, bless, and refresh the land in its perfect state through the river of life (47:1–12; cf. Ge 2:8–10; Rev 22:1–3). Tribal borders will be established, and land will be set aside for the priests, leaders, city, and the sanctuary. With Israel reestablished in the land of blessing, the Lord will reaffirm his eternal presence with them in a new name for the city (Jerusalem): "THE LORD IS THERE" (48:35). The Lord will be there forever!

1. The setting of the apocalyptic vision (40:1–4)

1–4 There are four essential elements in the literary setting of an apocalyptic vision: the date, the identity of the vision's recipient, the location of the vision's recipient, and noteworthy circumstances under which the vision was received.

The *date* of this apocalyptic vision has four aspects. (1) Ezekiel expressed it in terms of his normal calendrical system, using the reference point of Jehoiachin's deportation into Babylonian exile: 597 B.C. This vision was received in the twenty-fifth year of Jehoiachin's captivity, or in 573 B.C.

(2) The vision was received at the beginning of that year. Israel had two different calendars. The civil calendar began in the fall month of Tishri; the religious calendar began in the spring month of Nisan. The religious calendar is preferable since Ezekiel was a priest and the concerns of the apocalyptic vision relate to religious matters. Thus the date would be March/April 573 B.C.

(3) The vision was received on the tenth day of the month. If this is the month Nisan, then the tenth day is the very day the people may have begun to prepare for the Passover four days later. Whether they actually observed the Passover or not in exile is not known, but surely they would be contemplating Israel's redemption out of Egypt and the creation of their nation. This vision, then, would be an encouragement that the Lord would complete his purposes for the nation in the messianic kingdom.

(4) The vision was received in the fourteenth year after Jerusalem fell to the Babylonians, in 586 B.C. This also would corroborate the date of 573 B.C.

The second major element of the setting of an apocalyptic vision is the *identity of the vision's recipient*. Though Ezekiel's name is not given in these verses, the copious use of the first person pronoun in light of the context of the entire book certainly argues strongly that the recipient was Ezekiel.

The third aspect of the setting of this vision is the *location* in which it was received. Ezekiel saw the vision from a very high mountain in Israel, from which he could see a city to the south. Neither the mountain nor the city is identified. However, Ezekiel was taken into the city, where he then saw the temple's construction in detail. In light of the geography of Ezekiel's day, the city was most likely Jerusalem. To identify a high mountain to the north of Jerusalem, however, is not possible.

The final aspect of a literary setting of an apocalyptic vision is the *noteworthy circumstances* under which the vision was received. A divine messenger with the appearance of bronze was present. He was carrying both a measuring rod and a linen measuring cord. He exhorted Ezekiel to pay careful attention to all that he would be shown, because this vision was being given to him so that he might tell it in detail to the "house of Israel."

2. The apocalyptic vision (40:5–48:35)

a. The millennial temple (40:5–42:20)

A divine messenger guided Ezekiel through the temple complex, beginning on the outside and working gradually inward through the outer and inner courts to the temple sanctuary. He provided an abundance of details, especially dimensions. These plans and specific dimensions are accurate enough to enable plans to be drawn and models to be constructed with a fair degree of accuracy.

(1) The outer court (40:5–27)

5 Many dimensions of the temple are given in chs. 40–42. The normal cubit was the distance between the tip of the middle finger and the tip of the elbow—approximately eighteen inches. The handbreadth was the measurement of the hand's width at the base of the fingers—normally about three inches. The divine messenger guiding Ezekiel carried a measuring rod six cubits long. The long cubit was composed of one normal cubit plus a handbreadth, or eighteen inches plus three inches. Since the measurements in this portion of Ezekiel were made with this measuring rod, it can be assumed that the "cubit" in Ezekiel was normally the "long cubit" of twenty-one inches.

The examination of the temple complex began on the outside, where the messenger showed Ezekiel a wall that completely surrounded the complex. The wall was one rod high and one rod wide, or six long cubits for each dimension—approximately ten and one-half feet.

6–16 Ezekiel was taken to the eastern outer gate of the temple complex. The divine messenger explained the gate's design and dimensions in detail (see Fig. 1). The description began from the outside of the gate and worked inward. The gate was composed of seven steps (E) that led up to the gate from the outside. Perhaps these were the equivalent of the "entrance" mentioned in v.11. If so, the entrance steps measured ten cubits wide and thirteen cubits long. The north and south outer gates have the identical dimensions of the east gate (cf. vv.20–27). The gate's outer threshold (OT) measured ten cubits wide and six cubits deep. The entire gate sys-

tem resembled the multiple entry gates archaeologists discovered from the Solomonic period. There were several guard rooms (cf. 1Ki 24:28; 2Ch 12:11), or alcoves, on either side of the inner part of the Solomonic gate. In this gate there were three alcoves (A) on either side of the inside of the gate, each six cubits square with a wall (FW) one cubit high in front of each. The dimension of the walls (S) separating the three inner alcoves was five cubits. The gate's inner threshold (IT) was one rod deep (six cubits), like the outer threshold.

A "portico" (P; GK 395), or vestibule, on the inside of the gate faced the courtyard. It was eight cubits wide with a two-cubit doorjamb facing the temple. Verse 14 can be understood to give the total dimensions of the portico if all sides (both widths and both lengths) were measured. There would be a total of sixty cubits (eight cubits wide by twenty-two cubits long). On the other hand, if "porticoes" refers to doorjambs or pilasters, sixty cubits could be the height of each doorjamb of each gate. There were windows, or parapet openings (O), in each alcove and in the portico; but the number and exact location of each are uncertain. The only decoration mentioned was palm tree designs, found on the inner walls of the alcoves and/ or on the doorjambs.

The overall dimensions of the gate system were twenty-five cubits wide by fifty cubits long.

17–19 The courtyard (see Fig. 2) had a pavement strip (LP) the width of the east gate's length: fifty cubits. The pavement formed a border all around the outside edges of the outer court and was known as the lower pavement. Thirty rooms (R) were on this pavement around the outer court. The dimension of the outer courtyard from the inside of the outer eastern gate to the inner eastern gate was said to be one hundred cubits. The same dimension separated the north and south outer gate systems from their corresponding inner gates (40:23, 27).

20–27 The outer northern and southern gate systems were exactly identical with the outer eastern gate (cf. vv.6–16).

(2) The inner court (40:28–47)

28–37 In the examination of the inner court, the guide first discussed the gates, then the

Figure 1
Gate Systems for all Gates
of the Outer Court

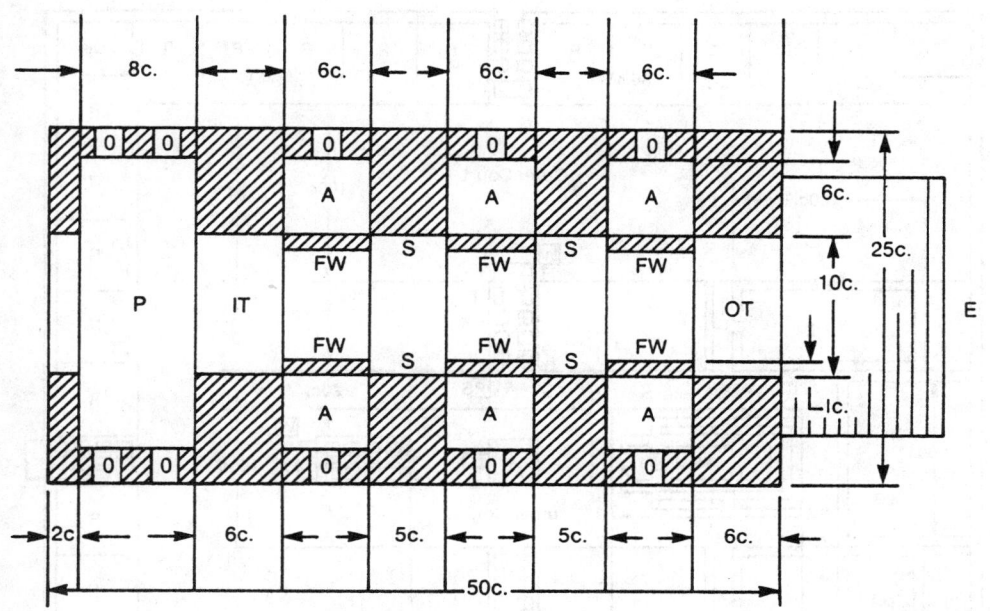

Key:

FW	Wall (barriers, borders, space) (40:12a)
A	Alcoves (side rooms, guard rooms) (40:7a, 10a, 12b)
P	Portico (portch, vestibule) (40:7c, 8–9, 14)
S	Walls separating alcoves (40:7b, 10b)
OT	Outer threshold of the gate (40:6, 11)
IT	Inner threshold of the porch (40:7c)
O	Windows (parapet openings) (40:16)
E	Steps (40:6b, 22b, 26a)

Overall height, length, and width of the gate (40:13–15)

rooms for preparation of the sacrifices, next the rooms for the ministering priests, and last the general dimension and character of the inner court.

The guide showed the three gates to the inner court to Ezekiel in a counterclockwise direction, beginning at the south gate. Each of these gates was identical in its dimensions and basic design with the three gates of the outer court. Two distinct alterations were made in the inner gate design over that of the outer gate. All inner gates had their porticoes facing outward toward the outer court rather than on the inside. In addition, each stairway leading up to an inner gate system had eight steps rather than seven. Verse 30 indicates that the portico dimensions of the inner gates

were five cubits by twenty-five cubits. However, this dimension does not harmonize with the dimensions of the porticoes in the outer gates; and the text states that the dimensions were the same between the inner and outer gate systems, excluding the two exceptions just mentioned. Perhaps the best solution is that the dimensions of the portico of the inner gates varies slightly from those of the outer gates.

38–43 As Ezekiel and the divine messenger were standing beside the northern inner gate system, the messenger described the rooms (W) and tables (T) to be used for the preparation of the sacrifices. There was a room located beside the doorjamb outside each inner court gate. This means each room (W) was in

Figure 2
Temple Complex

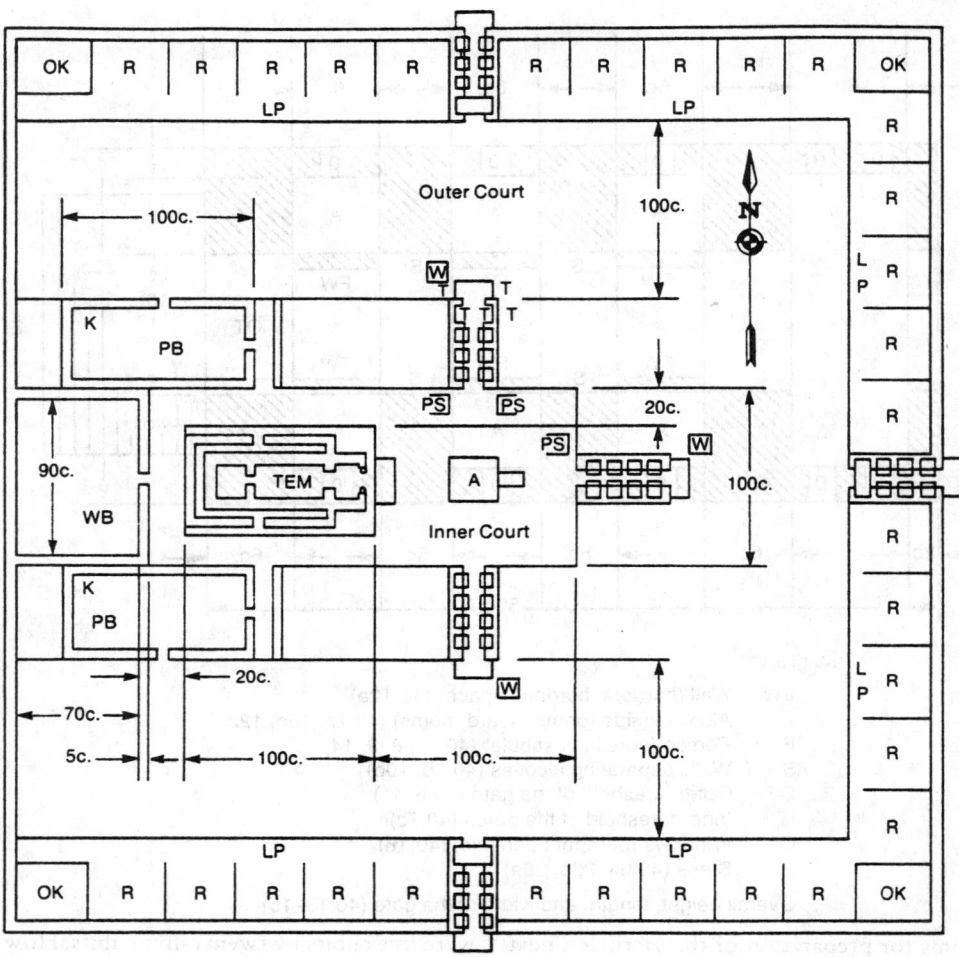

Key:

A	Altar (40:47b)
WB	Building of the separation yard (41:12, 13b, 15)
K	Kitchen for priests to boil sacrifices (46:19–20)
OK	Kitchens for priests to boil people's sacrifices (46:21–24)
LP	Pavement strip (40:17–18)
PB	Priests' chambers (42:1–14)
R	Rooms in outer court for storage or priests' quarters (40:17)
PS	Rooms for singers (priests) (40:44–46)
T	Tables for slaughter of sacrifices (two at each point) (40:39–43)
TEM	Temple proper (40:48–41:11, 13a, 14, 16, 23–26)
W	Rooms for washing offerings (40:38)
	Inner court (40:44–47a)
	Outer court (40:17–19, 23, 27, 39–43)
	Width from outer gates to inner gates (40:19, 23, 27)

the outer courtyard beside the stairs leading up to the portico of the inner gate. Here the burnt offerings were to be washed for ceremonial cleansing. Though the word for "gateway" is plural in v.38, it is singular in v.39. The implication is that the two tables on either side of each inner gate portico were for the slaughter of offerings. On these four tables (T) in each portico, the burnt offerings, sin offerings, and guilt offerings—the only sacrifices requiring an animal or bird to be killed—would be slaughtered. The significance of the offerings is discussed above in the introduction to this section and below where these sacrifices are mentioned in the worship ritual.

The northern inner gate had some furniture unique to it. Two additional tables (T) for slaughter of sacrifices were placed on either side of the stairs outside the north inner gate in the outer courtyard. This made a total of eight tables both outside and inside the north inner gate. Four additional small tables of dressed stone, one and one-half cubits square and one cubit high, on which the utensils for slaughtering the sacrifices would be laid, were distributed around the northern inner gate. Double-pronged hooks were placed around the portico's wall.

44–46 Inside the northern and eastern inner gates were rooms (PS) for the priests of the sons of Zadok. They were the only ones of the Levitical priesthood permitted to minister directly to the Lord. The exclusion of Levi's other descendants from this ministry is explained in ch. 44. The Hebrew states that the rooms were specifically for singers. Though other functions are mentioned for the priests who resided in these rooms, singing was a priestly function in OT temple worship (cf. 1Ch 16:4–6; 23:5; 2Ch 29). The rooms that faced south on the inside of the north inner gate housed the priests who ministered in the temple. The room that faced north on the inside of the east gate housed those priests who ministered primarily at the altar of sacrifice.

47 The inner court courtyard was one hundred cubits square. The altar of sacrifice (A; see ch. 43) was in front of the temple (TEM).

(3) The house of God (40:48–41:26)

48–49 The divine messenger moved next to the temple structure itself (see Fig. 3). The fourteen-cubit-wide entrance of the sanctuary was reached by a flight of stairs. Facing the entrance (EP) Ezekiel observed five-cubit-wide doorjambs (PJ) protruding three cubits from the inside of the temple wall on either side. Pillars (PL), perhaps similar to Joachin and Boaz of Solomon's and Herod's temples, stood in front of the doorjambs, one on either side. As Ezekiel stepped into the temple's portico (EP), he saw a room twenty-cubits wide by eleven cubits.

41:1–2 The outer sanctuary (OS), or Holy Place, consisted of a room twenty cubits wide by forty cubits long. Its ten-cubit-wide entrance (ET) was bounded on either side with six-cubit-wide doorjambs (TJ) on walls that protruded from the side walls of the chamber by five cubits on each side.

3–4 Ezekiel moved into the inner sanctuary (IS) through a six-cubit-wide entrance (EH) with two-cubit-wide doorjambs (HJ) on walls seven cubits wide. As Ezekiel viewed the twenty-cubit-square room he was told that this room was "the Most Holy Place." By narrowing the entrance ways to the portico (40:48), to the outer sanctuary (41:2), and to the inner sanctuary (41:3) from fourteen cubits, to ten cubits, to six cubits, respectively, the architect focused the worshiper's eyes on the Most Holy Place, the center of worship.

5–11 A six-cubit-thick wall (W) surrounded the entire temple. Next to this wall, but not attached to it, were ninety side rooms (SR), four cubits wide and constructed on three stories. The thirty rooms on each level became wider as one moved higher up through each story. Stairs joined the three stories from bottom to top. These side rooms (SR) had an outer wall (W) five cubits thick, and they all rested on a six-cubit-high foundation on either side of the temple proper. This foundation extended an additional five cubits beyond the temple's outer wall to the edge of the foundation. Entrances to these side rooms were only on the north and south sides of the inner court (see Fig. 2) of the temple structure. Twenty cubits separated these side rooms from the priests' chambers (PS in Fig. 2).

12–26 A separate building (WB in Fig. 2) was west of the temple proper, seemingly next to the western wall of the temple complex. Its function is unknown. The structure was seventy cubits wide by ninety cubits long with a five-cubit-thick wall all around. With its five-cubit wall on either side plus its ninety-cubit length, the building was exactly one hundred cubits across from north to south, exactly the same width as the inner court to the east of the temple proper.

The decorations of the temple structure consisted of windows all around the portico, the outer sanctuary, and the inner sanctuary. All the inside walls of each aspect of the temple structure were covered with a wood wainscoting up to the windows, and the windows were covered too. These wooden inner walls, as well as the outer walls, were carved with cherubim interspersed with palm trees. Each cherub had two faces, one each facing the palm tree on either side of it. The faces were those of a man and a lion. Though the cherubim may symbolize the guardianship of God's holiness, any significance of the palm trees is uncertain.

The only furniture in the temple was a wooden altar, three cubits high by two cubits square. The divine messenger called it "the table that is before the LORD." This altar was much smaller than the altar of sacrifice (cf. 43:13–17). Some have suggested that this was the altar of incense that sat before the veil of the Most Holy Place in the Mosaic system. The altar of incense symbolized the saints' prayers in the tabernacle.

Both the entrance to the outer sanctuary (ET in Fig. 3) and the entrance to the inner sanctuary (EH) had rectangular doors. These were double doors, hinged with two leaves for each door. The doors to the outer sanctuary were carved with cherubim interspersed with palm trees, similar to the outer walls.

The entire temple complex was of great beauty and symmetry.

(4) The priests' buildings (42:1–14)

1–9 There were two buildings (PB in Fig. 2) in the outer court just outside the inner court, one on the north and one on the south. The building was one hundred cubits long, east to west, and fifty cubits wide, north to south. The northern building lay parallel to the outer court pavement to the north and the inner court's north wall that it abutted. It was three-storied with many rooms and galleries on each floor. The two lower stories had pillars as structural supports. The rooms

on the third floor were smaller, though the third floor had larger galleries than the middle and ground floors. All rooms appeared to have doors on the north side. The lower floor had an entrance on the north with a ten-cubit wide and one-cubit long step in front of it (cf. vv.11–12). The building's lower floor also had an eastern entrance, in front of which was a wall parallel to the east end of the building. Perhaps this wall provided a separation from the rest of the activity of the outer court, giving privacy.

10–12 The southern building was similar to the northern building in every facet, providing perfect symmetry, which was a hallmark of the overall design (see the NIV note on v.10 for the reading of "south" instead of "eastward").

13–14 These two buildings provided a holy place where the ministering Zadokian priests could eat the holy offerings and change from their holy ministering garments to everyday clothes. The priests were to eat portions of the grain offerings, the sin offerings, and the guilt offerings. This building also provided a place to store these portions of the sacrifices. The priests would leave the priestly garments in these buildings. In doing so they would continue to distinguish between the holy and the profane.

(5) The measurement of the temple area (42:15–20)

15–20 The divine messenger brought Ezekiel outside the entire temple complex through the east gate. Ezekiel was shown the vast area that would be set aside for the sanctuary. It measured five hundred rods square (cf. NIV note), almost a square mile. Some immediately reject the term "rod" (16.5 feet) and replace it with "cubit," the standard of measure in these verses. However, such an alteration is contrary to 45:2, which declares the temple environs to be "500 . . . square." Neither the term "rod" nor "cubit" is stated. Ezekiel 45:2 does state that a border of fifty cubits provides an open space around the "500 . . . square" area. Ezekiel's explicit use of the term "cubit" seems to have been to distinguish cubits from the rods of the "500 . . . square" area as already revealed in 42:15–20. Some argue that an area five hundred rods square (about 1.5 miles square) would be too large and not fit the topography. But Zecha-

Figure 3
The Temple Sanctuary

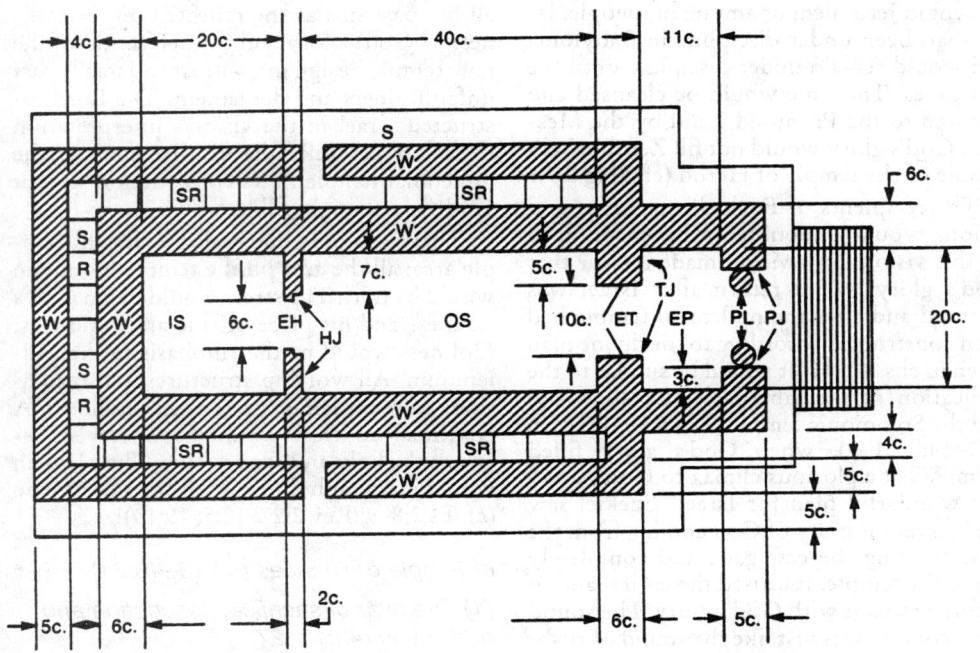

Key:

ET	Entry to the temple (outer sanctuary) (41:2a; cf. 41:23–25)
EH	Entry to the Most Holy Place (inner sanctuary) (41:3; cf. 41:23–25)
OS	Holy Place (outer sanctuary) (41:2b, 21b)
IS	Most Holy Place (inner sanctuary) (41:4)
EP	Potico (porch, vestibule) (40:48–49)
PL	Pillars (40:49)
HJ	Projecting wall (jamb, post) of the entry to the Most High Place (41:3)
PJ	Projecting wall (jamb, post) of the porch (40:48)
TJ	Projecting wall (jamb, post) of the temple proper (41:1)
SR	Side rooms of the temple sanctuary (41:5b–11a)
S	Space left around the temple (platform) (41:11b)
W	Wall of the temple (41:5a)
	Overall dimensions of the temple with yard on either side (41:13a, 14)
	Windows (41:16, 26) on the porch, side chambers, and decoration (41:16-20)

riah and other prophets demonstrate that the whole Palestinian topography will undergo geographical modifications at the beginning of the Millennium. No good reason appears to reject the term "rod" in these verses.

This large area provided a separation space between the holy (the temple complex and its worship) and the common (or profane) terrain of everyday life. Israel had frequently forgotten to make this distinction in her past history.

b. The return of the glory of God to the temple (43:1–12)

1–5 Ezekiel was then brought to the outer court's east gate where he looked out toward the east. Here he would see the most important aspect of this entire apocalyptic vision: God's glory returning to the temple!

The glory that Ezekiel saw had the same likeness of God's glory that he had seen in his inaugural visions on the river Kebar (chs. 1; 3) and that had departed from the temple during his announcement of destruction on Jerusalem (chs. 8; 10–11). Since Jerusalem's destruction, God's glory had not been present in Jerusalem or among his people. Israel had been under discipline in Babylonia and would remain under discipline until the end times. Then she would be cleansed and restored to the Promised Land by the Messiah. God's glory would not fill Zerubbabel's temple or the temple of Herod (cf. Hag 2:7).

The recipients of Ezekiel's messages and visions would undoubtedly be encouraged by this vision. This vision made it clear that God's glory would return after Israel was cleansed and after the millennial temple had been constructed according to the divine plan given in chs. 40–42. It would be similar to the dedication of the tabernacle (Ex 40:34–35) and the Solomonic temple (1Ki 8:10–11; 2Ch 5:13–14; 7:1–3), when God's glory filled them. What a glorious climax to God's good and wonderful plan for Israel! Ezekiel saw the marvelous glory of God coming from the east, entering the east gate, and completely filling the temple. It caused the entire land to become radiant with God's glory. The sound of its coming was just like the sound of rushing water Ezekiel had heard coming from the cherubim's wings in the previous visions of God's glory (cf. 1:24). God had indeed returned to dwell among his people!

6–12 The significance of this vision of God's glory was so important that the Lord himself interpreted it to Ezekiel. The temple was to be God's throne and residence among the Israelites forever. The promises of chs. 33–37 would be fulfilled when God's glory returned. The glory of God would fill the temple, and God's holiness would permeate the entire temple complex. This, in turn, would be instructive both for Ezekiel's contemporaries and for the house of Israel living in the Messianic Age. At that time Israel would never again defile the Lord's holy name (cf. 39:7) through her religious prostitution in the temple precinct (cf. 2Ki 23:7) and the burial of the corpses of kings in their high places. Israel had religiously defiled the Lord's name through her idolatrous practices. Therefore the Lord used this vision to exhort his people in Ezekiel's day to put away these defiling practices.

Ezekiel's contemporaries would be ashamed of their sins when they heard of this vision and saw the new temple design with the promised return of God's glory. Likewise, millennial Israel would be ashamed for all her past sins as she reflected on the holiness of God's glory and the perfection of the new temple design in contrast to Israel's past unfaithfulness and defilement. The Lord instructed Israel in the vision's interpretation to follow carefully the detailed plan of the millennial temple in its construction so that God's glory might fill it.

There was only one basic law for the temple area: all the area on the temple mountain would be holy. The stress would be on God's holiness and his place of rule and residency. Holiness would be the emphasis in the Millennium. All worship structures and regulations were to demonstrate God's holiness. A continual contrast would be observed between the holy and the profane. The Messiah would judge unholiness with the rod of iron (cf. Ps 2:8–9; Rev 2:27; 12:5; 19:15)!

c. Temple ordinances (43:13–46:24)

(1) The altar of sacrifice: description and dedication (43:13–27)

13–17 The basic design of the altar of sacrifice is clear (see Fig. 4). It was to be located in front of the sanctuary in the inner court (A in Fig. 2). The altar is described from the bottom to the top. The bottom portion (B in Fig. 4) of the altar was composed of a one-cubit-high base with a one-cubit-wide gutter around the altar. The gutter had a rim of one span length (approx. nine inches). On top of this base were three sections of the altar. Next to the base was a two-cubit-high section (I), sixteen cubits square with a one-cubit ledge around it. This ledge formed a gutter one cubit wide with a one-half-cubit-high rim. The middle section (E) was four cubits high and fourteen cubits square, including a one-cubit-wide ledge around it. The hearth (H), four cubits high and twelve cubits square, formed the altar's top portion. One horn (HA) projected from each of the four corners. Steps (S) led to the top on the east side, though the dimensions of the stairs are not given. These steps were in contrast to the altar of sacrifice under the Mosaic system, where it was forbidden to go up by steps on the altar (Ex 20:24–26). This millennial altar was very large: approximately thirty-one and one-half feet square at the base by approximately nineteen and one-quarter feet high!

18–27 After the altar of sacrifice was constructed, it would be necessary to cleanse and dedicate it. Cleansing was needed because everything associated with humankind partakes of sin and needs to be cleansed, especially if it is to be used in the worship of the Lord. A similar cleansing and dedication took place with the altar of sacrifice of the tabernacle (Ex 29:36–37; Lev 8:14–17) and the altar of Solomon's temple (2Ch 7:9).

The ritual cleansing and atonement for the altar took seven days. On the first day a special sin offering of a young bull was made by the Zadokian priests. They were to take some of the blood of the sacrifice and put it on the four horns of the altar, the four corners of the altar's upper ledge, and all around the rim. This sin or purification offering would cleanse the altar from its sinfulness, thereby making atonement for the altar. Atonement here has the idea of wiping away or cleansing, after which the altar would be holy (cf. Lev 8:14–15). The remainder of the sin offering was burned in a designated part of the temple area (cf. 42:20) but outside the sanctuary precinct per se (Lev 8:17).

On the second and succeeding five days, the priests offered a sin offering of a male goat without defect, to continue to purify the altar. After this ceremonial cleansing, the priests symbolized the altar's consecration by offering a young bull and a ram, both without defect and sprinkled with salt, as a burnt offering before the Lord. With these offerings each day for the prescribed seven days, the altar would be atoned for and cleansed (cf. Ex 29:36–37).

After the seven-day ceremonial cleansing and dedication of the altar of sacrifice, the priests would begin to present the burnt offerings and fellowship offerings on the altar for the people. Not only would the Lord then accept their offerings because they had properly consecrated the altar, but he also would accept the worshipers. What a glorious truth! Because of the Messiah's sacrifice, all who believe are accepted!

(2) Regulations for the east gate (44:1–3)

1–2 The outer east gate (cf. 40:6–16) was to remain closed permanently. This was done because of reverence for the gate's special sanctity, for it was the gate through which the Lord entered into the millennial precinct in his glory (cf. 43:1–4).

3 Only the "prince" (GK 5954) was permitted to enter this gate. He must enter and leave by way of the portico from the outer court only. His only function within that gate was to eat bread in the presence of the Lord, but exactly which meal or for what purpose is not stated.

The identity of this "prince" has been a puzzle. The English word "prince" connotes royalty. However, the Hebrew word is best translated "leader." This leader is not the Messiah, because he would make a sin offering for himself (cf. 45:22); such is not possible for the Lord Jesus (cf. Heb 4:15). In addition, this leader would have natural children (46:16), another impossibility for the Messiah. The leader was a man, but his identity remains unknown. He functions as the people's leader in their millennial worship, almost like a high priest, but not having the same role and function.

(3) The priests and the service of the temple (44:4–16)

4–5 The emphasis in this vision had been on God's glory and the resulting holiness that was required in all aspects of millennial worship. Ezekiel was brought again to see the Lord's glory filling the temple, and his immediate response was reverence and awe as he fell prostrate in worship. The Lord undoubtedly used this experience to impress again on Ezekiel the importance of holiness, for holiness must characterize the priests and their actions.

The priests would instruct the rest of the people in holiness, teaching holiness by their lives, their priestly function, and their word. For this reason Ezekiel was exhorted to watch and listen carefully to all the temple regulations, especially those concerning the entrances and exits. There the priests would contact both the common life in the people and the holiness of the temple's inner court and sanctuary. There they would meet and serve the people.

6–9 The religions of the ancient Near East frequently used foreign captives as temple servants to aid the priests. The Lord's rebuke of Israel in these verses reflected ancient Israel's adoption of this practice. This custom

Figure 4
Altar of Sacrifice

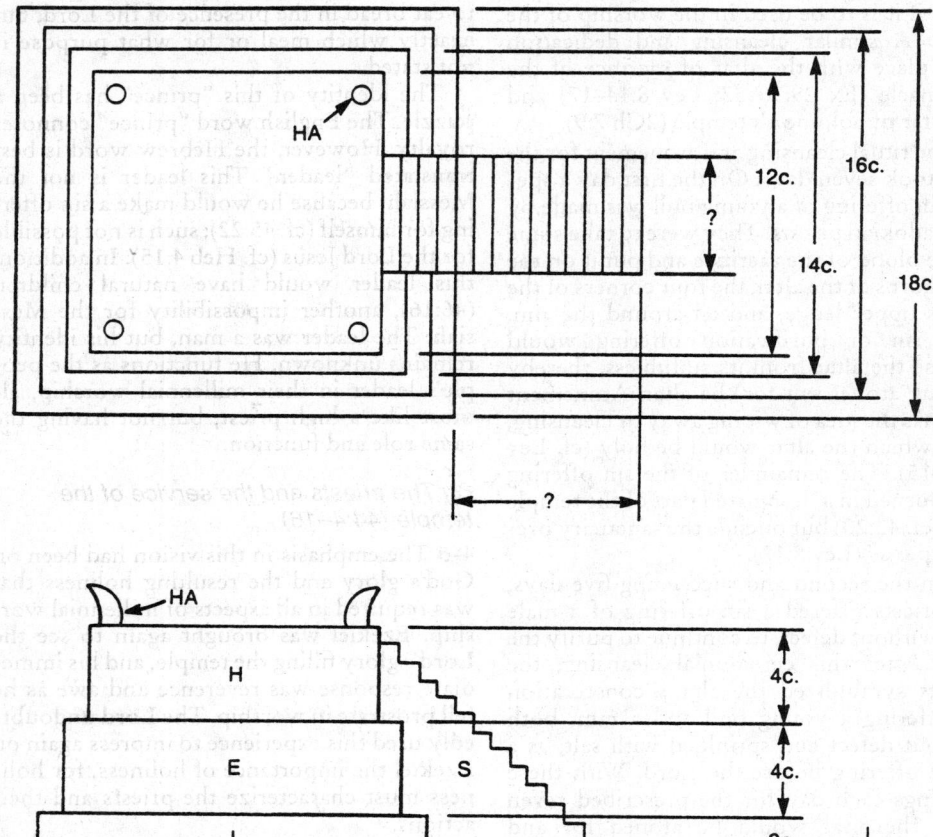

Key:

H	Altar hearth	(43:15–16)
E	Enclosure	(43:14, 17)
I	Interior	(43:14, 17)
B	Bottom	(43:13)
HA	Horns of the altar	(43:20)
S	Steps	(43:17b; cf. 40:47b)

was first observed in Israel when Joshua made the Gibeonites temple servants (Jos 9:23, 27). Israel seems to have continued this practice through the time of Ezra (Ezr 8:20). However, the Mosaic covenant stated that foreigners who were uncircumcised in flesh and heart were not to minister in the temple as priests, along with all other Israelites not of the Aaronic line (cf. Nu 3:10). Perhaps originally some of these foreigners had been circumcised both in the flesh and in the heart so that they could enter the temple area lawfully and make an offering (cf. Nu 15:14). Certainly Isa 56:3, 6 indicates that such would be possible in the messianic kingdom (cf. Zec 14:21). But Israel had broken the Mosaic covenant with the detestable practice of having foreign temple-servants not only entering the sanctuary but also taking charge of the temple duties. By their handling priestly functions related to the holy things, they had desecrated the temple. But these foreigners should never have been permitted to take over the priests' functions.

The Mosaic covenant called for all to be circumcised in their hearts as well as in the flesh, the sign of the Abrahamic covenant (cf. Lev 26:41; Dt 10:16; 30:6; Jer 4:4; 9:25). There must be a change of heart toward the Lord and his ways, a true circumcising of the hardness of the heart's foreskin. This was necessary for both Israelites and foreigners if they were to enter into a proper relationship with the Lord. Therefore, an explicit command was given: No foreigner, uncircumcised of heart and flesh, could enter the temple, not even those living in Israel. However, the implication was that any foreigner circumcised in heart and flesh could enter as any other person, but he could not function in any manner as a priest.

10–14 The Lord now clarifies who could minister in the millennial temple and in what manner. The Levites would be in charge of the temple gates, where they would slaughter the burnt offerings and other sacrifices for the people and assist them in their worship. The Levites would also be responsible for all work done in the temple, perhaps those duties previously handled by foreigners.

Limitations were placed on Levites' ministry. They would not be permitted to serve the Lord as priests nor would they be allowed to come near any of the Lord's holy things, especially his most holy offerings. They would serve neither in the inner court nor in the temple itself. The reason for this restriction was explicit. As a group they had strayed from the Lord in the past and had pursued idolatry. In so doing they had also led the nation into this sin (cf. ch. 8). They were to be held accountable for their past transgressions, even as they had been warned in Nu 18:23. They must bear sin's consequences and shame.

15–16 The descendants of Zadok were first placed into major priestly functions under Solomon (1Ki 2:26–35), though this had been foretold in 1Sa 2:35. They alone had remained faithful to their duties in the Lord's temple when all the rest of Israel had gone away from the Lord. Because of their faithfulness then, the Lord would give to them that singularly unique ministry before him in the millennial sanctuary. They alone would stand before the Lord to offer sacrifices. They alone would be permitted to enter the temple and come near the Lord's table to perform his service of worship (exactly which "table" is meant is not certain). Chapters 45–46 indicate that the sons of Zadok would bring the sacrifices for the prince and the people daily, on the Sabbaths, and at the appointed festivals. What a great privilege and blessing would be theirs because of their past faithfulness to God's laws!

(4) Ordinances for the Zadokian priesthood (44:17–31)

17–19 Various regulations and functions for the Zadokian priests are spelled out in the remainder of this chapter. The clothing worn when ministering highlights the holiness of their ministry. Linen was to be worn when these priests entered the inner court to serve (cf. Ex 28:42; Lev 16:4). The linen not only depicted purity by its whiteness, but its coolness kept the priests from perspiring and thereby becoming unclean. In addition to the outer linen garment, the priests wore linen undergarments and a linen turban.

When the priests left the inner court to go out among the common people, they were required to change their clothes (cf. Lev 6:11), leaving their linen garments in the sacred rooms so designated (42:1–14). In this way they would not improperly make the people holy with their ministering clothes.

Contact with a holy thing consecrates. A person or object enters into the state of holiness by touching a holy thing and thus becomes subject to the restrictions of holiness to which other holy people or objects are subject (Ex 29:37; 30:29; Lev 6:27; cf. 21:1–8). This rule concerning leaving the linen garments in the sacred rooms would aid in maintaining a clear distinction between the holy and the profane.

20–22 The Zadokian priests were not to shave their heads or allow their hair to grow long. It was to be trimmed properly. Shaving the head was often associated with pagan religion in which hair was offered to the gods to establish a relationship. Long hair could depict mourning. Priests were not to practice idolatry or pagan mourning rites (cf. Lev 10:6; 21:5, 10). As this hair regulation was a sign of holiness for the priests in the Mosaic system (Lev 21:6), so it would be in the millennial system.

No priest was to drink wine while ministering before the Lord (cf. Lev 10:9). He was to make sure that he had full control of himself when performing the Lord's service. This was holiness.

A Zadokian priest was permitted to marry an Israelite virgin or the widow of a priest. This would maintain the holiness of marriage. He could not marry any other widow or a divorced woman. This restriction, which had been true for the high priest in the Mosaic system, would now be applied to all priests (cf. Lev 21:7, 14).

23–24 The above regulations would enable the priests to teach the Israelites the difference between something holy and something common through the visual lessons of their priestly lives. In addition, these priests would serve as judges for any dispute, making their decision according to God's ordinances. They were always to keep God's laws and every decree concerning the appointed feasts and the Sabbaths, the sign of the Mosaic covenant.

25–27 There would be individuals entering the Millennium with natural bodies from the tribulation period. These, of course, would ultimately die physically, though physical life will be much longer during the Millennium (cf. Isa 65:20). A priest was defiled by coming near a dead person, and so this was forbid-

den, except in a case of a member of his immediate family (Lev 21:1–3). When a priest cared for a dead family member, he would be defiled; it would be necessary for him to be cleansed according to biblical guidelines (cf. Nu 19:11–19) and wait seven days, the period of cleansing. When a priest returned to minister in the inner court after defilement and cleansing, it would be necessary for him to offer a sin offering as a purification for himself.

28–31 All provisions for the priests would be made by the Lord. He would be their inheritance and their possession. No other possessions were to be given to them except those specified in these verses. The priests' food would be provided by the Lord through the people's offerings. The priests would eat from the grain offerings, the sin offerings, and the guilt offerings. They would also partake of everything devoted to the Lord by the Israelites, the best of all the firstfruits, all special gifts, and the ground meal of the people (cf. Nu 18:10–13). On "devoted" things, see comments on Lev 27:1–34, also v.28; Nu 18:14. The priests were not allowed to eat anything that had been torn by a wild animal or was found dead (cf. Lev 17:5; 22:8; Dt 14:21). The Israelites were promised blessing for their faithful giving to the priests in this way. There is always blessing in giving to the Lord!

(5) The sacred area of the Holy Land (45:1–8)

1–8 A specific portion of Israel's land in the Millennium would be set aside as a sacred area for the priests and the sanctuary. The entire area would be a contribution to the Lord by Israel. That land would not really belong to the priests but to the Lord. In this sense, also, the Lord would continue to be the priests' inheritance.

This contribution to the Lord for a holy area would measure twenty-five thousand rods by twenty thousand rods. The NIV translates "cubits" rather than "rods" as the standard of measure (see comment on 42:15–20). Actually no word for a standard is given in the text; this is because the standard of "rods" had already been given in 42:15–20. We can assume that Ezekiel understood this to be the measurement and only noted the exception to it in the measurement of a fifty-cubit-wide open area around the five hundred-square-rod sanctuary area.

This twenty-five thousand rods by twenty thousand rods area was further subdivided into two equal areas, twenty-five thousand rods by ten thousand rods. One was a sacred portion for the Zadokian priests who were to minister to the Lord in the temple (cf. 44:15–16; 48:9–12). Here they would place their houses. In the center of this area would be the five-hundred-rod square area for the sanctuary, the Most Holy Place. This five-hundred-rod-square area would have a fifty-cubit-wide border of open land all around it as a barrier to separate it from all else. This would stress the holiness of the sanctuary area.

The other twenty-five thousand rod by ten thousand rod area would belong to the Levites who would assist the Zadokian priests in the temple (cf. 44:10–14; 48:13–14). They would use the area for their towns. This entire area would run parallel to the portion for the Zadokian priests, immediately to the north (cf. 48:8, 21).

Another area of twenty-five thousand rods by five thousand rods, adjoining the Zadokian sacred area to the south, would provide for the city (cf. 48:15–19, 30–35). This city is most likely Jerusalem, though no name is given. The city area would belong to the entire house of Israel.

Finally, an area was allotted to the "prince" (see comment on 44:3). His portion was the land immediately to the east and west of the entire sacred area composed of the Levites' portion, the Zadokian priests' portion, and the city area (cf. 48:21–22). It would parallel the tribal boundaries of Judah and Benjamin.

Ezekiel concludes this section by declaring that Israel's millennial leaders would no longer oppress God's people as leaders had done in the past (cf. 11:1–13; 14:1–11; 20:1–23:49; 34:1–10). They would allow the people to possess their own land according to their tribes without attempting to confiscate land (cf. 48:1–29).

(6) The role of the prince in the Millennium (45:9–46:18)

9–12 The concluding verse of the preceding section implied that the leaders in Israel's past and in Ezekiel's day had seized property that was not theirs (cf. 46:18). Therefore, Ezekiel exhorts his contemporary princes (leaders) concerning their violence and oppression in which they used unjust and inaccurate scales and standards of measure. This kind of unrighteous conduct must stop in Ezekiel's day. It would not exist in the messianic kingdom.

The proper standards of measure are given. Just as linear measurements of the ancient Near East were not as accurate as those of today, so this was true of volume measurements. Ezekiel delineates the proper standard of volume measure in the terms of his day. An ephah (approx. one bushel) was a dry measure equivalent to a bath (approx. nine gallons), a liquid measure. Both were equivalent to one-tenth of a homer (approx. ninety gallons or eleven bushels), which was the basic standard of volume measure. Ezekiel also exhorts his contemporaries to make sure that their scales and measures were accurate according to this standard.

Likewise, Ezekiel clarifies the proper standard for weights. One shekel weight (approx. two-fifths of an ounce) consisted of twenty gerahs (approx. one-fiftieth of an ounce). Sixty shekels comprised one mina (approx. twenty-four ounces). It was important that the leaders of the people be just in all their business dealings.

13–17 Contrary to the unrighteous behavior of Israel's past leaders, Israel's "prince" (see comment on 44:3) in the Millennium would be faithful to the Lord's righteous requirements. One of his duties would be to make atonement for the people.

"Atonement" (GK 4105) is a word that carries many connotations. Most view this term theologically with a sense of expiation for sin of a person or a people. Such was the picture lesson of the Day of Atonement in the Mosaic system (cf. Lev 16). It has also been observed that the concept of atonement may stress purification, especially when atonement was made for things. In either case, the atonement rituals of the Mosaic system and those of the millennial system described in these chapters were picture lessons and reminders of humanity's sinfulness and their need for a complete cleansing from sin and forgiveness through the efficacious atoning sacrifice of the Messiah, Jesus Christ. The full and complete provision for forgiveness of sin was provided once and for all by Jesus Christ's shed blood.

The Israelites had made a special contribution of materials for the tabernacle's construction (cf. Ex 25:2–7; 35:5, 21, 24; 36:3, 6). In a similar manner Israel in the messianic kingdom would make a special contribution of grain, oil, and sheep to the prince, from which he would, in turn, make atonement for them (cf. Ex 30:13–15; Lev 1:4). The contribution from each Israelite was one-sixth ephah (about one-sixth bushel) out of each homer (approx. eleven bushels) of wheat or barley that was harvested, one-tenth of a bath (about one gallon) of oil from each cor (or liquid homer—approx. ninety gallons) of oil each would have, and one sheep from every flock of two hundred that had been fed on Israel's well-watered pastures.

From this contribution the prince would provide grain offerings, burnt offerings, and fellowship offerings for the people's atonement (cf. Lev 9:7; 10:17). The general statement of v.15 is further specified in v.17. The prince would bring burnt offerings, grain offerings, fellowship offerings, sin offerings, and drink offerings to make atonement for Israel at each of her festivals, her new moon celebrations, and her Sabbaths. These rituals of atonement were commemorative of the complete and finished saving work of Christ for sin through the sacrifice of himself (see introductory comments on chs. 40–48). They were in no way efficacious. What praise and worship they would give to the Lord for his gracious provision for sin as they viewed these sacrificial reminders in worship (cf. Rev 5:7–14)!

These acts of commemoration of atonement were limited to the weekly Sabbath, the new moons, and all appointed festivals of Israel (cf. Lev 23:1–41; Nu 28:1–29, 40). There is no special Day of Atonement in the Millennium. That special day had its full fruition in the special day of efficacious atonement provided by Christ on the cross. The people also were not asked to contribute any bulls, goats, or rams that would later be specified as the animals for sin and burnt offerings (cf. 45:21–25; 46:2–8, 11–12). Though the data are insufficient, perhaps these animals for the atoning sin and burnt offerings were provided by the prince (cf. vv.18, 22; 2Ch 31:3), not by the people, in order to symbolize that God alone could make that provision. The offerer in the Mosaic system was reminded of the substitute death for his own sins when he brought his own animal for his sin offering, except on the Day of Atonement, when all the sins of the nation were atoned for symbolically. In the Millennium the stress seems to be that God provides the substitute, insofar as the prince provided from his own resources the bulls, rams, and male goats.

18–20 It was also the millennial prince's annual duty to purify the temple sanctuary. On the first day of the first month (Nisan) of the religious year, the prince was to bring a sin offering of a young bull without defect to purify the temple sanctuary (cf. Lev 16:16, 33; 22:20). This was necessary because of humankind's sin that would defile the temple's holiness. Even the Zadokian priests, being human, could sin. Therefore the temple sanctuary had to be cleansed annually through this atoning (purifying) sacrifice as a reminder to all of the holiness of God and his sanctuary (cf. 2Ch 7:1–10; 29:20–24). In the ceremony the priest would take blood from the sacrificial bull and place it on the temple's doorposts (cf. 41:21—where the priests enter), on the four corners of the upper ledge of the altar of sacrifice, and on the gateposts of the inner court. This would be repeated on the seventh day of the month. Through this ceremony the temple was purified symbolically for the coming year so that all might continue to worship the Lord in holiness and purity.

21–25 The prince led in the observance of the Passover and the Feast of Tabernacles. These were the only two feasts specifically mentioned in the worship procedure of Ezekiel.

The Passover (cf. Ex 12:1–14; Lev 23:5–8; Nu 28:16–25) was observed in a manner similar to its observance under the Mosaic system. The Day of Passover would be celebrated on the fourteenth day of the first month (Nisan). The prince would provide a sin offering for himself and the people in commemoration of Christ's work. The Feast of Unleavened Bread would then continue for seven days, during which no one was to eat unleavened bread. Each day the prince would make a daily sacrifice of seven bulls and seven rams, all without defect, as a burnt offering to the Lord. In addition the prince would offer daily a male goat as a sin offering for the whole nation (cf. Nu 28:19–24). A grain offering of one ephah mixed with one hin of oil would accompany each burnt offering. These procedures followed closely those of the Mosaic system.

The Feast of Tabernacles began on the fifteenth day of the seventh month (Tishri) and lasted for seven days (cf. Lev 23:33–43; Nu 29:12–38). The same daily sacrifices made for Passover would be made also for the Feast of Tabernacles. This observance provided a continual reminder of God's gracious fulfillment of his promise to bring Israel securely and permanently into the Promised Land. Surely the Israelites would give praise and thanksgiving continually to God for this!

46:1–8 The Sabbath and the observance of the new moon would be part of the worship ritual during the Millennium. It may seem incongruous that the Sabbath, the sign of the Mosaic covenant (cf. Ex 31:13, 16–17), would be observed in the millennial kingdom when it is not observed during the church age under the new covenant. Is this a retrogression in God's purposes? Not if it is understood that all God's covenants would be fulfilled and operative in the messianic kingdom (cf. 37:15–28). The Mosaic covenant would find its fruition in the messianic kingdom in that Israel finally would be God's people and he would be their God in a relationship that was to exist under the Mosaic covenant. That the pictorial sacrifices had their reality in the work of Christ does not nullify the relationship of Mosaic covenant that is a holy one. The Mosaic covenant showed Israel how to live a holy life in a relationship with God, and that type of life is still valid under the new covenant (cf. Jer 31:33–34; Ro 8:4). Therefore, for the Mosaic covenant and the new covenant to be fulfilled side by side is not incongruous. Ezekiel, however, was looking at the situation only from his perspective under the Mosaic covenant.

Just as work was to be done for six days and on the Sabbath the Israelite was to rest, so for six days the inner court's east gate would remain closed but on the Sabbath it would be open for worship. On the Sabbath the prince would lead again his people in worship. He would enter the inner court's east gate and stand by the gate post, enjoying a position not possessed by the people. Though the specific post is not clear, it is likely the doorjamb of the portico, since the tables for the slaughter of offerings were in the portico. Here the prince would bring his

burnt offerings and fellowship offerings for the priests to sacrifice, since he could not enter into the inner court (cf. Nu 29:38). The burnt offering consisted of six male lambs and a ram, all without defect and each accompanied by a grain offering composed of one ephah of flour for the ram but as much as desired for the lambs. One hin of oil was to be mixed with each ephah of flour (cf. Nu 28:9–10). The makeup of the fellowship (thanksgiving) offering is not stated, since it was normally a freewill offering of whatever the offerer chose to bring. The prince would worship at the gate's inner threshold and then return in the same way as he entered. He would not enter the inner court. The people would worship at the east gate in the Lord's presence as the prince performed these sacrifices and worshiped within the gate.

The procedure for worship on the new moons was exactly the same for worship on the Sabbath except that the makeup of the burnt offering added a young bull along with the animals offered on the Sabbath (cf. Nu 28:11–15).

9–12 When Israel came to worship at the time of the appointed feasts (cf. Lev 23:37), the prince participated with the people, going in to worship and leaving whenever they did. The people entered through either the north or the south gate when they worshiped. They were not to return through the gate that they had entered but were to exit through the gate opposite from where they had entered. By entering one gate and leaving through its opposite, the flow of the festive crowd was regulated and confusion eliminated. Whether these gates were the outer or inner temple gates is not stated, though it would seem to be the inner court gates, since the people had normal access to the temple's outer court. If so, this is the first instance of others besides the priests entering the inner court. However, if the outer gates were in view, the arrangement of entering by one gate and leaving by its opposite would pertain only to these special days, probably because of the masses.

The sacrifices offered on these appointed feasts and festivals were specifically enumerated when each festival was discussed, or they were not specified. It is again stressed that a grain offering of one ephah of flour must accompany each bull or ram offered, and as much flour as desired must accompany the sacrifice of a lamb (cf. v.7). If the prince desired to make a freewill offering of a burnt offering of consecration or a fellowship offering of thanksgiving, the east gate was to be opened specially for this act of worship and then closed when he finished. This was the only exception to that gate remaining closed throughout the normal six days. The prince was to present his freewill offerings in the same manner as he made offerings on the Sabbath.

13–15 There were, therefore, three occasions for sacrifice: major festivals, freewill offerings of the priest, and daily offerings. In the daily offerings the prince also led the people. Each morning he would present a burnt offering of a one-year-old lamb without defect, accompanied by a grain offering of one-sixth ephah of flour and one-third hin of oil. Under the Mosaic system the daily burnt offering was offered both in the morning and in the evening. Here the offering was to be made only in the morning, though the reason was not stated. This daily burnt offering, which demonstrated the commitment of God's people to him, was to be a daily reminder of that commitment.

16–18 Inheritance was extremely important to the Israelite. Many laws had been established to guarantee that an Israelite retained family property. This concept continues in the messianic kingdom, at least in the case of the prince. Any inheritance given to one of his sons would remain with that son's descendants (that the prince has sons argues against his identity as the Messiah). Anything given to a servant would revert to the prince in the Year of Jubilee ("the year of freedom"; cf. Lev 25:10; 27:24). Ezekiel also stresses that the prince was not permitted to take other people's property and make it part of his inheritance as Israel's past leaders often did (cf. 34:3–4; 1Ki 21:19; Mic 2:1–2). No one was ever to be separated from his property.

(7) The priests' kitchens (46:19–24)

19–24 Ezekiel was brought out of the inner court to the north side of the outer court. He was led to the entrance of the building (PB in Fig. 2) that contained the rooms where the priests ate the most holy offerings and changed their garments (cf. 42:13–14). The rooms in this building faced north (42:1–5).

Here the divine messenger showed Ezekiel the place at the end of these sacred rooms where the priests would cook guilt offerings and sin offerings. Here they also baked the grain offerings and ate all the offerings. This way the priests would not have to take these offerings into the outer court to cook them and thereby consecrate the people (cf. 44:19).

There were four kitchens (OK in Fig. 2) in the four corners of the outer court, each forming a court in itself. Each of these kitchens was forty by thirty cubits. There was a stone ledge around the inside of each room under which fireplaces were built. These ample kitchen facilities enabled the priests (probably the Levites, cf. 44:10–14) to cook the people's sacrificial meals.

d. Topographical aspects of the Millennium (47:1–48:35)

It is appropriate to conclude this prophetic book with a discussion of the land of Israel during the Millennium. In the Abrahamic covenant God promised to give Canaan to Abraham and his descendants as their national land (Ge 12:7). The acquisition of that land was accomplished through Joshua's conquest. In the Mosaic covenant, God promised that Israel would appropriate the Abrahamic covenant blessings as the people obeyed the Mosaic covenant stipulations (Dt 7:12; 8:2). One of those blessings was the land of Canaan. However, throughout her history Israel consistently broke the Mosaic covenant, so that the people were removed from the Promised Land and scattered among the nations, especially Babylonia. Ezekiel prophesied of God's future promise to restore the people of Israel to their Promised Land, to cleanse them, and to give them a new heart, followed by salvation bliss in the land (36:24–40). Never again would Israel lose her land (ch. 39).

A fitting climax to the book, therefore, is to have Ezekiel describe the character of Israel's land during the Millennium with, perhaps, glimpses into the eternal state. The divine messenger would show Ezekiel the river that would heal the land. Then he would clarify Israel's boundaries and tribal allotments during the Millennium.

(1) The temple river (47:1–12)

1–12 Ezekiel was brought in his vision to the temple's entrance, where he saw water streaming eastward from under the south side of the temple-entrance threshold (41:2). The stream passed by the south side of the altar of sacrifice in the inner court, through the outer court, and out the temple complex along the south side of the outer eastern gate. The divine messenger took Ezekiel to explore the extent of this stream. The messenger used a measuring line to mark off four one-thousand-cubit intervals (approx. one-third of a mile each). At each one-thousand-cubit interval the messenger took Ezekiel out into the stream to examine its depth. The depth increased at each interval from ankle deep, to knee deep, to waist deep, and finally, at the four-thousand-cubit mark, to such magnitude that it could not be crossed. This river continued to flow southeasterly toward the Arabah, the desolate Jordan Valley rift that extends south to the Red Sea (modern Gulf of Aqabah). The river flowed into the Dead Sea and caused that sea to become alive.

The basic purpose of this divine river was to bring life. Many trees lined its sides. Every kind of fruit tree grew on both sides. Their leaves never withered and their fruit was perennial, bearing every month of the year because the divine river watered these trees. Their fruit provided food and their leaves provided healing. The entire Dead Sea and the Arabah were healed by these waters, causing the Dead Sea to swarm with marine life to the extent that fishermen fished its entire length from En Gedi to En Eglaim, catching a great variety of fish. The Arabah bloomed (cf. Isa 35:1–2, 6–7; Joel 3:18). Only the swamps and marshes were not healed; they were left to provide salt for the people. Everywhere else the river brought its life-giving power.

This river is similar to the rivers in the Garden of Eden and the eternal state. In Ge 2:8–10 God provided a river that gave life to the land in that perfect environment. That life-giving river dried up with the fall of humankind. In Ezekiel and Revelation, the full redemption of the land would be completed (cf. Ro 8:19–22). Once again the divine life-giving waters would flow from the source of God's residence, the temple, and heal the land.

The river in Rev 22:1–2 (cf. Zec 14:8) is similar to the one described in Eze 47. Though Rev 22:2 only mentions the tree of life on either side of the river, it seems that the word "tree" in that context is most likely used in a collective sense. No variance then exists with the trees in Ezekiel, only further clarification. As the tree of life was beside the river in the Garden of Eden, so the tree of life in abundance will be beside the life-giving river in the eternal state, if not in the Millennium. The variance between Ezekiel's account of this river and that of John in Revelation centers on the river's source. God is the source of both rivers; but Ezekiel saw the river issuing from the temple, whereas John saw the river coming from the throne of God and of the Lamb (a temple did not exist; cf. Rev 21:22). The river in Rev 22:2 also flowed down the city's street, which seems difficult, though not impossible, in the Ezekiel account. Regardless of whether the visions of Ezekiel and John speak of the same river (in the Millennium and the eternal state) or of two different rivers (one in the Millennium and one in the eternal state), both are similar in purpose. The source of the land's redemption and healing came from God and his throne. He would heal the land in the Millennium and in the eternal state. After all, the Millennium is the doorway to the eternal state.

(2) Divisions of the land (47:13–48:35)

13–14 Ezekiel first sets forth the manner in which the land would be distributed. It would be divided equally among Israel's twelve tribes. Two portions would go to Joseph in the form of tribal allotments for his two sons: Manasseh and Ephraim (cf. Ge 48:5–6, 22); the tribe of Joseph had been divided into two tribes to replace Levi. Thus there were twelve tribal land divisions of equal proportions. The tribe of Levi had become the priestly tribe, and in the Millennium they would have a special land for their residence (cf. 45:1–8; 48:8–14). The principle of equality would prevail. Any past abuses of inequity would be remedied.

The Lord reminds Israel that the reception of any portion of the Promised Land by a tribe was strictly on the basis of God's promise. None of them had done anything to deserve an allotment. God had promised the inheritance of this land in his covenant with Abraham (cf. Ge 12:7; 15:7, 18–21; 17:8).

15–20 Israel's national boundaries in the Millennium are similar to those of ancient Israel (cf. Nu 34:3–12). The borders followed known place names from Ezekiel's day and were given in such detail that they are without question to be taken literally.

The boundary started at the north, and each side is described in order clockwise. The north border started at an unspecified point on the Great (Mediterranean) Sea, though the remainder of the description suggests that that point might be around the mouth of the present-day Litanni River. This border followed an easterly direction in between the unknown boundaries of Damascus on the south and Hamath on the north to the site of Hazar Enan. The sites of Berothah, Sibraim, and Hazer Hatticon have not been located. Hamath and Zedad (perhaps modern Sadad southeast of Homs) as well as the area of Hauran have each received at least tentative identification.

The land's eastern border ran between the Hauran and Damascus districts to the Jordan River, where it followed the river south of the eastern (or Dead) sea. The southern border extended from Tamar (southwest of the Dead Sea) through Kadesh-barnea, to the wadi of Egypt (present day Wadi el-Arish), which it followed to the Great (Mediterranean) Sea. The western boundary was the Great Sea. By contrast, the land of God's people in the eternal state will have no sea, since the sea will no longer exist (Rev 21:1). Old Testament Israelite boundaries included two and one-half tribes in the Transjordan.

21–23 Further guidelines for the distribution of the land are given to treat the question of allotment as it relates to aliens in Israel's midst. Aliens who had settled within Israel in a given tribe and had borne children (indicating their permanency) were to be included in that given tribe when the land was distributed. These aliens were to be treated as if they were native Israelites. In this Israel would obey the Mosaic covenant (cf. Lev 19:34).

48:1–7 Each tribal area was declared to be equal, according to 47:14. Each would have parallel borders on the north and south and would stretch from the west boundary to the east boundary, in equal sizes, one next to the other. The allotments were listed for the tribes beginning at the north and progressing south. The order has no conformity to any other in Israel's history. The tribes that originated through Jacob's wives' handmaids were placed on the outer extremities, whereas the tribes from Rachel and Leah were in the center of the land (cf. Ge 35:23–26). The faithful tribes of the southern kingdom of Judah—Judah and Benjamin—would have the privileged positions next to the land's special sacred portion.

8–14 A portion of the land—25,000 rods wide (see comments on 42:15–20; 45:1–8) and having the same length as the tribal allotments from east to west—was set aside by the people as a special contribution to the Lord (cf. 45:1–8). This special portion was composed of four distinct parts: the sacred area given to the Zadokian priests (vv.9–12), the Levites' land (vv.13–14), the city land (vv.15–20), and the prince's land (vv.21–22).

The special contribution to the Lord for the sacred area of the Zadokian priests was 25,000 rods long on its north and south sides and 10,000 rods long on its east and west sides. The Lord's sanctuary would be in the center of this territory (cf. 45:4c).

To the north of this Zadokian portion would lie the Levites' land. This territory would have the same dimensions as that of the Zadokian priests mentioned above. The Lord did exhort the Levites to make sure that they did not sell, exchange, or in any way allow this land to pass to others because it belonged to the Lord. It was holy to him.

15–20 Land set aside for the city would be 25,000 rods long on the north and south sides and 5,000 rods long on the east and west sides. This land would be used for the city, houses, and pasture. The city would be in the exact center of this portion. It would be 4,500 rods square with a strip of land 250 rods wide all around it on each side. This land strip would be used for the city's pastureland. The city's total dimensions with its border would be 5,000 rods square (cf. v.15; 45:6). The remainder of the land on either side of the city would be used for growing food for the workers in the city. These two equal segments would be 5,000 rods long on the east and west sides and 10,000 rods long on their north and south sides. Workers from every tribe who lived in the city would farm this land.

The entire area that included the Levites' land, the Zadokian land, and the city land would form a combined area 25,000 rods square.

21–22 The land on either side of this 25,000-rod-square sacred area would be given to the prince (cf. 45:7–46:18). His land areas to the east and west of the sacred portion would extend to the national boundaries, east and west, as did all the tribal areas. The property of the Levites and priests, along with that of the city, would lie in the center of the prince's land. The entire sacred area and the prince's land would lie between the tribal allotments of Judah to the north and Benjamin to the south.

23–29 The tribal allotments of Israel's land south of the land's special portion are stated in these verses.

30–35 The city in the center of the 10,000 by 5,000 rod section south of the priests' sacred area is not named, but most likely it is Jerusalem (cf. Zec 14:8). In keeping with the dimensions given in vv.15–19, Ezekiel declares that the distance around the city, minus its pasture strip, would be 18,000 rods. The main emphasis in this section is on the city's twelve gates, each named after one of Israel's tribes (cf. Rev 21:12–13). There were three gates on each side of the city. The descendants of Leah were on the north and south sides. On the north the three gates were named Reuben (the firstborn), Judah (tribe of David), and Levi (tribe of priests). On the south the three gates were named Simeon, Issachar, and Zebulun. The three gates on the east were named after Rachel's two sons, Joseph and Benjamin, plus Dan, the son of Bilhah, Rachel's handmaid. The three gates on the west were named after the descendants of the two handmaids, Zilpah and Bilhah: Gad, Asher, and Naphtali.

The city was square, and the city in Revelation also is square (actually, it is a cube; cf. Rev 21:16). These likenesses between them have caused some to identify them with each other. However, additional data in Revelation should cause some hesitancy about a quick decision. If the two are not identical, they certainly demonstrate that the characteristics of the Millennium and those of the eternal state are similar.

Ezekiel concludes his great prophecy by giving the city a name, a name that the city would have from that day forward: "THE LORD IS THERE." The Lord would reside forever with his people. Never again would they be separated from him through discipline. Forever Israel would live as God's people and he as their God! This name would characterize God's city just as in Hebrew thought any new name gave a new character to its recipient.

The Old Testament in the New

OT Text	NT Text	Subject
Eze 1:4–10	Rev 4:8–8	Four living creatures
Eze 3:1–3	Rev 10:9–10	Eating a scroll
Eze 9:4	Rev 7:3	A mark on the forehead
Eze 14:21	Rev 6:8	Four dreadful judgments
Eze 20:41	2Co 6:17	Separate from the world
Eze 27:27–32	Rev 18:13–19	Destruction of a sinful city
Eze 36:22	Ro 2:24	God's name cursed among Gentiles
Eze 37:27	2Co 6:16	God living with us
Eze 38:1–39:16	Rev 20:8–9	God and Magog
Eze 39:17–20	Rev 19:17–21	Food for the birds
Eze 40:1–2	Rev 21:10	Vision of new Jerusalem
Eze 40:3	Rev 11:1	Measuring the temple
Eze 43:2	Rev 1:15	Voice of rushing waters
Eze 47:1, 12	Rev 22:1–2	Flowing waters and fruit trees
Eze 48:30–35	Rev 21:12–13	Twelve gates of the city

Daniel

INTRODUCTION

1. Purpose

The book of Daniel was written in the context of the Fall of Jerusalem and the deportation of the Jews to Babylonia. Despite decades of warning by numerous prophets, the people's flagrant apostasy and immorality finally brought to pass the destruction God had warned them about ever since the time of Moses (Dt 28:64; 29:28; 2Ch 36:16).

From a human viewpoint, it now seemed that the religion of the Hebrews had been completely discredited. The Lord appeared inferior to the gods of Assyria and Babylon. It was therefore essential at this time in Israel's history for God to display his power in such a way as to prove that he was the one true God and the sovereign Lord of history. So by a series of miracles he vindicated his position as the only true God over against his detractors and convinced the supreme rulers of Babylon and Persia that he, the Lord, was the greatest power both on earth and in heaven.

2. Authorship and Date

Many today deny that the prophet Daniel wrote this book, particularly the last six chapters. The most common argument is that the remarkably accurate "predictions" in Daniel (esp. ch. 11) were the result of a pious fraud, perpetrated by some zealous propagandist of the Maccabean movement, who wished to encourage a spirit of heroism among the Jewish patriots resisting Antiochus IV. Many modern scholars claim that every accurate prediction in Daniel was written after it had already been fulfilled, i.e., in the period of the Maccabean revolt (168–65 B.C.).

The clear testimony of the book itself, however, is that Daniel was the author (cf. 8:1; 9:2, 20; 10:2). Nor is there any question that Jesus also accepted Daniel as the author of this book (Mt 24:15; cf. Da 9:27 et al.). Furthermore, careful linguistic and historical analysis of the book supports a date much earlier than the second century B.C.

As to the date of the composition of Daniel, the first chapter refers to Daniel's capture in 605 B.C., and Daniel continued his public service until the first year of Cyrus (1:21), i.e., about 537 B.C. Daniel probably completed his memoirs c. 532 B.C., when he was about ninety years old. The appearance of Persian-derived governmental terms in Daniel strongly suggests that it was given its final form after Persian had become the official language of the government. Actually, the text of Daniel is in two languages: Hebrew (chs. 1, 8–12) and Aramaic (chs. 2–7). The Aramaic chapters pertain to the Babylonian and Persian empires, whereas the other six chapters relate to God's special plans for his covenant people.

3. Canonicity

Daniel should be regarded as having been inherently canonical from the very time it was first written and as having achieved recognition by God's people as the inspired word of God quite soon after its publication. It certainly would have found a ready reception among the exiles who returned to Judea under Zerubbabel because of its encouragement for them to trust in God's continuing providence in their behalf during the discouragements of those early years of recolonization. The discovery of several fragments of a second-century MS of Daniel in Qumran Cave I indicates that Jewish believers considered the book as inspired and authoritative.

4. Theological Values

The principal theological emphasis in Daniel is the absolute sovereignty of the Lord, the God of Israel. The book consistently emphasizes that the fortunes of kings and the affairs of humans are subject to God's decrees, and that he is able to accomplish his will despite the most determined opposition of the mightiest potentates on earth. The miracles recorded in chs. 1–6 clearly demonstrate God's sovereignty on behalf of his saints.

A second theological emphasis is the power of persistent prayer. Daniel and his companions were delivered from dangers and dilemmas by prayer. Especially impressive is Daniel's intense prayer on behalf of his nation for God to restore his people to their land at the end of the seventy years (9:2–19; cf. 10:12–14).

Another theological emphasis is the long-range purview of God's marvelous plan of the ages. Daniel predicts the precise year of Christ's appearance and the beginning of his ministry in A.D. 27 (cf. Da 9:25–26). Daniel was given the revelation of the eschatological Seventieth Week (9:26b–27), a week that we still eagerly look forward to.

Lastly, underlying the entire scenario is the indomitable grace of God. Even after the sternest warnings of the prophets had been disregarded and severe judgment of near total destruction had overtaken the nation in 587 B.C., the Lord never abandoned his people to the full consequences of their sin but in lovingkindness subjected them to an ordeal that purged them of idolatry. Then he allowed them to return to their homeland, thus setting the stage for the coming of the Messiah. The book of Daniel thus sets forth the pattern of God's persevering grace that characterizes the NT as well, that "God's gifts and his call are irrevocable" (Ro 11:29).

EXPOSITION

I. The Selection and Preparation of God's Special Servants (1:1–21)

1–2 Nebuchadnezzar, king of Babylon, first invaded Palestine in 605 B.C. and took captives back to Babylon. His second invasion was in 597 B.C. (cf. 2Ki 24:10–14). The third and final captivity took place in 587 B.C., when all the remaining people of Judah who had not escaped were taken to Babylon (for the significance of these dates, see the comments on ch. 9).

The first (i.e., 605) invasion was in the "third" year of the reign of Jehoiakim; this follows the Babylonian method of designating the years of a king's reign. According to the Jewish method of counting those years, 605 B.C. was his fourth regnal year (Jer 25:1).

Jehoiakim began his reign in 608, as an appointee of Neco king of Egypt, who officially changed his name from Eliakim ("El will establish") to Jehoiakim ("Yahweh will establish").

From the very beginning of this book, Daniel makes it clear that Nebuchadnezzar's success was not due to his own prowess but was the work of the one true God, who had brought about the complete collapse of the Judean monarchy. Thus the theme of God's absolute sovereignty is implied already here, a theme that dominates the entire book.

3–7 Nebuchadnezzar enlisted the most promising and gifted young men from Judah into his service, all of whom were assigned new names that contained the names of false gods of Babylon. A court official named Ashpenaz was put in charge of their physical and intellectual development. They were expected to follow the demanding course of study (cf. v.4) of the Chaldean curriculum.

Four of the Jewish youths accepted in the academy are singled out as having the courage to object to the food prepared for them and desiring to observe the dietary laws of the Torah (cf. Lev 11; Dt 14). Probably most of the meat items on the regular menu were from animals sacrificed to the gods of Babylon, and no doubt the wine from the king's table had first been part of the libation to these deities. Therefore even those portions of food and drink not inherently unclean had been tainted by contact with pagan cultic usage.

At the very beginning of their careers, therefore, these young worshipers faced a clear-cut issue of obedience and faith. Had they complied with their rulers, they would have displeased God, to whom they were surrendered body and soul. This early refusal to disobey God prepared them for future greatness as true witnesses for him in this pagan culture.

8–16 Daniel, spokesman for the four young Hebrews, determined to refuse the food from the king's table. Rather than break faith with God, he was willing to be expelled from the royal academy with the disgrace and danger that entailed.

But Daniel found "favor" (lit., "love or loyalty based on a mutual commitment"; GK 2876) with Ashpenaz and felt he could confide in him. Daniel proposed that the four

Hebrews be given "vegetables" ("herbs" or "garden plants") to eat and "water to drink" and that Ashpenaz see whether after a ten-day testing period all four of them did not look healthier than any of the other students. Such reversal of the laws of nutrition would require a miracle; yet Ashpenaz was willing to take the risk. The venture proved completely successful. No further objection could be raised against their simple diet.

17 Daniel and his friends were granted special wisdom by the Lord, not because of their diet, but because of his approval of their faith and commitment to his word. Daniel even mastered oneiromancy (the interpretation of dreams; cf. Joseph in the court of Egypt).

18–20 Ashpenaz proudly presented his students before Nebuchadnezzar for the final examinations. Out of the entire group of brilliant young men, the king found that the four Hebrews excelled vastly; so he gave them responsible posts in his government. "Magicians" (GK 3033) probably were those who used a chart or design to answer questions. "Enchanters" (GK 879) is derived from the Akkadian word for "soothsayer." The text does not state that the four Hebrews actually engaged in divination or conjuration (cf. Dt 18:10–12) but that they attained "wisdom and understanding," which implies that they surpassed the professional heathen diviners and conjurers. (Nowhere is there any indication that Daniel resorted to occult practices. He simply went to God in prayer, and God revealed the answer to him.)

21 Daniel's career in public service continued "until the first year of King Cyrus." Since Babylon was at first entrusted to Darius the Mede by King Cyrus (Da 5:31) after its fall in 539, and since Da 9 is dated in the "first year" of that Darius (9:1), Darius possibly remained as titular king till 538 or 537. If so, the "first year" of Cyrus king of Babylon would have been 537–536 B.C., which was probably the year when the forty-two thousand Jews returned to Palestine under Zerubbabel. If Daniel studied in the royal academy for three years, his first government appointment might have been around 601 B.C. Thus his whole term of service would have been about sixty-five years (601–536 B.C.).

II. Nebuchadnezzar's First Dream: God's Plan for the Ages (2:1–49)

A. The Babylonian Wise Men's Impotence (2:1–13)

1–3 Nebuchadnezzar was convinced that his remarkable dream contained a message of utmost importance. He ordered his experts in oneiromancy to reconstruct the dream itself and then to tell him its significance.

In addition to the magicians or diviners and the enchanters or conjurers, "sorcerers" (GK 4175) are mentioned, along with "astrologers." The word for "to practice sorcery" (or witchcraft) comes from Akkadian and strongly suggests necromancy as the original idea. "Astrologers" (GK 4169) translates a Sumerian term that is applied to a special class of astrologer-soothsayers. This fourth class of wise men acted as spokesmen for the whole group.

4–9 Verse 4 marks a transition from Hebrew to Aramaic in the text of Daniel, prefaced by the statement that the wise men spoke Aramaic with the king (see Introduction).

"O king, live forever!" represents a wish that the king would live on from one age to another (cf. 1Ki 1:31). The soothsayers' request for the king to reveal his dream to them was met with a surprising rejection. He wanted them to give its contents and then to explain the meaning. If they really had powers of divination, their gods would be able to pass the dream on to them. This would prove that they were not giving a purely human and essentially worthless conjecture as to the interpretation.

To his stringent demand, Nebuchadnezzar added a gruesome threat. Failure to reconstruct his dream would prove that the wise men were charlatans who deserved death for all the years they had deceived the king. They would be "cut to pieces" (cf. Eze 16:40; 23:47) and their estates utterly destroyed and left as refuse heaps. But if they should succeed, Nebuchadnezzar promised them wealth and honor far beyond what they already had. The "wise men" were powerless before the threats of punishment and the inducements of reward. They could only beg the king to change his mind and divulge his dream. This enraged him further as he accused them of stalling for time to find a way out of their dilemma. But no deception would help them, nor could they look for any unexpected turn of events to extricate them.

10–13 In desperation the wise men insisted that the king's demand was unreasonable, unprecedented, and beyond mortal ability. This defense convinced the king that his wise men were liars and deserved the penalty he had announced. So he issued a warrant for the arrest and execution of *all* the wise men (v.1), including the four young Hebrews.

B. Daniel's Intercession and Offer (2:14–23)

14–16 Arioch, the captain of the royal bodyguard, told Daniel why all the wise men had been condemned. At Daniel's request Arioch took him to Nebuchadnezzar to secure a stay of execution until Daniel had an opportunity to consult his God about the mysterious dream. The stage was set to show the reality, wisdom, and power of the one true God— the Lord of Israel. Daniel knew that he had to trust in God's faithfulness to do the impossible. If he succeeded, Nebuchadnezzar and all Babylon would be confronted with irrefutable proof that only Israel's God was real, sovereign, and limitless in his power.

17–23 Daniel, confident that God would answer his prayer, sought to make his prayer even more effective by enlisting his three companions in a concert of prayer. Verses 20–23 are a ringing manifesto of biblical faith over against the pretensions of pagan pride. Although the Babylonians may have triumphed on earth, the God of Israel was absolute Sovereign in heaven and on earth. His power is illustrated by his complete control over the events of history, bringing about the reversals of fortune that give history its unpredictability. God determines the time and duration of events. Thus he not only decreed the Fall of Jerusalem in 587 B.C.—an event future for Daniel in 602 B.C.—but also the exact number of years of the Captivity (cf. 9:2).

Daniel acknowledged that God *alone* bestows wisdom and discernment (v.21b). Only by his grace are humans able to achieve anything or to understand the "deep and hidden things" or what "lies in darkness." Thus, all the knowledge of Nebuchadnezzar's wise men could not give the king his dream and deliver them from imminent death.

Daniel closed his thanksgiving on a joyous note, expressing his confidence that the knowledge he had received of Nebuchadnezzar's dream was absolutely accurate. Acknowledging that the superhuman "wisdom" and "power" he was about to display as the interpreter of the king's dream had been granted in response to the collective prayers of him and his four companions, Daniel gave God all the glory.

C. Daniel's Recitation of the King's Dream (2:24–35)

24–25 Daniel assured Arioch, who was to execute the wise men, that he had the answer. Arioch, anxious to claim credit for himself in having discovered Daniel, hurried to tell Nebuchadnezzar his good news.

26–30 Capitalizing on Nebuchadnezzar's half-incredulous inquiry as to whether Daniel could actually describe his dream, Daniel pointed to the pagan seers' inability to unravel the mystery, thereby exposing the worthlessness of their theology and of polytheism in general. That the Lord's spokesman alone had the answer points unmistakably to the reality of the God of the Hebrews. Then Daniel told Nebuchadnezzar what he had seen in his dream.

First, Daniel reminded the king that preceding his dream, he was thinking about the future. Disclaiming any personal ability in transmitting this revelation and publicly giving God all the glory, Daniel implied that God had noticed the king's statesmanlike concern and had granted him a full answer to his thoughts on what was to come.

31–35 Daniel disclosed the main theme of the dream—the colossal image composed of a head of gold, breast and arms of silver, belly and thighs of bronze, and legs of iron, with feet of iron mingled with clay. This composite statue was then reduced to powder by a huge stone, and the powder was blown away by the wind. Where the image had stood, the rock grew to the size of a huge mountain that filled the whole scene.

D. Daniel's Interpretation of the King's Dream (2:36–47)

36–38 The golden head represented Nebuchadnezzar and the Babylonian Empire. The head came first in the explanation probably because "head" often means "beginning." To Nebuchadnezzar, his government was the ideal type and was therefore esteemed as highly as gold. He exercised unrestricted authority throughout Babylon. His word was law.

The first world-empire, then, was the Neo-Babylonian, over which Nebuchadnezzar ruled for about forty more years—from 605 to 562 or 560 B.C. But his empire did not last more than twenty-one years after his death. His son Evil-Merodach reigned only two years (562–560). Neriglissar reigned four years (560–556) and Labashi-Marduk only one (556). Nabonidus engineered a coup d'état in 555 and ruled till Babylon fell in 539.

39 The second empire (silver) is said to be "inferior" to Babylon. From Nebuchadnezzar's standpoint the restriction on the king's authority to annul a law once he had made it (6:12) was less desirable than his own unfettered power. The silver empire was to be Medo-Persia, which began with Cyrus the Great, who conquered Babylon in 539 and died ten years later. His older son, Cambyses, conquered Egypt but died in 523 or 522. After a brief reign by an upstart claiming to be Cyrus's younger son, Darius son of Hystaspes deposed and assassinated him and established a new dynasty. Darius brought the Persian Empire to its zenith of power but left unsettled the question of the Greeks in his western border, even though he did conquer Thrace. Xerxes (485–464) his son, in an abortive invasion in 480–479, failed to conquer the Greeks. Nor did his successor Artaxerxes I (464–424), who rather contented himself with intrigue by setting the Greek city-states against one another. Later Persian emperors—Darius II (423–404), Artaxerxes II (404–359), Artaxerxes III (359–338), Arses (338–336), and Darius III (336–331)—declined still further in power. This silver empire was supreme in the Near and Middle East for about two centuries.

The third empire (bronze) was even less desirable from Nebuchadnezzar's standpoint. This empire was the Greco-Macedonian Empire established by Alexander the Great. Though Greece was to "rule over the whole earth," its political tradition was more republican than its predecessor. Alexander began his invasion of Persia in 334, crushed its last resistance in 331, and established a realm extending from the border of Yugoslavia to beyond the Indus Valley in India—the largest empire of ancient times. After his death in 323, Alexander's territory was split into four realms, ruled over by his former generals (Antipater in Macedon-Greece, Lysimachus in Thrace-Asia Minor, Seleucus in Asia, and Ptolemy in Egypt, Cyrenaica, and Palestine). This situation crystallized after the Battle of Ipsus in 301, when the final attempt to maintain a unified empire was crushed through the defeat of the imperial regent Antigonus. The eastern sections of the Seleucid realm revolted from the central authority at Antioch and were gradually absorbed by the Parthians as far westward as Mesopotamia. But the remainder of the former Greek Empire was annexed by Rome after Antiochus the Great was defeated at Magnesia in 190 B.C. Macedon was annexed by Rome in 168, Greece was permanently subdued in 146, the Seleucid domains west of the Tigris were annexed by Pompey the Great in 63 B.C., and Egypt was reduced to a Roman province after the Battle of Actium in 31 B.C. Thus the bronze kingdom lasted about 260 or 300 years before it was supplanted by the fourth kingdom prefigured in Nebuchadnezzar's dream-image.

40–43 The fourth empire is symbolized by the legs of iron. From a despotic standpoint, the Roman Republic was of far less value than gold, silver, or bronze. Iron connotes toughness and ruthlessness and describes the Roman Empire that reached its widest extent under the reign of Trajan (98–117 A.D.), who occupied Rumania and much of Assyria for a few brief years.

A later phase of the fourth empire is symbolized by the feet and ten toes made up of iron and clay, a fragile base for the huge monument. The implication is that this final phase would be marked by a kind of federation rather than by a powerful single realm. The iron may represent the influence of the old Roman culture and tradition and the clay the inherent weakness in a socialist society based on relativism in morality and philosophy. This mixture results in weakness and confusion, foreshadowing the approaching day of doom. Within the scope of v.43 are disunity, class struggle, and even civil war, resulting from the failure of a hopelessly divided society to achieve an integrated world-order. Iron and clay may coexist but cannot combine into a strong and durable world power.

44–45a The final scene is of a rock cut from a mountain that rolls down and smashes against the great image's brittle feet (cf. v.34), toppling it over. The entire monument is then reduced to dust and swept away by the wind. Then the rock becomes a mountain (the fifth kingdom) that fills the earth. In contrast to the transitory nature of the four man-made empires, this God-established kingdom is destined to endure forever. Daniel 7 and parallel passages leave no doubt that this fifth realm is the kingdom ruled over by Christ.

45b–47 Daniel closed his interpretation of the dream by assuring Nebuchadnezzar that it was divinely inspired and absolutely trustworthy. Thus the God of heaven graciously granted the king knowledge of the future, unraveling the baffling mystery. The king could only respond by acknowledging Israel's Lord as "God of gods" (i.e., the Supreme God) and "Lord of kings" on earth, the true Lord of history. Moreover, the king acknowledged the Lord's supremacy in revealing the mysteries of the future, something no pagan god could do.

In token of his submission to Daniel's God, Nebuchadnezzar prostrated himself before Daniel and gave him an offering and incense. What a remarkable scene! The despot who but an hour before had ordered the execution of all his wise men was prostrating himself before this foreign captive from a third-rate subject nation! The king's praise to the Lord, however, does not necessarily mean that he doubted the existence of other gods, much less that he had experienced any sort of conversion.

E. The Promotion of Daniel and His Comrades (2:48–49)

48–49 As a result of Daniel's outstanding performance, Nebuchadnezzar put him in charge of all the diviners. He officially became "ruler" (lit., "chief of appointed officials"; GK 10715) over the whole bureau of "wise men." The king fulfilled his original promise (2:6) and loaded Daniel with gifts and honors, appointing him civil governor of the entire capital province of Babylon. Normally this would be reserved for a Chaldean nobleman of the master race. For a Jew to be so honored was unprecedented. Daniel requested that his three companions be given

high appointments too, thus strengthening his position.

III. The Golden Image and the Fiery Furnace (3:1–30)

A. The Erection of the Image (3:1–3)

1–2 Nebuchadnezzar forgot his new religious insights and had a statue made of gold (i.e., covered with gold leaf; there was not enough gold in all Babylon to make a statue so large of solid gold), undoubtedly reflecting the head in the dream-image. It is doubtful that the statue represented the king himself as there is no evidence that statues of Mesopotamian rulers were ever worshiped during the ruler's lifetime. More likely the statue represented Nebuchadnezzar's patron god, Nebo (or Nabu). Prostration before this god would amount to a pledge of allegiance to his viceroy, Nebuchadnezzar. The recent establishment of the Babylonian Empire as successor to Assyria made it appropriate for Nebuchadnezzar to assemble all the leaders of his domain and exact from them an oath of loyalty, certified by a ceremony of adoration of Babylon's god. Any who refused to comply were to be immediately executed in a superheated furnace.

3 The titles of the various ranks of government officials indicate a well-organized bureaucracy. "Satraps" were in charge of fairly large realms. "Prefects" were military commanders or more likely lieutenant governors. "Governors" were leaders of smaller territories. "Advisers" were "counsel-givers." "Provincial official" is a general term for a governmental executive.

B. The Institution of State Religion (3:4–7)

4–7 Nebuchadnezzar enlisted the royal musicians to furnish a proper setting for the ceremony. "All kinds of music" indicates that there were other instruments besides the six listed. This orchestra would give the signal for all to bow down and worship the golden statue, declaring their commitment to the Babylonian government and their willingness to incur divine wrath if they should ever break their oath of fealty. The nearby furnace was a grim reminder of the dreadful alternative to compliance. When the music struck up, all foreheads touched the ground—except three.

C. The Accusation and Trial of God's Faithful Witnesses (3:8–18)

8–12 After the public worship, some malicious men (called "Chaldeans" in the NIV note) reported to the king the disobedience of Shadrach, Meshach, and Abednego. These informers approached the king as members of the master race, denouncing the Jews. This heightens their reference to Daniel's three Hebrew associates in government service as "some Jews," with a contemptuous emphasis on their despised nationality. With a show of zeal for the king, the Chaldeans quoted his edict word for word and then related how these three recalcitrant Jews had dared to "pay no attention to" the express command of "King Nebuchadnezzar"; they had refused to bow down and worship the golden image!

13–18 Nebuchadnezzar became furious and ordered the offenders to be brought before him. Half incredulously he stared at them and asked whether they really had disobeyed his decree. Then he magnanimously gave them an opportunity to save themselves. He would order the musicians to play again so the three men might prove their loyalty and obedience by worshiping the image then and there. But Shadrach, Meshach, and Abednego loved the Lord more than life itself. Ready to lay down their lives for God's glory, the three refused to plead with Nebuchadnezzar to make an exception of them. They were confident that the Lord would deal with this king who thought he was sovereign on earth.

Nebuchadnezzar made the mistake of defying the Lord, saying, "Then what god will be able to rescue you from my hand?" Nebuchadnezzar had converted his confrontation with humans into a contest with the Lord God Almighty. Ungratefully he scoffed at the very God who had granted him success in battle (cf. Jer 27:6–8). Therefore he would undergo one humiliation after another, till he groveled in the dust before Israel's God.

The heroism of the three men went even further as they were ready to be burned up in the fiery furnace rather than betray their God. Scripture contains few more heroic words than "But even if he does not" (v.18). Interestingly, Scripture is silent as to Daniel's whereabouts at this time. Perhaps he was away on official business.

D. The Sentence Imposed and Executed (3:19–23)

19–23 Nebuchadnezzar had no recourse but to order the immediate execution of the three young Hebrews. In his rage he went to absurd lengths. No mortal could have survived an instant in the huge furnace, but the king insisted that it be heated to maximum intensity. So fierce was the fire that even to come near it was fatal. Equally absurd was Nebuchadnezzar's command for the three to be fully dressed with their hats on. Finally, they were "firmly tied" and thrown like logs into the furnace. Apparently there was no door to hide the inside from view. So apart from the swirling flames and smoke, the men were quite visible to an outside observer.

E. The Deliverance and the Fourth Man (3:24–27)

24–27 The dumbfounded Nebuchadnezzar saw the Hebrews walking upright in the flames without their bonds, and he saw a fourth person walking with them. After his officials confirmed that only three men had been thrown into the furnace, the king described the fourth one as resembling deity. All four persons in the furnace were walking around freely. Their divine companion in the flames had delivered Shadrach, Meshach, and Abednego from all harm.

Nebuchadnezzar commanded the three to come out of the furnace; so they climbed out—but not the fourth, who had apparently disappeared. To the officials' amazement neither the clothing nor the bodies of the three Hebrews gave any indication of having been in the fire. Their God had indeed been able to deliver them (cf. v.17).

F. Nebuchadnezzar's Second Submission to God (3:28–30)

28–30 Before such an awesome display of God's power, Nebuchadnezzar could only acknowledge his defeat. He hastened to praise the Lord and thereby confess his admiration for the courage and fidelity of the three Hebrews. To make amends Nebuchadnezzar decreed death and destruction for anyone saying anything against the God of Israel. Then Nebuchadnezzar promoted Shadrach, Meshach, and Abednego to a higher office in Babylon.

The Neo-Babylonian Empire
626-539 B.C.

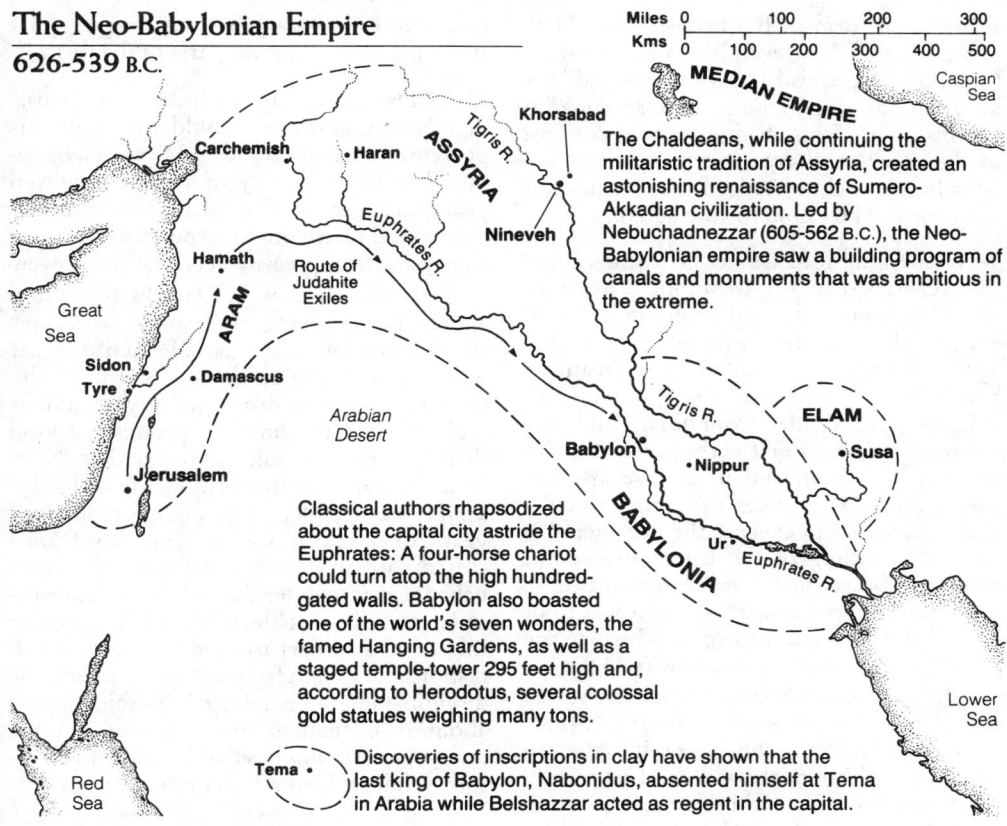

Miles 0 — 100 — 200 — 300
Kms 0 — 100 — 200 — 300 — 400 — 500

MEDIAN EMPIRE

Caspian Sea

Khorsabad

Carchemish • Haran

ASSYRIA

Euphrates R.

Nineveh

The Chaldeans, while continuing the militaristic tradition of Assyria, created an astonishing renaissance of Sumero-Akkadian civilization. Led by Nebuchadnezzar (605-562 B.C.), the Neo-Babylonian empire saw a building program of canals and monuments that was ambitious in the extreme.

Hamath • Route of Judahite Exiles

Tigris R.

Great Sea

ARAM

Sidon
Tyre • Damascus

Arabian Desert

ELAM

Babylon
• Nippur • Susa

Jerusalem

Classical authors rhapsodized about the capital city astride the Euphrates: A four-horse chariot could turn atop the high hundred-gated walls. Babylon also boasted one of the world's seven wonders, the famed Hanging Gardens, as well as a staged temple-tower 295 feet high and, according to Herodotus, several colossal gold statues weighing many tons.

BABYLONIA

Ur • Euphrates R.

Lower Sea

Red Sea

Tema •

Discoveries of inscriptions in clay have shown that the last king of Babylon, Nabonidus, absented himself at Tema in Arabia while Belshazzar acted as regent in the capital.

© 1985 The Zondervan Corporation

IV. Nebuchadnezzar's Second Dream and Humiliation (4:1–37)

A. The Circumstances of the Second Dream (4:1–7)

1–3 This chapter is unique in Scripture because it is composed under the authority of a pagan. Though he may have been intellectually convinced of the sovereignty and omniscience of the one true God, Nebuchadnezzar hardly had a true heart conversion. The decree showed his gratitude to the Lord for delivering him from insanity and restoring him to his throne. He wanted every person in his empire to share this knowledge and join him in giving glory to the God of heaven. Nebuchadnezzar frankly confessed his own arrogance in attributing to himself the glory for what the grace and power of God had done for him.

After blessing his subjects, Nebuchadnezzar exalted the miracle-working power and eternal sovereignty of the God of Israel. He made it clear that he had experienced this power both in his warning dream (explained by Daniel) and its pride-shattering fulfillment, his seven years of bestial insanity. These convinced him that God alone is the source of power, both in nature and in human affairs, and that no ruler possessed any authority except by God's permission. In contrast to the transient reigns of human rulers, the authority of God goes on forever.

4–7 The setting for the following event is the apparent security and prosperity of the king after vanquishing all his enemies and the occasion of another dream. Again (cf. 2:2) the king sent for his wise men, although on this occasion he told them the substance of the dream (cf. ch. 2). When they could not come up with any interpretation, once more the king turned to the one true expert, Daniel the seer.

B. The Description of the Dream (4:8–18)

8 Daniel's official court name is "Belteshazzar" ("Protect his life"), most likely an abbreviated form of Bel-belteshazzar ("Bel, protect his life") or even Nebu-belteshazzar ("Nebo, protect his life," if by "his god" the king was referring to the god whose name began his own, Nebu-chadnezzar). In contrast to the other soothsayers in his court, Nebuchadnezzar acknowledged that Daniel was truly inspired by God (or the gods).

9–18 The king told Daniel his dream about the great tree that grew to dominate the landscape for many miles and about its lush foliage and abundant fruit that provided shelter and nourishment for all sorts of creatures. Suddenly "a "holy one" (lit., "watchman"; GK 10620) descended from heaven and pronounced judgment on the tree, ordering it to be chopped down and its foliage stripped away. Verse 17 indicates that this particular class of angels can execute the judgments of God. The felling of the tree scattered the birds and beasts that were dependent on it. Only the stump was spared, and it was to be encircled with bands of iron and bronze and to remain in the grassy meadow (v.15a).

The symbolism changes from the stump to a man to a brute beast (vv.15b–16). "Mind" (GK 10381) refers to the inner self as the seat of moral reflection, the will, and pattern of behavior. The person this tree stump represents is to be transformed into an animal for seven "times," here undoubtedly years (see NIV note; cf. 7:25). The sentence was decreed from heaven so that the full sovereignty of the "Most High" might be demonstrated before all the world, and that people might realize that God chooses who is to wear the crown and sometimes selects the humblest and lowliest (cf. 1Sa 2:7–8; Job 5:11). (For a prideful person portrayed as a lofty tree, see Isa 2:12–13; 10:34; Eze 31:3–17.) By appealing to Daniel, the king showed his confidence in him and his God. So once again the honor of Daniel's God was at stake.

C. Daniel's Interpretation and Warning (4:19–27)

19–22 Daniel's loyalty to the king and his kindness to Daniel made it difficult to reveal the interpretation of the dream. At the king's insistence Daniel finally began to speak. After voicing the fruitless wish that the dream might apply to Nebuchadnezzar's worst enemies, Daniel explained that the mighty tree represented Nebuchadnezzar in all his military success, organizing an empire that stretched to the "distant parts of the earth."

23–27 Daniel came to the heart of the warning: Nebuchadnezzar would lose both his power to rule and his sanity. He would be reduced to the mentality of a beast for seven years, eating grass like cattle. This humiliation would teach him to respect God's sovereignty and to appreciate his glory and power.

Verse 26 closes with Daniel's prediction about the surviving tree stump: after his seven years of dementia, Nebuchadnezzar will be restored to his throne. Normally any monarch suffering from insanity would be replaced. But the unlikely promise of God that the throne would he restored to Nebuchadnezzar after the termination of his insanity was fulfilled. The prospect of seven years of insanity was terrible; so Daniel closed with an earnest admonition for Nebuchadnezzar to defer the evil day by immediately amending his life. If he would recognize that he was subject to God's moral law and responsible to him for good government, the discipline might be deferred. Nothing is said about Nebuchadnezzar's response, but the one-year delay implies that he made some effort to follow Daniel's recommendation.

D. The King's Punishment (4:28–33)

28–30 Though eager to avoid judgment, Nebuchadnezzar nevertheless retained his pride, taking all the credit for the achievements he owed to God's grace. Perhaps he refrained from boasting during his reprieve, but he never realized his indebtedness to God (see ZPEB, 4:395–99, for a description of Nebuchadnezzar's accomplishments).

31–32 After boasting that he had built Babylon the Great as a residence for himself by his own power (v.30), Nebuchadnezzar heard an unexpected word from God—he would experience the full weight of God's wrath and the punishment threatened in his fateful dream.

33 Nebuchadnezzar was abhorred even by his lowliest subjects and reduced to the state of a beast. His skin toughened into hide through constant exposure to the weather; his hair, matted and coarse, looked like eagle feathers; and his uncut fingernails and toenails became like claws. So the boasting king, a victim of a condition known as boanthropy, sank to a subhuman level.

E. The King's Repentance (4:34–37)

34–35 After seven years the Lord fulfilled his promise. By divine grace the humiliated king's reason returned. His first response was to praise, honor, and glorify God as the eternal, omnipotent Sovereign of the universe. Second, he honored him as the Ruler whose kingdom would never end. Third, Nebuchadnezzar acknowledged that humans are as nothing before God. Finally, Nebuchadnezzar saw that God is beyond the control of any human being and accountable to no one.

36–37 Now that he had begun to fear the Lord, Nebuchadnezzar was qualified for renewed leadership. The court and the army commanders were electrified to see that his reason had returned, and they thronged to congratulate him and hail him as their sovereign. "I was restored to my throne and became even greater than before" was his grateful testimony. The "head of gold" (2:38) had bowed in humble submission to the God of Daniel.

Through this event the Jews held captive in Babylon could not help but know that their Lord was the true and living God and that all the gods of the pagans were only idols. They knew for certain that the apparently limitless power of Nebuchadnezzar was under the control of the Lord God Almighty.

V. Belshazzar's Feast (5:1–31)

A. The Profanation of the Holy Vessels (5:1–4)

(As background for this episode, see ZPEB, 1:446, 515–16.)

1–4 Belshazzar the king conducted a state banquet for his nobles. In drunken bravado he decided to entertain them with the vessels from the temple in Jerusalem. Belshazzar and his guests taunted the Lord by praising their gods and drinking from the sacred goblets. Once again an arrogant Babylonian monarch defied the Lord God of Israel.

B. The Handwriting on the Wall (5:5–9)

5–6 Divine intervention came without announcement. Suddenly fingers appeared on the palace wall, wrote four words, and van-

ished. The party was over. The drunken Belshazzar stared at the words, terrified.

7–9 The king sent for his wise men to unravel the message. They could come up with nothing, despite inducements of riches and position. (Belshazzar could offer nothing higher than the third highest rank in the government since he himself was a viceroy under his father, Nabonidus.) As in Nebuchadnezzar's day, the wise men were baffled (cf. 2:2–11; 4:7).

C. The Queen Mother's Recommendation (5:10–16)

10 Daniel (who was probably about eighty-one by 539 B.C.) was not included among those summoned. Perhaps he was in semi-retirement, though ch. 8 indicates that he had been active as recently as the third year of Belshazzar (cf. v.1) but had not been enjoying good health (v.27). Evidently Belshazzar's administration had set him aside though he lived in Babylon. But the king's mother, likely a daughter of Nebuchadnezzar, thought of Daniel as soon as she saw the commotion in the banquet hall and urged the king to stop worrying.

11–12 The queen mother commended Daniel to the king, adding that Nebuchadnezzar had found him to be far superior to all the rest of his wise men (cf. 4:8), for Daniel could unravel mysteries and solve enigmas. Surely he was the right one for Belshazzar to consult. She referred to Nebuchadnezzar as Belshazzar's "father." Strictly speaking Nabonidus was his true father; but if Nabonidus had indeed married a daughter of Nebuchadnezzar to legitimize his usurpation of the throne, Nebuchadnezzar would have been Belshazzar's grandfather.

13–16 Belshazzar sent for Daniel at once, apparently meeting him for the first time. He explained his concern and asked Daniel to explain the mysterious writing. The king also enumerated the same rewards—including the position of "third highest ruler"—he had offered the other wise men.

D. Daniel's Interpretation (5:17–28)

17–24 Disclaiming all promotions, Daniel answered the king's request. Studying the inscription on the wall, Daniel prefaced his interpretation with the reason for the judgment it contained. He reviewed the experience of Nebuchadnezzar being humbled by the decree of the Lord. The young king should have remembered what these experiences had taught his grandfather about humility and respect for the Lord. Belshazzar's blasphemous conduct of profaning the Lord's holy vessels in his drunken orgy had led to the handwriting on the wall, proclaiming Belshazzar's doom.

25–28 Daniel then interpreted the four words. "Mene," meaning "numbered" or "measured," signified that the years of Belshazzar's reign had reached their end. "Tekel" is related to the word for "shekel," whose root idea is "to weigh." In Belshazzar's case, God found him deficient in his scales and therefore rejected him. "Peres" is derived from a root that means "to divide." Belshazzar's kingdom would be divided or separated from him and given to the Medes and Persians then besieging the city.

E. Daniel's Honor and Belshazzar's Demise (5:29–31)

29 Daniel's interpretation greatly disturbed Belshazzar, for it was spelling his imminent doom. Perhaps hoping to forestall judgment, the king fulfilled his promises to the letter, bestowing the royal chain of gold on Daniel and proclaiming him the third ruler in the kingdom.

30–31 But the time for repentance had run out. Belshazzar had gone too far in profaning the vessels of the temple. Destruction was closing in on Belshazzar and his kingdom even while Daniel's investiture was taking place. The Medo-Persian troops were moving along the exposed riverbed under cover of darkness and climbing the walls of the defenses throughout the city.

Verse 30 tersely reports that Belshazzar was slain that same night. The government of Babylon was then entrusted to Darius the Mede at the age of sixty-two. Thus was fulfilled Daniel's prediction that the Babylonian Empire would pass under the yoke of the Medo-Persian Empire, as kingdom number two in the four-kingdom series. (For the identity of Darius and further background to this chapter, see ZPEB, 2:26–29; cf. also EBC 7, in loc.)

VI. Daniel and the Lions' Den (6:1–28)

A. The Conspiracy Against Daniel (6:1–9)

1–3 One of Darius's first responsibilities was to appoint administrators over the territory won from the Babylonians. The 120 "satraps" must have been in charge of the smaller subdivisions. Over these 120 were three commissioners, of whom Daniel was chairman. Daniel's long experience and wide acquaintance with Babylonian government, combined with his superhuman knowledge and skill, made him a likely choice for prime minister.

4 Daniel encountered hostility in the new Persian government, no doubt because his enemies were race-conscious and did not appreciate the elevation of a Jewish captive. To be sure, King Cyrus was either looking favorably on the request of the Jews for release or had already promulgated the decree cited in Ezr 1:1–4. Though objects of Cyrus's charity, the Jews were nevertheless considered inferior, especially by their conquerors. Daniel's elevation to prime minister so disturbed his subordinates that they scrutinized his affairs, hoping to find something that marred his past. But their investigations proved fruitless; Daniel's integrity was beyond question.

5 The way to get Daniel was to force him to choose between obedience to his God and obedience to the government. A statute was needed that seemed merely political to Darius but was clearly religious for Daniel. So his enemies proposed that for one month all petitions be directed to Darius alone. This flattered him and also served to impress the captives that they were now under the Persians.

6–9 The government overseers came to the king "as a group" (i.e., an official delegation) to present their proposal, falsely implying that Daniel concurred with them. Darius had no reason to suspect that the other two royal administrators would misrepresent Daniel's position in this matter. The suggested mode of compelling every subject in the former Babylonian domain to acknowledge the authority of Persia seemed a statesmanlike measure that would contribute to the unification of the kingdom. The time limit of one month seemed reasonable. So Darius affirmed the decree.

B. Daniel's Detection, Trial, and Sentence (6:10–17)

10 The new ordinance mandated death by caged lions for noncompliance (v.12). When Daniel received notice of this new law, he faced a dilemma. Prayer and fellowship with the Lord had safeguarded him from the corrupting influences of Babylonian culture. To preserve his role in government and to save his own life, he would have to compromise his integrity by ceasing to pray to God or by praying privately. But faithful Daniel could not compromise. He would trust the Lord for deliverance. His habit had been to pray regularly toward Jerusalem, the focal point of his hopes and prayers for the progress of the kingdom of God. (Ch. 9 reveals Daniel's concern for Jerusalem and the Jews' restoration to their land.)

11–14 Apparently in collusion in order to make a public test case of Daniel, the hostile officials waited for him to pray and then burst in on him, catching him violating the new decree. They lost no time in reporting Daniel to Darius, reminding him that he had forbidden all petitions to anyone but himself during the thirty-day period. Darius acknowledged that the decree was still in force and that the "laws of the Medes and Persians" could neither be changed nor revoked. In reporting Daniel's disobedience to the king, the conspirators represented Daniel's praying thrice daily as willful disrespect to his king rather than as devotion to his God. Darius's response was not what the conspirators had expected. Indeed, he "was greatly distressed," probably realizing that he had been manipulated by Daniel's enemies. Throughout the day he tried his best to save Daniel's life.

15–17 By sunset the king resigned himself to comply with the conspirators' desire when they reminded him of his irrevocable decree. Concerned for his cherished minister, Darius went with Daniel to the lion pit. Before it was closed, Darius called down to Daniel, "May your God, whom you serve continually, rescue you!" For Darius these words voiced a tremulous hope (cf. v.20). A heavy stone was placed over the pit and secured with clay tablets bearing the king's royal seal and that of other officials.

C. Daniel's Deliverance and His Foes' Punishment (6:18–24)

18–24 Darius was a troubled man. Daniel's peril precluded the king from eating and entertainment. His anxious thoughts kept him awake till the first gray light of dawn, when he hastened to the lion pit, which was already unsealed. Darius's apprehensive call stressed his hope that the "living" God whom Daniel served had "been able to rescue [him] from the lions." Daniel's voice from the bottom of the pit, relating how God had sent his angel to shut the lions' mouths and to prove him guiltless, brought great joy to Darius. Not a scratch was found on Daniel. The evidence was incontrovertible—Daniel's God had "stopped the mouths of lions" (Heb 11:33).

Daniel's accusers were guilty of devising a decree to deprive the king of his most able counselor and of lying to the king when they had averred that "all agreed" (v.7) to recommend this decree. Therefore Darius ordered Daniel's accusers to be brought before him; he then cast them with their families into the same pit. The fate of the conspirators and their families is a masterly touch of poetic justice: "And before they reached the floor of the den, the lions overpowered them and crushed all their bones." Perhaps Darius consigned the families to death to minimize the danger of revenge against the executioner. Daniel's position as prime minister was now secure.

D. Darius's Testimony to God's Sovereignty (6:25–28)

25–27 Darius made a public proclamation giving glory to the God of the Hebrews, commanding all citizens of the realm to honor him. The sense of vv.26–27 is like the last clause of 3:29—"no other god can save in this way"—and like 4:3. Three emphases stand out in vv.26–27: (1) Daniel's God is alive and shows it by the way he acts in history, responding to the requirements of justice and the needs of his people; (2) God's rule is eternal (unlike the empires built by mortals); (3) God miraculously delivers his people, with wonders in heaven and on earth. Once again God acted redemptively to strengthen his people's faith in him.

28 The chapter ends on a positive note, highlighting Daniel's continuing usefulness in royal service throughout the rest of the reign of Darius and in the reign of Cyrus (cf. 1:21). After this, Daniel apparently retired from public service and gave himself to the study of the Scriptures and to prayer. He received the revelations of chs. 10–12 in the third year of Cyrus (cf. 10:1).

VII. The Triumph of the Son of Man (7:1–28)

A. The Four Beasts and the Succession of Empires (7:1–8)

1 In the latter part of his career, Daniel received a series of visions and revelations. The revelation in this chapter is dated "in the first year of Belshazzar king of Babylon." Nabonidus, his father, came to the throne in 556 B.C.; but he apparently entrusted to Belshazzar the "army and the kingship" of Babylon while he himself campaigned in north and central Arabia (so the Nabonidus Chronicle). It is uncertain whether the actual kingship of Babylon was immediately entrusted to Belshazzar at the commencement of his father's reign or whether his appointment as viceroy came later, as Nabonidus found himself detained in Arabia.

Verse 1 says that Daniel recorded only the "substance" of his memorable vision, though twenty-six verses may seem to us like a rather full report. Chapter 7 parallels ch. 2; both set forth the four empires, followed by the complete overthrow of all ungodly resistance, as the final (fifth) kingdom is established on earth to enforce the standards of God's righteousness. The winged lion corresponds to the golden head of the dream image (ch. 2), the ravenous bear to its arms and chest, the swift leopard to its belly and thighs, and the fearsome ten-horned beast to its legs and feet. Lastly, the stone cut out without hands that in ch. 2 demolishes the dream-image has its counterpart in the glorified Son of Man who is installed as Lord over all the earth. But ch. 7 tells us something ch. 2 does not—the Messiah himself will head up the final kingdom of righteousness.

2–3 "The great sea," possibly the Mediterranean, symbolizes the turbulent Gentile world (cf. Rev 13:1 and 21:1; cf. also Isa 57:20). Revelation 7:1 portrays the four winds as under the control of four mighty angels; in Rev 9:14, by the River Euphrates, they are bidden to release the winds on the earth so that one-third of humankind will

perish in war (v.15). Apparently the four winds represent God's judgments, hurling themselves on the ungodly nations from all four points of the compass. From the sea (Gentile nations) emerge in succession four fearsome beasts (namely, the empires of Babylon, Medo-Persia, Greece, and Rome), which apparently go on shore to perform their roles.

4 The first beast is a winged lion, whose eaglelike pinions are soon plucked so that instead of flying it stands on the ground. The lion was a symbol of Babylon, especially in Nebuchadnezzar's time, when the Ishtar Gate entrance was adorned with yellow lions. The final detail—"the heart of a man was given to it"—may refer to the restoration of Nebuchadnezzar's sanity after his seven-year dementia; plucking the lion's wings symbolizes the reduction of his pride and power at the time of his insanity (ch. 4).

5 The second beast—a hulking bear—apparently displaces the lion, though there is no mention of any conflict. The description of the bear suggests the alliance of two powers, one dominating the other—namely, Medo-Persia, with Persia dominating. One side of the bear was higher than the other, and it devoured three ribs from some other animal it had killed. This corresponds to the three major conquests the Medes and Persians made under Cyrus and his son Cambyses: the Lydian kingdom in Asia Minor (546), the Chaldean Empire (539), and Egypt (which Cambyses acquired in 525).

6 The third beast—the four-winged leopard with four heads—portrays the division of Alexander's swiftly won empire into four separate parts shortly after his death (see comment on 8:8). There is no way a quadripartite character can be the Persian Empire, for it remained unified till its end, under the onslaught of Alexander in 334–331.

7 The fourth beast is unlike any known to the human race, "terrifying and frightening and very powerful" (more fearsome than the preceding empires). Its teeth were of iron; hence it would be more crushing in its military power, exploitation, and repression than the other three. Another difference is the ten horns (conceivably two five-pronged antlers). There is an obvious correspondence between these horns and the ten toes of the

dream image (ch. 2), and the mention of iron in the teeth suggests the legs and toes of iron in that image. Thus the superior power of the colossus of Rome—as over against the less unified and weaker empires of Greece, Persia, and Babylon—is emphasized in the symbolism of this terrible fourth beast. Its ultimate form in a confederation of ten states is suggested by the horns (cf. note on 2:41).

8 In this latter-day, ten-state federation, a "little horn" emerges as the largest of them all, uprooting and destroying three adjacent horns (apparently subjecting the remaining six to vassalage). The contemporaneity of all ten of these states (or rulers) is virtually demanded, since six remain in subservience to the aggressive little horn. The victorious little horn's features symbolize an arrogant and vainglorious ruler rather than an entire kingdom (cf. ch. 4, where the Chaldean power is symbolized in the personality of Nebuchadnezzar whereas the bear and the leopard symbolize the Medo-Persian and Greek empires as entire realms). The final clause introduces the ruthless world dictator of the last days (cf. 2Th 2:3–4, 8). This little horn emerges from the fourth empire, unlike the little horn of ch. 8 (vv.9–11), which arises from the third empire (see comments on ch. 8).

B. The Kingdom of God and the Enthroned Messiah (7:9–14)

9–12 The fifth kingdom as the final form of world power overthrows and utterly destroys all the preceding empires erected by violence-worshiping men. Attention is directed to God, "the Ancient of Days" (cf. Eze 1:13). The fire represents the brilliant manifestation of his splendor as well as the fierce heat of his judgment. A lava-like "river of fire" depicts vast destructive power. An enormous crowd stands by as the heavenly court convenes for the examination and conviction of the rebellious little horn (i.e., the final world dictator) and his followers. The record books that are opened presumably contain the sins of the little horn and his adherents (cf. Rev 20:12–13). The blasphemous beast spews out his boastings against humans and God till the very moment he is dragged before the heavenly tribunal. Then his mouth is stopped as his physical life is taken and his body consigned to the flames of judgment.

The remnants of the world powers ("the other beasts") likewise come under judgment. They "were allowed to live for a period of time"; this may mean that the unbelieving world powers that precede the little horn are reserved for judgment by the returning Christ.

13–14 At this point Daniel saw the glorified Son of Man (v.13 is the most frequently quoted verse from Daniel in the NT). The personage who appears before God in the form of a human being is of heavenly origin. He comes to the place of coronation accompanied by the clouds of heaven and is clearly no mere human being in essence. The expression "like a son of man" identifies this final Ruler of the world not only as human, in contrast to the beasts (the four world empires), but also as the heavenly Sovereign incarnate. During his earthly ministry, the Lord Jesus maintained this same emphasis on his incarnate nature (that he was truly human as well as truly God). He repeatedly referred to himself as "the Son of Man" (i.e., that same one foretold in Da 7:13; see comment on Mark 8:31). Moreover, v.13 is the only place in the OT where "son of man" is used of a divine personage rather than a human being. Furthermore, Christ himself emphasized his return to earth accompanied by "clouds" (cf. Mt 24:30; 26:64; Mk 13:26; cf. also Ac 1:9–11; Rev 1:7). Nothing could be clearer than that Jesus regarded Da 7:13 as predictive of himself and that the two elements "like a son of man" and "with the clouds of heaven" combined to constitute a messianic title.

The messianic Son of Man is brought before the throne of the Ancient of Days to be awarded the crown of universal dominion. This picture refers to his appointment as absolute Lord and Judge by virtue of his atoning ministry as God incarnate—the One who lived a sinless life (Isa 53:9), paid the price for the redemption of the human race (Isa 53:5–6), and was vindicated by his bodily resurrection as Judge of the entire human race (Ac 17:31; Ro 2:16). So also his ascension into heaven means that he will be enthroned in glory (Ps 110:1; Ac 2:66) till all his enemies have been subdued (Heb 10:12–13).

The Son of Man is to be the supreme source of political power on earth after his earthly kingdom is established; all humans will worship and serve him. The outcome of human history will be a return of Adam's race under the rule of the divine Son of Man to loving obedience and subjection to the sovereignty of God (cf. Mt 28:18).

C. The Vision Interpreted by the Angel (7:15–28)

15–18 Despite the victorious conclusion of his dream, Daniel was distressed by his inability to understand several features of it. So he asked an angel standing nearby to explain some of these puzzling details. The angel gave a general reply (vv.17–18) to Daniel's first question, indicating that the four beasts represented the successive world empires that would dominate the Near East till the last days. But he added that the ultimate sovereignty over the world would be granted to "the saints of the Most High" (cf. v.27). The reason for emphasizing the participation of God's people in the final kingdom may be because it is a literal, earthly kingdom rather than a spiritual domain.

19–22 Daniel regarded the fourth beast with the greatest curiosity and dread. In particular he wondered about the ten horns and the little horn that emerged and overcame God's holy people. Despite the assurance that the ultimate victory would be the Lord's and that his people would finally prevail, Daniel was deeply concerned about their impending persecution.

23 The angel's answer (vv.23–27) centers on the career of the little horn (cf. 2Th 2:8–9; Rev 13:1–10) and his rise and fall at the second coming of Christ. In v.23 the angel refers to the Roman Empire, which will be markedly "different from" the three preceding empires. Its difference will not be in size (Alexander's empire far exceeded Trajan's) but in organization and unity, enabling it to endure for centuries beyond the lifetime of the preceding Near East empires. "The whole earth" refers (as in general OT usage) to the entire territory of the Near and Middle East that in any way relates to the Holy Land. The word translated "earth" (GK 10075), depending on context, might mean a single country or a region. Here it is the portion of the world included in the Roman Empire, or possibly the regions immediately adjacent to it. The Roman state is seen as devouring the surrounding nations bite by bite and thus acquiring an entire complex of subject kingdoms and nations.

24 The interpreting angel turned from the historic Roman Empire to its ultimate ten-horn phase (cf. 2:41–43) and the emergence of the final world dictator. He arises after ten horns have been set up and subdues three of these ten to his own direct rule. He will then subject the other seven states to vassalage.

25 The little horn will claim divine honors (even as he blasphemes the one true God). He will abandon all pretense of permitting freedom of religion and will revile the Lord of heaven and earth. By cruel and systematic pressure he will "oppress" (lit., "wear out") those with biblical convictions. Such continual and protracted persecution far more effectively breaks the human spirit than the single moment of crisis that calls for a heroic decision. It is easier to die for the Lord than to live for him under constant harassment and strain. This dictator will impose a new legal system, doubtless based on totalitarian principles in which the service of the government or the state will be substituted for the absolute standards of God's moral law. All opposition to the decisions and policies of the little horn will be adjudged treasonable and punishable by death. His program will include a revision of the calendar (implied by "to change the set times"). This was attempted during the French Revolution.

Significantly, the radical phase of the Beast's rule endures for "a time, times and half a time," or three and a half years. This is half of the seven years that mark the period of the little horn's career. Judging from 9:26–27, it appears that at the beginning of this final heptad of years the "ruler who will come" will "confirm a covenant with many for one 'seven' [but] in the middle of that 'seven'" will compel the offering of sacrifices to cease. Thus after the first three and a half years of his career, the Beast will abrogate his "covenant" with the religious establishment (cf. 12:11; Mt 24:15; 2Th 2:4). This would leave three and a half years for his program to be carried out unhindered by any rival theistic ideology.

26–27 The last two verses of the angel's explanation make it clear that a great day of judgment and destruction on the Beast's empire and on the whole wicked world will

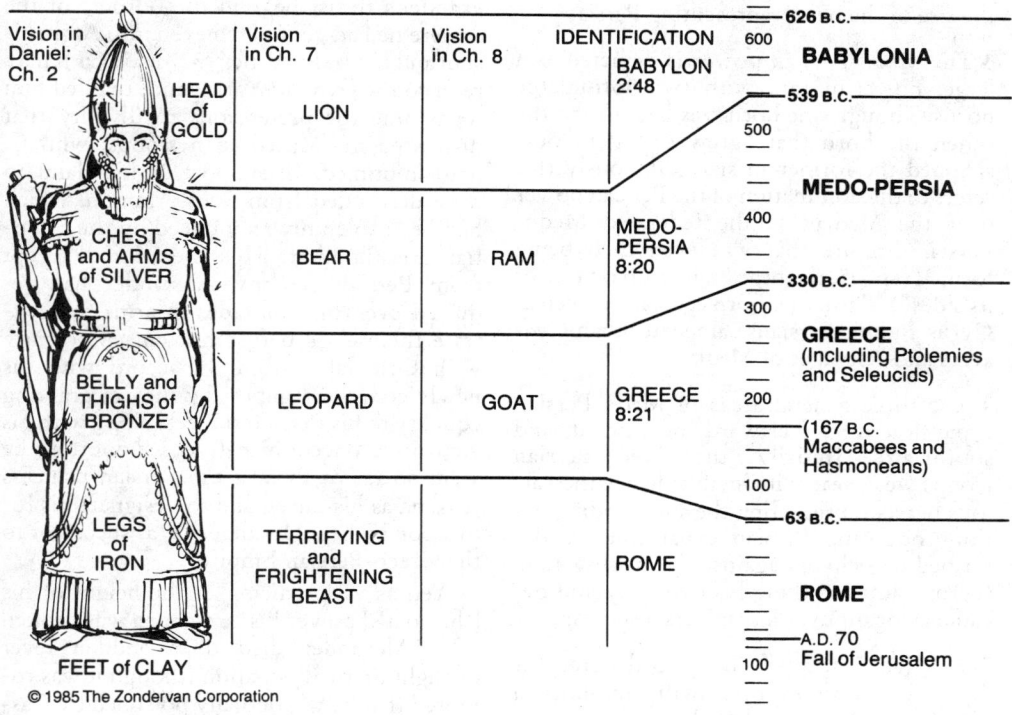

Identification of the Four Kingdoms

Vision in Daniel: Ch. 2	Vision in Ch. 7	Vision in Ch. 8	IDENTIFICATION
HEAD of GOLD	LION		BABYLON 2:48
CHEST and ARMS of SILVER	BEAR	RAM	MEDO-PERSIA 8:20
BELLY and THIGHS of BRONZE	LEOPARD	GOAT	GREECE 8:21
LEGS of IRON	TERRIFYING and FRIGHTENING BEAST		ROME
FEET of CLAY			

Chronology of Major Empires in Daniel

626 B.C. ———
600
BABYLONIA
539 B.C. ———
500
MEDO-PERSIA
400
330 B.C. ———
300
GREECE
(Including Ptolemies and Seleucids)
200
(167 B.C. Maccabees and Hasmoneans)
100
63 B.C. ———
ROME
A.D. 70
100 Fall of Jerusalem

© 1985 The Zondervan Corporation

usher in the seating of the Son of Man on the throne of absolute sovereignty and the commencement of the fifth kingdom (cf. ch. 2) administered by his faithful believers. No unsubdued, rebellious elements will be left among the surviving inhabitants of earth; "the sovereignty, power and greatness of the kingdoms under the whole heaven" will be granted to "the saints, the people of the Most High," indicating that the Son of Man (v.13) is to be equated with the Most High himself. In the final clause a clear difference is made between the plural "saints" and the singular "him," the one who is called "the Most High," whose kingdom will be everlasting— words not applicable to a finite human being.

28 Apparently Daniel experienced a tremendous emotional drain as a result of his extended interview with God's supernatural messenger (cf. Isa 6:5). His facial hue changed because of his inward concern about the severe trials awaiting his people. Yet these solemn disclosures were not proper matters to

divulge to anyone else; so apart from writing them down, he kept them to himself.

VIII. The Grecian Conquest of Persia and the Tyranny of Antiochus Epiphanes (8:1–27)

Here the text switches from Aramaic back to Hebrew (see Introduction).

A. The Vision of the Ram, the He-Goat, and the Little Horn (8:1–12)

1 This vision was granted Daniel two years after the previous one (cf. 7:1). It somewhat resembles it in subject matter and in manner of presentation, for it too portrays successive world empires as fierce beasts; and it also culminates in a tyrant described as a "little horn." Yet there are significant differences in detail between the two chapters, especially regarding the third and fourth kingdoms.

2 Daniel received this new vision either at the Babylonian capital itself or while on a diplomatic mission to Susa, the capital of Elam.

The scene Daniel saw in the vision was not Susa proper but rather the Ulai, a wide, artificial canal that flowed near the city. Appropriately enough, this furnished the setting for the rise of the beast representing Persia.

3 The Medo-Persian power is depicted as a large, powerful ram with two formidable horns. Though one horn was larger than the other, the horn that "grew up later" outstripped the former in size. Obviously this refers to the domination of the Persian power over the Median in the federated Medo-Persian Empire that was even then being formed (cf. 7:5, the bear "raised up on one of its sides"). The larger horn came later, even as Cyrus and his Persians came later than Cyaxeres and Astyages of Media.

4 The three general areas of Medo-Persian expansion were westward, northward, and southward. Initially the Medo-Persian troops were nearly invincible; hence the various beasts representing the surrounding nations opposing Persian expansion are described as helpless against the mighty ram. Cyrus had everything his own way and became arrogant over his universal success.

5–7 Verse 5 foretells coming disaster for Cyrus in the figure of a swift, one-horned goat that with one mighty charge shatters the horns of the Medo-Persian ram. First, the goat is described as coming from the west (i.e., Macedonia and Greece, as Alexander did in 334 B.C.). Second, he moves so fast that his hooves barely touch the ground as he charges all the way to the eastern limit of the Persian domain ("crossing the whole earth"). Third, this irresistible invading force is under the leadership of one man rather than a coalition of nations. In vain the ram attempts to withstand the charge of the goat, as the goat hurls himself against the ram—an implied prediction that the Macedonian-Greek forces would launch an unprovoked invasion such as took place in 334. The completeness of Alexander's victories is fittingly prefigured by this crushing attack on the ram.

Alexander's conquest of the entire Near and Middle East within three years stands unique in military history and is appropriately portrayed by the lightning speed of this one-horned goat. Despite the immense numerical superiority of the Persian imperial forces and their possession of military equipment like war elephants, the tactical genius of young Alexander proved decisive.

8 "The goat became very great" suggests Alexander's thrust beyond the borders of the empire he had conquered even into Afghanistan and the Indus Valley (327 B.C.). Or it may refer to the growth in arrogance that led him to assume the pretensions to divinity that distressed his Macedonian troops, who finally mutinied. In support of his claim to have descended from Zeus-Ammon, which had been solemnly announced by the Egyptian priesthood after his liberation of Egypt from Persian tyranny, Alexander had required even his comrades-in-arms to prostrate themselves before him, in conformity with Oriental custom. In accord with his newly conceived imperial policy of granting equality to his Persian subjects along with his victorious Macedonian-Greek supporters, he went so far as to take the Persian princess Roxana as his queen and to designate his future son by her, Alexander IV, as successor to the Greco-Persian Empire.

Yet, as v.8 predicts, "at the height of his [the goat's] power his large horn was broken off." Alexander died of a sudden fever brought on by dissipation (though it was rumored that he was actually poisoned by Cassander, the son of Antipater, viceroy of Macedonia) at Babylon in 323, at the age of thirty-three. Although efforts were made to hold the empire together—first by Antipater himself as regent for little Alexander IV (and for Philip III Arrhidaeus, his half-witted uncle), and then, after Antipater's death in 319, by Antigonus Monopthalmus, another highly respected general—the ambitions of such regional commanders as Ptolemy in Egypt, Seleucus in Babylonia, Lysimachus in Thrace and Asia Minor, and Cassander in Macedonia-Greece made this impossible. By 311 Seleucus asserted his claim to independent rule in Babylon, and the other three followed suit about the same time. Despite the earnest efforts of Antigonus and his brilliant son, Demetrius Poliorcetes, to subdue these separatist leaders, the final conflict at Ipsus in 301 resulted in defeat and death for Antigonus. The four ruthless and powerful generals named above became the "Diadochi" ("Successors"), who partitioned the Macedonian realm into four parts.

The prophecy "in its [the large horn's] place four prominent horns grew up toward the four winds of heaven" was fulfilled when Cassander retained his hold on Macedonia and Greece; Lysimachus held Thrace and the western half of Asia Minor as far as Cappadocia and Phrygia; Ptolemy consolidated Palestine, Cilicia, and Cyprus with his Egyptian-Libyan domains; and Seleucus controlled the rest of Asia all the way to the Indus Valley. While it is true that various vicissitudes beset these four realms during the third century and after (Pergamum, Bithynia, and Pontus achieved local independence in Asia Minor after the death of Lysimachus; and the eastern provinces of the Seleucid Empire achieved sovereignty as the kingdoms of Bactria and Parthia), nevertheless the initial division of Alexander's empire was unquestionably fourfold, as this verse and 7:6 (the four-winged leopard) indicate.

9–10 Verses 9–12 foretell the rise of a "small horn" from the midst of the four horns of the Diadochi. It is described as attaining success in aggression against the "south," or the domains of the Ptolemies. This evidently refers to the career of Antiochus IV Epiphanes ("the Manifest/Conspicuous One"; see comment on 8:23–25), who usurped the Seleucid throne from his nephew (son of his older brother, Seleucus IV) and succeeded in invading Egypt 170–169 B.C. His expeditions against rebellious elements in Parthia and Armenia were initially successful "to the east" as well, and his determination to impose religious and cultural uniformity on all his domains led to a brutal suppression of Jewish worship at Jerusalem and generally throughout Palestine (here referred to as "the Beautiful Land"; cf. 11:16, 41). This suppression came to a head in December 168 B.C., when Antiochus returned in frustration from Alexandria (Egypt), where he had been turned back by the Roman commander Popilius Laenas, and vented his exasperation on the Jews. He sent his general, Apollonius, with twenty thousand troops under orders to seize Jerusalem on a Sabbath. There he erected an idol of Zeus and desecrated the altar by offering swine on it. This idol became known to the Jews as "the abomination of desolation" (cf. 11:31), a type of a future abomination to be set up in the Jerusalem sanctuary in the last days (cf. Mt 24:15).

Some observations are in order concerning the relationship between the "little horn" (lit., "a horn from a small one") in 8:9 and the "little horn" in 7:8. The horn in ch. 7 emerged from the ten horns of the fourth beast, whereas this horn in 8:9 arises from the four-horned beast that represents the third kingdom, the empire of Alexander the Great (as all critics agree). Since the author of Daniel invests numbers with high significance, there is no possibility that he could have meant to equate a ten-horned beast with a four-horned one. The only plausible explanation is that the little horn arising from the third kingdom is a prototype of the little horn of the fourth kingdom. The crisis destined to confront God's people in the time of the earlier little horn, Antiochus Epiphanes, will bear a strong similarity to the one that will befall them in the final phase of the fourth kingdom in the last days (see Mt 24:15). In each case a determined effort is made by a ruthless dictator to suppress completely the biblical faith and the worship of the one true God. Rather than concluding that the little horn of ch. 7 is also intended as a prophecy of Antiochus Epiphanes (with a resultant identification of the fourth kingdom as the Greek or Seleucid Empire), we are to understand the relationship between the little horn of the Greek Empire and that of the latter-day fourth kingdom to be that of type and antitype, similar to that between Joshua and Jesus (Heb 4:8) and Melchizedek and Christ (Heb 7). In Da 11 both the typical little horn (Antiochus) and the antitypical little horn appear in succession, the transition from the one to the other taking place at 11:36, after which are predicted the circumstances of the destined death of the antitype that were not at all true of Antiochus Epiphanes himself. Therefore, the two figures cannot be identical, nor can the Greek Empire be equated with the fourth kingdom of Daniel's prophetic scheme.

Continuing with the predicted career of Antiochus (v.10), we encounter the remarkable statement that he will grow up to "the host of heaven" and will throw "some of the starry host down to the earth," where he will "trample on them." "Host" (GK 7372) is a term most often used of the armies of angels in the service of God (e.g., "LORD of hosts" in KJV) or else of the stars in heaven (cf. Jer 33:22). But it is also used of the people of God, who are to become as the stars in number (Ge 12:3; 15:5) and are spoken of as "the LORD's divisions" (Ex 12:41). Daniel 12:3 states that true believers (lit., "those who are wise") "will shine like the brightness of the heavens [lit., stars] for ever and ever." Since the Greek tyrant can hardly affect either the angels of heaven or the literal stars in the sky, it is quite evident that the phrase "the host of the heavens" must refer to those Jewish believers who will join the Maccabees in defending their faith and liberty. It is then implied here that Antiochus will cut down and destroy many of the Jews during the time of tribulation he will bring on them, when he will have "trampled on them."

From 171 or 170 B.C. and thereafter, Antiochus pursued his evil policy of securing control of the high priesthood and bringing increasing pressure on the Jewish hierarchy to surrender their religious loyalties in the interests of conformity to Greek culture and idolatry. Already in 175, at the beginning of his reign, he had expelled the godly high priest Onias III from office and replaced him with his Hellenizing younger brother, Jason. Before long a certain Jew named Menelaus, who was apparently also of the high priestly family, bribed Antiochus to depose Jason and appoint him high priest in his place. But while Antiochus was successfully campaigning in Egypt against Ptolemy VII (181-145 B.C.), Jason laid siege to Jerusalem in the hope of ousting Menelaus. In the process of dealing subsequently with Jason, Antiochus took occasion to storm Jerusalem and pillage the temple itself. Reinstalling Menelaus as high priest, Antiochus gave him the mandate to continue an aggressive policy of Hellenization. But in December of 168 (cf. above), he had Jerusalem again seized by treachery and subjected it to prolonged looting and massacre, and a year later he converted its sanctuary into a temple to Zeus (Dec. 16, 167). So it continued until that memorable day, three years later, when Judas Maccabaeus rededicated the sacred structure to the worship of God (Dec 14, 164 B.C.), an event celebrated as Hanukkah by the Jewish community.

11 This verse describes how the megalomania of Antiochus advances to such extremes that he will declare himself equal with God ("Prince of the host"). He will halt the regular morning and evening sacrifice. (This was the daily burnt offering ordained in Nu 28:3,

consisting of one lamb presented at sunrise and one at sunset, together with flour and oil [Nu 28:5].) This offering presented the atonement of the believing nation, whether or not any other sacrifice was brought before the Lord on that particular day. But the Seleucid tyrant commanded these offerings to be suspended in 168 and substituted a heathen sacrifice presented to an idol of Zeus, after the altar of the LORD had been destroyed and his temple pillaged and desecrated ("and the place of his sanctuary was brought low").

12 Judah's three-year tribulation period, during which the temple would be defiled and prostituted to heathen use, is now described. The phrase rendered "because of" is somewhat ambiguous. The verse as a whole probably should be rendered as follows:

> And on account of transgression [presumably the transgression of Jason and Menelaus and the pro-Syrian faction among the worldly minded Jews of the Maccabean period] the host [of God's people, the Jewish believers] will be given up [to the persecuting power of Antiochus IV] along with the [suspended] continual burnt offering; and the horn [Antiochus] will fling the truth [of scriptural faith and service of God] to the ground [by forbidding it on pain of death], and he will perform [his will, or carry out his program of enforcing idolatry] and will [for the three-year period] prosper.

B. Gabriel's Interpretation of the Vision (8:13–27)

13–14 There were two or possibly even three "holy ones" (GK 7705; i.e., heavenly beings) conversing about the prophetic meaning of the vision just described. Apparently the second angel ("another holy one") posed the question to the third ("to him") as to the duration of the terrible period when the temple and altar of the Lord would be desecrated (v.11). The answer given by the third angel was that this condition would last for "2,300 evenings and mornings." This period of time has been understood by interpreters in two ways, either as 2,300 twenty-four-hour days ("evening morning" meaning an entire day from sunset to sunset; cf. Ge 1) or as 1,150 days composed of 1,150 evenings and 1,150 mornings. In other words, the interval would either be 6 years and 111 days or 3 years and 55 days. Most evidence seems to favor the latter interpretation. The context speaks of the suspension of the "sacrifice," a reference to the "continual burnt offering" that was offered regularly each morning and evening. Surely there could have been no other reason for the compound expression than the reference to the two sacrifices that marked each day in temple worship.

Consequently, we are to understand v.14 as predicting the rededication of the temple by Judas Maccabaeus on 25 Chislev (or Dec. 14), 164 B.C.; 1,150 days before that would point to a terminus a quo of three years, one month, and 25 days earlier, or Tishri 167 B.C. While the actual erection of the idolatrous altar in the temple took place in Chislev 167, or one month and 15 days later, there is no reason to suppose that Antiochus Epiphanes's administrators may not have abolished the offering itself at that earlier date. Verse 14 simply specifies that when the 2,300 evenings and mornings have elapsed, "then the sanctuary will be reconsecrated." That certainly happened when the first Hanukkah was celebrated on 25 Chislev 164.

15–18 Some other heavenly being not otherwise specified commissioned Gabriel to explain the meaning of the vision to the swooning prophet. Gabriel was instructed to identify the coming world empires and the climactic events of the "time of the end." The overwhelming splendor of Gabriel's presence rendered Daniel completely helpless, but the angel's transforming touch restored him.

19–22 This passage furnishes a general summary of the rise of the second and third kingdoms. Gabriel gave no details about the Persian era beyond indicating its compound character as Medo-Persian. But he did identify the large single horn between the goat's eyes as the first king of the Greek Empire. This mighty conqueror was soon replaced by four other horns, which were the Diadochi (see comments on 7:8; 8:8). He added that none of these four would "have the same power" (i.e., of Alexander). History proved this true.

23–25 This passage depicts the rise of Antiochus Epiphanes, described as a "stern-faced king, a master of intrigue" (lit., "a master at understanding hidden things"), who will at

first enjoy much success. He will crush "mighty men" (presumably nobles and regional commanders who supported rival claimants to the throne) and also "the holy people" (i.e., the believing Jews).

Two noteworthy traits will characterize Antiochus's rule: (1) his treachery and intrigue, to catch his victims unawares and unprepared (as in Jerusalem in 168–167 B.C.); (2) his overweening pride, which led him to claim divine honors. The coins of Antiochus actually bore the title "God manifest." This clearly exhibited his character as the typical "little horn," a model for the antitypical "little horn" referred to in 7:8 (cf. 2Th 2:3–4).

While we are not told whether Antiochus made a formal claim to deity while enthroned in the court of the Jerusalem temple, he certainly did assume the right to determine what gods his subjects should worship, feeling that he was the earthly embodiment of the powers of heaven and that all rule and authority were given him. Like Nebuchadnezzar, he expected all his subjects to bow down to the great image he had set up. But he went even beyond Nebuchadnezzar in trying to abolish the ancestral religion of the Jews, forbidding them on pain of death to circumcise their children and making the possession of the Hebrew Scriptures a capital offense. By erecting the statue of Zeus Olympius (or Capitolinus) in the temple of the Lord and sacrificing swine on the altar, he committed the greatest possible sacrilege and affront to the Jewish people.

Yet v.25 predicts Antiochus's sudden destruction, not by human means, but by God's intervention. As a condign penalty for having taken "his stand against the Prince of princes" (the Lord God Almighty), Antiochus would be removed from the scene. He was. After making an unsuccessful attempt to pillage Nanaea, a wealthy temple in Elymais, he died of a sudden malady.

Ancient sources have somewhat diverse accounts of Antiochus's fatal illness. The author of 1Mc 6:4, 8–16 says that Antiochus withdrew to Babylon after his repulse at Elymais, that he became deathly ill after hearing of the victories of Judas Maccabaeus, and that he died many days later. But 2Mc 9:1–28 states that Antiochus had attempted to raid a temple in Persepolis (rather than Elymais), and that it was at Ecbatana that he heard the disturbing news of the Maccabean victories.

Then, as he was uttering dire threats of reprisal against them, he was seized with severe abdominal pains that never left him; and thus he fell out of the chariot in which he was riding. Finally, as a result of his severe injuries from the fall and the attack of worms on his bowels, accompanied by a revolting stench, he finally died with vain petitions on his lips, imploring the God of Israel to spare his life. The various accounts agree in stating that the tyrant met his end by a nonhuman agency. The question of Antiochus's death is of special importance in 11:45.

26–27 Chapter 8 closes with Gabriel's command for Daniel to keep confidential the predictions just revealed to him because they are related to "the distant future" (cf. 12:9). It is also significant that Gabriel states that the vision refers to "many days" (i.e., to many years in the future). (NIV's "distant future" is somewhat inexact but certainly should not be pressed to refer to the last days just before the Lord's return; the "many days" in this case obviously refers to the crisis years of 167–164 B.C.) Verse 27 describes the emotional strain the prophet felt following this encounter with the angel Gabriel. It drained him to the point of illness for several days. Even after he went back to the king's service, he kept brooding over the vision and its fulfillment. Perhaps what most disturbed Daniel was the prediction of the time of great tribulation appointed for the true people of God under the tyranny of the "little horn."

IX. The Vision of the Seventy Weeks (9:1–27)

A. Daniel's Great Prayer (9:1–19)

1–3 Daniel, a diligent student of Scripture, built his prayer life on God's Word. Significantly, even before any formal endorsement had been accorded them, he included Jeremiah's writings as inspired Scripture, even though Jeremiah had died only a few decades earlier. As Daniel studied Jer 25:11–13, he saw that God had appointed a period of seventy years for the captivity of Israel, at the end of which Babylon would be judged by God. Daniel was gripped by the words in Jer 29:10.

Since this episode took place in 539 or 538 ("the first year of Darius"; on the identity of Darius the Mede, see ZPEB, 2:29), less than fifty years had elapsed since the Fall of Jeru-

salem to Nebuchadnezzar (587 B.C.) or the destruction of the temple in 586. The earliest possible terminus a quo for the seventy years of exile would be Daniel's own captivity in Babylon (604 B.C.). While 538 might be three or four years short of the full seventy, it was not too soon for Daniel to begin praying. In view of the recent collapse of the Chaldean Empire and the benevolent attitude of Cyrus toward the religious preferences of his newly conquered subjects, Daniel was moved to claim the promise implied by the number seventy in Jeremiah's writings. So he implored the Lord to reckon those years from the year of his own exile and to ensure the reestablishment of Israel in the Land of Promise by seventy years from the first Palestinian invasion of King Nebuchadnezzar.

Although this passage does not actually mention the predictions concerning King Cyrus that were revealed to Isaiah back in the early seventh century, undoubtedly Daniel knew about them (cf. Isa 44:28; 45:1–2). Daniel must have been stirred when he first heard reports of the young king of Persia who made himself master of the entire Medo-Persian domain. When Cyrus finally launched his invasion of Mesopotamia and laid siege to Babylon itself, Daniel's heart must have leaped at seeing prophecy being fulfilled. Now that Cyrus had indeed attained the success that the Lord had promised him years before, Daniel besought the Lord to move the conqueror's heart to let the Hebrew exiles return to their land. Isaiah 45:4, 13 were promises that Daniel could claim at this critical time in Israel's history.

4–6 Verses 4–19 show how a true man of God should approach the Sovereign of the universe. Daniel made striking spiritual preparations for his ministry of intercession: he fasted, mourned, and clothed himself with sackcloth (v.3). Daniel realized he could not urge on God any merit of his nation, for they had forfeited all claim to divine mercy. By their persistent transgression of their covenant with God, their embracing of heathen idolatry and immorality, and their martyrdom of the prophets (cf. 2Ch 36:16), they had literally compelled him to bring on them the promised curses (cf. Lev 26:39–45; Dt 28:45–63; 30:1–5). They had richly deserved the destruction of their cities and the loss of their property, freedom, and native land; and they lacked any ground of merit on which to entreat God's favor. The only basis for Daniel's approach to God was his earnest desire for the Lord to glorify himself by displaying the riches of his mercy and grace in pardoning and restoring his guilty but repentant people to their land in fulfillment of his promise in Jer 25 and 29.

With these convictions Daniel devoted himself to a prayer of adoration and confession. In this chapter Daniel for the first time used the sacred Tetragrammaton, the covenant name of *Yahweh* (i.e., "LORD," v.2 and the preamble of v.4; GK 3378). Even though he found himself exiled from the sacred soil of Israel, Daniel boldly claimed the Lord's mercy as the covenant-keeping God of Israel. Although he addressed him as "Lord" in the opening sentence of his prayer and in v.7, Daniel addressed him directly as "LORD" in v.8 and referred to him by the same covenant name in vv.10, 13, and 14.

In his first words Daniel combined both aspects of God's nature, glorifying him as the "great and awesome God" and as the faithful, promise-keeping God. The Lord allowed his people to go down in utter defeat because they had forced his hand by flagrant and shameless sin.

As spokesman of his people, Daniel confessed their sin and wickedness and acknowledged that the Jews had succumbed to the surrounding cultures. They had been unwilling to repent at the warning of God's prophets. The whole nation had become involved in rejecting the Lord; there remained such a small remnant of faithful believers that Judah was not worth saving from the coming destruction. Daniel could find no excuse for their betrayal of their sacred trust.

7–11a Rather than appearing to be a chosen people (Dt 7:6), blessed of God in military success (Dt 28:7) and feared by the nations (Dt 28:10), Israel had been laid waste, its inhabitants killed or exiled. The Jews had become objects of scorn, deprived of property and freedom and derided for their claim to know the one true God. What made their disgrace even more shameful was their flagrant ingratitude toward their compassionate, forgiving God, whose pardon and mercy they ridiculed and rejected.

11b–14 Daniel exalted the justice of God (cf. Dt 28–32); it was more important for God to retain his integrity and uphold his moral law than for his guilty people to escape the consequences of their infidelity. Had God not fulfilled his word of judgment, little credence could be placed in his word of grace. The fall of Jerusalem, the destruction of the temple, and the Captivity vindicated the holiness and righteousness of God and demonstrated the sanctity of his moral law.

15–19 Daniel appealed to God's pity on the exiled nation and ruined Jerusalem, basing his appeal on God's honor and glory. Daniel was chiefly concerned about God's reputation in the eyes of the world. If the Lord allowed his sanctuary and Holy City to lie in ruins and his people to remain in exile, who among the surrounding nations would believe that the Lord was the true and holy Sovereign over all the universe? That, in Daniel's mind, was the worst thing about the tragedy of Jerusalem's fall and the Captivity—the pagans would conclude that the Lord was unable to protect his people against Babylon's gods. Moreover, since God had promised full pardon and restoration to his repentant people, the prophet felt emboldened to press the Lord for an early return of the Jewish captives to Palestine, that a new commonwealth of chastened believers might be established there and a testimony set up again for the one true God. Because of the purity of his motives and the earnestness of his desire, Daniel was heard and soon received his answer.

B. The Divine Answer: Seventy Heptads of Years (9:20–27)

20–23 The Lord's response came swiftly. Daniel had not even finished his prayer before Gabriel came to reveal God's will to his faithful servant. The term "the man" (GK 408) indicates that the archangel appeared in human form and spoke to Daniel as one man speaks to another. Daniel saw Gabriel approaching in "swift flight," and Gabriel responded to his prayer at the time of the evening sacrifice—i.e., at sunset. Evidently Daniel had prayed till late afternoon. Of course, no actual sacrifice could have been offered in Babylon—or in Palestine—without a new altar on the site of the destroyed temple. But devout Jews in Persia would have observed both sunrise and sunset as appropriate times of the day for offering adoration, praise, and supplication.

Gabriel began his teaching by encouraging Daniel; his faith was precious in God's eyes. The Lord is more eager to answer than we are to ask, and in Daniel's case there were powerful grounds for a speedy reply, reassuring him of the Lord's intention to bring to an end the seventy years of Israel's captivity.

24 This verse sets forth the approach of "seventy 'sevens'" of years during which God would accomplish his plan of national and spiritual redemption for Israel. The seventy "weeks" or "heptads" (lit., "units of seven," whether days or years) are 490 years (divided, as we shall see, into three sections). This was the time to elapse before the accomplishment of six great achievements for the Holy City and for God's covenant people. The first three relate to the removal of sin; the second three to the restoration of righteousness.

1. The first achievement is "to finish transgression." The culmination of the appointed years will witness the conclusion of human "transgression" (GK 7322) or "rebellion" against God—a development most naturally entered into with the establishment of an entirely new order on earth. This requires nothing less than the inauguration of the kingdom of God on earth. Certainly the crucifixion of Christ in A.D. 30 did not put an end to human iniquity or rebellion on earth.

2. The second achievement is "to put an end to sins." The Hebrew term for "sin" (GK 2633) refers to missing the mark or the true goal of life; it implies immorality of a more general sort rather than revolt against authority implied by "transgression." This achievement suggests the bringing in of a new society in which righteousness will prevail in complete contrast to the present condition of the human race.

3. The third achievement is "to atone for wickedness." This certainly points to the Crucifixion, which ushered in the final stage of human history before the establishment of the fifth kingdom (cf. 2:35, 44). At Pentecost Peter referred to "the last days" spoken of by the prophet Joel (cf. Ac 2:16–17). This implies that the "last days" began at the inauguration of the NT church at Pentecost. The Feast of Pentecost occurred just seven weeks after the Resurrection, which followed the Crucifixion by three days. The Crucifixion was the atonement that made possible the es-

tablishment of the new order, the church of the redeemed, and the coming millennial kingdom.

4. The fourth achievement is "to bring in everlasting righteousness." This clearly indicates an order of society in which righteousness, justice, and conformity to the standards of Scripture will prevail on earth, rather than the temporary periods of upright government that have occasionally occurred in world history till now.

5. The fifth achievement will be the fulfillment of the vision and "the prophecy," which serves as the grand and central goal of God's plan for the ages, that final stage of human history when the Son of Man receives "authority, glory and sovereign power" (7:14) so that all peoples will serve him. This fulfillment surely goes beyond the suffering, death, and resurrection of Christ to include his enthronement—on the throne of David—as supreme Ruler over all the earth.

6. The final goal to be achieved at the end of the seventy weeks is the anointing of "the most holy." This most likely refers to the consecration of the temple of the Lord, conceivably the millennial temple (cf. Eze 40–44).

Before the question of the seventieth week can be properly handled, the terminus ad quem of the seventy weeks must first be established. If all six goals of v.24 were attained by the crucifixion of Christ and the establishment of the early church seven years after his death, then it might be fair to assume that the entire 490 years of the seventy weeks were to be understood as running consecutively and coming to a close in A.D. 37. But since all or most of the six goals seem to be yet unfulfilled, it follows that if the seventieth week finds fulfillment at all, it must be identified as the last seven years before Christ's return to earth as millennial King.

25–26 Verse 25 is crucial. Only sixty-nine heptads are listed here, broken into two segments. The first segment of seven amounts to forty-nine years, during which the city of Jerusalem is to be "rebuilt with streets and a trench, but in times of trouble."

Verse 26 specifies the termination of the sixty-nine heptads: the cutting off of the Messiah. After the appearance of Messiah as Ruler—483 years after the sixty-nine weeks have begun—he will be cut off. This accords very well with a three-year ministry of the Messiah prior to his crucifixion. Verse 26 goes on to indicate that when Messiah is cut off, he will be bereft of followers; all of them will flee from him at the time of his arrest, trial, and death. (Or "nothing" may mean that he will die without any material wealth or resources.)

For the terminus a quo, notice that v.25 specifies the rebuilding of the city of Jerusalem with streets and moats, which will be completed within forty-nine years of the terminus a quo. The most likely fulfillment is the decree issued to Ezra in the seventh year of Artaxerxes I (i.e., 457 B.C.) (for other possibilities, see EBC, 7:113–16). Its text (Ezr 7:12–26) emphasizes restoring the temple and enforcing the Mosaic code. Yet Ezra understood the decree to include permission to rebuild the wall of Jerusalem. To be sure, he did not succeed in doing so; his attention was focused on urgently needed community reforms. Certainly he lacked the resources for so ambitious an undertaking; so the rebuilding never went beyond the talking stage. If this led to a delay of thirteen years in working on the walls, Nehemiah's disappointment (Ne 1:4) when in 446 he heard that no progress had been made seems all the more appropriate. Nehemiah no doubt had hoped for more tangible results from Ezra's leadership during his twelve years there.

If, then, the terminus a quo for the decree in v.25 be reckoned as 457 B.C. (the date of Ezra's return to Jerusalem), we may compute the first seven heptads as running from 457 to 408, within which time the rebuilding of the walls, streets, and moats was completed. Then from 408 we count off the sixty-two heptads (434 years) also mentioned in v.25 and come out to A.D. 26 (408 is 26 less than 434). But actually we come out to A.D. 27, since there is no year 0. If Christ was crucified on 14 Abib A.D. 30, as is generally believed (cf. EBC, 1:598–99, 607), this would come out to a remarkably exact fulfillment of the terms of v.25. Christ's public ministry, from the time of his baptism in the Jordan till his death and resurrection at Jerusalem, must have taken up about three years. The 483 years from the issuing of the decree of Artaxerxes came to an end in A.D. 27, the year of the "coming" of Messiah as Ruler. It was indeed "after the sixty-two 'sevens'"—three

years after—that "the Anointed One" was "cut off."

The second sentence of v.26 is perhaps more accurately rendered, "The people of a prince who shall come will destroy both the city and the sanctuary." (The reason for the ambiguity here is that the definite article is missing in front of "ruler" in the Hebrew, which would be necessary for the rendering "the people of the ruler.") Subsequent history shows this to be a clear reference to the destruction of Jerusalem by the Romans under Titus in A.D. 70, forty years after Calvary, or forty-three years after the end of the sixty-ninth "week"—if the 457 B.C. theory is correct for the commencement of the seventy weeks.

The next sentence or two indicate what is to happen after the destruction of Jerusalem: lit., "And the end of it will be in the overflowing, and unto the end there will be war, a strict determination of desolations" or "the determined amount of desolations." The general tenor is in striking conformity with Christ's own prediction (Mt 24:7–22). Notice that this entire intervening period is referred to before the final or seventieth week is mentioned in v.27. It is difficult to explain why this is so if the entire seventy weeks are intended to run consecutively and without interruption. It seems far more reasonable to infer that a long period of time of war and desolation is to intervene between the sixty-ninth week (when Messiah appears at his first advent) and the seventieth week, which is to usher in Christ's second advent.

27 This verse evokes the question, Who? The "ruler" in v.26 is the last eligible antecedent in the Hebrew text, which normally is to be taken as the subject of the following verb. If it was a ruler of the Roman people who was to destroy Jerusalem (in A.D. 70), then it would be a ruler of the Roman Empire—in its final phase, i.e., the ten-toes phase of ch. 2 and the ten-horned-beast phase of ch. 7— who will conclude this covenant. (Of course it could not be the same ruler, for a long period seems to be referred to in the last part of v.26; the earlier ruler must therefore be a type or forerunner of the "Roman" ruler of the last days.)

Who are "the many"? (The Heb. indicates "the many" rather than "many.") Apparently this refers to the true believers, presumably

Jewish believers in Christ. The foregoing thus indicates that the latter day ruler over the "Roman" people will "confirm" a "covenant" with the believing Jews for a stipulated period of seven years, permitting them to carry on their religious practices.

After about three and one-half years, the world dictator will break his agreement with the Jews. Possibly he will feel secure enough in his autocratic position to carry out his original, secret plan to impose an absolute dictatorship on all the people of his empire, especially the Jews. All pretense of religious toleration will be dropped as he aspires to display himself as the incarnation of all divine authority on earth (cf. 2Th 2:4).

The final statement of v.27 is difficult (see NIV note). The Hebrew has no word for "temple" or any verb for "set." A more literal translation is, "And on the wing of abominations (he is going to) commit abominations, and toward the end [or 'up until'] the predetermined (judgment) will be poured out upon him." In other words, the subject of "commit abominations" (lit. Heb.) is the Antichrist himself, carried over from v.26; and what we have here is more likely a construction like "he is about to commit abominations." It seems unjustified to supply a verb "to set." Since there is no word for "temple," it is more reasonable to understand "wing" as a figure for the vulture-like role of the Antichrist as he swoops down on his beleaguered victims.

The phrase "that causes desolation" (GK 9037) resembles "the abomination that causes desolation" in Da 11:31 and 12:11. Apparently these three passages were in Christ's mind when he predicted the final horrors of the Tribulation (cf. Mt 24:15). Furthermore, Jesus obviously regarded the fulfillment of this prophecy as yet future. It is simplest to take the "desolator" as the world dictator of the last days, who will resort to violence to carry through his ruthless policy of despotism. Revelation 13 indicates that he will remain in control of world affairs down to the End, enforcing his will by violent means till the final conflict of Armageddon. The dictator will hold sway till the wrath of God is poured out in fury on the God-defying world of the Beast (little horn or ruler). What is "poured out" may include the vials or bowls of divine wrath mentioned in Rev 16; but certainly what "is poured out on

him" points to the climax at Armageddon, when the blasphemous world ruler will be crushed by the full weight of God's judgment.

X. The Triumph of Persistent Prayer (10:1–21)

A. Daniel's Disturbing Vision and Prayerful Concern (10:1–3)

1–3 The "third year of Cyrus" identifies this vision as the latest recorded in the Book of Daniel. Since the reign of Darius lasted until 538 or 537, Cyrus's third year (at Babylon) would have been 535/534, probably just a few years before Daniel's death. (If he was born around 620 B.C., Daniel would have been ninety by 530.) The vision's message related to "a great war," portending troublesome times for the people of God. Daniel was so impressed by this revelation that he mourned and fasted for three weeks, giving himself to intense supplication and prayer (cf. v.12).

B. God's Delayed Messenger (10:4–14)

4–6 In early spring, Daniel received his answer through an angel while standing by the Tigris River, evidently there on some kind of official business. Verses 5–6 are probably the most detailed description in Scripture of the appearance of an angel (cf. Jdg 13:6; Lk 24:4; Ac 1:10). The angel (1) was dressed in linen, possibly the dazzling white apparel referred to in Lk 24:4; (2) he had a "gold" belt around his waist, possibly in the form of chain links, hinged panels, or gold thread embroidery; (3) his body glowed luminously; (4) his face flashed like lightning; (5) his eyes blazed like torches (cf. Rev 1:14); (6) his arms and legs (evidently uncovered) gleamed like burnished bronze; and (7) his voice was like the "sound of a multitude" (cf. Rev 10:1–3).

7–11 Although Daniel's companions did not see the vision, they sensed the angel's presence and fled in terror (cf. Ac 9:7; 22:9). Left alone with this awesome messenger, Daniel once again was emotionally overwhelmed (cf. 8:27). After hearing the angel speak to him, Daniel swooned. But the angel's touch soon aroused him. Daniel stood up, respectfully attentive to God's message. The remarkable greeting reassured him of God's love and concern for his faithful servants. Daniel's privileged status resulted from his

Ptolemies and Seleucids

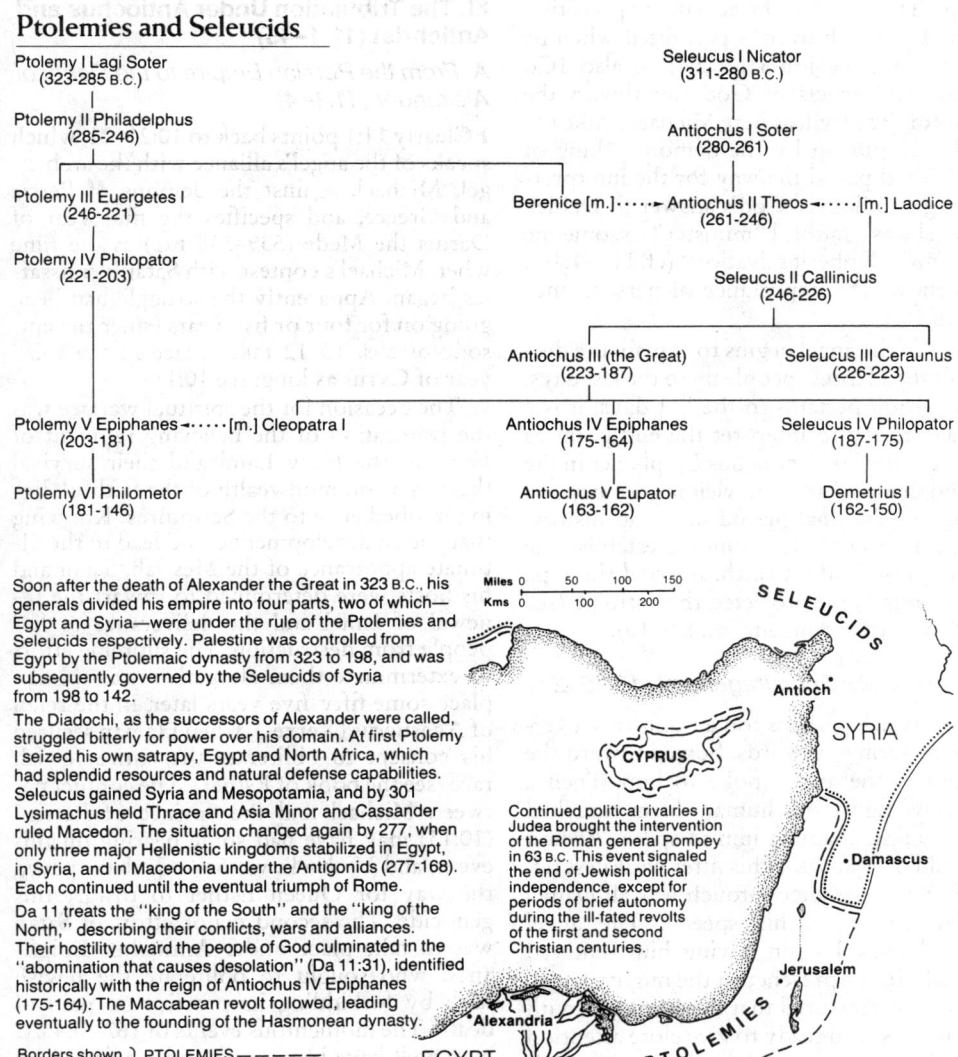

Ptolemy I Lagi Soter
(323-285 B.C.)

Ptolemy II Philadelphus
(285-246)

Ptolemy III Euergetes I
(246-221)

Ptolemy IV Philopator
(221-203)

Ptolemy V Epiphanes ◄·····[m.] Cleopatra I
(203-181)

Ptolemy VI Philometor
(181-146)

Seleucus I Nicator
(311-280 B.C.)

Antiochus I Soter
(280-261)

Berenice [m.]·····► Antiochus II Theos ◄·····[m.] Laodice
(261-246)

Seleucus II Callinicus
(246-226)

Antiochus III (the Great)   Seleucus III Ceraunus
(223-187)   (226-223)

Antiochus IV Epiphanes   Seleucus IV Philopator
(175-164)   (187-175)

Antiochus V Eupator   Demetrius I
(163-162)   (162-150)

Soon after the death of Alexander the Great in 323 B.C., his generals divided his empire into four parts, two of which—Egypt and Syria—were under the rule of the Ptolemies and Seleucids respectively. Palestine was controlled from Egypt by the Ptolemaic dynasty from 323 to 198, and was subsequently governed by the Seleucids of Syria from 198 to 142.

The Diadochi, as the successors of Alexander were called, struggled bitterly for power over his domain. At first Ptolemy I seized his own satrapy, Egypt and North Africa, which had splendid resources and natural defense capabilities. Seleucus gained Syria and Mesopotamia, and by 301 Lysimachus held Thrace and Asia Minor and Cassander ruled Macedon. The situation changed again by 277, when only three major Hellenistic kingdoms stabilized in Egypt, in Syria, and in Macedonia under the Antigonids (277-168). Each continued until the eventual triumph of Rome.

Da 11 treats the "king of the South" and the "king of the North," describing their conflicts, wars and alliances. Their hostility toward the people of God culminated in the "abomination that causes desolation" (Da 11:31), identified historically with the reign of Antiochus IV Epiphanes (175-164). The Maccabean revolt followed, leading eventually to the founding of the Hasmonean dynasty.

Borders shown ⎱ PTOLEMIES — — — —
c. 240 B.C. ⎰ SELEUCIDS ··············

Continued political rivalries in Judea brought the intervention of the Roman general Pompey in 63 B.C. This event signaled the end of Jewish political independence, except for periods of brief autonomy during the ill-fated revolts of the first and second Christian centuries.

© 1985 The Zondervan Corporation

complete absorption in the will and glory of the Lord. The angel called on Daniel to listen carefully to what he was about to receive. From the standpoint of 535 B.C., ch. 11 is full of confusing detail couched in vague terms, though the subsequent fulfillment in later times is amazingly accurate.

12–14 Daniel was told what happened in heaven when three weeks earlier he had begun to pray for an understanding of God's plan for Israel's future. Because Daniel had set his "mind to gain understanding and to humble [himself] before [his] God," the Lord commissioned his angelic messenger with the answer to Daniel's petition. The powers of evil apparently are able to hinder the delivery of the answers to requests God is minded to answer. God's response was immediate, but "the prince of the Persian kingdom"—apparently the satanic agent assigned to the Persian realm—vigorously opposed the actual delivery of the answer.

While God can override the united resistance of all the forces of hell, he accords to demons certain limited powers of obstruction and rebellion like those he allows human beings. The exercise of free will in opposition to the Lord of heaven is permitted when he sees fit (but see Job 1:12; 2:6; cf. also 1Co 10:13). The angels of God can thwart the agents of the Devil, as here Michael broke the hindrance put up by the demonic "king of Persia" and paved the way for the interpreting angel to deliver God's answer to Daniel. Michael was a faithful "minister" to someone who would "inherit salvation" (cf. Heb 1:14). This shows the importance of perseverance (cf. Lk 18:1).

In v.14 the angel begins to explain the destiny of the Hebrew people up to the last days. If the vision pertains to the last days, it is a mistake to try to interpret the end point as being the time of Antiochus Epiphanes in the second century B.C. The vision goes beyond his age to the final period in world history, before the Son of Man comes to establish the kingdom of God on earth. Beyond the type (Antiochus IV) is projected the antitype (see 11:40; also the comments on 8:9–10).

C. The Angel's Encouragement (10:15–21)

15–19 Daniel, perhaps too emotionally overcome to form any words, bowed toward the ground as the angel spoke to him. Then a heavenly figure in human form touched Daniel's lips, enabling him to speak. At first he could only speak of his utter weakness (cf. Isa 6:5), but the angel's touch was all Daniel needed to regain his speech. The angel touched Daniel again, giving him renewed strength. In the presence of the mighty angel, Daniel was reassured that the Lord was with him; he was then ready to give close attention to God's revelation of the future and write it down with utmost care.

20–21 The angel revealed that he was still in combat for the Lord and would soon return to the battlefield to fight against renewed attacks from the demon assigned to Persia. This antagonist would be succeeded by another satanic champion called the "prince of Greece." These battles between the warriors of heaven and those of hell most likely take place in heaven (cf. Rev 12:7) and result in the defeat of Satan. It is encouraging to know that God has mighty champions among the holy angels to defend the saints against the attacks of the Evil One.

XI. The Tribulation Under Antiochus and Antichrist (11:1–45)

A. From the Persian Empire to the Death of Alexander (11:1–4)

1 Clearly 11:1 points back to 10:20–21, which speaks of the angel's alliance with the archangel, Michael, against the demons of Persia and Greece, and specifies the first year of Darius the Mede (539–538 B.C.) as the time when Michael's contest with Satan's emissaries began. Apparently the struggle had been going on for four or five years (since the episode of chs. 10–12 takes place in the third year of Cyrus as king; see 10:1).

The occasion for the spiritual warfare was the restoration of the believing remnant of Israel to the Holy Land and their survival there as a commonwealth of the faithful, living in obedience to the Scriptures. Knowing that such a development could lead to the ultimate appearance of the Messiah, Satan and his hosts were determined to thwart the renewal of Israel and the deliverance of her people from destruction. The supreme effort to exterminate them altogether was to take place some fifty-five years later, in the reign of Ahasuerus (Xerxes), when Haman secured his consent to obliterate the entire Jewish race (see the book of Esther). The conflict between Michael and the "prince of Persia" (10:13) may have had some bearing on this event, and Michael's victory may have paved the way for Queen Esther to thwart this genocide. The second major effort of Satan was to take place under Antiochus Epiphanes, who sought to obliterate the Jewish faith by forbidding its practice on pain of death. The momentous events of 167–164 B.C. may well have been profoundly affected by this supernatural warfare between heaven and hell (see comments on 8:13–14).

2 Michael began to detail what God ordained for the future of the second commonwealth up until the crisis reign of Antiochus Epiphanes. The Persian king who invaded Greece was, of course, Xerxes, who reigned 485–464 B.C. The three kings who preceded him after the death of Cyrus were (1) Cambyses, Cyrus's elder son, who in the six or seven years of his reign (529–523) conquered Egypt; (2) then for a year or two an imposter named Gaumata or Bardiya (523–522), who passed himself off as Cyrus's younger son, Smerdis (who had been secretly murdered by his brother's agents); and (3) Darius the Persian (522–485), the son of Hystaspes, who in 522 assassinated the imposter and was elevated to the kingship in his place. Darius himself was of royal blood, being a cousin of Cyrus through his father, Hystaspes.

In 490 B.C. Darius attempted to conquer Athens to punish it for aiding the Ionian Greek cities in their abortive revolt against their Persian overlords. But his naval expedition came to grief at Marathon. As a result, Xerxes, Darius's son, not only inherited an obligation to wreak vengeance on Athens but also was motivated by the momentum of empire building to keep pushing westward to add yet another realm to the vast domain he had inherited from his father. Xerxes, however, sustained an even greater defeat than his father had. After his huge army (estimated at a million men) had subdued virtually all of Greece down to the Isthmus of Corinth and the city of Athens had been reduced to ashes, Xerxes' navy was soundly defeated by the united Greek fleet at Salamis in 480 B.C. This setback prompted him to retreat hastily to Asia. The land army of one hundred thousand men that he left behind was completely crushed in 479 by the allied forces of the Greeks at Plataea.

3–4 The next phase in world empires was the rise of Alexander the Great. Although v.3 does not make it altogether clear that this "mighty king" would inaugurate a new empire in place of the Persian one, v.4 leaves no doubt that he was the ruler predicted here. "After he has appeared" is better translated "As soon as he has appeared," which suggests that he would have a comparatively brief reign. Alexander's first clash with the Persians came at Granicus in 334, and his final overthrow of Persian power took place in 331 at Gaugamela. After that he pushed eastward to Afghanistan and the Indus River and Bahawalpur, beyond the farthest reaches of Persian conquest. There he was compelled by his battle-weary troops to return to Babylon in 327. Thus in seven or eight years he accomplished the most dazzling military conquest in human history. But he lived only four years more, dying in Babylon of a fever in 323 after one of his drunken bouts.

Verse 4 foretells the division of Alexander's domains among four smaller and weaker empires. After a period of imperial regency under Perdiccas (murdered in 321) and Antigonus (crushed at Ipsus in 301), the widespread domains of Alexander were parceled out to the four Diadochi (see comment on 8:8 for the history foretold here).

B. The Wars Between the Ptolemies and the Seleucids (11:5–20)

5–6 "The king of the South" was to be Ptolemy I (Soter), son of Lagus, whose ambitions extended far beyond the borders of Egypt (his charge from Alexander) to Palestine and the rest of Asia. Temporarily his naval forces captured Cyprus and important bases in Asia Minor, and there were even times when he wielded considerable influence over some of the city-states of the Greek mainland. But during the 280 years between Ptolemy I and Cleopatra VII (who met her end around 30 B.C.), the domain of the Ptolemies was mostly restricted to Egypt and Cyprus; they lost Palestine to the Seleucid king Antiochus III shortly before 200 B.C. "One of his commanders [who] will become even stronger than he" was Seleucus Nicator of the Seleucid Empire, who had served under Perdiccas and Antigonus in Babylon but had had a falling out with the latter in 316. Thereafter he defected to Ptolemy. After the defeat of Antigonus, he returned to Babylon (where he was well liked) with Ptolemy's sponsorship in 312, two years after which he assumed the title of king, so that 310 became the official starting date for the Seleucid Era. Since Seleucus secured control of Alexander's old domains all the way to the Indus on the east and to Syria and Phoenicia on the west, his authority far surpassed that of his sponsor, Ptolemy. Seleucus's dynasty endured till 64 B.C., when Pompey delivered the coup de grace to a truncated empire that had already lost Babylon and all its eastern dominions to the Parthians.

After Ptolemy I's death in 285, his son Ptolemy II (Philadelphus) continued the contest with the Seleucids till 252, when a treaty of peace was finally arranged with Antiochus II (Theos), under the terms of which Antiochus was to marry Berenice, the daughter of Philadelphus. This furnished a serious complication since Antiochus already had a wife, a powerful, influential woman named Laodice. She did not take kindly to being divorced, despite the obvious political advantages with Ptolemaic Egypt (v.6). Thus she organized a successful conspiracy, operating from her place of banishment after the divorce; and she managed to have both Berenice and her infant son assassinated. Soon afterward the king himself was poisoned (247 B.C.), and the pro-Laodice party engineered a coup d'etat that made her queen regent during the minority of her son, Seleucus II (Callinicus). Thus the prophecy was fulfilled concerning Berenice, that she would be "handed over," along with the nobles who supported her in Antioch.

7–12 Ptolemy Philadelphus died in 247 B.C., soon after the tragedy that had overtaken his daughter Berenice. But his capable son Ptolemy III (Euergetes) organized a great expeditionary force against Syria to avenge his sister's death. This war raged from 246 to 241, and Ptolemy captured and pillaged the Seleucid capital of Antioch and invaded its eastern domains as far as Bactria. Finally he returned to Egypt laden with spoil, but he did not see fit to add much of the Seleucid territory on a permanent basis. He did, however, shatter the Seleucid navy in the Aegean Sea and succeeded on other fronts as well, for he reunited Cyrenaica (at the western end of Libya), after twelve years of independence with the Ptolemaic domains. He also recovered all his father's conquests on the coasts of Asia Minor and temporarily gained control of portions of Thrace.

Verse 8 mentions the recovery of the idols and sacred treasures taken to Persia as booty by Cambyses in 524 B.C., the recovery of which moved the Egyptians to acclaim Ptolemy III as Euergetes ("Benefactor"). The verse concludes by alluding to the treaty of peace Ptolemy III made with Seleucus II in 240. Although there is no record of Seleucus II's attempting to invade Egypt proper, v.9 records his successful foray into Ptolemaic territory to regain control of northern Syria and Phoenicia, probably in the 230s.

Seleucus II (Callinicus) died in 226 and was succeeded by his son Seleucus III (Soter), who reigned for only three years (v.10). His principal efforts were directed against Asia Minor. The second son of Callinicus, Antiochus III, received the surname "the Great" because of his military successes. Coming to the throne in 223, he first had to suppress a revolt in the eastern provinces led by his trusted governor, Molon, who had set himself up as an independent king (220 B.C.). Antiochus III next launched an expedition against Phoenicia and Palestine (219–218) that ended in a serious setback at Raphia, where he was soundly beaten by the smaller army of Ptolemy IV (vv.11–12). In the peace that followed, Antiochus III ceded all Phoenicia and Palestine back to Ptolemy IV and left him in undisturbed possession of them till later. During the following years Antiochus attained his most brilliant successes in subjugating the rebellious provinces in the Middle East all the way to the Caspian Sea in the north and the Indus River on the east. These invasions absorbed all his energies from 212 to 204. But finally in 203, when Ptolemy IV died and was succeeded by Ptolemy V (Epiphanes), a mere boy of four, Antiochus saw his opportunity to strike at Egypt again.

13–19 Antiochus advanced once more against Phoenicia and Palestine with his battle-seasoned veterans and pushed all the way down to the fortress of Gaza, which fell in 201. Verse 14 continues: "In those times many will rise against the king of the South [i.e., Ptolemy V]. The violent men among your own people [i.e., the pro-Seleucid Jews] will rebel in fulfillment of the vision [i.e., this prophecy now being revealed], but without success." This refers to the counteroffensive launched by the powerful General Scopas of the Egyptian forces, who punished all the leaders in Jerusalem and Judah who favored the claims of Antiochus and were disaffected with the Ptolemaic government. But soon the war swept down from the north, and Scopas met with a severe loss at Panium (near Caesarea Philippi) in 200 B.C. From there he retreated to Sidon on the Phoenician coast, the "fortified city" of v.15.

When Scopas finally surrendered to Antiochus III at Sidon, the Holy Land ("Beautiful Land," v.16) was permanently acquired by the Antioch government, to the exclusion of Egypt. Antiochus did not pursue a general policy of destruction but simply exacted reprisals from the pro-Egyptian party leaders he captured. On his entrance into Jerusalem in 198 B.C., he was welcomed as a deliverer and benefactor.

More literally v.17 reads: "Then he will set his face to come with the power of all his kingdom, and equitable conditions shall be with him, and he will accomplish it. And he will give to him the daughter of women in order for her to corrupt [or 'destroy'] him [or possibly 'it,' referring to the kingdom of Egypt]." The clear intention of Antiochus was to bring the boy king Ptolemy V, who in 197 was ten or less, under the influence of his daughter, expecting her to maintain a strongly pro-Seleucid policy in Egypt. Then if Cleopatra gave birth to a son, he would become legal heir to both crowns, which conceivably might create a situation favorable to strong control in Egypt on the part of Antiochus himself, the maternal grandfather. However, after the marriage finally took place in 195, Cleopatra became completely sympathetic to her husband, Ptolemy V, and the Ptolemaic cause, much to her father's disappointment. Therefore when she gave birth to a royal heir (Ptolemy VI), her father gained no particular advantage or political leverage. When Ptolemy V died (181), Cleopatra became queen regent because the Egyptians all loved and appreciated her loyalty to their cause. But she herself died not long after, which meant the end of all possible Seleucid influence on Egyptian affairs. Antiochus himself had died in 187 B.C.

Soon after his victory over Scopas at Panium and Sidon, Antiochus III became involved in a new war front against Pergamum and the Aegean coastline island of Rhodes. As Antiochus's forces closed in on them, the Rhodians appealed to Rome for aid. Another important development was the arrival of Hannibal from exile in Macedonia to join Antiochus as a military adviser. The Roman government resented Antiochus's offer of asylum to their enemy. But Antiochus was not to be cowed, for he felt that he had the power to cope with Rome's military might. Therefore in 196 he crossed the Hellespont and the Aegean with his powerful navy and conquered considerable territory in Thrace. The "coastlands" (usually "islands") included all areas contiguous to the seacoast.

About this time the west-central Greek confederacy of the Aetolian League asked Antiochus for assistance against Macedon and the Peloponnesians. He therefore sent a modest naval force in 192 to land on the coast of central Greece and cooperate with the Aetolians. But the latter proved to be militarily ineffective, and the Macedonians joined forces with the Achaean League to oppose

Antiochus from both the north and the south. The Romans were only too happy to jump into the fray; so they joined their Greek allies to overwhelm the Seleucid command post at Thermopylae—the historic site of the Persian War in 480 B.C. As a result of this setback, Antiochus withdrew to Asia Minor in 191, especially since his navy was beaten in several engagements with the Roman fleet. During the winter of 190–189, the Roman troops followed him across to Asia and finally met him in a pitched battle at Magnesia, west of Sardis. Although Antiochus had an army of seventy thousand at his disposal to confront the Roman force of thirty thousand, he was badly defeated. Thus his "insolence" (v.18) met with disaster.

The Roman "commander" was none other than Lucius Cornelius Scipio Asiaticus, brother to Publius Cornelius Scipio Africanus, who had brilliantly defeated Hannibal at Zama in 202 B.C. After he compelled Antiochus to surrender, the commander dictated severe peace terms, which were included in the Treaty of Apamea, signed in 188. Antiochus was compelled to surrender not only all claims to Europe but also the greater part of Asia Minor as well: his boundary was to be the Taurus Range. Furthermore, he had to surrender his entire elephant brigade, all his navy, and twenty selected hostages. Finally, he was obliged to pay an indemnity of fifteen or twenty thousand talents over a period of several years. Antiochus's second son, who was named after him, was among the twenty hostages taken to Rome, where he spent the formative years of his life. He later became the dreaded persecutor of the Jews, Antiochus IV Epiphanes.

Antiochus the Great met an inglorious end in 187. Unable to meet the required indemnity payments out of his exhausted treasury, he resorted to pillaging—or attempting to pillage—the temple of Bel in Elymais. The local inhabitants were so incensed that they stormed his modest army with desperate bravery and succeeded in killing him and defending their temple (v.19).

20 The "tax collector" sent out by Seleucus IV (Philopator), the elder son of Antiochus, was apparently his special fund-raiser, Heliodorus. According to 2Mc 3:7–40, a certain traitorous Jew named Simon sent information to the king that the Jerusalem temple

contained sufficient treasure to meet all the king's needs. Impoverished as his treasury was (partly through the yearly indemnity payments to Rome of one thousand talents), Seleucus eagerly grasped at the prospect of plundering the temple and sent off Heliodorus to carry out this assignment. Only a frightful vision of mighty angels assaulting and flogging him kept Heliodorus from invading the temple and he returned home empty-handed. No other details are given here of the twelve-year reign of this rather ineffectual king, except that he did not die in battle or in a mob action as had his father, Antiochus. Yet Seleucus IV met an untimely end through poison administered by Heliodorus.

C. The Great Persecution Under Antiochus Epiphanes (11:21–35)

21 The tyrannical oppressor who did his utmost to destroy the Jewish religion altogether previously appeared in 8:9–12, 23–25 as the sinister "little horn" who would suspend the worship of God in the Jerusalem temple. Now he is introduced as a despicable tyrant who will shed much blood and enjoy power for a time. Verse 21 states that this tyrant "has not been given the honor of royalty." The young son of Seleucus IV, Demetrius I, was next in line to receive the crown. But since he had been sent to Rome as a replacement hostage for his uncle Antiochus (see comment on v.19), it was deemed best to put Antiochus in charge of the government as prince regent; he became Antiochus IV Epiphanes. This man was determined to set aside his nephew's claims altogether, even though he was already in his twenties and quite competent to rule. So Antiochus curried favor with governmental leaders and, by promises of promotion and large favors in return for their support, managed to secure approval for succession to the throne vacated by his poisoned brother. Fortunately Demetrius was still being held in Rome, where he was safe for the time being from assassination by his uncle's agents. Later on he was able to make good his claim to the throne, for he left Rome to lead an army against the son of Antiochus Epiphanes, Antiochus V (Eupator), in 162.

Epiphanes, that "contemptible person who has not been given the honor of royalty," converted his regency into royalty

soon after 175 and launched his own career as an ambitious and vigorous leader. The title "Epiphanes" ("the Illustrious One") also carries the meaning of "very evident" or "manifest." His coins show that he linked up *Epiphanes* with the added title *Theos* ("God"), thus yielding the combination "Illustrious God" or "God Manifest." Bearing in mind his role as a type of the Antichrist or Beast of the last days (who appears in ch. 7 as the "little horn," arising from the fourth kingdom), it becomes particularly meaningful to read about the future antitype in 2Th 2:3–4. Not only did Antiochus enthrone himself for adoration by the Jews as he sat in the court of the desecrated Jerusalem temple (in 168 B.C.), but he also claimed divine honors for himself on every major coin that he minted.

22–24 Verse 22 introduces the brilliantly successful beginning of Antiochus Epiphanes' reign, as he took up anew the struggle with Ptolemaic Egypt. Epiphanes threw his intended victims off guard by offering them his friendship and alliance. Then he would maneuver for an advantageous position till he could catch them by surprise. So it was with Ptolemy VI (Philometor), who had ascended the throne in 181 B.C. at the age of six, after the death of his mother, Cleopatra (see comment on v.17). But after he assumed power, he determined to recapture the regions of Palestine and Phoenicia that had been lost to Antiochus III. At first Ptolemy VII's invasion was successful, for he had challenged Antiochus with a large, well-equipped army. But eventually he encountered a serious reverse and became a prisoner of Antiochus Epiphanes.

The Egyptians gave up hope of regaining their king and appointed his young brother Physcon as king in his place. On learning this, Epiphanes craftily intervened on behalf of Ptolemy Philometor, his royal prisoner, and mounted an expeditionary force against Physcon's government in order to reestablish Philometor on his throne—as Antiochus's ally rather than his adversary. As the price of his help in expelling Physcon, Antiochus made a treaty of friendship and alliance with Philometor aimed at gaining a foothold in Egypt itself and ultimately uniting the two kingdoms under his own authority. The seriousness of this aim is attested by the issue of coinage (in the large and medium-sized bronzes, at least) that bore the same types as the corresponding Ptolemaic coinage (the head of Zeus on the front and the Ptolemaic eagle on the back) but with the legend "King Antiochus, God Manifest" rather than the usual Egyptian "Ptolemy the King." Although these Egyptian-type coins were presumably used in the Seleucid territory rather than in Egypt itself, they at least hinted at their potential claims to the Ptolemaic domains. Actually, Antiochus had penetrated Egypt itself all the way to Memphis, which he captured, along with Philometor himself.

Later on Antiochus's alliance with Philometor wore so thin that his reestablished protégé decided to make peace with Ptolemy Physcon, his defeated brother, because he felt he needed his help in dislodging Antiochus's troops from the border fortress of Pelusium. With Physcon as his associate, Philometor was able to raise a considerable army to expel the Seleucid army. But as soon as Epiphanes learned of this development, he again marched against Egypt, intending to subdue it once and for all. But this effort was forestalled by the intervention of the Roman fleet, which had been hurriedly dispatched to Alexandria in response to the urgent request of the embattled Ptolemies. The aggressive Roman commander Popilius Laenas met Antiochus marshaling his hosts for a siege of Alexandria and informed him that the Roman government ordered him to quit Egypt immediately or face the consequences of war with Rome. Remembering what had happened to his father at Magnesia and recalling his years as a young hostage in Roman captivity, it did not take Antiochus very long to give way before this mandate—especially after Popilius drew a circle around him with his staff and ordered him to make his decision before he stepped outside it. Even though Antiochus had for a time succeeded in destroying the power of "the prince of the covenant" (v.22)—Ptolemy Philometor—the remaining verses predicting his eventual failure found their fulfillment in this humiliation that took place near Alexandria in 169 B.C.

Verses 23–24 describe the above developments: "After coming to an agreement with him [i.e., Philometor], he will act deceitfully, and with only a few people [his initial invasion had been made by a small force] he will rise to power." The phrase "richest prov-

inces" apparently refers not only to Egypt itself but also to the eastern provinces all the way to Bactria, where successful campaigns were conducted by Eucratides, Antiochus's general. In 166, Antiochus conducted a full-scale muster of his armies at Daphnae, just outside Antioch, in celebration of the tenth anniversary of his rule—even after his expulsion from Egypt by Popilius Laenas.

25–28 Verses 25–26 refer to the earlier invasion of Egypt in 170, after Ptolemy had attempted an attack on Palestine. The king of the South's great army did not make him invincible because "of the plots devised against him" by Antiochus and his agents in Egypt. "Those who eat from the king's provisions will try to destroy him [i.e., Ptolemy Philometor]; his army will be swept away" probably refers to negotiations carried on by the two victors at the banquet table, apparently after Physcon had been defeated and expelled from Egypt, with the help of Antiochus's troops. At this stage these ostensibly cordial allies were already plotting against each other.

Quite clearly "the end" pertained to the permanent suspension of Antiochus's campaign to annex Egypt to his domains; it is explained by v.28: "The king of the North will return to his own country [i.e., to his capital of Antioch] with great wealth [from plundering Physcon's army], but his heart will be set against the holy covenant. He will take action against it and then return to his own country." The significant term here is "the holy covenant." Apparently this does not refer to the covenant between Antiochus and Ptolemy VII but seems to signify the religious establishment in Jerusalem or even the monotheistic Jewish population as a whole. It is here that the clash between Antiochus and the faith of Israel begins on a serious level.

The original friction had arisen over the question of the high priesthood. Early in his reign Antiochus IV had been approached by a younger member of the high priestly family named Jason, who promised the king that if he would depose from office the current, legitimate high priest, Onias III, then he—Jason—would pay the king a handsome bribe for this service. Antiochus was happy to accede to this request; Onias was removed and Jason installed in his place. But once the precedent of imperial interference had been set, still another brother, Menelaus, offered Antiochus a bribe still larger than Jason's if he would be installed in place of Jason. Antiochus had no scruples about supplanting one rascal by another, so long as he himself was enriched in the process. So in 172 B.C. Menelaus took Jason's place and set about selling some of the votive offerings and golden utensils of the temple to raise the cash necessary for the bribe. At this sacrilege the godly high priest Onias, though deposed, earnestly protested and so angered Menelaus that he had Onias killed. But this murder so angered the populace of Jerusalem that they became bitter against Menelaus and sent representatives to Antiochus himself to accuse Menelaus and his wicked brother Lysimachus. Antiochus did execute Andronicus, the agent of Menelaus who had murdered Onias. But a little later a courtier Menelaus had bribed persuaded Antiochus to act against the Jerusalemites. So instead of punishing Menelaus as he deserved, the king had the Jerusalem representatives put to death in Tyre, where the whole matter was being adjudicated (cf. 2Mc 4:30–50).

Later on (167 B.C.) Antiochus, following his bitter disappointment in Egypt, went and encamped near Jerusalem. He had a score to settle with Jason, who had taken the city in an effort to overthrow Menelaus. Acting on a false report that Antiochus had died in Egypt, Jason had organized a regiment of a thousand armed supporters for a coup d'état. He massacred a large number of citizens and shut Menelaus up in the Jerusalem citadel. Hearing of this, Antiochus decided to suppress the Jewish religion altogether and to exact stern reprisal from those who had taken up arms against his government. So he marched into Jerusalem with overwhelming forces, released Menelaus, and conducted a massacre in which eighty thousand men, women, and children were put to the sword (2Mc 5:11–14). Then he profaned the temple, accompanied by the despicable Menelaus, and robbed it of its golden vessels and other sacred objects (vv.15–21).

The date of this desecration and pillage of Jerusalem was Dec. 16, 168 B.C (see comments on 8:9–10)—a day of special significance, seeing that exactly four years later the patriot leader Judas Maccabaeus rededicated the temple to the worship of the Lord, having cleansed it from all its pagan defilements. But the actual suspension of the regular morning and evening sacrifices had apparently taken place 55 or 54 days prior to the desecration of the temple itself (if our interpretation of Da 8:14 is correct), because three years would total 1,095 or 1,096 days, and the 2,300 "evenings and mornings" (i.e., sacrifices) come out to 1,150 days. It seems, therefore, that during the earlier disturbances between Jason and Menelaus the regular daily offerings were suspended since the incumbent high priest was shut up in the Acra (Citadel) by Jason's troops. This, then, was the fulfillment of the prediction of 11:28 regarding Antiochus's "action" taken "against the holy covenant." This verse actually sums up the entire series of measures taken by Antiochus in suppressing the religious liberties of Judah, from 172 to 168 B.C.

29–30 The more exact chronology of Antiochus's later act of desecration is set forth in these verses. The "outcome" (v.29) was different this time because he was compelled by Popilius Laenas to withdraw from Egypt altogether. From the preceding discussion, it is evident that the followers of Menelaus, who made no protest as Antiochus removed the holy vessels from the Holy Place, are referred to here as "those who forsake the holy covenant." Menelaus and his followers were willing to suppress all religious scruples rather than cross the will of the tyrant who had put them in power.

31 In addition to the desecration already described, the abolition of the daily sacrifices to the Lord was made binding by the erection in the temple of the Lord of "the abomination [GK 9199] that causes desolation." Apparently this was a statue of Jupiter or Zeus Olympius because 2Mc 6:2 indicates that the temple itself was to be renamed the Temple of Zeus Olympius. Pagans invariably installed an image in the inner sanctuary of any temple dedicated to the worship of that deity. Even if the actual statue was not installed in the Jerusalem temple as early as Dec. 16 (25 Chislev), 168 B.C., an idolatrous altar was formally consecrated there at that time. Thus the same type of desecration overtook the second temple as befell the first temple in the evil days of Ahaz (735–715) and Manasseh (695–642; cf. 2Ki 16:10–16; 21:3–5). Interestingly, Christ's only explicit reference to "the prophet Daniel" as being the author of the book of Daniel occurs in the Olivet Discourse (cf. Mt 24:15), where he refers to "the abomination that causes desolation," the exact wording of the LXX for this verse (cf. Da 12:11).

32 Antiochus was a master in manipulating Jewish leaders who were divided in their loyalties, winning them over to his cause by glowing promises of preferment and reward. He already had as partisans for his cause a number of influential leaders in Jerusalem society and politics who were convinced of the expediency of a pro-Hellenic policy. These were doubtless "those who have violated the covenant"—i.e., their covenant relation with the Lord. First Maccabees 1:11–15 describes how certain "transgressors of the law" gathered about them a party of collaborators who were ready to throw off their Jewish loyalties and commitment to the Lord in their zeal to be accepted and find approval with their Syrian-Greek overlords.

The hope of Israel lay with committed believers who would risk their lives rather than betray their honor. A band of heroic patriots was stirred to action by a certain priest named Mattathias. He was the father of the valiant Maccabees: Judas, Jonathan, and Simon, each of whom later became "prince of Israel" during the victorious war of independence against the Seleucid government. These patriots, sparked by the zeal of the Hasidim movement, were the mainstay of the resistance that opposed the pro-Seleucid Jewish compromisers as well as Antiochus and his successors. They fulfilled the prediction of v.32: "The people who know their God will firmly resist him [i.e., Epiphanes]."

Later some of the Hasidim ("the godly, pious, loyal ones") became the sect of the Pharisees ("separated ones") who earnestly obeyed every regulation and oral interpretation of the Law. Later still a smaller group broke off and became out-and-out separatists rather than attempting, like the Pharisees, to reform the religious establishment from within. The Essenes, one group of whom made their headquarters at Qumran under the leadership of the unnamed "Teacher of Righteousness," believed in complete separation, abjuring the rationalism of the Sadducees and the materialism of the Pharisees.

Such were the offshoots of "the people who know their God."

33 During the persecution by Antiochus, the patriot leaders would preach to their fearful countrymen stirring messages of repentance and wholehearted commitment to the holy standards of the law of Moses and of the prophets, who upheld their sanctity during the ensuing centuries. They would summon their people to trust in the promises and power of the Lord instead of bowing to the demands of the pagan tyrant. Thus "those who are wise" would engage in a ministry of education and evangelism among their own countrymen, urging them first to get back to God and to pattern their lives according to Scripture. Then they were to answer the call to arms and hazard their very lives for the liberation of their land from the yoke of their God-hating persecutor. Yet the patriot leaders would have to endure great hardships and danger, and many would lose their lives and property, as the tyrant's forces turned their swords against them.

These predictions were fulfilled in 168 B.C., when the standard of revolt was raised by Mattathias, the leading priest in the city of Modein, located in the hills of Ephraim. After killing the officer of Antiochus who had come to enforce the new decree concerning idolatrous worship, Mattathias and his five sons (John Gaddis, Simon Thassi, Judas Maccabaeus, Eleazar Avaran, and Jonathan Apphus) led a guerrilla band that fled to the hills (1Mc 2:23–28) and attracted many adherents from other cities in the Judean province. A large number of the original patriots died in their first engagement with the king's troops because they refused to fight in their own defense on the Sabbath, the day on which they were attacked (1Mc 2:38). But revising their policy after this tragic slaughter, they decided to fight even on the Sabbath, if compelled to do so. Then they engaged in vigorous attacks on all their fellow Jews who had bowed to Antiochus's ordinance and forsaken their God. Not long afterward Mattathias died, entrusting the leadership of the Israelite forces to his own capable sons.

Judas Maccabaeus (originally he alone received the title "Hammer") assumed the military leadership and gained a brilliant victory over the forces of Apollonius, whom he slew in battle. Judas's second triumph involved routing an even larger army under Seron. A third army of formidable proportions came down from Syria under Lysias, Antiochus's deputy, equipped with a fearsome elephant corps. Thanks to the heroism of Judas's brother Eleazar, who managed to plunge his sword into an elephant's chest before it fell on him and crushed him to death, even this mighty host was put to flight by the Maccabean military forces. So the Maccabees fulfilled the predictions (cf. Mic 4:12–13; Zec 9:13; 10:8–9).

34 Presumably the "little help" refers to the relatively small numbers of compatriots who joined the Maccabean troops after the early successes of the original guerrilla band. They saw how they kept on fighting with great courage against overwhelming odds, even though they soon lost Mattathias and many of their first leaders. And then, because one Seleucid army after another fell before their onslaught, the Maccabean troops were able to intimidate many of their fellow citizens who had previously held back from the conflict. Particularly when the Hasidim began to round up those who had collaborated with the Seleucids and put them to death (1Mc 2:42) and Judas himself hunted out those in the various cities who had deserted Scriptural standards ("the lawless," as Maccabees calls them), goodly numbers of insincere followers attached themselves to the patriot cause, hoping to save their own skins. Such supporters, however, proved to be of more help to the enemy than to the cause of freedom when later invasions were launched against them by the successors of Antiochus Epiphanes after his death in 164.

35 The account of the Maccabean uprising concludes with a strong emphasis on the spiritual meaning of this heroic struggle for those who risked their lives for the survival of the commonwealth of Israel. In the first instance, v.35 refers to the terrible reverse that overtook the pitifully outnumbered army of Judas himself at the battle of Mount Azotus in 161. He chose to die bravely in battle rather than save his life through a strategic retreat (1Mc 9:1–19). After he had won this victory for King Demetrius I in 161, Bacchides followed it up with a systematic search for all Judas's leaders and supporters and did his best to wipe them out. But it was not long before the tide turned and Jonathan,

Judas's brother, was able to defeat the Syrian forces and compel them to retreat to Antioch. Thus the cause of freedom was maintained through vicissitudes of defeat and success, till finally a strong Jewish kingdom was founded by John Hyrcanus, son of Simon Maccabaeus (135–105), and enlarged to its fullest extent by his warlike son Alexander Jannaeus (104–78 B.C.).

D. The Latter-Day Counterpart Persecution (11:36–39)

36–39 With the conclusion of the preceding pericope at v.35, the predictive material that incontestably applies to the Hellenistic empires and the contest between the Seleucids and the Jewish patriots ends. Verses 36–39 contain some features that hardly apply to Antiochus IV, though most of the details could apply to him as well as to his latter-day antitype, "the Beast." All of ch. 11 to this point contains strikingly accurate predictions of the whole sweep of events from the reign of Cyrus (during which Daniel brought his career to a close) to the unsuccessful effort of Antiochus Epiphanes to stamp out the Jewish faith. This pattern of prediction and fulfillment is compelling evidence of the divine inspiration and authority of the Hebrew Scriptures, since only God could possibly foreknow the future and see to it that his plan would be precisely fulfilled as foretold by a prophet of God more than 360 years in advance.

Verse 36 contains material that can be applied to Antiochus IV as well as material that cannot be applied to him: "The king will do as he pleases [cf. 8:4; 11:3; 11:16—the latter two refer to Alexander and Antiochus the Great, respectively]. He will exalt and magnify himself above every god [hardly demonstrable of Antiochus, as we shall see] and will say unheard-of things against the God of gods [as Antiochus blasphemed against the Lord]. He will be successful until the time of wrath is completed [presumably referring to the wrath of God, who decreed this tribulation as a punishment for sin, possibly referring to the time between the desecration of the temple in 168 and its rededication in 164]." Yet as these words stand, they seem equally if not more appropriate to Christ's statement in Mt 24:21–22 predicting the Tribulation.

Although Antiochus entitled himself "God Manifest" on his coins, this is not necessarily tantamount to "magnifying himself above every god." In fact, he placed a statue, not of himself, but of Zeus Olympius (or possibly Jupiter Capitolinus), as the cult image in the Jerusalem temple, just as he represented Zeus enthroned on the reverse side of his coins, adorned with the title of *Nikephoros* ("Victory-winner"). Antiochus was evidently loyal to the Greek religious tradition that revered the entire Olympian set of gods.

The first clause of v.37—"He will show no regard for the gods of his fathers"—hardly fits Antiochus either. On the contrary, he compelled his Jewish subjects to worship the god of his fathers on pain of death. This statement seems more appropriate for a dictator of our modern age or the last days. The words "He will show no regard . . . for the one desired by women" are difficult. Some commentators see here an allusion to Tammuz or Adonis, the object of a special cult practiced by women from the second millennium B.C. and continued till the time of Antiochus. Yet there is no evidence in the historical records that Antiochus ever opposed or forbade this ancient practice. More literally the phrase reads "the love of women" or, better, "the desire of women," perhaps pointing to the cruelty Antiochus showed toward all of the women he was involved with.

The phrase "the gods [or 'God'] of his fathers"(v.37) might refer to the true God, who generally is referred to in the plural (though with a singular verb or adjective). Some commentators (esp. dispensational) take this phrase to refer to the God of the Hebrews and therefore deduce that the Antichrist himself will be an apostate Jew. While elsewhere in the OT the phrase "the God of your fathers" does indeed refer to the Lord himself, it does not necessarily follow that the Antichrist is a Jew, unless it can be demonstrated (as it surely cannot be) that the pagans never worshiped the god or gods (the plural would be more likely than the singular in the case of the heathen) of their own fathers.

Verse 37 emphasizes that this little horn will have no regard for any god. This hardly applies to Antiochus either, who exalted Zeus on the reverse side of his coinage and did everything to compel his Jewish subjects to sacrifice and bow down to his heathen gods. This therefore could only apply to his eschatological antitype, the Beast of the last days—who apparently will be an atheistic or ungodly dictator. Whether or not the Beast concedes the existence of gods in theory, he will certainly exalt himself above them in conducting his government. He will represent himself as the incarnation of the power and the will of the gods, if such there be. Thus there will be no appeal from his will to the will of heavenly deities who might outrank him or sit in judgment over him.

It is clear from v.38, however, that the Beast will not exclude all practice of religion: "Instead of them [i.e., the gods of his fathers], he will honor a god of fortresses; a god unknown to his fathers he will honor." This hardly refers to the well-known devotion Antiochus showed toward Zeus Olympius, for Zeus Olympius was certainly a god of his fathers. Rather, if this prediction relates to Antiochus, it would apply to some Roman deity whose cult he embraced as a youth while a hostage at Rome. Possibly this is a reference to Jupiter Capitolinus, the patron god of Rome itself, whose powerful protection Antiochus may have sought. In that case, he may have equated Zeus Olympius with Jupiter Capitolinus, as the deity to whom he dedicated the Jerusalem temple in 168 B.C.

But it must be conceded that "god of fortresses" does not clearly point to Capitolinus, and so this whole interpretation is thoroughly conjectural. Yet it is worth pointing out that the offering of votive gifts of silver, gold, and precious stones sounds more like an ancient, pre-Christian setting than a modern religious practice, except perhaps in the older traditions of medieval Christianity.

Verse 39 continues the account of the little horn and his conquests. Presumably this "foreign god" is the same one mentioned in v.38, even though the definite article is missing before "god." The application of this verse to Antiochus is hardly clear. Some take this in a completely futuristic sense.

E. The Triumph and Fall of Antichrist (11:40–45)

40 It is utterly hopeless to try to tie the details of the final paragraph of this chapter into the known career of Antiochus Epiphanes. As we have seen vv.36–39 contain important features irreconcilable with Antiochus. And

from v.40 on there is the greatest contrast between his career and that of the little horn, whose end is here described. Furthermore, the shift of scene to the last days seems to be doubly emphasized by the introductory words "At the time of the end" (lit., "And in the end time"). The transition between v.35 and v.36 is not so clearly indicated, for the latter verse is simply introduced with a Hebrew connective (lit., "Then the king will do as he pleases").

On the analogy of the struggle between the Ptolemies of Egypt and the Seleucids of Syria, we might expect to see in the final Near Eastern struggle a contest between a bloc of nations allied with Egypt, including Libya and Nubia (or Sudan) referred to in v.43, and a Syrian coalition, comprising a league of Middle Eastern nations. Yet if the antitype of Antiochus Epiphanes is referred to by the title "king of the North," which was applied to the Seleucid kings in the earlier narrative, then we cannot be altogether certain that we are dealing with a ruler located in either Syrian Damascus or Antioch (a city now under Turkish control). It may be that the eschatological counterpart is actually an Italian leader. The "ruler who will come" (9:26) will have to be a Roman or be somehow connected with the latter-day revival of the Roman Empire. The historical Roman Empire was mainly centered around the Mediterranean with its capital in Italy; so there is a good possibility that "the ruler who will come" will be from Europe rather than from the Near East. This is not beyond dispute, however, since at least one emperor of Rome, Elegabalus, was a Syrian or Phoenician; he reigned A.D. 218–22 and was succeeded by his cousin Severus Alexander, who was also Syrian or Phoenician, having been born in Acre.

The political cause of the clash between the two superpowers and their allies is not indicated, but the large amount of troops and armaments is clearly implied by the "chariots," "cavalry," and "fleet of ships." Presumably the warfare will be carried on by modern instruments of warfare—though to communicate with Daniel's generation, ancient equivalents are used here. Likewise, the ancient names of the countries or states occupying the region where the final conflict will be carried on are used in the prediction, though most of those political units will no longer bear these names in the last days.

Edom, Moab, Ammon, Assyria, and Babylon have long since ceased to exist as political entities, their places having been taken by later peoples occupying their territory.

"He will invade many countries and sweep through them like a flood" suggests the kind of spectacular success the Nazis had early in World War II. It also indicates that a large number of smaller, weaker nations will be drawn into the conflict between the two great powers of the North and the South and that Antichrist in particular will extend his authority with irresistible power.

41 This verse focuses on the Holy Land, the focal point for this terrible war. Israel will be ravaged by Antichrist's forces, as will many surrounding states, except those in the area of present-day Jordan, which for some unexplained reason (possibly because of their willing collaboration against Israel) will be spared from invasion. The "Beautiful Land" refers to the Holy Land from the standpoint of its special favor in the eyes of God rather than because of its natural beauty.

42–45 Apparently the king of the South will suffer defeat at the hands of Antichrist ("the king of the North," v.40), even though he had at first felt strong enough to initiate the conflict with the king of the North. Egypt will at last be defeated (v.42), whether or not it is completely and permanently added to Antichrist's realm. He will go on to capture all the reserves of silver and gold locked up in their vaults (v.43). Their loyal allies, the Libyans to the west and the Nubians (or Sudanese) to the south, will also be subjugated by him. At last his triumph over the powerful antagonists to the south will be consummated. But his satisfaction over this will be short-lived because (v.44) news of trouble in the Middle East will bring him out of Egypt in a fury to crush his opponents in Palestine. There, perhaps in the vicinity of Megiddo, he will encamp "between the seas" (v.45, i.e., the Dead Sea and the Mediterranean), within easy striking distance of Jerusalem itself. "The beautiful holy mountain" is Moriah, where the temple stood.

Verse 45 ends with an abrupt obituary: "Yet he will come to his end, and no one will help him." At the moment when Antichrist seems to be sweeping away all opposition, disaster overtakes him, like that which will overtake the pillaging and raping attackers of the Holy City (cf. Zec 14:12–3; Rev 19:19–20; cf. also Rev 16:16). This prediction of the location of the death of the Antichrist of Da 11:36–45 eliminates the figure of Antiochus Epiphanes, who died in Persia, after an unsuccessful raid on a temple in Elymais. There is no way the details of vv.40–45 can be fitted into the career of Antiochus Epiphanes.

XII. The Tribulation and Final Triumph of God's People (12:1–13)

A. The Great Tribulation (12:1)

1 "At that time" refers to the fortunes of God's covenant people during the career of Antichrist. The closing verses of ch. 11 deal exclusively with his military and political career, described in broad and general outline. But his internal policy toward the community of God's people within his empire has not been referred to thus far. Here we are told that it will be characterized by brutal oppression and persecution surpassing anything Israel—or perhaps any other nation—has ever experienced. Jesus enlarged on this prediction in the Olivet Discourse (see Mt 24:21), quite evidently taking this prophecy in Daniel as relating to the last days.

Michael is described as "the great prince who protects your people [lit.,who stands beside your people]" through this time of horror. Apparently God has assigned the special protection of his people to this mighty champion, and he will have a key part in protecting the people of Christ in the last days (Rev 17:6).

The faithful believers who are preserved through this harrowing ordeal are referred to as those whose names are "found written in the book." Evidently "the Book of Life" (cf. Ex 32:33) is the roster of professing believers who stand in covenant relationship with God, though apostates among them may have their name removed from this list (cf. Ps 69:28; see also Mal 3:16 and esp. Rev 20:12–15). Jesus himself was conscious of this heavenly register (Lk 10:20). Comparing these references, we find that the Book of Life contains the names of both the "elect" and those who profess faith in Christ but by their lives deny the authority and will of God. These latter will be deleted from the list of the redeemed.

In what sense will all those whose names are "found written" in the Lord's book "be delivered"? Will they be exempt from martyrdom at the hands of the Beast during the Great Tribulation? Probably not, since a great many of the true believers even back in the days of the Maccabean revolt were compelled to lay down their lives. The context of this passage seems to be definitely referring to the end times; and v.2 clearly refers to those who have already died but attain to the resurrection from the dead. They are delivered from the power of Satan and the curse of the "second death" (Rev 21:8).

B. The Resurrection and Judgment (12:2–3)

2 Those involved in the raising of the dead are said to "sleep in the dust of the earth"—i.e., they have experienced physical death (the first death implied in Rev 20:4–6) and have been buried. Yet they do not experience annihilation or a permanent imprisonment in the bonds of death so far as their body is concerned. That they will be awakened from "the dust of the earth" definitely points to bodily resurrection, not simply a renewal of the soul. They will then enter the next phase of their existence according to their faith or unbelief in their earthly life.

Resurrection is universal, whether believers or unbelievers, whether saved or lost. But in contrast to the resurrection of the saved, the resurrection of the unsaved will be neither a blessing nor a deliverance (cf. Jn 5:28–29). The unsaved will be exposed to "shame" and "contempt" (cf. Rev 20:11–15).

The word for "everlasting" (GK 6409) originally meant "lifetime," "era," or "age." When used of God, it takes on the connotation of endlessness (i.e., eternity; cf. Ps 90:2). Some thus argue that punishment in hell is only for a "lifetime" or "age." But if hell is not eternal, neither is God; for the same Hebrew and Greek words are used for both (cf. Rev 4:10; 20:10; 21:8).

3 At the judgment seat of Christ (cf. Isa 11:3 and Ro 2:16 for the identity of the Judge) the faithful children of God will be robed in the shining garments of their Redeemer's righteousness. True believers are here described as "those who are wise" and "those who lead many to righteousness." The term for "wise" (GK 8505) connotes acting sensibly or appropriately in view of the holy will of God and of the final day of judgment beyond the grave.

The parallel expression—"those who lead many to righteousness"—indicates that the fruit of a Christ-centered life is new believers won to the Lord. These faithful soul winners "will shine ... like the stars for ever and ever." He who will come like "a star ... out of Jacob" (Nu 24:17) will see his glory reflected in his followers.

Verses 2–3 clearly affirm the doctrines of resurrection and of eternity. The OT too embraces the expectation of resurrection glory (cf. Job 19:26; Pss 17:15; 73:23–24; Isa 25:8). In a sense the assurance of resurrection and eternal life is the capstone of OT revelation.

C. The Sealed Prophecies (12:4)

4 In the ancient Near East important documents were "closed up" and "sealed." The original document was kept in a secure place ("closed up") to conserve the interests and rights of all parties to the transaction. In Mesopotamian cultures these "documents" were clay tablets whose veracity was attested to by the cylinder seals the scribes rolled over the bottom section of the tablets. Once a document was thus sealed, it became official and unchangeable. The second tablet, the official copy, likewise was witnessed to by seal. Daniel was to certify by his personal seal to the faithfulness of the foregoing text as an exact transcript of what God had communicated to him through his angel. Thus this record would be preserved to the day when all the predictions would be fulfilled.

"Will go here and there" depicts movement like the strokes of an oar or a swimmer's arms. The verb stem connotes an intensity that may imply eagerness in moving quickly and excitedly back and forth. Here the meaning seems to be that many of God's people who pay heed to these prophetic sayings will eagerly seek to understand how they are presently being fulfilled or how they are going to be fulfilled in the future. As the predictions concerning the Persian and Greek kings are carried out during the fourth, third, and second centuries B.C., and those referring to the Roman conquest during the first century, so the distinction between the typical tribulation under Antiochus Epiphanes and the antitypical Great Tribulation in the end time will become clear. From this standpoint the knowledge of Bible

students greatly increased between the time of Daniel's sixth-century contemporaries and the period of Jerome, whose epoch-making commentary appeared around A.D. 400. Since Jerome's time there has been a corresponding increase of knowledge, especially with the rise of archaeology and the knowledge of ancient linguistics, to say nothing of the amazing developments leading up to the return of the Jewish people to their ancestral land since 1948.

D. The Prediction of the Three and One-Half Years (12:5–7)

5–7 On either side of the Tigris River (cf. 10:4), Daniel saw two "others," i.e., other angels besides the one who had been addressing him since 10:11. These two angels were personally interested in coming events in God's program of redemption (cf. Zec 1:12–13; 2:3–4; 1Pe 1:12). One angel asked the man in linen how long it would be till the remarkable prediction concerning the Antichrist (ch. 11) would be fulfilled. The man in linen, with a solemn oath and raised hands, said that the time interval would be "a time, times and half a time" (i.e., three and a half years), at the time when the power of the "holy people" of the end time would be broken. Apparently Antichrist will harass them to the point of utter defeat and extinction; then God will intervene in a mighty judgment on the invaders, and they will be utterly destroyed (cf. Zec 14:3). The three and a half years referred to here, which is exactly one-half the full seven years of the seventieth week in 9:27, would be the second half since it ends (in all probability) with the destruction of the Beast at the Battle of Armageddon.

E. The Final Commission to Daniel (12:8–13)

8–9 Daniel, confused by these predictions, asked for clarification of the mystifying prophecies, doubtless concerning the people of God whose power was to be "broken." The angel did not directly answer Daniel's question. Although the implication of victorious survival comes through quite clearly at the close of v.13, the answer of the angel relates to the faithful completion and custody of the prophetic scroll itself.

10 During this intervening period of time, the people of God will be refined in their faith

and purified in their motivation through the testings that they will endure. Moreover, the unbelieving world will not improve as a result of the testimony of the faithful but will increase in wickedness (cf. 2Ti 3:13; Rev 22:11). So we read that "none of the wicked will understand," though those who are "wise" in the Scriptures will comprehend quite fully what is going on during these times.

11–12 Verse 7 has supplied the approximate figure of three and a half years (i.e., 1,278 days; see comments at 9:24–26) for the length of the second, more intense phase of the Great Tribulation. But it appears from v.11 that the interval between the setting up of the "abomination that causes desolation" (subsequent to the abrogation of the covenant between Antichrist and Israel) and the final deliverance of Jerusalem from his hosts will come out more exactly to 12 more days than that, or a total of 1,290 days. For beleaguered saints enduring the horrors of the end time, the precise knowledge of the exact day of deliverance (cf. Mt 24:22) will be of great reassurance.

Verse 12 is one of the most enigmatic statements in this chapter. Between 1,290 and 1,335 days there is an interval of 45 days, or a month and a half. What is destined to take place in that short period can only be conjectured. It may be the time when the thousand-year earthly rule of Christ will be officially inaugurated, as he takes his seat on David's throne. The intervening time may well be devoted to repairing the devastation and burying the bodies left by the Armageddon campaign (cf. Eze 39:12). The believers who survive to that day and share in the glory of Jesus' coronation on earth are here acclaimed as "blessed" (GK 897). They are about to become citizens of the most wonderful society governed by the most wonderful ruler in all human history—the millennial kingdom of our Lord Jesus Christ!

13 The final verse of the book contains an encouraging word for the aged Daniel: "You will rest [i.e., his body will rest in the grave] and then at the end of the days you will rise [on the day of resurrection] to receive your allotted inheritance." Revelation 20:4 speaks of "thrones on which were seated those who had been given authority to judge." Then it goes on to say that those who died as martyrs will at that time "come to life" and reign with Christ a thousand years. Surely Daniel will be outstanding among the galaxy of judges and kings. Yet it is also true that those of us who are sincere and obedient believers will have a part in the supernatural glory of the Son of Man himself, who will assume supreme control over the entire earth (cf. Isa 11:9b; Zec 9:10b).

The Old Testament in the New

OT Text	NT Text	Subject
Da 7:3–7	Rev 13:1–2	Beasts from the sea
Da 7:10	Rev 20:12	Court books being opened
Da 7:13–14	Mt 24:30; 26:64; Mk 13:26; 14:62; Lk 21:27; Rev 1:13; 14:14	Coming Son of Man
Da 7:21	Rev 13:7	War against the saints
Da 7:24	Rev 17:12	Ten horns as ten kings
Da 7:25	Rev 12:14	Three times and a half
Da 7:27	Rev 11:15	An everlasting kingdom
Da 9:27	Mt 24:15; Mk 13:14	Abomination of desolation
Da 10:5–6	Rev 1:13–15	Vision of a man
Da 11:31	Mt 24:15; Mk 13:14	Abomination of desolation
Da 11:36	Rev 13:6	Blaspheming God
Da 12:4	Rev 10:4	Sealed words
Da 12:7	Rev 12:14	Three times and a half

Hosea

INTRODUCTION

1. Historical Background

Hosea, prophet to the northern kingdom of Israel, ministered in the stirring days just preceding the Fall of Assyria. When he began his work, one would not have thought the end was near. Jeroboam II (793–753 B.C.; cf. 2Ki 14:23–29) was the ruler, and a strong one. He had established approximately the same boundaries on the east and north of his country that had been held in the empire days of David and Solomon. This success had given him a remarkable position of influence along the entire Mediterranean coastland. Similarly, Uzziah, king of Judah, a contemporary of Jeroboam for thirty-seven years, had expanded his territory to a size nearly that of the southern boundary in the earlier period. Together Israel and Judah almost reduplicated the area held by Israel's two greatest rulers.

Before the accession of Jeroboam II, the situation had been quite a different one. Because of military attacks by Assyria and Syria, Israel had been brought to abject humiliation. During the reign of Jehoahaz (Jeroboam's grandfather), the strength of Israel's army had fallen to only "fifty horsemen, ten chariots and ten thousand foot soldiers." The king of Syria had "destroyed the rest, and made them like the dust at threshing time" (2Ki 13:7). Recovery had begun with Jeroboam's father, Jehoash, who had defeated the Syrians three times (2Ki 13:25). Jeroboam had then been able to continue this resurgence and bring the country to the strong position noted.

Because of this recovery, Hosea's generation knew of humiliating defeat and foreign oppression only through the memories of their fathers. By this time there had been peace for many years, and with it had come economic prosperity. The land was again producing abundantly (2Ch 26:10), and many people were becoming wealthy. Luxuries had become common. Building activity was flourishing (Hos 8:14), which led to a widespread feeling of pride (Am 3:15; 5:11; cf. Isa 9:10). Social and moral conditions developed that were wrong and degrading. Side by side with wealth, extreme poverty existed. Through dishonest gain and false balances, the strong took advantage of the weak (Hos 12:7; cf. Isa 5:8; Am 8:5–6). Justice seemed absent, and the courts apparently did little to help.

Religious conditions were no better. Though the pagan cult of Baal, brought into the land during the dynasty of Omri (1Ki 16:29–33), had been largely brought to an end (2Ki 10:19–28), many of its offensive features continued (Hos 2:8; 11:2; 13:1). Apparently sacred prostitution was still practiced (4:10–18). Also, the people still built "high places" and set up images and Asherah poles "on every high hill and under every spreading tree" (2Ki 17:7–12).

Amos had preceded Hosea in preaching against such sins, but the people paid little attention. Now it was Hosea's turn, and he courageously spoke out against the evils of the day.

After the reign of Jeroboam II, Israel's political fortunes declined rapidly. His son and successor, Zechariah (753 B.C.; cf. 2Ki 15:8–12), was killed by Shallum after reigning only six months. Shallum was in turn killed by Menahem after a rule of only one month (2Ki 15:13–15). Menahem (752–742 B.C.; cf. 2Ki 15:17–22) then ruled for ten years. The series of brief reigns resumed when his son Pekahiah (742–740 B.C.; cf. 2Ki 5:23–26) was killed by Pekah, one of his military leaders. Pekah was able to keep the throne for twenty years, until 732 B.C., with an overlapping reign of twelve years, from 752–740 (2Ki 15:27). His rule was marred by the crushing invasion of Tiglath-pileser III of Assyria in 733 B.C. The next Assyrian king, Shalmaneser V, marched into the region in 724 B.C. and put Samaria, its capital, under siege. The strong city held out for many months. Finally, however, when it capitulated in 722 B.C., many more Israelites were taken captive; and the sovereign days of Israel as a nation were over.

2. Authorship and Date

The author of this first book of the Minor Prophets was Hosea, son of Beeri (Hos 1:1). The book contains convincing evidence that he was a prophet to the northern kingdom of Israel. While occasionally mentioning Judah, his messages were directed mainly to Israel. Hosea refers to the ruler in Samaria as "our king" (7:5); and he uses a number of Aramaisms, suggesting that the Aramaic-speaking state of Syria immediately to the north had a close influence on Israel.

Hosea dates his ministry by listing four kings of Judah (Uzziah, Jotham, Ahaz, Hezekiah) and one of Israel (Jeroboam II), thus indicating his recognition that the Davidic line in Judah was the only legitimate one (2Sa 7:12–13). There are few clues to the date of his prophecies. For one thing, they were not given at the same time. The words about Hosea's marriage and also the earliest prophecies must have been delivered prior to the death of Jeroboam II, because in 1:4 Hosea refers to the coming vengeance on the "house of Jehu" (of which Jeroboam was a member). This came with the assassination of Jeroboam's son Zechariah six months after he began to reign (2Ki 15:8–12). Besides this, there are the references to contact with Assyria (e.g., 5:13; 8:9; 12:1), which point to the time of Menahem, who did negotiate with Tiglath-pileser III (2Ki 15:19–20). Finally, in 7:11 there is the reference to Israel's dealing with Egypt and Assyria, which suggests that it was written in the days when Egypt was pitted by Israel against Assyria.

Hosea himself lived till the reign of Hezekiah (728–686 B.C.). Because he did not specifically refer to Samaria's fall to the Assyrians in 722 B.C., he probably had completed his writing before that time, but he certainly witnessed the fall of the northern kingdom. As there is no indication that he was taken captive, he doubtless remained in the land. His ministry was a long one, extending at least from 753 to 715 B.C.

3. Hosea's Marriage

The marriage of Hosea has occasioned much discussion. In ch. 1, the Lord commanded him to take "an adulterous wife and children of unfaithfulness." In ch. 3, the Lord told Hosea to love a woman though she was an adulteress. Hosea did this and made a payment of money and barley. The different views regarding the marriage may be divided into four principal types. The *Hypothetical marriage* view sees the marriage as never happening but understands it as either a vision or an allegory symbolic of the relation of God to unfaithful Israel. The *Literal marriage with Gomer unchaste* view holds that the marriage did occur and that Gomer was already an unchaste person, possibly a temple prostitute. The *Spiritual infidelity* view is that the situation is one of spiritual rather than physical infidelity. Gomer became unchaste because, like the Israelites of Hosea's day, she became a worshiper of false gods.

The preferred view is the *Literal marriage with Gomer chaste* view, which holds that the marriage did indeed occur but that Gomer was chaste when married and only became adulterous later. Gomer was not a harlot at the time Hosea married her. Thus the ethical problem of his marrying an acknowledged harlot would not have existed. Perhaps the most convincing reason in favor of the preferred view is that it implies a significant parallel between Hosea's marriage and God's experience with Israel (cf. 1:2, 67, 9; 2:2–13). In the OT Israel is presented as having been chaste when espoused by God in the wilderness (Jer 2:2–3). Again and again God extended his love toward Israel, but she continually proved unfaithful herself to him.

4. Theological Values

The central thought of Hosea concerns God's covenant with Israel that the people had broken. God had loved his people and called them his "son" (11:1; cf. Ex 4:22). Through the passing years, however, they had wandered away from God; and the more he had called after them, the further they went from him (11:2). They fell deep into sin, breaking the covenant God had graciously made with them. Hosea repeatedly describes the sins committed both by the people (4:1–2, 9–19; 6:4–11; et al.) and by the religious leaders (4:5–10). He used the forceful illustration of his unhappy marriage relationship to impress these truths on the minds of his readers.

Hosea's principal significance lies in his sounding the call for Israel to repent of their sins. Other prophets, such as Elijah and

Elisha, had given earlier warnings. But Hosea's warning was the last one. God had been patient, but that patience was wearing thin and crushing punishment would soon be necessary. This punishment would come in the form of desolation of the land (4:3; 5:1–15) and exile for the people.

The prophet included a note of joy in this otherwise somber picture. Israel's future punishment would not spell the end; it would be followed by a glad time of restoration. Hosea characterized this time as one of true repentance on the part of the people (6:1–3) and of rich blessing at the hand of God (cf. 1:10; 2:14–15).

EXPOSITION

I. Israel's Infidelity Illustrated (1:1–3:5)

A. Historical Setting (1:1)

1 This verse concerns matters of the historical background of this prophecy (cf. Introduction).

B. Marriage and Children of Hosea (1:2–9)

2 For a discussion of "an adulterous wife," see Introduction. "Children of unfaithfulness" (lit., "of harlotries") means children who would become like their mother. Often the influence of parents will have this kind of result in their children. That the nation was "guilty of the vilest adultery in departing from the LORD" sets forth the parallel between Hosea's marriage and God's relation to Israel. Gomer was chaste at the time of her marriage but became unfaithful after her marriage; similarly, Israel became unfaithful after God chose her, and her descendants then followed in the same pattern of life.

3 Hosea obeyed God's command and married Gomer, though this was certainly not easy, knowing what Gomer would become. The text makes clear that the son that was now born was a proper son of the new marriage.

4 Three children were born to Hosea and Gomer, and each was given a symbolic name. "Jezreel" (the city where Jehu slaughtered the "house of Ahab," 2Ki 9:7–10:28) looks to a future day when "the blood" Jehu then shed would be avenged. Although Jehu had done well in carrying out God's directive (2Ki 9:1–10), he had sinned in killing more people than God had intended. The punishment for Jehu's sin was to be the cessation of Israel as a nation (which occurred in 722 B.C.).

5 The bow symbolized power; thus a broken bow symbolized the loss of power. The "Valley of Jezreel" lay north of the city of Jezreel. To the west it merged into the Esdraelon Valley, both scenes of major battles through history. The prediction here is that this valley would see a significant stage in Israel's final defeat, which came mainly in the campaign of Tiglath-pileser III (cf. Introduction).

6 "Lo-Ruhamah" means "not loved." Prophetically, God would no longer show love to Israel but would bring judgment on her. The reason Israel had continued this long was that God had favored them. "I should at all forgive them" may also be rendered "I will utterly take them away [GK 5951]," suggesting the idea that "I will no longer show love toward the nation of Israel, but will instead violently carry her away in judgment."

7 God would no more show love to Israel; yet he would continue to show love to Judah. These words were probably written during the reign of Uzziah in Judah—a "good" king (2Ki 15:3; 2Ch 26:4), the third of four "good" kings (Joash, Amaziah, Uzziah, Jotham). That God referred to himself by name ("the LORD their God") shows his desire to impress on Israel the name of their true God, whom they had forgotten. Judah's hope was fixed in the Lord and therefore Judah would be spared.

8–9 That Gomer had her third child after the second was weaned is a detail that shows the narrative is historical and not allegorical or spiritual. "Lo-Ammi" means "not my people." The people had departed from the Lord, going after other gods. Therefore Israel was disowned by God as his people; he would no longer be their God. The name Lo-Ruhamah spoke of not being loved; Lo-Ammi speaks of being fully disowned.

C. A Future Day of Hope (1:10–2:1)

10 Though in Hosea's day God was disclaiming the Israelites as his people, in a day to come God would make their number "like the sand on the seashore." God would carry out his promise to Abraham (Ge 22:17) despite the unfaithfulness of the people (cf. Ro 9:26).

11 By speaking of both the "people of Judah and the people of Israel," Hosea makes clear that the time of future hope would involve both nations. That the two peoples "will be reunited, and they will appoint one leader" is a clue to the identification of the hoped-for day. After the Babylonian exile, Israel was no longer divided into two nations, but they never attained true autonomy until May 1948. Another clue to the hoped-for day is found in the identity of "the land," which is best seen as Egypt, symbolizing the nations throughout the world among which the Israelites would be dispersed (cf. Dt 28:68; cf. 2:14–15). So this twentieth century has seen thousands of people returning to Palestine from this collective "land."

The statement "great will be the day of Jezreel" indicates that the day will in some sense be outstanding, and something will justify its being called "the day of Jezreel." In 2:22–23 Jezreel stands for Israel in the sense of the nation's being "sown" in the land by God for her rebirth and multiplication. This implies that the coming day would be "great" because it would see the nation reborn for a time of glory.

2:1 Hosea sets forth the spiritual relation between God and Israel in the future day of hope, which contrasts with his own day. At present that relationship was symbolized by the names Lo-Ruhamah and Lo-Ammi ("not loved" and "not my people"); but in the future day the appropriate names will be "my people" and "my loved one." "My people" is related to "brothers" and "my loved one" to "sisters" only because Lo-Ammi was a son's name and Lo-Ruhamah a daughter's (1:8–9).

D. Israel, the Adulterous Spouse (2:2–13)

2 Although the language of this section applies in good part to Hosea's unfaithful wife, it is primarily intended for Israel. The verb translated "rebuke" (GK 8189) means basically "to contend or strive." Here the meaning is to "strive with your mother in rebuke" for her life of sin. The mother is Israel as a nation, and the children are individual Israelites. Thus Israelites were being urged to call for their nation to return to faithful living before God.

The statement "she is not my wife" implies that Hosea had disowned his wife (see 3:1). Likewise God had disowned Israel, expressed in the symbolic name Lo-Ammi (1:9). The reference to her "breasts" may imply that she had laid bare her bosom to entice her lovers. So Israel, having turned from her own true God, was guilty of unblushing idolatry and voluptuous service to false gods.

3 If Israel did not change, she would be made as she was at birth—a naked, helpless child. The time of infancy was Israel's experience in the wilderness after the Exodus. God protected Israel at that time, but she herself would be like that parched and desolate land if she did not return to him.

4–5 Again Hosea draws a distinction between mother and children. The former again refers to the nation as a whole; the latter to individual Israelites. Israel as a nation was guilty and deserving of punishment, but so were individual Israelites. "Love" (GK 8163) would be shown to neither. "Children of adultery" refers to those who are called children because they practiced the sins of their mother (cf. 1:2).

The quotation in v.5 attributed to Israel, the Lord's unfaithful wife, applies equally to Gomer, Hosea's wife. As she was running after "lovers" who would give gifts to her, so Israel was running after the false gods of the surrounding nations. From these nations Israel was receiving gifts, which were no doubt the result of trade agreements. So the desire for trading benefits led Israel into going after other gods.

6 God threatened to keep her lovers from her by blocking "her path with thornbushes." In fact, he would use them to wall her in. The thornbushes symbolize all the warfare and hardship that God permitted to come on Israel in the following years (cf. Introduction; also Job 3:23; 19:8).

7 Though Israel's path would be blocked, she would still try to "chase after her lovers" in futility. "My husband as at first" is a reference to God. Israel, frustrated in chasing false gods, would finally recognize the supremacy of her own God, realizing that she was better off when following him than when pursuing strange gods. Only in the last days will Israel fully return to her "first husband."

8 The reason for Israel's unfaithfulness is that the people did not recognize God as the source of their benefits. They had used much silver and gold for images of false gods (e.g., Baal). Jehu had done much to eliminate Baal worship (2Ki 10:19–28), but it still persisted.

9 As a result of Israel's idolatry, God would punish her by taking away the "grain when it ripens," the "new wine when it is ready," and wool and linen. That is, because of their sin, the people would lack food and clothing (probably by rain being withheld).

10 "Expose her lewdness" is literally "uncover her shame" ("shame" means "withered state"; GK 5578). Israel would wither because God would withhold his bounty. Her "lovers" would thus come to despise her, not wanting to have dealings with one so distressed. No one would "take her out of" God's control, both because they would not care to and because God would not permit it.

11 Israel would no longer enjoy her "celebrations," "festivals" (the annual festivals of Passover, Pentecost, and Tabernacles), the monthly festival of the new moon, and the weekly Sabbaths. "Appointed feasts" probably refers to regular celebrations not covered by the other terms.

12 The "vines" and "fig trees" represent the finest of the land's products; God would destroy them because Israel had regarded them as "pay for her lovers." These would now become merely "thickets" for wild beasts to roam and eat in. In other words, the protective hedges would be taken away and cultivation stopped. These were fulfilled during Israel's last days. Her land was devastated by Assyrian forces; then, in 722 B.C., it was totally subjugated by them. God's warnings are never to be taken lightly.

13 The reason for these punishments now becomes more specific; it goes back to "the days" when Israel "burned offerings to the Baals." Such occurrences were mainly in the reign of Ahab and his sons; but even after Jehu had slaughtered the religious personnel of the Baals, idol worship continued to some degree. The remainder of the verse depicts activities of Israel in following the Baals, activities characteristic of a prostitute in her attempt to lure men.

E. The Blessing of Israel (2:14–23)

14 God, who withheld the blessings, cannot bestow them until Israel's sin has been punished. The word for "allure" (GK 7331) connotes persuasion by means of attractive benefits. The words "desert" and "Egypt" in v.15 point to a historical parallel with the time of Israel's journey from Egypt. As God persuaded Israel to leave Egypt and move on finally to the Promised Land, so in the final day he will persuade her to leave the Egypt of spiritual decline and move on to the Promised Land of blessed rest. In that day God will "speak tenderly to her" rather than in harsh words of vv.6–13.

15 In addition to speaking consolingly, God will give Israel's vineyards back to her. The Valley of Achor (cf. Jos 7:24–26) will in the future be "a door of hope." So Israel's future response in song-filled thanksgiving will be as when she entered Canaan the first time. In partial fulfillment, there was joyful praise when Israel returned from the Babylonian exile. But in the future there will be even greater praise, when the people return to their land and Christ is their king.

16 "My husband" is the symbolic name the people of God were to give him on returning to him. Israel will be spiritually revived so that she will recognize God to be her true husband and she his wife. No longer will she think of him as "my master" (lit., "my Baal").

17–18 In the coming day the Lord will remove Baal worship and all remembrance of the names of the Baals from Israel. Then God will be truly worshiped, Israel will be reconciled with God, and there will be peace on earth. The Lord will make a covenant with the beasts, the birds, and the little creatures of the ground (cf. Isa 11:6–9). Also the bow and sword (the two main weapons of war in Hosea's day) will be abolished, so that "all may lie down in safety" (cf. Isa 2:4; Mic 4:3).

19 God promises Israel that she will be betrothed to him forever. This betrothal involves several qualitative relationships, four being mentioned here: "righteousness and justice" (which indicate that all legal standards will be met in the betrothal) and "love and compassion" (which denote God's emotional concern for the new bride).

20 A fifth relationship—"faithfulness"—is also promised. The emphasis here is probably on Israel's faithfulness to God, though God's faithfulness is also present. That new relationship is no doubt the connotation of the statement "you [Israel] will acknowledge the LORD."

21–22 As a result of this beautiful coming relationship between the Lord and Israel, God will respond to the needs of the people. The skies are seen as pleading with God to send rain on the earth, to which God responds favorably; and the earth is seen as asking the heavens to send rain, and the heavens respond favorably. Hosea sees also the grain, the new wine, and the oil as asking the earth for its provisions—a request to which the earth responds favorably. Finally Jezreel is viewed as asking the grain, new wine, and oil to provide blessings, and these also respond favorably. Here "Jezreel" almost certainly means all Israel—a name that means "God plants" (cf. v.23, which clearly refers to Israel). The Valley of Jezreel was a center for production of food.

23 Israel (i.e., Jezreel), planted bountifully, will bring forth a large population (cf. 1:10–11). In contrast to Hosea's time, when the names "not loved" (Lo-Ruhamah) and "not my people" (Lo-Ammi) were appropriate (1:6, 8), the future day will find the opposite true. Love will be shown toward "Not my loved one," and "Not my people" will be called "You are my people" (cf. Ro 9:25). The Israelites, in turn, will respond, "You are my God." Thus vv.22–23 give response to all three of Gomer's children.

F. Gomer Loved Again (3:1–3)

1 After having dealt with the relations between God and Israel (1:9–2:23), the narrative now returns to the relations between Hosea and Gomer. Gomer had left Hosea following the birth of their third child. God tells his servant to take back his unfaithful wife. Gomer is called merely "woman," without a possessive suffix to indicate "your." That Hosea may have come to think of her as "some woman" would have made God's command the more difficult to carry out. But in taking her back, Hosea would be illustrating God's continuing love for Israel, who had turned to "other gods" and lusted after "raisin cakes" (delicacies of the day that represented the idolatrous worship of the Israelites).

2 It is unlikely that the price Hosea paid for Gomer was paid to her parents. After all, though estranged, Gomer was still Hosea's wife; and no payment was officially due. It was probably given to Gomer as a kind of bridal gift. The amount was not large. This gift (given as if for a new marriage) and its modest size show the emotional separation between Hosea and Gomer.

3 "Many days" points to an indefinite period of time. Hosea wanted Gomer to know that this time he intended their relationship to last indefinitely. She must resolve to live no longer as a prostitute.

G. Israel's Future Return to God (3:4–5)

For the third time in as many chapters, the future reconciliation between God and Israel is foreseen. The parallel with the Hosea/Gomer story continues.

4 Israel's time of separation from God is portrayed by her loss of three pairs of things: (1) "King or prince"; Israel will be without an autonomous rule. (2) "Sacrifice or sacred stones"; Israel will be without religious ceremonies (the "sacred stones" represent idolatrous worship, adopted from Israel's neighbors; cf. 2Ki 3:2; 10:26–28; 17:10). (3) "Ephod or idol"; the special devices used for searching into the future (cf. Ge 31:19–34; 1Sa 23:9; 30:7) will no longer be available.

5 After the "many days" of v.4, the Israelites "will return and seek the LORD their God." This will also involve seeking "David their king," and the Israelites will come "trembling" to the Lord. All this will occur in the "last days." For the complete fulfillment of these things, we must look once more to the millennial reign of Christ. The extent to which the Israelites sought God after the Babylonian captivity was limited and surely not with "trembling." While the people did cease from following false gods, their worship was cold and formal; and there was much sin among them. But in the Millennium the Jews will seek Christ (the David of the time, ruling on David's throne), and they will also truly seek after God in heaven (Isa 12:1–6; 66:23; Jer 33:11; Eze 20:40; et al.).

II. Israel's Indictment, Punishment, and Restoration (4:1–14:9)

A. Israel's Indictment (4:1–7:16)

1. A general indictment of the people (4:1–4)

1 Hosea exhorts the Israelites to listen because God was charging them with sinfulness. They were untrustworthy, failed to show compassion toward others, and lacked a true knowledge of the being and nature of God.

2–3 A list of the people's overt sins follows. The phrase "bloodshed follows bloodshed" (lit., "bloody deed touches bloody deed") suggests that violent crimes had become so common that one seemed immediately to follow another, as if touching it. These sins resulted in drought that came as a judgment, making the land dry up and the beasts and the birds "waste away" (cf. 1Ki 17–18). It had even brought death to the fish through the drying up of the streams and ponds.

4 Though conditions in Israel were shockingly bad, mutual charges and accusations could not remedy them. Accusing others only increased problems. But the people could accuse the priests, who, as vv.5–10 show, were blameworthy.

2. Sins of the priests (4:5–11a)

5 Hosea speaks directly to the priests (the mention of prophets implies that they were included in the indictment). Both groups, instead of being leaders for the right, had been stumbling day and night, committing sin. Jeroboam I had made priests "from all sorts of people" (1Ki 12:31; 13:33). Therefore, large numbers of true priests—and doubtless true prophets—had left the northern kingdom (2Ch 11:13–16). "Mother" refers to Israel (cf. 2:2–5) as the mother of individual Israelites.

6 The priests had not been teaching the people about God and his law (Dt 33:10; Eze 44:23; Mal 2:7), so the people were being "destroyed." Moreover, God removed the priests from their service because they themselves had rejected the knowledge of God and his law. The closing lines announce, in poetic format, that since they had "ignored" (GK 8894) the law, God would "ignore" their descendants.

7–8 The priests are still in view here. The greater their power became, the more they sinned. They were so given over to iniquity that Hosea said they were feeding on "the sins of" the people. This they did by enjoying the benefits of the people's sins, such as taking bribes and eating the sin offerings. As a result God would turn their "Glory" into "something disgraceful."

9 The aphorism "Like people, like priests" shows that the priests were no better than the people. Despite their priestly office, they would share the punishment of the people.

10–11a Though the priests "eat" the sins of the people, their appetite for evil remains insatiable. Though the people engage in ritual prostitution of the Canaanite fertility rites (done to enhance human and animal reproduction and to ensure good crops), they have no harvest. Israel's indulgence in these rites is a shameless example of the depth to which the people had fallen in forsaking the true God.

3. Sins of the people (4:11b–19)

11b–12 Attention turns to Israel, here called "my people." The priests had been the leaders in wrongdoing, but the people had followed them all too closely. The mention of "old wine and new" implies the sin of intoxication, which stole away the people's "understanding." Instead, they appealed for guidance to a mere "stick of wood." The "spirit of prostitution" prevalent in the land included the people and the priests (v.10). The reference to being unfaithful to their God suggests that the prostitution was primarily spiritual. The people were worshiping and looking for leading from false gods rather than from their own true God.

13 Mountaintops, hills, and groves of oak, poplar, and terebinth trees were favorite places for idolatrous worship (see Dt 12:2; Jer 2:20; 3:6; Eze 6:13). Middle Eastern religion in Hosea's time made cultic prostitution an important part of its practice; and because the Israelites had adopted other aspects of this kind of religion, their daughters and their daughters-in-law were prostituting themselves.

14 Yet even though the younger women were immoral, God would not punish them, because "the men" were consorting with harlots (the shrine prostitutes). Even-handed justice forbade punishment of the young women while the men were turning to prostitutes!

15 Though Hosea prophesied chiefly to the northern nation, here he warned the southern kingdom not to follow Israel in this abominable kind of worship. Judah must not, he declared, go either to Gilgal or Beth Aven for this purpose. Under Elijah and Elisha (2Ki 2:1; 4:38), Gilgal had been a center for prophetic instruction. Now, however, it had become a center of false worship (Hos 9:15; 12:11; Am 4:4; 5:5). Beth Aven is to be identified with Bethel (cf. Am 4:4; 5:5) and means "house of deceit"—a deliberate substitution by Hosea for Bethel ("house of God").

Bethel was the southern center of calf worship established by Jeroboam I (1Ki 12:28–29). Though God's people had been permitted to "swear" an oath in the name of the Lord (Dt 6:13; 10:20), Hosea now warned the people of Judah not to do this, probably because at this time such oaths were being sworn in connection with the false worship at Gilgal and Bethel.

16 The thought shifts back to the people of the northern nation. Hosea told them that if they acted like stubborn cows, they could not expect to be treated like obedient sheep.

17–18 The Ephraimites were the most influential tribe of the northern nation and were often referred to as representative of that nation. They were so far gone into idolatry as to have become incorrigible. They were, therefore, to be let alone till punishment came. Furthermore, as evidence of the depths of the Israelites' sin, the people are said to have continued their prostitution even after they had finished their drinks (with its lower inhibitions against sexual immorality). This was in part because "their rulers" influenced them through their love of "shameful ways."

19 The literal meaning of this verse is vivid: "A whirlwind has wrapped her [Ephraim] up in her wings," i.e., for the purpose of destruction. In other words, the people's "sacrifices will bring them shame." They will realize how ineffective their sacrifices have been, whether to false gods or to the Lord.

4. A warning to priest, people, and king (5:1–7)

1 Hosea demands attention from three groups of people: the priests (cf. ch. 4), the people of Israel, and the royal family. The "judgment" referred to is no doubt the one cited in v.2. The "snare" and the "net" were used to trap prey; and "Mizpah" of Gilead (cf. Jdg 10:17; 11:29) and Mount Tabor were likely places for hunting. The figure is of people being hurt, as if being hunted and trapped by the religious and civil leaders of the day.

2–3 That rebels were "deep in slaughter" reflects the plight of a people not only hunted but slaughtered. But God would discipline those responsible for this. The tribe of Ephraim in particular were foremost in fornication, for the Bethel altar was in their area—the center of a religion not only corrupt (see 4:10, 12) but also corrupting all Israel. God knew the whole sad story; nothing was hidden.

4 "Deeds" are the product of the state of one's heart. Because the hearts of the people desired prostitution (probably both spiritual and physical), their subsequent deeds did not allow a return to God.

5 The Israelites, steeped in the sin of idolatry, had grown arrogant against God. Ephraim, presumably the worst-offending tribe, was again singled out for censure. Judah too was indicted for wayward behavior (see vv.8–10).

6 To go with "flocks and herds to seek the LORD" means to search after God's favor through sacrifice. But without the evidence

Mount Tabor (seen here from the south) was one of the larger mountains in the northern kingdom of Israel.

of true faith, mere outward sacrifice will not do (cf. 6:6; 1Sa 15:22–23). Thus the people find only that God "has withdrawn himself from them."

7 In being "unfaithful" (GK 2338; cf. Jer 3:20; Mal 2:14), the people had produced "illegitimate children." That is, parents had reared their children in their own sinful ways rather than in the fear of God. The "New Moon festivals" were debased by hypocritical worship and thus, devoid of God's blessing, would bring about the ruin of people and fields alike.

5. A warning to Ephraim and Judah (5:8–15)

8–9 Hosea next warned Judah while continuing to warn Ephraim. A "trumpet" (GK 8795) was customarily used to sound a warning of impending danger. Both Gibeah and Ramah were important cities of Benjamin, strategic points on Judah's northern border. Beth Aven is probably another reference to Bethel (see comment on 4:15). Benjamin was especially being summoned to "lead on" in the conflict. (1) Because of its geographic proximity to Israel, Benjamin had to be especially watchful of Israel's influence on her. (2) Punishment would soon descend on Ephraim, making it a "waste." When that happened, the way would be opened for the invading army to descend immediately south on Benjamin (as Assyria eventually did). The last line shows the certainty of this.

10 Next Hosea turned to the reason for the coming punishment of Judah—its leaders were "like those who move boundary stones," which was tantamount to stealing property from neighbors (cf. Dt 19:14; 27:17). Property lines, indicated often only by stone markers, could be easily moved in a night. Judah's leaders, however, were not shifting physical property lines but spiritual ones established by God, changing the boundary between right and wrong, between true and false religion, between the true God and the idols.

11 Hosea turns back to Ephraim, saying that the tribe was "oppressed" and "trampled in judgment," looking on it as an accomplished fact. The reason is that the people had been intent on pursuing "idols." What may be in view here is Jeroboam's institution of calf worship on substitute altars at Bethel and Dan (1Ki 12:27–30).

12–13 A bold figure of speech describes the judgment referred to in v.11. It was not future but already on them. The people were being eaten—as if by moths and decay—by problems and troubles. On realizing the situation, Ephraim sought help from Assyria rather than from God—perhaps the time when Menahem paid tribute to Assyria (2Ki 15:19–20; cf. 2Ki 16:5–9). Ephraim's troubles were internal ones and indeed incurable.

14 Help could not come from Assyria, for God, mightier than this foreign country, was "like a lion" in bringing destruction on both Ephraim and Judah. His justice, like his love, works inevitably, irresistibly. His chastisement, already operating through the moth-like and decaying conditions, would be greatly accentuated through the coming devastation by Assyria—the very country whose aid had been sought. Tiglath-pileser III did come against Israel in two crushing campaigns (743 and 734–732 B.C.); later (722 B.C.) Shalmaneser V did much to bring Israel's history to an end (2Ki 17). Sennacherib came against Judah in 701 B.C. (2Ki 18:17–37).

15 When the punishment has been inflicted, God will withdraw to await the desired results. The people will admit their guilt and will search out his presence. The Assyrian-Babylonian captivity witnessed little of such a change of heart. Thus the language appears to reach into the Millennium (cf. 1:10–11; 2:14–23).

6. Words of repentant Israel (6:1–3)

For three verses Hosea gives the words of Israel in the day of her repentance. Israel as a nation has never yet prayed like this.

1–2 The people urge one another to return truly to God in the confidence that he who has punished them will heal them and bind up their wounds. The reference to "two days" and "the third day" means only that the restoration will come surely and quickly (cf. Job 5:19; Pr 6:16; 30:15, 18; Am 1:3, 6, 9; et al.)

3 Again the people admonish themselves, this time to "acknowledge the LORD." True knowledge of God provides the basis for faith and obedience. The people exhort

themselves to "press on" in obtaining this knowledge. And God, they can be sure, will respond to their persistence in seeking him; he will come to them as surely "as the sun rises," a coming as delightfully welcome as the "winter rains" and the "spring rains."

7. Continued indictment of the people (6:4–11)

After the inserted words of repentance, Hosea returns to his main theme of warning the people against their sin. He continues to address Ephraim and Judah. Probably, however, Ephraim is here to be understood once again as representing all Israel, not just one tribe.

4–5 In his strong indictment against both Ephraim and Judah, Hosea stresses that the love of the people for God was as unstable as the "morning mist" and "dew." The word "love" (GK 2876) connotes continued faithful love; but the people fell lamentably short when it came to sustaining it. As a result, God had sent his prophets to speak words of warning, which included predictions of doom and death. These "judgments" came clearly and ominously "like lightning" to the people.

6 The prophet sounds a note given also by the other eighth-century prophets (cf. Isa 1:11–17; Am 5:21–24; Mic 6:6–8): God desires true faith rather than empty sacrifice (cf. Mt 9:13; 12:7). This was not a denial of sacrifice as such but only of improper, faithless sacrifice. God had commanded the people to sacrifice, but the ceremony had to be marked by a proper attitude of heart; otherwise it was meaningless and worthless (cf. 5:6). The importance of "knowing God" is stressed as it had been in v.3.

7 Hosea begins to list a series of wrongdoings of the people, starting with the general sin of covenant breaking. The people were doing this knowingly, deliberately, just as Adam had in eating the forbidden fruit. "There" refers to Israel's land, covenanted to them by God, and perhaps especially to Bethel (see comment on 4:15; 5:11).

8–9 The list continues. Gilead is first noted as a "city of wicked men." This name is often applied to all the northern Transjordan area. The prophet next thought of the priests, who were acting in packs like highwaymen. Shechem lay on the road from the capital city, Samaria, to the religious center, Bethel. The thought is that the priests themselves, appointed by Jeroboam from "all sorts of people" (1Ki 12:31), were robbing and murdering pilgrims.

10–11 "House of Israel" no doubt stands for the Israelite nation, not to some special house of worship. The "horrible thing" singled out is the sin of prostitution. Judah seems never to have been far from Hosea's mind. Her "harvest" was her time of coming punishment ("harvest" elsewhere carries this sense; cf. Joel 3:13).

8. A ruinous domestic policy (7:1–7)

1–2 The first two lines speak of attempts by God to help and heal Israel—attempts that included sending prophets to warn and remonstrate. But the people's sins had thereby become more evident and exposed. The prophets' efforts had brought more sin to light, thus compounding the people's guilt. "Ephraim" continues to be mentioned as representative of the northern kingdom and Samaria, the capital city, is cited as the center of crime. Some of the sins are deceit, burglary, and street robbery by gangs. God knew about all this and saw it as engulfing the people, who themselves seem unaware that God knew about their sins.

3–4 An important reason for this sad situation is that the king and his princes were pleased with it. The sin of adultery is singled out for special mention—again primarily spiritual adultery, though physical adultery is also meant as part of the licentious worship of Baal. The people in their zeal for this sin were like a heated oven—a striking illustration of lust. The oven was so hot that after being unattended during an entire night, with a fresh tending of the fire in the morning, it had sufficient heat for baking at that time.

5–7 The prophet gives a striking example of the oven-inflamed sin of vv.3–4: the assassination of the king. It happened on a special day, a festival day. During the festivities the ringleaders planning the crime became drunk, and the king with them. In keeping the figure of the oven, the hearts of the plotters were hot with desire to perform their treacherous deed. Each time they were near the king, their hearts flamed up. They waited during the night, however, with their passion smoldering like the baker's fire, anticipating the morning. Then the blaze of passion stirred anew, and the terrible deed was done. Hosea mentions "rulers" (pl.; GK 9149) because he was describing an incident repeated several times in Israel's history (2Ki 15:10, 14, 25, 30). Though so many kings fell in this way, still no one in the land called to God for help.

9. A fatal foreign policy (7:8–16)

Having noted the weaknesses in Israel's internal affairs, Hosea next speaks of foreign relations, which he found equally wanting.

8–9 Outsiders were living among the Israelites, encouraged to do so by the Israelites themselves. They brought heathen gods and pagan ways of worship into the country. "A flat cake not turned over" is one that is overdone on one side and not baked on the other, thus being completely worthless. Unfortunately, the debilitating inroads of the foreigners, through their licentious cultic practices, were not recognized by Israel. As hair turning gray symbolizes aging, so Israel was becoming old and feeble without noticing it.

10 In spite of the sins mentioned in the previous verses, Israel had no thought of turning back to God and had no desire to seek him.

11 Hosea compares the people to "doves," which are proverbial for their naivete (cf. Mt 10:16). As doves, "easily deceived and senseless," may be lured by food into snares, so Israel was lured by both Egypt and Assyria as sources of assistance, only to be entrapped by them—especially by Assyria, which ultimately brought Israel down.

12 God is portrayed as a fowler throwing his net over Israel and pulling her down for correction. "Flocking together" may refer to the efforts of Israel's leaders to unite in seeking aid from Egypt and Assyria. "Catch" (GK 4334) means "to chastise"; this chastisement from God will come in full measure when he permits Assyria to devastate Israel.

13 The prophet characterizes the impending punishment as "woe" and "destruction," doubtless to come on the people by Assyria. God desperately wanted to redeem them, but they told lies about him, probably saying that he would not help them.

14–15 Though they bewailed their plight, the people were not truly turning their hearts to the Lord. They were gathering together in an attempt to get "grain and new wine," which had evidently become scarce under the divine correction. But instead of seeking them from God, they persisted in turning away from him. In fact, they went so far as to "plot evil" against God, even though he was the one who had trained and strengthened them. By "plot evil" the prophet meant their worship of foreign gods—in particular, the golden calves at Bethel and Dan.

16 The people were turning everywhere but to "the Most High," to their God who alone could help them. So they were like a warped bow, one that sends its arrows awry. The mention of the leaders who "fall by the sword" points to such men as Zechariah, Shallum, Pekahiah, and Pekah, all victims of assassination (see comment on vv.5–7). In the prosperous days of Jeroboam II, Israel had defied Egypt by boasting of her great strength. Now she would be ridiculed in Egypt because of the downfall of her leaders.

B. Israel's Punishment (8:1–10:15)

1. Warning of approaching judgment (8:1–14)

Hosea has been describing Israel's sin, but now he begins to speak primarily about punishment, the awful consequences of that sin.

1 God bids Hosea to trumpet a warning. An eagle (i.e., Assyria) was ready to descend on "the house of the LORD." As there was no temple in the northern kingdom to which this phrase could refer, it must refer to Israel as the people among whom God should and would dwell (cf. 9:15; Nu 12:7; Jer 12:7; Zec 9:8). The last two lines show why God would permit this "eagle" of punishment to come.

2–3 Though Israel would cry out that she knew God, this would be a cry of desperation rather than the cry of a believing heart. The people had rejected the "good" of truly knowing and serving God. Therefore their enemy would be permitted to pursue them.

4 The people had chosen their leaders, including their kings, without seeking guidance from God. Hence there was no continuing dynasty; in fact, nine different dynasties came to power in Israel. Furthermore, the people had made idols of silver and gold (a reference especially to the golden calves at Bethel and Dan, the extreme southern and northern points of Israel). The last two lines of this verse reemphasize the note of warning in v.1 by linking idol-making to destruction. Israel's destruction would come as a result of this sin.

5 "Throw out your calf-idol" is literally "your calf stinks." Here again the golden calves at Bethel and Dan, which were so odious to God, are in view. The rhetorical question at the close of the verse implies that there would never be a time when the idolatry of Israel would not be sinful.

6 The main reason why the calves were a stench before God was that they were manmade (1Ki 12:28). Therefore God would see that they were demolished. The calf idol is linked to Samaria only in the sense that Samaria, the capital city, represents the whole northern kingdom.

7–8 The figure of sowing and reaping, here in proverbial form, is common in the Bible (cf. 10:12–13; Job 4:8; Pr 22:8; Gal 6:7). The "wind" speaks of the emptiness of Israel's sin; the "whirlwind" speaks of God's impending destruction. That punishment had already begun: the stalks were not producing grain that could be milled into flour. God had apparently withheld the rain. Furthermore, if any stalks did produce grain, it was only for foreigners to snatch it up. Thus Israel, like the grain, was being swallowed up—i.e., losing her national identity and independence. So she was despised like worthless pottery.

9 The context shows that the Assyrian captivity was not in view here. Rather, Israel had "gone up to Assyria" in the sense of asking for aid. Hosea compared this to the solitary wandering of the wild donkey (cf. Jer 2:24). Wild donkeys are intractable; so Israel was stubborn in having her own way and repudiating God's guidance. Like a prostitute, she was selling herself to the heathen nations (cf. 2:5).

10 Hosea anticipates the full force of the Assyrian captivity on Israel. "Although" the people had looked to the nations for help, God would "gather them together" in order

to inflict this punishment on his people. As a result, their numbers would diminish under the oppression of the "mighty king." This most likely refers to the Assyrian ruler through whom God would bring the punishment (cf. Isa 10:8).

11 God had ordained the one altar at his central sanctuary as the place for the people to worship. With the division of the kingdom, Jeroboam had set up false altars at Bethel and Dan for religious sacrifices. Hosea made it clear that these were in no way a religious help to Israel but that God considered them only as altars for committing sin.

12 In the Pentateuch God had given the people "the many things" (lit., "ten thousand things") of his law so that they could know his will. But they had thought of his law as something "alien" or strange. Thus the fault lay with the people, not with God.

13 With the altars still in mind, Hosea says that God charged the people using these false altars to offer sacrifices that belonged to him (and therefore should have been offered in the proper place and manner). Furthermore, though God permitted certain parts of various sacrificial animals to be eaten, these people were apparently eating whatever they desired, and so were compounding their sin. In God's sight such offerings were only "meat," with no sacrificial value at all. So punishment would come in the form of a forced return to "Egypt"—a word used representatively for Assyria, where Israel was eventually taken.

14 An additional ground of Israel's punishment is that the people had forgotten their Maker and had instead put their confidence in fine palaces. Judah, too, had come to rely on fortified cities. Therefore, God would hurl fire on the cities and burn up the fortresses. This came with the Assyrian invasion not many years after Hosea's writing.

2. Assyrian captivity soon to come (9:1–9)

The message of warning continues, speaking more specifically about the coming captivity in Assyria.

1–2 The people of Israel were not to rejoice, nor were they to celebrate like other nations. They were the people of God, with standards much higher than those of the heathen with their false gods. The shame of Israel was that the people were denying their own supreme God and attributing their blessings to the heathen gods. This was spiritual adultery, analogous to the physical adultery practiced by prostitutes. The mention of "threshing floors" probably carries through the figure of prostitution, for the Canaanites frequently used threshing floors and winepresses as places for carrying out their fertility rites. God implies that because of insufficient rainfall the threshing floors and winepresses would fail to produce enough food for the people.

3 The people of Israel were soon to be taken captive from the land. The place of their captivity was first called "Egypt" (cf. 8:13) to show its general character, then "Assyria" was named as the actual place the people would be taken to (cf. 11:5). The food they were to eat there would be "unclean" because it would not be selected and prepared according to the Mosaic Law.

4–5 Moreover, the captive Israelites would not be able to present "wine offerings" or "sacrifices" because there would be no temple of the Lord in Assyria (Dt 12:5–14). Therefore, whatever sacrifices they did offer would be like "the bread of mourners" (cf. Dt 26:14)—unclean and unacceptable, like food touched by a mourner defiled by a dead body (Nu 19:22). Anyone eating the meat from such sacrifices would also be unclean. The rhetorical question in v.5 puts vividly the plight of Israel: captive in Assyria, without temple or sacrifices, and so unable to celebrate the commanded feasts and festivals.

6 Even if Israel is not utterly destroyed, the people will be taken captive; they will be gathered by Egypt (again used symbolically for Assyria; cf. v.3) and buried by Memphis (another symbol), an ancient capital of Egypt and a celebrated place of burial. Meanwhile, their own fine land ("treasures of silver") would revert to briars and thorns.

7–8 With eloquent power, Hosea announces the days of punishment that were coming on Israel and calls for understanding of it. Yet Israel had sunk so deep into sin that the people considered any prophet who warned them a madman and a fool. Since the prophets stood with God over Ephraim (the northern nation), the people, motivated by animosity, sought to entrap them. Hosea calls this "hos-tility in the house of his God" (the latter phrase being a reference to Israel; cf. comment on 8:1).

9 Hosea compares the sin of Israel to that of the men of Gibeah, who committed a heinous crime against the concubine of a Levite who was their guest (Jdg 19–20). This most shocking example of sin in the OT had led to civil war and brought the tribe of Benjamin to the brink of annihilation.

3. The fleeting glory of Israel (9:10–17)

The warning now turns to more general matters as Hosea speaks of punishments that would take place prior to the Assyrian captivity.

10 This is a poignant reference to Israel's earliest days as a nation, when God found her and chose her. Then she was like "grapes in the desert" and "the early fruit on the fig tree." Grapes, unusual in the desert, are a special delight when found there; the early figs are considered especially delicious. In other words, when God first found Israel in the desert (Dt 32:10), it was like finding such delicacies. Things soon changed, however. Already at Baal-peor, before even entering the Promised Land (Nu 25:3–18), the people slipped into the worship of the local Baal. This was not Israel's only time of sin, but it is singled out here because it was the first instance of their worship of Baal—worship they persisted in till it became their besetting sin.

11–12 The "glory" (GK 3883) God gave Ephraim (Israel), through making her a fine nation after he had found her in the desert, would fly away like a bird because of her recurring sin. "No birth, no pregnancy, no conception" is a terse way of saying that Israel's population would decrease. And even if children were born, they would die young before reaching adulthood (cf. Dt 32:25). God would turn his favor from Israel because of her unfaithfulness. This form of punishment would precede the captivity to Assyria, and the captivity itself would climax it.

13–14 God had given Israel a pleasant and advantageous location. All caravan trade between Egypt and countries to the north had to pass through her land, because the Mediterranean Sea was to the west and the desert to the east. She was like Tyre, for Tyre also had a situation highly advantageous for her maritime activities. Israel failed, however, to realize her potential because of her sin. Instead, her children would be led out to the "slayer"—a further factor in the diminishing of population through murders, civil strife, and warfare. Hosea's irony in v.14 is as unmistakable as it is powerful.

15 The severe treatment of Israel was because of "all their wickedness in Gilgal." By this time Gilgal had clearly become a center of false worship (cf. 4:15). The meaning of "hate" (GK 8533) in this context is defined by the words "I will no longer love them." It was not that God had a positive animosity toward Israel, but he had nothing favorable to say of them. Because of their "sinful deeds" and the rebellion of their leaders, God would expel them from his "house" (the congregation of Israel; see comments on 8:1; 9:8).

16 Hosea returns to the warning that Israel would be diminished in population, using again the figure of a plant (cf. v.10; 10:1; 14:8). The people would be withered right down to the root (cf. Mal 4:1) and thus rendered fruitless and hopeless.

17 In summary, God would reject the people because of their persistent disobedience. As a result they would become "wanderers among the nations"—another allusion to their coming captivity.

4. Guilt and coming captivity (10:1–8)

In this section Hosea speaks even more explicitly of the impending captivity of Israel.

1 Hosea begins by referring once more (cf. 9:10) to Israel's early history when the people were like a luxuriant vine. But as the "fruit" of prosperity "increased," they deteriorated spiritually. Pagan "altars" were built and "sacred stones" (or pillars) adorned. The people thus turned from the worship of the true God.

2 The word translated "deceitful" (lit., "smooth" or "flattering"; GK 2744) is elsewhere applied to lips or tongues that are insincere (cf. Pss 5:9; 12:3; Pr 5:3). Because the same is true here of the heart of a guilty peo-

ple, God would destroy both the altars and the sacred stones they had erected.

3 As a result, the people would be brought to admit that they had no king worthy of the name because they did not choose one who revered the Lord. The time referred to can only have been just before the captivity, when Israel's kings showed themselves ineffectual both in tackling Israel's problems and in coping with the Assyrian menace. The last two lines note despairingly that even if the land did have a truly capable king, things were so bad that he would be powerless to help.

4 Hosea enlarges on the idea of deceitfulness of heart (cf. v.2): promises had been made, false oaths taken, and contracts signed. The thought here mainly concerns agreements among the people themselves. With the denial of people's legal rights, "lawsuits" were springing up like "poisonous weeds" (cf. Dt 29:17) in a "plowed field."

5 The people of Samaria (representative of all Israel), seeing the ominous signs of the impending punishment, are said to be anxious about their "calf-idol" at Beth Aven (Bethel; cf. 4:15) rather than about their own sin. "Its people" (i.e., the Israelites identified as the people of this calf!) mourn concerning the matter, along with the idolatrous priests (cf. 2Ki 23:5) that serve it.

6–7 Hosea now speaks clearly of the Assyrian captivity. The shameful but materially valuable calf-idol would be carried to the victorious king of Assyria as tribute. And Israel would feel disgrace and humiliation. The word for "its wooden idols" is often translated "its counsel" (cf. NIV note). The former translation refers disdainfully to the calf as mere wood; the alternate translation to the "counsel" given by Jeroboam I when he had first established calf worship (1Ki 12:28). Not only the calf idol but also Samaria and its king would be taken, borne away to foreign Assyria, helpless as a twig on a river.

8 "The high places of wickedness" signifies the calf temple at Bethel (Beth Aven; cf. comments on 4:15; 5:8; 10:5). Destruction there by the Assyrians would be so complete that thorns and thistles would replace the buildings containing the altars (cf. Ge 3:18). Also, the people would cry in despair for the mountains and hills to fall on them, apparently to terminate their time of disgrace (cf. Lk 23:30; Rev 6:16).

5. Sin and punishment (10:9–15)

Hosea speaks more generally again, referring to both Israel's sin and her resulting punishment; he also gives a word of instruction. Mention of the Assyrian captivity reappears at the close of the section.

9–10 Once more the prophet refers to the sin at Gibeah (see comment on 9:9). Since that tragic occurrence, Israel has defiantly continued in the same basic sin, and the appropriate punishment—such as was meted out to the original offenders—has not yet been experienced but is now due. This punishment, at God's pleasure, would see nations gathering against Israel—a passing reference to the captivity. The "double sin" is probably the sins of forsaking God and of departing from the rule of David's house.

11 Ephraim (Israel) had been well trained in past days, like a heifer broken to the yoke. She had come, however, to enjoy only the work of threshing grain (pleasant to the heifer because she could then eat her fill of grain). But God would put a yoke of true work on her "fair neck" so that she would have to work hard in plowing and breaking up the hard soil. Judah is once more included (cf. 6:11; 8:14; et al.) as meriting the same treatment. "Jacob" suggests all twelve tribes.

12 Hosea pauses to give advice. The people should sow "righteousness" (i.e., treat each other in the right manner), and they would reap kindness in return. Thereby unplowed ground would be plowed (cf. v.11). Admittedly, just as plowing is hard work, so it would be hard for the people to change their lifestyle; but they must do so. Only by searching for the Lord and his righteousness would they be delivered from the coming punishment.

13 Instead of doing this, however, the people were planting (lit., "plowing") wickedness and reaping evil. Deceit and its baneful results (vv.2–4) therefore abounded. Because Israel had depended on her own strength and her many warriors, God would permit the roar of battle to come against the people.

14 The outcome would be the destruction of all Israel's fortifications through the Assyrian attack. To illustrate how bad the time would be, Hosea compares it with another horrible and tragic slaughter at Beth Arbel (difficult now to identify). Perhaps Shalman is Shalmaneser V, who played such a decisive part in the Assyrian action leading to Israel's captivity (2Ki 17:3–6).

15 So, concludes Hosea, Bethel, the calf-idol center, representative of all that was wicked in Israel, would experience the same fate as this Beth Arbel. In that day even the "king of Israel" would be "completely destroyed." Israel was facing a most foreboding future. Hosea prophesies that her destruction would occur from the very beginning of the day of battle; it is noteworthy that Israel's final king, Hoshea, was taken captive by the Assyrian conqueror Shalmaneser V before the actual siege of Samaria began.

C. Israel's Restoration (11:1–14:9)

1. God's love and Israel's rebellion (11:1–7)

The theme now changes from Israel's punishment to Israel's restoration. It is introduced by a moving contrast between God's steadfast love and Israel's persistent apostasy.

1 Once more (cf. 9:10; 10:1, 9) Hosea mentions the earlier history of Israel, this time looking back to the Lord's words in Ex 4:22–23: "Israel is my firstborn son. . . . 'Let my son go, so he may worship me.'" The reason Israel was God's son is that God had especially chosen him as his own (cf. Ge 12:2–3; cf. Mt 2:13–15).

2 God had multiplied the people of Israel and had shown his power in bringing them into the land of Canaan. Yet despite these evidences of his love, Israel forsook him and worshiped other gods (Jdg 2:11–13). So God disciplined them through numerous foreign oppressions to call them back; but the more he did so, the more they apostatized.

3–4 Here the tender figure of a parent teaching an infant to walk shows the Lord's compassion in disciplining Israel (Ephraim). But they were blind to his healing purpose in dealing with them. The poetic language continues in v.4. God had "led" (lit., "drawn"; GK 5432) them with cords of "human kindness" and "ties of love." He also had lifted "the yoke from their neck," just as an owner sometimes lifts the yoke away from the face of an ox so that it might eat more comfortably. So God had dealt gently with his people in spite of their sin.

5–6 A rhetorical question that implies an affirmative answer points to the impending captivity—the consequence of Israel's sin, which had been compounded because the people persisted in it despite God's continuing grace. When Egypt (i.e., Assyria; see comments on 8:13; 9:3) attacked, swords would bring death in the cities, the cities' defenses would be broken, and all the plans for survival would be frustrated.

7 In their apostasy the people of Israel were obdurate in their unfaithfulness. The remainder of this verse may best be taken to mean that the people would not listen to the prophets who were calling them to return to God but were choosing instead to remain in the mire of sin.

2. Restoration in the last days (11:8–11)

These verses are like a window into the heart of God. They show that his love for his people is a love that will never let them go. Like the beautiful final chapter of the book, these verses look forward, beyond the chastisement of the immediate future, to the Millennium, to the time, still distant, when Israel will truly return to her God and he will bless her once more.

8 Two poignant questions reveal the depth of God's love for his people. Despite the sure judgment that was soon to come on unfaithful Israel, he could not bear to give up his chosen people (here called Ephraim and Israel) forever. His enduring love precluded his treating them as he did Admah and Zeboiim, two cities that had been utterly destroyed along with Sodom and Gomorrah (cf. Dt 29:23).

9 In that future day God would not devastate his people Israel again, as he was about to do through the Assyrians. He is "God, and not man"—i.e., he is one whose ways transcend those of sinful humanity. Because he is holy, he does not let passion or bitterness govern his decisions. He promises wondrous blessing on the people, if they will follow him (cf. Dt 28:1–14). But in that future day of resto-

ration, he will not come against any city or land "in wrath," as he was about to do in Hosea's day.

10 Hosea gives God's reason for carrying out his promise of restoration in the coming day: The people "will follow the LORD." The metaphor of the lion's roar means that God's call to his people will sound so clearly throughout the earth that they will come "trembling" (i.e., "humbly") "from the west." The return of Judah from the Babylonian captivity was from the east. But this mention of "the west" sets off the future return from the earlier one (cf. Isa 11:11–12).

11 Hosea next compares the swiftness (i.e., the readiness and responsiveness) of the future return of his people to the flight of birds and doves. Egypt and Assyria are named because of Israel's years of bondage in Egypt and their impending captivity in Assyria. In this context Egypt and Assyria typify the many nations from which God's people will return in the future day. Then he will settle them "in their homes"—an assurance of their permanent residence in their land (cf. 2:19).

3. The folly of Israel (11:12–12:14)

This section, like ch. 3, reverts to the main theme of the book—Israel's unfaithfulness to her God. The book, however, will end on the contrasting note of Israel's future restoration.

12 God accuses the Israelites of surrounding him with deceit and dishonesty, as though attacking him. Once more Israel's sin is paralleled by Judah's rebellion against God, who is their "faithful Holy One."

12:1 Ephraim (Israel) is now said to "feed on the wind," meaning that her efforts were to no worthwhile purpose. One aspect of this effort was the treaties they made with Assyria and Egypt (cf. 2Ki 17:4; 18:21; Isa 30:7), which were seldom of benefit to Israel. "Lies and violence" were often involved in making them. Indeed, Israel, while making a treaty with Assyria, might at the same time be sending olive oil to Egypt in an effort to enlist her support against Assyria (cf. 2Ki 17:4).

2 Once more Hosea refers to Judah as being accused by God and facing retribution. "Jacob" is probably a reference to both Judah and Israel combined; he was the ancestor of all the Israelites and so becomes the subject of vv.3–4. All his descendants, the people of both the northern and the southern kingdoms, were guilty before God.

3 When Jacob was being born, he seized his brother's heel (Ge 25:24–26). Later he struggled with God himself at the brook Jabbok (Ge 32:25–29). He is an example for the people of Hosea's day to follow. His struggling with God was a time of triumph, for through it he received the Lord's blessing. Thus, the first occasion should be understood in the same way; Jacob's act in the womb of his mother was one in which the providential direction of God symbolized Jacob's desire for the birthright and blessing. Similarly, Israel in Hosea's time should be striving for God's favor and blessing rather than chasing the wind.

4 Hosea enlarges on Jacob's struggle at Jabbok, pointing out that Jacob overcame the angel because he wanted the blessing so much that he even "wept and begged" for it. Then the prophet shifts to Jacob's encounter with God at Bethel (Ge 35:1–15), when God confirmed the blessing already promised him. The implication is that God would do the same thing for Israel if she desired God's blessing as much as Jacob had.

5 Hosea now turns to God himself, the one who had blessed Jacob and wanted to do the same thing for Israel. His great name is given—the name that stands for him in all his excellency: "Lord God Almighty" (lit., "The Lord, the God of hosts"). Israel should always think of God in this way, and they could be sure that he would keep every promise he had ever made to them.

6 The people should repent and "return" (GK 8740) to God, to "maintain love and justice" in respect to one another, and to "wait" in expectancy for God to bring them the same kind of blessing he had brought Jacob. All this they were to do with the help of God. We work for God as God enables us (cf. Php 2:11–12); so only is God's work done.

7–8 Hosea next turns to a specific area of sin in Israel—"the merchant" using dishonest scales and loving "to defraud" customers. What a way to be remembered! Much of Israel's dealing with the nations of the day had involved trading and had been contaminated by deceit. As a result of these shady practices,

the people had been boasting of their wealth and declaring that no one could find them guilty of any sin. So they did not see themselves as deserving any punishment. Apparently they had devised loopholes in the law to justify what they had been doing. Hosea is probably speaking here of the reign of Jeroboam II, when Israel prospered greatly.

9 While the people were thinking themselves self-sufficient, God counters this thinking by reminding them that he had been the Lord their God from the land of Egypt. But now because of their sin, he would drive them out of their wealthy circumstances and make them "live in tents again," as they did at the Feast of Tabernacles (which commemorated the time they lived in the desert). This refers to the coming days of captivity. Because the Feast of Tabernacles was also a joyous occasion, the implication may be that even in their transient time of captivity God would again graciously provide for them—as indeed he did.

10 Hosea resumes his general theme. God, he recalls, had communicated his will to Israel through prophets, visions, and parables. The people therefore could not plead ignorance and were without excuse.

11 Gilead (east of the Jordan) and Gilgal (west of it) here represent the entire land. Rhetorical questions concerning both serve to underline their wickedness. The very idea of bulls being sacrificed at Gilgal indicates one of the ways in which wickedness was involved there, for it was the wrong place for such sacrifice (cf. 4:15; 9:15). As a result God would reduce the altars there to mere piles of stones on a "plowed field"—i.e., they would be useless and in the way.

12–13 In vv.3–4 Hosea had mentioned the blessing Jacob received; here he speaks of the hardship Jacob endured after running away from home. His point is that God had blessed this ancestor, even though things had happened at the time—the long years served for Rachel, the flight from Esau—that had not seemed like blessings. And God had similarly provided for Israel when he had brought them by a "prophet" (presumably Moses; cf. Dt 18:18) out of Egypt and cared for them.

14 This past history should have led Israel to a state of humility and submission before God, but it had not. Instead Ephraim (Israel) had "bitterly provoked him to anger" through her extensive sinning. Therefore Ephraim's "Lord" ("master"; GK 151) would leave the people in their "guilt of . . . bloodshed" (cf. Lev 20:9; Dt 19:10) and "repay" them for the insults rendered. Punishment would indeed come.

4. Israel's fall into sin (13:1–16)

Hosea continues to speak of Israel's unfaithfulness to God, but here he takes on a more historical approach.

1 Hosea has frequently referred to the whole northern nation as Ephraim, but in this verse the tribe of Ephraim is intended. In former years when Ephraim had spoken, the other tribes had listened with deference and respect. Ephraim had often asserted leadership, sometimes in improper ways (see Jdg 8:1–3; 12:1–6; 1Ki 12:25; cf. 11:26). Things had changed for Ephraim, however, since Baal worship (i.e., the calf worship at Bethel) had crept in. Though Jeroboam I had instituted calf worship as the worship of Israel's God (1Ki 12:26–33), doubtless elements of the Baal cult had come to be practiced there.

2–3 Spiritual death was the result of Baal worship. The people heaped sin on sin, owning and worshiping idols made from silver by clever craftsmen (cf. 8:4). The last two lines of v.2 admit of two renderings. Although NIV takes them to refer to "human sacrifice," this seems unlikely since no other indication is given that human sacrifices were practiced at Bethel or Dan. The more likely rendering is "In respect to the images [of the calves], they [leaders in this form of worship] are saying, 'Let those who would sacrifice do so by kissing the calf-idols.'" To kiss an image was to do homage to it (see 1Ki 19:18; cf. Ps 2:12). Jeroboam I had first bidden the people to give this homage, and leaders in the worship were continuing the practice. Persistence in this sin would lead to the disappearance of Israel (referred to in v.3 in four striking figures that suggest how surely and speedily it would happen).

4 Hosea again reminds Israel of what their covenant God had done for them in the Exodus. He then admonishes them to acknowl-edge God alone as their God and Savior. The admonition tallies with the tenor of the book.

5–6 Hosea goes on to remind the people how God had cared for them during those arduous desert days, a reminder that should also have stirred them to observe the admonition in v.4. God's care for the people involved his feeding them with manna, a thought that is probably intended to cover generally all of God's provisions. This satisfied the people, but then they "became proud" and forgot God (cf. Dt 8:11–20). This had happened in the desert, and it had been happening during the intervening centuries.

7–8 This brings Hosea again to his theme of coming judgment. God would pounce on the rebellious people like a lion and like a leopard, to bring punishment (cf. 5:14). The figure is apt, for in v.6 the people have been pictured as a flock under God's care. To intensify this theme, the figure of a bear crazed by the loss of her cubs is used, followed once more by the figure of a lion. The "wild animal" refers to all three as beasts of the field; they were all native to Palestine and known for their relentless manner of killing prey.

9–10 Israel would suffer destruction because she lived in opposition to God, who had helped her so much throughout history. Israel was not kingless, but she did not have as king one who could deliver the people from the Assyrian threat. Only God, their true "helper," whom they rejected, could do this. "Your rulers" (lit., "your judges") refers to the king's assistants. The last part of v.10 does not refer to the time of Samuel when the people asked for a king (1Sa 8:4–6), but to the occasion when the northern tribes wanted their own king after rebelling against Rehoboam (1Ki 12:16–20).

11–12 This verse can also be translated "I have been giving" you a king and "I have been taking him away." No one king apparently is in view here but the series of kings that had occupied Israel's throne since the kingdom's division. God had been allowing them to rule; but because of their unfaithfulness to him, he had also been setting them aside. Many had come to a violent end (see comment on 7:7). Thus was the guilt of Ephraim "stored up" and "kept on record" against the day of reckoning.

13 Hosea further delineates the punishment of Israel by likening her to a mother in labor and then to a son being born to the mother. This son, he says, was without wisdom because he did not come to the "opening of the womb" (cf. 2Ki 19:3; Isa 37:3) at the proper time for the birth. God, in other words, was bringing punishment on Israel so that the people might be reborn to follow him as he desired; but they were foolish in not grasping the opportunity. God had been using various disciplinary measures against Israel for years, but to no avail.

14 Like 11:8–11, this verse is parenthetical between v.13 and v.15. God breaks in to sound a note of encouragement and promise to the people. They had severe punishment ahead of them in Hosea's time, but a day would come when wondrous blessing would be their portion. Paul quoted v.14b at the triumphant climax of his great chapter on resurrection (1Co 15:55). One aspect of its fulfillment (that relating to the resurrection of the believer in a spiritual body) is to be found there. But since the context of ch. 13 relates to the earthly punishment of Israel, another aspect of v.14b must still be future—i. e., at the time of Christ's reign on earth during the Millennium (cf. 11:8–11).

Verse 14a speaks of the people being ransomed "from the power of the grave." The dreaded enemies of death and the grave will be shorn of their power against God's redeemed people. What glorious thoughts! The last line of v.14 literally reads, "Repentance is hidden from my eyes"; it is best taken with v.14 rather than with v.15, meaning that God will not change his mind about doing what this verse declares.

15–16 Though the people of Israel may thrive among their neighbors, eventually they will be dried up by an east wind from the desert. Because of this, springs and wells will fail. That time of thriving must be the time of Jeroboam II, when prosperity was marked. The destroying east wind must be Assyria—a power that came from the east and effected Israel's fall in 722 B.C. Moreover, Assyria did indeed plunder Israel's "storehouse" at that time. This invasion came as a result of the people's "guilt" of their rebellion against their God. The shocking brutalities described in v.16 are in keeping with what we know about the character of the Assyrians.

Here "Samaria," as the capital of the northern kingdom, represents all Israel.

5. Israel's repentance and God's blessing (14:1–9)

In beauty of expression these final words of Hosea rank with the memorable chapters of the OT. Like the rainbow after a storm, they promise Israel's final restoration. Here is the full flowering of God's unfailing love for his faithless people, the triumph of his grace, the assurance of his healing—all described in imagery that reveals the loving heart of God.

1–2 The people of Israel are not only invited to "return" (GK 8740) to their God; they are also reminded of their sins—God's forgiveness must be accompanied by awareness of sin. But they may not return to the Lord without bringing something; they must come to him with words that he puts, as it were, in their mouths. When they ask for forgiveness, the Lord will graciously receive them. The offering of "the fruit of our lips" is literally "we offer our lips as sacrifices of bulls" (cf. NIV note)—i.e., instead of offering bullocks we offer as our sacrifice our lips that utter prayer and praise to God (cf. Heb 13:15).

3 The offering of words—all of them words of repentance—continues. Israel was to admit that neither Assyria nor any military might (symbolized by "war-horses") could save her. Once and for all, she was to renounce man-made images as her "gods." Moreover, since God has compassion on the orphans (cf. Ex 22:22; Dt 10:18), Israel could expect him to have compassion also on her.

4 In response to Israel's penitent words, the Lord describes the wondrous blessings that he will bestow on them. Since the people had not repented and would not repent nationally in the way Hosea described until the future Great Tribulation, and since the blessings from God described in vv.4–8 will not be fully bestowed till the Millennium, the ultimate meaning of this passage must be eschatological—i.e., the time of the Millennium again (cf. 1:10–11; 2:14–23; et al.). Here we have God's grace in action—his healing of their "waywardness" and his loving them unconditionally. He had indeed turned his anger away from them.

5–6 Among the great biblical figures of speech are those that relate to trees and flowers—especially meaningful to dwellers in semiarid lands like Palestine. Here Hosea likens Israel in her time of future blessing to a lily, a cedar of Lebanon, and that most essential of all trees, an olive tree. The second and third lines of v.6 show the result of this healthy growth: the cedar will have the "splendor" or majesty of the olive tree and the "fragrance" of the cedar of Lebanon itself. So the nation of Israel will be admired throughout the world.

7 In the Hebrew the first two lines of this verse are literally "They who dwell in his shadow shall again make grain to live." The antecedent of "his" is the tree (representative of Israel nationally); and the antecedent of "they," individual Israelites. It is a promise

that the people of Israel in the future day will flourish and blossom like a vine, with their "fame" spreading abroad like the fame of Lebanese wine. How different from the situation of Israel in Hosea's day!

8 The rhetorical question here relates to the idolatry that had been Israel's besetting sin. In God's sight idols are absolutely nothing, and so shall they be for Ephraim (Israel). God, not the idols, is the one who will answer and "care for" Israel in her time of need. He is like a "green pine tree"; all their fruitfulness comes from him.

9 This verse is like a noble epilogue. The balance between the rhetorical questions, with their answers, and the dignity of the last sentence, with its concise parallelism, close Hosea's unique book on a note of solemn authority.

The Old Testament in the New

OT Text	NT Text	Subject
Hos 1:6, 9	1Pe 2:10	Not God's people
Hos 1:10	Ro 9:25–26	Now God's people
Hos 2:23	Ro 9:25–26; 1Pe 2:10	Now God's people
Hos 6:6	Mt 9:13; 12:7	Mercy, not sacrifice
Hos 10:8	Lk 23:30	Hills falling on us
Hos 11:1	Mt 2:15	My son from Egypt
Hos 13:14	1Co 15:55	Victory over death

INTRODUCTION

1. Background

Joel prophesied in Judah in the exciting and pivotal days of Uzziah (792–740 B.C.), the tenth king of the southern kingdom. Those were days of unparalleled prosperity. To the south Uzziah continued the control over Edom that Amaziah had effected (2Ki 14:22; 2Ch 26:2); he also seized the caravan routes that led from Arabia (2Ch 26:7). To the east he seems to have imposed tribute on the Transjordanian regions (v.8). To the west he moved with great success against the Philistines, taking Gath and the coastal plain, thus controlling the important trade routes (vv.6–7) and eliminating the slave-gathering raids into western Judah (3:4–8). A great military strategist, Uzziah's military preparedness included a total reorganization of the structure and equipment of the army (vv.11–15).

About 750 B.C., Uzziah contracted leprosy because of his intrusion into the priest's office, and he appointed Jotham, his son, as coregent and public officiator. Nevertheless, Uzziah continued to be the real power of the throne, for when Tiglath-pileser III invaded Syria in his first western campaign (743 B.C.), Uzziah was singled out as the leader of the anti-Assyrian coalition. Uzziah also turned his attention to the internal affairs of his country. Indeed, most of his military activity had economic goals. He also led the way in agricultural reorganization (2Ch 26:10).

In short, the era of the early eighth century B.C. was one of great expansion—militarily, administratively, commercially, and economically; it was a period of prosperity second only to that of Solomon's. It is small wonder, then, that Uzziah's fame should endure long after his death (2Ch 26:8b, 1:5b).

In such an era God raised up the great writing prophets, men of intense patriotism and deep spiritual concern. Their message took in the entire international scene from their own time to the culmination of God's teleological program.

2. Authorship

Little is known of the personal circumstances of the author, Joel ("The Lord is God"), except what can be gleaned from the book. The son of Pethuel, Joel lived and prophesied in Judah (cf. 2:32; 3:1, 17–18, 20). He was thoroughly familiar with the temple and its ministry (1:9, 113–14, 16; 2:14, 17) and was intimately acquainted with the geography and history of the land.

Joel was a man of vitality and spiritual maturity. As a keen discerner of the times, he delivered God's message to the people of Judah in a vivid and impassioned style.

3. Date

Since no date is given, conjectures have ranged from the ninth century B.C. to the Maccabean Period (i.e., either preexilic or postexilic). The preexilic date is the better of these two.

Three general positions have been advanced by those who assign a preexilic date to Joel–the ninth century, the eighth century, and the seventh century. The view that Joel prophesied in the early eighth century is to be preferred because it best fits all the data: (1) the nonmention of Assyria, Babylonia, and Persia, best explained by Assyria being in severe decline from 782 B.C. to 745 B.C.; (2) the position of Joel among the dated minor prophets (with Hosea, Amos, Jonah); (3) the contextual juxtaposition of six foreign nations in ch. 3; (4) the internal emphases; (5) the faithful reflection of the prevailing events, attitudes, and literary themes of the early eighth century B.C.; and (6) Joel's prophecy of the Day of the Lord, which may be connected with Amos's dating of his prophecy as two years before the earthquake of Uzziah's time (1:2; cf. Zec 14:5).

4. Occasion and Purpose

A locust plague without parallel had descended on Judah, ruining all the crops. All levels of society were disrupted. Worst of all, the agricultural loss threatened the continuance of the sacrificial offerings. In these circumstances Joel saw the judgment of God on Judah. The people in Uzziah's day had taken God and his blessings for granted. Faith had degenerated into an empty formalism and their lives into moral decadence. To Joel, the locust plague was a warning of a greater judgment that was coming unless the people repented and returned to fellowship with God. If they did, God would pardon them, restore the health of the land, and give them again the elements needed to offer the sacrifices.

5. Theological Values

As a man of faith in God, Joel imparted a reliance on the sufficiency of God and his prior claim on the believer's life. His basic tenet is that God is sovereignly guiding the affairs of world history toward his preconceived goal (1:15; 2:1-4, 25-32; 3:1-21). He alone is God (2:13)—a God of grace and mercy (2:13, 17), of love and patience (2:13), and of justice and righteousness (1:15; 2:23; 3:1-8). He calls for true worship from his followers, who have trusted him for salvation by grace through faith (2:32). Mere external worship is insufficient before the Lord (2:13, 18-19, 23, 26-27, 32).

Joel also taught that when sin becomes the dominant condition of God's people, they must be judged (1:15; 2:1, 11-13). God may use natural disasters (ch. 1) or political means (2:1-11) to chastise his people. If the people repent (2:12-13), they will be restored to fellowship with God (2:14, 19, 23), and nature too will be restored to blessings (2:23-27).

Joel's theology also contains teaching about the last things. Of central concern is God's role to his people Israel (1:6, 13-14; 2:12-14; et al.). While he may allow other nations to chastise Israel for her sins, God has reserved a remnant for himself (2:28-32). On them he will pour out his Spirit (2:28-29), to them he will manifest himself with marvelous signs (2:30-31), and them he will regather and bring to the Promised Land (2:32-3:1). He will gather for judgment those nations that have dealt so severely with his people (3:2, 12-13) and bring them to a great final battle near Jerusalem (3:9-16). On that awesome day (v.15), he himself will lead his people in triumph (vv.16-17) and usher in an era of unparalleled peace and prosperity (vv.17-21).

EXPOSITION

I. Joel's Present Instructions: Based on the Locust Plague (1:1–2:27)

A. The Occasion: the Locust Plague (1:1–4)

1-4 Joel begins his prophecy by identifying himself and his lineage and clearly declaring the divine source of his prophecy. Because the intensity of the locust plague was unprecedented, this message was to be handed down to the generations that followed. The four different Hebrew words for locusts that appear in v.4 probably are used to indicate the intensity of the plague and a successive series of locusts that had devastated the land.

B. The Instructions: Based on the Locust Plague (1:5–2:27)

1. Warnings in the light of the present crisis (1:5–20)

a. Joel's plea for penitence (1:5–13)

5-7 Joel begins his call for penitence with a solemn warning to three categories of pleasure seekers—the general citizenry, the farmers, and the priests. He tells them to awaken from their sleep of drunkenness (cf. Pr 23:35b). In so doing he calls attention to not only the debased nature of society but also the people's insensitivity to their own moral condition. Times of ease and prosperity, such as were experienced during the kingship of Uzziah, are unfortunately often times of spiritual, moral, and social corruption.

Joel condemns the misuse of wine, which had led to drunkenness, debauchery, and the loss of spiritual vitality. As a result, the locusts, like a powerful army, had stripped bare the vegetation of the land. These voracious insects had teeth like a lion's. The vine and the fig tree, symbols of God's blessing, lay stripped to the bark.

8-10 Far worse than the locust plague was the condition of the people's spiritual lives. The very worship of God was being compromised. Joel instructs the citizenry to mourn like an engaged virgin whose intended husband was taken from her before the wedding. How great would be her tragedy and sorrow! So also the people of Judah and Jerusalem should weep over the loss of vital religious experience through the devastation of the land. The loss of agricultural produce meant the early cessation of the meal (grain) and drink offerings. The cutting off of them should have been a warning to the people of their grave condition.

The observances of these offerings had degenerated in Joel's day into mere routine ritual (cf. Hos 6:6; Am 4:4–5). Still worse, the Israelites had made these times an occasion for drunkenness (Hos 2:5; Am 2:8). Therefore, as he had warned, God had taken away the privilege of offering that which symbolized purity of devotion. The cutting off of the sacrifices was a severe step of chastisement, though it should also have warned the people of their grave condition.

Joel notes that the priests, the ministers of the Lord, were mourning. The once productive fields were utterly laid waste (cf. Mic 2:4), and the very ground grieved like the priests (cf. Am 1:2). Grain (wheat after threshing), wine (the freshly squeezed fruit), and oil (the fresh juice of the olive) were all considered objects of God's blessing. These were being withdrawn as punishment for their sins (Hos 2:8–13).

11–12 Joel also calls on the farmers and vine keepers to "despair" (cf. Job 6:20; Isa 1:29; 20:5) and to "wail" (cf. v.5), lamenting the loss of the products of the field and of the vineyard and orchard, which symbolized the blessings of the relationship between God and Israel (see Ps 80:8–15; Isa 5:21–6; Jer 2:21; cf. Mt 21:18–21, 28–46). Joel also mentions other trees that were not only important to the economy but were symbols of spiritual nourishment, refreshment, joy, and fruitfulness in the life of the believer (cf. Dt 8:6–10; Ps 92:12; SS 2:3).

13 Joel closes this section with a special plea to the second specially affected segment of society—the priests. They were to gird themselves with sackcloth and to mourn and wail. The prophet demonstrates the urgency of the situation by pleading with them to spend the whole night in their garments of contrition and penitence (cf. Est 4:1–4), because of the loss of the daily sacrifices.

b. Joel's plea for prayer (1:14–20)

14–18 Because the locust plague warned of a still further and more drastic judgment, Joel calls for a solemn assembly for prayer. The priests were to convene the people at the temple for a solemn fast and a season of prayer (cf. Ne 9:1–3; Jer 36:9). The prophet was concerned that the people give a fervent cry of repentance and call on God for forgiveness, lest a greater judgment descend soon.

The reason for the repentant cry was that the Day of the Lord was at hand. The locust plague was a dire warning that the Lord's

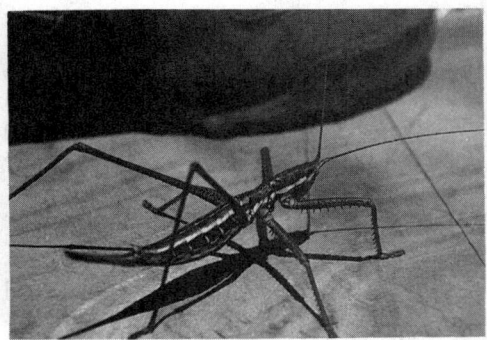

Invasions of giant locusts, "with teeth of a lion" and "fangs of a lioness," still occur in the Middle East today. These two pictures, taken in 1993, show the incredible size of the locusts and their destructive power.

judgment of Judah was imminent. That Day of the Lord was not to be one of vindication for Israel but was to signal its demise (Am 5:16–20). Not only was the Day imminent, it was certain—"like destruction from the Almighty."

The need for penitence and prayer ought to have been obvious from the terrible conditions. Their food had been cut off so that there could be no feasts or offerings of gladness. Worst of all, this had affected the worship in the house of "our God." The physical world too was a shambles. The unfructified grains lay shriveled under their hoes, the barns were desolate, and the granaries were trampled down. All the cattle were without pasturage.

19–20 As an example to the people, Joel breaks forth in a cry to the Lord who alone could forgive and deliver. He again speaks of the loss of pasturage as well as of the trees. What the locusts had not destroyed, a severe summer's heat and drought ruined.

Likewise, the beasts of the field were longing for God. They had to seek higher ground because of the loss of pasture and because the streams had dried up. Joel intimates that they were more sensitive to the basic issues at hand by their panting for God than were God's own people (cf. Isa 1:3). God's message was plain. The barrenness of the land reflected the dryness and decay of the hearts of the people. If their hearts remained unmoved and unrepentant, a worse judgment loomed ahead.

2. Warnings in the light of the coming conflict (2:1–27)

a. Joel's plea for preparation (2:1–11)

1 With the picture of the locust plague before him and the warning of judgment firmly in mind (1:15), Joel portrays a coming army—namely, the Assyrian army of the eighth and seventh centuries B.C. The appearance and activities of the locusts were analogous to a real army. The fitness of the image is seen in Joel's account: in the darkening of the day (vv.2, 10), in the suddenness of the locusts' arrival (v.2), in their horselike appearance (v.4), in the orderliness of the battle (vv.7–8), and in the ubiquitous nature of their devastation (vv.3, 9). Both locusts and armies are known to be the instruments of God's chastening (e.g., Dt 28:38–39; 1Ki 8:35–39; Isa 45:1; Am

4:9). Yet the imagery goes beyond a literal locust plague in 2:1–11 (e.g., vv.3, 6, 10), especially as amplified in the spiritual challenge based on this event in 2:12–27 (cf. vv.17, 20, 26–27).

Joel saw the invaders spread out before the walls of the city. Therefore he cried, "Blow the trumpet . . . sound the alarm!" The trumpet (GK 8795) was made from a ram's horn and was used from earliest times as a signal to battle (e.g., Jdg 3:27; 6:34) or (as here) a signal of imminent danger (e.g., Hos 5:8; 8:1; Am 3:6). "My holy hill" stresses the spiritual basis of the situation. At the sound of the alarm, all would tremble because of the fearfulness of the events that were to take place. It was the Day of the Lord, seen as having arrived in all its frightful consequences!

2–3a That "day" of judgment will be one of darkness and gloominess, of clouds and thick darkness (cf. Am 5:18–20). With the suddenness of dawn spreading over the mountains, a mighty army has appeared, which cast its shadow over the entire face of the land. This army was unrivaled in records prior to Joel's day, and even then Assyria's fall would be due as much to inner stresses as to the combined efforts of the Scythians, Medes, and Babylonians.

3b What had been a scene of beauty would become a picture of utter desolation. Nothing in the land would escape.

4–6 The double figure of locusts and armies must be kept in mind. On the one hand, the locusts had appeared like horses (cf. Job 39:19–20; Rev 9:7). Not only had their swiftness and orderly charge been like a well-disciplined cavalry unit, but their very form was horselike. The clamor of the locusts' flight had been like the din of the dreaded war chariot or the crackling of blazing stubble ignited by a wild fire. The regularity of their advance had been like that of men set in battle array. The awesomeness of their approach had caused great anguish of heart.

On the other hand, Joel relates the dreadfulness of that past scene to the coming devastation by the Assyrian army. He notes first the approach of the war horses, then the frightful war chariots as they crested over the mountain passes above the cities of Judah. He compared the swiftness and noise of their advance to wild fire. He notes the uniformity of the charge of the finely trained and unstoppable host. If the locusts had caused terror, how much more the human invaders!

7–9 The attack of that mighty army was like a locust swarm. They performed as heroic warriors: they climbed the walls of the city, rushed through its streets, and reached the innermost recesses of every place. The mighty men of war first rushed against, then over the walls. All the while each moved straightforward (cf. Jos 6:5), holding his rank and course. Joel depicts the invincibility of the invading soldiers as they unswervingly continued through the city's defenses. Their attack was powerful and swift; they rushed unrestricted throughout the city.

10–11 Joel brings this section to a close by explaining this army's sure success. Its leader was none other than the omnipotent and sovereign God himself. Utilizing epithets that were well-known to every Israelite since the Exodus, Joel depicts God as moving with great might before the Assyrian host, "his army." There were signs on earth (a great shaking) and in heaven (the luminaries darkened). Before the advancing army the thunderstorm raged. The sight of the Assyrian host ought to have been enough to strike terror into the hearts of the people. The accompanying signs of God's visible presence leading that powerful battle array would melt the stoniest of hearts. It was nothing else than the day of the Lord's judgment against his own. Who could endure his visitation?

b. Joel's plea and prescription (2:12–27)

12–14 By means of the introductory phrase "'Even now,' declares the LORD," Joel presents God's concern for his people. Joel pleads with the people for broken and contrite hearts (cf. Ps 51:17): "Return [GK 8740] to me." After reiterating his plea, Joel gives the grounds for its acceptance: God is a God of grace and mercy, who not only has compassion for all in their need (cf. Jnh 4:2), but is a God of love who has revealed himself in redemptive grace (cf. Ex 34:6). God is slow to anger, abundant in his righteous concern for the spiritual welfare of humankind, and willing to forgive people in their evil condition: "He relents from sending calamity."

Since judgment is conditioned on one's failure to meet God's standards, for a person to repent and meet God in his gracious provision is to avert the just judgment. From a human point of view, God would seem to have "changed his mind" or "repented concerning the evil" (cf. Ex 32:14; 2Sa 24:16). God might even restore the forfeited blessings and the fertility of the land so that the discontinued sacrifices might again be offered, this time out of a pure heart.

15–17 Joel issues another call for a solemn assembly (cf. 1:14), this time to convene the people in the light of the revealed invasion that stood so near. All must meet with God and listen to his commandments and act on them.

The priests were to be the first to experience repentance in their lives. Then they were to lead the people in doing the same. The main business was to implore the God of all grace to spare his people, not only for their good, but also that his inheritance be not a reproach before the world or his name be brought into disrepute because of what they had done.

18–19 God promises the repentant heart that his godly jealous love (as a husband for his wife) would move him to have pity on his people. He would immediately restore all that had been lost in the locust plague; they would be fully satisfied (cf. Dt 6:10–11; 8:7–10; 11:13–15) and would no longer be a reproach among the nations.

20 God also pledges to remove "the northern army," most likely a reference to a foreign invader (i.e., the Assyrians) descending from the north. This prediction is built on the incident of the locust plague. If the people would turn to God in genuine repentance, he would drive that army into a dry and desolate land, no doubt the desert west of the Dead Sea and south and southeast of Judah.

A further reason for this turned-about condition, despite her being the Lord's army, would be that Assyria's haughty pride would cause her to leave proper bounds (cf. Pss 35:26; 38:16; cf. also La 1:9), bragging and assuming that the great destruction she was effecting would be her own doing (cf. Eze 35:13; Da 8:4, 8, 11; 11:36–37).

21–27 Should the people truly repent, not only would God's promises of restoration, rest, and protection be theirs, but certain additional benefits would accrue. The message was one of comfort: "Be not afraid."

The first object of God's consoling words was the ground that had suffered so much. It would rejoice and be glad (cf. 1:16); for God himself, who does great things (v.20), would undertake for it. Next God's comfort was directed to the beasts of the field (cf. 1:18–20), who would have an abundance of food. Furthermore, the fig tree and the vine (cf. 1:7, 12), symbols of Israel's relation with her Lord, would bear again in full strength.

This leads to the third and central object of divine solace: Israel herself. The "people of Zion" (all true Israelites) were to rejoice and be glad in the Lord their God, for he would restore them in righteousness. He would send again the refreshing former and latter rains. The arrival of "autumn rain" (at the beginning of the rainy season, Oct-Nov) and the "spring rain" (Mar-Apr) on proper schedule would demonstrate the blessing of God on those with repentant hearts (cf. Dt 11:13–17; Jer 5:24–25; Hos 6:1–3).

Joel next mentions God's supplying the people's third need: renewed provisions—threshing floors filled with grain, vats overflowing with wine and oil. God would thoroughly restore the years that the devastating plague had caused them to lose (cf. 1:4, 10, 17; 2:19). Whereas the locust plague had brought on famine, the people would now experience the full satisfaction of an abundance of food (cf. 2:19). Therefore, they could praise God in the full knowledge of all that his revealed name signifies (cf. Ex 6:3; Dt 12:7; Pss 8:1–2; 66:8–15; 67:57; Am 5:8–9; 9:5–6).

The restored fellowship would be attested by God's renewed designation of them as "my people." They need never again "be shamed," whether by locusts (1:11), among the heathen (2:17), or before the whole world (cf. Isa 29:22; 49:22–23; 54:4). Best of all they would know the abiding presence of God himself, dwelling in their midst (cf. 2:17; 3:17, 21; Hos 11:9).

II. God's Future Intentions: the Eschatological Program (2:28–3:21)

A. The Promise of His Personal Provision (2:28–32)

Since the previous section dealt with the near future, presumably the events prophesied here lay still further beyond. Indeed,

these chapters disclose the Lord's eschatological interventions. Utilizing an apocalyptic style that was even then just emerging, Joel stresses two primary thoughts: the Lord's promise of personal provision in the lives of his own (2:28–32) and the prediction of his final triumph on behalf of his own at the culmination of human history (ch. 3).

1. The outpouring of the Spirit (2:28–31)

28–31 The Lord first promises that he will "pour out" (GK 9161) his Spirit. Hosea prophesied that the Lord must pour out his fury on an idolatrous Israel (5:10); Joel sees beyond this chastisement to the distant future (cf. Eze 36:16–38), when in a measure far more abundant than the promised rain (cf. 2:22–26) God would pour out his Holy Spirit in power. In those days (cf. Jer 33:15) that power would rest on all (i.e., human) flesh (cf. Isa 40:5–6; 66:23; Zec 2:12–13).

God's covenant people are primarily in view. Joel points out that what the Lord intended is that his Holy Spirit would be poured out on all believers, regardless of their age, sex, or status. It would be a time of renewed spiritual activity: prophesying, dreams, and visions (cf. Nu 12:6).

As visible signs of his supernatural intervention, God would cause extraordinary phenomena to be seen in nature. Although the heavens are mentioned first, the order that follows is one of ascending emphasis, beginning with events on earth (blood, fire, and smoke) and moving to signs in the sky (sun and the moon).

The earthly phenomena are no doubt principally concerned with the sociopolitical upheaval in that day: the blood and fire referring to warfare (cf. Nu 21:28; Ps 78:63; Isa 10:16; Zec 11:1; Rev 8:8–9; 14:14–20; et al.) and the rising smoke to gutted cities (cf. Jdg 20:38–40)—though God's activity in the natural world may also play a part (cf. Ex 19:9, 16–18; Rev 6:12, 17). These are to be recognized as well-known signs of the presence of a holy God (for blood, cf. Ex 7:17; 12:22–23; for fire, cf. Ex 3:2–3; 13:21–22; Eze 1:27; Ac 2:3; Heb 12:18; Rev 1:14; for smoke, cf. Ex 19:16–18; Isa 4:4–5; 6:4; Rev 15:8). The very signs speak of a redeemed and refined people eager to do God's will and to carry his message to a needy generation standing under his just judgment.

The heavenly phenomena are also portents of a miraculous nature. There will be a full eclipse of the sun by day (cf. 3:15; Am 5:18–20; 8:9; Zep 1:15); by night the moon will appear to be blood red, perhaps due to conditions caused by an accompanying earthquake (cf. Jer 4:23–24; Rev 6:12–13). All these will signal the advent of that great and terrible Day of the Lord. If the Day of the Lord in the Assyrian invasion would be "great" and "dreadful" (2:11), how much more the eschatological time designated "the great and dreadful day of the LORD"!

The Day of the Lord thus deals with judgment. As to the time of judgment, it could be present (1:15), the near future (Isa 2:12, 22; Jer 46:10; Eze 13:5; Am 5:18–20), the future-eschatological (Isa 13:6, 9; Eze 30:2–3; Ob 15; et al.), or the purely eschatological (Joel 3:14–15; Zec 14:1–21; 1Th 5:1–11; 2Th 2:2; 2Pe 3:10–13). The Day of the Lord, eschatologically speaking, also deals with deliverance for a regathered, repentant Israel (Joel 3:16–21; Zec 14:3; Mal 4:5–6). The NT further reveals that the eschatological Day of the Lord closes with the return of the Lord in glory (Rev 19:11–16) and the Battle of Armageddon (Rev 16:16; 19:17–21; cf. Eze 38–39), continues through the Millennium (Isa 2:1–4; 11:1–12:6; Mic 4:1–5; Rev 20), and culminates in the eternal state (2Pe 3:10–13; Rev 21–22).

2. The outworking of salvation (2:32)

32 Along with the outpouring of the Holy Spirit will be the outworking of salvation for those who truly trust God as Redeemer. To "call on the name of the LORD" is to call on him in believing faith (Pss 99:6; 145:18; Ro 10:3), which gives not only physical deliverance but a spiritual transformation and an abundant entrance into that great millennial period of peace and prosperity, when Judah and Jerusalem are once again spiritual centers for a redeemed Israel (cf. Hos 3:5; Mic 4:6–8).

Joel closes the chapter by balancing this thought with another truth. While salvation-deliverance will be the experience of the one who truly "calls on the name of the LORD" (cf. 2:26) in that day, it is God himself who will summon that remnant.

In Acts 2 Peter viewed Joel's prophecy as applicable to Pentecost (see Ac 2:16). Both his sermon and subsequent remarks are intimately intertwined with Joel's message (cf. Joel 2:30–31 with Ac 2:22–24; Joel 2:32 with

Ac 2:38–40). The intent of Joel's prophecy was not only the restoration of prophecy but that such a gift was open to all classes of people. The Spirit-empowered words of the apostles on Pentecost were evidence of the accuracy of Joel's prediction; they were also a direct fulfillment of Christ's promise to send the Holy Spirit; see Lk 24:49; Jn 14:16–18; 15:26–27; 16:7–15; Ac 1:4–5, 8).

Peter affirmed that Joel's "afterward" must be understood as "in the last days" (cf. Joel 2:28 with Ac 2:17). The point of Peter's remark in Ac 2:16 must be that Pentecost, as the initial day of that period known as "The Last [Latter] Days," will culminate in the return of Jesus and thus certifies the start and character of those final events.

It must also be noted that the outpouring of the Spirit is an accompanying feature of that underlying basic divine promise given to Abraham and the patriarchs, ratified through David, reaffirmed in the terms of the new covenant, and guaranteed in the person and work of Jesus the Messiah (cf. Ge 12:1–3; 15; 17; 2Sa 7:11–29; et al.). At Pentecost two streams of prophecy meet and blend together: Christ's prophetic promise is directly fulfilled; Joel's prophecy is fulfilled but not consummated. It awaits its ultimate fulfillment in the Day of the Lord and the events distinctive to the nation of Israel.

B. The Prediction of His Final Triumph (3:1–21)

1. The tribulation program (3:1–17)

a. The coming of judgment (3:1–8)

1–3 Joel has a new and important announcement. In those future times (cf. 2:29) in which God deals kindly with his covenant people (cf. Jer 33:15–18), he will gather all nations together (cf. Zep 3:8) and enter into judgment with them in the Valley of Jehoshaphat concerning the treatment of his own (cf. Ro 11:25–26).

Judah and Jerusalem will once again be the center of God's attention. The time involved in vv.1–17 is that of the Great Tribulation—a period of Jacob's trouble (cf. Jer 30:7 with Mt 24:21; Mk 13:19, 24) and of great affliction for Israel (Dt 4:30; Da 12:1), a period culminated by God's outpoured wrath against the sinful nations of earth (Isa 13:9, 13; 26:20–21; Zep 1:15–18; Ro 2:5–10; 1Th 1:10; 5:10–11; 2Th 1:6–7; Rev 6:16–17; et al.) and the return of Christ in glory and to judgment (Mt 24:27–31; Mk 13:24–27; Rev 19:11–21).

"The Valley of Jehoshaphat" (lit., "the valley of judgment"), where God enters into judgment with the nations, is not a known valley, as the wordplay makes clear. Joel subsequently called it "the valley of decision" (v.14). The broad valley in the Jerusalem area formed in connection with a cataclysmic earthquake will either be the scene of earth's final battles or will be the climactic stroke in them.

In v.2c, God rehearses the charges against the heathen nations. First, they had scattered his people among the nations, not only after the Fall of Jerusalem, but in their continued dispersion and persecution up to the end times. God himself would have to call his people back to his land (cf. Jer 50:17–26). Second, though the people had divided God's land (cf. Am 7:17), he had not renounced his claim to his people or to his land. Third, so cheaply were his people valued that the heathen had cast lots for them and, even worse, had sold a boy for a prostitute's hire and a girl so that they might drink a flask of wine.

4–8 Joel next records God's solemn promise of the sure execution of his judgment on the nations. He begins with God's question as to their purposes regarding himself. The districts of western Canaan, Tyre, and Sidon (well-known slave dealers in the ancient world) and the Philistine coast (often condemned with the Phoenicians by the prophets) are singled out as the primary enemies of Judah, who committed the most inhuman of all crimes—dealing in human merchandise. God warns them that if they would now add insult to injury by taking vengeance without cause against the Lord himself, they could be assured that God would most swiftly repay them in just kind.

The detailed charges against the nations are that they had taken the silver and gold of God's people (probably by plundering their handsomely furnished houses) to their palaces. Furthermore, they had sold the Jewish children into the hands of the Greek slave-traders, sending them far away.

God warns these enemies that he would righteously repay them in kind (cf. Isa 24:14–23; 2Th 1:6–8), while arousing his dispersed and captive people from the distant lands of their bondage. As he had warned them (v.4),

he would give those slave dealers a taste of their own medicine. Their people would in turn be sold into captivity by the children of Judah to the Sabeans who would send them far away.

Joel's prophecy, though intended for the end times, is also made historically applicable by being based on the current situation of his day. Not only would the great coalition of the future surely fall, but Uzziah's recapture of Ezion-Geber and his successes against the Philistines served as a warning of the dangerous position in which these allied commercial enemies of Joel's day stood.

b. The challenge in judgment (3:9–17)

9–12 The Lord's message is to be circulated among the nations (cf. Am 3:6–11). All the men of war were to assemble and prepare themselves in accordance with the proper spiritual rites before battle (cf. 1Sa 7:5–9), for in the final analysis theirs was to be the culmination of all holy warfare. The mighty men of battle were to be called up for duty (cf. 2:7). All segments of society and the economy were to be on a wartime footing. The basic agricultural tools were to be fashioned into weapons; weak and cowardly men were to count themselves as mighty men of war. The nations were soon to learn that the Lord too was mighty in battle (cf. Ex 15:3; Ps 24:8).

The surrounding nations are next commanded to come quickly and gather themselves together (cf. Pss 2:1–2; 110:1–3, 5–6) to that great final struggle that will culminate earth's present history (cf. Isa 17:12; 24:21–23; Mic 4:11–13; Zec 12:2–33; 14:1–3; Rev 16:14–16; 19:17–19). The thought of this climactic event causes the prophet to exclaim, "Bring down your warriors, O LORD!"—a reference to the angelic host (cf. Dt 33:2b–3; Pss 68:17; 103:19–20; Zec 14:5) of our mighty God. Whereas God's mighty ones had been the Gentile armies (ch. 2), God was now against those forces. Joel cries out for their just destruction.

The nations are bidden to come to the Valley of Jehoshaphat (see comment on v.2). The Lord had warned that he would enter into litigation with the enemies of his people; now he sits as judge to impose sentence on them (cf. Isa 28:5–6; Mt 25:31–46).

13–17 God is pictured as sending his reapers into the harvest field (cf. Rev 14:14–20) and to the winepress of judgment (Isa 63:3), for the nations are ripe for judgment; their wickedness is great and filled to overflowing. The confused and clamoring throng of nations and the tumultuous uproar and din of battle in this great day of reckoning are vividly portrayed (cf. Eze 38:21–23; Zec 14:13). The valley named Jehoshaphat (3:2, 12), in accordance with its purpose of being the place of final accomplishment, is now called "the valley of decision."

The accompanying signs in the natural world are depicted. What was applicable to the local scene of impending battle in the day of the Assyrian invasion (2:10b) is now seen in all its final intensity. The Lord comes forth out of Zion as a roaring lion (cf. Am 1:2). Because the nations had roared insolently against God's people (Isa 5:25–30), the Lord would be as a lion roaring after its prey in behalf of the returned remnant (cf. Hos 11:10–11 with Jer 25:30–33). Heaven and earth will tremble at his presence among the nations (cf. Ps 29; Isa 29:6–8; 30:30–31; Zec 14:37; Rev 16:16–18).

But the very manifestation of his coming, so fearful for the nations (cf. Rev 6:12–17), gives assurance of protection and strength for God's own (cf. Isa 26:20–21). As Israel had learned of God's sovereign concern for his people through judgment (cf. Eze 6:7), now she would know of his eternal compassion through her deliverance and his abiding presence with her (cf. 2:27). In contrast to the nations who would learn who God really is (cf. Eze 6:36–38; 39:6–7), Israel would know the redeeming power and the continuous enjoyment of his glorious presence with her forever (cf. Isa 49:22–26; Jer 24:7; Eze 34:27–30; Zec 2:8–9; et al.). Because the Lord himself is there (cf. 2:32; 3:21), Jerusalem will be everlastingly holy (cf. Isa 52:1; 60:14, 21; Zec 14:21; Rev 21:2). None but his own shall again set foot in it.

2. The millennial prosperity (3:18–21)

18 Joel looks beyond the great battle to the resultant millennial scene. He concludes his prophecy by contrasting the judgment of the nations—typified by Israel's most protracted antagonist, Edom, and by her most persistent source of spiritual defeat, Egypt—with the blessings that will rest on the repentant, restored, and revitalized people of God.

In glowing and hyperbolic terms, Joel describes the great fertility of soil of the coming Millennial Age. What had been cut off in the locust plague of Joel's day due to sin (1:5) will be commonplace in that era permeated by the presence of the Holy One (cf. 2:19–27; Isa 55:1). The formerly barren hills will flourish again with vegetation. The wadis, dried by the drought of God's judgment, will flow again, giving renewed vitality to the land, as God pours out his blessing on people of renewed spiritual vitality (cf. Isa 30:25–26; Eze 34:13–14).

In Jerusalem a fountain will issue forth from the house of the Lord. Ezekiel (47:1–12) reported that it will terminate in the Dead Sea, transforming it from salt water to fresh water. Zechariah (14:8) spoke of a great flow of water from Jerusalem emptying into both the Dead Sea and the Mediterranean Sea, a prophecy that, once incredible, now stands authenticated by recent geological discoveries.

Joel goes on to say that these waters will gush through the Wadi Shittim (see NIV note). The exact location of this place is uncertain and has occasioned many suggestions. Perhaps the best solution is to identify it with a barren valley east of Judah, where the Israelites suffered spiritual failure before making the last encampment prior to their entrance into the Promised Land (cf. Nu 25:1; 33:49; Jos 3:1).

19 Joel next contrasts the future condition of Judah and Jerusalem with that of Egypt and Edom, longtime adversaries of Israel. In contrast with their desolation, Judah and Jerusalem will be inhabited forever. All Judah's sins will be forgiven, and the Lord himself will abide in her midst forever (cf. Eze 48:35).

20–21 Joel's last prophetic view is a picture of Israel's everlasting felicity. The reason for this state of unending happiness is apparent. The Lord himself will "dwell" (GK 8905; related to the word "tabernacle," GK 5438) in her midst in all his glory (cf. 3:17; Zec 8:3–8). From the Hebrew word *shakan* used here, theologians have spoken of the Lord's "*shekinah* glory." Throughout the OT this *shekinah* glory designates the active presence *now* of the invisible God who transcends the universe he created. However, because of the spiritual and moral decay that had led to religious formalism and open idolatry, that glory left the temple and Jerusalem (Eze 10; 11:22–25) to return not at all till that day of God's future temple (Eze 43:1–12), when God would again redeem his people and dwell among a repentant, regenerated, and grateful people (Zec 2:10–13).

Before that millennial scene, the NT writers reveal that God has another "tabernacling" with people. His unique Son became flesh, dwelling among us (Jn 1:14) as the promised Immanuel (Isa 7:14). Having redeemed a lost humanity through his death and resurrection, and being ascended into heaven, he now dwells in his own whom he has taken into union with himself (Eph 1:15–2:21; Col 1:15–22, 27; 2:9–10). As the triumphant Redeemer, he has given to the church, his body, gifts of which it is steward (Eph 4:8–10). The believer's destiny is to enjoy God's presence forever (Rev 21:2–3).

The Old Testament in the New

OT Text	NT Text	Subject
Joel 2:28–32	Ac 2:17–21	God's Spirit poured out
Joel 2:32	Ro 10:13	Salvation in the Lord

Amos

INTRODUCTION

1. Background

In many ways the eighth century B.C. was unique in the history of Judah and Israel. It witnessed the toppling of the northern kingdom from the glory of economic prosperity and international influence to virtual subjugation by a foreign power. It also witnessed the near collapse of Judah, averted only by the steadying hand of King Hezekiah, who could do no more than slow Judah's progress toward certain ruin.

At the same time, however, the eighth century witnessed the rise of one of the most potent moral forces the world has ever known—the writing prophets. These men shared an overwhelming conviction that God had called them. They denounced the sins of their contemporaries and also looked far into the future as they spoke of deliverance for both Jew and Gentile.

The dawn of the eighth century brought new hope to Israel and Judah. Israel's subjugation to Damascus ended abruptly when the Assyrians under Adad-nirari III crushed Damascus in 802 B.C. The internal difficulties that had plagued Judah also ended with Uzziah's accession to the throne (792–740 B.C.). He built up a powerful army and increased Judah's mercantile activities. In the northern kingdom, Jeroboam II (793–753 B.C.) came to the throne at roughly the same time as Uzziah. This king of Israel restored much of the territory that had fallen to Damascus (2Ki 14:28).

The conquest of Damascus and the attendant quiescence of Assyria, coupled with the brilliant leadership of Uzziah and Jeroboam, brought Judah and Israel to heights of prominence second only to Solomon's golden age. The kingdoms prospered and expanded their borders. But as their economic well-being and national strength continued to foster their security, an internal decay was at work. It was primarily moral because it involved a basic violation of the covenant established by God at Sinai.

The covenantal stipulations required loyalty to God and love toward one's fellow human beings. Yet the idolatrous worship of their pagan neighbors had infiltrated the two kingdoms, producing a strange syncretistic worship. While pagan high places dotted the countryside and people disobeyed God by worshiping idols that stood within the cities, they continued to trust in such concepts as the "day of the LORD" (5:18) and aspects of Levitical worship (4:4–5). Furthermore, they violated the social legislation of the covenant. Amos was particularly vehement in denouncing lack of social concern.

The erosion of Israel's social structure showed itself primarily in a cleavage between the rich and the poor. The improved economic situation in Israel led to an increase of the wealthy, who not only neglected the poor, but used them to increase their own wealth. God's will, as it applied to the nation of Israel, was ignored, and this spurred the eighth-century prophets to action. Their protest largely contributed to the establishment of a believing remnant. The prophets preserved faith by assuring the people that God had not forsaken his promise.

2. Authorship and Date

Almost all agree that the prophecy of Amos is an authentic production of the man whose name it bears. The consonance of his message with the eighth-century milieu and his forthright style make it difficult to think otherwise. Little is known of him apart from the sketchy references in the superscription and the body of the prophecy. Amos lived and worked in Tekoa (1:1), a town ten miles south of Jerusalem. He was a shepherd and also tended sycamore trees (7:14). God then called him to be a prophet. His character, molded in the harsh terrain of the wilderness of Tekoa, enabled him to stand before the priest and the people, proclaiming the word God had given him.

We may best place the prophetic activity of Amos in the latter half of the reign of Jeroboam II (793–753 B.C.; cf. 7:10). It would certainly have taken some time for the affluence during Jeroboam's reign to lead to the social decay that was so widespread when Amos carried out his mission to the northern kingdom. But it is difficult to find a more exact time in which Amos's mission would fit. Jotham, Uzziah's son, acceded to the regency of Judah when Uzziah was stricken with leprosy (c. 750 B.C.). That 1:1 mentions only Uzziah and not Jotham may point to a time before Jotham's accession. The phrase "two years before the earthquake" (1:1) limits the date of the prophecy to a narrow period. This earthquake may have occurred around 760 B.C., according to excavations at Hazor. Thus it seems best to place the prophetic ministry of Amos shortly before 760 B.C.

3. Theological Values

Central in Amos's preaching is his belief in divine sovereignty. The Lord is the God of history. He effects the migrations of peoples (9:7) and controls the orderly progression of natural phenomena (4:3; 5:8). Yet within that sovereign domain, humankind has the freedom to bow in submission to the Lord or to reject him.

Amos affirmed the historical election of Israel (3:2). But he preached strongly against the perverted concept of election which held that God was unconditionally committed to the nation. Their election alone did not guarantee national blessing, for the sovereign God promised that the people of Israel would be his "treasured possession" (Ex 19:5) only if they obeyed him and kept his covenant.

A unique concept in Amos is his teaching about the Day of the Lord. Rather than being a day of national deliverance, it would be a time when the Lord would judge all sin, even in his own people. The gloomy portrayal of that day in this book reflects the fact that Amos's hearers were guilty of many transgressions. But Amos also predicted another coming Day, when hope will shine forth with glorious promise (9:13–15). This Davidic promise will be realized when David's kingdom is restored and Jews and Gentiles are united in the kingdom of David's Greater Son.

EXPOSITION

I. Superscription (1:1)

1 The prophecy is introduced by the formula "the words of Amos." Frequently this expression is used for collections of sayings or oracles (cf. 1:1; Pr 30:1; 31:1; Ecc 1:1).

The word translated "shepherd" (GK 5924) is not the usual word for shepherd; it implies that he was a breeder and supplier of sheep (2Ki 3:4). In Am 7:14 another word is used for shepherd to describe Amos's occupation (GK 1012); this word suggests that Amos kept cattle as well as sheep. Thus likely Amos was a breeder of various types of animals.

Amos's character and ideals were shaped by the desert. Being "neither a prophet nor a prophet's son" (7:14), he was not part of the prophetic movement in Judah. Undoubtedly his simple life in the desert led him to see more clearly the evils of city life.

The prophetic word of Amos concerned Israel, no doubt the northern kingdom. The numerous references to localities in the north as well as the encounter with Amaziah support this.

Uzziah (or Azariah), king of Judah, was an energetic king whose policies contributed to the resurgence of Judah in the eighth century. He rebuilt the city of Elath and strengthened the defenses of Jerusalem. Jeroboam II, king of Israel, was a vigorous leader. His greatest accomplishment was the expansion of Israelite territorial holdings into the Transjordan (2Ki 14:23–29).

II. Introduction to the Prophecy (1:2)

2 Verse 2 forms an appropriate introduction to the entire prophecy. The name "LORD" ("Yahweh"; GK 3378), which introduces the prophecy, connotes God's redemptive and covenantal concerns. The Exodus gave the name its greatest revelational content. Moses' first impression of God's character was the Lord's inviolable holiness (Ex 3:5). The awesome phenomena accompanying his appearance on Sinai (Ex 19:16–25) and the restrictions he placed on the people (Ex 19:10–15) enforced the concept of his holiness.

The prophet introduces a shocking note in depicting the Lord as roaring from Zion (cf. Joel 3:16). Linked with the roar of the Lord in Joel and here in Amos is the crashing of thunder (cf. Job 37:4). "Thunders" appears in a number of passages depicting God's intervention in history (Pss 18:13; cf. v.6; 46:6–11; Jer 10:13; 51:16; Joel 2:11). In some of these passages God's power is expressed in natural phenomena, most frequently in a violent thunderstorm.

The roar of the Lord is accompanied by cosmic changes. But instead of a storm, God's wrath causes a withering drought to destroy the green hills of Mount Carmel—a landmark of the northern kingdom.

III. The Prophetic Oracles (1:3–6:14)

A. Oracles of Judgment Against the Surrounding Nations (1:3–2:5)

A striking pattern runs through these oracles. The prophet begins with the distant city of Damascus and moves in ever-tightening circles till at last he pounces on Israel. One can imagine Amos's hearers approving the denunciation of these heathen nations and even applauding God's denunciation of Judah. But Amos plays no favorites; he swoops down on the unsuspecting Israelites as well.

1. The oracle against Syria (1:3–5)

3 Damascus represented the entire nation of Syria (Aram). From the time of Ahab till the dawn of the eighth century, there were hostilities between Israel and Damascus. Particularly embarrassing had been the incursion of Syria into Israelite territory during the reign of Jehu (2Ki 10:32–33).

The numerical motif—"for three sins ... even for four"—is common in Semitic literature (e.g., Job 5:19; 33:29; Pr 6:16; 30:15–31; Ecc 11:2; Mic 5:5–6) and is not always to be taken literally. Sometimes it denotes an indefinite number, as here. Amos cites only one crime of Damascus in this oracle.

The lack of immediate reference to a specific punishment following the statement "for three sins of" creates a feeling of dread uncertainty. The attention of the hearers would have been riveted on the prophet's words as they waited for the explicit judgment that comes in the last section of each oracle. The crime that provoked the judgment against Damascus was that the people had threshed Gilead with iron threshing sledges. Gilead, an extensive region east of the Jordan River, was known for its rich forests (Jer 22:6–7) and balm (Jer 8:22). Its richness, coupled with its being a frontier region, made it the object of numerous attacks by Ammon and Syria.

The incident Amos refers to here is probably the one recorded in 2Ki 13:1–9, where an incursion of the Syrians into Israel is described as making the army of Jehoahaz "like the dust at threshing time" (v.7). The threshing sledge was made of parallel boards fitted with sharp points. The metaphor implies extreme decimation and cruel or inhuman treatment.

4 The judgment the Lord decrees for Syria is "fire upon the house of Hazael." Hazael ruled Syria about 841 to 806 B.C. (cf. 2Ki 8:13). The Lord had revealed that Hazael would commit monstrous crimes against the Israelites (2Ki 8:12). When he came to the throne, he fought against Joram and Ahaziah at Ramoth Gilead, seriously wounding Joram (2Ki 8:28–29).

Ben-Hadad ("son of Hadad," an ancient storm god) is the name of two or possibly three kings of Syria. It may be a dynastic name. Ben-Hadad I, a contemporary of Baasha of Israel (909–886 B.C.) and Asa of Judah (911–870 B.C.), took large holdings from Baasha (1Ki 15:20). Each "Ben-Hadad" carried on continual hostilities against Israel. Likely the Ben-Hadad Amos had in mind was the son of Hazael (2Ki 13:3).

The "fire" is not a description of an isolated occurrence relating only to Damascus but appears in all the oracles except the one against Israel (2:6–16). It is perhaps a metaphorical representation of God's judgment (cf. 7:4).

5 The destruction of Damascus involved breaking the "gate of Damascus." Ancient gates were equipped with massive bars, sometimes of iron or bronze (1Ki 4:13). The breaking of the bar implies that the enemies had gained entrance to the city.

The identity of the places mentioned in this verse is difficult. The "Valley of Aven" was likely the plain between the Lebanon and Anti-Lebanon ranges. Beth Eden was probably an important city located on the Euphrates River. Kir is understood by Amos as the place of the national origin of the Syrians (9:7) and the place to which they would return. His prophecy was fulfilled when Tiglath-pileser took the people of Damascus captive and transported them to Kir (2Ki 16:9).

2. The oracle against the Philistines (1:6–8)

6–8 The prophet next turns to the Philistines, the perennial enemies of the Israelites who may have had their national origin in the Aegean area, probably Crete. They occupied the coastal plain in southwest Palestine and conducted numerous raids on the Israelites until their power was broken by King David.

Amos mentions four of the cities of the Philistine pentapolis in this oracle, excluding only Gath. Perhaps Gath never fully recovered from Uzziah's successful military campaign described in 2Ch 26:6, an event that occurred sometime between Amaziah's death (767 B.C.) and Amos's ministry (760 B.C.). Gath is excluded from all the lists of the Philistine cities cited after Amos (Jer 25:20; Zep 2:4; Zec 9:5–6).

The Philistines are denounced for the crime of enslavement—again a social crime. The event referred to was probably a series of border raids in which slaves were secured and sold to the Edomites. "Whole communities" were taken, thus underscoring the enormity of the crime. Likely the crime was committed against Israelites. The punishment to be inflicted on the Philistines was their absolute destruction.

3. The oracle against Tyre (1:9–10)

9–10 Amos has moved from Damascus in the northeast to the Philistine territory in the southwest. He moves next to Tyre, to the north of Israel and southwest of Damascus and thus closer to Israel than Damascus and

These are the ruins of the fortified Philistine city of Ashkelon, one of the cities of their pentapolis (cf. Jos 13:3).

the Philistine cities. Tyre was the most important city of Phoenicia at that time.

The crime of Tyre also involved enslavement of "whole communities," but to this Amos adds a reference to its "disregarding a treaty of brotherhood." This may refer to the pact made between Hiram, king of Tyre, and Solomon (1Ki 5:12; cf. "brother" in 1Ki 9:13). This relationship was strengthened by the marriage of Jezebel, daughter of Eth-baal, king of the Sidonians, to King Ahab (1Ki 16:31). While Jehu's purge of the family of Ahab (2Ki 10) interrupted the good relationship between the two states, Amos may have been referring to the generally amicable relations that characterized these nations over their long histories.

Tyre's security, however, was only temporary. It came under Assyrian hegemony during the long period of that empire's dominance but emerged from Assyrian control to enter a period of power and affluence. Later, Tyre was besieged by the forces of Nebuchadnezzar and never fully recovered. The massive efforts required for its defense greatly weakened the city.

4. The oracle against Edom (1:11–12)

11 The extensive, mountainous region of Edom lay southeast of the southern tip of the Dead Sea, east of the Arabah. It was one of the three Transjordanian kingdoms that included Ammon and Moab. Edom's crime was that "he pursued his brother with a sword" and "his anger raged continually"—a reference to the long-standing animosity of Edom toward the Israelites.

Edom was another name for Esau, the twin brother of Jacob. The Edomites and Israelites thus had close ethnic ties (cf. "brother" in Nu 20:14; Dt 23:7; Ob 12). The bitter relations between Jacob and Esau were perpetuated in the affairs of the two countries. In their desert journey the Israelites sought access to the king's highway that ran through Edom, but the Edomites refused passage and even sent a military force to block them (Nu 20:14–21). Later, the Edomites were enemies of Saul (1Sa 14:47), David (2Sa 8:14), and Jehoram (2Ki 8:20–22). Their greatest act of hostility against Israel occurred during the sack of Jerusalem by Nebuchadnezzar in 587 B.C. At that time the Edomites gloated over the destruction of their enemies and hindered the fugitives' escape, delivering many over to their captors (Ob 10–14).

The crime of Edom was in many ways similar to that of the other nations Amos speaks against—violence against one's fellow human beings. Amos emphasizes that the Edomites stifled "all compassion" (cf. Jas 4:11; 1Jn 2:9).

12 For these crimes the cities of Teman and Bozrah were to be destroyed. Teman, one of the largest cities of Edom, and Bozrah, a strong fortress city in the north of Edom, represent the whole country (cf. Isa 34:8; 63:1; Jer 49:13, 20; Eze 25:13; Ob 9). Edom became tributary to Tiglath-pileser III in 732 B.C. and was later overrun by the Nabataeans.

5. The oracle against Ammon (1:13–15)

13 Ammon lay northeast of the Dead Sea and north of Moab. The area was dominated by a vast expanse of desert, though the valley of the upper Jabbok in the north Ammon was fertile. The origin of the Ammonites (and the Moabites) was an incestuous relationship between Lot and his two daughters (see Ge 19:30–38). The Ammonites frequently sought to enlarge their territory, sometimes with the help of Moab and Syria (cf. Jdg 10:6–9). A serious threat to Israel by the Ammonites was quelled by the strong, personal leadership of Saul (1Sa 11:1–11). They were finally subdued in David's time (2Sa 12:26–31).

The crime Amos accuses the Ammonites of was like that of the other nations. They "ripped open the pregnant women of Gilead." Gilead was a mountainous region east of the Jordan, in the tribal territories of Gad and the half-tribe of Manasseh. This crime evidently took place in one of their attempts to expand their territorial holdings at Israel's expense (cf. 2Ki 8:12)—a crime that went far beyond necessary acts of war and is attributed to the Ammonites' insatiable desire for Israelite territory. Apparently it was a notorious event, and its mention would stir feelings of revulsion in Amos's hearers.

14–15 Rabbah was the capital of ancient Ammon. Ammon was to be destroyed by fire, to the accompaniment of the shouts of battle and "violent winds." The word translated "war cries" refers to the shout of the enemy "on the day of battle," a sound that would terrify the people as the enemy rushed to take the city. The word "winds" describes the great force with which the enemy would sweep over the city. The king of Ammon was to go into exile along with his officials. Ezekiel berated them for rejoicing at the fall of Jerusalem (Eze 25:1–7). Yet their rejoicing was to last only a little while, for they were caught up in the same turmoil that affected Israel. Nebuchadnezzar sacked the city of Rabbah and took large numbers of its citizens captive. Thereupon the Ammonites passed from history for good.

6. The oracle against Moab (2:1–3)

1 Moab (for their origin, see comment on 1:13) lay to the east of the Dead Sea, between Ammon and Edom. Antipathy between the Israelites and Moabites developed early when the king of Moab would not grant them permission to use the king's highway (Jdg 11:17). As a result the Moabites were excluded from the assembly of Israel (cf. Dt 23:3–4).

The Israelites camped in the plains of Moab before entering Canaan (Nu 22:1). The king of Moab engaged Balaam, the enigmatic seer, to curse them (Nu 22:4–6). There the Moabite women seduced the Israelites to join in their idolatrous worship (Nu 25:1–3). During a period of Israelite weakness, a coalition of Moabites, Ammonites, and Amalekites invaded Israel and subjugated them for eighteen years (Jdg 3:13–14).

Saul defeated the Moabites (1Sa 14:47), as did David (2Sa 8:2). During Solomon's reign Moab seems to have remained under Israelite dominion, for Solomon included Moabite women among his many wives (1Ki 11:1). But Mesha, king of Moab, rebelled against Israel after the death of Ahab (2Ki 1:1). Joram of Israel and Jehoshaphat of Judah, along with the king of Edom, made an abortive attempt to subdue them (2Ki 3). Later Hazael, an Aramean king, wrested from Jehu the disputed Moabite territory north of the Arnon (2Ki 10:32–33).

The crime Amos charges the Moabites with was their burning of the bones of the king of Edom. This may have taken place during the attempt of the coalition of the kings of Israel, Judah, and Edom to suppress the Moabite rebellion (2Ki 3). The expression "burn the bones" usually refers to the burning of the skeletal remains of a corpse (2Ki 23:20; cf. v.16; cf. also 1Ki 13:2; Eze 24:10) or the burning of the corpse itself (Am 6:9–10). Thus the crime of Moab involved the desecration of the body of an Edomite king.

2–3 The punishment of Moab was to be a fire that would consume Kerioth—a major city in Moab (cf. Jer 48:24). Amos uses vivid language to describe the conflict that would overthrow Moab. One can almost hear the "war cries" and "the blast of the trumpet."

Moab became subject to Tiglath-pileser III in 734 B.C. Later it was involved in a rebellion against Assyrian domination that was quelled by Sennacherib. During the period of Babylonian supremacy, Moab was forced to pay tribute to Babylon. The Moabites rebelled against Babylon shortly after 598 B.C. and were conquered by Nebuchadnezzar. Like Ammon, the nation of Moab disappeared from history.

It is significant that Amos here pronounces the punishment of the Lord on a social crime involving a non-Israelite. In his other oracles the crimes were, for the most part, against the covenant people. But Amos understands that an aspect of God's law transcends Israel. He affirms a moral law that extends to noncovenant nations, a law that would surely bring punishment if violated. The Moabites were held liable for the law of social responsibility—respect for human dignity and for the rights of all people.

7. The oracle against Judah (2:4–5)

4–5 Having pronounced judgment on various pagan nations, Amos next turns to Judah. Judah is condemned for rejecting the "law of the LORD." This is the first time this expression occurs in these oracles, and its significance is obvious. Those who stood in relationship to the covenant were judged on the basis of the light they possessed in God's law, not on the basis of a common moral consciousness.

"Led astray" connotes "to wander around" (GK 9494). It is used of straying animals and intoxicated persons. Judah had been led astray by "false gods." The expression "walked after them" frequently relates to following false gods. This sin of idolatry caused Judah to violate the law of the Lord. Like their fathers of old, they continued to bow down to the false gods of the pagans and to spurn the Creator.

Judah's punishment was to be similar to that of the other nations—destruction by the fire of war. It was inflicted when Jerusalem fell to the Babylonians in 612 B.C.

B. Oracles of Judgment Against Israel (2:6–6:14)

1. A lesson from history (2:6–16)

6 The Israelites were accused of selling "the righteous for silver" and "the needy for a pair of sandals." The word "righteous" parallels "needy," establishing a connection between them. The word "righteous" (GK 7404) connotes "righteousness," not in the sense of blamelessness, but rather in the basic sense of "rightness" or "justice." The needy are seen as being in the right, or as having a just cause (cf. Ex 23:7; Dt 25:1). This shows us something of the social conditions of that time when the poor had to fight for their just rights.

"They" applies to the oppressing classes, especially the judges and creditors who "sell the righteous." These people of power and influence were guilty of accepting bribes. They regarded the oppressed classes so lightly that they accepted such paltry bribes as a pair of sandals.

7 Amos further describes the oppression of the poor as trampling "on the heads of the poor." The word translated "trample" (GK 8635) may also have the sense of "pant," suggesting the rendering, "who pant after the dust of the earth on the head of the poor." This means either that the oppressing classes longed to see the poor brought to extreme anguish or that they were so avaricious that they craved even the dust that the poor had cast on their heads as a sign of sorrow (e.g., 2Sa 1:2; Job 2:12).

Israel's decadence was marked by sexual promiscuity. The word for "girl" is general and has no specific connotations. Most likely the sin depicted here relates to the ancient laws against incest (Lev 18:6–18; 20:17–21), as indicated by "profane my holy name" (cf. Lev 22:32, which culminates a lengthy section on personal and social purity). The use of one girl by both a father and a son was tantamount to incest in that the son uncovered the nakedness of his father and vice versa. Furthermore, the marital purity and faithfulness expected in a godly father were lacking, as both father and son engaged in deliberate acts of disobedience to God.

8 Amos pictures members of his society as sleeping by the altars on "garments taken in pledge." Clothing was valid collateral for securing debts. Hebrew law, however, required that such garments be restored to the owner each evening (Ex 22:26–27) as a covering during sleep. Many obviously disregarded this law. The placing of this practice "beside every altar" emphasizes the great disparity between religion and practice in Israel. This is further illustrated by the people's drinking in the "house of their god" the wine paid as fines.

9 Amos next recounts God's gracious acts during Israel's past. "Amorite" is sometimes used for the preconquest population of Canaan (Ge 15:16). The prophet reminds the people of God's destruction of the powerful Canaanites in the Conquest. The great height and strength of the Canaanites reflect a tradition begun at the return of the spies from their reconnaissance of Canaan (Nu 13:22–33). It points to their apparent invincibility and contrasts it with the might of the Lord. Amos's vivid metaphor of the fruit and the roots portrays the destruction of the Canaanites when the Israelites took the Promised Land.

10 Amos sees the Exodus and the forty years of wandering in the desert as expressions of the gracious power of the Lord. Thus there was no need for him to mention Israel's disobedience during that time. He simply points out that the Lord gave them "the land of the Amorites."

11–12 The raising up of prophets and Nazirites was another of God's gracious acts. These two groups ministered God's word to Israel and showed the Lord's care for their spiritual welfare. The word "Nazirite" (GK 5687) conveys the idea of "separate" and denotes the consecration practiced by this group. The Nazirites took special vows of separation (cf. Nu 6:1–12), abstaining from partaking of any product of the vine and vowing neither to cut their hair nor to touch a dead body. They were an influence for good in Israel. But now Israel was forcing them to drink wine and to violate their vows, and they were muzzling the prophets. This was tantamount to rejecting the word of the Lord.

13–16 Amos's rehearsal of Israel's rejection of the God who acted on their behalf—from Egypt to the present—leads to his statement of doom. The coming judgment is vividly expressed in a series of images rapidly moving from one familiar realm to another. First, Amos pictures the nation as being crushed under the wheels of a heavily laden cart. This reflects Amos's familiarity with the agricultural world. The other images include a swift runner, a strong man, and a warrior—all depicting Israel's inability to escape the impending destruction. The archer cannot stand. The brave warriors will flee with nothing left, their weapons and armor scattered behind as on a battlefield. In other words, the sword of the Lord that had fought for them would be turned against them. The oracle closes with an awesome note of finality—"declares the LORD."

2. A lesson based on cause and effect (3:1–12)

1 A summons to hear the "word of the LORD" introduces this oracle. It is directed against "the whole family I brought up out of Egypt" and thus seems to include Judah as well as Israel. Amos did not have high hopes for Judah (2:5), and he would never have exempted them from divine wrath because of their disobedience. The pronouncement of judgment, addressed primarily to the northern kingdom, warned Judah and Israel against thinking that their election by the Lord was sufficient ground for their national security; for God demanded personal obedience as well.

2 The statement "you only have I chosen of all the families of the earth" establishes Israel's elective privilege. The word "chosen" is literally "known" (GK 3359) and bears a special sense of intimacy. It includes the idea of God's sovereign activity whereby the object of that knowledge is set apart or chosen for a divine purpose (cf. Jer 1:5). Israel's privilege, however, incurred her punishment. Elective privilege entails responsibility. Because Israel failed to live up to her holy calling, she would be punished (cf. vv.11–12).

3–5 The words of judgment are preceded by a series of questions that culminate in an affirmation of Amos's prophetic authority. The first questions all anticipate a negative answer. Amos asks, Is it customary for two to walk together without agreeing to do so? Certainly not for an extended period of time. Does a lion roar when it is stalking its prey? Hardly. Is a bird ensnared without someone setting a trap or is a snare sprung unless something triggers it? Not likely.

6 To this point each question has begun with the effect followed by the cause. But now the order is reversed. Here the cause is the blast of the trumpet and the effect is the fear it brings to the city dwellers. The sound of the trumpet from a city wall warned of invaders, or the trumpet in the square heralded bad news. Ultimately the cause of the "disaster" coming to a city is "the LORD." The figures in these questions are not necessarily representations of Israel or her enemies but simply vivid analogies from life intended to illustrate the forthcoming conclusion (v.8).

7 "Plan" (GK 6051) has as its basic meaning the thought of "intimacy." It may connote a close relationship (Ge 49:6; Job 29:4; Ps 111:1; Jer 6:11) or the scheming of those united against others (Pss 64:2; 83:3). It may refer to something as intimate as a secret (Pr 11:13; 25:9) or close fellowship with a friend (Ps 55:14). When used of God, it refers to his secret council (Job 15:8) or the intimate relationship the righteous have with God in which he "makes his covenant known to them" (Ps 25:14) and takes them "into his confidence" (Pr 3:32).

8 "The lion has roared" sounds an alarm. There is indeed cause for fear—not from any lion or blast of a trumpet, but from the Lord's voice through his prophet. The Lord has spoken, and no one can contravene his word. So Amos is about to pronounce judgment on the people.

9 Amos summons the Egyptians and the Philistines of Ashdod to witness the oppression going on within Samaria. Amos may have chosen these nations because of their past oppression of Israel. It is as though Amos was asking these nations to view the violence being done by the rich and powerful against their poor neighbors in Samaria, a kind of oppression that even the pagan nations had never seen.

10 The Israelites were different from other aggressors because they plundered and looted in their own fortresses rather than in enemy territory. By oppressing the poorer classes, they had been plundering their own people; and Ashdod and Egypt were called to witness this evil. "They do not know how to do right," Amos declared of the Israelites. Their moral sense had become so warped that right and wrong were blurred.

11 "Therefore" logically connects the judgment segment of the oracle with the accusation stated in v.10. The following section of doom is a warning for those who flagrantly violated the covenant by treating a holy God lightly. Though the enemy who would overrun the land is not identified by Amos, historically we know it was Assyria.

12 Amos concludes the oracle with the analogy of a shepherd who retrieves the remains of an animal from the mouth of a lion. This reflects the Mosaic law, for a shepherd was required to produce the remains of an animal killed while in his care as proof that he did not steal it (Ex 22:13).

Amos goes on to describe how the Israelites, "those who sit in Samaria on the edge of their beds and in Damascus on their couches," would be "saved." As the remaining parts of the slaughtered animal attest to its destruction, so the broken remains of the wealth of Israel would be a pathetic witness to the complete destruction of that kingdom.

3. An oracle against the house of Jacob (3:13–15)

13 The command to hear is not addressed to Israel, for it goes on to say, "and testify against the house of Jacob." But this is best understood as a rhetorical statement, similar to 3:9 ("proclaim"), where Amos addresses imaginary witnesses either for dramatic effect or to establish a legal atmosphere with the Lord and Israel as adversaries (Isa 1:2; cf. Dt 32:1).

"House of Jacob" recalls Israel's heritage, especially the promise to the patriarchs that established the grounds on which the Lord would deal with his people. The covenant became the external structure of the eternal promise (Ge 15:12–20), providing the vehicle for obedience. Israel had betrayed the covenant and so had forfeited every right to its promised blessing.

14–15 As a result of Israel's disobedience, the "altars of Bethel" would be destroyed as well as the expensive homes of the people. Amos focuses on the two major aspects of Israel's disobedience: false religion and misuse of wealth and power. According to Israelite law, a fugitive could find refuge at the altar by grasping its horns (1Ki 1:50), but even this last refuge would be lost. The winter house and the summer house most likely refer to separate houses. The winter house would be destroyed along with the summer house.

4. The pampered women of Samaria (4:1–3)

1 The region of Bashan was known for its excellent cattle (Ps 22:12; Eze 39:18), to which Amos sarcastically likens the women of Samaria. He accuses these rich women of oppressing the poor, just as he had accused the male leaders of his society. They may not have been directly involved in mistreating the poor, but their incessant demands for luxuries drove their husbands to greater injustices. Their demand, "Bring us some drinks," creates a vivid picture of their indolence.

2–3 An oath in which the Lord "has sworn [GK 8678] by his holiness" introduces the judgment section of this oracle. The element in the oath formula by which one swears forms an external guarantee of the thing being affirmed (cf. Heb 6:16). When God takes an oath, that element usually relates to the nature of the thing sworn. For example, in Jer 44:26 the Lord swore by his great name, which signifies his reputation achieved by his mighty deeds, demonstrating his power and authority. Here the "holiness" of God is his absolute separation from anything secular or profane. God guarantees that the judgment will become a reality, because the holy God does not lie, nor can his holiness allow sin to go unpunished.

The Hebrew words used to describe Israel's judgment are obscure. Both "hooks" and "fishhooks" basically relate to some kind of thorn or hook. One form of the word underlying "hooks" is attested in Hebrew as "shields." Thus it may picture these indolent women, who lay on beds of luxury, being carried away on the enemies' shields. A more common meaning of the word "fishhooks" is "pot" or "receptacle." Its association with "fish" may mean a receptacle for carrying fish or a cauldron for boiling fish. At any rate, these women would be led in humiliating fashion through the breached wall of Jerusalem.

5. Sinful worship (4:4–5)

4 Amos addresses all the people in this shocking command: "Go to Bethel and sin." Bethel was the chief religious sanctuary of the northern kingdom. It once housed the ark and was one of the locations in Samuel's circuit (1Sa 7:16). Shortly after the division of the kingdom, Bethel was established as a sanctuary by Jeroboam I to provide an alternative center to Jerusalem (1Ki 12:26–29). In the time of Amos, Bethel was known as "the king's sanctuary" (7:13). It thus may have been the scene of royal as well as religious pomp.

The cultic worship practiced at Bethel combined concepts common to Canaanite religion, resulting in a syncretistic Israelite religion devoid of real allegiance to the covenant. Certainly, elements of Israel's religion were observed there (4:4–5; 5:21–23). But the idolatrous influences had left their mark. The heart—indeed, the very life of Israel's religion—had been destroyed; and the covenantal obligation of a heart response to God and a caring love for one's fellow humans were forgotten.

Gilgal was another Israelite sanctuary in Amos's time (5:5; cf. Hos 4:15; 9:15 12:11). Lest the people think that Bethel should be the only sanctuary that bore an onus, the prophet includes Gilgal.

The word "sin" connotes the basic concept of "rebellion." Little did these worshipers know that as they participated in the religious rites in order to maintain their relationship to the Lord, they were actually in rebellion against him. The morning sacrifices are probably not the continual burnt offering presented each morning and evening (Ex 29:38–41; Lev 6:8–13; Nu 28:3–4); rather, the context of Am 4:4–5 deals with the individual sacrifices of pilgrims to the cultic centers. The other aspects of worship mentioned (v.5)—the tithe, the thank offering, the freewill offering—are also individual obligations.

5 Possibly Amos represents the cultic practices prescribed for the pilgrimage to the cult centers that were current in his time, but it is also possible that he was using hyperbole to show the futility of offering many sacrifices and tithes. This seems to reflect the intent of the passage, because Amos said, "This is what you love to do." It is as though he was telling them that even if they sacrificed every morning and tithed regularly so that they had something to boast about, in the end they were only engaging in acts of rebellion against God.

6. A look to the past (4:6–13)

This section expresses the immanence of God in history. Amos relates a series of events from Israel's past that he interprets as God's intervention on her behalf. Terrible as these catastrophes were, they were designed by a loving God to alert Israel to her sin and to the certainty of judgment; yet the nation did not return to him (v.11). This section vividly illustrates God's permissive will that brings suffering so that his own may be brought closer to him (Heb 12:6).

6 This verse is literally, "I gave you cleanness of teeth" (see NIV note), an expression describing complete lack of food. The catastrophes mentioned are difficult to identify historically, though they reflect God's continuing activity in history on Israel's behalf.

7–8 The "withheld rain" is the latter rain, so important to the full development of the crops. That rain fell on some towns and not on others might show that God's hand was in the catastrophe. Nevertheless, the suffering that resulted did not lead to repentance.

9–10 Even the blighted gardens and dying trees did not remind the people of their spiritual responsibility; neither did God's judgment on individuals. The reference to plague and sword recalls the curse of Lev 26:25, which was to come on the nation if the people walked contrary to God. The "sword" refers to war and was a reminder of the long period of warfare with Syria (2Ki 13:3).

11 Amos compares the overthrow of certain Israelite cities to the fall of Sodom and Gomorrah, which are used as analogies of destruction in a number of passages (Isa 1:9; 13:19; Jer 50:40; Zep 2:9). Hence the picture is of the violence suffered by certain Israelite cities during the Syrian incursions. The analogy of the stick snatched from the fire probably describes the conquered towns that might have been lost forever but were "snatched" from the fire of conflict and restored to their inhabitants because of the intervention of some "deliverer" (see 2Ki 13:1–9).

Divine chastisement is that aspect of his dealing with his children in which he uses punishment to bring them back to him (cf. Job 33:19–33; Pr 3:11; cf. Heb 12:5–11). Of course, suffering does not always have this purpose. The point of vv.6–11 is that the Israelites had become spiritually hardened. Because Amos does not want his hearers to forget this, he stated five times, "Yet you have not returned to me" (vv.6, 8, 9, 10, 11).

The preceding verses contain a number of connections with Dt 28–29, where Moses set forth the blessings of obedience and the curses of disobedience. Thus Amos shows Israel that the catastrophes mentioned are evidence that God has chastised Israel in the past for her sins. The curses of Deuteronomy have been realized. Soon the ultimate curse will follow: "Then the LORD will scatter you among all nations from one end of the earth to the other" (Dt 28:64).

12 Judgment is impending, but Amos does not state what the judgment will be ("this" does not likely refer to the catastrophes of vv.6–11 because those are broader in scope than the captivity Amos elsewhere envisions as the impending judgment). The haunting uncertainty in Amos's words makes the threat of judgment even more ominous. Israel is to meet her God, not in a face-to-face sense, but as he intervenes in history to effect her destruction. The imperative "Prepare to meet your God, O Israel" has an aura of finality. When Israel meets her God, she will finally learn the nature of the coming judgment.

The command "Prepare" should not be understood as a plea for the people to repent. The die was cast. They had not turned to God when he chastised them (vv.6–11), and now Amos holds out no hope for their full-scale repentance. The people were to get ready for the national calamity about to befall them.

13 A hymnic element, portraying some aspects of the nature of the God the Israelites are to face in judgment, closes this section. The word "forms" refers to God's activity in

Creation and is paralleled by the word "creates." Not only does God form the mountains and create the wind, but he reveals to human beings "his thoughts." The word for "thoughts" (GK 8465) is never used of God, and it is unlikely that Amos believes that God revealed his thoughts to all people (cf. 3:7). It is best to speak of God's activity in searching the hearts of all humankind and revealing their secret thoughts and motives.

"High places" could refer to pagan religious sanctuaries (Jer 7:31), but more likely refers to mountains and hills. In ancient times possession of the heights of enemy territory meant that the enemy was virtually brought into subjection (Dt 33:29; Eze 36:2). The majestic metaphor of God striding over the hills and mountains shows his sovereignty over the earth (cf. Mic 1:37; 3:9–12). The awe this picture brings is heightened by the last line: "the LORD God Almighty" (lit., "LORD God of Hosts"). The "hosts" (GK 7372) are generally taken to be the heavenly bodies or the armies of heaven.

7. A lament for fallen Israel (5:1–3)

1–2 Amos next takes up a lament, mourning the fall of Israel. Amos was so certain that what he said would happen that he treated it as an accomplished fact. He saw Israel as a virgin whose life had been ended in the bloom of youth. He describes her hopelessness as "never to rise again" and her desolation as "deserted in her own land with no one to lift her up."

Israel's predicted fate stands in stark contrast to the promise God gave Abraham of numerous offspring (cf. Ge 12:15; 15:15). But Amos says that Israel was cut off as a virgin who had never borne children, and the enemy was soon to carry her off to his own land. This passage illustrates that the blessings of God's promise—which was irrevocable and eternal (Ge 13:15; 17:19; cf. Heb 6:13, 17–18)—were conditioned on the obedience of its recipients. Its eternality was guaranteed by God's sovereign activity in history and by the existence of a believing remnant in Israel whose obedience to the covenant stipulations marked them as the vehicle through whom God would keep his promises.

3 This verse depicts the finality of Israel's demise. As the cities sent out their defending armies to face the invader, they would be cut down. Only a handful of ragged, war-weary men will be left of Israel's proud army.

8. Seeking true values (5:4–17)

4 The word "seek" (GK 2011), when referring to the Lord, means to turn to him in trust and confidence (Pss 34:4; 77:2; Jer 10:21). Amos uses "live" (GK 2649) in a context of national collapse. Since he has spoken of Israel as a fallen nation, the meaning of national life or restoration seems appropriate for this word (cf. v.14). Thus it is hardly right to say that Amos confronts the people only with doom. He holds out a gracious invitation but looks only for calamity because he knows so many will not repent. His invitation may have been instrumental in leading some to seek the Lord, thus contributing to the establishment of the remnant.

5 The people are warned not to keep relying for help on the centers of cultic worship. When the invader came, these centers would fall just like all the cities of Israel.

Bethel was where Jacob had met the Lord (Ge 28:10–15) and where God had reiterated the promise to him (Ge 35). In Amos's day, however, Bethel stood for mere external religion (see comment on Am 4:4). The idolatry practiced there could only lead to continued separation from God and the ultimate destruction of the nation. The reference to Beersheba shows that Israelites continued to cross the border into the southern kingdom to worship at the sanctuary in Judah.

6 The name "house of Joseph" stands for the northern kingdom and reflects the descent of its largest tribe, Ephraim, from Joseph. The fire Amos speaks of is reminiscent of the judgment in the oracles of 1:3–2:11 and symbolizes the coming captivity. A clear alternative is offered to the people in the word "or." The choice is to "seek the LORD," with all the blessings and favor this will bring, or to experience ultimate doom.

7 "Justice" (GK 5477) connotes the fair and impartial administration of the requirements of the Mosaic law, which required concern for others (Ex 23:4–5; Dt 24:17–22). These concepts were being violated in Amos's day, for justice was being turned into "bitterness" (lit., "wormwood"; cf. Jer 9:15; La 3:15, 19; cf. Am 2:6–7).

8–9 In sublime words Amos depicts the Lord's creative power in making the constellations, establishing the succession of day and night, and summoning the vast oceans to cover so much of the land. But then he turns from the sovereignty of God in creation to his sovereignty in human history, as seen by his overthrowing military strongholds.

10 The accusation continues with Amos's description of his contemporaries' hating the one who reproves in the "court" (lit., "gate"; GK 9133); the city gate was where the legal proceedings were carried on (cf. vv.12, 15; see comment on Ru 4:1). The "reprovers" protested the injustices of the courts. They were hated, as were those who spoke the truth during the proceedings.

11 Amos next speaks vividly of the oppressive measures that exploited the poor and made the rich richer. These symbols of Israel's wealth and greed were to become the objects of God's wrath. A terrible calamity was to befall the nation (the reversal of Dt 6:10–11). As yet it has not been fully described; but each of Amos's allusions to it builds on the other until in ch. 9 it attains its fullest statement.

12–13 All these judgments result from the people's many sins—sins that entailed rebellion and failure to live up to God's standards. In the light of the corruption of the times, the prudent man said nothing, because anything he might have said would have been unavailing. Protest would only have made the situation worse and brought greater woe.

14 Amos exhorts the people to seek good and not evil as the way to life. To concern themselves with what is good was the only way the nation could be restored to "life." As a result "the LORD God Almighty" [see comment on 4:13] will be with you." This expression connotes the Lord's presence, not only to dispense national and individual blessing, but to defend and fight for his people (cf. Dt 31:8; Jdg 6:12).

15 The people were not only to stop seeking evil (v.14), they were to hate evil and love good. This alone would bring life, for the Lord might possibly have mercy on the "remnant of Joseph" (cf. v.6). "Remnant" (GK 8642) connotes a portion of something. Since Amos's exhortation in v.14 holds open the possibility of the nation's restoration based on their repentance, this similar appeal in v.15 must not be seen as fulfilled in some far-off future but refers to the possibility of the northern kingdom escaping from God's judgment—or at least a portion of the people escaping.

If these appeals for repentance do not seem to be in accord with Amos's pronouncements of inevitable doom elsewhere, it may be that while he saw no hope for the nation as a whole, he continued to hold out the gracious offer of deliverance, even though only a few would respond.

16–17 "Therefore" relates back to the accusation in vv.7–12 and introduces the judgment of the Lord. Amos pictures the people weeping as the Lord passed through their midst, judging the sin that he had so severely condemned.

9. The Day of the Lord (5:18–20)

18 This verse affords an insight into the popular theology in Amos's time. "The day of the Lord" is an important concept that runs through the prophetic writings. It refers to the complex of events surrounding the coming of the Lord in judgment to conquer his foes and to establish his sovereign rule over the world. The people were looking forward to that day. Apparently they understood it as the time when the Lord would act on their behalf to conquer their foes and establish Israel as his people forever. They regarded their election as the guarantee of the Lord's favor. But they failed to see the Day of the Lord as the time when God would judge all sin, even theirs. They named the name of the Lord but did not obey his precepts. For these people, Amos said, that coming day would be one of darkness.

19–20 Amos uses two metaphors to show the error of the popular concept of the Day of the Lord. A man flees from a lion only to meet a bear. Another enters his home, his place of security, but is bitten by a snake. The meaning is both clear and powerful. The Israelites saw the Day of the Lord as a comforting concept. But the faithless Israelites would find it to be a time of judgment for them. There would be no hope for them in that day, for it would bring not one ray of light.

10. Unacceptable worship (5:21–27)

21 The shock felt by the people when Amos attacked their comforting eschatology was followed by another shock. He turns to their worship and proclaims the Lord's hatred of their religious observances because they lacked the love, concern, and humble obedience to God that marks sincere profession of faith. Every aspect of their ritual was an act of disobedience because it ignored the heart of the law—love for God and concern for others.

22–23 The people may, Amos says, continue to bring sacrifices, but the Lord would not accept them. The "burnt offering" (GK 6592) is the offering that was entirely consumed. The "grain offering" (GK 4966) was any offering given as a gift to the Lord. The "fellowship offering" (GK 8968) was offered in part to the Lord and the rest was shared with the offerer, his family, and his friends. Even their songs were a source of revulsion to the Lord. God says they were to be put away from him.

24 The element that will transform the people's sterile worship into acceptable worship is "justice" (GK 5477) and "righteousness" (GK 7407), concepts that relate to the social order. Only when the personal concern of the law is incorporated into their social structure and "rightness" characterizes their dealings with others will their worship be acceptable. Justice and righteousness must "roll on like a river . . . like a never-failing stream." A momentary flow of these two qualities will not do.

25–27 The question in v.25 calls for a negative answer: no, the Israelites did not sacrifice then. Evidently the forty-year period (beginning with the defection of the Israelites at Kadesh; cf. Nu 14:33–34) was a time when obedience to the Levitical institutions had declined (Jos 5:5–6; see also Eze 20:10–26; Hos 9:10; 13:5–6).

Verse 26 is best understood as adversative: "But you have lifted." Israel disobeyed God and by her neglect of sacrifice turned to idolatry. Amos lists the implements of idolatrous worship of an unknown astral deity, an event far back in their history. In other words, v.24 calls for obedience, while the judgment section affirms their disobedience (vv.25–26)

and bases the predicted judgment (v.27) on their long history of unfaithfulness to God.

11. A warning to the complacent (6:1–7)

1–2 With masterly irony, Amos addresses the self-satisfied rich, secure in their affluence. The cities he mentions have not necessarily met their doom. Rather, the question has a sarcastic note: "Go to [these cities] and look. . . . Are they better off than your two kingdoms [Judah and Israel]?" It is as though he were echoing what the people of Israel were saying—"Look at the other countries: there is none greater than we." This is supported by the words "notable men of the foremost nation," which also has a note of sarcasm. Presumably the people of Amos's day were boasting of their national security and power. The prophet proclaims woe to those who felt secure in the strength of their nation. His parroting of their affirmations of self-assurance and national pride underscores their complacency and places their false pride in stark contrast to the doom he predicts in the subsequent context.

3 The people were unwilling to hear of the "evil day," the day of their demise predicted by Amos. Yet they were all too willing to make the poor miserable.

4–7 These verses describe the opulence of Israelite society. To Amos their luxuries were symbols of the oppression by which they aggrandized themselves. So those who amassed all this wealth would be the first to go into exile (v.7).

12. Pride before a fall (6:8–11)

8 The Lord swears by himself in the preface to this oracle of doom (see comment on 4:2–3). The parallelism of the oracle indicates that the "pride of Jacob" has to do with Israel's vaunted "fortresses" (likely a reference to the great houses of the people, the symbols of their misguided affluence; cf. 3:10, 15). The "city," evidently Samaria, and all its wealth would be delivered up to a conqueror.

9–11 The judgment (v.8) is vividly illustrated in vv.9–10. If ten men are in a house or fortress, they will die. When a relative of one of the dead comes to burn the corpses, should he find one person still alive, that person will not permit his mentioning the name of the Lord for fear that the Lord will turn his wrath on him. These verses reflect the responsibility of an individual for the burial of members of his family. Since cremation was not acceptable in ancient Israel, the reference is probably to the burning of corpses during a plague. Verse 11 is a powerful picture of the destruction that would surely come on oppressing Israel.

13. A grim paradox (6:12–14)

12–13 By two patently absurd questions, Amos introduces the scathing rebuke that follows. One expected the courts to dispense justice, but the rich and powerful dispensed poison instead and made bitter the fruit of righteousness. Those who did this are described as rejoicing in "Lo Debar" and "Karnaim," evidently the sites of recent victories in Jeroboam's incursion into Aramean territory. But Amos spells "Lo Debar" in Hebrew so that it means "no thing." Through this biting sarcasm he proclaims the utter futility of their burgeoning national influence. Karnaim means "horns" and, by extension, "strength." The people's pride and self-confidence were reflected in their boast that they took Karnaim by their own strength.

14 This verse specifies the judgment that would overtake the Israelites; a nation, not identified here by Amos, would oppress them from their northern border, "from the entrance to [cf. NIV note] Hamath" (cf. 2Ki 14:25), all the way to their southern border at the Wadi Arabah. This nation turned out to be Assyria.

IV. The Prophetic Visions (7:1–9:15)

A. The Vision of the Locusts, Fire, and the Plumb Line (7:1–9)

1 The first of the series of visions that occupy most of the rest of the book consists of three dramatic elements. The first is the threat of a locust invasion "as the second crop was coming" (i.e., just before the dry season). If the threat materialized, the people would be left without food till the next harvest. Apparently the king had the privilege of claiming the first mowing. The needs of the government were great, and the large military establishment had to be supported.

2–3 When Amos saw in his vision what devastation the locusts had brought, he prays that it will not happen, because Israel would not be able to survive it. "Jacob," he says, "is so small!" This appeal seems strange in view of Israel's extensive territory and economic prosperity. But Amos had seen an awesome display of the Lord's might in this vision; and, in comparison to that, the nation seemed small and helpless. Amos's prayer was answered. The Lord relented and the threat was revoked.

4–6 The second aspect of the vision involved the threat of fire—an all-consuming fire, lapping up the sea and land. Again Amos's prayer was answered, and the Lord relented, as he had done in the first part of the vision.

7–9 The third aspect of the vision is climactic and contains the didactic element of the vision. The Lord was seen standing by a plumb wall with a plumb line in his hand. The word "standing" connotes a posture of firmness and determination, thus providing a contrast to the change of heart attributed to the Lord in the first two parts of the vision.

A plumb line is a standard by which a wall's vertical trueness is tested. So the Lord was testing the people by a standard. In the first two visions, no standard was given. Therefore, the threatened judgment could be withdrawn. But after the plumb line vision, the Lord could not be accused of arbitrariness if he carried out the threats. The people had failed to live up to their privilege as the Lord's people. They had been called to be holy (Ex 19:6), but their repressive society violated the very standards of holiness itself. They gave lip service to the covenant of the Lord but ignored the social concerns woven into its fabric. When the test came, they were found wanting. The plumb line showed that the Lord was not an arbitrary judge.

The coming judgment would fall on the pagan sanctuaries of Israel and on the dynasty of Jeroboam. Thus the two major influences in Israelite life would perish.

B. Historical Interlude (7:10–17)

Amos's visions are momentarily interrupted by a passage that gives us important information about Amos himself. It may have been placed here because it actually followed Amos's public report of the preceding vision.

10–13 Amaziah, the priest of the sanctuary at Bethel, accuses Amos of conspiracy. The words reported by Amaziah are based on the threat recorded in v.9. Though Jeroboam's reaction is not given, it is presumably reflected in Amaziah's order to Amos. The word "seer" (GK 2602; a word associated with "prophet" in 2Ki 17:13) is legitimately used here, since Amos has just received a vision.

14–15 Amos's reply to Amaziah's order is not without its interpretive problems. Did Amos say, "I am not a prophet," or, "I was not a prophet"? The latter option seems best. Amos certainly denies any connection with professional prophetism and affirms that he is a prophet only by divine calling. Before that, he was merely a shepherd and a caretaker of sycamore-fig trees.

16–17 Amos's encounter with Amaziah ends with a prediction of dire judgment, despite the latter's insistence that Amos desist in his preaching against Israel. The judgment against Amaziah and his family was personal in nature. Amaziah's wife would be violated, perhaps by the invading soldiers, and his children killed. He would lose all he had and would die in a "pagan" ("unclean") country. So the priest, whose task it was to maintain the purity of the cult, would die in a Gentile land.

C. The Vision of the Summer Fruit (8:1–14)

1–2 While it is possible that Amos saw an actual basket of fruit and that the Lord used it as a means of revelation, its inclusion in this section of the book makes it more likely that it was another vision. The word for "ripe fruit" is similar to another word that Amos uses in the response of the Lord: "The time is ripe for my people." The basket of summer fruit, ordinarily associated with the joys and provisions of the harvest, becomes a mockery. The pleasant memories of past harvest festivals are shattered by the decisive words that the end time is near.

3 Just as the apparent promise of the ripe fruit was turned into the assurance of Israel's destruction, so the joyous temple hymns (cf. 6:5) would give way to the wailing of the populace of Israel when the wrath of the Lord fell on them. The last clause of v.3 is typical of the vivid staccato style of Amos: "Many, many bodies—flung everywhere! Si-

lence!" This final word calls for the reverence this appalling scene warrants.

4–6 This scene is followed by a recital of the social crimes of those whose disobedience to the Lord was responsible for the carnage. The merchants could not wait for the end of the holy days so that they could increase their wealth by giving short measure and raising prices. They even sold the sweepings to increase the weight! Yet these exploiters were careful to observe the Sabbath. Though the marketplace was deserted on the holy days, in the bustle of commerce their god—Mammon—was quite in evidence, and their true religious credo was Gain at Any Cost.

7–8 In the oath formula, the "Pride of Jacob" is best understood as an appellation for God (see comments on 4:2; 6:8). It is the Lord as the pride of Jacob who guarantees this oath. The judgment to follow will surely come because God does not allow his glorious name to be sullied. Verse 8 describes the convulsions the land would suffer. The striking metaphor of an earthquake represents the calamity Amos has referred to throughout the book.

9 "In that day" refers to the day of calamity and need not be understood as eschatological. It introduces a section that continues to describe the impending judgment. The setting of the sun at noon describes an interruption of the natural order that would cause terror and panic among earth's inhabitants. The upheaval predicted by Amos would be a disruption of the national life on such a scale that the fear and dread in the hearts of the people would be similar to the terror that a celestial cataclysm would cause.

10–13 The destruction to come on Samaria would cause bitter mourning. Amos describes the event in terms of a funeral for "an only son." He depicts a coming famine as no ordinary famine but one of the words of the Lord. He pictures people searching for God's word as starving people seek food or water. But they would not receive any word from the Lord. Since they had rejected the word and not realized its great value, they had lost it forever (cf. Lk 17:22; Jn 7:34).

14 The word "shame" has the primary meaning of "guilt" (cf. 2Ch 24:18; 33:23). Dan was the site of the worship of the golden calf under Jeroboam, and the "way to Beersheba" (NIV, "god of Beersheba") apparently refers to the pilgrimage to that site. The various shrines Amos refers to may indicate that a geographical split in the concept of the Lord was taking place. A similar split related to the Canaanite god Baal. Thus the worship of the Lord became idolatrous. Those whose confidence was in their distorted, pagan view of the Lord would fall.

D. The Vision of the Lord standing by the Altar (9:1–15)

1. The destruction of the temple (9:1–6)

1–4 Amos sees the Lord standing by the temple altar. He commands the temple to crumble, and it collapses on the people, destroying the whole nation. The temple was not a literal temple, for the collapse of such a building would affect only a few. Rather it represents the religion of the northern kingdom, which, in the end, brought about the destruction of its adherents. The decay of the social structure that resulted from their cold externalism could lead only to national ruin. The gross sin of idolatry could lead only to judgment. The god of "greed" is no respecter of persons and often turns his voraciousness on those who are his own. Amos allowed no escape for the nation.

5–6 The hymnic element is appropriate to the context because it sets forth the power of the Lord to carry out his threat. This hymn contains several elements common to other prophetic hymns, such as the reference to the heavens and the calling forth of the waters (5:8).

2. Israel and the other nations (9:7)

7 Cush was a territory roughly corresponding to Ethiopia and Nubia. Infrequently mentioned in the OT, this country seems to have been chosen because of its great distance from Israel. It lay at the outer extremities of the important nations of the ancient Near East. At the time of Amos, it was probably considered an insignificant region. Thus it would be shocking to the Israelites, who boasted of their election, to learn that in the eyes of the Lord they were no better than those obscure Cushites.

Furthermore, Israel was no different from the Philistines or Arameans, because the Lord governed the migrations of these peo-

ple just as he had led the Israelites from Egypt. Because of the Exodus, the Israelites assumed that the Lord was unalterably committed to them as a nation and that no other nation counted. But Amos destroys that false assumption by affirming the sovereignty of the Lord over all the nations.

3. The restoration of the Davidic kingdom (9:8–12)

8–10 The nation was to be destroyed, but not totally. Thus an element of hope is introduced at this point. The eighth-century prophets placed their hope of the future in a kingdom portrayed with obvious Davidic motifs (Isa 9:7; Mic 5:2). It is true that Amos held no hope for the nation of Israel. But that is not to say that he held out no hope for a preserved remnant. One important element of Amos's message was that the nation was not to be equated with the remnant; it was precisely that false hope that he attacked. A true remnant from Israel would remain (cf. Jer 30:11).

Verse 9 explains v.8 by the use of a metaphor. The concept of separation is inherent in the figure of sifting with a sieve. Amos had decreed that the nation was doomed to exile (7:17). The consonance of this with the "shaking" is apparent; a separation would be made between the destroyed kingdom and the remnant that remained.

11 "In that day" refers to the time when the sifting activity will be initiated, i.e., the period of the Exile (vv.9–10). This period was seen by the prophets as continuing until the coming of Messiah and so includes the Christian Era.

The word "tent" (GK 6109) refers to a rude shelter (a "hut") and pictures the "house" (cf. 2Sa 7:11) of David that was becoming a dilapidated shack; in Amos's time the Davidic dynasty had fallen so low that it could no longer be called a house. The continuation of that dynasty is envisioned in prophecy as continuing in the Messiah, who is often referred to in Davidic motifs (Isa 9:6–7; Jer 33:15, 17; Mic 5:2). Amos thus affirms the perpetuity of the Davidic house. The national upheaval that ultimately led to the fall of Judah and Israel and the overthrow of Judah's monarchy could not vitiate God's promise. The royal offspring would yet come. David's dynasty would be perpetuated in David's Greater Son.

The promise to David in 2 Samuel also carried with it the promise of an eternal kingdom (2Sa 7:12–13). While the Davidic dynasty is most prominent in Amos's prophecy, it is difficult to separate that concept from that of regnal authority or kingdom. Both are probably in view. The dynasty had not yet collapsed in Amos's time, but the seeds of its dissolution were present.

The Lord declared that he would restore that "tent." He would restore the "broken places" of the divided kingdom (the word "its" is plural). He would restore "his"—i.e., David's—"ruins" and "build it," referring to "the tent." The Davidic dynasty, represented by the tent, was, according to Amos, to be restored.

12 The NT, in Ac 15:17, follows the LXX here, reading "that the remnant of men may seek the Lord" instead of "possess the remnant of Edom." The subject of Ac 15:12–21, where this passage is quoted, is Gentile inclusion in the early church; James used this passage to support the rightness of Gentile inclusion. The phrase "that bear my name" always connotes that which is God's peculiar possession (Dt 28:10; 2Ch 7:14; Jer 14:9; 15:16). This is precisely James's argument.

Since the inclusion of Gentiles takes place, according to Amos, in the kingdom of the descendant of David, one may assume that that kingdom has been established in some way. It is invisible now but will appear in glorious power when Christ, David's Greater Son, returns. If this passage in Amos predicted only a future inclusion of Gentiles in the millennial kingdom, it is difficult to understand why James would have appealed to it for support of Gentile admission to the first-century church. It seems to be clearly relevant to the issues facing the early church. Then James obviously understood the restored Davidic monarchy to be represented, at least in its invisible sense, in the church in his time.

4. The blessings of the restored kingdom (9:13–15)

13 The reaper being overtaken by the plowman implies a great abundance of the produce of the field. Scarcely can the grapevines be planted than the grapes are ready for pressing. The great amount of wine in this time is pictured in the metaphor of new wine flowing from the hills. In other words, Amos sees a radical reversal of Israel's fortunes. He depicts a time when God's blessing will be poured out in unimaginable abundance.

14–15 The period of this abundance will witness the restoration of Israel to her land. Ruined cities will be rebuilt, and Israel will again flourish as a nation. Amos sees this restoration as being permanent. He maintains that Israel will be planted in her own land "never again to be uprooted." It is difficult to understand his words as finding fulfillment in the postexilic period. Not only were the economic conditions of that time not consonant with Amos's prediction, but its impermanence makes the identification doubly difficult.

It is also difficult to apply the concept of universal peace to the invisible kingdom, the church, unless the meaning of the prophet's language is severely restricted. If one understands the kingdom to have a present aspect as well as a future aspect, the problem becomes less difficult. The NT does teach a present, invisible aspect of the kingdom, which is the church. But the millennial kingdom is that aspect of the kingdom in which God's reign will be realized within the sphere of human history and natural order. It is in this aspect of the kingdom that Amos's prediction of the blessings of the kingdom may be placed.

The hope of Amos is not an isolated one that finds expression only in his book. Nor is it a purely prophetic tradition without relation to other OT traditions. It is an expression of one of the most important themes of OT theology: the promise. This promise, given to Abraham, reiterated to the patriarchs, reaffirmed to David, and expressed throughout the OT, affirms that God will mediate his redemptive blessings to Jews and Gentiles in a promised offspring or "seed." In the prophets, this offspring is clearly the Davidic Messiah, who in the NT is Christ. Amos affirms that God's promise has not ceased. In spite of the internal turmoil in the kingdom of his day, God would establish the Davidic monarchy; and through that monarchy God's blessing would come to "all peoples on earth" (Ge 12:3).

The Old Testament in the New

OT Text	NT Text	Subject
Am 5:25–27	Ac 7:42–43	Sin and judgment
Am 9:11–12	Ac 15:16–17	Restoration for everyone

Obadiah

INTRODUCTION

1. Background

Edom, established in the region around Mount Seir as far back as patriarchal times (cf. Ge 36), was a small kingdom that inhabited the Transjordanian highlands. Edom was well-established in the area south and east of the Dead Sea by the thirteenth century B.C. In the period of the monarchy, David brought Edom under subjection; relations were often hostile from then onward. Of particular interest in the context of Obadiah's work are two questions relating to Edom: (1) When might the hostility between Edom and Judah have produced the kind of Edomite perfidy expressed in vv.10–14? (2) When in Edom's history were Obadiah's words fulfilled? The first question will be dealt with in the commentary at v.14, while the latter question is addressed here.

Despite periods of subjugation to Judah, there is clear evidence that Edom still constituted an independent monarchy about 594–593 B.C. (cf. Jer 27:3), and it provided at least partial refuge to Judah's fugitives then (cf. Jer 40:11). Although Ammon and Moab, like Judah, were subsequently subjugated by Nebuchadnezzar (c. 582; cf. Eze 21:18–20, 28), no reference is made to Edom, which may therefore have followed Jeremiah's counsel to submit (Jer 27:6–7). Edom's continued existence in the sixth century is attested by excavations at Ezion-geber. Edom also figures in OT writings from the Exile, which bear witness to its continued existence (La 4:21–22; Eze 25:12–14; 35; Da 11:41).

By 312 B.C., it is certain that Petra was occupied by the Nabataeans, a nomadic Arabic tribe. There is evidence that this transition to Arabic influence was already established in the fifth century. Ammon and Moab are cited as enemies of Judah's interests in the time of Nehemiah (c. 444–432; Ne 2:10, 19; 4:3, 7; 6:1–15; 13:1–2, 23). Edom, however, is not named among Judah's traditional opponents, being replaced by the Arabs who played a dominant role under Geshem (Ne 2:19; 4:7: 6:1–2; cf. 2Ch 17:11; 21:16; 22:1; 26:7). A similar transition is evident at Ezion-geber, where Arabic names replace Edomite names on the fifth-century site, which was controlled by the Arabs during the Persian period (late sixth to the fourth centuries).

The destruction of Edom may therefore be located tentatively in the latter half of the sixth century. This is corroborated by Malachi, who described as past history the reduction of Esau's "mountains into a wasteland" and "his inheritance of the desert jackals" (c. 450, Mal 1:3–4; cf. Eze 32:29), though the prophet envisaged a continuing identity and national striving by Edom, even in exile (Mal 1:4–5).

2. Authorship and Date

Nothing is known of the author of Obadiah. The name, which means "servant of the LORD," is given to at least twelve other OT characters, none of whom seem obviously to be the author named in the book. Most attempts at correlation founder on the inability of scholars to date the book with certainty.

The date for the book of Obadiah continues to be much debated. The prophecy is clearly a response to a time when Jerusalem was overrun by foreign armies, a sack in which the Edomites were understood to have in some way collaborated (see v.15). If it was the 586 B.C. destruction under Nebuchadnezzar, and if Edom herself came under Nabataean control by the fifth century B.C., the date of the book is best left sometime after the 586 invasion of Zion.

EXPOSITION

I. The Message From the Lord (v.1)

1 Obadiah's prophecy opens with the formal announcement of a message from the Lord "about" or "against" (cf. Ps 137:7) Edom, a pattern repeated in the following lines. "Edom" represents an alternative name of

"Esau," the brother of Jacob (Ge 36:1, 8, 43; cf. Ob 6, 8–9, 18–19, 21). It also denotes the descendants of Esau (Ge 36:9, 16–17; cf. 36:31, 43), whose blood relationship with Israel is invoked repeatedly in the OT (Nu 20:14; Dt 23:7; Am 1:11; Mal 1:2; cf. Ob 10, 12); and it describes the land inhabited by them (Nu 20:23; 21:4; 34:3; cf. Ob 18–21).

The "message" (GK 9019) is evidently a supernatural revelation, being "from the LORD," corroborated by the prophecy's description as a "vision" (GK 2606; cf. Hab 1:1; 2:2–3). Such revelation was mediated primarily through the prophets. The plural "we" might indicate a prophetic group—perhaps including the believing community to which the revelation was to be mediated.

An "envoy" (GK 7495) is normally a human ambassador, sent to represent the authority of those whom he served. Verse 1 points to an envoy who represents one of the combatants ("let us").

The dual thrust of v.1 indicates two levels at which human history moves. The Lord is the ultimate mover, but there is also an international political alliance, motivated only by callous self-seeking (cf. vv.5–7). Even nations serve the overriding purposes of a God who sovereignly shapes human affairs through countless envoys of his own (cf. Ps 104:4). The "nations" are deaf to this realm, in which they serve unconsciously (cf. Isa 45:4–7).

II. The Abasement of Edom (vv.2–9)

A. Edom's Character (vv.2–4)

1. Edom's future smallness (v.2)

2 This verse introduces Edom's abasement, which is stressed by "small" and "despised." Edom's smallness is qualitative, corresponding to its despicable and debased character.

2. Edom's present pride (vv.3–4)

3–4 "Pride" (GK 2295) is derived from a verb meaning "to boil up, seethe"; the root of this word occurs three times in the account of Esau's squandered birthright. The essence of this "pride" is insubordination, rooted in an inordinate self-estimation: the proud man rejects authority, whether from God or another human being, and arrogates it to himself.

Edom's pride is grounded in its geographical location "on the heights," from which it draws its sense of security and self-sufficiency. Edom's natural defenses were impos-ing. Its main centers of civilization were situated in a narrow ridge of mountainous land southeast of the Dead Sea. This ridge exceeded a height of 4,000 feet throughout its northern sector, and it rose in places to 5,700 feet in the south. The frontiers of this lofty plateau were formed on the west by the Arabah, to which the land dropped over 4,000 feet within the space of a few miles. The northern border was similarly defended by the deep canyon of the Wadi Zered, and to the south the precipitous walls of the Wadi Hismeh mark the abrupt descent of the tableland to the desert. In addition to these natural fortifications, Edom was strongly defended by a series of Iron Age fortresses, particularly on the eastern frontier where the land descended more gradually to the desert.

Such was Edom's refuge "in the clefts of the rocks" (so SS 2:14; Jer 49:16), whose austere environment might well foster thoughts of invulnerability. "Sela" (see NIV note on v.3) is also the name of an Edomite settlement captured by Amaziah (c. 800–783, 2Ki 14:7). It is commonly associated with the subsequent Nabataean capital, Petra, whose name also signifies "rock" (cf. Mt 16:18).

Edom's sense of security "deceived" it. Although virtually impregnable to human forces, Edom was still utterly vulnerable before the wisdom and power of God. Edom's deceived pride is expressed in the confident question "Who can bring me down?" It is echoed in the unanticipated answer: "I will bring you down," a blunt statement that embodies the heart of the prophecy.

B. Edom's Calamity (vv.5–9)

1. Edom's ransacking (vv.5–6)

5–6 As "thieves" plunder a household, so "grape pickers" strip a vineyard. Yet in both cases they leave at least a pittance that escapes detection and despoliation. By contrast Esau will be "ransacked" with a terrible thoroughness that leaves nothing (cf. vv.8–9; Jer 49:9–10). This will be the work of the Lord's own judgment, from which nothing can remain "hidden." Whereas the Lord consistently promised to "leave" a remnant for Jacob, no such promise is extended to Edom.

2. Edom's entrapment (v.7)

7 Edom will be deceived by its "friends"; this deception is the expression of calculated

hostility as indicated by the verb "overpower" (GK 3523). "Deceived" epitomizes the treachery evoked by its juxtaposition to "friends." This deception is accompanied by rejection from its "allies," whose covenant loyalty is presupposed, when the Edomites seek help from or refuge with those allies. It is appropriate that Edom should be denied help and refuge as it had done to its brother Jacob's "survivors" (vv.10, 12, 14).

The third line is obscure in Hebrew. The meaning "they will make your bread a trap" yields good sense if "your bread" is interpreted as a synecdoche (i.e., a part for the whole): they make the friendship expressed and ratified when they ate your bread a trap.

3. God's initiative (vv.8–9)

8–9 "Declares the LORD" marks the opening of a new section, reverting to the perspective of God's initiative in the impending destruction of Edom. "In that day" frequently looks forward to a specific time appointed by God in his sovereignty, when he will intervene in human history in judgment and salvation. Both Edom's "wise men" and their "men of understanding" the Lord would destroy. The failure of Edom's traditional wisdom (cf. 1Ki 4:30; Job 1:1; 2:11; 4:1; Jer 49:7; La 4:21) amplifies further the theme of deception. Ultimately, Edom was deceived because the Lord gave her up to deception.

The term "Teman," generally taken to describe a region in the northern sector of Edom, clearly speaks of the population of "Edom" as a whole. No certainty exists regarding the historical outcome of this prophecy concerning Edom's demise at the hands of the "nations," but a great "slaughter" is in view.

III. The Charge Against Edom (vv.10–14)

A. The Reason for the Charge (v.10)

10 The noun "violence" (GK 2805) denotes both moral wrong and overt physical brutality (cf. Hab 1:2), both of which had characterized Edom's relations with Israel. This goes back to the very origins of the two nations, in the hatred of Esau for his brother Jacob (Ge 27:40–41). This hatred emerged again in Edom's hostility to Israel after the Exodus (Ex 15:15; Nu 20:14–21; Dt 2:4; Jdg 11:17–18); and Edom is numbered among Israel's "enemies . . . who had plundered them"

before they were defeated by Saul (1Sa 14:47–48). It is against this background of aggression that David's later campaigns are also to be understood (2Sa 8:13–14; 1Ki 11:15–16; 1Ch 18:11–13; Ps 60). All this culminated in Edom's exultation over the destruction of Jerusalem (Ps 137:7; La 4:21–22; Eze 25:12; 35:5, 15; 36:5; Joel 3:19).

B. The Explanation of the Charge (vv.11–14)

1. The charge defined (v.11)

11 The equating of Edom with the "foreigners" is intimated in the first two lines; the equality is stated in the last line. The correlation of these subjects, however, involves a definite contrast, based on the word "aloof," which differentiates sharply between the conduct of Edom and that of the rapacious "strangers." The latter actually "entered" Jerusalem and cast "lots" for its conquered property and probably for its citizens (cf. Joel 3:3; Na 3:10), while Edom did not participate in this looting (see also v.13). However, in the sight of God, there is little distinction in moral accountability between overt sin and an inner bias toward that sin that permits it to go unchecked (cf. Mt 5:21–32).

2. The charge repeated and amplified (vv.12–14)

The main emphasis of these verses is on Edom's hostile attitudes rather than on its physical violence at Jerusalem.

12 The initial Hebrew verb means to "look on" (GK 8011). Its connotations are varied, and either the sense of contempt ("look down on") or exultation ("gloat") is drawn from the context and parallel verbs. The verbs "rejoice" (GK 8523) and "boast" (GK 1540 & 7023) betray the perverted and reprehensible values of this typical enemy of Israel, for whom covenant loyalty to a brother meant nothing.

13 This verse echoes the description of the "foreigners" (v.11), attributing their conduct directly to Edom. However, v.11 has identified Edom with the foreigners only in intent, not explicitly in action; and it is at this level that Edom is accused of active participation in the sack of Jerusalem. While moving closer to participant status, Edom's historical role

was still primarily an attitudinal one ("look down").

14 The distinction between action and intent is virtually obliterated here since the verb "wait" (GK 6641) echoes the one action predicated clearly of Edom in v.11—"stood aloof." The verse describes Edom's treatment of Judah's "survivors," thereby corroborating the impression of detachment from the main scene of action in the city, since the "fugitives" would be fleeing away from the city. However, it also qualifies this detachment sharply, for it is accompanied by outright aggression against those fugitives.

The central concern of these verses is with the "day" that befell the people of Judah. This is portrayed as a major tragedy by the foreboding epithets that are applied to it and repeated with the crushing weight of a death knell (cf. Zep 1:14–16). "Trouble" (GK 7650; also v.12) and "destruction" (v.12; GK 6) both point to a national catastrophe of major proportion. Can we identify a specific catastrophe when Jerusalem was invaded, its property plundered, its people enslaved or slaughtered on a wide scale, and at the same time Edom participated as a mocking bystander and as a collaborator with the foreign invaders? Six periods in the history of Jerusalem and Judah present themselves for consideration, of which the last one (586 B.C.) corresponds to these criteria most closely (for a survey of the other five, see EBC, 7:350–51).

When this final invasion of Jerusalem by the Babylonians occurred, following Jehoiachin's previous capitulation to Nebuchadnezzar in 597 B.C., Edom still existed as an independent nation. On both occasions the city suffered seizure of its "wealth" and wholesale deportation of its population (2Ki 24:13–16; 25:4–17; 2Ch 36:18, 20). In 586 the city was virtually burned to the ground, including the temple (2Ki 25:9–10; 2Ch 36:19), and many of its inhabitants were massacred (2Ki 25:8–21; 2Ch 36:17; cf. Jer 6:1–9:22; Eze 4:1–7:27). There is specific reference to unsuccessful "fugitives" in the account of the king's escape with his retinue (2Ki 25:4–5). Of particular significance are the accounts of Edom's conduct at this time. It seems to have participated as an ally in a coalition of Palestinian states against Nebuchadnezzar (Jer 27:3; 40:11); yet it was later accused of taking vengeance on Judah (Eze 25:12) and of delivering the Israelites "over to the sword at the time of their calamity, at the time their punishment reached its climax" (Eze 35:5; cf. La 1:17). Edom was equally guilty at this time of rejoicing in Jerusalem's destruction (Ps 137:7; La 2:15–17; 4:21; Eze 35:11–15; 36:2–6); and it is therefore at this time that the prophetic announcements of Edom's annihilation reached a climax (Jer 9:26; 25:21; La 4:21–22; Eze 25:13; 32:29; 35:3–4; 7–9, 11, 14–15; 36:7).

IV. The Day of the Lord (vv.15–21)

A. The Judgment of Esau (vv.15–18)

15–16 The "day of the LORD," a theme of great significance in Israel's eschatology (cf. ZPEB, 2:46–47), gives final definition to the preceding references to a "day" in Obadiah. Edom's and Judah's downfall both constitute elements in the pattern of this "great and dreadful day of the LORD" (Joel 2:31). It signals the climactic establishment of God's rule in human history and, as such, brings judgment on all those enemies who oppose his dominion. Such a judgment engulfed apostate and rebellious Israel, most notably in the falls of Samaria and Jerusalem; it descended subsequently on "the nations" (those not bowing to God's sovereignty). This "day," then, defines the destiny of Edom and the nations in both vv.1–9 and vv.15–21. After the nations have had their "day" on the Lord's holy mountain, his "day" will come, with none to oppose its thrust. This "day" is, in the first instance, promised in terms that admit a preliminary fulfillment within history for the faithful remnant of Israel; and it is from this hope of restoration and blessing for a "holy" people that Obadiah derives his promise of "deliverance" and conquest for the "house of Jacob" (vv.17–21).

The opening line of v.15 therefore constitutes the core of Obadiah's prophecy, providing a theological framework for the preceding verses: the localized disasters befalling Edom and Jerusalem are not merely isolated incidents in a remote and insignificant war, for they mark the footsteps of the Lord himself as he approaches to set up a "kingdom that will never be destroyed" (Da 2:44). And the following verses are essentially a commentary on the implications of that impending "day." Verse 15 accordingly sets forth its guiding principle of retaliation: "As you have done, it will be done to you." The actions perpetrated by the nation addressed will correspond precisely to those perpetrated on her.

Verse 16 demonstrates the same equivalence as v.15 of past and future action ("drank," "will drink"; GK 9272). The metaphor of drinking is commonly used of the experience of judgment and humiliation (cf. Hab 2:15–16). Judah's suffering on God's "holy hill" in Jerusalem has been described as past in vv.10–14; for Edom and the nations, their suffering is still future at the time of Obadiah's prophecy.

17–18 "Mount Zion" denotes the place of God's rule in Jerusalem. It is therefore rendered "holy" (GK 7731) by his presence, and it demands a corresponding holiness of its inhabitants. As the visible expression of God's sovereign holiness, Mount Zion becomes the source of judgment on human sin (e.g., Isa 31:9; Joel 3:16; Am 1:2–2:16); and it is the final locus of God's judgment on the citizens of Judah (e.g., Isa 10:12; La 2:1–8; 4:2–16; Mic 3:12; cf. Ob 11–14, 16). However, the Lord's kingly rule is expressed equally by his salvation, which also emanates from Mount Zion (e.g., Pss 20:2; 53:6) and which restores to it the "holy" character consonant with his presence there. Obadiah's announcement of salvation belongs to this tradition.

"Deliverance" (GK 7129) implies escape from danger and widespread destruction (cf. Ge 14:13; Jdg 12:4–5; Ob 14). It is applied most consistently to God's gracious preservation and purification of a remnant in Israel particularly after the Fall of Jerusalem (cf. Ezr 9:8–13; Isa 4:2; 10:20; et al.). The final line expresses the outworking of this restoration. "Possess" (GK 3769) is associated preeminently with Israel's conquest of the Promised Land (e.g., Ex 6:8; Dt 3:8; 4:1, 22; et al.). Israel succeeded in this conquest because she obeyed the Lord, who entered the battle on behalf of his people and dispossessed the enemy before them. Israel therefore forfeited her control of the land through her subsequent disobedience; the prophets, however, held out to the nation the hope of repossessing the land on the same condition of an obedient and militant faith (e.g., Isa 54:3; 57:13; 60:21; 61:7; Eze 36:12; Am 9:12; cf. Gal 3:29; 1Pe 1:4); and it is to this hope that Obadiah

appealed in expectation of a "holy" community that would be able to appropriate it (cf. vv.19–21).

In keeping with the military associations of v.17, the "house of Jacob" is to annihilate the "house of Esau." The destructiveness of fire consuming stubble forms a repeated image of the relentless judgment predicted here (e.g., Ex 15:7; Isa 10:17; Joel 2:5; Mal 4:1). This prophecy will revive an earlier subjugation of Edom under Saul, David, and their successors, a yoke Edom later threw off. Edom's final submission is therefore still anticipated by the prophets (cf. Nu 24:18; Isa 11:14; Eze 25:13–14; Am 9:12). As in Isa 11:13–14, it will be accomplished by a reunited Israel—intimated by the parallel terms "Jacob" and "Joseph" (cf. Pss 77:15; 80:1; 81:4–5; Jer 3:18). Unlike the house of Jacob, the house of Esau can expect no "deliverance," no remnant; as the Edomites had thought to plunder and possess the land of Israel, cutting off its "survivors," so it will happen to them.

Verse 18 marks a progression in the judgment of Edom. The Lord had enlisted the heathen nations to eradicate Edom from its homeland in "the mountains of Esau" (cf. vv.8–9); now, however, his own people of Israel were to cooperate with him in destroying Esau altogether. Historical events support this progression. Edom was displaced from its country east of the Arabah in the sixth and fifth centuries, in a period of Judah's weakness; this was therefore executed by foreigners, culminating in Nabataean possession of that territory. In the same period the surviving Edomites were settling west of the Arabah, in the Negev (cf. Eze 35:10, 12; 36:2, 5). The postexilic region of Judah extended no farther south than Bethzur, north of Hebron. Hebron itself and the neighboring towns were all occupied by Edomite populations (cf. 1Esd 4:50; 1Mc 4:61; 5:65; Jub 38:8–9); and, by the end of the fourth century, their territory had acquired the Hellenistic name for Edom: Idumaea (i.e., Edom-aea).

However, the fortunes of Judah were revived under the Maccabees (c. 168–63 B.C.), and this era saw a resurgence of Jewish aspirations to possess its former lands. The Idumaeans were defeated in 166 B.C. by Judas Maccabaeus (cf. 1Mc 5:3, 65). Under John Hyrcanus (135–104 B.C.) this conquest of the

Idumaeans was completed (c. 125 B.C.), and they were compelled to submit to circumcision and to full observance of the Jewish law. They continued to haunt the Jews, however, for the family of Herod the Great was of Idumaean descent; but, eventually, they were consumed by the house of Jacob and lost their national identity and autonomy.

B. The Occupation of Edom (vv. 19–21)

19–20 Not only the term "possess" (see comment on vv.17–18), but also the ethnic and geographical references recall Israel's conquest of Canaan. The "Negev" was not always to be the home of the Edomites, dispossessed as they were from their own "portion," the "mountains of Esau" (cf. Dt 2:4–5); rather the reverse would be true. The "foothills," the low-lying region separating the Judean hills from Philistia, would extend itself westward. Even the northern territories of Ephraim and Samaria, lost to Assyria during the preexilic period, would again be part of Israel. Benjamin, the small tribe virtually absorbed by Judah in historic times, was to move east and north into Transjordan and possess the lush highlands of Gilead, while exiles in Canaan (note the antiquated name with its Exodus and Conquest overtones) and from Jerusalem would expand north to the Lebanese coast at Zarephath and south to the Negev.

"Sepharad" is not definitely identified but may refer to Sardis in distant Lydia; if so, it reflects an early colony of Jewish exiles (ZPEB, 5:342) who, with more local refugees, were expected to inherit portions of the Holy Land. In short, the land seen by Obadiah as promised to a reunited Israel in "the day of the LORD" is the land originally given to the Twelve Tribes. It was the inalienable bequest of the Lord to Abraham and his descendants (Ge 13:14–17; 26:2–5; 28:13–15), and neither Edomite treachery nor Assyrian-Babylonian dispersion could keep God's promises from their fulfillment.

The term "exiles" (GK 1661) is applied predominantly to the deported population of Judah after 586 B.C. (e.g., 2Ki 25:27; Isa 45:13; et al.). Such an application is clearly appropriate to the qualification "from Jerusalem": no other major deportation from that city is known, and that background is most suitable to the events described in vv.10–14. The "Israelite exiles" would therefore be the survivors from the northern kingdom of Israel, from which they were deported after the fall of Samaria (cf. 2Ki 17:6, 18, 20, 23; 18:11). On this evidence, not only Israel but also Judah had been destroyed as an independent nation; and Obadiah's prophecy is proclaimed with heroic faith to "the poorest people of the land" (2Ki 24:14; 25:12, 22–24; Jer 40–44), during an era of destitution and weakness in the exilic or postexilic period.

21 Verse 21 reiterates the theme of conquest, expressed in the verb "govern" (or "judge"; GK 9149). The noun "deliverers" (GK 4635) has similar connotations of military victory (cf. Hab 1:2; 3:13, 18). This conquest finds its source in Judah and specifically in its capital, "Mount Zion." The ultimate goal of the conquest had been to unite Israel, with centralized worship in the temple (Dt 12:1–28) and with centralized rule in dynastic monarchy (Dt 17:14–20; 2Sa 7). These were not to have autonomous functions, for they were the visible institutions of the theocracy through which the Lord himself was to rule as "king over Jeshurun" (Dt 33:5). Obadiah's vision of Mount Zion restored to its destined leadership of nations is grounded in these promises. It presupposes the existence of a nation obedient to its theocratic calling, which will "serve him without fear, in holiness and righteousness before him" (Lk 1:74–75; cf. v.17). And it finds its consummation in the true realization of that theocracy.

The "LORD" is indeed Israel's "king from of old" (Ps 74:12). He is in reality "the living God, the eternal King" (Jer 10:10), "the great King over all the earth" (Ps 47:2, 7). But the day is coming when that kingdom will be acknowledged universally, when every knee shall bow. It will be said to Zion, "The LORD, the King of Israel, is with you" (Zep 3:15); and they will say among the nations, "The Lord reigns" (Ps 96:10). Edom will be set aside, with "every pretension that sets itself up against the knowledge of God" (2Co 10:5); "And the kingdom will be the LORD's" (cf. 1Co 15:24–28; Rev 11:15; 12:10; 22:1–5).

Jonah

INTRODUCTION

1. Background

The book of Jonah is the fifth of the Minor Prophets (the Book of the Twelve). Jonah, the son of Amittai, from Gath Hepher in Galilee (cf. 2Ki 14:25; Jos 19:13) prophesied during or shortly before the reign of Jeroboam II (793–753 B.C.). This makes it virtually certain that we should place the story of the book in the period of Assyrian weakness between the death of Adad-nirari III in 782 B.C. and the seizing of the Assyrian throne by Tiglath-pileser III in 745 B.C. During this time, Assyria was engaged in a life and death struggle with the mountain tribes of Urartu and its associates of Mannai and Madai in the north, who had been able to push their frontier to within less than a hundred miles of Nineveh. The consciousness of weakness and possible defeat would go far to explain the readiness of Nineveh to accept the prophet's message.

Until the nineteenth century, Jonah was regarded as history. Liberal scholars today largely contend that the book is no more than a beautiful allegory or parable. Our Lord, however, referred to the story of Jonah as historical (Mt 12:38–41; Lk 11:29–30, 32). The main argument against the historicity of the book is, of course, the alleged impossibility of Jonah's surviving three days and three nights in the belly of the fish (1:17). There are sufficient, well-attested occurrences to show that survival is possible under these circumstances. Jesus placed the incident alongside the greater miracle of his own resurrection.

2. Date and Authorship

The information in the book clearly must have come from Jonah himself in the eighth century B.C. Since he is nowhere claimed as author, and since he is constantly referred to in the third person, the possibility cannot be dismissed that its present form comes from another hand.

3. Purpose

The purpose of Jonah's proclamation was to bring the Ninevites to repentance. The declaration of God's loving care was made,

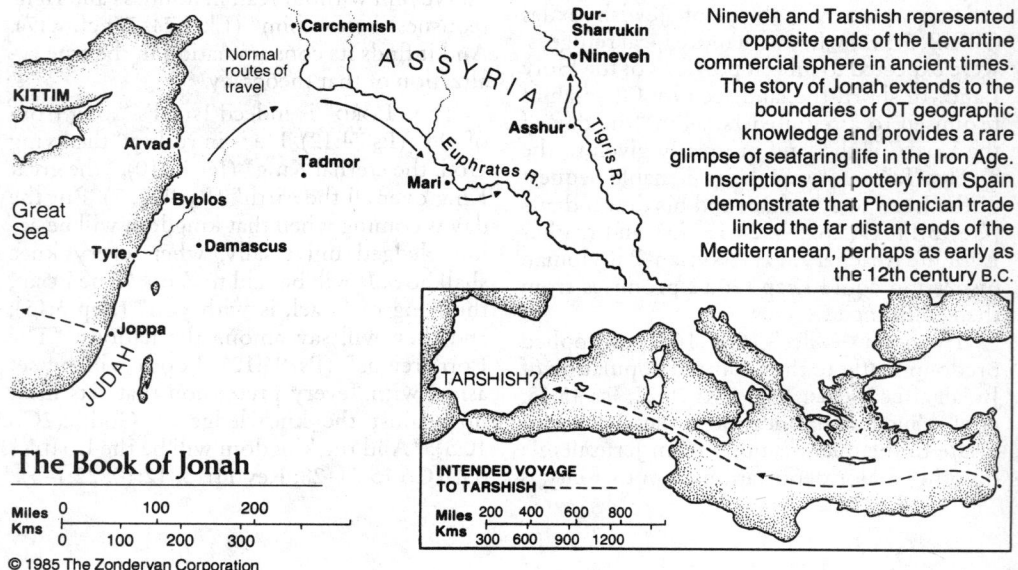

Nineveh and Tarshish represented opposite ends of the Levantine commercial sphere in ancient times. The story of Jonah extends to the boundaries of OT geographic knowledge and provides a rare glimpse of seafaring life in the Iron Age. Inscriptions and pottery from Spain demonstrate that Phoenician trade linked the far distant ends of the Mediterranean, perhaps as early as the 12th century B.C.

The Book of Jonah

Miles 0   100   200
Kms 0   100   200   300

© 1985 The Zondervan Corporation

INTENDED VOYAGE
TO TARSHISH – – – –

Miles 200 400 600 800
Kms   300 600 900 1200

1460

not to Nineveh, but to Jonah (4:11), and so to Israel. Taking the book as a whole, it is a revelation to God's people of God's all-sovereign power and care. It had a special relevance to Israel over which the shadow of Assyria was falling, and later to Judah, as it faced destruction at the hands of Babylon.

EXPOSITION

I. The Disobedient Prophet (1:1–2:10)

A. Jonah's Flight (1:1–3)

1 There is no indication how God communicated his will to Jonah. In many cases there must have been the overwhelming certainty of the divine message without any consciousness of how it had come. "Jonah son of Amittai" is the only prophetic name recorded for the North in the nearly forty years between the death of Elisha and the ministry of Amos (2Ki 14:25). Later rabbinic tradition claimed that Jonah was the widow's son brought back to life by Elijah (1Ki 17:17–24). So far as we know, Jonah was not picked because he was particularly suited to the task. When he fled, God could have turned to someone else; but since it is the sovereignty of God that is being particularly stressed, God held to his choice (cf. 1Co 9:16).

2 "The great city of Nineveh" goes back to early days after the Flood (Ge 10:11). Though it was not always the capital city of Assyria, Nineveh was always one of its principal towns. In the light of 4:11, it might be better to translate "great [GK 1524] city" as "big city"; for it is the number of its inhabitants that is being stressed. "Preach against it" indicates that God was particularly concerned with the Assyrians' self-confident pride (Isa 10:13) and cruelty (Na 3:1, 10, 19).

3 Apparently "Tarshish" comes from a Semitic root meaning "to smelt"; since there were a number of places with this name on the Mediterranean coast, probably Tartessus in Spain is intended. We need not go beyond Jonah's own words (4:2) to find his motive for not wanting to go to Nineveh, but this does not explain why he tried to run away.

Israel was involved in the battle of Qarqar in 853 B.C. and under Jehu paid tribute to Assyria in 841 B.C. If Assyria were to be spared now, it could only be that the doom pronounced at Horeb to Elijah (1Ki 19:15–18) should go into full effect. Sick at heart from the foreshortened view of the future, so common to the prophets in foretelling the coming judgments of God, Jonah wished to escape, not beyond the power of God, but away from the stage on which God was working out his purposes and judgments. "To flee from the Lord" is here probably the equivalent of "to flee from the Lord's land."

B. The Storm (1:4–6)

4 For the ancient Near East, the gods had created order by defeating the powers of chaos; but these had been tamed, not abolished, and so remained a constant threat. The embodiment of these lawless and chaotic forces was the sea, which people could not control or tame. Frequently God's control of the sea is used to stress his complete lordship over creation (cf. Pss 24:2; 33:7; 65:7; 74:13; et al.).

5–6 The crew were probably all Phoenicians, whose language differed only slightly from Jonah's; so the crew would have shared in a common religion and pantheon. In a developed polytheism, however, individuals tended to concentrate on favorite deities; in addition, all sorts of attractive foreign deities tended to be adopted by sailors.

Possibly Jonah's hurried flight to Joppa played a part in his sound sleep. The storm that can terrify the sailor can reduce the landsman to physical impotence and unconsciousness, as indeed "deep sleep" suggests. The captain's command to Jonah that he pray reflects the heathen concept that the amount of prayer is of importance (Mt 6:7) as well as that polytheists could seldom be sure which god had been displeased.

C. Jonah's Responsibility (1:7–10)

7 "Come, let us cast lots" assumes that Jonah had joined in the chorus of prayer. Though Jonah may have been terrified, he would hardly have realized, as did the sailors, that anything exceptional was happening. The lack of result from prayer and the rarity of such storms in the sailing season (cf. Ac 27:9) made the sailors conclude that someone on board must be responsible for their plight.

8 With the generosity of men who constantly risked their lives in their daily work, the sailors wanted to know whether Jonah was one who fully deserved his fate (cf. Ac 28:4), or whether there were extenuating circumstances that would justify their taking risks to try to save him.

9–10 In saying "I am a Hebrew," Jonah used the term by which an Israelite was known to his neighbors. In a polytheistic society, it was difficult to find a title that would more perfectly express the supremacy of the Lord than "the God of heaven." What terrified the sailors was the addition of "who made the sea and the land." They knew that Jonah was running away from the Lord (v.10), whom they knew to be the God of Israel. As Phoenicians they did not take seriously Jonah's claim that his Lord was superior to Baal. But now Jonah had claimed that the Lord was the Creator of the sea. Terrified they said, "What have you done!" It is an exclamation, not a question.

D. Jonah's Rejection (1:11–16)

11 The sailors found themselves in a new and unexpected position. They realized that they were not dealing with a heinous criminal. Here was a god's servant who had fallen out with his lord. In a culture where correct procedure in the service of the gods was essential, they sought to do the will of the Lord correctly. Only Jonah could guide them.

12 Jonah's answer to the distraught sailors was, in essence, "Hand me over to my God." Once the lot pointed to Jonah, he accepted that the storm was not simply a "natural phenomenon." So Jonah was willing to be handed over to his God. Jonah knew that God would not make the sailors pay for what had been an innocent act on their part. Jonah was confident that the sea would calm down once he was no longer in the ship.

13–14 Since the sailors' religious outlook could make no sense of a god of heaven's creating and controlling the sea—they probably did not even think of the sea as created but rather as a remnant of the original chaos—to throw Jonah overboard was equivalent to murdering him. They could not know for certain whether they were doing the Lord's will, and they feared that he might punish them for the death of his servant. So they tried hard to set him ashore, even though it involved great risk to the ship. When the increasing storm made this impossible, they prayed that they should not be held guilty of Jonah's death; for clearly the Lord had done as he pleased. When they called Jonah "innocent" (GK 5929), they were not impugning God's actions; they were merely stating that no human tribunal had passed sentence on him.

15–16 So far as the sailors knew, Jonah had been dealt with by his angry god. The immediate cessation of the storm after they threw Jonah overboard showed them that the Lord really had control of the sea. So "they offered a sacrifice to the LORD and made vows to him." There was a new respect for the God of Israel, a new understanding of his power. Because Jonah believed in the sovereignty of God, the sailors were brought to a realization of his power. But there is no evidence that their spiritual apprehension went further.

E. Jonah's Protection (1:17–2:1)

17 The sea did not change its nature when Jonah splashed into it. Jonah did not suddenly develop into a champion swimmer. But the necessary protection was there. There is no suggestion that the fish was a special creation for the purpose or that Jonah's preservation within it was miraculous. The power of God ensured that the fish was there at exactly the right time.

Why did God choose this means of preserving Jonah's life? God could easily have provided a piece of floating wreckage to which Jonah could have clung, until he washed up on the beach half-drowned. Miracle is not the gratuitous display of God's omnipotence, nor is it called out merely because of human need. Taken in its setting, it is probable that every miracle has spiritual significance (cf. the word "sign" in John's gospel). That must surely be the case here, especially since Jesus used this miracle to picture his own resurrection.

For the sailors the raising of the storm and its subsequent quieting were indubitable evidence of the Lord's control of chaos. Since "the fish" was at God's disposal, it meant that every force in the world, however potentially dangerous, was completely under God's dominance and control. So while in one way the fish is secondary in the revelation to Jonah, it was needed for the prophet to grasp that God's love is operative in a world that is entirely under divine control.

Once Jonah was on dry land again, he could make some kind of estimate of how long he had been in the fish. Yet to make any exact measure of the number of hours would have been impossible for him. Roused suddenly from a deep slumber, stupefied by the violence of the storm, and in all probability seasick, Jonah would have been in no position to know at what hour he was thrown overboard. Furthermore, on reaching the shore he would have needed time to collect his wits. Clearly, then, the term "three days and three nights" is intended as an approximation, not a precise period of seventy-two hours. The use by Jesus (Mt 12:40) should almost certainly be understood in the same way.

2:1 The popular idea that Jonah went straight from the deck of the ship into the fish's open mouth has no support from either the narrative or Jonah's prayer. He was half-drowned before he was swallowed. If he was still conscious, sheer dread would have caused him to faint—there is no mention of the fish in his prayer. He can hardly have known what caused the change from wet darkness to an even greater dry darkness. When he did regain consciousness, it would have taken some time to realize that the all-enveloping darkness was not that of Sheol (see next comment) but of a mysterious safety.

F. Jonah's Psalm of Thanksgiving (2:2–9)

2–4 "From the depths of the grave" is literally "from the belly of Sheol [GK 8619]." True, Sheol is often no more than a synonym for the grave; Jonah was not saying, however, that he thought he was buried but that he had gone to join the dead. The terrifying experience brought him to the realization of his plight and elicited the confession: "Yet I will look again." This is not a statement of salvation but of Jonah's determination to pray in spite of his banishment.

5–6 Jonah continued the description of his downward plunge into the deep, vividly illustrating the hopelessness of his situation. He was, as it were, beyond human help. The reference to the place of the dead as "the pit" (GK 8846) points to Jonah's expectation of certain death.

7–9 As he plummeted through the waters, Jonah realized that "his life was ebbing away." In these fleeting moments his thought turned to the Lord and his "holy temple." Remarkably, in spite of the position in which he found himself, Jonah had a mental picture of the despairing sailors calling in vain on their gods, while he, whom they thought had been lost, was awaiting the demonstration of his God's salvation.

G Jonah's Deliverance (2:10)

10 The literal Hebrew reads, "And the LORD spoke to the fish." Unlike the prophet, the fish responded promptly, as soon as it knew God's will. Where the fish spewed out Jonah is not indicated. No doubt the effect of the fish's gastric juices on Jonah's face and other exposed parts of his body must have been terrible.

II. The Obedient Prophet (3:1–4:11)

A. Jonah's Proclamation (3:1–4)

1 The expression "a second time" is completely vague. There are many examples in the Scriptures of no second chance. Indeed, we should rather ask why the second call came to Jonah. The answer seems to be the sovereignty of God, one of the main themes of this book.

2 God does not lay weight on Nineveh's political importance or on the magnificence of its buildings. "The message I give you" does not necessarily suggest that Jonah would have said otherwise. It is merely one more indication that we are dealing with the sovereignty of God.

3 "Now Nineveh was a very large city" (NIV note) most probably is the correct reading. "An important city" does not suit the context and introduces a note of particularity into a book where universality is constantly being implied. The stress on the importance and size of Nineveh is entirely justified. Its population was at least 120,000 (4:10), while Samaria, almost certainly larger than Jerusalem, had about 30,000.

"A visit required three days" is literally "a distance of three days." This could mean that it took three days to go either across it or around it; but it certainly does not mean what the NIV rendering might be taken to imply, that it would take three days to visit every part of it. Modern archaeology has shown that the inner wall had a length of almost eight miles.

4 Jonah was not necessarily proclaiming God's message as he went into the city. But sometime "on the first day," Jonah "proclaimed" his message. There may well have been something about Jonah, his bearing, his dress, or his "gastric juice tan" from the fish's belly as he strode toward the center of the city, looking neither to the right nor to the left, that drew many after him. When he finally stood and shouted, "Forty more days and Nineveh will be destroyed," the news spread like wildfire. The credibility of the message was underscored by the fact that at the time Assyria stood in considerable danger from its northern neighbors. But the word of the Lord worked the miracle, not Jonah or his commentary.

B. Nineveh's Repentance (3:5–10)

There now begins a subtle interplay on the two divine names. Up to this point, we consistently find the name "the LORD" (*Yahweh*; GK 3378), i.e., the name of the covenant-making God of Israel. Now alongside it we find the name "God" (*Elohim*; GK 466), the all-powerful One, the Creator, the Lord of nature. The obvious purpose is to bring home that Jonah had not been proclaiming the Lord to those who did not know him but that the supreme God, whatever his name, was about to show his power in judgment. There is not the slightest indication that Jonah had mentioned the God of Israel or had said that he came in his name. The Ninevites, however, recognized the voice of the supreme God, whatever name they may have given him, and repented.

5 We must picture the people, both those who heard Jonah and those to whom his words were reported, as saying spontaneously, "Let us fast!" Sackcloth was a standard, virtually obligatory, accompaniment of fasting. The coarsest of cloth, often made of goat's hair, sackcloth was the normal dress of the poor, prisoners, and slaves; it was worn by those who mourned (Eze 7:18). Prophets wore it, partly to associate themselves with the poor, partly perhaps as a sign of mourning for the sins of the people. When used by the Ninevites, it expressed their complete inability to contend with the divine decree and

with the recognition that they were the slaves of the supreme God.

6 There is no suggestion that Jonah made any effort to reach the royal presence; hence the news would have reached the king later than it did many of his subjects. He not only came down from his throne and sat on the ground—a feature of mourning rites—dressed in sackcloth like the meanest slave, but he sat in the dust, which means, presumably, in the open air, where he could be seen by his subjects. All this was done completely spontaneously. Then came the realization that this concerned everyone, and the decree was issued (v.7).

7 The king's courtiers and counselors sat in the dust around him and rapidly agreed on a decree that made the spontaneous response official. With the mourners were to be linked the domestic animals, a touch suggesting that it was indeed "Greater Nineveh" that was involved. Though we have no records from Mesopotamia of animals being so involved in mourning rites, there is nothing alien to the Oriental mind in it.

8 Anything and everything condemned by law and conscience is included under "evil ways." "Violence" (GK 2805) means a defiance of the law by one too strong to be brought to account. The Assyrians assumed that in virtue of their conquests they had been placed above lesser breeds and were entitled to ignore the dictates of conscience and compassion in their behavior to their neighbors. It is easy to slip into the concept that our position gives us the right to dominate others.

9–10 The operative phrase in these two verses is that God "had compassion" (GK 5714). We can know the character of God only from what he does and the words he uses to explain his actions. When he does not do what he said he would, we as finite beings can say only that he has changed his mind or repented, even though we should recognize, as Jonah did (4:2), that he had intended or desired this all along. "Compassion" is an inadequate rendering because it does not bring out the concept of a change. Thus "relent" is better. God's change was due to the change in the Ninevites.

2. Jonah's Displeasure (4:1–4)

1 We are so obsessed with pure doctrine that we are not satisfied when we meet obvious repentance but seek to ensure that it is accompanied by right doctrine. Jonah knew God well enough to understand that the person who really was repentant would be justified in God's sight. The literal translation here is "But it was evil to Jonah with great evil." The term "evil" (GK 8288 & 8317), which has been repeatedly applied to the Ninevites, now characterizes the prophet. By objecting to the character and actions of God, Jonah has effectively put himself out of fellowship with God, just like the evil and ignorant heathen. But God showed him the same compassion as he had shown Nineveh.

Why was Jonah so angry? Rabbinic literature suggests that on the basis of Dt 18:21–22 he would be regarded as a false prophet. True enough, once the first wave of terror had passed and destruction did not come, many in Nineveh must have asked themselves whether Jonah had really been a messenger of the gods. That was an unavoidable result of divine mercy. But it was recognized universally that a pronouncement of divine punishment might be averted by suitable penitence. Prophecy is conditional. So even if this motive played a part in Jonah's thinking, it must have been a minor one; and it does not explain why he ran away.

2 Jonah told God exactly why he was angry. He objected to God's sparing Nineveh. Jonah's motive could only stem from what Nineveh had meant in Israel's past and what he expected it to be in the future. (Compare the exultation over its fall in Na 2–3.)

The word "gracious" (GK 2843) is linked with "grace" and expresses God's attitude toward those who have no claim on him, since they are outside any and every covenant relationship. The Hebrew term translated "compassionate" (GK 8157) came to be linked with the word for "womb" and expressed the understanding and loving compassion of the mother to her child. We have here the male and female aspects of understanding, compassion, and favor united in the one God. "Love" (*hesed*; GK 2876) expresses God's behavior in the covenant relationship. There is no one term in English that adequately expresses the wide and rich range of meaning of this word. What is clear is that Jonah was

finding fault with God as he really is, not as he imagined him to be.

3 There can be little doubt that when Jonah asked God to take away his life, there is much more in what Jonah said than lies on the surface. He was virtually saying to God, "I have devoted my life to your service as your servant, as your prophet. But what I have experienced of you just does not make sense of the world order in which I find myself. Why should I go on living? For to leave your service would make my life purposeless. Once, in the past, you showed Elijah that there was a deeper purpose in life than he realized [1Ki 19:4]. Have you perhaps a similar message for me?"

4 "Are you right to be angry?" is a better translation than "Have you any right to be angry?" God was not rebuking Jonah; God was not even asking him what right he, a man, had to criticize God. Rather, he was suggesting to him that he might not be correct in his estimate of the position. Scripture has many examples of people who in agony tried to understand the ways of God and used language that others might consider blasphemous (cf. Jer 15:15–18; 20:7–18). God shows his compassion with all such people, including Jonah.

4. God's Rebuke of Jonah (4:5–9)

5 The usual view is that Jonah, hoping against hope, was waiting to see whether God might not change his mind again. But unless we are prepared to maintain that Jonah thought that Nineveh's repentance was merely superficial and transient and that therefore God might change his mind, the traditional view is alien to the picture of the prophet we have been slowly building up. It is far more probable that Jonah was expecting something to happen that would explain God's ways with humankind a little more clearly to him.

6 In the rest of this section, the divine name *Elohim* ("God"), which has been used consistently for God's dealings with Nineveh, is now used for his dealings with Jonah. The use of "Lord God" (*Yahweh Elohim*; see comment on 3:5–10) forms a link between the two usages, linking the God of creation (cf. Ge 1) and the God of revelation (cf. Ex 4). The Palestinian Jewish tradition identified the word traditionally rendered "gourd" with the castor oil plant. "Vine" is a safe rendering of this word. Though not stated, it is clear that the action Jonah took to "ease his discomfort" occurred in the hot season, when the daily maximum temperature in Mesopotamia is about 110 degrees Fahrenheit.

7 The repeated use of the verb "appointed" (GK 4948) of the fish (1:17), the vine (4:6), the worm (4:7), and the wind (4:8) stresses the divine initiative. The word for "worm" (GK 9357) implies something small. God uses both the great fish and the insignificant worm equally as instruments of his purpose.

8 "A scorching east wind" is normally called a "sirocco," which means "east wind." Obviously such a wind, blowing in from across the desert, withers all green growth. For Jonah there was no shelter, unless he was willing to reenter Nineveh. The shelter he had built did not exclude the wind and only partially broke the force of the sun's rays. Completely dispirited he in essence said, "I would be better off dead than alive."

9 As in v.4, it would be better to translate God's question by "Are you right to be angry about the vine?" and Jonah's answer by "I am." Why was Jonah so angry, or why did he feel such grief for the withered vine? God's answer in v.10 suggests that we take "Jonah was very happy about the vine" (v.6) to mean that sitting there in the burnt-up Tigris plain, shimmering in the heat, Jonah had felt real joy in the sight of the fresh, green plant. True enough, it increased his comfort, but that was secondary.

5. God's Mercy (4:10–11)

10 One of the greatest dangers besetting human beings is that they become such a part of their environment that they miss the pathos that pervades the universe. Paul describes it as a "groaning as in the pains of childbirth" (Ro 8:22), which comes from the futility caused by its bondage to decay. Jonah had apparently grown completely indifferent to the fate of God's creation outside Israel. We need hardly be surprised, for this attitude has

been common within the church, and indeed within some small local churches. So God placed his prophet on the level of an ordinary person. The discomforts of the summer heat, the attractiveness of the vine, and the destructiveness of the sirocco had nothing to do with Jonah's theology. He reacted to them as an ordinary man in the setting of nature.

Again the narrative changes to "the LORD." Once Jonah had realized his link with the rest of God's creation, God could declare the link between himself, the Creator, and his creation—not only humankind, made in the image and likeness of God, but also animals.

11 The meaning of "more than a hundred and twenty thousand people who cannot tell their right hand from their left" is difficult. It could refer either to the whole population of Nineveh or to the small children who do not yet know their right hand from their left. The former has been supported by archaeological considerations, which set the maximum population of Nineveh at 175,000 or less. Thus if only children were intended, far too high a total population would be involved—even if "Greater Nineveh" (cf. 3:2–3 is included.

We do not find in Scripture the sentimentalism about animals found in many classes of society today. Even so, Jonah had to understand that the fulfillment of his wishes about Nineveh would have involved the destruction not only of innocent human beings but also of "many cattle as well" that were dependent on people.

The curtain falls, and we are not told what, finally, Jonah did or said. Quite simply, the book contains a revelation of God's character and attitude toward his creation given to Jonah and through Jonah to Israel and to us. For Christians, the Son of Man's three days and three nights in the heart of the earth assure us of a love that embraces all, even in the darkest hour. We know that in Christ, God was reconciling the world to himself (2Co 5:18–19), and we will look with new eyes on those who have been reconciled. Christians cannot regard as enemies those whom God refuses to regard as his enemies.

The Old Testament in the New

OT Text	NT Text		Subject
Jnh 1:17	Mt 12:40		Three days and nights

Micah

INTRODUCTION

1. Background

Micah, like his contemporaries Isaiah and Amos, prophesied during the eighth century B.C., a time when Israel and Judah had risen to heights of economic affluence but had fallen to depths of spiritual decadence. Under the able leadership of Jeroboam II of Israel (786–746) and Uzziah of Judah (783–742), the territories of both kingdoms became almost as extensive as during the reign of Solomon. It was a time of great economic prosperity, fostered by the absence of international crises and by the mutual cooperation of both kingdoms. While Israel and Judah appeared to be strong externally, an internal decay was sapping their strength and threatening to destroy the social fabric of these two kingdoms. Canaanite religion had extended its influence among some of the people. And while Micah attacked the idolatry, it was not this aspect of Israel's condition that he emphasized most. It was rather the social injustices of the ruling classes.

The days of peace were destined to come to an end, however, as Assyria arose from a state of quiescence to occupy a threatening posture on the national scene. Under Tiglath-pileser III (745–727 B.C.), Assyria experienced a remarkable resurgence of power. At the same time Israel was being torn by internal strife and dissension. Finally, under the leadership of Shalmaneser V, Israel, the northern kingdom, was occupied; and several years later the city of Samaria fell to him and to Sargon II (721). In Judah, Ahaz's pro-Assyrian policies made Judah little more than a satellite of Assyria. Not till Hezekiah came to the throne (715) were sweeping religious—and most probably social—reforms instituted. Assyria continued to threaten Judah under Hezekiah's reign, but an attempt by Sennacherib to take Jerusalem was frustrated (2Ki 19:32–36; 2Ch 32:21; Isa 37:33–37). It was about a century after the death of

Hezekiah that Jerusalem would finally fall to the Babylonians.

2. Authorship

The superscription to the prophecy (1:1) asserts that Micah was the author. The prophet who bore that name was from Moresheth (probably Moresheth Gath) in Judah. This was a town in the general proximity of Isaiah's home, a factor that may explain certain similarities between the prophecies of both men. Little is known about Micah apart from what may be inferred from his prophecy. The book eloquently affirms his sensitivity to the social and religious wrongs of his time.

3. Date

The superscription (1:1) places Micah in the milieu of eighth-century B.C. prophetism. The reference to the destruction of Samaria (v.6) places the beginning of his prophetic career sometime before the capture of that city (722/721 B.C.); and this is in agreement with the superscription that fixes the beginning of his ministry in the reign of Jotham (750–731). The prophetic indictments of social and religious corruption fit well the time of Ahaz and could even be appropriate to the prereformation period of Hezekiah, who reigned 715–686 B.C. The reference to Micah's prophecy in Jer 26:18–19 fixes at least a portion of Micah's message in the time of Hezekiah.

4. Theological Values

While Micah may not have written a theology, he certainly based his pleas to the people on a consistent theology of God. The first theological emphasis is the sovereignty of God (1:2). To Micah the Lord acted within the nations to effect their destiny as well as the destiny of his own people. Micah understood the coming destruction of Samaria and Jerusalem to result from the Lord's punishing these centers of wickedness for their rebellion against him. However, only in the last days will God's activity regarding the nations reach its climax. Then the ultimate triumph and vindication of God's people will take place (4:11–13), and the nations will become subject to the rule of the Lord.

Another theological emphasis of Micah is the self-consistency of the Lord. He is immutably committed to his covenantal obligations. It is this theme, coupled with that of divine sovereignty, that gives such urgency to Micah's words. That God seems austere and unbending is only a partial picture of his self-consistency. He is consistent also with his nature, and that nature is to forgive (7:18–20). God will not give up his people altogether; he will forgive the sins of the believing remnant.

Micah's doctrine of the "remnant" (GK 8642) is unique among the prophets and is perhaps his most significant contribution to the prophetic theology of hope. The remnant is a force in the world, not simply a residue of people. It is a force that will ultimately conquer the world (4:11–13). By removing everything that robs his people of complete trust in him (5:10–15), the Ruler from Bethlehem will deliver his people.

The basis of the divine redemptive activity lies within the nature of God. The absence of a vicarious role in the redemptive work of the messianic King in Micah underscores the prophet's theological perspective, which is to assure us of the future exaltation and glory of the remnant; and this is done against the background of the humiliation the nation would soon endure. We may state this aspect of Micah's theology thus: The nation will suffer the shame of defeat and exile. But that is not the end, for certain triumph and glory lay ahead, not for the whole nation, but only for the remnant. The people of God will be delivered from affliction and exile by their King and will return with him, secure in his power. Thus Micah's focus is on the kingdom of the Lord and its manifestation in the world.

The kingdom is an expression of divine power and sovereignty within the sphere of the nations. The messianic King is depicted in close association with the Lord and embodies his might and authority. The work of the messianic King is presented by Micah almost entirely in terms of power. Even the tender act of caring for his own as a shepherd cares for his sheep is done in the strength of the Lord (5:4).

Micah spoke to a people whose disobedience had led them to ignominy and ruin. But he reminded them—and us—that the Lord is almighty; and, because he is consistent with his word and with his nature, the people of God will not fail to receive all he has promised them. Though we suffer shame now, glory and vindication lie ahead because the Lord will "be true to Jacob, and show mercy to Abraham" (7:20).

EXPOSITION

I. The Superscription (1:1)

1 According to the superscription, the prophetic activity of Micah spanned the reigns of three kings of Judah in the eighth century B.C. This period was one of great spiritual decline, especially for the northern kingdom; and the messages of Micah and the other eighth-century prophets, with their emphases on social justice and obedience to the laws of the Mosaic covenant, were a refreshing breeze in the arid climate of spiritual ignorance and disobedience.

The prophecy of Micah was directed primarily toward Samaria and Jerusalem, the capital cities of the northern and southern kingdoms (Israel and Judah). While Micah's message was applicable to all the inhabitants of these kingdoms, he singled out the capitals because the leaders of these centers of influence were largely responsible for the social ills of that time. In particular he singled out Jerusalem, not only because of the corruption of its leaders, but also because of its future glory—a central motif in the prophetic theology of hope.

II. The First Oracle: Israel's Impending Judgment and Her Future Restoration (1:2–2:13)

A. The Impending Judgment (1:2–7)

2 The opening statement of the prophecy consists of a summons to the nations to attend to the cosmic judgment scene so vividly described by the prophet in the subsequent verses. It is clear that the summons is directed to the nations.

Micah pictured God as coming from his dwelling place to "witness against" (GK 6332) the nations. This witness was effected in the cataclysmic destruction of the cities of

Samaria and Jerusalem. Micah, like Isaiah, saw the destiny of the nations as integrally related to the destiny of God's people. He deftly developed this theme throughout the prophecy.

The burning timbers and ruined houses of Samaria and Jerusalem would be an eloquent sermon to the people of the world that God does not allow sin to go unpunished, even in the case of his own people. God's destruction of Samaria and Jerusalem was to be a witness to the nations of God's hatred of sin and the harbinger of their own eventual destruction.

3–4 God's witness against the nations is depicted in a vivid anthropomorphic scene in which God comes forth from heaven to tread the high places of the earth and to bring about the destruction of Samaria and Jerusalem. In this representation, the prophet illustrates that God is not only transcendent above the world but immanent in it, and that he intervenes in history to effect his will.

The term "high places" (GK 1195) connotes several concepts. Aside from the basic meaning, it was used of pagan religious sanctuaries (Jer 7:31; Eze 20:29), the place of security and protection (Dt 32:13; Hab 3:19), and the place of military advantage (Dt 33:29; Eze 36:2). Apparently here Micah envisioned God as the majestic Sovereign who steps from heaven into the course of human events. Samaria and Jerusalem cannot stand before the might and power of the Conqueror who strides across the heights of the earth and before whom the pagan sanctuaries crumble as the mountains melt.The cataclysm that accompanied God's intervention in history is described in terms of a violent storm or earthquake (v.4). The language is metaphorical and describes the intensity of the destruction of Samaria and Jerusalem.

5 With telling force the prophet asserts that the national upheaval would be caused by the sins of the people of Israel. The close association between "high places" and "sin" in the mind of the prophet makes it clear that to him the incursion of non-Israelite religious practices was at the heart of the crisis of the house of Israel. Because of the influence of Canaanite religion, Israel was giving only lip service to the Lord; and the ethical demands of the law, with their resultant benign effect on the social structure of the nation, were being disregarded. This was the sin that led to estrangement from God and eventual captivity.

Literally the Hebrew here says, "Who is Jacob's transgression?" The prophet personified the cites of Samaria and Jerusalem, possibly because he wished to depict them as harlots.

6–7 Samaria was to become a ruin, a place with vineyards planted on her sloping sides amid the stones of her ruined buildings. The expression "lay bare her foundations" may echo the use of the word for uncovering one's nakedness (Lev 20: 11, 17–18, 20–21), a term used in the OT of prostitution (Eze 16:36; 23:18) and lewdness (2Sa 6:20; Hos 2:10). The imagery of the harlot appears where the wages Samaria received from the practice of prostitution would be burned. The prostitution referred to is idolatry, which the OT consistently regards as spiritual fornication.

The word translated "temple gifts" (GK 924) seems out of place in a sequence describing the destruction of idols and may reflect a Semitic root meaning "resemble"; hence it may refer to an image or idol. But the same word also connotes payment to a harlot, and Micah used the same word later in this verse (translated "the wages of prostitutes"). The wealth that accrued to Samaria from her idolatry would be taken away from her to be used again for the wages of prostitution—i.e., the invading Assyrians would transfer the wealth of Samaria to their own temples, where it would again be used for idolatrous worship.

B. The Prophet's Reaction to the Pronouncement of Judgment (1:8–9)

8–9 The prophet next laments the destruction of the great metropolis of Samaria by representing himself as wailing and going about unclothed as a sign of mourning. The judgment to come on Samaria was like an incurable wound, i.e., it was irreversible. But in its malignant course it had come to Jerusalem as well.

C. The Prophet's Warning and Summons to the People (1:10–16)

10 The phrase "Tell it not in Gath" is reflective of David's lament at Saul's death (2Sa 1:20). It warns the people not to weep lest the inhabitants of Gath, a Philistine city, learn of their impending destruction. In Beth Ophrah ("house of dust") the inhabitants are to roll in the dust as a sign of mourning (Jos 7:6; Job 16:15; Isa 47:1).

11–12 The people of Shaphir ("beautiful," "fair," "pleasant") are to experience something quite the opposite of what the name of their town means; they are to be reduced to shame and dishonor. Those who live in Zaanan ("come out") will not be able to come out from their city. Beth Ezel is unknown to us. The word *'etsel* means "beside," "contiguous to." We may paraphrase the name Beth Ezel as "nearby house." Perhaps the town was in close proximity to Jerusalem. That its "standing place" was to be taken away may indicate that this town would cease to exist. Thus a buffer between Jerusalem and the invading armies would be removed. The wailing is "because" Maroth ("bitter") will also endure God's punishment. All this is because God will punish his people, including Jerusalem.

13–14 The inhabitants of Lachish are to harness the team to the chariot and are to flee the coming destruction like steeds. The significance of Moresheth is difficult to determine. Its name in Hebrew is somewhat similar in sound to the word for "betrothed" and, since "parting gifts" were given to brides as dowries (1Ki 9:16), possibly the name was intended to connote that the town was soon to be parted from Judah as a bride parts from her family.

Aczib ("deception") will prove to be a deception to Judah. The word is used of a stream that has dried up (Jer 15:18); so this city will cease to exist.

15–16 The name Mareshah is somewhat similar to the root that means "to possess." Thus this town's name might have engendered associations with the word "conqueror." The glory of Israel, i.e., the people, will be forced to flee as David did to Adullam.

This section (vv.10–16) begins with words that recall David's lament at the death of Saul and ends with the name of the cave where David hid from Saul. These dark moments in David's life form a gloomy backdrop to the description of the fall of the towns Micah spoke of. Though he is never directly mentioned, the figure of a David bowed down by humiliation appears hauntingly in the tapestry of destruction. It is as if Micah saw in the

fall of each town and the eventual captivity of the two kingdoms the final dissolution of the Davidic monarchy. Like David, the glory of Israel would come to Adullam.

D. The Prophet's Indictment of the Oppressing Classes (2:1–5)

1–2 The oracle continues with a denunciation of the corrupt practices of the affluent and influential classes whose hold on society was so strong in Micah's day. The basis for the national crisis and the future collapse of the nation was Israel's disobedience to her God. Micah turned to the powerful ruling classes and began to vividly picture the intensity with which they sought to defraud the poor and become richer at the expense of the less fortunate. He pictured them lying awake at night devising their plans. At first light of day, they proceeded to put their schemes into action. They controlled the structure of society and had a free hand to perpetrate their deeds with impunity. They coveted the houses and lands of those who could not adequately defend themselves in this oppressive society.

3 The word "therefore" establishes the preceding catalog of wrongs as the basis for the "disaster" (GK 8288). Micah referred to the nation as a "people." He pictured the disaster as a burden from which they would be unable to save themselves (lit., "to remove their necks"). Micah saw the captivity as unavoidable. Because of the national humiliation, they would be unable to hold their heads high among the nations.

4 This verse contains a "mournful song" (GK 5631) or lament that is characteristic of the way the people would mourn the desolation of the land. This word is used of figurative prophetic accounts (e.g., Isa 14:4). In general, however, it is a "descriptive saying," "byword," or "proverb" that has popular appeal or significance. Because it is entirely in the first person, the song is clearly uttered by the house of Israel itself.

The lamentation concerns the fact that the land allotted to the people had changed hands. The land that had been Israel's exclusive possession had become the property of her enemies. The land was to be assigned to "traitors" (GK 8745) or, better, "to a rebel." Micah describes the enemy as a rebel, which is consistent with his view of the "nations that have not obeyed" (5:15).

5 The word "assembly" (GK 7736) may mean a "multitude" in general; here it connotes the assembly of people that is distinctly the Lord's, i.e., the covenantal community (Dt 23). Because of their blatant disregard for the obligations of the covenant, the oppressors had removed themselves from any inheritance in the congregation. Micah is saying that the corrupt people of his day would have no further participation in the covenant community.

E. The True Prophet Versus the False Prophets (2:6–11)

6 Micah quotes the false prophets of his day. "Do not prophesy," they said. The prohibition against prophesying is uttered by prophets, evidently the false, self-serving prophets of Micah's time. "Overtake" (GK 6047) never means that but always means "leave." Thus those false prophets appear to be saying: "Do not prophesy. Do not prophesy of these things; for as long as you do, disgrace will not leave us." The true prophets were apparently considered troublemakers whose powerful sermons disgraced the privileged classes and embarrassed the false prophets. As long as their prophetic protest continued, so the humiliation these corrupt leaders felt would continue.

7 The sense here indicates that one should not blame the continuing disgrace on the prophetic pronouncements of Micah. The subsequent questions imply that it is not of the nature of God only to punish or to reproach because, Micah continues, "my words [i.e., the words of the Lord through the prophet] do good to him whose ways are upright." If the ungodly people of his day would have lived according to the covenantal standards of the Lord, Micah's words would have had a benign effect on their lives as well as on the life of the nation; and the reproach and disgrace that they felt as he prophesied to them would have become a means of blessing.

8 But the people were not living according to the standards of the Lord, for Micah says, "Lately my people have risen up like an enemy." By their blatant disregard for the social concern demanded by the covenant, they were really rebelling against the Lord and evoking his anger. The acts of unbelievable hostility Micah cites describe the ways in which the poor were treated like an enemy. The people forcibly stripped off the outer garments of those who unsuspectingly passed by. The word "strip" (GK 7320) frequently has the sense of a "raid" that a marauding party would make against an enemy (Jdg 9:33; 1Sa 23:27), and it is used also of stripping for spoil (Hos 7:1). The peaceful and unsuspecting were suddenly bereft of some necessity of life by those who cared nothing for their victims' security or comfort.

9–10 The money hungry even treated the women cruelly. That only women are mentioned implies that they were probably widows forced from their homes. The children too were affected, for the Lord's blessing was taken from them forever. Because of the sin of the leaders of Micah's day, a whole generation would never see the glorious works of God but would live out their days in a strange land. Micah emphasized this as the intensity of his language rose to a sharp command. The people were to be banished because the land was irrevocably defiled.

11 The people of this time had an intense desire for the fruits of their affluent society, expressed in the terms "wine" and "beer." So if someone were to preach to them of greater affluence and prosperity, they would listen to him; and he would readily find acceptance among them. The implication is that Micah's message of doom was unacceptable to those who were basking in the affluence of the eighth century.

F. The Prophet's Statement of Hope (2:12–13)

12–13 The prophet turns abruptly to the statement of hope that ends the first oracle. In it he announces Israel's future restoration. The abruptness of the transition serves to place his message of hope in stark contrast to the message of the hypothetical preacher of v.11, who falsely preaches of continuing bright prospects for Israel. Micah's hope was not centered in his generation but in a remnant that would be led by their king from captivity to deliverance.

If studied in isolation from the total context of the prophecy, the passage may be understood simply as a prediction of the return from the captivity. But this is inadequate in view of the broader background of Micah's concept of the future. Micah envisioned a kingdom of eternal duration with the Lord as King (4:7). The Deliverer-King of 5:2–4 seems to be identical with the king of the present passage; he plays an important role in the restoration of God's people. In both passages the motif of the "flock" is prominent. The fulfillment of the great prophecy in 5:2–4 requires a ruler whose birthplace is Bethlehem and who will extend his influence to the ends of the earth and bring security to God's people. Micah's perspective of hope extends beyond a mere restoration from captivity to the messianic kingdom. It is only then that Israel's hope will be finally and consummately realized.

Micah depicts the "remnant" (GK 8642) as a flock of sheep penned up in an enclosure. In the next clause the figurative depiction of sheep gives place to the picture of a vast throng of people. The word translated "throng" (GK 2101) means "to murmur." It depicts the murmuring of the members of a community (Ru 1:19) and the resonating sound of the earth echoing to the noise of a loud shout (1Sa 4:5; 1Ki 1:45).

Suddenly a figure, called "the Breaker" (NIV, "One who breaks open the way"), appears in the narrative and goes up before the multitude. Led by the Breaker, the people burst through the gate of the enclosure to form a procession with their King at their head. Micah envisions a time when the kingdom of God will burst forth into sudden reality and the people of God will be manifested. He affirms that the strictures that now prevent the visible realization of the power and glory of God's kingdom and that blur the identity of God's people in the world will be shattered and the Breaker will lead his people to glory.

The parallelism of the last clause establishes a close relationship between the work of the Breaker and the King of 5:2–4. Both arise from the people (5:2) and bring deliverance to the people (5:4); the people they lead are likened to a flock (5:4); and both are intimately associated with the Lord (5:4). We may thus understand the Breaker to be Israel's King.

The last line of v.13 establishes a close connection between the Lord and the King.

It is the Lord whose strength and power are manifested in the reign of the King. The King reflects the strength and majesty of the Lord as does the figure of 5:4. The remnant, according to Micah, will receive its final glory and vindication only through the Messiah. He will arise from his people and lead them into the security of God's kingdom. This passage anticipates a later passage (4:7) in which Micah envisioned the remnant as a "strong nation" over which the Lord reigns.

III. The Second Oracle: The Prophet's Indictment of the Leaders of the House of Israel and Israel's Future Hope (3:1–5:15)

A. The Prophet's Indictment of the Rulers of Israel (3:1–4)

1 The second oracle begins, like the first, with a summons to hear the prophet's message. The summons was directed in this instance to the rulers of Judah and Israel. Micah begins this oracle with a devastating question. If any should know the meaning of "justice" (GK 5477), it is those who have the awesome responsibility of leadership. Here "justice" is used in the sense of fairness and equity in governmental administration.

2–4 The language of the prophet becomes vividly emotive as he describes the harsh treatment directed against the poor. He pictures the civil leaders as treating the exploited classes like animals being butchered and prepared for eating. The skin was torn from them and their flesh butchered. Because they had so treated the poor, the Lord would not hear these merciless authorities when they cried to him. Those who violate God's covenant cannot expect him to maintain the blessings of the covenant.

B. The Prophet's Indictment of the Religious Leaders of Israel (3:5–8)

5 Micah addresses another group of leaders in Israel, the false prophets of the time. The word "feeds" (lit., "bites"; GK 5966) is always used in the OT for the bite of a serpent—except where the root reflects the secondary connotation of paying interest on loaned money. Its primary use has led some to interpret the phrase as describing the harm inflicted on the people by the lying prophets, whose false message of peace was as harmful as a serpent's bite.

In this structure, however, "bite" is paralleled by "not put into their mouths," and "proclaim 'peace'" by "wage war." The parallelism thus determines that "bite" has to do with the action of putting something into the mouth. While the word is never used for "eating" in the OT, there is no reason why Micah could not have used this forceful figure to express the voracity with which these greedy prophets accepted the bribes given them for the performance of their prophetic activity.

6–7 The end would come for these religious hucksters. While they were basking in the sunlight of power and affluence, the sun would go down on their prophesying and the resultant night would be devoid of vision or divination. It would be a time in which false predictions of peace (v.5) would be discredited by the reality of the Captivity. These prophets would "cover their faces" (lit., "cover the beard"), an expression connoting deep mourning.

8 Micah contrasts his prophetic activity with that of the false prophets. He asserts that he was filled with power "with the [help of] the Spirit." The implication is that the false prophets were motivated by greed. The word "justice" (GK 5477) is used frequently in the OT prophetic books in the sense of true religion—i.e., the crystallization of the ethic of the law. Because Micah was not violating the covenantal standards, he stood in sharp contrast to the religious leaders who participated in and encouraged the social exploitation of their time. Because Micah was guiltless of his compatriot's crimes against their fellow Israelites, he could stand before his adversaries with the power of moral courage and a clear conscience. Thus he could fearlessly cry out against the sin of the house of Israel.

C. The Result of the Leaders' Corruption on the Nation (3:9–12)

9 The address to the leaders of the house of Jacob continues with a biting portrayal of their sins. Micah accuses them of despising justice. The word for "despise" (GK 9493) means utter abhorrence of something.

10–11 As the leaders discharged their duties, they did so with bloodshed and greed, motivated by their desire for personal gain. Characterized by avarice and violence, their whole system of government inevitably led to corruption. These leaders maintained a form of external religion based to some extent on the covenantal relationship. "Is not the Lord among us?" they asked. But they had lost sight of the ethical requirements of the covenant and felt that their historical relationship to the Lord would prevent the onslaught of misfortune. Yet a clear body of prophetic tradition made it obvious that God desired obedience, not allegiance to externals (1Sa 15:22; Ps 51:17). This optimistic but unfounded trust is described as "leaning on the Lord." It was a kind of trust, but one devoid of obedience to God.

12 Because of the actions of the corrupt religious and civil leaders, the predicted doom would become a reality. Again the "therefore" establishes that the cause of the Captivity was the disobedience of the people. While the name "Zion" originally referred to the Jebusite stronghold captured by David (2Sa 5:7), it became a synonym for the city of Jerusalem (Ps 149:2; Isa 4:3; 40:9; Am 6:1). Micah includes the destruction of the temple, the visible sign of God's presence, in his prophecy. The symbol of the people's empty religion would perish.

D. The Future Exaltation of Zion (4:1–8)

The chapter division at the end of ch. 3 is unfortunate because Micah continues to speak of Jerusalem. The mood changes, however, from gloom to sublime hope as Micah portrays the future glory of the city. The temple mount would be exalted in the latter days, and the city of Jerusalem would become the center of God's gracious activity to the peoples of the earth.

1 "In the last days" always denotes a period of time that is in the indefinite future (cf. esp. Da 10:4; Hos 3:5). Since the term is used in this context of the reign of the Lord, it is eschatological. That the prophet envisioned the exaltation of Jerusalem in association with the messianic kingdom is clear from 4:8 and 5:2–4, 7–9. So it appears that Micah looked for the fulfillment of this prophecy, not specifically in the return from the Captivity, but rather in that time when the messianic King would effect the will of God for his people and would restore the fortunes of Israel.

2 The object of the people's attraction to Jeru–salem is to be their desire for God's word that emanates from the city. Micah sees a change in the hearts of all peoples at this time when the law of the Lord will be received universally rather than by Israel and Judah alone.

3 The result of God's rule in this time will be that the nations of the world will experience peace. The prophecy is national and even universal in scope and looks forward to a time when the nations will come so fully under the peaceful influence of God's Word that war will be no more. Because of this, weapons of war will be fashioned into agricultural implements. The pastoral motif reflects the peace that Micah sees as the ruling element of the messianic kingdom (cf. Isa 11:6–10; Hos 2:15; Am 9:13–15). The close identification between the Lord and the messianic King is evident in the prophecy of Micah (see comments on Isa 2:2–4).

4 The peacefulness of this era is further described in pastoral imagery (cf. 1Ki 4:25; Zec 3:10). The people will dwell in peace and safety because of the word of the Lord of Hosts. The certainty of this event is established in Micah's mind because God has sovereignly declared that such will happen: "The LORD Almighty has spoken."

5 The reason for the people's safety and security is that they will walk in the name of the Lord forever. This means more than simply

"They will beat their swords into plowshares" (4:3). These farming tools were found at Gezer in 1972. Courtesy Tell Gezer Excavations.

adhering to religious requirements. It means to live in reliance on the strength of the Lord, relying on the might of his power. Unlike the nations, God's people will enjoy his strength forever. It will be otherwise with the nations, for the dominion of their gods will end when the people of the world submit to the rule of the Lord.

6–7 "In that day" refers back to the era of Jerusalem's exaltation (4:1). The future regathering of Israel in the time of Zion's exaltation is described differently from the way Micah described it earlier (2:12–13). Micah depicts those who are regathered as lame, referring to their weakness as a result of God's afflicting them; and he further describes them as exiles, connoting the shame of expulsion from one's homeland. The emphasis is on the misery and helplessness of the exiles and forms a striking contrast to the "strong nation" they are to become as a result of God's intervention on their behalf.

The returning people do not automatically comprise the remnant but are to be made into a remnant. To Micah the "remnant" is the repository of God's grace and promise as well as the force that will ultimately conquer the godless nations at the end time (5:8–15). Since the remnant is the beneficiary of God's promise, it cannot fail to experience ultimate vindication and glory. The nation the remnant is transformed into will have the Lord as its King forever. The center of God's governmental activity will be restored and exalted Zion.

8 The climax of this representation of Jerusalem's future glory is described in terms of its restoration as the seat of the "former dominion." The dominion soon to be lost in the dark time just ahead will be restored!

The phrase "watchtower of the flock" is in apposition with "stronghold ['*ophel*, GK 6754] of Zion" and synonymous with it. The "stronghold" was a fortified section of Jerusalem on the east side in the immediate area of the temple mount and the Kidron Valley. Since the expressions Micah uses have such close ties with the location of David's dominion, the words "former dominion" can mean little else than that the Davidic kingdom will in some sense be restored to Jerusalem. By asserting this, Micah stands firmly in the tradition of the preexilic prophets (Isa 9:17; Hos 3:5; Am 9:11).

E. The Future Might of Zion (4:9–13)

9 The writer shifts the reader's attention abruptly from the description of the future glory to the realities of the current crisis. The rhetorical questions are affirmations. Israel would have no king. She would be left without a counselor. The king was the Lord's anointed and stood as his vicegerent, mediating God's law to the people. The loss of Israel's ruler would lead many to question the veracity of God's promises as they related to the future of the nation and to the Messiah who was to come from Israel. The extreme anguish the nation was to endure through losing its national sovereignty is pictured as that of a woman in childbirth.

10 Micah saw the Captivity as taking place in three stages: leaving the city, sojourning in the open country, and arriving at the land of captivity. "Babylon" may typify world powers whose hostility to Israel was exhibited in so many ways and would continue to be shown until the time of Israel's restoration (cf. Ge 10:10; 11:4–9). The plural "enemies" indicates that "Babylon" had for Micah a broader significance than the empire soon to replace Assyria as the dominant world power.

The statement of hope that opened the chapter is reiterated and complemented by the truth that it is not a hope to be realized by an unrepentant people who have not paid for their sins. They are to suffer for their disobedience; but beyond that night of despair is the bright morning of Zion's glory, when God's people will be redeemed from the hand of their enemies.

11–13 The nations that exhibit hostility do this in ignorance; for as they gather to gloat over the misfortune of God's people, the nations do not know their part in God's plan for his people. The prophet pictures the nations as sheaves brought to the threshing floor; and only too late do they recognize that they are to be threshed and broken by Israel herself. The "horns of iron" symbolizes strength (cf. Dt 33:17; 1Sa 2:1). The wealth of the world is to be devoted to God, and all its might is to be under his dominion.

F. The Future King of Zion (5:1–4)

1 "Marshal your troops" is a summons for Jerusalem to gather troops for her defense. The expression "city of troops" depicts a warlike city. The implication is that Jerusalem, so renowned for its hostility toward the less fortunate, is to suffer siege because of its wrongdoing. The striking of the king on the cheek represents the most extreme of insults and marks the victory of Israel's enemies over her (1Ki 22:24). The king is called "judge" (GK 9149; NIV, "ruler"), depicting the judicial aspect of his office.

2 The statement of doom is followed by one of hope: the prediction of a king who will bring lasting security to Israel and whose influence will extend to the ends of the earth.

Ephrathah is the ancient name of Bethlehem (Ge 35:16, 19; 48:7; Ru 4:11) and distinguishes it from other towns named Bethlehem (cf. Jos 19:15). Its use identifies the town in which David was born (1Sa 17:12), thus establishing a connection between the messianic King and David.

The "ruler" (GK 5440) is represented as speaking here, and the close identification of the king with the purposes of God is thus implied. The ruler is the one whose activities stem from the distant past, yet whose coming is still future.

The word "origins" (GK 4606) comes from a word meaning "to go forth" or "to conduct one's activities" (cf. 2Ki 19:27). Beyond that the phrase has a military connotation referring to the departure of an army for battle (2Sa 3:25); it may thus speak of the kingly activities of the Messiah in terms of his might and power.

The terms "old" (GK 7710) and "ancient times" may denote "great antiquity" as well as "eternity" in the strictest sense. The context must determine the expanse of time indicated by the expressions. This word here can indicate only great antiquity, and its application to a future ruler—one yet to appear on the scene of Israel's history—is strong evidence that Micah expected a supernatural figure (cf. Isa 9:6; cf. also Isa 24:23; Mic 4:7). Only in Christ does this prophecy find fulfillment.

3 Because a ruler will eventually come to deliver Israel, God will give her up only temporarily. Israel will enter a period of absolute abandonment by God because of her sin (1:5–6; 2: 1–5; 3:4, 9–12; 4:10; 6:9–16), but a ruler will come who will end the period of

Israel's estrangement; therefore Israel will be given up only till that time.

Micah saw the period of abandonment continuing till "she who is in labor gives birth." The end of the period of Israel's estrangement from God is marked not only by the bringing forth of the ruler but also by the return to Israel of "the rest of his brothers." The brothers are those who share a common national heritage with the ruler (cf. 2Sa 19:13). The word "return" (GK 8740) implies an original identification with Israel. The need for their return indicates that they have been dispersed.

The gathering of those who comprise the remnant is an essential element in Micah's theology (2:12–13 and 4:6–7). The depiction of the future gathering of the remnant in 5:3 is presented in a captivity motif; the brothers have been dispersed—they are in exile.

4 The peaceful effect of the kingly reign of Messiah is described in pastoral terminology. Israel will be lovingly cared for by the messianic King who will carry out his regnal duties in the strength of God. The gracious benefits of his reign are to extend beyond national limitations, for the authority of the King is to be universal. This description of his power goes perfectly with the description of universal peace seen earlier (4:1–4) and complements it by affirming that the peace described there will be effected by the Ruler born in the insignificant town of Bethlehem. Isaiah called him the "Prince of Peace" (9:6).

G. The Future Peace of Zion (5:5–6)

5–6 The placid picture vanishes for a moment, and we hear the tramping boots of the invader. The events described here are difficult to place historically. If "Assyria" is understood as a figure of speech for all the world powers that oppress Israel, we may then understand the passage as a prophecy of Israel's ultimate victory over her foes. Micah uses the word "Assyria" typically in 7:12, where in the restoration people come to Israel from Assyria. Zechariah also uses "Assyria" and "Egypt" (10:10) to refer to the nations God's people will be gathered from when the kingdom is to be established. Significantly, the prophecy of Zechariah was written long after the fall of the Assyrian Empire. In the mind of Zechariah, Assyria (no longer a nation in his time) represented

more than the empire that brought down the northern kingdom.

The "seven shepherds" and "eight leaders" are to be understood as an indefinite number of leaders. The figure stresses the abundance of manpower Israel will enjoy when God accomplishes the work of gathering his people from the godless nations to establish them in the land under the Messiah.

H. The Future Vindication of Zion (5:7–9)

7 The "remnant" of believers trusting in the promises of God is to be transformed from an insignificant group to one of absolute dominance in the world, disseminating its faith and ideals throughout the earth. As the dew and showers "do not wait for man" but come from the Lord, so the remnant will be lifted to its place of sovereignty by the power of God.

8–9 Micah next pictures the remnant as a lion overcoming its prey. The vivid description does not mean that the remnant will achieve victory by bloodthirsty militaristic conquest. Micah rather pictures the relentless force with which a lion captures its prey—"and no one can rescue." The prophet indicates that the nations will not be able to withstand the burgeoning power of the remnant in the end time, with its ultimate triumph in the world.

I. The Future Purification of Zion (5:10–15)

10–13 If "in that day" refers to the period when the remnant will achieve victory over the nations (vv.7–9), then the prophet conceives of God as destroying the weaponry of the remnant and expunging their idolatrous practices after achieving the conquest. However, if it refers to Zion's exaltation in 4:1–4, the purification of the remnant will take place in the initial stages of the era of peace; and their rise to dominance over the nations is not to be by military might but by their total dedication to God, brought about as God removes everything that interferes with their total trust in him. The world will eventually be conquered, not by its own corruption or false ideologies, but by the gospel.

The implication of vv.10–15 is that the instruments of war and the elements of idolatrous worship are wrong. Horses and chariots are to be removed because they tend to undermine Israel's complete trust in God. The cities and defenses are to be destroyed as well as the elements of false religion. "Witch-craft" denotes the ways people sought control of natural forces or power over individuals. "Cast spells" connotes a type of sorcery and is always condemned in the OT (Dt 18:10; 2Ki 21:6). The foretelling of the future was an aspect of this type of divination.

Israel's images are to be destroyed as well. The word "images" (GK 6773) means idols carved from some material. The "sacred stones" were standing pillars, usually of stone, that represented pagan deities. Both terms used in this verse require manual structuring or fashioning; hence, Micah said, "You will no longer bow down to the work of your hands."

14–15 "Asherah," a Canaanite goddess who is called in mythological texts the "Creatress of the gods," was associated with all aspects of sexual life and thus with fertility in general. She was also a goddess of war. Sacred prostitution was an integral part of her cult. To Micah the "cities" were the centers of pagan worship. The repetition of "cities" (cf. v.11) throws into bold relief the inevitable captivity of the cities that were about to perish. The nations that do not yield to God will be subjugated so that the peace promised in 4:1–4 will never be threatened.

IV. The Third Oracle: God's Lawsuit With Israel and the Ultimate Triumph of the Kingdom of God (6:1–7:20)

A. God's Accusations Against His People (6:1–8)

1–2 The third oracle begins in the format of a legal controversy. The mountains are called as witnesses in the litigation. The enduring hills have mutely observed Israel's history from its very beginning; hence they are called "everlasting foundations." If they could speak, they would witness to the truthfulness of the Creator's claims.

3 Micah places the classic disputation form of the prophets in a legal context as he pictures God's pleading with his people. The passage takes on an atmosphere of pathos as God is pictured asking his people how he has wearied them. The Creator of those mountains seeks the cause of Israel's estrangement from him.

The word "burden" (GK 4206) signifies to wear down, to cause someone to become impatient, or to become physically tired. The Lord asks how he has caused them to become so weary of him that they have ceased to obey him. Their impatience cannot be due to inactivity on his part, for he has done much for them.

4 The deliverance from Egypt represents one of the first acts of redemption in which God demonstrated his saving love for the people. Moses was God's great prophet, the prototype of the line of prophets yet to come (Dt 18:15–22). Miriam was a prophetess (Ex 15:20); and Aaron, the progenitor of the Aaronic priesthood, was the representative of the people before God.

5 Micah cites the failure of Balaam to curse the people (Nu 22–24) as evidence of God's activity among them. Besides the failure of Balak to frustrate the progress of the people, the journey from Shittim to Gilgal witnessed the defeat of Midian, the crossing of the Jordan, and the conquest of Jericho. The recital of events stops abruptly as though the intent is to depict in one great sweep the progress of the nation from slavery in a foreign land to settlement in their own country.

"Righteous" (GK 7407) has the basic sense of "rightness" and can apply to the secular as well as religious spheres of life. Here the word underlines God's faithfulness to his standard, i.e., the covenant obligations. His great acts on behalf of Israel are more than simply coming to the aid of his people. They are manifestations of his righteousness as he maintains his faithfulness to the covenant promise.

6–7 The recital of Israel's history suddenly ends, and Micah speaks on behalf of the people, asking God what their responsibility is in the light of his faithfulness to the covenant. There is irony here as the prophet asks how one may come before the "exalted God." The word "exalted" (GK 5294) connotes "height" and speaks of God in his dwelling place in heaven. What is the proper way to worship him? With burnt offerings and calves a year old? Yearling calves were regarded as the choicest sacrifices. "Thousands of rams" suggests the large quantity of animals that one might offer to curry God's favor. But God is interested neither in the choicest animals nor in the number offered. Even great quantities of oil will not bring the worshiper into fellowship with God. The list reaches a shocking climax in the mention of the firstborn. Child sacrifice was carried out by certain Israelites on occasion (2Ki 3:27–16:3; Isa 57:5). The firstborn represents the most precious thing one could give to God. Again, this was not what God wants.

8 What God wants is a heart response to God demonstrated in the basic elements of true religion. God has told the people what is good. The Mosaic law differentiated between good and bad and reflected God's will in their religious and social lives. They were to act "justly" (GK 5477), here in the sense of "true religion," i.e., the ethical response to God that has a manifestation in social concerns as well. "To love mercy [GK 2876]" is freely and willingly to show kindness to others. "To walk humbly [GK 7570] with your God" means to live in conscious fellowship with him, exercising a spirit of humility before him. The prophet was not indicating that sacrifice was completely ineffectual and that simply a proper heart attitude to God would suffice. Rather, God has no interest in the multiplication of empty religious acts.

These ethical requirements do not comprise the way of salvation. Forgiveness of sin was received through the sacrifices. The standards of this verse are for those who are members of the covenantal community and delineate the areas of ethical response that God wants to see in those who share the covenantal obligations. These standards have not been abrogated for Christians, for the NT affirms their continuing validity. We are still called to the exercise of true religion (1Co 13:4; 2Co 6:6; Col 3:12; Jas 1:27; 1Pe 1:2; 5:5). Christians are in a covenant relationship with God in which the law has been placed within their hearts (Jer 31:33; cf. Heb 10:14–17), not abrogated. But our obedience is inspired by the indwelling Holy Spirit, not by the letter of the law.

B. The Sentence of Judgment (6:9–16)

9 The voice of the Lord suddenly sounds out. "Calling to the city" signifies the cry of alarm heard when disaster threatens a city. Micah adds that it is wise to fear God's name. The "rod" is the punishment that Israel would endure, and she was to "heed" it. The people were to attend to the fact that the invasion would come and that it was God who would

effect it through the instrumentality of the Assyrians.

10–13 The Hebrew says, literally, "Are there yet in the house of the wicked treasures of wickedness and the short measure that is cursed?" The question, of course, is rhetorical and affirms that the oppressing classes are still getting gain from their mistreatment of the poor and that the oppression has not ended. Hence the punishment is deserved and now imminent. Micah emphasizes social sins more than sins of idolatry, though ultimately they are closely intertwined in his thinking. The response to the question of v.11 was, of course, a resounding no! The society of Micah's time was characterized by violence, lying, and deceit. False promises were uttered and claims made that were not fulfilled. According to v.13, it was because of the people's sins that God was to bring ruin on them.

14–15 The land was to fall under the devastation of the sword and be totally unproductive. The greed that motivated the rich in that day would no longer be gratified because of the desolation of the land.

16 In their pagan religious practices, the people were no better than the generation of Omri, the notorious king who headed the dynasty that produced Ahab, the husband of Jezebel, and allowed Baal worship in Israel. "Therefore" indicates that Israel's disobedience to God would bring the three calamities the prophet was about to describe. She was to become a "ruin" (GK 9014). The Hebrew word means both "to be desolated" and "to be appalled." It may connote that which is an object of horror.

C. The Prophet's Lament of the Lack of Godly Fellowship (7:1–2)

Like a day that begins with a dark, foreboding sky but ends in golden sunlight, this chapter begins in gloom and ends in hope. Clouds of gloom have rolled in on the horizon of the prophet's life because of the disobedience of the people and the somber fate that awaited his nation. But rays of hope shine through the gloom.

1 This section begins with a lament as the prophet mourns the lack of godly fellowship in his time. The metaphor pictures the remnant as seeking for grapes and choice figs to satisfy its hunger, but it is as though it were the time of harvest when these have been picked and the hunger must go unsatiated.

2 The fruit in v.1 represents godly persons. The feeling of utter disappointment in seeking food and finding none conveys the feelings of the godly at the great lack of individuals who have remained faithful to God. The language describes the excesses that characterized the treatment of the "have nots" by the "haves."

D. The Prophet's Lament of the Corruption in His Society (7:3–6)

3 Micah describes the strong hold that those in responsible positions had on the throat of society. "The ruler demands gifts" means that the ruler insisted that justice be distorted for his gain. Power can corrupt if not guarded by the law of a higher Sovereign. The judicial system was corrupted by the lust for bribes. The controlling classes, i.e., the rich, simply dictated their desires; the implication is that they received them.

In the conspiracy of the ruling classes, the ruler sought, perhaps, for the indictment of an innocent person; the judge carried it out for a bribe; and the rich man was involved in the conspiracy by speaking "the desire of his soul" ("what they desire"). The word for "desire" (GK 2094) is always used in a bad sense and may mean "evil desire" but more commonly "calamity" or "destruction."

4 Micah describes even the best of the people as briers. If one sought mercy or sympathy from any of them—even those who appeared to be upright and respectable—they would prove to be hard and piercing. In keeping with his use of sudden, almost jarring, contrasts, Micah points to the coming judgment: "The day of your watchmen [GK 7595] has come." The watchmen were the prophets (Jer 6:17; Eze 3:19) who watched the course of their nation, saw its internal decay and decline, and, like watchmen who guarded the cities of ancient times, warned of the inherent danger. The day of the watchmen was the day of punishment—the Captivity.

5–6 Micah returns to the description of the wrongs of his society. In his day a man could not trust his friends or even his wife, and respect for one's parents had vanished.

E. The Godly Man's Attitude in the Midst of Discouragement (7:7–10)

7 The clouds of gloom begin to separate as the prophet describes the attitude of the godly person amid such difficult circumstances. Micah does not succumb to despair or lethargy. The word "watch" (GK 7595) means to "look" or "wait expectantly" (cf. v.4). The godly person will look expectantly for every evidence of God's working. By waiting for him to act in his own time, Micah finds peace in the knowledge of God's sovereign activity in the world. But Micah also expresses confidence that God will answer prayer.

8 Not only does he trust God to act and to answer prayer, but Micah trusts him to vindicate the faithful. Though the faithful are subjected to difficult experiences, they will one day rise to receive their heritage. There is vivid contrast between the people of God sitting in darkness and the gladdening effect of the light of God that will shine among them.

9 The remnant affirm their determination to wait till God pleads their cause and decides in their favor. They freely confess their sin in the awareness that the temporal punishment to be endured is just. However, the remnant can be confident of God's favorable action on their behalf; for they, unlike their guilty compatriots, stand on the ground of the covenant.

10 Ultimately the remnant will be exalted and the hostile nations of the world covered with shame and trampled like mud. This latter figure is used by Isaiah (10:6) of the invading Assyrians. Micah uses it of the conquest of the hostile powers in the day of Israel's exaltation.

F. The Assurance of Victory for the Kingdom of God (7:11–20)

1. Victory described in terms of the extension of the kingdom (7:11–13)

11–12 The remainder of the chapter is an exultant description of the eventual triumph of the remnant. The prophet envisions a great extension of the remnant's influence as he sees a future day when the nation will greatly increase in population by an influx of people from Gentile nations, symbolized by Assyria and Egypt. That the Gentiles are to become partakers of the promise through faith is a cardinal doctrine of both OT and NT (Ge 12:3; Am 9:11–12; Ro 9:30; Gal 3:6–9).

13 At the same time, however, the judgment of God will fall on the sinful world. Out of the decay of a crumbling society, Micah perceives the emergence of the kingdom of God.

2. Victory assured because of God's leadership (7:14–15)

14 The remnant will triumph because of their relationship to God. The text pictures them as dwelling alone, i.e., apart from the nations, in a forest. Bashan and Gilead were agricultural areas of great fertility that became symbols of plenty. The reference to them here is symbolic. This is a request that Israel's former years of blessing be restored by her Good Shepherd.

15 The Exodus was the central event in the prophetic theology of history. It could be repeated because to the prophets history was continually being fulfilled. The Exodus would occur again—but in a new and even greater way. To the prophets the Exodus was an event of more than historical interest. Because God is unchanging and his attributes timeless, his people could expect his acts to be repeated again and again in history.

3. Victory assured over the nations (7:16–17)

16 As a result of God's intervention on behalf of Israel, the nations will be humbled before God and his remnant. The power of the nations will be as nothing before the great power of Almighty God. To lay the hand on the mouth is to indicate reverence and awe. The deafness of the nations may be caused by the thunderous events that God brings about.

17 In the vindication of God and his remnant in the world, the nations are pictured as animals crawling from their dens and trembling before the Lord.

4. Victory assured because of God's nature (7:18–20)

18 The question "Who is a God like you?" points to the uniqueness of the Lord. The name "Micah" means "Who is like the LORD?" The words "sin" (GK 6411) and "transgression" (GK 7322) recall the affirmation of Ex 34:6–7, wherein the Lord proclaimed an essential aspect of his nature to be his willingness to forgive sin.

19–20 Because God's anger does not continue forever, the believing remnant can know that an end will come to their humiliation. After the great statement of forgiveness, the prophet recalls the promise given to Abraham and reaffirmed to Jacob. The remnant's optimism was rooted in the eternal promise sworn to Abraham and their "fathers" (Ge 13:15; 17:7–8, 13, 19; 48:4), and its elements are applicable to Christians (see 1Pe 2:5; cf. 2Co 6:16; Heb 8:10; Rev 21:3, 7). The promise is a continuum that guarantees an inheritance to all God's people. As God's people, our sins have been trodden underfoot. We, too, know the loving care of the Shepherd who feeds his flock in the strength of the Lord. Micah's concept of the remnant encompasses believers today.

The Old Testament in the New

OT Text	NT Text	Subject
Mic 5:2	Mt 2:6	Birth in Bethlehem
Mic 7:6	Mt 10:35; Lk 12:53	A divided household

INTRODUCTION

1. Background

The setting of Nahum's prophecy is the long and painful oppression of Israel by Assyria and the divine prospect of its end. Although God was the ultimate author of Israel's affliction, Assyria, the rod of God's anger, was the agent of his wrath; and the cup in the Lord's right hand was now coming around to her.

Assyria had long been central in God's affliction of his people, Israel. As early as the ninth century, Shalmaneser III (858–824 B.C.) exacted tribute from Jehu in one of his western campaigns (c. 824). However, Tiglath-pileser III (745–727) represents the first major scourge of Israel. He invaded that land during the reign of Menahem (752—732; cf. 2Ki 15:29; 1Ch 5:6, 26). This king extended his authority into Judah, where Ahaz (735–715) pursued a policy of submission to Assyria, thereby incurring the opposition of both Pekah, king of Israel (c. 740–732), who favored the anti-Assyrian coalition of his predecessor Ahab, and Isaiah, who denounced his faithlessness in depending on Assyria rather than on the Lord, when faced with Pekah's aggression (2Ki 16:5–18; 2Ch 28:16–25; Isa 7:1–25; 8:6–8). During Ahaz's reign, therefore, Judah was faced with the issue of submission or resistance to Assyria—an issue that confronted the nation for over a century and to which it responded in faith or fear according to its relationship to the Lord. Pekah was murdered by Hoshea (732–722), who adopted a vacillating pro-Assyrian policy. His fickle decision to rely on Egypt and repudiate his allegiance to Assyria provoked the invasion of Shalmaneser V (727–722), Tiglath-pileser III's successor.

Samaria fell after a long siege by Shalmaneser and his successor, Sargon II (721–705); the northern kingdom was destroyed and its population deported (2Ki 17:3–6). This catastrophe is explicitly attributed to the Lord's affliction of Israel for her sin (2Ki 17:20), as were the misfortunes of Ahaz in the same era (2Ch 28:19–20). Palestine experienced further depredations under Sargon II (Isa 20:1–6), before facing the full brunt of Assyria's hostility in the reign of Sennacherib (704–681). Hezekiah (728–687) had succeeded Ahaz and had abandoned Ahaz's pro-Assyrian policy (2Ki 18:7–8, 19–20). Sennacherib thereupon invaded Judah (701), conquered its fortified cities, and threatened Jerusalem, before the decimation of his army by a "wasting disease upon his sturdy warriors" (Isa 10:16; cf. 2Ki 18:13–19:37; 2Ch 32:1–31; Isa 36:1–37:38). The terrible distress preceding this deliverance was the Lord's chastening of his unfaithful yet beloved people (cf. Isa 5:26; 10:5–6, 11–12, 24–25; et al.).

The nation of Nineveh continued for another century, having times of both political stability and instability. Finally, as the power of Babylon began to climb during the reign of Nabopolassar (625–605), the Assyrian Empire began to crumble, and in 612 the siege and destruction of Nineveh were completed.

2. Authorship and Date

Little is known about Nahum himself. According to 1:1, he is "the Elkoshite." An Arab tradition places this village near Mosul in modern Iraq. Ancient writers, however, understood the prophet's home to be somewhere in Galilee.

From internal data it is possible to date the major blocks of material in Nahum. As a message of judgment, the book makes no sense if it was proclaimed following the collapse of the Assyrian empire in 612 B.C. On the other hand, references to the destruction of Thebes (No Amon) by the Nile (3:8) demand that the prophecy postdate that city's fall to Ashurbanipal in 663 B.C. Further consideration of the still formidable state of Assyrian power reflected in the book requires a date prior to the decline of that kingdom after about 626 B.C.

3. Theological Values

Theologically Nahum stands as an eloquent testimony to the particularity of God's justice and salvation. To the suffering remnant, there was little question that God would and did punish his own covenant people; but whether he was equally able and willing to impart justice to the powerful heathen nations surrounding Israel was untested. Among those nations, none was more cruel and arrogant than Assyria. The severity and kindness of God were both under scrutiny: the former as to whether it applied only selectively to his own people, and the latter in the context of God's ability and desire to bring about ultimate salvation for those who were faithful to him.

Into the situation of Israel's apostasy, Judah's vacillation, and Assyria's might came the word of the Lord: "The LORD is a jealous and avenging God . . . slow to anger and great in power; the LORD will not leave the guilty unpunished" (1:2–3). The vivid imagery of Nineveh's demise is eloquent testimony to the power of a God whose strength is never simply an abstraction. A theology of divine sovereignty and justice, applauded by all the nations, emerges from the specifics of Assyria's fall.

It is not merely divine retribution, however, that emerges from the picture. There is also good news to proclaim (1:15). Judah is called to celebration when the day of the Lord's wrath is fully understood and the remnant is prepared in righteousness. The corollary to the severity of God is his kindness, a mercy that includes covenant keeping and justice.

When the forces opposing God are so firmly ensconced and the flickering lamp of God's people is at the point of extinction, Nahum reminds us, as do the ruins of ancient Nineveh, that God himself is the ultimate Ruler. He will have the final word.

EXPOSITION

I. The Anger of the Lord (1:1–15)

A. The Judgment of the Lord (1:1–11)

The opening verses of Nahum form a prologue dominated by the revelation of God's eternal power and divine nature in creation (cf. Ro 1:20). This revelation is characterized preeminently by God's justice, expressed in retribution (v.2) and wrath (vv.2–3) that shake the entire creation (vv.3–6). The mercy of God, for all its reality, is a fleeting counterpart of this awesome display of majesty.

1. Awesome in power (1:1–6)

1–2 The adjective "jealous" (GK 7868) is used solely of God, primarily in his self-revelation at Sinai (Ex 20:5; 34:14). Against this covenantal background, it denotes the Lord's deep, fiercely protective commitment to his people and his exclusive claim to obedience and reciprocal commitment. Where this relationship of mutual commitment is threatened, either by Israel's unfaithfulness or by foreign oppression, the inevitable expressions of such jealousy are "vengeance" and "wrath," directed to restoring that relationship.

"Avenging" and "vengeance" (both GK 5933) are judicial in nature, expressing judgment and requital for infractions of law and morality, primarily those committed with presumption and impenitence. As a judicial function "vengeance" belongs supremely to God, the Judge of the whole earth, and to the ordained representatives of his authority. Consequently, human beings are forbidden to take the law into their own hands. Nineveh—despite God's use of her violence—had done just that. Now, just as she had devastated cities and populations, so it would happen to her. She had sown the wind and in her impenitence would surely reap the whirlwind.

Like jealousy, "wrath" (GK 5757) denotes intense and passionate feeling. It constitutes a divine characteristic that human beings must face whenever they break the proper limits of their relationship to God; to deny God's "wrath" is to deny the reality of judgment and the necessity of atonement. Verse 2 lays a foundation for the entire prophecy; all that follows is rooted in this revelation of the justice and burning zeal of the Lord exercised on behalf of his people.

3 The Lord's anger is balanced by his forbearance, which represents a restraint born of meekness and not of weakness; it is not to be misunderstood as passivity. Nor is it exercised indefinitely, for his power assures that "he will not leave the guilty unpunished." The forbearance of God had been extended to Nineveh a century earlier in response to her repentance (Jnh 3:10); but it was forfeited by her subsequent history of ruthless evil, making way for God's judgment instead.

The power and majesty of God are evidenced most dramatically in the forces of nature. "Whirlwind" and "storm" are often expressions of his judgment (cf. Ps 83:15; Isa 29:6). For all their grandeur, these mighty forces are dwarfed in the presence of the Lord, whom the highest heavens cannot contain; the tempest is but the disturbance caused as he marches by, and the dark storm clouds are merely dust stirred up by his feet.

4 The preceding description of the Lord's power is extended in the image of drought, consuming the fertile highlands of Palestine and their sources of water. "Bashan" in Transjordan, "Carmel" in northern Israel, and the "Lebanon" range on Israel's northern frontier are frequently represented together as the choicest forest and pasture regions of the Promised Land. Nevertheless, all are revealed as vulnerable; like the pride and strength of humankind, they are devastated and "wither" before the burning anger of the Lord. The drought depicted here is abnormally severe in its catastrophic effects on "sea" and "rivers."

5 Earthquake forms a third biblical manifestation of the Lord's power, causing the hills to "melt away." Such melting may be brought on by intense heat, a phenomenon associated with the earthquake at Sinai to which vv.2–3 allude. However, the verb "melt away" may also be applied to the effect of flooding.

6 This verse emphatically recapitulates the concept of anger, repeating the noun "wrath" that is stressed further by the kindred terms "indignation" and "fierce anger," and again describing the irresistible manifestation of this anger, before which the entire created world is subdued. This wrath is poured out "like fire"—fire is a common expression of the Lord's judgment. The section concluding with v.6 is deeply imbued with the recollection of God's covenant with Israel, also sharing with numerous poetic passages their various images of divine judgment and power (cf. Pss 11:6; 18:7–15; 29:3–9; Jer 23:29; Eze 38:19–22; Joel 2:1–11; et al.).

2. Just in execution (1:7–11)

7 The goodness of God forms a basic tenet of Israel's faith. Also, it repeatedly forms the basis for human faith, expressed in trusting obedience; where the goodness of God is impugned with success, faith soon crumbles. As an expression of covenant commitment to defend his people, the Lord himself is a "refuge" (GK 5057) or stronghold of protection. He "cares for" (lit., "knows"; GK 3359) the faithful, acknowledging their relationship to him and their claim on his goodness inherent in that relationship. The "trouble" from which he gives protection is graphically illustrated in Judah's sufferings at the hands of Assyria. It demanded a "trust" that was too often misplaced.

8 The goodness of God, like his patience, does not obviate his judgment, which is directed against those who refuse to submit to his rule, i.e., "his foes" and the oppressors of his loyal people. As long as evil exists, God's judgment, expressed here in terms of "flood" (cf. v.3; 2:6), is an inevitable expression of his goodness on behalf of the victims of evil; it banishes the enemy into "darkness" (i.e., death).

9 The utter finality of this sentence is stressed by "bring to an end." It is reinforced by the terse ambiguity of the final line: "trouble" will not arise again for God's people, for it will descend on those who trouble Israel in so conclusive a way that it need not arise again. The crime of these enemies is premeditated antagonism: they do not stumble into sin but actively "plot" against the Lord.

10 The means of judgment is portrayed here in metaphorical language. "Thorns" describes the spiny or prickly vegetation that proliferated in the semiarid climate of Palestine. They often grew as a tangled, impenetrable mass; as such, they were good for little more than burning. The Assyrians are portrayed as being "entangled among" or like such thorns, to which they correspond both in their worthless character and in their merited destruction.

The image of drunkenness reiterates these varied associations: a drunkard is good for nothing useful, and drunkenness is both a cause and consequence of judgment. The keynote of both lines, however, is helplessness. A drunkard is incapacitated from defending himself; the Assyrians would be no less vulnerable before the wrath of God.

Like thorns, stubble is without intrinsic value and is subject to be burnt; being "dry," it is an easy prey for the flames by which it is "consumed." Nineveh's destruction by fire is rooted in her helplessness to avert the disaster; and this in turn is due to her decadence, characterized by drunkenness.

11 The enemy is again defined as one who "plots" against the Lord, being specified further as a distinct individual from whom the rebellion emanates; such an individual is identified clearly in 3:18 as the "king of Assyria." The ruler envisaged here emerged from Nineveh in his opposition to the Lord. Sennacherib stands out as the most powerful aggressor to emerge from Nineveh against Judah. According to the Assyrian annals describing his Judean campaign (c. 701), he cruelly devastated forty-seven fortified cities including Lachish. That Nahum was referring primarily to Sennacherib's invasion is supported by his repeated reminiscences of Isaiah's prophecies relating to that era.

The intent of this plotting is "wickedness" (GK 1175), a noun often translated as "worthlessness" and implying a total lack of moral fiber and principle (e.g., Dt 13:13).

B. The Sentence of the Lord (1:12–14)

12 The opening clause of this verse is typical of the formula by which a messenger received or transmitted a message from his lord. The present decree is addressed to Judah and is essentially an oracle of salvation; it incorporates an announcement of judgment that is addressed directly to Assyria (v.14). The decree reverses the fortunes of the

This relief depicts King Assurbanipal dining in a garden in Nineveh. Courtesy Erich Lessing.

Assyrians. Although they had "allies," they would be "cut off." Although "numerous," the Assyrians would "pass away."

A similar reversal is decreed for Judah. To be "afflicted" (GK 6700) is to be humbled and oppressed. Such affliction is repeatedly the agent of God's chastisement, frequently being administered to his own people at the hands of foreign nations.

13 The continuing existence of such servitude is implied by the emphatic "Now" and by the future orientation of the promised deliverance from the "yoke" and the "shackles." This further supports dating Nahum's prophecy before Josiah's reign. Despite the devious and tragic analogy of the northern kingdom, the southern kingdom was still to experience political and religious revival in the reign of Josiah. And though its sins had made exile inevitable, this did not occur at Assyrian hands. The breaking of Assyria's yoke is strikingly affirmed by Nabopolassar, who was an unwitting instrument of the Lord's purposes (cf. Isa 45:4–5).

14 The "name" (GK 9005) of a population represented its living identity, perpetuated in its "descendants." The root underlying "descendants" (GK 2445) is used of physical and particularly dynastic succession. Thus Nahum implies the eradication of Nineveh's dynastic rule and of the nation whose cohesion derived from the Neo-Assyrian monarchy now centered at Nineveh. Nineveh's consignment to the grave reiterates the certainty of this extinction. This judgment is rooted in the charge that the city, for all its regal and religious grandeur, is "vile."

The Assyrian kings claimed to rule by the favor and authority of their "gods," whom they honored accordingly. Ashurbanipal, on a single cylinder, paid profuse homage to seventeen of the principal gods of the Assyrian pantheon. The judgment of Nineveh's king therefore demanded the destruction of the idolatrous religion on which his authority was founded. This was centralized in the "temple," which housed the "carved images" and "cast idols." These idols were normally made of precious wood plated with gold or of molten metal. The utter inefficacy of such "gods" was thus to be exposed in the destruction of their place of residence that they were powerless to protect.

C. The Purpose of the Lord (1:15)

15 The proclamation of "peace" (*shalom*; GK 8934) is replete with the promise of God's redemption and constitutes the most precise correlation of Nahum with Isaiah (e.g., Isa 9:6–7; 32:17; 53:5; et al.). The picture is one of joyous and complete restoration of the Lord's people and their legitimate worship. The reversal of fortunes is thus completed as Nineveh's flourishing religion is to be buried and the worship of oppressed Judah resurrected. The anticipated renewal of vital worship was accomplished in the reign of Josiah, after about 631 (2Ki 22:3–23:27; 2Ch 34–35).

As in Hezekiah's reign, this assertion of religious independence demanded that the "wicked" who opposed it be "destroyed." The verb "destroy" (GK 4162) is commonly used of cutting down an enemy in battle or of "cutting off" the name of the rebellious. The verb "invade" is similarly used of warfare.

II. The Fall of Nineveh (2:1–3:19)

The judgment of God decreed in ch. 1 is now worked out with terrifying actuality. Nahum 2:1–2 is transitional. On the one hand, it extends the dual perspective of judgment and mercy evident in 1:2–15. On the other hand, the military language and urgent imperatives of v.1 clearly anticipate the following battle.

A. Warning and Promise (2:1–2)

1 Nineveh's "attacker" (GK 7046) is more literally a "scatterer," a common figure for a victorious king (cf. Ps 68:1; Isa 24:1; Jer 52:8). In fulfillment of this prophecy, Nineveh was attacked in 614 B.C. by Cyaxares, king of the Medes (c. 625–585). A sector of the suburbs was captured, but the city was not yet taken. However, a subsequent alliance of Cyaxares with the Babylonian Nabopolassar led to their concerted attack on Nineveh in 612, a battle recorded in detail by the Babylonian Chronicle.

The Assyrians are mockingly called to action. Nineveh had in fact been well-equipped to withstand both siege and invasion. Sennacherib had spent no less than six years building his armory, which occupied a terraced area of forty acres. It was enlarged further by Esarhaddon and contained all the weaponry required for the extension and maintenance of the Assyrian empire. The royal "road" had been enlarged by Sennacherib to a breadth of seventy-eight feet, facilitating the movement of troops. However, the material resources would be of little avail if the "strength" (GK 3946) of the defenders could not be marshaled, and by the end of the seventh century it had been dissipated beyond retrieval.

2 This verse introduces the final reference to the salvation of God's people, whose "splendor" he will "restore." The noun "splendor" (GK 1454) implies elevation or exaltation. The comparison "like Israel" suggests restoration to the full stature promised to the nation and once occupied by it. The names "Jacob ... Israel" are usually synonymous, and they came to denote the Twelve Tribes descended from Jacob. After the kingdom was divided in two, usage varies; but the names are more commonly applied to the northern kingdom. Following the destruction of Samaria, the southern prophets reclaimed these names (Isa 14:1–4; et al.). Evidently "Judah" is envisaged here, though possibly the resurrection of Israel as a whole is promised (cf. Isa 9:1–8; 11:10–16; et al.). Such restoration is necessitated by the devastation of the land's "vines"—a mainstay of its economy, a source of its joy and fulfillment and indeed a symbol of the very life and identity of the nation. All this had been obliterated in the northern kingdom by the Assyrian "destroyers."

B. Nineveh's Destruction Detailed (2:3–3:19)

1. First description of Nineveh's destruction (2:3–3:1)

a. Onslaught (2:3–5)

3–4 The antecedent of "his" appears to be the "attacker" of v.1. It is possible that the "Lord" (v.2) is also intended, summoning an enemy against Nineveh as he had summoned the Assyrians against Judah (Isa 5:26–30; 10:5–6, 15). The attack is led by the invader's chariot forces, the most formidable wing of an army fighting in open terrain. The Neo-Assyrian "chariots" were built of various types of wood, for lightness and speed, with fittings of leather and of "metal" that would flash with reflected light. The chariots were fitted with a pole and yoke for the horses, normally a team of two, and with spoked wheels and a single axle. The Assyrian shields were either round or rectangular in shape, the latter being designed to cover most of the body. They were made of wood or wickerwork covered with leather, which could have been dyed "red." It is evident from the parallel passage in 3:2–3 that cavalry accompanied the chariots, a typical feature of Assyrian warfare; and both "shields" and "spears" might also be carried by the infantry. The conflict was located in the "streets" of Nineveh, denoting its suburbs outside the inner defensive "wall" that had not yet been reached.

5 The "picked troops" represent the shock troops directed to breach the "wall." The "protective covering" would describe the screen set up to protect them as they engaged in undermining and penetrating the wall. The stumbling of the "picked troops" is due, not to their weakness, but to the "corpses" of their victims, obstructing their advance.

b. Failing defenses (2:6–10)

6 This brief verse (five Heb. words) marks a decisive turning point in the campaign, as the main line of defense was broken and the heart of the city destroyed. The "river gates" envisaged are possibly those regulating the flow of water through the city. Indeed, the Akkadian term "gate of the river" was applied to a canal gate by Sennacherib. When "thrown open" by the enemy, who already controlled the suburbs where they were situated, the gates would have released a deluge of water, as a result of which the palace "collapses."

7–8 The survivors are "exiled" amid the mourning of the "slave girls," a not uncommon scene in Assyrian wall carvings depicting the agonies of their captives. The image of water depicts Nineveh's fate with vivid irony. Nineveh was a place of watered parks and orchards. As at the Flood, however, "water" became a source of death, overflowing its boundaries and bringing chaos to the inundated city. Unlike the Flood, this "pool" promised no respite as its waters "drained away."

9 The exaction of plunder had characterized the Neo-Assyrian Empire throughout its history. Those nations that submitted were drained of their resources, a fate suffered by Israel and Judah at various times. Thus Nineveh became the richest city throughout the ancient Near East. Now it was to suffer the same fate: its own people were to be led away; its "wealth" in "gold," "silver," and valuables was to be seized.

10 The defeat of the city is summarized forcefully. The inhabitants had failed to "brace" themselves (v.1) and instead "bodies tremble." The verb underlying "tremble" (GK 2714) is often applied to labor pains.

c. An interpretive analogy (2:11–12)

11 The mocking rhetorical question introduces an extended metaphor that interprets the horror of the preceding verses: Nineveh has ravaged Mesopotamia like a savage beast of prey and must be judged accordingly. Nineveh's kings compared themselves to lions in their terrible power, and its game parks sheltered such lions. Like a pride of such lions, Nineveh had been free to terrorize the land "with nothing to fear." Now, however an accounting was due for that ruthless spirit.

12 The root of "killed" (GK 3271), recurring in the nouns "kill" and "prey," is normally used of wild beasts that hunt and tear open their prey. The verb "strangle" (GK 2871) is equally apt to the image, as lions are represented as killing their prey in this manner in ancient Near Eastern art. Assyrian brutality matched and surpassed such displays of violence. The goal of the lion's violence was prey "for his cubs"; as the lion filled its "lairs with the kill," so Nineveh had been filled with foreign plunder.

d. Judgment from the Lord (2:13)

13 The climax is announced in the verdict of condemnation. "No prey" is a metonymy of effect: the taking of prey will be cut off with the extermination of the predator. The reference to "chariots" and to "messengers" recalls Sennacherib's "evil," plotted "against the Lord" (1:11; cf. Isa 37:9, 14, 24). This verse draws together the major motifs and vocabulary of Nahum's prophecy: the Lord's inexorable opposition to Nineveh; the destruction of its military resources; the role of "sword" and "fire" that "consume" the enemy; the cutting off of Nineveh and its "prey"; the termination of its cruelty, symbolized by the "young lions"; and the reversal of fortunes that awaits Assyria and Judah, exemplified in the fate of the "heralds."

e. The verdict announced (3:1)

1 The relation of this verse to its context is rendered uncertain by the interjection "Woe." Normally "woe" introduces a new section, suggesting here that v.1 belongs with 3:2–7. However, 3:1 is related thematically to 2:11–13 much more closely than to 3:4; it repeats the focal concept of killing in the noun "victims," an association reinforced by the parallel nouns "plunder" and "blood." And it also represents the city as "full (of plunder)," like the lion's den (2:12).

2. Second description of Nineveh's destruction (3:2–7)

a. Onslaught and failing defenses (3:2–3)

2–3 These verses resume the battle scene of 2:3–5, evoking the rapid movement and the sound of the onslaught led by the chariots. The term "cavalry" (GK 7305) may denote the mounted horsemen that are depicted accompanying chariots in Assyrian reliefs, or it may refer to the horses of the chariot corps. "Swords" were characteristic weapons of foot soldiers, being used in hand-to-hand combat; they did not form part of the regular equipment of horsemen or chariot crews. The "spears" also formed an integral part of the infantry's weapons.

As in 2:3–10, the defenders are annihilated by the attack: four times—using three different words—the verse refers to the corpses left in the wake of the invading army. Possibly the "people stumbling" are the fugitives; in view of 2:5, they are more likely to be the victors, impeded by the sheer mass of bodies.

b. An interpretive analogy (3:4)

4 The root underlying the word "harlot" (GK 2390) occurs three times in this verse (cf. "wanton lust," "prostitution"). The biblical references to "prostitution" imply treachery, infidelity, pollution, and lust. All are appropriate to this city that sacrificed any semblance of morality to personal interest. Of primary significance, however, is the prostitute's motive of personal gain and the ominous "alluring" that she exercises to attain it. As Ahaz had been lured into unholy relations with Assyria formerly (cf. 2Ki 16:7–18), so Nineveh had drained the life of those enticed by her smooth ways.

The harlot's practice of allurement and manipulation is abetted by "sorceries" and "witchcraft." Both sorcery and harlotry suggest an illicit, surreptitious yet deadly means; they correspond to the stealth of the hunting lion and are equally destructive. Nineveh is here seen as using both immoral attractions (the city was a center of the cult of Ishtar—herself represented as a harlot) and sorcery (Assyrian society was dominated by magic arts) as a means to enslave others.

c. Judgment from the Lord (3:5–6)

5–6 As the Lord's condemnation overthrows the city's brutality (2:13), so it annuls the demonic power that promotes that brutality. The same principle of reversal is effected: violence has been requited with violence (2:13); Nineveh's hidden arts are destroyed by exposure; as she enslaved "nations," so she will be bared to the "nations" (cf. Jer 13:26–27; Eze 16:37–41; Hos 2:3–5).

d. The verdict announced (3:7)

7 This section concludes on a note of mourning in response to the Lord's verdict—mourning occasioned by the presence of death. In v.1 death is foreshadowed in the city's sin; here it is an accomplished fact, and the witnesses respond in revulsion and amazement to the humiliated prostitute. The "ruins" of Nineveh reflect the Lord's determination to make a full "end" of it (1:8–9), and the fulfillment of this purpose is amply attested both inscriptionally and archaeologically. The debacle is still regarded as one of the greatest riddles of world history. Within eighty years, Nineveh, which had been raised to unrivaled prominence by Sennacherib and his successors, was obliterated from living memory. The Lord had purposed Nineveh's end, and the imperial city was never rebuilt. For the next three hundred years at least, there is no evidence that the site of Nineveh was even occupied.

3. Third description of Nineveh's destruction (3:8–11)

8 In Hebrew "Thebes" is "No Amon" ("the city of Amon"; cf. Jer 46:25; Eze 30:14–16). "Amon" was the chief god of the Theban pantheon and one of the principal deities of Egypt since the New Kingdom (c. 1580–1090 B.C.): the term "No" is derived from the Egyptian word for "city." Thebes, which lay on the Nile about four hundred miles south of modern Cairo, constituted the chief city of Upper, or southern, Egypt and was a leading center of Egyptian civilization. A place of temples, obelisks, sphinxes, and palaces, it was dominated by the mighty temples of Amon at Luxor and Karnak on the east bank of the Nile, opposite the funerary temples of the kings to the west. Its temples and palaces are said to have found no equal in antiquity, and they are still regarded by some as the mightiest ruins of ancient civilization to be found anywhere in the world.

As intimated above, the city lay on both banks of the Nile. The river was divided into the principal channels by the islands that interrupted its flow. Thebes could truly be described, therefore, as a city "with water around her." The term "river" (GK 3542) is normally translated "sea"; it is applied elsewhere to the Nile (Isa 18:2; 19:5; cf. Jer 51:36), and indeed the Nile is known as "the sea" to this day. The strategic location of Thebes made the river its natural or "outer" wall of "defense." In addition, it enjoyed the protection of a main, inner "wall," visualized again here as constituted by the surrounding waters or extending from them. It is thus equated with Nineveh, similarly defended by a "wall" and by water through its location on a great river (2:5–6, 8).

9 Thebes had intermittent periods of great glory as the capital of Egypt from Middle Kingdom times (c. 2160–1580) onward. After some indifferent periods, the establishment of an Ethiopian dynasty ("Cush") in the seventh century assured a continuing place for Thebes, with access to the strength of both Egypt and Ethiopia. The adjective "boundless" corresponds to "endless" (2:9), evoking the vast resources shared by the two cities and foreshadowing the "bodies without number" (v.3) that they were destined to share also.

"Libya" lay to the west of Egypt, with which it possessed similar ties: the long-lived Twenty-Second Dynasty had originated from Libya (c. 950–730), exemplified in the ruler Sheshonk I (Shishak; cf. 1Ki 14:25–26). "Put" is also to be located in North Africa on the basis of biblical references that associate it with Egypt and Ethiopia (cf. Ge 10:6; 1Ch 1:8; Jer 46:9; et al.). It is now commonly identified with the same area as Libya. Like Nineveh, Thebes was surrounded not only by natural defenses but by the confederate resources of a vast and ancient empire.

10–11 For all her strength, Thebes fell to the Assyrians (c. 664). The Ethiopian kings had provoked this attack by their policy of intrigue in Palestine. Rather than confront Assyria directly, they tended to incite the minor states to rebel against their Assyrian overlords, with a view to reestablishing Palestine as an Egyptian sphere of influence (cf. Isa 30:1–7; 31:13; 36:6; 37:9). As a result of such intrigue by Tirhakah (689–664; cf. Isa 37:9) with the prince of Tyre, Egypt was invaded by Esarhaddon in 675/674; the campaign was launched in earnest in 671, when the Egyptians were routed before the Assyrians who captured Memphis. Upper Egypt, including Thebes, surrendered; Tirhakah fled south to Ethiopia, and his rule was abrogated in Lower Egypt, which Esarhaddon fragmented under the rule of minor princes.

Esarhaddon died in 669 as he was marching to suppress further insurrection in Egypt, and Tirhakah immediately moved north into Egypt again: Thebes resumed its traditional allegiance to him, Memphis was seized, and Lower Egypt was again overrun. In 667 Ashurbanipal was in a position to take Egypt in hand, reversing the previous sequence of events. Memphis fell to his troops; Thebes surrendered with the rest of Egypt; Tirhakah fled south to Napata where he died. He was succeeded as king of Ethiopia by Tanutamon, who renewed the attempt to control Egypt. Again, Thebes reversed its allegiance, receiving him with acclaim. Memphis was taken, its Assyrian representatives were slaughtered, and Tanutamon gained temporary sovereignty over Egypt. The Egyptians were no match for the Assyrian army, however, which soon returned under Ashurbanipal in 664/663. Tanutamon fled south like his predecessors, the Delta was reconquered, and Thebes fell. Both Ashurbanipal and Esarhaddon had exercised restraint in their Egyptian foreign policy, as a means of securing loyalty in a distant country they could only with difficulty garrison effectively. Now, however, Ashurbanipal's patience was exhausted. Thebes was razed to the ground, in vengeance on its vacillating allegiance to Ethiopia (cf. 2Ki 17:3–6). His enraged and vehement attack on the city is documented in his annals. From that time on, Thebes has been largely a place of monuments to a glory and dominance now long departed. Both the Egyptian and the Assyrian sources, therefore, validate Nahum's description of a city scattered to the winds, its posterity cut off, its trained "nobles" plundered, and its leaders fleeing for refuge.

Verse 10 echoes the preceding announcement of judgment on Nineveh in the threat of "exile" (cf. 2:7) and of destruction in the streets (2:4); the human resources represented by its "nobles" suffered the same fate as Nineveh's "wealth" (2:9; cf. 3:3). And in v.11 this correlation is made explicit. Nineveh has been equated with Thebes in its defenses (v.8); it would surely be equated with Thebes in its downfall. The finality of this sentence is sealed by its further correspondence to 1:2–15. Nineveh would be "drunk" as decreed by the Lord (1:10). She would seek "refuge" (GK 5057) in vain, for she trusted in carved images and idols.

4. Fourth description of Nineveh's destruction (3:12–19)

a. Onslaught and failing defenses (3:12–14)

12–13 For Nineveh no refuge would be forthcoming. Her "fortresses" (probably walled cities) guarding the approach to Nineveh were ripe for destruction, being dislodged with as little effort as "figs" ready for harvesting. As the "gates" guarding entrance to the land, they were "open" to the enemy like those of Nineveh herself (cf. 2:6). This collapse is explained by the effeminate, weakened condition of her "troops."

14 The impending condition of "siege" demanded an independent supply of "water," since the enemy would cut off all external sources provided by the rivers flowing into the city (cf. 2:6). The Babylonian Chronicle corroborates this anticipation of siege, referring to a campaign that lasted three months. It also intimates that operations against the city had begun in 614 under Cyaxares (cf. 2:1), so that Nineveh was subject to intermittent siege for more than two years.

The word for "defenses" (GK 4448) can also mean "fortifications" or walls of the city. "Clay" was the principal building material of Mesopotamia, which lacked adequate resources in stone (cf. Ge 11:3). The walls of Nineveh, which were built of such "worked clay" bricks, averaged fifty feet in breadth, extending to over one hundred feet at the gates; they therefore demanded an enormous effort for their maintenance, as indicated here by the urgent and repeated references to the processes involved.

b. Interpretive analogy and judgment from the Lord (3:15–17)

15 Nineveh's conquest by fire, together with sword, is amply revealed in its ruins. The devouring fire evokes the destruction inflicted by "grasshoppers" or "locusts" (GK 746), which similarly "consume" all that lies in their path. Verses 15–17 develop this image of "locusts" (cf. Jer 51: 14, 27; Joel 1:4; 2:25) with intricate detail. The initial emphasis is on their omnivorous behavior, typical of locusts. The word "locusts" is related to the Hebrew word meaning "to increase, be many." The ability of the locust to proliferate in vast numbers underlies its menace to vegetation.

16 Like locusts, Nineveh's merchants proliferated beyond measure; and they likewise "strip" the land. The comparison to locusts introduces a further element: like locusts, these "merchants" also "fly away," unconcerned for the region they have exploited.

17 Nineveh's "officials," like her "merchants," are multitudinous as "swarms of locusts"; they "settle" within her boundaries for shelter and food, but they abandon her and "fly away" when tribulation comes. With remarkable artistry Nahum transforms the perspective of the prophecy. Judgment is executed from within by those claiming to serve Nineveh's interests as they flock to her (v.15); and her fall is explained in terms of the disloyalty of her own people. The Assyrians had based their empire on expediency and self-interest, multiplying power, wealth, and personnel like locusts for their own gratification. Now their empire was to succumb as a victim of the self-interest it had promoted— eaten away from within no less than it was devoured by the sword from without.

c. The verdict announced (3:18–19)

18–19 The collapse of effective loyalty penetrated even Assyria's aristocracy, represented by its "nobles" and "shepherds," or "rulers." Their "slumber" and "rest" foreshadow both their death and the inertia that occasions it.

The corollary of this failure is the scattering of the people, "with no one to gather them," like sheep without "shepherds." One of the striking phenomena of history is the disappearance of a nation that had existed for two thousand years!

The "king of Assyria" is addressed directly throughout vv.16–19; ultimately it was his fatal injury that accounted for his breakdown in authoritative government and military leadership. As anticipated by Nahum, the dynasty fell with the city. The "wound" could not be healed; the brief attempt by Ashur-uballit to keep the dynasty alive in Haran failed two years later. The injury was indeed fatal.

The book closes with the response of witnesses who heard of these events; the "endless cruelty" was ended!

For his anger lasts only a moment,
    but his favor lasts a lifetime;
weeping may remain for a night,
    but rejoicing comes in the morning.
(Ps 30:5)

Habakkuk

INTRODUCTION

1. Background and Date

Habakkuk's prophecy is set against a background of the decline and fall of the Judean kingdom (c. 626–586 B.C.). Although nothing is known of the prophet himself apart from the book bearing his name—the book is not dated in the usual manner (cf. Am 1:1; Zep 1:1; et al.)—the general background of Habakkuk is clear from the internal data. Verses 5–11 represent a period before 605, the year the Babylonians (the Chaldeans, 1:6; see NIV note) rose to power, and probably prior to the 612 destruction of Nineveh. By contrast it is sometimes argued that 1:12–17 and 2:6–20 must reflect a period after 612 B.C., when the power and rapacity of the Babylonians had become common knowledge to the prophet. The best solution seems to be to take the sections of the dialogue as representative of Habakkuk's spiritual struggles over a long period of time, possibly beginning as early as 626 and continuing as late as 590 or after.

During this period Judah enjoyed its last bit of prosperity under Josiah (d. 609 B.C.); Assyria's wound was revealed as fatal with the ultimate fall of Nineveh in 612; and the short-lived Babylonian Empire established its dominance over Palestine with Jerusalem a casualty and its people taken into exile in 586 B.C. Conditions during the life of the prophet would have progressed from excellent—with considerable material prosperity and even promise of spiritual revival—to the height of desperation as the net was drawn closer and closer around the hapless capital. There is no direct evidence from the book that Habakkuk lived past the destruction of Jerusalem (but cf. 3:16–19).

2. Authorship

Nothing is known of Habakkuk except his name, which does not lend itself to attempts at finding a Hebrew meaning. Of his temperament and personal situation we know only what may be inferred from the book. Literary dependencies and early canonical reception leave no doubt that Habakkuk's work was circulated and accepted early, but the details remain lost.

3. Occasion and Purpose

Habakkuk was unique among the prophets. He did not speak for God to the people but to God about his people. The similarity with the other prophets is in the setting. Violence and covenant violations abounded. The Lord should have arisen to correct the situation, but such had not been forthcoming, and the prayers of the righteous seemed in vain.

The Assyrians would naturally have been a threat to Judah; and apart from the problem of the future of God's covenant promises, the prophet would have expected Assyria to be "the rod of God's anger." The new element externally is the introduction of Babylonian power, with such awful potential consequences and with no clear vision of when and how the Lord would continue his commitments to the chosen line. But initially Habakkuk was more concerned with internal injustices and the Lord's apparent complacency toward the evil generation. It was God's reply (1:5–11) that catapulted the prophecy onto the international and eschatological level.

Chapters 2–3 carry us well beyond the last days of Judah to the future. Habakkuk himself was never told when or exactly how it would end, but 2:14, 20 assured him of the ultimate triumph of the Lord; and the psalm in ch. 3 shows that Habakkuk learned to live in the light of this fact.

4. Theological Values

Habakkuk's message (esp. 2:4) forms a basic point in three NT books (Ro 1:17; Gal 3:11–12; Heb 10:37–38). The theological value of Habakkuk, however, cannot be limited to a few, though crucial, NT quotations. The prophet asked deeply penetrating questions, and the answers are basic to a proper view of God and his relation to history. If God's initial response sounded the death knell for any strictly nationalistic covenant theology of Judah, his second reply outlined in a positive sense the fact that all history was hastening to a conclusion that was as certain as it was satisfying. In the interim, the righteous are to live by faith. The faith prescribed is still called for as a basic response to the unanswered questions in today's universe; and it is this theology for life that stands as Habakkuk's most basic contribution.

EXPOSITION

I. Habakkuk's Initial Lament (1:1–4)

These verses correspond closely to the psalms of lament or complaint; prominent features of this form in vv.2–4 include the questions addressed to the Lord, the urgent descriptions of dire need, and the sustained petition for deliverance (cf. Pss 10:1–13; 13:1–4; 22:1–21; 74:1–11; 80; 88). Habakkuk's prophecy is thus located clearly within the community of faith, exposed to many tribulations, yet oriented to the Lord as its help in trouble.

1–2 The question "How long" implies a situation of crisis from which the speaker seeks deliverance. The verb "listen" (GK 9048) normally carries connotations of an active response to what is heard; where that response is lacking, the righteousness of either the petitioner or the one addressed is called in question. The crisis in which Habakkuk called for help was "violence"; the response expected from the Lord was that he should "save."

"Violence" (GK 2805) denotes flagrant violation of moral law by which a person injures primarily one's fellow human beings (e.g., Ge 6:11). Its underlying meaning is one of ethical wrong, of which physical brutality is only one possible expression. To "save" (GK 3828) means to deliver from what oppresses or restricts. Such salvation is to be found ultimately only in the Lord, by those who are righteous toward him.

3 The concepts of "injustice" and "wrong" are correlated in ten other verses; NIV usually translates them as "evil" and "trouble." "Destruction" and "violence" are similarly correlated repeatedly in Scripture, associated with unjust oppression of the weaker members within a community (Jer 6:7; 20:8; Eze 45:9; Am 3:10). A third word-pair, "strife" and "conflict," evokes the anger and dissension born of conflicting and uncompromising wills (cf. Pr 15:18; 17:14; 26:20–21).

4 The disintegration of a society into factions is bound up with its rejection of the forces that bring it unity—"law" and "justice." The "law" (*torah*; GK 9368) may refer to any form of authoritative "teaching." When used in the singular without clear definition, as here, "law" signifies God's covenantal code established with Israel, given through Moses and mediated primarily through the Levitical priesthood in close conjunction with the king or other governing authorities. Its effectiveness was therefore "paralyzed" by the corruption of the religious and civil leadership of the nation. "Justice" (GK 5477) implies the exercise not merely of legal processes but of all the functions of government; it is through "justice" that law and order are represented, legislated, interpreted, and enforced.

II. God's First Response (1:5–11)

This passage is distinguished from vv.2–4 by a transition to the Lord as speaker. In form these verses resemble an oracle, yet scarcely the oracle of salvation that forms the turning point in certain other laments (e.g., Pss 12:5; 13:5–6; 22:23–24; et al.). They correspond more closely to an expanded announcement of judgment on God's people, the prophet's lament serving as the accusation on which this is based.

5 The Lord is now the speaker; he addresses a plural audience. The hearers, by implication Judeans, are treated as distinct from the "nations" (or Gentiles), at whom they are to "look." To be "amazed" is a human response to an event that utterly confounds all previous expectations; it runs counter to what the listeners "believe." The destruction of Jerusalem was such an event, creating both a national and a theological crisis among God's people.

6 This verse identifies both the speaker and the amazing work introduced in v.5—the Lord and Babylonia's rise to power. The latter ran counter to popular theology (cf. Jer 5:12; 6:14; 7:1–34; 8:11) but was fully in accord with the Lord's chastisement of his sinning people. Character produces conduct, and the Babylonian character is expressed by unprincipled rapacity ("ruthless and impetuous"). "The whole earth" suggests unrestricted scope for such behavior, which by implication would engulf Palestine also.

7 Verses 7–11 develop the description of the oppressors. Their character was rooted in a self-sufficiency that acknowledged no superior authority and no dependency, which was tantamount to self-deification. Thus they were "feared" and "dreaded," usurping the place of God. If God's people refuse to fear him, they will ultimately be compelled to fear those less worthy of fear. The source of Babylonian "law" and "honor" is exposed—it is self-generated.

8–9 The Babylonian "cavalry" are compared to three predators whose speed and power bring violent death to their prey. The "leopard" and the "wolf" recur, together with the lion, in Jer 5:6 as symbols of divine judgment on Judah. The "vulture" translates an ambiguous term that may also denote an eagle. The vulture is primarily a scavenger, feeding off carrion, whereas the eagle hunts and kills its prey. The imagery of the hunter better fits the historical context (cf. Dt 28:49–50).

Those who live by "violence" shall die by the violence of others. "Like a desert wind," describing the Babylonian advance, pictures the hot, scorching wind from the Eastern desert. "Like sand" creates a vivid portrait of numberless prisoners helplessly collected for deportation.

10 The Babylonians "deride kings" and "scoff at rulers," since they can "laugh" at their defenses. The "ramps," constructed primarily of earth, were a graded incline along which the cumbersome battering rams could be moved in besieging city walls. The "wicked" who "hem in" the "righteous" would themselves be hemmed in by the horrors of siege (cf. v.4).

11 The onrushing cavalry (vv.8–9) was checked by the siege warfare, in which it would not have participated. As the fortified cities fell and resistance crumbled, the cavalry's pent-up energy was released and its progress resumed. The Babylonians may "sweep past," but the final verdict was already in. "Guilty men" is followed immediately by the reason for the guilt: "whose own strength is their god." Such people acknowledge no accountability, seek no repentance, and offer no reparations, while violating the most fundamental order of created life.

III. Habakkuk's Second Lament (1:12–2:1)

This section has characteristics of a second lament, having many points of contact with 1:2–4 (see comment). These include invocation of the Lord's name (v.12), the urgent questions addressed to him (vv.13, 17), the description of the wicked oppressing the righteous (vv.13–17), and the issue of unrequited justice that this raises. The note of confidence expressed in v.12 is also typical of most laments—an attitude implicit in the prophet's perseverance and his insistence that his answers come from God.

12 Although "everlasting" (GK 7710) may refer to eternity, it more often denotes an unspecified point in past history and is applied repeatedly to God's former preservation of Israel. God's holiness is associated with his transcendent sovereignty and power, manifested in the past redemption of his people. Habakkuk's confidence of survival ("we will not die") reflects his knowledge of God's future commitment to his people in salvation history.

"Rock" (GK 7446) evokes the strength and reliability of "the LORD" as Israel's God, and the concepts of "judgment" and "punishment" are correlated repeatedly (cf. Isa 11:3–4). "Punish" (GK 3519) has an underlying judicial meaning of "establishing what is just or right." Frequently it signifies correction of an offender. Here "judgment" (GK 5477) implies the restoration of rule and authority through removal of the causes of disorder. As intimated in vv.7–8, the Israelites' rejection of God's authority mediated through the law merely exposed them to the harsher experience of his authority mediated through an alien people.

13 To "look on" (GK 8011) a matter can imply that it is viewed with acceptance. That the Lord refused to view "evil" and "wrong" in this manner was a basic tenet of Israel's faith (Pss 5:4; 34:16, 21). The evil apparently tolerated was that of the "treacherous," namely, those who are unreliable and break faith in relationship. The Lord's tolerance is implied because he was "silent," or uninvolved; the treachery was typically that of the wicked who "swallow up" the righteous as a wolf devours its prey.

Evidently the "wicked" corresponds to the fisherman in vv.15–17. The express purpose of fishing is to consume the prey. This is motivated by a boundless greed, gratified without principle and pursued by means of a far-flung, international aggression. The "righteous" correspond to the "nations," likened to fish (vv.14–17). This designation includes Judah, whose sin caused her to be numbered among the nations in judgment. Habakkuk's concern was his own people, as both the perpetrators and victims of injustice.

14 The presence of calamity and evil in the world is related without hesitation to God's sovereign control of human destiny. The comparison to "fish" implies a condition that is subhuman and vulnerable. The "sea creatures" are seen as equally helpless, lacking the organization or leadership normally expected in human society.

15 The "hook" and line were widely used for fishing. The "net" was used for hunting and fishing and so had a diversity of application (cf. Isa 19:8). The precise identification of the "net" and "dragnet" is not certain. They appear to correspond to the two main types of net, the throw-net and the seine. "Rejoice" and "be glad" are used with great frequency in religious contexts of worship and praise. They indicate not merely pleasure or merriment but a response affirming what is valued and honored. Again the Babylonians are exposed as exalting the images of their own power and dominance.

16 The verb "sacrifice" (GK 2284) denotes the slaughter of living creatures, usually in a context of worship and service offered to deity. To "burn incense" has the broad meaning of "burning," causing a sacrifice to smoke. The verb is used with various animal sacrifices (e.g., Ex 29:13, 18, 25) and specifically with incense (e.g., Ex 30:7; Nu 16:40). The prophet is complaining that the Babylonians were clearly guilty of according to their own power the honor and strength due to God alone.

The Babylonians' full-blown delusion of greatness is depicted by the swift violence of the "net" and the unyielding, wholesale spoliation of the "dragnet" (cf. vv.8–11). The vast catch they procured had the one purpose of providing "food" for the Babylonian lifestyle. The adjectives underlying "luxury" and "choicest" both have the meaning of "fat," suggesting prosperity. The prosperity of the wicked made them immune to any feeling of dependency or accountability. The metaphorical language barely veils the fact that the food consumed by the Babylonians consisted of nations and individual lives (cf. v.13).

17 Can injustice be tolerated indefinitely by a God of justice? The phrase "empty his net" is virtually identical with "draw his sword"; possibly a double entendre is intended here, since the sword symbolizes the military power of which the net has been the image. The verb underlying "without mercy" has the basic meaning of "sparing" or "removing from a situation." It is used of holding back or refraining from an action, and commonly of pity as the attitude that causes one to hold back or remove from harm. The Babylonians' unrestrained self-will produced in them a hard insensitivity, making them a pitiless threat to other nations.

2:1 The noun "watch" (GK 5466) denotes either the duty or act of watching or a place of observation where such a responsibility is fulfilled. Habakkuk's "watch" is evidently portrayed as being on the city walls, as indicated by the "ramparts." Mizpah, for example, was a typical fortified city of this preexilic period; it had a solid wall 1800 feet long, 12 feet thick on average and perhaps 36 feet high, thus posing a considerable obstacle to battering rams and attackers scaling it. It was built of stone with salients and recesses, being buttressed at its weak points with a total of ten towers; and it would have been crowned by a balcony and parapet. The gate was also guarded by two towers, being carefully designed and fortified in keeping with its strategic function.

It was at some point on such defenses as these that Habakkuk saw himself on duty. The verb "look" (GK 7595) is applied particularly to sentries or watchmen on city walls, who were to warn the citizens of danger. It is applied figuratively to the prophets, who as Israel's watchmen were to see the Lord's purposes and communicate them to their people—a fitting title for those called to be seers and visionaries. Thus, Habakkuk the prophet looked to God for revelation concerning the nations. His "ramparts" and "watch" were the place of responsibility assigned to him, to stand in the council of the Lord and to see his word. The noun "complaint" (GK 9350) denotes an argument by which one seeks to establish what is right and a rebuke or correction by which right is restored. Habakkuk needed to know how to respond to God's ways, both in his assessment of injustice and in his conduct amid the consequences of injustice. He revealed a mature wisdom in his determination that this response be shaped by what God himself would say.

IV. God's Second Response (2:2–20)

1. Prologue (2:2–3)

2 The noun "revelation" (GK 2606) denotes vision that is almost invariably supersensory in nature, and it is attributed especially to the prophets. The "revelation" was to be written down to preserve it for the future. To "make plain" (GK 930) may refer to clarity either in form (by engraving the words) or in content. The reference to the writing material favors the former. This prophecy has a lasting relevance and is to be guarded accordingly. The "tablets" may have been composed of stone, clay, or even metal. "Herald" is literally "the one who reads." Such might be done by a herald, whose role would then be to "run" with the message. Alternatively, "run with" may refer specifically to prophetic activity (cf. Jer 23:21). The context is concerned primarily with preservation of the revelation as a source of encouragement for the future, rather than with its geographical proclamation.

3 The directive to "write" is given because the revelation "awaits" a future fulfillment, at "the end"; its impact extends beyond the present and must therefore be transmitted by means of a permanent record. Indeed, this fulfillment may appear to "linger," suggesting a delay beyond what is expected or intended: the Lord's timetable differs from a human one (cf. 2Pe 3:1–10). The "end" implies the termination of a certain object, activity, or period of time. The immediate context of the "revelation" is the end of the Babylonian oppression, for which the prophet must "wait" (GK 2675).

There is an "appointed time" for the "revelation's" fulfillment, determined by the Lord; and it will not "prove false" or disappoint but "will certainly come." Thus the reader may run with confidence and perseverance the race marked out for him (cf. 1Co 15:58). The logical outcome of this "revelation" is that one should "wait."

2. Indictment (2:4–5)

4 With this verse, the prophet begins the content of the "revelation" referred to in vv.2–3. The verb "puffed up" carries the basic meaning of "swelling," here in the sense of arrogance and presumption. "His desires" translates *napsho* ("soul," "life"; cf. GK 5883), whose meaning includes also the idea of desire or appetite. "His" evidently refers to the Babylonians. The verb "to be upright" denotes what is straight or level. The "righteous" may be defined by his commitment to the demands of the "law."

"Faith" (GK 575) implies fairness, stability, certainty, or permanence. Hence it is commonly used of personal character and conduct, which is evidenced especially as reliability. God's reliability ("faithfulness") is parallel to his name "Rock," with its connotations of stability and security as a basis for reliance. This quality of reliability and stability is predicated of the "righteous," the only plausible antecedent of "his" in "his faith." It signifies that his commitment to righteousness is genuine and steadfast.

For a person to be faithful in righteousness entails dependent trust on God; such an attitude is clearly demanded in the present context of waiting for deliverance. And "faith" implies obedient commitment no less than trust. Contrary to appearances, the judgment of God is selective and awe-inspiring in its precision: in the midst of disaster, his grace overshadows the righteous and causes them to "live."

5 "Wine," like the Babylonians, is deceptive and unreliable ("betrays"); although drunk to enhance one's life, wine impoverishes, confuses, and destroys (cf. Pr 20:1; 23:20–21, 29–35). It is associated with arrogance, unfulfilled greed, and social injustice elsewhere in the OT (cf. Isa 5:8–30). The object of this betrayal is clarified by the references to "arrogance" and restless ambition, clearly the Babylonians. And, indeed, the Babylonian regime was to be overthrown in just the circumstances of drunken pride portrayed here (cf. Da 5:1–31).

Napsho ("greedy"; GK 5883) is also translated "his desire, throat, appetite." The greed is insatiable. "Grave" (Heb. *sheol*; GK 8619) is perhaps better translated "underworld" or "hell," a place depicted repeatedly as devouring its prey (Nu 16:30–34; Pr 1:12). The expression of this insatiable greed is political conquest. The dominant metaphor relates to the treachery of an addiction to wine, which, like political and military ambition, knows no limit of fulfillment and to which all other interests are sacrificed.

3. Sentence (2:6–20)

6a The opening line introduces the oracle of woe (vv.6–20), characterized as a type of proverb ("taunt"; GK 5442); as an ambiguous, allusive saying that requires interpretation ("ridicule"; GK 4886); and as a riddle or enigmatic saying translated "scorn" (GK 2648). The first two terms have certain limited associations with mockery. The dominant emphasis is not ridicule but didactic, exposing the Babylonians as an object-lesson.

6b–8 "Woe" (GK 2098) is commonly used to introduce a judicial indictment. The crime is specified, first, as unjust acquisition of wealth, achieved by "extortion" and plunder, and, more seriously, as the wholesale destruction of people and their environment in the pursuit of this wealth. The noun "extortion" (GK 6294) denotes the accumulation of pledges taken as security by a creditor; such a procedure often accompanied the exploitation and even enslavement of the poor (cf. 2Ki 4:1–7; Ne 5:1–13). The word "debtors" is defined as "the peoples who are left," i.e., the survivors within the conquered nations; and the sentence announced here was indeed executed by former victims of Babylon, the Medes and Persians (cf. Jer 25:25; 49:34–39; Eze 32:24–2.5; Isa 13:17–22; 21:2–10; Da 5:28).

9–11 The noun "gain" (GK 1299) is generally associated with rapacity and wrongdoing, associations that are stressed by "unjust." The verb translated as "plotted the ruin" implies the cutting off of life. The present section amplifies these accusations by exposing the self-interested purposes underlying such violence, namely, establishment of the Babylonian "realm" or dynastic house, by elevating it to the invulnerable security depicted by an eagle's "nest." However, this exercise of evil to escape "ruin" is futile, for one reaps what one sows. The sentence of judgment balances the crime: shame for self-exaltation, loss of life for destruction of life, a divided and discordant house for a secure house. And, indeed, despite all its impregnable defenses, Babylon was to fall in precisely such circumstances of division and deluded pride (cf. Da 5:1–30).

12–14 The third "woe" reiterates the indictment of ruthless self-aggrandizement achieved by "bloodshed," applying it to the construction of the Babylonian capital. The judgment pronounced on such an enterprise is inevitable: a civilization built up by the destruction of other civilizations and by the conscription of their labor for its own ends will itself be destroyed. The mainspring of human history is to be found, not in its events themselves, but in the revealed purposes of the Lord who directs it. The title "LORD Almighty" (lit., "LORD of armies") expresses the Lord's sovereign rule as king and commander over every created force, but primarily over Israel. It is associated repeatedly with his militant judgment of all that opposes his rule.

The underlying purpose for the preceding indictments is God's abiding intent that his "glory" (GK 3883) fill the whole earth as it has filled his house, and that humankind should know it fully—a "knowledge" that will be as the "sea" in its length, breadth, and depth. This entails the removal of all that rejects such "knowledge," of which the Babylonian character and aspirations are the very epitome. The phrase "glory of the LORD" is used of the visible presence of God, by which the preeminent value of his character and actions are revealed. It is associated most prominently with the tabernacle and temple, and especially with the cherubim above which the Lord is enthroned, ruling over Israel, his sovereign majesty being of the essence of his "glory." To know the Lord in such "glory" is therefore to abandon the Babylonians' proud autonomy and to honor him as Lord.

15–17 The fourth "woe" introduces a new accusation, expressed by the image of inducing drunkenness with its consequences. The figure is used repeatedly of God's judgment by which he prostrates human beings, confusing their faculties and thereby undermining their presumptuous claim to self-determination; and it is applied widely to the Babylonians as instruments of that judgment. However, the Babylonian motives in such judgment are entirely self-interested: they seek their own "glory" through their malicious humiliation of their "neighbors," in which there is no acknowledgment of God's sovereign determination. Once again, therefore, their evil motivation and conduct reap a corresponding judgment: they will succumb to the same drunken humiliation that they have administered to others.

The preceding crime is defined more literally as "destruction" and "violence" wrought on "Lebanon." Often associated with the territory of Israel, to whose people it was allotted by the Lord, "Lebanon" is used as a symbol of Israel, and more specifically of Israel as a victim of Babylonian aggression (Eze 17:3). In keeping with these connotations, the Babylonians' "violence" and "destruction" refer to their rape and despoliation of the region of Israel—an injustice requiting Israel's own "destruction and violence" (cf. 1:3, 9) while incurring a corresponding retribution for the Babylonians themselves.

18–20 The dominant motif of v.18 is its denunciation of "idols"; they are unable to "teach" truth to anyone, and they are therefore utterly unworthy of one's "trust." These artifacts of "wood" and "stone" are unable to "give guidance" because they are without "breath." It is therefore reprehensible folly for a person to call on them. By contrast the Lord is in his holy "temple," or "palace" (GK 2121), ruling and judging in sovereign power.

The futility of idols is contrasted repeatedly with the living God's unique claim to "trust" and obedience. Their insidiousness is suggested by their ability to usurp the place of God in human lives, claiming a trust that belongs to him alone, and "giving guidance" that can come from him alone. In view of the Lord's implacable opposition to all such usurpers, the mere reference to his presence constitutes an intimation of judgment—a judgment duly executed on Babylon and still operative against humanity's bent toward idolatry.

V. The Prayer of Habakkuk (3:1–19)

In its form and language, ch. 3 is closely related to the Psalms. Habakkuk's recollection of Israel's past history is typical of the praises, instruction, and supplications in the Psalms. More specifically, the passage resembles the psalms of lament. It shows particular affinities with Ps 18 and Ps 77. For an extended discussion on the relationship between the prayer of Habakkuk and the Psalms, see EBC 7:520–22.

1. Introduction (3:1)

1 The reference to "Habakkuk the prophet" marks a new section. The following verses are characterized as a "prayer," a title attributed elsewhere to five psalms of lament (Pss 17; 86; 90; 102; 142), and also to an early collection of Davidic psalms (cf. Ps 72:20). The associations with the psalmic literature are reinforced by the phrase "On shigionoth" (cf. "shiggaion" in the title of Ps 7). The precise meaning of the phrase is uncertain.

2. Prayer (3:2)

2 The orientation of Habakkuk's "prayer" is to the past. The noun "fame" (GK 9051) is normally used of secondhand information, suggesting a remoteness from the hearer's own experience to the persons or events referred to. The Lord's "deeds" envisaged here are his work at the Exodus—a primary anchor-point of Israel's recollection, faith, and hope. Habakkuk's appeal for "mercy" (GK 8163) is thus grounded in God's covenantal commitment to Israel, displayed in the Exodus and sealed at Sinai. However, it is also an admission of Israel's decline from the revelation of God's character and ways, made "known" at the Exodus: not only do the "deeds" of that epoch represent secondhand knowledge, but the need to "renew" them implies that their impact in redemption and revelation was facing extinction. Moreover, the imminence of "wrath" betrays the presence of sin, which the Lord is committed to judge in his people.

3. Theophany (3:3–15)

3 "Teman" was located in Edom, the land south and east of the Dead Sea, traditionally occupied by the descendants of Esau. The wilderness of "Paran" was a large, relatively diffuse area, lying between Kadesh Barnea to

the north and Mount Sinai to the south and bounded by Edom to the northeast and Egypt to the southwest. "Mount Paran" is generally thought to be situated to the east of this desert. The primary function of mentioning these locales is to evoke the revelation of God's law at Sinai. The noun "glory" (GK 2086) is used primarily of kingly authority, revealed preeminently in the Lord's sovereignty over creation and history. Thus God's "glory" covers "the heavens" in permeating them, being revealed in them as an expression of his majesty. God's "praise" denotes the power of his character and works, for which he is to be praised and which pervades his creation. The meaning of the expression "Selah" has been obscure to translators since early times; possibly it had a liturgical function, relating to music or prayer in the temple worship.

4 God's "glory" is as "the sunrise." "Splendor" (GK 5586) denotes the shining of various sources of light, including the sun, while "sunrise" translates the common noun "light." The noun "rays" normally means "horns," with the derived meaning of "projections," such as beams or rays of light. "Splendor" describes the radiance of God's presence in contexts that recall his theophanies at Sinai and in the wilderness. This radiance is generally manifested as intense fire, shrouded in clouds and darkness, an image very remote from that of the rising sun. "Sunrise" is used of lightning, which is a prominent characteristic of Sinai and later theophanies. On this understanding, the Lord is perceived as illuminating the world with the awe-inspiring radiance that characterized his descent on Mount Sinai. The "rays" are flashes of light manifested at the Lord's presence. The "hand" is a symbol of the Lord's power—a "power" manifested conspicuously in the forces of nature, which are "hidden" in his storehouses.

5 God's "power" is here revealed in judgment: almost invariably "plague" and "pestilence" are attributed directly to the sovereign agency and judgment of God. Accompanying him in the context of Sinai, they refer particularly to the plagues that devastated Egypt and which attended Israel's disobedience to the covenant given at Sinai.

6–7 The scope of this judgment embraces the "earth" as a whole, which is convulsed by earthquake and volcanic upheaval. The repercussions of such judgment and physical upheaval are reflected among the "nations." "Tremble" implies both emotional turmoil and abrupt physical dislocation. The "mountains" and "hills" are symbols of grandeur, permanence, and security in the "earth"; yet they are revealed as frail and temporary. Although they appear to be "age-old," in truth God alone is "eternal." The "nations" are exemplified more specifically by the tribes of "Cushan" and "Midian." The Midianites were localized in Transjordan; the word "dwellings" typifies their nomadic existence. The identity of "Cushan" is uncertain, but evidently it also denotes a nomadic group in similar "distress." This close parallelism suggests that "Cushan" was a nation related or even identical to "Midian" (cf. Ex 2:18–22; 18:1–5; Nu 12:1).

8 The Lord's "wrath" is directed against the "sea," evoking his display of power at the Red Sea. The correlation with that event is substantiated by the reference to "chariots" and "horses" and to the Lord's victory, or the salvation of his people.

9 All three Hebrew words in the second line of this verse are obscure, and they must be interpreted against the background of the first line. The noun "arrows" normally means "staffs" or "tribes," but the first of these meanings can be applied to the shaft of a weapon. Such an application is appropriate to "bow." "Many" translates a form derived from either a noun meaning "group of seven" or a verb meaning "to swear." The first alternative is suggested in the sevenfold volleys of arrows used in Israelite warfare. Although the issue is by no means clear-cut, "to swear" is preferable because vv.11–14 clearly echo Dt 32:39–43; v.9 is closely related to vv.11–14 by the correspondence of "uncovered" and "stripped"; it is therefore to be interpreted against the same Deuteronomic background. Thus, God's militant intervention is perceived as fulfilling the commitment sworn to Moses and Israel beyond the Jordan. A tentative translation of the entire line would be "The arrows of the promise are sworn."

The final line is also obscure, since it could be translated "you split the rivers to the earth." The noun "rivers" has associations with the Exodus. The verb "split" (GK 1324) is often applied to the division of the Red Sea, which allowed God's people to walk securely on the dry "earth." However, the vision of the earth "split" by floods of water is appropriate to the following verses with their undertones of the Creation and the Flood. The syntactical ambiguity is supported by the association of God's "bow" with the Flood (cf. Ge 9:13–14, 16) and by the similar juxtaposition of earthquake and flood in v.10. On this understanding "earth" may correspond to "mountains." Verse 8 would then deal with the Exodus and vv.9–11 more explicitly with the Flood, both motifs being integrated in vv.12–15.

10 The reference to "water" again evokes God's might revealed in driving back the Red Sea, as do the nouns "deep" and "torrents." This verse in particular draws on the language of Ps 77, where the Exodus is the explicit focus of recollection. Both passages envision that event in cosmic terms, as convulsing the "mountains" and the whole of nature. It is this awe-inspiring power of God, the Creator and Judge of all the earth, that is manifested in retribution and salvation at the Red Sea. As at the Cross, a universal cataclysm is compressed into a single, localized event in Israel's history; and that event, too, is destined to shake the universe.

11 The "sun" and "moon" are prominent symbols of God's created order, particularly of its permanence. Their inactivity indicates the interruption of that order. Here the picture is probably of an eclipse; they stay in their place and cease to give light. Moreover, darkness is appropriate to the context of storm in vv.9–11. Such an interruption of the created order typically accompanies the judgment of God; and this judgment, culminating in the eschatological Day of the Lord, is characterized consistently by darkness. The noun "glint" is used of lightning (cf. Ps 77:18), and the Lord's "arrows" are equated with lightning (Pss 18:14; 77:17–18). His "arrows" recur repeatedly as instruments of his judgment.

12 This verse recapitulates the motif of God's wrath, the noun "anger" being identical to "wrath" in v.8. It also recapitulates the military imagery of vv.8–9, 11. Habakkuk's vision embraces the conquest of the "nations" as an integral part of the Exodus and of Israel's subsequent destiny. The Lord may appoint the Babylonians to curse Israel, but they will surely inherit a curse themselves. Threshing implies violent shaking and crushing, which also characterizes the effects on the "earth" and mountains as the Lord "strode" by.

13 The military associations of "came out" are reiterated in the words "deliver" (GK 3829) and "save" (GK 3829), both derived from the same root as "victorious" (v.8) and "save" (1:2). This deliverance expresses the Lord's covenantal commitment to his "people" and to his "anointed one" (*mashiach*, "Messiah"). In the present context of the Exodus, "anointed one" appears to refer to Moses, who, like King David, combined in himself the messianic functions of shepherd, prophet, servant of God, and priest. The context of the Exodus also throws light on the identity of the "leader." Egypt represents an archetypal land of "wickedness," and the pharaoh as leader figures prominently as an agent of Israel's oppression. This understanding is reinforced by the associations of the noun "land" (GK 1074), normally translated "house," since Egypt is characterized as Israel's "house of bondage." The oppression in Egypt foreshadows subsequent oppression, and the deliverance at the Red Sea embodies the promise of subsequent deliverance.

14 This devastation is elaborated further here, the verb "pierced" echoing a meaning of "crushed," and the noun "head" being identical to "leader." It is accomplished by turning the enemy's "spear" (or "weapons") against himself. This is reminiscent of the overthrow of the pharaoh's horses and chariots and represents a fitting judgment on the Babylonians. Indeed, Babylon fell to Cyrus without opposition, its "leader" being betrayed by factions among his own subjects (cf. Da 5). The scene recalls the Babylonians' rapacity in the preceding chapters. This victory is wrought on behalf of the "wretched" (the "humble" or "afflicted"). This adjective denotes a condition of material or spiritual poverty.

15 Verse 15 reverts again to the language of v.8, thereby establishing the historical context of the intervening verses. The phrase

"great waters" represents a further allusion to the Exodus.

4. Response (3:16–19a)

16 The term "heart" (GK 1061) is applied in literal usage to the lower abdomen, particularly the womb or belly, as the seat of conception; it is used figuratively of the innermost thoughts and motives of man. As evidenced by the additional anatomical terms, the prophet was shaken and disabled throughout his being. The verb "pounded" echoes the same root in vv.2, 7, and occurs again in "trembled." The conspicuous repetitions indicate the cause of Habakkuk's inward upheaval: the imminence of God's "wrath" on Israel and, more acutely, the uncertainty of any time-frame that accompanies the subsequent judgment on the enemy. This is corroborated by the final, explanatory lines, which anticipate a "nation invading us" as an instrument of that "wrath." But they also anticipate for that nation its own "day of calamity." For Habakkuk to see such things that were veiled to his contemporaries was to experience distress. To see beyond them, to the Holy One who appointed them, was to demonstrate the greatness of faith and to find strength to "wait quietly" (cf. 2:3).

17 Israel's prosperity was dependent on the nation's obedience to the covenant and on the Lord's consequent blessing. Such prosperity was forfeited by disobedience and disloyalty to the covenant, thus incurring the Lord's chastening through natural and military disasters. In this vision of a devastated economy, Habakkuk acknowledges his nation's apostasy and the inevitability of judgment.

18 The faith demonstrated in v.16 reaches full expression (2:4). For Habakkuk it was "God" himself and his intervention as "Savior" (GK 3829) that motivated his longing and his joyful attaining. The basis of Habakkuk's faith, as of Paul's, was the revealed word of God (cf. Ro 10:17). The covenant that promised the invasion and devastation also gave assurance of restoration to God's favor and presence (cf. Dt 30:1–10; 32:34–43).

19a This verse is clearly dependent on Ps 18, in its affirmation of God-given "strength" and most notably in the image of "the feet of a deer ... on the heights." However, the phrase "go on the heights" is anticipated in Dt 33:29, which itself echoes Dt 32:13. Both passages envisage Israel's conquest and possession of the Promised Land.

5. Epilogue (3:19b)

19b The final line of the prophecy forms an editorial conclusion to ch. 3, expressed in the language of Psalms. The "director of music" probably had supervisory authority, particularly of the Levites in relation to the music of the temple service (1Ch 15:21; 23:4; 2Ch 2:2, 18; 34:12–13). The noun "stringed instruments" is translated "song" or music in common usage (cf. Job 30:9; Pss 69:12; 77:6).

The Old Testament in the New

OT Text	NT Text	Subject
Hab 1:5	Ac 13:41	Judgment for sin
Hab 2:3–4	Heb 10:37–38	Persevere in faith
Hab 2:4	Ro 1:17; Gal 3:11	The righteous live by faith

Zephaniah

INTRODUCTION

1. Author and Date

As far back as the early church fathers, the etymology of Zephaniah's name was disputed. One explanation understood the name to contain the root *saphan* (GK 7621; "to hide, shelter"). This etymology plus the common suffix *yah* (for "Yahweh") gives the meaning "Yah(weh) has hidden." Another suggestion derives the name "Zephaniah" from the root *sapah* (GK 7595; "to watch"); thus the name signifies something like "Watchman for Yah(weh)."

Three other men bore the name Zephaniah in the OT: a Levite descended from Kohath (1Ch 6:36–38); the second priest under the high priest Seraiah during the reign of King Zedekiah (2Ki 25:18–21; Jer 52:24–27); and the father of Josiah, an exile who returned from Babylon (Zec 6:10, 14).

The opening statement of the book indicates that Zephaniah prophesied "during the reign of Josiah son of Amon king of Judah" (640–609 B.C.). Zephaniah predicted the destruction of Nineveh (2:13–15), which took place in 612 B.C. The only question is whether his prophecy belonged to the earlier or later part of Josiah's reign. Scholars have argued for both options.

2. Background

After the wicked reigns of Manasseh (695–642 B.C.) and Amon (642–640 B.C.), the reformer king Josiah (640–609 B.C.) ascended the throne. For more than a half-century, during the reigns of his predecessors, apostate conditions had prevailed. It was during Josiah's reign that Zephaniah began warning the people of impending judgment. The fall of Samaria in 722 B.C. had been a solemn reminder of God's justice and power.

Manasseh and Amon had remained loyal vassals to Assyria, but under Josiah the nation of Judah experienced independence. The death of Ashurbanipal, king of Assyria (669–633 B.C.), probably coincided with Josiah's eighth year (2Ch 34:30), a time perhaps of Assyrian policy change. By the time Josiah was of age (628 B.C.), Ashurbanipal's son had died. Assyria was facing problems with Babylon and was no longer able to retain effective control in the west. Presumably about this time Josiah launched sweeping reforms and moved to take possession of the provinces into which Assyria had divided the territory of northern Israel.

The message of Zephaniah pictures the social, moral, and religious conditions in Judah at that time. The reforms of Josiah certainly included a purge of foreign cults and practices. Undoubtedly heading the list were Assyrian religious practices. Various astral deities and old Canaanite practices were removed (2Ki 23:4–25). Cult personnel—including prostitutes of both sexes—were done away with. The shrines of the north and their personnel—especially the rival temple of Bethel—were destroyed. Probably Josiah's most noteworthy reform policy was the centralization of worship in Jerusalem.

3. Message

The focal point of Zephaniah's message is the "day of the LORD." Zephaniah used the expression more often than any other prophet. The Day of the Lord would be a day of doom, because the people "have sinned against the LORD" (1:17). But he also held out a promise of shelter for those who sought the Lord (2:3). In ch. 1 Zephaniah centers God's word of judgment on Judah. In ch. 2, he predicts and pronounces judgment on the neighbors of Judah. In ch. 3, after a word concerning judgment on Jerusalem, he promises future glory for Israel's remnant.

EXPOSITION

I. Introduction (1:1)

1 The author gave us more information about his ancestry than any other prophet, tracing his pedigree back four generations. Perhaps this was because the good king Hezekiah was his great-great-grandfather (some feel the Hezekiah here is not the same one who had been king). The time of the prophecy was during the reign of Josiah king of Judah (see the introduction).

II. Day of Judgment (1:2–3:8)

A. Against Judah (1:2–2:3)

1. General warning (1:2–3)

2 Before focusing attention on Judah, Zephaniah issues a general warning of coming destruction in broad terminology. God is judge of the whole world, and especially of his people, Judah. The expression "face of the earth," used of the great Flood of Noah's time (Ge 6:7; 7:4), refers to more than just a local land, unless a specific limitation is added.

3 Language that pairs "men and animals" (sixth day of creation) and birds and fish (fifth day) and prefaces each with "sweep away" vividly sets forth the totality and intensity of a coming destruction.

2. Judgment for Judah (1:4–13)

4 When the Lord said he would "stretch out his hand against," he was indicating a special work of punishment (cf. Isa 5:25). The reference to the "remnant of Baal" would be to the forms of Baal worship still left in the land from Manasseh's detestable institution of it (2Ki 21:3, 5, 7). Josiah destroyed much of this; but pockets of Baalism still existed, necessitating judgment and eradication.

"Pagan and idolatrous priests" reflects the traces of idolatrous worship that yet remained despite official action against the cult. God intended a judgment that would totally eliminate Baalism. This was fulfilled in Judah by the Babylonian invasion.

5–6 These verses delineate and describe the persons involved in this pagan worship. Roof worship provided a clear view of the sky and a good place for altars. Josiah acted against this practice (2Ki 23:5), but obviously the evil practice still persisted. The religious syncretism reflected in swearing by the Lord and also by Molech was not new (cf. 1Ki 11:33). Finally listed are those simply and summarily described as the faithless and indifferent.

7 In view of the doom waiting, the prophet called all to silent attention before the Lord. "The day of the LORD" in view here is his day of reckoning, the time of God's judgment. "The LORD has prepared [his] sacrifice"—the people of Judah! "He has consecrated" the despised and dreaded Babylonians as his priests to slay this sacrifice. When sinners will not repent and offer themselves as living sacrifices, then he himself becomes the sacrifice and victim of his own sins.

8 The royal leaders who bore chief responsibility were singled out for special notice. They should have led the people in righteousness instead of evil. Those of royal blood bore responsibility for the conditions in Jerusalem. "Foreign clothes" seems to refer to dress that imitated or reflected Egyptian or Babylonian styles, indicative of a foreign inclination of the heart.

9 "Stepping [GK 1925] on the threshold" may reflect a cultic practice of pagan priests avoiding stepping on a defiled or sacrosanct threshold, deriving from when the head and hands of the Philistine god Dagon broke off and lay there (cf. 1Sa 5:5). More likely this passage refers to theft and plunder, which fits in nicely with the following couplet. Accordingly, the verb should be translated "leap on" (or "over") the threshold.

10 "That day" refers to the Day of the Lord, the time of great wailing and outcry. The Fish Gate was in the north wall, probably near the present Damascus Gate (cf. Ne 3:3; 12:39; 2Ch 33:14). This is the direction the enemy would come from. The "New Quarter" (lit., "second [town]") was probably near the Fish Gate. Huldah the prophetess lived there (2Ki 22:14). "The hills" probably refers to those within Jerusalem (Zion, Ophel, Moriah). The "loud crash" vividly depicts the city crashing down on the heads of its inhabitants.

11 "Market district" (GK 4847) translates an obscure Hebrew word. It seems to represent the area where merchants gathered, possibly somewhere in the depression of the Tyropean Valley. The choice of a Hebrew word that may mean "mortar" is especially appropriate since God was about to pound his people like grain in a mortar.

12 The "lamps" were clay oil-lamps commonly used at that time. The vivid imagery of "wine left on its dregs" was proverbial for indifference and callousness, as shown by the parallel: "who are complacent." In making the best wine, the liquid is poured from vessel to vessel, separating the wine from its dregs. If allowed to remain too long on its lees, the wine becomes harsh. So evil people rested complacently on harsh and evil influences and were securely settled in their wicked society. They concluded that the Lord would do "nothing, either good or bad," i.e., they denied God's providence, as though he brought about neither blessing nor judgment.

13 Because of their complacency and impudence, God would bring on the people the curses of the covenant: they would not enjoy their wealth, homes, and vineyards (cf. Lev 26:3–33; Dt 28:30, 39). He would fulfill his promises to his people—for good or bad.

3. Description of that day (1:14–2:3)

14 The Day of the Lord is called "great" (GK 1524; cf. Joel 2:11). This great day hung over the people like the famous sword of Damocles; it was right at hand, certain, and hastening to its goal. "Listen!" implies a "sound" or "noise" to be heard.

15 The dreadful character of the great day of the Lord is reflected in the words "distress," "anguish," "trouble," and "ruin." Then its ominous conditions are depicted by the use of "darkness," "gloom," "clouds," and "blackness."

16 The stark description continues so vividly that one feels he is present at the battle, seeing the clouds of smoke billowing upward and hearing the trumpet blasts from various parts of the city.

17 The deep distress was "because they have sinned against the LORD." The judgment the people would experience would cause them to stagger and stumble like the blind (cf. Dt 28:29). In addition, their life and entrails would be spilled out like dust and refuse, to be trampled underfoot by their enemy. God was against them.

18 To emphasize their desperate plight, the prophet warned the people that they could not buy their way out. Neither silver nor gold would protect them from the wrath of the Lord. This section closes with the universal terminology—"all who live in the earth."

2:1–2 Verse 1 opens with the invitation to "gather together" (GK 8006) in repentance and includes a derogatory note: "shameful nation." The "appointed time" refers to the Day of the Lord, the time of his giving vent to his holy wrath. This gathering together must take place before the judgment if it is to be averted. The reference to "chaff" indicates that the wicked nation would be scattered before the fierce anger of the Lord, as chaff is scattered before the wind.

3 Repentance must be manifested in works: seeking the Lord and doing what he commands. The "humble" must "seek the LORD," defined as seeking "righteousness" and "humility." Only the "humble of the land" are exhorted because nothing can be done with the rest. "Seeking the LORD" is essential to escape from judgment, but even with this the prophet said only, "Perhaps you will be sheltered" from the Lord's anger.

B. Against Gentiles (2:4–15)

1. Philistia (2:4–7)

4 The four cities—Gaza, Ashkelon, Ashdod, Ekron—represented the entire area of Philistia. Gaza and Ashkelon are summarily dismissed in judgment by a typical Hebrew synonymous couplet. Ashdod and Ekron are to be uprooted and emptied at midday—unusual since this hottest time is used for a siesta in the Orient. Undoubtedly the point being made is that judgment will fall on them when they least expect it.

5 "Kerethite" is a term used of the Philistines, perhaps originally of one branch of them (cf. Eze 25:16). David's bodyguard was made up of Kerethites and Pelethites (2Sa 8:18), usually considered two branches of the Philistines.

6–7 The once heavily settled seacoast of the Philistines would become a desolate place for shepherds and sheep pens. The lowly shepherd would be able to find a place for his sheep to graze where there was no sowing or reaping and where no civilization flourished. Eventually, however, it would be inhabited by the remnant of Judah. A note of hope for Judah is sounded in v.7. They will occupy the sites of their former enemy, the Philistines.

As Zephaniah predicted, Ekron was destroyed (2:4–5). This aerial shot shows what remains of this town—a huge fifty-acre site. Completely surrounding it can be seen the remnants of the wall. Courtesy Ilan Sztulman of the Tel Miqne-Ekron Excavations, 1988.

2. Moab and Ammon (2:8–11)

8 The encounter with Philistines dates back to the time of the patriarchs (Ge 20–21; 26). The confrontation with Moab goes back to the time of Moses (Nu 22–24). Conflicts with Ammon appear in Jdg 10:6–11:33; 2Sa 10:1–11:1; and Ne 2:10, 19; 4:3, 7. Because of the fall of the northern kingdom and the decline of the southern kingdom, the pride of the nations east of Israel increased greatly. They showed their enmity toward God's people on every opportunity. The insults and taunts mentioned here probably refer to the hostility assumed at various times and not to just one particular episode.

9 The comparison of Moab and Ammon to Sodom and Gomorrah is not surprising in view of their origin from Lots' daughters (Ge 19:30–38). "Weeds" and "salt pits" reflect desolation and sterility. To this day many rock-strewn ruins of ancient Moab and Ammon bear mute testimony to the truth of the prophet's words: "a wasteland forever." Only a remnant of God's people would be needed to plunder these ancient enemies, and only the survivors of Israel would inherit the ancient sites of Moab and Ammon.

10 "Pride" (GK 1454) is cited as the sin that led Moab and Ammon to insult and mock God's people (cf. Isa 16:6 and Jer 48:26, both of which refer to the pride of Moab).

11 The Lord destroys the gods by destroying the nations that depend on these gods; these deities have no real existence apart from the people who serve them (1Co 8:4–6). By revealing the unreal nature of these gods, he brings the nations to acknowledge him as the one true God.

3. Cush (2:12)

12 Having foretold God's judgment on nations east and west of Judah, Zephaniah next directs attention to nations south and north: Cush and Assyria. The "too" indicates that the Lord would bring Cush to an end just as he would Moab and Ammon.

Cush was located in the upper Nile region. Since Egypt had been under the rule of Cushite kings for years, the prophet's words probably included Egypt as well. Nebuchadnezzar was the Lord's sword that killed the Cushites: "I will strengthen the arms of the king of Babylon and put my sword in his hand" (Eze 30:24–25).

4. Assyria (2:13–15)

13 The prophecies against surrounding nations climax with Assyria, the strongest political factor and the most northerly nation of that time. The prediction of Nineveh's utter desolation while that Assyrian capital ruled the world testifies to the divine origin of Zephaniah's message. The prediction that God would leave Nineveh "dry as the desert" is remarkable in view of the fame of the city's great irrigation system.

14 Instead of marching armies and a prosperous population, the prophet predicted that flocks of sheep and goats and all kinds of creatures would be found at Nineveh. The renowned city would become fit only for herds and wild animals. The "owls" are depicted in another picture of desolation (Isa 34:11; cf. Ps 102:6). Nineveh's magnificent buildings, tumbled into debris, would become dwelling places for various creatures. Only doleful sounds would emerge from the doorways.

15 The city—complacent and carefree at the time of Zephaniah's prediction—would become a lair for wild beasts and an object of contempt for every passerby. She boasted in her self-sufficiency. But the inspired prophet predicted that she would become a ruin and a habitat for the creatures of the fields (cf. Isa 47:8; Rev 3:17).

C. Against Jerusalem (3:1–8)

1 After the series of predicted judgments against various surrounding nations, the prophet again focuses on Jerusalem and Judah. The guilty city harbored oppressors, rebels, and defiled people. These people often washed themselves with water and observed other ceremonies of external sanctity, outwardly appearing to be pure.

2 The continuing indictment of Jerusalem contains three specific charges: (1) she obeyed no one—not even the Lord; (2) she did not trust in the Lord; and (3) she did not draw near to her God, who was the only one who could provide direction and guidance for her.

3–4 Four classes of leaders represent the total leadership of the whole people. (1) "Officials" (GK 8569) were possibly the royal leaders who should have been characterized by justice and equity rather than by greed and avarice. (2) "Rulers" (GK 9149) also represented those in places of leadership, probably civil magistrates, who should have set an example for the rest of the people; instead, they are tagged as predatory and ravenous beasts. (3) "Her prophets" (GK 5566) are described as "arrogant" and "treacherous." The latter means "unfaithful," for they were unfaithful to the one they claimed to represent. (4) "Her priests" (GK 3913) represent the other religious leaders; they were profaning the sanctuary and violating the law. Their ordained function was to interpret the law and officiate at the sanctuary with reverence; they had done just the opposite.

5 In contrast to her misleading leaders "within her," the Lord in Israel's midst was a "righteous" standard against which the people were measured. His holy and righteous presence demanded judgment for sin and corruption. He is never implicated with iniquity—"he does no wrong." Moreover, he continuously—"morning by morning"—manifested his justice and righteousness before the people in his treatment of both Israel and the surrounding nations. Despite all this, the people were so calloused that they recognized no wickedness or felt no shame for what they had done.

6–7 As an object lesson, God reminded his people what he did to other nations. In view of these judgments, the Lord spoke imploringly to his people, declaring that judgment and punishment could have been averted and avoided. But trapped in the grip of sin, the people "were still eager to act corruptly."

8 "Therefore" anticipates a promise to pour out deserved judgment on the wicked people. Instead, the punishment was veiled; they were admonished to "wait [GK 2675] for me." The Lord promised "to pour out [his] wrath on them [the assembled nations]—all [his] fierce anger." He continued in strong language: "The whole world will be consumed by the fire of my jealous anger." This portrays a scene of great prophetic significance. The Lord had determined to gather the nations and kingdoms to pour out on them in great judgment his "wrath" and "fierce anger" and to consume them with "the fire of [his] jealous anger."

III. Day of Joy (3:9–20)

After the judgment thus described, the Lord will turn to himself a people of "purified lip" and united heart ("shoulder to shoulder"). The following verses describe the promises of blessing and restoration for God's people and the nations.

A. Return of a Scattered People (3:9–10)

9 The scattered people who return will bring offerings and experience purification. They will together call on the name of the Lord and worship and serve him. Before the scattering of the people at the tower of Babel, the world was unified by one language; but it was a world of rebellious people. In contrast, the new purified language will characterize a responsive people. The lips or language that had become impure through use in idol worship will become purified so that all may in unison call on the name of the Lord. To "call on the name of the LORD" is to turn to the Lord out of a sense of need. This kind of language may refer to the pre-Flood period (cf. Ge 4:26).

10 Cush, the southern extremity of the known world, represented the southern limits of the judgments. "The rivers" presumably indicates the Blue and the White branches of the Nile.

B. Restoration of a Sinful People (3:11–13)

11 "That day" refers to the time when Israel will be gathered together from the dispersion, as the Daughter of Zion (cf. v.14). They will not be put to shame because the very source of pride and haughtiness will be abolished: intolerable attitudes on "God's holy hill." Mount Zion is made holy by the presence of God.

12–13 Instead of the haughty, there will be the meek and humble, those "who trust in the name of the LORD." Their confidence and strength is derived from God himself. Further description of this remnant of Israel presents them as free from all deception, duplicity, and deceit, a probable allusion to their former idolatry. Thus they are fit to experience physical prosperity.

C. Rejoicing of a Saved People (3:14–20)

The messianic era is described vividly in this concluding passage. It will be a time of great joy; the Lord will be in the midst of his people. Fear and sorrow will be removed, and the Lord will restore their fortunes. It will be a time for singing and rejoicing.

14–15 An exhortation to "sing" and "rejoice" begins the conclusion to the prophet's message. "Daughter of Zion" refers here to the reassembled remnant of Israel; "Daughter of Jerusalem" is a parallel expression. In typical hymnic style the prophet follows the call to praise with the cause for praise: "The LORD has taken away your punishment . . . turned back your enemy. . . . [He] is with you; never again will you fear any harm."

16–17 In that wonderful messianic day, the remnant's hands will not "hang limp" because there will be no despair that slack hands symbolize. Since the Lord "is with" (lit., "in the midst of") his people, they need no longer be in fear; he is a "hero" who delivers or saves. The prophet continues his description of this saving God as one who "will take great delight in you" and "rejoice over you with singing."

18–19 The scattering of the people in judgment brought on sorrows as they yearned for the old assembly experiences at the appointed feasts, the festive meetings (cf. La 2:6). The Lord promises "at that time" to deal with all who oppressed Israel (cf. Isa 60:14). The pathetic condition of God's people is reflected in the references to the "lame" and "scattered." Undoubtedly these references apply to all in the Dispersion; all will be regathered and restored. But that is not the end of the story; also they will enjoy receiving praise and honor—even from the lands where they had been put to shame.

20 With a slight change in wording, the Lord repeats the promise just made, giving emphasis to it. It is supplemented with "when I restore your fortunes [cf. 2:7] before your very eyes." The work of redemption, as well as judgment, belongs to the Lord. He will accomplish his purposes with his people. This promise is the basis of their hope and joy.

Haggai

INTRODUCTION

1. Background

Everything in this brief prophecy hangs on this one imperative—build God's house (1:8)! The setting reflects much of the history of Israel—the days of the tabernacle, the beginning of the monarchy under Samuel, David's desire to build a dwelling for God, Solomon's building the temple, its destruction by Nebuchadnezzar, and the returning exiles who began to rebuild the temple in Jerusalem in 538 B.C. More immediately the setting of 1:8 begins with the rise of Cyrus.

In 559 B.C., Cyrus was only the king of An–shan, a district in Elam. He joined with Nabonidus, a weak successor of Nebuchadnezzar, to conquer Ecbatana, the capital of Media, in 550. Cyrus broke with Nabonidus and turned against him to capture Babylon in 539. Nabonidus had lost support because of his disinterest in Marduk and other traditional Babylonian deities. He failed also in his effort to secure Egyptian help against Cyrus. On the other hand, Cyrus, respectful of all deities, was probably welcomed to Babylon by the priests of the religion so unpopular with Nabonidus.

Nabonidus, the fourth king after the death of Nebuchadnezzar in 562 B.C., himself died in 539, after a seven-year reign. Belshazzar, his son, had evidently been coregent; but in fulfillment of Da 5:25–28, he too died. Cyrus, who had been king of Media and Persia since 549, now brought Babylon under his control. In the following year he made his famous edict (see Ezr 1:2–4; 6:3b–5), allowing all peoples to return to their native lands. The peaceful surrender of Babylon is recorded in both the so-called Nabonidus Chronicle and the Cyrus Cylinder. Ezr 5:13–14 describes the effect of Cyrus's decree on God's people.

According to Ezr 5:16, the foundations of the temple were laid by Sheshbazzar and his company, and Ezr 3:2 tells how the leaders built the altar and began sacrificing burnt offerings. Obviously, however, the work was not completed eighteen years later. Otherwise Haggai would not have preached his sermons.

Why did the enthusiasm of God's people wane? For one thing, during the seventy years in Babylon, most of the exiles had come to consider it their home (cf. Jer 29:5–7). Further, some may have been doing so well financially that they were reluctant to return to Jerusalem and face the dangers involved in rebuilding the temple. Those who did return in 538 B.C. were probably the poorer ones who had nothing to lose in such a venture.

The reconstruction project may have faltered also because of the unstable political situation that followed the death of Cyrus in 529 B.C. Cambyses came to the throne and reigned for seven years. His major accomplishment was bringing Egypt under Persian control. The passage of his armies through the land of Israel may have worked a hardship on the native population. Demands for food, water, clothing, and shelter may have greatly diminished the meager resources of a people engaged in a building project well beyond their means.

When Cambyses died in 522, there were several contestants for the throne; and one of them actually ruled for two months. He was the Pseudo-Smerdis, the real brother of Cambyses. In any event, Darius I, or Darius the Great, the son of a general named Hystaspes, became king and ruled until 486. He is the Darius of the book of Haggai. With him came the stability the Jews thought necessary for continuing the work on the temple. Even then it was the second year of his reign before Haggai appeared on the scene to stir them to action.

The biggest problem the returned exiles faced was the opposition from the Samaritans and others who lived in the land (cf. Ezr 4). At first the "enemies" offered to help build the temple, claiming that they had been sacrificing to God since the time of Esarhaddon, the Assyrian king whose policy of exchanging populations had brought them there. But

Zerubbabel, Joshua ("Jeshua" in Ezra), and the other leaders declined the offer and insisted on doing the work themselves. This antagonized those who had offered to help, and they continued to hinder the reconstruction project. They even secured temporary restraining orders and frustrated the plans of the faithful Jews throughout the reign of Cyrus and down to the reign of Darius (Ezr 4:5). At this point Haggai and Zechariah, who prophesied to the Jews in Judah and Jerusalem in the name of the God of Israel (Ezr 5:1), came on the scene.

2. Authorship

Haggai is unknown to us apart from his short book, the two isolated occurrences of his name in Ezra (5:1; 6:14), and an allusion in Zec 8:9. The word "Haggai" seems to be an adjective from the Hebrew word for "feast," and therefore the prophet's name may mean "festal." If the "i" ("y" in Hebrew) on the end suggests a shortened form of the name "Yahweh" (translated as "the LORD"), the prophet's name would mean "Feast of Yahweh."

If 2:3 indicates that Haggai saw Solomon's temple before it was destroyed, then he must have been at least seventy years old at the time of his prophecy. Since he was usually linked with Zechariah, and since his name comes first, Haggai was probably the older of the two. It is likely that he had returned to Jerusalem with Zerubbabel eighteen years earlier (in 538).

The lists of returnees in the opening chapters of Ezra do not mention Haggai; and we know nothing of his ancestry. Nor is there any information about his occupation other than that he was a prophet. The brief record of his ministry shows him as a man of conviction. Unique among the prophets, he was listened to, and his words were obeyed. In a mere four years the temple was complete.

3. Date and Place of Origin

Haggai dates his prophecies with precision. Four specific dates are mentioned (cf. 1:1, 15; 2:1, 10, 20), ranging from August 29 to December 18, 520 B.C. Thus the ministry of Haggai lasted less than four months. He obviously wrote in Jerusalem. His book refers to the house of God (the temple in Jerusalem). The command to go to the nearby mountains to fetch wood for the construction of the temple clearly implies this setting (1:8). Since neither Babylonia nor the adjoining part of Assyria has mountains, these references must be understood as the mountains of Judea.

4. Occasion and Purpose

Depending on how one calculates them, the seventy years of captivity may or may not have been over in 520 B.C. The exile connected with the final destruction of Jerusalem was in 586 B.C. (2Ki 25:8–11). Seventy years from that date would have been 516 B.C. Perhaps Haggai saw that date fast approaching and went to work to convince the people to get on with rebuilding the temple.

The constant oppression of hostile neighbors must have had a debilitating effect on the outlook of those trying to build for God. Against these odds and in the midst of this despair, Haggai chided the people to resume the task enthusiastically taken up so many years ago and subsequently dropped. His message was simply, "Build God's house." To support his case he contended that recent crop failures (1:9) and drought (1:10–11) were God's way of reminding them of their dependence on him.

Another of Haggai's purposes was to remind the people of spiritual priorities: they were God's kingdom on earth, the only witnesses to divine truth. If they proved faithless, it would damage God's reputation. Haggai kept before them the fact that they were God's representatives in the world.

5. Theological Values

Central to Haggai's theology was the temple. In his time it was more significant than the palace, and his dealings were more with priests than with princes. The temple and Mount Zion on which it sat represented God's dwelling on earth. Its destruction by Nebuchadnezzar amounted to the ultimate blasphemy. The only way to rectify this situation was to rebuild the temple.

Coupled with this concern for spiritual matters is Haggai's criticism of personal wealth and comfort. The people had finished building their own houses but had let the program of reconstruction on God's house lapse. Haggai was convinced that if the people expressed sincere devotion and obedient service to the Lord, the Lord would in turn bless them with better crops (see 2:10–19).

Of theological importance is the prophecy in 2:9. While this verse is nowhere quoted in the NT, most interpreters take it as a reference to the advent of the Messiah. The second temple was less sumptuous than Solomon's; but because it was to become the scene of some of Christ's ministry, it would actually have a greater glory than the first temple. The peace promised by the Lord in this prophecy would ultimately come through Christ.

EXPOSITION

I. A Call to Build the House of God (1:1–11)

1. Introduction (1:1–3)

1–3 These three verses introduce the book of Haggai, date the first oracle, and identify the addressees. The second year of King Darius was 520 B.C. The sixth month was Elul, and the first day of that month would be August 29, by modern reckoning.

The first message is addressed to "Zerubbabel son of Shealtiel" and "Joshua son of Jehozadak." This is the Zerubbabel who led the exiles back to Judea; he was the grandson of Jehoiachin (Jeconiah in Mt 1:12). Zerubbabel was, then, an heir to the Davidic throne; and it is understandable that the magnanimous Cyrus and Darius should allow such a man to be the governor of the province of Judea.

"Joshua son of Jehozadak" is spelled "Jeshua son of Jozadak" in Ezr 3:2, 8, et al. Apparently he was a direct descendant of Aaron the Levite, the first high priest. Joshua was then the high priest, the holder of the highest office in the religious hierarchy.

The actual message of Haggai begins with a quotation. The people were claiming that the time had not yet come for the Lord's house to be built. Exactly what lay behind this remark is not certain. Perhaps they thought that the seventy years of predicted captivity were not yet up and that they would be out of God's will if they built the temple before those years were past. If they counted the captivity from 586 B.C., then only sixty-six years had passed. If, however, they counted from 605 B.C. (the first invasion of Nebuchadnezzar), then the time was well past.

A second explanation relates to the opposition of the local population, mostly Samar-itans. Perhaps the returnees were saying that it was better to wait for more favorable times. In response to this, Haggai would have to say that the time is rarely just right to build the house of God—i.e., to do God's work. We can never expect the cooperation of the enemy in a truly spiritual task. Verse 3 is the introductory formula to Haggai's response to the people's claim that he had just quoted.

2. Ordering Priorities (1:4–11)

4 A rhetorical question opens Haggai's first sermon. A spiritual man might have answered, "No, it is not right that we live in paneled houses, while this house remains a ruin." But the people had put their own comfort before the building of the temple.

The word translated "paneled" (GK 6211) raises some questions. It apparently refers to an overlay of some kind, in some cases definitely wood. But it may be plaster (cf. KJV). It refers to an added measure of comfort the people thought they could not afford for the house of God.

5–7 The Hebrew idiom "put your heart on your roads" is aptly phrased by NIV's "Give careful thought to your ways." Verse 6 is a biting accusation that may reflect a drought and consequent famine conditions. Haggai broke into a kind of synonymous parallel poetry at this verse. The five pairs say essentially the same thing—all your effort is in vain.

(1) Pictured first is a lean harvest. It is a vicious cycle if from the precious little harvest of one year one feels obligated to save even more of it for next year's seed. Then if that next year is unproductive, the loss is even greater. Such was the desperate situation of these returned exiles.

(2) The next picture is of a person suffering from some disease where quantities of food fail to satisfy his needs. His metabolism somehow does not allow the food to be properly digested and turned into a healthy and strong body.

(3) The wine was so watery that it failed to provide the satisfaction and stimulus it ordinarily should. "Fill" (GK 8910) usually means inebriation. These people were unable to drown their sorrows because of the inadequate vintage.

(4) Their clothes were not sufficiently heavy to keep out the winter's damp chill (cf. Isa 28:20).

(5) Somehow the people's income failed to meet their expenses; money seemed to disappear through holes in their pockets. It is possible that inflation was working against solvency, as in our day.

All these figures speak of the hardship that befalls people who have not included the Lord in their plans and who are preoccupied with their own interests.

8 The first positive part of Haggai's initial message begins with three imperatives: "Go up . . . bring down . . . and build." The original temple was built with cedars from Lebanon (1Ki 5:5–6). It is uncertain whether this verse refers to the mountains far to the north or the lower but rugged hills around Jerusalem. The limited financial resources of the people would point to the more modest forests of the nearby hills. The reference to wood rather than stones may further indicate that only the interior work was left to be done.The two reasons the Lord gives for the people to obey and build the temple are that he may have pleasure and be honored in it. Proof of the people's devotion will come as they actually put their faith to work and finish the Lord's temple.

9 Agricultural and economic disaster result from God's withdrawal of his blessing because of the people's failure to do first of all what pleased him. The reference to God's blowing away what they brought home probably suggests that in the harvest was much chaff. The kernels or grains of wheat were so insubstantial that they simply disappeared with the chaff in the winnowing process. The harvest was poor because each man was busy with his own house, and no one cared for the house of God.

10–11 The first message of the prophet concludes pursuing the theme of economic catastrophe as the price for unfaithfulness in regard to building God's house. First, the heavens withheld their dew, and consequently the earth withheld its crops. Though ordinarily receiving more dew than the fields, even the mountains were denied it. Thus also the vineyards and olive orchards would be affected. Grain that supplied the staple bread, grapes that provided the basic beverage, and oil used for a number of things would all be in short supply. What a tragedy to have these three basic crops fail!

II. The People's Positive Response (1:12–15)

12 This verse records the positive reaction of the two leaders and the people to Haggai's initial sermon—they "obeyed" (GK 9048) and "feared" (GK 3707). The reason for this wholesome response was that the Lord had sent Haggai. Exactly what Haggai did to authenticate his message is unknown. Some charisma or ring of authority must have prompted this obedience and fear. A people who had been driven to their knees by the days of drought and famine would be all the more receptive to a word from God.

13–15 Haggai is named the "messenger" (GK 4855), and he brought this brief message from the Lord: "I am with you." These words were comforting and encouraging to a people oppressed by enemies and depressed by failing crops. By his divine aid this poor rabble could reconstruct a magnificent temple, repulse their enemies, seek and receive aid from an unbelieving monarch, and see dry ground bring forth food. Verse 14 records the results of that brief but strong reassurance. The Lord stirred the spirits of the two leaders (Zerubbabel and Joshua) and of the people, and they began to work on the temple. The date indicates that hardly three weeks had passed from Haggai's initial sermon to the people's obedience to his orders.

III. The Promised Glory of the New House (2:1–9)

1. Encouragement to Zerubbabel (2:1–5)

1–2 The twenty-first day of Tishri would correspond to October 17. This, the third date-formula of the book, marks the beginning of the second major oracle. The addressees are Zerubbabel, Joshua, and the "remnant of the people." "Remnant" (GK 8642) here means the population with the two leaders.

3–5 Verse 3 consists of three rhetorical questions. Some present may have been able to answer yes to the first question. They had seen the temple of Solomon in their childhood. They would have to be at least seventy years old because that temple was destroyed in 586 B.C., and Haggai was speaking some sixty-six years later (520 B.C.).

The next question addressed those who might have remembered Jerusalem before Nebuchadnezzar destroyed it. Their response may have been: "Although it certainly does not compare in opulence, it is the temple of the Lord, and we are happy to see it being built." There was no way these relatively poor exiles could have matched the extravagances of Solomon with his professional craftsmen working with imported woods and huge quantities of gold.

The third question virtually puts the discouraging sentiments into the mouths of the audience. They were all thinking it, and now Haggai says it. The new is inferior to the old, and that fact, along with the other discouraging circumstances, had thoroughly depressed the people and stifled their initiative.

Having brought the very problem of discouragement into focus, Haggai next offered the divine antidote: "Be strong . . . be strong . . . be strong . . . and work. For I am with you." The problem was essentially one of attitude. So the primary command was to take courage. When the people did that, the command to "work" would be fulfilled quite naturally. The most uplifting thing they could hear was that God was with them.

The message continues with a reminder that this is what God had covenanted with the people (v.5). After the reminder, the prophet gave the people a promise and a command: God's Spirit would remain with them, and "Do not fear." Undoubtedly fear gripped many returnees—fear that God had written an eternal "Ichabod" over Jerusalem, fear that no amount of praying or piety would induce him to bless them again, fear that the whole endeavor was in vain, fear that the political enemies would in fact win, fear that all was lost. Therefore the words of God through Haggai must have been a great source of strength and comfort.

2. The Glorious New House (2:6–9)

6–9 Verse 6 is the only verse in Haggai quoted in the NT (see Heb 12:26, 28–29); the author of Hebrews has made some interpretive comments on this verse. The first "shaking" took place at Mount Sinai, when God gave the law to Moses (Ex 19:16); the second shaking will come at the end of the world. But we who are in Christ have an unshakable

kingdom. The expression "a little while" (GK 5071) could mean anything from days to millennia (cf. Ps 2:12, where the same word occurs in a similar context).

"The desire of all nations" is beautifully messianic, though most modern translations do not support it. The problem centers on the words "the desired . . . will come." In Hebrew "desired" (GK 2775) is singular and "will come" is plural. Those who read "desired" as plural do not take the verse messianically but say that the "desired things" are the wealth of other nations brought to Jerusalem. They do not see the "desired one" as the Messiah. The reference to "glory" (GK 3883), however, tilts the interpretation toward a personal reference to the Messiah (cf. Isa 40:5; 60:1; Lk 2:32). But were the Gentile nations desiring him? Certainly the Gentiles who receive Christ as Savior view him as desirable. Can that, however, be said of them before their salvation? Despite this and other problems, a messianic view should not be wholly dismissed.

God's claim that "the silver" and "the gold" are his may be a response to the fears of the people—they were economically destitute. The drought and consequent famine had forced them to dip deeply into their meager resources. Subsequently they found no funds for the temple project. To a people discouraged because the temple they were building was so inferior to the one the Babylonians had destroyed, God promised that the glory of the present house would be greater than the glory of the former house. Certainly it would be a different kind of glory, for there was no way that the actual building was grander. The second temple was to be honored by the presence of Christ, a divine presence quite different from the Shekinah of the OT (see comments on Ex 24:15–17).

The second promise is that God will grant peace to the place. In fact, there have been few periods of enduring political peace in Palestine from this time on. But since Christ is the Prince of Peace (Isa 9:6), this too is probably a reference to his work and ministry (Mt 12:6; Ro 5:1). These people were plagued by enemies without and discouragement within. The promise of peace, which they thought of first in political terms, was a comforting one indeed!

IV. Blessings on a Defiled People (2:10–19)

1. The Past Defilement (2:10–14)

10–12 Haggai's third sermon came two months after the second: December 18, 520 B.C. The prophet asked, on behalf of the Lord, the priests a question about the law. Verse 11 introduces a hypothetical problem; v.12 states the question, which concerns second-degree contact of sacred meat with other food via the fold of a garment in which the meat is carried. The law spoke of the newly anointed altar's power to sanctify whatever touches it (Ex 29:37; cf. Mt 23:19). Leviticus 6:27 declares that the meat of the sin offering has the same power of contagiousness. The question Haggai posed is whether this holiness could be twice transmitted. Does the consecrated meat consecrate the garment? Can the garment in turn consecrate other foods such as bread, broth, wine, and oil?

The priests did not believe that such consecration could be so passed on. Holiness is not catching. This is the answer Haggai wanted, because he wished to show the people that it is easier to fall into sin than it is to fall into righteousness.

13–14 The question here is not, Is holiness infectious? but, Is defilement infectious? Leviticus 22:4–6 supplies the background: Uncleanness is contagious (cf. Nu 19:11–16). So the priests correctly answered in the affirmative to Haggai's question. The Lord declared, "So it is with this people and this nation."

The selfish attitude of putting personal comforts first had spread throughout the repatriated community. The people had encouraged one another to build their own houses and to wait for more propitious times to work on rebuilding God's house. When attitudes are wrong, nothing given to God is really acceptable. So whatever these people offered was defiled. From early times it was quite clear that God basically wanted hearts, not hands. He desired obedience rather than sacrifice.

2. The Future Blessing (2:15–19)

15–19 The third message of Haggai began with a twofold illustration: Is holiness or defilement contagious? Verse 15 begins the other half of the message, the required response of the audience. The building of the temple had begun twelve years earlier, but the prophet urged the people to review what the situation was before their initial response to his first message to get to work. This, then, is a promise passage. There has been a marked contrast between the past and the future. The turning point was the start of the rebuilding project.

In the days of their disobedience, lethargy, discouragement, and personal concern with selfish comforts, the people never had enough in the pantry or the barn to meet their needs. Instead, a person came to a silo or shed where he thought there was a pile of at least twenty "measures," but he found only ten. The same was true of the wine vat (v.16). These disastrous harvests and disappointing crops were the ways God was reminding his people of their duty to him.

"From this day on" means the date of Haggai's third message (cf. v.10). The mention of laying the foundation, however, poses a problem. First, Ezr 3:6, 10; 5:16 records that the foundation was laid about 537 B.C. Second, 1:1–15 indicates that the building was resumed three months earlier. Thus v.18 might be paraphrased: "From this day onward, the eighteenth of December, start thinking about how things have been for the last sixteen or eighteen years." Their resumption of work on the temple was the turning point; Haggai calls attention to the marked difference in the productivity of the land and the general blessing of God on the people's efforts.

Verse 19 focuses again on the barren years that had preceded their resumption of the temple (cf. v.16), evidently attributing them to God's punishment for the people's unconcern with the temple. There was, of course, no seed in the barn. The returned exiles were on the brink of agricultural disaster.

The very end of this little sermon contains this promise: "From this day on I will bless you." In the past it was touch and go. While the people were putting themselves first, they suffered the agonies of drought and famine. But when they put the Lord first, they began to enjoy his blessing. This was merely one way God chose to remind the people of his sovereignty over them. He who was concerned with the temple was also in control of the rain.

V. Zerubbabel, the Lord's Signet Ring (2:20–23)

20–23 The fourth oracle came on the same day as the preceding message. The words are directed to Zerubbabel alone. Haggai's apocalyptic language points to a day in the distant future. God promises to overthrow and destroy Gentile dominions. The description is in familiar terms. Because of the cosmic language, many interpreters link these predictions to the final overthrow of all unregenerate nations at the end of the age, at the second coming of Christ.

God's promise is expanded in v.23 to include Zerubbabel. Notice that he was called "my servant" (GK 6269). This was Isaiah's favorite designation of the Messiah (Isa 41:8; 42:1; 49:5–6; 50:10; 52:13; 53:11). Also, "chosen" (GK 1047) recalls references to the chosen people and the chosen One from among those people (cf. 1Ki 11:13; 1Ch 28:4; Ne 9:7; et al.). This promise to Zerubbabel must be understood messianically, for the Persians simply would not tolerate a man laying claim to the promises here stated. Zerubbabel was no more the Messiah than Moses, Joshua, David, Solomon, or Isaiah. But Zerubbabel was in the genealogy of Christ (cf. Mt 1:12–13) and pointed forward to him.

The mention of "signet ring" (GK 2597) deserves special attention. In ancient times the signet ring corresponded to the crown, the throne, or the scepter. Ahab, the wicked king of Israel, had one that his even more wicked wife Jezebel used to seal a letter, framing the innocent Naboth (1Ki 21:8). Darius used such a ring to seal the decree concerning the lions' den (Da 6:17). And King Xerxes also used such a ring to seal his decrees (Est 8:8). This token of authority would be granted to Zerubbabel much as it had been taken away from Jehoiachin king of Judah (cf. Jer 22:24 [Coniah]; cf. Mt 1:11–12). So Zerubbabel represents the resumption of the messianic line interrupted by the Exile, which had been ushered in by the unfortunate reign of three of Josiah's sons.

So the book of Haggai, which began on such a discouraging and depressing note, ends on an uplifting and promising one. Haggai's first message was one of indictment; his last one is of a great and blessed future for the people of God. As we now know, that future was much further away than either Haggai or Zerubbabel thought. But in the mind of God, it is as close and certain as tomorrow's rising sun.

The Old Testament in the New

OT Text	NT Text	Subject
Hag 2:6	Heb 12:26	One more shaking

Zechariah

INTRODUCTION

1. Historical Background

Zechariah's prophetic ministry took place in the time of Israel's restoration from the Babylonian captivity, i.e., in the postexilic period. Approximately seventy-five years had elapsed since Habakkuk and Jeremiah had predicted the invasion of Judah by the Neo-Babylonian army of King Nebuchadnezzar. When their "hard service" (Isa 40:2) in Babylonia was completed, God influenced Cyrus, the Persian king, to allow the Hebrews to return to their homeland and rebuild their temple (Isa 44:28).

The historical circumstances and conditions Zechariah ministered under were, in general, those of Haggai's time, since their labors were contemporary (cf. 1:1 with Hag 1:1). In 520 B.C. Haggai preached four sermons in four months. Zechariah began his ministry two months after Haggai had begun his. Thus the immediate historical background for Zechariah's ministry began with Cyrus's capture of Babylon and included the completion of the restoration, or second, temple.

Babylon fell to Cyrus in 539 B.C. Cyrus then signed the edict that permitted Israel to return and rebuild her temple (2Ch 36:21–23; Ezr 1:1–4; 6:3–5). According to Ezr 2, a large group (about fifty thousand) did return in 538–537 B.C. under the civil leadership of Zerubbabel (the governor) and the religious leadership of Joshua (the high priest). This group completed the foundation of the temple early in 536 B.C. (Ezr 3:8–13). But several obstacles arose that slowed and finally halted the construction (Ezr 4:1–5, 24). During the years of inactivity, Cyrus died in battle (529 B.C.); and his son Cambyses II, who was coregent with Cyrus for one year, reigned in his place (530–522 B.C.).

Political rebellion ultimately brought Darius Hystaspes to the throne in 522 B.C. His wise administration and religious toleration created a favorable climate for the Israelites to complete the rebuilding of their temple. He confirmed the decree of Cyrus and authorized resumption of the work (Ezr 6:6–12; Hag 1:1–2). The construction was resumed in 520 B.C., and the temple was finished in 516 B.C. For additional events in the history of the period, see the historical background of Ezra, Daniel, and Haggai.

2. Author, Date, and Unity

Like Jeremiah and Ezekiel, Zechariah was not only a prophet but also a priest. He was born in Babylonia and was among those who returned to Palestine in 538–537 B.C. under the leadership of Zerubbabel and Joshua (cf. Iddo, grandfather of Zechariah, listed in Ne 12:4).

At a later time, when Joiakim was high priest, Zechariah apparently succeeded Iddo (Zec 1:1, 7) as head of that priestly family (Ne 12:10–16). Since it was the grandson (Zechariah) who in this instance succeeded the grandfather (Iddo), it has been conjectured that the father (Berekiah, Zec 1:1, 7) died at an early age, before he could succeed to family headship.

Though a contemporary of Haggai, Zechariah continued his ministry long after him (cf. Zec 1:1 and 7:1 with Hag 1:1; see also Ne 12:10–16). Considering his young age in the early period of his ministry (Zec 2:4, "young man"), it is possible that Zechariah continued into the reign of Artaxerxes I (465–424 B.C.).

Some scholars have challenged Zechariah's authorship of chs. 9–14. All their arguments, however, have satisfactory alternative explanations, and other scholars have argued persuasively for the structural unity of the entire book. So there is no convincing reason to question its unity and authenticity.

3. Occasion and Purpose

At the time of his prophesying and writing, Zechariah was clearly back in Palestine; and his ministry was to the returned exiles (Zec 4:8–10; 6:10, 14; 7:2–3, 9; cf. Ne 12:1, 12, 16). The occasion is the same as that of the book of Haggai. Approximately fifty thousand former exiles had arrived in Jerusalem and the nearby towns in 538–537 B.C., with high hopes of resettling the land and rebuilding the temple (Ezr 2). Their original zeal was evident; immediately they set up the altar of burnt offering (Ezr 3:1–6). They resumed worship and restored the sacrificial ritual that had been suspended during the seventy years in Babylonia. The people then laid the foundation of the temple in the second month of the second year (536 B.C.) of their return (Ezr 3:8–13). But their fervor and activity soon met with opposition in various forms (Ezr 4:1–5; Hag 1:6–11). So the reconstruction of the temple ground to a halt and did not begin again till 520 B.C. (Ezr 4:24).

The chief purpose of Zechariah (along with Haggai) was to rebuke the people and motivate and encourage them to complete the rebuilding of the temple (Zec 4:8–10; cf. Hag 1–2), though Zechariah was clearly interested in spiritual renewal as well. Also, the purpose of the eight night visions is explained in Zec 1:3, 5–6: The Lord asked Israel to return to him; then he would return to them, and his word would continue to be fulfilled.

4. Theological Values

Zechariah is probably the most Messianic, apocalyptic, and eschatological of all the OT books. The prophet predicted Christ's first coming in lowliness (6:12), his humanity (6:12), his rejection and betrayal for thirty pieces of silver (11:12–13), his being struck by the sword of the Lord (13:7), his deity (3:4; 13:7), his priesthood (6:13), his kingship (6:13; 9:9; 14:9, 16), his second coming in glory (14:4), his building of the Lord's temple (6:12–13), his reign (9:10; 14), and his establishment of enduring peace and prosperity (3:10; 9:9–10). These messianic passages give added significance to Jesus' words in Lk 24:25–27, 44.

As for the apocalyptic ("revelatory") and eschatological aspect, Zechariah predicted the final siege of Jerusalem (12:1–3; 14:1–2), the initial victory of Israel's enemies (14:2), the Lord's defense of Jerusalem (14:3–4), the judgment on the nations (12:9; 14:3), the topographical changes in Israel (14:4–5), the celebration of the Feast of Tabernacles in the messianic kingdom age (14:16–19), and the ultimate holiness of Jerusalem and her

people (14:20–21). God (through Zechariah) intended that the apocalyptic material (primarily 1:7–6:8), combined with the judgment and salvation (or deliverance) oracles (primarily chs. 9–14), should function as an encouragement to his people to complete the rebuilding of the temple. Yet the then-current local scene becomes the basis for contemplating the universal, eschatological picture.

The prophet's name itself has theological significance. It means "the LORD [Yahweh] remembers." "The LORD," the personal, covenant name of God, is a perpetual testimony to his faithfulness to his promises (see comment on Ex 3:14–15). He "remembers" his covenant promises and acts to fulfill them. In Zechariah, God's promised deliverance from Babylonian captivity, including a restored theocratic community and a functioning temple—the earthly seat of the divine Sovereign—leads into even grander pictures of the salvation and restoration to come through the Messiah.

Finally, the book as a whole teaches the sovereignty of God in history, over people and nations—past, present, and future.

EXPOSITION

Part I (chs. 1–8)

I. The Introduction to the Entire Book (1:1–6)

A. The Date and the Author's Name (1:1)

1 The eighth month of Darius's second year was October-November 520 B.C. (cf. Hag 1:1). While it is clear that one of Zechariah's (and Haggai's) purposes was to encourage the Israelites to rebuild the temple, it is equally clear that Zechariah was also vitally interested in spiritual renewal.

At the time of Israel's return from the Babylonian exile, she had no king of her own to date events by. So Zechariah's prophecy—as well as Haggai's—had to be dated by the reign of Darius, king of Persia and suzerain of Judah. Thus the dating by a pagan king expresses that this is part of "the times of the Gentiles" (Lk 21:24).

That the word of the Lord "came" to Zechariah is indicative of the vitality of the divine word in the OT. God's word not only "comes," it also "comes true," or is fulfilled.

Dates of Haggai and Zechariah

The dates of Zechariah's recorded messages are best correlated with those of Haggai and with other historical events. All dates are B.C.

1.	Haggai's first message (Ezr 5:1; Hag 1:1–11)	Aug. 29, 520
2.	Resumption of the building of the temple (Ezr 5:2; Hag 1:12–15). The rebuilding seems to have been hindered from 536 to c. 530 (Ezr 4:1–5), and the work ceased altogether from c. 530 to 520 (Ezr 4:24).	Sept. 21, 520
3.	Haggai's second message (Hag 2:1–9)	Oct. 17, 520
4.	Beginning of Zechariah's preaching (1:1–6)	Oct./Nov., 520
5.	Haggai's third message (Hag 2:10–19)	Dec. 18, 520
6.	Haggai's fourth message (Hag 2:20–23	Dec 18, 520
7.	Tattenai's letter to Darius concerning the rebuilding of the temple (Ezr 5:3–6:14). There must have been a lapse of time between the resumption of the building and Tattenai's appearance.	519–518
8.	Zechariah's eight night visions (Zec 1:7–6:8)	Feb. 15, 519
9.	Joshua crowned (Zec 6:9–15)	Feb. 16(?), 519
10.	Repentance urged, blessings promised (Zec 7–8)	Dec. 7, 518
11.	Dedication of the temple (Ezr 6:15–18)	Mar. 12, 516
12.	Zechariah's final prophecies (Zec 9–14)	After 480(?)

The recipient of the divine revelation is identified as "the prophet" Zechariah. A "prophet" (GK 5566) is one called by God to be his spokesman. This is one reason the prophets spoke with such authority. The three names in the complete patronymic formula (Zechariah, Berekiah, Iddo) mean "the LORD remembers," "the LORD blesses," and "timely (?)." The latter indicates perhaps "the set time" when the Lord remembers and blesses.

Iddo was among the priests who returned to Jerusalem with Zerubbabel and Joshua (Ne 12:4, 16). Zechariah, who was born in exile, would have been quite young at the time of the return. Since Berekiah was his father, Zechariah was a "descendant" (i.e., "grandson," not "son" [GK 1201]) of Iddo (cf. Ezr 5:1 and 6:14). Like Jeremiah and Ezekiel, then, Zechariah was a priest before God called him to the prophetic office and ministry.

B. A Call to Repentance (1:2–6)

2–3 Because a holy and just God must deal with sin, Zechariah began his message by reminding his people of how angry their faithful, covenant God had been with the covenant-breaking sins of their unfaithful preexilic ancestors. Zechariah's hearers well knew that the Exile they had recently returned from was the direct result of God's wrath against their ancestors, and that the temple they were now rebuilding had been destroyed because of their sins. "Forefathers" is more literally "fathers"; but Semitic words for "father" (GK 3) can mean "grandfather," "forefather," or "ancestor."

The divine wrath is followed by the availability of divine grace. Repentance is one of the conditions for the personal experience of God's full blessing. Three times the call to repentance is said to be the authoritative declaration of "the LORD Almighty." Zechariah, then, came with the message and authority of Israel's divine King. As "the LORD Almighty," Israel's Lord is the controller of history who musters all the powers of heaven and earth to accomplish his will. The messianic King will also be a divine warrior or strong ruler (cf. "Mighty God" in Isa 9:6). If the people of Zechariah's day would only "return" (GK 8740) to the Lord or repent (i.e., change their course and go in the opposite direction from that of their forefathers), the Lord would return to them with a blessing instead of a curse. The emphasis is on personal relationship and allegiance.

4–6 "Forefathers" refers to the preexilic forefathers; and "earlier prophets" refers to the preexilic prophets who had warned of the approaching Babylonian exile—e.g., Isaiah, Habakkuk, Jeremiah, and Ezekiel.

"Evil ways" and "evil practices" stress the forefathers' wicked behavior in God's sight. In their failure to respond to the prophets, the people had not responded to God; for he is the one who had sent the prophets. The people had "mocked God's messengers, despised his words and scoffed at his prophets until the wrath of the LORD was aroused against his people and there was no remedy" (2Ch 36:16). Such brazen refusal to respond properly was the principal reason for the Fall of Jerusalem and the Babylonian exile.

Though the messengers may be gone, God's words live on to be fulfilled. These words are further defined as "decrees" (GK 2976)—the specific requirements of the law, including the threats and curses for breaking those laws. Although God's words were uttered by his servants the prophets, they were still his words. The designation "my servants" (GK 6269) is not demeaning, for it is a great privilege to serve the Lord, who is both Israel's King and the Sovereign of the universe.

In a bold personification God's words and decrees are pictured as "overtaking" (GK 5952) the disobedient forefathers. The question asked in v.6, of course, anticipates an affirmative reply. God's curse did, in fact, pursue and catch up with the wrongdoers, in direct fulfillment of Dt 28:15, 45. According to Dt 28:2, blessings too can "overtake." The choice is up to the subjects of the kingdom.

"Then they repented" (or "came to themselves," "changed their minds"; GK 8740) apparently refers to what happened to the preexilic forefathers and/or to their offspring during the Exile and immediately afterward (cf. Ezr 9–10; Da 9:1–19). They had to acknowledge that they had brought the divine discipline of the Exile on themselves because they had refused to "listen," or "pay attention," to the Lord. They also had to acknowledge that the Lord was just and righteous in his judgment, for he had done to them what their ways and practices deserved, all in accord with what he had "determined to do" (cf. La 2:17). The result was forgiveness and restoration, likewise in accord with his promise (cf. Dt 30:1–3; Isa 55:6–7; Jer 3:12; Joel 2:12–13).

II. A Series of Eight Night Visions (1:7–6:8)

A. The First Vision: The Horseman Among the Myrtle Trees (1:7–17)

7 In a series of eight apocalyptic visions on a single night, God revealed his purpose for the future of Israel—Judah and Jerusalem in particular, since Jerusalem was the seat of the Davidic dynasty and the place of the Lord's throne, i.e., the temple. As an encouragement to the people to persevere in the work of rebuilding the temple, God disclosed to them through his prophet his gracious purposes.

The setting is the time of Darius, and the date is February 15, 519 B.C., about three months after the call to repentance (cf. 1:1). On this same day five months earlier, the rebuilding of the temple had been resumed (cf. Hag 1:14–15). "The twenty-fourth day" was evidently a day in which God had special delight because of the obedience of his people.

8 The basic teaching of the first vision is that although God's covenant people are troubled while the oppressing nations are at ease, God is "jealous" (v.14) for his people and will restore them, their towns, and the temple. The Hebrew for "I had a vision" (GK 8011) is simply "I saw." From this comes the word "seer," another name for a prophet.

The vision portrayed a man on a red horse, standing among myrtle trees in a ravine. The "man" is identified as "the angel of the LORD" (v.11). In Rev 6:4 the red horse (cf. Zec 6:2) is associated with a sword, the instrument of war and death, which may also be the significance of the color here.

In Ne 8:15 myrtle trees, which are evergreen, are associated with the Feast of Tabernacles for making booths; and in Isa 41:19 and 55:13 they are included in a description of messianic kingdom blessing. Perhaps they speak of the hope and promise of the future, the restoration from Babylonian exile being but the initial stage in the progressive fulfillment of that promise. The trees are situated in a ravine. At the foot of the Mount of Olives are myrtle groves in the lowest part of the Kidron Valley. The ravine may picture Judah's lowly condition at the time; but there is a ray of light or hope for the future. Behind the horseman were red, brown, and white horses—presumably with riders on them, since they report to the angel of the Lord in v.11. These other riders or horses apparently represent angelic messengers (cf. v.10). White horses are associated with vengeance and triumph (cf. Rev 19:11, 14).

9–11 After Zechariah respectfully ("my lord") inquired about the meaning of the vision, the interpreting angel indicated that he would explain the meaning. It was, however, the horseman among the myrtle trees who did the explaining. The explanation is that the other horsemen are angelic messengers sent by the Lord on missions throughout the earth. Such angels are part of the Lord's "hosts."

The horseman among the myrtle trees, now specifically identified as "the angel of the LORD," served mainly as the captain of the Lord's host (the other horsemen). Elsewhere he is identified often with the Lord himself (cf. Ge 16:11, 13; 18:1–2, 13, 17, 22; et al.). The other horsemen report to him that the whole world is at rest and in peace.

Such a description of the Persian Empire is confirmed by the inscription and bas-relief that Darius had incised on a rock at Behistun, above the highway connecting Ecbatana and Babylon. The bas-relief portrays the surrender of those who had rebelled against the king, while the inscription tells in Persian, Elamite, and Babylonian the story of the political unrest in Persia during the first two years of Darius's reign, praising his feats of valor. Darius boasted that in nineteen battles he had defeated nine rebel leaders and had subdued all his enemies. So the empire was again virtually quiet by 520 B.C. While the Persian Empire as a whole was secure and at ease by this time, the Israelites in Judah were oppressed and, of course, still under foreign domination.

12 The angel of the Lord was moved to intercede for the people of Judah. He desired the completion of the process of restoration, which required the reconstruction of the temple, Jerusalem, and the other towns of Judah. The report of the horsemen must have disappointed God's chosen people because it told of rest and peace among the nations, when, instead, they were expecting the "shaking of all nations" (Hag 2:6–9, 20–23) as the sign of returning favor and full blessing to Zion. Through intercession the angel of the Lord prayed that in the "mercy" of God this situation would be rectified. The experience of God's disciplining anger for seventy years had been first predicted by Jeremiah (25:11–12; 29:10). This period may be calculated from 605 B.C. (the time of the first deportation from the land) to about 536 or 335 (the time when the first returnees were settled back in the land), or from 586 (when the temple was destroyed) to 516 (when the temple was rebuilt). Either way, the point is that the people wondered why God was still angry with them when the appointed time of their punishment had expired (or was almost over).

13–15 Although it was the angel of the Lord who had interceded, the Lord's answer came directly to the interpreting angel and through him to Zechariah. The answer contained words that promised kindness (or "good things") and comfort.

Zechariah was told to proclaim to the people that the Lord was "very jealous" (GK 7861 & 7863) for Jerusalem. In OT usage jealousy is but the intolerance of rivalry or unfaithfulness. When applied to the Lord, it usually concerns Israel and carries with it the notions of the marriage or covenant relationship and the Lord's right to exclusive possession of Israel. In this context the key idea is that of God's vindicating Israel for the violations against her. Actually, jealousy is part of the vocabulary of love; through such language the Lord showed his love for Israel.

In contrast to the Lord's jealous love for his people, he was "very angry" (GK 7911 & 7912) with the nations that treated them so harshly. The nations that God used to discipline his people included Assyria and Babylonia. They are characterized as feeling "secure"—i.e., they were arrogantly (or carelessly) at ease. The full charge against the nations is that "they added to the calamity" of the divine discipline, not only by going too far and trying to annihilate the Jews, but also by prolonging the calamity.

16–17 Because God had a jealous love for Israel and a jealous anger against her enemies, the promises in these verses would be fulfilled. The Lord promised to return to Jerusalem with "mercy" (GK 8171). The assurance that the temple ("my house") would be rebuilt expresses the divine mercy. The "measuring line" is that of those who were to reconstruct Jerusalem in a program of expansion (cf. 2:1–5).

Verse 17 anticipates a time when the towns of Judah (also "my towns," says the Lord) will "overflow" (or "spread out"; GK 7046) with prosperity. Thus the Lord would again "comfort Zion and choose Jerusalem." The temple, as the Lord's house, and Jerusalem, as the Lord's elect city in which his house and earthly throne were located, are inseparably linked in these verses.

B. The Second Vision: The Four Horns and the Four Craftsmen (1:18–21)

18–19 The second and third visions build on the concept of the comfort promised by presenting the manner in which God will execute his great anger against the nations that afflicted Israel (second vision) and by guaranteeing the prosperity and expansion promised Israel (third vision). The four "horns" are identified as the nations (or their rulers) that attacked Judah, Israel, and Jerusalem to scatter their people. When used figuratively, "horn" (GK 7967) usually symbolizes strength—either strength in general or the strength of a country or its king.

The Targum translates "four horns" as "four kingdoms." The kingdoms are claimed by some to be the four world empires of Da 2 and 7 (see the introduction to Daniel). Others suggest Assyria, Egypt, Babylonia, and Medo-Persia. Since the reference is to nations that have already "scattered" God's people, the latter view seems preferable. God's people are referred to under the all-inclusive designation "Judah, Israel and Jerusalem," i.e., the whole nation. Jerusalem is mentioned because it was the capital of the united nation of Israel.

20 The four "craftsmen" have been interpreted in at least two ways: (1) those who hold that the four horns symbolize the world empires of Da 2 and 7 (see vv.18–19) maintain that the craftsmen represent Medo-Persia, Greece, Rome, and the Messiah, since they are the destroyers of the preceding world empires (see Da 2:34–35, 44–45); (2) others believe that the craftsmen denote the nations God used to overthrow Israel's past enemies—nations such as Egypt, Babylonia, Persia, and Greece, or perhaps Persia alone. In any event, it is clear in Scripture that all Israel's enemies—past, present, and potential—will ultimately be defeated.

21 The prophet's inquiry this time concerns the function of the horns and craftsmen. The answer given (apparently by the interpreting angel) is that the horns came to scatter the people of Judah and render them helpless and powerless. The horns that did this to Israel, Judah, and Jerusalem have, by the time of Zechariah's prophecy, already been conquered and absorbed into the Persian Empire. The craftsmen are to be identified, then, at the very least with the world empire of Persia—and possibly with a few other nations as well. Their function was to terrify and throw down the powers that, in arrogant defiance of God, went beyond all bounds in punishing and scattering God's covenant people. In v.15 the nations "feel secure"; now they are to be terrified and overthrown.

C. The Third Vision: The Surveyor (2:1–13)

1 The scope of the restoration and blessing promised in this vision is such that its fulfillment must extend beyond the historical restoration period to the messianic kingdom era. The persons connected with the introductory part of the vision are Zechariah, a surveyor, the interpreting angel, and an unidentified angel. The "measuring line" (GK 7742) is a symbol of preparation for rebuilding and restoring Jerusalem and the temple, ultimately in the messianic kingdom. The restoration of the people, the temple, and the city immediately after the Babylonian exile was only the first stage in the progressive fulfillment of the promises that follow.

2–4a When Zechariah asked the surveyor where he was going, he replied that he was intending to measure the width and length of Jerusalem, evidently to mark out its boundaries. This would be the first step toward the restoration of the city and the realization of the promised blessing (cf. 1:16; Eze 40:5; Rev 11:1). When the interpreting angel started to leave, he was met by another angel and was instructed to convey the message to Zechariah, who, in turn, would naturally declare it to his people.

4b The measuring was done with expansion in view; now that purpose is to be achieved. The promise is given that Jerusalem will become so large and prosperous that it will expand beyond its walls. Indeed, it will overflow so much that it will be as though it had no walls. Evidently many of its people and animals will have to live in the surrounding unwalled villages (cf. Eze 38:11). Nothing like this has yet happened in the history of the city. The realization of the full scope of this prophecy must therefore still be in a future earthly kingdom.

5 Although Jerusalem will become so large and prosperous that many of its inhabitants will spill over beyond the walls into the suburbs, they will still be secure because of the divine protection and the divine presence. The "wall of fire" is reminiscent of the "pillar of fire" (Ex 13:21). Both are emblematic of God and his protection and guidance (in fact, both "fire" and "glory" recall the Exodus; Ex 13:22; 14:20; 40:34). There is the promise of the Lord's glorious presence in regal holiness and majesty. The Lord's "glory" (GK 3883) is his self-manifestation, which is here concerned with the final actualization of his rule. The future safety of Jerusalem and its people is guaranteed.

6–7 The land of the north is Babylon, north being the direction from which the Neo-Babylonian army had invaded Judah. The Jewish exiles who had not returned from Babylon in 538–537 B.C. were exhorted to do so at this time. The same Lord who had scattered them desired that they be restored and repatriated. The places of the Diaspora ("scattered"; GK 7298) included not only Babylon ("the north") but also Assyria, Egypt, Persia, and the neighboring countries ("the four winds of heaven"). "Zion" refers to the exiles from Zion in Babylon. "Flee" and "escape" imply that some imminent peril was coming on Babylon. The nature of that peril is historically uncertain.

"You who live in the Daughter of Babylon" refers to the Jews who had chosen to remain in Babylon. They were being called on to join the other returnees in Jerusalem, evidently to help them rebuild the temple and restore the city.

8 The opening words of the quotation ("After he has honored me and has sent me") are difficult. All the Hebrew has is "After glory [or honor; lit., weight or heaviness; GK 3883] he has sent me." Another problem is the identity of "me" both here and in v.9. While many think "me" refers to Zechariah, others maintain that it looks toward the messianic Servant-Messenger, the Angel of the Lord. The mission of this person is directed against the nations that have plundered God's chosen people. Such treatment of the Jews is condemned because harming them is like striking the apple of God's eye. "Apple" (lit., "gate") is the pupil, an extremely sensitive and vital part of the eye.

9 In a menacing gesture the Lord will raise his hand against Israel's enemies. The word "raise" (GK 5677) may also be rendered "wave." All it takes for God to punish his people's enemies is a wave of his hand. This is another evidence that the speaker here and in v.8 is deity. "My hand" refers to the display of God's infinite power, here exerted in behalf of God's people and against their enemies. God brings about a reversal of the fortunes of his people. The Jews, who were slaves of the nations that plundered them (v.8), will now plunder those nations (cf. Est 7:10; cf. also Gal 6:7–8). When all this happens, the people "will know that the LORD Almighty has sent" his messenger. The fulfillment will authenticate the message and ministry of the messianic Servant-Messenger.

10 The section begins with a call to joy, followed by the reason for such jubilation (cf. 9:9): the personal coming of God himself to live among his people in Jerusalem (Zion). This language is ultimately messianic—indirectly or by extension from God in general to the Messiah in particular. All passages that speak of a future coming of the Lord to his people or to the earth, or that speak of a future rule of the Lord over Israel or over the whole earth, are ultimately messianic, for to be fully and literally true, they require a future, literal messianic kingdom on the earth.

For further biblical development of the theological theme of God's dwelling or living among his people, see vv.11–13 and 8:3 (cf. also Jn 1:14; 2Co 6:16; Rev 21:3).

11–12 In the great messianic future, many nations "will be joined with the LORD" (or "will join themselves to the LORD"). Such an ingathering of the nations to the Lord echoes the promise in Ge 12:3 (cf. 18:18; 22:18). The result is that they too will become the people of God. All this will happen "in that day," which is frequently an abbreviation of the Day of the Lord (cf. Isa 2:12–21; 24–27; Joel 1:15; 2:28–3:21; Am 5:18–20; 9:11–15; Zep 1:7–2:2; Zec 14). The Messiah's advent is the turning point between the judgment and the blessing aspects of "that day." In the light of biblical usage, the eschatological Day of the Lord may be defined as earth's final period of time—the tribulation period, the Messiah's second advent to the earth (Rev 19), the messianic kingdom age (Rev 20), and the appearance of the new heavens and earth (Rev 21).

The conversion of many nations to the Lord does not abrogate the promise and purpose of God for Israel, his chosen and special covenant people. In keeping with that promise, v.12 indicates that the Lord will inherit Judah (both land and people) and will again choose Jerusalem (cf. 1:17), for many decisive events will yet take place there (e.g., 14:4).

The people of Judah are described as the Lord's portion in the "holy land." This is the only occurrence of the phrase "holy land" in Scripture (but cf. Pss 2:6; 15:1; Isa 48:2; Da 9:24; Mt 27:53; Rev 21:2). The temple, as the place of God's earthly throne, was by definition "holy" (Ps 65:4; Jnh 2:4). But that holiness extended beyond the temple and the holy city to the entire land. The root idea of the word "holy" (GK 7731) is "separate" or "set apart." Palestine is rendered holy (i.e., sacred) chiefly because it is the site of the earthly throne and sanctuary of the holy God, who dwells there among his covenant people.

13 All humankind was exhorted to be still before the Lord because, in a threatening gesture, he had roused himself from his holy dwelling and would judge the enemies of his people. He was about to break his apparent silence by acting in behalf of his elect (cf. Rev 5–6; 8). The first vision introduced the judgment (or curse) and blessing motif (1:1–17).

That motif is then developed in the second and third visions in an alternating cycle: judgment for the nations (1:18–21) but blessing and glory for Israel (2:1–5); judgment for the nations (2:6–9) but blessing for Israel—and for the nations (2:10–13).

D. The Fourth Vision: The Cleansing and Restoration of Israel (3:1–10)

1 In this apocalyptic vision the high priest Joshua—the same person as Jeshua in Ezra and Nehemiah—represents the sinful nation Israel (see especially comment on v.9). However, though Israel is presented in defilement, she is also cleansed and restored as a kingdom of priests for God. The revealer of the vision is either the interpreting angel or God himself (cf. 1:20). "Standing before the . . . LORD" is a technical designation for priestly ministry. Hence the scene is in the temple.

Although the scene is not basically a legal one, Satan's accusation invests it with a judicial character. The right side was the place of accusation under the law (Ps 109:6). Satan knows the purposes of God concerning Israel and therefore has always accused the Jews and accuses them still. The tool of his nefarious opposition to Israel has primarily been the Gentile nations—something that will be particularly true during the period of Daniel's seventieth "week." Satan is the accuser, not only of Joshua (i.e., Israel), but also of all believers. Undoubtedly the accusation here relates to the sin of Joshua (cf. vv.3–4) and is made in the hope that God will reject his people irrevocably. But this we know he will never do (cf. Jer 31:36–37).

2 Israel's defender was none other than the Lord himself. Since the speaker in this verse was quite clearly the Angel of the Lord, this is but another evidence of his deity. That God chose Jerusalem further proves that Joshua portrayed Israel as a nation. The quotation contains a double rebuke of Satan ("the accuser"). God's sovereign choice of Jerusalem in grace shows the unreasonableness of Satan's attack (cf. Ro 8:33). The reference to the stick is an additional indication that Israel, not Joshua, is ultimately in view. Israel was retrieved to carry out God's future purpose for her (cf. Am 4:11). The "fire" refers to the Babylonian captivity, though it may also look back to Israel's deliverance from Egypt (cf. Dt 4:20; 7:7–8; Jer 11:4) and forward to the rescue from the coming tribulation period (cf. Jer 30:7; Zec 13:8–9; Rev 12:13–17).

3 The reason for Satan's accusation is Israel's impurity. How can a holy God bless a filthy nation like Israel? The answer is that he can do so only by his grace. Joshua's clothes represent the pollution of sin (cf. Isa 64:6). To compound the problem, Joshua (i.e., Israel) was ministering in this filthy condition before the Angel of the Lord.

4 The removal of the filthy clothes (apparently by angels) may connote that Joshua was thereby deprived of priestly office. If so, he is reinstated in v.5. This seems to be a picture of the negative aspect of what God does when he saves a person—he takes away sin. Positively, he adds or imputes to the sinner his own righteousness. The act of causing sin to pass away represents justification, not sanctification.

Next, Joshua was to be clothed with rich garments—God's representative clothed in God's righteousness. The festive garments speak of purity, joy, and glory; but their chief significance is that they symbolize the restoration of Israel to her original calling (Ex 19:6; Isa 61:6). "I have taken away" (GK 6296) emphasizes the agent of the forgiveness. It is God who causes sin to be removed, ultimately on the basis of the messianic Servant's substitutionary death. The one who actually forgave sin here is the Angel of the Lord, thus identifying him as deity.

5 Joshua was crowned with a clean turban and clothed with rich garments, symbolic of divine righteousness. On the front of the turban were the words: HOLY TO THE LORD (Ex 28:36; 39:30). Again this is a foreview of Israel's future purging and reinstatement to her priestly function. "While the angel of the LORD stood by" indicates he was approving and directing Joshua's purging, clothing, and crowning.

6–7 Israel's originally intended position would finally be realized. "Walk in my ways" refers to the personal life and attitude toward the Lord. Personal or practical righteousness is in view. "Keep my requirements" speaks of the diligent and faithful fulfillment of official, divinely appointed, priestly duties.

An analysis of the three results of meeting these two conditions reveals Israel's earthly calling and her glory and ministry in the Messianic Age: (1) Israel will govern the house of God; (2) Israel will have charge of God's courts; and (3) Israel will have ready and free access to God in the priestly function, just as the angels ("these standing here").

8 The persons involved in this prediction were Joshua, his colleagues, and the Branch, the Servant of the Lord. Joshua and his fellow priests represented coming events and persons. They excited wonder because they were types of Israel in close association with someone to come. This coming one was called "my servant, the Branch"—two well-known OT appellations for the Messiah (e.g., Isa 11:1; 42:1; Jer 23:5). As Servant, the Messiah came into the world to do the will of the Father. Through his work, Israel will yet be redeemed and restored as a priestly nation, which Joshua and his associate priests typified.

9 Some interpret the "stone" as Israel. It seems best and more consistent, however, to take it as another figure of the Messiah. To the Jews at his first advent, the Messiah (Christ) was the stumbling stone and rock of offense (Isa 8:13–15; cf. Ps 118:22–23; Mt 21:42; 1Pe 2:7–8). Moreover, he is to be the smiting stone to the nations (Da 2:35, 45). At present he is the foundation and chief cornerstone of the church (Eph 2:19–22). The seven eyes speak of the fullness of the Holy Spirit or of the Godhead and are symbolic of infinite intelligence and omniscience.

The engraving on the stone is difficult to interpret. The early church fathers refer the "inscription" to the wounds of Christ. The passage possibly connotes a sealing action by God, or perhaps a beautifying activity. Next, the Lord (the Angel of the Lord?) purged and cleansed Israel from sin. "The sin of this land," not of Joshua but of the people of the land of Palestine, was taken away in a single day, symbolized by the removal of Joshua's filthy clothes (v.4). Prophetically, the one day is the once-for-all deliverance potentially provided at Calvary—to be actually and finally realized in Israel's experience at the second advent of her Messiah, when there will be cleansing and forgiveness for the nation as a whole (Zec 12:10–13:1; Ro 11:26–27).

10 The result of the action of vv.8–9 is peace and security for God's people. God's purpose for Israel will be realized in the theocratic kingdom, when Israel will enjoy contentment, peace, and prosperity (cf. 1Ki 4:25). "That day" is the eschatological time of Israel's cleansing and restoration as a kingdom of priests. This closing verse pictures Israel's future condition under divine favor and blessing when there will be no more curse. The vine and the fig tree speak of spiritual blessing and of agricultural blessing (cf. Isa 11:1–9; 35; 65:17).

E. The Fifth Vision: The Gold Lampstand and the Two Olive Trees (4:1–14)

1 The main purposes of the vision were (1) to encourage Joshua and Zerubbabel in the work of rebuilding the temple by reminding them of their divine resources and (2) to vindicate them in the eyes of the community. In this chapter the lampstand probably represents the idea of testimony (light bearing; cf. Mt 5:16; Rev 1:20). Zerubbabel and Joshua (the two olive branches) testified to God's power in completing the temple.

To prepare Zechariah to receive the fifth vision, the interpreting angel woke him from his ecstatic sleep of wonder and astonishment over the previous vision. The wakening obviously took place on the same night, further corroborating the view that Zechariah received all the visions during one night.

2 Though we do not know precisely how the lampstand looked, we do know what it signified. The seven "channels" (or "lips" or "spouts" for wicks) to each of the seven lamps (forty-nine spouts in all) would seem to stress the abundant supply of the oil, which in turn symbolizes the fullness of God's power through his Spirit (seven being the number of fullness or completeness; cf. v.6).

3 Possibly the two olive trees stand for the priestly and royal offices in Israel (cf. 6:13). Undoubtedly the two olive branches (vv.12, 14) represent Joshua-Israel (ch. 3) and Zerubbabel (ch. 4; cf. v.14). According to v.12, each olive tree has an olive branch beside a golden pipe that pours out golden oil. The olive oil is conducted directly from the trees to the bowl of oil at the top of the lampstand—without any human agency. Similarly, Zerubbabel and Joshua are to bear continual testimony for God's glory and are to do God's work—e.g., on the temple and in the lives of the people—in the power of his Spirit (v.6).

4–6 The purpose of this vision was to encourage Zerubbabel to complete the rebuilding of the temple and to assure him of the enablement of God's Spirit for the work. The answer to Zechariah's inquiry was postponed in order to emphasize the final verse of the chapter and, in the meantime, to focus attention on only one of the two olive branches, namely, Zerubbabel, and his special ministry. "These" refers to the two olive trees of v.3 (cf. v.11).

Verse 6 interprets the symbolism of the oil ("by my Spirit"). Just as there was a constant and sufficient supply of oil without human agency, so Zerubbabel's work on the temple and in the lives of the people was to be completed, not by human might or power, but by divine power—constant and sufficient. The work was dependent on God; he would provide the oil or strength of his Spirit. Such enablement was needed because of the opposition and apathy hindering the rebuilding (Hag 2:1–9).

7 Faith in the power of God's Spirit can overcome mountainous obstacles—indeed, can reduce them to "level ground." A defiant challenge was laid down against whatever would hinder the rebuilding of the temple. The figurative mountain could include opposition (Ezr 4:1–5, 24) and the people's unwillingness to persevere (Hag 1:14; 2:1–9). That the project would ultimately succeed is indicated by the assurance that Zerubbabel will experience the joy of helping put the capstone in place, thus marking the completion of the restoration temple.

8–9 The laying of the temple foundation refers back to what took place in 537–536 B.C. (Ezr 3:8–11; 5:16). The year was now 519, three years before the fulfillment of the prediction that Zerubbabel would complete the superstructure (Ezr 6:1–18). So then, a delay in the execution of God's will need not end in ultimate defeat. Finally, the completely restored temple (in 516 B.C.) would prove the divine commission of the speaker. "Me" apparently refers to the messianic Servant-Messenger (or the Angel of the Lord).

10 The opening question obviously implies that some of the people had a negative attitude toward the temple project and those

involved in it. In the context, the "day of small things" refers to the "day" of beginning the work on the temple and now continuing it. But God was definitely in this rebuilding program; by his Spirit (v.6) he was enabling Zerubbabel to finish the work. Perhaps the "despisers" were discouraged because they were a relatively small group, forgetting that God's work is usually accomplished through a remnant.

"Plumb line" (GK 643) may also be rendered "separated [i.e., chosen] stone," referring to the capstone of v.7. The parenthesis is probably a reminder to Zerubbabel and the people that God is omniscient ("seven eyes"). As such, he knows, sees, and governs the entire earth. He is in control of Israel's situation.

11–14 Zechariah repeated his question to be more specific. He desired an explanation of what he saw in vv.2–3. The answer to the prophet's inquiry is that the two olive branches are Zerubbabel, a member of the line of David, and Joshua. In the light of the context, they must be "the two who are anointed to serve the Lord" as God's appointed leaders. Both priest and ruler were anointed for service to the Lord and the covenant community. This combination of ruler and priest is evidently intended to point ultimately to the messianic King-Priest (cf. 6:13; Ps 110; Heb 7). Finally, since God was declared to be "the Lord of all the earth," he was master of all the circumstances in which Zerubbabel and the people found themselves.

F. The Sixth Vision: The Flying Scroll (5:1–4)

1–2 The scroll is not rolled up but flying (i.e., unrolled for all to read). Significantly, in the postexilic period there was a renewed interest in the study and teaching of the law (Torah). Not only was the scroll open for all to read, but it was also very large for all to see. Its message of judgment was not concealed from anyone. Such a bold, clear pronouncement of punishment for sin should have spurred the people on to repentance and righteousness.

3 The message and meaning of the scroll are revealed. Those who persisted in breaking the covenant (Ex 20) would experience the curse (punishment) for disobedience and unfaithfulness (Dt 21:26). Since the scroll was apparently inscribed on both sides, one side

must have contained the curse against those who violated the third commandment of the law while the other side contained the curse against those who broke the eighth commandment. The thief broke the eighth commandment, and whoever swore falsely violated the third commandment. These two representative sins—perhaps theft and perjury were the most common ones at this time—stand for all kinds of sin. The point is that Israel was guilty of breaking the whole law (cf. Jas 2:10). "Banished" (GK 5927) amounts to the notion of "purging" the land from chronic covenant-breakers. God has always required adherence, not only to the letter of the law, but also to its spirit.

4 "It" refers to the curse. There can be no hiding, no escape, from the judgment of that curse. God's word, whether promise or threat, is efficacious. "It" will enter and destroy the homes of the guilty. Even the privacy of their homes will afford them no refuge from divine judgment. The word "thief" recalls Ex 20:15, and "him who swears falsely by my name" recalls Ex 20:7. To judge from the materials used in the houses (cf. Hag 1:3–9), it was primarily the wealthy who were guilty of committing these sins.

G. The Seventh Vision: The Woman in a Basket (5:5–11)

5–6 The removal of wickedness is now vividly depicted. Not only sinners, but the whole sinful system must be removed—apparently to the place of its origin (Babylonia). What Zechariah saw this time was a measuring basket (lit., "an ephah," a measure that here stands for the container). An ephah is less than a bushel, so a normal ephah measuring basket (or barrel) is not large enough to hold a person. This one was undoubtedly enlarged—like the flying scroll—for the purpose of the vision. The basket represents the people's iniquity or crookedness that pervades the land.

7–8 The import of the measuring basket is now fully revealed: When the cover of lead was lifted from the basket, wickedness is exposed, personified by a woman (cf. Rev 17:3–5). Like the basket itself, the woman represents the sin of the people in Palestine, whose measure or cup of evil was full. The whole evil system was to be destroyed. The Hebrew word for "wickedness" (GK 8402), denoting moral, religious, and civil evil, is feminine, which may explain why the wickedness of the people is personified as a woman.

9 The fate of the woman (i.e., wickedness) is portrayed: She is to be removed from the land. Although some regard the two women, who now appear, as agents of evil (partly because the stork is an unclean bird, Lev 11:19), it seems preferable to regard them as divinely chosen agents. They, along with the wind (cf. Ps 104:3–4), thus demonstrate that the removal was the work of God alone. The simile "wings like those of a stork" is evidently intended to show that the winged women— carried along by the wind—were capable of supporting the woman in the basket over a great distance.

10–11 The destination of the women bearing the sin away was "Babylonia" (lit., "Shinar"). Shinar roughly corresponded to ancient Babylonia (cf. Ge 11:2; 14:1, 9). The evil will be put in a "house," perhaps referring to a temple or ziggurat. "Its place" may have in view a base or pedestal on which the basket and its contents are set up as an idol.

H. The Eighth Vision: The Four Chariots (6:1–8)

1 This last vision obviously corresponds to the first, though there are differences in details, such as in the order and colors of the horses. The Lord is again depicted as the one who controls the events of history. He will conquer the nations that oppress Israel. Since his war chariots claim victory in the north (v.8), total victory is certain. The chariots must serve basically the same symbolic function—they are vehicles of God's judgment on the nations. Such judgment is probably also the symbolic significance of the "bronze" mountains (cf. Nu 21:9). The two mountains most naturally refer to Mount Zion and the Mount of Olives, with the Kidron Valley between them.

2–3 The chariots seem to represent angelic spirits, while the variegated horses evidently signify divine judgments on the earth. Revelation 6:1–8 suggests that the red horses symbolize war and bloodshed; the black horses, famine and death; the white horses, victory and triumph; and the dappled horses, death by plagues and other judgments. White horses are clearly associated with vengeance

and triumph in Rev 19:11, 14. The four chariots may indicate that the angelic spirits are ready to embark on universal judgments (cf. "the four winds of heaven" [2:6], "the four corners of the earth" [Rev 7:1]).

4–6 "These" refers to the chariots, with the horses harnessed to them. The four chariots are identified as four spirits (i.e., angelic beings). Although the same Hebrew word can also mean "winds" (GK 8120), angelic "spirits" as agents of divine judgment seems more appropriate, particularly since they stand before God. The chariot with the black horses hitched to it goes toward the north country, primarily Babylonia, but also the direction from which most of Israel's formidable enemies invade Palestine. As the Hebrew text now stands, the chariot with the black horses is followed northward by the one with the white horses. However, with a slight change in the Hebrew text, the latter chariot would go toward the west, i.e., toward the islands and coastlands of the Mediterranean area. The south is principally Egypt but also the other main direction from which Israel's foes invade Palestine. Nothing is said of the east, possibly because the Arabian Desert lay in that direction. Similarly, nothing is said of the chariot with the red horses, but the latter are undoubtedly included among "the powerful horses" of v.7.

7–8 "Powerful" (GK 600) describes all the horses. All were eager to take the chariots (angelic spirits) on the mission of bringing divine judgment on the peoples of the earth. But the horses cannot begin until authorized to do so. "Those going toward the north country" designates either the black horses and their chariots or both the black horses and the white horses. The pronoun "my" in "my Spirit" indicates that the speaker is ultimately deity, i.e., either God or the messianic Servant-Messenger (the Angel of the Lord). Since conquest is announced in the north, victory is assured over all enemies.

III. The Symbolic Crowning of Joshua the High Priest (6:9–15)

9–10 The position of this actual ceremony after the eight visions is significant. The fourth and fifth visions were concerned with the high priest and the civil governor in the Davidic line. Zechariah here linked the message of those two visions to the messianic King-

Priest. In the fourth vision, Joshua was priest, here (v.13) the Branch was to officiate as priest. In the fifth vision, Zerubbabel was the governing civil official; here (v.13) the Branch was to rule the government. In 4:9 Zerubbabel was to complete the rebuilding of the temple; here (v.12) the Branch would build the temple. In 4:14 Zerubbabel and Joshua represented two separate offices; here the Branch was to hold both offices (v.13). Thus restored Israel is seen in the future under the glorious reign of the messianic King-Priest. The passage is typical-prophetical. Joshua served as a type of the Messiah, but at certain points the language transcends the experience of the type and becomes more directly prophetical of the antitype.

Verse 9 introduces a prophetic oracle. In the first part of v.10, representatives arrive from Babylon with gifts for the temple; and in the last part of the verse, Zechariah is told to meet them. The meeting takes place in the home of one Josiah, who was entertaining the returned exiles. In v.14 he is honored with the name "Hen."

11 In a coronation scene Zechariah was told to take the silver and gold brought from Babylon, to make a crown for royalty, and to put it on Joshua's head. It becomes obvious that the royal crowning of the high priest is a type of the goal and consummation of prophecy—the crowning and reign of the messianic King-Priest. Therefore Joshua, who was never a priest-king, was a type of the messianic Branch of v.12. According to v.13, the Branch would be a priest on his throne. Thus the fulfillment in the Messiah transcends Joshua's status and experience.

12 This verse predicts that the messianic Branch would appear as Joshua's antitype and would build the temple. The words were addressed to Joshua; yet it is clear that the language refers to the messianic "Branch" (GK 7542). Christ is pictured in Rev 19:12 as the majestic Sovereign of the universe, with "many crowns" on his head—an ornate crown with many diadems (cf. v.11). As the Branch, he would "branch out" (GK 7541) from his place. "His place" is most likely a reference to his humble and obscure origin, land, and people.

Verse 12 closes with the prediction that the Branch will build the temple of the Lord. Since the rebuilding of the restoration temple is to be completed by Zerubbabel (4:9–10), it is difficult to see how this could refer to that temple. Instead, it must have in view the temple of the Messianic Age (cf. Isa 2:2–4; Eze 40–43; Hag 2:6–9).

13 Not only will the messianic Branch build the temple, but he will also have regal splendor, will take his seat on his throne and rule, and will perfectly and harmoniously combine the two offices of king and priest. The clause at the end of v.12 is repeated at the beginning of v.13 to emphasize that "it is he," the Branch, not Joshua, who will build the temple. "Will sit" means "will sit enthroned." "His throne" refers to the promised Davidic throne (2Sa 7:16; Isa 9:7; Lk 1:32). No otherOT author makes it so plain that the coming Davidic king will also be a priest.

14 It was, in part, to keep the messianic hope alive that the crown was made for Joshua's symbolic crowning and then placed in the temple as a reminder of this hope. Historically, however, it was a memorial to the devotion of the embassy that came all the way from Babylon with such rich gifts for the temple. They, in turn, are typical of the group in v.15. "Hen" (meaning "gracious one"; see NIV note) is doubtless another name, and a very appropriate one, for Josiah (v.10), used on this occasion to honor him because he was so hospitable.

15 Gentiles will contribute materials for the construction of the messianic kingdom temple. When this happens, the people will know that the Lord has sent his messenger (Messenger?) to them. All this will happen if the people render absolute obedience to the Lord's word. "Those who are far away" must refer to Gentiles (cf. 2:11; 8:22; Isa 2:2–4; 56:6–7; 60:1–7; see also Eph 2:17). They will help build the temple by contributing their wealth (silver, gold, and other materials) to it (see also Isa 60:5–7). At the end of the verse, the conditional element—obedience—relates to the people's participation individually (cf. Dt 28:1–2, 15; 30:1–10). In the new covenant God will make with his people (Jer 31:33–34; Eze 36:26–27), he personally guarantees that the people will ultimately obey; his Spirit will enable them to do so.

IV. The Problem of Fasting and the Promise of the Future (7:1–8:23)

A. The Question by the Delegation From Bethel (7:1–3)

1 As early as 1:3–6 it was clear that Zechariah was interested in the spiritual renewal of the postexilic community. Here he deals further with this problem. The date is equivalent to December 7, 518 B.C., not quite two years after the eight night visions (1:7).

2–3 The occasion of the oracle is a question about fasting raised by a delegation from Bethel (cf. Ezr 2:28; Ne 7:32; 11:31). To judge from the foreign names—Sharezer and Regem-Melech—the members of the delegation had probably been born in Babylonia. They directed their question to the temple priests and the divinely appointed prophets—the latter would have included Zechariah—at Jerusalem. Their inquiry was reasonable. The fasts had been observed in exile, but should they be continued in these better times back in the homeland? Now that the temple was nearly rebuilt, it would seem that they were no longer necessary. Thus the mission of these Jews concerned a fast day instituted by the Jews in exile in commemoration of the destruction of Jerusalem. In the beginning there was doubtless sincere contrition in the observance of the day; now it had become a mere form. According to 8:19, the question included all the fasts commemorating the major events related to the fall and destruction of Jerusalem and the temple, namely, the "fasts of the fourth, fifth, seventh and tenth months."

B. The Rebuke by the Lord (7:4–7)

4–5 The Lord cast doubt on the people's sincerity when they previously had observed the fasts. They had turned a time that should have convicted them of their past and present sins into a rote ritual devoid of its divinely intended purpose—prayer and genuine repentance. They had also turned it into a time of self-pity for their physical condition. Since the question from the people of Bethel raised a larger issue touching the whole nation, the words here were addressed, not just to the people in Bethel, but to "all the people of the land [primarily Jews living in or near Jerusalem] and the priests." Priests also had to listen to God's word that came through the prophets. Since these fasts commemo-

rated events related to the destruction of Jerusalem and the temple in 586 B.C., the "seventy years" are to be reckoned from that time. Strictly speaking, sixty-eight years had transpired; seventy is thus a round number.

"Me" is set in obvious contrast with "yourselves": Was it really for me? Their fasting had become a mere religious form, not supported by obedience to the word of God (cf. Isa 58:1–7).

6–7 The reference to "the earlier prophets" shows that the problem is not lack of knowledge but lack of obedience. Without obedience and application, religious observance is meaningless. "At rest" and "prosperous" point to the preexilic situation when Jerusalem and the surrounding towns of Judah were bustling with life and the fields were being farmed—in contrast with their current condition resulting from disobedience, with only a partial restoration and without the full resumption of agriculture. "The Negev and the western foothills" were among the agricultural and grazing areas.

C. The Command to Repent (7:8–14)

8–9a With a solemn, authoritative message from God, the prophet focuses on the covenantal unfaithfulness, disobedience, and unrighteousness that first led to the Babylonian exile. He does this, hoping that the restored community will perceive the moral implications of their fasting and will let their forefathers' disobedience and its consequences serve as a warning to them. This section also explains why the people's fasting meant nothing to God. They were guilty of legalism: an external adherence to the letter of the law while disregarding the internal spirit—the true divine intent—of the law.

9b–10 With a series of social, moral, and ethical commands, the Lord gave the people four tests of their spiritual reality.

(1) "Administer true justice." "Justice" (GK 5477) denotes the rights and duties of each party arising out of the particular relation of fellowship in which they find themselves. Everyone has his own special "justice": the king, God, the priest, the firstborn son, the Israelites as a group, etc. The task of one who administers justice is to see that the good of everyone in the community is safeguarded.

(2) "Show mercy and compassion." While *hesed* (GK 2875) includes "mercy," it is really stronger than that. "Faithful love" would be a better rendering. Since "compassion" (GK 8171) is related to the Hebrew word for "womb," it focuses on a tender, maternal kind of love. Faithful love and tender compassion were to govern all relationships among the covenant people of God.

(3) "Do not oppress." Oppression is denounced so frequently that it is not necessary to multiply references. The most common victims of oppression are listed here as "the widow ... the fatherless, the alien ... the poor." These were the weakest, the neediest, the most defenseless, and the most disadvantaged members of their society—and the ones with the fewest legal rights.

(4) "Do not think evil." In the opening part of 8:17, the almost identical Hebrew is translated "do not plot evil against your neighbor." This excludes a spirit of hatred, vindictiveness, and revenge that devises wicked schemes for harming others. The clear inference is that the people of the restored community need to repent and to begin practicing this ethical teaching; otherwise their fasting is mere formalism, legalism, and hypocrisy.

11–12a The Lord had instructed his people to carry out the four commands of vv.9–10, but they refused ("they" referring to the preexilic forefathers, as the reference to "the earlier prophets" shows). The lesson to the Jews of the restoration period is clear: Do not be like your unrepentant, unfaithful, disobedient, covenant-breaking forefathers, or you will suffer a similar fate. One indispensable ingredient in true spirituality is a dogged attentiveness to familiar truths, but they did not "pay attention." "Stubbornly they turned their backs" echoes Dt 9:6, 13, 27 and characterizes the Israelite ancestors as a stiff-necked and stubborn people. The fact that they "stopped up their ears" seems to reflect the disciplinary dulling of their ears in Isa 6:10 (cf. Ac 28:27). The people even "made their hearts [including their minds and wills] as hard as flint." The specific kind of mineral is uncertain.

For the most part the people were recalcitrant and obdurate. Nor would they listen to the word of God in the law through the prophets. The latter were the secondary agents of divine revelation. The primary agent was the Spirit of God. Thus the words of the prophets were inspired by God's Spirit.

12b–13 The result of the forefathers' rejection of the command to change—i.e., to reform their ways and actions (Jer 7:3)—was the terrible experience of God's wrath manifested in the destruction of Jerusalem and the temple in 586 B.C. and in the ensuing exile to Babylonia. The motif of God's wrath is reminiscent of 1:2, 15. Dispersion was part of the curse for disobedience to the old (Mosaic) covenant (cf. v.14; Jer 11:11–14).

14 The scattering was one of the curses for covenant disobedience (Dt 28:36–37, 64–68), as was the desolation of the land (Dt 28:41–42, 45–52). "The nations" refers primarily to Babylonia and Egypt, though "all" may at the same time anticipate a future, more widespread Diaspora—the principle of progressive fulfillment again. "Behind them" means "after they were removed from it." "This is how" means "by their sins" (e.g., unbelief and disobedience). Because of such sins, "they made the pleasant land [Palestine] desolate."

D. The Restoration of Israel to God's Favor (8:1–17)

1–2 Zechariah here contrasts Israel's past judgment with her future restoration; she is to repent and live righteously because of the promise of her future restoration. This section is basically a salvation—or deliverance—oracle, the principal features of which are (1) the self-predication of God (v.2), (2) the message of salvation (vv.3–8), (3) the direct address (vv.9–17), and (4) the "do not be afraid" phrase (vv.13, 15). It is "the LORD Almighty" who stands behind this glorious prophecy (vv.1–4, 6–7, 14, 19–20, 23). Here the divine jealousy is directed toward the restoration of Israel.

3a On the Lord's returning to Zion and dwelling in Jerusalem, see comments on 1:16 and 2:10.

3b The blessed results of the Lord's return are now delineated. The first is a new character for Jerusalem, resulting in new epithets. The first is either "the City of Truth" or "the Faithful City." Either is possible, and both will be true. Furthermore, the temple mount will be called "the Holy Mountain" because of the Lord's holy presence there.

4–5 Other results of the Lord's return to dwell in Jerusalem are undisturbed tranquility, long life, peace, prosperity, and security. The weakest and most defenseless members of society will be able to live securely. Although it may be possible to regard historical references as stages in the progressive fulfillment of the passage, they certainly do not completely fulfill the scope of this grand prophecy as a whole. The final stage awaits the second advent of the Messiah.

6 Such things may have seemed too good to be true in the eyes of the Jewish "remnant" living "at that time," but the Lord Almighty did not so regard them. Nothing is too hard for him.

7–8 Although God's action is expressed in terms of saving, it is tantamount to regathering. "I will save my people" means "I will gather them from exile, bondage, and dispersion" (cf. Isa 11:11–12; 43:5–7; Jer 30:7–11; 31:7–8). "The east" and "the west" are best understood as opposites used to express totality, meaning "wherever the people are." Thus the regathering will be universal. Israel's predicted complete restoration to covenant favor and blessing rests on nothing less than the faithfulness, veracity, and righteousness of God. "To live in Jerusalem" need mean no more than "to go there frequently to worship."

"They will be my people, and I will be . . . their God" is covenant terminology, pertaining to intimate fellowship in a covenant relationship. Although Israel may go through a Lo-Ammi ("Not My People") stage, she will be fully restored as Ammi ("My People"; cf. Hos 1:8–2:1; 2:23). The theological principle involved is that God is a saving, forgiving, delivering, restoring God—one who delights to take "Not My People" and make them "My People." In the case of Gentiles, as in the church, he does this in his sovereign grace by grafting them into covenant relationship and blessing (Ro 11).

9 The immediate purpose of all this is to encourage Zechariah's audience to complete the rebuilding of the temple. The people addressed are those who had been listening to the preaching of, first, Haggai (1:1) and then

Zechariah (1:1; cf. Ezr 5:1–2), since 520 B.C. (it was now 518). The laying of the temple foundation is, accordingly, not the original one in 536. Although the foundation was restored in 536, the actual building of the superstructure was hindered from 536 to 530 (when it stopped altogether). Thus, the "founding" (almost in the sense of "building" or "rebuilding") of the temple did not begin in earnest till 520. "Let your hands be strong" is a way of saying "be encouraged" (Jdg 7:11).

10 The background for the verse appears to be the conditions described in Hag 1:6–11; 2:15–19. "Before that time" refers to the period prior to 520 B.C. (at least 530–520, if not 536–520). "No one could go about his business safely" is literally "No one could go out or come in safely." "Enemy" included the Samaritans (Ezr 4:1–5).

11–13 "But now" shows that the reasons for the people's discouragement have passed; God would now provide grounds for encouragement. In Hag 2:19, God through his prophet had predicted just such a reversal as we have here. The fecundity described is part of the covenant blessings for obedience promised in the Pentateuch (Lev 26:3–10; Dt 28:11–12) and in Eze 34:25–27. On the other hand, Israel's being an object of cursing among the nations is part of the covenant curses for disobedience threatened in Dt 28:15–68 and predicted in Jer 24:9; 25:18; 29:22. "As" God's old covenant people were an object of cursing, "so" God will save them; and they will be a blessing. Consequently, they are not to fear but to be encouraged.

14–15 These verses specify God's part in the people's restoration to favor and blessing. In the past God had "determined" (GK 2372) to bring disaster on them as covenantal discipline, but now he is "determined" to bless them (on God's determination, see Jer 4:28; 51:12). This is cause for not being afraid (cf. v.13).

16–17 Once again God's and Zechariah's interest in spiritual renewal comes to the fore. After the announcement of God's gracious action in vv.14–15 comes what he expects from his people in grateful response. Thus their obedience in the moral and ethical sphere has a gracious basis, just as the law itself did. Jerusalem will indeed be "the City of

Truth" (v.3) when its inhabitants are truthful and when true judgment is rendered in its courts. "Sound" (*shalom*; GK 8934) is probably best understood as descriptive of "judgment." The root idea of the word is "wholeness," "completeness," "soundness," though it is used principally of a state of "well-being," "health," "harmony," "peace," "security," and "prosperity."

The two positive injunctions are balanced by two negative ones. On the first negative command, see comment at 7:10b. The second prohibition has to do with perjury. "Do not love" perjury is another way of exhorting the people to hate it. God hates perjury and wicked schemes to harm others (cf. Pr 6:16–19). One theological rationale for ethics is awareness that God hates attitudes and actions contrary to his character. We must love what God loves and hate what he hates.

E. Kingdom Joy and Jewish Favor (8:18–23)

18–19 In this closing section of Part I, the Jews are told that there will be a reversal of their mourning and their position in the world. Returning at last to the question about fasting, the Lord announces through his prophetic messenger that there will come a time when it will cease. The people's mourning (expressed in fasting) will be turned into joy, for their low position among the nations will be changed. And they will be a source of blessing to Gentiles, for all the peoples of the earth will join them on pilgrimages to worship the Lord at Jerusalem.

The prophet announces that a day is coming when their fasts and mourning will give way to festivals (cf. Isa 65:18–19; Jer 31:10–14). Verse 19 closes with an exhortation to Zechariah's contemporaries to "love truth and peace."

20–22 As v.22 indicates, the "peoples" are Gentile nations. In view of the parallelism with "many peoples," "powerful nations" is perhaps better translated "numerous nations." Numerous Gentiles will make a pilgrimage to Jerusalem in order to seek and entreat the Lord (see also Isa 2:1–5; Mic 4:1–5).

23 "In those days" is equivalent to "in that day." "Ten" indicates a complete number. This verse closes with the reason for the Gentiles' desire to accompany the Jews on pilgrimages to Jerusalem: "We have heard that God is with you." Israel will be the means whereby God draws the nations of the earth to the Lord in the time of the messianic kingdom.

Part II (chs. 9–14)

V. Two Prophetic Oracles: The Great Messianic Future and the Full Realization of the Theocracy (9:1–14:21)

A. The First Oracle: The Advent and Rejection of the Messiah (9:1–11:17)

1. The advent of the messianic King (9:1–10:12)

a. The destruction of nations and preservation of Zion (9:1–8)

1–2a Part II of the book of Zechariah contains two undated oracles, though they probably belong to Zechariah's old age (shortly after 480 B.C.). More important than the date are the wide scope of the prophecies and the frequent emphasis on the end times, particularly the arrival of the great Messianic Era. Chapters 9–14 are almost exclusively eschatological.

The theme of Part II centers around the judgment and blessing that accompany the appearance of the messianic King. The mood of the first oracle is characterized by change. In the midst of judgment (9:1–7), Israel finds deliverance (9:8). Yet in the midst of blessing (9:9–10:12), Israel experiences sorrow (11:1–17). And when the messianic King comes, he is rejected! The judgment with which the first oracle begins commences north of Palestine and proceeds south down the west coast of Syro-Palestine (9:1–7). But Israel will be preserved for the advent of her Messiah (9:8). Thus this first section stands in sharp contrast with 1:11 and prepares the way for 9:9. It is probably best to understand 9:1–8 as a prophetic description of the Lord's march south to Jerusalem, destroying—as Divine Warrior—the traditional enemies of Israel.

As history shows, the agent of the Lord's judgment was Alexander the Great. After defeating the Persians (333 B.C.), Alexander moved swiftly toward Egypt. On his march he toppled the cities in the Aramean (Syrian) interior, as well as those on the Mediterranean coast. Yet, on coming to Jerusalem, he refused to destroy it. Verse 8 attributes this protection to the miraculous intervention of God.

In v.1, Hadrach is to be identified with Hatarikka, near Hamath. Damascus was the leading city-state of the Arameans. The last half of this verse can be rendered "For the eye of the LORD is on all mankind, as well as on the tribes of Israel" (see NIV note), though the most natural translation is that of NIV. The thought may be that the eyes of human beings, especially all the tribes of Israel, are toward the Lord (for deliverance).

2b–4 The Lord's word of judgment next came on the great Phoenician cities Tyre and Sidon, particularly the former. The judgment of Tyre and Sidon was also foretold in greater detail in Eze 26:3–14; 28:20–24. Ezekiel's prophecy against Tyre was remarkably fulfilled to the letter, first through Nebuchadnezzar, then through Alexander (see ZPEB, 5:832–35). By building a mole or causeway out to this island bastion, Alexander accomplished what Nebuchadnezzar could not do in thirteen years.

The last clause of v.2 may be either concessive ("though they are very skillful"; cf. Eze 28:5) or causal ("because they think they are so wise"; cf. Eze 28:4). Either way, their skill or wisdom is explained in v.3, which describes Tyre's island fortress (Isa 23:4) and the great wealth she acquired through commerce. "Stronghold" (GK 5190) refers to the seemingly impregnable island defenses of offshore Tyre, which was surrounded by a wall 150 feet high. The similes in the rest of the verse underscore Tyre's proverbial wealth. Despite her abundance and power, she will be destroyed.

5–7 Four of the five major Philistine cities are mentioned (Gath is omitted, evidently because it had lost all significance by this time). The Philistine cities were greatly alarmed at Alexander's inexorable advance. This was particularly true of Ekron, the northernmost city and the one that would suffer first; her "hope" that Tyre would stem the tide would meet with disappointment.

"Foreigners" probably refers to people of mixed nationality; they characterized the postexilic period (Ne 13:23–24). In v.6 the Lord explains that he is going to transform the Philistines by breaking their pride. Their "repulsive ritual" is described in the first half of v.7. The "blood" is that of idolatrous sacrifices, and "forbidden food" refers to polluted or ceremonially unclean foods. Obvi-

ously, other idolatrous practices are also included. Yet a Philistine remnant will belong to God and will become leaders in Judah. This interpretation is confirmed by the prediction that Ekron will be "like the Jebusites" in a good sense. When David conquered Jerusalem, he did not destroy the Jebusites; instead, they were absorbed into Judah (e.g., Araunah in 2Sa 24:16; 1Ch 21:18). So it will be with a remnant of the Philistines.

8 The verse begins with "But," setting it in contrast with the preceding judgments on the surrounding nations. "I" signals the fact that God was speaking through Zechariah. Just as God was to be a "wall of fire" around Jerusalem (2:5), so here he will "defend" his chosen people and land. "House" (GK 1074) stands for the land and people of Israel, among whom the Lord God had his earthly throne, so to speak, in the temple at Jerusalem. The defense is against the marauding forces of Alexander overrunning that area. "Never again" anticipates the second advent of the Messiah for its final, complete fulfillment. The word for "oppressor" is translated "slave driver" in Ex 3:7 et al.

b. The advent of Zion's King (9:9–10)

9a Verses 1–8 predicted the military campaigns of Alexander the Great as he advanced on a war-horse south from Aram (Syria), subjugating city after city. The scene depicts

In the Middle East today, the common folk still will use the donkey as a means of domestic transportation.

intense battle and war; yet it is the implements of war that the messianic King is said to remove from Israel in v.10. The language here is an echo of Zep 3:14. Zechariah first calls on Jerusalem's people to rejoice.

9b The prophet now gives the reasons for the rejoicing. The jubilation is over a new Sovereign. The first reason for joy, then, is the coming of the messianic, Davidic (note the "your") King. "To you" may be alternatively rendered "for you," i.e., "for your benefit." After announcing the King's coming, the prophet describes the King's character. (1) The King is righteous, conforming to the divine standard of morality and ethics, particularly as revealed in the Mosaic legislation. (2) He is also saving. (3) In contrast to most kings (such as Alexander), he is humble or gentle. (4) He is peaceful; this is the meaning of his riding on a colt, the foal of a donkey, though it possibly suggests both peace and humility. At any rate, he does not come on a war-horse. Although Jesus was acclaimed Messiah at his Triumphal Entry into Jerusalem (Mt 21:1–9; Mk 11:1–10; Lk 19:28–38; Jn 12:12–15), his own people nonetheless rejected him and his peace (cf. Lk 19:39–44 and, later, his crucifixion).

10 The first reason for rejoicing is the coming of the King (v.9). The second reason is the establishment of his kingdom—a kingdom of universal peace in Israel and among the nations and universal sovereignty. Again, in contrast with Alexander's empire, which was founded on bloodshed, the messianic King will establish a universal kingdom of peace. A shift begins from the foundation for peace (v.9) to the fact of peace. The progressive fulfillment reaches to the Messiah's second advent, when weapons of warfare will be either removed or converted to peaceful pursuits (cf. Isa 2:4; 9:5–7; 11:1–10; Mic 5:10–15). The chariot is related to Ephraim because it was characteristic of the army of the northern kingdom of Israel. An impressive sidelight on the removal of war-horses from Jerusalem is Zechariah's statement that the messianic King would enter the city riding on a donkey, an animal symbolizing peace, not war.

The chariot, the war-horse, and the battle bow represent the whole arsenal used in ancient warfare; so the passage implies the destruction of this whole arsenal. Not only will there be disarmament and peace in Israel, but

the messianic King will also proclaim "peace" (*shalom*; GK 8934) to the nations—a fulfillment of the Abrahamic covenant (cf. 14:16; Ge 12:3; 18:18; 22:18). "From sea to sea" has been variously explained as "from the Nile to the Euphrates" (cf. Ge 15:18; Ex 23:31), "from the Mediterranean to the Red Sea," and "from the Mediterranean to the Dead Sea." In any case, the Messiah's rule is to be universal. The same is implied in the phrase "from the River [Euphrates] to the ends of the earth" (cf. Ps 72:8–11; Isa 66:18). This will be the true "triumphal entry" (cf. 14:1–11; Mt 23:37–39).

c. The deliverance and blessing of Zion's people (9:11–10:1)

11–13 Although the Messiah's mission is to establish his kingdom of "peace," he must first conquer all enemies and deliver his people. This he sets out to do. Before he can reign in peace, he must fully deliver and restore Israel. The passage is filled with battle terminology: prisoners, fortress, bow, sword, arrow (vv.12–13), trumpet (v.14), and slingstones (v.15). Here the Messiah is depicted as a conquering King (Divine Warrior).

"You" is emphatic and refers to Zion (v.9). The "blood of my covenant with you" probably has in view the Mosaic covenant (Ex 24:3–8). "Prisoners" evidently refers to those still in the land of exile, Babylonia. The Lord will free them because he is bound to them by covenantal relationship. The "waterless pit" recalls Joseph's and Jeremiah's predicament (Ge 37:24; Jer 38:6–9). Those outside the land who have hope in the future, delivering King (vv.9–10) are exhorted to return. While "fortress" (GK 1315) may refer initially to Jerusalem (Zion) and Judah, the ultimate reference may well be to God himself, the only source of real security. "Twice as much" indicates full or complete restoration.

The basis for the hope is given in v.13. The verse is progressively fulfilled. The initial, partial fulfillment is apparently to be found in the conflict between the Maccabees ("Zion") and the Seleucids ("Greece"). But the final, complete fulfillment awaits the outworking of chs. 12 and 14 and 9:16–17. The point of the verse is that God's people will gain the victory over their enemies.

14–16 Here the sound of the trumpet is evidently a reference to thunder (cf. Ex 19:16–

19). God will come down to aid, protect, and deliver his covenant people. On the bowl used for sprinkling the corners of the altar, see Lev 4:7. Verse 16 plainly declares the divine deliverance of Zion's people. "That day" embraces the final eschatological era.

"His people" are the Lord's flock (cf. Ps 100:3). There is an apparent antithesis between the "slingstones" used to subdue Israel's enemies and the precious stones, or "jewels" (the saved, victorious remnant), that will sparkle in the Lord's land. The Hebrew for "crown" (GK 5694) is often used of the crown of the high priest. How appropriate, then, for Israel, restored as a priestly nation (see ch. 3)!

17 With Israel's deliverance comes blessing, including agricultural prosperity, because Israel's covenantal God controls the weather and the rain (10:1). The result is a land of peace, prosperity, and plenty. "They" is literally "he" (possibly the Lord), but the singular could be collective for the delivered remnant of the future. "Grain" and "new wine" are signs of prosperity.

10:1 This verse probably contains a veiled polemic against Baal and Baalism (cf. Jer 14:22; Am 5:8). The Lord, not Baal, is the one who controls the weather and the rain, giving life and fertility to the land. Therefore the people of God are to pray to him and trust in him. Some regard the spring rains as literal; others understand them as spiritual and typical. Perhaps both are in view. Certainly in the grand consummation of the Messianic Era, both the physical and spiritual realms will flourish (cf. Isa 55:1–12; Hos 6:3; Joel 2:21–32).

d. Warning and encouragement (10:2–4)

2 Zechariah warns Israel's idolatrous leaders but encourages the people. Prayer to God brings blessing (v.1), but trust in idols (or the false gods they represent) produces disappointment and sorrow. The "idols" (*teraphim*; GK 9572) are household gods (cf. Ge 31:19); they were used for divination during the period of the "judges" (Jdg 17:5; 18:5). "Diviners" were consulted to foretell the future. Since they "see visions" and "tell dreams," they were included among the false prophets. Resorting to diviners for information and guidance is specifically proscribed in

Dt 18:9–14, because God provided true prophets for his people (Dt 18:15–22).

Because diviners are unreliable, "they give comfort in vain"—e.g., when they wrongly promise rain and fruitful seasons. Similarly, because diviners speak lies, "therefore" the people are led astray like sheep without a shepherd. What the people need is spiritual leadership, but it is lacking (cf. Mk 6:34).

3–4 God threatens to judge the selfish, corrupt, unqualified leaders of the nation (cf. Eze 34:1–10). Since the earthly leaders are not taking proper care of the "flock," the Lord promises to care for them himself and to make them like a proud horse triumphant in battle. Verse 4 probably should be taken as messianic. So understood, the Messiah will come from Judah (cf. Ge 49:10; Jer 30:21). He is called (1) "the cornerstone" (cf. 3:9; cf. also Ps 118:22; Isa 28:16); (2) "the tent peg," a figure of a ruler as the support of the state (cf. Isa 22:23–24); and (3) "the battle bow," part of the Divine Warrior terminology (cf. Ps 45:5; Rev 19:11–16). From Judah will also come "every" divinely sanctioned king and ultimately the Messiah.

e. Israel's victory over her enemies (10:5–7)

5 The Lord promises to make Israel mighty and to reunite and restore the nation, causing the people to rejoice in him. Judah (i.e., its people) is probably the antecedent of "they." In the context "mighty men" has a military connotation: "valiant warriors." "Because" introduces the reason for their victory: supernatural help ("the LORD is with them") enables the infantry to overcome the cavalry (a symbol of power). God's people win against superior odds. Although the final fulfillment doubtless lies in the future, perhaps the first stage in the progressive fulfillment of the passage is to be found in the Maccabean victories.

6–7 There will be a reunification of south (Judah) and north (Joseph). The reason for their restoration is given as God's tender, motherly "compassion." The reason for their not continuing in a state of rejection is that the Lord is their covenantal God, bound to his people in a covenant relationship (cf. Ro 11). God's promise to answer them implies that they will pray to him for deliverance. Not only will Judah be like mighty men, but so also will Ephraim, resulting in great exuberance. For gladness associated with wine, see also Ps 104:15. The Lord is the secret, source, and sphere of this joy (Php 4:4).

f. Israel's complete deliverance and restoration (10:8–12)

8–9 The Lord promises to regather his people from distant lands. He will strengthen them, while the power of their ancient and traditional oppressors wanes. The word "redeem" (GK 1457) is often used for ransoming from slavery or captivity (see Isa 35:10; Mic 6:4; cf. 1Pe 1:18–19). "Before" seems to recall the situation in Egypt (Ex 1:6–20). Even in the Diaspora the Jews will remember the Lord. According to the meaning of Zechariah's name, "the LORD remembers" his covenant people and promises. Now the prediction is made that they will remember him. And they will also survive and return to the Promised Land.

10–12 Egypt and Assyria, the two ancient oppressors of God's chosen people, are probably intended to represent all the countries where the Israelites are dispersed. They evoke memories of slavery and exile. The promise of regathering is similar to that in Isa 11:11–16. "Gilead" lies east of the Jordan and "Lebanon" west of the Jordan—both in the territory of the old northern kingdom.

On the statement that "there will not be room enough for them," see v.8 and Isa 49:19–21; 54:2–3. Obstacles will be no barrier (v.11). The people "will pass through the sea of trouble"—as at the Red Sea, or Sea of Reeds. The "scepter" (i.e., "rule") of other great powers over them will cease. If the Ephraimites (northern kingdom) are still in view (see v.7), God is promising to do the same for them as he did for Judah (v.6), namely, to strengthen them. The source of the strength is the Lord himself. Walking "in his name" is probably equivalent to serving "as his representatives or ambassadors," though it may also mean that they will live "in keeping with his revealed character"—by divine enablement, of course.

2. The rejection of the messianic Shepherd-King (11:1–17)

a. The prologue (11:1–3)

1–3 Some interpret this little poem as a taunt song describing the lament over the destruction of the nations' power and arrogance (ch. 10), represented by the cedar, the pine, and the oak. Their kings are represented by the shepherds and the lions. So understood, vv.1–3 provide the conclusion for the preceding section. But others interpret the piece more literally as a description of the devastation of Syro–Palestine because of the rejection of the Messiah and Good Shepherd (vv.4–14). Verses 1–3 would then introduce the next section. The names in the text—Lebanon, Bashan, and Jordan—seem to favor this approach. Part of the fulfillment would be the destruction and further subjugation of that whole area by the Romans, including the fall of Jerusalem in A.D. 70 under Emperor Vespasian and General Titus, as well as the later fall of Masada. This action quelled one of several Jewish rebellions against Rome. Understood this way, the passage is in sharp contrast with what has just preceded in ch. 10, with its prediction of Israel's full deliverance and restoration to the covenant land. Now the scene is one of desolation for the land, followed by the threat of judgment and disaster for both land and people.

Lebanon was famous for its cedars, but they will be consumed. Jewish rabbis identified Lebanon here with the second temple (cf. 1Ki 6:15–18; 2Ch 2:8–9). The royal palace in Jerusalem was definitely referred to as "Lebanon" in Jer 22:23 (see 1Ki 7:2). The passage announces a judgment that would embrace both people and land, including Jerusalem and the temple. The pines and the oaks are to wail; for if the cedars do not survive the coming destruction, neither will they.

Bashan lay east of the Jordan and north of Mount Gilead. The Israelites took it from the Amorite king, Og, at the time of the conquest of Canaan (Nu 21:32–35). It was allotted to the half-tribe of Manasseh (Nu 32:33; Jos 13:30; 17:5). Bashan was renowned for its rich pastures and abundance of choice cattle (Dt 32:14; Eze 39:18). The oaks of Bashan are to wail because the "dense" (or better, "inaccessible") forest of Lebanon has been felled. How, then, can the lesser and more accessible trees escape?

The shepherds are wailing because the coming destruction will leave no pasture land for their flocks. Similarly, the lions are roaring because their lairs and food are gone, again because of the coming destruction.

b. The prophecy of the rejection of the Good Shepherd (11:4–14)

4–5 The reason for the calamity is the people's rejection of the messianic Shepherd-King. Just as the Servant in the Servant Songs (found basically in Isa 42; 49; 50; 53) is rejected, so here the Good Shepherd (a royal figure) is rejected. The same messianic King is in view in both instances. The purpose of this section, then, is to dramatize the rejection of the coming messianic Shepherd-King and the resulting rejection of Israel, ending in their judgment. "My God" indicates Zechariah's personal, intimate relationship with the Lord. What follows is addressed to him. Evidently he is instructed to act out the role of a good shepherd for the flock, i.e., Israel. The "slaughter" is explained in v.5, where the sheep (the Jews) are bought as slaves by outsiders. At least part of the fulfillment came in A.D. 70 and after. The sellers are their own shepherds—bad rulers or leaders.

6 "For" introduces the reason for the misery described in v.5, namely, the Lord's displeasure. The verse also interprets the parable of the flock. The "land" is Palestine. While the fulfillment may have been partially realized during the intertestamental period, it also seems to reach to Roman times; so one example of "king" would perhaps be the Roman emperor (cf. Jn 19:15), and those who "oppress the land" would include the Romans.

7–8a Zechariah carries out his divine instructions. In doing so, he becomes a type of the messianic Shepherd-King. He gives special attention to the "oppressed" (or "afflicted") of the flock. He also takes two staffs to ensure divine "favor" (GK 5840) on the flock and to ensure its "union" (GK 2482). Such unity (cf. Eze 37:15–28) is the result of the gracious leadership of the Good Shepherd.

Since so many interpretations have been given to the first part of v.8 (forty by one count), obviously no certainty is possible. "In one month" has been taken to refer to (1) a literal month, (2) a short period of time, and (3) a longer period of indefinite duration. One's conclusion on this matter will depend on one's identification of "the three shepherds." Four of the more popular interpretations are: (1) Eleazar, John, and Simon (the leaders of the three Jewish factions during the siege of Jerusalem by Titus in A.D. 70);

(2) Seleucus IV, Heliodorus, and Demetrius Soter (three Seleucid kings); (3) Jason, Menelaus, and Alcimus (high priests); and (4) three classes of leaders, such as prophet, priest, and king (or a lesser civil authority). This much is certain: The Good Shepherd will dispose of all unfit leaders.

8b–9 In spite of the ideal ministry of the Good Shepherd, the flock as a whole detested him. Similarly, he grew weary of them (cf. Isa 1:13–14) and terminated his providential care of the sheep so that they even ate "one another's flesh." According to Josephus, this actually happened during the siege of Jerusalem in A.D. 70 by the Romans.

10–11 A further consequence of the Shepherd's rejection is the cessation of his gracious favor. He revokes his covenant of security and restraint, by which he had been apparently holding back the nations from his people (cf. Eze 34:25; Hos 2:18). Now the nations (e.g., the Romans) will be permitted to overrun them. The last "it" evidently refers to Israel's affliction by the nations (cf. Mt 23:13, 23–24, 33–39). Faithful believers discern that what happens (e.g., the judgment on Jerusalem and the temple in A.D. 70) is a fulfillment of God's prophetic word—a result of such actions as those denounced in Mt 23, which led to the rejection of the Good Shepherd.

12–13 Now comes the final, outright rejection of the Good Shepherd, including even "severance" pay (his death is predicted in 13:7). "Give me my pay" speaks of the termination of the relationship; "keep it" is a more emphatic way of terminating the relationship. The "flock" (v.11) responds with thirty pieces of silver as the remuneration for the Shepherd's services. This sum was not only the price of a slave among the Israelites in ancient times (Ex 21:32) but also apparently a way of indicating a trifling amount. Next the Lord instructed Zechariah: "Throw it to the potter"—possibly a proverb. "So I took" indicates not only the prophet's obedience but also his continuing to "impersonate" the Good Shepherd by acting out this "parable." For the NT use of vv.12–13, see comments on Mt 26:14–15; 27:3–10.

14 The first staff, called "Favor," was broken (v.10). Now the second one, called "Union," is broken. This signifies the destruction or dissolution of the covenant nation, particularly of the unity between the south and the north. Yet even this new destruction and dispersion are not permanent; otherwise there would be no point in the promises of Israel's future deliverance, regathering, and restoration in the succeeding chapters.

c. The worthless shepherd (11:15–17)

15–16 With the Shepherd of the Lord's choice removed from the scene, a foolish and worthless shepherd replaces him. Zechariah acts out the role of such a bad shepherd, thus signifying that a selfish, corrupt, and greedy leader would arise and afflict the flock—the people of Israel. So the first oracle of Part II ends on a note of sorrow. "Again" doubtless refers to v.7, where Zechariah took two shepherd's staffs as the equipment of the Good Shepherd. The "equipment" would also include a bag for food, a pipe or reed for calling the sheep, a knife, and a case for setting and binding up broken bones. The bad shepherd is here characterized as "foolish" (GK 216), a word denoting "one who is morally deficient" (NIV note on Pr 1:7).

The reason for Zechariah's impersonation of a foolish shepherd is explained by the "For": God is going to raise up a shepherd who will not do what a good shepherd should; instead he will destroy the sheep. When one removes "not" from the sentence, one has an enlightening description of a truly effective pastoral ministry in the church today: (1) "care for the lost," (2) "seek the young," (3) "heal the injured," and (4) "feed the healthy." The bad shepherd will do none of these things. Instead of feeding the sheep, he will feed on them—preying on the unwary. He will even tear off their hoofs, apparently in search of the last edible morsel.

17 This same sinister figure is now called "the worthless [GK 496] shepherd" because of his diabolical deeds, such as deserting the flock, in contrast to the Good Shepherd (Jn 10:11–13). For this reason judgment is pronounced against him. While this counterfeit shepherd may have found a partial, historical fulfillment in such leaders as Bar Kokhba, who led the Jewish revolt against the Romans in A.D. 132–35 and was hailed as the Messiah, it seems that the final stage of the progressive fulfillment of the complete prophecy awaits the rise of the final Antichrist (cf. Eze 34:2–4;

Da 11:36–39; Jn 5:43; 2Th 2:3–10; Rev 13:1–8). The imprecation calls for his power ("arm") to be paralyzed ("completely withered") and his intelligence ("right eye") to be frustrated or nullified ("totally blinded"; cf. Rev 19:19–21; 20:10).

B. The Second Oracle: The Advent and Reception of the Messiah (12:1–14:21)

1. The deliverance and conversion of Israel (12:1–13:9)

a. The siege of Jerusalem (12:1–3)

1 Zechariah next encourages God's covenant people by contrasting initial judgment on them with their ultimate deliverance, restoration, and blessing. "In [or on] that day" appears sixteen times in the second oracle, placing it, for the most part, in the end times. The oracle basically revolves around two scenes: the final siege of Jerusalem and the Messiah's return to defeat Israel's enemies and to establish his kingdom fully.

It is surprising to be informed that the oracle concerns "Israel" instead of "Judah and Jerusalem," but it is clear that in chs. 12–14 "Israel" means the whole nation, not just the northern kingdom. The oracle begins by describing the Lord's creative power in the heavens, on the earth, and in human beings (Ge 2:7). Perhaps this description is a means of strengthening the royal and sovereign authority of the message.

2–3 Jerusalem is pictured as a cup that the nations gather around, eager to partake of its contents. But as they drink from her, they become intoxicated and reel. The end of v.2 indicates that the siege of Jerusalem will obviously affect Judah as well. Jerusalem is compared to a heavy, "immovable rock" that the nations attempt to move but only hurt themselves in the process. This, of course, will be due to special divine intervention and protection (vv.4–5). On the invasion of Jerusalem, "when all the nations of the earth are gathered against her," see also 14:2; Joel 3:9–16; Rev 16:16–21.

b. The divine deliverance (12:4–9)

4–6 In Dt 28:28, "panic" ("confusion of mind"), "madness," and "blindness" are listed among Israel's curses for disobeying the stipulations of the covenant. Now these curses are turned against Israel's enemies.

Special emphasis is laid on the horses to exalt God's power. On God's "watchful eye" over his people, see Pss 32:8 and 33:18. The wise leaders discern that the source of the people's strength is "the LORD Almighty." These faithful leaders are compared to a fire destroying wood and sheaves of grain; thus will they consume their enemies (cf. Jdg 15:3–5). By contrast Jerusalem and her people "will remain intact in her place."

7–9 In the coming deliverance there will be no superiority or inferiority or ranking of some above others in honor. Ultimately the Lord is the one who does the saving, the shielding or protecting, and the destroying of enemies. He will make the "feeblest" (lit., "the one who stumbles"; GK 4173) among them like David, who was celebrated as a great warrior. And the members of the Davidic dynasty will be "like God," which, in turn, is explained as being "like the Angel of the LORD going before them." God will be with them, will go before them, and will give them supernatural strength.

c. Israel's complete deliverance from sin (12:10–13:9)

10 Now there is movement from the physical deliverance, just described, to spiritual deliverance (cf. Dt 30:1–10). The Lord promises to "pour out" (GK 9161) his Spirit on his covenant people. The imagery is doubtless that of water as an emblem of the Holy Spirit. The recipients are the royal leaders and people of Jerusalem, representative of the inhabitants of the whole land. The content of the effusion is "a spirit of grace and supplication." While it is possible to construe "spirit" in the sense of "disposition," it seems preferable to follow the NIV margin note and see here a reference to the Spirit of God (cf. Isa 32:15; 44:3; 59:20–21; Jer 31:31, 33; Eze 36:26–27; 39:29; Joel 2:28–29). Because of the convicting work of God's Spirit, Israel will turn to the Messiah with mourning.

The most common meaning of the Hebrew preposition translated "on" is "to" (NIV note); there is no good contextual reason to depart from it here. The emphasis, then, is not on looking "on" (or "at") the Messiah literally but on looking "to" him in faith (cf. Nu 21:9; Isa 45:22; Jn 3:14–15). Some see this taking place at the second coming of Christ to the earth, or perhaps just

prior to his second advent. The object of the people's look of faith is identified as "the one they have pierced" (cf. Ps 22:16; Isa 53:5; Jn 19:34). John 19:37, which quotes this part of the verse, is but a stage in the progressive fulfillment of the whole. The final, complete fulfillment is yet future for Israel (Ro 11:25–27). The similes at the end of the verse accentuate the people's mourning (see Ex 11:5–6; Jer 6:26).

11 The convicting work of the Spirit of God will produce national contrition or repentance, led by the civil (royal) and religious leaders. The future weeping ("on that day") in Jerusalem is compared with "the weeping of Hadad Rimmon in the plain of Megiddo." Hadad-Rimmon is perhaps best taken as a place name (containing the names of ancient Semitic fertility gods) near Megiddo. So understood, the simile refers to the people of this town mourning the death of King Josiah (2Ch 35:20–27; see v.22 there for the plain of Megiddo and vv.24–25 for the mourning).

12–14 The expressions "each clan by itself" and "their wives by themselves" are doubtless intended to emphasize the sincerity of the mourning as true repentance. This is no purely emotional public spectacle. Nor are professional mourners involved. Individually and corporately, this is the experience of Lev 16 (the Day of Atonement) and Ps 51 (a penitential psalm) on a national scale. The mourning includes the royal house of David and the family of his son Nathan (2Sa 5:14), also the house of Levi and the family of Shimei son of Gershon, the son of Levi (Nu 3:17–18, 21), as well as "all the rest." While the repentance is led by the civil (royal) and religious leaders, it extends to every clan in the nation (cf. Isa 53:1–9).

13:1 Verse 1 contains new-covenant terminology. In Jer 31:33–34 God promised Israel: (1) enablement through his Spirit to obey his law (v.33a; Eze 36:26–27); (2) an intimate personal relationship and fellowship (v.33b); (3) a saving knowledge of himself (v.34a; Ro 11:26a); and (4) the forgiveness of sins (v.34b; Eze 36:25; Zec 3:4, 9; Ro 11:27). It is clear from the NT (e.g., Lk 22:20; 1Co 11:25; Heb 8–10) that the church—Gentiles and the spiritual remnant of Israel (Ro 11:1–16)—is today the recipient of the benefits promised to Israel in the new covenant. This is made possible only by God's sovereign, gracious grafting of Gentiles into that place of blessing (Ro 11:17–24). The cleansing referred to is related particularly to the fourth provision of the new covenant (see above) and is ultimately made possible through the atoning death of the pierced one (12:10).

2–3 Not only will there be personal internal cleansing—morally and spiritually—but also external cleansing, as the country is purged of "idols" and "false prophets," both of which were such a constant snare and source of deception to Israel (10:2–3; Jer 23:30–32; 27:9–10; Eze 13:1–14:11). God himself ("I") declares that he will rid the land of the names (i.e., the influence, fame, and even the very existence) of the idols. That false prophecy was still a problem in the postexilic period is clear from Ne 6:12–14. That both idolatry and false prophecy would once again be a problem in the future is evident also in Mt 24:4–5, 11, 15, 23–24; 2Th 2:2–4; Rev 9:20; 13:4–15. The "spirit of impurity" that inspired the false prophets to lie will also be removed. In that future day, if anyone dares to utter false prophecies ("lies"), his own parents—in obedience to Dt 13:6–9—will take the lead in executing him. The word "stab" (GK 1991; cf. "pierced" in 12:10) indicates that the feelings and actions shown in piercing the Messiah will be directed toward the false prophets.

4–6 Because of these stern measures, a false prophet will be reticent in identifying himself as such and will be evasive in responding to questioning. To help conceal his true identity, he will not wear "a prophet's garment of hair," such as Elijah wore (2Ki 1:8). To avoid being killed, he will deny being a prophet and will claim to have been a farmer from his youth. And if some suspicious person notices marks on his body and inquires about them, he will claim he received them in a scuffle with friends or as discipline from his parents during childhood. Apparently the accuser suspects that the false prophet's wounds were self-inflicted to arouse his prophetic ecstasy in idolatrous rites (as in 1Ki 18:28; cf. also Lev 19:28; 21:5; Dt 14:1; Jer 16:6; 41:5; 48:37).

7 Compared to the immediately preceding verses, the oracle now moves back to the time when Israel would be scattered because of her rejection of the true messianic Shepherd.

Then, after the announcement of the dispersion, the oracle seems to advance to a future period when Israel will undergo a special, purifying discipline, as silver and gold are refined (vv.8–9). The surviving remnant will be the Lord's people (v.9).

Death is announced against one whom God calls "my shepherd," i.e., the royal Good Shepherd—the true Shepherd of 11:4–14, in contrast with the foolish and worthless shepherd of 11:15–17. God also identifies him as "the man who is close to me." The expression eventually leads to Jn 10:30: "I and the Father are one" (cf. also Jn 1:1–2; 14:9).

In 11:17 it was the worthless shepherd who was to be struck; now it is the Good Shepherd (cf. 12:10). Apparently the one who wields the "sword" is God himself. In 12:10–14 the Messiah's death is presented as an act of Israel, but here it is the sovereign act of God (cf. Isa 53:10; Ac 2:23). When the Shepherd is struck, the sheep (cf. 10:3, 9) are scattered, in fulfillment of the curses for covenant disobedience (Dt 28:64; 29:24–25). This part of v.7 is quoted by Jesus not long before his arrest (Mt 26:31; Mk 14:27) and applied to the scattering of the apostles (Mt 26:56; Mk 11:50), but they are probably intended to serve as a type of the Diaspora that occurred in A.D. 70 and following. "The little ones" are the remnant (vv.8–9), "the oppressed" or "afflicted of the flock" (11:7, 11; cf. Isa 6:13; 66:22–24).

8–9 These verses apparently precede vv.1–6 chronologically. They depict a refining process for Israel. While what happened in A.D. 70 at the hands of the Romans may have been an initial stage in the progressive fulfillment, the final stage is yet future, for Israel as a whole is not in the proper covenant relationship with God described in v.9. The fact that a remnant will survive ("one-third") reveals God's mercy in the midst of judgment.

The survivors (cf. Jer 30:7) are those of 12:10–13:1; they will constitute the Jewish nucleus of the messianic kingdom and will evidently include the 144,000 of Rev 7:1–8 and 14:1–5. The calling on the Lord's name includes the "supplication" of 12:10. The verse closes with the covenant formula: "I will say, 'They are my people,' and they will say, 'The LORD is our God.'" Thus the new covenant will be fulfilled for Israel, and they will be restored to proper covenant relationship with the Lord (cf. also Eze 20:30–44, esp. v.37).

2. The Messiah's return and his kingdom (14:1–21)

a. The siege of Jerusalem (14:1–2)

1–2 The ultimate goal of all history is the Lord's personal appearance and reign. But before the literal and full manifestation of his kingdom, the earth must experience the throes of birth pangs. There is a return to the refining process as the nations gather at Jerusalem and ravish her. Although "a day of the LORD" is not the usual construction for "the day of the LORD," it doubtless means the same thing; "that day" occurs throughout the context (chs. 12–14). Perhaps this particular construction is used here to emphasize the fact that the "day" is distinctively the Lord's. Human beings are having their day now; a day of the Lord is yet to come. "Your" refers to Jerusalem.

"I" is a reminder that the sovereign God is in complete control. As the Lord of history and nations, he is the Prime Mover. The scene depicted here (contingents from all nations gathered to fight against Jerusalem) is probably the same as the one in Rev 16:16–21 (Armageddon). This eschatological verse alone—with its statement that "the city will be captured"—is sufficient to refute the notion popular in certain circles that "the times of the Gentiles" (Lk 21:24) were fulfilled as of the rebirth of the modern state of Israel. According to Lucan theology, after "the times of the Gentiles are fulfilled," Jerusalem will be trampled on no more. Since Zec 14:2 clearly indicates that Jerusalem will be "trampled on" again in the future, the "times of the Gentiles" would seem to extend to the Messiah's second advent, when those "times" will be replaced by the final, universal, everlasting kingdom of Da 2:35, 44–45. The rest of v.2 delineates some of the horrors that still await Jerusalem and its people. The fulfillment must still lie in the future. At that time all this will happen to fulfill the curses pronounced against covenant disobedience (Dt 28:30).

b. The tokens of the Messiah's return (14:3–8)

3–5 Just when it seems that all hope is gone, "then the LORD" himself appears as Divine Warrior and delivers his beleaguered people. But who is this "LORD"? When one compares this scene with Ac 1:9–12 and Rev 19:11–16, it appears certain that "the LORD" here is ultimately the Messiah. The passage, then, is indirectly messianic. "The day of battle" is any occasion when the Lord supernaturally intervenes to deliver his people, such as at the Red Sea (Ex 14:13–14). Acts 1:11–12 may well allude to the prophecy that "his feet will stand on the Mount of Olives," which is situated "east of Jerusalem." In the final days, when the Lord will stand on this mountain, it will split in two (perhaps due to an earthquake), creating a great valley running east and west. The purpose of the valley is to afford an easy means of rapid escape from the final anti-Semitic onslaught; the Mount of Olives has always constituted a serious obstacle to such an escape to the east.

The future escape of God's people is compared with the time when their ancestors "fled from the earthquake in the days of Uzziah king of Judah"—an earthquake so devastating and memorable that it is mentioned also in Am 1:1. In announcing the Lord's coming, Zechariah expresses his own personal faith in him ("my God"). "All the holy ones" will be in the Lord's retinue when he comes. These apparently include both believers and unfallen angels (see Mt 25:31; Rev 19:14).

6–8 The precise meaning of these verses is admittedly uncertain, but the general picture is clear. The eschatological aspect of the Day of the Lord described here will be characterized by cataclysmic phenomena, including cosmic signs (cf. Isa 13:9–10; Joel 2:31; 3:15; Am 5:18; Mt 24:29–30; Rev 6:12–14; 8:8–12; 9:1–18; 14:14–20; 16:4, 8–9). Because of the topographical, cosmic, and indeed, even cataclysmic changes, that day will be "unique" (GK 285). The situation itself cannot be classified as either day or night—"a day known [only] to the LORD." But after the judgment and suffering (possibly the refining of 13:8–9) are past, "there will be light" again, possibly symbolizing the ushering in of the new order.

Is the "living water" literal (physical) or figurative (spiritual)? It is probably best to view it as both literal and symbolic (cf. Pss 46:4; 65:9; Isa 8:6; Jer 2:13; Eze 47:1–12; Jn 4:10–14; 7:38; Rev 22:1–2). "The eastern sea" is the Dead Sea and "the western sea" is the Mediterranean.

c. The establishment of the Messiah's kingdom (14:9–11)

9 Statements like "The LORD will be king over the whole earth" stand at the very center of a truly biblical theology. When this comes true in the fullest sense, the prayer of Mt 6:9–10 will be answered. The time is coming when there will be no more idolatry, polytheism, or even henotheism, but only high, ethical monotheism (cf. Dt 6:4).

10–11 The land around Jerusalem is to be leveled while Jerusalem is to be elevated (see v.4). Geba was located almost six miles north of Jerusalem at the northern boundary of the kingdom of Judah (2Ki 23:8). As the text indicates, the Rimmon mentioned here is the one situated "south of Jerusalem" (this distinguishes it from other OT towns of the same name). It is usually identified with En Rimmon ("spring of the pomegranate tree," Ne 11:29; cf. Jos 15:32).

The term "Arabah" applied in part or wholly to the depression of the Jordan Valley, extending from Mt. Hermon, a 9100-ft. elevation in the Anti-Lebanon Range, and including both sides of the Jordan River, the Dead Sea, and the region slightly to the southwest as far as the head of the Gulf of Aqaba. That Jerusalem will thus be elevated is in agreement with Isa 2:2. The Benjamin Gate, the First Gate, and the Tower of Hananel were all at the northeastern part of the city wall, the Corner Gate was at its northwest corner, and the royal winepresses were just south of the city (cf. Jer 31:38). Furthermore, the city will be densely populated, never again to be depopulated through destruction. Finally, "Jerusalem will be secure" (see Jer 31:40).

d. The punishment of Israel's enemies (14:12–15)

12–15 The prophet next reveals how God will deal with the antikingdom forces of vv.1–3. (1) He will strike them with a "plague," just as he did the Assyrian army of King Sennacherib in 701 B.C. (Isa 37:36). (2) The Lord will strike the enemies of himself and his people with "great panic," causing them to "attack each other" (cf. Jdg 7:22; 1Sa 14:15–20; 2Ch 20:23). (3) The rest of the people of Judah will rally to defend the capital. The validity of this last point rests on the NIV rendering "at Jerusalem." Verse 14 ends with the Jews gathering the plunder, or spoils, of battle. Verse 15 adds that a plague similar to that in vv.12–13 will strike the beasts of burden, thus preventing their use for escape.

e. The universal worship of the King (14:16–19)

16 In spite of the awful decimation predicted in vv.12–15, there will be "survivors" (GK 3855)—a converted remnant from those nations—who will make an annual pilgrimage to Jerusalem "to worship the King" (see Isa 2:2–4; also Eze 40–48). "The Feast of Tabernacles" marked the final harvest of the year's crops (Lev 23:34–43). It was to be a time of grateful rejoicing (Lev 23:40; Dt 16:14–15; Ne 8:17). The people were to live in "booths" as a reminder that their ancestors lived in booths when the Lord brought them out of Egypt (Lev 23:42–43). Beginning with the period of Ezra and Nehemiah, the reading (and perhaps teaching) of "the Book of the Law of God" became an integral part of the festivities (Ne 8:18; cf. Isa 2:3). The festival seems to speak of the final, joyful regathering and restoration of Israel in full kingdom blessing, as well as of the ingathering of the nations. It may continue to have some significance (at least typically) in the eternal state (in the New Jerusalem on the new earth), since God will "live" (lit., "tabernacle"; GK 5012) with his people (Rev 21:3).

17–19 The prophet next unfolds what will happen to the recalcitrant nations that refuse to send delegations on this annual pilgrimage to worship the King in Jerusalem: The blessing of rain will be withheld from them (cf. Dt 28:22–24). This principle is illustrated with Egypt. Thus will all be punished who do not make the annual pilgrimage to Jerusalem to worship the King and to observe the thankful expressions associated with the Feast of Tabernacles, and thus will the King be universally worshiped.

f. "HOLY TO THE LORD" (14:20–21)

20–21 Here the nature of the messianic kingdom is depicted: It will be characterized by holiness (see 2:12). There will be holiness in public life ("the bells of the horses"), in religious life ("the cooking pots in the LORD's house"), and in private life ("every pot in Jerusalem and Judah"). Even common things become holy when they are used for God's service. So it is with our lives. In this way God's original purpose for Israel (Ex 19:6) will be fulfilled. "Cook" (GK 1418) means "cook the sacrifices." While the Hebrew for "Canaanite" can also mean "merchant" (possibly referring either to 11:5 or to the kind of activity condemned by Jesus in Mt 21:12–13), "Canaanite" seems the better translation, representing anyone who is morally or spiritually unclean—anyone who is not included among the chosen people of God (cf. Isa 35:8; Eze 43:7; 44:9; Rev 21:27).

The final scene of the book of Zechariah anticipates Rev 11:15, toward which all history is steadily moving—"the kingdom of the world has become the kingdom of our Lord and of his Christ, and he will reign for ever and ever"—and Rev 19:16—"On his robe and on his thigh he has this name written: KING OF KINGS AND LORD OF LORDS."

The Old Testament in the New

OT Text	NT Text	Subject
Zec 3:2	Jude 9	Rebuking Satan
Zec 4:1–2	Rev 11:4	Lampstand and olive trees
Zec 4:10	Rev 5:6	Seven eyes of God
Zec 6:1–6	Rev 6:2–8	Four different-colored horses
Zec 8:16	Eph 4:25	Speaking the truth
Zec 9:9	Mt 21:5; Jn 12:15	Palm Sunday
Zec 11:13	Mt 27:9–10	Thirty pieces of silver
Zec 12:10	Jn 19:37; Rev 1:7	Looking on one pierced
Zec 13:7	Mt 26:31; Mk 14:27	Striking the shepherd

Malachi

INTRODUCTION

1. Background

Unlike most other prophets, Malachi mentioned no datable persons or events in his brief prophecy. Any clues to the origin and time of his book must come from the text and its implications. Tradition, however, gives us some information. Malachi is and always has been placed last in the Minor Prophets, and there is an approximate chronological arrangement within the three major prophets and the twelve minor ones. In fact, the Talmud regularly classes Haggai, Zechariah, and Malachi together as the three postexilic prophets.

From the contents of Malachi, we deduce that the prophet wrote sometime after Ezra. Zerubbabel, the first governor after the return from the Babylonian exile, had, with the aid of the prophets Haggai and Zechariah, encouraged the people to rebuild the temple (515 B.C.). Ezra returned with another group of exiles in 458 B.C. Thirteen years later, Nehemiah returned and led the people in rebuilding the walls of the city of Jerusalem. In the twelfth year of his governorship, Nehemiah returned to Persia for an unknown period of time (cf. Ne 5:14; 13:6). It was during this interim, perhaps in 434 B.C., that Malachi took the helm of spiritual affairs in Jerusalem.

Some of the exiles had returned, the temple had been rebuilt, and the sacrificial system had been reestablished. Indeed, it had been functioning long enough to develop certain abuses against which Malachi contended at some length in his book.

In 1:8 another hint appears. The Persian word for "governor" (*pehah*; GK 7068) had been given to Nehemiah (Ne 5:14; 12:26), but the use here probably does not indicate Nehemiah because (1) his name is not given and its absence is hard to explain, and (2) the tone of the verse indicates a pagan ruler. Thus *pehah* in 1:8 likely refers to an interim governor who filled the office during Nehemiah's absence, so that Malachi's work preceded Nehemiah's second term as governor.

Many similarities exist between the thrust of Malachi's message and Nehemiah's reforms, such as mixed marriages (Ne 10:30; 13:23–27; Mal 2:11; cf. Ezra 9–10); corrupt priesthood (Ne 13:4–9; Mal 1:6–2:9); financial abuses (Ne 13:10–13; Mal 3:5–10). This is why the two are usually connected.

Thus the exiles had returned; the temple had been rebuilt; the city of Jerusalem had returned to a substantial degree of normalcy; and the inevitable lethargy, laxity, and leniency in spiritual matters had developed. A measure of comfort and security under Persian suzerainty encouraged the people of Judah to let their hands fall in their task of building their nation under God. To this declining state of affairs the last prophet of the OT addressed himself.

2. Authorship

Nothing is known of Malachi apart from his book. Even his name is in question. Some doubt that "Malachi" is a name and translate it as a title, meaning either "my messenger" or "the LORD's messenger." The suggestion has ancient support in the LXX. Some scholars affirm that the book is actually only the last of three sections of Zechariah, which was cut off in order to make the Minor Prophets amount to the sacred number twelve. The total obscurity of the author of the book is underlined by the absence of the name Malachi in all the rest of the Bible. Even in NT quotations, no name is given (Mt 11:10; Mk 1:2; Lk 7:27).

On the other hand, each of the other writing prophets is named in the opening verses of his book. If a man named Malachi did not write the book bearing this name, he would be the only exception. Moreover, Malachi is neither an unlikely name nor an unsuitable one for the author of this last book of the prophets. After all, Malachi was the Lord's messenger. His trumpet made no uncertain sound. Clearly and unmistakably he indicted his people and the priests for their sin and summoned them to righteousness.

3. Date

Malachi's book cannot be earlier than 516/515 B.C., because that was when the second temple was finished. Scholars have placed him anytime from then on through the administration of Nehemiah in Jerusalem. Ezra came to Jerusalem in 458 B.C. and Nehemiah in 445 (according to the traditional reckoning).

4. Occasion and Purpose

Apathy toward the temple ritual and especially toward the law of Moses had reached such proportions in postexilic Judah that God raised up the prophet Malachi to reprimand the people. The battle for truth and righteousness had waned because their obvious political enemies were gone. Yet this left room for the not-so-obvious enemies—namely, smugness, pride, and compromise.

The people in general and the priests in particular had lost their sense of "chosenness" (1:2). Not respecting his codes and regulations (1:6) showed they had stopped honoring God. Among them intermarriage with unbelievers was rampant (2:11). The view of domestic commitment was low, and divorce was the result (2:16). In 3:5 is a list of abuses and unacceptable practices: sorcery, adultery, perjury, fraud, oppression, and injustice. These were the things that occasioned Malachi's angry indictment.

No prophet or preacher who loves his people enjoys pointing out their sin or warning them of doom to come. So Malachi must have found his assignment, which was so packed with judgment of the people and the priests, a hard one. All the threats, challenges, encouragements, and promises were for the spiritual upbuilding of the repatriated exiles and their children. God and Malachi wanted a righteous nation, a pure and devoted priesthood, happy homes, God-fearing children, and a people characterized by truth, integrity, generosity, gratitude, fidelity, love, and hope.

5. Theology

The paramount theme of theology is the person and work of God himself. Malachi presents the sovereign Lord as the God of Israel and the God of the whole world. In 3:6 not only is the immutability of God affirmed—"I the LORD do not change"—but the corollary of the impossibility of his promises being nullified is also stated: "So you, O descendants of Jacob, are not destroyed." God has determined to maintain a people for himself; and it will happen—if not in Malachi's day, then in a later age.

Malachi was in accord with the great OT prophets in reminding the people he was addressing of the universality of God. God was concerned with all nations, not just Israel (cf. 1:5).

It may seem that Malachi was overly concerned with the proper execution of the ritual parts of the Hebrew religion (cf. 1:8, 13; 3:8), but a careful reading will show that he was actually concerned with what Jesus called the "more important matters of the law—justice, mercy and faithfulness" (Mt 23:23).

Malachi preached a God of justice who would condemn sinners but would also reward the righteous. Tithing would produce blessing (3:10); the righteous would be spared on that "day" (v.17). Those who revered God's name would bask in the "sun of righteousness" (4:2). So Malachi was a prophet of both malediction and benediction, because he preached a God who was altogether fair in his dealings with people.

Malachi's most notable contribution to the OT's corpus of messianic prophecy was his reference to the forerunner. The first allusion is in 3:1. "My messenger" there cannot be Malachi but rather some Elijah who would announce for the last time in the OT God's terms of repentance (4:5; cf. Mt 11:14; 17:12–13; Mk 9:11–13; Lk 1:17).

EXPOSITION

I. The Favor of the Lord (1:1–5)

1 This verse tells us the three barest minimum facts about the "oracle" (GK 5363): (1) it is from the Lord, (2) it is for Israel, and (3) Malachi is its agent.

2–3 The prophecy begins with the beautiful words "I have loved you." The popular attitude was that God had forsaken his people. Though the Exile might have prompted such feelings, one would think that the near miraculous turn of events that led to the repatriation of many of the Hebrews would have given the people cause to think about God's faithfulness. That return, though unaccompanied by the miracles of the Exodus from Egypt, was nevertheless viewed exultingly as the work of the hand of God. In the absence of any subsequent marvels, however, there came despair born of unfulfilled hopes.

The divine rejoinder to the people's question alludes to a crucial event in Isaac's family. While it is not baldly stated in Ge 25:23, in his sovereignty God chose Jacob over Esau, a choice that was tantamount to "hating" Esau. Paul used this to illustrate the doctrine of election (Ro 9:13). Malachi describes the result of God's rejection of Esau; his territory, ancient Edom, became a wasteland inhabited by desert jackals. In the fourth century B.C., the Nabataeans moved through Edom—driving the Edomites westward out of their centuries-old homeland—to the southern part of Judah. This area later came to be known as Idumea (cf. Mk 3:8).

4–5 These verses elaborate God's rejection of Esau's land (cf. Isa 11:14; 34:5–6; Jer 49:7–22; Eze 25:12–14; 35:15; Joel 3:19; Am 1:11; Obadiah). Of all the enemies of Israel, Edom was perhaps the most long-lived and consistent one. The enmity began with Amalek, an Edomite (Ex 17:8–16), and continued through the Exodus (Nu 14:44–45), into the period of the Judges (Jdg 3:12–13), and to the time of Saul (1Sa 15:1–3) and David (1Sa 27:8). Moreover, the enemies mentioned by Ezra (4:7) and Nehemiah (4:7) probably included Edomites (Amalekites), and this special curse would be an oblique kind of encouragement to the Israelites.

Though the Edomites in some small measure rebuilt their country, though never regaining its former territory or power, God spoke of his intention to see it perpetually cursed. This evidence of God's power beyond the borders of Israel will evoke from his people the doxology "Great is the LORD." This is the first of three or four such phrases throughout the book that speak of God's plans going beyond the boundaries of Israel (cf. 1:11, 14; 3:12; and perhaps 4:6).

II. The Failure of the Priests (1:6–14)
A. Disrespectful Service (1:6–7)

6–7 This first part of the indictment against the priests contains two more rhetorical questions. The first is God's: "Where is the respect due me?" The unwritten answer is that they had not been honoring the Lord. The servants at the temple, who were the closest to sacred things, had defaulted in the most central obligation of all—honoring God. And if the leadership failed, what could the people be expected to do? But spiritual leaders have often run the risk of treating sacred things as ordinary.

From the general charge of failing to honor the Lord, the prophet moved to this specific one: "You place defiled food on my altar." The priests countered this charge with a question. Then the prophet responded with an explanation of the charge: the priests say "that the LORD's table is contemptible."

B. Disqualified Sacrifices (1:8–9)

8 With four more questions, the prophet expanded the charge against the priests. Was it not wrong to sacrifice blind animals? Of course it was! The law forbade bringing lame, blind, blemished, or sick animals to the altar (Dt 15:21). The priests should have been reminding the people of these regulations. The second question is like the first. The third and fourth question ones clearly imply that such offerings would be unacceptable to the governor. The context probably implies that this governor was not Nehemiah but one of the Persian appointees who served before Nehemiah arrived in Jerusalem, or perhaps during his absence from it. Furthermore, animals were probably not brought to him as sacrifices but as a form of tax. Despite their generally favorable attitude toward the exiles, the Persians would not tolerate any cutting of corners by their subjects.

9 The closing verse of this section, where God speaks of himself in the third person, seems loaded with irony. Most modern translations understand it as one more of Malachi's ways of charging the priests with sin. The point is that God would not extend his favor when the gifts for thanksgiving and entreaty were given, because their shoddiness was an insult.

C. Disdainful Attitudes (1:10–14)

10 God, again speaking of himself in the first person (cf. v.9), wishes that the temple would go out of business. As long as it was not serving as a meeting place for God and his people, why should any perfunctory and self-deceiving rituals go on in it? Not only were the sacrifices ineffective, but the priests and the people were lulled into thinking that their deeds were winning God's approval. So why not shut the temple doors and be done with what was for the priests merely a nuisance? God could hardly have spoken his mind more clearly than he did in the last part of v.10: "I am not pleased with you . . . and I will accept no offering from your hands."

11 God told his faithless priests that he had others who in different places and in later times would bring acceptable offerings and give him with love and devotion the worship he demanded (cf. Heb 13:15–16; Rev 5:8). No doubt Christians are among those of the far-off nations living in the distant future, who in Malachi's day were thought to be without hope because they had no contact with the religion of Jerusalem (cf. 1Pe 2:9).

12–13 Once more the altar of the temple was called a "table" (GK 8947; cf. v.7). The priests were charged with profaning the Lord's name when they declared that his table was defiled and its food contemptible. The food, of course, was the grain and meat offerings the priests put on the Lord's table. It was true that certain species of animals and others that were blemished defiled the altar. But it was the priests' responsibility to keep such unacceptable offerings away from the altar. How strange that now they were the ones complaining of the defilement! Malachi put into words the thoughts of the priests. For them the holy service of God had become a bore, a labor of duty rather than of love, a yoke around their necks. The very men who were the mediators between God and his people (Ex 28:1, 43), the teachers of Israel (Lev 10:11; Dt 33:10; 2Ch 15:3), and the court of appeal (Dt 19:17–19) were, by their own choice, profaning their office and bringing shame on the name of the Lord. The question asked in v.13 lists the things that make animals unacceptable for sacrifice. "Should I accept [such animals from you]?" God asked.

14 God spoke drastically but realistically: "Cursed is the cheat." The opposite of "blessed" is "cursed," and the opposite of an honest person is a cheat. God is an absolute sovereign. If the people he chose reject him, as Lord, he will choose others—i.e., Gentiles, foreigners—who will revere his holy name.

III. The Rebuke of the Lord (2:1–9)

1–2 This section is aimed at the priests. The "curse" (GK 826 and 4423) idea relates to 1:14. The "blessings" are probably the very things that ultimately benefited the priesthood. Two of them are named in 3:11—pest-free crops and fruitful vines. The Levites lived off the tithes the people brought. When the nation as a whole suffered from drought or any other calamity, the perquisites of the priests dropped off proportionally.

3–6 "Offal" (GK 7302) was the internal waste of the sacrificial animal that normally was carried outside the camp. But here it is first used as a gross insult to the officiating priests; they and it would be carried away.

The word "covenant" (GK 1382) appears six times in this little book. The first three (2:4–5, 8) refer to God's covenant with Levi; then come references to the "covenant of the fathers" (v.10), the marriage covenant (v.14), and the new covenant (3:1). The covenant arrangement with the Levites was to endure unaltered. Obviously they were not meeting their responsibilities.

The description of what a priest should be simply did not fit the priests of Malachi's day. "Life and peace," "reverence," "true instruction," and "uprightness" were to be the hallmarks of those serving in the temple. There were to be the absence of falsehood on the lips and the ministry of turning many from sin. But in Malachi's day, instead of turning people from sin, the priests were, by their words and deeds, turning them to sin.

Throughout vv.4–6 Levi is spoken of ideally. What little we know of him is not so favorable; Jacob's "prophecy" in Ge 49:5–7 tells us something of what Jacob felt. Much more positive is the "blessing" of Moses on the ideal Levite (Dt 33:8–11) that Malachi was speaking of in this section. Doubtless many did their jobs conscientiously and with the required reverence and devotion.

7–8 The priests were the custodians of learning, both the preservers and the pioneers of scholarship. But those who sought to drink at those wells found them either dry or poisoned. Instead of turning people into "the way," the priests did the opposite. Such irresponsibility violated the covenant of Levi. Sins of omission were compounded with sins of commission. Malachi made it clear that God could tolerate the situation no longer.

9 The verdict comes. The sentence on the priests involved shame and humiliation. The regrettable part was that all priests were painted with the same brush, even though there must have been some conscientious ones among them. An additional feature of the indictment comes right at the end of this verse: the offenders had shown partiality in matters of the law.

So ends the section charging the Levitical priests with various misdemeanors and failures. From these specific targets of his wrath, God next turns to the people as a whole.

IV. The Unfaithfulness of the People (2:10–16)

The balance of ch. 2 deals with the same social evils Ezra and Nehemiah addressed: the problem of intermarriage with unbelievers and the subsequent divorces (Ezr 9:2; Ne 14:23–28). Hand in hand with this sin went a certain compromise of true religion.

10–12 The broad introductory statement is, of course, addressed to the people of Israel, not to the Moabites, Tyrians, Philistines, Syrians, or others with whom the intermarriage had taken place. Since Hebrew makes no proper-noun distinctions, the translators must decide whether "father" refers to God or to Abraham. In either case the point is clear: "We Jews should cooperate, work harmoniously, and marry within our own people." The implications of "breaking faith with one another" (cf. v.11) probably are broader than simply the matter of divorce. All betrayals, from the slightest unkindness to the grossest injustice, merit God's disapproval.

The mixture of the ideas of intermarriage and prostitution of the sanctuary is not unlike what Paul said in 2Co 6:14–16. Not to distinguish between Israelite women and heathen women—or between Christian spouses and unbelievers—is to deny the difference between the God of the Bible and the pagan deities. Malachi said there would be no exceptions to the rule: Intermarriage meant excommunication.

13 Apparently the people made a great display of grief over their spiritual barrenness. How exactly the lay people could be in a position to weep over the altar is uncertain. The people's sorrow, however, was for the wrong reason; they should have been bemoaning their sins rather than their lack of divine acceptance and consequent blessing.

14 We might consider the "Why" as another of Malachi's rhetorical questions. Having put the question in their mouths, the prophet proceeded to answer it. The reference to "wife of your youth" suggests that the men were divorcing their aging wives in favor of younger women.

15 This is the most difficult verse in the book grammatically. In effect it says that God made monogamous marriage and intends unions to last. Apparently the Israelites not only were marrying foreign women but were also divorcing their Israelite wives in the process. So they were really guilty of two sins—divorce and intermarriage with foreigners.

16 God succinctly gives his verdict: "I hate divorce." Many today would accuse Malachi of having a rigid view of marriage and divorce. But the covenant made between a man and a woman in the presence of a priest, the vicar of God, must be taken with utmost seriousness. "What God has joined together, let man not separate" was Jesus' way of saying it (Mt 19:6; Mk 10:9). Not even the man who is a part of that union may make such a separation.

V. The Coming Messenger of the Lord (2:17–3:5)

17 The question "Where is the God of justice?" points to the abuses in connection with worship and divorce. These have their roots in hearts destitute of the fear of God and culminate in avowed unbelief in the justice of Almighty God and his moral government of the world. God himself will answer their question, for 3:1 has "the LORD you are seeking will come to his temple." And 3:5 reads, "So I will come near to you for judgment." The first question in v.17 is "How have we wearied him [God]?" To this the prophet responds along now familiar lines. God was tired of hypocrisy, inverted morals, spiritual blindness, and obduracy.

3:1 This verse is quoted in the NT (Mt 11:10; Mk 1:2; Lk 7:27), all referring it to John the Baptist. Thus the one called "my messenger" is the forerunner of Christ, John the son of Zechariah and Elizabeth. The Lord who then follows is none other than Jesus Christ, the Son of God. The prophet's choice of the word "Lord" (*'adon*; GK 123) rather than "LORD" (GK 3378) points to this (cf. Ac 2:36; 1Co 12:3; Php 2:11). Significantly, the "me" establishes an identification between the first and second persons of the Trinity. Christ came to the temple, first as a baby to be dedicated, then at least yearly for the festivals. Most notably he came the last week of his life.

The phrase "whom you desire" is significant: Even in their sin the people longed for deliverance through the Messiah. Amos had people in his audience who "desired" the Day of the Lord; but he bluntly told them that the Day of the Lord would be darkness and not light (Am 5:18–20). So, too, Malachi asked, "Who can endure the day of his coming?" The coming Messiah would bring judgment—vindication and exoneration for the righteous but condemnation and punishment for the wicked. Like most OT prophets, Malachi, in his picture of the coming Christ, mingled the two advents. So while the birth and earthly ministry of Christ are in view in v.1, we already have the returning Judge in v.2. It could be said that the latter days began with Bethlehem and continued through the present, to be culminated in the eternal state. The Day of the Lord is any day God steps into history to do a special work, whether of judgment or deliverance. This passage speaks of purification and judgment.

2–4 Malachi continues his use of rhetorical questions as he asked in two ways, "Who will stand when he appears?" Christ's judgment, a Second Advent function, is likened to two purifying agents: fire for metals and soap for clothing. Just as these remove impurities, he will purify the latter-day Levites so that they will gleam and endure like "gold and silver." As a result of that process, God will have an approved and accepted priesthood to carry out the sacred ministry in a right spirit. Verse 4 does not mean that descendants of Levi and Aaron will function in any NT temple; it is, rather, symbolic of a cleansed and sanctified church (cf. 1Pe 2:5, 9; Rev 1:6; 5:10; 20:6). The soundest logical and theological reason for the abolition of the sacrificial system is found in Heb 9:23–10:14.

5 God simply says that he will at that time speedily bring to justice all sorts of malefactors. "Sorcerers" (GK 4175) is a category that takes in practitioners of the occult. "Adulterers" (GK 5537) includes any departure from God's ordained pattern of family life. Next come "perjurers" (lit., "false swearers"). This covers everything from "white lies" to perjury in a high court. The indictment against oppressors of widows and orphans reflects Malachi's interest in social justice. Like all true ministers of God, Malachi could not divorce responsibilities toward God from those toward other human beings. The number of laws in the Scriptures for the protection of aliens suggests it must have been common or easy to exploit expatriates among the Israelites. Hospitality was a requirement, any breach of which would come under the rubric of depriving aliens. All the offenders are categorized as those who "do not fear me." Their sin testified to a lamentable absence of that godly fear that is "the beginning of knowledge" (Pr 1:7).

VI. The Robbery and Riches of God (3:6–12)

A. The Neglect of the Tithe (3:6–9)

6–7 First there is a declaration of the immutability of God, the attribute of changelessness that ultimately preserves the nation from destruction. God keeps his promises to the patriarchs. He knows this evil generation will pass and that a God-fearing one will yet come to inherit the promises. God next explains why he does not answer the people's prayers: "You have turned away from my decrees." God is still pledged to give attention to those who earnestly seek him. The invitation to "return" (GK 8740), which could as well have been translated "repent" or "convert," was met with a cynical question: "How are we to return?" Malachi does not answer this question; his whole book and ministry tell how to get right with God.

8 Tithing (being fiscally responsible before God) is introduced by the blunt question "Will a man rob God?" Stealing means not only taking what is not yours but keeping back for yourself what belongs to someone else. In this case one-tenth of a man's income was due God; failure to pay that debt amounted to robbery (cf. Ac 5:1–11). The tenth of all produce as well as of flocks and cattle belonged to the Lord and was by him assigned to the Levites for their services (Nu 18:21, 24). It may be that the people's disobedience prompted some of the priestly grumbling that Malachi had earlier referred to. Nehemiah dealt with the same problem (Ne 10:32–39; 13:10). If Malachi predates the events of Ne 13, perhaps Malachi's words in v.8 had been heeded.

9 That God condemned the whole nation suggests that this "robbery" was a rather widespread abuse of his generosity. Most churches still fall under this indictment; their budgets are generally nowhere near ten percent of the members' income.

B. The Promise of Blessing (3:10–12)

10 The remedy for Israel was simply to start doing what was right—"bring the whole tithe into the storehouse." The temple served as a warehouse for the produce the Israelites brought. The Levites then distributed it for sacrificial purposes, for their own domestic needs, and for whatever emergencies arose. It should be emphasized that the OT tithe is not the upper limit. In the NT Christians are urged to "excel in this grace of giving" (2Co 8:7), remembering that they owe everything to the one who for their sake "made himself nothing" (Php 2:7; cf. 2Co 8:9). God offers his people the challenge of testing him. By this offer he virtually guarantees them a direct and abundant return on their investment. His "storehouse" of blessings is unlimited.

11–12 From a general statement of blessing, Malachi next specifies what form that blessing might take. Since he was dealing with an agrarian society, the "blessings" had to do with crops and the like. Then, as is always the case, there was a purpose for the blessing. Not merely would God's people be comfortable, healthy, and happy, but because of this the Lord's name would be honored. Whatever good happens to us should be turned into a testimony to the goodness of our God. Then unbelievers will note our blessedness and be drawn to our God.

VII. The Servants of the Lord (3:13–18)

A. The Faithless (3:13–15)

13–14 Once more, and for the last time, Malachi opens with a statement about what peo-

ple said, followed by a question in which they imply that the charge is unfounded. The third element then follows: an elaboration and explanation of the charge. The sin concerned lack of trust in God. By innuendo, if not by outright statement, God was represented as unfair and the keeping of the law a useless exercise.

15 This verse is a restatement of the age-old question so prominent in the book of Job: Why do the evil prosper and the righteous suffer? Malachi did not answer the complaint immediately.

B. The Faithful (3:16–18)

16 Malachi portrays God as listening to those who feared him. What they were saying, we do not know; perhaps it was an expression of love and worship. Then comes the remarkable statement that "a scroll . . . was written in his presence concerning those who feared the LORD." This idea of God's keeping written records appears frequently in Scripture (cf. Ex 32:32; Ps 69:28; Isa 4:3; Da 12:1; Lk 10:20; Php 4:3; Heb 12:23; Rev 3:5; 13:8; 17:8; 20:12, 15; 21:27). Perhaps the most beautiful expression of the idea is in Isa 49:16: "See, I have engraved you on the palms of my hands."

17–18 God's people will be his very own, and he will spare them. On that day, when all wrongs are rectified and all wickedness punished, it will be apparent that God does judge justly and that he does make a distinction between those who serve him and those who do not.

VIII. The Day of the Lord (4:1–6)

1 The eschatological theme of the Day of the Lord looms large in the OT prophets (c⁴ Isa 13:6; Jer 46:10; Joel 2:31; Zep 1:14–2:3) and also appears in the NT (cf. Mt 24:3–25:46; Ro 2:5; 2Pe 3:10; Rev 16:14). It continues into the second half of this somber verse in which Malachi alternately reproves and warns. The picture is cosmological. Fire will be the agent of destruction on that day as was water in Noah's day.

The word for "arrogant" (GK 2294) is a relatively rare one, but Malachi uses it also in 3:15. So those "blessed" arrogant ones of the former reference will now be burned as stubble (cf. Am 2:9). The mention of roots and branches indicates the complete termination of growth. As with the two extremities of a plant, all the wicked—without exception—will be destroyed.

2–3 Verse 2 focuses on the blessed future of the righteous. "Sun" is capitalized in the KJV, giving rise to the idea that the figure is messianic. No use is made of this figure, however, in the NT. Therefore most modern translations have not capitalized "sun." The righteous, now enlightened and healed, will gambol like calves, frisking about in their new-found freedom. An added reward is that the righteous will trample the wicked on that great judgment day (cf. Mic 2:12–13).

4 Malachi now gives two somewhat unrelated "appendixes" to the book. The first is an injunction to heed the law of Moses. Malachi began with an illustration from Genesis (Jacob and Esau) and spent most of the first half of the book reminding priests and people of the need to keep the Mosaic Law. Now, close to the end of his book, he gives another terse reminder of their continuing obligation to those laws.

5–6 The second "appendix" (vv.5–6) relates to Elijah's coming to announce the Messiah's arrival. Elijah, as has already been stated, was John the Baptist (Mt 11:14; 17:12; Mk 9:11–13; Lk 1:17). His ministry was to prepare for the Day of the Lord and to "turn the hearts of the fathers to their children" and vice versa, "before that great and dreadful Day of the LORD." The first Christmas was a day of the Lord. So were all the other days when God stepped into history and did something extraordinary. But all these are preparatory for "that great and dreadful day" when the curtain will drop on world history and the Lord, who came the first time as Savior and Friend, will come as King and Judge.

The mission of reconciling families has been successful insofar as people have come to Christ. Where this has not happened, God will "strike the land with a curse." "Land" probably refers to the Promised Land, where God's people were dwelling. Through the Exile the land had been denied them; now they had it back, but still only on probation. If they failed to honor that land and him who gave it to them, it would be denied them. Malachi has set before Israel the age-old alternatives: respond to the God who loves them (1:2), or suffer the terrible consequences (4:1, 6).

The Old Testament in the New

OT Text	NT Text	Subject
Mal 1.2–3	Ro 9:13	Love for Jacob, not Esau
Mal 3:1	Mt 11:10; Mk 1:2; Lk 7:27	Messenger sent ahead
Mal 4:5–6	Mt 17:10–11	Elijah comes

Index of Goodrick/Kohlenberger Numbers